THE TWENTY-FIRST MENTAL MEASUREMENTS YEARBOOK

EARLIER PUBLICATIONS IN THIS SERIES

EDUCATIONAL, PSYCHOLOGICAL, AND PERSONALITY TESTS (1933-1936)
THE NINETEEN THIRTY-EIGHT MENTAL MEASUREMENTS YEARBOOK
THE NINETEEN FORTY MENTAL MEASUREMENTS YEARBOOK
THE THIRD MENTAL MEASUREMENTS YEARBOOK
THE FOURTH MENTAL MEASUREMENTS YEARBOOK
THE FIFTH MENTAL MEASUREMENTS YEARBOOK
TESTS IN PRINT
THE SIXTH MENTAL MEASUREMENTS YEARBOOK
THE SEVENTH MENTAL MEASUREMENTS YEARBOOK
TESTS IN PRINT II
THE MONOGRAPH SERIES
THE EIGHTH MENTAL MEASUREMENTS YEARBOOK
TESTS IN PRINT III
THE NINTH MENTAL MEASUREMENTS YEARBOOK
THE TENTH MENTAL MEASUREMENTS YEARBOOK
THE ELEVENTH MENTAL MEASUREMENTS YEARBOOK
TESTS IN PRINT IV
BUROS DESK REFERENCE: PSYCHOLOGICAL ASSESSMENT IN THE SCHOOLS
BUROS DESK REFERENCE: ASSESSMENT OF SUBSTANCE ABUSE
THE TWELFTH MENTAL MEASUREMENTS YEARBOOK
THE THIRTEENTH MENTAL MEASUREMENTS YEARBOOK
TESTS IN PRINT V
THE FOURTEENTH MENTAL MEASUREMENTS YEARBOOK
TESTS IN PRINT VI
THE FIFTEENTH MENTAL MEASUREMENTS YEARBOOK
THE SIXTEENTH MENTAL MEASUREMENTS YEARBOOK
TESTS IN PRINT VII
THE SEVENTEENTH MENTAL MEASUREMENTS YEARBOOK
THE EIGHTEENTH MENTAL MEASUREMENTS YEARBOOK
TESTS IN PRINT VIII
PRUEBAS PUBLICADAS EN ESPAÑOL: AN INDEX OF SPANISH TESTS IN PRINT
THE NINETEENTH MENTAL MEASUREMENTS YEARBOOK
TESTS IN PRINT IX
THE TWENTIETH MENTAL MEASUREMENTS YEARBOOK
PRUEBAS PUBLICADAS EN ESPAÑOL II: AN INDEX OF SPANISH TESTS IN PRINT

THE TWENTY-FIRST MENTAL MEASUREMENTS YEARBOOK

JANET F. CARLSON, KURT F. GEISINGER,

and JESSICA L. JONSON

Editors

NANCY A. ANDERSON
Managing Editor

The Buros Center for Testing
The University of Nebraska-Lincoln
Lincoln, Nebraska

2021
Distributed by The University of Nebraska Press

LC 39-3422
ISBN 978-0-910674-68-3
ISSN 0076-6461

Manufactured in the United States of America.

The paper used in this publication meets the minimum requirements of American National Standard for Information Sciences—Permanence of Paper for Printed Library Materials, ANSI Z39.48-1984.

Note to Users

The staff of the Buros Center for Testing has made every effort to ensure the accuracy of the test information included in this work. However, the Buros Center for Testing and the Editors of *The Twenty-First Mental Measurements Yearbook* do not assume, and hereby expressly and absolutely disclaim, any liability to any party for any loss or damage caused by errors or omissions or statements of any kind in *The Twenty-First Mental Measurements Yearbook*. This disclaimer also includes judgments or statements of any kind made by test reviewers, who were extended the professional freedom appropriate to their task. The reviews are the sole opinion of the individual reviewers and do not necessarily represent any general consensus of the professional community or any professional organizations. The judgments and opinions of the reviewers are their own, uninfluenced in any way by the Buros Center or the Editors.

All material included in *The Twenty-First Mental Measurements Yearbook* is intended solely for the use of our readers. None of this material, including reviewer statements, may be used in advertising or for any other commercial purpose.

TABLE OF CONTENTS

INTRODUCTION

Consistent with all volumes of this long-running series, *The Twenty-First Mental Measurements Yearbook* (*21st MMY*) serves as a guide to the complex task of test evaluation, selection, and use. With its initial publication in 1938, Oscar K. Buros (1905-1978) provided a historic forum that would allow the emerging field of testing to improve in both science and practice.

Criteria for inclusion in this edition of the *MMY* series are that a test be (a) new or substantially revised since last reviewed in the *MMY* series, (b) commercially available, and (c) published in the English language. To be reviewed, a test must be documented with sufficient test development information and technical data to allow for a comprehensive evaluation.

THE TWENTY-FIRST MENTAL MEASUREMENTS YEARBOOK

The *21st MMY* primarily contains reviews of tests that are new or significantly revised since the publication of the *20th MMY* in 2017. Reviews, descriptions, and references associated with many established and older tests can be located in other Buros Center publications: previous *MMY*s, *Tests in Print IX*, and *Pruebas Publicadas en Español II: An Index of Spanish Tests in Print.* Criteria for review in this edition of the *MMY* remain that a test be (a) new or substantively revised since it was last reviewed in the *MMY* series, (b) commercially available from its publisher, (c) available in the English language, and (d) published with adequate developmental and technical documentation.

Content. The contents of the *21st MMY* include: (a) a bibliography of 192 commercially available tests, new or revised, published in English; (b) 362 critical test reviews of 183 tests by specialists selected by the editors on the basis of their expertise in measurement and, typically, the content of the test being reviewed; (c) a test title index with appropriate cross references; (d) an index of acronyms for easy reference when only a test acronym is known; (e) a classified subject index; (f) a publishers directory and index, including publisher addresses and other contact information with test listings by publisher; (g) a name index including the names of authors of all tests, reviews, or references included in this *MMY*; and (h) a score index to identify for users test scores of potential interest.

Appendix. Two separate listings appear in the *21st MMY* for users requiring additional information when a specific test cannot be otherwise located in the *Mental Measurements Yearbook* series. The first Appendix provides a list of tests that may meet review criteria but arrived too late for review in this volume. It is expected that many or all of these tests (plus additional tests received in the coming months) will be reviewed in *The Twenty-Second Mental Measurements Yearbook.* Test reviews completed prior to publication of the *22nd MMY* will be available electronically for a small fee from our ecommerce site, Test Reviews Online (buros.org). These reviews also will be available from electronic subscription services that carry our searchable database products. A second list in the Appendix includes titles of tests requested from publishers but not yet received as of this volume's publication. This listing includes tests that have been withheld by publishers specifically to prevent their being reviewed as well as tests from publishers who routinely make their instruments available for review but who have failed at this point to provide a new or revised test for evaluation. We at the Buros Center believe that to meet professional standards, test publishers should be willing to have their tests independently evaluated so that consumers are informed about the strengths and potential drawbacks of all measures under consideration for use.

Beginning with the *14th MMY* (2001), a new policy established the conditions that must be satisfied in order for a test to qualify for review. In order for a test to be reviewed in an *MMY,* the test publisher must provide an adequate developmental history and sufficient evidence describing the instrument's technical properties. Not all tests submitted for evaluation meet these criteria for review. A list of test titles of tests received (but not reviewed) first appeared in the Appendix of the *14th MMY*. The list continued to appear in subsequent yearbooks in order to make users aware of the availability of these tests, albeit without supporting documentation or reviews. This listing of tests received (but not reviewed) was dropped from the *20th MMY*, in favor of integrating bibliographic information about these tests into the primary content of the book. The *21st MMY* continues this practice. In effect, these listings are the current test entries from *Tests in Print IX* and thus provide considerably more detail than the test titles and publishers listed in earlier yearbooks. In place of a review, the following statement appears: "No review available. This test does not meet review criteria established by the Buros Center for Testing that call for at least minimal technical and development information."

Organization. The current *MMY* series is organized like an encyclopedia, with tests being ordered alphabetically by title. If the title of a test is known, the reader can locate the test information immediately without having to consult the Index of Titles.

TABLE 1
TESTS BY MAJOR CLASSIFICATIONS

Classification	Number	Percentage
Behavior Assessment	32	16.7
English and Language	29	15.1
Personality	29	15.1
Vocations	18	9.4
Neuropsychological	17	8.9
Miscellaneous	13	6.8
Intelligence and General Aptitude	13	6.8
Developmental	10	5.2
Speech and Hearing	8	4.2
Reading	7	3.6
Education	5	2.6
Achievement	4	2.1
Sensory Motor	4	2.1
Mathematics	3	1.6
Science	0	0.0
Fine Arts	0	0.0
Foreign Languages	0	0.0
Social Studies	0	0.0
Total	192	100.0

TABLE 2
NEW AND REVISED OR SUPPLEMENTED TESTS BY MAJOR CLASSIFICATION

Classification	Number of Tests	Percentage New	Percentage Revised
Achievement	4	25.0	75.0
Behavior Assessment	32	62.5	37.5
Developmental	10	30.0	70.0
Education	5	100.0	0.0
English and Language	29	41.4	58.6
Fine Arts	0	0.0	0.0
Foreign Languages	0	0.0	0.0
Intelligence and General Aptitude	13	30.8	69.2
Mathematics	3	66.7	33.3
Miscellaneous	13	53.8	46.2
Neuropsychological	17	58.8	41.2
Personality	29	69.0	31.0
Reading	7	42.9	57.1
Science	0	0.0	0.0
Sensory Motor	4	50.0	50.0
Social Studies	0	0.0	0.0
Speech and Hearing	8	50.0	50.0
Vocations	18	61.1	38.9
Total	192	54.2	45.8

The page headings reflect the encyclopedic organization. The page heading of the left-hand page cites the number and title of the first test listed on that page, and the page heading of the right-hand page cites the number and title of the last test listed on that page. All numbers presented in the various indexes are test numbers, not page numbers. Page numbers are important only for the Table of Contents and are located at the bottom of each page.

TESTS AND REVIEWS

The *21st MMY* contains descriptive information and reviews for 183 tests. Reviews were authored by 308 different professionals. As well, test descriptions are included for nine additional tests that did not meet review criteria. Statistics on the number and percentage of tests in each of 18 major classifications are contained in Table 1.

The percentages of new and revised or supplemented tests according to major classifications are found in Table 2. Overall, 104 of the tests included in the *21st MMY* are new and have not been reviewed in a previous *MMY* although some descriptions may have been included in *Tests in*

Print IX. The Index of Titles may be consulted to determine whether a test is new or revised.

Test Selection. As noted above, a new policy for selecting tests for review became effective with the *14th MMY* (2001). This policy requires at least minimal information be available regarding test development and technical properties. The requirement that tests have such minimal information does not assure the quality of the test; it simply provides reviewers with a minimum basis for critically evaluating the quality of the test. We select our reviewers carefully and let them and well-informed readers discern for themselves the essential features needed to assure appropriate use of a test. Some new or revised tests are not included because they were received too late to undergo the review process and still permit timely publication. A list of these tests is included in the Appendix, and every effort will be made to have them reviewed for *The Twenty-Second Mental Measurements Yearbook* and available before then through our ecommerce site, Test Reviews Online. These reviews also may be available in searchable databases available via subscription from EBSCO Information Services or Ovid Technologies at many university, medical, law, and research libraries.

There are some new or revised tests for which there will be no reviews although descriptive entries for these tests are provided in *Tests in Print IX* or will be included in a future edition of *Tests in Print*. The absence of reviews may have occurred for a variety of reasons including: the test materials were incomplete so reviews were not possible, the publisher advised us the test was out of print before reviews were completed, the test did not meet our criteria for documentation of technical and development information, or revisions were not substantial enough to warrant re-review.

Reviewer Selection. The selection of reviewers was done with great care. The objective was to secure measurement and content area specialists who would be independent and represent a variety of viewpoints. In addition, it was important to invite individuals who would write critical reviews competently, judiciously, fairly, and in a timely manner. Reviewers were identified by means of extensive searches of the professional literature, attendance at professional meetings, and recommendations from leaders in various professional fields. Perusal of reviews in this volume also will reveal that reviewers work in and represent a cross-section of the contexts in which testing is taught and tests are used: universities, public schools, businesses, community agencies, and healthcare settings, among others. These reviewers represent an outstanding array of professional talent, and their contributions are obviously of primary importance in making this *Yearbook* a valuable resource. A list of the individuals who contributed reviews to this volume is included at the beginning of the Index section.

Active, evaluative reading is the key to the most effective use of the professional expertise offered in each of the reviews. Just as one would evaluate a test, readers should evaluate critically the reviewer's comments about a test. The reviewers selected are competent professionals in their respective fields, but it is inevitable that their reviews also reflect their individual perspectives. The *Mental Measurements Yearbook* series was developed to stimulate critical thinking and assist in the selection of the best available test for a given purpose, not to promote the passive acceptance of reviewer judgment. That reviews of a particular measure sometimes differ represents the different perspectives that scholars may bring to a particular measure; indeed, reviews may be at variance with one another, but both yield important and accurate perspectives.

INDEXES

As mentioned above, the *21st MMY* includes six indexes invaluable as aids to effective use of this volume: (a) Index of Titles, (b) Index of Acronyms, (c) Classified Subject Index, (d) Publishers Directory and Index, (e) Index of Names, and (f) Score Index. Additional comment on each of these indexes appears below.

Index of Titles. Because the organization of the *21st MMY* is encyclopedic in nature, with the tests ordered alphabetically by title throughout the volume, the test title index need not be consulted to find a test if the title is known. However, the title index has some features that make it useful beyond its function as a complete title listing. First, it includes cross-reference information useful for tests with superseded or alternative titles or tests commonly (and sometimes inaccurately) known by multiple titles. Second, it identifies tests that are new or revised. Third, it may cue the user to other tests with similar titles that may prove useful. Titles of tests that were not reviewed because of insufficient technical documentation are included in the Index of Titles together with their corresponding test entry numbers. These test titles are preceded by an asterisk. As mentioned above, test entries for such tests contain all relevant descriptive fields (e.g., title, author, purpose, population, scores, acronym, publisher) in order to acquaint readers with basic information about a test that is known to exist. It is important to keep in mind that the numbers in this index, like those for all *MMY* indexes, are test numbers and not page numbers.

Because no *MMY* includes reviews of all tests currently in print, a particular test of interest may not be reviewed in this volume. To learn whether a commercially published test has been reviewed in this or an earlier volume of the *MMY*, users may access the Buros Center for Testing website (buros.org). A search of Test Reviews Online indicates whether a test has been reviewed and also indicates the yearbook in which the review can be found. The site also provides electronic access to reviews provided in recent *MMY*s (the most current reviews only) and test reviews that have been finalized since the publication of the most recent *MMY*. Thus, Test Reviews Online provides ready access, for a nominal fee, to the majority of current tests that have been reviewed in the *Mental Measurements Yearbook* series. In addition, *Tests in Print IX* provides cross references to reviews of still-in-print tests in the *MMY* series.

Index of Acronyms. Some tests seem to be better known by their acronyms than by their full titles. The Index of Acronyms can help in these instances; it refers the reader to the full title of the test and to the relevant descriptive information and reviews.

Classified Subject Index. The Classified Subject Index classifies all tests listed in the *21st MMY* into 14 of 18 major categories: Achievement, Behavior Assessment, Developmental, Education, English and Language, Fine Arts, Foreign Languages, Intelligence and General Aptitude, Mathematics, Miscellaneous, Neuropsychological, Personality, Reading, Science, Sensory-Motor, Social Studies, Speech and Hearing, and Vocations. (No tests in the Fine Arts, Foreign Languages, Science, or Social Studies categories are reviewed in the *21st MMY*.) Each test entry in this index includes test title, population for which the test is intended, and test number. The Classified Subject Index is of great help to readers who seek a listing of tests in given subject areas. This index represents a starting point for readers who know their general area of interest but do not know how to focus that interest in order to identify the best test(s) for their particular purposes.

Publishers Directory and Index. The Publishers Directory and Index includes the names and addresses of the publishers of all tests included in the *21st MMY* plus a listing of test numbers for each individual publisher. Also included are the telephone and FAX numbers, email, and Web addresses for those publishers who responded to our request for this information. This index can be particularly useful in obtaining contact information for publishers from whom one might wish to request further information or order testing products or catalogs after the test reviews have been read and evaluated. It also can be useful when a reader knows the publisher of a certain test but is uncertain about the test title, or when a reader is interested in the range of tests published by a given publisher.

Index of Names. The Index of Names provides a comprehensive list of names, indicating authorship of a test, test review, or reviewer's reference.

Score Index. The Score Index provides a listing of the scored parts of all tests reviewed or described in the *21st MMY*. Test titles are sometimes misleading or ambiguous, and test content may be difficult to define with precision. In contrast, test scores often represent operational definitions of the variables the test author is trying to measure, and as such they can define test purpose and content more adequately than other descriptive information. A search for a particular test is most often a search for a test that measures some specific attribute(s). Test scores and their associated labels often offer the best definitions of the variable(s) of interest. The Score Index is a detailed subject index based on the most critical operational features of any test—the scores and their associated labels.

HOW TO USE THIS YEARBOOK

A reference work like *The Twenty-First Mental Measurements Yearbook* can be of far greater benefit to a reader if some time is taken to become familiar with what it has to offer and how it might be used most effectively to obtain the information sought.

Step 1: Read the Introduction to the *21st MMY* in its entirety.

Step 2: Become familiar with the six indexes and particularly with the instructions preceding each index listing.

Step 3: Use the book by looking up needed information. This step is simple if one keeps the following procedures in mind:

1. Go directly to the test entry using the alphabetical page headings if you know the title of the test.

2. Consult the Index of Titles for possible variants of the title or consult the appropriate subject area of the Classified Subject Index for other possible leads or for similar or related tests in the same content area, if you do not know, cannot find, or are unsure of the title of a test. (Other uses for both of these indexes were described above.)

3. Consult the Index of Names if you know the author of a test but not the title or publisher. Look through the author's titles until you find the test you want.

4. Consult the Publishers Directory and Index if you know the test publisher but not the title or author. Look through the publisher's titles until you find the test you want.

5. Consult the Score Index and locate the test or tests that include the score variable of interest if you are looking for a test that yields a particular kind of test score.

6. If after following the above steps you are not able to find a review or description of the test you want, consult the Appendix to discover whether the test you seek was not reviewed or described because (a) the test was received late and is expected to be reviewed in the next edition of the *MMY*, or (b) the test publisher did not respond to our request for testing materials. You also may wish to consult *Tests in Print IX* or visit the Buros Center for Testing website (buros.org) and use the Test Reviews Online service to identify the yearbook that contains the description and any available reviews for a test of interest.

7. Once you have found the test or tests you are looking for, read the descriptive entries for these tests carefully so that you can take advantage of the information provided. A description of the information in these test entries is presented later in this section.

8. Read the test reviews carefully and analytically, as suggested above. The information and evaluations contained in the reviews are meant to assist test consumers in making well-informed decisions about the choice and applications of tests.

9. Once you have read the descriptive information and test reviews, you may want to contact the test publisher to order some or all of the test materials associated with a particular test so that you can examine it firsthand. The Publishers Directory and Index provides the information needed to contact test publishers.

Making Effective Use of the Test Entries. Although brief, the test entries include extensive information. For each test, descriptive information is presented in the following order:

a) TITLES. Test titles are printed in boldface type. Secondary or series titles are set off from main titles by a colon.

b) PURPOSE. For each test there is a brief, clear statement describing the purpose of the test. Often these statements are quotations from the test manual.

c) POPULATION. This field describes the groups for whom the test is intended. The grade, chronological age, semester range, or employment category is usually given. For example, "Grades 1.5–2.5, 2–3, 4–12, 13–17" means that there are four test booklets: a booklet for the middle of first grade through the middle of second grade, a booklet for the beginning of second grade through the end of third grade, a booklet for Grades 4 through 12 inclusive, and a booklet for undergraduate and graduate students in colleges and universities.

d) PUBLICATION DATE. The inclusive range of publication dates for the various forms, accessories, and editions of a test is reported.

e) ACRONYM. When a test is often referred to by an acronym, the acronym is given in the test entry.

f) SCORES. The number of part scores is presented along with their titles or descriptions of what they are intended to represent or measure.

g) ADMINISTRATION. Individual or group administration is indicated. A test is considered a group test unless it may be administered only individually.

h) FORMS, PARTS, AND LEVELS. All available forms, parts, and levels are listed.

i) MANUAL. Notation is made if no manual is available. All other manual information is included under Price Data.

j) RESTRICTED DISTRIBUTION. This designation is used only for tests that are made available to a special market by the publisher. Educational and psychological restrictions are not noted (unless a special training course is required for use).

k) PRICE DATA. Price information is reported for test packages (usually 20 to 35 tests), answer sheets, all other accessories, and specimen sets.

The statement "$17.50 per 35 tests" means that all accessories are included unless otherwise indicated by the reporting of separate prices for accessories. The statement also means 35 tests of one level, one edition, or one part unless stated otherwise. Because test prices can change very quickly, the year that the listed test prices were obtained is included. Foreign currency is assigned the appropriate symbol. When prices are given in foreign dollars, a qualifying symbol is added (e.g., A$16.50 refers to 16 dollars and 50 cents in Australian currency). Along with cost, the publication date and number of pages on which print occurs is reported for manuals and technical reports (e.g., 2009, 102 pages). All types of machine-scorable answer sheets available for use with a specific test are reported in the descriptive entry. Scoring and reporting services provided by publishers are reported along with information on costs. In a few cases, special computerized scoring and interpretation services are noted at the end of the price information.

l) FOREIGN LANGUAGE AND OTHER SPECIAL EDITIONS. This section concerns the availability of editions in languages other than English. It also indicates special editions (e.g., braille, large type) available from the same or a different publisher. Readers interested in a Spanish version of a particular test may wish to consult another Buros Center publication, *Pruebas Publicadas en Español II,* which provides descriptive listings of commercially published tests that are available in part or wholly in Spanish. Many of these tests are translations/adaptations of English language tests.

m) TIME. The number of minutes of actual working time allowed examinees and the approximate length of time needed for administering a test are reported whenever obtainable. The latter figure is always enclosed in parentheses. Thus, "50(60) minutes" indicates that examinees are allowed 50 minutes of working time and that a total of 60 minutes is needed to administer the test. A time of "40–50 minutes" indicates an untimed test that takes approximately 45 minutes to administer, or—in a few instances—a test so timed that working time and administration time are very difficult to disentangle. When the time necessary to administer a test is not reported or suggested in the test materials but has been obtained from a catalog or through correspondence with the test publisher or author, the time is enclosed in brackets.

n) COMMENTS. Some entries contain special notations, such as: "for research use only," "revision of the ABC Test," "tests administered monthly at centers throughout the United States," "online administration available," and "verbal creativity." A statement such as "verbal creativity" is intended to describe more fully the construct or constructs that the test claims to measure. Some of the test entries include factual statements that may imply criticism of the test, such as "2009 test identical with test copyrighted 1990."

o) AUTHOR. For most tests, all authors are reported. In the case of tests that appear in a new form each year, only authors of the most recent forms are listed. Names are reported exactly as printed on test booklets. Names of editors generally are not reported.

p) PUBLISHER. The name of the publisher or distributor is reported for each test. Foreign publishers are identified by listing the country in brackets immediately following the name of the publisher. The Publishers Directory and Index should be consulted for a publisher's address and other contact information.

q) SUBLISTINGS. Levels, editions, subtests, or parts of a test available in separate booklets are sometimes presented as sublistings with titles set in small capital letters. Sub-sublistings are indented, and titles are set in italic type.

r) CROSS REFERENCES. For tests that have been listed previously in a Buros Center for Testing (or a Buros Institute of Mental Measurements) publication, a test entry includes—if relevant—a final item containing cross references to the reviews, excerpts, and references for that test in those volumes. In the cross references, "T7:467" refers to test 467 in *Tests in Print VII*, "19:121" refers to test 121 in *The Nineteenth Mental Measurements Yearbook*, "8:1023" refers to test 1023 in *The Eighth Mental Measurements Yearbook*, "T3:144" refers to test 144 in *Tests in Print III*, "P:262" refers to test 262 in *Personality Tests and Reviews*, "2:1427" refers to test 1427 in *The 1940 Yearbook*, and "1:1110" refers to test 1110 in *The 1938 Yearbook*. In the case of batteries and programs, the paragraph also includes cross references—from the battery to the separately listed subtests and vice versa—to entries in this volume and to entries and reviews in earlier yearbooks.

ACKNOWLEDGMENTS

As we were preparing to complete this publication cycle, the world and the way we do business changed dramatically with the onset of a global pandemic. Nevertheless, our reviewers, publishers, and staff adapted, and together we persisted to bring *The Twenty-First Mental Measurements Yearbook* to fruition. This publication could not have been accomplished without the contributions of many individuals. The editors gratefully acknowledge the talent, expertise, and dedication of the staff at the Buros Center for Testing who have made this most recent volume in the *MMY* series possible.

Nancy Anderson, Managing Editor, played a vital role in this publication. Her substantial knowledge of testing and psychometrics, together with her expert editorial skills and experience, were critical to the development of this volume and made our job as editors easier and more palatable than it otherwise would be. She sorted out many inaccuracies, omissions, and inconsistencies as a matter of course, provided fine points on APA style, and alerted us to numerous errors that might occur save for her conscientious efforts to avert them. Her attention to detail and good humor throughout the process were greatly appreciated. As Managing Editor, Nancy was generally responsible for communications with test publishers to receive new and substantially revised tests and has been largely responsible for completion of the book.

Publication of this volume would not be possible without the perseverance of our Assistant Editor, Gary Anderson, who among many other duties continually updates the website, helps to manage voluminous testing materials and databases, communicates with all of our reviewers, and carefully proofreads each test review. We also wish to thank Jennifer Schlueter, Assistant Editor, for her assistance with numerous tasks related primarily to test acquisitions and communications with test publishers, layout, and proofreading. Her contributions and personable nature made many processes easier and more efficient. We are most appreciative of the important work performed by Anja Römhild who has ensured the integrity of our subscription database operations that serve hundreds of libraries worldwide. We are grateful for the ongoing assistance of Heather Snodgrass, Marketing and Communications Manager, in publicizing our work and doing so in a consistently cheerful manner. We would like to acknowledge the multifaceted assistance provided by Zoe McManaman, Office Assistant, and thank her for maintaining an efficient and warm office environment. We appreciate her energy and commitment to our mission. In addition, we would like to acknowledge other members of the Buros Center for Testing for their support and encouragement during the publication of this edition of the *MMY*. Tzu-Yun (Katherine) Chin, Theresa Glanz, Doug (Min Sung) Kim, Carina McCormick, and Maria Elena Oliveri have made generous contributions to discussions of our current and future directions. We appreciate the efforts of all permanent staff, each of whom contributes importantly to the development and production of our publications. We also enjoy the respect and collegiality of others within the University of Nebraska-Lincoln system. In particular, we wish to thank Michael Scheel, Chair of the Department of Educational Psychology, as well as Ralph de Ayala, former Chair of the Department of Educational Psychology, Sherri Jones, Dean of the College of Education and Human Sciences, and Beth Doll, former Interim Dean of the College of Education and Human Sciences, for their encouragement and support. Michael Fairchild, former senior web programmer, provided a great deal of data management and database development assistance, and his expert contributions were both valuable and appreciated. We extend our thanks to the University of Nebraska Information Technology Services staff for their work on our behalf in improving database-related operations.

This volume would not have been possible without the substantial efforts of our test reviewers. We are very grateful to the many reviewers (and especially to those Distinguished Reviewers recognized in this and previous editions of the *MMY* series) who have prepared test reviews for the Buros Center for Testing and, previously, for the Buros Institute of Mental Measurements. Their willingness to take time from busy professional schedules to share their expertise in the form of thoughtful test reviews is very much appreciated. We also extend our gratitude to the hundreds of reviewers who stood at the ready but were not invited to review this time, due to a lack of tests that matched their areas of expertise. The *Mental Measurements Yearbook* series would not exist without the concerted efforts of all reviewers.

The work of many graduate students helps make possible the quality of this volume. Their efforts include writing test descriptions, fact checking reviews, verifying references, proofreading, and innumerable other tasks. We thank our graduate research assistants, Henry Bass, Allen Garcia, Sara Gonzalez, Guadalupe Gutierrez, HyeSun Lee, Raul

Palacios II, Analay Perez, and Lindsey Sherd, for their assistance.

Appreciation is also extended to the members of our National Advisory Committee for their willingness to assist in the operation of the Buros Center for Testing and for their thought-provoking suggestions for improving the *MMY* series and other publications of the Center. During the period in which this volume was prepared, the National Advisory Council has included Deborah Bandalos, Jeffery Braden, Paula Kaufman, Scott Lilienfeld, Jennifer Randall, Michael Rodriguez, Joseph Salem, Jr., Jonathan Sandoval, Neal Schmitt, and Nancy Tippins.

The Buros Center for Testing is part of the Department of Educational Psychology of the University of Nebraska-Lincoln. We have benefited from the many departmental colleagues who have contributed to this work. In addition, we are grateful for the contribution of the University of Nebraska Press, which provides expert consultation and serves as distributor of our books, including those in the *MMY* series.

In recent years, volumes in the *MMY* series are published about once every three years. Throughout the development and publication process, we often reflect on changes that have occurred in the intervening years. During this past time period, the staff of the Buros Center for Testing was deeply saddened by the sudden loss of Dr. Scott Lilienfeld. We extend our sympathies to his family members, friends, close associates, professional colleagues, and students. Dr. Lilienfeld's career overlapped the mission of the Center in aiming to improve the science and practice of testing. His contributions as a member of our National Advisory Council were exceedingly valuable. Before he joined the Council, we were aware of his stellar professional reputation. During his service on the Council, we learned of his equally remarkable personal qualities—warmth, respect, and generosity among them. We miss him already, both personally and professionally.

SUMMARY

The *Mental Measurements Yearbook* series is an essential resource for both individuals and organizations seeking information critical to the evaluation, selection, and use of specific testing instruments. This edition contains 362 test reviews of 183 different tests.

Test reviews from recent *MMY* editions are available electronically through EBSCO Publishing or Ovid Technologies at many university, medical, law, and research libraries. Test reviews also are available directly from the Buros Center for Testing (buros.org) through our Test Reviews Online ecommerce site.

For over 80 years the *MMY* series has worked to support the interests of knowledgeable professionals and purpose of an informed public. By providing candid reviews of testing products, this publication also serves test publishers who wish to improve their instruments by submitting tests for independent review. Given the critical importance of testing, we hope test authors and publishers will carefully consider the comments made by reviewers and continue to refine and perfect their assessment products.

Janet F. Carlson
Kurt F. Geisinger
Jessica L. Jonson
January 2021

Tests and Reviews

[1]

Academic Achievement Battery.

Purpose: Designed to assess "the basic areas of achievement with a focus on reading comprehension."
Population: Ages 4-85.
Publication Date: 2017.
Acronym: AAB.
Scores, 6: Reading Composite (Letter/Word Reading, Reading Comprehension: Passages, Total), Total Academic Achievement Composite (Letter/Word Reading, Spelling, Reading Comprehension: Passages, Mathematical Calculation, Total).
Administration: Individual.
Price Data, 2020: $154 per print kit including manual (270 pages), Fast Guide (47 pages), 25 item booklets, 25 response booklets, stimulus card, and 5 standard form score reports; $88 per manual with Fast Guide (print or digital); $28 per 25 item booklets; $28 per 25 response booklets; $13 per stimulus card; $1 per online score report (minimum 5).
Time: (15-30) minutes.
Comments: Children in pre-kindergarten do not take Reading Comprehension: Passages; online scoring and reporting available; content is a subset of that contained in the Academic Achievement Battery Comprehensive Form (20:2).
Author: Melissa A. Messer.
Publisher: Psychological Assessment Resources, Inc.

Review of the Academic Achievement Battery by NICHOLAS F. BENSON, Associate Professor of School Psychology, and REBECCA J. TIPTON, Graduate Student, Baylor University, Waco, TX:

DESCRIPTION. The Academic Achievement Battery (AAB) Standard Form is a standardized, norm-referenced test of academic achievement appropriate for ages 4 to 85. The AAB Standard Form consists of a subset of content from the comprehensive version of the AAB (20:2). Whereas the comprehensive version was designed to assess all areas of academic achievement defined by the 2004 authorization of the Individuals with Disabilities Education Act, the primary goal of developing the standard form was to provide a "quick and easy-to-administer" (manual, p. 1) assessment of academic skills with an emphasis on reading comprehension. The AAB Standard Form consists of the following subtests: Letter/Word Reading, Spelling, Reading Comprehension: Passages, and Mathematical Calculation. Two composites, the Reading Composite and the Total Academic Achievement Battery Composite, can be derived based on performance with these subtests. The Spelling subtest and a portion of the Mathematical Calculation subtest may be group-administered. The remaining subtests are administered individually. The AAB Standard Form reportedly can be completed in 30 minutes or less, with scoring requiring an additional 5 to 10 minutes. The AAB is administered in a paper and pencil format; online scoring and reporting are available.

DEVELOPMENT. Items for the Letter/Word Reading subtest were developed to assess a wide range of skills, including simple letter recognition; identification of basic, high frequency vocabulary words; identification of general academic words; and identification of domain-specific academic terms. Items for the Spelling subtest were developed to assess a range of skills from writing upper and lowercase letters to spelling words of increasing difficulty. Items for the Mathematical Calculation subtest were developed to assess a wide range of skills ranging from counting to advanced skills (e.g., applying exponents, simplifying square roots). Finally, items for the Reading Comprehension: Passages subtest were developed by adapting nonfiction passages from Wikipedia and several topic-specific web sites. The format for responding to these passages is a sentence identification technique that involves syntactical analysis. Specifically, readers must determine where sentences end and draw lines denoting the end of each sentence. Notably, readers are not required to semantically analyze the passages, draw conclusions, or make inferences.

Expert and bias panels reviewed all AAB items. Feedback was combined with results from statistical item analysis to inform decisions regarding item revision and deletion. Expert feedback also was used to inform the development of the scoring rubrics and skill analysis procedures.

Initial pilot testing of the items included 133 individuals ages 4 to 83. Classical item analysis and Rasch modeling were used to calibrate item difficulty. Item difficulty indices were used to re-order items according to difficulty and were used in concert with feedback from the expert and bias panels to inform item removal. Next, start points and basal and ceiling rules were established. The refined version was administered to a second pilot sample of 280 individuals, ages 4 to 70. Data were collected in both the fall and spring, and results were compared to determine whether the items were sensitive to growth over time. Item analysis procedures were repeated. Results were used to reorder items as well as to establish new start points, basal rules, and ceiling rules for the standardization version.

Subsequent to the standardization process, subtest and composite discrepancy scores were developed. Ipsative analysis and interpretation are encouraged by the test author, and the manual provides tables to assist in the identification of statistically significant and normatively rare discrepancies. Tables also are provided to assist with identification of discrepancies between intellectual ability as operationalized by IQ values and levels of academic achievement. Using these tables, users can identify statistically significant and normatively rare discrepancies between AAB scores and IQ values from the Reynolds Intellectual Assessment Scales, Second Edition (RIAS-2; Reynolds & Kamphaus, 2015; see 138, this volume); the Wechsler Intelligence Scale for Children, Fourth Edition (WISC-IV; Wechsler, 2003; 16:262); and the Wechsler Adult Intelligence Scale, Fourth Edition (WAIS-IV; Wechsler, 2008; 18:151). Tables are provided to facilitate both simple difference and predicted-regression models for determining discrepancies. The test manual also includes tables that allow users to determine statistically significant changes in scores over time. Additionally, skill analysis maps that allow examiners to track academic subskills and a summary form to determine the percent of items answered correctly for each subskill were developed.

TECHNICAL.

Standardization. Normative data were collected from January 2013 to March 2014. The norm sample was drawn from 30 states. A total of 137 examiners collected data, although it is unclear from how many sites participants were drawn. Rather than the sounder approach of random stratified sampling, a statistical weighting procedure was used that involved random duplication and deletion of cases to match the norms with U.S. Census Bureau data with respect to salient demographic variables (e.g., ethnicity, socioeconomic status, geographic region). The total sample consisted of 1,447 individuals; the weighting procedure effectively decreased the sample size to 1,274 for the age-based norms. Although 16 of the 32 age groups defined by the test author consisted of students younger than 12, approximately 25% of the sample consisted of students younger than 12. Thus, only about 320 students in the normative sample were younger than age 12. If these students were assigned equally to each age group, there would be 20 students per norm block used to derive age-based norm-reference scores. Conversely, 75% of the sample makes up the 16 groups that are ages 12 years and older. If these participants were assigned equally to each age group, there would be 59.6 people per group.

Using the grade-based norms (pre-K through Grade 12), there are 48-56 students per norm block. As a result, norm-referenced comparisons are made relative to a small number of students. This concern was addressed using continuous norming, a regression technique used to estimate predicted means and standard deviations for each age-based and grade-based norm block. These predicted means and standard deviations were subsequently used to calculate normalized standard scores.

Reliability. Coefficient alpha was used to estimate internal consistency. Except for the Reading Comprehension: Passages subtest, all estimates for subtests were above .90. Estimates for Reading Comprehension: Passages were based on test-retest correlations corrected for attenuation. Resulting coefficients were .88 based on the age-based sample and .81 based on the fall and spring grade-based samples. Estimates for the Reading Composite were .93 for the age-based sample and .91 for both grade-based samples; estimates for the Total Academic

Achievement Battery Composite were .97 for the age-based sample and .97 and .96 for the fall and spring grade-based samples, respectively. Test-retest reliability was examined using 147 participants from the standardization sample who were tested twice with an interval of 7 to 49 days between testing sessions. Test-retest reliability coefficients were .89 for the Reading Composite and .96 for the Total Composite, suggesting excellent temporal stability. Test-retest coefficients for Spelling and Mathematical Calculation exceeded .90. Coefficients for Reading Comprehension: Passages and Letter/Word Reading were somewhat lower at .81 and .89, respectively.

Validity. The user's manual includes a discussion of efforts to ensure the validity of score interpretation and uses. These efforts included the author's review of academic standards prior to writing items as well as comments from expert panels regarding the face validity and appropriateness of items and subtests. Age-based subtest intercorrelations are presented. For ages 4-18, coefficients range from .27 for Mathematical Calculation and Letter/Word Reading to .71 for Spelling and Letter/Word Reading. For ages 19 and older, coefficients range from .26 (Mathematical Calculation and Reading Comprehension: Passages) to .84 (Spelling and Letter/Word Reading). Notably, although they are summed when obtaining the Reading Composite, the correlations between Letter/Word Reading and Reading Comprehension: Passages were only .40 for ages 4-18 and .35 for ages 19 and older. Results from exploratory or confirmatory factor analysis are not reported to support the proposed structure of the test. No evidence is provided to demonstrate that test items function similarly across identifiable groups (e.g., racial/ethnic groups, gender). Additionally, it is unclear whether the subtests and composites are calibrated similarly across identifiable groups.

Correlations among AAB scores and scores from four tests of academic achievement and three tests of intelligence were included for comparison in the manual. Patterns of correlations among AAB scores and scores from other tests of achievement suggest that the AAB generally measures similar constructs as extant tests of academic achievement. A notable exception is the Reading Comprehension: Passages subtest, which correlated more modestly (i.e., from .32 to .63) with scores from other measures of reading comprehension.

The AAB was administered to clinical samples, and scores were compared to those from a nonclinical sample to determine the extent to which the AAB discriminated between these groups. The largest effects were found for individuals diagnosed with intellectual development disorder, with Cohen's *d* values ranging from 1.67 for the Reading Comprehension: Passages subtest to 3.14 for the Mathematical Calculation subtest. Cohen's *d* values for individuals diagnosed with a specific learning disorder were large, ranging from 1.09 for the Reading Comprehension: Passages subtest to 1.68 for the Total Academic Achievement Battery Composite. Cohen's *d* values for individuals diagnosed with attention-deficit/hyperactivity disorder were small, ranging from 0.07 for the Letter/Word Reading subtest to 0.41 for the Mathematical Calculation subtest. Finally, Cohen's *d* values for individuals diagnosed with a speech/language impairment ranged from 0.22 for Letter/Word Reading to 0.93 for the Total Academic Achievement Battery Composite.

COMMENTARY. The primary goal of developing the AAB Standard Form was to provide a quick assessment of academic achievement with an emphasis on reading comprehension. The instructions for administration are clearly stated and easy to follow. The skill analysis maps and summary form might prove useful when planning instruction. Tables are included to facilitate identification of discrepancies between intellectual ability and academic achievement, although one of the intelligence tests is now outdated (i.e., the WISC-IV) and another (i.e., the WAIS-IV) is currently being revised. The use of Rasch modeling to calibrate item difficulty seems to be a strength, although technical issues such as model estimation methods and the criteria used to evaluate model fit are not reported and discussed in the manual. Further, limited evidence of validity is presented to support the interpretation and use of scores.

Most AAB Standard Form subtest and composite scores display good reliability and convergent validity (i.e., they relate strongly with similar measures designed to assess the same academic skills). The Reading Comprehension: Passages subtest is less reliable than the other subtests and correlates only modestly (i.e., coefficients from .32 to .63) with scores from other measures of reading comprehension. This modest evidence of convergent validity likely reflects the fact that the Reading Comprehension: Passages subtest is limited to syntactical processing (i.e., readers must determine where sentences end and draw lines denoting the end of each sentence). In contrast, the comparison measures require semantic processing (e.g., drawing conclusions, making inferences). Additionally, although the Reading Comprehension: Passages and Letter/Word Reading scores are summed when obtaining the Reading Composite, the correlation coefficient for these subtests is only .40 for examinees ages 4-18. Thus, although the AAB Standard Form was designed to emphasize reading comprehension, caution is recommended when using the AAB Standard Form for this purpose.

No evidence is provided to demonstrate that test items function similarly across identifiable groups (e.g., racial/ethnic groups, gender). Additionally, it is unclear whether the subtests and composites are calibrated similarly across identifiable groups. Although a bias panel reviewed items, the absence of bias must be established statistically. Research with clinical samples does suggest that composite and subtest scores are useful to identify academic deficits typically displayed by individuals with disabilities.

SUMMARY. The AAB Standard Form is an abbreviated measure of achievement suitable for a wide age range. It was designed to align with contemporary curricular standards as well as with a subset of the academic domains defined in the 2004 authorization of the Individuals with Disabilities Education Act. The AAB comprises four subtests: Letter/Word Reading, Spelling, Reading Comprehension: Passages, and Mathematical Calculation. The AAB Standard Form reportedly can be completed in 30 minutes or less. Although the AAB Standard Form was designed to emphasize reading comprehension, caution is recommended when using the AAB Standard Form for this purpose.

REVIEWERS' REFERENCES

International Reading Association Common Core State Standards Committee. (2012). *Literacy implementation guidance for the ELA Common Core State Standards* [White paper].

National Council of Teachers of Mathematics. (2013, August). Supporting the Common Core State Standards for Mathematics. Retrieved from https://www.nctm.org/ccssmposition/

National Governors Association Center for Best Practices, Council of Chief State School Officers. (2010). Common Core State Standards. Washington, DC: Authors.

Reynolds, C. R., & Kamphaus, R. W. (2015). Reynolds Intellectual Assessment Scales, Second Edition. Lutz, FL: Psychological Assessment Resources.

Wechsler, D. (2003). Wechsler Intelligence Scale for Children, Fourth Edition. San Antonio, TX: Pearson.

Wechsler, D. (2008). Wechsler Adult Intelligence Scale, Fourth Edition. San Antonio, TX: Pearson.

Review of the Academic Achievement Battery by BETHANY A. BRUNSMAN, Assessment/Evaluation Specialist, Lincoln Public Schools, Lincoln, NE:

DESCRIPTION. The Academic Achievement Battery (AAB) was designed to be a quick measure of basic reading and math skills. Results are intended to be used to plan interventions and as part of decisions about special education services for school-aged students, for placement and accommodations decisions for college students, and for decisions about disability and vocational services for adults. The AAB consists of Letter/Word Reading (75 items), Spelling (68 items), Reading Comprehension: Passages (13 passages), and Mathematical Calculation (60 items). Subscale scores are available for these tests along with a Reading Composite (comprising Letter/Word Reading and Reading Comprehension: Passages) and Total Academic Achievement Battery Composite (Total Composite). The AAB is intended for English-speaking children and adults ages 4 to 85. Pre-K students do not take the Reading Comprehension: Passages test, so a Reading Composite score is not available for them. The AAB is a subset of the AAB Comprehensive Form (20:2), so it can be used first, and the clinician can then decide whether to administer the rest of the longer form.

The Letter/Word Reading subtest requires examinees to read letters and words aloud to the examiner. For the Spelling subtest, the examiner reads letters and words to the examinee, who writes them down. Reading Comprehension: Passages consists of passages, ranging from three to 15 sentences without punctuation (commas or periods) or beginning of sentence capitalization. Examinees must mark the end of each sentence. The shorter passages tend to be narrative, whereas the longer, more complex passages used with older examinees tend to be expository non-fiction. The Mathematical Calculation subtest contains two parts: (a) orally administered counting and addition items and (b) a timed section of written calculation problems.

The AAB is a paper-and-pencil test that takes 15-30 minutes to administer and 5-10 minutes to score by hand. Spelling and Mathematical Calculation: Part 2 may be administered to groups of students. All other subtests require individual administration. The manual specifies that professionals with training in assessment, including psychologists, school counselors, special education teachers, and licensed professional counselors are qualified to administer the AAB. It is important for those administering the test to read the manual or fast guide carefully so they can apply administration guidelines, including starting, basal, reverse, and discontinuation rules for correct scoring.

Examinees begin different tests at different points based on their grade levels. Students in Grades 4 and higher skip the Letter Reading, Letter Writing, and Math: Part 1 tests and receive credit for correct answers on all of these items unless they miss all of the first three items in the subsequent tests (Word Reading, Word Writing, and Math: Part 2). The examiner can record specific information about wrong answers that is not used in scoring but can be used to interpret results diagnostically. Scores are determined by summing correct responses and then using conversion tables to translate them to age- or grade-based standard scores. There is an additional weighting step for the Reading Comprehension: Passages subtest. Fall and spring norms are available. Confidence intervals are based on grade- or age-level norm group error rates. Percentile ranks, stanines, normal curve equivalents, and age and grade equivalents are also available through conversion tables. Directions and conversion tables for conducting analyses of patterns in incorrect answers ("skills analysis"), discrepancies among subtest scores, change over time, and relationships of scores with several ability measures are also provided. Hand scoring is somewhat complicated, but well explained in the test manual and fast guide. The manual states that scoring is quick, but it would be time consuming for a teacher to do the scoring by hand for a large number of students. A fee-based online scoring option exists. The examiner can enter raw scores, and the online system generates score reports.

DEVELOPMENT. Content for the items was based largely on the Common Core State Standards (National Governors Association Center for Best Practices, 2010) and the National Council of Teachers of Mathematics Principles and Standards for School Mathematics (NCTM, 2000). The test development process included item writing, pilot testing/refinement, and item and bias review prior to norms development. No information is provided regarding the qualifications of the item writers. The test manual contains some information about the item reviewers—who were described as curriculum experts in reading, writing, and math and a school psychologist—and bias review panel—six people with backgrounds in clinical psychology, school psychology, educational measurement, and pharmacy—but it is not sufficient to determine their level of expertise, and the specific item review training provided is not described. The bias review panel did include diversity (i.e., members were Caucasian, Hispanic, and Indian), but some ethnic/race groups were notably absent, and no experience with students with disabilities was mentioned for either review group. The item review panel developed content specifications to evaluate content coverage for each of the subtests, but it appears from the description that these specifications were developed after the items were written and pilot tested. The content specifications are also used as part of the skills analysis when interpreting scores.

A pilot study included 133 participants, ages 4 to 83. The mean age of pilot participants was 26 years. Item statistics from this study were used to eliminate some items and reorder items within the tests based on difficulty. A second pilot (refinement) study included 280 participants, ages 4 to 70 years, with a mean age of 21 years. It is not clear how many of the participants in either pilot study were in the school-aged population. The specific process used to develop the basal, discontinuation, and reverse rules is not described in the test manual, but the author states that data from the refinement pilot informed these decision rules. Additionally, Reading Comprehension: Passages was revised. In the pilot version, this test also included multiple-choice items with each passage. These items were changed to open-ended items after the first pilot and then dropped after the refinement study. The manual reports that correlation coefficients of .54-.87 were observed between scores based on the multiple-choice items and the current task involving indicating the end of sentences.

TECHNICAL.

Standardization. The standardization sample was collected between January 2013 and March 2014 in 30 states and included 1,274 participants ages 4 to 65+ for the age-based norms and 1,447 individuals ages 4 to 19 for the school-based norms, 737 of whom were included in the fall norms and 710 in the spring. Although the norm sample generally mirrored the 2012 U.S. Census (except for geographical representation), the sample is relatively small, with only about 50 students per grade-level group and age-level groups ranging from 18 to 113 participants. No information about disabilities represented in the norm group is provided. This information is particularly important because one purpose of the test is to inform interventions and services for people with disabilities, and there may be individuals with other types of disabilities besides learning or intellectual (e.g., visual or orthopedic impairments) that may impact performance on the test. A continuous norming procedure along with a weighting procedure designed to correct small discrepancies between the samples and the Census population were used to develop the age- and grade-based norms. All of the standard scores for the norm groups were close to a mean of 100 and a standard deviation of 15 as the test author intended. The Reading Comprehension: Passages test had no participants at any age or grade who fell below a standard score of 70.

Ability-achievement discrepancy scores comparing scores on the AAB with scores on the Wechsler Intelligence Scale for Children, Fourth Edition (WISC-IV; Wechsler, 2003; 16:262); the Wechsler Adult Intelligence Scale, Fourth Edition (WAIS-IV; Wechsler, 2008; 18:151); and the Reynolds Intellectual Assessment Scales, Second Edition (RIAS-2; Reynolds & Kamphaus, 2015; see 138, this volume) are available. The samples for these students were small, however, and the age distribution of participants is not reported.

Reliability. Alpha coefficients for scores from the standardization sample ranged from .74 to .98 for scores on the subtests and from .91 to .97 on the Reading and Total Composite scores. Scores on the Reading Comprehension: Passages and Mathematical Calculation subtests were slightly less consistent than scores on other measures. Test-retest reliability of scores for a sample of 147 individuals tested twice over a 7- to 49-day interval ranged from .81 on Reading Comprehension to .96 on the Total Composite. These internal consistency and test-retest reliability estimates are within the acceptable range in the opinion of this reviewer.

Validity. The test manual describes several sources of evidence of validity of using scores to identify needs of school-aged and adult populations. Concurrent evidence was examined using the following achievement measures: Wide Range Achievement Test 4 (Wilkinson & Robertson, 2006; 18:157); Wechsler Individual Achievement Test, Third Edition (Wechsler, 2009; 18:153); Kaufman Test of Educational Achievement—Second Edition (Kaufman & Kaufman, 2004; 16:124); and Woodcock-Johnson Tests of Achievement, Third Edition (Woodcock, McGrew, & Mather, 2007; 15:281). Sample sizes for these correlations are small (52 or less), and samples are not adequately described to determine age representation. The relationship between Reading Composite scores on the AAB Standard Form and reading comprehension or reading composite scores on these other measures was relatively strong (ranging from .60 to .88) as were the correlations between the AAB Standard Form Total Composite and total composites on other measures (ranging from .64 to .83). The relationships of the subtests with other similar measures (e.g., word recognition, spelling, passage comprehension, math computation) was much more mixed. The AAB Spelling and Letter/Word Reading subtest scores had the strongest relationships. Spelling correlations ranged from .70 to .88, and Letter/Word Reading correlations ranged from .49 to .86. Reading Comprehension: Passages and Mathematical Calculation showed much weaker relationships. Correlations ranged from .22 to .63 for Reading Comprehension: Passages and from .13 to .85 for Math Calculation.

Additional concurrent validity studies examined the relationships between AAB scores and subscores and several intelligence tests. Sample sizes for these studies were larger than for the achievement test studies, but still were relatively small (*N*s = 75-253). These studies also provided normative data for these relationships.

The test author also compared scores on the AAB Standard Form for students with specific learning disabilities, intellectual disabilities, attention-deficit/hyperactivity disorder, and speech and language impairments with those of people in the norm group. Sample sizes ranged from 33 to 68. Score patterns for individuals with these disabilities were generally what would be expected.

COMMENTARY. The processes used to develop the AAB were generally sound. More specific information about the qualifications of the item writers and reviewers would help test users be more confident about score interpretations, as would larger samples in the standardization and validity studies. Sample sizes for the norms calculations were too small, particularly with respect to representation of individuals in specific ethnic/racial groups. For this reason, caution should be used in interpreting scores for students in minority groups. Because only one form of the test is available, change scores should be interpreted carefully.

This reviewer has concerns about whether Reading Comprehension: Passages measures reading comprehension. Not enough evidence was provided that the task of dividing paragraphs into sentences is related to the aspects of reading comprehension as defined in state and national standards (e.g., literal and inferential comprehension, vocabulary knowledge and usage, understanding of cause and effect). Moreover, the validation studies showed weak relationships with some other measure of reading comprehension.

Accessibility and fairness of the test for some students with disabilities and for the growing population of English learners are also concerns. Specific recommendations for accommodations for students with disabilities are not included in the test manual. If test users are left to use their own judgment about what accommodations will compromise the constructs being measured, the accessibility of the AAB may be limited, and score interpretations may be compromised for some examinees. Defining the target population for the AAB as English speaking also limits the utility of the test for both school-aged and adult populations. "English speaking" is not defined in the manual, and because English learners were not included in the standardization sample, it is not clear how scores would be interpretable for these individuals.

SUMMARY. The AAB may provide useful information to inform decisions about instruction and supports for individuals with disabilities. The evidence of validity of score interpretations for the Reading Composite and Total Composite scores is stronger than that for the subscale scores. Because the norm sample is small, other sources of data should be used in conjunction with the AAB scores, and caution should be exercised when interpreting scores of ethnic minorities and individuals with physical disabilities. The AAB would not be practical as a reading screening instrument for K-12 classrooms because of the time required for administration and scoring and the lack of alignment with reading standards. Also, it should not be used with English learners.

REVIEWER'S REFERENCES

Kaufman, A. S., & Kaufman, N. L. (2004). Kaufman Test of Educational Achievement—Second Edition. San Antonio, TX: Pearson.

National Council of Teachers of Mathematics. (2000). Principles and standards for school mathematics. Reston, VA: NCTM.

National Governors Association Center for Best Practices, Council of Chief School Officers. (2010). Common Core State Standards. Washington, DC: Authors.

Reynolds, C. R., & Kamphaus, R. W. (2015). Reynolds Intellectual Assessment Scales, Second Edition. Lutz, FL: Psychological Assessment Resources.

Wechsler, D. (2003). Weschler Intelligence Scale for Children, Fourth Edition. San Antonio, TX: Pearson.

Wechsler, D. (2008). Weschler Adult Intelligence Scale, Fourth Edition. San Antonio, TX: Pearson.

Wechsler, D. (2009). Weschler Individual Achievement Test, Third Edition. San Antonio, TX: Pearson.

Wilkinson, G. S., & Robertson, G. J. (2006). Wide Range Achievement Test 4. Lutz, FL: Psychological Assessment Resources.

Woodcock, R. W., McGrew, K. S., & Mather, N. (2007). Woodcock-Johnson III Normative Update. Rolling Meadows, IL: Riverside.

[2]

Adaptive Behavior Diagnostic Scale.

Purpose: Designed as "a norm-referenced, interview-based rating scale ... to estimate adaptive behavior skills in children and young adults."
Population: Ages 2-21 years.
Publication Date: 2016.
Acronym: ABDS.
Scores, 4: Conceptual Domain, Social Domain, Practical Domain, Adaptive Behavior Composite.
Administration: Individual.
Price Data, 2020: $142 per complete kit including manual (125 pages), Rating Scale Reference Card, and 25 record booklets; $48 per 25 record booklets; $95 per manual.
Time: (25-45) minutes.
Authors: Nils A. Pearson, James R. Patton, and Daniel W. Mruzek.
Publisher: PRO-ED.

Review of the Adaptive Behavior Diagnostic Scale by LEAH M. NELLIS, Dean and Professor, School of Education, Indiana University Kokomo, Kokomo, Indiana, and BRANDON J. WOOD, Doctoral Student, Indiana State University, Terre Haute, IN:

DESCRIPTION. The Adaptive Behavior Diagnostic Scale (ABDS) is a measure of adaptive behavior designed for use with individuals ages 2 to 21 years. It was designed primarily to assess the presence and magnitude of adaptive behavioral functioning for the purpose of identification and eligibility decision making. Additionally, the ABDS was designed to inform the planning of interventions, services, and programs. The ABDS was also developed for use in research on adaptive behavior and intervention effectiveness.

Adaptive behavior is defined by test authors as an "individual's ability to deal with the demands of everyday life in whatever context he or she lives, learns, works, and plays" (manual, p. 1). This definition aligns with that of the *Diagnostic and Statistical Manual of Mental Disorders-Fifth Edition* (*DSM-5*; American Psychiatric Association, 2013) and the American Association on Intellectual and Developmental Disabilities (AAIDD; Schalock et al., 2010). The ABDS was developed to assess three domains of adaptive behavior—Conceptual, Social, and Practical. Each domain includes 50 items rated on a scale of 0 to 4. Scores on the rating scale are associated with corresponding descriptive labels and explanations to help the rater accurately assess an individual's adaptive functioning and assign a rating. Descriptions for the rating scale are as follows: 0 = *cannnot do*, 1 = *can do–but does not*; 2 = *can do–only with help*; 3 = *can do by self–some of the time*; and 4 = *can do by self–almost all of the time or did when younger*. A reference card outlining the rating scale is provided, and the test authors recommend that it be given to respondents before beginning administration. The ABDS also includes a list of 17 "interfering behaviors" that the respondent can indicate as being present or problematic.

The ABDS is described as an interview-based rating scale that is to be completed by a respondent knowledgeable about an individual's level of functioning in the three domains of adaptive behavior based on multiple, regular direct observations over an extended period of time (defined as several weeks). According to the ABDS manual, the method of administration differs for professional and family/parent respondents. Professionals, such as teachers and clinicians, complete the ABDS on their own, as a rating scale. The test authors strongly recommend administering the scale as an interview to parents or family members although, if absolutely necessary, it can be completed as a rating scale using additional guidelines.

Administration begins with the first item in each domain and continues until five consecutive items are rated as 0 = *cannot do*. Administration procedures and guidelines are provided. The test authors suggest that the examiner can elaborate on specific items or answer questions in an effort to ensure that the respondent understands the nature of the item. However, examiners are cautioned against altering the nature or intent of an item. Completion time ranges from 25 to 45 minutes. Supplemental raters can be used if the primary rater has not observed a particular skill/behavior or has not observed it sufficiently (e.g., frequency or duration) to provide a rating and denotes a "*Don't know*" response. Information about both the primary and supplemental rating is recorded on the record form. The test authors recommend that an interview method be used to obtain supplemental ratings; however, they note that if fewer than three items need to be rated by a second respondent, ratings can be completed without an interview.

Ratings are converted to normative scores which include domain index scores, a composite index score, percentile ranks, and age equivalents. Index scores have a mean of 100 and a standard deviation of 15. Six descriptive classifications (*above average, average, low average, low, very low*, and *extremely low*) are provided to aid with interpretation. The test manual includes several case study examples to assist examiners with score interpretation and intervention planning.

DEVELOPMENT. The ABDS was developed to assess adaptive functioning in the domains of Conceptual, Social, and Practical skills. To develop items, the test authors divided each of these three domains into subdomains and corresponding skills. Items were then generated to assess these skills. The subdomains and skills were determined by a "close study of the life skills, transition, and adaptive behavior literature" (manual, p. 58). According to information provided in the test manual, the initial item pool consisted of 235 items for two subdomains (Communication and Functional Academics in the Conceptual domain), 160 items for one subdomain (Social) in the Social domain, and 490 items for eight subdomains (Community Use, Health, Home Living, Leisure, Safety, Self-Care, Self-Direction, and Work) in the Practical domain. This totals 885, although a table in the test manual and the narrative report a total of 974 initial items. These items were used in a pilot study with 90 typically developing individuals ages 3 to 14 years, 27 individuals with intellectual disabilities ages 2 to 21 years, and 31 individuals with autism spectrum disorder ages 2 to 21 years. Mean differences between the typically developing individuals and individuals with known adaptive behavior impairments were analyzed to reduce the number of items to 425.

The 425 items were administered to the normative sample. Responses were analyzed using exploratory factor analysis (EFA), which confirmed the three domains and permitted item assignment to domains based on "items with the strongest correlations representing different levels of difficulty ... that provided the best representation of the skills that are identified by the three domains" (manual, p. 58). Results of the EFA are not included in the test manual. Item-to-domain alignment for the final version of the ABDS is reported in the test manual, although the process for determining this final breakdown is not fully described.

TECHNICAL. The normative sample for the ABDS consisted of 1,061 individuals from 11 states representing the four geographic regions in the United States. Data were collected from fall 2010 through spring 2014 and involved parents and teachers as respondents. The sample is reported to be nationally representative of the school-age population. The sample was 51% male, 78% White, and 20% Hispanic; 53% had a parent education level of high school graduate with some college. Seven distinct categories of disabilities were used to capture data about exceptionality status. The data approximate U.S. figures with, perhaps, an underrepresentation of specific learning disabilities and an overrepresentation of intellectual disability.

Total raw scores are reportedly normally distributed for individuals up to age 10 years. The test authors note that because of ceiling effects, the ABDS is not well suited for use with high-ability populations. Ceiling effects were noted for examinees 9 years old and older on the Conceptual and Social domains and for those 14 years old and older on the Practical domain. Additionally, floor effects were noted for all domains at the youngest age ranges (2-0 to 2-5) as index scores below 70 were not attainable. Normative tables are provided at 3-month intervals for ages 2-0 to 6-11; 6-month intervals for ages 7-0 to 15-11; 1-year intervals for ages 16 and 17; and a 4-year interval for ages 18-0 to 21-11 combined.

Internal consistency reliability was evaluated using coefficient alpha, which was calculated for 17 age intervals using data from the entire normative sample. Averaged alpha coefficients across the age groups were .94 and above for all domain scores and the Adaptive Behavior Composite. Only two coefficients were below .90: Conceptual domain at age 2 years and Practical domain at age 4 years. Alpha coefficients also were reported for subgroups (e.g., gender, race/ethnicity, and exceptionality area) with all at .91 or higher.

Test-retest data were presented for 46 individuals without disabilities in two age groups: 2 to 12 years (*n* = 22) and 13 to 21 years (*n* = 24). The ABDS was completed twice by each individual with an approximate intervening time of two weeks. Subtest standard scores were then correlated. For the combined sample, correlation coefficients were .94 for the Adaptive Behavior Composite, .92 for the Conceptual domain, .93 for the Social domain, and .89 for the Practical domain. The lowest correlation coefficient was .79 for the Practical domain for the 13- to 21-year age group. The test authors interpret these data as evidence of acceptable test-retest reliability. Two members of the publisher's staff independently scored 50 rating scales selected at random from the normative sample. The resulting scores were correlated yielding coefficients of .99 for domains and the composite score, suggesting acceptable evidence of interscorer reliability.

Evidence of content-description, criterion-prediction, and construct-identification validity was provided and summarized in the test manual. The test authors discuss evidence of content validity resulting from the use of a common rating scale/interview format, the previously described process for item development and selection, item analysis, and differential item functioning analysis. The point-biserial correlation technique was used to determine the discriminating power of each test item. Using a criterion of .20, the test authors report data for each domain at 17 age intervals that well exceed the criterion. Item difficulty was analyzed to identify items that are too easy or too difficult using a range of 15% to 85% as acceptable and to arrange items in order of difficulty. Median percentage of difficulty ranged from 6% (Conceptual domain, 2 years) to 97% for multiple domains/ages. The test authors note that these data align with the previously mentioned ceiling effects and the purpose of the instrument to assess limitations in adaptive functioning. Logistic regression was used to investigate differential item functioning for three groups: male versus female, African American versus non-African American, and Hispanic versus non-Hispanic. Using a significance level of .001 and moderate or large effect size, three items were identified for possible removal, all of which involved the African American versus non-African American comparison. The items demonstrated moderate effect sizes and were not removed. The test authors assert that the ABDS items possess "no bias in regard to gender, race, and ethnicity" (manual, p. 65).

Criterion-predictive validity evidence was examined by correlating ABDS scores with Vineland-II Adaptive Behavior Composite scores. It was unclear which form of the Vineland-II was used for this analysis. The composite scores of the two instruments yielded a corrected correlation of .77 indicating a very large relationship. The diagnostic accuracy of the ABDS domain and composite indexes was analyzed through the use of specificity and sensitivity indexes. A composite score with a cutoff at 70 demonstrated the best classification accuracy when predicting the intellectual disability category (.98) with a sensitivity of .85 and a specificity of .99. Evidence of construct validity was also provided showing positive relationships between ADBS scores and chronological age and intelligence. Factor analysis also provided support for the domain structure of the ABDS.

COMMENTARY. The ABDS reflects the current definition and conceptualization of adaptive behavior thus offering a valuable tool for practitioners and clinicians in a variety of settings. Detailed explanations for the points on the rating scale are clear and offer much potential for helping respondents who complete the ABDS via a non-interview format assign more accurate and meaningful ratings. The detailed guidance for involving and documenting the input of supplemental raters is also a valuable addition that is not present in many other similar scales.

One substantial limitation with the development and validation of the ABDS is the apparent lack of attention to its use for culturally and linguistically diverse populations. No information was provided about the English proficiency level of subgroups in the normative sample or guidance regarding the use of the ABDS with non-English-speaking respondents or bilingual individuals. Although analyses were conducted to investigate group differentiation, those analyses appear to be insufficient to address questions about the use of the tool with individuals from culturally and linguistically diverse backgrounds. This issue is significant for use in school settings in particular.

Although the test authors caution against the use of the ABDS with high-ability populations, it is unclear how the restricted distribution of scores impacts the utility of the tool to measure growth in response to intervention.

SUMMARY. The ABDS provides a measure of adaptive behavior that can be administered in either an interview or rating scale format, depending on the respondent. It provides an assessment of the three domains of adaptive behavior—Conceptual, Social, and Practical—and yields domain indexes as well as an overall Adaptive Behavior Composite. The ABDS is best suited for use as a tool to assess limitations in adaptive behavioral functioning to assist with eligibility decision making. The administration procedures and materials are clear and easy to use. Additional research on the utility of the ABDS with culturally and linguistically diverse populations is needed to provide further evidence of reliability and validity.

REVIEWERS' REFERENCES

American Psychiatric Association. (2013). *Diagnostic and statistical manual of mental disorders* (5th ed.). Washington, DC: Author.

Schalock, R., et al. (2010). *Intellectual disability: Definition, classification, and systems of supports* (11th ed.). Washington, DC: American Association on Intellectual and Developmental Disabilities.

Review of the Adaptive Behavior Diagnostic Scale by NATASHA SEGOOL, Associate Professor, and NATALIE POLITIKOS, Associate Professor, Department of Psychology, University of Hartford, West Hartford, CT:

DESCRIPTION. The Adaptive Behavior Diagnostic Scale (ABDS) is a 150-item rating scale that assesses three core domains of adaptive behavior—Conceptual, Social, and Practical—in children ages 2-21. Adaptive Behavior is defined in the test manual as "an individual's ability to deal with the demands of everyday life in whatever context he or she lives, learns, works, and plays" (p. 1). This definition includes social competence, receptive and expressive language, functional academics, and ability to care for oneself. It aligns with recognized adaptive behavior definitions by the American Association on Intellectual and Developmental Disabilities and the *Diagnostic and Statistical Manual of Mental Disorders-Fifth Edition* (*DSM-5*; American Psychiatric Association, 2013).

The most common use of the ABDS is for the assessment and identification of intellectual disabilities in school-aged children. It also may be useful in assessing adaptive skill deficits in children with learning disabilities, attention-deficit/hyperactivity disorder, mental health concerns, or physical disabilities. It aligns with a companion instrument, the Adaptive Behavior Planning Inventory (ABPI), that can be used to design, implement, and monitor adaptive behavior interventions. Examiners should have training in test development, administration, and interpretation. Qualified examiners include school psychologists, social workers, educational diagnosticians, and special educators.

The ABDS can be completed in 25–40 minutes. It uses an interview-style format for family members and a paper-and-pencil format for professional raters such as teachers. When completed as an interview, standard procedures permit examiners to rephrase items as questions and to ask follow-up questions. Respondents should have directly observed the adaptive behavior on a regular basis over an extended period of time. When the primary respondent is unable to answer all questions, supplemental respondents must be identified to complete missing items, or the examiner must estimate ratings based on the available information. Brief instructions are present for supplemental respondents to complete up to three items using a paper-and-pencil format; however, no specific directions are provided for how examiners are to infer ratings if they are unable to identify supplemental respondents.

The ABDS is answered using a 5-point Likert-type scale ranging from *cannot do* to *can do by self–almost all of the time or did when younger*. Each rating is concisely described on a laminated reference card that can be given to respondents during the interview. Respondents are asked to respond regarding the individual's usual behavior rather than his or her best or worst performance. Each of the three domains reaches a ceiling when five consecutive items are scored 0. Once the scale is complete, administrators must add item ratings to calculate raw scores. Appendices in the test manual are then used to convert raw scores to index scores for each domain. The sum of the three index scores is converted into the Adaptive Behavior Composite (ABC) score. Finally, index scores are converted into percentile ranks and described descriptively and as age equivalents.

DEVELOPMENT. The ABDS was developed using a pilot and a norming study. The initial pilot study involved 974 items generated using a literature search of life skills, transition, and adaptive behavior research. Ninety typically developing individuals and 58 individuals with intellectual disabilities or autism spectrum disorder, and who had adaptive behavior impairments completed the pilot. Items found to best discriminate between the two groups were retained in a revised scale comprising 425 items that was administered to the normative sample of 1,061 individuals ages 2–21. Exploratory factor analysis (EFA) was used to select the items with the strongest correlations and different levels of difficulty and assign them into the three adaptive skill domains; item difficulty analyses were used to order items.

TECHNICAL.

Standardization. The ABDS was standardized on 1,061 participants in 11 U.S. states, with at least one state in the West, Northeast, South, and Midwest. Demographic data suggest that participants generally represent national demographics with respect to gender, race/ethnicity, family income, and parental education. Comparison of the sample with National Center for Education Statistics data on the proportion of children within each disability category was not presented. Data were collected from at least 100 participants in each age interval (2-year groupings from ages 2 to 17 and a 4-year grouping for ages 18-21). Each interval generally appears representative of the U.S. population, though there is an undersampling of students with disabilities for ages 2-7 years and ages 14-15 years.

Reliability. The three ABDS domains demonstrated strong internal consistency, with alpha coefficients ranging from .89 to .98 across 17 age intervals. The test authors provide a clear explanation of standard errors of measurement when discussing internal consistency and provide examples for calculating an individual's domain scores with 68%, 95%, and 99% confidence intervals. Two-week test-retest reliability was assessed using a small sample of 46 children without disabilities. Overall, test-retest reliability estimates (*r*s = .79-.98) for the three adaptive behavior domains were strong, with somewhat lower values among younger children. Finally, interscorer reliability was reported to be very strong (*r* = .99) when evaluated by having two members of the test publisher's staff calculate scores using 50 test protocols. Interrater reliability, which includes more than correct scoring, should also be examined, especially because the ABDS is completed using an interview format.

Validity. Content validity evidence was examined by describing the qualitative process of identifying possible items using an exhaustive literature review and using EFA to select items. The test authors provide a summary of median item difficulty at 17 age intervals to illustrate that as age increases, the proportion of items passed increases. A ceiling effect begins at age 9 for the Conceptual and Social domains and at age 14 for the practical domain. Differential item functioning (DIF) analyses were used to examine items for bias. Seven items demonstrated DIF. Of these, three yielded moderate effect sizes, indicating that these three items were answered differently for African American versus non-African American participants. The test authors concluded that there was no bias in the scale and retained these items.

Criterion validity evidence was evaluated by examining the strength of correlations between the Vineland-II Adaptive Behavior Composite and the ABDS domain scores (*r*s = .61-.65) and the ABC (.77) using a sample of 28 participants. Further, differences between the mean composite scores on the Vineland-II and ABDS were not significant, suggesting that the ABDS and Vineland-II composites result in similar evaluations. The diagnostic accuracy of the scale in identifying intellectual disabilities was also assessed. Using the *DSM-5* criteria of < 70 for one of the domains or the ABC, the ABDS demonstrated sensitivity of .92 and specificity of .97, suggesting it does a good job identifying those with and without an intellectual disability. The test authors clearly state that the ABDS should be used as part of a comprehensive assessment and that converging data must be used in identifying any disability.

Construct validity was evidenced through (a) large correlations (*r*s = .79-.87) between the mean domain scores and age to show that adaptive skills increase with age; (b) demonstrating that typically developing participants score in the average range whereas individuals with autism spectrum disorder or intellectual disability do not; (c) a moderate correlation coefficient (.63) between IQ and the ABC; (d) strong correlations (*r*s = .71-.73) between the three domains; (e) the three domains loading onto a single factor; and (f) median item discrimination values ranging from .34 to .81.

COMMENTARY. The ABDS is unusual in its design as a single-form interview assessing adaptive skills. Unlike established assessments such as the Vineland-II or ABAS-II, which have multiple different rating forms for caregivers/teachers and parents and for individuals of different ages, the ABDS uses a single interview form for rating individuals ages 2-21. Strengths of the ABDS include its development using a comprehensive review of theory, research, and other adaptive behavior assessments and strong evidence of internal consistency and construct validity. In these reviewers' opinion, four weaknesses deserve mention. First, the test authors note several times that the ABDS is aligned with the ABPI, which can be used to design, implement, and monitor adaptive behavior interventions. However, no evidence supporting the use of the ABDS with the ABPI is provided. Second, although the test authors acknowledge that age equivalents have been extensively criticized, they provide them, noting that some schools mandate their use and that they aid in determining entry points on the ABPI. Given concerns about misinterpretation of age equivalents, it is recommended that they be removed from the examiner record booklet. Third, the three items identified as potentially biased should be considered for removal. Finally, the rating scale itself is mildly challenging to read and score with small font, long rating descriptions, and small scoring squares for recording subtotals. [Editor's note: The test publisher advises that although the logistic regression procedure revealed three items with moderate effect size differences between African American and non-African American examinees, the differences in standard score means reported for these subgroups were within 1 standard error of measurement, an indication that the groups performed equally well.]

SUMMARY. The ABDS is a 150-item scale assessing three areas of adaptive functioning: Conceptual, Social, and Practical. The scale is easy to score and provides index scores in the three domains as well as a composite score of overall adaptive behavior. The scale is completed by one respondent who has directly observed the person's adaptive behaviors. It was normed using 1,061 participants from 11 states. The test authors present solid evidence of internal consistency, criterion validity, and construct validity. The ABDS appears to be a promising measure of adaptive behavior. Future research on the scale's use with the ABPI and evaluating interrater reliability in recording interview responses is encouraged.

REVIEWERS' REFERENCE

American Psychiatric Association. (2013). *Diagnostic and statistical manual of mental disorders* (5th ed.). Washington, DC: Author.

[3]

Adaptive Employee Personality Test.

Purpose: Designed as a personality assessment for use "in global high-volume screening, professional-level assessment, and leadership development."

Population: Prospective employees and job candidates.

Publication Date: 2017.

Acronym: ADEPT-15.

Scores, 21: 15 personality aspects in 6 styles: Task (Drive, Structure), Adaptation (Conceptual, Flexibility, Mastery), Achievement (Ambition, Power), Interaction (Assertiveness, Liveliness), Emotional (Composure, Positivity, Awareness), Teamwork (Cooperation, Sensitivity, Humility).

Administration: Individual or group.

Price Data: Available from publisher.

Foreign Language Editions: Available in Afrikaans, Arabic, Czech, French, Spanish, German, Haitian-Creole, Hebrew, Hindi, Hungarian, Indonesian, Indonesian-Malay, Italian, Japanese, Korean, Marathi, Polish, Portuguese, Romanian, Russian, Chinese-Simplified, Chinese-Traditional, Swahili, Tagalog, Thai, Turkish, and Vietnamese.

Time: (25) minutes.

Comments: Computer adaptive test; administered online.

Authors: Anthony S. Boyce (test and technical manual), Pat Caputo (test), Jeff Conway (test), and John F. Capman (technical manual).

Publisher: Aon Hewitt.

Review of the Adaptive Employee Personality Test by JOHN K. HAWLEY, Engineering Psychologist, U.S. Army Research Laboratory, Ft. Bliss Field Element, Ft. Bliss, TX:

DESCRIPTION. The Adaptive Employee Personality Test (ADEPT-15) is a broad-based personality assessment tool developed by consulting firm Aon Hewitt for use in global high-volume screening, professional-level assessment, and leadership development. The ADEPT-15 is appropriate for use early in the recruitment process to screen applicants prior to more resource-intensive selection activities such as resume screening and interviews. It can also be used as an on-boarding tool to highlight potential employee developmental areas. These might include enhancing "self-insight" and "facilitating introspection" (manual, p. 72) regarding how personality influences day-to-day behavior on the job.

Technical documentation (provided in the ADEPT-15 Technical Report, 2nd ed., 2017) notes that test development followed two critical paths: The first involved developing a personality model based on the "latest personality and leadership research" (manual, p. 5) that would be useful in the company's world-wide consulting practice. The second step required developing and validating a computer adaptive test (CAT) to "accurately and efficiently assess the aspects of personality defined in the model" (manual, p. 5). The resulting Aon Hewitt Personality Model consists of 15 aspects of personality, 10 of which map directly to the well-established and generally accepted five-factor model (FFM) of personality. Five additional personality aspects reflecting traits judged critical to successful job performance in leadership roles, but "not captured in the traditional FFM" (manual, p. 5) also are included in the assessment tool. These additional aspects are Humility, Awareness, Power, Ambition, and Mastery. The 15 personality traits comprising the ADEPT-15 are grouped into six higher-order personality styles, denoted as Task, Adaptation, Achievement, Interaction, Emotional, and Teamwork. The technical documentation for the ADEPT-15 provides additional description and information on the test's component personality traits and styles.

The ADEPT-15 requires examinees to respond to multidimensional forced-choice items consisting of paired statements. "Items are scored and tailored to each candidate on the basis of both the multi-unidimensional pairwise preference (MUPP) and generalized graded unfolding model (GGUM) item response theory (IRT) models" (manual, p. 5). This approach results in an assessment tool that has some favorable psychometric properties, is resistant to faking and impression management, and allows for secure and efficient administration. The test consists of a 100-item assessment, which can be completed in about 25 minutes and taken using any web-connected device. The ADEPT-15 is also designed to be modular. This feature supports the administration of shorter, tailored versions of the test consisting of subsets of the available personality dimensions. Test reports are straightforward to interpret and available in a variety of formats. Formats range from a one-page Selcction report intended for recruiters and managers, to a multiple-page Styles report providing personality information related to person-job fit. A one-page Aspects report for use by qualified coaches to facilitate employee learning and development also is available. The Aspects report is focused on an examinee's results on each of the 15 personality aspects addressed in the ADEPT-15.

DEVELOMENT. "Prior to designing and developing a personality assessment tool, a clear conceptualization of the personality model targeted for assessment is required" (manual, p. 11). As noted, the conceptual foundation for Aon Hewitt's personality model is the well-researched and widely accepted FFM of personality. The test development team also identified and included personality traits not captured using the FFM, but particularly relevant for managerial and leadership assessment—the core of Aon Hewitt's consulting practice. The result was the Aon Hewitt Personality Model consisting of 15 personality constructs organized into six higher-order personality styles.

Given the personality traits targeted for assessment, ADEPT-15 development proceeded in the standard fashion. The test development process consisted of personality statement writing and initial review, statement calibration, and final statement and item (statement pair) review and screening. All of these developmental procedures were performed or supervised by PhD-level industrial-organizational psychologists. The test development team also performed a number of additional studies and test refinement activities related to issues such as statement and item social desirability, test length, the number of items per personality dimension, statement exposure constraints, and the number of items necessary to estimate reliably trait scores across all 15 personality dimensions. A final total of 1,470 unique personality statements was selected and calibrated to target the 15 personality aspects underlying the assessment. Monte Carlo simulation studies were used to inform final ADEPT-15 test parameters and confirm that a 100-item assessment was capable of accurately recovering normative trait scores.

TECHNICAL. ADEPT-15 norms are provided for 18 countries and five regions. A global norm is also provided. All norms are based on results from professional, managerial, and executive level employees with college degrees. Follow-on comparisons indicated there were no substantive differences between selection (pre-employment takers) and developmental (on-board takers) samples. Thus, country, region, and global norms combine results from both selection and developmental samples.

Reliability information is reported in terms of test-retest reliability as opposed to traditional test theory estimates of reliability such as coefficient alpha or split-half indices. Test technical documentation asserts that the assessment's multidimensional forced-choice adaptive format supports this choice. Test-retest reliability estimates for the 15 personality dimensions obtained from a sample of 112 "honest" (manual, p. 30) test takers completing the assessment once and then again after a 2-week delay ranged from .44 to .73. Test-retest reliability coefficients by personality dimension in this range are indicative of at best moderate overall reliability. Reliability coefficients are much stronger when considered at the Style or personality composite level. Style reliability values ranged from .66 to .77. The test's technical documentation asserts that moderate reliability coefficients at the aspect level are an artifact of removing the social desirability response bias inherent in most other types of personality tests.

Validity evidence for the ADEPT-15 is addressed in terms of the three traditional components of validity evidence: content, construct, and criterion-related. Content evidence of validity is based on the comprehensive manner in which the ADEPT-15's underlying personality construct (the Aon Hewitt Personality Model) was defined and the rigorous way in which personality statements and items consistent with that model were developed and screened. Construct evidence of validity was investigated in terms of the underlying factor structure of the instrument and the test's relationship with other tests measuring both similar and dissimilar constructs. Results indicated that the ADEPT-15's underlying factor structure is consistent with theoretical expectations. Factor structure results can provide end users with information regarding the potential incremental validity the aspects can provide over and above each other in predicting relevant performance criteria. The personality aspects assessed in the ADEPT-15 demonstrated some substantial correlations with external measures of similar constructs and exhibited strong discriminant validity versus unrelated constructs—including cognitive ability. Criterion-related evidence of validity is provided in terms of results from 21 concurrent criterion-related validation studies based on 6,200 job incumbents from 16 organizations across five countries and 36 different jobs or job families. The job performance criteria used across all of these studies were based on an up-front job analysis mapping of ADEPT-15 personality aspects to job competencies followed by supervisor performance ratings of incumbent performance in most of those areas. Criterion-related results indicated that the ADEPT-15 is moderately predictive of a test taker's on-the-job performance, although the percentage of high correlations was rather modest.

COMMENTARY. The ADEPT-15 is based on a personality assessment foundation provided by the well-known and widely researched FFM of personality. The test development team extended the underlying FFM foundation by adding personality dimensions relevant to Aon Hewitt's consulting practice but not addressed in the FFM. The ADEPT-15 is easy to administer and relatively short (100 items requiring about 25 minutes to take), and interpretation of test results is straightforward. The test was developed and validated in accord with generally accepted practices within the field of industrial-organizational psychology. Test reliability assessed in terms of test-retest reliability indices is in the moderate to acceptable range. Construct-related evidence of validity indicates that the test adequately measures what it was intended to measure—the personality dimensions defined in Aon Hewitt's Personality Model. Convergent and discriminant validity results indicate that test results correlate with results from conceptually similar instruments, while not being correlated with unrelated constructs. One particularly desirable aspect of the ADEPT-15 is that personality results are not confounded with cognitive ability. Criterion-related evidence of validity indicates that test scores are correlated with independent supervisor ratings of on the job performance in jobs relying on managerial skills and leadership abilities. In this reviewer's opinion, the detailed technical documentation provided with the test, and providing the basis for this review, represents a primer on how a personality assessment tool such as the ADEPT-15 should be developed.

SUMMARY. Aon Hewitt's ADEPT-15 personality assessment test was developed to support the company's world-wide human resources consulting practice specializing in managerial and leadership positions. The conceptual foundation of the test is the well-known and widely researched five-factor model (FFM) of personality. This FFM foundation is supplemented with additional personality dimensions related to managerial and leadership performance. The test is easily administered using any web-connected device and relatively short both in terms of time and the number of items. Test results are reported in a straightforward manner. Results from the ADEPT-15 can be used for any of the purposes suggested in the accompanying technical documentation. These uses primarily involve selection and follow-on development for high-level employees.

Review of the Adaptive Employee Personality Test by STEVEN V. ROUSE, Professor of Psychology, Pepperdine University, Malibu, CA:

DESCRIPTION. The Adaptive Employee Personality Test (ADEPT-15) was developed by Aon Hewitt Consulting (an international human resources company) to provide a measure of several different personality traits relevant in workplace settings for both career development and applicant selection purposes. This online-administered omnibus inventory assesses 15 different traits, rationally clustered into six broader categories: Adaptation, Task, Teamwork, Emotional, Interaction, and Achievement. The test development team considered 10 of these traits to be related to traits from the five-factor model of personality, but five were created to assess traits that were considered by the development team to be important in work settings but not fully situated in the five-factor model, such as Ambition and Mastery.

Although the ADEPT-15 item pool includes a total of 1,470 statements, only a small portion of these statements are included in any specific administration. Using computer adaptive testing (CAT) technology based on item response theory (IRT), the test system presents the test taker with a series of forced-choice pairs, in which each option of the pair reflects a different trait. During an administration, the test taker is presented with 100 pairs of forced-choice options; after each set of five pairs, the test system selects new statements to pair with each other, balanced for social desirability ratings and reflecting the high or low level of each trait suggested by the test taker's previous responses. This approach allows for an efficient assessment of 15 traits based on 100 responses, and the administration process is clear and user-friendly.

Feedback for each of the 15 scales is provided in the form of normally distributed stanine scores (that is, ranging from 1 to 9), with the ends of each continuum anchored by a small number of brief descriptors. For example, Ambition is described as a measure of the dimension "contented vs. striving," with low levels anchored by the phrases "good work-life balance, less concerned with career progression" and the high end anchored by the phrases "career-focused, goal-oriented, obsessive." Reports of scores are available both in brief forms providing just the scores and descriptors, or longer interpretive forms that provide five or six bullet-point interpretive comments and two or three brief interpretive paragraphs for each score. The reports are clear and easy to read and understand.

DEVELOPMENT. A rigorous item development process was used to create the large pool of statements available for each administration. The development team followed a multistep process, in which trait-relevant statements were written; independently evaluated to ensure a range of high, medium, and low levels of each trait; reviewed to retain an eighth-grade reading level; and independently reviewed for relevance to the particular trait. Two specific aspects of the initial statement development process were notable. First, the development team also had each item reviewed specifically to consider language that might be biasing in regard to age, gender, race, ethnicity, and disability. Second, items were retained only if they were successfully translated into Spanish and back-translated without losing meaning.

After the creation of the initial statement pool, data were collected from online samples in order to assess IRT parameters such as discrimination indices, and statements were removed if these initial statistics suggested poor psychometric functioning. New data were collected for each remaining statement to assess the degree of social desirability bias. Based on these data sets (and data representing social desirability levels of trait strength levels for each of the 1,470 statements), the test system algorithmically selects pairs of statements to present in 100 forced-choice items.

TECHNICAL.

Standardization. The ADEPT-15 normative samples for some international regions are very large: 14,605 participants for Asia; 5,197 for South America; 3,258 for North America; 929 for the Middle East; and 486 for Europe. Although these samples can be broken down to provide country-level norms, in some cases these divisions result in relatively small samples, such as a sample of 192 for the United Kingdom. Although the test development team conscientiously reported demographic data for the various samples used for initial development and validation purposes, the manual neglects to provide information about gender, age, race, ethnicity, educational attainment, or any other demographic variables for these normative samples, preventing the test user from being confident in the representativeness of these samples.

Reliability. The manual correctly notes that internal consistency estimates are not meaningful for tests that use CAT technology because only a fraction of the statements for each trait are used in a given administration, and each statement is paired against another statement reflecting a different trait. However, 2-week test-retest correlations for the 15 scales were reported, and they ranged from .44 to .73, with a median of .66. Because IRT methods were used for the development of the statement pool, standard IRT statistics such as item information indices would have been helpful for evaluating psychometric strength.

Validity. Several lines of validation evidence were provided by the test development team. First, correlations were provided between each score and extant scores judged to measure comparable personality traits; these correlations, corrected for unreliability, ranged from .28 to .80, with a median of .65. Second, because of their frequent use in workplace settings, scores from the Hogan Personality Inventory (HPI; Hogan & Hogan, 2007) and the Motives, Values, and Preferences Inventory (MVPI; Hogan & Hogan, 2010) were correlated with the most relevant ADEPT-15 scores. These values ranged from .08 to .48 for the HPI and from .13 to .53 for the MVPI. Third, discriminant validation was demonstrated in the negligible correlations between ADEPT-15 scores and measures of cognitive ability, with correlations between -.15 and .11 indicating the expected independence between personality traits and cognitive ability. Fourth, the structure of the ADEPT-15 was validated by the results of a confirmatory factor analysis, with fit indices suggesting that the 15 scales were appropriately grouped into six different clusters. Finally, 21 different criterion-related studies were conducted to determine the degree to which ADEPT-15 scores correlated with real-world indicators of job performance in areas ranging from consumer retail to hotel management. For each performance variable, specific ADEPT-15 scores were identified as most relevant, and a composite score was created by combining these scales; these composite scores were correlated with the performance variable scores.

COMMENTARY. Several positive characteristics differentiate the ADEPT-15 from other omnibus personality inventories developed for workplace settings. First, it benefits from a rigorous test development process. Second, the IRT and CAT methods take advantage of modern psychometric developments. Third, the forced-choice format distinguishes the test from commonly used Likert-based measures, and this method is likely to make the test less susceptible to response bias. Fourth, it benefits from a large and internationally diverse normative sample. Fifth, care was taken to utilize fair language.

SUMMARY. The ADEPT-15 is an internet-administered computerized adaptive measure of 15 personality traits that are relevant to workplace performance. Developed using rigorous contemporary methods and using a forced-choice format, it is a promising addition to the field of applied personality assessment.

REVIEWER'S REFERENCES

Hogan, R., & Hogan, J. (2007). *Hogan Personality Inventory manual.* Tulsa, OK: Hogan Assessment Systems.

Hogan, R., & Hogan, J. (2010). *Motives, Values, Preferences Inventory manual.* Tulsa, OK: Hogan Assessment Systems.

[4]

ADHD Rating Scale-5.

Purpose: Designed to "provide clinicians with a method to obtain parent and teacher ratings regarding the frequency of each of the symptoms of ADHD based on DSM-5 criteria."

Population: Ages 5-17.

Publication Dates: 1998-2016.

Scores, 3: Inattention, Hyperactivity-Impulsivity, Total.

Administration: Individual.

Levels, 2: Child (ages 5-10), Adolescent (ages 11-17).

Forms, 2: Home, School.

Price Data, 2020: $131.25 per manual (2016, 136 pages) including reproducible forms (may be copied at no extra cost for repeated use).

Foreign Language Edition: Home forms available in Spanish.

Time: [5] minutes.

Authors: George J. DuPaul, Thomas J. Power, Arthur D. Anastopoulos, and Robert Reid.

Publisher: Guilford Publications, Inc.

Cross References: For reviews by Jill Ann Jenkins and Cederick O. Lindskog of an earlier edition based on DSM-IV criteria, see 15:7.

Review of the ADHD Rating Scale–5 by LAURIE FORD, Associate Professor, and ROCHELLE PICARDO, Master's Student, School Psychology, University of British Columbia, Vancouver, BC, Canada:

DESCRIPTION. The ADHD Rating Scale–5 is an 18-item paper and pencil rating scale that aims to provide information about symptoms suggestive of attention-deficit/hyperactivity disorder (ADHD) in children and adolescents. Completed by either the child's parent or teacher, this instrument has different versions for home and school, as well as forms for children (ages 5-10) and adolescents (ages 11-17). The Home Version is available in English and Spanish; the School Version is available only in English. As with the previous edition, the scale is intended for use as part of a comprehensive assessment of ADHD that may include additional components such as diagnostic interviews, direct observations, and direct child testing (Barkley, 2015; DuPaul & Stoner, 2014). The items on the ADHD Rating Scale–5 were adapted directly from the *Diagnostic and Statistical Manual of Mental Disorders* (5th ed.; *DSM-5*; American Psychiatric Association, 2013) to allow clinicians to translate the information obtained from this scale to *DSM-5* diagnostic criteria for ADHD, a very useful feature for diagnosis.

In both versions of the ADHD Rating Scale–5, there are two symptom subscales, Inattention and Hyperactivity-Impulsivity, each comprising nine items. Respondents rate their responses to items regarding the frequency of behavior on a 4-point scale from 0 (*never or rarely*) to 3 (*very often*). Each version of the scale yields a Total score and scores for the Inattention and Hyperactivity-Impulsivity subscales. In addition to the symptom subscales, the ADHD Rating Scale–5 includes items reflecting six domains of impairment that are common among children with ADHD: relationships with significant others, peer relationships, academic functioning, behavioral functioning, homework functioning, and self-esteem. Each of the six impairment items is rated once after rating Inattention symptom items and again after rating Hyperactivity-Impulsivity symptom items. Informants are asked, "How much do the above behaviors cause problems for your child/this student?" Responses are recorded on a 4-point scale from 0 (*no problem*) to 3 (*severe problem*). No information is provided in the test manual regarding how long it takes to complete or score the measure.

DEVELOPMENT. Limited details specific to the development of this edition are provided in the test manual. However, the primary development efforts for the ADHD Rating Scale–5 are anchored in the previous edition. The test authors do not include details about the previous edition (i.e., the ADHD Rating Scale–IV) in the manual for the current edition but acknowledge the basic format of the test follows the previous edition. Content was updated to reflect changes in ADHD diagnosis with publication of the *DSM-5*. A review of the ADHD Rating Scale–IV provides information about the instrument's original development (Jenkins, 2003). The major focus of the ADHD Rating Scale–5 was to create items that parallel *DSM-5* diagnostic criteria. Changes to this edition also included changes in the wording of some items. For example, wording of some items for adolescents was adjusted so that the items would be more developmentally appropriate to that age range. In addition, given the renewed emphasis on the importance of functional impairment in the assessment of ADHD in determining the impact on functioning in the home and school settings, items reflecting impairment due to inattention symptoms and impairment due to hyperactive-impulsive symptoms were added. Two different normative samples, one for parent ratings and one for teacher ratings, were also added.

TECHNICAL.

Standardization. The normative sample for the ADHD Rating Scale–5, Home Version was a representative sample of 2,079 parents and guardians who completed symptom and impairment ratings for one of their children, selected at random using a web-based survey. The parents and guardians were 59.1% White and non-Hispanic, married (78.3%) with at least a high school education level (86.4%), employed (72.3%), and recruited from metropolitan (86.4%) and non-metropolitan (13.6%) areas of the United States. The sample for the Home Version is representative of the U.S. population in terms of age, sex, race/ethnicity, family income, and geographic distribution. The School Version was normed on 1,070 teachers, each of whom completed symptom and impairment ratings for two (one boy, one girl) randomly selected students in their class via web-based survey. Predominately White and non-Hispanic (87.3%), the teachers had a mean years of teaching experience of 17.88, and they were recruited from across the United States. The majority of the students they rated were in general education classrooms (83.2%); 54.8% were from White, non-Hispanic backgrounds. Some racial and ethnic differences in parent and teacher ratings were reportedly found, but normative data were not presented by race or ethnic group because there was an insufficient number of participants for the normative data to be stratified by age, gender, and racial/ethnic group. These differences are discussed in the test manual and should be reviewed and taken into consideration when interpreting the data. Normative data for both the Home and School Versions are provided for eight gender-by-age groups (5-7 years; 8-10 years; 11-13 years; 14-17 years).

A rich discussion of the gender, age, and race/ethnic group difference prevalence rates and the utility of the impairment ratings is provided in the test manual. This information is very useful in understanding the context of the rates provided. The prevalence rates used in the ADHD Rating Scale–5 are higher than the prevalence described in the *DSM-5*. The test authors indicate, and this reviewer agrees, that this is likely because the rates seen in the normative sample are based on the ADHD symptom rating plus impairment from one informant (teacher or parent), and not from all of the *DSM-5* criteria. As a result, the test authors indicate that the rates on the measure may be best thought of as the upper limits of the prevalence of ADHD in the general population. This is an important consideration when interpreting test results.

Reliability. The internal consistency reliability for Total, Inattention, and Hyperactivity-Impulsivity scores across both versions (Home and School) and age groups (child/adolescent) of the ADHD Rating Scale–5 is strong with alpha coefficients ranging from .89 to .97. Test-retest reliability was calculated from data obtained approximately six weeks apart and was also satisfactory overall. However, the Pearson product-moment correlations for each of the three scores (Total, Inattention, and Hyperactivity-Impulsivity) varied depending on the version and age group. Correlation coefficients varied from .61 to .93, with the lowest value observed for ratings of Hyperactivity-Impulsivity on the Home Version for adolescents. Interrater agreement coefficients between parent and teacher ratings of children were in the moderate range, with coefficients as follows: Total score = .68; Inattention = .77; Hyperactivity-Impulsivity = .48. For ratings of adolescents, interrater agreement was mixed, with coefficients as follows: Total score = .38; Inattention = .46; Hyperactivity-Impulsivity = .01. In general, the teacher ratings have greater stability over time than the parent ratings in most areas, but differences in stability across the two ratings are noted across the age range of the test. The differences in the parent and teacher ratings point to the importance of having both parent and teacher ratings.

Validity. Support for the predictive validity of the ADHD Rating Scale–5 was provided with both clinic- and school-based studies. The results of studies in both settings indicate that the Inattention subscale differentiated children with ADHD/Inattentive and ADHD/Combined from a control group. The Hyperactivity-Impulsivity subscale differentiated children with ADHD/Combined from controls and from children with ADHD/Inattentive. The predictive value of parent and teacher ratings varied depending on the setting. Although parent and teacher ratings were both significantly predictive of diagnostic status in the clinic-based studies, teacher ratings were better at predicting ADHD presentation than parent ratings. The school-based study found equal contributions by parents and teachers with regard to the Inattention subscale, but parent ratings on the Hyperactivity-Impulsivity subscale were more accurate than teacher ratings.

Factor analytic studies detailed in the test manual provide good support for the structure of the various scales, versions, and domains with greater support for the two subscales (Hyperactivity-Impulsivity, Inattention) than any further breakdown. Criterion validity was evaluated by calculating Pearson product-moment correlations between the ADHD Rating Scale–5 Home Version and the Conners 3rd Edition (Conners 3) Parent rating scale, and the School Version and the Conners 3 Teacher rating scale. Correlation coefficients between the ADHD Rating Scale–5 Home Version and the Conners 3 Parent rating scale ranged from .01 to .85, with 28 of the 36 values calculated achieving statistical significance. Correlations between the School Version and the Conners 3 Teacher rating scale were more robust, as evidenced by coefficients ranging from .46 to .89; all 45 values calculated achieved statistical significance. Moreover, on both versions of the ADHD Rating Scale–5, Inattention symptom ratings were more strongly related to Conners Attention related factors (e.g., DSM-Inattentive, Inattention) than with Hyperactivity-Impulsivity related factors. In contrast, Hyperactivity-Impulsivity ratings on the

ADHD Rating Scale–5 were more strongly related to Conners Hyperactivity-Impulsivity related factors than to Attention related factors.

COMMENTARY. The ADHD Rating Scale–5 represents an update of the ADHD Rating Scale–IV and is, overall, a brief, easy-to-score, and useful tool for supplementing comprehensive assessments of ADHD. It is an efficient rating scale, and the two versions, Home and School, are important assets. Its items and scales align well with *DSM-5* criteria for ADHD diagnosis and provide reliable and valid information about ADHD symptoms in children and adolescents.

The standardization sample parallels other norm-referenced and standardized instruments. The test authors point to the representativeness of the sample across a number of variables and geographic regions, but the informants are largely White and educated with parents typically married and teachers very experienced. Although this sample may be representative of the larger U.S. population, it may be less representative of the demographics of parents who have children with ADHD and teachers with these students in their classrooms as some research points to higher incidence of ADHD reported in single parent homes and by less experienced teachers. On every score derived from teacher ratings (Total, Inattention, and Hyperactivity-Impulsivity), African American children received higher scores than their White and Hispanic counterparts; differences between White and Hispanic children were not significant. On scores derived from parent ratings, African American children and White children received significantly higher total scores than Hispanic children; on the Inattention subscale, White children received significantly higher scores than Hispanic children; and on the Hyperactivity-Impulsivity subscale African American children received significantly higher scores than White and Hispanic children. Such differences raise concerns that this instrument is not yet sensitive to potential respondent bias in rating ADHD symptoms in children from diverse backgrounds. Some care may be warranted when interpreting the scores of students from culturally and linguistically diverse backgrounds. However, the foundation of the technical characteristics reported indicate as a brief measure used in the context of a larger comprehensive assessment with both parents and teachers the measure likely would be very beneficial.

SUMMARY. The ADHD Rating Scale–5 is a rating scale that is easy to use and score and that provides useful, *DSM-5* specific information about ADHD symptoms in children and adolescents. It has demonstrated utility in both clinic and school settings. The test authors have provided strong support for the psychometric properties of the instrument, which are discussed in the user-friendly test manual. The opportunity for ratings from both parents and teachers and for both children and adolescents is a strength of the measure. The ADHD Rating Scale–5 demonstrates satisfactory reliability and good support for its validity. It will be of primary interest to clinicians familiar with *DSM-5* criteria for ADHD who are looking for a rating scale to help them collect information based directly on these criteria to complement their comprehensive assessment of children and adolescents.

REVIEWERS' REFERENCES

American Psychiatric Association. (2013). *Diagnostic and statistical manual of mental disorders* (5th ed.). Washington, DC: Author.

Barkley, R. A. (Ed.). (2015). *Attention-deficit hyperactivity disorder: A handbook for diagnosis & treatment* (4th ed.). New York, NY: Guilford.

DuPaul, G. J., & Stoner, G. (2014). *ADHD in the schools: Assessment and intervention strategies* (3rd ed.). New York, NY: Guilford.

Jenkins, J. A. (2003). [Test review of the ADHD Rating Scale–IV]. In B. S. Plake, J. C. Impara, & R. A. Spies, (Eds.), *The fifteenth mental measurements yearbook* (pp. 19-23). Lincoln, NE: Buros Institute of Mental Measurements.

Review of the ADHD Rating Scale–5 by TRACY L. PASKIEWICZ, Lecturer, School Psychology Program, University of Massachusetts-Boston, Boston, MA:

DESCRIPTION. The ADHD Rating Scale–5 is an informant-based measure developed to provide clinicians with a method of obtaining parent and teacher ratings regarding the frequency of ADHD symptoms based on *DSM-5* diagnostic criteria. It is appropriate for children and adolescents ages 5-17; there is a Home Version to obtain parent ratings and a School Version to obtain teacher ratings. The Home Version is available in both English and Spanish. Both versions include items that are based on the diagnostic criteria for attention-deficit/hyperactivity disorder (ADHD) as outlined in the *Diagnostic and Statistical Manual of Mental Disorders* (5th ed.; *DSM-5*; American Psychiatric Association, 2013). Separate forms exist for children (ages 5-10) and adolescents (ages 11-17), reflecting *DSM-5* criteria of slightly different symptom descriptors for these age groups.

Informants are asked to rate the target individual's behaviors over the previous 6 months (or since the beginning of the school year, if a teacher has known the student less than 6 months). Ratings are provided on a 4-point Likert scale reflecting frequency of symptomatic behaviors: *never/rarely, sometimes, often, very often.*

The instrument includes two subscales with items that assess inattentive as well as hyperactive-impulsive symptoms. Also, there are impairment scales included in the questionnaire. These impairment items cover the *DSM-5* requirement for impairment in at least one functional area (e.g., relationships with family members/teachers, relationships with peers, academic functioning, behavioral functioning, homework functioning, self-esteem). Raw scores are converted to percentile scores based on the child's gender and age. Three scores are derived: Inattention, Hyperactivity-Impulsivity, and Total. Cutoff points are recommended for screening and identification purposes.

The test manual provides information about development and standardization, collection of normative data, factor structure, psychometric properties, and interpretive uses.

DEVELOPMENT. The current edition of the *DSM* describes ADHD as a two-dimensional disorder, reflecting problems with inattention or problems with hyperactivity and impulsivity (or both). In addition, there is a requirement for impaired functioning across two or more settings (e.g., home, work, school). The ADHD Rating Scale–5 manual includes information regarding instrument development, including confirmatory factor analyses to examine the fit of the instrument to the theoretical two-factor *DSM* model. On reviewing the test items, they closely describe symptoms of ADHD as listed in the *DSM-5*. The development of the Spanish version for parents underwent a thorough translation and expert review process as described in the test manual.

TECHNICAL.

Standardization. Data from two separate normative samples were collected; the same children were not included in both the parent ratings and the teacher ratings. No information was provided in the test manual regarding whether children in the samples had a confirmed diagnosis of ADHD.

The normative sample of the Home Version was drawn via probability-based sampling of addresses from the U.S. Postal Service. The sample consisted of 2,079 parents/guardians (1,131 women, 948 men). The sample was predominantly White, non-Hispanic (64.1%) and was drawn from all regions of the United States. English was spoken in most (89.4%) households. The sample reflects a more affluent segment of the population (median income from $60,000 to $75,000). The children rated in this sample ranged in age from 5 to 17 and come from White, non-Hispanic (53.9%); Black, non-Hispanic (13.1%); Asian, non-Hispanic (5.7%); Hispanic (23.4%), and other (3.9%) backgrounds. The test authors contend this sample is representative of the U.S. population in terms of child age, sex, race/ethnicity, family income, and geographic distribution.

The normative sample of the School Version was drawn with assistance from a national research firm. The sample consisted of 1,070 teachers (766 women, 304 men) who were predominantly White, non-Hispanic (87.3%). The teacher sample was recruited from all regions of the United States and included general and special education teachers. The students in this sample (N = 2,140, with equal male/female distribution) ranged in age from 5 to 17 and were enrolled in Grades K-12. A majority of students attended general education classrooms (83.2%) and were from White, non-Hispanic (54.8%); Black, non-Hispanic (12.7%); other non-Hispanic (7.0%); Hispanic (24%); or biracial (1.5%) backgrounds. Teachers were asked to provide symptom ratings for one randomly selected boy and one randomly selected girl on their roster. The test authors contend the sample of teacher ratings is representative of the U.S. population.

Reliability. The normative samples were used to examine internal consistency reliability. For the School Version, alpha coefficients were very high: .94-.97 for subscales and the Total score. For the Home Version, alpha coefficients were high to very high: .89-.95 for subscales and the Total score.

Additional samples selected from suburban school districts in eastern Pennsylvania, eastern Nebraska, and southern New Jersey were used to evaluate test-retest reliability and interrater agreement. The teacher sample consisted of 64 students, and the parent sample consisted of 34 students; both samples were predominantly White. To assess test-retest reliability, raters completed the ADHD Rating Scale–5 on two occasions approximately six weeks apart. For the teacher sample, the resultant Pearson product-moment correlation coefficients ranged from .90 to .93 for subscales and the Total score on the Child Form and from .77 to .91 on the Adolescent Form. For teacher ratings of impairment, test-retest coefficients using Spearman rho correlations ranged from .62 to .88 on the Child Form and from .69 to .92 on the Adolescent Form.

Test-retest reliability estimates for the parent sample were mixed. For the Child Form, Pearson product-moment correlations ranged from .80 to .87 for subscales and the Total score, and Spearman rho correlations ranged from .62 to .90 for the impairment ratings. Results were lower for parent ratings on the Adolescent Form, with correlation coefficients of .61 to .70 for subscales and the Total score and .14 to .81 for impairment ratings.

Interrater agreement was examined using both parent and teacher ratings for 41 students; on the Child Form, coefficients were in the low to moderate/acceptable range (.48-.77) for symptom subscales and the Total score. Agreement between parent and teacher impairment ratings were mixed, with some results quite low (.11-.60). On the Adolescent Form, coefficients for the symptom subscales and the Total score ranged from .01 (Hyperactivity-Impulsivity) to .46 (Inattention). For the impairment ratings, coefficients ranged in magnitude from .06 to .77.

Validity evidence. As described earlier, confirmatory factor analysis (CFA) was used to provide evidence about the adequacy of the structure of the instrument and to examine fit with the *DSM-5* theoretical two-factor model. According to the analyses, the two-factor model demonstrated acceptable fit and is the preferred model for interpretation. In addition, CFA was used to evaluate the structure of the impairment scales. On the impairment scales, respondents (parents and teachers) are asked to assess the extent to which problems with inattention or hyperactivity-impulsivity impair a child's functioning. A six-factor model that combined items across the source of impairment was the best-fitting model for both Home and School Versions. These results suggest respondents are able to identify the existence of impairment in separate domains (e.g., relationships with peers, academic functioning), but are less able to pinpoint the source of the impairment (i.e., inattention or hyperactivity-impulsivity).

The aforementioned samples from suburban school districts in eastern Pennsylvania, eastern Nebraska, and southern New Jersey were used to examine criterion-related validity evidence. Criterion measures involved direct observation of classroom behavior and academic performance for a subsample of 32 students (for the teacher rating scales) and 45 students (for the parent rating scales). Classroom behavior was observed using the Behavior Observation of Students in Schools (BOSS; Shapiro, 2011). The results indicated that all three symptom rating scores (i.e., Inattention, Hyperactivity-Impulsivity, Total) on the ADHD Rating Scale–5 were significantly correlated with direct observations of classroom off-task behaviors. Symptom ratings on the ADHD Rating Scale–5 were compared with classroom work samples; the results indicated negative relationships between teacher ratings and academic performance. Additional criterion measures included the Conners 3rd Edition (Conners 3; Conners, 2008) and the Impairment Rating Scale (IRS; Fabiano et al., 2006). When teacher ratings on the ADHD Rating Scale–5 were compared with the Conners 3 Teacher rating scales, Pearson correlation coefficients ranged from .46 to .89, with all values achieving statistical significance. The strongest correlations were found with Conners 3 scores closely related to ADHD symptoms. When parent ratings on the ADHD Rating Scale–5 were compared with the Conners 3 Parent rating scales, Pearson correlation coefficients ranged from .01 to .85, with most achieving statistical significance. Again, the strongest correlations were found with Conners 3 scores closely related to ADHD symptoms.

Discriminant validity evidence was provided based on the previous version of the measure, the ADHD Rating Scale–IV. A clinical sample of 92 children—mostly boys, mostly White—who had been referred to a hospital clinic for evaluation was used in the analysis. The criterion measures included a diagnostic interview and a number of rating scales, including the ADHD Rating Scales–IV. Children were assigned to a diagnostic group or a control group on the basis of their scores on these assessments. The results indicated that parent and teacher ratings of Inattention and Hyperactivity-Impulsivity on the ADHD Rating Scale–IV corresponded with diagnostic group assignment.

The test authors pose important questions related to the instrument's predictive validity, specifically: Does this instrument differentiate children with ADHD from those without? Can it distinguish children with the two most common presentations of ADHD (Inattentive and Combined type)? Using logistic regression analyses and the ADHD Rating Scale–IV, the authors came to three important conclusions. First, the Inattention subscale of the ADHD Rating Scale–IV differentiated children with ADHD Inattentive type from controls, and children with ADHD Combined type from controls. Second, the Hyperactivity-Impulsivity subscale differentiated children with ADHD Combined type from controls and from ADHD Impulsive type. Third, teacher ratings are extremely important in predicting ADHD presentation; teacher ratings were better than parent ratings at predicting ADHD presentation status; however, information from both teachers and parents is preferable to a single-informant approach.

Finally, the test authors discuss diagnostic sensitivity and specificity; in other words, they examined the utility of the instrument in diagnosing ADHD and screening out those who do not have the disorder. Again, the clinical utility studies reported are from the previous version of the scale, but the information presented is nonetheless helpful for the user to understand how cutoff points were set for screening and diagnosis in the development of this instrument.

Bias and fairness. A number of important factors should be considered when interpreting test scores across gender, racial, ethnic, and cultural groups. According to the normative samples, both parent and teacher ratings of ADHD symptoms vary significantly as a function of gender, age, and race/ethnicity of the child being rated. Specifically, teachers report more frequent symptoms in boys. Both parents and teachers report more frequent symptoms in younger age groups. Thus, children being evaluated should be compared against norms based on that child's gender and age. The effect of race/ethnicity was also significant: African American children scored higher (i.e., were rated as having more frequent symptoms) than those in other racial/ethnic groups. Users should be cautious about using cutoff scores with children who belong to racial/ethnic minority groups, especially African American children. This caution is reiterated several times throughout the test manual.

The test authors spend considerable time discussing ADHD prevalence rates as a result of parent ratings, teacher ratings, or multi-informant ratings. Rates of ADHD are considerably higher when based on teacher symptom ratings relative to parent symptom ratings. Prevalence rates drop when impairment is considered along with symptom report. Thus, users of the ADHD Rating Scale–5 should pay close attention to ratings of impairment.

COMMENTARY. Overall, the ADHD Rating Scale–5 has good psychometric properties, and the validity evidence is solid, especially for White, middle-class (or higher) children. Clinicians can confidently use this instrument to provide data regarding the frequency of ADHD symptoms and the severity of ADHD symptom-related impairment. The combination of teacher and parent ratings predicts ADHD diagnosis adequately. This measure is available in Spanish for parents who would be at a disadvantage in completing the scale in English. The test manual is well organized and presents data clearly for the user to judge clinical utility of the instrument.

Although the normative samples are representative of the U.S. population, the test authors may wish to oversample children from more diverse backgrounds in terms of racial/ethnic group and socioeconomic status so clinicians can use this instrument confidently with members of diverse groups. The authors advise caution in using this instrument for making diagnostic decisions for African American children; this represents a substantial limitation of the instrument and does not resolve the dilemma of overidentification/overpathologizing in this population. Case examples are provided in the test manual, including a child from a racial/ethnic minority group with the relevant cautions noted.

Another limitation is noted regarding the teacher rating scale, which instructs teachers to describe behavior over the previous 6 months (or since the beginning of the school year if the teacher has known the student for less than 6 months). The validity of ratings provided by teachers who have known the child fewer than 6 months is not addressed in the test manual. The normative samples for the parent rating scale and the teacher rating scale are different; the same children were not included in both samples. What is missing is information on how different raters (e.g., different teachers) view symptoms *in the same child.* The manual includes a helpful chart with optimal cutoff scores for screening, diagnosing, and ruling out ADHD when both parent and teacher ratings are available; however, these recommendations are made based on findings from a study using a previous version of the scale. Therefore, these recommendations may not be applicable with the ADHD Rating Scale–5.

With regard to this scale's utility in school settings, based on development studies, the ADHD Rating Scale–5 appears to be most useful in a school setting as a screening measure to be included in a multi-gate assessment process. The test authors do not support the practice of using teacher and parent ratings alone or in combination when making diagnostic decisions about the presence of ADHD. Rather, the authors recommend using teacher and parent ratings in conjunction with other methods, such as informant ratings of symptom-related impairment, diagnostic interviews, and direct observations, in making diagnostic decisions about ADHD.

SUMMARY. Practitioners working in schools and clinic settings, as well as researchers, will find the ADHD Rating Scale–5 a helpful tool for identifying symptom frequency and identifying whether symptoms cause impairment in important areas of functioning. Caution should be used with individuals from racial/ethnic minority groups, as clinicians should be aware of the potential for overidentification (especially in African American boys). The best use of this instrument may be as a screener, or as part of a multi-source, multi-method comprehensive assessment.

REVIEWER'S REFERENCES

American Psychiatric Association. (2013). *Diagnostic and statistical manual of mental disorders* (5th ed.). Washington, DC: Author.

Conners, C. K. (2008). Conners 3rd edition. Toronto, Canada: Multi-Health Systems.

Fabiano, G. A., Pelham, W. E., Jr., Waschbusch, D. A., Gnagy, E. M., Lahey, B. B., Chronis, A. M., ... Burrows-MacLean, L. (2006). A practical measure of impairment: Psychometric properties of the Impairment Rating Scale in samples of children with attention deficit hyperactivity disorder and two school-based samples. *Journal of Clinical Child and Adolescent Psychology, 35,* 369-385.

Shapiro, E. S. (2011). *Academic skills problems fourth edition workbook.* New York, NY: Guilford.

[5]

Adult SASSI–4.

Purpose: Designed to "identify individuals who have a high probability of having a substance use disorder."
Population: Ages 18 and older.
Publication Dates: 1983-2016.
Acronym: SASSI-4.
Scores: 11 scales: Face Valid Alcohol, Face Valid Other Drugs, Symptoms, Obvious Attributes, Subtle Attributes, Defensiveness, Supplemental Addiction Measure, Family vs. Controls, Correctional, Prescription Drug Scale, Random Answering Pattern, plus Probability of Having a Substance Use Disorder (High or Low).
Administration: Individual.
Price Data, 2020: $265 per large starter kit including 100 questionnaires and profiles, scoring key, and user guide/manual (2016, 126 pages); $150 per small starter kit including 25 questionnaires and profiles, scoring key, and user guide/manual; $200 per 100 questionnaires and profiles; $85 per user guide/manual; $65 per 25 questionnaires and profiles; $30 per audio recording; $12.50 per online questionnaire administration and scoring (quantity discounts available); $12 per scoring guide.
Foreign Language Edition: Spanish version available.
Time: (15) minutes.
Comments: May be administered via paper and pencil with hand scoring; online administration available; audio CD available for people with special needs regarding vision or literacy.
Authors: The SASSI Institute, Inc. (inventory); Linda E. Lazowski, Kristin S. Kimmell, and Scarlett L. Baker (user guide/manual).
Publisher: The SASSI Institute.
Cross References: For reviews by Ephrem Fernandez and David J. Pittenger of the third edition, see 15:252; see T5:2553 (6 references); for reviews by Barbara Kerr and Nicholas A. Vacc of an earlier edition, see 12:381 (1 reference); see also T4:2623 (1 reference).

Review of the Adult SASSI–4 by SHERI BAUMAN, Professor of Counseling, Department of Disability and Psychoeducational Studies, University of Arizona, Tucson, AZ:

DESCRIPTION. The Adult SASSI–4 is the fourth iteration of a measure designed to detect the probability that an individual has a substance use disorder even when the individual attempts to conceal the problem. The SASSI–4 (Substance Abuse Subtle Screening Inventory) is aligned with the *Diagnostic and Statistical Manual of Mental Disorders* (*DSM-5*; American Psychiatric Association, 2013) diagnostic categories for substance use disorders (SUD) and is available in a paper-and-pencil format or online. The SASSI is available in a Spanish version (Spanish SASSI; 20:165), and an American Sign Language (ASL) substance abuse screener also has been derived (SAS-ASL; 20:170). The reading level of the Adult SASSI–4 is estimated to be fourth to fifth grade. The inventory takes less than 15 minutes to administer, with a scoring time for the hand-scored version of one or two minutes.

The inventory is printed on one sheet, with one side containing 74 true/false items that comprise the "subtle" part of the inventory. The other side includes demographic information, 13 items inquiring about frequency of alcohol use or symptoms (response options: *never, once or twice, several times, repeatedly*), and 18 items related to use of other drugs, including prescription drugs. The clinician selects the time frame to be used by the respondent (your entire life, the past 6 months, the past 12 months, the 6 months before ___, and the 6 months after ___).

The true/false items are scored using a transparency that indicates which items should be counted for each scale. The Face Valid scales are sums of the endorsed responses. The results are recorded on a profile form (one side for females, the other for males) that includes the decision rules by which the examiner determines whether the individual has a high or low probability of having a substance use disorder. The specifiers for severity (*mild*, *moderate*, or *severe*) are determined by the number of symptoms endorsed.

The inventory provides scores for the following scales: Random Answering Pattern (RAP), which alerts the clinician that results may not be valid; Prescription Drug Scale (Rx); Face Valid Alcohol (FVA); Face Valid Other Drugs (FVOD); Symptoms (SYM); Obvious Attributes (OAT); Subtle Attributes (SAT); Defensiveness (DEF); Supplemental Addiction Measure (SAM); Family vs. Controls (FAM); and Correctional (COR). The DEF score is used when a respondent's result is indicative of low probability of having a substance use disorder. If the DEF score is above the cutoff, it suggests the possibility of a false negative.

DEVELOPMENT. The SASSI–4 is based on a research version of the SASSI–3 with 15 new items. The development sample consisted of 620 adults and the validation sample of 625 adults recruited by clinicians (qualified by the SASSI institute to use the measure) who agreed to participate and who also submitted a clinical diagnosis (of substance abuse or other psychiatric disorders) based on *DSM-5* criteria. The development and validation groups did not differ on any demographic variable.

TECHNICAL. The properties of the SASSI–4 are based on studies conducted by the SASSI Institute and reported in the test manual and in an article by the test manual's primary author (Linda Lazowski) and an independent clinical practitioner (Brent Geary). No additional research on the SASSI–4 could be located at the time of this review. Readers should keep this in mind when evaluating the technical properties of the instrument.

Standardization. The majority (64%) of the 1,245 respondents were from substance use treatment programs and various criminal justice services. Almost 76% of the sample was classified as having a high probability of having a substance use disorder, 48% of whom were classified as *severe*. An independent sample of 40 participants (70% female, mean age 61.9 years, 95% White) was used to examine test-retest reliability. A sample of 120 independent respondents (79% male, mean age 42.2 years, 77% White) was used in the "fake good" experiment. Participants with elevated RAP scores were excluded from analysis.

Reliability. Internal consistency was appropriately measured using the omega coefficient using all items that are included in the decision rules for determining probability of having a substance use disorder (i.e., RAP, DEF, FAM, and COR items were not included). Omega for the overall scale was .97; the range of values for individual scales was .70 to .96. Test-retest reliability over an 8- to 60-day interval was reported to be .99 for the overall scale and ranged from .78 to .99 for individual scales.

Validity. The developers report criterion evidence of validity, which compared the results of the SASSI–4 classification with those given by the clinicians. For participants given both lifetime prevalence and past year instructions, there was 92% agreement on the classification. The test authors also used discriminant function analysis to determine that the SAT scale alone correctly classified 82.1% of cases even under "fake good" instructions. Also reported with high values are data on specificity, sensitivity, positive and negative predictive value, and correct classification. Values are presented for each criterion stratified as any SUD (n = 625), lifetime SUD (n = 480), and past year SUD (n = 145), as well as four SUD severity levels, three other mental health conditions, and two levels of opioid or sedative use. Across all strata, sensitivity ranged from 78% to 98%, specificity from 86% to 98%, positive predictive value from 83% to 98%, negative predictive value from 76% to 96%, and correct classification from 86% to 97%.

COMMENTARY. The contribution of this measure is the proclaimed ability to detect the probability that an individual has a substance use disorder even when the individual is unaware of, or denies, the problem. The test authors state that the measure is empirically derived rather than based on theory. The absence of a theoretical framework makes it difficult to assess construct evidence of validity, and the absence of independent studies on this version limits the reviewer's ability to evaluate the measure.

The SASSI measures have been widely used since the first edition. The SASSI–4 is a revision to align the classification more closely with *DSM-5* criteria, to add a measure of prescription drug abuse, and to make some changes to the items. The lead author of the only published study at the time of this review is also an author of the test manual. The test authors report extremely high rates of sensitivity, specificity, positive predictive value, and negative predictive value. They also report excellent reliability (test-retest and internal consistency) and criterion evidence of validity.

Independent researchers identified several concerns with previous versions of the SASSI.

There are no new data to determine whether these concerns have been addressed in the most recent edition. For example, Gray (2001) conducted factor analytic studies of the SASSI–3 and found that the fit of the measurement model to the data was poor. Laux et al. (2016) found only moderate agreement between SASSI–3 classification and counselor diagnosis. Based on their extensive analysis, Laux and colleagues recommended that cutoff scores used in the decision rules be differentiated by population (e.g., criminal justice, inpatient treatment). Feldstein and Miller (2007) reviewed existing literature on the measure (36 articles) and tested the claims made by the SASSI Institute. They concluded that the high coefficients for test-retest reliability and internal consistency reported by the institute were not replicated in other studies. They also observed that the SASSI decision rules demonstrated moderate convergence with other measures of substance abuse (most of which are available at no cost). Feldstein and Miller noted that other studies have reported lower rates of sensitivity and specificity than those found by the SASSI researchers. Perez and Wish (2011) found that the SASSI–3 over-classified incarcerated men as substance abusers; although sensitivity was high, specificity for men was 28%, and for women 63%.

The representativeness of the samples used to develop the SASSI–4 is questionable, as African Americans and especially Hispanics/Latinos were under-represented in the development and validation samples. Studies of previous versions of the measure found that ethnic minorities are more often classified as having a high probability of a substance use disorder than Whites and also have higher scores on the DEF, RAP, and COR scales. These findings suggest that there may be bias in the measure when used with minority populations.

Finally, the SASSI–4 is described as a screening instrument, which means it should detect examinees who need more in-depth assessment. Yet in the test manual, the authors provide considerable clinical interpretation, including case studies, that appear to extend the use beyond screening.

SUMMARY. The SASSI–4 is a popular screening inventory that was designed to detect substance use problems even in those who are motivated to conceal the problem. The test authors suggest that the addition of the subtle scales (not obviously related to substance disorders) increases the accuracy of the classification (high or low probability of having a substance use disorder), although research on previous versions has questioned that assertion. The Adult SASSI–4 includes supplemental scales to detect invalid responding and a new scale that assesses misuse of prescription medication. The test manual provides high values for all psychometric properties, but there are no studies to date that evaluate those properties independently. The availability of a Spanish SASSI is a plus; its accuracy is reported by the test publisher as 84%. There is also an ASL substance use screener for hearing impaired clients (accuracy of 87% reported) whose literacy skills preclude the use of the standard versions.

REVIEWER'S REFERENCES

American Psychiatric Association. (2013). *Diagnostic and statistical manual of mental disorders* (5th ed.). Washington, DC: Author.

Feldstein, S. W., & Miller, W. R. (2007). Does subtle screening for substance abuse work? A review of the Substance Abuse Subtle Screening Inventory (SASSI). *Addiction, 102,* 41-50.

Fernandez, E. (2003). [Test review of the Substance Abuse Subtle Screening Inventory–3]. In B. S. Plake, J. C. Impara, & R. A. Spies (Eds.), *The fifteenth mental measurements yearbook.* Lincoln, NE: Buros Institute of Mental Measurements.

Gray, B. T. (2001). A factor analytic study of the Substance Abuse Subtle Screening Inventory (SASSI). *Educational and Psychological Measurement, 61,* 102-118.

Laux, J. M., DuFresne, R. M., Arnekrans, A. K., Lindinger-Sternart, S., Roseman, C. P., Wertenberger, A., ... Schultz, J. (2016). Assessing the accuracy of the Substance Abuse Subtle Screening Inventory–3 using DSM-5 criteria. *The Professional Counselor, 6,* 121–133.

Lazowski, L. E., & Geary, B. B. (2016). Validation of the Adult Substance Abuse Subtle Screening Inventory–4 (SASSI–4). *European Journal of Psychological Assessment.* Advance online publication. http://dx.doi.org/10.1027/1015-5759/a000359

Lazowski, L. E., & Miller, G. A. (2007). SASSI: A reply to the critique of Feldstein & Miller (2007). *Addiction, 102,* 1001-1002.

Miller, W. R., & Feldstein, S. W. (2007). SASSI: A response to Lazowski & Miller (2007). *Addiction, 102,* 1002-1004.

Perez, D. M., & Wish, E. D. (2011). Gender differences in the validity of the Substance Abuse Subtle Screening Inventory (SASSI–3) with a criminal justice population. *International Journal of Offender Therapy and Comparative Criminology, 55,* 476-491.

Pittenger, D. J. (2003). [Test review of the Substance Abuse Subtle Screening Inventory–3]. In B. S. Plake, J. C. Impara, & R. A. Spies (Eds.), *The fifteenth mental measurements yearbook.* Lincoln, NE: Buros Institute of Mental Measurements.

Review of the Adult SASSI–4 by TONY CELLUCCI, Professor and Director of the Psychology Training Clinic at East Carolina University, and KIRK MOCHRIE, Doctoral Candidate in Clinical Health Psychology at East Carolina University, Greenville, NC:

DESCRIPTION. The Adult SASSI–4 is the latest version of a screening instrument designed to help human service practitioners better identify and assess adult clients (ages 18 years and older) with a high probability of having a substance use disorder (SUD). Dr. Glenn Miller originally developed the Substance Abuse Subtle Screening Inventory (SASSI) as a screening tool, and the test manual clearly states that a more thorough evaluation is needed to make an SUD diagnosis. It is argued that the SASSI can help identify individuals with substance use difficulties who might benefit from a variety of early intervention and other targeted services. The user's guide and manual first describe the rationale and utility of this instrument, followed by a discussion of the item types, history and development of the SASSI, and recommended uses. Next, a guide to presenting the instrument to clients is included with instructions for scoring and interpretation. The SASSI scales are outlined in detail with 10 sample client profiles to help guide practitioners in interpretation. Finally, the test manual concludes with supporting research and appendices with normative data and conversion scores. The Adult SASSI–4 can be administered via paper and pencil (with hand-scoring template) or online; an audio CD is available for people with reading difficulties.

The questionnaire is composed of two parts and is reported to take 15 minutes or less to administer. Part one consists of 74 true/false questions, which respondents are instructed to respond to just "the way you feel." This section contains both face valid and subtle items. Part two includes 31 questions directly related to alcohol and other drug use and/or associated negative consequences, which are responded to on a 4-point scale: *never, once or twice*, *several times,* or *repeatedly*. The administrator can specify the time frame (i.e., lifetime, past year, past 6 months, or other specified 6 months) to be considered in answering these questions. There is also a brief demographic section.

The Adult SASSI–4 includes a total of 11 scales. Four assess alcohol and other drug abuse with face valid questions: Face Valid Alcohol (FVA) and Face Valid Other Drugs (FVOD) scales from side two along with a new scale assessing Prescription Drug (Rx) misuse, and the Symptoms (SYM) scale, measuring substance misuse behaviors and symptoms. In addition, four scales contain subtle items used in the decision rules to screen for SUDs. These include the Obvious Attributes (OAT) scale, which measures endorsement of personal limitations; the Subtle Attributes (SAT) scale, measuring characteristics of substance misuse that are not easily recognized; the Defensiveness (DEF) scale, measuring the likelihood of minimizing substance use problems; and the Supplemental Addiction Measure (SAM) scale, which measures substance use symptoms. Further, two scales provide information about an individual's family history (FAM) of substance use and information regarding criminal justice or Correctional (COR) violations, although these scales are not used in screening. Finally, a validity scale is included to detect a Random Answering Pattern (RAP). A profile form records a respondent's scale profile with separate T score norms for male and female clients. The test manual describes each of the above scales (6-20 items) and 10 associated decision rules used in scoring.

DEVELOPMENT. The SASSI–4 was based on previous versions of the measure; the SASSI–3 was published in 1997, and the profile sheets and decision rules were revised in 2013 to reflect changes in the fifth edition of the *Diagnostic and Statistical Manual of Mental Disorders* (*DSM-5*; American Psychiatric Association, 2013) related to substance use. The items from the SASSI–3 were retained; in addition, the SASSI–4 contains a new scale (Rx for Prescription Drug abuse) and additional subtle and symptom indicators. However, the latter specific items added are not explicitly stated in the test manual. A new validation study of the provisional SASSI–4 was also conducted (Lazowski & Geary, 2016).

The SASSI's FVA and FVOD items were originally developed by the Indiana Division of Addiction Services with experts in substance use assessment proposing a large pool of potential questions. There was no theory underlying the selection of items, which were chosen using an empirical keying approach that identified items separating clients with SUDs from controls. Items were refined by analyses assessing "fake good" instructions and choosing items that minimized effects of demographic variables.

TECHNICAL. Technical information related to the SASSI–4 is provided in the user's guide and in the validation article by Lazowski and Geary (2016).

Standardization. The SASSI–4 was developed using a total sample of 1,245 individuals from nine U.S. Census Bureau regions and two Canadian provinces who were administered the provisional version online. They were recruited from substance use treatment programs, criminal justice programs, private practices, behavioral health facilities, driving while intoxicated and department of transportation screening and education programs, and social services agencies. The sample was divided into two subsamples including development (*N* = 620)—those used to derive new decision rules for the SASSI–4 scoring—and cross-validation (*N* = 625)—an unexamined set of cases for cross-validating the newly derived decision rules. The development sample included 620 individuals (74% Caucasian) with a mean age of 34.4, 62% male, and varied marital status (51% single, 21% married, 15% divorced). Regarding educational level,

41% of the sample reported one or more years of postsecondary education, 40% had a high school degree or equivalent, and 18% had less than a high school degree. Forty-eight percent were employed, 34% not employed, 9% student/homemaker, and 8% retired due to disability. In terms of diagnoses, 49% were diagnosed with a severe SUD, 12% moderate, 14% mild, and 24% were criterion negative. The cross-validation sample was equivalent to the development sample on all variables including the ratio of cases diagnosed as having or not having an SUD. Finally, a normative sample (N = 551) of U.S. and Canadian community respondents (237 males and 314 females) not in treatment for substance use was drawn to derive standard scores.

Reliability. Internal consistency estimates (coefficient omega) for the scales ranged from .70 to .96 with higher coefficients for the face valid alcohol and other drug scales than other attributes; lower internal consistency would be expected given the actuarial nature of these scales. Test-retest reliability estimates based on a small sample (n = 40) over 1-8 weeks (M = 22.8 days) ranged from .78 (DEF) to .99.

Validity. The validation focus was on the accuracy of the SASSI–4 as a screening tool as evaluated against the criterion of clinician diagnosis using *DSM-5* symptom criteria. In the cross-validation sample, the SASSI–4 had a 92% overall accuracy rate (sensitivity 92.8%, specificity 90%) in identifying individuals who have a low or high probability of an SUD (Lazowski & Geary, 2016). Accuracy was somewhat lower (86.4%) among respondents with a DEF score of 8 or more. For the new prescription drug abuse scale, overall accuracy was reported to be 94% with sensitivity of 87.4% and specificity of 98%.

Using all 10 decision rules reportedly increased incremental accuracy (13%) compared to using only the first two rules based on face valid scales. However, there is a debate in the literature as to the utility of the subtle items of the SASSI in detecting substance use problems (Feldstein & Miller, 2007; Lazowski, & Miller, 2007; Miller & Feldstein, 2007).

No data are presented related to concurrent evidence of validity of individual scale scores relative to other substance abuse measures, either direct (e.g., Michigan Alcoholism Screening Test [MAST] and Drug Abuse Screening Test [DAST]) or indirect (e.g., MMPI-2 MacAndrew Alcoholism Scale [MAC], Addiction Potential Scale [APS]). Perhaps the constructs underlying the subtle scales could be clarified by comparing them to other measures of response style (e.g., DEF compared to MMPI-2 K scale).

The reported analyses indicate that demographics did not appreciably affect accuracy. However, for ethnicity, decision rules were least accurate among African Americans (88%) and demonstrated the highest false positive rate (20%). It would be of interest to examine differential item and scale functioning among minority groups. There was also a small age effect in the combined sample indicating less accuracy among those under 21 years, which the test authors attribute to the possible reluctance on the part of clinicians to diagnose SUD in this age group.

COMMENTARY. The SASSI–4 appears to be an efficient tool for assessing substance use behaviors and identifying individuals with a low or high probability of having an SUD. The test manual is readily comprehendible and gives detailed explanations and example interpretations. The current version appears improved over its predecessors, with reasonable internal consistency estimates and the addition of a new prescription abuse scale (Rx). Although the test manual provides evidence of incremental validity for using the full set of decision rules, more independent research on these items is needed. Moreover, factor analysis of the scales would be useful in delineating the constructs measured by the instrument, along with correlating selected scales with other external criteria.

Also, while impressive, the accuracy estimates are not easily evaluated apart from the *DSM-5* diagnostic criteria, which require only two of 11 criteria to be identified as having an SUD, thus providing a broad target. Some authors have suggested that the low *DSM-5* threshold results in elevated prevalence estimates (Martin, Steinley, Vergés, & Sher, 2011). Although the SASSI–4 appears to be a sensitive screening tool among populations with a high percentage of substance abuse clients, there is a need for more research with diverse samples in terms of substance use symptomatology. Practitioners should be careful not to over identify individuals as having SUDs versus situational misuse and adhere to the test authors' caution that the SASSI–4 should *not* be used as a stand-alone diagnostic instrument.

SUMMARY. The SASSI–4 provides a systematic screening tool for identifying individuals with a low and high probability of having an SUD, and it is considered reliable and useful for that purpose. More research might be conducted with diverse populations, on the factor structure of the scales, and on the utility of subtle items, as well as to compare it to other substance use measures.

REVIEWERS' REFERENCES

American Psychiatric Association. (2013). *Diagnostic and statistical manual of mental disorders* (5th ed.). Washington, DC: Author.

Feldstein, S. W., & Miller, W. R. (2007). Does subtle screening for substance abuse work? A review of the Substance Abuse Subtle Screening Inventory (SASSI). *Addiction, 102,* 41-50. doi:10.1111/j.1360-0443.2006.01634.x

Lazowski, L. E., & Geary, B. B. (2016). Validation of the Adult Substance Abuse Subtle Screening Inventory–4 (SASSI–4). *European Journal of Psychological Assessment.* Advance online publication. http://dx.doi.org/10.1027/1015-5759/a000359

Lazowski, L. E., & Miller, G. A. (2007). SASSI: A reply to the critique of Feldstein & Miller (2007). *Addiction, 102,* 1001-1002. doi:10.1111/j.1360-0443.2007.01861.x

Martin, C. S., Steinley, D. L., Vergés, A., & Sher, K. J. (2011). The proposed 2/11 symptom algorithm for DSM-5 substance-use disorders is too lenient. *Psychological Medicine, 41,* 2008-2010. doi:10.1017/S0033291711000717

Miller, W. R., & Feldstein, S. W. (2007). SASSI: A response to Lazowski & Miller (2007). *Addiction, 102,* 1002-1004. doi:10.1111/j.1360-0443.2007.01860.x

[6]

ALEKS PPL (Placement, Preparation and Learning).

Purpose: Designed as an adaptive placement and course preparedness assessment for mathematics in higher education and to provide individualized remediation to students.

Population: Undergraduate students.

Publication Date: 2013.

Acronym: ALEKS PPL.

Scores: Total score (used for placement); plus information on performance across all topics.

Administration: Group.

Parts, 2: Placement Assessment, Prep and Learning Module.

Price Data: Available from publisher.

Time: 60-90 minutes for administration.

Comments: Administered online; assessment uses "adaptive, open-response questioning" to cover 314 topics in 30 questions or fewer; cut scores provided for class placement (from Basic Math to Calculus I); Prep and Learning Module designed "to help students refresh and learn new math topics"; assistive listening system available for visually impaired students.

Author: ALEKS Corporation.

Publisher: McGraw-Hill Education.

Review of ALEKS PPL (Placement, Preparation and Learning) by MARY L. GARNER, Professor Emeritus of Mathematics, Kennesaw State University, and Visiting Assistant Professor of Mathematics, Oglethorpe University, Atlanta, GA:

DESCRIPTION. ALEKS PPL (Assessment and Learning in Knowledge Spaces—Placement, Preparation and Learning) is a computerized, adaptive mathematics test that can be used to determine a student's readiness to be placed in basic math/prealgebra, beginning algebra, intermediate algebra, college algebra, precalculus, or calculus I. The student is exposed to 30 free-response questions or fewer drawn from a bank of items or problem types covering 314 topics. Areas that can be assessed range from basic arithmetic to trigonometry. Each item is a collection of "instances" in which the parameters of the problem are selected randomly, or a different context is selected for a word problem. According to Falmagne and Doble (2013), one item may have thousands of instances. A sample of specific items is included in a paper by Doble, Matayoshi, Cosyn, Uzun, and Karami (2019).

Scoring procedures vary according to the context and can be established in collaboration between the institution using the assessment and ALEKS PPL researchers. For example, in a research study by Doble et al. (2019), the authors used the percentage of the 314 items that are in the student's knowledge state. In using the ALEKS PPL at the University of Illinois for placement purposes, Reddy and Harper (2013) used the proportion of items demonstrated as a score. Although such scores are an oversimplification that may not reflect the knowledge state of the student (two students with the same score may have different knowledge states), the test also generates a series of analyses for students and administrators. For example, the student obtains a profile describing what the student knows, what he or she does not know, and what topics the student is ready to learn next. If the student is unhappy with the placement score, the student can then move through a series of modules designed to help the student master the material he or she has not learned, in order of increasing difficulty. The student can then retake ALEKS PPL for placement purposes.

DEVELOPMENT. ALEKS PPL is built on a theory first developed by mathematicians Jean-Claude Falmagne and Jean-Paul Doignon in 1985. Knowledge space theory is a formal axiomatic approach to building assessments; it posits that a student's knowledge in a specific domain (defined by the items) can be visualized as a network of knowledge states that range from knowing nothing to knowing all the material in the domain. Each knowledge state consists of a subset of the items in a domain. In ALEKS PPL, with 314 items, there are 2^{314} possible subsets or knowledge states. However, not all knowledge states are actually feasible. Doble et al. (2019) report there are 10^{23} states in ALEKS PPL. Unlu, Schrepp, Heller, Hockemeyer, Wesiak, and Albert (2013) state that the structure of a knowledge space is built by first describing possible knowledge spaces and then testing those spaces against data using some fit measures. They also state requirements for the population on which the knowledge structure is tested. A description of how the domain of ALEKS PPL and its knowledge spaces were constructed is not provided in the test materials reviewed or on the test publisher's website.

TECHNICAL. There was no description provided in the materials reviewed regarding exactly how the ALEKS PPL was developed or how the knowledge space was determined.

Reliability was addressed by Doble et al. (2019). Their conclusion was that "the ALEKS PPL assessment has variability" (p. 278) based on conditional standard errors of measurement that differ among knowledge categories and that the variability is greatest for scores in the range of those for precalculus and calculus placement. They hypothesized that the method of determining the score could be causing variability and recommended the testing of other methods for scoring the assessment, such as a weighted sum based on the degree to which items are useful in predicting success in future courses.

The validity of ALEKS PPL is reflected in reports of the usefulness of the software in both placement and remediation from the University of Illinois, University of Colorado-Boulder, Utah Valley University, Ohio University, University of California–Long Beach and Santa Cruz, and Iowa Central Community College. Universities report higher passing rates for students under ALEKS PPL than other placement methods. They also report that by using ALEKS learning modules, students can refresh their skills before enrolling in certain courses. These reports can be accessed from the test publisher's website.

COMMENTARY. An axiomatic system for describing and assessing the state of knowledge in a certain domain is an intriguing mathematical proposition. As stated by Unlu et al. (2013), the theory is quite new and "there is a high potential for further developments of Knowledge Space Theory" (p. 147). The researchers go on to say, "The methodology in this field has still to mature" (p. 191). There is limited evidence provided for the validity of ALEKS PPL as a placement test; however, a number of universities have described positive experiences with the test. There seem to be many assumptions made in the ALEKS PPL that this reviewer believes need questioning, including the following: (a) a person's knowledge can be described by a network of ordered knowledge states that consist of sets of items that describe the domain; (b) the different instances of the items are equivalent; (c) the items test what is important to know and are not prone to careless errors; (d) the items work similarly for different populations of students; (e) all high school mathematics worth learning consists of regurgitation of algorithms; (f) the assessment is valid and reliable even under very different scoring routines.

SUMMARY. ALEKS PPL is an assessment that can be used for placement and remediation in high school and college mathematics courses. Its theoretical basis is in an axiomatic theory of how to describe the knowledge of a student within a specific domain. There is no doubt that many mathematicians would be attracted by the application of a rigorous axiomatic method to educational assessment, but much work needs to be done. The validity and reliability of scores from the assessment need further examination. The nature of the items and how they were developed are not described in the test materials. Nevertheless, the University of Illinois and other universities have successfully used ALEKS PPL and recommend that other mathematics departments follow their lead.

REVIEWER'S REFERENCES

Cosyn, E., Doble, C., Falmagne, J.-C., Lenoble, A., Thiéry, N., & Uzun, H. (2013). Assessing mathematical knowledge in a learning space. In J.-C. Falmagne, D. Albert, C. Doble, D. Eppstein, & X. Hu (Eds.), *Knowledge spaces: Applications in education* (pp. 27-50). New York, NY: Springer.

Doble, C., Matayoshi, J., Cosyn, E., Uzun, H., & Karami, A. (2019). A data-based simulation study of reliability for an adaptive assessment based on knowledge space theory. *International Journal of Artificial Intelligence in Education, 29*, 258-282. https://doi.org/10.1007/s40593-019-00176-0

Falmagne, J.-C., & Doble, C. (2013). Overview. In J.-C. Falmagne, D. Albert, C. Doble, D. Eppstein, & X. Hu (Eds.), *Knowledge spaces: Applications in education* (pp. 3-26). New York, NY: Springer.

Reddy, A. A., & Harper, M. (2013). Mathematics placement at the University of Illinois. *PRIMUS, 23*(8), 683-702. doi:10.1080/10511970.2013.801378

Unlu, A., Schrepp, M., Heller, J., Hockemeyer, C., Wesiak, G., & Albert, D. (2013). Recent developments in performance-based knowledge space theory. In J.-C. Falmagne, D. Albert, C. Doble, D. Eppstein, & X. Hu (Eds.), *Knowledge spaces: Applications in education* (pp. 147-192). New York, NY: Springer.

Review of the ALEKS PPL (Placement, Preparation and Learning) by JAMES P. VAN HANEGHAN, Professor, Department of Counseling and Instructional Sciences, University of South Alabama, Mobile, AL:

DESCRIPTION. The ALEKS PPL (Placement, Preparation and Learning) is a computer adaptive test of mathematics knowledge that helps determine the "knowledge state" of the student. Knowledge states can roughly be defined as the configuration of items mastered by the student as a function of the entire set of mathematics knowledge. The system uses powerful computing to take 314 item topics covered in high school mathematics and create a finite, although huge, network of knowledge states that takes advantage of the sequential structure of mathematics content to provide an estimate of what the student is likely to be ready to master as he or she signs up for college mathematics courses. The system provides a way for students, teachers, and professors to see the pattern of strengths and weaknesses a student has in mathematics. Through the preparation and learning modules, the student can then proceed in an orderly manner to master pre- and co-requisite concepts for upcoming classes or learn new concepts within the context of a class.

ALEKS PPL is accessed through a web-based system for administering tests and instruction. The system offers flexible administration options. There are options for collecting data, examining the validity of cut scores, and offering post-assessment modules to further prepare for courses. The test scoring system and the modules assigned are based on theoretical connections generated from the mathematical model of the system.

The placement testing can be proctored or not, and there are tools for students to use in solving problems. There are no multiple-choice questions. Students have to solve the problems posed (although they can say they do not know the answer). There is a calculator tool and other supports for entering fractions and mathematical copy. Students take a tutorial in how to use the tools prior to taking the assessments. The placement test is offered as a computer-adaptive test, where students answer up to 30 different problems depending upon the patterns of correct and incorrect answers. That pattern provides insight into the student's knowledge state. The placement test generates both percentage correct item scores and information about strengths and weaknesses in various domains. The system has a set of default placements based on evidence collected in the system, experience of the developers, and consultation with subject matter experts. These placements can, in theory, predict success in various courses. The data tools on the site provide opportunities for institutions that use the system to alter placement recommendations. There are also default preparation and learning modules automatically assigned based on the pattern of scores. This default pattern can be overridden so that students can choose preferred learning modules. Cycles of follow-up testing and completion of modules can systematically work students through material. Hence, the system provides formative and summative assessments of the mastery of students that can be used to tailor instruction.

DEVELOPMENT. The development of the ALEKS system has spanned several decades of work in mathematics, computing, and expert analysis. The focus has largely been on the development of the mathematical models that appear to use combinatorics and set theory to understand how problem types are related. The process of development involved experts, their own work over the years, and recognized standards to create a body of items that emerged into a system that addresses 314 problem types in high school mathematics. What Falmagne and Doignon (2011) have accomplished is to develop a mathematical theory of how success or failure on the various problem types identifies where students are in a particular knowledge space that combines the patterns of competencies associated with the various item types in their system. Knowledge spaces were developed through mathematical models using conditional probabilities of solutions to one problem given patterns of solutions to one or more prerequisite problems. The research also involved querying experts concerning their opinions on whether individuals who could solve prerequisite problems would be able to solve a subsequent problem. As they accumulated data over decades, they were able to tweak the model and also address problems with new solutions. Artificial intelligence-based decision processes are approached through probability models that calculate and recalculate probabilities associated with a particular knowledge state after each assessment. The model also has led to some interesting concepts that are mathematically and possibly psychologically interesting. For example, the idea of inner and outer fringes provides insights into the leading edge of a student's competence. That is, the outer fringe reflects the knowledge state that can be acquired by mastering one additional problem type. This outer fringe notion connects with ideas about Vygotsky's (1978) concept of a zone of proximal development. The inner fringe is defined by the impact of removing one already mastered problem type. It may reflect the most recent and perhaps most fragile knowledge state of the student. The ideas are interesting and mathematically definable. Additional research to explore them further would prove interesting.

TECHNICAL. Given that the development of the system has been so different from typical test development, it is not a simple task to evaluate the reliability and validity of the ALEKS system. There is no test manual that pulls together all of the evidence. ALEKS does not address a single construct, but addresses expectations of performance based on configurations of prior performance. Evidence that would support reliability would be analyses of whether the pattern of assessment results for individuals was consistent across retesting (within certain parameters). Such data exist in the system but are not formally presented in any one publication. Doble, Matayoshi, Cosyn, Uzun, and Karami (2019) attempted to simulate retest iterations by using probabilities derived from students' learning spaces to predict what would happen on a second assessment. Given that the assessment is computer adaptive, ending up in the same place through different problem sets should yield evidence that the test results have some reliability. Doble et al. examined more than 700,000 cases and found high correlations between actual and simulated scores (mean correlation = .96).

As for validity, the evidence centers around the predictability of mathematics performance on individual problems and in whole courses from ALEKS assessments. Falmagne, Cosyn, Doble, Thiery, & Uzun (n.d.) examined whether an extra problem presented at random during an assessment would be accurately predicted to be answered correctly or incorrectly by the knowledge state predicted from the assessment. If someone is predicted to miss the problem, can it predict that state? Likewise, if someone is predicted to get the problem correct, can the knowledge state predict that outcome? Falmagne et al. found that there was an average tetrachoric correlation of .67 between the predicted and actual response on the extra problem. Hence there was some evidence of this short-term predictive validity.

Mathematics course placement data provide additional evidence because incorrect placement has significant consequences for students. Students placed in courses that are too easy might spend more money and time on material they have already mastered. Students placed in courses that are too difficult may fail and lose their sense of efficacy to succeed in mathematics. The University of Illinois, as well as others, report improvements in placement success using ALEKS (Reddy & Harper, 2013). The data that are presented on the test publisher's website tend to be more informal and case by case. Data on elements such as whether ALEKS placement accuracy varies by gender, race, or ethnic background are not systematically presented. Case studies presented with the test materials suggest some accuracy with the placement of students into courses, but data presented in a systematic study based on the large database of ALEKS data would provide stronger support. Likewise, there are reports concerning the success of programs using the system to improve mathematics learning, providing some validity evidence for its use as a tool for teaching and learning (e.g., see Falmagne, Albert, Doble, Eppstein, & Hu, 2013). One study suggested the system's potential in lessening the achievement gap between racial/ethnic groups (Hu, Xu, Hall, Walker, & Okwumabua, 2013). Very little of the evidence supporting these components of ALEKS' use has appeared in peer-reviewed journals. Evidence needs to be brought together into a systematic meta-analysis that can present a more rigorous defense of inferences. An analysis of the massive amount of data collected by the system on the web would provide stronger evidence about the strengths and weaknesses of the system in its practical application.

COMMENTARY. Much work has been done in building and refining the mathematical model surrounding the ALEKS system. There is a trove of data that can be used to explore the system and its implications for student success in mathematics (and other areas that ALEKS has moved into). There is no question that the ALEKS system presents an interesting and useful model for conceptualizing mathematics learning. What would make the case stronger for this system is a more comprehensive set of research that focuses on evaluating rigorously the impact of the system and its consequential validity (Messick, 1989).

SUMMARY. As Mislevy (2016) points out, complex systems such as ALEKS stretch and sometimes break our traditional thinking about assessment. They also provide us with new ways of thinking about assessment by introducing new concepts to explore and consider. The ALEKS system presents a complex and demonstrably useable system for mathematics placement and for learning mathematics by college and university students. More systematic research on the application side that matches the rigorous mathematics analysis on the development side of ALEKS is needed to maximize its potential and valid use.

REVIEWER'S REFERENCES

Doble, C., Matayoshi, J., Cosyn, E., Uzun, H., & Karami, A. (2019). A data-based simulation study of reliability for an adaptive assessment based on knowledge space theory. *International Journal of Artificial Intelligence in Education, 29,* 258-282. https://doi.org/10.1007/s40593-019-00176-0

Falmagne, J.-C., Albert, D., Doble, C., Eppstein, D., & Hu, X. (Eds.). (2013). *Knowledge spaces: Applications in education.* New York, NY: Springer.

Falmagne, J.-C., Cosyn, E., Doble, C., Thiéry, N., & Uzun, H. (n.d.). Assessing mathematical knowledge in a learning space: Validity and/or reliability. Retrieved from https://www.aleks.com/paper_psych/Validity_in_L_Spaces.pdf

Falmagne, J.-C., & Doignon, J.-P. (2011). *Learning spaces: Interdisciplinary applied mathematics.* New York, NY: Springer.

Hu, X., Xu, Y. J., Hall, C., Walker, K., & Okwumabua, T. (2013). A potential technological solution for reducing the achievement gap between white and black students. In J.-C. Falmagne, D. Albert, C. Doble, D. Eppstein, & X. Hu (Eds.), *Knowledge spaces: Applications in education* (pp. 79-92). New York, NY: Springer.

Messick, S. (1989). Validity. In R. L. Linn (Ed.), *Educational measurement* (3rd ed., pp. 13-103). New York, NY: American Council on Education/Macmillan.

Mislevy, R. J. (2016). How developments in psychology and technology challenge validity argumentation. *Journal of Educational Measurement, 53*(3), 265-292. https://doi.org/10.1111/jedm.12117

Reddy, A. A., & Harper, M. (2013). ALEKS-based placement at the University of Illinois. In J.-C. Falmagne, D. Albert, C. Doble, D. Eppstein, & X. Hu (Eds.), *Knowledge spaces: Applications in education* (pp. 51-68). New York, NY: Springer.

Vygotsky, L. S. (1978). Interaction between learning and development. In M. Cole, V. John-Steiner, S. Scribner, & E. Souberman (Eds.), *Mind in society: The development of higher psychological processes* (pp. 79-91). Cambridge, MA: Harvard University Press.

[7]

Areas of Worklife Survey [Fifth Edition Manual].

Purpose: Designed for use "as an element within an organizational survey" to assess six areas of worklife.
Population: Employees.
Publication Dates: 2000-2011.
Acronym: AWS.
Scores, 6: Workload, Control, Reward, Community, Fairness, Values.
Administration: Individual or group.
Price Data, 2020: $50 per electronic copy of Fifth Edition Manual (2011, 32 pages) including review-only copy of the AWS form; $15 per individual report; $200 per group report; $2.50 per remote online survey license or license to reproduce (minimum 50); $60 per printed manual.
Time: [15] minutes.
Comments: Short version available "for large projects in which participants have a great amount of questions to respond to for the survey being administered ... should not be used for individual assessment"; may be combined with Maslach Burnout Inventory (see 87, this volume).
Authors: Michael P. Leiter and Christina Maslach.
Publisher: Mind Garden, Inc.

Review of the Areas of Worklife Survey [Fifth Edition Manual] by CAROL EZZELLE, Director, Psychometrics, National Board for Professional Teaching Standards, Arlington, VA:

DESCRIPTION. The Areas of Worklife Survey (AWS) is a 28-item survey assessing organization contexts of burnout. The survey statements gauge job-person fit as degree of experienced congruence between a person and six domains, or areas, of his or her job environment (Maslach & Leiter, 1997). The six areas of worklife and number of survey items corresponding to each are: Workload (5), Control (4), Reward (4), Community (5), Fairness (6), and Values (4). The intended use of the AWS is as part of an organizational survey. Demographics and additional items can be added to the AWS, and a short form (18 items to be used only for group assessment) is also available. Average individual completion time is 15 minutes.

Respondents indicate their agreement with each item, or statement, using a 5-point Likert-type scale ranging from 1 (*strongly disagree*) to 3 (*hard to decide*) to 5 (*strongly agree*). Six separate scores are produced upon scoring the statements; scores are not combined to form a total. Negatively worded statements are reverse scored, and the test manual contains easy-to-understand, comprehensive instructions on scoring. The higher the score on each scale, the greater the job-person fit or match; the lower the score, the greater the mismatch between job and person.

The test authors cite research to support that the larger the gap between the person and job environment, the greater likelihood of burnout. Conversely, when the person and the job environment have greater match, then work engagement is the likely outcome.

The AWS is available for administration via either paper or online licenses. Translated surveys are available for the following languages: Finnish, French (Canadian), Japanese, Korean, Polish, Spanish, Turkish, and Vietnamese. Sample items are provided on the test publisher's website. Both individual and group reports are available.

DEVELOPMENT. The development of the AWS was initiated by reviewing studies containing correlates of burnout and job stress. These reviews led to the identification of six key domains: Workload, Control, Reward, Community, Fairness, and Values (Maslach & Leiter, 1997, 1999; Leiter & Maslach, 1999). The Areas of Worklife Survey Manual and Sampler Set provides considerable information about these six areas and research citations supporting the identification of the domains for the AWS.

The items were developed from staff surveys conducted by the Centre for Organization Research & Development. The scale showed high correlations with the three burnout dimensions measured by the Maslach Burnout Inventory-General Scale (MBI-GS).

TECHNICAL. The AWS is a survey intended to measure survey assessing organization contexts of burnout as a function of the job-person fit in six areas of a person's job environment. The manual provides a chapter on statistical properties of the AWS including descriptive statistics for each scale, quartiles, correlations among its scale and scales of the MBI-GS subscales, and evidence of reliability and validity. The normative sample (*N* = 22,714) was drawn from Canada, the United States, Italy, Spain, Finland, Germany, Mexico, Turkey, and China. Alpha coefficients for scales ranged from .67 (Workload) to .83 (Control). Test-retest reliability coefficients from administrations 1 year apart (*N* = 456) provided evidence of consistency of all six scale scores. Coefficients ranged from .51 (Reward) to .62 (Workload). Face validity is evidenced by the clarity of the survey statements, response scale, and general organization of the survey. Principal components analysis supported a six-factor structure with all items loading on an appropriate factor. A validity study examined the relationships between the AWS's six scale scores and written comments provided by participants in a hospital study. Results showed that presence of a written complaint was most strongly related with scores on the scale for which the complaint was most relevant. Differences in AWS scale scores for gender and job position (frontline, supervisor, manager) are also examined in the test manual.

COMMENTARY. The AWS is a brief survey assessing job-person fit in six key areas of worklife. It can provide useful diagnostic information to organizations wishing to address job burnout. The survey comprises 28 clearly written survey statements and an easy to understand response scale. Employees will find the survey easy to complete, and survey administrators, if not using the online version, will find the survey easy to score.

The printed survey materials provided for this review would have benefitted from the inclusion of sample score reports, the options for normative score data, and information on how to use the individual and group score reports. Based on the test publisher's website, the reports appear to have ample information regarding interpreting the AWS scores.

SUMMARY. The AWS is a brief survey assessing job stressors that contribute to burnout. It is intended to be used as part of an organizational survey. The AWS comprises clearly written survey statements and an easy to understand response scale. It is administered and scored either in a paper- or online-based format. Administration time is approximately 15 minutes.

Strengths are the survey's accessibility to a variety of employees, ease in administration and scoring, and ability to assess job-person fit in a variety of contexts that are related to job burnout and, conversely, work engagement.

REVIEWER'S REFERENCES

Leiter, M. P., & Maslach, C. (1999). Six areas of worklife: A model of the organizational context of burnout. *Journal of Health and Human Resources Administration, 21,* 472-489.

Maslach, C., & Leiter, M. P. (1997). *The truth about burnout.* San Francisco, CA: Jossey-Bass.

Maslach, C., & Leiter, M. P. (1999). Burnout and engagement in the workplace: A contextual analysis. In T. Urdan (Ed.), *Advances in motivation and achievement* (Vol. 11, pp. 275-302). Stanford, CT: JAI Press.

Review of the Areas of Worklife Survey [Fifth Edition Manual] by MELANIE E. LEUTY, Associate Professor, Department of Psychology, University of Southern Mississippi, Hattiesburg, MS:

DESCRIPTION. The Areas of Worklife Survey (AWS) is a self-report instrument measuring six areas of an employee's fit with his or her job for use in organizational surveys to provide diagnostic information to organizations interested in dealing with burnout. The AWS contains 28 items that assess six different domains: Workload, Control, Reward, Community, Fairness, and Values. Briefly, the domains are defined as follows: Workload pertains to the demands and amount of work to be done (5 items); Control refers to a worker's ability to work autonomously and have access to needed equipment and space and influence over decisions (4 items); Reward assesses receiving recognition for one's work (4 items); Community pertains to the social environment such as the availability of support and sense of collegiality (5 items); Fairness measures perceptions of fairness in decision-making, treatment from supervisors, and allocation of resources (6 items); Values assesses the match between the individual's and the organization's values (4 items). Item responses are indicated by agreement with statements using a 5-point scale ranging from 1 = *strongly disagree* to 5 = *strongly agree.* Most scales have items that are worded positively and negatively.

Scores are derived by averaging the item scores for each scale after reverse scoring eight items where the wording was negatively related to the scale. No total score is produced as such a score would not be meaningful. Average scale scores greater than 3 (3 = *hard to decide*) are indicative of a match between the person and the job on that domain whereas scores lower than 3 indicate a poor fit between the person and the job, indicating a possible stressor.

The AWS is available for use on paper or for online administration and has been translated into a number of languages. The manual notes that a subset of 18 items comprise a short version with three items assessing each domain when brevity is needed for more basic research or longer projects.

DEVELOPMENT. Previous research, as reviewed in the test manual, has documented that mismatch between an individual and his or her job relates to burnout. This concept, known as person-job fit, is part of a long history of research on person and environment interactions in the workplace. The AWS was developed to offer a broader assessment of person-job fit with the assumption that greater congruence with one's job is expected to relate to work engagement, whereas a misfit, or low congruence, likely is more related to burnout. The domains assessed on the AWS were theoretically derived given empirical evidence of these particular workplace factors relating to burnout. For instance, the inclusion of the Workload and Control scales was based on the Demand-Control theory of job stress (Karasek & Theorell, 1990), which asserts that having too many demands and/or little control over one's work relates to higher stress, with evidence finding that less control and higher demands correlate to higher exhaustion (an aspect of burnout).

AWS items were developed by the Centre for Organizational Research and Development from staff surveys and selected given a consistent factor structure across initial samples and high correlations with the three dimensions of burnout assessed by the Maslach Burnout Inventory-General Scale (MBI-GS; Schaufeli, Leiter, Maslach, & Jackson, 1996). No further information is reported in the test manual about the process of development for the full or short versions of the AWS.

The current version of the AWS (dated 2011) is a revision of the 2006 version, containing 29 items, although the first version of the measure appears to have been published in 2000 (Leiter & Maslach, 2000). Revisions to the 2006 version included deleting an item from the Workload scale that referenced fatigue that was beyond the intended construct of workload demands and deleting an item from the Values scale that had poor factor loadings in some translated versions. One item was added to the Control scale to increase inter-item correlations on some translated versions.

TECHNICAL.

Standardization. Normative data on the AWS were drawn from large samples from the United States (*N* = 5,428), Canada (*N* = 6,501), Italy (*N* = 6,077), Spain (*N* = 1,826), and Finland (*N* = 1,705); smaller samples from Mexico (*N* = 261), China (*N* = 235), Germany (*N* = 190), and Turkey (*N* = 185); and 306 participants who did not identify their nationalities. Of those reporting demographic information, there were 13,884 women and 6,815 men. Ages reported ranged from 18 to 60+ years (with sample sizes reported for five age groups). Supervisory status included frontline workers (*N* = 8,339), supervisors (*N* = 997), and upper management (*N* = 983). Occupations represented include hospital (*N* = 15,260) and university (*N* = 4,338) employees as the majority, with additional data from public service workers, retail employees, postal workers, teachers, nursing home workers, and those not reporting occupation (*N* = 645). The test manual provides quartiles, means, standard deviations, skewness, and kurtosis for each of the six domains for the total normative sample. Tables containing descriptive data for the six scales by gender and position (i.e., frontline, supervisor, manager) are available, noting significant difference across scales. Differences in scale scores by age have been found (Leiter & Maslach, 2003a) as well. No information is reported in the test manual regarding the ethnicity or employment tenure (which may be useful for comparison) of the normative sample.

Reliability. Internal consistency reliability (coefficient alpha) for the normative sample is reported for the six scales as follows: Workload (.67), Control (.83), Reward (.78), Community (.80), Fairness (.80), and Values (.73). Test-retest correlations for a sample of health care workers (*N* = 456) are favorable, ranging from .51 (Reward) to .62 (Workload) although the time period of the delay was simply listed as "over" one year (manual, p. 17). Alpha coefficients also are reported for scales on the 18-item short version, ranging from .48 (Workload) to .76 (Reward).

Validity Evidence. Contributing to content evidence of validity, principal components analysis of the 28 items is reported. Notably, all items have loadings above an absolute value of .50 on their respective scales with the exception of the last item on the Workload scale (-.468), and low cross loadings on other scales (e.g., all below an absolute value of .31).

Limited evidence to evaluate construct validity is presented in the test manual. Although the test authors report that the impetus for creating the AWS was to assess broad areas of person-job fit, most items do not appear to be assessing fit per se but rather one's evaluation of the environment regardless of whether the individual perceives this aspect as matching his or her preferences. The exception is the Values scale, on which items are worded to appear to tap into a person's fit with the organization's values. Adding to this criticism, no comparisons between AWS scales and measures of fit are reported. What is reported are data from qualitative responses, mostly complaints, obtained from a subsample of 1,443 individuals from a hospital study (Leiter & Maslach, 2003b). The authors coded these responses into 21 categories that were associated with one of the six scales and then assigned a binary code as to whether a participant provided a response to one of these. These scores were then correlated with participant's AWS scores. These correlations were mostly small in magnitude (i.e., < .14), but with few exceptions, complaints demonstrated the highest correlations with their respective scales. Correlations between the six AWS scales also are reported in the manual with most being low to moderate, ranging from .09 (Workload and Values) to .52 (Fairness and Values).

Supportive criterion-related evidence of validity is available. Correlations with the MBI-GS are reported in the manual, with all six scales being negatively related to the Exhaustion (r = -.23 to -.49) and Cynicism (r = -.19 to -.36) components of burnout and positively related to the efficacy component (r =.01 to .31). The results were expected, although some of these correlations are quite low. Conversely, Alarcon and Lyons (2011) report positive correlations between the AWS scales and facets of work engagement (r = .05 to .55) and overall job satisfaction (r = .29 Workload to .60 Values). Maslach and Leiter (2008) found the AWS, particularly low scores on the Fairness dimension, predicted burnout a year later.

COMMENTARY. The AWS is a brief tool designed to assess a number of different organizational dimensions of which an individual fits with his/her job. Its strengths include its brevity, including availability of a short form; ease of use; and translations into a number of languages. With the exception of the Workload scale, all reliability meet or exceed .70. The Workload scale, in both the 28- and 18-item versions, has less than ideal internal consistency and may need further revision, especially given the lower factor loading (-.468) of one item. However, other samples have found adequate reliability for the previous version of this scale (Maslach & Leiter, 2008). Additionally, a very large normative sample was used, and descriptive data for some useful demographic factors (e.g., gender and position) are reported.

Despite these strengths at this time, there is limited construct evidence of validity reported to support that scales are measuring the intended constructs or person-job fit. However, as an overarching goal in the development of the AWS was to assess organizational factors that promote burnout, correlations between the AWS scales and MBI-GS scales, as well as Engagement, do support this purpose.

SUMMARY. The AWS was developed to be used to assess the match between an individual and six organizational factors known to relate to burnout. Reliability and evidence of validity is mostly favorable, but limited evidence of validity is available in the test manual. This deficit appears to be an omission of the manual more than that of available research because available studies provide support for using the AWS to predict burnout and work engagement or to assess intervention outcomes. Caution is suggested for use other than this purpose.

REVIEWER'S REFERENCES

Alarcon, G. M., & Lyons, J. B. (2011). The relationship of engagement and job satisfaction in working samples. *The Journal of Psychology, 145*, 463-480.

Karasek, R., & Theorell, T. (1990). *Stress, productivity, and the reconstruction of working life.* New York, NY: Basic Books.

Leiter, M. P., & Maslach, C. (2000). Areas of Worklife Survey. Wolfville, NS, Canada: Center for Organizational Research & Development.

Leiter, M. P., & Maslach, C. (2003a). Areas of worklife: A structured approach to organizational predictors of job burnout. In P. L. Perrewe & D. C. Ganster (Eds.), Research in Occupational Stress and Well Being Series: Vol. 3. Emotional and physiological processes and positive intervention strategies (pp. 91-134). Oxford, UK: Elsevier.

Leiter, M. P., & Maslach, C. (2003b). *A mediation model of job burnout.* Unpublished manuscript.

Maslach, C., & Leiter, M. P. (2008). Early predictors of job burnout and engagement. *Journal of Applied Psychology, 93*, 498-512.

Schaufeli, W. B., Leiter, M. P., Maslach, C., & Jackson, S. E. (1996). The Maslach Burnout Inventory—General Survey. In C. Maslach, S. E. Jackson, & M. P. Leiter (Eds.), *MBI manual* (3rd ed.). Palo Alto, CA: Consulting Psychologists Press.

[8]

Arizona Articulation and Phonology Scale, Fourth Revision.

Purpose: Designed to evaluate "articulatory and phonological skills."

Population: Ages 18 months through 21 years.

Publication Dates: 1963-2017.

Acronym: Arizona–4.

Scores, 7: Word Articulation Total, Sentence Articulation Total, Word-Sentence Articulation Critical Difference, Percentage of Speech Improvement, Level of Articulatory Impairment, Phonology, Level of Phonological Impairment.

Administration: Individual.

Price Data, 2020: $289 per kit (print or digital) including manual (2017, 226 pages), 25 word/sentence articulation forms, 25 phonology coding forms, and easel; $104 per manual (print or digital); $147 per stimulus

book (print easel or digital images and print and digital administration guides); $42 per 25 word/sentence articulation forms; $42 per 25 phonology coding forms; $389 per print/digital combination kit.
Time: 5-20 minutes each for administration of Word Articulation and Sentence Articulation, plus 5-10 minutes each for scoring; 5-20 minutes for completion of Phonology.
Comments: Previously titled Arizona Articulation Proficiency Scale; Word Articulation and Sentence Articulation may be administered together or separately; online scoring and reporting available.
Authors: Janet B. Fudala and Sheri Stegall.
Publisher: Western Psychological Services.
Cross References: For reviews by Steven Long and Roger L. Towne of the third revision, see 16:15; see also T5:175 (12 references) and T4:191 (4 references); for reviews by Penelope K. Hall and Charles Wm. Martin of the second edition, see 11:17 (12 references); see also T3:200 (8 references); for reviews by Raphael M. Haller and Ronald K. Sommers, and an excerpted review by Barton B. Proger of the revised edition, see 8:954 (6 references); see also T2:2065 (2 references), 7:948 (2 references), and 6:307a (2 references).

Review of the Arizona Articulation and Phonology Scale-Fourth Revision by SHARI L. DeVENEY, Associate Professor of Special Education and Communication Disorders, University of Nebraska at Omaha, Omaha, NE:

DESCRIPTION. The 2017 revision of the Arizona Articulation and Phonology Scale (Arizona-4) is a norm-referenced instrument designed to evaluate American English speech sound production skills of individuals ages 1:6 to 21:11 years. The assessment is administered individually to determine the presence of articulatory and phonologically based speech sound disorders (SSDs). Although previous versions of the assessment tool have focused on articulatory-based SSD, the fourth revision's expanded application incorporates identification of phonologically based SSDs. The current edition includes three norm-referenced tests: Word Articulation, Sentence Articulation (with a more restricted normed age range, 3:0-21:11), and Phonology. Examinee responses, derived from naming, repeating, or reading stimuli presented with either a printed test easel or in digital format, may be elicited through line-drawn colored picture stimuli for the Word Articulation and Phonology tests and through word/sentence orthographic representation for all three norm-referenced tests. The inclusion of the orthographic stimuli presentation option allows for age-appropriate presentation to older children, adolescents, and adults who are readers. The Arizona-4 is one of the only commercially available norm-referenced speech sound assessment tools to offer this presentation option, making its use preferable for speech-language pathologists (SLPs) working primarily with students/young adults in the upper portion of the normed age range.

Administration time for the word and sentence tests is estimated at 5-20 minutes. Phonology consists of the first 41 of 48 target responses to the Word Articulation test transferred to the Phonology coding form. Scoring the articulation and sentence portions is estimated to take 5-10 minutes, whereas scoring Phonology is estimated to take an additional 5-20 minutes. Consequently, for most examiners, administration and scoring of all three norm-referenced sections will be a 15- to 50-minute task with variability depending on numerous factors including familiarity with the assessment tool and characteristics of the examinee. Several supplemental non-standardized sections also are available, completion of which would add to the estimated administration and scoring time.

The assessment tool may be scored manually or online using the test publisher's platform. The online scoring option is another new feature of the current edition. Consistent with previous versions, scoring involves the examiner judging the accuracy of target consonant and vowel productions. The word and sentence record form provides space for phonetic transcription of errors, full words, and/or sentences; however, scoring of these sections is based on accurate/inaccurate judgments of consonants produced in initial/final position and vowels, negating the need for phonetic transcription proficiency. Still, the descriptive content that phonetic transcription provides would be advantageous to record to assist in the determination of similarities/patterns across errors produced and in planning intervention. Each sound error is assigned a numerical value (range = 0.5-5.0) reflecting its frequency of use in American speech, for which higher values are assigned to more frequently used sounds. The numerical values are used to calculate total scores for word and sentence articulation. Phonology scoring involves identification of 11 phonological error patterns, 10 of which are developmental and one, initial consonant deletion, that is considered to be an uncommon error pattern (Bankson & Bernthal, 1990; Bauman-Waengler, 2016). The number of target words and types of phonological error patterns are comparable to, yet below, those represented in the third edition of the Khan-Lewis Phonological Analysis (KLPA-3; Khan & Lewis, 2015), a test for identifying preschool phonological patterns often used by American SLPs. The KLPA-3 consists of 60 target words (Arizona-4 has 41) and 12 core phonological error patterns along with 12 supplemental processes (Arizona-4 has 11 total). For this section of the Arizona-4, the number of occurrences for each phonological error pattern is used to calculate a Phonology raw score.

Instructions, illustrations, and reference tables for scoring all three norm-referenced tests are presented in the examiner's manual in a user-friendly, explicit, and clear format. Gender specific normative information is available up to age 5:11.

DEVELOPMENT. The Arizona-4 is the fourth revision of the assessment tool first published in 1963. The theory and rationale underlying the Arizona-4, which is grounded in the "intelligibility model of speech communication" (manual, p. 104), remains consistent with the original instrument. The test authors described the rationale as "the more frequently a misarticulated sound is heard, the more difficult it is to understand the speaker" (manual, p. 104). The Arizona's unique weighted scoring method is aligned with this notion of frequency relative to listener-perceived speech intelligibility. As previous reviewers of this assessment tool have noted, although the sound frequency reference source forming the basis of the scoring system is fairly dated (Barker, 1960), the overall scoring system continues to present a well thought through, useful representation of American English sound frequency.

Differences between the third revision (Fudala, 2000) and the Arizona-4 are numerous, substantive, and positive. These differences include an expanded number of stimulus items in Word Articulation (increased from the 42 items in the third revision back to the 48 items that were included in the second revision); transition to uniformly colored picture stimuli illustrations from previous black-and-white line drawings; updated normative data that include an expansion of the standardized age range from 18:11 to 21:11; scoring guidance specific to dialectal variations of English including African American vernacular and Spanish-influenced English; inclusion of standardized assessment for phonologically based SSDs; inclusion of a standardized sentence-level task that allows for direct comparison to targeted single-word productions; a change in the scoring system such that numeric values of vowels are reduced compared to consonant values (currently representing 29.5% of score values compared with 44.5% previously); and incorporation of technological options for presentation of stimulus material, scoring, and report generation.

From this reviewer's viewpoint, the inclusion of the Phonology section represents the most substantial difference between the Arizona-4 and its predecessors. The development was a threefold process beginning with a review of existing research, analysis of error patterns assessed using existing stimuli from the Arizona-3, and solicitation of feedback from professional examiners. Next, a pilot study including 104 participants ranging in age from 2 to 9 years was conducted to determine the ease of naming current and alternative target words using updated color picture stimuli. Finally, decisions were made regarding target words to be retained for the test's standardization process such that target words were readily nameable; represented the pre-determined 11 phonological error patterns; and did not show evidence of bias regarding gender, ethnicity, socioeconomic status, or disability.

TECHNICAL. The Arizona-4 was standardized using a sample of 3,192 cases across the target age range, 1:6-21:11, collected by 63 data collectors across 29 states in the four major geographic regions recognized by the U.S. Census. Data were gathered by both students and licensed SLPs. The test authors detailed reasonable requirements for data collectors to observe in order to participate (e.g., submission of first five completed record forms for research staff review and feedback). Efforts were made to align the demographic characteristics of the standardization sample with the 2012 U.S. Census figures across gender, race/ethnicity, parent education level, and geographic region. The sample included individuals with mild disabilities, but not severe (e.g., excluded those with intellectual deficits and/or moderate to severe autism spectrum disorder) such that 7% of the sample had a diagnosed disability including 3% with speech-language impairment. The test authors included information about dialectal differences of the speakers sampled. The breakdown is as follows: 79% Standard American English, 9% African American vernacular, 7% Spanish-influenced English, 4% Southern English, and 1% Asian-influenced or other dialects of English. Whether this breakdown was consistent with Census figures was not addressed.

Evidence of reliability was well documented in the examiner's manual. Three approaches were incorporated to estimate the reliability of the Arizona-4:

internal consistency using the split-half method; test-retest reliability within a 2-week interval; and interrater reliability between research assistants, between research assistants and field examiners, and between field examiners. For all of these measures, reliability coefficients were high across age ranges and across each of the three norm-referenced tests, with values ranging from r = .85 to 1.00.

Numerous approaches were employed to examine evidence of test score validity. Sources of evidence included content, response process, construct, convergence, and detection of clinical groups. These are discussed extensively in the examiner's manual. Of note, convergent evidence of validity showed the Arizona-4 correlated with other SSD identification assessment tools, including the Goldman-Fristoe Test of Articulation-Second Edition (GFTA-2; Goldman & Fristoe, 2000). Coefficients between Arizona-4 Word Articulation scores and scores on the GFTA-2 Sounds-in-Words test were .77 for a subset of the standardization sample (n = 55) and .85 for the clinical sample. For Arizona-4 Phonology and the KLPA-2 (Kahn & Lewis, 2002) standard score, coefficients were .76 for the standardization sample subset and .65 for the clinical sample. It should be noted that GFTA and KLPA are now in third edition, as of 2015.

COMMENTARY. This latest revision of the Arizona was substantial compared with previous versions and increased the clinical utility for a more diverse sample of speakers including those presenting with phonologically based SSDs, those with dialectal variations of American English, and those between the ages of 19 and 21 years. Consistent with previous versions of the assessment tool, the latest edition is easy to administer and score. Several unique features separate the Arizona-4 from other commercially available SSD assessment tools and further extend its usefulness: vowel assessment inclusion, options available for stimulus item presentation (e.g., orthographic symbols for examinees who are readers, digital format availability), and potential for identification of both articulatory and phonologically based SSDs.

SUMMARY. The Arizona-4 is a well-designed and comprehensive assessment tool representing a substantial improvement over the previous version. This assessment tool is appropriate for a wide variety of individuals and now includes an expanded focus inclusive of phonologically based SSDs. However, SLPs working primarily with young children suspected of frequent phonological process use may find the KLPA-3 a preferable alternative for identification of a larger scope of developmental phonological error patterns.

REVIEWER'S REFERENCES

Bankson, N. W., & Bernthal, J. E. (1990). Bankson-Bernthal Test of Phonology. San Antonio, TX: Special Press.

Barker, J. O. (1960). A numerical measure of articulation. *Journal of Speech and Hearing Disorders, 25,* 79-88.

Bauman-Waengler, J. (2016). *Articulation and phonology in speech sound disorders: A clinical focus* (5th ed.). Boston, MA: Pearson.

Fudala, J. B. (2000). Arizona Articulation Proficiency Scale, Third Revision. Torrance, CA: Western Psychological Services.

Goldman, R., & Fristoe, M. (2000). Goldman-Fristoe Test of Articulation—Second Edition. Circle Pines, MN: American Guidance Service.

Kahn, L. M., & Lewis, N. P. (2002). Kahn-Lewis Phonological Analysis—Second Edition. Circle Pines, MN: American Guidance Service.

Kahn, L. M., & Lewis, N. P. (2015). Kahn-Lewis Phonological Analysis—Third Edition. Bloomington, MN: Pearson.

Review of the Arizona Articulation and Phonology Scale, Fourth Revision by REBECCA J. McCAULEY, Professor, Department of Speech and Hearing Science, The Ohio State University, Columbus, OH:

DESCRIPTION. The Arizona Articulation and Phonology Scale, Fourth Revision (Arizona-4) comprises three tests and five supplemental tasks designed to aid in the evaluation of speech production in English. Two of these tests examine articulatory skills—one in single words (the Word Articulation test; normed for ages 18 months through 21 years) and the other in connected speech (the Sentence Articulation test; normed for ages 3 through 21 years). The third test (the Phonology test; normed for ages 18 months through 21 years) uses phonological processes to describe misarticulations made on the items from the Word Articulation test as well as seven additional items.

Purposes for which the Arizona-4 is intended include description of articulatory ability compared to a normative group, description of intelligibility, comparison of performance in single word versus connected speech, treatment planning, and progress monitoring over time. Materials for the Arizona-4 include a test manual, self-standing stimulus book, alternative digital stimulus images, record forms for the two articulation tests, and a coding form for the Phonology test. Each of the two articulation tests requires about 5 to 20 minutes for administration and 5 to 10 minutes for scoring; the Phonology test requires 5 to 20 minutes of coding based on responses to the Word Articulation test. Total scores for each articulation test are reported on a scale of 1 to 100, with each target sound weighted by a value equivalent to its frequency of occurrence in American speech. In addition, standard scores, severity ranges, percentile ranks, and test-age equivalents can be reported. For the Phonology test, raw and standard scores are available. The technical manual is well organized, easy to read, and contains numerous examples as well as guidance designed to help address dialectal variation, especially that related to African American and Spanish-influenced English.

DEVELOPMENT. The Arizona-4 has predecessors dating to the late 1950s. One of the innovative features of the original Arizona, maintained through to this fourth revision, is the use of the total score for articulation reflecting the frequency of occurrence of individual sounds in American speech with the goal of approximating the effects of production errors on intelligibility. The expected frequency of occurrence used to create the scoring systems in all versions of the Arizona has been based on frequencies obtained from a study of 500 telephone conversations in New York City (French, Carter, & Koenig, 1930), with empirical support from high correlations (>.90) between expert judgments of children's speech samples and their performances using closely related scoring systems (Barker, 1960; Barker & England, 1962). Changes that resulted in the Arizona-4 version of the scoring system included increasing the relative contribution of consonants to the total score, with corresponding decreases in the contribution of vowels, as well as several other small adjustments that are described in the test manual. Other changes made to the Arizona-3 to arrive at the current edition included updating the Word Articulation test, creating the Sentence Articulation and Phonology tests, and collecting data for new norms and new reliability and validity analyses.

TECHNICAL.

Standardization. Data for standardization of the Arizona-4 were obtained by trained data collectors from 3,192 individuals, ages 1:6 to 21:11 years, in 29 states across the four major geographic regions used in the U.S. Census. Demographic characteristics of the sample matched those of the U.S. population to within about 5% in terms of gender, ethnicity, geographic region and parental educational level (as a proxy for socioeconomic status). Although test takers with serious disabilities were excluded, 7% of the standardization sample had a diagnosed disability and 8% had a language other than English as their home language. Dialect variability is also described.

Reliability. Reliability was examined using three approaches: internal consistency, test-retest, and interrater. Internal consistency, which reflects the extent to which items are correlated with each other and therefore may reflect the extent to which they are measuring the same construct, was reasonably high for ages covered by the typically developing standardization sample (split-half correlation coefficients of .87 to .98) as well as for the clinical sample (coefficients were .88 or higher).

Test-retest reliability coefficients estimated over a time interval averaging 2 weeks were also high (.94 or higher) for 94 cases whose demographic characteristics generally approximated the gender, ethnicity, age, parent's education, and geographic area of the entire standardization sample. Differences in the amount of change between Time 1 and Time 2 for the three major tests in the instrument yielded only small effect sizes as measured by Cohen's *d*.

Interrater reliability was assessed using two raters—one administering and scoring the test and the other who only scored the test for 97 cases from the standardization sample. Intraclass correlation coefficients (ICCs), which examine the amount of variability related to test takers' performances versus that related to raters' scoring, were obtained for the Word Articulation and Sentence Articulation tests and were excellent, at .90 and .85, respectively. For the Phonology test, interrater agreement as measured by ICCs was acceptable to excellent (r = .85 to 1.00) across three pairings: two research assistants (n = 50), two field examiners (n = 97), and a research assistant and a field examiner (n = 3,192).

Validity. Validity evidence offered in support of the Arizona-4 encompasses most of the sources described in the *Standards for Educational and Psychological Testing* (American Educational Research Association, American Psychological Association, & National Council on Management in Education, 2014). With regard to content-related evidence, the authors report extensive examinations of the test items' relevance, content coverage, and developmental appropriateness.

Demonstrations that the test performs as expected based on the construct it measures included studies of developmental changes of scores across age, correlations between the three component tests, and expert judgment of intelligibility. Separately for boys and girls, the test authors plotted raw mean scores against age and showed patterns similar to those expected based on the developmental literature. Correlations between Word Articulation and Sentence Articulation showed a strong correlation with moderate correlations between those two tests and the Phonology test. When field examiners for the Arizona-4 made judgments of intelligibility along a 6-point scale, correlations between those judgments and Word Articulation were .78 and between those judgments and Sentence Articulation were .66. Exact agreements between those ratings and the two articulation tests were 73% and 77%, respectively.

Other data used to effectively support the validity of the tests included comparisons of the Word Articulation test with the earlier Arizona-3 and with the Goldman-Fristoe Test of Articulation—Second Edition (GFTA-2; Goldman & Fristoe, 2000) and the Phonology test with the Khan-Lewis Phonological Analysis—Second Edition (KLPA-2; Khan & Lewis, 2002), a companion to the GFTA-2. Finally, a comparison of 50 individuals with and without diagnosed speech sound disorders was used to examine the diagnostic accuracy of the Arizona-4. All of the component tests of the Arizona-4 showed significant differences between groups with large effect sizes. A range of diagnostic accuracy scores (i.e., sensitivity, specificity, positive predictive values, and negative predictive values) were calculated and were impressive for several cut points. Although highly desirable in a diagnostic test, such data are rarely reported in tests of this kind.

COMMENTARY. Although this reviewer is not convinced that the test's continuing use of frequency of occurrence data for phonemes taken from a small sample in 1930 remains the best source of such information, the Arizona-4 has undergone significant and impressive revision and study since the publication of the Arizona-3 (Fudala, 2000). With the addition of the Sentence Articulation test and the Phonology test, the Arizona-4 has gone beyond its earlier history as an articulation test to be useful for examining speech sound disorders across a broader range of severity. Extensive attention to the technical features of this instrument's revision, especially reliability and validity, make it one of the most thoroughly supported tests available, especially for diagnosis.

SUMMARY. In summary, this extensively updated and well-studied assessment tool has much to recommend it for the assessment of children and adults suspected of having articulation or phonological speech sound disorders.

REVIEWER'S REFERENCES

American Educational Research Association, American Psychological Association, & National Council on Measurement in Education. (2014). *Standards for educational and psychological testing.* Washington, DC: American Educational Research Association.

Barker, J. O. (1960). A numerical measure of articulation. *Journal of Speech and Hearing Disorders, 25,* 79-88.

Barker, J., & England, G. (1962). A numerical measure of articulation: Further developments. *Journal of Speech and Hearing Disorders, 27,* 23-26.

French, N. R., Carter, C. W., & Koenig, W. (1930). The words and sounds of telephone conversations. *The Bell System Technical Journal, 9,* 290-324.

Fudala, J. B. (2000). Arizona Articulation Proficiency Scale, Third Revision. Torrance, CA: Western Psychological Services.

Goldman, R., & Fristoe, M. (2000). Goldman-Fristoe Test of Articulation—Second Edition. Circle Pines, MN: American Guidance Service.

Khan, L. M., & Lewis, N. P. (2002). Khan-Lewis Phonological Analysis—Second Edition. Circle Pines, MN: American Guidance Service.

[9]

Assessment for Persons With Profound or Severe Impairments–Second Edition.

Purpose: Designed for "identifying abilities or behaviors that examinees with severe or profound impairments can demonstrate, identifying abilities or behaviors that should be taught next, and monitoring examinee progress."

Population: Infants through adults who are thought to be profoundly or severely impaired and functioning within the birth-through-24-month age level.

Publication Dates: 1984-2019.

Acronym: APPSI-2.

Scores: 5 domains assessed in 2 content areas: Foundational Learning Components (Alertness Domain, Preferences Domain); Developmental Components (Problem-Solving Prerequisites Domain, Communication Domain, Social-Emotional Domain).

Administration: Individual.

Forms, 7: Alertness Domain Record Form, Stimulus Preference Record Form, Reward Preference-Choice Record Form, Reward Preference-Approach Record Form, Problem-Solving Prerequisites and Communication Domains Record Booklet, Social-Emotional Domain Record Form, Goal Attainment Scaling Record Form.

Price Data, 2020: $271 per complete kit including manual (2019, 39 pages), 25 of each record form and an object kit with mesh bag; $39 per manual; $27 per 25 record forms (Alertness Domain, Goal Attainment Scaling, Social-Emotional Domain, Reward Preference-Choice, Reward Preference-Approach, or Stimulus Preference); $31 per 25 Problem-solving Prerequisites and Communication Domains record booklets; $39 per object kit.

Time: 16-60 minutes for administration, depending on domains used.

Comments: Domains may be administered individually or as a group in any order.

Authors: Sharon Bradley-Johnson and C. Merle Johnson.

Publisher: PRO-ED.

a) ALERTNESS DOMAIN RECORD FORM.

Purpose: Designed "to record the frequency of an examinee's alert states."

Scores: 6 alertness categories: Sleep, Drowsy, Alert, Self-Stimulation, Fussy to Agitated, Seizures.

Comments: Sleep-Pattern Questionnaire (optional) may be used "to obtain information on the examinee's sleep routines."

b) STIMULUS PREFERENCE RECORD FORM.
Purpose: Designed "to identify and record the types of stimuli likely to evoke a response from the examinee."
Scores: Preferences for 3 types of stimuli: Visual Stimulus, Auditory Stimulus, Presence Stimulus.
c) REWARD PREFERENCE-CHOICE RECORD FORM.
Purpose: Designed "to identify objects and edibles an examinee prefers."
Population: Examinees able to indicate their choices.
d) REWARD PREFERENCE-APPROACH RECORD FORM.
Purpose: Designed "to identify objects and edibles an examinee prefers."
Population: Examinees unable to indicate their choices.
e) PROBLEM-SOLVING PREREQUISITES AND COMMUNICATION DOMAINS RECORD BOOKLET.
Purpose: Designed "to assess abilities ranging from visual attending and grasping to vocal and nonvocal communication abilities."
Scores: Criterion-referenced item scores for 12 first-year abilities and 11 second-year abilities.
f) SOCIAL-EMOTIONAL DOMAIN RECORD FORM.
Purpose: Designed "to assess the vocal and nonvocal abilities used to initiate interaction and respond appropriately to the initiations of others."
Scores: Criterion-referenced scores for 18 items.
g) GOAL ATTAINMENT SCALING RECORD FORM.
Purpose: Designed "to aid instructional decision making and for evaluating examinee progress on abilities assessed on any or all APPSI-2 domains."

Cross References: For reviews by Carolyn Mitchell-Person and Lawrence J. Ryan of the previous edition titled Assessment for Persons Profoundly or Severely Impaired, see 15:18; for reviews by Karen T. Carey and Joe Olmi of an earlier edition titled Preverbal Assessment Intervention Profile, see 11:301.

Review of the Assessment for Persons With Profound or Severe Impairments—Second Edition by LISA L. PERSINGER, Assistant Professor, Northern Arizona University, Flagstaff, AZ:

DESCRIPTION. The Assessment for Persons With Profound or Severe Impairments—Second Edition (APPSI-2) is an individually administered, standardized test that is intended to aid in instructional planning and progress monitoring for individuals with severe and profound disabilities whose mental age is estimated to be below 24 months. This test is a third-generation instrument whose prior versions include the Assessment for Persons Profoundly or Severely Impaired (APPSI; 1994) and the Preverbal Assessment-Intervention Profile (1984). The test has standardized administration procedures for five developmental domains; however, no specific standard scores are derived. Rather, the instrument is intended to assist with identification of the examinee's abilities and behaviors within each domain in order to target instruction. The test authors report that four principles guided the substantial revision of the instrument to its current form. Those principles included (a) create an assessment system comprehensive enough to drive individualized instruction, (b) provide a system of assessments that can be used for progress monitoring, (c) provide an assessment that takes idiosyncratic needs of examinees into account, and (d) create an assessment that reflects the examinee's abilities as well as identifies those abilities to be targeted in instruction.

The test can be administered in 15 minutes to 1 hour depending upon how many domains are assessed. Administration should be expected to be conducted over multiple days in order to sample the targeted behaviors and obtain adequate information about the examinee. The five domains that can be assessed are Alertness, Preferences, Problem-Solving Prerequisites, Communication, and Social-Emotional. Alertness and Preferences are considered foundational learning components whereas Problem-Solving Prerequisites, Communication, and Social-Emotional are developmental components. The scoring procedure for each domain is described in the test manual and repeated on the corresponding domain form. Domains may be administered in any order or combination. The Preferences domain has three separate record forms to help differentiate procedures to assess an examinee's choice between items versus hierarchical preference regarding stimuli that help to establish an understanding of what is rewarding to the examinee.

The APPSI-2 kit comes with visual and auditory stimulus materials. These materials should be supplemented with additional materials customized based on the examinee's known interests. These follow a standard preference assessment procedure in applied behavior analysis. There is also an optional Sleep-Pattern Questionnaire in the appendix of the test manual that is associated with the Alertness domain. Administration of domains is linked to a Goal Attainment Scaling record form that can be used for recording goals derived from the examinee's documented abilities and instructional needs and tracking progress.

The Alertness domain is scored during multiple observations in the morning and afternoon on different days with interval recording of different states including sleep, drowsy, alert, self-stimulation, fussy to agitated, and seizure activity. Percent of intervals observed during which the state was predominant are computed across all four observations. With the exception of the Preferences domain, the other domains are scored item by item with + if the behavior occurred, 0 if not, and NP when the behavior is not physically possible for the examinee. Each record form has ample space for qualitative notes and a summary of observed abilities. The test authors provide helpful guidelines for planning instruction based on information obtained through administration of the APPSI-2 with multiple observations over time.

Administration is standardized, though examiners are also encouraged to be flexible and provide needed adaptations and repeated assessment with the goal of obtaining accurate information about the examinee. Examiners should have training in individual assessment and systematic direct observation procedures.

DEVELOPMENT. The test authors provide minimal information about development of the APPSI-2. In the test manual they report that they considered test reviews of the APPSI, their own personal experiences, review of research about the domains, and feedback from the APPSI users. There is no description of piloting of the instrument. Rather, a validity chapter in the manual provides an overview of the sources for research review supporting each domain construction.

TECHNICAL. The APPSI-2 is not a norm-referenced measure, and as such, there is no standardization sample. The focus of technical adequacy presented in the test manual is on content validity of results in each domain. This discussion is a significant improvement over the prior version of the instrument, which did not include any validity discussion (Mitchell-Person, 2003). The test authors cite and describe development of the Preferences domain procedures based on classic and contemporary behavior analytic literature. Problem-Solving, Social-Emotional, and Communication domains are evaluated in relation to eight different developmental assessment instruments as well as a review of contemporary research about typical child development with items organized by age in the record forms. The Goal Attainment Scaling form development is rooted in associated literature. There is no information provided in the test manual about reliability. The authors make clear the need to probe the examinee on items when scoring is unclear and to assess on different occasions to ensure that the most accurate information about an examinee is obtained. These author recommendations are the most relevant to understanding how to reduce bias and increase the validity of an individual examinee's results. It would be helpful if the test authors placed this discussion in the validity section of the manual and related the discussion to industry standards articulated in the *Standards for Educational and Psychological Testing* (American Educational Research Association, American Psychological Association, & National Council on Measurement in Education, 2014).

COMMENTARY. The APPSI-2 represents a substantial revision of the APPSI. The addition of the Goal Attainment Scale form and explanation for its use are helpful because it adds a direct link between the domain measures and the instructional goals and progress monitoring. The addition of the Preferences domain assessment enhances the benefit of this instrument for instructional planning. The theoretical model of this instrument is not described in the test manual, though it appears that the Communication and Problem-Solving domains remain rooted in a Piagetian framework, whereas the new domain of Preferences is clearly derived from a behavioral perspective. The instrument is likely to provide relevant functional information that can be used to develop goals and reinforcement plans for instructional purposes. Evidence of content validity is presented, but there is no evidence of any form of reliability nor piloting of the new instrument with the target population. At a minimum, evidence of interrater reliability would provide valuable information about this instrument. The psychometric weaknesses should be addressed.

SUMMARY. The APPSI-2 was designed to be an individually administered measure of key developmental and learning components to facilitate development of relevant and targeted instruction for individuals with severe and profound impairments whose mental age is below 24 months. Although this is a complex population of individuals, this instrument is laid out well and easy to follow for an examiner who is both informed and experienced in working with this population. The test is likely to yield very helpful information regarding instructional planning in Communication, Social-Emotional, and Problem-Solving developmental domains informed by the examinee's Alertness and Preferences. Additionally, the Goal Attainment Scaling form facilitates progress monitoring. Overall, despite concerns about inadequate presentation of technical adequacy, this instrument has face validity. Research addressing needed aspects of technical adequacy will be helpful to further evaluate the APPSI-2.

REVIEWER'S REFERENCES

American Educational Research Association, American Psychological Association, & National Council on Measurement in Education. (2014). *Standards for educational and psychological testing*. Washington, DC: AERA.

Mitchell-Person, C. (2003). [Test review of the Assessment for Persons Profoundly or Severely Impaired]. In B. S. Plake, J. C. Impara, & R. A. Spies (Eds.), *The fifteenth mental measurements yearbook*. Retrieved from http://marketplace.unl.edu/buros/

Review of the Assessment for Persons With Profound or Severe Impairments—Second Edition by MARTIN J. WIESE, Licensed Psychologist/Certified School Psychologist, Lincoln Public Schools, Lincoln, NE:

DESCRIPTION. The Assessment for Persons With Profound or Severe Impairments—Second Edition (APPSI-2) is designed to provide a standard assessment to assist with designing effective individualized instructional programs and for use in monitoring individual progress. It is intended for use with preverbal individuals at any age whose cognitive functioning is within the severe or profound range (birth through 24 months) due to cognitive disability, severe autism, brain trauma, or multiple impairments. With this successor to the Assessment for Persons Profoundly or Severely Impaired (APPSI; 1994) the test authors attempted to address, in part, reviewers' concerns about a lack of psychometric properties and administration and scoring complexities (Mitchell-Person, 2003; Ryan, 2003).

The APPSI-2 kit contains an examiner's manual, seven different examiner record forms (plus an optional sleep pattern questionnaire), and manipulatives. The various record forms are used to assess different domains including Alertness, Preferences, Problem-Solving, Communication, and Social-Emotional. Manipulatives are used during administration to elicit responses from the examinee. Items within the Alertness and Preferences domains are used to assess an individual's foundations or readiness for learning. The remaining three domains are considered developmental and represent the skills necessary to control the immediate environment and enhance the individual's quality of life. A Goal Attainment Scaling record form is used to identify and record up to four instructional goals for the examinee and to track progress.

Section one of the examiner's manual presents an introduction to the APPSI-2, explaining its underlying framework, selection of content areas assessed, suggested uses for the test, and examiner qualifications. Section two of the manual provides general administration procedures, estimates of testing time, and instructions for completing the record forms. A table is provided to help the examiner decide which domains are most relevant to answer the referral questions. Depending on the information needed, all or portions of the APPSI-2 can be administered in any order. Each of the domain record forms has separate directions, but all generally follow a standard format and include identifying information, summary of observations or results, and space to record notes or additional information.

Guidelines for planning instruction are provided in section three of the examiner's manual. This section provides ways to interpret the APPSI-2 results in order to increase the effectiveness of instruction and improve learning. Examples of how to use the APPSI-2 to facilitate learning and demonstrate progress are provided. The final section of the test manual concludes with a short discussion of content evidence of validity.

DEVELOPMENT. The APPSI-2 was developed to help educators and therapists design effective individualized instructional programs and/or monitor individual progress. The developers state four goals for the APPSI-2: create a standardized comprehensive assessment to guide instruction for individuals with severe or profound disabilities, provide several ways to evaluate instruction, allow for the different needs of the individuals assessed, and accurately depict their abilities and needs. The APPSI-2 is not norm-referenced, and no standardization data are provided. Items from each domain were selected and included based on a review of research studies and methods as well as scrutiny of eight norm-referenced tests of infant/toddler cognitive development and communication skills.

TECHNICAL. Very limited psychometric information is provided, perhaps no more than that reported in the previous version of the test. There is minimal information about standardization, test construction, or domain item selection. No estimates of test reliability or internal consistency are provided. An assessment of interrater reliability would be one way to bolster the APPSI-2 psychometric properties by quantifying the agreement between two observers who make independent ratings about test takers' behaviors and responses to stimuli presented.

The test authors explain that "because the APPSI-2 is not norm-referenced, most types of technical adequacy do not apply" (examiner's manual, p. 25). An individual's performance in the measured domains is not designed for conversion to standard scores of any kind and is not compared to a reference group. The only psychometric properties provided are found in section four of the examiner's manual where the test authors include a discussion of content validity evidence for the APPSI-2, including the format of the instrument and item content within each domain.

COMMENTARY. The APPSI-2 is better described as a structured observation system (rather than a test) that is useful in observing and recording specific behaviors that are displayed (typically over the course of two observation periods or two different trials). As the test authors intended, the APPSI-2 may be most helpful in identifying the presence or absence of rudimentary communication skills on which to build. Other uses also come to mind. For example, the APPSI-2 may prove useful in identifying optimal environmental conditions before attempting standardized assessment or perhaps in adding qualitative descriptions of behavior during cognitive or educational assessment. The APPSI-2 may be helpful if used as part of a functional behavioral analysis and subsequent development of behavior intervention plans. The APPSI-2 also could be used in conjunction with measures of adaptive functioning to better identify individual strengths or weaknesses in functional skills.

SUMMARY. The APPSI-2 is not a standardized test per se, but if used as a systematic observational system it may be helpful as an aid in designing individualized instruction and monitoring progress of persons who have severe or profound cognitive impairments.

REVIEWER'S REFERENCES

Mitchell-Person, C. (2003). [Test review of Assessment for Persons Profoundly or Severely Impaired]. In B. S. Plake, J. C. Impara, & R. A. Spies (Eds.), *The fifteenth mental measurements yearbook.* Retrieved from http://marketplace.unl.edu/buros/

Ryan, L. J. (2003). [Test review of Assessment for Persons Profoundly or Severely Impaired]. In B. S. Plake, J. C. Impara, & R. A. Spies (Eds.), *The fifteenth mental measurements yearbook.* Retrieved from http://marketplace.unl.edu/buros/

[10]

The Assessment of Basic Language and Learning Skills–Revised.

Purpose: Designed to identify "language and other critical skills that are in need of intervention in order for a child to become more capable of learning from his everyday experiences."
Population: Children with autism or other developmental disabilities.
Publication Dates: 2006-2010.
Acronym: ABLLS-R.
Scores, 25: Basic Learner Skills (Cooperation and Reinforcer Effectiveness, Visual Performance, Receptive Language, Imitation, Vocal Imitation, Requests, Labeling, Intraverbals, Spontaneous Vocalizations, Syntax and Grammar, Play and Leisure, Social Interaction, Group Interaction, Follow Classroom Routines, Generalized Responding), Academic Skills (Reading Skills, Math Skills, Writing Skills, Spelling), Self-Help Skills (Dressing Skills, Eating Skills, Grooming, Toileting Skills), Motor Skills (Gross Motor Skills, Fine Motor Skills).
Administration: Individual.
Price Data, 2020: $64.95 per set of ABLLS-R Protocol and ABLLS-R Guide (2010, 153 pages); quantity discounts available.
Foreign Language Editions: Available in French, Hebrew, Japanese, Norwegian, Russian, and Spanish.
Time: Administration time not reported.
Comments: Provides "criterion-referenced information regarding a child's current skills that can serve as a basis for the selection of educational objectives"; also includes curriculum guide for an educational program for children with language delays; web-based version (WebABLLS) available.
Authors: James W. Partington.
Publisher: Behavior Analysts, Inc.

Review of the Assessment of Basic Language and Learning Skills–Revised by CATHLEEN CARNEY THOMAS, Assistant Professor, Communication Disorders and Sciences, Indiana State University, Terre Haute, IN:

DESCRIPTION. The Assessment of Basic Language and Learning Skills–Revised (ABLLS-R) is an individually administered measure of the skills necessary to communicate successfully and learn from everyday experiences. The test author suggests it will be useful for providing criterion-referenced information regarding a child's current skills as well as acting as a tracking system for these skills. There are two manuals for the test. The ABLLS-R Protocol is used to score performance and serves as a basis for selection of educational objectives and as a tracking system. The ABLLS-R Guide provides instructions for scoring as well as strategies to aid professionals in using the information to develop an individualized educational program (IEP) and to select goals for the child. The performance protocol reviews 544 skills from 25 domains arranged from simple to complex. Protocols are completed by anyone who has frequent contact with the child, and it is suggested that respondents be parents, teachers, or therapists. The majority of the information comes from those who regularly interact with the child; the second source of information comes from observing the child, and the third source of information comes from formal presentation of the tasks. The protocol includes a notes section to record brief accounts of the child's particular issues in performance.

The administration instructions are practical and parent-friendly. Each skill has a maximum score that varies from one skill to the next. The maximum score is always 1, 2, or 4. For skills with a maximum of 2, the child scores a 0, 1, or 2. For skills with a maximum of 4, the child scores a 0, 1, 2, 3, or 4. A score of zero means that the child does not meet the criterion. Scores are assigned by circling the number that represents the level of performance as specified in the *criteria* column. The protocol is subdivided using letters of the alphabet to correspond to a particular skill. The top row of scores for each item is for the initial skills assessment, and the remaining rows are for up to three updates. Scores are recorded and transferred to a tracking grid. The score determines the number of boxes that should be shaded on the grid. There is an open circle to the left of each task number that is to be filled in for those items on which the child received a score of zero. The assessment does not compare the child's score to a statistical score of children of the same age, as the measure is not norm-referenced. The author does not describe how long it will take to administer the assessment or transfer scores to the grid. Because the information is gathered over a period of time and by several examiners, the administration time will vary with each student and be dependent on student behavior.

DEVELOPMENT. In developing the ABLLS-R, the author wanted an assessment that would (a) identify the skills that are in need of intervention in order for the child to learn language, (b) provide a method for identifying specific skills in a variety of other important areas including self-help, academic, and motor skills, and (c) act as a curriculum guide for an educational program for a child with language delays and provide a method for visually displaying the acquisition of new skills on the tracking system. The test author states the first version of the ABLLS (1998) is based on Skinner's book *Verbal Behavior* and a review of the skills of typically developing kindergarten-age children; revisions were made in 2006 to the original version. The revisions to the original were made with input from professionals. Changes were made to 18 of the original 25 sections with modifications presented in tables in the guide that delineate changes from the original version. Substantive changes included modification of the scoring criteria, inclusion of new items, and a reordering of sequences of tasks. Partington added tasks to account for the child's motivation to respond, ability to attend, ability to generalize, and ability to spontaneously use these skills in and out of the educational setting.

Little information is provided about the development of the ABLLS-R. No information is given as to how the word lists are chosen or how common the word lists are to the child other than "items familiar to the home." For example, the child may not have access to many of the items chosen for the assessment. There is limited information on the ordering of items on the protocol. The test author acknowledges that there may be skills learned out of order and suggests that ordering is not important to the overall score of the assessment.

TECHNICAL. The ABLLS-R materials themselves do not include information about development, standardization, or technical properties of the assessment. However, the test author has published articles related to some of these matters (e.g., Partington, Bailey, & Partington, 2016, 2018; Usry, Partington, & Partington, 2018). Prospective users of the ABLLS-R should consult these resources for additional information about test-retest and internal consistency reliability (Partington et al., 2016), interrater reliability and content validity (Usry et al., 2018), and educational programming uses (Partington et al., 2018). In addition, Malkin, Dixon, Speelman, and Luke (2017) evaluated evidence of criterion validity by examining the correspondence among the ABLLS-R, a second language assessment, and an adaptive behavior scale.

Partington et al. (2016) used reports from parents and professionals about a sample of 50 neurotypical children to examine test-retest reliability and internal consistency of the ABLLS-R. Reports were completed using the online version of the ABLLS-R beginning when children were as young as 6 months of age and continuing at 3-month intervals until children reached 6 years of age. The researchers reported average test-retest correlation coefficients of .84 for 3-month intervals and .77 for 6-month intervals. As expected, longer test-retest intervals produced lower coefficients (.62 and .54 for 9 months and 12 months, respectively). Internal consistency estimates were mostly high and very high (alpha coefficients for 18 of the 25 skill areas were .90 or higher; 6 of 25 coefficients were between .80 and .89; only one value was below .80).

Usry et al. (2018) examined content validity evidence of the ABLLS-R using two panels of experts who evaluated the 544 items in terms of how essential the item is to a thorough understanding of skills of children with autism spectrum disorder. At least five out of six panel members rated 81% of the items as "essential." The researchers also evaluated interrater reliability by producing videotapes of assessments of specific skills reflected in 86 ABLLS-R items. Members of the expert panel, trained in how to score the ABLLS-R, viewed all 86 video clips and scored the items. Interrater reliability was very high, with an intraclass correlation coefficient of .95 reported.

COMMENTARY. The ABLLS-R is an assessment that relies on input from several sources and, thus, takes place over a period of time. Ultimately, it assesses skills in a variety of domains taking into account the whole child's performance. The assessment shows promise as a tool for use in developing goals for a child's academic/educational program. In addition, the ABLLS-R Protocol provides space for recording data from repeated administrations, which facilitates tracking progress toward IEP goals. One strength of the assessment is the inclusion of parents as respondents. Parent ratings and reports are vital to understanding a child's development and do not preclude the inclusion of other respondents, some of whom may lack previous knowledge of a particular child's language or skill development. These respondents may provide input on other skills and domains evaluated by the ABLLS-R. One disadvantage of the ABLLS-R is that some of the skills (especially in the areas of spelling and math) typically are not mastered until children are older than the age of 5. Also, some test users may prefer—or be more familiar with—assessments that are norm referenced with more tightly controlled procedures for administration. Scoring can be tedious but can be completed in multiple sessions.

The language skills included on the ABLLS-R Protocol are not necessarily listed in the order in which they typically develop. In addition, some skills that typically develop early are foundational for the development of later language skills, making it impossible to teach these skills out of order. The scores do not indicate the inter-relationship of the skills. Consequently, using results to develop IEP objectives will need to involve professionals with the requisite knowledge about how important particular skills may be to the advancement of other skills. Of note is the ordering of the intraverbal summary. The child is expected to respond to questions of what, where, who/whose, when, which, how, and why. Yet some research in the areas of child language development and language comprehension (Parnell, Patterson, & Harding, 1984) found that children between the ages of 3 and 6 responded to wh questions in order of difficulty; from easiest to most challenging, the order was: where, which, what+be, who, what+do, when, whose, why, and what happened.

The test author indicates that prosody is an important language skill for children to master and has distilled this task into components of (a) repeating sounds fast and slow, (b) repeating sounds loudly and softly, and (c) repeating sounds in high and low pitch. However, these skills are only indirectly related to prosody, which refers to the aspects of stress, intonation, and rhythm. Gerken and McGregor (1998) provide an overview of the development of these suprasegmentals in typical and disordered children, concluding that intonation develops before stress. Notably, these elements are not included in the ABLLS-R assessment.

In administering assessments such as the ABLLS-R, it is important to note that the reliability of children's responses may be affected by unintentional cues and feedback. For example, Chapman, Klee, and Miller (1980) found that mothers frequently used gestures to gain and direct their child's attention and timed their actions to align with their child's responses. Ultimately, these pseudo-successes could lead to an overestimation of a child's skills. Further study of a sample of children could be conducted during a task analysis to identify possible social and environmental cues and to evaluate the effect of such cues on ABLLS-R scores.

The ABLLS-R would benefit from additional validation research, especially in the areas of language development and communication involving both typically and atypically developing children. Although some work has been published that delineates differences and similarities of scores obtained by these two groups of children for developmental tests and the ABLLS-R, similar research is needed for tests of language development and the ABLLS-R.

SUMMARY. The ABLLS-R was developed as an individually administered criterion-referenced measure of skills necessary for learning, generalizing, and participating in academics. It is designed to facilitate the collection and compilation of relevant information from a variety of respondents and to provide a comprehensive assessment of an individual child's language and learning skills. The assessment would be of interest to educational practitioners for use as a guide to help them elicit and measure performance in several language and learning skill domains. The ABLLS-R meets its stated goal of offering a means for tracking skills of individual students over time, thus providing an advantage over many other assessments currently in use in educational settings. The documentation included in the test materials provides little evidence to support the ordering or importance of tasks on the assessment, and evidence of its technical properties must be accessed elsewhere. The ABLLS-R should not be used as a stand-alone assessment, though it may prove helpful in developing goals for a child's academic/educational program.

REVIEWER'S REFERENCES

Chapman, R., Klee, T., & Miller, J. (1980, November). *Pragmatic comprehension of skills: How mothers get some action*. Paper presented at the annual meeting of the American Speech-Language-Hearing Association, Detroit, MI.

Gerken, L., & McGregor, K. (1998). An overview of prosody and its role in normal and disordered child language. *American Journal of Speech-Language Pathology, 7*, 38-48.

Malkin, A., Dixon, M. R., Speelman, R. C., & Luke, N. (2017). Evaluating the relationships between the PEAK Relational Training System—Direct Training Module, Assessment of Basic Language and Learning Skills—Revised, and the Vineland Adaptive Behavior Scales—II. *Journal of Developmental and Physical Disabilities, 29*, 341-351.

Parnell, M. M., Patterson, S. S., & Harding, M. A. (1984). Answers to wh-questions: A developmental study. *Journal of Speech and Hearing Research, 27*, 297-305.

Partington, J. W., Bailey, A., & Partington, S. W. (2016). A pilot study examining the test-retest and internal consistency reliability of the ABLLS-R. *Journal of Psychoeducational Assessment, 36*, 405-410.

Partington, J. W., Bailey, A., & Partington, S. W. (2018). A pilot study on patterns of skill development of neurotypical children as measured by the ABLLS-R: Implications for educational programming for children with autism. *International Journal of Contemporary Education, 1*, 70-85.

Usry, J., Partington, S. W., & Partington, J. W. (2018). Using expert panels to examine the content validity and inter-rater reliability of the ABLLS-R. *Journal of Developmental and Physical Disabilities, 30*, 27-38.

Review of the Assessment of Basic Language and Learning Skills–Revised by REBECCA GOKIERT, Associate Professor, and CHELSEA DURBER, PhD Candidate, School and Clinical Child Psychology, Department of Educational Psychology, University of Alberta, Edmonton, Alberta, Canada:

DESCRIPTION. The Assessment of Basic Language and Learning Skills–Revised (ABLLS-R) is a criterion-referenced skills assessment that identifies for individual children language intervention objectives that might form the basis of a child's individual education plan (IEP). Specifically, clinicians have used the ABLLS-R to assess the skills of children with autism spectrum disorder (ASD). The ABLLS-R is administered once to establish a child's baseline skill set and then repeated yearly to update and document the child's skill development. Although the first administration is lengthy, subsequent administrations are much easier. The ABLLS-R system consists of two books: the *ABLLS-R Protocol*, which is used to record the scores for each child, and the *ABLLS-R Scoring Instructions and IEP Development Guide*, which provides instructions for scoring the protocol and strategies for parents, educators, and other professionals to develop an IEP for a child. An online version of the ABLLS-R called the WebABLLS provides online versions of the protocol and guide book, tracking of assessment data, reports, and worksheets. The website indicates that the ABLLS-R is available in several languages (English, French, Japanese, Hebrew, Russian, and Spanish).

The ABLLS-R comprises 544 task items across 25 sub-skill areas that make up four broad skills: (a) Basic Learner Skills (Cooperation and Reinforcer Effectiveness, Visual Performance, Receptive Language, Imitation, Vocal Imitation, Requests, Labeling, Intraverbals, Spontaneous Vocalizations, Syntax and Grammar, Play and Leisure, Social Interaction, Group Interaction, Follow Classroom Routines, and Generalized Responding); (b) Academic Skills (Reading, Math, Writing, and Spelling); (c) Self-Help Skills (Dressing, Eating, Grooming, Toileting); and (d) Motor Skills (Gross Motor and Fine Motor). Several sources of information are used to determine an individual's score on each task item. The majority of information is gathered from one or more individual(s) who regularly interact with the child (i.e., parent, teacher, speech and language pathologist). Additionally, a child's skill acquisition can be evaluated by directly observing the child or having the child complete a task to assess whether they possess a specific skill. In the protocol book, each task item is presented as a unique row with the same column headers: task number, score range (the range of scores for most items is 0–*can't do the task* to 4–*mastery*, but some items are scored from 0 to 2–*mastery*, and 0 to 1–*mastery*), task objective, question that can be asked about a child's skill, examples of responses, criteria for each score, and notes. Ratings are transferred to tracking system grids, in which the scorer shades in the number of boxes that corresponds to a child's score for each task item. There is no reported administration time, but given the number of task items and sources of information, it may take several days to weeks to complete the assessment. Once the tracking system grids are completed, it is recommended that a child's clinical team (i.e., parents, educators, behavior specialists, psychologists) develop and implement an IEP that addresses the skills most important for the child to develop. The test author recommends focusing on developing the skills in the Basic Learner Skills section, as they are most valuable in supporting a child's learning without highly individualized and specialized instructions. It is also recommended that the *Teaching Language to Children with Autism or Other Developmental Disabilities* (Sundberg & Partington, 1998) companion book be used as it provides useful information regarding how to interpret assessment information and translate it into an educational plan.

DEVELOPMENT. The ABLLS Protocol and Guide were first published in 1998 and are based conceptually on the behavior analysis of language presented by B. F. Skinner (Skinner, 1957). Additionally, the test author reports that much of the assessment is based on Spradlin's early work and the *Parsons Language Sample,* as it was the first program that used Skinner's analysis (Spradlin, 1963). The most recent revision, ABLLS-R, was published in 2010. There is no information in the ABLLS-R Guide that describes how the assessment was developed, task items were selected, or scoring criteria determined. However, the guide describes the variety of skill areas that are assessed by the ABLLS-R and how they reflect Skinner's behavioral analysis of language. These skill areas include language, motivation to respond, attending to verbal and nonverbal stimuli, and ability to generalize skills and spontaneously use skills. The guide also states that revisions to the original version were made with input from many professionals across the fields of education, speech and language pathology, and behavior analysis. In addition, substantive changes were made in 18 of the 25 skills sections in the ABLLS-R Protocol, and a narrative description of the changes is provided in an appendix of the ABLLS-R Guide. The changes included modifications to the scoring criteria for some items; addition of new task items; reordering of some of the task items; and changing some wording in the task objectives, questions to determine skill levels, and examples in order to improve clarity.

TECHNICAL. The ABLLS-R was not designed to compare a child's skills to those of a defined group or provide age norms; it is a criterion-referenced skills assessment that provides information on where a language intervention should begin and on what language objectives an intervention should focus. There is no technical information about the ABLLS-R in the guide or the protocol. Three recently published articles were reviewed to report on the psychometric properties of the ABLLS-R (Malkin, Dixon, Speelman, & Luke, 2016; Partington, Bailey, & Partington, 2016; Usry, Partington, & Partington, 2018).

Reliability. Two recent studies examined test-retest, internal consistency, and interrater reliability of the ABLLS-R (Partington et al., 2016; Usry et al., 2018). Internal consistency and test-retest reliability were established for a sample of 50 neuro-typical children (29 females and 21 males, age range 6 to 72 months). Parents completed the ABLLS-R on their child across five time points: time 1 (T1) baseline assessment and then four subsequent time points (i.e., 3, 6, 9, and 12 months). The overall alpha coefficient for the 25 skill areas was .70, with 18 of the 25 skill areas demonstrating an alpha coefficient ≥ .90 (Partington et al., 2016). All of the Pearson's correlation coefficients for T1 and the 3-month assessment were ≥.70, with the exception of the Requests skill area, which was .68. Of the 25 skill areas, 18 yielded a correlation coefficient for the T1 and 6-month assessment of over .70. Nine of the 25 coefficients for the T1 and 9-month assessment were .70 or above, whereas three of the 25 coefficients between T1 and the 12-month assessment were above .70. The test authors state, "One could predict this finding as children continuously acquire skills, which likely accounts for the systematic decreases observed in the retest correlations" (Partington et al., 2016, p. 408). Usry et al. (2018) evaluated interrater reliability. A panel of five experts received excerpts from the *ABLLS-R Scoring Instructions and IEP Development Guide.* They then received 86 different ABLLS-R items that corresponded to 86 video clips of children with ASD and were asked to score the items. Intraclass correlations demonstrated strong interrater reliability with ICC (2, 5) = .95 (95% CI [.94-.97]; $p < .001$).

Validity. Content and criterion evidence of validity was demonstrated by grounding the tool in B. F. Skinner's behavioral analysis of language. Additionally, Usry et al. (2018) recruited a panel of six experts to review each of the 544 ABLLS-R items on a 3-point Likert scale (3 = *essential*, 2 = *useful, but not essential*; 1 = *not necessary*). The panel rated 441 items (81%) as *essential.* Malkin and colleagues (2017) reported convergent evidence for the ABLLS-R by comparing it to the Promoting the Emergence of Advanced Knowledge Relational Training System–Direct Training Module

(PEAK–DT), and the Vineland Adaptive Behavior Scales, Second Edition (Vineland-II). All comparisons were completed with 21 children diagnosed with ASD. A strong significant correlation was found between the PEAK-DT and the ABLLS-R (r = .951, p < .001); moderate correlations were found between the PEAK-DT and Vineland-II (r = .453, p < .05), and the ABLLS-R and Vineland-II (r = .563, p < .05).

COMMENTARY. The ABLLS-R is a criterion-referenced skills assessment that is useful for identifying when to begin a language intervention and the language objectives that would be best suited to an IEP. The ABLLS-R can be completed by anyone who has studied the protocol and has direct contact with the child (i.e., parent, teacher, speech and language pathologist, behavior analyst), thereby making the ABLLS-R quite an accessible measure. The tool draws its strength from its conceptual grounding in B.F. Skinner's behavioral analysis of language and the extensive assessment of 544 skills across several areas (Basic Learner, Academic, Motor, and Self-Help). A strength of the assessment is that it may be used several times for one child to establish baseline and subsequent skill development on a yearly basis, which can inform continued modifications to an IEP for a child. The guide contains detailed instructions on scoring and strategies for developing an IEP, with two rich case examples that describe the process along with sample scored protocols and IEPs. One weakness of the assessment is the lack of empirical evidence regarding psychometric properties. No information on the technical aspects of the assessment is reported in the protocol or the guide; however, a few recent articles provide evidence of reliability and convergent evidence of validity. These articles indicate that the ABLLS-R can yield reliable scores (Partington et al., 2016), has excellent interrater reliability (Usry et al., 2018), and has moderate to strong correlations with other assessments that measure similar constructs (Malkin et al., 2017). Continued research on the clinical and educational utility of the ABLLS-R is needed. For a recent article focused on the use of ABLLS-R to study patterns of skill development in neurotypical children and the implications for educational programming for children with autism, review Partington, Bailey, and Partington (2018).

SUMMARY. The ABLLS-R was designed as a criterion-referenced assessment of several language and learning skills. The ABLLS-R results, when used by a child's clinical team (i.e., parents, educators, behavior specialists, psychologists) to develop and implement an IEP, can address language skills that are most important for the child to develop or enhance in order to participate successfully in learning. Although the assessment provides detailed strategies for using the results to build an IEP, it is also recommended that the *Teaching Language to Children with Autism or Other Developmental Disabilities* (Sundberg & Partington, 1998) companion book be used. The ABLLS-R Guide provides information on the revisions that were made from the original ABLLS, but information on how criteria were established and task items were selected are not provided. Furthermore, there is no information about the psychometric properties of the assessment in the guide, and anyone using the ABLLS-R needs to review the academic literature, which is not always readily available to all users (e.g., parents and educators). Overall, the ABLLS-R is a comprehensive tool, and with emerging studies on the psychometric properties and clinical and educational utility, proving useful for determining objectives for language intervention.

REVIEWERS' REFERENCES

Malkin, A., Dixon, M. R., Speelman, R. C., & Luke, N. (2017). Evaluating the relationships between the PEAK Relational Training System–Direct Training Module, Assessment of Basic Language and Learning Skills–Revised, and the Vineland Adaptive Behavior Scales–II. *Journal of Developmental and Physical Disabilities, 29*, 341–351. http://doi.org/10.1007/s10882-016-9527-8

Partington, J. W., Bailey, A., & Partington, S. W. (2016). A pilot study examining the test-retest and internal consistency reliability of the ABLLS-R. *Journal of Psychoeducational Assessment, 36*, 405-410. http://doi.org/10.1177/0734282916678348

Partington, J. W., Bailey, A., & Partington, S. W. (2018). A pilot study on patterns of skill development of neurotypical children as measured by the ABLLS-R: Implications for educational programming for children with autism. *International Journal of Contemporary Education, 1*, 70-85.

Skinner, B. F. (1957). *Verbal behavior.* New York, NY: Appleton-Century-Crofts.

Spradlin, J. E. (1963). Assessment of speech and language of retarded children: The Parsons language sample. *Journal of Speech and Hearing Disorders Monograph, 10*, 8-31.

Sundberg, M. L., & Partington, J. W. (1998). *Teaching language to children with autism or other developmental disabilities.* Pleasant Hill, CA: Behavior Analysts, Inc.

Usry, J., Partington, S. W., & Partington, J. W. (2018). Using expert panels to examine the content validity and inter-rater reliability of the ABLLS-R. *Journal of Developmental and Physical Disabilities, 30*, 27-38.

[11]

Assessment of Story Comprehension.

Purpose: Designed as a curriculum-based measure to help identify children who need supplemental and intensive language intervention and for use in progress monitoring.

Population: Ages 3-5.

Publication Date: 2019.

Acronym: ASC™.

Scores: Total score only.

Administration: Individual.

Forms, 6: Parallel forms (1-6).

Price Data, 2020: $65 per set including manual (142 pages), 10 record forms, and downloadable materials, including scoring guides and fidelity checklists; $35 per manual; $30 per 10 record forms.

[11] Assessment of Story Comprehension

Time: 3-4 minutes for administration of each story.
Authors: Trina D. Spencer and Howard Goldstein.
Publisher: Paul H. Brookes Publishing Co., Inc.

Review of the Assessment of Story Comprehension by STEPHEN T. SCHROTH, Professor of Early Childhood Education/Gifted & Creative Education and Graduate Programs Director, Towson University, Towson, MD:

DESCRIPTION. Understanding that reading comprehension is among the most important skills determining academic success and that reading comprehension relies on a child's decoding abilities and language comprehension, developers designed the Assessment of Story Comprehension (ASC) to assess these skills in early childhood so that appropriate instructional programs and supports may be put into place. The ASC evaluates children's language comprehension abilities (i.e., vocabulary knowledge, inference making, knowledge of syntax and grammar, and background knowledge) to facilitate decision making related to language interventions for young children. With early and appropriate assessments, potential problems may be identified and suitable language interventions implemented to prepare children for the rigors of the primary grades and to reduce the risk of later reading failure.

The ASC consists of a user's manual and consumables (i.e., administration and scoring forms). The test manual is written in clear and concise language and provides an introduction to the ASC, an overview of its components, instructions for administration and scoring, and suggestions for using the test results. The ASC's administration and scoring forms are distributed in packets of 10 booklets, each of which permits administration of the six assessments that comprise the ASC. Early childhood professionals, including teachers, special education specialists, paraprofessionals, school psychologists, and speech-language pathologists are qualified to administer the ASC.

The ASC is best viewed as a curriculum-based measure (CBM), designed to assist educators in making data-based decisions that link interventions to classroom testing. As the ASC is time efficient and easy to administer, it can be used to screen all children in a class up to three times per year. Children who receive low scores on the ASC should be provided with supplemental language instruction, whereas those with high scores do not need intervention. The ASC has six parallel forms, allowing for administration every 4 to 6 weeks for those children to whom intervention services are being provided. Such progress monitoring permits teachers to assess the effectiveness of instruction and to recognize improvement in children's language abilities.

DEVELOPMENT. When developing the ASC, the authors attempted to conform to CBM principles because they intended to develop an instrument that could help identify children in need of instructional support in the areas of language comprehension and vocabulary and to provide a tool for monitoring progress subsequent to the implementation of classroom-based interventions. During test development, the authors focused on the need to ensure the assessment was authentic and did not test language separate from child-relevant contexts. The ASC monitors children's ability to comprehend stories, an authentic and socially significant outcome. To do well on the ASC, children must be able to (a) understand the words and linguistic composition of the story, (b) understand the questions asked, and (c) integrate background knowledge and information derived from the story to make inferences.

The ASC was developed as six parallel forms for repeated use. Forms that were determined statistically to be easier were paired with more challenging forms in the final version; thus, the forms are grouped 1-2, 3-4, and 5-6 for screening in fall, winter, and spring, respectively. The higher score from the two forms should be used for determining whether intervention is needed. For progress monitoring, forms are to be used one at a time.

Written with standardized administration and scoring procedures, the ASC was intended to be simple and easy to use. To that end, each form appears on two facing pages in the administration and scoring booklet, and specific scoring guidelines are employed. Each form contains eight items, of which three are factual questions, and five are inferential questions. Raw scores are easily calculated. Administration to one student takes 3-4 minutes, and scoring can be completed in an additional 2-4 minutes.

TECHNICAL. The ASC was standardized using 237 preschool children with a mean age of 3 years 8 months. The group was 34% Caucasian, 31% Latino/Hispanic, 18% Native American, 3% African American, 1% Asian American, 10% multiethnic, and 3% other. English was the primary language for 84% of the sample; 9% of the sample had an individualized education program (IEP). No information was provided about where the sample data were collected nor when the assessment was piloted.

Alpha coefficients were calculated to estimate internal consistency among all items within each form, individual items across forms (e.g., first item on all forms), and all items on all forms. The mean coefficient across forms was .83 with a range of .79 to .86. The mean coefficient for individual items was .81 with a range of .71 to .89. The overall alpha coefficient for all items on all forms was .83, with a coefficient of .96 when totals from each of the forms were used as items.

Parallel form reliability was examined using Pearson correlations among all forms with coefficients ranging from .65 to .83. Test-retest reliability was estimated by comparing the two best scores from three different testing sessions for a single child "close in time" (manual, p. 7). The mean correlation coefficient was .78. A mean correlation coefficient of .78 also resulted from an examination of alternate form reliability using a random selection of forms administered within a single session.

The test manual includes a detailed fidelity checklist for each form for use in training and monitoring examiners. Studies of the ASC have shown administration fidelity (e.g., script delivered exactly or with only minor paraphrasing, prompts used correctly) to be high, with a mean of 99.6% of the items on the checklist administered correctly (range 78.6% to 100%). Scorer reliability as assessed by examiner agreement with the scoring keys using two sample sets of responses provided in the test manual was typically above 90% (mean 92%; range 52% to 100%). Reliability also was examined through kappa coefficients for individual items that ranged from .60 to .94.

To provide evidence of validity, scores from the ASC were correlated with scores from the Clinical Evaluation of Language Fundamentals Preschool—Second Edition (CELF Preschool-2), a standardized norm-referenced assessment of general language skills. The correlation between the CELF Preschool-2 and the ASC yielded a coefficient of .81, with $p < .001$. The test authors also reported that studies have shown the ASC is sensitive to growth related to the effects of two different language interventions. In one study, a significant improvement was observed in scores on the ASC inferential questions following implementation of a story-based curriculum for preschoolers. In the second study, scores of students in classrooms using a narrative retelling intervention were significantly higher than those of students who did not receive the intervention over a 7-month period.

COMMENTARY. The ASC provides an easy-to-administer and score assessment that is inexpensive and accessible. The hand-scorable survey booklet and professional manual are attractive and well designed. Its key strengths include an ethnically diverse standardization sample, strong reliability data, and evidence of validity. The standardization sample reflects diversity but not in proportion to U.S. demographics. Further studies should be conducted with samples that better represent the U.S. preschool population as a whole, especially with regard to African American and Asian American children. Overall, the strength of the ASC lies in its ability to assess story comprehension in children ages 3 to 5 years, and then to monitor progress, indicating when comprehension has meaningfully improved. Additional studies with more diverse groups should provide more support for use.

SUMMARY. The ASC was designed to be an individually administered measure of a child's listening comprehension abilities and to provide information related to readiness for the language demands of kindergarten. The assessment meets its goal of assessing language comprehension abilities and monitoring how these skills respond to intervention, indicating when such comprehension has meaningfully improved. Inexpensive and easy to administer, the ASC provides preschool teachers, administrators, and other early educators a valid and reliable tool to be used to monitor story comprehension and track a given child's response to classroom interventions. Although recommended, the instrument would be improved by additional evidence of validity and better representation of the standardization sample, especially with regard to African American and Asian American children.

Review of the Assessment of Story Comprehension by AMY N. SCOTT, Associate Professor in the Counseling and School Psychology Program, University of the Pacific, Stockton, CA:

DESCRIPTION. The Assessment of Story Comprehension (ASC—pronounced "ask") is an individually administered measure of language comprehension and vocabulary development for preschool-age students. The test authors indicate that the test provides a curriculum-based measurement (CBM) that evaluates language comprehension skills in a "child-friendly" (manual, p. 13) context. It can be used as a screening measure to identify children in need of intervention, and it also can be used to monitor progress of children receiving interventions. When used as a screening instrument, the test authors indicate that two forms (e.g., Form 1 and Form 2) should be administered to ensure a valid assessment. With six available forms, the measure can be used up to three times a year to serve the purpose of screening. If it is used for progress monitoring, only one form is administered at a time, allowing for six possible administrations over the course of a year. Students should be given each test form only once regardless of whether it is used for screening or progress-monitoring purposes. The test authors note that an exception is that the six stories could be used during the year when the child is 3 years old and then again during the year that the child is 4 years old. Each form takes 3-4 minutes to administer. Materials needed include the form, a clipboard, and a pencil.

Administration consists of reading the passages aloud to the child, asking the child the questions on the form (both factual and inferential), and recording the child's answer verbatim in the space provided. All of the information needed to complete the administration is on the form. Fidelity checklists are available for each form of the assessment; the test authors encourage the use of the fidelity checklists both as one learns the assessment and to ensure one administers it correctly over time.

Each form contains eight items. Items 1-7 are scored on a 0-1-2 scale, and Item 8a is scored on a 0-2-3 scale. If the child receives 0 points on 8a, then 8b is administered and scored on a 0-1 scale. Basic and extended scoring guides are provided in the test manual along with practice scoring sets that contain a key. Each form has 17 possible points with higher scores indicating stronger language comprehension skills. According to the test manual, 3-year-olds who obtain scores below 6 and 4-year-olds who obtain scores below 11 should receive intervention for language comprehension and vocabulary development. The test authors also note that children who score 15 or higher are typically ready for kindergarten. The ASC was developed in tandem with Story Friends, an intervention curriculum, but the measure can be used with other interventions as well. By purchasing the test manual, users may access additional materials online including the practice sets, basic and extended scoring guides, and fidelity checklists.

DEVELOPMENT. An iterative process was used to develop the stories and the questions. Each story is structured consistently with a character, setting, problem, feeling, attempt to solve the problem, consequence, and resolution. The stories all have the same number of complex linguistic features and a less common word (to measure vocabulary development). Inferential and factual comprehension questions are presented in an alternating sequence, so as to not discourage children from attempting to answer. The test authors indicate that most preschool students should be able to answer the factual questions. To make the six forms parallel, the question order and the types of questions are consistent for each form; only the content changes based on the specific story.

TECHNICAL. The standardization sample consisted of 237 preschool children (mean age = 3 years 8 months), 84% of whom spoke English as their dominant language. The children were from ethnically and racially diverse backgrounds, and 9% of the children were participating in an individualized education program (IEP).

Parallel form reliability coefficients (including three forms that were dropped for the final version of the measure) were reported to range from .65 to .83, and coefficients associated with test-retest reliability demonstrated a mean of .78. Internal consistency estimates (alpha coefficients) among the items on each form ranged from .79 to .86 (mean = .83). The alpha coefficient was .96 when the totals from each form were compared, indicating high consistency across forms. As a result of examining the technical adequacy of the forms, three forms were eliminated, leaving the test with the current six forms. The forms are purposefully paired (1-2, 3-4, 5-6) for screening purposes because some forms produced slightly higher results than other forms. The test authors report that the test demonstrated strong concurrent evidence of validity with the Clinical Evaluation of Language Fundamentals Preschool—Second Edition ($r = .81, p < .001$).

COMMENTARY. The ASC is an easy to administer and short test of story comprehension. Although the test authors contend that this test may be used as a screening and progress-monitoring measure, to use this measure as both in practice would likely prove difficult. If a preschool child were screened following the directions (i.e., using Forms 1 and 2), that would leave four forms remaining to be used throughout the year for progress monitoring. Most students in need of interventions would need to be monitored more than four times during the school year to ensure that the intervention was working. The measure may be appropriate for students who enter preschool already identified as needing intervention in this area, as six forms likely would allow for progress monitoring to take place every 4-8 weeks. Use of the ASC as a screener seems more appropriate, as with the six forms, screening could be completed three times during the school year. However, if a student were identified as needing intervention, a different measure likely would need to be used to monitor progress. The ASC also may be beneficial for researchers, as it may be used three to six times during the course of a school year, an ideal amount for a time-limited research study. Additional parallel forms would increase the utility of this measure. The standardization sample was small, and there was no indication of which regions of the United States contributed participants to the sample. Additionally, the test authors indicate that use of this measure has not been examined with special populations, yet they recommend its use for those with disabilities who may be receiving language interventions (i.e., language impairment, autism spectrum disorder, developmental disabilities, English language learners). Additional research should be conducted with this measure to ensure its appropriateness for special populations. The test authors are commended for the amount of training materials provided. The scoring guides are easy to use, and the fidelity checklists are thorough. Additionally, the practice scoring sets ensure that examiners are able to score the items correctly to obtain reliable and valid results.

SUMMARY. The ASC is a short, easy-to-administer and easy-to-score measure of preschool language comprehension. Although the test authors indicate that it can be used for screening and progress monitoring, it is not practical to think that it can do both for a single student as there are only six parallel forms, two of which must be used for each screening period. A larger standardization sample that includes children with a variety of disabilities and students who are English language learners is highly recommended to increase the utility of this measure. For a preschool teacher who is explicitly teaching language comprehension, this measure would likely serve as a formative and/or summative measure of children's learning.

[12]

Athletic Milieu Direct Questionnaire.

Purpose: Developed as a screening test for eating disorders/disordered eating among female college athletes.
Population: Female college athletes.
Publication Date: 2018.
Acronym: AMDQ.
Scores: OK versus Eating Disorder/Disordered Eating.
Administration: Group.
Price Data, 2020: $25 per manual (2018, 33 pages); $5 per test administration.
Time: Administration time not reported.
Comments: Companion to the Physiological Screening Test (PST; see 120, this volume); developed based on the third and fourth editions of the Diagnostic and Statistical Manual of Mental Disorders; administered online; scoring completed by test publisher.
Authors: David R. Black and Daniel C. Coster.
Publisher: Creative Solutions Press.

Review of the Athletic Milieu Direct Questionnaire by SANDRA HAYNES, Chancellor, Washington State University Tri Cities, Richland, WA:

DESCRIPTION. The Athletic Milieu Direct Questionnaire (AMDQ) was developed to screen female collegiate athletes for eating disorders or disordered eating, the former based on diagnostic criteria and the latter to describe detrimental eating behaviors employed to lose weight. As such, the test was specifically designed to address the unique performance requirements and the environment of collegiate athletics for women. The test authors make clear in several areas of the manual that the purpose of the assessment is for screening—creating opportunities for early intervention or prevention of an eating disorder or disordered eating—and that it is not for use as a diagnostic tool.

The test is computerized for group administration and takes approximately 20 minutes to complete. Individual administration is allowed if the participant needs such an accommodation or if the measure is used during a counseling session. It appears that the test was not administered individually during test development. The manual provides highly detailed instructions for test administration hygiene including basic information about the testing environment, the number of required proctors for different group sizes, and the purpose of standardization of procedures. The importance of fidelity to these instructions is emphasized repeatedly. The test administrator is described as the person in athletics responsible for assessment of athletes who also has experience using computers and administrating objective tests in a classroom setting.

Scores are generated electronically and available 5 to 7 business days after completion. Participants' scores fall into one of three categories: ED for scores indicative of an eating disorder, DE for scores indicative of disordered eating, or OK for scores that are not indicative of eating disorders or disordered eating. However, scores are only reported as ED/DE or OK. It is unclear whether reporting only ED/DE or OK applies to all users or a subset such as testers, participants, and other people who need to know.

DEVELOPMENT. The AMDQ was developed based on evidence from the literature that eating disorders and disordered eating have a higher prevalence in student athletes, especially female athletes. The AMDQ items were initially constructed using diagnostic criteria from the *Diagnostic and Statistical Manual of Mental Disorders* (3rd ed., rev.; *DSM-III-R;* American Psychiatric Association [APA], 1987; 4th ed., text rev.; *DSM-IV-TR*; APA, 2000) and the literature on how athletics affect eating behaviors.

The test administration manual states that the original set of questions was given to 20 female high school seniors to ascertain whether they believed the questions would prompt an "honest answer or an answer that would conform to socially acceptable norms" (manual, p. 20). Items were re-evaluated based on this feedback and some were revised and some were eliminated. After this revision, the test was given to a different group of 39 female high school seniors with the same instructions. Again, some items were modified or eliminated based on the students' feedback. Final revisions were made after receiving input from three experts in the field of eating disorders in athletics. The test manual states that these efforts were used to select appropriate questions and reduce response bias.

The test authors note that they did not use *DSM-5* (APA, 2013) criteria even though the test was developed after the fifth edition of the diagnostic manual was released. They justify this by stating that the criterion for eating disorders had not changed substantially across the three editions of the diagnostic manual. The test authors also note that the study took several years (at least two decades) to complete and that the *DSM-5* was not available through most of the instrument's development.

TECHNICAL. Limited data are provided in the test administration manual about how the AMDQ was standardized or evaluated for reliability and evidence of validity as required by the *Standards for Educational and Psychological Testing* (American Educational Research Association, American Psychological Association, & National Council on Measurement in Education, 2014). For this review, the publisher provided an article titled "Evaluation of a Screening Test for Female College Athletes with Eating Disorders and Disordered Eating" from the *Journal of Athletic Training* (2000). The article's four authors include two of the manual's authors, Black and Coster. All technical data presented for this review were gleaned from this article as they were absent from the test manual.

In the test manual, the authors define the measure as a standardized test by virtue of the explicit instructions for administration, as this is a definition of a standardization. In the article provided, the authors note that the use of only one sample from a major university may make the test less generalizable. The AMDQ was pilot tested on 175 female athletes from a wide variety of sports at a large Division I university.

Test-retest reliability was examined during pilot testing by administering the test to the same group of 175 participants 2-4 weeks apart. No numerical data are provided on the results of this reliability study.

Content evidence of validity was assessed with the review completed by the three experts described above, and corrections in the test were made until all were in agreement on all items. Criterion evidence of validity was estimated by comparing self-report data on height, weight, and percent body fat to actual measurements. Again, no numerical data are provided on the results of these validity studies.

COMMENTARY. The efficacy of the AMDQ was difficult to assess given the test administration manual alone. Without the provision by the publisher of the article titled "Evaluation of a Screening Test for Female College Athletes with Eating Disorders and Disordered Eating," a thorough review could not have occurred. Even still, data regarding test development were absent. In the article provided by the publisher, the authors note that, "... the pilot test clearly met psychometric standards for test construction, and detailed results can be obtained by contacting the authors" (Nagel, Black, Leverenz, & Coster, 2000, p. 432). Not including these data in the test manual is not adequate. In addition, the manual is poorly written and, as the title of the test manual suggests, aimed almost solely at ensuring fidelity in test administration.

The test manual refers to events that took place during research in the publisher-provided article. Rather than adding to the clarity of the test construction process, these references create confusion. For example, the test manual indicates that the length of time it took to complete structured diagnostic interviews and for the certification of interviewers was a barrier to using the *DSM-5* (APA, 2013) criteria. No detail was provided as to how an interview was used as a method for test development. When reading the article, the reader realizes it was used for research purposes only.

SUMMARY. Results from the research by Nagel, Black, Leverenz, and Coster (2000) demonstrate the greater efficacy of the AMDQ as compared with other measures of eating behavior such as the Eating Disorders Inventory (EDI) and the Bulimia Test-Revised (BULIT-R). These findings suggest that the AMDQ is a viable screening instrument for ED/DE in Division I female athletes. The poorly written manual that does not meet with standards set forth by the American Educational Research Association, American Psychological Association, and the National Council on Measurement in Education (2014) is inadequate for discernment of the test's psychometric features and thus for proper discernment regarding test use.

REVIEWER'S REFERENCES

American Educational Research Association, American Psychological Association, & National Council on Measurement in Education. (2014). *Standards for educational and psychological testing*. Washington, DC: American Educational Research Association.

American Psychiatric Association. (1987). *Diagnostic and statistical manual of mental disorders* (3rd ed., rev.). Washington, DC: Author.

American Psychiatric Association. (2000). *Diagnostic and statistical manual of mental disorders* (4th ed., text rev.). Washington, DC: Author.

American Psychiatric Association. (2013). *Diagnostic and statistical manual of mental disorders* (5th ed.). Washington, DC: Author.

Nagel, D. L., Black, D. R., Leverenz, L. J., & Coster, D. C. (2000). Evaluation of a screening test for female college athletes with eating disorders and disordered eating. *Journal of Athletic Training, 35,* 431-440.

Review of the Athletic Milieu Direct Questionnaire by JOHN A. MILLS, Professor of Psychology, Indiana University of Pennsylvania, Indiana, PA:

DESCRIPTION. The Athletic Milieu Direct Questionnaire (AMDQ) is described on the cover of its manual as a "screening test for female collegiate athletes with eating disorders/disordered eating." This new measure is a 56-item, web-based instrument that is designed to screen female college athletes for disordered eating as defined by the fourth edition of the *Diagnostic and Statistical Manual of Mental Disorders* (*DSM-IV-TR*; American Psychiatric Association [APA], 2000). The AMDQ is intended for use by professionals in college and university athletic departments who are "responsible for assessments of female collegiate athletes ... and those on committees deciding on the selection of screening tests to be used with this specific population" (manual, p. 1). Administration of the measure is realized by gathering female athletes in facilities with appropriate computing capabilities to respond in a group setting that requires an estimated administration time of 20 minutes (though the test is not timed). Individual administrations at other times are permissible. Respondent results are computer scored by the test publisher, and each respondent is classified as either eating disordered/disordered eating (ED/DE) or not (OK) in accordance with *DSM* criteria. Based on the classifications, the procedure provides three options. Option 1 includes the possibility that individuals classified as ED/DE could be "immediately referred to a healthcare provider with expertise in ED/DE among athletes" (manual, p. 17). Option 2 is to repeat the screening, with the possibility of a referral of athletes who test positive. Option 3 is to use a different test, such as the Physiological Screening Test, whose authors include the AMDQ authors and which also was developed for athletes.

DEVELOPMENT. The test authors readily acknowledge the limitations of self-report of disordered eating. Items used in the instrument were created from questions in standardized diagnostic interviews, items from three prior tests, and items that describe the impact of the athlete's training environment on weight management and eating (Nagel, Black, Leverenz, & Coster, 2000). In two data collection sessions, the original items were piloted and interviews were conducted with 149 participants to confirm written responses and to obtain physiologic measures. Respondents were classified as having anorexia nervosa, bulimia nervosa, or an eating disorder not otherwise specified on the basis of responses to an established interview protocol.

TECHNICAL. The most recent technical scholarship pertaining to the AMDQ provided to this reviewer was a 2000 article that described the development of the inventory. The AMDQ is mentioned very briefly in the 2008 position statement of the National Athletic Trainers' Association (Bonci et al., 2008) without specific comments on the psychometric properties of the instrument. Technical elements of the AMDQ were repeated in reviews by Knapp, Aerni, and Anderson (2014) and by Pope, Gao, Bolter, and Pritchard (2015), but it appears (and Pope et al. affirmed) that there has not been empirical support reported for the psychometric properties of the measure subsequent to the 2000 work. The authors of the AMDQ reported that content validity, test-retest reliability, and criterion validity were examined, but the analyses that supported their arguments are not readily apparent. The data for sensitivity and low false-negatives were encouraging (approximately 80% and 20%, respectively), and accuracy appears to be good. The instrument also has been praised for the use of interviews in the validation process. However, these analyses have not been seen elsewhere because the instrument does not appear to have received the same attention as other measures and has not been discussed in other studies (Knapp, Aerni & Anderson, 2014).

COMMENTARY. The authors of the AMDQ developed the instrument in a context of expressed deep concern for the well-being of the potential participant population and in concert with appropriate colleagues. The measure addresses a number of concerns associated with assessing the target population in the specific context in which significant health risk may be found. The method of assessment is efficient and convenient, and may be realized within existing procedures that are likely to be present in collegiate athletic programs.

The AMDQ attempts to evaluate an area of athlete risk in which there are two broad domains of respondent concern for the nature of reactions to their individual responses. First, it is not unlikely that college athletes who are at risk for problems with eating will be strongly motivated to obscure the realities of their problem for personal reasons. Next, athletes are likely to know that there is risk to their medical eligibility if certain difficulties or levels of difficulty are discovered. While the test developers indicate that results are not to be distributed to persons who determine eligibility or participation, the existence of the data presents a serious dilemma for the person to whom such data might be released. Even if the safeguards against untoward disclosure are secure, the *perception* of such safeguards is likely to be distorted by athletes.

The arguments for careful attention to the eating health of female college athletes are irrefutable. Given the potential difficulties with social desirability and perceptions of institutional behavior, one may appreciate that implicit or covert measurement is a means to enhance the ecological validity of the measure. In fact, covert measurement is consistent with the discussion provided in Nagel et al. (2000), but these authors include the test developers as well as professionals who appear to be institutionally affiliated with the authors. The covert approach to assessment is directed in the administration procedures. Specifically, Page 1 of the test manual states, "Test administrators and proctors should NOT reveal that this is a screening test for eating disorders/disordered eating among female collegiate athletes." This directive is inconsistent with Section 4.1 of the Code of Professional Responsibilities of the National Council on Measurement in Education (NCME) to which the test authors refer. Even when the high calling for attention and the means of implementing a program to respond to the problem are comprehensively described, there is no recommendation of covert investigation (e.g., Bonci et al., 2008). Section 4.1 states that it is a responsibility of those who administer assessments to "Inform the examinees about the assessment prior to its administration, including its purposes, uses, and consequences; how the assessment information will be judged or scored; how the results will be kept on file; who will have access to the results; how the results will be distributed; and examinees' rights before, during, and after the assessment" (NCME, 1995). It is not clear that the administration procedures are designed to realize these goals in a credible fashion. [Editor's Note: The discussion above relates to the ethical principle of informed consent. Although the test authors reference the NCME Code, the AMDQ items are aligned directly with symptoms of psychological disorders, making the American Psychological Association's Ethical Principles of Psychologists and Code of Conduct (2017) relevant to this discussion. We note that Standard 9.03 of the APA Code states that informed consent is implied for routine testing that occurs as part of an educational, institutional, or organizational activity. As a screening measure intended for group administration to all female college athletes, the AMDQ appears to qualify as routine.]

This reviewer cautiously agrees with test authors that the use of *DSM-IV-TR* (APA, 2000) rather than the more current *DSM-5* (APA, 2013) could be defensible and was necessary because of the constraints of research timing and the fact that it is a screening test and only a "general indicator" of ED/DE (manual, p. 20). However, the *DSM-5* is more than 5 years old, and the test authors should be active in updating the items to ensure consistency with evolving *DSM* standards. Changes in criteria from the *DSM IV-TR* to the *DSM-5* are known to alter the diagnosis that would be assigned to some persons, so this could be significant to the validity of the measure (e.g., Call, Walsh, & Attia, 2013).

SUMMARY. The Athletic Milieu Direct Questionnaire is a 56-item, web-based screening instrument that examines the self-reports of female college athletes pertaining to their eating behavior and the atmosphere of their training program related to weight management and eating. The measure is administered in groups of any size or to individuals, and the scoring method provides two categories of results and a method of rapid referral to a suitable health-related university professional for follow-up. Results are based on *DSM-IV* criteria, but strong psychometric properties and clinical utility are claimed.

REVIEWER'S REFERENCES

American Psychiatric Association. (2000). *Diagnostic and statistical manual of mental disorders* (4th ed., text rev.). Washington, DC: Author.

American Psychiatric Association. (2013). *Diagnostic and statistical manual of mental disorders* (5th ed.). Washington, DC: Author.

Bonci, C. M., Bonci, L. J., Granger, L. R., Johnson, C. L., Malina, R. M., Milne, L. W., Ryan, R. R., & Vanderbunt, E. M. (2008). National Athletic Trainers' Association position statement: Preventing, detecting, and managing disordered eating in athletes. *Journal of Athletic Training, 43*(1), 80-108.

Call, C., Walsh, B., & Attia, E. (2013). From DSM-IV to DSM-5: Changes to eating disorder diagnoses. *Current Opinion in Psychiatry,* 26, 532-536. doi:10.1097/YCO.0b013e328365a321

Knapp, J., Aerni, G., & Anderson, J. (2014). Eating disorders in female athletes: Use of screening tools. *Current Sports Medicine Reports, 13,* 214-218.

Nagel, D. L., Black, D. R., Leverenz, L. J., & Coster, D. C. (2000). Evaluation of a screening test for female college athletes with eating disorders and disordered eating. *Journal of Athletic Training, 35,* 431-440.

National Council on Measurement in Education. (1995). *Code of Professional Responsibilities in Educational Measurement.* Retrieved June 20, 2019 from https://www.ncme.org/resources/library/professional-responsibilities

Pope, Z., Gao, Y., Bolter, N., & Pritchard, M. (2015). Validity and reliability of eating disorder assessments used with athletes: A review. *Journal of Sport and Health Science, 4,* 211-221.

[13]

Attention Deficit Hyperactivity Disorder School Observation Code.

Purpose: "Designed for observing child behavior in three school settings: classroom, lunchroom, and playground."
Population: School-aged children.
Publication Date: 1996.
Acronym: ADHD SOC.
Administration: Individual.
Forms, 2: Classroom, Lunchroom/Playground.
Price Data, 2020: $31 per observation code kit including manual (89 pages), 25 Classroom code sheets, 25 Lunchroom/Playground code sheets, Classroom training code sheets, and Lunchroom/Playground training code sheets.
Time: Minimum observations of 45 minutes on 2 different days or 30 minutes on 3 different days.
Authors: Kenneth D. Gadow, Joyce Sprafkin, and Edith E. Nolan.
Publisher: Checkmate Plus, Ltd.

a) CLASSROOM.

Scores, 5: Interference, Motor Movement, Noncompliance, Nonphysical Aggression, Off Task.

b) LUNCHROOM/PLAYGROUND.

Scores, 5: Appropriate Social Behavior, Physical Aggression, Nonphysical Aggression, Noncompliance, Verbal Aggression.

Review of the Attention Deficit Hyperactivity Disorder School Observation Code by A. ALEXANDER BEAUJEAN, Associate Professor of Psychology and Neuroscience, Baylor University, Waco, TX:

DESCRIPTION. The Attention Deficit Hyperactivity Disorder School Observation Code (ADHD SOC) is an instrument designed to code direct observation of the behaviors children exhibit constitutive of ADHD, oppositional defiant disorder (ODD) and conduct disorder (CD). The test developers do not indicate any particular age or grade ranges for whom the instrument can be used, but based on the studies reported in the technical manual it appears most appropriate for students in elementary and middle school grades. The recommended uses for the instrument are screening evaluations for identifying children suspected of having ADHD and determining changes in behaviors after implementing an intervention for ADHD.

The ADHD SOC can be used in three types of school settings: unstructured (playground), semi-structured (lunchroom), and structured (classroom). It comes with two types of paper-and-pencil code sheets: one for classrooms and the other for both lunchrooms and playgrounds. There are five topographically defined target behaviors on both sheets. There is some overlap in target behaviors across the code sheets, but they are not the exact same. The behaviors for the classroom setting are: (a) Interference (i.e., disruption of classroom functioning); (b) Motor Movement (i.e., inappropriate motor activity); (c) Noncompliance (i.e., failure to respond appropriately to teacher directives); (d) Nonphysical Aggression, including Object (i.e., inflict physical damage on object), Symbolic (i.e., threaten, attempt to hurt, or interfere with others nonverbal and without contact), and Verbal (i.e., attempt to hurt someone nonphysically); and (e) Off Task (i.e., failure to attend to assigned academic activity). The five target behaviors for the lunchroom/playground sheet are: (a) Appropriate

Social Behavior (i.e., positive verbal/nonverbal social interactions); (b) Physical Aggression (e.g., unwanted negative physical contact); (c) Nonphysical Aggression, which includes both Object Aggression and Symbolic Aggression; (d) Verbal Aggression; and (e) Noncompliance.

Across all settings, the recommended method for recording behavior is time-sampling using 15-second intervals for 90 minutes total, distributed evenly across two or three days. Target behaviors are coded using partial- or whole-interval recording. The developers recommend conducting two or three observations for every target student; three observations are needed for medication evaluations.

Almost any adult who is "mature, tactful, and able to adhere to expectations about professional confidentiality" (manual, p. 61) should be able to learn the ADHD SOC coding procedures. The test developers indicate it generally takes 20-25 hours to learn them. There are two ways to learn the coding system: using a special trainer and self-teaching. The technical manual provides instruction for both methods.

DEVELOPMENT. The ADHD SOC developers originally created the code for use in their studies on the effects of stimulant medication in children with ADHD. To do so, they borrowed aspects of some already-existing behavior codes, but simplified the target behavior definitions to make them easier to learn and use. In addition, they also wanted to have a single instrument that would be suitable for multiple school settings, relatively easy to use, and able to assess a wide range of behaviors.

TECHNICAL. Measurement data for direct observation instruments differ from other types of instruments (Hintze, 2005; Merrell, 2003). Broadly conceived, reliability is still paramount, although the focus is on observer agreement regarding behavior occurrence. This agreement is inextricably tied to the definition of the concepts the instrument is designed to measure and their criterial behaviors (Baker & Hacker, 1982).

Conceptually, the ADHD SOC developers sought to create an observation code that captures the behaviors indicative of ADHD (i.e., symptoms). To make the case that they did this, they provide a crosswalk for how the target behaviors relate to ADHD symptoms in the *Diagnostic and Statistical Manual of Mental Disorders* (4th ed.; *DSM-IV*; American Psychiatric Association, 1994). The crosswalk indicates that the target behaviors capture 16 of the 18 ADHD symptoms in the *DSM-IV*, with some of the symptoms captured by multiple target behaviors. The aggressive target behaviors do not relate to any ADHD symptoms but do capture many *DSM-IV* symptoms for ODD and CD.

The technical manual provides two types of reliability information: interobserver agreement and temporal stability. Interobserver agreement information is given by the kappa statistic from two separate studies. Across both studies, kappa values ranged from .60 to .94, although these may be underestimates (see review in Briesch et al., 2018). For temporal stability, the developers reported correlations of target behavior occurrence in elementary school children diagnosed with ADHD across three days. The Pearson correlation coefficients among the classroom behaviors ranged from .27 to .72, with higher values typically seen between consecutive days and lower correlations typically seen between non-consecutive days. The correlations for the lunchroom and playground tended to be much lower, with coefficients that ranged from -.43 to .68, although most of them hover around zero. Intraclass correlations (ICCs) across all three days ranged from .33 to .57 for classroom observations and from -.20 to .24 for the lunchroom and playground settings.

The developers did not collect data from a norming sample, and so do not provide norm-referenced scores or normative information for target behavior occurrences. Instead, they provide a set of recommended procedures for acquiring comparison information from "typical" peers and calculating the difference between behavior occurrence from the target student and peers (i.e., deviation scores). The technical manual provides an overview of the diagnostic utility for the deviation scores, but more detail is provided elsewhere (Nolan & Gadow, 1997). A combined deviation score for the Interference and Off Task target behaviors yielded the most accurate classifications, with sensitivity and specificity proportions both exceeding .80. These results are consistent with the mean occurrence differences between children with and without ADHD provided in the technical manual.

There is information about the coding system's sensitivity to change in the form of mean differences for groups of students taking different doses of methylphenidate (including a placebo condition). In general, the average number of occurrences for classroom target behaviors was lower in the dose conditions than placebo condition, although the difference for Nonphysical Aggression was not statistically significant. Results for lunchroom and playground environments were inconsistent. There tended to be fewer target behavior occurrences in the dose conditions than placebo condition, but the variability in occurrences was large, rendering most of the mean differences not statistically different.

One study reported in the technical manual examined behavior differences between students identified with specific learning disability and emotional disturbance (ED). The only differences found were that students with an ED exhibited more Noncompliance (across all settings) and Nonphysical Aggression (classroom setting only) than did students with learning disabilities.

COMMENTARY. The ADHD SOC has many positive features. It provides a way to code behaviors constitutive of ADHD both between students (e.g., target student and peers) and within-student (e.g., across times or school settings). Although the *DSM* is now it its fifth edition, the ADHD symptoms did not change across editions, so the *DSM-IV* behavior crosswalk is still applicable. The instrument is relatively simple to use, the training required to learn the instrument is relatively minimal, and the resulting behavior codes demonstrate moderate to high between-observer consistency. The measure is inexpensive to purchase, and the developers give purchasers permission to make photocopies of all the code sheets, meaning the initial cost of the instrument will be the total cost for most instrument users. Moreover, there are a few reviews of it already published (e.g., Briesch, Volpe, & Floyd, 2018), which are generally positive.

Despite the positive aspects of the instrument, there are some concerns. First, the target behaviors for both sheets are defined broadly. This makes it easier to code behaviors, but clumps disparate behaviors together, such as indicating that the ADHD symptoms of reluctance to engage in tasks requiring sustained mental effort and difficulty organizing tasks are both manifestations of Noncompliance (Martel, Levinson, Langer, & Nigg, 2016). Second, including aggressive target behaviors on both code sheets seems ill-advised. These behaviors only capture symptoms associated with ODD and CD, and most of the research in the technical manual concerns ADHD only. Thus, there is little evidence that coding aggressive target behaviors will aid in identifying students with ODD or CD or is sensitive to interventions focusing on either disorder's symptoms.

Third, the target behaviors on the lunchroom/playground sheet seem to vary substantially across observations. Other behavior observation systems appear to produce more temporally stable results in playground settings (Leff & Lakin, 2005). Thus, those who want to observe behavior outside of classrooms may want to investigate alternative coding systems.

SUMMARY. The ADHD SOC developers have created a simple and easy-to-use instrument for coding behaviors children exhibit constitutive of ADHD in classroom settings. This instrument could provide information to school personnel to aid in making eligibility decisions or monitoring progress. Given the currently available information, other uses of the instrument should be undertaken cautiously.

REVIEWER'S REFERENCES

American Psychiatric Association. (1994). *Diagnostic and Statistical Manual of Mental Disorders* (4th ed.). Washington, DC: Author.

Baker, G. P., & Hacker, P. M. S. (1982). The grammar of psychology: Wittgenstein's *Bemerkungen über die philosophie der psychologie. Language & Communication, 2*, 227-244.

Briesch, A. M., Volpe, R. J., & Floyd, R. G. (2018). *School-based observation: A practical guide to assessing student behavior*. New York, NY: Guilford.

Hintze, J. M. (2005). Psychometrics of direct observation. *School Psychology Review, 34*, 507-519.

Leff, S. S., & Lakin, R. (2005). Playground-based observational systems: A review and implications for practitioners and researchers. *School Psychology Review, 34*, 475-489.

Martel, M. M., Levinson, C. A., Langer, J. K., & Nigg, J. T. (2016). A network analysis of developmental change in ADHD symptom structure from preschool to adulthood. *Clinical Psychological Science, 4*, 988-1001.

Merrell, K. W. (2003). *Behavioral, social, and emotional assessment of children and adolescents* (2nd ed.). Mahwah, NJ: Erlbaum.

Nolan, E. E., & Gadow, K. D. (1997). Children with ADHD and tic disorder and their classmates: Behavioral normalization with methylphenidate. *Journal of the American Academy of Child & Adolescent Psychiatry, 36*, 597-604.

Review of the Attention Deficit Hyperactivity Disorder School Observation Code by TAWNYA MEADOWS, Pediatric Psychologist, Geisinger Health System, and McKENNA COSOTTILE, Postdoctoral Fellow, Geisinger Health System, Danville, PA:

DESCRIPTION. The Attention Deficit Hyperactivity Disorder School Observation Code (ADHD SOC) is a measure of systematic direct observation using partial time sampling interval recording, developed in 1996. The intended purposes of the observation assessment are to screen for ADHD, measure responses to medication, inform special education services, formulate treatment plans, and monitor responses to intervention. The ADHD SOC is designed for its users to observe children's behavior across five primary behavioral categories in the classroom, lunchroom, and playground. The specific behaviors observed are different in the classroom than the lunchroom and playground. In the classroom, behaviors of focus are Interference, Motor Movement, Noncompliance, Nonphysical Aggression, and Off Task. In the lunchroom and playground, behaviors of focus are Appropriate Social Behavior, Noncompliance, Nonphysical Aggression, Physical Aggression, and Verbal Aggression. Each behavior is recorded only once in any 15-second interval if it occurs. The test authors note that some situations may warrant the use of additional or alternative code categories and provide suggestions of other behaviors to consider. The ADHD SOC is not intended as a norm-referenced test; rather, scores are calculated based on comparisons to observations of typically developing peers. The test kit includes a manual, classroom code sheets, and lunchroom/playground code sheets. The user can make additional copies of these code sheets.

To train observers to use the ADHD SOC, the test authors recommend using one of two strategies. One, raters may code videotapes of behavior until they reach a certain minimum agreement with an established expert. The authors recommend that once a novice rater reaches minimum agreement with a defined expert on video coding, one or more observers and the expert should rate behavior in the lunchroom, classroom, and playground of a local school. Ratings should be conducted until a predetermined minimum agreement is met. Of note, the publishing company does not provide training videos. The alternative training strategy recommended is for raters to train themselves independently using instructional materials. Although the test authors identify the people who might serve as raters, the manual does not specify educational requirements of the raters, nor does it specify skills needed to accurately perform and interpret the ADHD SOC. Training time is estimated to be 20-25 hours.

When screening a child suspected of having attention- deficit/hyperactivity disorder (ADHD), a three-step procedure is recommended. The rater is to select a minimum of three typical gender-matched peers of the target child to serve as a comparison group. The rater alternates coding observations of the target child and a member of the comparison group each for one minute. The rater should observe the class for 45 minutes on two different days or 30 minutes on three different days. Once the observations are complete, the rater is to determine a screening score for ADHD. This score is calculated by subtracting the mean rate of occurrence of Off Task and Interference behaviors in the peer group from the mean rate of occurrence of Off Task and Interference behaviors in the target child. This result is then divided by the standard deviation of the peer group. If the sum of the deviation scores for Interference and Off Task behaviors is greater than 1.5, the child receives a screening score for ADHD. No standardized scores are provided.

DEVELOPMENT. ADHD SOC was developed as a screening tool and to evaluate the effects of intervention for children diagnosed with ADHD and related behavioral disorders in the school setting. The test authors indicate the ADHD SOC was developed from the Code for Observing Social Activity (COSA; Sprafkin et al., 1983), a behavior observation code the authors and others previously created to measure disruptive child behaviors. In developing the ADHD SOC, the authors also incorporated target behaviors described in other coding systems that had demonstrated strong discriminant validity. In creating the ADHD SOC, the authors intended to create an observation code that was more user-friendly than other existing codes for observing behavior. The ADHD SOC can be used to identify children with symptoms of ADHD and/or other behavioral concerns in the classroom.

TECHNICAL. The test authors did not collect normative data for the ADHD SOC as it is challenging to create a valid standard for normal conduct. They acknowledge that what is regarded as normal varies across school contexts and depends on classroom factors such as teachers. Instead, the test authors encourage comparing the target child's behavior to the behaviors of other children in the classroom whom teachers have identified as non-hyperactive or typically developing.

The test manual indicates a "considerable amount of information is available" (manual, p. 24) about interobserver reliability; however, the test authors only provide ratings from two representative studies. These results indicate reasonable reliability, with Cohen's kappa estimates ranging from .60 to .94 (Gadow et al., 1995a; Nolan & Gadow, 1994). The test manual cites several studies that evaluated the validity of the ADHD SOC by comparing ADHD SOC ratings to behavioral observations of typically developing children and parent/teacher ratings of behavior concerns in target children. In an examination of 34 elementary school children diagnosed with ADHD, Nolan and Gadow (1994) found very few significant correlations between ADHD SOC categories. Significant correlations that were found were associated with coefficients in the low to moderate range, indicating minimal overlap between behavioral categories. Results from this study also indicated that the ADHD SOC shared moderate to high correlations with parent- and teacher-reported ratings of child behavior (Nolan & Gadow, 1994). Earlier research found moderate correlations only between certain behavioral codes from the ADHD SOC and specific behavioral factors from teacher rating forms (Sprafkin & Gadow, 1987). Research indicates that the ADHD SOC successfully differentiates children with behavior disorders from children with learning disabilities (Sprafkin & Gadow, 1987) and children with diagnoses of attention-deficit disorder from peers perceived as typically developing (Gadow et al., 1992; Gadow et al., 1995b).

COMMENTARY. The ADHD SOC is a user-friendly coding system that allows for observation of target behaviors in the school setting. Its main strengths are that it utilizes direct behavior observations to code occurrences of target behaviors, provides clear operational definitions of target behaviors, appears relatively easy to learn and administer, and to learn, and can be completed in a relatively short period of time. Scoring and interpretation appear to be more complicated. The code does not use standardized norms but instead relies on comparing behavioral observations of target children to typically developing peers. Minimal guidance is provided for the selection of comparison children, and no discussion is offered regarding potential rater bias in rating target and comparison children simultaneously.

Although the test authors describe behavior observation strategies used in previous research, they do not provide a thorough rationale for the target behaviors included in the ADHD SOC. There are no pilot data reported on initial development or refinement of the tool. They also do not explain their rationale for a 15-second partial interval coding system, as other described codes utilized 10-, 20-, or 30-second intervals. Although the authors recognize several challenges of selecting control peers, they do not provide ready solutions. The test authors do provide a reasonable description of the primary behavior categories, including clear operational definitions of each behavior. The test authors also describe and provide alternate coding options as well.

Although reasonable reliability, convergent, and discriminant validity are described in the test manual, there are several important limitations worth noting. First, the ADHD SOC has not been used in diverse samples. Most studies using the ADHD SOC had small samples comprising predominantly male participants (Sprafkin & Gadow, 1987) and children with diagnoses of attention-deficit disorder (Gadow et al., 1992; Gadow et al., 1995b; Sprafkin & Gadow, 1987). [Editor's Note: ADHD is diagnosed twice as often in males as it is in females, per *DSM-5* (p. 63).] Moreover, specific demographics are not provided for the samples. It is therefore difficult to determine the extent to which results from the ADHD SOC generalize beyond the demographics for which the measure has been studied. Additionally, psychiatric diagnoses were based on criteria from previous (i.e., third and fourth) editions of the *Diagnostic and Statistical Manual of Mental Disorders* (American Psychiatric Association, 1980, 1994). Whereas this would have been appropriate for the time of the studies, these diagnostic criteria and classification of ADHD have changed in the past 20 years. Current approaches to ADHD assessment generally include parent and teacher rating scales. There has been no research comparing the reliability of behavior rating scales to systematic observations such as the ADHD SOC. Finally, it must be noted that the most recent reference in the test manual is from 1996 with the oldest reference dating to 1938. It would be highly beneficial for this manual to be updated by synthesizing recent research developments from the field of ADHD.

SUMMARY. Direct observation is one of the most widely used assessment procedures in the school setting. The ADHD SOC provides systematic direct observation using partial time sampling interval recording. There are many similar behavior observation methods on the market such as the Behavioral Observation of Students in Schools (BOSS; Shapiro, 1996), Systematic Screening for Behavior Disorders: Peer Social Behavior Code (Walker & Severson, 1990), Classroom Observation Code (Abikoff & Gittelman, 1985), and the State-Event Classroom Observation System (Saudargas, 1997). There is a paucity of research on this instrument beyond that conducted by the test authors for the purpose of test development, which occurred more than 25 years ago. The observation system appears relatively user friendly, as it is generally completed in less than one hour. Interpreting results is less clear and, if following the advice of the test authors, requires some comfort and familiarity with statistical calculations. The instrument appears to have adequate reliability and evidence of validity. The demographics for which this instrument was validated appear somewhat restricted, thereby limiting generalization.

REVIEWERS' REFERENCES

Abikoff, H., & Gittelman, R. (1985). The normalizing effects of methylphenidate on the classroom behavior of ADDH children. *Journal of Abnormal Child Psychology, 13,* 33-44.

American Psychiatric Association. (1980). *Diagnostic and statistical manual of mental disorders* (3rd ed.). Washington, DC: Author.

American Psychiatric Association. (1994). *Diagnostic and statistical manual of mental disorders* (4th ed.). Washington, DC: Author.

Gadow, K. D., Nolan, E., Sprafkin, J., & Sverd, J. (1995a). School observations of children with attention-deficit hyperactivity disorder and comorbid tic disorder: Effects of methylphenidate treatment. *Journal of Developmental and Behavioral Pediatrics, 16,* 167-176.

Gadow, K. D., Paolicelli, L. M., Nolan, E. E., Schwartz, J., Sprafkin, J., & Sverd, J. (1992). Methylphenidate in aggressive hyperactive boys: II. Indirect effects of medication treatment on peer behavior. *Journal of Child and Adolescent Psychopharmacology, 2,* 49-61.

Gadow, K. D., Sverd, J., Sprafkin, J., Nolan, E. E., & Ezor, S. N. (1995b). Efficacy of methylphenidate for attention-deficit hyperactivity disorder in children with tic disorder. *Archives of General Psychiatry, 52,* 444-455.

Nolan, E. E., & Gadow, K. D. (1994). Relation between ratings and observations of stimulant drug response in hyperactive children. *Journal of Clinical Child Psychology, 23,* 78-90.

Saudargas, R. A. (1997). *State-event classroom observation system (SECOS) observation manual.* Knoxville, TN: University of Tennessee.

Shapiro, E. S. (1996). Direct observation: Manual for the Behavioral Observation of Students in Schools (BOSS). In *Academic skills problems workbook.* New York, NY: Guilford.

Sprafkin, J., & Gadow, K. (1987). An observational study of emotionally disturbed and learning-disabled children in school settings. *Journal of Abnormal Child Psychology, 15,* 393-408.

Sprafkin, J., Grayson, P., Gadow, K. D., Nolan, E. E., & Paolicelli, L. M. (1983). Code for Observing Social Activity. Stony Brook, NY: State University of New York.

Walker, H. M., & Severson, H. H. (1990). Systematic Screening for Behavior Disorders (SSBD). Longmont, CO: Sopris West.

[14]

Bankson Expressive Language Test–Third Edition.

Purpose: Designed to "help identify children who present with an expressive language disorder," to provide information on the examinee's strengths and weaknesses, and to monitor changes in expressive language development.

Population: Ages 3-0 to 6-11.

Publication Dates: 1977-2018.

Acronym: BELT-3.

Scores, 3: Lexical Semantics, Morphology and Syntax, Expressive Language Index.

Administration: Individual.

Price Data, 2020: $199 per complete kit including examiner's manual (2018, 84 pages), picture book, and 25 record booklets; $51 per examiner's manual; $101 per picture book; $47 per 25 record booklets.

Time: 25-30 minutes for administration.

Authors: Nicholas W. Bankson, Michelle Mentis, and Jennifer R. Jagielko.

Publisher: PRO-ED.

Cross References: See T5:241 (4 references) and T4:241 (3 references); for reviews by Ronald B. Gillam and Roger L. Towne of the Bankson Language Test–2, see 11:26 (4 references); for a review by Barry W. Jones of the Bankson Language Screening Test, see 9:107 (1 reference).

Review of the Bankson Expressive Language Test—Third Edition by LAUREEN J. McINTYRE, Speech-Language Pathologist and Associate Professor of Educational Psychology & Special Education, University of Saskatchewan, Saskatoon, Saskatchewan, Canada:

DESCRIPTION. The Bankson Expressive Language Test—Third Edition (BELT-3) is an individually administered test assessing children's (3-0 to 6-11 years of age) expressive language skills with three components: an examiner's manual, a picture book, and an examiner record booklet. This test, comprising two subtests (Lexical Semantics, Morphology and Syntax), aims to: (a) identify children with expressive language disorder, (b) give test users beginning information on a child's expressive language strengths and weaknesses, (c) keep track of a child's expressive language development in relation to peers, and (d) provide researchers a tool to use when studying children's expressive language and/or the "success of language instruction programs" (manual, p. 3). The BELT-3 is estimated to take 25 to 30 minutes to administer, and testing may be extended to more than one session (i.e., for younger children, if easily distracted).

Basic testing procedure suggestions are highlighted in the examiner's manual with regard to administering and scoring the test. Within the subtests, groups of items targeting similar language forms are organized into testlets (e.g., testlets of naming, categories and functions, and antonyms and synonyms are grouped under the Lexical Semantics subtest) to "reduce examinee fatigue and administration time" (manual, p. 6). Administration instructions and allowable prompts for each testlet are clear, easy to follow, and provided in the examiner record booklet so test users do not have to refer to the examiner's manual during testing. Ceiling rules for each testlet (three consecutive incorrect items) allow test users to discontinue item administration and move to the next testlet in a timelier manner. Normative scores (i.e., subtest scaled scores, percentile ranks, age equivalents) are derived from the examinee's raw scores, and composite scores and descriptive terms are derived from subtest scaled scores (i.e., Expressive Language Index and a percentile rank; *impaired or delayed* ranging to *gifted or very advanced*).

DEVELOPMENT. There are two previous editions of the BELT-3: the Bankson Language Screening Test (BLST; Bankson, 1977) and the Bankson Language Test—2 (BLT-2; Bankson, 1990). The BELT-3 authors seek to address test users', reviewers' (e.g., Gillam, 1992; Towne, 1992), and their own critiques of the previous edition to improve the BELT-3 by collecting new normative data; reducing test administration time; making picture items more visually attractive; expanding the developmental range and increasing the complexity or difficulty of items in both subtests; enhancing the reliability studies being conducted; and undertaking new and extensive studies of test bias (e.g., differential item functioning and subgroup comparisons), subtests and composites (e.g., floors, ceilings, item gradients), and criterion-prediction validity (e.g., diagnostic accuracy analyses). The authors of the BELT-3 extended the Lexical Semantics subtest to ensure items span a wider developmental range by adding not only items that address the naming of adjectives and synonyms, but also items that incorporate more advanced vocabulary. In addition, the test authors added items in the Morphology and Syntax subtest to increase the complexity of grammatical structures being assessed (e.g., simple declarative, compound, and complex sentence forms). However, although the authors outline what they term the BELT-3 model as targeting the domains of language form and content, there are no additional details in the test manual as to what specific language theory was used to guide test development (i.e., how the construct of expressive language was defined, how the test authors determined the items that needed to be included in each subtest).

TECHNICAL.

Standardization. The test authors discuss following a strict qualification process when choosing field examiners (e.g., verified qualifications and experience), employing specific procedures to ensure data quality control for the normative sample (e.g., reviewing collected examiner record booklets for errors), and selecting the normative sample itself (e.g., representative of geographic region, race, gender, exceptionality status). The sample included 684 children ranging in age from 3-0 years to 6-11 years across "29 states and 199 different zip codes" (manual, p. 19). There are no Canadian norms for this test.

Reliability evidence. In an effort to enhance the reliability studies being conducted related to this new version of the test, the authors report three types of reliability coefficients for the subtests and composite: (a) internal consistency reliability (.83 for Lexical Semantics, .92 for Morphology and Syntax, .93 for the composite); (b) test-retest reliability over an approximately two-week period (.91 for Lexical Semantics, .88 for Morphology and Syntax, .91 for the composite); and (c) scorer difference reliability or examiner scoring variability (.99 for Lexical Semantics, Morphology and Syntax, and the composite). The reported values for the composite met the recommended .90 minimum standard suggested by Nunnally and Bernstein (1994); Reynolds, Livingston, and Willson (2009); and Salvia, Ysseldyke, and Witmer (2017), according to the test authors.

Validity evidence. Three sources of validity evidence are reported for the subtests and composites of the BELT-3, including (a) content-description evidence (e.g., rationale for test item selection; conventional item analyses; analyses of item gradients, floors, and ceilings; and analyses of test bias), (b) criterion-prediction evidence (e.g., correlations with the standard scores of other criterion tests of expressive language ability, comparisons with means and standard deviations of other expressive language tests, and studies of the ability of test scores to differentiate between children with poor or severely disordered expressive language skills and those with better than average expressive language skills), and (c) construct-identification evidence (e.g., identifying constructs thought to explain test performance and stating and logically or empirically verifying related hypotheses such as that raw scores should increase with age or that the subtests should correlate well because both were developed to assess expressive language.

COMMENTARY. The BELT-3's straightforward instructions make this an easy test to administer in a relatively short period of time. As an assessment tool that can give test users a snapshot of a child's expressive language skills, it shows promise for use in research studies and by clinicians needing a quick measure of expressive language ability. The test authors appropriately caution test users about some of the issues they need to consider when interpreting test results, such as offering a reminder that single assessment tools are best used as part of a comprehensive assessment and not in isolation. Further discussion of the theory the test authors used to guide how they defined the construct of expressive language and the resulting representative test items they included in their subtests would further enhance descriptions of this tool's development. A clear effort is made to ensure children's scores on this test can be "compared to a representative sample of peers in this country" (manual, p. 26). In addition, test users are given additional reliability (i.e., internal consistency, stability over time, and test error related to examiner scoring variability) and validity evidence (i.e., studies of test bias, subtests and composites, and criterion-prediction validity) to demonstrate the quality and usefulness of the BELT-3. As with any assessment tool, additional reliability and validity evidence resulting from studies conducted by a variety of authors and researchers and not solely the authors of this test will provide further support of the test's utility.

SUMMARY. The BELT-3 was created to assess children's expressive language skills. The revisions made and additional reliability and validity evidence provided by the test authors have resulted in an assessment tool that has the potential to provide both clinicians and researchers an overview of children's expressive language skills in a relatively brief manner. The next step in the BELT-3's evolution would be for additional reliability and validity evidence to be collected and shared by a wide variety of test users and researchers.

REVIEWER'S REFERENCES

Bankson, N. W. (1977). Bankson Language Screening Test. Baltimore, MD: University Park Press.

Bankson, N. W. (1990). Bankson Language Test—2. Austin, TX: PRO-ED.

Gillam, R. B. (1992). [Test review of Bankson Language Test—2]. In J. J. Kramer & J. C. Conoley (Eds.), *The eleventh mental measurements yearbook* (pp. 53-55). Lincoln, NE: Buros Institute of Mental Measurements.

Nunnally, J. C., & Bernstein, I. H. (1994). *Psychometric theory* (3rd ed.). New York, NY: McGraw-Hill.

Reynolds, C. R., Livingston, R. B., & Willson, V. (2009). *Measurement and assessment in education* (2nd ed.). Boston, MA: Pearson Education.

Salvia, J., Ysseldyke, J. E., & Witmer, S. (2017). *Assessment in special and inclusive education* (13th ed.). Boston, MA: Cengage Learning.

Towne, R. L. (1992). [Test review of Bankson Language Test—2]. In J. J. Kramer & J. C. Conoley (Eds.), *The eleventh mental measurements yearbook* (pp. 55-56). Lincoln, NE: Buros Institute of Mental Measurements.

Review of the Bankson Expressive Language Test—Third Edition by CAROL WESTBY, Consultant, Bilingual Multicultural Services, Inc., Albuquerque, NM:

DESCRIPTION. The Bankson Expressive Language Test—Third Edition (BELT-3) is a standardized, norm-referenced expressive language assessment for children ages 3 years 0 months through 6 years 11 months. The BELT-3 is intended for the following uses: (a) to identify students with expressive language disorder, (b) to provide data regarding strengths and weaknesses in individual children, (c) to document changes in expressive language development, and (d) to be used in research involving children's oral language development. The BELT-3 evaluates two aspects of expressive language: Lexical Semantics and Morphology and Syntax. The Lexical Semantics subtest evaluates expressive vocabulary including nouns, verbs, and adjectives as well as word knowledge of categories, object functions, antonyms, and synonyms. The Morphology and Syntax subtest evaluates production of pronouns; inflectional and derivational morphemes (plural nouns and verb forms—present progressive, third person singular, irregular past tense, regular past tense, auxiliaries, copula, modals); comparatives and superlatives; expanded phrases (e.g., adjective + noun); simple declarative, compound, and complex sentences; and question forms. Each subtest comprises several "testlets," similar items that are grouped together. Many of the longer testlets have ceiling rules that permit the testlet to be discontinued. This structure reduces child fatigue and test administration time. The testlets for synonyms and antonyms are auditory only; all the other testlets make use of a book with colored pictures. The children depicted in the pictures represent a range of races/ethnicities. The majority of the testlets begin with examples so children know the types of responses they are expected to give. Scaled scores, age equivalents, and percentile ranks are available for both subtests and the Expressive Language Index standard score, which is based on the raw scores from both the lexical and morphology/syntax subtests.

DEVELOPMENT. In developing the BELT-3, the test authors considered reviews of the Bankson Language Test—2 (BLT-2; Bankson, 1990). They maintained the organization of the BLT-2 but updated words and pictures to make them more contemporary, and they modified and expanded the scope and content of the items to better capture expressive language development in children in the 3- to 6-year age range. Many child language tests include a range of language items, even though some items might not discriminate between typically developing children and children with language impairment, and they sample only one instance of the concept. The items on the BELT-3 are those that research has shown to be difficult for children with language disorders to acquire, and hence they best differentiate children with language disorders from typically developing children. Furthermore, several instances of each language concept are elicited. Prompts were modified to provide a more functional context for elicitation of the target forms.

TECHNICAL.

Standardization. The BELT-3 was normed on a sample of 684 children, ages 3 through 6, from 29 states and 199 ZIP codes. The BELT-3 normative sample was representative of the U.S. population in terms of parent income and educational level, gender, race, and Hispanic status. Seventy-two percent of children were White, 15% were Black/African American, 5% were Asian/Pacific Islander, 1% were American Indian/Eskimo/Aleut, and 7% were multiracial. Twenty-four percent were Hispanic. A small percentage of children with disabilities was included in the norming sample.

Reliability. The BELT-3 manual provides reliability information for content sampling, test-retest, and scorer difference. Alpha coefficients were used to estimate internal consistency of the test items, or how closely the items were related, at each age level. Coefficients of .70 or higher are considered acceptable. Average coefficients for the subtests exceeded .80, and the average coefficient for the Expressive Language Index was reported as .93.

Test-retest reliability was determined by retesting 101 children from the normative sample approximately two weeks after the first testing. Children were divided into two age groups: 3-0 to 4-11 (n = 36) and 5-0 to 6-11 (n = 65). For the combined age groups the Morphology and Syntax subtest demonstrated a reliability coefficient of .88 (good reliability), and the Lexical Semantics subtest and Expressive Language Index both demonstrated a reliability coefficient of .91 (excellent reliability). Coefficients ranged from .94 to .96 for the younger group and from .86 to .89 for the older group.

Scorer difference reliability refers to the amount of variance in test scores that is due to variability in scoring. Two members of the test publisher's research staff independently rescored 50 protocols drawn randomly from the normative sample. Resulting coefficients for both subtests and the index were .99.

Validity. The BELT-3 manual presents information on content, criterion-prediction, and construct-identification evidence of validity. Content evidence of validity refers to the degree to which the test items are representative of the behavior being measured. The test authors approached content validation in four ways: (a) explaining how the selection of items was based on what research has shown are language forms that are difficult for children with language disorders, (b) reporting how the discriminating power of items was determined and how items that did not sufficiently discriminate were discarded, (c) analyzing floors, ceilings, and item gradients, and (d) describing research dealing with bias and analyzing how different racial/ethnic groups performed on the test items. Tests that do not have sufficiently low floors or sufficiently high ceilings fail to accurately identify students with very low or very high abilities. BELT-3 subtest floors and ceilings had excellent adequacy; fewer than 3% of examinees with very low or very high abilities would fail to be accurately identified. There was some variation in test performance among the ethnic/racial groups, but the magnitude of the differences was trivial to small, making it possible to conclude that the BELT-3 scores pose little or no bias toward Hispanic, Black/African American, or Asian/Pacific Islander populations.

Criterion-prediction evidence of validity is critical for accurately identifying students who have language impairment. The BELT-3 scores demonstrated large to very large correlation coefficients with scores on several well-established language tests: the Expressive Language Index of the Test of Expressive Language (TEXL; Carrow-Woolfolk & Allen, 2014), the Expressive Language Index of the Test of Early Language Development-Fourth Edition (TELD-4; Hresko, Reid, & Hammill, 2018), and the Expressive Communication component of the Preschool Language Scales, Fifth Edition (PLS-5; Zimmerman, Steiner, & Pond, 2011). To demonstrate diagnostic accuracy, the test authors computed sensitivity, specificity, and receiver operating characteristic/area under the curve (ROC/AUC) values for several standard index scores. Based on the data reported, the test authors recommend an Expressive Language Index cut score of either 88 (sensitivity .70; specificity .83) or 90 (sensitivity .75; specificity .73), which is considered fair and corresponds to an overall ROC/AUC value of .83, which is considered good.

To evaluate construct-identification evidence of validity, the test authors explored (a) the relationships of BELT-3 scores to chronological age, (b) the ability of the test to differentiate between groups with known expressive language disorders and those with typical language, (c) the correlation between the two subtests, and (d) the correlation of items on each subtest to the total score. When comparing scores of children with and without diagnosed language impairment, the magnitude of effect sizes for difference scores for both subtests and the composite was large. Articulation disorders without comorbid conditions are not expected to have a significant impact on expressive language ability, and indeed, the magnitude of effect size differences between children with and without articulation disorders was small. The Lexical Semantics and Morphology and Syntax subtests demonstrated a correlation coefficient of .73, indicating the two subtests are related but yet are measuring somewhat different aspects of language.

COMMENTARY. Since 2001, the American Speech-Language-Hearing Association (ASHA; 2016) has advocated for the use of the International Classification of Functioning (ICF; World Health Organization, 2001; 2007) in all clinical and research work in speech-language pathology. In the BELT-3 examiner's manual, the authors reference the ICF as a framework for comprehensive evaluations, and they mention a range of procedures that should be part of a comprehensive assessment. They state that the BELT-3 should be considered one piece of a comprehensive evaluation. They do not, however, clearly explain the role of the BELT-3 in the ICF assessment framework. Within the ICF framework, the BELT-3 evaluates a child's capacity at the activity level, that is, the child's ability to carry out a task in a structured context. In so doing, its intent is to provide a diagnosis of a possible impairment in function. The BELT-3 does not evaluate a child's ability to use language to perform or participate in naturalistic life situations.

The BELT-3 has fair sensitivity and specificity to make diagnostic decisions if cut scores of 88 or 90 are used. In many states, however, children in educational settings must have standard scores below 77 or 70 to be eligible for speech and language services. At a standard score of 70 on the BELT-3, sensitivity is .30 and specificity is 1.00. This may be problematic for speech-language pathologists using the BELT-3 in school settings. If they are permitted to conduct additional evaluations with or to qualify only those children with standard scores below 70, many children who are highly likely to have a language disorder will be denied services. This problem is not unique to the BELT-3 (although sensitivity is especially low on the BELT-3 at a standard score of 70). A number of language tests now recommend cut scores between 80 and 90. These test data illustrate the need for speech-language pathologists to educate administrators about the appropriate use and interpretation of standardized tests—specifically, that the use of the same cut score across all tests is inappropriate.

SUMMARY. The BELT-3 is a standardized norm-referenced test designed to assess the expressive language ability of children ages 3-0 through 6-11. It is intended to be a mechanism for beginning a review of a child's language skills, not as a comprehensive language assessment. The test items were carefully selected to best discriminate between children with and without language disorders, and several instances of each skill are elicited. Comprehensive data on reliability and validity studies are provided.

REVIEWER'S REFERENCES

American Speech-Language-Hearing Association. (2016). *Scope of practice in speech-language pathology.* Retrieved from www.asha.org/policy

Bankson, N. W. (1990). Bankson Language Test—2. Austin, TX: PRO-ED.

Carrow-Woolfolk, E., & Allen, E. A. (2014). Test of Expressive Language. Austin, TX: PRO-ED.

Hresko, W. P., Reid, D. K., & Hammill, D. D. (2018). Test of Early Language Development—Fourth Edition. Austin, TX: PRO-ED.

World Health Organization. (2001). *International classification of functioning, disability and health: ICF.* Geneva, Switzerland: Author.

World Health Organization. (2007). *International classification of functioning, disability and health: Children and youth version: ICF-CY.* Geneva, Switzerland: Author.

Zimmerman, I. L., Steiner, V. G., & Pond, R. E. (2011). Preschool Language Scales, Fifth Edition. San Antonio, TX: Pearson.

[15]

Barkley Sluggish Cognitive Tempo Scale—Children and Adolescents.

Purpose: A parent-completed rating scale designed to assess symptoms of attention-deficit/hyperactivity disorder, executive functioning deficits, and functional impairments in major life activities.

Population: Ages 6 to 17.

Publication Date: 2018.

Acronym: BSCTS-CA.

Scores, 4: SCT Daydreamy, SCT Sluggish, SCT Total, SCT Symptom Count.

Administration: Individual.

Price Data, 2020: $123.75 per manual (128 pages) including reproducible forms.

Time: 5-10 minutes for administration.

Comments: Interview form available for use with individuals who cannot read, have visual impairments, or are non-English speakers.

Authors: Russell A. Barkley.

Publisher: Guilford Press.

Review of the Barkley Sluggish Cognitive Tempo Scale—Children and Adolescents by JANE E. BOGAN, Associate Professor of Education, Wilmington College, Wilmington, OH:

DESCRIPTION. The Barkley Sluggish Cognitive Tempo Scale—Children and Adolescents (BSCTS-CA) is an individually administered rating scale designed to measure concentration deficits, or symptoms of sluggish cognitive tempo (SCT), in the daily life activities of children and adolescents as observed by their parents. The test author advises that the rating scale should be used in conjunction with other data sources such as achievement tests, transcripts, and other evaluation tools. The rating scale is easy to administer, with only 12 items on which parents rate their child/adolescent. It takes approximately 5-10 minutes to complete the rating scale. An included interview form may be used if the parent cannot read, cannot read English, or has a visual impairment that would prevent him/her from completing the rating scale. The interview form contains the same items; the parent responds to each item with *yes* or *no*.

Four scores are computed; percentile ranks can be determined for each by using the gender and age charts in the administration manual. The first score is SCT Daydreamy. The scores of the five items in Section 1 on the rating scale are added to get this score. The second score is SCT Sluggish. This score is computed by summing the scores of the seven items in Section 2 of the rating scale. The third score is SCT Total. The total score in Section 1 is added to the total score in Section 2 to compute SCT Total. Finally, SCT Symptom Count is computed by summing the number of statements in both Sections 1 and 2 that were rated as 3 (*often*) or 4 (*very often*).

DEVELOPMENT. The BSCTS-CA originated as part of a national survey measuring attention-deficit/hyperactivity disorder (ADHD) symptoms, deficits in executive functioning, and functional impairments in major life activities. The first chapter of the administration manual presents a review of research on the evidence distinguishing SCT from ADHD. The review examines the history of the two disorders, symptoms, diagnostic procedures, and treatments. However, research distinguishing SCT from ADHD is minimal with the test author reporting fewer than 70 studies involving children and fewer than 20 studies involving adults.

A factor analysis of the items on the original national survey identified items that loaded on symptoms different from ADHD. Those distinct items then became the items used in the BSCTS-CA. The original version included 14 items; the last two (slow to complete tasks and lacks initiative/effort fades) equivalently loaded on both the ADHD inattention dimension and the SCT dimension. Because they could not be used to differentiate SCT and ADHD, they were eliminated from the final version of the BSCTS-CA. The interview form does not include normative information because it is intended to accommodate parents struggling with literacy and to get more detailed qualitative information on SCT symptoms.

TECHNICAL. The standardization sample for the BSCTS-CA included 1,922 parents who had children between the ages of 6 and 17 with equal representation of males and females in each of 12 age groups from across the United States. People selected to participate who did not have access to the web-based survey were provided with a laptop and an Internet service provider at no cost. Participants were paid for completing the survey. Demographic characteristics are reported in the administration manual for both children and parents. Three groups were overrepresented in the initial sample: White respondents, those with a bachelor's degree or higher, and fathers. As a result, 122 White males (rating 61 male children and 61 female children) with at least a bachelor's degree were randomly dropped from the sample, resulting in a normative sample of 1,800 parents and their children. Parent ages ranged from 18 to 68 years. Other demographic characteristics reported include sex, biological relationship, parent education level, ethnicity, household income, parent marital status, parent employment status, and geographic region (Northeast, Midwest, South, West). Additionally, parents reported any developmental or psychiatric diagnoses and the treatment status of the children. Based on the data from the normative sample, the appendix of the BSCTS-CA manual includes four profile sheets with raw scores and associated percentile ranks for males ages 6-11, males ages 12-17, females ages 6-11, and females ages 12-17.

The test author provides reliability information that includes internal consistency estimates (alpha coefficients) for the three subscale scores. The coefficients for SCT Daydreamy, SCT Sluggish, and SCT Total were .87, .91, and .93, respectively. Test-retest reliability was evaluated by re-assessing a subset of the original sample participants 3-5 weeks after initial completion of the scale. There were 86 parents completing the second administration of the scale with at least five children in each age level from 6 through 17 years. Pearson product-moment correlation coefficients across the two administrations were .79 for SCT Daydreamy, .82 for SCT Sluggish, and .84 for SCT Total; all coefficients were significant at $p < .001$. Scores from the two administrations were compared using a paired samples t-test, and results indicated no significant change in the three subscale scores across the 3- to 5-week span.

Much of the evidence supporting the validity of the BSCTS-CA comes from the national survey and from studies of other rating scales of SCT. Construct validity evidence was evaluated by comparing the BSCTS-CA items to items identified in prior studies as assessing SCT. Because the items are the same, the construct evidence of validity is considered acceptable by this reviewer. Convergent evidence of validity was discussed in the administration manual, and the test author stated that the instrument "would be expected to show high correlations with other rating scales using most or all of these 12 SCT symptoms" (p. 54). The correlations to provide the convergent evidence of validity were not actually calculated. The BSCTS-CA administration manual states that there is no current evidence on the relationship of the rating scale to measures of IQ but that previous research using SCT scales with similar items found ratings to be low and inconsistently related to IQ. The test author uses those findings as discriminant evidence of validity for the BSCTS-CA. Regression analysis of the national SCT survey given to a U.S. normative sample (Barkley, 2013) and a survey of executive functioning administered to a U.S. sample found minimal association between the two instruments. Criterion evidence of validity was presented using analyses of data from the national U.S. survey; comparisons were made between groups of children reporting specific psychiatric and developmental conditions and groups of children who did not report those conditions. Overall, evidence of validity presented in the administration manual appears to be adequate.

COMMENTARY. The BSCTS-CA is a brief and easy-to-administer rating scale that parses out a specific set of characteristics that are frequently folded into measures of ADHD. The key strengths of this rating scale include the brevity of the instrument and the provision of an interview format to accommodate the potential language and/or literacy barriers of parents completing the rating scale. Scoring is relatively easy. The normative sample appears to match the categories of the U.S. Census fairly accurately. The validity analyses provide limited evidence for the technical adequacy of this specific instrument, instead relying on data analyses and evidence from an earlier iteration of the survey or other studies on similar instruments. The BSCTS-CA would benefit from additional validity evidence specifically related to this iteration of the rating scale. Additionally, the theoretical model would benefit from further research to better discriminate between SCT and characteristics of inattentiveness seen in ADHD.

SUMMARY. The BSCTS-CA was designed to be an individually administered measure of sluggish cognitive tempo in children and adolescents as observed and rated by their parents. The rating scale distinguishes between daydreamy and sluggish characteristics as evidenced by the scores derived from the data. Although some evidence of reliability and validity is included, much of it is implied based on data analyses from studies of similar instruments, from a study of a previous iteration of this instrument, or from the informal comparison of this instrument to other instruments. It is recommended that additional data on reliability and validity based on this instrument be provided as well as further research to distinguish between SCT and inattentiveness that occurs in ADHD.

REVIEWER'S REFERENCE

Barkley, R. A. (2013). Distinguishing sluggish cognitive tempo from ADHD in children and adolescents: Executive functioning, impairment, and comorbidity. *Journal of Clinical Child & Adolescent Psychology, 42,* 161-173.

Review of the Barkley Sluggish Cognitive Tempo Scale—Children and Adolescents by ROSEMARY FLANAGAN, Independent Practice, Garden City, NY:

DESCRIPTION. The theoretical underpinnings of the Barkley Sluggish Cognitive Tempo Scale—Children and Adolescents (BSCTS-CA) are presented via an extensive review and analysis of the literature. Barkley concluded there are sufficient data supporting the existence of a separate disorder of attention, distinct from the inattentive and hyperactive-impulsive types of attention-deficit/hyperactivity disorder (ADHD); this provides the basis for developing a scale to measure it. Data for the development of the BSCTS-CA were gathered via a national survey assessing executive functioning deficits, symptoms of ADHD, and functional impairments in major life activities. Items address the extent to which a child's state of mind appears spacey, confused, or unfocused, as well as the extent to which his or her mental alertness and physical arousal, stamina, or psychomotor activity appear to be diminished. BSCTS-CA items were derived from parental ratings of symptom frequency. Factor analysis resulted in items measuring sluggish cognitive tempo (SCT) falling in two domains: daydreamy and sluggish; the final version of the scale consists of 12 items. An interview-based parent rating scale, reflecting the typicality or atypicality of parental complaints rather than the child's standing in the normal distribution, is available for assessment based on deficit measurement. Currently, SCT is not recognized as a separate diagnostic entity.

Both formats of the BSCTS-CA (Parent Rating Scale or Parent Interview) are included in the test manual and are reproducible; no other materials are needed to administer the scale. The 12-item Parent Rating Scale yields ratings on a 4-point scale (1 = *never or rarely*, 4 = *very often*). Data are converted to percentile ranks for the Daydreamy, Sluggish, and Total scores and an SCT Symptom Count. The Parent Interview yields descriptive information according to a yes/no format as well as the SCT Symptom Count. The interview format is for use with individuals who cannot read or who have other impairments.

Scoring the forms is accomplished by summing the numerical responses and scores for each scale. Tables provided in an appendix of the test manual facilitate the conversion of raw scores and symptom counts to percentile ranks. Norms are available for ratings of children ages 6-11 and 12-17, with separate norms for males and females.

DEVELOPMENT.

Norms. The nationally representative standardization sample consisted of 1,922 parents of children ages 6-17; adjustments were made to correct overrepresentation of White, college-educated males, as compared to Census data for year 2000 so as to have a sample of 1,800 raters. The ages of respondents ranged from 18 to 63, with a mean age of 42.3 years. Educational attainment of parents was similar to Census data for high school completers and those with some college attendance. Fewer individuals had less than a high school education, with more having an associate's, bachelor's, or graduate degree as compared to the Census. Similarly, median household income for the standardization group was approximately $20,000-$35,000 higher than the median household income reported in the year 2000 census. Data on geographic dwelling area indicate 18%, 28%, 31%, and 23% of participants were from the Northeast, Midwest, South, and West, respectively. Sample breakdown according to race/ethnicity was similar to Census data. Ratings for equal numbers of males (n = 75) and females (n = 75) for each of 12 age groups (6, 7, 8, 9, 10, 11, 12, 13, 14, 15, 16, 17) comprise the standardization sample. Seventy-seven percent of the youngsters rated by parents did not carry any special education label or psychiatric diagnosis. This sample was a general population sample that included those with special education, medical, or psychiatric history.

Participants were chosen via a web-based program that randomly selected respondents by address and telephone number. Because invitations were sent to parents by postal mail or telephone, laptops and internet connections were provided for those who did not have access so that the survey could be completed online. Reminder email messages were sent, and respondents were paid, with a second payment made for providing data for test-retest reliability.

TECHNICAL.

Reliability. Internal consistency reliability data are based on the original sample of 1,922 participants. Alpha coefficients were .87, .91, and .93 for the Daydreamy, Sluggish, and SCT Total scores, respectively. Test-retest reliability estimates for a sample of 86 participants completing two administrations over a 3- to 5-week interval were .79, .82, and .84 for Daydreamy, Sluggish, and SCT Total, respectively.

Validity. The development of the BSCTS-CA followed from literature review and investigations demonstrating that SCT is distinct from ADHD. These data along with their interpretation are carefully explained in the test manual and are offered as evidence of validity. Validity evidence falls into the following categories: factor analytic, discriminant or divergent, and criterion.

Data from 32 items—14 items for SCT and 18 items for ADHD based on *DSM-IV-TR* (American Psychiatric Association [APA], 2000) and *DSM*-5 (APA, 2013)—were analyzed using principal components analysis with a varimax rotation. The factor loadings are substantial and are available for inspection in the test manual. The factors are believed to assess ADHD Inattention, ADHD Hyperactivity-Impulsivity, SCT Sluggish, and SCT Daydreamy. Two items thought to belong to the SCT Sluggish factor had their highest loading on the factor assessing ADHD Inattention and were not included in the published version of the scale; the items address slow task completion and limited sustained initiative. The BSCTS-CA comprises five items loading on the SCT Daydreamy factor (item factor loadings ranged from .534 to .696) and seven items loading on the SCT Sluggish factor (item factor loadings ranged from .547 to .851).

The percentages of normative sample respondents who endorsed each possible response (1 = *never or rarely*, 4 = *very often*) on the 32 items subjected to factor analysis are reported in the test manual. The data are believed to illustrate which symptoms never or rarely occur as compared to those occurring sometimes to very often for both kinds of ADHD and SCT. These data also show that parents rated ADHD inattentive as occurring more frequently than ADHD hyperactive-impulsive, which was rated as more commonly occurring than both SCT Daydreamy and SCT Sluggish, an expected finding.

Discriminant evidence of validity comes from several sources. A meta-analysis (Becker et al., 2016) showed strong support for SCT as distinct from ADHD across factor analytic studies based on data from 19,000 individuals. SCT also has been shown to be distinct from academic achievement (DuPaul & Langberg, 2015). The inattentive type of ADHD explains considerably more of the variance in executive functioning as measured by the Barkley Deficits in Executive Functioning Scale—Children and Adolescents than either the hyperactive-impulsive type of ADHD or SCT, again showing that SCT differs from ADHD (Barkley, 2012).

Criterion evidence of validity is based on the differences in the pattern of overlap between ADHD symptoms and SCT symptoms across an array of childhood disorders; the test manual contains extensive data for inspection. Moreover, some elevation of SCT symptoms was found to be evident in some disorders after controlling for ADHD.

COMMENTARY. The BSCTS-CA was developed to assess sluggish cognitive tempo. The test manual describes how SCT differs from ADHD based on factor analytic data. Researchers need a good scale to measure SCT in order to document it as a disorder in its own right and to select participants for treatment studies that can lead to the development of interventions for SCT. Additional research may be needed to ascertain the utility of the scale. Use of the scale by clinical practitioners for diagnostic purposes appears premature, given that SCT is not yet recognized as a diagnostic entity, although there may be clinical utility for identifying treatment targets as part of intervention planning. The scale also may be of use to prescribers of medications for treating ADHD, given the symptom overlap between ADHD and SCT.

SUMMARY. The BSCTS-CA is an instrument that assesses sluggish cognitive tempo as distinct from ADHD. Test construction procedures are appropriate, and there is good evidence of psychometric soundness. The instrument is readily completed by parents, scoring is completed by hand and interpretation is straightforward. Research is needed to establish scale utility.

REVIEWER'S REFERENCES

American Psychiatric Association. (2000). *Diagnostic and statistical manual of mental disorders* (4th ed., text rev). Washington, DC: Author.

American Psychiatric Association. (2013). *Diagnostic and statistical manual of mental disorders* (5th ed.). Washington, DC: Author.

Barkley, R. A. (2012). Barkley Deficits in Executive Functioning Scale—Children and Adolescents (BDEFS-CA). New York, NY: Guilford Press.

Becker, S. P., Leopold, D. R., Burns, G. L., Jarrett, M. A., Langberg, J. M., Marshall, S. A., ... Willcutt, E. G. (2016). The internal, external, and diagnostic validity of sluggish cognitive tempo: A meta-analysis and critical review. *Journal of the American Academy of Child and Adolescent Psychiatry, 55*, 163-178.

DuPaul, G. J., & Langberg, J. M. (2015). Educational impairments in children with ADHD. In R. A. Barkley (Ed.), *Attention-deficit hyperactivity disorder: A handbook for diagnosis and treatment* (4th ed., pp. 169-190). New York, NY: Guilford Press.

[16]

BASC-3 Flex Monitor.

Purpose: Designed as a tool "for monitoring the status of behavioral and emotional functioning ... that can be used to measure the effectiveness of intervention programs at a group or individual level."
Population: Ages 2-18.
Publication Dates: 2009-2016.
Scores: Total score only.
Administration: Individual or group.
Levels, 3: Preschool (ages 2-5), child (ages 6-11 or 8-11), adolescent (ages 12-18).
Forms: Teacher, parent, and self-report forms available for 5 behavior types: Inattention/Hyperactivity (teacher, parent), Internalizing Problems [teacher, parent, self-report (ages 8-18)], Disruptive Behaviors (teacher, parent), Developmental Social Disorders (teacher, parent), School Problems [self-report (ages 8-18)].
Price Data, 2020: $65.50 per kit including digital manual (2016, 55 pages) and 10 Q-global reports; $58.50 per digital manual; $1.30 per report.
Foreign Language Editions: Parent and self-report forms available in Spanish.
Time: Approximately 5 minutes to complete each standard form.
Comments: Custom forms can be created using the online item bank; available only through test publisher's Q-global online platform.
Authors: Cecil R. Reynolds and Randy W. Kamphaus.
Publisher: Pearson.
Cross References: For reviews by Anthony T. Dugbartey and Rosemary Flanagan of a previous edition titled BASC-2 Progress Monitor, see 20:16.

Review of the BASC-3 Flex Monitor by RONALD A. MADLE, Retired School Psychologist (formerly Shikellamy School District and Penn State University), Mifflinburg, PA:

DESCRIPTION. Services in schools have increasingly focused on providing and documenting positive academic and behavioral changes in children. The BASC-3 Flex Monitor is designed to monitor such changes in children with behavioral or emotional disorders formally and efficiently. It was developed specifically as an adjunct to the Behavior Assessment System for Children, Third Edition (BASC-3; 20:18) as a progress-monitoring tool. The Flex Monitor is best used to track changes in behavioral and emotional functioning, particularly when monitoring the effectiveness of intervention.

The BASC-3 Flex Monitor is available on the test publisher's online system for administering, scoring, and reporting test results. When digital administration is not possible, paper forms can be printed and completed for later entry. Many types of individuals can complete the forms, but each site should have someone qualified in psychometrics, test design, and psychological and educational testing standards to assure proper interpretation of results. Raters select the response corresponding to the frequency of the behavior (*never, sometimes, often, almost always*). All items must be completed before a form can be scored and a report generated.

The BASC-3 Flex Monitor includes standard forms corresponding to the five behavior types comprising the major BASC-3 scales (Inattention/Hyperactivity, Disruptive Behaviors, Internalizing Problems, Developmental Social Disorders, and School Problems) for various raters (teacher, parent, and self) and ages (preschool, child, and adolescent). Each 8- to 18-item form can be completed in about 5 minutes and provides a single Total Score. In addition, custom forms can be designed from more than 700 BASC-3 items using a drag-and-drop approach. Parent- and self-report forms are available in Spanish as well as English. When a customized scale is constructed, a reliability coefficient may be calculated. A coefficient of .80 or higher is suggested for typical monitoring purposes. General age-based T-score norms (based on a nationally representative sample) are automatically provided.

Reports are compiled online with up to 10 administrations of a single form type. Reports include information on the subject, raters, form types, dates, and so forth, followed by a profile with a graph of Total Scores in T scores with a goal zone representing non-problematic scores. There also is a table of T scores with changes and significance levels from both the initial value and the last measured value. The same descriptive cutoffs (i.e., *average, at-risk, clinically significant*) as in the BASC-3 are used. Although not a requirement for a Flex Monitor report, the test authors recommend establishing a baseline of at least three observations.

DEVELOPMENT. The BASC-3 Flex Monitor was developed concurrently with the BASC-3. A pool of more than 700 items remained after some items were eliminated based on expert reviews, item bias analysis, and inappropriateness for monitoring (e.g., validity scale items). Spanish language forms were reviewed by 10 bilingual professionals in different regions of the country to ensure accurate and appropriately worded translations.

The Flesch-Kincaid Readability Index was used to estimate readability. Parent items had a median of 4.9, or about a fifth-grade reading level. The median reading index for the self-report items (2.2) was approximately second-grade level.

TECHNICAL.

Standardization. Standardization data were obtained from a large, representative sample of children and adolescents across the United States stratified by demographic characteristics including gender, race/ethnicity, parent education level, geographic region, and representation in special education and gifted programs based on 2013 U.S. Census data. Data were mostly collected using digital methods; 30% of forms were submitted using paper-and-pencil. Consent was obtained for self reports, teacher ratings, and parent ratings. More than 9,000 forms, both English and Spanish, were obtained from 311 examiners in 44 states as part of the overall BASC-3 project.

The final standardization sample consists of 4,400 overall ratings from 1,700 teachers; 1,800 parents; and 900 self-reports (ages 8-18). There were 300 ratings for each age band (2-3, 4-5, 6-7, 8-11, 12-14, and 15-18), except for teacher ratings at ages 2-3, which had only 200 ratings. The demographic characteristics closely approximated 2013 U.S. Census Bureau information. Dominant special education classifications were included for each form type.

Total raw scores were obtained for each scale by summing the responses from participants in the standardization sample, including reverse scoring for positively worded items. Raw scores were converted to T scores with a mean of 50 and standard deviation of 10.

Reliability. High internal consistency, as represented by coefficient alpha, shows the degree to which items measure the same construct. Standard form alpha coefficients are good to excellent, with most being in the upper .80s or higher. Predictably, scales with highly salient and observable items (e.g., disruptive, overactive behaviors), those for older individuals, and teacher ratings yielded the highest coefficients. More subtle or subjective behaviors, such as those in the Developmental Social Disorders and Internalizing Problems forms, tend to be lower. Standard errors of measurement to permit estimation of confidence intervals are mostly between two and four T-score points.

Test-retest reliability was estimated over an average interval of 3 weeks in samples ranging from 72 to 129 participants across a variety of demographic groups. Both raw test-retest correlation coefficients and coefficients corrected for restriction of range are presented. The corrected values are uniformly high for the individual scales (.81 to .92), although a few uncorrected coefficients for more subjective areas such as Internalizing Problems in adolescents rated by teachers were moderate (e.g., .66). Effect sizes computed for various scales revealed negligible differences in the means across the two ratings.

Validity. Construct evidence of validity focused on relationships with relevant BASC-3 scales. Comparisons show the agreement between various forms (age and rater) of the BASC-3 and corresponding Flex Monitor scales provides support for the constructs measured by the BASC-3 Flex Monitor.

Across all forms and levels, the BASC-3 Flex Monitor scores correlated with the corresponding BASC-3 composites in an expected manner. For example, scores from Inattention/Hyperactivity and Disruptive Behavior were highly correlated with the BASC-3 Externalizing Problems composite (coefficients from .75 to .87 and from .90 to .95, respectively). Other particularly notable correlations emerged between the BASC-3 Flex Monitor Internalizing Problems scale and the BASC-3 Internalizing Problems composite (coefficients ranged from .86 to .96), as well as between the BASC-3 Flex Monitor Developmental Social scale and the BASC-3 Adaptive Skills composite (coefficients ranged from -.78 to -.87). The School Problems Scale on the child and adolescent Flex Monitor self-report forms correlated highly with the BASC-3 School Problems composite and the Inattention/ Hyperactivity composite with coefficients of .70-.74 and .87-.91, respectively.

COMMENTARY AND SUMMARY. Overall, the BASC-3 Flex Monitor appears to provide a useful approach for tracking changes in child and adolescent behavior in response to interventions or simply over time. It is a sensible addition to instruments available for monitoring responses to treatment interventions.

The Flex Monitor is easily administered and scored across a wide age range. Reading levels for the scales are appropriate, and instructions are clear. The psychometric characteristics of the standard forms are strong. The content representation of the items for all forms of the instrument is broad and comprehensive. A distinct strength of this instrument is its brevity and ease of completion for tracking mid- to higher-level constructs as opposed to single, discrete behaviors. The brevity of the scales permits selection of students for small-group or classroom-based interventions without administering broad-based, time-consuming behavior rating scales.

Although the BASC-3 Flex Monitor may be an improvement over the earlier BASC-2 Progress Monitor (BASC-2 PM), there are several areas where the Flex Monitor might be improved. First, more information on reliability and validity is needed in the test manual. For example, information on interrater reliability at the scale level would be useful. In addition, inclusion of the "true" score range on the report printout might be a desirable feature. Generally, the BASC-2 PM report provided more information than the BASC-3 Flex Monitor report.

Although not addressed in the test manual, it would be desirable to include control conditions at the single-subject level, such as reversal designs or multiple baseline designs across behaviors, settings, or subjects to more definitively attribute changes to the applied interventions. This would, in addition, help rule out possible artificial changes caused by expectations. Various studies have shown ratings are more susceptible to this influence than are observationally based behavioral assessments (Madle, Neisworth, & Kurtz, 1980).

REVIEWER'S REFERENCES

Madle, R. A., Neisworth, J. T., & Kurtz, P. D. (1980). Biasing of hyperkinetic behavior ratings by diagnostic reports: Effects of observer training and assessment method. *Journal of Learning Disabilities, 13,* 30-33.

Reynolds, C. R., & Kamphaus, R. W. (2015). Behavior Assessment System for Children, Third Edition. San Antonio, TX: Pearson.

Reynolds, C. R., & Kamphaus, R. W. (2009) BASC-2 Progress Monitor. San Antonio, TX: Pearson.

Review of the BASC-3 Flex Monitor by LIA SANDILOS, Assistant Professor, and SAMANTHA RUSHWORTH, M.S., Temple University, Philadelphia, PA:

DESCRIPTION. The BASC-3 Flex Monitor is a multidimensional rating system used to track students' behavioral and emotional functioning over time. The Flex Monitor is available in forms for parent raters and teacher raters of children and adolescents ages 2-18 and self-report for ages 8-18. The BASC-3 Flex Monitor standard forms allow respondents to rate five types of behaviors: Inattention/Hyperactivity, Internalizing Problems, Disruptive Behavior, Developmental Social Disorders, and School Problems. In comparison to the BASC-3 rating scales, the BASC-3 Flex Monitor serves as a brief, efficient tool for monitoring progress in specific areas of behavioral and emotional functioning.

The BASC-3 Flex Monitor allows for the administration of either standard forms or customized forms. All forms are created and administered digitally (printed PDF versions also can be obtained) and scored through the test publisher's online platform. The test authors report that the scales can be easily used in multi-tiered systems of support at the schoolwide, small-group, and individual levels. The purpose of the custom forms is to individualize the assessment based on the specific behavioral issues of interest. The test authors indicate that standard or custom forms should be chosen based on intervention, screening results, diagnosis, classification, and/or observation. Consistent with the use of other progress-monitoring tools, the test authors suggest three administrations of a BASC-3 Flex Monitor rating scale to determine a student's baseline behaviors prior to implementing an intervention. To create the Flex Monitor forms, users indicate the rater type and age of student. Users can choose to use standard items for a given behavior type, or they can individually select items to create a customized form.

The test authors indicate that users of the assessment should obtain ratings using multiple forms (parent, teacher, self) and ratings from more than one teacher for optimal information. Each administration of the assessment provides a new score in order to determine the student's change in behavior. Specifically, score reports include T scores, which are scaled scores with a mean of 50 and a standard deviation (*SD*) of 10. Scores falling within 1 *SD* of the mean are considered average as compared to the representative population of same-age peers, but higher or lower scores may be considered desirable depending on the types of items used. Score reports provide descriptions of scores based on standard deviations from the mean. If a high score is more desirable (e.g., adaptive skills) classification categories consist of *very high*, *high*, *average*, *at-risk*, and *clinically significant*. If a low score is more desirable (e.g., disruptive behaviors), classification categories consist of *very low*, *low*, *average*, *at-risk*, and *clinically significant*. When comparing scores to determine change over time, statistically significant differences in scaled scores are tested using the standard error of the difference.

DEVELOPMENT. Items included on the BASC-3 teacher, parent, and self-report scales formed the initial item pool for the BASC-3 Flex Monitor. Given that the Flex Monitor is intended as a progress-monitoring tool, the initial pool was reviewed to determine the appropriateness of each item for monitoring change in emotional or behavioral functioning. Any items deemed inappropriate for monitoring change were removed from the Flex Monitor item pool, resulting in 700 Flex Monitor items. An analysis of Flex Monitor item readability indicated that the median Flesch-Kincaid Reading Index level for parent forms is fifth grade, and the median level for student forms is second grade. Spanish language forms also are available. After bilingual developers translated English items, 10 bilingual reviewers provided feedback on item wording and clarity.

TECHNICAL. The same normative sample was used for the BASC-3 Flex Monitor as was used in the development and standardization of the BASC-3. Standardization took place from April 2013 to November 2014. Participants were recruited from daycare facilities, schools, and clinics, and more than 9,000 forms were administered in 44 states. The normative sample includes 1,700 teacher forms; 1,800 parent forms; and 900 self-report forms stratified by parent education, race/ethnicity, and geographic region based on figures from the 2013 U.S. Census. In descriptive tables in the test manual, the test authors compare percentages from the BASC-3 Flex Monitor norming group and the U.S. population. The test authors note that standard scores calculated from the normative sample will not include cases with missing responses, and they report that most items have five or fewer individuals with missing responses. Within the age-based normative groups, genders are combined.

When creating a custom form, the Flex Monitor provides internal consistency reliability if the user selects five or more items. This internal consistency is based on data gathered from the BASC-3 standardization sample. The test authors recommend that users create scales with coefficients of .80 or higher. Whether reliability is prioritized when creating a custom form is up to the discretion of the test user. For the standard forms, the test authors note that teacher forms, forms for reporting on older ages, and reports of externalizing behaviors have the highest internal consistency reliability. Values for the teacher forms across ages and behavior types ranged from .81 to .95. Parent-form coefficients were .77 to .90, and coefficients for the self-report forms were .84 to .88. Test-retest reliability was examined at every level (preschool, child, adolescent) of the three forms. Samples ranged from 72 participants (teacher, preschool level) to 129 participants (self-report, adolescent) with an average of 3 weeks between administrations. Test-retest coefficients across parent, teacher, and self-report forms are relatively high (corrected *r*s = .81 to .92).

To evaluate the convergent and discriminant evidence of validity for the constructs measured by the BASC-3 Flex Monitor standard forms and the BASC-3, correlational analyses were conducted. Overall, correlation coefficients ranged from moderate to high in magnitude and were in predictable directions. Across teacher and parent ratings, Inattention/Hyperactivity and Disruptive Behaviors on the Flex Monitor demonstrated high correlations with the Externalizing Problems composite of the BASC-3 (coefficients ranged from .75 to .95). The Internalizing Problems composite was highly correlated across both measures as well, with coefficients ranging from .95 to .96, .92 to .95, and .86 to .87 for teacher, parent, and self-report ratings, respectively. As expected, the Flex Monitor Developmental Social Disorders had a high negative correlation with the Adaptive Skills composite of the BASC-3 (coefficients from -.78 to -.87 across teacher and parent ratings). Additionally, the Flex Monitor School Problems composite demonstrated the highest correlation coefficients (.87 for adolescents and .91 for children) with the Inattention/Hyperactivity index of the BASC-3 self-report, as expected given that the Flex Monitor School Problems composite includes questions related to ADHD symptomatology. No associations with measures other than the BASC-3 are reported in the Flex Monitor manual.

COMMENTARY. The BASC-3 Flex Monitor represents an innovative and efficient way to monitor student behavior in an individualized manner and within a multi-tiered framework of support (Albers & Kettler, 2014). The measure is used in conjunction with the BASC-3 and is fairly easy to customize and use in the test publisher's online system. Additional benefits of the measure include the establishment of readability level, the creation of Spanish and English versions for parent- and self-report, and the ability to determine statistically significant changes in ratings over time. However, with efficiency and individualization come some limitations to reliability and validity. The overall psychometric soundness of the Flex Monitor is understandably difficult to assess given that users can create customized forms; however, this reviewer believes more information could be provided with regard to the standard Flex Monitor forms. Within the development section, the authors do not include details about the supporting theory behind the specific constructs included in the BASC-3 Flex Monitor, perhaps because the test user is expected to have access to this information in the BASC-3 documentation, as the framework of the BASC-3 is echoed in the Flex Monitor. By extension, convergent evidence of validity is limited to that obtained from the BASC-3. Report of a pilot study of the Flex Monitor could be particularly useful given that this measure is somewhat experimental in nature and leaves to the discretion of the user whether to create a custom form and, if so, to ensure the creation has reasonable reliability coefficients.

SUMMARY. The BASC-3 Flex Monitor is a progress monitoring tool that allows for but does not require customization of the rating scales to be used within a multi-tiered systems of support model. Teacher, parent, and self-report forms are available to assess the behavioral and emotional functioning of students ages 2-18. Standard and customized forms can be used to assess the following behavior types: Inattention/Hyperactivity, Internalizing Problems, Disruptive Behavior, Developmental Social Disorders, and School Problems. Efficiency and individualization are benefits of the measure, but there are some potential concerns about the reliability of customized forms created by users. Although preliminary validity evidence is reported in the test manual, more information about development and pilot work as well as convergent associations with other behavioral outcome measures would help to substantiate its use for progress monitoring and assessment of responses to intervention efforts.

REVIEWERS' REFERENCE

Albers, C. A., & Kettler, R. J. (2014). Best practices in universal screening. In P. L. Harrison & A. Thomas (Eds.), *Best practices in school psychology: Data-based and collaborative decision making* (pp. 121-131). Bethesda, MD: NASP Publications.

[17]

Batería IV Woodcock-Muñoz.

Purpose: A Spanish-language psychoeducational assessment system designed for use in forming "a broad-based assessment of cognitive abilities, achievement, and comparative oral language abilities."

Population: Spanish speakers ages 2-95.

Publication Dates: 1982-2019.

Acronym: Batería IV.

Administration: Individual.

Parts, 2: Pruebas de Habilidades Cognitivas (Tests of Cognitive Abilities), Pruebas de Aprovechamiento (Tests of Achievement).

Price Data, 2019: $2,141 per complete battery, including cognitive abilities kit and achievement kit.

Comments: Parallel Spanish version of Woodcock-Johnson IV; online scoring available; some cluster scores require administration of select tests from the Batería III Woodcock-Muñoz or Woodcock-Johnson IV Tests of Oral Language.

Authors: Richard W. Woodcock, Criselda G. Alvarado, Fredrick A. Shrank, Kevin S. McGrew, Nancy Mather, Ana F. Muñoz-Sandoval (test), and Barbara J. Wendling (examiner's manuals).

Publisher: Riverside Insights.

a) PRUEBAS DE HABILIDADES COGNITIVAS (TESTS OF COGNITIVE ABILITIES).

Purpose: Designed to assess "different aspects of cognitive ability."

Acronym: Batería IV COG.

Scores, 29: 7 Standard Battery tests: Vocabulario Oral (Oral Vocabulary), Series Numéricas (Number Series), Atención Verbal (Verbal Attention), Pareo de Letras Idénticas (Letter-Pattern Matching), Procesamiento Fonético (Phonological Processing), Rememoración de Cuentos (Story Recall), Visualización (Visualization); 7 Extended Battery tests: Información General (General Information), Formación de Conceptos (Concept Formation), Inversión de Números (Numbers Reversed), Pareo de Números Idénticos (Number-Pattern Matching), Repetición de Palabras sin Sentido (Nonword Repetition), Cancelación de Pares (Pair Cancellation), Rapidez en la Identificación de Dibujos (Rapid Picture Naming); 15 clusters: Habilidad Intelectual General (General Intellectual Ability), Habilidad Intelectual Breve (Brief Intellectual Ability), Gf-Gc Combinado (Gf-Gc Composite), Compresión-Conocimiento (Comprehension-Knowledge), Razonamiento Fluido (Fluid Reasoning), Memoria de Trabajo a Corto Plazo (Short-Term Working Memory), Velocidad de Procesamiento Cognitivo (Cognitive Processing Speed), Procesamiento Auditivo (Auditory Processing), Almacenamiento y Recuperación a Largo Plazo (Long-Term Storage and Retrieval), Procesamiento Visual (Visual Processing), Razonamiento Cuantitative (Quantitative Reasoning), Destreza Numérica (Number Facility), Rapidez Perceptual (Perceptual Speed), Vocabulario (Vocabulary), Eficicencia Cognitiva (Cognitive Efficiency).

Price Data: $1,432 per Cognitive Battery kit with case including examiner's manual (2019, 168 pages), test book, 25 record booklets, 25 answer booklets, and scoring transparencies.

Time: Approximately 35 minutes for administration of the Standard Battery; 5 minutes per additional test.

b) PRUEBAS DE APROVECHAMIENTO (TESTS OF ACHIEVEMENT).

Purpose: Designed to measure achievement in "three curricular areas—reading, mathematics, and written language."

Acronym: Batería IV APROV.

Scores, 30: 13 tests: Identificación de Letras y Palabras (Letter-Word Identification), Problemas Aplicados (Applied Problems), Ortografía (Spelling), Compresión de Textos (Passage Comprehension), Cálculo (Calculation), Expresión de Lenguaje Escrito (Written Language Expression), Análisis de Palabras (Word Attack), Lectura Oral (Oral Reading), Fluidez en Lectura de Frases (Sentence Reading Fluency), Fluidez en Datos Matemáticos (Math Facts Fluency), Fluidez en Escritura de Frases (Sentence Writing Fluency), Rememoración de Lectura (Reading Recall), Números Matrices (Number Matrices); 17 clusters: Lectura (Reading), Lectura Amplia (Broad Reading), Destrezas Básicas en Lectura (Basic Reading Skills), Comprensión de Lectura (Reading Comprehension), Fluidez en la Lectura (Reading Fluency), Matemáticas (Mathematics), Matemáticas Amplias (Broad Mathematics), Destrezas en Cálculos Matemáticos (Math Calculation Skills), Resolución de Problemas Matemáticos (Math Problem Solving), Lenjuage Escrito (Written Language), Lenguaje Escrito Amplio (Broad Written Language), Expresión Escrita (Written Expression), Aprovechamiento Breve (Brief Achievement), Aprovechamiento Amplio (Broad Achievement), Destrezas Académicas (Academic Skills), Fluidez Académica (Academic Fluency), Aplicaciones Académicas (Academic Applications).

Price Data: $925 per Achievement Battery with case, including examiner's manual (2019, 162 pages), test book, 25 record booklets, 25 answer booklets, and scoring transparencies.

Time: 40 minutes for administration of Tests 1 through 6, with Test 6 requiring 15-20 minutes; 5-10 minutes for administration of Tests 7-13.

Cross References: For reviews by Beth Doll and Courtney LeClair and by Arturo Olivárez, Jr. and Allison Boroda of the Batería III Woodcock-Muñoz™, see 17:14; for reviews by Robert B. Frary and Maria Prendes Lintel of the Bateria Woodcock-Munoz—Revisada, see 13:27; for reviews by Jack A. Cummings and by Steven W. Lee and Elaine Flory Stefany of the Woodcock-Johnson Psycho-Educational Battery—Revised, see 12:415 (36 references); see also T4:2973 (90 references) and T3:2639 (3 references); for reviews by Jack A. Cummings and Alan S. Kaufman of an earlier edition of the Woodcock-Johnson Psycho-Educational Battery, see 9:1387 (6 references).

Review of the Batería IV Woodcock-Muñoz by S. KATHLEEN KRACH, Assistant Professor of School Psychology, Florida State University, Tallahassee, FL:

DESCRIPTION. The Batería IV Woodcock-Muñoz consists of two parts: the Pruebas de habilidades cognitivas (Batería IV COG; Tests of Cognitive Ability) and the Pruebas de aprovechamiento (Batería IV APROV; Tests of Achievement). Both parts of the Batería IV are Spanish translations or adaptations of their respective subparts of the Woodcock-Johnson IV (WJ IV; Schrank, McGrew, & Mather, 2014). According to the Batería IV manual, the WJ IV COG/Batería IV COG were designed to measure an individual's overall cognitive ability as well as any specific Cattell-Horn-Carroll (CHC) based cognitive processes. The WJ IV ACH/Batería IV APROV was designed to measure an individual's achievement in math, reading, and writing.

The original Woodcock-Johnson Psycho-Educational Battery (WJ; Woodcock & Johnson, 1977-1978) was translated and renormed into a Spanish version, the Batería Woodcock Psico-Educativa en Español (Woodcock, 1982). Reviews of the original Batería expressed concerns about insufficient psychometric data and problematic norms (Lintel, 1998). The second version, the Batería Woodcock-Muñoz—Revisada (Batería-R; Woodcock & Muñoz-Sandoval, 1996), was created to accompany the WJ-Revised (WJ-R; Woodcock & Johnson, 1989). Reviewers considered the Batería-*R* to be far superior to any other Spanish translated test at that time (Frary, 1998). The third version of the Batería was called the Batería III (Muñoz-Sandoval, Woodcock, McGrew, & Mather, 2005) and accompanied the WJ III (Woodcock, McGrew, & Mather, 2001). The Batería III was well reviewed and described as the best Spanish test on the market (Doll, 2007; Olivarez & Boroda, 2007), but as with the Batería, the Batería III reviewers expressed continued concerns about normative sampling issues.

Reviews of the WJ IV (Canivez, 2017; Madle, 2017) were mostly positive. The main concern was that the factor analytic data were incomplete/inconclusive regarding the construct evidence of validity of the CHC factors described in the test manual. In addition, one reviewer expressed a concern that the scoring software removed the transparency of the score conversion procedures potentially making it more difficult to calculate out-of-level estimates.

DEVELOPMENT AND TECHNICAL. For technical specifications related to the development of the instruments, please see reviews of the WJ IV (Canivez, 2017; Madle, 2017). Given that the Batería IV uses the same norms and many of the same items as the WJ IV, the concerns and comments listed in the WJ IV reviews should also be considered applicable to the Batería IV. Therefore, the following technical review focuses only on the conversion process between the WJ IV and the Batería IV. It does not focus on the development of the WJ IV.

The conversion process included several steps. First, the authors determined which tests needed a simple translation versus a more intensive adaptation. For certain tests, the test directions and/or items were directly translated with no other changes. Translated tests on the Batería IV COG are Test 2–Number Series, 3–Verbal Attention, 4–Letter-Pattern Matching, 7–Visualization, 9–Concept Formation, 10–Numbers Reversed, 11–Number-Pattern Matching, 13–Visual-Auditory Learning, and 14–Picture Recognition. Translated tests on the Batería IV APROV are Test 5–Calculation, 8–Oral Reading, 10–Math Facts Fluency, and 13–Number Matrices.

Other tests had to be significantly adapted because a direct translation was not appropriate. These adapted tests on the Batería IV COG are Tests 1–Oral Vocabulary, 5–Phonological Processing, 6–Story Recall, 8–General Information, and 12–Nonword Repetition. Adapted tests on the Batería IV APROV are 1–Letter-Word Identification, 2–Applied Problems, 3–Spelling, 4–Passage Comprehension, 6–Writing Samples, 7–Word Attack, 9–Sentence Reading Fluency, 11–Sentence Writing Fluency, and 12–Reading Recall. Many tests that were translated or adapted for the Batería III were unchanged for the Batería IV.

According to the Batería IV manuals, the WJ IV and the Batería IV use the same norming sample. This original norming group was designed to reflect the population of individuals within the United States. Instead of collecting Spanish norms, the authors performed calibration studies for the following tests that were new or contained new items: Batería IV COG Tests 5A—Phonological Processing (Word Access), 5C—Phonological Processing (Substitution), 6—Story Recall, and 12—Nonword Repetition and Batería IV APROV Tests 8—Oral Reading and 12—Reading Recall.

The calibration studies were conducted with 601 native Spanish speakers (ages 2 to 81 years) living in 10 states in the United States of America;

400 of the participants were ages 2 to 19 years. The largest percentage of participants (70.1%) were of Mexican heritage. Puerto Ricans (5.5%) made up the next largest group; also included were individuals from El Salvador (2.8%), Guatemala (2.0%), Cuba (1.5%), and the Dominican Republic (0.8%). According to the 2010 U.S. Census, countries of origin for Hispanics living in the United States are proportioned differently from the Batería IV sample: Mexicans (63%), Puerto Ricans (9.2%), Cubans (3.5%), Salvadorans (3.3%), and Dominicans (2.8%).

Following the collection of data from the calibration sample, items were calibrated using Rasch equating procedures. Extreme outliers were removed. Items were sorted to ensure that the item presentation order was consistent with item difficulty. Reliability coefficients were calculated for the tests that were included in the calibration study: Batería IV COG Phonological Process (.80-.91), Story Recall (.95-.96), and Nonword Repetition (.85-.94) as well as Batería IV APROV Oral Reading (.89-.92) and Reading Recall (.94-.97). Reliability coefficients were provided for the other tests, but they were derived from the WJ IV sample. No equivalency data were presented between the WJ IV and Batería IV.

COMMENTARY. Given that the Batería IV uses the same norms and many of the same items as the WJ IV, any strengths and/or weaknesses discussed in the WJ IV review should be applied to the Batería IV as well. Therefore, for a complete review of the Batería IV, readers should refer to the issues and problems discussed by the reviewers of the WJ IV (Canivez, 2017; Madle, 2017). In addition, a few issues specific to the Batería IV are worth noting. The first is that the documentation regarding the translation and calibration of the WJ IV to the Batería IV is lacking. For example, the test authors write that many of the tests from the Batería III were reused, altered or renamed for the Batería IV. They did not state the extent that each subtest stayed the same or was altered between the two versions or why these alterations were made.

Another issue is that only six tests (22% of the 27 possible) went through the calibration process described in the manual. Of the subtests that were newly calibrated, two were from the six new tests on the Cognitiva and two were from the four new tests on the Aprovechamiento. That means that only 40% of the new subtests went through the calibration process. In addition, specific calibration data were not provided. The test developers state the rules used to decide sufficient calibration, but specific numbers are not provided so that readers of the test manuals can make determinations for themselves.

Another concern related to calibration is that two-thirds of the sample members were age 19 or younger. For those who work with children, the sample may be sufficient. However, the use of the Batería IV for anyone over age 19 does not seem well supported. In addition, the sample of Spanish speakers overrepresents some countries of origin (and underrepresents others) compared with U.S. Census figures. Although this disproportionate representation is a concern, it is nice to see that the test authors recruited the Spanish speakers from within the United States. Whether the test can or should be used in other countries is not supportable at the present time.

The largest problem is the lack of equivalency data between the Batería IV and the WJ IV. Equivalency studies should include data between versions such as correlations, mean score differences, and differences in shapes of score distributions (APA, 1986). These data were not provided.

SUMMARY. The reviewers of the Batería III (Olivarez & Boroda, 2007; Doll, 2007) described it as the best Spanish test available at that time. Overall, even with the concerns discussed in this review, the Batería IV continues to be one of the best tests available for working with Spanish speakers in the United States. However, other test developers have been busy creating tests in multiple languages. There is now more competition for the title of "best" than there has ever been in the past.

REVIEWER'S REFERENCES

American Psychological Association, Committee on Professional Standards, & Committee on Psychological Tests and Assessment. (1986). *Guidelines for computer-based tests and interpretations.* Washington, DC: Author.

Canivez, G. L. (2017). [Test review of Woodcock-Johnson IV]. In J. F. Carlson, K. F. Geisinger, & J. L. Jonson (Eds.), *The twentieth mental measurements yearbook.* Lincoln, NE: Buros Center for Testing.

Doll, B. J. (2007). [Test review of Batería III]. In K. F. Geisinger, R. A. Spies, J. F. Carlson, & B. S. Plake (Eds.), *The seventeenth mental measurements yearbook.* Lincoln, NE: Buros Institute of Mental Measurements.

Frary, R. B. (1998). [Test review of Batería Woodcock-Muñoz—Revisada. In J. C. Impara & B. S. Plake (Eds.), *The thirteenth mental measurements yearbook.* Lincoln, NE: Buros Institute of Mental Measurements.

Lintel, M. P. (1998). [Test review of the Batería Woodcock Psico-Educativa en Español]. In J. C. Impara & B. S. Plake (Eds.), *The thirteenth mental measurements yearbook.* Lincoln, NE: Buros Institute of Mental Measurements.

Madle, R. A. (2017). [Test review of Woodcock-Johnson IV]. In J. F. Carlson, K. F. Geisinger, & J. L. Jonson (Eds.), *The twentieth mental measurements yearbook.* Lincoln, NE: Buros Center for Testing.

Muñoz-Sandoval, A. F., Woodcock, R. W., McGrew, K. S., & Mather, N. (2005). Batería III Woodcock-Muñoz. Rolling Meadows, IL: Riverside.

Olivarez, A., & Boroda, A. D. [Test review of Batería III]. In K. F. Geisinger, R. A. Spies, J. F. Carlson, & B. S. Plake (Eds.), *The seventeenth mental measurements yearbook.* Lincoln, NE: Buros Institute of Mental Measurements.

Schrank, F. A., McGrew, K. S., & Mather, N. (2014). Woodcock-Johnson IV. Rolling Meadows, IL: Riverside.

U.S. Census Bureau (2010). *Decennial census.* Retrieved from https://www.pewresearch.org/hispanic/2011/05/26/us-hispanic-country-of-origin-counts-for-nation-top-30-metropolitan-areas/

Woodcock, R. W. (1982). Batería Woodcock Psico-Educativa en Español. Rolling Meadows, IL: Riverside.

Woodcock, R. W., & Johnson, M. B. (1977-1978). Woodcock-Johnson Psycho-educational Battery. Rolling Meadows, IL: Riverside.

Woodcock, R. W., & Johnson, M. B. (1989). Woodcock-Johnson Psycho-Educational Battery—Revised. Rolling Meadows, IL: Riverside.

Woodcock, R. W., McGrew, K. S., & Mather, N. (2001). Woodcock-Johnson III. Rolling Meadows, IL: Riverside.

Woodcock, R. W., & Muñoz-Sandoval, A. F. (1996). Batería Woodcock-Muñoz—Revisada. Rolling Meadows, IL: Riverside.

Review of the Batería IV Woodcock-Muñoz by ARTURO OLIVÁREZ, JR., Professor, Educational Leadership & Foundations Department, University of Texas at El Paso, El Paso, TX:

DESCRIPTION. The Batería IV Woodcock-Muñoz is a comprehensive Spanish-language psychoeducational assessment system made up of two exam batteries: the Batería IV Woodcock-Muñoz: *Pruebas de habilidades cognitivas* (Batería IV COG) and the Batería IV Woodcock-Muñoz: *Pruebas de aprovechamiento* (Batería IV APROV). The tests included in the Batería IV are adaptations or direct translations of tests from the Woodcock-Johnson IV (WJ IV; Schrank, McGrew, & Mather, 2014). The battery of tests is best suited for use with examinees from 5 to 95 years of age, but select tests may be used with children as young as 2 years of age. Test developers used native Spanish speakers to calibrate data and equate it to that of the nationally representative WJ IV normative sample of English-speaking test takers.

The Batería IV is based on the Cattell-Horn-Carroll (CHC) theory of cognitive abilities version 2 (McGrew, LaForte, & Schrank, 2014). The Batería IV follows an organization similar to previous versions with minor modifications as to the inclusion or exclusion of certain tests. The Batería IV COG includes all 10 tests from the WJ IV Tests of Cognitive Abilities Standard Battery plus four tests from the Extended Battery and the Oral Language Battery (WJ IV OL). The Batería IV APROV includes all 11 tests from the WJ IV Tests of Achievement Standard Battery (Schrank et al., 2014) plus two additional tests from the WJ IV Extended Battery. Each battery (i.e., Batería IV COG and Batería IV APROV) contains one easel-style stimulus book, record forms, response booklets, an examiner's manual, scoring guides, and access to the online scoring and reporting system and an online training video. Compared to the WJ IV COG and WJ IV ACH, which each have two stimulus books, only one book is needed for the Batería IV COG and the Batería IV APROV. Overall, the Batería IV COG has 14 tests, and the Batería IV APROV has 13 tests.

A summary of updates for the Batería IV COG includes: a larger emphasis on the core set of tests (1-7); a new Gf-Gc composite score; a revised cluster composition to increase cognitive complexity; the addition of several important narrow abilities; co-norming with Batería IV APROV tests; and the use of web-based scoring and reporting. For the Batería IV APROV, updates include: the removal of audio-recorded tests; qualitative observation checklists; co-norming with Batería IV COG tests; four new tests (*Lectura oral*, *Rememoración de lectura*, *Expresión de lenguaje escrito*, and *Números matrices*), and five new clusters (*Lectura*, *Lenguaje escrito*, *Fluidez en la lectura*, *Matemáticas*, and *Aprovechamiento breve*).

The administration instructions and scoring procedures are delineated for the examiner with training videos that should enhance proper use of basal and ceiling rules for both the Batería IV COG and Batería IV APROV tests. Several chapters in the examiner's manual are dedicated to the importance of appropriate administration, scoring, and interpretation of test results. In addition, the manuals are replete with useful information regarding the norming, representative sampling, and calibration procedures for the Batería IV.

DEVELOPMENT. As with previous versions of the Batería, the Batería IV is a parallel Spanish version of the WJ IV battery. Many of the included tests are direct translations, whereas others are adaptations of the English versions. As before, the Batería IV is modeled after the WJ IV battery's underlying CHC theoretical framework with only seven factors or broad abilities rather than nine factors. Similar to previous versions, the Batería IV is designed to be a comprehensive assessment system to evaluate individuals' general and specific cognitive abilities as well as their academic achievement across grade and age levels. Other equally important aspects of development include the Batería's enhanced diagnostic capabilities for describing cognitive performance and understanding the nature of individual learning problems by using information derived not just from the set of broad abilities, but also from the set of narrow abilities tests and clusters.

The Batería IV and the WJ IV rely on the same set of norms that yield scores such as standard scores and percentile ranks for both age- and grade-level groupings. Application of Rasch model equating procedures allowed for the calibration of test items from both tests by placing items onto a common metric or scale, called the *W*-scale. In other words, examinees who received a *W*-scale score from the English form of a test in the WJ IV can be directly compared to examinees who took the Spanish form of the same test in the Batería IV. The test takers' normed scores can mirror their relative standings in a distribution of their same language peers of the same age or grade.

Although many important results from the WJ IV norming sample and calibration studies may be applicable to the Batería IV, the actual calibration study for this battery involved only six tests that were administered to 601 native Spanish-speaking individuals between the ages of 2 and 81 years. Information in the test manual indicates these tests were new or contained new items whereas other adapted tests were not included because adequate item data from previous calibration studies were available. Examinees in the present study were selected from all regions of the United States with an even representation across gender and parents' educational attainment. However, there was an overrepresentation of individuals with a Mexican background (70.1%) and a resulting underrepresentation of other national groups. Most comparability and equating standards involved in the development of the Batería IV tests were represented as adhering to the *Standards for Educational and Psychological Testing* (American Educational Research Association, American Psychological Association, & National Council on Measurement in Education, 2014).

TECHNICAL. Similar to previous versions, the WJ IV serves as the blueprint for the Batería IV, and it relies on the same norming sample for psychometric property purposes including calibration and equating of selected test items from the norming sample of Spanish speakers. Specific to the calibration and equating of items, less than one-tenth of 1% of the total responses for most Batería IV tests were classified as "misfits" and removed during the Rasch calibration phase.

The developers of these scales relied on both classical true-score and Rasch-based theories to guide their final item selection by identifying content-relevant and biased items using common psychometric procedures. The test developers used the Rasch iterative-logit method to examine differential item functioning or bias for the tests in the calibration study across male and female test takers. The test manual reports the percentage of items that were more difficult for males and those more difficult for females on each of the tests. The Batería IV COG Test 6 (*Rememoración de cuentos*), with 159 items calibrated, yielded the largest percentages with 3.1% of the items being more difficult for males and 7.5% being more difficult for females.

Split-half reliability analyses for the Batería IV COG and APROV tests (for single-point items), Rasch model reliability information (for multiple-point items), and Mosier's formula for composite reliability (for clusters) were presented in an appendix of the respective examiner's manuals. Data indicate each of the COG and APROV tests and clusters have very high stability and internal consistency reliability values. The median reliability coefficients across several age groupings for the COG set ranged from .85 (*Prueba 5: Procesamiento fonético* and *Prueba 7: Visualización*) to .95 (*Prueba 6: Rememoración de cuentos*). For the COG clusters, the smallest median reliability value (.90) was obtained for the *Destreza numérica* cluster, and the largest value (.97) was observed for the *Habilidad intelectual general* cluster. For the APROV tests and clusters, similar results were observed with the majority of the tests and clusters producing more than adequate reliability values. Median reliability values for the 10 nonspeeded tests ranged from .79 (*Prueba 6: Expresión de lenguaje escrito*) to .97 (*Prueba 12: Rememoración de lectura*) across the age groups examined. For the APROV clusters, the median reliability values ranged from .88 (*Expresión escrita*) to .98 (*Aprovechamiento amplio*). Overall, the Batería IV tests and clusters appear to exhibit rather high levels of internal consistency reliability.

In terms of validity evidence for the Batería IV COG and APROV, the test developers point to the parallel nature of the cognitive and achievement tests from the WJ IV battery and the Batería IV tests. Thus, developers implied a "transferring" of psychometric properties from the WJ IV to the Batería IV. All aspects regarding content or substantive evidence of validity, internal structure, and construct evidence of validity are presumably inherited by the Batería test, and test users are directed to review and evaluate the WJ IV technical manual regarding most validity issues. A service bulletin (i.e., Assessment Service Bulletin Number I [Laforte et al., 2019]) addressing the Batería tests' validity issues includes similar information (i.e., representativeness of content, process, construct coverage, and developmental patterns) to that found in the WJ IV technical manual. This manual provides extensive evidence across age groups as to the intercorrelations within tests and clusters, intercorrelations with other intelligence measures such as the WISC-IV (Wechsler, 2003), internal structure, model fit statistics as to the specific test item-to-factor correspondence, cross-validation studies, and exploratory multidimensional scaling analyses. Therefore, if one is to rely on the psychometric work performed on the WJ IV tests and clusters, then one should be confident that there exists ample evidence put forth as to the various aspects of construct validity for the Batería IV. However, users must have access to the English technical manual and determine for themselves the weight of the validity evidence presented by developers. Users must critically judge the degree to which these validity data are applicable to these translated/adapted Spanish test forms.

COMMENTARY. There is no doubt as to the need nowadays for cognitive and achievement assessment to be readily available for diverse populations of non-English speaking individuals where clear evidence as to their critical thinking, communication, literacy, numeracy, and technology skills are needed. The Batería IV set of tests provides a measurement instrument that is hardly matched by any other similar battery. Its close alignment to the WJ IV battery provides a strong level of assurance as to its overall validity, especially with the current improvements to the CHC theoretical framework applicable to both the cognitive and achievement tests. The improvements made to the tests themselves, administration manuals, and web-based scoring and interpretations are a testament to the developers' commitment to continue providing diagnosticians, counselors, and parents with the most accurate and robust set of academic interpretation for diagnostic and placement decisions. In terms of some persisting or troublesome issues with this version of the battery, there is a need for the developers and technical personnel to continue their focus on the overall country of origin representation of the norming sample. More than 70% of the identified individuals were of Mexican descent, leaving other nationalities either under- or not represented. There is a need, minimally, for intercorrelation analyses of the tests and clusters themselves using the norming sample (n = 601) and including basic classical testing concepts such as item difficulty and discrimination from such norming sample. Also, there appears to have been no attempt to conduct similar psychometric procedures (e.g., exploratory and confirmatory factor analyses, structural equation modeling) with the Spanish-speaking norming sample. Finally, there is still a need to conduct follow-up analyses from previous Batería versions as to the observed misidentification and misplacement of test takers into special education programs as a way to justify the need for newer and more expensive versions of the tests.

SUMMARY. Overall, the reviewer finds this new version of the Batería IV more user-friendly with a reduced number of tests and clusters to accomplish similar outcomes in assessment, interpretation, and decision-making by professionals. The online scoring system facilitates this ease of use and interpretation, but it does add an additional burden for the need for examiners new to the system to be trained with the online scoring dashboard. This reviewer can recommend, with a reasonable level of confidence, that the test takers' performance on both cognitive and achievement tests and some clusters can yield accurate and valid representations of these latent traits.

REVIEWER'S REFERENCES

American Educational Research Association, American Psychological Association, & National Council on Measurement in Education. (2014). *Standards for educational and psychological testing.* Washington, DC: American Educational Research Association.

LaForte, E. M., Wendling, B. J., Mather, N., Schrank, F. A., & McGrew, K. S. (2019). Batería IV Woodcock-Muñoz. *Technical Abstract* (Batería IV Assessment Service Bulletin No. 1). Itasca, IL: Riverside Insights.

McGrew, K. S., LaForte, E. M., & Schrank, F. A. (2014). *Technical manual.* Woodcock-Johnson IV. Rolling Meadows, IL: Riverside.

Schrank, F. A., McGrew, K. S., & Mather, N. (2014). Woodcock-Johnson IV. Rolling Meadows, IL: Riverside.

[18]

Behavior Rating Inventory of Executive Function, Second Edition.

Purpose: Designed to assess "everyday behaviors associated with executive functions in the home and school environments."

Population: Ages 5-18.

Publication Dates: 1996-2015.

Acronym: BRIEF2.

Scores, 14-16: 10 clinical scale scores: Inhibit, Self-Monitor, Shift, Emotional Control, Initiate (Parent and Teacher forms only), Working Memory, Plan/Organize, Task-Monitor (Parent and Teacher forms only), Organization of Materials (Parent and Teacher forms only), Task Completion (Self-Report form only); 4 index scores: Behavior Regulation Index, Emotion Regulation Index, Cognitive Regulation Index, Global Executive Composite; 3 validity scale scores: Inconsistency, Negativity, Infrequency.

Administration: Individual or group.

Forms, 6: Parent, Teacher, Self-Report core forms and screening forms.

Price Data, 2019: $435 per hand-scored kit including professional manual (2015, 341 pages) with fast guide, 25

Parent Forms, 25 Teacher Forms, 25 Self-Report Forms, 25 Parent Scoring Summary/Profile Forms, 25 Teacher Scoring Summary/Profile Forms, and 25 Self-Report Scoring Summary Profile Forms; $128 per manual; $79 per 25 forms (Parent, Teacher, or Self-Report); $34 per 25 scoring summary/profile forms (Parent, Teacher or Self-Report); $61 per 25 screening forms (Parent, Teacher or Self-Report).

Foreign Language Edition: Spanish versions available for the Parent and Self-Report core and screening forms.

Time: (10-15) minutes.

Comments: Completed by parents and teachers of school-age children (5 to 18 years) and by adolescents ages 11 to 18 years. Administered via paper and pencil or computer.

Authors: Gerard A. Gioia, Peter K. Isquith, Steven C. Guy, and Lauren Kenworthy.

Publisher: Psychological Assessment Resources, Inc.

Cross References: For reviews by Corine Fitzpatrick and Gregory Schraw of the original edition (Parent and Teacher forms), see 15:32; for reviews by Stephen L. Benton and Sheryl Benton and by Manuel Martinez-Pons of the original BRIEF–Self-Report Version, see 16:28.

Review of the Behavior Rating Inventory of Executive Function, Second Edition by RYAN J. McGILL, Assistant Professor of School Psychology, William & Mary School of Education, Williamsburg, VA:

DESCRIPTION. The Behavior Rating Inventory of Executive Function, Second Edition (BRIEF2) is the first revision of the BRIEF (Gioia, Isquith, Guy, & Kenworthy, 2000), the first published rating scale assessing self-regulatory abilities in children and adolescents. The BRIEF2 maintains many of the essential properties of the BRIEF with numerous scales designed to provide "a window into the everyday behavior associated with specific domains of self-regulated cognitive problem solving, behavioral functioning, and emotion regulation" (manual, p. 26). The BRIEF family of instruments relies on a bi-level model of executive functioning in which specific functions are embedded within a broader network of cognitive/affective domains. The BRIEF2 is a substantive revision and re-standardization with a larger and more representative normative sample and more concise scales. Separate co-normed parent, teacher (63 items each), and self-report (55 items) forms are available.

The BRIEF2 parent and teacher forms include nine clinical scales (Inhibit, Self-Monitor, Shift, Emotional Control, Initiate, Working Memory, Plan/Organize, Task-Monitor, Organization of Materials) that combine to form three first-order index scores (Behavior Regulation Index [BRI], Emotion Regulation Index [ERI], Cognitive Regulation Index [CRI]) and an omnibus second-order Global Executive Composite (GEC) score. The self-report form yields the same index and composite scores as the parent and teacher forms with a slightly different configuration of seven clinical scales. Additionally, all three forms contain several validity indices (Negativity, Infrequency, Inconsistency) to help clinicians identify questionable responding by raters.

DEVELOPMENT. The goal for the revision noted in the test manual was to enhance the clinical and research utility of the scale without substantively altering the structure of the instrument. Specific enhancements include improving psychometric properties with new statistics (i.e., change indices, base rate tables) to support clinical interpretation, the addition of an Infrequency scale to help identify unusual responding, and greater parallelism in item content and order across the forms. It also should be noted that no new items were added as part of the revision, although some items were deleted to make the scales more concise and to help decrease the frequency of nonresponse by raters.

The BRIEF2 was standardized and validated for use with boys and girls ages 5-18 years (parent and teacher forms) and boys and girls ages 11-18 years (self-report form). The test manual indicates that test items were written at approximately a fifth-grade reading level, and each form can be completed in less than 10 minutes. Rating forms are accompanied by the BRIEF2 Professional Manual and a Fast Guide that contain standardized oral instructions for raters. In addition, the manual includes several case studies to aide users with clinical interpretation. A supplemental Interpretive Guide (Isquith, Gioia, Guy, & Kenworthy, 2017) is also available and contains additional case studies and intervention recommendations.

TECHNICAL.

Standardization. The BRIEF2 Professional Manual presents extensive and detailed information about the normative sample. Sample sizes ranged from 803 (self-report form) to 1,400 (parent and teacher forms) participants. The standardization sample was obtained through stratified proportional sampling across key demographic variables (age, gender, race/ethnicity, parent educational level as a proxy for socioeconomic status, and geographic region). Inspection of the demographic tables reported in the manual reveal a close match to the 2013 U.S. Census data.

Separate norms are provided for boys and girls across four age groups (two age groups for self-report). Inspection of the raw score conversion tables provided in the test manual revealed the presence of item gradient violations for several of the clinical scales. For example, the average gradient for the Initiate scale on the teacher rating form for girls ages 11-13 years was 4.8 points, exceeding established guidelines (Bracken, 1987). According to Wasserman and Bracken (2012), inadequate item density across the distribution of a latent trait reduces the sensitivity and discrimination of a test. Whereas the ceilings for all scales and index scores were adequate, virtually all scales demonstrated floor effects. However, it should be noted that this is less of a concern for rating scales such as the BRIEF2 in which lower scores are indicative of intact abilities.

All score scale, index, and composite scores on the BRIEF2 are expressed as T scores (M = 50, SD = 10, range = 35 to ≥ 90), though users should be aware that the percentile ranks associated with those scores may vary from scale to scale due to skew in the distributions. According to the manual, T scores between 60 and 64 are considered to be *mildly elevated*, scores between 65 and 69 are considered *potentially clinically elevated*, and scores at or above 70 are considered *clinically elevated* and significant.

In terms of interpretation, the manual outlines an interpretive strategy. In addition, clinicians are encouraged to utilize BRIEF2 scores to develop hypotheses about individual strengths and weaknesses that can be explored in follow-up testing. To wit, a series of procedures is described that includes assessing the validity indices, interpreting clinical scale and index scores, interpreting profile shape and scatter, and comparing the results obtained across multiple informants. Like many psychoeducational instruments, it is suggested that the GEC score can only be validly interpreted if an examiner first determines that there are no significant differences among the index scores, though the use of this popular interpretive heuristic has been questioned (McGill, 2016).

Reliability. Three methods of estimating reliability of BRIEF2 scores are reported in the test manual: internal consistency, test-retest stability, and interrater agreement. Internal consistency was estimated using alpha coefficients. Average coefficients across the forms were moderate to strong, ranging from .80 to .98, and estimates were invariant across several demographic characteristics. Temporal stability was assessed using a subsample of the normative sample with retest intervals that ranged from 2.8 to 3.7 weeks. Test-retest correlation coefficients for the parent (.67 to .92), teacher (.76 to .90), and self-report (.61 to .85) forms were moderate to strong. As expected, interrater reliability coefficients ranged from low to moderate on all of the rating forms although higher levels of agreement were observed for the scores obtained from parent dyads.

Validity. Consistent with the *Standards for Educational and Psychological Testing* (American Educational Research Association, American Psychological Association, & National Council on Measurement in Education, 2014), evidence of validity was structured around the areas of test content, internal structure, and relations with other variables. To examine the structure of the BRIEF2, item-total correlations, scale intercorrelations, and confirmatory factor analysis (CFA) results were reported. The CFA relied exclusively on the use of constrained analyses (i.e., rival models were not examined). The first CFA examined relationships at the item-level in order to establish the latent structure of the clinical scales. Then a second CFA commenced using the clinical scale scores as measured variables to examine higher-order structure using a three oblique (correlated) factors model. Results from both analyses generally supported the theoretical model posited in the test manual for all of the rating forms.

Numerous comparative studies of the BRIEF2 in relation to other behavioral rating scales and intelligence tests were reported in the test manual, and evidence of convergent and divergent validity was inconsistent. Whereas the zero-order correlations between scale and index scores from the BRIEF2 and other attention-related indices on rating scales were moderate to strong, relationships with some reference scores on intelligence tests were less robust. For example, correlations between the Working Memory scale on the BRIEF2 and the Working Memory Index on the WISC-IV/WAIS-IV were -.08 and -.27, respectively, for the parent and teacher forms. Relationships between BRIEF2 scores and external measures of achievement were not reported. Special groups and matched controls were compared to test for specific group differences. Mean scale, index, and composite score differences between the groups were typically what one would expect, with individuals diagnosed with various subtypes of attention-deficit/hyperactivity disorder, learning disabilities, and autism spectrum disorder scoring higher than matched groups of typically developing peers. To buttress these findings, additional diagnostic efficiency statistics were provided to support the use of specific clinical scales for differential diagnosis.

COMMENTARY. As with any test, the BRIEF2 has strengths and weaknesses. Whereas extensive psychometric information is provided in the test manual, there are a few notable omissions. In particular, it remains unclear to this reviewer how the instrument should be interpreted. Given the strong correlations and linear redundancy between the scale and index scores, it seems relevant to ask whether sufficient variance is captured by all of the scores that are presented to clinicians as capable of being interpreted. In fact, the GEC score was not included in any of the structural models that were examined even though some recent CFA studies (e.g., Roth et al., 2013) have supported a three-stratum model with the GEC score at the apex. As previously noted, strong latent factor correlations were observed in all of the first-order models that were reported in the test manual, which imply the presence of a higher-order dimension (Gorsuch, 1983). Unfortunately, this dimension was not explored. As noted by Reise, Moore, and Haviland (2010), data from behavioral rating scales are rarely univocal, often containing variance that can be sourced to multiple latent dimensions and attributes producing interpretive ambiguity. Given that users of the BRIEF2 are encouraged to use the clinical scales as a primary means to conduct profile analysis, it is important to determine how much unique information is captured by those scores apart from a more general construct that may explain variance in all of the BRIEF2 measures. This information is vital given the well documented issues with psychoeducational profile analysis in general (Youngstrom, 2013).

Additionally, information regarding the relationship between BRIEF2 scores and performance measures of executive functioning (e.g., Trail Making and n-back tasks) is absent. This omission is curious given the fact that the BRIEF was originally developed as "an index of ecological validity for findings on performance measures of executive function in the clinic setting" (Isquith et al., 2017, p. 21). In particular, this information would be useful for helping clinicians to select appropriate measures for follow-up testing and other useful procedures for validating the inferences generated from BRIEF2 data.

SUMMARY. Overall, the BRIEF2 has many strengths. The test materials are of exceptional quality, and the rating forms are easy to administer and score. The test manual contains a wealth of psychometric information and for the most part, the technical properties of the instrument are quite exceptional. The use of a larger and more representative normative sample addresses one of the more prominent issues noted in previous reviews of the BRIEF, and the use of diagnostic efficiency statistics to help inform clinical utility is noteworthy. In the test manual it is made clear that the BRIEF2 should not be used as a stand-alone measure for diagnosing executive dysfunction. Users who heed this advice and interpret BRIEF2 scores with appropriate caution within the context of a comprehensive assessment battery will likely find the instrument to be a useful addition to their clinical toolkit.

REVIEWER'S REFERENCES

American Educational Research Association, American Psychological Association, & National Council on Measurement in Education. (2014). *Standards for educational and psychological testing*. Washington, DC: American Educational Research Association.

Bracken, B. A. (1987). Limitations of preschool instruments and standards for minimal levels of technical adequacy. *Journal of Psychoeducational Assessment, 5*, 313-326. doi:10.1177/073428298700500402

Gioia, G. A., Isquith, P. K., Guy, S. C., & Kenworthy, L. (2000). Behavior Rating Inventory of Executive Function. Lutz, FL: Psychological Assessment Resources.

Gorsuch, R. L. (1983). *Factor analysis* (2nd ed.). Hillsdale, NJ: Erlbaum.

Isquith, P. K., Gioia, G. A., Guy, S. C., & Kenworthy, L. (2017). *Behavior Rating Inventory of Executive Function, Second Edition: Interpretive guide.* Lutz, FL: Psychological Assessment Resources.

McGill, R. J. (2016). Invalidating the full scale IQ score in the presence of significant factor score variability: Clinical acumen or clinical illusion? *Archives of Assessment Psychology, 6*, 49-79. Retrieved from http://www.assessmentpsychologyboard.org/journal/index.php/AAP

Reise, S. P., Moore, T. M., & Haviland, M. G. (2010). Bifactor models and rotations: Exploring the extent to which multidimensional data yield univocal scale scores. *Journal of Personality Assessment, 92*, 544-559. doi:10.1080/00223891.2010.496477

Roth, R. M., Lance, C. E., Isquith, P. K., Fischer, A. S., & Giancola, P. R. (2013). Confirmatory factor analysis of the Behavior Rating Inventory of Executive Function-Adult Version in healthy adults and application to attention-deficit/hyperactivity disorder. *Archives of Clinical Neuropsychology, 28*, 425-434. doi:10.1093/arclin/act031

Wasserman, J. D., & Bracken, B. A. (2012). Fundamental psychometric considerations in assessment. In I. B. Weiner, J. R. Graham, & J. A. Naglieri (Eds.), *Handbook of psychology: Assessment psychology* (2nd ed., Vol. 10, pp. 50-81). Hoboken, NJ: Wiley.

Youngstrom, E. A. (2013). Future directions in psychological assessment: Combining evidence-based medicine innovations with psychology's historical strengths to enhance utility. *Journal of Clinical Child & Adolescent Psychology, 42*, 139-159. doi:10.1080/15374416.2012.736358

Review of the Behavior Rating Inventory of Executive Function, Second Edition by JEFFREY H. SNOW, Associate Professor of Pediatrics, University of Arkansas for Medical Sciences, Little Rock, AR:

DESCRIPTION. The Behavior Rating Inventory of Executive Function, Second Edition (BRIEF2) is a rating scale designed to assess executive functions for use with children and adolescents ages 5-18. The test consists of parent, teacher, and self-report forms. The self-report form is for ages 11-18. The parent and teacher forms consist of 63 items that are rated using the following scale: N = *never*, S = *sometimes*, and O = *often*. The rater is instructed to complete the inventory based on observations over the past 6 months and to complete all items. Each item is numerically converted using the following scale: N = 1, S = 2, and O = 3. The parent and teacher forms consist of the following nine scales: Inhibit, Self-Monitor, Shift, Emotional Control, Initiate, Working Memory, Plan/Organize, Task-Monitor, and Organization of Materials. Raw scores are summed for each scale and converted to T scores. The measure also yields three index scores: Behavior Regulation Index (Inhibit, Self-Monitor), Emotion Regulation Index (Shift, Emotional Control), and Cognitive Regulation Index (Initiate, Working Memory, Plan/Organize, Task Monitor, Organization of Materials). Raw scores for each of these indices also are converted to T scores. There is also a Global Executive Composite that represents the sum of all scale scores with subsequent conversion to a T score. The parent and teacher forms include three validity scales: Inconsistency, Negativity, and Infrequency. These are scored using item raw scores and compared to the validity indicators.

The BRIEF2 has a self-report form, which was not available in the first edition of this measure. The self-report form consists of 55 items and uses the same rating format and scoring system described. This form consists of the following seven scales: Inhibit, Self-Monitor, Shift, Emotional Control, Task Completion, Working Memory, and Plan/Organize. The self-report form yields the following three index scores: Behavior Regulation Index (Inhibit, Self-Monitor), Emotion Regulation Index (Shift, Emotional Control), and Cognitive Regulation Index (Task Completion, Working Memory, Plan/Organize). The self-report form also yields a Global Executive Composite and the same three validity scales as the parent and teacher forms.

The BRIEF2 is a well-constructed measure that is easy to administer and score. The instructions are clear and written on the front page of each rating form, and there are supplemental instructions provided in the test manual. The test authors suggest it should take raters less than 10 minutes to complete the form. Raw scores are documented on a page beneath the rating and then are transferred to a scoring summary sheet, which provides a scoring summary table and areas for the validity scales. Ratings can be scored by hand or by using computer scoring services. The test manual is easy to navigate when converting raw scores to T scores. The test authors also published the BRIEF2 Interpretive Guide (Isquith, Gioia, Guy, & Kenworthy, 2017), which provides an overview of executive functions, fundamentals relative to the BRIEF2 including test development, reliability/validity information, use of screening forms, basic/enhanced interpretation guidelines, and suggestions for intervention with executive functions.

DEVELOPMENT. The original BRIEF was published in 2000 and was formulated based on a developmental neuropsychological assessment model put forth by Holmes-Bernstein and Waber (1990). Items for this measure were developed from clinical interviews with parents and teachers and organized into a developmental model of executive functions. The test authors used a framework that defines executive functions as a multidimensional construct responsible for goal-directed behavior and cognitive activity. Soon after the publication of the BRIEF, the authors published the BRIEF Self-Report in order to provide a parallel measure to assess adolescents' self-perceptions of executive functions. The test authors noted the utility of the rating scale format to assess the complexity of executive functions and refined the measure further in developing BRIEF2.

The test authors report improvements with this new version. The BRIEF2 employed a large standardization sample matched to the U.S. Census figures by age, gender, ethnicity, parent education level, and geographic region. The scales are more concise, which reduces the time burden placed on raters, and demonstrated increased sensitivity to executive functions with certain clinical groups. The BRIEF2 has improved internal structure within scales as supported by factor analysis. This included improved empirical scale structure with separate Task-Monitor and Self-Monitor scales. The revision demonstrates increased parallelism of item content with the original version, with most items shared among the forms. The test authors included an Infrequency scale to help determine validity of the rating. With this version, there are new 12-item screening parent, teacher, and self-report forms. There were no new items added on the clinical scales, which allows for consistency of research data collection between the two versions. Additionally, the test authors report new statistics to support interpretation of profiles.

TECHNICAL. The standardization of the BRIEF2 utilized sampling to approximate the U.S. population. The test authors used the key demographic variables of gender, race/ethnicity, age, parent education, and geographical region. All states were included in the standardization. The normative sample consisted of 3,603 ratings for children and adolescents ages 5-18 years across the parent, teacher, and self-report forms. With the parent form, ratings were obtained for 1,400 participants comprising 687 males and 713 females. The teacher form used 1,400 respondents rating 681 males and 719 females. For the self-report form, there were 803 respondents with 396 males and 407 females.

The test authors provide reliability data for the BRIEF2. Internal consistency reliability coefficients are reported for the parent, teacher, and self-report forms. These data are provided for the standardization sample and a clinical sample. Across forms and samples, coefficients ranged from .71 to .94 for the scales, .84 to .98 for the indices, and .94 to .98 for the GEC. Internal consistency estimates are also provided by gender and age for each of the three forms. Across forms, coefficients range from .70 to .95 for the scales, .86 to .98 for the indices, and .96 to .99 for the GEC. Interrater reliability is also reported. For parent-teacher comparisons, the mean correlation coefficient was .64 for typical developing individuals and .34 for a clinical sample. For parent-adolescent raters, the mean correlation coefficient was .62 for typical developing individuals and .30 for the clinical sample. The mean correlation coefficient was .77 for typical developing individuals and .59 for a clinical sample for parent-parent comparisons. The test authors calculated test-retest data using 2.9-, 2.8-, and 3.7-week intervals for parent, teacher, and self-report. Using a subsample of the standardization sample, the mean coefficient was .79 for the clinical scales on the parent form, and coefficients for the indices and the GEC were all above .80. For the teacher form, the mean coefficient was .82 for the scales, and all coefficients were above .80 for the indices and the GEC. For the self-report form, the mean coefficient was .74 for the scales, and all coefficients were .75 or higher for the indices and the GEC. The test authors also report data comparing the BRIEF and BRIEF2. The correlation coefficients ranged from .60 to .97, with most being above .80.

The test manual describes several studies concerning validity of BRIEF2 scores and their uses. To examine evidence based on content, 12 experienced pediatric neuropsychologists assigned items to a primary scale and, if needed, a secondary scale. The test authors also assigned items to scales. The results showed high interrater agreement. To examine internal structure, correlations were calculated between total scores and the scale items; obtained coefficients were moderate to strong. The test authors also examined intercorrelation of scales, which generally yielded moderate coefficients. This result suggests some overlap in terms of assessing executive functions, but also provides evidence that the scales measure different constructs. The test authors also conducted confirmatory factor analysis, and the results supported the three-factor model. Comparisons of the BRIEF2 with other rating scales and intelligence measures are also reported. Generally, the results showed low to moderate correlations with some values in the moderately high range, indicating some relationship among the measures, but also supporting that the BRIEF2 is assessing different constructs. Finally, the test authors explored patterns with different clinical populations, and results consistently showed significant differences when individuals from diagnostic groups were compared to typically developing individuals.

COMMENTARY. The release of the original BRIEF represented one of the most significant contributions to pediatric neuropsychology, and the BRIEF2 will continue that tradition. Practitioners in this field realize that issues with executive functions are a prevalent problem with most clinical groups. The BRIEF2 will continue to provide an objective measure giving important information in different environments. The measure is easy to administer and score, and its authors provide information concerning interpretation of profiles. The addition of the self-report and introduction of the screening measures provides additional information and other means to assess executive functions in children and adolescents. The test authors provide compelling reliability and validity data, and the BRIEF2 is an invaluable measure for clinical and research purposes.

SUMMARY. The BRIEF2 is a rating scale designed to assess executive functions in children and adolescents. The test was designed using developmental models and excellent empirical methods. The test authors provide good reliability and validity data as well as information designed to improve interpretation. Pediatric neuropsychologists should definitely include this measure with any clinical groups or research protocols.

REVIEWER'S REFERENCES

Holmes-Bernstein, J., & Waber, D. P. (1990). Developmental neuropsychological assessment: The systemic approach. In A. A. Boulton, G. B. Baker, & M. Hiscock (Eds.), *Neuromethods: Neuropsychology* (Vol. 17, pp. 311-371). Clifton, NJ: Humana.

Isquith, P. K., Gioia, G. A., Guy, S. C., & Kenworthy, L. (2017). *Behavior Rating Inventory of Executive Function, Second Edition: Interpretive guide.* Lutz, FL: PAR.

[19]

BEST Plus 2.0.

Purpose: "Designed to assess the English language proficiency ... [and] interpersonal communication" of adult English learners.
Population: English language learners ages 16 and older who are not enrolled in secondary school.
Publication Dates: 2003-2016.
Scores, 3: Listening Comprehension, Language Complexity, Communication.
Administration: Individual.
Levels, 3: 1, 2, and 3 (for print-based version).
Forms, 3: D, E, and F (for print-based version).
Restricted Distribution: Training and certification required for test administrators.
Price Data, 2017: $40 per 20 print-based test booklets (Form D, E, or F); $25 per picture cue book (Form D, E, or F); $25 per test administrator guide (2016, 152 pages); $15 per software (USB); $1.75 per computer-adaptive test administration (volume discounts available); training price data available from publisher.
Time: 5-25 minutes for administration, depending on examinee's ability.
Comments: Administered as face-to-face oral interview; computer-adaptive version and semi-adaptive print-based version available; scores can be converted to Student Performance Levels and to National Reporting System ESL Educational Functioning Levels.
Author: Center for Applied Linguistics.
Publisher: Center for Applied Linguistics.
Cross References: For reviews by S. Kathleen Krach and Annita Ward of an earlier version, see 17:27.

Review of the BEST Plus 2.0 by PRISCILLA M. DANIELSON, Speech/Language Pathologist & AT/AAC Specialist, Linguistic Solutions, LLC, Royal Oak, MD:

DESCRIPTION. BEST Plus Version 2.0 is an individually administered, standardized test designed to assess English language proficiency and interpersonal communication skills of adult English learners. A face-to-face interview procedure is employed. Scored responses must be in English. The test was not designed to measure language expression or comprehension of language-impaired individuals and is not recommended for individuals presenting visual impairments. BEST Plus 2.0 is an update to the original BEST Plus, which was developed and published in 2003.

There are two versions of the test: a computer-adaptive version and three forms of a print-based version. Assessment begins with warm-up items related to demographics and a series of locator questions associated with personal, occupational, and public domains of language. The purpose of the warm-up and locator questions is to determine the appropriate level at which to begin testing on the print-based forms, which are preset. Items on both versions are scored by the examiner according to a strict, leveled rubric within the categories of Listening Comprehension, Language Complexity, and Communication. Following administration of the print-based forms, scores are entered into computer software, which generates a score report. On the computer-adaptive version, scores are entered following each item, resulting in the selection of the next item. Administration of the computer-adaptive version ends automatically when enough information has been gathered regarding the examinee's functioning level, and a report is generated. Administration is expected to take 5 to 20 minutes.

The scoring software generates a scaled score reflecting performance and difficulty level within a range of 88 to 999 with 500 as the center. Scaled scores can be converted to Student Performance Levels (SPLs; Grognet, 1997) and National Reporting System (NRS) ESL Educational Functioning Levels (EFLs; U.S. Department of Education, 2016). BEST Plus Version 2.0 also provides diagnostic raw scores for the subscales of Listening Comprehension, Language Complexity, and Communication. These scores are reported on the score report along with the associated SPL score averages as determined from the original field testing of students for the BEST Plus. The administrator's guide provides outcome measure definitions of NRS ESL Functioning Level descriptors.

The test administrator's guide also provides reference sheets, explanations within the scoring rubric, and copies of the training PowerPoint slides. The test authors provide guidance regarding pre- and post-testing administrations, suggesting that a minimum of 60 hours of instruction be provided before post-testing occurs, with exceptions acknowledged for state policies and funding guidelines.

DEVELOPMENT. BEST Plus 2.0 is an updated version of the BEST Plus, which was developed by the Center for Applied Linguistics (CAL) and originally published in 2003. The stated intent was to assess adult language learners' ability to process and express conversational language. The test authors wanted the test results to differentiate the levels of English language proficiency associated with SPLs. Additionally, the authors wanted BEST Plus to provide data that aligned with NRS and could be used to evaluate the progress of English language learners within and across programs.

TECHNICAL. Standardized test administration is a priority for the BEST Plus 2.0. The test materials provide consistent administration guidelines, prompts, and cues. Scoring is based upon a consistent rubric with in-depth explanation of answer types. Test administrators are required to undergo 6 hours of training with suggested follow-up familiarization with testing procedures and processes.

The BEST Plus Version 2.0 revision included field testing new and revised items and analyzing and revising warm-up questions on the print-based forms to better ensure students would be placed in the appropriate test level within the print-based forms.

Development of new items was undertaken to replace BEST Plus items that had been identified during a bias and sensitivity review. New items were field-tested with operational BEST Plus items so that examinees received both new and old items. A total of 112 new items were exposed to examinees using the computer-adaptive version of the test with each item being seen by an average of 194 examinees. Following statistical analysis, 90 new items were added and tied psychometrically to the BEST Plus measurement scale. An additional 21 items were modified.

Statistical analysis (paired-sample *t*-tests) of data from 84 students completed in 2010 using the computer-adaptive and print versions of the BEST Plus revealed some locator items on the print version were placing examinees in lower test levels, resulting in ceiling effects on one of the print forms. Item difficulty for old and new locator questions was expressed along a logit scale using the Rasch model to determine which locator items should be retired or added to BEST Plus 2.0. Following the revisions, three groups of examinees (*n*s = 32-34) each took both the computer-adaptive version and one of the print-based forms. Correlation coefficients between the print versions and the computer-adaptive versions were .86-.89, and paired-sample *t*-tests showed no significant differences between scores from the different test formats.

In 2012 CAL completed a standard-setting study to provide new cut scores linking BEST Plus results to revised NRS EFLs for English as a second language. The study reflected judges' ratings of 21 videotaped, full test administrations. Statistical analysis followed a modified Body of Work procedure (Kenyon & Fidelman, 2009; Kingston, Kahl, Sweeney, & Bay, 2001). Judges rated student performance twice with discussion of initial ratings being permitted. Analysis of judges' ratings revealed less scatter across NRS levels following the second rating. In 2013 CAL utilized an expert external advisory board to review the new cut scores and provide policy advice for implementation and use. According to the test publisher's website, the new cut scores were implemented in 2016.

The test authors evaluated reliability using an operational data set collected from multiple testing sites between 2011 and 2013. Statistical methods defined in Livingston and Lewis (1995) and Young and Yoon (1998) were employed to estimate classification accuracy and data consistency, as well as to estimate a Cohen's kappa statistic between the NRS classifications and the performance scores on the BEST Plus. Indices ranged from 0 to 1, with scores closer to 1 indicating higher consistency and accuracy of agreement. Overall accuracy and consistency of classification indices for the operational dataset and EFL revealed an estimate for accuracy of .557, an estimate of consistency of .460, and Cohen's kappa statistic of .346. Further analysis using observed and modeled scores revealed that the BEST Plus scores appear to provide the strongest reliability for accurately achieving NRS classification at cut points. The accuracy and consistency of classifying performance into the same NRS EFL level for observed and modeled scores was more variable. Interrater reliability using a sample of 49 students from a single adult ESL program was evaluated using descriptive statistics and Pearson correlations. These analyses revealed relatively high rater consistency when using the scoring rubric for the computer-adaptive and print versions of the BEST Plus.

Five expert reviewers participating in a content alignment study assessed validity. The purpose of this study was to align BEST Plus 2.0 items to the NRS EFLs and to establish that BEST Plus 2.0 items fully encompassed the descriptors of the NRS EFLs. A supplemental content alignment study was conducted via a mailed survey for reviewers to assign 17 new test items to NRS EFLs. An intraclass correlation coefficient (ICC; Shrout & Fleiss, 1979) was used to measure the degree of consistency between the expert reviewers at the item level, achieving an ICC of .96. Using the BEST Plus, the test authors also assessed the relationship between learner instructional hours and two measures: NRS EFL gains and score gains on the BEST Plus. Data sets included pre-test scores, post-test scores, and instructional hours completed for 2,960 adult learners. The first assessment revealed 77% percent of the learners made at least a single Educational Functioning Level gain following instruction. Gains in performance were most notable following 20 or more hours of instruction. The test authors provided additional statistics and data to respond to concerns associated with item exposure, item drift, and item overlap that can be seen with computer-adaptive tests.

COMMENTARY. BEST Plus Version 2.0 is a well-developed, standardized measure of English language proficiency and interpersonal communication skills of adult English learners. Using a computer-adaptive version or one of three forms of a print-based version, trained test administrators can evaluate proficiency within the subscales of Listening Comprehension, Language Complexity, and Communication. Testing and grading processes reflect attention to test administrator training, development of grading rubrics, standardization of question formats, pre- and post-testing guidelines, and content analysis to provide scaled scores, which can be converted to Student Performance Levels (SPLs) and the National Reporting System (NRS) ESL Educational Functioning Levels. Administration time is not excessive. The test authors have provided evidence to support the reliability and validity of test items, versions, and associations with SPLs and NRS EFLs using multiple statistical methods. Statistical analyses most often were associated with the BEST Plus; however, the test authors have begun incorporating items from BEST Plus 2.0 as questions have been developed and data sets have become available. Due to the evaluative measurements this test attempts to provide, it is strongly recommended that validity and reliability analyses continue as larger data sets evolve in order to effectively monitor for changes in performance levels and item difficulties.

SUMMARY. BEST Plus Version 2.0 appears to be an improvement upon the BEST Plus, which was carefully designed to measure English proficiency of adult English learners. Subscales associated with Listening Comprehension, Language Complexity, and Communication are included within the test design. Performance scores can be converted to SPLs and NRS EFLs to provide additional information regarding leveled performance relative to program placement and progress. The test meets its goal of assessing proficiency of English comprehension and use within interpersonal and everyday communication. The test is interactive and relies on an interview procedure. The test maintains a strict standardized assessment and scoring process accessible via computer-adaptive and print versions. Measures of validity and reliability were applied to support item consistency and relativity, as well as leveled scoring processes that provide useful information for establishing performance levels upon entering an instructional program and determining the effectiveness of program instruction.

REVIEWER'S REFERENCES

Grognet, A. G. (1997). *Performance-based curricula and outcomes: The mainstream English language training project (MELT)—Update for the 1990s and beyond.* Denver, CO: Spring Institute for International Studies.

Kenyon, D., & Fidelman, C. (2009, April). *Standard setting with the modified body of work method.* Paper presented at the annual meeting of the National Council on Measurement in Education, San Diego, CA.

Kingston, N. M., Kahl, S. R., Sweeney, K. P., & Bay, L. (2001). Setting performance standards using the body of work method. In G. J. Cizek (Ed.), *Setting performance standards: Concepts, methods, and perspectives* (pp. 219-248). Mahwah, NJ: Erlbaum.

Livingston, S. A., & Lewis, C. (1995). Estimating the consistency and accuracy of classifications based on test scores. *Journal of Educational Measurement, 32,* 179-197.

Shrout, P. E., & Fleiss, J. L. (1979). Intraclass correlations: Uses in assessing rater reliability. *Psychological Bulletin, 86,* 420-428. doi:10.1037/0033-2909.86.2.420

U.S. Department of Education, Office of Vocational and Adult Education, Division of Adult Education and Literacy. (2016, February). *Implementation guidelines: Measures and methods for the National Reporting System for adult education.* Washington, DC: Author. Retrieved from http://www.nrsweb.org/docs/ImplementationGuidelines.pdf

Young, M. J., & Yoon, B. (1998, April). Estimating the consistency and accuracy of classifications in a standards-referenced assessment (CSE Tech. Rep. No. 475). Los Angeles, CA: University of California, Los Angeles; National Center for Research on Evaluations, Standards, and Student Testing.

Review of the BEST Plus 2.0 by JORGE E. GONZALEZ, Professor, and JACQUELINE ANDERSON, Doctoral Student in School Psychology, the University of Houston, Houston, TX:

DESCRIPTION. BEST Plus 2.0 is an individually administered oral interview designed to assess English language proficiency of English learners ages 16 and older through real-life interpersonal communication. BEST Plus 2.0 scores can be converted to Student Performance Levels and to the National Reporting System ESL Educational Functioning Levels. The test provides information for placement decisions, assessment of student progress, program evaluation, and diagnosis. Two administration formats are available: a computer-adaptive format and a semi-adaptive print format with three parallel forms for pre- and post-testing.

Potential examiners must take a 6-hour training workshop and gain approval from a Center for Applied Linguistics (CAL) certified trainer before administering the test. For the computer-adaptive version, the administrator asks the examinee questions presented on the computer screen, listens to the student response, uses the test's scoring rubric to determine a score for the item, and enters the score into the computer. The computer estimates the examinee's ability based on answers to prior questions and selects the next item from the 250-item pool. The computer-adaptive test ends when the Best Plus 2.0 software determines that enough items have been administered to assess the examinee's English functioning level accurately. In the print-based version, test questions have been pre-selected and are organized according to three levels. The test administrator begins by asking the examinee locator questions to determine which level should be administered. The examiner records scores in a test booklet using the same rubric employed in the computer-adaptive version and generates a score report by entering the item scores into the computer at the end of the test. Administration takes 5 to 20 minutes.

BEST Plus 2.0 is scored on three dimensions: Listening Comprehension, Language Complexity, and Communication. Performance is reported on a scale ranging from 88 to 999 with a mean of 500. Exam scores can be interpreted using two sets of proficiency level descriptors: Student Performance Levels (SPLs) and the National Reporting System (NRS) ESL Functioning Level Descriptors. SPLs range from 0 (corresponding to a BEST Plus 2.0 scale score range of 88-329) to 10 (corresponding to a range of 796-999). NRS ESL levels range from Beginning ESL Literacy (with a BEST Plus 2.0 scale score of 88-361) to Exit Criteria from NRS (with a score of 565 or higher).

DEVELOPMENT. The BEST Plus 2.0 technical report is described as "a companion to the *BEST Plus Technical Report: Development of a Computer-Assisted Assessment of Oral Proficiency for Adult English Language Learners,* published in September 2005" (technical report, p. 1). The 2005 report was not included in the BEST Plus 2.0 test kit provided to the reviewers. BEST Plus represented a revision of the oral interview portion of the Basic English Skills Test (BEST). Results of a bias and sensitivity review of the BEST Plus were used to develop new items for the BEST Plus 2.0. In the end, 111 of the original 258 items were replaced or modified.

The BEST Plus print-based forms were developed in an effort to make the testing environment for the two formats as similar as possible. Results from 84 examinees who took the test in both formats showed no significant differences in scores between the computer-adaptive version and two of the print forms; however, scores were significantly different between one of the print forms and the computer-adaptive version, as ceiling effects were observed for some examinees using the print form. Test developers revised locator questions for BEST Plus 2.0 to include more difficult items and improve level placement on the print forms. Subsequent comparability studies showed no statistically significant differences between scores on the computer-adaptive version and any of the three print forms. Correlational analyses produced coefficients of .87-.89 between the computer-adaptive and print forms, suggesting examinees' results will be similar across test formats.

TECHNICAL.

Classification accuracy and consistency. Data from examinees (n = 1,353) who took the BEST Plus between 2011 and 2013 were used to examine consistency of the BEST Plus NRS classifications (i.e., NRS Levels 1-7). Statistical analyses using the observed test scores as well as statistical models of true scores and hypothetical scores from a parallel form of the test indicated the percentage of examinees who would be classified in the same language proficiency level by both the administered test and either the true score distribution (accuracy) or the distribution using the parallel form (consistency). Results showed an overall estimate for accuracy of .557 and an overall estimate for consistency of .460. Cohen's kappa was .346. Additional analyses indicated the percentage of examinees accurately and consistently placed into each EFL according to the modeled distributions. Accuracy estimates ranged from .282 for Level 3 (High Beginning ESL) to .821 for Level 7 (Exit from NRS); consistency estimates varied from .217 for Level 3 to .687 for Level 7. Finally, accuracy and consistency were examined for each cut point between levels. Using the modeled true score distribution, the percentage of examinees accurately placed above and below a cut point ranged from .873 for cut point 2/3 (Low/High Beginning ESL) to .961 for cut point 6/7 (Advanced ESL/Exit from NRS). The false positive and false negative indices indicated a low probability of examinees being classified to a level higher (false positive) or lower (false negative) than their true ability. Using the modeled parallel form distribution, the percentage of test takers consistently placed above and below the cut points ranged from .826 at cut point 2/3 to .942 at cut point 6/7.

Interrater reliability. Interrater reliability was examined using two teams of raters, one scoring the computer-adaptive items and one scoring a print version of the BEST Plus 2.0. Each student (n = 49) was tested using both administration formats. Correlations between raw scores of three rater pairs on the computer-adaptive version demonstrated coefficients that ranged from .93 to .98 with a total score coefficient averaged across the three pairs of .98. For the print-based version of the test, correlation coefficients ranged from .85 to .98 between rater pairs with an average total score correlation of .96 across the three pairs. Further analyses on the scaled scores from the print version showed an average correlation coefficient of .94 across the three rater pairs.

Validity. In 2014 the test publisher conducted a content alignment study using five adult ESL experts who served as reviewers. Each BEST Plus 2.0 item was mapped to one NRS EFL based on judgments of the expert panel. Following the NRS EFL assignments, items were then mapped onto skills used to describe 28 component descriptor statements that underlie the NRS EFLs. All warm-up items and items projected to make up the item bank for BEST Plus 2.0 were reviewed. The resulting interclass correlation coefficient (ICC) among the five reviewers of .96 indicates that reviewers were consistent in assigning NRS levels to the items.

Between 2012 and 2013, CAL examined the relationship between scores on the BEST Plus and examinee instructional hours attended to show how many hours of instruction are needed for learners to show a gain on the test in terms of an NRS EFL. Results showed that about 77% of the sample (n = 2,960) demonstrated a level gain on their post-test scores, and about 86% of the learners gained at least 20 points on their BEST Plus scale score. Comparisons of pre- and post-test mean scores showed statistically significant ($p < .001$) improvements after 20 or more hours of instruction.

To maintain the integrity of the item bank, test developers examined efforts to guard against overusing items. Descriptive analyses showed that strategies to control item use have been effective. Item drift analyses also showed that as a whole, items have remained stable over the years that the program has been operational, and little evidence of an association between item exposure and item drift was found. Because the BEST Plus is used for pre- and post-testing, developers in 2014 examined the incidence and effects of item overlap using the computer-adaptive version of the BEST Plus 2.0. Thirty-three examinees took the test in one room and were immediately retested in a different room. Results indicated that examinees likely would be re-administered no more than three items in back-to-back administrations. Moreover, findings revealed that exposure to overlapping items did not increase the score from the first to the second administration, suggesting that exposure to a few overlapping items does not affect observed scores.

Interpretation of test results was re-examined in 2012 with a new standard-setting study to link BEST Plus results to revised NRS EFLs, replacing the original cut scores that were linked to an earlier adult English language education proficiency scale, the Student Performance Levels (SPLs). Ten judges participated in the standard-setting study. Analyses of the data showed different judges' consistency in associating scale scores with the NRS EFLs across the 2002 and 2012 standard-setting studies. Following the 2012 standard-setting study, an external advisory board of field experts reviewed the new cut scores and unanimously agreed they should be put into effect. According to the test publisher's website, the new cut scores took effect in July 2016.

COMMENTARY. The BEST Plus 2.0 is an individually administered scripted oral interview designed to assess the English language proficiency of adult learners using everyday interpersonal communication. It is available in both a computer-adaptive format and a semi-adaptive print format. Scores are linked to Student Performance Levels and to the National Reporting System ESL Educational Functioning Levels. Its key strengths are robust psychometric properties, its standard-setting procedures, the detailed analyses conducted to guard against item exceptionalities (e.g., drift), and strong reliability evidence. The test authors have been very attentive to establishing the psychometric strengths of the BEST Plus 2.0. Readers of the technical manual will, however, have difficulty determining whether the psychometric studies were conducted using the older BEST Plus or BEST Plus Version 2.0. One must read carefully to determine to which of the versions the analyses pertain. Additionally, the technical report was described as a companion to the *BEST Plus Technical Report: Development of a Computer-Assisted Assessment of Oral Proficiency for Adult English Language Learners* (2005), which was not included in the test kit, making it difficult to fully understand item development. Moreover, it is not always easy to follow whether the analyses and results pertained to the print version or the computer-adaptive version of the test.

SUMMARY. BEST Plus 2.0 is designed to assess the English language proficiency of adult English learners "who may or may not have received an education in their native language or English, but who need to use English to function in day-to-day life in the United States" (technical manual, p. 1). The computer-adaptive version and the semi-adaptive print version have been found to be comparable. The test appears psychometrically robust. More attention should be directed at clarifying which version and format of the test is the focus of the psychometric analyses and other studies conducted with the BEST Plus and BEST Plus 2.0.

[20]

Beta–4.

Purpose: "Designed to assess nonverbal intellectual ability by drawing on various facets of intelligence including fluid, spatial, and nonverbal reasoning; visual information processing; and processing speed."
Population: Ages 16-99+.
Publication Dates: 1934-2016.
Scores, 6: Coding, Picture Absurdities, Clerical Checking, Picture Completion, Matrix Reasoning, BETA-4 IQ.
Administration: Individual or group.
Price Data, 2020: $267.75 per kit including manual (2016, 66 pages), 25 response booklets, and scoring key; $171.50 per 25 response booklets; $64.25 per manual; $42.75 per scoring key.
Foreign Language Edition: Spanish administration available.
Time: Subtests are timed as follows: Coding, 2 minutes; Picture Absurdities, 3 minutes; Clerical Checking, 2 minutes; Picture Completion, 2.5 minutes; Matrix Reasoning, 5 minutes.
Comments: Spanish administration directions are included in the test manual.
Authors: C. E. Kellogg and N. W. Morton.
Publisher: Pearson.
Cross References: For reviews by C. G. Bellah and Louise M. Soares of the third edition, see 16:33; for information regarding the previous edition, see T5:2212 (3 references) and T4:2255 (4 references); for reviews by Louis M. Hsu and Mark D. Reckase of the Revised Beta Examination, Second Edition, see 9:1044; see also T2:447 (29 references); for a review by Bert A. Goldman, see 6:494 (13 references); see also 5:375 (14 references); for reviews by Raleigh M. Drake and Walter C. Shipley, see 3:259 (5 references); for reviews by S. D. Porteus and David Wechsler, see 2:1419 (4 references).

Review of the Beta–4 by PHILLIP L. ACKERMAN, Professor of Psychology, Georgia Institute of Technology, Atlanta, GA:

DESCRIPTION. The Beta–4 consists of five tests that the manual describes as providing an assessment of "...nonverbal intellectual ability by drawing on various facets of intelligence including fluid, spatial, and nonverbal reasoning; visual information processing; and processing speed" (p. 1). The five tests are Coding (a symbol-digit test), Picture Absurdities, Clerical Checking, Picture Completion, and Matrix Reasoning. The target population for this test includes adults; a stated age range is 16 to 99+ years. The test may be administered individually or in groups, and instructions are provided for separate administrations in English and Spanish. The test can be administered in 25-30 minutes total time, which includes instructions, practice problems, and 14.5 minutes of actual test completion time across the five tests. The test content is essentially unchanged from the Beta III, which was the last revision of the test, though the instructions have been simplified from a third-grade to a second-grade level. The test uses a paper-and-pencil format and is scored by hand.

The test manual indicates that the intended population for the test includes individuals in correctional environments, persons with "literacy issues or language differences" (p. 2) and those with low cognitive ability—the latter is justified on the basis of the "exceptionally low test floor" (p. 3). The Beta–4 is also described as being used in industrial settings with unskilled workers and with "occupational rehabilitation and job training programs" (p. 3). The test manual indicates that with training and supervision, the measure may be administered by technicians and paraprofessionals.

DEVELOPMENT. The Beta–4 is the latest revision of a test that was originally designed for assessing the intellectual ability of individuals with "low literacy and extreme unfamiliarity with English" more than 100 years ago (Yoakum & Yerkes, 1920, p. 16). The original Beta test consisted of seven subtests, including assessments of perceptual speed abilities (number checking and digit-symbol), spatial abilities (cube analysis and a form board test called geometrical construction), pictorial completion (similar to the Stanford-Binet), and reasoning, as embodied in a series test with Xs, Os, and blanks. The noteworthy aspect of the original Beta test was that it was the test developers' intention that test instructions not require spoken language and that the manner of the test could be conveyed in "pantomime and demonstration" (Yoakum & Yerkes, 1920, pp. 16-17). The original Army Beta test was first modified for civilian use (see Porteus, 1941; Wechsler, 1941) and has been modified at various times in subsequent decades (e.g., Drake, 1949; Goldman, 1965; Hsu, 1985; Soares, 2005). In the earliest Revised Beta, most of the current test content was established (with the elimination of the Cube Analysis and Maze tests). Most of the remaining tests are similar in content to those original tests (e.g., the Digit-Symbol, Number Checking, Pictorial Completion tests are similar to the current Beta–4 tests).

Numerous criticisms have been made by various investigators of the Beta test, even in the earliest reviews in the *Mental Measurements Yearbook* series. Concerns were raised about the overall content of the test, the speededness of the test, adequacy of the pictures used as test items, norms, indicators of validity, and so on. Some of these concerns have been addressed in subsequent editions of the test, but one could reasonably argue that the overall construction and content of the test is fundamentally unchanged from its original design.

TECHNICAL.

Standardization. The Beta–4 was standardized on a representative sample of 1,035 examinees, with 130 examinees in each of various adolescent and adult age bands, but only 75 examinees in each of the 65-74 and 75-99+ age groups. It is not clear from the test manual, but it appears that the standardization sample examinees were all administered the test in English. Scaled-score tables for each of the five tests are presented for each age group separately. The scaled scores for all the tests are summed, and that value is translated to an IQ equivalent score and a percentile rank. Confidence intervals also may be determined. Thus, the IQ score is the result of an unweighted sum of the five component tests. It is notable, however, that for the Picture Absurdities test, there are apparent ceiling effects, so that the maximum test score matches a lower scaled score than can be achieved on the other tests. The smaller samples of older adults, along with the lack of a specific analysis of age-related score differences (which would especially be expected among the oldest sample), suggest that the test may be inadequately standardized for older adults.

Reliability. Because the component tests are short and speeded, internal consistency reliability estimates were deemed inappropriate indicators of test reliability. The only evidence presented for the reliability of the test was based on a test-retest design and a sample of 227 examinees who were tested twice over a 10- to 89-day interval (mean of 32 days). As noted in earlier reviews, such a design is susceptible to practice effects. (The mean at first testing was 100.5, but the mean at second testing was 106.6.) Test-retest reliability was reported to be r = .91, which might be expected to be an overestimate of reliabilities that would be based on re-testing with significant time delays between administrations because of memory effects for specific test items and overall practice effects.

Validity. The manual importantly notes that the Beta–4 is a brief test that is not aimed at obtaining a full assessment of intellectual abilities and therefore should be considered mostly for the purpose of rapid initial assessment that could be followed up with a more intensive assessment of intelligence. There are no item-level analyses reported for the tests, and no assessments of test bias or other such considerations. Evidence of validity is based largely on intercorrelations among the five tests, correlations with an earlier version of the test (Beta III), and the performance tests (but not the verbal tests) from the Wechsler Adult Intelligence Scale—Fourth Edition. For these evaluations, the Beta–4 appears to provide results that are consistent with the notion that it assesses nonverbal aspects of intelligence, at least as traditionally conceptualized. One set of results, however, does raise concerns about what it is the Beta–4 actually assesses. In the current revision of the test, it is linked with the Wechsler Fundamentals: Academic Skills battery, which includes tests of several abilities. The correlation between the Beta–4 IQ score and the Wechsler Numerical Operations test of r = .70 is consistent with the stated construct, but correlations between the Beta–4 and several verbal tests (Reading Comprehension, r = 59; Word Reading, r = .58; and Reading composite, r = .65) suggest that, for better or worse, the Beta–4 may be tapping more verbal-related abilities than seem to be conceptualized by the test developers. It is possible that, even with the simplified instructions for this test, there is still a non-trivial component of verbal understanding capabilities that influence test performance (a phenomenon noted by Carroll, 1982, in describing the evolution of intelligence test assessments over the last century).

Additional evidence regarding test validity is provided from comparisons of several special groups, including a correctional sample, intellectual disability sample, attention-deficit/hyperactivity disorder sample, samples of Spanish speakers and English language learners, and specific learning disorder samples. No criterion-related evidence of validity is provided for the Beta–4 test, a shortcoming that has been described in reviews of previous revisions, although the manual describes correlations with some other tests as criterion-related.

COMMENTARY. As noted by earlier reviewers, the claim that the Beta test has "a long and distinguished history" is only partially true. The fact that the test has survived for more than 100 years in a form roughly similar to the initial development of the test indeed indicates a long history, perhaps surpassed by just a handful of other tests (which, the Beta test is partially based upon, such as the Binet-Simon scales). The "distinguished" part of the description provided by the test authors has been the most contentious element. The test was roundly criticized in the literature as being an inadequate measure of intelligence even before the publication of the first *Mental Measurements Yearbook* in 1938, and that criticism has continued for subsequent revisions of the test. The current version represents a relatively modest revision of the Beta III, such that most of the concerns previously expressed about some aspects of the test (e.g., the design of various items), the overall content of the test, and the interpretation of the test scores, remain relevant concerns for the Beta–4. Minor improvements have been made in the documentation of test norms and validity indicators, but the lack of documented criterion-related evidence of validity and concerns about discriminant validity (from verbal intelligence tests) represent significant shortcomings in any test. These issues are especially significant because they represent ongoing concerns that have been associated with several decades of *Mental Measurements Yearbook* reviews of previous revisions of the test.

SUMMARY. The Beta–4 represents an incremental change from the most recent version of the test (Beta III). Based on the fact that the entire test represents a very brief and limited sample of ability, from the evidence presented, it seems to have adequate construct evidence of validity for some aspects of nonverbal intelligence in a format that can be used in certain circumstances, such as with the targeted correctional population. However, it is limited by the speededness of the tests and the limited coverage of the underlying abilities that make up nonverbal intelligence. The lack of extensive reliability and criterion-related evidence of validity, the paucity of age-related information for older adults, and the limited information on results from Spanish speakers, together suggest that the test is useful mainly as an initial screening instrument for low-literacy English speakers and not as a definitive assessment of nonverbal intellectual abilities beyond that population. Although there is a long history of developments and use for the Beta test, its shortcomings largely have not been overcome in its current revision.

REVIEWER'S REFERENCES

Carroll, J. B. (1982). The measurement of intelligence. In R. J. Sternberg (Ed.), *Handbook of human intelligence* (pp. 29-120). Cambridge, UK: Cambridge University Press.

Drake, R. M. (1949). [Test review of Revised Beta Examination]. In O. K. Buros (Ed.), *The third mental measurements yearbook* (pp. 339-341). Highland Park, NJ: Gryphon Press.

Goldman, B. A. (1965). [Test review of Revised Beta Examination]. In O. K. Buros (Ed.), *The sixth mental measurements yearbook* (pp. 769-771). Highland Park, NJ: Gryphon Press.

Hsu, L. M. (1985). [Test review of Revised Beta Examination, Second Edition]. In J. V. Mitchell, Jr. (Ed.), *The ninth mental measurements yearbook* (pp. 1276-1278). Lincoln, NE: Buros Institute of Mental Measurements.

Porteus, S. D. (1941). [Test review of Revised Beta Examination]. In O. K. Buros (Ed.), *The 1940 mental measurements yearbook* (pp. 240-241). Highland Park, NJ: Gryphon Press.

Soares, L. M. (2005). [Test review of Beta III]. In R. A. Spies & B. S. Plake (Eds.), *The sixteenth mental measurements yearbook* (pp. 144-145). Lincoln, NE: Buros Institute of Mental Measurements.

Wechsler, D. (1941). [Test review of Revised Beta Examination]. In O. K. Buros (Ed.), *The 1940 mental measurements yearbook* (pp. 241-242). Highland Park, NJ: Gryphon Press.

Yoakum, C. S., & Yerkes, R. M. (1920). *Mental tests in the American Army*. London, England: Sidgwick & Jackson.

Review of the Beta–4 by MARTIN J. WIESE, School Psychologist, Lincoln Public Schools, Lincoln, NE:

DESCRIPTION. The Beta–4 is a nationally standardized test of intellectual ability that uses a nonverbal format. It is intended for use as a quick and reliable measure of nonverbal intelligence. Administration time is estimated to be 25 to 30 minutes, and the test can be administered individually or in a group setting with test takers ages 16 to 99+. Following the third edition (Beta III; Kellogg & Morton, 1999) the test authors updated the normative sample, provided new evidence of validity and several new group studies, and linked the Beta–4 to academic achievement using the Wechsler Fundamentals: Academic Skills test (Pearson, 2008). The Beta-4 includes five tests: Coding, Picture Absurdities, Clerical Checking, Picture Completion, and Matrix Reasoning.

Each test begins with practice/teaching items followed by the scored test items. All tests are presented in a single response booklet and will seem familiar to examiners with knowledge of other intelligence tests such as the Wechsler tests. There are strict time limits ranging from 2 to 5 minutes for each test, and a timing device is required. Administration instructions are read to the examinee before practice items and allow an opportunity to ask questions if the directions are not understood. An appendix to the test manual provides language directions in Spanish.

The Coding test requires the examinee to write numbers that go with symbols row by row without skipping items for 2 minutes. Picture Absurdities items present four pictures grouped together, and the examinee must mark out one picture that doesn't make sense. Two examples and two practice items are presented to ensure the directions are understood. Clerical Checking requires the examinee to compare two pictures or series of numbers and determine whether they are the same or different (equal or not equal). Picture Completion asks the examinee to determine what essential element is missing from a picture and use a pencil to draw it where it belongs. Lastly, Matrix Reasoning requires the examinee to study a 2 x 2 matrix of designs with one item missing and then select the correct solution from five choices.

A scoring template is provided, and all items are scored 1 (correct) or 0 (incorrect) to obtain a raw score for each test. Raw scores are converted into scaled scores (ranging from 1 to 19). The sum of scaled scores is then converted into a Beta–4 IQ standard score with a mean of 100 and standard deviation of 15. A table is used to obtain the Beta–4 IQ percentile rank and confidence intervals.

The examiner's manual includes an introductory section, administration and scoring procedures, standardization procedures, normative information, interpretive considerations, and a section on the technical properties of the test.

DEVELOPMENT. The Beta–4 was developed in stages including conceptualization, three pilot studies, national try out study, and, lastly, collecting data for standardization. The standardization data were collected from a national sample of the U.S. English-speaking population ages 16 through 99+.

The normative sample included 1,035 individuals from four major geographic regions. The sample characteristics were compared to U.S. Census data from 2014 with regard to age, gender, geographic area, race/ethnicity, and educational level. The authors provide a table demonstrating a close correspondence between the obtained normative sample and the 2014 U.S. Census proportions. For individuals younger than 21, examinees with several special education needs were included to reflect proportions found in the general population. These special education classifications included attention-deficit/hyperactivity disorder, gifted and talented, intellectual disability, and specific learning disability.

TECHNICAL. The Beta–4 manual and the online Beta–4 manual supplement report evidence of test score reliability and validity. Test-retest stability is used to estimate score reliability. Reliability was calculated for all ages and two age bands (i.e., the lower and upper ends of the age range) using a sample of 227 individuals tested 10-89 days apart (mean of 32 days). The test-retest reliability coefficient for the Beta–4 IQ across all ages was .91 with a standard error of measurement of 4.50.

The test manual provides validity evidence based on examination of test content, response processes, internal structure, relations with other variables, special group studies, and consequences of testing. The Beta–4 tests were developed using methods similar to those used to develop Perceptual Reasoning and Processing Speed subtests of the Wechsler Adult Intelligence Scale—Fourth Edition (WAIS-IV) and appear to sample the same domains. Response frequencies for item response errors were examined to identify and modify problematic items. Intercorrelation among the various tests was used to examine the internal structure of the test. All tests demonstrated correlation coefficients with the overall Beta–4 IQ of .60 to .65 and correlations with each other of .40 to .60. Confirmatory factor analysis results indicate a two-factor model provides a good fit and is consistent with the expectation that the test measures fluid reasoning and processing speed components.

The test authors compared Beta–4 scores with other measures of intellectual ability and an achievement test. The Beta–4 scores of 198 individuals were compared with their results from the Beta III. The corrected (for range restriction) correlation coefficient between the IQ scores from the two editions is high (r = .80), indicating the Beta III and Beta–4 scores are consistent with each other. The mean Beta–4 IQ score was approximately 3 points less than the mean Beta III IQ score, which the authors attributed to the Flynn effect (Flynn, 2007).

The Beta–4 and the WAIS-IV (Wechsler, 2008) were administered to a nonclinical sample (N = 188) in counterbalanced order. As predicted, the Beta–4 IQ and WAIS-IV Full Scale IQ scores were highly correlated (r = .76). Correlations between Beta–4 and WAIS-IV subtest scores also provide evidence that the two tests measure similar cognitive constructs (perceptual reasoning and processing speed). The Beta–4 may also be used with school-aged individuals (16 to 21 years), and the test authors correlated the Beta–4 with the Wechsler Fundamentals: Academic Skills test with a nonclinical sample (*N* = 54). Nonverbal intelligence tests generally share less overlap with achievement than verbal intelligence tests, and, as expected, the nonverbal Beta–4 scores demonstrated lower correlation coefficients with this measure of academic achievement (correlation coefficients of .20 to .68 between subtests and .65 between the Beta–4 IQ score and the Reading composite).

The results of several special group studies also are presented in the test manual. Samples from correctional facilities, individuals with mild or moderate intellectual disability, persons with attention-deficit/hyperactivity disorder, Spanish speakers, English as a second language learners, and individuals with a specific learning disorder were administered the Beta–4 and compared to matched control groups. The results are consistent with predicted findings and previous research supporting the validity of using the Beta–4 with these populations. Finally, the test authors address evidence of validity based on the consequences of testing by discussing their evaluations of item bias and the percentages of individuals in special group studies who score below certain levels.

COMMENTARY. The Beta test has a well-established history, and various editions have been in use since the World War I era. The authors of this fourth edition of the Beta have addressed some criticisms (Soares, 2005) of the previous version. The Beta–4 manual now includes information on special group studies (intellectual disability, attention-deficit/hyperactivity disorder, Spanish speakers, English as a second language learners, specific learning disorder, and individuals in correctional settings). In addition, the standardization group is better described and disaggregates the sample by education level, race/ethnicity, and gender. Also, examinees from each group were selected from four geographic regions roughly proportionate to Census percentages.

Even so, some concerns remain. The pictures in the Picture Absurdities test are relatively small and congested on the page. The addition of color would also make the test more engaging and appear less dated. The test scoring template remains somewhat cumbersome and mildly confusing to use. As noted in an earlier review (Bellah, 2005), no information is provided on item analysis, and test reliability is again limited to test-retest reliability because split-half and coefficient alpha estimates are deemed inappropriate by the authors.

SUMMARY. Language-reduced or nonverbal intelligence tests provide a useful adjunct to the traditional assessment of cognitive ability. The Beta–4 requires no reading or verbal responses and can be administered to individuals with minimal literacy skills or limited language proficiency. Relatively brief verbal directions and teaching/practice items allow for adequate understanding of the task requirements. The Beta–4 has a large nationally representative normative base, and the manual provides evidence of reliability and validity of scores from the instrument. The Beta–4 will likely be most useful as a cognitive screener to determine whether in-depth intellectual assessment is required.

REVIEWER'S REFERENCES

Bellah, C. G. (2005). [Test review of Beta III]. In R. A. Spies & B. S. Plake (Eds.), *The sixteenth mental measurements yearbook.* Retrieved from http://marketplace.unl.edu/buros/

Flynn, J. R. (2007). *What is intelligence? Beyond the Flynn effect.* New York, NY: Cambridge University Press.

Kellogg, C. E., & Morton, N. W. (1999). *Beta III manual.* San Antonio, TX: Pearson.

Pearson (2008). Wechsler Fundamentals: Academic Skills. Bloomington, MN: Author.

Soares, L. M. (2005). [Test review of Beta III]. In R. A. Spies & B. S. Plake (Eds.), *The sixteenth mental measurements yearbook.* Retrieved from http://marketplace.unl.edu/buros/

Wechsler, D. (2008). Wechsler Adult Intelligence Scale—Fourth Edition. San Antonio, TX: Pearson.

[21]

Bilingual English-Spanish Assessment.

Purpose: Designed to "identify phonological and/or language impairment in bilingual and English language learner (ELL) children."

Population: Latino/a children ages 4-0 to 6-11 who speak English, Spanish, or both.

Publication Date: 2018.

Acronym: BESA.

Scores: 8 in each language (English and Spanish): Phonology, Morphosyntax (Cloze, Sentence Repetition), Semantics (Receptive, Expressive), Language Composite.

Administration: Individual.

Price Data, 2020: $550 per complete kit, including test manual, stimulus book, 20 English test forms, 20 Spanish test forms, 20 BIOS forms, and 20 ITALK forms; $80 per 20 test forms (English or Spanish); $35 per 20 ITALK forms; $35 per 20 BIOS forms.

Time: (60) minutes per language for complete battery.

Comments: Can be administered as a complete battery or as separate tests; administrator should be an experienced Spanish-English bilingual speech-language professional; test publisher advises that if administering the test in both languages, administration should be conducted on separate days; Pragmatics Activity is included to help establish rapport with test taker.

[21] Bilingual English-Spanish Assessment

Authors: Elizabeth D. Peña, Vera F. Gutiérrez-Clellen, Aquiles Iglesias, Brian A. Goldstein, and Lisa M. Bedore.
Publisher: Paul H. Brookes Publishing Co., Inc.

a) BILINGUAL INPUT-OUTPUT SURVEY.
Purpose: Designed to provide an assessment of the child's language exposure history and current use of Spanish and English in the home and at school.
Acronym: BIOS.
Forms, 2: Home, School.
Scores, 12: Spanish School Input, Spanish School Output, English School Input, English School Output, Spanish Home Input, Spanish Home Output, English Home Input, English Home Output, Average Spanish School Input/Output, Average English School Input/Output, Average Spanish Home Input/Output, Average English Home Input/Output.
Time: (5-15) minutes.
Comments: To be administered "prior to the assessment to guide whether to test children in Spanish, English, or both."

b) INVENTORY TO ASSESS LANGUAGE KNOWLEDGE.
Purpose: Designed as a parent and teacher interview to "identify child's perceived level of performance in Spanish and English" in five areas of speech and language: Vocabulary, Grammar, Sentence Production, Comprehension, Phonology.
Acronym: ITALK.
Forms, 2: Home, School.
Scores: Total score only in English and Spanish.
Time: (10) minutes.
Comments: Administer before assessment to "provide a summary of parent and teacher concerns that can be used to guide target areas of assessment."

Review of the Bilingual English-Spanish Assessment by JOSEPH R. ENGLER, Associate Professor of School Psychology, and VINCENT C. ALFONSO, Dean, School of Education, Gonzaga University, Spokane, WA:

DESCRIPTION. The Bilingual English-Spanish Assessment (BESA) is designed to be a comprehensive assessment of speech and language abilities. The BESA is intended to be used to assess speech and language abilities of children who are Spanish-English bilingual and whose ages range from 4 years through 6 years. The BESA can be administered in English, Spanish, or both. Prior to assessing the child, the examiner completes two parent/teacher interviews called the Inventory to Assess Language Knowledge (ITALK) and the Bilingual Input-Output Survey (BIOS). The ITALK addresses the child's production of each language whereas the BIOS assesses the child's history and exposure to each language. The scores derived from the ITALK are compared to a cut score to determine whether the child warrants a comprehensive speech and language evaluation, and results can be used to determine specific areas for assessment. The score derived from the BIOS is used to determine whether the child should be tested in Spanish, English, or both. During these interviews, the test authors suggest that the examiner gains a better perspective of parent and/or teacher concerns.

After the interviews are completed, the examiner administers a Pragmatics activity followed by a series of three standardized norm-referenced tests assessing Phonology, Morphosyntax, and Semantics. The administration typically begins with a Pragmatics Activity. The Pragmatics activity involves collectively engaging in a real-world activity with the child. The test authors state that this allows the examiner to build rapport with the child while observing his/her use of language. The Pragmatics activity is not scored but rather provides the examiner with qualitative information regarding the child's use of language. The Phonology subtest consists of showing the examinee a picture from the stimulus book and asking the examinee to identify/name the picture. There is a series of prompts to use if the examinee does not spontaneously identify/name the picture. The Morphosyntax subtest consists of two parts: the first part is a cloze activity, and the second part involves sentence repetition. The cloze activity evaluates different components of language depending on the language in which the examiner is assessing. The Cloze and Sentence Repetition scaled scores are combined to form an aggregate Morphosyntax standard score. The Semantics subtest measures both receptive and expressive language. The Receptive and Expressive scaled scores are combined to form a Semantics standard score. Each of the aforementioned subtests yields a scaled score that is used to derive a standard score, age equivalent, and percentile rank. If administering the BESA in English and Spanish, the test authors suggest using the highest standard score of the two. In addition to individual scores for the three subtests assessed, the Morphosyntax and Semantic standard scores can be aggregated to form an overall Language Index standard score.

Collectively, the BESA takes approximately one hour to administer per language. The test includes a user-friendly protocol, and the test manual is easy to follow. The stimulus book contains pictures that are colorful and are likely to gain the examinee's attention. The scoring guidelines are clear, and the scores are easy to compute.

DEVELOPMENT. The test authors state that the BESA was developed from a review of the literature most salient to phonology, morphosyntax, and semantic development in bilingual children with and without language impairments. In addition, the authors noted that they drew on their own clinical experiences when creating the BESA. The authors cite several studies that assisted in the creation of items. Within each of the subtests, the authors reported "a large number of items for each domain was generated and tested" (manual, p. 83). Through item analysis, the authors derived their final item set for inclusion based on each item's ability to differentiate between those with or without language impairments. The test manual, however, does not appear to inform the reader as to how many items were originally generated and why phonology, morphosyntax, and semantic constructs were chosen for inclusion in the test. The test authors attempted to justify these constructs for inclusion in the Theoretical Background section of the manual (p. 6); however, much of the literature cited appears to be empirically supported rather than theoretically driven.

With regard to the Pragmatics activity, the test authors reported that the activity is based on "Fey's (1986) model of assertiveness and responsiveness" (manual, p. 2). The authors did not explain in detail what that model entails and how it was relevant to the creation of the activity.

TECHNICAL. The standardization sample for the BESA consisted of 756 children residing in the United States. The majority of the sample was from the South (47%), although participants from the East (29%) and West (24%) also were included. The test authors reported that the majority of the test data were collected from three states (California, Texas, and Pennsylvania); residents of Georgia and New Jersey also were included in the overall sample. Data from the sample were collected across seven variables, only one of which (geographic region) included U.S. Census data for comparison purposes. Due to the restricted representation of the overall sample, norms may not be representative of the larger population.

Internal consistency of the BESA, evaluated by coefficient alpha, ranged from .75 to .96 and from .83 to .96 across English and Spanish subtests, respectively. Alpha coefficients across languages and subtest domains were .83 or higher, with the exception of the Semantics subtest (English) where values were notably lower, ranging from .75 to .82. Split-half reliability coefficients ranged from .86 to .97 and from .87 to .96 across English and Spanish subtests, respectively. These reviewers regard these values as adequate to good (Alfonso & Flanagan, 2009). Interrater agreement was reported to be 95% or higher for subtests in both languages.

The test authors provide content evidence of validity through a literature search and their own experiences, citing several studies for the development of each subtest. It may have been more helpful to have independent expert reviews of the content material. The authors provided construct evidence of validity by documenting increases in language acquisition by age, implementing factor analyses, and demonstrating differences between those with and without language impairments. Overall, there was evidence to support consistency between the constructs in English and Spanish as well as divergence of scores between those with and without language impairments. The test authors provided the latter using raw scores, whereas it may have been more appropriate to demonstrate this feature using standard scores.

To provide criterion evidence of validity, the test authors correlated scores from the BESA with language samples and standardized test results. The obtained correlations make sense, in that the test authors indicated that they expected stronger correlations to emerge when performance on the Semantics and Morphosyntax subtests were compared to language samples and to standardized test scores than when the Phonology subtest and the Pragmatics activity were used in the comparisons. The predicted pattern emerged for both the English and Spanish subtests. For the English version, correlation coefficients between the Morphosyntax subtest and language samples ranged from .38 to .65 and were from .35 to .72 for standardized tests, which included the Test of Narrative Language, Test of Language Development, and the Expressive One-Word Picture Vocabulary Test-2000 (EOWPVT-2000). For the Semantics subtest, the corresponding values ranged from .41 to .56 (language samples) and from .42 to .82 (standardized tests). For the Spanish version of the BESA, correlation coefficients between the Morphosyntax subtest and language samples ranged from .32 to .53, and a coefficient of .28 was demonstrated with the EOWPVT-Spanish Bilingual Edition. For the Semantics subtest, the corresponding values ranged from .30 to .41 (language samples) with a value of .41 with the standardized test. It should be noted that raw scores, once again, were used in these comparisons. It is recommended that scaled or standard scores be used instead, as raw scores can be misleading.

Classification accuracy was examined and used to show evidence that the BESA accurately discriminates between those with and without language impairment. The test authors suggest 80% as a minimally acceptable level for both sensitivity and specificity. With a few exceptions, subtests across all ages met this criterion. The exceptions for specificity occurred for the Semantics subtest at age 4 on the English (78.5%) and Spanish (78.3%) versions. The exceptions for sensitivity occurred for the Semantics subtest at age 5 on the Spanish version (72.0%) and for the Phonology subtest at age 6 on the Spanish version (66.7%).

COMMENTARY. The test authors are to be commended for their research and work in this area as bilingual standardized norm-referenced tests are lacking for early childhood. The BESA is an easy test to administer and score, and it demonstrates promise in the area of Spanish-English bilingual assessment. The users of the BESA would likely benefit from a more detailed description of how to interpret test results. For example, the test manual provides details about obtaining scores; however, it does not go into depth regarding what the scores mean and how those scores can be used for further programming needs. It would be helpful if the test manual provided a description of what each subtest and/or composite measured as well as qualitative descriptors (i.e., labels) for ranges of scores. The norms for the BESA could be strengthened by including greater geographic diversity in the sample. Additionally, the test authors are encouraged to provide tables that demonstrate the match with U.S. Census data across all demographic variables. The reliability or consistency of the BESA is an overall strength. The test authors described several methods used to provide evidence of validity of BESA scores and uses. When correlating BESA scores with scores from other standardized tests, it is suggested that standard scores be used rather than raw scores.

SUMMARY. The BESA was designed to provide a comprehensive measure of speech and language abilities for children who are Spanish-English bilingual. The test accomplishes this goal and does so by imbedding opportunities to build rapport with children and include parent/teacher input in the overall assessment process. Because the normative sample appears to have been based more on convenience than representativeness of the population, the ability to generalize the results of the assessment is lacking.

REVIEWERS' REFERENCE

Alfonso, V. C., & Flanagan, D. P. (2009). Assessment of preschool children: A framework for evaluating the adequacy of the technical characteristics of norm-referenced instruments. In B. A. Mowder, F. Rubinson, & A. E. Yasik (Eds.), *Evidence-based practice in infant and early childhood psychology* (pp. 129-166). Hoboken, NJ: Wiley.

Review of the Bilingual English-Spanish Assessment by TRACY PASKIEWICZ, Lecturer of School Psychology, University of Massachusetts-Boston, Boston, MA:

DESCRIPTION. The Bilingual English-Spanish Assessment (BESA) is a set of tools for the assessment of speech/language ability in Spanish-English bilingual children, ages 4:0-6:11 years. The measure consists of questionnaires for caregivers and educators, a structured observation/interaction activity (to evaluate pragmatic language), and three standardized, norm-referenced subtests in two languages. The intended users are bilingual (Spanish-English) speech/language professionals. Examiners must have knowledge of bilingual language acquisition. Eligible examinees for this assessment are children of Hispanic/Latinx heritage living in the United States who speak English, Spanish, or both.

The purpose of this instrument is to document language exposure in Spanish and English; gather parent and teacher concerns about language proficiency and use; and assess Phonology, Morphosyntax, and Semantics in Spanish and English. The test authors state that results can be used to (a) identify language impairment in bilingual and monolingual Latinx children; (b) document progress in speech/language intervention; (c) ascertain the dominant language in domains of Phonology, Morphosyntax, and Semantics; and (d) conduct research.

Results yield scaled and standard scores for each domain (Phonology, Morphosyntax, Semantics). The questionnaires provide qualitative data to determine language(s) of testing and to develop an assessment strategy. The instrument offers some flexibility regarding which components should be used as well as the order of administration. According to the test manual, administration should take 1 hour (for a single language) or up to 2 hours (if testing in both languages). The test authors recommend testing on different days if assessing in both Spanish and English.

Components of the BESA include the following:

Bilingual Input-Output Survey (BIOS): This survey helps identify when and in what context the child uses Spanish and English. The examiner conducts an interview with caregivers (e.g., parents, teachers) to document language exposure history on a year-to-year basis of the child's life. The survey provides the examiner with information about the child's language history over time, as well as current use and exposure to each language across settings. Survey results determine percentages of input and output in both Spanish and English, to help examiners decide which language(s) to assess.

Inventory to Assess Language Knowledge (ITALK): This interview documents teacher and parent concerns regarding language proficiency and use. It addresses a child's use of Spanish and English in the areas of vocabulary, grammar, sentence production, comprehension, and phonology. The ITALK provides information about proficiency in both languages and helps guide decisions regarding which language(s) to use for the direct assessment. Guidelines for interpreting scores are presented in the test manual.

Pragmatics activity: This activity is based on Fey's (1986) model of assertiveness and responsiveness. It provides users with observational data on social/pragmatic communication and offers an opportunity to establish rapport with the child. It is used for descriptive/qualitative information only; there are no standardized scores associated with this component.

Phonology subtest: This is a standardized, norm-referenced assessment of phonological skills at the single word level, with the intended purpose of differentiating typical from atypical phonological skills in Spanish and English.

Morphosyntax subtest: This is a standardized, norm-referenced assessment of morphemes and sentence structures expected to be difficult for children with language impairment.

Semantics subtest: This is a standardized, norm-referenced assessment of semantics through analogies, properties, categories, functions, linguistic concepts, and similarities/differences. Scoring of this subtest permits code switching. (Child earns credit for correct responses in either language.)

The BESA yields up to six sets of scaled and standard subtest scores (Spanish/English Phonology, Morphosyntax, and Semantics). In addition, Morphosyntax and Semantics each yield two scaled scores: Cloze and Sentence Repetition; Receptive and Expressive language. Finally, the Language Index Composite score represents a weighted score based on a combination of subtest data. Descriptive/qualitative information is obtained from the Pragmatics activity. Percentile ranks and age-equivalent scores are also available for the norm-referenced subtests. The test manual includes detailed descriptions of the various score types and the benefits and limitations of each. The test authors recommend interpreting test scores within the context of observations of speech/language use for ecological validity. Finally, the test authors recommend that truly bilingual children with mixed language dominance should be tested in both Spanish and English in order to make the most accurate diagnostic decisions.

DEVELOPMENT. The test authors begin with a comprehensive literature review regarding normal bilingual acquisition, variation in bilingual acquisition as a function of exposure, and language impairment in bilingual individuals. This important theoretical background justifies the need for such an assessment. It is important for users to understand that the elements that discriminate children with language impairment from typically developing peers may be different in Spanish and English. The pragmatic language activity is based on a specific model of assertiveness and responsiveness proposed by Fey (1986).

The test manual describes procedures for selecting final items for this instrument. Tryout studies included a longer, "experimental" version of the test, from which final items were selected. The test authors developed and tested items in order to identify those that differentiate language and/or speech impairment in Spanish and English. Items that best differentiated typical development from language impairment were retained on the final, normed version of the test. Empirical evidence of validity—specifically related to identifying language impairment—includes studies of item discrimination. Items judged to be poor discriminators were dropped from the final, normed version of the instrument.

TECHNICAL.

Standardization. The test manual describes procedures for drawing the normative sample. The norms are based on a sample of 756 children, ages 4:0-6:11. Approximately half were tested in both languages. Data from 198 children diagnosed with language impairment were used for validity studies.

The sample was drawn from five states: California, Texas, Pennsylvania, Georgia, and New Jersey. The authors note that future editions will be designed to encompass all geographic regions of the United States. Children with exposure to several different dialects of Spanish (e.g., Cuban, Dominican, Mexican) are included in the sample, and percentages of each dialect are listed. The sample was nearly 70% Mexican; the test authors indicate the distribution of dialects is representative of the Hispanic/Latinx population in the United States. The authors provide other demographic data for the normative sample, including age; geographic region (West, South, East); degree of language exposure (Functional Monolingual English, Bilingual Dominant English, Balanced Bilingual, Bilingual Dominant Spanish, and Functional Monolingual Spanish); dialect; gender; parental level of education; and economic status (as determined by eligibility for free/reduced lunch). All children in the normative sample resided in the United States.

Reliability. The test authors cite evidence of generally high internal consistency for each of the subtests. (Alpha coefficients ranged from .83 to .96 for Spanish subtests and .75 to .96 for English subtests.) Data from a tryout sample showed significant correlations between results from students tested in kindergarten and again in first grade, suggesting stability over time. Studies of interrater reliability provide evidence of high (95-100%) agreement in scoring protocols and the Pragmatics activity. Confidence intervals and standard errors of measurement (*SEMs*) are presented as a way to illustrate precision of test scores. Generally, the *SEMs* increase with increasing age on this measure, suggesting a decrease in the instrument's reliability as a function of increasing age. Overall, the reliability data suggest stability and consistency in test scores.

Validity evidence. The validity studies for the BESA focus on a single purpose: to identify language impairment in bilingual and monolingual Hispanic/Latinx children. Construct validity evidence includes score associations with age. The test authors state that they expected older children to perform better, overall, than younger children (as a function of language development). The results show moderate to large gains as a function of increasing age in both languages. The test authors expected children with language impairment to score lower than typically developing children; this was, in fact, the case. Finally, principal components factor analyses were completed for the Spanish and English tests, separately. The English test yielded five factors, as the Cloze and Sentence Repetition items loaded on separate factors, whereas the Spanish test yielded four factors. Ultimately, a four-factor solution was chosen to represent the BESA.

Criterion-related validity evidence includes independent validity samples separate from the norm group. Analyses included correlations with other measures, including language sample measures and other standardized tests (i.e., Test of Narrative Language, Test of Language Development–Primary, Expressive One-Word Picture Vocabulary Test-2000 for the English version and Expressive One-Word Picture Vocabulary Test-Spanish Bilingual Edition for the Spanish version). Correlation coefficients between BESA subtests and language samples ranged from .15 to .65 and from .09 to .53 for English and Spanish versions, respectively. Coefficients between BESA subtests and standardized tests ranged from .08 to .82 and from .27 to .41 for English and Spanish versions, respectively. The test authors indicate the results suggest BESA subtests assess constructs that are similar to other language measures.

Consequential validity evidence examines the diagnostic accuracy of this measure. The test authors evaluated the instrument's sensitivity and specificity as well as classification accuracy. These validity studies examined children previously identified as having language impairment. The results suggest classification accuracy ranging from fair to good, with an overall assessment of "adequate" per the test authors. Across ages, subtests, and language versions, all but four sensitivity and specificity values exceeded the 80% criterion proposed by the test authors. Three involved the Semantics subtest, two of which approached the criterion (78.5% and 78.3%).

Bias analyses included the test authors' process for reducing bias in the development of test items and activities. The authors explain that the greatest opportunity to obtain a potentially biased result would be found on the Pragmatics activity; however, because this activity gathers qualitative data only and does not yield standardized scores, this opportunity is minimized. Individual item bias was evaluated through statistical methods (item discrimination values). These analyses found no differences on individual item performance by sex/gender, but there were significant differences by region. Specifically, children from the Eastern region of the United States had difficulty with certain items that children from other regions did not. This finding suggests, according to the test authors, that children from the Eastern United States may be misclassified more often than children from other regions of the country.

COMMENTARY. The test authors provide an excellent rationale regarding the need for the BESA, citing the cultural and linguistic appropriateness of a battery specifically designed for bilingual children or those who are English learners. The common practice of translating tests from English—in the absence of Spanish/English tests—may emphasize language forms that are not diagnostically relevant in Spanish. Perhaps one of the most important functions of the BESA is the systematic assessment process involved in identifying language exposure in both languages, which results in a preference for assessment in Spanish or English (or both). The BESA manual offers specific guidelines for practitioners regarding how to evaluate bilingual children. This test offers a much more psychometrically sound practice than translating tests from English. Though the measure is primarily used by bilingual speech/language professionals, broader applications may be useful for helping other evaluators (e.g., psychologists, educators) decide how to proceed and in which language(s) with other assessments.

The test manual is well-organized and comprehensive. It includes appendixes of acceptable and unacceptable responses for all items, taking into account regional variations and dialects. It contains a review of the literature pertaining to normal bilingual language acquisition and variations of bilingual language proficiency as a function of exposure as well as a description of language impairment features in bilinguals and English learners. This manual can serve as an authoritative source on appropriate methods and procedures for testing bilingual children. The authors certainly satisfy a need for an assessment with a single norm group that can be administered in Spanish or English or both. This measure contributes to the overall body of knowledge of typical development versus pathology in bilinguals or English learners.

This reviewer sees four areas of concern in the BESA. First, the measure has quite a narrow age range (4:0-6:11). If this tool is meant to be used in schools, it may be helpful to expand the age range, as concerns for language acquisition and proficiency exist in younger and older children as well. Next, though the reliability estimates are very good overall, the standard error of measurement (*SEM*) increases as a function of age; the confidence interval for a particular subtest at a particular age group approaches one standard deviation. If cut points are used for diagnostic purposes, the authors may wish to include discussion of this issue in the interpretation section of the manual. Third, though the norm group may indeed represent the Hispanic/Latinx population in the United States, given the significant variability in regional dialects, the test authors may wish to consider developing regional norms as well. For example, a norm group that is 70% Mexican may be more appropriate for a Mexican-American child in California than a Puerto Rican child living in New York City. Finally, the authors cite several purposes for the BESA, but the validity evidence is limited to a single purpose: identification of language impairment. The authors should provide validity evidence for other proposed purposes (e.g., progress monitoring) if the BESA can be used in this way.

SUMMARY. The BESA is a well-developed measure that fills a need for bilingual speech/language professionals and offers the unique contribution of a single measure normed in both Spanish and English for those children who are exposed to both languages. As this population is increasing across the United States, instruments such as the BESA will hold a prominent place in a practitioner's toolbox. Although the test authors offer several purposes, validity evidence supports the single purpose of identifying language impairment in Hispanic/Latinx bilingual children of a young age. The test authors could focus future work on expanding the age range of this measure, developing regional norms that consider the influence of regional Spanish dialects, and norm-referencing the pragmatic language assessment.

REVIEWER'S REFERENCES

Fey, M. E. (1986). *Language intervention with young children.* San Diego, CA: College-Hill Press.

Leonard, L. B. (2014). Specific language impairment across languages. *Child Development Perspectives, 8*(1), 1-5.

[22]

Brown Executive Function/Attention Scales.

Purpose: "Designed to evaluate executive functions related to attention-deficit/hyperactivity disorder (ADHD)."

Population: Ages 3 years and older.

Publication Dates: 1991-2019.

Acronym: Brown EF/A Scales.

Scores, 7: Activation, Focus, Effort, Emotion, Memory, Action, Total.

Administration: Individual.

Levels, 4: Early Childhood (Ages 3-7), Child (Ages 8-12), Adolescent (Ages 13-18), Adult (Ages 19 and older).
Forms, 8: Parent (Early Childhood, Child, Adolescent), Teacher (Early Childhood, Child), Self-Report (Child, Adolescent, Adult).
Price Data, 2020: $347.90 per online kit including print manual, 5 parent forms, 5 teacher forms, and 1 year online scoring subscription; $328.50 per digital only kit with digital manual and 50 online score reports; $324.40 per hand scoring starter kit including manual (2019, 176 pages),and 5 copies each of the teacher, parent and self-report forms and answer sheets (all ages); $193.80 per print manual; $173.40 per digital manual; $88.80 per 25 forms (specify rater and age level); $15.30 per 25 scoring sheets (specify rater and age level); $3.90 per online score report with administration.
Time: 10-15 minutes for completion of each form.
Comments: Computer administration available; updated version of the Brown Attention-Deficit Disorder Scales and the Brown Attention-Deficit Disorder Scales for Children and Adolescents.
Author: Thomas E. Brown.
Publisher: Pearson.
Cross References: For reviews by Karen E. Jennings and William K. Wilkinson of the Brown Attention-Deficit Disorder Scales for Children and Adolescents, see 15:42; for reviews by Nadeen L. Kaufman and Alan S. Kaufman, by E. Jean Newman, and by Judy Oehler-Stinnett of the Brown Attention-Deficit Disorder Scales, see 14:54.

Review of the Brown Executive Function/Attention Scales by S. KATHLEEN KRACH, Assistant Professor of School Psychology, Florida State University, Tallahassee, FL:

DESCRIPTION. The Brown Executive Function/Attention Scales (Brown EF/A Scales) is a follow-up to the Brown Attention-Deficit Disorder Scales (Brown ADD Scales; Brown, 1996) and the Brown Attention-Deficit Disorder Scales for Children and Adolescents (Brown ADD Scales for Children; Brown, 2001). As with the previous versions, the current version uses a rating scale format. The Brown EF/A Scales has eight separate forms: self-report (ages 8-12, 13-18, 19 and older), parent (ages 3-7, 8-12, 13-18), and teacher (ages 3-7, 8-12). Each form has a paper administration/paper scoring option and a digital administration/digital scoring option. The test author describes the goals of the assessment as screening for and diagnosing attention-deficit/hyperactivity disorder (ADHD) along with associated executive functioning deficits. In addition, the test author suggests that the instrument can be used for progress monitoring.

Each form provides a Total Composite score as well as scores for the following subscales: Activation, Focus, Effort, Emotion, Memory, and Action. Activation is described as "organizing, prioritizing, and activating to work"; Focus as "focusing, sustaining, and shifting attention to tasks"; Effort as "regulating alertness, sustaining effort, and adjusting processing speed"; Emotion as "managing frustration and modulating emotions"; Memory as "utilizing working memory and accessing recall"; and Action as "monitoring and self-regulating action" (manual, p. 2). The test author states that subscales and items were selected to measure the diagnostic criteria outlined in the *Diagnostic and Statistical Manual of Mental Disorders* (5th ed.; *DSM-5*; American Psychiatric Association [APA], 2013); however, he does not go so far as to make direct links between the two. On the surface, the subscales appear to align diagnostically as follows: inattention symptoms—Focus, Effort, and Memory; hyperactivity and impulsivity symptoms—Emotion, Action, and Activation.

The test author states that the Total Composite is the most valuable score used in decision making. After interpreting the composite score, the emphasis shifts to score profiles (and not to individual subscales). The test manual provides eight examples of interpreting patterns of scores. Higher T scores are seen as problematic for the composites and the subscales. Normative data are provided for males, females, and combined.

DEVELOPMENT AND TECHNICAL. The Brown EF/A Scales is not simply a revision of the Brown ADD Scales or the Brown ADD Scales for Children. Instead, the author started with a new theoretical perspective related to the assessment of ADHD. Therefore, technical information from prior versions is not relevant for the current instrument.

Normative data were collected for 1,950 forms between 2017 and 2018. Many of the forms were completed on the same individual (e.g., 232 children were evaluated by both parents and teachers). The sample was stratified based on the U.S. Census by age and socioeconomic status (educational level), ethnicity/race, and geographic region. The sample included approximately equal numbers of males and females.

Reliability coefficients were provided for internal consistency (coefficient alpha), test-retest (7- to 28-day interval), and interrater (parent-teacher, self-teacher, and self-parent). Internal consistency and test-retest reliability coefficients were above .70 for all subscales, forms, and raters; most were above .85. Interrater coefficients for the Total Composite ranged from .45 to .67.

Content validity was addressed through using literature to define the subscales and items representing each construct. A confirmatory factor analysis conducted on the normative sample data indicated six factors (matching the six subscales); however, the Emotion cluster factor loadings were somewhat weak, especially for the youngest age groups. Convergent validity evidence was evaluated through both predictive (clinical group) and concurrent (BASC-3, BRIEF2, and Conners 3) comparisons. Concurrent validity coefficients all fell within the expected range; for example, the BASC-3 Overall Executive Functioning Index correlated with the Brown EF/A Scales Total Composite at .67 on the teacher form and .69 on the parent form. With the BRIEF2 Global Executive Composite, correlation coefficients were .95 for the parent form and .86 for the teacher and self-report forms. Predictive validity findings indicate that those with clinical diagnoses of ADHD prior to completing the scales went on to obtain Brown EF/A Total Composite scores around 1.5 standard deviations higher than matched controls from the normative sample.

COMMENTARY. A few areas of concern were noted when administering the Brown EF/A Scales. First, the hand-scoring worksheet is cumbersome and difficult to use; because of this, hand-scoring procedures may be prone to human error. It may be best to use the digital version instead of the paper version to ensure accuracy. However, use of the digital version also may be problematic because no equivalency studies (paper to digital) were included in the test manual. This is problematic given that research is inconclusive for rating scale equivalency across formats (Patalay, Deighton, Fonagy, & Wolpert, 2015); this is especially true for rating scales completed by children (Schulenberg & Yutrzenka, 1999).

The other main issue is that the norming tables were not differentiated sufficiently based on age. For example, ages 3 through 5 are combined in a single group. This was the case for ages 19 and above as well. There are significant developmental differences in executive functioning at younger ages (Espy, Kaufmann, McDiarmid, & Glisky, 1999) and older ages (Lin, Chan, Zheng, Yang, & Wang, 2007) that may not be reflected in the T scores provided. Given this, it may be best to limit the use of the Brown EF/A Scales to children ages 6 through 18.

SUMMARY. The Brown EF/A Scales shows a strong theoretical link between the content assessed and the diagnosis of ADHD. The psychometric data presented by the author support the use of this instrument for measuring executive functioning; the test author clearly links executive functioning constructs to ADHD. The multiple forms for different ages and raters are appropriate and useful. However, given the lack of normative comparison differentiation at the younger and older ages, for those groups the scores should be interpreted with caution. In addition, although the test author discusses using the instrument for progress monitoring, this use is not recommended based on this reviewer's evaluation of the materials available at this time (Coffee & Ray-Subramanian, 2009). Overall, the use of the Brown EF/A Scales as a screener and/or a diagnostic tool seems supported for children and adolescents.

REVIEWER'S REFERENCES

American Psychiatric Association. (2013). *Diagnostic and statistical manual of mental disorders* (5th ed.). Washington, DC: Author.

Brown, T. E. (1996). Brown Attention-Deficit Disorder Scales. San Antonio, TX: The Psychological Corporation.

Brown, T. E. (2001). Brown Attention-Deficit Disorder Scales for Children and Adolescents. San Antonio, TX: The Psychological Corporation.

Coffee, G., & Ray-Subramanian, C. E. (2009). Goal attainment scaling: A progress-monitoring tool for behavioral interventions. *School Psychology Forum, 3*, 1-12.

Espy, K. A., Kaufmann, P. M., McDiarmid, M. D., & Glisky, M. L. (1999). Executive functioning in preschool children: Performance on A-not-B and other delayed response format tasks. *Brain and Cognition, 41,* 178-199. doi:10.1006/brcg.1999.1117

Lin, H., Chan, R. C., Zheng, L., Yang, T., & Wang, Y. (2007). Executive functioning in healthy elderly Chinese people. *Archives of Clinical Neuropsychology, 22,* 501-511. doi:10.1016/j.acn.2007.01.028

Patalay, P., Deighton, J., Fonagy, P., & Wolpert, M. (2015). Equivalence of paper and computer formats of a child self-report mental health measure. *European Journal of Psychological Assessment, 31,* 54-61. doi:10.1027/1015-5759/a000206

Schulenberg, S. E., & Yutrzenka, B. A. (1999). The equivalence of computerized and paper-and-pencil psychological instruments: Implications for measures of negative affect. *Behavior Research Methods, Instruments, & Computers, 31,* 315-321. doi:10.3758/BF03207726

Review of the Brown Executive Function/Attention Scales by RAMA K. MISHRA, Neuropsychologist, Addictions and Mental Health, Medicine Hat Regional Hospital, Alberta, Canada:

DESCRIPTION. The Brown Executive Function/Attention Scales (Brown EF/A Scales) are described as "a set of rating scales designed to evaluate executive functions related to attention-deficit/hyperactivity disorder (ADHD) in individuals ages 3 years and older" (manual, p. 1). The instrument is a significant revision of the Brown Attention-Deficit Disorder Scales (Brown ADD Scales; Brown 1996, 2001). These scales can be used for screening, as part of a comprehensive evaluation, or for monitoring progress from treatment for attention-deficit/hyperactivity disorder (ADHD).

The scales consist of parent and teacher rating scales for ages 3 to 7; parent, teacher, and self-report scales for ages 8 to 12; parent and self-report scales for ages 13-18; and a self-report scale for ages 19 and older. The number of items ranges from 56 to 58, and each scale is expected to be completed by the raters in 10-15 minutes. Items are rated on a 4-point scale: *N* = *No Problem* (score of 0), *L* = *Little Problem*, *M* = *Medium Problem*, and *B* = *Big Problem* (score of 3). The scales can be hand scored or scored using the test publisher's online platform for a nominal cost.

The Brown EF/A Scales provide T scores with a mean of 50 and standard deviation of 10 to describe the "relative extremeness of a score" (manual, p. 19). They also provide percentile ranks to "describe the frequency (or infrequency) of a score" (p. 19). The descriptive classifications of the T-score ranges are as follows: 54 and below = *typical* (unlikely significant problem), 55-59 = *somewhat atypical* (possibly significant problem), 60-69 = *moderately atypical* (significant problem), 70 and above = *markedly atypical* (very significant problem).

The Brown EF/A Scales manual provides a list of distinguishing features that include the test author's conceptualization of six subscales or clusters of executive function deficits in ADHD; items that differentiate individuals with ADHD from others; emphasis on symptoms that are more severe rather than more frequent; multiple perspectives from self, parent, and teacher ratings; and close association with diagnostic criteria contained in the *Diagnostic and Statistical Manual of Mental Disorders* (5th ed.; *DSM-5*; American Psychiatric Association [APA], 2013).

DEVELOPMENT. Brown indicated that his research over the past 30 years demonstrated that ADHD is "a complicated problem involving the chronic impairment of the brain's executive functions" (manual, p. 41). The items on the Brown EF/A Scales are grouped into six clusters or subscales representing his model of executive function impairments. These clusters include (a) organizing, prioritizing, and activating to work, termed *Activation*; (b) focusing, sustaining, and shifting attention to tasks, named *Focus*; (c) regulating alertness, sustaining effort, and adjusting processing speed, named *Effort*; (d) managing frustration and modulating emotions, termed *Emotion*; (e) utilizing working memory and accessing recall, named *Memory*; and (f) monitoring and self-regulating action, termed *Action*.

The development of the test as described in the test manual involved four phases. In the initial phase extensive consultation and review of literature occurred, and parameters of the theorized clusters were defined. In the second phase, items relevant to the age and developmental stage of the clients were developed for each scale; response format was chosen; effort was made to lower the reading level across all scales, particularly for the child self-report scale; and items were updated to reflect current use of idioms as much as possible.

In the third phase, a pilot study was conducted in the spring of 2017 to evaluate the psychometric properties of the items. The pilot study included a nonclinical sample (73 parent forms, 47 teacher forms, and 67 self-report forms) as well as a clinical sample of individuals diagnosed with ADHD (67 parent forms, 39 teacher forms, and 63 self-report forms). All intended age levels were represented in the pilot study; the nonclinical group was 51% males, and the clinical group was 63% males. The test results were analyzed using classical test theory models, and items that demonstrated low sensitivity or that were redundant were removed while ensuring that adequate cluster coverage was maintained. For the final phase, the standardization study included rating forms with 56 items for the 3- to 7-year age group, 58 items for the 8- to 12-year age group, and 57 items for both the 13- to 18-year age group, and the 19 and older age group.

TECHNICAL. The standardization included a nonclinical stratified sample of 1,950 self, parent, and teacher forms representing U.S. Census data with respect to gender, age group, race/ethnicity, geographical region, and parental education for normative information. The test author reports a "close correspondence between the normative sample and the 2016 U.S. Census proportions" (manual, p. 46). The normative sample also included 2% to 8% individuals in special education categories including gifted and talented, speech and language impaired, and specific learning disability to reflect the U.S. population.

Additionally, a clinical sample of 359 individuals diagnosed with ADHD (inattentive, hyperactive/impulsive, and combined type) was used to examine reliability and validity.

Several reliability estimates were provided. Internal consistency was estimated using coefficient alpha, which was between .96 and .98 for the composite scores across all age groups, and between .74 and .95 for all six clusters across all age groups for the normative sample. Similarly, the alpha coefficients were between .94 and .97 for the composite scores and between .70 and .92 for the six clusters across all age groups for the clinical sample.

Test-retest reliability coefficients for the same rater with an interval of 7 to 28 days were between .79 and .94 for the composite scores for all forms and between .71 and .95 for the six clusters across all age groups. All but one of the standard difference values for the composite score, calculated as the difference between the first and second testing and divided by the pooled standard deviation, were less than ±.15, further evidence of stability of scores over time.

Interrater reliability coefficients were reported to be .48 for the composite scores between parent and teacher, .45 between self-report and teacher, and from .60 to .67 between self-report and parent across the various age groups of children. The cluster level interrater reliabilities ranged from .35 to .52 between parent and teacher, from .32 to .46 between self-report and teacher, and from .54 to .72 between self-report and parent.

Several validity estimates were reported for the Brown EF/A Scales. Intercorrelation coefficients obtained between the clusters and composite scores were presented as evidence of internal structure. For the normative sample, the estimates were between .52 and .96 for the parent form, between .49 and .96 for the teacher form, and between .59 and .95 for the self-report form. For the clinical sample, intercorrelations were between .31 and .93 for the parent form, between .16 and .91 for the teacher form, and between .27 and .92 for the self-report form.

The covariance structure analysis or confirmatory factor analysis showed reasonable factor loadings across all forms and age groups for all six clusters, with the highest factor loadings for Activation, Focus, and Effort clusters (.88 to .97) and the lowest for the Emotion cluster (.63 to .83).

Evidence of validity was also demonstrated by the strength of the relationship between scores obtained from the Brown EF/A Scales and those from other instruments designed to measure similar constructs. For example, correlations between the parent rating scales from the Brown EF/A Scales and parent rating scales from the Behavior Assessment System for Children, Third Edition (BASC-3; Reynolds & Kamphaus, 2015) were moderate to high for the Attention Problems Scale (.58 to .72) and Overall Executive Functioning (.56 to .71), but lower for the Emotional Control Index (.28 to .67). As expected, the Emotion cluster of the Brown EF/A Scales had a moderate relationship (.67) with the Emotional Control Index of the BASC-3. For the teacher rating scales, the highest correlation coefficients were obtained for the ADHD Probability Index (.43 to .69) and the Attentional Control Index (.24 to .76). Coefficients for the Emotional Control Index were lowest overall (.02 to .67). The self-report forms had the highest correlations with Attention Problems (.58 to .76) Inattention/Hyperactivity (.57 to .77), and the Functional Impairment Index (.66 to .81) and the lowest correlations with Hyperactivity (.44 to .72).

Similarly, the Brown EF/A Scales had high correlations across all forms and age groups with the corresponding scales from the Conners 3rd Edition (Conners 3; Conners, 2008). For example, the parent form had high correlations with Inattention (.48 to .84) and Hyperactivity/Impulsivity (.52 to .84) and low correlations with Peer Relations (.02 to .41). The teacher form had high correlations with Inattention (.52 to .90) and Executive Functioning (.47 to .88) and low correlations with Peer Relations (.29 to .44). The self-report had the highest correlations with Learning Problems (.70 to .79) and Inattention (.52 to .82) and the lowest correlation with Family Relations (.38 to .48).

Finally, Brown EF/A Scales demonstrated moderate to high correlations with the Behavior Rating Inventory of Executive Function, Second Edition (BRIEF2; Gioia, Isquith, Guy, & Kenworthy, 2015). For example, the parent form had the highest correlations with the Global Executive Composite (.73 to .95), the Emotion Regulation Index (.81 to .92), and the Shift scale (.79 to .90) and the lowest correlations with the Task Monitor scale (.10 to .48). The teacher form had the highest correlations with the Global Executive Composite (.52 to .86), the Cognitive Regulation Index (.46 to .87) and the Working Memory scale (.47 to .86) and the lowest correlation with the Emotional Control scale (.24 to .55). Interestingly, the self-report had moderate to high correlations with all subscales and composite scales with the highest correlations with Global Executive Composite (.74 to .86), Emotion Regulation Index (.69 to .82) and Cognitive Regulation Index (.63 to .81).

Evidence of criterion validity was presented by comparing the clinical group with a diagnosis of ADHD and the control group with no clinical diagnosis matched with respect to such demographic characteristics as gender, age, education, and ethnicity. Across all forms, the ADHD groups scored significantly higher on the six clusters and the Total Composite than the matched controls (p < .01).

Finally, evidence of validity was presented by examining diagnostic accuracy using *DSM-5* (APA, 2013) criteria. Values for five base rates at four different cutoff scores—55, 60, 65, and 70, representing 0.5, 1.0, 1.5, and 2.0 standard deviations (SDs) from the mean, respectively—are presented in corresponding tables in the test manual. The test author reported that a Total Composite cutoff score of 60, or 1.0 SD above the mean, provided the best balance between sensitivity and specificity with most values above .75.

COMMENTARY. Brown Executive Function/Attention Scales is one of the most robust tests available in the market for clinicians to identify executive functioning deficits in ADHD and monitor treatment effectiveness across the lifespan. This scale is easy to use. It can be hand scored or scored using a web-based platform for a nominal price. It allows input from the clients, parents, and teachers for children and adolescents up to age 18 years for added clinical utility.

Brown EF/A Scales is based on Brown's 30 years of research and a theoretical model of six clusters of executive functioning deficits in individuals with ADHD. It has impressive internal consistency and test-retest reliability results. The interrater reliability is somewhat low, but comparable to other rating scales. Brown has provided extensive validity data including intercorrelations of scores, confirmatory factor analysis supporting the six clusters, correlations with similar measures, criterion group comparison, and diagnostic accuracy.

The rating scale for 19 years and older has a self-rating version only, unlike many adult rating scales with collateral or informant rating scales, namely Behavior Rating Inventory of Executive Function-Adult (Roth, Isquith, & Gioia, 2005). It would have been useful to include an informant rating scale, particularly for young adults, as the perception of an informant might be different and clinically useful. Similarly, teacher rating scales for ages 13 to 18 would provide useful information about how the child is functioning at school and should have been included in addition to the parent rating scale to provide a perspective parents cannot provide.

Further validity studies with respect to sensitivity and specificity using other diagnostic groups such as individuals with affective difficulties (e.g., depression, anxiety), brain injury, developmental disorders (e.g., intellectual and autism spectrum disorder), and others who present some degree of attentional difficulties would be useful for differential diagnosis of ADHD and clinical management.

SUMMARY. Brown Executive Function/Attention Scales provide increased psychometric properties and clinical utility to the users of the Brown ADD Scales, a measure that was very popular among many users. Strong reliability, validity, and diagnostic accuracy of this scale would be particularly useful for clinicians and researchers.

Clinicians interested in using this tool for diagnostic purposes might like to identify evidence of retrospective childhood attentional difficulties, particularly for the adult clients, available in other rating scales such as the Clinical Assessment of Attention Deficit-Adult (Bracken & Boatwright, 2005), which also provides information on response bias such as Infrequency, Positive Impression, and Negative Impression. In addition to a thorough clinical interview based on *DSM-5* (APA, 2013) diagnostic criteria and cognitive assessment, multiple rating scales could be used along with the Brown Executive Function/Attention Scales to maximize diagnostic accuracy.

REVIEWER'S REFERENCES

American Psychiatric Association. (2013). *Diagnostic and statistical manual of mental disorders* (5th ed.). Washington, DC: Author.

Bracken, B. A., & Boatwright, B. S. (2005). Clinical Assessment of Attention Deficit-Adult. Lutz, FL: Psychological Assessment Resources.

Brown, T. E. (1996). *Brown Attention-Deficit Disorder Scales manual.* San Antonio, TX: The Psychological Corporation.

Brown, T. E. (2001). *Brown Attention-Deficit Disorder Scales for Children and Adolescents manual.* San Antonio, TX: The Psychological Corporation.

Conners, C. K. (2008). Conners 3rd Edition. Toronto, Canada: Multi-Health Systems.

Gioia, G. A., Isquith, P. K., Guy S. C., & Kenworthy, L. (2015). Behavior Rating Inventory of Executive Function, Second Edition. Lutz, FL: Psychological Assessment Resources.

Reynolds, C. R., & Kamphaus, R. W. (2015). Behavior Assessment System for Children, Third Edition. San Antonio, TX: Pearson.

Roth, R. M., Isquith, P. K., & Gioia, G. A. (2005). Behavior Rating Inventory of Executive Function—Adult Version. Lutz, FL: Psychological Assessment Resources.

[23]

California Older Adult Stroop Test.

Purpose: A Stroop Test adaptation "designed to minimize errors due to decreased visual acuity or color naming difficulty secondary to confusion or cataracts."

Population: Ages 60 and older.

Publication Date: 2010.

Acronym: COAST.

Scores, 9: Color (Time, Self-Corrected Errors, Total Errors), Word (Time, Self-Corrected Errors, Total Errors), Interference (Time, Self-Corrected Errors, Total Errors).

Administration: Individual.

Price Data, 2020: $50 per PDF manual (17 pages); $60 per paper manual; $10 per license to reproduce.
Time: Approximately 15 minutes for administration.
Authors: Nancy A. Pachana, Bernice A. Marcopulos, Ruth E. Yoash-Gantz, and Larry W. Thompson.
Publisher: Mind Garden, Inc.

Review of the California Older Adult Stroop Test by CARLTON S. GASS, Neuropsychologist, TMH Physician Partners Neurology Specialists, Tallahassee Memorial Healthcare, Tallahassee, FL:

DESCRIPTION. The California Older Adult Stroop Test (COAST) is an individually administered test designed for individuals over the age of 60, and is used to measure speed of mental processing, divided attention, and mental flexibility. It is a test of executive functioning and has been shown to be sensitive to frontal lobe damage. The test is an adaptation of the popular Stroop Color Word Test (Golden, 1978) designed to improve its validity as applied to older persons who commonly have problems with visual acuity, confusion with color naming, differentiating blue from green, and fatigue. The stimulus cards were modified in ways that help eliminate the unwanted impact of perceptual errors and mental fatigue.

The test has clinical application with inpatients and outpatients, as well as research value with various populations. The test consists of three parts that are always presented in the same sequence. All trials are timed. In Part A, the examinee is presented with a card that has colored squares only (red, yellow, and green) in a 5-column, 10-row array. This is half the length of the traditional test. The examinee is timed while naming the colors across all the rows as quickly as possible. In Part B, the examinee is presented with a card with the words *red, yellow,* and *green* printed in a 5 x 10 array in all capital letters, in black ink, and in a larger font than in previous versions. The examinee's reading speed is timed. In Part C, the card has the words *red, yellow,* and *green* printed in colored ink, again in a 5 x 10 array and in all capital letters. The instruction is "Do not read the words, but name the color of the ink they are printed in (as fast as you can)." On a score sheet, the examiner records the time to completion as well as the corrected and uncorrected errors. Test administration typically requires less than 5 minutes. For each of the three parts, scores consist of total time to completion of the 50 items, total number of self-corrections, and total number of errors.

DEVELOPMENT. The test authors recognized that color confusion, small type face, and the length of most versions of the Stroop Color Word Test often inappropriately interfered with older examinees' ability to complete the task. In one study, Pachana, Thompson, Marcopulos, and Yoash-Gantz (2004) found that about 20% of older adults have difficulties distinguishing blue and green. They further demonstrated that color confusion was significantly reduced by eliminating blue stimuli. Other changes are also helpful. For example, larger type likely reduced problems created by impaired visual acuity. The length of the task was reduced by 50%, likely reducing the possible impact of fatigue.

TECHNICAL. Six experimental groups completed the COAST and provide bases for comparison. Means and standard deviations for scores (times and errors) are presented for persons with Type II diabetes (n = 124), outpatients with depression (n = 39), inpatients with psychiatric disorders (n = 38), inpatients with dementia (n = 51), community volunteers (n = 86), and family caregivers (n = 72). In addition, means and standard deviations are provided for select demographic variables (i.e., age, education, and occupation) and scores from cognitive tests/subtests (i.e., digit span, vocabulary, similarities, digit symbol, trails B, logical memory [immediate and delayed], visual reproduction [immediate and delayed], and global cognitive functioning). The reader is advised to calculate z-scores in order to derive percentile ranks. The role of gender was described as negligible, and no cross-cultural data are presented.

Practice effects were assessed in healthy adults and adults with non-insulin-dependent Type II diabetes who were "in good general health" (manual, p. 8). Three test administrations were conducted at 1- to 2-month intervals. Sample sizes were not reported. Effects were negligible for color reading and word reading trials. However, a practice effect of unspecified magnitude was found for the interference trial, leading the test authors to recommend against repeat administration within 3 months, and ideally 6 months, of testing. Test-retest correlation coefficients between times to completion across the three administrations were acceptable, ranging from .72 to .91. Error and self-correction scores were much less stable (correlation coefficients ranged from .04 to .37 and from .02 to .50, respectively), raising concerns about their utility.

Discriminative validity evidence was examined by comparing the mean scores of healthy adults and patients with Type II diabetes. Unfortunately, no *t* test or ANOVA results were reported. The test manual does not report sample sizes. However, it cites a study involving 33 diabetics and 18 controls (Pachana, Thompson, Marcopulos, & Yoash-Gantz, 2004). Applying a *t* test to compare the mean time to completion on the Interference trial, this reviewer found $t = 0.96, p = 0.35$ (2-tailed). The test authors suggest validation support (manual, p. 8), despite the absence of reported statistically significant mean differences. The test manual also cites Pachana et al. (2004), which showed that dementia inpatients performed worse than controls on the COAST. The manual does not report the statistical data that are presented in the 2004 study. Convergent validation evidence was sought by correlating COAST scores and scores from the Golden (1978) version of Stroop ($n = 34$). Validation was clearly supported for Interference time ($r = .89$), partially supported for Word Reading ($r = .72$), and not supported for Color Naming ($r = .50$); the test manual suggests a more favorable conclusion (p. 10).

COMMENTARY. The COAST is a modified version of the Stroop Color Word Test (Golden, 1978) that is expected to reduce the unwanted impact of perceptual errors and mental fatigue in older examinees. Changes in the stimulus cards appear to be favorable. Elimination of the blue stimuli reduced errors that were attributed to failed blue-green discrimination (Pachana et al., 2004). What is lacking is an adequate set of age- and education-based norms using a large healthy sample. Without stratified norms, there is no way a clinician can clearly determine whether a score is truly abnormal. In addition, the test manual should include scaled scores or percentile ranks rather than requiring the clinician to compute *z* scores and perform a conversion to percentile ranks.

The COAST has spotty validation support. Pachana et al. (2004) showed that it can differentiate healthy adults from patients with dementia, but this is unimpressive. A test is not necessary for making such a gross differentiation. The test manual further appeals to the reader to visually inspect raw scores (in Table 1) and reach the conclusion that non-insulin-dependent Type II diabetics who reported being in good general health performed "slightly worse" (p. 8) than healthy adults when, in fact, it appears that the score differences were not statistically significant and could be attributable entirely to chance.

The COAST evaluates cognitive flexibility. Perhaps a more appropriate comparison sample would consist of individuals with known mild brain dysfunction. In addition, rather than simply comparing mean score differences between healthy adults and persons with mild brain dysfunction, validation studies should assess the COAST's receiver operating characteristics and diagnostic classification accuracy as applied to individuals. Data regarding its sensitivity, specificity, false positives, and false negatives would be far more informative. Finally, given the high incidence of psychological conditions in neuropsychological referrals, research including non-brain-damaged psychiatric samples is warranted.

SUMMARY. The COAST is a well-conceived version of the Stroop Color Word Test (Golden, 1978) that holds promise for use with older examinees. At present, the test has limited validation support, and further research is warranted. The clinical utility of the instrument is limited by the absence of a sufficiently large standardization sample composed of healthy adults with norms that are stratified by age and education.

REVIEWER'S REFERENCES

Golden, C. J. (1978). Stroop Color and Word Test. Chicago, IL: Stoelting.

Pachana, N. A., Thompson, L. W., Marcopulos, B. A., & Yoash-Gantz, R. (2004). California Older Adult Stroop Test (COAST): Development of a Stroop test adapted for geriatric populations. *Clinical Gerontologist, 27*(3), 3-22. doi:10.1300/J018v27n03_02

Review of the California Older Adult Stroop Test by TAMARA McKENZIE-HARTMAN, Defense and Veterans Brain Injury Center, James A. Haley VA Hospital, Tampa, FL:

DESCRIPTION. The California Older Adult Stroop Test (COAST), published in 2010, is intended for adults age 60 or older. It is modeled after the original Stroop Color Word Test, which is a commonly used measure of executive functioning that involves cognitive flexibility, information processing speed, and focused attention (Lezak, Howieson, Bigler, & Tranel, 2012). A number of Stroop tests with varying instructions, stimuli (i.e., varying trials, number of items, number of colors), and scoring methods have been developed over the past several decades, though no one version appears dominant. According to the test authors, the COAST was "designed to minimize errors due to decreased visual acuity or color naming difficulty secondary to confusion or cataracts" (manual, p. 5), which often come with advancing age.

Much like the original Stroop (1935), the COAST includes three stimulus cards, each containing 10 rows of five items each. The test is presented in three parts and always in the same order. Prior to starting the test, the examiner must be certain that the examinee can read and is able to distinguish the three colors (red, yellow, and green). If the examinee cannot read or has trouble identifying the words or the colors, the test is discontinued. In the first part (Card 1-Color Task), the examinee is shown the stimulus card with colored squares only and asked to name the colors aloud, going from left to right on the card, as fast as he/she can. The examiner records the time it takes to complete the stimulus card, while also keeping track of the examinee's self-corrected and uncorrected errors.

In the second part (Card 2-Word Task), the examinee is presented with the stimulus card with the words *red, yellow,* and *green* printed in black ink in all capital letters. The examinee is instructed to read the words aloud (going from left to right), as fast as possible until the end of the stimulus card is reached. Again, the examiner records the time to complete the task as well as self-corrected and uncorrected errors.

In the last part (Card 3-Interference Task), the stimulus card with the words *red, yellow,* and *green* presented in capital letters in colored ink is shown. The examinee is instructed to "name the color of the ink each word is printed in," and to not read the words. The task is practiced until the examiner is sure that the examinee comprehends it. Once the examinee understands the task, he or she is instructed to name the color of the ink, and not to read the words, as fast as possible until the end of the stimulus card. The examiner again records time and self-corrected and uncorrected errors.

There are nine total derived scores. Three scores are obtained on each of the three COAST stimulus cards: time, self-corrected errors, and total errors.

DEVELOPMENT. The COAST was developed secondary to research suggesting that peripheral factors such as administration length, print size, and stimuli colors of the traditional Stroop task may be contributing to poorer performance, rather than true cognitive changes, among some older adults. Research on normal aging indicates that older individuals have increased difficulty distinguishing colors near the end of the visible spectrum of light (i.e., blue and green) due to changes within the eye including retinal degeneration, yellowing from cataracts, decreased lens transparency, cloudy intraocular fluid, or loss of visual accommodation.

Pilot testing between the COAST and the Golden (1978) version of the Stroop test was completed with a group of non-insulin-dependent Type II diabetics (n = 33), and healthy age-matched controls (n = 18). Neither group differed on completion time or error rate; however, participants who had a higher error rate on the color or color-word interference task, had the most errors on blue and green items and consequently longer completion times (Pachana, Thompson, Marcopulos, & Yoash-Gantz, 2004). Although other studies looking at the Golden Stroop have found similar trends between aging, dementia, and increased errors secondary to blue-green color confusion, a similar pattern has not been established on the COAST, even after controlling for error rate on the Stroop. Another analysis using standard neuropsychological measures found a strong association between completion time and error rate even after controlling for age and performance on memory measures, thereby supporting that the blue/green color confusion among healthy older adults is a significant phenomenon (Pachana et al., 2004).

Given the importance of discriminating between normal aging and true decline in cognitive ability, the developers were led to create a test designed to be minimally influenced by decreased visual acuity. As such, more easily distinguished colors of red, yellow, and green were used for the COAST. Stimuli print size also increased, leading to 50 stimuli on the page (versus the traditional 100), which also accommodated changes in visual acuity and fatigue.

TECHNICAL. The test manual indicates that the COAST is appropriate for use with both inpatient and outpatient adults and includes normative data (means and standard deviations) for Type II diabetics (n = 124), outpatients with depression (n = 39), psychiatric inpatients (n = 38), inpatients with dementia (n = 51), and healthy controls (community volunteers, n = 86; caregivers, n = 72). Age and education were found to be associated with overall performance (i.e., slowing) on the COAST, and slower cognitive processing secondary to advancing age has been consistently documented in the literature (Lezak et al., 2012). Similarly, significant differences in performance due to dementia, when compared to healthy controls, were also noted on the COAST, and are also consistently documented in other studies evaluating Stroop tasks. No gender differences were noted by the test authors when controlling for age and education, though there appears to be variability with this assertion according to other researchers. Across studies however, there is widespread consensus that those with the presence of a dementing illness perform poorer on the COAST and Stroop-like tests than healthy controls (Pachana et al., 2004).

Test-retest correlation coefficients were obtained with a combined sample of reportedly healthy community volunteers and Type II diabetics (n = 90); there were no between group differences. The test manual reports that correlation coefficients between time to completion (r = .72 to r = .91), self-corrected errors (r = .50 to r = .02), and uncorrected errors (r = .37 to r = .04) across three time intervals reflect stability of the measure over time. A small sample of long-term care residents with degenerative dementia (n = 15) was used to establish test-retest reliability over a 1- to 2-day interval among those with stable cognitive impairment (time to complete, r = .82 to .95; self-corrected and uncorrected errors, r = .47 to 1.00).

Practice effects were calculated using a two (i.e., healthy volunteer, diabetic) by three (administration time point) MANOVA. The test authors indicate that there were not any practice effects for the color (Card 1) or word (Card 2) trials of the COAST, a finding validated by three separate administrations at 1- to 2-month intervals (Pachana, Marcopulos, Yoash-Gantz, & Thompson, 1997). In contrast, the test authors did find a practice effect for the interference trial (Card 3) and caution against re-administration at a period of less than 3 months. The test manual suggests that the measure be re-administered at 6-month intervals, ideally, to avoid practice effects.

Construct validity evidence was demonstrated based on comparisons between the COAST and the Golden (1978) version of the Stroop. Correlation coefficients of completion time among all three trials on both measures ranged from r = .50 to r = .89 (Pachana et al., 1997).

COMMENTARY. The COAST is a brief and easily administered task. It appears to be an acceptable version of the Stroop test, particularly when trying to account for visual changes associated with normal aging. Strengths of the measure include evidence in support of construct validity, large print, short format, and removal of the blue/green stimuli that older adults have found to be confusing. Scoring is straightforward and accomplished by referencing normative data in the test manual and calculating standard scores. However, once scores are obtained, the manual does not provide guidance with respect to interpretation.

Although the test manual indicates that the measure is intended for older adults (i.e., over age 60), normative data are based on small convenience samples with limited variability in terms of cognitive functioning, visual ability, or age. Additional data with greater variability in age, visual ability, and cognitive functioning are needed. Similarly, normative data also would be strengthened by including a more ethnically and geographically diverse sample, as well as by including norms for specific neurological (i.e., multiple sclerosis, Parkinson's disease, type of dementia) and psychiatric (i.e., anxiety) populations. In general, reliability and validity evidence for the COAST appears acceptable.

SUMMARY. The COAST was designed to be a more precise measure of executive functioning (as compared to existing Stroop tests), for older adults who have been found to experience changes in vision with increasing age. The test appears to meet this goal, though additional data are needed to increase the normative sample and strengthen its representativeness.

REVIEWER'S REFERENCES

Golden, C. J. (1978). Stroop Color and Word Test. Chicago, IL: Stoelting.

Lezak, M. D., Howieson, D. B., Bigler, E. D., & Tranel, D. (2012). Stroop tests. In *Neuropsychological assessment* (5th ed., pp. 416-418). New York, NY: Oxford University Press.

Pachana, N. A., Marcopulos, B. A., Yoash-Gantz, R., & Thompson, L. W. (1997). California Older Adult Stroop Test (COAST): Pilot test results for subjects with non-insulin-dependent Type II diabetes mellitus and age-matched controls. In G. M. Habermann (Ed.), *Looking back and moving forward: 50 years of New Zealand psychology* (pp. 171-178). Wellington, New Zealand: New Zealand Psychological Society.

Pachana, N. A., Thompson, L. W., Marcopulos, B. A., & Yoash-Gantz, R. (2004). California Older Adult Stroop Test (COAST): Development of a Stroop test adapted for geriatric populations. *Clinical Gerontologist, 27*(3), 3-22. doi:10.1300/J018v27n03_02

Stroop, J. R. (1935). Studies of interference in serial verbal reactions. *Journal of Experimental Psychology, 18,* 643-662.

[24]

California Verbal Learning Test–Third Edition.

Purpose: Designed to assess "the strategies and processes involved in learning, recalling, and recognizing verbal information."

Population: Ages 16-90.

Publication Dates: 1983-2017.

Acronym: CVLT 3.

Scores, 77: 16 core scaled scores: Trial 1 Correct, Trial 2 Correct, Trial 3 Correct, Trial 4 Correct, Trial 5 Correct, List B Correct, Short Delay Free Recall Correct, Short Delay Cued Recall Correct, Long Delay Free Recall Correct, Long Delay Cued Recall Correct, Total Intrusions, Long Delay Yes/No Recognition Total Hits, Long Delay Yes/No Recognition Total False Positives, Recognition

Discriminability, Recognition Discriminability Nonparametric, Forced Choice Recognition Hits; 4 standard scores: Trials 1-5 Correct, Delayed Recall Correct, Total Recall Correct, Total Recall Responses; 33 process scaled scores: Trial 5 Semantic Clustering (Chance Adjusted), Trials 1-5 Semantic Clustering (Chance Adjusted), Trials 1-5 Serial Clustering (Chance Adjusted), Trials 1-5 % Recall Primacy, Trials 1-5 % Recall Middle, Trials 1-5 % Recall Recency, Trials 1-5 Recall Consistency, Trials 1-5 Learning Slope Analysis, Trials 1-2 Learning Slope Analysis, Trials 2-5 Learning Slope Analysis, Trials 1-5 Recall Discriminability, Trials 1-5 Intrusions, Short Delay Free Recall Semantic Clustering (Chance Adjusted), Short Delay Free Recall Discriminability, Short Delay Cued Recall Discriminability, Long Delay Free Recall Semantic Clustering (Chance Adjusted), Long Delay Free Recall Discriminability, Long Delay Cued Recall Discriminability, Delayed Recall Discriminability, Delayed Recall Intrusions, Free Recall Intrusions, Cued Recall Intrusions, Total Novel Intrusions, Total Across/Within Trial Repeated Intrusions, Total Repetitions, Total Target Repetitions, Total Recall Discriminability, Cued Recall Discriminability, List A vs. List B Recognition Discriminability, List A vs. Novel/Prototypical Recognition Discriminability, List A vs. Novel/Unrelated Recognition Discriminability, Response Bias, Response Bias Nonparametric; 6 contrast scaled scores: List B Correct vs. Trial 1 Correct, Short Delay Free Recall Correct vs. Trial 5 Correct, Long Delay Free Recall Correct vs. Trial 5 Correct, Long Delay Free Recall Correct vs. Short Delay Free Recall Correct, Long Delay Free Recall Correct vs. Recognition Discriminability, Long Delay Free Recall Discriminability vs. Recognition Discriminability; 18 base rates: Cued Recall Novel Intrusions, Cued Recall Across/Within Trial Intrusions, Cued Recall Target Category Errors, Novel Intrusions/Total Intrusions Ratio, Novel Cued Recall Intrusions/Total Cued Recall Intrusions Ratio, Targets/Targets + Intrusions Ratio, Targets/Targets + Target Repetitions Ratio, List B False Positives, List B/Shared False Positives, List B/Nonshared False Positives, Novel/Prototypical False Positives, Novel/Unrelated False Positives, Recall Critical Items, Yes/No Recognition Critical Items, Noncategory Intrusions, Across-List Intrusions, Synonym/Subordinate Intrusions.
Administration: Individual.
Forms, 3: Standard Form, Alternate Form, Brief Form.
Price Data, 2020: $417.20 per complete print kit including manual (2017, 280 pages) and 25 record forms (Standard/Alternate/Brief); $430 per online kit including 1-year online subscription; $135.70 per print manual; $101 per digital manual; $104.60 per 25 record forms (Standard or Alternate); $83.70 per 25 Brief record forms; $40 per 1-year online subscription (includes unlimited score reports; reduced prices available for longer subscriptions); $2.30 per individual online score report.
Time: Approximately 45 minutes for administration including delay intervals.
Comments: Administered and scored via paper and pencil or online.
Authors: Dean C. Delis, Joel H. Kramer, Edith Kaplan, and Beth A. Ober.
Publisher: Pearson.

a) BRIEF FORM.

Scores, 26: 13 core scaled scores: Trial 1 Correct, Trial 2 Correct, Trial 3 Correct, Trial 4 Correct, Short Delay Free Recall Correct, Long Delay Free Recall Correct, Long Delay Cued Recall Correct, Total Intrusions, Long Delay Yes/No Recognition Total Hits, Long Delay Yes/No Recognition Total False Positives, Recognition Discriminability, Recognition Discriminability Nonparametric, Forced Choice Recognition Hits; 4 standard scores: Trials 1-4 Correct, Delayed Recall Correct, Total Recall Correct, Total Recall Responses; 4 process scaled scores: Trials 1-4 Intrusions, Free Recall Intrusions, Cued Recall Intrusions, Total Repetitions; 5 base rates: Forced Choice Recognition Hits, Recall Critical Items, Yes/No Recognition Critical Items, Noncategory Intrusions, Synonym/Subordinate Intrusions.
Time: Approximately 25 minutes for administration including delay intervals.

Cross References: For reviews by Anita M. Hubley and Cederick O. Lindskog of the second edition, see 16:41; see also T5:376 (35 references); for a review by Ray Fenton of the Research Edition, see 13:42 (57 references); see also T4:364 (12 references).

Review of the California Verbal Learning Test—Third Edition by MARY (RINA) M. CHITTOORAN, Associate Professor, School of Education, Saint Louis University, St. Louis, MO:

DESCRIPTION. The California Verbal Learning Test—Third Edition (CVLT 3) is an individually administered standardized measure that assesses how adults, ages 16-90, recognize, recall, and learn verbal information. The test comes in three forms: Standard, Alternate, and Brief, and involves several kinds of tasks: immediate free recall, short delay free recall, long delay free recall, and an optional forced choice recognition. The test manual states that the CVLT 3 may be used by a range of professionals including neuropsychologists and psychologists as an aid to identify verbal learning deficiencies or as an adjunct to more comprehensive forms of assessment. Test materials include a spiral-bound, 264-page paperback manual with technical information and normative data as well as test booklets for each of the three forms. Time required for administration varies from 25 to 45 minutes, depending on which form of the test is being used.

Administration of the CVLT 3 may be in a traditional paper-and-pencil format or can be achieved through the test publisher's digital platform, an approach that significantly simplifies scoring. The test can be scored manually or automatically, and performance is recorded as verbal responses and as raw scores. An examinee's verbal learning can be represented by core scaled scores, process scaled scores (which allow an examiner to record information that may not be readily available using numbers alone), contrast scaled scores, standard scores (with a mean of 100 and a standard deviation of 15), an overall Verbal Learning Index, base scores (cumulative percentages), and percentile ranks.

DEVELOPMENT. The CVLT 3 and its predecessors, the CVLT and the CVLT-II, were developed out of a need to assess verbal learning and memory in adults. The initial version of the CVLT was one of the first clinical measures to use principles of cognitive science "to quantify multiple processes of learning and memory" (manual, p. 1). Refinements, which included improved examinee instructions and refined lists of target words, were instituted and implemented on each subsequent version of the test.

TECHNICAL. An independent study of the CVLT-II determined the equivalence of the CVLT-II paper-and-pencil form and the digital administration format; therefore, all standardization data for the CVLT 3 were collected using the digital platform between June 2016 and February 2017. This standardization sample included 700 adolescents and adults, 16 to 90 years, with all participants being paid an incentive for study participation. The gender distribution for those under 60 was equal, whereas that of participants over 60 matched Census figures gathered in 2015. Race and ethnicity reflected Census data, as well. Education ranged from 0 to 8 years of schooling to a bachelor's degree plus. Finally, geographic representation was determined by dividing the United States into four major geographic regions, with the number of participants reflecting the number of residents in that area. The test manual includes a number of tables that provide information about the standardization sample.

Internal consistency and test-retest reliability coefficients were determined by the test authors to be less useful for this type of test and population; therefore, alternate form reliability was selected as evidence of both test stability and equivalence of measures. Alternate form reliability of the CVLT 3 Standard Form and its Alternate Form was examined with a sample of 213 adults with a mean age of 50.9, with approximately equal numbers of males and females. Reliability of the index scores was good, ranging from .75 to .83 with trial-based coefficients being lower (delayed recall ranged from .56 to .71). Alternate form reliability of the Standard Form and the Brief Form with an equivalent sample yielded similar but lower coefficients for the index scores (as might be expected given the brevity of this form) ranging from .66 to .79; delayed recall coefficients ranged from .43 to .67.

The test manual reports that construct evidence of validity of CVLT scores has been demonstrated in numerous studies over the decades; therefore, the test authors chose to compare the CVLT 3 with the CVLT-II as evidence of validity, given that the target lists and the yes/no distractor items were the same. A random sample (n = 594) was selected from the CVLT-II standardization sample and matched with the CVLT 3 standardization sample on variables related to age, gender, ethnicity, and education. Results suggested equivalence between the two tests, with sample means being slightly higher on the CVLT-II and differences showing up in lower age ranges. Factor analysis with a group of non-clinical individuals (n = 698) was conducted as further evidence of validity; five factors (General Verbal Learning, Response Discrimination, Organizational Strategies, Acquisition Rate, and Primary Recency Effects) were extracted, showing equivalence with the factor solution obtained on a similar examination of the CLVT-II. The test manual also uses data from the forced choice recognition trial to address examinee effort and subsequent performance validity of the CVLT 3. The test manual includes a chapter on the meaning and clinical utility of various constructs upon which this measure is based, for example, immediate recall and free recall. Finally, the test manual offers information on the performance of the CVLT and the CVLT-II as examined in the literature from 1999 to 2017 with summaries of studies in areas like demographics and various conditions such as traumatic brain injury and schizophrenia.

COMMENTARY. The CVLT, in its various iterations, has been a welcome addition to the testing landscape since the 1980s. It has a long and impressive history of use with various populations, is carefully conceptualized and developed, and has been evaluated by researchers in several disciplines; in fact, the test manual states that more than 5,000 studies of earlier versions of the CVLT 3 have been published since the measure was first introduced in 1987. The test is firmly situated in the literature on assessment, memory, and verbal learning and as such, has a sound theoretical foundation. When the test was first developed, it was based on the recognition that memory is complex and cannot be represented by a unitary score. Instead, memory functioning in adults takes on different forms, based on the particular type of neurological or psychiatric conditions displayed by the examinee. The CVLT 3 is unique in that it does not just assess how much verbal learning occurs, it also assesses exactly *how* that learning occurs. More specifically, it provides qualitative information about examinees' error patterns, the kinds of learning strategies employed, and ways in which memory breaks down under testing conditions.

Test materials, including the manual and the various record forms, are neat and well organized, comprehensive, relatively inexpensive, and are laid out in pleasing shades of green, purple, blue, and white. Users are provided with detailed information on the test and its development, as well as administration, scoring, and interpretation information. In addition, extensive norms tables are provided for all three forms of the test. Information on standardization is comprehensive and detailed, reliability estimates are superior, and evidence of validity is generally good, with a unique emphasis on performance validity, a phenomenon that has seen considerable growth in neuropsychological assessment. The test manual provides several examples of scoring for various subtests that would be useful to clinicians. The Standard Form and the Alternate Form are useful in cases where retesting is necessary. The Brief Form offers a quick way to screen for potential problems with verbal learning that can then be followed up with more comprehensive measures of functioning in specific areas of concern.

SUMMARY. The California Verbal Learning Test—Third Edition appears to be one of the few published measures of its kind in that it assesses not just how much, but how verbal information is recognized and learned under conditions of immediate, short delay, and long delay free recall. It is suitable for use with a wide range of adolescents and adults with both typical and atypical functioning, and its development and technical merits are superior. As such, the CVLT 3 is highly recommended as a measure of verbal learning that can be used as an adjunct to other measures of verbal functioning, such as tests of intelligence and academic achievement.

Review of the California Verbal Learning Test—Third Edition by RICHARD RUTH, Associate Professor of Clinical Psychology, The George Washington University, KATHERINE MARSHALL WOODS, Assistant Professor of Clinical Psychology, The George Washington University, and RACHEL FENTON, graduate student in clinical psychology, The George Washington University, Washington, DC:

DESCRIPTION. The California Verbal Learning Test—Third Edition (CVLT 3) is a revised version of a test widely used in assessing neuropsychological questions (Strauss, Sherman, & Spreen, 2006). Acknowledging its conceptual grounding in Kaplan's (1988) process approach to neuropsychological assessment, its purpose is to evaluate "the strategies and processes involved in learning, recalling, and recognizing verbal information" (manual, p. 1).

In its previous versions, the CVLT and the CVLT-II (Delis, Kramer, Kaplan, & Ober, 1987, 2000), this test has won acclaim for helping clinicians and researchers not only to assess whether verbal learning and memory problems may be present, but also to delineate specific process variables involved in verbal learning and memory relevant to diagnosis, educational planning, medical decision-making, measuring rehabilitation progress, and other applications. The CVLT and CVLT-II have been widely researched and found to meet high standards of internal consistency, test/retest reliability, and construct and predictive validity.

The CVLT 3 offers two alternate forms in addition to a brief form. On both full-length forms, lists of target words are administered, following standardized instructions, over five trials. Then, a second list of words is administered, as an interference condition. Next, recall of the first list of words is assessed on free and cued recall, and re-assessed after a specified delay. Finally, the test taker is asked to recognize which word in a series of word pairs appeared on the original list of words.

The test manual describes administration instructions in clear language, readily accessible to working clinicians and researchers. Instructions also are printed on the answer sheets to facilitate the examiner's task.

The CVLT 3 is available in both paper-and-pencil and digital versions. When the paper-and-pencil version of the test is given, the examiner records correct and incorrect responses as well as qualitative and process information on the nature of errors—such as intrusion errors—on a well-designed, user-friendly answer sheet. On the digital version, this information is recorded on a well-designed tablet interface.

Raw scores can be converted to standard scores using detailed tables in the test manual. However, the procedure for calculating the more than 30 process scores by hand is, the test's authors acknowledge, cumbersome, so many relevant process scores realistically can be obtained only by using the digital version of the test, whose software calculates these scores in minutes.

The CVLT 3 is administered individually. Estimated administration time, including the required delay interval, is 45 minutes. The test may be administered by measurement professionals with training and experience sensitizing and equipping them to interpret process results from a complex neuropsychological instrument.

The brief version of the CVLT 3 can be used as a screening instrument. It yields a narrower set of standard and process scores.

DEVELOPMENT. The developers of the CVLT 3 made changes thoughtfully, based on evolutions in contemporary neuropsychological thinking and appraisal of cumulative experience with the CVLT and CVLT-II. Target words on the word lists were not revised because these have proven effective for the test's intended purposes. The principal changes involve a national, Census-matched standardization and norming sample; introduction of intrusion and yes/no recognition measures to enhance the test's differential neuropsychological diagnostic capacity; options for both paper-and-pencil and digital administration and scoring; use of standard scores rather than *z*-scores to facilitate comparing CVLT 3 scores with scores on other tests given as part of the variety of kinds of batteries to which the CVLT 3 can usefully contribute; and availability of scores adjusted for age, education, and binary gender.

The CVLT 3 was developed by an impressive, multidisciplinary team including professionals with expertise in psychometrics, research design and methodology, programming, digital media development, and design, as well as recognized experts in neuropsychology. The result is a handsome, user-friendly product that, importantly, is designed and structured to minimize chances of administration and scoring errors owing to awkward or cumbersome formatting.

TECHNICAL. The CVLT 3 standardization and norming sample of 700 adolescents and adults matched 2015 U.S. Census Bureau figures (the latest such figures available) for race, ethnicity, binary gender, education, and geography, a stratification that impresses as reasonable and comparable to or exceeding the technical parameters of other sophisticated neuropsychological tests. Age cohorts were 16-19, 20-29, 30-44, 45-59, 60-69, 70-79, and 80-90. Gender cohorts were equal for males and females for persons 16-59, and congruent with proportions in the population for those over 60, consistent with relevant demographic realities in the U.S. population. Educational level cohorts were those with 0-8 years of schooling, 9-11 years of schooling and no high school diploma, a high school diploma or equivalent, some college or technical schooling short of completion of a bachelor's degree, and a bachelor's degree or greater academic achievement, stratification that seems reasonable and consistent with that of other major neuropsychological tests. Racial/ethnic groups studied were African Americans, Asians, Hispanics, "other racial/ethnic examinees," and Whites, based on proportions of the English-speaking population within each age band according to the 2015 U.S. Census data. Proportionate representation of persons from the Midwest, Northeast, South, and West was achieved. As characteristics of these demographic categories can bear directly on verbal learning and indirectly on verbal memory functions, this representativeness is a welcome technical feature of the CVLT 3.

The test manual, acknowledging that test/retest reliability in persons with progressive memory problems may be difficult, assesses reliability by providing information about alternate form reliability and Brief Form compared to Standard Form reliability. Demographic characteristics of the stratified sample used in the reliability studies were considered with care, seem reasonable, and are reported in the test manual. Age-adjusted alternate form and Standard/Brief Form reliability estimates, using Cohen's Formula 10.4 and corrected for variability in the standardization sample, are reported for a broad variety of CVLT 3 standard and process scores. Coefficients vary across a wide range (from .15 to .83 for alternate form and from .14 to .80 for Standard/Brief Form comparisons) with often lower reliability for process scores and somewhat higher values (.60s to .70s range) for many standard scores, as is not uncommonly found in other neuropsychological measures. Future appraisal of the internal stability of CVLT 3 scores, beyond issues of internal stability relevant to the reliability of scores, would be welcome.

CVLT 3 validity is appraised in part by comparing performance on the CVLT-II, a measure with demonstrated evidence of validity, with performance on the CVLT 3. In a study with an impressive sample size (n = 594), score levels were found to be largely equivalent, with CVLT-II scores slightly higher than CVLT 3 scores, as is not uncommon when tests are re-normed. This beginning is promising, but less than fully satisfying, especially given known problems with ecological validity and predictive validity in neuropsychological tests (Chaytor & Schmitter-Edgecombe, 2003). It is hoped that future studies can appraise CVLT 3 external validity directly.

Factor analyses were conducted to provide construct evidence of validity for the CVLT 3, using a nonclinical sample (n = 698) and studying 18 key CVLT 3 variables, a strategy designed to overcome problematic artifactual findings in previous factor-analytic studies of memory tests. These analyses employed random sampling and matching procedures that established equivalence of the current and previous versions of the test. These results offer users of the CVLT 3 confidence in the evidence of the revised measure's robust construct validity, an important consideration in many applications of this test.

Chapter 6 of the CVLT 3 manual provides a thorough review of the extensive literature on the CVLT and the CVLT-II. This literature provides robust evidence of these tests' clinical utility, which is offered as implied evidence of the tests' reliability and validity. However, as research on the CVLT 3 is not included, it cannot yet be concluded that it will yield similar results.

COMMENTARY. The CVLT 3 is a carefully, thoughtfully revised version of a well-known test of clinically relevant verbal learning and memory functions, with impressive psychometric qualities and broad, proven utility for a wide variety of clinical applications. Review of the CVLT 3 convinces these reviewers that its revisions were made reasonably and thoughtfully and hold potential to improve further the appeal of this measure for researchers and clinicians and its broad employ. The test materials are well-constructed and user-friendly. The major change is that clinicians will have to consider whether the paper-and-pencil version of the test will yield the process scores they need to address questions of differential diagnosis and treatment/intervention planning with adequate precision, specificity, and nuance. For many applications, switching to the digital version of the test will be necessary.

Potential users of the CVLT 3 will be well advised to bear in mind a few cautions that arise from aspects of the measure's development and some of its technical qualities as they apply this robust and widely useful measure. First, some populations with disorders the test is designed to help detect and assess were excluded from the standardization and norming study—as examples, people with active physical or psychological problems that could depress CVLT 3 performance; people with intellectual disabilities; and people on medications that could affect cognitive functioning. The practical difficulties of including such populations in the test development process are acknowledged with respect. However, the result of this decision is that a clinician or researcher working with such populations will only be able to infer, and will not be able to know from direct, empirically derived data, what process variables may play roles in the verbal learning and memory functions of persons from such populations.

A second caution involves another aspect of the population on which the CVLT 3 was standardized and normed. In a commendable attempt to avoid inadvertent bias, the standardization and norming studies recruited and utilized a geographically diverse, age-stratified sample of 700 persons, in percentages matching the distribution of racial/ethnic groups in updated U.S. Census data. However, for some racial/ethnic groups, this process resulted in questionable representation. For example, the assumption was made, incorrectly, that African Americans, Asian Americans, Hispanic populations, and Native Americans lack various dimensions of internal diversity that need to be captured. Inferring from the percentages reported and the number in the sample, some cells appear to have been too small for parametric analysis. Again acknowledging with respect the considerable difficulty those developing tests often encounter in their committed attempts to recruit robust, racially/ethnically diverse samples in the test development process, these technical features of the CVLT 3 will need to be borne in mind when clinicians use the measure with members of racial/ethnic minority groups. Clinical appraisal of cultural and ecological factors that may affect obtained CVLT 3 scores and process observations will be necessary, given the evidence that persons from diverse racial/ethnic groups do not all perform similarly on many neuropsychological tests (Ardila, 2007), especially when, as with U.S. ethnic/racial group members, the cultural differences involve dimensions of cultural individualism vs. collectivism (Chiao et al., 2013; Park & Huang, 2010).

Third, while the developers of the CVLT 3 are to be strongly commended for including optional gender norms in their scoring system, the gender norms for the CVLT 3 incorporate gender-binary criteria. The embedded assumption is that the CVLT 3 will be unlikely to be used to evaluate transgender and gender-nonconforming populations. However, tests such as the CVLT 3 are widely used with such populations, both to help assess whether candidates for hormone replacement therapies and gender assignment surgeries possess verbal learning and memory skills felt necessary for compliance with medical, surgical, and post-surgical care (Keo-Meier & Fitzgerald, 2017) and to help assess the learning-related problems that have been found to be particularly prevalent in transgender and gender-nonconforming populations (Berg & Edwards-Leeper, 2018; Sandil & Henise, 2017). The American Psychological Association has adopted practice guidelines that ask all psychologists to avoid cisgender-normative assumptions and related practices (American Psychological Association, 2015). It is especially salient that this be held in mind with the use of the CVLT 3, given recent estimates that the transgender and gender-nonconforming population may be up to 12 times larger than was previously estimated, especially in rising generations (Johns et al., 2019).

As with all new tests whose applicability and robust psychometric properties make it likely they will be widely and rapidly adopted, there is room for further development of some technical aspects of the CVLT 3. Work to establish further evidence of the internal stability and external/ecological validity of test scores can enhance the informed use of the instrument. Whether research findings using the CVLT and CVLT-II will be replicated with the CVLT 3—and, if not, whether the changes have to do with changes in presenting neuropsychological profiles in clinical populations or qualities of the CVLT 3 itself—remains to be clarified. As with the cautions mentioned in this review regarding the use of the CVLT 3 with persons with disabilities, persons with active medical or psychological symptomatology, racial/ethnic minority populations, and transgender and gender-nonconforming persons, it is hoped these questions can be elucidated with future research using the CVLT 3.

The reviewers wish to be clear that they are raising concerns to be held in mind when clinicians and researchers employ the CVLT 3 for some applications, and not broader or more fundamental criticisms of this justly highly regarded test. The CVLT 3 is a well-conceptualized, well-developed, psychometrically robust test that will be a valuable tool in the armamentarium of many kinds of measurement professionals; and, as with all tests, such professionals will have the training to use the CVLT 3 with both its considerable contributions and appropriate cautions taken into consideration.

SUMMARY. The CVLT 3, an updated version of an established, highly regarded, and widely used test of verbal learning and verbal memory functions, will continue to be useful to clinicians addressing neuropsychological issues in a variety of settings. Offering a mix of standard scores assessing intactness vs. compromise of verbal learning and verbal recall, and more than 30 process scores bringing into focus how a test taker accomplishes, fails to accomplish, or faces challenges in accomplishing the functions the test targets, the test incorporates valuable advances in its conceptual foundations and constituent elements that will enhance its capacity to continue to be useful in differential diagnosis, intervention planning, and other applications.

Some concerns have been discussed regarding the exclusion from the standardization and norming studies of persons with some of the conditions the test aims to help assess, the as-yet undemonstrated assumption that the CVLT 3 will replicate findings from studies that have used the CVLT and the CVLT-II, the development of norms for racial and ethnic minority populations, and the use of gender-binary norms that embed cisgender assumptions. It is not uncommon for such concerns to arise with the revision of a major neuropsychological test that strives for wide clinical usage and good ecological and predictive validity. It is hoped that research that takes up these concerns will enhance the clinical utility of the CVLT 3.

REVIEWERS' REFERENCES

American Psychological Association. (2015). Guidelines for psychological practice with transgender and gender nonconforming people. *American Psychologist, 70*, 832-864.

Ardila, A. (2007). The impact of culture on neuropsychological test performance. In B. P. Uzzell, M. Ponton, & A. Ardila (Eds.), *International handbook of cross-cultural neuropsychology* (pp. 23-44). Mahwah, NJ: Erlbaum.

Berg, D., & Edwards-Leeper, L. (2018). Child and family assessment. In C. Keo-Meier & D. Ehrensaft (Eds.), *The gender affirmative model: An interdisciplinary approach to supporting transgender and gender expansive youth* (pp. 101-124). Washington, DC: American Psychological Association.

Chaytor, N., & Schmitter-Edgecombe, M. (2003). The ecological validity of neuropsychological tests: A review of the literature on everyday cognitive skills. *Neuropsychology Review, 13*, 181-197.

Chiao, J. Y., Cheon, B. K., Pornpattananangkul, N., Mrazek, A. J., & Blizinsky, K. D. (2013). Cultural neuroscience: Progress and promise. *Psychological Inquiry, 24*, 1-19.

Delis, D. C., Kramer, J. H., Kaplan, E., & Ober, B. A. (2000). California Verbal Learning Test, Second Edition. San Antonio, TX: The Psychological Corporation.

Delis, D. C., Kramer, J. H., Kaplan, E., & Ober, B. A. (1987). California Verbal Learning Test. San Antonio, TX: The Psychological Corporation.

Johns, M. M., Lowry, R., Andrzejewski, J., Barrios, L. C., Demissie, Z., McManus, T., ... Underwood, J. M. (2019). Transgender identity and experiences of violence victimization, substance use, suicide risk, and sexual risk behaviors among high school students—19 states and large urban school districts, 2017. *MMWR Morbidity and Mortality Weekly Report, 68*, 67–71.

Kaplan, E. (1988). The process approach to neuropsychological assessment. *Aphasiology, 2*, 309-312.

Keo-Meier, C. L., & Fitzgerald, K. M. (2017). Affirmative psychological testing and neurocognitive assessment with transgender adults. *Psychiatric Clinics of North America, 40*, 51-64.

Park, D. C., & Huang, C. M. (2010). Culture wires the brain: A cognitive neuroscience perspective. *Perspectives on Psychological Science, 5*, 391-400.

Sandil, R., & Henise, S. (2017). Making psychology trans-inclusive and trans-affirmative: Recommendations for research and practice. In R. Ruth & E. Santacruz (Eds.), *LGBT psychology and mental health: Emerging research and advances* (pp. 47-67). Santa Barbara, CA: Praeger.

Strauss, E., Sherman, E. M. S., & Spreen, O. (2006). *A compendium of neuropsychological tests: Administration, norms, and commentary* (3rd ed.). New York, NY: Oxford University Press.

[25]

The Camden Memory Tests.

Purpose: Designed "to fulfill a clinical need that was not met by existing memory tests."
Population: Ages 85 and younger.
Publication Date: 1996.
Scores: 5 tests: Pictorial Recognition Memory Test, Topographical Recognition Memory Test, Paired Associate Learning Test, Short Recognition Memory Test for Words, Short Recognition Memory Test for Faces.
Administration: Individual.
Price Data, 2019: $450 per set of all 5 tests including manual and 5 packs of scoring sheets.
Time: Administration time not reported.
Comments: "Tests are intended to be presented as individual memory tests, not as a battery."
Author: Elizabeth K. Warrington.
Publisher: Routledge Psychology.

Review of The Camden Memory Tests by ELIZABETH E. MacDOUGALL, Associate Professor of Psychology and Counseling, Hood College, Frederick, MD:

DESCRIPTION. The Camden Memory Tests are a collection of five individually administered memory tests developed for clinical use. The test manual states that these tests were designed to be easier and shorter than most available memory tests and to be standardized and validated for use with older adults. The test author emphasizes that "pragmatic" considerations were given top priority in developing these tests (manual, p. 2). Additionally, the test author notes these tests will "add to the neuropsychologist's armamentarium for the assessment of neurological and neuropsychiatric patients" (manual, p. 1). Although bundled as a package, The Camden Memory Tests are not intended to be used as a battery but, rather, as five individual memory tests assessing pictorial recognition memory (CPRMT), topographical recognition memory (CTRMT), paired associate learning (CPALT), recognition memory for words (CSRMT-W), and recognition memory for faces (CSRMT-F). The test manual describes the CPRMT as an extremely simple test of recognition memory for pictorial material (photographs of scenes in Camden, London), and it is recommended as a warm-up for patients who might be anxious or who are having difficulties with attention/concentration. The test author also suggests that it may be useful with patients who are motivated to fake bad, as most people are not able to judge the difficulty level of the test. The CTRMT is an alternative to the test author's Recognition Memory Test (RMT) for Faces (Warrington, 1984). She argues that topographical stimuli are ecologically valid, in a similar way as faces, with neural networks that can be dissociated. The test stimuli are 30 color photographs of streets, parks, and buildings. The test author developed the CPALT to try to overcome the problems with ceiling and floor effects found on a similar paired-associates test on the Wechsler Memory Scale. As such, the CPALT includes word-pairs of "equivalent and moderate difficulty" (manual, p. 4). Finally, the CSRMT-W and the CSRMT-F are short but slightly more difficult versions of Warrington's (1984) standard RMT, with greater sensitivity for identifying memory dysfunction in younger individuals.

The manual for The Camden Memory Tests is extremely short, but it is sturdy with laminated pages that will undoubtedly last longer than most typical standard paper manuals. All administration materials are supplied, and the stimulus materials/books are sturdy and attractive. An appendix in the test manual provides straightforward verbatim administration instructions for each test, and scoring is simple and clear on the record forms. The test manual contains tables with means and standard deviations for each test by age band, which may facilitate transformation of a patient's raw score into a *z* score. Additionally, another appendix provides percentile ranks by age band to facilitate the interpretation of raw scores. However, the test manual provides no explicit guidelines for the interpretation of test scores, nor does it address the education, training, or credentials recommended for individuals wishing to administer, score, and interpret the tests. In addition, the test manual provides no information about approximately how long it takes to administer each test.

DEVELOPMENT. The test author clearly states that practical clinical considerations guided the development of The Camden Memory Tests. It appears that the test author modeled each test after existing memory tests, with the goal of making each test shorter than the test after which it was modeled. Although Warrington mentions creating five "easy" memory tests, the CSRMT-W and the CSRMT-F are described as more difficult than the standard RMT (Warrington, 1984). The test manual provides only very limited additional information about the development of each individual test and references no theory associated with the development of these tests.

TECHNICAL. Two standardization samples included participants recruited from organizations and businesses in England and screened for previous medical conditions that might negatively affect cognition. Exclusion criteria included those with a history of such conditions, as well as those who had not been educated in the British school system. An initial sample of 424 participants completed three of the Camden Memory Tests: the CPRMT, the CTRMT, and the CPALT. Normative data from this sample are presented in four age bands: under 40, 40-54, 55-70, 71-85. A second sample of 122 participants completed the remaining two of The Camden Memory Tests, the CSRMT-W and the CSRMT-F. Normative data from this sample are presented in three age bands: under 50, 50-69, 70-85. The samples are described in a table in the test manual, but demographic information about the samples is limited to means and standard deviations for ages of participants in each age band, along with means and standard deviations for their reading IQ equivalents (as measured by the North American Reading Test). The test author also provides separate norms (means and standard deviations) for each test for patients with right-sided, left-sided, and diffuse brain lesions. Cutoff scores based on the 5th percentile identify a "significant deficit" (manual, p. 2).

The test author presents no score reliability evidence for any of the Camden Memory Tests. In addition, this reviewer could find no manuscripts investigating the score reliability of The Camden Memory Tests since their publication in 1996.

The test author makes no reference to content, convergent, or discriminant evidence of validity. She states that "validation studies" were conducted "to establish the task sensitivity and task selectivity" (manual, p. 1) by examining group differences between patients with preexisting unilateral or diffuse brain damage and normal controls. The 96 participants with "lateralized cerebral lesions" are described as 32 females and 64 males "with proven unilateral cerebral lesions, 48 of the right hemisphere and 48 of the left hemisphere" (manual, p. 2). No additional information is provided about from where these participants came or what condition/circumstance led to their diagnoses. A table in the test manual presents means and standard deviations for age, reading IQ equivalent, prorated verbal IQ, and prorated performance IQ for participants with right vs. left lesions. No other demographic information is provided for this sample. A second validation sample included 60 patients (20 females; 40 males) with "established neurological conditions that are known to cause bilateral brain damage (e.g., cortical degenerative conditions)" (manual, p. 2). A table in the manual presents means and standard deviations for age, reading IQ equivalent, and prorated full scale IQ, broken down by severity of their brain damage based on an analysis of the discrepancy between reading IQ equivalents and full-scale IQ: no significant intellectual impairment, mild intellectual impairment, moderate intellectual impairment. The test author provides no other demographic information for this sample and no rationale or empirical support for this discrepancy formula. The test manual provides no statistical evidence to support the sensitivity, specificity, positive predictive value, or negative predictive value of the tests. In addition, this reviewer could find no manuscripts investigating test score validity of The Camden Memory Tests since their publication in 1996.

COMMENTARY. The test author appears to have achieved the goal of developing memory tests that are shorter—and, in several cases, easier—than many of the memory tests used by neuropsychologists in 1996. In addition, the test materials are durable and reasonably well-designed, with clear and straightforward administration and scoring procedures. On the other hand, score reliability and validity evidence are all but completely absent. In addition, for the tests to be useful outside of London, a more representative normative sample is required. Although the test author states that she developed The Camden Memory Tests specifically to assess memory functions in older adults, it does not appear that any special effort was made to gather a standardization sample of older adults, nor was there a targeted effort to use older adult clinical validation samples. In fact, the average age of individuals in the unilateral brain lesion groups (right and left) was 49, and the average age of patients in the diffuse brain lesion groups was 51 to 56. In addition, although most memory problems in older adults are caused by Alzheimer's disease, only 60 patients with "diffuse" brain disease comprised the clinical validation sample, and their brain disease was vaguely described as being caused by "established neurological conditions" for which "cortical degenerative conditions" was given as an example (manual, p. 2). If the diffuse brain damage group did consist primarily of individuals with Alzheimer's disease, the average age of these individuals (50s) would suggest that many were experiencing early-onset Alzheimer's disease, which is much more rare than late-onset Alzheimer's disease and presents differently, with "relatively greater deficits in attention, executive functions, praxis, and visuospatial functions" than late-onset Alzheimer's disease (Mendez, 2017, p. 263).

SUMMARY. Health professionals across many disciplines benefit from well-designed, standardized, and validated cognitive tests. Whereas the ease and brevity of The Camden Memory Tests make them potentially useful for qualitative data-gathering, the limitations in the description of the standardization sample combined with no evidence of score reliability and extremely limited evidence of score validity render them inappropriate for quantitative assessment.

REVIEWER'S REFERENCES

Mendez, M. F. (2017). Early-onset Alzheimer disease. *Neurologic Clinics, 35*, 263-281. doi:10.1016/j.ncl.2017.01.005

Warrington, E. K. (1984). *Recognition Memory Test manual.* Berkshire, UK: NFER-Nelson.

Review of The Camden Memory Tests by BRADLEY MERKER, Division Head, Neuropsychology, Henry Ford Health System, and DANA R. CONNOR, Staff Neuropsychologist, Henry Ford Health System, Detroit, MI:

DESCRIPTION. The Camden Memory Tests include five standalone tests, which are intended to be used as individual memory tests. According to the test author, these tests overcome the limitations of available memory tests, which tend to be fairly demanding and lengthy to administer. As such, the individual memory tests were designed to be brief, standalone tests that could complement or corroborate data from other standard memory tests.

The five Camden Memory Tests are the Pictorial Recognition Memory Test (CPRMT), the Topographical Recognition Memory Test (CTRMT), the Paired Associate Learning Test (CPALT), the Short Recognition Memory Test for Words (CSRMT-W), and the Short Recognition Memory Test for Faces (CSRMT-F). Each test involves stimulus presentation, at a rate of one every 3 seconds, and a simple orienting task during stimulus presentation to ensure that attention is focused on each stimulus. The presentation is immediately followed by a recognition memory trial, without an intervening delay. The CPALT has an additional retention trial immediately following the first retention trial, on which the examinee is provided corrective feedback following each response. The test materials do not indicate how long it takes to administer each test, and recognition trials are unpaced; these reviewers administered the measure in less than 10 minutes per test.

Although the test manual and stimulus booklets appear somewhat outdated, the manual provides clear administration instructions. The verbatim task instructions are succinct and likely would be easy for most examinees to understand. A single record form is used for all five tests. For the four tests involving forced-choice recognition (either two or three response options), shaded cells indicate correct responses, which assists with efficient scoring. The CPALT requires that verbatim responses are written on the record form. The correct response is not indicated on the record form for this test, which requires either scoring as you go (correct or incorrect) or referencing back to the stimulus pairs when scoring later.

DEVELOPMENT. The five Camden Memory Tests were developed using well-validated constructs of assessing memory, while addressing limitations of standard memory measures [e.g., Wechsler Memory Scale (Wechsler, 1945); Recognition Memory Test (RMT; Warrington, 1984)]. According to the test author, the CPRMT was developed to be very simple, with minimal attentional demands, to allow for testing patients "unable to cope with more stringent task demands" (manual, p. 2). A secondary aim for this test was to provide an exceptionally easy measure for detecting possible poor effort/task engagement, as unsophisticated examinees likely would have difficulty accurately assessing the difficulty level. The CTRMT was developed to be an ecologically valid test of nonverbal memory. A three-choice pictorial format with very similar distractor items was used to minimize the effects of verbal mediation. The CPALT was developed given that paired-associate learning is well-documented to discriminate between normal and disordered memory, with particular impairments seen in amnestic individuals. The test author critiqued existing paired-associate tasks for having both too easy and too hard items and aimed to develop a test using word pairs of equal and moderate difficulty. Finally, the CSRMT-W and CSRMT-F were developed to provide a briefer alternative to the longer, standard RMT, as well as to increase the difficulty level in comparison to existing easy recognition memory tests, with the hope that they would have greater sensitivity in a younger population.

Unfortunately, the test manual contains little explanation regarding how the number of stimulus items was selected, how the rate of stimulus presentation was selected, how each picture or word was chosen, and how the level of item difficulty was assessed. Additionally, it is unclear from the test manual whether pilot testing was conducted.

TECHNICAL. Two standardization samples were tested in the development of The Camden Memory Tests. All participants were volunteers from organizations and businesses, and those with medical conditions that could compromise cognitive function were excluded. Unfortunately, there is no description of the specific exclusion criteria in the test manual. The first sample comprised 424 participants, who were tested on three of The Camden Memory Tests (CPRMT, CTRMT, and CPALT). Outside of age, demographic information is not provided. Normative data for these three tests are provided separately by age (under 40; 40-54; 55-70; 71-85). The second sample comprised 122 participants who were tested on the two other Camden Memory Tests (CSRMT-W and CSRMT-F). This sample was striated into slightly broader age bands (under 50; 50-69; and 70-85), and, similarly to the first sample, no additional demographic information is provided. The mean IQ for the age groups of each sample ranged from 100.2 (*SD* = 13.4) to 105.4 (*SD* = 12.6). In the absence of information about the sex or race/ethnicity of the samples, it is unclear how representative the samples are of the intended British urban population.

Two experimental samples also were tested to provide evidence of validity for the test scores. The first experimental sample consisted of 96 patients (32 female, 64 male; mean age of 49.6 years) with known unilateral cerebral lesions (48 left hemisphere lesions, 48 right hemisphere lesions, no additional information provided related to localization or etiology). The mean IQ measures (verbal and performance) were in the middle of the average range for both the left and right hemisphere groups. This experimental group was administered three of The Camden Memory Tests (CTRMT, CPALT, and CPRMT).

The tests' abilities to differentiate between normal and lesion groups were variable. The CTRMT was found to have a clear effect of laterality, as the right lesion group performed significantly worse than the left lesion group. The CPALT was also found to differentiate well between the left lesion group, who performed significantly worse on this task, and the right lesion group, whose performances were similar to that of the standardization samples. However, the CPRMT was found to be "easy" for both the normative group and the lesion group, who tended to obtain high scores on this test. Of those who did score below a 5% cutoff, there was no difference in failure rates between the left and right lesion groups.

The second experimental sample consisted of 60 patients with established diffuse brain disease (20 females, 40 males, no information provided related to etiology). The group was subdivided into three groups based on the discrepancy between their reading and full scale IQ score: (a) No intellectual impairment (*N* = 20); (b) Mild intellectual impairment (*N* = 17); (c) Moderate intellectual impairment (*N* = 23). This experimental group was administered two of The Camden Memory Tests (CSRMT-W and CSRMT-F).

Regarding performance on the CSRMT-W and CSRMT-F, the test manual did not state whether these tests significantly differentiated between normal and diffuse brain disease groups. However, a review of the included data tables suggests a difference in scores between the experimental and standardization groups. The test author reported that within the experimental group, mean scores declined with the severity of the dementia, and the number of patients with a significant deficit score increased.

Regarding criterion evidence of validity, the experimental groups were also administered the standard RMT in order to compare the tests' relative sensitivity. The sensitivity of the new, shorter CSRMT-W and CSRMT-F was reported to be "nearly as great" (manual, p. 5) as the longer, standard

RMT. Patterns of performances on the CTRMT and CPALT were reported to be similar to those of the RMT. In contrast, patients' performances on the CPRMT were significantly higher than their performances on the RMT.

Other forms of evidence of validity and reliability are not provided in the test manual. For instance, there was no report of differential validity across gender, racial, or ethnic groups.

COMMENTARY. The Camden Memory Tests include five brief and easy-to-administer tests of verbal and nonverbal memory, with several noteworthy weaknesses. Specifically, reliability and validity evidence to support the use of test scores is quite limited. Comparisons to similar clinical measures would be beneficial in establishing convincing criterion evidence of validity (e.g., comparing the CPALT to the Wechsler Verbal Paired Associates subtest). Additionally, the test manual and stimuli appear somewhat outdated, and should stronger psychometric evidence become available, an update with inclusion of interpretive recommendations and case studies would be welcomed.

Review of the normative data tables reveals that there is a significant ceiling effect. This finding suggests the tests may be too easy for the average individual and/or is a function of the test format of immediate recognition trials with no interval delay. Thus, given the ease of the tests, clinicians seeing individuals with only mild or subtle cognitive deficits may find the tests to have little clinical utility. For those suspected of having significant cognitive impairment, the tests may yield more clinically useful information.

Although the CPALT appears to be a promising measure of paired associate learning, there is an unfortunate test material issue. When administering the retention trials of the CPALT, the stimulus pages with the first word of the pair are slightly transparent and allow the keen examinee to see the correct word pair on the following feedback page. In order to investigate whether this is a practical concern, these reviewers administered the retention trial to a volunteer without any exposure to the word pairs previously, and she scored at the 75th percentile (missing only two answers because a portion of the correct response was obscured). The possibility of false negatives calls into question the validity of the CPALT.

Lastly, given the ease of these tests and their novelty, the tests could potentially be very good measures of effort and task engagement. Future research using the tests as performance validity measures is strongly recommended.

SUMMARY. The Camden Memory Tests were designed to fulfill a need for simple, brief, and effective tools to assess the memory of patients by addressing the limitations of existing memory tests. The CTRMT is a promising topographical memory task that offers the advantage of increased ecological validity (as compared to other nonverbal memory measures), as well as evidence of right hemisphere lateralization. As such, the CTRMT may be a useful addition to neuropsychologists' assessment toolkit. The CSRMT-W and CSRMT-F may be useful in screening memory difficulties in a younger neurological population, given that test items were designed to be more challenging than other standard, brief measures.

In contrast, although the theoretical concept of the CPRMT is reasonable, significant ceiling effects render the test too easy to be useful in assessing suspected memory impairment, and yet not adequately validated to be useful in assessing for suboptimal task engagement. Finally, although these reviewers acknowledge the limitations of currently available paired-associate tasks, we do not recommend the CPALT given the above-mentioned administration concerns.

REVIEWERS' REFERENCES

Warrington, E. K. (1984). Recognition Memory Test. Windsor, UK: NFER-Nelson.

Wechsler, D. (1945). Wechsler Memory Scale. New York, NY: Psychological Corporation.

[26]

Career Exploration Inventory: A Guide for Exploring Work, Leisure, and Learning, Fifth Edition.

Purpose: Designed to help participants explore and plan three major areas in their lives—work, leisure activities, and education or learning.

Population: Ages 18-73.

Publication Date: 1992-2015.

Acronym: CEI.

Scores: 16 occupational categories: Agriculture and Natural Resources, Architecture and Construction, Arts and Communication, Business and Administration, Education and Training, Finance and Insurance, Government and Public Administration, Health Science, Hospitality/Tourism/Recreation, Human Service, Information Technology, Law and Public Safety, Manufacturing, Retail and Wholesale Sales and Service, Scientific Research/Engineering/Mathematics, Transportation/Distribution/Logistics.

Administration: Group.

Price Data, 2020: $69.95 per 25 12-panel foldout inventories; manual (2015, 64 pages) available as free download from test publisher's website.
Time: Administration time not reported.
Author: John J. Liptak.
Publisher: JIST Career Solutions, a division of Kendall Hunt.
Cross References: For reviews by Bert A. Goldman and Douglas J. McRae of the original edition, see 13:49.

Review of the Career Exploration Inventory: A Guide for Exploring Work, Leisure, and Learning, Fifth Edition, by RICHARD T. KINNIER, Professor of Counseling and Counseling Psychology, Arizona State University, Tempe, AZ:

DESCRIPTION. The Career Exploration Inventory (CEI) is an interest inventory that is self-administered, self-scored, and self-interpreted. It contains seven steps that instruct participants to identify past, present, and future interests in work, leisure, and learning activities. The CEI also provides many exploratory questions and useful resources. The instructions are clear and easy to follow. An accompanying workshop manual provides an extensive and detailed guide for counselors on when and how to use the CEI.

In the first step of the CEI, participants are asked to write down their past, current, and future work, leisure, and learning/training experiences. Next, they are asked three questions about any similarities in their work, leisure, and learning interests and whether any interests stayed the same over the past, present, and their predicted futures. The first step ends with participants being instructed to choose the three activities they most enjoy and would like to be part of their career. This section is thought-provoking and clarifying for respondents. The main part of the CEI (steps 2–4) asks participants to identify their interests in 128 activities. For each of the 128 activities, participants are instructed to circle the letter *P* if it was a past interest, the letter *C* if it is a current interest, and the letter *F* if they predict it will be a future interest. By adding the circles, each activity could get a score of 0, 1, 2, or 3. This section is nicely formatted so that each row contains activities that are associated with broader interest areas (e.g., "Agriculture and Natural Resources"). The CEI is self-scoring (step 3) and self-interpreting (step 4). The layout and directions for scoring and interpretation are clear and simple. In step 5, participants are instructed to refer to the "Work, Leisure, and Learning Activities Guide" printed on the inventory and fill in a worksheet with their specific interests. The guide is nicely organized with hundreds of specific occupations, activities, and education/training areas. The guide is adjacent to the worksheet, which makes it easy for participants to read and then write down their specific interests. The last two steps (6 and 7) offer participants suggestions, more resources to consult, guiding questions, and a final worksheet for "Creating an Action Plan" and developing short, medium, and long-range goals. One of the main positives of the CEI, in the opinion of this reviewer, is the layout. All of the sections are on one big page (22 by 26 inches). The big page folds up (with six sections) into a booklet that is 8.5 by 11 inches. The layout makes the inventory self-contained and easy to follow.

DEVELOPMENT. The creator of the CEI (John Liptak) presents a good theoretical rationale for the instrument. In the professional manual, he cites the work of theoreticians such as Super, Maslow, Bolles, Seligman, and others to make the case that a balanced life of enjoyment of work and leisure is important for obtaining life satisfaction. Liptak's goal was to create a measure "that could be used in career counseling, in leisure counseling, or in a holistic approach" across the life span (manual, p. 13).

This reviewer believes that Liptak did an impressive job in constructing the CEI. An initial pool of 700 items was created from existing career and leisure interest inventories. Expert judges were used in the creation of items and interest categories. Several qualitative pilot studies were conducted to improve the format and clarity of the CEI. Field studies were conducted to obtain quantitative data on reliability and validity. This CEI version is the fifth edition of the measure. Each edition brought more revision and refinement, which is commendable.

TECHNICAL. Norms are based on adult (ages 18 to 65) samples. However, participants' scores are most meaningful in comparison with their other scores, not in comparison with other people. (The interpretation is, thus, ipsative.) Therefore, it is recommended that raw scores be used. The test author points out that the use of raw scores also eliminates possible sex bias in interpretation.

With regard to validation of the inventory, content evidence of validity is claimed based on the care taken to develop the items with expert consultation and pilot studies. Five independent judges were employed to improve the form of the items and determine their placement into interest categories. Item analysis (yielding alpha reliability coefficients) was conducted on the items within each category, resulting in the reduction of items in each category from 12 to eight. Alpha coefficient for the eight items within the interest areas ranged from .56 to .84. These values compare favorably with other interest inventories in the opinion of this reviewer. Concurrent validity of the CEI was addressed by comparing participants' top three scores on the interest categories with their favorite activities. Percentage of "hits" ranged from 69% to 79%. The test author claims that several other studies provide construct evidence of validity of the inventory. These studies found correlations between scales of the CEI and similar scales from the Self-Directed Search, the Myers-Briggs Type Indicator, and the Transferable Skills Scale. Reliability was evaluated with a test-retest study (N = 55) over a 3-month period. Coefficients for the 15 interest categories included in the original inventory ranged from .80 to .92 (median = .82). The scales, which expanded to 16 in the fourth edition, thus seem stable over time. Overall, the CEI shows good validity and reliability, in the opinion of this reviewer.

COMMENTARY. The CEI is nicely formatted. Directions are clearly written and easy to follow. Scoring and interpreting are facilitated by the excellent formatting and clear instructions. The listing of hundreds of occupations, activities, and learning areas, all subsumed under 16 interest areas, is impressive and helpful for participants. The process of test construction and examinations of validity and reliability suggest that the CEI is a good measure when compared with similar interest inventories. The professional manual contains good information but is poorly organized in certain chapters. This reviewer recommends that the next edition improve the organization of that manual.

Counselors should recognize that career interest measures are crude estimates that do not yield precise guides for final career choices. The CEI is no exception. The following brief critique is offered as an illustration. The CEI asks participants to circle whether an activity is an interest, rather than asking them to rate how much or how little they like an activity. Rating on an interval scale seems a more precise reflection of how humans feel about most things. Also, the CEI gives equal weight to the past, present, and future. A past interest that is no longer an interest is essentially not an interest, and predicting future interests is like most predictions—difficult and unreliable. Thus, dichotomous choices and responses about the past and future are problematic. The CEI mostly remedies this lack of precision by presenting scores in broad categories—low, average, and high.

A positive feature of the CEI is that it provides participants with thoughtful questions and helpful resources. Counselors and participants should not expect any clear and final career choice to emerge from the results of any interest inventory. Rather, the results should serve to provide some good ideas and a general guide for the ongoing, lifelong process of career development.

SUMMARY. The CEI is a self-administered, self-scored and self-interpreted career-related interest inventory. It is well-formatted. Directions are clearly written for taking, scoring, and interpreting the measure. The CEI also offers good clarifying questions and helpful resources for participants. The CEI was impressively developed. The reliability and validity evidence for the CEI puts it on a par with other interest inventories.

It bears repeating that no interest inventory yields a simple and final answer for a career choice. Career development is a complicated, life-long process that is influenced not only by interests, but also by abilities, values, motivation, and interpersonal issues. The CEI does not address those variables. It does offer participants and their counselors relevant and useful information, ideas, and resources. As such, the CEI, like other respected interest inventories, can be one of the many tools used during the process of career counseling.

Review of the Career Exploration Inventory: A Guide for Exploring Work, Leisure, and Learning, Fifth Edition, by JULIA Y. PORTER, National Certified Counselor, National Certified School Counselor, Mississippi Licensed Professional Counselor, Ocean Springs, MS:

DESCRIPTION. The Career Exploration Inventory (CEI) helps individuals explore interests in work, leisure, and learning activities by responding to 128 items grouped into 16 interest areas: (1) Agriculture and National Resources, (2) Architecture and Construction, (3) Arts and Communication, (4) Business and Administration, (5) Education and Training, (6) Finance and Insurance, (7) Government and Public Administration, (8) Health Science, (9) Hospitality, Tourism, and Recreation, (10) Human Service, (11) Information Technology,

(12) Law and Public Safety, (13) Manufacturing, (14) Retail and Wholesale Sales and Service, (15) Scientific Research, Engineering, and Mathematics, (16) Transportation, Distribution, and Logistics. The CEI uses a unique item response format where the inventory user circles *P* for past interest, *C* for current interest, and *F* for future interest for items that the user enjoys doing. There is also an option to not respond to an item if users have not enjoyed the described activity in the past, do not currently enjoy doing it, or do not think they would like to do it in the future. The CEI is designed to be self-administered, self-scored, and self-interpreted following seven steps: (1) Exploring Work, Leisure, and Learning Activities; (2) Taking the Inventory; (3) Adding Your Total Score; (4) Interpreting Your CEI Scores; (5) Exploring the Work, Leisure, and Learning Activities Guide; (6) Researching Career, Leisure, and Learning Options; and (7) Creating an Action Plan. Instructions and worksheets for each of the seven steps are included in the 12-panel foldout inventory. The CEI may be administered to individuals or to groups and is available in a paper-and-pencil format and a web-based format. Administration time of the inventory by itself excluding exploration activities is usually 20-30 minutes. Inventory administration and exploration activities may be completed in one day or may be completed using several shorter sessions over several days.

To calculate the score, the number of circles in each row is counted and entered on the "subtotal" line for that row. Two rows of items are used to measure each of the 16 interest areas. The subtotals for the two rows related to the same interest area are added to get the score for that interest area. Scores between 0 and 5 indicate *low interest*, between 6 and 18 *average interest*, and between 19 and 24 *high interest*.

DEVELOPMENT. The CEI is based on Liptak's Leisure Theory of Career Development, which is based on Super's Life Span, Life Space theory of career development and McDaniels's concept of Career Equals Work Plus Leisure (C = W + L) (manual, p. 21). Liptak's holistic view of career development views individuals' lives and career paths as a combination of their work and leisure roles. Work roles include "all paid employment," and leisure roles comprise "everything else including recreational activities, hobbies, learning, volunteering, self-maintenance, and family activities" (Liptak, 2015, p. 30).

Through research, Liptak identified a pool of 700 items related to work and leisure that was narrowed to 204 items based on each of the item's applicability to both work and leisure. The 204 items were placed into 17 interest categories. A panel of five expert judges then reviewed the items and their placement into interest categories. Based on the judges' recommendations, two of the interest categories were combined with other categories, which reduced the number of interest categories to 15. A pilot test was conducted (*N* = 30), and a coefficient alpha correlational analysis was run on the data to select eight items for each of the 15 categories. Three qualitative pilot studies (*N* = 15) were conducted to evaluate the inventory's format, clarity, and utility. The CEI was then field-tested (*N* = 210). Based on results from the pilot studies, a career exploration guide, which in the fifth edition of the CEI is called the Work, Leisure, and Learning Activities Guide, was added to the inventory. This guide gives examples of related occupations, related leisure activities, and related education and training for each of the 16 interest categories. In the fourth edition of the CEI, the "interest categories" were renamed "interest areas" and included 16 career clusters used by the Department of Education and the New Guide for Occupational Exploration. Occupational titles and job groups on the fourth edition of the CEI were revised based on the O*NET (Occupational Information Network) and remain in place for the fifth edition.

Also based on data from pilot studies, Creating An Action Plan was added as Step 7 to help users develop a career plan that includes interaction between their work and leisure interests.

Ongoing research on the CEI includes norms studies for high school and college students.

TECHNICAL. The CEI was normed with two groups from the United States: unemployed/underemployed adults (*N* = 104) in Pennsylvania and employed adults (*N* = 106) in Virginia. Ages of the total sample of 210 volunteer participants ranged from 18 to 73; the sample consisted of 85 males and 125 females.

Each participant's top three scores on the interest categories in the areas of work, educational courses, and leisure activities were compared with their favorite work and leisure activities from the past, present, and future to establish concurrent validity. Construct evidence of validity was collected by determining the number of times the

CEI accurately measured sustained interest from the past, in the present, and anticipated for the future. CEI "coefficient alpha analysis consistency measures ranged from .56 to .84. Subjects' top scores for their interest categories were consistent with their work and leisure activities 43% to 51% of the time. The CEI correctly identified sustained, developmental interests for work (54%) and leisure (67%)" (manual, p. 50). Test-retest reliability was established by re-administering the CEI to a portion of the original sample (N = 55) approximately 3 months after the initial field testing with results ranging from .80 to .92.

COMMENTARY. The CEI is unique because it uses one instrument to explore career, leisure, and educational training across the life span (past, present, and future) at the same time. The CEI workshop manual includes a narrative, agenda, and reproducible worksheets that can be used in conducting group assessments. This manual would be especially useful for new test administrators. The CEI professional manual contains additional information about the development and validation of the CEI. Both manuals are easy to read and use. Although training is not required to administer the CEI, the test developer recommends that administrators take the inventory themselves before administering it to others.

An advantage of the 12-fold panel test instrument is having all the information from the CEI assessment results collected together for future reference. A disadvantage of this format is that the 12-fold panel requires more desk space than a traditional paper-sized assessment booklet. This additional space requirement would be important when administering the CEI in a group setting. The Work, Leisure, and Learning Activities Guide provided in Step 5 is an excellent resource for helping users explore the 16 interest areas as they relate to occupations, leisure activities, and related education and training. There are some activities included in the CEI that require the user to flip back and forth from one side of the panel to the other when the panel is fully opened, which may be challenging for some users. In Step 6 of the instrument, a list of resources is provided for further exploration of assessment results.

SUMMARY. Offered in a paper-and-pencil version and a web-based version, the CEI is used to help individuals explore their career, leisure, and learning interests from the past, in the present, and for the future and to examine how these interests can contribute to the lifestyle they desire. The CEI is self-administered, self-scored, and self-interpreted using a developmental, free response item format. Seven steps are included in the inventory to help respondents explore items that apply to work, leisure, and learning across the life span. An expert panel, pilot tests, and field-testing were used to establish the reliability and validity of the CEI. Training is not required for test administration. Two manuals (a workshop manual and a professional manual) provide guidance for administering and interpreting the CEI. CEI results may be helpful in developing a career plan that includes selecting jobs, identifying leisure activities, and selecting educational training.

REVIEWER'S REFERENCE

Liptak, J. J. (2015). *Career Exploration Inventory workshop manual* (5th ed.). St. Paul, MN: JIST Publishing.

[27]

Career Exploration Inventory EZ, Second Edition.

Purpose: Designed to "help people explore their career and job alternatives based on their interests."
Population: Working and unemployed adults, students, and youth.
Publication Date: 2011.
Acronym: CEI-EZ.
Scores, 16: Agriculture and Natural Resources, Architecture and Construction, Arts and Communication, Business and Administration, Education and Training, Finance and Insurance, Government and Public Administration, Health Science, Hospitality/Tourism/Recreation, Human Service, Information Technology, Law and Public Safety, Manufacturing, Retail and Wholesale Sales and Service, Scientific Research/Engineering/Mathematics, Transportation/Distribution/Logistics.
Administration: Group.
Price Data, 2020: $64.95 per 25 inventories; administrator's guide (10 pages) can be downloaded from test publisher's website.
Time: [20] minutes.
Comments: "Designed for self-administration and interpretation"; based on the Career Interest Inventory, Fourth Edition.
Author: John J. Liptak.
Publisher: JIST Career Solutions, a division of Kendall Hunt.

No review available. This test does not meet review criteria established by the Buros Center for Testing that call for at least minimal technical and development information.

[28]

Checklist for Autism Spectrum Disorder-Short Form.

Purpose: Designed as a semi-structured diagnostic interview for use in autism screening.
Population: Ages 1-17.
Publication Date: 2017.
Acronym: CASD-SF.
Scores: Total score only.
Administration: Individual.
Price Data, 2020: $98 per kit including manual (28 pages) and 25 interview forms; $78 per manual; $32 per 25 interview forms.
Time: (5) minutes.
Author: Susan Dickerson Mayes.
Publisher: Stoelting Co.

Review of the Checklist for Autism Spectrum Disorder—Short Form by DAMIEN C. CORMIER, Associate Professor of Educational Psychology, University of Alberta, Edmonton, AB, Canada, and AGNES FLANAGAN, Graduate Student in School and Clinical Child Psychology, Educational Psychology, University of Alberta, Edmonton, AB, Canada:

DESCRIPTION. The Checklist for Autism Spectrum Disorder—Short Form (CASD-SF) is described as an instrument to be used in the screening for and diagnosis of autism spectrum disorder (ASD) as outlined in the *Diagnostic and Statistical Manual of Mental Disorders* (5th ed.; *DSM-5*; American Psychiatric Association [APA], 2013). The CASD-SF manual specifies that, when used for the purpose of screening for ASD, the CASD-SF can be completed independently by parents and teachers. When used for the purpose of diagnosing ASD, it should be administered to a parent by a qualified clinician who has training and experience in the diagnosis of ASD.

The CASD-SF is intended to be used to assess ASD symptoms in children and adolescents, ages 1 to 17. The checklist includes a total of six symptoms to be carefully considered by those completing the form. The CASD-SF is one double-sided page in length with demographic information and two of the six items appearing on the front side of the form. The remaining four items are found on the back side of the form. Under each of the six items identifying broad ASD symptoms (e.g., limited reciprocal interaction) are lists of subitems that focus on specific behaviors that are associated with each of the broad ASD symptoms. The number of subitems ranges from two to 11 with one item, Stereotypies, being the exception with no subitems listed. If *any* of the behaviors described in the subitems are characteristic of the behaviors exhibited by the child or adolescent being assessed, then the item is checked. The subitems are considered present/endorsed if the behaviors they describe are currently occurring or have occurred in the past, even if, in the case of the latter, the behaviors are no longer present.

A single score is generated from the six CASD-SF items. Every time an item is checked, a point is counted toward the total score—referred to on the CASD-SF form as the Total Number of Symptoms Checked (range = 0 to 6). A single point is always assigned if one or more of the subitems is checked; no additional points are assigned based on the number of subitems checked. The CASD-SF manual identifies a threshold value of 3 or more points as a score "indicating autism" (p. 1).

DEVELOPMENT. The CASD-SF is the first abbreviated version of the original Checklist for Autism Spectrum Disorder (Mayes, 2012). The CASD-SF underwent two stages of development. First, a clinical sample of 607 children and adolescents diagnosed with autism (*n* = 469) or attention-deficit/hyperactivity disorder (ADHD; *n* = 138) was drawn from a child psychiatric diagnostic clinic. The purpose of the first stage was to determine the subset of items from the CASD that differentiated between the two diagnostic groups with 100% accuracy. The second stage of development involved a cross-validation of the six items identified in the first phase with an independent sample of children with ASD (*n* = 336) or ADHD (*n* = 61). Tables are presented in the test manual to compare the diagnostic accuracy and score distributions between the development and cross-validation samples as well as the standardization sample from the full-length instrument (i.e., the CASD) using the six items used in the CASD-SF.

TECHNICAL. The CASD-SF manual presents some information related to the instrument's psychometric properties. Internal consistency was calculated from the CASD standardization sample of 1,417 children (alpha = .79) and from the development sample of 607 children (alpha = .87). As mentioned above, the cross-validation and diagnostic accuracy information are the two primary areas of focus in the description of the psychometric properties of the CASD-SF. When the criteria from the CASD-SF were applied to the CASD standardization sample, the overall diagnostic accuracy for the CASD-SF was 96.4%.

When individual raters were considered, the test author reported that all (100%) of the children with autism were correctly identified as having autism using psychologist scores on the CASD-SF items, whereas fewer mothers (88.7%) and a limited number of teachers (58.9%) correctly identified children and adolescents with autism using the CASD-SF criteria.

The CASD-SF manual reports three concurrent validity studies. The first was completed to determine the level of agreement between the CASD-SF and the Childhood Autism Rating Scale. The sample included 329 children with autism and 46 children with ADHD, oppositional defiant disorder, and/or anxiety disorder. The agreement between the two instruments was 97.9% in the autism group and 95.7% in the group of children with other disorders. The second study measured the level of agreement between the CASD-SF completed by a parent and the Autism Diagnostic Interview-Revised. Results revealed a 96.3% agreement in a sample of 27 adolescents with suspected autism. The third study examined the agreement between psychologist, mother, and teacher CASD-SF scores extracted from completed CASD scores. Scores from 168 children with autism and 40 children with ADHD were compared using an ANCOVA to control for differences on key variables (e.g., age, sex, race). CASD-SF scores were significantly higher ($p < .0001$) for children with autism than children with ADHD for each of the raters. Further, CASD-SF clinician scores were significantly higher than mother scores, and mother scores were significantly higher than teacher scores. For children who did not have autism, CASD-SF mother scores were significantly higher than clinician and teacher scores.

COMMENTARY. The CASD-SF has a number of strengths and weaknesses. The instrument's strengths include its straightforward layout and presentation. The procedure to administer and score the CASD-SF is simple. The test manual is easy to read and includes answers to useful questions, such as "Who should be evaluated using the CASD-SF?" and "What sources of information should be used?" Another important strength of this test is its strong diagnostic accuracy when completed by a clinician. Finally, its alignment with *DSM-5* criteria that conceptualizes ASD as a single spectrum disorder is a benefit to clinicians who seek information about a potential ASD diagnosis. As such, this instrument demonstrates good potential for contributing meaningful information to the assessment process when hypotheses regarding neurodevelopmental disorders are generated by clinicians.

Some of the strengths of the CASD-SF are countered by several weaknesses. The test author describes the instrument as being useful as both a screening and a diagnostic measure. There appears to be a misalignment between the stated diagnostic purpose of the instrument and the approach used in its development, which places greater emphasis on distinguishing between ADHD and autism compared to other possible co-morbid disorders (e.g., intellectual disability). The justification for the test author's approach is implied by noting that many children with ASD also have ADHD. If the measure is indeed intended to serve the dual purposes of screening and diagnosis, each purpose should be clearly identified, and reliability and validity evidence should be presented to support the specific use.

Second, the development sample appears to be limited considering the instrument's stated age range. For example, it would be beneficial to see greater emphasis placed on the developmental levels within the sample. A breakdown of the development data with respect to reliability, validity, and diagnostic accuracy for specific age ranges (e.g., 1-3, 4-6, 7-12, and 13-17 years old) would be beneficial. This level of detail may help to identify certain age ranges where the CASD-SF is perhaps most useful. In addition, the description of the development sample suggests an over-representation of White children and adolescents, although the standardization sample was nationally representative. It would be helpful to have relevant Census information presented to compare how the development and normative samples align with proportions that are observed in the population of interest.

Third, the information related to reliability is limited. The procedure that was used to generate the cut-score "indicating autism" (p. 1) is well described. Data related to precision of measurement (e.g., standard errors of measurement, confidence intervals) are not reported in the test manual. Based on the reported internal consistency of the instrument (alpha coefficients were .87 and .79 for the development and standardization samples, respectively), it would be reasonable to consider the CASD-SF as being useful for low stakes decisions (i.e., screening). Current standards suggest that, when instruments are intended to be used to make high-stakes decisions in educational contexts, these values should be at or above .90 (Salvia, Ysseldyke, & Bolt, 2012), although the relatively low number of items on the scale likely affects the resulting values. Of note, classification accuracy in the standardization sample was 96.4%. Confidence in the interpretation of a clinical measure intended for diagnostic applications could be enhanced by including data on test-retest and interrater reliability.

Fourth, the test author presents evidence of concurrent validity that appears to be strong for clinical decision-making when the CASD-SF is completed by a clinician. Evidence of concurrent validity from parent and teacher raters is weaker. (As noted in the test manual, ratings from those respondents should be used only for screening or in conjunction with information from other sources.) Furthermore, the validity section of the CASD-SF manual does not discuss validity specifically from construct or content perspectives. A broader scope of validity evidence would increase confidence that inferences drawn from the scores produced by the CASD-SF are appropriate. In addition, it appears that no teachers completed the CASD-SF in the development or normative samples. According to the CASD-SF manual, approximately half of the forms were completed independently by a parent and half by a clinician. Additional validity evidence should be gathered to support the use of the CASD-SF for the purpose of diagnosis of ASD.

SUMMARY. The CASD-SF is a brief, simple instrument that aligns with the diagnostic criteria in the *DSM-5*. The development procedure for the CASD-SF suggests that the instrument has relatively good diagnostic accuracy when it is used by a trained clinician. However, some limitations regarding reliability and validity evidence lead to some hesitation with respect to establishing the utility and appropriateness of the CASD-SF as a diagnostic instrument. Some of the concerns relate to the high-stakes nature of making an ASD diagnosis. Based on the current evidence, the CASD-SF appears to be a reasonable screening instrument when completed by clinicians. Additional reliability and validity evidence should be collected to strengthen its utility as a screening measure that is completed by parents and teachers.

REVIEWERS' REFERENCES

American Psychiatric Association. (2013). *Diagnostic and statistical manual of mental disorders* (5th ed.). Washington, DC: Author.

Mayes, S. D. (2012). Checklist for Autism Spectrum Disorder. Wood Dale, IL: Stoelting.

Salvia, J., Ysseldyke, J. & Bolt, S. (2012). *Assessment: In special and inclusive education* (12th ed.). Belmont, CA: Cengage.

Review of the Checklist for Autism Spectrum Disorder—Short Form by TIFFANY L. HUTCHINS, Associate Professor, Communication Sciences and Disorders, University of Vermont, Burlington, VT:

DESCRIPTION. The Checklist for Autism Spectrum Disorder—Short Form (CASD-SF) is a criterion-referenced measure/semistructured parent interview intended for the screening and identification of autism spectrum disorder (ASD) in children between the ages of 1 and 17 years. The CASD-SF comprises six items: limited reciprocal interaction, narrow or unusual range of interests and play behaviors, upset with change, stereotypies, sensory disturbance, and atypical vocalizations or speech. Each of these items, in turn, comprises a set of more specific subitems, usually in the form of a short list of example behaviors. For instance, the item atypical vocalizations or speech contains 11 subitems including unusual, repetitive vocalizations and sounds; idiosyncratic jargon as if talking in own language; and excessively repetitive speech and questions. If any one of the subitems is deemed present (at the current time or any time in the past), the higher-order item is also scored as present. Scores on the CASD-SF range from 0 to 6. A score of 3 or higher is taken as an indicator of ASD.

When a child is referred for diagnostic assessment, the recommended procedure for administering the CASD-SF is to obtain parent and teacher responses before meeting with the child's parent so the clinician can compile parent and teacher responses ahead of time. These data are then used to facilitate the semistructured parent interview that is the CASD-SF. The test manual states that if parent and teacher data cannot be collected prior to the clinic appointment, the CASD-SF can still be administered as part of a diagnostic assessment. During the interview, "Parents should be directly asked about each CASD-SF item to clarify and confirm prior information and to obtain additional information if needed to score the item" (manual, p. 5). A limited set of examples of interview questions, requests for additional information, and guidance for gearing questions to the child's developmental level are provided in the test manual. The CASD-SF interview is estimated to take about five minutes. When parents or teachers complete the CASD-SF independently and there is no clinician-directed interview, the data should be used only for screening purposes (a recommendation in response to the comparatively less robust psychometric properties associated with the CASD-SF under these conditions).

DEVELOPMENT. The CASD-SF was developed to provide a brief instrument equally effective in diagnosing autism as the original 30-item Checklist for Autism Spectrum Disorder (CASD). The test manual states that "the 30 CASD items were statistically analyzed to determine the smallest subset of items that differentiated between children with autism and children with other disorders" (p. 1), although the precise statistical procedures for identifying the resulting six items are not described. The CASD-SF cut score (3 or higher) was established using a sample of 469 children with ASD and 138 children with ADHD, some of whom also had other comorbid disorders, resulting in 100% accuracy in differentiating children with autism from those without. Informal inspection of the content of the CASD-SF by this reviewer suggests good content coverage and content relevance, but a more formal discussion of content evidence of validity should be included in any revisions of the test manual.

TECHNICAL.

Standardization. The standardization sample included 925 typically developing children, 437 children with disorders other than ASD, and 55 children with ASD, whose CASD-SF scores were extracted from the 30-item CASD. Other than a general characterization of the ASD group as representing a wide range in terms of language, intelligence, and symptom severity, specific characteristics of this group are not provided, and it is unclear whether or which concomitant diagnoses/conditions were represented in the ASD group. The test manual states that 785 of the CASDs used in the standardization sample were completed independently by the parent, and 632 were completed by clinicians in collaboration with parents (i.e., as is intended and required for diagnostic purposes). Demographic information is reported for the variables of age, child gender, race/ethnicity, region, urban/rural living, and maternal and paternal education.

Crucially, the clinician-informants who provided data for the standardization sample were trained in administration of the CASD. Although the test manual refers to videotapes and the involvement of qualified clinicians with expertise in evaluating autism, no citations or other information are available to evaluate the nature and extent of training required. Training expectations for new users are not specified. Similarly, whether claims of validity based on psychometrics involving the standardization sample will generalize to new (untrained) users is not addressed.

Reliability. Data for internal consistency are reported as alpha coefficients. Results indicated an alpha of .79 for the standardization sample and .87 for the development sample. These data would suggest that the CASD-SF taps a unitary construct (presumably autistic symptomology), but it is not clear that there should be an assumption of homogeneity of content for the samples tested because each consisted of mixed groups (i.e., the standardization sample comprised typically developing children, children with ASD, and children with disorders order than ASD; the development sample comprised children with ASD and children with disorders other than ASD). As such, the test author should consider computing an alpha coefficient using a sample consisting only of children with ASD. No data are offered in support of the tool's test-retest reliability.

Validity. Validity data were drawn from a variety of sources. Both "Standardization" and "Psychiatric" (consisting of "Development" and "Cross-Validation") samples were involved in various comparisons, but the samples and data collection procedures for each are underspecified. Of particular concern are the training of raters, the contexts for data collection, and the nature of the ASD group. With regard to the latter, it is unclear whether the children in any of the autism groups were diagnosed with concomitant conditions, which has important implications for diagnostic tests.

Two pieces of criterion-related evidence of validity are offered. The first is the level of diagnostic agreement between the CASD-SF and the Childhood Autism Rating Scale (CARS; Schopler, Reichler, & Renner, 1986). The CARS is similar to the CASD-SF in that it is a scale to be used by trained clinicians following direct observation of a child. In a sample of children with ASD (n = 329) and a sample of children with ADHD, oppositional defiant disorder, and/or anxiety disorders (n = 46), the CARS and CASD-SF agreed 97.9% of the time when identifying ASD and 95.7% of the time when identifying other disorders. The second piece of evidence involves the level of diagnostic agreement between the CASD-SF and a highly recognized systematic caregiver interview known as the Autism Diagnostic Interview-Revised (ADI-R; Rutter, LeCouteur, & Lord, 2003). In this comparison involving 27 adolescents, results showed 96.3% agreement when identifying ASD.

Data for the diagnostic accuracy of the CASD-SF when compared to the CASD are also reported. Data from the standardization, cross-validation, and original development samples were excellent (> 96%) with sensitivity ranging from 95.5% to 100% and specificity ranging from 90.2% to 100%. Because the CASD-SF was extracted from the larger CASD measure, these estimates are artificially inflated. Estimates of the diagnostic accuracy of the CASD-SF when compared to other reputable assessments (e.g., the Autism Diagnostic Observation Schedule [ADOS]; Lord, Luyster, Gotham, & Guthrie, 2012) would constitute more compelling evidence for diagnostic accuracy.

Data for interrater agreement are provided in the validity section of the manual. Significant differences were reported such that psychologists' scores were significantly higher than parents' scores, which were significantly higher than teachers' scores. With regard to diagnostic accuracy using criterion cutoffs, 100% of the psychologists identified ASD using the CASD-SF, the accuracy of parents was somewhat less (88.7%), and the accuracy of teachers was characterized as unacceptable (58.9% true positive rate and 41.1% false negative rate). Interpretation of these data are complicated, however, in that the administration procedures varied across respondents: Scores for psychologists' data were extracted from the larger CASD, which, in turn, had been administered in the context of a comprehensive diagnostic evaluation that included "parent interview; behavior and autism rating scales ¼ observations of the child during psychological testing; and a review of early intervention and school records" (manual, p. 15). By contrast, parent and teacher respondents simply completed the CASD-SF independently.

Although "diagnostic validity for the CASD-SF [when] completed by clinicians following standardized procedures is excellent and is comparable to validity for the 30-item CASD" (manual, p. 19), the explicit purpose of the CASD-SF is to serve as a "brief, cost effective" measure that is "easy to administer and score" (manual, p. 2). Because all clinician data in support of the validity of the CASD-SF were drawn from data collected as part of a full diagnostic evaluation, the validity of the CASD-SF when used under variable conditions is unknown and threatens the generalizability of validity evidence.

COMMENTARY. The strengths of the CASD-SF include its brevity and face validity, and the evidence for the criterion-related validity and diagnostic accuracy are promising. On the other hand, test-retest reliability and more rigorous tests of diagnostic accuracy are sorely needed. With regard to the latter, the sensitivity and specificity of the CASD-SF when compared to a diagnostic process that includes a gold standard of assessment is desirable. A more detailed description of the standardization sample is also needed as is a larger ASD sample. Finally, the test manual would benefit from revision to improve organization and to include detailed descriptions of groups and data collection procedures including the nature and extent of the training of raters and interviewers used to collect data for the standardization sample.

SUMMARY. The CASD-SF is a six-item version of the original 30-item CASD that "offers an even quicker assessment that streamlines diagnosis" (manual, p. 2). The instrument provides a framework for interviewing caregivers to identify the presence or absence of hallmark characteristics of ASD. The CASD-SF is grounded in a sound theoretical perspective and decades of clinical experience, but it needs stronger empirical support for use in high-stakes accountability decisions. Despite its promise, the CASD-SF cannot be recommended for clinical use without additional supportive psychometric evidence. Preparation of a more comprehensive test manual is also recommended. Clinicians seeking a validated ASD assessment that makes use of caregiver informant data also may consider the Gilliam Autism Rating Scale—Third Edition (Gilliam, 2014), the Social Responsiveness Scale, Second Edition (Constantino & Gruber, 2012), and the aforementioned (but considerably lengthier) ADI-R.

REVIEWER'S REFERENCES

Constantino, J. N., & Gruber, C. P. (2012). Social Responsiveness Scale, Second Edition. Torrance, CA: Western Psychological Services.

Gilliam, J. E. (2014). Gilliam Autism Rating Scale—Third Edition. Austin, TX: PRO-ED.

Lord, C., Luyster, R. J., Gotham, K., & Guthrie, W. (2012). Autism Diagnostic Observation Schedule, Second Edition. Torrance, CA: Western Psychological Services.

Rutter, M., LeCouteur, A., & Lord, C. (2003). Autism Diagnostic Interview-Revised. Torrance, CA: Western Psychological Services.

Schopler, E., Reichler, R. J., & Renner, B. R. (1986). The Childhood Autism Rating Scale. Torrance, CA: Western Psychological Services.

[29]

Child/Home Early Language & Literacy Observation Tool.

Purpose: "Designed to measure the quality of the language and literacy environment" in home-based child care settings.

Population: Home-based care settings for children from birth to age 5.

Publication Date: 2007.

Acronym: CHELLO.
Scores, 3: Literacy Environment Checklist, Group/Family Observation, Overall.
Administration: Individual child care settings.
Parts, 3: Literacy Environment Checklist, Group/Family Observation, Provider Interview.
Price Data, 2020: $50 per set including user's guide (100 pages), and 1 CHELLO Tool (observation record form); $30 per user's guide; $25 per 5 CHELLO Tools.
Time: 90-120 minutes for observation.
Comments: Provider Interview can be completed after the observation to supplement information in the Group/Family section; companion tool to Early Language & Literacy Classroom Observation Tool, Pre-K (ELLCO Pre-K; 19:55).
Authors: Susan B. Neuman, Julie Dwyer, and Serene Koh.
Publisher: Paul H. Brookes Publishing Co., Inc.

Review of the Child/Home Early Language & Literacy Observation Tool by JEFFERY P. BRADEN, Professor of Psychology, Dean, College of Humanities and Social Sciences, North Carolina State University, Raleigh, NC:

DESCRIPTION. The Child/Home Early Language & Literacy Observation Tool (CHELLO) is intended to assess the quality of the literacy (and, to a lesser extent, oral language) environment provided to preschool children in their homes or other caregiving settings. The CHELLO was developed to complement the Early Language & Literacy Classroom Observation Tool, Pre-K (ELLCO Pre-K; Smith, Brady, & Anastasopoulos, 2012), which assesses the literacy and language environment of preschool classroom settings (see reviews by Krach, 2014 and Smith, 2014). Both tools were developed to help professionals interested in improving preschool children's acquisition of literacy and language skills assess and improve literacy environments. As such, the CHELLO and ELLCO Pre-K aim to enhance preschool children's opportunities to learn, especially children who may come from low-income environments.

The CHELLO has three main sections: a Literacy Environment Checklist, a Group/Family Observation, and a Provider Interview. Items within the Checklist are scored based on whether the features are present or absent, whereas items from the Observation are scored from 5 (*exemplary*) to 1 (*deficient*) using a rubric. The subtotals from the Checklist and Observation are summed to provide the Overall CHELLO Score; the Interview responses are narrative and used for descriptive purposes, to supplement the observations.

DEVELOPMENT. The CHELLO (and the ELLCO Pre-K) were developed as part of the federally funded Project Great Start Professional Development Initiative, which aimed to enhance professionals' ability to improve the quality of home and school environments to support literacy. The CHELLO authors drew from research linking features of children's home environments (e.g., number of books; objects inviting language-mediated play; caregiver support for linguistic interactions; structure and organization of activities) to children's literacy outcomes. These features became the core items of the CHELLO and were refined throughout the project and eventually piloted with 98 home-based observations and interviews. About half of the total home environments (n = 55) were targeted to improve the literacy environments, whereas the others (n = 43) were observed only (i.e., a no-treatment control group). The CHELLO manual did not specify whether researchers randomly assigned homes to control or treatment groups.

TECHNICAL.

Standardization. The CHELLO is a criterion-referenced instrument in which items are keyed to reflect ideal literacy environments (i.e., high/present scores indicate high-quality environments; low/absent scores indicate lack of literacy and language supports). There is neither a normative sample nor norm-referenced scores.

Reliability. Interobserver agreement for 20 homes (in which pairs of observers did blind observations) was rated at 91% agreement for the Literacy Environment Checklist; one assumes this is exact agreement on the total score rather than average agreement across the 22 items. Additionally, the exact agreement (again, one assumes for the total score) is 49% for the Group/Family Observation, and 42% of raters were within 1 point of each other (i.e., perfect or near agreement is 91%). Internal association measures are good; correlations among the Checklist and Observation subsections are all positive and statistically reliable; the internal consistency of the total Checklist is good (alpha coefficient = .82), and the internal consistency of the Observation total and subscales is excellent (alpha coefficients ≥ .90). The internal consistencies for Checklist subscales vary more widely, with Books being good (.78) but Resources lacking support (.42).

Validity. The forms of validity most relevant to the CHELLO are content validity (i.e., the claim that items are sensitive to the quality of the home literacy environment) and treatment or consequential validity (i.e., the CHELLO is "sensitive to interventions specifically designed to improve home-based care" [manual, p. 3]). The literature review provides support for the content validity of the CHELLO, although some critics might note the potential for bias (i.e., higher scores indicate features most often associated with higher SES homes). It is unclear whether such bias can (or should) be avoided; that is, lower SES homes may be less likely to be able to afford/provide children's books in good condition, but given the importance of such books for literacy development, it may be appropriate to include the items. No specific description of bias review (e.g., empaneling experts to review items for bias) is mentioned.

The second major validity claim is that the CHELLO can guide caregivers to improve the literacy and language opportunities they provide to preschool children. Some relevant evidence is presented to support this claim, as means for treatment and no-treatment controls diverge following intervention with caregivers (i.e., the treatment group shows reliable improvement over pre-treatment means, whereas the control group does not). However, the test authors fail to report the statistics that would most directly support their claim (e.g., How many of the non-treatment homes improved beyond the threshold for a reliable change index vs. how many of the treatment homes did so?), and they fail to note that all means for both groups increased. Likewise, the report of positive correlations between the overall CHELLO Score and children's achievement scores is argued as evidence that better literacy environments produce higher literacy achievement, but fails to acknowledge that correlation is not causation (e.g., the positive associations between achievement and CHELLO scores may be due to SES generally, and not the literacy environment in particular).

COMMENTARY. Although the CHELLO is imperfect, its authors do (much) more than most in conducting and reporting intervention outcomes. The content of the instrument was not independently validated nor specifically reviewed for bias; however, the items appear sound, and the link between assessment and intervention is direct and explicit. The instructions for scoring are clear, and the inclusion of photographs shows examiners how to score environmental characteristics. Case studies included to guide interventions are logical and helpful.

It is unfortunate that the CHELLO has been virtually ignored since its publication (this reviewer found only one study not by the original team that cited the CHELLO; Chao & Lin, 2015). In contrast, this reviewer found more than 30 publications citing the ELLCO Pre-K. What is particularly ironic in this outcome is that the researchers generally argue that the home environment is more important for literacy and language development than classrooms (e.g., the "thirty-million word gap" described by Hart & Risley, 1995), and the CHELLO data strongly suggest it is easier to change the literacy environment of homes relative to classrooms. It would appear that, despite what appears to be a promising tool for assessing, intervening, and improving the quality of preschool children's home/caregiving environments, researchers and professionals ignore non-school environments in their efforts to improve children's literacy. Or, to put it differently, the CHELLO provides a promising approach to illuminate and improve children's literacy and language, but professionals—like the drunk who looks for a lost wallet only under the illumination of the street lamp—have yet to look beyond preschool classrooms for pathways to improve the literacy and language of low-income children.

SUMMARY. The CHELLO offers a practical tool to assess the language and literacy environments in preschool children's homes/caregiving environments. It is well-aligned with the research literature, and its outcomes clearly suggest ways to improve home (and, through the companion ELLCO Pre-K, classroom) literacy environments. It is surprising and unfortunate that the CHELLO has not received attention since its publication. Although the evidence provided to support the instrument may be incomplete, it is a promising and potentially important tool for improving the home literacy environments of preschool children.

REVIEWER'S REFERENCES

Chao, P.-Y., & Lin, C.-C. (2015). Young children's storybook searching with a visualized search interface. *The Electronic Library, 33*, 610-624.

Hart, B., & Risley, T. R. (1995). *Meaningful differences in the everyday experience of young American children.* Baltimore, MD: Paul H. Brookes Publishing Co.

Krach, S. K. (2014). [Test review of the Early Language & Literacy Classroom Observation Tool, Pre-K]. In J. F. Carlson, K. F. Geisinger, & J. L. Jonson (Eds.), *The nineteenth mental measurements yearbook* (pp. 244-246). Lincoln, NE: Buros Center for Testing.

Smith, J. K. (2014). [Test review of the Early Language & Literacy Classroom Observation Tool, Pre-K]. In J. F. Carlson, K. F. Geisinger, & J. L. Jonson (Eds.), *The nineteenth mental measurements yearbook* (pp. 246-247). Lincoln, NE: Buros Center for Testing.

Smith, M. W., Brady, J. P., & Anastasopoulos, L. (2012). Early Language & Literacy Classroom Observation Tool, Pre-K. Baltimore, MD: Paul H. Brookes Publishing Co.

Review of the Child/Home Early Language & Literacy Observation Tool by IHEOMA U. IRUKA, Chief Research Innovation Officer and Director, HighScope Educational Research Foundation, Ypsilanti, MI:

DESCRIPTION. The Child/Home Early Language & Literacy Observation Tool (CHELLO) evaluates the quality of the language and literacy environment in home-based settings, such as family, friend, and neighbor care. The CHELLO comprises three tools. The first is the Literacy Environment Checklist, which examines the availability of literacy resources and the organization of the setting (i.e., structure), such as whether there is a book reading area or whether books are available for children. There are 22 items covering the areas of books, writing, and resources. The second tool is the Group/Family Observation, which examines the instructional supports and affective quality of the learning environment (i.e., process), such as the environment being intentionally organized to interest children and providers showing attachment toward children. There are 43 items covering the area of physical environment for learning, support for learning, and adult teacher strategies. The third tool within the CHELLO is the Provider Interview, which is intended to supplement information gathered during the observation using the Literacy Environment Checklist and the Group/Family Observation. Some of the questions asked include the types of activities and experiences the providers seek to deliver in their programs and how they focus on children's strengths and challenges to plan language and literacy activities. Items in each area of the Literacy Environment Checklist and the Group/Family Observation are scored and then summed to obtain a score in each area. Together, the tools of the CHELLO are said to "provide a profile of the environment and the language and literacy supports in home-based settings" (manual, p. 11).

It is important that observers are familiar with home-based settings and knowledge about children's development, especially for children birth to age 5. Observers familiar with home-based settings recognize these settings as uniquely and vastly different from center-based programs in many ways, including group size, child-staff ratio, mixed age group, familiarity between provider and child, and use of the space. Furthermore, it is important to keep the Provider Interview informal and open-ended to help ensure the provider is candid and likely to provide detailed information to help score aspects of the tools.

DEVELOPMENT. A history of the development of the CHELLO is contained in the user's guide. The development of the CHELLO came about through the Project Great Start Professional Development Initiative based in Michigan. The study examined the effects of professional development on the quality of home- and center-based programs focusing on children's language and literacy. Prior to this work, there was a tool to measure the quality of center-based programs' language and literacy environments, called the Early Language and Literacy Classroom Observation Toolkit, Research Edition (ELLCO; Smith & Dickinson, 2002). Initial efforts to adapt the ELLCO for home-based programs proved to be unsuccessful due to the uniqueness of the home-based setting, creating the need to develop a new measure for home-based programs, which resulted in the CHELLO. Based on observations and a review of the literature, the developers of the measure identified aspects of the home-based environment that were observable and associated with high quality programs. They included: providers' engagement with children in conflict resolution through language, contingent responses of children based on providers' deep familiarity with children in their care, caregivers setting up activities based on children's interests and abilities, strong parent-provider relationships, and thoughtful and flexible use of the physical space to support children's learning. To ensure comparability between home- and center-based settings, the developers wrote 20 items that were comparable between the CHELLO for home-based programs and ELLCO for center-based programs.

TECHNICAL.

Reliability. Psychometric evidence for this measure came from the Project Great Start Professional Development Initiative, an intervention program that included 158 providers in the treatment group (55 were home-based providers), and 103 providers in the control group (43 were home-based providers). The treatment group received 6 credit hours of professional development intervention for a total of 90 hours, and the control group received no training.

Reliability evidence is based on three sources: interrater agreement, scale intercorrelations, and internal consistency. Interrater reliability was based on 20 home-based settings that were independently observed by a pair of data collectors. Interrater reliability was 91% within 1 point for the Literacy Environment Checklist and the Group/Family Observation. Internal correlations examined the relationships among the major subscales. For example, providers who scored high on the Support for Learning were also likely to score high on the Adult Teaching Strategies within the Group/Family Observation (r = .72). Internal consistency (alpha coefficients) for the Literacy Environment Checklist and the Group/Family Observation total scores were .82 and .97, respectively. Alpha coefficients for subscales ranged from .42 to .78 and from .90 to .94, respectively.

Validity. Validity evidence for the CHELLO was based on stability and sensitivity to change as well as predictive validity related to outcomes. Through the Project Great Start Professional Development Initiative the test authors demonstrated significant change in the treatment group's scores from fall to spring, and they improved significantly in all areas compared to the control group. During the same time period, the control group showed some change, but significantly less than the treatment group in all areas assessed by the CHELLO.

The CHELLO also showed significant relationship to children's receptive language, language-oriented math concepts, and phonological awareness. Correlation coefficients ranged from .33 (receptive language) to .25 (phonological awareness). There was no relationship to letter-identification (coefficient was .14), which the developers note is not measured by the CHELLO.

COMMENTARY. The CHELLO seems to be a well-conceived research-based instrument with reliability and validity evidence based on a convenience sample. There is also some comparability of the CHELLO for home-based providers and the ELLCO for center-based providers, which is especially important for early childhood programs that seek to improve both types of settings. There are also positive and consistent associations with children's language-oriented measures such as the Peabody Picture Vocabulary Test, Third Edition and the PALS Nursery Rhyme. It also seems to have strong interrater reliability. With the proliferation of quality tools for center-based programs, this tool offers an important and distinct alternative for the early childhood field in that it focuses on the uniqueness and strengths of home-based settings. The test authors should be commended for including structural and process features of the environment, as is typical in other observation tools. The potential for use of this tool in home-visiting programs is also of value. The simplicity and clarity of the instruction and scoring methods make it a tool that can be easily understood and used by a variety of individuals, which is an asset for early care and education programs that may have few staff with extensive technical evaluation and research knowledge. Attention should be paid, however, to the instruction about how best to select and train observers. The test developers provide much useful information on how to support and strengthen children's language and literacy in home-based settings.

Although there are several strengths to the CHELLO, there are also several concerns. First, this tool does not seem to be culturally responsive as there are no questions about the diversity of books and whether the books match children's culture and language. Second, the technology section is dated, which is expected given the year when this measure was developed, so there are no items about tablets, smartphones, apps, social media, and so on. Third, the psychometric evidence for this measure is primarily from a Michigan-based intervention program in urban settings with a convenience sample. It is unclear whether the sample was representative of early childhood programs in the United States or, minimally, the state of Michigan. It is unclear whether this tool would be generalizable to home-based programs in rural settings. Third, there was no information about the providers or the children to whom they provide services such as education level, experience, or other demographics. Having some basic information about providers would help test users to gauge the validity of the instrument's scores if it were to be noted that more experienced and educated providers engage in more language-rich activities in their programs. Finally, to strengthen overall validity evidence, the test authors should attend to construct evidence. Along this point, there seems to be a need for the authors to conduct a confirmatory factor analysis to establish the presence of two factors as there is evidence that some items in the Literacy Environment Checklist correlated more strongly with items from the Group/Family Observation. For example, the Books area from the Literacy Environment Checklist had a higher correlation with the Physical Environment for Learning area of the Group/Family Observation (r = .68) than with the Writing Materials area of the Literacy Environment Checklist (r = .52).

SUMMARY. The CHELLO is a well-conceived tool with some evidence of the reliability and validity of its scores, based on research involving a convenience sample. It incorporates research indicating the essential elements for a language-rich early care and education environment in a home-based setting. For early childhood systems and programs seeking to improve the language and literacy inputs in home-based programs, this tool provides good information that can support professional development in different areas from structural and organization aspects to more instructional aspects. Its alignment with an existing center-based tool also makes it compelling for those seeking to improve language and literacy practices in multiple settings. However, potential users should consider whether the tools are culturally responsive, up-to-date, and demonstrate sufficient psychometric evidence for their planned use.

REVIEWER'S REFERENCE

Smith, M. W., & Dickinson, D. K. (2002). Early Language and Literacy Classroom Observation Toolkit (Research ed.). Baltimore, MD: Paul H. Brookes Publishing Co.

[30]

Choosing Outcomes & Accommodations for Children (COACH): A Guide to Educational Planning for Students with Disabilities, Third Edition.

Purpose: Designed to help teams plan individualized education programs for students with disabilities.
Population: Students ages 3-21 with disabilities who have intensive special educational needs.
Publication Dates: 1985-2011.
Acronym: COACH.
Scores: Item scores only.
Administration: Individual.
Parts, 2: Part A: Determining a Student's Educational Program; Part B: Translating the Family-Identified Priorities into Goals and Objectives.
Price Data, 2020: $49.95 per manual (2011, 232 pages) with CD.
Time: Completion time varies based on a number of factors; approximately 60-85 minutes for Step 1 (Family Interview) and 45-60 minutes for Step 2 (Additional Learning Outcomes) with additional time required for Steps 3-6.
Comments: "Designed to be used with a student's family, special educator, and general educator(s) together."
Authors: Michael F. Giangreco, Chigee J. Cloninger, and Virginia S. Iverson.
Publisher: Paul H. Brookes Publishing Co., Inc.
Cross References: See T5:553 (1 reference); for a review by Jay Kuder and David E. Kapel of a previous edition titled C.O.A.C.H.: Cayuga-Onondaga Assessment for Children with Handicaps, Version 6.0, see 11:73.

Review of Choosing Outcomes & Accommodations for Children, Third Edition by ABIGAIL BAXTER, Professor, Department of Leadership and Teacher Education, University of South Alabama, Mobile, AL:

DESCRIPTION. Choosing Outcomes & Accommodations for Children, Third Edition (COACH3) is designed to help families and school personnel collect information that can be used to develop individualized educational programs (IEPs) for students receiving special education services. The COACH3 was designed for students with disabilities between the ages of 3 and 21 who have more complex support needs. The COACH3 can also be used in transition planning from grade to grade. COACH3 is used prior to IEP development to help families and school personnel better understand students' strengths and needs. The COACH3 has six foundational principles that team members must value. They relate to effective ways to work together, inclusion and effective instruction, meaningful curriculum, family involvement, valued lifespan outcomes, and coordination of services and supports.

The COACH3 is a two-part assessment process: Part A: Determining a Student's Educational Program and Part B: Translating the Family-Identified Priorities into Goals and Objectives. Each part consists of three separate steps. For Part A, the steps are (1) Family Interview, (2) Additional Learning Outcomes, and (3) General Supports. For Part B, the three steps are (4) Annual Goals, (5) Short-term Objectives, and (6) Program-at-a-Glance. The first two steps in Part A are further divided. Step 1, the Family Interview, helps the family identify learning outcomes by considering the 83 learning outcomes contained in the COACH3; an iterative process leads to the choice of four to six outcomes that are most appropriate for the child. Step 2 guides the team through a consideration of potential general education outcomes. In Step 3, the team identifies supports the student needs in multiple domains. Steps 4 and 5 identify annual goals and objectives, respectively. Step 6 summarizes information about curricular and support needs of the student throughout his or her school day.

The complete COACH3 process is well described in the assessment manual, and each step and substep is fully explained with examples. For each step, the manual details its purpose, materials needed, directions, and helpful hints and provides examples of completing the student record. The administration times for the six steps vary. In the COACH3 manual, estimated time ranges are given for Steps 1-3 and 6. Time estimates are difficult to determine because of the idiosyncrasies of individual planning teams, but according to the information in the manual, completion of all steps could take approximately 4 hours. A planning team comprising family and school representatives implements the COACH3, but the composition of these teams is not prescribed. It is recommended that the complete COACH3 (Parts A and B) be used the first time a team plans for a specific child. The next year, the team can decide to use the existing Part A, to complete Part A again, to revisit parts of Part A, or to re-validate the existing Part A depending on changes that exist. The COACH3 does not have a specific examiner. Instead, the team process is guided by a facilitator who is an individual familiar with the process of using the COACH3. There are no scoring procedures for the COACH3; rather, the information gathered is used to develop the IEP.

DEVELOPMENT. The COACH3 is the ninth version of the COACH since 1985; it is the third edition with the current publisher. The COACH3 is based on evidence-based approaches to educational planning such as collaborative teamwork, family involvement, problem-solving approaches, and appropriate curriculum selection. According to the assessment manual, field-testing has led to revisions; however, the details of the data and their impact on subsequent revisions are not detailed. The manual does summarize revisions made to the COACH3. These changes include updating the foundational principles; reorganization of the manual; inclusion of a CD-ROM that includes the manual, PDF versions of all forms, examples, and supplemental materials; and an updated and streamlined student record form. The COACH3 manual provides a great deal of information about the theoretical assumptions and underpinnings of the instrument. For each of the guiding principles, the manual details the research literature supporting the principle. Each of the steps in the COACH3 process is also supported by the research literature, and the linkages are discussed in the manual.

TECHNICAL. The nature of the COACH3 does not lend itself to typical psychometric analyses. A search of the literature using EBSCO identified a case study in which COACH3 was used. Even though the COACH3 is not a norm-referenced assessment tool, it would be improved by the addition of psychometric analyses that support its use. Specifically, content validation of the learning outcomes, reliability studies for the scales and questionnaires, and consequential validity studies investigating the use of the COACH3 and IEP development would make this tool stronger. It is important to be able to demonstrate that use of the COACH3 has a positive impact on IEPs and subsequently on the learning of students with significant support needs and their families and teachers.

COMMENTARY. The COACH3 is a well-developed process that can be used when developing an IEP for students with disabilities who have extensive support needs. The COACH3 is based on a theoretical model that values family involvement and family-school partnerships. Use of the COACH3 should lead to the development of an individualized plan that will meet the student's educational and functional skill needs as well as provide the opportunity for team members to develop relationships that will effectively support the student throughout the school year. The COACH3 helps families focus on potential goals and outcomes for the student and to identify the most salient outcomes for the IEP team to focus upon. The COACH3 also helps school personnel to better understand the student's needs and abilities in many ecological contexts in addition to school. However, there is no empirical evidence pointing to improved processes or outcomes related to the use of the COACH3.

Initially, the COACH3 requires a substantial investment of time for families and school personnel, and the student record form is extensive. Not all members of all IEP teams will be able to commit to use of the COACH3 prior to developing IEPs. However, the COACH3 is an excellent tool to use when families and school personnel need a multifaceted assessment that leads to a complete understanding of the student and his or her needs. In light of the 2017 U.S. Supreme Court ruling in Endrew v. Douglas County School District, educators may be in search of assessment tools that will help them better understand the needs of students with more significant support needs in order to develop IEPs with individualized, meaningful, and sufficiently ambitious goals toward which students will be able to make progress. The COACH3 can ably provide the needed information and facilitate IEP development for these students.

SUMMARY. The COACH3 is an all-encompassing assessment tool that helps teams prepare for developing IEPs that meet the academic and functional needs of students with more extensive support needs. In terms of face validity, the COACH3 appears to have been developed to well meet the goals it has set out for itself. However, consistent with a previous review (Kuder & Kapel,

1992) the COACH3 lacks psychometric information on standardization, reliability, and validity. In addition, information about the initial selection of items and item refinement would be helpful. These data should be available to justify to IEP teams that the extra planning time required by the COACH3 is worthwhile.

The COACH3 represents an additional layer of assessment that is used for developing IEPs. In addition to assessments detailing students' academic and functional skills, the COACH3 is a way for teams to develop IEPs that meet current standards. The COACH3 should lead to better family participation and ownership of IEPs. School personnel also will benefit from a more holistic view of the child, his or her needs, and involvement of the family in the child's education.

REVIEWER'S REFERENCES

Endrew F. v. Douglas County School District Re-1, 137 S. Ct. 988 (2017).

Kuder, J., & Kapel, D. E. (1992). [Test review of C.O.A.C.H.: Cayuga-Onondaga Assessment for Children with Handicaps, Version 6.0]. In J. J. Kramer & J. C. Conoley (Eds.), *The eleventh mental measurements yearbook* (pp. 194-196). Lincoln, NE: Buros Institute of Mental Measurements.

Review of Choosing Outcomes & Accommodations for Children, Third Edition by JENNIFER N. MAHDAVI, Professor of Special Education, Sonoma State University, Rohnert Park, CA:

DESCRIPTION. The authors of Choosing Outcomes & Accommodations for Children, Third Edition (COACH3) refer to it as a "planning tool" rather than as an assessment. Designed for use in the service of individuals with severe disabilities ages 3-21, COACH3 has two objectives: to determine elements that should be included in a student's educational program and to transform educational priorities into individualized education or transition plan (IEP or ITP) goals and objectives. These objectives are accomplished through a two-part process. The first part focuses on determining priorities for the student of interest through an interview with the family of the individual with disabilities conducted with education-related service providers present. This process acknowledges the voice of the family as primary in planning the child's education. Once a maximum of four priority areas have been selected from the family interview, the student's team works collaboratively to ensure that general education and school-based outcomes are integrated with broader priorities to be included in the student's IEP/ITP. The final element of the collaborative interview process is to identify the general supports that the student needs to pursue successfully the identified priorities. In the second part of the COACH3 process, the priorities and supports are translated into IEP/ITP goals and objectives, and a short description of the IEP/ITP itself is created.

COACH3 is a flexible, non-standardized activity that takes two to three hours to complete. The assessment manual makes clear that using COACH3 must involve an interactive, collaborative process rather than a mere completion of forms.

DEVELOPMENT. COACH3 was developed in alignment with six explicitly stated principles regarding best practices in educating students with significant disabilities. These principles are: (1) all students can learn and deserve appropriate curriculum, (2) access to inclusive instructional settings is vital, (3) curricular choices must be based on valued life goals, (4) family involvement in educational planning is crucial, (5) education requires collaborative teamwork, and (6) services must be coordinated to be effective. Each principle is supported by relevant research, cited in the COACH3 manual, regarding best practices in education for individuals with disabilities.

Beyond stating that these six principles guided the development of COACH3, the manual offers little further information about how interview items were selected, tested, or refined. Interview directions mention that questions were drawn from previous research in which families raised their major concerns for their children with disabilities. Each family interview item is phrased in an open-ended way, allowing for responses that span an individual's age, level of ability, and needs.

Families may choose to address several broad topics through the interview process. Each of these topics is under the umbrella of "valued life outcomes," that would make the "child's life a good life" (manual, p. 128). These outcomes are categorized as safety/health, home, relationships, self-determination, and activities. Each area is considered according to what is age-appropriate, as well as what the family believes is most important.

A further element of the assessment asks families and service providers to collaboratively select school-related curriculum areas, such as communication, personal management, or academics, to explore further. In each area, the team rates the student's skill as *early/emerging* (E), *partial* (P), or *skillful* (S). No rubric is provided to guide these ratings aside from a brief percentage range (E = 1-25%), which offers little on which to base an evaluation.

The final elements of the COACH3 process require the team to use interview and ratings data to rank all potential learning outcomes that emerged for the benefit of the student, and to select up to six to develop into IEP/ITP goals. Guided IEP goal development, in the form of organizers with prompts that emphasize the context for learning the skill and specify the level of support that will be necessary to achieve it, are provided. Development of the organizers is not described, but they appear to align with best practices used by special educators.

TECHNICAL. Because COACH3 is not designed as nor intended to be a standardized or norm-referenced measure, no discussion of reliability or validity is provided in the manual. One may assume that families would reliably identify their priorities for their children. One also may assume that the interview items accurately reflect the needs of individuals with more severe disabilities, as the items are rooted in the well-supported six principles serving as the foundation for the instrument.

There are no scores, per se, nor directions for coding interview responses. The instrument could be viewed as a semi-structured interview. As such, it offers guidelines for organizing and prioritizing concerns that emerge during qualitative data collection.

COMMENTARY. In a review of a previous version of COACH, the directions were criticized as confusing and hard to follow (Kuder & Kapel, 1992). This problem has been rectified in the current edition. The COACH3 manual provides an informative overview of the tool, with each page of the form providing comprehensible instructions. The format of the instrument leads the administrator smoothly through each step of the process. In addition, the previous review questioned including sensory needs in the interview priorities; this element does not appear in the current version of the instrument.

The COACH3 is presented in a paperbound book with a CD. The book contains directions, rationale, and forms. On the CD, both printable and fillable PDFs are provided for the team to use. Adding online access to these forms would be useful as so many people now work on tablets or computers that do not have CD drives.

Families and professionals who work with individuals with severe disabilities in school settings will find a great deal of value in the COACH3. It provides a discussion scaffold for all of the people involved with a child to come together to identify priorities and goals to make his or her life better. The authenticity of the items, combined with respect for what families believe and care about, make this an especially powerful tool for use in IEP and ITP development. It should not be the only method of assessment selected, but it can help distill an array of concerns and priorities to their most important essence.

SUMMARY. Despite the absence of technical documentation that is discussed in many psychological or academic assessments, COACH3 is a valuable instrument for use in IEP and ITP programming. The forms and interview questions may make it easier for families and professionals to discuss and come to consensus about educational or transition-planning priorities for an individual with severe disabilities. The measure can facilitate difficult conversations in a respectful way if used by a skilled interviewer. IEP and ITP team members may find the COACH3 an effective scaffold for discussions about meaningful life outcomes for children with severe disabilities.

[Editor's note: The COACH3 publisher advises that some peer-reviewed research about the instrument (e.g., a validation study using national experts, a cross-cultural review, and a use and impact study) has been published and that the research is summarized in the following source: Shepherd, K. G., Giangreco, M. F., & Cook, B. G. (2013). Parent participation in assessment and in development of individualized education programs. In B. G. Cook & M. Tankersley (Eds.), *Research-based practices in special education* (pp. 260-272). Boston, MA: Pearson.]

REVIEWER'S REFERENCE

Kuder, J., & Kapel, D. E. (1992). [Test review of C.O.A.C.H.: Cayuga-Onondaga Assessment for Children with Handicaps, Version 6.0]. In J. J. Kramer & J. C. Conoley (Eds.), *The eleventh mental measurements yearbook* (pp. 194-196). Lincoln, NE: Buros Institute of Mental Measurements.

[31]

Clarity Well-Being Measures.

Purpose: Designed as measures of well-being, defined as "the self-appraisal of positive health status across six dimensions of life experience."
Population: Ages 16 and older.
Publication Date: 2018.
Administration: Individual.
Forms, 3: Clarity Well-Being Scales, Clarity Well-Being Scale, Clarity Health Assessment Scales.
Price Data: Available from publisher.
Time: 5-10 minutes for administration of each measure.
Comments: Administered and scored online.
Authors: Kevin L. Moreland and Barry Schlosser (test); Paul Turner, David Avila and Daniel Turner (manual).
Publisher: Clarity Health Assessment Systems, Inc.

a) CLARITY WELL-BEING SCALES.
Acronym: CWBS-18.
Scores, 8: Physical Well-Being, Emotional Well-Being, Mental Well-Being, Social Well-Being, Life Satisfaction, Life Direction, Total Well-Being, Brief Well-Being.
b) CLARITY WELL-BEING SCALE.
Acronym: CWBS-6.
Scores, 1: Brief Well-Being.
c) CLARITY HEALTH ASSESSMENT SCALES.
Acronym: CHAS-24.
Scores, 9: Physical Well-Being, Emotional Well-Being, Mental Well-Being, Social Well-Being, Life Satisfaction, Life Direction, Total Well-Being, Brief Well-Being, Brief Distress.

Review of the Clarity Well-Being Measures by JAMES P. DONNELLY, Professor, Department of Counseling & Human Services, Director of Measurement & Statistics, Institute for Autism Research, Canisius College, Buffalo, NY:

DESCRIPTION. The Clarity Well-Being Measures comprise a set of three scales of subjective well-being. They are said to be written at a sixth-grade English language reading level, appropriate for age 16 and above, completed in 10 minutes or less, and accessed via computer or mobile device. The three versions of the scale vary in length (6, 18, 24 items). The 24-item version produces scores on Physical, Emotional, Mental, Social, and Total Well-Being; Life Satisfaction; Life Direction; and Brief Distress. The 18-item version is the same as the 24-item version but without the distress scale. The six-item scale generates a Brief Well-Being score. Items are rated on a 9-point frequency scale (*never* to *always*), and raw scores are converted to T-scores. Scoring is automatic on a secure server with text and graphic output. User access to the web site is structured at administrator and participant levels. Upon invitation from a test administrator, individuals can complete the assessments on multiple occasions, enabling tracking of changes over time. Administrators can enroll and manage participants, utilize analytic tools, and export data. Cost/access options are obtained directly from the test publisher, Clarity Health Assessment Systems, Inc. The analytic tools include Matrix Analysis and Outlier Analysis. The Matrix Analysis plots scores on a two-dimensional graph of Distress vs. Well-Being. Outliers are defined as greater than one standard deviation from the mean of pooled development samples. The user's guide provides brief narratives describing psychological characteristics of high and low scorers on the subscales. Supplementary scales were developed to provide a more complete assessment of life context in clinical settings. These supplementary scales are not included in this review but were used by test developers in evaluation of the well-being scales. The user's guide provides information on scale content, interpretation, and test development as well as a supplementary psychometric report.

DEVELOPMENT. Version history is referred to by number (e.g., Generation 5). A supplementary manuscript provided by the test publisher (Ayers, Bathe, Moreland, & Schlosser, 1998, 2018) indicates that development was initiated in 1981 by Barry Schlosser. His goal was to define subjective well-being as not merely the absence of symptoms, but the presence of a positive state of being, consistent with emerging models of related constructs (Schlosser, 1990, 1996). Schlosser described item sources as positive health studies, his own experience, martial arts/Taoist philosophy, and dictionaries. The first psychometric analysis included internal consistency reliability and convergent/discriminant validity correlations, assessed in a sample of 195 female undergraduates. Generations 2 and 3 were developed by Schlosser and Moreland (Schlosser, 1996). Generation 4 was produced by Moreland and Schlosser with two graduate students (Ayers et al., 1998, 2018). The psychometric efforts resulting in the Generation 4 measure included more items and samples described as 130 adults representing diverse individuals and settings, 63 diverse and non-traditional community college students, and 162 high school students in an affluent community. The Ayers et al. report indicates that the final Generation 4 scale included 50 items. The evolution of the scale from Generation 4 to Generation 5 is not described.

TECHNICAL. The standardization sample of the current version is a combination of the prior Generation 2-4 samples. The intended reference population is described as age 16 to adult. Appendices summarize scale descriptive statistics, demographics, internal consistency reliability, correlations, and discriminant validity indicators. There is no comprehensive discussion of all of the sampling methods utilized in the various subsets that were pooled. However, the Schlosser (1990) article and the Ayers et al. (1998, 2018) report describe what appear to have been convenience and purposive sampling strategies in a variety of settings that included "senior centers, colleges and universities, professional meetings, and businesses" (no page number in the text). The descriptive statistics show large sample sizes (over 800) for the Physical, Emotional, Mental, and Social Well-Being scales but a smaller sample size (*n* = 247) for the Life Satisfaction and Life Direction scales. This discrepancy is not addressed in the user's guide except as a note in one of the appendices, citing changes in item sets over time. Minimums, maximums, means, and standard deviations for raw and T-scores are presented. Demographics are provided for the larger sample, including age, gender, education, and race/ethnicity. The most frequently occurring demographic characteristics are: female (61.8%), White (74%), well-educated (77% at least some college) and relatively young (*M* = 37, 59% less than 40 years old). There are no data on geographic location or other sociodemographic variables. There is no analysis by sample characteristics. The user's guide presents T-score interpretation, which assumes a normal distribution. On this basis, T-scores above or below one standard deviation from the mean are considered high or low. Five histograms showing score distributions are included in an appendix, including for the Brief Well-Being (six-item) scale and the Brief Distress (six-item) scale. Both appear to be slightly skewed, but skewness and kurtosis statistics are not presented for any of the distributions.

An appendix in the test manual provides reliability evidence for the Generation 5 scales. Alpha coefficients are given for the subscales, the Brief Well-Being and Brief Distress scales, Total Well-Being, and two Impact of Life scales. As with the summary statistics, larger sample sizes were reported for the Physical, Emotional, Mental, and Social Well-Being scales (over 800) with smaller samples for the others (*ns* = 192-693). All except two of the reliability estimates are greater than .80, the exceptions being the Brief Distress scale (.76) and the Life Satisfaction scale (.78). Alpha coefficients also are presented for a 50-item "Comprehensive Well-Being: Gen 5 Database" scale and six subscales (four well-being subscales as well as Life Satisfaction and Life Direction). All coefficients were .89 and higher. According to the test publisher, the 50-item scale was developed for research purposes (D. Turner, personal communication, June 28, 2019). The Ayers et al. (1998, 2018) report includes a test-retest reliability assessment based on 70 participants, who were mainly female (*n* = 52) and White (*n* = 64), with an average education level of 16 years and an age range of 19-80 years (*M* = 48, *SD* = 18). The retest occurred on average 415 days after the initial assessment, with generally high test-retest correlation coefficients (.67-.84).

Two forms of validity evidence are presented in appendices. First, a table of scale intercorrelations again based on different sample sizes for different scales, with greater than 800 for the four well-being subscales and smaller numbers for the Life Satisfaction and Life Direction subscales. Correlations with other Clarity scales (positive/negative image, impact of life events) are also provided in this table. Correlations assessing the relationship of the 24-, 18-, and 6-item versions of the Well-Being scale to one another are extremely high at .96, .97, and .98 (*N* = 247). The correlations within the six subscales range from moderate to high (.46-.74).

A second table shows strong negative relationships between the three summary well-being scores and the Brief Distress score (*r* = -.78, -.79, -.79). Another form of discriminant validity evidence is presented as a breakdown of life events and Comprehensive Well-Being scores. Percentages of the sample who experienced a stressful life event (13 events; medical procedures, legal difficulties, etc.) at the highest and lowest 15% of the Comprehensive Well-Being score distribution are provided. A similar table is presented based on the Brief Distress scale scores. There is no formal analysis, but the pattern of differences is presumably in the expected direction, with higher well-being associated with less frequent stressful life events and greater distress associated with more frequent stressful events. A similar analysis was reported by Ayers et al. (1998, 2018) with the addition of *t*-tests. These analyses were based on the same sample of 70 participants described in the test-retest reliability analysis. There are no analyses of reliability or differential item/scale functioning across demographic groups.

COMMENTARY. The Clarity Well-Being scales originated in the early 1980s, a period of blossoming theory and research in affect, well-being, and quality of life, all of which have continued to evolve. Since 1981 more than 250,000 articles have been published on "subjective well-being" (Google Scholar, April, 2019) and more than 2,000 measures can be found in a quality of life measures database (PROQOLID, https://eprovide.mapi-trust.org/about/about-proqolid) and the NIH PROMIS site (http://www.healthmeasures.net/index.php). Scale development of the Clarity measures was vigorous in the early stages in the 1990s, as content was carefully refined. The test-retest correlation coefficient obtained with a limited sample over a relatively long period is less than compelling, given that the measure is intended to be used in treatment planning and outcome evaluation. A more carefully controlled and theoretically derived retest interval with a defined clinical population would provide important information about score consistency and sensitivity to change. Overall confidence in the validity evidence is limited by the absence of the following: tests of assumptions of the analyses, clear reporting on sampling strategies and generalizability, evidence of normal distributions associated with the T-score conversion and interpretation, evidence of validity of outlier and matrix analyses, norms related to specific populations (e.g., psychotherapy clients, age groups), construct validity tests of the current measures with external measures and methods, detail on changes from Generation 4 to 5, analysis of differential item functioning, and structural studies such as factor analysis.

SUMMARY. The Clarity Well-Being Measures provide brief computer-based assessments of subjective well-being aimed at clinical use in assessment, treatment planning, and outcome evaluation of older adolescents and adults. The system has evolved over nearly four decades and survived the loss of two key contributors (assessment expert Kevin Moreland and user's guide author and clinical expert Paul Turner). Strengths include the formative item and scale evaluation in the early phase of development and the simple computer interface in the current version. With so many alternatives in modern well-being assessment, the future utility of this system will depend on addressing limitations noted above and taking additional steps to comply with current test standards concerning validity, reliability, generalizability, and documentation (American Educational Research Association, American Psychological Association, & National Council on Measurement in Education, 2014).

REVIEWER'S REFERENCES

American Educational Research Association, American Psychological Association, & National Council on Measurement in Education. (2014). *Standards for educational and psychological testing*. Washington, DC: American Educational Research Association.

Ayers, W., Bathe, S., Moreland, K. L., & Schlosser, B. (1998, 2018). *Clarity Well-Being Scales: Development, reliability, concurrent and predictive validity*. Unpublished manuscript.

Schlosser, B. (1990). The assessment of subjective well-being and its relationship to the stress process. *Journal of Personality Assessment, 54*, 128-140.

Schlosser, B. (1996). New perspectives on outcomes assessment: The philosophy and application of the subjective health process model. *Psychotherapy, 33*, 284-304.

Review of the Clarity Well-Being Measures by MICHAEL G. KAVAN, Professor of Family Medicine and Professor of Psychiatry, Associate Dean for Student Affairs, Creighton University School of Medicine, Omaha, NE:

DESCRIPTION. The Clarity Well-Being Measures comprise a set of three instruments designed to measure "overall subjective well-being and its well-being sub-dimensions: Physical, Emotional, Mental, Social, Life Satisfaction, Life Direction" (publisher communication, included as cover sheet to user's guide). The three assessments include the Clarity Health Assessment Scales (CHAS-24), which yields a Total Well-Being score, well-being scores for the six dimensions of Physical Well-Being, Emotional Well-Being, Mental Well-Being, Social Well-Being, Life Satisfaction, and Life Direction, and a Brief Distress score; Clarity Well-Being Scales (CWBS-18), which yields a Total Well-Being score and well-being scores for each of the six previously noted dimensions; and the Clarity Well-Being Scale (CWBS-6), which yields an index score of positive health status titled Brief Well-Being.

The Clarity Well-Being Measures are available as web-based measures only. The Clarity instruments are designed for people 16 years of age and older. The user's guide notes that items are written at the sixth-grade reading level. All Clarity instruments are designed to be administered and used by professionals with appropriate training and experience in the use of psychometric assessments with the supervisor of the assessment having a Doctorate in Psychology. For all instruments, examinees are asked to respond to each item based on a 9-point Likert-type scale ranging from 0 (*never*) to 8 (*always*). The Clarity instruments have no time limit but typically can be completed in "a matter of minutes" (user's guide, p. 6). Testing should be completed in a single sitting. Clarity instruments are designed for repeated administrations but should not be given more than once per day. Raw scores are converted to T-scores for Total Well-Being and each of the well-being, Brief Distress, and Brief Well-Being dimensions. Examinee scores are displayed in a T-score bar graph, and scores from multiple administrations may be displayed on a T-score tracking graph.

Scores may be interpreted objectively or subjectively. Objective interpretation involves examining respondent T-scores relative to the mean, noting trends in repeated measures over time, and comparing well-being and distress scores with the incidence of actual life events reported within the current, Generation 5, adult composite database of 824 people. Subjective interpretation involves interviewing respondents about the accuracy and meanings of their raw scores and graphed T-score results, inquiring as to items marked with the highest and lowest ratings, and asking about observable patterns in their graphs. The website allows respondents to see immediate results on a bar graph and to see previously completed single assessments and multiple scores across time on a T-score tracking graph. A matrix analysis is also available for the CHAS-24 in which well-being and distress may be plotted and outlier scores explored with respondents.

DEVELOPMENT. Information regarding the development of the Clarity Well-Being Measures comes from a supplemental manuscript (Ayers, Bathe, Moreland, & Schlosser, 1998, 2018) that accompanied the user's guide provided by the test publisher. This manuscript describes the development of Generation 4 of the Clarity Well-Being Scales and notes that the CWBS "traces it lineage" (Ayers et al., 1998, 2018, p. 2) to Schlosser (1990) and the Well-Being Scale-36 (WBS-36). The test authors also refer to the Quality of Life Inventory (QOLI) (Frisch et al., 1992) as the CWBS's "most recently published predecessor" (Ayers et al., 1998, 2018, p. 5). The WBS-36 items focus on strictly positive indicators of health status and were generated from the literature on positive aspects of health, Schlosser's own experiences of well-being, martial arts/Taoist philosophies, and dictionaries. The QOLI is based on the assumption that an individual's overall life satisfaction is based largely on the sum of satisfactions in various life areas that are then weighted accordingly. The development of the CWBS was motivated by the authors' belief that current subjective well-being measures were conceptually vague and inconsistent in terminology, psychometrically weak, and not appropriate for many populations due to their reliance on restricted samples for validation. The CWBS Generation 4 and its scale development is based on analyses from Generation 3 data and is chronicled in the supplemental manuscript. The 142-item Generation 3 instrument was administered to 130 adults, 62 college students, and 162 high school students. For the most part, an item was eliminated if it had a significant relationship with demographic variables, lowered the scale's alpha coefficient, had high correlations with any scale other than the scale it was written for, or if it was deemed redundant. Remaining items were combined to form a single set of scales that included 32 items. Apparently, items were added to boost the alpha value and to assure broad content representation, resulting in a 50-item "Comprehensive" scale intended for research purposes (D. Turner, personal communication, June 28, 2019). Descriptive statistics are provided within the user's guide for the current Generation 5 version of the Clarity measures and represent a merging of data from Generations 2, 3, and 4.

TECHNICAL. The user's guide provides descriptive statistics for the current Generation 5 database. The standardization sample consisted of 824 persons with a mean age of 37.19 years (range 16 to 91 years); 61.8% female; ethnicity of 74% White, 10.7 Black, 5.7% Hispanic, 2.1% Asian, and 2.4% Other; and educational level across the spectrum. No other information is provided within the user's guide on this sample.

In terms of reliability, alpha coefficients for the "Comprehensive Well-Being from the full database" (user's guide, Appendix B) was .97. Alpha coefficients for the six dimensions of well-being in the 50-item Comprehensive scale ranged from .89 (Life Satisfaction) to .93 (Social Well-Being). Alpha coefficients for the Clarity Well-Being Scales (CHAS-24 and CWBS-18) were .94 for the Total Well-Being Score with dimension scores ranging from .78 (Life Satisfaction) to .89 (Emotional Well-Being). Coefficients for the Brief Well-Being and Brief Distress scales were .86 and .76, respectively. The user's guide provides data on the intercorrelations of the various scales. The data make use of Generation 2, 3, and 4 samples that were used to construct the Generation 5 database. The Comprehensive Well-Being from the full database correlates .98 with the 18-item Well-Being Scales and .96 with the Brief Well-Being score, whereas the Total Well-Being score correlates .97 with the Brief Well-Being score. The six dimensions show moderate intercorrelations ranging from .46 (Social Well-Being and Physical Well-Being) to .74 (Social Well-Being and Life Direction; Life Satisfaction and Life Direction). Limited additional reliability data are provided within the user's guide. The supplemental manuscript that accompanied the user's guide contains additional reliability data, but data are limited to the Generation 2 and 3 versions of the instrument.

In terms of validity, the user's guide provides contrast group study results in which well-being and distress scores are compared with various life events such as "Had a medical procedure or surgery" or "Sexual problem(s)." Data are provided for the highest 15% and lowest 15% in the well-being group for the Comprehensive Well-Being scores and the Brief Distress scores. All results are in the predicted direction, though examinee perception for events such as "Began a new job or school or changed careers" may not necessarily be the same for each respondent. No other validity data are provided within the user's guide.

COMMENTARY. The Clarity Well-Being Measures comprise several web-based instruments designed to measure subjective well-being in people 16 years of age and older. The measures are quick and easy to complete. Scoring is accomplished online and displayed in a T-score bar graph, and scores from multiple administrations may be displayed on a T-score tracking graph. Reliability for the Total Well-Being and well-being dimensions are strong. Although the user's guide suggests that the instruments have test-retest reliability, no such information is provided within the guide. One has to go to the supplemental manuscript to see test-retest reliability data from previous versions of the Clarity measures.

In regard to validity, the user's guide notes that "the instruments accurately measure their target constructs" (p. 6). Although the user's guide provides comparative data between well-being and distress scores for various life events, no other data are provided within the guide that would support these validity claims. As with the reliability data, additional information is provided within the supplemental manuscript on concurrent and predictive validity for Generations 2 and 3, but not the current Generation 5 iteration.

The technical data supporting the use of these measures is fairly solid for previous generations of these measures; however, limited data are available to support the use of the current Clarity Well-Being Measures beyond research purposes. Although the Clarity measures hold promise, one is reminded that the subjective measurement of well-being is just that—subjective. Cooke, Melchert, and Connor (2016) found little or no consensus as to what constitutes well-being or how it should be measured. In addition, even if one could adequately define well-being, the measurement of well-being is a crowded market as demonstrated by Linton, Dieppe, and Medina-Lara's (2016) recent review of 99 self-report measures for assessing this concept; the Clarity measures were not included as part of their review. They concluded that no one measure is recommended, but instead "the most appropriate measure of well-being will depend on the dimensions of well-being of most interest, in coordination with psychometric guidance" (p. 14).

SUMMARY. The Clarity Well-Being Measures include a set of three instruments designed to measure overall subjective well-being and several well-being sub-dimensions including Physical, Emotional, Mental, and Social Well-Being, along with Life Satisfaction and Life Direction. They are web-based instruments that are quick and easy to take. For the most part, reliability is strong, but limited validity data are available for the current Generation 5 version. As a result, the Clarity Well-Being Measures would benefit from additional studies examining test-retest reliability and validity across the spectrum before one can confidently use them in a clinical setting.

REVIEWER'S REFERENCES

Ayers, W., Bathe, S., Moreland, K. C., & Schlosser, B. (1998, 2018). *Clarity Well-Being Scales: Development, reliability, concurrent and predictive validity.* Unpublished manuscript.

Cooke, P. J., Melchert, T. P., & Connor, K. (2016). Measuring well-being: A review of instruments. *The Counseling Psychologist, 44*, 730-757.

Frisch, M. B., Cornell, J., Villanueva, M., & Retzlaff, P. J. (1992). Clinical validation of the Quality of Life Inventory: A measure of life satisfaction for use in treatment planning and outcome assessment. *Psychological Assessment, 4*, 92-101.

Linton, M-J., Dieppe, P., & Medina-Lara, A. (2016). Review of 99 self-report measures for assessing well-being in adults: Exploring dimensions of well-being and developments over time. *BMJ Open, 6*(7), e010641.

Schlosser, B. (1990). The assessment of subjective well-being and its relationship to the stress process. *Journal of Personality Assessment, 54*, 128-140.

[32]

Classification of Violence Risk.

Purpose: "An interactive software program designed to estimate the risk that an acute civil psychiatric patient will be violent to others over the next several months after discharge into the community."

Population: Acute psychiatric civil inpatients ages 18 to 60.

Publication Date: 2005.

Acronym: COVR.

Scores, 1: Estimate of Violence Risk (probability, frequency, and categorical).

Administration: Individual.

Price Data, 2020: $405 per kit including manual (48 pages), software program with quick start guide (CD-ROM), and 10 administrations; $1,246 per 100 administrations; $686 per 50 administrations; $374 per 25 administrations; $65 per manual.

Time: (10) minutes.

Comments: Computer administered and scored.

Authors: John Monahan, Henry J. Steadman, Paul S. Appelbaum, Thomas Grisso, Edward P. Mulvey, Loren H. Roth, Pamela Clark Robbins, Steven Banks, and Eric Silver.

Publisher: Psychological Assessment Resources, Inc.

Review of the Classification of Violence Risk by SARA BENDER, Associate Professor of Psychology, Central Washington University, Ellensburg, WA:

DESCRIPTION. Throughout history, many have suggested the presence of a mental health diagnosis may predispose individuals to engage in acts of violence. Although conclusions from research dedicated to this purported association are variable, this belief persists throughout American culture, as seen in media portrayals of mental health, and as reflected in public policies, such as those pertaining to the civil commitment process. Mental health professionals maintain responsibility for protecting the public from those whom may be classified as dangerous to others by recognizing such circumstances and initiating involuntary hospitalization procedures when warranted. In most jurisdictions, civil commitment is pursued in cases of suspected likely imminent harm to self or others, or in circumstances of grave disability. Within these guidelines, mental health professionals are tasked with trying to predict an individual's propensity to engage in violent acts, either to self or others. The purpose of the Classification of Violence Risk (COVR) is to aid mental health professionals in this process.

The COVR was developed as a tool to aid clinicians in predicting in-patient psychiatric patients' likelihood to engage in dangerous behaviors aimed at others following discharge from an acute hospitalization. The COVR is an interactive software program that produces a report gauging patients' potential risk for violence based on the responses to a series of questions answered via a brief interview with a clinician. The software requires clinicians to provide demographic information, including marital status, a Global Assessment of Functioning (GAF) score, and number of previous hospitalizations. The clinician must also identify whether the current hospitalization is voluntary or involuntary. Questions pertaining to reason for admission as well as diagnoses are also presented.

After preliminary patient information is entered into the program, the clinician conducts a structured interview with the patient, entering the individual's response to each question as it occurs. The COVR interview typically takes about 10 minutes to complete and includes questions pertaining to prior arrest records, drug use, intention to engage in and actual completion of violent acts toward self and others, and past parental abuse. Questions are closed-ended in that patients are directed to select from yes/no answers or to select a Likert-type response. The iteration of the interview is dependent on the patient's replies. The software places patients in a low-risk category or high-risk category as the interview progresses based upon their responses. Subsequent probing questions are automatically generated by the software based on patients' previous answers. The COVR repeats an assessment of risk across 10 different iterative classification trees, each addressing a different key risk factor. If patients are unwilling or unable to participate in the interview, or if the responses are perceived to be untruthful, the clinician may enter data based on available documentation and/or his or her judgment. The tool was developed to assess patients between the ages of 18 and 60, regardless of race, ethnicity, geographic region, or associated diagnosis.

Upon interview completion, the COVR software generates a report estimating the patient's risk of violent behaviors, which includes the probability of engaging in violent acts, likely frequency of violent acts, and categorical risk level in which the patient is anticipated to fall. The probability and frequency profiles provide estimates that the patient will engage in violent behaviors in the several months following discharge. These estimates are provided with a 95% confidence interval. The categorical designation communicates the patient's likely risk as *very low, low, average, high,* or *very high.* The test developers caution COVR users that the instrument is to be used as a tool to aid in clinical judgment, not to replace it. This warning is reiterated on COVR score reports.

DEVELOPMENT. The COVR was developed over a period of 18 years, following the release of the results from the MacArthur Violence Risk Assessment Study, which attempted to scientifically predict violence potential and provide clinicians with an actuarial instrument to predict such risk. The MacArthur Risk Study is often credited as more accurate in its approach to predicting violence across psychiatric patients than other published risk assessments. Its structure, which involves five tree-based models, is also critiqued as overly complex and laborious to complete by hand. Thus, a movement toward leveraging software to assist with the use of multiple models was a natural progression in risk assessment strategies.

The COVR was developed in eight stages. First, developers reviewed past violence risk assessment studies and noted that most were limited in their scope in terms of populations studied, environments examined, and data collection sources. Next, the developers conducted an in-depth review of the available scholarly literature and supplementary sources to identify personal factors, contextual factors, and clinical factors that are often correlated with violence. A new instrument was developed to measure each of these factors, mirrored after previously validated assessments. Third, rather than rely on a regression approach typical to aggression assessments, COVR developers pursued tree-based methods, recognizing that "factors that are relevant to the risk assessment of one individual may not be relevant to the risk assessment of another individual" (manual, p. 2). Within tree-based methods, the questions asked within a particular assessment are contingent on previous answers provided, thus prioritizing risk factors and facilitating a risk assessment based on the individual's unique combination of responses. Fourth, COVR developers established two thresholds for individuals based on the responses provided within the assessment: high risk and low risk. Individuals falling between these two risk groups were defined as average risk. Next, the average risk group was further analyzed to determine the presence of additional factors that could further classify the group, resulting in iterative classification trees. Sixth, COVR developers established several risk profiles based on potential combinations of risk estimates grounded in the potential ordering of previously identified risk variables that could contribute to violence risk. Seventh, software was developed to classify patients' violence risk level based on the established classification trees. Finally, developers used the COVR software with patients at two civil commitment sites and confirmed that it may be useful to clinicians in discharge planning.

TECHNICAL. Instrument developers identify two efforts substantiating the COVR: a development study and a validation study. The development study (the MacArthur Violence Risk Assessment Study) leveraged a classification tree methodology to assess 1,136 psychiatric patients using more than 100 previously identified potential risk factors for violence. Data were collected via personal interviews, hospital records, police reports, and collateral information provided by those in patients' lives. Via the classification tree methodology, patients' responses to questions determined subsequent queries, eventually leading to one's placement into one of five risk classes. Researchers then followed participants for 20 weeks post-discharge into the community, assessing for violence as predicted. They found, "For risk classes 1 through 5, the percentage of individuals with two or more violent acts was 0.0, 1.6. 9.7, 21.6, and 36.5, respectively ($p < .0001$)" (manual, p. 36), demonstrating a strong correspondence between one's estimated risk level and propensity to engage in violent acts. Further, of the 134 risk factors studied, 70 demonstrated statistically significant bivariate relationships with subsequent community violence ($p < .05$) (MacArthur Research Network, 2001) thus suggesting the method of risk assessment leveraged within the study to be highly effective, especially in comparison to other risk assessments.

In the validation study, test authors conducted COVR evaluations with 700 individuals, placing them in one of the established five risk categories. A follow-up sample consisted of 157 participants: 102 designated as low risk and 55 classified as high risk. Among those classified by the COVR as low risk, 91% had no reported acts of violence in the 20 weeks following discharge, whereas 9% ($n = 9$) had at least one. Among those classified as high risk, 19 (35%) engaged in at least one violent act post discharge, and 36 (66%) had no reports of violence. The high-risk group's rate of violence was significantly different from that of the low-risk group, suggesting that the COVR demonstrates strong predictive ability. Researchers then broadened their criteria for violence and re-examined the data. Whereas the revised criteria did not change results for the low-risk group (i.e., 9% still had a reported violent act), the number of high-risk participants with violent acts during the follow-up period increased to 27, or 49% of the sample.

McCusker (2007) noted that clinicians considering using the COVR would be most invested in the instrument's positive predictive power (PPP), or the individual's probability of being positive for a characteristic given a positive test score, and negative predictive power (NPP), which records the opposite. PPP and NPP are established by using sensitivity and specificity values. Per the information provided in the test manual, sensitivity rates dropped from .96 in the development study to .68 in the validation study before increasing to .75 in the revised validation study. Similarly, specificity dropped from .86 in the development study to .72 in the validation study and increased to .77 in the revised validation study (McCusker, 2007). McCusker (2007) reported PPP of .35 and NPP of .91 in the original validation study and PPP of .49 and NPP of .91 when the violence criteria were revised. These differences in rate should be considered in light of the population evaluated and the protections in place for that populace. The differences in results between the development sample and the validation sample also may have been impacted by variation in the recruitment criteria (age range, for example) rather than any other factor. It is also worth noting that all participants in both studies were offered Federal Confidentiality Certificates. This effort allowed participants the security of knowing their responses could not be reported to authorities, thus likely influencing their willingness to provide honest responses. Stone and colleagues (2000) warn that those without such protections in place may not be forthcoming in their responses, thus compromising the predictive validity of the COVR results. Doyle, Shaw, Carter, and Dolan (2010) used the COVR in their own examination of 93 acute psychiatric patients. Their analysis did not confirm the instrument's ability to predict future violent acts upon discharge. Instead, they found several other demographic variables to be more accurate predictors of violent acts. They called for additional cross-validation of the COVR.

Literature suggests that the mere classification of a patient into a high-risk category may affect his or her violence trajectory. By receiving this designation, a patient is likely to receive additional clinical support, which, in turn, may mitigate potential acts of violence (McCusker, 2007). This outcome further complicates the process of assessing and interpreting the COVR's predictive value as well.

COMMENTARY. The COVR is a brief instrument to administer and may assist clinicians in evaluating patients' propensity to engage in future violent behaviors, which could inform discharge planning. One of its key strengths is that its authors recognize that predictive factors associated with behaviors vary by individual. Its inductive approach to predicting the propensity to engage in future violence is notable as well. Further, the software is easy to navigate, and the resulting score reports are simple to decipher. Despite its potential utility, there are several limitations associated with the COVR. First, the test manual indicates that the instrument is to be used by physicians, medical students, psychologists, psychology interns, and nurses. There is no indication regarding whether the tool is appropriate for use by other professionals who may be tasked with discharge planning processes such as social workers, counselors, or other mental health professionals. The COVR also requests a GAF score. The validity of the GAF as an assessment of functioning has been called into question in recent literature due to its lack of reliability and clinical utility (APA, 2013). In addition, the COVR is based upon the original MacArthur Risk Study, which some have critiqued for its sample, methodology, and findings. Critics of that study suggest that individuals included in the original sample likely engaged in considerable violent behavior, thus skewing the data. They also call into question whether the comparison group was appropriate, whether the analysis of behaviors across diagnoses was comprehensive, whether the results are generalizable, and whether the conclusions regarding the relationship between treatment and violence reduction were accurate (Torrey, Stanley, Monahan, & Steadman, 2008). The instrument's developers also identify some additional considerations, including the reliability of self-report, whether clinical review is necessary, and how the COVR might actually inform risk communication as well as the strength of the relationship between risk assessment and risk management. With these points in mind, the test's developers reiterate throughout the professional manual (and on all score reports), that the COVR is to be used as a tool to supplement clinical judgment of potential risk, not to replace it. As such, the COVR should be pursued as one element of a more comprehensive assessment and discharge practice.

SUMMARY. The COVR is an interactive software system designed to assist clinicians in estimating inpatient psychiatric patients' violence risk. Clinicians should be discerning when deciding whether to use the COVR. It may serve as a solid initial guide in assessing a patient's potential risk but should not be relied upon in place of clinical judgment.

REVIEWER'S REFERENCES

American Psychiatric Association. (2013). *Diagnostic and statistical manual of mental disorders* (5th ed.). Washington, DC: Author.

Doyle, M., Shaw, J., Carter, S., & Dolan, M. (2010). Investigating the validity of the Classification of Violence Risk in a UK sample. *International Journal of Forensic Mental Health, 9*(4), 316-323.

MacArthur Research Network on Mental Health and the Law. (2001, April). Executive summary. Retrieved from http://www.macarthur.virginia.edu/mentalhome.html

McCusker, P. J. (2007). Issues regarding the clinical use of the Classification of Violence Risk (COVR) assessment instrument. *International Journal of Offender Therapy and Comparative Criminology, 51*(6), 676-685. doi.10.1177/0306624X0729927

Monahan, J., Steadman, H. J., Appelbaum, P. S., Grisso, T., Mulvey, E. P., Roth, L. H., ... Silver, E. (2006). The Classification of Violence Risk. *Behavioral Sciences & the Law, 24*, 721-730.

Stone, A., Turkkan, J., Bachrach, C., Jobe, J., Kurtzmna, H., & Cain, V. S. (Eds). (2000). *The science of self-report.* Mahwah, NJ: Erlbaum.

Torrey, E. F., Stanley, J., Monahan, J., & Steadman, H. J. (2008). The MacArthur Violence Risk Assessment Study Revisited: Two views ten years after its initial publication. *Psychiatric Services, 59*(2), 147-152.

Review of the Classification of Violence Risk by GEOFFREY L. THORPE, Professor Emeritus of Psychology, University of Maine, Orono, ME:

DESCRIPTION. The Classification of Violence Risk (COVR) is an interactive computer software program designed to help mental health professionals make accurate predictions about the danger to others posed by psychiatric inpatients being considered for discharge. The COVR is the result of extensive research on classification models and data from patient self-report, information from collateral contacts, and police and clinical records, and was developed from empirical findings that were refined in eight stages over 18 years. The materials received from the test publisher consist of a professional manual and a CD-ROM with printed instructions on installation and activation of the software, which guides the evaluator through a brief review of the clinical record and a 10-minute structured interview of the patient. A printable report is generated that classifies the patient's violence risk in five probability ranges (estimates of the likelihood of violence), five frequency ranges (estimates of the percentage of similar patients who will commit a violent act), and five risk categories: *very low, low, average, high,* and *very high*.

DEVELOPMENT. The developers of the COVR and authors of its professional manual remind us that (a) the clinical judgments of professionals based on unadorned traditional interviews and mental status examinations have failed to produce empirically valid predictions of patients' risk of future violence, whereas (b) prospective studies have demonstrated the predictive accuracy of indicators drawn from actuarial data. Accordingly, the developers identified an array of violence risk factors from archival data, selected those with the strongest predictive validity, and explored and tested "classification tree" assessment models in which the answers to key questions direct further questioning along appropriate lines.

The empirical basis for the COVR was established by a development study and a validation study. The development study (MacArthur Violence Risk Assessment Study; Monahan et al., 2001) was informed by the data from 1,136 psychiatric inpatients who were assessed for 106 violence risk factors and followed for 20 weeks post-discharge. At the end of the follow-up interval, patients were classified dichotomously as having, or having not, acted violently in the community after discharge from the hospital. Values for that binary variable were compared with those for each of the 106 potential risk factors in an iterative series of chi-square analyses. The risk factor with the most statistically significant value for chi-square would be used to divide the sample into two groups, and then "the recursive partitioning approach was extended [with additional risk factors] in an iterative fashion" (manual, p. 29).

Two thresholds or cutoff scores were derived, one for selecting high-risk and the other for selecting low-risk patients. The results for the group of patients classified between the two thresholds ("average risk" individuals) were re-analyzed to produce a series of successive refinements that could reveal any systematic differences between the average risk patients and those in the other categories. Five risk classes were identified and 10 "iterative classification tree" models were constructed.

The classification tree methodology led to a branching program in which the items evaluated would differ from patient to patient; responses to previous items would determine the items to be considered subsequently. The COVR software calculates a patient's level of risk as determined by the 10 models, each of which is distinguished by the first variable to be presented in its tree. The results for a given patient can be presented in terms of how many models indicate a given level of overall risk.

The validation study examined a new sample of 157 patients who were hospitalized in, or had recently been discharged from, facilities in Worcester, Massachusetts, and Philadelphia, Pennsylvania, and subsamples of patients who had been followed prospectively. The COVR and its component classification tree models identified those categorized as high- or low-risk for violence. The rate of actual violence in the community was 9% in the low-risk group and 35 to 49% (depending on the criterion used) in the high-risk group.

TECHNICAL. The 10 iterative classification tree models, each marked by the first risk factor listed in its tree, initially divided patients into *low risk, average risk,* and *high risk* groups. Examples of risk factors are "seriousness of arrest" and "anger reaction." Within a model, a given patient would receive a score of -1 (*low risk*), 0 (*average risk*) or +1 (*high risk*). A composite risk score ranging from -10 to +10 was assigned to each patient by adding the scores on all 10 models. The percentage of patients within the successive composite risk categories who in fact acted violently after discharge increased with almost perfect monotonicity. All models taken together predicted violence better than any single model, but stepwise logistic regression analyses led to the selection of the five most discriminating models.

The 939 patients in the development study committed 355 acts of violence during the 20-week follow-up interval. The two highest risk categories of the five identified by the COVR contained almost 18% of the sample but were associated with 67% of the violent acts.

COMMENTARY. A substantial body of research on violence risk assessment has been reported extensively in the professional literature by subsets of the list of COVR developers since 1994 if not earlier. Several of their articles on actuarial risk assessment, the classification tree approach, and risk communication appeared in 2000 alone, and the work has continued. The highlights of this literature as of 2005 have been summarized and distilled in the COVR professional manual, which serves as an accessible guide to the test user and a professional resource to the researcher. Among the information on reliability and validity tabulated and summarized in the manual one element stands out: the near-perfect monotonicity in the relationship between the categories reflecting increasing risk levels and the percentages of former patients in those categories actually acting violently during the 20-week follow-up interval. The predictive validity of the COVR was established for the composite risk scores from the 10-model and the five-model groupings, and for the five risk classes or categories.

Moving from one level to another in the iterative decision trees upon which the COVR results are based is managed by the software program itself and does not depend on the judgment or decision-making competencies of test administrators. Comparing the groups of patients found at the end of each of the possible branches of a decision tree would represent a challenging research task because of the many proliferations. In the example of the tree beginning with "seriousness of arrest" (none, minor, and major; manual, Fig. 1, p. 7), Iteration #1 ends in nine descriptors: two low-risk, two high-risk, and five indeterminate. Patients with any of the indeterminate descriptors move on to Iteration #2, ending in five descriptors: one low-risk, one high-risk, and three indeterminate. The shortest branch is Iteration #1: seriousness of arrest "high" and Recent Violent Fantasies "high" (high-risk group), and the longest is Iteration #1: Seriousness of Arrest "none," Motor Impulsiveness "low," Father Used Drugs "no," Legal Status "involuntary;" Iteration #2: Schizophrenia "no," Anger Reaction "high," Employed "no," and Legal Status "involuntary" (high-risk group).

The COVR software was easily installed, entering the data was a straightforward process, and the resulting score report presented information clearly. The facts that the minimum requirements for the use of this software include Windows XP, Vista, or 7 and an NTFS file system, and that the most recent copyright date is 2008, suggest that a revision and update may be overdue.

SUMMARY. The COVR is an interactive computer software program for processing information that can predict the risk of violence presented by current psychiatric inpatients. It is the result of extensive research on predictors of violence risk that can be identified from current clinical records and the results of a brief structured interview with a patient. The developers of the COVR used a classification tree model to assess different combinations of risk factors as predictive evidence of validity in accurately distributing patients among five levels of probability, frequency, and category of risk for future violence. The software loads and installs easily, and the format for entering data is convenient. The data to be entered are drawn from the current clinical record and a brief structured interview of the patient. Computer platforms and the professional research literature have advanced since the latest copyright dates of the professional manual (2005) and the CD-ROM (2008), so updates are warranted. The COVR can be recommended as a convenient clinical tool with well-researched psychometric properties.

REVIEWER'S REFERENCE

Monahan, J., Steadman, H. J., Silver, E., Appelbaum, P. S., Robbins, P. C., ... Banks, S. (2001). *Rethinking risk assessment: The MacArthur study of mental disorder and violence.* New York, NY: Oxford University Press.

[33]

Clinical Assessment of Pragmatics.

Purpose: A video-based test battery designed to evaluate the pragmatic language skills and social language development of children and young adults.
Population: Ages 7 through 18.
Publication Date: 2019.
Acronym: CAPs.
Scores, 10: 6 subtest scores: Instrumental Performance Appraisal, Social Context Appraisal, Paralinguistic Decoding, Instrumental Performance, Affective Expression, Paralinguistic Signals; 3 index scores: Pragmatic Judgment Index, Pragmatic Performance Index, Paralinguistic Index; Core Pragmatic Language Composite.
Administration: Individual.
Price Data, 2020: $237 per kit including manual (122 pages), USB with audio-video scenes, and 25 examiner record forms; $81 per manual; $105 per USB with audio-video scenes; $53 per 25 examiner record forms. All materials also available digitally.
Time: 45-55 minutes for administration.

Comments: Subtests may be administered separately.
Author: Adriana Lavi.
Publisher: Western Psychological Services.

Review of the Clinical Assessment of Pragmatics by KATHY L. COUFAL, Professor, Speech-Language Pathology, University of Nebraska-Omaha, Omaha, NE:

DESCRIPTION. The Clinical Assessment of Pragmatics (CAPs) is an individually administered assessment of pragmatic language skills and social language development of children and adolescents. This norm-referenced, video-based measure is designed to measure six pragmatic language constructs in children and young adults ages 7:0 through 18:11. The CAPs is intended to provide a standardized measure of six areas of pragmatic abilities and social language skills based on examinees' responses to examiner questions regarding video vignettes. The six areas are each evaluated by subtests, which include: (a) Instrumental Performance Appraisal, (b) Social Context Appraisal, (c) Paralinguistic Decoding, (d) Instrumental Performance, (e) Affective Expression, and (f) Paralinguistic Signals. Each video consists of short scenarios performed by professional actors depicting social situations. The video format is new, designed to replace pictorial stimuli, and intended to be more appropriate for assessing pragmatic abilities. The test is intended for use by speech-language pathologists and other professionals with the education and experience appropriate to administering a psychometric measure that includes judgment of examinees' linguistic and social development.

The purposes of the CAPs are to provide comprehensive information addressing four goals: (1) to identify and determine the degree of pragmatic language deficits, (2) to develop a profile of strengths and weaknesses among the pragmatic domains assessed, (3) to document progress and monitor treatment efficacy, and (4) to assess skills for use in research investigations. The test author describes the videos as depicting "true-to-life interactions ... which might occur in environments with which the participants could be expected to be familiar" (manual, p. 2). The characters in the videos represent a variety of ethnic and cultural backgrounds interacting in life-like contexts that are considered relevant. Vocabulary is appropriate to the age range of examinees and is presented in dialogues that are controlled for speaking rate and clarity. Test materials include a memory stick that contains the videos, examiner's manual, and scoring forms. Administration of the test requires arranging the computer to allow both the examiner and the examinee to view the monitor while seated in a quiet environment without distractions. Administration time is 45-55 minutes for the full version, which can vary considerably depending on variables such as age of examinee, language proficiency, attention to tasks, and the number of subtests administered.

The test manual describes each of the subtest purposes and rationale for inclusion, which is intended to help the examiner determine specific areas of strength and weakness and to plan interventions. The test author's aim is to draw distinctions between pragmatic judgment and pragmatic performance. Subtests are developed to assess pragmatic judgment as related to receptive pragmatic skills to "allow a more detailed grasp of an individual's ability to understand social situations" (manual, p. 6). Pragmatic performance is defined as "congruent to an individual's expressive pragmatic skills and is measured through the response given in social situations" (manual, p. 7). By measuring both judgment and performance, the intent is to derive a more complete profile of pragmatic abilities.

The CAPs yields four types of scores: raw scores, scaled scores, percentile ranks, and index/composite scores. Subtest scaled scores are combined to form index scores for three skill areas and an overall composite. Index scores and percentile ranks for Pragmatic Judgment, Pragmatic Performance, and Paralinguistics are derived from three subtests; the Core Pragmatic Language Composite is derived from the scaled scores of all six subtests.

The theoretical underpinnings for the CAPs are well documented and provide research that grounds the test author's rationale for the content and format of the instrument. Overall the conceptual framework for the CAPs is explained in the test manual, which is a strength of this instrument. One area of omission in the test manual is more detailed instructions for the examiner on how to compute indices in the three areas requiring specific subtests. Although examiners can determine which subtests to include from the assessment scoring form (shaded boxes indicate which scores to include in the computation) and from a sample record form that appears in the test manual, this information should be stated explicitly and clearly denoted in the appendix where conversion tables are presented.

DEVELOPMENT. The rationale and theoretical foundations for developing the CAPs are well articulated in the test manual. The author refers to seminal works in the area of pragmatics, such as those of Grice (1975), Hymes (1971), and Prutting and Kirchner (1987), as defining the aspects of pragmatics that are targeted in the assessment. The elements of the assessment are discussed, followed by directions for administration and scoring. Another chapter provides descriptions of the six subtests, which the author states were designed and constructed based on the theoretical underpinnings defined in an earlier chapter. This chapter also discusses the definition and application of the different scores derived from the CAPs. The test author links the various subtests and scores to the theoretical foundations: "The theory that the CAPs test was founded on explains that pragmatics can be conceptualized as an integrative interaction between pragmatic judgment, pragmatic performance, and paralinguistic cohesion. The CAPs subtests were combined in such a way as to form composites to represent these domains" (manual, p. 21).

TECHNICAL. Standardization and normative information are presented in the test manual. The standardization sample consisted of 914 examinees, ages 7:0-18:11, selected to match U.S. Census data. Participants were recruited from 14 geographically varied states and included members of three clinical groups: autism spectrum disorder (ASD; *n* = 18), specific language impairment (SLI; *n* = 27); and other (*n* = 92). Within each age group, the sample was stratified by gender, race or ethnic group, Hispanic origin, and geographic region.

Reliability. Coefficient alpha was used to examine internal consistency. Averaged across ages, coefficients were .89 to .91 for subtests and .95 for the composite. Interrater reliability was established by randomly selecting 24 examinee responses and having five raters score the responses. The resulting correlation coefficients were determined to be high (.90 or above). Test-retest reliability was investigated using a sample of 48 randomly selected examinees who took the test twice with a 16- to 20-day interval between administrations. Correlation coefficients were .80 to .92 for subtests and .94 to .95 for the composite.

Validity. Content evidence of validity was based on the reviews of 27 speech-language pathologists' expert opinions. Reviewer ratings for each of the six subtests are reported, leading the test author to conclude that the content is consistent with the theoretical intent of the CAPs. Construct evidence is presented as well and should be considered carefully by examiners, especially as related to the intercorrelations among subtests and the clinical validity examination, which involved differences between three clinical groups and a group of typically developing children. Inclusion criteria for the typically developing group (*n* = 80) were the following: normal hearing, age-appropriate speech and language development, demonstrated school success, and general education placement in public school. Those in the ASD group (*n* = 88) had a medical diagnosis according to the *Diagnostic and Statistical Manual of Mental Disorders* (5th ed.; *DSM-5;* American Psychiatric Association, 2013) and attended public school where they were in general education placements at least 3 hours daily. Those in the SLI (*n* = 61) and pragmatic language impairment (PLI; *n* = 64) groups had scores on two standardized tests of language that placed them at least 1.5 standard deviations below the mean for their chronological age and were in general education at least 4 hours per day. Exclusion criteria are further explained in the test manual. Results showed the ASD and the PLI groups scored significantly lower on all subtests than the SLI and typically developing groups. Further, no significant score differences were observed between the SLI group and the typically developing group, a finding the test author suggested is evidence of the CAPs' utility in assessing pragmatic language deficits.

COMMENTARY. The CAPs provides an approach to pragmatic assessment that replaces static pictures with more realistic video prompts. This is a promising addition to the clinical battery of assessments in the area of communication development. It is intended for use with a wide range of ages and backgrounds. It has the beginnings of normative data for use in identifying and differentiating among the elements of pragmatic performance that may be delayed or otherwise impairing effective communication. Overall, the sample size is very small given the scope of the population intended for inclusion.

There are some timing concerns with the management of the video prompts, as the vignettes do not always advance promptly following the examiner's selection. The administration instructions state that the video prompts cannot be replayed. This raises a concern. It is realistic that in "real-time" pragmatic situations an exchange does not have "instant replay" ability; however, this measure evaluates the examinee's ability to receive, process, integrate, analyze, and explain the pragmatic aspects of a vignette that can be less than 10 seconds long. Further, prompts are used to clarify or expand responses that are ambiguous or not provided using first-person pronouns in targeted subtests. Failure of the examinee to respond within 10 seconds of an item administration results in a score of zero. All examinee responses are judged and scored for each item before advancing to the next item presentation. Examples are provided on the record form of responses that align with the point values. The examiner is not instructed to record examinee responses for later review or as clinical data to be used for scoring or intervention planning, and insufficient space is provided on the scoring form for such purposes. Such transcription can be a valuable source of information and critical analysis and would enhance the value of the assessment data.

Videos are introduced by a narrator identifying each of the characters in the videos. A distraction occurs when the same actor is named differently in videos that are in succession. For example, the two males in the Instrumental Performance Appraisal vignettes are both referred to as "Tom" but are clearly not the same person (one is Hispanic, and one is Black/African American). Because the vignettes occur in succession and this continues to occur in multiple videos throughout the test, it may be a distraction for the examinee. Each character should be given his or her own name, and this should be maintained consistently throughout the test. Similarly, "Cindy" and "Jane" are referred to interchangeably, and at times a third character who is portraying Cindy's sister is referred to as "Jane." Again, this may be a distraction that could contribute to poor performance or inappropriate responses to the examiner's questions. Although the test author states the contexts for the videos are realistic settings, the same room is labeled as one character's bedroom and a different person's living room and at times changes across all the characters without any changes to the room setting. This is not realistic and, again, may introduce distractions that can have negative impact on performance. Finally, varying length of the vignettes may present performance challenges for examinees who are experiencing language or pragmatic challenges. For example, one vignette is approximately 4 seconds long whereas others are close to 1 minute. Vignettes cannot be replayed. Of course, the examiner needs to ensure the examinee is attending before playing each video, but a child anticipating the video will be longer or that there will be more to the story may miss important cues, thus negatively influencing performance.

The current version lacks technical scrutiny and has a relatively small standardization sample for the scope of the instrument. The test author and publisher provide the examiner with descriptive data, but considering the instrument is intended for use in research, it lacks the necessary technical foundations. The norms need to be strengthened using a larger sample, more independent raters for establishing reliability and validity with the increased sample population, and detailed analysis of the comparisons among subgroups of examinees. The test manual will be greatly improved with more detailed recommendations to assist examiners in the administration, scoring, and interpretation of results. Much is left to the examiner to determine, which makes the test more challenging. The benefit of specific administration details would enhance usability as would some changes to the record form to allow for transcribing examinee responses.

SUMMARY. The CAPs is designed as a clinical assessment of pragmatic abilities using video prompts rather than static picture stimuli. It is grounded in theoretical constructs that define the elements of pragmatics and align with the subtests of the CAPs. In this reviewer's opinion, the instrument lacks sufficient sample size and critical analysis among the many subgroups within the norming population and the six subtests of the instrument. Further expansion of the instrument would enhance examiner confidence in the results and scoring. It should be used cautiously and supplemented with other standardized measures of communication, observation of performance in naturally occurring contexts, and structured ethnographic interviews with familiar communication partners.

REVIEWER'S REFERENCES

American Psychiatric Association. (2013). *Diagnostic and statistical manual of mental disorders* (5th ed.). Washington, DC: Author.

Grice, H. P. (1975). Logic and conversation. In P. Cole & J. Morgan (Eds.), *Studies in syntax and semantics III: Speech acts*. New York, NY: Academic Press.

Hymes, D. (1971). On communicative competence. In J. Pride & J. Holmes (Eds.), *Sociolinguistics*. Harmondsworth, UK: Penguin.

Prutting, C. A., & Kirchner, D. M. (1987). A clinical appraisal of the pragmatic aspects of language. *Journal of Speech and Hearing Disorders*, 52(2), 105-119.

Review of the Clinical Assessment of Pragmatics by CAROL WESTBY, Consultant, Bilingual Multicultural Services, Inc., Albuquerque, NM:

DESCRIPTION. The Clinical Assessment of Pragmatics (CAPs) is a standardized, norm-referenced test of pragmatics for students ages 7 years 0 months through 18 years 11 months. The CAPs is intended for the following uses: (a) to identify pragmatic language deficits and determine the degree of the deficits, (b) to determine strengths and weaknesses within several pragmatic domains, (c) to document progress in pragmatic language skills and measure treatment efficacy, and (d) to analyze social pragmatic skills in children and young adults for research purposes.

The CAPs uses videos of teenagers from diverse backgrounds engaging in true-to-life social interactions to evaluate two aspects of students' pragmatic skills: pragmatic judgment or appraisal (their ability to comprehend social situations) and pragmatic performance (their ability to express themselves appropriately in various social situations). On Pragmatic Judgment subtests, students are asked to judge the appropriateness of social interaction by answering, "Did anything go wrong on this video?" and "What went wrong?" On the Pragmatic Performance subtests, students are asked "What would you say and how?" Three areas of judgment/appraisal and performance are assessed for a total of six subtests: instrumental intent (judgment: awareness of basic social routines, such as introductions, requesting information, asking permission; and performance: using social routine language in these situations), affective intent (judgment: ability to read social contextual cues, infer what others are thinking, and interpret figurative language; and performance: ability to appropriately express emotions such as regret, sorrow, empathy, and encouragement verbally and nonverbally), and paralinguistic cohesion (judgment: ability to detect a speaker's intent by recognizing meaning of facial cues, tone of voice, prosody, and gestures; and performance: ability to use facial expressions, tone of voice, prosody, and gestures to express a variety of communicative intents). Each item is scored on a 0 to 2 or 0 to 3 scale, with 0 indicating an incorrect response and 1 to 3 indicating a correct response with increasing detail in the explanations or specificity in the language and behaviors used. Examples of scored responses are available for all items.

The six subtests are grouped into three indexes: Pragmatic Judgment; Pragmatic Performance; and Paralinguistic, which includes the paralinguistic subtests plus the expressing affective intent subtest. Scaled scores and percentile ranks are available for each of the six subtests; standard scores and percentile ranks are available for the overall Core Pragmatic Language Composite and the three indexes. The test form also includes a Conversational Adaptation Checklist designed to note information obtained through observation or interviews of parents or teachers. The categories and specific items on the checklist mirror the content of the video stimuli.

DEVELOPMENT. This test was developed to address the issue that many students diagnosed with autism or social communication disorder exhibit pragmatic difficulties in activities of daily living, yet do well on a number of the standardized tools designed to evaluate pragmatics. Current tests of pragmatics typically use static, two-dimensional pictures to elicit description of emotions and potential reasons for emotions, report expected social rules or violation of social rules, explain what is meant when a person uses figurative language or sarcasm, or suggest what should be said in a situation. These tests are not so much assessments of the ability to use pragmatic skills, but rather of cognitive knowledge of pragmatic rules. Although such factual knowledge (or pragmatic judgment) is foundational for appropriate pragmatic behaviors, this knowledge does not ensure that persons can interpret the relevant cues in real-life situations and organize an appropriate response. The intent of the CAPs is to evaluate students' abilities to interpret and use language in context. By responding to video stimuli, students demonstrate their ability to consider multiple contextual cues to interpret the purpose and appropriateness of communication in a specific situation and to organize responses that incorporate appropriate language, facial expression, gestures, and tone of voice.

TECHNICAL.

Standardization. The CAPs was normed on a sample of 914 students across eight age groups in 14 states. The standardization sample was selected to match the U.S. Census data regarding gender, race/ethnicity, parents' educational level, and geographic region. Of the total sample, 2% were diagnosed with autism spectrum disorder and 3% with specific language impairment.

Reliability. The CAPs manual presents reliability information related to internal consistency, standard errors of measurement (*SEM*), interrater reliability, and test-retest. Alpha coefficients were used to estimate the internal consistency of the test items—how closely the items in each area, at each age level, and for gender and each racial/ethnic group were related. Generally speaking, coefficients of .70 or higher are considered acceptable. All alpha coefficients for the CAPs were in the high

.80s and .90s. To evaluate interrater reliability, five speech-language pathologists were trained on item-by-item scoring rules and procedures and then independently evaluated 24 randomly selected test administrations. The interrater reliability coefficients for all subtests were between .90 and .97. Test-retest reliability was examined for the six subtests and the composite score by randomly selecting and retesting 48 of the original 914 children within 16 to 20 days of the original testing. Retest coefficients for all subtests were above .80 and for the composite exceeded .90. The *SEM* was 1 point for nearly all subtest scores at all age levels and 3 for the composite score at all age levels.

Validity. The CAPs manual provides information related to multiple sources of validity evidence. Content evidence of validity was examined by having 27 experienced speech-language pathologists with at least 5 years of experience with assessment of children with autism and pragmatic language impairment watch all videos and answer five questions regarding how each of the subtests related to test content and whether they believed the test was an adequate measure of pragmatic language skills. Criterion evidence of validity was assessed by correlating four of the CAPs subtests with four other well-known tests that assess pragmatic skills (Comprehensive Assessment of Spoken Language, CASL, Carrow-Woolfolk, 1999; Test of Pragmatic Language, TOPL, Phelps-Terasaki & Phelps-Gunn, 1992; and the Social Language Developmental Test [Elementary and Adolescent Editions], SLDT, Bowers, Huisingh, & LoGiudice, 2008, 2010). The test author reports that the two paralinguistic subtests were not correlated with other assessments because their content and design are unique. The CAPs instrumental intent judgment and performance subtests were highly correlated with the CASL Pragmatic Judgment subtest with coefficients of .96 and .87, respectively. The CAPs affective intent judgment and performance subtests correlated with the SLDT at .86 and .74, respectively. The correlations between the TOPL and the CAPs affective judgment and performance subtests were lower (.62 and .54, respectively). To demonstrate clinical/diagnostic validity for autism, the test author reports sensitivity ranges from .90 to 1.0 and specificity ranges from .85 to .97. Diagnosis of autism was based on the *Diagnostic and Statistical Manual of Mental Disorders* (5th ed.; *DSM-5*; American Psychological Association, 2013), but because level of autism was not reported, the degree to which the CAPs identifies higher-functioning students is unknown. Means and standard deviations of CAPs subtest scores are reported for three clinical groups—autism spectrum disorder (ASD), pragmatic language impairment (PLI), and specific language impairment (SLI)—and a demographically matched typically developing group. As expected, both the ASD and PLI groups scored significantly ($p < .001$) lower than the SLI group and the typically developing group on all subtests. The ASD group also scored significantly lower than the PLI group on all subtests except the judgment portion of instrumental intent.

COMMENTARY. Many children and adolescents who exhibit pervasive social language deficits in daily life activities attain average scores not only on tests measuring semantic, morphological, and syntactic skills, but also on tests designed to assess pragmatic skills. School systems frequently will not qualify students for special education services unless their performance on standardized tests is 1.5–2.0 standard deviations below a test mean. At this time, the CAPs is the only standardized pragmatic test to use video/audio stimuli for all tasks. This makes it unique and enables it to address issues in pragmatic assessment that have not been taken into account previously. Although the CAPs has good face validity for identifying deficits in high-functioning students with autism or social communication disorder, unfortunately, the test manual provides limited justification from the research on pragmatics and autism/social communication disorder to explain the rationale for the six subtests and why video/audio stimuli are likely to improve the abilities to assess pragmatic skills in higher functioning students. Such research literature is available.

Vermeulen (2012) suggested that persons with autism have context blindness—they have difficulty responding to multiple pieces of information at the same time; they are insensitive to context that affects face perception, emotion recognition, the understanding of language and communication, and problem solving. Tests of pragmatics that use static picture stimuli provide minimal contextual information. Furthermore, with static picture stimuli, students see a facial expression and a body stance and have quite a bit of time to process components of the scene. In actual interactions (and videos of interactions), students must interpret facial expressions, gestures, and tone of voice simultaneously within microseconds. Hence, although videos still do not provide all the same contextual information as real-life situations, they do require the rapid simultaneous processing of multiple cues.

SUMMARY. The CAPs is a standardized, norm-referenced test using video stimuli designed to assess the pragmatic skills of students ages 7:0 through 18:11. Because it requires the ability to rapidly and simultaneously interpret multiple cues in social situations and to integrate language, facial expressions, gestures, and tone of voice to produce appropriate and effective responses in realistic social situations, it may better identify social deficits in students with average or above average skills in cognition and structural language than pragmatic tests that employ static pictures or language vignettes only as stimuli.

REVIEWER'S REFERENCES

Bowers, L., Huisingh, R., & LoGiudice, C. (2008). Social Language Development Test—Elementary. East Moline, IL: LinguiSystems.

Bowers, L., Huisingh, R., & LoGiudice, C. (2010). Social Language Development Test—Adolescent. East Moline, IL: LinguiSystems.

Carrow-Woolfolk, E. (1999). Comprehensive Assessment of Spoken Language. Torrance, CA: Western Psychological Services.

Phelps-Terasaki, D., & Phelps-Gunn, T. (1992). Test of Pragmatic Language. Austin, TX: PRO-ED.

Vermeulen, P. (2012). *Autism as context blindness*. Shawnee Mission, KS: AAPC.

[34]

Cognistat [2016 Manual].

Purpose: Designed to assess "five major domains of cognitive functioning" for screening and quantifying neuropsychological problems.
Population: Ages 12 and older.
Publication Dates: 1983-2016.
Administration: Individual.
Forms, 4: Paper, off-line, online, and short forms available.
Time: Approximately 20 minutes for administration.
Comments: Formerly titled The Neurobehavioral Cognitive Status Examination.
Authors: Jonathan Mueller, Ralph Kiernan, J. William Langston, and Richard J. Flanagan.
Publisher: Cognistat, Inc.

a) COGNISTAT PAPER.
Scores, 11: Level of Consciousness, Orientation, Attention, Language (Comprehension, Repetition, Naming), Constructional Ability, Memory, Calculations, Reasoning (Similarities, Judgment).
Price Data, 2019: $575 per starter kit including manual (2016, 96 pages), 25 test booklets, stimulus booklet, and set of 8 tokens; $475 per 25 test booklets; $75 per manual; $35 per stimulus booklet; $35 per set of 8 tokens.
Foreign Language Editions: Available in Chinese, Czech, Finnish, French, Hebrew, Japanese, Norwegian, Spanish, and Swedish.
Comments: The original paper-and-pencil test.

b) COGNISTAT ACTIVE FORM.
Scores, 12: Same as *a*) above, plus Mild Cognitive Impairment (MCI) Index.
Price Data: $525 per starter kit including unlimited active forms for 1 month, stimulus booklet, and set of 8 tokens; $425 per 25 tests; $35 per stimulus booklet; $35 per set of 8 tokens.
Foreign Language Editions: Available in French and Spanish.
Comments: An off-line, computer-assisted version of the original paper-and-pencil test.

c) COGNISTAT ASSESSMENT SYSTEM.
Acronym: CAS-II.
Scores, 12: Same as *b*) above.
Price Data: $525 per starter kit including manual, 25 online tests, stimulus booklet, and set of 8 tokens; $425 per 25 online tests; $35 per stimulus booklet; $35 per set of 8 tokens.
Foreign Language Editions: Available in Czech, French, and Spanish.
Comments: A computer-assisted, online version of the original paper-and-pencil test; creates an electronic data record (EDR) for the patient, which allows for data sharing and longitudinal analysis.

d) COGNISTAT FIVE.
Purpose: "Designed to screen rapidly for the presence of delirium/confusion or cognitive deficits due to mild cognitive impairment (MCI) or dementia."
Population: Ages 18 and older.
Publication Dates: 1983-2016.
Scores, 4: Memory, Orientation, Constructions, Mild Cognitive Impairment (MCI) Index.
Administration: Individual.
Price Data: $295 per starter kit including 100 tests (paper or digital), manual (2016, 38 pages), stimulus booklet, and Guide to MCI Index Scores; $350 per 100 tests (paper or digital); $35 per set of 8 tokens; $20 per Guide to MCI Index Scores.
Foreign Language Edition: Available in French.
Time: Approximately 5 minutes for administration.
Comments: Abbreviated version of the full Cognistat test; available in paper and digital computer-assisted (online and off-line) formats.
Authors: Jonathan Mueller, Ralph Kiernan, and Richard Flanagan.

Cross References: For reviews by Charles J. Long and Faith Gunning-Dixon and by Steven R. Shaw of an earlier (1995) edition, see 14:81.

Review of the Cognistat [2016 Manual] by KAREN T. CAREY, Provost, University of Alaska Southeast, Juneau, AK:

DESCRIPTION. The Cognistat is a cognitive screening test designed to assess five major ability areas including language, spatial skills, memory, calculations, and reasoning. There are six formats for the test, which was normed on adolescents, adults, and three age groups of seniors. The six formats include a traditional paper-and-pencil test; the Cognistat Active Form, a computer-assisted offline PDF version of the original; the Cognistat Assessment System, a web-based version of the original; and the Cognistat Five, a rapid version available as a PDF, an online, or a paper-and-pencil version. The Cognistat Five is especially designed for individuals with delirium, confusion, mild cognitive impairment, and dementia. The first three versions mentioned above take 15 to 20 minutes to administer, and the Cognistat Five takes approximately 5 minutes to administer. Individuals taking the Cognistat do not have interaction with the computer versions; the computer versions provide guidance, analysis, and scoring for the administrator. All versions can be administered by health care professionals, including nurses, other therapists (e.g., occupational therapists), and clinical assistants. Training videos are available online at the Cognistat website.

All versions are used in a face-to-face setting with the patient, and the examiner records the patient's responses on a protocol (either on paper or digitally). The patient's general information, any factors that may influence his/her test performance (e.g., neurological conditions, dizziness, exhaustion), and any medications the patient may be taking are recorded. Questions are then asked of the patient related to Orientation to time and place; Attention (digit repetition); Memory Registration (four words are given to the patient who must repeat all four words on two consecutive trials); Language, which includes a speech sample (the patient is shown a picture and asked to tell the examiner what is happening in the picture), a Comprehension section (six items are placed in front of the patient and he/she is asked to complete a series of commands), a Repetition section (the patient repeats a series of phrases and sentences), and a Naming section (a series of pictures is shown to the patient, and he/she names each item); Constructional Ability (the patient is shown two drawings for 10 seconds and then asked to draw them from memory and to complete three block designs with red and white squares); Memory (repeating the four words from the Memory Registration section); Calculations (a series of arithmetic problems are presented to the patient that he/she must complete in 20 seconds or less); and Reasoning, including Similarities (e.g., identifying how two items are alike) and Judgment (e.g., "what if" questions). The protocol has additional space for the patient's impression of his/her responses (recorded by the examiner) and the examiner's observations. Scores are summed for each domain. A graphic profile illustrates the patient's strengths and weaknesses.

The Mild Cognitive Impairment (MCI) Index may be obtained on the computerized versions and identifies the degree of risk for mild cognitive impairment and dementia. The MCI Index provides a rating for patients on a 7-point scale ranging from 0 to 6, where 0 reflects *no indication of cognitive impairment* and 6 *strongly suggests dementia.*

DEVELOPMENT. The Cognistat was originally known as the Neurobehavioral Cognitive Status Examination (NCSE) and was developed by Drs. Ralph Kiernan, Jonathan Mueller, and J. William Langston in 1979. Minimal information is provided in the test manual related to the development of the Cognistat, and the user is directed to two articles appearing in the *Annals of Internal Medicine* (1987). In the articles the tool is described as a "screening examination that assesses in a brief fashion, uses independent tests to evaluate functioning within five major cognitive ability areas…" (Kiernan, Mueller, Langston, & Van Dyke, 1987, p. 481). Schwamm, Van Dyke, Kiernan, Merrin, and Mueller (1987) conducted a comparative study of three different measures: NCSE (i.e., Cognistat), the Cognitive Capacity Screening Exam (CCSE), and the Mini-Mental State Examination (MMSE) with 30 individuals diagnosed with brain lesions. Results indicated that the NCSE was significantly more sensitive than the other measures due to the use of individual subtests and graded items used to assess the five major cognitive areas.

TECHNICAL. The Cognistat was normed on 60 volunteers from the developers' own non-professional staff, in two age groups (20-30 and 40-66). Results on the subtests indicated minimal variability among the participants, and there were no significant differences between the age groups. A validity study was conducted with 59 participants between the ages of 70 and 92 years (Harris, Van Aelstyn, Kurn, & Kiernan, 1991) with no known medical or physical conditions. Results indicated a slightly larger standard deviation than had been observed in younger populations, but scores were within normal limits. A further study conducted by the test authors with 30 neurosurgical patients diagnosed with brain lesions (ages 25 to 88 years) found that scores obtained by this population fell far below the standardization groups, and 28 of the 30 patients had below average scores on at least one subtest.

In terms of reliability, the test authors state that because the Cognistat is a screening tool, the range of performance among the normal population is very small. Test-retest reliability would simply result in the same scores over and over. Split-half reliability scores also would be of limited value as there are so few items on the test. Finally, the test authors note, "The meaning of reliability studies in pathologic populations that are notoriously unstable is even less clear" (manual, p. 36).

COMMENTARY. The Cognistat can be a useful screening tool for individuals with possible cognitive impairments but it should be viewed as just that—a screening tool. A more thorough assessment of an individual's cognitive impairments would be required. The test authors note on the protocol that, "Not all brain lesions produce cognitive deficits that will be detected by Cognistat. Average Range scores, therefore, cannot be taken as evidence that brain pathology does not exist. Similarly, scores falling in the Mild, Moderate, or Severe range of impairment do not necessarily reflect brain dysfunction." In addition the test manual lists a number of cautions related to the interpretation of scores that should be heeded by the examiner.

The test manual provides information about 10 detailed cognitive status profiles. Cases described include cerebral infarction, encephalitis, alcohol abuse, dementia, and mild cognitive impairment. In addition, a list of references that reflect studies conducted on the use of the Cognistat with different populations is provided.

SUMMARY. The Cognistat was designed to be a face-to-face screening tool to assess neurocognitive functioning in five domains that may be due to dementia, brain injury, stroke, or other cognitive conditions. Administration is straightforward, and the online versions provide additional information for the examiner. Little information is provided in the test manual in terms of test development and standardization or technical properties, including reliability and validity. An administrator should not rely on the Cognistat for making any type of diagnosis.

REVIEWER'S REFERENCES

Harris, M. E., Van Aelstyn, C., Kurn, S. J., & Kiernan, R. (1991). Performance of normal elderly on the Neurobehavioral Cognitive Status Examination, and related findings in Alzheimer's disease. *Archives in Clinical Neuropsychology,* 6, p. 191.

Kiernan, R. J., Mueller, J., Langston, J. W., & Van Dyke, C. (1987). The Neurobehavioral Cognitive Status Examination: A brief but differentiated approach to cognitive assessment. *Annals of Internal Medicine,* 107, 481-485.

Schwamm, L. H., Van Dyke, C., Kiernan, R. J., Merrin, E. L., & Mueller, J. (1987). The Neurobehavioral Cognitive Status Examination: Comparison with the Cognitive Capacity Screening Examination and the Mini-Mental State Examination in a neurosurgical population. *Annals of Internal Medicine, 107,* 486-491.

Review of the Cognistat [2016 Manual] by MARY (RINA) M. CHITTOORAN, Associate Professor, School of Education, Saint Louis University, St. Louis, MO:

DESCRIPTION. The Cognistat (with the 2016 manual) is an individually administered screening measure of cognitive functioning in five major domains: receptive and expressive language, pattern construction, calculations, memory, and reasoning. It can be used by professionals in fields such as geriatrics and neuropsychology to describe and quantify cognitive functioning and neuropsychological deficits in individuals age 12 and older. The Cognistat comes in six forms, including paper, online, and computer-assisted offline versions, several of which are available in multiple languages.

Test materials include a manual with information about the philosophical underpinnings of the Cognistat, normative data, and instructions for administration, as well as test protocols, a stimulus booklet, and a set of small plastic tiles. Examiners are required to provide six common items, such as an eraser, for one of the subtests. Training needs for administration, scoring, and interpretation are minimal, and the test manual indicates that trained health care professionals can administer the Cognistat in 5-20 minutes, depending on which form of the test is being used.

The Cognistat uses the "screen and metric" (manual, p. 10) approach to test administration, so that the examinee is first presented with a screening item in each area of functioning except memory. A pass on that item indicates adequate functioning in that area and the examiner is directed to the next area of cognitive functioning. Failure on the screening item necessitates further testing in that area. Performance on the Cognistat may be reported as pass or fail and as numerical scores ranging from 0 to 3, depending on the item. Certain test items also allow the examiner to assess an examinee's performance qualitatively; for example, a score of 2 is assigned to an abstract response on the Similarities subtest, whereas a concrete response would be assigned a score of 1. Raw scores on the Cognistat can be plotted on a Cognitive Status Profile that offers examiners a visual representation of strengths and weaknesses in the following areas: Level of Consciousness, Orientation (Person, Place, and Time), Attention, Language (Comprehension, Repetition, and Naming), Constructional Ability, Memory, Calculations, and Reasoning (Similarities and Judgment). The profile shows the average range of functioning, as well as mild, moderate, and severe cognitive impairment for each of the cognitive areas. Also available on computerized versions of the Cognistat is the Mild Cognitive Impairment (MCI) Index which uses expert system technology to guide clinical decision-making. The MCI assesses the degree of risk for mild cognitive impairment and dementia based on a consideration of the patient's "memory and constructional skills ... adjusted for age and education" (manual, p. 9). Index levels range from 0 (*no indication of cognitive impairment*) to 4 (*raises the question of a dementia syndrome*) to 6 (*strongly suggests a dementia syndrome*).

DEVELOPMENT. The present-day Cognistat is the successor to the Neurobehavioral Cognitive Status Examination (NCSE). The measure was developed in 1979 and has been in almost continuous use since then. The measure is based on the idea that cognitive functions are discrete and therefore need to be assessed individually, using specific tasks that target those areas. It is also based on the presumption that the assessment areas are those most susceptible to brain dysfunction and that assessment in those areas may be the first step in a more comprehensive assessment in cases where impairment is strongly suspected. The Cognistat authors argue against a global score of functioning that may mask weaknesses in one or more individual areas; instead, the test provides domain-specific scores that may be particularly informative in the beginning stages of cognitive decline.

TECHNICAL. The 2016 Cognistat manual provides initial standardization information about 60 participants who were selected from staff members at the authors' places of employment and divided into two age groups: 20-30 years and 40-66 years. All participants had a normal medical and neurological history and none were on medications or substances that might have affected test results. Mean differences across both groups were small and not statistically significant. An independent study conducted with 263 adolescents ranging from 12 to 19 years of age yielded norms that can be used with examinees in this age range.

Information about validity is presented for a geriatric population consisting of 59 individuals with a mean age of 77.6 years. Once again, these participants were volunteers with normal histories; however, there were statistically significant differences between this group and the original standardization group in construction, memory, and similarities, the three areas that tend to be most influenced by cognitive decline in old age. Thirty neurosurgical patients (mean age = 54.2 years) with documented brain lesions also were assessed using the Cognistat prior to neurosurgery. Mean scores fell far below the scores of the standardization sample as well as the geriatric group, and 28 of the 30 participants had below average scores on at least one Cognistat subtest. The test manual also reports an independent validity study of 123 typically functioning individuals that resulted in varying profiles across different age groups, with participants between the ages of 75 and 84 years doing more poorly than those in the 65-74 age range, as might be expected. Finally, the test manual offers a comparison of scores on the Cognistat and another neuropsychological battery for 13 patients who took both measures; results showed a high degree of comparability between the Cognistat and the other measure.

The test authors mention the importance of reliability and provide a justification for not providing coefficients, citing issues such as brevity of the measure and the historic unreliability of test-retest data in normal and pathological populations. No other reliability information is provided.

COMMENTARY. The Cognistat has been in regular use for more than 35 years as of this writing. It has been translated into numerous languages and is used all over the world. Its authorship by two medical doctors and two PhDs recognizes its interdisciplinary nature as well as its potential utility for a range of disciplines. The online and offline versions of the measure are a welcome addition to the paper forms and facilitate administration, scoring, and interpretation. The materials are relatively inexpensive and easy to use, and the 96-page manual includes a good deal of information about the test and the record form as well as instructions about how to administer and interpret the test. The manual also includes several pages of references categorized by discipline, some of which refer to the more than 300 studies that have been conducted using various versions of the Cognistat. The record form also conveniently includes space to comment on factors that could influence test performance, including pain, mania/psychosis, and central nervous system (CNS) active medications that the patient might be taking.

The screen and metric approach is a quick and efficient way to administer the Cognistat given that it saves time and limits frustration for patients who may struggle with some of the tasks presented.

The Cognitive Status Profile offers a quick snapshot of an individual's functioning, and the inclusion of 10 cases with completed profiles, such as patients with aphasia and dementia, is likely to be very helpful for clinicians.

Despite the positive features described here, there are some concerns surrounding the Cognistat. The most important of these has to do with the relative lack of technical information that is included in the test manual. For example, although the manual provides a rationale for the Cognistat and the types of scores that are available, it would be very helpful to know more about test development. How did the authors come up with the test items? Were they based on clinical practice, on the literature, or both? Was the first draft of the measure revised, perhaps subsequent to content expert review or piloting of the instrument? Perhaps this information is available somewhere in the history of the Cognistat, but it should be included in the test manual. Some standardization information was provided, but it would be useful to have more details about patients in the standardization groups. Validation studies are reported, but they are not described using the usual terms associated with validity. Further studies that examine the predictive ability of the Cognistat would be helpful as would studies that examine the equivalence of the Cognistat and other measures like it, perhaps the Mini-Mental State Examination. Also, given that reliability information is absent, it is difficult to determine whether the Cognistat is a reliable measure. The authors do comment on the futility of studying the reliability of the Cognistat, but perhaps an attempt could have been made to study interrater reliability or the comparability of short and long forms of the Cognistat. There are numerous studies included in the test manual; perhaps some of those could have been summarized and added to the section on the technical merits of the measure. Finally, it must be noted that the screen and metric approach has its advantages; however, it is subject to the limitations inherent in such an approach, that is, the high likelihood of a number of false positives or false negatives.

The Cognistat record form is plagued by tiny, crowded font and too much print on each page. Although this reviewer appreciates the effort to save paper, it also makes the record form difficult to use. One other minor concern relates to the fact that the pages of the record form could be numbered for easier access.

In addition to the Cognistat Paper, this reviewer also examined the Cognistat Five, which is a brief version of the Cognistat that is designed to be administered in 5 minutes. This measure assesses only orientation, memory, and construction, given that these areas are most susceptible to cognitive decline. The Cognistat Five can be a good first step in neuropsychological assessment but must be followed up by more comprehensive assessment if deficits are noted. Further, given the fact that the test manual does not provide evidence of the comparability between the Cognistat Five and the longer version of the Cognistat, caution should be exercised in using the measures interchangeably.

The reviewer also accessed the Cognistat Assessment System (CAS-II), which is the online version of the paper measure. Positive features of the CAS-II included an online version of the manual, automatic scoring, convenient Help buttons, the automatic generation of a Cognitive Status Profile, a number of norms tables, and the MCI Index. One minor, but somewhat frustrating concern had to do with the fact that Firefox was the only web browser that allowed the examiner to accurately register a "new patient's" date of birth. It might, therefore, be a good idea to include information about the technology requirements in the test manual itself.

As part of the review of this measure, the reviewer conducted a trial administration of the Cognistat Paper with an 86-year-old female who was experiencing memory loss and some mental confusion. Medical records indicated that she had, unbeknownst to her, suffered a minor stroke in the recent past. Test administration, scoring, and interpretation proved to be a simple matter; further, the examinee's scores on the Cognistat showed impaired functioning in the Memory subtests and no impairment in the other areas, as might well have been expected, given her history.

SUMMARY. The Cognistat (with the 2016 manual) is one of the few published measures of its kind in that it (a) provides a screening measure of cognitive impairment in five primary functional areas in adolescents and adults, and (b) has a long and successful history of use not only in the United States but in other countries, as well. The Cognistat is highly recommended as a screening measure of cognitive impairment in adults. It also can serve as a basis for decisions about comprehensive assessments of individuals who exhibit impaired cognitive functioning in one or more areas assessed by this measure.

[35]

Communication Activities of Daily Living–Third Edition.

Purpose: Designed to measure "functional communication abilities in adults with neurogenic disorders of language."
Population: Adults ages 18 and older with neurogenic language disorders.
Publication Dates: 1980-2018.
Acronym: CADL-3.
Scores: Total score only.
Administration: Individual.
Price Data, 2017: $248 per kit including manual (2018, 42 pages), picture book, 25 record booklets, and 25 response forms; $97 per picture book; $69 per manual; $49 per 25 record booklets; $33 per 25 response forms.
Time: Approximately 30 minutes for administration.
Comments: Administration requires four $1 bills and two quarters supplied by the examiner.
Authors: Audrey Holland, Davida Fromm, and Linda Wozniak.
Publisher: PRO-ED.
Cross References: For reviews by Carolyn Mitchell Person and Katharine Snyder of the second edition, see 14:84; for a review by Rita Sloan Berndt of an earlier edition titled Communicative Abilities in Daily Living, see 10:69 (2 references).

Review of Communication Activities of Daily Living—Third Edition by MARY BOYLE, Professor of Communication Sciences & Disorders, Montclair State University, Montclair, NJ:

DESCRIPTION. Communication Activities of Daily Living—Third Edition (CADL-3) is designed to assess functional everyday communication abilities of adults ages 18 and older with neurogenic disorders of language who were premorbidly fluent in English. Its aim is to provide information about an individual's ability to communicate, verbally and/or nonverbally, in everyday situations by presenting the individual with a series of plausible communication activities, each supported by appropriate contextual material (e.g., photographs, computer screenshots, text material) and asking the individual to respond to a specific question or command. The third edition has retained the format, scoring, and administration procedures of the second edition. The test authors updated several features of the test in this edition to make the test more contemporary and efficient, specifically: picture stimuli are mostly photographs instead of drawings; items that address basic use of technology (e.g., mobile phones, email) have been added; the new edition was normed on a new standardization sample; all administration instructions are included in the examiner record book; and reliability and validity studies have been expanded.

The CADL-3 is meant to be administered by certified speech-language pathologists who have formal training in assessment and experience in evaluating and treating individuals with neurogenic communication disorders. The test authors report that testing can be completed in approximately 30 minutes, but there is no time limit for administering the test. It is acceptable to provide breaks during administration, but the test authors recommend that the test be completed in a single session. Test takers should have adequate hearing and vision, whether corrected or uncorrected, to follow a conversation at normal volume and to read a newspaper.

The test consists of 50 items. Materials consist of an examiner's manual, a picture book, an examiner record booklet, and an examinee response form used for three of the test items. The test authors recommend that examiners practice administering the test before using it for an actual assessment in order to develop a system for recording responses and to develop a natural presentation style. Instructions for administering the test are straightforward, and the materials are easy to manipulate during testing. Complete instructions for administering each item are in the examiner record booklet, which contributes to smooth and efficient administration.

Seven categories of communication activities are addressed in the CADL-3. Reading, Writing, or Using Numbers assesses basic contextual reading and writing of numbers and includes calculations involving money, time, and dates. Social Interactions requires communication of information and intent as well as use of simple social conventions like greetings. Contextual Communication items require the test taker to consider the context supplied by the examiner when responding. Nonverbal Communication includes interpreting symbols like traffic signs and facial expressions. Sequential Relationships involves performing sequences of actions or interpreting cause-effect relationships. Humor, Metaphor, and Absurdity requires interpretation of figurative language and understanding humor. Internet Basics involves skills required to find information on the Internet.

The scoring system for the third edition has not changed. General scoring guidelines and a description of the scoring system are included in the examiner's manual. This information is repeated in the examiner record booklet, which also contains scoring criteria for each item alongside the instructions for administering the item. The CADL-3 uses a 3-point scoring system. A score of 0 points is given for responses that are clearly incorrect. A score of 1 point is awarded when a response is partially correct or when a test taker does not respond within 5 seconds but then responds correctly when the item is readministered. A score of 2 points is given when a response clearly and completely answers the question, whether verbally or nonverbally (e.g., with a gesture or by drawing) or when the test taker spontaneously requests repetition of an item within 5 seconds and then answers correctly. Including scoring criteria for each item is a strength of the test, because it reduces idiosyncratic decision making by the examiner.

The test authors recommend that examiners develop a system for recording responses that captures their nature and modality, since this information is important for counseling, planning treatment, and measuring change over time. They provide some suggestions, such as using "G" to code gestured responses or writing a brief note to capture the gist of a response. Identifying the response modalities is helpful in determining the test taker's communicative strengths and/or in choosing areas that could potentially improve with treatment.

Results on the CADL-3 can be reported as raw scores, percentile ranks, or index scores. The raw score is the sum of the scores obtained on the 50 test items, with a maximum possible raw score of 100. The raw score can be converted into a percentile rank or an index score using a table provided in the examiner's manual. The examiner record book also provides a table indicating the relationship of raw scores to percentile ranks and a corresponding two-headed arrow with anchors of *low* and *high*, which the examiner can use to indicate a test taker's corresponding level of functional communication. Index scores are provided despite the test authors' report that the CADL-3's distribution of raw scores was not normal and that, therefore, the resulting index scores cannot be compared to normalized standard scores of other tests and should not be used for clinical interpretations.

The test authors caution that the CADL-3 is meant to be one part of an assessment. It can provide valuable information about an individual's communication functioning, but it cannot, by itself, diagnose a communication disorder or provide a complete picture of an individual's language and communication abilities.

DEVELOPMENT. The original edition of this test was developed to assess communication abilities of individuals with aphasia in everyday situations. The second edition expanded the scope of the normative sample by including individuals with traumatic brain injury, intellectual disability, and Alzheimer's disease, as well as individuals with aphasia. Items for all editions were selected based on questions about the communication of neurologically healthy individuals: How do they demonstrate comprehension? What functional communication activities do they engage in? What do they read? What do they write? How do they use numbers for communication? How do they communicate that they cannot or do not wish to communicate? What strategies do they use to clarify miscommunication?

TECHNICAL. The CADL-3 was standardized on a clinical sample and a comparison sample. The clinical sample consisted of 115 adults ages 29 to 102 years with neurogenic language disorders caused by stroke, traumatic brain injury, dementia (including primary progressive aphasia), or other types of brain insult. There is no information regarding time since onset, time since diagnosis, whether the sample included individuals who had more than one neurologic diagnosis, or whether there were any exclusionary criteria (e.g., medical diagnosis of depression or other illness). The sample included individuals from 13 states in the United States and from three Canadian provinces. The comparison sample consisted of 49 adults ages 24 to 96 without language or cognitive impairments from 13 states in the United States.

The examiner's manual provides the number of individuals in each age decade for both samples, along with comparison data from the adult population in the United States regarding geographic area, gender, race, and Hispanic status. In general, compared to the United States adult population, the clinical sample included more individuals from the Northeast and fewer from the Midwest, the South, and the West, and it included more males (62%) than females (38%). The clinical sample was generally comparable to the adult population of the United States in terms of race and Hispanic status.

Regarding the CADL-3's reliability, coefficient alpha was used to estimate the internal consistency of test items. The resulting coefficient of .94 indicates very strong internal consistency. The standard error of measurement (*SEM*) was calculated for the index score, which is problematic given that the distribution of raw scores was not normal and the test authors appropriately cautioned against using index scores for clinical interpretation or for comparison to results on other standardized tests. As a result, it is hard to know why one would choose to use the index scores or how to interpret the *SEM* associated with them.

There are problems with the evaluation of test-retest reliability of the CADL-3. The test authors rightly describe time sampling error, typically determined by calculating test-retest reliability, as the extent to which an individual's test performance might change as a result of the passage of time. Establishing test-retest reliability, which is also referred to as the stability of a measure, is an important component of a test's standardization. It is assessed by administering the test at two time points between which nothing that might change a person's performance on the test, like deteriorating health or participation in a treatment program, takes place. A test that is not stable from one administration to another under these conditions cannot confidently be used to evaluate a person's ability on the domain being assessed or to reflect a true change in ability on that domain that might result from treatment (Bennett & Miller, 2010; Herbert, Hickin, Howard, Osborne, & Best, 2008). The CADL-3's test-retest reliability was assessed with 22 individuals who were part of a month-long intensive outpatient aphasia treatment group. They were tested before treatment and 4.5 weeks later, after treatment had concluded. This methodology is unusual in the context of assessing test-retest reliability because of the intervening treatment. Indeed, a *t*-test revealed a statistically significant difference between the scores obtained before and after treatment, although the effect size was small. Thus, the correlation coefficient reported in the examiner's manual does not reflect cleanly the stability of scores obtained on the CADL-3. Given the magnitude of the reliability coefficient (.94, corrected for range effects) and the fact that all study participants (n = 22) experienced the intervention, the evidence supports the stability of the CADL-3 as a measure that can be used to assess an individual's functional communication ability or to assess change in that ability.

To assess scorer difference reliability, two trained individuals independently scored 50 CADL-3 protocols randomly drawn from the clinical sample. Although the statistic and method used to determine the correlation coefficient are not specified, the coefficient reported (.99) indicates very strong agreement between scorers.

The methods used to develop the CADL-3 support its content validity. Additional evidence of content validity comes from results of an item analysis, which showed that item discrimination and item difficulty were largely within limits that are considered acceptable. Concurrent validity evidence was assessed by comparing raw scores of 69 individuals on the CADL-3 with their Aphasia Quotients from the Western Aphasia Battery–Revised (WAB-R; Kertesz, 2007), which provides an index of aphasia severity. The test authors do not specify what statistic was used to determine the relationship between these two measures, but they report an uncorrected coefficient of .74 and a corrected coefficient of .78.

Construct evidence of validity was assessed by determining whether people with diagnosed neurogenic communication disorders performed differently in comparison to the neurologically healthy sample. The results of a *t*-test revealed that there was a statistically significant difference in scores for the two groups.

COMMENTARY. The CADL-3 is a test that provides an efficient method of evaluating the functional communication abilities of adults in everyday situations. This aspect of communication is not fully addressed by other assessments. Its strengths are its careful development, its clear administration procedures, and the detailed guidelines that are provided for scoring each test item. In future development of the CADL, the test authors might consider clearer and more transparent reporting of reliability assessment procedures and an evaluation of test-retest reliability that is not compromised by the occurrence of treatment between testing sessions.

SUMMARY. The CADL-3 was designed to assess functional everyday communication abilities of adults with neurogenic language disorders. The item selection, administration procedures, and detailed scoring guidelines help it to meet this goal. Currently, it is the only assessment that provides an efficient standardized method of assessing communication in everyday situations. However, some technical aspects of the test (e.g., reliability) need further attention.

REVIEWER'S REFERENCES

Bennett, C. M., & Miller, M. B. (2010). How reliable are the results from functional magnetic resonance imaging? *Annals of the New York Academy of Science, 1191*, 133-155.

Herbert, R., Hickin, J., Howard, D., Osborne, F., & Best, W. (2008). Do picture-naming tests provide a valid assessment of lexical retrieval in conversation in aphasia? *Aphasiology, 22*, 184-203.

Kertesz, A. (2007). Western Aphasia Battery–Revised. San Antonio, TX: Pearson.

Review of Communication Activities of Daily Living—Third Edition by RAMA K. MISHRA, R. Psych. Neuropsychologist, Addictions and Mental Health, Medicine Hat Regional Hospital, Medicine Hat, Alberta, Canada:

DESCRIPTION. Communication Activities of Daily Living—Third Edition (CADL-3) is the latest edition of this instrument intended to measure "functional communication abilities" of adults and older adults (18 to 90+ years of age) "with neurogenic disorders of language" (manual, p. 1). The original version, published in 1980, was primarily intended to be used for individuals with aphasia. However, it has been used for individuals with other neurological disorders to determine their level of communication abilities.

The second version of the measure (CADL-2) was published in 1999 and eliminated the role-playing format and use of such devices as audiocassettes and manipulatives that were used in the first edition. New normative data also were collected and included individuals with Alzheimer's disease, traumatic brain injury, and intellectual disability. Additionally, test items were dropped from 68 to 50 to improve efficiency.

The third edition is essentially an extension of the second edition, with improved test items reflecting current use of technology. More attention also was given to enhance reliability and validity of the test.

The 50 items on the CADL-3 include questions from seven categories: reading, writing or using numbers; social interactions; contextual communication; nonverbal communication; sequential relationships; humor, metaphor, and absurdity; and Internet basics. Responses are scored on a 3-point scale, 0, 1, or 2. The record booklet provides scoring guidelines with examples for each of the three scores for each item. The test kit contains the examiner's manual, stimulus book, record booklets, and patient response forms, all in paper format. The examiner needs to supply some paper money and coins for use with one of the items. The total score obtained by the patient is converted to a percentile rank and index score, which has a mean of 100 and a standard deviation of 15, using the table provided in the examiner's manual.

DEVELOPMENT. Information in the test manual indicates most CADL-3 items also appeared in the CADL-2. Items for the CADL-2 were written based on item categories identified by the test authors and endorsed by field-test examiners who were experienced speech–language pathologists. For the CADL-3, the test authors changed some items to make them more meaningful to current uses of technology. For example, items involving the use of a landline telephone were dropped in favor of cell phone usage, and "items that show rudimentary familiarity with the Internet were added" (manual, p. 20). The number of items that were changed from the CADL-2 is not specified in the test manual.

The 50 items on the CADL-3 were categorized into one or more of the seven categories identified above as follows: 26 items involve reading, writing, or use of numbers; 16 involve contextual communication; 13 involve social interactions; 10 involve nonverbal communication; seven involve sequential relationships; four items involve humor, metaphor, and absurdity; and three involve Internet basics.

TECHNICAL. CADL-3 was normed on a clinical sample of 115 adults between the ages of 29 and 102 with language disorder due to such conditions as traumatic brain injury, stroke, dementia, and primary progressive aphasia. Most of these individuals were recruited through three specialty clinics—two in the state of Maryland and one at Dalhousie University in Halifax, Canada. The examinees were reported to be residents of 13 U.S. states and three Canadian provinces. An additional sample of 49 adults between the ages of 24 and 96, without any language or cognitive deficits, was recruited through the test publisher's website as a control group. The demographic characteristics of the clinical sample and the control group, along with U.S. population statistics, are presented in tables contained in the examiner's manual.

The CADL-3 authors reported that even though stroke patients comprised 83% of the clinical sample, there was no significant difference between the stroke patients and patients with other conditions in their CADL-3 total score. Therefore, the test authors conducted reliability and validity studies using the entire sample.

The test authors reported a test retest reliability coefficient of .94 over a 4.5-week period using a subsample of 22 examinees who were part of an intensive treatment group. Interscorer reliability was reported to be very high with a correlation coefficient of .99 for a group of 50 patients randomly drawn from the clinical sample whose protocols were scored by two raters independently. Internal consistency also was reported to be quite impressive with an alpha coefficient of .94 for the entire clinical sample. A Spanish version of the test published recently using the same 50 items demonstrated high reliability estimates with a test–rest reliability coefficient of .90 and an alpha coefficient of .95 (Roca, Ivern, Bruna, & Velasco, 2018).

Several validity estimates were reported in the test manual. The test authors suggest that the new edition is timely and covers a broad range of content areas identified by site examiners who were licensed speech-language pathologists with experience working with adults with neurological disorders. They also presented item discrimination indexes in the form of point-biserial coefficients of each item with the total score. The test authors describe the discriminating power of the items as satisfactory as reflected by median discrimination coefficients that fell between .21 and .70, except for one item (with a .16 discrimination coefficient). The test authors also calculated the passing percentage for each item to represent item difficulty and reported that the median difficulty for all items ranged from .45 to .99, indicating an acceptable range of difficulty of the test.

Criterion-prediction evidence of validity was evaluated by correlating CADL-3 raw scores with Aphasia Quotients from the Western Aphasia Battery-Revised, which were obtained from the study patients' case files. The correlation coefficient was reported as .78.

Construct-identification evidence was examined using a three-step approach. First, the test authors identified constructs that presumably accounted for performance on the test. Second, they developed hypotheses based on these constructs. Finally, they presented statistical evidence to support their hypotheses. One piece of evidence came from a significantly lower score (t = -12.89, p < .001) by examinees with aphasia (M = 100, SD = 15), compared to examinees without aphasia (M = 119, SD = 2). The corresponding effect-size correlation (r) of .75 was reported to be "very large" (manual, p. 24). The test authors also suggest that item discrimination indexes of .21 to .70 for 49 of the 50 items, as noted above, indicated a valid assessment of communication difficulty due to aphasia by CADL-3.

COMMENTARY. The current edition of the CADL, published 19 years after the previous edition, included much needed item revisions due to changes in contemporary use of technology such as cell phones, the Internet, and email. Improvements in item selection have been made using several item analysis techniques as well. Other improvements include an updated stimulus book with colorful pictures, new standardization samples, and enhanced reliability and validity studies. Thus, the test authors have made substantial improvements to the previous edition, making the CADL-3 a very useful tool for the assessment and monitoring of communication activities of neurologically impaired patients. The test authors have addressed some of the concerns identified by reviewers of the previous edition (Person, 2001; Snyder, 2001). However, use of a larger sample with a broader range of communication skills would provide more meaningful interpretation of the percentile ranks. Currently, change of 1 point in the raw score corresponds to a change in percentile rank of as much as 5 points as the distribution of raw scores is fairly skewed. For example, a raw score of 77 is equivalent to a percentile rank of 43, whereas a raw score of 78 is equivalent to a percentile rank of 48.

Use of this tool to make a diagnosis of aphasia is still quite limited, as sensitivity and specificity have not been adequately established using a control group of non-aphasic patients with neurogenic disorders. A review of 161 language tests revealed that only six tests, including CADL-2, had adequate psychometric properties; all of them used normal/healthy individuals, as opposed to non-aphasic patients, as their control group (Rohde, Worrall, Godecke, O'Halloran, Farrell, & Massey, 2018). In CADL-3, the control group also consisted of normal individuals similar to CADL-2. Hopefully, future editions would address these issues and also make this test available for portable electronic devices, as electronic health records could become a reality in the very near future.

SUMMARY. The CADL-3 is an invaluable tool to assess and monitor functional communication in adult patients with neurological and intellectual disorders. A Spanish edition of the test is already available (Roca et al., 2018). Hopefully other translations will become available in the future to help individuals in other countries. Obviously, further standardization would be necessary to determine item difficulty and relevance to each linguistic group when such versions become available. Nevertheless, this instrument is an excellent addition to the battery of tools available for the study of aphasia in neurologically impaired individuals when used in conjunction with other psychological and neuropsychological instruments.

REVIEWER'S REFERENCES

Person, C. M. (2001). [Test review of Communication Activities of Daily Living Scale, Second Edition]. In B. S. Plake & J. C. Impara (Eds.), *The fourteenth mental measurements yearbook* (pp. 288–290). Lincoln, NE: Buros Institute of Mental Measurements.

Roca, C., Ivern, I., Bruna, O., & Velasco, M. (2018). Communication Activities of Daily Living (CADL-3) version Espanola. Adaptacion al contexto espanol y analisis de fiabilidad. *Revista de Logopedia, Foniatria y Audiologia, 38*, 6-13.

Rohde, A., Worrall, L., Godecke, E., O'Halloran, R., Farrell, A., & Massey, M. (2018). Diagnosis of aphasia in stroke populations: A systematic review of language tests. *PLoS ONE 13(3)*: e0194143. https://doi.org/10.1371/journal.pone.0194143

Snyder, K. (2001). [Test review of Communication Activities of Daily Living Scale, Second Edition]. In B. S. Plake & J. C. Impara (Eds.), *The fourteenth mental measurements yearbook* (pp. 290–291). Lincoln, NE: Buros Institute of Mental Measurements.

[36]

Community Oriented Programs Environment Scale [Fourth Edition Manual].

Purpose: Designed to "assess the social environments of community-based psychiatric treatment programs, day programs, sheltered workshops, rehabilitation centers and community care homes."
Population: Patients and staff of community oriented psychiatric facilities.
Publication Dates: 1974-2009.
Acronym: COPES.
Scores, 10: Involvement, Support, Spontaneity, Autonomy, Practical Orientation, Personal Problem Orientation, Anger and Aggression, Order and Organization, Program Clarity, Staff Control.
Administration: Individual or group.
Forms, 4: R (Real), I (Ideal), E (Expectations), S (Short).
Price Data, 2019: $50 for manual, including review-only copy of test form; $2.50 per remote online survey license or license to reproduce (minimum 50); $10 per Social Climate Scales user's guide.
Foreign Language Editions: Translations available in French, Italian, Japanese, Norwegian, Spanish, and Swedish.
Time: Administration time not reported.
Comments: A part of the Social Climate Scales.
Author: Rudolf H. Moos.
Publisher: Mind Garden, Inc.
Cross References: See T5:637 (3 references), T4:605 (11 references) and T3:542 (6 references); for a review by Richard I. Lanyon of the original edition, see 8:525 (17 references). For a review of the Social Climate Scales, see 8:681.

Review of the Community Oriented Programs Environment Scale [Fourth Edition Manual] by JAMES T. AUSTIN, Program Lead, Assessment Services for Center on Education and Training for Employment, The Ohio State University, Columbus, OH:

DESCRIPTION. This review covers the 2009 revision of the Community Oriented Programs Environment Scale (COPES), first published by Rudolf Moos in 1974 as one of a battery of social climate self-report measures for use across community mental health agencies. The test materials provided to this reviewer were supplemented with published research literature (for example a "refinement" of the COPES to measure social climate of therapeutic residential youth care in Norway; Leipoldt, Kayed, Harder, Grietens, & Rimehaug, 2018). The last review completed for the COPES appeared in *The Eighth Mental Measurements Yearbook*; therefore, only the initial edition would have been available for review by Lanyon (1978).

The COPES is a 100-item self-report measure that uses a true/false response format. Following brief instructions, several variables (date, name or ID, and background-demographic) are requested before the items are presented. Items are scored according to a key on 10 non-overlapping scales that span three underlying constructs: Relationship dimensions (first 3 scales), Personal Growth dimensions (middle 4 scales), and System Maintenance dimensions (last 3 scales). Among the settings proposed for use of the COPES are community residential facilities, halfway or sober houses, sheltered workshops, and rehabilitation centers; populations include clients-patients ("members") and staff. Scores on the forms describe the social perception of the environment from multiple perspectives. (Forms R, I, and E refer to Real, Ideal, and Expectations; S refers to the Short form of 40 items.) The test manual is organized in seven sections: (1) Introduction and Rationale; (2) Forms of the COPES (R, I, E, S); (3) Administration and Scoring; (4) Applications for Clinicians, Consultants, and Program Evaluators; (5) Development, Normative Samples, and Psychometric Characteristics; (6) Research Applications and Validity; and (7) References. Two appendices contain Spirituality/Religiosity subscale items and scoring directions and tables for converting raw scores to standard scores.

DEVELOPMENT. Rudolf Moos, the developer of the COPES and other social climate scales, is prolific in mental health research, measurement, and practice. He has provided continuity in conceptualization and guidance of his social climate paradigm for some 50 years.

The COPES manual provides a model for profiling community treatment programs and relating their social climate to client-patient outcomes. The COPES first appeared in the *Journal of Abnormal Psychology* (Moos, 1972), and then was published for widespread use 2 years later (1974). Revisions followed in 1988, 1996, and 2009 (the current edition). A battery of social climate measures (i.e., the Social Climate Scales) developed by Moos and coworkers is described in the user's guide (2003 edition of the Social Climate Scales is the third and latest); the battery represents a recognition by Moos and mental health researchers that the perception of environment or therapeutic milieu could be described and related to therapeutic outcomes. Both mental health and substance abuse programs can be evaluated with the COPES.

The development of the COPES leading to initial publication in 1972 began with an earlier Moos scale, the Ward Atmosphere Scale (WAS; Moos & Houts, 1968). Although Lanyon (1978) critiqued the COPES development process as poorly described and merely shifting the WAS to a new setting, Moos did describe a content-oriented approach involving the use of staff and patients as subject matter experts (with respect to community organizations). There were, however, no tabulated judgments of content. The WAS items were reworded and expanded to 130 items that were field tested with samples across various transition institutions in the community (21 programs). Scales (10 of 12 retained) were constructed using four criteria (internal consistency, avoidance of extremes, reduction of acquiescence bias by equalizing true and false responses within a scale, and low correlations with halo response set scale administered with the COPES trial version).

The fourth edition was published in 2009 and includes six new/revised items listed in the test manual as well as in the instrument itself to avoid confusion. Explanation of the revisions is provided in the test manual with twofold logic that program practices have evolved and new data were available (Timko & Moos, 1996 is cited in text but not found in the reference section of the manual). A fifth criterion for scale development was added but without specificity ("low" scale intercorrelations). It is noted in the test manual (p. 27) that norms are based on the "initial" version of the COPES (assumed 1974). Administration and scoring (Section III) are described on a single page in the test manual, and users are directed for additional information to the user's guide for the Social Climate Scales (Moos, 2003). In terms of suggested applications, (Section IV), there are profiles at the individual client-patient or staff member level, as well as aggregate profiles that describe community programs. Suggested applications involve score interpretations that should be supported with evidence. The bibliography lists studies conducted with the COPES across the United States and around the world.

TECHNICAL. Information on the quality of evidence offered to support reliability, validity, and test norms can instill confidence or doubt among users of measurement tools. This information is found in Section 5 of the COPES manual, from development through cross-cultural samples. (Six of the seven parts are reviewed here; development was presented above.)

The test manual states that the "main" (p. 27) normative data for Form R is based on 219 community programs (*N* = 5,531) for clients and 206 programs for staff (*N* = 1,282); the union of these two sets would be informative (i.e., the number of programs that have data for both members and staff). Then the total norms are decomposed into additional samples that followed the initial sample (1974). This reviewer inferred that the total norms were constructed by aggregating an initial sample of 54 programs, described in terms of program type (frequencies were variable), with subsequent samples of 36 (1995), 15 (1998), 26 (1989), and 80 other programs from a "range of evaluation projects" (manual, p. 27). It is valuable to know the program type breakdown for the "main" normative sample so that the applicability of the norms is clearer.

Specific norms are provided in a series of tables, one of which provides, by clients (members) and staff, subscale means and two standard deviations, one based on programs (aggregated), and one based on members (individual). A table note indicates that the number of programs used to produce these norms is a reduced set. (Some program data were not used.) Table 3 provides norms for a British sample, but the reported sample sizes are small and may not inspire confidence. Table 4 provides norms from samples of 125 programs (clients/members) and 105 programs (staff) for Form S (Short; first 40 items from full length COPES with four items per subscale); standard deviations are based on subsets of the programs used to calculate the means. Table 5 provides values for Form I (Ideal), based on numbers of respondents but without programs; the standard deviations are again calculated on subsets of respondents (without explanation). Table 6 provides the subscale means and standard deviations for Form E (Expectations), based on a sample of 188 members measured before admission. The norms section of the test manual was difficult to follow.

A description of the programs would have helped to communicate the information, and samples of programs are lower than typical norms.

Reliability information is presented and discussed in the third and fourth parts of Section 5, together with tables that provide estimates of internal consistency and various correlations (items with their subscales and average inter-item correlations). In Table 7, mean internal consistency values for members and staff of .67 and .71 are based on samples that vary slightly, presumably due to missing data. Item-subscale correlations average .36 and .37 for members and staff, while average interitem correlations are .17 and .18 for members and staff. Table 8 presents subscale intercorrelations, with clear variability, although the test manual notes that the averages are between .25 and .30 for both members and staff. A note in the text indicates that Form I correlations (for a small sample of 15 programs, with no sample size information) range from .35 to .55, while subscale estimates of internal consistency were between .70 and .88. Profile stabilities are provided.

Retest reliability and profile stability are reported in the fourth part of Section 5, with various retest intervals (4-6 months to 24 months) and number of programs or re-administration as related to average profile correlations (overall range is .60 to .98), with the highest value found for members at the longest interval of 2 years. Of note, average profile correlations for members were consistently higher than those for staff.

Sections that follow provide reliability estimates for a 12-item Spirituality/Religiosity subscale based on a separate sample of 15 programs and 3,300+ members or staff. Means and standard deviations are presented as are correlations of the Spirituality/Religiosity subscale with the standard 10 COPES subscales.

Methodological and statistical issues are treated briefly in the sixth part, with the following topics: 2- or 4-point response, factor dimensions (a 1973 study reported by Wilkinson using many of the Social Climate Scales that found a large factor named Value was not cited), personal characteristics and program perceptions, and construct validity. The seventh and final part of Section 5 addressed cross-cultural samples and relevant psychometrics but provided only descriptive information. (Note that a United Kingdom sample did yield norms as mentioned above.)

Validity, the sine qua non, is addressed in Section 6 of the test manual using research applications as the apparent vehicle. (Evidence of construct validity was noted in a brief part of Section 5 and consisted of citation of a research study.) This approach is different from measurement validity frameworks in common use, and was also noted in the earlier review by Lanyon (1978). The measurement framework that was available at the time of the revision that created the fourth edition of COPES, the 1999 *Standards for Educational and Psychological Testing* (American Educational Research Association [AERA], American Psychological Association [APA], & National Council on Measurement in Education [NCME]), was noteworthy for beginning to move away from a tripartite division (content, criterion, and construct validity) to a construct-focused, evidence-based approach with five categories of evidence: content, response process, internal structure, external relationships, and consequences. The approach taken by Moos in this manual is different.

The validity section leads with a conceptual framework presented in five panels or blocks of constructs: (1) objective program characteristics that interact with (2) clients' personal factors and predict (3) social climate as a core component, (4) clients' in-program outcomes (satisfaction, participation), and (5) clients' community adaptation. Asserting that social climate can be measured at both the individual and program level implies that aggregation is warranted.

The validity treatment continues with a discussion of describing and comparing programs, including narrative review of mostly published studies organized by settings: substance abuse, psychiatric, rehabilitation, therapeutic community, group home and day treatment, community versus hospital programs, schizophrenia (Soteria Project), cross- cultural findings (although developed in the United States there are publications dealing with applications in other countries and cultures [i.e., Norway]), supported housing, and consumer-operated self-help programs. From this narrative discussion of applications comes a typology of six community programs resulting from a cluster analysis reported in Moos (1997) but not otherwise described (two other citations are provided). Three other settings are briefly discussed before moving on to the third subsection on determinants of program climate in five categories: institutional context, physical features, policies and services, aggregate client and staff characteristics, and social climate. These categories seem similar to the "panels" presented earlier in the validity and research applications section, and a dynamic system is asserted although much of the research seems to be cross-sectional in nature.

Impact of program climate is discussed in the fourth part of the validity section, which corresponds to a focus on external relationships (here outcomes or criteria) from the 1999 *Standards* (AERA, APA, & NCME). The categories of outcomes enumerated begin with morale or satisfaction, in-program symptoms, dropout and attrition (withdrawal), symptom reduction, and substance abuse. Dual diagnosis patients are also mentioned, and the section continues with additional types of outcomes—many of the paragraphs discuss a small number of studies, often a single report. The overall impression is one of a large body of coordinate research, but the text makes for difficult reading without going to the primary sources. The mass of research suggests to this reviewer that a quantitative summary would be of great value if it could be assembled.

COMMENTARY. This scale has been used in many published research studies over time dating back nearly five decades, and the presentation is voluminous. Some evidence of a construct is developed, and there is reliability evidence (mostly internal consistency, some stability). The norms and evidence of validity are not as well established, and this was noted in the earlier review by Lanyon (1978), who sounded a warning if the scale were to be used without additional validity evidence. This warning was somewhat heeded based on the quantity of evidence reviewed (research was conducted by Moos as well as by others) but also presumes that the research is high-quality and sound. The studies were insufficiently described to serve as a strong validity foundation in the measurement sense. A quantitative synthesis might be helpful, as would better tabulation of the studies cited. The norms seem to be based on small samples (of institutions and of members/staff) without extensive demographic information that would help in interpretation of results at the individual client-patient level. Validity evidence could be better organized using the newer categories of evidence and an argument-based strategy.

SUMMARY. The COPES is a scale developed and revised several times since its initial publication in 1974. It addresses an important aspect of mental health research and practice: the milieu or environment as perceived by program participants and by staff. A rational approach using internal consistency was used by Moos to develop the scale as a replicate of his earlier in-patient (hospital ward) atmosphere scale, leading Moos to develop a battery of scales to evaluate perceptions of social climate. Norms are based on relatively small samples of programs and participants. Validity evidence is asserted through citation of empirical studies and their results, but without using integrated validity frameworks available at the time of last revision (2009) and since revised into the 2014 *Standards for Educational and Psychological Testing* (AERA, APA, & NCME). This reviewer believes that it is possible to provide stronger validity evidence for the COPES so that score interpretations at both individual and aggregate levels are supported.

REVIEWER'S REFERENCES

American Educational Research Association, American Psychological Association, & National Council on Measurement in Education. (1999). *Standards for educational and psychological testing.* Washington, DC: American Educational Research Association.

American Educational Research Association, American Psychological Association, & National Council on Measurement in Education. (2014). *Standards for educational and psychological testing.* Washington, DC: American Educational Research Association.

Lanyon, R. I. (1978). [Test review of Community Oriented Programs Environment Scales]. In O. K. Buros (Ed.), *The eighth mental measurements yearbook* (pp. 752-753). Highland Park, NJ: Gryphon Press.

Leipoldt, J. D., Kayed, N. S., Harder, A. T., Grietens, H., & Rimehaug, T. (2018). Refining the COPES to measure social climate in therapeutic residential youth care. *Child Youth Care Forum, 47,* 173-197.

Moos, R. H. (1972). Assessment of the psychosocial environments of community-oriented psychiatric treatment programs. *Journal of Abnormal Psychology, 79,* 9-18.

Moos, R. H. (1973). Conceptualizations of human environments. *American Psychologist, 28,* 652-665.

Moos, R. H. (1974). *Community-Oriented Programs Environment Scale manual.* Palo Alto, CA: Consulting Psychologists Press.

Moos, R. H. (1997). *Evaluating treatment environments: The quality of psychiatric and substance abuse programs* (2nd ed.). New Brunswick, NJ: Transaction.

Moos, R. H. (2003). *Social Climate Scales: A user's guide.* Menlo Park, CA: Mind Garden.

Moos, R. H., & Houts, P. S. (1968). Assessment of the social atmosphere of psychiatric wards. *Journal of Abnormal Psychology, 73,* 595-604.

Moos, R., & Otto, J. (1972). The Community-Oriented Programs Environment Scale: A methodology for the facilitation and evaluation of social change. *Community Mental Health Journal, 8,* 28-37.

Timko, C., & Moos, R. H. (1998). Determinants of the treatment climate in psychiatric and substance abuse programs: Implications for improving patient outcomes. *Journal of Nervous and Mental Disease, 186,* 96-103.

Wilkinson, L. (1973). An assessment of the dimensionality of Moos' Social Climate Scale. *American Journal of Community Psychology, 1,* 342-350.

Review of the Community Oriented Programs Environment Scale [Fourth Edition Manual] by ANDREW COX, Professor Emeritus, Troy University, Phenix City, AL:

DESCRIPTION. The Community Oriented Programs Environment Scale (COPES) is an individually or group administered inventory assessing the social environment that characterizes various mental health, psychiatric, rehabilitation, health, or other community treatment programs. The inventory is part of a family of social climate scales. Moos (2003) provides additional information regarding the nature and use of each scale.

The COPES is a 100-item true/false measure that has three forms measuring client and staff views of a community treatment program. The three forms are the: Real form (Form R), measuring client and staff views of their current treatment program; Ideal form (Form I), assessing client and staff preferences relative to an ideal community oriented treatment program; and Expectation form (Form E), assessing client expectations about their treatment program. Short form (Form S) with 40 true/false questions is also available. Further information relative to the use of each form is described within the test manual.

There are 10 subscales measuring actual, preferred, and expected social climate within a rated community treatment program. The 10 subscales underlie three dimensions: Relationship, Personal Growth, and System Maintenance. Subscales and their relationship to these dimensions are described within the test manual.

Staff and (i.e., client member) responses are converted to raw scores that can be converted to standard scores by referring to respective norms for program members/clients and staff. Profile forms are available for compiling client and staff perceptions. The test author indicates that the scale can be used in international settings to include Sweden, Australia, and Canada, but normative data for these international groups are not provided. Descriptive data are available for a United Kingdom normative group.

DEVELOPMENT. The initial item pool was developed through interviews and observations with clients and staff within representative sets of programs. Selected items were adapted from the Ward Atmosphere Scale (Moos, 1996). The resulting 130-item initial form was administered to 373 clients and 203 staff in 21 community treatment programs. From this initial form, a final inventory form was developed to include 10 dimensions with nine to 10 items each. Items were selected for the final form on the basis of item correlation with its respective subscale, acquiescence response considerations, low to moderate intercorrelations, and item discriminative ability. A final normative sample consisting of clients in 219 community programs and staff within 206 community programs was developed. It is unclear whether the normative sample for the current edition comprises a new or expanded sample or the same sample developed for the original COPES. Dates for such data collection are not reported within the test manual. The manual reports additional samples drawn from 36 residential psychiatric facilities, 15 substance use treatment facilities, 26 homeless programs, and more than 80 other community programs. Dates and characteristics for such sample selection are not specified. The data were drawn from various research studies, the results of which were published from 1982 through 2006 and are referenced within the test manual. The test manual also mentions data obtained from a new sample of psychiatric and substance abuse programs but provides no further details.

TECHNICAL. The final normative sample for the COPES consisting of members and staff within community programs (n = 219 and n = 206, respectively) are described in the previous section of this review. The test author also refers to subsequent samples as detailed in research studies, but descriptive data or uses of these additional samples are not described. No descriptive data regarding the sample are provided within the current version of the test manual. Such data as gender, age, ethnicity, or similar characteristics are not included. The test manual also provides a scoring key for deriving a Spirituality/Religiosity subscale together with means and standard deviations for this scale.

Tables are provided within the test manual's appendix to convert client and staff raw scores into standard scores for Form R and the Short form (Form S) for each subscale. Norms are arranged to allow comparison of clients to staff as well as individual client and staff profiles. Though means and standard deviations are provided for Forms I and E, standard score conversions are not provided for these forms, which limits the use of the instrument. Form R descriptive statistics that include means and standard deviations for the United Kingdom sample are provided, but this information is not provided for other international or cross-cultural samples.

Reliability estimates are reported in terms of internal consistency and test-retest estimates. Internal consistency coefficients range from .58 to .78 for members and .60 to .79 for staff with a mean of .67 for members and .71 for staff. Average item-subscale correlation coefficients ranged from .28 to .45 (mean .36) and from .30 to .45 (mean .37) for members and staff, respectively. Moderate to moderately high internal consistency is suggested by these coefficients.

Item-subscale correlations and intercorrelations among subscale scores are also presented as reliability evidence. Test-retest reliability coefficients range from .81 to .98 for clients for time periods of 4 to 6 months through 24 months. Lower correlation coefficients were found for staff with values ranging from .60 to .81 for similar time periods. Adequate test-retest reliability appears to be present with moderate to high correlation coefficients depending upon the reference group used for comparison. Average subscale intercorrelations ranged from .25 to .30. The test author characterizes the scale's 10 subscales as distinct but moderately related.

The test author describes evidence of validity in terms of construct validation using an early 1995 sample of individuals residing in learning disability residences. Correlation using the scale dimensions is presented as evidence of construct validation. The test author also offers a conceptual framework as evidence of construct validation, but research evidence supporting this framework is not described. Overall, COPES validation evidence is limited, suggesting that additional work on scale validation is needed. An earlier review by Lanyon (1978) of the original COPES version reached a similar conclusion.

COMMENTARY. The COPES could serve a useful role in assessing the climate that may be found within community based treatment programs based upon members and staff perceptions, a useful addition to other social climate scales. The scale could be useful for administrative and program evaluation, particularly in researching program strengths and weaknesses. This instrument would serve an end result in providing suggestions for program improvement. Item analysis procedures would provide useful information for program evaluators and administrators. Treatment providers could also use the inventory to obtain data concerning perceptions of program recipients and staff.

The test manual needs to provide more details regarding the nature of the normative sample relative to age, gender, ethnicity and similar characteristics. The manual is also unclear about whether the 1996 inventory version has new normative data or is an extension of the original sample. Providing dates or time periods associated with data collection would clear up this confusion.

The test manual provides examples of the use of the COPES with various treatment programs. This is useful in providing ideas as to how the inventory could be used within program evaluation. A large portion of the test manual is devoted to summarizing older as well as more recent research completed with the COPES. This literature provides some insight into scale differentiation between staff and members and could be useful to program evaluators and administrators. Program evaluators might wish to compare individual program findings to those obtained by others. Some attention to cross-cultural studies is found within this review.

Reliability evidence for the inventory appears to be adequate. However, validation evidence is sparse with more work needed within this area. Considerable research appears to have been conducted with this measure, some being longitudinal in nature. The test developers could consider meta-analytic studies to establish construct and other validation support.

Although means and standard deviations are provided for Form I (Ideal) and Form E (Expectations), it would be helpful to have standard score equivalents for these forms as well.

The COPES is most suitable for use in program evaluation and administration and is best used in conjunction with interview, observation, or program developed surveys. The Moos (2003) publication should be considered an essential reference for users of the COPES.

SUMMARY. The COPES is an individually or group administered inventory assessing various dimensions of the social climate within community based treatment and health provision facilities. It provides insight into staff and client perceptions of the facility relative to 10 qualities (subscales) within three dimensions. The instrument could serve a useful role within this program dimension. It would be of primary interest to program evaluators and administrators seeking to identify, remediate, or improve selected aspects of their program's treatment milieu. A large body of research exists using this instrument within program evaluation. Reviewing this literature in conjunction with administrators' or program evaluators' program results may prove useful. However, the COPES continues to demonstrate limited evidence of validity. For this reason, it is recommended that its results be supplemented with other program evaluative data. It would not be recommended as a tool with clinical utility for those users primarily interested in practice aspects of community treatment. Such a role appears to be beyond the purposes espoused for this instrument.

REVIEWER'S REFERENCES

Lanyon, R. I. (1978). [Test review of the Community Oriented Programs Environment Scale]. In O.K. Buros (Ed.), *The eighth mental measurements yearbook* (pp. 752- 753). Highland Park, NJ: Gryphon Press.

Moos, R. H. (1996). *Word Atmosphere Scale manual: Third edition.* Menlo Park, CA: Mind Garden.

Moos, R. H. (2003). *The social climate scales: A user's guide.* Menlo Park, CA: Mind Garden.

[37]

Comprehensive Assessment of Spoken Language, Second Edition.

Purpose: Designed "to provide an in-depth assessment of an individual's oral language skills."
Population: Ages 3-21.
Publication Dates: 1999-2017.
Acronym: CASL-2.
Scores, 20: 14 test scores: Receptive Vocabulary, Antonyms, Synonyms, Expressive Vocabulary, Idiomatic Language, Sentence Expression, Grammatical Morphemes, Sentence Comprehension, Grammaticality Judgment, Nonliteral Language, Meaning from Context, Inference, Double Meaning, Pragmatic Language; 6 index scores: Receptive Language Index, Expressive Language Index, Lexical/Semantic Index, Syntactic Index, Supralinguistic Index, General Language Ability Index.
Administration: Individual.
Forms, 2: Comprehensive Form (ages 3-21), Preschool Form (ages 3-6).
Price Data, 2020: $635 per complete kit including 10 Comprehensive Forms, easel 1, easel 2, easel 3, manual (2017, 368 pages), and access to test publisher's online scoring system; $163 per any one easel (1, 2, or 3); $146 per manual; $55 per 10 Comprehensive Forms; $50 per 10 Preschool Forms.
Time: 5-10 minutes for administration of individual tests; 30-60 minutes for administration of all tests needed to calculate the General Language Index, depending on age of examinee.
Comments: Administered via paper and pencil or online; tests may be administered separately or in combination.
Author: Elizabeth Carrow-Woolfolk.
Publisher: Western Psychological Services.
Cross References: For reviews by Katharine A. Snyder and Gabrielle Stutman of the original edition, see 15:58.

Review of the Comprehensive Assessment of Spoken Language, Second Edition by MAURA JONES MOYLE, Associate Professor, Department of Speech Pathology and Audiology, Marquette University, Milwaukee, WI:

DESCRIPTION. The Comprehensive Assessment of Spoken Language, Second Edition (CASL-2) is an individually administered in-depth assessment of oral language for individuals ages 3 to 21 years. Its purposes are to diagnose language delays or disorders, identify specific strengths and weaknesses in oral language skills, and measure English proficiency in English language learners. The CASL-2 consists of 14 tests, each of which may be administered as stand-alone assessments (i.e., Receptive Vocabulary, Antonyms, Synonyms, Expressive Vocabulary, Idiomatic Language, Sentence Expression, Grammatical Morphemes, Sentence Comprehension, Grammaticality Judgment, Nonliteral Language, Meaning from Context, Inference, Double Meaning, Pragmatic Language). Test scores can be combined into one summary score of general language functioning (i.e., General Language Ability Index) and five additional index scores measuring various aspects of oral language (i.e., Receptive Language Index, Expressive Language Index, Lexical/Semantic Index, Syntactic Index, Supralinguistic Index). The CASL-2 evaluates four types of language knowledge (i.e., lexical/semantic, syntactic, supralinguistic, pragmatic) and two types of language performance (i.e., auditory comprehension, oral expression).

DEVELOPMENT. The theoretical foundation of the CASL-2 is Integrative Language Theory (ILT; Carrow-Woolfolk, 1988), which describes language as consisting of two primary dimensions: knowledge and performance. Knowledge comprises four categories of language structures: lexical/semantic (e.g., vocabulary), syntactic (e.g., grammar, morphology), supralinguistic (e.g., inferencing, humor, figurative language), and pragmatic (e.g., functional, social use of language). Performance includes the major processes of language comprehension (i.e., receptive language) and language production (i.e., expressive language). ILT is based upon a modular view of language (e.g., Fodor, 1983), which posits that language consists of independent cognitive units that interact during language comprehension and expression. Although the modular theory of language has been challenged (e.g., Bates, 1994), most standardized language tests are designed to isolate the structures and processes of language in order to evaluate them separately.

The CASL-2 includes several revisions of the original CASL (Carrow-Woolfolk, 1999). Updates consisted of expanding the age range for nine tests, collecting a new normative sample that provides age- and grade-based norms, improving scoring criteria to increase scoring reliability and offer alternate responses for nonstandard English dialects, deleting items that were outdated or not useful, and updating the artwork to full-color illustrations. The revised record form includes an Item Analysis Worksheet for each test to facilitate a qualitative analysis of an examinee's responses. In addition, the Paragraph Comprehension test from the CASL was eliminated based on user feedback. Instead, a separate assessment was designed for individuals ages 5 to 21 titled the Oral Passage Understanding Scale (OPUS; Carrow-Woolfolk & Klein, 2017). The OPUS was standardized simultaneously with the CASL-2.

A pilot study using the 14 CASL-2 tests was conducted on a diverse sample of 972 typically developing individuals, ages 3:0 to 21:11. The responses collected during the pilot study were used to develop preliminary scoring criteria for those tests that elicit open-ended responses. For each CASL-2 test, items were analyzed to assess item difficulty and potential biases against groups of interest (e.g., gender, ethnicity). Items that showed evidence of bias or other problems were eliminated. The resulting items were used for the national standardization and validation study.

TECHNICAL. The CASL-2 was normed on 2,394 children ages 3:0 to 21:11 residing in 29 states. The demographics of the sample reflect the 2012 U.S. population in terms of gender, race/ethnicity, and parent educational level (an index of socioeconomic status). Individuals with mild disabilities who spent the majority of their time in general education classrooms were included in the standardization sample, whereas individuals with severe developmental disabilities were excluded. More data were collected for preschoolers and young children than for adolescents and adults, given that normative age ranges tend to be smaller at younger ages when language development is most rapid. Age-based norms are provided for individuals 3-21 years, and grade-based norms are provided for Grades K-12. Responses gathered during standardization were used to establish the final scoring criteria for each subtest, develop alternative scoring rules for nonmainstream dialects, determine basal and ceiling rules, and derive several types of scores (i.e., standard scores, index scores, test-age equivalent scores, and grade equivalent scores).

Data from a clinical sample of 271 individuals were also collected. To be included, individuals needed to be diagnosed with a disorder and receiving clinical services. Clinical diagnoses included language disorder, hearing impairment, autism spectrum disorder, social (pragmatic) communication disorder, intellectual disability, learning disability, and developmental delay.

Information describing evidence of validity and reliability is provided in the test manual. Reliability of the CASL-2 was assessed in several ways. First, internal consistency was estimated using a split-half method that resulted in correlation coefficients that ranged from .85 to .99 for individual tests and were .95 or greater for index scores. Similar results were observed for the clinical sample. These results suggest that the CASL-2 exhibits strong internal consistency. Test-retest reliability was evaluated by re-administering the CASL-2 to 145 individuals 2 weeks after the first administration. The resulting correlation coefficients ranged from .73 to .94 for individual tests (median .85). Reliability was higher between index scores, with coefficients ranging from .88 to .96 (median .92). The results suggest fair to excellent stability in test scores. Interrater reliability was assessed by having two raters separately score responses from 60 individuals. Interclass correlation coefficients ranged from .86 to .97, with a median of .92, suggesting good to excellent interrater reliability.

Construct validity evidence reflects the degree to which a test supports the theoretical framework that served as the foundation for the design. Construct evidence for the CASL-2 was developed in two ways. First, a factor analysis was performed. The results supported two- and three-factor models as predicted by the ILT's modular view of language, versus a one-factor undifferentiated model of language. Second, the intercorrelations between tests were examined. The resulting correlation coefficients ranged from .42 to .93, with less similar tests exhibiting lower coefficients than more similar tests. In addition, the correlations between the 14 tests were weaker than the correlations for internal consistency reliability. The test author states that these results suggest that the tests measure unique aspects of language, thus justifying each as a stand-alone measure that can be interpreted separately.

Convergent validity evidence is used to support the extent to which a measure relates to other measures with similar constructs. The CASL-2 was compared to several language measures, including the CASL; the OPUS; the Oral and Written Language Scales, Second Edition (OWLS-II; Carrow-Woolfolk, 2011); and the Clinical Evaluation of Language Fundamentals, Fifth Edition (CELF-5; Wiig, Semel, & Secord, 2013). The correlation between the General Language Ability Index scores of the CASL and CASL-2 was strong (.90) for the 52 individuals who were administered both measures. Correlations between other index scores were moderate to high (.51 to .84). Correlations between the OPUS and CASL-2 were also strong for 953 individuals (i.e., correlations between index scores ranged from .71 to

.77). Similarly, relationships between CASL-2 and OWLS-II scores were moderate to strong for 71 individuals (i.e., correlations between index scores ranged from .73 to .89). In addition, the CASL-2 General Language Ability Index exhibited a strong relationship (.89) with the CELF-5 Core Language score for 58 individuals.

Sensitivity (i.e., ability to detect true disorders) and specificity (i.e., ability to correctly rule out disorders) were reported using various CASL-2 General Language Ability Index standard scores. Based on the results, the test author suggests that a cutoff score of 85 provides the best balance of sensitivity (.74) and specificity (.84). This level of sensitivity is below what is recommended by Plante and Vance (1994), who state that standardized tests should have sensitivity and specificity levels of at least .80 for clinical purposes.

Clinical validity evidence for the CASL-2 was examined by comparing scores between typically developing individuals and those from various special populations (i.e., language disorder, hearing impairment, autism spectrum disorder, social/pragmatic disorder, intellectual/learning disability, and developmental delay). In all comparisons, clinical groups performed significantly below the typically developing group, with large effect sizes.

COMMENTARY. The CASL-2 provides a comprehensive measure of language skills for individuals ages 3 to 21. The instructions are easy to follow, and administration and scoring are straightforward. Each of the 14 tests can serve as stand-alone assessments or be combined into six different index scores, providing flexibility in administration depending on the purposes of the evaluation. Standard scores, percentile ranks, confidence intervals, test-age equivalent, and grade equivalent scores are provided. In addition, norms are available based on both age and grade. The CASL-2 includes several improvements over the CASL, such as full-color pictures, updated norms, and more evidence of reliability and validity.

The test author reports the sensitivity and specificity of the CASL-2 for various cutoff scores. A cutoff score of 85 provided the best balance of sensitivity and specificity; however, a standard score of 85 is just one standard deviation below the mean (i.e., the low end of the normal range). The criteria for diagnosing language disorder is usually much lower in most clinical settings.

SUMMARY. The Comprehensive Assessment of Spoken Language, Second Edition (CASL-2) is an individually administered comprehensive language assessment for individuals ages 3 to 21 years. Its primary purposes are to identify language disorders, describe strengths and weaknesses in oral language abilities, and measure English proficiency in English language learners. The CASL-2 assesses the language processes of auditory comprehension and oral expression. It also assesses lexical/semantic, syntactic, supralinguistic, and pragmatic language knowledge. The CASL-2 is based on the Integrative Language Theory, which views language as modular. The CASL-2 has undergone several updates and improvements since the original version. Evidence supporting the validity and reliability of its scores as language assessments is provided.

REVIEWER'S REFERENCES

Bates, E. (1994). Modularity, domain specificity and the development of language. *Discussions in Neuroscience, 10,* 136-149.

Carrow-Woolfolk, E. (1988). *Theory, assessment, and intervention in language disorders: An integrative approach.* Philadelphia, PA: Grune & Stratton.

Carrow-Woolfolk, E. (1999). Comprehensive Assessment of Spoken Language. Circle Pines, MN: American Guidance Service.

Carrow-Woolfolk, E. (2011). Oral and Written Language Scales, Second Edition. Torrance, CA: Western Psychological Services.

Carrow-Woolfolk, E., & Klein, A. (2017). Oral Passage Understanding Scale. Torrance, CA: Western Psychological Services.

Fodor, J. A. (1983). *The modularity of mind.* Cambridge, MA: The MIT Press.

Plante, E., & Vance, R. (1994). Selection of preschool language tests: A data-based approach. *Language, Speech, and Hearing Services in Schools, 25,* 15-24.

Wiig, E. H., Semel, E., & Secord, W. A. (2013). Clinical Evaluation of Language Fundamentals—Fifth Edition. San Antonio, TX: Pearson.

Review of the Comprehensive Assessment of Spoken Language, Second Edition by DIANA B. NEWMAN, Associate Professor (Retired), Communication Disorders, Southern Connecticut State University, New Haven, CT:

DESCRIPTION. The Comprehensive Assessment of Spoken Language, Second Edition (CASL-2) is an individually administered standardized assessment used to evaluate auditory comprehension and expressive language skills in individuals 3-21 years of age who are considered proficient in English. The CASL-2 is organized as a battery of four components: Lexical/Semantic, Syntactic, Supralinguistic, and Pragmatic. There are 14 stand-alone tests, each measuring a specific language skill in one of these components. Lexical/Semantic tests include Receptive Vocabulary, Antonyms, Synonyms, Expressive Vocabulary, and Idiomatic Language. The Syntactic component includes measures of Sentence Expression, Grammatical Morphemes, Sentence Comprehension, and Grammaticality Judgment. The Supralinguistic tests include Nonliteral Language, Meaning from Context, Inference, and Double Meaning. The Pragmatic component is assessed with a Pragmatic Language test. Test format includes both multiple-choice and open-ended questions with preferred and acceptable responses provided on the record form. None of the tests require reading or writing, as the stimuli are presented in one of three easel books with full-color illustrations. There are two record forms (the Preschool Form for ages 3-6, and the Comprehensive Form for ages 3-21).

The evaluator should be trained and experienced in the administration and interpretation of psychoeducational assessments. Interventions based on the CASL-2 should be planned by a speech-language pathologist, child psychologist or educational specialist. Each test typically takes 5-10 minutes to administer and 5 minutes to score. Age-related starting points, basals, and ceilings are provided.

In addition to deriving norm-referenced scores, examiners may further review results of each test using its accompanying Item Analysis Worksheet. Test scores may be combined to derive index scores representing skills in six broad areas of spoken language. These include the General Language Ability Index, Receptive Language Index, Expressive Language Index, Lexical/Semantic Index, Syntactic Index, and Supralinguistic Index.

The test publisher offers free online scoring and reporting features; however, online administration is not available, so paper protocols are still necessary.

DEVELOPMENT. Consistent with the purpose of the original CASL (Carrow-Woolfolk, 1999), the CASL-2 provides an in-depth assessment of an individual's oral language skills based on Integrative Language Theory (ILT). The ILT hypothesizes that language reflects two dimensions: knowledge and performance. Language knowledge, also referred to as the structures of language, represents the form and content of language and is defined by four elements, lexical/semantic, syntactic, supralinguistic, and pragmatic. Although these structures are integrated simultaneously when we speak and/or listen, ILT posits that each may be considered as a separately functioning component that may be measured individually. Language performance represents the major processes by which an individual receives and expresses language. For oral language these include auditory comprehension, oral expression, and retrieval.

The CASL-2 consists of 14 of the original CASL tests, with changes made in some of the names, items, and age ranges. All artwork was updated to full-color illustrations. The scoring criteria for open-ended format questions were amended to increase the reliability of coding and scoring across examiners. Alternative scoring guidelines for individuals who speak African American English or a similar dialect were added.

The functionality and psychometric properties of these 14 updated tests were examined in a pilot study of 972 typically developing individuals from a diverse range of age, race/ethnicity, and parent educational level. Responses for each test were analyzed together using the Rasch one-parameter model. Items with bias or problems with model fit were deleted. The Rasch estimate of item difficulty was used to determine the final item order for the standardization and validation version.

TECHNICAL. Standardization was conducted using the data collected from a normative sample of 2,394 children and young adults. The sample was largely representative of the 2012 U.S. Census data in terms of gender, race/ethnicity, region, and parents' educational level. A clinical validation sample of 271 individuals with a clinical diagnosis and receiving special services was also collected. Responses were analyzed using the Rasch one-parameter model. Items that met the parameters of model fit and did not show bias were selected for the final test form. Age-based and grade-based (fall and spring) test and index standard scores were derived as well as test-age and grade-equivalent scores.

Reliability was evaluated using estimates of internal consistency, test-retest reliability, and interrater reliability. Internal consistency evaluated by split-half reliability coefficients for the standardization sample by age range for each of the tests was high, ranging from .85 to .99; coefficients for index scores were also high at .95 or greater. Similar results were found for the clinical samples. Reliability coefficients and standard errors of measurement were used to determine confidence intervals at 90% and 95% and are presented in the normative tables. Reliability was also examined using a 2-week test-retest paradigm involving 145 individuals, balanced for gender, age, ethnicity, and parents' educational level. The coefficients for the individual tests ranged from .73 to .94 with a median of .85, while those for index scores ranged from .88 to .96 with a median of .92. All effect sizes were considered small, indicating negligible changes in the average performance of the test-retest sample over time. In addition, intraclass correlation coefficients were calculated to determine the extent of agreement between a pair of raters who separately scored responses to open-ended questions of 60 participants randomly selected from the standardization sample. The intraclass correlation coefficients ranged from .86 to .97 with a median of .92, suggesting strong agreement between different raters who used written instructions to score the tests.

The test author provides evidence regarding the CASL-2's construct validity, convergent validity, and validity based on clinical groups. Confirmatory factor analyses support the structure of the test's organization (construct), that is, one consistent with its basis in the ILT. Intercorrelations between tests and between indices were found to be moderate (.42) to high (.93), suggesting that each CASL-2 test assesses a distinct aspect of oral language and therefore can be scored and interpreted separately. Evidence of convergence was derived from comparisons between the CASL-2 and the Oral Passage Understanding Scale (OPUS; Carrow-Woolfolk & Klein, 2017); the Oral Language Composite of the Oral and Written Language Scales, Second Edition (OWLS-II; Carrow-Woolfolk, 2011); and the original version (CASL). Observed correlation coefficients for the CASL-2 General Language Ability Index and these tests were .77, .89, and .90, respectively. However, all were developed by Carrow-Woolfolk using the ILT framework. Perhaps, then, the strongest evidence of convergent validity would be the .89 correlation found between the General Language Ability Index of the CASL-2 and the Core Language score of the Clinical Evaluation of Language Fundamentals, Fifth Edition (CELF-5; Wiig, Semel, & Secord, 2013), a test based on a framework other than ILT. Finally, when using a cutoff standard score of 85 or higher, the differences between the standard scores of the group with a clinical diagnosis and their corresponding matched control group were statistically significant and clinically meaningful, with a sensitivity ≥ .74 and specificity ≥ .84.

COMMENTARY. The CASL-2 is well normed and has strong psychometric properties. The examiner's manual provides extensive guidance to assist in the interpretation of the CASL-2 test scores. Likely of most help is a table that outlines each test with a description of the processing involved, the number and format of the items, the skills measured, and what is suggested by poor performance. The manual also discusses how to examine for differences between test or index scores, how to use the CASL-2 to identify language disorders, and how to conduct qualitative analysis of responses for each test, a very useful, though often neglected, aspect of assessment. Several in-depth case examples will also be appreciated by test users.

At first glance, the 54-page CASL-2 record form appears overwhelming and even clumsy with its fold-out layout. However, not all pages/tests necessarily will be used with a given individual. Thought should be given to also providing individual index booklets with forms only for those tests needed. Or, better yet, online test protocols or even full administration could be considered. In today's environmentally conscious society, the excessive paper waste should be addressed even before any possible third edition.

The response format and scoring methods vary across the CASL-2 tests. Although these variations allow for a deeper insight into an individual's language strengths and weaknesses, they require sufficient study of the test manual and practice prior to administration, especially for novice examiners.

The CASL-2 was intentionally designed to minimize the influence of memory on the language structures assessed. However, there is no test in the CASL-2 that examines verbal memory, which is widely accepted as an integral part of both auditory comprehension and oral expression (specifically, retrieval).

Finally, the CASL-2 provides alternative correct responses for speakers of African American English or similar dialect. Yet given the significant number of individuals in the United States of Latino or Asian backgrounds, the examiner also must be aware of and consider the possible influence of Latino or Asian languages (or, in fact, any other language) on English syntax.

SUMMARY. The CASL-2, like the original CASL, is based on the Integrative Language Theory (ILT), which posits that language reflects two dimensions: knowledge (structures) and performance. Fourteen stand-alone tests are categorized into one of four structures: Lexical/Semantic, Syntactic, Supralinguistic, and Pragmatic. Six norm-referenced index scores—General Language Ability, Receptive Language, Expressive Language, Lexical/Semantic, Syntactic, and Supralinguistic—are derived from combinations of standard scores from individual tests. The CASL-2 can provide information in a targeted area of concern or a comprehensive profile of an individual's spoken language. Either way, the CASL-2 is suitable for use in diagnosis and intervention planning.

REVIEWER'S REFERENCES

Carrow-Woolfolk, E. (1999). Comprehensive Assessment of Spoken Language. Circle Pines, MN: American Guidance Service.

Carrow-Woolfolk, E. (2011). Oral and Written Language Scales, Second Edition. Torrance, CA: Western Psychological Services.

Carrow-Woolfolk, E., & Klein, A. (2017). Oral Passage Understanding Scale. Torrance, CA: Western Psychological Services.

Wiig, E. H., Semel, E., & Secord, W. A. (2013). Clinical Evaluation of Language Fundamentals—Fifth Edition. San Antonio, TX: Pearson.

[38]

Comprehensive Executive Function Inventory Adult.

Purpose: Designed to "measure behaviors associated with executive function in adults."
Population: Ages 18 and older.
Publication Date: 2017.
Acronym: CEFI Adult.
Scores, 12: Attention, Emotion Regulation, Flexibility, Inhibitory Control, Initiation, Organization, Planning, Self-Monitoring, Working Memory, Full Scale, plus Consistency Index and Negative Impression.
Administration: Individual.
Forms, 2: Self-Report, Observer.
Price Data, 2019: $280 per online kit including manual (2017, 242 pages), 25 Self-Report forms, 25 Observer forms, automatic scoring, and automatic report generation; $213 per handscored kit including manual, 25 Self-Report forms, and 25 Observer forms; $92 per manual; $65 per 25 print Observer forms; $65 per 25 print Self-Report forms; $4 per online Observer form; $4 per online Self-Report form.
Foreign Language Edition: Spanish forms available.
Time: (10-15) minutes.
Comments: Administered and scored via paper and pencil or online.
Authors: Jack A. Naglieri and Sam Goldstein.
Publisher: Multi-Health Systems, Inc.

Review of the Comprehensive Executive Function Inventory Adult by JOHN J. BRINKMAN, Professor of Psychology and Counseling, and EMILY LAUTZENHEISER, Assistant Professor of Psychology and Counseling, University of Saint Francis, Fort Wayne, IN:

DESCRIPTION. The Comprehensive Executive Function Inventory Adult™ (CEFI Adult™) is an individually administered 80-item multi-informant assessment used to evaluate executive functioning strengths and weaknesses in individuals age 18 or older. Assessments are conducted either through self-report of experiences in the previous 4 weeks or by a person who has known the individual for at least 4 weeks. The CEFI Adult provides an overall Full Scale score, as well as scores for each of the nine individual scales. The test items are written at a fourth-grade reading level; the test instructions are written at a seventh-grade level. The measure is available for both English and Spanish speakers and is normed for use with individuals in the United States and Canada.

The CEFI Adult consists of a Self-Report Form and an Observer Form, as well as a technical manual. Only one form needs to be completed to conduct the assessment. The CEFI Adult can be completed on paper or online via the test publisher's site. The paper forms can be hand scored using a two-part response and scoring form, or they can be scored online. If the assessment is completed and/or scored online, computer-based interpretive reports are available.

The test manual is well-written and organized, with concise summaries preceding each section of the manual. The format of both forms is straightforward. The directions instruct the respondent "to answer each statement that follows the phrase, 'During the past four weeks, how often did you/the individual...'" The respondent is instructed to circle his/her response using the following response scale: *never*, *rarely*, *sometimes*, *often*, *very often*, and *always*. Each response is symbolized on the forms by the first letter of each word (i.e., N, R, S, O, V, A). The examiner should ensure that the respondent answers each question, only provides one response per question, and completes the assessment independently. If a respondent is unable to read the items, the examiner may read them aloud as long as the respondent marks his/her own responses.

The scoring sheet converts the response scale to a 0-5 scale and automatically transfers the respondent's item scores to the scoring sheet. The examiner then transfers item scores to blank spaces that correspond to each scale, transfers one set of numbers to the results page, sums raw scores for each scale and then totals the scale raw scores into the CEFI Adult Full Scale raw score. The examiner then consults multiple age-band-dependent appendices in the test manual to obtain scale standard scores, confidence intervals, and prorated scores (if items were omitted by the respondent), then consults a second set of tables to determine whether the standard scores are statistically significant. Scores that fall within statistical significance are considered executive function strengths or executive function weaknesses because they are not average. The test giver must also calculate the Negative Impression score as well as the Consistency Index score.

DEVELOPMENT. The CEFI Adult is intended to serve as a single data point used for evaluation and treatment planning, based on a single construct of executive functioning. The CEFI Adult was piloted with 165 items that assessed cognition, behavior, emotions, and rater response bias. Following the pilot study, a statistical and practical analysis was used to reduce the number of items to 120. The final CEFI Adult assessment was created via an item analysis that reduced the number of items to 80. Exploratory factor analyses were then used for both the items and the scales, to confirm that the CEFI Adult's unidimensional construct accurately assesses executive functioning. Through factor analyses, the nine individual scales were developed, along with a Negative Impression scale to screen for overly negative responses and a Consistency Index to screen for inconsistent responses. Of note, when the Consistency Index was developed, item-pair correlations were calculated for both forms of the assessment. Correlations between item pairs were consistently lower for the Self-Report Form (a range of .51-.68) than for the Observer Form (a range of .70-.75). Because the items on the forms are identical, this may indicate that observers are more likely to consistently interpret like items.

TECHNICAL. Norming for the assessment included individuals from the general population. Ten percent of the norming sample comprised individuals diagnosed with attention-deficit/hyperactivity disorder (ADHD), autism spectrum disorder, bipolar disorder, generalized anxiety disorder, major depressive disorder, post-traumatic stress disorder (PTSD), or major neurocognitive disorder (i.e., dementia). Individuals were included from every U.S. state and Canadian province. An effect size study was conducted between the paper form and the online form. Cohen's *d* effect size ratios indicated minimal differences between the two types of administration. Thus, data from both administrations were combined for the norming of the CEFI Adult.

Data from 3,320 ratings (evenly split between the Self-Report Form and Observer ratings) were included in the normative sample. For the Observer Form, the sampling group comprised mostly relatives of the individual being rated; the sample was 69% White, 49% male, 50% with at least a bachelor's degree, and an average age of 49. The CEFI Adult norms were developed primarily based on demographic data of the individuals who completed the Self-Report Form. The sample was matched to the 2010 U.S. Census with regard to race/ethnicity, age, gender, education level, and geographic region via a stratified sampling plan. Analyses of variance (ANOVAs) were conducted using normative data to establish generalizability across racial/ethnic groups. Cohen's *d* effect sizes of .13 and .10 for the Self-Report Form and -.01 and -.12 for the Observer Form for the Black and White and Hispanic and White test takers, respectively, demonstrated a minimal relationship between race/ethnicity and Full Scale scores on either form.

The CEFI Adult was evaluated for internal consistency, test-retest reliability, and interrater reliability. Alpha coefficients were used to evaluate internal consistency for the Full Scale and each of the nine individual scales. For both forms of assessment, internal consistency coefficients exceeded .96 across all age groups on the Full Scale. Reliability coefficients for the Observer Form were all well above .80 for each scale. Lower reliability was demonstrated for some scales on the Self-Report Form, including Attention (.74 for age groups 18-22 and 23-29 and .77 for age group 75+), Emotion Regulation (.75 for age group 75+), Planning (.75 for age group 18-22), Self-Monitoring (.76 for age groups 45-64 and 75+), and Working Memory (.73 for age group 18-22).

Both the Self-Report Form and Observer Form demonstrated high test-retest reliability for 2- to 4-week intervals and 2- to 3-month intervals. However, for the 2- to 4-week interval, the Observer Form demonstrated higher reliability across the Full Scale and the nine individual scales, with the exception of Organization (.87 compared to .90 on the Self-Report Form). For the 2- to 3-month interval, the Self-Report Form demonstrated higher reliability across all scales, with the exception of Self-Monitoring (equal coefficients of .86 on both forms). Thus, the Self-Report Form may be more reliable with a longer amount of time between tests, whereas the Observer Form may be more reliable with a shorter amount of time between tests.

Interrater reliability estimates for the Observer Form yielded a Full Scale coefficient of .78; the only scale to achieve a coefficient of at least .80 was Inhibitory Control. Lower coefficients were demonstrated for Initiation (.58), Planning (.68), and Working Memory (.66). Overall, interrater reliability of the Observer Form appears moderate at best.

Validity was examined with attention to content, construct, and criterion-related evidence. The test authors reviewed theory, literature, and their own clinical experiences, which informed the creation of the nine scales. Construct validity and criterion-related validity studies were performed to confirm that the CEFI Adult measures the single (unidimensional) construct of executive functioning. To establish construct validity, exploratory factor analyses were conducted for the items and scales using normative data. A congruence analysis was used to determine similarity of scales across demographics. The exploratory factor analyses were conducted using *psych* R packages and oblimin rotation to determine correlation. Pearson product-moment correlations were also used to determine the association between scales. The item-level factor analysis concluded that one factor explained the data, confirming the test authors' premise that executive function can be assessed as a unidimensional construct; factor loadings ranged from .35 to .85, well above the minimum .32. The scale-level factor analysis demonstrated stronger results, with factor loadings ranging from .79 to .95. Congruence coefficients were calculated across demographic groups (i.e., gender, age, racial/ethnic group, and clinical status) to further establish the unidimensional nature of the assessment; the results demonstrated high congruence with a range of .993 to .999. Lastly, correlation coefficients were calculated for the Full Scale to determine the relationship between the Self-Report and Observer Forms (after using Cook's distance to identify and remove outliers); a corrected coefficient of .53 was obtained.

To provide criterion-related validity evidence, univariate analyses of variance were conducted using data from individuals previously diagnosed with clinical disorders (i.e., ADHD, generalized anxiety disorder, a mood disorder, or dementia). Data from this group were compared to the norm group for the Full Scale on both forms and consistently demonstrated statistically significant differences between the clinical group and the norming group. These results indicate that the Full Scale is appropriately sensitive to differences between clinical and general populations.

Scores on the CEFI Adult were compared to scores from the Behavior Rating Inventory of Executive Function—Adult Version (BRIEF-A), another assessment that evaluates executive functioning, and to scores from the Wechsler Adult Intelligence Scale—Fourth Edition (WAIS-IV), a measure of general intelligence. Validity coefficients demonstrated that the CEFI Adult is somewhat comparable to the BRIEF-A, with corrected correlation coefficients between individual scales ranging from .19 to .66 for the Self-Report Form and from .23 to .77 for the Observer Form. Coefficients between the CEFI Adult Full Scale score and the BRIEF-A Global Executive Composite were .67 for the Self-Report Form and .76 for the Observer Form. Additionally, the CEFI Adult and WAIS-IV scales demonstrated very low corrected correlations (a range of .00 to .24 across both forms), appropriately indicating that the CEFI Adult does not measure general intelligence.

COMMENTARY. Overall, the CEFI Adult is a simple self-report or observational assessment that quickly provides a single data point in the evaluation of and treatment planning for individuals with suspected deficits in executive functioning. The CEFI Adult is well normed to align with the 2010 U.S. Census and underwent several reliability and validity studies. The technical manual provides ample data to support the use of the assessment. The CEFI Adult can be used in multiple ways including supporting diagnoses and creating treatment plans, as well as implementing interventions and monitoring progress or outcomes.

Although the CEFI Adult is a well-designed assessment of executive functioning, limitations have been identified. First, responses to certain items may be highly subjective. A second limitation is related to reliability of scores obtained on either form. Interrater reliability coefficients for the Observer Form demonstrated only moderate reliability, whereas the Self-Report Form demonstrated moderate internal reliability estimates across the scales, especially when compared to the Observer Form. Finally, the CEFI Adult did not demonstrate strong criterion-related validity when compared to another assessment that also evaluates executive functioning. Although the authors attributed the moderate correlation coefficients that emerged to the idea that the two tests measure executive functioning in different ways, no clarification was provided for those differences.

SUMMARY. The CEFI Adult authors developed an assessment to be used in evaluating executive functioning, either through self-report or through observation for individuals ages 18 and older. The assessment adequately measures an individual's executive functioning strengths and weaknesses. Despite some of the limitations identified related to subjective responses, mixed evidence of reliability, and criterion validity, the strength of this test lies in its ability to identify strengths and limitations of executive functioning for patients diagnosed with a range of disorders that may impact executive functioning including attentional, developmental, neurocognitive, and psychiatric disorders.

Review of the Comprehensive Executive Function Inventory Adult by DAVID M. HULAC, Associate Professor, University of Northern Colorado, Greeley, CO:

DESCRIPTION. The Comprehensive Executive Function Inventory Adult (CEFI Adult) is a pair of rating scales, each with 80 questions designed to assess behaviors that are thought to represent an individual's executive functioning abilities. The Self-Report Form is completed by the individual undergoing assessment; the Observer Form is designed to be completed by a significant other such as a spouse, life partner, or other individual who is familiar with the client. Executive functioning represents a variety of cognitive abilities that allow an individual to pursue goal-oriented behavior. Deficits in executive functioning underlie a variety of emotional problems such as depression and anxiety, behavioral disorders such as attention-deficit/hyperactivity disorder (ADHD), and neurocognitive problems such as dementia. The use of rating scales addresses a problem of ecological validity. Many traditional psychological testing environments have few distractions. An individual with an executive functioning difficulty may be able to succeed in an environment with distractions removed but may struggle in natural settings where distractions are more likely.

The 10 scores on the CEFI Adult are reported as standard scores with a mean of 100 and a standard deviation of 15. The test publisher requires that examiners qualify as Level B test users, meaning they have had graduate-level training in tests and measurement. The average completion time is 10-15 minutes.

DEVELOPMENT. In developing the CEFI Adult, 165 items were created that addressed cognitive, behavioral, and emotional domains. These items were then pilot-tested with 300 self-reporting individuals and 269 observers. Final items were then selected based on the items' ability to differentiate individuals (e.g., those with ADHD from those with major depression), items that exhibited sufficient variance, and items with sufficient clinical utility.

TECHNICAL. The standardization sample included 3,320 raters with equal numbers completing the Self-Report and Observer forms. The participants roughly corresponded with demographic data from the 2010 U.S. Census in terms of geographic region, gender, race, Hispanic status, educational exceptionality status, household income, and parent education. Ratings of individuals with clinical diagnoses such as ADHD, autism spectrum disorder, bipolar disorder, generalized anxiety disorder, major depressive disorder, post-traumatic stress disorder, and major neurocognitive disorder (dementia) made up 10% of the sample for each form. An additional 321 individuals who had been diagnosed with ADHD, a mood disorder, generalized anxiety disorder, or dementia comprised a clinical sample. The test authors provide extensive tables of demographic data for the normative sample by age, race, and disability status. Raw scores are converted to standard scores by comparing an examinee's performance against other adults from the same age group in the normative sample.

The CEFI Adult provides both online and paper-and-pencil administration and scoring options. Analyses of data from a general population sample showed almost no difference between scores from online and paper administrations, so the norms reflect combined administrations methods. The test manual reports estimates of reliability across all ages and for the clinical sample. Internal consistency estimates for the Full Scale score on both forms ranged from .97 to .99. Test-retest estimates for the Full Scale over a 2- to 4-week period were .93 for the Self-Report Form (n = 152) and .94 for the Observer Form (n = 135). Interrater reliability was examined using 79 rater pairs and yielded a correlation coefficient of .78 for the Full Scale.

A variety of validity studies were conducted. First, the test authors evaluated whether there was a disparate impact of a client's race or ethnicity on the scores obtained from the instrument. The relative ratios for Black and Hispanic versus White respondents ranged from .90 to 1.09, exceeding the .80 threshold that signifies disparate impact. Correlations between Full Scale scores on the Self-Report Form and the Observer Form were .53, which the test manual describes as moderate, but not so large as to produce redundancy. Two concurrent validity studies were conducted, one using the Behavior Rating Inventory of Executive Function–Adult Version (BRIEF-A), a measure of executive functioning, and the Wechsler Adult

Intelligence Scale–Fourth Edition (WAIS-IV), a measure of intellectual ability. The corrected correlation coefficient of .67 with the BRIEF-A was moderately high, whereas the .15 correlation coefficient with the WAIS-IV suggested that the two instruments measure different constructs.

Finally, construct validity evidence was provided by an exploratory factor analysis. This analysis suggested a single unidimensional factor of executive functioning. This one-factor solution held across a variety of dimensions including race, gender, age, and clinical status.

COMMENTARY. The CEFI Adult provides a reliable method of evaluating behaviors that appear to reflect executive functioning abilities. The test authors provide solid evidence that these abilities are not related to general intelligence. The administration time of 10-15 minutes is reasonable, and the test provides opportunities for both the client and an individual who has known the client well to respond. The questions across both forms are similar, which allows a clinician to gain multiple viewpoints on a client's executive functioning abilities. Although the factor structure evidence suggests that the Full Scale score may provide the best estimate of an individual's executive skills, a clinician may find the subscales useful for possible targets of intervention or accommodation.

The test authors do not provide diagnostic accuracy information to help understand the sensitivity and specificity of the instrument. This information would help an evaluator know the likelihood of an executive functioning problem based on the scores that are observed. As the authors state in the test manual, it is only appropriate to use this information together with other data when making an evaluation. The CEFI Adult does not provide direct links to interventions. However, there is some evidence to suggest that the CEFI Adult may be used to monitor an individual's progress when undergoing interventions linked to executive functioning. Future research should investigate the diagnostic accuracy of the CEFI Adult with individuals with clinical, behavioral, and mental health problems. Other research ideas include comparing CEFI Adult results with adaptive measures to determine the relationship between executive functions and social skills and other self-care problems.

SUMMARY. The CEFI Adult provides a moderately reliable measure of behaviors related to executive functioning that may be useful for clinicians who are interested in identifying the degree of executive dysfunction in an individual with a variety of mental health disorders.

[39]

Contextual Probes of Articulation Competence—Spanish.

Purpose: Designed to assess the phonological skills of Spanish-speaking children and to "assist in planning intervention and/or monitoring phonological change during intervention."

Publication Dates: 2006-2009.

Acronym: CPAC-S.

Administration: Individual.

Price Data, 2019: $241 per complete kit including examiner's manual (2006, 121 pages), client words and sentences lists, assessment flip easel, and normative data manual (2009, 68 pages); $199 per test kit without normative data manual; $115 per normative data manual.

Comments: Based on the Contextual Probes of Articulation Competence in the Secord Contextual Articulation Test designed for English speakers. Developed for use by bilingual speech-language pathologists; if the examiner is not bilingual, he/she may collaborate with a trained interpreter. The administrator must know the examinee's country of origin and the primary dialect spoken in the home as scoring will depend on dialect; online scoring system available to aid in accounting for dialectical variations.

Authors: Brian Goldstein and Aquiles Iglesias.

Publisher: PRO-ED.

a) QUICK SCREEN.

Purpose: A 17-item screener designed to assess articulatory and phonological performance by making an "immediate link between the client's errors and the consonant and phonological probes."

Population: Spanish speakers from preschool to adult.

Scores: Phonemic Inventory Errors, Phonological Patterns Exhibited.

Time: 5-10 minutes for administration of screener; 3-5 minutes for administration of each phonological probe.

Comments: Criterion-referenced; errors and patterns that are noted in scoring guide clinicians in determining which of the corresponding probes should be administered.

b) FULL ASSESSMENT.

Purpose: Designed to provide a comprehensive analysis of phonological skills.

Population: Spanish-speaking children ages 3-8.

Scores: Phonemic Inventory Errors, Whole Word and Segmental Accuracy (Whole Words, Consonants, Syllable-Initial, Syllable-Final), Phonological Patterns (Syllabic Patterns [Final Consonant Deletion, Cluster Reduction Deletion, Unstressed Syllable Deletion, Initial Consonant Deletion], Substitution Patterns

[Velar Fronting, Stopping, Palatal Fronting, Liquid Simplification, Flap/Trill Deviation, Assimilation], Other Pattern).

Time: 20-25 minutes for administration of assessment; 3-5 minutes for administration of each phonological probe.

Comments: As a criterion-referenced assessment, errors and patterns that are noted in scoring guide clinicians in determining which of the corresponding probes should be administered; norm-referenced total score (number of correctly produced consonants [initial and final]) also may be derived.

Review of the Contextual Probes of Articulation Competence–Spanish by JOSEPH R. ENGLER, Associate Professor of School Psychology, Gonzaga University, and JENNA M. WHITE, Graduate Student, School Psychology, Gonzaga University, Spokane, WA:

DESCRIPTION. The Contextual Probes of Articulation Competence–Spanish (CPAC-S) is designed to assess the phonological and articulation abilities of Spanish-speaking individuals from preschool through adulthood, with normative data for the full assessment included for preschool and early elementary ages (i.e., 3:0 to 8:11). Data collected during test administration can be used to identify appropriate follow-up probes (included in the test kit) that can be utilized for collecting pretest/posttest data, progress monitoring, and designing appropriate goals. Information regarding the use of the CPAC-S is found within an examiner's manual and a normative data manual.

The CPAC-S includes two main components: a 17-item screener and a 64-item full assessment. The screener is intended to provide baseline data reflecting an individual's abilities prior to administering the full assessment. The full assessment provides a more in-depth understanding of an individual's phonological and articulation skills. The full assessment also may be used to guide the examiner's selection of probes for future use. Test users are encouraged to use the CPAC-S as either a criterion-referenced or norm-referenced test, depending on the purpose of assessment. The test authors provide an estimated testing time for the full assessment of 20-25 minutes.

Administration of the norm-referenced full assessment begins with two trial items that ensure the examinee can identify or imitate words. The normative data manual instructs examiners to proceed to the full assessment if the examinee is able to identify the trial items or imitate them; however, it is unclear whether proceeding to the full assessment is contingent upon successful word identification or imitation or whether the full assessment is administered regardless of the examinee's performance on trial items. Upon proceeding to the full assessment, the examinee is shown a picture and asked, "*¿Qué es esto?*/What is this?" Examinee responses are transcribed and recorded using the International Phonetic Alphabet. Any distortion, substitution, omission, or addition errors on targeted sounds are noted.

Upon test completion, the examiner determines the total raw score. To begin, the examiner subtotals the number of correctly produced consonants (initial and final sounds) at the bottom of each of the five response pages. Then, the examiner adds all response page totals to get an aggregate total raw score. The aggregate total raw score is transformed into a standard score using tables provided in the normative data manual. Confidence intervals and percentile ranks may also be determined. For further analysis, the examiner is encouraged to document sounds produced by the examinee on a separate page of the record form with sections for Phonemic Inventory, Whole Word & Segmental Accuracy, and Phonological Patterns. Examiners are referred to an online tool on the test publisher's website that accounts for dialectal variations, scores an examinee's responses, and generates all normative data when working with an individual who speaks with an unfamiliar dialect (normative data manual, p. 7).

DEVELOPMENT. The CPAC-S was standardized and normed with five criteria in mind. The test authors developed the measure to (a) include the 64 words and pictures from the criterion-referenced full assessment; (b) include norms for ages 3:0 to 8:11 using Spanish speakers from the United States, Puerto Rico, and Mexico; (c) be sensitive to dialectal variations; (d) test all consonant phonemes found in Spanish dialects; and (e) include an online analyzer. Developers piloted the test in the United States, Puerto Rico, and Mexico and received feedback from the original testers. Based on this feedback, the test authors made modest modifications, and the international standardization of the CPAC-S commenced. Although the test authors thoroughly communicate the importance of considering the many dialectal variations in the Spanish language both in administration and scoring of the CPAC-S, it is unclear how dialect was accounted for when creating norms for the broad target population.

TECHNICAL. The normative sample consisted of 1,127 children between the ages of 3:0

and 8:11 from the United States, Puerto Rico, and Mexico. The sample was compared to U.S. Census data on the following demographic characteristics: region, gender, ethnicity, and socioeconomic status. There was an overrepresentation of children from the Midwest and underrepresentation of children from the West. In addition, Puerto Rican children were overrepresented, and Mexican children were underrepresented. With regard to socioeconomic status, based on mother's education level, there was a slight underrepresentation of mothers who did not finish high school and overrepresentation of mothers with four or more years of university education. Test users should consider this information to ensure that the child they are testing is adequately represented in the normative sample. The remaining characteristics matched the U.S. Census data relatively well.

The test authors provided three forms of evidence for reliability of the CPAC-S. The first involved calculating internal consistency using coefficient alpha across age groups. Alpha coefficients ranged from .89 to .97, which is considered adequate to good across ages 3:0 to 8:11 (see Alfonso & Flanagan, 2008). The test authors also provided evidence of test-retest reliability. In total, 32 children were included in the test-retest sample with an interval ranging from 14 to 30 days. The resultant reliability coefficient (.94) indicates an acceptable degree of temporal stability. That said, these reviewers would recommend that the test authors describe the demographics of the sample to ensure that it is representative of the target population. It also would be preferable to use a larger sample. The final evidence of reliability was provided through interrater reliability. Interrater reliability was very high, with coefficients ranging from .98 to .99.

The authors of the CPAC-S describe two sources of evidence of validity. The first involves concurrent evidence in which the test authors compared the CPAC-S and another Spanish articulation test. In sum, 21 children completed both tests, and the comparison yielded a high correlation coefficient of .96. The second form of evidence involved the sensitivity and specificity of the CPAC-S, which were assessed by comparing scores obtained by a control group to those from a clinical sample. Results showed acceptable levels of correct classifications at cutoffs of -1 standard deviation (93% correct) and -1.5 standard deviations (89% correct).

Overall, the evidence of reliability as presented in the normative data manual is considered a relative strength of the test by these reviewers. In contrast, the evidence of validity appears relatively weak, primarily because there is not enough of it.

COMMENTARY. The test authors are commended for their research and work in the area of test development for Spanish-speaking individuals. Moreover, the test authors are commended for clearly articulating the importance of taking dialect into account when assessing examinees. The CPAC-S is an easy test to administer and score. Additionally, the test provides useful quantitative and qualitative information that can assist examiners in the interpretation of test performance. That said, there are several weaknesses of the test that should be noted. First, the use of two manuals for the CPAC-S was difficult for these reviewers to follow. For example, it may be clearer for test users to have one manual that includes all pertinent information for the test. Second, the test is purported to be used for screening, full assessment, and progress monitoring. However, the test manuals do not clearly articulate the rationale and evidence needed to support its use for each purpose. As such, it is recommended that the test authors more clearly define the intended use of the test. Third, the standardization sample was not representative of the U.S. population for several demographic characteristics. As a result, the ability to generalize the results of the assessment may not be indicated. Fourth, the test authors cite McCauley and Swisher (1984) as the standard employed for providing reliability and validity evidence. As a result, the evidence to support these areas was not aligned with current standards and expectations. The test authors are encouraged to use the current *Standards for Educational and Psychological Testing* (American Educational Research Association, American Psychological Association, & National Council on Measurement in Education, 2014) as a conceptual framework for providing such data.

SUMMARY. The CPAC-S was designed to assess the phonological and articulation abilities in Spanish-speaking individuals. The test accomplishes this goal through either the 17-item screener or 64-item full assessment. The lack of representativeness of the standardization sample calls into question the generalizability of the test. In addition, presenting the CPAC-S as a broad test (e.g., screener, full assessment, progress monitoring) without providing supporting data for each of these intended uses compromises the validity of the test.

As such, the CPAC-S is not recommended for clinical use as a norm-referenced test at this time. That said, the CPAC-S shows promise when used as a criterion-referenced test and is better supported for that purpose.

REVIEWERS' REFERENCES

Alfonso, V. C., & Flanagan, D. P. (2009). Assessment of preschool children. In B. A. Mowder, F. Rubinson, & A. E. Yasik (Eds.), *Evidence based practice in infant and early childhood psychology* (pp. 129-166). Hoboken, NJ: Wiley.

American Educational Research Association, American Psychological Association, & National Council on Measurement in Education. (2014). *Standards for educational and psychological testing.* Washington, DC: AERA.

McCauley, R. J., & Swisher, L. (1984). Psychometric review of language and articulation tests for preschool children. *Journal of Speech and Hearing Disorders, 49,* 34-42.

Review of the Contextual Probes of Articulation Competence—Spanish by ALBERT VILLANUEVA-REYES, Program Director & Professor of Speech-Language Pathology, Gannon University, Ruskin, FL:

DESCRIPTION. The Contextual Probes of Articulation Competence—Spanish (CPAC-S) is an individually administered instrument designed for bilingual (Spanish/English) speech-language pathologists to assess the phonological skills of Spanish-speaking individuals. It is appropriate for clients in the age range from preschool through adults, although the assessment component is designed specifically for children. The instrument is designed to probe production of all Spanish phonemes in a variety of phonetic and phonological contexts, examine performance across different speech production levels, and help plan intervention. The test authors state that the instrument "evolved out of a need for an assessment tool that was flexible enough so that clinicians could use it with a variety of clients, regardless of their verbal output level or knowledge of specific lexical items, and thorough enough so that clinicians could use it as a prescriptive tool" (manual, p. 2). It can be used either as a quick screener with 17 items for Spanish speakers from preschool to adult or as a full assessment instrument with 64 items for children ages 3:0 to 8:11. The target words are of three types: disyllabic words, consonant clusters, and multisyllabic words. The test allows for scoring of the individual's phonetic inventory, whole word accuracy, segmental accuracy, and percentage-of-occurrence of phonological patterns. The instrument also contains 17 consonant probes that "examine articulatory consistency according to syllabic function in a representative sample of Spanish phonetic contexts" (manual, p. 30). These probes can be coordinated with the assessment component to help clinicians choose intervention targets.

The CPAC-S was originally designed as a criterion-referenced assessment, and the screener is still intended for that purpose. The full assessment also may be used as a criterion-referenced tool, but a norm-referenced Total score also may be derived. Information on the development of norms is contained in a separate normative data manual.

Administration instructions are clear and easy to follow. According to the test authors, administration of the screening tool takes approximately 5 to 10 minutes, whereas the full assessment takes approximately 20 to 25 minutes. In addition, each probe takes about 3 to 5 minutes. Both in the screener and in the full assessment, pictures are presented for the examinee to name, and the examiner records phonetic transcriptions of each of the examinee's productions. If the examinee cannot name the picture, the examiner is to prompt the test taker using a sentence also provided in the instrument. The consonant probes are administered after the assessment portion. This section allows the evaluation of error sounds in a wide range of phonotactic contexts, which can validate results and provide a greater understanding of the client's productions.

DEVELOPMENT. In developing the Contextual Probes of Articulation Competence—Spanish (CPAC-S) the authors sought to develop a "comprehensive clinical management program" (manual, p. 1) that would (a) probe production of all Spanish phonemes in a variety of phonetic and phonological contexts, (b) examine performance across different speech production levels (e.g., prevocalic and postvocalic word contexts, clusters, and sentences), and (c) help plan intervention. The CPAC-S was based on the Contextual Probes of Articulation Competence in the Secord Contextual Articulation Tests (Secord & Shine, 1997) designed for English speakers. The target words in this instrument conform to the phonological properties of Spanish, and allow the clinician to obtain immediate feedback on the intactness of the client's phonological system. According to the manual, the phonological processes, described by the test authors as phonological patterns, targeted in the instrument are largely those described in Shriberg and Kwiatkowski's *Natural Process Analysis.*

Prior to collecting normative data, two trial items were created to ensure examinees understand the picture-naming task. The test authors also created a comprehensive list of potential dialectal variations to facilitate the differentiation of acceptable pronunciations and true misarticulations. A list of phonetic symbols was included to aid examiners with transcription. Data from a pilot study involving 10 examiners in the United States, Mexico, and Puerto Rico indicated that all 64 items from the original full assessment were appropriate and elicited the desired responses. Based on examiners' transcriptions, the most prevalent dialectal variations were identified and used to determine acceptable responses in the final stage of development.

TECHNICAL. A total of 1,127 children from 20 states in the United States and its territories, including the District of Columbia and Puerto Rico, as well as Mexico, were included in the normative sample. Sample sizes were sufficient for representative norms to be developed, with more than 150 children in yearly intervals between the ages of 3:0 and 8:11. Demographic data were presented for the sample according to geographic region/country, gender, ethnicity, and socioeconomic status. In categories where the sample differed from the population (e.g., children from the South and the Midwest were overrepresented while children from the West were underrepresented), the test authors contend the differences had little impact on the normative data as evidenced in the means of the various groups. Raw score means are reported for the normative sample by age, ethnicity, socioeconomic status, and region of the country. Independent samples *t*-tests were conducted to determine whether significant differences occurred among the groups. One significant comparison was observed for region (South vs. Puerto Rico), and one significant comparison was observed for ethnicity (Mexican vs. Puerto Rican). Effect sizes calculated using Cohen's *d* were small in both cases.

The standardization procedure included collecting evidence to support concurrent validity, diagnostic validity (specificity and sensitivity), internal consistency, test-retest reliability, and interrater reliability. In addition, the test authors suggest that face validity was ensured by including all Spanish phonemes on the test in accordance with their percentages of occurrence in the language and by including a representative sample of the most commonly occurring phonological processes (patterns).

Internal consistency (coefficient alpha) was reported for each age level and ranged from .89 to .97. As concurrent validity evidence, scores from the CPAC-S were correlated with scores from the Spanish Articulation Measures test using a sample of 21 children. Results showed the instruments are highly and significantly correlated, with Pearson's r = .96 (p < .001) and Spearman's rho = .96 (p < .001). Specificity was reported as 94% for a cutoff score 1 standard deviation below the mean; sensitivity was reported as 91%.

Correlations between test and retest scores were very high, with a reported Pearson's r of .94 and Spearman's rho of .92. The interval between test administrations was 14-30 days for the 32-person sample. Interrater reliability was examined using three speech-language pathologists trained to administer the CPAC-S. Correlations (Pearson's r) among the three raters (taken in pairs) were very high, ranging between .98 and .99, accounting for between 97% and 98% of the variance. The administration of the CPAC-S is described in sufficient detail to enable test users to duplicate the administration and scoring procedures used during test standardization.

COMMENTARY. The CPAC-S is a relatively brief and easy test to administer that can be quite appropriate for speakers of some Spanish dialects. Its administration requires that the clinician know the country of origin of the client being tested and the primary dialect spoken at home. Knowledge of phonetics and phonological processes is required of the clinician, as the examiner needs to phonetically transcribe the client's responses and analyze them. The examiner also needs a good understanding of Spanish dialectal variations, especially those described in the instrument (Mexican and Caribbean). Scoring is not too difficult. The acceptable dialectal variations described in the instrument need to be revised in order to improve its accuracy. The Caribbean particularities, for example, that are described in the instrument cannot be generalized for all dialects in that region. Similarly, the instrument describes not too accurately the allophonic particularities of the region. For example, it indicates that in the Puerto Rican dialect, the /s/ in final context of syllable is omitted, whereas in reality, such sound is aspirated (/s^h/). Similarly, the instrument indicates that the production of /R/ instead of /r/ in initial syllable context is acceptable in Puerto Rico, which is somewhat misguided. In general, the instrument describes relatively well the particularities of the dialects it addresses, but this reviewer suggests careful revision by native speakers of these dialects. Moreover, the instrument provides an incomplete description of phonemes and allophones of spoken Spanish, which seems to be limited to Mexico and the Caribbean but does not completely address the phonetic repertoires of these regions. Spanish phonemes such as /θ/, /ʒ/, and allophone /ŋ/ are not included in the instrument's list. Finally, although the test authors claim that the instrument works with the most common phonologic processes for Spanish, other important processes must be incorporated into it.

SUMMARY. The CPAC-S is designed to identify articulatory and phonological problems in Spanish-speaking individuals, mostly children between the ages of 3:0 and 8:11. The instrument meets the goals of testing production of Spanish phonemes for some dialects in a variety of phonetic and phonological contexts, examining performance across different speech production levels, and helping plan intervention. The instrument is based on good design and standardization processes. Unfortunately, its application is limited to dialects of Mexico and the Caribbean, which does not ensure that there will be no difficulties with the use of the instrument with these dialects.

REVIEWER'S REFERENCE

Secord, W. A., & Shine, R. E. (1997). Secord Contextual Articulation Tests. Greenville, SC: Super Duper.

[40]

Coping Operations Preference Enquiry.

Purpose: Designed to measure a person's preference for using each of five coping mechanisms, or mechanisms of defense.
Population: Adults.
Publication Dates: 1962-1978.
Acronyms: COPE, FCPE.
Scores, 5: Denial, Isolation, Projection, Regression, Turning-Against-the-Self.
Administration: Individual or group.
Forms, 2: Male, Female.
Price Data, 2016: $50 per PDF manual (1978, 24 pages including test forms and scoring keys), including review-only copy of test form; $2 per Remote Online Survey License or License to Reproduce (minimum 50).
Time: [10] minutes.
Comments: Previously included in The FIRO Scales (7:78).
Authors: Will Schutz.
Publisher: Mind Garden, Inc.

No review available. This test does not meet review criteria established by the Buros Center for Testing that call for at least minimal technical and development information.

[41]

Coping Resources Inventory [Revised].

Purpose: Developed to assess a person's resources for coping with stress.
Population: Middle school-age to adult.
Publication Dates: 1987-2004.
Acronym: CRI.
Scores, 6: Cognitive, Social, Emotional, Spiritual/Philosophical, Physical, Total.
Administration: Individual or group.
Price Data, 2020: $50 per manual (2004, 55 pages), including review-only copy of the CRI form; $2.50 per online administration license (minimum 50); $200 per Group Report; $2.50 per Remote Online Survey License (minimum 50); $15 per Individual Report; $15 Report About Me.
Foreign Language Edition: Available in Portuguese.
Time: (10) minutes.
Authors: M. Susan Marting and Allen L. Hammer.
Publisher: Mind Garden, Inc.
Cross References: See T5:697 (6 references); for reviews by Roger A. Boothroyd and Larry Cochran of the original edition, see 12:95 (1 reference); see also T4:649 (2 references).

Review of the Coping Resources Inventory [Revised] by NATALIE POLITIKOS, Associate Professor, and NATASHA SEGOOL, Associate Professor, Department of Psychology, University of Hartford, West Hartford, CT:

DESCRIPTION. The Coping Resources Inventory [Revised] (CRI) is a 60-item instrument that identifies resources inherently available to individuals for managing stress and is recommended by the test authors for a wide range of ages. The CRI defines coping resources as "those resources inherent in individuals that enable them to handle stressors ... or to recover faster from exposure" (p. 2). This definition is based on models that emphasize that the amount of and types of resources individuals have intrinsically can act to allow for greater resilience in the face of stressors. The CRI seeks to focus on adaptive skills rather than deficits as they pertain to the coping process. Resources are assessed in five domains: Cognitive, Social, Emotional, Spiritual/Philosophical, and Physical. The test authors acknowledge that younger clients may have difficulty responding to the Spiritual/Philosophical items.

The CRI can be used in clinical and educational settings for treatment planning for individuals who are coping with stress-related problems as well as to identify individuals at risk who would benefit from counseling or medical intervention. Furthermore, the CRI can be used as a program evaluation tool and research instrument for the purpose of gathering data on coping resources among various populations. The CRI also can be used as a framework for creating workshops tailored to specific groups and as a planning tool for use with high school health classes. Although the test authors do not explicitly define the qualifications of examiners, it is recommended that examiners have training in test development, administration, and interpretation of tests.

The CRI can be completed in approximately 10 minutes. It can be administered individually or to groups and can be administered in three different ways: paper and pencil format, online survey directly administered by the test publisher, or digitally by a third party online survey company. Examinees are asked to respond to 60 items by indicating "how often they have engaged in the behavior described in the item over the past six months" (manual, p. 5). If respondents are unsure about the meaning of an item, they are instructed to provide a response based on their understanding. Furthermore, alternate instructions may be provided for individuals experiencing a specific condition, such as pregnancy or illness, when information is sought about resources present during the special condition versus the typical condition.

The CRI is completed using a 4-point scale with the following anchors: *never or rarely*, *sometimes*, *often*, *always or almost always*. Examinees mark responses on a separate answer sheet, and examiners are provided with five scoring keys, one for each of the five scales. Scoring instructions are located in the Coping Resources Inventory Instrument and Scoring Guide. To obtain raw scores, the sum of the item responses for each scale is calculated. There are six items with negative wording; hence, points for those items must be reversed as part of the scoring process. Examiners can derive five scale scores as well as a Total Resource score calculated by summing the five scale scores. Higher scores indicate the presence of higher amounts of the resource. Raw scores are converted to standard scores with a mean of 50 and standard deviation of 10. Norms are available for males and females; however, they are not age specific. Ipsative and normative interpretation of the CRI profile is outlined and recommended by the test authors.

DEVELOPMENT. The CRI was developed using pilot studies and item analyses. In the initial stage of development, a pool of 150 items was developed and content experts were consulted. Through pilot studies and item analyses, the number of items was reduced to 93 and, as the instrument has been revised, items were included based on item-to-scale correlations and response frequencies. This 93-item scale was used with 300 individuals including high school students, college students, and adults; inclusion criterion for item-to-scale correlations was set to .30 as a minimum. Sixty items emerged as having met the necessary criteria and were selected for inclusion in this version of the CRI.

TECHNICAL.

Standardization. The CRI was standardized using 843 participants who ranged in age from 14 to 83 years and comprised adults, college students, and high school students. The sample included 327 males and 491 females. Review of demographic data suggests that the standardization sample was small, lacked diversity, and did not generally represent national demographics. Hence, interpretations based on the normative data should be made with caution.

Reliability. The five CRI scales and the Total Resource scale had low to moderate item-to-scale correlations with median coefficients ranging from .37 to .46. The test authors discuss an exception related to a single item involving fatigue on the Physical scale that demonstrated a correlation coefficient of .11 with the Physical scale and reflects low consistency among items on this scale for the high school sample (N = 242). The corrected item-to-scale correlation for this group was r = -.26, which indicates that items reflecting physical fatigue might be a result of involvement in physical activity rather than an indicator of low resources in that area. Alpha coefficients were computed for the five scales and the Total Resource scale. The Total Resource scale demonstrated high internal consistency, with alpha coefficients ranging from .89 to .94. The test authors provided results from a number of groups including males, females, adults, high school students, and college students. Internal consistency estimates indicated homogeneity within the scales. Six-week test-retest reliability was assessed using a sample of 115 high school students and identical forms of the CRI. Moderate test-retest reliability coefficients (.60-.78) for the five scales and the Total Resource scale were observed. The lowest values were noted for the Spiritual/Philosophical (.60) and Emotional (.62) scales.

Validity. Validity for coping measures is not easy to establish. To examine predictive validity, the authors of the CRI studied its ability to predict stress using a sample of 108 junior high school students. This sample was administered both the CRI and Elkind's Stress Test for Children (Elkind, 1981), which is a measure of life events. The Personal Stress Symptom Assessment (PSSA; Numeroff, 1983), a measure of frequency of physical and psychological symptoms, was administered to the same population 12 weeks later. The CRI Total Resource score emerged as a significant incremental predictor of stress symptoms (R^2 change = .15, $p < .0001$). When evaluating the five scales of the CRI, the Physical and Cognitive scales surfaced as significant univariate incremental predictors.

Convergent validity evidence was examined using a multitrait-multimethod procedure. A sample of 83 adults was administered the CRI and also was asked to complete self-ratings of coping resources based on a short description of each construct. Moderate to high validity coefficients emerged, ranging from .61 for the Spiritual/Philosophical scale to .80 for the Physical scale.

Gender differences were examined through univariate F tests, and data suggest that women reported significantly higher resources in the following CRI scales: Social ($F = 71.40, p < .0001$; Emotional ($F = 40.44, p < .0001$); Spiritual/Philosophical ($F = 7.87, p < .01$). Women reported significantly lower resources than men on the Physical scale ($F = 6.69, p < .01$); however, there was only approximately a 1-point difference in actual score on the Spiritual/Philosophical and Physical scales, so real implications may not be evident. A higher level of resources on the Social scale is supported by research that shows that women tend to have a stronger focus on interpersonal relationships (Lowenthal, Thurnher, & Chiriboga, 1975).

COMMENTARY. The CRI is unique in its focus on identifying resources currently available to individuals experiencing stress. Whereas other stress and coping measures seek to assess deficits that contribute to the experience of stress, the CRI emphasizes the need to focus on those resources inherent to each individual that may assist in coping with stressors. Strengths of the CRI include a theoretically based development and approach, ease of administration and scoring, and strong internal consistency. Weaknesses include the small sample used for standardization as well as the lack of diversity of said sample. Age-specific norms are not provided. The test authors refrain from specifying the age group with which this instrument should be used, stating that it can be used with a "wide range of ages" (manual, p. 5). More specificity is necessary to ensure that this instrument is used with the appropriate population. In addition, clinical norms might be helpful to clinicians working with specific populations. Item-to-scale correlation coefficients were quite low, and the test authors are encouraged to consider revising item wording or content to obtain more satisfactory item-to-scale correlations.

SUMMARY. The CRI is a 60-item instrument designed to assess the coping resources inherently available to each respondent. Rather than focusing on deficits, this instrument focuses on the adaptive traits of individuals that may be helpful in coping with stress. The inventory is easy to administer with three administration options available that include paper and pencil or digital options. The CRI is easy to score and provides five scale scores as well as a Total Resource score. It was normed using 843 participants ages 14-83, and norms are available for males and females. Due to the small size and the lack of diversity of the sample, results should be interpreted cautiously. The test authors present good evidence of internal consistency, predictive validity, and convergent validity. The CRI is an interesting instrument that focuses on positive and adaptive skills to guide clinicians in their work with clients experiencing stress.

REVIEWERS' REFERENCES

Elkind, D. (1981). *The hurried child.* Reading, MA: Addison-Wesley.

Lowenthal, M. F., Thurnher, M., & Chiriboga, D. (1975). *Four stages of life.* San Francisco, CA: Jossey-Bass.

Numeroff, R. (1983). *Managing stress: A guide for health professionals.* Rockville, MD: Aspen.

Review of the Coping Resources Inventory [Revised] by CYNTHIA A. ROHRBECK, Associate Professor of Psychology, and MEAGAN RYAN, Clinical Psychology Doctoral Student, The George Washington University, Washington, DC:

DESCRIPTION. The Coping Resources Inventory (CRI) is a self-report measure that assesses strategies that teens and adults (ages 14-83) use when they are confronted with a stressor. Respondents are told to choose the response that best describes them in the last 6 months using a 4-point Likert scale (never or rarely, sometimes, often, always or almost always). The 60 items include six reverse-coded items. Items are summed, and higher scores indicate greater coping resources. The CRI, which can be completed in about 10 minutes, is available in paper-and-pencil and online formats. It includes five subscales—Cognitive, Social, Emotional, Spiritual/

Philosophical, and Physical—each with 9-16 items. The Cognitive scale reflects the extent to which individuals maintain a positive self-concept; the Social scale assesses the amount of available social support; the Emotional scale reflects the degree to which individuals can accept and express a range of emotions; the Spiritual/Philosophical scale assesses the degree to which individuals' actions are guided by stable and consistent values; and the Physical scale reflects the individual's ability to maintain a healthy lifestyle. Raw scores are converted to standard scores with a mean of 50 and standard deviation of 10; conversion tables are provided in the test manual. Individual scores also can be compared to (limited) norms for males and females. The CRI can be hand scored with templates or scored online. It was developed for use in educational and treatment settings and in coping research.

DEVELOPMENT. A pool of 150 possible items was constructed based on clinical experience, the stress and coping literature, previously published instruments, and content experts. Pilot studies and preliminary item analyses reduced this number to 93. Those items were administered to a heterogeneous sample of 300 people, which included high school and college students as well as adults. The inclusion criterion for item-to-scale correlations was ≥.30 for that sample. This standard reduced the number of items to 74. Two more items were eliminated due to lack of variability, and other items were dropped due to problems with content validity and possible confounding with outcome measures. The remaining 60 items comprised the final version of the CRI.

TECHNICAL. In a sample of 749 junior high and high school students, college students, and adults, the item-to-scale correlation coefficients ranged from .11 to .67. One item demonstrated an item-to-scale correlation of .11 possibly due to the junior high and high school students, for whom fatigue was positively correlated with physical coping, while it was negatively associated for adults and college students. Test-retest data were obtained from a sample of 115 high school students over a period of 6 weeks. The CRI seems to be relatively stable, with correlation coefficients from .60 to .78. A sample of junior high school students provided evidence for predictive validity; the CRI Total score significantly predicted stress symptoms after controlling for life events.

The test manual provides a review of studies showing evidence for convergent and discriminant validity (up to 2004). Research shows that "healthy" or "trained" participants had more resources than "ill" or "untrained" participants. Women have scored significantly higher on the Total score and the Social and Emotional scales than men. Other observed differences were significant, but perhaps not clinically meaningful: women scored higher on the Spiritual/Philosophical scale and lower on the Physical scale.

Norms were based on 232 junior high and high school students, 175 college students, and 436 adults. The test manual includes forms to plot scores and compare them to male and female norms. Age and ethnic group norms are not provided. Means and standard deviations are provided for additional specialized samples including nursing students, active seniors, and so on. As noted in the test manual, it is important to consider individual contexts when interpreting scores given the small size and lack of diversity of the normative sample.

COMMENTARY. The CRI provides a measure of five different types of coping resources and a total score for a large age range. Subscales are internally consistent. Most items appear appropriate; however, there are some items on the Physical scale that seem overly specific and less clearly reflective of a coping resource. The CRI has shown strong evidence of validity, including concurrent, discriminant, and predictive validity. The test authors suggest caution when using the scale with adolescents as they have shown lower reliabilities (especially on the Physical subscale), and may have difficulty understanding items on the Spiritual/Philosophical scale. In addition, as the test authors acknowledge, normative samples were small and lacked diversity. When compared to other coping measures, the CRI is less theory-based than some (e.g., the COPE) and has been used less often than the COPE or Ways of Coping, which are predominant in the research literature (Kato, 2015).

SUMMARY. The CRI is an individually completed 60-item measure that assesses individual resources available for coping with stressors. Subscales include Cognitive, Social, Emotional, Spiritual/Philosophical, and Physical; subscale scores can be added together for a Total score. The CRI takes about 10 minutes to complete and is appropriate for teens and adults. It has evidence of reliability and validity and can be used in applied and research settings.

REVIEWERS' REFERENCE

Kato, T. (2015). Frequently used coping scales: A meta-analysis. *Stress and Health, 31*, 315-323.

[42]

Crisis Stabilization Scale.

Purpose: Designed as a clinician-rated instrument to "track progress and stabilization for adolescents in crisis, inform clinical decisions, and indicate treatment or program effectiveness."
Population: Adolesents in crisis.
Publication Date: 2014.
Acronym: CriSS.
Scores, 2: Coping, Commitment to Follow-Up.
Administration: Individual.
Price Data, 2020: $50 per PDF manual including review-only copy of form (31 pages); $60 per paper manual; $2.50 per Remote Online Survey License or License to Reproduce (minimum 50).
Time: Approximately 10 minutes for administration.
Comments: Completed by clinician; previously titled Goal Attainment Scale of Stabilization.
Author: Richard S. Balkin.
Publisher: Mind Garden, Inc.

Review of the Crisis Stabilization Scale by ROGER A. BOOTHROYD, Professor, Department of Mental Health Law and Policy, Louis de la Parte Florida Mental Health Institute, College of Behavioral and Community Sciences, University of South Florida, Tampa, FL:

DESCRIPTION. The Crisis Stabilization Scale (CriSS) is a 25-item clinician-reported measure developed to identify "the extent to which adolescents in crisis meet therapeutic goals consistent with client stabilization" (Balkin, 2013, p. 261). The scale was previously published in the literature under the name Goal Attainment Scale of Stabilization (GASS) but was renamed "to clarify the utility and value of the CriSS in clinical situations" (manual, p. 3). The test author noted that a self-report form for adolescents is available for research purposes but that no psychometric data are available associated with this form of data collection.

Items on the CriSS comprise two subscales—Coping (18 items) and Commitment to Follow-up (7 items)—and are aligned with a counseling model specifically developed for adolescents in crisis (Balkin, 2004; Balkin & Roland, 2007). For each item, the clinician rates the client's progress in attaining stated goals on scales from -2 to +2 where -2 *denotes the least favorable outcome*, -1 *outcome is less than desired or expected*, 0 means *attained desired or expected outcome*, +1 *outcome is more than desired or expected*, and +2 *denotes the most favorable outcome*. It is a little confusing that the description of the scale options on the actual form differs from the description presented in the test manual (e.g., the ratings as described in the test manual range from *below attainment* of stated goal to *above expected attainment*).

Although originally developed to be individually administered and hand-scored by clinicians using either a norm-referenced or criterion-referenced approach, there are now several other options available for administering the CriSS, including the test publisher's online platform or through the use of an outside survey company.

The test author recommends the CriSS for use by health and behavioral health professionals as a psychological screening tool, for supporting clinical decisions, monitoring treatment progress, and assessing treatment and program effectiveness. It is recommended that when used by an agency or for program evaluation, the meaning of the item response scale be discussed with potential raters and several practice cases be assessed. The first case is discussed, then rated, and rating differences are discussed. The second case is then rated without prior discussion.

DEVELOPMENT. As previously noted, the CriSS was originally developed and published under the name Goal Attainment Scale of Stabilization (GASS) in 2013 but was renamed by the current publisher, Mind Garden, in 2014.

Balkin and Roland (2007) indicated that items were originally created to be consistent with published research on problem identification, process coping skills, and commitment to follow-up treatment. Once the items were generated, four content experts assessed each item by rating the extent to which the item represented a clear measure of the stated goal. This review process resulted in items on the CriSS being assigned to two subscales: (a) Coping, which relates to the youth's ability to commit to safety, identify problems, and process coping skills; and (b) Commitment to Follow-up, which assesses the youth's willingness to continue treatment (Balkin, 2004; Balkin & Roland, 2007). The items were originally constructed so that scoring could be used in goal attainment scaling, although unlike goal attainment scaling, the goals are pre-stated and are general in nature. The scoring system was also adapted to generate "T-like scores" (manual, p. 5) with a mean of 50 and a standard deviation of 10.

TECHNICAL.

Standardization and Scoring. For norm-referenced scoring, the 18 items on the Coping scale are summed. Raw scores on this scale can range from -36 to +36 and are converted to T scores using the norm tables provided in an appendix in the test manual. Interpretation is based on the corresponding percentile column that was generated from a fairly specific normative sample of 435 adolescents ages 11 to 18 who were admitted to an acute care unit in the North-Central or Southern United States. This sample was fairly evenly split on gender (55.3% female, 45.7% male), but most participants were White (78.4%) or African American (17.9%). The youth's primary diagnoses were predominantly mood disorders (76.6%) and disruptive behavioral disorders (15.3%). In a similar manner, the seven items on the Commitment to Follow-up scale are scored and interpreted.

A potential concern with the use of these T scores for interpretation is that in an earlier study by Balkin and Roland (2005), gender was found to be a significant predictor of client stabilization. The study's authors concluded that "gender differences should be considered in both diagnosis and treatment of adolescents" (p. 644). Given this finding, non-gender-specific norms should be used with caution as they may result in some misleading interpretations.

For criterion-referenced scoring and interpretation of the CriSS, the 18 items on the Coping scale are again summed. As with the normative scoring approach, the resulting scores can range from -36 to +36. This score is compared to the corresponding goal attainment scaling ("T-like") score column presented in an appendix and interpreted as 30 indicating *far below what was expected*, 40 *below what was expected*, 50 *as expected*, 60 *above what was expected*, and 70 *far above what was expected*. Scoring of the Commitment to Follow-up scale is completed in a similar fashion.

The test manual does not provide any information for scoring the CriSS when missing data are present. This may be due to the fact that the CriSS is completed by clinicians and thus it is assumed that there will be no missing data. However, Balkin (2013) noted, "MLM in Mplus (Version 6) was used to handle missing data (<1%)" (p. 264). Although the amount of missing data was small in this study, if the CriSS is used for research purposes, guidelines should be provided on how to handle missing data and at what level missingness becomes problematic.

Reliability. Internal consistency reliability estimates were derived from 435 adolescent clients, ages 11 to 18, who were admitted to an acute care unit. Alpha coefficients were .98 for the Coping scale and .95 for the Commitment to Follow-up scale (Balkin, 2013). These internal consistency reliability estimates are similar to those reported for the Coping (alpha = .97) and Commitment to Follow-up (alpha = .94) scales based on an earlier version of the GASS assessing 98 youth admitted to an acute care program (Balkin & Roland, 2007). Interrater reliability between clinician raters is reported at $r = .77$. No test-retest reliability estimates are available.

Validity. An exploratory factor analysis (EFA) of the CriSS was conducted using a random sample of 125 youth from the normative sample. A two-factor solution accounting for 73.0% of the total variance resulted with the first factor consisting of 18 items addressing Coping and the second factor containing seven items reflecting Commitment to Follow-up. The two scales were moderately to highly correlated ($r = .68$), indicating that the latent constructs underlying the two scales share a substantial amount of conceptual overlap.

To validate the factor structure, a confirmatory factor analysis (CFA) was performed on the remaining 310 youth from the normative sample using maximum likelihood estimation. The results supported the two-factor hypothesized model generated in the EFA. The mean scores for the Coping and Commitment to Follow-up scales from the EFA and CFA samples were compared and did not yield significant differences across the two samples. No criterion-predictive forms of validity evidence are provided. One might expect that scores on the CriSS would exhibit meaningful convergence with improvement on measures of youth symptomatology and/or functioning, or that discharge scores on the CriSS would differentiate youth who are readmitted to acute care versus those who are not.

COMMENTARY. The CriSS is a renamed version of the Goal Attainment Scale of Stabilization (Balkin, 2013). The measure was originally developed for use by clinicians to assess the extent to which the youth they were treating were making progress on treatment goals, particularly goals related to Coping and Commitment to Follow-up. The psychometric data for this measure are limited and based on a standardization sample of 435 youth admitted to inpatient settings in geographically limited regions of the United States. In addition, the sample consists primarily of youth who are White and who have a diagnosis of mood disorder.

Data on validity are limited to content evidence and an examination of the measure's factor structure. Although the test author suggests the CriSS can be used in private or community-based settings, the lack of psychometric data based on youth treated in other therapeutic settings suggests the CriSS should be used and interpreted with caution in those settings. In addition, the use of this measure as a general research tool is yet untested, as is the self-report youth form.

SUMMARY. The CriSS is a 25-item clinician-rated measure designed to assess the extent to which youth have attained treatment goals in terms of Coping and Commitment to Follow-up. To date, few studies have been conducted using and/or assessing the psychometric properties of the CriSS. Although the test author indicates that it may be used in community-based settings and private practices, the only psychometric data available are based on a limited sample of youth admitted to acute care.

REVIEWER'S REFERENCES

Balkin, R. S. (2004). Application of a model for adolescent acute care psychiatric programs. *Dissertation Abstracts International, 64*(7-A), 2391.

Balkin, R. S. (2013). Validation of the Goal Attainment Scale of Stabilization. *Measurement and Evaluation in Counseling and Development, 46*, 261-269. doi:10.1177/0748175613497040

Balkin, R. S. (2014). *The Crisis Stabilization Scale: Manual and sampler set.* Menlo Park, CA: Mind Garden, Inc.

Balkin, R. S., & Roland, C. B. (2005). Identification of differences in gender for adolescents in crisis residence. *Journal of Mental Health, 14*, 637-646. doi:10.1080/09638230500347707

Balkin, R. S., & Roland, C. B. (2007). Reconceptualizing stabilization for counseling adolescents in brief psychiatric hospitalization: A new model. *Journal of Counseling & Development, 85*, 64-72. doi:10.1002/j.1556-6678.2007.tb00445.x

Review of the Crisis Stabilization Scale by ANNETTE S. KLUCK, Assistant Provost for Women's Initiatives and Professor of Counseling Psychology, and SAMANTHA CHACE, Doctoral Student in Counseling Psychology, Auburn University, Auburn, AL:

DESCRIPTION. The Crisis Stabilization Scale (CriSS) is a clinician rating form, which the test author describes as a norm-based and criterion-referenced measure for use in assessing stabilization and progress of adolescents in acute psychiatric settings using a goal attainment framework. The test manual describes the measure and includes samples of the CriSS and a self-rating form (CriSS-SR) that the author suggests can be completed by the adolescent. However, the manual provides no information about the psychometric properties of the CriSS-SR or any established scoring technique, and the test author notes that adolescents' self-report may not be valid and reliable.

The CriSS is designed to be completed by mental health clinicians or within mental health agencies that treat adolescents in crisis. The measure itself contains directions regarding how to complete the clinician rating form. However, the test manual offers only limited information about qualifications of test users or extent of contact with the adolescent needed prior to using the CriSS. Beyond training in psychiatric risk assessment with adolescents, the rater would need to have spent sufficient time with the adolescent and family members to evaluate the extent to which the adolescent is stabilized before the CriSS can be completed. Specifically, items require evaluation of "work" completed by the adolescent and the extent to which the expected outcome was attained. The test manual includes some guidelines for training when the CriSS is used for program evaluation and recommends licensure for independent clinicians using the CriSS. The completion of the CriSS by a qualified clinician who has worked with the adolescent for a sufficient amount of time is likely to be quick (5-10 minutes), but may take substantially longer if the clinician does not have experience directly treating the adolescent and working with the adolescent's family because the clinician would need to, at a minimum, engage in a clinical interview to adequately answer questions about the adolescent and thc family.

Administration and scoring can be done online or by hand. The CriSS has two norm-referenced subscales (a total score is not used). The Coping subscale is described as a measure of the extent to which the adolescent has attained the expected outcomes for safety, problem solving, and coping skills. The Commitment to Follow-up subscale is described as a measure of the extent to which the adolescent has attained the expected outcome for awareness of need and ability and willingness to access resources in a less restrictive care environment. Scoring is rather simple as described in the test manual, and a table to convert raw scores to T scores is provided. The test manual also offers a non-normed approach to scoring in which the adolescent receives a score meant to indicate the degree to which goals have been attained. Although interpretations are offered for this scoring approach, the manual provides no psychometric support to support this approach to interpretation (computation of the mean and comparing it to the scale used for rating would provide interpretative information that would have more psychometric support than the descriptions offered).

DEVELOPMENT. Items were developed to support goal attainment scaling. The test manual specifies that items (presumably all of them) were evaluated by four content specialists. The manual does not provide information about the specialists. The cutoff applied to the specialists' ratings allowed for less than 100% agreement despite the small number of experts involved. No information was provided in the test materials about the number of items that did not meet the criteria, but experts appeared to have some difficulty correctly placing the items into the original four categories. As a result, the commitment to safety and coping skills items were merged, "as commitment to safety could be viewed as a coping mechanism" (manual, p. 6).

TECHNICAL. The normative sample for the CriSS comprised 435 adolescents (240 females and 195 males), ages 11-18, who had been admitted to inpatient, acute care psychiatric facilities in the Southern or North Central regions of the United States. Admission to the participating facilities required patients to present as a danger to themselves or others. The majority of the sample identified as White (78.4%), followed by African American (17.9%), Latino/a (2.1%), "Other" (1.4%), and Asian (0.2%); 1.1% of the sample did not indicate ethnicity. Latino/a and Asian youth are notably underrepresented in the norming sample (see Child Trends, 2016). Diagnostic categories (based on *DSM-IV-TR* criteria) represented by the adolescents comprising the norming sample (diagnoses were reported for 406 of the adolescents) included mood disorder, disruptive behavior disorder, substance abuse disorder/dependency, psychosis, anxiety disorder, and "other."

Reliability coefficients reported in the CriSS manual reveal subscales that were internally consistent (Coping alpha = .98; Commitment to Follow-up alpha = .95). After clinicians using the CriSS in a program, agency, or institutional setting followed a procedure recommended by the test author to increase interrater reliability, acceptable interrater reliability between clinicians' scores was reported (r = .77). Test-retest reliability estimates were not reported.

The test manual reports that content validity evidence for the CriSS was assessed by the aforementioned four content experts. Exploratory factor analysis and confirmatory factor analysis (CFA) were used to examine the internal structure of the CriSS. Exploratory factor analysis with an oblique rotation supported a two-factor solution with factor loadings for all items exceeding .70 for the primary factor. Although each item loaded most strongly onto its hypothesized factor, cross loadings were high, with a difference of less than .20 between factor loadings for nine of 25 items. The two subscales were moderately to strongly correlated (r = .68). The CFA supported strong loadings on the assigned factors, and the two-factor solution fit better than a single-factor solution. However, some fit indices for the two-factor solution were below recommended cutoffs (Schreiber, Nora, Stage, Barlow, & King, 2006). No information about criterion-related or incremental validity is provided.

COMMENTARY. The CriSS requires clinical skill and knowledge of the adolescent to complete. The structure and format of the test manual is not clear and requires careful review for critical information (such as qualifications of test users), and clear administration guidelines are lacking. Although the manual reports strong reliability coefficients for the subscales, the evidence for validity is more limited. In addition, the methods used to examine the factor structure do not reflect best practices in measurement development with regard to EFA and CFA (Costello & Osborne, 2005; Schreiber et al., 2006). For example, the use of eigenvalues to determine the number of factors in EFA is no longer considered best practice (parallel analysis is an example of a more preferred method; Costello & Osborne, 2005), and multiple fit indices (X^2/df ratio, CFI, and TLI) do not meet recommended cutoffs for acceptance (see Schrieber et al., 2006). The information about the norming sample is limited, making it difficult to know how well any individual client is represented within the norming group. Because young adolescents can differ substantially from older adolescents (Knight & Zerr, 2010), establishing measurement equivalence across age groups is critical for a tool that may be used to determine whether an adolescent in crisis is sufficiently stabilized to move to a less restrictive psychiatric care environment. In addition, if the CriSS is to be used (as suggested in the test manual) with individuals outside of the adolescent age range (represented in the norming sample), the measure should be normed on younger and older psychiatric inpatient groups. Without a test of criterion-related validity or incremental validity, it is difficult to know whether this tool provides improvement over, or performs as well as, clinical judgment in assessing whether adolescents in psychiatric crisis are sufficiently stabilized to be placed in a lower level of care. Similarly, the lack of comparison studies and evaluation of the incremental validity of this tool over existing outcome measures prohibit explicit recommendation for use of the CriSS in program evaluation.

SUMMARY. Until evidence supporting the criterion-related validity and documenting comparability or superiority to other tools is available, clinicians should avoid use of the CriSS as the sole source for their clinical decision making and should prioritize other measures with more substantial psychometric support in making clinical decisions. Additional evaluation of the measure in new, clearly described (including number of male and female adolescents of each age with each type of diagnosis), and representative samples is needed. In addition, evaluation of the interrater reliability without the use of training of raters is needed given that the measure was developed, at least in part, to be used by independent clinicians who are unlikely to train with another rater. Finally, additional evaluation of the validity of the CriSS including evaluation of incremental validity for determining the extent to which adolescents are sufficiently stable and have made progress in treatment is warranted before use in high-stakes situations such as evaluating need for continued intensive treatment during crises.

REVIEWERS' REFERENCES

Child Trends. (2016). Racial and ethnic composition of the child population: Indicators of child and youth well-being. Retrieved from https://www.childtrends.org/wp-content/uploads/2016/07/60_Racial-Composition.pdf

Costello, A. B., & Osborne, J. W. (2005). Best practices in exploratory factor analysis: Four recommendations for getting the most from your analysis. *Practical Assessment, Research & Evaluation, 10*(7), 1-9. Retrieved from http://pareonline.net/getvn.asp?v=10&n=7

Knight, G. P., & Zerr, A. A. (2010). Introduction to the special section: Measurement equivalence in child development research. *Child Development Perspectives, 4*, 1-4. doi:10.1111/j.1750-8606.2009.00108.x

Schreiber, J. B., Nora, A., Stage, F. K., Barlow, E. A., & King, J. (2006). Reporting structural equation modeling and confirmatory factor analysis results: A review. *The Journal of Educational Research, 99*, 323-337. doi:10.3200/JOER.99.6.323-338

[43]

The DATA Model for Teaching Preschoolers with Autism.

Purpose: Designed "to augment existing early childhood curriculum-based assessments to provide a broad view of child behavior, including those behaviors and skills associated with the core deficits of ASD [autism spectrum disorder]."

Population: Young children with autism spectrum disorder.

Publication Date: 2017.

Acronym: DATA Model.

Scores: Skills assessed in 6 domains: Adaptive, Executive Functioning, Cognitive, Communication, Social, Play.

Administration: Individual.

Price Data, 2020: $64.95 per book (473 pages), including Skills Checklist, instructional programming sheets and lesson plans, Family Interview Survey, and more; $30 per 5 Skills Checklists.

Time: "The DATA Model Skills Checklist is usually completed within four to six extended day sessions and one or two classroom observations."

Comments: Based on applied behavior analysis. The Project DATA model was developed to include five core components: "integrated early childhood experience; extended, intensive instruction; technical and social support for families; collaboration and coordination among all providers working with the child and family; quality-of-life influenced curriculum." The DATA Model Skills Checklist "is designed to provide more in-depth information on the specific programming needs of children with ASD."

Authors: Ilene Schwartz, Julie Ashmun, Bonnie McBride, Crista Scott, and Susan R. Sandall.

Publisher: Paul H. Brookes Publishing Co., Inc.

Review of the DATA Model for Teaching Preschoolers with Autism by RENÉE M. TOBIN, Professor of Psychological Studies in Education, Temple University, Philadelphia, PA, and MICHAEL MATTA, Adjunct Professor of Psychological Diagnosis, University of Milano-Bicocca, Milan, Italy:

DESCRIPTION. The DATA Model for Teaching Preschoolers with Autism (Developmentally Appropriate Treatment for Autism) is designed to enrich existing curriculum-based assessment in inclusive school settings by providing a framework for implementing an evidence-based teaching approach for children ages 3-5 years with autism spectrum disorder (ASD). The test manual includes overviews of inclusive early childhood programming, applied behavior analysis, instructional strategies and instructional program development, data-based decision making, family and community collaboration, and the DATA Model approach to teaching and implementation. In relevant chapters, the manual infuses examples of data sheets with and without graphing, instructional program sheets, lesson plans, surveys, and skills checklists that may be adapted to suit the unique needs of preschoolers. These operative sheets allow for the assessment of children's functional needs, the establishment of behavioral objectives, the development of tailored interventions in order to improve specific skills, and the ongoing evaluation and monitoring of developmental progress.

First, in terms of assessment measures within the DATA Model, the DATA Model Skills Checklist allows qualified practitioners to evaluate preschoolers with ASD on six domain areas: Adaptive, Executive Functioning, Cognitive, Communication, Social, and Play. Each area is assessed through multiple items on a 3-point scale, from *never meets criterion* (0) to *always meets criterion* (2). The checklist is usually completed in four to six extended day sessions (see Development section) and one or two observations in class. The test authors suggest that this scale should be completed at least twice during the school year.

Second, Section II of the test manual contains instructional programs to guide lesson planning and teaching skills within the six domains and subdomains assessed by the initial checklist. Each lesson plan form provides space to list settings and materials, teaching directions and strategies, behavioral prompts and responses, instructional sets, and data collection methods.

Third, data sheets are provided to record and keep track of target interventions and changes in individual behavioral patterns over time using Daily, Weekly, and Monthly Data Sheets. The test authors place particular emphasis upon the external environment and its role in promoting positive change. Hence, the flexible interview forms allow for the gathering of information about activities, interactions, and routines between caregivers and children with ASD, while also providing opportunities to examine changes across consecutive meetings (via the Family Interview Survey and Home Visit Notes).

Lastly, an Implementation Checklist is provided to assess the community in which the intervention program is developed and implemented. Within this context, the test authors recommend putting in place the DATA program only after examining environmental strengths and weaknesses.

DEVELOPMENT. The DATA Model is an applied behavior analysis (ABA) approach to intervening with preschoolers with ASD. Based on this theoretical and methodological framework, the DATA Model is built on five core components: integrated early childhood experience; extended, intensive instruction; technical and social support for families; collaboration and coordination among all providers working with the child and family; and quality-of-life influenced curriculum. The test authors' two central tenets are that "children with ASD are children first" and "student failure is instructional failure" (manual, p. 8).

First, within the DATA Model, preschoolers with ASD receive support to interact with typically developing peers for 20-25 hours per week. Evidence-based behavioral strategies are placed to meet individual needs and promote interactions between children with and without disabilities in the school environment.

Second, tailored instruction is provided individually or in small groups within the program, which is organized in "extended instructional days" (manual, p. 71). During these sessions, teachers provide discrete trial training, choice making, model-question, time delay, and incidental teaching to target specific children's needs.

Third, monthly meetings at each student's home allow specialists to help families in their daily environment. Additionally, a multidisciplinary team provides approximately six evening events per year for parent education during which they can learn the principles of ABA and talk informally with other parents.

Fourth, particular emphasis is placed on the collaboration and coordination among preschool teachers and staff implementing the DATA Model. All the children receive an individualized education program (IEP), which may include extra therapeutic services (e.g., hippotherapy, private speech therapy).

Fifth, the philosophy behind the DATA Model is to produce consistent and positive changes in children's lives. Thus, each intervention aims to promote autonomy, success, and interpersonal effectiveness in school and at home. The forms and procedures detailed in the test manual are designed to flexibly facilitate children's development.

TECHNICAL. The DATA Model provides clinical background and a theoretical foundation, but it is not a traditional psychometric tool. It is intended as a guide to a developmentally appropriate, evidence-based, criterion-referenced approach to assessing and intervening with preschoolers with ASD. As such, the test authors do not address technical aspects of the measures in the DATA Model manual.

COMMENTARY. The DATA Model has some considerable strengths. First, preschoolers with ASD represent the most appropriate population who can benefit from this kind of tailored intervention program. Indeed, empirical evidence has shown that early support for young children is crucial for obtaining positive effects (Dawson, 2008) and that children with ASD have unique presentations that require customized interventions (Linstead et al., 2017). Second, the DATA Model places emphasis on multiple levels of the environment. Hence, the system aims to reorganize school programs, interactions with peers, and the child's life at home and in the community deeply. Third, the DATA Model authors tested the effectiveness of this intervention system, and their preliminary data were published in a peer-reviewed journal article (Schwartz, Thomas, McBride, & Sandall, 2013). Children who participated for one year in Project DATA showed significant improvements in autism symptomatology, in the size of receptive vocabulary, and in many developmental skills (such as fine and gross motor, cognitive, and social communication and interactions) relative to pre-intervention.

This system also has some minor weaknesses. Although the test manual is explicitly addressed to "teachers, applied behavior analysts, parents, and other educators" (manual, p. ix), substantial training in ABA theory and techniques is required to understand and implement each step of the model effectively. Moreover, the DATA Model manual is 473 pages long with various forms infused throughout as opposed to including all forms in the appendix or in a separate forms manual (though forms can be downloaded via a website provided in the manual).

SUMMARY. The DATA Model is designed to examine deficits in behaviors of preschoolers with ASD and to provide flexible intervention programs that require the collaborative efforts of a multidisciplinary team. From this point of view, the DATA Model represents a promising early treatment for ASD, and it may prevent the manifestations of more severe symptoms. One published article is not sufficient to demonstrate its effectiveness, but the test authors' interests to validate their system through empirical evidence is commended and encouraged.

It is important to note that the system is based on ABA methodology. Although this foundation is a strength of the program, teachers, educators, and even psychologists who are not familiar with basic principles and techniques of this approach may have a difficult time implementing this system in schools or in communities without substantial training. Thus, these reviewers recommend using the DATA Model only under the supervision of ABA specialists.

REVIEWERS' REFERENCES

Dawson, G. (2008). Early behavioral intervention, brain plasticity, and the prevention of autism spectrum disorder. *Development and Psychopathology, 20*, 775-803.

Linstead, E., Dixon, D. R., Hong, E., Burns, C. O., French, R., Novack, M. N., & Granpeesheh, D. (2017). An evaluation of the effects of intensity and duration on outcomes across treatment domains for children with autism spectrum disorder. *Translational Psychiatry, 7*, e1234.

Schwartz, I., Thomas, C. J., McBride, B., & Sandall, S. (2013). A school-based preschool program for children with ASD: A quasi-experimental assessment of child change in Project DATA. *School Mental Health, 5*, 221-232.

Review of The DATA Model for Teaching Preschoolers with Autism, by GEORGETTE YETTER, Associate Professor, School Psychology, Oklahoma State University, Stillwater, OK:

DESCRIPTION. The DATA Model for Teaching Preschoolers with Autism is a behavior-analytic framework designed to guide educators such as classroom teachers, paraprofessionals, and behavior analysts to effectively instruct very young children with autism spectrum disorder (ASD) in public school settings. The Developmentally Appropriate Treatment for Autism (DATA) program initially was developed at the University of Washington in 1997. It provides a comprehensive system for assessing the functional life skills of children with ASD, developing an appropriate curriculum for them, identifying effective instructional strategies to teach them, and tracking their growth over time.

Behavior-analytic strategies are well established as state-of-the-art for teaching individuals with ASD (Foxx, 2008). These strategies include discrete-trial instruction, incidental teaching, and visual support and prompting strategies. The DATA program recommends that children receive at least 20 hours per week of instruction, with roughly 10 hours interacting with neurotypical children and 10 hours in segregated settings that more intensively address their individual needs. The program emphasizes family involvement in the child's education, offering information, social support, and individual technical assistance in addressing the child's behavior at home. The primary goal of instruction is to enhance the child's quality of life.

The DATA program defines a structured curriculum consisting of an ordered sequence of functionally important skills in six major areas: Adaptive Behavior, Executive Functioning, Cognition, Communication, Social Functioning, and Play Skills. The DATA manual specifies systematic procedures for quantifying, collecting, graphing, and organizing information (i.e., data) about a child's skill levels across the six skill areas. It includes numerous forms to guide educators in gathering information to help them efficiently organize, summarize, and analyze these data and to develop and revise the child's instructional goals. These forms also can be downloaded from a dedicated webpage.

On first entering a DATA Model program and at regular intervals (at least twice a year and each time a new individualized family service plan or individualized education plan is written for the child), a child's functional skills are assessed comprehensively across all six major areas. This comprehensive assessment process is facilitated using the DATA Model Skills Checklist. The DATA Model Skills Checklist is intended to be used in conjunction with a comprehensive early childhood curriculum-based assessment and with the Project DATA Family Interview. It includes 23 Adaptive Behavior items, 22 Executive Functioning items, 25 Cognition items, 25 Communication items, 22 Social Functioning items, and 17 Play Skills items. Teachers rate Skills Checklist items on a 0 to 2 scale, where 0 indicates that the child *does not/never meets the criterion*, 1 indicates that the child *inconsistently/sometimes meets the criterion*, and 2 indicates that the child *consistently/always meets the criterion*. An additional eight items, rated on a *yes* or *no* scale, ask teachers to indicate any behaviors that interfere with the child's participation and learning.

The DATA Model Skills Checklist requires considerable time to complete. Whereas some items can be scored based on direct observation of the child in classroom activities, other items require direct testing. The test manual states that the Skills Checklist "is usually completed within four to six extended day sessions and one or two classroom observations" (p. 46). The materials needed to administer the direct-test items are not included with the DATA manual and must be acquired separately, but the manual lists all the materials needed (for example, 30 pictures with actions, three different cause-and-effect toys). Using the Skills Checklist, together with other curriculum-based instruments and family input, a child's team of educators can gain a comprehensive understanding of his or her skills across the six major areas of the DATA Model. For each skill, the DATA manual provides an Instructional Program Sheet that defines the skill (e.g., "Drinks from an open cup"), breaks it down into its component parts (e.g., "puts hands on cup," "picks up cup"), and lists the sequence of steps to be used for teaching it. This information is used to develop instructional goals, an instructional program, and individualized lesson plans for the child.

The DATA manual offers Lesson Plans to guide instruction for each skill. Teachers complete Lesson Plan forms (included in the test manual) to specify what materials they will use to teach the skill to the target child, where they will teach it, what directions or cues they will give the child, how they will prompt the child to answer, and what responses they will require the child to produce. Teachers use their own judgment to decide whether to teach a given skill in a naturalistic setting (such as in a classroom with typically developing peers) or in a more decontextualized setting (such as sitting at a table and working one-on-one with a teacher). Teachers prepare and maintain an individual binder for each child in the program that contains all assessment data and instructional information. The binder is updated daily.

DEVELOPMENT. The DATA Model Skills Checklist is a curriculum-based assessment, designed to measure the functional skills the test authors identified as most important for very young children with ASD. No additional information is provided in the test manual describing its development.

TECHNICAL AND COMMENTARY. As a curriculum-based assessment, the DATA Model Skills Checklist is not standardized or norm-referenced. Therefore, issues pertaining to standardization, reliability, and validity do not pertain to this measure.

The DATA Model is similar to The Assessment of Basic Language and Learning Skills—Revised (Partington, 2010), when used in combination with the Assessment of Functional Living Skills (Partington & Mueller, 2012) in that both systems are behavior analytic and well constructed. Both systems offer a structure for identifying learning goals for young children with ASD, together with a curriculum-based assessment to evaluate and document changes in skill levels over time. Both systems are staff-intensive; the DATA program has a recommended teacher-to-student ratio no higher than 2 to 1, and both systems require that staff have some applied behavior analysis (ABA) training. The DATA program is unique, however, in that it offers specific recommendations and suggestions for program implementation in public school settings. The test manual devotes a chapter to discussing potential strategies school teams can adopt to try to obtain the resources needed to implement the DATA approach in their community.

SUMMARY. The DATA Model is a well-constructed framework designed to guide teams of professional educators in implementing an effective ABA system to teach young children with ASD. If practical challenges can be surmounted, a potentially large number of children who may not otherwise have access to ABA services would be able to receive state-of-the-art instruction.

REVIEWER'S REFERENCES

Foxx, R. M. (2008). Applied behavior analysis treatment of autism: The state of the art. *Child and Adolescent Psychiatric Clinics of North America, 17*, 821-834.

Partington, J. W. (2010). The Assessment of Basic Language and Learning Skills—Revised (ABLLS-R). Pleasant Hill, CA: Behavior Analysts, Inc.

Partington, J. W., & Mueller, M. M. (2012). The Assessment of Functional Living Skills (AFLS). Pleasant Hill, CA: Behavior Analysts, Inc.

[44]

Decision-making and Self-regulation Assessor.

Purpose: Designed to measure "a person's decision-making competence, decision-making style and ability to self-regulate."
Population: Adults.
Publication Date: 2015.
Acronym: DASA.
Scores, 12: Mental Energy, Self-Discipline, Procrastination, Advancement Focus, Protection Focus, Decision Avoidance, Spontaneous Choice, Deliberation, Option Generation, Decision-Making Confidence, General Self-Regulation, Decision-Making Competence.
Administration: Individual.
Price Data, 2020: £30 per manual (52 pages); £76 per online administration with Technical Report & Personal Insight Report (subscription discounts available).
Time: Approximately 10 minutes to complete questionnaire and 15 minutes for total testing process.
Comments: Administered online.
Author: Chris Dewberry.
Publisher: Hogrefe Ltd [United Kingdom].

Review of the Decision-making and Self-regulation Assessor by CARRIE A. CHAMP MORERA, Coordinator of Admissions Assessment, Milton Hershey School, Hershey, PA:

DESCRIPTION. The Decision-making and Self-regulation Assessor (DASA) is a norm-referenced, self-report instrument, usually administered individually, that measures the ability to self-regulate, decision-making style, and decision-making self-confidence. It was developed for use with individuals older than age 18. The DASA has multiple uses including personnel selection, counseling, personal development, team building, and coaching.

The DASA comprises 54 self-report items across nine scales. Each scale comprises six items. The Mental Energy scale measures the extent to which people believe they feel lively and energized, persevere on tasks until they are completed, and are resistant to tasks that sap mental energy. The Self-Discipline scale assesses the ability to avoid distractions and delay gratification. The Procrastination/Decision Avoidance scale measures the extent to which people delay acting on urgent tasks and instead focus on less urgent tasks. The Advancement Focus scale evaluates the likelihood that people choose to engage in activities that allow them to demonstrate success and accomplishments. The Protection Focus scale measures the extent to which people attempt to avoid risk and maintain the status quo. The Spontaneous Choice scale measures perceived ability to accept or reject multiple options with little to no thought. The Deliberation scale assesses the extent to which people consciously think matters through when making choices. The Option Generation scale evaluates people's perceived ability to generate alternative options when choices are necessary rather than accepting the immediate options. Finally, the Decision-Making Confidence scale measures the extent to which people believe they make better decisions than others make.

The instrument yields percentile ranges and T-scores, with a mean of 50 and a standard deviation of 10. The test author also provides five score bands (*very low, quite low, average, quite high,* and *very high*) as he suggests these descriptors are easily understandable by test takers. Although the test manual notes that conversion to other standard scales is supported, no further details are provided.

The test author reports that it takes 15 minutes for the testing process, with 10 minutes to complete all 54 items. The instrument requires a minimum reading age of 12. The test taker rates each item on a 5-point scale indicating the level of agreement. All items are administered using the test publisher's online platform. The DASA manual is the only printed material for this instrument as all administration and accompanying testing materials are online.

DEVELOPMENT. The development of the DASA started with an extensive literature review of psychological dimensions related to individual decision-making and self-regulation, including theories in cognitive psychology, social psychology, organizational psychology, and personality theory. The test author determined that self-report was an effective way to measure these dimensions and that a small number of items could measure them effectively as the concepts are narrow. Item analyses and exploratory analyses were used through the draft versions of the instrument to refine it to items measuring decision-making ability. Existing self-regulation models set the stage for the development of the DASA and a three-factor model (proactive cognition, choice, and the planned and self-disciplined control and implementation of actions) was developed. Then, a prototype was constructed with 10 scales. After further research, the DASA was fundamentally revised and also included recent developments in research on self-regulation.

TECHNICAL. The standardization sample for the DASA consisted of 1,435 working people in the United Kingdom with a mean age of 49 years. Individuals who participated in this study were selected as a random sample from approximately 600,000 individuals who were registered online with a U.K. company specializing in internet-based surveys. Reported demographic characteristics of the normative sample include gender, ethnicity, and education (demographic statistics were not collected for 2.5% of the sample). Whether the normative sample is representative of the United Kingdom as a whole is unknown.

Data collected for the psychometric analyses for the DASA were from participants who completed the instrument online on whatever computer was available to them at the time and in whatever social situation, such as work or home, they desired. The only control was that participants were over 18 years old. Formal administration by an examiner was not provided, so information regarding participants' motivation to complete the items honestly, amount of time taken to complete the assessment, and adherence to administration procedures could not be ascertained.

Standard scores, percentiles, and broad classifications were developed for the DASA. The instrument is scored online and yields two types of computer-generated reports. A technical report is available that provides graphs and scores for the nine scales and two composite scores for General Self-Regulation and Decision-Making Competence. A personal insight report is also available for coaching and development. This report provides feedback on all of the scales and the two derived scores.

Overall, DASA scores evidence a good degree of reliability, which was examined relative to three sources of error. First, internal consistency among the items on the test was examined. Coefficient alpha values for the nine scales ranged from .84 to .93, which is a desirable level. Second, test-retest reliability, which reflects the extent to which an examinee's test performance is constant over time, was measured. The DASA has acceptable test-retest reliability; test-retest correlation coefficients for a sample of 228 participants ranged from .77 to .89 across an 8-week interval with a reasonably normal distribution of scores. Finally, item response theory was used to analyze DASA items. Results of these analyses concluded that the reliability is at least .80 on each scale in 95% of the people who complete it. The 5% who obtain either unusually high or low scores are measured on each scale at a reliability of .70 or greater. These reliability results are positive, particularly given the remote online testing used to conduct the DASA reliability studies.

The DASA provides three types of evidence validity: content, construct, and criterion-related. The test author demonstrated content validity through an extensive literature search on individual differences in decision-making and self-regulation, including a review of existing measures available to assess these areas or areas closely related. These efforts concluded that the DASA is supported by extensive theory and research across multiple areas such as organizational psychology, cognitive psychology, and social psychology. Construct evidence was based on confirmatory factor analysis of the DASA model, which illustrated good fit through chi-square analysis. Similarly, DASA has been compared with other instruments that either measure the same or similar constructs; good convergent validity (.64 to .84) was found for alternative scales available for five dimensions measured by the DASA. Finally, criterion-related validity evidence was obtained through two studies that included the Spontaneous Choice and Decision Avoidance scales and provide support that these dimensions predict real-world decision-making outcomes. A strong correlation was found between DASA raw scores and age; DASA mean raw scores also increased with age. Although initial research using the DASA is promising, additional research is needed to strengthen validity evidence for this instrument, particularly when it is used with other populations.

COMMENTARY. The test author states, "The DASA is the first dedicated measure of an individual's capacity to self-regulate and make sound decisions" and "measures how people actively manage themselves and make their own choices" (manual, back cover). Although research presented in the test manual supports these claims, measurement in these areas are still in their infancy. Dimensions on the DASA are similar to several constructs of executive functioning (see McCloskey & Perkins, 2012); research in this area could determine whether there is a relationship between these areas as well as implications for practice and future revisions to the DASA. Additional research is needed to refine measurement of these constructs. For example, how do scores on the DASA in the U.K. compare to scores in other countries? How do scores on the DASA with working adults compare to non-working adults? Exploration to determine whether this scale is appropriate for use with adolescents and how it can be applied to this population for preparation to enter the work force or future educational training appears warranted. The test author may wish to consider a more diverse group in the normative sample for a future revision.

The DASA is completed, scored, and interpreted using an online testing platform, and the manual is the only written material provided to test users. It is notable that the manual does not provide instructions on how to locate or access the online testing platform. Furthermore, the testing platform is not fully described in the manual. Although the online administration is described as quick, efficient, and convenient, it can be expensive to administer and score if the user pays per individual administration. If the user plans to use the instrument often, purchasing a subscription may be more cost effective. Additionally, the test author could make a paper-and-pencil version of the assessment available for situations in which access to a computer is unavailable.

A strength of the DASA is that it is research-based and includes dimensions such as Mental Energy, Self-Discipline, Option Generation, and Decision-Making Confidence that reportedly are not measured by other scales. All scales on the instrument are clearly defined; however, the test manual does not specify which items comprise each scale. Furthermore, the manual states that the same set of items comprise both the Procrastination and Decision Avoidance scales as they are highly correlated; this results in the same score for both areas. This can be confusing, but the test author chose to separate these scales as different feedback can be provided to the test taker for both areas.

SUMMARY. Overall, the DASA is an adequate self-report measure of decision-making and self-regulation. Given that the instrument was normed on a U.K. population of working adults who have access to a computer and that limited demographic information is provided on the norm group, users need to be cautious about the measure's use and interpretation. Due to the limitations of this instrument, this reviewer would rely less on the scores provided and instead utilize qualitative interpretation. Each dimension on the DASA is well defined, and the test author offers feedback for each dimension that can be provided to the test taker. Feedback provided from this instrument can used for coaching, personal development, and consideration in personnel selection.

REVIEWER'S REFERENCE

McCloskey, G., & Perkins, L. A. (2012). *Essentials of executive functions assessment.* Hoboken, NJ: Wiley.

Review of the Decision-making and Self-regulation Assessor by ANNETTE S. KLUCK, Assistant Provost for Women's Initiatives & Professor of Counseling Psychology, and KATHERINE O'NEIL, Doctoral Student in Counseling Psychology, Auburn University, Auburn, AL:

DESCRIPTION. The Decision-making and Self-regulation Assessor (DASA) is a norm-referenced, self-report questionnaire developed to assist test users in personnel and counseling-related contexts to assess self-regulation, decision-making style, and decision-making competence among normal adults. The DASA was designed to reflect research and theory on regulatory stages in decision-making processes with an emphasis on agency and variations in volitional behavior rather than trait constructs.

Administration of the DASA is clear and only available online. The DASA can be administered under direct supervision or remotely and typically requires 10-15 minutes to complete. DASA items average a seventh-grade reading level. Scoring is completed via the test administration platform (hand scoring is unavailable), and users receive two reports: a personal insight report that can be given to the test taker and a technical report that includes item-level information for use by test users. The DASA yields 11 distinct norm-referenced scores (the Procrastination and Decision Avoidance scales are identical and produce identical scores despite having different names). Nine scores reflect three directly measured domains: Energy and control within self-regulation (Mental Energy, Self-Discipline, and Procrastination); Regulatory focus (Advancement Focus and Protection Focus); and Decision-making style (Decision Avoidance, Spontaneous Choice, Deliberation, Option Generation, and Decision-Making Confidence). The final two scores (General Self-Regulation and Decision-Making Competence) are composites derived from scores on the other scales.

DEVELOPMENT. The test author sought to create a brief assessment tool to evaluate a person's decision-making competence, decision-making style, and ability to self-regulate because theory and research suggest that these dimensions are critical to decision-making processes. The test manual describes use of research on decision making and self-regulation throughout the item development process as evidence of content validity, and the author returned to the literature to guide multiple iterations of questions and scale development. Specific information about the process of generating and eliminating items is limited. All reverse-keyed items were ultimately removed to improve internal reliability of the scales. The test manual describes use of item and principal components analyses with orthogonal rotation to develop nine scales with six items each. The test manual provides no specific information regarding the "hundreds of test takers" who took earlier versions of the DASA before the one used for standardization (p. 25). Scales that had inadequate criterion-related validity were dropped, and the Mental Energy scale was added during the development process. Aspects of decision-making reflecting values were considered outside the purview of the test and not included.

TECHNICAL. A total of 1,435 adults (above 18 years of age) in the United Kingdom, recruited using a U.K. internet survey company, comprised the standardization sample. No individuals from clinical settings were included. The sample included slightly more women (n = 722) than men (n = 677; 36 participants did not specify gender). The majority of the sample was White (82.2% identified as White British, 7.0% identified as White/Other). The mean age was 49, and the sample had a fairly even distribution of educational backgrounds with individuals without college or post-secondary degrees well represented (60.3% of the sample had less than a college degree).

The test manual describes several studies supporting the reliability of the DASA. Internal consistency estimates using the full standardization sample ranged from very good to excellent (alpha coefficients $\geq$ .84) for the directly measured scales. Test-retest reliability coefficients (N = 228) for an 8-week interval were acceptable to good (.77 to .89) for the directly measured scales.

Construct and criterion-related evidence of validity provided in the test manual offers modest support for the use of the DASA in explaining decision making and self-regulation. In a principal components analysis (which the manual misrepresents as an exploratory factor analysis, p. 34), DASA items loaded onto components representing their assigned scales for the directly measured scales. However, potential cross-loadings cannot be examined because loadings on other factors were not reported. It is similarly unclear whether the confirmatory factor analysis (which produced good model fit) was conducted using the same sample (which would be expected to produce good model fit and would not yield a test of cross-validation of the structure of the measure). Intercorrelations of the nine directly measured DASA scales tended to be weak to modest with the strongest correlations being .40-.50, suggesting the scales are sufficiently distinct.

The test author presents as evidence of discriminant validity associations between the directly measured DASA scales and the Big Five factors. In an unspecified sample, most coefficients were small or moderate, but three coefficients exceeded .50 (the test manual does not clearly indicate which relationships are statistically significant). Despite these findings, the patterns of relationships (based on inspection of the magnitude of the correlations) fit with what would theoretically be expected based on the Big Five factors (McCrae & Costa, 2005). The manual reviews results from tests of convergent validity that were conducted for five of the directly measured DASA scales (other than analyses with the Big Five, no evaluation of Mental Energy, Self-Discipline, Option Generation, or Decision-Making Confidence was reported). The pattern of correlations for tests of convergent validity within an unspecified sample revealed that directly measured DASA subscales were strongly related to measures of similar constructs (rs ranged from .64 [for Advancement Focus] to .84 [for Procrastination/Decision Avoidance]), supporting the construct-related validity of the DASA. The aforementioned correlations of DASA scales with Big Five factors provide additional validity support (based on patterns of correlation coefficients > .30 that match theoretical expectations) for Mental Energy (which relates to emotional stability), Self-Discipline (which relates to conscientiousness and emotional stability), and Decision-Making Confidence (which relates to conscientiousness and emotional stability). No evidence is offered or available that specifically supports the convergent or discriminant validity of the Option Generation subscale. Evidence supporting the criterion-related validity, as it relates to applied decision making, is limited to the Spontaneous Choice and Decision Avoidance/Procrastination scales. The test manual provides no information for reliability or validity for the two composite scales.

COMMENTARY. The DASA is easy to administer if one has access to the internet, and the generated reports are user friendly. The emphasis on developing a measure of habits for decision making and self-regulation produced a unique measure that helps test takers gain greater self-understanding and identify goals for behavioral change. Moreover, careful attention to research and theory in identifying constructs of the measure is a strength. Despite some psychometric support for the DASA overall (e.g., acceptable reliability coefficients were reported, patterns of correlations with other measures that support convergent validity), criterion-related validity evidence for some scales is lacking. As such, use of those scales for understanding and behavioral goal setting would be premature. Furthermore, the use of principal components analysis and lack of detail about the principal components analysis and confirmatory factor analysis is not consistent with standards of practice for these techniques (Costello & Osborne, 2005; Schreiber, Nora, Stage, Barlow, & King, 2006). Thus, it is difficult to have confidence in the construct validity evidence provided in the test manual, which is a major limitation of the test.

Although the limited available reliability and validity evidence (e.g., convergent validity) appears to support the use of some DASA scales in contexts where the primary goal is increased self-understanding, the test manual provides no test of criterion-related validity using job performance/dismissal. Furthermore, despite a statement in the manual that random responding was rare in unpublished studies (p. 4), the manual does not address potential issues with invalid responding that often results from efforts in impression management. Together with the lack of evidence of such criterion-related validity, there is insufficient psychometric support to recommend use of the DASA in personnel selection, and the DASA should not be used in contexts where decisions based on DASA scores could harm test takers.

The sizable norming sample for the DASA is a strength; however, limited representation of racial minority groups raises questions about the appropriateness of the norms for individuals from diverse backgrounds. In addition, the test manual provided no information about measurement equivalence for individuals of diverse backgrounds and age groups (no indication of age range was reported). Test users should be wary of using the test for individuals outside of middle adulthood (the DASA should not be used with minors) and individuals who do not identify as White. Until evidence supporting the measurement equivalence and adequacy of the U.K. norms is available for individuals from other countries, test users should not use the DASA outside of the United Kingdom except for research purposes.

SUMMARY. The DASA is a self-report measure that yields 11 separate scores reflecting decision-making processes and self-regulation tendencies. The measure may have potential in aiding test takers to gain self-understanding and to set behavioral goals, and test takers may find the personal insight report appealing. However, the current limited psychometric support of the measure proscribes its use in contexts where test takers may be harmed (e.g., personnel selection, diagnosis, assigning of work conditions/tasks). In addition, test users should have a clear understanding of how the lack of strong psychometric information for some scales and lack of clarity about the factor structure limit what can be concluded about an individual based on DASA scores even when using the DASA to promote self-understanding. As such, the DASA appears most appropriate for use as a tool to facilitate further evaluation of goals and challenges around decision making and self-regulation and should not be used on its own for counseling or personnel decisions.

REVIEWERS' REFERENCES

Costello, A. B., & Osborne, J. W. (2005). Best practices in exploratory factor analysis: Four recommendations for getting the most from your analysis. *Practical Assessment, Research & Evaluation, 10*(7), 1-9. Retrieved from http://pareonline.net/getvn.asp?v=10&n=7

McCrae, R. R., & Costa, P. T., Jr., (2005). *Personality in adulthood: A five-factor theory perspective* (2nd ed.). New York, NY: Guilford.

Schreiber, J. B., Nora, A., Stage, F. K., Barlow, E. A., & King, J. (2006). Reporting structural equation modeling and confirmatory factor analysis results: A review. *The Journal of Educational Research, 99*, 323-337. doi:10.3200/JOER.99.6.323-338

[45]

Depression Anxiety Stress Scales.

Purpose: "Designed to measure the negative emotional states of depression, anxiety, and stress."
Population: Adolescents and adults.
Publication Date: 1995.
Acronyms: DASS, DASS21.
Scores, 3: Depression, Anxiety, Stress.
Administration: Individual or group.
Forms, 2: Regular, short.
Price Data, 2019: AUS$55.00 per manual (2nd edition, 1995, 48 pages); questionnaire available as free download from test publisher's website.

Foreign Language Editions: Information about translations carried out by others is available from the test publisher's website.
Time: Administration time not reported.
Comments: Earlier version titled Self-Analysis Questionnaire; DASS21 is a half-length version of the DASS.
Authors: Sydney H. Lovibond and Peter F. Lovibond.
Publisher: Psychology Foundation of Australia.

Review of Depression Anxiety Stress Scales by TONY CELLUCCI, Professor and Director of the ECU Psychological Assessment and Specialty Services (PASS) Clinic, East Carolina University, Greenville, NC:

DESCRIPTION. The Depression Anxiety Stress Scales (DASS) is a set of three self-report scales developed in Australia to better define and measure the negative emotion states of depression, anxiety, and stress among adults. The three scales are each composed of 14 items measuring four to seven core components of that emotion. Respondents rate the degree to which each item statement applies to them over the past week on a 4-point (0-3) severity/frequency scale. The scales were designed for use in research, screening, and clinical settings although they are considered dimensional constructs rather than diagnostic per se. The scales are said to be helpful in both distinguishing and measuring the severity of these emotional states but may not capture associated symptoms or reflections of the emotions such as loss of appetite or suicidal ideation in depression. A brief form consisting of a half-length version (DASS-21) is also available. Administration and scoring are straightforward with scoring templates (multiply DASS-21 totals by 2) and associated percentile profile sheets provided. These may be freely duplicated along with the instrument. In addition to publishing an informative manual that is available for purchase, the test publisher has constructed a website listing frequently asked questions, translations, and publications (Psychology Foundation of Australia, 2018).

DEVELOPMENT. The test manual provides a good description of the development of the DASS, which the authors describe as simultaneous multiscale dimensioning. Their aim was to develop separate scales identifying the full range of the core features of depression and anxiety, establish psychometric adequacy, and distinguish these constructs as much as possible by removing any item overlap. Nonclinical samples (e.g., university students, blue- and white-collar employees) were used in the development process based on continuous view of these emotional states. Initially, items were selected a priori to tap core symptoms of either depression or anxiety versus control items, and item correlations were examined. This process was followed by multiple groups factor analysis retaining the most discriminating items for the two factors; a third factor termed Stress was identified by items that appeared to tap chronic nonspecific arousal (e.g., restlessness, irritability). Factors were replicated in independent samples (total n = 1,750) using both exploratory and confirmatory analyses. Validity studies were carried out using the self-report scales with 152 psychiatric outpatients and a variety of health patient groups (e.g., myocardial infarction and patients with insomnia) as well as nurses in training reporting on nonwork life Stress (STR).

TECHNICAL. Since the publication of the DASS manual, there has been considerable research on these scales, particularly the DASS-21, in the literature.

Standardization. The test manual provides normative data based on multiple nonclinical samples consisting of 1,044 men and 1,870 women ranging in age from 17 to 69 years. Means and standard deviations are provided by sex and for four age cohorts; sex differences were small, and there was a trend for higher scores among young adults. Sinclair et al. (2012) reported normative information for the DASS-21 based on a U.S. adult sample (n = 503) selected based on sample matching to population 2004 Census data. The means and standard deviations (Depression [DEP] 5.7 [8.2], Anxiety [ANX] 4.0 [6.3], and Stress [STR] 8.1 [7.6]) were said to be consistent with a prior U.K. sample (Henry & Crawford, 2005). Although the scale distributions are somewhat positively skewed, available normative data can be used to calculate standard scores or estimated percentile rank (see Crawford et al., 2009). In addition, there is a developing cross-cultural literature on the DASS-21, suggesting national differences should be considered (Scholten, Velten, Bieda, Zhang, & Margraf, 2017).

Reliability. Consistent with their development, the internal consistency estimates for these scales are excellent. The test manual reports alpha coefficients for the full scales to be DEP (.91), ANX (.84), and STR (.90) with only small reductions for the 7-item versions (DEP .81, ANX .73, and STR .81). Internal consistency of the DASS-21 was higher in the U.S. (DEP .91, ANX .80, and STR .84) and other samples (Sinclair et al., 2012).

High reliability estimates (>.90) are also reported for clinical samples (Ronk, Korman, Hooke, & Page, 2013). There are no reported data in the test manual on temporal stability over short time frames.

Validity. Regarding content validity, the test manual states that initial item selection was made by a group of clinical researchers selecting items differentiating depression and anxiety without explicit reference to existing scales and later compares DASS item content to other literature sources. Discriminant validity evidence was shown by comparing various patient groups to the nonclinical sample. Outpatients predictably scored higher, and there was general correspondence in the rank ordering of factor loadings. Of note, items (e.g., appetite, sleep difficulties) often included in clinical descriptions of depression were not found to contribute to the DASS Depression factor, an outcome that the test authors attribute to these being nonspecific reactions to psychological disorders.

Despite noted differences in development, the test authors also compared the DASS scales with the Beck Inventories using a student sample. As expected, there were higher correlations between associated constructs (Depression with BDI .74 and Anxiety with BAI .81); the other correlations, including intercorrelations between DASS scales, were on the order of .50-.60. Several other analyses related to validity evidence are provided in the test manual. Myocardial infarction and insomnia patient groups scored in the intermediate range on DASS scales with the latter scoring significantly higher than normal on the STR scale. Nurses in training showed higher scores on ANX that declined progressively across four years.

Subsequent research also has supported the validity of the DASS-21 scales. Weiss, Aderka, Lee, Beard, and Björgvinsson (2015) reported that the DASS-21 DEP scale correlated .86 with the Center for Epidemiological Studies Depression Scale (CES-D-10) in an acute psychiatric setting; DASS-21 ANX and STR measures were more strongly related to the 7-item Generalized Anxiety Disorder Scale (GAD-7) (.76-.80) than the Penn State Worry Questionnaire-Abbreviated (PSWQ-A) (.34). In their general population sample, Sinclair et al. (2012) found that most items had the highest item-scale correlations with their intended scale, albeit with a few exceptions and relatively high interscale correlations. Factor analytic studies used to assess construct validity confirm a three-factor model although there is also considerable shared variance between scales suggesting an overarching negative affect factor (Henry & Crawford, 2005; Sinclair et al., 2012). Finally, several investigators have demonstrated the sensitivity of the DASS-21 to treatment effects suggesting its utility for outcome monitoring especially in patients experiencing symptoms of depression or anxiety (Ng et al., 2007; Ronk, Korman, Hooke, & Page, 2013).

COMMENTARY. The DASS scales provide a viable instrument for assessing depression, anxiety, and stress as differential emotional states ranging on a continuum of severity. Test users would benefit from understanding the core components assessed within each scale described in the test manual. The scales have demonstrated adequate internal consistency, and the test developers have been at least partially successful in distinguishing these constructs even though the scales remain intercorrelated. Factor analytic research seems to support a hierarchical model including overall negative affect and subfactors, although further research may be needed to confirm this structural model. Although there is developing cross-cultural literature on the DASS, one limitation is the absence of information regarding possible differential item functioning across gender and ethnicity within populations.

The scales also appear applicable to clinical groups but only as part of an evaluation as the DASS is not a diagnostic instrument and it is likely important to assess excluded vegetative and behavioral symptoms of depression including suicidal ideation. Nevertheless, DASS scale scores are consistent with other clinical measures and may be useful in case formulation and treatment monitoring. Readers are reminded that reliability and validity estimates may differ across different groups. For example, Wood, Nicholas, Blyth, Asghari, and Gibson (2010) reported lower internal consistency estimates for the ANX scale in a sample of elderly pain patients due to their frequency of somatic complaints, and such overlapping symptoms in medical populations should be considered (Nanthakumar et al., 2017).

SUMMARY. The DASS is an important addition to the literature on measuring emotional states. The brevity of the DASS-21 and its public availability no doubt both contributed to its increasing use. There is sufficient supportive data to warrant its use in research on emotional distress, as an epidemiological measure, and as a screening tool in general populations, as well as with clinical groups with the cautions noted above.

REVIEWER'S REFERENCES

Crawford, J. R., Garthwaite, P. H., Lawrie, C. J., Henry, J. D., MacDonald, M. A., Sutherland, J., & Sinha, P. (2009). A convenient method of obtaining percentile norms and accompanying interval estimates for self-report mood scales (DASS, DASS-21, HADS, PANAS, and sAD). *British Journal of Clinical Psychology, 48*, 163-180. doi:10.1348/014466508X377757

Henry, J. D., & Crawford, J. R. (2005). The short-form version of the Depression Anxiety Stress Scales (DASS-21): Construct validity and normative data in a large non-clinical sample. *British Journal of Clinical Psychology, 44*, 227-239. doi:10.1348/014466505X29657

Nanthakumar, S., Bucks, R. S., Skinner, T. C., Starkstein, S., Hillman, D., James, A., & Hunter, M. (2017). Assessment of the Depression, Anxiety, and Stress Scale (DASS-21) in untreated obstructive sleep apnea (OSA). *Psychological Assessment, 29*, 1201-1209. doi:10.1037/pas0000401

Ng, F., Trauer, T., Dodd, S., Callaly, T., Campbell, S., & Berk, M. (2007). The validity of the 21-item version of the Depression Anxiety Stress Scales as a routine clinical outcome measure. *Acta Neuropsychiatrica, 19*, 304-310. doi:10.1111/j.1601-5215.2007.00217.x

Psychology Foundation of Australia. (2018). Depression Anxiety Stress Scales (DASS). Retrieved from http://www2.psy.unsw.edu.au/dass/

Ronk, F. R., Korman, J. R., Hooke, G. R., & Page, A. C. (2013). Assessing clinical significance of treatment outcomes using the DASS-21. *Psychological Assessment, 25*, 1103-1110. doi:10.1037/a0033100

Scholten, S., Velten, J., Bieda, A., Zhang, X. C., & Margraf, J. (2017). Testing measurement invariance of the Depression, Anxiety, and Stress Scales (DASS-21) across four countries. *Psychological Assessment, 29*, 1376-1390. http://dx.doi.org/10.1037/pas0000440

Sinclair, S. J., Siefert, C. J., Slavin-Mulford, J. M., Stein, M. B., Renna, M., & Blais, M. A. (2012). Psychometric evaluation and normative data for the Depression, Anxiety, and Stress Scales-21 (DASS-21) in a nonclinical sample of U.S. adults. *Evaluation & the Health Professions, 35*, 259-279. doi:10.1177/0163278711424282

Weiss, R. B., Aderka, I. M., Lee, J., Beard, C., & Björgvinsson, T. (2015). A comparison of three brief depression measures in an acute psychiatric population: CES-D-10, QIDS-SR, and DASS-21-DEP. *Journal of Psychopathology and Behavioral Assessment, 37*, 217-230. doi:10.1007/s10862-014-9461-y

Wood, B. M., Nicholas, M. K., Blyth, F., Asghari, A., & Gibson, S. (2010). The utility of the short version of the Depression Anxiety Stress Scales (DASS-21) in elderly patients with persistent pain: Does age make a difference? *Pain Medicine, 11*, 1780-1790. doi:10.1111/j.1526-4637.2010.01005.x

Review of the Depression Anxiety Stress Scales by CARL ISENHART, Psychologist, Phoenix VA Health Care System, Phoenix, AZ:

DESCRIPTION. The Depression Anxiety Stress Scales (DASS) is a self-report measure of depression, anxiety, and stress (over the past week). It can be administered individually or in a group. Clients respond to each item by circling a number from 0 to 3 to indicate the degree to which the symptom applies. The DASS is hand scored using a scoring template, then the scores are summarized on a profile sheet that provides a *z*-score and a percentile rank. The instrument can be used with adolescents and adults. There are two forms: the original 42-item scale and a 21-item short form.

DEVELOPMENT. The DASS was developed as a clinical test for practitioners and also as a research instrument. The test authors described five stages in the scale's development. First, in a research project reported by Wilson (1982), "clinical researchers" identified 37 items that assessed depression or anxiety, but not both. The preliminary samples included 125 clients seeking services for depression at a university clinic. Item analysis was conducted using confirmatory factor analysis and simultaneous multiscale dimensioning, which confirmed the presence of Depression and Anxiety items (but also suggested the presence of a third scale, later labeled Stress).

Second, these items were administered to a group of 950 first-year university students, and protocols with the highest combined Depression and Anxiety scores (n = 504) were retained and subjected to factor analysis. This analysis again identified the Depression and Anxiety scales and also confirmed a third group of items consisting of themes of tension and stress (i.e., nonspecific arousal).

In the third stage, the three scales were administered to university students in psychology, medicine, and adult education classes, along with employees at a major airline, bank, railway workshop, and a naval dockyard. Multiple groups factor analysis was conducted and confirmed the three-subscale structure. In the fourth stage, the three scales were administered to 152 psychiatric patients; subsequent analyses confirmed the factor structure. Finally, in the fifth stage, the scales were administered to a variety of clinical samples, including myocardial infarction patients and people with insomnia.

TECHNICAL. In addition to the information presented in the test manual, there have been a number of research studies, using both clinical and nonclinical participants (including a nonclinical sample [n = 1,771] from the United Kingdom [Crawford & Henry, 2003]) that support the psychometric properties of the DASS. A summary of the results from these studies will be used to review the technical aspects of the instrument.

Standardization. The DASS was standardized on 1,044 male and 1,870 female university students in psychology, medicine, and adult education classes, along with employees at a major airline, bank, railway workshop, and a naval dockyard.

Reliability. The reliability research consistently shows very high alpha coefficients for each of the three scales, all typically in the .90s with two reports in the low- to mid-.80s (for Stress and Anxiety). In addition, Crawford and Henry (2003) reported an alpha of .97 for a "total score" (p. 122) for all three scales. Also, Brown, Chorpita, Korotitsch, and Barlow (1997) reported 2-week test-retest reliability coefficients of .71, .79, and .81 for Depression, Anxiety, and Stress, respectively.

Validity. DASS has been subjected to a number of factor analytic studies, which have reported consistent and robust support for the three-factor model. Consistently, items selected for the Depression scale load onto one factor labeled Depression and have relatively low loading on the other two factors. A similar pattern is seen with the Anxiety and Stress scales. There were some reports of a few items that double-loaded, typically with the Stress and Anxiety scales, but typically the identified dimensions were stable.

Convergent and discriminant validity evidence has been demonstrated by administering the DASS along with the Beck Depression Inventory (BDI) and the Beck Anxiety Inventory (BAI). In all studies (Antony, Bieling, Cox, Enns, & Swinson, 1998; Brown et al., 1997; P. F. Lovibond & Lovibond, 1995) the BDI had the highest correlation with the DASS Depression scale (coefficients ranged from .74 to .77) and lower correlations with the Anxiety (coefficients ranged from .49 to .58) and Stress (coefficients ranged from .60 to .62) scales. The BAI had the highest correlations with the DASS Anxiety scale (coefficients ranged from .81 to .84), moderate correlations with the Stress scale (coefficients ranged from .58 to .64), and low correlations with the Depression scale (coefficients ranged from .40 to .54). Two studies (Brown et al., 1997; Crawford & Henry, 2003) administered the DASS and the Positive and Negative Affect Schedule (PANAS). All three DASS scales were found to have negative correlations with the PANAS-Positive subscale (coefficients ranged from -.18 [Anxiety] to -.48 [Depression]) and positive correlations with the PANAS-Negative subscale (coefficients ranged from .57 [Depression]) to .72 [Stress]). Expected and similar patterns were seen with other tests: the Hospital Anxiety and Depression Scale, the Personal Disturbance Scale, the Penn State Worry Scale, and the trait version of the State-Trait Anxiety Inventory.

Other studies compared the DASS scales to different diagnostic groups. Antony et al. (1998) found that clients diagnosed with major depressive disorder (MDD) scored significantly higher on the Depression and Stress scales than did the groups with anxiety disorders. Also, clients with panic disorder scored significantly higher on the anxiety scale than did clients diagnosed with MDD, obsessive-compulsive disorder (OCD), or social or specific phobias. Similarly, Brown et al. (1997) found that clients with a mood disorder scored significantly higher on the Depression scale than any of the other diagnostic groups (i.e., panic disorder, generalized anxiety disorder [GAD], OCD, and social or simple phobias), whereas clients with simple phobias scored significantly lower on the Depression scale than the other groups. They found that clients diagnosed with panic disorder scored significantly higher on the Anxiety scale than any other group, while clients with simple phobias scored significantly lower on the Anxiety scale than the other groups. Finally, they found that clients with GAD and mood disorders scored significantly higher on the Stress scale (except for the OCD group).

Finally, Crawford and Henry (2003), using a nonclinical sample from the United Kingdom, found that demographics (e.g., age, occupation, education, and gender) had "very modest" impacts on the DASS scales. Page, Hooke, and Morrison (2007) found that there may be a ceiling effect for Depression in that some clients may "max out" the scale, and therefore their score may not be a true representation of the severity of their depression.

COMMENTARY. There are a number of strengths to this test. It appears to provide reliable and valid scores for three relatively independent dimensions of depression, anxiety, and stress, all integrated into one test. It is easy to administer and score (although a computerized process of administering and scoring the instrument would be a true advancement), and the interpretation is straightforward. It can be used as a clinical instrument and as a research tool. There needs to be further research on the possible ceiling effect of the Depression scale (keeping in mind the study reporting this concern was completed with a nonclinical sample in the United Kingdom). As that issue is being studied, caution should be exercised when providing services to clients with high Depression scores or when working with populations who commonly have high levels of co-occurring depression.

SUMMARY. The DASS appears to be a good test to assess depression, anxiety, and stress in clinical and research settings. Its reliability is supported by high alpha coefficients (high enough to possibly suggest some redundancy in the scales) and good test-retest results. The validity of its scores and their uses has been supported by a number of factor analytic studies and by evidence of convergent and discriminant validity using both other instruments and comparing the scales across different diagnostic groups. The DASS does not appear to be unduly influenced by test takers' demographic features. One caveat is the possibility of a ceiling effect with the Depression scale. Therefore, given the potential risks associated with underestimating a client's depression, additional monitoring and assessment could be warranted for clients with elevated Depression scores.

REVIEWER'S REFERENCES

Antony, M. M., Bieling, P. J., Cox, B. J., Enns, M. W., & Swinson, R. P. (1998). Psychometric properties of the 42-item and 21-item versions of the Depression Anxiety Stress Scales in clinical groups and a community sample. *Psychological Assessment, 10,* 176-181.

Brown, T. A., Chorpita, B. F., Korotitsch, W., & Barlow, D. H. (1997). Psychometric properties of the Depression Anxiety Stress Scales (DASS) in clinical samples. *Behaviour Research and Therapy, 35,* 79-89.

Crawford, J. R., & Henry, J. D. (2003). The Depression Anxiety Stress Scales (DASS): Normative data and latent structure in a large non-clinical sample. *British Journal of Clinical Psychology, 42,* 111-131.

Lovibond, P. F., & Lovibond, S. H. (1995). The structure of negative emotional states: Comparison of the Depression Anxiety Stress Scales (DASS) with the Beck Depression and Anxiety Inventories. *Behaviour Research and Therapy, 33,* 335-343.

Page, A. C., Hooke, G. R., & Morrison, D. L. (2007). Psychometric properties of the Depression Anxiety Stress Scales (DASS) in depressed clinical samples. *British Journal of Clinical Psychology, 46,* 283-297.

Wilson, P. H. (1982). Combined pharmacological and behavioural treatment of depression. *Behaviour Research and Therapy, 20,* 173-184.

[46]

Detroit Tests of Learning Abilities–Fifth Edition.

Purpose: Designed to assess "a selected group of cognitive abilities."
Population: Ages 6-0 to 17-11.
Publication Dates: 1935-2018.
Acronym: DTLA-5.
Scores, 21: Acquired Knowledge (Humanities/Social Studies, Science/Mathematics, Total), Verbal Comprehension (Word Opposites, Word Associations, Total), Nonverbal Problem Solving (Geometric Matrices, Geometric Sequences, Total), Reasoning Ability; Verbal Memory (Sentence Imitation, Word Span, Total), Nonverbal Memory (Design Reproduction, Reversed Letters, Total), Processing Speed (Trail Making, Rapid Naming, Total), Processing Ability; General Cognitive Ability.
Administration: Individual.
Price Data, 2020: $593 per kit including manual (2018, 241 pages), picture books 1 and 2, 25 record booklets, and 25 response booklets; $168 per picture book 2; $150 per picture book 1; $101 per manual; $88 per 25 record booklets; $86 per 25 response booklets.
Time: 60-80 minutes for administration of the entire battery.
Comments: Subtests may be administered separately; scoring is completed online; previously titled Detroit Tests of Learning Aptitude.
Authors: Donald D. Hammill, Ronnie L. McGhee, and David J. Ehrler.
Publisher: PRO-ED.
Cross References: For reviews by Jeffrey K. Smith and Ross E. Traub of the fourth edition, see 14:113; see also T5:798 (27 references); for reviews by William A. Mehrens and G. Michael Poteat of the third edition, see 12:107 (4 references); see also T4:752 (7 references); for reviews by Arthur B. Silverstein and Joan Silverstein of the second edition, see 10:85 (15 references); see also 9:320 (11 references), and T3:691 (20 references); for a review by Arthur B. Silverstein of an earlier (1975) edition, see 8:213 (14 references); see also T2:493 (3 references), and 7:406 (10 references); for a review by F. L. Wells of an earlier (1939) edition, see 3:275 (1 reference); for reviews by Anne Anastasi and Henry Feinburg and an excerpted review by D. A. Worcester and S. M. Corey of the original edition, see 1:1058.

Review of the Detroit Tests of Learning Abilities—Fifth Edition by RUSSELL N. CARNEY, Professor Emeritus of Psychology, Missouri State University, Springfield, MO:

DESCRIPTION. The Detroit Tests of Learning Abilities—Fifth Edition (DTLA-5) is the current version of this individually administered test of cognitive abilities first published in 1935. The test is designed for English-speaking students ages 6 years 0 months through 17 years 11 months. With an administration time ranging from 60-80 minutes, the test battery yields 12 subtest scores regarding 12 specific cognitive abilities. Based on disjoint pairs of the 12 subtests, six subdomain composite scores also are derived: Acquired Knowledge, Verbal Comprehension, Nonverbal Problem Solving, Verbal Memory, Nonverbal Memory, and Processing Speed. These scores, then, lead to two domain scores, Reasoning Ability and Processing Ability, and finally, to an overall, global measure termed General Cognitive Ability (i.e., *g*).

Test materials include a 241-page examiner's manual and two stimulus books, one containing stimuli for the Geometric Matrices and Geometric Sequences subtests and the other containing stimuli for the Design Reproduction, Reversed Letters, and Rapid Naming subtests. Both are designed as easel books. Other materials include a 24-page student response booklet and a 14-page examiner record booklet. Finally, there is an online scoring and report system that allows for data entry, generates all scores, and yields both a Standard Summary Report and a Detailed Narrative Report, which can aid in interpretation.

Subtest scores are reported as standard scaled scores (M = 10; SD = 3); composite scores are reported as index scores (M = 100; SD = 15). Confidence intervals (90% and 95%) are also provided. Other provided scores include user-friendly percentile ranks as well as the more problematic age equivalent scores. Finally, seven qualitative phrases are provided to describe ranges of scores, from a low of *impaired or delayed* (i.e., scaled score 1-3; index score < 70) to a high of *gifted or very advanced* (i.e., scaled score 17-20; index score > 129).

The test manual lists six principal uses for the DTLA-5: (a) to identify children who are significantly below average in cognitive abilities, (b) to predict future achievement, (c) to identify strengths and weaknesses, (d) to aid in research, (e) to identify gifted individuals, and (f) to measure the extent of injuries to cognitive functioning.

Examiners should have at least some training in assessment and are encouraged to study the manual and practice administering the test beforehand. Instructions for administration appear prior to each subtest in the examiner record booklet. Although age-range rules suggest the entry points for most of the subtests, the examiner can adjust this process based on prior knowledge about the examinee. Further, the test manual notes that any parts of the test (e.g., subtests, composites, etc.) can be administered independently if desired.

DEVELOPMENT. In developing the DTLA-5, the test authors sought to update and improve the qualities of this long-standing test. The test manual describes the four prior editions (1935, 1985, 1991, 1998), and in particular, describes how the fifth edition's development followed from criticisms of the fourth. With that in mind, the test manual for the DTLA-5 describes its development and subsequent improvements in terms of (a) having a better theoretical model; (b) eliminating and adding subtests; (c) deriving norms from a new sample; (d) improving floors, ceilings, and item gradients; (e) conducting studies that showed little to no bias; (f) presenting supportive criterion-prediction validity evidence; (g) presenting supportive construct-identification validity evidence; (h) including electronic scoring; and, finally, (i) changing *Aptitude* to *Abilities* in the test title.

TECHNICAL. The test was normed on a representative sample of 1,383 students from 30 states, ages 6 years 0 months to 17 years 11 months who were administered the test sometime during a 5-year period (2011 through 2015). The sample was stratified so as to approximate characteristics of the U.S. population in terms of "gender, race, Hispanic status, exceptionality status, educational level of parents," household income, and geographic region (manual, p. 50). Each of the 12 age groups (i.e., age 6, age 7, ... age 17) included more than 100 children (*ns* = 104-135).

Two types of reliability estimates are described. First, coefficient alpha was used to examine internal consistency. This measure of reliability was applied to 10 of the 12 subtests (and alternate-form reliability was used for the two speeded subtests). Such reliability estimates were provided in the test manual for the 12 age groups. Averaged across ages, all coefficients were deemed adequate (above .80), except for the Rapid Naming subtest (.79). Further, all of the averaged composite score estimates (except Processing Speed, .87), were .90 or higher. Reliabilities of .90 or higher are recommended when test scores are used to make high stakes decisions. Impressively, the average coefficient for the General Cognitive Ability score was listed as .98. Based on these reliability coefficients, corresponding standard errors of measurement (*SEM*s) are reported.

To compute test-retest reliability, 209 students (ages 6-17) were selected. This group was tested twice, with about a two-week interval between administrations. Their scores were correlated and corrected for range effects. Corrected reliability coefficients for subtests ranged from .72 to .90 (with most in the .80s), and for subdomains from .80 to .92. Domain and global composite results were all higher than .90.

Test validity can be defined as "the degree to which evidence and theory support the interpretations of test scores for proposed uses of tests" and is said to be the "most fundamental consideration in developing tests and evaluating tests" (American Educational Research Association [AERA], American Psychological Association [APA], & National Council on Measurement in Education [NCME], 2014, p. 11). In the test manual, citing Anastasi and Urbina (1997), developers provide three types of evidence of validity: content-description, criterion-prediction, and construct identification.

Content-description validity has to do with how well the test samples content that is representative of the behavior domain in question. Five lines of evidence for content validity are provided. First, the test developers argue that the structure of the DTLA-5 fits with current models of intelligence. Four tables are provided illustrating how the DTLA-5's subtests align with each of four theories, including Cattell, Horn, and Carroll's CHC model (Carroll, 1993). Second, they describe the rationales for each of the 12 subtests and how their content was selected. Third, the authors suggest that item selection criteria, based on conventional item analysis—item difficulty (*p*) and discrimination—provide evidence for content-description validity. Items on subtests were selected with item difficulties between .15 and .85, with the average being .50, and with item discrimination (point-biserial correlations) set at .30 or higher. Fourth, their analysis of floors, ceilings, and item gradients detailed in the test manual suggests that: (a) the test has acceptable floors (for measuring those with low ability, as is often the case in special education assessment) and ceilings (for those with high ability, as in gifted programs), and that (b) item gradients were adequate. Fifth, an examination of potential test bias using differential item functioning and demographic subgroup comparisons (e.g., gender, race,) generally found little or no systematic bias in the test.

Criterion-prediction validity relates to how well the test predicts particular outcomes. Corresponding DTLA-5 composite scores were correlated with scores from several well-known tests: the Cognitive Assessment System-Second Edition, the Primary Test of Nonverbal Intelligence, the Universal Nonverbal Intelligence Test-Second Edition, the Stanford-Binet Intelligence Scales—Fifth Edition (SB5), the Wechsler Intelligence Scale for Children—Fourth Edition (WISC-IV), the Wechsler Intelligence Scale for Children—Fifth Edition (WISC-V), and the Woodcock-Johnson III Tests of Cognitive Abilities. Using Hopkins' (2002) descriptors for ranges of correlation coefficients, of 27 averaged correlation coefficients (corrected for attenuation), seven were deemed very large, 12 were deemed large, and eight were deemed moderate. As a specific example, the DTLA-5's General Cognitive Ability score correlated with the WISC-IV Full Scale IQ score at .84 (very large). These findings tend to support the notion that the DTLA-5 is assessing cognitive abilities similar to comparable, well-respected measures. Further, they examined the relationship of DTLA-5 scores to general achievement, as measured by the Diagnostic Achievement Battery-Fourth Edition (2014), the Kaufman Test of Educational Achievement-Second Edition (2004), and the Woodcock-Johnson III Tests of Achievement (2001). Again, their findings supported the validity of the DTLA-5 as a measure of general achievement.

Construct-identification validity consists of the extent to which a test measures its stated theoretical construct(s). In this regard, maximum likelihood confirmatory factor analysis (CFA) was conducted to examine the DTLA-5's fit with a hierarchical theoretical model at four age levels, using five indexes of fit. Here again, the test manual suggests that the findings supported factor structure of the DTLA-5. Item discrimination values were also mentioned as supporting construct validity. All in all, the test authors concluded that the DTLA-5 is a valid instrument for its stated purposes and that examiners should use it with confidence.

COMMENTARY. Although Smith (2001) found the DTLA-4 a well-designed test of cognitive abilities, he criticized the fact that 16 composite scores were produced from just 10 initial subtests. In the DTLA-5, this pattern is reversed, with more subtests than composites. Another criticism was that the DTLA-4 produced a difficult-to-interpret score called the Optimal Composite, based on the examinee's highest four scores (Smith, 2001). The DTLA-5 does away with that problematic score. Other authors criticized three of the DTLA-4's subtests due to their poor psychometric properties (Salvia & Ysseldyke, 2001; Sattler, 2001), and those subtests were dropped in the fifth edition.

Traub (2001) wrote that the DTLA-4 might, indeed, function well for its stated purposes, but that the authors needed to better document the psychometric properties of the test via the manual. In that regard, the DTLA-5's 241-page test manual describes the psychometric properties of the DTLA-5 in more detail (e.g., it includes a 64-page chapter documenting validity evidence). Both Smith (2001) and Traub (2001) criticized the DTLA-4's use of Jensen's (1980) delta scores to determine item bias. In the DTLA-5, logistic regression was used to identify differential item functioning to investigate item bias.

Finally, throughout the well-written test manual, the authors refer to classic measurement authors often, and in particular, seem to have valued and followed the guidelines presented in the *Standards for Educational and Psychological Testing* (AERA, APA, & NCME, 2014). They are to be commended for this approach. Based on evidence presented in the test manual, the DTLA-5 appears to be a reliable instrument and one that has demonstrated validity for the purposes advertised.

SUMMARY. The DTLA-5 is an individually administered assessment battery, yielding an overall measure of General Cognitive Ability, domain scores in Reasoning and Processing, and other useful composite (and subtest) scores for children ages 6-0 to 17-11. The fifth edition appears to have been carefully revised in light of prior criticisms and following industry guidelines. As summarized in the test manual, they "eliminated and added subtests, created and modified composites, and enhanced the statistical properties of the test" (p. xx). As a result, the DTLA-5 appears to be an improved instrument that should be helpful to those charged with assessing the learning abilities (and disabilities) of children and youth.

REVIEWER'S REFERENCES

American Educational Research Association, American Psychological Association, & National Council on Measurement in Education. (2014). *Standards for educational and psychological testing*. Washington, DC: American Educational Research Association.

Anastasi, A., & Urbina, S. (1997). *Psychological testing* (7th ed.). Upper Saddle River, NJ: Prentice Hall.

Carroll, J. B. (1993). *Human cognitive abilities*. Cambridge, England: Cambridge University Press.

Hopkins, W. G. (2002). A scale of magnitudes for the effect statistics. In *A new view of statistics*. Retrieved from http://www.sportsci.org/resource/stats/effecctmag.html

Jensen, A. R. (1980). *Bias in mental testing*. New York, NY: Free Press.

Salvia, J., & Ysseldyke, J. E. (2001). *Assessment* (8th ed.). Boston, MA: Houghton Mifflin.

Sattler, J. M. (2001). *Assessment of children: Cognitive applications* (4th ed.). San Diego, CA: Jerome M. Sattler.

Smith, J. K. (2001). [Test review of the Detroit Tests of Learning Aptitude—Fourth Edition.] In B. S. Plake & J. C. Impara (Eds.), *The fourteenth mental measurements yearbook* (pp. 382-383). Lincoln, NE: Buros Institute of Mental Measurements.

Traub, R. E. (2001). [Test review of the Detroit Tests of Learning Aptitude—Fourth Edition.] In B. S. Plake & J. C. Impara (Eds.), *The fourteenth mental measurements yearbook* (pp. 384-386). Lincoln, NE: Buros Institute of Mental Measurements.

Review of the Detroit Tests of Learning Abilities—Fifth Edition by DAMIEN C. CORMIER, Associate Professor of Educational Psychology, University of Alberta, Edmonton, AB, Canada, & ANDREA ANTONIUK, Graduate Student in School and Clinical Child Psychology, Educational Psychology, University of Alberta, Edmonton, AB, Canada:

DESCRIPTION. The Detroit Tests of Learning Abilities—Fifth Edition (DTLA-5) is a comprehensive test of cognitive abilities that can be administered to children and adolescents between the ages of 6 years 0 months and 17 years 11 months. The DTLA was previously known as the Detroit Tests of Learning *Aptitude*, and the first edition of the test was published in 1935 (Baker & Leland, 1935). Although it has undergone another significant revision, the purpose of the DTLA-5 remains consistent with its previous editions: to measure cognitive abilities broadly. The DTLA-5 examiner's manual describes six uses for this instrument. They include diagnostic considerations related to learning and development, answering research questions related to cognitive ability, and identifying students who have particularly strong cognitive abilities.

The DTLA-5 test model is hierarchical, with General Cognitive Ability being identified as the global composite score that is produced from this test. This composite is produced from 12 subtests that are categorized based on domains and subdomains. Below General Cognitive Ability are two domain scores: Reasoning Ability and Processing Ability. The subdomains associated with the Reasoning Ability domain, as well as their respective subtests, are (a) Acquired Knowledge (subtests: Humanities/Social Studies, Science/Mathematics); (b) Verbal Comprehension (subtests: Word Opposites, Word Associations); and (c) Nonverbal Problem Solving (subtests: Geometric Matrices, Geometric Sequences). The subdomains associated with the Processing Ability domain and their respective subtests are (a) Verbal Memory (subtests: Sentence Imitation, Word Span); (b) Nonverbal Memory (subtests: Design Reproduction, Reversed Letters); and (c) Processing Speed (subtests: Trail Making, Rapid Naming). To measure each of the domains and subdomains, the DTLA-5 kit includes an examiner's manual, two picture books, a student response booklet, and an examiner record booklet. Another important component of the DTLA-5 is the online scoring and reporting system, which is required to produce scores from the examinee's recorded responses.

The DTLA-5 is intended for English-speaking children and adolescents. The average administration time for the full battery is 60 to 80 minutes. The authors of the DTLA-5 recommend administering the subtests in the order stated in the examiner record booklets. Seven subtests contain both basal and ceiling rules, whereas three subtests have ceiling rules only. Nine subtests have start points for various age levels. Scoring is relatively simple with point values being assigned to correct and incorrect responses to individual items. The online scoring system produces scaled scores, composite index scores, percentile ranks, age equivalents, and confidence intervals. The system also reports strengths, weaknesses, and score summaries.

DEVELOPMENT. The DTLA-5's normative sample included a stratified sample of 1,383 students from 30 states and 354 ZIP codes. Sampling occurred between 2011 and 2015, inclusively, with a minimum of 100 respondents in each age group. The DTLA-5 authors determined that the normative sample was representative of the general population based on comparisons with those reported in the *Statistical Abstracts of the United States* published by ProQuest LLC and the *Digest of Education Statistics, 2014* published by the National Center for Education Statistics.

TECHNICAL. The DTLA-5 manual presents a number of statistics to demonstrate the reliability of the scores produced by the measure.

The values for coefficient alpha for all subtests except for the two timed tests, Trail Making and Rapid Naming, are reported by age in the DTLA-5 manual. The reliability of the timed tests was calculated as appropriate using alternate-forms reliability. Across all the subtests and age ranges, the average (as calculated using a Fisher's *z* transformation) reliability coefficients range from .73 to .94, with an average coefficient for all but one subtest exceeding .80 for all age groups (the Rapid Naming average = .79). The average coefficients for the domain composite scores are .97 for Reasoning Ability and .95 for Processing Ability. The DTLA-5's General Cognitive Ability score has an average coefficient value of .98.

Across all subtests and age intervals, the average standard error of measurement (*SEM*) for the DTLA-5 subtests is 1, and the average *SEM* for the subdomain composites ranges from 3 to 5. The domain composites' average *SEM* is 3, and the global composite's average *SEM* is 2. Test-retest reliability was examined using a 209-examinee sample assessed on a 2-week test-retest schedule. For all age groups, coefficients for subtest performance ranged from .72 to .90, whereas subdomain coefficients ranged from .80 to .90, and coefficients for domain and global scores exceeded .90.

The DTLA-5 manual summarizes a great deal of evidence in support of its general purpose to measure cognitive abilities broadly. The DTLA-5 was not designed to be mapped onto a single theory of cognitive abilities; instead, the manual describes how the test's content aligns with a number of contemporary theories of intelligence and cognition. The influences referenced in the design of DTLA-5 include Anastasi and Urbina's Continuum of Developed Abilities (Anastasi & Urbina, 1997); the Cattell-Horn-Carroll Theory of Cognitive Abilities (Schneider & McGrew, 2012); Salvia, Ysseldyke, and Witmer's abilities (Salvia, Ysseldyke, & Witmer, 2017); and Dehn's memory classification (Dehn, 2008).

Criterion-related evidence of validity was gathered by correlating the DTLA-5 with seven other cognitive assessments, including the Wechsler Intelligence Scale for Children–Fifth Edition, the Woodcock-Johnson III Tests of Cognitive Abilities, and the Universal Nonverbal Intelligence Test—Second Edition. The results of the numerous comparisons made suggest that the DTLA-5 correlated as expected with other measures of cognitive abilities. In addition, the structure of the DTLA-5 was supported by evidence of expected intercorrelations among its subtests as well as strong factor loadings within domains and subdomains. Finally, when tested for potential item bias, negligible differential item functioning (DIF) was observed for all subtests, which suggests an absence of test bias. In addition, subgroup performance analyses identified no meaningful gender or race biases.

A number of approaches were used to gather construct-related evidence of validity. First, performance on the DTLA-5 (i.e., raw scores) was expected to correlate with age. Correlation coefficients were generally large or very large. Second, students with exceptionalities were expected to perform differently on the DTLA-5 when compared to students without exceptionalities. The trends across various exceptionality groups (e.g., gifted and talented, ADHD, learning disabilities) were in line with the performance that is expected from these groups with respect to cognitive abilities. For example, students identified as gifted and talented tended to perform better on individual subtests than a matched sample. Performance on the DTLA-5 was also expected to be predictive of academic achievement. DTLA-5 performance demonstrated a strong or very strong association with a variety of standardized tests of academic achievement, such as the Kaufman Test of Educational Achievement—Second Edition. The scores from the DTLA-5 were also strongly correlated with performance on several measures of written language (e.g., Test of Silent Contextual Reading Fluency–Second Edition*)*, as well as measures of spoken language (e.g., Test for Auditory Comprehension of Language–Fourth Edition*)*.

COMMENTARY. The DTLA-5 includes everything that would be expected from a contemporary comprehensive test of cognitive abilities. Based on the information provided in the DLTA-5 examiner's manual, it is evident that a great deal of care and attention went into the development of the latest edition of this test. For example, the rationale for the change made to the test name was clearly explained and well justified. Overall, the test demonstrates strong psychometric properties and appears to be well designed to meet its stated purposes. The examiner's manual is comprehensive but easy to read and not overwhelming in its presentation of important psychometric information. The primary characteristic that distinguishes the DTLA-5 from other standardized, norm-referenced tests of cognitive abilities is the approach to developing its structure and content. This test draws from a relatively broad array of expert- and empirically driven foundations that are relevant to learning. Consequently, it appears to be a relevant and appropriate component of a comprehensive psycho-educational assessment process.

Despite the DTLA-5's many strengths, a few weaknesses are also worth noting. First, the testing time is relatively lengthy with a range of 60 to 80 minutes. Developers of many other comprehensive tests of cognitive abilities have reduced the total administration time in their most recent versions to below 60 minutes. In addition, the record form could be more user friendly, especially for a new examiner. For example, the large blocks of text that appear in the directions section may make it difficult for a new examiner to ensure that he or she is conforming to the standardized administration without having to read the entire section in its entirety during administration. The small font used on the form also may prove challenging for some examiners. Finally, the visual aids that are included in the stimulus books are entirely in black and white (i.e., no color images). This could be considered a strength to avoid any issues with color perception that may occur with some examinees, but it also may lead to the tasks being less engaging for young examinees. The latter may be particularly relevant considering the relatively lengthy administration time.

SUMMARY. Overall, the DTLA-5 is a well-developed, comprehensive measure of the cognitive abilities that are relevant to learning. The test can be used to measure functioning within a wide range of ability levels. The quality of the normative sample and reliability and validity evidence appears to be adequate to support its stated purposes. The overall usability of the DTLA-5 is strong: the examiner's manual is well-written and easily accessible to its intended audience, the administration and scoring are similar to those of other measures of cognitive abilities, and the scores produced appear to be beneficial in making a number of useful interpretations. The DTLA-5 has very few weaknesses. Potential users, however, may want to consider the administration time and the format of the visuals, depending on the individual characteristics of the students they are assessing.

REVIEWERS' REFERENCES

Anastasi, A., & Urbina, S. (1997). *Psychological testing* (7th ed.). Upper Saddle River, NJ: Prentice Hall.

Baker, H. J., & Leland, B. (1935). Detroit Tests of Learning Aptitude. Indianapolis, IN: Bobbs-Merrill.

Dehn, M. J. (2008). *Working memory and academic learning: Assessment and intervention.* Hoboken, NJ: Wiley.

Salvia, J., Ysseldyke, J. E. & Witmer, S. (2017). *Assessment in special and inclusive education* (13th ed.). Boston, MA: Cengage.

Schneider, W. J., & McGrew, K. S. (2012). The Cattell-Horn-Carroll model of intelligence. In D. P. Flanagan & P. L. Harrison (Eds.), *Contemporary intellectual assessment: Theories, tests, and,* issues (3rd ed., pp. 99-144). New York, NY: Guilford.

[47]

Developmental Assets Profile.

Purpose: Designed as a group-level examination of "young people's own sense of their strengths, supports, and skills that are essential for success in school and life."

Population: Students in Grades 4 to 12.

Publication Dates: 2005-2016.

Acronym: DAP.

Scores, 17: External Assets (Support, Empowerment, Boundaries and Expectations, Constructive Use of Time), Internal Assets (Commitment to Learning, Positive Values, Social Competencies, Positive Identity), Composite Assets Score, plus 5 asset contexts (Personal, Social, Family, School, Community).

Administration: Group.

Price Data, 2020: $250 per site report, including up to 100 surveys; $2 per additional survey (beyond the included 100); $250 per aggregate report (encompassing multiple sites); $150 per individual data file of all youth surveyed.

Foreign Language Editions: Available in Spanish and selected other languages; contact test publisher for information.

Time: 10 minutes or less for completion.

Comments: User's guide (September 2016, 45 pages) available for download from survey publisher's website; data analyzed and report provided by survey publisher; minimum of 30 surveys required for report.

Author: Search Institute.

Publisher: Search Institute.

Review of the Developmental Assets Profile by FRANK BERNT, Professor of Teacher Education, Saint Joseph's University, Philadelphia, PA:

DESCRIPTION. The Developmental Assets Profile (DAP) was designed to assess developmental assets or strengths for youth ages 11-18 years. Developmental assets are described as "positive experiences and qualities identified ... as being essential to healthy psychological and social development" (Search Institute, 2005, p. 2).The instrument consists of 58 items scored on a 4-point rating scale (0 = *not at all or rarely*; 3 = *extremely or almost always*). The inventory yields subscores for eight separate Asset categories divided into four External (Support, Empowerment, Boundaries and Expectations, and Constructive Use of Time) and four Internal categories (Commitment to Learning,

Positive Values, Social Competencies, and Positive Identity). Items are also scored to yield five Context scores (Personal, Social, Family, School, and Community), though these subscales appear to receive less attention in the test materials than the Internal and External categories.

The reading level for the DAP, based upon the Flesch-Kincaid Index, is Grade 5.7 (93% of items were assessed to be at an eighth-grade reading level or below). The DAP is designed principally for written administration to groups, though it also may be administered orally or as a mailed survey. Instructions for administration are detailed and straightforward. The test authors report that the DAP is completed by most participants in 10 minutes or less. They also provide a very detailed user's guide (Search Institute, 2016) that lays out practical steps for designing and conducting the survey and for interpreting and communicating findings.

Instructions for hand scoring are available; there is also an option for internet-based data entry and automatic scoring. The user's manual provides clear, detailed instructions for screening completed DAP forms for validity and completeness and also for error-free hand scoring. Subscale scores are computed by averaging the scores for completed items on that subscale and multiplying by 10 (yielding scores ranging from 0 to 30). Qualifications for use include having a general background in standardized assessment and a basic understanding of data analysis, preferably at the master's level (Search Institute, 2005, p. ii).

The primary intended uses of the DAP are for research and program evaluation, most particularly in the fields of education, medicine, social work/services, counseling, and therapy. The test authors provide clear guidelines for each intended use with particular emphasis on the instrument's utility for program evaluation.

DEVELOPMENT. The test authors describe development of the DAP as driven by a need for an instrument that would "complement and extend the utility of existing asset measures" (Search Institute, 2005, page i)—particularly, the Search Institute Profiles of Student Life: Attitudes and Behavior (A&B) survey. The added values of the DAP are that it is much shorter, it yields individual measures (rather than aggregate reports), and it is sensitive to changes in reported assets over time. The assumption is that possession of such assets will serve as protective factors and contribute to positive development and empowerment of young adolescents (Search Institute, 2005, p. 2).

TECHNICAL. The authors of the DAP describe a thorough and intentional process of test development in the user's manual, involving the use of adolescent focus groups, exploration of a variety of possible response scaling types, and a three-phase process (initial design, pilot testing, and field trials). The description is detailed, transparent, and very credible. The test authors state that development is ongoing (Search Institute, 2005, p. 32), although this reviewer's sense is that attention has (probably rightly) turned from intensive study of psychometric properties to actual practical applications (see below).

The introduction to the Interpretation section of the user's manual argues in favor of a "theoretical" (or more criterion-related) approach to interpreting scores, although it still also provides extensive statistical data to support a norm-based approach. The section begins with a description of Interpretive Ranges, arguing (conceptually rather than statistically) for four a priori category ranges: *Excellent* (scores 26-30); *Good* (21-25); *Fair* (15-20); and *Low* (0-14).

Statistical norms for the DAP were developed using the original field test, conducted with more than 1,300 students in Grades 6 through 12 in Minnesota and followed by a second field test using a sample of more than 1,100 students in Grades 6 through 8 in Oregon. More detailed and updated norms are presented for more data using 2,621 youth in Minneapolis (Search Institute, 2017); however, additional studies of the instrument's reliability and validity were not reported.

Initial field tests (reported in the user's manual) yielded internal consistency estimates averaging .81 (alpha coefficients) for Asset category scores and .88 for Context scales (and .93, .95, and .97 for Internal, External, and Total Assets scales, respectively). Only the Constructive Use of Time subscale was noted as questionable, with an alpha coefficient of .59. The test authors' explanation for this subscale's lower internal consistency was plausible, as one would not expect these items from different contexts to be highly correlated. In addition, having only four items on the scale may have set a ceiling on reliability.

To assess test-retest reliability, a sample of 225 students from the first field test completed the DAP twice, with a 2-week interval. Reliability coefficients for subscales were more than satisfactory: average r = .79; Internal, External, and Total Assets rs were .86, .84, and .87, respectively. It was noted that test-retest reliability estimates differed significantly by gender and age, with estimates for females being significantly higher than for males and higher for older than for younger participants on 13 of the 16 subscales. In addition, a subsample of 161 students was retested 1 year after the initial test administration, and stability for the eight scales was relatively high: average r = .61, range .52-.67 (Search Institute, 2005, p. 34).

The vast majority of the discussion of validity in the user's manual focuses upon concurrent and convergent evidence, specifically upon DAP's correlations with the A&B survey upon which it was based. There was a high positive correlation between the DAP's Total Assets scale and the A&B survey's total number of assets (r was .82), based on the Minnesota field test sample. All reported correlations were described as "robust" (Search Institute, 2005, p. 36) and were consistent across gender and grade level categories. There is little reported beyond the correlations between the DAP and the A&B survey. Exceptions are explorations of the correlations between the Positive Identity subscale and both the Rosenberg Self-Esteem Scale and Harter's Global Self-Worth Scale. The correlations between the DAP and the Rosenberg and Harter scales were moderately high, r = .70 and r = .72, respectively. To support criterion evidence, the test authors report that participants in a "more asset-rich" middle school scored significantly higher on Constructive Use of Time, Empowerment, and Community subscales than did their counterparts in a "less asset-rich" middle school. It should also be noted that Internal, External, and Total Assets scores were positively correlated (r ranged from .46 to .65) with thriving and self-reported grades scores and negatively correlated (r ranged from -.47 to -.49) with an index of risk behaviors (Search Institute, 2005, p. 64).

COMMENTARY. The Developmental Assets Profile appears to be "a strengths-focused assessment tool with strong psychometric properties" (Haggerty, Elgin, & Woolley, 2011, p. 26) that has been successfully used as a program evaluation tool in a wide number of settings including empowering adolescent girls in rural Bangladesh (Scales et al., 2013); a wilderness program for urban youth (Norton & Watt, 2014); structured programs and youth sports (Strachan, Côté, & Deakin, 2009); emergency shelters (Heinze, 2013); and afterschool leadership development programs, in which the DAP was used as an independent variable (Thompson, Corsello, McReynolds, & Conklin-Powers, 2013). Other measures have been developed more recently, perhaps most notably the Social and Emotion Health Survey for Secondary School Students (Furlong, You, Renshaw, Smith, & O'Malley, 2014); however, that measure is clearly targeted for an older adolescent population than the DAP.

SUMMARY. The DAP provides a valuable counterbalance to extensive research done in the area of adverse childhood experiences (Anda, Butchart, Felitii, & Brown, 2010), inasmuch as DAP focuses precisely upon the buffer mechanisms that may mitigate the negative effect of adverse childhood experiences.

A review of published studies using the DAP leaves the impression that use of the DAP has not continued to increase in recent years. This is somewhat surprising, given renewed interest in affective outcomes and in socio-emotional learning by educational leaders (National Conference of State Legislatures, 2018). This reviewer's sense is that the DAP would be well-suited for use in more mainstream educational settings, not as a sole measure of student learning, but certainly as one important tool in a toolbox of effective mechanisms for assessing efforts to strengthen and empower middle school children.

Finally, while the emphasis certainly seems to be upon using the DAP primarily for program evaluation, additional study of its psychometric qualities—especially alongside other measures—as well as its use as a basic research tool should be encouraged. There is room for meta-analyses and other approaches to synthesize and integrate what has already been learned. That said, while the Search Institute's focus is clearly upon spreading the DAP's use primarily for program evaluation purposes, its construction, instructions, and detail to test validation clearly establish it as an excellent tool for that purpose and for purposes of research as well.

REVIEWER'S REFERENCES

Anda, R. F., Butchart, A., Felitii, V. J., & Brown, D. W. (2010). Building a framework for global surveillance of the public health implications of adverse childhood experiences. *American Journal of Preventive Medicine, 39* (1), 93-98. doi:10.1016/j.amepre.2010.03.015

Furlong, M. J., You, S., Renshaw, T. L, Smith, D. C., & O'Malley, M. D. (2014). Preliminary development and validation of the Social and Emotional Health Survey for Secondary School Students. *Social Indicators Research, 117*, 1011-1032. doi:10.1007/s11205-013-0373-0

Haggerty, K., Elgin, J., & Woolley, A. (2011). *Social-emotional learning: Assessment measures for middle school youth.* Seattle, WA: Social Development Research Group, University of Washington: Commissioned by the Raikes Foundation.

Heinze, H. J. (2013). Beyond a bed: Support for positive development for youth residing in emergency shelters. *Children and Youth Services Review, 35* (2), 278-286.

National Conference of State Legislatures. (2018). *Social and emotional learning.* Retrieved May 4, 2019 from http://www.ncsl.org/research/education/social-emotional-learning.aspx

Norton, C. L., & Watt, T. T. (2014). Exploring the impact of a wilderness-based positive youth development program for urban youth. *Journal of Experiential Education, 37* (4), 335-350. doi:10.1177/1053825913503113

Scales, P. C., Benson, P. L., Fraher, K., Syvertsen, A. K. Dershem, L., Makonnen, R., Nazneen, S., & Titus, S. (2013). Building developmental assets to empower adolescent girls in rural Bangladesh: Evaluation of Project Kishoree Kontha. *Journal of Research on Adolescence, 23* (1), 171-184. doi:10.1111/j.1532-7795.2012.00805.x

Search Institute. (2005). *Developmental Assets Profile: User manual.* Minneapolis, MN: Author.

Search Institute. (2016). *User guide for the Developmental Assets Profile.* Minneapolis, MN: Author.

Search Institute. (2017). *Strengths and support in the lives of Search Institute sample youth: Based on the results from the Developmental Assets Profile.* Minneapolis, MN: Author.

Strachan, L., Côté, J., & Deakin, J. (2009). An evaluation of personal and contextual factors in competitive youth sport. *Journal of Applied Sport Psychology, 21*(3), 340-355.

Thompson, R. B., Corsello, M., McReynolds, S., & Conklin-Powers, B. (2013). A longitudinal study of family socioeconomic status (SES) variables as predictors of socio-emotional resilience among mentored youth. *Mentoring & Tutoring: Partnership in Learning, 21*(4), 378-391.

Review of Developmental Assets Profile by THOMAS P. HOGAN, Emeritus Professor of Psychology, University of Scranton, Scranton, PA:

DESCRIPTION. The Developmental Assets Profile (DAP) aims to assess self-reported standing with respect to assets as defined in Search Institute's framework of experiences, relationships, behaviors, and values. The framework encompasses 40 such assets, 20 external and 20 internal. DAP does not purport to tap each of the 40 assets, but its organization relates to categories of these assets. The instrument falls generally into what contemporary sources call social-emotional learning (SEL). DAP manuals identify its target group variously as individuals in Grades 4-12 or ages 11-18. It is intended for reporting scores for both individuals and groups.

DAP consists of 58 items. Each begins "I ...", "I am ...", or "I have ..." followed by short completions, such as "feel safe" or "parents who help me" (not actual items). Items use a common 4-point response scale: *not at all or rarely, somewhat or sometimes, very or often, extremely or almost always,* with response points for scoring of 0, 1, 2, and 3. The test manual gives a Flesch-Kincaid readability index of 5.7 for the 58 items.

DAP scores are organized into three categories (called Asset categories). First, there are four scales (Support, Empowerment, Boundaries and Expectations, Constructive Use of Time) summing to an External Assets score. Second, there are four scales (Commitment to Learning, Positive Values, Social Competencies, Positive Identity) summing to an Internal Assets score. The Internal and External Assets scores sum to a Total Assets score. Third, there are five scales (Personal, Social, Family, School, Community) called Context scores. Each scale within the Internal and External Assets categories comes from unique item sets within the 58 DAP items (i.e., none of the items contribute to more than one scale). In contrast, items for the Context scores overlap entirely with the Internal and External Assets scales, simply being different combinations of the items. The Context scales do not sum to a total score. Scores for individual areas are obtained by averaging responses (0, 1, 2, 3), then multiplying by 10, after applying certain rules for missing items, double marks, and other anomalies, yielding scores that range from 0 to 30. Internal and External Assets scores are obtained by averaging separate scale scores. The overall Total score is the sum of the Internal and External Assets scores, thus ranging from 0 to 60. DAP manuals refer to the scores as "scales." They are not scales in the sense of some type of conversion or standardization; they are simply raw scores based on summing responses.

DAP can be administered either online or in paper form. The DAP paper form consists of a two-sided sheet containing identification information, instructions for responding, the 58 DAP items, and space for marking responses. Instructions refer to "now or within the past three months" as the relevant time frame. Manuals state that typical completion time is about 10 minutes; for group administrations, including time to distribute materials and ensure understanding of directions, about 20 minutes is recommended.

Descriptions of the DAP for this review come from the following sources: an 80-page "user manual" (Search Institute, 2005; the 2005 manual); a 45-page "user guide" (Search Institute, 2016; the 2016 guide); a 63-page "strengths and supports" document (Search Institute, 2017; the 2017 document); and description of DAP on the Search Institute website. The 2016 guide is listed as "revised and updated," presumably referring to the 2005 manual. The 2017 document provides examples of the types of reports prepared by Search Institute for a group. None of the documents show examples of the types of reports for individuals. Oddly, this document also refers (just once, on page 11) to two versions of DAP, one for Grades 4-6 and another for Grades 6-12. This is the only reference to two versions of the instrument.

DEVELOPMENT. DAP has its origin in the Search Institute framework of "developmental assets," an assortment of values, experiences, and behaviors considered important for success in school and life. The Search Institute offers programs for developing these assets. It identifies 40 such assets. And it offers a longer survey, consisting of 156 items and requiring 40-50 minutes, called the Search Institute Profiles of Student Life: Attitudes and Behaviors (A&B survey). DAP is described as being complementary to the A&B survey, and obviously requires much less administration time.

DAP manuals provide very little information about the process of developing or trying out items. Manuals simply state that items were intended to measure assets within the Search Institute framework and that there was some pilot testing, without further description. From the 2005 manual to the 2016 guide, there were no revisions in items or test structure.

TECHNICAL. Data for technical characteristics of DAP come from two samples. The first consists of approximately 1,300 students in Grades 6-12 from one public school district in Minnesota. The second consists of approximately 1,100 students in Grades 6-8 from two schools in Oregon. Information provided about these samples is limited to gender and minimal information about race/ethnicity; for example, the Minnesota group is broken down by White and non-White and the Oregon group by several categories but not a Black/African American category. Although DAP materials give the target population as Grades 4-12, neither sample includes students in Grades 4 or 5, and data for Grades 9-12 come only from one school district in Minnesota. The Search Institute 2016 guide refers to reliability data from eight communities but provides no further information (e.g., grade/age, gender, race/ethnicity, socioeconomic status) about these samples other than state.

The 2005 manual provides internal consistency (coefficient alpha) reliability estimates for each of the scales separately for the Minnesota and Oregon samples. Results for individual scales range from as low as .50 to the lower .90s, with an average of .81. Alpha coefficients for total scores (Internal, External, and Total) center in the mid-.90s. For the eight community studies mentioned in the 2016 guide, alpha coefficients are given only for the internal and external subscores, not for the total scores or context scales. Values ranged from .44 to the upper .80s with an overall median of .78. A sample of 225 students completed the DAP twice with a 2-week interval between sessions, yielding test-retest reliability coefficients averaging .79 for subscores and .86 for total scores. A sample of 161 students completed DAP with a 1-year interval, yielding stability coefficients generally in the mid-.60s.

Validity evidence derives from correlations between DAP and the A&B survey, plus self-reported grades, for "more than 1,300 youth in grades six through 12" (Search Institute, 2005, p. 36), presumably the Minnesota group. Correlation coefficients for DAP scales and various indices from the A&B survey and grades tend to be moderate. The 2005 manual also reported correlation coefficients around .70 between one of the DAP scales (Positive Identity) and two measures of self-esteem (Rosenberg's Self-Esteem Scale and Harter's Global Self-Worth Scale) based on a sample of 320 public school students in Grades 6-12. Correlations of these two measures with the other DAP scales are not reported. Finally, the test manual reports mean scores on DAP for a middle school judged more asset-rich versus a middle school judged less asset-rich. The manual reports the differences as significant; effect sizes are not reported. Mean differences on individual scales average about two points on the 0-30 scales. The manuals provide neither information about correlations among the DAP scales themselves nor other indexes of overall structure (e.g., factor structure). DAP manuals do not address the issue of fairness.

DAP's 2005 manual argues for criterion-referenced (what it calls "theoretical") interpretation of scores rather than norm-referenced interpretation. For all scales, the manual gives score ranges corresponding to four levels (low, fair, good, and excellent), with comparable raw score ranges for each. The manual also provides what it calls preliminary norms based on combining all the cases from the Minnesota and Oregon samples. These norms are presented as quartile points.

COMMENTARY. In general, DAP materials leave much to be desired. Lack of information about the two pilot testing groups is a major shortcoming for virtually all of the data presented in the manuals. The *Standards for Educational and Psychological Testing* (American Educational Research Association, American Psychological Association, & National Council on Measurement in Education, 2014) refers repeatedly to the need for careful description of groups used for determination of reliability, validity, and norms. DAP clearly fails to meet these requirements. Failure to provide any data for Grades 4-5, despite recommending use in those grades, is inexcusable. The 2005 manual refers to more studies to come, including provision of more representative norms, but the 2016 guide provides no new information; it simply repeats the presentation of the 2005 analyses.

DAP manuals do not provide a forthright assessment of the instrument's psychometric quality. For example, the 2005 manual refers to the "relatively high" (p. 33 and p. 41) internal consistency of scales when the data show some coefficients in the .40s and .50s. In numerous places, DAP materials simply state that it is "a reliable and valid" assessment. In this reviewer's opinion, such statements are clearly overgeneralizations. Some of the scales have good reliability; some do not. Other than serving as a kind of opinion poll for individual items, it is difficult to discern what constructs DAP might be measuring. Lack of any exploration of the structure of the DAP items and scales is a significant deficiency. The 2005 manual states in a number of places (e.g., pp. 35, 39, 40) that there are no relevant assessments (other than the A&B survey) against which to validate DAP. That is not true. There are many extant instruments touching on constructs very similar to DAP's, as illustrated in the extensive lists provided by American Institutes for Research (AIR; 2019); Collaborative for Academic, Social, and Emotional Learning (CASEL; 2019); and RAND Education and Labor (2019).

SUMMARY. For organizations or schools using the Search Institute developmental program, the DAP might merit use, with considerable caution, in Grades 6-12, but not at all in Grades 4-5. For others seeking an assessment in the general area of social-emotional learning, the DAP cannot be recommended. Several more well-developed and better-documented instruments are available. On the face of it, the DAP items and the general notion of assessing self-perceived assets make sense. With considerable additional work, DAP might be a useful addition to the array of SEL assessments, but that work needs to be done.

REVIEWER'S REFERENCES

American Educational Research Association, American Psychological Association, & National Council on Measurement in Education. (2014). *Standards for educational and psychological testing*. Washington, DC: American Educational Research Association.

American Institutes for Research. (2019). Stop, Think, Act: Ready to Assess (2nd ed.). Retrieved from https://www.air.org/resource/are-you-ready-assess-social-and-emotional-development

Collaborative for Academic, Social, and Emotional Learning. (2019). CASEL Assessment Guide. Retrieved from https://measuringsel.casel.org/assessment-guide/

RAND Education and Labor. (2019). RAND Education Assessment Finder. Retrieved from https://www.rand.org/education-and-labor/projects/assessments.html

Search Institute. (2005). *Developmental Assets Profile: User manual.* Minneapolis, MN: Author.

Search Institute. (2016). *User guide for the Developmental Assets Profile.* Minneapolis, MN: Author.

Search Institute. (2017). *Strengths and supports in the lives of Search Institute sample youth: Based on the results from the Developmental Assets Profile.* Minneapolis, MN: Author.

[48]

Developmental Behavior Checklist 2.

Purpose: Designed to assess "emotional and behavioral problems in children, adolescents, and adults who have intellectual and developmental disability."
Population: Ages 4 and older.
Publication Date: 2018.
Acronym: DBC2.
Administration: Individual.
Forms, 3: Parent, Teacher, Adult.
Price Data, 2019: $155 per online child kit including online manual (2018, 88 pages), 25 uses of the online parent form, and 25 uses of the online teacher form; $122 per online adult kit including online manual and 25 uses of the online adult form; $9 per 5 uses of the online form (Parent, Teacher, or Adult), volume discounts available; $83 per online manual.
Time: Approximately 20 minutes for completion of each form.
Comments: Administered online or via paper and pencil form; all scoring must be completed online.
Authors: Kylie Gray, Bruce Tonge, Stewart Einfeld, Christian Gruber, and Amber Klein.
Publisher: Western Psychological Services.

a) DEVELOPMENTAL BEHAVIOR CHECKLIST 2–PARENT FORM.
Population: Ages 4-18.
Acronym: DBC2–P.
Scores, 6: Disruptive, Self-Absorbed, Communication Disturbance, Anxiety, Social Relating, Total.

b) DEVELOPMENTAL BEHAVIOR CHECKLIST 2–TEACHER FORM.
Population: Ages 4-18.
Acronym: DBC2–T.
Scores, 6: Same as *a)* above.

c) DEVELOPMENTAL BEHAVIOR CHECKLIST 2–ADULT FORM.
Population: Ages 18 and older.
Acronym: DBC2–A.
Scores, 6: Disruptive, Communication and Anxiety Disturbance, Self-Absorbed, Depressive, Social Relating, Total.

Review of the Developmental Behavior Checklist 2 by RYAN J. KETTLER, Associate Professor, Rutgers University, New Brunswick, NJ, and LEAH DEMBITZER, Assistant Professor, Concordia College New York, Bronxville, NY:

DESCRIPTION. The Developmental Behavior Checklist 2 (DBC2) is a rating scale that assesses emotional and behavioral difficulties in individuals with intellectual and developmental disabilities (IDD). The measure contains three forms: (a) the DBC2-P for parents and caregivers of individuals ages 4 to 18, (b) the DBC2-T for teachers of individuals ages 4 to 18, and (c) the DBC2-A for adults who are rating other adults ages 18 and older. There is some variation in the number of items per form, from 94 items on the DBC2-T to 107 items on the DBC2-A; all items are rated on a 3-point scale. The test yields a Total Score and five subscale scores in the form of T scores that take into account the categories of IDD (i.e., mild, moderate, severe, profound). In addition, each form contains "flagged" critical items. For the child versions, the five subscales are Disruptive, Self-Absorbed, Communication Disturbance, Anxiety, and Social Relating. For the adult version, the subscales are Disruptive, Communication and Anxiety Disturbance, Self-Absorbed, Depressive, and Social Relating. In addition, three scores provide information about the range and intensity of the difficulties: Mean Item Score, Proportion of Items Checked, and Intensity Score.

The test authors provide examples of some applications of the DBC2 including (a) to complement an initial assessment in a clinical setting, (b) for use as a pre- and post-measure for intervention monitoring, (c) to provide standardized documentation of behavior for service planning purposes, and (d) for use as a screening tool to identify individuals at risk for emotional and behavioral difficulties.

Administration. The DBC2 is administered electronically on the test publisher's online platform or on paper. Administration is untimed and is generally completed within 20 minutes. The professional manual provides instructions for administration and guidelines for interpreting the results and cautions that the DBC2 is intended for use by practitioners in mental health or related fields with relevant assessment qualifications.

Scoring. The DBC2 is scored online, and a score report is generated automatically. Raw scores, T scores, and ranges of concern are provided for the Total Score and the subscales. A 95% confidence interval and clinical cutoff score are provided for the Total Score. All T scores also are presented on a plotted chart, and flagged items that have been endorsed are listed along with the Mean Item Score, Proportion of Items Checked, and Intensity Score. There is an option to generate a report for monitoring progress based on multiple administrations at different points in time as well as an option to compare forms from different respondents. Results from the DBC2-P and DBC2-T can be compared; the DBC2-A can be compared only with other DBC2-A forms. Up to five specific items can be selected to administer and include in a daily Item Level Progress Monitoring Report.

DEVELOPMENT. The first iteration of the DBC was developed by coding the descriptive data from the developmental and psychological assessment of 1,000 children with intellectual disabilities in Australia. The descriptive data were consolidated into 135 descriptions, which were then reviewed by four experts (psychiatrists and psychologists), and 95 descriptions were retained. The DBC was then written in parent-friendly language, and a highly parallel teacher form was developed as well. The subscales were derived through exploratory factor analytic procedures and confirmed with confirmatory factor analytic procedures. The 106 items on the adult form were developed through the coding of 660 clinical files and the evaluation of items on the DBC-P form. Factor analytic procedures were used to determine the factor structure. In developing the DBC2, the authors indicated minimal changes were made to the subscale structure based on Jackson's (1971) method of review of subscale structure. On the parent and teacher forms, three items were moved among subscales for the DBC2 revision, five items were deleted, and four items were added to a subscale. For the adult form, seven items were moved among subscales, four were deleted, and two items were added to a subscale.

TECHNICAL.

Standardization. Norming samples were collected for both the child population (for the DBC2-P and the DBC2-T) and the adult population (for the DBC2-A). Both samples included only persons diagnosed with IDD.

The child norming sample was based on 1,154 ratings of 593 children ages 4 to 18. The sample was acceptably matched to the U.S. population regarding ethnicity/race, parents' educational levels, and geographic region. Frequencies and percentages of the sample were available for groups labeled as Asian, Black/African American, Hispanic/Latino, Native American, White, Multiple, and Other. The sample included more male children (n = 350, 59.0%) than female children (n = 243, 41.0%). The sample included an even balance of children with mild (n = 186, 31.4%), moderate (n = 181, 30.5%), and severe IDD (n = 165, 27.8%), with a somewhat lower proportion in the profound category (n = 61, 10.3%).

The adult norming sample was based on 330 individuals with IDD, ages 18 to 89, rated once each by a caregiver or relative. This sample also was acceptably matched to the U.S. population regarding ethnicity/race, although Asians were somewhat underrepresented (1.5% of the sample compared to 5.1% of the population) and Native Americans were somewhat overrepresented (4.5% versus 0.7%). Frequencies and percentages of the sample were also available for groups labeled as Black/African American, Hispanic/Latino, White, Multiple, and Other. By geographic region, the sample was only moderately matched to the U.S. population; as the test authors noted, mismatch with geographic region is unlikely to impact the functioning of this measure. The sample included slightly more male adults (n = 185, 56.1%) than female adults (n = 145, 43.9%). The sample included an even balance of individuals with mild (n = 128, 38.8%) and moderate (n = 121, 36.7%) IDD, with somewhat lower proportions in the severe (n = 49, 14.8%) and profound (n = 32, 9.7%) categories.

Because large effect sizes were observed between degree of IDD and DBC2 scores, scores are provided using subsamples of degree of IDD (e.g., mild, moderate) as well as the entire child and adult samples as reference groups. These scores for subsamples are based on much smaller samples. In addition to the U.S. norming samples, the test authors provided information on the original Australian sample.

Reliability. Reliability evidence is provided in three forms: coefficient alpha, test-retest stability, and cross-informant agreement. Alpha coefficients exceeded .94 at the Total Score level for all three forms, regardless of whether the calculation was based on the full sample or a category-specific subsample. For the child forms, alpha coefficients were higher for the Disruptive and Self-Absorbed subscales (coefficients ranged from .87 to .95 across forms and samples) than for the other three subscales (coefficients ranged from .61 to .85 across forms and samples). For the adult form, coefficients were higher for the Disruptive subscale (range of .92 to .94 across samples) than for the Communication and Anxiety Disturbance and Self-Absorbed subscales (range of .83 to .87 across samples), which were higher than for the Depressive and Social Relating subscales (range of .71 to .81 across samples). Based on an interval of 1 to 3 weeks, test-retest stability was in the very high to nearly perfect range; rs ranged from .84 to .99, and effect sizes for score changes ranged from 0.01 to 0.16. Cross-informant agreement was presented for the child form using interclass correlations, which ranged from .53 to .97. Additional reliability evidence was provided from the original DBC, based on the rationale that the DBC2 has the same items and Total Score and very similar subscales as the original measure.

Validity Evidence Based on Content. The test authors based item development for the original DBC on qualitative analysis of behavioral disorders within files of persons already diagnosed with IDD. No quantitative nor evaluative review of DBC2 content, in either pilot or final form, was reported. A focus group of parents of children with autism spectrum disorder endorsed the original DBC as the best of four measures of behavior with regard to several accessibility and content validity characteristics (Chandler et al., 2016).

Validity Evidence Based on Internal Structure. The five subscales of the original DBC for children were derived using exploratory factor analysis, then subsequently validated through confirmatory factor analysis (Einfeld & Tonge, 1995) and other factor analytic studies (Dekker, Nunn, Einfeld, Tonge, & Koot, 2002). To develop the DBC2, its authors used a process that favors maximizing item-to-total correlations within subscales (Jackson, 1971). Although items were moved between subscales to create the second edition, no additional evidence of internal structure (e.g., confirmatory factor analysis, correlations among subscales) was reported for the DBC2.

Validity Evidence Based on Relations to Other Variables. Evidence based on relations to other variables was not collected for the DBC2; psychometric evidence from the original DBC was included in the test manual. Convergent validity evidence for the DBC (child version) Total Score has been found with positive correlations with measures of behavioral difficulties in the very large range (rs = .72 to .86). Discriminant validity has been found with negative correlations in the nonexistent range (r = -.06) to medium range (r = -.43) with measures of adaptive behavior (Dekker et al., 2002). DBC-P total scores also correlated in the very large range (r = .81) with independent ratings of the severity of emotional and behavioral difficulties (Einfield & Tonge, 1995), and scores were found to be higher for children with previous clinical diagnoses based on the *Diagnostic and Statistical Manual of Mental Disorders* (4th ed., text rev.; *DSM-IV-TR*; American Psychiatric Association, 2000; Dekker, Nunn, & Koot, 2002).

Convergent validity evidence also has been reported for the DBC-A. The Total Score has been found to correlate in the large to very large range (*r*s = .61 to .77) with measures of behavioral difficulties.

COMMENTARY. Across forms, the arguments for interpretation of DBC2 scores are limited. Although the norming samples for the measures are acceptable (593 children and 330 adults), interpretation is recommended based on specific category of IDD, for which the samples are smaller (165 to 186 for mild, moderate, and severe IDD) and much smaller for profound IDD (n = 61) yielding potentially less accurate normative scores. The Total Score is internally consistent enough for interpretation as part of high-stakes decision making, as are some of the subscales across forms of the DBC2. Communication Disturbance on the DBC2-P and DBC2-T and Depressive and Social Relating on the DBC2-A are subscales that may be appropriate to use as part of low-stakes decision making. Anxiety and Social Relating on the DBC2-P and DBC2-T are not internally consistent enough to be used as part of decision making. Evidence of test stability was strong.

The lack of several types of evidence of validity is problematic. Evidence based on response processes was not included; including a validity index on the scales could have partially addressed this evidence. The lack of evidence based on internal structure is problematic given the re-organization of several items between subscales; evidence for the DBC internal structure is not sufficient for the revision. In the same area, a correlation matrix of subscale scores would provide some evidence if it indicated there exists substantial divergence among the various scales. The evidence based on relations with other variables presented is acceptable for the Total Score; the evidence based on subscales of the original DBC is not entirely relevant because of the shifting of items for the DBC2 revision.

SUMMARY. The DBC2 may be an appropriate test for some of its proposed applications. The biggest limitations of the assessment are the following: the DBC2 normative subsamples by IDD category are small, several subscales are not internally consistent, and validity evidence is based largely on the previous version of the measure. The Total Score and the more internally consistent subscales may be used to complement an initial assessment and for intervention monitoring. Those scores also may be used for standardized documentation, although interpreters should be mindful of whether they are using the full sample (yielding a likely more accurate normative score across categories of IDD) or the category-specific subsample (yielding a likely less accurate normative score specific to category). Typical evidence of the validity of screening scores, such as classification accuracy for predicting criteria, was not provided for the DBC2.

REVIEWERS' REFERENCES

American Psychiatric Association. (2000). *Diagnostic and statistical manual of mental disorders* (4th ed., text rev.). Washington, DC: Author.

Chandler, S., Howlin, P., Simonoff, E., O'Sullivan, T., Tseng, E., Kennedy, J., ... Baird, G. (2016). Emotional and behavioural problems in young children with autism spectrum disorder. *Developmental Medicine & Child Neurology, 58*(2), 202-208.

Dekker, M. C., Nunn, R., Einfeld, S. E., Tonge, B. J., & Koot, H. M. (2002). Assessing emotional and behavioural problems in children with intellectual disability: Revising the factor structure of the Developmental Behavior Checklist. *Journal of Autism and Developmental Disorders, 32*(6), 601-610.

Dekker, M. C., Nunn, R., & Koot, H. M. (2002). Psychometric properties of the revised Developmental Behavior Checklist scales in Dutch children with intellectual disability. *Journal of Intellectual Disability Research, 46*(1), 61-75.

Einfeld, S. E., & Tonge, B. J. (1995). The Developmental Behaviour Checklist: The development and validation of an instrument to assess behavioral and emotional disturbance in children and adolescents with mental retardation. *Journal of Autism and Developmental Disorders, 25*(2), 81-104.

Jackson, D. N. (1971). The dynamics of structured personality tests: 1971. *Psychological Review, 78*(3), 229-248.

Review of the Developmental Behavior Checklist 2 by LAURA L. PENDERGAST, Associate Professor, and STEPHANIE JOSEPH, Doctoral Student, Temple University, Philadelphia, PA:

DESCRIPTION. The Developmental Behavior Checklist 2 (DBC2) is a rating scale that is intended to assess emotional and behavioral problems among individuals (children, adolescents, and adults) with intellectual and developmental disability (IDD). The measure's authors make a compelling argument that emotional and behavioral problems may manifest differently in individuals with IDD and that other measures may not sufficiently identify the challenges children and adults with IDD experience. The DBC2 includes forms for ratings by parents and teachers and by adults who are rating other adults. Forms can be completed online or on paper in approximately 20 minutes. All forms, regardless of administration format, are scored online. The test developers state that the DBC2 "can be used for clinical, educational, and research purposes" (manual, p. 3) but note that, if used diagnostically, the DBC2 should be used in conjunction with other comprehensive assessment tools. DBC2 scores should be interpreted by professionals with "relevant training and experience in psychological and educational assessments, as well as training or experience in child development, psychology, psychiatry, or other mental health professions" (manual, p. 3).

The parent form of the DBC2 includes 96 items and is intended for parents/guardians of children ages 4 to 18. The teacher form includes 94 items and is intended for teachers or teachers' aides of children ages 4 to 18. The version for adults rated by others includes 107 items and can be completed by parents or other long-term adult caregivers for individuals ages 18 and older. Raters respond to each item using a 3-point scale (0 = *not true as far as you know*; 1 = *somewhat true or sometimes true*; 2 = *very true or often true*).

For the parent and teacher versions of the DBC2, subscale scores (reported as T scores) are available for the following subscales: Disruptive, Self-Absorbed, Communication Disturbance, Anxiety, and Social Relating. The form for adults rated by caregivers includes the following subscales: Disruptive, Communication and Anxiety Disturbance, Self-Absorbed, Depressive, and Social Relating. Additional scores that can be calculated are a Mean Item Score, Proportion of Items Checked, and an Intensity Score (IS).

DEVELOPMENT. The original version of the DBC (Einfeld & Tonge, 1995) was developed using a sample from Australia. The items for the DBC parent and teacher versions were derived from the reviews of case files of 5,000 children and adolescents with IDD. Subsequently, 7,000 children with intellectual disabilities in Australia were given what the test authors describe as comprehensive developmental and psychological assessments, and both parents and teachers provided ratings for the children. In regard to psychometric properties, the original version of the scale demonstrated a test-retest reliability coefficient of .72. The interval between testing was not reported. Concurrent validity with similar measures was established, and cut scores were derived using receiver operating characteristics (ROC) analyses. Structural validity of the original version was based on principal components analysis of a polychoric correlation matrix with oblique rotation. A five-factor solution was identified with the parent version and applied to the teacher version. An independent research team (Bontempo et al., 2008) conducted a confirmatory factor analysis, and its findings supported the general structure and two of the factors (Disruptive/Antisocial and Self Absorbed) but raised concern about the remaining three factors. The test authors state that the adult version of the original DBC followed a similar development process.

According to the test developers, the primary purpose for revising the DBC was to increase the extent to which the scale can be used internationally. Therefore, the revised version included child and adult reference samples from the United States. Additionally, minor wording changes were made to items to increase consistency with American English.

The normative samples for the DBC2 were from the United States. Participants in the child/adolescent sample were 593 individuals ages 4 to 18, the majority of whom were rated by both a parent and a teacher (581 teacher ratings, 573 parent ratings). The samples included individuals from across the spectrum of severity of IDD (mild to profound; *ns* = 61-186). Participants from throughout the United States were included. Of the total sample, 58.5% were White, 17.6% Latino, 14.2% African American, 3% Asian, and 1.9% Native American. The adult sample was composed of 330 adults ages 18 to 89 (*ns* = 32-128 for profound to mild disability status). The demographics of the adult sample were similar to the child sample. In both the child and adult samples, participants had a mean IQ score between 40 and 60. All individuals in the sample had a diagnosis of IDD and were currently receiving some form of treatment.

TECHNICAL.

Reliability. In these reviewers' opinion, interrater reliability was acceptable and consistent with what is commonly found in behavioral rating scales with relatively low correspondence between parent and teacher forms (interclass correlation coefficients of .76 for the Total Score and from .64-.80 for the subscales in the total sample). Test-retest reliability was evaluated over a period of 1 to 3 weeks with samples ranging in size from 29 to 42. Coefficients ranged from .86 to .98 for the parent and teacher forms and from .82 to .99 for the adult form. Internal consistency estimates for the Total Score and for the majority of the subscale scores on the DBC2-P and DBC2-T were sufficient (.80-.99). However, for some subgroups, particularly those with more severe IDD, reliability fell below .70 for the Anxiety and Social Relating subscales. The authors do note in the test manual that the Total Score has stronger psychometric support than the subscale scores (as is true with most measures).

Validity. In regard to validity, the scale developers described using the Jackson method developed in 1971 (Jackson, 1971) to evaluate consistency between the original and revised versions of the scale. Aside from the Jackson method, no analyses of validity evidence specific to the DBC2 were reported in the test manual. Instead, the developers relied primarily upon validity analyses from the original DBC, which had differently worded items and, more importantly in these reviewers' view, a culturally different sample. No invariance or measurement equivalence studies were reported in the test manual. Likewise, cut scores from the original DBC were retained, and no new analyses were conducted to evaluate whether those cut scores were applicable in a United States population and with the revised items. In addition, the purposes for which practitioners should use the three supplementary scores (i.e., Mean Item Score, Proportion of Items Checked, and Intensity Score) are not clearly described, and psychometric support for the scores is not discussed in the manual.

COMMENTARY. The DBC2 is a tool that appears to fill an important need. As noted by the measure's authors, behavioral and emotional symptoms often manifest differently among individuals with IDD. The success of interventions for emotional and behavioral symptoms among those with IDD is dependent upon the ability to accurately assess symptoms with this population. The development of the DBC2 is a promising step in that direction.

In regard to psychometric properties, fairly extensive analyses were conducted on the original DBC. Those findings largely supported the reliability, structural validity evidence, and concurrent evidence of validity of the original version of the DBC with an Australian sample—although independent researchers have raised some concerns about some of the subscale scores (Bontempo et al., 2008). For the revised version, the DBC2, reliability analyses were conducted with the new sample, and those generally supported the use of the scale, particularly the Total Score.

No validity analyses of the DBC2 were reported. Moreover, no analyses examining the measurement invariance/equivalence of the two versions of the scale or the two samples (United States and Australian) were reported. Yet, the cutoff scores for the original DBC were applied to the revised version without supporting evidence for such a decision. Despite the fact that the test authors describe the item changes as minor, neither the equivalence of the two versions nor the cultural equivalence of the United States and Australian samples should be assumed without evidence. Numerous researchers have written about the critical need to establish measurement invariance prior to using a measurement tool with a new cultural group (e.g., Chen, 2008; Pendergast, von der Embse, Kilgus, & Eklund, 2017; Vandenberg & Lance, 2000). In addition, the sample sizes used with the United States sample were quite small–particularly for the adult version. Finally, data were collected in treatment centers; thus, individuals in the DBC2 normative sample were likely to have been receiving treatment and may differ in important ways from individuals with IDD who may not be receiving treatment. Collectively, these issues raise concern regarding the extent to which the DBC2 is ready for use by practitioners.

SUMMARY. In summary, the DBC2 appears to be a promising tool that has the potential to support practitioners in addressing an important area of need. It is reasonably priced and relatively quick to administer, and online scoring is available. Unfortunately, virtually no validity analyses of the revised version that used a United States normative sample have been reported in the test manual. Therefore, while the DBC2 may be promising, further research and validation of scores from the revised version are necessary before the DBC2 can be recommended for use in school or clinical settings.

REVIEWERS' REFERENCES

Bontempo, D. E., Hofer, S. M., Mackinnon, A., Piccinin, A. M., Gray, K., Tonge, B., & Einfeld, S. (2008). Factor structure of the Developmental Behavior Checklist using confirmatory factor analysis of polytomous items. *Journal of Applied Measurement, 9*(3), 265-280.

Chen, F. F. (2008). What happens if we compare chopsticks with forks? The impact of making inappropriate comparisons in cross-cultural research. *Journal of Personality and Social Psychology, 95*, 1005–1018.

Einfeld, S. L., & Tonge, B. J. (1995). The Developmental Behavior Checklist: The development and validation of an instrument to assess behavioral and emotional disturbance in children and adolescents with mental retardation. *Journal of Autism and Developmental Disorders, 25*(2), 81-104.

Jackson, D. N. (1971). The dynamics of structured personality tests: 1971. *Psychological Review, 78*, 229–248.

Pendergast, L. L., von der Embse, N., Kilgus, S. P., & Eklund, K. R. (2017). Measurement equivalence: A non-technical primer on categorical multi-group confirmatory factor analysis in school psychology. *Journal of School Psychology, 60*, 65-82.

Vandenberg, R. J., & Lance, C. E. (2000). A review and synthesis of the measurement invariance literature: Suggestions, practices, and recommendations for organizational research. *Organizational Research Methods, 3*, 4–70.

[49]

Devereux Early Childhood Assessment for Preschoolers, Second Edition.

Purpose: Designed to evaluate within-child protective factors and to identify children who may be exhibiting emotional and behavioral problems.

Population: Ages 3-0 to 6-0.

Publication Dates: 1999-2012.

Acronym: DECA–P2.

Scores, 5: Initiative, Self-Regulation, Attachment/Relationships, Total Protective Factors, Behavioral Concerns.

Administration: Individual.

Price Data, 2020: $229.95 per kit including manual (2012, 136 pages), strategy guide (2012, 402 pages),

2 copies of Building Your Bounce: Simple Strategies for a Resilient You (2013, 80 pages), 20 family guides, 1 copy of Flip It: Transforming Challenging Behavior (2011, 94 pages), and 40 record forms.
Foreign Language Edition: Rating form available in Spanish.
Time: Administration time not reported.
Comments: Revision of the Devereux Early Childhood Assessment; online administration and scoring available; ratings by teachers and parents; rater needs to observe child's behavior for at least 4 weeks.
Authors: Paul A. LeBuffe and Jack A. Naglieri.
Publisher: Kaplan Early Learning Company.
Cross References: For reviews by Eric S. Buhs and Mary M. Chittooran of the original edition titled Devereux Early Childhood Assessment, see 15:81.

Review of the Devereux Early Childhood Assessment for Preschoolers, Second Edition by TRACY THORNDIKE, Associate Professor of Special Education and Education Leadership, Western Washington University, Bellingham, WA:

DESCRIPTION. The Devereux Early Childhood Assessment for Preschoolers, Second Edition (DECA–P2) is part of the Devereux family of assessments (e.g., DECA–I/T for infants and toddlers, Devereux Student Strengths Assessment for children Grades K-8) and is designed to measure resilience-related strengths as well as screen for behavioral concerns in children ages 3-5 (i.e., third birthday until the sixth birthday). The DECA–P2 is a standardized, norm-referenced behavior rating scale that may be completed by parents and by professionals working in early childhood settings (e.g., preschools, childcare centers). Raters use a 5-point rating scale (i.e., 0 = *never* to 4 = *very frequently*) to indicate the frequency with which they have observed 27 positive behaviors. From these ratings, four scale scores may be derived: three representing the individual within-child protective factors Initiative, Self-Regulation, and Attachment/Relationships and one representing overall Total Protective Factors. An additional 11 items make up a fifth scale assessing Behavioral Concerns. Raw scores are converted to percentile ranks and finally to standard scores (i.e., T-scores with a mean of 50 and a standard deviation of 10) for interpretation. Results for a single child on all five scales may be displayed on an Individual Child Profile, and T-score values may then be compared to cut scores tied to descriptive categories to determine areas of strength, typical behavior, and areas of need. Because a child's behavior often differs across environmental settings and in the presence of different adults, different norms are provided for scores derived from parent ratings versus those based on teacher observations. Whole classroom/group profiles also may be generated if examining the relative strengths and needs of a group of children is desired. The DECA–P2 is available in both English and Spanish and in both an online and paper version.

DEVELOPMENT. Development of the DECA–P2 began with a review of items from the original Devereux Early Childhood Assessment (DECA; LeBuffe & Naglieri, 1999) coupled with feedback from various stakeholders including DECA program users, the DECA revision advisory board, and staff at the Devereux Center for Resilient Children. Several original items were removed, other items were revised to improve clarity and/or reduce the reading level required, and new items were written to assess a potential new protective factor, "approaches to learning." Ultimately, 59 items were included in the standardization edition of the DECA–P2.

The initial standardization sample consisted of 4,964 protocols, 2,133 of which were filled out by parents or other relatives living with the child and 2,831 completed by teachers or other professionals working in early childcare or educational settings. Participants were recruited from all geographic regions of the U.S. with efforts made to adequately represent the United States population of young children in terms of gender, race/ethnicity, and socioeconomic status. Data were collected using both the online and paper versions of the rating form. To avoid overlap with the infant/toddler version of the DECA, the initial sample was trimmed by removing records for all 2-year-olds. A final standardization sample of 3,553 protocols (1,416 completed by parents, 2,137 by teachers) that matched the demographic characteristics of 3- to 5-year-olds (i.e., third birthday through sixth birthday) found in the 2010 U.S. Census was created by randomly dropping cases from overrepresented groups.

Organization of items into scales was informed by factor analysis. As with the original DECA (1999), protective factor items loaded onto three factors (i.e., Initiative, Self-Regulation, and Attachment/Relationships) with solutions for parents and teachers looking very similar. New items related to "approaches to learning" did not constitute a new factor; these items loaded onto the original three protective factors. The final Behavioral

Concerns scale consisted of items chosen based on (a) their psychometric properties (e.g., reliability, item-total correlations) and (b) the breadth of concerning behaviors represented. Development of the DECA–P2 resulted in one 38-item rating form that may be used by raters with different types of relationships to a child (i.e., parent, teacher).

TECHNICAL. The sample upon which norms are based is representative of the U.S. population of children ages 3-5 years in terms of race/ethnicity, socioeconomic status (defined as eligibility for food stamps), and geographic region, and includes an equal number of males and females. Parents in the sample were somewhat more highly educated than is typical of parents generally (Makun & Wilson, 2011).

No age trend was observed in these data, so scores of all preschool-aged children can be interpreted relative to the same set of norms. Although girls' scores on the protective factor scales are somewhat higher than boys' and their scores on the Behavioral Concerns scale somewhat lower, these score differences reflect real gender differences in children's behavior. Consequently, both boys' and girls' scores can be compared to the same set of norms. Different norms are provided for scale scores derived from parent ratings and those derived from teacher ratings. Parents and teachers have different types of relationships with children and interact with them in different settings with differing expectations for behavior. Therefore it is useful to compare a child's scores to those of other children observed by the same type of rater in the same type of setting to determine whether that child's behavior is typical or represents an area of strength or need.

To obtain norms, raw score frequency distributions for each protective factor scale and the Behavioral Concerns scale were fitted to normal probability standard scores then smoothed. From there, T-scores were computed and cutoffs for interpretive categories were assigned.

Multiple approaches were used to assess the reliability of scale scores on the DECA–P2. In each case, estimates were calculated separately for different types of raters (i.e., parents, teachers). Internal consistency estimates for the Total Protective Factors scale were .92 for parents and .95 for teachers. Coeffcients for the individual protective factor scale scores ranged from .79 to .94 with median internal consistency estimates of .88 and .92 for parent and teacher raters, respectively. Internal consistency estimates for the Behavioral Concerns scale were .80 for parents and .86 for teachers. Test-retest data show high correlations between the ratings given by both parents and teachers over an approximately one-week interval, indicating that there is virtually no fluctuation for scale scores over short spans of time. Additional analysis showed that the actual T-scores obtained by children at pre- and post-test were almost identical, further bolstering evidence for the assertion that DECA–P2 scores are stable in the absence of intervention. Finally, interrater reliability was explored by comparing the scores derived from the ratings of pairs of parents living in the same home and of professionals working in the same educational setting. Correlations between the scores of paired raters demonstrated coefficients that ranged from a low of .36 to a high of .77 indicating that, in general, the same type of rater observing a particular child in the same environment tended to rate that child's behavior very similarly.

Results from numerous studies providing a variety of types of evidence establish a strong case for the validity of multiple score-based inferences derived from ratings of child behavior on the DECA–P2. Alignment of items with the breadth and boundaries of the domains of early childhood social-emotional competence and emotional and/or behavioral disturbances found in the relevant research literature and in the opinions of established content area experts constitutes content-related evidence. Large and statistically significant score differences were observed between children diagnosed or otherwise identified by a professional as having an "emotional or behavioral disturbance (EBD)" (manual, p. 63) and those not so identified on both the Total Protective Factors scale and the Behavioral Concerns scale. Further a Total Protective Factors score of less than or equal to 40 or a Behavioral Concerns scale score of greater than or equal to 60 (i.e., the cut scores used to identify an area of potential need) placed a majority of children into the correct EBD or non-identified group. Another study explored the appropriateness of the DECA–P2 for use with children from racial and ethnic minority groups. Differences in DECA–P2 scale scores between children grouped according to these construct irrelevant variables would undermine the validity of the assessment. However, when comparing scores from Black/African American and White children and from Hispanic and Non-Hispanic children, effect sizes were small or very small. These results indicate that similar interpretations of DECA–P2 scores are appropriate regardless of a child's racial or ethnic group membership. Taken together, these findings constitute considerable criterion-related evidence of validity. Finally, to develop convergent construct-related evidence, a series of studies explored the relationships between DECA–P2 scale scores and scores on other assessments of similar constructs. A sample of 45 parents and 56 teachers rated children on the DECA–P2, the Preschool Behavioral and Emotional Rating Scale (PreBERS) and the Conners Early Childhood scale (Conners EC) in a single observation setting with the order of assessments counter-balanced. T-scores on the DECA–P2 Total Protective Factors and Behavioral Concerns scales were correlated with standard scores on the PreBERS Strength Factor scale and the Conners EC Global Index (an indicator of social, emotional, and behavioral concerns) for both parents and teachers. The patterns of correlations were in the expected directions and moderate in magnitude, suggesting that scale scores on the DECA–P2 tap into similar strengths and concerns measured on other, established assessments of these constructs but also provide some unique information.

COMMENTARY. The DECA–P2 yields psychometrically sound measures of a child's social-emotional competencies and screens for behavioral concerns. A single rating form for both parents and teachers facilitates communication between families and professionals in educational settings because all informants observe and rate the same behaviors. Items are written in plain language, minimizing reading demands and need for rater inference about an item's meaning. This, coupled with the availability of forms in both English and Spanish, means that informants from a broad array of backgrounds can provide reliable and valid information about a child.

Administration and scoring of the DECA–P2 could not be easier. The multi-page record form makes score calculation simple, and instructions for building child profiles and interpreting patterns of strengths and needs are exceptionally clear. The meaning of each scale score is explained in family-friendly terms, and guidelines to help professionals communicate test results to families are included in the test manual. Users interested in more advanced applications such as program evaluation or calculation of percentage delay, required in some states to establish sufficient risk to access early prevention or intervention services, will find additional support material online. Overall, this assessment is remarkably user-friendly.

A major strength of the DECA–P2 is that it functions as part of an integrated preschool programming system that includes an extensive strategy guide for professionals working in early childhood educational settings. The system as a whole is designed to promote healthy social and emotional development in young children through strengthening protective factors related to resilience both at school and at home. As such, it aligns well with national and state standards for early childhood education and would help programs satisfy evidentiary requirements for funding and/or accreditation. Guidelines for using the DECA–P2 and its companion strategy guides in the context of a multi-tiered service delivery model are provided in the technical manual. Consequently, assessment results can assist teachers and other early education staff members in identifying areas of need to inform goal setting and selection of strategies to strengthen particular protective factors and/or decrease behavioral concerns at the universal, targeted, and expanded intervention levels. Additional testing following implementation of strategies allows for evaluation of the effectiveness of those interventions in achieving their intended purposes for both individual children and groups. New to this revision is the availability of individual item level analysis to facilitate the development of individual goals (e.g., individualized family service plan [IFSP] goals) by more easily pinpointing specific behaviors for intervention.

SUMMARY. The DECA–P2 has been substantially revised from its predecessor with changes to 25% of the content, modified scale names, and new norms based on a sample representative of the current population of the United States (Humes, Jones, & Ramirez, 2011; Makun & Wilson, 2011). The ease of administration, scoring, and score interpretation remain the same. The scores are reliable, and the validity of proposed score-based inferences is well supported. The DECA–P2 functions as part of an integrated preschool programming system with companion guides to support early childhood educators and families working to build resilience and decrease risk in young children. The clear connections between the behaviors rated on the DECA–P2 and the strategies for positively influencing those behaviors found in the programming guide make clear its appropriateness and utility in the context of contemporary standards-driven early childhood education, particularly for those settings utilizing multi-tiered models of instruction and support.

REVIEWER'S REFERENCES

Humes, K. R., Jones, N. A., & Ramirez, R. R. (2011, March). *Overview of race and Hispanic origin: 2010.* Retrieved from https://www.census.gov/prod/cen2010/briefs/c2010br-02.pdf

LeBuffe, P. A., & Naglieri, J. A. (1999). Devereux Early Childhood Assessment. Lewisville, NC: Kaplan Early Learning Company.

Makun, P., & Wilson, S. (2011, March). *Population distribution and change: 2000 to 2010.* Retrieved from https://www.census.gov/content/dam/Census/library/publications/2011/dec/c2010br-01.pdf

Review of the Devereux Early Childhood Assessment for Preschoolers, Second Edition by GEORGETTE YETTER, Associate Professor, School Psychology, Oklahoma State University, Stillwater, OK:

DESCRIPTION. The Devereux Early Childhood Assessment for Preschoolers, Second Edition (DECA–P2), a revision of the Devereux Early Childhood Assessment (LeBuffe & Naglieri, 1999), is a standardized, norm-referenced behavior rating scale for children ages 3-0 to 5-11. It is designed to be completed by home-based caregivers, such as parents and other family members, and by early childhood professionals, such as preschool teachers and child care providers. The DECA–P2 aims to identify children's social-emotional strengths (i.e., competencies or protective factors) and weaknesses (i.e., problem behaviors or behavioral concerns). A guidebook (Cairone & Mackrain, 2012) provides information about activities parents and teachers can engage in to strengthen children's social-emotional competencies and reduce problem behaviors in accordance with child resilience and social-emotional learning paradigms (e.g., Durlak, Weissberg, Dymnicki, Taylor, & Schellinger, 2011; Masten, Best, & Garmezy, 1991).

The DECA–P2 contains 38 items. There is a single version of the scale, designed to be completed by both parents and teachers. Using a 5-point Likert-type format, the rater indicates the frequency with which he or she has observed the target child engaging in specific behaviors over the past 4 weeks. A scoring sheet is attached to the form. Scoring is straightforward and can be completed in 5 to 10 minutes.

The DECA–P2 contains three 9-item protective factor scales (Initiative, Self-Regulation, and Attachment/Relationships), a composite Total Protective Factors scale, and a single 11-item Behavioral Concerns scale. After raw scores are computed on the scoring sheet, they are circled on a separate Individual Child Profile sheet, which allows for scores to be graphed easily and converted to T-scores and percentile ranks. A Classroom/Group Profile sheet also is provided to allow educators to evaluate and graphically display the strengths and weaknesses of groups of children. The Individual Child Profile provides separate conversion tables for parent and teacher raters. Protective factor scores are classified as *strengths* for T-scores of 60 or above, *typical* for T-scores of 41 to 59, and as *areas of need* for T-scores of 40 or below. Behavioral Concerns scores are classified as *typical* for T-scores of 59 or below and as *areas of need* for T-scores of 60 or above. An accompanying book, *Promoting Resilience in Preschoolers* (Cairone & Mackrain, 2012), offers specific strategies parents and teachers can use to enhance a child's initiative, self-regulation, and attachment and relationships. These strategies address healthy daily routines and activities, effective learning environments, positive interactions with children, and supportive parent-teacher partnerships.

DEVELOPMENT. Initial development of the DECA–P2 items was carried out by soliciting feedback from experts and clinicians on items contained in the DECA (LeBuffe & Naglieri, 1999) and by revising and deleting items based on this feedback. New items were written following a review of the childhood resilience and social-emotional learning literature. The resulting 59-item pilot instrument was administered to 1,416 home caregivers and 2,137 teachers of young children.

The three protective factor scales were derived using exploratory factor analysis, using a varimax rotation. No rationale was provided for using varimax rotation, which assumes that the resulting factors are expected to be uncorrelated. On the resulting protective factor scales, numerous items load on multiple scales at the .3 level. The final protective factor scales are substantially intercorrelated, with Pearson *r*s ranging from .53 to .69 (parents) and from .56 to .68 (teachers). Such substantial correlations raise questions about the distinctiveness of the three PF scales and about the adequacy of the scale derivation procedures. The items included in the Behavioral Concerns scale were not selected using factor analysis, but according to "their psychometric properties (e.g., reliability and item-total correlations) and their representation of a wide range of behaviors" (manual, p. 46).

TECHNICAL.

Standardization. The norm sample consisted of 3,553 children ages 3 years 0 months to 5 years 11 months, of whom 28% were 3-year-olds, 49%

were 4-year-olds, and 23% were 5-year-olds. Sample demographics approximated those of the U.S. population according to the 2010 Census by geographic region, sex, race, Hispanic ethnicity, percentage of children in poverty, and parent education.

Reliability. Internal consistency estimates of the DECA–P2 scale scores are good to excellent, with alpha coefficients ranging from .79 to .92 for parent ratings and from .85 to .95 for teacher ratings. Test-retest reliability over a period of 6 to 8 days was good to excellent, with correlation coefficients ranging from .78 to .88 for parent ratings (n = 53) and from .80 to .95 for teacher ratings (n = 37).

Interrater reliability was computed for a sample of 31 children rated by two parents and for a sample of 52 children rated by two educators. Overall interrater reliabilities were quite variable. Adjusted correlation coefficients ranged from .39 (Self-Regulation) to .76 (Attachment/Relationships) for ratings of the same child by two parents, with a median coefficient of .51 (Total Protective Factors). Adjusted correlation coefficients ranged from .36 (Attachment/Relationships) to .77 (Initiative) for ratings of the same child by two educators, with a median correlation coefficient of .70 (Behavioral Concerns). The test manual provides no information on agreement between parents' and educators' scores for a given child. The parent and educator samples differed in racial/ethnic composition. Whereas the children rated by two parents were primarily White and Asian, those rated by two educators were more racially diverse, and one-third were Black. The lack of demographic representativeness leaves questions about the interrater reliability of this instrument unanswered.

Validity. Criterion-related evidence of validity was examined in several ways. The test developers investigated the degree to which scale scores distinguished a sample of children previously identified as having "an emotional or behavioral disturbance [EBD], ... including AD/HD" (n = 125) from a demographically matched sample of non-identified children (n = 126). Large statistically significant group differences (p < .01) were evident for all scale scores (d = .58 to 1.09; Cohen, 1992).

The developers also explored the ability of the Total Protective Factors and Behavioral Concerns scales to predict whether a given child was drawn from the EBD or non-EBD group. Fifty-eight percent of children with Total Protective Factors T-scores of 40 or lower were correctly classified as EBD, and 75% of those with T-scores over 40 were correctly classified as non-EBD. Similarly, 70% of children with Behavioral Concerns T-scores of 60 or above were correctly classified as EBD, and 68% of those with T-scores below 60 were correctly classified as non-EBD.

Racial and ethnic differences in scale scores were analyzed. According to Cohen's (1992) criteria, small differences were evident in parent ratings of Black children and White children on the Attachment/Relationships and Behavioral Concerns scales. On average, parents of Black children rated their children lower in Attachment/Relationships and lower in Behavioral Concerns than did parents of White children. Small differences were evident in teacher ratings of Black children and White children on the Self-Regulation, Attachment/Relationships, Total Protective Factors, and Behavioral Concerns scales. On average, teachers rated Black children as lower in Self-Regulation, Attachment/Relationships, and Total Protective Factors and higher in Behavioral Concerns. Overall, both parents and teachers rated Hispanic children slightly lower than non-Hispanics in Attachment/Relationships. Racial-ethnic differences were negligible on all other scales. In sum, small racial/ethnic differences are evident in the majority of DECA–P2 scale scores. Further research is needed to explore the meaningfulness of these differences.

The convergent and discriminant validity of the scale scores were explored with 45 parents and 56 teachers. The Total Protective Factors and Behavioral Concerns scale scores were compared with the Strength Factor scale score on the Preschool Behavioral and Emotional Rating Scale (PreBERS; Epstein & Synhorst, 2009). As expected, the Total Protective Factors score evidenced large positive correlations with the PreBERS Strength Factor scale (corrected r = .63 for parents; corrected r = .78 for teachers). The Behavioral Concerns scale showed moderate to moderately large negative correlations with the PreBERS Strength Factor scale (corrected r = -.32 among parents and corrected r = -.70 among teachers). The Total Protective Factors and Behavioral Concerns scale scores also were compared with the Global Index scale score from the Conners Early Childhood scale (Conners EC; Conners, 2009). As anticipated, the Total Protective Factors scores showed moderate negative correlations with the Conners EC (corrected r = -.34 for parents; corrected r = -.41 for teachers). The Behavioral Concerns scale showed moderately large positive correlations with the Conners EC among both parents (corrected $r = .60$) and teachers (corrected $r = .64$). These results support the validity of the DECA–P2's Total Protective Factors and Behavioral Concerns scale scores.

COMMENTARY. The DECA–P2 sets out to evaluate young children's social-emotional strengths (protective factors) in accordance with resilience and attachment theories. It also includes a short, general measure of social-emotional weaknesses (behavioral concerns). A clearly written accompanying manual provides appropriate guidance for parents and teachers to build on these areas of strength by restructuring their interactions with the child. Although the DECA–P2 produces separate scores for three specific protective factors, users are advised to formally interpret only the Total Protective Factors composite and Behavioral Concerns scales and to interpret the individual protective factors scales only informally, due to questions about the distinctiveness of the protective factors scales.

SUMMARY. The DECA–P2, together with its accompanying manual, is a strengths-based instrument with reasonable evidence of the validity of its scores and their uses. This scale has the potential to be useful to help parents and teachers better understand young children's social-emotional strengths and needs and to develop interventions to benefit them.

REVIEWER'S REFERENCES

Cairone, K. B., & Mackrain, M. (2012). *Promoting resilience in preschoolers: A strategy guide for early childhood professionals* (2nd ed.). Villanova, PA: Devereux Foundation.

Cohen, J. (1992). A power primer. *Psychological Bulletin, 112,* 155-159.

Conners, C. K. (2009). *Conners Early Childhood manual.* Toronto, Canada: Multi-Health Systems.

Durlak, J. A., Weissberg, R. P., Dymnicki, A. B., Taylor, R. D., & Schellinger, K. B. (2011). The impact of enhancing students' social and emotional learning: A meta-analysis of school-based universal interventions. *Child Development, 82,* 405-432.

Epstein, M. H., & Synhorst, L. (2009). *Preschool Emotional and Behavioral Rating Scale examiner's manual.* Austin, TX: PRO-ED.

LeBuffe, P. A., & Naglieri, J. A. (1999). Devereux Early Childhood Assessment. Lewisville, NC: Kaplan Early Learning Company.

Masten, A. S., Best, K. M., & Garmezy, N. (1990). Resilience and development: Contributions from the study of children who overcome adversity. *Development and Psychopathology, 2,* 425-444.

[50]

Devereux Student Strengths Assessment—Second Step Edition.

Purpose: A rating scale designed to assess social-emotional competencies of children in the Second Step program and for evaluating the program's impact.
Population: Children in kindergarten through Grade 5.
Publication Date: 2011.
Acronym: DESSA-SSE.
Scores, 5: Skills for Learning, Empathy, Emotion Management, Problem Solving, Social-Emotional Composite.
Administration: Individual or group.
Price Data: Available from publisher.
Time: Approximately 5 minutes for administration.
Comments: The 36 items on the DESSA-SSE are a subset of those on the 72-item Devereux Student Strengths Assessment (DESSA; 18:41); ratings completed by parent or family member, teacher, after-school program staff, or staff from social service, mental health, or child welfare program.
Authors: Paul A. LeBuffe, Jack A. Naglieri, & Valerie B. Shapiro.
Publisher: Aperture Education.

Review of the Devereux Student Strengths Assessment—Second Step Edition by ERIC S. BUHS, Associate Professor of Educational Psychology, University of Nebraska-Lincoln, Lincoln, NE:

DESCRIPTION. The Devereux Student Strengths Assessment—Second Step Edition (DESSA-SSE) is a shortened version of the previously published Devereux Student Strengths Assessment (DESSA; LeBuffe, Shapiro, & Naglieri, 2009; 18:41) measure of children's social-emotional competency. The DESSA-SSE is a standardized, 36-item behavior rating scale for use with children in kindergarten through fifth grade. Items are rated by teachers (or other educational personnel) and/or parents and caregivers using a 5-point, Likert-type scale of behavior frequency. The instrument includes four subscales that are nine items each: Skills for Learning, Empathy, Emotion Management, and Problem Solving. The measure was developed to evaluate social-emotional skill needs and outcomes for the well-established Second Step intervention program (Committee for Children, 2011) designed to improve disruptive behavior, anxiety, social-emotional outcomes, and academic performance. The test authors suggest that the DESSA-SSE is useful more broadly as a needs assessment of social-emotional competence identifying children who may benefit from similar interventions.

DEVELOPMENT. The DESSA-SSE includes a subset of 36 items drawn from the original 72-item DESSA. As such, the only development description provided is that of the original DESSA. A large pool of 765 items was first developed using items from the research literature on resilience, social-emotional learning, and positive youth development. Items were also drawn from the Devereux Early Childhood Assessment (DECA; LeBuffe & Naglieri, 1999; 15:81). This pool was initially reduced through elimination of duplicate items and removal of non-behavioral/

non-observable content, resulting in a pool of 156 items. Items were written to reduce observer inference and to require the lowest reading level possible for raters.

Data drawn from a pilot study of 428 students in kindergarten through eighth grade (including 25% with identified emotional/behavioral disorders) were used to eliminate items with low item-total correlations, items that did not differentiate between the disordered and typical groups, and those that were rated as unclear or not applicable. The resulting set of 81 items was used during standardization. Developers assigned items to the four hypothesized subscales (i.e., the four skill areas of the Second Step intervention), and the resulting subscales were examined for item-total correlations and age trends. Items with low correlations to subscale scores and those that showed age trends were eliminated. This process produced the final set of four 9-item scales: The Skills for Learning scale targets attention and listening; the Empathy scale describes prosocial behaviors and perspective-taking skills; Emotion Management taps emotional control and coping; and Problem Solving targets children's ability to handle social conflicts and personal challenges. No follow-up exploratory or confirmatory factor analyses were reported. Standard scores from the four scales are summed to create an overall Social-Emotional Composite score as an estimate of children's overall ability.

TECHNICAL.

Standardization. The DESSA/DESSA-SSE was standardized using a nationwide sample of 2,494 children designed to be representative of the U.S. population for the age group. Ratings were provided by 778 teachers and teacher aides; 1,244 parents/caregivers; and 472 staff from after-school programs. Sample proportions are provided by gender, geographic region, and ethnic group and indicate that the sample was reasonably representative of the U.S. population. The American Indian/Alaska Native, Asian, and Native Hawaiian/Pacific Islander groups, while proportionally representative, remained small (n = 41, 65, and 14, respectively). The African American and Hispanic groups were substantially larger (n = 481 and 450, respectively), but no ethnic-group score comparisons were made in analyses of potential score differences. The test authors used free and reduced lunch status to estimate that 22% of the children in the sample were living at or below the poverty level, approximating the national level of 25%.

Scale means are presented by gender and grade level and also by rater source (parents vs. teachers). The test authors judged that data indicated only minor differences across grade level and subsequently combined data for norm development. Analyses of mean scores by scale showed scores differed by rater source and, thus, separate norms are presented for scores drawn from parents vs. teachers. Gender differences also emerged in scale means. Girls consistently scored .5 to 5 points higher than boys, indicating slightly higher social-emotional competence; however, the magnitude of the differences—which were said to reflect natural differences in behavior—were small or medium, and, thus, separate norms were not developed. Most of the standardization data include data from students in Grades 6-8 (i.e., not the targeted age group for the DESSA-SSE), somewhat confusing the interpretation of the sample characteristics and scale means. Potential score differences across ethnic groups were not explored.

Reliability. Internal reliability estimates (alpha coefficients) for the four scales indicated acceptable reliability and ranged from .82 to .87 for parent-rated scores and from .90 to .93 for teacher-rated scores. The composite score internal reliability was estimated at .96 using data drawn from the parent raters and .98 for the teacher raters. Test-retest reliability estimates using an interval of 4 to 8 days for the scale scores were high and ranged from .84 to .86 for the parent-rated scores and from .90 to .94 for the teacher-rated scores. The composite scores for parent and teacher raters were correlated at .87 and .95, respectively. Data were also gathered from a subsample of pairs of raters familiar with the child (e.g., two parents, or a teacher and a teacher aide), and scores were examined for interrater reliability. Coefficients were again high, ranging from .68 to .76 for parents and from .68 to .85 for teachers on the subscales. Coefficients were .77 and .81 on the Social-Emotional Composite for parents and teachers, respectively. In sum, the reliability data indicated acceptable reliability for the subscale and composite scores.

Validity. Content-related evidence of validity was judged to be good by the test authors based on the extent of the conceptual support for the item sets gathered from existing research and the content coverage provided by the nine items assigned to each scale. Criterion-related evidence of validity was examined via score comparisons between a sample of children recruited from students receiving special education services under the seriously emotionally disturbed label (SED, n = 78). This sample was matched on age, gender, and type of rater to a group of students from the norming sample. Demographic characteristics were similar across the groups. Scores were compared to evaluate the premise that students in the SED group would score lower than those in the normative group, and analyses confirmed that all scores were lower for the SED group. External evidence of validity (e.g., correlation of DESSA-SSE scores with scores from similar measures) was not assessed.

COMMENTARY. The DESSA-SSE was developed for use with the Second Step intervention program as a means of evaluating important social-emotional skills and program-specific outcomes for elementary-aged children. Second Step is an established intervention program and has demonstrated positive effects in most of the published research examining the program outcomes (e.g., Low, Cook, Smolkowski, & Buntain-Ricklefs, 2015). As such, the items and scales developed for this measure provide a well-designed set of indicators for the important, strengths-based set of social-emotional skills targeted by the intervention. The measure benefits from the thorough development strategy used for its parent measure, the well-established DESSA, and from the extensive development and research associated with the Second Step program.

Broader use of the measure, independent of the Second Step program, is probably best confined to use in similar intervention efforts or evaluations of student competency. Investigators seeking scales tapping social-emotional constructs common to social development research may find that the scales are not precise indicators of accepted construct definitions (e.g., executive function, prosocial behavior). However, this was neither the goal of the test authors nor the measure development strategy. It is also important to note that many of the items included in the DESSA-SSE tap a broader set of skills and behaviors that are commonly associated with children's executive function (i.e., adaptive, goal-directed behaviors such as working memory, inhibition, behavior regulation, and managing attention). This may be a strength of the measure in that executive function has been consistently associated with a range of important adjustment outcomes such as academic skills and social relationships (Allan, Hume, Allan, Farrington, & Lonigan, 2014; Bierman & Motamedi, 2015). As a result, the Social-Emotional Composite score that this measure includes should be predictive of broader school adjustment. It is unfortunate, however, that this potential use (and source of external validity information) was not examined as part of the test development process nor was it discussed in the handbook materials. Measure development also lacked fine-grained examination of potential socioeconomic status and ethnic group differences in scale scores and resulting norms—an unfortunate omission because scores for this skill set may differ for groups of students experiencing higher levels of economic stress (Mistry, Vandewater, Huston, & McLoyd, 2002).

SUMMARY. The DESSA-SSE is, overall, a well-developed measure of an important set of social-emotional behaviors and competencies that are tied directly to the popular Second Step intervention program. The scores provided by the instrument should prove useful both in identifying elementary school-aged children in need of skill development in these areas and as a means to measure intervention effects.

REVIEWER'S REFERENCES

Allan, N. P., Hume, L. E., Allan, D. M., Farrington, A. L., & Lonigan, C. J. (2014). Relations between inhibitory control and the development of academic skills in preschool and kindergarten: A meta-analysis. *Developmental Psychology, 50*, 2368-2379.

Bierman, K. L., & Motamedi, M. (2015). SEL programs for preschool children. In J. A. Durlak, C. E. Domitrovich, R. P. Weissberg, & T. P. Gullotta (Eds.), *Handbook of social and emotional learning: Research and practice* (pp. 135-150). New York, NY: Guilford.

Committee for Children. (2011). *Second Step: Skills for social and academic success.* Seattle, WA: Author.

LeBuffe, P. A., & Naglieri, J. A. (1999). Devereux Early Childhood Assessment. Lewisville, NC: Kaplan Press.

LeBuffe, P. A., Shapiro, V. B., & Naglieri, J. A. (2009). Devereux Student Strengths Assessment. Lewisville, NC: Kaplan.

Low, S., Cook, C. R., Smolkowski, K., & Buntain-Ricklefs, J. (2015). Promoting social–emotional competence: An evaluation of the elementary version of Second Step. *Journal of School Psychology, 53*, 463-477.

Mistry, R. S., Vandewater, E. A., Huston, A. C., & McLoyd, V. C. (2002). Economic well-being and children's social adjustment: The role of family process in an ethnically diverse low-income sample. *Child Development, 73*, 935-951.

Review of the Devereux Student Strengths Assessment—Second Step Edition by KARA M. STYCK, Assistant Professor of School Psychology, Department of Psychology, Northern Illinois University, Dekalb, IL, and ESTHER H. YI, Doctoral Student in School Psychology, Department of Psychology, Northern Illinois University, Dekalb, IL:

DESCRIPTION. The Devereux Student Strengths Assessment—Second Step Edition (DESSA-SSE) is a standardized behavior rating scale intended to measure strengths-based social-emotional competencies of children in Grades K-5. It was adapted from the Devereux Student Strengths Assessment (DESSA; LeBuffe, Shapiro, & Naglieri, 2009; 18:41) and is similar in its screening and progress-monitoring functions to the Devereux Student Strengths Assessment-mini (DESSA-mini; Naglieri, LeBuffe, & Shapiro, 2014; 20:73). The DESSA-SSE was uniquely constructed to align with the skills taught in the social and emotional learning (SEL) program Second Step (Committee for Children, 2011). As such, it is purported to be able to evaluate the impact of Second Step (or other SEL programs) on student outcomes. Parents, teachers, after-school program staff, and staff from social service, mental, or child welfare programs are eligible raters to complete the DESSA-SSE. It takes approximately five minutes to complete, and raters are asked to consider only behaviors that they have directly observed within four weeks of the administration date.

DESSA-SSE items are rated using a 5-point ordinal scale ranging from *never* to *very frequently*. The DESSA-SSE user is directed to tear off the perforated strip at the left edge of the record form and to complete all scoring on the attached carbonless scoresheet upon completion. T scores and percentile ranks are provided for four subscales from which norm-referenced score interpretations can be made: (a) Skills for Learning, (b) Empathy, (c) Emotion Management, and (d) Problem Solving. In addition, a total Social-Emotional Composite score can be derived from the sum of the four subscales (i.e., T scores) to provide an overall estimate of a child's social-emotional competency, which implies a hierarchical underlying structure. T scores can be used to interpret these subscores individually and together as part of an individual student profile and a classroom/program profile that illustrate social-emotional competency strengths and areas in need of improvement.

DEVELOPMENT. The DESSA-SSE consists of a subset of 36 items drawn from the DESSA. Development of the DESSA followed a series of steps. First, characteristic behaviors of resilient children were identified from a review of the literature on resilience, SEL, and positive youth development as well as a review of other strength-based assessments (i.e., the Devereux Early Childhood Assessment; LeBuffe & Naglieri, 1999a, 1999b). The review resulted in an initial pool of 765 items, which was further reduced to 156 by combining redundant items and deleting items that were problematic (i.e., not measurable, subjective, or unmodifiable). The items were pilot tested on 428 students in kindergarten through eighth grade, 25% of whom had been "identified as having significant emotional or behavioral disorders" (manual, p. 4). An additional 75 items were eliminated due to having item-total correlations lower than .60, being unable to differentiate students with and without emotional or behavioral disorders by at least half a standard deviation, or being rated as unclear or not applicable by at least 20% of raters. The final set of 81 items was used in the national standardization edition of the DESSA.

Initial item-scale assignments for the DESSA-SSE were made "based on their relationship to the definitions and descriptions" (manual, p. 8) of the four skill areas in the Second Step intervention program: (a) Skills for Learning, (b) Empathy, (c) Emotion Management, and (d) Problem Solving. Item content mapping was then reviewed by the Research and Program Development staff of the Committee for Children. An unnamed number of items were deleted/substituted based on the committee's feedback. Next, corrected item-total correlations were examined to verify that each item correlated highly with its corresponding scale, and items with scores that increased with age were eliminated to remove the need for age norms. These procedures resulted in a final set of 36 items (i.e., nine items per subscale).

TECHNICAL.

Standardization. The DESSA-SSE was constructed using the standardization sample of the DESSA. The standardization sample of the DESSA comprised 2,494 children in kindergarten through eighth grade who closely resembled the demographic characteristics (i.e., age, gender, geographic region of residence, race, ethnicity, and socioeconomic status) of the K-8 student population of the United States in 2006. It included 1,250 ratings completed by teachers, teacher aides, and after-school or other program staff and 1,244 ratings completed by parents and other adult relatives living in the home. Data were collected by paper and online and were analyzed together due to the absence of statistical differences between the two administration formats. Separate norms for teacher and parent raters are provided due to the presence of significant mean differences in subscores and the Social-Emotional Composite score across rater types in the standardization sample. However, separate norms are not provided for grade or gender as there was no evidence in the standardization sample that DESSA-SSE scores increased across grade, and significant gender differences were assumed to represent "real disparities in how boys and girls behave" (manual, p. 10) as opposed to implicit rater bias.

Reliability. Internal consistency, test-retest, and interrater reliability of DESSA-SSE scores were reported in the test manual. Alpha coefficients were used to calculate internal reliability for a sample of 978 parent ratings and 1,098 teacher ratings drawn from the DESSA-SSE standardization sample. Coefficients for the four DESSA-SSE subscales ranged from .82 to .87 and from .90 to .93 for parent and teacher raters, respectively. For the Social-Emotional Composite, coefficient alpha was .96 for parent raters and .98 for teacher raters. Short-term test-retest reliability of DESSA-SSE subscales was based on a sample of 54 parents and 38 teachers who rated the same child on two occasions over a period of 4 to 8 days. All test-retest correlations were statistically significant ($p < .01$). Test-retest correlation coefficients for the four DESSA-SSE subscales ranged from .84 to .86 and from .90 to .94 for parent and teacher raters, respectively. Test-retest correlation coefficients for the Social-Emotional Composite were .87 and .95 for parents and teachers, respectively. Short-term stability was also assessed by inspecting mean differences in DESSA-SSE scores over the 4- to 8-day test-retest interval. Mean differences between scores were less than 1 T score point. Interrater reliability of DESSA-SSE subscales was examined using a sample of 51 parent-parent pairs and 51 teacher-teacher aide pairs. Correlations between rater pairs were statistically significant ($p < .01$) with coefficients ranging from .68 to .76 and from .68 to .85 for parents and teachers, respectively, on the four DESSA-SSE subscales. Correlations between rater pairs on the Social-Emotional Composite were .77 for parents and .81 for teachers.

Validity. Content, internal structure, and criterion-related validity evidence for DESSA-SSE scores was reported in the test manual. Content and internal structure evidence was established during the DESSA-SSE item development as noted in the development section of this review. The validity of item content was based on a review of the definitions and descriptions of the Second Step program as well as feedback from the Research and Program Development staff of the Committee for Children. The internal structure of the DESSA-SSE was evaluated by ensuring corrected item-total correlations were greater than .60 during the item development stage. Criterion validity was assessed by evaluating the degree to which mean DESSA-SSE scores were significantly different between a sample of 78 children receiving special education services for emotional disturbance and a sample of 78 children in regular education who were matched on rater type, gender, and age. Scores for children who were receiving special education services for emotional disturbance were significantly ($p < .001$) lower on average than scores for children in the comparison group, and these differences were large (*d*-ratios ranged between .90 to 1.5).

COMMENTARY. The DESSA-SSE is an abbreviated version of the DESSA aligned with the skills targeted in Second Step and intended to be used to screen and monitor the progress of children who participate in Second Step or other SEL intervention programs. It is noteworthy that the standardization sample closely resembles the demographic characteristics of the K-8 student population of the United States when the DESSA was developed. However, these Census data are now more than a decade old. Important aspects of test score reliability and validity also were not evaluated in the development of the DESSA-SSE. For example, the standard error of measurement was computed from internal consistency reliability studies and does not account for systematic variance in scores due to rater effects (e.g., raters providing systematically high/low ratings due to differences in severity/leniency; Splett et al., 2018). Furthermore, external and structural validity evidence was sparse. Evidence was not gathered to assess the degree to which scores obtained from the DESSA-SSE relate concurrently to or predict scores of other measures of dis/similar constructs, and factor analyses were not conducted to explore and confirm the hypothesized underlying hierarchical structure of DESSA-SSE item scores (Messick, 1995). Consequently, exactly what constructs the DESSA-SSE truly measures remain unknown. Finally, the diagnostic utility of subscores to accurately discriminate between individuals with and without emotional disturbance (Swets, Dawes, & Monahan, 2000) was not investigated nor were items evaluated across participant demographic groups (e.g., gender, race, ethnicity) for the presence of differential item functioning.

SUMMARY. The DESSA-SSE is a strengths-based behavior rating scale that measures the social-emotional competencies of children in kindergarten through fifth grade. It serves an important role within the Second Step program (and potentially other SEL intervention programs) as a brief rating scale that can be used to assess children's progress. However, the norms are more than a decade old, which may impact the generalizability of reliability and validity studies, and more information about the reliability and validity of DESSA-SSE score interpretations is needed to substantiate its continued use as a screening and progress monitoring tool.

REVIEWERS' REFERENCES

Committee for Children. (2011). *Second step: Skills for social and academic success.* Seattle, WA: Author.

LeBuffe, P. A., & Naglieri, J. A. (1999a). *Devereux early childhood assessment technical manual.* Lewisville, NC: Kaplan Press

LeBuffe, P. A., & Naglieri, J. A. (1999b). *Devereux early childhood assessment user's guide.* Lewisville, NC: Kaplan Press.

LeBuffe, P. A., Shapiro, V. B., & Naglieri, J. A. (2009). *The Devereux student strengths assessment (DESSA), technical manual and user's guide.* Lewisville, NC: Kaplan Press.

Messick, S. (1995). Validity of psychological assessment: Validation of inferences from persons' responses and performances as scientific inquiry into score meaning. *American Psychologist, 50,* 741–749.

Naglieri, J. A., LeBuffe, P. A., & Shapiro, V. B. (2014). *Devereux student strengths assessment mini (DESSA-mini) technical manual and user's guide.* Lewisville, NC: Kaplan Press.

Splett, J. W., Smith-Millman, M., Raborn, A., Brann, K. L., Flaspohler, P. D., & Maras, M. A. (2018). Student, teacher, and classroom predictors of between-teacher variance of students' teacher-rated behavior. *School Psychology Quarterly, 33,* 460-468. doi:10.1037/spq0000241

Swets, J. A., Dawes, R. M., & Monahan, J. (2000). Psychological science can improve diagnostic decisions. *Psychological Science in the Public Interest, 1,* 1–26.

[51]

Diagnostic Adaptive Behavior Scale.

Purpose: Designed to provide information "for the evaluation of limitations in adaptive behavior, ... one of the three criteria for a diagnosis of intellectual disability."
Population: Ages 4 to 21.
Publication Date: 2017.
Acronym: DABS.
Scores, 4: Conceptual Skills, Social Skills, Practical Skills, Total.
Administration: Individual.
Levels, 3: 4-8 Years, 9-15 Years, 16-21 Years.
Price Data, 2020: $155 per user's manual (144 pages) and 25 interview forms; $120 per manual; $50 per 25 forms; $1 per scored protocol; volume discounts and membership discounts available.
Time: Administration time not reported.
Comments: Scored via test publisher's online platform.
Authors: Marc J. Tassé, Robert L. Schalock, Giulia Balboni, Henry (Hank) Bersani, Jr., Sharon A. Borthwick-Duffy, Scott Spreat, David Thissen, Keith F. Widaman, and Dalun Zhang.
Publisher: American Association on Intellectual and Developmental Disabilities.

Review of the Diagnostic Adaptive Behavior Scale by A. ALEXANDER BEAUJEAN, Associate Professor of Psychology and Neuroscience, Baylor University, Waco, TX:

DESCRIPTION. The Diagnostic Adaptive Behavior Scale (DABS) is a standardized instrument designed to aid in identifying individuals ages 4–21 years who have significant adaptive behavior limitations. It was devised specifically for diagnostic purposes rather than for programming or identifying areas of needed support. There are three age-based interview forms: 4–8, 9-15, and 16–21 years. Each form has three 25-item content domains (Conceptual, Social, Practical) for a total of 75 items. Estimated completion time is not provided but should take approximately 30–45 minutes.

The DABS is administered face-to-face via a semistructured interview, presumably as part of an intellectual disability (ID) evaluation. The interviewer asks caregivers of a person suspected of having an ID about the frequency with which the individual typically exhibits certain behaviors. Responses are recorded on the interview form using one of four options. In addition, a "no score" (NS) option is available when respondents have no information about a behavior, but the option should be used rarely because it increases resulting scores' standard error of measurement (*SEM*).

DABS interviewers typically are helping professionals with at least a bachelor's degree who have experience with developmental disabilities and conducting individual assessments. Respondents should have extensive knowledge of the person's typical behaviors across a variety of settings over an extended period of time. Self-reports are not allowed. Interviewing multiple respondents for each individual is suggested but not required.

Users score the DABS forms online; hand scoring is not possible. Scoring costs are not included in the price of the interview forms. The scoring software produces an interpretive report that includes standard scores and confidence intervals for each content domain as well as a Total Score. In addition, the report indicates whether the person meets criteria for a significant adaptive behavior limitation. Users must print or save reports locally because the online program does not store them.

DEVELOPMENT. DABS was developed to follow the American Association on Intellectual and Developmental Disabilities' (AAIDD) guidelines for diagnosing an ID (Schalock et al., 2010), which require significant adaptive behavior limitations. The AAIDD defined adaptive behavior as a collection of conceptual, social, and practical skills that people perform in their everyday lives. They defined a significant adaptive behavior limitation as "performance that is approximately two standard deviations below the mean of either (a) one of the following three types of adaptive behavior: conceptual, social, or practical or (b) an overall score on a standardized measure of conceptual, social, and practical skills" (manual, p. 6).

In creating the DABS, the authors first generated a large item pool by reviewing the scientific literature and other published adaptive behavior instruments. Then, they culled the items using three stages: (a) removing redundant stems, (b) removing items clinicians classified as either not pertinent for children/adolescents or belonging to a domain other than Conceptual/Social/Practical, and (c) removing the worst performing items from field testing. Field testing was done with 474 respondents, 26% of whom had a child with an ID. Item responses were factor analyzed and calibrated using item response theory (IRT). The test authors selected the final items based on (a) how well they related to other items in the same domain, (b) number of other items in the same *subdomain* (i.e., content area within a domain), (c) how often they elicited an NS response, and (d) how much information they provided about adaptive behavior limitations.

Within each content domain, some items are repeated across multiple forms. This allows for estimating IRT-based person scores (thetas) on a common metric within each content domain and then linking the scores across forms. The Total Score is derived from the three theta estimates. The authors re-calibrated the items using the full standardization data and converted the theta and Total Score estimates to standard scores with a mean of 100 and standard deviation of 15.

TECHNICAL. The standardization sample consisted of 1,058 respondents, 12% of whom had a child with an ID. Because the field-testing sample was included in the standardization sample, only 584 respondents were new. They were purposively selected so that the children's demographic characteristics roughly matched the 2000 U.S. Census with respect to geographic region and ethnic composition; the number of males and females was roughly the same. The interviewers and respondents were relatively homogenous. Most interviewers had graduate degrees (71%) or were currently in graduate school (17%), and more than 40% of them were psychologists. Approximately 80% of the respondents were parents, the majority of whom were mothers.

The number of children at each age ranged from 21 to 91, with younger ages tending to have larger sample sizes. These numbers are low. The test authors' solution was to use local regression methods (i.e., LOESS) to estimate smoothed values for the theta means and standard deviations at each age.

Three different reliability estimates are provided: (a) internal consistency (i.e., coefficient alpha from the standardization sample); (b) test-retest reliability (i.e., Pearson correlation among scores for 30 respondents across an average of 22 days); and (c) interrespondent reliability (i.e., response agreement across 21 different pairs of respondents for the same child), which was estimated using intraclass correlations (ICCs). Noticeably lacking is information about inter-interviewer reliability (i.e., response agreement for the same respondent across different interviewers), making any influence of interviewer effects currently unknown.

Internal consistency and test-retest reliability estimates were all > .90 except for the Social domain (r = .78). ICC values ranged from .61 to .87, which approximate those from other adaptive behavior instruments (e.g., Salekin, Neal, & Hedge, 2018). The scores' *SEM* values were estimated using an undisclosed method of combining these reliability estimates with item calibration information.

Validity evidence consists of (a) Pearson correlations with scores from the Vineland Adaptive Behavior Scales, Second Edition (Vineland-II) in a small sample (n = 28), and (b) growth curve plots for the IRT-based person scores gathered from the standardization sample. In addition, utility information is provided for the standard scores using the standardization sample. Utility information is paramount for the DABS because it was designed for making diagnostic decisions. Noticeably lacking is information about differences across demographic subgroups (e.g., sex, race, ethnicity).

All the Vineland-II scores positively correlated with all the DABS scores, with coefficients of .25-.78 between DABS and Vineland-II domains and .84 for the total score. Most of the correlations' confidence intervals overlapped; thus, all that can be said is that the DABS and Vineland-II scores are all positively correlated. Growth curve plots show that theta and Total Score values generally increase across ages for individuals without any known disabilities. Individuals with an ID generally had lower scores than individuals without a disability, but there was overlap across all four scores (i.e., some individuals with ID demonstrated more adaptive behaviors than some individuals without a disability).

A cutoff of 70 + 2 *SEM* (i.e., 76 for domain scores; 74 for the Total Score) was used to assess utility. Sensitivity and specificity values are commendable (sensitivity range: .81–.98; specificity range: .89–.91); nonetheless, meeting diagnostic criteria based on a single respondent's observations only minimally increases the probability of having an ID because the prevalence rate is so low. Thus, obtaining information from multiple respondents should likely be required instead of being an option.

The test authors state that all DABS standard scores are comparable in classifying individuals with and without an ID (manual, p. 66). Yet, Balboni et al. (2014) reported that the average Social and Practical scores for individuals with an ID were greater than the diagnostic cutoff across multiple ages; this pattern was not present for the Total Score or Conceptual score. Thus, the scores may not work interchangeably in identifying individuals with significant adaptive behavior limitations.

COMMENTARY. The DABS is a psychometrically sophisticated instrument designed to follow the AAIDD's definition of adaptive behavior impairment and aid clinicians in making diagnostic decisions. To that end, the DABS met its authors' goals. At the same time, the DABS does not reach its full potential for assessing adaptive behavior limitations. Although IRT was used throughout the creation and calibration processes, DABS administration does not make full use of it. For example, using item parameter values to implement some type of adaptive testing could have reduced most administration times and increased the likelihood of interviewing multiple respondents. Likewise, the DABS scores do not use all the information available from IRT calibration (e.g., Woodcock, 1999). For example, because IRT models make item and person scores directly comparable, the test authors could have provided more of a criterion-based understanding of adaptive behavior limitations—something many of the DABS authors have previously discussed (Tassé et al., 2012).

DABS standard scores are reported on the same scale used for intelligence test scores. This practice is shared by several other standardized adaptive behavior scales (e.g., Vineland-3, Adaptive Behavior Assessment System, Third Edition, among others). The concern for this reviewer is that the practice may prompt users to believe that the scores can be used to assess differences between individuals or within a single individual (e.g., clinical profile analysis) instead of solely for diagnostic decision making. In addition, it may lead to a false impression that scores from these instruments can be compared directly to intelligence test scores.

Another concern about the DABS involves scoring. Because users cannot score the forms by hand, they must pay a fee each time a form is scored. Ideally, there would be some method for temporarily storing responses, thereby allowing users who find they made a data entry error to make edits instead of having to purchase another score report. Granted, a change of this sort introduces additional security and privacy concerns, but it is something offered by electronic scoring systems for other instruments.

SUMMARY. The DABS is a semistructured interview for assessing adaptive behavior in children/adolescents, and the scores can be used to identify significant adaptive behavior limitations. The DABS is similar to other adaptive behavior instruments in terms of administration and scoring. The sophisticated psychometrics employed for item selection and calibration assisted in the development of a measure with fewer items. However, the complex psychometrics were not used to their full potential, yielding a measure that differs only minimally from other adaptive behavior instruments. Consequently, practitioners interested solely in making dichotomous (diagnostic) decisions about adaptive behavior limitations using an interview format likely will find the DABS worth adding to their library.

REVIEWER'S REFERENCES

Balboni, G., Tassé, M. J., Schalock, R. L., Borthwick-Duffy, S. A., Spreat, S., Thissen, D., ... Navas, P. (2014). The Diagnostic Adaptive Behavior Scale: Evaluating its diagnostic sensitivity and specificity. *Research in Developmental Disabilities, 35,* 2884-2893.

Salekin, K. L., Neal, T. M. S., & Hedge, K. A. (2018). Validity, interrater reliability, and measures of adaptive behavior: Concerns regarding the probative versus prejudicial value. *Psychology, Public Policy, and Law, 24,* 24-35.

Schalock, R. L., Borthwick-Duffy, S. A., Bradley, V. J., Buntinx, W. H. E., Coulter, D. L., Craig, E. M., ... Yeager, M. H. (2010). *Intellectual disability: Definition, classification, and systems of supports* (11th ed.). Washington, DC: American Association on Intellectual and Developmental Disabilities.

Tassé, M. J., Schalock, R. L., Balboni, G., Bersani, H., Borthwick-Duffy, S. A., Spreat, S., ... Zhang, D. (2012). The construct of adaptive behavior: Its conceptualization, measurement, and use in the field of intellectual disability. *American Journal on Intellectual and Developmental Disabilities, 117,* 291-303.

Woodcock, R. W. (1999). What can Rasch-based scores convey about a person's test performance? In S. E. Embretson & S. L. Hershberger (Eds.), *The new rules of measurement: What every psychologist and educator should know* (pp. 105–127). Mahwah, NJ: Erlbaum.

Review of the Diagnostic Adaptive Behavior Scale by BRIAN F. FRENCH, Professor of Educational Psychology, and DAVID ALPIZAR, Doctoral Candidate, Educational Psychology, Washington State University, Pullman, WA:

DESCRIPTION. The Diagnostic Adaptive Behavior Scale (DABS) contains 75 items to assess adaptive behaviors in individuals ranging in age from 4 to 21 years. Scores help identify individuals who exhibit significant limitations in conceptual, social, and practical skills required for daily functioning. Limited skills in these areas is one criterion used for diagnosing an intellectual disability (ID). Items are scored on a 4-point scale by an interviewer based on respondent answers. Respondent responses reflect direct observation and knowledge of the assessed individual's behavior. To improve the accuracy of ratings, multiple respondents are suggested to capture functioning in different settings. The interviewer should use clinical judgment to evaluate respondent accuracy.

The interviewer completes administration of the assessment with the respondent(s), with no average time per assessment indicated. The interviewer should be a professional (a) with at least a bachelor's degree, (b) who has worked in the ID realm, (c) who has assessment experience, and (d) who is sensitive to cultural differences. The respondent(s), with whom the interviewer must build rapport, should be adults who are familiar with the daily behaviors of the assessed individual for an extended time. Item response theory (IRT) based scores are available in an individual scoring report via an online platform; hand scoring is not possible. The test manual provides clear technical and practical information about score interpretations written for the competent clinician.

DEVELOPMENT. The DABS is aligned with the *Diagnostic and Statistical Manual of Mental Disorders* (5th ed.; *DSM-5*; American Psychiatric Association [APA], 2013) definition of adaptive behavior, which is based on a tripartite model including conceptual, social, and practical skills domains. The DABS development rests on 20 years of theoretical and empirical work, with the goal to improve the diagnostic criteria for adaptive behavior assessment. In Phase 1 of development, 12 standardized assessments were reviewed. An initial pool of 2,000 items was created and then reduced to 1,180 after eliminating redundancy. An international expert panel (N = 31) used the Q-sort technique to map the items to the three skill domains. In Phase 2, the field-test items (n = 260) were selected based on item alignment agreement between judges by domain (i.e., Conceptual n = 94; Social n = 86; Practical n = 80). A large representative sample (n = 474) was used to develop the three age-based forms for 4-8 years (132 items), 9-15 years (192 items), and 16-21 years (128 items). In Phase 3, on a nationally representative sample, the item set was finalized via IRT-based analyses, scales were linked across age, and reliability and validity information was collected. This process resulted in 75 items per form with 25 items capturing each domain. The development process generally followed professional guidelines (American Educational Research Association, American Psychological Association, & National Council on Measurement in Education, 2014) with well-articulated criteria at each development decision point.

TECHNICAL.

Standardization. The DABS standardization was based on 1,058 individuals from 46 states, including 474 from the calibration sample. The standardization sample was based on U.S. Census 2000 data. Overrepresentation (African American 17.1% vs. 12.3%) and modest underrepresentation (Hispanic 9.5% vs. 12.5%; White 71.5% vs. 75.1%) of the national sample were noted regarding ethnicity. Demographic comparisons for income and education level were not provided. The target sample (n = 125) was labeled ID-related, with 61.6% identified as ID and 38.4% identified as developmentally delayed. The interviewer sample had professional training, with 71% holding an advanced degree. The majority were employed as psychologists (42%) or in an undisclosed profession (28%) and were mainly Caucasian (80%). Respondents were primarily mothers (70%) of the individual assessed, Caucasian (74%), and with a college degree (65%).

Reliability. Reliability evidence was presented for the total and domain scores. Coefficient alpha internal consistency estimates were high (≥ .94), meeting standards for score use for individual decisions (Nunnally & Bernstein, 1994). Test-retest reliability was reported for 30 individuals (Caucasian 77%, diagnosis of ID and/or autism spectrum disorder in 70% and 37%, respectively) after 7 to 51 days from initial testing with values greater than .91 for all scores except for the Social Skills domain (.78). Interrespondent reliability was estimated for paired respondents (n = 21) with correlations ranging from .63 to .90, and intraclass correlation coefficients ranging from .61 to .87 across domains. Values meet acceptable standards. Finally and appropriately, the standard error of measurement for scores was provided, but details about estimation were not documented.

Validity. In a traditional checklist fashion, validity evidence for DABS scores was evaluated. Content validity evidence was examined through a review of existing measures and a panel of content experts with clearly articulated criteria for item-domain alignment and definitional consistency with theory and practice (e.g., *DSM-5*). A bifactor model to support the scores is mentioned, but no internal structure evidence (e.g., factor analysis) was provided in the test manual. Evidence deriving from associations with other variables was provided via correlations between the DABS and the Vineland Adaptive Behavior Scales, Second Edition. Correlation coefficients were as high as .84 (total DABS score with total Vineland-II score) to as low as .25 with scores that should not correlate highly (DABS Conceptual with Vineland Socialization). There is some potential confusion of the labels used for evidence presented (e.g., convergent and concurrent; divergent vs. discriminant, Messick, 1989, p. 35) that can be clarified. The test manual documents the accuracy of DABS scores for differentiating between age groups and diagnostic criteria. For example, decision accuracy information is strong, and specificity and sensitivity values are in the acceptable range to support diagnostic use. Lower scores occur for individuals with ID-related diagnoses compared to non-diagnosed peers, with effect sizes greater than 2.0, aligned with ID diagnostic criteria specified in the test manual. Such evidence is critical, given this group differentiation is aligned with the test developer's theoretical framework and score use. The manual presents such results statistically and graphically, which is welcomed. There is no evidence documented for score fairness across diverse groups. Finally, the test manual provides an extensive section on IRT item calibration, which the technically interested and savvy user will appreciate.

COMMENTARY. The DABS has great promise as a tool for clinicians to use in an assessment battery to identify limitations in adaptive behaviors. The DABS key strengths are (a) content based on the *DSM-5* definition of adaptive behavior, (b) use of IRT to drive item development and scoring, (c) an online scoring and reporting platform, (d) strong evidence of score reliability, and (e) a solid foundation of components to construct a validity argument. Practitioners should find the platform and reports helpful and the technical manual easy to follow.

A lack of information and diversity with regard to the standardization sample hinders enthusiasm for the normative information. This ranges from a lack of justification of the use of the 2000 U.S. Census data for representation and over and under representation of groups, to a lack of reported demographic information. Also, approximately one-third of the standardization sample was from the calibration sample. No discussion about how such issues may have influenced the validity evidence is offered.

A major weakness involves fairness issues. The test manual advises the user to be sensitive to cultural differences when administrating the assessment. However, no information was offered regarding how this was examined in the standardization process or what influences culture might have on the assessment process. Although assessment of fairness through differential item functioning was mentioned in the test manual, not all items were evaluated, and group comparisons lacked description. The study of fairness and cultural influences of scores warrants additional attention, especially given the composition of the interviewer, respondents, and individuals in the development process.

Although much of the information presented to support the development and use of the DABS is documented in the test manual, there is a general need for revising the manual for both accuracy of information and updated validity language. The addition of a validity framework of the test authors' choice and clarifying the validity language aligned with cited work would increase understanding of the evidence.

SUMMARY. The Diagnostic Adaptive Behavior Scale is designed to determine whether a person age 4 to 21 has significant limitations in adaptive behaviors, which are important to the diagnosis of ID. Items and skill domains are grounded in theory and empirical evidence. Reporting procedures are clear for a professional's use in combination with clinical judgment. The test manual documents appropriate psychometric information to support the intended score use. Specifically, evidence to support classification accuracy based on cutoff points for adaptive behaviors is provided. Caution is offered with score use across cultural groups. Additional detail discussing fairness and invariance issues, especially given the small standardization sample sizes for certain groups, is needed. The validity argument could be strengthened in the future with a clearly defined validity inference framework nested in a clearly articulated assessment framework. That said, the DABS, in current form, can provide an important piece of information in the assessment process, generally, and in the ID assessment process, specifically.

REVIEWERS' REFERENCES

American Educational Research Association, American Psychological Association, & National Council on Measurement in Education. (2014). *Standards for educational and psychological testing.* Washington, DC: American Educational Research Association.

American Psychiatric Association. (2013). *Diagnostic and statistical manual of mental disorders* (5th ed.). Washington, DC: Author.

Messick, S. (1989). Validity. In R. L. Linn (Ed.), *Educational measurement* (3rd ed., pp. 13-104). New York, NY: American Council on Education and Macmillan.

Nunnally, J. C., & Bernstein, I. H. (1994). *Psychometric theory* (3rd ed.). New York, NY: McGraw-Hill.

[52]

Early Screening Inventory, Third Edition.

Purpose: Designed "to help identify potential developmental delays or antecedents to developmental disabilities ... that may warrant special education services."
Population: Ages 3:0-5:11.
Publication Dates: 1976-2019.
Acronym: ESI-3.
Scores: Total score only.
Administration: Individual.
Levels, 2: Preschool (Ages 3:0-4:5), Kindergarten (Ages 4:6-5:11).
Price Data, 2020: $189 per preschool or kindergarten kit, including examiner's manual (2019, 234 pages), manipulatives, 25 record forms (preschool or kindergarten), and 25 parent questionnaires in bag; $78.80 per print manual; $44.25 per 25 record forms; $36.80 per 25 parent questionnaires; $33.70 per manipulatives kit; $76.50 per digital manual; $1.30 per Q-global parent questionnaire report; $1.60 per Q-global score summary report (subscriptions and volume discounts available).
Foreign Language Edition: Spanish versions of record forms, parent questionnaires, and the administration and scoring chapter of the test manual are available.
Time: 15-20 minutes for administration.
Comments: Supplemental parent questionnaire available that is designed to "provide an overview of a number of conditions, problems, and events that could constitute risk factors for typical development"; computer administration and scoring available.
Authors: Samuel J. Meisels, Dorothea B. Marsden, Laura W. Henderson, and Martha Stone Wiske.
Publisher: Pearson.
Cross References: For reviews by Ernest Kimmel and Kathleen D. Paget of the 1997 edition of the Early Screening Inventory—Revised, see 14:135; see also T5:889 (1 reference); for reviews by Denise M. Dezolt and Kevin Menefee of the Early Screening Inventory, see 11:122 (1 reference).

Review of the Early Screening Inventory, Third Edition by JOHN D. HALL, Professor of Psychology and Counseling, Arkansas State University, State University, Arkansas:

DESCRIPTION. The Early Screening Inventory, Third Edition (ESI-3)) is a revision of the Early Screening Inventory-Revised (ESI-R; Meisels, Marsden, Wiske, & Henderson, 2008). The ESI-3 is a brief, individually administered developmental screening instrument for ages 3:0-5:11 available in English and Spanish. Administration is untimed and takes 15-20 minutes. The total score reflects performance across three domains: (a) Visual-Motor/Adaptive, (b) Language and Cognition, and (c) Gross Motor. Results assist in determining whether a child merits referral for more in-depth assessment and whether the child may need special education services to perform successfully in school. The revision includes updated 2018 norms to validate cut scores; the addition of a web-based administration, scoring, and reporting option; and an updated Parent Questionnaire with more social-emotional learning content. Although paper and pencil administration and scoring are still available, the purchase of the web-based system allows for administration on any computer or smart device. This system generates reports that include research-based intervention activities for the child. A trainer's manual and additional resources for administration and scoring also are available for purchase.

The examiner qualification for the ESI-3 is level A. Qualification at this level by this test publisher call for training and experience in testing children whose ages and linguistic and cultural backgrounds are like those who will be screened as well as expertise in using development screeners. Individuals with less experience may administer the ESI-3 under supervision of qualified examiners following training. The trainer's manual and additional training resources are useful in these situations.

As noted in the test manual, the three domains include a variety of tasks, which are composed of one to four items. Some tasks include practice items. The Visual-Motor/Adaptive domain consists of four tasks: Block Building, Copy Forms, Draw a Person, and Visual Sequential Memory. The Language and Cognition domain also has four tasks: Number Concept, Verbal Expression, Verbal Reasoning, and Auditory Sequential Memory. Finally, the Gross Motor domain consists of five age-specific tasks: Jump, Walk on the Line, Balance, Hop, and Skip.

The test kit includes the examiner's manual, which provides administration directions in English and Spanish plus recording and scoring guidelines. The manual also includes information on instrument development, technical characteristics (e.g., reliability and validity), and interpretation. Twenty-five age- and language-specific record forms are included. The Preschool Record Form is for ages 3:0-4:5, and the Kindergarten Record Form is for ages 4:6-5:11. Both are available in English and Spanish. Items are arranged by domain with space to record and score responses. For each domain, the tasks and items appear in the order of administration. Examiner directions and instructions are clear and listed on the record forms. The last page of the forms includes space for notes pertaining to speech development, test observations, and steps for calculating the Total Screening Score and decision (i.e., Refer, Rescreen, or OK) based on the provided age-specific cut scores. Children who score in the Refer category merit further assessment to determine whether there are developmental concerns that warrant intervention. Children who score in the Rescreen category should be rescreened in 8-10 weeks unless they are 3 years of age. In this situation, they should be rescreened at age 3:6. Children who score in the OK category are considered to be developing normally. Also included in the kit are required manipulatives. The examiner must provide a few basic materials. Finally, the kit includes 25 supplemental Parent Questionnaires available in English and Spanish. The Parent Questionnaire contains five sections: (a) Child Information; (b) Family; (c) Preschool/Childcare History; (d) Medical History; and (e) Social, Emotional, Language, and Self-Help Skills. Responses provide an overview of issues that also could be risk factors for development. This form can be used prior to the administration of the ESI-3 for observing potential difficulties during the screening.

DEVELOPMENT. According to the test authors, the ESI-3 was developed from and closely resembles the ESI-R. The design and item content were not changed from the ESI-R as developmental skills remain consistent. Expert review involved professional educators including a group of 20 in two states who evaluated the usability of both the paper and the web-based versions. Furthermore, a pilot study was conducted in 2017 with a local sample (*N* = 30) of English-speaking children ages 3:0–5:11 who had no history of developmental delays or other diagnoses to determine the feasibility of using the web-based administration and scoring system. These results validated the use of the online system.

Standardization data were collected in 2018 from both normal and developmentally delayed populations. This testing was conducted by 82 qualified examiners in 32 states. The standardization sample consisted of a normative group representative of the U.S. population of children ages 3:0-5:11, according to 2016 Census Bureau figures. To qualify, children had to display typical development and take the screener without modifications. The sample included 180 English-speaking children and 30 Spanish-speaking children stratified by age, sex, race/ethnicity, geographic region, and parent/caregiver educational level. Concerning English and Spanish results, there was not a significant difference between the raw score mean values when matched sample English and Spanish administrations were compared. This resulted in the cut scores being the same for the ESI-3 screener in English and Spanish. Frequency distributions, means, and standard deviations were obtained for each 6-month age band. A comparison of these data with raw score means and standard deviations from the ESI-R normative sample showed minimal change. In terms of final development, it was determined that new cut scores should be created for most of the age bands to maintain and improve sensitivity and specificity.

TECHNICAL. The test authors note that the ESI has had strong reliability and validity dating to 1982. Local reliability coefficients for the ESI-3 applicable for both English and Spanish versions are reported for cut scores for each age group. These reliability estimates were high and averaged .88 with standard errors of measurement of 2.41 for Refer vs. Rescreen and 2.40 for Refer vs OK. Internal consistency was examined using split-half reliability coefficients corrected with the Spearman-Brown formula. The average reliability coefficients for the English and Spanish versions were high. Specifically, the average value was .81 for preschool and .86 for kindergarten.

Content evidence of validity was evaluated by literature review, user feedback, and expert review. Evidence for criterion validity was based on data from clinical and special group studies. A nationwide study of 82 children ages 3:0-5:11 diagnosed with developmental delays was conducted. Reported demographic characteristics of the sample included age, parent educational level, race/ethnicity, geographic region, and sex. A matched control sample was selected so that each child in the above group was matched to a typically developing child from the normative validation sample based on demographic characteristics and primary language. Group comparison statistics were computed using effect size (Cohen's *d*) comparing the developmentally delayed sample to the matched control sample. The effect sizes were large for the preschool form (d = 1.42) and the kindergarten form (d = 1.57), demonstrating that the ESI-3 effectively discriminates between developmentally delayed children and typically developing children. In terms of sensitivity, defined as the probability that a child who has a developmental delay will test positive for it and specificity, the probability that a child who does not have a developmental delay will test negative, the ESI-3 appears to have average to excellent sensitivity and specificity. More specifically, across ages, sensitivity was .84 (Refer and Rescreen group), and specificity was .95 (Refer group).

COMMENTARY. The ESI-3 appears to provide scores that are reliable and valid for screening young children to determine whether they need more in-depth assessment and whether they present with developmental delays that merit intervention. The screener is brief and straightforward to administer, and the examiner's manual and record forms are well developed. More research is needed to examine the decision consistency of the instrument, which is defined as the extent to which the observed classification of examinees would be the same across replications of the testing procedures (e.g., American Educational Research Association, American Psychological Association, & National Council on Measurement in Education, 2014). Furthermore, future validity studies with the ESI-3 are warranted. Finally, the ESI-3, like most developmental screeners, focuses primarily on select pre-academic child variables (e.g., visual-motor, gross motor, concepts, and language) with limited direct assessment of social-emotional functioning and parent/family functioning. There remains a need for screening practices with young children to include the assessment of these other key variables, as they also link to educational success (e.g., Barnett, Hall, & Bramlett, 1990).

SUMMARY. The ESI-3 is clearly an improvement over the ESI-R in terms of updated norms and Parent Questionnaire content. The Parent Questionnaire, which includes items pertaining to social, emotional, language, and self-help skills, may be useful in the problem-identification process. The optional web-based administration and scoring system, which allows for time efficient assessment and provides reports with intervention recommendations, is also a strength of the instrument. The trainer's manual and additional resources should prove to be useful in situations where individuals with less assessment knowledge and skills are used under the supervision of an experienced examiner. In sum, the ESI-3 will continue to be an important instrument for identifying those children at risk for developmental delays and in need of further assessment and intervention.

REVIEWER'S REFERENCES

American Educational Research Association, American Psychological Association, & National Council on Measurement in Education. (2014). *Standards for educational and psychological testing.* Washington, DC: American Educational Research Association.

Barnett, D. W., Hall, J. D., & Bramlett, R. K. (1990). Family factors in preschool assessment and intervention: A validity study of parenting stress and coping measures. *Journal of School Psychology, 28,* 13-20.

Meisels, S. J., Marsden, D. B., Wiske, M. S., & Henderson, L. W. (2008). Early Screening Inventory—Revised. Bloomington, MN: Pearson.

Review of the Early Screening Inventory, Third Edition by CARL J. SHEPERIS, Dean of the College of Education and Human Development, Texas A&M University-San Antonio, San Antonio, TX, and JORDAN AUSTIN, Doctoral Student, University of North Carolina, Greensboro, Greensboro, NC:

DESCRIPTION. The third edition of the Early Screening Inventory (ESI-3) is a screening instrument designed to assess development across three domains: (a) Visual-Motor/Adaptive, (b) Language and Cognition, and (c) Gross Motor. The primary purpose of the ESI-3 is to assist in the identification of children who may need additional assessment for developmental concerns. The ESI-3 is not a diagnostic test, and, as such, children who score below test cut scores should be referred for more in-depth assessment.

The ESI-3 can be administered to children ages 3 years 0 months to 5 years 11 months, and the instrument is available in both English and Spanish. The administration instructions are clear and easy to follow; administration and scoring processes can be conducted through the use of the test publisher's web-based administration and scoring platform. Prior to administration, if possible, the examiner should collect and review the information provided by the Parent Questionnaire (also available in both English and Spanish) to allow for any indicated concerns or difficulties to be more closely observed during administration.

Each of the three aforementioned developmental domains is assessed through a variety of tasks; for some tasks, the administration is dependent on the child's chronological age. The Visual-Motor/Adaptive domain assesses perceptual and fine motor skills as well as short-term memory. The Language and Cognition domain indicates a child's skill and ability to understand and use language to express his or her own ideas and thoughts. Lastly, the Gross Motor domain assesses overall readiness to accomplish specific motor tasks, such as speaking, writing, reading, and perceptual learning.

Within each of the tasks is a total of one to four items, and each item is scored and summed to generate a Total Screening Score. Because there are separate scoring sheets for preschool and kindergarten, the ESI-3 allows for age-specific cutoff scores to determine whether the child meets criteria for a referral or a rescreen.

The ESI-3 is an untimed assessment; administration is reported to take 15 to 20 minutes. All ESI-3 examiners should have experience or training in administration and interpretation of developmental screening inventories, as well as familiarity and experience with testing children whose ages and linguistic and cultural backgrounds are similar to those of the children to be screened with the ESI-3. No specific degrees, licensures, or certifications are required to administer the ESI-3. Novice teachers, professionals, and students of child development can administer the ESI-3 with appropriate supervision, and a training manual is available to assist with this process.

DEVELOPMENT. The ESI-3 is a revision of the Early Screening Inventory—Revised (ESI-R; Meisels, Marsden, Wiske, & Henderson, 2008), which originated due to a need for a valid and reliable screening instrument distinct from school readiness or intelligence tests. The latter assessment categories measure only current levels of achievement and performance, whereas the ESI-3 focuses instead on tasks that all children with normative development should be able to perform (Meisels, Henderson, Liaw, Browning, & Ten Have, 1993). Changes in the ESI-3 include updated normative data and Parent Questionnaire, as well as compatibility with the test publisher's online platform.

The ESI-3 is a well-respected instrument with versions in use since 1975. Although the third edition of the ESI includes updated normative data, the instrument maintains the same content and structure as the ESI-R. With the new edition of the ESI, the test authors conducted a pilot study to determine the feasibility of administering the instrument via the test publisher's software platform. The pilot study employed a sample of 30 children between the ages of 3:0 and 5:11. The primary finding from the pilot study was that the web-based administration provided a more efficient assessment process than the paper-and-pencil version.

Like the ESI-R, the ESI-3 manual provides a thorough guide for administering and scoring the instrument with extensive examples to guide the user. The addition of the web-based platform has increased the ease of administration and scoring beyond that of the earlier versions of the ESI. The software is able to generate score reports that include suggested intervention strategies for the classroom and home environment.

TECHNICAL. For the standardization study, the ESI-3 authors sampled 180 English-speaking and 30 Spanish-speaking children with an effort toward better representation of the U.S. population of children ages 3:0 to 5:11. In contrast to the ESI-R, the test authors were purposeful in their assessment of Hispanic children, especially those who speak English as a second language. However, the demographic information presented in the test manual is difficult to interpret because the authors appear to have combined the data for the English and Spanish administrations of the instrument in their presentation of results. The authors indicated that they did not meet the self-established sampling criterion (i.e., within 5% of the U.S. population demographics) because 14% of the sample was administered the Spanish version of the instrument. This rationale is not clearly explained and leaves these reviewers with questions about the adequacy of the representation of Hispanic children in the English version of the ESI-3.

Although the test authors conducted a re-standardization process with a small sample of Spanish-speaking children, they reported that the English and Spanish versions resulted in equal cut scores based on their analysis using the Rasch model of item response theory (IRT). The small sample size with Rasch analysis raises some concerns about the power of the statistical analysis and the potential for incorrectly ordered parameters.

The test authors noted only small differences in their comparisons of raw score means between the ESI-R and the ESI-3. They opted to develop new cut scores for most of the age bands in the interest of improving sensitivity and specificity. However, the authors did not delineate their process for determining the new cut scores. Although these reviewers found the technical manual for the ESI-3 to be less clear than the previous versions, the ESI has a strong history, and the new cut scores have the same degree of diagnostic accuracy as previous versions.

Because the test authors used Rasch modeling in their analyses, they calculated measures of local reliability by comparing the local standard error of measurement (*SEM*) at each age group with the standard deviation for each age group. The resulting local reliability estimates ranged from .82 to .90 with the average being .88 for children approaching cut scores. The standard errors of measurement for the ESI-3 are a narrow band ranging between 2.11 and 2.71 across age groups. In addition to local reliability estimates and *SEM*, the test authors calculated split-half reliability, with averages for the combined English and Spanish versions being .81 for the preschool age group and .86 for the kindergarten age group.

The ESI has a history of adequate evidence of validity. However, the test authors provided little information about validity for the ESI-3 based on test content. Instead, the authors focused on response processes in their analyses. They also conducted a study using 82 children identified as having developmental delays in the standardization sample and compared them with a matched sample group of children who did not have developmental delays. Based on the group comparisons, the authors found a large effect size (i.e., 1.42 for the preschool group and 1.57 for the kindergarten group) demonstrating the ability of the instrument to discriminate between those who have developmental delays and those who do not. It is also important to note that the ESI-3 has a strong degree of sensitivity and specificity for identifying those who are at risk and those who should be referred for further screening. Across ages, the positive predictive power (PPP) of the ESI-3 is .36 and .54 for the Refer and Rescreen and the Refer cut scores, respectively. This means that there is an acceptable potential for false positives during the screening process.

COMMENTARY. The ESI is an instrument with a long history of research to support its use. For this version of the instrument, the test authors combined the technical information for both English and Spanish versions into one section of the test manual but neglected to clearly differentiate the data in a meaningful way. In some instances, they provided clear differentiations among the English, Spanish, and combined language formats whereas in other instances (e.g., the validation study), they did not identify the version of the instrument being used. As such, the technical elements of the manual could be further revised to provide greater clarity about the data surrounding each version of the instrument. Further studies of the ESI-3 may prove useful for understanding similarities and differences between English and Spanish versions of the instrument.

SUMMARY. The ESI-3 remains similar to previous versions in terms of content and structure. The instrument has a strong history of clinical utility, and the data support its use in practice. Although the manual lacks some clarity in terms of the technical development of the ESI-3 across English, Spanish, and combined versions, there is evidence of strong reliability and validity for the instrument's scores. The addition of web-based administration and standard reports will provide greater utility for users in early childhood settings.

REVIEWERS' REFERENCES

Chen, W. H., Lenderking, W., Jin, Y., Wyrwich, K. W., Gelhorn, H., & Revicki, D. A., (2014). Is Rasch model analysis applicable in small sample size pilot studies for assessing item characteristics? An example using PROMIS pain behavior item bank data. *Quality of Life Research, 23*(2), 485-493. doi:10.1007/s11136-013-0487-5

Meisels, S. J., Henderson, L. W., Liaw, F.-R., Browning, K., & Ten Have, T. (1993). New evidence for the effectiveness of the Early Screening Inventory. *Early Childhood Research Quarterly, 8*(3), 327-346.

Meisels, S. J., Marsden, D. B., Wiske, M. S., & Henderson, L. W. (2008). Early Screening Inventory—Revised [2008 Edition]. San Antonio, TX: Pearson.

[53]

Emotional Disturbance Decision Tree–Self-Report Form.

Purpose: Designed to "assist in the identification of children who qualify for the federal Special Education category of Emotional Disturbance (ED)."

Population: Ages 9-18.

Publication Date: 2016.

Acronym: EDDT-SR.

Scores, 13: Inability to Build or Maintain Relationships Scale, Inappropriate Behaviors or Feelings Scale, Pervasive Mood/Depression Scale, Physical Symptoms or Fears Scale, Total Score, Resilience Scale, Attention-Deficit Hyperactivity Disorder Cluster, Possible Psychosis/Schizophrenia Cluster, Social Maladjustment Cluster, Level of Severity Cluster, Motivation Cluster, plus 2 validity scores (Infrequency, Inconsistency).

Administration: Individual or group.

Price Data, 2020: $223 per introductory kit including 25 response booklets, 25 reusable item booklets, 25 score summary booklets, and professional manual (192 pages); $83 per professional manual; $87 per 25 response booklets; $46 per 25 reusable item booklets; $33 per 25 score summary booklets; $19 per multi-rater summary form.

Foreign Language Edition: Spanish version available.

Time: [20] minutes.

Comments: Intended for use with the Emotional Disturbance Decision Tree (18:48) and/or the Emotional Disturbance Decision Tree–Parent Form (19:60).

Author: Bryan L. Euler.

Publisher: Psychological Assessment Resources, Inc.

Review of the Emotional Disturbance Decision Tree—Self-Report Form by JEFFREY A. ATLAS, Director, Mental Health Services, SCO Family of Services, Queens, NY:

DESCRIPTION. The issue of self versus other reporting is not unique to the area of individual mental measurements. Late 20th-Century cultural anthropology came to recognize the different perspectives offered by social groups in their self-descriptions versus ethnographer depictions, a distinction that came to be referred to as "emic-etic," modelled on the linguistic contrast of phonemes and phonetics as meaningful sounds of one's language versus universal acoustic transcriptions. Fieldwork came to incorporate in some quarters the presentation of studies to indigenous peoples, including review of film, for input and corrective additions. For Bryan L. Euler's latest contribution to the Emotional Disturbance Decision Tree measure, a self-report edition is offered for use when paired with earlier teacher and/or parent forms to round out special education considerations and to identify children's resilience and motivation. Although not expressly delineating means of child and adolescent feedback of findings, the model is a perspectivist one that seeks to incorporate interview, observation, and multiple clinical ratings in pre-evaluation and full evaluation of students for special education designation.

The Emotional Disturbance Decision Tree—Self-Report (EDDT-SR) comprises 136 statements that are anchored in Likert-like endorsements of *never, sometimes, frequently,* and *almost always*, with numerical scoring using integers of 0-3, in some cases reverse-scored. The phrasing is accessible to the target group of 9- to 18-year-olds, and couched in an informal vernacular that may engage the interest of a majority of questionnaire respondents. Similar to other instruments by this test publisher, the answer form is superimposed on a convenient carbonless tear-away copy, which permits rapid computation of aggregate raw scores. A score summary booklet carries an EDDT-SR Total Score as well as two validity checks for Infrequent and Inconsistent responses, followed by summaries of four Emotional Disturbance (ED) Characteristic Scales; a Resilience Scale; syndrome cluster scores for Attention-Deficit/Hyperactivity Disorder (ADHD), Social Maladjustment, and Possible Psychosis/Schizophrenia; and cluster scores for Severity and Motivation. The summary booklet includes a T score comparative profile of ED scales and a criteria table to aid in referral decisions drawing from the series of EDDT measures.

The four ED scales, conceived as operationalizations of federally described characteristics of emotional disturbance, are carried over from the original EDDT completed by teachers and a later one completed by parents. They are Inability to Build or Maintain Relationships, Inappropriate Behaviors or Feelings, Pervasive Mood/Depression, and Physical Symptoms or Fears.

DEVELOPMENT. Items were written with an aim to be concrete and relevant to students' experiences. Initial item-scale assignments were drawn from the teacher and parent scales and subjected to further empirical analysis. Frequency distributions of item endorsement among a normative sample of 614 children and a combined clinical sample of 118, together with item-total correlations, were reviewed. Those items bearing low item-total correlations were eliminated. Internal consistency correlation coefficients contributed to the final selection of scale and cluster items.

An Infrequency score was developed by grouping three self-evident or atypical items whose endorsement might suggest haphazard or compromised responses to the scale. Using a 99th percentile standardization sample cutoff, including an additional emotional disturbance sample of 162 individuals, a cumulative score of 2 was deemed to constitute an acceptable test protocol, whereas a score of 3 or higher was deemed to indicate questionable response validity. Six other item couplets that would be mutually incompatible if endorsed comprise the Inconsistency score, with a summed point difference score of 10 or above constituting a greater than 99% outlier and an inconsistent protocol.

TECHNICAL.

Standardization. The EDDT-SR normative sample included 614 site-recruited children ages 9-18 with good approximation of 2014 U.S. Census norms across gender, ethnicity, geographic region, and parent education stratification percentages. The average age and grade levels of the normative sample were 13.51 years and 7.92, respectively. A similar age- and grade-level emotional disturbance sample of 162 children, with demographics similar to reported educational statistics, constituted the comparison sample.

Although regression analyses showed negligible age or gender effects, three age groupings of 9-11, 12-14, and 15-18, consistent with preadolescent to adolescent stages, were established across male and female categories. Raw score distributions of items were converted to T scores with a mean of 50 and standard deviation of 10. Norms tables for the ED Characteristic Scales are provided with descriptors of *normal* (T score 0-54), *mild at risk* (T score 55-59), *moderate clinical* (T score 60-69), *high clinical* (T score 70-79), and *very high clinical* (T score at or above 80).

Raw scores for four clinical samples within a combined clinical group (N = 118) were converted to percentile ranks with qualitative labels of *normal* (at or less than 1st percentile), *mild at risk* (2nd to 24th percentile), *moderate clinical* (25th to 74th percentile), and *high clinical* (at or above the 75th percentile). The cluster scores for ADHD, Possible Psychosis, Social Maladjustment, and Severity, all presented as supplemental screeners, received respective normative sample basal-level designations of 91.2%, 93.6%, 70.5%, and 43.3%, differentiating the normative group from the corresponding clinical sample for the involved cluster.

The strength factor of Resilience follows respective scalar T score and descriptive additive item cluster designations. The strength factor of Motivation is scored by adding raw scores.

A newly featured index of the EDDT series uses standard errors of measurement and difference to provide for significance of reliable change scores over time, for instance in response to intervention.

Reliability. In the normative and emotional disturbance samples, internal consistency of items across the scales and clusters yielded alpha coefficients that ranged from .74 to .93, with the exception of a .55 value for the Severity Level cluster for the normative sample.

Although test-retest reliabilities in subsamples of normative (n = 68) and ED (n = 25) students were moderate to high (.77 to .97) for the scales, the preponderance of males (88%) in the ED subsample and the extended range of days for the retest (5-69 for the normative subsample) render this aspect of the measure difficult to evaluate conclusively.

Estimates of interrater reliability for EDDT parent to self-report (n = 100) and teacher to self-report (n = 110) adduced significant, low to moderate correlation coefficients, in line with different behavior settings and general under-reporting from the vantage point of child and adolescent self-reports. Parents' and children's reports for items suggesting Possible Psychosis did not correlate significantly (r = .15), nor did teacher and children's reports of Fears (r = .16).

Validity. Significant intercorrelations were found among the scales and clusters for the normative and ED samples, primarily in the moderate range, suggesting consistency in the internal structure of the instrument.

Moderate convergent validity evidence was demonstrated in comparing the EDDT-SR with the Behavior Assessment System for Children, Second Edition Self-Report of Personality (BASC-2 SRP; Reynolds & Kamphaus, 2004). For example, an EDDT-SR normative subsample (n = 46) Total Score correlated with the BASC-2 SRP Attention Problems Scale at .49, while the correlation between an emotional disturbance subsample (n = 50) and the BASC-2 SRP Attention Problems Scale was .49 as well.

Moderate criterion validity evidence emerged from comparison between the EDDT-SR ADHD subsample (n = 27) and Conners 3 (Conners, 2008) scores, with a correlation coefficient between the EDDT-SR ADHD cluster score and the Conners 3 DSM-IV Hyperactive/Impulsive scale of .56.

Mean scores for the psychosis subsample (n = 28) for the Possible Psychosis cluster were more than five times those obtained for a matched normative subsample, suggestive of high discriminant validity evidence. It may be recalled, however, that children's and parents' reports did not demonstrate good interrater reliability for this cluster.

COMMENTARY. The question of children's "true score," for instance in identifying instantiation of psychotic symptomatology, looms behind evaluation of the EDDT-SR's efficacy. Given a sound inventory of items pertaining to psychological decompensation, one may be inclined to look beyond the poor agreement with the EDDT-PF cluster and rely on the child's "emic" report of experience, particularly as regards positive symptoms, as a guide toward further diagnostic assessment.

The reliance on percentile conversion tables is a more troubling aspect of the EDDT-SR as, similar to the parental form, there is an inordinate degree of scale scores at or above the 99th percentile, bringing into question the necessity of so many items. Visual inspection of 24 pages of tables in just one appendix indicates that more than half of the raw scores in the tables register at or above such a cutoff, suggestive of a low ceiling.

The test author repeatedly invokes use of the EDDT-SR only in combination with the parent and teacher versions, as well as with other measures and in the context of observations and interviews of students. This is wise counsel, but practitioners will have to consider the practicality of this instrument given the larger investment of resources and time needed for administration and scoring of the full EDDT series.

SUMMARY. The Emotional Disturbance Decision Tree-Self Report Form appears to be a useful adjunctive instrument for school psychologists in pre-evaluation and full evaluation of 9- to 18-year-olds being considered for federally mandated special education designation and services. It provides a wealth of data in operationalization of behavioral and mood categories central to special education, while screening for more specific disorders such as ADHD and psychosis. Youth displaying isolated social maladjustment, aside from special education characterization categories and placement, are separable in this assessment component. The Severity and, secondarily, Motivation clusters provide for consideration of cases in which there may be questions to balance in terms of indications for placement and/or suitability of special services/special education versus other intervention strategies. Potentially such assessment procedures can serve differential diagnostic purposes to ameliorate educational groupings in which symptomatic students are grouped with more antisocial youth with differing essential challenges and needs.

The self-report format is a welcome addition to the EDDT series, while a continued low ceiling issue reinforces the acknowledgement that this instrument may find its best use as one component of the full series. The EDDT series may be seen as more helpful when used with other measures that, in comparison, may have a higher degree of specificity with regard to identifiable psychological conditions.

REVIEWER'S REFERENCES

Conners, C. K. (2008). Conners 3rd Edition. North Tonawanda, NY: Multi-Health Systems.

Reynolds, C. R., & Kamphaus, R. W. (2004). Behavior Assessment System for Children, Second Edition. Circle Pines, MN: American Guidance Service.

Review of the Emotional Disturbance Decision Tree—Self-Report Form by JOSEPH C. KUSH, Professor, Duquesne University, Pittsburgh, PA:

DESCRIPTION. The Emotional Disturbance Decision Tree—Self-Report Form (EDDT-SR) is a standardized, norm referenced scale designed to assist school psychologists, diagnosticians, and multidisciplinary teams in the identification of children and adolescents who qualify for the federal special education category of emotional disturbance (ED). The scale is designed to be used with two supplemental scales, one completed by parents (EDDT Parent Form; EDDT-PF) and one completed by classroom teachers (EDDT Teacher Form; EDDT-TF). A multi-rater summary form is available to summarize the data gathered from these multiple sources. However, even when all three EDDT components are administered, they are not intended to be a stand-alone diagnostic instrument, but rather sources of information to be added to a more comprehensive evaluation.

The EDDT-SR is administered individually, in a paper and pencil format, and takes approximately 20 minutes to complete and 10 minutes to score. The technical manual contains detailed information for examiners to assist with developing rapport as well as detailed suggestions for how to intervene if students appear not to comprehend questions or appear to answer questions in a random fashion. Additionally, examiners are instructed to scan the response booklet at the end of the administration for skipped items or multiple responses and to ask the student to amend his or her responses. Scoring is based on a 4-point Likert scale.

The EDDT-SR is intended for use by children and adolescents ages 9 through 18, throughout the United States. The technical manual indicates it can be used with youth "from a broad range of racial/ethnic and sociodemographic contexts" (p. 15). Spanish versions of the item and response booklets are available for use with Hispanic/Latino populations.

Consistent with guidelines from the *Standards for Educational and Psychological Testing* (American Educational Research Association, American Psychological Association, & National Council on Measurement in Education, 2014), use of the EDDT-SR requires either professional training in psychology or a related field, or licensure from an agency/organization that requires appropriate training in the ethical and competent use of psychological tests. This typically includes school psychologists, educational diagnosticians, and clinical or counseling psychologists.

DEVELOPMENT. The EDDT-SR was standardized in 2015 using a sample of 614 children ages 9 through 18 years. Demographic characteristics are provided, and the normative sample demographics appear to align with U.S. population characteristics in terms of gender, ethnicity, geographic region, and parental level of education. Data from a second clinical sample of 162 children found eligible for special education under the federal ED criteria were also collected and again, demographic characteristics of the sample are comparable with U.S. averages with regard to ethnicity and race. Reflecting the fact that male students are overrepresented in ED classrooms, the clinical sample was approximately 63% male—comparable with U.S. special education rates (i.e., 74.7%) but well above the level of inclusion in the normative sample (54.4%).

Items comprising the EDDT-SR were drawn from the already existing parent and teacher forms as well as from rational/empirical analysis. The manual indicates that questions were aligned with the federal definition of emotional disturbance, but it is not clear how the alignment was performed and by whom. After initial questions were revised, the item-total correlations were calculated, and an unspecified number of questions were eliminated. The technical manual indicates that "some items were retained even if they fell below the desired level of reliability because they were seen as critical to a particular area of the federal ED criteria" (manual, p. 61). This process resulted in a final version of the scale that consisted of 136 items. In addition to a Total Score, the measure produces scores for five scales, five clusters, and two validity scales.

Four Characteristic Scales directly align with ED diagnostic criteria taken from the Individuals with Disabilities Education Act, 2004 (IDEA, 2004): inability to build or maintain satisfactory interpersonal relationships, inappropriate behaviors or feelings under normal circumstances, a general or pervasive mood of unhappiness or depression, and a tendency to develop physical symptoms or fears. The fifth scale assesses resilience. Additionally, four cluster scores can be calculated (Attention-Deficit/Hyperactivity Disorder [ADHD], Possible Psychosis, Social Maladjustment, and Level of Severity) as well as a Motivation cluster that includes three domain scores (Tangible/Consumable, Independence/Escape, Positive Attention). A three-item Infrequency score is designed to identify individuals who respond in an atypical fashion, and six item pairs comprise the Inconsistency scale. Tables are provided so that raw scores from the five characteristic scales can be converted to T scores, confidence intervals, and percentile ranks. Separate tables are provided for male and female students and for each of three age groupings.

TECHNICAL. Internal consistency and test–retest reliability coefficients are reported in the technical manual for each of the scales and clusters. Alpha coefficients for the normative sample are acceptable for the total sample and for males and females. Internal consistency coefficients ranged from .69 to .95 for the scales (median alpha for the total sample = .84) and from .55 to .90 for the clusters (median = .80). Similar data were reported of the ED sample, also evidencing acceptable internal consistency, with values ranging from .77 to .92 for the scales (median = .86) and .78 to .91 for the clusters (median = .88). Test-retest reliability was computed on modest sample sizes (normative n = 68; ED n = 25) following a 2-week average interval and produced values for scales of .77 to .95 in the normative sample and from .81 to .97 in the ED sample.

Because the EDDT-SR is objectively scored, differences in scoring that result among multiple raters would reflect arithmetic errors. However, the technical manual does present interrater reliability data based on similarities and differences between the self-report form and the teacher and parent forms. As would be expected, these values are highly variable with reliability coefficients between the parent and self-report forms ranging from .40 to .59 for the scales and from .15 to .51 for cluster scores. These low to moderate values are not unique to the EDDT family; it is quite common for many behavior rating scales, and rating scales of emotional disturbance in particular, to produce discrepant scores when a student's self-report is compared to the ratings of his/her parent or teacher. The EDDT-SR technical manual discusses this phenomenon and points out the necessity for a comprehensive psychoeducational battery to include data from multiple sources and across multiple settings.

Convergent validity evidence is presented in the technical manual by comparing the EDDT-SR scores of 46 students from the normative sample and 50 students from the ED sample with scores on a comparable behavioral rating scale, the BASC-2 Self-Report of Personality. Moderate to moderately highly correlation coefficients (.60 to .80) were produced across composite and most scale and cluster scores for both the normative and ED samples. Additional convergent validity data were reported by comparing EDDT-SR performance with other behavior rating scales (e.g., BASC-2 Parent Rating Scale, Conners Self-Report Form, Conduct Disorder Scale, and Pediatric Behavior Rating Scale Parent Version) across children with a variety of special education needs, including specific learning disabilities, ADHD, social maladjustment, and psychosis. Correlations with each of these scales are reported, typically evidencing low to moderate correlation coefficients. These data should be viewed as preliminary as the clinical samples each included only approximately 30 students.

COMMENTARY. The EDDT-SR directly aligns with criteria from the Individuals with Disabilities Education Act, 2004 (IDEA, 2004) for the identification of individuals with emotional disturbance with most questions derived directly from the federal definition. Questions are behaviorally anchored and require little, if any, interpretation. This feature will be seen as a strength by some; however, clinicians looking for a scale to assist with the identification of underlying pathology may regard the atheoretical nature of the EDDT-SR as a weakness.

Possibly the greatest weakness of the EDDT-SR is that no factor analytic data are provided to support the construct validity of the scale. As a result, it remains unknown whether the theorized scales do in fact provide distinct and discreet information, separate from what is yielded by the Total Score.

SUMMARY. The EDDT-SR is a self-report instrument designed to assess the identification of children and adolescents who will qualify for special education under the emotional disturbance category outlined in the Individuals with Disabilities Education Act (IDEA, 2004). Questions appear face valid and align well with the federal definition of ED, and the scale is designed to be combined with companion scales that collect behavior ratings from the students' parents and teachers. The development of the norms and reliability evidence are adequate, but the lack of exploratory or confirmatory factor analytic findings may limit the diagnostic utility of the scale. The EDDT-SR is most appropriate for use as a screening tool, with emphasis placed on the Total scale score.

REVIEWER'S REFERENCES

American Educational Research Association, American Psychological Association, & National Council on Measurement in Education. (2014). *Standards for educational and psychological testing*. Washington, DC: American Educational Research Association.

Individuals with Disabilities Education Act, 20 U.S.C. §1400 (2004).

[54]

Emotional Processing Scale.

Purpose: Designed to "identify, quantify and differentiate different types of emotional processing styles in normal healthy individuals and those with psychological disorders."
Population: Ages 18 and older.
Publication Date: 2015.
Acronym: EPS.
Scores, 6: Suppression, Signs of Unprocessed Emotion, Controllability of Emotion, Avoidance, Emotional Experience, Total.
Administration: Individual.
Price Data, 2020: £163 per kit including manual, norms booklet, and 25 test booklets; £64 per manual (2015, 106 pages); £45 per norms booklet-version 1; £65 per 25 booklets/scoring forms.
Time: 5-10 minutes for administration.
Authors: Roger Baker, Peter Thomas, Sarah Thomas, Mariaelisa Santonastaso, and Eimear Corrigan.
Publisher: Hogrefe Ltd [United Kingdom].

Review of the Emotional Processing Scale by ROGER A. BOOTHROYD, Professor, Department of Mental Health Law and Policy, Louis de la Parte Florida Mental Health Institute, College of Behavioral and Community Sciences, University of South Florida, Tampa, FL:

DESCRIPTION. The Emotional Processing Scale (EPS) is a 25-item self-assessment measure designed to assess "mechanisms and processes involved in emotional processing and whether there are signs of unprocessed emotional material" in the week prior to rating (manual, p. 23). The test authors articulate a broad set of aims for the scale ranging from theory development, to assessing clinical response, to conducting research on emotional processing. Development began in 1998 with the current version being completed and used internationally in 2004. Since 2004, the scale has been translated into a number of languages (the test manual reports the number both as 13 and as 15), and validity studies have been conducted in a number of different cultural and client diagnosis samples. In 2012, norms were constructed for 13 different cultures and/or diagnostic subgroups of respondents.

Items on the EPS comprise five subscales of five items each in addition to a total emotional processing score. The subscales are as follows: Avoidance, associated with experiential or internal avoidance of stimuli that produce an emotional response; Emotional Experience, related to one's internal emotional experiences; Suppression, associated with controlling one's emotional states; Signs of Unprocessed Emotion, associated with "persistent, intrusive, inadequate resolution" (manual, p. 33) to an emotional event; and Controllability of Emotion, reflecting one's perception of control over his or her emotional feelings. Respondents answer each item using a 10-point Likert-type scale ranging from 0 = *completely disagree* to 9 = *completely agree*. In addition, there are two free-response questions.

The EPS takes a respondent between 5 and 10 minutes to complete. It can be hand-scored and interpreted by the test administrator using the scoring sheet attached to each EPS form. The five items comprising each subscale are summed and divided by 5 to obtain the subscale score (i.e., mean for the subscale). The resulting means are interpreted using a profile chart and percentile ranks using a standardization sample of healthy United Kingdom adults. Additional conversion tables are provided in the norms booklet for other populations. For example, the accompanying norms manual provides gender specific (and some combined) T scores as well as T scores and percentile ranks for 13 discrete diagnostic and cultural samples. The test authors note that a minimum of three items must be answered on a subscale to generate a "valid" (manual, p. 36) subscale score.

A digital version of the EPS is available online through the test publisher's platform. After logging in, respondents complete a Personal Data Screen and then are instructed to think through the past week in terms of where they were, what they did, who they interacted with, and how they were feeling. In addition, respondents are given several practice examples with instructions that they must double enter their responses to continue to the next question. Respondents may change their answers by returning to previous questions. Although the average completion time is only 10 minutes and the scale is typically completed in one sitting, respondents have the option to complete the EPS in more than one session. The interface is fairly straightforward and easy to use. Once completed, a five-component individualized technical report is provided through email. The report includes: (1) the respondent's profile summary, (2) a table of subscale scores (raw and normative values), (3) a detailed summary for each subscale (scale meaning and respondent normative data), (4) an item-level analysis (item score and response time), and (5) response statistics. This interface seems like it would be quite valuable in clinical applications, but its usefulness in research applications is less clear.

DEVELOPMENT. The test manual provides a detailed history of the development of the EPS from a pre-pilot initial item pool containing 302 items, through the various versions of the EPS, to the current 25-item version that was finalized in 2004, the fourth version in its history. Separate studies were conducted to collect data on each of the three prior versions of the EPS, and each time items were added and deleted based on the results of factor analyses, the emerging model of emotional processing, and the ability of the items and subscales to differentiate among clinical diagnostic groups.

TECHNICAL.

Standardization and scoring. Given that EPS is part of an international collaboration of some 80 researchers, gender specific and combined norms have been developed for 13 different diagnostic and cultural groups. These norms are reported in a comprehensive supplemental norms booklet. All of the norms tables were based on a minimum sample size of 75 respondents, which can be rather small when analyzed by gender. Brief descriptions of each standardization sample are provided in the norms booklet. Examination of the norms highlights a number of significant differences in scores associated with gender, age, diagnostic group, and culture. Therefore, users must ensure that interpretation is based on the use of the appropriate normative sample.

As previously noted, the EPS is scored by calculating the mean of the completed items comprising each subscale with a minimum of three items answered to obtain a valid score. These raw scores can be compared to the appropriate norms table to obtain the percentile rank and T score associated with the mean score.

Reliability. Internal consistency reliability estimates based on alpha coefficients are reported for four different samples and the total sample (N = 3,657). For the total scale, alphas ranged from .92 to .96 across the four samples with a value of .95 for the total sample. Internal consistency estimates for the five subscale scores ranged from .74 to .92 across samples, indicating the items are conceptually similar. Two studies examined the test-retest reliability of the EPS. Baker et al. (2010) reported subscale test-retest reliabilities ranging from .48 for the Unprocessed subscale to .84 for the Experience subscale over a 4- to 6-week interval. However this study was based on the 53-item version of the EPS (with data extracted for the 25 items on the final version) and only included 17 respondents. The second study was by Santonastaso (2011) and involved 48 respondents to the Italian translation of the EPS. Test-retest reliability estimates over an unspecified interval ranged from .52 for the Suppression subscale to .81 for the Experience subscale. In short, more research needs to be conducted to more rigorously establish the test-retest reliability of this scale.

Information on the average interitem correlations is provided for the same five samples used in the internal consistency analyses. The average interitem correlation coefficients ranged from .36 and .70 for subscales and from .31 to .49 for the total scale, indicating that the items contribute unique information and are not redundant. The interitem correlations are highest on the Suppression subscale (.52-.70), suggesting some of these items may be somewhat redundant whereas the average interitem correlations among the Avoidance scale items are much lower (.36-.41) indicating these items may be less cohesive. This observation is supported by the fact that the Avoidance scale has the lowest internal consistency reliability of the five subscales.

Factor structure. The factor structure of the EPS was examined using data from two independent samples, one from Baker et al. (2010) and the other comprising a combined sample from other studies. Both analyses used maximum likelihood estimators with a Promax rotation to allow for correlated factors. With few exceptions, cutoffs for factor loading values were not specified, only the loadings for the items comprising a subscale are presented in the test manual making it somewhat difficult to fully compare the results of the two analyses. The test authors concluded that the factor structure of the EPS replicated itself well across the two analyses. However, the Baker et al. (2010) study was based on the 53-item version of the EPS (of which only the 25 items from the final version were analyzed), the total sample was presumably based on administration of the 25-item version, and both samples involved only English-speaking respondents. Therefore, additional factor analytic studies are needed to determine the extent to which the EPS has a stable factor structure across subpopulations and cultural groups.

Interscale correlations. Interscale correlations are presented for three samples and the total sample. A review of the correlations indicates they are high with most exceeding .60 and many approaching .70. These results suggest that the five subscales have a high degree of conceptual overlap.

Discrimination. Data are presented in the test manual documenting the fact that the EPS subscale scores can meaningfully differentiate between healthy respondents and both pain and psychological samples or respondents. Examination of the means seems to suggest that the healthy subpopulation has better emotional processing skills compared to the other two subgroups although the specific pairwise comparisons are not reported in the test manual. Presentation of the magnitude of these differences (i.e., effect sizes) would be helpful.

Concurrent validity. Correlations between total score on the EPS and other commonly used measures are presented from several studies as evidence of the concurrent validity of the EPS. For example, the correlation coefficient between the EPS total score and the Toronto Alexithymia Scale (Bagby, Parker, & Taylor, 1994) was .70. Coefficients were .55 with the Symptoms of Anxiety and Depression scale score (from the Foulds & Bedford Delusions-Symptoms-State Inventory; Bedford, Foulds, & Sheffield, 1976) and .79 with the General Health Questionnaire (Goldberg, 1978). These results indicate the EPS correlates moderately to strongly with other theoretically related measures.

Sensitivity to change. Several studies are summarized in the test manual that examined the ability of the EPS to detect change resulting from intervention. Pre- to post-intervention improvements in emotional processing were found to be correlated significantly with similar changes in a number of other commonly used measures such as the Brief Symptom Inventory.

COMMENTARY. The EPS was developed on a strong theoretical framework, and its development has been ongoing for many years. In addition, the EPS is currently being used internationally by many investigators, and a substantial amount of data has been and continues to be collected from a variety of subpopulations and cultures.

However, a concern with some analyses presented in the test manual is that they are based on different sample sizes even within the same subpopulation, yielding different results that can be confusing. For example, the mean score for Item 21 in the Healthy subsample (N = 2,764) is reported initially as 3.68 (SD = 2.69). In contrast, the mean score for Item 21 from the same Healthy subpopulation presented elsewhere in the manual (N = 3,703) is 2.93, which is quite different from 3.68. Mean score differences on other items are much smaller, but the magnitude of this difference represents an effect size on the order of .28, a meaningful difference. It also raises the question about the 939 respondents (25.4%) not included in the first analysis. Also the psychometric analyses are based only on respondents completing the English version of the EPS. This raises additional questions regarding the extent to which these analyses reflect the psychometric properties of the 13 (or 15) translations of the EPS. In addition, the lack of gender specific norms on the Profile Chart of the EPS form is a concern given that the test authors stated in previous research that gender is an important factor associated with emotional processing.

Despite these concerns, given the substantial international network of researchers using the EPS, opportunities likely will exist as more data become available to conduct psychometric analyses to deal with some of these concerns. Until this occurs, users should exercise some caution and attempt to understand whether and how these differences might impact decision making.

SUMMARY. In summary, the EPS is a 25-item self-administered measure designed to assess respondents' emotional processing. The scale has a long developmental history and has been administered to respondents representing a diverse group of clinical and cultural subpopulations. Although extensive psychometric analyses have been conducted, variability in the subsamples examined may create some issues for EPS users that need to be considered when interpreting results.

REVIEWER'S REFERENCES

Bagby, R. M., Parker, J. D. A., & Taylor, G. J. (1994). The twenty-item Toronto Alexithymia Scale-I: Item selection and cross-validation of the factor structure. *Journal of Psychosomatic Research, 38,* 23-32. https://doi.org/10.1016/0022-3999(94)90005-1

Baker, R., Thomas, S., Thomas, P. W., Gower, P., Santonastaso, M., & Whittlesea, A. (2010). The Emotional Processing Scale: Scale refinement and abridgement (EPS-25). *Journal of Psychosomatic Research, 68,* 83-88.

Bedford, A., Foulds, G. A., & Sheffield, B. F. (1976). A new personal disturbance scale (DSSI/sAD). *British Journal of Social and Clinical Psychology, 15,* 387-394.

Derogatis, L. R., & Melisaratos, N. (1983). The Brief Symptom Inventory: An introductory report. *Psychological Medicine, 13,* 595-605. http://dx.doi.org/10.1017/s0033291700048017

Goldberg, D. (1978). *Manual of the General Health Questionnaire.* Windsor, UK: NFER.

Santonastaso, M. (2011). *Cross-cultural comparison of emotional processing: A quantitative psychological study of healthy patients and chronic-pain patients from England, Italy and Japan.* (Unpublished doctoral dissertation). Bournemouth University, UK.

Review of the Emotional Processing Scale by ANDREW A. COX, Professor Emeritus, Counseling, Rehabilitation, and Interpreter Training, Troy University, Phenix City, AL:

DESCRIPTION. The Emotional Processing Scale is a 25- item self-assessment that measures emotional processing mechanisms and processes. It is designed for use with test takers 18 years of age and older. Respondents rate their emotional processing for 1 week prior to the rating using a 0 to 9 Likert-type scale with visual, numerical, and written anchor points. The answer sheet also provides sections where respondents can provide additional information regarding their emotions. The scale requires 5 to 10 minutes for response time.

The scale has five subscales of five items each and a total emotional processing score. Subscales are Suppression, Signs of Unprocessed Emotion, Controllability of Emotion, Avoidance, and Emotional Experience. The instrument appears to be based upon well referenced and empirically supported theoretical concepts as detailed within the test manual. There is a focus upon Rachman's and Foa's emotional processing concepts describing the manner in which distressing cognitive input is absorbed and processed.

The test manual details easy to follow scoring directions. The scale can be hand-scored, and SPSS syntax is provided for computer scoring. Norms tables provide raw score conversions to T scores and percentile ranks. Cutoff scores for all subscales and the total score are provided to facilitate clinical usage of the instrument. Combined gender and gender-based norms are provided.

A variety of normative tables are provided within the norms booklet. These include healthy United Kingdom and international populations to include Polish, Portuguese, Indian, Egyptian, and Japanese samples; English speaking samples including the United States, Canada, and Australia; chronic pain; youthful offenders; addictions, eating disordered, and general psychological problem mental health; and pregnant women populations. Limited data with small population samples are reported for attention disorders, traumatic brain injury, long term abstinence from addiction, childhood sexual abuse, cancer patient, and non-epileptic attack disorder.

DEVELOPMENT. The scale's initial development emanated from a research project involving cognitive therapy with panic disorder patients that was later expanded to include individuals with depressive disorders. The readable and well organized test manual provides a chronology and details regarding the scale's development. Scale development is supported through recent research studies.

The inventory was initially piloted with a form containing 101 items selected from a pool of 136 items. Two additional pilot forms were used, with the final 25 items selected over a 4-year period. Piloting was completed with a total of 1,300 research participants. Additional item development input was obtained from international collaborators, increasing the sample size to 7,113 participants.

Factor analytic studies were used to identify and clarify the structure of the scale. The test authors appear to have gone to great lengths to develop a psychometrically sound assessment scale that also differentiated different diagnostic groups.

TECHNICAL. The scale was normed on 6,402 respondents with some samples selected from healthy English speaking populations in the United Kingdom, United States, Canada, and Australia. Other samples comprising the normative sample included those with various psychological and medical conditions drawn from medical practice, residential and inpatient treatment, university, and community settings. The test manual describes gender, age, and educational characteristics for the normative sample. There are no data reported regarding ethnicity.

Internal consistency (alpha) coefficients for the subscales ranged from .74 to .92 with full-scale coefficients of .92 to .96. Split-half reliability coefficients ranged from .88 to .92. Results from preliminary test-retest reliability studies are reported. One study (Baker et al., 2010) retested 17 individuals (nine women, eight men) on the 25 items of the final version of the EPS at an interval of 4 to 6 weeks. Correlation coefficients ranged from .48 to .84 for the subscales; the coefficient for Total EPS was .74. The test authors acknowledge that additional test-retest reliability research is needed. The test manual also reports other item statistics via tables to include means and standard deviations for the scale's various normative groups and subscales.

Relative to validity, interscale correlations of .51 to .69 were reported for the subscales in a study with 4,024 participants. The test authors indicate that subscales share common elements but also distinguish healthy emotional processing as compared to various diagnostic groups. The test authors suggest that this study supports expectations relative to the scale.

Concurrent validation studies are reported comparing the EPS to other emotional control, alexithymia, anxiety, depression, postnatal depression, general health, and self-esteem inventories. Adequate concurrent validation evidence appears to be present.

A study providing predictive validity evidence for the EPS is described. The study involved 974 pregnant women who completed the EPS and other measures at 13 and 34 weeks' gestation and again 6 weeks after giving birth. Results indicated that the EPS scores contributed meaningfully to the prediction of postpartum depression. Results from a second study involving cancer survivors suggested that the EPS may be able to detect symptoms of posttraumatic stress disorder among cancer survivors.

COMMENTARY. The test manual details the use and application of the EPS within various clinical settings. The chronology of the scale's development is a positive feature. It is thought that this scale could play a viable role in emotional processing research, psychosocial treatment evaluation and development, and enhancement of personal insight on emotional processing styles of test respondents. The test manual details the use and potential use of the scale within research settings.

The test manual details the psychometric qualities of the scale in an easy-to-read format allowing potential test users to evaluate the instrument's usage within their settings. The test authors also address areas for additional work to include developing norms for older adults, young males, and different professional, occupational, and ethnic groups. There is also a need to address the meaning associated with low scores on this measure.

The test authors also indicate a need for more cross cultural studies; the scale has several language translations that would facilitate such research. One of two limitations identified for this scale concerns the lack of information provided within the manual relative to ethnicity represented by the standardization sample. Such information should be provided and may be essential for test users anticipating use of the EPS within culturally diverse settings.

The English speaking international normative sample is based upon healthy university student respondents, a second limitation identified for this scale. This normative group needs to be expanded to other representative groups within North America and Australia to promote the usage of the EPS to settings outside of the United Kingdom and Europe.

SUMMARY. The EPS appears useful in research on emotional processing. It is based upon a well-researched model to explain the scale's constructs. It has some utility in clinical settings where the target of intervention may include assessment of changes in emotional processing or identification of emotional processing styles.

If the test authors carry out the research agenda relative to the future development of the scale as described within the manual, such should improve the psychometric qualities as well as the clinical utility of the inventory. The scale presents evidence of adequate reliability and concurrent validation. Some evidence that the scale assesses aspects of theoretical constructs upon which it is based is presented. Further evidence of construct validation should be shown through research efforts with this scale.

More information regarding ethnicities represented in the scale's normative sample along with further research regarding cross cultural groups is required. If used with English speaking respondents in Australia, Canada, and the United States, test users should be aware that the normative sample for these groups was based upon university student samples. Accordingly, test users should carefully consider whether their intended respondents were represented adequately within the scale's normative sample. Other than these considerations, the scale appears to be a useful addition to emotional processing instruments for use in research and clinical settings.

REVIEWER'S REFERENCE

Baker, R., Thomas, S., Thomas, P. W., Gower, P., Santonastaso, M., & Whittlesea, A. (2010). The Emotional Processing Scale: Scale refinement and abridgement (EPS-25). *Journal of Psychosomatic Research, 68*, 83-88.

[55]

Employee Screening Questionnaire–2.

Purpose: Designed as "a personality-based selection measure" to assess "employees' propensity to engage in both positive as well as counterproductive work behaviors."
Population: Prospective employees.
Publication Dates: 2001-2009.
Acronym: ESQ2.
Scores, 15: Customer Service, Productivity, Accuracy, Commitment/Job Satisfaction, Promotability, Alcohol and Substance Abuse, Unauthorized Sick Days, Driving Delinquency, Lateness, Loafing, Sabotage of Production or Property, Safety Infractions, Theft, Risk of Counterproductive Behavior, Overall Hiring Recommendation.
Administration: Individual or group.
Price Data, 2020: $248.50 per fax-in scoring including technical manual (2009, 47 pages), 1 reusable test booklet, and 10 fax-in answer sheets; $22 per online test administration including scoring and report; $2.50 per reusable test booklet.
Foreign Language Editions: Available in French, Portuguese, and Spanish.
Time: (15-20) minutes.
Author: Douglas N. Jackson.
Publisher: SIGMA Assessment Systems, Inc.

a) EMPLOYEE SCREENING QUESTIONNAIRE–CALL CENTER.
Acronym: ESQ-CC.
Scores, 13: Same as above minus Driving Delinquency, and Bogus Sick Days replaces Unauthorized Sick Days.
Comments: Alternate form specifically for use in call centers.

Cross References: For reviews by Paul M. Muchinsky and Frank Schmidt of the original edition, see 16:86.

Review of the Employee Screening Questionnaire—2 by CHARLES A. SCHERBAUM, Professor of Psychology, Baruch College, City University of New York, New York, NY:

DESCRIPTION. The Employee Screening Questionnaire—2 is a personality inventory for use in employee selection contexts to identify individuals who are likely to engage in counterproductive work behaviors as well as those who are likely to perform well on the job. The second version of this measure contains 27 forced choice item quartets that assess the personality dimensions of dependability, methodicalness, industriousness, extraversion, agreeableness, and independence. In each quartet, the individual selects the statements that are the most and least descriptive of the four options. The data on these personality dimensions are combined to create five scales of positive work behaviors (e.g., Customer Service, Productivity), eight scales of counterproductive behaviors at work (e.g., Theft, Loafing), a scale of the overall Risk of Counterproductive Behaviors, and an Overall Hiring Recommendation. The technical manual provides sufficient detail on the procedures for administering the assessment. Paper-and-pencil and online administration options are available; all scoring is completed by the test publisher. It is recommended that the assessment be proctored. The test publisher provides a score report with the individual's percentile score on each of the scales and the Overall Hiring Recommendation. The technical manual notes that the scores should not be shared with the test taker. In addition to the technical manual, the test publisher provides a user's guide to aid in proper administration of the assessment and interpretation and use of the scores.

DEVELOPMENT. The development of Employee Screening Questionnaire—2 is conceptually based on the five-factor model of personality and draws on the item pools from the Six-Factor Personality Questionnaire, the Personality Research Form, and the Jackson Personality Inventory-Revised. The technical manual provides information on the process that was used to create the original Employee Screening Questionnaire as well as the revised version as reviewed here. This description includes the process used to create the forced choice version of the assessment. There is little description of the process by which the 15 work-related scale scores were created, how they relate to the personality items, or how the "pass" score on the assessment was established. It appears the scales were created using self-reported positive and negative work behaviors (e.g., self-reported theft), not objective data (e.g., actual theft). Data are presented on the relationship between the original items and other personality measures as well as evidence on the degree to which the forced-choice version minimizes faking. The Employee Screening Questionnaire-2 manual describes the changes made to the assessment for the second edition such as moving the locations of some statements within the 27 item quartets, replacing some of the statements, and updating the scoring algorithm.

TECHNICAL. The technical manual includes discussion of the results of two criterion-related validity studies using the Employee Screening Questionnaire—2. Elsewhere in the technical manual, research is referenced for the original version of the assessment. The two criterion-related studies using the Employee Screening Questionnaire—2 report a number of correlations between the Employee Screening Questionnaire—2 scale scores and self-reports of the corresponding outcomes (e.g., the Loafing scale correlates with self-reported loafing). The correlations are generally in the .20 to .30 range with the Loafing and Risk of Counterproductive Behavior scales showing higher correlations (as high as the .50's). Correlations are not reported for several of the scales due to the lack of the counterproductive behavior being reported. Low base rates are common with counterproductive behaviors. Given that the data in these studies are self-reported counterproductive behaviors, it is not known how well this assessment predicts actual counterproductive behaviors. The manual reports analyses on the frequency of self-reported counterproductive behaviors and the pass/fail score on the Employee Screening Questionnaire—2. The results generally show that those who fail to reach the passing score on the measure have higher reported levels of counterproductive behaviors. The report does not describe what constitutes a passing or failing score. No results on group score differences are reported in the test manual.

COMMENTARY. The research literature on personality assessment in recent years has focused on the use of forced-choice items as a way to improve validity, better model the underlying response process, and minimize faking. Very little of this research and current thinking is leveraged in the technical manual including independent studies that have examined the Employee Screen Questionnaire (e.g., O'Neill et al., 2017). An update of the technical manual with more current perspectives on personality assessment and its use in employee selection would be welcomed. Although the development of the personality items is well described, the technical manual included very little information about the development of the scale scores in this assessment. Interpreting the validity evidence without this information is difficult.

SUMMARY. Based on the available evidence, there is some support for using the Employee Screening Questionnaire—2 in employee selection contexts. However, the existing evidence is limited and requires a number of assumptions (e.g., self-reported counterproductive behaviors are a good proxy for actual counterproductive behaviors). Additional studies providing further criterion-related validity evidence and evidence of score differences are needed.

REVIEWER'S REFERENCE

O'Neill, T. A., Lewis, R. J., Law, S. J., Larson, N., Hancock, S., Radan, J., . . . Carswell, J. J. (2017). Forced-choice pre-employment personality assessment: Construct validity and resistance to faking. *Personality and Individual Differences, 115,* 120-127.

Review of the Employee Screening Questionnaire-2 by CHOCKALINGAM VISWESVARAN, Professor of Psychology, Florida International University, Miami, FL:

DESCRIPTION. The Employee Screening Questionnaire-2 (ESQ2) is designed to assess personality traits that correlate with productive and counterproductive work behaviors. It is presented as a personality-based integrity assessment. Psychometric integrity tests have been found to predict job performance and counterproductive work behaviors in multiple samples (cf. Ones, Viswesvaran, & Schmidt, 1993, 2012). These integrity tests are classified as overt or clear purpose tests if the test intention is clear to test takers and personality-based integrity tests if the stress is on the measurement of personality traits that assess integrity (Sackett, Burris, & Callahan, 1989). ESQ2 focuses on measuring five personality facets and a dependability facet that includes assessments of integrity, risk taking and responsibility. ESQ2 is a refinement of an earlier version ESQ that was reviewed in *The Sixteenth Mental Measurements Yearbook* (Muchinsky, 2005; Schmidt, 2005). There is also a version of the ESQ that is focused on assessments for call center employees (ESQ-CC). The ESQ2 consists of 27 tetrads and provides 13 specific scores in addition to (a) Risk of Counterproductive Behaviors and (b) an Overall Hiring Recommendation. ESQ2 scores are reported as percentiles—high percentile scores for positive work dimensions are desirable whereas low percentile scores are desirable for dimensions that assess counterproductive behaviors.

DEVELOPMENT. The test manual spends 12 pages on how the scales were developed. Ten of the 12 pages focus on ESQ construction, and the last two pages address how the ESQ was refined to ESQ2. This review provides the steps taken in the construction of ESQ and then notes the changes made for ESQ2. ESQ was developed as an assessment of five personality factors (extraversion, agreeableness, independence, methodicalness, and industriousness) and a dependability factor (that is comprised of integrity, risk taking, and responsibility). The developmental steps for the five factors, the integrity facet of the dependability factor, and the other two facets of the dependability factor (risk taking and responsibility) are different.

To develop the five personality factors of the ESQ, the test authors started with a pool of 2,500 items. Items were chosen so that they do not overlap across scales. Other considerations for item retention included (a) shorter items, (b) their correlation with the factor scores, and (c) correlation with peer ratings for the relevant factor the item was designed to assess. The five factor scores were then correlated with peer ratings of the respondent on the same factor. Finally, the five scales were administered to 4,040 job applicants and item means were computed. The frequency of endorsements was coupled with desirability ratings of the items to complete the forced-choice scales for the five personality factors.

To assess the integrity facet of the dependability factor, a series of steps was undertaken. First, a sample of 432 items assessing a wide range of personality and psychopathological content was administered to 69 prison inmates and 166 non-prisoners. Items that differentiated the two groups at the .001 statistical significance level (n = 140) were factor-analyzed, and four factors were identified. Of these four factors, two factors were deemed relevant to integrity. The substantive content of these two factors along with *DSM* criteria for defining "antisocial personality" were used to write an initial pool of 120 items to measure the integrity facet. The 120 items were administered to 102 adults, and factor analyses suggested two factors. The first factor reflected ethical behaviors in morally demanding situations, and the second reflected self-control in situations where aggression can be elicited. The two factors were labelled honesty and self-control. Scores from the two factors were correlated with three experimental measures: (1) a self-rating of bipolar traits linked to integrity; (2) a job preference rating on eight hypothetical jobs, four of which had integrity implications; and (3) advice given on nine ethical dilemmas. Evidence is presented that scores from the honesty scale correlated with these three criteria whereas the self-control scale did not yield statistically significant correlations with any of the three criteria. Based on these item analyses as well as desirability ratings, 20 items were chosen to assess integrity and were administered to 4,040 job applicants. Based on further item analysis, eight items were chosen for assessing the integrity facet of the dependability scale. Items were drawn from the Jackson Personality Inventory-Revised (JPI-R) to assess the other two facets of the dependability scale—responsibility and risk taking.

The test manual states that the ESQ was used to assess "tens of thousands of job applicants" (p. 31) between 2002 and 2008 (actual number not provided; mean age 29.87 years; 28% male, 31% female, 41% gender unreported; 57.2% took the test online). In the space of one page in the manual, it is noted that the following refinements to ESQ resulted in ESQ2: (1) the locations of 19 of the 108 statements on the scale were changed based on endorsement rates to reduce applicant ability to fake; (2) 17 new statements (14 of which came from the JPI-R, the Personality Research Form, and the Six Factor Personality Questionnaire) were substituted into the ESQ to enhance validity and minimize group differences; (3) the algorithm to generate the 15 scale scores was changed based on responses from 943 job incumbents and self-report measures of counterproductivity, job satisfaction, and other work-related assessments; and (4) new norms were generated based on responses from 5,000 job applicants across the United States. This reviewer believes that this section of the manual needs to be substantially elaborated before an evaluative review and meaningful evaluations can be made.

TECHNICAL. The section of the test manual on the empirical evaluation of the ESQ2 is also short and needs expansion. This section does not report any estimates of reliability, but in another section of the manual the internal consistency reliability (coefficient alpha) of the ESQ-CC scales is reported based on a sample of 163. In the sections describing the ESQ2, a table based on data from 163 respondents is presented with correlations between the 16PF factors and the five personality factors and dependability factor of the original ESQ. It is not clear whether the reliability data and convergent correlations with the 16PF are based on the same sample. No reliabilities are reported for the 15 scale scores generated in the original ESQ. Also reported is a table summarizing the intercorrelations among the six factors of ESQ2 (five personality factors and the dependability factor) based on 5,415 job applicants. The correlations are low in magnitude (.01-.38), suggesting that the six factors of ESQ2 are largely independent.

Validity evidence for ESQ2 is based on a sample of 943 job incumbents at a nationwide retailer in the United States. Of the 943 incumbents, 506 were in entry-level positions and the rest were in managerial levels. All 943 incumbents were assessed on the ESQ2 and provided self-ratings of counterproductive workplace behaviors. A 19-item measure of counterproductive behaviors by Bennett and Robinson (2000) was used for the self-ratings and supplemented by four items to tap some ESQ2 outcomes. All respondents also completed a job satisfaction measure. In addition, managers completed a self-reported inventory for risk of derailment whereas entry-level incumbents completed the Honesty-Humility scale of the HEXACO Personality Inventory (Lee & Ashton, 2004). Correlations between nine ESQ2 scale scores and the corresponding self-report measures are provided in a table in the test manual and range from .23 (Sabotage of Production or Property) to .51 (Risk of Counterproductive Behavior). Correlations between the ESQ2's Overall Hiring Recommendation and the HEXACO scale and risk of derailment measure were .38 and -.49, respectively. A similar analysis was conducted with a sample of 217 call center employees.

COMMENTARY. The detailed description of the item generation and scale construction is commendable. The same cannot be said about the clarity of studies assessing the reliability and validity of the most recent version of the ESQ. Further, if "tens of thousands of job applicants" (manual, p. 31) have taken this measure, it might be possible for the authors to present the validity evidence from this database (e.g., criterion-related validity using external criteria such as supervisory ratings). Also, if the ESQ was revised to construct the ESQ2 to reduce group differences, data should be presented on such group differences (cf. Ones & Viswesvaran, 1998). In fact, if the database is as extensive as claimed in the test manual, the authors can provide empirical tests of predictive bias, measurement equivalence across formats (e.g., online), and non-linearity of predictor-criterion relationships.

If ESQ and ESQ2 have been used so extensively by employers, normative data should be tailored to job-specific applicant pools (Ones & Viswesvaran, 2003). Reliability estimates should be reported for the scale scores generated by ESQ2, and not just for the five personality factors and the dependability factor. In addition to coefficient alpha, test-retest estimates over appropriate time periods are needed. When reporting the validity coefficients between ESQ2 scale scores and self-reported criterion measures, the full correlation matrix should be reported.

SUMMARY. The ESQ2 and ESQ-CC have developed from well-established personality tests and programs of personality research, the authors of which are distinguished scholars in the field of personality assessment and pioneers of personality psychology. With such foundations, and based on the exemplary care in item and scale construction detailed in the test manual, this assessment should be evaluated very favorably. This reviewer would also encourage the test authors to summarize all available data (and more details) on all their samples in a revised manual.

REVIEWER'S REFERENCES

Bennett, R. J., & Robinson, S. L. (2000). Development of a measure of workplace deviance. *Journal of Applied Psychology, 85*(3), 349-360.

Lee, K., & Ashton, M. C. (2004). Psychometric properties of the HEXACO Personality Inventory. *Multivariate Behavioral Research, 39,* 329-358.

Muchinsky, P. M. (2005). [Test review of Employee Screening Questionnaire]. In R. A. Spies & B. S. Plake (Eds.), *The sixteenth mental measurements yearbook* (pp. 364-365). Lincoln, NE: Buros Institute of Mental Measurements.

Ones, D. S., & Viswesvaran, C. (2003). Job-specific applicant pools and national norms for personality scales: Implications for range-restriction corrections in validation research. *Journal of Applied Psychology, 88,* 570-577.

Ones, D. S., & Viswesvaran, C. (1998). Gender, age, and race differences on overt integrity tests: Results across four large-scale job applicant data sets. *Journal of Applied Psychology, 83,* 35-42.

Ones, D. S., Viswesvaran, C., & Schmidt, F. L. (1993). Comprehensive meta-analysis of integrity test validities: Findings and implications for personnel selection and theories of job performance [Monograph]. *Journal of Applied Psychology, 78,* 679-703.

Ones, D. S., Viswesvaran, C., & Schmidt, F. L. (2012). Integrity tests predict counterproductive work behaviors and job performance well: Comment on Van Iddekinge, Roth, Raymark, and Odle-Dusseau (2012). *Journal of Applied Psychology, 97,* 537-542.

Sackett, P. R., Burris, L. R., & Callahan, C. (1989). Integrity testing for personnel selection: an update. *Personnel Psychology, 42,* 491-526.

Schmidt, F. (2005). [Test review of Employee Screening Questionnaire]. In R. A. Spies & B. S. Plake (Eds.), *The sixteenth mental measurements yearbook* (pp. 364-365). Lincoln, NE: Buros Institute of Mental Measurements.

[56]

The Encouragement Index.

Purpose: Designed to help people "develop a picture of [their] strengths and opportunities for improvement in the leadership practice of Encouraging the Heart."
Population: Persons in leadership roles.
Publication Date: 2011.
Score: Total score only.
Administration: Group.
Price Data, 2016: $12 per assessment; $91 per facilitator's guide (2011, 78 pages); $19.95 per revised workbook (2011, 119 pages).
Time: Administration time not reported.
Comments: Focuses on the leadership practice Encourage the Heart from the Five Practices of Exemplary Leadership® in the Leadership Practices Inventory, Fourth Edition (see 86, this volume).
Authors: James M. Kouzes and Barry Z. Posner.
Publisher: The Leadership Challenge, A Wiley Brand.

No review available. This test does not meet review criteria established by the Buros Center for Testing that call for at least minimal technical and development information.

[57]

Executive Functions Test–Elementary: Normative Update.

Purpose: "Designed to identify weaknesses in language-based executive function."
Population: Ages 7-0 to 12-11.
Publication Dates: 2014-2017.
Acronym: EFT-E: NU.
Scores, 5: Attention and Immediate Memory-Verbal, Attention and Immediate Memory-Verbal and Nonverbal, Working Memory and Flexible Thinking, Shifting, Executive Function Index.
Administration: Individual.
Price Data, 2020: $213 per kit including manual (2017, 86 pages), picture book, and 25 record booklets; $96 per picture book; $73 per manual; $49 per 25 record booklets.
Time: 45-60 minutes for administration.
Authors: Linda Bowers and Rosemary Huisingh.
Publisher: PRO-ED.

Review of the Executive Functions Test–Elementary: Normative Update by MAURICIO A. GARCIA-BARRERA, Associate Professor, Department of Psychology, University of Victoria, B.C., Canada:

DESCRIPTION. The Executive Functions Test–Elementary: Normative Update (EFT-E: NU) is "designed to identify weaknesses in language-based executive function" (manual, p. 2) in English-speaking children ages 7-0 through 12-11. It includes four subtests: Attention and Immediate Memory-Verbal (emphasizes attention to detail during a verbal memory task), Attention and Immediate Memory-Verbal and Nonverbal (examines attention to detail, problem-solving, and inference skills during a task that involves seeing illustrations and hearing passages), Working Memory and Flexible Thinking (examines problem solving and the ability to make inferences about somebody else's behavior based on short passages), and Shifting (examines ability to shift between naming categories after being primed in a specific category). Administration takes 45-60 minutes. The test yields the four subtest scores as scale scores (mean 10, SD 3), a composite score (the Executive Function Index [EFI]) that is presented as a standard score (mean 100, SD 15), percentile ranks, and age equivalents. The EFT-E: NU floors and ceilings were examined and deemed to meet the criteria for very good to excellent range proposed by Bracken (1987; as cited by the test authors in the test manual). Adequate item difficulty gradients were achieved by smoothing the normative tables.

The test authors list four major uses of the test: identification of impairment, profile analysis (i.e., patterns of strengths and weaknesses), development of strategies for remediation, and use in research settings. Qualified users include "speech-language pathologists, school psychologists, educational diagnosticians, and professionals in related fields" (manual, p. 4). Knowledge of language disorders is a requisite for administration. The test manual includes simple scoring instructions (1 point for correct answers or 0 points for incorrect answers).

DEVELOPMENT. Most of the information about the development of the EFT-E: NU is included in the validity studies, and this reviewer failed to identify literature referring to this instrument outside of that which is cited in the test manual. The original version of the test was not reviewed in earlier editions of the *Mental Measurements Yearbook.* The test authors state that the main objective of a normative update is "rebalancing an existing dataset by reducing overrepresented demographic subgroups and increasing underrepresented subgroups to reflect the demographic characteristics of the current population" (manual, p. ix). The updates included a new stratification of the normative sample, inclusion of scale scores for the four subtests (two of which changed names from the original version), recalculation of the EFI composite, new reliability and validity analytics, including analysis of sensitivity and specificity, and re-organization of the test manual. According to the test authors, no item content was changed, but the norm tables were updated as needed. [Editor's note: The test publisher advised the Buros Center for Testing that nine items linked with three picture plates were removed from the previous version. This information was omitted from the EFT-E: NU manual and will be included in manual reprints, according to the test publisher.]

TECHNICAL. Data for this normative update of the EFT-E were collected by 731 speech language pathologists from 647 participants across 41 states, fairly evenly distributed by age (1-year intervals) from 7 to 12 years, averaging close to 107 participants per age group. Demographic distribution (gender, race, Hispanic status, geographic region, and exceptionality status) followed closely the reports on school-age populations in the *Statistical Abstract of the United States 2015* (ProQuest, 2014, as cited by the test authors).

Reliability of the EFT-E: NU test scores was estimated using alpha coefficients per subtest and composite and by age group and demographic clusters. Across age groups, alpha coefficients ranged from .67 to .96 with a consistent pattern of higher reliability coefficients for the EFI composite and lower values for the Shifting subtest (which has the fewest items and the largest standard errors of measurement). For demographic subgroups, alpha coefficients were consistently high across variable clusters and ranged from .72 to .97, again consistently demonstrating lower alpha values for Shifting, and the highest values for the composite score. A test-retest study with an average interval of 2 weeks was conducted using 76 children. Test-retest reliability estimates were high overall, ranging from .85 to .99, with the EFI composite consistently higher than several of the other scores. Practice effects were examined, and the effects noted were negligible (.00) to small (-.23 to -.50 effect size [Cohen's *d*]). Scorer difference reliability was evaluated using 15 randomly selected test forms scored by six trained examiners. The average reliability coefficient reported was .93.

Evidence of validity of test scores was extensively examined. Content-description evidence was addressed by the test authors who reviewed the literature with an emphasis on the interactions between language and executive functioning. Several executive function components were addressed initially (e.g., self-monitoring, inhibition/impulsivity, planning, problem solving) but were "discarded because the items did not show a strong age progression" (manual, p. 36). Furthermore, item discrimination and item difficulty parameters met the criterion established a priori (≥ .20 and passing percentages between 15% and 85%, respectively). Differential item functioning (DIF) analysis was implemented using all item scores from typically developing participants from the normative sample, and between three dichotomous groups: male versus female, Black/African American versus non-Black/African American, and Hispanic versus non-Hispanic. A few items (ranging from 1 to 2 per subtest) demonstrated bias favoring a particular group, and one item showed moderate DIF, favoring males. The item was retained. To further examine test fairness, means were calculated for each mainstream group (Whites, males, females) and three minority groups (Hispanics, Blacks/African Americans, and Asians/Pacific Islanders), and normality of score distributions was observed. A second study compared subgroups of participants against matched control groups and demonstrated little or no evidence of bias for gender (Cohen's *d* effect sizes from -.23 to .05), little or no bias against Black/African American children (Cohen's *d* between -.05 and -.30), some bias against Asian/Pacific Islander children (Cohen's *d* between -.44 and .57), and little or no bias against Hispanic children (Cohen's *d* between -.19 and .09).

Criterion-prediction evidence was examined by investigating the precision of the EFT-E: NU scores in correctly identifying children with known executive function impairments. Three groups were included in the analysis: children diagnosed with autism spectrum disorder (ASD; n = 130, 36% female), children diagnosed with learning disabilities (LD; n = 155, 47% female), and children with specific language impairments (SLI; n = 172, 44% female). Sensitivity and specificity indexes for the ASD and LD groups were deemed adequate when criteria recommended in the literature were applied. For the SLI group, criteria cutoffs for sensitivity were not met, and the rate of false positives was too high.

Construct-identification evidence of validity was evaluated along several avenues, including (a) analysis of developmental trends based on age (raw scores should increase with age, and they did), (b) differences between clinical groups with known executive impairments versus non-clinical groups, which were identified, (c) inter-subtest score correlations (coefficients ranged from .66 to .82), (d) principal components exploratory factor analysis, which identified a one-factor solution, and (e) median item-total correlations, which ranged from .30 to .53.

COMMENTARY. It is this reviewer's opinion that the EFT-E: NU is a valuable instrument for several reasons, including that it relies on a multidimensional approach to the definition of executive functions, emphasizes the identification of specific deficits in test performance, relies on strong indicators of reliability, includes a rich and detailed examination of validity evidence for the test results that includes a detailed examination of test bias, has a test manual that is quite instructive on psychometrics and test development, and has friendly administration and scoring procedures. Its utility in the assessment of executive impairments in school-age children seems overall to be robust. A strong feature of the test manual is the inclusion of a chapter on informal analysis of subtest performance, which details the skills needed to succeed on the test and describes common error patterns and potential remediation strategies for parents, interventionists, and teachers.

Some aspects of the psychometric development could be improved in future iterations of this test, including examination of the instrument using confirmatory factor analysis as it is quite possible that the one factor derived from the exploratory analysis relates to overall verbal ability more than executive abilities, and the involvement of a more clearly defined panel of experts in the item development process. Also, it was not clear to this reviewer how the Attention and Immediate Memory-Verbal subtest contributes to a better understanding of executive functioning. Rather, it seems to serve as an aid in clarifying the contribution of attention/short-term memory to learning. This is somewhat problematic as this subtest includes the largest proportion of items contributing to the composite (36% of the test item pool). The construct of executive function is briefly reviewed in the first chapter of the test manual, using a collage of pieces from definitions and approaches from the literature. However, there is no cohesive theory or statistical model presented as support for the five components evaluated by the test: attention, immediate memory (verbal and nonverbal), working memory, flexible thinking, and shifting. Inhibition is cited as a relevant component for executive functioning, which is consistent with current developments in the field (e.g., Miyake & Friedman, 2012), but it is vaguely and only indirectly measured (perhaps via attentional control) in the test.

SUMMARY. The EFT-E: NU was designed to be an individually administered test examining four language-based executive functions, namely, attention and immediate memory using verbal and non-verbal items, working memory and flexible thinking, and shifting, offering a novel perspective into the assessment of executive functioning in children ages 7-12. Administration and scoring are parsimonious and well guided by the test manual and the examiner record booklet. This version of the test includes updated norms based on a rebalancing of the original normative sample, and the test scores demonstrated robust psychometric properties. Overall, the EFT-E would benefit from a stronger theoretical approach to the concept of executive functions, including using confirmatory factor analysis of a more robust model than the one-factor model supported by the principal component analysis. Evidence of convergent and discriminant validity of the test results would add considerable value to the validity analysis.

REVIEWER'S REFERENCE

Miyake, A., & Friedman, N. P. (2012). The nature and organization of individual differences in executive functions: Four general conclusions. *Current Directions in Psychological Science, 21*, 8-14.

Review of the Executive Functions Test–Elementary: Normative Update by DENISE E. MARICLE, Professor, Doctoral Program in School Psychology, and BRITTANY McGEEHAN, Doctoral Candidate in School Psychology, Texas Woman's University, Denton, TX:

DESCRIPTION. The Executive Functions Test–Elementary: Normative Update (EFT-E: NU) is an updated version of the Executive Functions Test–Elementary (Bowers & Huisingh, 2014). The EFT-E and the EFT-E: NU individually measure language skills that affect executive functions such as inhibition, working memory, and cognitive flexibility. The EFT-E: NU provides updated norms for the EFT-E, but more importantly includes revised psychometric analyses including item analysis, reliability, validity evidence, and the application of standardized scores for subtests and composites. According to the test manual, the EFT-E: NU was designed to yield specific information about children's executive function skills in relation to their language abilities. The test authors state that the test helps to identify children who are significantly behind their peers in language-based executive functioning abilities, determine the degree of the problem, and discover patterns of executive functioning strengths and weaknesses within individual children.

The EFT-E: NU was designed for children ages 7 years 0 months through 12 years 11 months. Examinees must be English speakers and able to understand the directions of the test. Thus, this test would not be appropriate for English language learners or children with cognitive impairments. This test is intended for use by speech language pathologists or other trained professionals familiar with language disorders, such as psychologists or special education teachers. Test materials include the examiner's manual, a picture book easel, and the examiner record booklet.

The test consists of four subtests: Attention and Immediate Memory-Verbal, Attention and Immediate Memory-Verbal and Nonverbal, Working Memory and Flexible Thinking, and Shifting. The Attention and Immediate Memory-Verbal subtest evaluates a test taker's ability to attend to and recall details of what he or she hears. The examiner verbally administers a short passage and asks three follow-up questions. Children must accurately remember details from each of 12 passages that are read aloud to the child. In order to receive credit, the child must recall specific details of the passage. The subtest "tests how well the child can attend to and comprehend the passage content, retain details from the passage, comprehend questions asked about the passage, and verbally provide the answers to the questions" (manual, p. 36). The task does not require the child to use inference or to problem solve, rather it focuses on the child's ability to attend to, store, and retrieve information. Using a similar format, the Attention and Immediate Memory-Verbal and Nonverbal subtest measures the child's ability to correctly respond to questions about verbally and visually presented material. This task includes 10 passages that are read aloud while a picture is simultaneously presented to the child. Questions asked of the child require the incorporation of information seen in the picture and heard in the passage to formulate a response. The test purportedly taps the ability to attend to information, identify problems, make inferences, and plan and recall visual/verbal details or information. It is unclear how this subtest measures verbal and nonverbal attention and immediate memory, as the directions do not specify that the picture should be taken away before the questions are asked. The Working Memory and Flexible Thinking subtest is designed to measure the ability to problem solve and make inferences regarding another person's behavior. Children are read a short passage and asked two follow-up questions. The task requires the child to store the passage information in order to solve the problems and to think flexibly about the situation to give a plausible answer. The Shifting subtest measures the ability to shift one's thinking about categorical information quickly and accurately. Children are given four items and the name of the category to which they belong. The child is then given a category name and asked to name an item in a similar category.

The administration instructions are provided in the examiner record booklet and are fairly clear and easy to follow. The script is bolded in purple, clearly indicating what the examiner should say to administer each question. Examiners are instructed to avoid spending too much time on specific items, and all items must be administered. The child must respond verbally to each item. Items may not be repeated, re-worded, or paraphrased by the examiner. The examiner should encourage a response if no response is made after 10 seconds have elapsed. If none is offered, the examiner is to score the item as incorrect and present the next item. However, the EFT-E: NU does not have hard time limits for acceptable response periods. The test authors report testing will take 45 to 60 minutes. The test manual instructs examiners to score items during administration. Any response that is not indicated in the examiner record booklet must be transcribed verbatim. A score of 1 results from an exact, precise answer. A score of 0 indicates a vague or imprecise answer was given. No prompts are allowed. Scoring instructions are straightforward and easy to understand.

Derived scores include the following four types of normative scores: age equivalents, percentile ranks, subtest scaled scores, and a composite index score. The composite score is a sum of the scaled scores for the four subtests (Attention and Immediate Memory-Verbal, Attention and Immediate Memory-Verbal and Nonverbal, Working Memory and Flexible Thinking, and Shifting). The composite standard score is called the Executive Function Index (EFI).

DEVELOPMENT. In developing the EFT-E: NU, the authors sought to build a test that would identify the role of language in executive functions. In their discussion of test development, the authors report that literature in the broader fields of speech-language pathology, psychology, autism, and neuropsychology was reviewed. The goals of this review were "to gather information on executive function development in typically developing students and to determine how language skills affect or interact with this development" (manual, p. 36). No rationale was provided for the age range of 7 years 0 months to 12 years 11 months. As is the case for most normative updates, the EFT-E: NU update involved rebalancing the existing dataset and did not include revisions to item content or items. [Editor's note: The test publisher advised the Buros Center for Testing that nine items linked with three picture plates were removed from the previous version. This information was omitted from the EFT-E: NU manual and will be included in manual reprints, according to the test publisher.]

TECHNICAL. The examiner's manual provides information regarding technical aspects of the EFT-E: NU. The information provided is clear and easy to read, albeit limited. The standardization sample for the EFT-E: NU consists of 647 children in 41 states. The age breakdown was as follows: 120 7-year-olds, 122 8-year-olds, 93 9-year-olds, 100 10-year-olds, 101 11-year-olds, and 111 12-year-olds. Stratification of selected demographic categories at each age interval (geographic region, gender, race, Hispanic status, and exceptionality status) indicated the data largely conformed to national expectations (delineated in the 2015 *Statistical Abstract of the United States*) for the age groups included in the test's norms. Data were weighted to improve representativeness of the normative sample. Subtest scaled scores were developed via continuous norming and "used polynomial regression to fit the progression of means, standard deviations, skewness and kurtosis across ages" (manual, p. 10). According to the test manual, the "resulting data were smoothed somewhat to allow for consistent progression across age levels" (manual, p. 10) and to produce a normal distribution of derived scores and percentile ranks.

The examiner's manual provides reliability and validity evidence supporting the EFT-E: NU. To establish reliability, three types of correlation coefficients (coefficient alpha, test-retest, and scorer difference) were calculated. Internal consistency reliability was investigated using alpha coefficients (Cronbach, 1951). Alpha coefficients for the composites were calculated at six age intervals using data from the normative sample and applying Guilford's (1954) formula. Averages for subtests and composites were computed using Fisher z-transformations. The test manual provides coefficient alpha results by age group and for selected subgroups. Coefficients ranged from .67 to .97 with the majority falling above .80, suggesting adequate internal consistency. Time sampling error (e.g., the extent to which test performance changes due to the passage of time) was estimated using the test-retest method. A sample of children (n = 76), ages 7 years 0 months through 12 years 11 months from 26 states, participated. The retest interval was about two weeks. Corrected correlation coefficients for the subtests and composites were .85 or higher for each of three age groups and ≥ .90 for the combined sample, suggesting that the test demonstrates strong temporal stability. In a study examining scorer differences, six trained examiners scored the same 15 test forms individually. The resulting average coefficient across all test items was .93, suggesting that the test has good interscorer reliability for properly trained examiners.

To provide content evidence of validity for the EFT-E: NU, the test authors began the test development process by reviewing the relevant literature in speech-language pathology, psychology, neuropsychology, and autism. The goal was "to gather information on executive function development in typically developing students and to determine how language skills affect or interact with this development" (manual, p. 36). The test authors then drafted items that they believed assess executive functions through a variety of language tasks. Items were subjected to item analysis procedures (item discrimination, item difficulty, and differential item functioning). Predictive criterion evidence of validity was based on diagnostic accuracy analyses examining the precision with which the EFT-E: NU scores accurately identified students known to possess executive functioning deficits. Three disability groups were chosen as being reflective of executive function deficits: autism spectrum disorder (ASD), specific learning disability (SLD), and speech language impairment (SLI). Using sensitivity and specificity values, the test authors reported that the ASD and SLD groups were accurately identified. However, because the actual executive functioning of these groups was not measured, it cannot be known whether the test scores reflected additional or other characteristics present in the groups. Finally, the test manual presents information on construct identification validity, which is defined by the test authors as the degree to which the underlying traits of the test can be identified. However, the description appears to relate more to the concept of content evidence rather than construct evidence, in that no evaluation of convergent or discriminant construct evidence was applied or discussed. Finally, the test authors report that the EFT-E: NU subtest scaled scores were analyzed using principal components exploratory factor analysis to evaluate the underlying latent constructs of the measure. A single factor was extracted (e.g., all subtests loaded on one factor and were highly correlated), which they labeled as measuring verbal executive functioning ability.

COMMENTARY. The EFT-E: NU was designed to yield specific information about children's executive function skills in relation to their language abilities. The EFT-E: NU does appear to measure language ability such as language comprehension, memory for auditorily presented contextual information and reasoning or problem-solving with auditorily provided information. However, it does not provide enough evidence to conclude that it measures actual executive functions such as working memory, attention, contextual reasoning, or inhibition. Its key strengths are a readable, easily understood manual; clear and simple administration; and in-depth information regarding the necessary skills that a child must have to perform each task as well as common error patterns and possible remediation strategies. The test authors appear to have taken appropriate steps with regard to item analysis and in evaluating the reliability of the instrument. However, validity support appears to be lacking. No evidence is provided that the instrument actually measures or relates to executive functions, or that the four identified subtests measure language-based executive functions uniquely. In fact, the EFA conducted by the test publishers resulted in a one-factor solution, suggesting that all of the items and the four subtests measure a single construct, which may or may not be related to executive functions. Given that the test authors have divided the measure into four distinct subtests that they indicate measure different aspects of language-based executive functions, a one-factor solution should have raised questions about the structure of the measure. Additionally, to provide construct evidence of validity and support the hypothesis that the measure evaluates executive functioning using a language format, convergent and discriminant validation studies should have been conducted and reported. Finally, the instrument is limited in its application in terms of age range (e.g., it can only be used over the 6-year age range of 7-0 to 12-11) and types of children (e.g., English speakers only; children in the average range cognitively).

SUMMARY. The Executive Functions Test–Elementary: Normative Update (EFT-E: NU) is an updated version of the Executive Functions Test–Elementary (Bowers & Huisingh, 2014). The EFT-E: NU was designed to yield specific information about children's executive function skills in relation to their language abilities. The ETF-E: NU was designed for children ages 7 years 0 months through 12 years 11 months. This test is intended for use by speech language pathologists or other trained professionals familiar with language disorders such as psychologists or special education teachers. The EFT-E: NU does appear to measure language ability such as language comprehension, memory for auditorily presented contextual information, and reasoning or problem-solving with auditorily provided information. However, it does not provide enough evidence to determine conclusively that the instrument measures actual executive functions such as working memory, attention, contextual reasoning, or inhibition. Reliability evidence for the EFT-E: NU appears to be good, but validity evidence is limited, and what is provided does not adequately support the validity of the EFT-E: NU as a measure of language-based executive functioning skills.

REVIEWERS' REFERENCES

Bowers, L., & Huisingh, R. (2014). Executive Functions Test-Elementary. Austin, TX: PRO-ED.

Cronbach, L. J. (1951). Coefficient alpha and the internal structure of tests. *Psychometrika, 16*, 297-334.

Guilford, J. P. (1954). *Psychometric methods* (2nd ed.). New York, NY: McGraw Hill.

[58]

Expressive Vocabulary Test, Third Edition.

Purpose: Designed to assess expressive vocabulary and word retrieval for children and adults.

Population: Ages 2-6 to 90+.

Publication Dates: 1997-2019.

Acronym: EVT-3.

Scores: Total score only.

Administration: Individual.

Forms, 2: A, B.

Price Data, 2020: $405 per complete kit (A & B) including manual (2019, 345 pages), 2 stimulus books (A & B), and 25 of each record form (A & B); $225 per individual kit (A or B); $99 per manual; $99 per

stimulus book (A or B); $49 per 25 record forms (A or B); $40 per 1-year scoring subscription; $4.50 per digital administration (A or B).
Time: Approximately 10-20 minutes for administration.
Comments: Co-normed with the Peabody Picture Vocabulary Test, Fifth Edition (see 117, this volume) to allow comparison of a test taker's expressive and receptive vocabulary skills; available in print and digital formats.
Author: Kathleen T. Williams.
Publisher: Pearson.
Cross References: For reviews by Theresa Graham and Natalie Rathvon of the second edition, see 18:51; for reviews by Frederick Bessai and Orest Eugene Wasyliw of the original edition, see 14:143.

Review of the Expressive Vocabulary Test, Third Edition by SHARI L. DeVENEY, Associate Professor of Special Education and Communication Disorders, University of Nebraska at Omaha, Omaha, NE:

DESCRIPTION. The 2019 Third Edition of the Expressive Vocabulary Test (EVT-3) is a norm-referenced, individually administered assessment tool designed to evaluate expressive vocabulary (i.e., productive use of words) and word retrieval (i.e., word-finding skills) for a wide variety of Standard American English speakers. The instrument is administered orally and normed for use with children ages 2:6 to adults over 90 years. Scoring relies on two types of expressive word knowledge, labels and synonyms, reflected in examinee responses. The EVT-3 is similar to the second edition (EVT-2) in many ways, as it includes the same general assessment tool kit components (two self-standing easels for presentation of colored line-drawn pictures associated with stimulus words for Forms A and B, A and B record forms, and a manual); continued co-norming with the Peabody Picture Vocabulary Test, now in its fifth edition (PPVT-5; Dunn, 2019; 117, this volume); the same total number of test items, n = 190, for both forms; and consistency in overall purpose and recommended applications. The test author noted that the updated EVT includes a number of shared items between the test's two forms as well as with the two forms of the PPVT-5 (Dunn, 2019); an updated normative sample; new artwork; and a new qualitative item analysis specific to science, technology, engineering, and mathematics (STEM) vocabulary use. Although the total number of words per test form remains consistent with the second edition, the EVT-3 has 13 new stimulus items and 38 omitted items compared with the previous edition. These numerical differences are mediated by the inclusion of shared stimuli across test forms.

Test administration begins with two training items and continues with seven possible age-determined start points for all but the lowest start point, which begins at Item 1, confirmed through basal establishment (three consecutive accurate responses, a change from five in the second edition). Responses are evaluated for accuracy dichotomously (i.e., correct/incorrect), and these two categories, as well as exemplar responses of each, are clearly noted on the record form for each test item. Prompts are noted for the examiner with a "Q" for "query" on each item's example incorrect response(s). Although the test author cautions examiners against "over-querying that would potentially cue the examinee toward a correct response" (manual, p. 18), guidelines regarding a maximum number of queries per item are not provided; this decision is left to the examiner's professional judgment. Administration continues until a ceiling is reached with six consecutive incorrect responses (an increase from five in the second edition) or until an examinee reaches the last test item. Although the EVT is not a timed test, the test author advises an approximately 10-second time limit for each item. Because of this limited response time for individual test items, the requirement of single-word responses, and the age-determined start points that negate the need to proceed through the tool in its entirety, typical EVT-3 administration time is relatively short, 11-21 minutes on average, based on the age of the examinee.

Examiner qualifications are rather broad and inclusive of a wide variety of professionals with a range of backgrounds. Converting examinee responses to a raw score is a quick, straightforward, and intuitive endeavor. Raw scores are easily translated to standard scores, percentile ranks, normal curve equivalents, stanines, age equivalents, and growth scale values. Four qualitative item analyses are available to facilitate descriptive investigations of vocabulary use. These include item analyses for home compared to school vocabulary development; parts of speech; a three-tier model of lexical acquisition adopted from Beck, McKeown, and Kucan (2013); and STEM-related terminology use. For further qualitative inquiry, examiners can compare EVT-3 and PPVT-5 scores, interpret differences, and consider production and comprehension test performance differences on crossover (i.e., shared) vocabulary items between the EVT-3 and PPVT-5.

The EVT-3 is now available through digital platforms for administration, scoring, and generation of narrative reports.

DEVELOPMENT. The goal in developing the latest EVT iteration was to improve test content such that it continues to support professional practice and represents current Standard American English usage without sacrificing the test's nature or universality of included vocabulary constructs. To that end, the EVT-3 developmental steps involved solicitation of feedback from EVT-2 users regarding administration, picture stimuli, and scoring as well as that of international test developers regarding culture differences and a review of current literature on vocabulary development and expressive vocabulary deficits. A panel of school psychologists and speech-language pathologists with expertise assessing individuals from diverse populations reviewed vocabulary targets and picture stimuli for the presence of potential bias. Items identified by more than one panel member as suggesting bias were not included in the pilot research. Based on these steps, 36 new items were piloted with a sample of 217 individuals identified as having typical development and ranging in age from 2:6 to 21:11. From this pilot research, examiner directions, scoring guidelines, and verbal and visual stimuli, among other test constructs, were established for the standardization phase of development.

TECHNICAL.

Standardization. The sample for standardization included 2,720 individuals in the U.S. ranging in age from 2:6 to over 90 years who were not diagnosed with language or hearing deficits and who were fluent English speakers. Although the vast majority of the 28 age-based groups sampled included 100 individuals, the groups representing ages 71:0-80:11 and 81:0-90:11 included only 60 each. Efforts were made to match the demographic characteristics of the sample to the latest U.S. Census Bureau data with particular emphasis placed on demographic aspects deemed most likely to influence vocabulary development (e.g., race/ethnicity, parent/caregiver education level). The sample was stratified based on age, gender, race/ethnicity, geographic region, and parent/caregiver education level.

Reliability. As with previous EVT versions, consistency of the EVT-3 was assessed through estimates of internal consistency using split-half reliability, alternate form reliability, and test-retest reliability. Internal consistency reliability coefficients ranged from .94 to .99, indicating a high degree of consistency across all age groups. Alternate form reliability coefficients ranged from .86 to .92 indicating consistency of examinee performance across the two testing forms. Test-retest reliability coefficients ranged from .87 to .93 when examinees across the age range were administered Form A twice on average about one month apart. As previous reviewers of the EVT have noted, evidence of interscorer reliability was not included for EVT-3. As others have commented and this reviewer agrees, the omission presents a possible oversight given the potential for variability across examiners' use of queries when presented with incorrect item responses.

Validity. Evidence of test score validity for the EVT-3 was addressed through various means including content relevance and breadth, analysis of response processes, correlation of other standardized assessments with the EVT-3, and investigation of its ability to differentiate performance of individuals from several special populations compared to individuals with typical expressive vocabulary skills. The test author also included information regarding specificity and sensitivity of the measure as a diagnostic tool. For content validity, consistent with criticism offered regarding the validity of EVT-2, this reviewer acknowledges that although test items (including new vocabulary content and updated artwork) were reviewed by content and bias experts and EVT-2 users, the author does not offer explicit empirical evidence indicating the validity of the test's single-word verbal response format and specific use of colored line-drawn picture stimuli, some of which are repeated to elicit different responses during the same test form. The test correlates highly with the EVT-2 (coefficients ranged from .80 to .90) and moderately to highly (coefficients were between .49 and .82) with several other assessment tools targeting vocabulary and language skills, the majority of which typically are used in diagnostic evaluations with pediatric populations. The assessment tool was shown to discriminate the performance of special populations with clinical effect sizes that were large (for individuals with language delay, specific language impairment, and learning disability in reading and/or writing) to moderate (for individuals diagnosed with autism spectrum disorder and those with hearing impairment). Diagnostic accuracy was addressed through examination of sensitivity and specificity for identification of several language-related conditions including language delay, specific language impairment, and learning disability in reading and/or writing. Based on these results, the test author described the EVT-3 as a "good" screening measure for these diagnostic categories (manual, pp. 52-54).

COMMENTARY. Strengths of the EVT-3 include ease and convenience of administration and scoring, varied opportunities for supplemental analyses of examinee performance, continued co-norming with the PPVT, and availability of digital formats. Enhanced information regarding diagnostic accuracy of the assessment is beneficial to examiners working with pediatric clinical populations. Continued challenges related to the EVT-3 include the scope of the reliability analysis, which does not include interscorer reliability, and the validity evidence, which is weighed heavily toward pediatric populations.

SUMMARY. Given the limited scope of the EVT-3, which measures only one aspect of expressive language, this assessment tool should be used as part of an assessment battery to evaluate language ability and not as a stand-alone measure. Use with pediatric populations seems better supported than its use with adults, particularly elderly populations.

REVIEWER'S REFERENCES

Beck, I. L., McKeown, M. G., & Kucan, L. (2013). *Bringing words to life: Robust vocabulary instruction* (2nd ed.). New York, NY: Guilford Press.

Dunn, D. M. (2019). Peabody Picture Vocabulary Test, Fifth Edition. San Antonio, TX: Pearson.

Review of the Expressive Vocabulary Test, Third Edition by JEFFREY K. SMITH, Professor of Education, University of Otago, Dunedin, New Zealand:

DESCRIPTION. The Expressive Vocabulary Test, Third Edition (EVT-3), is an individually administered test of expressive vocabulary and word retrieval ability. It is norm-refenced and designed to assess children from the age of 2 years 6 months through adulthood. It can be used in conjunction with the Peabody Picture Vocabulary Test, Fifth Edition (PPVT-5), which is a companion measure with joint norming data. It has a variety of clinical and school-based purposes, including screening for expressive language, screening of preschool children, and understanding reading difficulties, among others. It provides a norm-referenced score presented in a variety of scales, and does not require extensive training to use, although the test manual recommends that the individual be trained in administering individual assessments. The EVT-3 is a revision of previous forms of the assessment and includes some items from those previous forms in addition to newly developed items. There are two forms (A and B) of the EVT-3 available, each with 190 items, ordered from the least to most difficult. Examinees start on a predetermined item based upon their age and continue taking items until they have missed six in a row. Their raw score is then the total number of items answered correctly. Each item has an illustration along with a spoken direction or question to the examinee that requires a brief verbal response. If an examinee gives a word that is close to an acceptable answer, an additional prompt is provided, for example, "Can you tell me a better word?"

DEVELOPMENT. This is the third form of the Expressive Vocabulary Test; it relies heavily on previous versions, which seems appropriate, as they were professionally developed and have been in use for more than 20 years. The test was originally developed in the 1990s as a companion measure to the PPVT and can be used with the PPVT-5 for diagnostic purposes. Underlying the development of the EVT-3 are several concepts, including the evolving nature of vocabulary in use over time and the importance of vocabulary that is related to academic subjects. The fundamental idea behind the EVT-3 is to measure expressive vocabulary, that is, the words that an individual can retrieve and express, as opposed to recognize. The EVT-3 focuses on spoken vocabulary; no writing or reading is involved in the measure. Examinees are asked to look at a picture and respond to a prompt that requests that they say what the picture represents or provide another word (synonym) for the image. A total of 36 new items were developed for the EVT-3 and pilot-tested on a sample of 217 examinees by a group of trained professionals. The test manual states that items were analyzed via classical test theory (CTT), item response theory (IRT), and diffential item functioning (DIF) analysis, and modifications and refinements of items were made.

TECHNICAL. The standardization sample for the EVT-3 consisted of 2,720 individuals for the development of norms, with additional samples taken for reliability and validity studies. Samples of 100 were obtained for age bands ranging from 2 years 6 months to 70 years 11 months with sample sizes of 60 for subsequent age bands. Stratification of the sample included age, sex, race and ethnicity, region of the country, and educational level of parent and/or caregiver. Data are reported for education levels, race and ethnicity, and region of the country sampled. Raw scores are translatable into standard scores; test-age equivalents; and "growth scores," Rasch-model-generated scores that are interval in nature and can be used to evaluate growth over time and changes in growth. Additionally, the EVT-3 was normed with the PPVT-5 so that differences between the two measures can be calculated for diagnostic purposes.

Reliability of the EVT-3 was assessed using internal consistency, alternate forms, and test-retest reliability estimates. All three approaches produced extremely high reliability coefficients, which is not surprising given the very tightly defined nature of the construct being measured. Internal consistency reliability coefficients were in the mid to high .90s for all of the age ranges covered by the measure, and alternate forms and test-retest reliability estimates were in the mid .80s and low .90s. Validity was assessed using a variety of sources of evidence, including content, criterion-related, and differences between known groups. The EVT-3 shows moderate to strong correlations (validity coefficients ranging from .49 to .90) with a variety of other measures of vocabulary and discriminates between children known to have language impairment issues, specific learning disabilities, autism spectrum disorder, and hearing issues and those who have not been identified as having those issues. The EVT-3 manual presents detailed analyses of studies demonstrating the utility of the instrument. The only thing that the EVT-3 does not appear to have been assessed for statistically is gender or racial/ethnic bias. The test author reports a content analysis conducted to look for issues related to such bias, and differential item functioning analysis, typically used in bias studies, is mentioned, but there are no bias studies reported for this edition of the EVT.

The EVT-3 manual contains an extensive and accessible discussion of how to obtain and interpret the various scores available with the instrument. It also presents several case studies as exemplars of how to use the EVT-3 and contains special sections on working with examinees who are color blind or have hearing loss.

COMMENTARY. The EVT-3 is a professionally developed and presented measure of expressive vocabulary that appears to be easy to use and interpret and that is based upon a solid history of development. The pictures used in the measure are easy to interpret, and the directions provided are clear. The quality of the technical material presented is among the best that this reviewer has seen in decades of reviewing for the *Mental Measurments Yearbook* series, in particular, the extensive information regarding reliability and validity. Again, the only shortcoming noted was a lack of research presented concerning potential issues of bias. Given the potential for real language differences among various racial/ethnic groups, it would be good to see such research in a future manual or technical report. That is an important concern, but this reviewer wishes to emphasize that the overall technical quality of the EVT-3 appears to be exceptionally strong.

SUMMARY. The EVT-3 is a professionally developed and researched measure of expressive vocabulary that appears easy to administer, score, and interpret and has strong norming data from the age of 2 years 6 months onward through adulthood and old age. It provides ample evidence of its quality, including extensive studies of children with a range of disabilities. The third edition is based on successful prior editions and has a strong theoretical foundation. The measure can be recommended for the uses described in the test manual, in particular the identification of learning issues and the assessment of growth in expressive vocabulary development.

[59]

The Fairy Tale Test, 2nd Edition.

Purpose: A projective test designed to help assess personality variables in children.
Population: Ages 6-12 years.
Publication Dates: 2003-2013.
Acronym: FTT.
Scores, 30: Desire for Material Things, Desire for Help, Desire for Superiority, Oral Needs, Need for Affiliation, Need to Give and/or Receive Affection, Need for Approval, Need for Protection, Sexual Preoccupation, Bizarres, Oral Aggression, Instrumental Aggression, Impulsive Aggression, Aggression as Defense, Aggression as Dominance, Aggression as Envy, Aggression as Jealousy, Aggression as Retaliation, Relationship with Mother, Relationship with Father, Fear of Aggression, Anxiety, Depression, Ambivalence, Self-Esteem, Morality, Sense of Property, Sense of Privacy, Adaptation to Fairy Tale Content, Repetitions.
Administration: Individual.
Price Data, 2020: $193 per complete kit including manual (2013, 298 pages), 21 test cards, and 10 recording sheets; $111 per manual; $48 per 21 test cards; $34 per 10 recording sheets.
Time: (45) minutes.
Comments: Norms based on sample of children from regions of India.

[59] The Fairy Tale Test, 2nd Edition

Authors: Carina Coulacoglou.
Publisher: Hogrefe Ltd [United Kingdom].
Cross References: For reviews by Frederic J. Medway and Peter Zachar of the original edition (norms based on sample of children from Greece), see 16:90.

Review of The Fairy Tale Test, 2nd Edition by ROSEMARY FLANAGAN, Adjunct Faculty, SUNY Old Westbury, Old Westbury, NY:

DESCRIPTION. The Fairy Tale Test, 2nd Edition (FTT) is a picture story narrative measure that examines personality variables rather than relationships with individuals in and outside the family. The test author, Coulacoglou, indicates that fairy tales are used because these are considered a superior form of expression in India (location of the current norming) and are free of religious or moral constraints. Fairy tale characters are symbolic and unchanging throughout the tale, which commonly has a happy ending. Fairy tales have been examined by numerous figures in the psychoanalytic community from theoretical (examining the structure of the psyche) and clinical (working through conflict) perspectives. Thus, fairy tales may be a vehicle for examining and understanding that which is out of the child's awareness. FTT interpretation and analysis are according to psychodynamic theories of the ego and object relations. Thirty variables are assessed and are classified into five personality groupings: Impulses, Desires and Needs, Ego Functions, Emotional States, and Object Relations. Extensive operational definitions and descriptions of each of the 30 variables are provided in the test manual.

DEVELOPMENT. The FTT was originally developed and standardized on Greek children. The initial standardization occurred between 1989 and 1993 (*N* = 800); the standardization for the current edition occurred between 2001 and 2003 (*N* = 873). The first standardization sample was composed of children ages 7-12; the current standardization sample is composed of children ages 6-12. There are 21 cards, designed to be presented as seven sets of three, with numbering on the back to indicate which story line the cards belong to. A record form for recording the child's responses and tabulating scores is available. The original versions of Little Red Riding Hood and Snow White and the Seven Dwarfs are used, along with adaptations designed to elicit responses with more significant content. The cards are designed such that multiple themes and conflicts are elicited in the seven card sets. There are depictions of scenes from both fairy tales, as well as cards that are character specific for both fairy tales. Depictions of a witch and a giant have been added to broaden the possible range of information elicited. The quantitative data were factor analyzed, resulting in an 11-factor solution, which in turn was reanalyzed to yield a four-factor solution. The occurrence of defense mechanisms in the narrative data obtained from the norm sample is reported as percentages.

Administration. The FTT (2nd ed.) is administered in a standard manner. It must be ascertained that the child is familiar with fairy tales and the characters in the tales. If the child is unfamiliar with the tales, these stories are read to the child, and the test is rescheduled; the premise is that the fairy tale will become part of the child's unconscious. The actual testing involves the child telling the fairy tales to the examiner. In the next step, seven sets of three cards are presented in turn. The child is asked to respond to standard questions designed to elicit the child's apperception of what is taking place in the picture, the thoughts and feelings of the characters, and the story outcome. Specific directions and examples for examiner guidance are provided in the test manual. The standard questions are printed on the record form.

Scoring. The process for rating responses is detailed and complex. Because responses are rated from the viewpoint of the figure the child identifies with, the entire protocol should be perused first in order to make that determination. Some variables are rated on a 3-point scale from 1 (*low*) to 3 (*high*) in terms of their intensity, although there are some exceptions. Relationships with Mother or Father parent as well as Self-Esteem are rated *positive* (+1) or *negative* (-1); Bizarre responses and Repetitions are scored 1. Adaption to Fairy Tale Content is rated 0 if the child tells a story without action or gives meaningless or incomplete responses. Direction is provided for rating responses of greater complexity (e.g., identifying with more than one figure). Specific direction for rating responses to questions is provided. Many scoring examples reflecting each possible rating are provided in the test manual's appendices.

Interpretation. Interpretation is qualitative and quantitative. Quantitative interpretation is according to normalized T scores (mean = 50; standard deviation = 10). T scores between 40 and 60 are considered within normal limits; scores greater than 70 (2 *SD* above the mean) are considered highly significant. Examiners are urged to distinguish between low normal (T = 40-50) and high normal (T = 50-60) scores. Percentile scores are also available. Qualitative interpretation considers the following variables: continuity of responses in a card set; responses in the first person; interactions between the three figures (i.e., three cards presented); contamination responses (incorporating an unrelated theme); and over-involvement responses (incorporating the child into the story), which involve an evaluation of ego integration and function. Qualitative interpretations of defense mechanisms are extensive, a feature that distinguishes the FTT (2nd ed.) from other narrative measures for youth, such as the Roberts-2 (Roberts, 2005). The defense mechanisms observed in the FTT (2nd ed.) are Denial, Undoing, Negation, Splitting, Compensation, Devaluation, Projection, Rationalization, Repression, Displacement, Reaction Formation, Aggression Turned Inwards, Acting Out, Reversal, and Identification with the Aggressor. Case studies in the test manual illustrate the interpretive process.

TECHNICAL.

Standardization and Norms. The standardization sample of Indian children numbers 1,355 participants who were assessed individually. Sampling was stratified, and norms are available by gender for three age groups (7-8 years, 9-10 years, and 11-12 years) and four regions of India (Bangalore, Delhi, Kolkata, and Mumbai). Socioeconomic status was categorized as *low, middle*, and *high*; religious denominations were Christian, Hindu, Muslim, and Zoroastrian Parsi.

Psychometric properties. No internal consistency data are reported mainly because the stimulus cards are not equivalent. There is no report of test-retest reliability, as it is unlikely that the exact same responses will be provided on two occasions. These omissions are appropriate for projective measures (Anastasi, 1988). A limitation of concern is that there is no report of interrater reliability for the quantitative scoring in the test manual. Validity data are limited to construct evidence based on factor analyses elucidating the structure of the FTT (2nd ed.) and comparisons between factor scores and defense mechanisms. A first-order factor analysis led to the identification of 11 factors; each is described in the test manual according to developmental trends and gender. A second-order factor analysis reduced 11 factors to four factors, which were subsequently compared to defense mechanisms. Factor 1 comprises Over-control against Defensive Aggression, Self-Concept and Depression, and Primary Emotional Needs. Factor 2 is composed of Emotional Deprivation and Profitable Aggression. Factor 3 comprises Social Needs, Impulsive Aggression vs. Fearfulness, Assertiveness, and Helpfulness as Defense Against Envy. Factor 4 consists of Moral Consciousness, Autonomy, Over-control against Defensive Aggression, and Self-Concept and Depression. (The first-order factors called Over-control against Defensive Aggression Self-Concept and Depression loaded on two second-order factors.) Components of each of the second-order factors are described in the test manual in terms of an operational definition, developmental trends, and gender differences. The same data were scored for the presence of defense mechanisms, providing additional evidence of validity. Defense mechanisms varied by age and gender, with 27.9% providing evidence of Undoing, 17.2% showing Denial, 15.1% showing Negation, 12.3% showing Splitting, 12.3% showing Projection, and 6.9% showing Rationalization. These data taken together are offered as construct evidence of validity.

COMMENTARY. The FTT (2nd ed.) is a picture story test grounded in psychodynamic theory that has been standardized in India; the earlier version was standardized in Greece. Standardization data from other cultures would be desirable. Although the availability of norms offers some control for variation in examiner skill and provides anchor points for what is typical and what is not, increased examiner skill will likely result in richer and more effective qualitative interpretations.

SUMMARY. The FTT (2nd ed.) is a projective picture story technique using fairy tales as the test stimuli. Administration procedures are similar to other narrative measures. Scoring is complex and may require some examiner judgment. Interpretation is qualitative and quantitative, according to a psychodynamic framework. Some evidence of construct validity is provided; no reliability data are reported. Little other information is available on psychometric properties, as it is difficult to apply these concepts to test stimuli that elicit a wide variety of responses, none of which represents a singular correct response. The FTT (2nd ed.) should prove useful to skilled examiners, although test utility may be limited with beginning examiners.

REVIEWER'S REFERENCES

Anastasi, A. (1988). *Psychological testing* (6th ed.). New York, NY: Macmillian.
Roberts, G. E. (2005). Roberts-2. Torrance, CA: Western Psychological Services.

Review of the Fairy Tale Test, 2nd Edition by WILLIAM K. WILKINSON, Consultant Psychologist, Boleybeg, Galway, Republic of Ireland:

DESCRIPTION AND DEVELOPMENT. The first edition of the Fairy Tale Test (FTT) was reviewed by Medway (2005) and Zachar (2005) in *The Sixteenth Mental Measurements Yearbook*. The FTT is now in its second edition (2013). The FTT purpose, administration, scoring, and materials are the same as those of the original version, so potential users should refer to the existing reviews for additional information.

As the FTT is a projective technique for children, there are core issues the prospective user needs to understand. One issue is the assumption of knowledge and familiarity with the fairy tale content. The use of fairy tales is compelling and represents a unique projective method. However, it is likely that fairy tales are more culturally embedded than many other projective methods. Therefore, it could be argued that the quality of projective responses would be dependent on familiarity with the stories, which raises the question: Are children in non-European/non-Western countries (and even within Europe/West) familiar with the stories used in the FTT, specifically those of Snow White and Little Red Riding Hood? To address this concern, the test user records each respondent's re-telling of the two stories on page two of the test booklet. The test author advises that if the test user believes that the child's knowledge is insufficient, the test can be rescheduled once the child has read/listened to the stories.

Standardization in different countries will partially address the issue of unique individual and cultural exposure to the core fairy tales by providing normative data in order to evaluate an individual's responses against those of similar age children in the same geographical location. The test author's mention of completed and ongoing standardization of the FTT in countries like India (which is the feature of the second edition manual), China, and Russia are commendable and would serve as a starting point for users in these locations.

The second core issue is that the FTT user must be psychodynamically trained and oriented. The administration of the FTT requires responses to all 21 stimulus cards with the child asked what each character thinks and feels and why. Subsequently, each series of three cards (which are presented in a prescribed order) has several unique follow-up questions. Responses are recorded verbatim on the record form. Regarding quantitative scoring, there are examples of responses to each card and questions for each of the 30 scored variables. Information about how responses link to the 30 measured variables is provided in the test manual. The majority of variables have intensity ratings from 1 to 3, with several domains rated dichotomously (e.g., -1 or +1 scores for Relationship with Mother, Relationship with Father, and Self-Esteem). Scores of 0 are possible for only one scale—Adaption to Fairy Tale Content—which can occur when responses do not describe an action or cannot be categorized in the scoring system. Finally, Bizarre responses and Repetitions are scored 1 with examples provided in the test manual.

One can see how this system of administration and scoring requires training in psychodynamic processes. Probes and clarification prompts require knowledge of the foundational tenets of ego psychology. As the FTT is a projective technique, knowledge of basic psychoanalytic theory (e.g., defense mechanisms, ego functions) is vital. The FTT is not recommended for use by non-psychodynamically oriented professionals.

Once the test is completed, the scores for each of the 30 variables are transferred to page one of the response booklet. These raw scores are then converted to T scores for three age bands.

TECHNICAL. The standardization sample for the second edition of the FTT consisted of 1,355 children ages 7 to 12 years living in four regions of India: Bangalore, Delhi, Kolkata, and Mumbai. Gender, religion, and socioeconomic status also were reported. Norms are presented separately by gender and age group (7-8 years, 9-10 years, and 11-12 years) for each of the four regions.

In terms of technical/statistical development, projective techniques have had an uneasy relationship with psychometrics. The enterprise of projection is aligned to, and deeply grounded in, psychodynamic theory, with its rich qualitative features. Capturing theoretical constructs like Need for Approval or Oral Needs is difficult from an operationalization standpoint. In reviewing the psychometric properties of the FTT, the previous reviewers refer to interrater reliability and test-retest reliability coefficients that are not provided in the second edition of the FTT manual. The only technical information presented in the current manual is factorial evidence in which 29 variables (one is omitted) resulted in 11 clusters on first rotation, with a second rotation of the 11 clusters reduced to four principal categories: Defensiveness, Profitable Aggression, Helpfulness & Sociability versus Aggression, and Moral Consciousness. The total amount of variance accounted for was not provided. As reported in the Medway (2005) review, the FTT factor analytic study yielded eight factors, at least some of which (e.g., Reality Contact) have different interpretations than those that emerged in the second edition. In future research, it would be interesting to compare the different factor structures across countries.

COMMENTARY. When an instrument is updated, the test author typically explains the reasons for the new edition (e.g., updated research findings, critiques of previous materials). However, no explanation is offered to support the development of the second edition of the FTT, which appears to have resulted solely from the Indian standardization effort.

Data from the large sample of Greek children used in standardizing the first edition are not included in the second edition. The test author notes that the test has also been standardized in Russia, Turkey, and China (as well as India). However, these standardization samples also are not included in the second edition. It is certainly admirable to engage in international standardization, but this reviewer believes it is insufficient to roll out a new edition of an instrument on a country by country basis. In this reviewer's opinion, Indian norms would be better published as a supplement to the existing test manual and/or made available to users on the dedicated webpage.

Although use of the FTT will remain limited in countries in which it has not been standardized, it may have potential as a child-based projective technique. The projective hypothesis and its associated methods are key elements of psychodynamic practice. Heretofore, projective methods for children were sentence completion, drawings, and stimulus cards involving story telling. The FTT is novel in that the materials are based on common tales (Little Red Riding Hood, Snow White), characters from these stories (dwarfs, wolves, witches), and characters common to many tales (e.g., giants). The child is asked a series of questions about the cards, so the story-telling element is reduced to several questions (and follow-up probes).

Overall, however, the parameters and language regarding background knowledge of the featured fairy tales are extremely vague. In future editions, it is recommended that Little Red Riding Hood and Snow White be subjected to content analysis in terms of story form/details, with a set criterion of recalled information so the test user has clear operational definitions of knowledge, recall, and familiarity. In discussing the development of the FTT, the test author mentions key episodes from various scenes. Recall of these key events could be quantified to provide some clarity with regard to the child's background knowledge of the material.

The FTT is not recommended for use in countries in which it has not been standardized, including the United States, Canada, England, and Ireland. The second edition is new only in that the Indian standardization sample is complete, with Indian norms published in the test manual. Some key information from the first manual is not re-published in the second edition. A child's background knowledge of the two key fairy tales is left for the user to decide. The test author appropriately delimits the use of the test as a therapeutic tool for psychodynamically oriented child psychologists (e.g., to formulate treatment goals, evaluate response to intervention). The FTT has numerous research applications, and it is hoped that standardization will continue and include potentially large Western samples.

SUMMARY. The FTT provides a unique projective method for psychoanalytically oriented practitioners. The second edition is based entirely on a new Indian standardization sample. In the single area of psychometric duplication with the first edition, a factor analytic study produced a different number of factors, with different interpretations from those mentioned in the original test manual. A key recommendation from earlier reviews regarding U.S. standardization was not mentioned in the new FTT manual.

REVIEWER'S REFERENCES

Medway, F. J. (2005). [Review of the Fairy Tale Test]. In R. A. Spies & B. S. Plake (Eds.), *The sixteenth mental measurements yearbook* (pp. 381-383). Lincoln, NE: Buros Institute of Mental Measurements.

Zachar, P. (2005). [Review of the Fairy Tale Test]. In R. A. Spies & B. S. Plake (Eds.), *The sixteenth mental measurements yearbook* (pp. 384-386). Lincoln, NE: Buros Institute of Mental Measurements.

[60]

Family Child Care Environment Rating Scale–Third Edition.

Purpose: "Designed to assess the overall quality of early childhood programs" in family homes with items that address "provisions in the environment to ensure protection of children's health and safety; appropriate stimulation through language and activities; and warm, supportive interactions."

Population: Family child care programs serving children from birth to 12 years.
Publication Dates: 1989-2019.
Acronym: FCCERS-3.
Scores, 40: 33 items in 6 subscales: Space and Furnishings (Indoor Space Used for Childcare, Furniture for Routine Care/Play/Learning, Arrangement of Indoor Space for Child Care, Display for Children), Personal Care Routines (Meals/Snacks, Diapering/Toileting, Health Practices, Safety Practices), Language and Books (Talking with Children, Encouraging Vocabulary Development, Responding to Children's Communication, Encouraging Children to Communicate, Provider Use of Books with Children, Encouraging Children's Use of Books), Activities (Fine Motor, Art, Music and Movement, Blocks, Dramatic Play, Nature/Science, Math/Number, Appropriate Use of Screen Time, Promoting Acceptance of Diversity, Gross Motor), Interaction (Supervision of Gross Motor Play, Supervision of Play and Learning [Non-Gross Motor], Provider-Child Interaction, Providing Physical Warmth/Touch, Guiding Children's Behavior, Interactions Among Children), Program Structure (Schedule and Transitions, Free Play, Group Time), plus Total Score.
Administration: Individual family child care homes.
Price Data, 2020: $25.95 per spiral bound manual with complete assessment (2019, 104 pages).
Time: 180 minutes minimum for observation.
Authors: Thelma Harms, Debby Cryer, Richard M. Clifford, and Noreen Yazejian.
Publisher: Teachers College Press.
Cross References: For reviews by Edward E. Gotts and Lisa F. Smith of the revised edition, see 20:89; for a review by Annette M. Iverson of an earlier edition titled Family Day Care Rating Scale, see 11:141.

Review of the Family Child Care Environment Rating Scale—Third Edition by SANDRA I. PLATA-POTTER, Associate Professor, Early Childhood Education, University of Mount Olive, Mount Olive, NC:

DESCRIPTION. The Family Child Care Environment Rating Scale—Third Edition (FCCERS-3) is part of a group of assessment tools known as the Environment Rating Scales (ERS). FCCERS-3 is designed to assess, by means of observation, the quality of a family childcare environment within a home. The focus is to assess the interactions between individual children and other children, the physical environment, instruction, and childcare provider. Because the caregiver in a family childcare home can provide care for children from birth to 12 years old, including the provider's own children, the assessment is designed to take a wide age range into consideration, whereas a center-based facility has similar-aged children grouped together in a classroom. The FCCERS-3 consists of items that are designed "to assess provisions in the environment to ensure protection of children's health and safety, appropriate stimulation through language and activities, and warm, supportive interactions" (manual, p. 2). Items, which are made up of indicators, are grouped within six subscales. FCCERS-3 relies on observation and what is being said during interactions between the child and his or her environment in order to score the indicators. The assessor does not interview the childcare provider because the focus of the assessment is to observe. Prior to starting the FCCERS-3, the assessor should become familiar with the indicators and items that will be scored. The assessor also should be familiar with or have on hand the appropriate handouts that list the expectations for gross motor play and equipment, nutrition, and health; these can be obtained from the website listed in the instructions. Before beginning the observation, the assessor should ascertain that every age group of children being cared for is represented during the assessment. Throughout the observation, the children and the caregiver are to be followed. On the occasion that children go to different areas, the assessor is to go where the caregiver is, as long as the caregiver is interacting with a child or children.

Indicators within each item are scored *yes*, *no*, or, on occasion, *N/A* for not applicable. Based on these responses, the item is scored from 1 to 7. Each item is presented on facing pages in the spiral-bound manual/record booklet. One page contains the item and its indicators, and the other contains clarifying notes. The scale range for the item is presented horizontally across the top of the page with four descriptors as follows: 1 = *inadequate*, 3 = *minimal*, 5 = *good*, 7 = *excellent*. Indicators are grouped in four corresponding columns below. After each indicator is scored, the item is scored based on the responses to the indicators. An even-numbered score (2, 4, or 6) means the item met all of the previous column's indicators and at least half of the next column's indicators. For example, an item meeting all indicators listed under 1 and 3 and at least half of the indicators listed under 5 would be assigned a score of 4. Scores for the items in each subscale are averaged to obtain subscale scores. To compute a total score, the scores of all items scored are averaged. Scoring of indicators and items is to be completed during the 3-hour observation period.

DEVELOPMENT. FCCERS-3 is a revision of the FCCERS-R. The development of the FCCERS-3 relied on current research as well as an extensive review of organization position statements (e.g., National Association for the Education of Young Children's [NAEYC] revision of *Developmentally Appropriate Practice: Focus on Preschoolers*, NAEYC and the Fred Rogers Center for Early Learning and Children's Media) and performance standards (e.g., *Caring for Our Children: National Health and Safety Performance Standards*) as cited in the test manual. Caring for children in a home environment increases the complexities of child care, due to the fact that the caregiver is tasked with meeting the needs of numerous children from different age groups, at different developmental levels, and with different backgrounds. Even though the thinking is that providing care in a home environment benefits the children, the challenges not only increase, but also are different than if the children were in a classroom with peers who fall in the same age bracket. Because the purpose of the assessment tool is to assess and describe the quality of the family childcare environment, development and refinement of the FCCERS-3 relied on research, known best practices, and real-life experiences. The number of items to be scored in FCCERS-3 was reduced to 33, down from 38 in the FCCERS-R. Some of the items that were dropped entailed teacher report or activities that were not usually observed (e.g., nap time). According to the test authors, the FCCERS-3 includes a component that places more emphasis on language, science, and mathematics. The 33 items in the FCCERS-3 are focused on what can be observed while the assessor is present. A large dataset (n = 1,218) that used FCCERS-R was used to help fine-tune the indicators in FCCERS-3. To begin, small pilot trials were conducted, followed by a more sizable field test that consisted of 63 family child care homes (FCCHs) in four states from four different parts of the country. Experienced assessors were used, and baseline reliability of 85% or higher was attained.

TECHNICAL. The test authors state that because of the field test sample size, how the sample was selected, and the geographic locations, normative data were not provided. However, as the data become available, they will be posted on the website given in the assessment manual. Because the FCCERS-3 uses items and indicators as part of the assessment process, reliability was examined for both indicators and items. Indicator reliability, which considered the exact match across all indicators, was 85.5%. Item reliability was 62.2% for exact agreement, and 86.4% for agreement within 1 point. The scale authors pointed out that the personnel used to test reliability were proficient in the use of ERS; new assessors would most likely need extensive training. The instructions provide an ample amount of research evidence demonstrating both reliability and validity for scores from the measures that make up the ERS.

COMMENTARY. FCCERS-3 is focused on the interactions that are actually observed while the assessors are present and not on self-report. Observation plays an important role in the early childhood field because it is a common method used in assessments. Moreover, the test authors relied on research and position statements related to family child care homes in order to improve this tool. The authors extensively reviewed a plethora of material so as to provide a better and up-to-date assessment tool. The only drawback with regard to the FCCERS-3 and the other ERSs is that the first list of indicators is written in a way that raters may find confusing. The indicators are worded so that an answer of *yes* is actually a negative indicator, with all the other indicators needing an answer of *yes* for a positive indicator. This can cause confusion that requires the assessor to stop and think about how the indicator is worded to arrive at the correct scoring. It would be helpful if an explanation for this approach were provided.

SUMMARY. FCCERS-3 is designed to assess and assure that a family child care home where children spend a good portion of their day provides a learning environment that meets the child's developmental needs. The assessment tool takes into account that child care within a home can include children whose ages fall within a wide range. The test authors have demonstrated a level of due diligence to review the literature and position statements that would contribute to improving this tool, which has been in use extensively nationally and internationally. This type of support for the assessment tool is clearly presented in the instructions, providing readers what they need to review and be informed. The FCCERS-3 has some significant differences from the FCCERS-R, in that the FCCERS-R consisted of 38 items and the FCCERS-3 consists of 33 items. One significant difference is that the FCCERS-3 requires that assessors score only what is actually observed, thereby not relying on self-report to score an item. Although the assessors who participated in field testing the FCCERS-3 were experienced, the instructions provide detailed explanations to assist those with less experience in scoring correctly.

Review of the Family Child Care Environment Rating Scale—Third Edition by GLEN E. RAY, Professor of Psychology, Auburn University at Montgomery, Montgomery, AL:

DESCRIPTION. The Family Child Care Environment Rating Scale—Third Edition (FCCERS-3) is a substantial update to the previous version (FCCERS-R) with regard to content areas covered and the administration of the measure. The FCCERS-3 is based on rater observations and is designed to evaluate the quality of child care homes with children ranging in age from birth to 12 years. This latest version consists of 33 total items divided into six subscales: Space and Furnishings, Personal Care Routines, Language and Books, Activities, Interaction, and Program Structure. The test authors have based what they mean by quality of the child care home on "research evidence from a number of relevant fields ..., professional views of best practice, and real experiences from ... providers" (manual, p. 2). According to the authors this revision "is designed to improve the prediction of child outcomes through an increased emphasis on language interactions and science/mathematics in ongoing activities" (manual, p. 4).

Unlike previous versions, the FCCERS-3 is based entirely on rater observations conducted over a pre-determined 3-hour time sample. The Parents and Provider subscale in the previous version, which was based in part on post-hoc reports as opposed to concurrent observations, has been eliminated, and other individual items from various subscales have either been eliminated or modified. There also is more emphasis placed on observing how providers use available materials to foster children's learning and less emphasis placed on access to materials compared to earlier versions.

The FCCERS-3 is flexible and can be used in both small and large homes. In larger homes with separate groups of children who may not interact often, observations can be made separately. The 3-hour continuous time sample to be used is clearly indicated as "the most active time of the day" (manual, p. 9) when most children would be in attendance. Observers are encouraged to schedule the observation in collaboration with the child care provider to determine the best observing time for that particular home. Observers are expected to make notes and calculate how long the children being observed are engaged in various activities. Observers also must move around in the same space used by the children in order to hear and see the provider-children interactions. Specific observer guidelines are provided to ensure that observers navigate through the interactive space (inside and outside the home) with minimal disruption to the everyday activities of the home. Observers will need to be familiar with and have with them additional information to accompany the FCCERS-3 with regard to health and safety items (e.g., Revised USDA Meal Guidelines for ERS). Access links to these additional materials are provided in the test manual. Scoring of all the indicators and the items is to be completed when administering the FCCERS-3 and before leaving the home.

With the one exception of a short provider interview needed to complete the front page of the FCCERS-3, all scores are based solely on the observations made within the 3-hour time sample. Subscales are composed of items that are, in turn, composed of indicators of quality. Indicators are scored as either *yes*, *no*, or *N/A*. Items are scored from 1 (*inadequate*) through 7 (*excellent*) or N/A (*not applicable*) based on how the indicators for that particular item are scored. All indicators for each item are to be scored before an item score can be determined. Subscale scores can be calculated by summing all item scores in a particular subscale and then dividing by the number of items scored. An overall score on the FCCERS-3 is computed as the sum of all item scores divided by the number of items scored. The scoresheet for the FCCERS-3 provides a template to create a graphic representation based on the scoring profile of all items and subscales to assist with interpretation and to highlight strengths as well as areas that may be in need of improvement.

DEVELOPMENT. The FCCERS-3 is a revision of the Family Child Care Environment Rating Scale-Revised (FCCERS-R) and is part of a larger "family" of Environment Rating Scales (ERS) that are designed to evaluate the quality of early childhood programs (manual, p. 3). Changes in the FCCERS-3 have been made with regard to the content to be observed and with regard to improving accuracy in administration. Items and indicators, including the placement of indicators have been revised or added to various subscales, and one subscale (Parents and Provider) was omitted from this latest version. These changes were based on current literature and empirical research using the FCCERS-R. According to the test authors, these changes were made to "reflect current research, knowledge, and practice in the field" (manual, p. 2).

TECHNICAL. The test authors report that the Environment Rating Scales (ERS), of which the FCCERS-3 is a part, have been extensively researched and shown to produce reliable and valid scores. There also is evidence that the scales are technically sound when used with international samples. A field test was conducted including 63 family child care homes (FCCHs). The field test had two experienced raters independently rate the FCCH at the same time. Looking at indictor reliability of the FCCERS-3, the average reliability between the two trained observers (percent agreement) was 85.5%. For item reliability, exact agreement occurred 62.2% of the time, and observers were within 1 point of each other 86.4% of the time. To account for chance agreement between raters, Cohen's kappa was also calculated. Overall, the mean weighted kappa was .64 with a range of .43-.96 depending on the item. For interclass correlations at the item level, the mean coefficient was .96, and coefficients ranged from .76 to 1.00. At the subscale level, interclass correlation coefficients were .96 for the full scale with subscales ranging from .73 to .92. Internal consistency (coefficient alpha) of the full measure was .97 with individual subscales ranging from .74 to .93. Normative data are not presented with the manual but will be made available through the test publisher's website when available.

COMMENTARY. The FCCERS-3 is a well-developed observation-based measure designed to assess the quality of FCCHs. The FCCERS-3 is a member of a larger family of measures that have well-established psychometric properties. As such, the instrument being evaluated here is the product of decades of research, application in the field, and systematic refinement. In addition to updating the content and increasing the accuracy of the administration/scoring, a main goal of this edition was to increase the predictive power of the measure. This was accomplished by focusing more on cognitive development (language, math, science). The pilot testing conducted thus far has focused on observer agreement and reliability concerns. As noted by the test authors, it will be interesting to determine whether future research with the new measure allows for greater prediction of various developmental outcomes compared to the previous version.

SUMMARY. The FCCERS-3 is a well-designed assessment of the overall quality of FCCHs. Observer reliability for the measure has been demonstrated. The Environment Rating Scales instruments have been shown to provide scores that are considered valid, and subsequent research investigating validity issues is planned for this specific measure. The instrument is administratively flexible, and scoring/interpretation are straightforward. This instrument appears to be a high-quality measure of the quality of FCCHs.

[61]

Family Environment Scale [Fourth Edition Manual].

Purpose: Designed to measure family member perceptions of "actual, preferred, and expected family social environments."

Population: Ages 11 and older.

Publication Dates: 1974-2009.

Acronym: FES.

Scores: 10 in 3 dimensions: Relationship (Cohesion, Expressiveness, Conflict), Personal Growth (Independence, Achievement Orientation, Intellectual-Cultural Orientation, Active-Recreational Orientation, Moral-Religious Emphasis), System Maintenance (Organization, Control).

Administration: Individual or group.

Forms, 3: Real (Form R), Ideal (Form I), Expectations (Form E).

Price Data, 2020: $60 per print manual (2009, 188 pages); $50 per digital manual; $100 per group report (Real Form); $15 per individual report (Real Form); 2.50 per online survey (all forms; minimum of 20); $2.50 per online survey license (all forms; minimum 50); $2.50 per printable survey (all forms; minimum 50).

Foreign Language Editions: Translated materials available in Arabic, Chinese (traditional), Creole (Haitian), Danish, Dutch, Farsi (Form R), Finnish, French, Greek, Hebrew, Hindi, Italian, Japanese, Korean, Malay (Form R), Norwegian (Form R), Polish, Portuguese, Slovenian (Form R), Spanish (Form R), Swedish, Tagalog (Form R), and Thai.

Time: 15-20 minutes for administration.

Comments: Component of the Social Climate Scales; online administration and scoring available; a children's version for ages 5-11 is published separately.

Authors: Rudolf H. Moos and Bernice S. Moos.

Publisher: Mind Garden, Inc.

Cross References: For reviews by Jay A. Mancini and Michael J. Sporakowski of the third edition manual, see 14:146; see also T5:1010 (138 references); for reviews by Julie A. Allison and Brenda H. Loyd of the second edition, see 12:151 (76 references); see also T4:961 (136 references); for reviews by Nancy A. Busch-Rossnagel and Nadine M. Lambert of an earlier edition (1981 manual), see 9:408 (18 references); see also T3:872 (14 references); for a review by Philip H. Dreyer of the original edition, see 8:557 (4 references). For a review of the Social Climate Series, see 8:681.

Review of the Family Environment Scale by MARY M. CLARE, Professor Emerita, Lewis & Clark College, Portland, OR:

DESCRIPTION. The Family Environment Scale (FES) was introduced 46 years ago when Rudolf Moos asserted that social environments have personalities that affect the individuals within them. With the FES, Moos' focus was families. Since its first publication in 1974, the FES has garnered scholarly attention such that the current manual contains nearly 50 pages of references in which the scale has been cited in professional literature.

In the context of contemporary psychometric complexity as enabled by technical agility, the simplicity of this longstanding instrument is refreshing, grounding the clinician in data very close to families themselves. Individuals respond to 90 *true/false* questions to indicate their perspective on the Real (R), Expected (E), or Ideal (I) family. Self-report data, including from young family members (see 30-item Children's Version, published separately) are thus immediately available from clients with quick clinical summary for therapeutic application.

DEVELOPMENT. Based on social interviews and content of other Social Climate Scales (Moos, 2003), the original FES was developed to include items calling forward responses to the three theoretical family emphases: interpersonal relationships within the family, personal growth (e.g., in educational and moral/religious spheres), and family structure or organization. Subscales were subsequently designated within each area of emphasis—first conceptually and then according to frequency of response consistent with the designation. Original normative samples included 1,432 "normal" and 788 "distressed" families for Forms R and E, and 1,746 individuals for Form I. Additional norms have been more recently derived based on smaller samples of African-American and Latino parents, single parents, and African-American adolescents.

TECHNICAL. The FES shows the most strength in construct evidence of validity, particularly as reflected in longitudinal clinical case data (often up to 10-year follow up) reported first in 1998 (Moos, Cronkite, & Moos, 1998). Reliability data from the original samples are adequate to strong. Given space considerations, this reviewer chooses to refer readers to other reviews of the FES so as to devote more space to the commentary that follows.

COMMENTARY. The FES stands on history. It is grounded in theory that has withstood the test of time. Although its greatest promise is as a clinical tool, there are considerations that would be wise to take into account when using this instrument.

Sensitivity of item content. Based on close review of the test manual, it is unclear whether the items themselves have undergone any revision over the life of the FES. Meanwhile, vernacular, lifestyles, and contemporary values have shifted. Although comparisons certainly may be made between respondents using these questions, their sensitivity to contemporary worldviews and values may be quite a bit lower, several decades later.

Currency of underlying data. It is difficult to tell when the cases reported in the test manual were active. A brief review of the extensive reference listings revealed an article published in 1998 reporting 10-year outcomes. The age of the data upon which technical features like reliability and validity are based, if 10 years or older, could reduce the accuracy of those metrics.

Validity of scales. As mentioned above, scale designations were initially established based on theory. Metrics supporting the scale categories were originally generated according to frequency of response similarity (all *true*, all *false*) across items within those categories. It is unclear whether similar measurements have been taken more recently to ensure ongoing fit of assigned scales with respondents' interpretation of item prompts. The current manual reports factor analytic research between 1989 and 2002. Among these studies were findings revealing factor clusters interpreted to indicate family climate conceptually linked with the three emphases of cohesion, social activity (intellectual, recreational, moral-religious), and organization/control. Additional inquiry toward explicit validation of the FES scale and subscale structures would be valuable.

Representativeness of diverse families. In his review of the original FES in 1978, Dryer commented, "The norms developed for the test so far are particularly good for the study of traditional, middle class families, but more information is needed about the response patterns of families representing lower SES groups, minorities, and single parents." Similar observations have appeared in each subsequent review (Busch-Rossnagel, 1985; Loyd, 1995; Mancini, 2001). Addition of norms specific to African-American, Latino, and single-parent families occurred in the 2002 revision. The current manual reports impressive translation of the FES into 18 languages for use in European, Asian, and African countries, and briefly recounts research related to the experiences of various immigrant families in the context of acculturation. Yet, here in the fourth set of reviews of this instrument in the *Mental Measurements Yearbook* series, the limitation related to validity across all families continues. This is, in part, because of the age of the item language together with the appearance that the typologies assigned to families have not been updated since these normative groups were formed (Billings & Moos, 1982). Notably absent are norms for families with same-gender parents or families with gender-diverse children. With regard to gender diversity, the demographic information requested on the FES answer sheet provides only "male" or "female" as options for designating gender. Heteronormative family structure is also assumed with the prompt for indicating family position as "mother (wife), father (husband), son or daughter." Additional use restrictions for the FES would be with immigrant families, Native American families, and family homes composed of multiple generations not represented by sample pools.

Best suited for clinical applicability. In the context of the above considerations, clinicians will find the FES to have great potential for supplementing work with families who seek support in meeting their children's developmental needs and for responding well to profound stressors and transitions linked with physical challenges, or with psychiatric or addictive disorders. These areas of investigation have produced the richest of evidence of FES utility. In her 1985 review of the FES, Nadine Lambert offered a matter-of-fact summary indicating that the normative data underlying the FES were not for diagnosis of family function, but for comparison of perspectives within families. She indicated the importance of respecting this limitation and resisting judgments about the "relative worth of family environments" based on FES results. This reviewer endorses Lambert's (1985) observation. The strength of the FES remains as a tool for comparing responses across family members as a method for promoting family exploration of strengths, needs, and opportunities for therapeutic change.

SUMMARY. The most impressive effect of the FES over the years is its facilitation of clinical service to families stressed by mental illness, substance dependence, and other profound transitions. Going forward, and as indicated in the test manual's section on future directions, there are rich possibilities, given the years the FES has been clinically applied, for deriving subtle insights into the ways family members affect and are affected by each other. The scale's utility is substantial for clinical work with both healthy and challenged family constellations. At the same time, the challenge is significant for keeping current with item content as well as responsiveness to the vast diversity in healthy family composition and function. The evolution of a dynamic FES would be well worth the effort, in particular, in support of positive clinical outcomes.

REVIEWER'S REFERENCES

Billings, A. G., & Moos, R. H. (1982). Psychosocial theory and research on depression: An integrative framework and review. *Clinical Psychology Review, 2*(2), 213–237.

Busch-Rossnagel, N. A. (1985). [Test review of the Family Environment Scale]. In J. V. Mitchell, Jr. (Ed.), *The ninth mental measurements yearbook*. Retrieved from http://marketplace.unl.edu/buros/

Dryer, P. H. (1978). [Test review of the Family Environment Scale]. In O. K. Buros (Ed.), *The eighth mental measurements yearbook*. Retrieved from http://marketplace.unl.edu/buros/

Lambert, N. M. (1985). [Test review of the Family Environment Scale]. In J. V. Mitchell, Jr. (Ed.), *The ninth mental measurements yearbook*. Retrieved from http://marketplace.unl.edu/buros/

Loyd, B. H. (1995). [Test review of the Family Environment Scale, Second Edition]. In J. C. Conoley & J. C. Impara (Eds.), *The twelfth mental measurements yearbook*. Retrieved from http://marketplace.unl.edu/buros/

Mancini, J. A. (2001). [Test review of the Family Environment Scale, Third Edition Manual]. In B. S. Plake & J. C. Impara (Eds.), *The fourteenth mental measurements yearbook*. Retrieved from http://marketplace.unl.edu/buros/

Moos, R. H. (2003). *The social climate scales: A user's guide* (3rd ed.). Menlo Park, CA: Mind Garden.

Moos, R. H., Cronkite, R. C., & Moos, B. S. (1998). Family and extrafamily resources and the 10-year course of treated depression. *Journal of Abnormal Psychology, 107*(3), 450–460.

Review of Family Environment Scale [Fourth Edition Manual] by MARK D. SHRIVER, Professor, Psychology, Munroe-Meyer Institute, University of Nebraska Medical Center, Omaha, NE:

DESCRIPTION. This 2009 manual represents the fourth edition of the Family Environment Scale (FES), which has been available and used extensively in many research and clinical applications since 1974. The FES manual lists hundreds of references to research and related literature on the use of the FES. The primary purpose of the FES is to provide an assessment of an individual's perceptions of a family's social environment. The FES can be used in clinical practice with individuals or families and for program evaluation.

The FES has 90 *true/false* items divided into 10 subscales assessing three dimensions of families:

Relationship, Personal Growth, and System Maintenance. The there are three forms of the FES, all of which have the same content items, but the items are phrased slightly differently across the forms to assess current or future perceptions of raters. The Real (R) Form measures raters' perceptions of their current family environment. The Ideal (I) Form measures raters' preferences about what the rater perceives may be an ideal family environment. The Expectations (E) Form measures raters' future expectations about family environment for those who may be entering a new family situation (e.g., foster care, blended family). The rater uses a separate scoring sheet to mark either *true* or *false* for each item on the scale. Raw scores are converted to standard scores with a mean of 50 for each of the subscales using a chart provided in the test manual. In addition, a Family Incongruence Score can be computed based on differences in subscale scores between dyads within a family. It appears that respondents are typically older children, adolescents, or adults of typical cognitive functioning. A Children's Version of the FES, published separately and described in a different manual, is not reviewed here.

DEVELOPMENT. Items on the FES were developed based on interviews with different types of families and previous scales developed by the same authors to match the authors' "general formulation of three sets of social climate dimensions" (manual, p. 27), namely interpersonal relationships, personal growth, and family structure. There were initially 200 items that were subsequently culled to 90 items based on the responses of 1,000 individuals in 285 families recruited locally by the test authors and labeled "normal." An additional 42 families labeled "distressed" by the test authors also were included. No indication of how these labels were operationalized is provided. Recruitment took place from three church groups, newspaper advertisements, and high school students. A sample of racial minority families was obtained "in part from African-American and Latino research assistants" (manual, p. 27). Additional demographics of this sample are not provided. The final 90 items were selected based on psychometric properties to ensure an equal number of items between subscales, to enhance variability of responding, to demonstrate higher internal consistency of subscales, and to achieve low-to-moderate correlations among subscales. Perhaps because of the decade in which the FES was developed and the initial sample of respondents (i.e., church groups), items related to moral-religious emphasis appear primarily to reflect a Judeo-Christian framework.

TECHNICAL.

Standardization. Normative data for Form R and Form E are based on 1,432 normal and 788 distressed families, including the initial 285 and 42 families, respectively, that completed the pilot form. It is reported that families were drawn from all areas of the country and included different types of family structure, racial minority groups, and ages, but no demographic data are provided on the sample. Normative data for Form I were collected from "1,746 individuals who were from normal and distressed families or were professional family therapists" (manual, p. 31), but no specific demographic information is provided. It is not clear when these data were collected. If they were collected during the initial development of the measure, they may be decades old. Similarly, it is not clear the extent to which the demographics of the normative group represent those of the current national population.

Reliability. Internal consistency (coefficient alpha) estimates are provided for Form R subscales for a sample of 1,067 respondents presumably from the standardization study. A citation to a 1990 study by the test authors is provided, suggesting this study was conducted in the 1980s. Internal consistency estimates ranged from .61 to .78. Corrected average item-subscale correlation coefficients for the same sample ranged from .27 to .44. Test-retest reliability estimates across intervals of 2 months and 4 months were reported for samples of 47 and 35 individuals, respectively. No information about these samples is provided. Test-retest reliability coefficients were low to moderate, ranging from .68 to .86 for 2 months and from .54 to .91 for 4 months. For a sample combining psychiatric patients and case controls, subscale stability scores were calculated for 1 year, 3-4 years, 6 years, and 9-10 years and ranged largely from the .50s to .70s. Overall, the reliability of the subscales is varied and largely moderate, suggesting caution if using the FES for progress monitoring over time or with treatment, or in interpretation of subscale profiles. Means and standard deviations for special groups of families (different numbers, one-parent, African-American, and Latino) are provided in the appendices to the test manual, but no information on the reliability of test scores for these special groups is provided. The test authors do caution that for African-American and Latino families, "Results should be interpreted with caution because the samples are small, the families were drawn primarily from middle class populations, and the groups were not matched on family background factors such as size and socioeconomic status" (manual, p. 37).

Validity. The test authors report results from factor analytic studies of the FES, most of which appear to have been conducted in the 1990s. These studies indicate factor structures of two to four or more dimensions. The test authors note that the factor structure of the FES depends on the researchers' "conceptual considerations; aspects of the sample such as its diversity; and decisions about statistical procedures" (manual, p. 39). The authors note that they attempted "to build content and face validity into the FES" during the initial development of items (p. 41). The authors review "some evidence of the subscales' construct and discriminant validity" (p. 41) over the next 66 pages of the test manual by describing research using the FES for various applications. Much of the research appears to have taken place in the 1980s and 1990s and appears focused on using the FES in research studies with different samples of families with particular child or adult problems. Descriptions of how these different samples are scored or profiled on the FES relative to normal families or in response to treatment for the respective problems is provided. Although it is clearly evident that the FES has been used in many research studies, it is not clear that data from these studies provide construct evidence of validity for FES scores. In other words, evidence is not clearly provided demonstrating that the data from the subscales actually represent the construct purportedly measured by the subscale.

COMMENTARY. The test manual is not particularly well organized and appears to rely largely on research conducted by others on the applications of the scale. This approach can be fine, but it is not clear how studies were chosen to be included in the test manual and whether the studies represent accurately the totality of the evidence base for the FES. In addition, the test authors note that they "have taken some liberties in reviewing and integrating literature on the FES" (manual preface) because researchers have adapted scales, employed new labels, provided new names for factors, or used only parts of scales. In short, the research cited is not necessarily on the same scale the clinician may be using. In addition, much of the research is quite dated and likely was conducted using earlier versions of the FES, so it is not clear whether the research is applicable to the current version. Similarly, normative data appear to be based on families from at least 20 years ago or more. Given what appear to be ongoing changes in family structure and dynamics over the past decades, it is unclear how this measure keeps pace or accurately represents the current diversity of families in the United States or internationally. Future editions of this measure and manual will benefit from a clear organization of the manual with emphasis on providing the potential user current and well-organized information about revisions that have occurred with the latest edition, current samples for normative comparison, updated information on reliability, and validity evidence specific to the subscales' constructs.

SUMMARY. The FES has a long history in research on family structure and dynamics. There are a paucity of measures available for researchers and clinicians for this purpose. The FES is grounded in a relatively coherent conceptual heuristic that may be useful for researchers and clinicians alike. However, the reliability and validity evidence for scores obtained from the subscales is not well presented and appears questionable. Thus, caution should be used in interpreting scores from this measure. Additional caution appears warranted when interpreting scores in that the normative group for comparison is dated, narrowly sampled, and may not be representative of the current population of families.

[62]

Family-Supportive Supervisor's Behaviors.

Purpose: Designed to address "how supervisors can help workers ease the stress of work and non-work life."
Population: Working adults.
Publication Date: 2014.
Acronym: FSSB.
Scores, 4: Emotional Support, Instrumental Support, Role Modeling, Creative Work-Family Management.
Administration: Individual or group.
Price Data: Available from publisher.
Time: (5) minutes.
Authors: Leslie B. Hammer and Ellen E. Kossek.
Publisher: Mind Garden, Inc. [Editor's note: The publisher of this test changed after the review was written. The test is now published by Work Life Help.]

Review of the Family-Supportive Supervisor's Behaviors by WARREN BOBROW, President, All About Performance LLC, Los Angeles, CA:

DESCRIPTION. The Family-Supportive Supervisor's Behaviors (FSSB) instrument is designed to be used to begin, track, and assess organizational change efforts to ease the stress of work and non-work life. The measure consists of two 14-item forms that are rated on a 5-point Likert-type scale from *strongly disagree* to *strongly agree*. The first form asks the participant how supportive his/her supervisor is of work-life balance. The second asks the supervisor to rate his/her support of the employee's work-life balance. There are four scales on each form: Emotional Support (four items), Instrumental Support (three items), Role Modeling (three items), and Creative Work-Family Management (four items). All items are worded in a positive direction, and the scale scores are derived from the average of the responses. The scale scores are categorized into *low, medium,* and *high* bands using a table presented in the test manual. The manual also provides a narrative description of each category for each subscale.

DEVELOPMENT. Items for the FSSB were developed via focus groups and reviews of the literature. Twenty-eight initial items were given to a sample (size unknown), and results were statistically analyzed in several steps to determine the items to be retained. Based on the item analyses, the scale was reduced to 18 items. Following a subsequent study, four items were found not to correlate well with other items in their subscales, and the FSSB was further reduced to 14 items.

The test manual does not provide a reference that explicitly gives a rationale for the four subscales. The statistical information provided does not support the multiple dimensions, as the median correlation between subscales is .64 (with a range of .62 to .74). The manual also indicates that the second-order factor analysis suggests the use of a single total scale score.

Most of the items are behaviorally based, so a before-and-after comparison could be made after participants received the training prescribed in the manual.

TECHNICAL. The normative sample included 360 employees at a grocery chain in the Midwestern United States, 239 nursing home employees, and 105 food manufacturing employees. Although data also were collected from 79 grocery store supervisors, those results were not included, and no normative data are provided for the supervisor version. Means and standard deviations are reported for the three employee groups separately and combined. Cutoff classifications for low, medium, and high scores are provided for the combined group. It should be noted that the cutoff between the *low* and *medium* score categories for the Role Modeling subscale is different (i.e., slightly higher) than that for the other three subscales, despite similar means and standard deviations. There is no explanation or histogram to explain this difference.

Demographic information (gender, race, age, marital status, and caretaker status) is provided for the grocery store sample only. The manual does not provide any statistical tests of group differences based on these variables. One can imagine that such findings would be useful data in providing proper training for participants. Researchers who would want to use the instrument would find this analysis valuable as well. The categories of data regarding caretaker status (i.e., children living at home, providing care for another adult, providing care for child and an adult) only add up to 66%, leaving one to wonder what other categories are part of this variable.

Reliability coefficients were calculated based on the grocery store employee data. The alpha coefficient for the entire scale was reported to be .94, with coefficients ranging from .73 to .90 for the subscales.

The criterion-related evidence for validity for the FSSB is moderate. There are significant correlations between the overall score and some self-report outcomes variables (work-family conflict, family-work positive spillover, job satisfaction and intent to turnover), but not others (family-work conflict and work-family positive spillover). Not surprisingly, moderate to moderately high correlations were found with other measures of general supervisor support (coefficients ranged from .55 to .74).

No data are provided that indicate correlations between the survey and similar measures (e.g., King et al., 1995), so the construct-related evidence of validity cannot be evaluated.

Given that data from the normative sample were gathered in 2009 or earlier, it would be useful to see the correlation between scores and measurable organizational outcomes, such as absenteeism and turnover rather than self-report measures only. Such results would provide important data as to whether a company would want to invest in using the instrument and subsequent training.

COMMENTARY. The FSSB is designed to measure family supportive supervisor behaviors on four different dimensions with the results being used to provide training to supervisors to become more supportive. The data do not support a four-factor model that is reported in the manual. The complexity of the constructs is also called into question due to subsequent research (Hammer, Kossek, Bodner, & Crain, 2013), which indicates that supervisor support can be measured with four, rather than 14, items. Although 14 items are not onerous to most survey respondents, four would likely lead to greater participant satisfaction.

It is unclear why this instrument would be given to measure both employee and supervisor perceptions of supervisor behaviors when data are not presented on how the supervisors evaluate themselves. There is no information provided on what a user should do if there are differences between the supervisor and employee scores. The manual does not indicate how these two sets of scores should be integrated.

SUMMARY. The test developers have created an instrument to begin a discussion about the degree to which supervisors behave in a way that indicates family support levels in an organization. As the assessment is low stakes (e.g., not involved in hiring or firing decisions), it does not have to meet a high psychometric bar. Rather, participants can view their level of support, at least through the eyes of their employees, and participate in training with a goal of improving. However, if supervisors who are rated in the *high* category on the scales do not need to participate in training, this could be a cost savings to the company. If this is the case, more diligence should be applied to creating the cutoff scores.

REVIEWER'S REFERENCES

Hammer, L. B., Kossek, E. E., Bodner, T., & Crain, T. (2013). Measurement development and validation of the Family Supportive Supervisor Behavior Short Form (FSSB-SF). *Journal of Occupational Health Psychology, 18*(3), 285-296.

King, L. A., Mattimore, L. K., King, D. W., & Adams, G. A. (1995). Family Support Inventory for Workers: A new measure of perceived social support from family members. *Journal of Organizational Behavior, 16*(3), 235-258.

Review of the Family-Supportive Supervisor's Behaviors by PHILIP J. MOBERG, Associate Professor, Northern Kentucky University, Highland Heights, KY:

DESCRIPTION. The Family-Supportive Supervisor's Behaviors (FSSB) instrument is an individual- or group-administered rating measure of four supervisor behavior types for use by employees or supervisors in work settings. A single-sentence instruction precedes 14 behavioral statements that exemplify supervisor Emotional Support, Instrumental Support, Role Modeling, and Creative Work-Family Management. The test is available in digital or printed format. Examinees respond using a 5-point Likert scale. The FSSB manual provides instructions for computing individual scores and interpretations of *low, medium,* and *high* values. The publisher provides digital scoring and an FSSB Personal Report that reviews how an employee rates a supervisor.

The FSSB manual describes (a) the background literature, (b) interventions and training programs, (c) administration and scoring, (d) scale interpretation, (e) test construction and development, (f) reliability and validity assessment, (g) FSSB research, (h) references, and (i) observer- and self-rating forms.

DEVELOPMENT. To construct the FSSB instrument, the authors wrote 28 items to represent four dimensions of supervisor support deduced from reviews of prior theory, the research literature, and content analysis of four employee and supervisor focus group discussions and four individual interviews with district managers of a grocery chain in the Northeastern United States (see Hammer, Kossek, Anger, Bodnar, & Zimmerman, 2011).

To collect initial response data, the test authors distributed a survey form of the 28 items to 585 staff members at a university in the Northwestern United States (see Hammer et al., 2009). Using a subset of the responses (n = 123), the authors assessed the psychometric properties and retained items if (a) less than 10% of respondents marked "not applicable," (b) item intercorrelations were moderate to strong within dimensions but weaker extradimensionally, (c) item-total correlations exceeded .60, (d) coefficient alpha exceeded .70, (e) item difficulty values ranged from .30 to .70, and (f) item discrimination exceeded .30. By applying these criteria, the authors reduced the initial 28-item pool to 18 items.

Citing inadequate available sample size to conduct an exploratory factor analysis of the remaining 18 items, the authors instead applied principal axis factoring to conduct four independent exploratory factor analyses of each item subset that comprised a dimension: Emotional Support (five items), Instrumental Support (four items), Role Modeling (three items), and Creative Work-Family Management (six items). Empirical evidence of the scale's internal structure and extent to which the 18 items represent four distinct but related dimensions is not provided (Furr & Bacharach, 2014).

Following a second study involving employees of a Midwestern United States grocery chain, results "suggested that four items did not correlate well with the other items within their FSSB dimensions and the factors representing those dimensions" (manual, p. 10). The authors omitted these four items based on this correlation criterion and due to lack of conceptual clarity. The magnitude of the omission criterion and actual correlation values were not specified.

Although the test authors do not specify which items were dropped, by comparing the number of items on the dimensions of the initial 18-item scale with that of the reduced set of 14 items, it is evident that Emotional Support was reduced from five items to four; Instrumental Support, from four items to three; and Creative Work-Family Management, from six items to four. Items for the Role Modeling dimension were unchanged (i.e., three items on both versions). In the absence of an exploratory factor analysis of the full 18-item scale, it is not known whether the four omitted items may have correlated with another dimension. Exploratory factor analysis of the preliminary 18-item scale that empirically supports the hypothesized four-factor structure and reduction from 18 to 14 items would strengthen the meaning of FSSB dimensions.

The test manual states that the authors conducted a "second-order factor analysis" (p. 10) on the four support dimensions to assess the presence of a superordinate factor. A second-order factor analysis necessarily requires that an obliquely-rotated, first-order factor analysis of item-level data be conducted to produce the interfactor correlation matrix needed for second-order analysis. Thus, it would be more appropriate either to describe both analyses or to describe this step as a factor analysis of scores on the four dimensions. The manual adds that, "All factor loadings for the first-order and second-order factors were statistically significant" (p. 10), but reports no values for "first-order" loadings and only a value range for "second-order" loadings. One or two factor-loading tables presented in the test manual would illuminate dimensionality.

The test manual (Table 3, p. 11) reports factor loadings and error variances for a multilevel confirmatory factor analysis model reported as Study 2 in Hammer et al. (2009). First-order factor loadings are reported for items on each subordinate dimension, along with second-order factor loadings for dimensions on a superordinate construct. Unfortunately, the manual does not report fit indices for this confirmatory model, forcing the reader to refer to Hammer et al. (2009) for evidence.

As a rough index, the ratio of χ^2 = 294.92 to df = 178 produces a value less than 2.00, suggesting a good fit to the data (Tabachnick & Fidell, 2013). Because sample size is known to impact the value of χ^2, it is customarily disregarded as an indicator of model fit, however. Hammer et al. (2009) reports values for the comparative fit index (CFI = .97), root mean square error of approximation (RMSEA = .04), and standardized root mean square residual (RMSR = .05), suggesting that the proposed model provides a good fit to the observed data. It is important to note that, although multiple indicators of good fit are reported, they do not preclude the possibility that alternative models also may explain relations observed in the data.

TECHNICAL. The FSSB manual provides norms (i.e., means and standard deviations) for each dimension and the overall scale. The initial normative sample (N = 360) is composed of the grocery chain employees and is characterized as 92% White, 73% female, 55% married or living as married, 41% with children living at home, 16% providing care for another adult, and 9% providing care for a child and an adult. The mean age of this sample is 38 years, but range and standard deviation are not reported, producing an unknown distribution of adult ages in this sample.

The manual also includes means and standard deviations for two additional samples, nursing home employees (N = 239) and food manufacturing employees (N = 104 or 105), but demographic characteristics are not provided for either of these samples. Thus, the reader cannot compare sample characteristics or estimate the likelihood that these samples represent their respective populations.

Reliability. Alpha reliability coefficients based on data from the grocery employee sample are reported for the 14-item aggregate (.94) and the Emotional Support (.90), Instrumental Support (.73), Role Modeling (.86), and Creative Work-Family Management (.86) subscales.

Validity. Convergent evidence of validity is provided in the test manual. Bivariate correlations of FSSB full-scale scores with scores on measures of general supervisor support (r = .74) and supervisor support behaviors (r = .68) are provided (N = 358 to 360).

The authors assessed criterion evidence for validity by examining correlations of the FSSB total scale score with measures of work-to-family, family-to-work, and job outcomes. Total score was positively related to family-work positive spillover and job satisfaction and negatively related to turnover intention and work-family conflict but unrelated to work-family positive spillover and family-work conflict.

COMMENTARY. The FSSB is designed to be an individual- or group-administered measure of four dimensions of family-supportive supervisor behavior for use work settings. Scoring is conducted by the test user or test publisher, is straightforward, and is accompanied by score interpretation.

Due to ambiguity about internal structure, it is unclear that the test meets its goal of assessing employee perceptions of four distinct, but related types of supervisor support behaviors (i.e., Emotional Support, Instrumental Support, Role Modeling, and Creative Work-Family Management). By factor analyzing dimension scores without first factor analyzing item-level data, the authors imposed a theory-based correlated factor structure on the data without empirical evidence or at least without sharing such information. The meaning of the FSSB measure would be illuminated by conducting an initial exploratory factor analysis with oblique rotation of the FSSB items to identify factor structure, determine items that form each factor, and allow the factors to correlate. A second exploratory factor analysis of interfactor correlations then could be conducted to examine the higher-order factor structure suggested by the confirmatory factor analysis.

Because the FSSB manual appears to omit information describing samples, methods, statistical analyses, and results that guided scale development and subsequent interpretation, and does not clearly distinguish analyses describing the 18-item scale versus the reduced 14-item instrument, potential users are compelled to search Hammer et al. (2009) for clarification. A concise, but detailed description of scale development reported as Studies 1 and 2 in Hammer et al. (2009) could be added to the test manual to enhance reader understanding and minimize the need to refer to Hammer et al. (2009) for evidence.

SUMMARY. The FSSB is an easily administered scale that offers potential utility by expanding coverage of family supportive supervisor behaviors. Norms would be strengthened by expanding sample diversity in age, ethnicity, job level, and industry type. It appears to this reviewer that stronger evidence of internal structure is needed to buttress the assertion that supervisor support comprises four correlated dimensions that reflect one common overarching factor.

This reviewer believes that the authors could strengthen the FSSB measure by conducting an exploratory factor analysis of the initial 18-item scale to identify the factors that emerge, rather than impose a theory-based factor structure without empirical evidence. Although confirmatory factor analysis suggests a good fit to the data, an exploratory factor analysis of the hypothesized four-factor structure would provide a more rigorous test of the theory and enhance confidence in the meaning of the construct measure.

REVIEWER'S REFERENCES

Furr, R. M., & Bacharach, V. R. (2014). Psychometrics: An introduction (2nd ed.). Thousand Oaks, CA: Sage.

Hammer, L. B., Kossek, E. E., Anger, W. K., Bodner, T., & Zimmerman, K. L. (2011). Clarifying work-family intervention processes: The roles of work-family conflict and family-supportive supervisor behaviors. *Journal of Applied Psychology, 96*(1), 134-150.

Hammer, L. B., Kossek, E. E., Yragui, N. L., Bodner, T. E., & Hanson, G. C. (2009). Development and validation of a multidimensional measure of Family Supportive Supervisor Behaviors (FSSB). *Journal of Management, 35*(4), 837-856.

Tabachnick, B. G., & Fidell, L. S. (2013). *Using multivariate statistics* (6th ed.). Boston, MA: Pearson.

[63]

Feifer Assessment of Mathematics.

Purpose: "Designed to isolate, measure, and quantify various subtypes of developmental dyscalculia to better explain why an examinee may have difficulty acquiring fundamental math skills."

Population: Students in prekindergarten through college.

Publication Date: 2016.

Acronym: FAM.

Administration: Individual.

Price Data, 2020: $593 per comprehensive kit including manual (231 pages), Fast Guide (55 pages), 10 record forms, 10 response forms, stimulus book 1, stimulus book 2, and 5 online interpretive reports; $220 per stimulus book (1 or 2); $120 per manual and Fast Guide (print or digital); $59 per 10 record forms; $27 per 10 response forms; $6 per online interpretive report.

Comments: Subtests and indexes may be administered independently; online scoring and reporting available.

Authors: Steven G. Feifer (test and manual) and Heddy Kovach Clark (manual).

Publisher: Psychological Assessment Resources, Inc.

a) PREKINDERGARTEN.

Scores, 13: Procedural Index (Forward Number Count, Numeric Capacity, Sequences, Object Counting), Verbal Index (Rapid Number Naming, Linguistic Math Concepts), Semantic Index (Spatial Memory, Perceptual Estimation, Number Comparison), FAM Total Index.

Time: Approximately 35 minutes to administer full battery.

b) GRADES K-2.
Scores, 18: Procedural Index (Forward Number Count, Backward Number Count, Numeric Capacity, Sequences, Object Counting), Verbal Index (Rapid Number Naming, Addition Fluency, Subtraction Fluency, Linguistic Math Concepts), Semantic Index (Spatial Memory, Perceptual Estimation, Number Comparison, Addition Knowledge, Subtraction Knowledge), FAM Total Index.
Time: Approximately 50 minutes to administer full battery.
c) GRADES 3-COLLEGE.
Scores, 22: Procedural Index (Forward Number Count, Backward Number Count, Numeric Capacity, Sequences), Verbal Index (Rapid Number Naming, Addition Fluency, Subtraction Fluency, Multiplication Fluency, Division Fluency, Linguistic Math Concepts), Semantic Index (Spatial Memory, Equation Building, Perceptual Estimation, Number Comparison, Addition Knowledge, Subtraction Knowledge, Multiplication Knowledge, Division Knowledge), FAM Total Index.
Time: Approximately 60 minutes to administer full battery.
d) SCREENING FORM.
Purpose: "Designed to identify children at risk for dyscalculia by measuring the underlying processes of math."
Scores, 4: Linguistic Math Concepts, Sequences, Number Comparison, FAM Screening Index.
Price Data: $315 per Screening Form kit including manual, Fast Guide, 25 Screening Form record forms, 25 Screening Form response sheets, Screening Form stimulus book, and 5 online score reports; $120 per Screening Form stimulus book; $94 per 25 Screening Form record forms; $20 per 25 Screening Form response sheets; $2 per online Screening Form score report.
Time: Approximately 15 minutes for administration.

Review of the Feifer Assessment of Mathematics by RANDY G. FLOYD, Professor of Psychology, and ALLYSON K. TOPPS, Doctoral Candidate, University of Memphis, Memphis, TN:

DESCRIPTION. The Feifer Assessment of Mathematics (FAM) measures math skills and the neurodevelopmental components that support their acquisition. It comprises 19 subtests administered individually to those in prekindergarten through college. The test kit includes a professional manual, two stimulus books, examiner record forms, examinee response forms, and a fast guide that focuses on subtest administration and scoring. Across grade levels, eight subtests are administered, and depending on the grade level, one to 10 additional subtests are administered. Examination time ranges from 35 to 60 minutes.

The FAM yields three index scores and a total score. The Procedural Index is yielded from four or five subtests and measures counting, ordering and sequencing numbers, and symbolic memory. The Verbal Index is computed from two to six subtests and measures fluency in fact retrieval and linguistic underpinnings of mathematics. The Semantic Index is yielded from three to eight subtests and measures quantitative knowledge as well as visual-spatial operations and memory. The Total Index score is yielded from all subtests administered. Norm-referenced scores are standard scores (M = 100, SD = 15), and confidence intervals, percentile ranks, z-scores, and normal curve equivalents can be employed.

In addition to the full battery, a screening form is available that includes three subtests; it can be completed in 15 minutes. Its materials are distinct from the FAM, but all subtests are included in the full FAM. It yields subtest scores and a total score, titled the Screening Index, which is scaled like the Total Index.

The professional manual provides details for subtest administration and scoring, and the examiner record forms contain instructions for examinees, rules for administration and scoring, and checklists for recording behaviors. The spiral-bound stimulus books include directions to examiners on one side and stimuli for examinees on the other. Subtests employ start rules, reverse rules, and stop rules that are similar to those used in other prominent achievement tests. Timing requirements increase the difficulty of administration, with most subtest items imposing a 15-second time limit on examinees. In addition, some subtests require precise exposure to stimuli (e.g., 2 seconds exposure to images). Furthermore, subtests presented in the examinee response form have a 60-second time limit, and other fluency subtests have a 30-second time limit. Scoring occurs by hand or through access to the test publisher's online assessment platform. The FAM provides skills, error, and behavior analyses for some subtests.

DEVELOPMENT. The FAM was designed based on a neuropsychological approach to testing, and its items were developed to address subtypes of learning disability (LD) in math (sometimes called dyscalculia). An iterative process of item reviews by expert panels, statistical analysis, and refinement followed. Pilot testing of items was conducted, and item difficulty, discrimination, and statistical bias were evaluated using both classical test theory and item response theory. Items were reviewed for offensiveness and potential bias based on gender, ethnicity, and religious background.

TECHNICAL. Norms were based on data from 1,061 students. Normative data were collected from fall 2013 to fall 2014 across 36 states, based on the 2013 U.S. Census Bureau data. How participants were recruited was not reported, but examiners were selected based on their experience, access to potential participants, and demographic factors. Quality control procedures, such as protocol review, were implemented by site coordinators. The norming sample appeared representative, based on gender, ethnicity, and parent education level, across grade levels. Sample weighting procedures and continuous norming procedures were employed.

The FAM offers grade-based norms, and norms for subtests are presented in 16 blocks representing grades in one-grade-level increments from prekindergarten to Grade 12 and two-year increments for college students. There are 61 to 76 students associated with each norm block, which is lower than what has been recommended (100 per level). Norm blocks were not divided into smaller segments (e.g., fall and spring) to represent developmental change across the school year better. Norms for index scores are presented in three groups: prekindergarten, kindergarten to Grade 2, and Grade 3 and above.

Subtests demonstrate floor and ceiling violations and do not measure low levels and high levels of targeted skills with accuracy. Raw scores of 1 and the highest raw scores for subtests did not uniformly produce norm-referenced scores that were at least two standard deviations below or above the scale mean (Bracken, 1987). Floor violations were apparent for 17 subtests, and ceiling violations were apparent for seven subtests. In total, seven subtests demonstrate both floor and ceiling violations.

The median alpha coefficients for subtests ranged from .71 to .93 across grade levels. Alpha coefficients were typically above .80 for all subtests except for Numeric Capacity and Perceptual Estimation, and coefficients for eight other subtests were typically above .90. Reliability coefficients for index scores were higher than those for subtests and ranged from .87 to .97 across grade levels; the Total Index was uniformly the most reliable index. Only the Procedural Index and Semantic Index for the prekindergarten sample yielded values less than .90. Internal consistency coefficients for the Screening Index ranged from .89 to .95.

Test-retest reliability was assessed across 7 to 46 days with 137 students sampled relatively equally across four broad grade levels. Attenuation-corrected coefficients for subtests ranged from .61 to .91; only four subtests yielded coefficients lower than .80. It is rare to see the attenuation-correction method employed for test-retest reliability evaluation, as the method assumes the subtests are perfectly reliable at initial and follow-up testing; thus, it leads to inflated coefficients. Uncorrected and range-corrected correlations were not reported for subtests, but frequent larger-than-expected standard deviations mean that range-corrected correlations would likely be diminished in magnitude in most cases. No test-retest reliability coefficients were reported for FAM index scores, but attenuation-corrected coefficients for the Screening Index ranged from .88 to .94. To assess interscorer reliability, two trained individuals scored a set of 35 protocols independently; the resulting correlation was 1.0 for each subtest.

Neither correlations between subtests nor results from factor analysis were reported, so the index scores associated with the three subtypes of dyscalculia are supported primarily by evidence based on content. Validity evidence based on relations with other variables was most prominent and impressive. Some participants in the norming sample completed other achievement tests, including the Process Assessment of the Learner-Second Edition: Diagnostic Assessment for Math (PAL-II Math), the KeyMath-3 Diagnostic Assessment (KeyMath-3), and the Academic Achievement Battery (AAB). FAM subtests correlated positively with PAL-II Math scores, but the correlations varied widely in magnitude, with the strongest correlations evident between measures targeting the same operation. Correlations between FAM and KeyMath-3 subtest scores were generally moderate. Correlations between FAM and AAB math subtest scores were generally positive and moderate in magnitude but also included some negative and negligible values; correlations between FAM indices and AAB math composites were generally moderate.

Other norming sample participants completed the Feifer Assessment of Reading (FAR) and the Child and Adolescent Memory Profile (ChAMP). Correlations between FAM and FAR subtest scores were weak to moderate and generally less than .40. Correlations between the FAM and ChAMP scores were generally negligible and weak. Similar findings were evident for correlations between FAM and Reynolds Intellectual Assessment Scales, Second Edition (RIAS-2) subtest scores. Some exceptions included higher correlations between FAM speeded naming and fluency subtests and the RIAS-2 Speeded Naming Task. Correlations between FAM and RIAS-2 indices were positive but generally weak; it appears that the FAR Procedural Index most closely aligns with the constructs measured by intelligence tests. Similar patterns of correlations were evident for the Screening Index.

Scores from adolescents from four clinical groups, including intellectual developmental disorder (ID), attention-deficit/hyperactivity disorder (ADHD), and LD in math, were compared with those from demographically matched samples. Results were as expected. Those with ID demonstrated the lowest scores, and those with LD in math demonstrated somewhat lower scores than their matched comparisons. Even smaller differences were found between the ADHD sample and their matched comparisons. A diagnostic accuracy analysis using the Total Index to predict membership in the group with an LD in math revealed that a cut score of 85 balanced sensitivity and specificity. When the Screening Index was evaluated, similar patterns were evident.

COMMENTARY. The FAM targets the measurement of the subtypes of dyscalculia to explain why students may struggle with math skill development. Its materials are well constructed and easy to use, and it may serve as a viable narrow-band math test to supplement omnibus achievement tests or for focused assessments. The FAM draws on relatively recent normative data, which is a relative strength, and its total scores were subjected to diagnostic accuracy analysis, which is underused during the test validation process. The reliability and validity evidence presented to support the FAM is satisfactory but warrants further study. Specifically, no test-retest reliability coefficients are reported for index scores, and little evidence based on internal structure was evident.

Several other weaknesses are apparent. The FAM includes grade-level norm blocks encompassing fewer than 80 participants, and smaller and more developmentally sensitive divisions, as seen in many other achievement tests, were not employed. Its ability to measure low and high levels of math skills is limited, as numerous floor and ceiling violations are evident. The complexity of the subtest administration (mainly related to timing) also increases the risk of errors, especially with inexperienced examiners. Time limits applied to items may also increase the anxiety of students who feel less confident about their math skills.

SUMMARY. The FAM has potential applicability to various populations who struggle with math skills and concepts. Its development followed neuropsychological research examining the underpinnings of number sense, counting, math fact retrieval, and sequencing, and its professional manual presents a wealth of information about dyscalculia. However, its small norming sample, narrow range of item scaling on some subtests, and limited evidence based on internal structure present potential problems in its use.

REVIEWERS' REFERENCE

Bracken, B. A. (1987). Limitations of preschool instruments and standards for minimal levels of technical adequacy. *Journal of Psychoeducational Assessment, 4*, 313-326.

Review of the Feifer Assessment of Mathematics by MARY L. GARNER, Professor Emeritus of Mathematics, Kennesaw State University, Visiting Assistant Professor, Oglethorpe University, Atlanta, GA:

DESCRIPTION. The Feifer Assessment of Mathematics (FAM) is designed to determine whether students have specific learning disabilities in mathematics where those learning disabilities are defined by the test authors based on their interpretation of neuropsychological studies. The test can be administered to students from preschool to college. The FAM includes 808 items spread across 19 subtests. Within each subtest, the examiner begins with an item appropriate for the examinee's grade level and moves forward or backward in the test depending on the examinee's success. Some subtests are timed; on untimed subtests, the examiner usually stops when the examinee gets four items in a row incorrect. The authors state that a preschooler could complete the appropriate subtests in 35 minutes; a kindergartner through second grader in 50 minutes; and a third grader to college student in 1 hour.

Based on neuropsychological research connecting brain activity with performance on foundational mathematical tasks, the three types of developmental dyscalculia defined by the test authors are procedural, verbal, and semantic. The procedural type of dyscalculia "represents one or more deficits in the ability to count, order, or sequence numbers and/or sequence mathematical procedures (e.g., remember the algorithm) when problem solving" (manual, p. 7). Subtests associated with the procedural type of learning deficit are Forward Number Count (FNC; 30 items), Backward Number Count (BNC; 30 items), Numeric Capacity (NCA; 16 items; remembering a set of numbers), Sequences (SEQ; 39 items; filling in the missing word or number in a sequence), and Object Counting (OC; 24 items). The set of tasks and number of items associated with the verbal type of learning deficit are Rapid Number Naming (RNN; 91), Addition Fluency (AF; 60), Subtraction Fluency (SF; 60), Multiplication Fluency (MF; 60), Division Fluency (DF; 60), and Linguistic Math Concepts (LMC; 50). The items included in the AF, SF, MF, and DF subtests are simple two-digit operations, and examinees complete as many as possible in 30 seconds each. In the LMC subtest, the examinee chooses from a set of four possible descriptions of a mathematical term. The set of tasks and number of items associated with the semantic type of learning deficit are Spatial Memory (SM; 32), Equation Building (EB; 30), Perceptual Estimation (PE; 26), Number Comparison (NC; 40), Addition Knowledge (AK; 40), Subtraction Knowledge (SK; 40), Multiplication Knowledge (MK; 40), and Division Knowledge (DK; 40). The items in the AK, SK, MK, and DK subtests consist of equations such as "3 + __ = 5" in which the examinee must identify the missing number. The EB subtest consists of familiar word problems from the mathematics curriculum with the examinee choosing from four possible responses.

The raw score on each subtest is converted to a grade-based standard score, with a mean of 100 and standard deviation of 15. Subtest standard scores within each type of learning deficit are then summed. Standard scores for those sums are generated according to three grade groups: preschool, kindergarten to Grade 2, and Grade 3 and above. The standard scores for the Procedural Index, the Semantic Index, and the Verbal Index are then summed to produce a Total Index, which also is converted to a standard score using the same three grade groups. Confidence intervals (90% and 95%) are provided for each standard score, along with percentiles, stanines, *z*-scores, and normal curve equivalents. Reliable change scores are also provided so teachers can determine whether a change in a student's score is significant or due to chance.

In addition to the full battery, a screening form is available consisting of three subtests, one from each of the three types of dyscalculia: Sequences, Linguistic Math Concepts, and Number Comparison. Each subtest score is converted to a standard score. Those standard scores are summed to produce a Screening Index, which is converted to a standard score for all grades.

DEVELOPMENT. The technical manual does not indicate who created the items but states that they were designed in accordance with brain-based studies. The items were then reviewed by a panel of two people whose expertise in mathematics is not explicitly stated. The items were revised and then reviewed again by the panel of two people. Classical test theory and Rasch measurement theory were used to analyze pilot data from a sample of 403 examinees to explore item quality and difficulty. Details of those analyses are not included in the test manual. The panel of two people then conducted a final review of the items, and a second panel of five people reviewed the items for bias. The rationale for the scoring procedures on each test is not described.

TECHNICAL. The norming sample consisted of 1,061 individuals across 16 grades from prekindergarten to college, with college freshmen and sophomores grouped together and college juniors and seniors grouped together. Each grade level included 61 to 76 participants. Each subtest was normed within each grade level. The sample was designed according to the 2013 U.S. Census to be representative of grade, gender, ethnicity, and parent education level. Discrepancies between the U.S. Census proportions and the sample proportions were addressed by weighting each participant score in the sample. Continuous norming was used. Sums of standard scores on subtests within each type of dyscalculia were then normed according to the three aforementioned grade groups: preschool, kindergarten to Grade 2, and Grade 3 and above. The standard scores for the Procedural Index, the Semantic Index, and the Verbal Index were then summed, and that sum also was normed according to the three groups.

Evidence for construct-based validity was presented in the form of correlations with grade, math tests, achievement tests, memory tests, intelligence tests, and reading tests. Internal consistency was demonstrated through coefficient alphas. To demonstrate criterion evidence of validity, the authors described the result of administering FAM to individuals with an intellectual developmental disorder, attention-deficit/hyperactivity disorder, and learning disabilities.

COMMENTARY. Although an internet search indicates that the two people who reviewed test items at multiple stages of development are connected with mathematics or mathematics education, some of the questions seem poorly worded. For example, the wording of each item on the Equation Building subtest is incorrect. The subtest includes questions such as "There were 5 kittens in a box, and Amy took 2 kittens out. Which equation shows how many kittens were left in the box?" The possible answers are "5 + 2", "2 – 5", "5 – 2", or "5 ÷ 2." None of those possible answers is an equation. An equation expresses a relationship (equality) between two mathematical expressions. In the Linguistic Math Concepts subtest, "calculus" is defined inaccurately. In any case, is "calculus" a key word for students to define? How were the key terms determined?

The computational fluency subtests (AF, SF, MF, DF) are associated with the Verbal Index because "math facts can be learned, memorized, and reinforced as a mere byproduct of language and, in some cases, completely independent of any quantitative value" (manual, p. 6). Admittedly, multiplication tables can be memorized, but there is no evidence provided that addition and subtraction facts are memorized in the same manner, rather than visualized.

The test authors state that "The FAM was designed to explain developmental dyscalculia from a brain-based educational perspective in order to better inform intervention decision making" (manual, p. 7). They provide two case studies to illustrate the use of the test, but in both cases, recommendations based on the test results were vague. No evidence is provided to suggest the recommendations actually produce a change in scores.

SUMMARY. The FAM includes 808 items across 19 subtests, with different procedures for administering and scoring each subtest and an array of standardized scores based on samples as small as 61. The test can serve pre-kindergarten to college. It has much face validity, with items requiring counting, recognizing sequences, connecting quantities with symbols, estimating quantities, knowing definitions of math terms, performing basic operations, and even identifying how to solve word problems. However, the link between the test and recommended interventions is unsubstantiated. It is an ambitious and interesting test, but is it worth using?

[64]

Feifer Assessment of Reading.

Purpose: "Designed to examine the underlying cognitive and linguistic processes that support proficient reading skills ... [to help] users determine not only the presence of a reading disorder but also the specific dyslexia subtype."

Population: Students in prekindergarten through college.

Publication Date: 2015.

Acronym: FAR.

Administration: Individual.

Price Data, 2020: $619 per comprehensive kit including manual (2015, 252 pages), Fast Guide, 10 examiner record forms, 10 examinee response forms, 3 stimulus books, set of 3 scoring templates, and storybook; $146 per any one stimulus book (1, 2, or 3); $120 per professional manual and fast guide; $59 per 10 examiner record forms; $27 per 10 examinee response forms.

Comments: Subtests and indexes may be administered independently; online scoring and reporting available.

Authors: Steven G. Feifer (test and manual) and Rebecca Gerhardstein Nader (manual).

Publisher: Psychological Assessment Resources, Inc.

a) PREKINDERGARTEN.

Scores, 13: Mixed Index (Phonological Index [Phonemic Awareness, Positioning Sounds], Fluency Index [Rapid Automatic Naming, Verbal Fluency, Visual Perception]), Comprehension Index (Semantic Concepts, Word Recall, Print Knowledge), FAR Total Index.

Time: Approximately 35 minutes to administer full battery.

b) GRADES K-1.

Scores, 16: Mixed Index (Phonological Index [Phonemic Awareness, Isolated Word Reading Fluency, Oral Reading Fluency, Positioning Sounds], Fluency Index [Rapid Automatic Naming, Verbal Fluency, Visual Perception, Orthographical Processing]), Comprehension Index (Semantic Concepts, Word Recall, Print Knowledge), FAR Total Index.

Time: Approximately 60 minutes to administer full battery.

c) GRADES 2-COLLEGE.

Scores, 19: Mixed Index (Phonological Index [Phonemic Awareness, Nonsense Word Decoding, Isolated Word Reading Fluency, Oral Reading Fluency, Positioning Sounds], Fluency Index [Rapid Automatic Naming, Verbal Fluency, Visual Perception, Irregular Word Reading Fluency, Orthographical Processing]), Comprehension Index (Semantic Concepts, Word Recall, Morphological Processing, Silent Reading Fluency), FAR Total Index.

Time: Approximately 75 minutes to administer full battery.

d) SCREENING FORM.

Purpose: "Designed to identify children at risk for developmental dyslexia by measuring the underlying processes of reading."

Scores, 4: Phonemic Awareness, Rapid Automatic Naming, Semantic Concepts, FAR Screening Index.

Price Data: $320 per Screening Form kit including manual, fast guide, 25 examiner record forms, and Screening Form stimulus book; $133 per stimulus book; $101 per 25 record forms.

Time: 15-25 minutes for administration.

Review of the Feifer Assessment of Reading by CARLEN HENINGTON, Professor of Educational and School Psychology, Mississippi State University, Mississippi State, MS:

DESCRIPTION. The Feifer Assessment of Reading (FAR) examines "underlying cognitive and linguistic processes that support proficient reading" (manual, p. 1) in individuals in prekindergarten through college. The FAR applies a neuropsychological approach to evaluate dyslexia subtypes to inform development of reading intervention. Fifteen subtests are used to assess phonological development, orthographical processing, decoding, morphological awareness, reading fluency, and comprehension. The FAR also can be used to measure changes in reading ability (i.e., progress monitoring) and to facilitate intervention development.

Using the premise that reading disorders arise from a variety of neurocognitive pathologies, the test authors propose fou general subtypes of reading disorders with contributions of brain regions and psychological constructs: (a) dysphonetic dyslexia—inability to use a phonological route to bridge letters and sounds; (b) surface dyslexia—the ability to sound out words but not recognize words in print due to difficulty with orthographical input (manifested as letter transpositions and difficulty reading irregular words), orthographical processing (manifested as difficulty in determining whether a string of letters is a word and impacting comprehension), or orthographical output (manifested as difficulty in reading aloud when matching orthography to a phonological lexicon); (c) mixed dyslexia–the most severe subtype that results in difficulties across the language spectrum (e.g., poor phonological processing, slower rapid and automatic word recognition, illogical error patterns, inconsistent language comprehension); and (d) reading comprehension deficits—a deficit in the ability to derive meaning from printed material despite an ability to decode words. The subtests are organized using a gradient model of brain functioning (e.g., neurogenic regions are related to various cognitive processes) and basic brain-behavior principles (i.e., Goldberg, 1990; Luria, 1980).

The FAR includes the following indices: The Phonological Index, in which the primary modality is auditory and an ability to process sounds is required, is composed of five subtests: (a) Phonemic Awareness—rhyming, blending, segmenting, and manipulation (modifying a specific sound); (b) Nonsense Word Decoding—decoding individual nonsense words; (c) Isolated Word Reading Fluency—reading phonetically consistent words; (d) Oral Reading Fluency—reading rate and accuracy; and (e) Positioning Sounds—identifying missing sounds. The Fluency Index, in which the primary modality is visual and attention is a component, is composed of five subtests: (a) Rapid Automatic Naming—timed naming of different objects, letters, or stencils of letters; (b) Verbal Fluency—timed naming without visual stimuli (i.e., animals, letters); (c) Visual Perception—quick identification of a printed backward letter in a group of letters or words; (d) Irregular Word Reading Fluency—reading phonologically irregular words; and (e) Orthographical Processing—recall of a letter or group of letters in a word or nonword. The Comprehension Index in which the modality is semantic (i.e., understanding language/word meaning), is composed of five subtests: (a) Semantic Concepts—antonyms and synonyms; (b) Word Recall—recall of a list of words with and without semantic cues as a memory aid; (c) Print Knowledge—response to a series of preliteracy questions; (d) Morphological Processing—selection of a morpheme that best completes an incomplete word; and (e) Silent Reading Fluency—answering a series of literal and inferential questions after reading silently. Consistent with the expected severity of reading deficits, the Mixed Index is composed of all subtests in the Phonological and Fluency indices. The FAR Total Index is composed of all subtests. The FAR Screening Index estimates functioning on each main index (Phonological, Fluency, and Comprehension).

No specific license is required of administrators; however, knowledge of measurement and psychometric concepts and training and skills in assessment are necessary. Test materials include three stimulus books, a story book (*Bears are Beary Fun*), a response form, and an examiner record form. Administration directions are straightforward and are facilitated by the use of icons to prompt the administrator about required materials, timed tasks, and start points. Each subtest requires 1 to 10 minutes to administer. Administration of the full battery takes 35 to 75 minutes, depending on grade level. The more simple screening requires 15 to 20 minutes for administration. Some items across indices have practice items to promote understanding of the skill. The professional manual includes a useful two-page guide for administration. There is also a pronunciation guide and icon legend. Start, stop, reverse, and pre-basal rules are clearly described.

Instructions for scoring are easily understood, and optional skills and/or error analyses are available for all subtests except Print Knowledge. Error analyses group errors into three broad categories (*acceptable, elevated, highly elevated*) by grade level. Hand scoring is reported to take 15 to 20 minutes. Data also may be entered into the test publisher's online platform, which generates a report of summary scores, profiles, and a brief score interpretation of subtests and indices. A series of tables is used to obtain standard scores (M = 100; SD = 15), index scores, percentiles, and confidence intervals.

The test manual includes a chapter on interpretations of scores and the implications of specific difficulties with brief suggestions for interventions for such difficulties. For purposes of interpretation, discrepancies and significance levels between scores can be calculated. The test authors suggest a five-level system of interpretation beginning with the Total Index score, then moving to specific index scores, followed by targeted subtest interpretations and comparisons. Optional behavioral observations and skills and error analyses round out the five levels.

DEVELOPMENT. Words used in the initial development were created from a variety of sources (e.g., dictionaries, word lists) with selection of items and foils based on the inclusion of the 44 recognized phonemes and seven phoneme types; synonyms/antonyms; a balance of missing parts within a word (e.g., roots, prefixes, suffixes); and inclusion of English words coming from multiple cultures (e.g., Spanish, French). Reading passages were examined for readability using appropriate readability indexes. A panel of experts reviewed items and administered every item to a child in each of three age groups (4-7 years, 8-12 years, and 13-21 years). Results from this prototype sample (N = 21) were used to revise and eliminate items for the pilot test. Data from the pilot sample (N = 393) were analyzed to examine item discrimination, item bias, and optimal time allotted for timed subtests. Items were refined and re-examined by the expert panel with regard to difficulty and quality. A second panel of five people with backgrounds in school psychology and other relevant disciplines also reviewed items for item bias.

Standardization was conducted in 2013-2014 across 30 states. The normative sample consisted of 1,074 individuals across 16 age groups. Post-stratification weighting procedures (Gelman & Carlin, 2001; Lynn, 1996) were used to achieve better representation between the sample and the U.S. population. A three-step continuous norming procedure was described in which the grade-based normative tables were constructed. These tables, along with others showing confidence intervals, percentiles, and age and grade equivalents are located within the appendices of the test manual. Additional appendices offer further analyses, such as change scores, error analysis, and skill analysis.

TECHNICAL. The FAR has a high degree of internal consistency with median alpha coefficients for the seven untimed subtests ranging from .89 to .95. Analysis of test-retest reliability (conducted with 127 individuals across age ranges with 7 to 34 days between administrations) yielded coefficients ranging from .66 to .95, with most in the .80 to .90 range. Median standard errors of measurement (*SEMs*) ranged from 3.1 to 8.1. Interscorer reliability was evaluated across 35 randomly selected protocols and showed correlations from .87 to 1.00. These results collectively demonstrate relatively strong internal consistency and stability across subtests, at least over a short period of time. With regard to construct evidence of validity, in correlations with other achievement and cognitive tests, results, with exceptions, show coefficients with acceptable magnitude and range. In an examination of predictive evidence of validity, a series of analyses with relatively small samples (ranging from 28 to 59) was performed. These analyses related to the diagnosis of clinical populations with intellectual disabilities, attention-deficit/ hyperactivity disorder, and learning disabilities and show the FAR distinguishes between those with and without learning disabilities and predicts a learning disability with a high degree of accuracy. No peer-reviewed publications examining reliability and validity of the FAR were cited in the test manual.

COMMENTARY. The FAR, based on a neuropsychological approach to reading, encompasses assessment of specific subtypes of dyslexia and measures aspects of reading. A strength is the relatively brief but comprehensive assessment of phonological development, orthographical processing, decoding, morphological awareness, reading fluency, and comprehension across a wide range of ages. The knowledge regarding these skills can be used to develop targeted interventions to address those specific skills. Although the test authors indicate the FAR can be used to "isolate, measure, and analyze specific cognitive processes involved in reading" (manual, p. 6), insufficient empirical support for such conclusions is provided.

SUMMARY. The developers of the FAR have produced a useful tool for those who seek to conduct a relatively brief, comprehensive evaluation of reading skills. The materials are user friendly, and administration and scoring are straightforward. Resulting reading profiles will likely assist in understanding the specific issues that are impacting the reading ability of students. There is a need for additional studies to validate the FAR, in that the studies conducted by the authors involved relatively small samples. The best use of the FAR is to identify and monitor individuals' specific deficits in the specific subtypes of reading impairment.

REVIEWER'S REFERENCES

Gelman, A., & Carlin, J. B. (2001). Poststratification and weighting adjustments. In R. M. Goves, D. A. Dillman, J. L. Eltinge, & R. J. A. Little (Eds.), *Survey nonresponse* (pp. 289-302). New York, NY: Wiley.

Goldberg, E. (Ed.). (1990). *Contemporary neuropsychology and the legacy of Luria.* Hillsdale, NJ: Erlbaum.

Luria, A. R. (1980). *Higher cortical functions in man* (2nd ed.). (B. Haigh, Trans.) New York, NY: Basic Books.

Lynn, P. (1996). Weighting for non-response. In R. Banks, J. Fairgrieve, L. Gerrard, T. Orchard, C. D. Payne, & A. Westlake (Eds.), *Survey and statistical computing 1996: Proceedings of the second ASC international conference.* (pp. 205-214). Chesham, England: Association for Survey Computing.

Review of the Feifer Assessment of Reading by JENNIFER N. MAHDAVI, Professor of Special Education, Sonoma State University, Rohnert Park, CA:

DESCRIPTION. The Feifer Assessment of Reading (FAR) is a standardized, norm-referenced test of reading skills, based on a neuropsychological theory of dyslexia subtypes. The purpose of the FAR is twofold: to help practitioners determine which neurological subtype of dyslexia an individual has and to use that information to select the most appropriate reading interventions. The FAR test package includes an extensive manual, three stimulus books, a story book, protocols, and a "fast guide" to describe administration and scoring procedures quickly. The full battery of subtests recommended varies by the examinee's grade level (pre-kindergarten through college) and requires 35-75 minutes to administer.

FAR contains 15 subtests clustered within four composites: Phonological, Fluency, Mixed (Phonological with Fluency), and Comprehension. A Total Index score also is derived. FAR norms are grade based and presented as standard scores (mean = 100, *SD* = 15). Also available are age- and grade-equivalents, confidence intervals, percentile ranks, stanines, *z* scores, and normal curve equivalents. The test can be hand scored, or, for an additional fee, input to the test publisher's online scoring system.

Examiners must be experienced and trained to administer and interpret academic or psychological tests. Start and stop rules for each subtest are noted on the examiner record form.

DEVELOPMENT. Dyslexia is a type of learning disability that specifically involves difficulty with reading and language; poor or dysfluent word reading, decoding, and spelling are hallmarks of dyslexia. According to the FAR manual, neuropsychology has further distinguished dyslexia into four subtypes, the etiology of each of which is located in a different region of the brain. These four subtypes provide the theoretical foundation for the FAR and its subtests. The dysphonetic type manifests as deficits in phonologic ability, leading children to read by sight rather than by matching sounds to letters for decoding. For those with surface dyslexia, phonemic awareness is well-developed, but little attention is paid to the orthographic features of text. Mixed dyslexia involves difficulty with both phonologic and orthographic elements of reading. The fourth type of deficit is in reading comprehension, in which children can read words but not interpret their meaning. Each subtype requires a different intervention to help an individual with dyslexia develop reading skills.

With this model of dyslexia to guide test development, indices or composites were developed in three areas. Phonological consists of primarily auditory items and those that match sounds to words in subtests such as Phonemic Awareness and Nonsense Word Decoding. The second area is Fluency, with visual, orthographic, and working memory tasks with a fluency component, such as Rapid Automatic Naming, and Irregular Word Reading Fluency. The Comprehension Index involves semantic subtests, such as Morphological Processing and fluency measures like Silent Reading Fluency.

Word lists for the subtests were derived from a variety of dictionaries, guides to words children should read at various ages, and vocabulary books. Care was taken to prevent words from being duplicated across subtests. For phonemic measures, pictures were included to assist young children, and care was taken to include all phoneme types, such as long vowels, diphthongs, and blends. For fluency tests, passages were leveled using the Flesch-Kincaid Reading and Grade-Level Formulas to account for text complexity as well as word/syllable difficulty. Both fiction and nonfiction passages were selected.

Rapid naming measures were developed to include objects, letters, and stencils.

Once initial items were selected and ordered for each subtest, seven experts from the fields of psychology and speech-language pathology reviewed them for developmental appropriateness, difficulty, appropriateness of alternate answers/foils, and content. Each expert also administered all items to three children. This initial testing was used to revise the measure for more extensive pilot testing with nearly 400 individuals.

Classical test theory and Rasch analyses were conducted on the results of the pilot testing to assess how well items distinguished individuals who performed well from those who performed poorly. Standard item analyses appear to have been conducted. Further analyses were performed to determine whether items were answered differentially by individuals from different ethnic or gender groups; those that did were determined to be biased and changed or dropped from the final version. Bias was further examined by a panel of five individuals who evaluated whether items were offensive or biased against any demographic groups.

TECHNICAL.

Standardization. The standardization sample included 1,074 individuals from 30 states, representing ages/grades from pre-kindergarten through college. The sample was matched closely to U.S. Census data for gender, ethnicity, grade/age, and parent education level. Individuals from the South were slightly overrepresented, with the Midwest slightly underrepresented; statistical tests showed that these differences were not significant. Statistical weighting was used after the sample was stratified to correct other discrepancies in representation.

When using the FAR to analyze the performance of African American (n = 148) or Hispanic (n = 247) individuals, administrators should use caution. When the small number of total individuals in these groups is further divided among the 16 grade levels, there are only 8-17 individuals to represent each ethnicity at each grade level. As well, individuals with disabilities were not represented in the stratification of the norming group (at least the numbers of individuals with disabilities is not provided), so their results should also be interpreted with caution.

Reliability. Measures of reliability were calculated for all subtests. Internal consistency was examined for the seven non-timed subtests using coefficient alpha. Median coefficients were between .89 and .95, which are strong indicators of internal consistency. Test-retest reliability was examined using a subset of 127 participants from the standardization sample and a range of 7-34 days between testing. Median test-retest correlations ranged from .67 for Word Recall (which the authors note is subject to variability due to individuals' inabilities to remember words over time), and .95 for Print Knowledge and Oral Reading Fluency. Interscorer reliability checks were conducted on 35 randomly selected record forms. Two expert scorers re-scored each subtest, with all resultant reliability coefficients except one being .98 or above. (The coefficient for Verbal Fluency was .87.)

The standard errors of measurement (*SEM*s) reported range from a strong 0.5 to a worrying 12.2 points. With many reported *SEM*s approximating half of a standard deviation, the variability for some measures, such as Word Recall (*SEM*s 6.0-12.2, median 8.1) call the reliability of some subtests into question. Users of the FAR would be wise to carefully examine the reliability data of each subtest for individuals at various ages; several demonstrate higher *SEM*s for older individuals than for younger people.

Validity. The subtests of the FAR are designed to represent the test authors' theorized four domains of reading deficits: dysphonetic dyslexia, surface dyslexia, mixed dyslexia, and comprehension deficit. Content evidence of validity was established by a team of reviewers, including neuropsychologists, speech-language pathologists, and clinical psychologists, who examined items in subtests to ensure that each one represented the authors' theoretical framework for reading. Strong internal consistency was also cited in the test manual as support for the measure's content validity.

Construct evidence of validity was estimated by correlating FAR scores with those from other tests. Three reading measures were selected for comparisons: Process Assessment of the Learner—Second Edition: Diagnostic Assessment for Reading and Writing (PAL-II RW), Gray Silent Reading Tests, and Gray Oral Reading Tests—Fifth Edition (GORT-5). Examination of the correlations between subtests on FAR and these other reading measures reveals few correlations greater than .60 and many around or below .30. Composite scores from the PAL-II RW, which combine specific subtests, provide the highest correlations with various

FAR measures, such as the Orthographical Coding Composite with Isolated Word Reading (ISO, .70), and Irregular Word Reading (.76) and the Phonological Coding Composite with ISO (.82) and Semantic Concepts (.76). GORT-5 measures most strongly correlating with those from FAR are Rate and Fluency. Correlations with an intelligence test, Reynolds Intellectual Assessment Scales, Second Edition, were low to moderate, indicating that reading skills are largely not a component of aptitude.

Analyses were conducted to determine whether individuals from different groups would score differently on the measures. Three clinical groups were composed and compared to individuals in the standardization sample. As predicted, people with disabilities achieved lower scores across the FAR subtests, composites, and total scores than did their typically developing peers. On the Total Index, individuals with intellectual disabilities (n = 28) scored an average of 48.7 points lower; individuals with attention-deficit/hyperactivity disorder (n = 36) scored 6.8 points lower; and those with learning disabilities (n = 59) scored 39 points lower.

COMMENTARY. A test that "is based on the premise that treatments for reading disorders vary by dyslexic subtype" (manual, p. 6) should include individuals who have been diagnosed with dyslexia as a means to test whether the measure can differentiate individuals with dyslexia from those with other reading difficulties. Individuals with disabilities were not included in the standardization sample but were assessed later to examine differences between known groups as well as to suggest cut scores to identify individuals with learning disabilities. However, the absence of individuals with disabilities in the original norming sample means that the group may not accurately reflect the broadest spectrum of students (Reynolds & Suzuki, 2013), particularly the students for whom the test was purportedly designed.

The reliability estimates and evidence of validity appear to be adequate. However, this reviewer questions the reliance on only 11 individuals to comprise the item selection and bias review panels.

Stimulus books in the test package do not have the usual A-frame shape that allows students to see their stimuli while the examiner is able to look at prompts, directions, or scripts to aid administration. Having the "fast guide" open might be helpful to the examiner, along with many repetitions of practice administering the test.

SUMMARY. Given the concerns raised about the FAR in this review, professionals should not use it to make important clinical decisions about individuals with disabilities. However, the error analysis features of the test may make it useful for diagnosing reading difficulties and selecting appropriate instructional strategies for individual students.

REVIEWER'S REFERENCE

Reynolds, C. R., & Suzuki, L. (2013). Bias in psychological assessment: An empirical review and recommendations. In J. R. Graham, J. A. Naglieri, & I. B. Weiner (Eds.), *Handbook of psychology: Assessment psychology* (2nd ed., Vol. 10, pp. 82-113). Hoboken, NJ: Wiley.

[65]

Five Factor Wellness Inventory [2nd Edition Manual].

Purpose: Designed to "assess characters of wellness as a basis for helping individuals make choices for healthier living."
Population: Elementary students, high school students, and adults.
Publication Dates: 2005-2014.
Acronym: FFWEL, 5F-WEL.
Scores, 28: Wellness (Creative Self [Thinking, Emotions, Control, Positive Humor, Work], Coping Self [Realistic Beliefs, Stress Management, Self-Worth, Leisure], Social Self [Friendship, Love], Essential Self [Spirituality, Self-Care, Gender Identity, Cultural Identity], Physical Self [Exercise, Nutrition]), Local Context, Institutional Context, Global Context, Chronometrical Context, Life Satisfaction Index.
Administration: Individual or group.
Levels, 3: Elementary, Teen, Adult.
Forms, 3: FFWEL-E, FFWEL-T, FFWEL-A2.
Price Data, 2020: $50 per PDF manual, including review-only copy of forms and scoring key (2014, 88 pages); $15 per individual report; $2.50 per Remote Online Survey License or License to Reproduce (minimum 50).
Foreign Language Editions: Translations available from test publisher.
Time: (10-20) minutes.
Comments: Original adult form (Form A) was revised in 2014 to alter one item on the Self-Care scale; 2nd edition manual includes norms for teenagers and adult norms.
Authors: Jane E. Myers and Thomas J. Sweeney.
Publisher: Mind Garden, Inc.
Cross References: For reviews by Gerald E. DeMauro and Susan Lonborg of the original version, see 17:74.

No review available. This test does not meet review criteria established by the Buros Center for Testing that call for at least minimal technical and development information.

[66]

Flow Scales.

Purpose: Designed "to assess flow in two ways: general tendency to experience flow, as well as particular incidence (or non-incidence) of flow characteristics during a particular event."
Population: Ages 12 and older.
Publication Date: 2010.
Administration: Individual or group.
Price Data, 2020: $50 per PDF manual (85 pages including sample forms and scoring information); $60 per print manual; $2.50 per Transform Survey Hosting (minimum 20); $2.50 per Remote Online Survey License (minimum 50); $2.50 per License to Reproduce (minimum 50).
Foreign Language Editions: Various forms available in Chinese, Croatian, Dutch, German, Hebrew, Indonesian, Italian, Japanese, Macedonian, Norwegian, Portuguese, Russian, Spanish, Swedish, and Turkish.
Authors: Susan A. Jackson, Robert C. Eklund, and Andrew J. Martin.
Publisher: Mind Garden, Inc.

a) LONG FLOW SCALES.
Purpose: Designed to "provide a detailed assessment of the dimensional flow model."
Scores, 10: Challenge-Skill Balance, Merging of Action and Awareness, Clear Goals, Unambiguous Feedback, Concentration on the Task at Hand, Sense of Control, Loss of Self-Consciousness, Transformation of Time, Autotelic Experience, Total.
Forms, 2: General (adaptable to a wide range of settings), Physical (to be used in sport and performance settings).
Time: (10) minutes.

1) *LONG Dispositional Flow Scale-2.*
Acronym: DFS-2.
2) *LONG Flow State Scale-2.*
Acronym: FSS-2.

b) SHORT FLOW SCALES.
Purpose: Designed to "provide a flow assessment that focuses on a holistic concept of flow as one coherent experience ... drawn from the nine flow dimensions."
Scores: Same as *a)* above.
Time: (5) minutes.

1) *SHORT Dispositional Flow Scale.*
Acronym: S DFS.
2) *SHORT Flow State Scale.*
Acronym: S FSS.

c) CORE FLOW SCALES.
Purpose: "Designed to describe what it is like to be in flow from the perspective of the person in flow."
Score: Total score only.
Time: (5) minutes.

1) *CORE Dispositional Flow Scale.*
Acronym: C DFS.
2) *CORE Flow State Scale.*
Acronym: C FSS.

Review of the Flow Scales by COLLIE W. CONOLEY, Professor, and MARGARET P. BOYER, Doctoral Student, University of California-Santa Barbara, Santa Barbara, CA:

DESCRIPTION. The Flow Scales measure the amount of flow—that is, the optimal state for performing an activity—as defined by Csikszentmihalyi (1990). The assessments were developed for both researchers and practitioners to assess individuals 12 years of age and older. The purpose of the set of measures is to assess flow in any activity; however, the validation is almost exclusively based upon sports and exercise assessments.

The set of Flow Scales includes: Long Dispositional Flow Scale-2 (DFS-2)–Physical; Long Dispositional Flow Scale-2 (DFS-2)–General; Long Flow State Scale-2 (FSS-2)–Physical; Long Flow State Scale-2 (FSS-2)–General; Short Dispositional Flow Scale (S DFS); Short Flow State Scale (S FSS); Core Dispositional Flow Scale (C DFS); Core Flow State Scale (C FSS).

The dispositional scales assess a person's general tendency toward flow for a specified activity. Dispositional forms should be administered at a time not close to the activity assessed. The state scales assess a person's experience of a just-completed activity. State forms should be administered immediately after performing the activity being assessed. The general forms assess any non-physical type of activity specified by the administrator, whereas the physical form assesses a physical activity such as a sport or other movement-based performance.

The long scales (36 items) contain nine subscales based upon Csikszentmihalyi's (1990) conceptualization of flow having nine components: Challenge-Skill Balance, Action-Awareness Merging, Clear Goals, Unambiguous Feedback, Concentration on Task, Sense of Control, Loss of Self-Consciousness, Time Transformation, and Autotelic Experience. The long scale forms provide subscale scores and a total score.

The short scales (nine items) provide a single score with one item measuring each of the nine subscales of the longer version. The individual items may not be used to represent the subscales. The Short Flow Scale has four versions that mirror the Long Flow Scales.

The core scales (10 items) differ from the short and long scales by using questions that do not correspond to the nine-component model. The core scales rely upon the descriptions that elite athletes have reported experiencing during a flow state. The amount of flow is measured by the extent to which respondent experiences match athlete experiences.

The test manual provides clear information about the scoring of the forms.

DEVELOPMENT. The items of the initial Long Flow Scale were developed to assess each of Csikszentmihalyi's (1990) nine dimensions of flow. The test manual describes the initial item pool as generated from earlier flow measures (e.g., Begly, 1979; Csikszentmihalyi & Csikszentmihalyi, 1988; Privette, 1984; Privette & Bundrick, 1991) and qualitative research (e.g., Jackson, 1992, 1995, 1996). A panel of seven experts reduced the initial pool to 54 items that included six items per subscale. A series of analyses of data from athletes rating athletic performances led to the original 36-item measure. Confirmatory factor analyses adequately supported the nine dimensions. However, the Time Transformation dimension did not relate or contribute to the overall flow score. Additionally, concurrent validity studies found that Lack of Self-Consciousness and Time Transformation did not reliably correlate with Motivation, which led to validity concerns for these subscales.

As a result, a revised Long Flow Scale (DFS-2 & FSS-2) was developed by adding a pool of 13 items to the 36 original items to replace the underperforming items. The form was studied using 597 physical activity participants from 17 to 72 years old with about half the sample identifying as male. The study examined the long physical activity version of the State (n = 391) and Dispositional (n = 386) Flow Scales. Using structural equation modeling, the 36 items best representing the nine dimensions of flow were selected. Selection of statistically ambiguous items was determined by conceptual considerations. Five new items were deemed a reasonable fit and included in the final pool of items (Jackson & Eklund, 2002).

TECHNICAL.

Standardization. The manual provides aggregate descriptive data to help contextualize the amount of flow a particular individual experiences in comparison to groups of individuals in a variety of physical activities or creative and performing arts. Unfortunately, the demographic composition of the comparison sample is not provided, and the standardized scoring tables are not organized by demographic groupings. Therefore, differences across age, gender, and ethnic/racial groups are unknown. Additionally, it is unclear whether the descriptive data are based upon the original or revised measures.

Reliability. Reliability of the flow assessments was based upon evaluations of internal consistency. The revised long forms demonstrated good reliability with a mean alpha across studies approximating .85 (.85 and .87 for FSS-2; .85 and .82 for DFS-2). The coefficient alpha average for the short forms was within the acceptable range of reliability at approximately .77 (.77 and .78 for FSS; .81 and .74 for DFS).

Confirmatory Factor Analysis. The validity of the revised long forms was examined using confirmatory factor analysis (CFA). An initial problem with the evaluation of the CFA fit as reported in the test manual was the use of .90 as the acceptable coefficient for non-normed fit index (NNFI) instead of the customary .95 (Hu & Bentler, 1999).

Validity indicated by CFA for the revised Long Flow Scales is based upon two studies that reveal acceptable to just short of acceptable fit. The initial confirmatory factor analysis reported in the test manual for the FSS-2 (n = 422) and the DFS-2 (n = 574) focused on physical activity, with the sample ranging in age from 16 to 82 and 48% identifying as male. The model fit did not meet all the requirements for acceptable fit but was very close. The combination of subscales into a total score yielded a somewhat weak fit. The Time Transformation dimension and the Loss of Self-Consciousness dimension were identified as not fitting well on the global flow factor for both versions (state and dispositional). The test authors hypothesize that the Loss of Self-Consciousness subscale may be problematic when performance must include awareness of self-presentation, as in figure skating. This suggests that the user may wish to select subscales thoughtfully based upon the activity measured.

The second CFA evaluated the FSS-2 and DFS-2 using 897 participants from 27 physical activities ranging from highly competitive sports to casual exercise activities. The age range was 16 to 82 (M = 26.3, SD = 11.1) with 48% of the sample identifying as male. The goodness of fit values were similar to those in study one, with the fit statistics in the acceptable range for the nine dimensions. The Total score fit was marginal for the FSS-2 and fell just short for the DFS-2.

The third CFA evaluated the revised Long and Short Flow Scales physical activity measures with larger samples that included 1,653 participants from 58 physical activities ranging from highly competitive sports to casual exercise activities. The mean age was 26 (SD = 10.6), and 62% of the sample identified as female (Jackson, Martin, & Eklund, 2008). The CFA nine factor fit coefficients for the Dispositional and State Long Flow measures met criteria, and the higher-order model had acceptable fit. The State Short Flow measure did not meet acceptable criteria for fit (Hu & Bentler, 1999). The test authors suggest that, when examining fit across activities, some dimensions may not fit some activities as well as other activities (Jackson, Martin, & Eklund, 2008).

Concurrent Validity for the Revised Long and Short Flow Measures. Both the state and dispositional forms of the Long (36 items) and Short (nine items) revised Flow Scales were examined (Jackson, Martin, & Eklund, 2008). The Long and Short Dispositional Flow Scales were moderately correlated with measures of intrinsic motivation (long form r = .34; short form r = .50), perceived competence (long form r = .38; short form r = .61), sport self-concept (long form r = .31; short form r = .47), and anxiety (long form r = -.36; short form r = -.51). The Long and Short Flow State Scales were moderately correlated with measures of intrinsic motivation (long form r = .30; short form r = .41), positive well-being (long form r = .42; short form r = .56), and psychological distress (long form r = -.28; short form r = -.42), but not fatigue (long form r = -.03; short form r = -.07).

Oddly, the short forms were more highly correlated with the target constructs than the long forms. The average Pearson's correlation coefficient between the Short Dispositional Flow Scale and the target constructs was .50, whereas the average for the long form was .34. Similarly, the average correlation coefficient for the Short Flow State Scale with the target constructs (excluding the uncorrelated fatigue measure) was .46, whereas the average for the long form was .34.

Core Flow Scale Validity. The Core Flow Scale assesses the subjective experience of flow for a specified activity by asking participants to indicate the extent to which they feel similarly to descriptions of flow offered by elite athletes. The core flow form demonstrated a high internal consistency reliability alpha of approximately .92 on average across samples. Multi-group CFA assessed invariance across participation in sport, mathematics, and extracurricular activity for students ages 12-18 (Martin & Jackson, 2008). The results suggested invariance except for the RMSEA coefficients, which were higher than accepted criteria (.08 to .11). Similar groups (general school, mathematics, and extracurricular activity) were used to explore concurrent validity by correlating Core Flow Scale scores with scores from measures of participation, enjoyment, self-evaluation of performance, aspirations, adaptive cognitions, adaptive behaviors, impeding/maladaptive cognitions, and maladaptive behaviors. The mean correlation of the target constructs with the Core Flow Scales was strong for general school (r = .61) and mathematics (r = .49), but not for extracurricular activity (r = .17).

COMMENTARY AND SUMMARY. The Flow Scales were developed to measure the amount of flow, or the optimal state for performing an activity, in individuals 12 and older. The scales have received substantial research attention, primarily in the area of sports activities. The Flow Scales were well supported for careful use. There was greater support for the use of the long form subscales rather than the use of a total score. Therefore, the reviewers recommend using the total score of long forms cautiously, as certain activities are not associated with all subscales or are associated with specific subscales to varying degrees. The user is urged to consider the use of subscales rather than the total score, especially for the Flow State Scale experiences of just-completed activities. The total score from the Short Dispositional Flow Scales attained strong support in the validation research.

A few shortcomings were noticed in the test manual, which generally was full of important information. Unfortunately, recommended uses for the Core Flow measure were not clear. The test manual did not specify when the Core Flow assessment of dispositional flow should be used in place of the revised Long or Short Dispositional Flow Scales.

Of specific concern were the unexamined demographic differences within the samples. Differences across age, gender, and ethnic/racial groups are unknown and unaccounted for in the standardized scoring tables.

Additionally, the test manual does not specify clearly when validity evidence is associated with the revisions of the measure versus the initial version. Finally, the test manual uses a lower criterion for model fit than is typically accepted in the literature, which may confuse the reader.

REVIEWERS' REFERENCES

Begly, G. (1979). A self-report measure to assess flow in physical activities. (Unpublished master's thesis). Pennsylvania State University, Pennsylvania.

Csikszentmihalyi, M. (1990). *Flow: The psychology of optimal experience.* New York, NY: Harper & Row.

Csikszentmihalyi, M., & Csikszentmihalyi, I. S. (Eds.) (1988). *Optimal experience: Psychological studies of flow in consciousness.* New York, NY: Cambridge University Press.

Hu, L.-T., & Bentler, P. M. (1999). Cutoff criteria for fit indexes in covariance structure analysis: Conventional criteria versus new alternatives. *Structural Equation Modeling: A Multidisciplinary Journal, 6*(1), 1–55.

Jackson, S. A. (1992). Athletes in flow: A qualitative investigation of flow states in elite figure skaters. *Journal of Applied Sport Psychology, 4,* 161-180.

Jackson, S. A. (1995). Factors influencing the occurrence of flow states in elite athletes. *Journal of Applied Sport Psychology, 7,* 138-166.

Jackson, S. A. (1996). Toward a conceptual understanding of the flow experience in elite athletes. *Research Quarterly for Exercise and Sport, 67,* 76-90.

Jackson, S. A., & Eklund, R. C. (2002). Assessing flow in physical activity: The Flow State Scale-2 and Dispositional Flow Scale-2. *Journal of Sport and Exercise Psychology, 24,* 133-150.

Jackson, S. A., Martin, A. J., & Eklund, R. C. (2008). Long and short measures of flow: The construct validity of the FSS-2, DFS-2, and new brief counterparts. *Journal of Sport and Exercise Psychology, 30,* 561-587.

Martin, A. J., & Jackson, S. A. (2008). Brief approaches to assessing task absorption and enhanced subjective experience: Examining 'short' and 'core' flow in diverse performance domains. *Motivation and Emotion, 32,* 141-157.

Privette, G. (1984). Experience questionnaire. Pensacola, FL: The University of West Florida.

Privette, G., & Bundrick, C. M. (1991). Peak experience, peak performance, and flow: Correspondence of personal descriptions and theoretical constructs. *Journal of Social Behavior and Personality, 6,* 169-188.

Review of the Flow Scales by MICHAEL J. SCHEEL, Professor, Educational Psychology, University of Nebraska-Lincoln, Lincoln, NE:

DESCRIPTION. The Flow Scales require respondents to report subjective experiences of flow in an activity of their choosing. Items on the scales cover nine dimensions of a flow state as specified by Csikszentmihalyi (1990). These dimensions include Challenge-Skill Balance, Merging of Action and Awareness, Clear Goals, Unambiguous Feedback, Concentration on the Task at Hand, Sense of Control, Loss of Self-Consciousness, Transformation of Time, and Autotelic Experience. An optimal and idiosyncratic combination of skill and challenge is posited to produce flow states. Less than optimal experiences are derived from too little or too much skill of the individual in relation to the challenge of the specified activity. Jackson (1993) defines flow as "an experience that stands out as being better than average in some way, where the individual is totally absorbed in what she or he is doing, and where the experience is very rewarding in and of itself" (manual, p. 5).

The six scales described in the test manual are grouped into "the triad of flow scales" (manual, p. 10). Each of the three types (i.e., multidimensional, or long; unidimensional, or short; and core) is represented by state and dispositional instruments. State scales are intended to measure experience of flow after completion of an activity. Dispositional scales assess the general tendency to experience flow and frequency of flow experiences. When completing a scale, the respondent specifies the activity (e.g., tennis, ballet, rock climbing) and writes it at the top of the protocol. State scales present Likert-type items of agreement (i.e., 1 = *strongly disagree,* 2 = *disagree,* 3 = *neither agree or disagree,* 4 = *agree,* and 5 = *strongly agree*). Dispositional scales present Likert-type items of frequency (i.e., 1 = *never,* 2 = *rarely,* 3 = *sometimes,* 4 = *frequently,* 5 = *always*). Flow State Scale-2 (FSS-2) and the Dispositional Flow Scale-2 (DFS-2), considered the long scales, each contain 36 items and are designed to provide comprehensive assessments of the nine dimensions of flow. Each of the nine dimensions comprises four items. Item means are calculated in scoring the dimensions and the Total score. The test authors recommend using dimension scores over total scores because the long Flow Scales were designed to be multidimensional instruments.

The Short Flow State Scale (S FSS) and the Short Dispositional Flow Scale (S DFS) assess unidimensional flow. These short scales provide a global assessment of flow. Items are derived from the long scales and were chosen for the short scales based on their ability to capture the holistic concept of flow. Nine single items in the short form are used to represent each of the dimensions. The Total scale score is the mean of the nine item scores.

The Core Dispositional Flow Scale (C DFS) and the Core Flow State Scale (C FSS) represent the third of the triad of flow scales. The state scale measures the nature of the flow experience immediately after the target activity, and the dispositional scale measures the frequency of flow experiences with the target activity. These 10-item scales are designed to capture the phenomenon of the flow experience. The core scales are scored by summing the scores of the 10 items and then dividing by 10 to obtain one core flow score.

Pairing state and dispositional scales provides a context to use in thinking about flow experiences, to allow comparisons of dispositional and state responses, and to focus the respondent on activities conducive to flow experiences. Dispositional responses are hypothesized to remain stable across time. A timeframe (e.g., over the last year) for thinking about flow experiences with particular activities can be added to the instructions. Respondents might also be asked to think about peak experiences.

DEVELOPMENT. The Flow Scales have been translated into French, Japanese, Greek, Finnish, Spanish, Hungarian, and Hindi. The DFS-2/FSS-2 is also referred to as the Long Form-Physical. The physical version contains words referring to movement and performance and is intended for use with sporting and performance activities.

Recently, a Long Form-General version was developed for non-physical wider use beyond sport and performance settings. The Long Form-General is recommended when both physical and non-physical activities are being assessed. Data in the test manual were collected from the original Long Form-Physical version.

Items were initially written based on Csikszentmihalyi's (1990) nine hypothesized dimensions of flow, and qualitative study findings of elite performers' experiences helped in writing items (Jackson, 1992, 1995, 1996). A self-report measure of 54 items was written to represent the nine flow dimensions. An expert panel was used to review the items, and refinement of scales and items led to the final 36-item scale.

TECHNICAL.

Descriptive Data. Aggregate descriptive data are available in the test manual for the DFS (Long Dispositional Flow Scales) and FSS (Long Flow State Scales) drawn from the activities of yoga, physical activity, creative and performing arts, sports, and exercise. Data also are presented from a large composite sample. Sample sizes are large, ranging from 142 respondents in the FSS yoga sample to 3,184 in the DFS yoga sample. No data are available for aspects of demographic diversity (e.g., age, gender, race/ethnicity).

For the Short Flow Scale, dispositional data for sport, exercise, music, and work activities are provided, and state data are offered for sport, exercise, and yoga activities. A large school extracurricular activity sample (n = 2,202) is provided for the Core Flow Dispositional Scale; a smaller sample of sport activity (n = 220) is used for the Core Flow State Scale. Thus, aggregate descriptive data are available for comparisons of individual scores for a specific activity, but diverse characteristics such as gender, culture, and age have not been considered. Finally, the Jackson and Eklund (2002) study could be useful in expanding the dimensions of the sample. They conducted a large validation study of the DFS-2 and FSS-2 that included a sample of 897 participants in which age (ranges from 16 to 82), gender, and 27 activities (e.g., running, dance, yoga, triathlon, Australian rules football, basketball, American football, rugby, track and field, soccer, and non-competitive activities) were represented.

Standardized scoring tables are available in the test manual. These tables display mean item raw scores and corresponding T scores, making it possible for individuals to compare state and dispositional long scale scores for physical activity and yoga. In like manner, state and dispositional core and short scale mean item scores with corresponding T scores are offered in test manual tables for extracurricular and physical activities. Individuals are instructed to use raw scores for interpretation if their sample or the activity being evaluated is deemed to markedly deviate from those in the tables.

Reliability Evidence. Internal consistency reliability was strong with alpha coefficients ranging from .72 to .91 with a mean of .85 for the FSS and from .70 to .88 with a mean of .81 for the DFS (Jackson et al., 1998). Jackson and Eklund (2002) found equally strong reliability coefficients for the FSS-2, ranging from .80 to .90 with a mean of .85 and for the DFS-2, ranging from .81 to .90 with a mean alpha coefficient of .85.

Validity Evidence for Long Scales. Confirmatory factor analyses (CFA) were used to analyze a nine-factor solution and a higher-order model with a global flow factor for both a 54-item and a 36-item scale. The 36-item scale was retained because the fit of the nine-factor solution was stronger and demonstrated approximately equal reliability with the longer version. Jackson and Marsh (1996) examined the higher-order factor model with one global flow factor, finding all nine factors loading on the global flow factor with values ranging from .39 (Time Transformation) to .91 (Sense of Control).

The DFS was developed after the FSS. The nine-factor structure and the higher-order global flow factor were confirmed through both individual and simultaneous evaluations of the FSS and DFS (Marsh & Jackson, 1999). All but the Time Transformation factor loaded reasonably well (greater than .40) on the global flow higher-order factor. Time Transformation demonstrated essentially no relationship with global flow. Matching factors between the DFS and the FSS all correlated above .55 except the Loss of Self-Consciousness factor. This finding provided comparative evidence of similar structure and construct validity evidence between the DFS and FSS. Subsequent research findings indicate that the Loss of Self-Consciousness and Time Transformation factors are only weakly related to the global flow factor (Jackson & Marsh, 1996; Kowal & Fortier, 1999; Marsh & Jackson, 1999; Vlachopoulos, Karageorghis, & Terry, 2000). Consequently, the DFS-2 and FSS-2 were developed using five replacement items (Jackson & Eklund, 2002). Despite scale improvements, higher-order factor loadings remained low for Loss of Self-Consciousness and Time Transformation. The explanation given for the Loss of Self-Consciousness low factor loading was that many performers such as figure skaters must maintain high awareness of how they present themselves since performances are partly judged by self-presentation. Time Transformation was thought not to relate strongly with global flow for activities requiring awareness of time such as a wrestling competition or a basketball game.

Construct evidence of validity was further explored through assessment of relationships between flow and variables posited to be related to flow. Perceived ability, intrinsic internal motivation, and anxiety were chosen for their theoretical relevance to flow; using the original flow questionnaire, each was found to be a significant predictor of flow (Jackson, Kimiecik, Ford, & Marsh, 1998). In subsequent investigations, positive engagement, post-exercise revitalization, and tranquility (Karageorghis, Vlachopoulos, & Terry, 2000) as well as physical and mental skills and the psychological skills of negative thinking, activation, emotional control, relaxation, goal-setting, and imagery (Marsh, Hey, Johnson, & Perry, 1997; Thomas, Murphy, & Hardy, 1999) were found to be related significantly to flow.

Conspicuously absent from validity studies were examinations of the influence of context, more specifically aspects of culture, gender, and age. Validity studies investigating the interaction of flow activities and gender, culture, and age would provide the opportunity to further contextualize flow experiences.

Validity Evidence for the Short Flow Scales. Using CFA, the nine-dimensional structure of flow was preserved in the Short Flow Scales. Alpha reliability was also found acceptable for the S DFS (.81 and .74) and the S FSS (.77 and .78) using two different data sets (Jackson & Eklund, 2002). Short scale items correlated at acceptable levels with long scale factors for the dispositional (r = .66 to .83) and the state scales (r = .65 to .82).

Validity Evidence for the Core Flow Scales. Core Flow Scale items were designed to capture the phenomenological experience of flow. Wording of items was derived from elite performers' statements of flow experiences. Diverse samples from core general school flow, mathematics flow, extracurricular flow, and flow in sport were used to conduct CFA resulting in acceptable factor loadings (Martin & Jackson, 2008). Core flow scores for general school, mathematics, and extracurricular activity generally correlated highly with motivation and engagement correlates. Differences were also noted. For instance, enjoyment differed in its correlation with general school (r = .71), mathematics (r = .58), and extracurricular (r = .13), indicating variability of flow experiences dependent on the type of activity. Discriminant validity between Core and Short Flow Scales was also explored, yielding a correlation coefficient of .72 that indicated significant overlap between the two types of scales. Noted in the test manual, 50% of the variance in this correlation is unexplained, indicating there are also differences in the constructs being measured by the two scales.

COMMENTARY. The utility of the Flow Scales lies in their ability to quantify optimal experience and functioning. The three types of scales allow for the examination of relationships between flow and other constructs (e.g., hope, self-efficacy, anxiety, personality). The scales make it possible to assess flow in activities in which the quality of the experience or performance is important such as yoga, music, athletics, dance, chess, and even computer games.

All three types of scales (i.e., long, short, and core) demonstrate strong psychometric properties through extensive study of evidence supporting validity and reliability of test scores. The theorized nine-factor structure of the flow construct was supported through factor analytic studies. Short Flow Scales assess all nine dimensions of flow through single items. The Short Flow Scales allow for rapid assessment of flow without significantly sacrificing validity or reliability. Core Flow and Short Flow Scales were found to evaluate different but related constructs. Test developers explain the core scales are meant to measure "in the zone" (manual, p. 40) experiences.

Validity and reliability evidence is available only for the Physical version of the long scales. The recently developed General version assesses flow in non-physical activities but lacks validity and reliability evidence needed to compare the physical and non-physical versions of the scales. Some dimensions of flow may not apply with some activities due to the nature of flow.

SUMMARY. The Flow Scales have captured the elusive construct of flow. The three types of scales (i.e., long, short, and core), all having state and dispositional versions, provide great versatility in measuring flow in research and as a tool to compare individual flow experiences to aggregated samples. The standardized scoring tables allow for comparison of individual item scores to descriptive data obtained from several samples. The Flow Scales have successfully captured the nine dimensions of flow identified by Csikszentmihalyi so that each aspect of the flow experience can be assessed as well as the global flow factor. Non-physical scales have been developed to parallel the physical scales and await research to establish similar high levels of validity evidence and reliability as observed in the physical scales. Various flow activities have been considered, and standardized scoring tables established. Culture, gender, and age in interaction with flow activities have not as yet not been explored, hampering generalizability. Overall, extensive research has contributed to the validation of the Flow Scales and has solidly established the measurement of flow, producing an excellent tool to assess flow experiences.

REVIEWER'S REFERENCES

Csikszentmihalyi, M. (1990). *Flow: The psychology of optimal experience.* New York, NY: Harper & Row.

Jackson, S. A. (1993). *Elite athletes in flow: The psychology of optimal sport experience.* (Unpublished doctoral dissertation). University of North Carolina-Greensboro.

Jackson, S. A. (1992). Athletes in flow: A qualitative investigation of flow states in elite figure skaters. *Journal of Applied Sport Psychology, 4,* 161-180.

Jackson, S. A. (1995). Factors influencing the occurrence of flow states in elite athletes. *Journal of Applied Sport Psychology,* 7, 138-166.

Jackson, S. A. (1996). Toward a conceptual understanding of the flow experience in elite athletes. *Research Quarterly for Exercise and Sport, 67,* 76-90.

Jackson, S. A., & Eklund, R. C. (2002). Assessing flow in physical activity: The Flow State Scale–2 and Dispositional Flow Scale-2. *Journal of Sport and Exercise Psychology, 24,* 133-150.

Jackson, S. A., Kimiecik, J. C., Ford, S. K., & Marsh, H. W. (1998). Psychological correlates of flow in sport. *Journal of Sport and Exercise Psychology, 20,* 358-378.

Jackson, S. A., & Marsh, H. W. (1996). Development and validation of a scale to measure optimal experience: The flow state scale. *Journal of Sport and Exercise Psychology, 18,* 17-35.

Kowal, J., & Fortier, M. S. (1999). Motivational determinants of flow: Contributions from self-determination theory. *Journal of Social Psychology, 139,* 355-368.

Marsh, H. W., Hey, J., Johnson, S., & Perry, C. (1997). Elite athlete self-description questionnaire: Hierarchical confirmatory factor analysis of responses by two distinct groups of elite athletes. *International Journal of Sport Psychology, 28,* 237-258.

Marsh, H. W., & Jackson, S. A. (1999). Flow experiences in sport: Construct validation of multidimensional hierarchical state and trait responses. *Structural Equation Modeling, 6,* 343-371.

Martin, A. J., & Jackson, S. A. (2008). Brief approaches to assessing task absorption and enhanced subjective experience: Examining 'short' and 'core' flow in diverse performance domains. *Motivation and Emotion, 32,* 141-157.

Vlachopoulos, S. P., Karageorghis, C. I., & Terry, P. C. (2000). Hierarchical confirmatory factor analysis of the Flow State Scale in exercise. *Journal of Sports Sciences, 18,* 815-823.

[67]

Functional Behavior Assessment of Absenteeism and Truancy.

Purpose: Designed as a set of tools to provide "school teams with a clear process for identifying students who are chronically absent, gathering relevant data, and designing a corresponding function-based intervention."

Population: Students in Grades K-12.

Publication Date: 2013.

Acronym: FBAAT.

Scores: No formal scores.

Administration: Individual.

Levels, 2: Basic, Comprehensive.

Price Data, 2020: $225 per kit including manual (2013, 128 pages), CD of fillable forms (reproducible), 5 of each consumable booklet (Core Checklist, Additional Data Sources, Summary Core Checklist/Global Overview/Behavior Intervention Plan), copy of Absenteeism and Truancy: Interventions and Universal Procedures; $60 per copy of Absenteeism and Truancy: Interventions and Universal Procedures; $30 per 5 sets of consumable booklets (each set consists of 3 booklets).

Time: Untimed.

Authors: William R. Jenson, Jessica Sprick, Randy Sprick, Holly Majszak, Linda Phosaly, Cal Evans, Daniel Olympia, and Cristina Teplick.

Publisher: Ancora Publishing.

a) BASIC.

Parts, 3: Core Checklist, Summary Core Checklist, Behavior Intervention Plan.

b) COMPREHENSIVE.

Parts, 5: Core Checklist, Summary Core Checklist, Additional Optional Assessments (On-Task Observation, Classroom Observation, Interviews [Teacher, Parent, Student], Discipline Referrals, ABC Tracking Sheet, Academic Screening/Oral Reading Fluency), Global Overview, Behavior Intervention Plan.

Review of the Functional Behavior Assessment of Absenteeism & Truancy by ADAM LEKWA, Assistant Research Professor, Rutgers, the State University of New Jersey, New Brunswick, NJ:

DESCRIPTION. The Functional Behavior Assessment of Absenteeism & Truancy (FBAAT) is an assessment framework intended to help guide teams of educators in the collection and use of information about the conditions surrounding problematic behaviors related to absenteeism and truancy for students in the K-12 context. As an assessment framework, the FBAAT is not a test, per se, but rather comprises a collection of assessment materials and brief intervention protocols. The FBAAT may be administered by a single individual but is intended by its authors for use by small multi-disciplinary teams of K-12 educators, who might include school psychologists, special education teachers, school counselors, or others. The qualitative and quantitative information generated through administration of the FBAAT is intended to help teams identify the function or functions of a problematic behavior as well as to plan and evaluate interventions linked to functions identified.

The FBAAT materials include consumable forms (a total of five sets are included); each is also available digitally on a CD that accompanies the test kit. A book by the FBAAT authors, *Absenteeism & Truancy: Interventions and Universal Procedures,* accompanies the assessment kit with a collection of ideas and brief procedural descriptions of 25 behavior interventions linked to the set of potential behavioral functions assessed by FBAAT; this book also may be purchased separately.

Basic administration of the FBAAT involves, at a minimum, completion of its Core Checklist (112 items) and Core Summary sheet, in which responses to the Core Checklist are aggregated and summarized. The FBAAT is intended to be administered by education professionals such as school psychologists, counselors, or other general or special educators. This basic administration process may be carried out through a meeting between the FBAAT administrator and a primary informant—a person of sufficient familiarity with the target student that he or she can respond to at least 80% of the items in the Core Checklist.

The first 11 items in the Core Checklist are used to determine the severity of a student's problematic truancy; responses to each item are either "Yes" or "No." The remaining 101 items seek descriptive information about potential setting events, antecedents, topology of the student behaviors, and consequences organized by a set of common behavioral functions. Responses to the first 11 items on the Core Checklist are used to determine whether a student is Type 1 truant (often younger children with truancy typically related to health conditions) or Type 2 truant (often older students with truancy as one part of a learned behavioral pattern). Recommended action for students of either type involves a range of school-based intervention strategies, as well as parent training. Responses to the larger body of descriptive items for setting events, antecedents, and the topology of the behavior are summarized in writing. Responses to items on the potential functions of the behavior are summarized by rank-ordering each behavioral function category according to the number of its items endorsed with a "Yes" by the respondent; interventions aligned with the function with the greatest number of items endorsed are thus indicated.

A more comprehensive administration augments the Core Checklist and Summary sheet with a range of optional procedures including any one or more of the following: (a) direct observation of student behavior; (b) observation of the classroom environment; (c) interviews with the student, the student's parents, or the student's teachers; (d) a discipline records review; and (e) informal screening of academic skills through reviews of records or brief, informal curriculum-based measurement of the student's skill in reading. Information gathered from these additional procedures is meant to expand upon and add depth to responses in the Core Checklist for purposes of intervention planning. These optional procedures also include guidance for monitoring a student's progress (in school settings) throughout implementation of intervention to target truancy-related problem behaviors.

The test authors do not list an expected range of administration time requirements for FBAAT, but users should expect administration time to vary as a function of administrator and informant familiarity with the student who is the subject of assessment, as well as the extent of supplemental FBAAT assessment activities selected. These supplemental assessment procedures may be carried out over a short span of time for intervention planning and a longer span of time—a number of weeks—for progress monitoring. Likewise, the test authors do not outline specific training requirements, but users of FBAAT should have completed at least introductory training in behavioral assessment and intervention for children to obtain maximum benefit from use of this assessment.

DEVELOPMENT. The authors of FBAAT provide no information about its development. The items of the Core Checklist were not reported to have been piloted or to have undergone a process of evaluation and improvement before publication. The authors did provide references to empirical research in support of the interventions linked to hypothesized functions of student behavior. Overall, the design and intended uses of the FBAAT, as described by its authors, appear to be oriented toward behaviorist theory and human ecological theory (e.g., Bronfenbrenner, 1994/1997). In a similar way, users of the FBAAT might note that the procedures involved in FBAAT loosely align with a framework of behavioral consultation originated by Bergan and Kratochwill (1990) and expanded by Sheridan and Kratochwill (2007) in which a consultant (ideally the individual who leads administration of FBAAT) works with consultees (teachers and parents) to understand and change the behavior of a student.

TECHNICAL. The primary element of the FBAAT—the Core Checklist—consists of a set of 112 items. Specific details about the validity of the scores yielded by these items are not provided. Similarly, reliability and validity information is not provided about the supplemental assessment protocols (observation or interviews) included in FBAAT. Although the reliability of FBAAT data for determining levels of behavior, functions of behavior, and (optionally) rates of change in behavior could be challenged, the level of reliability required for intervention planning and evaluation is less stringent than that which would be required for high-stakes decision making (e.g., Salvia, Ysseldyke, & Bolt, 2012). The observational methods advocated by the authors of FBAAT, including counts of the frequency or durations of behaviors, are consistent with those described in educational psychological literature on systematic direct observation; researchers who have incorporated such measures frequently report adequate to strong levels of interrater agreement in the use of such methods (see, for reference, Hintze, Volpe, & Shapiro, 2002).

The FBAAT is not a psychometric instrument, per se, but is rather an assessment framework developed to guide school practitioners through the assessment of conditions that surround truancy and absenteeism. Thus, the traditional range of psychometric indices are not applicable in the usual way. In this instance, future users or researchers might conceptualize reliability of FBAAT data as consistency in responses between multiple primary informants for the same student and might consider hypothesized functions and outcomes of selected interventions as forms of validity evidence.

COMMENTARY. Behaviors associated with problematic absenteeism and truancy can be challenging for school-based professionals to address. This can be due, in part, to the potential severity of underlying problems but also to the fact that the pattern of behavior itself often is not observable directly. For this reason it is helpful for educators to have guidance around planning and organizing behavioral assessment that leads directly to function-based intervention. The format of the FBAAT as an assessment framework rather than a rating scale is advantageous in that it facilitates a more direct link between data and decision making.

That said, although the main strength of FBAAT is in facilitation of behavioral analysis and intervention planning, much of the outcome of this process will rely upon users' own knowledge of, and experience in, behavioral assessment and intervention. For example, the Core Checklist ultimately guides users to interventions based on hypothetical functions of identified problem truancy behaviors, but no procedures or suggestions are provided to direct FBAAT users in the integration of important information about potential setting events and antecedents of the behavior. Similarly, only minimal guidelines are provided for collection and interpretation of direct observational data, or direct assessment of student academic skills when indicated. Therefore the utility of the information obtained from administration of FBAAT will depend on the prior training and experience of the FBAAT administrator.

The materials provided within FBAAT should be regarded as exemplars meant to provide procedural guidance and ideas for assessment and intervention. Users of FBAAT who have previous training and some experience with functional behavior assessment will find the materials and structure of the FBAAT to be a helpful scaffold. Yet in many cases, practitioners will already have access to instruments or other materials intended to provide reliable and valid data about the same patterns of behavior. Individuals with advanced training and considerable experience in this domain likely would not require the assessment materials included in FBAAT, but might yet find the materials to be helpful for guiding or enhancing consultee intervention implementation.

SUMMARY. The FBAAT is an assessment framework that was designed to assist teams of educators in assessing the conditions surrounding problematic behaviors associated with truancy or chronic absenteeism. The FBAAT was not designed to evaluate truancy behaviors along a particular scale, but rather to help (a) organize information already known to students' teachers and parents or (b) guide the collection of additional, unknown information in an effort to indicate intervention strategies that are likely to be aligned with maintaining functions and effective in promoting behavioral improvement. The FBAAT could be useful as an aid to increase likelihood of successful behavior intervention implementation.

REVIEWER'S REFERENCES

Bergan, J. R., & Kratochwill, T. R. (1990). *Behavioral consultation and therapy.* New York, NY: Plenum Press.

Bronfenbrenner, U. (1997). Ecological models of human development. In M. Gauvain & M. Cole (Eds.), *Readings on the development of children* (2nd ed., pp. 37-43). New York, NY: Freeman. (Reprinted from *International encyclopedia of education,* Vol. 3, 2nd ed., pp. 1643-1647, by T. Husén & T. N. Postlethwaite, Eds., 1994, New York, NY: Pergamon)

Hintze, J. M., Volpe, R. J., & Shapiro, E. S. (2002). Best practices in the systematic direct observation of student behavior. In A. Thomas & J. Grimes (Eds.), *Best Practices in School Psychology* (4th ed., Vol. 2, pp. 993-1006). Washington, DC: National Association of School Psychologists.

Salvia, J., Ysseldyke, J., & Bolt, S. (2012). *Assessment: In special and inclusive education.* Belmont, CA: Wadsworth/Cengage Learning.

Sheridan, S. M., & Kratochwill, T. R. (2007). *Conjoint behavioral consultation: Promoting family-school connections and interventions* (2nd ed.). New York, NY: Springer.

Review of the Functional Behavior Assessment of Absenteeism & Truancy by JUSTIN A. LOW, Associate Professor of Counseling and School Psychology, University of the Pacific, Stockton, CA:

DESCRIPTION. The Functional Behavior Assessment of Absenteeism & Truancy (FBAAT) consists of a series of checklists, forms, and tracking sheets to help identify students who are chronically absent, determine the function of absenteeism, and develop intervention plans. The assessment system is likely appropriate for children in kindergarten through Grade 12, although the intended target population is not specified in the FBAAT manual.

The FBAAT system may be administered by a professional or team of professionals affiliated with a school, law enforcement, mental health, or court system. It is divided into two sections, the first of which includes the assessment materials and test manual, and the second of which includes suggested interventions and procedures to reduce truancy. The assessment measures include three booklets, which begin with the Core Checklist. The Core Checklist is administered to a school staff member most familiar with the identified student and includes questions designed to help the team determine dynamics underlying the student's absenteeism and the context surrounding the absenteeism. The Core Checklist is followed by the Summary Core Checklist (Booklet 3), which consolidates information gathered during the administration of the Core Checklist and helps the assessment team understand the function of absenteeism. The assessment team may then proceed to develop a Behavior Intervention Plan (Booklet 3) or gather additional information using Booklet 2—Additional Data Sources. These additional data sources include an On-Task Observation form to determine whether the student has difficulties with a specific teacher or class; a Classroom Observation form to measure whether the classroom is engaging and predominantly marked by positive or negative interactions; Parent, Teacher, and Student Interview forms to gather information about the function of the absenteeism from a variety of perspectives; a Discipline Records Review to identify patterns in the student's discipline referrals; and an ABC Tracking Sheet to track antecedents, behaviors, and consequences related to absenteeism across multiple occurrences. The FBAAT manual also provides guidance on screening for academic and oral reading fluency problems. Assessment teams that gather additional data using Booklet 2 then complete the Global Overview form to consolidate the information gathered throughout the assessment.

Much of the data gathered through the FBAAT is qualitative and includes open-ended and yes/no responses. These data are summarized in the Summary Core Checklist or the Global Overview. Many of the summarizations are qualitative; however, a few tables require the assessor to tally the number of "Yes" responses to determine the type of the student's truancy and the function of the student's behavior. Guidelines are provided to help interpret the number of "Yes" responses.

DEVELOPMENT. The FBAAT manual does not include a section on the development of the various measures included in the assessment system. The test authors did not provide information regarding how the assessment measures were developed, why items on checklists and forms were included or excluded, or whether the assessment was piloted. The authors do, however, explain the purpose of each of the checklists and forms included in the assessment, some of which are tied to research. For example, they explain that the On-Task Observation form may be useful in an assessment of absenteeism because poor on-task behavior is related to difficulties with a class or teacher that, in turn, is related to absenteeism.

The FBAAT is not a norm-referenced assessment; however, some criteria are included to guide assessors in making decisions. For example, after completing the Core Checklist, assessors count the number of "Yes" responses and make a decision whether the student is a Type 1 (acute-onset, health-related) or Type 2 (slow-onset) Truant. No information is provided regarding how the criteria were established or the prevalence of either type of truancy in the population.

TECHNICAL. The test authors did not provide information regarding technical aspects of the FBAAT. There is no discussion of a standardization sample, and no evidence of reliability or validity appears in the test manual.

COMMENTARY. The FBAAT is a compilation of checklists, forms, and data summarization guides designed to provide a comprehensive functional behavior assessment of absenteeism. The assessments included in the FBAAT indeed have the potential to guide assessment teams in gathering information from a wide variety of data sources and perspectives. Other helpful features of the assessment system are the summarization forms that help assessors conceptualize the data and the accompanying manual that provides interventions and procedures designed to reduce truant behavior. Unfortunately, no technical information is provided to establish the reliability or validity of the assessment system as a whole, although individual forms appear to be based on well-established assessment procedures. For example, the ABC Tracking Sheet helps assessors identify antecedents and consequences of truant behavior, the general practice of which is a well-established assessment technique (Anderson, Rodriguez, & Campbell, 2015). Given the inclusion of several similarly recognized techniques, the FBAAT can be conceptualized as a series of assessments based on well-established techniques that have been geared toward absenteeism. Nevertheless, the FBAAT would greatly benefit from information detailing the development of the assessment, evidence of reliability, and evidence of validity. For example, evidence that interventions provided in the manual result in reduced truancy would be helpful in establishing the validity of the entire assessment system (i.e., the assessment measures and the accompanying manual of interventions and procedures).

SUMMARY. The FBAAT consists of a series of checklists, forms, and tracking sheets to help identify, determine the function of, and develop intervention plans for absenteeism. These checklists and forms help assessors approach the assessment of absenteeism from multiple perspectives using multiple approaches to data collection. Many of these assessment tools appear to be based on well-established functional behavior assessment techniques; however, the authors do not discuss the development of the assessment nor do they discuss evidence of reliability or validity. Therefore, before this assessment system can be recommended for use, the authors need to provide discussions of the development and technical characteristics of the test. Until that time, users may wish to use elements of this assessment that can be linked to evidence-based practices in functional behavior assessment and intervention.

REVIEWER'S REFERENCE

Anderson, C. M., Rodriguez, B. J., & Campbell, A. (2015). Functional behavior assessment in schools: Current status and future directions. *Journal of Behavioral Education, 24*(3), 338–371.

[68]

Functional Behavior Assessment of Bullying.

Purpose: Designed as "a series of assessment tools for bullying behavior" leading to "evidence-based interventions ... for students who exhibit bullying behavior and who may themselves be targets of bullying."

Population: Students in Grades K-12.
Publication Date: 2017.
Acronym: FBA of Bullying.
Scores: No formal scores.
Administration: Individual.
Levels, 2: Basic, Comprehensive.
Price Data, 2020: $295 per kit including manual (2017, 132 pages), 5 of each consumable booklet (Core Checklist, Additional Data Sources, Summary Core Checklist/Global Overview/Behavior Intervention Plan), access to downloadable assessment and intervention forms, and copy of Bullying Solutions: Universal and Individual Strategies (2017, 715 pages); $95 per copy of Bullying Solutions: Universal and Individual Strategies.
Time: Untimed.
Authors: William R. Jenson, Jessica Sprick, Cristy Coughlin, Elaine Clark, and Julie Bowen (assessment); Jessica Sprick, William R. Jenson, Randy Sprick, and Cristy Coughlin (Bullying Solutions guide).
Publisher: Ancora Publishing.

a) BASIC.

Parts, 3: Core Checklist, Summary Core Checklist, Behavior Intervention Plan.

b) COMPREHENSIVE.

Parts, 5: Core Checklist, Summary Core Checklist, Additional Optional Assessments (ABC Tracking Sheet, Time-Sampling Observation, Climate Observation, Interviews [Parent, Teacher, Referred Student, Student Targeted], Discipline Referrals), Global Overview, Behavior Intervention Plan.

Review of the Functional Behavior Assessment of Bullying by MICHELE CASCARDI, Professor, and CHELSEA PEARSALL, Graduate Assistant, Department of Psychology, William Paterson University, Wayne, NJ:

DESCRIPTION. The Functional Behavior Assessment (FBA) of Bullying is a comprehensive package of assessment methods and recording forms to monitor chronic bullying behavior and evaluate the function of a student's chronic bullying behavior. The ultimate goal of the FBA of Bullying is to guide the development of function-based interventions for implementation and monitoring in a school setting. Materials include nine measures and recording forms: three are required, and six are optional. Required measures and forms are the Core Checklist, the Summary Core Checklist, and the Behavior Intervention Plan. The optional measures are the ABC Tracking Sheet, Time-Sampling Observation Form, Climate Observation Form, multiple interview forms (student, teacher, parent), Discipline Records Review Form, and Global Interview Form. Measures may be administered by a "competent professional or team of professionals" (manual, p. 14) who speak the same language as the student, teacher, and parent. Ideally, the FBA of Bullying is conducted shortly after an incident of bullying behavior. The three required measures evaluate factors maintaining the chronic bullying behavior and intervention techniques specific to the identified maintaining factors. The optional components provide more detailed and comprehensive evaluation of the function of the student's bullying behavior. The Core Checklist, Summary Core Checklist, and Behavior Intervention Plan are the three required components for a basic FBA of Bullying. A comprehensive FBA of Bullying includes the three required and six optional components.

Required Measures. The three required measures include a two-part Core Checklist comprising 97 yes/no items, which are to be completed by a professional. Part One consists of contributing factors, antecedent factors, behaviors, and consequences associated with the student's chronic bullying behavior. Contributing factors include items on mood and setting, whereas items about antecedent factors focus on specific aspects of the bullying incidents: time and location of the behavior, individuals involved in the behavior, and the type of activity taking place when bullying behavior occurs. Behavioral items measure specific bullying behaviors, internalizing behaviors, and other misbehaviors. Finally, social, emotional, and tangible consequences (e.g., peer or adult attention) of bullying behavior are measured in legal, home, and school settings. In Part Two, the informant provides information about the function (attention seeking/social rewards, material rewards, escape or avoidance) or reasons (skill deficits) for the bullying behavior. "Yes" responses to the Core Checklist are tabulated on the Summary Core Checklist in an organized manner. Responses to Part One are recorded in designated sections on the Contributing Factors sheet: setting events, antecedents, behaviors, and consequences. All "yes" responses on Part Two are recorded in the Function Table so that the function of chronic bullying behavior can be determined. The final section of the Summary Core Checklist provides space for recording the planned intervention strategies. The Behavioral Intervention Plan is a three-part method used to determine intervention strategies. In Part Onc, FBA findings are summarized, and potential intervention strategies are documented. Specific interventions that align with the function of chronic bullying behavior are refined in Part Two, and steps for implementing the intervention are outlined in Part Three.

Optional Measures. There are six optional measures. The ABC Tracking Sheet provides a systematic method for recording data on chronic bullying behavior, including consequences of this behavior across multiple places, individuals, and activities. The occurrence of five types of bullying behavior and misbehavior may be tracked: physical, verbal, relational, cyber, and other. The purpose of this tracking sheet is to provide a consolidated snapshot of chronic bullying behavior to reveal behavioral patterns.

The Time-Sampling Observation Form provides a systematic method for recording direct observations of bullying behavior in 15-minute intervals. Real-time occurrences of bullying behavior are recorded every 10 seconds. Using a coding key, observers quantify the rate, type (e.g., verbal, physical, relational, or cyber), and consequences (e.g., encouraging/neutral, discouraging, or mixed) of bullying behavior for the student referred for bullying (target student), peers, and student who is the object of bullying (referred student).

The Climate Observation Form provides a systematic method for recording observations of environmental factors that could affect the target student's motivation and choices for bullying behavior. Observations are made regarding students' behaviors, warnings of prohibited behavior, and the supervisor's proactive behaviors. Observational data are recorded every 10 seconds during a 12-minute interval. The observer quantifies the percentage of time the target student engages in inappropriate behavior and the supervisor engages in proactive behaviors.

Multiple interview forms are available to guide interviews with students (both referred and target), parents, and staff as needed. The targeted student interview consists of 17 questions on the occurrences and times of bullying, the student's perceptions about the bullying events, and his/her peer group behavior. Interviews with the referred student, parents, and staff members consist of 34-38 questions, depending on the individual interviewed. Questions include setting events, antecedents, behaviors, corrective consequences, and motivating consequences.

The Discipline Records Review Form allows the evaluator to record the existing discipline referrals for the referred student. For the most recent three incidents of bullying, more detailed information is recorded, including date/time, location, individuals involved, activity taking place at time of incident, behavior prompting referral for discipline, action taken (disciplinary or otherwise), and the function of behavior during each incident.

When all required and optional measures of the FBA have been used, the evaluator compiles and integrates all data using the Global Overview Form.

The *Bullying Solutions Universal & Individual Strategies* book is a compendium of recommendations from best-practice research to reduce school-wide and individual bullying behavior.

DEVELOPMENT. The FBA of Bullying system is based on research demonstrating that function-based interventions result in more rapid and sustained behavior change (Dunlap & Fox, 2011) than other interventions.

TECHNICAL. At present, there are no psychometric data available on the FBA of Bullying; thus, it is not yet known whether the methods accurately identify the function of chronic bullying behavior or result in more efficacious interventions to prevent school-wide or individual bullying.

COMMENTARY. The FBA of Bullying provides a straightforward and comprehensive method for completing a functional behavior assessment of chronic bullying behavior. This system provides school or related professionals the tools to conduct a thorough and comprehensive evaluation of the contributing factors, setting events, antecedents, consequences, and function of bullying behavior. The FBA of Bullying provides forms for summarizing and synthesizing information to guide the development of a function-based behavior intervention plan to target the chronic bullying. Additionally, the *Bullying Solutions* compendium provides an exhaustive list of evidence-based universal and individual strategies to reduce chronic bullying behavior. Despite the intuitive appeal of the FBA of Bullying, further research is needed to evaluate evidence of validity and reliability of this system.

SUMMARY. The FBA of Bullying includes three required measures and six optional measures used to identify the function of chronic bullying behavior and an associated behavior plan for school-aged children and adolescents. The accompanying *Bullying Solutions* book provides an exhaustive list of universal and individual strategies derived from best-practice research. At the present time, there are no normative data, and evidence of validity and reliability of the FBA of Bullying are unknown. However, the FBA of Bullying is based on empirically supported research in the effectiveness of function-based behavior change and can be administered by any school or other related professional.

REVIEWERS' REFERENCE

Dunlap, G., & Fox, L. (2011). Function-based interventions for children with challenging behavior. *Journal of Early Intervention, 33*, 333-343. doi:10.1177/1053815111429971

Review of the Functional Behavior Assessment of Bullying by SUSAN M. SWEARER, Willa Cather Professor of Educational Psychology, University of Nebraska–Lincoln, Lincoln, NE:

DESCRIPTION. The Functional Behavior Assessment of Bullying (FBA of Bullying) is designed to help educators determine the function of bullying behavior for school-aged youth. There are two components: (a) the Functional Behavior Assessment manual with accompanying forms and (b) *Bullying Solutions: Universal & Individual Strategies*, a resource book with strategies that educators can select based on the assessed function of the bullying behavior. The test authors note that the assessment can be completed by "school psychologists, behavior specialists, counselors, social workers, teachers, and administrators" as well as "juvenile court personnel, probation officers, and mental health professionals" (manual, p. 14). The Core Checklist (Booklet 1) includes a series of questions designed to determine the function of a student's bullying behavior. The Core Checklist queries about contributing factors (i.e., academic, family), antecedents to bullying, description of the behaviors exhibited by the student, consequences of bullying, the function of the bullying (i.e., attention seeking/social rewards, acquisition of tangibles, escape/avoidance), and general deficits. The additional data sources checklist (Booklet 2) includes a tracking sheet for recording antecedents, behaviors, and consequences for bullying; observation recording sheets; staff, parent, and student interview protocols; and a sheet for use in a disciplinary records review. The assessment results and plan (Booklet 3) includes the Summary Core Checklist, an overview of data collected, and the behavior intervention plan that is developed based on all the data collected. Sample data collected in the booklets are provided in the FBA of Bullying manual.

DEVELOPMENT. The FBA of Bullying was created to augment school-wide bullying prevention and intervention strategies. These strategies are described in the included *Bullying Solutions: Universal & Individual Strategies* book. The authors note several considerations that underlie the system. First, "Bullying is a complex and difficult issue to address" (manual, p. ix); second, "Purely punitive approaches are unlikely to make a difference in changing the behavior of a student who chronically bullies" (p. ix); third, "Many reactive school-based efforts to address individual bullying problems are ineffectual, while some well-intentioned but misguided efforts have the potential to make chronic bullying problems much, much worse" (p. x); and fourth, "Intervention strategies in the *Bullying Solutions* book are derived from best-practice research in changing behaviors that are often related to bullying behavior" (p. x). Finally, the test authors state, "The procedures in this manual are designed to help you develop a reasonable hypothesis about factors contributing to a student's chronic bullying behavior. Because of the above considerations and the complexities and many factors that may be related to bullying, any conclusions and procedures derived through the FBA process represent the practitioner's best efforts rather than a guarantee of behavioral change" (p. x). The FBA of Bullying system was developed to help school personnel understand the function of bullying behavior in order to develop individual interventions to help drive behavior change and stop the bullying behavior.

TECHNICAL. Because the FBA of Bullying system is an individualized approach to understanding the function underlying the bullying behavior displayed by an individual student, no standardization sample, normative data, reliability data, nor validity data are described or reported. The test authors could conduct research examining the reliability and validity of the FBA of Bullying; however, this work has not yet been done. There are many assessment tools for bullying behavior that have been compiled by the Centers for Disease Control and Prevention (Hamburger, Basile, & Vivolo, 2011) that could be used in a research study to determine reliability and evaluate evidence of validity for this approach.

COMMENTARY. The FBA of Bullying uses multiple sources (i.e., school personnel, parent, student) and multiple methods (i.e., observation, interviews, records reviews) to address chronic bullying behavior and to create a behavior intervention plan for chronic bullies. Given that some researchers report that as many as 30% of students in a given school may be bully perpetrators (Bradshaw, Sawyer, & O'Brennan, 2007), this system offers a comprehensive model for developing function-based interventions for bullying. The FBA of Bullying and the *Bullying Solutions: Universal & Individual Strategies* book provide a comprehensive assessment approach that guides the universal and individual strategies designed to intervene in bullying behaviors with the goal of stopping these behaviors.

SUMMARY. The FBA of Bullying system was designed to help school personnel identify students who engage in chronic bullying behaviors and to determine the function of the bullying behaviors. In identifying the function of the behavior, interventions can be tailored to address these functions, thereby creating more targeted and meaningful interventions. Although the FBA of Bullying is comprehensive and fits with a multi-tiered system of support for behavior and a positive behavioral interventions and support model, it is also a time-consuming approach that might be challenging to use in low-resourced schools. In order to implement the FBA of Bullying system according to the directions, it would take a skilled adult to complete the checklists, observations, and interviews. In reality, there are few school personnel who have the time to implement complex assessments and interventions with fidelity. The FBA of Bullying would take a lot of time that many school personnel just do not have. It will be important for the test authors to examine reliability and validity evidence related to this approach and to provide evidence for its effectiveness. The FBA of Bullying is a roadmap for assessing and developing functional interventions for bullying. It is not yet known whether this model is effective.

REVIEWER'S REFERENCES.

Bradshaw, C. P., Sawyer, A. L., & O'Brennan, L. M. (2007). Bullying and peer victimization at school: Perceptual differences between students and school staff. *School Psychology Review, 36*(3), 361-382.

Hamburger, M. E., Basile, K. C., & Vivolo, A. M. (2011). *Measuring Bullying Victzmization, Perpetration, and Bystander Experiences: A Compendium of Assessment Tools.* Atlanta, GA: Centers for Disease Control and Prevention, National Center for Injury Prevention and Control.

[69]

Glaspey Dynamic Assessment of Phonology.

Purpose: Designed to measure a child's speech sound production, speech adaptability, and potential for learning phonemes and phonological patterns.
Population: Ages 3-0 through 10-11.
Publication Date: 2019.
Acronym: GDAP.
Scores, 61: Syllables, Glides, Nasals, Stops, Velars, Stridents, Interdentals, Liquids, Clusters, Initial Position Phonemes Score, Final Position Phonemes Score, Overall Score, plus 49 individual item scores.
Administration: Individual.
Price Data, 2020: $225 per kit including manual (2019, 192 pages), test plates, and 25 record forms; $75 per manual; $100 per test plates; $50 per 25 record forms.

[69] Glaspey Dynamic Assessment of Phonology

Time: 5-80 minutes for administration, depending on the number of targets administered and the adaptability of the child.
Author: Amy M. Glaspey.
Publisher: Academic Therapy Publications.

Review of the Glaspey Dynamic Assessment of Phonology by PRISCILLA M. DANIELSON, Speech/Language Pathologist and AT/AAC Specialist, Linguistic Solutions, LLC, Royal Oak, MD:

DESCRIPTION. The Glaspey Dynamic Assessment of Phonology (GDAP) is an individually administered dynamic assessment described as a measurement of speech sound production and speech adaptability for children ages 3 through 10 years. The measure was designed to evaluate speech sounds and changes over time using a hierarchy of cues and linguistic environments. The measure's goal is to evaluate current correct speech sound production as well as potential for learning by using assistance, cues, and scaffolding to plan for improved individualized intervention. The GDAP is reported to be useful for diagnostic, prognostic, and progress monitoring purposes. The test author suggests that this measure also could be used to assess discrete improvements following treatment using scoring patterns characteristic of the test as methods for assessing progress within a session. The measure incorporates Vygotsky's social development theory, stimulability and speech adaptability to speech sound production and errors observed (Vygotsky, 1978). The measure examines "a child's potential for learning phonemes and phonological patterns through a systematic presentation of instructions, models, cues, and linguistic environments" (manual, p. 9).

To complete the test, it is expected that the child can produce sounds, words, and sentences or connected speech. The test comprises 49 items arranged in sets of three test plates and presented using an easel-back flipbook. The test author suggests that administration resembles activities occurring during speech treatment. Token reinforcement is allowed. The pictures are colored items or scenes representing phoneme targets. The scoring form allows for scoring correct production of a single item at the levels of isolation, word, sentence, and connected speech. Within each level, performance is scored following varying degrees of stimulability support. The measure also allows for monitoring correct sound production in the initial and final position of words within a connected speech sample collected prior to administration of the test items and scored using the Phonemic Inventory. If a sound is produced correctly in either position two times in the connected sample, testing of that sound in the position(s) noted is not suggested. The measure employs a "15-point scale of speech adaptability that combines and manipulates six linguistic environments and four clinical cues" (manual, p. 13). Initially, sounds are assessed within six linguistic contexts, ranging from isolation to connected speech. If a child's production is correct, the assessment moves to a more complex context. If the child's production is incorrect, the context is reduced in complexity. The GDAP manual specifies cues that may be used to encourage correct production of targets across linguistic contexts. Cues are provided in response to error production with increasing articulatory support. The cue range includes (a) spontaneous production without support; (b) verbal instruction about articulatory placement and verbal model; (c) verbal instruction and verbal model plus prolongation or segmentation; and (d) verbal instruction, verbal model, and prolongation, or segmentation plus tactile cues. The results of the assessment reflect syllable patterns, phonemes, and consonant cluster productions. Test items assess 24 phonemes of standard American English appearing in initial or final positions of words. Phonemes are organized by Sound Classes: Glides, Nasals, Stops, Velars, Stridents, Interdentals, and Liquids. Sound clusters emphasize /l/, /r/, and /s/ in the initial and final positions. Vowels are not assessed.

The GDAP is described as appropriate for students ages 3:0 to 10:11. Caution is advised when administering to students who have language deficits or hearing impairments impacting picture labeling. The normative sample comprised English-speaking children. Testing time is estimated to be between 5 and 80 minutes, with breaks permitted during testing as needed. A standup easel with pictures facing the examinee is employed. The GDAP uses a decision matrix for scoring; therefore, there are no ceilings, basals, or age-based starting points. It is recommended that a speech sample be obtained prior to testing to determine whether a particular phoneme needs to be assessed. It is suggested that the GDAP can be re-administered to evaluate therapy progress. The test manual provides specific and annotated directions for administration and scoring of the connected speech sample, Phonemic Inventory, and test items. Because the GDAP is a dynamic measure, the annotated cues for determining the highest level of correct phonemic production should be helpful to both inexperienced and experienced clinicians. The annotated responses mirror therapeutic cues for stimulability. The GDAP may be administered and scored by hand or by using the test publisher's online platform. When using the paper scoring form, the clinician follows the decision matrix for the appropriate cue according to the child's performance on each individual item. When using the computer assisted administration, the computer moves the clinician through the decision matrix as the administrator scores each item. Clinicians provide increased levels of support and increased environmental complexity based upon the child's performance.

The GDAP provides scaled scores for all Sound Classes in 2-month intervals for ages 3:0 through 6:11, in 3-month intervals for ages 7:0 through 8:11, and in 6-month intervals for ages 9:0 through 10:11. Standard scores are derived for Initial and Final Position Phonemes as well as Overall scores. Percentile ranks, *z*-scores, T scores and stanines also may be derived.

DEVELOPMENT. The GDAP was developed over approximately 20 years, beginning as a strategy for collecting data following treatment with children presenting sound disorders. The original measure was expanded upon for dissertation studies at the University of Washington and included more linguistic environments, more cues, and improved instructions. A refined 21-point scale emerged as the Scaffolding Scale of Stimulability (Glaspey & Stoel-Gammon, 2005, 2007). Further research and refinements resulted in a 15-point version (Glaspey, 2012; Glaspey & MacLeod, 2010; MacLeod & Glaspey, 2014). For the current standardization version, illustrations were created for all test items and a computer-based administration format was developed. The standardization version employed the 15-point scoring system for 49 items, and item difficulty and item discrimination were analyzed. The test author examined differential item functioning (DIF) for the following groups: gender, ethnicity (i.e., African American/non-African American; Caucasian/non-Caucasian; Asian American/non-Asian American), Hispanic origin, residence (urban/rural), and region of the country. Results revealed 14 instances of significant levels of DIF for 10 items. It was noted that effect sizes in all cases were negligible (Gómez-Benito, Hidalgo, & Padilla, 2009), suggesting that test items are free from bias associated with the variables examined.

TECHNICAL. The standardization sample for the GDAP included 880 children ages 3:0 years through 10:11 who were tested at one of 88 sites in 37 states. All 95 examiners were speech-language pathologists (SLPs). Background data collected included speech diagnosis, basic demographic information, household income and parents' educational level, class placement, disability status, and community characteristics. The sample was designed to approximate the population according to 2010 U.S. Census figures. The sample was obtained from the South (37.2%), West (25.6%), North Central (21.1%), and Northeast (16.1%). The predominant ethnicity was White/Caucasian (79.6%) followed by Black/African-American (9.4%), Asian-American (4.1%), and American-Indian/Alaska Native (1.4%). Two or more ethnicities were reported by 5.6% of the sample, and 21.1% of the sample was of Hispanic origin. Of the total sample, 14.6% reported one or more disability status categories. The most prevalent disability was speech/sound disorder (10.0%) followed by autism spectrum disorder (3.6%), cochlear implant/hearing impairment (1.5%), and Down syndrome/genetic developmental condition (1.0%).

The test author evaluated reliability in terms of internal consistency estimates and test-retest reliability. To assess internal consistency, alpha coefficients were computed for Sound Classes, Initial and Final Position Phonemes, and the Overall score for age ranges included in the standardization sample. Historically, alpha coefficients between .70 and .95 have been regarded as indicating acceptable homogeneity of test items. Across ages, average alpha coefficients ranged from .68 to .93 for individual Sound Classes and from .89 to .95 for Initial Position Phonemes, Final Position Phonemes, and the Overall score. Additional analysis revealed that 20 (of 72) of the reported alpha coefficients for individual ages at the Sound Class level fell below .70. The test author suggested that a ceiling effect may have impacted Sound Class scores and that test users should report confidence intervals when reporting those scores. Overall the test developer reported strong evidence of internal consistency for the GDAP.

Test-retest reliability was assessed with 61 children and an average interval between test sessions of 8 days. Corrected correlations ranged from .95 to .99 for Sound Classes, Initial Position Phonemes, Final Position Phonemes, and the Overall score. No significant differences in mean scores were observed at the Sound Class level, Initial Position Phonemes, Final Position Phonemes, or Overall score, suggesting temporal stability of GDAP scores. Using correlational analyses, the test developer demonstrated that computer and paper administrations correlated between .94 and .99 for individual Sound Classes, Initial Position Phonemes, Final Position Phonemes, and the Overall score. The test authors compared scores calculated from the Phonemic Inventory with administration scores, finding that Phonemic Inventory scores predicted 88.4% of test item scores with a range between 66.5% and 98.5%. Additionally, correlations and mean comparisons between predicted GDAP scores based on Phonemic Inventory performance and observed GDAP scores yielded correlation coefficients that ranged from .73 to .99 with nearly perfect effect sizes. It is suggested that the Phonemic Inventory does a fair job of predicting what items on the GDAP to administer. It is this reviewer's recommendation that examiner judgment be used when attempting to fairly and thoroughly assess student mastery of individual sounds when using the Phonemic Inventory as a predictor. In summary, it appears from the reliability metrics applied that scores generated by the GDAP are relatively stable, reliable, and consistent across ages using either paper or computer administration.

The test author provided four types of validity evidence. The first, content, was well represented by the consistent and clear test instructions, number of phonemes and phoneme classes assessed, variety of item complexity, and age ranges assessed. Criterion evidence was also examined. Based upon discrimination values, it appeared that the GDAP sufficiently diagnosed speech sound disorders without results being used as criterion cutoffs. An additional form of validity evidence consisted of comparing the GDAP to another assessment of speech sound production, specifically the Goldman-Fristoe Test of Articulation, Third Edition (GFTA-3; 20:96). Correlation coefficients were statistically significant with a large effect size and a significant difference in means. Thus, the GDAP and GFTA-3 appear to assess related, but different, articulation and phonology skills. The final evaluation of validity involved correlating raw score performance with chronological age to assess the underlying assessment construct. These correlation coefficients were statistically significant with moderate to large effect sizes. Thus, the GDAP appears to provide a useful measure of articulation and phonological weaknesses in children.

COMMENTARY AND SUMMARY. The Glaspey Dynamic Assessment of Phonology (GDAP) is an individually administered dynamic assessment of speech sound production and speech adaptability for children ages 3:0 to 10:11. Its purpose is to evaluate current correct speech sound production as well as to assess potential for learning using assistance, cues, and scaffolding to plan for improved individualized intervention. The scoring form allows for scoring correct production of a single item at the levels of isolation, word, sentence, and connected speech with varied degrees of stimulability support. Overall the test developer reported strong evidence of internal consistency and evidence of validity indicating that GDAP scores provide valid measures of the skills assessed. This reviewer recommends using examiner judgment to assess mastery of individual sounds when using the Phonemic Inventory as a predictor.

REVIEWER'S REFERENCES

Glaspey, A. M. (2012). Stimulability measures and dynamic assessment of speech adaptability. *Perspectives on Language Learning and Education, 19,* 12-18.

Glaspey, A. M., & MacLeod, A. A. N. (2010). A multi-dimensional approach to gradient change in phonological acquisition: A case study of disordered speech development. *Clinical Linguistics & Phonetics, 24,* 283-299. doi:10.3109/02699200903581091

Glaspey, A. M., & Stoel-Gammon, C. (2005). Dynamic assessment in phonological disorders: The Scaffolding Scale of Stimulability. *Topics in Language Disorders, 25*(3), 220-230.

Glaspey, A. M., & Stoel-Gammon, C. (2007). A dynamic approach to phonological assessment. *Advances in Speech-Language Pathology, 9*(4), 286-296.

Gómez-Benito, J., Hidalgo, M. D., & Padilla, J. L. (2009). Efficacy of effect size measures in logistic regression: An application for detecting DIF. *Methodology, 5*(1), 18-25. doi:10.1027/1614-2241.5.1.18

MacLeod, A. A. N., & Glaspey, A. M. (2014). A multidimensional view of gradient change in velar acquisition in three-year-olds receiving phonological treatment. *Clinical Linguistics & Phonetics, 28*(9), 664-681. doi:10.3109/02699206.2013.878855

Vygotsky, L. S. (1978). *Mind in society: The development of higher psychological processes.* (M. Cole, V. John-Steiner, S. Schribner, & E. Souberman, Eds.). Cambridge, MA: Harvard University Press.

Review of the Glaspey Dynamic Assessment of Phonology by RHEA PAUL, Professor and Chair, Department of Communication Disorders, Sacred Heart University, Fairfield, CT:

DESCRIPTION. The Glaspey Dynamic Assessment of Phonology (GDAP) is designed to assess children's current speech sound production and potential for learning new sounds and sound patterns. The test kit contains a stimulus book with simple pictures and detailed instructions for assessing each target word in a variety of linguistic contexts (single word, phrase, sentence, connected speech), an administration manual with detailed instructions and psychometric information, and test forms in a canvas carrying case. Target words include a range of speech sounds (e.g., glides, nasals, stops, velars) in both initial and final positions. The assessment can take from 5 to 80 minutes to administer, depending on the child's level of language, and it is appropriate for children ages 3:0 through 10:11. Scores are calculated for each sound type and for each position (initial, final) as well as overall. Standard scores, percentile ranks, and reliable change index values that reflect a significant increase in scores between two test administrations are provided.

DEVELOPMENT. Test development is described in detail in the administration manual. Careful attention has been paid to the choice of target words for testing and to the sequence of prompts to be presented. There is not a strongly established research literature for the decisions made; rather, they are based primarily on clinical experience. A few words might not meet the stated standard of being identifiable in pictures by an average 3-year-old. However, if the child cannot name a picture independently, the procedures call for the examiner to say the target word and ask the child to repeat it.

The unique aspect of the GDAP is its use of dynamic assessment, which involves not only asking a child to produce a particular sound, syllable, or word to name a picture (static assessment), but also providing, in cases when the child is unable to produce the target correctly, several levels of prompting in an attempt to elicit the form. A hierarchy of prompts—from independent production to modeling, prolongation/segmentation, and tactile cues—is provided for each sound in each context. Administration is guided by graphically presented instructions in the stimulus manual that lay out the sequence of prompts, subsequent stimuli, and point value for every sound and pattern tested. This method expands the traditional concept of stimulability to yield a gradient of 15 points that represent the number of prompts provided to the child to produce the target sound in the most complex linguistic environment of which she or he is capable. The higher the number of points, the greater the level of prompting required; thus, higher numerical scores indicate less accurate and independent function. The administration manual provides a thoughtful discussion of dynamic assessment and explains both how and why it applies to the testing of speech sound production.

TECHNICAL. The assessment's psychometric properties are discussed in the administration manual. Item difficulty and item discrimination indices are provided, which substantiate the sequence of presentation of prompts. Differential item functioning, as a source of potential bias, was investigated and determined to be negligible, suggesting the test is relatively unbiased regarding gender, ethnic, and geographic diversity. The test was standardized on a sample (N = 880) that approximated demographically the distribution of the 2010 U.S. Census.

Internal consistency estimates of reliability (coefficient alpha) averaged across ages ranged from .68 to .95. Temporal stability (test-retest reliability) was at or above .95 for all ages over a 1- to 21-day interval (average of 8 days). Stability of scores on paper versus computer administration were in the same range. Standard errors of measurement (*SEM*s) and confidence intervals at each age are provided for each sound class and position. *SEM*s for Sound Class scores ranged from 0.38 to 2.56 and were higher for Initial and Final Position Phonemes (2.12 to 7.50) and for the Overall score (1.59 to 5.08).

Several forms of validity evidence are reported. The administration manual cites measures of item difficulty, item discrimination, item reliability, and differential item functioning as evidence of content validity. Diagnostic accuracy was evaluated by reporting specificity (ranging from 0.80 to 1.00) and sensitivity (ranging from 0.08 to .77) for specific standard scores and by plotting receiver operating characteristic (ROC) curves. Area under the curve (AUC) measurements based on these plots revealed an overall value of .88 with diagnostic accuracy for individual ages ranging from .85 to .93. These values are typically considered in the "good" to "excellent" range. Positive and negative predictive power values also were reported. Criterion-related validity was assessed by comparing the GDAP Overall score to the Sounds in Words score on the Goldman-Fristoe Test of Articulation, Third Edition. Correlation coefficients were .60 and .67 (uncorrected and corrected, respectively), which are considered "large." These measures would appear to substantiate the GDAP's utility as a measure of speech sound production.

In addition to reporting the psychometric properties described above, the administration manual does an especially good job of explaining, in clear and simple terms, the meaning of each statistic and how it is calculated. This information can serve as a comprehensible introduction or a quick refresher on the interpretation and significance of test properties in general, in addition to supporting the strengths of this particular test.

COMMENTARY. The advantage of this form of testing is that it provides a much richer level of information about the child's strengths and needs. Results provide clear guidance for developing an intervention approach that will meet the child at his or her current level of functioning and will provide the appropriate level of support to promote growth to the next level. Dynamic assessment is considered especially valuable in assessing children from culturally and linguistically different (CLD) backgrounds (e.g., Orellana, Wada, & Gillam, 2019) in that it evaluates the child's ability to learn language skills rather than what she or he already knows. Given the large number of children in U.S. schools who come from CLD backgrounds, the GDAP serves as a useful alternative to more traditional articulation tests for children for whom English is not their first language. (Examinees must, however, be proficient in English.) As might be expected, though, this method of testing requires more skill and training for the examiner than more traditional articulation tests that simply require the child to name a picture and the examiner to score the production as right or wrong. Although instruction for using the system of prompts is provided in both the administration manual and in the stimulus book, it is difficult to gain an adequate understanding of how the prompting hierarchy was used during test administration without studying the video provided on the test publisher's website. Even then, it would take multiple practice administrations for an examiner to feel confident in using the prompt hierarchy accurately, reliably, and smoothly.

SUMMARY. The GDAP is a carefully developed and well-constructed test of child speech sound production that meets contemporary standards for test quality. Its use of a dynamic assessment approach has advantages in providing not only information about the child's errors in production, but also information about how to effectively stimulate correct production in a therapy program by virtue of examining speech sounds in a range of increasingly complex linguistic contexts. Compared to a more static assessment, this more elaborate form of testing does require more training and practice on the part of the examiner in order to administer it effectively.

REVIEWER'S REFERENCE

Orellana, C. I., Wada, R., & Gillam, R. B. (2019). The use of dynamic assessment for the diagnosis of language disorders in bilingual children: A meta-analysis. *American Journal of Speech-Language Pathology, 28,* 1298-1317. https://doi.org/10.1044/2019_AJSLP-18-0202

[70]

Goldman-Fristoe Test of Articulation–Third Edition, Spanish.

Purpose: Designed "to measure the speech sound abilities in the area of articulation in Spanish-speaking children, adolescents, and young adults."
Population: Ages 2-0 through 21-11.
Publication Date: 2017.
Acronym: GFTA-3 Spanish.
Scores, 6: Total scores in two sections: Sonidos-en-palabras, Sonidos-en-oraciones; 4 supplemental measures: Phonetic Error Analysis, Vowel Error Observations, Intelligibility, Estimulación de consonants y sínfones.
Administration: Individual.
Parts, 2: Sonidos-en-palabras (all ages), Sonidos-en-oraciones (ages 4-0 through 21-11).
Price Data, 2020: $348 per kit including manual (2017, 253 pages), stimulus book, and 25 record forms; $243.80 per stimulus book (print or digital); $119 per manual (print or digital); $65 per 25 record forms; $35 per 1-year online score report subscription; $1.55 per individual online score report.
Time: 13 minutes, on average, to administer Sonidos-en-palabras; 14 minutes to administer Sonidos-en-oraciones.
Comments: The GFTA-3 Spanish is the first edition of the GFTA in Spanish; administrators must have native or near native proficiency in Spanish; online administration and scoring available; the English edition (GFTA-3; 20:96) should be used when examining individuals whose primary language is English.
Authors: Ronald Goldman and Macalyne Fristoe.
Publisher: Pearson.

Review of the Goldman-Fristoe Test of Articulation—Third Edition, Spanish by REBECCA J. McCAULEY, Professor, Department of Speech and Hearing Science, The Ohio State University, Columbus, OH:

DESCRIPTION. The Goldman-Fristoe Test of Articulation—Third Edition, Spanish (GFTA-3 Spanish) includes two brief, individually administered tests for examining speech sound production skills—one using individual words (Sonidos-en-palabras) and the other, connected speech (Sonidos-en-oraciones). Despite its description as a third edition, this test is actually the first measure designed by these authors for Spanish-speaking examinees. Materials consist of a test manual (written primarily in English), a stimulus book, and a protocol that serves as a record form for both Sonidos-en-palabras and Sonidos-en-oraciones. The manual is thorough and easy to read. The stimulus book contains pictures for eliciting 50 words (Sonidos-en-palabras) as well as two sets of picture stimuli for eliciting connected speech (Sonidos-en-oraciones). The two stories used in Sonidos-en-oraciones differ in visual style and phonemic content to be appropriate for children ages 4:0 to 6:11 and individuals from 7:0 to 21:11. Digital options are available for both tests. Words and picture stimuli were selected so that they would be known and used by speakers from a variety of regions and cultural backgrounds and probably would *not* be associated with regional variations in pronunciation or word choice.

The test authors list several purposes for the GFTA-3 Spanish: identification of a speech sound disorder; examination of consonant singletons, /r/ and /l/ clusters, and vowels; comparison of productions in single words versus connected speech; rating of intelligibility; use in determining eligibility for services; treatment planning; and progress monitoring. For all of these uses, potential users are advised to interpret test results in conjunction with results from other tools to provide a more comprehensive basis for decision making. Each test is estimated to take 13-14 minutes to administer, with longer times for younger children. The GFTA-3 Spanish should be administered, scored, and interpreted by Spanish-speaking speech-language pathologists (SLPs), with "native or near native proficiency in Spanish" (manual, p. 5). Standard scores, percentile ranks, age equivalent scores, and growth scale curves are used, as appropriate, to report results of the Sonidos-en-palabras for ages 2:0 to 21:11 and of Sonidos-en-oraciones for ages 4:0 to 21:11.

DEVELOPMENT. Although the test shares the name of a well-known and widely used test for American English speech production, items for the GFTA-3 Spanish were developed independently. After surveying SLPs from the United States and Puerto Rico, test developers created items that were then reviewed by customers and experts for content and potential bias. An initial pilot study to look at a very early version of the test was conducted in San Antonio, Texas, using 34 bilingual or monolingual Spanish speakers in three age groups—2:0 to 3:11, 5:0 to 5:11, and 7:0 to 17:11—all from homes in which caregivers were born in Mexico, the Caribbean, or other region (South America, Central America, other). The pilot study helped identify target words and stories, stimulus representational formats (realistic versus cartoon), and specific instructions for a tryout version of the two tests. The actual test tryout, designed to finalize the selection of single word and story items, was conducted with a sample of 262 individuals, ages 2:0 to 6:11 and 7:11 to 21:11, who were fluent Spanish speakers from the U.S. and Puerto Rico but with parents coming from a variety of Hispanic countries. Prior to participating in the item tryout, examiners were screened for Spanish language skills and knowledge of the Spanish phonological system. In addition to the final selection of items, results of the tryout led to the selection of specific error analyses incorporated in the final standardization research study and the final versions of test materials.

TECHNICAL.

Normative data. The standardization sample consisted of 860 bilingual or monolingual speakers fluent in Spanish, with additional individuals used for validity and reliability studies. Norms for Sonidos-en-palabras were based on performances of individuals from 2:0 to 21:11, whereas those for Sonidos-en-oraciones were based on performances of individuals 4:0 to 21:11. At least 100 individuals were included in each 12-month age interval between 2:0 and 7:11 and for each 24-month interval between ages 8:0 to 12:11. Ninety-one individuals were studied for the development of norms for ages 13:0 to 21:11.

Participants in the standardization sample were described as speaking a wide variety of Spanish dialects, with participants living in the United States, Puerto Rico, and Mexico. Education, race/ethnicity, and geographic region were reported for the standardization sample as a whole, but no comparison of these data to broader U.S. Hispanic demographics was offered. Therefore, it is hard to determine whether the sample is representative of the larger population. The standardization data were used to conduct a final item analysis that included examination of item difficulty, discrimination, differential item functioning, ease and reliability of scoring, and examiners' feedback to arrive at the final composition of the Sonidos-en-palabras and Sonidos-en-oraciones tests. These several studies constitute a very serious program of test development.

Reliability. For Sonidos-en-palabras, internal consistency was examined using data from the entire standardization sample. For Sonidos-en-oraciones, internal consistency was examined separately for participants ages 4:0 to 6:11 and 7:0 to 21:11 because of their different, age-appropriate elicitation stimuli. Resulting reliability coefficients and standard errors of measurement (*SEMs*) were reported by age and gender and reached levels generally regarded as good to excellent. For Sonidos-en-palabras, alpha coefficients ranged from .78 to .98 across genders and age intervals. *SEMs* ranged from 2.12 to 7.04 and overall were 4.48 and 4.30 for females and males, respectively. For Sonidos-en-oraciones, alpha coefficients ranged from .77 to .95 across genders and age intervals. *SEMs* ranged from 3.35 to 7.19 and overall were 4.92 and 4.44 for females and males, respectively.

Test-retest reliability was examined by having 80 individuals, ages 2:6 to 7:11 (mean age = 4.2 years with 43 males and 37 females), retake the test, on average within 2-3 days of their initial test. The reliability coefficient for Sonidos-en-palabras was .93 for participants ages 2:6 to 7:11 and for Sonidos-en-oraciones was .85 for participants ages 4:0 to 7:11. Although the first of these coefficients surpasses the .90 level usually recommended for tests of speech sound disorders (e.g., Flipsen & Ogiela, 2015), the second approaches, but does not meet the criterion. Data were provided about the total sample's composition in terms of race and parent education. However, data were not provided in terms of dialect, and it is unclear how many individuals were studied at each age level—unfortunate omissions given the specificity of reliability data to the sample on which it is obtained.

Validity. Validity evidence was drawn both from studies specifically conducted to provide such evidence as well as from the series of initial studies used to arrive at the test's final form. The test manual describes steps taken during the development of the test to ensure content relevance and coverage and avoid bias, thereby providing validity evidence based on content. In addition, the test manual points to evidence suggesting that the scores for both tests perform as expected when age differentiation is examined using both total raw scores as well as scores related to selected individual sounds for which there are relatively language-independent expectations of earlier versus later acquisition.

For 29 typically developing children (ages 3:0 to 7:11), scores on Sonidos-en-palabras items were compared to scores on a similar Spanish-language test, the Articulation Screener of the Preschool Language Scales–Fifth Edition Spanish (Zimmerman, Steiner, & Pond, 2012). The moderate positive correlation coefficient (.70, corrected; correction not specified) that was obtained provided further empirical evidence of validity, as did results from a study of 34 Hispanic individuals (ages 4:0 to 8:11) with diagnosed speech sound disorder (SSD) whose performances were compared to matched controls without that diagnosis. The relatively high sensitivity (.88) and specificity (.91) values obtained from these data at a cut score 1 standard deviation below the mean suggest that the Sonidos-en-palabras test performs well both in terms of correctly identifying the disorder status of children with SSD as well as those without. One concern, however, is that all except one of the children in the SSD group had been diagnosed with an articulation, rather than phonological, disorder. Thus, this evidence is more supportive of the validity of the test for this subgroup than for the subgroup of children with a phonological SSD, which is a smaller, but usually more broadly affected, subgroup.

COMMENTARY. The GFTA-3 Spanish is a brief and easy-to-administer test designed to help meet the important need for valid methods of identifying speech sound impairments in individuals who speak Spanish, either mono- or bilingually. Normative data were provided for individuals for two tests—one using single words, with norms from 2:0 to 21:11, and the other using connected speech, with norms for ages 4:0 to 21:11. Internal validity seemed good for both as did test-retest reliability, with the limitation that the latter data were obtained for age ranges that stopped at 7:11, despite the wide age range for which the test was intended. Considerable content and other evidence was offered for validity, including extensive item analyses and a study of age differentiation; however, concurrent validity evidence was limited to the test that used single words for a similarly limited age group. Therefore, the GFTA-3 Spanish provides strongest support for the use of Sonidos-en-palabras for children between the ages of 2:0 and 7:11. Further, lack of detailed information about the regional dialects and monolingual versus bilingual status found in the different normative subgroups and in the other psychometric data suggest that individual clinicians should inspect test stimuli closely to determine whether the test is likely to be useful for the individuals they serve. Norm-referenced tests for preschoolers and young school-age children that might be considered as competitors can be identified in McLeod and Verdon (2014) or McLeod (2012).

SUMMARY. In summary, with its two tests (Sonidos-en-palabras and Sonidos-en-oraciones), the GFTA-3 Spanish presents a valuable addition to the relatively small group of tests that can be used to evaluate speech sound production abilities of Spanish-speaking monolingual and bilingual children and adults. Nonetheless, further evidence of reliability and validity is needed, and clinicians will particularly want to inspect the test's content for congruence with the dialect of the individuals they serve.

REVIEWER'S REFERENCES

Flipsen, P., Jr., & Ogiela, D. A. (2015). Psychometric characteristics of single-word tests of children's speech sound production. *Language, Speech, and Hearing Services in Schools, 46*, 166-178.

McLeod, S. (2012). *Multilingual speech assessments*. Bathurst, NSW, Australia: Charles Sturt University. Retrieved from http://www.csu.edu.au/research/multilingual-speech/speech-assessments

McLeod, S., & Verdon, S. (2014). A review of 30 speech assessments in 19 languages other than English. *American Journal of Speech-Language Pathology, 23*, 708-723.

Zimmerman, I. L., Steiner, V. G., & Pond, R. E. (2012). Preschool Language Scales—Fifth Edition Spanish. Bloomington, MN: Pearson.

[71]

Hardiness Resilience Gauge.

Purpose: Designed to assess an individual's "ability to cope with stress and unexpected situations" across settings.
Population: Ages 18 and older.
Publication Date: 2018.
Acronym: HRG.
Scores, 4: Challenge, Control, Commitment, Total Hardiness.
Administration: Individual.
Restricted Distribution: Certification or pre-qualification required.
Price Data: Available from publisher.
Time: 5-10 minutes for completion.
Comments: Administered and scored online.
Author: Paul T. Bartone.
Publisher: Multi-Health Systems, Inc.

Review of the Hardiness Resilience Gauge by JANET HOUSER, Provost and Professor, and MICHAEL CAHILL, Assistant Provost, Regis University, Denver, CO:

DESCRIPTION. The Hardiness Resilience Gauge (HRG) is an online tool designed to measure the capability of an individual to cope with stress. The outcome is a normalized set of scores from which an administrator can provide an interpretation and development plan for the respondent.

The test author suggests that the HRG may be used with a variety of populations. Examples of workplace use include employee selection, employee development, and identifying those in need of early intervention for occupational stress. The author notes the tool also may be used with students and athletes ages 18 and older. The HRG is not intended as a sole instrument from which to base decisions. Rather, the HRG should be a complement to other methods of evaluation, such as interviews and observation.

The HRG is administered online via the test publisher's web portal. Respondents are notified via an email triggered by the test administrator. Completion of the instrument is reported to take 5-10 minutes. The tool is made up of 28 items that measure three areas used to predict an individual's resilience: Challenge is defined as "seeing change and new experiences as exciting opportunities to learn and develop"; Control is "belief in one's ability to control or influence events and outcomes"; and Commitment is "a tendency to see the world and day-to-day activities as interesting, meaningful, and having purpose" (online user's handbook, "What Does the HRG Measure?"). These three subscales are aggregated into a Total Hardiness score.

Results are generated via the administrator's web portal account, and reports include detailed scoring of the three subcategories as well as the Total Hardiness score. It is highly recommended that the administrator not simply provide the report to the examinee, but rather guide the respondent through the results and interpretation.

DEVELOPMENT. This is the first iteration of the Hardiness Resilience Gauge (HRG). The HRG was initially conceptualized as a doctoral research effort that resulted in 1984 in the Dispositional Resilience Scale (DRS), a 76-item hardiness assessment. The DRS was refined four times based on psychometric analysis, including reliability analysis, item-scale correlations, and factor analysis. These revisions resulted in a 15-item assessment across three subscales of Challenge, Control, and Commitment that was the foundation of the HRG.

The HRG was derived as an effort to improve upon the DRS. Specifically, three goals were addressed to create the HRG. First, although the DRS had acceptable internal consistency reliability, there was a desire to improve overall reliability. This need was accomplished by including additional items. Additional items also helped to measure the hardiness subscales more precisely. A second goal was to ensure the construct measured was theoretically intended, specifically in the Challenge scale. To achieve both goals, 21 additional items were added to the instrument, and seven of the original 15 items were modified. The third goal was to collect data from a large representative sample to enable comparison of individual scores with those from a general population. These 36 items were administered to a sample of 2,016 respondents, primarily to assess the three subscales and to ensure the most psychometrically sound items were retained. The test manual does not identify how the respondents were recruited. The test author considered response distribution, item-total correlation, confirmatory factor analysis results, and item-response theory analysis as criteria for psychometric appropriateness. After applying these criteria, 28 items were selected for the final HRG.

TECHNICAL. Test developers screened the data collected from 2,016 respondents for patterns of inconsistency or questionable validity and excluded a number of respondents. From those that remained, the normative sample (*N* = 1,500) was selected to match within 1% of 2016 U.S. Census values for race/ethnicity and geographic region and was equally proportioned across five age groups by gender. Education and employment status varied across the sample. Descriptive data about the sample's gender, age, racial/ethnic groups, geographic region, education level, and employment status are provided in the user manual.

The test author provides evidence of strong internal reliability, with a coefficient alpha measurement for Total Hardiness of .93. The three subscales of Challenge, Control, and Commitment had alpha reliability coefficients of .85, .84, and .89, respectively, all seen as acceptable to these reviewers (Shultz, Whitney, & Zickar, 2014). Evidence for consistency of scores over time was analyzed based on 168 individuals tested 2 to 4 weeks following the initial assessment. The test-retest correlation for Total Hardiness was reported as a Pearson rho coefficient of .81; the subscales of Challenge, Control, and Commitment yielded coefficients of .80, .74, and .79, respectively, all believed by these reviewers as within acceptable ranges.

Evidence of the author's assessment of validity is provided. The author assessed the scale structure and correlation of the HRG with other theoretical associations. Confirmatory factor analysis was conducted using data from the normative sample. The author tested the expected hierarchical model of factors, a one-factor model, and a three-factor model. The three-factor model was rotated and reported as a three-factor orthogonal model. All three models yielded a significant chi-square association; however, the one-factor alternative model and the hierarchical model resulted in a CFI of .96 and .98, respectively, whereas the three-factor alternative model had a CFI of .53. A CFI greater than .90 is generally accepted as appropriate model fit. The hierarchical HRG model resulted in a root mean squared error of approximation (RMSEA) of 0.08, whereas the one-factor alternative and three-factor alternative resulted in an RMSEA of 0.10 and 0.38, respectively. A smaller RMSEA (i.e., 0.05 to 0.08), generally is considered an indication of acceptable fit (Shultz, Whitney, & Zickar, 2014). It would appear, then, that the validity of the subscales is strongly fit to the theoretical constructs; the rotated analysis assuming no correlation, on the other hand, is not a fit. This finding provides construct evidence of the validity of the instrument.

The test author further used parallel measures to gather criterion-related evidence of validity. The HRG was correlated with accepted measures of coping styles, burnout, satisfaction, challenging situations, and work-related outcomes. Correlations ranged from medium to large and were strongest between the HRG and life/relationship satisfaction measures (*r* = .32 to .56) and the HRG and assessments of the ability to thrive, overcome, and cope with difficult situations (*r* = .38 to .58).

Despite the recommended use with potential employees, no predictive evidence of validity was provided.

COMMENTARY. The HRG appears to be a reliable and valid measure of an individual's hardiness and resilience. Extensive refinement and testing over three decades has produced a breadth of data about the instrument development process and its psychometric evaluation. Scoring is automated, although it is strongly suggested that a facilitator receive training to successfully prepare, evaluate, and follow-up with a respondent. The norms were developed using a group that was diverse in terms of race/ethnicity and gender. Caution should be given to applying results of the assessment to individuals outside the United States due to the derivation of the normative samples to match the U.S. Census.

The HRG could be useful for inferential research, sequential testing, individual development, and creating interventions to promote hardiness. It is strongly suggested that the HRG be used as part of a broader engagement with individuals and to plan out the purpose of the engagement. The test author points out that the HRG is not useful for diagnosis of clinical conditions, and these reviewers agree with this conclusion. There is inadequate predictive evidence of validity to suggest its use for employee selection.

SUMMARY. The HRG was designed to measure hardiness and resilience for individuals in high-stress occupations or circumstances. Its rigorous development and strong validity indicators support its use for these purposes. The test meets its goal of measuring how individuals respond to challenge, control, and commitment. The administration manual is thorough and well-constructed, although it does require some persistence to find and match results with narrative. The manual gives a step-by-step interpretation guide. This measure is overall a strong instrument that has been rigorously tested for reliability and validity, enabling confident use by researchers and organizations.

REVIEWERS' REFERENCE

Shultz, K. S., Whitney, D. J., & Zickar, M. J. (2014). *Measurement theory in action: Case studies and exercises* (2nd ed.). New York, NY: Routledge/Taylor & Francis.

Review of the Hardiness Resilience Gauge by JEAN POWELL KIRNAN, Professor of Psychology, The College of New Jersey, Ewing, NJ, and NINA E. VENTRESCO, Graduate Student, Lehigh University, Bethlehem, PA:

DESCRIPTION. The Hardiness Resilience Gauge (HRG) is a measure of an "individual's level of hardiness and their ability to cope with stressful and unexpected situations" (Bartone, 2018). The instrument yields a Total Hardiness score and subscale scores for the three key characteristics that hardy people possess: Control, Commitment, and Challenge.

The HRG is primarily used to (a) identify individuals who possess hardiness in recruitment and selection contexts, and (b) foster hardiness in coaching and training contexts.

According to the HRG author, this versatile instrument is especially appropriate for use in settings defined by stress or uncertain circumstances (e.g., health, military, law enforcement). Administration is online, requiring about 5 to 10 minutes; the interface is clean, and user instructions are straightforward. Using a 4-point Likert scale (ranging from *not at all true* to *completely true*), respondents indicate the degree to which each of 28 statements is descriptive of themselves. The majority of the items are positively worded, which can potentially lead to a response set of acquiescence. There is no method included to detect intentional or unintentional dishonesty in responding.

Score reports are available for download almost immediately. In addition to one's scores, the nine-page report contains information about the construct of hardiness and discrepancies between one's various scores (deemed "balance"), as well as individualized strategies for developing one's hardiness, balancing one's hardiness scores, and promoting hardiness in others. The final two pages of the report provide worksheets for personal development such as using hardiness to improve leadership and creating SMART (specific, measurable, achievable, relevant, time bound) goals to develop hardiness. A welcome addition to the manual would be sample reports showing various hardiness profiles as well as sample development plans.

DEVELOPMENT. Formerly known as the Dispositional Resilience Scale (DRS), the HRG has been adapted several times over the course of 30 years. The development section of the test manual focuses somewhat narrowly on this evolution, and would benefit from additional description of the tool's theoretical underpinnings. For example, the test author notes that hardiness was first conceptualized by Kobasa (1979), but neglects to discuss that the three components of the HRG were determined by Kobasa and colleagues and have empirical support.

The instrument's current revision was conducted with specific goals relative to its immediate predecessor, the 15-item DRS. These goals focused on (a) adding items to improve the reliability of the subscales and more thoroughly assess the constructs, (b) strengthening the construct evidence of validity of the Challenge subscale, and (c) obtaining a normative sample representative of the general population.

During this process, certain DRS items were modified and 21 new items were added, yielding an instrument with 36 items. Statistical analyses using response distributions, item-total correlations, factor analysis, and item response theory reduced the number of items to the 28 in the current HRG (i.e., 10 Challenge, 10 Commitment, and eight Control items). The test manual would benefit from additional detail describing how new items were generated and which specific statistical criteria were applied for item retention decisions. The item generation and selection process, as presently described, could have been more thorough. For example, it may have been beneficial to have subject matter experts (external to the development team) review the proposed items and/or match them to their assigned constructs.

TECHNICAL. In 2018, a normative sample was recruited consisting of 1,500 adults in the United States, stratified to model the 2016 U.S. Census (age, gender, race/ethnicity, and region). The recruitment process is not explained. The test publisher provides information on the distribution of the sample across education and employment levels, but the sample was not stratified for education. If the measure was completed online, the sample may not represent the population on other characteristics, such as socioeconomic status (SES).

All four HRG scales are reported as standardized scores with a mean of 100 and a standard deviation of 15. Behavioral examples are provided for low scores (< 90) and high scores (> 110), but not for mid-range scores (90-110). These cutoffs are based on quartiles derived from the normative sample with the bottom 25% scoring < 90, the middle 50% scoring from 90 to 110, and the top 25% scoring > 110. Reportedly, it is best if all three component scores are in the mid- to high range and in balance with each other. Balance is defined as no more than a 10-point difference in subscale scores. However, no empirical evidence is provided to support this interpretation.

Reliability was evaluated using both internal consistency and test-retest methods. Strong evidence of internal consistency was demonstrated with coefficient alpha values of .93 for Total Hardiness and .85, .84, and .89 for the subscales of Challenge, Control, and Commitment, respectively. Test-retest reliability was calculated from a subset of 168 respondents who took the HRG a second time 2 to 4 weeks after the initial administration (a relatively short time period). Moderate evidence was found with a coefficient of .81 for the Total score and .80, .74, and .79 for the subscales of Challenge, Control, and Commitment, respectively. The reliability findings affirm one of the goals in revising the instrument as the earlier scales reported substantially lower reliability coefficients for both methods (Bartone, 2007; Windle, Bennett, & Noyes, 2011).

The majority of the validity evidence for the HRG focused on the demonstration of construct-related evidence. Factor analysis confirmed the hierarchical factor structure of the three components of Challenge, Control, and Commitment. Additional construct evidence was provided by comparing the HRG with other psychological measures. Overall, the HRG demonstrated expected positive correlations with measures of coping, efficacy, and satisfaction and expected negative correlations with traits such as cynicism and burnout.

Positive correlations are also reported with responses to challenging situations (defined as thriving, overcoming, and coping) and job success in an attempt at demonstrating criterion-related evidence of validity. However, none of these criteria was independently obtained; instead, they were self-reported by the respondents. Additionally, the criteria were each measured using a single Likert scale item. These criteria could be improved through the use of actual behaviors, supervisor/peer ratings, or established scales rather than relying on self-report to single items. This procedure is especially problematic for the correlation with job success, which some might interpret as demonstrating sufficient evidence for the use of the HRG in personnel decisions. Correlating a self-report of hardiness with a self-report of job success does not meet appropriate standards for use as a selection, placement, or promotion tool.

The test author claims that the HRG has "cross-cultural applicability and utility" because the normative sample matched U.S. Census data, and, "Earlier versions of the HRG have been used successfully in multiple countries" (Bartone, 2018). This claim is dangerous, as there is no evidence to suggest that the normative sample for the HRG included international participants or non-English speakers. Although earlier versions of the measure were used in other countries, evidence of this use is not provided, nor can test users assume the new measure will retain any cross-cultural properties.

The use of measures in the workplace whether for selecting, training, or development should be reviewed for differences across various marginalized or legally protected groups. Comparison of mean scores showed that neither racial minorities nor women are negatively impacted by the HRG. Using Cohen's *d*, the only meaningful difference between Caucasian and Hispanic scores is found for the Challenge subscale, where Hispanics score higher. A comparison of Black and Caucasian respondents revealed small differences for Total Hardiness, Control, and Commitment, and a medium difference for Challenge, with Black respondents consistently scoring higher. No gender differences in any scores were found. Thus, the use of the HRG will not exclude individuals from these protected groups and may in fact favor racial minorities. Due to the lack of group mean differences, the test author determined that separate norm data would not be needed to interpret scores.

COMMENTARY. The HRG is a quick, user-friendly measure of an individual's ability to handle stressful situations effectively. The instrument is grounded in theory and has a long history of development and improvement with ongoing research and revisions. This most recent revision made progress toward the stated goals related to the normative sample and improvements in reliability and construct-based validity, yet some areas of concern remain. Questions remain regarding the recruitment of the normative sample and its representativeness on certain variables (e.g., education, SES). Validity evidence could be improved with comparisons to other established measures of resilience or behavioral evidence of resilience rather than reliance on non-standardized measures and self-report. Documentation of test development and claims for cross-cultural applications are vague and seem to rely on evidence from earlier versions of the instrument.

SUMMARY. The HRG is a brief, straightforward measure of resilience, a trait that is critical for individuals who find themselves in stressful situations. The measure holds greatest promise for use in personal development, career counseling, training, and coaching. Its use as an adjunct tool in personnel decisions such as hiring and promotion cannot be recommended due to the lack of acceptable criterion-related evidence and the self-report nature and transparency of the measure.

REVIEWERS' REFERENCES

Bartone, P. T. (2007). Test-retest reliability of the Dispositional Resilience Scale-15, a brief hardiness scale. *Psychological Reports, 101*, 943-944.

Bartone, P.T. (2018). *Hardiness Resilience Gauge User's handbook* [digital]. Retrieved from MHS Assessments Talent Assessment Portal.

Kobasa, S. C. (1979). Stressful life events, personality, and health: An inquiry into hardiness. *Journal of Personality and Social Psychology, 37*, 1-11. doi:10.1037/0022-3514.37.1.1

Windle, G., Bennett, K. M., & Noyes, J. (2011). A methodological review of resilience measurement scales. *Health and Quality of Life Outcomes, 9*, 8.

[72]

HELP® 3–6 (2nd Edition).

Purpose: Designed as "a curriculum-based assessment" of developmental skills/behaviors for use in identifying "strengths and needs, and the services appropriate to meet those needs" as well as in documenting growth and progress, at home and in educational settings.
Population: Children ages 3-6 years.
Publication Dates: 1987-2010.
Scores: Item scores in 6 developmental areas: Cognitive, Language, Gross Motor, Fine Motor, Social, Self-Help.
Administration: Individual.
Price Data, 2020: $57.95 per Assessment Manual (2010, 400 pages); $62.95 per Activities at Home book; $39.95 per Curriculum Guide; $3.50 per charts; $3.50 per checklist; $3.50 per Assessment Strands; volume discounts available.
Time: Administration time not reported.
Comments: Adaptation of Behavioral Characteristics Progression (BCP; T9:234); upward extension of HELP Strands (Hawaii Early Learning Profile): Ages 0-3 (T9:930); "criterion-referenced"; formerly titled Help for Preschoolers.
Author: VORT Corporation.
Publisher: VORT Corporation.
Cross References: For reviews by Harlan J. Stientjes and Gerald Tindal of the original edition titled Help for Special Preschoolers Assessment Checklist: Ages 3-6 (1987) see 11:158.

No review available. This test does not meet review criteria established by the Buros Center for Testing that call for at least minimal technical and development information.

[73]

Hoffman Organicity Test.

Purpose: Designed "to determine the presence of organic brain disorder."
Population: Individuals thought to have a brain disorder.
Publication Dates: 1975-2016.
Acronym: HOT.
Scores: Total score only.
Administration: Individual.
Price Data, 2020: $109 per kit including digital manual (2016, 33 pages), printable design sheet, printable scoring sheet, and audio recording.
Time: Approximately 5 minutes for administration.
Author: Norman E. Hoffman.
Publisher: VG Press.

Review of the Hoffman Organicity Test by LEIGH J. BEGLINGER, Department of Adult Neuropsychology, St. Luke's Rehabilitation Hospital, Boise, ID:

DESCRIPTION. The Hoffman Organicity Test (HOT) is an individually administered screening test designed to differentiate organic brain disorders from non-organic disorders and schizophrenia. The original Hoffman Test for Organicity (HTO) was developed and copyrighted in 1975 by Norman Hoffman, PhD, and has undergone revisions in 1995 and 2016. The test author notes that it can be difficult to distinguish between psychotic behaviors stemming from organic illnesses and those associated with schizophrenia. The test is based on the premise that disorders of rhythm frequently occur with organic brain impairment. The test manual outlines three purposes of the test: to determine whether brain damage exists in a patient identified as psychotic; to differentiate organic and non-organic syndromes; and to serve as a valid diagnostic procedure to facilitate treatment for those with cerebral damage. The test is presented as a screening form to differentiate "organic from psychiatric patients" and to identify who would need referral for further assessment. Specifically, the HOT was designed to assess visual motor perception, recent memory recall, and associative integration.

The test requires the examinee to pair rhythmic patterns with geometric designs following a brief sample and learning demonstration (to ensure there is no auditory perceptual difficulty). There are 34 audio pattern items presented (four distinct rhythms paired with four pictures of shapes). The test takes 5 minutes to administer and is a revision of the previous HTO, which required 10 minutes and had both rhythm reproduction and shape pairings components utilizing actual instruments on a transportable apparatus. The revised version uses digital audio files on a flash drive. The test manual notes that a person's prior musical ability does not influence results of the test. A total score is obtained by summing the number of errors made during the test. A cutoff at 7 or higher indicates organic syndromes.

DEVELOPMENT. The HOT was developed based on the premise that organic syndromes disrupt a person's ability to perceive rhythm through any number of bodily systems, including speech, vision, and walking. These disruptions result in disability. The test author also indicates that many individuals with organic impairments are unable to tolerate a lengthy evaluation so he sought to create a short valid screening tool. The development of the original HTO was based on a sample of 221 participants matched by age and IQ. The participants were diagnosed by a psychiatrist, psychologist, or neurologist (the test manual does not state whether these diagnoses were independent from the study) with the following disorders: organic (n = 63), schizophrenia (n = 50), and non-organic with no known neurological or psychiatric disability (n = 108). The organic group scored highest, followed by individuals with schizophrenia; the non-organic group was the least impaired. A cutoff score between 6 and 7 was recommended with the most accurate predictions for individuals between 10 and 59 years of age. Test-retest reliability was assessed in 58 participants averaging a 2-week inter-test interval. Pearson correlation coefficients between the scores obtained for the two administrations were .92 for Part I and .96 for Part II. Fifty-seven of fifty-eight (98%) reached the same classification over the two administrations. In a validation study, the HTO correctly classified 25/25 in the organic group, 26/28 in the schizophrenia group, and 25/25 of the non-organic group.

The revision eliminates the rhythm reproduction component of the test on the apparatus, which was noted by users to be too noisy and bulky to use in clinical practice and as such was mainly used by music therapists. It is also noted that Part I of the test (rhythm reproduction) did not contribute meaningfully to the determination of organicity.

TECHNICAL.

Standardization. In the revised version of the HOT, the sample size was 44 individuals matched on age (n = 25 non-organic and n = 19 organic). Participants were drawn from several private practices in Florida, tested as outpatients and chosen for the organic group "with a definite diagnosis of organic brain syndrome" (manual, p. 13; no further details were given, other than the etiologies were unknown but it appears they had vascular and Alzheimer's dementia). Participants were not permitted to be taking any medications, so as to eliminate possible medication side effects.

Although the test author notes in the test manual that the disorders most commonly seen in psychiatric settings, and thus most geared for this type of screening task, are those associated with diffuse, progressive conditions such as arteriosclerosis, dementia, alcoholism, and cardiovascular insufficiency, the development sample appears to contain little breadth in terms of these specific diagnoses. Further, there is no information describing the sample, beyond a figure with ages grouped into three categories. At a minimum, a table with participants' age, gender, ethnicity/race and some disease characteristics would be helpful, especially if it included information such as diagnoses, number of years with the disease (severity), functional status, and so forth.

Reliability. Test-retest reliability was determined by administering the HOT to organic and non-organic groups 2-3 weeks apart. The groups were examined separately and together. Collapsed across groups, the correlation coefficient was high (r = .93). Similarly, the correlation coefficient for the organic group alone was high (r = .91), but only moderate in the non-organic group (r = .50).

Validity. Evidence of validity was demonstrated with concurrent evidence (comparing the HOT to the Bender Gestalt Test [BGT]) and construct evidence (examining group differences on the HOT and BGT). The Spearman rank correlation between the HOT and the BGT was .87 in the organic group and .11 in the non-organic group. For construct evidence, a Mann Whitney U test was used to assess the differences between the performance of the organic and the non-organic groups on the HOT and BGT. Both were significant at $p < .001$. There are no data presented that examine validity evidence of HOT scores across ages, genders, cultural groups, or diagnoses.

COMMENTARY. Strengths of the HOT include the novel approach to detection of disease through rhythm patterns and learning, short time and ease of administration, and that it appears to be a culture- and language-free instrument. Also, in the validation study the same examiner was used for all participants, the examiner was blind to the participant classification groups, and order of test administration between the HOT and BGT was counterbalanced.

Despite the above strengths, there are a number of significant weaknesses that raise concern about the usefulness of the HOT. First, the rationale for why such a test is needed is not convincing, and much of the information in the test manual appears outdated. Many of the references cited date to the 1960s and '70s, with none newer than the mid-1990s. The term *organicity* itself is no longer in favor, and it is unclear in what circumstances a provider would use this test. The test author indicates that impaired rhythmic functions indicate an organic disorder and not a psychiatric disorder without providing support from the current literature for this claim. As a counterpoint, there is now literature supporting neurological and structural abnormalities in individuals with schizophrenia. Second, the test author suggests the HOT can be used for a wide range of ages (early childhood to geriatric) without supporting evidence. As the test author points out, the development of the test was based on a small, non-randomized sample as a pilot project. Additionally, participants were eliminated if they were taking medication, which makes it unclear how the data would generalize to a clinical population. The test author notes that it is important to identify those with diffuse progressive conditions, such as vascular disease and those with alcohol-related impairments, but those patient populations were not necessarily included in the normative samples. Third, the test manual is poorly written and confusing. It is unclear whether the same cutoff is being used with the revision as in the original 1975 study. The test manual does not include the tables, figures, and some of the appendices, which are available by request from the test author. Even so, the test manual is still lacking in organization and would benefit from significant editing for completeness and ease of use. It is unclear why two pages out of the 21 comprising the test manual are devoted to lengthy discussion of the various scoring systems of the BGT. This space may have been better devoted to review of recent literature in clinical populations and developing a rationale for the HOT. Finally, the test author makes unfounded claims about how the HOT could be used to localize lesions, identify children early for intervention, and eliminate the need for lengthy neuropsychological testing.

SUMMARY. The HOT is a screening measure designed to differentiate organic brain disorders from non-organic disorders and schizophrenia. Although the test itself is novel and interesting and does appear to correlate well with the Bender Gestalt, it is significantly limited by a small sample size without necessary details about who comprises the sample, unconvincing rationale and clinical need for the test, and broad and unfounded claims about the validity of the measure and its potential for localization of brain impairment and use with both geriatric and early childhood patients. The test manual would benefit from a complete overhaul to include all tables and figures. In addition, it appears that the text has been assembled from other source documents and is confusing, and there are frank errors on the record form that need to be edited. There are no peer-reviewed publications using this measure to support or expand on what is provided in the test manual. In its current form, the HOT cannot be recommended for use. It is hoped that the author will address the test's weaknesses to determine whether sound pattern recognition and learning may be clinically useful and, if so, in which populations.

Review of the Hoffman Organicity Test by RICHARD RUTH, Associate Professor of Clinical Psychology, RUPA KALAHASTHI, Graduate Student in Clinical Psychology, and LILITH ANTINORI, Graduate Student in Clinical Psychology, The George Washington University, Washington, DC:

DESCRIPTION. The Hoffman Organicity Test (HOT) is a second, revised version of a test intended to "determine the presence of organic brain disorder" (manual, p. 5). It is specifically intended to help clinicians screen individuals from psychiatric populations for the presence of indicators that may appear to be psychotic symptoms but instead may be signs of global neuropsychological dysfunction. The test was developed by Norman E. Hoffman.

The HOT is administered individually. Typical administration time is estimated to be 5 minutes. The test is readily hand scored. The person taking the test is asked to listen to a series of rhythmic patterns on an audio recording and to match the rhythms, according to algorithms presented in standardized instructions, with designs on an answer sheet. The rhythms increase in length and complexity over the course of the test.

Test materials include a test manual; the audio recording, available as a computer audio file; a sheet of designs; and an answer sheet. The test yields a single total score, based on the number of rhythms and designs matched correctly according to the algorithms presented. Although the test manual makes reference to conversion of raw scores to standard scores, the conversion tables are not included in the test manual and must be requested from the test author.

DEVELOPMENT. The impetus for the development of the HOT and its predecessor was an observation by music therapists, with whom the test developer—a psychologist—collaborated, that accurate integrative association of rhythmic patterns with other kinds of perceptual data is impaired in persons with neuropsychological compromise. Hoffman first attempted to operationalize this observation by creating a formal test, in 1975, known as the Hoffman Test for Organicity (HTO; Hoffman, 1975).

Hoffman's experience with the HTO, as described in the HOT manual, revealed two problems to him: (a) the machinery necessary for the (pre-digital era) administration of the audio stimuli was too cumbersome for ordinary clinical use, and (b) the standardized administration instructions, in an attempt to be clear and explicit, proved repetitive in a way that confused some examinees with clearly documented organic impairments.

The HOT has attempted to address these observed difficulties. HOT audio stimuli can be administered using desktop or laptop computers, and there are now less wordy and repetitive instructions. The HOT was then tried out on what seems to have been a small, local sample of 44 participants (19 with organic conditions, 25 without) in the test development phase.

Although the test manual suggests that the HOT yields excellent results in distinguishing individuals with and without organic brain damage; the relatively small test development and norming study sample; the lack of geographic diversity in the sample; and the lack of data in the test manual about educational backgrounds, ethnicity, socioeconomic status, presence or absence of sensory deficits, and presence or absence of intercurrent medical conditions among the sample participants bring into serious question the adequacy of the HOT development and norming processes.

TECHNICAL. The test manual provides limited information related to the technical properties of the HOT, relying to a substantial extent on evidence offered to support the earlier version of the measure. The HOT was standardized using a sample of 44 individuals, 19 of whom were diagnosed with an organic brain disorder and 25 of whom were diagnosed with a non-organic disorder. The subsamples were drawn from private practice settings in Broward County, Florida, and were matched on age. No other demographic information about the sample is provided in the test manual.

Test-retest reliability estimates were developed using individuals from the standardization sample (n = 44) who were retested at intervals of 2 to 3 weeks. Across both groups, a Spearman rank-order correlation coefficient of .93 emerged. Separately, the coefficients were .91 for the organic group and .50 for the non-organic group.

Concurrent evidence of validity derived from comparisons of HOT scores to scores obtained on the Bender Gestalt Test (BGT; Bender, 1993), which yielded Spearman rank-order correlation coefficients of .87 and .11 for the organic and non-organic groups, respectively. Construct evidence of validity was based on an examination of group differences in performance on the HOT and the BGT, which were evaluated using a Mann Whitney U test. Results indicated significant ($p < .001$) performance differences in the predicted direction between the two groups.

COMMENTARY. All tests, historically and in contemporary times, have their origins in a clinician's attempts to pursue observations seen clinically with systematic rigor. In this sense, Hoffman's attempt to investigate his observation that there appears to be an association between problems with rhythmic integration and the presence of covert, global neuropsychological compromise in persons thought to have a primary mental illness is commendable and forms a hypothesis worth pursuing.

The HOT presents several types of substantive technical concerns. A beginning point involves the test manual's literature review. Consistent with its use of the outdated concept of *organicity* as part of the HOT's title, the manual references primarily an older generation of publications and measures. For example, it makes repeated reference to the Bender Gestalt Test (Bender, 1938; 1993), rather than the updated versions, the Bender Visual-Motor Gestalt Test-II (Brannigan & Decker, 2003) and the Koppitz-2 (Reynolds, 2007). This is not simply a question of preference for newer vs. older terminology. The shift within clinical psychology and neuropsychology has been from an understanding of organicity as a unidimensional concept to an understanding that all psychological phenomena have meaningful and diverse neuropsychological substrates. This shift has been essential to the scientific flowering and clinical contributions of contemporary neuropsychology as reflected in newer generations of neuropsychological tests that provide nuanced assessment of both global and specific/localized neuropsychological compromise. Hoffman seems not to have considered fully that these developments would have merited being taken into account in conceptualizing the clinical and scientific issues that became salient in developing the HOT.

Hoffman notes that dysrhythmias as markers of neuropsychological compromise are intrinsic to clinicians' intuitive understanding but largely lack a basis of research support, something he hopes research and clinical work using the HOT can help provide. However, his statement ignores important bodies of contemporary research involving the neuropsychology of rhythm in healthy (Clynes, 1982) and clinical (e.g., Wilson, Pressing, & Wales, 2002) populations. Since 1980, and in recognition of the scientifically validated importance of dysrhythmias, neuropsychologists have assessed rhythmic functions with the Rhythm scale of the Luria-Nebraska Neuropsychological Battery (Golden, Hammeke, & Purisch, 1980) and with other neuropsychological test instruments.

The HOT manual addresses validity primarily via concurrent evidence using scores on other measures that assess global neuropsychological compromise and comparing them to HOT scores. However, these comparisons involve outdated measures that are no longer in widespread use. Also, the limitations in the size and diversity, including diagnostic and symptom-expression diversity, in the test development and norming study samples preclude meaningful estimation of reliability, essential to the development of a psychometrically robust test (American Educational Research Association [AERA], American Psychological Association [APA], & National Council on Measurement in Education [NCME], 2014). No effort seems to have been made to correlate HOT performance with neuroimaging or neurological findings, something often undertaken as part of the development of contemporary neuropsychological tests.

The lack of inclusion of standard score conversion tables and adequate technical supporting data in the HOT manual poses a substantial technical concern. Without these, a clinician or researcher potentially interested in using the HOT cannot independently appraise the adequacy of the derived scores, including whether they are normally distributed, cover a sufficient range in the norming sample, or show floor or ceiling effects relevant to potential diagnostic issues. The field's standards require such independent appraisals for professionals planning to utilize standardized tests for specific clinical and research purposes (AERA, APA, & NCME, 2014).

Similarly, the test manual does not provide data allowing a potential test user to appraise whether the number of HOT test items is sufficient or possibly excessive; whether the test items are at the same or different levels of difficulty and, if the levels are different, by the same or varying increments; and, other than by clinical observation, whether the person taking the test grasped and retained the instructions and was or was not confused by them. Given the presumed deficits in the target population the HOT is intended to identify, these omissions further weaken its utility.

Standardized tests gain their power, utility, and acceptance—and avoid pitfalls of inadvertent bias—through the demanding obligation to meet consensually developed scientific and professional standards. These include thorough, critical appraisal of relevant prior literature; thorough description in published test manuals of how items, scores, and scales are developed and their technical properties; trying out the test on a development, standardization, and norming sample large and diverse enough to meet the needs of clinicians and researchers to know whether the test can be used appropriately with the populations with whom they intend to work; and determining and publishing meaningful estimates of reliability and evidence of validity. In each of the areas, the HOT falls short.

It can be helpful to add tests that appraise the same function to one's armamentarium. Both the Bender-II (Brannigan & Decker, 2003) and the Screening Test for the Luria-Nebraska Neuropsychological Battery (Golden, 1987), among other well-validated neuropsychological instruments, screen for the presence or absence of global neuropsychological dysfunction in psychiatric populations, as Hoffman notes was his objective in developing the HOT. Having another instrument available that addresses the same target function can be useful to monitor progress or re-evaluate functioning. This was Hoffman's explicit hope in developing the HOT. Perhaps, with further development, the HOT could become such an instrument. However, due to the marked limitations in its technical and psychometric properties at present, it cannot yet be recommended for clinical or research purposes.

SUMMARY. The HOT is intended to help clinicians and researchers identify persons, primarily among the population of persons with severe and persistent mental illnesses, who may have primary, previously undetected neuropsychological compromise. It attempts to do so by determining whether persons taking the test have difficulty associating rhythmic patterns with visual designs, a sign meant to differentiate these populations.

At this time, because of the noted limitations in its technical development and psychometric properties, the HOT cannot be recommended for clinical or research purposes. The test's potential utility awaits the development of an instrument better aligned with the profession's current standards for test development, justification for its derived scores, reliability, validity, and applicability to more demographically and clinically diverse populations.

REVIEWERS' REFERENCES

American Educational Research Association, American Psychological Association, & National Council on Measurement in Education. (2014). *Standards for educational and psychological testing.* Washington, DC: American Educational Research Association.

Bender, L. (1938). A visual motor Gestalt test and its clinical use. New York, NY: American Orthopsychiatric Association.

Bender, L. (1993). Bender Visual Motor Gestalt Test. San Antonio, TX: The Psychological Corporation.

Brannigan, G. G., & Decker, S. L. (2003). Bender Visual-Motor Gestalt Test, Second Edition. Itasca, IL: Riverside Publishing.

Clynes, M. (Ed.). (1982). *Music, mind, and brain: The neuropsychology of music.* New York, NY: Plenum.

Golden, C. J. (1987). Screening Test for the Luria-Nebraska Neuropsychological Battery: Adult and Children's Forms. Torrance, CA: Western Psychological Services.

Golden, C. J., Hammeke, T. A., & Purisch, A. D. (1980). Luria-Nebraska Neuropsychological Battery. Torrance, CA: Western Psychological Services.

Hoffman, N. E. (1975). Hoffman Test for Organicity. West Palm Beach, FL: Proof Press.

Reynolds, C. R. (2007). Koppitz Developmental Scoring System for the Bender Gestalt Test, Second Edition (Koppitz-2). Austin, TX: PRO-ED.

Wilson, S. J., Pressing, J. L., & Wales, R. J. (2002). Modeling rhythmic function in a musician post-stroke. *Neuropsychologia, 40,* 1494-1505.

[74]

Inclusive Classroom Profile, Research Edition.

Purpose: "Designed to assess the quality of daily inclusive classroom practices that support the developmental needs of children with disabilities in early childhood settings."

Population: Inclusive classrooms serving children ages 2-5 years.

Publication Date: 2016.

Acronym: ICP™.

Scores, 13: 12 item scores (Adaptations of Space/Materials/Equipment, Adult Involvement in Peer Interactions, Adults' Guidance of Children's Free-Choice Activities and Play, Conflict Resolution, Membership, Relationships Between Adults and Children, Support for Communication, Adaptations of Group Activities, Transitions Between Activities, Feedback, Family-Professional Partnerships, Monitoring Children's Learning) plus Total score.

Administration: Individual classrooms.

Price Data, 2020: $70 per set including manual (71 pages) and 5 forms; $35 per manual; $35 per 5 forms.

Time: 2.5 to 3 hours for classroom observation plus approximately 20 minutes for interview and documentation review.

Comments: The observation portion of the assessment must be completed on the same day and within 3 hours. A follow-up teacher interview and documentation review are required.

Author: Elena P. Soukakou.

Publisher: Paul H. Brookes Publishing Co., Inc.

Review of the Inclusive Classroom Profile, Research Edition by LESLIE R. HAWLEY, Research Assistant Professor, Nebraska Center for Research on Children, Youth, Families and Schools, University of Nebraska-Lincoln, Lincoln, NE:

DESCRIPTION. The Inclusive Classroom Profile (ICP) is a structured observation protocol designed to assess the quality of inclusive practices that support children with disabilities. The ICP is designed to be used in inclusive early childhood classrooms serving youth ages 2-5 years. The instrument has been designed for use as a classroom quality assessment tool, a quality improvement tool, and/or a research instrument. ICP administration includes direct observation of individual classrooms, a teacher interview, and a documentation review. The observation portion of the assessment requires 2.5-3 hours of direct observation of the classroom environment (e.g., physical environment, daily routines, and activities both inside and outside the classroom). Assessment usually takes place in a single session, but it is possible to bridge multiple sessions from the same day (e.g., morning and afternoon) for an observation. Interview and document review portions of the assessment require about 20 minutes of time with the lead teacher when he or she is not supervising other activities. Observers are provided with structured interview questions aligned to specific quality indicators. The documentation review process includes reviewing documents such as the program's inclusive policies, screening and progress monitoring assessments, procedures for communicating with families, and individual intervention plans.

In addition to the Total score, 12 individual items (practices) are scored on the ICP: (a) Adaptations of Space, Materials, and Equipment, (b) Adult Involvement in Peer Interactions, (c) Adults' Guidance of Children's Free-Choice Activities and Play, (d) Conflict Resolution, (e) Membership, (f) Relationships Between Adults and Children, (g) Support for Communication, (h) Adaptations of Group Activities, (i) Transitions Between Activities, (j) Feedback, (k) Family-Professional Partnerships, and (l) Monitoring Children's Learning. Depending on the item, information can be gathered using observation, interview, or document review. Items are assessed on a 7-point rating scale, from *inadequate* to *excellent*. Within each item are a series of dichotomous quality indicators. Scoring is a two-step process in which users rate each of the quality indicators and then provide an overall rating for an item based on which combination of quality indicators is met. Quality indicators provide examples of practices at each level of quality. Each item has a supplementary page in the manual, which includes additional detail on criteria for rating indicators. Criterion information provides users with a reminder of the objective of the item and guidance for rating indicators. Assessors create a total score by summing all individual item ratings and dividing by the number of items rated as part of the ICP assessment. The manual instructs assessment users to map the total scores onto the rating scale (i.e., ratings range from 1 [*inadequate*] to 7 [*excellent*]) for interpretation. It is recommended that observers be familiar with the scale's items, general administration, and scoring procedures prior to administering the ICP.

Individual assessors are encouraged to complete training from a certified/approved ICP trainer prior to administering and scoring the instrument. A component of the ICP training program is reliability training where individuals conduct observations alongside an ICP trainer. This portion of the training provides the opportunity for a face-to-face debrief session with the trainer to compare and discuss observations and ratings. During training, individuals are provided support in applying the protocol scoring criteria and reaching satisfactory level of rater agreement.

DEVELOPMENT. The development of the ICP was an iterative process that included exploratory research, conceptualization, item generation, expert review, and pilot testing. Early research was guided by (a) multiple case study research (e.g., observation of inclusive classrooms, interviews with early childhood staff and administrators), (b) a literature review, and (c) research on early childhood inclusion. In the conceptualization phase, the ICP developer identified a broad set of research goals for all children participating in early childhood programs. According to the ICP manual, goals identified in the conceptualization phase were found to be aligned with the 2009 joint position statement on high-quality inclusive programs by the Division of Early Childhood (DEC)/National Association for the Education of Young Children (NAEYC).

A multilayered approach was taken by the ICP developer to generate items for the protocol. Item generation involved the following steps: (1) triangulating case study data with literature to generate quality dimensions, (2) operationalizing each dimension into measurable indicators, (3) applying specific criteria to each of the quality indicators, and (4) mapping the quality indicators on the 7-point quality continuum. The final component of the ICP development process was expert review. An early childhood practitioner and experts from early childhood education, special education, and measurement reviewed the content and structure of the ICP. Each of the ICP items was rated in terms of importance by the expert team. Experts also completed open-ended questions regarding instrument content, structure, and administration. Information gathered from the expert review was used to revise the instrument for formal pilot and field-testing.

TECHNICAL. The ICP manual provides information on two field test studies using the instrument. The first study was conducted with 45 inclusive preschool classrooms in the United Kingdom, and the second included 51 inclusive preschools in the United States.

In the U.K. study, the 45 inclusive preschool classrooms included a sample of 112 children with an identified disability (Soukakou, 2012). Children with an identified disability ranged in age from 30 months to 72 months (M = 50 months). The manual author and a trained researcher familiar with early childhood program quality assessment administered the observation protocol. Rater agreement was assessed using a separate set of 10 classrooms, and the results showed raters that were fairly consistent. According to Soukakou (2012), weighted kappa scores ranged from .45 to .93, with a mean of .79. Reliability of the ICP items was evaluated using coefficient alpha, yielding a coefficient of .79. ICP factor structure was tested using exploratory and confirmatory factor analysis (EFA and CFA, respectively). EFA evidence combined with theory suggested a one-factor solution that was later tested using CFA (Soukakou, 2012). CFA results demonstrated acceptable fit for a one-factor solution (χ^2 = 35.164, df = 35, p = .460, CMIN/df = 1.005, RMSEA = .010, NNFI = .998, and CFI = .998). Soukakou (2012) reports that two of the items (i.e., membership and transitions) demonstrated low factor loadings (i.e., .20 and .18, respectively), but items were retained for conceptual reasons. Evidence of the instrument's relationship to other measures of program quality was also explored. Total ICP scores were moderately correlated (r = .62) with scores from the Early Childhood Environment Rating Scale—Revised Edition (ECERS-R; Harms et al., 2005).

The other pilot study took place in 51 inclusive preschool classrooms in North Carolina. Soukakou et al. (2014) indicates that classrooms varied on demographics such as the number of children with a disability, child-teacher ratios, whether children received the majority of services in their classroom, and lead teachers' academic and applied experience. According to the ICP manual, the four assessors who completed the protocol all had experience conducting program quality assessments for North Carolina's Star Rated License. The mean intraclass correlation (ICC) for item level interrater reliability was .71 (range .11-.99; Soukakou et al., 2014). As noted in Soukakou et al. (2014), raters had low agreement (ICC = .11) on Item 3, Adult Guidance of Children's Play, but the item was retained because other sources of evidence (e.g., factor loadings) provided support for inclusion. Evidence of internal consistency was evaluated using coefficient alpha, with a resulting coefficient of .88. An EFA was conducted to examine the factor structure of the ICP. Evidence from the factor loadings (ranged from .34 to .84), scree plot, and parallel analysis suggests evidence for a single-factor solution (Soukakou et al., 2014). Additional construct evidence was collected by examining the relationship between total scores on the ICP and the ECERS-R (r = .48). Mean differences between the different types of programs included in the sample (e.g., Head Start, public pre-K, developmental delay) were found to be significant [$F(3, 47) = 13.77, p < 0.05$] and accounted for a large amount of variance (R^2 = .47) in ICP scores. Additional evidence was collected to evaluate the usability and quality of the training by soliciting feedback from the assessors. Using a 5-point scale (with 5 indicating more positive impressions), results indicate that assessors felt the ICP contained important constructs (M = 5), would recommend the instrument to others (M = 5), and found it relatively easy to administer (M = 4). Ratings on the training session indicated it was fairly useful (M = 3.75) and provided adequate preparation for conducting observations (M = 4).

COMMENTARY. The ICP observation tool fills a need for assessing access and participation for all children. Extensive efforts were undertaken during development to ensure the tool was based on applied and empirical research, and would be relevant to users (e.g., early childhood staff and administrators). Additionally, empirical efforts to date have provided evidence for the factor structure and a moderately strong relationship to other classroom observation tools. In theory, scores from the ICP protocol can provide guidance on the quality of inclusion practices by providing information that can be used for quality assessment, improvement, and research. Although the ICP has strong potential for use in these multiple roles, more evidence needs to be collected on the validity and utility of scores. The initial convergent evidence from the two populations of youth (i.e., U.K. and U.S.) is promising, but it is not enough to substantiate claims that scores can be used for multiple purposes. Additionally, the time requirements for ICP training and observation may be potential barriers for use in applied settings. Further research will need to explore the trade-off between validity, utility, and feasibility in applied settings. Overall, the development efforts and pilot studies provide a good foundation of evidence for scores from the ICP. Additional research and evaluation efforts will be able to expand on this strong foundation to continue to build a case for the validity of scores from the ICP.

SUMMARY. The Inclusive Classroom Profile (ICP) is a structured observation protocol designed to assess the quality of inclusive practices in early childhood classrooms. Current research on the instrument is limited to only a few studies; yet, there is promising convergent evidence using different populations of youth. As a whole, the instrument development efforts and pilot studies provide a good foundation of evidence, but further research is needed to explore the validity of ICP scores for use with quality assessment, improvement, and research.

REVIEWER'S REFERENCES

Harms, T., Clifford, R M., & Cryer, D. (2005). Early Childhood Environment Rating Scale-Revised Edition. New York, NY: Teacher's College Press.

Soukakou E. P. (2012). Measuring quality in inclusive preschool classrooms: Development and validation of the Inclusive Classroom Profile (ICP). *Early Childhood Research Quarterly, 27*, 478-488.

Soukakou, E. P., Winton, P. J., West, T. A., Sideris, J. H., & Rucker, L. M. (2014). Measuring the quality of inclusive practices: Findings from the Inclusive Classroom Profile pilot. *Journal of Early Intervention, 36*, 223-240.

Review of the Inclusive Classroom Profile, Research Edition by ANNA HICKEY, Assistant Professor of Clinical Pediatrics, SIU School of Medicine, and HEATHER POTTS, Advanced Doctoral Student, Syracuse University, Psychology Intern, SIU School of Medicine, Springfield, IL:

DESCRIPTION. The Inclusive Classroom Profile (ICP) is a criterion-based measure intended to assess the ability of classroom practices to meet the needs of diverse learners and children with disabilities ages 2-5 years. The ICP is designed to provide information to guide quality improvement within classrooms and can also be used to compare practices across classrooms/settings. The ICP requires 2.5-3 hours of direct observation of student and teacher behavior in different activities, during which the observer makes notes to be referenced for later scoring. Approximately 20 minutes are required to complete a structured interview with the lead teacher as well as a documentation review of inclusive policies, procedures for family communication, child intervention plans, and means of monitoring progress.

The ICP assesses 12 classroom practices determined to be indicators of high-quality inclusive teaching: Adaptations of Space/Materials/Equipment, Adult Involvement in Peer Interactions, Adults' Guidance of Children's Free-Choice Activities and Play, Conflict Resolution, Membership, Relationships Between Adults and Children, Support for Communication, Adaptations of Group Activities, Transitions Between Activities, Feedback, Family-Professional Partnerships, and Monitoring Children's Learning. Each classroom practice indicator receives a score on a 7-point response scale (1 = *inadequate*; 7 = *excellent*). The response scale for each classroom indicator includes yes/no questions that are used as benchmark criteria to aid in scoring. Scores are determined based upon whether the majority of students with disabilities and/or teachers meet the criteria of that response scale point. The ICP provides individual quality scores for the 12 classroom practices, along with an overall classroom Total score that averages scores across all individual item ratings.

DEVELOPMENT. Development of the ICP proceeded in five phases. Exploratory research was first conducted via a literature review of international early childhood education practices as well as case studies (observations and interviews). Conceptualization of the measure then proceeded with a review of guidelines from the Division of Early Childhood/National Association for the Education of Young Children (DEC/NAEYC), which emphasize access to a wide range of learning environments and activities, active participation and engagement in the classroom community, and systems-level supports including professional development, resources, and teacher-family collaboration. In the item generation phase, findings from case studies, the literature review, and the DEC/NAEYC guidelines were synthesized to identify the key dimensions of quality inclusive practices. Each dimension was then operationalized with measurable indicators of quality, and explicit criteria were developed on which indicators would be rated. Subsequently, an expert review of the measure was completed by a panel of five reviewers including professors and practitioners in early childhood education and special education, as well as researchers knowledgeable in measure development. Reviewers rated the importance of each quality indicator on a 5-point scale (mean scores indicated that all items were viewed as *important* or *very important*) and provided open-ended feedback on the content, structure, and administration of each quality indicator. Finally, pilot testing was conducted in five classrooms in the United Kingdom, which informed additional revisions to items and scoring procedures for clarity purposes as well as to reflect a wider range of inclusive activities for children with diverse abilities (Soukakou, 2012).

TECHNICAL.

Standardization. The ICP is a criterion-referenced measure with no normative data. Field testing for validation/reliability was first conducted in 45 inclusive preschool classrooms (both private and government-run) from three counties in the United Kingdom; this sample included 112 children identified with disabilities (Soukakou, 2012). The ICP author and one other trained observer completed all the observations using the

ICP as well as the Early Childhood Environment Rating Scale-Revised Edition (ECERS-R), the ECERS-Extension (ECERS-E), and the Caregiver Interaction Scale (CIS). A second study included 51 inclusive preschool classrooms across 46 counties in North Carolina; this sample included 150 children identified with disabilities (Soukakou, Winton, West, Sideris, & Rucker, 2014). Programs were recruited to reflect a range of program types (child care, pre-kindergarten, Head Start, developmental delay) and program quality as previously measured on the ECERS-R as required by the state of North Carolina. Observations were conducted by four trained observers. When a recent ECERS-R rating was available, those results were used in the study, but when not available, the ECERS-R was also completed but during a separate observation from the ICP. Neither the ICP manual nor the specific studies referenced in the manual (Soukakou, 2012; Soukakou et al., 2014) provide information about the geographic locations (i.e., rural, suburban, urban) of the classrooms, socioeconomic factors, or the racial/ethnic characteristics of students and teachers.

Reliability. Interrater reliability was computed based on observations in a subset of 10 classrooms in the U.K., with weighted kappa coefficients for individual items ranging from .45 to .93 and a mean kappa coefficient of .79. Internal consistency was adequate, with a coefficient alpha value of .79. In the North Carolina sample, a subset of nine classrooms was used to compute interrater reliability, with intraclass correlations for most individual items being adequate or better (rs ranging from .51 to .99) but one showing low agreement between raters (r = .11). The mean intraclass correlation was adequate (r = .71). Internal consistency was good, with a coefficient alpha value at .88.

Validity. An exploratory factor analysis was conducted using the North Carolina data and supported a one-factor solution to reflect a single dimension of inclusive practices. A confirmatory factor analysis and parallel analysis then showed good fit with the one-factor model, with factor loadings ranging from .34 to .84.

Convergent evidence of validity was reported using data from the U.K. study, with moderate correlations between the ICP and the ECERS-R total score (r = .62) and most individual items (r = .38-.55). Convergent evidence of validity was also found in moderate correlations with the CIS (r = .49 for Positive Relationships and r = -.33 for Detachment). Divergent evidence of validity was reported with low correlations (r = .04-.08) between the ICP and items measuring gender and race equality (from the ECERS-E) as well as materials for activities (from the ECERS-R), constructs not directly measured with the ICP. In the North Carolina study, observers also provided ratings of perceived value and ease of administration to support the social validity of the ICP.

COMMENTARY. The ICP offers a potentially useful addition to instruments currently available for assessment of inclusive classroom practices, specifically providing a framework for assessing those practices that enable young children with disabilities to access classroom activities, form meaningful relationships with adults and peers, and progress toward their individualized goals. Although the measure certainly holds promise with regard to quality improvement efforts, the validity evidence in this regard is lacking. Specifically, as of yet there is no published evidence (in the ICP manual or otherwise) suggesting that data derived from the ICP can be linked to meaningful interventions or positive classroom and child outcomes.

The ICP manual also appears to be lacking and slightly inconsistent in its description of procedures used for standardization and establishment of psychometric properties, requiring the reader to refer to the original published studies for clarification. Even in the original studies, there is no information available regarding major demographic characteristics of the samples, which leaves some question as to the generalizability of the measure. Sampling methods and rationale for using samples in small subsections of the U.K. and U.S. are also unclear. In addition, both the manual and original studies seem to omit information regarding some psychometric properties. For example, specific weighted kappa coefficients are not reported for each individual item on the ICP; instead only a range and a mean kappa coefficient are cited (Soukakou, 2012). Furthermore, the procedures for establishing interrater reliability are not clearly outlined (e.g., unknown whether all four observers were represented in the interrater reliability sampling; Soukakou et al., 2014). Interestingly, the authors contradict the use of the weighted kappa coefficient used in their 2012 study as they described their reasons for using the intraclass correlation in the 2014 study, though both analyses arguably could be considered appropriate with the nature of the ICP's ordinal data (e.g., see Hallgren, 2012).

At a more practical level, the ICP provides detailed descriptors to help guide observations and ratings, but the descriptors and benchmarks themselves appear to be quite cumbersome. The observation itself takes approximately 2.5 to 3 hours, but the process of reviewing notes and calculating scores requires additional time and is contingent upon the evaluator's fluency with the measure. When observing a classroom with more than one student identified as having a disability, there is also a substantial demand for divided attention, as the observer must make note of supports in place for all students with disabilities. Thus, it is not surprising that a thorough didactic training including observed reliability checks is recommended prior to using the ICP.

SUMMARY. The ICP is an observational tool that provides a useful guide for assessing inclusive practices to support students with disabilities in early childhood classrooms. However, as a fairly new measure, the evidence supporting its reliability and validity remains limited, particularly with regard to its clinical utility in supporting quality improvement efforts. To the reviewers' knowledge, the ICP does measure unique dimensions that are not included in other commercially available assessments. Therefore, pending additional research, the ICP could prove to be a useful criterion-based measure of inclusive practices for schools to consider.

REVIEWERS' REFERENCES

Hallgren, K. A. (2012). Computing inter-rater reliability for observational data: An overview and tutorial. *Tutorials in Quantitative Methods in Psychology, 8*, 23-34. doi:10.20982/tqmp.08.1.p023

Soukakou, E. P. (2012). Measuring quality in inclusive preschool classrooms: Development and validation of the Inclusive Classroom Profile (ICP). *Early Childhood Research Quarterly, 27*, 478-488. doi:10.1016/j.ecresq.2011.12.003

Soukakou, E. P., Winton, P. J., West, T. A., Sideris, J. H., & Rucker, L. M. (2014). Measuring the quality of inclusive practices: Findings from the Inclusive Classroom Profile pilot. *Journal of Early Intervention, 36*, 223-240. doi:10.1177/1053815115569732

[75]

Infant-Toddler Developmental Assessment–Second Edition.

Purpose: "Designed to improve early identification of children who are developmentally at risk and who may be in need of monitoring or intervention services."
Population: Birth to 3 years.
Publication Dates: 1995-2016.
Acronym: IDA-2.
Scores: Criterion-referenced scores in 8 domains: Gross Motor, Fine Motor, Relationship to Inanimate Objects, Language/Communication, Self-Help, Relationship to Persons, Emotions and Feeling States, Coping Behavior.
Administration: Individual.
Parts: 6 phases: Referral and Data Gathering; Parent Interview; Health Review; Developmental Observation and Assessment (the Provence Birth-to-Three Developmental Profile); Integration and Synthesis; Share Findings, Completion, and Report.
Price Data, 2020: $587 per complete kit including administration manual (2016, 145 pages), study guide (2016, 155 pages), 25 parent report forms, 25 health recording guides, 25 record forms, and a manipulatives kit in canvas carrying case; $395 per kit without manipulatives and carrying case; $111 per administration manual; $193 per manipulatives kit; $48 per 25 parent report forms; $48 per 25 health recording guides; $80 per 25 record forms; $111 per study guide.
Time: Varies.
Foreign Language Edition: Parent report forms and record forms are available in Spanish.
Comments: Conducted by a transdisciplinary team of two (or more) professionals; "the Provence Profile is designed to be used within the context of the complete assessment process and never used as a standalone test."
Authors: Sally Provence, Joanna Erikson, Susan Vater, Kyle Pruett, Jennifer Rosinia, and Saro Palmeri.
Publisher: PRO-ED.
Cross References: For reviews by Melissa M. Groves and E. Jean Newman of the original edition, see 13:146.

Review of the Infant-Toddler Developmental Assessment–Second Edition by MICHELLE S. ATHANASIOU, Professor of School Psychology, and ANNABEL W. LI, Graduate Student, University of Northern Colorado, Greeley, CO:

DESCRIPTION. The Infant-Toddler Developmental Assessment–Second Edition (IDA-2) is an individually administered, criterion-referenced instrument designed to identify children ages birth to 3 years who could benefit from developmental monitoring or early intervention services. The family-centered and comprehensive approach used by the IDA-2 makes it especially useful for devising individualized family service plans (IFSPs). The IDA-2 includes an administration manual, a study guide that provides detailed instructions related to the entire assessment process, record forms (i.e., IDA-2 Record, Health Recording Guide, Caregiver Report), and a manipulatives kit. Several necessary items are not included in the kit (i.e., bottle, blanket, soft animal toy, cracker/cookie, hat or cap, favorite toy, pacifier if used). Examiners will need to ask parents to make these items available.

The IDA-2 process is a comprehensive one that includes six phases: (1) referral and data gathering; (2) parent interview; (3) health review; (4) developmental observation and assessment (using the Provence Profile); (5) integration and synthesis; and (6) sharing of findings, completion, and report.

At least two core members of a multidisciplinary team should collaborate throughout the assessment process. Parental input regarding the child's developmental competencies, as well as reports of developmental and health history are integrated into the family-centered process, including scoring of developmental items. The Provence Profile assesses children's development in eight domains through both structured and naturalistic observations: Gross Motor, Fine Motor, Relationship to Inanimate Objects, Language/Communication, Self-Help, Relationship to Persons, Emotions and Feeling States, and Coping Behavior. Performance age can be calculated and compared to chronological age to determine the typicality of development and possible need for services. Percent delay also can be calculated, which is useful for eligibility determinations. Finally, certain items serve as "marker" skills that are typical of development at specific ages. Seven of the eight domains assessed have designated markers. For five of these domains, failure on two or more marker items below a child's chronological age, combined with the examiner's qualitative judgment of the child's performance, can lead to a determination that the child's development is *of questionable concern, delayed,* or *problematic* in the respective domains. Two domains require failure on only one marker item, coupled with examiner's judgment, to prompt such concerns. The Health Recording Guide and the Caregiver Report allow IDA-2 practitioners to gather information regarding the child's health, which is crucial in understanding developmental delay.

DEVELOPMENT. The IDA-2 was developed based on 35 years of research, systematic observation, and clinical experience with infants and toddlers. Items in each domain are presented hierarchically and grouped into age ranges at which the skills are typically exhibited. Content was selected based on what is known about development from reliable and valid psychological and developmental scales and related literature. There appears to be no specific theory guiding the eight domains identified and item criteria. The test authors discuss the use of an "interdisciplinary, interagency consultant group" (manual, p. 109) whose members reviewed and field-tested content and procedures in 1984. The work of this group prompted revisions by the test authors, but the nature and scope of such revisions are not specified.

TECHNICAL. Psychometric properties of the IDA-2 are based on studies with Provence Profile scores of the IDA from a sample of 100 children between birth and 3 years. Numbers of children at each 6-month age level varied, with only eight children ages 13-18 months, and nine children at ages 1 to 6 months. Other age ranges included 18 to 24 children. Data were collected from the IDA assessments conducted by practitioners at 23 service agencies. The test authors did not specify the criteria for choosing the 100 children from those records and did not specify the qualifications of the examiners who administered the IDA assessments. Because items on the IDA and IDA-2 are identical, the test authors suggest that statistical evidence of the IDA's validity applies to the IDA-2.

Several aspects of validity are discussed in the IDA-2 manual. Content-description evidence was based on a study of the original IDA that examined percentage agreement of developmental age as assessed by the IDA and other tests of development (e.g., Bayley Scales of Infant Development [Bayley, 1969], Vineland Adaptive Behavior Scales [Sparrow, Balla, & Cicchetti, 1984]). Agreement on developmental age between the IDA and the other scales ranged from high (84%) to very high (100%). There was a generally high overlap of items across the IDA and the other scales. Although calculated developmental age was similar among the instruments, these comparisons involved only the original IDA and other older and/or since revised instruments, at least one of which lacks validity evidence (i.e., Hawaii Early Learning Profile, Furuno et al., 1979). Criterion-prediction studies raise similar concerns. For example, with regard to concurrent validity evidence, data were gathered using the original IDA and other dated instruments. Furthermore, a reported study of predictive validity evidence involved asking personnel from 12 agencies whether they found referrals of young children based on IDA data to be appropriate. This question seems to provide information related to the social validity of the IDA, rather than its predictive validity.

With regard to construct-identification evidence, IDA-2 authors reported relationships of original IDA scores to chronological age, as well as relationships among IDA domains. With regard to the former, criterion scores across all Provence domains were shown to increase with age, which the test authors offer as support for the instrument's ability to measure development. However, these findings were based on a small sample, and results demonstrated a small change and large variability in the Language/Communication domain at two age intervals. There appear to be issues with the specificity in this domain at ages 19 to 30 months. Mean scores on this domain increased from 28.1 (*SD* = 9.7) for ages 19 to 24 months to only 32.7 (*SD* = 11.0) for ages 25 to 30 months over a developmental period during which speech and language would be expected to grow significantly. Such large standard deviations suggest significant variability in performance. Domain intercorrelations ranged from moderate to moderately high, with some correlations suggesting relatively small amounts of shared variance (e.g., Self-Help for children 0-18 months; Emotions and Feeling States for children 19-36 months). Other coefficients are very high, especially at 0-18 months (i.e., median intercorrelation .915). This might suggest that items/domains are not measuring unique constructs. The test authors attribute the lower intercorrelations noted for ages 0 to 18 months compared to ages 19 to 36 months to greater variability in development during the first 18 months. In fact, per the coefficients presented in the manual, the intercorrelations are much higher for those 0-18 months than for those 19-36 months.

Reliability. Internal consistency and interrater reliability were examined. For internal consistency, alpha coefficients exceeded generally accepted standards for reliability of instruments used clinically (i.e., .80). The two exceptions were Self-Help and Coping Behavior for children 19 to 36 months, for which coefficients were .77 and .78, respectively. It should be noted that these subtests are the shortest in the instrument, with 19 and 26 items, respectively. Reliability coefficients for these subtests may be influenced by this brevity. With regard to interrater reliability, a small study involved three professionals who worked in pairs to assess nine children ages 2 months to 36 months. Agreement ranged from 91% to 95% for seven domains and was 81% for Language/Communication. Another study included 36 IDA practitioners who had been trained for 1 to 6 years. The interrater agreement of these practitioners' recommendations for services based on a case developed by program staff and scored by the IDA authors was high, ranging from 78% for family mental health services to 97% for early intervention services. It should be noted that, in addition to the small sample sizes for these studies, neither was conducted using the IDA-2.

COMMENTARY. The IDA-2 is a comprehensive measure, including procedures for all aspects of developmental assessment and eligibility determination. It encourages a family-centered process, assessment of skills in natural environments, involvement of a multidisciplinary team, and incorporation of health history and caregiver reports of development. The IDA-2 includes most materials needed for administration, although several items specific to an individual child (e.g., child's favorite toy) must be provided by the family. The study guide provides an in-depth description of all phases of the IDA-2 assessment and is a valuable tool for practitioners. Although most of the record forms are self-explanatory, the Provence Profile worksheet in the IDA-2 Record is not user-friendly and might be difficult for some novice practitioners to use. Most problematic with this scale is the fact that no psychometric data are presented for the IDA-2; rather, all studies were conducted using the original IDA. Although items have not changed from the original IDA, the revised edition needs investigating, especially given that most studies reported included small samples and most were conducted circa 1988. Relatedly, other than changes to the organization of the manual and study guide, it is unclear how the IDA-2 differs from the original version.

SUMMARY. The IDA-2 is a comprehensive measure of infant/toddler development designed to provide information for intervention planning and eligibility determination. The instrument reflects best practice in early childhood assessment. The primary problem with this instrument is the lack of current psychometric data, which is imperative for making informed decisions about the appropriateness of the IDA-2 in clinical use. It is unfortunate that updated data were not included as part of the revision of the IDA manuals.

REVIEWERS' REFERENCES

Bayley, N. (1969). Bayley Scales of Infant Development. San Antonio, TX: Psychological Corporation.

Furuno, S., O'Reilly, K. A., Hosaka, C. M., Inatsuka, T. T., Allman, T. L., & Zeisloft, B. (1979). Hawaii Early Learning Profile. Palo Alto, CA: VORT.

Sparrow, S. S., Balla, D. A., & Cicchetti, D. V. (1984). Vineland Adaptive Behavior Scales. Circle Pines, MN: American Guidance Service.

Review of the Infant-Toddler Developmental Assessment–Second Edition by IHEOMA U. IRUKA, Chief Research Innovation Officer and Director, HighScope Educational Research Foundation, Ypsilanti, MI:

DESCRIPTION. The Infant-Toddler Developmental Assessment–Second Edition (IDA-2) is a comprehensive "family-centered assessment that addresses the health and development of children from birth to 3 years of age" (manual, p. 1). The IDA-2 was developed to improve the early identification of children who are developmentally at risk and may need monitoring or intervention services through a holistic and family-centered approach that takes into account the multifaceted nature of early development. The IDA-2 incorporates multiple steps within six phases: referral and data gathering; parent interview; health review; developmental observation and assessment (also known as the Provence Profile); integration and synthesis; and share findings, completion, and report.

In addition to an administration manual (with summary information about the steps and phases), the IDA-2 includes a study guide (with more detailed information about the steps and phases), the IDA-2 Record (Provence Profile to assess children's competency in eight domains), Caregiver Report (report from the caregiver about child birth history, health and social experience, and so forth), Health Recording Guide (form for practitioners and clinicians to record and organize health information), supplemental forms (for requesting health information, evaluation of services), and the Provence Profile manipulatives kit. The eight domains assessed in the Provence Profile are Gross Motor, Fine Motor, Relationship to Inanimate Objects, Language/Communication, Self-Help, Relationship to Persons, Emotions and Feeling States, and Coping Behavior.

The IDA-2 can be used by practitioners who have "completed their basic academic and clinical programs" (manual, p. 4). Practitioners include early childhood special educators, nurses and nurse practitioners, physicians, speech-language clinicians, physical and occupational therapists, and others with similar credentials. The IDA-2 is designed to be conducted by a transdisciplinary team of two or more professionals credentialed in a developmental discipline in diverse settings including Early Head Start, infant mental health programs, health centers, birth-to-3 systems, and rehabilitation centers. A delay is present based on any difference between the child's chronological age and performance age. Chronological ages of children who are born premature are adjusted based on the number of days and months the child was premature.

DEVELOPMENT. The IDA is based on the complexity and interdependence of many factors that influence young children's health, development, and well-being, especially in the first three years of life. These factors are biological, such as the maturation of the central nervous system; environmental; and social/emotional, such as the child's relationship to parents and other adults. Foremost is that children's development is complex, and each child has his or her own biology and makeup, which includes genetic makeup, the prenatal environment, and unique circumstances of labor and delivery. Children's development is a set of sequences and phases that build upon each other and work along multiple interrelated lines. Thus, development must be examined holistically across interdependent areas such as motor, language, cognitive, and social-emotional. The external environment serves to support and promote children's development and includes the parent or primary caregiver as well as other adults and community agents. Issues of vulnerability and risk also frame how children's development is examined. Vulnerability is a state of physical fragility that has a biological or genetic origin. Risks are physical and psychosocial environmental factors that impact children's development. A single risk is not determinative; rather it is the "cumulative effect of multiple risk factors in combination with biological vulnerability that point to the long-term adverse effects on healthy development" (manual, p. 3).

The items and procedures for the Provence Profile came about through an interdisciplinary, interagency group in 1984 that consisted of five physicians, four psychologists, three pediatric nurse practitioners, three speech-language clinicians, an occupational therapist, a social worker, and a special educator. The IDA-2 is an update of the IDA. Organizational changes were made to the study guide and the administration manual. Items comprising the Provence Profile (the criterion-referenced instrument used in the IDA and also in the IDA-2) are the same, but the descriptions and directions have been clarified and arranged to be more user-friendly.

TECHNICAL.

Data for establishing the psychometric evidence for the Provence Profile are based on 100 children, birth to 3 years, from IDA practitioners from 23 agencies: 27 children were from 1-12 months, 29 children from 13-24 months, and 44 children from 25-36 months. Scoring is based on whether behavior was observed (which was viewed as more accurate) or reported by a parent (which was regarded as less accurate because behavior was not directly observed by the practitioner).

Reliability. Reliability information is based on examinations of interitem consistency (coefficient alpha) and interrater reliability. Interitem consistency estimates for the Provence Profile domains were high, ranging from .90 to .96 (for children from birth to 18 months) and from .77 to .96 (for children from 19 to 36 months). Interrater reliability involving three clinical supervisors assessing nine children from ages

2 months to 36 months showed agreement ranging from 81% to 95%.

Validity. Validity evidence for IDA-2 scores is based on content-description, criterion-prediction, and construct-identification. Content-description validity evidence was derived from the input of the interdisciplinary, interagency group described above. This group reviewed the test content, and some of them field-tested the entire process with teams of two clinicians who evaluated two children. Furthermore, the items of the Provence Profile were compared to items on other widely used developmental assessments, including the Bayley Scales of Infant Development (Bayley), The Hawaii Early Learning Profile (HELP), the Learning Accomplishment Profile (LAP), and the Vineland Adaptive Behavior Scales (Vineland). Items common to the Provence Profile and these other assessments were evaluated regarding the developmental age levels associated with each. Results ranged from 84% agreement on developmental age (Bayley) to 100% (Vineland). An examination of criterion-prediction validity in 1994 using the Vineland and the Bayley showed that the Bayley identified fewer children as being in need of services than the Vineland or the Provence Profile. Construct-identification validity evidence was based on the improvement of scores by age and strong relationships between the items. For example, scores for the Gross Motor domain increased from an average of 7.8 (1- to 6-month-olds) to 41.8 (31- to 36-month-olds). Correlation coefficients between domains of the IDA-2 ranged from .53 to .97 (children birth to 18 months) and .23 to .83 (children 19 to 36 months).

COMMENTARY. The IDA-2 provides an intentional, comprehensive, and family-centered approach to holistically examine children's development. This tool provides a holistic approach to evaluating children with a clear understanding of children's development and the importance of integrating information acquired through multiple methods including observations, parent interview, and review of existing health information. It also takes into account children's prenatal environment and current environment, both of which are critical to understanding factors that may support or impede children's normal developmental trajectory. The test authors focus on all aspects of children's development from gross and fine motor to language development and coping behaviors, which speaks to their understanding of the interrelatedness between children's skills in the first three years of life. Their detailed phases and steps, which are clearly described in the study guide, provide a clear way for clinicians to use the tool. Beyond just describing the phases and steps, the test authors provide a thorough description of the purpose and conceptual overview of the process, so users of the tool have a clear understanding to ensure fidelity of implementation of these effective practices. The Provence Profile, which is part of Phase 4, demonstrated reliability and validity evidence and is very much aligned with current assessments for young children.

Although there are many strengths to this tool, the areas of concern include the possibly lengthy process of implementation and the time it may take to get to a comprehensive diagnosis. This may be an especially lengthy and expensive process in clinics with limited resources. Although the developers present adequate validity and reliability information, much of the evidence comes from data collected more than 20 years ago. No items were updated for the IDA-2, which is somewhat surprising considering new information about child development, the proliferation of new technology and social media, and many children being in out-of-home care environments. It is unclear the extent to which children who provided the basis for the psychometric information are similar to the current population of children in the United States, such as the nine children (and three clinicians) used to establish interrater reliability.

SUMMARY. The strength of the IDA-2 is its use within an interdisciplinary team of well-trained clinicians that takes a step-by-step approach to gathering comprehensive information about children's strengths and areas of concern. This assessment seems to provide a valid and holistic view of children's development through multiple methods and sources and thoughtful integration by trained professionals. Potential users of this instrument should consider the skills and time needed to engage in this assessment process, which is very child- and family-centered. The IDA-2 provides a clear indication of children's strengths and delays across various domains. The IDA-2 covers the same areas as most assessments in this age group but seems to assess children through a holistic process based on child development and family-centered practices. There is concern about whether there is a need to examine the items of the Provence Profile, which has not been updated since its development in 1984, and to standardize the measure using a sample representative of U.S. children who have developmental delays or are at-risk for such delays.

[76]

Infant/Toddler Environment Rating Scale, Third Edition.

Purpose: Designed to assess programs for very young children in group care settings.
Population: Child care programs for infants and toddlers ages birth to 36 months.
Publication Dates: 1990-2017.
Acronym: ITERS-3.
Scores, 7: Space and Furnishings, Personal Care Routines, Language and Books, Activities, Interaction, Program Structure, Total.
Administration: Individual classrooms/programs.
Price Data, 2020: $25.95 per rating scale (2017, 102 pages) including administration and scoring instructions and score sheet and profile form that may be photocopied.
Time: 3 hours to observe and rate.
Authors: Thelma Harms, Debby Cryer, Richard M. Clifford, and Noreen Yazejian.
Publisher: Teachers College Press.
Cross References: For reviews by Karen Carey and Joseph C. Kush of the revised edition, see 17:89; see also T5:1264 (6 references); for reviews by Norman A. Constantine and Annette M. Iverson of the original edition, see 12:188.

Review of the Infant/Toddler Environment Rating Scale, Third Edition by THOMAS J. GROSS, Assistant Professor, and GRANT A. HACHERL, School Psychology Graduate Assistant, Psychology Department, College of Education and Behavioral Sciences, Western Kentucky University, Bowling Green, KY:

DESCRIPTION. The Infant/Toddler Environment Rating Scale, Third Edition (ITERS-3) was developed from the ITERS-Revised Edition. The ITERS-3 was created to facilitate systematic observations of classrooms for children birth to 36 months. The test manual includes all forms for the assessment, such as rating scales and scoring forms. It also provides an introduction to the ITERS-3 as well as administration and scoring procedures. An overview section within the test manual gives items and corresponding score indicators that are checked off to determine subscale item ratings. Administration instructions detail the overall guidelines for observing, using the scoresheet, and completing the profile graph. A list of terms is provided for user clarity.

The ITERS-3 contains six subscales that are to be completed during a 3-hour observation. The Space and Furnishings subscale includes items regarding indoor space; furnishings for care play, and learning; room arrangement; and display for children. The Personal Care Routines subscale has indicators for meals/snacks, diapering/toileting, health practices, and safety practices. The Language and Books subscale contains items related to talking with children, encouraging vocabulary development, responding to children's communication, encouraging children to communicate, staff use of books with children, and encouraging children's use of books. The Activities subscale contains items for fine motor, art, music and movement, blocks, dramatic play, nature/science, math/number, appropriate use of technology, promoting acceptance of diversity, and gross motor. The Interaction subscale has items for supervision of gross motor play, supervision of play and learning (non-gross motor), peer interaction, staff-child interaction, providing physical warmth/touch, and guiding children's behavior. The Program Structure subscale contains items for schedule and transitions, free play, and group play activities.

All items within the subscales are scored on a Likert-type scale from 1 (*inadequate*) to 7 (*excellent*). Each item consists of a number of indicators that can be checked *yes*, *no*, or *NA* (i.e., not applicable) where permitted. Sets of indicators are assigned to the point values 1, 3, 5, and 7 with whole number values between them. The scoresheet provides space for note taking and qualitative observations as well as space for subscales' total scores, number of items scored, and item averages on each subscale. All of the item scores are summed and averaged to create a total mean score. The profile page allows users to graph scores for individual items, average subscale scores, and the total mean score.

DEVELOPMENT. The test authors identified seven areas of substantial changes on the ITERS-3 from the ITERS-R. The focus of the ITERS-3 is toward teacher use of materials, which is in contrast to the previous version's emphasis on amount and quality of materials. The ITERS-3 extends the type of classroom to include children from birth to 36 months. Further, teacher reports were removed, and the current version focuses on the 3-hour observation. There are now six subscales, and the items were reduced from 39 to 33. The Parents and Staff scale from the ITERS-R was removed due to its reliance on staff report. The Language and Books scale is a six-item extension of the ITERS-R Listening and Talking scale, where the teacher use of language for instruction has been given more indicators. Additional items were added to the Interaction scale to reflect the role of relationships, and an additional item was added to the Activities scale to reflect instruction for math in early childhood education. The ITERS-3 authors assert that the current form of the assessment is a better predictor of youth outcomes.

TECHNICAL. The scale authors state that the ITERS-R and the Early Childhood Environment Rating Scale, Third Edition (ECERS-3) have well-established evidence of concurrent and predictive validity, and that the ITERS-3 keeps the basic properties of the ITERS-R; therefore, reliability between trained observers was the focus of the initial field studies. The test authors do call for more research and direct readers to the website of the Environment Rating Scales Institute to look for future research, as it becomes available.

Fifty-three classrooms in the United States were sampled from Georgia (15), Pennsylvania (16), Washington (18), and North Carolina (4). Classrooms were selected with the goal of having one-third low-quality programs, moderate-quality programs, and high-quality programs as evaluated by state licensing and Quality Rating and Improvement System data. Specific criteria were not mentioned in the test manual. Initially, nine raters were trained to be at 85% agreement, within one point for each item, with a "gold standard trainer." The raters were then paired to conduct observations in each classroom.

Indicator reliability is the percentage of scores that matched exactly for each indicator by the two assessors, and it was used to pilot indicators and items. The mean reliability was 86.9% across indicators; however, no standard deviation was reported. Some indicators fell below the criterion of 75% reliability, and the number of indicators was reduced from 476 to 457.

Item reliability was assessed for the 33 items, to which the indicators are anchored. Exact agreement was 60.6%, with 86.1% within one point (range from 69.8% to 94.4%). A weighted Cohen's kappa was used to assess agreement as well. Kappa coefficients ranged from .38 to .75, or minimal to moderate, and six items had weak (.40 < kappa < .50) interrater correspondence (McHugh, 2012). The test authors reported editing items to improve reliability based on these data. However, it was not stated whether the altered items were assessed for reliability.

Two-way mixed model intraclass correlations (ICC) were also calculated between raters' scoring of the subscales, and it was found that Full Scale scores demonstrated excellent reliability (.92) with good reliability for the overall subscale mean (.87), and for each subscale (ICC range = .76 to .94; Koo & Li, 2016). Internal consistency was estimated by computing alpha coefficients for the scales. The alpha coefficients were adequate or better for the Full Scale score (.91), subscale mean (.87), and each subscale (range = .76 to .94).

COMMENTARY. The ITERS-3 is designed to require only one 3-hour observation. There are 33 items and approximately 14 indicators per item on average. Having a large number of indicators to choose from could help raters more clearly determine which rating to choose for an item. However, this system also requires raters to refer to the test manual throughout the observation, as the scoresheet provides the indicator numbers, but not the definitions. In general, this could be cumbersome for an individual using the ITERS-3 in a field-based setting. Further, the current data available for the ITERS-3 are based on ratings assigned by trained individuals. It is yet to be determined how necessary the training is to accurately rate and score the assessment, but the test authors suggest that extensive training likely is needed. It might be seen as cost prohibitive for some to educational agencies or time consuming and impractical for practitioners if specialized training is necessary.

Overall, the current classroom sample for developing the ITERS-3 is small (N = 53) and potentially difficult to generalize to other classrooms from a broad range of geographic areas. Nonetheless, the test authors did provide reliability analyses for the indicators, items, subscales, and Full Scale score. The overall appraisal of quality (i.e., Full Scale score) and subscales are the most reliable measures, which could be viewed as the most interpretable measures in the assessment. The variability at the indicator and item level might make consistently interpreting indicators or items difficult. Still, it should be noted that evidence of concurrent or criterion validity for the ITERS-3 has not yet been published. It might not be appropriate to assume that a previous version of an assessment will measure the same constructs, considering changes to items and scales were made by the test authors. The authors did recommend that more research should be completed, but assuming validity from a previous version of an assessment could be premature without empirically demonstrating their correspondence between versions on psychometrically meaningful dimensions.

SUMMARY. The ITERS-3 was developed to provide an observational assessment of early childhood classrooms. It is a revision of an earlier version that focuses on the observational period, rather than requiring a substantial amount of information from teacher report. The overall score and subscales could be adequate for drawing conclusions about early childhood classroom quality. However, difficulty with administration, narrow reliability data, and unanswered questions regarding validity could limit the ITERS-3 use.

REVIEWERS' REFERENCES

Koo, T. K., & Li, M. Y. (2016). A guideline of selecting and reporting intraclass correlation coefficients for reliability research. *Journal of Chiropractic Medicine, 15,* 155-163.

McHugh, M. L. (2012). Interrater reliability: The kappa statistic. *Biochemia Medica, 22,* 276-282.

Review of the Infant/Toddler Environment Rating Scale, Third Edition by ANNA HICKEY, Assistant Professor of Clinical Pediatrics, SIU School of Medicine, and SAMANTHA DEHAAN SULLIVAN, Advanced Doctoral Student, Illinois State University and Practicum Student, SIU School of Medicine, Springfield, IL:

DESCRIPTION. The Infant/Toddler Environment Rating Scale, Third Edition (ITERS-3) is an observational measure that assesses environmental aspects of group child care settings for infants and toddlers ages birth to 36 months. The ITERS-3 comprises 33 items designed to assess the overall quality of a classroom by evaluating the physical environment as well as methods teachers use to support children's learning, health, safety, and social-emotional development. Items are organized into six subscales: Space and Furnishings, Personal Care Routines, Language and Books, Activities, Interactions, and Program Structure. Ratings are based on a 3-hour observation, with flexibility to adjust the observation time to evaluate select aspects of the environment that did not naturally occur during the observation period. The test manual provides guidance as to how assessors should navigate variabilities in classroom schedule and structure across settings and ways to minimize the observer's impact on the environment.

The ITERS-3 scoring instructions are clear, and operational definitions are provided for terms used throughout the scale to increase objectivity during the observation. The assessor is not permitted to use teacher reports to supplement observations but is encouraged to take notes to assist in scoring items after the observation is complete. Individual items are rated on a 7-point scale (1 = *inadequate*; 7 = *excellent*) with *yes/no* quality indicators for four of the ratings. An outlined scoring system allows the assessor to rate items based on the number of quality indicators scored *yes* or *no*, which is intended to enhance objectivity in measurement. Item ratings are averaged to compute the six subscale scores, and a scoring profile is used to evaluate the scatter across items within each subscale. A total mean score is computed by averaging the scores of all 33 items on the scale.

DEVELOPMENT. Earlier editions of the ITERS and its parent Environment Rating Scale (ERS) were conceptually grounded in early childhood and developmental theory. The ITERS-3 maintains a holistic perspective of child development and education, such that multiple domains (physical, social, emotional, cognitive) are considered essential to fostering children's development in early childhood care settings. The ITERS-3 was revised from the updated ITERS-R (Harms, Cryer, & Clifford, 2006) to include an extended age range up to age 36 months. Revisions were guided by data available from the ITERS-R, current health and safety standards, ongoing communication with practitioners, and experience in the field. The current literature on early childhood education, trends and challenges in educational practices, and child development were also considered. The Parents and Staff scale from the ITERS-R was removed due to restriction in range of scores and reliance on teacher report, as opposed to direct observation. A greater emphasis was placed on strategies to foster cognitive development. Changes were made in the placement and description of item indicators, and new indicators were added to improve reliability in measurement scaling.

Small scale pilot testing of the ITERS-3 was followed by a more thorough field test including 53 classrooms in Georgia, North Carolina, Pennsylvania, and Washington. Classrooms were selected to represent varying levels of quality based on previous data available through state licensing and the Quality Rating and Improvement System, though the final sample included a relatively small portion of high-quality classrooms. Two trained assessors observed and provided ratings on the classroom environment during the same 3-hour observation period, and additional examination of select materials and routines was allowed outside this window for specific indicators. After field testing, indicators with less than 75% reliability (i.e., percentage of matching scores by two independent raters) were clarified or removed, resulting in a total of 457 indicators for the 33 items.

TECHNICAL.

Standardization. Normative data are not available for the ITERS-3 due to the small sample size, sampling method, and limited geographic representation. The test authors state that these data may be available on the Environment Rating Scale Institute (ERSI) website if a larger, more representative sample can be obtained in the future.

Reliability. Reliability estimates were computed based on data gathered during the field study. The test authors reported a high level of internal consistency for the Full Scale (alpha = .91) and moderate to high internal consistency for individual subscales, with alpha coefficients ranging from .76 to .94. Interrater reliability was reported in various forms. Across specific *yes/no* indicators and assessor pairs, a mean of 86.9% agreement was achieved. Exact agreement on item ratings was achieved for 60.6% of paired ratings, and agreement within one point was achieved for 86.1% of paired ratings. Weighted kappa coefficients for item ratings ranged from 0.376 to 0.753, with the mean weighted kappa coefficient of .600 considered adequate by the test authors. Seven items required revisions due to low interrater reliability. Intraclass correlations (ICC) were also computed using absolute agreement, two-way mixed model of average estimates, with ICCs ranging from 0.637 to 0.943 for individual items (mean ICC = 0.83) and from 0.764 to 0.940 for subscales (mean ICC = 0.87). The ICC for the Full Scale was 0.915.

Validity. The test authors reference many studies that demonstrate the relation between various ERS measures that evaluate the quality of early childhood programs and other measures of program quality and outcomes for children's cognitive, language, and social-emotional development. The ITERS-3 is purported to maintain the basic properties of earlier versions of the test, which has well-established evidence of concurrent and predictive validity. Thus, the main focus of the test authors' field study was to evaluate and establish the reliability of the instrument. The authors acknowledge the need for further research concerning evidence of predictive validity of the ITERS-3 ratings on child outcomes using a larger sample size.

COMMENTARY. The ITERS-3 is the latest addition to the ERS observation tool family and is described as an improvement in terms of its focus on observational methods (as opposed to gathering some evidence through interview), clarity in item and indicator descriptions, and extended age range. Most item descriptions and indicators are clearly outlined, yet there remains a need to access and review more detailed guidelines in order to provide ratings on certain subscales. These supplemental materials are available on the ERSI website.

Although psychometric evidence has been reported for the previous renditions of the ERS and ITERS, the evidence supporting the reliability and validity of these latest changes has yet to be established. Preliminary reliability data suggest strong internal consistency and variable interrater agreement depending upon the statistics used. Weighted kappa coefficients, for example, were described as acceptable but actually reflected a wide range of low to substantial interrater agreement across items. Of particular concern is the fact that additional changes to the items and indicators were made *after* the reliability study was conducted, and no new data were collected prior to the measure being published. The test authors clearly acknowledge a need for larger-scale studies to more fully establish the reliability and validity of the measure across a broader sample of the population.

Some presentations of the ITERS-3 reliability data are also misleading. Specifically, reporting the percentage of agreement on indicators and items may overestimate the degree of interrater reliability, largely due to the inability to account for rate of agreement that is expected by chance (e.g., see Hallgren, 2012, for a review). In addition, the means of computing the ICC for individual items seems to have been appropriate, but there remains some question as to the appropriateness of calculations using the subscale and Full Scale scores, both of which are derived from averaging individual item scores. These ICC values were also remarkably similar to the alpha coefficients reported for the subscale and Full Scale scores.

SUMMARY. The ITERS-3 is an observational measure intended to assess the child care and classroom environments of children from birth to 36 months. Its predecessors have strong theoretical and conceptual foundations as well as a large body of research supporting their reliability and validity. However, the current version is lacking in psychometric data supporting its use, particularly considering the claim that substantial changes were made from previous editions and that additional changes were made to items after the reliability studies were completed. No data supporting the validity of scores from the ITERS-3, specifically, were reported in the test manual. The authors indicate that additional evidence of psychometric quality will be available on the ERSI website as further research is conducted. At this time, the lack of current psychometric evidence is a concerning feature of the newly revised measure, and until additional research is available, its use should be limited to those contexts in which other sound data in making accountability and evaluative decisions are available.

REVIEWERS' REFERENCES

Hallgren, K. A. (2012). Computing inter-rater reliability for observational data: An overview and tutorial. *Tutorials in Quantitative Methods for Psychology, 8,* 23-34. doi:10.20982/tqmp.08.1.p023

Harms, T., Cryer, D., & Clifford, R. M. (2006). Infant/Toddler Environment Rating Scale–Revised Edition, Updated. New York, NY: Teachers College Press.

[77]

Internet Addiction Test and Internet Addiction Test for Families.

Purpose: Designed "to measure the presence and severity of Internet and technology dependence."
Population: Adolescents and adults.
Publication Date: 2017.
Acronym: IAT.
Scores, 7: Salience, Excessive Use, Neglect Work, Anticipation, Lack of Control, Neglect Social Life, Total.
Administration: Individual or group.
Price Data, 2020: $110 per combo pack including Internet Addiction Test manual (29 pages) containing reproducible copies of the response and interpretation forms and Internet Addiction Test for Families manual (32 pages) containing reproducible copies of the Parent-Child Internet Addiction Test response and interpretation forms and the Problematic and Risky Media Use in Children Checklist; $60 per Internet Addiction Test manual.
Foreign Language Editions: Available in Chinese, French, Italian, Korean, and Turkish.
Time: 5-10 minutes for self-administration; 15 minutes for oral administration.
Author: Kimberly S. Young.
Publisher: Stoelting Co.

a) INTERNET ADDICTION TEST FOR FAMILIES.
Purpose: Designed "to be administered to adults to assess Internet addiction within their children."
Acronym: IAT-F.
Price Data: $60 per manual containing reproducible copies of the Parent-Child Internet Addiction Test response and interpretation forms and the Problematic and Risky Media Use in Children Checklist.

1) *Parent-Child Internet Addiction Test.*
Population: Parents of adolescents, ages 12-18.
Acronym: PCIAT.
Scores, 4: Attention, Social Behavior, Aggressive Behavior, Total.

2) *Problematic and Risky Media Use in Children Checklist.*
Population: Parents of children ages 3-11.
Scores: Total score only.

Review of the Internet Addiction Test and Internet Addiction Test for Families by RYAN L. FARMER, Assistant Professor, Oklahoma State University, Stillwater, OK:

DESCRIPTION. The Internet Addiction Test and the Parent-Child Internet Addiction Test (PCIAT) are 20-item tests to be completed by the client and the client's guardian (e.g., parent, teacher), respectively. All items are presented on a 5-point scale from rarely to always; alternatively, examinees can indicate that an item does not apply to their life or the life of the child. The IAT is designed for adolescents and adults, whereas the PCIAT is intended for parents of persons ages 12 to 18. Both instruments aim to measure "characteristics and behaviors associated with compulsive use of the Internet" (IAT manual, p. 11). The PCIAT comes as part of the IAT for Families (IAT-F), which also includes the Problematic and Risky Media Use in Children Checklist. The checklist contains eight yes-or-no items regarding children ages 3 to 11 and is designed to provide information about how children use technology and associated devices. The IAT and both components of the IAT-F can be individually or group administered either as a rating form or with items read aloud. The three measures include a practice question and comprehension check that assesses examinee understanding of the directions; if the examinee fails the practice question twice, testing is discontinued. Additionally, each component includes a personal information page that obtains examinee identifying information as well as information about the types of Internet sites the examinee uses.

The IAT and PCIAT produce a Total score with a maximum of 100, with higher levels indicating greater severity of Internet dependency. The test author provides cut points to facilitate users' interpretation of severity (i.e., 0-30 = *none*; 31-49 = *mild*; 50-79 = *moderate*; 80-100 = *severe*). Additionally, the IAT provides six domain scores: Salience, Excessive Use, Neglect Work, Anticipation, Lack of Control, and Neglect Social Life. The PCIAT provides three domain scores: Attention, Social Behavior, and Aggression. For both the IAT and PCIAT, domain scores are calculated by averaging the scores of the items that contribute to a particular domain. The test author recommends that domain scores be interpreted consistent with the scale that examinees used to respond to the items. The checklist has a maximum score of 8, and the test author advises that "answering yes to at least three of these behaviors in children ... indicates that they are exhibiting risky or problematic behaviors associated with excessive screen and device use" (IAT-F manual, p. 19).

The administration instructions for the three instruments are clearly written and easy to follow. The IAT, PCIAT, and checklist each may be completed in 15 minutes or less, and summing of the Total score is quick and easy. The test author provides a domain interpretation guide to facilitate scoring of domains for the IAT and PCIAT, making the process efficient and potentially reducing calculation errors.

DEVELOPMENT. In developing the IAT and PCIAT, the test author sought to create a test that would sample Internet addiction behaviors that are similar to those of established addictions (e.g., gambling) to facilitate classification efforts of Internet addiction disorders and to aid in pre-employment screening (see IAT manual, p. 10). The Internet Addiction Questionnaire (IADQ; Young, 1998) was first developed to facilitate diagnosis. Research using the IADQ expanded upon the research literature and helped to identify associated features of Internet addiction including excessive use of the Internet, neglect of responsibilities, withdrawal, and covert Internet behaviors. Research exploring features that differentiate compulsive versus normal Internet users (e.g., Greenfield, 1999) illuminated classification elements beyond excessive use to include preoccupation with the Internet, covert Internet-related behavior, preference of Internet-related behaviors over social or non-Internet activities, use of the Internet to escape, and functional impairment. The IADQ was adapted in light of extant research. The IAT, and subsequently the PCIAT, were direct results.

In contrast to the IAT and PCIAT, the checklist was developed to provide clinicians with a survey of a child-client's media use in general. The test author cites the absence of a standard tool for collecting data regarding young children's use of (a) Internet and computers, (b) television and movies, (c) video games, (d) mobile media, (e) music, (f) reading and print media, and (g) social media. In addition to collecting basic information about the duration of time spent with such devices, the checklist is used to assess behavioral impairments related to media use, such as tantrums or aggression when asked to stop using devices.

TECHNICAL. The IAT and IAT-F manuals do not report standardization procedures or data resulting from such procedures. The test author describes the six IAT domain scores as having high to moderate reliability based on independent research (Widyanto & McMurran, 2004) but does not report alpha coefficients or other reliability estimates within the test manual. Widyanto and McMurran (2004) reported adequate or better alpha reliability for Salience (.82), Excessive Use (.77), Lack of Self-Control (.76), and Neglect Work (.75) whereas Anticipation (.61) and Neglect Social Life (.54), were below the .70 criterion for adequate reliability (Hunsley & Mash, 2018). Coefficient alpha reliability for the Total score was not presented but was available via a literature search as .92-93. No reliability estimates were reported for the PCIAT or the checklist.

Evidence of validity to support the use of scores from the IAT and IAT-F is limited. The test author describes an exploratory factor analysis (N = 86) of the IAT conducted by Widyanto and McMurran (2004) in which factors representing the six domains were identified. However, alternative factor structures published in the literature have identified unidimensional (Khazaal et al., 2008; Korkeila, Kaarlas, Jääskeläinen, Vahlberg, & Taiminen, 2010), two-factor (Korkeila et al., 2010), and three-factor structures (Chang & Law, 2008). Similar structural ambiguity is present for the IAT with younger populations (e.g., Watters, Keefer, Kloosterman, Summerfeldt, & Parker, 2013). The test author does not provide empirical support for the factor structure of the PCIAT.

External evidence of validity is provided for the IAT in the form of weak correlations (r between .004 and .344) between scores and behaviors of interest such as an individual's average use of the Internet and personal use of the Internet. Most factors demonstrated significant correlations with at least one behavior. For example, Salience was significantly correlated with personal use (.321; $p < .01$) and average use (.263; $p < .05$), Lack of Self-Control was significantly correlated with personal use (.223; $p < .05$), and Neglect Social Life was significantly correlated with duration of use (.261, $p < .05$) and personal use (.216; $p < .05$). The Total score was significantly correlated with average use (.217; $p < .05$) and personal use (.299; $p < .01$).

No data are provided to support the diagnostic utility of the three instruments. The validity evidence reported in the IAT and IAT-F manuals as well as the conflicting data presented in the extant literature suggest that these instruments fall short of the desired level of validity evidence called for in the *Standards for Educational and Psychological Testing* (American Educational Research Association, American Psychological Association, & National Council on Measurement in Education, 2014) and in published accounts (Hunsley & Mash, 2018).

COMMENTARY. The IAT and IAT-F may be useful in situations warranting specific assessment of behaviors related to Internet addiction. However, a clear theoretical model for the scale and supporting evidence are lacking at this time. First, the test was adapted from the IADQ to model the *Diagnostic and Statistical Manual of Mental Disorders* (4th ed.; American Psychiatric Association, 1994) gambling criteria; five domains were then added based on exploratory factor analysis. Given that the test was developed to "measure the severity of Internet addiction" (IAT manual, p. 10), that the EFA upon which the six domains were extracted was conducted with a small sample and has not been replicated, the conflicting factor structures reported in the literature, and the inadequate reliability of two domain scores, it is unclear how best to interpret the IAT. Due to a deficit of research, no such analysis can be provided for the components of the IAT-F.

Second, total and domain score reliability estimates are not provided in the examiner's manual of either the IAT or the IAT-F. Although reliability estimates can be obtained from external publications for the IAT, this is not true for either component of the IAT-F. Based on Hunsley and Mash's (2018) criteria, only the IAT's Total score (see Jelenchick, Becker, & Moreno, 2012) and four of the six domain scores meet the minimum criteria for reliability (alpha coefficients of .70 or greater). More so, it is problematic that a clinician must conduct a literature search to obtain initial estimates.

Finally, the test author suggests that the IAT and related scales are intended for use in the diagnosis or risk assessment of Internet addiction and that they also may be used for screening purposes or in professional situations. However, the author offers minimal validity evidence for the scale, no diagnostic utility for the scale, and no data suggesting that the scale has adequate predictive ability for use in a professional sector. Cut points are provided in both the IAT and IAT-F manuals, but it is unclear how these cut points were determined; the test author refers to published validity evidence but provides no citations.

SUMMARY. The test author has developed scales that have greatly facilitated research on Internet addiction. More so, they can be administered, scored, and interpreted efficiently. The author wisely based the development of the IAT on established methods used in the assessment of related disorders. However, theoretical ambiguity and limited psychometric evidence severely limit the current utility of the scales for clinical practice. There is continued doubt as to whether the IAT or the scales included within the IAT-F provide incremental utility beyond conducting a targeted clinical interview related to Internet-use behaviors.

REVIEWER'S REFERENCES

American Educational Research Association, American Psychological Association, & National Council on Measurement in Education. (2014). *Standards for educational and psychological testing*. Washington, DC: American Educational Research Association.

American Psychiatric Association. (1994). *Diagnostic and statistical manual of mental disorders* (4th ed.). Washington, DC: Author.

Chang, M. K., & Law, S. P. M. (2008). Factor structure for Young's Internet Addiction Test: A confirmatory study. *Computers in Human Behavior, 24*, 2597-2619.

Greenfield, D. N. (1999, August). *Internet addiction: Disinhibition, accelerated intimacy, and other theoretical considerations*. Paper presented at the 107th annual meeting of the American Psychological Association, Boston, MA.

Hunsley, J., & Mash, E. J. (2018). *A guide to assessments that work* (2nd ed.). New York, NY: Oxford University Press.

Jelenchick, L. A., Becker, T., & Moreno, M. A. (2012). Assessing the psychometric properties of the Internet Addiction Test (IAT) in US college students. *Psychiatry Research, 196*, 296-301.

Khazaal, Y., Billieux, J., Thorens, G., Khan, R., Louati, Y., Scarlatti, E., ... Zullino, D. (2008). French validation of the Internet Addiction Test. *CyberPsychology & Behavior, 11*, 703-706.

Korkeila, J., Kaarlas, S., Jääskeläinen, M., Vahlberg, T., & Taiminen, T. (2010). Attached to the web—harmful use of the Internet and its correlates. *European Psychiatry, 25*, 236-241.

Watters, C. A., Keefer, K. V., Kloosterman, P. H., Summerfeldt, L. J., & Parker, J. D. A. (2013). Examining the structure of the Internet Addiction Test in adolescents: A bifactor approach. *Computers in Human Behavior, 29*, 2294-2302.

Widyanto, L., & McMurran, M. (2004). The psychometric properties of the Internet Addiction Test. *CyberPsychology & Behavior, 7*, 443-450.

Young, K. S. (1998). Internet addiction: The emergence of a new clinical disorder. *CyberPsychology & Behavior, 1*, 237-244.

Review of the Internet Addiction Test and Internet Addiction Test for Families by SUZANNE YOUNG, Professor of Educational Research, University of Wyoming, Laramie, WY:

DESCRIPTION. The Internet Addiction Test (IAT) and Internet Addiction Test for Families (IAT-F) were published in 2017. The purpose of the IAT is to assess Internet addiction in adults and adolescents; similarly, the IAT-F is used for adults to assess Internet addiction in children. The IAT-F consists of the Parent-Child Internet Addiction Test (PCIAT) and the Problematic and Risky Media Use in Children Checklist.

The IAT should be administered by a professional or paraprofessional who has clinical experience. The test, which can be completed in 5 to 15 minutes, can be administered individually or in groups, either self-administered or with verbal assistance from the examiner. The examinees must be able to read and comprehend the instructions and test items, which are designed for reading at a minimum of seventh grade reading level. If examinees are unable to understand instructions, the examiner is expected to administer directions verbally. The test includes a cover page with personal information as well as information about the amount of time spent on various Internet activities. The cover page is followed by a 20-item set of statements related to Internet addiction. The examinee is asked to rate each item on a frequency scale from *rarely* (1) to *always* (5). Scoring is accomplished by totaling all ratings, yielding an overall score that ranges from 0 to 100. The total score provides an indication of the severity of Internet addiction and problems with Internet use and is interpreted as *normal, mild, moderate*, or *severe*. In addition, average scores for six groups of items are calculated so that the examiner may further assess Internet addiction. The six groups of items are the following: Salience (5 items), Excessive Use (5 items), Neglect Work (3 items), Anticipation (2 items), Lack of Control (3 items), and Neglect Social Life (2 items). The averages for each group of items are rounded to the nearest whole number and interpreted by using the anchor descriptors for the scale (*rarely, occasionally, frequently, often,* and *always*). The examiner interprets the scores along with consideration of other disorders that may be present.

The PCIAT is completed by a parent (or another adult) of children 12 to 18 years old, either individually or in groups. The test is either self-administered or administered orally, for those with difficulties in understanding the written instructions and items. Similar to the IAT, the examiner must determine whether respondents can understand the written information; if respondents are unable to understand the information, the test should be administered orally. The test requires 5 to 10 minutes if self-administered and approximately 15 minutes if administered orally. Examinees are first asked to complete the child's personal information and to estimate the percentage of time that the child spends on the Internet engaging in certain types of activities such as instant messaging, emailing, and shopping. The PCIAT items are rated using a scale from *rarely* (1) to *always* (5). It includes 20 items, and the examiner computes a total for all 20 items as an indication of the severity of the child's overall Internet addiction. The test manual provides a description for four ranges of Total scores (*none, mild, moderate,* and *severe*). In addition to the total score, the test items are associated with three different domains: Attention (6 items), Social Behavior (8 items), and Aggressive Behavior (8 items). The examiner averages the scores for each domain, rounds to the nearest whole number, and interprets the averages using the anchors on the frequency scale (*rarely, occasionally, frequently, often,* and *always*). The examiner interprets the scores along with consideration of other disorders that may be present as well as the child's environment at school and at home.

The Problematic and Risky Media Use in Children Checklist is designed to assess screen or device use for children ages 3 to 11. It is completed by parents or other adults, individually or in small groups. Similar to the PCIAT, respondents' reading abilities should be evaluated to determine whether the checklist should be self-administered or administered verbally. Respondents are asked to complete the personal information sheet for the child and then to complete the checklist. They choose *yes* or *no* for each of the eight items on the checklist; three or more items that are checked *yes* indicate problematic or risky behavior, potentially leading to Internet addiction in adolescence. Both the PCIAT and the Problematic and Risky Media Use in Children Checklist should be administered by a qualified clinician if the tests are being used for diagnosis. If the goal is for screening, they may be administered by others such as parents or teachers.

DEVELOPMENT. The IAT was developed based on the Internet Addiction Diagnostic Questionnaire (IADQ) along with research on compulsive online behaviors. The IADQ was developed in the late 1990s by Kimberly Young (Young, 1998) and initially titled Diagnostic Questionnaire (DQ) to screen for addictive Internet use. The IADQ was based on the fourth edition of the *Diagnostic and Statistical Manual of Mental Disorders* (*DSM-IV;* American Psychiatric Association [APA], 1994) criteria for pathological gambling.

To further support the development of the IAT, research on compulsive online behavior suggests that Internet addiction is related to other psychiatric disorders such as substance use disorder, attention-deficit/hyperactivity disorder, depression, hostility, and aggression (Ko, Yen, Yen, Chen, & Chen, 2012). Internet addiction appears to be difficult to assess for several reasons, most importantly because use of the Internet is integrated into many practical daily life activities. Items on the IAT were developed to differentiate normal use from compulsive use.

The PCIAT and the Problematic and Risky Media Use in Children Checklist were developed for use in clinical assessments of children. They were adapted from the IAT so that adults could provide perspectives on a child's Internet use. Items on the PCIAT are very similar to items on the IAT; the checklist items are less comprehensive and simpler to assess. Both assessments allow the examiner to determine whether the child's behavior is addictive or has potential to be addictive.

TECHNICAL. Validity and reliability aspects of the IAT are presented in the test manual. Content evidence of validity is supported due to the thorough grounding of the items in the literature as well as the *DSM-IV* (APA, 1994). The test author provides additional information based on a validation study conducted by Widyanto and McMurran (2004). Widyanto and McMurran used a sample of 86 volunteer participants, 29 males and 57 females, who were contacted personally or via the Internet. Using a principal components extraction method with a varimax rotation, a factor analysis yielded six factors: Salience, Excessive Use, Neglect Work, Anticipation, Lack of Self-Control, and Neglect Social Life. The six factors explained 68.16% of the variance, with Salience explaining the most variance at 35.8%. Alpha coefficients were determined for each factor and ranged from .54 to .82, indicating the factors were at least moderately internally consistent. Correlations were found among the six factors, the Total score, Internet use, and participant age. The six factors were positively correlated with each other, with the strongest correlation of .62 between Salience and Excessive Use and the weakest correlation of .23 between Neglect Social Life and Neglect Work. Correlations between the Total score and the amount of use suggested higher general and personal Internet use were related to an increase in problems with respondents' Internet use. Overall, the study's authors suggest that the IAT has strong potential as a reliable and valid measure of Internet addiction but that it needs further testing due to the small volunteer sample.

The test manual for IAT-F offers no technical data for consideration. However, because both the PCIAT and the Problematic and Risky Media Use in Children Checklist are based on the IAT, by extension there is some content evidence of validity. The reference list in the test manual provides support for research on addiction in children and adolescents, including Internet addiction, but research on the valid and reliable use of the PCIAT and the Problematic and Risky Media Use in Children Checklist is not available from the test author.

COMMENTARY. The IAT is designed for users to assess the degree to which they are addictive Internet users, use that may be described as *normal*, *mild*, *moderate*, or *severe* in its addiction. The test manual provides information on how to administer, score, and interpret results of the test. A validation study supports the technical aspects of the test for a small volunteer sample of Internet users; the authors of the study suggest that further research is necessary.

The manual for the PCIAT and the Problematic and Risky Media Use in Children Checklist also provides detailed information about administering, scoring, and interpreting the two tests that together comprise the Internet Addiction Test for Families (IAT-F). The test author notes that the two tests are adapted from the IAT but otherwise provides no validity or reliability information.

SUMMARY. The IAT and the IAT-F provide test administrators an opportunity to assess Internet addiction in children, adolescents, and adults. The IAT has been studied and used extensively, but it is lacking in psychometric data. Psychometric data for the PCIAT and the Problematic and Risky Media Use in Children Checklist are not available. Additionally, the manuals for the IAT and the IAT-F contain a number of errors that can and should be easily corrected. In spite of these limitations, Internet addiction is a serious concern, especially with young children and adolescents, and Young's tests of Internet addiction hold great promise as strong assessments in both formal and informal settings. In summary, this reviewer highly recommends the continued development of the IAT and the IAT-F and cautions users to interpret results in combination with other sources of information.

REVIEWER'S REFERENCES

American Psychiatric Association. (1994). *Diagnostic and statistical manual of mental disorders* (4th ed.). Washington, DC: Author.

Ko, C.-H., Yen, J.-Y., Yen, C.-F., Chen, C.-S., & Chen, C.-C. (2012). The association between Internet addiction and psychiatric disorder: A review of the literature. *European Psychiatry, 27*(1), 1-8. doi:10.1016/j.eurpsy.2010.04.011

Widyanto, L., & McMurran, M. (2004). The psychometric properties of the Internet addiction test. *CyberPsychology & Behavior, 7*, 443-450.

Young, K. S. (1998). Internet addiction: The emergence of a new clinical disorder. *CyberPsychology & Behavior, 1*, 237-244.

[78]

Iowa Gambling Task, Version 2.

Purpose: Designed to detect impaired decision making that is mediated by the prefrontal cortex.

Population: Ages 8 and older.

Publication Dates: 1992-2016.

Acronym: IGT2.

Scores, 5: Block Net, Total Number of Cards Selected From Each Deck, Total Money, Reaction Time, Net Total.

Administration: Individual.
Price Data, 2020: $693 per software kit including software download, professional manual (2016, 101 pages), and administration card; $624 per software download; $172 per software upgrade CD-ROM; $69 per professional manual with administration card (print or digital).
Time: 10-15 minutes for administration.
Comments: Administered and scored via computer.
Author: Antoine Bechara.
Publisher: Psychological Assessment Resources, Inc.
Cross References: For reviews by Anita M. Hubley and Matthew E. Lambert of the original edition, see 18:62.

Review of the Iowa Gambling Task, Version 2 by ANTHONY T. DUGBARTEY, Adjunct Associate Professor, Department of Psychology, University of Victoria, Victoria, British Columbia, and Forensic Psychiatric Services Commission, Victoria, British Columbia, Canada:

DESCRIPTION. The Iowa Gambling Task, Version 2 (IGT2) is an individual, computer-administered test designed to measure decision making among individuals whose ages range from 8 to 80 years. No prior experience with a computer is required for this neuropsychological task, which takes approximately 10 to 15 minutes to complete. An examiner is required to be present at all times during the administration of the test, and the test instructions must be read from a card to the examinee.

Using four decks of cards labeled A through D, with each deck containing 60 cards, the examinee uses a computer mouse to click on the card from any one of the four decks he or she chooses. The examinee is given $2,000 facsimile money at the start of the test and is instructed to win as much money as possible by selecting from among the four decks, one at a time. Unbeknownst to the examinee, two of the decks are structured so as to have higher immediate win magnitudes, but also have larger net losses in the long term. The examinee receives feedback on the reward or loss, as applicable for each card selected, as well as the overall running tally. To succeed in this task, the examinee must look beyond the immediacy of substantial payoffs that also carry large risky losses, and then choose strategically from the decks that may seem less attractive in the short term but are ultimately more advantageous in the long term. Essentially, the task probes the degree to which the examinee can learn—initially through trial and error—in choosing the safer and modest yielding decks over the unpredictably higher yielding but inherently riskier decks.

The graphical layout of the test is quite attractive in simulating a casino platform. Colored bars on the computer screen provide ongoing feedback about money won (green bar) or lost (red bar).

The IGT2 is designed to mimic real-life risky decision making among clinical populations in a controlled psychometric testing environment. In fact, while it has now been extended to diverse clinical populations, the IGT was specifically designed for use with populations of patients who have sustained impairments to the frontal lobes of the brain, which hitherto were silent to traditional neuropsychological tests of reasoning and decision making. The test results, therefore, are intended to add to the complement of tests and examination procedures for determining brain dysfunction. As such, the IGT2 is not meant to be used as a stand-alone test of brain functioning.

What is new in the IGT2 is the downward extension of the test by about a decade to children 8 years and older, with associated normative data for children and adolescents from 8 to 17 years. In essence, therefore, anyone who has proficiency with the IGT would have little difficulty with the IGT2.

DEVELOPMENT. The developer of the IGT2 and its predecessor, the Iowa Gambling Task (IGT; Bechara, 2007), owes the inspiration for developing this test to Antonio Damasio's somatic marker hypothesis (see Damasio, 1996). As such, this test originally was developed to measure those decision-making deficits that occur as a consequence of lesions to the medial orbitofrontal cortical and ventro-medial cortical regions of the prefrontal cortex (i.e., mOFC and vmPFC respectively). The IGT2 manual indicates that the test also is appropriate for use with a broader clinical population ranging from patients with focal brain damage to various impulse control disorders and diverse neuropsychiatric conditions. Earlier, research versions of what is now the IGT2 were not computerized: The four actual decks of cards were laid out on the desk in front of the examinee, who was handed various pre-programmed financial reward and punishment contingencies for each card that he or she chose from the four decks (Bechara, Damasio, Damasio, & Anderson, 1994). From these humble beginnings came the development of the computerized version, which made test administration and scoring far easier and added the ability to generate a lot more data, such as reaction times in making advantageous versus disadvantageous decisions.

TECHNICAL. The standardization sample for the IGT2 consisted of a downward extension of 453 healthy youth ages 8 to 17 years, of which 51% were male. The adult standardization sample was unchanged from the earlier version of the IGT and included 932 healthy adults ages 18 and older (45.3% males and 54.7% females). The technical psychometric properties of the IGT2 for adults were not updated from the previous version of the IGT. This essentially means the reviews of the IGT by Hubley (2010) and Lambert (2010) in *The Eighteenth Mental Measurements Yearbook* continue to apply and are not reiterated here. The information in this section is limited to the addition of the downward age extension that forms the sole rationale for the test author coming up with the IGT2. In fact, the test author indicates that "the only difference between the two versions is the addition of normative data for children and adolescents ages 8 to 17, [and so] the results of research using the IGT also apply to the IGT2" (manual, p. 29).

In the main, the standardization sample for the downward age extension of the IGT2 provides a fairly good representation of ethnocultural groups as reflected by the U.S. Census. Caucasian White, African American, and Hispanic participants made up 64.2%, 13.7%, and 15.2% of the sample, respectively. Normative data are provided according to three age groups: 8 to 10 years, 11 to 13 years, and 14 to 17 years. Although the initial regression analyses showed that age for this youth sample had minimal predictive effect on IGT2 scores in accounting for up to only about 3% of the variance, age-based norms were nonetheless developed because of mounting evidence that decision making under ambiguity for children and adolescents may be qualitatively different from that of adults (Cassotti, Aïte, Osmont, Houdé, & Borst, 2014).

Separate norms are not available for different cultural or linguistic groups on the IGT2, which the test author suggests is a nonverbal test that may be easily modified to use different currencies other than the dollar as necessary.

Reliability. No reliability indices are reported for the IGT2 in the test manual. The IGT2's predecessor also lacked reliability estimates, as was astutely identified by Hubley (2010) and Lambert (2010), and this current version did nothing to rectify this omission. A significant challenge that almost effectively precludes applying internal consistency reliability estimates like split-half or alpha coefficients with the IGT2 is that the task is structured such that there can be large variabilities in deck experiences across card selections. At the very least, this reviewer believes temporal stability estimates ought to have been obtained, but they were not. A study that provides a glimpse into the reliability of the IGT used a rather narrow age range of 19- to 22-year-old university students to show a 3-week test-retest reliability of .35 (Xu, Korczykowski, Zhu, & Rao, 2013). In another study, this time with a 1-hour test-retest reliability examination of the IGT, Schmitz and colleagues (2020) found a correlation of .28 to .36 among healthy community residents ranging in age from 18 to 35 years. In comparing the IGT with two other tasks of risk-taking and impulsive behaviors—the Balloon Analogue Risk Task (BART) and Delay Discounting Task (DDT)—Xu and colleagues (2013) concluded that the IGT had a significantly lower test-retest reliability estimate relative to the BART and DDT. In sum, these independent test-retest reliability indices with the IGT are quite low.

Validity. There were some significant gaps in the validity evidence, and one must be cautious in reviewing validity evidence when no reliability indices are described. No updated validity studies are described for the adult population on the IGT2, which fundamentally relies on validity evidence provided for the previously published version. Although a few selected studies using such other executive control tests as the Stroop task, Trail-Making Test B, Continuous Performance Test, and rating scales of executive function have been included in the IGT2 manual, the test author cautions that the IGT measures a construct so unique that one should expect mixed results when the IGT is compared with extant tests of executive function. A factor analytic study (Buelow & Blaine, 2015) that employed two tests of decision making in addition to the IGT—the BART and the Columbia Card Task—appears to show quite convincingly that the neuropsychological construct of risky decision making, which the IGT and IGT2 purport to measure, is still poorly understood.

There are no new validity indices specifically generated by the test author for the IGT2 with the younger population of children and adolescents between the ages of 8 and 17 years. What is described in the validity chapter of the test manual is basically a literature review by researchers attempting to answer miscellaneous questions with the IGT in various clinical populations and life circumstances. The IGT2 author noted that in some of these studies it appeared that modified, perhaps even simplified, versions of the IGT were used. As such, the methodological differences in several of these studies would hamper a clear determination of the validity evidence applicable to the IGT/IGT2. Of note as well, several of the conceptual and methodological challenges of the IGT2 affect empirical determination of test score validity. One such criticism is that because the IGT is so difficult and healthy young examinees frequently perform at floor level (Steingroever et al., 2012), poor task performance cannot be taken to mean impaired decision-making abilities (Schmitz, Kunina-Habenicht, Hildebrandt, Oberauer, & Wilhelm, 2020).

In an interesting attempt to provide concurrent evidence of validity, Xu and colleagues (2013) showed rather low correlation of the IGT with both the BART (-.25) and the DDT (.28). A clever attempt to document construct evidence of validity led Schmitz and colleagues to develop a variant of this task, which they called the Berlin Gambling Task (BGT). Even with the BGT, Schmitz and colleagues concluded that both gambling tasks had such low reliability that they could not provide evidence of the tasks' validity.

COMMENTARY. The IGT2 has two principal strengths. One is its explicit basis in a clearly articulated theoretical framework of the somatic marker hypothesis. The second is the laudatory attempt to measure the uncertainty of real-life decision making in a formal and standardized psychometric manner. All of the weaknesses that bedeviled the IGT, with the exception of the lack of normative data for children and adolescents, are present in the IGT2. One must wonder, therefore, why the IGT2 has been re-branded as "Version 2," when there is nothing much new for adults in this current version. A supplement monograph that includes the new norms for younger populations may have sufficed. Even the four case examples from the IGT have been retained, and among the three additional case examples that have been included in the IGT2, the youngest is 18 years of age.

A criticism levelled against the previous version of the IGT2 remains appropriate with the current version: Depicting IGT2 performance in table form with various concurrent, construct, and predictive validity coefficient correlations for various population groups would have been very helpful. No such tables are offered in the IGT2 manual.

The IGT2 is a missed opportunity for addressing some of the emerging, substantive criticisms of this potentially useful task. For example, Gansler and his colleagues (2011), in an elegant convergent and discriminant validity study, have suggested that various aspects of the IGT/IGT2 may have more robust attentional and general intellect components than executive functioning. Others, such as Steingroever and colleagues (2013), in criticizing the very assumptions of the IGT/IGT2 about performance by healthy populations, go as far as to conclude this task is not ready for use as a tool for measuring decision-making deficits in clinical populations.

On a more practical note, researchers of youth gambling may question the probity of administering the IGT2 to children, as doing so may represent a potentially unhealthy socialization to gambling (see for example, Pitt et al., 2017).

SUMMARY. Barely a decade after the IGT was published in 2007, a second version was released that made only one notable modification: addition of normative data for youth ages 8 through 17 years. There are no changes in the task design, technical validation updates, or item compositions of the IGT with adults to warrant it being described as a second version. The researcher or clinician who uses the IGT only with adults would be rather disappointed to discover after upgrading to the IGT2 that no substantive improvements have been made. Those who intend to use the IGT2 with children and adolescents may be pleased to see the norms for that age group, but also quite disappointed about the lack of hard data with respect to the underlying psychometric properties.

REVIEWER'S REFERENCES

Bechara, A. (2007). Iowa Gambling Task. Lutz, FL: Psychological Assessment Recources.

Bechara, A., Damasio, A. R., Damasio, H., & Anderson, S. W. (1994). Insensitivity to future consequences following damage to human prefrontal cortex. *Cognition, 50,* 7-15.

Buelow, M. T., & Blaine, A. L. (2015). The assessment of risky decision making: A factor analysis of performance on the Iowa Gambling Task, Balloon Analogue Risk Task, and Columbia Card Task. *Psychological Assessment, 27,* 777-785.

Cassotti, M., Aïte, A., Osmont, A., Houdé, O., & Borst, G. (2014). What have we learned about the processes involved in the Iowa Gambling Task from developmental studies? *Frontiers in Psychology, 5,* 1-5.

Damasio, A. R. (1996). The somatic marker hypothesis and the possible functions of the prefrontal cortex. *Philosophical Transactions of the Royal Society of London: Biological Sciences, 351,* 1413-1420.

Gansler, D. A., Jerram, M. W., Vannorsdall, T. D., & Schretlen, D. J. (2011). Does the Iowa Gambling Task measure executive function? *Archives of Clinical Neuropsychology, 26,* 706-717.

Hubley, A. M. (2010). [Test review of the Iowa Gambling Task]. In K. F. Geisinger, R. A. Spies, J. F. Carlson, & B. S. Plake (Eds.), *The eighteenth mental measurements yearbook* (pp. 273-275). Lincoln, NE: Buros Institute of Mental Measurements.

Lambert, M. E. (2010). [Test review of the Iowa Gambling Task]. In K. F. Geisinger, R. A. Spies, J. F. Carlson, & B. S. Plake (Eds.), *The eighteenth mental measurements yearbook* (pp. 275-278). Lincoln, NE: Buros Institute of Mental Measurements.

Pitt, H., Thomas, S. L., Bestman, A., Daube, M., & Derevensky, J. (2017). Factors that influence children's gambling attitudes and consumption intentions: Lessons for gambling harm prevention research, policies and advocacy strategies. *Harm Reduction Journal, 14,* doi:10.1186/s12954-017-0136-3.

Schmitz, F., Kunina-Habenicht, O., Hildebrandt, A., Oberauer, K., & Wilhelm, O. (2020). Psychometrics of the Iowa and Berlin Gambling Tasks: Unresolved issues with reliability and validity for risk taking. *Assessment, 27,* 232-245.

Steingroever, H., Wetzels, R., Horstmann, A., Neumann, J., & Wagenmakers, E-J. (2013). Performance of healthy participants on the Iowa Gambling Task. *Psychological Assessment, 25,* 180-193.

Xu, S., Korczykowski, M., Zhu, S., & Rao, H. (2013). Risk-taking and impulsive behaviors: A comparative assessment of three tasks. *Social Behavior and Personality, 41,* 477-486.

Review of the Iowa Gambling Task, Version 2 by JENNIFER M. STRANG, Neuropsychologist, Washington DC Veterans Affairs Medical Center, Washington, DC:

DESCRIPTION. The Iowa Gambling Task, Version 2 (IGT2) is a computer-administered measure of decision-making ability that is identical to the original IGT, but extends the age range by including normative data for children and adolescents ages 8 to 17 years. The original IGT was designed to fill the gap in the neuropsychological repertoire with regard to measurement of decision-making impairments characteristic of individuals suffering damage to the medial orbitofrontal (mOFC) and ventromedial (vmPFC) regions of the prefrontal cortex. These individuals typically perform normally on measures of intellectual functioning, memory, language, and attention, yet struggle with adaptive functioning—often secondary to deficits in decision making.

Administration, scoring, and interpretation of the IGT2 are identical to the IGT. The examinee is seated in front of a computer, and the examiner reads a lengthy, standardized set of instructions. Administration takes 10 to 15 minutes. The goal of the task is to win as much money as possible while minimizing loss. The examinee is presented with four decks of 60 cards each and a beginning balance of $2,000. Using a mouse, the examinee clicks on a card from any deck, and a message is displayed indicating the amount of money the examinee has won or lost. A green bar at the top of the screen lengthens or shortens depending on the amount of money won or lost. After money has been added or subtracted, the card disappears and the examinee selects another card. The standard administration consists of 100 trials. The four decks are labeled A', B', C', and D'. Choosing a card from decks A' and B' results in a large immediate gain; however, at unpredictable points, a gain is followed by a high penalty, so that ultimately, these decks are disadvantageous. Decks C' and D', considered to be advantageous, result in smaller immediate gains but also smaller eventual losses. The frequency of punishment and average loss per punishment vary by deck. There are a number of optional settings, including intertrial interval (i.e., the interval between two consecutive card selections), number of trials, and monetary options (e.g., the starting amount and currency can be altered). However, normative data are based on a standardized administration; therefore, the test author recommends using the default settings for general clinical purposes, and it is not entirely clear why one would choose to use the optional settings.

The examiner generates a score report by clicking on the View Reports button. Two normative standards, demographically corrected and U.S. Census-matched, are available. The test author recommends using the demographically corrected norms for diagnostic purposes and the U.S. Census-matched norms when determining an examinee's capacity for everyday functioning. Similar to the original IGT, the primary IGT2 scores include: total net score (number of cards chosen from the advantageous decks); block net scores (number of advantageous choices for each block of 20 cards); number of cards selected from each deck; total money (total amount of money won minus the total amount of money borrowed); and reaction time (amount of time it takes an individual to choose a card). The test manual includes several case examples to aid interpretation of results, though interpretation is not necessarily straightforward. For instance, one of the case examples achieved IGT2 scores that qualified as "nonimpaired." The test manual explains that the individual made a slightly higher number of selections from the disadvantageous decks (51) relative to the advantageous decks (49), and his scores on the Wisconsin Card Sorting Test indicated impairment in executive function. Although his IGT2 scores were in the nonimpaired range, the scores were at the very low end. Ultimately, this individual was believed to have "at least a mild compromise in decision making" (manual, p. 12).

DEVELOPMENT. A gambling task was chosen to assess decision making because it "mimics real-life decision making so closely" and "resembles real-world contingencies" (manual p. 2). The original version of the IGT, which was administered manually before being computerized to improve the speed and accuracy of scoring, is described in two previous reviews in *The Eighteenth Mental Measurements Yearbook* (2010). The test author notes that the principles of the computerized IGT (and therefore the IGT2) remained the same as the manual version with two exceptions: a change in the schedule and magnitude of reward and punishment and the use of 60 cards in each deck instead of 40. Initial studies, cited in the test manual, indicated that individuals using the computerized version believed that the computer was generating the reward and punishment schedules, making it impossible to "win." Therefore, the schedule change was implemented to ensure that the computerized scores were identical to those generated by the manual version. Additionally, the number of cards in each deck was increased from 40 to 60 to minimize possible depletion of cards. Several studies are cited in the test manual indicating that IGT performance is consistent regardless of the use of real versus facsimile money, the use of varying intertrial time delays, and manual versus computerized administration.

TECHNICAL. The test manual includes standardization and normative information for the IGT (Bechara, 2007), as well as the new standardization and normative information for children and adolescents. Briefly, in the original IGT, demographically corrected normative data were derived from a group of 932 nonimpaired adult participants gathered from multiple sites. The normative sample was well matched to the U.S. population for age and gender; however, the standardization sample appears to have a relatively higher education level than the general U.S. population. Additionally, the degree to which the standardization sample matches the U.S. population in terms of ethnicity is not reported. Data for a 2003 U.S. Census-matched sample (N = 264), derived from a subset of the demographically corrected sample, also are presented. Regression analyses indicated that gender, age, and education accounted for minimal variance in IGT scores. Despite the minor effect of demographic characteristics, age- and education-based scores were developed based on prior research regarding the differential effects of development and education on cognitive test performance. Continuous and categorical norming methods were used to derive non-normalized T scores and percentiles ranks.

The IGT2 sample consisted of 453 nonimpaired children ranging in age from 8 to 17 years. The sample was well matched to the U.S. population for age and ethnicity. Other than demographic information, no additional details about the sample (e.g., geographic location of data collection sites, testing procedures) are provided. Similar to the adult sample, demographic characteristics had little effect on IGT2 scores; nonetheless, age-based norms were derived to reflect developmental differences in cognitive test performance demonstrated in prior research. As with the adult sample, continuous and categorical norming methods were used to derive T scores and percentile ranks. In both samples, scores were classified as *Impaired* (T score range 0-39), *Below Average* (T score range 40-44), and *Nonimpaired* (T score range ≥ 45), with percentages in each category grossly equivalent to the percentages predicted from the normal distribution.

The absence of reliability data is discussed in previous IGT reviews and persists in the current version. The test manual presents construct evidence of validity for the original IGT. However, such evidence is limited by the fact that there are no other available executive function measures that capture the construct of decision making. Indeed, construct evidence is mixed, with some studies showing nonsignificant correlations between various IGT scores and other measures of executive function (e.g., Wisconsin Card Sorting Test), and other studies finding significant correlations between certain IGT scores and other commonly used executive function measures (e.g., Stroop task). Evidence for use of the IGT with different age groups and clinical populations, factors impacting IGT performance, and neuroimaging studies examining the relationship between IGT performance and adolescent prefrontal cortex activity also are presented. The test author asserts that "the results of research using the IGT also apply to the IGT2" because "the only difference between the two versions is the addition of normative data for children and adolescents ages 8 to 17" (manual, p. 29). All of the validity evidence reported in the IGT2 manual is from research using the IGT.

COMMENTARY. Strengths of the IGT2 include its expanded norms, brevity, ease of administration and scoring, engaging game-like format, reasonably sized child/adolescent normative sample well matched to the U.S. population for age and ethnicity, and empirical evidence supporting its use with multiple clinical populations. Furthermore, to the knowledge of this reviewer, it continues to be the only commercially available measure of decision making. The absence of reliability data is a significant weakness. Theoretically, decision-making capacity would be considered a relatively stable construct; therefore, the validity of the IGT would be enhanced if good reliability were demonstrated. Additionally, all validity evidence reported for the IGT2 is from research conducted with the original IGT. Logistically, the administration includes a rather lengthy set of instructions that could potentially be difficult for individuals with working memory deficits to process and retain. Finally, interpretation is not necessarily straightforward, especially when scores hover near the border of what is classified as impaired decision making and the nonimpaired range of functioning.

SUMMARY. The IGT2 extends the age range of the original IGT to children and adolescents ages 8 to 17 years. It is a unique measure that fills the gap in the neuropsychological repertoire with regard to measurement of decision-making capacity. The IGT2's many strengths include its expanded norms; brevity; ease of administration and scoring; engaging game-like format; reasonably sized, demographically matched child/adolescent normative sample; and empirical evidence supporting its use with multiple clinical populations. The absence of reliability evidence continues to be a significant weakness. Furthermore, construct evidence of validity appears mixed and was not updated for the IGT2. Lastly, the interpretive guide is, in some cases, misleading and ultimately calls into question the relevance of the T score distribution categories. In all, the IGT2 is recommended as an adjunct to a comprehensive assessment of neurocognitive functioning, and caution is urged in drawing conclusions about decision-making capacity in the absence of additional supporting data.

REVIEWER'S REFERENCE

Bechara, A. (2007). Iowa Gambling Task. Lutz, FL: Psychological Assessment Resources.

[79]

IPT English Early Literacy Test, Third and Fourth Editions.

Purpose: Designed to "assess the skill development of English learners in kindergarten and first grade on the continuum of literacy development."

Population: Students in Kindergarten and Grade 1 who speak English as a second language.

Publication Dates: 2000-2017.

Administration: Small groups of no more than five students.

Price Data, 2020: $455 per test set including 50 Reading test booklets, 50 Writing test booklets, and examiner's manual; $209 per 50 Reading test booklets; $159 per 50 Writing test booklets; $133 per examiner's manual; $86 per technical manual.

Foreign Language Edition: Spanish version available for "students who speak Spanish as a first language, heritage language, or second language."

Comments: Assesses students' developmental stages of reading and writing; designed for "initial identification, program placement, progress monitoring, and redesignation in school." Test items did not change between the third and fourth editions, but norms were updated.

Author: Nathalie Longree-Guevara.

Publisher: Ballard & Tighe, Publishers.

a) READING.

Scores, 9: Visual Recognition, Letter Recognition, Phonemic Awareness-Initial Sounds, Phonics-Initial Blends and Digraphs (Grade 1 only), Reading Vocabulary, Reading for Life Skills, Reading for Understanding Sentences, Reading for Understanding Stories (Grade 1 only), Total Reading.

Time: (15-30) minutes.

b) WRITING.

Scores, 5: Copy Letters, Write a Word and Copy the Sentence, Write a Story, Spelling (Grade 1 only), Total Writing.

Time: (5-30) minutes.

Cross References: For reviews by Merith Cosden and Patti L. Harrison of an earlier edition, see 17:94.

Review of the IPT English Early Literacy Test, Third Edition and IPT English Early Literacy Test, Fourth Edition by SANDRA T. ACOSTA, Associate Professor of Bilingual Education, Educational Psychology, Texas A&M University, College Station, TX:

DESCRIPTION. The IPT English Early Literacy Test is a paper-and-pencil, norm-referenced test for assessing reading and writing skills of kindergarten and first grade students whose first language is not English. The two subtests—Reading and Writing—are untimed tests that can be administered to small groups of no more than five students. The purpose of the IPT English Early Literacy Test is to assess early literacy in English using a developmental framework of three stages or levels to indicate progression on a continuum. The Reading subtest levels are pre-, beginning, and early reading; Writing subtest levels are pre-, beginning, and early writing. Uses for the test include assessing and monitoring annual progress of English learners (ELs) and identifying early literacy skills that are less developed. Test results should not be interpreted as designating non-English, limited English, or competent English readers or writers.

The Reading subtest consists of 61 items organized into eight skill categories: Visual Recognition, Letter Recognition, Phonemic Awareness—Initial Sounds, Phonics–Initial Blends and Digraphs (administered only to first graders), Reading Vocabulary, Reading for Life Skills (recognition of common symbol and word signs), Reading for Understanding Sentences, and Reading for Understanding Stories (first grade only). Test administration ranges from 15 to 30 minutes. The Writing subtest consists of

19 items organized into four skill categories: Copy Letters, Write a Word and Copy the Sentence, Write a Story, and Spelling (first grade only). Test administration ranges from 5 to 30 minutes.

In addition to the test administration script, the test publishers, Ballard and Tighe, provide procedures for administering and scoring the subtests in three training formats: online, face-to-face, and train-the-trainer workshops. Subtest scores are reported as raw scores, standard scores derived from *z*-scores, percentile ranks, and normal curve equivalents.

DEVELOPMENT. The IPT English Early Literacy Test estimates two facets of English early literacy—Reading and Writing—but not English language proficiency. The test authors provide a view of early literacy development in which the three stages of literacy development are operationally defined by the tasks the child is able to perform. For example, beginning readers are able to recognize most uppercase and lowercase letters. Each facet was parsed into three standards (levels) using cut scores (for standards setting see Kane, 2001; Loomis & Bourque, 2001). The procedures for determining how cut scores were derived are not described in the test manual. Item development appears to have been drawn primarily from the previous edition of the IPT English Early Literacy Test with input and recommendations from practitioners and expert panels. Scoring for the Reading subtest uses a dichotomous (correct/incorrect) format. Conversely, the Writing subtest uses two scoring formats: dichotomous and holistic rubric-based (for story writing only). Test items were selected during field testing that occurred in two time periods, fall (kindergarten) and spring (kindergarten and first grade).

TECHNICAL.

Standardization. For the IPT English Early Literacy Test, Third Edition, the spring 2009 norming sample for Reading comprised 754 students ranging in age from 5 to 8 years. For Writing, the sample consisted of 736 students ranging from 5 to 9 years of age. The samples were drawn from 10 states representing the major geographic areas of the United States—West, South, Central, and East. The demographic characteristics of the Reading and Writing samples, respectively, were as follows: *grade*: K (45%, 45%), first (55%, 55%); *gender*: male (50%, 51%), female (50%, 49%); *race/ethnicity*: Asian (9%, 9%), Black (34%, 31%), Hispanic (41%, 41%), White (16%, 18%), Other (< 1%, < 1%); *economically disadvantaged*: no (47%, 46%), yes (53%, 54%); *home language*: English (50%, 50%), Spanish (36%, 36%), Other (14%, 7.5%); and *country of birth*: U.S. (89%, 89%), outside U.S. (11%, 11%).

To evaluate the distribution of the standardization sample, teachers rated student participants' general, oral, reading, and writing abilities. Field tests were conducted during spring and fall of 2009. The kindergarten field tests were conducted again in the fall of 2010 (n = 464) because the earlier field test "did not meet Ballard & Tighe's quality criteria for demographic variation" (technical manual, p. 7). The fall 2010 data replaced those collected in fall 2009. The test publisher did not describe the process for selecting the standardization sample in the technical manual.

In 2016, the test was renormed, resulting in the IPT English Early Literacy Test, Fourth Edition. The test items did not change. The 2016 Reading norms were based on a sample of 422 students (fall kindergarten n = 131; spring kindergarten n = 154; first grade n = 137). Of the total sample, 58% did not specify ethnicity; the remainder of the sample was Asian (2%), Black (3%), Hispanic (35%), White (1%), or multi-ethnic (2%). The 2016 Writing norm sample included 507 students (fall kindergarten n = 131; spring kindergarten n = 184; first grade n = 192). Reported ethnicity was similar to the Reading sample with two exceptions: 65% of the sample did not provide ethnicity, and 30% identified as Hispanic.

Reliability. Internal consistency estimates for the spring 2009 sample were between .42 and .81 across Reading (Parts 1 through 7) and .89 for Total Reading in kindergarten and between .47 and .85 across Reading (Parts 1 through 8) and .92 for Total Reading in Grade 1. For Writing, alpha coefficients were .84 and .56 for Parts 1 and 2, respectively, and .82 for Total Writing in kindergarten and between .50 and .90 (for Parts 1, 2, and 4) and .85 for Total Writing in Grade 1. Alpha coefficients for the fall 2010 sample of kindergarteners ranged from .56 to .89 across Reading (Parts 1 through 7) with a value of .89 for Total Reading. For Writing, the coefficients were .79 and .69 for Parts 1 and 2, respectively, and .80 for Total Writing. The Rasch model was used to estimate reliability for the 2016 norms. Coefficients for the Reading and Writing tests were .85 and .77, respectively.

Interrater reliability was evaluated as part of the spring 2009 field test using a process in which Part 3 of the Writing tests that were completed by kindergarten (n = 328) and Grade 1 (n = 404) students were rated by two trained independent raters. The resultant intraclass correlation coefficients were .91 and .88 for kindergarten and Grade 1 students, respectively. Exact agreement between raters was found in about 86% of the cases, and agreement within 1 point was found in approximately 13% of cases. A second interrater reliability study was conducted in which two independent raters each rated Part 3 for 249 tests takers, all kindergarteners, in the fall 2010 sample, yielding an intraclass correlation coefficient of .92. Exact agreement between raters was found in about 94% of the cases, and agreement within 1 point was found in approximately 5.2% of cases. Interrater reliability information was not provided for the 2016 normative sample (i.e., the IPT English Early Literacy, Fourth Edition).

Validity. Validity evidence derived from three sources: alignment to the TESOL English language proficiency standards in reading and writing that occurred during test development, content evidence matrices (one for reading and one for writing), and construct evidence. The content evidence matrices list the parts associated with each facet of the test (reading or writing), together with descriptions of the skills associated with each part and the corresponding test items that evaluate the specified skills. Part/total scale correlations for the spring 2009 sample are provided to support construct evidence of validity. Correlation coefficients ranged from .35 to .89 and from .17 to .65 for Reading and Writing, respectively. Additional construct evidence was provided in the form of teacher opinions of reading and writing abilities, which indicated that higher teacher ratings of ability were associated with higher scores on the IPT English Early Literacy Test, Third Edition.

COMMENTARY. The strength of the IPT English Early Literacy Test is its practicality (i.e., short test, ease of administration, small group testing format). The primary weakness of the test involves the incomplete description of its development. For example, the standard-setting process for determining the cutoff scores for the three categories is vague and imprecise. Another concern is the absence of generally accepted statistical analyses to support the test publisher's claims of the appropriate uses of the test scores (e.g., measuring change and growth).

SUMMARY. The IPT English Early Literacy Test, a paper-and-pencil, norm-referenced test, assesses the early literacy skills of ELs in reading and writing. Using a criterion-referenced approach to score interpretation, test scores are classified into three literacy categories: pre-, beginning, and early reading/writing. The test publisher advises that the three categories do not correspond to language proficiency levels, and scores should not be used for initial identification or redesignation (exit process from EL status). Additionally, the IPT English Early Literacy Test is a descriptive test, and scores should not be interpreted as diagnostic. The test's limitations with regard to usage, utility, and limited range within the three categories should be carefully considered. Consequently, it is not recommended as a test for assessing student growth. It is recommended with caution as a screening test for evaluating kindergarten and first grade English learners' emergent literacy skills in reading and writing.

REVIEWER'S REFERENCES

Baker, C. (2001). *Foundations of bilingual education and bilingualism* (3rd ed.). Clevedon, England: Multilingual Matters.

Kane, M. T. (2001). So much remains the same: Conception and status of validation in setting standards. In G. J. Cizek (Ed.), *Setting performance standards: Concepts, methods, and perspectives* (pp. 53–88). Mahwah, NJ: Erlbaum.

Loomis, S. C., & Bourque, M. L. (2001). From tradition to innovation: Standard setting on the National Assessment of Educational Progress. In G. J. Cizek (Ed.), *Setting performance standards: Concepts, methods, and perspectives* (pp. 175–217). Mahwah, NJ: Erlbaum.

Review of the IPT English Early Literacy Test, Third Edition and Fourth Edition by HONGLI LI, Assistant Professor, Georgia State University, Atlanta, GA:

DESCRIPTION. The IPT English Early Literacy Test, Third Edition and the IPT English Early Literacy Test, Fourth Edition are designed to assess literacy skill development of English learners in kindergarten and first grade. The Fourth Edition of the test provides a normative update based on data collected in 2016; test items and test materials were unchanged. The 2016 norms and other technical information are included in an appendix to the test manual. The tests have been aligned to the current TESOL standards and many state standards. The test developers state that this test is intended to guide instruction rather than to make proficiency determinations. Thus, the test results should not be used to make inferences regarding whether a student is non-, limited, or competent in his or her literacy skills. Instead, the test focuses on students' developmental stages. As a result of taking this test, students' literacy skills can be classified into one of three categories. The score categories are pre-reading, beginning reading, and early reading based on the Reading test and pre-writing, beginning writing, and early writing based on the Writing test.

The Reading test consists of eight parts: Part 1 (Visual Recognition), Part 2 (Letter Recognition), Part 3 (Phonemic Awareness-Initial Sounds), Part 4 (Phonics-Initial Blends and Digraphs), Part 5 (Reading Vocabulary), Part 6 (Reading for Life Skills), Part 7 (Reading for Understanding Sentences), and Part 8 (Reading for Understanding Stories). Parts 4 and 8 are for first graders only. The Writing test consists of four parts: Part 1 (Copy Letters), Part 2 (Write a Word and Copy the Sentence), Part 3 (Write a Story), and Part 4 (Spelling). Part 4 is for first graders only.

The IPT English Early Literacy Test must be administered by a teacher or other qualified district personnel. The test is administered to small groups of students (no more than five at a time), typically in two sessions. The testing can be broken up into more sessions if necessary. The Reading test takes from 15 to 30 minutes, and the Writing test takes from 5 to 30 minutes. The administration procedure described in the examiner's manual is easy to follow. The examiner's manual also provides detailed information on the scoring procedure and score interpretations.

DEVELOPMENT. Similar to the rest of the IPT family of tests, the third and fourth editions of the IPT English Early Literacy Test are designed to respond to state and federal legislation that requires initial language proficiency assessment of non-native English-speaking students. The test developers believe that there are different components of early reading or writing skills, so different parts of the test can provide important descriptive information. One test was developed to serve students in kindergarten and first grade. However, because kindergarteners and first graders are undergoing rapid development, accommodations are provided to differentiate between expected competencies for kindergarteners and first graders. For example, kindergarteners do not need to answer Parts 4 and 8 of the Reading test and Part 4 of the Writing test. To ensure diverse membership among kindergarteners in the fall cohort, a fall 2010 field test for kindergarteners was carried out in addition to the spring 2009 field test, which included both kindergarteners and first graders. As a result, there are three norming groups for the third edition of the test, one for fall kindergarteners, one for spring kindergarteners, and one for spring first graders. The 2016 renorming effort provides three additional sets of norms that parallel those just listed.

In the spring 2009 field test, the norming sample involved 754 participants in kindergarten and first grade from 10 states. Fifty percent of participants identified their primary language as English, and 36.3% of participants reported Spanish as their primary language. In the fall 2010 field test, 464 kindergarteners were tested within the first 30 days of their enrollment using the IPT English Early Literacy Reading Test, and an additional 330 kindergarteners were tested using the IPT English Early Literacy Writing Test. English was the primary language for 47.4% of the students who took the Reading test and 48.8% of the students who took the Writing test. Spanish was the primary language for 43.1% of the students who took the Reading test and 47.3% of those who took the Writing test. Overall, these norming samples appear diverse in terms of ethnicity.

The data from the 2016 renorming study were collected from 422 students in kindergarten and first grade. In some respects, the demographic data are less clear than those in the previous cohorts because many responses are coded as "unspecified." For example, 42.4%, 58.1%, and 56.4% of responses for gender, ethnicity, and primary language, respectively, are presented as "unspecified" in the tables describing the sample characteristics for the Reading test. For the Writing test, the percentages are similar, at 52.9%, 64.5%, and 62.3%. The unspecified composition of the norming samples makes it impossible to evaluate the extent to which the sample reflects the population for whom the test is intended. Although the examiner's manual says that the test is nationally normed, the norming samples appear to be convenience samples drawn from 10 U.S. states. Both the examiner's manual and the technical manual suggest that the IPT English Early Literacy Test is to be used with students who speak English as a second language. However, in the two early field tests (Spring 2009 and Fall 2010), about half of the participants were students whose primary language was English. In the 2016 renorming sample, only 2.1% (Reading) and 2.2% (Writing) reported English as their primary language; however, the large percentage of "unspecified" primary language noted previously leaves the question of representativeness unanswered. The test developers need to clarify the target population and ensure the representativeness of the norming samples. A similar point was raised in a prior review of the earlier version of the IPT

English Early Literacy Test in which 82% and 55% of norming sample participants were English native speakers (Harrison, 2007).

TECHNICAL. The technical manual provides detailed information about item and test characteristics based on results from the three field tests. A large majority of the students who participated in the 2009 and 2010 field tests had "moderate" reading, writing, or general academic ability based on their teachers' opinions. However, the Reading test appears to be particularly easy for both spring kindergarteners and first graders, based on item difficulty indices. For example, the proportion of spring 2009 kindergarteners passing Parts 1, 2, and 3 of the Reading test (averaged across items) exceeded .90. Similarly, for spring 2009 first graders, the proportion passing all Reading parts, except Part 8, exceeded .90. If the IPT English Early Literacy Test is too easy for students, it may not be able to provide rich developmental information as the test is designed to do.

Raw scores, standard scores, percentile ranks, and normal curve equivalents are provided for fall kindergarteners, spring kindergarteners, and first graders separately. The conversion tables are straightforward and easy to follow. In addition, students' ability can be classified into three categories (pre-, beginning, and early). The classification for the Reading test is based on the total Reading score, and the classification for the Writing test is based on scores obtained from each part.

The technical manual provides reliability estimates in the form of internal consistency and interrater reliability coefficients. Alpha coefficients for the total Reading score and the total Writing score were .89 and .82, respectively, for kindergarteners and .92 and .85, respectively, for first graders in the 2009 and 2010 norming samples. Alpha coefficients varied widely across the parts comprising both Reading and Writing. The 2016 norming study used Rasch modeling to estimate internal consistency of the test, which is reported as .85 for Reading and .77 for Writing. In addition, Part 3 of the Writing test is a productive writing item scored using a rubric. Sufficiently high interrater reliability was established with the rubrics and rater training materials, as reflected by intraclass correlation coefficients of .91 and .88 for kindergarten and first grade students, respectively, in spring 2009.

The technical manual provides evidence to support content, construct, and concurrent validity of test scores. Content evidence is presented in the form of a matrix listing the domains covered by the test items. Construct evidence is presented in the form of correlations between scores from the different parts and the total score, using data from the 2009 and 2010 field tests. The correlation coefficients are generally moderate to moderately high, ranging overall between .35 and .94, with more than 80% of the reported coefficients exceeding .50. However, the Reading test, Part 1 (Visual Recognition) demonstrated low correlations (coefficients ranged from .13 to .49, overall) with other parts, with the lowest values associated with kindergarten students. This raises the question of whether visual recognition should be included as part of the reading construct. Evidence to support the concurrent validity of test scores is presented in the form of how well the test results agree with teachers' opinions. Notably, the reliability and the validity of teachers' opinions of students' ability is unknown.

COMMENTARY. The IPT English Early Literacy Test, Third Edition and the IPT English Early Literacy Test, Fourth Edition are part of the IPT family of tests designed to respond to the assessment needs of English learners. The test developers followed professional standards in terms of test development, field testing, and validation. The examiners' manual and the technical manual provide sufficient information in terms of the test administration and scoring procedures, norming, item and test characteristics, and validity evidence. Both the Reading test and the Writing test show high reliability. The validity evidence provided in the test manual is more limited. Also, none of the norming samples have been shown to be nationally representative. In particular, half of the students in the 2009 and 2010 norming samples reported English as their primary language, which runs counter to the test developers' claim that the tests are designed to evaluate English learners. Because the 2016 norming study included demographic data that were often "unspecified," it is not possible to gauge the representativeness of this more recent sample of test takers. Thus, this reviewer questions whether the norming tables provided are appropriate for use with students whose primary language is not English.

SUMMARY. The IPT English Early Literacy Test (Third and Fourth Editions) are intended to assess the skill development of English learners in kindergarten and first grade. The test developers have considered the developmental differences of kindergartners and first graders and have accommodated such differences. The test demonstrates high reliability and has garnered some validity evidence. The administration and scoring procedures are straightforward and easy to follow. In order for the tests to realize their full potential, the test developers need to clarify the target population and align the norming samples with this target population.

REVIEWER'S REFERENCE

Harrison, P. L. (2007). [Test review of IPT Early Literacy Test]. In K. F. Geisinger, R. A. Spies, J. F. Carlson, & B. S. Plake (Eds.), *The seventeenth mental measurements yearbook*. Retrieved from http://marketplace.unl.edu/buros/

[80]

IPT English Reading & Writing Tests, Third Edition.

Purpose: Designed to "assess students' reading and writing skills in English in order to identify English language learners who need language support ... for purposes of placement, progress monitoring, and redesignation."
Population: Students in Grades 2-12 whose native language is not English.
Publication Dates: 1992-2015.
Scores, 10: Reading (Vocabulary, Vocabulary in Context, Reading for Understanding, Reading for Life Skills, Language Usage, Total), Writing (Conventions, Write a Story, Write Your Own Story, Total).
Administration: Group.
Levels, 3: IPT 1, IPT 2, IPT 3.
Foreign Language Edition: Spanish version available for "students who speak Spanish as a first language, heritage language, or second language."
Time: (45-75) minutes for Reading; (25-60) minutes for Writing.
Comments: Administered via paper and pencil or online.
Authors: Beverly Amori, Enrique F. Dalton, and Phyllis L. Tighe.
Publisher: Ballard & Tighe, Publishers.

a) IPT 1.
Population: Students in Grades 2-3.
Forms, 2: 1C, 1D.
Price Data: $455 per test set including 50 Reading test booklets, 50 Writing test booklets and examiner's manual (2015, 130 pages); $78 per technical manual (2015, 114 pages).

b) IPT 2.
Population: Students in Grades 4-6.
Forms, 2: 2C, 2D.
Price Data: $455 per test set including 50 Reading test booklets, 50 Reading Test answer sheets, 50 Writing test booklets, Reading test scoring template, and examiner's manual (2015, 142 pages); $78 per technical manual (2015, 128 pages).

c) IPT 3.
Population: Students in Grades 7-12.
Forms, 2: 3C, 3D.
Price Data: $455 per test set including 50 Reading test booklets, 50 Reading Test answer sheets, 50 Writing test booklets, Reading test scoring template, and examiner's manual (2015, 141 pages); $78 per technical manual (2015, 113 pages).

Cross References: For reviews by James Dean Brown and Alan Garfinkel of an earlier edition titled IDEA Reading and Writing Proficiency Test, see 13:142.

Review of the IPT English Reading & Writing Tests, Third Edition by CAROL EZZELLE, Director, Psychometrics, National Board for Professional Teaching Standards, Arlington, VA:

DESCRIPTION. The IDEA Proficiency Test (IPT) Reading & Writing Tests, Third Edition, are group administered, standardized, and nationally normed assessments of English language reading and writing ability for students in Grades 2-12 whose native language is not English. The IPT 1 is designed for students in Grades 2-3, the IPT 2 is designed for students in Grades 4-6, and the IPT 3 is for students in Grades 7-12.

The purpose of the tests is to measure "students' reading and writing skills in English in order to identify English language learners who need language support in reading and writing for purposes of placement, progress monitoring, and redesignation" (technical manual for IPT 1, p. 1). The tests are not intended to assess specific course content or skills that are above average for grade levels.

The IPT 1, IPT 2, and IPT 3 Reading tests each assess five domains consisting of the number of items in parentheses: Vocabulary (10), Vocabulary in Context (10), Reading for Understanding (13), Reading for Life Skills (10), and Language Usage (10). The IPT 1, IPT 2, and IPT 3 Writing tests each assess three domains: Conventions (10), Write a Story (two open-ended items), and Write Your Own Story (one open-ended item). The three levels of the IPT Reading and Writing tests have been aligned to Teaching English to Speakers of Other Languages (TESOL) standards and individual state standards.

Each test is untimed. Large font, single color, and clear graphics result in user-friendly test materials. Web-based versions are also available. All multiple-choice items have four answer choices. Tests are scored either by hand or machine. Open-ended writing items are scored by human raters trained in using the scoring rubrics.

The examiner's manuals for the IPT 1, IPT 2, and IPT 3 are each thorough; they contain step-by-step instructions for preparing for, administering, and scoring the tests; training raters for the open-ended Writing test items; and using results for instructional groupings, using profile templates for individual and group profiles, and improving instruction.

DEVELOPMENT. The tests of English language reading and writing ability were based in research and analysis of reading and writing curricula, learning materials, tests, and literacy standards. Items from the original IPT Reading and Writing tests were reviewed, and based on criticisms and comments from teachers' and language professionals' review, items were identified for improvement or replacement with newly developed items. Multiple cycles of reviews by practitioners and item field tests were conducted to ensure a well-functioning test. The test publisher updated norms in 2007 and again in 2014.

TECHNICAL. The technical manual contains information on the purpose, structure, and development of the IPT Reading and Writing tests as well as demographic information about the normative sample and reliability and validity evidence. Psychometric properties of the measure support its intended use with students who are at or below grade level in English language reading and writing, and not with students above grade level.

Score types include raw scores as well as normative scores including scaled scores, percentile ranks, and normal curve equivalents. Scores from writing test parts are weighted. Raw scores in reading and writing are classified as Non-, Limited, and Competent Reader or Writer, and also can be classified into one of five IPT Proficiency Levels: Beginning, Early Intermediate, Intermediate, Early Advanced, or Advanced. Based on results from the IPT English Reading & Writing Tests and the IPT Oral English Test (see 81, this volume), a student's overall English language proficiency can be classified as either Fluent English Proficient or Limited English Proficient. Results can help identify a student's English language strengths and weaknesses. Parallel forms support the use of the IPT measures in pre- and post-testing.

In 2014, the renorming study resulted in updated cutoff scores for Non-, Limited, and Competent English Reading and Writing classification categories. The scores for designating a student as Non-, Limited, or Competent were identified through the use of analysis that maximized the classification accuracy for Non- and Limited while providing a "reasonable" (technical manual for IPT 1, p. 44) cutoff score for classifying students as Competent.

Descriptive statistics by domain within each test form, including alpha coefficients (.69–.88 for Reading subtests; .94–.96 for total Reading; .73–.75 for Writing Conventions) and alternate forms reliability (.38–.81 for Reading subtests; .69–.89 for total Reading; .37–.68 for Writing Conventions) are reported in the technical manual. For the open-ended writing test items, interrater agreement and correlation coefficients were calculated.

The technical manual also provides a summary of content, construct, and criterion/concurrent validity evidence for the IPT Reading and Writing tests as a measure of English language reading and writing ability for students in Grades 2-12 whose native language is not English. Evidence of content validity includes item mapping to subtest areas and objectives being assessed. Evidence of construct validity is provided by an examination of correlations between various subtest scores within each test form that indicate related yet different skills are being measured. Evidence of criterion validity is provided by (a) correlations of subtest scores with teacher ratings of students' reading and writing abilities, and (b) crosstabulation of teachers' classification of student achievement by the IPT's classification of student achievement. Rubric development utilizing committees of experts and practitioners and extensive research provided validity evidence for the scoring of the open-ended items on the Writing test.

COMMENTARY. The uses of the IPT English Reading & Writing Tests encompass (a) evaluating the reading and writing skills of English language learners in basic school settings, (b) testing language minority students for initial identification and redesignation, (c) providing placement information for instructional programs, (d) monitoring progress and growth in English language development, and (e) providing diagnostic information for program planning. The examiner's manuals and technical manuals are thorough and well-organized in supporting the uses of the tests. Available reports are presented on the test publisher's website. The program will continue to benefit from its updated norms and by gathering further evidence of validity for the tests' uses.

SUMMARY. The IPT English Reading & Writing Tests have validity and reliability evidence supporting their use as effective, group-administered, standardized tests evaluating the reading and writing skills of English language learners in Grades 2-12. Multiple score types, classification categories, and report types readily aid teachers, schools, and districts to support instruction for English language learners.

Review of the IPT English Reading & Writing Tests, Third Edition by BO ZHANG, Professor, Department of Educational Psychology, University of Wisconsin-Milwaukee, Milwaukee, WI:

DESCRIPTION. The IPT English Reading & Writing Tests are a series of tests that measure English language ability for students from Grades 2 to 12 whose native language is not English. The series is divided into three levels: IPT 1 for Grades 2-3, IPT 2 for Grades 4-6, and IPT 3 for Grades 7-12. Each level of the IPT series assesses three curricular areas (Reading, Writing, and Oral Language). The intended uses of the IPT tests include (a) to identify English language learners (ELLs), (b) to determine the strengths and weaknesses of ELLs, and (c) to re-designate ELL status (technical manual, p. 1). Test authors recommended using the Reading and Writing tests along with the Oral Language tests to render the above decisions. These tests should not be used to assess language learning in specific classrooms as the IPT tests are not aligned with any particular school curriculum, nor should they be used to assess reading and writing competencies of a non-ELL population as the IPT test items tend to be too easy for those students. IPT has an online version, but this review is for the paper and pencil version of the Reading and Writing tests only.

All IPT English Reading tests consist of five sections: Vocabulary, Vocabulary in Context, Reading for Understanding, Reading for Life Skills, and Language Usage. Altogether there are 53 Reading items for IPT 1 and IPT 2 and 55 items for IPT 3. All IPT English Writing tests share the following three components: Conventions, Write a Story, and Write Your Own Story. The Conventions subtest has 10 items, Write a Story has two writing tasks, and Write Your Own Story has one writing task. All items are multiple-choice except for the latter two writing components. The IPT tests are power tests in that no time limit is imposed on a section or on the whole test. Students are allowed to complete the test at their own pace. As a general estimate, the Reading and Writing tests take 45-75 and 25-60 minutes, respectively.

An examiner's manual accompanies the IPT English Reading & Writing Tests for each level. Each level has two parallel forms (C and D). The examiner's manual provides step-by-step instruction on how to administer the tests and provides details on how to score the tests and interpret test results. Along with the raw score, IPT reports the following norm-referenced scores: scaled score, percentile rank, and normal curve equivalent (NCE) for both Reading and Writing tests. In addition, for both tests, designation category (three levels) and proficiency level (five levels) are reported. To facilitate the scoring of the two subjectively scored writing tasks, a highly descriptive holistic scoring rubric is provided. Additionally, writing samples are included for teachers to practice the use of the rubric.

DEVELOPMENT. The current IPT Reading and Writing forms (C and D) were developed from the original forms, A and B. Items in the old forms were revised and replaced with new items. All items were then reviewed by practitioners and pilot tested by students. The final versions of the new forms were tested with large samples in 2001, consisting of "3,324 students in 178 schools and 76 school districts in 25 states" (technical manual, p. 5). Sample sizes for the Reading tests were approximately 1,500 for each level; sample sizes for the Writing tests were smaller, at around 250. Item and test characteristics were reported based on these samples. Item analysis showed that a majority of items were easy. For instance, for the IPT Reading tests, the average difficulty values were .80, .74, and .75 for IPT 1C, 2C and 3C, respectively. Item discrimination values were not reported.

TECHNICAL. The IPT English Reading & Writing Tests Forms C and D were first standardized in 2002 and were re-normed in 2007 and 2014. The most recent norms (2014) used the following samples: 1,219 for IPT 1–Reading; 980 for IPT 1–Writing; 1,422 for IPT 2-Reading; 1,116 for IPT 2–Writing; 1,360 for IPT 3–Reading; and 993 for IPT 3–Writing. Large samples like these promote the establishment of stable norms. Demographic information for the normative samples was provided regarding gender, grade level, ethnicity, and primary language. For primary language, about 40% of students at all grade levels selected Spanish. As none of the samples was compared to the actual ELL population, it is hard to gauge their representativeness. Further complicating the issue of representativeness is the fact that a large percentage of respondents (e.g., 46% for IPT 1) did not indicate their primary language. Normative tables are provided for each grade from 2 to 12. Practitioners can easily obtain norm-referenced scores using these conversion tables. Readers of the normative tables will note that the IPT tests are easy for many students because many students are English proficient. Thus, one finds high raw scores for many test takers. For example, with a raw score scale that runs from 0 to 53 for Grade 3 Reading, a score of 50 on Form 1C corresponds to a percentile rank of 57.

Reliability coefficients were high for IPT Reading tests. Coefficient alpha was .96 for both forms of IPT 1, .94 and .95 for the two forms of IPT 2, and .94 and .95 for the two forms of IPT 3. All the subscales on the Reading tests also demonstrated relatively high reliability coefficients. Some of them were higher than .80, indicating that these subscale scores may be used separately. Alternate form reliability coefficients were strong too: .85 to .89 for IPT 1, .69 to .79 for IPT 2, and .82 to .85 for IPT 3. In addition, test-retest reliability coefficients were high for all Reading tests over an interval of approximately two weeks: .87 for IPT 1 Form C, .83 for IPT 2 Form C, and .94 for IPT 3 Form C. Alternate form reliability coefficients for the subscales were lower than those reported for internal consistency. To summarize reliability information, users should have confidence in using all forms of the IPT Reading tests as consistent measures of ELL students' reading competence.

For the Writing tests, reliability evidence was reported separately for each task. For the 10-item Writing Conventions subtest, internal consistency, alternate form, and test-retest reliability coefficients were mostly in the .60 or .70 range for all levels. Reliabilities of the two writing subtests were evaluated by interrater reliability. The agreement and correlation between ratings from two raters were computed. They were all at moderate levels, ranging from .65 to .82. For example, for the Write a Story subtest on Form 1C, the correlation between two ratings was .78 for task 1 and .77 for task 2. Two raters had exact agreement for 67.6% and 70.5% of the students, respectively. Similar results were reported for the Write Your Own Story subtest. Although correlation and percent agreement estimate reliability for each task, more advanced statistical techniques, such as generalizability theory analysis, can be employed to estimate the overall reliability of two writing tasks.

Regarding validity, the test authors present three types of validity evidence: content, construct, and criterion/concurrent. For content validity, the evidence is illustrated in a table that describes the competencies or concepts assessed under each subtest along with the item number for each competency. Although it is clear that the stated competencies are assessed and the alignment between item content and the corresponding competency is apparent for some items, the content of the table itself should be evaluated by content experts. Such a panel of experts would be able to evaluate how well the selected competencies have been covered in each subtest and how well each test item aligns with the target competency.

The test authors suggest that construct evidence for an educational test like IPT Reading and Writing is hard to obtain. Tests like IPT are usually organized by curriculum areas such as vocabulary and vocabulary in use but there is no construct as such. The test authors present the intercorrelations among the Reading subtests as construct evidence; these coefficients were quite high, ranging from .50 to .87. Although the exact meaning of these intercorrelations is unclear, one can probably conclude that these subtests have measured one common construct.

For criterion evidence, the external criterion was the teacher's opinion of reading and writing abilities. Students were rated by teachers using a 5-point scale of *very low, low, average, high average,* and *superior*. Overall, teacher rating and IPT Reading and Writing scores were moderately correlated, with coefficients ranging from .54 to .65. Because the IPT tests are used to identify and re-designate English language learners, one important aspect of the validity of their scores lies in their accuracy in placing students into these proficiency levels, such as certifying whether a student has met the ELL requirement. Statistically, this amounts to testing the validity of the cutoff scores set for each category. For the IPT Reading and Writing tests, cut scores were set for three competence levels: Non-English Readers (NER), Limited English Readers (LER) and Competent English Readers (CER). These scores were set to "maximize the classification accuracy for Non- and Limited English Readers (NER and LER), while providing a reasonable cutoff for classifying Competent English Readers" (technical manual for IPT 1, p. 44). In other words, cutoff scores were selected to minimize the classification error for NER and LER, the two classifications that would prompt further ELL instruction.

The test authors provide validation information for the cutoff scores for the Reading tests by comparing them to teacher opinion of oral ability. The validity of this comparison may be questionable. First, the comparison is not direct, as reading is different from oral language. Second, different competence levels were used: three for reading but four for oral English, making the comparison hard to interpret. Lastly, only moderate association was found between the two measures. Overall, it is hard to evaluate how much this comparison has enhanced the validity evidence of the selected cutoff scores.

COMMENTARY. The IPT tests demonstrate many strengths. Technically, reliability for the Reading tests is very strong not only for the whole test but also for many of the subtests. This enables a wide range of test score use, such as considering subtest scores within a comprehensive diagnostic framework. Practically speaking, the tests are easy to use. They are relatively brief. The test booklets are easy for students to follow, and the examiner's manuals are convenient for teachers to use. Another major strength lies in the recency and relevancy of the norms. These tests were normed in 2014 using large, relevant samples.

Evidence of validity can be improved. First, more validity evidence should be reported. Judging by the test design and test items, the IPT English Reading & Writing Tests show strength in content evidence that could be evaluated more rigorously. The criterion-related validity evidence can be enhanced in a few ways. One can compare this test to other tests for the same purpose, such as those from WIDA (WIDA, 2018). A high correlation between them would provide direct convergent evidence of validity. The cutoff scores need stronger support. One shortcoming of the current cutoff scores is that their relationship with the designated performance levels is unclear. Take the IPT 1 Reading for second grade as an example. Classification error may have been minimized for the cutoff scores of 25 and 45, but no evidence was provided for how such scores indicate limited or no competence. A more meaningful cutoff score could be established through standard setting, about which no information was reported.

Reliability of the Writing tests can be strengthened. An overall reliability measure of writing competence will enhance the utility of the general writing score.

SUMMARY. For school districts and ELL teachers looking for a general measure of English language competence for ELLs, the IPT tests present a compelling option. These tests are easy to use, offer a variety of test scores, have recent norms, and enjoy considerable technical soundness. Reliability is very high for the Reading tests and moderately high for the Writing tests. Validity evidence also looks promising, though more direct evidence is highly desirable.

REVIEWER'S REFERENCE

WIDA. (2018). *ACCESS for ELLs.* Retrieved from https://www.wida.wisc.edu/assess/access

[81]

IPT Oral English Test.

Purpose: Designed to "evaluate students' oral proficiency in English" for program placement, progress monitoring, and/or redesignation after completion of a language development program.

Population: Students in pre-kindergarten through Grade 12 who speak English as a second language.

Publication Dates: 1983-2010.

Scores, 8: Vocabulary, grammar, Comprehension, Verbal Expression, Listening Skills, Speaking Skills, Basic Interpersonal Communication Skills, Cognitive Academic Language Proficiency.

Administration: Individual.

Foreign Language Edition: Spanish version available for "students who speak Spanish as a first language, heritage language, or second language."

Comments: Administered via paper and pencil or online.

Publisher: Ballard & Tighe, Publishers.

a) PRE-IPT ORAL ENGLISH, FOURTH EDITION.

Population: Ages 3-5.

Price Data, 2020: $414 per paper-based test set including 50 test booklets, story board with story pieces and box, examiner's manual (2010, 37 pages), 50 test level summaries in English, and 50 test level summaries in Spanish; $175 per 50 online test credits (story board [$89] and story pieces [$89] required for online administration; examiner's manuals provided free online); $64 per technical manual.

Time: (15-20) minutes.

Author: Robin Stevens.

b) IPT I.

Population: Students in kindergarten to Grade 6.

Forms, 2: G, H.

Price Data: $399 per paper-based test set including 50 test booklets, 1 book of test pictures, examiner's manual (2010, 50 pages), 50 test level summaries in English, and 50 test level summaries in Spanish; $175 per 50 online test credits (picture book [$160 for Form G or Form H] required for online administration; examiner's manuals provided free online); $64 per technical manual.

Time: 14 minutes for average administration time.

Authors: Corie De Anda and Bill Eilfort.

c) IPT II.
Population: Students in Grades 6-12.
Scores, 9: Same as above plus Morphology.
Forms, 2: E, F.
Price Data: $399 per paper-based test set including 50 test booklets, 1 book of test pictures, examiner's manual (2010, 48 pages), 50 test level summaries in English, and 50 test level summaries in Spanish; $175 per 50 online test credits (picture book [$160 for Form E or Form F] required for online administration; examiner's manuals provided free online); $64 per technical manual.
Time: 14 minutes for average administration time.
Authors: Bill Eilfort and Corie De Anda.

Cross References: For reviews by Emilia C. Lopez and Salvador Hector Ochoa of an earlier edition titled IDEA Oral Language Proficiency Test, see 14:171; see also T5:1234 (5 references).

Review of the IPT Oral English Test by STEVEN H. LONG, Associate Professor, Marquette University, Milwaukee, WI:

DESCRIPTION. The IPT Oral English Test is an assessment of English listening and speaking proficiency. It comes in three separate versions: Pre-IPT, intended for preschool children ages 3-5; IPT I, for elementary school children in Grades K-6 grade; and IPT II, for middle and high school children in Grades 6-12. The three versions share a common design. They all yield information about eight components of language: Vocabulary, Grammar, Comprehension, Verbal Expression, Listening Skills, Speaking Skills, Basic Interpersonal Communication Skills, and Cognitive Academic Language Proficiency (IPT II also includes Morphology). The test is intended primarily for the evaluation and appropriate educational placement of children learning English as a second language. Results also can be used to identify general strengths and weaknesses within the eight components that are tested and to periodically assess student progress toward greater proficiency. The format of the test requires the abilities to follow auditory directions and to respond in English. With the exception of a few pointing responses, children must speak intelligibly. The test is therefore not suitable for those with serious phonological problems.

The first version of the IPT Oral English Test was published in 1983. Subsequently new authors have continued development of the test, and the norms have been updated three times: in 1997, 2004, and most recently in 2009. [Editor's note: The test publisher advised that norms based on data collected in 2017 are now available.] Other small changes, based on user feedback and critical review, have been made to the test picture and verbal stimuli to assure that they are current, appropriate, and still achieving their psychometric purpose of measuring a child's language proficiency. In the latest version the original three-level ordinal scale of proficiency (Non-English Speaking, Limited English Speaking, Fluent English Speaking) has been expanded by creating three categories within the Limited English level (Early Intermediate, Intermediate, Early Advanced). The result, then, is a five-level scale that the test authors believe is more discriminating and can help in the evaluation of student progress.

The IPT Oral English Test is administered, scored, and interpreted in ways that should be familiar to any professional accustomed to giving standardized tests. Pre-IPT, the preschool version of the test, uses as props eight two-dimensional cutout figures that must be positioned and moved on a flat "park scene." The examiner asks the child questions related to these figures and also instructs the child to position and move them in certain ways in order to evaluate auditory comprehension. It requires some rehearsal by the examiner in order to make this interaction natural and thereby obtain the best possible responses from a child. The versions for school-age children, IPT I and IPT II, use picture easels and questions read from the test booklet in order to elicit responses.

To administer and score the test takes from 15 to 20 minutes for Pre-IPT and an average of 14 minutes for the other versions. If a student is uncomfortable or appears unwell, the test can be stopped and resumed on another day. The test is administered by question levels that increase in difficulty. Test responses must be scored in real time as each level has a ceiling expressed as a given number of errors. The Pre-IPT has a single test booklet that is used for every administration. IPT I and IPT II come with two different booklets (G/H or E/F) that should be alternated in successive administrations in order to reduce any learning effect. To elicit responses, verbal prompts are read verbatim to the student. Many of the questions also provide a second prompt that can be given if the first one does not elicit an adequate response. If a student responds with an answer that seems relevant to the question but is not one of the words or phrases listed as acceptable in the test booklet, the examiner prompts a revision from the student ("Can you think of another word that means about the same thing?"). The test booklets provide alternate prompts for some questions and scoring guidelines for all of them but, given the number of items, examiners should review the booklets prior to attempting to give the test. Details about how to manage and score more problematic answers are contained in the examiner's manual.

The examiner's manuals, one for each of the three versions, describe the administration and scoring of the IPT Oral English Test, provide normative information, and offer guidelines for interpreting the results. Raw scores, the total number of correct responses, are converted to standard scores, percentile ranks and normal curve equivalents. The latter scores, used mainly for research, are derived from percentile ranks, but have equal intervals and so should be used to compute group averages or gain scores. The test manual offers general guidelines for administration and scoring of the test. Specific prompts and criteria that must be satisfied in order to award a point to scoreable items are provided in the test booklets. A set of appendices contains information regarding: (a) the specific speaking skills that are expected at each proficiency level; (b) the linguistic content at each level under the headings of vocabulary, grammar, comprehension, and verbal expression; (c) the skill areas tapped by each test item; (d) and the pragmatic functions addressed by each test item. Collectively, this information can be used to interpret test results and can aid in identifying potential areas of instructional need.

DEVELOPMENT. The IPT Oral English Test was developed to address needs created by the emergence of bilingual education in the late 1960s. It draws on several educational and cognitive models such as Cummins' (1984) distinction between Basic Interpersonal Communication Skills (BICS) and Cognitive Academic Language Proficiency (CALP) as well as Bloom's (1956) hierarchical taxonomy of cognitive skills. To these models the test authors added a general linguistic framework identifying the domains of vocabulary, grammar, comprehension, verbal expression, and morphology. All of these components are analyzed developmentally, though the authors do not cite specific sources for the way in which they scale specific language behaviors. The language behaviors, ordered developmentally in terms of a series of levels and distributed among the components of the authors' model, are then evaluated via specific items on the test.

TECHNICAL. The 2009 norms for the IPT Oral English Test were developed using three samples of students: 735 ages 3-5 for the Pre-IPT; 1,130 and 1,128 ages 4-14 for the IPT I Forms G and H, respectively; and 670 and 646 ages 11-21 for the IPT II Forms E and F, respectively. The samples were drawn from five (Pre-IPT) to as many as 14 (IPT I) states and the District of Columbia. The demographics of the samples were broadly similar. All samples were balanced for gender, combined students mainly born in the U.S. with a smaller number born in other countries, and included roughly a third from economically disadvantaged families. Spanish and English were the primary languages spoken in the great majority of students' homes, though numerous other languages were represented in smaller numbers. The biggest difference among the three normative samples was in their ethnic composition. The Pre-IPT sample was predominantly Hispanic (70.9%) and White (17.9%). The IPT I sample had a smaller majority of Hispanic students (51.9%) and almost equal percentages of Black (21.3%) and White (19.6%) students. The IPT II sample comprised mostly Hispanic students (45.2%), slightly more White students (23.4%), and almost equal numbers of Black (14.9) and Asian/Pacific Islander (13.5%) students.

The validity and reliability analyses parallel one another for all three versions of the IPT Oral English Test. The test authors present item difficulty data to show that correct responses declined from lower to higher item numbers thereby showing evidence of content validity and justifying the organization of the test into developmental levels, each of which have ceiling criteria. Further analysis showed a positive relationship between proficiency levels obtained on the test and teacher ratings of students' English oral ability. Spearman rho coefficients ranged from .41 to .69. In contrast, the relationship between test proficiency levels and age was only .13 for the Pre-IPT sample. This age analysis was not done for the IPT I and II samples. Overall, the correlation results indicate that the IPT Oral English Test demonstrates evidence that supports the construct validity of its scores.

Coefficient alpha was used to evaluate content sampling error, or internal consistency reliability of the test. The test authors consider coefficients of .80 to be minimally reliable, and the coefficients for the IPT Oral English Test scores at the different age and grade intervals ranged from .95 to .99. This evidence suggests that the internal consistency of the test is very good. The test authors also provide data regarding the standard error of measurement

(*SEM*) for test scores. The *SEM* is used to estimate the band of scores within which an individual's true score probably lies (confidence interval). The *SEM* across eight age and grade intervals ranged from 2.08 to 2.79 points, indicating that the *SEM*s are relatively similar across age groups. No data were reported for either test-retest or interrater reliability.

COMMENTARY. The test authors provide evidence that items in the three versions of the IPT Oral English Test increase in difficulty as students progress to higher proficiency levels. As a result, there is a clear developmental trend that appears to justify the test's use in assigning children to developmental stages in the acquisition of English. It also supports a transition from use of the Pre-IPT to subsequent use of IPT I and IPT II. They appear to represent a continuous hierarchy of content difficulty. What is less clear is how the IPT Oral English Test can or should be used in instructional planning. The test documentation provides a breakdown of its items according to the various linguistic and educational domains they target. However, the test authors did not employ explicit developmental models of lexical, morphological, or syntactic learning (e.g., Crystal, 1982) in creating the test hierarchy. This makes it difficult to apply the test results to teaching English in a principled way.

The lack of interrater reliability data is concerning because of the student population targeted by the IPT Oral English Test, often referenced as English language learners. Because the test is likely to be used with children who are ethnically different from the examiner and may speak a nonstandard dialect of English this creates a higher risk of measurement error (Craig, 2016). Without an assessment of interrater reliability, one can only speculate on how great that error might be.

SUMMARY. The IPT Oral English Test assesses students' English oral proficiency via their ability to respond nonverbally and verbally to a series of listening and speaking tasks. The test aims to help in educational placement, provide a profile of skills in different educational and linguistic domains, and monitor progress across repeated administrations. The test has been revised and renormed several times since the first edition appeared in 1983. Administration is straightforward but requires real-time scoring because of ceilings. The IPT Oral English Test shows good validity and internal consistency evidence but has not been evaluated for interrater reliability. The lack of a clear developmental model behind the test suggests that English teaching goals should not be based solely on test results. Care should be taken when comparing results obtained from the same student at different times by different examiners.

REVIEWER'S REFERENCES

Bloom, B. S. (Ed.). (1956). *Taxonomy of educational objectives: The classification of educational goals, handbook 1: Cognitive domain.* New York, NY: David McKay.

Craig, H. K. (2016). *African American English and the achievement gap: The role of dialectal code switching.* Abingdon, UK: Routledge.

Crystal, D. (1982). *Profiling linguistic disability.* London, UK: Edward Arnold.

Cummins, J. (1984). *Bilingualism and special education: Issues in assessment and pedagogy.* San Diego, CA: College-Hill Press.

Review of the IPT Oral English Test by WILLIAM LORIÉ, Principal, Capital Metrics, Washington, DC:

DESCRIPTION. The purpose of the IPT Oral English Test is to evaluate students' oral proficiency in English for identification of English language learners (ELLs), ELL progress monitoring, and ELL re-designation upon language development program completion. The IPT tests are designed to address listening and speaking skills, specifically targeted to four areas of language: vocabulary, grammar, comprehension, and verbal expression. Test scores are directly translated to levels of oral proficiency in English, labeled A through F (the IPT levels) and described in examiner's manuals.

This review covers the English language print versions of the following tests: Pre-IPT Oral English Test (Ages 3-5, Fourth Edition), IPT I Oral English Test (Grades K-6, Forms G and H), and IPT II Oral English Test (Grades 6-12, Forms E and F).

Regardless of age/grade level, the IPT is administered individually and scored item-by-item by the test administrator. After the completion of a section labeled by the IPT level of its constituent items, a number-correct error score is tallied for the section, and either testing stops and the test taker is assigned to a level according to that score, or testing continues to the next section. Although the IPT I and IPT II examiner's manuals reference optional diagnostic answer sheets and scannable answer sheets, these were not available to the reviewer and thus their use cannot be commented upon. The default administration forms provided are straightforward and easy to use by a trained and qualified examiner. The published testing times—15-20 minutes for the Pre-IPT and 14 minutes on average for the IPT I and IPT II—appear accurate, given the nature of the questions and expected responses, and the test lengths.

The Pre-IPT is administered using a picture board and individual picture pieces. Manipulation of these pieces is required for many of the items, either by the examiner or the test taker. The IPT I and IPT II have a greater variety of prompt types and include picture cards that are referenced by the examiner and test taker for some of the items.

Norms are provided by form and for specific age- or grade-band groupings of students: 3-year-olds, 4- and 5-year-olds (together), Kindergarten (Initial Identification), Grades K-1, Grades 2-6, Grades 6-8, and Grades 9-12.

DEVELOPMENT. The IPT tests are grounded in the passage of the Bilingual Education Act in 1968. According to the technical manuals, the IPT tests have been available since 1979 with the start of field testing for the IPT I. The IPT II and the Pre-IPT were subsequently developed. When new IPT test form are developed, items are drafted to align with an oral proficiency skills framework informed by work in oral language skills research. Items undergo expert review, piloting, revision, and field testing for each form. Attention is paid to the balance of vocabulary, grammar, comprehension, and verbal expression items across levels of the tests. The most recent forms and set of norms were developed using field testing conducted in spring and fall 2009. [Editor's note: The test publisher advises that the norms have been updated based on data collected in 2017. This review was written before those data were available.]

Demographic characteristics of these samples, with sizes ranging from 167 (Pre-IPT, 3-year-olds) to 580 (IPT I, Form G, Grades 2-6), are documented in detail, with gender, ethnicity, primary language, country of birth, socioeconomic status, migrant status, disability, and teacher opinion of test taker general academic, English oral, English reading, and English writing skills among the variables tabulated.

TECHNICAL.

Standardization. Although characteristics of the field test participants support the claim that all students in the standardization samples are ELLs, the basis for the selection of the participating states, districts, schools, and students is not documented in the test manuals. There is no comparison of the sampled groups to any reference populations (for example, ELLs in the U.S.) or even to a sampling target. If any weighting was applied, for example to approximate a uniform distribution across grades for norms spanning several grades, such weighting is not documented in the technical manuals. Otherwise, the norms appear to have been set using established procedures for norming, although the sample sizes are somewhat low for this purpose.

Reliability. The number of items administered to a test taker and the test taker's true score are dependent on each other, due to the IPT's test continuation/discontinuation rules. This complicates the estimation of internal consistency reliability (i.e., alpha coefficients), which normally requires responses from all test takers to all items. The technical report does not explain how reliability was estimated. Moreover, all items for a given test taker are scored by the same person. Such a design can inflate reliability coefficients because scoring could be affected by judgments of test taker performance on previous items (a halo effect), thus inducing a systematic dependency among item scores. The reliabilities of the magnitudes reported for the IPT (.94 through .99) would typically have much to commend them. In this case, they should be interpreted with caution.

Test reliability is affected by consistency between raters (administrators); however, technical manuals for the IPT do not report estimates of rater consistency. Without interrater reliability coefficients, it is difficult to contextualize the alpha reliabilities reported.

The IPT I and IPT II each have two forms, although alternate forms reliability coefficients are not provided, and it is not clear whether such analyses have been conducted.

Validity. Directions to the examiner include guides for scoring each item. On some of the vocabulary items, examiners are directed to accept "any appropriate response." The Pre-IPT examiner's manual elaborates on this instruction, with respect to vocabulary: "[T]he words that the student uses must be appropriate to the situation and acceptable in regular English usage. For example, when describing a frayed pair of tennis shoes, appropriate responses would include *frayed* or *worn*, along with many others, but not *broken* or *holey*" (p. 14, italics in original). It is not unreasonable for otherwise well-trained examiners to differ on the acceptability of certain responses, such as *used*, *messed-up*, and *not useful*, in this context. With respect to comprehension and verbal expression, the manual again calls upon examiner judgments. Reliance on these judgments might introduce a potential source of error due to non-standardization. Investigation of this possible threat to validity is not reported in any of the technical manuals.

The reported magnitudes and patterns of intercorrelations among total test scores and teacher opinions of English oral, reading, and writing ability are as expected for all forms, and offer supportive evidence for convergent and discriminant validity.

All the external validation evidence presented for the IPT is in the form of crosstabulations of IPT proficiency level or IPT designation with teacher opinion of test taker English oral ability. The reported Somers' *D* and Spearman's rho coefficients support concurrent measures criterion-related validity claims.

COMMENTARY. The IPT is an easy-to-administer and score test of oral English proficiency useful for ELL identification, monitoring, and re-designation. The IPT is purposely built to a blueprint informed by language learning theory and research.

The principal source of external support for inferences about IPT test takers' oral English proficiency is the opinion of teachers of students who participated in field testing. Additional studies incorporating other (not necessarily concurrent) measures would strengthen assurance that the test is meeting its goals.

The IPT seems highly reliable, but it must be noted that the reported alpha coefficients do not consider possible halo and administrator effects.

There is no evidence supporting inferences from the norm sample to a well-defined external population, but the norms may be used if such inferences are not intended.

According to the widely accepted *Standards for Educational and Psychological Testing* (American Educational Research Association, American Psychological Association, & National Council on Measurement in Education, 2014), the use of subscores is premised on evidence of their uniqueness and distinctness from each other and from total scores. No such evidence is provided in the Pre-IPT or IPT technical manuals or other available materials. As such, while it may be that the IPT can help educators identify specific areas of weakness, reviewing item responses, subscores, or response profiles in order to identify weaknesses cannot be recommended.

SUMMARY. The IPT Oral English Test was designed to evaluate students' oral proficiency in English for identification of English language learners (ELLs), ELL progress monitoring, and ELL re-designation upon language development program completion.

There is a basic level of validation research supporting the IPT's stated purpose. That support is limited in its accounting of potential sources of error, and does not include predictive studies that could have measured, for example, the extent to which IPT-based designations appeared to be accurate.

Use of the IPT cannot be recommended for comparisons to a national population, or a general population of English language learners. The IPT cannot be recommended for diagnosing areas of strength or weakness *within* oral English proficiency.

Test users in need of an oral English proficiency measure should conduct due diligence in selecting the most appropriate test. For those whose purpose is limited to ELL identification, monitoring, and re-designation, the IPT is a candidate test to consider. Those in need of national norms and/or diagnostic information should look to alternatives.

REVIEWER'S REFERENCE

American Educational Research Association, American Psychological Association, & National Council on Measurement in Education. (2014). *Standards for educational and psychological testing*. Washington, DC: American Educational Research Association.

[82]

Jail Screening Assessment Tool.

Purpose: Designed as a semi-structured interview to assess an inmate's current level of functioning and to identify those who require mental health services.
Population: Individuals entering correctional institutions.
Publication Date: 2005.
Acronym: JSAT.
Scores: No formal scores; management recommendations made in 6 areas: Suicide/Self-Harm Risk, Violence Risk, Victimization Risk, Mental Health Issues, Placement Recommendations, Referrals.
Administration: Individual.
Price Data, 2020: $70 each per 1-24 copies of manual (141 pages), which includes coding form; $55 each per 25 copies or more.
Time: Approximately 20 minutes per interview.
Authors: Tonia L. Nicholls, Ronald Roesch, Maureen C. Olley, James R. P. Ogloff, and James F. Hemphill.
Publisher: Mental Health, Law, and Policy Institute, Simon Fraser University [Canada].

Review of the Jail Screening Assessment Tool by SEAN REILLEY, Licensed Psychologist, Eastern State Hospital, Lexington, KY:

DESCRIPTION. The Jail Screening Assessment Tool (JSAT) is a semistructured interview for adults entering jail that provides screening data for identification of mental health needs and recommendations for referrals, placement, and management of risks for violence toward others, self-harm and/or suicide, and victimization. A well-utilized screening protocol in Canadian jails, the JSAT can be completed in less than 20 minutes by individuals with advanced training and experience in acute psychiatry, correctional populations, psychological assessment techniques (including conducting semistructured interviews), and additional JSAT administration training.

The JSAT manual includes tabbed sections that provide the user a brief literature review of mental health concerns in jails and commonly encountered ethical and professional issues in this population. An empirical foundation for the JSAT interview domains (Identifying Information, Legal Situation, Violence Issues, Social Background, Substance Use, Mental Health Treatment, Suicide and Self-Harm Issues, and Mental Health Status) is provided along with a separate recommendations section detailing management and placement considerations. Following informed consent considerations, JSAT interview questions are administered in ascending fashion. Some judgment is needed to determine whether follow-up inquiries and prompts (provided in the test manual) are needed to better understand and code a given response. Responses to JSAT interview questions are coded on the double-sided coding form using guidelines found in the test manual. The order of the JSAT Coding Form departs chronologically from the suggested order of administration in the manual, although it is not difficult to discern where to correctly code items. No specific summary scores are yielded at the completion of the JSAT. Rather, the particular benefit of the JSAT is as a structured professional judgment tool. That is, the examiner obtains interview responses as part of a systematic review of evidence-based variables in multiple domains; augments them with data from file review and clinical observations; attempts to identify specific mental health issues, risks for suicide/self-harm, violence, and victimization; and makes referrals and placement recommendations within the jail. The clinical management recommendations are coded on the front of the JSAT Coding Form, and additional comments or clarifications based on the screening can be made by the examiner.

DEVELOPMENT. The JSAT is an extension of a brief manual used for structured mental health screening in Canadian jails that was developed from empirical and clinical work in the 1990s by staff at the Mental Health, Law, and Policy Institute at Simon Fraser University. The original publication, the *Manual for the Mental Health Screening Interview and Coding at Surrey Pretrial Services Center*, was used to conduct screening interviews for mental health concerns and risks for violence, self-harm, suicide, and victimization among adults undergoing admission to jails in British Columbia. Inmates who screened positive for a serious mental health concern were referred to a licensed professional for comprehensive assessment. As interest in the screening program grew across Canada, the United States, and other English-speaking areas, a decision was made to update the original manual to ensure the integrity of the screening program and to revise and update items reflective of current scientific evidence and theory as well as practice developments in the field. As such, the JSAT and the JSAT Coding Form were subsequently published in 2005 for mental health screening in jails while balancing needs for (a) valid and reliable screening; (b) efficiency; and (c) risk management considerations for placement, safety management, and treatment needs. Specific modifications and enhancements to the JSAT guidelines and manual are not detailed well in the test manual. An exception occurs in the description of the mental health [symptom] status items, which use a modified version of the Brief Psychiatric Rating Scale (BPRS; Overall & Gorman, 1962), titled the BPRS Expanded Version 4.0. The expanded scale utilizes a 3-point rating system reflecting an absence of the mental health symptom, possible presence, or definitive presence. No total BPRS summary scores are yielded by the current version of the JSAT.

TECHNICAL. Data concerning sizes of the standardization samples are not reported in the test manual, in favor of more general descriptions. Preliminary validation data are provided from two studies of male and female inmates. For the study involving male inmates, nurses and supervised graduate students working at the facility completed an earlier version of the procedures described in the JSAT manual for 303 men representing sampling of every second inmate. One to four days later, the inmates completed the Structured Interview for DSM (SCID) and were rated on the Brief Psychiatric Rating Scale (BPRS) and the Global Assessment of Functioning scale (GAF). Overall, mental health referrals generated from both sets of evaluators occurred in 30% of inmates, which generally aligns with mental health rates reported in correctional settings. Of those referred for services, 84% (true positive rate) were found to have a mental health disorder according to blind evaluation using the SCID. Specificity was found to be 67% for the JSAT. Perhaps related to differences in graduate coursework, differences emerged between the two sets of evaluators. Inmates screened and referred for mental health services by nurses did not differ in their mental status relative to inmates not referred for services. However, inmates screened and referred by supervised graduate students did have significantly different mental status scores as measured by the BPRS and GAF compared to inmates not referred for services.

In the validation studies with female inmates, a sample of 91 inmates completed the JSAT and an expanded version of the BPRS with supervised graduate students. A slightly higher rate of mental health referrals (37%) emerged, and referred inmates had higher BPRS ratings relative to non-referred inmates. A second validation study used stratified sampling to identify 15 referred and 14 non-referred inmates for mental health services based on the JSAT. An interviewer blind to the JSAT screening status completed the Structured Clinical Interview for DSM-IV Non-Patient Edition (SCID-I/NP) with both groups of inmates, and the overall kappa value was considered fair to moderate at 0.45. Further, the JSAT demonstrated adequate, albeit slightly lower, sensitivity (i.e., true positive rate of 71.6%) than results from the male inmate study and slightly higher specificity (i.e., true negative rate of 75%).

Given that the JSAT includes mental status screening items ranging in mental health severity, preliminary SCID analyses are reported in both male and female inmate studies that examine the rate of referrals for specific clinical concerns. Across studies, the JSAT was found to have a high rate of referrals for psychotic disorders (100%) and for individuals identified to be at least a medium suicide risk (96-100%). Future work is needed to evaluate evidence of predictive validity of JSAT results for a fuller range of mental health concerns covered by the instrument (e.g., violence and victimization risk). The degree of convergence of the JSAT with other comparable screening instruments is not currently addressed in the test manual. Estimates of interrater agreement are also needed given differing educational and experience backgrounds of screeners with some notable differences between nursing and graduate students in one of the validation studies.

COMMENTARY. The JSAT appears to be a potentially valuable, structured professional judgment tool for mental health screening in jails by mental health staff with requisite training and professional experience as outlined in the test manual. As a semistructured interview, it is longer and covers more clinically relevant domains than alternative, briefer screening instruments; however, it does not provide psychometric summary scores and requires some inference on the part of the interviewer. The benefit of the JSAT is as a structured professional judgment tool where the examiner systematically reviews multiple domains of evidence-based variables, provides rapid assessment of common mental health symptoms using a modified version of the commonly used BPRS, and reviews other sources of data. The ultimate goal is to make recommendations regarding mental health referrals, placement, and risk management. The need for examiners with appropriate training and educational experience may have some fiscal implications for institutions. Interrater reliability evidence is needed to bolster the accuracy of screening data obtained, given that some inference is required by interviewers and they may have significantly different educational backgrounds and training experiences. The length of the screening interview also may pose some challenges for jails and other correctional facilities with higher volumes of inmates needing to be screened. Initial Canadian validation studies are supportive of the JSAT as a measure used in Canadian jails, although these data use small to medium samples with examiners often trained by the test's co-authors. The JSAT at present does not specifically address some mental health concerns relevant to female inmates nor has it been validated in all offender populations. As the measure is intended for use in jails with male and female inmates in Canada, the United States, and other English-speaking areas, additional validation and reliability work is suggested to determine its applicability and generalizability.

SUMMARY. The developers, to their credit, have produced a potentially valuable semistructured interview for mental health screening of adult inmates by mental health staff with specific recommended graduate coursework and professional experiences. The benefit of the JSAT in its current form is as a structured professional judgment tool. That is, the examiner uses the JSAT systematically to review multiple domains of evidence-based variables in different domains and completes a rapid assessment of mental health symptoms in order to arrive at a set of referral decisions for addressing potential mental health and risk-related needs. In order for this instrument to become a gold standard, careful, continued validation and reliability work will be required to solidify its applicability equally to male and female inmates in English-speaking institutions and to determine its potential in other offender populations and as an international structured professional judgment tool via translation. As a whole, the JSAT is recommended for screening purposes at jails in English-speaking institutions at this time by mental health evaluators with requisite educational and professional experiences as stipulated in the test manual.

REVIEWER'S REFERENCE

Overall, J. E., & Gorman, D. R. (1962). The Brief Psychiatric Rating Scale. *Psychological Reports, 10,* 799-812.

Review of the Jail Screening Assessment Tool by DONNA S. SHEPERIS, Associate Professor, Department of Counseling, Palo Alto University, Los Altos, CA, and YE LUO, Assistant Professor, Department of Counseling and Higher Education, College of Education, University of North Texas, Denton, TX:

DESCRIPTION. The Jail Screening Assessment Tool (JSAT) is a semistructured interview intended to facilitate a comprehensive intake for inmates entering a correctional setting. The overarching goal of the JSAT is to identify those individuals who might need further mental health assessment and care. Although the test manual does not specify when this interview should occur, the nature of the questions indicate that the interview could occur when the inmate first enters the system or after an inmate has been in the system for some time. Inmates are asked questions related to the eight domains of Identifying Information, Legal Situation, Violence Issues, Social Background, Substance Use, Mental Health Treatment, Suicide/Self-Harm, and Mental Health Status. Each domain has a list of questions ranging from three to 28 discrete items with specifiers and follow-up questions also provided. Most of the data collected are nominal in terms of yes/no answers to questions such as whether there is a history of aggression. Further narrative data are sought with follow-up questions to uncover what happened, whether the person was charged, and whether the person was disciplined or transferred as a result of the charge.

The assessment authors state that corrections facilities in Canada have reported that the interview takes 15-20 minutes to conduct. Because this is an interview, no scores are generated. The developers provide a coding form to assist interviewers in tracking their questions and determining follow-up questions based on the answers given. The manual also includes suggestions about how to reduce the length of the tool to meet certain circumstances such as when adding the JSAT to a lengthy pre-existing jail intake. The authors of the tool recommend using the JSAT to help screen inmates for further mental health evaluation. In addition, it is suggested by the authors that this tool can assess functioning, predict psychological adjustment to the correctional setting, identify additional mental health needs, and recognize opportunities for referral for additional interventions.

DEVELOPMENT. Development information is briefly described in the test manual. The JSAT questions were primarily built upon the Historical, Clinical, and Risk Management Scales 20 (HCR-20; Webster, Douglas, Eaves, & Hart, 1997). Aside from reporting that the JSAT interview procedure was rooted in the empirical literature and informed by the experience of operating and evaluating a model mental health program for mentally ill inmates at multiple institutions in Canada, the manual authors do not elaborate on the procedures of question development and revision. Based on the information provided in the JSAT manual, it seems that the tool is designed to evaluate multiple mental health concerns. The tool embodies the structured professional judgment (SPJ) model, an approach in which clinical judgment is guided by a standardized procedure. The authors note the SPJ approach can potentially help clinicians make appropriate referral decisions. However, the developers did not specify theories or underlying assumptions that support the construction of JSAT questions.

TECHNICAL. The test manual includes limited technical data. No norms or scores are presented due to the fact that the JSAT comprises a semistructured interview rather than a psychometric test. The authors present two studies regarding validation and reliability evidence. In the first study (Tien et al., 1993), 303 male inmates, selected by choosing every second inmate from the overall pool, were interviewed using an older version of the JSAT. Interviewers also completed three other rating scales (a) the Structured Clinical Interview for DSM assessments (SCID; American Psychiatric Association [APA], 1987), the Global Assessment of Functioning scale (GAF; APA, 1987), and the

Brief Psychiatric Rating Scale (BPRS; Lukoff, Nuechterlein, & Ventura, 1986). Researchers reported the percentage of those referred for mental health services who then received mental health diagnoses (i.e., the true positive rate/sensitivity) was 84%. Those who met criteria for referral scored significantly differently on the GAF and the BPRS from those not referred. The results supported that the earlier version of the JSAT was sensitive in screening mental health needs among male prisoners.

The second study (Nicholls, Lee, Corrado, & Ogloff, 2004) occurred in two stages. In Stage I, 97 female inmates (mean age = 30) were interviewed using the JSAT and the BPRS. Participants were predominately White (Caucasian, 64.9%; Aboriginal, 25.8%). Researchers reported similar findings: Participants whose JSAT results prompted referrals for mental health services scored significantly higher than those who were not referred. In Stage II, a group described in the test materials as a stratified sample of 29 women was recruited among participants in Stage I to be interviewed with the SCID. Researchers reported the true positive rate/sensitivity of the JSAT to be 70.6%. In addition, Nicholls et al. reported fair (Fleiss, 1981) to moderate (Landis & Koch, 1977) interrater reliability (kappa = .45) for the sample. In a similar study conducted in Australia, researchers reported that the JSAT demonstrated a true positive rate/sensitivity of 74.7% among detainees of police stations (Baksheev, Ogloff, & Thomas, 2012). Most participants were men (90.7%) and Caucasian (81.2%).

COMMENTARY. A strength of the JSAT is that it is adaptable to the setting, interviewer, and interviewee. The semistructured interview allows users to alter the administration as needed to obtain information relevant to the mental health of the inmate. The ability to refer inmates for appropriate care is a defined need within corrections systems that the JSAT attempts to fill. As a screening tool, the JSAT seems to be adequately sensitive in identifying inmates' mental health needs for referral, as supported by the studies cited. Because participants in those studies were predominately White, it remains unclear how effective the tool would be if administered among ethnic minorities. Although called an assessment, the JSAT is actually a guided interview. There is no description of item development procedures or any reflection of best practice instrument design.

With regard to administration, the JSAT is only as good as the person administering the tool. By relying on the SPJ approach, the JSAT relies heavily on the expertise of the interviewer. SPJ models are widely used in criminal and correctional settings but remain a controversial and subjective method of data collection (Baird, 2017). The test manual provides a coding form that offers a way to track the questions asked, responses provided, and interpretations by the examiner. It does not serve to code, score, or evaluate any material from the interview. The manual glosses over the technical development and psychometric properties of the JSAT, making it difficult to evaluate objectively. Validity and reliability data are largely absent in the test materials and must be discovered in subsequent studies. The test authors provide a brief literature review in the manual establishing the need for the instrument but fail to provide basic technical data and instrument design information expected in an assessment manual.

The JSAT questions are presented in the manual along with helpful narrative information to aid the interviewer throughout the process. The test authors assert that the interviewer is tasked with conducting the assessment to identify needs, share those needs with appropriate correctional or other personnel, and recommend potential referrals or interventions. To that end, they provide a section of recommended potential courses of action that may be appropriate. Throughout the manual, the authors strongly suggest the use of the JSAT as a means of early intervention for mental health services.

SUMMARY. The JSAT is best understood as a semistructured interview or guided questionnaire that may be helpful in identifying mental health needs of inmates in correctional settings. The quality of JSAT results is largely dependent upon the expertise of the interviewer due to the use of an SPJ approach. There is no foundation in psychometric principles and instrument design that would provide information about validity and reliability as is customary in psychometric tests but not in measures such as the JSAT where clinical utility is a major concern. At this point, it is best used as a questionnaire and with caution about how responses are interpreted.

REVIEWERS' REFERENCES

American Psychiatric Association. (1987). *Diagnostic and statistical manual of mental disorders* (3rd ed., rev.). Washington, DC: Author.

Baird, C. (2017, February). *A question of evidence, part two: Structured professional judgment models* (Brief 5). Madison, WI: National Council on Crime & Delinquency.

Baksheev, G. N., Ogloff, J., & Thomas, S. (2012). Identification of mental illness in police cells: A comparison of police processes, the Brief Jail Mental Health Screen and the Jail Screening Assessment Tool. Psychology, Crime & Law, 18, 529-542. doi:10.1080/1068316X.2010.510118

Fleiss, J. L. (1981). *Statistical methods for rates and proportions* (2nd ed.). New York, NY: Wiley.

Landis, J., & Koch, G. G. (1977). The measurement of observer agreement for categorical data. *Biometrics, 33*, 159-174.
Lukoff, D., Nuechterlein, K. H., & Ventura, J. (1986). Manual for Expanded Brief Psychiatric Rating Scale (BPRS). *Schizophrenia Bulletin, 12*(4), 594-602.
Nicholls, T. L., Lee, Z., Corrado, R. R., & Ogloff, J. R. P. (2004). Women inmates' mental health needs: Evidence of the validity of the Jail Screening Assessment Tool (JSAT). *International Journal of Forensic Mental Health, 3*(2), 167–184. https://doi.org/10.1080/14999013.2004.10471205
Tien, G., Ogloff, J. R. P., Roesch, R., Wilson, D., Grant, F., & Mah, B. (1993). *Surrey pretrial mental health project: Evaluation report for the management committee.* Vancouver, BC, Canada: British Columbia Forensic Psychiatric Services Commission.
Webster, C. D., Douglas, K. S., Eaves, D., & Hart, S. D. (1997). HCR-20: Assessing Risk for Violence (Version 2). Burnaby, BC, Canada: Mental Health, Law, and Policy Institute, Simon Fraser University.

[83]

Job Search Attitude Inventory, Fifth Edition.

Purpose: Designed to "make job seekers more aware of their self-directed and other-directed attitudes about their searches for employment."
Population: Adult and teen job seekers and career planners.
Publication Dates: 2002-2015.
Acronym: JSAI.
Scores, 5: Luck vs. Planning, Uninvolved vs. Involved, Help from Others vs. Self-Help, Passive vs. Active, Pessimistic vs. Optimistic.
Administration: Individual or group.
Price Data, 2020: $69.95 per 25 inventories; administrator's guide (2015, 19 pages) may be downloaded at no charge.
Time: (20) minutes.
Comments: Self-administered, self-scored, and self-interpreted.
Author: John J. Liptak.
Publisher: JIST Career Solutions, a division of Kendall Hunt.
Cross References: For reviews by John W. Fleenor and Thomas R. O'Neill of the second edition, see 16:120.

Review of the Job Search Attitude Inventory, Fifth Edition, by JOHN K. HAWLEY, Engineering Psychologist, U.S. Army Research Laboratory, Ft. Bliss Field Element, Ft. Bliss, TX:

DESCRIPTION. The Job Search Attitude Inventory (JSAI) is a short, self-report attitude inventory intended to "make job seekers more aware of their ... attitudes about their searches for employment" (administrator's guide, p. 1). According to the administrator's guide, the JSAI "compares the inventory takers' attitudes about the job search process with those of professional counselors trained in teaching job search techniques" (p. 1). The inventory consists of 40 job-search-related attitude statements. Inventory takers respond to each statement using a four-point Likert scale: *strongly agree, agree, disagree,* and *strongly disagree.* The inventory is self-administered by job seekers either alone or in a group setting. The inventory response form is designed to be used in paper-and-pencil mode, but an online version is also available. There is no time limit for administering the JSAI; the average administration time was reported to be approximately 20 minutes. The inventory is intended to be self-scoring, which provides the person taking the inventory and the administrator with immediate results. A scoring profile, information to interpret the profile results, suggestions for improving the taker's job search attitude, and suggestions for improving the taker's job search process are also provided.

The 40 attitude statements used in the JSAI are organized in terms of five scales determined on the basis of research and expert judgment to be related to success in the job search process. These scales are (a) Luck vs. Planning: planning for a job search versus relying on luck to find a job; (b) Uninvolved vs. Involved: how involved the individual is in his or her search for a job; (c) Help from Others vs. Self-Help: depending on outside agencies for help finding a job versus relying on oneself; (d) Passive vs. Active: how much control the individual thinks he or she has in searching for a job; (e) Pessimistic vs. Optimistic: how optimistic the respondent is in being able to find a job.

Items are grouped into five sections on the response sheet for easy scoring by the person taking the inventory. Scoring is done very simply by adding the response scores for each item in each of the five scale sections and recording the total. Scores on each of the scales range from 8 to 32. Respondents interpret their scores according to how high they scored on each scale: The higher a respondent's score, the more positive his or her attitude toward searching for a job. Guidelines for interpreting scale score results are provided on the response sheet.

DEVELOPMENT. The conceptual rationale for the JSAI is based on a study conducted to determine the most important determinants of a successful job search campaign (Helwig, 1987). Helwig's study indicated that personal motivation and positive job search attitudes are as important or more important in finding employment than job search skills and techniques. Employment counselors participating in Helwig's study (n = 1,121) rated "knowledge of the importance of personal responsibility in finding a job" as the most important of the job search behaviors considered. This work and related research on job search behaviors suggested that an individual's success in finding a job is largely determined by that individual's attitudes toward the job search process and perceptions of eventual success in the search process. The JSAI was developed to assess these aspects of job search success.

An initial set of items reflecting the JSAI's underlying job search attitudinal construct was developed based on material from case studies, interviews with unemployed adults, research reported in journal articles, and descriptive material from job search training/coaching programs. Based on this review, the first four scales making up the JSAI were defined. A pool of 50 attitude statements was then developed to represent the four scales. Three professional job search counselors reviewed, revised, and refined the draft attitude statements. A sample of unemployed adults then completed a draft version of the inventory. Based on trial results, a final pool of 32 attitude statements addressing the four initial job search attitude scales comprising the JSAI was selected. Eight more attitude statements representing the fifth scale, Pessimistic vs. Optimistic, were added subsequently, resulting in the current 40-item, five-scale version of the JSAI.

TECHNICAL. As noted, the JSAI was developed to assess job seeker attitudes toward the job search process and perceptions of their eventual success in finding a job. Final versions of JSAI items were based on the results of a trial application to a sample of adult job seekers in combination with the expert judgment of professional job search counselors.

Reliability indices for the JSAI are expressed in terms of coefficient alpha measures of internal consistency; response stability, assessed in terms of test-retest correlations; and split-half correlations. All of these indices were computed using adult respondents and are reported by scale. Alpha coefficients for the JSAI scales ranged from .85 to .91 (n = 135). Test-retest scale correlations ranged from .60 to .76 over a 3-month period using a sample of 107 people. Split-half reliability indices ranged from .53 to .81 (n = 135). All of these reliability indices were computed using an early version of the JSAI consisting of the four initial scales. Reliability data are not provided for JSAI editions four and five following the addition of the fifth scale, Pessimistic vs. Optimistic.

Several types of validity evidence are discussed in the administrator's guide. Content evidence of validity is based on the fact that items were specifically developed to reflect the underlying attitudinal construct, relevant academic literature, and the expert judgment of professional employment counselors.

Construct evidence of validity, discussed in terms of what the administrator's guide terms concurrent validity, is based on interscale correlations. These correlations are generally low. Magnitudes ranged from .11 to .58. The administrator's guide notes that this evidence "supports the independence of the scales" (p. 11). No evidence is provided concerning the JSAI's predictive validity assessed in terms of the relationship between inventory scores and later job search success.

Normative data provided for selected groups of respondents are presented in the administrator's guide as construct evidence of validity. Normative inventory results are expressed as means and standard deviations for selected groups of takers including males and females, (criminal) offenders, persons transitioning from welfare to work, college students, and youth (takers ages 12-18). In this respect, normative results across selected groups are compared, contrasted, and discussed.

COMMENTARY. The JSAI is easy to administer and score. Moreover, interpretation of inventory results is relatively straightforward. The inventory was developed in accord with some generally accepted practices within the field of industrial-organizational psychology for instruments of its type. Inventory reliability assessed in terms of various aspects of internal consistency and response repeatability is in the moderate range. Criterion-related evidence of validity is sparse. Interscale correlations are not typical concurrent evidence of validity. Rather, they are more construct related, pertaining to the instrument's underlying structure (i.e., so-called structural validity). Moreover, no evidence pertaining to the relationship between inventory results and future job search success are provided. In this reviewer's opinion, this omission represents an obvious gap in the validity evidence provided in the administrator's guide. It would seem to be a relatively straightforward proposition to report the relationship between JSAI results and later job search success. Construct-related evidence of validity also is addressed in a somewhat non-standard manner. The discussion of normative inventory results by selected group provided in the administrator's manual does not directly pertain to the underlying construct issue of validity: Is the inventory measuring what it is intended to measure?

In this reviewer's opinion, the JSAI is potentially useful in a job search program when administered and interpreted by a professional employment counselor and used in combination with other job search related data and tools. Potential job search data and tools that might be used in combination with the JSAI include information on the local job situation; respondent vocational interests assessed through the use of a validated interest inventory; and the respondent's job qualifications assessed in terms of education, training, and special skills. This reviewer does not dispute that a respondent's job search attitude as assessed using the JSAI is important. However, eventual success in a job search depends on more than a positive attitude toward the job search process. Available job opportunities and person-job match also are important considerations.

SUMMARY. The JSAI was developed to assess a job seeker's attitude toward the job search process and perceptions of success in that effort. The inventory is easily administered and scored, and the results are readily interpretable. If the JSAI taker responds truthfully, results can reasonably be used for the purpose and in the settings suggested in the administrator's guide. Users should be cautioned, however, that the JSAI might best be used under the supervision of a professional employment counselor and in combination with other indicators of the kinds of work a job seeker should reasonably pursue.

REVIEWER'S REFERENCE

Helwig, A. A. (1987). Information required for job hunting: 1,121 counselors respond. *Journal of Employment Counseling, 24*(4), 184-190.

Review of the Job Search Attitude Inventory, Fifth Edition by LARRY KORTERING, Professor of Special Education, Appalachian State University, Boone, NC:

DESCRIPTION. The Job Search Attitude Inventory, Fifth Edition (JSAI) is a brief inventory that provides feedback on one's job search attitude. The inventory includes 40 individual items, each placed into one of five scales representing self-directed job search attitudes: Luck vs. Planning, Uninvolved vs. Involved, Help from Others vs. Self-Help; Passive vs. Active, and Pessimistic vs. Optimistic. The inventory uses a 4-point Likert-like scale (*strongly agree, agree, disagree,* and *strongly disagree*) to record responses.

The protocol suggests the inventory offers an opportunity to help individuals improve their job search process. Initially, individuals use the Likert-like rating to express their level of agreement for each of 40 item stems. Color coding is then used to assist individuals in calculating their raw scores for each of the five scales. Then respondents identify the respective score range for each of five scales (low, average, or high). Low to average ratings suggest potential areas of challenge affecting one's job search attitude. The protocol provides descriptive information to assist the individual in better understanding the respective scales and corresponding implications for one's job search attitude. The descriptive information then facilitates a final step (Further Exploration) where respondents record their scores (i.e., ratings of one's attitude) for each of the five scales and then note ideas for improving in each scale area (i.e., What Can I Do to Improve?). Additional sources of information from the test publisher are at the end of the protocol.

The inventory is set up for either individual or group administration. The total respective raw scores for each scale are ranked as follows: Scores between 8 and 16 suggest respondents believe they need assistance from others and lack the proper mindset for effectively seeking a job; scores between 17 and 23 suggest one is not completely dependent on others in the job search, but could initiate more control over the process; and scores between 24 and 32 suggest one believes his or her job search process is a function of his or her planning and effort. The author of the inventory suggests that higher scores indicate a more positive attitude about searching for a job.

The test author posits that the most important consideration in working with someone involved in a job search is the person's attitude toward unemployment and the job search process. Intuitively, it seems reasonable that respondents may benefit from an opportunity to better understand their job search attitude in the context of gaining insight into how to improve their job search, but this reviewer was unable to find empirical support for this suggestion. The inventory, at best, provides an indirect inference into one's attitude toward unemployment, and it remains unclear how this assessment offers insight into this concept.

DEVELOPMENT. The JSAI includes a 19-page administrator's guide with information on its development. At its heart, the instrument reflects a belief that enhancement of one's self-esteem, meaning in life, and career or life purpose improves self-directed motivation in a search for employment. This belief is in contrast to one who tends toward learned helplessness or a victim-oriented mentality. In support of the JSAI, the author references as the foundation Helwig's (1987) study involving counselors from one state reviewing comments from a group of unemployed adults. Helwig noted that, based on his sample, an individual's attitude toward unemployment and the job search itself were the most important factors affecting the success of one's job search. Helwig's study used a series of interviews with a sample of unemployed adults that generated 50 potential items related to the job search process. A set of 1,121 professional counselors then reviewed the items for categorization into one of four scales: Luck vs. Planning, Uninvolved vs. Involved, Help from Others vs. Self-Help; Passive vs. Active. The JSAI incorporates the items and their respective categorization. For an earlier version, the author used responses from a sample of 135 adults to establish adequate intercorrelations among the initial four constructs (currently five in the addition of the Pessimistic vs. Optimistic scale).

The author provides dated references (1977 to 2014) to support the theoretical basis for the JSAI. This basis includes expert opinion as support for the important concepts of learned helplessness, self-directed and other-directed job seekers, attitudes, models for enhancing job search attitudes, and job search mindset. This evidence provides indirect support for this type of instrument and insight into the construction of the JASI and its corresponding scales. As to the constructs, the concept of learned helplessness suggests that a lack of belief in one's ability to affect his or her job search outcomes subjects the person to a passive job search at the mercy of luck and others. Self-direction in the job search process allows one to take responsibility for what happens and sets the stage for success. It is apparently believed that attitudes, based on the early work of Bandura (1977), are another aspect of a successful job search with core beliefs influencing the success of seeking a job. In terms of models for enhancing job search attitudes, the manual suggests the JSAI fits with cognitive behavioral theory, solution focused therapy, and motivational interviewing.

The fifth edition of the JSAI is the most recent version of the instrument. The author noted changes in items on all five scales to reflect societal and world of work changes, updated validity information incorporating a fifth scale (Pessimistic vs. Optimistic) that was added in the fourth edition, an updated norm reference group (adults in Slovenia), and a revised worksheet to help one focus on goal setting and self-direction. The author does not provide a listing of specific items that changed; however, the new scale has eight items that are consistent in format with the rest of the items. For the updated norms with scores from adults in Slovenia, the test author cites a master's thesis study that offers the score range and corresponding means and standard deviations for a sample of 203 adults (58% female) for each of the five scales in the fourth edition. The revised worksheet seems appropriate in the sense of helping individuals use their results to reflect on their job search and implement a more effective one.

TECHNICAL. The manual provides information on the normative sample and technical aspects for the JSAI. As to the normative sample, the current edition appears to rely on aspects of earlier editions. Means and standard deviations are presented for a group of 190 adults (102 males, 88 females) who took the fourth edition of the inventory. Similarly, means and standard deviations are provided for earlier versions of the inventory before the fifth scale was added.

In terms of technical aspects, the manual offers limited information. A major concern relates to the lack of clarity as to which information applies to the fifth edition. For example, each of the tables with reliability and validity data have four scales, not five, suggesting the information applies to one or more earlier editions. Similarly, earlier reviews of the second edition (see Fleenor, 2005 and O'Neill, 2005) summarized reliability and validity information and reported identical information to that in the current manual. More specifically in terms of reliability, based on a sample of 107 adults, test/retest scores over a 3-month period ranged from .60 (Uninvolved v. Involved) to .76 (Passive vs. Active). For a sample of 135 adults, the split-half index of reliability ranged from .53 (Uninvolved vs. Involved) to .81 (Passive vs. Active), and alpha coefficients ranged from .85 (Luck vs. Planning) to .91 (Help from Others vs. Self Help).

Under the heading of validity, the test author provides intercorrelations for the original four scales with magnitudes ranging from .11 (Passive vs. Active and Help Others vs. Self Help) to .58 (Uninvolved vs. Involved and Luck vs. Planning). These data suggest the constructs are relatively independent. Additional information under validity includes data on means and standard deviations for respective groups, including the initial samples representing 135 adults, 554 offenders, 296 welfare-to-work clients, 535 college students, and 308 youth ages 12–18. A minor concern with the means and standard deviations is the range of means across the various groups. For illustration, the highest mean score was over 26 (Help from Others vs. Self-Help across each of the five samples) while a low score was 16 (Passive vs. Active for the sample of 308 youth). Despite this range, the rating for the five constructs is the same in terms of implication.

In combination, these data suggest adequate reliability and independent constructs, while offering insufficient evidence for validity in this reviewer's opinion. Relative to validity, the manual only offers theoretical support. Under validity, the manual does provide means and standard deviations for several different samples, but there is no concurrent or construct validity data.

COMMENTARY. The JSAI is an efficient tool for assessing one's job search attitude but lacks a solid evidential base. From a practical standpoint, it seems prudent to spend a few minutes helping individuals to better understand their attitudes toward the job search process, and this inventory helps. This practical use is the relative strength of this inventory, and the activity sheet offers a process for facilitating understanding of results. An obvious weakness is a lack of current independent research and previous research that is the basis for the inventory. For the former, a literature search of pertinent major databases yielded no results in terms of peer-reviewed research using any editions of the JSAI. A similar concern lies with the previous research that supports the assessment's approach to quantifying one's job search attitude. The manual presents data that appears identical to that presented in the Fleenor (2005) and O'Neill (2005) reviews of the second edition from 2002.

A major challenge to the theoretical basis for the JSAI relates to a reliance on limited and dated references for support. In addition, the limited theoretical references fail to unite the scales into the construct of job search attitude.

SUMMARY. The JSAI offers promise as a practical measure to stimulate self-motivation toward improving one's job search process. It is largely self-directed with a suggestion that a counselor provide assistance with implementing insight from the worksheet. The practicality, ease of use, and efficient time frame are the relative strengths of the JSAI. The major weakness continues to be, as reported earlier by Fleenor (2005) and O'Neill (2005), the insufficient information on the psychometric properties of the instrument. Furthermore, the measure would benefit from independent research involving the most recent edition along with a consideration of the emerging role that the Internet and technology play into today's job search (see e.g., Liu, Huang, & Wang, 2014).

REVIEWER'S REFERENCES

Fleenor, J. W. (2005). [Test review of Job Search Attitude Inventory, Second Edition]. In R. A. Spies & B. S. Plake (Eds.), *The sixteenth mental measurements yearbook* (pp.503-505). Lincoln, NE: Buros Institute of Mental Measurements.

Helwig, A. A. (1987). Information required for job hunting: 1,121 counselors respond. *Journal of Employment Counseling, 24,* 184-190.

Liu, S., Huang, J. L., & Wang, M. (2014). Effectiveness of job search interventions: A meta-analytic review. *Psychological Bulletin, 140,* 1009-1041.

O'Neill, T. R. (2005). [Test review of Job Search Attitude Inventory, Second Edition]. In R. A. Spies & B. S. Plake (Eds.), *The sixteenth mental measurements yearbook* (pp.505-506). Lincoln, NE: Buros Institute of Mental Measurements.

[84]

Kane Learning Difficulties Assessment.

Purpose: A self-report rating form "designed to map individual learning strengths and weaknesses, provide students with a comparative sense of their academic skills, and identify students at risk for LD [learning disabilities] and ADHD [attention-deficit/hyperactivity disorder] who may require further assessment."
Population: Students enrolled in postsecondary education.
Publication Date: 2016.
Acronym: KLDA.
Scores, 24: Reading (Physiological, Processing and Comprehension), Listening (Listening-Processing, Attention), Concentration and Memory, Writing (Writing-Processing, Spelling, Note-Taking, Copying), Mathematics (Mathematics-Processing, Symbolic Understanding), Time (In-class and Testing, Procrastination), Organization and Self-Control (Organization, Task-Focus), Anxiety/Pressure, Oral Presentation, Overall Academic Risk.
Administration: Individual or group.
Price Data, 2020: $149 per digital kit including professional manual (46 pages), e-manual, and 25 online administrations and score reports; $149 per hybrid kit including professional manual, 25 item/response booklets, and 25 online score reports; $86 per replacement set including 25 item/response booklets and 25 online score reports; $66 per professional manual (print or digital); $2 per online administration; $2 per score report.
Time: 15 minutes or fewer for administration.
Comments: Administered via paper and pencil or digitally using the test publisher's online platform; all scoring must be performed using test publisher's online platform.
Authors: Steven T. Kane (test and professional manual) and Heddy Kovach Clark (professional manual).
Publisher: Psychological Assessment Resources, Inc.

Review of the Kane Learning Difficulties Assessment by RUSSELL N. CARNEY, Professor Emeritus of Psychology, Missouri State University, Springfield, MO:

DESCRIPTION. In the professional manual, Kane and Clark describe the Kane Learning Difficulties Assessment (KLDA) as a "normed self-report rating form for college students that evaluates difficulties with reading, writing, mathematics, listening, concentration, memory, organization, time management, oral presentation, self-control, and anxiety" (p. 1). It is designed to identify students' strengths and weaknesses, and hence can serve as a quick (15 minute) screening instrument for college-age individuals who might be at risk for a diagnosis of learning disabilities (LD) or attention-deficit/hyperactivity disorder (ADHD). As such, the instrument may be useful for advisors, counselors, psychologists, and others working with post-secondary students in academic settings. No special training or qualifications are required to administer the test, and it can be administered either individually or in a group setting, via paper or by using the test publisher's online assessment platform.

The KLDA consists of a 120-item rating form that yields nine scales, 14 subscales, and an Overall Academic Risk score (OAR). The 120 statements describe various learning difficulties that are rated using five descriptors as follows: *agree completely, agree somewhat, neutral, disagree somewhat,* or *disagree completely*. Agreement with a statement endorses a particular difficulty. In the printed form, a cover page asks for identifying and demographic information and is followed by two pages (front and back) listing 30 to-be-rated statements per page.

All scoring is accomplished online using the test publisher's platform. With paper forms, student responses must be entered manually. Two reports are generated: a Score Report for the administrator and a Student Feedback Report. Scores reported include the students' mean ratings and corresponding percentile ranks for each of the 24 scores. Here, the higher the percentile rank, the more a weakness is indicated. Besides student scores, the reports include helpful suggestions regarding interpretation, interventions, and accommodations.

The mean ratings for a student are plotted on 24 number lines (labeled 1.00 to 5.00; this time with the right side indicating a weakness), with shaded bands representing 1 standard deviation (*SD*) above or below the mean for each scale. Generally, scores falling to the right of these bands may indicate significant problem areas. The test manual gives some guidance as to how to interpret student scores and provides three case illustrations.

DEVELOPMENT. Initially, a comprehensive review was conducted regarding the topics of learning disabilities and learning skills. Further, relevant professionals, such as academic advisers, counselors, specialists in learning disabilities, and disability service providers were consulted. This research led to the generation of 200 statements related to the problems of at-risk college-age learners. The initial version consisted of 186 items and was pilot tested on 207 diverse students at two universities in California. Factor analysis with Varimax rotation was used to refine the items and clarify subscales, yielding a 123-item version. These items were then administered to a different sample of 183 college students. Factor analysis with Varimax rotation was again used to identify the structure of the instrument.

TECHNICAL. To standardize the rating scale, the 123-item instrument was put online. Over a 4-year period (2011-2015), 4,207 college students completed the measure. Eventually, 981 postsecondary students (*not* diagnosed with learning disabilities) became the normative sample. Some items were removed or revised, and the KLDA was reduced to 120 items. Based on statistical analysis, variables such as ethnicity, age, gender, and so forth, were said to "not meaningfully affect KLDA scores" (manual, p. 12), and thus the same norm group is used for all students.

Two types of reliability are documented in the manual: internal consistency and test-retest. Internal consistency reliability estimates are designed to get at how well the items comprising a particular scale hang together (i.e., correlate). Coefficient alpha was used to examine internal consistency within each scale and subscale. Reported values ranged from .79 to .95 on scale scores, with most being in the .90s. Subscale coefficients ranged from .71 to .91. As expected, larger coefficients tended to occur in scales or subscales based on more items. Overall, the average alpha coefficient based on the scales and subscales (i.e., for the Overall Academic Risk score) was .86.

A second measure of reliability was test-retest. Test-retest reliability evaluates the stability of the scores for individuals over time. For this estimate of reliability, a sample of 36 students completed the KLDA, and then took it again 30 days later. Performance on the two administrations was then correlated for the students' OAR scores. The resultant reliability coefficient was .87.

The manual provides content and construct evidence of validity. Content evidence of validity has to do with whether the instrument samples the correct content and is built into the instrument during its development. Evidence here includes the fact that a review of the literature was initially conducted and that experts were consulted during the selection of item statements. Further, the test authors suggest that internal consistency estimates (described earlier) also provide content evidence of validity.

Validity based on construct evidence has to do with whether the instrument gets at the theoretical construct(s) or characteristics it is supposed to assess and is demonstrated by various lines of evidence. First, the factor analysis used in the KLDA's development shows "the degree to which the internal structure conforms to theory and the intended constructs" (manual, p. 14). Another line of evidence is how well individual items correlate with total scores for each scale and subscale to which they contribute. According to the test manual, "Average item-total correlations were moderate to strong" (p. 14). Within subscales, average correlations ranged from .49 to .69, and within scale scores correlations ranged from .53 to .71. On individual item-total correlations, a majority fell between .50 and .82.

Further, scale and subscale intercorrelations were reported and characterized (based on $r \geq .10$ = small, $r \geq .30$ = medium, and $r \geq .5$ = large). Using those descriptors, scale and subscale intercorrelations were termed large, ranging from .69 to .97. Intercorrelations between scales went from .19 to .88, and the OAR score correlations with scale and subscale scores ranged from .43 to .90. The manual concludes that these "results provide solid evidence of domain overlap between scores measuring similar constructs [i.e., convergent evidence] and less overlap between scores measuring dissimilar constructs [i.e., divergent evidence]" (p. 16).

Criterion-related evidence of validity is determined by correlating scores with related outside criteria. The manual describes two such studies. In one (Kane, Walker, & Schmidt, 2011), a sample of students was taken from a university's learning disabilities clinic. Those with either an LD or ADHD diagnosis were compared to a sample of students who were not so diagnosed. Using logistic regression with the OAR score as predictor, the authors found it to be "strongly associated" with an LD or ADHD diagnosis ($p < .0001$; manual p. 16). For example, an OAR score of 4.0 (to the right of the shaded band) yielded a probability of an LD or ADHD diagnosis of 60.7%. This study provides evidence that the OAR score is useful in identifying students who may receive an LD/ADHD diagnosis.

In a second validity study reported in the manual, Kane, Roy, and Medina (2013) examined how well the OAR score predicted: "(a) attitude toward academic success, (b) odds of LD diagnosis, and (c) self-reported LD severity" (p. 17). Data came from a large, initial sample (N = 775) that had taken a version of the instrument online. Again using logistic regression models with the OAR score as predictor, the findings were that students with higher OAR scores (a) felt they were "less likely to succeed academically," (b) were "more likely to be diagnosed with LD," and were (c) "more likely to report the severity of their LD as significant" (manual, p. 17).

COMMENTARY. First, it is important to note that, as with all self-report measures, the KLDA is dependent upon the insight and honesty of the individuals completing it. Also, with all the 120 statements worded in the same negative direction, the KLDA rating scale might at times suffer from response bias on the part of examinees. However, putting those self-report rating scale issues aside, the KLDA seems to be a potentially useful instrument. This endorsement is supported by the 46-page professional manual, which is clearly written, covers critical topics, and includes reasonable evidence for reliability and validity. The evidence for reliability and validity is acceptable, especially in that this instrument is modest in its screening-oriented purpose. That is, it is not designed to diagnose, to measure intelligence, or to predict college success per se. Rather, it is simply a screening device that *may* prompt further testing. The instrument certainly has good face validity, in that the straightforward statements appear to fit well within the various scales and subscales to which they contribute. Published in 2016, the KLDA is still a relatively new instrument. As recommended in the *Standards for Educational and Psychological Testing* (American Educational Research Association, American Psychological Association, & National Council on Measurement in Education, 2014), future researchers may provide additional evidence for validity. For example, it would be interesting to examine the correlation between students' scores on the KLDA and scores on some measure of academic self-concept. One would expect positive correlations between the two.

SUMMARY. The Kane Learning Difficulties Assessment is a straightforward, relatively brief (120-item) self-report instrument that should be helpful as an initial screening device for college students presenting academic difficulties—especially with those suspected of having learning disabilities or ADHD. Research described in the test manual provides reasonable evidence of reliability and validity for the purposes described.

REVIEWER'S REFERENCES

American Educational Research Association, American Psychological Association, & National Council on Measurement in Education. (2014). *Standards for educational and psychological testing.* Washington, DC: American Educational Research Association.

Kane, S. T., Roy, S., & Medina, S. (2013). Identifying college students at risk for learning disabilities: Evidence for use of the Learning Difficulties Assessment in post-secondary settings. *Journal of Postsecondary Education and Disability, 26*, 21-33.

Kane, S. T., Walker, J. H., & Schmidt, G. R. (2011). Assessing college-level learning difficulties and "at-riskness" for learning disabilities and ADHD: Development and validation of the Learning Difficulties Assessment. *Journal of Learning Disabilities, 44*, 533-542.

Review of the Kane Learning Difficulties Assessment by RYAN J. KETTLER, Associate Professor, Rutgers, The State University of New Jersey, New Brunswick, NJ, and LEAH DEMBITZER, Assistant Professor, Concordia College-New York, Bronxville, NY:

DESCRIPTION. The Kane Learning Difficulties Assessment (KLDA) is a self-report rating form for college students ages 17 and older. It contains 120 self-statements rated on a 5-point Likert scale. The test yields scores for Overall Academic Risk (OAR), as well as for nine scales (Reading, Listening, Concentration and Memory, Writing, Mathematics, Time, Organization and Self-Control, Anxiety/Pressure, Oral Presentation) and 14 subscales (Physiological, Processing and Comprehension, Listening-Processing, Attention, Writing-Processing, Spelling, Note-Taking, Copying, Mathematics-Processing, Symbolic Understanding, In-class and Testing, Procrastination, Organization, Task-Focus). The listed uses of the KLDA are to (a) identify self-perceived student learning strengths and weaknesses, (b) provide normative information about perceived student academic skills, and (c) screen for individuals at-risk for learning disability (LD) or attention-deficit/hyperactivity disorder (ADHD) classification.

Administration. The KLDA is administered either individually or to groups and either by paper-and-pencil or online using the test publisher's platform. Administration is untimed and is generally completed in less than 15 minutes. The professional manual provides instructions for administration and guidelines for interpreting the results. No specific qualifications are required for administration.

Scoring. The KLDA is scored online, and a Score Report and Student Feedback Report are automatically generated. Scores are provided for the OAR, as well as for each scale and subscale. Scale and subscale scores are means of their constituent items and range from 1.00 to 5.00 with higher scores indicating higher academic risk. The OAR score is the average of the nine scale scores and the 14 subscale scores. Students with OAR scores exceeding 3.5, especially including those with scores exceeding 4.0, are recommended to be referred for further assessment. The Score Report includes percentile ranks and average bands to facilitate comparison of student scores to the normative sample. The Student Feedback Report contains scores, interpretive statements, and suggested interventions and accommodations.

DEVELOPMENT. The KLDA was developed via literature review and expert review (LD specialists, disability service providers, academic advisors, counselors, and psychologists) to delineate the constructs, scales, and subsequent pool of 200 items. Items were written at a sixth-grade reading level and were piloted twice with college students (n = 207 and n = 183). Following each study "non-contributory or confusing items" (manual, p. 11) were discarded based on factor-analytic findings.

TECHNICAL.

Standardization. The norm sample was sufficiently large (N = 981) and was acceptably matched to the U.S. college population regarding age, gender, ethnicity/race, high school GPA, and college GPA. Frequencies and percentages of the sample were available for groups labeled as White, African American, Hispanic, and Other. The sample included relatively small numbers of students from vocational schools, technical colleges, and community colleges (n = 98, 10.0%), or from graduate schools (n = 115, 11.7%), as well as relatively small numbers of students whose highest level of education was reported as less than high school (n = 14, 1.4%), college graduate (n = 72, 7.3%), or graduate degree (n = 57, 5.8%). Contextualizing individual performance against the mean performance of an American student at a 4-year college or university (n = 768, 78.3%), whose highest level of education is either high school graduate (n = 468, 47.7%) or some college (n = 367, 37.4%), can be done with confidence. Small total numbers and percentages of persons from other groups render inferences to these populations more tenuous.

Reliability. Reliability evidence is provided in two forms: coefficient alpha and test-retest stability.

Coefficient alpha met or exceeded .90 for seven of nine scales and exceeded .80 for nine of 14 subscales. The test authors report the mean alpha coefficient of the 23 scores (i.e., nine scale alphas and 14 subscale alphas) as a reflection of the reliability of the OAR score (mean alpha = .86). Test-retest stability was acceptable (r = .87) for the OAR score. The estimate was based on a sample of 36 students and a 30-day interval between test administrations.

Validity Evidence Based on Content. The test authors based their content evidence of validity on the development of items for the scale from literature review and surveying or experts. No quantitative or evaluative review of the items, in either their final form or a pilot form, was reported.

Validity Evidence Based on Internal Structure. Validity evidence based on internal structure is provided in the form of an exploratory factor analysis (EFA), item-total correlations, and correlations among scales and subscales of the KLDA. Two EFAs with Varimax rotations were conducted on pilot versions of the assessment; results were not reported except that some items were removed.

Individual item-total correlations ranged from .23 to .82. This range is acceptable particularly because items contribute to multiple scores.

All correlations among scale and subscale scores of the KLDA were positive and equaled or exceeded .09. Correlations among scales of the KLDA equaled or exceeded .70 in 13 of 36 combinations, including four for which the correlations exceeded .80. Correlations among subscales nested within the same scales of the KLDA exceeded .70 in five of 11 combinations, including three for which the correlations equaled or exceeded .80. These findings indicate that while it is defensible to combine scores from the scales and subscales into an overarching composite score, a large proportion of the scores from the KLDA overlap to the extent they may not represent independent constructs.

Validity Evidence Based on Relations to Other Variables. Evidence based on relations to other variables was provided in the form of a known groups study (Kane, Walker, & Schmidt, 2011) and a correlational study with several self-reported student characteristics (Kane, Roy, & Medina, 2013). In the known groups study, students (N = 267) seeking assessment for possible LD or ADHD classification underwent a battery of assessments and were diagnosed based on the *Diagnostic and Statistical Manual of Mental Disorders, Fourth Edition–Text Revision* (DSM-IV-TR; American Psychiatric Association, 2000). Results of logistic regression indicated OAR scores of the diagnosed students corresponded with expected profile patterns and were higher than scores for a comparison group of students without diagnoses. Classification accuracies were reported across a range of cut scores, only one (2.8) of which yielded sensitivity (66.7), specificity (63.8), and hit rate (64.7) in the moderate range or higher. Although not directly reported, sensitivity at the suggested cut score of 3.5 was very low, and at the other suggested cut score of 4.0 was almost nonexistent (1.9%). Classification accuracy indices were likely depressed by the presumably restricted sample.

Kane, Roy, and Medina (2013) used logistic regression to examine the relationship between the OAR score and several characteristics among anonymous students (N = 775) completing an online version of the KLDA. Students with higher scores reported being less likely to succeed academically, being more likely to be diagnosed with LD, and being more likely to report the severity of their LD as significant, compared to students with lower scores.

COMMENTARY. The OAR score may contribute to LD/ADHD identification to an acceptable degree, although it is difficult to know based on information provided in the test manual. Two scoring choices are worth noting. Rather than basing the OAR score on a summation of all items or a subset of items, the developers average scores from the nine scales and 14 subscales, within which many of the items are cross-nested. Items are thus differentially weighted in a way that is not explained by theory underlying the measure. The test authors recommend interpreting the OAR score first, as the putative most reliable and valid indicator of risk. Whether this assumption is true is unclear, because an overall coefficient alpha is not reported for the OAR score and because subscale scores are not included in estimates of test-retest reliability or validity.

The second scoring issue is that the KLDA does not include any validity scales to ensure student self-raters respond truthfully and accurately. This deficiency is a limitation because the scale is likely to be completed by students who may desire to be identified as having disabilities (that is, to "fake bad," perhaps to attain accommodations). Without validity scales, it is difficult to determine whether findings from research studies are likely to generalize to use in practice.

Scores from most KLDA scales are internally consistent enough to contribute to making high or low stakes decisions. Most subscale scores are internally consistent enough to contribute to making low stakes decisions.

More validity evidence is needed supporting inferences from the KLDA. Expert review of items in their final form would contribute to content evidence. A confirmatory factor analysis of the measure in its final form would contribute to internal structure validity evidence. The provided evidence of correlations among scale scores and subscale scores indicates the measure may be unidimensional. Information on evidence of relations with other variables is limited; for the three studies described, more information on operationalizing the criterion variables and on the effect sizes of the observed relationships would be helpful.

SUMMARY. The KLDA may be an appropriate measure for some of its stated purposes. The biggest limitation of the assessment is the OAR is not fully supported by reliability and validity evidence and many other scores correlate too highly with each other. Thus, the measure may contribute to finding some student learning strengths and weaknesses and academic skills, though not as many as the 24 reported scores imply. Also, the OAR score may be a useful screen for individuals at risk for LD and ADHD, although it is difficult to know whether the reported classification accuracies are acceptable. More detailed information about the OAR would be helpful in evaluation for this purpose.

REVIEWERS' REFERENCES

American Psychiatric Association. (2000). *Diagnostic and statistical manual of mental disorders* (4th ed., text rev.). Washington, DC: Author.

Kane, S. T., Roy, S., & Medina, S. (2013). Identifying college students at risk for learning disabilities: Evidence for use of the Learning Difficulties Assessment in post-secondary settings. *Journal of Postsecondary Education and Disability, 26,* 21-33.

Kane, S. T., Walker, J. H., & Schmidt, G. R. (2011). Assessing college-level learning difficulties and "at riskness" for learning disabilities and ADHD: Development and validation of the Learning Difficulties Assessment. *Journal of Learning Disabilities, 44,* 533-542.

[85]

Kaufman Assessment Battery for Children, Second Edition Normative Update.

Purpose: Designed to measure the "processing and cognitive abilities of children and adolescents."
Population: Ages 3 through 18.
Publication Dates: 1983-2018.
Acronym: KABC-II NU.
Scores, 7-23: Sequential (Number Recall, Word Order, Hand Movements, Total), Simultaneous (Block Counting, Conceptual Thinking, Face Recognition, Pattern Reasoning [Ages 5 and 6], Rover, Story Completion [Ages 5 and 6], Triangles, Gestalt Closure, Total), Planning [Ages 7–18 only] (Pattern Reasoning, Story Completion, Total), Learning (Atlantis, Rebus, Atlantis Delayed, Rebus Delayed, Total), Knowledge (Expressive Vocabulary, Riddles, Verbal Knowledge, Total), Nonverbal Index, Mental Processing Index, Fluid-Crystallized Index.
Administration: Individual.
Price Data, 2020: $995 per complete kit including 4 easels, KABC-II manual (2004, 236 pages), Normative Update manual supplement (2018, 155 pages), stimulus and manipulative materials, 25 record forms, and soft-sided nylon briefcase; $100 per KABC-II manual and Normative Update manual supplement package; $85 per Normative Update manual supplement; $80 per 25 Normative Update record forms; $2.20 per online score report.
Time: (25-70) minutes.
Comments: Nonverbal scale available for hearing impaired, speech-and-language disordered, and non-English-speaking children (an adaptation that examiners can make when verbal concerns are present); Normative Update data were collected using the original KABC-II materials with no changes to either the test content or structure; the test publisher advises that users of the KABC-II can continue to use their test materials along with the Normative Update manual supplement and Normative Update record forms.
Authors: Alan S. Kaufman and Nadeen L. Kaufman.
Publisher: Pearson.
Cross References: For reviews by Jeffery P. Braden and Sandye M. Ouzts and by Robert M. Thorndike of the second edition, see 16:123; see also T5:1379 (103 references) and T4:1343 (114 references); for reviews by Anne Anastasi, William E. Coffman, and Ellis Batten Page of the original edition, see 9:562 (3 references).

Review of the Kaufman Assessment Battery for Children, Second Edition Normative Update by KATHY J. BOHAN, Associate Professor of Educational Psychology-School Psychology, Northern Arizona University, Flagstaff, AZ:

DESCRIPTION. The Kaufman Assessment Battery for Children, Second Edition Normative Update (KABC-II NU) is a supplement to the KABC-II, offering users updated normative samples representing current U.S. population demographics. No changes were made to the administration, scoring, and interpretation guidance. This review focuses on the information in the KABC-II NU manual supplement (Kaufman & Kaufman, 2018).

The stated purpose of the KABC-II NU is to provide comparison data representative of a more diverse U.S. population (e.g., language diversity, race/ethnicity, socioeconomic status, educational levels) and changing educational environments (e.g., curriculum rigor, technology integration). Updated norms also address concerns of the Flynn effect (Flynn, 1987), the inflation of older cognitive ability scores as intellectual levels change over time. The manual supplement also apprises users of how the KABC-II aligns with more recent theoretical models of intelligence and neuropsychological assessment; updates somewhat evidence of reliability and validity; provides an illustrative case study; and offers guidance on often encountered administration, scoring, and interpretation questions.

DEVELOPMENT. In 2004, the KABC-II was released, offering major revisions to the original assessment battery published in 1983. The KABC-II provided users with the option of interpreting results using the Cattell-Horn-Carroll (CHC) psychometric theory of cognitive abilities or Luria's neuropsychological theory. Additional supplementary subtests were included to produce a Crystallized Ability scale, a measure of a child or adolescent's acquired knowledge. Examiners are generally encouraged to interpret results using the Fluid-Crystallized Index (FCI) global scale, aligned to CHC theory. The test authors suggest that the Lurian MPI global score may be a more appropriate global score for children whose background would suggest that including measures of acquired knowledge would not adequately represent their cognitive abilities. The KABC-II also offers a Nonverbal Index (NVI) useful for assessing children with limited English proficiency, moderate to severe speech or language disabilities, or hearing impairments. The KABC-II is appropriate for children and adolescents ages 3:0 to 18:11. The 18 subtests combine to produce a global score based on specific core subtests depending upon the child's age. As previously stated, the KABC-II NU updates norms and offers information about how to interpret results integrating recent changes in CHC theory.

TECHNICAL. The KABC-II was originally normed with 3,025 children and adolescents. The new norm sample is significantly smaller (N = 700). The revised normative data were collected in 2017 using a sample of children and adolescents stratified by race/ethnicity, parent education level, and geographic region. Experienced examiners from four geographic regions consistent with U.S. Census reports were recruited, trained, and monitored throughout the standardization process.

For each year of age from 3 to 14, fifty children were included. In the age ranges of 15-16 years and 17-18 years, 50 adolescents were included in each group. For the KABC-II NU, the parent education variable was defined differently than in the KABC-II normative sample. For children in two-parent families, the average educational attainment was calculated rather than using the highest level of the mother's education. Approximately equal numbers of females and males were included in each age group. Children representing special education eligibility categories were included in the normative sample consistent with the U.S. population overall. However, these children were not directly recruited into the sample, resulting in the age groups representing lower proportions of children in special education classifications compared to the U.S. Census data or the KABC-II sample. The battery developers report that further analyses of the results of the children with clinical diagnoses did not vary significantly from the original KABC-II results.

Inferential norming procedures were used to determine best fit curves that aligned to the theoretical and developmental expectations of a given age group. Results were smoothed to address any irregularities and produce an approximation to a normal distribution. The derived scale scores corresponding to mid-interval percentiles were converted to scaled scores with a mean of 10 and a standard deviation of 3. Similarly, the composite scores were converted to standard scores with means of 100 and standard deviations of 15.

For reliability, the manual describes similar correlations across gender, racial/ethnic, parent education, and special education eligibility groups as was attained from the larger KABC-II sample. The KABC-II NU global scores' split-half reliability coefficients were in the mid- to upper .90s (FCI and MPI) and the low to mid-.90s (NVI). Core subtests also produced good internal consistency values across age ranges with core subtests showing higher values and supplementary subtests producing somewhat lower averages. Average subtest coefficients ranged from .83 to .97 for ages 3-6 and from .79 to .96 for ages 7-18. Composite score reliability averages across ages 7-18 were .98 (FCI) and .97 (MPI), nearly identical to means from the KABC-II normative sample of .97 (FCI) and .95 (MPI). Composite correlation coefficients for ages 3-6 were also high at .97 (FCI) and .96 (MPI).

When comparing individual standard scores on the KABC-II NU norms, approximately half of the children's FCI, MPI, and NVI composites were three to four points lower than the same scores on the KABC-II, consistent with expectations suggesting that these changes occurred from the

Flynn effect. The majority (90%) of the individual scores were within six standard score points. The test developers remind users that individual differences will vary and to use caution in making inferences across scales based solely on group differences.

The manual supplement provides updated evidence of concurrent and discriminate validity through studies comparing KABC-II NU with other measures. For example, the KABC-II NU FCI correlates at .72 with the Wechsler Intelligence Scale for Children-Fifth Edition (WISC-V) Full Scale IQ, somewhat lower than the previous correlation between the WISC-V and the KABC-II, which was .81 (Wechsler, 2014). The correlation coefficient with the Kaufman Test of Educational Achievement-Third Edition (KTEA-3) Academic Skills Battery Composite was .74, nearly identical to the results obtained in the KABC-II validation study (.75).

COMMENTARY. The test developers are commended for providing a normative update using the same cognitive battery. The revised norms address Flynn effect concerns while maintaining a familiar instrument for practitioners and researchers to use. Some reviewers of the KABC-II have criticized the interpretation approach of choosing theories based on background information about the child or adolescent or examiner preference. These reviewers consider it illogical to use the same subtests and composite scores, with the exception of including the subtests that contribute to the Knowledge/Gc composite, when CHC interpretation is chosen (Braden, 2005; Thorndike, 2005). Others find the interpretative options to be a strength of the measure, offering examiners a cross-battery assessment approach with an engaging set of subtests that measures broad and narrow abilities (Bain & Gray, 2008). The addition of a new table in the KABC-II NU manual supplement assists examiners with interpreting results aligned with revised CHC Broad and Narrow Ability Constructs for both the KABC-II NU and the KTEA-3 (Schneider & McGrew, 2018). Examiners should consider how the provided crosswalk of subtest results with current CHC theory understanding contributes to meaningful interpretation and recommendations.

The manual supplement includes an illustrative case study. This case study gives users an example of how to integrate findings into a psychoeducational evaluation report. However, as noted by other reviewers, the KABC-II does not offer guidance on how results connect to interventions (Braden, 2005; Thorndike, 2005). A helpful appendix in the manual supplement offers administration, scoring, and interpretation considerations to address common examiner errors and frequently asked questions.

SUMMARY. As a highly respected clinical instrument, the KABC-II has been translated into several languages and is used internationally by practitioners and researchers. The KABC-II NU retains the familiar and child-friendly subtests for use across the 3- to 18-year age range. The normative update affords current demographic comparisons as well as strong evidence of validity and the reliability of results. Examiners are strongly encouraged to use the manual supplement to report scores as well as to consider provided information for formulating implications of findings based on more current understanding of CHC theory.

REVIEWER'S REFERENCES

Bain, S. K., & Gray, R. (2008). Test Reviews: Kaufman Assessment Battery for Children, Second Edition. *Journal of Psychoeducational Assessment, 26*(1), 92-101.

Braden, J. P. (2005). [Test review of Kaufman Assessment Battery for Children, Second Edition]. In R. A. Spies & B. S. Plake (Eds.), *The sixteenth mental measurements yearbook.* Lincoln, NE: Buros Institute of Mental Measurements.

Flynn, J. R. (1987). Massive IQ gains in 14 nations: What IQ tests really measure. *Psychological Bulletin, 101,* 171-191.

Kaufman, A. S., Kaufman, N. L., Drozdick, L. W., & Morrison, J. (2018). *Kaufman Assessment Battery for Children, Second Edition, Normative Update manual supplement.* Bloomington, MN: Pearson.

Thorndike, R. M. (2005). [Test review of Kaufman Assessment Battery for Children, Second Edition]. In R. A. Spies & B. S. Plake (Eds.), *The sixteenth mental measurements yearbook.* Lincoln, NE: Institute of Mental Measurements.

Schneider, W. J., & McGrew, K. S. (2018). The Cattell-Horn-Carroll Theory. In D. P. Flanagan & E. M. McDonough (Eds.), *Contemporary intellectual assessment: Theories, tests, and issues* (4th ed.). New York, NY: The Guilford Press.

Wechsler, D. (2014). *Wechsler Intelligence Scale for Children—Fifth Edition technical and interpretive manual.* Bloomington, MN: Pearson.

Review of the Kaufman Assessment Battery for Children, Second Edition Normative Update by TIMOTHY R. KONOLD, Professor of Research, Statistics, and Evaluation, University of Virginia, Charlottesville, VA:

DESCRIPTION AND DEVELOPMENT. The Kaufman Assessment Battery for Children, Second Edition Normative Update (KABC-II NU) is an individually administered battery of 18 core and supplemental subtests designed for measuring processing and cognitive abilities in youth between 3:0 and 18:11 years of age. The normative update retains the same materials as the original KABC-II, and the same subtests can be combined to form five specific index scores and three global index scales. The number of subtests administered varies as a function of the examinee's age and the theoretical framework under which the scores are to be interpreted. The index scores can be situated within one of two theoretical and interpretive frameworks that align with either Luria's theory of neuropsychological processes or the Cattell-Horn-Carrol (CHC) theory of cognitive abilities. New to the normative update is a refreshed CHC theoretical model that is based on recent empirical work by Schneider and McGrew (2018).

Four index scores are named in accordance with either Luria's theory (or the CHC theory). These include Planning (Gf Index–Fluid Reasoning), Sequential (Gsm Index–Short-Term Memory), Simultaneous (Gv Index–Visual-Spatial Processing), and Learning (Glr Index–Long-Term Storage and Retrieval). A fifth index score pertaining to Knowledge/Crystalized Ability can be obtained when users adopt a CHC interpretive framework. In addition to these index scores, users can obtain up to three global index scores: Nonverbal Index (NVI), Mental Processing Index (MPI), and Fluid-Crystalized Index (FCI). Users are encouraged to adopt the MPI for culturally diverse examinees and the NVI for examinees with language concerns. However, when contrasts were investigated between Caucasian, African American, and Hispanic students, recent research (Scheiber & Kaufman, 2015) indicated that the FCI may be less biased than the NVI or the MPI in predicting student achievement.

Administration times for the core subtests vary as a function of the examinee's age and whether users elect Luria's or the CHC interpretive framework, with estimates ranging from 25 to 60 minutes and 30 to 75 minutes, respectively. According to the test authors, scores from the KABC-II NU are intended to be useful in evaluations related to "SLD, known or suspected neurological disorders, attention-deficit/hyperactivity disorder (ADHD), intellectual disabilities/developmental delays, speech-language difficulties, emotional/behavioral disorders, autism spectrum disorders, reading/math disabilities, intellectual giftedness, and hearing impairment" (normative update manual supplement, p. 14). Normative frameworks for score interpretations are provided in the form of scaled scores (M = 10, SD = 3), standard scores (M = 100, SD = 15), confidence intervals, percentile ranks, and age equivalents.

TECHNICAL. The KABC-II (2004) was standardized on a nationally representative sample of 3,025 youth ages 3-18 years. The normative update was based on a national sample of 700 English-speaking youth who were evaluated over a seven-month period that began in January 2017. The sample was stratified in accordance with 2015 U.S. Census proportions with respect to race/ethnicity (i.e., African American, Asian, Hispanic, White, and Other), four parent education levels ranging from *11 years or less* to *16 years or more*, and four major U.S. geographic regions. The sample was also representative of the 14 age groups with which the KABC-II can be used. Approximately 50 youth were tested within each of the 1-year intervals that ranged from 3:0-3:11 to 14:0-14:11 and the 2-year intervals of 15:0-16:11 and 17:0-18:11. Each group consisted of approximately equal numbers of males and females.

Portions of the sample were also administered the Kaufman Test of Educational Achievement, Third Edition (KTEA-3; 20:105) and the Wechsler Intelligence Scale for Children—Fifth Edition (WISC-V; 20:205) for purposes of validation. As was the case with the 2004 standardization, very reasonable efforts were made to ensure that examiners were well trained with the instrument and had extensive experience testing children. In addition, several procedures were adopted to guard against potential data entry and scoring errors and to otherwise ensure data integrity.

Given the relatively small number (n = 50) of participants within each age group, scaled subtest scores were derived through inferential norming procedures in which various polynomial regressions were evaluated to gauge their fit to the data. The best fitting curves were used to generate population estimates of distributional characteristics related to means, standard deviations, and skewness. These in turn were used to construct theoretical distributions for each age group that allowed for percentiles to be identified at each raw score point. Percentiles were then transformed into scaled scores, and irregularities were removed through smoothing. The resulting subtest scores ranged from 1 to 19 (M = 10, SD = 3).

Reliability. Estimates of reliability are useful in gauging the extent to which scores are free from random error that can arise from sources that are unrelated to the construct that is intended to be measured. Reliability estimates are provided in the forms of internal consistency and standard errors of measurement. Average Spearman-Brown corrected split-half internal consistency estimates were appreciable. In the 3- to 6-year age group, these estimates ranged from .83-.97 across the subtest scores, .91-.98 across the index scores, and .94-.97 across the global index scores. Estimates were equally strong within the 7- to 18-year age group with ranges of .79-.96, .91-.97, and .95-.98, respectively.

Standard errors of measurement convey measurement precision around individual scores. Among children ages 3-6 years, these estimates were 0.55-1.31 across subtest scores, 2.45-4.50 across index scores, and 2.60-3.82 across global index scores. Within the 7- to 18-year age group these ranges were 0.63-1.40, 2.72-4.65, and 2.27-3.39, respectively. In contrast to the earlier version of the KABC-II (2004), test-retest reliability estimates were not provided in the normative update.

Validity. Validity refers to the accumulation of evidence to support the interpretation of test scores for their intended purpose. The normative update provides rather limited validity evidence, and does so only in the form of intercorrelations among subtests and index scores, correlations among KABC-II NU and KABC-II scales, and KABC-II correlations with measures located on the WISC-V and KTEA-3. For additional sources of validity evidence, users are encouraged to consult the KABC-II manual, where results from restricted factor analysis and clinical studies are presented, and other published studies on the KABC-II that can be found in the literature.

Correlations among same-named subtests and index scores on the KABC-II NU and KABC-II were all very high (*rs* > .95), as would be expected. Mean differences between these two versions were found present on the global index scales. On average, scores on the MPI and FCI were about 3-4 points lower in the normative update sample, as would be expected from the Flynn effect (Flynn, 1987). KABC-II NU scale associations with WISC-V scores are provided from a sample of 79 youth ages 7-16, and with KTEA-3 scores from a sample of 99 youth ages 4-18. These values were reasonable and were similar to those obtained with the original KABC-II standardization sample.

COMMENTARY. A 2017 national survey of more than 1,300 practicing school psychologists ranked the KABC-II as the fourth-most-used cognitive assessment in the United States (Benson et al., 2019). The normative update differs from the 2004 release of the KABC-II in at least three important ways. One is that the normative update manual supplement provides a nice illustrative case study for a hypothetical student. Second, discussion of the CHC theory and operational components have been updated to reflect more contemporary research in this evolving framework of cognitive abilities. Third, and perhaps most notably, the normative tables have been updated on the basis of a new sample of 700 participants. Normative interpretations of ability measures figure prominently into psychoeducational assessments, and the authors do a very nice job in the introduction of the updated manual reminding users of the importance of refreshing norms. Examples of these reasons include changing demographics in the United States in general and in schools in particular, changes in prevalence rates of individuals without U.S. citizenship residing in the United States, changes in language diversity, changes in economic diversity, changes in technology, and the Flynn effect (i.e., anticipated increases in ability scores over time). Beyond these updates, the KABC-II remains unchanged with respect to materials and subtests.

A number of concerns were raised in earlier reviews of the 2004 release (Braden, 2005; Thorndike, 2005), many of which appear to remain in the normative update. One concern focused on the many claims for how the KABC-II can be used in psychoeducational assessments (see last paragraph of Description and Development section above) that lack empirical demonstrations of its utility for these purposes and descriptions of how KABC-II scores could be used for these purposes in a clinical setting. A second concern was that there was no mention of the Cognitive Assessment System (CAS; Naglieri & Das, 1997) in the original KABC-II manual even though the CAS was specifically created to assess the PASS (Das, Naglieri, & Kirby, 1994) theory of cognitive functioning that is founded within Luria's processing model. Although the normative update does now include theoretical descriptions of how the KABC-II links to the PASS theory, it was a missed opportunity not to include associations between the KABC-II and the CAS as part of the validity studies presented in the normative update.

The normative update provides very limited new evidence to support the validity of the KABC-II scores in this new sample. As noted above, users are encouraged to consult the KABC-II manual or other published studies for this information. Although the content of the exam has not changed, it is unclear whether the same results would hold in this new sample that is nearly 15 years removed from the original KABC-II sample. As the test authors note on pages 1-3 of the normative update manual supplement, there have been many changes in the composition and characteristics of youth over this time.

The test authors note that there is much published research on the KABC-II. However, many clinicians are unlikely to have access to these sources given journal costs. A summary of these studies would have been a helpful addition to this update.

SUMMARY. Given the demographic changes that have occurred in the U.S. landscape and new ways of learning through technology that have taken place over the past 15 years, the KABC-II update brings an important refresh to the normative interpretation of scores. The update also places score interpretations in the context of more contemporary CHC theories of cognitive abilities. At the same time, validity evidence from this and other more recently evaluated samples is needed. For example, recent factor-analytic research on the 2004 standardization sample of the KABC-II failed to substantiate the four-factor solution advocated for use through index scores (McGill & Spurgin, 2017). Users should be on the lookout for whether this remains the case in studies conducted with the more recent normative update sample.

REVIEWER'S REFERENCES

Benson, N. F., Floyd, R. G., Kranzler, J. H., Eckert, T. L., Fefer, S. A., & Morgan, G. B. (2019). Test use and assessment practices of school psychologists in the United States: Findings from the 2017 National Survey. *Journal of School Psychology, 72,* 29-48.

Braden, J. P. (2005). [Test review of Kaufman Assessment Battery for Children, Second Edition]. In R. A. Spies & B. S. Plake (Eds.), *The sixteenth mental measurements yearbook.* Retrieved from http://marketplace.unl.edu/buros/

Das, J. P., Naglieri, J. A., & Kirby, J. R. (1994). *Assessment of cognitive processes: The PASS theory of intelligence.* Needham Heights, MA: Allyn & Bacon.

Flynn, J. R. (1987). Massive IQ gains in 14 nations: What IQ tests really measure. *Psychological Bulletin, 101,* 171-191.

McGill, R. J., & Spurgin, A. R. (2017). Exploratory higher order analysis of the Luria interpretive model on the Kaufman Assessment Battery for Children-Second Edition (KABC-II) school-age battery. *Assessment, 24,* 540-552.

Naglieri, J. A., & Das, J. P. (1997). Cognitive Assessment System. Itasca, IL: Riverside.

Scheiber, C., & Kaufman, A. S. (2015). Which of the three KABC-II global scores is the least biased? *Journal of Pediatric Neuropsychology, 1,* 21-35.

Schneider, W. J., & McGrew, K. S. (2018). The Cattell-Horn-Carroll theory of cognitive abilities. In D. P. Flanagan, & E. M. McDonough (Eds.), *Contemporary intellectual assessment: Theories, tests and issues* (4th ed., pp. 73-163). New York, NY: Guilford Press.

Thorndike, R. M. (2005). [Test review of Kaufman Assessment Battery for Children, Second Edition]. In R. A. Spies & B. S. Plake (Eds.), *The sixteenth mental measurements yearbook.* Retrieved from http://marketplace.unl.edu/buros/

[86]

Leadership Practices Inventory, Fourth Edition.

Purpose: Designed "as a measure of the frequency of specific leadership behaviors ... to help leaders gain perspective into how they see themselves as leaders, how others view them, and what actions they can take to improve their effectiveness."
Population: Individuals at all organizational levels; primarily used at middle management level.
Publication Dates: 1990-2013.
Acronym: LPI.
Scores, 5: Model the Way, Inspire a Shared Vision, Challenge the Process, Enable Others to Act, Encourage the Heart.
Administration: Group.
Forms, 2: Self, Observer.
Price Data: Available from publisher.
Time: (10-20) minutes.
Comments: Observer form can be completed by up to 10 people for 360-degree feedback; administered via paper and pencil or online.
Authors: James M. Kouzes and Barry Z. Posner.
Publisher: The Leadership Challenge, A Wiley Brand.

a) STUDENT LEADERSHIP PRACTICES INVENTORY, SECOND EDITION.
Population: High school and college students.
Publication Date: 2013.
Acronym: Student LPI.
Price Data: $6 per print Self Assessment; $4 per print Observer Instrument.

Cross References: See T5:1448 (1 reference); for reviews by John M. Enger and L. Carolyn Pearson of an earlier version titled Leadership Practices Inventory—Individual Contributor [Second Edition], see 14:204; for reviews by Jeffrey B. Brookings and William J. Waldron of The Team Leadership Practices Inventory, see 13:317; for reviews by Frederick T. L. Leong and Mary A. Lewis of an earlier version (1992) of the Leadership Practices Inventory, see 12:213; see also T4:1411 (2 references).

No review available. This test does not meet review criteria established by the Buros Center for Testing that call for at least minimal technical and development information.

[87]

Maslach Burnout Inventory [Fourth Edition Manual].

Purpose: "Designed to capture feelings of burnout."
Population: Adults.
Publication Dates: 1981-2016.
Acronym: MBI.
Administration: Individual or group.
Forms, 5: Human Services, Medical Personnel, Educators, General, Students.
Price Data, 2020: $60 per print manual (2016, 79 pages); $50 per digital manual; $15 per individual report; $200 per group report; $2.50 per Transform survey hosting (minimum 20); $2.50 per remote online survey license or license to reproduce (minimum 50).
Foreign Language Editions: Human Services Survey, Educators Survey, and General Survey are available in Spanish; information about additional translations available from test publisher.
Comments: Online administration and scoring available.
Authors: Christina Maslach (manual and all forms), Susan E. Jackson (manual and all forms), Michael P. Leiter (manual, General Survey, Student Survey), Wilmar B. Schaufeli (General Survey, Student Survey), and Richard L. Schwab (Educators Survey).
Publisher: Mind Garden, Inc.

a) HUMAN SERVICES SURVEY.
Population: Individuals who work in human services.
Publication Date: 1981.
Acronym: MBI-HSS.
Scores, 3: Emotional Exhaustion, Depersonalization, Personal Accomplishment.
Time: 10-15 minutes for administration.
b) MEDICAL PERSONNEL SURVEY.
Population: Medical personnel.
Publication Date: 2016.
Acronym: MBI-HSS (MP).
Scores, 3: Same as *a*) above.
Time: 10-15 minutes for administration.
c) EDUCATORS SURVEY.
Population: Teachers, administrators, other staff members, and volunteers who work in any educational setting.
Publication Date: 1986.
Acronym: MBI-ES.
Scores, 3: Same as *a*) above.
Time: 10-15 minutes for administration.
d) GENERAL SURVEY.
Population: Adults working in occupations other than human services and education.
Publication Date: 1986.
Acronym: MBI-GS.
Scores, 3: Exhaustion, Cynicism, Professional Efficacy.
Time: 5-10 minutes for administration.
Comments: "Focuses on the performance of work in general regardless of the specific nature of that work."
e) GENERAL SURVEY FOR STUDENTS.
Population: College and university students.
Publication Date: 2016.
Acronym: MBI-GS (S).
Scores, 3: Same as *d*) above.
Time: 5-10 minutes for administration.

Cross References: For reviews by Robert Fitzpatrick and Claudia R. Wright of the third edition manual, see 16:140; see also T5:1590 (69 references) and T4:1552 (30 references); for reviews by David S. Hargrove and Jonathan Sandoval of the second edition, see 10:189 (34 references); for reviews by Jack L. Bodden and E. Thomas Dowd of the original edition, see 9:659 (8 references).

Review of the Maslach Burnout Inventory [Fourth Edition Manual] by MICHAEL G. KAVAN, Professor of Family Medicine and Professor of Psychiatry, Associate Dean for Student Affairs, Creighton University School of Medicine, Omaha, NE:

DESCRIPTION. The Maslach Burnout Inventory (MBI) is a set of five related, but distinct, self-report forms designed to measure an individual's experience with burnout. The MBI Human Services Survey (MBI-HSS) is the original version and includes 22 items designed to measure feelings of burnout among human services workers who spend significant time interacting intensely with clients. The MBI Human Services Survey for Medical Personnel (MBI-HSS [MP]) includes 22 items and is designed to measure burnout in medical personnel. It is identical to the MBI-HSS except that the term "recipients" is replaced with "patients." The MBI for Educators Survey (MBI-ES) is similar and replaces the term "recipient" with "student." The MBI General Survey (MBI-GS) is a 16-item version for occupations that have limited direct personal contact with service recipients, and the MBI General Survey for Students (MBI-GS [S]) is a 16-item version designed to assess burnout in college and university students.

The MBI may be administered with no special qualifications other than that the person should not be a supervisor or administrator with direct authority over the respondent. The MBI may be administered in paper- and- pencil format or as an online survey. For all forms except the MBI-GS (S), examinees are asked to respond to each item based on whether they "ever feel this way about *your* job" or in the case of the MBI-GS (S) "*your* academic work" on a 7-point scale from *never* to *every day*. All MBI versions take 10 to 15 minutes to complete except the MBI-GS and the MBI-GS (S), which take 5 to 10 minutes. One set of scoring keys are provided for the MBI-HSS, MBI-HSS (MP), and MBI-ES, and another set for the MBI-GS and MBI-GS (S). Scores are summed to arrive at a total and an average score for each scale. For each version, users are reminded that each scale score should be interpreted separately and that the item scores should not be combined to form a single burnout score. Scores may be interpreted for individual respondents, or group data may be aggregated. Means and standard deviations may be calculated and compared to those provided within the test manual or to local norms. Online scoring and reports for individuals and organizations are also available through the test publisher.

DEVELOPMENT. The MBI Human Services Survey (MBI-HSS) is the original version of the MBI and was developed to "capture feelings of burnout" (manual, p. 12) among people working in professions where intense interactions with clients can be emotionally draining and lead to burnout. MBI items were designed to measure hypothetical aspects of a syndrome described as "burnout." The test authors conducted interviews and administered surveys to gather information about attitudes and feelings that characterize workers who are burned out.

A 47-item preliminary form of the MBI was administered to a sample of 605 health and service occupation workers. A factor analysis revealed 10 factors accounting for most of the variance. Items that had a single factor loading greater than .40, a large range of responses, a low percentage of "never" responses, and a high item-total correlation were retained, which reduced the total items to 25. This 25-item version was administered to a new, unidentified sample of 420 examinees. Results of a factor analysis were noted to be similar to the first. Twenty-two items performed consistently across three factors (i.e., Emotional Exhaustion, Depersonalization, and Personal Accomplishment) and now make up the current MBI-HSS.

The test authors have since developed several other versions. The MBI for Medical Personnel (MBI-HSS [MP]) was developed due to the high risk of burnout among physicians, nurses, and other medical personnel. The test authors provide limited information about its development and recommend that users assess the factor structure and scale reliabilities prior to using the results. The MBI for Educators (MBI-ES) was developed for teachers, but no information is provided within the test manual on its development. The MBI General Survey (MBI-GS) was developed for occupations with limited direct contact with service recipients and focuses more on the general performance of work. A 28-item survey was administered to samples in Canada, Holland, and Finland, and after a series of regression and factor analyses, 16 items were selected and make up three scales titled Exhaustion, Cynicism, and Professional Efficacy. The three-factor structure was confirmed with managers, clerical and maintenance workers, technologists and therapists, and nurses. An MBI General Survey for Students (MBI-GS [S]) is available for college and university students; however, the test authors note that "its psychometric properties are not yet documented" (manual, p. 2).

TECHNICAL.

Standardization. Test users are encouraged to interpret test scores as absolute values or by comparing scores to those from a larger group to determine a person's relative degree of burnout. Group data must be calculated locally or through the test publisher's online service. The test manual provides means and standard deviations for the MBI-HSS subscales across the occupational subgroups of social services (n = 1,538), medicine (n = 1,104), mental health (n = 730), and others (n = 2,897). No demographic information is provided for these groups. No normative data are provided for the MBI-HSS (MP). For the MBI-ES, norms and standard deviations are provided for the summative scores for primary and secondary school teachers (n = 4,163) and for postsecondary teachers (n = 635) with no additional demographic information. The MBI-GS scale means and standard deviations are provided for 28,018 respondents of the Schaufeli database, 19,782 respondents of the Leiter database, and then a combination of these. Demographic information is broken down by database and by gender, country, and occupation; however, no information is provided on the age, race, or ethnicity of respondents. Those using the online scoring service may obtain reports for the MBI-HSS, MBI-HSS (MP), MBI-ES, and MBI-GS that include normative data for their particular sample of users. No normative data are provided for the MBI-GS (S).

Reliability. For the MBI-HSS, coefficient alpha was .90 for Emotional Exhaustion, .79 for Depersonalization, and .71 for Personal Accomplishment in "early samples"; .79 for Emotional Exhaustion, .61 for Depersonalization, and .73 for Personal Accomplishment in a sample of 1,849 intensive care nurses; and .85 for Emotional Exhaustion, .58 for Depersonalization, and .71 for Personal Accomplishment in a sample of 705 Spanish professionals. Test-retest reliability coefficients for a sample of 53 graduate students who took the MBI-HSS 2 to 4 weeks apart were .82 for Emotional Exhaustion, .60 for Depersonalization, and .80 for Personal Accomplishment. Other studies found test-retest correlations of .74, .72, and .65, respectively, over an 8-month interval; .59, .50, and .63, respectively, over a 6-month interval; and .75, .64, and .62, respectively, over a 3-month interval for these subscales. A three-wave study of 258 Dutch nurses found reliability coefficients ranging from .66 to .71 for the Emotional Exhaustion scale, and from .55 to .64 for the Depersonalization scale. Finally, a study involving 316 staff nurses found a significant difference in means for the Emotional Exhaustion scale only over a one-year testing interval.

For the MBI-ES, alpha coefficient ranged from .87 to .90 for Emotional Exhaustion, .74 to .76 for Depersonalization, and .72 to .84 for Personal Accomplishment in 492 teachers and were .85, .63, and .79, respectively, in a sample of 771 Greek Cypriot teachers. Test-retest reliability for 248 teachers over two separate administrations of the MBI-ES 1 year apart were .60 for Emotional Exhaustion, .54 for Depersonalization, and .57 for Personal Accomplishment.

For the MBI-GS, alpha coefficients were .88 for Emotional Exhaustion, .76 for Cynicism, and .76 for Professional Efficacy for 12,140 employees from a variety of unspecified organizations; .83, .79, and .74, respectively, for a sample of 2,431 working adults; .86, .75, and .83, respectively, for 9,055 forest industry employees; and from .87 to .90, .74 to .80, and .70 to .77, respectively, for 3,312 employees from four unspecified occupational groups. Test-retest reliabilities were .72 for Emotional Exhaustion, .61 for Cynicism, and .58 for Professional Efficacy in 694 police officers, air traffic controllers, journalists, and construction managers over a 6-month interval; .74, .67, and .71, respectively, for a sample of 219 nurses over a 2-week interval; and .65, .60, and .67, respectively, in a sample of 1,018 Dutch civil service employees over a 1-year interval. No reliability data are provided in the test manual for the MBI-HSS (MP) or MBI-GS (S).

Validity. For the MBI-HSS, several studies are cited within the test manual demonstrating a relationship between the Emotional Exhaustion and Depersonalization scales and mental health co-worker ratings of being emotionally or physically drained, between the Emotional Exhaustion scale and spousal ratings of police officers' upset, anger, tension, anxiety, exhaustion, and complaints about work, and between the Personal Accomplishment scale and police officer spousal ratings of being cheerful and doing work that was a source of pride. Higher scores on MBI-HSS Emotional Exhaustion and Depersonalization and lower scores on Personal Accomplishment were related to higher caseloads for public contact employees. Physicians spending most or all of their time in direct patient contact scored higher on Emotional Exhaustion versus those with more varied duties. The test manual also cites a meta-analytic review that found job demands were related to the three dimensions of burnout measured in the MBI. MBI-HSS scores were also predictive of police officers' and public contact workers' intention to quit. Research across multiple studies suggests that Emotional Exhaustion is most strongly associated with intentions to leave one's profession. Other studies found that Emotional Exhaustion, Depersonalization, and Personal Accomplishment scores were related to relationships with co-workers, supervisors, patients, and families; sleep problems and the use of alcohol and drugs; physical well-being; and general job satisfaction. The MBI-HSS does not appear to be influenced by social desirability as evaluated by the Crowne-Marlowe Social Desirability Scale.

Evidence of validity for the MBI-ES scores is demonstrated through its predicted relationships between the three scales and job conditions for teachers, co-worker harassment, student misbehavior, and having more special needs students in class. A meta-analysis of public school teachers demonstrated that workplace demands were associated with Emotional Exhaustion, whereas workplace resources were associated with lower Depersonalization and higher Personal Accomplishment scores. The MBI-ES scales also were noted to be predictive of less improvement in the quality of the teacher-child relationship and literacy skills of students.

MBI-GS Exhaustion scores were related to job conditions such as control, opportunities for growth, and job demand overload in teachers, whereas Cynicism and Professional Efficacy were correlated with a lack of growth opportunities. Firefighters with positive relationships with their supervisor had lower levels of Exhaustion and Cynicism. In aircraft maintenance technicians, perceived control over accidents was related to Professional Efficacy, and hazard-related training was negatively related to Exhaustion and positively related to Professional Efficacy. Professional Efficacy also has been shown to be related to satisfaction, organizational commitment, job involvement, and access to resources. Exhaustion, and to a lesser degree Cynicism, were related to job turnover in nurses and work-to-family interference in Dutch governmental workers. All three scales were related to various physical health parameters; however, burnout was not significantly associated with physiological markers of stress. The MBI-ES demonstrated low to moderate correlations with indicators of occupational stress (suggesting it is related, but not the same entity); moderate correlations with turnover intention; and nonsignificant, low, or moderate correlations with overwork or fatigue. Separate studies found that the MBI-GS composite score correlated .79 with the composite score from the Shirom-Melamed Burnout Measure; the Exhaustion scales of the MBI-GS and the Oldenburg Burnout Inventory (OLBI) correlated .60, .65, and .72; and the MBI-GS Cynicism scale correlated .60, .48, and .67 with the OLBI Disengagement scale. No validity data are provided for the MBI-HSS (MP) or the MBI-GS (S).

COMMENTARY. The MBI encompasses several instruments designed to measure burnout in professionals in the human services industry, medical personnel, educators, workers who are not human service providers or educators, and college students. The MBI instruments are easily administered and scored. Factor analyses generally demonstrate a three-factor solution with most items loading on the appropriate scales for the MBI-HSS, MBI-ES, and MBI-GS. In general, the MBI-HSS, MBI-ES, and MBI-GS demonstrate good internal reliability, although reliability coefficients for the Depersonalization scale are generally lower. Test-retest reliabilities across forms are reasonable for an instrument measuring feelings likely to vary due to changing conditions. Numerous studies are cited throughout the test manual concerning validity evidence for the MBI instruments with most pointing to reasonable and predicted relationships between MBI scale scores and measures hypothesized as being related to burnout. It is unfortunate that no reliability or validity data are provided for the MBI-HSS (MP) or MBI-GS (S).

Despite its solid reliability and validity, a conundrum exists regarding what to make of MBI scale scores. The test authors note that the MBI is a research instrument and that scale scores should be calculated and interpreted separately and not combined for a single burnout score. Unfortunately, limited normative data and guidance on how to interpret scores often results in researchers and clinicians either making judgments on the relative status of an examinee compared to group data or by inappropriately using single scale scores (e.g., Emotional Exhaustion or Depersonalization) or a total score to do just that. Questions also arise as to what the MBI truly measures. Is it burnout, solely, or some combination of factors such as burnout, depression, stress, or fatigue? The test authors address the issue of burnout and depression within the test manual noting that burnout and depression are linked, but distinct, entities. Others (e.g., Bianchi, Schonfeld, & Laurent, 2015) suggest a more "fragile" connection, and even Maslach and Leiter (2016) agree that burnout and depression appear to be linked but that this relationship is "complex." In addition to the interpretation issue, the MBI has been faulted for not considering "nonprofessional confounders" of burnout such as child care demands, the support of partners, life events, financial issues, and factors such as excessive technology (Eckelberry-Hunt, Kirkpatrick, & Barbera, 2018).

Previous reviews of the MBI (Wright, 2005) noted that the MBI suffered from the currency of data, a lack of validity support for the MBI-GS, and limited normative data, especially as related to underrepresented populations. The former two issues have been addressed; however, technical data for underrepresented populations is still lacking.

SUMMARY. The MBI includes a series of instruments that purport to measure burnout in human services employees, medical personnel, educators, non-human service and education employees, and college students. The MBI forms are easy to use and score. The MBI demonstrates good reliability and validity evidence with scores being related to factors predicted to be associated with burnout. The MBI was developed as a research instrument and, as such, it is quite good. Although the test authors caution users about inappropriately using MBI scores, the burnout literature is replete with instances in which MBI scores have been inappropriately used to determine burnout in employment and clinical settings. The MBI would benefit from psychometric studies designed to provide more guidance on its appropriate use, technical data on the MBI-HSS (MP) and MBI-GS (S), and additional normative data across forms that are based on a more heterogeneous population.

REVIEWER'S REFERENCES

Bianchi, R., Schonfeld, I. S., & Laurent, E. (2015). Burnout–depression overlap: A review. *Clinical Psychology Review, 36*, 28-41.

Eckleberry-Hunt, J., Kirkpatrick, H., & Barbera, T. (2018). The problems with burnout research. *Academic Medicine, 93*, 367-370.

Maslach, C., & Leiter, M. P (2016). Understanding the burnout experience: Recent research and its implications for psychiatry. *World Psychiatry, 15*(2), 103-111.

Wright, C. R. (2005). [Review of the Maslach Burnout Inventory, Third Edition]. In R. A. Spies & B. S. Plake (Eds.), *The sixteenth mental measurements yearbook* (pp. 582-585). Lincoln, NE: Buros Institute of Mental Measurements.

Review of the Maslach Burnout Inventory [Fourth Edition Manual] by DEBORAH M. POWELL, Associate Professor, University of Guelph, Guelph, Ontario, Canada:

DESCRIPTION. The Maslach Burnout Inventory (MBI) assesses burnout, which the test authors define as a syndrome that consists of three types of feelings and that indicates "a crisis in one's relationship with work" (manual, p. 21). The MBI Fourth Edition Manual includes information about five versions that are appropriate for different types of respondents and settings: (a) Human Services, MBI-HSS, which is the original published scale; (b) Medical Personnel, the MBI-HSS (MP); (c) Educators, the MBI-ES; (d) General, the MBI-GS; and (e) Students, the MBI-GS (S). The three types of feelings that make up the burnout syndrome for the HSS and ES versions are Emotional Exhaustion, Depersonalization, and Personal Accomplishment. The Emotional Exhaustion scale assesses feelings of being emotionally overextended and exhausted by one's work. The Depersonalization scale measures an unfeeling and impersonal response toward clients/patients, and the Personal Accomplishment scale assesses feelings of competence and successful achievement in one's work with people. The latter scale is sometimes reverse coded as diminished personal accomplishment. For the GS version, the three types of feelings are Exhaustion, Cynicism, and Professional Efficacy.

The original scale, the MBI-HSS (MP), and the MBI-ES each have 22 items: nine items for Emotional Exhaustion, five items for Depersonalization, and eight items for Personal Accomplishment. The MBI-GS and MBI-GS (S) have 16 items: five for Exhaustion, five for Cynicism, and six for Professional Efficacy. Initially items were rated on frequency and intensity, but research showed strong correlations between the two, so now items are rated only on a 7-point frequency scale (0 = *never* to 6 = *every day*). Each version takes 10-15 minutes to complete (5-10 minutes for educators and students) and is generally done in electronic form but can be completed in paper form. The test authors state that burnout is not a dichotomous variable that is either present or not (there is no set cutoff for "burnout"), but rather is a continuous variable ranging from low to high. As such, the MBI is not a clinical diagnostic tool. The MBI can be used as a tool for basic research (e.g., for investigating the nature, causes, and consequences of burnout) or in applied settings for investigating work units, including before/after measures for intervention evaluation. A scoring key for the scales is provided in the test manual, or test administrators can use the test publisher's online platform to generate reports. Scores can be reported as either an average or a sum for each factor, and the test authors make clear that each scale is a separate factor that should not be combined to form an overall burnout score. Test users can obtain reports from the test publisher that compare respondents' scores to normative data. Alternatively, test users can interpret respondents' scores with respect to the rating scale (e.g., 5.5 indicates feeling Emotional Exhaustion several times a week on average but not every day).

DEVELOPMENT. The MBI Human Services Survey (MBI-HSS) is the original version of the MBI. The items were "designed to capture feelings of burnout among people working in job settings characterized as human services, where professionals in a variety of specific occupations spend considerable time interacting intensely with their clients" (manual, p. 12). The test authors describe how they conducted their exploratory research, including interviews and surveys, to gather ideas about the attitudes and feelings that characterize burned out workers. The test authors also describe a process of consulting items in other existing measures for content material (although the specific measures that were consulted are not listed in the manual).

The initial development of the instrument included administering 47 items to 605 people in health and service occupations. The items were then subjected to principal components analysis with varimax rotation; 10 factors seemed to best account for the variance in the 47 items. Next, several selection criteria were applied to select the best items, including: (a) the item had to have a single factor loading higher than .40, (b) the item had to have a range of responses including a low percentage of "never" responses, and (c) the item had to display a high item-total correlation coefficient. This process reduced the scale to 25 items. The 25-item form was then administered to a new sample of 420 people, and 22 items were retained. Those 22 items loaded onto one of three factors, which each had eigenvalues greater than 1. The factor analysis results are presented in the test manual. The Emotional Exhaustion factor has nine items that clearly load on one factor. The Depersonalization scale has five items, some of which have a bit of a cross loading. (For example, one item has a factor loading of .55 on the Depersonalization factor and a .37 loading on Emotional Exhaustion.) The Personal Accomplishment factor has eight items, some of which also have a bit of a cross loading. (For example, one item has a loading of -.30 on Emotional Exhaustion versus .43 on Personal Accomplishment.) These cross loadings are consistent with the factors being correlated.

TECHNICAL. The three-factor structure of the MBI has been replicated in multiple studies conducted by independent researchers. The factors are correlated (e.g., correlation coefficients of .52 between Depersonalization and Emotional Exhaustion, -.22 between Emotional Exhaustion and Personal Accomplishment, and -.26 between Personal Accomplishment and Depersonalization). The test authors report alpha coefficients ranging from .71 (Personal Accomplishment), to .79 (Depersonalization), to .90 (Emotional Exhaustion). The test manual also reports on three studies that have examined test-retest reliability, and the correlation coefficients reported, such as .74, .72, and .65 for an

8-month interval (Lee & Ashforth, 1993), and .59, .50, and .63 for a 6-month interval (Leiter, 1990), seem consistent with a construct that is described as an enduring state.

A number of studies are cited to provide convergent evidence of validity for the test scores. For example, in a sample of 845 public contact employees, employees with larger caseloads demonstrated higher scores on Emotional Exhaustion and Depersonalization and lower scores on Personal Accomplishment. In a meta-analysis, Lee and Ashforth (1993) found that job demands were related to the three dimensions of burnout. In another meta-analysis, Alarcon (2011) found that the MBI correlated with role ambiguity, role conflict, and workload. Alarcon (2011) also reported correlations with turnover intentions. Burnout also has been found to be associated with physiological health complaints (Kim, Ji, & Kao, 2011) and sleep, appetite, and health disturbances (Jourdain & Chênevert, 2010).

In terms of evidence of discriminant validity, the test authors report correlation coefficients of -.23 between Emotional Exhaustion and job satisfaction, -.22 between Depersonalization and job satisfaction and .17 between Personal Accomplishment and job satisfaction, suggesting that burnout is not overlapping with job satisfaction.

Means and standard deviations from two large databases that included thousands of respondents and covered many countries and a variety of occupations are presented in the test manual. If desired, users can request reports that include the normative data that are appropriate for their respondents. In many research applications of the MBI, users would more likely use average or total scores, without reference to norms.

COMMENTARY. The MBI has been used in hundreds of research studies since its first version appeared in 1981. The scale has reasonable internal consistency, good test-retest reliability, and correlates with other variables (e.g., depression, job satisfaction, turnover intentions) in the expected directions. An interesting feature of this inventory is that the original factor structure was developed based on exploratory factor analyses, and the test manual does not cite any additional refinement of the three-factor model of burnout. There are unequal numbers of items to assess each factor, and there appears to be no reason for that difference, other than it is how the original factor analysis worked out. It is unclear whether the factor with the most items is the most important, or the broadest, or whether there is another reason why the Emotional Exhaustion factor has more items. It would be useful for future research to investigate the construct further, to determine whether all factors are equally important. As an example of further construct exploration, Jourdain and Chênevert (2010) suggested that job demands are positively associated with Emotional Exhaustion, which in turn causes an increase in Depersonalization. In other words, one of the factors of burnout might happen before the others. These types of processes seem worth investigating further.

SUMMARY. The MBI is a psychometrically sound inventory of burnout that has been used in hundreds of research studies. It is used primarily for research purposes, rather than clinical diagnoses, and can be used in a variety of research and applied settings, such as testing the effectiveness of interventions. The three-factor structure was initially developed through exploratory factor analysis, rather than theory-driven, but the factor structure seems consistent in numerous studies conducted both by the original authors and independent researchers.

REVIEWER'S REFERENCES

Alarcon, G. M. (2011). A meta-analysis of burnout with job demands, resources, and attitudes. *Journal of Vocational Behavior, 79,* 549-562.

Jourdain, G., & Chênevert, D. (2010). Job demands-resources, burnout and intention to leave the nursing profession: A questionnaire survey. *International Journal of Nursing Studies, 47,* 709-722.

Kim, H., Ji, J., & Kao, D. (2011). Burnout and physical health among social workers: A three-year longitudinal study. *Social Work, 56,* 258-268.

Lee, R. T., & Ashforth, B. E. (1993). A longitudinal study of burnout among supervisors and managers: Comparisons between the Leiter and Maslach (1988) and Golembiewski et al. (1986) models. *Organizational Behavior and Human Decisions Processes, 54,* 369-398.

Leiter, M. P. (1990). The impact of family resources, control coping, and skill utilization on the development of burnout: A longitudinal study. *Human Relations, 43,* 1067-1083.

[88]

Matrigma.

Purpose: Designed as a non-verbal measure of general mental ability for use in workplace selection and recruitment.
Population: Prospective employees.
Publication Date: 2017.
Scores: Total score only.
Administration: Individual or group.
Forms: 5 parallel forms (A, B, C, D, E).
Price Data: Available from publisher.
Foreign Language Editions: Available in more than 20 languages.
Time: 40 minutes.
Comments: Administered online.
Authors: Assessio (test); Hunter Mabon and Anders Sjöberg (technical manual).
Publisher: Assessio [Sweden].

Review of the Matrigma by ESTHER KAUFMANN, Senior Lecturer and Researcher, University of Zurich (Switzerland), Institute of Education, Zurich, Switzerland:

DESCRIPTION. Matrigma is an online test of general mental ability (GMA) specifically designed to aid in the selection of prospective employees. Cultural and linguistic factors are less likely to bias test scores due to the test's non-verbal, non-numerical format. According to the test authors, the measure is inappropriate for assessing manager and employee development or for use in career guidance, team building, or coaching, and it is not designed for use in clinical contexts. The test is distributed by the company Assessio in Stockholm, Sweden. Currently, there are five parallel versions available in more than 20 languages (e.g., English, German).

The test can be administered in an individual or group setting and can be conducted with or without supervision. In the unsupervised version, test takers receive an invitation email with a link to the test, and the Assessio company provides technological assistance via email. However, unsupervised tests should either be re-administered with onsite supervision, or the test score should be supplemented with results from an additional GMA test. Test administrators are responsible for fulfilling the test's technological (e.g., internet connection) and environmental (e.g., a quiet place) requirements.

Test takers are first provided with a clear, easily understandable introduction to the test, followed by three example tasks. Test takers are then presented with 30 tasks, ordered by difficulty. Each task is presented on a separate, standardized screen. During each task, test takers are presented with a series of geometrical figures or matrices. Test takers must then identify connections, fill in missing information, grasp the relationship between the different objects, or find similarities across the figures. Test takers have 40 minutes to complete as many tasks as possible. A clock indicates the remaining time available. When they have finished the test, test takers are informed whether they missed or skipped any tasks and, if time allows, they have the opportunity to return to any incomplete items. They then submit their responses to the online system.

After responses have been submitted, the online system automatically creates a standardized report for each test taker. The report includes an easy-to-understand text description and graphical display of the individual's test score (between 0 and 10), and whether his/her performance is *relatively high*, *average*, or *low*. High scorers (7–10) are likely to manage well in complex jobs that make strong demands on their problem-solving abilities. Average scorers (3–6) are assumed to manage well in jobs that make moderate problem-solving demands. Generally, people with scores of 2 or lower are assumed to manage better in less demanding, less complex jobs, though a highly conscientious approach may compensate for low GMA. The individualized report is sent to each test taker via email. Test takers have the opportunity to ask questions if they have difficulty interpreting their score.

DEVELOPMENT. Matrigma is based on the intelligence testing tradition, which traces its development to Galton (see Jensen, 1998). Although the use of GMA tests for employee selection sometimes has been criticized in the past, meta-analyses have now indicated that GMA test scores are a good predictor of employees' work performance (see Schmidt & Hunter, 1992).

Matrigma is based on a one-parameter item response theory approach (see Rasch, 1960). The raw score distribution of Matrigma is transformed to the standard scale C. This transformation is useful for communicating test results in a user-friendly way, as scores range from 0 to 10.

A first tryout edition of Matrigma including 33 matrix tasks was evaluated based on a sample of 78 students (78% women). Across the scale and within the score subcategories (0 to 10), reliability was fairly high. GMA scores from the Predicting Job Performance test (tasks include logical series, number series, and analogies, see Sjöberg, Sjöberg, & Forssén, 2006) were available for a subsample of participants. Comparison of participants' scores on both tests provided evidence of construct validity.

A second, follow-up edition included four additional items and also a parallel version (B). This edition was evaluated based on a sample of 352 Nordic adults. The sample consisted of 42% women, and 53% of participants had three or more years of higher education (versus 20% in the Swedish general population). Fairly high reliability values were confirmed across and within the 11 test subsections (C-transformed scales). The stability of test scores was evaluated after 30 days (r = .68) and after 8 weeks (r = .66), both times based on samples with overrepresentations of women (74% and 67%, respectively). The results indicated reasonable retest stability, although this time frame is relatively short. Comparison of test scores with scores from the Wechsler Adult Intelligence Scale (WAIS III; Wechsler, 1997) and Raven's Progressive Matrices (RPM Advanced; Raven, 1960) provided construct/convergent evidence of validity. Comparison of scores on the different GMA measures also indicated that the Matrigma (A, B) had a similar level of difficulty as the RPM Advanced, but was somewhat more difficult than the WAIS III. Matrigma scores were significantly related to test takers' age and educational level, but were unrelated to their gender. Thus, there was evidence that the Matrigma slightly overestimated the GMA of younger relative to older and more highly educated relative to less educated test takers. Four concurrent studies of validity compared Matrigma scores with job performance based on samples of call center advisors and bank and retail employees. For example, one of the validity studies found that managers' Matrigma scores were meaningfully related to their job performance as rated by two immediate superiors. A psychometric meta-analysis (see Schmidt & Hunter, 2015) of the four validity studies indicated that, overall, Matrigma scores were related to job performance (r = .36).

TECHNICAL.

Standardization. The third (current) edition of Matrigma includes five versions (A through E) and was evaluated based on a sample of 4,606 test takers. The sample was largely Nordic in origin, and 45% were women. About a third (36%) had completed high school, 33% had a bachelor's degree, and 28% had a master's degree; 2% of the sample had less than secondary education, and 2% had more than a master's degree. As in previous evaluations, test scores were moderately and negatively related to test takers' age and positively related to their educational levels.

Reliability. The internal reliability (coefficient alpha) of all test editions is relatively high, ranging from .80 to .85. However, reliability for scores of zero is unsatisfactory, meaning that results for participants who score zero should be interpreted with caution. There are no results regarding the retest stability for the latest test edition, but analyses revealed that the retest stability of previous editions was satisfactory.

Validity. No validity information is available specifically for the current test edition. However, analyses revealed that previous editions demonstrated satisfactory predictive and concurrent evidence of validity.

COMMENTARY. All in all, evaluations support the use of the Matrigma for employee selection. In addition to being a valid measure of GMA and a meaningful predictor of job performance, the online test has several advantages over more traditional GMA measures, such as an automatic check for missing or skipped items and automatically generated and individualized feedback. Supervision is suggested to help test takers understand the received feedback.

A number of caveats to the overall positive results should be noted. In particular, scores on the first Matrigma edition should be treated with caution because its evaluation was based on a small, selective sample. The evaluations of the second and third editions were based on larger, more gender-balanced samples. Overall, in the absence of a different item functioning (DIF) analysis, it is also unknown how test taker characteristics (e.g., gender) may seem to affect test scores. Additionally, both the second and third evaluation samples consisted entirely or largely of Nordic test takers. Hence, further evaluation with people from other cultural backgrounds is necessary to assess the usefulness of the instrument outside of Scandinavia. The results of four carefully conducted individual studies and a state-of-the-art meta-analysis demonstrate the concurrent validity of the second edition, specifically, that Matrigma is highly useful for predicting job performance. Still, it should be noted that conclusions are based on just four studies. Finally, although the Matrigma is an online test, there is currently no available information in the test manual regarding which technological systems are needed in order to conduct the test without technical problems or bias, nor regarding whether participants can check that they can successfully access the test before the test begins.

SUMMARY. The Matrigma is an online and non-verbal, non-numerical test of GMA for use in employee selection. The test successfully assesses GMA and meaningfully predicts job performance. The test considers test takers' needs by suggesting additional onsite supervision and by providing test takers with individualized feedback about their performance. Overall, this online test is a good supplement to traditional GMA measures (e.g., RPM), but further evaluation of its validity with samples other than Nordic test takers is needed if the test is to be used outside Scandinavia.

REVIEWER'S REFERENCES

Jensen, A. R. (1998). *The g factor: The science of mental ability.* Westport, CT: Praeger.

Rasch, G. (1960). *Probabilistic models for some intelligence and attainment tests.* Copenhagen, Denmark: Paedagogiske Institut.

Raven, J. C. (1960). *Guide to the Standard Progressive Matrices.* London, England: H. K. Lewis.

Schmidt, F. L., & Hunter, J. E. (1992). Development of a causal model of processes determining job performance. *Current Directions in Psychological Science, 1*, 89–92.
Schmidt, F. L., & Hunter, J. E. (2015). *Methods of meta-analysis: Correcting error and bias in research findings* (3rd ed.). Thousand Oaks, CA: SAGE.
Sjöberg, A., Sjöberg, S., & Forssén, K. (2006). *Predicting Job Performance: Manual.* Stockholm, Sweden: Assessio.
Wechsler, D. (1997). Wechsler Adult Intelligence Scale-Third Edition. London, England: The Psychological Corporation.

Review of the Matrigma by CHARLES A. SCHERBAUM, Professor of Psychology, Baruch College, City University of New York, New York, NY:

DESCRIPTION. The Matrigma from Assessio is designed to measure general mental ability using non-verbal, graphical matrix-style items. The test was developed to be used for employee selection in a variety of occupations. There are currently five forms of the test with 30 items on each form. The administration instructions are available in multiple languages. The technical manual provides sufficient detail on the procedures for administering the test. The test administration process includes several practice items. The test is administered online and is available for proctored or unproctored contexts. The test is timed at 40 minutes. The administration platform scores the test responses and provides several scoring reports. Test scores are reported on a standardized metric called the C-scale with scores from 0 to 10. The manual notes that the C-scale scores can be used to rank job applicants to make selection decisions.

DEVELOPMENT. The Matrigma was initially developed in 2007 and has undergone a major extension between 2015 and 2016. The current technical manual (2017 edition) does not explicitly describe the construct(s) measured by the test or the types of items included. One must deduce this information from the sections on the history of general mental ability (GMA) and its prediction of job performance as well as from the sections about the research on the test. The technical manual provides little information about the process used to create the matrix items on the initial version of the Matrigma. Additional items were developed by creating variations on the initial items. According to the technical manual, a small number of items were removed from the test during the initial and subsequent item development. Item response theory item statistics and item characteristic curves were used to retain or remove items from the test as well as to establish the psychometric equivalence of the different forms of the test.

TECHNICAL. The technical manual includes several studies evaluating different forms of the Matrigma and updating the norms. Despite the extensive work developing and updating norms, a final norms table is not included in the technical report. However, this information is shown graphically in the score reports. Although the nationality of the test takers in these studies is not reported, the language selected for the instructions is listed. To date, the majority of test takers completed the test with instructions in a European language. Norms are not reported by language of the instructions.

The development of the test was based on a Rasch item response theory (IRT) model. With this model, it is possible to estimate reliability for each score level. The technical manual includes the reliability estimate for each of the 11 possible scores on the C-scale metric collapsing across all forms of the test based on a sample of 4,606 collected in 2016. Seven of the reliability estimates are .80 or higher, and five are above .90. The exception is the extreme lower and upper scores which have reliability estimates in the .70 range or lower. Reliability estimates at the extreme ends of a score distribution are often considerably lower. The IRT reliability estimates at each score level are not reported separately for each version of the Matrigma, but the classical test theory (CTT) reliability estimates for each test form are reported. The CTT reliability estimates range from .80 to .85. Test-retest reliability estimates are reported using the initial forms of the Matrigma. The correlation coefficient in one study with 4 weeks between administrations was .68. In a second study with 8 weeks between administrations, the correlation coefficient was .66.

Given the use of the Rasch model, which does not include item discrimination, there are no item discrimination indices reported. The item difficulty estimates on the raw score metric of the test indicate that an average score is around 60% correct. No evidence is reported for the factor structure of the test items.

The technical manual reports four studies with criterion-related evidence of validity and a meta-analytic summary of these studies. The results of the meta-analysis include an uncorrected correlation coefficient of .25 with job performance (N = 490). This estimate is in line with other uncorrected estimates of the relationship between GMA and job performance (e.g., Bobko, Roth, & Potosky, 1999). It is important to note that each of the four studies uses a different type of performance measure (i.e., supervisor overall performance ratings, supervisor competency ratings, objective performance indicators). The technical manual includes several different forms of evidence to establish the relationship between the Matrigma and other tests of GMA (e.g., factor analysis with other tests, comparison of test characteristic curves from independent samples). However, only one small sample study (n = 54) reports the correlation between the Matrigma and another test that uses matrix items to measure GMA. This correlation coefficient was .63. The initial research shows some evidence that the test is related to job performance and similar tests of GMA that use matrices. However, this evidence comes from a limited number of small sample studies.

Analyses from several samples report on group differences in test scores, but no differential item functioning analyses are reported. The group differences results indicate that there are no differences based on gender, but that younger and more educated test takers receive higher scores on the Matrigma. No results are presented for race/ ethnicity or country of origin.

COMMENTARY. The technical development efforts to date have been based on modern test theory, which is a positive feature of this measure in the opinion of this reviewer. The conceptual development is primarily rooted in the scientific literature for crystalized intelligence tests. However, the Matrigma uses a test format that is more closely associated with fluid intelligence tests. At this point, there is little evidence comparing this measure to similar, but more established measures of GMA that use matrix items. The score differences based on age need to be considered carefully given the potential risk of differential employment outcomes for older applicants.

SUMMARY. Based on the available evidence, there is some support for using the Matrigma in employee selection contexts. However, the existing evidence is limited at this point. Additional studies providing additional criterion-related validity evidence and evidence of the relationship with other GMA tests that use matrix items is needed.

REVIEWER'S REFERENCE

Bobko, P., Roth, P. L., & Potosky, D. (1999). Derivation and implications of a meta-analytic matrix incorporating cognitive ability, alternative predictors, and job performance. *Personnel Psychology, 52*(3), 561-589.

[89]

Mayer-Salovey-Caruso Emotional Intelligence Test–Youth Research Version.

Purpose: "Designed to assess emotional intelligence among pre-adolescents and adolescents ... an ability-based scale that measures how well people perform tasks and solve emotional problems, rather than a self-report of one's emotional skills."

Population: Ages 10-18 years.

Publication Date: 2014.

Acronym: MSCEIT-YRV.

Scores, 7: Experiential Emotional Intelligence Quotient (Perceiving Emotions, Facilitating Thought, Total), Strategic Emotional Intelligence Quotient (Understanding Emotions, Managing Emotions, Total), Total Emotional Intelligence Quotient.

Administration: Individual or group.

Price Data, 2020: $363 per kit including manual (56 pages), 5 item booklets, 25 response forms, and 25 scored data sets; $198 per online kit including manual, online administration, and 25 scored data sets; $111 per 5 item booklets; $56 per manual; $62 per 25 response forms; $6.25 per scored data set.

Time: 20-30 minutes to complete.

Comments: Online administration and scoring available; after the test reviews were written, the test publisher advised that this instrument is a research version, and, as such, usage should be limited to research contexts.

Authors: John D. Mayer, Peter Salovey, and David R. Caruso.

Publisher: Multi-Health Systems, Inc.

Review of the Mayer-Salovey-Caruso Emotional Intelligence Test—Youth Research Version by LAURA L. PENDERGAST, Assistant Professor of School Psychology, Temple University, and MARIAH N. DAVIS, Doctoral Student of School Psychology, Temple University, Philadelphia, PA:

DESCRIPTION. The Mayer-Salovey-Caruso Emotional Intelligence Test—Youth Research Version (MSCEIT-YRV) was designed to measure emotional intelligence among youth ages 10-18. The test authors define emotional intelligence as "the ability to perceive emotions, to access and generate emotions so as to assist thought, to understand emotions and emotional knowledge, and to regulate emotions so as to promote emotional and intellectual growth" (Mayer & Salovey, 1997; as cited in the test manual). They describe the MSCEIT-YRV as "an ability-based scale that measures how well people *perform tasks* and *solve emotional problems* rather than a self-report of one's emotional skills" (manual, p. 1).

The MSCEIT-YRV yields a Total Emotional Intelligence Quotient (Total EIQ) and two area subscores: Experiential EIQ and Strategic EIQ. Four "branch" scores are also included. Experiential EIQ includes two branches, Perceiving Emotions and Facilitating Thought. Strategic EIQ includes two branches, Understanding Emotions and

Managing Emotions. Each branch has its own skill-based assessment strategy. The test authors note the four branches map onto the four-branch model of emotional intelligence (Mayer & Salovey, 1997; as cited in the test manual).

The MSCEIT-YRV can be administered, typically in 20-30 minutes, by users who have "completed graduate-level courses in tests and measurements or have received equivalent documented training" (manual, p. 4). Online and paper formats are available with the option of group or individual administration. The test authors encourage use of the MSCEIT-YRV in research contexts. With regard to other applications, they indicate that school psychologists and counselors "may find the assessment results helpful" in understanding student behavior and that the tool "could be valuable to clinicians" in conjunction with other measures but not as a diagnostic tool (manual, p. 3).

DEVELOPMENT. The MSCEIT-YRV was developed based on the theoretical framework posited by Mayer, Salovey, and Caruso (2016) that suggested four branches involved in emotional intelligence (Perceiving Emotions, Facilitating Thought, Understanding Emotions, and Managing Emotions), and an extensive review of the literature. The MSCEIT-YRV resembles the adult version but was modified to be more appropriate for youth (e.g., pictures of children, rather than adults, are incorporated; language has been modified). An expert panel was recruited and a veridical scoring method used to assign point values for responses.

A pilot version of the MSCEIT-YRV containing 184 items was created and examined based on a development sample (n = 2,000). Detailed demographic information about this development sample is not provided in the test manual, although the test authors report that the sample was predominantly (75%) White and Hispanic, 46.4% male, and 13.2 years old on average.

The test authors report 83 items were removed after piloting, resulting in a final scale with 101 items. Items were evaluated and removed based on findings from item-total correlations, exploratory factor analysis (EFA), and "interpretation issues." Minimal information about the technical procedures used in the EFAs was provided in the test manual. Thus, it is not possible to evaluate the appropriateness of these analyses and the decisions based on them.

TECHNICAL.

Standardization. The normative sample included 1,000 youth ages 10-18 (50% female) from the United States and Canada that was relatively diverse in race/ethnicity and socioeconomic status. The test authors examined mean differences in scores based on age and gender. However, no information about measurement invariance of scores across age, race, or gender was provided. If it is not clear that the measure is invariant across groups, then mean comparisons may be premature (e.g., Chen, 2008).

Reliability. According to the test manual, internal consistency (coefficient alpha and split-half reliability), test-retest reliability, and standard error of measurement were assessed during the test's development (standard errors of measurement ranged from 4.81 to 8.35 for the EIQ standard scores). Regarding internal consistency, estimates are reported separately by gender and age and for the combined sample. Alpha coefficients for the four branches were between .61 and .84. Estimates for the Total EIQ across all groups ranged from .81 to .90, placing them above the conventional research cutoff (.70). Test-retest reliability estimates over a 10- to 29-day interval were generally sufficient (> .78). However, the sample used for this analysis was quite small (n = 32) and demographically quite different from the full normative sample. For example, 9.4% of the normative sample was Hispanic as opposed to 84% of the test-retest sample.

Validity.

Content Evidence. The MSCEIT-YRV is grounded in theory. Item content was reviewed using a clear and logical process. Scoring procedures were supported through a veridical approach. The evidence presented in the test manual appears to support the content validity of the MSCEIT-YRV.

Structural Evidence. The test manual discusses the test's internal structure beginning with a presentation of intercorrelations between subscales. Next, it is noted that "Because this shortened test is comprised of fewer scales, it is unable to determine structurally valid subareas of emotional intelligence; however, it is still possible to test whether the MSCEIT-YRV—and its four branches—all reflect an overall factor" (manual, p. 34). Subsequently, the test authors used confirmatory factor analysis to examine a single emotional intelligence factor without looking at the other factor scores specifically.

Concurrent and Predictive Evidence. No evidence was presented in the test manual that examined the association of MSCEIT-YRV scores with other measures. However, the test manual states, "Because emotional intelligence is associated with daily functioning, it is presumed to be lower in individuals with various psychiatric or psychological conditions" (manual, p. 35). Mean differences between the general population (i.e., matched subgroup of the normative sample) and individuals with learning disorders (n = 34), anxiety disorders (n = 25), and mood disorders (n = 29) were examined. It is unclear how the diagnostic categories were established. The differences generally fell in expected directions and were not probed further. For example, classification accuracy using receiver operating characteristics/area under the curve analyses was not examined.

COMMENTARY. The MSCEIT-YRV has a number of strengths. It is theoretically grounded and examines emotional intelligence beyond self-report—a necessary and important benefit. It has a variety of other benefits that make it particularly useful to researchers, such as the option for online and group administration and the generation of data within an Excel spreadsheet.

These strengths must be considered in light of some psychometric limitations. Most notably, the structural validity of the MSCEIT-YRV has not been sufficiently established. With modern analytical methods, many techniques can be used to examine structural validity with a smaller number of items and item-level data (e.g., item response theory analyses, categorical factor analyses with correlated errors to account for similarities between item types, bifactor modeling approaches). Thus, structural analyses for the branch and area scores likely could be conducted. Further, it seems that the Total EIQ score might be a higher-order factor score (or general factor within a bifactor model), but no analyses examining this possibility are presented in the test manual. The incorporation of a general EIQ factor, and the intercorrelation between subscales, suggest that a higher-order or bifactor model might best approximate these data. This is especially important given evidence from the adult version of the MSCEIT suggesting that the factor structure may differ from that originally proposed by the test authors (Palmer, Gignac, Manocha, & Stough, 2005; Rossen & Kranzler, 2009; Rossen, Kranzler, & Algina, 2008). Finally, numerous analyses were conducted examining mean differences in MSCEIT-YRV scores based on age and gender, but in the absence of evidence of measurement invariance, the finding of mean differences is not informative, as it is unclear whether such differences are the result of true differences or differences in the validity of measurement (Chen, 2008).

Regarding validity evidence based on associations with other variables, it should be noted that research suggests that scores on the MSCEIT-YRV are positively correlated with school achievement, cognitive assessment, and other measures of emotional intelligence and negatively correlated with disciplinary referrals and emotional outbursts (Peters, Kranzler, & Rossen, 2009). Current research using the MSCEIT-YRV that supports its psychometric qualities examines EI in youth with ADHD (Climie et al. 2017) and those on the autism spectrum (Boily, Kingston, & Montgomery, 2017). Thus, additional validity evidence has become available since the test manual was published in 2014.

SUMMARY. Test users considering the MSCEIT-YRV should fully consider its strengths and weaknesses relative to their intended purpose. There are clear advantages for researchers (ease and speed of administration, price, established correlations with key outcome measures). The test manual mentions potential use by practitioners in schools and clinical settings; however, research presented in the technical manual supporting the use of the scale for these purposes is relatively sparse. A significant weakness of the MSCEIT-YRV is that structural validity, a foundational component of validity, is insufficiently established, and there is not a clear consensus in the literature regarding the factor structure of other versions of this scale (e.g., Palmer et al., 2005). Users should proceed with a degree of caution when interpreting scores until such evidence becomes available.

REVIEWERS' REFERENCES

Boily, R., Kingston, S. E., & Montgomery, J. M. (2017). Trait and ability emotional intelligence in adolescents with and without autism spectrum disorder. *Canadian Journal of School Psychology, 32*, 282–298. https://doi.org/10.1177/0829573517717160

Chen, F. F. (2008). What happens if we compare chopsticks with forks? The impact of making inappropriate comparisons in cross-cultural research. *Journal of Personality and Social Psychology, 95*, 1005-1018. doi:10.1037/a0013193

Climie, E. A., Saklofske, D. H., Mastoras, S. M., & Schwean, V. L. (2017). Trait and ability emotional intelligence in children with ADHD. *Journal of Attention Disorders*. Advance online publication. https://doi.org/10.1177/1087054717702216

Mayer, J. D., Caruso, D. R., & Salovey, P. (2016). The ability model of emotional intelligence: Principles and updates. *Emotion Review, 8*, 290–300. https://doi.org/10.1177/1754073916639667

Palmer, B. R., Gignac, G., Manocha, R., & Stough, C. (2005). A psychometric evaluation of the Mayer-Salovey-Caruso Emotional Intelligence Test Version 2.0. *Intelligence, 33*, 285–305. https://doi.org/10.1016/j.intell.2004.11.003

Peters, C., Kranzler, J. H., & Rossen, E. (2009). Validity of the Mayer–Salovey–Caruso Emotional Intelligence Test: Youth Version–Research Edition. *Canadian Journal of School Psychology, 24*, 76–81. https://doi.org/10.1177/0829573508329822

Rossen, E., & Kranzler, J. H. (2009). Incremental validity of the Mayer-Salovey-Caruso Emotional Intelligence Test Version 2.0 (MSCEIT) after controlling for personality and intelligence. *Journal of Research in Personality, 43*, 60–65. https://doi.org/10.1016/j.jrp.2008.12.002

Rossen, E., Kranzler, J. H., & Algina, J. (2008). Confirmatory factor analysis of the Mayer-Salovey-Caruso Emotional Intelligence Test V 2.0 (MSCEIT). *Personality and Individual Differences, 44*, 1258–1269. https://doi.org/10.1016/j.paid.2007.11.020

Review of the Mayer-Salovey-Caruso Emotional Intelligence Test—Youth Research Version by LIA SANDILOS, Assistant Professor, and KAIYLA DARMER, Doctoral Student, Temple University, Philadelphia, PA:

DESCRIPTION. The Mayer-Salovey-Caruso Emotional Intelligence Test—Youth Research Version (MSCEIT-YRV) is an individually administered measure of emotional intelligence intended for use among youth 10 to 18 years of age. The MSCEIT-YRV measures the "capacity to reason using feelings and the capacity to enhance thought with feelings" (manual, p. 1). The test authors emphasize that the MSCEIT-YRV is an applied measure that evaluates the use of emotions when solving problems and performing tasks rather than a measure that focuses on self-perceptions. Also, as the title indicates, the measure is considered a research version and should not be used for diagnostic purposes. The assessment can be administered online (completion time is 20-30 minutes) and is scored through the test publisher's online portal. To avoid creating emotional bias within the respondent, it is recommended that administration procedures establish a neutral test environment. Upon completion of the assessment, the respondent receives an Excel file containing a score report. Currently, there are no computerized interpretative reports available to respondents. A paper version of the assessment is also available from the test publisher. The scores from the paper version must be entered online; there are no scoring guides available within the test manual.

The assessment contains several sections (101 items), all requiring the respondent to engage in different tasks. The first section is Branch 1: Perceiving Emotions. In this section, the respondent rates the extent to which certain emotions are present in a facial prompt. The second section, Branch 2: Facilitating Thought, requires respondents to match sensory experiences (e.g., color, temperature, and speed) to emotions. For the third section, Branch 3: Understanding Emotions, respondents answer three types of multiple-choice questions involving defining emotions, determining which emotions would follow a specific event, and indicating which emotions would be combined to create a multidimensional emotional state. In the fourth section, Branch 4: Managing Emotions, respondents are presented scenarios in which they must determine which actions to take in order to achieve a specific emotional state.

The MSCEIT-YRV produces three primary emotional intelligence scores: Experiential Emotional Intelligence Quotient (EIQ), Strategic EIQ, and Total EIQ. The Experiential EIQ is the mean of Branches 1 and 2 (titled Area 1). This score represents the respondent's ability "to perceive, respond to, and feel emotions accurately, and to use such perceptions in reasoning processes" (manual, p. 15). Strategic EIQ is the mean of Branches 3 and 4 (titled Area 2). This score reflects the respondent's ability "to understand emotional concepts, to reason with them, and to strategize how to manage emotional reactions in oneself and in situations involving others" (manual, p. 16). Total EIQ is the mean of the two area scores.

DEVELOPMENT. The MSCEIT-YRV was piloted with 184 items. The pilot items were based on the original MSCEIT (adult version) and followed the theoretical four-branch framework: Perceiving Emotions, Facilitating Thought, Understanding Emotions, and Managing Emotions. Within the test manual, the authors cite a variety of sources consulted in the development of these four branches. These sources include empirical and theoretical papers related to emotions, emotion regulation, emotional intelligence, and coping, as well as the Merriam-Webster Dictionary and the American Pediatric Association (see full list of sources on pages 19-21 of the test manual). The test authors adapted the original MSCEIT to include age-appropriate images, stories, and language for the youth research version. Further, they used several criteria for selecting images to reflect the diversity of experiences and perceptions of the intended participants, such as ensuring that the images included a range of weak to strong emotions from both male and female faces between ages 11 and 17 and from a variety of racial/ethnic backgrounds.

The pilot items were administered to 2,000 respondents. Fifty-two percent of the respondents were female, and 46.4% of the respondents were male (1.6% did not report gender). The mean age of participants was 13.22 years (range of 10-18 years). Seventy-five percent of the sample identified as White or Hispanic. Data from the pilot study were used for item revision and reduction as well as to establish the scoring system.

The MSCEIT-YRV was developed with a "veridical" scoring system, meaning that scores are either correct or incorrect based upon standards developed by five independent experts in emotion research (manual, p. 21). The scorers used a 3-point scale to determine the accuracy of a response (2 = *plainly correct,* 1 = *response is possibly correct,* and 0 = *response is plainly incorrect*). Scores are placed on a normal curve with an average of 100 and a standard deviation of 15. The EIQ score range is as follows: < 85 is *below average*, 85-115 is *average*, > 115 is *above average*.

TECHNICAL. Data collection for the standardization of the MSCEIT-YRV took place between 2007 and 2010. Ultimately, results from 1,000 participants (500 male, 500 female) were chosen for the normative database. These data were collected from the four U.S. Census regions (13 states) and also included Canada (3.5%). As a first step in the standardization process, the test authors analyzed the data to determine whether there were trends across gender and age levels. Findings revealed that males and females did not differ significantly at the youngest age level (10-12 years), but significant gender differences were present at the older age ranges (13-15, 16-18) with females scoring higher.

The MSCEIT-YRV generally demonstrates reliability coefficients within an acceptable range (median alpha is .77), with Branch 1 most frequently displaying slightly lower levels of internal consistency (.66). The researchers found excellent test-retest reliability with coefficients ranging from .78 to .99 when examinees were tested twice with a mean retest interval of 18.6 days. It is important to note that the test-retest sample size was relatively small (n = 32).

As evidence of validity, the test developers examined correlations to determine whether there was an expected moderate relationship among the four branches. The correlation coefficient between Understanding Emotions (Branch 3) and Managing Emotions (Branch 4) was the largest at r = .60. The correlation coefficient between Perceiving Emotions (Branch 1) and Facilitating Thought (Branch 2) failed to reach significance at r = .04. Confirmatory factor analysis also was conducted to assess the measure's structural validity. Factor loadings for the four branches ranged from .30 to .85, with Branch 1 exhibiting the smallest loading. Regarding model fit, CFI (.954) and GFI (.980) generally fell within acceptable ranges but TLI fell below .90 at .86, and RMSEA was above .10 (.137), indicating poor fit (Hu & Bentler, 1999; Kline, 2013). These results raise questions about error in the fit of the existing four-branch factor structure and the likelihood of model replication with other samples. No evidence of criterion-referenced or convergent validity was provided in the test manual.

The test authors note that existing literature indicates that individuals with various psychological and psychiatric conditions will demonstrate lower levels of emotional intelligence. This phenomenon was explored with the MSCEIT-YRV by examining scores from "110 individuals with varying clinical diagnoses" (manual, p. 35), which included learning disorders, anxiety disorders, mood disorders (bipolar disorder, depression), and a variety of other disorders (attention-deficit/hyperactivity disorder, post-traumatic stress disorder, autism spectrum disorder, etc.). The race/ethnicity of the clinical sample was largely White (72.7%). The test developers found that the clinical group did score significantly (p < .05) lower than the non-clinical group on Branches 3 (Understanding Emotions) and 4 (Managing Emotions), Area 2 (Strategic EIQ), and Total EIQ. Within the clinical group, respondents with learning disorders scored lower on all branches except Branch 1 (Perceiving Emotions) than respondents with mood or anxiety disorders.

COMMENTARY. Overall, the test authors have established some preliminary validity and reliability evidence for the MSCEIT-YRV. Limitations to validity evidence include suboptimal model fit (e.g., RMSEA > .10, TLI < .90), no concurrent and predictive associations with other measures of emotional access/regulation or social skills, and a lack of exploration of psychometrics across race/ethnicity, language proficiency, or socioeconomic status. Examination of cultural, linguistic, and economic differences is particularly important given that the test requires a high level of vocabulary knowledge, especially at the oldest ages (16-18). Given the high reading level, the test developers might consider an audio version that provides a voice-over in addition to text. Additionally, an initial script to further standardize administration procedures and a clear scoring guide included in the test manual would also be useful additions to the assessment.

SUMMARY. The Mayer-Salovey-Caruso Emotional Intelligence Test—Youth Research Version is an applied measure of emotional intelligence for youth between 10 and 18 years of age. The measure was developed using the four-branch theory of emotional intelligence and was adapted from the original MSCEIT (adult version). The 101-item measure contains a variety of tasks including interpreting facial expressions, defining emotions and matching emotions to other sensory words, determining emotions linked to an event, and deciding what actions might lead to certain emotions. The technical information provided in the test manual offers preliminary support for the measure's reliability and evidence of the validity of its scores. Continued research is needed to establish further support for the inferences made from the MSCEIT-YRV scores with students who have varied reading and language proficiency levels, as well as with students from different cultural and socioeconomic backgrounds.

REVIEWERS' REFERENCES

Hu, L., & Bentler, P. M. (1999). Cut off criteria for fit indices in covariance structure analysis: Conventional criteria versus new alternatives. *Structural Equation Modeling, 6*, 1-55.

Kline, R. B. (2013). *Principles and practice of structural equation modeling* (3rd ed.). New York, NY: Guilford Press.

[90]

McCloskey Executive Functions Scale.

Purpose: "Designed to assess teacher perceptions about students' use of executive functions ... to facilitate the identification of executive function strengths, executive function deficits, and executive skill deficits in children."

Population: Ages 5-18.

Publication Date: 2016.

Acronym: MEFS.

Scores, 55: 31 Self-Regulation Executive Functions in 7 clusters: Attention (Perceiving, Focusing, Sustaining), Engagement (Initiating, Energizing, Inhibiting, Stopping, Pausing, Being Flexible, Shifting), Optimization (Monitoring, Modulating, Correcting, Balancing), Efficiency (Sensing Time, Pacing, Using Routines, Sequencing), Memory (Holding/Working, Storing/Retrieving), Inquiry (Gauging, Anticipating, Estimating Time, Analyzing, Evaluating), Solution (Generating, Associating, Organizing, Planning, Prioritizing, Deciding); 7 cluster scores in Academic Arena; 7 cluster scores in Self/Social Arena; 2 composite scores: Self-Realization, Self-Determination; plus Inconsistency (validity scale).

Administration: Individual.

Price Data, 2020: $365 per complete online kit including printed manual (140 pages), 25 parent online forms and reports, and 25 teacher online forms and reports; $325 per complete online kit including online pdf manual, 25 parent forms and reports, and 25 teacher forms and reports; $75 per 25 online forms and reports (parent or teacher); $75 per printed manual.

Time: (12-15) minutes.

Comments: Administered and scored using the test publisher's online platform; ratings may be completed on paper and entered online for scoring.

Author: George McCloskey.

Publisher: Schoolhouse Educational Services.

Review of the McCloskey Executive Functions Scale by RIK CARL D'AMATO, Distinguished International Research Professor in School Psychology and Clinical Neuropsychology, the Chicago School of Professional Psychology, Chicago, IL, and ELIZABETH M. POWER, Assistant Professor, Department of School Psychology, the College of Saint Rose, Albany, NY:

[The first reviewer would like to acknowledge the equal contributions of the second reviewer.]

DESCRIPTION. The McCloskey Executive Functions Scale (MEFS) is an individually administered, user-friendly, web-based rating scale designed to assess teacher perceptions about students' executive functions. According to the test author, "the main function of the MEFS is to facilitate the identification of executive function (EF) strengths, executive function deficits, and executive skill deficits in children" (manual, p. 1). The rating scale is designed to be used with children ages 5 to 18 years. Teachers are asked to assess observable aspects of either academic or self/social functioning that occur within their classrooms. Teachers circle a rating option that best describes the student on 110 Likert-type questions. The MEFS consists of two parts, and rating options vary depending on the section. Part One rating options/descriptions range from 5 (*almost always does it on own without prompting*) to 0 (*unable to do it even with assistance*). Part Two rating options/descriptions range from 3 (*does this very often*) to 0 (*never does this*). According to the test author, the scale can be completed in 12 to 15 minutes. The ratings are compiled to generate a report that includes a brief narrative and several score tables with standard scores, T scores, and/or percentile ranks. Additionally, descriptive categories are provided according to a percentile rank range (e.g., 39th–62nd percentile rank = average), and a strengths and weaknesses (deficits) item analysis is provided for Self-Regulation Executive Functions (SREF) and Self-Realization and Self-Determination Executive Functions. The test manual provides very detailed and specific directions regarding how to access the online MEFS account, complete rating forms, and generate reports.

DEVELOPMENT. The Development, Standardization, and Norming chapter in the MEFS manual provides specific information related to initial item development and selection, initial item tryout, formal item tryout, procedures used to select items for standardization, and data collection procedures used during standardization. The entire chapter on test development provides intricate details of the standardization process in an extremely organized fashion. It is clear that the test author wants readers to understand how decisions were made during initial and formal stages of standardization. The initial item pool was developed using the Holarchical Model of Executive Functions (HMEF), a multidimensional theoretical model based on work from multiple disciplines. The model is used to conceptualize and organize executive functions at multiple tiers, including self-regulation, self-realization and self-determination, self-generation, and trans-self integration (latter two tiers not captured by this assessment). A major difference between this rating scale and other tests measuring similar constructs is the author's goal of allowing the evaluator to view which items and how many of them were rated as strengths or deficits. These strengths and weaknesses are made apparent on the report, using a color coding system to "signify the level of functioning and whether the executive function is an executive function strength, an executive function deficit, or an executive skill deficit" (manual, p. 35). Executive skill deficits refer to the fact that the rater is asked to provide not only the *frequency* with which a child engages in certain behaviors, but also the *degree* to which the child needs assistance/prompts to carry out tasks. This is a distinction that seems significant and critical, but is, of course, often only found in adaptive measures.

TECHNICAL. During standardization, data were collected on 1,127 participants from 167 communities in 29 U.S. states. For final item selection and norming purposes, 127 participants were removed from the sample, resulting in a total of 1,000 with 200 participants (100 male, 100 female) in each of the five age groups. The demographic characteristics of the sample closely match that of the 2010 U.S. Census. Of the 1,000 participants, 18.7% consisted of children with various disabilities. According to the test author, a lower percentage of children diagnosed with only attention-deficit/hyperactivity disorder (ADHD) were used during standardization due to the unknown comorbidity of ADHD and other childhood disorders, such as learning disabilities. During standardization, the test author considered academic skills rankings and gender differences when grouping children.

Reliability was evaluated using traditional internal consistency reliability coefficients (alpha coefficients and split-half method), standard error of measurement, and test-retest reliability. Alpha coefficients were exceptionally high for all five age groups with no value below .86. However, the test author noted that some of the high alpha coefficients should be interpreted with caution in this case as they may overestimate a scale's reliability. Split-half reliability was examined by dividing the MEFS into two equal halves. The test author reported that all but two median coefficients are above .90. The standard error of measurement varies between 2.6 and 5.4. A test-retest study involved 42 teachers and students. A second administration occurred from 0 to 62 days after the first administration with a mean interval of 16.6 days. The test-retest sample was balanced in terms of gender, race/ethnicity, academic ability, age, and disability status. The majority of correlations fell in the mid-.80s with the exception of Self/Social Arena of Attention Cluster (.79), Academic Arena for Memory (.78), and Self-Realization (.67).

With regard to validity, the test author presents a refreshing perspective on the provision of evidence. Instead of describing the "traditional, but now outdated, format" (manual, p. 43) of content, criterion-related, and construct validity, test score validity evidence for the MEFS can be evaluated through the following: (a) evidence based on test content, (b) evidence based on response processes, (c) evidence based on internal structure, (d) evidence based on relations to other variables, and (e) evidence based on the consequences of testing. There is a large emphasis on the research basis of the MEFS content; trial use of the scales in clinical settings; feedback from experts, clinicians, and those who completed the scale; and empirical analyses of item content. It is clear that the test author cares that readers understand how the test content was created and has changed over the years. Internal consistency analyses revealed high values for all age groups, and developmental age progression of teacher ratings is consistent with research-based expectations. Upon initially reading that specific headings related to content, criterion-related, and construct validity would not be explicitly discussed, it was assumed that this section might be met with controversy. However, it is made clear in various sections where/how outdated validity conceptualizations fit within the current framework (e.g., criterion-related validity under "Evidence Based on Relations to Other Variables," manual, p. 53).

COMMENTARY. The MEFS is a brief and easy-to-use rating scale for teachers to complete regarding students' executive functions displayed in classroom settings. Directions are clear and simple to understand. The web services appear easily accessible and cost-effective. Another positive feature is the measure's Inconsistency index, which reflects the degree to which teachers have been consistent in their responses. Nonetheless, it is unclear whether frustrated teachers may over-rate student deficits. Given the number of years that the test author has spent researching and writing about executive functions, it is not surprising that this tool is impressively well-researched. The manual not only provides detail related to the assessment process, but also provides interesting research as it relates to populations of children with ADHD, how executive functions manifest across development and gender, and more. The case studies provide notable details and demonstrate how the instrument can be used in various settings, especially schools. There are multiple rating scales that help assess for individuals' executive functions, but none of the other measures is as exhaustive as the MEFS. Given the utility of the measure, hopefully in the future a parent version will become available. Additionally, the test author might consider adding an alternate form for intervention monitoring purposes. This measure is unique in many ways, including the array of executive functions considered and that it enables the identification of executive function strengths, executive function deficits, and executive skill deficits. This measure can be used for progress monitoring, benchmarking, differential diagnosis, and classroom management. It is uniquely designed to aid in individualized rehabilitation and therapeutic management, and it is especially friendly when writing individualized education programs.

SUMMARY. The MEFS is designed to be an individually administered, web-based measure of teacher perceptions about students' use of executive functions for children ages 5 through 18 years. The MEFS is based on the test author's model of executive functions, which is a conceptual and empirical framework that integrates multiple disciplines. The tool allows for assessment of a wide array of executive functions within the domains of Self-Regulation, Self-Realization, and Self-Determination. Although there are multiple executive function rating scales available, none appears to be as impressively designed or have as much utility as the MEFS. The test meets its goal of assessing executive functions across development and is recommended for use within various settings. Future research will determine whether the MEFS becomes the instrument of choice for executive functions.

Review of the McCloskey Executive Functions Scale by MAURICIO A. GARCIA-BARRERA, Associate Professor, Department of Psychology, University of Victoria, B.C., Canada:

DESCRIPTION. The McCloskey Executive Functions Scale (MEFS) is a rating scale with 110 Likert-type items designed for the assessment of self-regulation, self-realization, and self-determination in children ages 5 through 18. According to its author, the MEFS enables the characterization of a child's executive function strengths and weaknesses, as well as executive skill deficits, and facilitates clinical diagnosis by complementing other sources of information. Furthermore, the test author suggests that when used over time, the MEFS also informs developmental change.

This instrument is designed to be purchased, downloaded, and completed online. Psychologists and other qualified users (defined as practitioners with graduate level training in educational or psychological testing and measurement) must first register and create an account in order to purchase the instrument. Individualized links are generated for third-party informants such as "teachers or clinicians that are familiar with the child" (manual, p. 15), although throughout the test manual and on the form, teachers are the main named raters. Teachers receive an automated e-mail message inviting them to complete a rating form online. Paper forms can be printed, and responses are then entered online for scoring. Instructions are clear and streamlined. Incomplete ratings (e.g., with unanswered items) are flagged and cannot be scored; in fact, teachers are asked to "respond to each item even if you must guess" (instructions on form, manual p. 119). The rating form is divided into two parts, each with a different set of Likert-type anchors. Overall, completion of the rating scale takes about 15 minutes. Complete MEFS reports can be generated and stored electronically or printed. The 12-page report is quite comprehensive. Inconsistency indicators are provided first, followed by scores for Self-Regulation clusters and their 31 components, further divided by arena (i.e., Academic and Self/Social). Scores for Self-Realization and Self-Determination are also provided. For the report, users can select T scores or other standard scores.

DEVELOPMENT. The MEFS is an instrument supported by the Holarchical Model of Executive Functions (HMEF; McCloskey, Perkins, & VanDivner, 2009). In this model, executive function represents "a set of mental capacities that can be used to direct, cue, coordinate, and integrate multiple aspects of perception, emotion, cognition, and action" (manual, p. 3). The HMEF is "holarchically organized" in tiers representing a range of "different levels of mental management" (manual, p. 4), including self-regulation, self-realization and self-determination, self-generation, and, at the top, trans-self integration. Thirty-one self-regulation capacities are clustered into seven executive functions/skills: Attention, Engagement, Optimization, Efficiency, Memory, Inquiry, and Solution. Each of the executive capacities represents both a function (associated with awareness) and a skill (which directs perception, feelings, thoughts, and actions). According to the test authors, these executive capacities are differentially engaged in a range of arenas: intrapersonal (self-control in relation to one's internalized states), interpersonal (self-control in relation to others), environment (self-control in relation to one's surroundings), and within a symbol system arena (self-control in relation to processing, storage, and use of symbol-based information).

The MEFS was developed in phases between 2010 and 2015. An initial pool of 256 items created by the test author was reduced to 146 items after consultation with practitioners during the initial tryout. A formal item tryout conducted by the test publisher examined ratings from 109 participants. Rasch item response theory (IRT) analysis yielded a final blueprint of 112 items, plus six redundant items used for the validity scale. All items use positive or neutral wording. Standardization of the MEFS was conducted between 2014 and 2015. Because teachers had difficulty with the self-generation component of the scale, it was eliminated altogether, yielding a final set of 110 items, 93 of them evaluating self-regulation and 17 evaluating self-determination and self-realization within the Self/Social (combined) and Academic Arenas.

TECHNICAL. The MEFS was standardized using a sample of 1,127 examinees rated by 255 teachers (88.6% female) located across 29 states of the U.S. From the initial sample, 127 clinical subjects were removed, yielding a final sample of 1,000 students, distributed in five groups of 200 stratified by age range (5-6, 7-8, 9-10, 11-13, and 14-18). The sample was 50% female, and 18.7% of the sample included children with disabilities. Efforts were made to closely match the 2010 U.S. Census for race representation. Socioeconomic status was not included; instead, three levels of academic skill were used as a proxy. Norms are not provided in the examiner's manual; rather, they are applied in the automatically generated report, so online administration and scoring is the only option available. Gender differences were identified; thus, gender-specific norms are used in computing the scores.

Reliability was evaluated using examination of internal consistency (split-half and coefficient alpha) as well as a test-retest approach. All alpha coefficients were above .85. The test-retest study was conducted using ratings obtained from 42 teachers with the second administration taking place 0 to 62 days after the first administration (mean interval = 16.6 days). Pearson correlation coefficients were calculated and corrected for attenuation; these ranged from .67 (Self-Realization) to .90 (Engagement cluster for the Academic arena).

Evidence of test score validity was evaluated using findings from the standardization process, including the item development process, development of the HMEF theory, and empirical analysis of item content (i.e., Rasch IRT analysis), all used as evidence based on test content. The test author asserts that factor analysis has become an "almost monolithic approach" to demonstrate evidence based on internal structure, suggesting that it places less attention on the meaningfulness of item-scale relationships and clinical utility (manual, p. 46); instead, he asserts that high internal consistency, adequacy of developmental progression of teacher ratings (i.e., higher expectations as children mature), cluster correlations, dissociation between arenas and executive components, and differential rating patterns between clinical and non-clinical samples are robust indicators of internal structure validity. To acquire criterion-related validity evidence, a series of small studies compared MEFS ratings with subtest scores from the NEPSY-II (*N* = 22; Korkman, Kirk, & Kemp, 2007), subtest scores, the teacher form from the Behavior Rating Inventory of Executive Function (*N* = 40; BRIEF; Gioia, Isquith, Guy, & Kenworthy, 1996), and academic competence ratings by teachers in the standardization sample. Consistent with the literature (e.g., Toplak, West, & Stanovich, 2013), behavioral ratings obtained with the MEFS demonstrated low to moderate correlation coefficients with the NEPSY-II scales, while stronger associations between the MEFS and BRIEF were observed, particularly with the Behavior Regulation Index and its subscales. Academic competence was assessed by asking the question "How would you characterize this child's academic ability?": *above average*, *average* or *below average* (manual, p. 66). The three levels of academic competence corresponded quite well with the level of executive function and skills, and analysis of variance results showed significant differences between levels.

COMMENTARY. It is this reviewer's opinion that the MEFS is a valuable instrument for several reasons: (a) it relies on a multidimensional approach to the definition of executive functions, (b) it emphasizes the identification of deficits as much as strengths using a broad range of Likert-type anchors, (c) the ratings are related to more than one context (i.e., Self/Social and Academic arenas) enhancing its ecological validity, (d) it relies on strong indicators of reliability, and (e) it includes a rich and detailed interpretative report in addition to analysis of clinical samples and a detailed case study to illustrate the instrument's clinical utility. There are some aspects of psychometric development that could be improved in future iterations of the scale, including analysis of the scores' sensitivity and specificity to correctly classify clinical samples, examination of the correspondence between the HMEF theory and the structure of the instrument using confirmatory factor analysis, and the use of a more clearly defined panel of experts weighing in on the item development (i.e., the MEFS relies extensively on the author's theory, research, and clinical experiences; consultation was present but not externally led). The HMEF theory is promising, but it is also complex. Its major pitfall is that—despite some disclaimers from the test author—its language suggests a definition of executive function as the operations of a homuncular system (e.g., "... the Executive Function manager recognizes...," "... an effective Executive Function manager who is aware...," "... an effective Executive Skills manager who is prepared..."; manual, p. 7), a conceptual approach that has been criticized in the literature (e.g., Alvarez & Emory, 2006; Stuss & Alexander, 2000). The test author seems involved in a remarkable personal quest to create a theory and an instrument that offers a superior approach to existing models and rating scales.

SUMMARY. The MEFS is a web-based rating scale to be completed by teachers and designed for the assessment of executive functions and skills. The scale facilitates the identification not only of deficits but also of strengths in executive functioning in two broad contexts including Social/Self and Academic. As such, this scale offers a multidimensional approach to the assessment of executive functions. Online completion makes it easier to administer, and the output report facilitates some aspects of the interpretation. On the downside, the model supporting the construct is so complex that only a portion of it can be represented by the scale. Given the strong association with the model, the MEFS will benefit from factor analysis and external validation studies.

REVIEWER'S REFERENCES

Alvarez, J. A., & Emory, E. (2006). Executive function and the frontal lobes: A meta-analytic review. *Neuropsychology Review, 16*, 17-42.

Gioia, G. A., Isquith, P. K., Guy, S. C., & Kenworthy, L. (1996). Behavior Rating Inventory of Executive Function. Lutz, FL: Psychological Assessment Resources.

Korkman, M., Kirk, U., & Kemp, S. (2007). NEPSY-II- Second Edition. San Antonio, TX: Pearson.

McCloskey, G., Perkins, L. A., & Van Divner, B. (2009). *Assessment and intervention for executive function difficulties.* New York, NY: Taylor & Francis.

Stuss, D. T., & Alexander, M. P. (2000). Executive functions and the frontal lobes: A conceptual view. *Psychological Research, 63*, 289-298.

Toplak, M. E., West, R. F., & Stanovich, K. E. (2013). Practitioner review: Do performance-based measures and ratings of executive function assess the same construct? *Journal of Psychology and Psychiatry, 54,* 131-143.

[91]

Memory Validity Profile.

Purpose: Designed for use by "clinicians who administer cognitive, academic, or neuropsychological assessments to children, adolescents, and young adults" to detect "whether an examinee is providing valid test scores."
Population: Ages 5-21.
Publication Date: 2015.
Acronym: MVP.
Scores, 3: Visual, Verbal, Total.
Administration: Individual.
Price Data, 2020: $223 per introductory kit including professional manual with fast guide, 25 record forms, and stimulus book; $77 per professional manual with fast guide; $126 per stimulus book; $50 per 25 record forms.
Time: (5-7) minutes.
Comments: Conormed with the Child and Adolescent Memory Profile (20:34).
Authors: Elisabeth M. S. Sherman and Brian L. Brooks.
Publisher: Psychological Assessment Resources, Inc.

Review of the Memory Validity Profile by CARLTON S. GASS, Neuropsychologist, TMH Physicians Partners Neurology Specialists, Tallahassee Memorial Healthcare, Tallahassee, FL:

DESCRIPTION. The Memory Validity Profile (MVP) is a brief and easy-to-administer test designed to assess performance validity in examinees ages 5 to 21 years. It is the first stand-alone performance validity test with age adjusted cutoff scores designed for, nationally standardized on, and validated for use with children, adolescents, and young adults. Applicable across a variety of settings, the MVP assists the clinician in deciding whether an examinee's test scores are based on test adherence and truthful responding, as opposed to noncompliance, malingering, or suboptimal effort. Using the MVP, clinicians can better estimate whether obtained test results are a valid reflection of an examinee's abilities. The MVP requires 5-7 minutes to administer, uses colorful stimuli, and has easy-to-learn instructions. It is the first performance validity test to be co-normed with a comprehensive memory battery, the Child and Adolescent Memory Profile (ChAMP; Sherman & Brooks, 2015).

The MVP test kit includes a professional manual, a fast guide for quick reference, a stimulus book for the visual subtest administration, and 25 record forms. The three-page record forms include the instructions for test administration in bold print.

The Visual subtest has two parts, each containing eight items. For each item, the examiner instructs the examinee to remember a blurred picture shown for 2 seconds. This is followed by a 4-second presentation of a blank page, then a page with three blurred choices (the target and two foils). The examinee is asked to point to the originally shown picture. Part two is very similar, except that it consists of more heavily blurred items. The Verbal subtest also has two parts each consisting of eight items. The examinee is told to remember a single-digit number and 4 seconds later given three numbers (the target and two foils) from which to choose the original number. In part two, the eight target items are two-letter combinations (e.g., w-s), each chosen from among three options.

Scoring is quick and simple. Only raw scores are used. On the answer sheet of the record form, correct responses appear in bold with shading, and are scored 1 point. Incorrect responses are scored as 0. The scoring ranges for the Visual and Verbal subtests are 0-16, with a potential Total score of 32. The cover page of the record form has the score summary for Visual, Verbal, and Total scores with cutoffs for ages 5, 6-10, 11-15, and 16-21. The MVP Total score is the primary score for interpretation, though the Visual and Verbal scores are provided as secondary options when visual or language impairments preclude an examinee from completing the entire test. A Total score suggests invalidity if it is less than 14 for examinees age 5, below 23 for children ages 6–10, below 25 for ages 11-15, and below 27 for ages 16–21.

The MVP was developed primarily for use by psychologists, educational diagnosticians, and other professionals in related areas who are trained in standardized testing.

DEVELOPMENT. The use of adult versions of performance validity tests is potentially problematic with children, especially younger children and those with intellectual disabilities. Evidence based on adult versions suggests that younger children do more poorly than older children and adults. Intellectually challenged children have difficulties with the cognitive demands of many performance validity tests. The absence of such tests with age-based norms, age-adjusted score cutoffs, and simplified stimulus materials are considerations that led to the development of the MVP. The MVP is the only performance validity test with a large standardization sample that provides cutoff scores adjusted for age.

A stepwise process was used to develop the MVP, including two independent expert panel reviews of test items, local pilot testing, bias review, and refinement testing. Cutoff scores were established using a three-step process. First, MVP Total scores with frequency rates of 0% were determined for each age group in the standardization sample. Second, age-adjusted cutoffs were studied using a subset of the standardization sample that was instructed to produce invalid test scores to ensure that 100% of this sample scored at or below the cutoffs. Third, the age-adjusted cutoffs were examined using a clinical sample of 198 youth to ensure that the percentages of positive scorers were consistent with the base rates reported in the performance validity test literature. Cutoff scores were selected that would allow no more than a 5% false detection rate in the clinical sample.

TECHNICAL. The standardization sample consists of 1,221 healthy persons ages 5 to 21 years in 35 U.S. states. The sample was divided into 15 age groups, with each group consisting of 66 to 89 individuals. Sampling was designed to reflect the 2012 U.S. Census with regard to age, gender, ethnicity, and parental education level. In the test manual, four tables describe the demographic characteristics of the normative sample. Statistical analyses revealed that age was related to scores on the Verbal subtest but not on the Visual subtest. Scores were not related to gender, ethnicity, or parental education.

Reliability was initially assessed by examining internal consistency and stability over a time period ranging from 10 days to 141 days (mean = 60 days). Alpha coefficients in the clinical sample (n = 198) were .85 (Visual), .84 (Verbal), and .89 (Total). Test-retest reliability coefficients based on a sample of 99 individuals from the standardization sample were .51 (Visual), .36 (Verbal), and .41 (Total). These values were attenuated by a severe range restriction and ceiling effect, as most participants scored 100%. Therefore, percent of classification agreement in labeling *valid* or *invalid* was examined. Agreement was 100%.

Construct validity evidence was based on correlations of the two subtest scores with the Total score. In the clinical sample, correlation coefficients were .64 (Visual) and .92 (Verbal). In the invalid performance sample (n = 45), correlation coefficients were .96 (Visual) and .95 (Verbal). Divergent validity was established by showing that MVP scores were weakly related to scores on tests of memory, intelligence, executive functioning, and achievement. Coefficients were generally less than .30. Convergent validity evidence was demonstrated by showing high correlations with the Test of Memory Malingering (TOMM; Tombaugh, 1996). In the invalid performance sample, the MVP Total score showed strong correlations with TOMM Trial 1 (r = .83) and TOMM Trial 2 (r = .81).

Predictive validity was assessed by measuring the false positive rate within the sample of 198 clinical cases including traumatic brain injury, attention-deficit/hyperactivity disorder, and academic disabilities. Only 3.5% of this sample was flagged as having a suspected invalid profile. Discriminative validity was examined by comparing the mean scores of 45 examinees instructed to underperform with those of a matched control sample. The results showed excellent discrimination, yielding effect sizes as high as d = 6.10 for the MVP Total score (p < .01). Overall, the age-adjusted cutoff scores for the MVP Total, Visual, and Verbal scores flagged 0% of the standardization sample, less than 5% of the clinical sample, and 100% of the invalid performance sample.

COMMENTARY. The authors of the MVP sought to design a convenient forced choice test of performance validity that is particularly suited for a younger population of examinees, including children. They succeeded in this task. The MVP is highly convenient, simple, and quick to administer and score. It has an excellent standardization sample with age-based cutoffs that accurately assess performance validity in examinees ages 5 to 21. The test manual is well-organized and reveals the detailed approach used by the authors to construct the test and to provide psychometric support for its clinical application.

The use of a simulation paradigm to assess the MVP's classification accuracy provided supportive data that are likely inflated. The simulators used in the validation study performed below chance (TOMM < 18) in over 60% of cases! That is, the participants performed worse than random responding. Such a high frequency of extreme faking greatly exceeds that observed in real assessment settings. Thus, whereas evidence suggests that the MVP is excellent at detecting flagrant malingering, its utility in detecting the more commonly observed subtle manifestations of incomplete effort remains unclear. This problem might be magnified in teenagers and young adults for whom the tasks might be too easy. For this reason it is arguable that this scale is best suited for grade schoolers and young teenagers (Favreau, Tross, Wolff, & Piehl, 2017).

SUMMARY. The Memory Validity Profile (MVP) is a quick, easy-to-use performance validity test with age-adjusted cutoff scores designed for, nationally standardized on, and validated for use with children, adolescents, and young adults. It has adequate reliability and validity data for psychometric support. Clinicians should find it useful in their clinical work, especially with children and younger adolescents. The MVP appears to be useful in detecting flagrant malingering. However, its sensitivity to more subtle forms of performance invalidity such as incomplete effort, especially in older adolescents and young adults, remains unclear.

REVIEWER'S REFERENCES

Favreau, Z., Tross, B., Wolff, M., & Piehl, J. J. (2017). Test review of the Memory Validity Profile (MVP). *Journal of Pediatric Neuropsychology*. doi:10.1007/s40817-017-0037-0

Sherman, E. M. S., & Brooks, B. L. (2015). Child and Adolescent Memory Profile. Lutz, FL: Psychological Assessment Resources.

Tombaugh, T. N. (1996). Test of Memory Malingering. North Tonawanda, NY: Multi-Health Systems.

Review of the Memory Validity Profile by ILYSE O'DESKY, Associate Professor of Psychology, Kean University, Union, NJ; Chief of Psychology, Saint Barnabas Medical Center, Livingston, NJ; Director, Neuropsychological Testing Center, Springfield, NJ; and ZANDRA GRATZ, Professor of Psychology, Kean University, Union, NJ:

DESCRIPTION. It has been estimated that some degree of malingering or exaggeration of symptoms occurs in 39% of mild head injury cases, in 30% of disability assessments, and in 29% of personal injury cases (Mittenberg, Patton, Canyok, & Condit, 2002). Therefore, it is often necessary to determine whether a patient is putting forth his or her best effort during an evaluation, and this test was developed to serve this need. As indicated by its authors, the Memory Validity Profile (MVP) was developed in order to determine "whether an examinee is actually engaged in the testing process and is providing valid test scores that can later be interpreted as a valid reflection of that examinee's abilities" (manual, p. 1). Whereas many clinicians use validity tests or tests of malingering in forensic evaluations, they are also useful in clinical evaluations as they provide a concrete assessment of the integrity of the results obtained as opposed to solely qualitatively assessing a patient's engagement in the testing process.

According to the professional manual, this test is specifically designed to be used by "psychologists, educational diagnosticians, and other professionals in related areas who are trained in individual testing" (p. 6). The test can be administered in 5 to 7 minutes and it has a visual section and verbal section resulting in an overall score reflecting the child's engagement and performance validity during testing. Moreover, given the fact that it has both verbal and visual components, it can be used with children who have specific sensory impairments. Answer sheets clearly identify cutoff scores below which validity may be an issue. To provide more information, the test authors suggest test users consider not only the cutoff scores but also chance level performance as a second criterion to denote possible feigning. This suggestion is consistent with standard practice in the field and with other tests of malingering. The test manual also presents several case studies to illustrate the manner in which the MVP can be part of an overall assessment.

Consistent with other tests of malingering, the MVP uses a forced-choice design in order to determine the examinee's willingness to put forth a good effort on the test. Unlike most testing in this area (e.g., Test of Memory Malingering), the MVP was designed specifically to be used with children (ages 5 to 21 years). The test materials are colorful and engaging, and the short administration time makes it ideal to add to a session in which there is any concern that a child may not be putting forth his or her best effort.

DEVELOPMENT. As noted in the test manual, two versions of the MVP, each including verbal and nonverbal items, were reviewed by pediatric neuropsychology and school psychology practitioners. This panel examined items for functionality, range of difficulty, visual appeal confounds and/or bias. Their feedback was used to develop a single pilot version of the MVP, which was administered to a small sample (n = 98). Also, a bias review panel examined the pilot test items to identify items that may be biased or offensive to different groups based on gender, ethnicity, or religion. Based on these data, the MVP was revised, including adding additional blurring of visual items and more letter pairing to give the appearance of difficulty. The revised test was administered to 196 youngsters. MVP authors' review of data determined that the revisions of the MVP were successful and no "meaningful" differences were evident by race and gender. However, specific data were not included in the test manual. Also noted in the manual (p. 19), the MVP was revised again based on the performance of individuals in the standardization, clinical, and invalid samples. In particular, the easiest items, having the least discrimination were removed from the final version.

TECHNICAL. The standardization sample included 1,221 participants, ages 5 to 21. This sample adequately reflected U.S. Census (2012) data with regard to gender and ethnicity. Also collected were data from a clinical sample and a sample of youngsters instructed to feign memory problems (the invalid sample). This procedure is consistent with other tests in this field as well. As noted earlier, the MVP was modified post-standardization sample. This may be of concern in that the test experienced by the standardization sample is not identical to the final version. However, because traditional norms (e.g., percentile ranks) are not used or available, concern is limited. Rather, age adjusted cutoff scores are offered. Cutoff scores identified for four age groups (5, 6-10, 11-15, and 16-21) were set at a point at which none of the standardization sample fell at or below the cutoff and all of the invalid sample fell at or below the cutoff. These data were then examined to ensure the rate of identification in the clinical sample was no more than 10%, as recommended by Binder, Larrabee, and Millis (2014).

As noted by the test authors, reliability and validity estimates need to be interpreted in view of the low variability of MVP scores, particularly in the standardization sample. As expected, alpha coefficients based on the standardization sample are low (Visual .46, Verbal .61, and Total .64). Among the clinical sample, alpha coefficients range from .84 to .89, while those of the invalid sample range from .78 to .88. The test-retest coefficient from 99 participants with a mean interval of 60 days was

.41 for the Total score; although low, this is likely a result of the restriction of range. Dependability of classification relative to cutoff scores was also examined and resulted in 100% agreement.

Validity evidence was evaluated in several ways. Expertise of MVP developers and committees supports the content validity of the measure. Intercorrelations between subtests and total MVP scores are offered as evidence of construct validity; however, interpretation of these data is limited in that significant differences between coefficients are not explored. Considerable criterion-related validity evidence is reported based on correlations between the MVP and several measures of memory, executive function, and academic functioning. Across comparisons, MVP appears to have little to no variance in common with these other measures. The invalid sample also took the TOMM (Test of Memory Malingering; Tombaugh, 1996). In this sample, the correlation between measures was high, as the coefficient exceeded .80. Comparisons of classifications based on the MVP and TOMM support the acceptability of the cutoff scores. Given that one of the measures, the Child and Adolescent Memory Profile (Sherman & Brooks, 2015), has a validity scale, comparison of classification (valid or not valid) between the two validity measures would have been of interest. In addition, comparisons between the MVP and TOMM among youngsters (clinical and non-clinical) not instructed to feign memory issues would have been of value.

COMMENTARY. The MVP demonstrates reasonable estimates of reliability and validity. This is suggested despite two caveats including the test being modified (items removed) post-standardization and the ceiling effect demonstrated during the standardization process, which limits the magnitude of classical measurement indices. The MVP authors suggest a second examination of invalid scores based on chance level performance which may be useful. That is, those who score below the cutoff score and the level of chance responding (33.3%) may be purposefully giving incorrect answers and not simply inattentive. Beyond this, as is evident in the case examples and recommended by the *Standards for Educational and Psychological Testing* (American Educational Research Association, American Psychological Association, & National Council of Measurement in Education, 2014), the test authors emphasize the need to consider a wide array of information in order to conclude that a score is invalid.

While the test authors rightly point out that this type of measure is useful in order to determine whether an examinee is "feigning or exaggerating" (manual, p. 2) any difficulty, another advantage to this type of test should be considered. If there is a concern that the child may not be putting forth a good effort because of insecurity regarding his or her overall cognitive ability, or if the child is anxious about being judged due to a generally high degree of anxiety, this test may be useful in increasing the child's confidence so that he or she is more willing to put forth a good effort on subsequent testing.

SUMMARY. This test is a well-designed measure to determine whether an examinee is appropriately engaged in the evaluation process. It provides a concrete measure of a patient's engagement as opposed to the typical qualitative assessment examiners use to determine if a patient is putting forth a good effort during testing. As a result, this test appears to be very useful for filling a need of appropriate validity testing specifically with children. This is especially important given the fact that there has been a recent increased awareness of traumatic brain injury in children due to sports-related mild traumatic brain injury resulting in more testing of a population that may exaggerate symptoms for some type of perceived gain.

REVIEWERS' REFERENCES

American Educational Research Association, American Psychological Association, & National Council on Measurement in Education. (2014). *Standards for educational and psychological testing.* Washington, DC: American Educational Research Association.

Binder, L. M., Larrabee, G. J., & Millis, S. R. (2014). Intent to fail: Significance testing of forced choice test results. *The Clinical Neuropsychologist, 28,* 1366-1375.

Eglit, G. M. L., Lynch, J. K., & McCaffrey, R. J. (2017). Not all performance validity tests are created equal: The role of recollection and familiarity in the Test of Memory Malingering and Word Memory Test. *Journal of Clinical and Experimental Neuropsychology, 39,* 173-189.

Mittenberg, W., Patton, C., Canyock, E. M., & Condit, D. C. (2002). Base rates of malingering and symptom exaggeration. *Journal of Clinical and Experimental Neuropsychology, 24,* 1094-1102.

Sherman, E. M. S., & Brooks, B. L. (2015). Child and Adolescent Memory Profile. Lutz, FL: Psychological Assessment Resources.

Tombaugh, T. (1996). Test of Memory Malingering. North Tonawanda, NY: Multi-Health Systems.

[92]

Mini-ICF-APP Social Functioning Scale.

Purpose: Designed "to assess the extent to which a patient's activities and capacities are limited in terms of performance and ability, along with what is hindering the patient."

Population: Adults with mental disorders.

Publication Date: 2014.

Acronym: Mini-ICF-APP.

Scores, 13: Adherence to Regulations, Structuring of Tasks, Flexibility, Competency, Judgment, Endurance, Assertiveness, Contact with Others, Group Integration, Intimate Relationships, Spontaneous Activities, Self Care, Mobility.

Administration: Individual.
Price Data, 2020: £127 per complete kit including reference manual (2014, 70 pages), short manual with U.K. data, 50 forms, and case; £65 per reference manual; £52 per short manual; £46 per 50 scoring forms.
Foreign Language Edition: Originally published in German.
Time: (10-15) minutes.
Authors: Michael Linden, Stefanie Baron, Beate Muschalla, and Andrew Molodynski (U.K. Adaptor).
Publisher: Hogrefe Ltd [United Kingdom].

Review of the Mini-ICF-APP Social Functioning Scale by CATHERINE A. FIORELLO, Professor of School Psychology, Temple University, and LINDA RUAN, Doctoral Candidate in School Psychology, Temple University, Philadelphia, PA:

DESCRIPTION. The Mini-ICF-APP Social Functioning Scale is a clinician/observer rating scale designed to assess abilities or limitations in activities in adults with mental health disorders. It is derived to match the framework of the World Health Organization's International Classification of Functioning, Disability, and Health (ICF). The developers suggest the Mini-ICF-APP can be used to evaluate the patient's current level of functioning and for progress monitoring over time. Administration takes approximately 10 minutes.

The Mini-ICF-APP was originally developed in German; Italian and English versions are now available. This review is of the English version, which was adapted and validated in the United Kingdom. Administration of the Mini-ICF-APP requires a single scoring form, which consists of 13 items, each describing an area of functioning (i.e., Adherence to Regulations, Structuring of Tasks, Flexibility, Competency, Judgment, Endurance, Assertiveness, Contact with Others, Group Integration, Intimate Relationships, Spontaneous Activities, Self Care, and Mobility). Observers use a 5-point Likert-type scale (*0 = no impairment, 1 = mild impairment, 2 = moderate disability, 3 = severe disability, 4 = complete disability*) to rate the ability of the patient on each item within the previous 2 weeks. Two types of raw scores can be derived: the individual dimensional score, which can inform whether and where the patient is restricted, and a global score, which is the sum of ratings across all items. The total score can range from 0 to 52, with higher scores indicating greater levels of impairment.

The Mini-ICF-APP kit consists of a reference manual translated from the original German, a short manual specific to the U.K. Edition, and a packet of scoring forms. A link to an online tutorial video is provided by the test publisher after the kit is purchased. The reference manual contains information about the purpose, theoretical background, and psychometric properties of the original Mini-ICF-APP in addition to a variety of example cases. The short manual provides administration and scoring instructions, information about the psychometric properties of the U.K. Edition, and five case studies. The video provides a description of each item, a video of a patient interview to practice scoring, and an explanation of the correct scoring for the sample case.

Assessors should be practitioners experienced with mental disorders (e.g., clinical psychologists, physicians, psychotherapists, social workers, occupational therapists, physical therapists) and have information regarding the patient's functioning relative to expected performance in their environment.

DEVELOPMENT. The Mini-ICF-APP is designed to facilitate assessment of the level of impairment or disability in patients with mental illness. The items were derived from the Activities and Participation sections in the ICF, and the test manual details those links. The constructs in the ICF were operationalized to make them measurable. The descriptions of each item are general, and the rater is expected to take into account the patient's age, gender, cultural and ethnic background, educational status, and so on, when considering the patient's expected level of functioning. The reference manual gives clear examples of each functioning level for each item, and the training video reinforces how the ratings should be made.

TECHNICAL. Psychometric studies reported in the reference manual are based on the original 12 items (excluding Judgment) of the German Mini-ICF-APP using a sample of 213 patients from the Rehabilitation Center of the German Pension Insurance Association. The English Mini-ICF-APP consists of 13 items, and psychometric studies of this version were completed using a community sample of 105 adults with mental health problems from the Oxford Health NHS Foundation Trust from February to September 2011 (Molodynski et al., 2013).

Reliability. For the 13-item scale, coefficient alpha was reported as .87 for rater 1 at time one, .86 for rater 2 at time one, and .91 for rater 1 at time two (Molodynski et al., 2013), indicating adequate internal consistency.

The 13-item scale demonstrated strong test-retest reliability, with an intra-class correlation coefficient of .83, and linear regression coefficient of 1.03, $p < 0.001$ (Molodynski et al., 2013).

For the 12-item Mini-ICF-APP, interrater reliability was reported between trained and untrained assessors, yielding moderate correlations (*r*s from .47 to .79) for the items and the global score ($r = .70$). Interrater reliability for two trained assessors was stronger (*r*s from .71 to .99) for items and the global score ($r = .92$). For the 13-item scale, the intra-class correlation was .89 and the linear regression coefficient was .94, $p < 0.001$, suggesting good interrater reliability (Molodynski et al., 2013).

Validity. Development of the items from the ICF descriptors provides evidence of adequate content validity. Construct validity was examined using a *t*-test to determine the relationship between the Mini-ICF-APP total score and employment status, and results indicate a positive relationship $p < .001$ (Molodynski et al., 2013).

As evidence of criterion-related validity, Spearman correlations between the 12-item Mini-ICF-APP and the Groningen Social Disability Schedule II were examined and revealed low to moderate relationships. Pearson correlations between the 13-item Mini-ICF-APP total score with other measures of psychological symptoms and social functioning revealed evidence of convergent validity (Endicott Work Productivity Scale, $r = .74$; Brief Psychiatric Rating Scale, $r = .70$), and divergent validity (Personal and Social Performance Scale, $r = -.82$; Social and Occupational Functioning Assessment Scale, $r = -.77$) (Molodynski et al., 2013).

COMMENTARY. The Mini-ICF-APP is a well-designed, brief clinician rating scale used for measuring the degree of impairment or disability in adults with mental disorders. The Mini-ICF-APP kit is attractive and easy to carry and provides a short manual, reference manual, and rating forms. A training video is also provided. The Mini-ICF-APP is fast to administer, taking approximately 10 minutes, and the manuals and video provide clear and complete instructions for administration.

Although the Mini-ICF-APP is a well-developed instrument, structural validity is not well established. Molodynski and colleagues (2013) reported examining the factor structure of the Mini-ICF-APP using principal component factor analysis with varimax rotation, but results were not reported. Hence, it is unclear whether the scale is unidimensional or multidimensional and whether interpretation at the item level is appropriate.

SUMMARY. The Mini-ICF-APP is a brief observer rating scale that assesses 13 areas of impairment due to mental disorders and can be used for treatment planning and progress monitoring. In designing the Mini-ICF-APP, the developers matched the instrument to the ICF. Though the Mini-ICF-APP demonstrates strong reliability and evidence of validity, structural validity has yet to be established. The manuals and training video are well laid out and helpful in learning the instrument. The Mini-ICF-APP is a brief measure that appears promising and is easy to administer and straightforward to score.

REVIEWERS' REFERENCE

Molodynski, A., Linden, M., Juckel, G., Yeeles, K., Anderson, C., Vazquez-Montes, M., & Burns, T. (2013). The reliability, validity, and applicability of an English language version of the Mini-ICF-APP. *Social Psychiatry and Psychiatric Epidemiology, 48*, 1347–1354. https://doi.org/10.1007/s00127-012-0604-8

Review of the Mini-ICF-APP Social Functioning Scale by KATHLEEN TORSNEY, Professor of Psychology, William Paterson University, Wayne, NJ:

DESCRIPTION. The Mini-ICF-APP Social Functioning Scale (Mini-ICF-APP) provides an assessment of occupational and social functioning in adults with mental illnesses. The scale involves observations of a patient's current capacity levels and degree of change during an individually administered semi-structured interview. The semi-structured interview addresses the social history of the patient and covers the topics of daily activities, relationships, social supports, hobbies/interests, work, and self-care. The score reflects the following categories of behavior: Adherence to Regulations, Structuring of Tasks, Flexibility, Competency, Judgment, Endurance, Assertiveness, Contact with Others, Group Integration, Intimate Relationships, Spontaneous Activities, Self Care, and Mobility. The assessment typically takes 10-15 minutes to complete. The measure includes a short manual specific to the U.K. version of the scale, a longer reference manual that is a translation of the original German manual, score sheets, and a 1 hour and 18 minute video training program. The manuals provide case studies with suggested ratings on the Mini-ICF-APP. The video contains three parts: an overall introduction to the measure, including the domains and scoring; a detailed video of an interview with an actor portraying a patient and the scoring domains; and a thorough explanation of the domain scoring of the interview with the patient depicted in the video. The scores reflect how the individual may fulfill the role functions needed in their lives and are indicated as 0 = *no impairment*, 1 = *mild impairment*, 2 = *moderate disability*, 3 = *severe disability*, and 4 = *complete disability*. A maximum score of 52 indicates high disability, and the minimum score of 0 suggests no disability. The test authors sought to determine how much a mental illness can impair social functioning to more effectively provide needed treatment and social supports to patients. The measure may be used by professionals in the fields of psychiatry, rehabilitation, social medicine, and psychotherapy. The measure builds upon the work of the International Classification of Functioning, Disability and Health (ICF; World Health Organization [WHO], 2001), which describes and evaluates disabilities. The test authors note that the measure may be used in routine clinical or research practice.

DEVELOPMENT. The Mini-ICF-APP was designed to provide a standardized classification of functioning and disability based on the ICF (WHO, 2001), which was developed to be compatible with the International Classification of Diseases, Tenth Revision (ICD-10; WHO, 1992) and which outlines degrees of functioning and disability. The assessment of activity and participation restrictions associated with mental illnesses emerged relatively recently. Some measures such as the Global Assessment Scale and the Global Assessment of Functioning Scale assess the impact of illnesses on functioning, but the results do not specify how disability—especially mental illness—affects participation and impacts functioning. The original version of the Mini-ICF-APP was developed in German, and revisions have since been published in English (in the United Kingdom) and in Italian. Molodynski et al. (2013) established the reliability and validity of the English language version.

TECHNICAL.

Standardization. The test authors noted that the Mini-ICF-APP does not rely on norms or standardized samples because it is an individual assessment intended to identify one's strengths and weaknesses. The original Mini-ICF-APP was standardized in Germany. Participants were 213 patients in the department of behavioral therapy and psychosomatics at the German Pension Insurance Association. Women comprised 70% of the sample, and the average age of the sample was 45 years. Within the sample 41% were not able to work; 61% had been diagnosed with neuroses, stress, and somatic symptom disorders; 29% were diagnosed with affective disorders; and 10% were diagnosed with personality disorders. The sample was assessed during a 6-week inpatient treatment program at the clinic. The patients were tested within 1 week of admission to the clinic, by physicians or psychotherapists, and by a trained interviewer. The therapists were given an overview of the assessment in advance, but they did not receive specialized training. The test authors employed the Symptom Checklist-90-R and the Questionnaire on Work-Related Behavioural and Experiential Patterns. Patients were diagnosed using the ICD–10 taxonomy. Approximately 60% and 30% of the sample were found to have mild and moderate disabilities, respectively, according to the Mini-ICF-APP results. The areas of disability that were most impaired were Flexibility, Structuring of Tasks, and Endurance, whereas areas of Self Care, Mobility, and Adherence to Regulations were less impaired.

Psychometric properties of the U.K. Edition of the Mini-ICF-APP were examined using a sample of 105 English-speaking patients undergoing treatment for various mental disorders in 2011. The sample was stratified to include at least 30 patients with primary diagnoses of schizophrenia, anxiety disorders, and depression. A subgroup of patients (n = 47) was interviewed on two separate occasions (interval not specified), and another subgroup (n = 45) was interviewed by two researchers to determine test-retest and interrater reliability estimates, respectively. The researchers also recorded employment status and sick leave status in an effort to provide evidence bearing on construct validity.

Reliability. The U.K. Edition demonstrated high levels of internal consistency with alpha coefficients ranging from .86 to .91. In addition, all 13 items correlated highly with the total score. Test-retest reliability was good with an intra-class correlation coefficient (ICC) of .83 for the total score, and interrater reliability was also strong (ICC was .89). A linear regression study of the test-retest reliability evidenced a coefficient of 1.03, $p < 0.001$. An interrater reliability study using linear regression yielded a coefficient of .94, $p < 0.001$, which suggests high levels of reliability between the first and second raters. The measure correlated highly with other instruments that assess illness disability and functioning. The test authors note that additional research should determine whether the subscales could yield more specific information about an individual's impairment. For the German version, interrater reliability estimates were statistically significant at $p < .001$. For a trained interviewer and an untrained interviewer, correlation coefficients ranged from .47 to .79, and between two trained interviewers, coefficients ranged from .71 to .99.

Validity. The test authors of the U.K. Edition conducted a validation study of the Mini-ICF-APP with 105 individuals living in the United Kingdom. Validity studies show that scores on the Mini-ICF-APP were highly correlated with scores from other measures of functioning and mental health, including the Endicott Work Productivity Scale, the Personal and Social Performance Scale, the Social and Occupational Functioning Assessment Scale, and the Brief Psychiatric Rating Scale. The authors of the Mini-ICF-APP conducted an independent samples t-test and found that scores from the Mini-ICF-APP correlated significantly with employment status, $p < 0.001$. A study examining concurrent validity evidence for the Italian Mini-ICF-APP indicated that its scores provided a valid means for evaluating the degree of functioning in persons with chronic schizophrenia and related disorders (Pinna, Fiorello, Tusconi, Guiso, & Carpiniello, 2015). The total Mini-ICF-APP score significantly correlated with total scores of the Clinical Global Impression-Schizophrenia scale (CGI-SCH), Positive and Negative Syndrome Scale (PANSS), Mini Mental State Examination (MMSE), and several items of the Brief Assessment of Cognition in Schizophrenia scale (BACS). Rucci and Balestrieri (2015) found that the Italian Mini-ICF-APP demonstrated significant convergent and discriminant validity evidence. Their factor analytic study revealed that factor scores were significantly higher among individuals with schizophrenia than those with bipolar disorders.

COMMENTARY. The Mini-ICF-APP is an extremely well-designed and comprehensive tool for assessing activity and participation limitations arising from mental illnesses. The video training guide is extremely helpful and well designed. The test manual provides case studies with suggested scoring, and the video outlines scoring in a semi-structured interview with an actor portraying a patient with a mental illness. The test authors suggest questions for assessing the categories, and the resulting flexibility may prevent a patient from being judged too harshly without considering the individual nature of his or her situation. Even so, cultural considerations may affect how individuals in the person's environment relate to the patient, as when questions probe areas in which culture-to-culture variations have been well established. In addition, although the manual notes that "the assessor must gain an overview of the individual's 'uniform standard environment' or social reference group in relation to the case—e.g., social/ethnic group, gender, occupation and education, degree of professional education and so on" (reference manual, p. 13), no specific guidelines are offered in the test manual for how that might be accomplished. It is suggested that the test authors provide more detailed information in the test manual about how the interviewer may gain information about cultural, ethnic, and socioeconomic factors. The Mini-ICF-APP is an extremely useful measure to address needs for supports in employment among persons with mental illness (Rowland et al., 2014).

SUMMARY. The Mini-ICF-APP is a very well-designed and thorough measure for the assessment of social and occupational functioning of adults with mental illnesses. The publisher of the U.K. Edition produced a very clear, well-organized, and helpful video for conducting the semi-structured interview and scoring the items. The test authors sought to avoid using norms to emphasize the individualized nature of the instrument, but it is important to specifically consider the role of gender, ethnicity, socioeconomic status, culture, and environment to better understand the social and occupational needs of an individual. The test manual indicates that it is important to be mindful of cultural issues, but it does not specifically outline how one would identify cultural factors and address them. It is suggested that a more detailed method of examining the impact of culture, ethnicity, gender, and socioeconomic status be included in the test manual. Overall, the Mini-ICF-APP is an excellent tool for the assessment of social functioning and treatment planning for persons with mental illnesses.

REVIEWER'S REFERENCES

Molodynski, A., Linden, M., Juckel, G., Yeeles, K., Anderson, C., Vazquez-Montes, M., & Burns, T. (2013). The reliability, validity, and applicability of an English language version of the Mini-ICF-APP. *Social Psychiatry and Psychiatric Epidemiology, 48*, 1347-1354. doi:10.1007/s00127-012-0604-8

Pinna, F., Fiorillo, A., Tusconi, M., Guiso, B., & Carpiniello, B. (2015). Assessment of functioning in patients with schizophrenia and schizoaffective disorder with the Mini-ICF-APP: A validation study in Italy. *International Journal of Mental Health Systems, 9*, 1-10.

Rowland, J. P., Yeeles, K., Anderson, C., Catalao, R., Morley, H., & Molodynski, A. (2014). Is it possible to measure social and occupational functioning in a CMHT? *Progress in Neurology and Psychiatry, 18*(5), 21-25.

Rucci, P., & Balestrieri, M. (2015). Exploratory factor analysis of the Mini instrument for the observer rating according to ICF of Activities and Participation in Psychological disorders (Mini-ICF-APP) in patients with severe mental illness. *Journal of Psychopathology/Giornale Italiano Di Psicopatologia, 21*(3), 254-261.

World Health Organization. (1992). *International Classification of Disorders and Related Health Problems* (10th rev., ICD-10). Geneva, Switzerland: Author.

World Health Organization. (2001). *International Classification of Functioning, Disability and Health.* Geneva, Switzerland: Author.

[93]

Minnesota Multiphasic Personality Inventory–Adolescent–Restructured Form.

Purpose: "A broad-spectrum instrument designed to assess the psychological functioning [patterns of personality and psychopathology] of adolescents."
Population: Ages 14-18.
Publication Date: 2016.
Acronym: MMPI-A-RF.
Scores, 48: 6 Validity Scales: Variable Response Inconsistency (VRIN-r), True Response Inconsistency (TRIN-r), Combined Response Inconsistency (CRIN), Infrequent Responses (F-r), Uncommon Virtues (L-r), Adjustment Validity (K-r); 3 Higher-Order (H-O) Scales: Emotional/Internalizing Dysfunction (EID), Thought Dysfunction (THD), Behavioral/Externalizing Dysfunction (BXD); 9 Restructured Clinical (RC) Scales: Demoralization (RCd), Somatic Complaints (RC1), Low Positive Emotions (RC2), Cynicism (RC3), Antisocial Behavior (RC4), Ideas of Persecution (RC6), Dysfunctional Negative Emotions (RC7), Aberrant Experiences (RC8), Hypomanic Activation (RC9); Personality Psychopathology Five (PSY-5) Scales: Aggressiveness-Revised (AGGR-r), Psychoticism-Revised (PSYC-r), Disconstraint-Revised (DISC-r), Negative Emotionality/Neuroticism-Revised (NEGE-r), Introversion/Low Positive Emotionality-Revised (INTR-r); 25 Specific Problems (SP) Scales [5 Somatic/Cognitive Scales: Malaise (MLS), Gastrointestinal Complaints (GIC), Head Pain Complaints (HPC), Neurological Complaints (NUC), Cognitive Complaints (COG); 9 Internalizing Scales: Helplessness/Hopelessness (HLP), Self-Doubt (SFD), Inefficacy (NFC), Obsessions/Compulsions (OCS), Stress/Worry (STW), Anxiety (AXY), Anger Proneness (ANP), Behavior-Restricting Fears (BRF), Specific Fears (SPF); 6 Externalizing Scales: Negative School Attitudes (NSA), Antisocial Attitudes (ASA), Conduct Problems (CNP), Substance Abuse (SUB), Negative Peer Influence (NPI), Aggression (AGG); 5 Interpersonal Scales: Family Problems (FML), Interpersonal Passivity (IPP), Social Avoidance (SAV), Shyness (SHY), Disaffiliativeness (DSF)].
Administration: Individual.
Price Data, 2020: $535.25 per kit including manual (280 pages), 25 answer sheets, 5 sets of profile forms, 5 sets of answer keys, and 5 softcover test booklets in a tote bag; $180.25 per Q-global (web-based) Interpretive Report kit including manual, user's guide, 1 softcover test booklet, 3 answer sheets, and 3 Q-global administrations; $64 per print manual; $49.50 per user's guide for reports-print; $25.75 per 5 test booklets; $38.75 per 25 hand-scoring answer sheets; $68 per audio CD; $32 per 25 hand-scoring profile forms (5 available); $51.25 per answer key (5 available); $45.25 per digital manual; $45.50 per mail-in interpretive report; $36.90 per Q Local (software based) interpretive report; $36.90 per Q-global interpretive report; $23.25 per mail-in score report; $17.60 per Q Local score report; $17.60 per Q-Global score report.
Foreign Language Edition: Test booklets and audio CD available in Spanish.
Time: 20-35 minutes for computer administration; 30-45 minutes for paper and pencil administration.
Comments: A restructured form containing 241 items that are a subset of the 478 MMPI-A items; computer administration and scoring available.
Authors: Robert P. Archer, Richard W. Handel, Yossef S. Ben-Porath, and Auke Tellegen.
Publisher: University of Minnesota Press; distributed by Pearson.
Cross References: For reviews by Charles D. Claiborn and Richard I. Lanyon of the MMPI-A, see 12:23.

Review of the Minnesota Multiphasic Personality Inventory–Adolescent–Restructured Form by STEPHANIE STEIN, Department Chair, Central Washington University, Ellensburg, WA:

DESCRIPTION. The Minnesota Multiphasic Personality Inventory–Adolescent–Restructured Form (MMPI-A-RF) is an individually administered broad-spectrum self-report questionnaire intended to assess adolescent psychopathology. The test authors are refreshingly candid in clarifying that the MMPI-A-RF is a pathology-seeking instrument, not one intended to assess normal adolescent functioning. This inventory has 241 *true/false* items, which are summarized on 48 scales, including Validity scales (6), Higher-Order (H-O) scales (3), Restructured Clinical (RC) scales (9), Specific Problem (SP) scales (25), and Personality Psychopathology Five (PSY-5) scales (5). In addition, the test authors have identified 53 critical items that, if endorsed, suggest the need for follow-up questions. The MMPI-A-RF comes with a manual for administration, interpretation, scoring, and technical data; printed test booklets; 1-page fill-in-the-blank answer sheets; 51 separate scoring templates; and five separate profile sheets.

Although the measure is intended for 14- to 18-year-olds, the test authors suggest that the MMPI-A-RF could be appropriate for some 12- to 13-year-olds if they can handle the reading level, which, for most items, is estimated to be fifth to seventh grade. They do note, however, that no adolescents under age 14 were included in the normative sample. The administration of the instrument is simple and straightforward, with scripted instructions provided. The adolescent can complete the MMPI-A-RF on a computer or with paper and pencil; computer administration is recommended. The inventory takes 20 to 35 minutes to complete on the computer and 30 to 45 minutes using the printed booklet and answer sheet. If necessary, the MMPI-A-RF can be completed over several testing sessions, which may be preferable if the test taker has a short attention span.

Scoring can be completed by hand or by computer. Inventories scored by computer provide either a Score Report or an Interpretative Report for Clinical Settings. Hand scoring requires a set of transparent plastic templates that are laid on the answer sheet. The responses that align with the particular template are counted, and the raw score is entered for the specific scale. Raw scores are converted to nongendered T scores, which are then plotted on five separate profile sheets.

DEVELOPMENT. The MMPI-A-RF is a revision of the MMPI-A (Butcher, Williams, Graham, Archer, Tellegen, Ben-Porath, & Kaemmer, 1992) and based on scales from the MMPI-2-RF (Ben-Porath & Tellegen, 2008). The rationale for the development of this inventory was to resolve some limitations of the MMPI-A, including considerable overlap of items between the scales and the resulting excess of intercorrelations between the scales and diminished discriminant validity. In addition, the MMPI-A-RF has approximately half the number of items as the MMPI-A (478 items), making it more appropriate in length for adolescent concentration and attention span. The development sample for the MMPI-A-RF, based on archival data from the MMPI-A for 14- to 18-year-olds, included 9,286 boys and 5,842 girls from inpatient, outpatient, correctional, and school settings. Four subgroups in the development sample were identified, based on gender and younger (14-15) or older (16-18) age groups.

The three-tiered structured scales from the MMPI-2-RF were used as a template for the development of the MMPI-A-RF scales, with the MMPI-A items that matched those from the MMPI-2-RF used as initial seed scales. An ongoing process of statistical item analysis, expert review of content, and exploratory factor analyses were used to develop the RC scales. One of the main goals in this development process was to develop a Demoralization (RCd) scale. The construct of demoralization represents non-specific, generalized feelings of distress and unhappiness; this construct is thought to result in the high levels of heterogeneity in the MMPI-A Clinical scales. Once the RCd scale was developed, exploratory factor analyses were used to identify the distinctive elements of the MMPI-A Clinical scales without the influence of the demoralization factor. The result of the analyses led to the development of the Restructured Clinical (RC) scales of the MMPI-A-RF.

In addition, principal component analyses of the Basic Clinical scales from the MMPI-A resulted in the development of three Higher-Order (H-O) scales, representing broad measures of psychopathology. Next, the Specific Problem (SP) scales were developed to assess MMPI-A content not otherwise covered in the RC scales, as well as other areas of psychological functioning considered clinically relevant. Factor analyses were conducted on the preliminary SP scales to minimize the association between these scales and Demoralization. The PSY-5 scales, which represent the five-factor personality model developed by Harkness and McNulty (1994), are the final set of substantive scales. The PSY-5 scales on the MMPI-A-RF were developed through a repetitive process of item selection by expert raters and item-criterion analyses. Finally, in addition to the substantive scales, the MMPI-A-RF has six Validity scales, including three inconsistent responding indicators (VRIN-r, TRIN-r, and CRIN), an over-reporting indicator (F-r), and two under-reporting indicators (L-r, K-r).

TECHNICAL. The standardization sample for the MMPI-A-RF is a subgroup of 1,610 adolescents from the MMPI-A normative sample. The resulting sample of 805 boys and 805 girls was predominantly White (76.3%), followed by Black (12.4%), Asian and American Indian (both 2.9%), Hispanic (2%), and other/not reported (3.5%). The test authors theorize that the under-representation of Hispanic adolescents may be due to the requirement that participants have at least a sixth-grade reading level, which could exclude students who do not speak English as their primary language. The average age of the sample was 15.56 years with a standard deviation of 1.18. Although the adolescents in the standardization sample ranged from Grade 7 to Grade 12, adolescents in Grades 9-12 comprised more than 75% of the sample. The majority had parents in professional or managerial occupations, and the most common parent educational attainment was college graduate. No information is provided on geographical representation of the sample.

Evidence for reliability includes internal consistency coefficients, test-retest reliability coefficients, and standard error of measurement

(*SEM*). Many of the alpha coefficients for the three Validity inconsistency scales are lower than what typically would be considered acceptable because of the lack of variability in the scores following the elimination of invalid protocols in the MMPI-A. Alpha coefficients for these Validity scales ranged from .04 (school sample, girls) on the TRIN-r to .60 (MMPI-A-RF normative sample, boys) for the CRIN. The three remaining Validity scales demonstrated alpha coefficients ranging from .42 (school sample, girls) on the L-r to .77 (inpatient sample, boys) on the F-r. Test-retest coefficients on all of the Validity scales are less variable, ranging from .51 on the F-r Scale to .78 for the VRIN-r Scale. The test-retest interval was not reported in the test manual.

For the substantive scales, the broad H-O scales, not surprisingly, had the highest reliability coefficients (alphas of .70 to .92; test-retest .64 to .85). Alpha coefficients on the mid-level RC scales ranged from .45 to .90, with the lowest alphas in RC9 and the highest in RCd. Test-retest reliability coefficients for the RC scales ranged from .56 (RC8) to .82 (RCd). Of the 25 SP scales, alphas ranged from .28 (SPF, inpatient boys) to .84 (SAV, inpatient girls). Test-retest coefficients for the SP scales ranged from .24 (BRF) to .73 (SFD). Finally, the PSY-5 scales demonstrated internal consistency alphas ranging from .57 (AGGR-r, normative sample, boys) to .85 (DISC-r, school boys and INTR-r, school girls). The *SEM* for many of the scales fall in the range of 5 to 7. Overall, test administrators should be most cautious about the reliability of the low-item SP scales like BRF (three items), SPF (four items), and IPP (four items).

The MMPI-A-RF manual provides extensive correlation tables in support of validity claims. The Validity scales on the MMPI-A-RF were correlated with the Validity scales on the MMPI-A under three conditions. Specifically, test developers compared the two instruments after having half of the normative sample results adjusted with computer-generated random responses on 70% of the items. They did the same with computer-generated fixed true (acquiescent) responses and fixed false (counter-acquiescent) responses. As expected, the VRIN-r and CRIN were highly correlated (.76 and .80) with the VRIN from the MMPI-A on the random response analysis. Similarly, the TRIN-r was highly correlated with the TRIN on the fixed-true analyses (.93) and the fixed-false analyses (.85). In other comparisons, an over-reporting analysis between F-r and the MMPI-A F, F1, and F2 revealed high correlations (.99, .98., and .98). In addition, an under-reporting analysis compared the L-r and L (.81) and the K-r and K (.80).

The substantive scales on the MMPI-A-RF were correlated with several other instruments assessing a variety of populations outside of the normative sample. Comparisons with the Record Review Form (based on clinical records) for adolescents in acute inpatient psychiatric settings revealed fairly modest correlations. However, these correlations were generally in the expected direction, with "Oppositional Behavior" negatively correlated with Emotional/Internalizing Dysfunction (EID) and positively correlated with Conduct Problems (CNP). Similarly, the correlations with the Adolescent Client Description Form (Forbey & Ben-Porath, 2003) for adolescents in a residential treatment facility were unimpressive (few above .20), but usually in the expected direction. In contrast, comparisons between the H-O scales and the Child Behavior Checklist and Youth Self-Report (Achenbach & Rescorla, 2001) for adolescents with a "forensic predisposition" revealed generally moderate to strong correlations. Correlations between these Achenbach scales and the RC, SP, and PSY-5 scales were weak to moderate, though. With this same population, correlations with the Disruptive Behavior Rating Scale (DBRS; Barkley & Murphy, 1998) and a mental status form were modest.

In addition, all of the scales on the MMPI-A-RF were correlated with all of the MMPI-A scales and subscales for the development samples, resulting in moderate to strong correlations. Finally, all of the scales on the MMPI-A-RF were compared with one another for the entire normative sample and the development samples. One rationale for presenting the intercorrelation tables was to demonstrate that each H-O scale was correlated with the RC, SP, and PSY-5 scales associated with the specific H-O scale in the interpretation guidelines. For example, the interpretation guide for the Thought Dysfunction (THD) Scale says that "specific manifestation of thought dysfunction will be indicated by elevations on RC6, RC8, and PSYC-r" (Archer et al., 2016, p. 75). Sure enough, the correlations between THD and the above scales were .93, .69, and .81 for the normative sample of boys and even higher for the inpatient boys' sample (.93, .74, and .86). Similar patterns of correlations were found for the normative and inpatient samples of girls. However, these strong correlations are a bit less impressive when one realizes that items on the THD are often also a part of one or more of the other three scales.

COMMENTARY. The MMPI-A-RF is a welcome alternative to the MMPI-A. It has half the number of items, which makes it much more appropriate for adolescent attention spans. The MMPI-A-RF also was designed to isolate the nonspecific distress (demoralization) factor that led to excessively high intercorrelations on the MMPI-A. As a result, the RC scales are more independent from one another than the clinical scales on the MMPI-A, which increases the discriminant validity of the measure for identifying specific concerns as opposed to globalized dysfunction. In other words, the absence of demoralization saturation results in less multiple-scale elevations, which should make interpretation more clear-cut and straightforward. The test manual is thorough, informative, and extremely detailed (72,792 correlation coefficients presented in just the validity section alone). The reliability of the inventory varies, with the broad H-O scales demonstrating acceptable to good reliability and the smallest SP scales revealing much weaker reliability. The test has decent convergent and divergent validity with well-established behavioral measures (e.g., Achenbach scales) when assessing psychopathology in adolescents. The main weakness of the MMPI-A-RF is that it does not include updated norms from the MMPI-A. The test authors' argument that adolescents and their response patterns have not changed much since the late 1980s is unconvincing. A final minor concern is that the hand-scoring for the MMPI-A-RF is time-consuming, laborious, and prone to error. Using computerized administration and scoring is recommended instead.

SUMMARY. The MMPI-A-RF, a revision of the MMPI-A structured after the MMPI-2-RF, is designed to assess psychopathology in adolescents ages 14-18. The rationale for the restructured format of the scales is logical, and the process of scale development appears to be thorough and statistically sound. The inventory has acceptable psychometric properties, though it would be helpful to have more comparisons with other psychometrically sound instruments to provide additional evidence to support construct validity. Collecting current normative data from a diverse, representative sample of adolescents would make this good instrument even better. Even without updated norms, though, clinicians will likely find the MMPI-A-RF to be a good replacement for the MMPI-A. It is recommended that clinicians interested in switching from the MMPI-A to the MMPI-A-RF review the research by Stokes, Pogge, and Archer (2018) for a detailed and informative comparison of the two instruments.

REVIEWER'S REFERENCES

Achenbach, T. M., & Rescorla, L. A. (2001). *Manual for the Achenbach System of Empirically Based Assessment school-age forms and profiles.* Burlington, VT: University of Vermont, Research Center for Children, Youth, & Families.

Barkley, R. A., & Murphy, K. R. (1998). *Attention-deficit hyperactivity disorder: A clinical workbook* (2nd ed.). New York, NY: Guilford Press.

Ben-Porath, Y. S., & Tellegen, A. (2008). *Minnesota Multiphasic Personality Inventory-2-Restructured Form (MMPI-2-RF): Manual for administration, scoring, and interpretation.* Minneapolis, MN: University of Minnesota Press.

Butcher, J. N., Williams, C. L., Graham, J. R., Archer, R. P., Tellegen, A., Ben-Porath, Y. S., & Kaemmer, B. (1992). *Minnesota Multiphasic Personality Inventory-Adolescent (MMPI-A): Manual for administration, scoring, and interpretation.* Minneapolis, MN: University of Minnesota Press.

Forbey, J. D., & Ben-Porath, Y. S. (2003). Incremental validity of the MMPI-A content scales in a residential treatment facility. *Assessment, 10*(2), 191-202. doi:10.1177/1073191103010002010

Harkness, A. R., & McNulty, J. L. (1994). The Personality Psychopathology Five (PSY-5): Issues from the pages of a diagnostic manual instead of a dictionary. In S. Strack & M. Lorr (Eds.), *Differentiating normal and abnormal personality* (pp. 291-315). New York, NY: Springer.

Stokes, J. M., Pogge, D. L., & Archer, R. P. (2018). Comparisons between the Minnesota Multiphasic Personality Inventory-Adolescent-Restructured Form (MMPI-A RF) and MMPI-A in adolescent psychiatric inpatients. *Psychological Assessment, 30*(3), 370-382.

[94]

Minnesota Multiphasic Personality Inventory–2 [2001 Manual Revision].

Purpose: "Designed to assess a number of the major patterns of personality and emotional disorders."
Population: Ages 18 and over.
Publication Dates: 1942–2001.
Acronym: MMPI-2.
Scores, 75: 7 Validity Indicators: Cannot Say (?), Lie (L), Infrequency (F), Correction (K), Back F (FB), Variable Response Inconsistency (VRIN), True Response Inconsistency (TRIN); 10 Clinical Scales: Hypochondriasis (Hs), Depression (D), Conversion Hysteria (Hy), Psychopathic Deviate (Pd), Masculinity-Femininity (Mf), Paranoia (Pa), Psychasthenia (Pt), Schizophrenia (Sc), Hypomania (Ma), Social Introversion (Si); 15 Supplementary Scales: Anxiety (A), Repression (R), Ego Strength (Es), MacAndrew Alcoholism Scale-Revised (MAC-R), Overcontrolled Hostility (O-H), Dominance (Do), Social Responsibility (Re), College Maladjustment (Mt), Gender Role-Masculine (GM), Gender Role-Feminine (GF), 2 Post-Traumatic Stress Disorder Scales (PK & PS); Marital Distress Scale (MDS), Addiction Potential Scale (APS), Addiction Admission Scale (AAS); 15 Content Scales: Anxiety (ANX), Fears (FRS), Obsessiveness (OBS), Depression (DEP), Health Concerns (HEA), Bizarre Mentation (BIZ), Anger (ANG), Cynicism (CYN), Antisocial Practices (ASP), Type A (TPA), Low Self-Esteem (LSE), Social Discomfort (SOD), Family Problems (FAM), Work Interference (WRK), Negative Treatment Indicators (TRT);

3 Si subscales: Shyness/Self-Consciousness (Si1), Social Avoidance (Si2), Alienation-Self and Others (Si3); 28 Harris-Lingoes Subscales: Subjective Depression (D1), Psychomotor Retardation (D2), Physical Malfunctioning (D3), Mental Dullness (D4), Brooding (D5), Denial of Social Anxiety (Hy1), Need for Affection (Hy2), Lassitude-Malaise (Hy3), Somatic Complaints (Hy4), Inhibition of Aggression (Hy5), Familial Discord (Pd1), Authority Problems (Pd2), Social Imperturbability (Pd3), Social Alienation (Pd4), Self-Alienation (Pd5), Persecutory Ideas (Pa1), Poignancy (Pa2), Naivete (Pa3), Social Alienation (Sc1), Emotional Alienation (Sc2), Lack of Ego Mastery, Cognitive (Sc3), Conative (Sc4), Defective Inhibition (Sc5), Bizarre Sensory Experiences (Sc6), Amorality (Ma1), Psychomotor Acceleration (Ma2), Imperturbability (Ma3), Ego Inflation (Ma4).

Administration: Group or individual.

Price Data, 2020: $1,060.25 per hand-scoring introductory kit with 10 softcover test booklets including manual (2001, 221 pages), Restructured Clinical Scales monograph (2003, 123 pages), reusable answer keys, answer sheets, and profile and record forms in tote bag; $49 per 10 reusable softcover test booklets; $75 per reusable hardcover test booklet; $64 per 50 hand-scorable answer sheets and profile forms; $68 per audio CD; $70.50 per manual; price data available from publisher for various scoring options and interpretive reports.

Foreign Language Editions: May be administered in Spanish, Hmong, and French (Canadian).

Time: (90) minutes.

Comments: May be administered via computer, audio CD, or paper and pencil.

Authors: James N. Butcher, W. Grant Dahlstrom, John R. Graham, and Auke Tellegen (test booklet); James N. Butcher, John R. Graham, Yossef S. Ben-Porath, Auke Tellegen, and W. Grant Dahlstrom (2001 manual).

Publisher: Published by University of Minnesota Press; distributed by Pearson.

Cross References: See T5:1697 (600 references) and T4:1645 (504 references); for reviews by Robert P. Archer and David S. Nichols based on the 1989 manual of the MMPI-2, see 11:244 (637 references); see also 9:715 (339 references) and T3:1498 (749 references); for reviews by Henry A. Alker and Glen D. King of the original version, see 8:616 (1,188 references); see also T2:1281 (549 references); for reviews by Malcolm D. Gynther and David A. Rodgers, see 7:104 (831 references); see also P:166 (1,066 references); for reviews by C. J. Adcock and James C. Lingoes, see 6:143 (626 references); for reviews by Albert Ellis and Warren T. Norman, see 5:86 (496 references); for a review by Arthur L. Benton, see 4:71 (211 references); for reviews by Arthur L. Benton, H. J. Eysenck, L. S. Penrose, and Julian B. Rotter, and an excerpted review, see 3:60 (76 references); for reviews by Shawn K. Acheson and Geoffrey L. Thorpe of the MMPI-2-RF, see 20:121.

Review of the Minnesota Multiphasic Personality Inventory-2 [2001 Manual Revision] by JEFFREY A. ATLAS, Director, Mental Health Services, SCO Family of Services, Queens, NY:

DESCRIPTION. The Minnesota Multiphasic Personality Inventory, currently in its second edition and 2001 manual revision (MMPI-2), and attendant Buros *Mental Measurements Yearbook* (*MMY*) reviews over 75 years provide a veritable timeline for the history of western psychology and psychiatry. There are echoes of Freudian psychology in scales of Conversion Hysteria, Repression, Ego Strength, Lack of Ego Mastery, and Ego Inflation. Refinements inventorying Need for Affection, Alcoholism, Posttraumatic Stress, Marital Distress, and Gender Roles trace evolving areas of concern in American psychology. Fundamental clinical syndromes that seem to be obtained cross-culturally and historically include measures of Depression and Schizophrenia. The coverage of this 567-item true-false index is encyclopedic, thus its use as the foremost personality psychometric despite an administration time of approximately 90 minutes, with hand-scoring requiring upwards of another hour (computer scoring and interpretive reports optional). Previous reviewers of the MMPI have included pioneers in test development (Arthur Benton in the third and fourth *MMY*s), personality theory (H. J. Eysenck in the third *MMY*), and a school of psychotherapy (Albert Ellis in the fifth *MMY*). There is much to appreciate and digest.

A central, recurrent question that courses through this history is that of the validity of endorsed self-report statements in veridically identifying personality patterns and abnormal behavior. The MMPI-2 test materials furnished for the present review included the revised manual, a separate Restructured Clinical Scales monograph (2003) of a scale-shortened and modified version of the test, a Symptom Validity Scale monograph (2009), Personality Psychopathology Five (PSY-5) Scales monograph (2002), test booklets, answer sheets, reusable answer keys, profile forms, audio cassettes in English and Spanish, and a Spanish-language test booklet, all conveniently packaged in a tote bag.

Test takers are supervised, individually or in groups, while completing the inventory, which may be administered in staggered sessions if there is interruption for other procedures. Sixth-grade reading level is required; the audio cassettes furnish an alternate form of test administration for those with lower reading proficiency. Test monitors or supervisors are advised to provide minimal redirection to maintain standardization of inventory completion, encouraging querying examinees to just answer the question as they understand it.

Minimum qualifications for use of the MMPI-2 are cited as a "graduate-level course in psychological testing" as well as a "graduate-level course in psychopathology" (manual, p. 7). It may be stated that, at 52 pages, the brevity of the instruction and summary portion of the (2001) manual presents a daunting challenge for a beginning-level psychodiagnostician when contrasted with the 160 accompanying pages of references and extensive data scales, tables, and figures. The test manual perhaps relies too heavily on references to outside articles, which themselves may comprise more than 10,000 papers on the MMPI series. Comfort with use of the MMPI with adults and select clinical populations likely is an ongoing, but potentially quite rewarding, professional process for practitioners.

DEVELOPMENT. Items for the original scale were designed by Hathaway and McKinley (1943), a psychologist and psychiatrist, respectively, at The University of Minnesota, to differentiate hospital patients manifesting "neurotic" hypochondriacal disorder from nonpatient visitors on the basis of answers to a group of statements canvassing "some personal experience, belief, attitude, or concern" (manual, p. 1). This principle of contrasting and cross-validating item responses for successive studies of Psychasthenia, Depression, Conversion Hysteria, Hypomania, Paranoia, Schizophrenia, Psychopathic Deviate, Masculinity-Femininity, and Social Introversion by 1956 comprised the current roster of MMPI-2 Clinical scales. It should be noted that development of different classifications of MMPI items, up through the later versions, employed combinations of varying scale construction approaches, summarized by Harkness and McNulty in the PSY-5 monograph (p. 1) as including "empirical, rational, internal, Item Response Theory (IRT), and hybrid approaches."

The import of this approach is readily apparent in Item 1, of the order, "I like (electronics) magazines" (fictive). The fact that this one statement bears empirical "scale memberships" in Masculinity-Femininity, Repression, Overcontrolled Hostility, and Gender Role-Feminine illustrates how basic, seemingly innocuous, and atheoretical formulations were predictive of (patient) group membership, albeit less so of the specific nosological categories. Even where items bore more direct relation to defining features of disorders, such as the positive symptoms of Schizophrenia (derealization, delusions, auditory hallucinations, paranoia), the extra weight of correlating to other syndromes such as Psychasthenia (Obsessive-Compulsive Disorder) led to high clinical scale overlap, due in part to a common factor of Demoralization (one scale of the MMPI-2-RF).

The MMPI-2 validity scales offer another tempering and, in the case of K (Correction), moderating factor. The success of these scales may be attested to by psychometricians and test developers over many years analogizing their variable response set or inconsistent response adjustments to the "Lie Scale" of the MMPI. While the "L scale" more generally was aimed at assessing a defensive test-taking mind set (manual, p. 20), cumulatively the seven response Validity indicators are designed to determine "protocol acceptability." Omitted or "Cannot say" counts above 30 indicate a protocol "may be invalid." Variously high elevations of T scores for "Infrequent" F scale responding, infrequent responding to the back portion of the test (Back F), "faking good" Lie scale reporting, "faking bad" psychopathology (F-p responding), and "Superlative Self-Presentation" S scores each similarly suggest the invalidity of a protocol. A "K" scale score indicating the degree of defensive responding may invalidate protocols, but also functions through additive fractions as a "correction" that adjusts raw scores on five of the clinical scales.

Complementing these early validity scales are two that were added for the MMPI-2 and concern Variable Response Inconsistency (VRIN; paired items answered inconsistently—that is, in opposite directions) and True Response Inconsistency (TRIN; paired items opposite in content answered inconsistently—that is, in the same direction). High VRIN scores may signal errors or random responding, whereas high TRIN scores may suggest acquiescent or non-acquiescent response sets (excessive "yea- or nay-saying," manual, p. 16).

The original MMPI clinical scale interpretation rested upon the empirical distinctions between select groupings of individuals, for instance hypochondriacal and "normal" group Minnesotan visitors to a hospital. MMPI-2 "content component" scales were developed by a "combined rational/empirical procedure" to provide the 15 content scales. A "rational" item selection approach to identifying Depression, for instance, would involve test participants identifying from the MMPI pool items that more directly assess the construct, such as "not (having) lived according to one's principles." The test authors refer to external studies that further demonstrate empirical correlates of the item pools. To facilitate finer-grained content interpretation, the MMPI-2 features "content component scales" for 12 of the 15 content scales, "constructed through a series of empirical and rational analyses designed to identify meaningful and discernible" themes (manual, p. 33), for instance differentially identifying Lack of Drive and Suicidal Ideation in Depression.

Supplementary scales were added to the MMPI-2 to delineate major factor analytic dimensions (Anxiety and Repression) and include interim and later-developed scales of clinical importance. The MMPI items for additional Supplementary scales were derived from journal articles that empirically contrasted various client groups or choosing items significantly associated with select group scores on other measures. The latest addition to the Supplementary scales, described in the MMPI-2 revised manual and included in a separate monograph, are the Personality Psychopathology Five (PSY-5) scales, expressly delineating "characteristic traits" of personality such as Aggression, Psychoticism, Disconstraint, Negative Emotionality/Neuroticism, and Introversion/Low Positive Emotionality. The PSY-5 was developed using a procedure the authors call "Replicated Rational Selection" (PSY-5 manual, p. 16). Personality constructs were developed by a series of studies eventuating in 201 lay "judges" evaluating "psychological distances" between personality descriptors that were then subjected to latent root analyses and the extraction of five principal components comprising the five scales. "Independent item selectors" (114 college volunteers) then examined MMPI-2 items, and trial scales were constructed for each construct. Item reviewers culled difficult-to-key items and items tapping multiple dimensions, with the final scale psychometrically analyzed to ensure placement of items in the one most highly correlated PSY-5 scale (PSY-5 monograph, pp. 16-17).

TECHNICAL.

Standardization. The 1989 MMPI-2 revision entailed testing of 2,600 individuals ages 18 to 85 (1,138 men and 1,462 women). Ethnic backgrounds of individuals included in the sample (manual tables, p. 4) hew reasonably close to 1990 census data, with the exception of the MMPI-2's overrepresentation of Native Americans. The inclusion of Black participants is significant given earlier controversies surrounding reported high scores of African Americans when compared to the Minnesotan samples of the original MMPI. Age and educational distributions of the MMPI-2 normative sample are adequate, with the exception of overrepresentation of college and post-graduate individuals, a finding the test authors reference as not having significant impact on scores.

Reliability. Reliability data are furnished for 82 men and 111 women drawn from the MMPI-2 normative sample retested after an average interval of 8.58 days. Retest coefficients for the Clinical, Content, and Supplementary scales (manual, p. 124) are moderate (e.g., .54 for Schizophrenia in females) to very high (e.g., .89 and .88 for Anxiety Content scales, respectively for males and females, .91 for each for the Anxiety Supplementary scale). Alpha coefficients assessing internal consistency are somewhat low and quite variable, ranging on the Clinical scales from .34 to .85 for males and from .37 to .87 for females, with lows on Paranoia of .34 and .39 for males and females, respectively (manual, p. 125). The alpha coefficients associated with the Supplementary scale of Overcontrolled Hostility registered only .34 and .24 for males and females, respectively.

Test-retest reliability estimates over a 1-week interval are presented (FBS manual, p. 6) for 193 men and women from a "subset of the normative sample" who completed a developmental version of the MMPI "used to construct the MMPI-2." The VRIN and TRIN coefficients for the normative sample are in the moderate range (.52 and .45 respectively) with very low alpha coefficients (.11 to .29) across studies of community mental health center outpatients, psychiatric inpatients (community hospital), psychiatric inpatients (VA hospital), medical patients, chronic pain patients, and disability claimants.

One-week (n = 193) reliability and 5-year (n's varying from 897 to 998) stability coefficients for the PSY-5 scales (PSY-5 manual, p. 19) were significantly high.

Validity. Correlation coefficients were calculated between the PSY-5 scales and numerous external scales, most comprehensively the Symptom Checklist-90-R (SCL-R-90; Derogatis, 1983) for 403 men and 605 women attending a community mental health center (PSY-5 manual, p. 23). The PSY-5 Aggression scale correlation coefficients with SCL-90-R Hostility and Paranoid Ideation were low (.19-.41). The Psychoticism scale demonstrated moderate to high correlation coefficients (.41-.65) with SCL-90-R scales for Somaticization, Obsessive-Compulsive, Interpersonal Sensitivity, Depression, Anxiety, Hostility, Phobic Anxiety, Paranoid Ideation (.65 and .63, respectively, for men and women), and Psychoticism (.61 and .63, respectively, for men and women). The Disconstraint scale correlated with SCL-90-R Hostility at only .24 and .05, respectively, for men and women. The Negative Emotionality/Neuroticism scale correlated moderately (.43-.65) with SCL-90-R Somaticization, Obsessive-Compulsive, Interpersonal Sensitivity, Depression, Anxiety, Hostility, Phobic Anxiety, Paranoid Ideation, and Psychoticism. PSY-5 Introversion/Low Positive Emotionality correlated in the low to moderate range (coefficients were .34-61) with SCL-90-R Somaticization, Obsessive-Compulsive, Interpersonal Sensitivity, Depression, Anxiety, Hostility, Phobic Anxiety, Paranoid Ideation, and Psychoticism.

COMMENTARY. The MMPI-2, with 2001 manual revision, 2009 Symptom Validity (FBS) Scale monograph, and 2002 Personality Psychopathology Five (PSY-5) Scales monograph is a noteworthy update of an historic personality test. While it has had demonstrable use in differentiating clinical and normal groups in successive categories of problem behavior since its inception, it has been less successful in the particular task of differential identification of nosological syndromes (diagnostic specificity). This was a major contention of Benton's (1949) earlier critique, along with the elaborate length of the scale, in Benton's phrasing of the time "send[ing] a man to do a boy's work." Ellis (1959) similarly wondered about the MMPI's validity for individual diagnoses and whether a clinical psychologist "in equal or less time, [might not] get more pertinent, incisive, and depth-centered 'personality' material from a straightforward interview," and be "worth his salt."

The plethora of research studies cited in the current manuals suggest a more level playing field in comparing MMPI-2 and clinician-rated assessments of psychopathology and improvements with therapy, and from its earliest days, the MMPI has been offered as just one component, along with clinical interview and consideration of historical data, in proffering a diagnosis. The PSY-5 scales improve the test's precision in identifying personality patterns having overlap with other shorter, if less comprehensive, scales.

The extensive, and somewhat cumbersome validity scales may be valuable in and of themselves in forensic, medical, or personnel screening instances to assess malingering or defensive self-presentation. When hand scoring the protocols, those cases deemed invalid early may make scoring of the remaining MMPI-2 scales seem like an arduous and arid task when contrasted with the flexibility a diagnostician may possess in meeting a patient or individual where they are. Armed with different amounts of Thematic Apperception Test (Murray, 1943) cards, Rorschach (Rorschach, 1921) inkblots for which one may vary depth of inquiry, or even having at hand a full or brief form of, say, a self-report depression scale may yield information of greater utility than the MMPI-2.

SUMMARY. The MMPI-2 [2001 Manual Revision] remains the unparalleled psychometric instrument for comprehensive, quantifiable screening and assessment of personality and psychopathology. In individual clinical practice it is best viewed as augmentative to differential diagnostic interviewing and auxiliary sources of information. Given the thousands of articles pertaining to the MMPI series, this latest iteration is likely to continue the instrument's unique standing as a source of ongoing research and clinical investigation with practical application across hospital, outpatient, and forensic settings.

REVIEWER'S REFERENCES

Benton, A. L. (1949). [Test review of Minnesota Multiphasic Personality Inventory, Revised Edition]. In O. K. Buros (Ed.), *The third mental measurements yearbook.* Highland Park, NJ: The Gryphon Press.

Derogatis, L. R. (1983). *SCL-90-R: Administration, scoring, and procedures manual for the R (revised) version.* Towson, MD: Clinical Psychometric Research.

Ellis, A. (1959). [Test review of Minnesota Multiphasic Personality Inventory, Revised Edition]. In O. K. Buros (Ed.), *The fifth mental measurements yearbook.* Highland Park, NJ: The Gryphon Press.

Hathaway, S. R., & McKinley, J. C. (1943). *Manual for administering and scoring the MMPI.* Minneapolis, MN: University of Minnesota Press.

Murray, H. A. (1943). *Thematic Apperception Test manual.* Cambridge, MA: Harvard University Press.

Rorschach, H. (1921). *Rorschach-Test.* Bern, Switzerland: Verlag Hans Huber AG.

Review of the Minnesota Multiphasic Personality Inventory-2 [2001 Manual Revision] by PETER ZACHAR, Professor of Psychology, Auburn University Montgomery, Montgomery AL:

[This review greatly benefitted from the knowledge and thoughtful advice of Dr. Mark Waugh.]

DESCRIPTION. Starke R. Hathaway and J. Charnley McKinley began developing the Minnesota Multiphasic Personality Inventory (MMPI) in the 1930s as an instrument for use in diagnostic assessment. Its history can be delineated by several milestones, five of which are discussed here.

First, it quickly became evident that the test had shortcomings as a diagnostic instrument. The MMPI, however, was saved by a shift in which interpretations emphasized any empirical correlates and only empirical correlates of the scales (Meehl, 1945, 1954). Reformulated as an instrument for systematically providing information about the nature of a person's psychological distress and dysfunction, the MMPI became a mainstay of psychological assessment in which psychologists use their expertise to answer a wide range of referral questions about an individual's psychological functioning. The popularity of the MMPI played a leading role in psychological assessment becoming an important specialization for clinical psychologists, eclipsing the activity of assigning individuals a psychiatric diagnosis.

A second milestone was marked by the practice of basing interpretations on code types, for example, a type based on the person's two highest, clinically significant scale scores (Guthrie, 1956; Hathaway & Meehl, 1956). Each MMPI basic clinical scale was developed by selecting items that discriminated between a group of patients with a known diagnosis and a contrast group of non-patients (the empirical-keying approach). As a consequence, elevations on the basic clinical scales are a function of the diagnostic construct of interest, common co-occurring symptoms shared by people in the same diagnostic group, indicators of general psychiatric distress that discriminate between patients and non-patients, and potentially construct-irrelevant items selected on the basis of chance correlations. Code types are handy simplifying tools. To illustrate, if a person's two highest scores are on Scale 2 and Scale 7, they can be labeled a 27/72 type, and the interpretation can emphasize the empirical correlates of that particular configuration.

A third milestone was the introduction of homogeneous content scales (Harris & Lingoes, 1955; Welsh, 1956). The purpose of the content scales was to reduce the symptomatic noise, creating more construct-pure scales for which the interpretation of elevations is more specific. The most comprehensive application of this approach was championed by Jerry Wiggins for the MMPI (Wiggins, 1966; Wiggins, Goldberg, & Apelbaum, 1971) and by Jane Loevinger (1957) and Douglas Jackson (1971) for test construction in general (but anticipated by work on construct validity by Cronbach and Meehl, 1955).

A fourth major milestone was the restandardization of the MMPI, introduced in 1989 as the MMPI-2 (Butcher, Dahlstrom, Graham, Tellegen, & Kaemmer, 1989). The restandardization project included: collecting new norms to better represent the current U.S. population than did the original Minnesota sample, revising outdated or offensive items and adding new items, introducing three new scales to evaluate profile validity, constructing all new content scales (Butcher, Graham, Williams, & Ben-Porath, 1990), revising the list of critical items that are sensitive to severe distress (Koss & Butcher, 1973; Lachar & Wrobel, 1979), and adjusting for variation in skewness across the clinical scales by making the standardized scores more uniform so that the percentile rank of the scores across the scales did not vary (Tellegen & Ben-Porath, 1992). The MMPI-2 also prioritized maintaining continuity with the original MMPI. This principle was followed in order to preserve the enormous research base and, to a lesser extent, clinical lore associated with the MMPI.

A fifth major milestone was the introduction of the restructured clinical scales in 2003 (Tellegen et al., 2003). In the 1989 restandardization, maintaining continuity between the MMPI and the MMPI-2 led to what some would consider problems with the MMPI being replicated in the MMPI-2. In addition to within-scale item heterogeneity, because the scales measure the same general psychiatric distress factor using shared items, scale scores rise and fall together. Some thinkers believe that another problem is that the basic clinical scales measure diagnostic constructs that are unfamiliar to users because they are not represented in the current nosology. This last problem may be less bothersome to those who are more familiar with the history of psychiatric nosology and less inclined to be Whiggish about current developments.

To address these perceived problems, Tellegen and colleagues used principal components analysis to restructure the basic clinical scales. They began by isolating an analogue of the general distress factor (called Demoralization). For those eight basic clinical scales that measure psychopathology, the researchers partialed out the Demoralization factor and then identified the next most important factor on each basic clinical scale that did not overlap with any other scale. In effect, this began a project of transforming the MMPI-2 into a homogeneous content-scale-based inventory. In 2008, a completely separate inventory called MMPI-2 Restructured

Form (MMPI-2-RF; Ben-Porath & Tellegen, 2008a, 2008b; 20:121) was introduced.

DEVELOPMENT. This review addresses the 2001 revision of the MMPI-2 manual (Butcher, Graham, Ben-Porath, Tellegen, & Dahlstrom, 2001) and also reviews various iterative changes since 2001.

When the MMPI-2 was published in 1989, the validity and clinical scales profile form included only the four standard validity scales of the MMPI (Cannot Say, L, F, and K). Two new validity scales, the Variable Response Inconsistency (VRIN) and True Response Inconsistency (TRIN), were considered experimental and thus optional. A third new validity scale, the Back F (F_B), was also optional. Subsequent to the MMPI-2 of 1989, Arbisi and Ben-Porath (1995) developed another new validity scale, which they named Infrequency Psychopathology (F_P). It assesses reporting of symptoms rarely endorsed by psychiatric inpatients. On the original MMPI, the Infrequency scale (F) assessed the reporting of symptoms rarely endorsed in non-patient populations, but in addition to over-reporting, F is elevated by actual distress (Nichols, 2001). F_P was designed to assess for over-reporting only.

As of 2001, the MMPI-2 profile includes all the new validity scales (VRIN, TRIN, F, F_B, F_P, L, and K), plus an additional validity scale, named Superlative Self-presentation (S), which was developed to detect the tendency to present oneself in an unrealistically positive light in employment settings (Butcher & Han, 1995). In addition, the 2001 manual reinserts Gough's (1956) F-K index as an indicator of profile invalidity.

The 2001 manual introduces 27 subscales for the content scales, paralleling the Harris-Lingoes subscales for the basic clinical scales. Developed by Ben-Porath and Sherwood (1993), they are called the content component scales.

An MMPI tradition has been to use the item pool to develop scales for additional constructs such as ego strength (Barron, 1956) and personality disorders (Morey, Waugh, & Blashfield, 1985) and to classify them under the term *supplementary scales*. Just prior to and after the publication of the MMPI-2 in 1989, a few supplementary scales were included on the validity and basic scale profile form. The 2001 manual has 20 supplementary scales including new and/or revised scales and puts them all on a separate supplementary scales profile form.

The most discussed new supplementary scales are the Personality Psychopathology Five (PSY-5) scales. Many psychologists believe that the quantitative structure of normal human personality is best described by a five-factor model. Extreme values on these factors may represent maladaptive or disordered conditions. Item reduction methods using personality disorder symptoms, however, often replicate only four of the normal personality factors (Livesley, 2003; Widiger & Simonsen, 2005). Depending on the analysis, additional factors emerge that have no clear analogue among the five factors (Shedler & Westen, 2004; Skodol et al., 2011).

The PSY-5 constructs were originally derived from items for measuring both normal personality and disordered personality (Harkness, 1992; Harkness & McNulty, 1994). Leading the way on replicating only four normal personality factors with personality disorders, the PSY-5 constructs partially represent four of the five normal personality constructs, and there is an additional construct—Psychoticism—that is not captured by the five-factor model. Once these constructs were identified, measures of them using MMPI items were developed (Harkness, McNulty, & Ben-Porath, 1995).

One important innovation of the 2001 MMPI-2 manual involves a self-correction. A suspicion about the veridicality of self-report was a fundamental theoretical perspective in the original MMPI. Some of the items on the basic clinical scales have face validity for the construct being measured and are "obvious." Those items that do not have face validity were called "subtle." Let us use as an example Scale 2 (Depression). If examinees wanted to present themselves as more depressed than they are or less depressed than they are, they likely would alter their response to the obvious items on Scale 2, but not to the subtle items because the subtle items do not appear to be depression indicators. So, a large difference between scores on the obvious and subtle items might suggest some attempt at distortion (Wiener, 1948). In retrospect, the subtle items on Scale 2 do not appear to be depression items because they are not. They may be items that assess occasional comorbid depression symptoms (like anxiety), but also may be items for which inclusion on the scale capitalized on chance correlations due to the large number of items used to develop the basic clinical scales, and likely would have been eliminated with adequate cross-replication of the original item selection procedures (Graham, 1993; Weed, Ben-Porath, & Butcher, 1990). The 2001 manual makes no mention of the obvious versus subtle distinction and does not describe how to score these subscales.

The 2001 manual also puts increased importance on a different self-correction. The Adjustment Validity scale (K) measures a defensive tendency to not acknowledge current distress. Traditionally, it has been used to correct scores on some basic clinical scales by adding points to those scales in proportion to the assessed level of defensive responding (McKinley, Hathaway, & Meehl, 1948). This is called the K-correction. Like other MMPI scales, K seems to measure more than one thing (Nichols, 2001). For example, moderate elevations on the K scale can represent resiliency, meaning that for some people their measured level of distress on the MMPI-2 is artificially increased in proportion to their degree of resiliency. This would reduce, rather than increase, the validity of the basic clinical scales thus "corrected" (Barthlow, Graham, Ben-Porath, Tellegen, & McNulty, 2002). The 1989 manual included tables of non-K-corrected T scores, but as of 2001, users have the option of generating non-K-corrected validity and clinical scale profiles. The MMPI scales that are not corrected can be compared most directly to the non-K-corrected T scores.

The 2001 manual introduces translations for speakers of Spanish, French Canadian, and Hmong (a Southeast Asian group with a large community in Minnesota). After 2001, the cassette tapes for special administrations were replaced by CDs.

The MMPI-2 is often used in personnel selection for occupations where public safety is a concern such as pilots and police officers. After 2001, to conform to laws regarding gender not being considered in personnel selection, non-gendered norms became available. Differences between scores using gendered and non-gendered norms are small (Ben-Porath & Tellegen, 2008a).

Lees-Haley, English, and Glenn (1991) developed a scale called the Fake Bad Scale (FBS) with the goal of detecting non-credible reporting of physical and neurocognitive symptoms in personal injury evaluations. Subsequent to 2001, it was renamed the Symptom Validity Scale and has been added to the validity and clinical scales profile (Ben-Porath, Graham, & Tellegen, 2009).

A final change since the publication of the 2001 manual is the incorporation of the restructured clinical scales into the standard package of materials. Tellegen et al. (2003) argue that those basic clinical scales that remain elevated in the transition to the restructured profiles are good targets to emphasize as more important.

TECHNICAL. The 1989 test manual stated that test takers need an eighth-grade level of reading comprehension. The 2001 manual lowers the required reading level to the sixth grade. The 2001 manual is described as a guide for interpretation, and the way it is organized makes it more useful in that respect. For example, the descriptions of the basic clinical scale and content scale correlates are integrated with the Harris-Lingoes and content component subscales.

More substantively, the descriptions of high and moderate scores have been revised, appearing to be more behavioral, less psychodynamic. For eight of the 10 basic clinical scales, average and low scores are not interpretable. Thus, most MMPI scales represent unipolar scales rather than bipolar scales. The 2001 manual also adds a brief mention of using 2- and 3-point code types to guide interpretation.

When the MMPI-2 was published in 1989, norms for adolescents were not available, and professionals were advised to test adolescents using the original MMPI. By 2001 norms for use with adolescents (age 14-18) were available with the publication of the MMPI-Adolescent (MMPI-A; Butcher et al., 1992). Unless 18-year-olds are living independently, the 2001 manual recommends that they be tested with the MMPI-A.

The 1989 manual provided descriptive statistics and reliability estimates with respect to 1-week (roughly) test-retest reliability coefficients and alpha coefficients for the basic clinical, content, and supplementary scales. Standard errors of measurement were computed using the test-retest coefficients. The test manual did not discuss the small number of validity coefficients reported.

The 2001 manual presents the same reliability data, although inexplicably the retest coefficients are different despite both manuals using the same data sets. As might be expected, the more homogeneous content scales and restructured clinical scales are more reliable than the heterogeneous basic clinical scales and several of the supplementary scales. For all scales, reliability coefficients are typically higher in clinical samples. Other than describing the "correlates" of the clinical scales (which do not distinguish between quantitative associations and clinical lore), the 2001 manual does not report validity coefficients, which is a shortcoming. It would be preferable to follow the lead of the MMPI-2-RF, which has both a shorter administrative and interpretation manual and a longer technical manual to document evidence of validity.

COMMENTARY. The MMPI-2 is a widely used inventory with a long and venerable tradition (Butcher, 2000a; Dahlstrom & Dahlstrom, 1980; Welsh & Dahlstrom, 1956). Many people have spent their careers digging into the details of this instrument, and anyone who is not a specialist to that degree should—and appropriately—be daunted when wading into the many controversies and debates about the MMPI, both historical and contemporary. This reviewer proceeds with caution, putting more emphasis on topics relevant to theoretical issues in the conceptualization of psychopathology.

The elephant in the room is what to do about an MMPI-3 because after nearly 30 years, new norms need to be developed. As with the MMPI-2, the collection of new normative data also presents an opportunity to improve the inventory in other ways.

Improve in what way? The current trend in the development of the MMPI is to emphasize homogeneous scales as opposed to the more heterogeneous scales that the empirical-keying approach tends to produce. Anyone who prefers more homogeneous and conceptually driven scales may emphasize slightly different validators than those who are committed to the traditional empirical-keying approach, and vice versa.

Butcher (2000b) argues that an attractive feature of the MMPI's empirical-keying approach is that the placement of an item on a scale is not constrained by one's conceptual grasp of the construct being measured. Someone more committed to a conceptually driven approach would argue that this feature is not desirable in the long run. For instance, one of the Harris-Lingoes subscales for Scale 6 (Paranoia) is named Naiveté. The converse of naiveté is cynicism. The MMPI-2 Cynicism content scale and the MMPI-RF RC3 (Cynicism) scale both include several Naiveté items that are reverse scored (Ben-Porath & Tellegen, 2008; Butcher, Graham, Williams, & Ben-Porath, 1990). On other modern psychological inventories, the empirical correlates for paranoia indicate that it is positively correlated with higher cynicism (Clark, 2005; Millon, Millon, Roger, & Grossman, 2009; Morey, 2007). But on MMPI Scale 6 (Paranoia), the more one answers in the naive direction, the higher one's score on Scale 6 (Paranoia) even though as a group these Naiveté items are negatively correlated with Scale 6 (Paranoia) (Ward, Kersh, & Waxmonsky, 1998). To make these items measures of the construct of paranoia, conceptually driven approaches might reverse score them.

Hathaway (1956) claimed that Scale 6 was a weak scale when it was first developed and that he and his colleagues were never able to fix it. They decided not to eliminate items just because their manifest content seemed to have no relation to the constructs being measured. From a more conceptual perspective, the next step would be to try to understand why those items are keyed so counterintuitively. This process of defining and redefining constructs is what Cronbach and Meehl (1955) meant by bootstrapping toward increased validity. Without a conceptual grasp of the "why" here, it is possible that the MMPI Scale 6 lacks construct validity evidence with respect to clinical paranoia.

Those who remain committed to the empirical-keying approach might disagree. For one, maximizing content purity may not be a single best option (Streiner, 2003). One of the nice things about the MMPI-2 is that it is pretty sensitive to psychiatric distress. For instance, on some prominent psychological inventories, a person can produce moderate scores on several scales. Although none of the scale elevations may cross the clinical significance threshold, overall, the person may have a high number of symptoms and be in substantial distress. The heterogeneous MMPI-2 basic clinical scales seem to be less subject to such false negatives.

Such sensitivity may be a function of the MMPI-2 cutoffs for clinical significance being slightly lower for some clinical scales than those used for some other psychological tests. However, psychological test scales developed to have a simple structure in which items are highly correlated with their own scale and minimally correlated with other scales may be creating idealized constructs (e.g., pure depression) that do not accord with complex clinical realities. If a patient's clinical presentation includes common co-occurring symptoms not classified under the idealized construct, demarcating the threshold for clinical significance with respect to the idealized construct alone might increase the risk of false negative decisions about how much distress is present.

From the standpoint of an empirical-keying approach, the composition of the MMPI basic scales suggests an alternative conception of psychopathological kinds in which the threshold for maladjustment takes into account both the features that cohere in the idealized construct of interest (e.g., depression) and a set of commonly occurring auxiliary features (e.g., generalized anxiety and somatic complaints). Together they form an extended symptom network (Cramer, Waldorp, van der Maas, & Borsboom, 2010). A scale targeting a broader network also might be useful as long as what Clark and Watson (2019) call the conglomerate construct is more informative than the linear combination of its components.

In this reviewer's opinion, there may be some value in preserving something of the MMPI traditional approach to psychopathology in the form of scales that are sensitive to real-world clinical complexity (Caldwell, 2006). Such scales can also be decomposed into purer constructs if need be. Nevertheless, to advance our conceptual understanding of psychopathology, any robustly construct-irrelevant items should be fixed. That is, keep some anxiety and somatic items on a depression scale but do not score more naïve and more trusting responses as more paranoid.

One long-standing challenge in interpreting the MMPI-2 is the ambiguity of F scale elevations. TRIN and VRIN are important additions, but they do not eliminate the ambiguity with the F scale. For example, there is some limited evidence that outpatients with borderline features conceptualized as an indicator of personality disorder severity can produce elevations on F (Archer, Ball, & Hunter, 1985; Bell-Pringle, Pate, & Brown, 1997). If so, such test takers are vulnerable to being labeled as "faking" by examiners, especially in forensic settings. This would be a radical move and not undertaken lightly, but this reviewer has cause to wonder whether it might be better to drop the ambiguous F scale in favor of the less ambiguous, improved validity scales such as F_p.

In 1989 computers were not in widespread use. The potential for computer administration was noted, but the manual cautioned that administration could take at least an hour and a half during which no other processing could be carried out on that unit. By 2001 computers were more ubiquitous, and the test manual dispenses with the suggestion that test takers be shown how to use the keyboard to enter answers. The 2001 manual recognizes that, ideally, the MMPI should be scored by computer because it eliminates the possibility of errors being made in scoring.

We are even further along now. Although hand scoring the MMPI using templates is still an option, besides the risk of making errors in scoring, there are too many scales now to score efficiently by hand. The only advantage to the templates is cost saving over the long run. Computer scoring should be the only option, but making this ideal more practical would require making computer administration more affordable.

Computer-based scoring also offers the possibility of providing information that would be too laborious to calculate by hand, such as using shading to indicate confidence intervals on each scale for the population being tested. More thought could be given to taking full advantage of the information processing capacities of today's computers. The next MMPI manual should also explain how all the information available on the computer printouts is both calculated and interpreted.

SUMMARY. Many incremental improvements have been made in the 2001 manual revision of the MMPI-2 and beyond. New validity scales are included on the profile forms, and additional subscales and supplementary scales have been added to help users better interpret elevations on the various clinical scales. The practice of scoring subscales composed of subtle items has been discontinued, and the potentially invalid use of the K-correction has become optional. Some psychologists, however, believe that other problems with the MMPI have been replicated in the MMPI-2, possibly as an unintended consequence of maintaining continuity. Future developments of the inventory should not conservatively preserve features of the test that its own developers may have seen as provisional and temporary, and advances in psychometrics and the conceptualization of psychopathology should be incorporated in the next revision, but hopefully that revision will also be a recognizable MMPI-3, and not an MMPI-RF-2.

REVIEWER'S REFERENCES

Arbisi, P. A., & Ben-Porath, Y. S. (1995). An MMPI-2 infrequent response scale for use with psychopathological populations: The Infrequency-Psychopathology Scale, F(p). *Psychological Assessment, 7*(4), 424-431.

Archer, R. P., Ball, J. D., & Hunter, J. A. (1985). MMPI characteristics of borderline psychopathology in adolescent inpatients. *Journal of Personality Assessment, 49*(1), 47-55.

Barron, F. (1956). An ego-strength scale which predicts response to psychotherapy. In G. S. Welsh & W. G. Dahlstrom (Eds.), *Basic readings on the MMPI in psychology and medicine* (pp. 226-234). Minneapolis, MN: University of Minnesota Press.

Barthlow, D. L., Graham, J. R., Ben-Porath, Y. S., Tellegen, A., & McNulty, J. L. (2002). The appropriateness of the MMPI-2 K correction. *Assessment, 9*(3), 219-229.

Bell-Pringle, V. J., Pate, J. L., & Brown, R. C. (1997). Assessment of borderline personality disorder using the MMPI-2 and the Personality Assessment Inventory. *Assessment, 4*(2), 131-139.

Ben-Porath, Y. S., Graham, J. R., & Tellegen, A. (2009). *The MMPI-2 symptom validity (FBS) scale.* Minneapolis, MN: University of Minnesota Press.

Ben-Porath, Y. S., & Sherwood, N. E. (1993). *The MMPI-2 content component scales.* Minneapolis, MN: University of Minnesota Press.

Ben-Porath, Y. S., & Tellegen, A. (2008a). *Minnesota Multiphasic Personality Inventory-2 Restructured Form®: Manual for administration, scoring, and interpreting.* Minneapolis, MN: University of Minnesota Press.

Ben-Porath, Y. S., & Tellegen, A. (2008b). *Minnesota Multiphasic Personality Inventory-2 Restructured Form®: Technical manual.* Minneapolis, MN: University of Minnesota Press.

Butcher, J. N. (2000a). *Basic sources on the MMPI-2.* Minneapolis, MN: University of Minnesota Press.

Butcher, J. N. (2000b). Dynamics of personality test responses: The empiricist's manifesto revisited. *Journal of Clinical Psychology, 56*(3), 375-386.

Butcher, J. N., Dahlstrom, W. G., Graham, J. R., Tellegen, A., & Kaemmer, B. (1989). *Minnesota Multiphasic Personality Inventory-2: Manual for administration and scoring*. Minneapolis, MN: University of Minnesota Press.

Butcher, J. N., Graham, J. R., Ben-Porath, Y. S., Tellegen, A., & Dahlstrom, W. G. (2001). *MMPI-2 (Minnesota Multiphasic Personality Inventory-2): Manual for administration, scoring, and interpretation*. Minneapolis. MN: University of Minnesota Press.

Butcher, J. N., Graham, J. R., Williams, C. L., & Ben-Porath, Y. S. (1990). *Development and use of the MMPI-2 Content Scales*. Minneapolis, MN: University of Minnesota Press.

Butcher, J. N., & Han, K. (1995). Development of an MMPI-2 scale to assess the presentation of self in a superlative manner: The S Scale. In J. N. Butcher & C. D. Spielberger (Eds.), *Advances in personality assessment, Vol. 10.* (pp. 25-50). Hillsdale, NJ: Erlbaum.

Butcher, J. N., Williams, C. L., Graham, J. R., Archer, R. P., Tellegen, A., Ben-Porath, Y. S., & Kaemmer, B. (1992). *The Minnesota Multiphasic Personality Inventory-Adolescent (MMPI-A)*. Minneapolis, MN: University of Minnesota Press.

Caldwell, A. B. (2006). Maximal measurement or meaningful measurement: The interpretive challenges of the MMPI-2 restructured clinical (RC) scales. *Journal of Personality Assessment, 87*(2), 193-201.

Clark, L. A. (2005). *Schedule for Nonadaptive and Adaptive personality (SNAP): Manual for administration, scoring, and interpretation*. Minneapolis, MN: University of Minnesota Press.

Clark, L. A., & Watson, D. (2019, March 21). Constructing validity: New developments in creating objective measuring instruments. *Psychological Assessment*. Advance online publication.

Cramer, A. O. J., Waldorp, L. J., van der Maas, H. L. J., & Borsboom, D. (2010). Comorbidity: A network perspective. *Behavioral and Brain Sciences, 33*(2-3), 137-150.

Cronbach, L. J., & Meehl, P. E. (1955). Construct validity in psychological tests. *Psychological Bulletin, 52*(4), 281-302.

Dahlstrom, W. G., & Dahlstrom, L. E. (1980). *Basic readings on the MMPI.* Minneapolis, MN: University of Minnesota Press.

Gough, H. G. (1956). The F minus K dissimulation index for the MMPI. In G. S. Welsh & W. G. Dahlstrom (Eds.), *Basic readings on the MMPI in psychology and medicine* (pp. 321-327). Minneapolis, MN: University of Minnesota Press.

Graham, J. R. (1993). *MMPI-2: Assessing personality and psychopathology* (2nd ed.). New York, NY: Oxford University Press.

Guthrie, G. M. (1956). Common characteristics associated with frequent MMPI profile types. In G. S. Welsh & W. G. Dahlstrom (Eds.), *Basic readings on the MMPI in psychology and medicine* (pp. 145-150). Minneapolis, MN: University of Minnesota Press.

Harkness, A. R. (1992). Fundamental topics in the personality disorders: Candidate trait dimensions from lower regions of the hierarchy. *Psychological Assessment, 4*(2), 251-259.

Harkness, A. R., & McNulty, J. L. (1994). The Personality Psychopathology Five (PSY-5): Issues from the pages of a diagnostic manual instead of a dictionary. In S. Strack & M. Lorr (Eds.), *Differentiating normal and abnormal personality.* (pp. 291-315). New York, NY: Springer.

Harkness, A. R., McNulty, J. L., & Ben-Porath, Y. S. (1995). The Personality Psychopathology Five (PSY-5): Constructs and MMPI-2 scales. *Psychological Assessment, 7*(1), 104-114.

Harris, R. E., & Lingoes, J. C. (1955). *Subscales for the MMPI: An aid to profile interpretation.* Unpublished manuscript, Langley Porter Clinic, University of California.

Hathaway, S. R. (1956). Scales 9 (masculinity-femininity), 6 (paranoia) and 8 (schizophrenia). In G. S. Welsh & W. G. Dahlstrom (Eds.), *Basic readings on the MMPI in psychology and medicine* (pp. 104-111). Minneapolis, MN: University of Minnesota Press.

Hathaway, S. R., & Meehl, P. E. (1956). Psychiatric implications of code types. In G. S. Welsh & W. G. Dahlstrom (Eds.), *Basic readings on the MMPI in psychology and medicine* (pp. 136-144). Minneapolis, MN: University of Minnesota Press.

Jackson, D. N. (1971). The dynamics of structured personality Tests: 1971. *Psychological Review*, 78(3), 229-248.

Koss, M. P., & Butcher, J. N. (1973). A comparison of psychiatric patients' self report with other sources of clinical information. *Journal of Research in Personality, 7*, 225-236.

Lachar, D., & Wrobel, T. A. (1979). Validating clinicians' hunches: Construction of a new MMPI critical item set. *Journal of Consulting and Clinical Psychology, 47*, 277-284.

Lees-Haley, P. R., English, L. T., & Glenn, W. J. (1991). A Fake Bad Scale on the MMPI-2 for personal injury claimants. *Psychological Reports, 68*(1), 203-210.

Livesley, W. J. (2003). Diagnostic dilemmas in classifying personality disorder. In K. A. Phillips, M. B. First, & H. A. Pincus (Eds.), *Advancing DSM: Dilemmas in psychiatric diagnosis* (pp. 153-189). Washington, DC: American Psychiatric Association.

Loevinger, J. (1957). Objective tests as instruments of psychological theory. *Psychological Reports, 3*, 635-694.

McKinley, J. C., Hathaway, S. R., & Meehl, P. E. (1948). The Minnesota Multiphasic Personality Inventory: VI. The K Scale. *Journal of Consulting Psychology, 12*(1), 20-31.

Meehl, P. E. (1945). The dynamics of "structured" personality tests. *Journal of Clinical Psychology, 1*(4), 296-303.

Meehl, P. E. (1954). *Clinical versus statistical prediction.* Minneapolis, MN: University of Minnesota Press.

Millon, T., Millon, C., Roger, D., & Grossman, S. (2009). *Millon Clinical Multiaxial Inventory-III (MCMI-III): Manual.* Bloomington, MN: Pearson.

Morey, L. C. (2007). *Personality Assessment Inventory (PAI): Professional manual.* Lutz, FL: Psychological Assessment Resources.

Morey, L. C., Waugh, M. H., & Blashfield, R. K. (1985). MMPI scales for DSM-III personality disorders: Their derivation and correlates. *Journal of Personality Assessment, 49*(3), 245-251.

Nichols, D. H. (2001). *Essentials of MMPI-2™ assessment.* New York: John Wiley & Sons.

Shedler, J., & Westen, D. (2004). Dimensions of personality pathology: An alternative to the five-factor model of personality. *American Journal of Psychiatry, 161*, 1743-1754.

Skodol, A. E., Clark, L. A., Bender, D. S., Krueger, R. F., Morey, L. C., Verheul, R., ... Oldham, J. M. (2011). Proposed changes in personality and personality disorder assessment and diagnosis for DSM-5 part I: Description and rationale. *Personality Disorders: Theory, Research, and Treatment, 2*(1), 4-22.

Streiner, D. L. (2003). Being inconsistent about consistency: When coefficient alpha does and doesn't matter. *Journal of Personality Assessment, 80*(3), 217-222.

Tellegen, A., & Ben-Porath, Y. S. (1992). The new uniform T scores for the MMPI—2: Rationale, derivation, and appraisal. *Psychological Assessment, 4*(2), 145-155.

Tellegen, A., Ben-Porath, Y. S., McNulty, J. L., Arbisi, P. A., Graham, J. R., & Kaemmer, B. (2003). *The MMPI-2 restructured clinical (RC) scales: Development, validation, and interpretation.* Minneapolis, MN: University of Minnesota Press.

Ward, C. L., Kersh, B. C., & Waxmonsky, J. N. (1998). Factor structure of the paranoia scale of the MMPI-2 in relation to the Harris-Longoes subscales and Comrey factor analysis. *Psychological Assessment, 10*(2), 292-296.

Weed, N. C., Ben-Porath, Y. S., & Butcher, J. N. (1990). Failure of Wiener and Harmon Minnesota Multiphasic Personality Inventory (MMPI) subtle scales as personality descriptors and as validity indicators. *Psychological Assessment: A Journal of Consulting and Clinical Psychology, 2*(3), 281-285.

Welsh, G. S. (1956). Factor dimensions A and R. In G. S. Welsh & W. G. Dahlstrom (Eds.), *Basic readings on the MMPI in psychology and medicine* (pp. 264-281). Minneapolis, MN: University of Minnesota Press.

Welsh, G. S., & Dahlstrom, W. G. (Eds.). (1956). *Basic readings on the MMPI in psychology and medicine.* Minneapolis, MN: University of Minnesota Press.

Widiger, T. A., & Simonsen, E. (2005). Alternative dimensional models of personality disorder: Finding a common ground. *Journal of Personality Disorders, 19*(2), 110-130.

Wiener, D. N. (1948). Subtle and obvious keys for the Minnesota Multiphasic Personality Inventory. *Journal of Consulting Psychology, 12*(3), 164-170.

Wiggins, J. S. (1966). Substantive dimensions of self-report in the MMPI item pool. *Psychological Monographs: General and Applied, 80*(22), 1-42.

Wiggins, J. S., Goldberg, L. R., & Apelbaum, M. (1971). MMPI content scales: Interpretation norms and correlations with other scales. *Journal of Consulting and Clinical Psychology, 37*(3), 403-410.

[95]

MINT–Measuring Integrity.

Purpose: Designed as a "personality-based integrity test" for "making personnel decisions based on candidates' likelihood of demonstrating CWB [counterproductive work behavior]."

Population: Prospective employees.

Publication Date: 2017.

Acronym: MINT.

Scores, 3: Interpersonal Orientation, Task Orientation, Integrity.

Administration: Individual or group.

Price Data: Available from publisher.

Foreign Language Editions: Available in Danish, Estonian, Finnish, Hungarian, Latvian, Lithuanian, Norwegian, Russian, Slovak, Spanish, Swedish, and Thai.

Time: [15] minutes.

Comments: Administered online.

Authors: Assessio (test); Sofia Sjöberg and Anders Sjöberg (technical manual).

Publisher: Assessio [Sweden].

Review of MINT-Measuring Integrity by MATT VASSAR, Clinical Assistant Professor of Psychiatry and Behavioral Sciences, Oklahoma State University Center for Health Sciences, Tulsa, OK, and MICHAEL BIBENS, Ph.D. Student, Oklahoma State University Center for Health Sciences, Tulsa, OK:

DESCRIPTION. MINT-Measuring Integrity (MINT) is designed to evaluate the likelihood that a job candidate will demonstrate counterproductive work behavior (CWB). This test, which was developed in Sweden and is available in 13 languages, is intended for use as a screening tool—ideally in the hiring process—for businesses hiring personnel. MINT is monitored by a trained test administrator who delivers the test on-site or via email to each job applicant. The test comprises 60 items that assess one general factor (Integrity) and two lower-order factors (Task Orientation and Interpersonal Orientation). Integrity consists of three personality dimensions: Conscientiousness, Agreeableness, and Emotional Stability. The MINT is scored using a C-scale format from 0-10, which is separated into three categories: *low* (0-2), *average* (3-6), and *high* (7-10). Integrity is inversely related to CWB. Task Orientation and Interpersonal Orientation C-scores are not placed into these categories; rather, scores from these lower-order factors display the extent to which a candidate applies both attributes in the workplace. All factors are scored independently.

DEVELOPMENT. During development, Emotional Stability was deemed by the authors of the instrument to play a larger role in Integrity than Conscientiousness or Agreeableness. The underlying model therefore places Emotional Stability at the top of the hierarchy, whereas Conscientiousness and Agreeableness are lower-level factors (Markon, Krueger, & Watson, 2005). Initially 206 items were written in Swedish and separated into four categories: Emotional Stability, Extraversion, Agreeableness, and Conscientiousness. Each category contained 50 items, with the exception of Conscientiousness which contained 56 items. The scale was distributed to a representative sample of the Swedish population (N = 650). Three hundred completed questionnaires were returned. Extraversion items (n = 50) were removed in accordance with Ones, Viswesvaran, and Dilchert (2005), who concluded that Extraversion should not be considered as part of a theoretical model of integrity. Items were also removed from Conscientiousness (n = 23), Agreeableness (n = 15), and Emotional Stability (n = 14), leaving a total of 104 items. A qualitative examination of each item ensued by comparing items of corresponding constructs from the Hogan Personality Inventory (Hogan & Hogan, 1997a) and the Hogan Descriptive Scales (Hogan & Hogan, 1997b). Correlations between items and Five-Factor Model (FFM) dimensions on the NEO-PI-R personality inventory were calculated. These calculations excluded 22 items owing to weak correlation with their corresponding FFM dimension, leaving 30 Conscientiousness items, 29 Agreeableness items, and 23 Emotional Stability items. Each item was then correlated with the dimension on the NEO-PI-R to which it belonged theoretically. Twenty-three Conscientiousness, 25 Agreeableness, and 23 Emotional Stability items remained after excluding those based on weak item-to-dimension correlations. Using item response theory, a one-parameter Rasch-model was used to exclude items of similar difficulty and discrimination. After this analysis, additional items were removed to avoid overlapping content and to reach the a priori target of 20 items per scale.

The Norwegian translation comprised 206 items and used the same methodology as that used for the Predicting Job Performance test (Sjöberg, Sjöberg, & Forssén, 2006) adapted at the same time. A total of 537 participants served as a representative sample of the Norwegian population. Each participant was also given the NEO-PI-R. In total, 237 surveys were returned. Items that fulfilled the same criteria as the 60 items in the Swedish version were adopted into the Norwegian translation. The technical manual (2017 edition) does not include information about the development of versions in other languages.

TECHNICAL. The initial norm group comprised 300 participants. Distribution of the norm group by age, sex, and education level closely matched the distribution of the Swedish population in these categories. In October 2011, the norm group was updated to include 22,207 participants and the MINT was expanded to four languages (Swedish, Norwegian, English, and Finnish). In December 2014, the norm group was updated to 124,499 participants and the MINT expanded to 13 languages.

Internal consistency reliability was estimated using an equation that sums the true variance and covariance and divides by total variance. This metric was used instead of coefficient alpha because the MINT was operationalized from a congeneric measurement model. In cases of congeneric models, alpha may be underestimated. Internal consistency estimates were .98 for the composite MINT score (i.e., Integrity), .93 for Interpersonal Orientation, and .94 for Task Orientation. Additional data from the global norm sample suggest internal consistency estimates of .92 for the MINT composite, .89 for Interpersonal Orientation, and .84 for Task Orientation. Test-retest reliability was estimated using two samples: the first, a sample of 97 (72 female; 25 male) masters-level psychology students from Stockholm University (mean age = 23, *SD* = 5); the second, a sample of 129 (91 female; 38 male) Norwegian grocery store workers (mean age = 35, *SD* = 12). For the student sample, test-retest estimates were .85 for the composite MINT score, .80 for Interpersonal Orientation, and .87 for Task Orientation over a 30-day interval. For the grocery worker sample, test-retest estimates were .88 for the composite MINT score, .77 for Interpersonal Orientation, and .75 for Task Orientation over an 8-week interval. Thus, these findings support high internal consistency for both composite and lower-order scale scores and adequate stability over time.

Confirmatory factor analysis was used to evaluate the internal structure of scale scores. A hierarchical model was tested in which the structure of the MINT was operationalized using two indicators for each of three personality dimensions (Emotional Stability, Agreeableness, and Conscientiousness). Interpersonal Orientation and Task Orientation were modeled as lower-level factors. Several goodness-of-fit indices are reported (RMSEA = .065, GFI = .983, TLI = .981, CFI = .991), all within acceptable ranges. Emotional Stability was confirmed as a major component of the Integrity factor, as indicated by factor loadings of .89 and .91. Since the time of initial structural analysis, the test developers have gathered data from 124,499 respondents using the 13 language versions. Multigroup confirmatory factor analysis was conducted to test for measurement invariance across 10 of the 13 language versions and found evidence of stability across versions even in the most restricted model in which equality constraints were imposed on measurement error terms.

Concurrent evidence of validity of MINT scale scores was provided by negative correlation with the Demoralization subscale of the Minnesota Multiphasic Personality Inventory-2 and the Inventory of Interpersonal Problems. Lower-level factors, Interpersonal Orientation and Task Orientation, were found to be correlated with the Antisocial Behavior subscale of the Minnesota Multiphasic Personality Inventory-2 and Job Involvement, a work-related attitudes scale in the hypothesized directions. The MINT was also correlated with portions of the Hogan Development Survey using data collected from the test publisher's Norwegian database, as well as scores from Measuring and Assessing Individual Potential, Matrigma (which measures general cognitive ability using progressive matrices), and ServiceFirst (a measure of service potential) collected from a sample of approximately 200 Norwegian grocery store workers. In general, results indicated correlations in the hypothesized directions; however, some relationships were not statistically significant. The test manual also reports concurrent validity data from a subsample of the grocery worker study from which test-retest reliability was estimated and from a sample of retail employees. Forty-four employees from the grocery store sample were included for analysis, and results suggested that Integrity scores were positively related with job performance (r = .19) and negatively related to CWB (r = -.28), although correlations were low to modest. In a Norwegian retail sample of 68 employees, managerial performance ratings had a low correlation with Integrity (r = .13; rho = .18) and Interpersonal Orientation (r = .24; rho = .33), and no correlation with Task Orientation (r = -.05; rho = -.07), where rho is the estimate after adjusting for measurement error. Additional studies have provided supporting predictive evidence for the validity of MINT scale scores using manager performance ratings and self-reported ratings of job satisfaction and performance in Swedish traffic controllers. MINT scores predicted higher job performance as rated by managers (operational validity coefficient = .32) and by self-report (operational validity coefficient = .67); however, the operational validity coefficient was lower for self-reported job satisfaction (.07). Operational validity estimates of MINT scores with exam grades based on a sample of 79 students from Stockholm University were also lower (.17). Overall, these findings support that the MINT is adequately operationalized and may be used as a predictive tool for relevant employee outcomes.

COMMENTARY. The MINT has extensive psychometric validation. Reliability estimates are satisfactory, and validity estimates are generally good. The internal scale structure adheres to the theoretical model. The scale is available in 13 languages, although some sample sizes for specific languages listed in the test manual were quite small. Additional invariance testing by language will likely continue as the MINT gains popularity. This testing would be a welcome addition. Future invariance testing should consider stratification by gender and occupation type.

SUMMARY. The MINT was designed to assess the likelihood that a job candidate will demonstrate counterproductive work behavior. The test meets its goal of evaluating Integrity, and evidence suggests that it may be useful as a predictive test for counterproductive work behavior prior to hiring a new employee.

REVIEWERS' REFERENCES

Hogan, R., & Hogan, J. (1997a). Hogan Personality Inventory. Tulsa, OK: Hogan Assessment Systems. Swedish version: *Hogans Personlighetsinventorium*. Stockholm, Sweden: Psykologiforlaget AB, 2002.

Hogan, R., & Hogan, J. (1997b). Hogan Development Survey. Tulsa, OK: Hogan Assessment Systems. Swedish version: Hogans Deskriptiva Skalor. Stockholm, Sweden: Psykologiforlaget AB, 2002.

Markon, K. E., Krueger, R. R., & Watson, D. (2005). Delineating the structure of normal and abnormal personality: An integrative hierarchical approach. *Journal of Personality and Social Psychology, 88*, 139-157.

Ones, D. S., Viswesvaran, C., & Dilchert, S. (2005). Personality at work: Raising awareness and correcting misconceptions. *Human Performance, 18*, 389-404.

Sjöberg, A., Sjöberg, S., & Forssén, K. (2006). *Predicting Job Performance manual.* Stockholm, Sweden: Assessio AB.

Review of MINT—Measuring Integrity by CHOCKALINGAM VISWESVARAN, Professor of Psychology, Florida International University, Miami, FL:

DESCRIPTION. MINT—Measuring Integrity (MINT) is designed to assess the potential for counterproductive work behaviors and for selecting from a pool of job applicants employees who are less likely to disrupt the workplace. Integrity assessments have been shown in multiple studies to predict productive and counterproductive behaviors, and meta-analytic cumulation of this literature supports the criterion-related evidence of validity of such assessments (Ones, Viswesvaran, & Schmidt, 1993, 2012). Integrity assessments that rely on items that ask test takers about their past infractions and where the purpose of the items is clear to test takers (i.e., that integrity is being assessed) are referred to as clear-purpose or overt integrity tests. Integrity assessments that rely on items that assess personality traits hypothesized to relate to counterproductive behaviors and where the purpose of the test (i.e., to assess integrity) is not clear are referred to as personality-based integrity tests (Sackett, Burris, & Callahan, 1989). MINT is a personality-based integrity test designed to assess counterproductive work behaviors (CWBs).

A noteworthy feature of MINT is the careful attention paid to the underlying theory in explicating both the Integrity construct and the construct domain of counterproductive behaviors. The authors place Integrity in the personality domain as tapping into Emotional Stability, Agreeableness, and Conscientiousness. In this conceptualization, the overall factor of Integrity does not derive equal contributions from the three personality factors—the greatest contribution comes from Emotional Stability. In addition to the overall score of Integrity, MINT also provides scores for Interpersonal Orientation and Task Orientation. The former reflects the Agreeableness aspects and the latter the Conscientiousness aspect of personality. MINT also is based on a clearly defined model of counterproductive behaviors. The authors used the Sackett and DeVore (2001) model in which CWBs are grouped as those directed toward the organization (CWB-O) and those directed toward individuals (CWB-I). In addition, 11 categories of counterproductive behaviors as identified by Gruys and Sackett (2003) are grouped into either CWB-I or CWB-O.

DEVELOPMENT. The initial item pool for the development of MINT was a set of 206 items written in Swedish with 50 items to assess each of the personality dimensions of Emotional Stability, Agreeableness, and Extraversion and 56 items to measure Conscientiousness. These items along with the Swedish version of the NEO-PI-R were administered to a representative sample of the Swedish population. Of the 650 questionnaires distributed, 300 completed responses were obtained. Of the respondents, 59% were women, and the sample was representative of the population in terms of both age and educational level (although the sample had more respondents with university degree—29%—compared with 16% in the population).

The test authors removed from consideration all Extraversion items (as they were not part of the Integrity construct), and items from the other three factors that were used in another scale to measure job performance. As such, 23 of the Conscientiousness items, 15 of the Agreeableness items and 14 of the Emotional Stability items were removed. This choice is surprising, as the construct of Integrity has been shown to predict not only CWBs but also job performance. A qualitative comparison of the remaining 104 items was done to ensure the items reflected the personality dimension by comparing them to items of that personality dimension from other personality inventories. Correlations were computed between each item and the personality dimension (that the item was supposed to assess) in the NEO-PI-R. Items that correlated weakly or items that correlated with multiple dimensions of the NEO-PI-R were eliminated. This correlational analysis resulted in the retention of 23, 25, and 23 items for the Conscientiousness, Agreeableness and Emotional Stability scales, respectively. A one-parameter Rasch model was used to delete items with similar difficulty as the authors wanted the items to discriminate test takers across a range of scores. Twenty items were retained for each of the three dimensions for a total of 60 items. A confirmatory factor analysis was conducted where an overall Integrity factor loaded on to all three personality dimensions. The CFA also specified two other latent factors—Interpersonal Orientation and Task Orientation, which were paired to Agreeableness and Conscientiousness. A hierarchic nested factor analyses conducted in which the three factors contributed to the overall Integrity factor but the residuals from Agreeableness and Conscientiousness were related to Interpersonal and Task Orientation. The test manual reports acceptable fit indices.

TECHNICAL. The test authors reject coefficient alpha as a suitable measure of internal consistency but employ a congeneric model and report internal consistency coefficients of .98 for the general Integrity factor, and .93 and .94 for the factors of Interpersonal Orientation and Task Orientation, respectively. Although not explicitly stated in the test manual, this reviewer assumes that these estimates are based on the same 300 respondents used to develop the scales. In another study involving 97 students from Stockholm University, the 1-month test-retest reliability coefficients are reported as .85, .80, and .87 for the overall factor, Interpersonal Orientation and Task Orientation, respectively. The manual also reports 8-week test-retest reliability estimates using a sample of 129 employees of a Norwegian grocery chain (using a Norwegian version of the test) of .88, .77, and .75 for the overall Integrity, Interpersonal Orientation, and Task Orientation scores.

Validity evidence is provided in terms of correlations between the three scores generated by MINT (overall Integrity, Interpersonal Orientation, and Task Orientation) and several self-report measures such as the Demoralization and Antisocial behavior scales of the MMPI-2, a measure of job involvement, and two factor scale scores from the Hogan Development Survey. Other personality-based tests of the Five Factor Model of personality and a customer service inventory are also used in the validation studies. The manual reports that a non-significant correlation was found between MINT scores and a measure of general cognitive ability.

Criterion-related evidence of validity is reported on a sample of 47 applicants to the job of rail traffic controller in Sweden. The criterion included (a) the average of operational manager and line manager ratings on 19 items focusing on problem-solving skills, interpersonal skills, and work commitment, (b) self-ratings of performance on a 5-item scale assessing commitment, confidence, and competence, and (c) a measure of job satisfaction. The overall Integrity scores from the MINT correlated .25 with supervisor-rated performance, .48 with self-ratings, and .05 with job satisfaction. In another sample involving 79 students, the overall Integrity scores correlated .11 with grades.

The Norwegian version of the test was validated for both job performance and CWB (both assessed by supervisors). On a sample of 101, the overall Integrity scores correlated .19 with supervisor-rated job performance. On a sample of 44 employees, the coefficient was -.28 for prediction of CWB. Finally, a concurrent validity study with data from 68 warehouse workers and truck drivers in Norway showed a correlation of .13 between MINT Integrity scores and performance ratings.

COMMENTARY. The test manual reports further developments since 2011 when the test was made available in different languages, including English. A table is provided summarizing data collected until December 2014 that indicates more than 124,000 job applicants have taken this test in several languages (e.g., Danish, English, Finnish, Latvian, Lithuanian, Russian, Spanish, Thai). A table summarizes the multigroup measurement equivalence across 10 languages with sufficient sample sizes for a CFA. This reviewer would recommend that a more detailed description of this vastly superior database be given and used as the central piece of the manual (rather than the sample of 300 respondents currently presented).

With data from more than 100,000 job applicants, the test authors should be able to report more detailed analyses of demographic group differences and whether there are Age X Gender interactions as has been found in other integrity tests (cf. Ones & Viswesvaran, 1998). Further, the validity evidence accumulated from this large sample should be incorporated into the test manual.

SUMMARY. Measuring integrity in job applicants is a central piece of personnel selection, and MINT provides a psychometrically sound, construct driven approach to help organizations achieve this objective. Its availability in multiple languages is another asset. The manual, however, should be updated to incorporate all available empirical data.

REVIEWER'S REFERENCES

Gruys, M. L., & Sackett, P. R. (2003). Investigating the dimensionality of counterproductive work behavior. *International Journal of Selection and Assessment, 11*, 30-42.

Ones, D. S., & Viswesvaran, C. (1998). Gender, age, and race differences on overt integrity tests: Results across four large-scale job applicant data sets. *Journal of Applied Psychology, 83*, 35-42.

Ones, D. S., Viswesvaran, C., & Schmidt, F. L. (1993). Comprehensive meta-analysis of integrity test validities: Findings and implications for personnel selection and theories of job performance. *Journal of Applied Psychology, 78*, 679-703.

Ones, D. S., Viswesvaran, C., & Schmidt, F. L. (2012). Integrity tests predict counterproductive work behaviors and job performance well: Comment on Van Iddekinge, Roth, Raymark, and Odle-Dusseau (2012). *Journal of Applied Psychology, 97*, 537-542.

Sackett, P. R., Burris, L. R., & Callahan, C. (1989). Integrity testing for personnel selection: An update. *Personnel Psychology, 42*, 491-529.

Sackett, P. R., & Devore, C. J. (2001). Counterproductive behaviors at work. In N. Anderson, D. S. Ones, H. K. Sinangil, & C. Viswesvaran (Eds.), *Handbook of industrial, work & organizational psychology* (Vol 1., pp. 145-164). London, England: Sage.

[96]

Multidimensional Emotional Intelligence Assessment.

Purpose: Designed as a "self-report measure of that part of emotional intelligence conceived as a set of relatively stable and distinct personality-type traits bearing on the perception, control, and use of emotions in the self and others."
Population: Ages 16 and older.
Publication Date: 2006.
Acronym: MEIA.
Scores, 11: Recognition of Emotion in the Self, Regulation of Emotion in the Self, Recognition of Emotion in Others, Regulation of Emotion in Others, Nonverbal Emotional Expression, Empathy, Intuition vs. Reason, Creative Thinking, Mood Redirected Attention, Motivating Emotions, Infrequency (validity scale).
Administration: Individual or group.
Price Data, 2020: $70 per technical manual (Version 1.2.1; 2006, 69 pages), 2 test administrations, account set up, and technical support; $35 per basic report including online administration, scoring, and report.
Time: Approximately 20 minutes for completion.
Comments: Administered and scored online.
Authors: Robert P. Tett, Alvin Wang, and Kevin E. Fox.
Publisher: SIGMA Assessment Systems, Inc.

a) MULTIDIMENSIONAL EMOTIONAL INTELLIGENCE ASSESSMENT-WORKPLACE.
Purpose: Designed as "a parallel measure [of the MEIA] ... for use in work settings."
Acronym: MEIA-W.
Price Data: $55 per online scoring including technical manual (2006, 69 pages), 1 test administration, account set up, and technical support.

Review of the Multidimensional Emotional Intelligence Assessment and Multidimensional Emotional Intelligence Assessment–Workplace by JEAN POWELL KIRNAN, Professor of Psychology, The College of New Jersey, Ewing, NJ:

DESCRIPTION. The Multidimensional Emotional Intelligence Assessment (MEIA) and the Multidimensional Emotional Intelligence Assessment–Workplace (MEIA-W) are self-report measures of emotional intelligence (EI). The MEIA is designed for use in research or counseling, whereas the MEIA-W is intended for use in the workplace. The MEIA and MEIA-W yield 10 subscores, six of which represent central facets of EI: Recognition of Emotion in Self, Regulation of Emotion in Self, Recognition of Emotion in Others, Regulation of Emotion in Others, Nonverbal Emotional Expression, and Empathy. The remaining four subscores represent proximal EI outcomes of Intuition vs. Reason, Creative Thinking, Mood Redirected Attention, and Motivating Emotions, which can also be viewed as applications or utilizations of EI.

Using a 6-point Likert scale, respondents indicate the degree to which they agree with each of several statements (150 for MEIA; 144 for MEIA-W). The items are straightforward and written clearly with many being reverse worded, an effective technique to minimize response acquiescence.

The score report for the MEIA includes a general description of EI as well as scores for the respondent. EI scores are presented as percentiles (combined, male, and female), along with a one-sentence description and a color-coded "range." The three range designations are: *develop,* printed in red and indicating a weak tendency; *enhance,* appearing in orange and representing a moderate tendency; and *refine,* printed in green and indicating a strong tendency. In addition to describing the importance of each subscore, the report addresses over and underutilization. Laypeople often assume that the more EI the better, when, in fact, too much regulation or recognition of emotions can be problematic.

The score report for the MEIA-W is much more detailed (20 pages) than for the MEIA (3 pages) as each of the 10 components has a full-page interpretation with percentile (combined), range, fuller description of the component, over and underutilization, and suggestions for action steps. Both reports emphasize that no measure is completely accurate and that the MEIA/MEIA-W should never be used alone but rather combined with other information (interviews, behavioral assessments, personality measures) for interpretation and decision making. This warning is prudent for any self-report measure that, by its nature, assumes the respondent is able and willing to answer honestly. Only the MEIA has an additional Infrequency score designed to identify haphazard responding. The use of an infrequency score or other indicator of the accuracy of responses is common in self-report measures, and it is unclear why the MEIA-W does not include this additional scale.

The MEIA-W has 144 items, but a reference in the Brief Interpretation Guide for MEIA-W (p. 1) states that there are 122 items. The sample score report (p. 5) states, "The MEIA-W is developed specifically for the workplace setting or context. As a context-specific measure it captures workplace tendencies more accurately than a general measure." However, a comparison of the items reveals that they are very similar with minor wording changes such as using "co-worker" instead of "people." Aside from the smaller number of items, reflecting the lack of the Infrequency scale, the differences between the two measures are minimal.

The purpose of the MEIA-W is cited as "self-development," and it is recommended that test takers share the results with someone who is familiar with their workplace situation. This person might be an HR representative, supervisor, co-worker, or career coach. The test publisher appropriately cautions that the MEIA-W only can be used in the selection or promotion process following local validation of the measure using relevant performance outcomes.

DEVELOPMENT. The research on EI, while abundant, is plagued by the large number of competing theoretical models and the subsequent challenge of defining and measuring the construct (Roberts, Schulze, & MacCann, 2008). A common delineation is the view of EI as an ability rather than a disposition. The test publisher specifically states that the MEIA/MEIA-W are intended to measure the personality domain and that ability should be measured via other assessments. Indeed, most measures consider EI as a personality construct rather than a cognitive dimension.

The test manual makes reference to several published studies on the development of the MEIA. One of these articles (Tett, Fox, & Wang, 2005) provides detail on the reason for the development of the scale and how it differs from existing measures of EI. This information would be useful to include in the test manual as there are many EI measures available. In brief, the MEIA was developed specifically to provide a measure for each of the 10 components of EI identified by Salovey and Mayer (1990), to improve subscale reliability and distinctiveness, to address issues of social desirability in item selection, and to expand the range of personality traits employed to demonstrate convergent and discriminant validity.

The MEIA was developed over several years using both rational and empirical methods. Construction began with the development of items that represented the constructs defined in Salovey and Mayer's model (1990). An initial pool of 307 items was developed by a team of psychology professors and subsequently peer-reviewed. Items were retained only if they were correctly categorized by subscale. The resulting measure included 122 items that were combined with a social desirability scale and an infrequency scale and tested on a sample of 158 American college students. Data from this sample were analyzed for item-total correlations, item–scale correlations, alpha coefficients, and item-item correlations. The instrument was correlated with scales from the Jackson Personality Inventory–Revised (JPI-R) as well as a desirability measure. Strong support was found for convergent validity, and moderate support was found for divergent validity leading to additional revisions. New items were written, combined with items that survived the first series of analyses, and tested on a sample of 191 American college students. Similar analyses were conducted, and general support found, for the construct validity of the MEIA. According to the test manual, additional studies led to minor refinements and a final measure with 12 items in each of the 10 subscales; however, the current instrument contains 150 items. Even after allowing for additional Infrequency scale items, it is unclear how to reconcile this discrepancy.

There is little information in the test materials on the development of the MEIA-W. The test manual notes that the MEIA-W is a "close duplicate of the original MEIA" as the items are "simple work-related versions of the original items" (manual, p. 45). A comparison of the two measures confirms that there is little difference.

TECHNICAL. Raw scores on the MEIA are converted to standard scores using normative data, but the source and composition of this normative sample are unclear. In the introduction to the test manual (p. 1), reference is made to a normative sample consisting of 332 American college students; yet, later in the manual (p. 9) the normative group is described as 3,448 participants, which was reduced to 3,258 after removing those with high Infrequency scores. Of the 2,641 participants who reported their gender, the sample was predominantly female (65%). Of the 2,179 who reported race/ethnicity, 84% were Caucasian, with only about 3% reporting as Black and 3% as Hispanic. The average age of the sample was 32 years, and respondents represented a wide range of industries. No information is provided as to when or how the sample was recruited, raising concerns for representativeness in terms of education and socioeconomic status (an especially concerning issue if the survey was completed online). A comparison of mean scores for men and women revealed differences on four of the subscales with men scoring higher on Regulation of Emotion in Self and women scoring higher on Empathy, Nonverbal Emotional Expression, and Intuition vs. Reason. The test publishers consider these differences to be modest and suggest the use of the combined norms to determine percentile ranks when interpreting scores. No information is reported regarding other group differences, which would be difficult to evaluate, given the small sample sizes of ethnic minorities.

Reliability was examined using both test-retest and internal consistency methods. A sample of 68 college students completed the MEIA twice over a 4- to 6-week period. Moderate evidence of consistency over time was found with correlation coefficients ranging from .67 to .88. The test publishers suggest that this is acceptable for personality measures, which is broadly true, but .67 is rather weak. Moderate evidence of internal consistency was reported with alpha coefficients and the entire normative sample of 3,448. This analysis yielded coefficients ranging from .74 to .91. Estimates of internal consistency generally yield stronger coefficients than test-retest measures. Although acceptable, internal consistency estimates in the mid .70s might be improved upon.

The validity evidence for the MEIA draws from content, criterion, and construct validity methods. Content evidence was the focus of the original item development. Items were specifically written to represent the 10 components of EI as delineated by Salovey and Mayer (1990). Items were categorized by peer item writers, and only those that were correctly classified into the intended components were retained. Criterion-related evidence of validity was demonstrated via the MEIA's relationship with standardized measures of satisfaction and adaptability with supportive findings. Consideration might be given to testing additional criteria such as biographical outcomes and performance measures to strengthen criterion validity evidence.

Construct evidence of validity was demonstrated during the development of the MEIA by correlating the 10 subscales with dimensions measured in the JPI-R. Additional studies correlated the MEIA with the Big Five personality dimensions and the Hogan Personality Inventory (HPI). The data provide broad support for the constructs measured by the MEIA. Additionally, a principal components analysis revealed meaningful clusters of subscale scores and supported a three-factor structure of self-orientation, emotional sharing, and other orientation.

The test manual reports "preliminary norms" (p. 45) for the MEIA-W, but the sample used is unclear, being referred to as "over 600 working adults" (p. 45) and later as "1,750 people" (p. 46). The sample of 1,750 is further described as roughly equal in terms of male and female, average age of 40 years, mostly Caucasian (84%), and from a variety of industries. Similar to the description of the MEIA normative sample, there is no information on how the sample was recruited. A comparison of mean scores for men and women revealed similar patterns as noted above for the MEIA. Again, the test publishers recommend the use of the combined norms to determine percentile ranks. This is the only normative reference in the score report for the MEIA-W to avoid the use of sex-based norms in the workplace.

Content validity evidence was not demonstrated specifically for the MEIA-W but is assumed to extend from the MEIA as the items in the MEIA-W are "simple word changes" relative to the original MEIA items (manual, p. 47). Construct validity evidence was demonstrated in a sample of 50 employees from two worksites by correlating MEIA-W scores with subscores from the Hogan Personality Inventory–Short Form and the Personnel Assessment Form. The analyses generally support construct validity of the test scores and their usage and demonstrated similar patterns found with the MEIA. Criterion evidence of validity was provided from a study comparing the MEIA-W scores of 116 workers from two different organizations with their supervisor's ratings on an array of performance criteria. The subscores of Regulation of Emotion in Others and Nonverbal Emotional Expression demonstrated the strongest relationships with performance.

Additional analyses were conducted to determine the incremental and structural validity of the MEIA-W. The MEIA-W was shown to add uniquely to the prediction of several performance outcomes relative to measures of cognitive ability and various personality traits, albeit within a small sample (N = 50). The component structure of the MEIA-W was tested on a sample of manufacturing workers, publishing workers, and MBA students. The three-factor solution noted above for the MEIA was replicated here, although there were some unexplained differences when comparing the student subsample with workers.

COMMENTARY. The MEIA/MEIA-W have a sound foundation in EI theory and demonstrate strong evidence of reliability and validity. Similar to existing measures of EI, the MEIA/MEIA-W assess awareness and regulation of emotions in self and others. Unlike other measures, social desirability was controlled for in the development of the MEIA/MEIA-W, and the measures include supplemental subscales that assess the four proximal outcomes. Alternative measures of EI often have a provision for "other" report in addition to self-report, which the MEIA/MEIA-W do not provide (Consortium for Research on Emotional Intelligence in Organizations, 2018). Given the recommendation that the MEIA-W results should be reviewed with a trusted colleague or mentor, this might be an area of future development. The MEIA-W looks like a workplace measure (face validity) and has demonstrated criterion validity with workplace outcomes. However, the need for a separate measure of EI is not clear. Would the MEIA be equally effective? A statistical comparison of scores on the two measures should be undertaken to answer this question.

SUMMARY. Both the MEIA and the MEIA-W provide evidence of sound psychometric properties. The MEIA is appropriate for research and counseling where it would be part of a larger assessment that includes other measures. Although the MEIA-W is valid for use in the workplace, there is little evidence to suggest that it provides different results from the MEIA. The lack of development information for the MEIA-W and mere wording changes between the two measures suggest that the MEIA-W, while effective, may be redundant with the MEIA.

REVIEWER'S REFERENCES

Consortium for Research on Emotional Intelligence in Organizations. (2018). Emotional intelligence measures. Retrieved from http://www.eiconsortium.org/measures/measures.html

Roberts, R. D., Schulze, R., & MacCann, C. (2008). The measurement of emotional intelligence: A decade of progress? In G. J. Boyle, G. Matthews, & D. H. Saklofske (Eds.), *The SAGE handbook of personality theory and assessment* (pp. 461-482). Los Angeles, CA: SAGE.

Salovey, P., & Mayer, J. D. (1990). Emotional intelligence. *Imagination, cognition and personality*, *9*(3), 185-211.

Tett, R. P., Fox, K. E., & Wang, A. (2005). Development and validation of a self-report measure of emotional intelligence as a multidimensional trait domain. *Personality and Social Psychology Bulletin*, *31*(7), 859-888.

Review of the Multidimensional Emotional Intelligence Assessment and the Multidimensional Emotional Intelligence Assessment—Workplace by MARK E. SIBICKY, Professor of Psychology, Marietta College, Marietta, OH:

DESCRIPTION. The Multidimensional Emotional Intelligence Assessment (MEIA) is a 150-item self-report multidimensional personality trait measure of emotional intelligence (EI). The MEIA developers define EI as "intraindividual consistency and interindividual uniqueness in the capacity and willingness to perceive, understand, regulate, and express emotions in the self and others" (manual, p. 4). The assessment consists of 10 subscales, six of which comprise core factors that load onto three broader fundamental areas: (a) emotional sharing, represented by the core factors of Empathy and Nonverbal Emotional Expression; (b) other orientation, with core factors of Recognition of Emotions in Others and Regulation of Emotion in Others; and (c) self-orientation, consisting of the core factors of Recognition of Emotion in Self and Regulation of Emotion in Self. The remaining four scales of the MEIA measure proximal EI outcomes that are conceived of as preferences and applications of EI in terms of life goals and decisions. Proximal EI outcomes are represented by four scales: Intuition vs. Reason, Creative Thinking, Mood Redirected Attention, and Motivating Expression.

Test administration requires respondents (age 16 or older) to log into a website and respond to self-descriptive items on a 6-point (*strongly disagree* to *strongly agree*) Likert rating scale. Test completion requires approximately 20 minutes, after which the test administrator can obtain a score report. Score reporting is given in percentiles for each of the six core and four proximal scales. A table provides additional score interpretation information, including labeling the respondent's scores as being in the *develop* range (weak to low tendency), *enhance* range (moderate tendency), or *refine* range (strong to high tendency). The MEIA technical manual provides detailed background information and research on MEIA scale construction and measurement properties. The developers suggest the primary use of the MEIA would be for researchers looking for multiple-personality-dimensional assessments of EI rather than seeking a single overall score of respondent EI (something more common among "ability" measures of EI).

Given the widespread popularity of EI, it is not surprising there is also a workplace version of the MEIA, known as the MEIA-W. The MEIA-W is slightly shorter (i.e., 144 items), and items have been re-worded for a workplace setting. For example, items ask about respondents' emotions regarding their job and co-worker interactions. The MEIA-W test manual contains additional information about score interpretation and suggestions about using MEIA-W scores for employee development and improvement.

DEVELOPMENT. For decades, EI has been of interest to both researchers and those wishing to apply the concept to real-world settings (e.g., work, school). Yet, debate continues over how EI should be conceptualized and measured. For the most part, EI measures fall into two categories (Zeidner, Roberts, & Matthews, 2008), one of which conceptualizes EI as a mental-emotional ability and most often uses performance measures to produce a single global EI score. The second category takes a personality trait perspective toward EI and uses self-report measures common to personality trait measures. Interestingly, the developers of the MEIA based the MEIA on Salovey and Mayer's (1990) original ability model of EI, but constructed the MEIA using a multidimensional personality trait approach. According to the test developers, this approach not only lends itself to self-report measurement, but also allows the MEIA to capture both core personality traits and some ability aspects of EI.

TECHNICAL. The MEIA was normed on a sample of 3,258 people (930 males, 1,711 females, 617 unreported). The average age of respondents was 32; most who reported race/ethnicity were White (84%), and members of the group were employed in a variety of jobs. Internal consistency estimates for MEIA scale items were moderately high to high, with reported alpha coefficients ranging from .74 to .91. Test-retest reliability was assessed over a 4- to 6-week period with a smaller sample of college students (N = 68). Correlation coefficients for the 10 scales ranged from .67 to .88. Slight differences in responding emerged between men and women; however, the test developers noted similar response patterns and suggest the MEIA results can be used for both sexes.

An important issue for any self-report measure involves respondents distorting or faking responses in socially desirable ways. The developers of the MEIA/MEIA-W attempted to minimize response distortions by avoiding positive and negative language in favor of neutral wording. More importantly, they attempted to account for social desirability effects by using the Marlowe-Crowne scale of social desirability while conducting validity studies. Although they found some evidence for the role of social desirability in responses, it seems these effects are no greater than those found in other self-report trait measures of EI.

A second issue is predictive and incremental validity. Gardner and Qualter (2010) investigated the predictive and incremental validity of several trait measures of EI, including the MEIA. They found the Trait Emotional Intelligence Questionnaire (TEIQue; Petrides, 2009) to be a slightly better predictor of the psychological criteria used in the study (e.g., loneliness, alcoholism, life satisfaction) but concluded the MEIA was adequate and equal to other trait measures of EI.

The MEIA-W was normed on a sample of 1,750 respondents (651 males, 603 females, 496 unreported) with an average age of 40 and representing a diverse range of occupations. The MEIA-W demonstrates psychometric properties similar to those of the MEIA. Because the MEIA-W is intended for use in the workplace, a key question is how well it predicts worker performance. The test manual describes a validity study that compared supervisor performance ratings of 116 workers and their MEIA-W scores. The findings are not particularly strong, with the most consistent predictors of supervisory ratings being the subscale scores of Regulation of Emotion in Others, and Nonverbal Emotional Expression. The test developers themselves suggest the need for additional research on the predictive validity of the MEIA-W, especially in the context of specific occupations and organizational contexts. Additional research is also needed that investigates faking or other forms of response distortions on the MEIA-W, which, unlike the MEIA, does not include the Infrequency scale designed to detect random response sets.

COMMENTARY. For many years, EI has been a topic of great interest and considerable debate, both among researchers and those seeking to apply EI in real-world settings. Yet any debate has not hindered the development of EI measures, and today the MEIA/MEIA-W exist in a crowded field of EI measures, both ability- and trait-based. The strengths of the MEIA/MEIA-W are (a) easy test administration and scoring; (b) a test manual providing substantial background information on scale construction, reliability and validity data, and information about score interpretation; and (c) both measures were developed from a conceptual theory of EI, and the measures were constructed using established methods common to self-report personality trait tests. Overall, the psychometric properties of the MEIA are adequate and within the range of other measures of EI. Although perhaps not as popular among researchers as the TEIQue (Petrides, 2009), the MEIA appears equal to or better than some other measures of EI (see Siegling, Saklofske, & Petrides, 2015).

Although the MEIA-W shares many of the qualities of the MEIA, caution is recommended when applying MEIA-W scores, or any measure of EI in the workplace. More than a decade ago, Zeidner, Roberts, and Matthews (2008) voiced concern over the use and sometimes misuse of EI measures. These concerns still ring true today and include the need for more research demonstrating (a) long-term reliability and predictive performance validity of EI measures when used for a specific occupation or organizational context, (b) the possible susceptibility of EI trait measures to response distortion and faking, and (c) the need to demonstrate the effectiveness of EI training programs or self-reflection feedback (e.g., MEIA-W scoring manual) intended for EI improvement.

SUMMARY. The MEIA and MEIA-W provide an easy-to-use self-report assessment of EI using a multidimensional personality trait approach (although conceptually based on an ability model of EI). The manuals for the MEIA and MEIA-W provide clear and detailed information on test construction and score interpretation. Although the MEIA is one of many trait EI measures, there is research suggesting it could benefit researchers looking for a multidimensional (i.e., trait and ability) measure of EI. Given a persistent lack of agreement in the field over whether EI measures can significantly predict worker performance within specific occupations, caution is recommended in using the MEIA-W (or any trait measure of EI) in the workplace.

REVIEWER'S REFERENCES

Gardner, K. J., & Qualter, P. (2010). Concurrent and incremental validity of three trait emotional intelligence measures. *Australian Journal of Psychology, 62*, 5-13.

Petrides, K. V. (2009). *Technical manual for the Trait Emotional Intelligence Questionnaires (TEIQue)*. London, England: London Psychometric Laboratory.

Salovey, P., & Mayer, J. D. (1990). Emotional intelligence. *Imagination, Cognition and Personality, 9*, 185-211.

Siegling, A. B., Saklofske, D. H., & Petrides, K. V. (2015). Measures of ability and trait emotional intelligence. In G. J. Boyle, D. H. Saklofske, & G. Matthews (Eds.), *Measures of personality and social psychological constructs* (pp. 381-414). London, England: Academic Press.

Zeidner, M., Roberts, R. D., & Matthews, G. (2008). The science of emotional intelligence: Current consensus and controversies. *European Psychologist, 13*(1), 64-78.

[97]

Multidimensional Everyday Memory Ratings for Youth.

Purpose: Designed to assess "essential aspects of real-world memory abilities, including everyday memory and learning ... aspects of executive functioning that impact memory, as well as working memory and attention."
Population: Ages 5-21.
Publication Date: 2017.
Acronym: MEMRY.
Scores, 7: Learning, Daily Memory, Executive/Working Memory, Everyday Memory Index, plus 3 validity scales (Inconsistency, Maximizing, Implausibility).
Administration: Individual or group.
Forms, 3: Parent and Teacher Forms (Ages 5-19); Self-Report Form (Ages 9-21).
Price Data, 2020: $334 per kit including professional manual (130 pages), fast guide, 25 of each form (parent, teacher, self-report), and 25 of each scoring summary form (parent, teacher, self-report); $110 per professional manual and fast guide; $55 per 25 forms (specify parent, teacher, or self-report); $30 per 25 scoring summary forms (specify parent, teacher, or self-report).
Time: (5) minutes per form.
Comments: Administered via paper and pencil or online.
Authors: Elisabeth M. S. Sherman and Brian L. Brooks.
Publisher: Psychological Assessment Resources, Inc.

Review of the Multidimensional Everyday Memory Ratings for Youth by DENISE E. MARICLE, Professor, Doctoral Program in School Psychology, and AMY SKINNER, Doctoral Candidate in School Psychology, Texas Woman's University, Denton, TX:

DESCRIPTION. The Multidimensional Everyday Memory Ratings for Youth (MEMRY) is a rating scale designed to measure everyday memory in children, adolescents, and young adults. The MEMRY was intended to be a quick, reliable screening tool for clinicians to evaluate real-world functional memory deficits. Parent, teacher, and self-report forms are used to measure everyday memory and learning and certain aspects of executive functioning, working memory, and attention. The MEMRY was co-normed with the Child and Adolescent Memory Profile (ChAMP; Sherman & Brooks, 2015; see reviews by Maricle, Caldwell, & Spurgin, 2017; and Jarratt, 2017) and the Memory Validity Profile (MVP; Sherman & Brooks, 2015; see 91, this volume).

The MEMRY parent and teacher forms are designed for ages 5 to 19 years, and the self-report form can be completed by 9- to 21-year-old individuals. This measure can be used with typically developing youth as well as those who demonstrate developmental, memory, or learning problems.

The MEMRY kit consists of the Professional Manual, a Fast Guide, self-scoring protocols (parent, teacher, and self-report), and scoring summary forms for each type of protocol (e.g., parent, teacher, self). The parent and teacher protocols consist of 31 statements to which the respondent answers *rarely or never* (R), *sometimes* (S), *often* (O), and *almost always* (A). The self-report form consists of 30 statements requiring similar Likert ratings.

The MEMRY consists of three clinical scales (Learning, Daily Memory, and Executive/Working Memory), three validity scales (Inconsistency, Maximizing, and Implausibility), and a single overall composite index of memory (Everyday Memory Index). The Learning scale assesses the ability to encode and retain information necessary for learning under repeated learning or repeated practice expectations. The Daily Memory scale provides information about memory for discrete aspects of visual and auditory memory in everyday life, as well as recall of remote events, names of people, and names of things. The Executive/Working Memory scale is a measure of problems with attentional and executive components of memory such as working memory, concentration, memory organization, and prospective memory. The validity scales were designed to flag protocols that are likely to reflect inconsistent, exaggerated, or implausible responses. The Inconsistency scale indicates the degree to which items endorsed in a particular manner by individuals comprising the standardization sample were endorsed similarly by the rater. The scale attempts to identify erratic response patterns due to carelessness, inattention, or random responding. The Maximizing scale is intended to identify severe symptomology that may indicate a tendency to over report or exaggerate symptoms. The Implausibility scale identifies raters who endorse atypical symptoms not normally seen in children with or without clinical conditions. It was designed to identify feigning, falsification, or careless/random responding. The composite, the Everyday Memory Index, provides an estimate of overall memory problems in daily life.

Administration of the MEMRY takes approximately 5 minutes for each form. The forms are equivalent to approximately a third-grade reading level. The MEMRY can be administered either online or with paper and pencil. The online administration is through a link emailed from the test publisher's online assessment platform. All rating forms should be administered for the child in order to reveal areas of agreement or disagreement amongst the raters. For the paper version, once the rating form has been filled out, the clinician tears off the perforated strips along the top of the form and peels away the answer sheet, which allows the clinician to view the scoring sheet. This sheet is used to calculate the raw scores for the Learning, Daily Memory, and Executive/Working Memory scales. The numbers on the scoring sheet correspond to the answers given by the rater. For example, 1 corresponds to *rarely or never* and 4 corresponds to *almost always*. The item scores in each column are summed and then entered into the boxes at the bottom of the columns. T Scores and percentile ranks can be obtained using conversion tables provided in appendices in the test manual. The online version is scored using the test publisher's web platform. Additionally, items from the paper form can be entered easily into the system for scoring. A score report is generated that delineates scores for the clinical and validity scales and Everyday Memory Index as well as scale discrepancies and a profile of the clinical scores.

DEVELOPMENT. The goal in the development of the MEMRY was to provide clinicians with a practical yet easy-to-use screening tool that would be relevant to everyday functioning. This measure was developed via a multistep process including a review of scientific literature on memory. Pilot testing was conducted on an identical set of 82 parent and teacher items and 74 self-report items. The self-report items were similar to those of the parent and teacher items except the wording was modified to reflect first-person language. This national pilot testing included 149 parent, 104 teacher, and 147 self-report cases. An adequate representation of each demographic group (age, gender, and race/ethnicity) was sought to ensure a strong representation of the current population. Multiple statistical analyses (descriptive statistics, item-total correlations, and alpha coefficients) were conducted on the pilot instrument. Ultimately, on both the parent and teacher form, 65 items were retained, 12 items were deleted, and five new items were added. This resulted in a 70-item form for standardization. The self-report form saw the most revision, with 34 items retained, four items removed, 20 items revised, and 16 new items added. This final self-report form effectively mirrored the 70-item form of the parent and teacher versions. Following standardization of this version of the MEMRY, the final clinical item pool (reflecting the current version of the measure) was selected using classical test theory (CTT) and Rasch analyses. The test manual reports that items were examined using item discrimination techniques such as item-total correlations and Rasch infit mean squares. Items meeting minimum criteria for both (i.e., $r > .30$; mean square values ≤ 1.2) were retained. In all, 33 items were retained for the parent and self-report forms and 32 items for the teacher version. An exploratory factor analysis was then conducted to assist with the final selection of clinical items. A three-factor solution accounted for 52% of the variance in the parent form, 64% of the variance in the teacher form, and 47% of the variance in the self-report form. Items that loaded on a single factor with a loading greater than .40 were retained, resulting in 26 clinical items on the parent and teacher forms and 25 clinical items on the self-report form.

TECHNICAL. It is important to note that the versions of the parent, teacher, and self-report forms that were standardized were the 70-item revised pilot measures and not the final 30-31 item versions of the test. A national sample was collected from 32 states. Participants were targeted based on age, gender, and race/ethnicity to ensure a sample representative of the U.S. population. The parent sample consisted of 1,080 parents of children ages 5 to 19, the teacher sample consisted of 450 teachers of students between the ages of 5 and 19, and the self-report sample consisted of 845 youth ages 9 to 21. The test authors used analysis of raw score distributions across ages in the standardization sample to establish four age groups (ages 5-7, 8-11, 12-15 and 16-19 years) for the parent and teacher forms. Three age groups were established for the self-report form (9-11, 12-15, 16-21). A series of ANOVAs was conducted on each sample to examine the effect of demographic characteristics such as age, gender, ethnicity, geographic region, and parental education. Statistically significant effects were found for region suggesting fewer representative cases from the Northeast and Midwest for parent and self-report samples; however, region accounted for only a small percentage of the variance of the scores. It does not appear that further standardization was completed on the final (30+ item) versions of the MEMRY that were published.

The test manual reports internal consistency, test-retest stability, percent agreement on retest, and effects of repeat administration on test scores in support of reliability. Reliability analyses were conducted on the standardization sample and a clinical sample consisting of children with various clinical diagnoses. Internal consistency refers to the consistency of the items within a test, and high coefficients represent more homogenous measures. Tables in the test manual report internal consistency coefficients by form and age group for the MEMRY scales and index. Alpha coefficients for the self-report form for the three scales and the composite using the all ages group fell in the moderately high range at .86 (Learning), .85 (Daily Memory), .85 (Executive/Working Memory), and .93 (Everyday Memory Index). When examined by age levels and the three different respondent forms, alpha coefficients were more variable as one would expect. For example, across ages and forms the coefficients for the Daily Memory scale ranged from .68 to .92; across all ages for the parent form, coefficients ranged from .71 (Daily Memory) to .93 (Everyday Memory Index). Similar variation was seen in the clinical sample with the most significant concern for these analyses being the sample sizes for the various clinical groups (n = 16-35). Test-retest reliability reflects the stability of performance over time. Test-retest reliability was assessed in two ways: test-retest correlations and percent agreement for clinical classification (i.e., having a T score in the same score range at Time 1 and Time 2). The test-retest analysis included 34 parent, 34 teacher, and 39 self-report respondents. Reliability coefficients across an approximately two-week interval ranged from .70 to .95 varying by respondent and scale, with the teacher form showing the strongest reliability in the test-retest scenario. Across all three forms, percent agreement for clinical classification between the two test administrations was 87%-97%.

The test manual reports construct, criterion, and concurrent evidence of validity as a means of establishing validity of MEMRY scores and their uses. The results of intercorrelations and exploratory factor analysis were used to support the construct validity of the MEMRY. All intercorrelations among the scales were statistically significant ($p <$ .01) and substantial in magnitude, ranging from .43 to .94 across all forms and samples (standardization and clinical). The test manual is somewhat unclear about which version of the test was subjected to analyses. Convergent and discriminant evidence of validity was based on a subset of the standardization sample who concurrently completed relevant measures of memory, executive functions, and academic skills. Correlations with objective measures of memory (i.e., Child and Adolescent Memory Profile [Sherman & Brooks, 2015a] and the Test of Memory and Learning, Second Edition [Reynolds & Voress, 2007]) were generally significant but low and negative or showed inverse relationships. Similar negative or inverse correlations were found with the California Verbal Learning Test Children's Version (Delis, Kramer, Kaplan, & Ober, 1994) and the Rey Complex Figure Test and Recognition Trial (Meyers & Meyers, 1995). Although one might expect some degree of convergence with objective measures of memory, the test authors posit that the MEMRY measures different aspects of memory than those assessed by objective measures of memory. Significant and positive correlations were found between the MEMRY parent form and the Behavior Rating Inventory of Executive Function (BRIEF; Gioia, Isquith, Guy, & Kenworthy, 2000) parent form with a large correlation between the MEMRY Everyday Memory Index and the BRIEF Global Executive Composite (r = .78). The test authors attribute these moderate to high correlation coefficients between the BRIEF and the MEMRY as being the result of both measures assessing aspects of executive functions.

COMMENTARY. The MEMRY rating scale is a quick, efficient screener of everyday behavioral manifestations related to memory functioning that can assist clinicians in determining an appropriate plan for further testing of memory abilities. It is best used in a limited capacity to screen for further assessment needs. Although the test authors are to be applauded for their desire to create a rating scale that can effectively screen for real-world functional memory problems, the MEMRY has some serious flaws. Information regarding the scale's development, standardization, reliability, and validity is provided, but the procedures were difficult for these reviewers to follow, as explanations were incomplete, and often the information was confusing. For example, exactly what version was standardized? From the information provided it would seem that it was the revised pilot version of the test and not the final version of the test that has actually been published. This issue trickles down into the concerns regarding reliability and validity. What version of the test were the reliability and validity statistics completed on? It appears to these reviewers that reliability and validity studies were conducted on the standardization sample, which utilizes a different version of the MEMRY. If so, then we do not really know the reliability and validity evidence of this final published version of the test. [Editor's note: The test publisher clarified that all reliability and validity analyses were conducted using the final, published versions of the measure.] Finally, regardless of which version the validity studies were conducted with, there is some concern with moderate to high positive correlations with a similar rating scale measuring executive functions, and negative or inverse correlations with scales measuring objective memory abilities. Perhaps what the MEMRY is actually measuring is the behavioral manifestation of executive functioning, which may or may not be related to memory functions. These psychometric concerns lead to a more theoretical concern regarding whether a small number of behavioral statements completed by others or through self-report adequately measures everyday memory functioning.

SUMMARY. The MEMRY was designed to be a quick, reliable screening tool to measure memory in children, adolescents, and young adults. Parent, teacher, and self-report ratings of the behavioral manifestations of memory functions are used to measure everyday memory. The test authors are to be applauded for their desire to create a rating scale that can effectively screen for real-world functional memory problems. Unfortunately, the MEMRY has some serious flaws. Given the limitations of the MEMRY, it should be used only in a limited capacity as a screening tool.

REVIEWERS' REFERENCES

Delis, D. C., Kramer, J. H., Kaplan, E., & Ober, B. A. (1994). California Verbal Learning Test-Children's Version. San Antonio, TX: Pearson.

Jarratt, K. P. (2017). [Test review of Child and Adolescent Memory Profile]. In J. F. Carlson, K. F. Geisinger, & J. L. Jonson (Eds.), *The twentieth mental measurements yearbook* (pp. 144-147). Lincoln, NE: Buros Center for Testing.

Maricle, D., Caldwell, K., & Spurgin, A. (2017). [Test review of Child and Adolescent Memory Profile]. In J. F. Carlson, K. F. Geisinger, & J. L. Jonson (Eds.), *The twentieth mental measurements yearbook* (pp. 141-144). Lincoln, NE: Buros Center for Testing.

Meyers, J. E., & Meyers, K. R. (1995). Rey Complex Figure Test and Recognition Trial. Lutz, FL: Psychological Assessment Resources.

Reynolds, C. R., & Voress, J. K. (2007). Test of Memory and Learning, Second Edition. Austin, TX: PRO-ED.

Sherman, E. M. S., & Brooks, B. L. (2015a). Child and Adolescent Memory Profile. Lutz, FL: Psychological Assessment Resources.

Sherman, E. M. S., & Brooks, B. L. (2015b). Memory Validity Profile. Lutz, FL: Psychological Assessment Resources.

Review of the Multidimensional Everyday Memory Ratings for Youth by JEREMY R. SULLIVAN, Professor of Educational Psychology, University of Texas at San Antonio, San Antonio, TX:

DESCRIPTION. The Multidimensional Everyday Memory Ratings for Youth (MEMRY) was designed to provide behavioral ratings of memory skills that have relevance for everyday functioning (i.e., ecological validity). The MEMRY includes parent-report (31 items), teacher-report (31 items), and self-report (30 items) forms to allow for multisource assessment. These behavior ratings are meant to complement information gained through more performance-based memory tasks, and may be especially useful in assessing the functional impact of memory problems in school, home, and social contexts. The test authors note that in addition to incorporating the MEMRY into a comprehensive psychoeducational evaluation, the test has utility for screening purposes to determine whether more thorough memory assessment is necessary. The MEMRY is part of a larger family of memory scales that also includes the Child and Adolescent Memory Profile (Sherman & Brooks, 2015a) and the Memory Validity Profile (Sherman & Brooks, 2015b). The parent- and teacher-report forms are normed for ages 5 to 19 years, and the self-report form can be used with individuals ages 9 to 21 years.

The MEMRY can be administered using traditional paper forms or online via the test publisher's web platform, and can be administered either individually or in a group setting. Test materials include the professional manual, rating forms, scoring summary forms, and a Fast Guide that briefly summarizes administration and scoring procedures. The rating forms are straightforward and efficient, with instructions for respondents on one side and the items on the other side. Following completion, the rating forms can be opened by the examiner and scored using a carbonless scoring sheet. The scoring summary forms provide instructions and tables to facilitate scoring and interpretation by the examiner, including analyzing scale discrepancies and using the Reliable Change Index to detect statistically significant differences in scores across repeated administrations (e.g., to monitor progress or assess effectiveness of an intervention).

The items describe various problems with memory, learning, and attention, and the respondent is asked to rate the frequency of these behaviors using a 4-point scale (*rarely or never, sometimes, often, almost always*). Scores on the MEMRY include the Everyday Memory Index as the total score, which is the sum of the three clinical scales: Learning (capacity to encode, retain, and recall information), Daily Memory (visual and auditory memory of people, objects, and events encountered in everyday life), and Executive/Working Memory (problems with attention, organization, and executive function). As noted in the test manual, "The capacity to assess executive functioning and working memory is an important component that allows clinicians to differentiate between problems caused by learning and memory failures versus failures due to problems with working memory and attention, one of the most common referral questions for clinicians assessing children and adolescents" (p. 11). Higher scores on the clinical scales represent more problems compared to the normative sample. T scores of 65 and higher are interpreted as clinically elevated, whereas T scores below 65 are within the normal range. Validity scales on the MEMRY include Inconsistency (based on discrepancies within pairs of similar items), Maximizing (endorsement of unusually severe symptoms or deficits), and Implausibility (endorsement of unusually severe symptoms or deficits that would be extremely rare even in clinical populations).

The test manual begins with a discussion of why memory is an important construct to assess in children and adolescents who are experiencing learning or behavior problems, followed by a review of important terms and concepts related to memory assessment. The manual includes a chapter on interpretation and recommendations based on MEMRY scores (although the test authors note that more research is necessary to establish the validity of connecting MEMRY scores to these specific recommendations) and a chapter with four case examples to illustrate the interpretation process. Appendices contain the norms tables necessary for converting raw scores to T scores and percentile ranks, in addition to standard error of measurement values needed to calculate 90% confidence intervals. Overall, the test manual seems to provide sufficient guidance on administration, scoring, and interpretation. The step-by-step interpretation guidelines will be especially welcomed by novice examiners, particularly the guidelines related to the validity scales and understanding possible reasons for agreement/disagreement across different raters.

DEVELOPMENT. Item development was based on a review of the literature on memory, the test authors' clinical experience, and expert review. The authors attempted to develop items specifically related to six different aspects of memory: "auditory, visual, general, procedural, prospective, and working memory/executive" (manual, p. 31). Initial items were pilot tested, and items were retained, revised, eliminated, or created based on item characteristics. This process resulted in 70-item versions of all three forms (parent, teacher, and self) for standardization. Following the gathering of standardization data, item discrimination indices were used to reduce the parent and self-report forms to 33 items, and the teacher form to 32 items. Exploratory factor analyses were conducted with these remaining items. Across all three forms of the test, factor analyses supported a three-factor solution, which the test authors labeled Learning, Daily Memory, and Executive/Working Memory. Once items were removed based on loadings below .40 and loading on multiple factors, the parent and teacher forms included 26 clinical items and the self-report form included 25 clinical items. As expected, the clinical scale score distributions are positively skewed, given the items' focus on problematic behaviors and deficits.

The remaining items on the final versions of the rating scales contribute to the validity scales. The test manual includes a separate chapter on the development of the validity scales. For example, a sample of youth instructed to feign memory problems produced MEMRY T scores significantly higher than those produced by a matched control group, and this pattern was replicated with parent ratings. The Maximizing and Implausibility scales were able to distinguish a significant proportion of these feigned protocols. Similarly, the Inconsistency scale was largely successful at identifying MEMRY profiles that were randomly generated by the test authors.

TECHNICAL.

Standardization. Standardization data were gathered from parents (*n* = 1,080 for the parent form), teachers (*n* = 450 for the teacher form), and youth (*n* = 845 for the self-report form) from 32 states. The test manual provides detailed tables describing these samples. In describing the parent sample, the test manual states that "although some statistically significant effects were found, age, gender, ethnicity, and parental education accounted for a very small percent of the variance in MEMRY scores and had no meaningful effect on the normative scores" (p. 32). Similar statements are included in the descriptions of the teacher and self-report samples, but specific results of statistical tests are not provided to allow readers to reach their own conclusions about the influence of demographic variables. In general, demographic characteristics of the sample appear to adequately match those of the U.S. Census. Based on the age groups sampled and the raw score distributions in these standardization samples, the parent and teacher forms are normed for ages 5 to 19 (with norms grouped by ages 5 to 7, 8 to 11, 12 to 15, and 16 to 19) and the self-report form is normed for ages 9 to 21 (with norms grouped by ages 9 to 11, 12 to 15, and 16 to 21). The test manual describes how the authors used continuous norming procedures to develop the normative tables used to convert raw scores to T scores.

Reliability. Score reliability was assessed with internal consistency and test-retest reliability analyses. With regard to internal consistency, alpha coefficients are provided for different age groupings among the parents, teachers, and youth in the standardization sample, and also for various clinical samples (e.g., attention-deficit/hyperactivity disorder [ADHD], autism spectrum disorder, learning disabilities, traumatic brain injury). With all age groups combined in the standardization sample, alpha coefficients for the Learning, Daily Memory, and Executive/Working Memory scales ranged from .71 to .92 for the parent form, .90 to .94 for the teacher form, and .85 to .86 for the self-report form. Coefficients for the Everyday Memory Index were consistently in the .90s for all age groups and forms. Generally speaking, alpha coefficients for the clinical samples were similar to those for the standardization sample.

Test-retest reliability was assessed using test-retest correlation coefficients and stability of clinical classification (i.e., scoring in the same T score range on two different administrations). The test-retest sample included 34 parents, 34 teachers, and 39 youth from the standardization sample, and the average interval between administrations was approximately two weeks (although there was a rather wide range, from 8 to 36 days). Across the three forms, test-retest correlation coefficients ranged from .70 to .93 for the subscales and from .86 to .95 for the Everyday Memory Index. Using the Everyday Memory Index, percent agreement for clinical classification ranged from 87.2% to 95.0% across forms, with similar results for the subscales. Thus, youth rated as functioning in the clinically elevated range on the first administration tended to stay in that range upon second administration (although it should be noted that there were only two categories used in this analysis: T scores below 65 and T scores of 65 or greater).

Validity. The test manual describes several types of evidence of validity to support potential uses and interpretations of the MEMRY; this review will be selective due to space constraints. Construct evidence of validity is provided by examining intercorrelations among MEMRY scales and results of factor analysis. For example, correlations among the scales were classified as medium to large, and all were statistically significant. Intercorrelation coefficients and factor loadings were quite similar across the standardization and clinical samples, and exploratory factor analyses supported the three-factor structure of the MEMRY items.

Concurrent evidence of validity is provided by correlations of MEMRY scores with scores on rating scales designed to measure similar constructs in addition to scores on performance-based measures of memory, intellectual ability, and academic functioning. All correlations with the Test of Memory and Learning, Second Edition (TOMAL-2) index scores were in the negative direction, as would be predicted. For both the parent and self-report forms, the strongest correlation coefficients with the TOMAL-2 scales were found for the Learning scale, followed by the Everyday Memory Index. Smaller and mostly nonsignificant correlation coefficients were observed for the Daily Memory and Executive/Working Memory scales. It should be noted that the sample sizes for these correlations were small (29 for the parent form and 22 for the self-report form). Interestingly, scores on the Executive/Working Memory scale did not correlate significantly with any scores on the California Verbal Learning Test, Children's Version or the Rey Complex Figure Test, although, again, these coefficients were based on small sample sizes (ranging from 22 to 30). With regard to correlations with the Wechsler Intelligence Scale for Children-Fourth Edition (WISC-IV) index scores, across parent, teacher, and self-report forms, Learning was the scale most consistently significantly correlated with the WISC-IV scores. The Executive/Working Memory scale was not significantly correlated with WISC-IV Working Memory for any of the MEMRY forms. When correlating MEMRY scores with scores on the Behavior Rating Inventory of Executive Function (BRIEF) parent form, all three of the MEMRY scales and the Everyday Memory Index were consistently and significantly correlated with the Metacognition Index and the Global Executive Composite scores of the BRIEF. Further, MEMRY scales generally were correlated with appropriate BRIEF subscales (e.g., Daily Memory was significantly correlated with Plan/Organize, Executive/Working Memory was significantly correlated with Working Memory).

Criterion evidence of validity is provided by clinical group studies, showing youth with particular diagnoses were rated as presenting more impairment on MEMRY scales compared to a matched group from the standardization sample. As one example, for the ADHD comparisons, youth in the ADHD group were rated as significantly more impaired on all four MEMRY scales than youth in the control group, and this pattern was observed across parent, teacher, and self-report forms. Similar results were found with autism spectrum disorder, math disability, language disability, and intellectual disability groups.

COMMENTARY. The MEMRY is a brief and straightforward rating scale, and appears to be easy to administer and score. The items seem to measure behaviors that have relevance to everyday functioning, and the multiple forms allow for multisource assessment. The validity scales also offer the possibility of detecting response patterns that would suggest caution when interpreting clinical scale scores.

A common criticism of newly published tests involves small sample sizes for reliability and validity analyses. This criticism applies somewhat to the MEMRY, as some of the clinical samples used for the internal consistency analyses were quite small (although it is still useful to see that alpha coefficients were generally similar across different clinical groups), as were some of the samples used in the validity analyses. Similarly, the concurrent evidence of validity was somewhat mixed when compared to the other sources of reliability and validity evidence. On the other hand, the test manual generally does an excellent job of describing the demographic characteristics of the various samples used in these analyses, and the test authors transparently note the limitations associated with small sample sizes.

Lastly, although the test authors do provide a list of possible interventions based on scores on the different MEMRY scales, not much evidence is presented to suggest that scores can be used to develop particular interventions. The recommended interventions are welcome, but most potential users of the MEMRY would probably appreciate a more empirically based discussion of interventions (the test authors acknowledge that more research is required to evaluate these possible interventions).

SUMMARY. The MEMRY is likely to be of interest to school psychologists, clinical psychologists, and neuropsychologists given its focus on functional impact across multiple settings/raters. In light of the brevity and relatively narrow scope of the MEMRY scales, this test may be most appropriate when the examiner needs to efficiently gather behavioral information on a limited set of constructs. If the examiner wants to explore functioning on a broader range of constructs related to memory, learning, and executive function, more comprehensive rating scales will be necessary, such as the Behavior Rating Inventory of Executive Function, Second Edition (Gioia, Isquith, Guy, & Kenworthy, 2015), Comprehensive Executive Function Inventory (Naglieri & Goldstein, 2013), or Children's Psychological Processes Scale (Dehn, 2012). When used in conjunction with more performance-based measures, the MEMRY may be most useful in helping to differentiate memory problems from other behavioral or learning problems, and in describing how deficits identified with performance-based measures may manifest in everyday settings/contexts.

REVIEWER'S REFERENCES

Dehn, M. J. (2012). Children's Psychological Processes Scale. Stoddard, WI: Schoolhouse Educational Services.

Gioia, G. A., Isquith, P. K., Guy, S. C., & Kenworthy, L. (2015). Behavior Rating Inventory of Executive Function, Second Edition. Lutz, FL: Psychological Assessment Resources.

Naglieri, J. A., & Goldstein, S. (2013). Comprehensive Executive Function Inventory. North Tonawanda, NY: Multi-Health Systems.

Sherman, E. M. S., & Brooks, B. L. (2015a). Child and Adolescent Memory Profile. Lutz, FL: Psychological Assessment Resources.

Sherman, E. M. S., & Brooks, B. L. (2015b). Memory Validity Profile. Lutz, FL: Psychological Assessment Resources.

[98]

Multiple Auditory Processing Assessment-2.

Purpose: Designed to "provide information about auditory processing skills in individuals with reported functional listening difficulties."

Population: Ages 7-14.

Publication Dates: 2007-2018.

Acronym: MAPA-2.

Scores, 15: Monaural-Selective Auditory Attention Test, Speech in Noise for Children (SINCA), Tap Test, Pitch Pattern Test, Dichotic Digits, Competing Sentences, Duration Pattern Test (supplemental), Gap Detection Test (supplemental), Dichotic Advantage (supplemental), Monaural Domain, Temporal Domain, Binaural Domain, Overall Score, SINCA Estimated Signal-to-Noise Ratio, Gap Detection Estimated Gap Threshold.

Administration: Individual.

Price Data, 2020: $215 per kit including administration manual (2018, 122 pages), 25 records forms, administration CD, and 25 Scale of Auditory Behaviors forms; $80 per manual; $75 per administration CD; $45 per 25 record forms; $15 per 25 Scale of Auditory Behaviors forms.

Time: Approximately 30 minutes for administration and 5-10 minutes for scoring.

Comments: Includes Scale of Auditory Behaviors, a rating scale completed by parents and teachers to assess frequently reported listening-related behaviors.

Authors: Ronald L. Schow, J. Anthony Seikel, Jeff E. Brockett, and Mary M. Whitaker.

Publisher: Academic Therapy Publications.

Review of the Multiple Auditory Processing Assessment–2 by DAVID P. HURFORD, Director of the Center for Research, Evaluation and Awareness of Dyslexia, and Professor, Psychology and Counseling, Pittsburg State University, Pittsburg, KS:

DESCRIPTION. The Multiple Auditory Processing Assessment—2 (MAPA-2) was designed to evaluate children ages 7-0 through 14-11 years who are suspected of having auditory processing difficulties. An auditory processing disorder (ADP) is present when an individual with normal hearing thresholds and at least average intelligence levels has difficulties involving listening skills.

Best practices indicate that the evaluation of APD should include a functional approach that addresses the individual's tested listening abilities and gathers information regarding the situations in which these listening difficulties occur. The MAPA-2 meets these demands and comprises subtests that tap the three most commonly used domains for assessment: monaural low-redundancy speech, auditory temporal processing, and dichotic speech. It also gathers information regarding the child's auditory behaviors via the Scale of Auditory Behaviors (SAB) questionnaire. The parent/guardian, teacher, speech and language pathologist, or audiologist completes the SAB, providing information concerning the child's listening skills, learning abilities, attentional capacity, and organizational skills in various situations.

The MAPA-2 consists of the following subtests within the following domains: Monaural Domain consisting of the Monaural-Selective Auditory Attention Test (MSAAT) and the Speech in Noise for Children (SINCA) subtest, Temporal Domain consisting of the Tap Test and the Pitch Pattern Test, and Binaural Domain consisting of the Dichotic Digits and Competing Sentences subtests. Two supplemental subtests, Duration Pattern Test and Gap Detection Test, are provided as well as a strategy for examining the child's Dichotic Advantage. The diotic condition is supplemental to the Dichotic Digits subtest and is administered only if the Dichotic Advantage score is desired.

Administration of the MAPA-2 typically is completed within approximately 30 minutes. The test authors recommend that the MAPA-2 not be administered more than once within a 4- to 6-month period. Exceptions to this guideline include verification of potential changes in listening skills or modifications to medications. The record form has sections for demographic information and raw scores, scaled scores, percentile ranks, and confidence intervals for subtests, domains, and the Overall score.

The subtests, along with their brief instructions and scoring rules, are contained within the record form. All of the stimulus materials for the MAPA-2 are provided via a CD. Information concerning when to begin each track is provided for each subtest. If the MAPA-2 is not administered within a sound booth, headphones are required. The test authors recommend the use of any Koss model headphones with a flat response curve.

DEVELOPMENT. The MAPA consisted of five subtests assessing three domains, three supplementary subtests, and the SAB. The MAPA-2 includes six subtests assessing three domains. There are two supplemental subtests in addition to the diotic condition that can be used to calculate the Dichotic Advantage score.

The MAPA-2 was standardized with 748 children and adolescents ages 7-0 to 14-11 from 27 states. The sample was consistent with the demographics of the United States in terms of gender, ethnicity, Hispanic origin, parent education, region, type of community, and disability. The sample had a larger percentage of children who had specific language impairment than the national average (7.49% vs. 2.70%) and a smaller percentage of children with auditory processing disorder (1.74% vs. about 5.0%). To be included in the norming sample, children must have passed an auditory threshold test examining frequencies within the range of speech.

The SAB consists of 12 items and was standardized using 716 members of the MAPA-2 normative sample. It consists of questions examining the observation of difficulties in listening, auditory issues, learning, or attention. The response format includes five Likert scale alternatives ranging from *frequent* to *never*. The SAB produces a total raw score that can be converted to a scaled score, standard score, and percentile rank. Confidence intervals are provided by age.

TECHNICAL. Reliability was assessed with internal consistency and temporal stability (test-retest), as well as examination of standard errors of measurement. Internal consistency was evaluated with alpha coefficients for subtests, domains, and Overall score by age level. Alpha coefficients by age ranged from .40 to .95. Averaged across ages, alpha values were .59 to .93 for subtests, .73 to .93 for domains, and .92 for the Overall score. Of the 64 alpha coefficients reported for subtests, 22 were below an acceptable level (.70). Of the low coefficients 14 were reported for the MSAAT and the SINCA, and three of the four lowest alpha coefficients were reported for the Gap Detection Test for ages 11 through 14 years. As a result, the test authors recommend providing confidence intervals for the MSAAT and SINCA subtests and the Monaural Domain to which they contribute.

Test-retest reliability was evaluated by assessing 33 children between 13 and 22 days (average of 16 days) after the first administration. Correlation coefficients corrected for range restriction ranged from .57 to .87 for subtests. Coefficients for domains and the Overall score ranged from .82 to .98. The test authors cite Hopkins (2002) to support their conclusion that the test-retest correlations are acceptable; however, test-retest correlation coefficients less than .70 are generally considered to be questionable. These values notwithstanding, the children in the test-retest study performed significantly better on the second administration for half of the MAPA-2 subtests.

Lastly, reliability was assessed by examining the standard errors of measurement (*SEMs*) for each subtest by age. The test authors report the *SEM* for the scaled and standard scores. Estimating the *SEM* from the raw score data reported in the test manual, the *SEMs* for the raw scores and the standard scores were not appreciably different and were both acceptable.

The case for reliability for the MAPA-2 is sufficient with the exception of the MSAAT and SINCA subtests. The test authors suggest reporting only confidence intervals for these two subtests.

Examination of internal consistency of the SAB resulted in alpha coefficients that ranged from .92 to .97 with an average of .95. Interrater reliability results indicated that the average standard score for parents was 100.3 and the average standard score for professionals was 103.8, a difference that is statistically significant ($p < .001$). The correlation coefficient for the interrater reliability estimate was .67, which is generally considered a relatively weak relationship for interrater reliability. In this reviewer's opinion, it would have been useful to present raw score means as well as standard score means.

Evidence of validity for MAPA-2 test scores and their uses was assessed with attention to content, convergent, and construct source. The MAPA-2 includes mechanisms that have been used for decades to evaluate auditory processing. The subtests are also aligned with the recommendations of the American Speech-Language-Hearing Association and the American Academy of Audiology to evaluate the presence of APD. As a result, the subtests used in the MAPA-2 are well established measures for evaluating auditory processing.

Convergent evidence of validity was examined by comparing subtest performance on the MAPA-2 with subtests from the TAPS-4: A Language Processing Skills Assessment (TAPS-4; see 165, this volume) with 172 children between the ages of 7-0 and 14-11. The TAPS-4 evaluates phonological processing, auditory memory, and listening comprehension. Corrected correlation coefficients between the Overall and domain scores ranged from .32 to .92. The weakest linkage between the MAPA-2 and TAPS-4 domains were for the Monaural Domain and the Listening Comprehension composite. This finding is not surprising given that the TAPS-4 subtests that contribute to the Listening Comprehension composite evaluate the participant's ability to process oral directions and to comprehend oral language without background noise whereas the subtests that contribute to the Monaural Domain of the MAPA-2 include information with competing auditory stimulation. In addition, the mean differences between standard scores of the two tests were generally quite small with a range between 0.00 and 3.06 and an average of 1.09. The comparisons that were statistically significant were small and likely to be of no practical significance.

Construct evidence of validity was examined using age differentiation, group differentiation, and confirmatory factor analysis. Age differentiation was examined by correlating subtest performance and age for the 748 children in the normative sample. The skills assessed with the MAPA-2 should become stronger with age, resulting in strong, positive correlations. Although the reported correlations were positive, many were relatively weak. The correlations ranged from .24 to .61. Correlations of the three domain scores and the Overall score with age were stronger (i.e., Monaural = .57, Temporal = .50, Binaural = .58, Overall = .65).

One way to further evidence construct validity is to examine potential differences between groups of children who should theoretically perform differently on measures of auditory processing due to their group characteristics. Children with learning disabilities (n = 29), specific language impairment (n = 40), auditory processing disorder (n = 14), and attention-deficit hyperactivity disorder (ADHD; n = 41) were matched with an equal number of children who did not have diagnoses. Theoretically, the matched sample should perform at or nearly at the standardized average, which was generally the case. The only group to perform significantly poorer on the Monaural Domain than its matched counterpart was the APD group. All of the diagnostic groups performed significantly poorer than their matched groups on the Temporal Domain except for the ADHD group, which was also the case for the Binaural Domain and the Overall score. The ADHD group performed similarly to its matched group on the Monaural and Temporal Domains and the Overall score; however, there are discrepancies between the reporting of the ADHD group's data in the test manual. The test authors state that the ADHD group performed significantly worse than their matched group on the Binaural Domain, but the tabular data presented in the manual suggest the opposite. [Editor's note: The test publisher advised the Buros Center for Testing that the means and standard deviations in the tabular data referenced here were reversed for the ADHD group and the matched sample. The test publisher confirmed that the ADHD group performed significantly worse than the matched sample.]

Exploratory factor analysis examines the correlations, known as loadings, between the variables of a test and the factors to which they contribute. Variables that load on a factor together define the nature of the factor. The exploratory factor analysis resulted in three factors with each of the variables loading well on their factors. For the Monaural Domain, the MSAAT and SINCA loadings were .48 and .71, respectively, with the other subtest loadings ranging from .06 to .19. For the Temporal Domain, the Tap and Pitch Pattern loadings were .63 and .68, respectively, with the other subtest loadings ranging from .05 to .44. For the Binaural Domain, the Dichotic Digits and Competing Sentences loadings were .51 and .77, respectively, with the other subtest loadings ranging from .04 to .19. The exploratory factor analysis supported the theoretical relationship between the subtests and their domains.

Confirmatory factor analysis examines the appropriateness of the fit of the theoretical framework underlying the MAPA-2 (Monaural, Temporal, and Binaural Domains) and the actual data collected using the MAPA-2. The results indicated a strong fit as the Bentler comparative fit index, which should be above 0.95, was 0.97. In addition, the root mean square error of approximation was .07, and acceptable levels range between .05 and .08. Lastly, a chi-square analysis produced significant results ($p < .001$).

Validity evidence regarding the SAB was evaluated with content validity, convergent validity, and construct validity. The items on the SAB are consistent with the behaviors often reported in children with APD. Exploratory factor analysis resulted in loadings of .67 to .88 on a single factor. Convergent validity was examined by comparing the results of the SAB with the MAPA-2. The corrected correlation coefficients between the SAB and the MAPA-2 Monaural Domain, Temporal Domain, Binaural Domain, and Overall Scores were .10, .25, .37, and .45, respectively, which are generally relatively to very weak. Even though the correlation coefficients are relatively weak, it would be anticipated that they would be given the nature and purpose of the two instruments. The SAB was also examined in terms of potential group differences. Children with learning disabilities (n = 22), specific language impairment (n = 33), APD (n = 11), and ADHD (n = 40) were matched to an equal number of children who did not have diagnoses. All diagnosis groups performed significantly differently than their matched counterparts. The results were reported with standard scores rather than raw scores, which this reviewer would have found more illuminating.

COMMENTARY. The MAPA-2 provides raw scores, scaled scores, domain standard scores, confidence intervals, percentile ranks, and an Overall score. In addition, estimated Signal-to-Noise Ratio, Dichotic Advantage, and Estimated Gap Threshold can be calculated if the appropriate supplementary subtests are administered.

The test manual is clearly written and provides adequate information regarding the nature of the subtests and how to administer them. In addition, there is adequate information regarding the nature of raw scores, subtest scaled scores, domain and Overall standard scores, confidence intervals, and percentile ranks. The conversion of raw scores to scaled scores for each subtest is straightforward and nicely explained. The appendices also provide information regarding the nature of differences between subtests so that adequate comparisons can be made.

The stimulus materials for the MAPA-2 are all provided on a prerecorded compact disc. The clarity and presentation of the stimuli is very good.

One of the difficulties with the original version of this test (MAPA) was its inconsistency. That problem might have been lessened, but the MAPA-2's reliability is still less than desirable. Several of the subtests are very challenging and require not only good listening skills, but also very good attentional capacity. The challenging nature of these subtests will generate performance that is likely variable, leading to inconsistency within subtests and relatively poor internal consistency. This is precisely what was reflected by the alpha coefficients. Validity estimates were also lower than expected, but this is likely due to the issues reported with reliability. The exploratory and confirmatory factor analyses provided solid evidence of validity.

SUMMARY. The MAPA-2 is an evaluation instrument designed to evaluate auditory processing skills in children ages 7-0 through 14-11 years who are suspected of having auditory processing difficulties. The MAPA-2 comprises six subtests that contribute to three domains and an Overall score. There are also two supplementary subtests that allow for the calculation of the Dichotic Advantage score. The MAPA-2 provides scaled scores, confidence intervals, and percentile ranks for each subtest, domain, and the Overall score. The MAPA-2 has only one form, and the test authors recommend that the MAPA-2 not be re-administered any earlier than a 4- to 6-month interval. The psychometric properties of the MAPA-2 appear adequate, with some only marginally so.

REVIEWER'S REFERENCE

Hopkins, W. G. (2002). A scale of magnitudes for effect statistics. In *A New View of Statistics*. Retrieved from http://sportsci.org/resource/stats/effectmag.html

Review of the Multiple Auditory Processing Assessment–2 by ELLEN L. JACOBS, Director, Reading and Speech Clinic, Baker City, OR:

DESCRIPTION. The Multiple Auditory Processing Assessment–2 (MAPA-2) is a standardized test designed to measure auditory processing and listening skills in children and adolescents ages 7-14. The test is individually administered via CD by a trained professional and can be used in a clinical audiometry environment or by using headphones and an audio player. With the inclusion of eight different subtests in three domains (Monaural, Temporal, Binaural) and a 12-item parent- or teacher-completed questionnaire of listening behaviors, it meets the criteria for a comprehensive assessment of auditory processing recommended by the American Speech-Language-Hearing Association (ASHA, 2005) and the American Academy of Audiology (AAA, 2010). Also, a single subtest or domain of MAPA-2 can be administered as a screener or to document progress over time.

The Monaural Domain consists of two subtests that assess the individual's ability to use low-redundancy information. For the Monaural-Selective Auditory Attention Test, the individual repeats a list of monosyllabic words heard, first without competition, and second, while a competing high-interest story is presented in the same ear. For Speech in Noise for Children (SINCA), the examinee repeats pairs of monosyllabic words heard while steady background pink noise plays in the same ear at progressively decreasing signal-to-noise ratios.

The Temporal Domain includes two subtests that evaluate the individual's ability to use acoustic information over time. On the Tap Test, the examinee reports the number of taps heard when a series of rapidly presented tapping noises is played in both ears. Pitch Pattern requires the individual to report what is heard when a series of four high and low tones is presented at different rates and patterns to both ears.

The Binaural Domain consists of two subtests that assess the individual's ability to use unique information presented to each ear simultaneously. Dichotic Digits requires the individual, after hearing a set of six digits presented in both ears, to repeat all digits in any order. The digits can be presented under two different conditions, dichotic and diotic. On Competing Sentences, the individual repeats both sentences heard when a different sentence is presented in each ear concurrently.

Two supplemental subtests are available for testing skills in the temporal area. For Duration Pattern, the individual reports the pattern heard after a series of four short and long tones is presented in different patterns to both ears. For Gap Detection, the individual reports the number of clicks heard (one or two) after hearing a series of click pairs with randomly ordered intrastimulus intervals.

The full MAPA-2 can be administered in 30-40 minutes. Testing procedures and examiner qualifications are clearly described, and scoring is easy and straightforward. Raw scores are reported as scaled scores and percentile ranks for subtests and as standard scores and percentile ranks for the domains and the Overall score. Additional qualitative analyses are provided: SINCA Estimated Signal-to-Noise Ratio estimates the amount of background noise the individual can locate, Dichotic Advantage determines whether the examinee demonstrates an expected dichotic advantage, and Gap Detection Estimated Gap Threshold determines the shortest time interval in which an individual can hear two consecutively presented tones. Significant changes in scores over time can be documented with the reliable change index.

The Scale of Auditory Behaviors (SAB) consists of 12 items to be rated by a parent and by a professional who knows the examinee well. Items are scored on a 5-point Likert scale indicating the frequency with which problem auditory behaviors are observed. SAB raw scores are converted to scaled scores and percentile ranks.

DEVELOPMENT. In response to the need for a standardized testing tool that meets the ASHA and AAA guidelines for screening and evaluating auditory processing disorder (APD), more than 25 years of extensive research went into test development. The research yielded three beta versions of MAPA (Domitz & Schow, 2000); the first published version, called MAPA Version 1.0 (Schow, Seikel, Brockett, & Whitaker, 2007); and, finally, the MAPA-2. MAPA Version 1.0 included five subtests across the three domains, three supplementary tests, and the SAB. Each of the five tests was examined in at least one factor analytic study that demonstrated its loading on one of the three domains.

In developing the MAPA-2, an extensive review process resulted in the decision to revise the measure and to add content. Changes were made to improve test-retest reliability of the SINCA, add a way to analyze the Dichotic Advantage, improve the structure of the Dichotic Digits subtest, revise the scoring on the Tap and Gap Detection subtests, and update instructions for both MAPA-2 and the SAB.

TECHNICAL. The norming sample for MAPA-2 consisted of 748 children and adolescents ages 7 years 0 months to 14 years 11 months. Standardization took place at 51 sites in 27 states across the United States. The sample's distribution of parent education/socioeconomic status, gender, ethnic representation, and disorder/impairment was similar to that of the United States population according to 2010 Census data. The sample included 109 individuals who represented one or more of the following disability status categories: specific learning disability/dyslexia, attention-deficit hyperactivity disorder, APD, and specific language impairment. Thirteen of the 109 were in the APD category.

The age distribution of the normative sample is presented in 1-year intervals. The recommended criterion of at least 100 participants in each subgroup within the sample (McCauley & Swisher, 1984, as cited in Friberg & McNamara, 2010) is met for the 7- and 8-year-old groups only. It is nearly met for the other age groups, which all have at least 90 participants except the 14-year-old group, which has 78 participants. Raw score to scaled score conversions are provided for all MAPA-2 subtests in 6-month intervals for ages 7-0 through 10-11 and in 12-month intervals for ages 11-0 through 14-11. Dividing the 1-year-interval age groups in two effectively reduces the sample size for each subgroup in ages 7-0 through 10-11.

Reported alpha coefficients overall suggest strong evidence for internal consistency of MAPA-2. Average coefficients across ages ranged from .73 to .93 for the domains and the Overall score. Although the majority were above an acceptable range, 22 of the 64 alpha coefficients for individual ages at the subtest level fell below .70. Thus, the test authors stress the importance of using confidence intervals when reporting and interpreting subtest results.

Temporal stability was evaluated with a sample of 33 children who were re-tested by the same examiner between 13 and 22 days after the first test administration. Test-retest correlation coefficients ranged from .82 to .98 for the domain and Overall scores. Significant increases in scores occurred in four subtests, two domains, and in the Overall score on the second administration of the test. Therefore, the test authors emphasize the importance of waiting 4 to 6 months before re-administration to minimize practice effects. Inter-examiner reliability data are not provided; however, administration via CD likely would reduce variability in administration.

The test authors provide content and construct validity evidence to support the use of the MAPA-2 in evaluating auditory processing skills. Exploratory and confirmatory factor analyses support the three-domain structure, suggesting that the individual skills assessed combine to measure auditory processing and listening skills. Additional validation was based on a comparison with the TAPS-4: A Language Processing Skills Assessment (TAPS-4; see 165, this volume) and on relations to other variables (chronological age and differences between groups with attention-deficit/hyperactivity disorder, learning disability, specific language impairment, and APD). Results provide evidence of construct validity: MAPA-2 scores correlated with TAPS-4 scores, improved with age, and were significantly lower for the disability groups.

COMMENTARY. The MAPA-2, used alongside the SAB, meets the criteria for a comprehensive assessment of auditory processing as set forth by ASHA and the AAA. The MAPA-2 is based on the theoretical model of APD accepted by ASHA (2005) and aims to identify it—after ruling out higher order language, cognitive, and related factors—through documentation of poor performance in one or more of the skills listed in ASHA's current description of the nature of APD. Inclusion of individuals with APD in the norming sample may limit the test's sensitivity as far as identifying individuals with milder auditory processing issues (Peña, Spaulding, & Plante, 2006). Also, it may be less sensitive for examinees in some of the age brackets, due to some less-than-adequate subgroup sample sizes in the normative sample.

SUMMARY. The MAPA-2 is an individually administered standardized test of auditory processing and listening skills for children and adolescents. It was developed to meet the need for a screening and diagnostic tool that follows ASHA and AAA guidelines for identifying auditory processing disorder. It is the only standardized nationally normed test that examines skills in three critical domains of auditory processing and includes a standardized behavior listening checklist. Reliability data suggested strong evidence for internal consistency of the MAPA-2 Overall and domain scores. Content and construct validity studies support the use of the MAPA-2 for preliminary diagnostic and research purposes. Caution is advised when interpreting test results for the purpose of an APD diagnosis. In addition, the sensitivity of the test for some examinees may be reduced because of less-than-adequate normative sample sizes for their age groups.

REVIEWER'S REFERENCES

American Academy of Audiology. (2010). *Clinical practice guidelines: Diagnosis, treatment and management of children and adults with central auditory processing disorder.* Retrieved from https://www.audiology.org/publications-resources/document-library/central-auditory-processing-disorder

American Speech-Language-Hearing Association. (2005). *(Central) auditory processing disorders—The role of the audiologist* (Position statement). Retrieved from https://www.asha.org/policy/PS2005-00114/

Domitz, D. M., & Schow, R. L. (2000). A new CAPD battery—Multiple Auditory Processing Assessment: Factor analysis and comparisons with SCAN. *American Journal of Audiology, 9*(2), 101-111.

Friberg, J. C., & McNamara, T. L. (2010). Evaluating the reliability and validity of (central) auditory processing tests: A preliminary investigation. *Journal of Educational Audiology, 16,* 4-17.

Peña, E. D., Spaulding, T. J., & Plante, E. (2006). The composition of normative groups and diagnostic decision making: Shooting ourselves in the foot. *American Journal of Speech-Language Pathology, 15,* 247–254.

Schow, R. L., Seikel, J. A., Brockett, J. E., & Whitaker, M. M. (2007). Multiple Auditory Processing Assessment. St. Louis, MO: Auditec.

[99]

Naglieri Nonverbal Ability Test–Third Edition.

Purpose: Designed as a "nonverbal measure of general ability" for "students of all ability levels for whom a language-free assessment is required," as well as for use in "the identification of gifted and talented students, especially those from underrepresented groups."
Population: Students in kindergarten through Grade 12.
Publication Dates: 1996-2016.
Acronym: NNAT3.
Scores: Total score only.
Administration: Group.
Restricted Distribution: Sold only to accredited/approved schools and districts.
Levels, 7: A (Kindergarten), B (Grade 1), C (Grade 2), D (Grades 3-4), E (Grades 5-6), F (Grades 7-9), G (Grades 10-12).
Forms: Levels A through D have parallel forms (Form 1, Form 2).
Price Data: Available from publisher.
Foreign Language Edition: Directions for administration and home report are available in Spanish.
Time: (30) minutes.
Comments: Administered online or via paper and pencil; Items in Levels A-D are new; items in Levels E-G are the same as in the NNAT2, but they have been re-normed; "Norms are also provided for children aged 4:0-4:11 so that NNAT3 Level A may be used with high-ability preschoolers. However, because of its difficulty, the test is not appropriate for general use with children younger than 5 years old."
Authors: Jack A. Naglieri.
Publisher: Pearson.
Cross References: For reviews by Russell N. Carney and Mary (Rina) M. Chittooran of the second edition, see 20:128; for reviews by Terry A. Stinnett and Michael S. Trevisan of the original edition, see 14:252.

Review of the Naglieri Nonverbal Ability Test—Third Edition by NICHOLAS F. BENSON, Associate Professor of School Psychology, and REBECCA J. TIPTON, Graduate Student, Baylor University, Waco, TX:

DESCRIPTION. The Naglieri Nonverbal Ability Test—Third Edition (NNAT3) is a standardized, norm-referenced test of intelligence appropriate for ages 5:0 through 17:11 and for high ability preschoolers ages 4:0 through 4:11. It can be group administered using either a paper-based format or an online, computer-based format. Administration typically can be completed in 35-45 minutes. The NNAT3 is considered a nonverbal test because the stimuli are visual (i.e., consist of various shapes, colors, and visual patterns), which presumably reduces language demands. However, directions for completing the test are administered both pictorially and verbally. The test manual notes that the directions should be administered in the language most appropriate for the students, although the directions are only available in English and Spanish.

The NNAT3 is a unidimensional intelligence test, meaning that it was designed to measure a single ability: general intelligence or simply *g* (Spearman, 1904). Although the structure of intelligence is not unidimensional, *g* is almost always the largest source of variance when accounting for individual differences in performance with cognitive tasks. The Naglieri Ability Index (NAI) is on a normalized standard score scale that ranges from 40 to 160 with a mean of 100 and a standard deviation of 16. Scores such as the NAI tend to be useful, albeit imperfect, measures of *g* (Kranzler, 2002). It is suggested in the test manual that the NNAT3 can be used to assist with identifying gifted children, particularly those whose knowledge and verbal abilities are presumed to be negatively impacted by social, economic, and/or educational disadvantage. The manual also notes that the NNAT3 is fair and appropriate when assessing the intelligence of students with limited English proficiency, hearing impairments, language impairments, or motor impairments.

DEVELOPMENT. The NNAT3 is the most current revision of the Naglieri Nonverbal Intelligence Test, originally developed in 1996 as an expansion and revision of the Matrix Analogies Test Expanded and Short Forms.

The item format of the NNAT3 follows the tradition, first introduced by J. C. Raven in 1936, requiring examinees to complete a visual pattern by selecting the correct response option among several geometric shapes (Lohman, 2005a). The NNAT3 is divided into seven levels labeled A to G that are administered based on grade level (e.g., children in kindergarten are administered Level A items; students in Grades 10 to 12 are administered

Level G items). Each level consists of 48 items, arranged so that easier items are presented before more difficult items.

The NNAT3 includes new items for Levels A-D. Items and content did not change for Levels E-G. Items were reviewed by color experts and examined using software that simulates color blindness to ensure that the items could be perceived correctly by individuals with various types of color blindness. Classical item analysis procedures were applied separately at each age and grade level, and Rasch modeling was used to calibrate item difficulty across the entire sample. A linear transformation of Rasch ability scores was used to convert raw scores into scale scores. A student's NAI score, percentile rank, stanine, and norm curve equivalent are obtained using the converted scaled score and chronological age. Notably, administration mode was found to impact scores, necessitating separate raw score to scale score conversion tables for the paper-based and computer-based formats.

Two parallel forms were developed for Levels A-D. A 48-item equating form with items from both forms was used to allow the forms to be linked using common item equating. Additionally, adjacent levels of the NNAT3 contain some common items so that levels are vertically linked and on a common scale. The norms for the NNAT3 are age-based, and a student can be administered items at a level that is higher or lower than the level recommended based on grade level provided the student's chronological age falls within the valid age range for that level.

TECHNICAL.

Standardization. Normative data were collected during the 2014-2015 school year for Levels A-D and from February to May of 2016 for Levels E-G. The norm sample for Levels A-D was drawn from 113 schools and preschools in 27 states, whereas the norm sample for Levels E-G was drawn from 59 schools in 23 states. Rather than the sounder approach of random stratified sampling, a statistical weighting procedure was used that involved random duplication and deletion of cases to match the norms with U.S. Census Bureau data with respect to salient demographic variables (e.g., ethnicity, socioeconomic status, geographic region). The number of duplicated cases and demographic information regarding these duplicated cases is not provided in the test manual, although it is noted that the weighting process reduced the size of the norm samples from 10,225 to 9,992 at Levels A-D and from 9,583 to 8,579 at Levels E-G.

Reliability. Coefficient alpha is reported for the NAI at Levels E-G. At Levels A-D the reliability of the NAI was estimated using the marginal reliability method. This method utilizes the standard error of measurement and standard deviation of Rasch ability scores to obtain coefficients that correspond closely to coefficient alpha. Estimates for Levels A-D range from .80 to .88 while estimates for Levels E-G range from .81 to .89. Evidence of test-retest reliability is not provided so it is unclear how stable NAI scores are over time. Estimates of alternate-form reliability are provided at Levels A-D, with an average coefficient of .79 for both alternate forms (i.e., Form 1 and Form 2) and alternate modes (i.e., paper-based and computer-based administrations).

Validity. Evidence to support the validity of score interpretation and use is limited. At Levels A-D a sample of 368 students was administered both the NNAT3 and the previous edition of the test in a counterbalanced fashion. The weighted mean correlation for all levels was .78. Also at Levels A-D, a sample of 366 students was administered both the NNAT3 and the Otis-Lennon School Ability Test, Eighth Edition (OLSAT 8). Correlations, which were adjusted for range restriction on the NNAT3, ranged from .17 for the NAI and the OLSAT 8 Verbal score at Level A to .62 for the NAI and the OLSAT 8 Total score at Level C. The test manual does not include results from exploratory or confirmatory factor analysis to support the proposed structure of the NNAT3. Further, neither evidence to support the predictive validity of the NAI nor diagnostic efficiency statistics are provided. Notably, the manual for Levels E-G does not present any evidence of validity.

COMMENTARY. The NNAT3 was designed to measure *g*. Although other abilities may affect cognitive performance, there is little evidence to support the clinical interpretation of abilities other than *g* (e.g., Benson, Beaujean, McGill, & Dombrowski, 2018). Thus, it has been suggested that the applied measurement of intelligence should focus on *g* (e.g., Canivez, 2013; Kranzler & Floyd, 2013). Most tests of intelligence provide excellent measures of *g*. Although it is likely that the NNAT3 provides a reasonable measure of *g* based on decades of research regarding the item format as well as research regarding previous versions of the test, additional evidence is needed to support the use of the NAI when making high-stakes decisions. Evidence of temporal stability is not provided, and estimates of internal consistency fall below the minimum value of .90 recommended by some authors when using scores from tests of intelligence for making high-stakes decisions (Kranzler & Floyd, 2013). Further, the administration format can be problematic, as the impact of test session behavior on the obtained score is difficult to determine for group- and computer-based administrations. Conversely, the item format, and especially the computer-based format, seemingly minimizes the impact of scoring errors.

All NNAT3 items have a similar format. Spearman (1939) suggested that *g* is best measured using tasks that are sufficiently diverse in content as not to be redundant. Restricting test content may result in a measure that fails to capture important aspects of intellectual functioning. As noted by Braden (2000), "Nonverbal tests may fail to elicit a sufficiently broad range of intellectual processes" (p. 7). While it may be necessary to omit linguistic and knowledge demands to minimize bias for some students (e.g., students with English deficiencies, hearing impairments, or language impairments), doing so may result in a measure that underrepresents the construct. Indeed, verbal ability has been found to be the best predictor of academic success across all racial/ethnic groups and all levels of English language proficiency (Lohman, 2005b).

Notably, presenting nonverbal stimuli to students does not guarantee that the NNAT3 is an unbiased measure of intelligence across identifiable groups (e.g., racial/ethnic groups, students with and without disabilities); this determination must be established statistically. The *Standards for Educational and Psychological Testing* (American Educational Research Association, American Psychological Association, & National Council on Measurement in Education, 2014) describes bias as any construct-irrelevant source of variance that produces systematic differences in test scores between identifiable groups of examinees. No evidence is provided to demonstrate that test items function similarly across identifiable groups or that *g* is calibrated similarly across identifiable groups. No evidence is provided to show that the NNAT3 is superior to other tests of intelligence at identifying gifted students whose knowledge and verbal abilities are presumed to be negatively impacted by social, economic, and/or educational disadvantage. Additionally, no evidence is provided to show that the NNAT3 is fair and appropriate when assessing the intelligence of students with limited English proficiency, hearing impairments, language impairments, or motor impairments. The NNAT3 is designed to accomplish laudable goals; given an absence of empirical data, however, it is unclear whether these goals are met.

SUMMARY. The Naglieri Nonverbal Ability Test—Third Edition (NNAT3) is the most current version of the NNAT, a norm-referenced, unidimensional test of intelligence. The NNAT3 employs a nonverbal format and is intended to measure *g*. The assessment is composed of multiple levels (A-G) that are administered by grade level. The NNAT3 can be administered quickly and efficiently, and it likely provides a reasonable measure of *g* that is appropriate for some purposes. However, in the absence of additional evidence of reliability and validity, these reviewers caution against its use for high-stakes decisions such as determining eligibility for gifted education programs. If the NNAT3 is used for identifying gifted students, these reviewers recommend that rather than using the NAI to exclude students from gifted education programs, the score should instead be used to assist with identifying students for whom performance on a comprehensive measure of intelligence likely represents an underestimate of *g* due to the negative impact of linguistic and knowledge demands.

REVIEWERS' REFERENCES

American Educational Research Association, American Psychological Association, & National Council on Measurement in Education. (2014). *Standards for educational and psychological testing*. Washington, DC: American Educational Research Association.

Benson, N. F., Beaujean, A. A., McGill, R. J., & Dombrowski, S. C. (2018). Revisiting Carroll's survey of factor-analytic studies: Implications for the clinical assessment of intelligence. *Psychological Assessment, 30*(8), 1028-1038. http://dx.doi.org/10.1037/pas0000556

Braden, J. P. (2000). Editor's introduction: Perspectives on the nonverbal assessment of intelligence. *Journal of Psychoeducational Assessment, 18*, 204–210.

Canivez, G. L. (2013). Psychometric versus actuarial interpretation of intelligence and related aptitude batteries. In D. H. Saklofske, C. R. Reynolds, & V. L. Schwean (Eds.), *The Oxford handbook of child psychological assessments* (pp. 84–112). New York, NY: Oxford University Press.

Kranzler, J. H. (2002). Commentary on "Is *g* a viable construct for school psychology?". *Learning and Individual Differences, 13*(2), 189-195.

Kranzler, J. H., & Floyd, R. G. (2013). *Assessing intelligence in children and adolescents: A practical guide*. New York, NY: Guilford Press.

Lohman, D. F. (2005a). Review of Naglieri and Ford (2003): Does the Naglieri Nonverbal Ability Test identify equal proportions of high-scoring White, Black, and Hispanic students? *Gifted Child Quarterly, 49*, 19-28.

Lohman, D. F. (2005b). The role of nonverbal ability tests in identifying academically gifted students: An aptitude perspective. *Gifted Child Quarterly, 49*, 111-138.

Spearman, C. (1904). "General intelligence," objectively determined and measured. *The American Journal of Psychology, 15*, 201-292. doi:10.2307/1412107

Spearman, C. (1939). Thurstone's work re-worked. *Journal of Educational Psychology, 30*, 1-16. doi:10.1037/h0061267

Review of the Naglieri Nonverbal Ability Test–Third Edition by RANDY G. FLOYD, Professor of Psychology, and PATRICK J. McNICHOLAS, Doctoral Candidate, University of Memphis, Memphis, TN:

DESCRIPTION. The Naglieri Nonverbal Ability Test–Third Edition (NNAT3) is an individual- or group-administered, brief nonverbal ability test. It was developed to measure general ability across a wide range of students (K-12), including those from diverse backgrounds or with disabilities that may confound scores on traditional verbal-based ability tests. It can be administered electronically via computer or in paper format in 35 to 45 minutes.

The NNAT3 includes Levels A-D for ages 5 years 0 months to 11 years 5 months and Levels E-G for ages 9 years 9 months to 17 years 11 months; there are manuals supporting both series of levels. (Level A also may be used with high ability preschoolers, ages 4 years 0 months to 4 years 11 months.) Items employ visual designs and geometric shapes in colored arrays and require examinees to select the correct answer from five options. During computer-based administration, questions are presented one at a time, and students respond by clicking the answer. During paper-based administration for Levels A-D, items are presented in a scannable printed booklet, and students respond by marking in the booklet. At Levels C and D, reusable printed booklets also are available, and a scannable answer document is used. Paper administration for Levels E-G involves reusable booklets only. The booklets include 28 pages, offer instructions and three sample items, and present two items per page.

Across administration formats, performance yields a total score referred to as the Naglieri Ability Index (NAI; M = 100, SD = 16). Additional score options include scaled scores, percentile ranks, stanines, and normal curve equivalents. Scaled scores, supported by vertical linking methods, may be used to compare scores across Levels A-D and across Levels E-G. Confidence intervals are not reported for the NAI.

Administration and scoring of the NNAT3 is relatively simple. Individuals with minimal training in testing and assessment can administer and score the measure, but they should be knowledgeable about ideal testing practices and specific administration guidelines. The computer version and paper version are identical in terms of instructions and time allotted.

DEVELOPMENT. NNAT3 items were based on the previous versions of the test. Levels A-D each include two forms with different items. In developing these alternate forms, 480 new items, organized into four levels based on estimated item difficulty, were generated. The graphical specifications for these new items were the same as those used for the NNAT2, but the colors employed were changed to be discernable by examinees who experience color blindness. A national tryout of these items was completed to evaluate their difficulty and discrimination (using both classical item analysis and item response theory [IRT] methods) and distractor functioning, and they were divided across forms. Items for Levels E-G are the same as those from the NNAT2; only the norms have been updated.

TECHNICAL. Norms for Levels A-D were based on 10,225 students from 113 schools and preschools across 27 states, and norms for Levels E-G were based on 9,583 students from 59 schools across 23 states. Schools were chosen to be representative of the U.S. school population with respect to ethnicity, socioeconomic status, geographical region, urbanicity, and type of school. Data for Levels A-D were collected during the 2014-2015 school year, and all tests (except those completed as part of a validity study) were administered via computer. Specially designed Pre-K forms were administered individually, and Levels A and B were administered to small groups. Data for Levels E-G were collected during early 2016, and all tests were administered via computer. Sample weighting was employed to match the norming sample to population estimates; cases were deleted or duplicated until the desired sample characteristics were obtained. The weighted norming sample (N = 9,992 and N = 8,579 for Levels A-D and E-G, respectively) generally matches the 2013 U.S. Census statistics and appears representative. The same general findings were evident for the weighted norming sample for Levels E-G; however, there appears to be oversampling of urban students and undersampling of rural students. Continuous norming procedures do not appear to have been employed.

For Levels A-D, norms for ages 4:0-9:11 were organized into blocks with 1-month intervals, and for ages 10:0-11:5, blocks with 3-month intervals. There are approximately 65 to 333 participants associated with each age-based norm block. For Levels E-G, norms were organized into nine norm blocks of 3-month intervals for ages 9:6-17:11; approximately 198 to 275 participants are associated with each norm block. There are no ceiling or floor violations associated with a standard administration, following the criteria that (a) the maximum raw score should be associated with a norm-referenced score that is at least two standard deviations above the mean and (b) a raw score of 1 should be associated with a norm-referenced score that is at least two standard deviations below the mean. Some floor violations were evident for age levels too young for valid administration.

Across Levels A-D, IRT-based reliability coefficients, representing internal consistency, for the NAI ranged from .80 to .88 for both forms. Across Levels E-G and Grades 5-12, alpha coefficients and odd-even split-half reliability coefficients were reported. The alpha coefficients ranged from .81 to .89, and the split-half reliability coefficients were slightly higher in most cases. Overall, reliability values are notably lower than many total scores from individually administered intelligence tests. Some school psychologists typically consider the standard for internal consistency reliability to be at least .90.

An alternate-form reliability study compared forms, completed at 4-week intervals, at each level for Levels A-D. Range-corrected coefficients were relatively low in magnitude, with a range of .70 to .83 for the Form-1-to-Form-2 comparison and a range of .69 to .86 for the Form-2-to-Form-1 comparison. Another alternate-form reliability study compared online and paper versions while controlling for form. Again, coefficients were uniformly lower than .90, with a range of .72 to .81 for the online-to-paper comparison and a range of .77 to .84 for the paper-to-online comparison.

Validity evidence supporting the NNAT3 is limited; three studies that focused on Levels A-D examined evidence based on response processes and relations with other variables. In an extension of the study described previously, results from large samples completing Levels A-D revealed that the paper format yielded slightly higher total scores than the online format at each level. As a result, separate raw-score-to-scaled-score conversion tables are employed for the two administration formats, making online and paper scaled scores more comparable. A prior study using the NNAT2 was summarized to support use of the same methods for Levels E-G, but no specific results were reproduced in the NNAT3 manual.

In a comparison of levels A-D from the NNAT2 and NNAT3, uncorrected correlations between total scores ranged from .68 to .75 for levels A-C when the NNAT2 was completed first. When the NNAT3 was completed first, the correlations across levels A-D ranged from .73 to .75. The average weighted mean of range-corrected correlations across administrations based on level (considering only cases completing the NNAT3 first for Level D) ranged from .76 to .79. These values seem strikingly low considering the almost identical structure of the two tests. Range corrected correlations between the NAI and the Otis-Lennon School Ability Test, Eighth Edition (OLSAT 8) School Ability Index scores ranged from .41 to .62 across Levels A-D. The NAI also demonstrated range-corrected correlations from .17 to .55 (Mdn = .46) with the OLSAT 8 Verbal score and from .51 to .61 (Mdn = .57) with its Nonverbal score. Higher correlations between these two ability tests—especially the NNAT3 NAI and OLSAT 8 Nonverbal score—were anticipated.

The NNAT3 manual included no new validity evidence for Levels E-G, only alluding to very limited evidence from the comparable NNAT2 Levels E-G. Across all levels of the NNAT3, there was no evidence of comparisons across students from targeted populations (e.g., those requiring a language-free assessment) or students with identified clinical or educational conditions (e.g., gifted and talented students). Because the NNAT3 is frequently used as a screener for gifted and talented students, classification accuracy studies should be conducted.

COMMENTARY. The NNAT3 is a nonverbal test measuring general ability that is appropriate for students at any grade level. It may be particularly useful for students who experience language and cultural barriers that could undermine performance when completing traditional tests. It can be completed using a computer-based or a paper-and-pencil format in a relatively short amount of time (35 to 45 minutes) and in group settings. It is also easy to administer and score. Its alternate forms for Levels A-D are noteworthy, and its application of vertical linking methods within levels was innovative.

Despite the NNAT3's strengths, the internal consistency reliability of the NAI is lower than typically expected, and no test-retest reliability results were reported. Other evidence (e.g., from alternate-form reliability studies and comparisons of the NNAT2 and NNAT3 scores) also suggests more general problems associated with reliability, which undermines the construct evidence of validity for the NNAT3. These problems are amplified as confidence intervals are not reported. For a test designed to identify students who are gifted and talented and more accurately assess those who experience language and cultural barriers, there is limited research using the NNAT3 to support these design goals.

SUMMARY. The NNAT3 is a nonverbal test designed to obtain an estimate of general ability. It can be administered to many students simultaneously and is easy to administer and score. Its psychometric properties should be stronger, so it should be used only cautiously as a screener for intellectual giftedness. Users also should be aware of its wider standard deviation (16) than tests typically employ.

[100]

Nelson-Denny Reading Test Forms I & J.

Purpose: "Designed to measure the reading vocabulary, reading comprehension, and reading rate of high school-level and college-level students."
Population: Ages 14-0 through 24-11.
Publication Dates: 1929-2019.
Acronym: NDRT I & J.
Scores, 3-4: General Reading Ability (Vocabulary, Comprehension, Total), Reading Rate (supplemental).
Administration: Individual or group.
Forms, 2: I, J.
Price Data, 2020: $302 per complete kit including examiner's manual (2019, 184 pages), 25 Form I test booklets, 25 Form J test booklets, and 50 self-scorable answer sheets; $57 per examiner's manual; $77 per 25 test booklets with administration instructions (Form I or Form J); $91 per 50 self-scorable answer sheets; $91 per 50 online administrations; $302 per computer administered kit with 50 administrations.
Time: 15-minute time limit for Vocabulary subtest; 20-minute time limit for Comprehension subtest; approximately 45 minutes total for administration.
Comments: Administered and scored online or via paper and pencil.
Author: Vivian Vick Fishco.
Publisher: PRO-ED.
Cross References: For reviews by Alice Corkill and by Darrell L. Sabers and Amy M. Olson of CD-ROM Version 1.2 (Forms G and H), see 17:132; See T5:1767 (9 references); for reviews by Mildred Murray-Ward and Douglas K. Smith of the paper and pencil version of Forms G and H, see 13:206 (52 references); see also T4:1715 (30 references); for reviews by Robert J. Tierney and James E. Ysseldyke of Forms E and F, see 9:745 (12 references); see also T3:1568 (38 references); for reviews by Robert A. Forsyth and Alton L. Raynor of Forms C and D, see 8:735 (31 references); see also T2:1572 (46 references); for reviews by David B. Orr and Agatha Townsend and an excerpted review by John O. Crites of Forms A and B, see 6:800 (13 references); for a review by Ivan A. Booker, see 4:544 (17 references); for a review by Hans C. Gordon, see 2:1557.

Review of the Nelson-Denny Reading Test Forms I & J by MICHAEL B. BUNCH, Senior Vice President, Measurement Incorporated, Durham, NC:

DESCRIPTION. The Nelson-Denny Reading Test Forms I & J (NDRT) is the latest edition of a familiar test that was first published in 1929. This timed 35-minute test can be administered either individually or to groups of students. The NDRT assesses Vocabulary, Comprehension, and Reading Rate for students in Grades 9-12 and college, as did its predecessors. Norms are available for both age (14-0 to 24-11) and grade (9 to 16). According to the examiner's manual, the purpose of the test is "to identify adolescents and adults who are significantly behind or above their peers in reading ability" (p. 3). The test publisher also points out that scores "can be used to qualify students for placement in remedial or accelerated classes or programs or to confirm the results of other reading tests" (p. 3).

The 15-minute Vocabulary subtest consists of 80 target words for which the student must select one of five possible matches. For Comprehension, students are given 20 minutes to read seven brief passages (approximately 600 words for the first passage and 200 for each of the next six) and answer a total of 38 five-choice multiple-choice items. The first passage is longer because it is used to measure Reading Rate—the number of lines of that passage a student can read in exactly 1 minute. The format of each of the three sections is the same as in the previous edition. Vocabulary and Comprehension subtest scores are combined to form the General Reading Ability Composite.

DEVELOPMENT. The test publishers created an initial item bank based on passages from 11 different sources, including four technical/scientific sources. These passages were selected not only to represent the humanities but physical and social sciences as well. Two rounds of item analysis yielded the final set of items to be assigned to the two forms.

TECHNICAL. The examiner's manual combines directions for administration and scoring/interpreting with documentation of norming, reliability, and validity. Directions for administration are exemplary and quite thorough as are directions for scoring and interpreting the tests. This section of the manual includes examples with ample explanation.

The grade-based norms were based on a sample of 3,487 students in 36 states. By grade, sample sizes were 305 to 405. Age-based norms were based on a sample of 4,010 students in 37 states. By age, sample sizes were 240 to 361 per year for ages 14-17; 1,287 for ages 18-19; and 1,472 for ages 20-24. Samples included students from both public and nonpublic schools as well as gifted students and students with disabilities. Four appendices to the examiner's manual contain complete percentile rank and scale score lookup tables, and two provide age and grade equivalent lookup tables.

Reliability analyses include calculation of internal consistency, alternate-forms reliability, test-retest reliability, and standard errors of measurement (*SEMs*). Results of reliability analyses are presented in 12 tables in the test manual. These tables show the subtests to be highly reliable.

For validity, the publisher focused on test construction rationale and approach, correlation of scores from Forms I and J with those of similar tests (including NDRT Forms G and H), internal structure of the tests, floor and ceiling effects, differential item functioning, and discrimination among groups of known ability. There is also a section on diagnostic accuracy. The validity chapter contains 38 tables.

COMMENTARY. This review focuses on the contents of the NDRT Forms I & J and the test's technical underpinning and does not address its online delivery system. Specifically, it addresses test and item development, norming, reliability, and validity. Comparisons to similar tests are also included where appropriate.

To make the test relevant to high school and college-level students, the publisher selected vocabulary words and passages from a wide variety of age- and grade-appropriate texts and conducted a series of pilot and standardization analyses. Although the description of these activities is quite good, the publisher does not document how the items were reviewed for content and bias and how the final pool of items was divided between Forms I and J. In reviewing the Vocabulary items, for example, it was clear that there are differences in the grade levels of the two sets. Form I has far more target words from Grade 9 reading lists, and Form J has far more target words from Grade 8 reading lists. Form I and Form J Vocabulary items are not of equal difficulty, as revealed in comparison of their raw score to percentile rank conversion tables. These differences are smoothed out, however, in the conversion of raw scores to scale (index) scores through equipercentile equating, rendering index scores equivalent across forms. The Comprehension passages and items are more similar across the two forms, as reflected not only in passage topics and item types but in raw score to percentile rank conversions as well.

Grade- and age-based norms are based on nationwide samples of 3,487 students and 4,010 students, respectively. Comparable tests have sample sizes of around 2,500. Although the NDRT norms are fairly representative of high school and college-age students, gifted and talented students are overrepresented, and students with disabilities are slightly underrepresented. Private schools are greatly overrepresented at both the high school and 2-year college levels. Moreover, there is nothing in the examiner's manual to help users compare percentile ranks and scale scores on Forms G and H to those on Forms I and J as they transition from one edition to the next. The examiner's manual also includes raw score to grade equivalent tables. Given the fact that a difference of 2-3 raw score points (and sometimes a single point) translates into a whole grade equivalent, the use of grade equivalents should be discouraged.

Both forms (I and J) demonstrate better than acceptable levels of reliability. Indeed, several types of reliability, including test-retest, are documented. In addition, the examiner's manual provides standard errors of measurement, which range from 3 to 5 scale score points for Vocabulary, 5-7 points for Comprehension, 4-8 points for Reading Rate, and 3-5 points for General Reading Ability.

Documentation of validity is quite extensive and includes content, criterion, and construct evidence. As noted above, the description of item development is quite good except for the fact that it does not specify how the final set of items was apportioned across forms. The discussion of bias conflates the term "bias," which is associated with human judgment, with differential item functioning (DIF), a statistical procedure, and fails to justify the inclusion of an item that demonstrated significant DIF. The general population of students consistently outscored Black and Hispanic students by about half a standard deviation. No score differences were noted between males and females. NDRT scores correlate very highly with scores on several other reading tests (e.g., Gray Oral Reading Tests—Fifth Edition, Wechsler Individual Achievement Test—Third Edition). Perhaps the most important criterion-related validity evidence comes from comparison of known groups. NDRT scores predict known reading disabilities quite well, showing a 77% hit rate at three different cut scores.

SUMMARY. The NDRT has been around for 90 years. The publisher knows its market and its competition well. The examiner's manual reveals a considerable amount of effort to justify the use of the instrument and reliance on scores derived from it to make decisions about students' reading abilities and to differentiate it from its competitors. For a 35-minute test, it does rather well. Compared to other reading tests with similar purposes, the NDRT stands up well, despite a number of rather minor technical deficiencies.

Review of the Nelson-Denny Reading Test Forms I & J by M. DAVID MILLER, Professor of Research and Evaluation Methods, University of Florida, and JIEHAN LI, Graduate Student in Research and Evaluation Methods, University of Florida, Gainesville, FL:

DESCRIPTION. The Nelson-Denny Reading Test (NDRT) Forms I & J is the fifth edition of the NDRT designed to measure reading vocabulary, reading comprehension, and reading rate for high school and college students. The NDRT can be administered in groups or individually. Tests can be administered online or using paper and pencil. Clear and simple administration directions make it possible for anyone who can read and follow the administration procedures to administer the test. Interpretation directions are provided and can be done by anyone understanding basic test statistics and having a general knowledge of testing at a level taught in college courses in school psychology, special education, counseling, or other related disciplines.

The NDRT examiner's manual suggests three possible uses for the test: (a) identifying adolescents and adults who are significantly behind or above their peers in reading ability and determining the magnitude of the discrepancies, (b) placement in remedial or accelerated classes/programs, and (c) conducting research.

Because multiple forms of the NDRT are available, raw scores are neither useful nor reported. Scores include index scores (M = 100, SD = 15), percentile ranks, and grade and age equivalents for each of the three subtests. Vocabulary and Comprehension index scores are summed to form a General Reading Ability index. Score interpretations also include statistically significant versus clinically meaningful difference scores for Vocabulary and Comprehension for grade- and age-based scores.

DEVELOPMENT. The NDRT Forms I & J were developed with a consideration of the critiques of Forms G & H. (e.g., Murray-Ward, 1998; Smith, 1998). The major changes in response to critiques and user feedback include the development of new norms; new vocabulary items and comprehension passages; new studies of bias; new studies of validity evidence (criterion-prediction and construct-identification); and a new online administration, scoring and reporting system.

The development of the Vocabulary items, using the same task format as in previous editions (multiple-choice sentence completion), drew on an initial bank of 258 items using vocabulary words selected from various high school and college textbooks (listed in the examiner's manual). After two pilot studies, the pool was reduced to 193 items with 80 items selected for each of the final forms. The Comprehension subtest consists of seven reading passages and 38 multiple-choice items. The task format is the same as in previous editions, and passages were drawn from the same textbooks as those used for the Vocabulary items. Reading Rate is measured on the first, longest passage of the Comprehension subtest (1 minute reading).

Median values are reported for classical item statistics, including difficulty and discrimination. Reasonable item statistics were obtained by grade level and age for the Vocabulary and Comprehension items on both forms. Based on critiques of Forms G & H, studies were also conducted on passage readability and passage dependence for the Comprehension subtest. In addition, new studies of floors, ceilings, and item gradients were conducted and showed reasonably consistent measurement across grade and age ranges.

Grade-based norms were developed from a weighted national sample of 3,487 students. The age-based scores were developed from a sample of 4,010 students weighted to reflect a representative age-based population. The sample approximated the population according to geographic region, gender, race, Hispanic status, exceptionality status, parent educational level, and household income.

TECHNICAL. Test developers have been comprehensive in collecting technical data to aid in the interpretation and use of scores. The data include extensive consideration of the three foundational components of the *Standards for Educational and Psychological Testing* (American Educational Research Association [AERA], American Psychological Association [APA], & National Council on Measurement in Education [NCME], 2014): validity, reliability, and fairness. Within each foundational component, multiple studies were conducted.

Validity. Many types of evidence of validity are reported with a strong emphasis on content, criterion-prediction, and construct-identification. The content evidence process is broadly described and rigorous as part of the test development process, providing strong evidence of the validity of the content and the format of the tests. However, there is no evidence of external review of the content during test development or of the final forms. Future studies should consider including external reviewers who would provide unbiased reviews for content evidence of validity.

Relationships with multiple criteria also provide strong evidence for the validity of NDRT Forms I & J. As hypothesized, the forms have moderate to strong positive correlations with assessments including the Test of Silent Contextual Reading Fluency—Second Edition, the Test of Silent Word Reading Fluency—Second Edition, the Gray Oral Reading Tests—Fifth Edition, the Wechsler Individual Achievement Test—Third Edition, and the NDRT Forms G & H. The NDRT Forms I & J also performed well in diagnostic accuracy analyses. Using a cutoff score of 90 on the General Reading Ability index, the assessment identified students with learning disabilities correctly (sensitivity index = .69) and was correctly identifying students with no diagnosis (specificity index = .85).

A series of construct-based hypotheses were also examined. The data show that Vocabulary and Comprehension scores increased with age and grade level while Reading Rate was relatively static. The assessment also had means as expected for exceptionality subgroups (e.g., gifted and talented, attention-deficit/hyperactivity disorder, learning disabilities). The assessment also correlated positively with written language, intelligence, and other measures of ability. Thus, the reading constructs were consistent with hypotheses about reading.

Reliability. The test developer conducted multiple reliability studies of the NDRT Forms I & J including internal consistency (coefficient alpha), alternate form-immediate, test-retest, and alternate form-delayed. Internal consistency coefficients were calculated for each of the 10 grade and six age intervals in the normative sample. The internal consistency estimates exceeded the minimal reliability criterion specified in the examiner's manual (.80) for the Vocabulary and Comprehension subtests and for the composite. Grade-based alphas ranged from .80 to .95 for the Vocabulary and Comprehension subtests and from .90 to .96 for the composite. Age-based alphas ranged from .83 to .95 for Vocabulary and Comprehension and from .92 to .96 for the composite. For the speeded Reading Rate subtest, the test author estimated internal consistency from test-retest reliability results and reported coefficients of .72 to .92 for the grade-based sample and .71 to .83 for the age-based sample. The lowest coefficients in both samples were reported for high school students and those ages 17 and younger, respectively.

A sample of students completed Forms I & J in a counterbalanced order to estimate alternate-form reliability corrected for the effect of range. Again, reliability estimates were calculated at 10 grade levels and six age levels. Results were similar to the internal consistency estimates. Alternate-form reliability coefficients for Vocabulary, Comprehension, and the composite exceeded .80 for all groups. Coefficients were lower for Reading Rate for younger and lower grade level cohorts.

Test-retest and alternate form–delayed reliability coefficients from a sample of 128 examinees were estimated. The test-retest reliabilities were relatively large for all grade-based groups on all subtests and the composite. Most of the alternate form-delayed reliabilities were high for grade- and age-based groups. These coefficients ranged from the high .70s through the low .90s.

Fairness. Fairness studies included differential item functioning and mean comparisons of scores from demographic subgroups. Using logistic regression analyses, only one item was identified with differential item functioning by gender, race, or ethnicity that had a moderate or larger difference (less than expected by chance). With regard to mean differences, trivial and nonsignificant differences were found for gender and most racial/ethnic groups. There were small significant differences for the Black/African American and Hispanic examinees. These differences suggest that demographic differences are relatively small compared to many other tests and are unlikely to be due to factors in the test itself.

COMMENTARY. The NDRT Forms I & J are able to serve as useful measures of Vocabulary, Comprehension, and Reading Rate that have effectively responded to criticisms of the previous edition. The assessment provides extensive and strong psychometric evidence that is consistent with the *Standards for Educational and Psychological Testing (*AERA, APA, & NCME, 2014) with their emphasis on validity, reliability, and fairness. The preponderance of evidence supports the validity, reliability, and fairness of NDRT Forms I & J scores for their proposed uses and interpretations. However, there are cautions that should be considered when using any test, including this assessment. With regard to validity, the content evidence rests on the selection of certain textbooks to define the Vocabulary and Comprehension items. As part of an external content review, users should review the textbooks selected and the items developed before adopting them with a focus on the local intended uses and interpretations. In addition, the diagnostic evidence, which may be key to the placement of students in remedial or accelerated classes, focuses only on the diagnosis of populations with learning disabilities. Further evidence would be needed when working with other populations (e.g., ADHD, gifted).

Reliability evidence supports the use and interpretations of scores from the NDRT Forms I & J. The examiner's manual reports a criterion for minimal reliability of .80; however, this cutoff is arbitrary. For high stakes uses (e.g., placement), higher reliabilities should be used. The cutoff value of .80 would generate some concerns to professional users about the use of the Reading Rate scores for high school students. For lower stakes uses and interpretations (e.g., research), results would suggest that the NDRT has adequate reliability for all subtests and all cohorts.

Fairness data show that the NDRT Forms I & J can be used with demographically diverse populations. Future studies could include expert review of Comprehension passages for cultural sensitivity.

SUMMARY. The authors of the NDRT Forms I & J have updated their previous forms to provide a useful and interpretable measure of reading Vocabulary and Comprehension as well as Reading Rate. Psychometric evidence provides a strong case for the validity, reliability, and fairness of the assessment.

REVIEWERS' REFERENCES

American Educational Research Association, American Psychological Association, & National Council on Measurement in Education. (2014). *Standards for educational and psychological testing.* Washington, DC: American Educational Research Association.

Murray-Ward, M. (1998). [Test review of the Nelson-Denny Reading Test, Forms G and H]. In J. C. Impara & B. S. Plake (Eds.), *The thirteenth mental measurements yearbook* (pp. 683-685). Lincoln, NE: Buros Institute of Mental Measurements.

Smith, D. K. (1998). [Test review of the Nelson-Denny Reading Test, Forms G and H]. In J. C. Impara & B. S. Plake (Eds.), *The thirteenth mental measurements yearbook* (pp. 685-686). Lincoln, NE: Buros Institute of Mental Measurements.

[101]

NEO Personality Inventory-3 (UK Edition).

Purpose: Designed to measure "the five broad domains of personality and specific salient traits, or facets, associated with each domain."

Population: Ages 16 and older.

Publication Dates: 2006-2015.

Acronym: NEO-PI-3 (UK Edition).

Scores, 35: 30 facets in 5 domains: Neuroticism (Anxiety, Angry Hostility, Depression, Self-Consciousness, Impulsiveness, Vulnerability), Extraversion (Warmth, Gregariousness, Assertiveness, Activity, Excitement Seeking, Positive Emotions), Openness (Fantasy, Aesthetics, Feelings, Actions, Ideas, Values), Agreeableness (Trust, Straightforwardness, Altruism, Compliance, Modesty, Tender-Mindedness), Conscientiousness (Competence, Order, Dutifulness, Achievement Striving, Self-Discipline, Deliberation).

Administration: Individual or group.

Price Data, 2020: £350 per complete print kit including manual (2015, 81 pages), norms booklet, item booklets, response sheets, profile sheets, and feedback charts; £61 per manual; £105 per Technical Report and Personal Insight Report (includes online administration); £90 per Technical Report (includes online administration); £114 per Primary Colours Leadership Report (includes online administration); subscription discounts available; £109 per NEO Cards.

Time: Administration time not reported.

Comments: A U.K. adaptation of the U.S. version of the NEO Personality Inventory-3 (19:116); administered online or via paper and pencil.

Authors: Robert R. McCrae and Paul T. Costa, Jr. (test); UK adaptation by Wendy Lord.

Publisher: Hogrefe Ltd [United Kingdom].

Cross References: For reviews by Nicholas F. Benson and Annette S. Kluck of the U.S. version, see 19:116.

Review of the NEO Personality Inventory-3 (U.K. Edition) by KATE HATTRUP, Professor of Psychology, San Diego State University, San Diego, CA:

DESCRIPTION. The NEO Personality Inventory-3 (U.K. Edition; NEO-PI-3) is an adaptation of the well-known NEO-PI-3 for use with respondents from the United Kingdom. It measures dimensions of the Five Factor Model (FFM), which represent aspects of normal personality derived from the lexical approach to identifying salient personality characteristics. Like the U.S. edition, the U.K. edition provides scores on 30 facets, consisting of six subdimensions for each of the five major domains. Unlike the U.S. edition, the U.K. edition manual also identifies 10 aspects of the Big Five domains, which represent a level of generalization that lies between the facets and domains, and also two meta-factors, which represent a higher level of generality than the five domains. Specific scales are not yet available for these factors. The measure includes 240 items, each rated on a 5-point scale ranging from *strongly disagree* to *strongly agree*. Items were re-ordered to create a reduced-length version of the measure, consisting of the first 120 items, by identifying the two positively and two negatively keyed items that best predicted the facet scores in item analyses. One of the main goals in revising the NEO-PI-R to create the NEO-PI-3 was to reduce the reading requirements of the test; the revision also provides norms for younger examinees between the ages of 12 and 18. Although the U.K. edition retained all but two of the 37 new items written for the U.S. edition of the NEO-PI-3, and is intended for use with respondents as young as 16, norms for the U.K. edition are not available for examinees younger than 18.

The NEO-PI-3 U.K. Edition can be administered online or in person. Administration takes 30-40 minutes (Kluck, 2014), although the test manual advises setting aside one hour to introduce the measure and sufficient time for examinees to respond to the items. Unlike the U.S. edition, the test manual for the U.K. edition does not provide a table of easy-to-understand definitions of words used in the measure to assist examinees while they are responding to the items. Alternative terms for some of the facets are provided for use when giving feedback about test scores.

Scoring is done automatically for the online version and can easily be done by hand for the paper-and-pencil version. Raw scores and T scores can be obtained for the 30 facets and five domains, and T scores can be plotted to reveal profiles. Information about examinees' response styles may be obtained or deduced such as (a) how examinees responded to questions in terms of whether they tried to answer honestly and accurately, whether they answered all of the items, and whether they entered responses in the correct areas, and (b) whether the respondent gave the same rating for many consecutive items. The online scoring platform also provides a detailed narrative report for examinees.

DEVELOPMENT. The NEO-PI scales have been translated into more than 50 languages, and considerable factor analytic evidence supports the model underlying the NEO-PI across national boundaries, even in languages that bear little similarity to English. Nevertheless, it is desirable to standardize the measure in different contexts, and norms are provided for the U.K. edition based on samples of working adults from various regions of the United Kingdom. In developing the U.K. edition, the test authors also revised several items in the NEO-PI-3 U.S. edition in an effort to anglicize the measure. First, items were translated, when necessary, from U.S. English to U.K. English. Second, the reading level was reduced by simplifying the wording of some items. Third, some items were revised slightly to better reflect the facet to which they were assigned. Fourth, some items were revised to improve "political correctness" (manual, p. 30; i.e., reduce bias), and finally, some items were modified to improve their relevance to today's world.

In developing the new U.K. edition, 261 new and original items from the NEO-PI-R U.K. Edition were administered to a pilot sample of 1,289 participants, ages 18-70 years, who were broadly representative of the U.K. working population according to the 2011 Census. Of the 37 new items that were written for the U.S. edition, all but two were retained for the U.K. edition, with some modifications to 14 of them. An additional 34 modifications were made to items in the NEO-PI-R U.K. Edition, 25 of which were regarded by the test authors as minor and nine of which were considered more substantial. Item order was also revised as noted above.

TECHNICAL. The final set of 240 items was administered to 696 individuals from the U.K. working population, of which 656 provided scores used in developing norms. The sample was stratified by region and included a wide range of education levels, industries, and occupations representative of the overall U.K. 2011 Census. The five domain and 30 facet scores were normalized and rescaled to T scores using the percentile equivalent method. Norms are therefore available for the U.K. working population ages 18-70, and also separately for a subgroup (N = 353) of managerial and professional workers. Separate norms are provided for men and women within the overall U.K. working population. Separate norms are not provided for the shorter-length version of the NEO-PI-3 U.K. Edition. [Editor's note: The test publisher advised the Buros Center for Testing that a third normative group of international managerial and professional adults (N = 422) was added after materials were received for this review.]

Internal consistency reliability coefficients were calculated from data provided by the standardization sample and compare favorably with the values reported for the NEO-PI-3 U.S. Edition. Alpha coefficients ranged from .88 to .94 for the domain scales, and from .60 to .86 for the facet scales. Nine of the facet scales have alpha values below .70. McDonald's omega estimates of reliability are provided for the facets and range from .60 to .86. Standard errors of measurement and 95% confidence intervals are also provided for the domain and facet scales.

Alternate forms reliability coefficients were calculated in a sample of 159 examinees who obtained scores on the U.K. editions of both the NEO-PI-R and NEO-PI-3. For the domain scales, these values ranged from .88 to .91 and for the facet scales from .72 to .87. This implies that findings from the U.K. edition of the NEO-PI-R can generalize to a substantial degree to the newer version.

Test-retest reliability was examined for a sample of 112 U.K. examinees using the pilot version of the measure and a 4-week retest interval. Coefficients ranged from .74 to .85 for the domain scales and from .76 to .90 for the facet scales. These values are lower than those reported for the domain scales with the U.S. Edition (.91-.93 for domain scales and .70-.91 for facet scales). Evidence of longer-term stability can be generalized from U.S. data, with the Manual reporting retest reliabilities for a six-year interval ranging from .68 to .83 for the N, E, and O scales, and retest reliabilities for a 3-year interval ranging from .63 to .79 for brief versions of the A and C scales. Overall, the retest reliability coefficients support the conclusion that the NEO-PI-3 U.K. Edition measures stable traits.

Factor analytic evidence played a central role in the development of the FFM and the NEO-PI scales and continues to figure prominently with the NEO-PI-3 U.K. Edition. Using the U.K. standardization sample, target rotation showed excellent fit with the normative NEO-PI-R structure, with factor congruence coefficients between .95 and .98. Of the 30 facets, all but one (O3: Openness to Feelings) loaded highest on the intended domain. However, many items had large secondary loadings on unintended factors. Analyses of the NEO-PI scales with confirmatory factor analysis (CFA) has consistently failed to support the intended structure (e.g., Furnham, Guenole, Levine, & Chamorro-Premuzic, 2013). Using the U.K. standardization sample and exploratory structural equation modeling (ESEM), good fit of the hypothesized model was obtained by allowing facets to freely load on unintended domains, with many of these secondary loadings being high. Finally, CFAs were performed with the U.K. standardization sample for each of the five domains, comparing the fit of single factor models for each domain with models that separated the facets into two aspects for each domain. Better fit was achieved when the aspects were modeled; in fact, the single factor model did not result in acceptable fit for three of the five domains. Overall, analyses with CFA do not provide support for the facets or the domains; acceptable model fit can be achieved only by testing models that are more complex than the hypothesized structure or models that allow a lot of cross-loadings among items.

The test manual does not report criterion-related validity evidence for the revised U.K. edition; therefore, evidence must be extrapolated from U.S. samples and previous versions of the NEO-PI scales. This evidence is largely supportive, and the manual summarizes substantial evidence supporting the use of the NEO-PI scales in a variety of contexts, such as employee staffing, occupational psychology, behavioral health and well-being, and counseling. The NEO-PI scales have been used in more published studies of the relationship between personality and job performance than any other commercial measure of the FFM, with results largely supporting its criterion-related validity (Prewett, Tett, & Christiansen, 2013). At the same time, the lack of normative data for occupation-specific samples creates challenges for test score interpretation in applied settings (Prewett et al., 2013).

COMMENTARY. The NEO-PI scales are the most widely used measures of normal personality across the world (Simms, Williams, & Nus, 2017; Weiner & Greene, 2017), and research conducted with the scales has contributed to widespread acceptance of the FFM more generally (Weiner & Greene, 2017). In this sense, there is some truth to the test publisher's claim that the NEO-PI scales are a "gold standard" for measuring the FFM. Nevertheless, several of the criticisms of other versions of the NEO-PI apply to the new U.K. edition. For instance, reviewers of the NEO-PI scales (e.g., Kluck, 2014; Weiner & Greene, 2017) note that the lack of validity scales is problematic, despite the test authors' tendency to dismiss these concerns (Kluck, 2014). Evidence shows that respondents can distort answers in a socially desirable fashion, that they tend to do so in high stakes testing contexts, and that distortion is not consistent across examinees

(Griffith & Robie, 2013; Prewett et al., 2013). As a consequence, faking reduces the quality of hiring decisions made with personality measures, although there is no consensus about whether validity scales and measures of social desirability should be used to adjust test scores (Griffith & Robie, 2013). Moreover, because the norm samples for the U.K. edition of the NEO-PI-3 consisted of working adults, with an unknown number being job applicants, interpretation of score levels obtained from non-working adults, job applicants, students, and younger respondents might be somewhat difficult. New insights from research on insufficient effort responding (e.g., Huang, Liu, & Bowling, 2015), which can sometimes inflate or attenuate correlations among measures, should also be considered in future studies of the NEO-PI scales.

Although the five domain scores in the NEO-PI-3 are well-supported by exploratory factor analysis, far less support has been observed with CFA. Good fit requires relaxing the simple structure underlying the hypothesized model by freely estimating secondary loadings. Results of CFA also do not consistently support the presumed structure when testing each domain separately, unless the additional aspects are modeled for each domain. Some of these difficulties probably stem in part from limitations of the specific items, which a previous review discussed in some detail (Juni, 1995). Although the latest edition of the measure is an improvement, several double-barreled items remain, and others ask the respondent to indicate how the respondent is perceived by others.

SUMMARY. The NEO-PI-3 U.K. Edition is the latest revision of the well-known NEO-PI scales for use with respondents from the United Kingdom. It is based on a very large body of empirical evidence and an impressive record of ongoing research leading to continual improvements in the measure. New evidence presented in the test manual regarding the 10 personality aspects and two meta-factors is an example of the kind of ongoing research that has contributed to the continued relevance of the measure. Although findings regarding this edition of the test are somewhat limited compared to other versions of the NEO Inventories, the U.K. edition is close enough to previous versions to generalize core findings to the present measure. Improvements are still needed in the measure's factor structure, in solutions for dealing with response distortion, and in the normative information required for test score interpretation in various contexts.

REVIEWER'S REFERENCES

Furnham, A., Guenole, N., Levine, S. Z., & Chamorro-Premuzic, T. (2013). The NEO Personality Inventory–Revised: Factor structure and gender invariance from exploratory structural equation modeling analyses in a high-stakes setting. *Assessment, 20(1)*, 14-23.

Griffith, R. L., & Robie, C. (2013). Personality testing and the "F-word": Revisiting seven questions about faking. In N. D. Christiansen & R. P. Tett (Eds.), *Handbook of personality at work* (pp. 253-280). New York, NY: Routledge.

Huang, J. L., Liu, M., & Bowling, N. A. (2015). Insufficient effort responding: Examining an insidious confound in survey data. *Journal of Applied Psychology, 100*(3), 828-845.

Juni, S. (1995). [Review of the NEO Personality Inventory]. In J. C. Conoley & J. C. Impara (Eds.), *The twelfth mental measurements yearbook* (pp. 863-868). Lincoln, NE: Buros Institute of Mental Measurements.

Kluck, A. S. (2014). [Review of the NEO Personality Inventory-3]. In J. F. Carlson, K. F. Geisinger, & J. L. Jonson (Eds.), *The nineteenth mental measurements yearbook* (pp. 481-483). Lincoln, NE: Buros Center for Testing.

Prewett, M. S., Tett, R. P., & Christiansen, N. D. (2013). A review and comparison of 12 personality inventories on key psychometric characteristics. In N. D. Christiansen & R. P. Tett (Eds.), *Handbook of personality at work* (pp. 191-225). New York, NY: Routledge.

Simms, L. J., Williams, T. F., & Nus, E. (2017). Assessment of the Five Factor Model. In T. A. Widiger (Ed.), *The Oxford handbook of the Five Factor Model* (pp. 353-380). New York, NY: Oxford University Press.

Weiner, I. B., & Greene, R. L. (2017). NEO Personality Inventory-3. In *Handbook of personality assessment* (pp. 287-307). Hoboken, NJ: Wiley.

Review of the NEO Personality Inventory–3 (U.K. Edition) by JANET V. SMITH, Assistant Vice President for Institutional Effectiveness, Pittsburg State University, Pittsburg, KS:

DESCRIPTION. The U.K. edition of the NEO Personality Inventory–3 (NEO-PI-3) is an adaptation of the U.S. NEO-PI-3 using a language and normative sample of relevance to individuals in the United Kingdom. In all other respects, the instrument appears very comparable to the U.S. version. The NEO-PI-3 U.K. Edition is a 240-item self-report measure designed to assess the "Big Five" domains of personality: Neuroticism (N), Extraversion (E), Openness to Experience (O), Agreeableness (A), and Conscientiousness (C). In addition to a score for each of the five broad domains, the instrument yields 30 facet scores that provide a more in-depth understanding of personality. According to the test manual, formal validity scales are deliberately not included in the NEO-PI-3, but users can check validity of scores by assessing a test taker's attitude toward the test, as well as by acquiescence/nay-saying and random responding. Despite criticism of previous versions of the NEO, social desirability scales are also deliberately omitted; the test authors cite research indicating lack of effectiveness as the reason for this exclusion.

Ideally, the NEO-PI-3 U.K. Edition is administered and scored online, although it is also available in paper-and-pencil format. Online administration can be from remote locations. Test takers are advised to allow 1 hour for completion of the test, although typical completion time is considerably less. Both a technical report for the test administrator and a personal insight report for the test taker are available. The required reading age is 16 or above. The NEO-PI-3 U.K. Edition is one of a number of versions of the NEO inventories. The test manual provides a description of characteristics associated with both high and low scores on NEO facet scales and the five broad domains. Limited information is provided on interpretation of combinations of scales. The test manual provides a description of applications of NEO inventories in general. These include use in occupational, behavioral medicine and health, clinical/counseling, and research settings.

DEVELOPMENT. The NEO-PI-3 U.K. Edition is based on the U.S. version of the NEO-PI-3, with minor modifications in item language and content. According to the test manual, development of the NEO inventories is based on factor analysis of ratings of trait adjectives, resulting in identification of the Big Five fundamental dimensions of personality. Each of the five factors, or domains, is made up of intercorrelated traits of a more specific nature, referred to as facet scales. Domain scores are obtained by summing relevant facet scale scores. The test manual provides a brief history of the development of the NEO inventories, with key aspects including basis in the psychological literature and rational scale construction, using factor analysis as the basis for item selection.

TECHNICAL. Comprehensive psychometric data that are specific to the U.K. edition of the NEO-PI-3 are provided in the test manual. Norms are based on a sample of 656 individuals ages 18-70, also referred to as the U.K. working norm group. Key demographic information for this group is provided in the manual, including gender, educational level, ethnic group, occupation, industry sector, geographic region, and employment status. According to the manual, the normative sample is similar to 2011 U.K. census data, although no specific data are provided for comparison. In addition, a managerial and professional norm group is available that is based on 353 respondents. The test manual includes findings on the effect of age, gender, and education on U.K. edition scores. Gender-specific norms are an option. [Editor's note: The test publisher advised the Buros Center for Testing that a third normative group of international managerial and professional adults (N = 422) was added after materials were received for this review.]

Overall, reliability of the NEO-PI-3 U.K. Edition appears consistent with the U.S. version. Internal consistency coefficients for the domain scales range from .88 to .94. As would be expected, internal consistency for the individual facet scales is lower, with coefficient alpha values that range from .60 to .86. Internal consistency estimates for nine of the 30 facet scales fall below .70. Test-retest reliability is based on a pilot version of the NEO-PI-3 U.K. Edition, with a sample size of 112 test takers and a 4-week interval between tests. Reliability coefficients range from .74 to .85 for the domain scores and from .76 to .90 for the facet scores. Test-retest reliability coefficients are above .80 for all but five of the facet scores.

Factor structure was verified by performing target rotation and exploratory structural equation modelling techniques on the U.K. standardization data. Findings confirmed the five-factor model. Factor congruence coefficients were significant and ranged from .95 to .98. In addition, facet scales had significant variable congruence for all but one scale, Openness to Values, which was also the facet scale with the lowest internal consistency coefficient. Evidence of convergent and discriminant validity relies on previous studies with other NEO instruments rather than the NEO-PI-3 U.K. Edition. In support of this reliance, the test manual includes data showing equivalence of the U.K. versions of the NEO-PI-3 and the NEO-PI-R, with domain scale correlation coefficients ranging from .88 to .91 and facet scale correlations ranging from .72 to .87 based on a sample of 159 individuals.

COMMENTARY. The NEO-PI-3 U.K. Edition is designed to measure five broad personality domains and accompanying traits or facets. With a total of 35 scores, the test provides a wealth of information regarding personality characteristics that may be useful in a variety of settings. As with previous versions, there is no formal assessment of evidence supporting the interpretation of profiles, although it is important to note this is a deliberate choice on the part of the test authors, based on their review of relevant research. The test manual is comprehensive and well organized. Both the technical and personal insight computer-generated reports are also well organized and user-friendly, with the personal insight report written in lay language for test takers to easily comprehend.

The test is very comparable to the U.S. version, but language has been anglicized and item content appears appropriate for use with a U.K. population. The test has been normed with individuals from all regions of the United Kingdom, and the test manual provides extensive information on key demographic variables, reportedly consistent with 2011 census data. Of note, the normative sample is homogenous with regard to ethnic group, with 91.9% of individuals identified as White. The NEO-PI-3 U.K. Edition replaces the NEO-PI-R U.K. Edition and is a marked improvement over the previous version. The NEO-PI-3 U.K. Edition provides useful data on reliability and validity specific to this instrument, rather than relying on psychometric properties of the equivalent U.S. version, as was the case for the previous version. In general, coefficients for both internal consistency and test-retest reliability are acceptable. The five-factor structure is confirmed, with high loadings of facet scales on the designated domain scale and with very few facet scales loading significantly on more than one domain. Less established is evidence supporting convergent and discriminant validity of test scores, as reliance is exclusively on research with previous versions of the instrument.

SUMMARY. The NEO-PI-3 U.K. Edition is an easily administered and scored self-report inventory used to measure five broad personality domains. As well as a description of personality traits in these five domains, the instrument yields useful information on an additional 30 facets of personality. Scales and accompanying descriptors focus on normal personality traits, and the instrument is neither designed nor appropriate for diagnosis of psychopathology. The U.K. edition appears very comparable to the U.S. version, except the test manual includes psychometric properties specific to the U.K. version. The current version represents a major improvement over the previous U.K. version of the instrument.

[102]

Neonatal Behavioral Assessment Scale, 4th Edition.

Purpose: Designed to assess an infant's behavioral and neurological status.
Population: Ages 3 days through 2 months.
Publication Dates: 1973-2011.
Acronym: NBAS.
Scores: 53 in 3 domains: Behavioral (Response Decrement to Light, Response Decrement to Rattle, Response Decrement to Bell, Response Decrement to Foot, Animate Visual, Animate Visual and Auditory, Inanimate Visual, Inanimate Visual and Auditory, Animate Auditory, Inanimate Auditory, Alertness, General Tone, Motor Maturity, Pull-to-Sit, Defensive, Activity Level, Peak of Excitement, Rapidity of Build-up, Irritability, Lability of States, Cuddliness, Consolability, Self-Quieting, Hand-to-Mouth, Tremulousness, Startles, Lability of Skin Color, Smiles), Supplementary (Quality of Alertness, Cost of Attention, Examiner Facilitation, General Irritability, Robustness/Endurance, State Regulation, Examiner's Emotional Response), Reflex (Plantar Grasp, Babinski, Ankle Clonus, Rooting, Sucking, Glabella, Passive Resistance—Legs, Passive Resistance—Arms, Palmar Grasp, Placing, Standing, Walking, Crawling, Incurvation, Tonic Dev. Head/Eyes, Nystagmus, Tonic Neck Reflex, Moro).
Administration: Individual.
Price Data, 2020: £55 per hardcover book (2011, 200 pages).
Time: (12-20) minutes.
Comments: A 53-item rating scale of infant behavior and reflexes; not for use with infants recovering from illness or premature birth; to be administered by clinicians trained in neonatal behavior.
Authors: T. Berry Brazelton and J. Kevin Nugent.
Publisher: Mac Keith Press [United Kingdom].
Cross References: For reviews by Carol M. McGregor and Hoi K. Suen of the third edition, see 14:255; see also T5:1770 (17 references), T4:321 (9 references), 9:157 (9 references), and T3:311 (31 references); for a review by Anita Miller Sostek and an excerpted review by Stephen Wolkind of an earlier edition titled Brazelton Neonatal Behavioral Assessment Scale, see 8:208 (15 references).

Review of the Neonatal Behavioral Assessment Scale, 4th Edition by MICHELLE ATHANASIOU, Professor of School Psychology, and KRISTEN STODDARD, Doctoral Student, University of Northern Colorado, Greeley, CO:

DESCRIPTION. The Neonatal Behavioral Assessment Scale, 4th Edition (NBAS) is intended to foster attachment and encourage differentiated care through the identification of patterns of newborn behavior and development. Appropriate for teaching and intervention, this instrument provides caregivers insight into the way their newborn infant responds to the environment outside the uterus and contributes to the caregiver/child relationship. The test is appropriate for term infants from birth through 2 months old (and for preterm infants under certain conditions). Ideally, development is tracked over time, but the NBAS is more feasibly used as a snapshot during the first few days of life. Additionally, although not the main focus of the test, the instrument may detect possible neurological abnormalities.

Test materials include a hardcover manual within which is a reproducible scoring form. The assessment materials alluded to in the book (i.e., rattle and bell) are not included. The NBAS includes 28 behavioral items scored on a 9-point scale (response and orientation to stimuli, motor control, alertness, and mood), 18 neurological status items scored on a 4-point scale (i.e., reflexes), and seven supplementary items also scored on a 4-point scale and designed to reveal subtle signs of stress in high-risk infants (e.g., quality of alertness, cost of attention). The test authors refer to 20 neurological status items in one place in the manual, but the scoring form, item descriptions, and scoring criteria only list 18.

The NBAS is a criterion-referenced measure in which infants' behaviors are scored based on the quality of developmental skills exhibited. Each item contains unique scoring guidelines adapted specifically to the behavior measured; therefore, numerical scores across items cannot be directly compared, and no total or subscale scores are provided. Results demonstrate the degree to which an infant may deviate from what is typical, according to extensive research conducted on newborn development. Examiners are encouraged to involve caregivers in the administration process.

Following test administration and scoring, a narrative behavioral summary can be provided to the caregiver. This summary includes the infant's strengths and areas for growth. A consultation between the examiner and the caregiver(s) is strongly recommended to discuss practical strategies to address the areas for growth. This process is discussed in the manual, with guidelines as to how the consultation session should flow, and an example of a behavioral summary is provided. Per the test authors, certification on the NBAS is required to assure examiner proficiency and attune examiners to the art of eliciting the best performance of each infant. The test authors refer to many centers around the world that provide this training.

DEVELOPMENT. Original development of the NBAS followed findings of child development researchers in the 1960s and 1970s. This research characterized newborns as competent and complex with individualized behaviors. Within this view, infants have the ability to elicit caregiving, and insight about their ability to self-regulate and be social can be drawn from their behaviors. This knowledge, along with Brazelton's and colleagues' clinical work with infants, formed the basis of their work toward systematically observing and coding newborn behavior for the purposes of describing developmental competencies and difficulties.

NBAS item content was designed to allow for measurement of newborns' progress through hierarchical developmental challenges related to self-regulation over the first two months of life (i.e., regulation of autonomic state, followed by regulation of state behavior, motor behavior, and affective interactive behavior). Items related to such regulation were written in a way that could be coded for contemporaneous description and documentation of developmental progression, and the supplementary items have been added since the first edition of the scale. Later editions focused on guidelines for clinical uses, and the current edition includes chapters written by researchers and clinicians highlighting various uses of the NBAS in research and clinical practice. The content of the scale itself remains unchanged from earlier editions.

NBAS content was developed based on the culmination of then-current research and professional judgment based on extensive clinical experience. Little mention of pilot testing or revision of scale items is made in the NBAS manual. Recent work with the scale is focused on updated guidelines for usage in research and clinical practice, rather than content revision.

TECHNICAL. Although the test has been criticized for its inability to predict later development, the test authors explain that the test in isolation is not intended to make long-term predictions, as this is contrary to the theory of the reciprocal nature of the caregiver-child relationship and the role of an individual's environment. However, some studies have shown associations between certain NBAS scores and early childhood behavior (see Redshaw, 2011), suggesting possible predictive ability. Face validity is a strength of the NBAS, given item content that samples crucial aspects of newborn behavior and development. The test authors also highlight extensive item and factor analyses (see Redshaw, 2011). Concurrent evidence of validity is not addressed in the test manual.

The test authors explain that test-retest reliability measures are not appropriate for the NBAS, given the environmental and state changes and the rapid developmental growth that are nearly constant for a newborn. Instead, they emphasize the interrater reliability among certified examiners. Studies have shown interrater agreement ranging from .84 to .99 (see Redshaw, 2011).

COMMENTARY. The NBAS appears theoretically sound and aligns with current research on newborn development. Many studies, as interpreted by the test authors, have shown positive effects of the NBAS on maternal confidence and self-esteem, parent-infant interaction, and developmental outcome (see Brazelton & Nugent, 2011). Certification training is designed to produce competent examiners who are comfortable working with newborns and able to elicit best performance. Certified examiners are required to demonstrate administration accuracy. Furthermore, they are competent to conduct consultations with parents through which scores on the NBAS can be interpreted and strategies for addressing areas for infant growth can be shared. The NBAS has been used in 24 cultures spanning five continents.

A past criticism of the NBAS is still of some concern, namely that the instrument can take up to 20 minutes to administer. The test authors lament the suggestion by some that 20 minutes is too much to ask, given the benefits of findings for infants and their families. However, it may be difficult to find a 20-minute period during which the infant is in the required state for item administration. Examiners concerned about length and timing issues might consider the Newborn Behavioral Observation (NBO; Nugent, Keefer, Minear, Johnson, & Blanchard, 2007). The NBO is described as a relationship-building tool that can screen for worrisome behaviors that subsequently can be more thoroughly examined by the NBAS.

Logistical considerations related to NBAS administration might be somewhat problematic. Access to infants is easiest in a hospital setting before discharge, and the test authors state that it is best to wait until the infant is at least 2 days old—the time at which infants are often taken home. Furthermore, the test is ideally intended to be administered more than once, yet access to the infant is greatly reduced after the typically small window of time at the hospital.

Certification upkeep is a barrier to widespread implementation of the NBAS. Certification must be renewed every three years, and examiners must be sure to assess a healthy term infant after every five research examinations to avoid observer drift. Although these measures seem reasonable given the nature of the test, they do serve as hurdles to universal administration, as the test authors desire.

SUMMARY. The Neonatal Behavioral Assessment Scale, 4th Edition appears to be a beneficial and widely used measure of newborn behavior that positively affects the caregiver/child relationship, maternal mental health, and child development. Although the test manual does not include information about concurrent evidence of validity, the NBAS seems to have adequate interrater reliability. The nature of the test and its intended population limit the extent to which predictive validity evidence has been examined. Administrator certification is designed to ensure fidelity of instrument use and reliable measurements. Time constraints are still of some concern with the NBAS when considering working with newborns. Logistics and certification upkeep serve as barriers to widespread implementation.

REVIEWERS' REFERENCES

Brazelton, T. B., & Nugent, J. K. (2011). The Neonatal Behavioral Assessment Scale (NBAS)–Background and conceptual basis. In T. B. Brazelton & J. K. Nugent (Eds.), *The Neonatal Behavioral Assessment Scale* (4th ed.). London, England: Mac Keith Press.

Nugent, J. K., Keefer, C. H., Minear, S., Johnson, L. C., & Blanchard, Y. (2007). *Understanding newborn behavior and early relationships: The Newborn Behavioral Observation (NBO) system handbook.* Baltimore, MD: Paul H. Brookes Publishing.

Redshaw, M. (2011). Using the NBAS in research. In T. B. Brazelton & J. K. Nugent (Eds.), *The Neonatal Behavioral Assessment Scale* (4th ed., pp. 79-93). London, England: Mac Keith Press.

Review of the Neonatal Behavioral Assessment Scale, 4th Edition by LESLIE R. HAWLEY, Research Assistant Professor, Nebraska Center for Research on Children, Youth, Families and Schools, University of Nebraska-Lincoln, Lincoln, NE:

DESCRIPTION. The Neonatal Behavioral Assessment Scale (NBAS) is a neurobehavioral scale designed to assess the behavioral and neurological status of infants ages 3 days through 2 months. The 53-item rating scale is designed to be administered by clinicians trained in neonatal behavior. NBAS can be used for healthy preterm (37 weeks gestational age) infants, but it is not designed for use with premature birth infants requiring neonatal intensive care or those recovering from illness. Administration is estimated to take 12-20 minutes. Items fall into three broad domains: Behavioral (28 items), Supplementary (7 items), and Reflex (18 items). Behavioral items, scored on a 9-point scale, include: Response Decrement to Light, Response Decrement to Rattle, Response Decrement to Bell, Response Decrement to Tactile Stimulation of the Foot, Orientation Inanimate Visual, Orientation Inanimate Auditory, Orientation Inanimate Visual and Auditory, Orientation Animate Visual, Orientation Animate Auditory, Orientation Animate Visual and Auditory, Alertness, General Tonus, Motor Maturity, Pull-to-Sit, Defensive Movements, Activity Level, Peak of Excitement, Rapidity of Build-Up, Irritability, Lability of States, Cuddliness, Consolability, Self-Quieting, Hand-to-Mouth, Tremulousness, Startles, Lability of Skin Color, and Smiles. Supplementary items, scored on a 9-point scale, include: Quality of Alertness, Cost of Attention, Examiner Facilitation, General Irritability, Robustness and Endurance, State Regulation, and Examiner's Emotional Response. Reflex items, scored on a 4-point scale, include: Plantar Grasp, Babinski, Ankle Clonus, Rooting, Sucking, Glabella, Passive Movements—Arms, Passive Movements—Legs, Palmar Grasp, Placing, Standing, Walking, Crawling, Incurvation (Gallant Response), Tonic Deviation of Head and Eyes, Nystagmus, Tonic Neck Reflex, and Moro.

Training is required to effectively administer and score the scale. NBAS training curricula may vary across training sites around the world, but all trainings should include two major components: preparation/training phase and reliability phase. In the reliability phase, trainees and trainers jointly observe and score a baby using the NBAS. Following a debrief session with the trainer, the trainer provides a demonstration examination that is jointly scored by the trainer and trainee, followed by another debrief. Next, trainees administer the NBAS, and the trainer and trainee score independently. Scores are reviewed for consistency with the goal of achieving 90 percent agreement. On the 9-point scale items (Behavioral and Supplementary), examiners should agree within 1 point, and there should be 100 percent agreement on 4-point items. Certification lasts for three years and must be renewed if the user wishes to use the NBAS in research settings. Trainees are encouraged to familiarize themselves with items, administration, and scoring procedures and to learn to be comfortable and confident in handling newborns.

Examiners need to be able to draw out a baby's "best performance," using responses and cues of the infant. Examiners are trained to score items only if the infant is in the appropriate state. NBAS uses a more flexible approach to administration with no fixed order of administration to "draw out the full richness of the infant's repertoire of behavior" (manual, p. 10). Behavioral and reflex items can be grouped into administrative "packages," which follow an established order based on level of intensity or degree of stimulation. Packages include: (a) habituation, (b) motor-oral, (c) truncal, (d) vestibular, and (e) social interactive. The social interactive package can be administered only when the baby is in an alert state, so it is considered a moveable package. NBAS does not provide a single score; rather, item-level scores can be summarized across different dimensions or clusters. The test manual emphasizes that the NBAS can be used by a clinician to gather information about an infant's current level of functioning while also providing a blueprint to help parents better understand their child.

DEVELOPMENT. According to the test manual, the NBAS is designed to assess the integration of autonomic, motor, state, and social interactive behavioral systems in newborn infants. The NBAS considers infant development in terms of integrated competencies and is based on the assumption that newborns are social organisms capable of interacting with caregivers from the beginning. The main breakthroughs for this line of thinking were due to the clinical experience of T. Berry Brazelton, whose research in the early 1960s led to the first iteration of the NBAS, the Cambridge Neonatal Scales (Brazelton & Freedman, 1971). The next iteration of the scale appeared in 1983 and included supplementary items adapted from a Kansas version of the instrument and the Assessment of Premature Infant Behavior (Als, Lester, Tonick, & Brazelton, 1982). A third edition of the NBAS was released in 1996 with new guidelines for clinical uses. The most recent version of the NBAS is the fourth edition, which expands on the previous editions and highlights the range of research and clinical contexts for using the NBAS.

NBAS items cover four domains of neurobehavioral functioning: autonomic/physiological regulation, motor organization, state organization and regulation, and attention/social interaction. NBAS can be used to describe the current status of the individual infant's functioning as the integration across systems over time and potential influence from environmental factors. NBAS development has focused on its potential as a form of intervention as well as a research tool (Nugent, 1985).

TECHNICAL. According to the test manual, when data have been collected on interrater reliability, agreement between raters has ranged from .84 to .99 (e.g., Azuma, Malee, Kavanagh, & Deddish, 1991; DiPietro and Larson, 1989; Osofsky & O'Connell, 1977). The test manual provides rubrics and guidelines for scoring individual items but does not provide specific instructions for summarizing items. According to the manual, the most commonly used system for summarizing NBAS scores uses seven clusters: (a) habituation, (b) orientation, (c) motor, (d) range of state, (e) regulation of state, (f) autonomic stability, and (g) reflexes. Yet, a recent study by Costa et al. (2010)

used factor analysis with principal component analysis and found evidence for four components. Two studies cited in the test manual (Gyurke, Reich, & Holmes, 1988; McCollam, Embretson, Mitchell, & Horowitz, 1997) have examined the effects of scoring method. Gyurke et al. found that different scoring methods all detected differences between medically at-risk and healthy infants. McCollam et al. found psychometric evidence to support the use of the original scoring approach (i.e., summarizing by six factors excluding reflexes) over alternative scoring approaches.

The test manual cites a broad range of studies that have used NBAS scores to understand individual differences in term infants by examining aspects such as infant feeding, sex differences in infant behavior, maternal mental health, clinical problems, and cross-cultural and cross-species comparisons (e.g., Boatella-Costa, Costas-Moragas, Botet-Mussons, Fornieles-Deu, & De Cáceres-Zurita, 2007; Hart, Boylan, Carroll, Musick, & Lampe, 2003; Hernandez-Reif, Field, Diego, & Ruddock, 2006; Paludetto et al., 2002; Redshaw, 1989). NBAS scores have been used in cross-cultural settings across Europe, Asia, Africa, and North and South America (e.g., Lester & Brazelton, 1982; Nugent, Lester, & Brazelton, 1989, 1991; Super & Harkness, 1982). Studies examining the effects of maternal substance misuse and alcohol consumption on infant behavioral and development have utilized NBAS scores (e.g., Eyler, Behnke, Conlon, Woods, & Wobie, 1998; Tronick et al., 2005). The test manual also references the use of NBAS scores in studies that measured effects of preterm birth and low birthweight on infant development (e.g., Anderson et al., 1989; Feldman & Eidelman, 2006; Ohgi et al., 2002; Ohgi, Takahashi, Nugent, Arisawa, & Akiyama, 2003; Stjernqvist & Svenningsen, 1990; Wolf et al., 2002).

NBAS scores have been used as a form of intervention as well as a research tool to examine aspects related to maternal self-confidence and self-esteem, parent-infant interaction, and developmental outcomes (e.g., Kaaresen, Rønning, Ulvund, & Dahl, 2006). A meta-analysis of NBAS-based parenting interventions found that intervention processes have small to moderate beneficial effects on parental quality (Eiden & Reifman, 1996). NBAS scores have also been used to examine long-term outcomes by evaluating potential links between newborn and later behavior (e.g., Canals, Hernández-Martínez, & Fernández-Ballart, 2011; Lundqvist-Persson, 2001; Ohgi et al., 2003).

COMMENTARY. The NBAS is a widely used tool to assess infant functioning. A major strength of the instrument is its extensive history and evidence supporting use of its scores as a form of intervention and a research tool. Despite the extensive use of the NBAS, there are weaknesses with the instrument. As mentioned in the test manual, there are tension points with traditional standardized assessments in terms of consistency and fidelity of administration. NBAS training allows for flexibility of item administration to elicit the infant's "best performance," yet this flexibility is at odds with standardized approaches. The test manual also highlights limitations related to establishing and maintaining reliability across time and between examiners. The lack of specific guidance for summarizing the 53 items is another limitation of the instrument. These limitations make it difficult to evaluate NBAS relative to other traditional standardized assessments. Yet, the potential benefits of the information gleaned from the NBAS outweigh some of its faults. The NBAS provides an important tool for physicians and parents to understand and explore strengths and weaknesses of an infant. Physicians and parents can use information learned through the administration of the NBAS to monitor infant development and/or seek additional screening measures (if needed).

SUMMARY. The Neonatal Behavioral Assessment Scale (NBAS) is a neurobehavioral scale designed to assess infants ages 3 days through 2 months. NBAS scores have been used extensively in cross-cultural research and clinical settings to understand infant behavior. Although there are limitations to the NBAS as a traditional standardized assessment, the potential benefits of the information learned from the NBAS outweigh these limitations. NBAS scores provide important feedback for physicians and parents so they can monitor strengths and weaknesses in infant development.

REVIEWER'S REFERENCES

Als, H., Lester, B. M., Tonick, E. Z., & Brazelton, T. B. (1982). Manual for the Assessment of Preterm Infants' Behavior (APIB). In H. E. Fitzgerald, B. M. Lester, & M. W. Yogman (Eds.), *Theory and research in behavioral pediatrics* (pp. 65-132). New York, NY: Plenum Press.

Anderson, L. T., Coll, C. G., Vohr, B. R., Emmons, L., Brann, B., Shaul, P. W., Mayfield, S. R., & Oh, W. (1989). Behavioral characteristics and early temperament of premature infants with intracranial hemorrhage. *Early Human Development, 18*, 273-283.

Azuma, S. D., Malee, K. M., Kavanagh, J. A., & Deddish, R. B. (1991). Confirmatory factor analysis with preterm NBAS data: A comparison of four data reduction models. *Infant Behavior and Development, 14*, 209-225.

Boatella-Costa, E., Costas-Moragas, C., Botet-Mussons, F., Fornieles-Deu, A., & De Cáceres-Zurita, M. L. (2007). Behavioral gender differences in the neonatal period according to the Brazelton scale. *Early Human Development, 83*, 91-97.

Brazelton, T. B., & Freedman, D. G. (1971). The Cambridge Neonatal Scales. In G. B. A. Stodinga & J. J. van der Werften Bosch (Eds.), *Normal and abnormal development of brain and behaviour* (pp. 104-132). Leiden, Netherlands: Leiden University Press.

Canals, J., Hernández-Martínez, C., & Fernández-Ballart, J. D. (2011). Relationships between early behavioural characteristics and temperament at 6 years. *Infant Behavior and Development, 34*, 152-160.

Costa, R., Figueiredo, B., Tendais, I., Conde, A., Pacheco, A., & Teixeira, C. (2010). Brazelton neonatal behavioral assessment scale: A psychometric study in a Portuguese sample. *Infant Behavior and Development, 33*, 510-517.
DiPietro, J. A., & Larson, S. K. (1989). Examiner effects in the administration of the NBAS: The illusion of reliability. *Infant Behavior and Development, 12*, 119-123.
Eiden, R. D., & Reifman, A. (1996). Effects of Brazelton demonstrations on later parenting: A meta-analysis. *Journal of Pediatric Psychology, 21*, 857-868.
Eyler, F. D., Behnke, M., Conlon, M., Woods, N. S., & Wobie, K. (1998). Birth outcome from a prospective, matched study of prenatal crack/cocaine use: I. Interactive and dose effects on health and growth. *Pediatrics, 101*, 229-236.
Feldman, R., & Eidelman, A. I. (2006). Neonatal state organization, neuromaturation, mother-infant interaction, and cognitive development in small-for-gestational-age premature infants. *Pediatrics, 118*, e869-e878.
Gyurke, J. S., Reich, J. N., & Holmes, D. L. (1988). An examination of the effectiveness of multiple summary scoring procedures of the BNBAS in detecting group differences. *Infant Mental Health Journal, 9*, 201-208.
Hart, S., Boylan, L. M., Carroll, S., Musick, Y. A., & Lampe, R. M. (2003). Brief report: Breast-fed one-week-olds demonstrate superior neurobehavioral organization. *Journal of Pediatric Psychology, 28*, 529-534.
Hernandez-Reif, M., Field, T., Diego, M., & Ruddock, M. (2006). Greater arousal and less attentiveness to face/voice stimuli by neonates of depressed mothers on the Brazelton Neonatal Behavioral Assessment Scale. *Infant Behavior and Development, 29*, 594-598.
Kaaresen, P. I., Rønning, J. A., Ulvund, S. E., & Dahl, L. B. (2006). A randomized, controlled trial of the effectiveness of an early-intervention program in reducing parenting stress after preterm birth. *Pediatrics, 118*, e9-e19.
Lester, B. M., & Brazelton, T. B. (1982). Cross-cultural assessment of neonatal behavior. In D. Wagner & H. Stevenson (Eds.), *Cultural perspectives on child development* (pp. 20-53). San Francisco, CA: W. H. Freeman.
Lundqvist-Persson, C. (2001). Correlation between level of self-regulation in the newborn infant and developmental status at two years of age. *Acta Paediatrica, 90*, 345-350.
McCollam, K. M., Embretson, S. E., Mitchell, D. W., & Horowitz, F. D. (1997). Using confirmatory factor analysis to identify newborn behavior structure with the NBAS. *Infant Behavior and Development, 20*, 123-131.
Nugent, J. K. (1985). *Using the NBAS with infants and their families: Guidelines for intervention.* White Plains, NY: March of Dimes Birth Defects Foundation.
Nugent, J. K., Lester, B. M., & Brazelton, T. B. (1989). *The cultural context of infancy, Vol. 1. Biology, culture, and infant development.* Norwood, NJ: Ablex.
Nugent, J. K., Lester, B. M., & Brazelton, T. B. (1991). *The cultural context of infancy, Vol. 2. Multicultural and interdisciplinary approaches to parent-infant relations.* Norwood, NJ: Ablex.
Paludetto, R., Mansi, G., Raimondi, F., Romano, A., Crivaro, V., Bussi, M., & D'Ambrosio, G. (2002). Moderate hyperbilirubinemia induces a transient alteration of neonatal behavior. *Pediatrics, 110*, e50-e50.
Ohgi, S., Fukuda, M., Moriuchi, H., Kusumoto, T., Akiyama, T., Nugent, J. K., ... Saitoh, H. (2002). Comparison of kangaroo care and standard care: Behavioral organization, development, and temperament in healthy, low-birth-weight infants through 1 year. *Journal of Perinatology, 22*, 374-379.
Ohgi, S., Takahashi, T., Nugent, J. K., Arisawa, K., & Akiyama, T. (2003). Neonatal behavioral characteristics and later behavioral problems. *Clinical Pediatrics, 42*, 679-686.
Osofsky, J. D., & O'Connell, E. J. (1977). Patterning of newborn behavior in an urban population. *Child Development, 48*, 532-536.
Redshaw, M. E. (1989). A comparison of neonatal behaviour and reflexes in the great apes. *Journal of Human Evolution, 18*, 191-200.
Stjernqvist, K., & Svenningsen, N. W. (1990). Neurobehavioural development at term of extremely low-birthweight infants (< 901G). *Developmental Medicine & Child Neurology, 32*, 679-688.
Super, C. M., & Harkness, S. (1982). The infant's niche in rural Kenya and metropolitan America. In L. Adler (Ed.), *Cross-cultural research at issue* (pp. 47-55). New York, NY: Academic Press.
Tronick, E. Z., Messinger, D. S., Weinberg, M. K., Lester, B. M., LaGasse, L., Seifer, R., ... Liu, J. (2005). Cocaine exposure is associated with subtle compromises of infants' and mothers' social-emotional behavior and dyadic features of their interaction in the face-to-face still-face paradigm. *Developmental Psychology, 41*, 711-722.
Wolf, M. J., Koldewijn, K., Beelen, A., Smit, B., Hedlund, R., & Groot, I. D. (2002). Neurobehavioral and developmental profile of very low birthweight preterm infants in early infancy. *Acta Paediatrica, 91*, 930-938.

[103]

Neuropsychological Assessment of Adults with Visual Impairment.

Purpose: Designed as a neuropsychological test battery for adults with visual impairments.
Population: Individuals 16 and older who are visually impaired.
Publication Date: 2017.
Administration: Individual.
Price Data, 2020: $1,195 per kit including manual (2017, two volumes: manual, 118 pages; manual appendix, 102 pages, includes reproducible record forms), Adapted Token Test, Digit Symbol boards, pattern board and pegs, 50 Pattern of Search test forms, Pattern of Search Test, object assemblies (ball, block, doll, hand), tactile block design, and Tactual Formboard Test; $130 per manual.
Comments: All tests in the battery may be administered separately.
Authors: John T. Gallagher and Katherine A. Burnham.
Publisher: Stoelting, Co.

a) ADAPTED TOKEN TEST.
Purpose: Designed to assess receptive language and immediate retention.
Scores: Total score only.
Price: $28 per set of objects.
Time: Up to 20 minutes for administration.
Comments: Adapted from The Token Test to replace tokens with geometric shapes and modify instructions to replace color specifications with shape specifications.

b) REY AUDITORY VERBAL LEARNING TEST.
Purpose: Designed to assess memory and word recognition.
Acronym: RAVLT.
Scores, 23: 9 trial summary scores (A1, A2, A3, A4, A5, A6, A7, B1, B2), 6 word recognition scores, Total Items Recalled A, Total Items Recalled B, Total Recall, Source Errors, Total Accurate Recall, Overall Score, Delayed Memory, Learning.
Time: Administration time not reported.
Comments: Adapted to include Wechsler Vocabulary subtest, recall for List B, and modified scoring for recognition procedure.

c) TACTUAL FORMBOARD TEST.
Purpose: Designed to assess spatial functioning and memory.
Acronym: TFBT.
Scores, 10: Dominant Hand, Non-Dominant Hand, Both Hands 1, Memory 1/Location 1, Both Hands 2, Memory 2/Location 2, Rotated, Exploration of Space, Overall Spatial Awareness, Spatial Memory.
Price: $100 per test.
Time: 8 minutes maximum per trial (timed).
Comments: Adapted from the Tactual Performance Test.

d) AUDITORY CANCELLATION TEST.
Purpose: Designed to assess sustained attention.
Scores, 2: Omission Errors, Commission Errors.
Time: Approximately 4 minutes for administration.

e) SUBTESTS OF HAPTIC INTELLIGENCE SCALE FOR ADULT BLIND.
Purpose: Designed to assess nonverbal functioning.
Acronym: HIS.
Comments: Adapted from the Haptic Intelligence Scale for Adult Blind to remove or update items perceived to be outdated and to reduce time constraints.

1) *Digit Symbol.*
Scores, 1-2: Total, Incidental Memory (optional).
Price: $80 per Digit Symbol boards.
Time: 2 minutes maximum (timed).

2) *Block Design.*
Scores: Total score only.

Price: $200 per tactile block design set.
Time: 3 minutes maximum per design (timed).
3) *Object Assembly.*
Scores: Total score only.
Price: $100 per ball or block; $150 per doll or hand.
Time: 5 minutes maximum per object (timed).
4) *Pattern Board.*
Scores: Total score only.
Price: $55 per pattern board and pegs.
Time: 30-60 seconds per pattern (timed).
f) MICHIGAN NONVISUAL MATHEMATICS TEST.
Purpose: Designed to assess mathematical ability in individuals with no sklls in mathematics code designed for the visually impaired.
Scores, 9: Information, Decimals, Accuracy, Fractions/Percentages, Addition/Subtraction, Multiplication/Division, Reasoning, Story Problems, Total.
Time: Administration time not reported.
Comments: Administered orally.
g) PATTERN OF SEARCH TEST.
Purpose: Designed to assess "planning ... considered to be an executive function" and spatial understanding.
Acronym: POS.
Scores, 3: Thoroughness, Plan, Total.
Price: $85 per test; $52.50 per 50 forms.
Time: 2-3 minutes for administration.
Comments: Adapted from the Plan of Search subtest originally intended to be included in the Haptic Intelligence Scale for Adult Blind.

Review of the Neuropsychological Assessment of Adults with Visual Impairment by MATTHEW E. LAMBERT, Private Practice, Granbury, TX:

DESCRIPTION. The Neuropsychological Assessment of Adults with Visual Impairment is a 10-test neuropsychological battery designed to assess cognitive abilities in individuals 16 years and older with either partial or total acquired visual impairment. The test assesses receptive language and immediate retention, verbal memory and word recognition, spatial memory and functioning, sustained auditory attention, nonverbal intellectual functioning, nonvisual mathematical ability, and executive functioning involving planning and spatial understanding. Tests can be administered individually or as part of a comprehensive battery. No composite scores are obtained from administering the entire battery. Traditional measures of cognitive, sensory, and motor functioning also are expected to be administered as part of the evaluation.

Test materials, along with educational and administration manuals, are provided in a wheeled carrying case. Individual tests can be purchased separately. The educational manual is an instructional textbook to educate professionals about conducting evaluations of adults who are visually impaired. Test development or adaptation for individuals with visual impairments, understanding vision function and visual disorders, and cognitive abilities relevant to visual impairments are discussed in the educational manual. The administration manual contains reproducible test forms, administration and scoring instructions, interpretation guidelines, normative data, and limited psychometric data.

DEVELOPMENT. Principles underlying the assessment are included in the preface to the educational manual. Development of the measure evolved over the first author's 30-year career working at the Michigan Bureau of Services for Blind Persons Training Center and primarily involved adapting previously developed tests for sighted individuals to a visually impaired population. The test authors state that test adaptations require standardization and statistical development and acknowledge that research presented for their assessment will "fall short of the usual test development and reporting standards" (Gallagher & Burnham, 2017, p. 8). They indicate that limited options for use with this population led them to publish "so that others might use and research these techniques" (Gallagher & Burnham, 2017, p. 8). Sighted-population norms were applied to some adapted tests with the justification that experience will support using pre-existing norms. Underlying constructs for adapted tests were assumed to be the same as for the non-adapted tests.

The 20-item Adapted Token Test is taken from the original 22-item Token Test (DeRenzi & Vignolo, 1962). The original colored squares and circles are replaced by blocks, discs, and cylinders. Instructions were adapted for individuals with visual impairments, with multistep procedures for the final three items. The Rey Auditory Verbal Learning Test (RAVLT) uses Lezak's recognition format (Lezak, 1976) and is adapted to include a List B recall, new recognition trial scoring, and inclusion of the Wechsler Vocabulary subtest to assess incidental verbal memory and incidental learning strength versus effortful learning. The Tactual Formboard Test (TFBT) is adapted from the Halstead-Reitan Neuropsychological Test Battery's Tactual Performance Test (Reitan & Wolfson, 1985). The adaptations involved placing the formboard flat on a table; eliminating board orientation; increasing the number of trials from three to fivc, including a trial with the board rotated 90 degrees; shortening the time per trial to 8 minutes; adding another memory trial; altering orientation to the memory trials by flipping the board; and adding two new scores. The Auditory Cancellation Test is an adaptation of a visual cancellation task (Mesulam, 1985) and requires indication when a specific letter occurs in a spoken letter string. Omission and commission errors are scored and interpreted. Four subtests from the Haptic Intelligence Scale for Adult Blind (Shurrager & Shurrager, 1964) are included: Digit Symbol, Block Design, Object Assembly, and Pattern Board. The first three were deemed to be aspects of nonverbal haptic intelligence comparable to performance subtests in the Wechsler Adult Intelligence Scale. The Michigan Nonvisual Mathematics Test was developed within the training center for the visually impaired to screen for mathematical ability and multiple mathematical skills and concepts at a sixth grade or higher level. Finally, the Pattern of Search Test (POS) is derived from "Plan of Search" tests first included in the Stanford-Binet Intelligence Scale Form LM (Terman & Merrill, 1973). A page is placed over a board containing five small holes with a goal of finding all holes while using a ballpoint pen to tactually scan the page. Complete visual obstruction is required. Plan and Thoroughness scores are generated on a 0 to 5 scale with the Plan score multiplied by 12 and Thoroughness rated for each of 12 squares on the test form. Planning is viewed as an executive function. The Plan and Thoroughness scores can be summed to produce a Total score.

TECHNICAL. Most test development participants were students at the Michigan training center; the remainder were referred from across Michigan. Members of the standardization sample were said to be representative of the Michigan state population and the visually impaired population although 17- to 20-year-olds, men, and African Americans were overrepresented. Elderly individuals were underrepresented. Individuals with severe mental illness, cognitive deficiencies, or severe physical disabilities were excluded.

Although test development occurred over 30 years, only data from the 20 years prior to publication were included. More than 1,500 records were reviewed, and 526 were selected for inclusion in psychometric studies. Not all 526 records included all tests, as assessments were tailored to individual test takers' needs. Data were most prevalent for the Tactual Formboard Test, Haptic Intelligence Scale tests, and the RAVLT. Means and standard deviations are presented for nearly all test scores across four age groups: 16-24 years, 25-44 years, 45-64 years, and 65 years and older, the exceptions being the Adapted Token Test, the Auditory Cancellation Test, and the Michigan Nonvisual Mathematics Test, for which means and standard deviations are reported for the entire age group.

Reliability data are absent for most tests. Limited psychometric data for the Adapted Token Test are presented for 34 participants with the lowest 10% reported to have a score of less than 7, and neurologically impaired adults under age 65 reportedly performed more poorly on all measures, although the differences did not reach statistical significance. Significant differences between neurologically and non-neurologically visual-impaired were noted across six RAVLT scores. TFBT normative data included a greater number of males, and approximately 30% were African American. Only two to five participants were 65 years old or older. Reliability for 314 participants was estimated by correlating the mean completion time per piece for two different trials. The resulting correlation coefficient was deemed acceptable ($r = .75$). Significant differentiation between participants who are visually impaired with and without concordant neurological dysfunction was found for three of six test scores. One score significantly ($p = 0.005$) predicted participants' success managing independent travel. Combination with a POS score, however, produced better accuracy in predicting independent travel. No significant differences were identified comparing adults who are visually impaired with and without neurological impairments for the Auditory Cancellation Test. Despite this, interpretive statements were suggested for cases in which five or more commission or seven or more omission errors occurred. Data from the original Haptic Intelligence Scale for Adult Blind national standardization sample were said to be nonapplicable to the Michigan sample and should not be used with the present measure. Even so, scaled score equivalents of raw scores were presented based on the original norms. All subtests were said to show age-related performance declines, although the sample sizes for those 65 and older ranged from one to seven, depending upon the subtest. The Michigan Nonvisual Mathematics Test was designed to assess mathematical skills taught in the sixth grade or earlier. Data from 68 individuals (mean age = 37 years; mean education = Grade 12) with visual impairments were included, and scores for the top and lowest 25% were presented. Excellent interrater reliabilities (all *r*s were above .99) for the POS Plan, Thoroughness, and Total scores were demonstrated between highly trained raters. Significant differences between individuals who are visually impaired with and without neurological impairments were not found. Yet, the Thoroughness score was significantly related to travel independence (p = 0.0494). As previously noted, combination of the Thoroughness score with a TFBT score improved prediction of someone being an independent traveler.

COMMENTARY. Despite acknowledging shortcomings in test development, the authors of the Neuropsychological Assessment of Adults with Visual Impairment suggest future research will provide additional support for the measure. Yet, professionals without an extensive background evaluating individuals who are visually impaired would lack sufficient clinical experience necessary to effectively interpret the tests that are included in the battery. The lack of psychometric data underpinning the assessment only exacerbates this reality. Additionally, the development sample does not represent the broader group of adults with visual impairments with whom it may be used, necessitating further psychometric development. Finally, there is a dearth of information regarding the meaning of observed differences in performance between adults with visual impairments with and those without neurological dysfunction. This deficiency limits the utility of the assessment in practice. Although the measure is a contribution to evaluating this population, it is not fully realized in its current form.

SUMMARY. The Neuropsychological Assessment of Adults with Visual Impairment presents a model for neuropsychological evaluation of adults who are visually impaired. The battery is limited by a lack of psychometric foundation for its tests, a restricted sample used in its development, and the lack of interpretive specificity to be drawn from the test results. The measure should be used now only by professionals well-versed in working with individuals who are visually impaired. Additional psychometric research is needed before it can become a widely used and foundation technique with this population.

REVIEWER'S REFERENCES

De Renzi, E., & Vignolo, L. A. (1962). The Token Test: A sensitive test to detect receptive disturbances in aphasics. *Brain, 85*, 665-668.

Gallagher, J. T., & Burnham, K. A. (2017) *Neuropsychological Assessment of Adults with Visual Impairment*. Wood Dale, IL: Stoelting.

Lezak, M. D. (1976). *Neuropsychological assessment*. New York, NY: Oxford University Press.

Mesulam, M. (1985). Tests of Directed Attention and Memory. Philadelphia, PA: FA Davis.

Reitan, R. M., & Wolfson, D. (1985). *The Halstead-Reitan Neuropsychological Test Battery: Theory and clinical interpretation*. Tucson, AZ: Neuropsychological Press.

Shurrager, H. C., & Shurrager, P. S. (1964). Haptic Intelligence Scale for Adult Blind. Chicago, IL: Stoelting.

Strauss, E., Sherman, E. M. S., & Spreen, O. (2006). *A compendium of neuropsychological tests: Administration, norms, and commentary*. (3rd Edition). New York, NY: Oxford.

Terman, L. M., & Merrill, M. A. (1973) *Stanford-Binet Intelligence Scale: Manual for the third revision, 1973 norms*. Boston, MA: Houghton Mifflin.

Review of the Neuropsychological Assessment of Adults with Visual Impairment by ROMEO VITELLI, Psychologist, Private Practice, Toronto, Ontario, Canada:

DESCRIPTION. While not a formal neuropsychological test battery in its own right, the new Neuropsychological Assessment of Adults with Visual Impairment assessment kit published by Stoelting represents one of the best new resources for the neuropsychological assessment of adults who are visually impaired. Given that assessing this population has long been problematic, the subtests and accompanying manual provided in this kit represent an excellent new resource both in terms of testing clients with visual impairments and providing a thorough overview of the existing literature in this largely neglected area.

With more than 6 million people in the United States alone reporting visual disability (not all of whom meet criteria for legal blindness), the need for better neuropsychological tests for this population has been long-recognized. Although previous tests have been developed for use with people who are visually impaired, including the Cognitive Test of the Blind, the Haptic Intelligence Scale for the Adult Blind, and the Vision Independent System, they have been used primarily to supplement existing tests, and their validity has been compromised as a result. As well, many of these tests have gone out of print with no new tests to take their place.

The comprehensive manual written by John T. Gallagher of the Borgess Medical Center and Katherine A. Burnham of Western Michigan University represents a culmination of Dr. Gallagher's 30 years of experience in testing adults with visual impairments coupled with assistance from Dr. Burnham. Along with a description of the core tests provided, the test manual provides an encyclopedic overview of the problems that examiners often face when testing individuals who are visually impaired. The coverage includes a thorough review of the human visual system; different kinds of visual perceptual disorders; and a discussion of how these disorders may impact the assessment of key neuropsychological domains such as intelligence, language, verbal and episodic memory, attention, and executive functioning. The test manual appendix provides an administration guide, record and summary forms, and scaled conversion tables for normative data.

Along with the test manual and appendix, the assessment kit includes 10 subtests to be used with individuals who are visually impaired. Most of these subtests have been taken from pre-existing neuropsychological measures and have been specially adapted to accommodate people with visual impairments. They include:

Adapted Token Test. This measure is used for assessment of receptive aphasia and verbal comprehension. Instead of colored chips as with the standard version, the adapted version uses a series of three-dimensional objects with different geometric shapes. Participants are tested on their ability to understand and carry out increasingly complex tasks.

Rey Auditory Verbal Learning Test (RAVLT). Nearly identical to the standard version, the main differences are the additions of a delayed recall for the interference list and a comparison to incidental recall from the Wechsler Vocabulary subtest.

Tactual Formboard Test (TFBT). Developed from the Halstead-Reitan Tactual Performance Test, the TFBT calls for the manual insertion of three-dimensional objects with different shapes into a formboard containing niches for each object. Participants are tested for the time required to complete the test for the dominant hand, non-dominant hand, both hands, and both hands with the board rotated.

Auditory Cancellation Test. Designed to measure selective attention, this test involves having examines listen to a series of letters read by the assessor and respond by tapping on the table whenever they hear a specific letter. Scoring is based on the number of letters missed (both omissions and commissions).

Digit Symbol Test. Adapted from the Digit Symbol subtest found in different versions of the Wechsler Adult Intelligence Scale, the modified test uses a tactile format. A reference key is provided with six shapes composed of raised dots. Test takers identify shape and number of dots by touch using a practice trial and then attempt to identify the shapes on 40 items while being timed. There is also an optional incidental memory procedure that can be used with this test.

Block Design. Developed from the Wechsler Block Design subtest, this test uses four 3-dimensional blocks with patterns made up of rough and smooth surfaces that can be identified by touch. Examinees are instructed to use the provided blocks to match sample patterns of increasing complexity within a 3-minute period.

Object Assembly. Based on the Wechsler Object Assembly subtest, test takers assemble four items from provided pieces based on touch alone within the allowed time period.

Pattern Board. Examinees are provided with a square board with 24 holes for round pegs and a fixed peg in the center. After the examiner inserts pegs into the board that the examinee is instructed to learn by touch, the pegs are removed and the examinee then attempts to reproduce that pattern from memory. Test takers are timed over 10 trials with the patterns becoming increasingly complex.

Michigan Nonvisual Mathematics Test. Used for the past 20 years to assess arithmetic ability in individuals who are visually impaired, this test consists of a series of oral questions measuring skills in different areas of mathematics.

Pattern of Search Test. Designed to measure planning ability and executive functioning, this subtest is based on the Plan of Search test developed for the Haptic Intelligence Scale and uses a tactile format allowing test takers to develop a pattern of search that can be scored independently, along with number of errors.

Throughout testing, a blindfold is needed for test takers with some vision to ensure comparability of results. The test manual also offers alternatives such as use of a small curtain setup and allows for special needs the test taker might have (such as the presence of a guide dog). Alternative versions of the tests are suggested for test takers with prior familiarity to the standard tests.

The response sheets for the different subtests are designed for easy hand scoring, and the test manual contains a chapter on report writing as well as examples and case histories to provide a guide for the proper administration, scoring, and reporting of test results.

DEVELOPMENT. Most of the subtests included in the assessment kit are already well-validated. Those subtests developed specifically for this test including the Tactual Formboard Test, Auditory Cancellation Test, Adapted Token Test, and Michigan Nonvisual Mathematics Test, were developed over the past 30 years by Dr. Gallagher and his colleagues and tested on patients referred for evaluation across the state of Michigan as well as a large sample of students at the Michigan Bureau of Services for Blind Persons Training Center. The demographic characteristics of the more than 500 test takers whose results were used for research, including standardization and case studies appears to be fairly representative of Michigan's population, although the test authors acknowledge that some age groups are overrepresented (young adults) and some are underrepresented (elderly adults), which may skew the results. Also, not all tests are administered to every test taker. For example, the Adapted Token Test is given only if there is a question of receptive aphasia.

TECHNICAL. The test manual presents data collected over the past 20 years by Dr. Gallagher and his colleagues. The test authors acknowledge that the research included in the test manual and appendix falls short of the usual test development and reporting standards (American Educational Research Association, American Psychological Association, & National Council on Measurement in Education, 2014). Nevertheless, they released the kit in its current form to encourage research and clinical use.

Although no formal reliability and validity data are presented, case studies comparing many of the assessment kit subtests to more formal neuropsychological measures such as relevant subtests of the Weschler Adult Intelligence Scale—Third Edition highlight the distortions that can result from using tests that fail to take visual impairments into account.

COMMENTARY. Given that the neuropsychological assessment of adults with visual impairments has been a largely neglected area up to now, the new Neuropsychological Assessment of Adults with Visual Impairment assessment kit represents a valuable resource for research and clinical testing. Despite the limited validity and reliability data available for the kit in its current form, many of these subtests have been the focus of extensive research that has indicated that they provide scores representing valid measures of different aspects of cognitive functioning. Some of the tests have been specially adapted for use in the kit. In addition, demographic data are provided to help guide researchers and clinicians work effectively with this population. Still, as the test authors point out, clinicians need to employ their own best judgment in how the assessment kit should be used. As for researchers exploring visual impairment in different populations, including elderly patients and low birth-weight children, the development of this assessment kit helps circumvent the problems that often result from using tests that fail to take visual impairments into account.

SUMMARY. While not a formal neuropsychological test battery in its own right, the new Neuropsychological Assessment of Adults with Visual Impairment assessment kit is a culmination of 30 years of research with adults who are visually impaired. The test manual, appendix, and subtest materials are unique resources for clinicians and researchers as well as a guide to the assessment, interpretation, and communication of test results for clients who have been traditionally neglected by test publishers. The test manual also provides a comprehensive overview of the current state of testing individuals with visual impairments and the kind of research that still needs to be done. Despite the lack of psychometric rigor seen in more established commercial tests, this kit represents a starting point for clinicians and researchers who work with this population.

REVIEWER'S REFERENCE

American Educational Research Association, American Psychological Association, & National Council on Measurement in Education. (2014). *Standards for educational and psychological testing*. Washington, DC: American Educational Research Association.

[104]

Neuropsychology Behavior and Affect Profile–Dementia.

Purpose: Designed to assess "symptoms of a neurodegenerative process, such as dementia, by measuring changes in emotional levels and in behavior."
Population: Ages 15 and older.
Publication Dates: 1989-2009.
Acronym: NBAP–D.
Scores, 10: Indifference (Before, Now), Inappropriateness (Before, Now), Pragnosia (Before, Now), Depression (Before, Now), Mania (Before, Now).
Administration: Individual.
Forms, 2: Self, Other.
Price Data, 2020: $50 per digital manual including review-only copy of form; $2.50 per remote online survey license or license to reproduce (minimum 50).
Time: Administration time not reported.
Authors: Linda D. Nelson, Paul Satz, and Louis F. D'Elia.
Publisher: Mind Garden, Inc.
Cross References: For a review by Surendra P. Singh of an earlier edition, see 14:258.

Review of the Neuropsychology Behavior and Affect Profile–Dementia by D. ASHLEY COHEN, Forensic Neuropsychologist, CogniMetrix, San Jose, CA:

DESCRIPTION. The Neuropsychology Behavior and Affect Profile–Dementia (NBAP-D) is designed to be administered to individuals with a suspected or previously diagnosed dementing condition. There is a companion form covering identical topics, to be completed by someone close to the patient, ideally someone who lives with the patient. This test would likely be individually administered, although a group administration would not be precluded.

The test authors note that neuropsychological assessments, even those that are fairly extensive, do not evaluate the behavioral and emotional functioning of patients. Test results can be used along with other neuropsychological measurements performed to provide a fuller picture of the individual; the NBAP-D also can be given at successive assessments to evaluate changes in emotional and behavioral status.

There are 66 questions presented as a column of statements printed toward the middle of a page of the response form, each describing behavioral or emotional experiences in first-person vernacular. To the left side of the page are two columns, with the heading over both "Before." On the right side are two columns labeled "Now." For each statement, the test taker can mark "agree" or "disagree" under each heading. The version meant for the family member is the same, except the questions are worded beginning "The patient ..."

Assuming that both patient and caregiver complete the test forms, four scores are obtained: (a) how the patient believes he or she was prior to the onset of the disorder; (b) how the patient assesses himself or herself presently; (c) how the caregiver believes the patient was prior to the onset of the disorder; (d) how the caregiver assesses the patient currently.

Five scales make up the NBAP-D: (a) Indifference, (b) Inappropriateness, (c) Pragnosia, (d) Depression, (e) Mania. The test authors specify these scales were rationally derived and were selected because these conditions are known to be associated with neuropsychological changes brought about by various dementing conditions.

The NBAP-D is designed for use with persons ages 15 and older who have at least 8 to 10 years of education, and a sixth-grade reading level. Central to completion of the test is a determination of date of onset of the dementing condition. This date is important because it serves as the dividing line between "Before" and "Now." Examinees are urged to make their "best guess" (manual, p. 16) regarding that date. The date offered by test takers could vary widely in accuracy for a variety of reasons. Caregiver reports may help establish a more reliable date of onset.

The test kit contains a manual, Self and Other record forms, a key to determining scale scores, and a Profile Form. There are 12 items in the Indifference scale; 7 for Inappropriateness; 12 in Pragnosia; 11 for Depression; and 24 items for Mania. No rationale is given for twice the number of Mania questions than for any of the other scales. The test is untimed; the authors estimate approximately 20 minutes for most persons to complete it.

The clinician calculates scores by summing the number of "agree" responses for each of the five scales, doing so for both the "Before" and "Now" columns. Therefore, there are 10 raw scores. There is a separate form to aid in this process, requiring the clinician to go through the response booklet to locate the items making up each scale, then transfer those responses to the summary form. Such a scoring scheme makes the test less costly, but increases the possibility of errors in transcribing item responses.

Having the total number of affirmative answers for each scale, the psychologist locates the scale being scored in a table in the test manual, then notes the percent score. Note that this is not a percentile score. This score merely indicates that if the respondent recorded six out of 12 "agree" responses, that patient answered that scale at 50%. The test manual states that any scales answered more than 50% "agree" should be considered elevated. Appendices are available for obtaining T-scores for three different groups: elderly controls, vascular dementia patients, and demented outpatients (with "Before" and "After" scores for each).

The test can be administered by any trained, competent individual, but must be interpreted by a neuropsychologist or other professional with comparable training. The test authors state, and it is important to note, that the NBAP-D should be given and interpreted as part of a full neuropsychological evaluation of the patient (that is, the NBAP-D is not meant to be a stand-alone instrument).

DEVELOPMENT. The Neuropsychology Behavior and Affect Profile–Dementia (NBAP-D) is a revision of the Neuropsychology Behavior and Affect Profile published in 1994. The first author of the current version credits Paul Satz as originating the test, which was first developed for patients with brain injuries and now focuses on patients with dementia.

TECHNICAL.

Standardization. A total of 145 persons comprise the normative sample. There were 42 elderly controls, 42 vascular dementia patients, and 61 demented outpatients. This reviewer could not locate data on the gender or educational makeup of the sample; it is unknown whether either of those factors proved to be significant with the NBAP-D. Percentage of various ethnic groups were listed for the validation studies.

Reliability. It does not appear that overall reliability was examined with a sample that included all groups for whom the test is appropriate. Three studies examined internal consistency using individuals with vascular dementia (n = 70), probable Alzheimer's disease (n = 61), and Down syndrome (n = 34). Across studies, alpha coefficients were reported as moderate to moderately high, ranging from .49 to .89. On the "Before" subscales, coefficients ranged from .70 to .82 for the vascular dementia group and from .49 to .78 for the probable Alzheimer's group. Coefficients for the "Now" subscales were .66-.82, .68-.82, and .56-.89 for the vascular dementia, probable Alzheimer's, and Down syndrome groups, respectively. A test-retest reliability study was conducted using persons with Down syndrome (n = 19) who were tested 1 year apart, on average. Adequate to very good correlation coefficients (.48 to .83) were found.

Validity. Two validity studies are described in the test manual. First, discriminant validity was examined using 42 participants from the vascular dementia group and comparing them to a matched sample of healthy, elderly controls. Three of the five scales (Indifference, Pragnosia, and Depression) demonstrated evidence of discriminant validity, as significant differences (p < .05) were observed between the scores of the two groups. The second validity study examined evidence of criterion validity in adults with Down syndrome (n = 34). Dementia status was determined by the Dementia Questionnaire for Mentally Retarded Persons (a 1995 test from the Netherlands, as cited in the NBAP-D manual). Of the five scales, Pragnosia (pragmatic language functioning) had the highest percentage of persons correctly classified, 80%.

COMMENTARY. Perhaps the thorniest issue faced by the NBAP-D is one common to most tests in which individuals with a presumed mental impairment are asked to rate or evaluate themselves in specific areas. The present reviewer has explored the area of "awareness of deficits" in individuals with traumatic brain injuries and neuropsychological impairment from chronic substance abuse, among others, and can attest that attempting to determine an individual's level of ability or customary behavior in any specific area is a murky endeavor.

Some persons do not know how they perform. Others know, but report their abilities as much higher or lower for impression management reasons. Many believe that they know—and think they are giving an honest appraisal—but consistently present their abilities as better or worse than they are in fact, as a manifestation of their neuropsychological disorder. The test authors provided a brief discussion of the somewhat analogous difficulties of reliability of the caregiver reports, and urge caution in interpretation.

Some of the questions perhaps could be written a bit more simply, for easier comprehension by a greater number of test takers. A few questions are ambiguous. Many of the test items use the word "seem." Often it adds nothing to the item, and occasionally its use makes the test item potentially more difficult to interpret. Finally, there is a self-recursiveness to a few items, essentially requiring respondents to reflect on their ability to self-reflect.

SUMMARY. The NBAP-D is designed to be used in evaluating change over time across five areas of behavioral and emotional functioning in persons who have a dementing condition. It is meant to be part of a larger and more comprehensive neuropsychological evaluation, not to be used by itself.

The test has some weaknesses, discussed above. To their credit, the test authors present the NBAP-D as a test that continues being developed. It is hoped they continue to expand it and conduct more reliability and validity studies with larger sample sizes.

The instrument has a number of challenges to resolve, such that if it were one of many tests available in a crowded subfield (e.g., measuring reading comprehension in elementary school children), it may not be highly recommended. However, because the area it assesses is so under-studied (precisely because there are so many obstacles to test construction in this field), there are so few measures available, and the issues it addresses are so important to millions of patients and their families, the NBAP-D is an important addition to neuropsychological assessment.

Review of the Neuropsychology Behavior and Affect Profile–Dementia by A. SMERBECK, Assistant Professor of Psychology, Rochester Institute of Technology, Rochester, NY:

DESCRIPTION. The Neuropsychology Behavior and Affect Profile–Dementia (NBAP-D) is a 66-item survey designed to assess changes in dementia patients' psychological functioning as compared to their premorbid state. Each item consists of a statement that the respondent rates dichotomously ("agree" or "disagree") for both the present time and before the onset of dementia. No items are reverse-scored. There are two forms, Self and Other, to be completed by the patient and an informant, respectively. The 66 items form five non-overlapping scales: Indifference (12 items), Inappropriateness (7 items), Pragnosia (12 items; impaired pragmatic communication), Depression (11 items), and Mania (24 items). Each of the five scales yields two subscale scores: a retrospective Before score and a current-functioning Now score. To score the NBAP-D, the clinician uses a worksheet to circle the items marked "agree" and tallies the total number in each scale. The raw frequency can be converted to a percentage of the total number of items in the scale; a table is provided for ease of use. For interpretive purposes, the test manual suggests that any subscale with greater than 50% "agree" ratings be considered elevated. The percentage scores can then be transformed into T-scores using the tables provided. The test offers three sets of normative data for conversion to T-scores: two types of dementia and a healthy control group. Norms are provided for the Other form only. The test manual emphasizes the importance of comparing the Before and Now scores, although it provides no specific guidelines as to how to do so. Formal psychometric training is not required to administer and score the NBAP-D, but is necessary for interpretation.

DEVELOPMENT. The test authors state that the five scales comprising the NBAP-D are "rationally derived" (manual, p. 6) and speculate that certain scales should be associated with impairment of certain brain areas, but offer no references from the literature to support this argument. The manual does not specify how NBAP-D items were developed. The test authors provide a citation to a 1989 paper about the original Neuropsychology Behavior and Affect Profile that offers some description of item development (Nelson et al., 1989). According to this article, a group of six experts developed a pool of 106 items to fit the five intended scales. A group of six doctoral-level professionals then sorted the items into the pre-set groups; only items that were correctly sorted by at least 80% of participants were retained, leaving a final tally of 66 items. However, it is never stated explicitly in the manual that these items comprise the current NBAP-D; the original form was not created to be specific to dementia, but rather to all individuals with acquired neurocognitive impairments, and did not include a self-report option.

TECHNICAL.

Standardization. All technical data, including norms, are based on a series of studies described in the test manual, which are derived from data published in three journal articles (Nelson, Mitrushina, Satz, Sowa, & Cohen, 1993; Nelson et al., 1989; Nelson, Scheibel, Ringman, & Sayre, 2007). Of note, key data appear to come from an uncited article (Nelson, Mitrushina, et al., 1993)—discussed further below. In several instances, the articles provide useful information that is missing from the test manual, such as the relationships between the informants and participants; that information is not considered in this review unless otherwise specified. Four samples were studied: a group of elderly controls (EC), vascular dementia patients (VDP), demented outpatients (DOP), and adults with Down syndrome (DS). The manual does not provide dates of data collection, but the EC and DOP group data were first published in 1989, the VDP data in 1993, and the DS data in 2007. In all cases, only Other form data (i.e., data from informants) were provided.

No inclusion or exclusion criteria for any group were provided in the test manual. Of note, the manual describes the DOP group as having "probable Alzheimer's disease" (p. 11). When the group data were first published, the sample was characterized as diagnosed with "presenile or senile dementia," by two independent clinicians, specifically allowing for either an insidious or abrupt/stepwise disease course (Nelson et al., 1989). As such, the user should consider the DOP sample a general dementia group.

Normative data are provided for three groups: EC (n = 42), VDP (n = 42), and DOP (n = 61). The EC and VDP groups are matched pairs taken from a larger sample of 88 EC participants and 70 VDP participants. Some demographic statistics are provided for each larger group, but not for the subgroup of 42 that makes up the normative sample. For the EC group, the manual provides mean age, mean years of education, and marital status. For the VDP group, the manual provides mean age and racial breakdown. For the DOP group, the manual provides the group's mean age, mean years of education, marital status, and percentage of Caucasians. For all demographic data, means are provided without standard deviations or ranges. No group provides breakdown by sex.

Reliability. Three forms of reliability are important for establishing the psychometric adequacy of the NBAP-D: internal consistency, test-retest, and interrater. The test manual provides internal consistency reliability data for three populations (VDP, DOP, and DS). Alpha coefficients from these studies demonstrated variable ranges: Indifference (.70-.82), Inappropriateness (.59-.75), Pragnosia (.49-.75), Depression (.56-.81), and Mania (.70-.89). Test-retest reliability is presented only for the Now subscales of the NBAP-D via the DS sample. Nineteen cases were drawn from a sample of 34 participants for retesting following a delay that ranged from approximately 6 months to 2 1/2 years (Nelson et al., 2007). Reliability coefficients for two scales fell below the common .70 criterion (Indifference at .48 and Depression at .57), whereas the other three fell above it (Inappropriateness at .79, Pragnosia at .72, and Mania at .83). Sample size is reported as 34 for these data, although presumably only 19 cases were used. No test-retest data are provided for the Before subscales. No data are provided on interrater reliability.

Validity. Validity is often divided into three major domains based on the source of evidence evaluated: content, criterion-related, and construct. With regard to content validity, little specific evidence is provided in the test manual, though as noted above, a cited study (Nelson et al., 1989) may provide some basic information.

With regard to criterion validity, the test manual states that its goal is to assess "changes" in psychological functioning that may occur with dementia. To do so, the test authors would need to demonstrate that the NBAP-D's Before scores are an accurate measure of premorbid functioning. No such evidence is presented in the test manual. Two tables compare the Other-rated Before and Now scores for the VDP and DOP groups, but no statistical analyses (i.e., paired *t*-tests) are provided to assess whether any derived changes are statistically significant. Furthermore, the VDP group study cites a 1993 paper that does not appear to include the relevant data (Nelson, Cicchetti, et al., 1993), whereas the data are present in an uncited paper from the same year (Nelson, Mitrushina, et al., 1993). The manual draws from the latter, uncited paper to present a table showing significant differences between the VDP and EC groups on the Now subtests. This is expected and contributes to the validity of the instrument. However, the uncited paper reports that the two groups also differed significantly on the Before (i.e., pre-stroke) scales (Nelson, Mitrushina, et al., 1993). This finding strongly suggests that informants could not provide an unbiased estimate of Before functioning.

Another study attempted to establish predictive criterion evidence by using NBAP-D Now scores to predict adult Down syndrome (DS) patients' status on a dementia rating questionnaire. The DS group began with 34 participants, 19 of whom were retested an average of 1 year later, as noted in the Reliability section. The manual text regarding the predictive validity study indicates that NBAP-D scores obtained at Time 1 were used to predict dementia scores at Time 2. However, the table of results suggests a sample size of 34 participants in the predictive analysis, which is not possible, as only 19 participants would have had data points at Time 2. As per the published article, only two participants were considered non-demented at Time 1 and demented at Time 2, making interpretation of the data difficult (Nelson et al., 2007). Nonetheless, the test manual states that the NBAP-D Pragnosia scale has an 80.00% correct classification rate. A *p*-value is provided for this assertion; it is unclear what statistical test was performed as classification rate is not an inferential statistic. Lastly, it should be noted that there is no whole number that can divide into either 19 or 34 to yield 80.00%; this indicates a calculation or reporting error related to a key finding.

The final element of validity is construct evidence. For a multiscale measure such as NBAP-D, this is often demonstrated by correlating the novel measure with an established one, using the pattern of strong and weak correlations to argue for each scale's convergent and divergent validity. No such evidence is provided in the test manual. The only construct evidence of test score validity offered compares the Other form Now subtest scores of VDP and EC groups, finding statistically significant differences on the Indifference, Pragnosia, and Depression scales (but not Inappropriateness or Mania). No literature is provided as to why these three scales, but not the other two, should elevate in response to vascular dementia and, as noted previously, in the original publication, these groups were found to be different on both the Before and Now subscales (Nelson, Mitrushina, et al., 1993).

No reliability or validity data are presented for the Self form.

COMMENTARY. Affective and behavioral changes can present significant challenges in the lives of adults with dementia. The NBAP-D attempts to fill this gap by providing an assessment tool that compares pre-morbid and current functioning across five domains and two respondent types. Administration and scoring are relatively straightforward. The items are easy enough to understand and appear representative of their intended constructs. However, the test manual is disorganized, and key information is erroneous or absent. It is difficult to have confidence in the manual when tables are mislabeled, incorrect citations are provided, and basic demographic data are omitted. There are no normative or psychometric data provided regarding the Self form, and the manual confusingly fails to highlight this fact. With regard to the Other form, the normative groups are small, poorly characterized, and do not appear to be representative of the larger population. Reliability coefficients vary; only the Mania and Indifference scales consistently fall at or above .70. Evidence of validity is lacking. There is no evidence that the Before subscales accurately assess premorbid functioning and thus no evidence that the NBAP-D assesses change over time. Although the items appear intuitively to assess their intended constructs, sufficient evidence of construct validity is not provided.

SUMMARY. The NBAP-D offers an intuitively appealing approach for measuring change in non-cognitive functioning among adults with dementia, a domain badly in need of new assessment tools. Unfortunately, the Other form lacks adequate normative and validity data to argue for its use, while the Self form provides no psychometric data at all. This test may be used qualitatively to investigate changes in a patient's functioning, and may be a good starting point for conversations between clinicians and clients, but it should not be used as a quantitative or psychometric test.

REVIEWER'S REFERENCES

Nelson, L. D., Cicchetti, D., Satz, P., Stern, S., Sowa, M., Cohen, S., ... Van Gorp, W. (1993). Emotional sequelae of stroke. *Neuropsychology, 7*(4), 553-560.

Nelson, L. D., Mitrushina, M., Satz, P., Sowa, M., & Cohen, S. (1993). Cross-validation of the Neuropsychology Behavior and Affect Profile in stroke patients. *Psychological Assessment, 5*(3), 374-376.

Nelson, L. D., Satz, P., Mitrushina, M., Van Gorp, W., Cicchetti, D., Lewis, R., & Van Lancker, D. (1989). Development and validation of the Neuropsychology Behavior and Affect Profile. *Psychological Assessment, 1*(4), 266-272.

Nelson, L. D., Scheibel, K. E., Ringman, J. M., & Sayre, J. W. (2007). An experimental approach to detecting dementia in Down syndrome: A paradigm for Alzheimer's disease. *Brain and Cognition, 64*(1), 92-103. doi:10.1016/j.bandc.2007.01.003

[105]

NIH Toolbox–Cognition Domain.

Purpose: Designed to assess several aspects of cognitive functioning including attention, language, episodic memory, executive function, working memory, and processing speed.

Population: Ages 3-85.

Publication Dates: 2012-2018.

Administration: Individual.

Levels, 2: Ages 3-6, Ages 7-85.

Price Data, 2020: $499.99 per annual subscription fee for administration and scoring of tests in all 4 NIH Toolbox domains (Cognition, Emotion, Motor, Sensation).

Foreign Language Editions: Available in Spanish.

Comments: Administered and scored via iPad app; full hardware and software requirements available from test publisher.

Authors: Sandra Weintraub, Sureyya S. Dikmen, Robert K. Heaton, David S. Tulsky, Philip D. Zelazo, Patricia J. Bauer, Noelle E. Carlozzi, Jerry Slotkin, David Blitz, Kathleen Wallner-Allen, Nathan A. Fox, Jennifer L. Beaumont, Dan Mungas, Cindy J. Nowinski, Jennifer Richler, Joanne A. Deocampo, Jacob E. Anderson, Jennifer J. Manly, Beth Borosh, Richard Havlik, Kevin Conway, Emmeline Edwards, Lisa Freund, Jonathan W. King, Claudia Moy, Ellen Witt, and Richard C. Gershon.

Publisher: National Institutes of Health.

a) EARLY CHILDHOOD COGNITION BATTERY.

Population: Ages 3-6.

Scores, 5-9: 5 Early Childhood Battery scores: Early Childhood Composite (Picture Vocabulary, Flanker Inhibitory Control and Attention, Dimensional Change Card Sort, Picture Sequence Memory); 4 supplemental scores: Pattern Comparison Processing Speed, Flanker Inhibitory Control and Attention with Developmental Extension (Experimental), Dimensional Change Card Sort with Developmental Extension (Experimental), List Sorting Working Memory.

Time: Approximately 20 minutes for administration of 4 core battery subtests.

b) COGNITION BATTERY.

Population: Ages 7-85.

Scores, 10-12: Fluid Cognition Composite (Flanker Inhibitory Control and Attention, Dimensional Change Card Sort, Picture Sequence Memory, List Sorting Working Memory, Pattern Comparison Processing Speed), Crystallized Cognition Composite (Picture Vocabulary, Oral Reading Recognition), Cognitive Function Composite; 2 supplemental scores: (Oral Symbol Digit, Auditory Verbal Learning [Rey]).

Time: Approximately 30 minutes for administration of 7 core battery subtests.

Review of the NIH Toolbox–Cognition Domain by SHAWN K. ACHESON, Clinical Neuroscience Services of WNC, Durham, NC:

DESCRIPTION. The NIH Toolbox is a battery of psychological and neurobehavioral instruments administered via iPad. The Toolbox covers considerable ground including measures of cognition, sensation (perception and acuity), motor function, and emotion. The focus of this review is limited to measures within the cognition domain. The Toolbox was developed through the National Institutes of Health (NIH) to provide basic science and clinical investigators a comprehensive battery of royalty-free instruments for use in epidemiological, intervention, and prevention studies. In so doing, the Toolbox provides a norm-referenced set of measures to improve study outcomes across time and studies; increases opportunity for broader assessment of cognition, emotion, motor, and sensation; reduces costs associated with test publisher's royalties and equipment; and increases availability of state-of-the-art measures that require fewer highly experienced examiners to administer.

The battery as a whole, though not every individual test, is designed for use with individuals ages 3 to 85 years. The cognition battery includes measures across six domains including attention, episodic memory, working memory, language, executive function, and processing. The standard battery is intended for individuals ages 7 through 85. The Early Childhood Cognition Battery is a subset of the standard battery sans any measure of working memory or processing speed. The standard battery requires an estimated 30 minutes; the early childhood battery can be completed in approximately 20 minutes. Standardized scores are provided for each measure as well as three summary scores (Cognitive Function Composite, Fluid Cognition Composite, and Crystallized Cognition Composite). All measures in the cognition battery are scored and converted to standard scores locally without need for Wi-Fi or cellular connection. This capability is helpful in those contexts where connectivity is limited. Overall, the layout, instructions, and administration procedures are fairly straightforward. There are extensive web-based resources including a YouTube channel for learning to use and administer the Toolbox.

DEVELOPMENT. The NIH Toolbox was the product of NIH's Blueprint for Neuroscience Research and was supported by the 15 NIH institutes that incorporate neuroscience into their portfolios. This endeavor began in 2004. Where appropriate, NIH measures were validated against "gold standard" instruments. Several instruments, including the Picture Vocabulary Test, use item response theory to maximize the efficiency of the evaluation. IRT measures were calibrated against large samples. In all, validation and calibration samples included more than 16,000 participants. Most of the individual measures in the cognitive battery are simple variations on familiar themes. For example, the Picture Vocabulary Test will be well familiar to those with experience using the Peabody Picture Vocabulary Test and similar measures. Despite that familiarity, use of IRT and computer-aided testing strategies make the NIH Toolbox Picture Vocabulary Test considerably more efficient.

Details concerning the specific strategies used to select individual tests or specific items are not provided in the test manuals. Instead, this information appears to be distributed across a number of published monographs and journal articles. This type of distribution of information makes it a challenge for reviewers and potential test adopters to access such information easily. Even a cursory review of these monographs makes it clear that subject matter experts invested considerable time and effort on the development of each task and the stimuli within.

TECHNICAL. The technical attributes of the NIH Toolbox are something of a mixed bag and should be carefully considered. First and foremost, it must be recognized that the NIH Toolbox is a set of research instruments. The battery was not developed for use as a clinical instrument for informing diagnoses or shaping treatment recommendations for individual participants. As such, there are different standards for reliability and validity. In a research context, the comparison of group means (e.g., treatment vs. control) or group mean change over time (e.g., pre- vs. post-) is of greater interest than the diagnostic utility of an individual's score.

Standardization typically is not a requirement for purely research-based instruments. For example, flanker tasks have been used effectively in various experimental paradigms for nearly 50 years without benefit of normative data. The fact that normative data are available for the NIH Toolbox is purely a benefit. Nonetheless, normative data for the cognition battery in English and Spanish were established using a nationally representative sample of more than 4,800 individuals. Norm-referenced scores are available in 1-year increments from ages 3 to 17 and then approximately in decade increments (18-29, 30-39, 40-49, 50-59, 60-69, 70-79, and 80-85). However, there are no details concerning the demographic makeup of the normative data beyond the description of the sample being nationally representative.

Reliability and validity of the NIH Toolbox are difficult to appreciate. The Administrator's Manual and the Scoring and Interpretation Guide are absent any technical information concerning reliability and validity, and there appears to be no technical manual that summarizes this work as might be expected of a traditional clinical instrument. Were this intended to be a traditional clinical battery, this omission would represent an epic failure. However, the NIH Toolbox is not intended to be a traditional clinical instrument. As a battery of common tests to be used in the context of research, every publication adds to the body of evidence concerning reliability and validity. As evidence of this, the test publishers provided for review a stack of published monographs and peer-reviewed publications that provide such technical information. In most circumstances, reliability estimates are at least acceptable if not excellent.

Validity is somewhat more complicated. Comparison of Toolbox measures to "gold standard" measures leaves something to be desired both in the selection of the gold standard and with regard to the magnitude of association. In the younger age groups, convergent validity for the Dimensional Change Card Sort (DCCS) task was established by correlation with the Wechsler Preschool and Primary Scale of Intelligence—Third Edition Block Design subtest in 3- to 6-year-olds and the Delis-Kaplan Executive Function System (D-KEFS) Inhibition score for 8- to 15-year-olds. Those correlations were .69 and .64, respectively. This reviewer's primary criticism is the choice of gold standard measures. The DCCS is essentially a task-switching measure that has relatively little in common with block design and inhibitory control as measured by the D-KEFS Inhibition score. In light of that, the modest correlations are to be expected. The greatest asset of many Toolbox measures lies in their individual construct evidence of validity. These results are often either not reported or located in places where it might be overlooked. As an example, the DCCS "designed by Zelazo and colleagues ... based on Luria's seminal work on rule use, has been used extensively to study the development of EF in childhood, and indeed, it may be the most widely used measure of EF in young children" (Zelazo et al., 2013). This very important statement is made in the description of the measure, not in a section on scale validity.

COMMENTARY. Overall, the NIH Toolbox-Cognition Domain is a collection of empirically sound measures with deep historical and experimental roots. Reliability is generally well established. Validity is also reasonably well established, though its greatest strengths often require searching on the part of the user. The implementation of the measures in a portable electronic platform is outstanding. However, considerable effort should be given to a more concise and centralized reporting of the technical details. A downloadable technical manual would go a very long way toward making the NIH Toolbox-Cognition Domain the go-to measure for research. Toolbox developers are also encouraged to establish a database of published research findings, including those relating to reliability and validity. Such a document would allow researchers to compare their clinical samples to previously published clinical samples using the Toolbox, which will help to clarify discrepancies in findings across studies, labs, time, and investigators. One final comment that is of increasing importance in the field of neuropsychology concerns performance and symptom validity. Although there is little reason to suspect widespread malingering among research participants, measures of symptom and performance validity can help in removing research participants who may not have been fully compliant or well engaged in the research process. Inclusion of such procedures should be considered in future iterations of the Toolbox.

SUMMARY. The NIH Toolbox-Cognition Domain is a collection of seven core measures spanning six domains and normed for individuals ages 3 through 85. Overall, reliability and validity are appropriate for the battery's intended purpose, though that information is sometimes challenging to find in the absence of a formal technical manual. The NIH Toolbox-Cognition Domain stands as a major contribution to the field and should go a long way toward improving the quality of research involving neurocognitive functioning.

REVIEWER'S REFERENCE

Zelazo, P. D., Anderson, J. E., Richler, J., Wallner-Allen, K., Beaumont, J. L., & Weintraub, S. (2013). NIH Toolbox Cognition Battery (CB): Measuring executive function and attention. *Monographs of the Society for Research in Child Development, 78*(4), 16-33.

Review of the NIH Toolbox–Cognition Domain by MARK A. ALBANESE, Director of Testing and Research, National Conference of Bar Examiners, Professor Emeritus, University of Wisconsin-Madison, and MENGYAO ZHANG, Research Psychometrician, National Conference of Bar Examiners, Madison, WI:

DESCRIPTION. The NIH Toolbox–Cognition Domain is a set of brief and efficient measurement tools that is part of a larger set of similarly designed instruments evaluating not only cognition, but also sensory, motor, and emotional health across the lifespan. Compared with traditional neurological measures, the NIH Toolbox is unique in its ability to report normative scores for a broad spectrum of neural functioning across a wide age range, providing users with a common metric for describing different aspects of neurological and behavioral developments in children and adults. The NIH Toolbox results can be useful neurobehavioral outcomes for longitudinal epidemiologic studies and prevention or intervention trials.

The Cognition Domain consists of two test batteries, each recommended for a different age group: The Cognition Battery is for ages 7–85, and the Early Childhood Cognition Battery is for ages 3–6. The Cognition Battery contains seven core tests measuring important cognitive functioning in areas of executive function, attention, episodic memory, working memory, language, and processing speed. Individual tests include Flanker Inhibitory Control and Attention (Flanker), Dimensional Change Card Sort (DCCS), Picture Sequence Memory Test (PSMT), List Sorting Working Memory (List Sorting), Picture Vocabulary Test (PVT), Oral Reading Recognition (Reading), and Pattern Comparison Processing Speed (Pattern Comparison). Among those tests, Flanker, DCCS, PSMT, and PVT comprise the Early Childhood Cognition Battery, with adjustments made to test items and instructions for young children. All tests are available in English and Spanish (NIH Toolbox en Español–Cognition Domain), along with norms developed separately for English and Spanish speakers. For examinees with certain disabilities, the Cognition Domain offers several substitute tests, including the Auditory Verbal Learning Test as an alternative for PSMT and the Oral Symbol Digit Test, which can be substituted for Pattern Comparison.

The Cognition Domain is administered via the NIH Toolbox iPad app with minimal or no extra equipment and materials. This highly portable test platform provides many user-friendly features, including internet-free administration, automatic scoring and report generation, secure data storage and exporting, and multichannel customer support. The app is freely downloadable from the Apple app store, with an annual fee to receive updates and unlimited administration and scoring of the overall NIH Toolbox and several other NIH-funded measures. Access to the Cognition Domain is restricted to professionals with appropriate education, training, and experience to use the tests responsibly. Eligible users should learn how to administer the tests through the administrator's manual, an online training course (eLearning), and/or interactive workshops. Documents, manuals, and guides on the administration, scoring, and interpretation are clear and instructional. The seven core tests can be administered in at most 35 minutes. Most tests take less than five minutes to administer, except for PSMT and List Sorting, each of which requires approximately seven minutes. Two language tests (PVT and Reading) are delivered in a computerized adaptive testing (CAT) mode, where the assortment of questions administered is individualized depending upon examinee performance and other relevant factors. The other tests are given in a conventional fixed mode (fixed forms or time). Users may choose to administer tests individually, create new combinations of tests, or customize the administration order of selected tests. It is important to note that normative data reported for Cognition Domain tests were based upon administration of all seven core tests in the suggested order. It is not clear how well the norms extend to other forms of administration.

All Cognition tests are scored automatically on the app. Different types of scores are derived for individual tests. For example, theta scores (mean = 0, standard deviation = 1) are computed using item response theory (IRT) for the two language tests and PSMT. Alternatively, scores that combine accuracy and reaction time are generated for Flanker and DCCS. Despite the heterogeneity of these scores, the same types of normative data are reported for scores from all core tests, including uncorrected standard scores, age-corrected standard scores, and fully corrected scores (fully "corrected" or adjusted for age, gender, race/ethnicity, and education). The uncorrected and age-corrected scores are scaled to have a mean of 100 and a standard deviation of 15, whereas fully corrected scores are scaled to have a mean of 50 and a standard deviation of 10. Normative data allow users to compare examinee performance to the entire English- or Spanish-speaking normative samples, to a particular age cohort, or to peers with similar demographics. The two supplemental tests generate raw scores only, and users may refer to the technical manuals for descriptive statistics obtained during standardization. The two batteries yield composite scores by standardizing the average of uncorrected, age-corrected, or fully corrected scores on all or a subset of tests. The Cognition Battery creates three composite scores: Cognitive Function (including all seven tests), Crystallized Cognition (including two language tests), and Fluid Cognition (including the remaining five tests). The Early Childhood Cognition Battery produces a single composite, Early Childhood (including all four tests). National percentiles associated with age-corrected scores are also reported on the app, offering users another straightforward way to interpret test performance.

DEVELOPMENT. The Cognition Domain was developed through a large-scale interdisciplinary collaboration. Subdomains (i.e., executive function, attention, episodic memory, working memory, language, and processing speed) were determined through systematic literature reviews, expert consultations, surveys, and interviews involving researchers and clinicians who specialized in different aspects of cognitive functioning in children and adults. After subdomains of the Cognition Domain were selected, experts with varying backgrounds and desired specialties were involved in the design of individual tests. Multiple pilot studies were performed to refine the tests. Working groups then evaluated the content and administration procedures to ensure they are appropriate for use with examinees of different cultural, ethnic and racial backgrounds, young children, older adults, and people with disabilities. A universal translation method was employed to translate tests and instructions from English into Spanish. Preliminary Rasch calibrations of PVT and Reading were conducted before standardization, serving as a basis for developing IRT-based item banks and CAT administration. Later, item calibrations for those tests were updated using separate normative samples for English and Spanish speakers. IRT methodology was also applied to calibrating PSMT, but it is unclear whether calibrations were independently done in different language groups. Refinements made to the tests during development are documented in a series of monographs. Additional changes were made after standardization, most notably capability of administration via the app. The test authors claim that with correction, "the web-based normative scores can also be applied to results obtained from the app" (brochure, p. 3). However, details for this equivalency research were described in a very limited fashion.

TECHNICAL. Separate studies were conducted for providing reliability and validity evidence as well as normative data. Reliability data and validity evidence came from 476 examinees distributed across age, sex, race/ethnicity, and education strata, with a deliberate overrepresentation of ethnic minorities, young children, and older adults.

Reliability. Internal consistency of composite scores (coefficient alpha) ranged from .77 to .84 in adults. Test-retest reliability estimates (intraclass correlation coefficients [ICCs]) for the seven core tests were based upon a subgroup of 155 examinees who were retested over intervals of 7–21 days and were found to range from .76 to .97 in children and from .73 to .90 in adults. ICCs for Crystallized, Fluid, and total composites were all around .90, except for Fluid in adults (.79). These values suggest good to excellent score consistency but should be interpreted with caution given the small and presumably heterogeneous samples. Reliability estimates for the supplemental tests and the Early Childhood composite are not provided.

Validity. The relevance and appropriateness of test content was based upon reviews by content experts and stakeholders (e.g., potential "end users") as well as reviews of literature and databases. In validation studies, Pearson correlations between Cognition tests and well-established measures of the same construct (e.g., subtests of the Wechsler Preschool and Primary Scale of Intelligence—Third Edition [WPPSI-III]; the Wechsler Adult Intelligence Scale—Fourth Edition [WAIS-IV]; and the Peabody Picture Vocabulary Test, Fourth Edition [PPVT-4]) provided evidence supporting the convergent validity of scores. For example, in the children's sample, correlations between scores from the PPVT-4 and the NIH Toolbox Picture Vocabulary and Oral Reading Recognition tests yielded coefficients of .90 and .87, respectively (Bauer & Zelazo, 2013). In the adult sample, the correlation coefficient between the NIH Toolbox List Sorting Working Memory test and WAIS-IV Letter-Number Sequencing was .57 (Tulsky et al., 2014), and the coefficient between the Toolbox Pattern Comparison Processing Speed test and the WAIS-IV Processing Speed Composite was .54 (Carlozzi et al., 2014). Discriminant validity evidence for adults was supported by low correlations between the Cognition tests or composites and selected well-established measures of a different construct (e.g., .06s between Flanker/DCCS and PPVT-4). For young children, the discriminant validity evidence was generally weak (e.g., .70s between Flanker/DCCS and PPVT-4). The authors attribute this pattern to the lack of differentiation of cognitive abilities during early childhood and the absence of direct gold standards for some Cognition tests. Disattenuated correlations that correct for measurement error may be considered in future studies.

Confirmatory factor analysis was used to provide evidence of validity based on the internal structure of the Cognition Battery. A five-factor model tapping the vocabulary, reading, episodic memory, working memory, and executive/speed dimensions best fit data from older children and adults, whereas a model having only language and general fluid dimensions best fit data from young children, reflecting the brain development and neural differentiation across childhood. These findings support the construct validity argument, but generalizability is weakened by small sample sizes and inaccurate representativeness of the population because of deliberate over-sampling of selected subgroups.

Standardization. The current norms were developed separately for English and Spanish speakers, following similar standardization processes (Casaletto et al., 2015; Casaletto et al., 2016). The normative samples included 3,955 examinees for the English version and 904 examinees for the Spanish version. Examinees were recruited using a stratified sampling strategy from the healthy, community-dwelling U.S. population ages 3 to 85. Unlike the English-speaking sample, the Spanish-speaking sample did not recruit children ages 8 to 17, primarily due to "the scarcity of such school-aged monolingual Spanish-speaking children in the United States" (Casaletto et al., 2016, p. 13), making its use with school-aged Spanish-speakers very limited. Web-based test data and demographic information collected during standardization were used to develop norms for different types of scores, inform modifications of test items and administration procedures, and support research on the relationship between demographics and test performance.

COMMENTARY. The Cognition Domain is a novel set of measurement tools that quickly assess some of the most essential cognitive processes in adults as well as children as young as 3 years old. Its newly released app-based platform is easy to use and cost effective. Application of IRT and especially CAT has helped reduce practice effects. Users will find the real-time assessment reports very concise but useful, where different types of scores have their most applicable research or clinical scenarios.

Empirical evidence for reliability and validity is clearly addressed for individual tests and the Cognition Battery. To resolve the sample size and representativeness issues in an earlier validation study, the test authors mention several plans for using the normative samples to further examine reliability and validity properties, but actual results are not presented. Additionally, details about IRT-related analyses based on the normative samples are needed. For instance, information about whether the PSMT was calibrated using IRT during standardization is needed, and if so, what model, procedure, and software were used; what psychometric analyses and guidelines were involved in the development and maintenance of item banks; how was item parameter drift evaluated and, if it is found, what actions should be taken?

The Cognition Domain was originally designed to assess normal cognitive functioning, not to screen for disease. Standardization processes were obtained from healthy, normal examinees. Recent validation studies suggest its clinical potential in that Cognition test scores may be useful in diagnosing or monitoring early stages of neurological problems (e.g., Hackett et al., 2018; Tulsky et al., 2017).

SUMMARY. The NIH Toolbox-Cognition Domain is a set of computerized measurement tools that quickly evaluate cognitive health across the lifespan. Suitably trained and certified professionals can easily administer the tests and batteries and interpret scores. National norms are available, incorporating demographic and cultural factors. The Cognition Domain is suitable for use in a variety of research and clinical settings. Its full value, especially as part of clinical diagnostic and therapeutic evaluation, is promising and may be better demonstrated with further research.

REVIEWERS' REFERENCES

Bauer, P. J., & Zelazo, P. D. (2013). NIH Toolbox Cognition Battery (CB): Summary, conclusions, and implications for cognitive development. *Mongraphs of the Society for Research in Child Development, 78*(4), 133-146.

Carlozzi, N. E., Tulsky, D. S., Chiaravalloti, N. D., Beaumont, J. L., Weintraub, S., Conway, K. & Gershon, R. C. (2014). NIH Toolbox Cognitive Battery (NIHTB-CB): The NIHTB Pattern Comparison Processing Speed test. *Journal of the International Neuropsychological Society, 20,* 630-641.

Casaletto, K. B., Umlauf, A., Beaumont, J., Gershon, R., Slotkin, J., Akshoomoff, N., & Heaton, R. K. (2015). Demographically corrected normative standards for the English version of the NIH Toolbox Cognition Battery. *Journal of the International Neuropsychological Society, 21,* 378–391.

Casaletto, K. B., Umlauf, A., Marquine, M., Beaumont, J. L., Mungas, D., Gershon, R., ... Heaton, R. K. (2016). Demographically corrected normative standards for the Spanish Language version of the NIH Toolbox Cognition Battery. *Journal of the International Neuropsychological Society, 22,* 364–374.

Hackett, K., Krikorian, R., Giovannetti, T., Melendez-Cabrero, J., Rahman, A., Caesar, E. E., ... Isaacson, R. S. (2018). Utility of the NIH Toolbox for assessment of prodromal Alzheimer's and dementia. *Alzheimer's & Dementia, 10,* 764–772.

Tulsky, D. S., Carlozzi, N., Chiaravalloti, N. D., Beaumont, J. L., Kisala, P. A., Mungas, D., ... Gershon, R. (2014). NIH Toolbox Cognition Battery (NIHTB-CB): List Sorting Test to measure working memory. *Journal of the International Neuropsychological Society, 20,* 599-610.

Tulsky, D. S., Carlozzi, N. E., Holdnack, J., Heaton, R. K., Wong, A., Goldsmith, A., & Heinemann, A. W. (2017). Using the NIH Toolbox Cognition Battery (NIHTB-CB) in individuals with traumatic brain injury. *Rehabilitation Psychology, 62,* 413–424.

[106]

NIH Toolbox–Emotion Domain.

Purpose: Designed to assess emotion in four subdomains: Psychological Well-Being, Social Relationships, Stress and Self Efficacy, and Negative Affect.
Population: Ages 3-85.
Publication Dates: 2012-2018.
Administration: Individual.
Levels, 5: 3 for Self-Report, 2 for Parent-Report.
Forms, 2: Self-Report, Parent-Report.
Price Data, 2020: $499.99 per annual subscription fee for administration and scoring of tests in all 4 NIH Toolbox domains (Cognition, Emotion, Motor, Sensation).
Foreign Language Editions: Available in Spanish.
Time: 1-2 minutes to complete each measure/survey.
Comments: Administered and scored via iPad app; full hardware and software requirements available from test publisher.
Authors: John M. Salsman, Zeeshan Butt, Paul A. Pilkonis, Jill M. Cyranowski, Nicholas Zill, Hugh C. Hendrie, Mary Jo Kupst, Morgen A. R. Kelly, Rita K. Bode, Seung W. Choi, Jin-Shei Lai, James W. Griffith, Catherine M. Stoney, Pim Brouwers, Sarah S. Knox, and David Cella.
Publisher: National Institutes of Health.

a) SELF-REPORT BATTERY.

1) *Ages 8-12.*
Scores, 15: 11 survey scores: Positive Affect, General Life Satisfaction, Emotional Support, Friendship, Loneliness, Perceived Hostility, Perceived Rejection, Self-Efficacy, Anger, Fear, Sadness; 4 summary scores: Negative Affect, Psychological Well-Being, Social Satisfaction, Negative Social Perception.
Time: 11-22 minutes for completion.

2) *Ages 13-17.*
Scores, 15: 12 survey scores: Positive Affect, General Life Satisfaction, Emotional Support, Friendship, Loneliness, Perceived Hostility, Perceived Rejection, Perceived Stress, Self-Efficacy, Anger, Fear, Sadness; 3 summary scores: Negative Affect, Social Satisfaction, Negative Social Perception.
Time: 12-24 minutes for completion.

3) *Ages 18-85.*
Scores, 20: 17 survey scores: Positive Affect, Life Satisfaction, Meaning, Emotional Support, Instrumental Support, Friendship, Loneliness, Perceived Hostility, Perceived Rejection, Perceived Stress, Self-Efficacy, Anger-Physical Aggression, Anger-Hostility, Anger-Affect, Fear-Affect, Fear-Somatic Arousal, Sadness; 3 summary scores: Negative Affect, Social Satisfaction, Psychological Well Being.
Time: 17-34 minutes for completion.

b) PARENT-REPORT BATTERY.

1) *Ages 3-7.*
Scores, 13: 10 survey scores: Positive Affect, General Life Satisfaction, Positive Peer Interaction, Social Withdrawal, Peer Rejection, Empathic Behaviors, Anger, Fear-Over Anxious, Fear-Separation Anxiety, Sadness; 3 summary scores: Psychological Well-Being, Anxiety, Negative Psychosocial Functioning.
Time: 10-20 minutes for completion.

2) *Ages 8-12.*
Scores, 13: 11 survey scores: Positive Affect, General Life Satisfaction, Positive Peer Interaction, Social Withdrawal, Peer Rejection, Empathic Behaviors, Perceived Stress, Self-Efficacy, Anger, Fear, Sadness; 2 summary scores: Psychological Well-Being, Negative Peer Relations.
Time: 11-22 minutes for completion.

Review of the NIH Toolbox-Emotion Domain by FRANCIS STASKON, Senior Analyst, Walgreen Co., Deerfield, IL, and, EDWARD WITT, Manager, Walgreen Co., Deerfield, IL:

DESCRIPTION. The NIH Toolbox-Emotion Domain is a set of instruments for use as outcome measures in longitudinal and epidemiologic studies as well as in prevention or intervention trials across the lifespan. The Emotion Domain includes measures that assess those feelings, thoughts, and behaviors that influence a given individual's general health and well-being. To this end, the instruments cover four theoretically critical subdomains for emotional health: negative affect, psychological well-being, stress and self-efficacy, and social relationships. The Negative Affect subdomain measures the constructs of fear, sadness, and anger; the Psychological Well-Being subdomain measures positive affect, life satisfaction, and meaning and purpose; the Stress and Self-Efficacy subdomain measures perceived stress and self-efficacy; and the Social Relationships subdomain measures social support, companionship, social distress, and positive social development. Given human developmental changes, domain constructs are measured with self-report versions validated for adults 18 years or older, ages 13-17, and ages 8-12; proxy parent-report versions are available for children ages 8-12 and 3-7.

During an assessment, participants are asked about their thoughts, feelings, and behaviors whereas parental instructions ask questions about the target child's feelings and behaviors. Depending upon the instrument, responses are framed within the past 7 days, past 2 weeks, past month, or true of you (or child), agreement with, or satisfaction with. Participant responses are recorded on scales ranging from 3 to 8 points. Each instrument yields an uncorrected T score that compares to the entire NIH Toolbox normative pediatric or adult sample, making the measure useful for gauging overall performance or monitoring change over time. Corrected T scores for age and gender are also provided for children (ages 3-17) in the Emotion Domain, which is useful given that different age groups are administered different instrument items and that maturational differences are known between the genders. These patient-reported outcomes (PRO) T scores have a mean of 50 with a standard deviation of 10. Scores beyond one standard deviation are interpreted as either better than average or problematic based on the direction of the score for a given attribute. Percentile ranks associated with each PRO T score can be referenced in a supplemental table.

Fixed forms in English and Spanish are available online. Additionally, the NIH Toolbox iPad app, which provides access to all Toolbox domains as well as scoring and reporting, requires an annual licensing fee. Free documentation for test administrators and eLearning videos are available online.

In the iPad app (v1.20.2456), 69 Emotion Domain instruments are provided across age groups along with five preset batteries (ages 18-85, ages 8-12, and ages 13-17; parental proxy reports for children ages 3-7 and 8-12). Subdomain instruments can be selected individually or combined per assessment with a preset battery; other optional instruments are available outside of the emotion bank. All measures in the emotion battery are self-paced, with individual instruments taking about 2 minutes to complete and a battery requiring up to 30 minutes. Customized batteries are available in the app only when created by the assessor. The app generates reports containing raw scores, thetas, standard errors, and uncorrected T scores or, for children, corrected T scores. Subdomain total scores are reported only as T scores. If the same participant is assessed more than once on a given instrument, longitudinal reports with graphics can be generated. Exported reports provide additional fields for tracking participants and administration details.

DEVELOPMENT. The NIH Toolbox-Emotion Domain was funded by a larger NIH coalition called Blueprint for Neuroscience Research. The NIH Toolbox also includes Cognitive, Motor, and Sensation Domains. In addition, the emotion battery includes items from a set of commonly used published legacy scales (too numerous to be detailed in this review) that were reformatted and calibrated for the Emotion Domain item bank. Measures for all four NIH Toolbox domains were developed at the same time among domain teams and normed together, allowing for comparisons across completed and future studies. The NIH Toolbox was made available online in 2012 and released as an iPad app in 2015 to aid assessment in field settings with customization capabilities and for use as a stand-alone application.

Methodologically, the NIH Toolbox invokes the successful approach taken by the NIH PROMIS® initiative, where classical test theory (CTT) methods were used to establish which items create a theoretical dimension followed by the generation of item calibrations using item response theory (IRT) information for reliability and error measurement. Validation was, in part, obtained from multiple differential item functioning (DIF) statistics comparing age groups and gender for all measures, as well as education level or primary language, where relevant. For convergent validity evidence, correlations with included legacy scales or PROMIS® instruments were calculated and evaluated.

TECHNICAL. In the initial validation and calibration studies, participants were recruited from the databases of the Toluna internet survey company, which also provided eligibility screening. All participants were community dwelling and available only through the internet panel. The norming studies included in-person samples of both English- and Spanish-speaking adults. The Spanish versions of the NIH Toolbox were created through application of the rigorous nine-step Functional Assessment of Chronic Illness Therapy translation methodology (Victorson et al., 2013). For the norming studies (Babakhanyan, McKenna, Casaletto, Nowinski, & Heaton, 2018), a weighted sample reflected the demographics of the 2010 U.S. Census for English speakers after applying a ranking procedure based on a participant's age, gender, education, and race/ethnicity. The resultant normalized T scores represent an individual's emotional score compared to the average English-speaking person in the United States. For the Spanish-speaking cohort, sample-based T scores without Census-weighted corrections are used to compare the individual to a normative cohort of Spanish-speaking adults.

In all item calibration and total score studies, reported reliability estimates are good for all instruments. Salsman et al. (2013, 2014), Pilkonis et al. (2013), and Kupst et al. (2015) reported CTT statistics for comparing legacy items and new measures to ensure a single construct was established (e.g., item-total correlations, alpha coefficients > .70). Once the new measure was calibrated, the IRT reliability of the resulting two parameters was based on the information function converted to a reliability function > .70. (A majority of measures display reliabilities > .90.)

Validity of items per construct was investigated with exploratory factor analysis and nonparametric multidimensional scaling. The underlying factor was confirmed, and local item dependencies were addressed with confirmatory factor analysis (using multiple fit criteria) followed by item fit information for a two-parameter graded response IRT model used for item calibrations. Differential item functioning (DIF) analyses were then conducted comparing groups based on age, education, and gender for adults and age and gender for children. For more than a majority of individual measure calibrations, convergent validity correlations were moderate to strong, and DIF analyses were rarely significant. However, as reported by Salsman et al. (2013), the convergent validity coefficients with legacy measures for the proxy pediatric measures are moderate (.10-.30), suggesting proxy measures for children are still limited as informant measures. Kupst et al. (2015) was not able to validate a unidimensional emotional regulation and coping scales among child participants. And, the stress and self-efficacy subdomain is not represented by a composite score for adults or children (Paolillo et al., 2018).

COMMENTARY. Overall, the NIH Toolbox-Emotion Domain is a suite of instruments that have a coherent rationale and cutting-edge set of assessment processes available in traditional fixed forms or with computer-adaptive testing (CAT) options in the iPad app. Given the project's size, scope of topic, sophisticated psychometric analysis, and open access for fixed forms, it is unparalleled. This project also establishes the use of IRT methods in measuring health status across domains and different age groups. In addition, the retooling of many prior established emotion-related measurement scales into the new instruments provides replication and brings simplicity to the constructs being measured.

Given the complexity of all the NIH Toolbox domains, the assessor's familiarity with the underlying rationale, standardized process, and interpretation of the results requires training made available from the NIH websites, documentation, and scheduled workshops. However, these reviewers noted several inconsistencies between the administrator's manual, brief information provided on the website, and the iPad scoring guide. Specifically, there are inconsistencies regarding which measures are included per subdomain, the number of items per measure, and the availability of a CAT version.

The NIH criteria that a lifespan perspective be taken per subdomain assessed does not appear to be fully established across all instruments and age groups. Some of the measures (emotion regulation and coping for children) did not meet IRT model calibration requirements of a single dimension (Kupst et al., 2015). And, as discussed in Paolillo et al. (2018) regarding summary scores, the underlying factor structures were different across ages in several emotional subdomains. This limits use of the emotion battery to track emotional functioning as assessed by different age-based versions of the instrument. In short, assessors should be aware that constructs assessed by instruments with the same name are not necessarily equivalent across different age groups.

SUMMARY. The NIH Toolbox-Emotion Domain instruments are a significant advancement in the available measures needed to examine the emotional health status of individuals from ages 3 through 85 across four subdomains with some noted limitations. The assessment results for comprehensive batteries are obtained within 30 minutes and easily interpreted with the use of standardized T score norms (corrected for children's ages). Supporting documentation addresses only the statistical interpretation of scores, although the test authors acknowledge a need to work toward identifying clinically meaningful thresholds. The iPad app allows assessors to customize the battery of instruments, either among emotion subdomains or with other NIH Toolbox health domains.

REVIEWERS' REFERENCES

Babakhanyan, I., McKenna, B. S., Casaletto, K. B., Nowinski, C. J., & Heaton, R. K. (2018). National Institutes of Health Toolbox Emotion Battery for English- and Spanish-speaking adults: normative data and factor-based summary scores. *Patient Related Outcome Measures, 9,* 115-127. doi:10.2147/PROM.S151658

Kupst, M. J., Butt, Z., Stoney, C. M., Griffith, J. W., Salsman, J. M., Folkmon, S., & Cella, D. (2015). Assesment of stress and self-efficacy for the NIH Toolbox for Neurological and Behavioral Function. *Anxiety, Stress, & Coping, 28*(5) 531-544. doi: 10.1080/10615806.2014.994204

Paolillo, E. W., McKenna, B. S., Nowinski, C. J., Thomas, M. L., Malcarne, V. L., & Heaton, R. K. (2018). NIH Toolbox® emotion batteries for children: Factor-based composites and norms. *Assessment.* Advance online publication. doi: 10.1177/107319111866396

Pilkonis, P. A., Choi, S. W., Salsman, J. M., Butt, Z., Moore, T. L., Lawrence, S. M.... Cella, D. (2013). Assessment of self-reported negative affect in the NIH Toolbox. *Psychiatry Research, 206,* 88-97. doi:10.1016/j.psychres.2012.09.034

Salsman, J. M., Butt, Z., Pilkonis, P. A., Cyranowski, J. M., Zill, N., Hendrie, H. C., ... Cella, D. (2013). Emotion assessment using the NIH Toolbox. *Neurology, 80*(Suppl. 3), S76–S86. doi:10.1212/WNL.0b013e3182872e11

Salsman, J. M., Lai, J.-S., Hendrie, H. C., Butt, Z., Zill, N., Pilkonis, P. A., ... Cella, D. (2014). Assessing psychological well-being: Self-report instruments for the NIH Toolbox. *Quality of Life Research, 23*(1), 205–215. doi:10.1007/s11136-013-0452-3

Victorson, D., Manly, J., Wallner-Allen, K., Fox, N., Purnell, C., Hendrie, H., ... Gershon, R. (2013). Using the NIH Toolbox in special populations: Considerations for assessment of pediatric, geriatric, culturally diverse, non-English-speaking, and disabled individuals. *Neurology 80*(Suppl. 3), S13-S19. doi:10.1212/wnl.0b013e3182872e26

Review of the NIH Toolbox-Emotion Domain by MATT VASSAR, Clinical Assistant Professor, Oklahoma State University Center for Health Sciences, COLE WAYANT, Doctoral Candidate, and ASHLEY KEENER, PhD, Research Assistant, Tulsa, OK:

DESCRIPTION. The National Institutes of Health (NIH) Toolbox for Assessment of Neurological and Behavioral Function comprises four domains: Sensation, Motor, Cognition, and Emotion. The Emotion Domain was specifically created in response to the need to measure positive and negative emotion across an individual's life. The test authors clarify that emotion is an affective state of consciousness in which negative and positive constructs, such as joy and fear, are experienced. The NIH Toolbox is designed for use in prospective epidemiological or otherwise clinical research. There were four original, theoretical subdomains of the Emotion Domain (Psychological Well-Being, Social Relationships, Stress and Self-Efficacy, and Negative Affect). Exploratory and confirmatory factor analyses (EFA and CFA, respectively) on a normative sample supported a three-factor model, with each subdomain comprising multiple first-order factors. All first-order factors within a subdomain are assessed using one of five measurement batteries, chosen based on the respondent's age and whether a proxy report is required. Individual measures within each battery are administered either as a fixed form, where all items are asked sequentially, or as a computer-adaptive testing (CAT) form, where an algorithm determines which item should be administered next based on the respondent's previous answers. In addition, supplemental measures are available that offer alternative formats (e.g., fixed form instead of CAT) or additional measures not included in the preset batteries. All individual emotion measures within a battery take 1-2 minutes to complete.

DEVELOPMENT. The NIH Toolbox was developed when 15 institutes, centers, and offices of the NIH that provide support for neuroscience research formed a coalition to develop instruments, resources, and training opportunities to accelerate discovery in neuroscience research. During development of the Toolbox, literature reviews, database searches, and a request for information from NIH-funded researchers helped to identify subdomains for inclusion. Existing free-for-use measures were identified and considered for inclusion, and new items were developed when existing measures were unavailable. Validation of the battery of instruments occurred across a wide age range from samples of 450-500 participants. These studies compared NIH Toolbox responses with those from instruments regarded as gold standards, when possible. For tests using item response theory, calibration samples comprised several thousand participants. Altogether, data were collected from more than 16,000 participants during field testing, calibration, and validation.

TECHNICAL. Normative data for the adult and children's emotion batteries were based on samples of 1,036 English-speaking adults ages 18–85 and 2,916 English-speaking children ages 3-17 (Babakhanyan, McKenna, Casaletto, Nowinski, & Heaton, 2018; Paolillo et al., 2018). Separate norms were derived for a Spanish version (NIH Toolbox en Español–Emotion Domain) using samples of 408 adults and 496 children ages 3-7.

Score reliability for the emotion batteries—in particular, internal consistency reliability—has been extensively evaluated. In the English-speaking adult cohort, internal consistency reliability ranged from .84 for the Psychological Well-Being and Social Satisfaction subdomains to .86 for the Negative Affect subdomain. For the Spanish-speaking adult cohort, internal consistency reliability ranged from .82 for the Psychological Well-Being subdomain to .86 in the Negative Affect subdomain. In the normative sample for English-speaking children (Paolillo et al., 2018), factor-based composites were established by exploratory factor analysis. Results suggested a three-factor solution with marginal to satisfactory alpha estimates of .67, .68, and .76 for Psychological Well-Being, Anxiety, and Negative Psychosocial Functioning, respectively. Additional empirical studies have reported internal consistency estimates of scales that comprise each subdomain, suggesting adequacy in most cases. For example, O'Connell and Killeen-Byrt (2018) reported an alpha coefficient of .94 for the Perceived Loneliness subscale and .89 for Perceived Stress in a mixed gender sample of 790 Irish students.

For the six measures recommended for the sadness, fear, and anxiety scales, convergent and discriminant evidence of validity was provided for a mixed gender sample of 748 adults (Pilkonis et al., 2013); correlations ranged from .37 to .81.

In a validation sample of 2,551 adults (18+ years), the greatest convergence across the three subdomains of Negative Affect, Psychological Well-Being, and Social Relationships was found between the NIH Toolbox Positive Affect scale and the Positive and Negative Affect Schedule-Positive subscale (r = .92). The greatest divergence (r = -.80) was observed between the NIH Toolbox Friendship scale and the UCLA Loneliness Scale (Salsman et al., 2013). In the pediatric sample used for item calibration and validation (*n* = 1,525; 13-17 years), convergent/divergent validity estimates ranged from -.55 (NIH Toolbox Pediatric Friendship and Monitoring the Future–Loneliness Scale) to .96 (NIH Toolbox Pediatric Positive Affect and Positive and Negative Affect Schedule for Children–Positive Subscale) across the two subdomains of Psychological Well-Being and Social Relationships. Overall, Salsman et al. (2013) acknowledged that some relationships were modest to weak when examining convergence across several NIH Toolbox and comparison measures and recommended a more comprehensive treatment of these psychometric issues in future studies.

Factor analytic studies have been conducted to examine the emotion battery's construct validity evidence. An EFA was conducted in a stratified sample of English-speaking (*n* = 636) and Spanish-speaking (*n* = 208) adults (Babakhanyan et al., 2018). Results supported a three-factor solution: Negative Affect, Social Satisfaction, and Psychological Well-Being. Additionally, the authors conducted a CFA with English-speaking (*n* = 400) and Spanish-speaking (*n* = 200) adults and found that a revised three-factor model was the most parsimonious and best fitting model. Specifically, anger-physical aggression and fear-somatic arousal were the lowest weighting scales on the Negative Affect subdomain and were excluded from the final model. A measurement invariance analysis was also conducted and found that a three-factor model was equivalent between English- and Spanish-speaking adults (Babakhanyan et al., 2018).

COMMENTARY. The NIH Toolbox-Emotion Domain is a comprehensive test that shows promise. One of its greatest strengths is its thorough approach to one's mental health status by examining both positive and negative affect in addition to social functioning. Norms could be strengthened by determining whether cultural variations influence an individual's emotional health and what effect, if any, they have on test scores. Additionally, studies that examine various clinical populations and more severe psychopathologies will better inform the battery's evidence of criterion validity. Given one of the primary objectives of the NIH Toolbox is to examine health status over time, evidence supporting test-retest reliability of the emotion measures should be obtained.

SUMMARY. The NIH Toolbox-Emotion Domain was designed to measure the full spectrum of emotional life by including both positive and negative emotions. The instrument displays much promise for both clinical and research work given its user-friendly iPad administration, nationally representative norms, and comprehensive nature. The battery meets its goals of assessing negative affect, social satisfaction, and psychological well-being in several populations including both adults and children. However, factor structures have been shown to vary across age groups and administration (i.e., self or proxy report); therefore, there may be limitations to using the available batteries for tracking emotional functioning across different age-based versions of the instrument.

REVIEWERS' REFERENCES

Babakhanyan, I., McKenna, B. S., Casaletto, K. B., Nowinski, C. J., & Heaton, R. K. (2018). National Institutes of Health Toolbox Emotion Battery for English- and Spanish-speaking adults: Normative data and factor-based summary scores. *Patient Related Outcome Measures, 9,* 115–127. https://doi.org/10.2147/prom.s151658

O'Connell, B. H., & Killeen-Byrt, M. (2018). Psychosocial health mediates the gratitude-physical health link. *Psychology, Health & Medicine,23*(9), 1145–1150. https://doi.org/10.1080/13548506.2018.1469782

Paolillo, E. W., McKenna, B. S., Nowinski, C. J., Thomas, M. L., Malcarne, V. L., & Heaton, R. K. (2018). NIH Toolbox® Emotion Batteries for Children: Factor-based composites and norms. *Assessment.* Advance online publication. https://doi.org/10.1177/1073191118766396

Pilkonis, P. A., Choi, S. W., Salsman, J. M., Butt, Z., Moore, T. L., Lawrence, S. M., ... Cella, D. (2013). Assessment of self-reported negative affect in the NIH Toolbox. *Psychiatry Research, 206*(1), 88–97. https://doi.org/10.1016/j.psychres.2012.09.034

Salsman, J. M., Butt, Z., Pilkonis, P. A., Cyranowski, J. M., Zill, N., Hendrie, H. C., ... Cella, D. (2013). Emotion assessment using the NIH Toolbox. *Neurology, 80*(Suppl. 3), S76–S86. https://doi.org/10.1212/WNL.0b013e3182872e11

[107]

NIH Toolbox–Motor Domain.

Purpose: Designed to assess motor performance including dexterity, strength, balance, locomotion, and endurance.

Population: Ages 3-85.

Publication Dates: 2012-2018.

Scores, 4-5: 9-Hole Pegboard Dexterity, Grip Strength, Standing Balance, 4 Meter Walk Gait Speed (Ages 7 and older), 2-Minute Walk Endurance.

Administration: Individual.

Price Data, 2020: $499.99 per annual subscription fee for administration and scoring of tests in all 4 NIH Toolbox domains (Cognition, Emotion, Motor, Sensation).

Foreign Language Edition: Available in Spanish.

Time: Approximately 3-7 minutes for administration of each subtest; approximately 20 minutes for administration of full battery.

Comments: Administered and scored via iPad app; full hardware and software requirements available from test publisher; additional equipment needed for administration of subtests includes 9-hole pegboard with replacement pegs, digital hand dynamometer, iPod Touch (5th generation or later), balance pad, gait belt, measuring tape, masking tape, two cones, and chair.
Authors: David B. Reuben, Susan Magasi, Heather E. McCreath, Richard W. Bohannon, Ying-Chih Wang, Deborah J. Bubela, William Z. Rymer, Jennifer Beaumont, Rose Marie Rine, Jin-Shei Lai, and Richard C. Gershon.
Publisher: National Institutes of Health.

Review of the NIH Toolbox-Motor Domain by PHILLIP L. ACKERMAN, Professor of Psychology, Georgia Institute of Technology, Atlanta, GA:

DESCRIPTION. The NIH Toolbox-Motor Domain consists of five tests designed to measure domains of motor activity "related to daily functioning and quality of life" (scoring guide, p. 16). The domains are locomotion (a 4-meter walk gait speed assessment), balance (a measure of standing balance), dexterity (a 9-hole pegboard test), strength (using a hand dynamometer), and endurance (distance traveled in a 2-minute timed walk). The test battery is designed to be administered within a brief period (approximately 20 minutes), and the stated target population is ages 3-85. (The gait speed test is not part of the battery for examinees ages 3-6.) The test is administered individually. In addition to the annual license fee for access to the test battery and scoring/report software, which are available via an iPad app, the examiner must have or purchase a number of different components, including an Apple iPad, a Jamar® 9-hole peg test kit, a Jamar® Plus+ digital hand dynamometer, an AIREX Balance Pad Elite, a Scott Gait Belt, measuring tape, two cones, colored masking tape, and an iPod Touch (used to measure sway during the balance test).

According to a brochure from the test publisher, the stated goal of the larger NIH Toolbox for Assessment of Neurological and Behavioral Function is to provide "state-of-the-art tools to enhance data collection in large cohort studies and to advance the neurobehavioral research enterprise." There is no traditional test manual per se; rather, there is the brochure about the larger NIH Toolbox, of which the Motor Domain is one part; an *Administrator's Manual;* and a *Scoring and Interpretation Guide for the iPad.*

The NIH Toolbox app is downloaded from the Apple store for use on the iPad. The app requires the test user to enter demographic information for each participant and then select whether to administer the entire Motor Domain battery or specific tests within the battery. Instructions to the test administrator are provided on the iPad screen, along with timing and entry of data from off-line devices (e.g., timing, grip strength). Instructions are largely the same for participants under the age of 7 and over the age of 7. After the tests are complete, scores may be exported to a variety of different sources in a format that can be opened easily in standard spreadsheet software.

Data include raw scores, T scores, and "fully corrected" T scores for each component of the battery. (No total scores are provided.) Interpretations for most of the tests are suggested on the basis of the fully corrected T scores (which are reported to be adjusted for "gender, age, ethnicity, and education differences" (scoring manual, p. 17). The NIH Toolbox as a whole, which is available in both English and Spanish, was reportedly normed using a nationally representative sample of more than 4,800 people. The test publisher suggests education is used as a proxy for socioeconomic status in adjusting the scores, but the relevance of education or SES to the Motor Domain is unclear. Regardless, the test user is told that corrected T scores below 30 (i.e., 2 standard deviations below the mean) indicate some level of motor dysfunction. For the dexterity test, test users are told that they can make "raw score comparisons between the dominant and non-dominant hand" (p. 16), but no information is provided for standard errors of measurement for the raw scores or difference scores on which to determine the meaningfulness of such comparative differences.

DEVELOPMENT. The development of the Motor Domain battery is described in an article by Reuben et al. (2013). The article explains that decisions about what domains to include in the battery were based on a field survey of 62 researchers and in-depth interviews with nine "motor-function experts" (p. S66). Multiple off-the-shelf tests were administered to two samples (a sample of "51 participants aged 4 to 78 years" at a rehabilitation institute or a university sample of "70 participants aged 3 to 85 years" (p. S66), although each of the existing tests was only administered to small samples (3-14 individuals for each test). The next phase (validation) included a convenience sample of 340 "English speaking participants who did not use assistive devices for walking" (p. S68), between the ages of 3 and 85.

TECHNICAL.

Standardization. No information about the standardization sample was included in the provided manuals. Associated articles mention standardization samples of 1,320 adult participants (Bohannon & Wang, 2018) and 2,706 children (Bohannon, Wang, Bubela, & Gershon, 2017) for some of the individual tests in the Motor Domain.

Reliability. Reliability was reported as test-retest reliability (delayed, with a period of 7 to 21 days) for each test on a total sample of 340 participants, ranging from 3 to 85 years. However, for each test, the test-retest reliability estimates were obtained for subsamples (ages not provided) of 50-54 individuals. Reliability coefficients ranged from .64 (4-m walk test) to .98 (grip strength-left).

Validity. The validity data provided are from subsamples of the 340 participants who also were used for the reliability analysis. Sample sizes ranged from 75 to 332 individuals. Each motor domain test was correlated with one or more similar tests (e.g., the 9-hole pegboard was correlated with performance on the BOT-Dexterity Scale and the Purdue Pegboard), thus the validation was aimed at determining convergence. Correlation coefficients between the motor domain tests and comparative tests were generally in the range of .60-.70. No information was provided about the discriminant validity of the various measures. In addition, there were no reports of intercorrelations among the five tests in the battery, nor were there any external criterion validation data provided.

COMMENTARY. The iPad interface for the tests appears to be designed with the user in mind. Accessing the options in the app was straightforward, and there were numerous sources of additional information provided for administering the tests and exporting the data for later analysis. The fact that the test battery was not entirely self-contained, in that the user is expected to source additional apparatus items separately from the test battery, may pose an inconvenience for some users.

It is important to acknowledge that the developers of the NIH Toolbox-Motor Domain intend for these tests to be used for research purposes. The selection process that was used for the choice of tests and design appears to be well thought out and implemented. Available information indicates that the test may have reasonable levels of test-retest reliability, and, given that the tests appear to be exact duplicates or minor modifications of existing measures, they appear to have acceptable levels of convergence with similar measures. It is also useful to note that the developers acknowledge that these tests are just a subsample of possible measures of motor abilities, though they do not provide information about how representative these measures may be of the larger domain of motor skills/abilities (e.g., see Fleishman & Quaintance, 1984).

Still, there are major shortcomings for these tests and the documentation provided to the user. Instructions to the participant appeared to be highly similar or identical, regardless of the age of the participant. It is unclear how this was determined to be appropriate for the very young children who are included in the target population. Interpretative information is provided only in the context of normative scores (reportedly corrected for an odd assortment of variables for motor tests, such as education), and mostly with a single cutoff of 2 standard deviations below the mean, for which no other clinical justification is provided. The kinds of information about the standardization sample and results, reliability, and validity that one normally expects (and is advised by the *Standards for Educational and Psychological Testing* [American Educational Research Association, American Psychological Association, & National Council on Measurement in Education, 2014]) is not provided in a test manual, but must be obtained piecemeal from journal articles for the individual tests.

SUMMARY. The NIH Toolbox-Motor Domain provides an integrated approach to the assessment of five different aspects of motor abilities using modern technology in the form of an iPad and various traditional apparatus devices. The tests are brief and probably can be administered by examiners without extensive training. In theory, these tests also could be used with examinees across a wide range of ages. The shortcomings of the tests and the documentation suggest that the battery is still a work in progress, and there remain significant concerns about the scope of the assessments in the context of the wider nomological network of motor ability constructs or the relevance of the battery for diagnostic or application purposes. At this point, other than providing comparison means, standard deviations, and similar descriptive statistics for a particular research sample that could be compared to other research samples or the existing norms, it is difficult to determine additional uses for this battery of tests.

REVIEWER'S REFERENCES

American Educational Research Association, American Psychological Association, & National Council on Measurement in Education. (2014). *Standards for educational and psychological testing.* Washington, DC: American Educational Research Association.

Bohannon, R. W., & Wang, Y.-C. (2018). Four-meter gait speed: Normative values and reliability determined for adults participating in the NIH Toolbox study. *Archives of Physical Medicine and Rehabilitation, 100,* 509-513.

Bohannon, R. W., Wang, Y.-C., Bubela, D., & Gershon, R. C. (2017). Handgrip strength: A population-based study of norms and age trajectories for 3- to 17-year-olds. *Pediatric Physical Therapy, 29(2),* 118-123.

Fleishman, E. A., & Quaintance, M. K. (1984). *Taxonomies of human performance.* Orlando, FL: Academic Press.

Reuben, D. B., Magasi, S., McCreath, H. E., Bohannon, R. W., Wang, Y.-C., Bubela, D. J. ... Gershon, R. C. (2013). Motor assessment using the NIH Toolbox. *Neurology 80*(Suppl. 3), S65-S75.

[108]

NIH Toolbox–Sensation Domain.

Purpose: Designed to assess the sensory processes of Pain, Olfaction, Vision, Audition, and Taste.
Population: Ages 3-85.
Publication Dates: 2012-2018.
Scores, 2-6: Words-in-Noise (ages 6-85), Regional Taste Intensity (ages 12-85), Visual Accuity (ages 3-85), Odor Identification (ages 3-85), Pain Intensity (ages 18-85), Pain Interference (ages 18-85).
Administration: Individual.
Price Data, 2020: $499.99 per annual subscription fee for administration and scoring of tests in all 4 NIH Toolbox domains (Cognition, Emotion, Motor, Sensation).
Foreign Language Edition: Available in Spanish.
Time: 1-6 minutes for administration of each measure; approximately 24 minutes for administration of entire battery.
Comments: Administered and scored via iPad app; full hardware and software requirements available from test publisher.
Authors: Susan E. Coldwell, Karon F. Cook, Pamela Dalton, Winnie Dunn, Rose Marie Rine, Rohit Varma, Steven G. Zecker, and NIH Toolbox Sensation Team.
Publisher: National Institutes of Health.

Review of the NIH Toolbox–Sensation Domain by ANITA M. HUBLEY, Professor of Measurement, Evaluation, and Research Methodology, University of British Columbia, Vancouver, British Columbia, Canada:

DESCRIPTION. The NIH Toolbox was introduced in 2012 and adapted for the iPad in 2015 (administrator's manual, 2006-2018). One of four sets of brief measures assessing cognitive, motor, emotional, and sensory functions, the Sensation Domain assesses olfaction, vision, audition, taste, and pain. It is not intended as a diagnostic tool (Gershon et al., 2013). At this time, only the core Sensation Domain tests are included on the iPad app, which is used to display stimuli, record responses, and automatically score the tests.

The 4- to 5-minute Odor Identification Test assesses the ability to identify different odors using scratch-and-sniff cards. Children ages 3-9 years identify five odors whereas individuals ages 10-85 years identify nine odors by choosing a response from among four picture options. Higher scores indicate better olfactory functioning.

In the 3-minute static Visual Acuity Test, letters ("optotypes") are presented on an iPad positioned at eye level 3 meters away. Using both eyes together, individuals ages 3-85 years identify letters one at a time that get progressively smaller. Gold standard ETDRS charts are used for individuals aged 8 and older, whereas children ages 3-7 years are tested with the letters H, O, T, and V. The test is scored in LogMAR units, which range from 1.6 (worst) to -0.3 (best); Snellen equivalents ranging from 20/640 to 20/10 also can be obtained.

The 6-minute Words-in-Noise (WIN) Test measures the ability of individuals ages 6-85 years to hear words in a noisy environment (i.e., in multitalker babble). Each ear is tested separately with five one-syllable words spoken by a female speaker at each of seven levels of background noise (i.e., noise:word ratios). Percent correct out of a total raw score of 35 is computed and translated into a threshold score in decibels of signal-to-noise ratio (dB S/N); scores range from 26.0 to -2.0 dB S/N, with higher scores indicating more difficulty.

The 6-minute Regional Taste Intensity Test evaluates the taste sensitivity of individuals ages 12-85 years to bitter (quinine) and salty solutions in the mouth generally and on the tip of the tongue. Respondents rate intensity using a generalized labeled magnitude scale (gLMS) ranging from *strongest imaginable* to *no sensation*. A score from 0 to 100 on a semi-logarithmic scale is obtained for the four items; lower scores indicate lower perceived taste intensity.

Pain is assessed in adults ages 18 years and older using two measures. The single-item Pain Intensity Survey asks respondents to rate their level of pain in the past 7 days on a 10-point scale (from *no pain* to *worst imaginable pain*). The computer-adaptive Pain Interference Survey uses 4-12 items rated on a 5-point scale (from *not at all* to *very much*) to ask how pain has interfered with enjoyment of various daily activities over the past 7 days. The surveys take approximately 1 minute each. The Pain Intensity Survey simply reports a raw score ranging from 0 to 10. For the Pain Interference Survey, an item response theory (IRT) theta score is computed and converted to a T score; higher scores indicate greater pain interference.

DEVELOPMENT. Literature reviews, interviews with experts, and requests for information from NIH-funded researchers were used to select the Sensation subdomains for inclusion as well as criteria for test inclusion, creation, and norming (Nowinski, Victorson, Debb, & Gershon, 2013). Selection criteria included test brevity, ease of use by nonclinical personnel, psychometric soundness (with a preference for measures already normed for the broad target population), lack of intellectual property constraints, and applicability across the life span, diverse settings, and different groups. Separate teams of experts were created for each sensation, but numerous other teams (e.g., pediatric, geriatric, epidemiology/biostatistics, technology, multicultural, accessibility) also reviewed these tests (Gershon et al., 2013; Victorson et al., 2013).

TECHNICAL. As noted in the Sensation Domain technical manuals, which are available from the NIH Toolbox website, a large national standardization study was conducted with 4,859 individuals ages 3 to 85 years who were representative of the 2010 U.S. Census based on ethnicity, race, socioeconomic status, and gender. Of this sample, 2,917 children and 1,038 adults were administered the tests in English whereas 496 children and 408 adults were administered the tests in Spanish. Norms are reported for each age from 3 to 17 years and for age ranges 18-29, 30-39, 40-49, 50-59, 60-69, and 70-85 years. Beaumont et al. (2013) reported the plans for norming, but there is no post-norming report that clarifies to what extent the actual norming process may have differed from these plans, the sample sizes for each specific test, or details about the versions of the tests included in the norming process. Normative data are provided for all of the tests except the single-item Pain Intensity Survey. The scoring guide indicates the levels at which a referral for further testing is warranted, although it is noted for the Odor Identification Test and Pain Interference Survey that "additional work remains to examine the predictive validity ... and to identify clinically meaningful thresholds" (scoring guide, pp. 24 and 25). Wilson et al. (2010) presented normative data for the WIN Test for children ages 6-12 years, but these data may be based on an earlier version of the test.

Limited reliability evidence appears to be available and only for three tests in the Sensation Domain. For the Visual Acuity Test, same-day test-retest reliability intraclass correlations (ICCs; $N = 292$) were .91 for HOTV in 3- to 12-year-olds and .89 for ETDRS for individuals ages 7 and older (Varma et al., 2013). Test-retest reliabilities, using ICCs, on two 35-word versions of the WIN Test were .89 with 48 older adults with mild-to-severe hearing loss over intervals ranging from 14 to 89 days and .91 for 48 older adults with moderate-to-severe hearing loss over intervals ranging from 21 to 130 days (Wilson & McArdle, 2007). For the Odor Identification Test, 1-week test-retest reliability, using Pearson's r, was unacceptably low at .45 for 106 children ages 3-9 years and .58 for 480 children and adults ages 10-85 years (Dalton et al., 2013).

There is also very limited available validity evidence for the Sensation Domain tests. A study of 445 individuals ages 10-69 years reported that the Odor Identification Test tracked smell identification performance across age in a similar manner to the Brief Smell Identification test and the University of Pennsylvania Smell Identification Test (Dalton et al., 2013). The correlation coefficient between computerized and standard lightbox ETDRS Visual Acuity Test performance was .80 for both 7- to 17-year-olds ($n = 143$) and 36 adults ages 18 and older (Varma et al., 2013). A study of adults with strokes, spinal cord injuries, or traumatic brain injuries found some, but not all, findings on the Sensation tests matched predictions (Carlozzi et al., 2017). More validation work (e.g., Wilson, 2011; Wilson, Carnell, & Cleghorn, 2007; Wilson & Cates, 2008) has been conducted with the WIN Test, and this evidence is supportive, but it has primarily focused on adults and a comparison of young adults with normal pure-tone thresholds to older adults with hearing loss.

COMMENTARY. To use the Sensation Domain tests, test users need to have or obtain an iPad, Bluetooth wireless keyboard, and wireless headset as well as numerous additional materials, particularly for the Regional Taste Intensity Test. Key strengths of the NIH Toolbox tests are the use of multiple expert teams to consider, develop, and evaluate potential tests for inclusion as well as the careful attention paid to test administration. The test publisher provides online training materials with brief quizzes and very useful YouTube videos demonstrating test administration.

There are two critical weaknesses at present. The first weakness is that there is relatively little psychometric evidence available for these tests, and what does exist takes some effort to find. Greater efforts are needed in obtaining a critical mass of reliability and validity evidence to support the use of these tests (see Nowinski et al., 2013). The second weakness is the very poor documentation of ongoing modifications to the various subdomains and tests as well as the rationale for these decisions, norms as they relate to the specific tests, and reliability and validity evidence of specific tests. Sometimes the rationale for the choice of a core subdomain or test is clear (e.g., visual acuity, Varma et al., 2013), but often it is not. As examples, no clear rationale has been presented for why: (a) the core measure of audition was changed from a pure-tone thresholds test (Zecker et al., 2013) to word recognition-in-noise, (b) pain intensity asks about "average" rather than "worst" pain (Cook et al., 2013), (c) there was a change from testing bitter taste intensity for those ages 12-85 years and sucrose preference for those ages 5-85 years (Coldwell et al., 2013) to testing bitter and salty taste intensity in those aged 12-85 years, (d) there was a change from six items that best discriminated among different levels of pain interference (Cook et al., 2013) to 4-12 items selected via computer-adaptive testing (CAT) in the iPad version (administrator's manual, 2006-2018), or (e) the Visual Acuity test uses a distance of 9.84 feet (3 meters) according to the administration manual when it was normed at a distance of 12.5 feet (3.81 meters) (Li et al., 2014). It is very difficult to determine what changes have been made to individual tests over time, when those changes took place, and the degree to which those changes affect the applicability of the norms and available reliability and validity evidence.

At present, the test publisher has provided separate technical manuals on its website for each test. These documents are mostly redundant with one another, provide little technical detail, and are dated around 2012. The test publisher needs to prepare a single, coherent, comprehensive technical manual that (a) details the development of each test; (b) clarifies the current status of the Sensation Domain core tests, supplemental tests, and any batteries of tests; (c) describes the normative study that took place in more detail as well as any subsequent normative studies; and (d) summarizes and critically evaluates all reliability and validity evidence relevant to the current versions of the Sensation Domain tests, rather than directing test users to various articles in the literature.

SUMMARY. The NIH Toolbox-Sensation Domain tests provide a standardized set of relatively inexpensive and brief measures of specific aspects of olfaction, vision, audition, taste, and pain that require minimal expertise to administer. The use of teams with considerable and varied expertise to identify Sensation subdomains and tests that would meet key criteria (e.g., brevity, applicability across the life span, psychometric soundness) was exceptional. Thus, the specific tests included in the NIH Toolbox–Sensation Domain are highly promising but there is currently very limited reliability and validity evidence to support their use. A comprehensive and current technical manual as well as stronger and more extensive psychometric evidence are essential before the NIH Toolbox-Sensation Domain tests can be recommended for research or clinical use.

REVIEWER'S REFERENCES

Beaumont, J. L., Havlik, R., Cook, K. F., Hays, R. D., Wallner-Allen, K., Korper, S. P., ... Gershon, R. C. (2013). Norming plans for the NIH Toolbox. *Neurology, 80*(Suppl. 3), S87-S92.

Carlozzi, N. E., Goodnight, S., Casaletto, K. B., Goldsmith, A., Heaton, R. K., Wong, A. W. K., ... Tulsky, D. S. (2017). Validation of the NIH Toolbox in individuals with neurologic disorders. *Archives of Clinical Neuropsychology, 32*, 555-573.

Coldwell, S. E., Mennella, J. A., Duffy, V. B., Pelchat, M. L., Griffith, J. W., Smutzer, G., ... Hoffman, H. J. (2013). Gustation assessment using the NIH Toolbox. *Neurology, 80*(Suppl. 3), S20-S24.

Cook, K. F., Dunn, W., Griffith, J. W., Morrison, M. T., Tanguary, J., Sabata, D., ... Gershon, R. C. (2013). Pain assessment using the NIH Toolbox. *Neurology, 80*(Suppl. 3), S49-S53.

Dalton, P., Doty, R. L., Murphy, C., Frank, R., Hoffman, H. J., Maute, C., ... Slotkin, J. (2013). Olfactory assessment using the NIH Toolbox. *Neurology, 80*(Suppl. 3), S32-S36.

Gershon, R. C., Wagster, M. V., Hendrie, H. C., Fox, N. A., Cook, K. F., & Nowinski, C. J. (2013). NIH Toolbox for assessment of neurological and behavioral function. *Neurology, 80*(Suppl. 3), S2-S6.

Li, C., Beaumont, J. L., Rine, R. M., Slotkin, J., & Schubert, M. C. (2014). Normative scores for the NIH Toolbox Dynamic Visual Acuity Test from 3 to 85 years. *Frontiers in Neurology, 5*, Article 223.

Nowinski, C. J., Victorson, D., Debb, S. M., & Gershon, R. C. (2013). Input on NIH Toolbox inclusion criteria: Surveying the end-user community. *Neurology, 80*(Suppl. 3), S7-S12.

Varma, R., McKean-Cowdin, R., Vitale, S., Slotkin, J., & Hays, R. D. (2013). Vision assessment using the NIH Toolbox. *Neurology, 80*(Suppl. 3), S37-S40.

Victorson, D., Manly, J., Wallner-Allen, K., Fox, N., Purnell, C., Hendrie, H., ... Gershon, R. (2013). Using the NIH Toolbox in special populations: Considerations for assessment of pediatric, geriatric, culturally diverse, non-English-speaking, and disabled individuals. *Neurology, 80*(Suppl. 3), S13-S19.

Wilson, R. H. (2011). Clinical experience with the Words-in-Noise Test on 3,430 veterans: Comparisons with pure-tone thresholds and word recognition in quiet. *Journal of the American Academy of Audiology, 22*(7), 405–423.

Wilson, R. H., Carnell, C. S., & Cleghorn, A. L. (2007). The Words-in-Noise (WIN) test with multitalker babble and speech-spectrum noise maskers. *Journal of the American Academy of Audiology, 18*(6), 522–529.

Wilson, R. H., & Cates, W. B. (2008). A comparison of two word-recognition tasks in multitalker babble: Speech Recognition in Noise Test (SPRINT) and Words-in-Noise Test (WIN). *Journal of the American Academy of Audiology, 19*(7), 548–556.

Wilson, R. H., Farmer, N. M., Gandhi, A., Shelburne, E., & Weaver, J. (2010). Normative data for the Words-in-Noise test for 6- to 12-year-old children. *Journal of Speech, Language, and Hearing Research, 53*(5), 1111–1121.

Wilson, R. H., & McArdle, R. (2007). Intra- and inter-session test, retest reliability of the Words-in-Noise (WIN) test. *Journal of the American Academy of Audiology, 18*(10), 813–825.

Zecker, S. G., Hoffman, H. J., Frisina, R., Dubno, J. R., Dhar, S., Wallhagen, M., ... Wilson, R. H. (2013). Audition assessment using the NIH Toolbox. *Neurology, 80*(Suppl. 3), S45-S48.

Review of the NIH Toolbox-Sensation Domain by RYAN J. McGILL, Assistant Professor of School Psychology, William & Mary School of Education, Williamsburg, VA:

DESCRIPTION. The NIH Toolbox-Sensation Domain is a core component of the National Institutes of Health Toolbox for Assessment of

Neurological and Behavioral Function, a multidimensional set of brief tests designed to assess cognitive, sensory, motor, and emotional functioning that can be used by researchers and clinicians in a variety of settings to measure outcomes in clinical trials and longitudinal or epidemiological studies. The battery, which can be administered in English or Spanish, has been validated across the lifespan, and norms have been developed for various measures for participants ages 3 to 85 years. In a brochure from the test publisher, it is noted that use of measures from the NIH Toolbox ensures that "assessment methods and results can be used for comparisons across existing and future studies" (National Institutes of Health & Northwestern University, 2017, p. 2) and that the Toolbox functions as a sort of "common currency" for neuroscience research.

Sensation is defined in the test administrator's manual as the "biochemical and neurologic process of detecting incoming impulses as nervous system activity" (p. 187). The Sensation Domain contains six measures (Words-in-Noise Test, Visual Acuity Test, Odor Identification Test, Pain Intensity Survey, Pain Interference Survey, and Regional Taste Intensity Test) that assess functioning in audition, vision, olfaction, perceived pain, and taste, respectively. Each measure is delivered exclusively through the NIH Toolbox iPad app. In order to use NIH Toolbox measures, users must download the app and purchase a 12-month subscription ($499) that provides access to all measures in the Toolbox. It should be noted that several Sensation measures require users to purchase additional iPad accessories and assessment materials (~$1,000) that are not covered in the cost of the yearly subscription. For example, to administer the Regional Taste Intensity Test, clinicians must obtain the necessary laboratory equipment to produce standardized quinine and sodium chloride solutions that are administered to the tip of an examinee's tongue as well as the whole mouth during the administration of that test. Detailed lists of required Toolbox equipment and materials are provided in appendices in the administrator's manual, which is located on the NIH Toolbox website.

DEVELOPMENT. The genesis of the NIH Toolbox can be traced to 2004 when the NIH formed a coalition called the Blueprint for Neuroscience Research. The goal of the coalition was to develop a set of new standardized assessment tools that could be used by researchers across the country to facilitate discoveries in neuroscience research. In 2006, a large-scale grant was awarded to a team of 250 scientists from nearly 80 academic institutions to develop Toolbox measures. Many of the Sensation measures were adapted from existing technologies or surveys (e.g., San Diego Odor Identification Test, Patient-Reported Outcomes Measurement Information System [PROMIS®] Pain Interference Survey). Each measure was uniquely calibrated and formatted for standardized digital administration using item response theory and computer adaptive testing procedures. This process allows users to assess various Sensation abilities in a relatively short amount of time without sacrificing psychometric integrity.

The NIH Toolbox was officially released in 2012 and designed to be administered through a web-based data collection platform. In 2015 an iPad app was developed to supplant the web platform, and access to the online assessment center was eventually closed. During the migration to the iPad app, internal validation studies were conducted to establish the equivalency of Sensation Domain scores across platforms. Results of those studies indicate that score corrections are not needed for that domain. Although Toolbox measures have undergone a continuous validation process since their development, inspection of test technical manuals reveals that no significant modifications have been made to any of the Sensation Domain measures since their initial validation.

The age ranges for Sensation Domain measures vary by test. Whereas performance measures can generally be administered from ages 3 to 85, the pain surveys can be administered only to examinees 18 and older. All six measures can be administered in approximately 30 minutes, and most of the tests can be delivered with the iPad placed directly in front of the examinee with the assessor seated next to them. Verbal directions for each test are provided on the iPad screen, and modifications are available for younger examinees. Several measures require additional time to prepare assessment materials and iPad accessories (e.g., Regional Taste Intensity Test, Visual Acuity Test). With the exception of the pain measures, all of the tests require users to identify and respond to various sensory stimuli. For example, examinees are asked to identify words spoken through earphones amidst increasing levels of background noise and letters that gradually decrease in size on a conventional visual array. The *Scoring and Interpretation Guide for the iPad*, technical manuals for all of the Sensation tests, the administrator's manual, and a comprehensive eLearning module can be accessed at the NIH Toolbox website.

TECHNICAL. Although technical manuals are available online for each test in the Sensation Domain, conventional reliability and validity information is not reported in these documents. Instead, readers are directed to a panoply of research articles reporting results from validation studies typically including 400-500 participants across the age ranges of the tests. This reviewer was provided with a detailed list of Sensation Domain articles by the test publisher, and the information provided below was extracted from the articles on that list. (These references are also available at the Toolbox website.)

Standardization. The technical manuals for each Sensation measure briefly describe the NIH Toolbox total standardization sample, and users are directed to Beaumont et al. (2013) for more details about the sampling plan. The standardization sample contains 4,859 English- and Spanish-speaking participants, ages 3-85, and it is reported that the sample was representative of the U.S. population based on key demographic variables from the 2010 U.S. Census. Whereas Beaumont and colleagues (2013) outline numerous desired characteristics for the normative sample that are consistent with best-practice standards, the actual obtained results on many key demographic variables are not reported in available technical documentation, so users are unable to independently evaluate the degree to which obtained estimates match many of the intended parameters.

Primary Toolbox measures were administered to participants at 10 sites across the United States. Separate norms are provided for males and females (disaggregated by primary language) for 21 age brackets (each year from ages 3-17, then 18-29, 30-39, 40-49, 50-59, 60-69, and 70-85). The raw scores for each test are tabulated automatically by the app during the course of administration, and a score report is generated at the conclusion of the assessment with raw scores transformed into various normative scores. For performance measures, age-corrected standard scores that compare examinees' performance to other examinees their age (M = 100, SD = 15), uncorrected standard scores that compare an examinee's performance to the total normative sample (M = 100, SD = 15), fully corrected T scores that correct for age and other key demographic variables (M = 50, SD = 10), and percentile ranks are available. For patient-reported outcome (PRO) measures, such as the pain surveys, uncorrected T scores (M = 50, SD = 10) are reported. Two of the Sensation measures report scores that are idiosyncratic to those tests. For the Words-In-Noise Test, the obtained raw score for each ear is converted to a decibels of signal-to-noise ratio (dB S/N) score ranging from -2.0 to 26.0 with lower scores indicative of better performance. Additionally, for the Visual Acuity Test, the raw score is transformed logarithmically into a conventional Snellen Visual Acuity score. In terms of clinical interpretation, practitioners are encouraged to interpret most of the Toolbox scores primarily as screening indicators. For example, in the scoring and interpretation guide, it is recommended that examinees who obtain a Snellen equivalent score of 20/40 or worse should be referred to an eye care professional for additional testing.

Although descriptive statistics, disaggregated by age, are provided for each normative age bracket in respective test technical manuals, raw score to normative score conversions are not available. Therefore this reviewer was unable to evaluate whether the item gradients at each age are sufficient. The relatively small number of items in each of the Sensation measures raises concern about potential item density issues within the scales. According to Wasserman and Bracken (2013), inadequate item density across the distribution of a variable reduces the sensitivity and discrimination of a test. No normative information is reported for either of the shortened pain surveys.

Reliability. Within the reference list provided, three studies were found to report conventional reliability evidence. Test-retest reliability coefficients for the Odor Identification Test reported by Dalton et al. (2013) ranged from .45-.57, which are considered low. In contrast, Rine and colleagues (2012) report strong test-retest estimates (.84-.91) for the Visual Acuity Test in the form of intraclass correlation coefficients (ICCs). Finally, Mennella, Lukasewycz, Griffith, and Beauchamp (2011) report low to moderate (.42-.65) internal consistency estimates also in the form of ICCs. It should be noted that the use of ICCs with these data may be problematic given the skew that is likely in the underlying distributions. As noted by Bobak, Barr, and O'Malley (2018), the ICC coefficient assumes that data are normally distributed, and when this assumption is violated, reliability estimates may be inflated.

Validity. Similar to reliability, validity evidence for the Sensation Domain varies by test. Whereas content validity for the measures was established largely via a series of articles published in a special issue of *Neurology* in 2013, compelling structural validity evidence was unable to be located. To date, construct evidence of validity is largely limited to concurrent evidence in the form of correlations with existing measures for the Visual Acuity Test and the Regional Taste Intensity Test and evidence of developmental differences for the former as well as for the Odor Identification Test. Available diagnostic utility studies have been mixed. In a comprehensive study of NIH Toolbox measures with neurologic patients, Carlozzi et al. (2017) found that individuals with Traumatic Brain Injury were at risk for olfactory dysfunction. However, Abasaeed and colleagues (2018) found that scores from the Regional Taste Intensity Test did not differ among patients receiving stem cell transplantation over the course of treatment, raising concern about the sensitivity of the measure.

COMMENTARY. As with any test, the NIH Toolbox-Sensation Domain has strengths and weaknesses. The iPad app provides an innovative platform for clinical assessment and, in terms of assessment, has few flaws. Most of the measures require minimal training or advanced setup, although users are encouraged to supplement the administrator's manual with available video demonstrations to facilitate assessment fidelity. Clinicians unfamiliar with basic laboratory techniques will likely need additional practice preparing assessment materials for the Regional Taste Intensity Test. Many of the embedded links in the app to technical documentation on the Toolbox website are broken, which makes it difficult to access those materials. Thus, users will likely have to consult the website via a conventional computer in order to ascertain the psychometric properties of the instrument more fully.

In spite of the conventional appeal of the measures, reliability and validity evidence for the tests, in its present form, remains underdeveloped. Whereas extensive validation work has been conducted on other Toolbox domains, the validation network for the Sensation Domain measures presently consists of a small series of articles mostly using preliminary versions of the tests. In some cases, stimuli and assessment methods differ significantly from current versions of the measures (e.g., Smutzer, Desai, Coldwell, & Griffith, 2013). As a result, it is unclear whether this information generalizes to the Sensation tests presently available in the iPad app. Even so, it is believed that the development of the current delivery system will be instrumental for furthering existing validation efforts, and it is anticipated that additional research on the measures should follow. As that information accumulates, users would benefit from a reformatting of the technical manuals to include this information rather than directing readers to research articles that may be difficult for clinicians to locate.

SUMMARY. Overall, the NIH Toolbox-Sensation Domain has many strengths. For the most part, the app is an excellent technological innovation and is of exceptional quality. Whereas the technical documentation for many of the measures remains underdeveloped, it is more than adequate to support their use in research settings, which is the fundamental goal underlying the development of the NIH Toolbox. Clinicians looking to replace existing instrumentation in clinical practice settings should employ Sensation Domain measures with caution until additional validity evidence is presented, in particular diagnostic validity evidence indicating that the measures have adequate sensitivity and specificity to identify targeted pathologies.

REVIEWER'S REFERENCES

Abasaeed, R., Coldwell, S. E., Lloid, M. E., Soliman, S. H., Macris, P. C., & Schubert, M. M. (2018). Chemosensory changes and quality of life in patients undergoing hematopoietic stem cell transplantation. *Supportive Care in Cancer, 26,* 3553-3561. doi:10.1007/s00520-018-4200-7

Beaumont, J. L., Havlik, R., Cook, K. F., Hays, R. D., Wallner-Allen, K., Korper, S. P., ... Gershon, R. C. (2013). Norming plans for the NIH Toolbox. *Neurology, 80*(Suppl. 3), S87-S92. doi:10.1212/WNL.0b013e3182872e70

Bobak, C. A., Barr, P. J., & O'Malley, A. J. (2018). Estimation of an intra-class correlation coefficient that overcomes common assumption violations in the assessment of health measurement scales. *BMC Medical Research Methodology, 18,* 93. doi:10.1186/s12874-018-0550-6

Carlozzi, N. E., Goodnight, S., Casaletto, K. B., Goldsmith, A., Heaton, R. K., Wong, A. W. K., ... Tulsky, D. S. (2017). Validation of the NIH Toolbox in individuals with neurologic disorders. *Archives of Clinical Neuropsychology, 32,* 555-573. doi:10.1093/arclin/acx020

Dalton, P., Doty, R. L., Murphy, C., Frank, R., Hoffman, H. J., Maute, C., ... Slotkin, J. (2013). Olfactory assessment using the NIH Toolbox. *Neurology, 80*(Suppl. 3), S32-S36. doi:10.1212/WNL.0b013e3182872eb4

Mennella, J. A., Lukasewycz, L. D., Griffith, J. W., & Beauchamp, G. K. (2011). Evaluation of the Monell forced-choice, paired-comparison tracking procedure for determining sweet taste preferences across the lifespan. *Chemical Senses, 36,* 345-355. doi:10.1093/chemse/bjq134

National Institutes of Health, & Northwestern University (2017). NIH Toolbox® for Assessment of Neurological and Behavioral Function brochure. Retrieved from https://www.healthmeasures.net/images/nihtoolbox/NIH_Toolbox_brochure_June_2017.pdf

Rine, R. M., Roberts, D., Corbin, B. A., McKean-Cowdin, R., Varma, R., Beaumont, J., ... Schubert, M. C. (2012). New portable tool to screen vestibular and visual function—National Institutes of Health Toolbox initiative. *Journal of Rehabilitation Research and Development, 49,* 209-220. doi:10.1682/JRRD.2010.12.0239

Smutzer, G., Desai, H., Coldwell, S. E., & Griffith, J. W. (2013). Validation of edible taste strips for assessing PROP taste perception. *Chemical Senses, 38,* 529-539. doi:10.1093/chemse/bjt023

Wasserman, J. D., & Bracken, B. A. (2013). Fundamental psychometric considerations in assessment. In I. B. Weiner, J. R. Graham, & J. A. Naglieri (Eds.), *Handbook of psychology: Assessment psychology* (2nd ed., vol. 10, pp. 50-81). Hoboken, NJ: Wiley.

[109]

O*NET Career Values Inventory, Third Edition: Based on the "O*NET Work Importance Locator" Developed by the U.S. Department of Labor.

Purpose: Designed to allow users to rank six work values and relate them to specific careers.

Population: Youth and adults.
Publication Dates: 2002-2012.
Scores, 6: Achievement, Independence, Recognition, Relationships, Support, Working Conditions.
Administration: Individual or group.
Price Data, 2020: $68.95 per package of 25 consumable booklets; volume discount available. Administrator's guide (2012, 8 pages) available for download from publisher's website.
Time: (30) minutes.
Author: JIST/EMC Publishing.
Publisher: JIST Career Solutions, a division of Kendall Hunt.
Cross References: For reviews by Kathy Green and Richard E. Harding of an earlier edition, see 16:173.

No review available. This test does not meet review criteria established by the Buros Center for Testing that call for at least minimal technical and development information.

[110]

Offender Reintegration Scale, Second Edition.

Purpose: "A self-report assessment designed to measure the concerns and potential barriers faced by offenders and ex-offenders" regarding re-entry into society.
Population: Offenders in various statuses, including incarceration, work release, probation, or parole.
Publication Dates: 2008-2016.
Acronym: ORS.
Scores, 5: Basic Needs, Job Search, Family, Wellness, Career Development.
Administration: Individual or group.
Price Data, 2020: $61.95 per 25 scales; administrator's guide (2016, 17 pages) may be downloaded at no charge.
Time: (20) minutes.
Comments: Self-administered, self-scored, and self-interpreted.
Author: John J. Liptak.
Publisher: JIST Career Solutions, a division of Kendall Hunt.
Cross References: For reviews by Michael G. Kavan and Romeo Vitelli of the original edition, see 19:121.

Review of the Offender Reintegration Scale, Second Edition by ROCHELE CADE, Assistant Professor, Graduate Counseling Department, University of Mary Hardin-Baylor, Belton, TX:

DESCRIPTION. The Offender Reintegration Scale (ORS), Second Edition is an assessment designed to identify the concerns, potential barriers, and skill deficits of juvenile and adult offenders in regard to successful reentry into society. It is a self-report assessment intended for use with offenders in correctional settings by a variety of correctional professionals (parole and probation officers) or mental health professionals (rehabilitation counselors, pre-release counselors).

The ORS, Second Edition consists of 60 statements that cover concerns related to Basic Needs, Job Search, Family, Wellness, and Career Development. The assessment is in the form of a trifold booklet and uses a different color for each area of concern. Offenders completing the assessment first respond to basic demographic questions on the cover and then circle their level of concern for each statement on a 4-point scale (1 indicating *no concern* and 4 indicating *great concern*) on the inside pages. Scoring by hand includes totaling the scores for each scale and then plotting them on a profile contained in the booklet. Offenders then interpret their scores as *high* (37-48), *average* (24-36), or *low* (12-23). Next, offenders are directed to identify suggestions in the booklet that would address their concerns. For example, if Job Search was an identified concern, an offender could choose to learn how to use electronic search tools to find a job. The final step in the booklet directs offenders to make an action plan by listing their own ideas for how they will be a productive and successful member of society. There are no special training or educational requirements for administration or scoring. The ORS can be administered in individual or group format. The reading level of the assessment is not reported.

The 17-page administrator's guide is in its second edition, and the table of contents includes theoretical background, description, changes to the second edition, administration, interpretation, and development of the ORS. The guide incorporates an illustrative case of James, a 41-year-old male nearing release after a 5-year prison sentence.

DEVELOPMENT. The test author developed the ORS to fill the need for a quick, reliable inventory to help offenders identify their concerns about release and to aid in the development of a reentry plan. Following a literature review, "a large pool of items that were representative of the five major scales on the ORS was developed and later revised" (administrator's guide, p. 12). These items were reviewed for clarity; style; appropriateness in identifying concerns; and reference to sex, race, culture, and ethnicity. The test author identified adult prison populations to complete the ORS as part of item standardization, but no other information is given about the population. In the guidelines for development section of the administrator's guide, there is a statement that the "norms developed for the ORS show an age range from 21-65" (p. 11). Aside from these two brief statements, no other information is provided about the norm group. Although the administrator's guide includes a section titled theoretical background, this section does not include a theory or theoretical framework that guided the development of the ORS or its five scales. The test author does indicate that several broad purposes of the Second Chance Act, P.L. 110-199 are integrated in the ORS.

The administrator's guide describes changes from the first edition to the second edition of the ORS. These changes included moving items to different scales "to enhance the inter-scale reliability" (p. 8); renaming the *Lifeskills* scale the *Wellness* scale; removing and replacing similar statements and those "nebulous in nature" (p. 8); adding items that have become more prominent concerns; removing stereotypical and career-focused images from the front of the test booklet; updating language to be inclusive and representative in relationships and technology; and revising the score interpretation section of the form to reduce the reading level. The list of changes ends with the test author stating that the ORS was "tested to ensure the accuracy of the changes" (p. 8), but no details are provided regarding what happened or how.

TECHNICAL. Internal consistency reliability estimates (split-half correlations) and interscale correlations are included in the administrator's guide for a sample of 48 adults about which no information is provided. Split-half correlation coefficients ranged from .87 to .94. Interscale correlations ranged from .063 (Family and Basic Needs) to .564 (Job Search and Career Development). The test author reported that the .564 correlation, which is significant at the .01 level, "was expected because both of these scales deal with employability" (administrator's guide, p. 13).

The administrator's guide includes evidence of validity in the form of means and standards deviations on the five scales reported for offenders recently released (n = 129), offenders in work release (n = 136), offenders currently in prison (n = 167), and all offenders (N = 432). There is no other construct, concurrent, criterion, or predictive evidence of validity reported.

COMMENTARY. The author designed the ORS for measuring a range of concerns, ease of use, administration, scoring and interpretation with applicability for juvenile and adult offenders returning to society. The intended audience does not have an age range or consideration of offense(s) of the offender. As previously observed by Vitelli (2014), some offenders (sex offenders) or offenses (felonies, violent offenses) may require additional considerations and challenges upon release, and a specialized version of the assessment may be needed. Examiners can have difficulty determining whether the assessment is appropriate for an offender given that no age range or reading level is specified and no norm group information is included. A substantial amount of relevant content related to the psychometric properties of the ORS is absent from the administrator's guide. Split-half correlations and interscale correlations are included, but test-retest reliability is not examined. There is minimal information regarding the validity of scores generated from the assessment. Whether the ORS influences successful reentry of offenders was questioned by Kavan (2014) in a review of the first edition of the assessment, and this question remains unanswered in the second edition of the administrator's guide. Future research to support the predictive validity of the ORS is warranted.

SUMMARY. The ORS is a brief assessment used to identify the reentry needs of adult and juvenile offenders. Examiners will likely appreciate its ease of use and straightforward administration, scoring, and interpretation. However, the lack of information related to age range, reading level, evidence of psychometric properties, and the normative sample in the administrator's guide limits the utility of the ORS.

REVIEWER'S REFERENCES

Kavan, M. G. (2014). [Test review of Offender Reintegration Scale]. In J. F. Carlson, K. F. Geisinger, & J. L. Jonson (Eds.), *The nineteenth mental measurements yearbook* (pp. 499-501). Lincoln, NE: Buros Center for Testing.

Vitelli, R. (2014). [Test review of Offender Reintegration Scale]. In J. F. Carlson, K. F. Geisinger, & J. L. Jonson (Eds.), *The nineteenth mental measurements yearbook* (pp. 501-503). Lincoln, NE: Buros Center for Testing.

Review of the Offender Reintegration Scale, Second Edition by JEFFREY A. JENKINS, Professor of Justice Studies, Roger Williams University, Bristol, RI:

DESCRIPTION. The Offender Reintegration Scale (ORS), Second Edition is a revision of the Offender Reintegration Scale first published in 2008. It is intended for use by those who work with or make decisions regarding inmates about to reenter society after a period of incarceration. It is designed to assess "concerns and potential barriers" they may face upon reentry (administrator's guide, p. 3).

The ORS, Second Edition is composed of 60 items relating to an inmate's anticipated release from prison and expectations regarding aspects of life after prison. The items are presented as 4-point Likert scales on which a respondent indicates *great concern* (4 points), *some concern* (3 points), *little concern* (2 points), or *no concern* (1 point) to each of the statements presented. The items are grouped on the instrument according to the scales they measure. Responses to each item are recorded on a three-page trifold booklet on which a profile and action plan also may be created.

The respondent's profile is summarized in five areas involving an inmate's release and re-establishment in society. These are Basic Needs, Job Search, Family, Wellness, and Career Development, each of which is composed of 12 items resulting in a scale score. Higher scores on each scale reflect more concern by the inmate about the topic assessed. The Basic Needs scale addresses areas of life after release such as finding a place to live, being able to purchase food and clothing, affording transportation, and earning money. Job Search involves such topics as an inmate's understanding of the world of work, conducting a job search, and how to present oneself in job interviews. The Family scale relates to the inmate's ability to interact and communicate with family and friends as well as how they may be perceived as a former inmate in the family setting. The Wellness scale reflects the inmate's concerns about such issues as managing stress, substance abuse, mental health, and general wellbeing. Finally, the Career Development scale examines an inmate's concerns about beginning or continuing an occupation, aptitudes and interests, and educational requirements and opportunities.

Examinees or their counselors sum the item scores within each scale and write the total in a box on the instrument. These five scores can then be placed on a profile by circling the total number corresponding to the inmate's score on each scale. These scale scores are classified on the profile as *high* (a scale score from 37 to 48), *average* (a scale score from 24 to 36), or *low* (a scale score from 12 to 23). These descriptors reflect a respondent's degree of concern with the topic measured by each scale. A description and interpretive guide for the scores is also provided in the instrument booklet itself. The administrator's guide gives further assistance for interpretation as well as an explanatory illustrative case showing a profile and its interpretation.

DEVELOPMENT. The original ORS was published in 2008, in recognition of the "need to assist offenders in the transition from prison to the community" (administrator's guide, p. 3). Based on a review of the literature regarding prisoner reentry, the test author concluded that prisoners "simply aren't prepared for the barriers they will face" and that the ORS would address the need to assess and address the extent of inmates' concerns about these barriers. Therefore, the ORS was designed to provide a short assessment to help inmates understand their "needs, barriers, and skills deficits" prior to reentry (p. 6). The areas measured by each scale reflect potential barriers or difficulties that were identified in the research literature reviewed, and a "large" pool of items was developed (p. 12). These items were pilot-tested on adult prison populations, and 12 items were selected to best represent each scale.

The second edition of the ORS incorporates what the administrator's guide describes as "major" changes to the instrument (p. 8). These include the following: (a) movement of some items from one scale to another to improve reliability; (b) adoption of the name *Wellness* in place of the former scale named *Lifeskills* to better describe item content; (c) redrafting or removal of items that were too similar in wording to other items or were too vague; (d) removal of pictures on the cover of the instrument because they were deemed to be stereotypical; (e) updating item language to be more reflective of modern changes in family makeup; (f) addition of items that have become more prominent concerns of inmates (e.g., obtaining a driver's license); (g) changes in the instructions to reduce the reading level and amount of reading required; (h) revisions to items to reflect technology available to inmates.

TECHNICAL. The administrator's guide contains a brief description of the reliability and validity of the ORS, Second Edition based on research samples of respondents gathered by the test author. Split-half reliability estimates for each scale, ranging from .87 to .94, are reported for a sample of 48 respondents. These estimates appear to be the same split-half coefficients (with the same sample size) as were previously reported for the first edition of the ORS, with the new scale name *Wellness* substituted for the name in the first edition, *Lifeskills*. Interscale correlations are also reported, ranging from .063 to .564, to demonstrate varying levels of "independence" among the scales (administrator's guide, p. 13). While these would seem to be better construct evidence of validity than reliability (as reported), they also are based on the same sample of 48 participants as the split-half coefficients. As noted, the research sample appears to have been from a study involving the original ORS, not the second edition. No further reliability information is reported, nor is any information provided about how the research sample was obtained.

Validity evidence is reported in the administrator's guide as scale means and standard deviations for three groups of respondents: those incarcerated (n = 167), those in work release programs (n = 136), and those recently released from prison (n = 129). The scale means and standard deviations for the entire sample (N = 432) also are reported. The guide notes that there are some mean differences among the three groups on various scales and that the results were similar to those reported as validation of the first edition. Other than stating that these descriptive statistics are evidence of validity, no argument is made to show how mean differences among these groups establish validity. No additional information about validity is provided.

COMMENTARY. As a measure of inmate concerns relating to life after prison, the ORS, Second Edition appears to be useful. The need for the instrument is justified by the reality of the differences between prison and life after release, and its rationale and item development are supported by research in the field. The instrument is easy to use by both test administrators and respondents.

Scoring is straightforward, and interpretation of the scale results does not require specialized training and could lead to productive decision-making upon an inmate's reentry to society.

Nonetheless, the ORS, Second Edition is not without shortcomings. Foremost among these is the lack of evidence for the instrument's technical characteristics. Although the instrument does have some face validity, this is insufficient for an instrument that focuses on scale scores for decision making. It also appears that the instrument has content evidence of validity, based on the literature relating to reintegration and the barriers faced by offenders, but no systematic presentation of the domains of inmate concerns and their relationship to the items on the instrument is given. Moreover, the evidence presented in the administrator's guide in support of validity does not explain or address either the construct or criterion-related aspects of validity of the instrument. The guide's comparison of mean scale scores among current inmates, those in work release, and those who have been released does not demonstrate that the instrument measures inmate concerns; it merely shows that there are differences among the groups in whatever is being measured. Because the instrument purports to measure inmate concerns, more compelling evidence that this is true is needed.

Regarding reliability, the split-half coefficients reported appear to be for the first edition of the ORS, not the second. This is problematic given that the second edition makes many item changes and additions. Reliance on the reliability coefficients from the prior edition is not warranted.

SUMMARY. The ORS, Second Edition is an updated version of the ORS, which was created to fill a need in understanding and addressing the concerns faced by inmates upon their release and return to society. As an exploratory measure of inmate concerns about returning to society, the ORS, Second Edition may be beneficial by helping inmates think about the barriers they may face and express their thoughts about them. Without further information about the validity and reliability of scores from the instrument, however, users should be cautious in relying on the scale profile the instrument creates to make decisions about areas in which inmates should focus their attention upon release or in their consideration of barriers that may lie ahead.

[111]

Oral Language Acquisition Inventory, Second Edition.

Purpose: Designed to "identify, organize, and address the particular needs of students who are not performing at their expected age or grade level in reading and writing, including English language learners."
Population: Students in preschool through Grade 6.
Publication Date: 2011.
Acronym: OLAI-2.
Administration: Individual.
Levels, 2: Pre-K–Grade 3; Grades 4-6.
Forms: 3 for each level: A, B, C.
Price Data, 2020: $283.10 per complete kit, including manual (2011, 118 pages) with art cards, 25 of each PreK-3 record form (A/B/C), and 25 of each Grades 4-6 record forms (A/B/C); $184.70 per PreK-3 kit or Grades 4-6 kit; $110.50 per manual; $31.70 per package of 25 record forms (PreK-3 or Grades 4-6 A, B, or C).
Foreign Language Edition: The Spanish materials for the original OLAI are still available; both the

assessment and the instructional guide may be used with OLAI-2.
Time: Approximately 20 minutes for administration.
Comments: Formative, criterion-referenced assessment that includes an intervention program.
Author: Lance M. Gentile.
Publisher: Pearson.

a) PRE-K–GRADE 3.
Scores, 4: Phonemic Awareness, Print Concepts, Repeated Sentences, Story Retelling.
b) GRADES 4-6.
Scores, 4: Phonemic Awareness, Repeated Sentences, Expository Reading, Expository Writing.

Review of the Oral Language Acquisition Inventory, Second Edition by GABRIEL M. DELLA-PIANA, Professor Emeritus in Educational Psychology, College of Education, University of Utah, Salt Lake City, UT:

DESCRIPTION. The Oral Language Acquisition Inventory, Second Edition (OLAI-2) is the latest edition of an individually administered, formative, criterion-referenced (not normed), measure of language, literacy, and learning behavior that includes an intervention program and is designed for students in preschool through Grade 6. Its primary purpose is to provide a tool for professionals in schools and other settings to identify students who are performing below grade level in reading and writing, including English language learners, and to help develop appropriate instruction for those students. Test results are intended to inform instruction but not to label students or to be used as a sole measure for diagnosing a student.

The OLAI-2 contains four sections for each of two grade levels (PreK-Grade 3 and Grades 4-6), and three test forms are included for each level for repeated assessment throughout the school year. In the Phonemic Awareness section (both levels), the examiner reads aloud a sentence and then rereads each word slowly in order to emphasize all the individual sounds contained in each word and asks the student to identify and say each sound. In Print Concepts (PreK-Grade 3), students are asked questions about "how text works" (manual, p. 3), such as how to position a book for reading. Repeated Sentences (both levels) requires students to repeat sentences read to them by the test administrator. In Story Retelling (PreK-Grade 3), the administrator reads aloud a story with accompanying picture cards. Examinees are then asked to retell the story using the cards. Expository Reading and Expository Writing (Grades 4-6) involve reading passages and answering questions about them and summarizing in writing what is happening in a picture, respectively. A Learning Behavior rating follows each section for student coping behavior during that section as, roughly, positive interaction, resistant, or apparently immobilized. In addition, scores are classified into one of three relative stages of language acquisition: least experienced, basic, and most experienced.

The "Introduction" and "Administration and Scoring" chapters in the test manual detail user qualifications including recommendations to users to be familiar with assessment materials, practice at least one administration of each form, and consult with others as needed for interpretation, particularly if the administrator's own judgment does not yield a consistent pattern. The estimate of 20 minutes for administration and scoring seems reasonable for an experienced test administrator with most students.

The test manual includes a chapter titled "Interpretation to Intervention," which is intended to guide the movement from interpretation to a summary plan for instruction. For example, a least experienced rating in Phonemic Awareness "indicates an overall need to address multiple types of phonologic and phonic skills during instruction" (manual, p. 30), whereas a least experienced rating in Repeated Sentences "indicates a need to address basic syntactic structures during language and literacy development activities" (manual, p. 31). These activities may include practicing hearing, seeing, and repeating such structures "in meaningful conversations with a professional who knows how to prompt for them" (manual, p. 31). The "Oracy Instruction" chapter complements these guidelines by specifying goals and integrating strategies for literacy instruction and learning or coping behavior. These are very broad recommendations, referenced but not clearly tied to theory and research, and will require expert knowledge and experience to interpret and integrate with other information (because the OLAI-2 is not a stand-alone measure), and to guide instruction. Because teachers are to be among users, it would be useful to examine Brookhart (2011) on assessment knowledge and skills for teachers.

DEVELOPMENT. Test development and changes in testing and instructional plans for the OLAI-2 were based on the test author's research, tryout, practical experience, and feedback from observing and working with students and professionals. The need for the original OLAI was based on cited research on lack of language development in preschool and school-age children; limited life and language experiences for many children; frequent school emphasis on drill-and-skill instruction with little integrated language and literacy instruction; and inappropriate balance of children's hours spent on reading and writing compared with television, movies, computer games, phoning, and texting. The development research, experience, and assessed context of schools led to shortening the test and other changes in the second edition. Whereas the OLAI age range went through third grade, the OLAI-2 extended the range through sixth grade. Other changes include fewer sentences in the Repeated Sentences section, and a reduction in the relative stages of language acquisition from five to three in analysis of test results. Story Retelling now uses three pictures instead of four, and scoring was simplified by reducing the number of structures in the retelling. Learning Behavior is scored for each section. Case studies were added, and three types of discourse skills are now assessed: telling a story (narrative), reading informative (expository) text, and writing informative text. Argumentation is not included, although it is a major type of discourse.

TECHNICAL. The OLAI-2 is not a norm-referenced test. The process used to standardize administration and scoring is not described in the test manual. Test users are advised to become familiar with the test materials and administration procedures via practice administrations, as noted previously. In addition, the test author recommends consultation with an experienced examiner especially for those lacking training and experience in individual testing.

A "Research Evidence" chapter summarizes some of the test author's research and reports findings from two outside studies. A key purpose of the OLAI-2 is to serve as a tool for professionals "to help identify and provide appropriate instruction for students whose experiences have not adequately prepared them for the ever-increasing language and learning demands required in school and the global economy" (manual, p. 1). The validity evidence claim in support of that declared purpose is that research leading to and furthering OLAI development "supports the founding principles of the OLAI and the constructs underlying its measures" (manual, p. 51). Content-related evidence of validity is reported in the test manual and includes a detailed description of test development, a cited research base, and alternative domains considered. Evidence related to the consequences of the testing itself on the student and on instruction or the curriculum is not formally addressed or analyzed.

A validity argument in the form of integrating various strands of evidence into a coherent account of the degree to which existing evidence and theory support the interpretation of test scores for the proposed construct and intended use of informing instruction is not presented. As well, there is no validity evidence described for assessing cognitive processes underlying test responses. However, the test manual references a process used for item reviews and iterative revision that may include such validity evidence. Although there is considerable description, there is no statistical study of internal structure of the test. The test manual presents convergent evidence of relationships to the California English Language Development Test (CELDT) using total scores (88.3% agreement within 1 score point using a 5-point range), offering support for the construct. No discriminant validity evidence is reported on measures different from the test construct.

COMMENTARY. The above analysis, in part, supports the OLAI-2 as a potentially useful tool (or set of tasks) in the hands of experienced professionals, though validity evidence is lacking for some intended constructs. Furthermore, two threats to validity (construct-irrelevant variance and construct underrepresentation) should be examined. For example, the objective of Story Retelling is "to measure and analyze the ability to link sentences in sequence to develop a logical narrative with a clear beginning, middle, and ending" (manual, p. 3). However, the procedure for Story Retelling involves asking the student to "try to use the same words I said, so it sounds like a story in a book" (PreK-Grade 3 record form, p. 5). This process may introduce unrelated factors such as memory or hearing ability that affect performance but are unrelated to the construct of interest. Similarly, the goal of Repeated Sentences is to "measure the degree of control of the grammatical and sound structures most commonly found in written text" (record form, p. 3). Scoring instructions, however, say, "Score 1 point for each verbatim response [which] requires a student to repeat each word in a sentence accurately and in the proper sequence" (manual, p. 25). Such a scoring procedure may not adequately represent the target construct as operationalized.

Because the main purpose of the assessment is to inform instruction, the test manual should include more detailed guidelines than those currently offered for moving from scoring and interpretation to instruction using other information, as the OLAI-2 is not intended for use as a stand-alone test. User qualifications should specify the need for supervised practice in scoring, interpretation, and providing recommendations. Though a formative measure, validity evidence might be gathered for cognitive processes underlying the measures. Finally, in this reviewer's opinion, argumentation discourse should be included in the test along with narrative and expository discourse.

SUMMARY. The OLAI-2 is a potentially useful set of tasks that experienced professionals in language and literacy might adapt to use as a formative assessment of some aspects of language development and a rough measure of coping behavior of students engaged in these kinds of tasks. In its current stage of development there is a lack of key sources of validity evidence to support intended use for informing instruction. Mainly, the task scoring and validity evidence do not match some of the constructs. The test author cautions that the OLAI-2 is not to be used as a sole measure for diagnosis but does not provide guidance for the demands of integrating its results with other measures. The challenges of interpretation and use for instructional planning go well beyond the testing information yielded and assistance provided. The question for the prospective user is, "Why should I use this set of tasks rather than also consult a source like *The Mental Measurements Yearbook* to probe for additional possibilities and, ultimately, test selection?"

REVIEWER'S REFERENCE

Brookhart, S. M. (2011). Educational assessment knowledge and skills for teachers. *Educational Measurement: Issues and Practice, 30*(1), 3-12.

Review of the Oral Language Acquisition Inventory, Second Edition by DAVID P. HURFORD, Director of the Center for Research, Evaluation and Awareness of Dyslexia and Professor, Psychology and Counseling, Pittsburg State University, Pittsburg, KS:

DESCRIPTION. Like its predecessor, the Oral Language Acquisition Inventory, Second Edition (OLAI-2) is an assessment instrument designed to evaluate language, literacy, and learning behavior with the goal of informing instruction. A primary purpose of the OLAI-2 is to provide information concerning the student's language, literacy, and learning behavior skills. From this information, appropriate instructional techniques can be developed to assist the student to further develop his or her language and learning skills. The test manual provides not only descriptions of the OLAI-2 and its sections, but also information and activities concerning oracy instruction and how the OLAI-2 informs that instruction.

The OLAI-2 consists of the following sections: Phonemic Awareness, Print Concepts, Repeated Sentences, and Story Retelling for children in prekindergarten to Grade 3 and Phonemic Awareness, Repeated Sentences, Expository Reading, and Expository Writing for children in Grades 4 through 6. The Expository Reading section includes two subsections, Intrapersonal Questions and Extrapersonal Questions. Intrapersonal Questions require answers based on the child's prior knowledge, and Extrapersonal Questions require answers that must be determined from information contained within the OLAI-2 text samples. Expository Writing also contains two subsections, Conventions and Content. Conventions evaluates the child's spelling, punctuation, and grammatical skills, and Content addresses the child's ability to provide a main idea, detail that is related to the main idea, and a concluding statement about the content of the theme.

Learning behavior is identified as *flexible, fight,* or *flight* behavior. If the student responds positively to the evaluator and the tasks, he or she is considered to be exhibiting flexible behavior. If the student is confrontational or avoids engagement of the tasks, he or she is considered to be exhibiting fight behavior. If the student avoids or "flees" from the test environment, he or she is considered to be exhibiting flight behavior. The examiner identifies and records the student's learning behavior for each task on the OLAI-2 after completion of that task.

The OLAI-2 has no time limits, and administration typically is completed within 20 minutes. There are two version of the record form, one for prekindergarten to Grade 3 and one for Grades 4 through 6; each version has three different forms for repeated assessment. The record form has sections for demographic information (e.g., name, sex, grade, age, teacher's name, assessment date, reason for assessment) and for recording the scores. For the PreK-Grade 3 record form, the scores reflect number of correct responses, except for the Phonemic Awareness section and the word count for Story Retelling, which are reported as percent correct. For Grades 4-6, scores are reported as number correct, except for the Phonemic Awareness section, which is reported as percent correct. The items for each section along with their brief instructions and scoring rules are contained within the record form. Test administrators are encouraged to audio record the entire assessment; audio recording is required for Story Retelling.

DEVELOPMENT. The OLAI was developed based on language and literacy development theory and how to use those theories to aid in the language and literacy development of children who are English language learners or children who have delayed language development. The test was developed using qualitative research methods including observations of teacher-student interactions, interviews, and analyses of classroom work in an effort to gain insight into the nature of instruction that should be developed for individual students. To determine the effectiveness of such instruction, it is recommended that the OLAI-2 be administered at the beginning, middle, and end of the school year. The test author indicates that the OLAI-2 is a criterion-referenced assessment, but as discussed below, no formal evaluation of its criterion-referenced abilities was examined for the OLAI-2.

Changes to the second edition include an age extension to sixth grade, shorter administration time, and the incorporation of instructional activities into the test manual.

TECHNICAL. Because the OLAI-2 is criterion-referenced, there is neither a normative sample nor normative data. The test author references two studies that provide some information regarding the psychometric properties of the original OLAI. One study (Romeo, Gentile, & Bernhardt, 2008) involved 117 first, second, and third grade bilingual students and OLAI Repeated Sentences and Story Retelling. Interrater reliability was reported to range between 80% and 90%. The second study (Goldenberg & Rutherford, 2009) compared students' language levels based on OLAI Repeated Sentences and Story Retelling scores to those based on scores from the California English Language Development Test (CELDT) in 120 elementary and 42 middle grade students. Exact agreement was observed with 43.8% of participants, and agreement within one score point was observed with 88.3% of participants. The test manual offered no additional information regarding the participants in the second study. Of note, the research evidence provided in the test manual evaluated the OLAI rather than the OLAI-2.

Content evidence of validity is assessed in the test manual. The various sections of the OLAI-2 have been used for quite some time to evaluate language and literacy development.

In summary, a convincing case for the psychometric properties of the OLAI-2 was not provided. Information related to reliability provided few details regarding the methods employed and results obtained. Some evidence of validity was provided regarding test content and the relationship of test scores with other variables (i.e., the CELDT). However, the criterion evidence involved classifications based on only two sections of the test, and both studies involved the OLAI and not the OLAI-2.

COMMENTARY. The OLAI-2 manual provides information not only concerning the administration of the OLAI-2, but also information about how to translate the results of the OLAI-2 to intervention strategies to help the student to develop his or her language and literacy skills. In addition, the test manual provides information concerning oracy instruction including modeling, changing negative responses, multisensory learning, additional suggestions for English language learning students, and oracy instructional activities. Given the lack of evidence concerning psychometric properties, one could argue that the administrator cannot be entirely confident that oracy intervention is necessary or what precisely that intervention should be. In fact, the test manual provides tables so students' performance on the OLAI-2 can be classified into Stage I (least experienced), Stage II (basic), or Stage III (most experienced) with regard to their language and literacy skills. However, the values in the table do not appear linked to data or research to support the rubric. For example, a student is classified as *least experienced* if he or she accurately identifies less than 30% of the sounds in the Phonemic Awareness section, *basic* if he or she accurately identifies between 30% and 40% of the sounds, and *most experienced* if he or she accurately identifies more than 40% of the sounds.

Those administering the OLAI-2 may find the description of Phonemic Awareness and how to administer that section confusing. For example, in the test manual, the Phonemic Awareness section is described as providing a "stimulus sentence to measure a student's knowledge of sound-symbol relationships." Knowledge of sound-symbol relationships is phonics, not phonemic awareness. Phonemic awareness refers to the ability to identify sounds in spoken words, that is, to be aware of phonemes. The actual Phonemic Awareness section is a measure of phonemic awareness as it asks the student to indicate by telling the administrator the sounds that the student hears in each word of a sentence. However, if the student does not understand the requirement of this task, the administrator is instructed to model segmenting the words into their individual phonemes. For example, the administrator is instructed to ask, "Can you say the /m/ in my?" which is essentially providing the answer for the child. Further, the instructions request that the administrator "repeat this prompt for each sound in each word." There are no instructions to count the item as incorrect before doing so. If the student responds with /m/ when asked to "say the /m/ in my," it appears that the item would be scored as correct. As a result, it is entirely possible for a student to score 100% on this task while not being able to engage in the skill of phonemic awareness. The scoring of this section needs further clarification.

SUMMARY. The OLAI-2 is an evaluation instrument designed to evaluate the language, literacy, and learning behavior of students between prekindergarten and sixth grade. It was developed to identify English language learners and students who have poorly developed language ability and to assist them to become more competent with the oracy instructional materials that are provided with the test manual.

The OLAI-2 manual recommends examining students' abilities at the beginning, middle, and end of the school year and provides three different forms to do so. Unfortunately, the test author provides no psychometric evidence of the OLAI-2's ability to identify children's language, literacy, and learning behaviors. Therefore, the results of the OLAI-2 do not allow for making conclusive statements or recommendations concerning language, literacy, or learning behaviors.

REVIEWER'S REFERENCES

Goldenberg, C., & Rutherford, S. (2009). *Assessing English language proficiency.* Unpublished manuscript, Stanford University.

Romeo, K., Gentile, L., & Bernhardt, E. (2008). Sentence repetition and story retelling as indicators of language proficiency in young bilingual children. In *57th yearbook of the National Reading Conference* (p. 298).

[112]

Oral Passage Understanding Scale.

Purpose: Designed to assess "listening comprehension by measuring the ability to listen to orally presented passages and recall information about them."
Population: Ages 5-21.
Publication Date: 2017.
Acronym: OPUS.
Scores, 7: Inference, Memory, Lexical/Semantic, Syntax, Passage Synthesis, Total.
Administration: Individual.
Price Data, 2020: $295 per kit including manual (133 pages), 10 record forms, easel, and access to test publisher's online evaluation system; $163 per easel; $88 per manual; $43 per 10 record forms.
Time: (10-20) minutes.
Comments: Administered via paper and pencil or digitally; may be used alone or as a companion to the Comprehensive Assessment of Spoken Language, Second Edition (see 37, this volume).
Authors: Elizabeth Carrow-Woolfolk and Amber Klein.
Publisher: Western Psychological Services.

Review of the Oral Passage Understanding Scale by STEVEN H. LONG, Associate Professor, Marquette University, Milwaukee, WI:

DESCRIPTION. The Oral Passage Understanding Scale (OPUS) provides an assessment of auditory comprehension based on the ability to recall and interpret information from short stories read to the listener. It is intended for students from 5 to 21 years of age. The OPUS yields information about five components of listening comprehension: Inference, Memory, Lexical/Semantic, Syntax, and Passage Synthesis. The test can assist in the diagnosis of a deficit or in the assessment of strengths and weaknesses based on item and passage analysis. It also can be used in combination with the Comprehensive Assessment of Spoken Language, Second Edition (CASL-2; Carrow-Woolfolk, 2017; see 37, this volume), a companion test by the first author. Together the two tests can provide repeated measures to monitor progress during treatment. The format of the OPUS requires the abilities to listen attentively to short passages and to respond in intelligible English to a series of examiner questions. It is not recommended for English language learners who, by definition, lack English proficiency. It also may not be suitable for students with significant attentional deficits or speech that is not easily understood.

Any professional familiar with standardized test administration and principles of psychometric interpretation should be able to use the OPUS. The element that requires the most care is the rate and tone to use when reading test passages to the student. The test authors provide audio samples online that model appropriate reading style. However, they emphasize that these audio recordings should be used solely for training and should not substitute for the live voice reading during the test.

The OPUS instructions ask the examinee to listen as the examiner reads aloud brief passages that are fictional, nonfictional, or narrative. The Student then responds to a series of questions regarding the passage that he or she has just heard. At the simplest level the passage contains 25 words and a mean of 6.2 words per sentence; the most complex passage contains 125 words and a mean of 25 words per sentence. To administer the test takes 10-20 minutes. Scoring and interpretation require additional time, although there is an online program where student responses can be entered securely in order to generate automatically the test's analysis forms. The OPUS is administered individually. Reading passages cannot be repeated, but questions can be repeated once if requested. Passages are grouped in item sets labeled A to F that increase in complexity. The starting place for the test is determined by the student's age. Each item set has a basal of two or more correct answers on the first two passages and a ceiling of at least two errors in the item set as a whole. In no case are more than two item sets administered. A set of neutral prompts may be used if the student provides an unclear or ambiguous response (e.g., "I missed your answer—say it again?" "Can you please explain what you mean?"). Scoring requires the examiner to apply the response criteria for each item. These criteria are clearly stated in the test easel that contains both the passages and the question items. If the examiner is uncertain how to score a particular response it should be recorded exactly in the test booklet and scored later.

The examiner's manual describes the administration and scoring of the OPUS, provides normative information, and offers guidelines for interpreting the results. The raw score is the total number of correct responses in the final item set given after the application of any basal or ceiling. This score is then converted to an ability score based on the item set used and from there to a standard score, percentile rank, and age or grade equivalent by means of tables provided. A separate chapter on test interpretation provides information and guidelines for the analysis of difficulties that may have been caused by a particular type of reading passage or item question. Two case studies are presented, one of which includes data from both the CASL-2 and the OPUS to illustrate how their findings can complement one another.

DEVELOPMENT. The OPUS is based on the Integrative Language Theory of the test's first author (Carrow-Woolfolk & Lynch, 1981). The CASL was first developed in 1999 to assess "differential skill levels of specific Lexical/Semantic, Syntactic, and Supralinguistic tasks" (manual, p. 1). The OPUS aims to assess the integration of those same skills in the context of a listening comprehension exercise. In principle, then, the two tests can be used together to evaluate a student's skills in more discrete, isolated language tasks and compare that performance to a task that requires their integration and that simulates the natural context of the classroom.

TECHNICAL. The OPUS was normed on a sample of 1,517 persons ages 5 to 21. The original normative sample included children 3 and 4 years of age, but these participants were removed when it was found that many in that age group could not answer even the lowest level questions on the test. The sample also was reduced by randomly removing individuals in oversampled categories. The demographics of the resulting normative sample closely resemble those of the 2012 U.S. census with regard to gender, race/ethnicity, education level of parents, and region. The sample included native English speakers as well as bilingual individuals who were judged to be "fully proficient in English" (manual, p. 5).

The test authors present three types of correlation coefficients to demonstrate the reliability of the OPUS: internal consistency, test-retest, and interscorer. Coefficients calculated using Rasch-based ability estimates were used to examine the internal consistency reliability of the test. The coefficients for OPUS scores across age intervals from 5 to 21 ranged from .82 to .91. The internal consistency of results obtained from a smaller clinical sample (N = 204) was .88. Taken together, these results suggest that the internal consistency of the OPUS is adequate to good. Test-retest reliability was assessed using 141 students who were retested 1-3 weeks after initial testing. The correlation coefficient between scores was .85, and comparison of the means from the two test administrations yielded a small effect size of .25., indicating good test-retest reliability. The reliability of scorer differences was examined by having two raters score the responses from 48 randomly selected students who had been part of the normative sample. The students were selected to produce a subsample balanced for age, gender, ethnicity, and parental education. The resulting correlation coefficient was .91, suggesting good interrater reliability.

The test manual presents evidence of validity under three categories: construct validity, discriminative validity, and detection of skill deficits. With regard to construct validity, the test authors first demonstrate graphically that the distribution of ability scores in the normative sample closely mirrors the distribution of test items scaled by difficulty. Thus, they argue, the OPUS represents a continuous range of task difficulty and shows that student performance corresponds closely to that range. Next, the scores from individuals in the normative sample were correlated with scores from three other tests also intended to measure language skills. Two of these tests, the CASL-2 (Carroll-Woolfolk, 2017) and the Oral and Written Language Scales, Second Edition (OWLS-II; Carroll-Woolfolk, 2011) were developed by the first author of the OPUS and were guided by the same model of language. Not surprisingly, therefore, the OPUS correlates highly with both. Correlations of OPUS scores with the subtests and indices of the CASL-2 yielded coefficients that ranged from .56-.77, with higher values observed for indices (.71-.77). The three OWLS-II composites correlated with OPUS scores with coefficients from .60-.74. In addition, the OPUS results were compared to those from another language test with different authors, the Clinical Evaluation of Language Fundamentals—Fifth Edition (CELF-5; Wiig, Semel, & Secord, 2013). This comparison yielded an equally strong correlation coefficient of .73.

Discriminative validity or "the capacity of test scores to distinguish between groups of participants who are expected to differ in the ability being measured" (manual, p. 48) was examined by comparing OPUS results from individuals with disabilities and matched controls. For students with seven different types of disabilities, significant *t*-test differences and large effect sizes (1.53-2.72) were found. This finding indicates the ability of OPUS scores to differentiate between typically developing students and those with many types of developmental disabilities.

Conditional probability analyses were used to evaluate the OPUS's sensitivity (correct identification of children with language disorder) and specificity (correct identification of children with normal language). The test authors present results at five different standard score cutoff levels from a low of 70 to a high of 90 and discuss how test users might use the sensitivity and specificity data to best achieve their clinical objectives.

COMMENTARY. The test authors provide evidence that the OPUS offers a series of graded listening exercises that challenge a student's ability to attend, integrate information, make use of contextual clues, and store and recall discrete facts in order to answer questions from the examiner. They further demonstrate with multiple analyses that the OPUS provides scores that are reliable and valid for their intended uses, and that the test is not biased with regard to gender, ethnicity, or socioeconomic status. Because the OPUS is a test of *integrated* listening comprehension, a poor result may be difficult to interpret without additional evaluation of language subskills. For this reason the test authors describe in the examiner's manual the combined use of OPUS with the CASL-2, which provides more information on specific language subskills. Other language tests (e.g., the CELF-5) might also be used in conjunction with the OPUS. When considering the use of the OPUS it is important to remember that (a) it requires focused attention to both the passages, which cannot be repeated, and the question items, and (b) it requires full proficiency in English as well as speech that can be readily understood. These criteria may render the OPUS inappropriate for certain students.

SUMMARY. The OPUS assesses a student's listening comprehension through a series of questions about passages that have been read aloud. By design, the test aims to evaluate the ability to integrate lexical, syntactic information with that inferred from context. Administration and scoring are uncomplicated, although the examiner must attend to basal and ceiling criteria. Evidence suggests that the OPUS provides reliable and valid scores when used with students proficient in English. A complete evaluation of auditory comprehension problems likely will require additional testing that examines more specific language subskills.

REVIEWER'S REFERENCES

Carrow-Woolfolk, E. (2011). Oral and Written Language Scales, Second Edition. Torrance, CA: Western Psychological Services.

Carrow-Woolfolk, E. (2017). Comprehensive Assessment of Spoken Language, Second Edition. Torrance, CA: Western Psychological Services.

Carrow-Woolfolk, E., & Lynch, J. I. (1981). *An integrative approach to language disorders in children.* San Antonio, TX: The Psychological Corporation.

Wiig, E. H., Semel, E., & Secord, W. A. (2013). Clinical Evaluation of Language Fundamentals—Fifth Edition. San Antonio, TX: Pearson.

Review of the Oral Passage Understanding Scale by PATRICIA A. PRELOCK, Professor and Dean, College of Nursing and Health Sciences, University of Vermont, Burlington, VT:

DESCRIPTION. The Oral Passage Understanding Scale (OPUS) is a norm-referenced measure of listening comprehension or the ability to listen to information heard orally and to remember that information. It is specifically designed for children and young adults, 5 to 21 years of age. Based on Carrow-Woolfolk and Lynch's (1981) integrative approach to language disorders, the OPUS measures oral listening and information recall when orally presented with passages. In addition, it assesses memory skills important to listening comprehension. Listening, information recall, and memory are highly relevant skills to classroom success as well as success in social situations.

The OPUS is recommended as a companion test to the Comprehensive Assessment of Spoken Language, Second Edition (CASL-2; Carrow-Woolfolk, 2017; see 37, this volume) as it provides greater information about an individual's listening comprehension than the CASL-2, thus, creating a more comprehensive profile of the individual's ability. It also may be used independently if the expected assessment does not require more specific information about an individual's spoken language abilities.

Assessment of an individual's understanding of spoken language is important, as the ability to listen impacts the ability to make sense of what one hears and experiences in everyday life from talk in the classroom to talk on the radio, television, podcasts, video, and in social conversations. Recognizing the value of using material encountered in everyday life, Carrow-Woolfolk and Klein designed the OPUS to represent material one might listen to on a daily basis, creating 17 passages with seven to 10 comprehension questions each. There are six different item sets, each with five passages, containing fictional, nonfictional and/or narrative content ordered by difficulty. A range of language skills are probed including: (a) Lexical/Semantic—understanding of word meaning; (b) Syntax—understanding of grammatical morphemes; (c) Inference—understanding information as applied to background knowledge, discernment of explicit ideas from implicit ones, understanding figurative or nonliteral language and the capacity to predict what might come next; (d) Memory—understanding information without context as well as details related to the context; and (e) Passage Synthesis—understanding overall meaning of what was heard using skills for integrating memory and language.

Administration takes 10 to 20 minutes, and item set selection is based on the age of the examinee. A passage is read aloud, and the examinee responds to a series of questions. Responses are scored, added, and converted to a standard score with a mean of 100 and standard deviation of 15 for both age and grade level, leading to an overall score for listening comprehension. Notably, audio files for the 17 passages are available on the test publisher's website to train the examiner in delivering each passage using a standard pace and intonation. Free online scoring and an assessment report are also available on the website, although registration is required to enter scores into the WPS Online Evaluation System™.

DEVELOPMENT. The OPUS was developed as a companion tool to the CASL-2 with a focus on multiple variables impacting listening comprehension. The examiner reads aloud passages taken from published works or created to reflect what individuals might hear in day-to-day communication. Material was drawn from both fiction and nonfiction sources and ordered by complexity. Of the 29 passages used in the development of the OPUS, 23 came from published works or the public domain, and six were written specifically for the OPUS. Using a model for Integrative Language Theory, the test authors wrote items to assess understanding of semantic, syntactic, and supralinguistic information as well as memory and the ability to synthesize passage meaning. Examinees are assessed using "probed recall" requiring them to pull from memory the relevant information in response to questions posed (manual, p. 36).

A pilot study was conducted to assess the functionality of the passages and test items prior to standardizing the tool. An expert panel determined that three of the 29 passages were too difficult for the targeted age range, so the pilot used 26 passages. For the pilot, participants comprised 288 individuals ages 3 years 0 months to 21 years 11 months. The test authors reviewed passing rates for items across ages to determine difficulty level and to ensure sufficient item representation across age and ability. This review led the test authors to make several changes including deleting items, creating new items, removing seven passages, writing six new passages (including two easy passages for the youngest age group), shortening a passage to facilitate comprehension, and modifying the order of passage delivery based on difficulty level.

TECHNICAL.

Standardization. The OPUS was normed using 1,517 individuals, ages 5 to 21, representing four main regions of the country (Northeast, Midwest, South, and West). The sample was stratified by race/ethnicity, geographic region, gender, and parent education level. Notably, the test authors randomly removed individuals who represented demographic categories that were oversampled. The sample remained overly representative of younger age groups (i.e., 5 to 12 years for which norms are presented in 3- or 6-month increments). The youngest population sampled included 3- and 4-year-olds, but the test questions were too difficult to achieve consistent responses, so these ages were dropped. Stratified variables were aligned with the U.S. Census Bureau (2012) with a slight under-representation of the Asian population. Notably, children with severe disabilities were excluded from the sample, but those with mild disabilities who spent the majority of their educational program in the general education classroom were included. A clinical sample included 204 individuals who were receiving services and had one of the following clinical diagnoses: autism spectrum disorder, developmental delay, hearing impairment, intellectual disability, receptive and/or expressive language disorder, and social communication disorder. Diversity was surprisingly strong, matching the U.S. Census statistics with overrepresentation of males as is typical in clinical groups.

Reliability. Three types of reliability were evaluated for the OPUS including internal consistency, test-retest, and interrater. Reliability coefficients for internal consistency of the items across age groups were strong with a range of .82 to .91 for the normative sample and .88 for the clinical sample.

Test-retest reliability was also strong with a reliability coefficient of .85 using a sample subset (n = 141) similar to that of the larger normative sample in major demographic characteristics. The test-retest interval was between 1 and 3 weeks.

To assess interrater reliability, 48 randomly selected protocols were drawn from those completed by participants in the normative sample. A high level of agreement was achieved between raters with an intraclass correlation of .91.

Validity. Evidence of validity was evaluated in two primary areas: construct validity and discriminative validity. Two methods were used to evaluate construct validity. Rasch analysis was used to compare the difficulty of items to the overall abilities of the examinees. Results indicated good item coverage across ability levels and the age ranges sampled. Convergent validity evidence was based on comparisons of the OPUS with three tools that measure similar constructs (i.e., Comprehensive Assessment of Spoken Language, Second Edition [CASL-2], Oral and Written Language Scales, Second Edition [OWLS-II], and Clinical Evaluation of Language Fundamentals—Fifth Edition [CELF-5]). Because the same sample was used for norming the CASL-2 and the OPUS, a large comparison sample was available (N = 953) yielding a strong correlation (.77) between the General Language Ability Index on the CASL-2 and the overall score on the OPUS. This high but not overly high correlation supports the intention of the test authors for these two measures to be used as companion pieces with "overlapping but different constructs" (manual, p. 48). Correlations with the OWLS-II yielded coefficients that were moderate (.60) for the Oral Expression scale to high (.74) for the Listening Comprehension scale. Correlation with the CELF-5 was also strong, as indicated by a coefficient of .73.

Evidence of discriminative validity, the strength of the test in distinguishing different populations, was examined using the clinical sample of 204 individuals and randomly pulling matched controls from the normative sample. Effect sizes were large (1.53-2.72), indicating that the clinical sample's performance was significantly different from that of the matched controls.

Sensitivity and specificity analyses were also conducted for various cutoff scores used to detect a clinical difference in listening comprehension. The OPUS was effective in identifying 79% of the cases that received a clinical diagnosis (sensitivity) and in identifying 87% of the cases who were drawn from the normative sample (specificity) when using a cutoff standard score of 85.

COMMENTARY. OPUS is founded in Integrative Language Theory, which the first author has applied to the development of several language assessments over the past 30 years (Carrow-Woolfolk, 1988, 1994, 1999; Carrow-Woolfolk & Lynch, 1981). Its development is guided by sound principles for assessment, which has characterized the previous work of the first author. The test requires training to ensure that delivery of the oral passages models appropriate tone and pacing. It is also important to be familiar with the information needed to assign a correct response. The test authors provide a comprehensive outline in the test manual of item information for each passage including the item text, type, information needed to score the item as correct, and identification of those language skills that would be observed in a correct response. The value of the

OPUS lies in its more comprehensive approach to examining listening comprehension across variables using real content an individual might experience in the classroom and in their day-to-day interactions. This reviewer suspects, however, that many of the passages would be challenging for clinical populations with working memory problems, difficulty with inferential versus factual information, and weak semantic knowledge. Notably, however, the use of a clinical sample is of value as it both discriminates performance from the normative sample and provides data regarding likely response performance for individuals with receptive and/or expressive language difficulties, autism spectrum disorder, hearing impairment, social communication disorder, learning disability, developmental delay, and intellectual disability. Data tables and scoring are clear, and case studies are provided. As this is a newly published test, there is no available research at this time examining the validity or reliability of the measure for assessing and monitoring listening comprehension following intervention in clinical populations.

SUMMARY. The OPUS is a new tool that will require some use before an assessment of clinical and therapeutic utility can be made. It is a more comprehensive approach to listening comprehension than its companion, the CASL-2, and other available language measures that examine more individual components of listening. The standardization sample is closely representative of the diversity of the U.S. population, and psychometric properties of the OPUS give it strength with some caution that there could be some individuals missed as well as some over identified as having a listening comprehension problem. The test authors should be commended for their careful development of the final passages selected and for including a clinical sample that gives the measure broader application across several disability categories. There are opportunities for this test to support intervention planning and progress monitoring, but it will require targeted research to assess the validity of the tool as an outcome measure across clinical populations.

REVIEWER'S REFERENCES

Carrow-Woolfolk, E. (1988). *Theory, assessment, and intervention in language disorders: An integrative approach*. Philadelphia, PA: Grune & Stratton.

Carrow-Woolfolk, E. (1994). *Learning to read: An oral language perspective of beginning reading*. San Antonio, TX: The Psychological Corporation.

Carrow-Woolfolk, E. (1999). Comprehensive Assessment of Spoken Language. Circle Pines, MN: American Guidance Service.

Carrow-Woolfolk, E. (2017). Comprehensive Assessment of Spoken Language, Second Edition. Torrance, CA: Western Psychological Services.

Carrow-Woolfolk, E., & Lynch, J. I. (1981). *An integrative approach to language disorders in children*. San Antonio, TX: The Psychological Corporation.

[113]

Ortiz Picture Vocabulary Acquisition Test.

Purpose: Designed to assess "general language competence, as indicated by receptive vocabulary acquisition, and to assist in the identification of language impairments in both [native] English speakers and [English] learners."
Population: Ages 2-6 to 22-11.
Publication Date: 2018.
Acronym: Ortiz PVAT.
Scores, 14: Vocabulary Acquisition and Development Total, Vocabulary Type Analysis [Parts of Speech Total (Noun, Verb, Adjective, Adverb, Preposition), Word Types Total (Basic Interpersonal Communicative Skills: Emergent, Intermediate, Advanced; Cognitive Academic Language Proficiency: Emergent, Intermediate, Advanced)].
Administration: Individual.
Forms, 2: Parallel forms A and B.
Price Data, 2020: $495 per complete kit, including downloadable software for a single user across unlimited devices, digital manual, and 50 test uses.
Foreign Language Editions: Task instruction script available in Arabic, Chinese, Russian, Spanish, and Vietnamese.
Time: (10-15) minutes.
Comments: Administered via Windows computer or iPad; scored online.
Author: Samuel O. Ortiz.
Publisher: Multi-Health Systems, Inc.

Review of the Ortiz Picture Vocabulary Acquisition Test by CHARLES BARRETT, School Psychologist, Loudoun County Public Schools, Ashburn, VA:

DESCRIPTION. The Ortiz Picture Vocabulary Acquisition Test (Ortiz PVAT) is an individually administered test of vocabulary knowledge for native English speakers and English learners between the ages of 2 years 6 months and 22 years 11 months. Unlike other tests of vocabulary knowledge or acquisition, the Ortiz PVAT follows an electronic administration via desktop, laptop computer, or tablet. Each item consists of the audible presentation of a vocabulary word, in English, accompanied by four pictures. Respondents are asked to select the picture that corresponds to the vocabulary term using a mouse or a touchscreen or by saying the number that corresponds to the picture. Because the Ortiz PVAT includes normative data for both English speakers and English learners, evaluators can assess the degree to which respondents' knowledge of English vocabulary is commensurate with same-age peers with a similar language background. Particularly relevant to school-based practitioners, including school psychologists and speech pathologists, the instrument helps to determine the degree to which students' functioning is related to language difference (e.g., second language acquisition) or disorder (e.g., receptive language disorder, specific learning disability).

Due to its digital format, administration of the PVAT is relatively simple and straightforward. Potential examiners should review the iOS and Windows system requirements. Upon completion of the assessment, which typically takes 10 to 15 minutes, a detailed report is generated that provides the following information: raw score, standard score, percentile rank, stanine, age equivalent, and descriptive classification. Additionally, interpretation and instructional level statements are provided as well as intervention recommendations. The report offers users an item analysis based on parts of speech (nouns, verbs, adjectives, adverbs, and prepositions) regarding the number presented, number correct, and percent correct. Last, the report provides similar information (i.e., number presented, number correct, and percent correct) for the following word types: Emergent Basic Interpersonal Communicative Skills (BICS), Intermediate BICS, Advanced BICS, Emergent Cognitive Academic Language Proficiency (CALP), Intermediate CALP, and Advanced CALP.

DEVELOPMENT. The Ortiz PVAT was developed over 6 years and included multiple phases: conceptualization and initial planning, item generation and development, pre-pilot phase, pilot phase, standardization phase, and final test construction. The first stage included a systematic literature review in the areas of language development and assessment (e.g., assessing vocabulary and second language acquisition). During the item generation and development phase, target words were selected to represent various parts of speech as well as BICS and CALP progression. According to the test developer, stock images were selected to avoid bias toward any cultural group and to maintain balance related to gender and ethnic diversity.

Data were collected during the pre-pilot phase from 278 English speakers between the ages of 2 years 6 months and 22 years 11 months who were representative of the U.S. population in terms of gender, geographic region, race/ethnicity, and parental education level. Of the 474 items that were used during this phase, 381 were retained for the pilot phase based on item analyses and expert panel feedback.

During the pilot phase, 861 English speakers and 513 English learners were included in the sample. Additionally, clinical populations (N = 89) representing the following conditions were included: language disorder, language delay, speech-sound communication disorder, autism spectrum disorder, intellectual disability, attention-deficit/hyperactivity disorder (ADHD), and learning disabilities.

After revisions, deletions, and the development of additional items to increase the number of easier words and to balance the parts of speech represented, 367 items were used in the standardization phase. Data were collected from 1,530 English speakers and 1,190 English learners. After item analysis using both classical test theory and item response theory, 292 items were retained for the final test construction phase, which included ordering items by difficulty, establishing basal and ceiling rules, and creating two parallel forms.

TECHNICAL.

Standardization. The technical manual, which is only available online, provides the following data for the English speaker and English learner samples: age, gender, parental education level, and geographic region. Race/ethnicity is provided for the English speaker sample. For the English learner sample, data related to language spoken (organized into four categories: Spanish and Spanish Creole, Indo-European, Asian and Pacific Islander, and other) and exposure to English are provided. Gender was evenly balanced in both samples, and the other variables were stratified to closely match 2014 U.S. Census Bureau figures.

The English speaker sample included 90 individuals from each of 17 age groups between 2 years 6 months and 22 years 11 months. Males and females were evenly balanced in each age group, and careful consideration was given to balance gender stratification in the following ways: Age x Gender x Race/Ethnicity; Age x Gender x Parental Education Level; Age x Gender x Geographic Region. The English learner sample included 70 individuals from each of the 17 age groups. Males and females were almost evenly balanced (49.2% male participants and 50.8% female participants). The technical manual reports the following information about the English learners: Age x Gender x Language Spoken; Language Spoken x Length of Exposure to English (years); Language Spoken x Percentage of Life Exposed to English; Age x Gender x Parental Education Level; and Age x Gender x Geographic Region. Such detailed analyses are helpful to clinicians who are working with students from a multitude of racial/ethnic and socioeconomic backgrounds.

A variety of analyses included in the technical manual showed no statistically significant differences in test scores based on examinees' gender (in both samples), race/ethnicity (in the English speaker sample), or language spoken (in the English learner sample). Significant differences were found between groups in both samples based on parental education level. Small effect sizes (*d* = .02 to .34) were observed, indicating that children whose parents had more education (i.e., some college or a college degree) scored higher than those whose parents had less (i.e., high school graduate or less).

Reliability. Acceptable levels of reliability were reported for both English speakers and English learners. Alternate forms reliability coefficients were .99 for both groups using data from the standardization sample. Test-retest reliability was examined over a 2- to 4-week interval and yielded corrected (for variability and restriction of range) coefficients of .75 and .81 for English speakers (*n* = 72) and .72 and .76 for English learners (*n* = 73).

Validity. Broadly speaking, validity is not a matter of "yes" or "no," but rather the extent to which the instrument accurately measures or accomplishes that which it has been purported to assess. The test manual includes evidence of validity based on test content, internal structure, relationships with other variables, response processes, and consequences of testing. Extensive detail is included about the extent to which the research team and test developers approached constructing this instrument to benefit educators working with English speakers and English learners. Specifically, this process included systematic literature reviews of language development, assessment, second language acquisition, and vocabulary assessment to inform test formulation.

Validation studies showed the Ortiz PVAT is sensitive enough to reflect true differences in ability between individuals with receptive impairment and those with expressive impairment related to language disorder versus general impairment in vocabulary or language ability. Most effect sizes ranged from medium to large when comparing the general and clinical populations with diagnoses that involve or may involve receptive language abilities. Said another way, the Ortiz PVAT produces clear and expected differences in receptive language functioning in clinical versus nonclinical populations as seen in the following examples (nonclinical sample was a randomly selected subsample of 52 members of the English speaker norm group):

Individuals with intellectual disability (*n* = 31) scored more than 15 points lower than those without intellectual disability; large effect sizes were observed for both Form A (*d* = 1.16) and Form B (*d* = 1.21).

Medium effect sizes of .66 and .60 for Forms A and B, respectively, were detected for those with a language disorder (receptive or mixed receptive-expressive language-related impairment; *n* = 47), who scored approximately 10 points lower than the nonclinical sample.

Medium effect sizes (Form A: *d* = .51; Form B: *d* =.48) were detected for those with a language delay (*n* = 30), whose scores were approximately 7 points lower than those of the nonclinical sample.

Individuals with autism spectrum disorder (ASD; *n* = 37) scored lower on the Ortiz PVAT than those without ASD, but the difference was small and nonsignificant (Form A: *d* = .37; Form B: *d* = .30). The test authors noted that although persons with ASD may have language deficits compared with the general population, those deficits may not involve receptive vocabulary ability. Further analysis showed individuals with ASD and receptive impairment (*n* = 15) scored lower than those with ASD and expressive impairment (*n* = 22); however, small sample sizes limited additional interpretation.

As hypothesized by the test authors, no statistically significant differences were found between the nonclinical sample and those with specific learning disability with impairment in reading (*n* = 31; Form A: *d* = .25; Form B: *d* = .30), ADHD (*n* = 31; Form A: *d* = .13; Form B: *d* =.11), or expressive language disorder (*n* = 52; Form A: *d* = .06; Form B: *d* =.07).

As convergent evidence of validity, the Ortiz PVAT demonstrated moderate-to-large correlation coefficients with the Peabody Picture Vocabulary Test, Fourth Edition (PPVT-4), another assessment of receptive language functioning. In samples of English speakers (*n* = 116) and English learners (*n* = 102), correlation coefficients between scores on the Ortiz PVAT and the PPVT-4 were .59-.63 and .60-.69, respectively. Corrected coefficients were slightly higher, .63-.67 and .62 to .71, respectively.

COMMENTARY. From a practical perspective, the Ortiz PVAT technical manual includes multiple case studies (assessment of an English speaker suspected of having a speech or language impairment; assessment of an English learner suspected of having a specific learning disability; and progress monitoring of an English learner suspected of deficits in verbal ability and language) to illustrate the appropriate clinical uses of the instrument as well as detailed information about score interpretation. Step-by-step interpretation guidelines are offered related to the following: establishing context and determining validity, interpreting scores, reviewing instructional needs and intervention recommendations, examining performance by vocabulary type, and evaluating change over time. Particularly beneficial for clinicians working in applied settings, the intervention recommendations are further delineated into the following broad categories: instructional level recommendations, instructional strategies, practical strategies for intervention, and behaviors to avoid. Based on the skill or experience level of the teacher or interventionist serving English speakers or English learners, these concrete suggestions are helpful to better serve the varied needs of students/clients, which is the foremost goal of assessment. Relatedly, and especially salient in the contemporary culture of multitiered system of support such as response to intervention that is rapidly being adopted in many states, local schools, and school jurisdictions, the test authors provide guidelines related to the examinee's rate of progress (i.e., much less than expected, less than expected, expected, and more than expected) and intervention recommendations.

SUMMARY. The Ortiz PVAT has many noteworthy elements. First, the administration time is relatively short (10-15 minutes), and the test is presented digitally. Next, verbal responses, which could pose significant challenges for English learners and those with a variety of expressive language deficits, are not required. Second, the availability of normative data for English speakers and English learners is valuable for making appropriate comparisons between students of similar age and language background. The test author's careful research and data collection efforts were evident as various subgroups, including English learners that were stratified by parental education level, region, age, gender, language spoken, and exposure to English, were generally commensurate with the U.S. population. Reliability and validity data indicate that the instrument provides stable, consistent scores over time and measures the constructs that it purports to assess.

The Ortiz PVAT joins several existing instruments or subtests that already assess this domain with adequate reliability and evidence of validity (e.g., Differential Ability Scales—Second Edition: Naming Vocabulary; Kaufman Assessment Battery for Children, Second Edition: Expressive Vocabulary; Peabody Picture Vocabulary Test, Fourth Edition). Depending on referral concerns, practitioners are encouraged to carefully consider the unique predictive validity of vocabulary knowledge for academic success in the absence of confounding factors (e.g., quality of instruction and exposure to educationally rich environments).

Review of the Ortiz Picture Vocabulary Acquisition Test by MICHAEL S. MATTHEWS, Professor of Gifted Education, Department of Special Education and Child Development, University of North Carolina at Charlotte, Charlotte, NC:

DESCRIPTION. The Ortiz Picture Vocabulary Acquisition Test (Ortiz PVAT) is an individually administered assessment of receptive vocabulary in English that is designed both for native speakers and English learners of diverse backgrounds. The test can assess general language competence, help to determine school readiness in young children, and assist in the identification of language impairments among both English learners and native speakers. The Ortiz PVAT does not require examinees to read, write, or produce verbal responses, and its minimal task instructions are available in five common languages in addition to English. As the test author observes (online test manual, Chapter 2), vocabulary is strongly correlated with a number of other important variables, and its assessment is an important component of many other measures of intelligence and language development.

The Ortiz PVAT is delivered via a software application (app) for devices running either iOS or Windows operating systems. The user downloads the app, which is compatible with older system software back to iOS 9 and Windows 8.1, via the relevant app store. The app is not available for iPhone or the Mac computer. It can be used with either a mouse or a touchscreen interface; this reviewer tried it exclusively on an iPad.

Testing and score reporting are fully computerized, so once started, there is little the examiner needs to do to complete the assessment besides monitor it. As such, it can be administered by a wide range of individuals, although the test publisher states B-level qualification is necessary to interpret test results. The test administrator does not need to be bilingual.

Practice items at the beginning (plus additional optional ones) allow for setting the volume of the pre-recorded spoken prompt to a comfortable level and ensuring that the examinee understands the task request, which is to select the one picture among the four presented that most closely reflects the target word. Target words represent nouns, verbs, adjectives, adverbs, and prepositions as well as different levels of English language proficiency and are arranged in order of increasing difficulty.

A screener automatically selects the appropriate basal level for examinees ages 6 and older, or a lower starting level can be selected manually via the custom administration option. Testing is discontinued after the examinee has missed five prompts in any 10 consecutive items. On completion, the app uploads data to the test publisher's online portal (i.e., MHS Online Assessment Center+) where the examiner-generated score reports can then be saved or shared as PDF files. Scores can be generated as an assessment report on a single administration or as a progress report evaluating change over time in a single examinee's performance. Standard scores provided in either report are scaled to the widely used metric of a mean of 100 and standard deviation of 15, with the mean and confidence interval indicated visually on a bell curve. Score reports also include raw score, percentile rank, stanine, age equivalent, and a seven-point proficiency classification, as well as interpretation guidelines, recommendations for appropriate instructional level, and strategies for promoting future growth.

DEVELOPMENT. Rather than developing a separate measure for each different language (see e.g., Matthews, 2014), the Ortiz PVAT instead offers two different sets of norms, with the English learner norms adjusted for examinees' exposure to English (ranging from 1% to 99%). Dual norming samples then allow the same test items and instructions to be administered with students who are monolingual native speakers and those who are learning English as an additional language. Other design considerations include the online platform for delivery and reporting, stimuli chosen for relevance and ecological validity, and statistically equated A/B alternate forms to allow for repeat assessments.

In addition to general developmental considerations, the Ortiz PVAT is based in the developmental distinction between Basic Interpersonal Communication Skills (BICS) and Cognitive Academic Language Proficiency (CALP; see Cummins, 1979). The influence of family socioeconomic status on early reading ability and affect toward reading are recognized by their inclusion in the standardization process.

TECHNICAL.

Standardization. Development began with a review of literature and selection of 474 target words selected using frequency lists and a dictionary of English words. Selection considerations included providing a range of difficulty levels, word categories, and parts of speech as well as inclusion of terms relevant to both BICS and CALP. A set of 1,422 distractor terms was also selected, along with stock images corresponding to both sets of words. Each item was constructed using four images, corresponding to a target word plus three distractors arranged in a 2x2 grid, along with a spoken prompt of the target word.

The standardization process was extensive. Via panel review (five experts), a pre-pilot phase (278 native English speakers representative of the U.S. population), and a pilot phase (stratified samples of 861 native English speakers and 513 English learners), the standardization version consisted of 367 items. Individuals with a clinical diagnosis that might affect performance (seven categories) were included in both the pilot and standardization phases.

The standardization version was administered to samples of 1,530 English speakers and 1,190 English learners, stratified to the U.S. Census population on geographic region, parent education level, race/ethnicity (for English speakers only), and (for English learners only) exposure to English and home language, and balanced for gender and age group representation. Lastly, using classical test theory and item response theory, the final item pool was pared to 292 items. These items in turn were arranged into two parallel forms of 167 items each, with the first 10 items plus every fifth item thereafter shared across the A and B forms.

Reliability. The online test manual (Chapter 8) provides evidence supporting four aspects of reliability. Alternate-form reliability coefficients were very high—above .99—for both English speakers and English learners. Marginal reliability coefficients (similar to coefficient alpha) also were very high, at .98 for the pooled English learner and English speaker sample for both the A and B forms, and .99 for the clinical sample on both forms. Test information curves (online manual, Figure 8.1) indicate high precision and low error. Corrected test-retest reliability coefficients for the two forms and norming populations (four groups in total) over 13 to 31 days ranged from .72 to .81, with negligible effect sizes for the standardized mean difference values, indicating the measured values were stable over time.

Validity. Validity evidence includes the examiner's evaluation of the administration (e.g., attentiveness of the examinee to the test tasks). Content evidence of validity for the final version's items was supported by the expert review during standardization, through which a number of less appropriate items were discarded. Validity of the measure's internal structure was supported by factor analysis showing that a one-factor solution, consistent with theory suggesting a unidimensional construct, provided as effective an explanation as a two-factor solution loading into easier vs. more difficult items. Criterion-related evidence of validity was supported by depressed scores obtained by a sample of participants with various clinically diagnosed disorders expected to impair receptive language ability. Moderate positive correlations between Ortiz PVAT performance and scores on the Peabody Picture Vocabulary Test, Fourth Edition, ranging from .63 to .67 for English speakers and .62 to .71 for English learners, also provide evidence of criterion-related validity. In another more distal comparison, moderately strong correlation coefficients of .55 to .65 were observed for 70 individuals who completed the Ortiz PVAT and the Verbal Comprehension Index of the Wechsler Intelligence Scale for Children. Lastly, in considering fairness, bias was not observed across groups by gender or race/ethnicity, and differences by parent education level were relatively small and in the expected direction (i.e., higher parent education was associated with greater vocabulary among their children).

COMMENTARY. Overall the Ortiz PVAT is a well-developed measure with strong evidence of reliability and validity and one that provides a straightforward experience for the examinee. The supporting materials are comprehensive with strong coverage of the salient issues in assessing bilingual learners and clear descriptions of the measure's development and psychometric properties.

This reviewer wishes children identified as academically gifted (my area of research) had been addressed as an additional group within the norming sample. There are few measures available to answer the questions so often asked regarding ways to identify high ability among preschool-aged children, and English learners remain among the most under-identified population in gifted education programming (e.g., Matthews & Peters, 2018). The measure's capability to assess young children and also those learning English would be quite useful in this regard.

This reviewer's only real complaint is that the initial setup is somewhat cumbersome. A web search for MHS Assessments goes to an order page, but the link lower down the page labeled "MHS Online Assessment Center" does not access the measure; farther below this is the "MHS Online Assessment Center+" button that is actually the correct link. It is helpfully labeled "Now Available! Login here to access The Ortiz PVAT or assessments purchased for the improved and redesigned MHS Online Assessment Center+".

Once logged in on the MHS site, the app is supposed to be downloaded by clicking a link to the app store, but this reviewer had trouble getting the download link to work and had to search manually in the app store to locate it. Once both the site and app are open, the user has to go back and forth between the app and web page to enter examinees, administer the test, and generate reports. The account access times out quickly, necessitating repeatedly typing in one's login credentials to regain access. It is unfortunate that the Ortiz PVAT app is not presently available for the Mac laptop or iPhone, as these platforms would allow for additional flexibility.

SUMMARY. The Ortiz PVAT is a well-designed measure of receptive vocabulary that is straightforward for examinees to use and closely grounded in best practices for assessing English learners. Its strengths include suitability with a wide age range, strong psychometric properties, and independence from any specific home language children may speak. Although the user interface can be somewhat clunky from the examiner's end, once mastered it will save time and effort in test administration and record keeping.

REVIEWER'S REFERENCES

Cummins, J. (1979). Cognitive/academic language proficiency, linguistic interdependence, the optimum age question and some other matters. *Working Papers on Bilingualism, 19,* 121-129.

Matthews, M. S. (2014). [Test review of the Expressive One-Word Picture Vocabulary Test—4: Spanish-Bilingual Edition]. In J. F. Carlson, K. F. Geisinger, & J. L. Jonson (Eds.), *The nineteenth mental measurements yearbook* (pp. 295-297). Lincoln, NE: Buros Center for Testing.

Matthews, M. S., & Peters, S. J. (2018). Methods to increase the identification rate of students from traditionally underrepresented populations for gifted services. In S. I. Pfeiffer, E. Shaunessy-Dedrick, & M. Foley-Nicpon (Eds.), *APA handbook of giftedness and talent* (pp. 317-332). Washington, DC: American Psychological Association.

[114]

Overall Assessment of the Speaker's Experience of Stuttering [2016 Manual].

Purpose: Designed to "provide speech-language pathologists with a measure of the overall impact of stuttering on a person's life."

Population: Individuals 7 and older who stutter.

[114] Overall Assessment of the Speaker's Experience of Stuttering [2016 Manual]

Publication Dates: 2008-2016.
Acronym: OASES.
Scores, 5: General Information, Your Reactions to Stuttering, Communication in Daily Situations, Quality of Life, Overall Impact.
Administration: Individual or group.
Forms, 3: School-Age, Teenage, Adult.
Price Data, 2020: \$55 per print manual (2016, 60 pages); \$61 per printable electronic manual; \$45 per 25 record forms; \$51 per 25 printable electronic record forms.
Foreign Language Editions: Available in Dutch, German, Hebrew, Portuguese (Brazil), and Spanish.
Time: 15-20 minutes for administration.
Authors: J. Scott Yaruss and Robert W. Quesal (manual and test forms); Craig E. Coleman (School-Age and Teenage forms).
Publisher: Stuttering Therapy Resources, Inc.
a) SCHOOL-AGE.
Population: Ages 7-12.
Acronym: OASES-S.
b) TEENAGE.
Population: Ages 13-17.
Acronym: OASES-T.
c) ADULT.
Population: Ages 18 and older.
Acronym: OASES-A.
Cross References: For reviews by Sandra D. Haynes and by Jeanette Lee-Farmer and Joyce Meikamp of the original edition, see 18:83.

Review of the Overall Assessment of the Speaker's Experience of Stuttering [2016 Manual] by ROBIN L. EDGE, Associate Professor, Brooks Rehabilitation Department of Communication Sciences and Disorders, Jacksonville University, Jacksonville, FL:

DESCRIPTION. The Overall Assessment of the Speaker's Experience of Stuttering (OASES) is a criterion-referenced self-report measure designed to assess "the overall impact of stuttering on a person's life" by examining "the entirety of the stuttering disorder from the perspective of the individual who stutters" (manual, p. 1). The test authors operationalize the "entirety of the disorder" as the four sections on the OASES: general information, the respondent's reactions to stuttering, communication in daily situations, and quality of life. Earlier versions of the OASES were designed for adults; the current version has added forms for teenagers (OASES-T; ages 13-17) and school-aged children (OASES-S; ages 7-12). The instrument's intended goal is to provide speech-language pathologists with a measure of the impact stuttering has on a person's life. The test authors state it can be used to inform both clinicians and individuals who stutter about the impacts of the disorder.

The test authors designed the OASES to be used at various points throughout assessment and treatment in clinical and research settings. It was developed to be used primarily by speech-language pathologists (SLPs), but also can be used by other professionals working with an SLP. The adult version (OASES-A) has 100 items, the OASES-T has 80 items, and the OASES-S has 60 items. Each item is rated using a 5-point Likert response scale with higher values signifying greater negative impact. Participants are not timed when completing the measure, and the test manual reports a typical completion time of less than 20 minutes for adults and teenagers and a 20-minute completion time for children. Although the test is self-report, clinicians can assist respondents with reading or understanding the questions. Speakers are instructed to complete the instrument based on their current feelings and experiences with stuttering.

All three forms of the OASES use the same scoring procedures, response scales, and impact ratings. Respondents are instructed to mark *not applicable* (*N/A*) if an item does not apply to them. Unscorable items should be assessed by the clinician, preferably while the speaker is still available to clarify omitted or unclear responses. Excessive omissions or responses that indicate a person's lack of attention are not to be scored. Impact scores are calculated for each subsection by counting the points rated in each section and dividing that by the number of questions completed in each section. This value corresponds to an impact rating ranging from *mild* (1) to *severe* (5). The technical manual provides score interpretation based on "data and experience gained through the validation of the instrument and through input provided by many expert clinicians and individuals who stutter" to assist clinicians (p. 13).

DEVELOPMENT. The initial OASES was developed based on the World Health Organization's (WHO's) *International Classification of Impairments, Disabilities, and Handicaps* (*ICIDH*; 1980), but speakers' and environmental reactions were added as a result of the inadequacy of the *ICIDH* to describe the impact stuttering has on these factors for a person who stutters' experience of disability and handicap (Yaruss, 1998). The development of the OASES occurred in four stages. Initially, a pool of items was created and reviewed by researchers and clinicians with expertise in stuttering treatment and by focus groups of people who stutter. Drafts of the instrument were tested, revised, and retested until the final items were selected for use in the OASES (now the OASES-A), and scoring procedures and interpretation guidelines were developed. The adult version was adapted for use with children and adolescents.

The initial item pool was developed from a review of other instruments that measure "communication attitudes" in people who stutter (Brutten & Shoemaker, 1974; Cooper, 1993; Erickson, 1969; Ornstein & Manning, 1985; Watson, 1988; Woolf, 1967), a review of the American Speech-Language-Hearing Association's *Functional Assessment of Communication Skills for Adults* (Frattali, Thompson, Holland, Wohl, & Ferketic, 1995), and quality of life measures from other fields, as detailed in the OASES manual. A focus group of 20 SLP fluency specialists and 30 people who stutter assessed the questions to determine whether they accurately represented the stuttering experience. Post focus groups, the items were condensed, and three try-out instruments were created to correspond with the *ICIDH* framework and adaptations: Speaker's Reactions to Stuttering (SRS), Functional Communication and Stuttering (FCS), and Quality of Life and Stuttering (QOL-S). The SRS, FCS, and QOL-S were then administered to 39 adults who stutter. Based on the data and statistical analysis from this pilot study, the instrument was revised for a second pilot study of 71 people who stutter. Statistical analyses of central tendency, distribution of responses, and internal consistency reliability were conducted. Alpha coefficients ranged from .93 to .96, indicating a high degree of internal consistency within each measure. Correlations between instruments ranged from .76 to .83, leading the test authors to conclude that they measured different constructs. Five people who stutter completed this version of the measure twice over a 2-week period, and items that were inconsistent were considered for revision. Content was again revised upon the transition from the *ICIDH* to the *International Classification of Functioning, Disability and Health* (WHO) in 2001. First, the SRS, FCS, and QOL-S were combined into one measure. Second, the general information section was added to assess speakers' perceptions of impairment. The resulting 100-item instrument became the OASES-A.

To adapt the adult version for younger populations, the 100 OASES-A items were reviewed and revised for use with children ages 7-17 (Coleman, Yaruss, & Quesal, 2004; Yaruss, Coleman, & Quesal, 2006). Pilot data were collected from more than 40 children who stutter and their families, and it was found that one instrument could not adequately evaluate children ages 7-17. This instrument was divided into two tests (OASES-T and OASES-S), and standardization data were collected.

TECHNICAL.

Standardization. The standardization sample for the OASES-A comprised 173 people who stutter who were recruited predominately from a National Stuttering Association mailing list. The sample closely matched the 3:1 male-to-female ratio of people who stutter (Bloodstein & Bernstein Ratner, 2008). Ethnicity information was not presented by the test authors, but the measure has been translated into "approximately 30 languages, with numerous validation and publication projects ongoing or completed" (manual, p. 36). The OASES-T was standardized using 45 teenagers (37 males, eight females) ages 13-0 to 17-11. The OASES-S standardization sample included 75 school-aged children (63 males, 12 females) ages 7-0 to 12-11. Minimal unusable responses were found in these sample data. Central tendencies and distributions of item responses were analyzed for each item to identify ceiling and floor effects, skewness, and kurtosis, and results are presented in the test manual for all three versions of the OASES.

Reliability. Internal consistency reliability and test-retest reliability were assessed during the development of the OASES. Internal consistency reliability provides a measure of how well the items in an instrument assess the same construct. The even-odd split-half method was used with all three versions of the OASES, and the ranges were .94-.99, .88-.98, and .67-.95 for the adult, teen, and child versions, respectively, across sections and overall. For reference, a value of 1.0 indicates perfect internal consistency. The standard error of measurement (*SEM*) is the average amount a person's observed score differs from his or her true score. It provides a measure of the extent to which a score is affected by measurement error. Observed scores within 1 *SEM* have a 68% probability of including the person's true score. The *SEM* for the impact scores of the three OASES versions are .08-.17 (OASES-A), .08-.21 (OASES-T), and .11-.25 (OASES-S).

Test-retest reliability indicates the consistency of a person's performance across time. This type of reliability is evaluated by giving the measure to the same respondent twice within a short amount of time. Using the data from these two administrations, statistical correlations are calculated and can range from 0 to 1. (The higher the number the more consistent the score.) The OASES-A used 14 people to calculate test-retest reliability estimates whereas 10 were given the OASES-T, and 20 the OASES-S, 7-14 days apart. Test-retest correlation coefficients across sections and overall were .89-.95, .92-.99, and .90-.97 for adults, teens, and children, respectively.

Validity. Authors claim the OASES has content evidence of validity as it was developed and revised using the WHO ICF framework. The test authors evaluated construct evidence of validity by conducting correlations between the impact scores on each section within the same version of the test. The closer the number is to 1, the more highly the two sections are correlated or related. The sections are moderately correlated for all three OASES versions, ranging from .67 to .85 on the OASES-A, .58 to .79 on the OASES-T, and .18 to .73 on the OASES-S (excluding the correlations with the Overall Score). Some correlation between these sections is expected as stuttering is a multifactorial disorder that can be affected by various factors that intersect. The three OASES-A tryout instruments (SRS, FCS, and QOL-S) were administered to 71 participants, together with the Erickson S24 (Andrews & Cutler, 1974), an instrument designed to assess interpersonal communication attitudes toward stuttering among older adolescents. Correlation coefficients between the tryout instruments and the Erickson S24 ranged from .68 (QOL-S) to .83 (SRS), offering further evidence of validity for the OASES-A scores.

COMMENTARY. The biggest strength of the OASES is that it is the first stuttering measure to address the impact of the entire disorder using the WHO-ICF framework. It is the culmination of multiple versions of the test including content revisions after pilot data and focus groups. Reliability and validity testing were conducted using a small number of participants, especially the OASES-T and OASES-S versions. Although the small samples should not discourage users from the instrument's use, they should be noted when drawing conclusions about obtained results. Continued psychometric testing of all three versions of the OASES would strengthen the instrument substantially.

SUMMARY. The OASES is a criterion-referenced, self-report measure of the effect of the entire stuttering disorder on a person's life. There are three forms of the OASES: Adult (OASES-A), Teenage (OASES-T), and School-Age (OASES-S). The measure has four sections (A/T/S): General Information (20/15/15 items), Your Reactions to Stuttering (30/25/20 items), Communication in Daily Situations (25/20/15 items), and Quality of Life (25/20/10 items). It is the only measure developed using the WHO ICF framework intended to quantify the impact the entire stuttering disorder has on a person. The instrument can be given multiple times to assess change over time as well as to help clinicians select therapy goals. It is easy to score and interpret. Although there are other stuttering measures that assess social, emotional, and/or cognitive variables in people who stutter, this is the first tool to integrate the effects of the disorder in a single instrument. Although it was standardized using small samples, it fills a void in the assessment of stuttering; therefore, its use should be considered.

REVIEWER'S REFERENCES

Andrews, G., & Cutler, J. (1974). Stuttering therapy: The relation between changes in symptom level and attitudes. *Journal of Speech and Hearing Research, 34,* 312-319.

Bloodstein, O., & Bernstein Ratner, N. (2008). *A handbook on stuttering* (6th ed.). Clifton Park, NY: Thompson/Delmar Learning.

Brutten, G., & Shoemaker, D. (1974). *Speech Situation Checklist.* Carbondale, IL: Speech Clinic, Southern Illinois University.

Coleman, C., Yaruss, J. S., & Quesal, R. W. (2004, November). *Assessment of the Child's Experience of Stuttering (ACES).* Poster presented at the annual convention of the American Speech-Language-Hearing Association, Philadelphia, PA.

Cooper, E. B. (1993). Chronic perseverative stuttering syndrome: A harmful or helpful construct? *American Journal of Speech-Language Pathology, 2,* 11-15.

Erickson, R. L. (1969). Assessing communication attitudes among stutterers. *Journal of Speech and Hearing Research, 12,* 711-724.

Frattali, C., Thompson, C. K., Holland, A. L., Wohl, C. B., & Ferketic, M. M. (1995). *American Speech-Language-Hearing Association Functional Assessment of Communication Skills for Adults.* Rockville, MD: American Speech-Language-Hearing Association.

Ornstein, A. F., & Manning, W. H. (1985). Self-efficacy scaling by adult stutterers. *Journal of Communication Disorders, 18,* 313-320.

Watson, J. B. (1988). A comparison of stutterers' and nonstutterers' affective, cognitive, and behavioral self-reports. *Journal of Speech and Hearing Research, 31,* 377-385.

Woolf, G. (1967). The assessment of stuttering as struggle, avoidance, and expectancy. *British Journal of Disorders in Communication, 2,* 158-171.

World Health Organization (1980). *International classification of impairments, disabilities, and handicaps: A manual of classification relating to the consequences of disease, published in accordance with resolution WHA29.35 of the Twenty-ninth World Health Assembly, May 1976.* Geneva, Switzerland: Author.

World Health Organization (2001). *International classification of functioning, disability and health: ICF.* Geneva, Switzerland: Author.

Yaruss, J. S. (1998). Describing the consequences of disorders: Stuttering and the International Classification of Impairments, Disabilities, and Handicaps. *Journal of Speech, Language, and Hearing Research, 41,* 249-257.

Review of the Overall Assessment of the Speaker's Experience of Stuttering [2016 Manual] by KENNETH MELNICK, Associate Professor in the Communication Sciences and Disorders Department, Worcester State University, Worcester, MA:

DESCRIPTION. The Overall Assessment of the Speaker's Experience of Stuttering (OASES) is designed to examine the impact that stuttering has on a person's life as reported from the client's perspective. It may be administered to school-aged children (OASES-S, 60 questions; ages 7-12 years), teens (OASES-T, 80 questions; ages 13-17 years), and adults (OASES-A, 100 questions; ages 18+

years). The test may be individually or group administered. Administration time is 15-20 minutes. There are four sections, each containing a series of questions formatted on a 5-point Likert scale, including (a) general information about stuttering, (b) speaker's reactions to stuttering, (c) difficulty in communicating in daily situations (i.e., how difficult speaking is), and (d) quality of life (i.e., how stuttering interferes with daily activities). Points for questions within each section are added. Summing a section's points and dividing by the number of questions answered within that section yields an impact score for that section. Summing the total points on the measure and dividing by the number of questions answered generates an overall impact score. Impact scores for individual sections and overall correspond to five impact ratings (i.e., 1.00-1.49 = *mild,* 1.50-2.24 = *mild-moderate,* 2.25-2.99 = *moderate,* 3.0-3.74 = *moderate-severe,* and 3.75-5.00 = *severe*). Questions within sections may be omitted or identified as not applicable (*N/A*); however, sections should not be scored if 25% or more of questions are omitted (or marked *N/A*). If this occurs, an overall impact score cannot be generated. Suggested interpretations for each section's impact score and overall impact score are provided in the technical manual. Impact scores/ratings may be conveyed in diagnostic reports for overall therapy purposes, and individual questions within sections may be helpful to both clients and clinicians when planning interventions or conducting research.

DEVELOPMENT. The OASES was developed to evaluate the impact stuttering has on a person's life. Initial development of the test was based on the *International Classification of Impairments, Disabilities, and Handicaps* (World Health Organization [WHO], 1980). The rationale for using this method was to ensure a test that was relevant to the experiences of people who stutter, including not just the symptoms of the disability, but the impact those symptoms have on a person's life. When the revision of *International Classification of Impairments, Disabilities, and Handicaps* was released (*International Classification of Functioning, Disability and Health* [WHO, 2001]), the OASES was modified to reflect both negative and positive aspects of stuttering. The test was designed to parallel the framework of the World Health Organization for describing human health experience and the *International Classification of Functioning, Disability and Health.* The test was originally designed for adults and later adapted for use with school-aged children (i.e., OASES-S) and teenagers (OASES-T). The OASES was created in stages, including (1) creation of an initial corpus of questions, (2) analysis of questions by researchers and speech-language pathologists who specialize in stuttering, (3) evaluation of numerous drafts and analyses of the test, and (4) final product. The test was developed so that it could be scored quickly following administration.

TECHNICAL. The OASES was standardized by administering the test primarily to members of the National Stuttering Association, the largest self-help organization for people who stutter in the United States. In all, 173 tests (31.5%) were returned. Ages ranged from 18 to 78 years. The ratio of males to females was 3:1, which closely mirrored the distribution of males to females in the population of adults who stutter (Bloodstein & Bernstein Ratner, 2008). Analysis ensured questions were answered correctly (e.g., skipped sections and sections in which the same answer was given to all items in the section were excluded). Questions were analyzed for ceiling and floor effects, skewness, and kurtosis; the vast majority yielded normal distributions with minimal skewness or kurtosis. Interitem correlation coefficients did not exceed .90. After the initial test was created, follow-up interviews with 29 adults occurred, resulting in slight modification of wording to some of the questions. The most current version of the test (i.e., published by Stuttering Therapy Resources) reflects additional minor wording changes after years of test usage and experience of the test authors and feedback from speakers, researchers, and clinicians. The OASES-T and OASES-S were standardized with 45 and 75 participants, respectively. Analyses for these two tests were performed in a fashion similar to the OASES-A. As the negative impact of stuttering tends to worsen with age, it follows that a smaller percentage of participants received higher ratings (i.e., relatively more negative impact score) in the OASES-T compared to the OASES-A and that the smallest percentage of higher ratings was observed in the OASES-S.

An item analysis was performed on every test question on every OASES test to ensure each item had an appropriate distribution. Internal consistency reliability and test-retest reliability were evaluated for all OASES tests. Internal consistency reliability coefficients were between .94 and .99 for each section of the OASES-A, between .88 and .98 for each section of the OASES-T, and between .67 and .95 for each section of the OASES-S. Test-retest reliability was examined using sample sizes of 14, 10, and 20 for adults, teenagers, and school-aged children, respectively. Over a 7- to 14-day period, coefficients were between .89 and .95 for each section of the OASES-A, between .92 and .99 for each section of the OASES-T, and between .90 and .97 for each section of the OASES-S.

Content and construct evidence of validity was also evaluated. Content evidence was supported through the test's development based on the WHO's *International Classification of Functioning, Disability and Health.* However, it was also supported by consultation with expert reviewers in the field as well as analysis of test items in empirical research studies. Construct evidence of validity indicated that the different sections of the tests measured different constructs. Another measure used to evaluate attitude toward communication, the Erickson S24 (Andrews & Cutler, 1974), was well correlated (r = .83) with the Speaker's Reaction to Stuttering component of the OASES-A.

COMMENTARY. Many recommend that stuttering assessment and treatment include affective and cognitive components (Beilby, 2014; Guitar, 2014; Manning & DiLollo, 2018) as the impact of stuttering on a person goes well beyond the surface features (e.g., stuttering-like behaviors such as sound repetitions). Only after identification of these parameters can treatment be maximized. The test authors chose to base the OASES on the WHO framework and *International Classification of Functioning, Disability and Health* to better align with other health sciences in evaluating the entirety of the disorder. Although the tests associated with all ages assessed by OASES were standardized, the adult sample (OASES-A) was most robust (n = 173), followed by the school-age version (OASES-S; n = 75). The teenage version (OASES-T) had the smallest sample (n = 45).

SUMMARY. The OASES provides a terrific supplement to the assessment of stuttering as it provides valuable insight into the impact that stuttering has on the individual. This information can facilitate intervention, with continued re-administration of the measure furthering the therapeutic process. Because intrinsic components of stuttering (e.g., anxiety, embarrassment, shame [Manning & DiLollo, 2018]) have been shown to be present and to negatively affect children, teenagers, and adults who stutter (Guitar, 2014), the OASES is an important tool for the speech-language pathologist to have when evaluating people of all ages who stutter.

REVIEWER'S REFERENCES

Andrews, G., & Cutler, J. (1974). Stuttering therapy: The relation between changes in symptom level and attitudes. *Journal of Speech and Hearing Disorders, 39,* 312-319.

Beilby, J. (2014). Psychosocial impact of living with a stuttering disorder: Knowing is not enough. *Seminars in Speech and Language, 35(2),* 132-143.

Bloodstein, O., & Bernstein Ratner, N. (2008). *A handbook on stuttering* (6th ed.). Clifton Park, NY: Thomson Delmar Learning.

Guitar, B. (2014). *Stuttering: An integrated approach to its nature and treatment* (4th ed.). Baltimore, MD: Lippincott Williams & Wilkins.

Manning, W. H., & DiLollo, A. (2018). *Clinical decision making in fluency disorders* (4th ed.). San Diego, CA: Plural Publishing.

World Health Organization (1980). *International classification of impairments, disabilities, and handicaps: A manual of classification relating to the consequences of disease, published in accordance with resolution WHA29.35 of the Twenty-ninth World Health Assembly, May 1976.* Geneva, Switzerland: Author.

World Health Organization (2001). *International classification of functioning, disability and health: ICF.* Geneva, Switzerland: Author.

[115]

The Parent Empowerment and Efficacy Measure.

Purpose: Designed to measure parent functioning using a strengths-based approach.
Population: Parents or caregivers of pre- and primary-school-aged children.
Publication Date: 2014.
Acronym: PEEM.
Scores, 3: Efficacy to Parent, Efficacy to Connect, Total Empowerment.
Administration: Individual.
Price Data: Available from publisher.
Time: Administration time not reported.
Comments: Administered via paper and pencil or online.
Authors: Kate Freiberg, Ross Homel, and Sara Branch.
Publisher: Griffith University [Australia].

Review of the Parent Empowerment and Efficacy Measure by MICHAEL K. CRUCE, Nationally Certified School Psychologist, Educational Service Unit #6, Milford, NE:

DESCRIPTION. The Parent Empowerment and Efficacy Measure (PEEM) was developed to assist family service providers with usable information about caregivers' abilities to provide a positive home environment as well as to look at their strengths and resourcefulness in managing the trials associated with being a parent. The authors of the PEEM saw a need for providers to have data that would allow them to make sound decisions concerning the treatments they implement. Designed as both an outcome measure for program evaluation and as an instrument to allow professionals to work with caregivers on parental confidence, the PEEM was developed to assist therapists and social workers in treatment planning to strengthen parental efficacy in caregivers of children ages 5-12. The scale consists of 20 items and measures two factors: Efficacy to Parent (11 items) and Efficacy to Connect (nine items). The PEEM provides cutoff scores and can be administered on paper or online. Caregivers are asked to reflect on their current level of parent empowerment on a 10-point scale, with 10 being a perfect match, and to rate themselves on how effective they believe they are as a parent.

DEVELOPMENT. The PEEM was developed through the 10-year Pathways to Prevention Project, which consisted of a research-based, cooperative partnership between a university, a community agency, and primary schools located in a socially disadvantaged area in Australia. The goal of this project was to develop a prevention framework that would reduce antisocial behaviors and emphasize positive childhood development. The researchers paid special attention to the challenges associated with parental stress, and a focus on family empowerment was emphasized. The PEEM was developed to fill a gap in the literature regarding parental efficacy and the ability to seek out supports in the community. The desire of the test authors was to develop a survey that would focus on caregivers' sense of competency as a parent and their ability to confidently rise to the challenges associated with parenting. They designed an instrument to assess these skills that would be brief, have a positive focus, be easily accessible to professionals, result in a low likelihood of misinterpretation, and have practical value in guiding decisions about services needed for parents. The individual items of the PEEM were refined after a review of the literature on parental efficacy.

The PEEM's items are all positively worded items, so no reverse scoring is necessary. The instrument should take 10 minutes or less to complete. Although a paper version is available, the authors emphasize the use of an online version called A Parent's Voice, which reads the questions, is highly interactive and visually engaging, and scores the assessment automatically. As items are rated on a scale of 1 to 10, the PEEM provides a total score that ranges from 20 to 200. Cut-off scores are provided to determine significance. The average score on the PEEM is 154, with a standard deviation of 24, so scores that fall below 130 would indicate low perceived parental efficacy. Additionally, two subscale scores can be obtained: Efficacy to Parent (range = 11-110, average score = 87) and Efficacy to Connect (range = 9-90, average score = 67).

Parents from 11 schools (n = 866) took part in the standardization of the PEEM. From four of the schools, assessments were collected during two administrations 4 weeks apart, and those packets included several additional measures that were used for analysis of convergent validity and test-retest reliability. Families from the other seven schools were given the PEEM once in an informational packet. Families were offered an incentive to participate in the data collection consisting of a raffle where they could win shopping vouchers or movie passes. Parents (n = 474) also completed the Marlowe-Crowne Social Desirability Scale (MCDS; Reynolds, 1982) to evaluate possible response bias due to the positive wording of the PEEM.

TECHNICAL. The standardization sample consisted of parents (n = 866) with children in the 5-12 age range. A variety of households with differing socioeconomic status took part in the standardization. Students attended one of 11 different primary schools in Australia. Most of the respondents were female (n = 744), and 153 indicated that they were single parents. Eighteen of the raters identified as being a grandparent or a guardian of the child. Within the sample, 513 caregivers stated that they only had one child in primary school, although most had one to five children in their households, with an average of 1.5 (SD = .70). The ethnic makeup of the standardization sample was not provided in the test materials.

The PEEM was initially developed based on two hypothesized factors of parental efficacy. Principal factor analysis with Oblimin rotation was undertaken and resulted in a two-factor solution being the most optimal. The two factors were identified as Efficacy to Parent and Efficacy to Connect (with services/people) (Frieberg, Homel, & Branch, 2014). Sampling adequacy was within the recommended value at 0.94, and a test of sphericity was significant and further supported the hypothesized factors. The PEEM yields high overall internal consistency with an alpha coefficient of .92 for one general dimension of parental efficacy. Coefficients for the two individualized factors were satisfactory at .88 and .85. Test-retest reliability was estimated at .84 using a sample of 200 that was pulled from the original standardization sample. To determine convergent validity, Pearson's correlation coefficients were used to compare the PEEM to other instruments that would measure the same types of constructs. With the three assessments used for comparison, correlation coefficients were strong and positive (r = .59, .61, and .66 with measures of efficacy, wellbeing, and family empowerment, respectively). With regard to concurrent validity evidence, the test developers compared parents in the sample with no history of child concerns to those who had sought out services and supports for their children. ANOVA (one-way, between groups) was used to compare the two samples and indicated that those who had sought services scored significantly below the comparison group.

COMMENTARY. The Parent Empowerment and Efficacy Measure (PEEM) is an interesting, simple, and useful assessment tool that appears to fill a gap in the existing literature on parental efficacy. Evidence supports that the PEEM assesses the constructs that it intends to and is sensitive to changes in performance, which makes it useful at the level of treatment planning. After rapport has been established with a parent, the PEEM can be introduced early in service coordination as a tool for planning and progress monitoring. The test authors have noted that it is important to let parents know that this is simply a tool to assist in treatment planning and not meant to be an evaluation of their parenting skills. The positive wording of individual items has the potential to allow caregivers to more freely express their beliefs about their parenting without excessive worry about judgment of their skills from others.

One could administer a follow-up PEEM 3 to 6 months after the first to gauge improvements in parenting efficacy. The PEEM appears to be sensitive enough to detect changes in parenting efficacy over time and could be used to monitor progress and outcomes quickly and easily by front-line service providers. Paying close attention to the subscale scores would allow the treatment provider to make specific suggestions as to the direction of service, and this would be an appropriate use of the PEEM. Low values on a subscale or even on a single question could indicate a need for more education, support, and service to be provided to enhance that particular skill.

SUMMARY. Although the PEEM focuses on parenting efficacy strengths, it also delivers the ability to determine specific parenting needs that can be treated, evaluated, and further monitored by the same instrument. Treatment planning can be evaluated broadly or at the individual item level. The speed of information collection with the PEEM and its easy scoring make its utility appealing. The test authors' development of an online version, which saves staff time for administration and scoring, further adds to its practicality. The online version is also less intimidating for those with lower literacy skills due to the use of a voice over, and it is more interactive than a routine form that must be completed at an intake or follow-up visit.

REVIEWER'S REFERENCES

Freiberg, K., Homel, R., & Branch, S. (2014). The Parent Empowerment and Efficacy Measure (PEEM): A tool for strengthening the accountability and effectiveness of family support services. *Australian Social Work, 67*(3), 405-418.

Reynolds, W. M. (1982). Development of reliable and valid short forms of the Marlowe-Crowne Social Desirability Scale. *Journal of Clinical Psychology, 38*(1), 119-125.

Review of the Parent Empowerment and Efficacy Measure by KEITH F. WIDAMAN, Distinguished Professor of the Graduate Division, University of California, Riverside, CA:

DESCRIPTION. The Parent Empowerment and Efficacy Measure (PEEM) is a brief, easily administered measure for service providers to use to help demonstrate the efficacy of intervention programs with families. The PEEM is a 20-item questionnaire that can be administered in a short time and was designed within a strength-based approach to family empowerment. The research program within which the PEEM was developed was one of intervention with families under stress, with interventions having a goal of promoting positive child development and preventing youth antisocial behavior. Interventions with families were not programmed in a "one size fits all" approach, but rather in a more open-ended form that was adapted to the needs of individual families. The primary goal of the intervention was to enhance participants' personal development, to empower them to gain greater control of their lives, and to help them function more effectively in the parenting role.

Administration instructions are clear and easy to follow. The PEEM can be administered as a paper-and-pencil self-report measure or through an online portal. It takes about 10 minutes to administer the measure. An additional 5 minutes or so might be needed to score the instrument by hand, and the online portal should allow automatic scoring and score reporting. The instructions for scoring the instrument were clear, with an overall Total Empowerment score computed as the simple sum of the 20 items. Subscores for Efficacy to Parent (sum of 11 items) and Efficacy to Connect (sum of nine items) also may be computed. No normative data or norming tables were provided.

DEVELOPMENT. The PEEM was developed because intervention staff were dissatisfied with existing instruments that assessed family empowerment. According to the test authors, a suitable measure of family empowerment should have four attributes: It should (a) be brief, (b) have a positive focus, (c) be accessible, and (d) have practical value. Concerning brevity, an instrument should be concise, administrable by non-specialists, and easy to score. In having a positive focus, the instrument should highlight personal strengths and capabilities to be fostered, without stressing difficulties or deficits. The goal of accessibility involves creating an instrument with items worded in simple and unambiguous language so the measure does not appear forbidding and would be acceptable to families who might be concerned about biased perceptions of their familial situations. Finally, practical value would be demonstrated if the scores from the measure could be used to guide delivery of services to individuals and could be used to document success of intervention services.

The PEEM was designed to provide an assessment of overall parental sense of capacity to engage confidently with challenges of being a parent. In addition to an overall sense of control, the measure was expected to cover two subdomains: confidence in being a parent and capacity to connect with formal or informal networks. With these goals in mind, a set of 20 items was developed, each item answered on a 1-to-10 scale, with 1 representing *definitely not like me* and 10 representing *definitely describes me very well*. All items are worded in the positive direction, so a higher score on each item indicates more positive feelings of empowerment.

TECHNICAL. All technical data are contained in an article by Freiberg, Homel, and Branch (2014). The sample on which the PEEM was evaluated consisted of 866 parents of 5- to 12-year-old children enrolled in 11 primary schools in high (n = 290), medium (n = 228), or low (n = 348) socioeconomic status (SES) areas in Australia. Survey packets included a cover letter, the PEEM, at least one other scale to provide validity information for the PEEM, and a short demographic information questionnaire. At four of the 11 schools, survey packets were distributed on two occasions about 4 weeks apart to allow estimation of test-retest reliability. More than 85% of respondents were female, and approximately 80% were parents in two-parent families. Education levels of respondents reporting their highest education level indicated that just over one third had a university degree; more than 50% had a high school, trade, or other certificate; and about 12% had not completed high school. Thus, respondents represented a wide range of parental education levels. On a more negative note, the sample appears to have been one of convenience, with no documentation of how representative the sample was of the broader population.

Given the 20-item PEEM measure with items each scored on a 1-to-10 scale, overall scores could range from 20 to 200. In the sample, obtained scores ranged from 51 to 199, with a mean of 154 and standard deviation of 24. Thus, sum scores tended to be negatively skewed, with a mean score considerably above the midpoint of the scale. That is, with a mean of 154, the average item score was 7.7, which is decidedly above the midpoint of the scale (which would be 5.5). Freiberg et al. (2014) reported that total PEEM scores did not vary significantly in mean level across SES groups, but no other normative trends (e.g., as a function of offspring age, parent education level) were reported.

A principal factor analysis of the 20 PEEM items yielded a single general factor that accounted for almost 86 percent of the variance (presumably estimated common variance). A two-factor rotated solution led to one factor that reflected Efficacy to Parent (11 items) and another that reflected Efficacy to Connect (nine items). These two rotated factors demonstrated a correlation coefficient of .78, so they were rather highly related. Simple sum scores were extremely highly correlated with regression estimate factor scores, so the simple sum scores were used in all later analyses.

The total score on the PEEM demonstrated high internal consistency reliability, with an alpha coefficient of .92. The alpha coefficients for the two factors, Efficacy to Parent and Efficacy to Connect, were also substantial, at .88 and .85, respectively. Test-retest reliability across a 4-week interval (n = 200) was reported for the total score and was fairly good at r = .84; test-retest reliability estimates were not reported for the separate factors.

Validity evidence was provided in several ways. First, the mean for the development sample (mean = 154; n = 866) was significantly higher statistically than the mean for a sample of families in a program for families under stress (mean = 148; n = 178). Considering the standard deviation of 24 in the development sample, however, this difference was not large in a practical sense. Convergent validity evidence was evaluated by correlating PEEM scores with other instruments measuring similar constructs. PEEM scores yielded correlations of .66 with scores on the Family Empowerment Scale and .61 with scores on the Parenting Sense of

Competence Scale. The correlation with a measure of confident wellbeing, the Warwick-Edinburgh Mental Wellbeing Scale, was also fairly strong at .59. The significant, but relatively low, correlation of -.27 between total PEEM scores and scores on the Marlowe-Crowne Social Desirability scale suggests that the PEEM is not strongly affected by bias to present a favorable impression. However, because all PEEM items are worded in the positive direction, acquiescence response bias may well be a problem and could not be examined.

COMMENTARY. The PEEM is a relatively new instrument to assess family or parenting empowerment in the context of evaluating treatment efficacy. Administration procedures were fairly well described as were the methods for obtaining raw scores on the instrument. Information on psychometric properties, including reliability and validity, was encouraging, but rather preliminary, having been based on a single sample of respondents of unknown representativeness and across a relatively restricted set of collateral measures. Potential effects of bias were limited to the evaluation of bias due to social desirability, and other forms of bias, such as acquiescence response bias, should be evaluated.

SUMMARY. The PEEM was designed to be an easily administered measure of family and/or parenting empowerment. The instrument meets its goals of ease of administration and ease of computing raw scores. The psychometric properties of PEEM scores are certainly encouraging, but they should be replicated across additional, more representative samples. As a result, the PEEM, at its present level of development and technical evaluation, cannot be recommended as a well-standardized measure of family empowerment yielding scores with clear interpretation, although its use in research studies might be supported.

REVIEWER'S REFERENCE

Freiberg, K., Homel, R., & Branch, S. (2014). The Parent Empowerment and Efficacy Measure (PEEM): A tool for strengthening the accountability and effectiveness of family support services. *Australian Social Work, 67*, 405-418. doi:10.1080/0312407X.2014.902980

[116]

PDD Behavior Inventory [Including 2017 Manual Supplements: Adolescent Normative Data and Autism Spectrum Disorder Decision Tree].

Purpose: Designed to assist in the assessment of children and adolescents who have been diagnosed "with any one of the previously identified pervasive developmental disorders, now identified as autism spectrum disorder in the Diagnostic and Statistical Manual of Mental Disorders, 5th Ed."

Population: Ages 1-6 to 18-5 with adolescent normative data; ages 1-6 to 12-5 with Autism Spectrum Disorder Decision Tree (ASD-DT) form.

Publication Dates: 1999-2017.

Acronym: PDDBI.

Scores: 61 (parent form), 59 (teacher form): 34-36 Approach/Withdrawal Problems scores: Approach/Withdrawal Problems Composite, Repetitive/Ritualistic/Pragmatic Problems Composite, Sensory/Perceptual Approach Behaviors (Visual Behaviors, Non-Food Taste Behaviors [parent/caregiver form only], Non-Food Taste or Smell Behaviors [teacher form only], Touch Behaviors [parent/caregiver form only], Noise Making Behaviors [teacher form only], Proprioceptive/Kinesthetic Behaviors, Repetitive Manipulative Behaviors, Gait-Based (Walking) Kinesthetic Behaviors [teacher form only]), Ritualisms/Resistance to Change (Resistance to Change in the Environment, Resistance to Change in Schedules/Routines, Rituals), Social Pragmatic Problems (Problems with Social Approach, Social Awareness Problems, Inappropriate Reactions to the Approaches of Others), Semantic/Pragmatic Problems (Aberrant Vocal Quality When Speaking, Problems with Understanding Words, Verbal Pragmatic Deficits); Extended form only: Arousal Regulation Problems (Kinesthetic Behaviors, Reduced Responsiveness, Sleep Regulation Problem [parent/caregiver form only]), Specific Fears (Sadness When Away From Caregiver/Other Significant Figure/or in New Situation [parent/caregiver form only], Anxiousness When Away From Caregiver/Other Significant Figure/or in New Situation [parent/caregiver form only], Auditory Withdrawal Behaviors, Fears and Anxieties, Social Withdrawal Behaviors), Aggressiveness (Self-Directed Aggressive Behaviors, Incongruous Negative Affect, Problems When Caregiver or Other Significant Figure Returns From Work/an Outing/or Vacation, Aggressiveness Toward Others, Overall Temperament Problems); 22 Receptive/Expressive Social Communication Abilities scores: Receptive/Expressive Social Communication Abilities Composite, Expressive Social Communication Abilities Composite, Social Approach Behaviors (Visual Social Approach Behaviors, Positive Affect Behaviors, Gestural Approach Behaviors, Responsiveness to Social Inhibition Cues, Social Play Behaviors, Imaginative Play Behaviors, Empathy Behaviors, Social Interaction Behaviors [parent/caregiver form only], Social Imitative Behaviors), Expressive Language (Vowel Production [parent], Basic Vowel Production [teacher], Consonant Production at the Beginning/Middle/and End of Words, Basic Consonant Production at the Beginning/Middle/and End of Words [teacher], Diphthong Production [parent], Basic Diphthong Production [teacher], Expressive Language Competence, Verbal Affective Tone, Pragmatic Conversational Skills); Extended form only: Learning/Memory/Receptive Language (General Memory Skills,

Receptive Language Competence, Associative Memory Skills [teacher form only]); plus Autism Composite, SOCPP-SOCAPP Discrepancy Score, SEMPP-EXPRESS Discrepancy Score.
Administration: Individual or group.
Forms, 4: Parent/Guardian or Teacher, Standard or Extended.
Price Data, 2020: $438 per comprehensive kit including professional manual (2005, 545 pages), ASD-DT manual supplement (2017, 37 pages), adolescent normative data manual supplement (2017, 110 pages), 25 parent rating forms, 25 teacher rating forms, 25 parent score summary sheets, 25 teacher score summary sheets, 50 profile forms, 25 ASD-DT record forms, carrying case, and certificate for 5 online score reports; $124 per professional manual; $32 per manual supplement (ASD-DT or adolescent normative data); $105 per 25 rating forms (parent or teacher); $31 per 25 score summary sheets (parent or teacher); $46 per 50 profile forms; $32 per 25 ASD-DT record forms; $4 per online administration; $3 per online score report.
Foreign Language Edition: Parent form available in Spanish.
Time: 30-45 minutes for administration of extended forms; 20-30 minutes for administration of standard forms.
Comments: Ratings from both parents and multiple teachers/school personnel is desirable; the ASD-DT form should be used in conjunction with the parent or teacher extended form, and only with children ages 1-6 to 12-5.
Authors: Ira L. Cohen and Vicki Sudhalter.
Publisher: Psychological Assessment Resources, Inc.
Cross References: For reviews by Karen Carey and by Kathryn E. Hoff and Renee M. Tobin of the original version, see 17:142.

Review of the PDD Behavior Inventory [Including 2017 Manual Supplements: Adolescent Normative Data and Autism Spectrum Disorder Decision Tree] by KAREN MACKLER, District Psychologist, Lawrence Public Schools, Lawrence, NY:

DESCRIPTION. The PDD Behavior Inventory (PDDBI) is a checklist completed by a parent or teacher familiar with a student suspected of having a pervasive developmental disorder according to the diagnostic criteria of the *Diagnostic and Statistical Manual of Mental Disorders* (4th ed.; *DSM-IV;* American Psychiatric Association [APA], 1994). Reviews of the PDDBI by Karen Carey (2007) and by Kathryn E. Hoff and Renee M. Tobin (2007) were published in *The Seventeenth Mental Measurements Yearbook* (17:142). Although the original measure (1999) will be referenced here, this review focuses on the Adolescent Normative Data Manual Supplement and the Autism Spectrum Disorder Decision Tree (ASD-DT), published in 2017.

The test kit contains a manual complete with normative scoring tables, parent and teacher rating forms and scoring sheets, and profile sheets that can be used with either form. One manual supplement contains adolescent normative data; a second describes the Autism Spectrum Disorder Decision Tree. Copies of the decision-making tree also are included.

The PDDBI originally was normed on children ages 1:6 to 12:5. Both the parent and teacher forms can be presented in standard form or extended form. The rating booklets contain the expanded form, but responders may be instructed to stop at a designated point, yielding scores for only the standard form. Both forms include demographic questionnaire items; the questions are much more detailed in the parent form.

Questionnaires may be scored manually or by computer. The score summary sheet guides the clinician through the process. The profile form generates a graphic representation of a child's profile. The standard form takes 20-30 minutes to complete versus 30-45 minutes for the extended form. Manual scoring takes another 15-20 minutes.

The PDDBI was designed less as a diagnostic measure and more as an aid for assessing growth in a targeted area following intervention or for assisting with placement decisions, staffing ratios, evaluating educational programs, and so on.

The inventory provides domain/composite scores, an Autism Composite score and discrepancy scores between deficits and abilities. Deficits are assessed in areas typically considered characteristic of children on the autism spectrum. Domains include Approach/Withdrawal Problems and Receptive/Expressive Abilities. Within the Approach/Withdrawal Problems domain, scores are calculated for Sensory/Perceptual Approach Behaviors, Ritualisms/Resistance to Change, Social Pragmatic Problems, Semantic/Pragmatic Problems, Arousal Regulation Problems (extended), Specific Fears (extended), and Aggressiveness (extended). Within the Receptive/Expressive Social Communication Abilities domain, scores are calculated for Social Approach Behaviors; Expressive Language; and Learning, Memory, and Receptive Language (extended). From these scores, composite scores are calculated, leading to a Repetitive, Ritualistic, and Pragmatic Problems composite score; an Approach/Withdrawal Problems composite score (extended); an Expressive Social Communication Abilities composite score; and a Receptive/Expressive Social Communication Abilities composite score (extended).

Cluster scores can be obtained for specific behaviors within each subcategory. For example, under Ritualisms/Resistance to Change, one could look at resistance to change in the environment, resistance to change in schedules/routines, and rituals. Raw scores are converted to percentile ranges and categorized as *low, moderate, high,* or *very high.*

The Adolescent Normative Data Manual Supplement provides data that allow clinicians to use the existing PDDBI with individuals up to 18:5 years. The age range was restricted to students who are still involved in school settings.

The Autism Spectrum Disorder Decision Tree (ASD-DT) is based on an algorithm created by Cohen et al. (2016) and is presented as a way to increase the utility of the PDDBI to be more diagnostic in addition to its use as a progress-monitoring tool. The Decision Tree is not a primary diagnostic measure but could be used as a Level 2 screener with children suspected as being at-risk for autism spectrum disorder (ASD). The tree is to be used for children ages 1:6 to 12:5 and uses the data from the extended form. The tree includes information about potential deficits, possible diagnoses, and further assessments recommended for 11 classification nodes that range from *atypical ASD* to *ASD not likely, with typical social skills.*

DEVELOPMENT. The behaviors assessed on the PDDBI were chosen to correspond to typical deficits in social communication skills, as such deficits are a hallmark of ASD. Item development included skills that were characteristic of both low-functioning and high-functioning individuals. Each domain was developed independently so that each may be used as a stand-alone assessment tool measuring growth in a particular area. Pilot and field-testing of the original measure led to inclusion of several additional domains.

Standardization was based on a sample of 369 parents and 277 teachers of children ages 1:6 to 12:5. Confirmation of a diagnosis of autism was based on results from the Autism Diagnostic Interview–Revised (ADI-R), the Autism Diagnostic Observation Schedule–Generic (ADOS-G), or diagnosis by an experienced examiner according to the *DSM-IV*.

The adolescent norms were based on ratings by 147 parents and 101 teachers of adolescents ages 12:6 to 18:5 years. All raters completed the extended form. Most of the sample participants had confirmed diagnoses on the autism spectrum, again based on ADI-R or ADOS-G results. Compared to the original sample, more cases in the adolescent sample were diagnosed with Asperger's disorder.

The ASD-DT was created using the domain T scores from the extended forms of the PDDBI, leading to the creation of different nodes, rather than having an overall cutoff score indicating the presence or absence of ASD. The development sample included 660 children whose parents and/or teachers completed extended form questionnaires. The children were ages 1:5 to 13:0. Three groups emerged based upon these data: typically developing, children with ASD, and children who had other developmental issues with ASD ruled out. It should be noted that highly educated Caucasian mothers completed most of the parent forms. The teacher inventories were completed by special education teachers, teaching assistants, behavior analysts, and speech/language pathologists. Male children made up 84% of the ASD group.

TECHNICAL. Technical information is reported here for the Adolescent Normative Data Manual Supplement and the ASD-DT. Readers are referred to previous reviews for reliability and validity information for the PDDBI.

For the adolescent norms, internal consistency was computed for the domain and composite scores for both the parent and teacher rating scales (standard and extended versions). For the parent form, alpha coefficients ranged from .78 to .96 for Approach/Withdrawal Problems and from .92 to .98 for Receptive/Expressive Social Communication Abilities. For the teacher form, alpha coefficients ranged from .80 to .95 on the Problems section and from .93 to .98 on the Abilities section.

Internal structure was assessed on both the parent form and the teacher form. Most of the domain and composite scores were significantly correlated with each other. There were some differences noted between the parent form and the teacher form. The scores suggest that different processes may be at work due to different structures in play, based upon environment. For example, a lack of structure in the home may be linked to a parent endorsing anxiety or irritability. In summary, results supported the inclusion of each of the domains in the PDDBI.

Construct evidence of validity included an examination of whether the factor structure of the original standardization was applicable to this second set of data. Results indicated that the two-factor structure that emerged in the original sample holds for this set of data as well. Analysis also supports the inclusion of specific ASD symptoms in the fifth edition of the *Diagnostic and Statistical Manual of Mental Disorders* (*DSM-5;* APA, 2013) regarding social communication deficits and repetitive/ritualistic behaviors.

Criterion-related evidence of validity involved comparisons with two tools not used in the original studies. The Approach/Withdrawal Problems domain and composite scores were compared with scores from the Aberrant Behavior Checklist (ABC). The ADI-R also was used. Parents are the responders for both of these measures. Strong correlations were found between the ABC and the Approach/Withdrawal Problems domain and composite scores. The ADI-R also provided evidence validity for the domains. Overall, adequate reliability and evidence of validity were present in the adolescent extension of the PDDBI.

Data were also collected to examine evidence of validity for the ASD–DT. Developmental validity was investigated by looking at classification accuracy for three age groups (toddlers, preschool, and primary school). For the parent form, classification accuracy (sensitivity and specificity) improved from around 80% to 90% for the primary school cohort versus the preschool and toddler groups. The trend for the teacher form was similar, though less pronounced. This suggests that as behaviors become more consistent with age, they are easier to define.

Criterion-related evidence of validity was examined using the Vineland Adaptive Behavior Scales (Sparrow, Balla, & Cicchetti, 1984) or the Vineland Adaptive Behavior Scales-II (Sparrow, Cicchetti, & Balla, 2005). Results indicated that for minimally verbal ASD and atypical ASD subgroups, skills were impacted along all adaptive areas, whereas for those in the verbal ASD subgroup, adaptive scores were lowest in self-care and social skills. The Griffiths Mental Development Scales was also used in 80 cases, and results offered criterion evidence of validity for the various classifications.

Finally, the test authors assert that the decision tree has clinical validity, as it was able to accurately classify children in three age groups as having or not having ASD with percent correctly classified in the 80s for the parent form. In the study, no typically developing children were classified incorrectly. Overall, the accuracy of classification was above 80% for the parent rating scale.

COMMENTARY. The PDDBI is a user-friendly inventory that can be used as part of a battery of tests and interviews to screen for autism spectrum disorder. The PDDBI has adequate statistical properties to be of use in monitoring the progress of selected targeted behaviors, which is how the authors originally intended the tool to be used. Each domain can stand alone as a separate entity, which allows a clinician to collect data and graph growth. The adolescent norms will be helpful in this area, as diagnosis becomes less of an issue with age, but intervention and growth continue to be the focus.

The paperwork associated with the measure is a bit overwhelming, with the clinician flipping pages over and generating multiple scores. Use of the computer scoring option likely would decrease much of the paperwork and provide the graphs, but this feature was not specifically assessed by this reviewer. For those with a background in data collection and progress monitoring, this concern may be less of an issue.

The demographic data requested on the parent inventory is also a bit daunting in nature, and it is suggested that a clinician sit with a parent and assist in completing the form. Parents often feel that these types of questions are too invasive and leave out critical information.

The ASD-DT is a helpful tool as it adds practical information to the data that can be used to make intervention decisions. The tree lays out possible diagnoses and suggests further assessments that could be administered. This feature could be especially helpful for new clinicians and for giving parents concrete information that they may not get from a medical office.

SUMMARY. The PDDBI is a useful tool for screening ASD in an at-risk population. The ability to use each domain as a stand-alone measure is helpful for progress monitoring of specific intervention goals, and with the inclusion of adolescent norms, children may be followed into their teen years while they are still part of a school program. The ASD-DT is helpful for clinicians and parents who are looking for a differential diagnosis in terms of where to focus intervention and treatment. Further assessments are suggested, which also may be helpful to a planning team and to families.

REVIEWER'S REFERENCES

American Psychiatric Association. (2000). *Diagnostic and statistical manual of mental disorders.* (4th ed., text revision). Washington, DC: Author.

American Psychiatric Association. (2013). *Diagnostic and statistical manual of mental disorders* (5th ed.). Washington, DC: Author.

Carey, K. (2007). [Test review of PDD Behavior Inventory]. In K. F. Geisinger, R. A. Spies, J. F. Carlson, & B. S. Plake (Eds.), *The seventeenth mental measurements yearbook.* Lincoln, NE: Buros Institute of Mental Measurements.

Cohen, I. L., Liu, X., Hudson, M., Gillis, J., Cavalari, R. N. S., Romanczyk, R. G., & Gardner, J. M. (2016). Using the PDD Behavior Inventory as a Level 2 screener: A classification and regression trees analysis. *Journal of Autism and Developmental Disorders, 46*(9), 3006-3022.

Hoff, K. E., & Tobin, R. M. (2007). [Test review of PDD Behavior Inventory]. In K. F. Geisinger, R. A. Spies, J. F. Carlson, & B. S. Plake (Eds.), *The seventeenth mental measurements yearbook*. Lincoln, NE: Buros Institute of Mental Measurements.

Sparrow, S. S., Balla, D. A., & Cicchetti, D. V. (1984). Vineland Adaptive Behavior Scales: Interview Edition, Survey Form Manual. Circle Pines, MN: American Guidance Service.

Sparrow, S. S., Cicchetti, D. V., & Balla, D. A. (2005). Vineland Adaptive Behavior Scale-II. Circle Pines, MN: American Guidance Service.

Review of the PDD Behavior Inventory [Including 2017 Manual Supplements: Adolescent Normative Data and Autism Spectrum Disorder Decision Tree] by TRACY THORNDIKE, Associate Professor of Special Education and Education Leadership, Western Washington University, Bellingham, WA:

DESCRIPTION. The PDD Behavior Inventory (PDDBI) is an age-normed, informant-based assessment designed to measure behaviors commonly associated with autism spectrum disorder. Originally normed for children ages 1 year 6 months through 12 years 5 months, the age range was extended through 18 years 5 months with the addition of adolescent norms in 2017. The instrument may be used to assess both adaptive and maladaptive behaviors in children and adolescents already diagnosed with any of the pervasive developmental disorders in the taxomony of the *Diagnostic and Statistical Manual of Mental Disorders* (4th ed.; *DSM-IV;* American Psychiatric Association [APA], 1994) or with autism spectrum disorder (ASD) as specified in DSM-5 (APA, 2013). The norms represent typical functioning of children and adolescents with ASD making the PDDBI useful in evaluating a change in functioning over time such as gauging the degree of response to intervention for this population.

There are separate inventories for parent and teacher respondents, and each is available in two versions: a standard version with 124 items grouped into six domains and an extended version with 180 items for teachers and 188 items for parents grouped into 10 domains. The standard version contains only the domains uniquely associated with ASD whereas the extended version provides information about behaviors that co-occur with other disorders. Raters use a 4-point scale (i.e., 0 = *does not show the behavior* to 3 = *usually/typically shows the behavior*) to indicate the frequency with which they have observed the behavior described in each item. Examples are provided to help illustrate ways in which a particular behavior might be displayed. The standard version takes approximately 20-30 minutes to complete whereas the extended version takes approximately 30-45 minutes.

Scoring consists of summing ratings on individual items to create cluster scores and then summing across sets of clusters to create domain scores. Raw domain scores are then transferred to score summary sheets for calculation of composite scores after which both domain and composite scores are converted to T scores with 90% confidence intervals prior to interpretation. Three composite scores may be computed for the standard version with an additional two for the extended version. Three discrepancy scores also may be calculated from sets of composite scores. Cluster level raw scores may be compared to age-normed percentile tables with cutoffs with verbal descriptors to determine the severity of a particular type of behavior relative to what is typical for same-age peers with ASD. Those scoring the rating forms and interpreting scores on the PDDBI should be well versed in pervasive developmental disorders/ASD as well as in the interpretation of standard scores.

Professionals familiar with ASD as defined in the *DSM-5* (APA, 2013) may use the newly available supplemental Autism Spectrum Disorder Decision Tree (ASD—DT; Cohen, 2017) in conjunction with results from the extended version of either the parent or teacher inventory for children ages 1:6 to 12:5 years as a Level 2 screener for ASD. This supplement also may be used as part of a comprehensive evaluation to aid in the differential diagnosis of ASD versus other disorders with overlapping patterns of symptoms. The PDDBI, with or without the Decision Tree, is not intended for use as a stand-alone diagnostic tool or Level 1 screening instrument.

DEVELOPMENT.

Development of the PDDBI. Developers initially identified key domains of behavior commonly associated with ASD. Individual behaviors were organized by type (i.e., cluster) with similar clusters of behaviors grouped into domains. Behaviors selected to represent clusters within each domain came from the test authors' own observations from working with children with ASD as well as those suggested as important in the literature on social communication, ASD, and complex language development as well as some behaviors that may be useful in differentiating ASD from other conditions. Effort was made to include items that would be applicable across a wide range of functioning on the autism spectrum. Initial pilot testing consisted of

306 items measuring seven domains. Analyses of the psychometric properties and factor structure of the items guided subsequent revisions over the course of 9 years. These revisions resulted in a substantially shorter inventory and led to the current structure of 10 domains (in the full extended version).

Domains in the final version of the PDDBI are conceptualized as existing along two main dimensions: Receptive-Expressive Social Communication Abilities (three domains) and Approach/Withdrawal Problems (seven domains). Composite scores for both may be calculated from the extended version of either the parent or teacher rating form. Higher scores on the social communication dimension indicate greater levels of competence whereas higher scores on the approach/withdrawal problem behavior dimension indicate greater degrees of impairment relative to what is typical for children and adolescents with ASD. Three other composite scores based on a smaller number of domains, including an Autism Composite score, can be computed from both the standard and extended version of either rating form. Higher T scores on the Autism Composite indicate an individual is more severely impacted by problem behaviors associated with ASD with fewer meaningful social communication skills than is typical.

Development of the ASD—DT. Parents and/or teachers of 660 children referred for evaluation at a number of child development and behavior research clinics in New York State completed the PDDBI extended version. Based on clinical evaluation, 535 children were classified as having ASD, 76 with other non-ASD developmental problems, and 49 as typically developing. Protocols were divided into three separate datasets for use in developing, testing, and validating the decision tree. Developers used CART, "a computer algorithm that generates a decision tree to predict group membership" (Cohen, 2017, p. 21) to create classification groups.

TECHNICAL.

Standardization. Standardization and norming were carried out separately for parent and teacher raters of children ages 1:6 to 12:5 years and for those of adolescents ages 12:6 to 18:5. For the child age range, the sample consisted of 369 parents and 277 teachers of children all with a confirmed diagnosis of a pervasive developmental disorder using *DSM-IV* (APA, 1994) criteria. An additional 147 parents and 101 teachers of adolescents on the autism spectrum ages 12:6 to 18:5 years comprised the second norming sample. The adolescent sample contained a higher proportion of individuals with "higher functioning" diagnoses (i.e., Asperger's or PDD-NOS vs. autism) than did the child sample. Both samples were generally representative of the demographics of the population of individuals commonly diagnosed with ASD in the United States (i.e., overwhelmingly white, non-Hispanic, and male, with relatively well educated parents).

To establish age norms, the child age range was divided into nine age categories and the adolescent age range into three categories. Age-adjusted T scores for each domain and composite area were derived separately for the parent and teacher rating forms using a three-parameter nonlinear growth/loss model (i.e., the Hill equation). Distributional characteristics of the derived T scores for both norming samples were as expected for all domains and composites with mean T scores close to 50 with standard deviations close to 10 for both the parent and teacher rating forms.

Percentile tables with descriptors of qualitative ranges (e.g., moderate) were also created to aid in the interpretation of cluster scores. Raw cluster scores capture the presence and severity of individual behaviors (e.g., flaps hands, flicks fingers) of a particular type (e.g., proprioceptive/kinesthetic behaviors). Scores for each cluster were divided into four categories based on their frequency of occurrence in the norming samples and their clinical utility and meaningfulness in guiding intervention.

Reliability of scores. Alpha coefficients are presented for each age range and each type of rating form (i.e., parent vs. teacher) in the child sample at the domain and composite score levels. For both rating forms at both the domain and composite levels, values were mostly in the moderate to high range (.80s and .90s), indicating acceptable levels of internal consistency for the types of decisions that would be informed by these scores. When values were calculated for each rating scale collapsed across age, all domain values were .80 or higher, and all composite values were .91 or higher in the child sample. Internal consistency data were not presented for each of the three age ranges in the adolescent sample. However, for both rating scales, values of .78 or higher at the domain level and .92 or higher at the composite level were observed for the adolescent sample when collapsed across all age ranges.

Short- and longer-term stability of scores over time were explored for both the parent and teacher versions of the PDDBI for the child age range over intervals ranging from two weeks to approximately one year. Stability coefficients for parent ratings over a 12-month interval ranged from .38 for the Social Pragmatic Problems domain to .91 for both the Expressive Social Communication Abilities Composite and the Receptive/Expressive Social Communication Abilities Composite. At 2-week and 6-month intervals with two different samples of teachers, ratings were stable over time with correlation coefficients between .58 and .99 at the domain level and between .65 and .99 at the composite level. No studies of score stability over time are presented in the adolescent norm supplement manual.

Interrater reliability is briefly discussed in the original technical manual. The magnitude of correlations varied substantially by domain and type of composite score with greater agreement observed for those domains/composite scores that included verbal behaviors. In general, somewhat higher agreement was observed between teachers than between teachers and parents. Again, no data were presented for the adolescent norming sample.

Evidence of validity. Multiple lines of evidence to support the validity of proposed inferences derived from PDDBI scores are presented in the main and supplemental technical manuals. The pattern of intercorrelations among domain and composite scores generally supported the proposed two area/factor (e.g., social communication skills vs. approach and/or withdrawal behaviors that create problems) internal structure for both the parent and teacher rating forms. Principal components factor analysis with varimax rotation supported a two-factor solution in both the original child and subsequent adolescent standardization samples. Significant mean differences for children of different ages were found for domains and composites that reflect abilities that are developmental in nature. Criterion-related evidence in the form of associations of scores on the PDDBI with scores on other measures is presented for both the child and adolescent age ranges. In general, results of these validation studies support the proposed interpretations of PDDBI domain and composite scores. Any discrepancies between expected and observed results in the validation studies are well explained in the technical manuals.

Classification and validity evidence for the ASD—DT. Indicators of classification accuracy, representing the ability of the ASD—DT to distinguish among those in each of the three diagnostic categories (i.e., ASD, other, non-ASD developmental problem, typically developing), exceeded 80% sensitivity for both parent and teacher raters. ASD—DT forms based on ratings from parents had the highest levels of sensitivity and specificity. Specificity was poor when the ASD—DT was based on teacher ratings alone, but this result may have been an artifact of some very small sample sizes in the validation study.

Discrimination accuracy was greater for primary school aged children (91% sensitivity and 87% specificity based on parent informants) than for toddlers (79% and 81%, respectively) or preschoolers (79% and 80%, respectively). Analyses of mean differences on various adaptive functioning scales (e.g., Communication and Daily Living Skills from the Vineland) and measures of cognitive function (i.e., Griffiths Mental Development Scales) among children given different classifications on the ASD—DT support criterion-related evidence of validity of ASD—DT informed classifications.

COMMENTARY. The Centers for Disease Control and Prevention now estimates autism prevalence at one in every 59 individuals (Baio et al., 2018). Consequently, the need for psychometrically sound measures that can screen for and facilitate the diagnosis of ASD as well as track response to intervention in those already diagnosed with ASD is more critical than ever. The PDDBI has a long track record of successful use for the latter purpose and when used in concert with the new ASD—DT shows promise as a Level 2 screener and aid in differential diagnosis, thus expanding the utility of the PDDBI.

That said, demographic disproportionality in ASD diagnosis is well documented (e.g., Burkett, Morris, Manning-Courtney, Anthony, & Shambley-Ebron, 2015; Durkin et al., 2010; Nowell, Brewton, Allain, & Mire, 2015). Authors of the PDDBI/ASD—DT claim their tools are "appropriate for use with children and adolescents from a broad range of racial/ethnic and socioeconomic contexts" (Cohen & Sudhalter, 2005, p. 5). However, the standardization samples for the PDDBI and the development/validation sample for the ASD—DT lacked diversity compared to the general population (Humes, Jones, & Ramirez, 2011) on these and other potentially important demographic variables. Given the proposed expansion of use of the PDDBI to include screening and diagnosis, the assertion that ratings will be unaffected by demographic characteristics of raters and children/adolescents being rated needs to be verified with data from samples sufficiently large to yield stable estimates. In future revisions, the test authors may wish to review the reading level and degree of understanding of formal linguistic conventions required of raters to ensure that the language is accessible to a wider range of raters, particularly those who are not extremely well-educated. Terms like "idiosyncratic" that appear in item examples and "past participle" and "indefinite adjective" found in item-level behavior statements seem more sophisticated than one could reasonably expect of a parent with a typical level of education who is living in the United States. Until then, as suggested in the *Standards for Educational and Psychological Testing* (American Educational Research Association, American Psychological Association, & National Council on Measurement in Education, 2014), users are encouraged to exercise caution when interpreting scores based on ratings of children/adolescents by parents and teachers who differ demographically from the populations sampled in the studies described in the technical manuals and related research articles.

SUMMARY. The PDDBI provides reliable and valid scores that serve as measures of both adaptive and maladaptive behaviors commonly seen in individuals with ASD. Age-normed on children and adolescents diagnosed with ASD, the PDDBI is perhaps uniquely useful in tracking changes in behavior over time among people with ASD. The addition of the Autism Spectrum Disorder Decision Tree, to be used in combination with the PDDBI extended version (parent or teacher rating form), expands the utility of the PDDBI to the diagnostic arena. The ASD—DT shows good sensitivity and specificity, particularly when based on the ratings of parent informants for school-aged children. As with any norm-referenced assessment, users are urged to carefully consider the characteristics of the norming and standardization samples to determine whether they adequately represent the population about whom the user intends to make decisions.

REVIEWER'S REFERENCES

American Educational Research Association, American Psychological Association, & National Council on Measurement in Education. (2014). *Standards for educational and psychological testing.* Washington, DC: AERA.

American Psychiatric Association. (2013). *Diagnostic and statistical manual of mental disorders* (5th ed.). Washington, DC: Author.

American Psychiatric Association. (1994). *Diagnostic and statistical manual of mental disorders* (4th ed.). Washington, DC: Author.

Baio, J., Wiggins, L., Christensen, D. L., Maenner, M. J., Daniels, J., Warren, Z., ... Dowling, N. F. (2018, April). Prevalence of autism spectrum disorder among children aged 8 years: Autism and developmental disabilities monitoring network, 11 sites, United States, 2014. *Surveillance Summaries, 67* (6), 1-23. Retrieved from http://dx.doi.org/10.15585/mmwr.ss6706a1

Burkett, K., Morris, E., Manning-Courtney, P., Anthony, J., & Shambley-Ebron, D. (2015). African American families on autism diagnosis and treatment: The influence of culture. *Journal of Autism and Developmental Disorders, 45*, 3244-3254.

Durkin, M. S., Maenner, M. J., Meaney, F. J., Levy, S. E., DiGuiseppi, C., Nicholas, J. S., ... Schieve, L. A. (2010). Socioeconomic inequality in the prevalence of autism spectrum disorder: Evidence from a U.S. cross-sectional study. *PLoS ONE, 5*(7). doi:10.1371/journal.pone.0011551

Humes, K. R., Jones, N. A., & Ramirez, R. R. (2011, March). *Overview of race and Hispanic origin: 2010.* Retrieved from https://www.census.gov/prod/cen2010/briefs/c2010br-02.pdf

Nowell, K. P., Brewton, C. M., Allain, E., & Mire, S. S. (2015). The influence of demographic factors on the identification of autism spectrum disorder: A review and call for research. *Review Journal of Autism and Developmental Disorders, 2*, 300-309.

[117]

Peabody Picture Vocabulary Test, Fifth Edition.

Purpose: Designed to assess receptive vocabulary for children and adults.
Population: Ages 2-6 to 90+.
Publication Dates: 1959-2019.
Acronym: PPVT-5.
Scores: Total score only.
Administration: Individual.
Forms, 2: A, B.
Price Data, 2020: $405 per complete kit (A & B) including manual (2019, 343 pages), 2 stimulus books (A & B), and 25 of each record form (A & B); $225 per individual kit (A or B); $99 per manual; $99 per stimulus book (A or B); $49 per 25 record forms (A or B); $40 per 1-year scoring subscription; $4.50 per digital administration (A or B); $1.10 per digital score summary report (quantity discounts available).
Time: Approximately 10-15 minutes for administration.
Comments: Co-normed with the Expressive Vocabulary Test, Third Edition (see 58, this volume) to allow comparison of a test taker's receptive and expressive vocabulary skills; available in print and digital formats.
Author: Douglas M. Dunn.
Publisher: Pearson.
Cross References: For reviews by Joseph C. Kush and Steven R. Shaw of the fourth edition, see 18:88; for reviews by Frederick Bessai and Orest Eugene Wasyliw of the third edition, see 14:280; see also T5:1903 (585 references) and T4:1945 (426 references); for reviews by R. Steve McCallum and Elisabeth H. Wiig of the revised edition, see 9:926 (117 references); see also T3:1771 (301 references), 8:222 (213 references), T2:516 (77 references), and 7:417 (201 references); for reviews by Howard B. Lyman and Ellen V. Piers of the original edition, see 6:530 (21 references).

Review of the Peabody Picture Vocabulary Test, Fifth Edition by GARY L. CANIVEZ, Professor of Psychology, Department of Psychology, Eastern Illinois University, Charleston, IL:

DESCRIPTION. The Peabody Picture Vocabulary Test, Fifth Edition (PPVT–5) is the fifth version of a popular measure of receptive vocabulary for children and adults (ages 2 years 6 months to 90+ years) that originated in 1959 (Dunn, 1959). It is a major revision of the Peabody Picture Vocabulary Test, Fourth Edition (PPVT–4; Dunn & Dunn, 2007). The PPVT–5 measures English vocabulary word knowledge (nouns, verbs, attributes) and was co-normed with the Expressive Vocabulary Test, Third Edition (EVT–3; Williams, 2019; see 58, this volume) for broad assessment and comparisons of receptive (listening) versus expressive (spoken) vocabulary skills in clinical and school applications (screening, diagnosis, research). It includes a detailed manual, two stimulus books (Forms A and B), and two record forms (A and B). In addition to the traditional administration and scoring, the test publisher provides digital administration, scoring, and reporting via two tablets on the Q-interactive platform and computerized scoring and reporting of traditional administration on the Q-global platform.

As an individually administered measure of receptive vocabulary, the PPVT–5 requires the examinee to choose one of four pictures corresponding to the word verbally presented by the examiner. It is untimed (although examiners are instructed to prompt a response after approximately 10 seconds), and median completion time ranged from 11 to 16 minutes during standardization. Administration is relatively simple, and scoring is objective. The test manual specifies guidelines for proper administration and scoring by professionals or paraprofessionals, but interpretation is reserved for properly trained professionals. The test manual provides useful descriptions of various testing environments, cultural diversity, and testing individuals with special needs to maximize valid assessment.

Detailed instructions for administration are provided in the test manual and include training items to teach the examinee how to respond and determine whether they may be properly assessed, starting points based on age, the basal rule (and reverse order testing), and the ceiling (discontinue) rule. Item administration is clearly presented instructing the examiner to say, "Put your finger on [word]," "Show me [word]," "Point to [word]," "Where is [word]?" and so forth. Additional instructions are provided for encouraging responses, guessing, and handling unclear responses. Additional accommodations are provided to facilitate assessment of very young children or those with physical disabilities that would prevent them from pointing. The two stimulus books are well organized with tabs marking training pages and item start points by age for efficient presentation and include high-quality images. The two record forms are well designed for easy completion and include color coding of correct responses and pronunciation guides for the most difficult words.

Scoring the PPVT–5 is well described and illustrated with figures as is the process of transforming raw scores to standard scores (M = 100, SD = 15) with 90% and 95% confidence intervals, percentile ranks, normal curve equivalents, stanines, age equivalents (four major limitations explicitly described in the test manual), and growth scale values. Graphical presentation and qualitative descriptions are also provided and illustrated. Statistical significance of growth scale values across time can be determined as can differences between standard scores on the PPVT-5 and the EVT-3. When significant differences are observed between the PPVT-5 and the EVT-3, population base rates are provided for judging rarity.

DEVELOPMENT. The development of the PPVT–5 began with a survey of PPVT–4 users regarding test administration instructions, item words, and pictures. International test developers in various countries reviewed items for cultural differences. This feedback provided guidance for PPVT–5 item development. Newly created items (N = 109) were examined for content and bias (gender, culture/ethnic, region, socioeconomic) through review by a panel of experts, and items identified by more than one panel member as potentially biased were eliminated. Pilot research was conducted on new items with a sample of 217 typically developing children using classical test theory (CTT), item response theory (IRT), item logistic regression, and differential item functioning (DIF) to assess adequacy for inclusion. All item stimulus art was replaced with newly created images designed for digital presentation. The test manual lists the number of items within 20 different content categories (actions, adjectives, animals, body parts, buildings, household objects, etc.) within Forms A and B, each containing 251 items for standardization.

TECHNICAL.

Standardization. Standardization of the PPVT–5 included digital administration by 217 examiners in 44 states who met specified criteria and were approved following submission of a practice test for quality control. The standardization sample was demographically representative of the U.S. population as per U.S. Census estimates in 2017, stratified by key variables of age, sex, race/ethnicity, geographic region, and parent education level (proxy for SES); the sample included English-speaking individuals ages 2 years 6 months to 90+ years. A table in the test manual presents normative sample percentages for demographic variables of education, race/ethnicity, and region by age group and U.S. population percentages for comparison. There are no tables presenting percentages of education by race/ethnicity, education by region, or race/ethnicity by region, which would be useful. The normative sample included 2,720 participants meeting inclusion criteria for standard administration without modifications. It was noted that during standardization, participants first completed the PPVT–5 Form A followed by the EVT–3 Form A *or* the PPVT–5 Form B followed by the EVT–3 Form B, but it is unclear whether all 2,720 participants were administered *both* Forms A *and* B of the PPVT–5 and EVT–3, and if so, whether any form of counterbalancing was used and what the inter-form test interval was. If the standardization sample was randomly bifurcated such that 1,360 participants were administered PPVT–5 and EVT–3 Forms A and 1,360 participants were administered PPVT–5 and EVT–3 Forms B, it would reflect a sizable reduction in normative samples of *each* form and should be explicitly stated.

Each PPVT–5 form was reduced to 240 items for norm development using statistical analyses and feedback from examiners. As with other tests published by Pearson, such as the Wechsler Intelligence Scale for Children—Fifth Edition (WISC–V; Wechsler, 2014), "inferential norming" (manual, p. 33) was used in which distributions of means, standard deviations, and skewness for each age group were examined from first- through fourth-order polynomial regressions with comparison to theoretical distributions and growth curves that produced percentiles for conversion to standard scores (M = 100, SD = 15). Distribution irregularities were reportedly corrected through smoothing, but the smoothing method (statistical vs. hand/visual) was not noted. One-parameter IRT (Rasch) models were used to produce ability scores that were rescaled into growth scale values (M = 500, SD = 25) for score comparisons across time. Critical values for statistical significance were produced using p = .10 without explicit justification.

Reliability. Three types of reliability estimates for PPVT–5 scores are reported: internal consistency, alternate form, and test-retest stability. Strong evidence was provided in each case. Internal consistency estimates by age group were produced by Spearman-Brown corrected split-half correlations ranging from .94 to .98 (M = .97) and used for producing standard errors of measurement and confidence intervals. These should be considered best-case estimates because they do not consider other major sources of error such as long-term temporal stability, administration errors, or scoring errors (Hanna, Bradley, & Holen, 1981) known to influence test scores in clinical assessments, although given the ease of administration and scoring of the PPVT–5, such sources of error are likely less problematic than intelligence tests. Estimated true score confidence intervals (90% and 95%) are provided in the test manual and present increasingly asymmetrical confidence intervals the further from the mean the score is due to regression to mean effects. However, obtained score confidence intervals are appropriate (Glutting, McDermott, & Stanley, 1987; Sattler, 2008) when the assessment question is concerned with estimating the true score of the individual at the time of the evaluation (rather than the long-term estimate).

Alternate forms reliability (equivalence) was assessed with 273 participants in three age groups using counterbalancing of forms with random assignment of the first form administered and test intervals ranging from 0 to 34 days (mean and/or median not disclosed). Equivalence estimates were good (M = .86): .81 for ages 2:6-11:11 (n = 132), .86 for ages 12:0-24:11 (n = 75), and .89 for ages 25:0-90:11 and older (n = 66). Effect sizes (Cohen's d) for mean differences between the two forms were trivial (.06-.07).

Short-term test-retest stability was investigated for 213 participants in three age groups with a mean retest interval of 30 days (range not disclosed). Stability coefficients (M = .84) were good: .86 for ages 2:6-11:11 (n = 96), .75 for ages 12:0-24:11 (n = 62), and .89 for ages 25:0-90:11 and older (n = 55). Effect sizes for mean differences between the two administrations were trivial to small (Cohen's d = .08-.32, M = .16).

Validity. Support for validity of PPVT-5 scores was focused on evidence based on test content, response processes, relationships with other variables, and special group studies (distinct group differences). Review of literature, test user feedback, and expert reviews were reported as sources of evidence for test content. Empirical and qualitative methods were noted for assessing evidence based on response processes in pilot testing of new items as well as standardization items. Evidence based on relationships with other variables (convergent and discriminant validity) included comparisons of PPVT–5 scores with scores from the PPVT–4 (M = .79), with language based tests such as the EVT–3 (M = .76), CELF Preschool–2 (*rs* ranged from .61 to .75), and CELF–5 (*rs* ranged from .68 to .73), and with the Kaufman Test of Educational Achievement–Third Edition Brief (KTEA–3 Brief) (*rs* ranged from .42 to .46). These results illustrate expected convergent and discriminant relationships.

Special group studies (distinct group differences) examined differences in PPVT–5 performance of individuals identified with language delay (N = 120), specific language impairment (N = 100), specific learning disability in reading and/or writing (N = 162), hearing impairment (N = 70), or autism spectrum disorder (N = 118) with matched (age, sex, race/ethnicity, parent educational level) samples of typically developing individuals. Mean differences were large with typically developing youth showing average PPVT–5 scores and special groups scoring significantly lower with large effect sizes (Cohen's d): language delay (d = 1.93), specific language impairment (d = 1.68), specific learning disability (d = .90), hearing impairment (d = .89), and autism spectrum disorder (d = .81).

Diagnostic Utility (Accuracy). The test author keenly recognized that special group studies or group differences are necessary but not sufficient indicators of clinical utility and provided extensive description of diagnostic accuracy methods and the variety of important indicators for judging such accuracy described by Kessell and Zimmerman (1993). Using the language delay (N = 120), specific language impairment (N = 100), and specific learning disability in reading and/or writing (N = 162) special groups and their matched samples, the test author reported the diagnostic accuracy of PPVT–5 scores across three cut scores (85, 77, and 70, corresponding to 1, 1.5, and 2 *SD*s below the mean) as well as five different base rates, which are known to affect diagnostic utility statistics. Discussion of positive results focused primarily on sensitivity and specificity estimates, but in the context of correctly identifying those who truly have or do not have a disorder or condition, it is the positive and negative predictive power estimates presented that are more important.

COMMENTARY. The PPVT–5 is well designed and normed, and incorporation of digital administration via Q-interactive may be a useful adaptation. However, the test manual did not include evidence for the equivalence of scores produced from the digital versus the traditional method of administration, and such support is essential. Also, while the inclusion of diagnostic accuracy was welcome and refreshing and it was acknowledged that base rates and cut scores affect such estimates, one method that should be considered in future studies and revision is the use of receiver operating characteristic (ROC) curve analysis (Swets, 1996; Treat & Viken, 2012), which is not affected by base rates or cut scores. As a very narrow measure of receptive vocabulary the test's value will mostly be for screening or supplementing assessments; however, vocabulary knowledge is an important component of speech and language and reading, and a narrow aspect of general intelligence. Speech and language pathologists, school psychologists, early childhood specialists, reading specialists, and clinical psychologists will find the PPVT–5 familiar and useful given preliminary supportive evidence for reliability, validity, and diagnostic utility. Such positive results should be replicated and extend these preliminary results.

SUMMARY. The present revision represents a well-designed, relatively inexpensive, easy-to-use measure of receptive vocabulary that has good norms and ample preliminary evidence for score reliability, validity, and utility. As such the PPVT-5 is an excellent revision that should provide users confident assessment of receptive vocabulary for comparison to other skills and attributes in screening, clinical assessment, and research.

REVIEWER'S REFERENCES

Dunn, L. M. (1959). Peabody Picture Vocabulary Test. Circle Pines, MN: American Guidance Service.

Dunn, L. M., & Dunn, D. M. (2007) Peabody Picture Vocabulary Test, Fourth Edition. San Antonio, TX: Pearson.

Glutting, J. J., McDermott, P. A., & Stanley, J. C. (1987). Resolving differences among methods of establishing confidence limits for test scores. *Educational and Psychological Measurement, 47,* 607-614.

Hanna, G. S., Bradley, F. O., & Holen, M. C. (1981). Estimating major sources of measurement error in individual intelligences scales: Taking our heads out of the sand. *Journal of School Psychology, 19,* 370-376.

Kessel, J. B., & Zimmerman, M. (1993). Reporting errors in studies of the diagnostic performance of self-administered questionnaires: Extent of the problem, recommendations for standardized presentation of results, and implications for the peer review process. *Psychological Assessment, 5,* 395–399. doi:10.1037/1040-3590.5.4.395

Sattler, J. M. (2008). *Assessment of children: Cognitive foundations* (5th ed.). San Diego, CA: Author.

Swets, J. A. (1996). *Signal detection theory and ROC analysis in psychological diagnostics: Collected papers.* Mahwah, NJ: Erlbaum.

Treat, T. A., & Viken, R. J. (2012). Measuring test performance with signal detection theory techniques. In H. Cooper, P. M. Camic, D. L. Long, A. T. Panter, D. Rindskopf, & K. J. Sher (Eds.), *APA handbook of research methods in psychology, Volume 1: Foundations, planning, measures, and psychometrics* (pp. 723–744). Washington, DC: American Psychological Association.

Wechsler, D. (2014). *Wechsler Intelligence Scale for Children-Fifth Edition technical and interpretive manual.* San Antonio, TX: Pearson.

Williams, K. T. (2019). Expressive Vocabulary Test, Third Edition. San Antonio, TX: Pearson.

Review of the Peabody Picture Vocabulary Test, Fifth Edition by THERESA GRAHAM LAUGHLIN, Adjunct Faculty, Nebraska Methodist College of Nursing, Omaha, NE:

DESCRIPTION. The Peabody Picture Vocabulary Test, Fifth Edition (PPVT-5) is a norm-referenced assessment tool designed to measure receptive vocabulary of Standard American English for individuals ages 2 years 6 months to 90 years and older. A feature of the PPVT-5 is that it was co-normed with the Expressive Vocabulary Test, Third Edition (EVT-3; Williams, 2019). The PPVT-5 includes two parallel forms, A and B, consisting of 240 items on each form. The current edition was updated to include items that are shared between PPVT-5 Forms A and B. In addition, some items are shared between the PPVT-5 and the EVT-3, which contributes to the comparability of the two instruments. All of the artwork has been newly drawn to be "familiar to individuals of various ages and from diverse regional and cultural backgrounds" (manual, p. 1). Finally, the norming tables have been updated to represent demographic changes in the United States. Using pictures and verbal prompts, the PPVT-5 can be used as a screening tool to identify receptive language disorders in children and adults, to examine preschoolers' vocabulary development, to provide a tool for reevaluation, and to understand reading difficulties. The PPVT-5 is also available on a digital platform for both administration and scoring. Intervention reporting is available on the digital platform but is not included in this review.

The PPVT-5 materials include an examiner's manual, stimulus books with pictures for Forms A and B, and examiner record forms for Forms A and B. The examiner's manual provides information on administration, scoring, and interpreting the test. In addition, it describes the development and standardization of the current version of the PPVT-5 and includes evidence of reliability and validity. The appendices provide information on age equivalents and testing examinees with hearing loss. Finally, information is provided on item analyses on subsets of items in the areas of home versus school vocabulary, parts of speech, and STEM vocabulary.

The PPVT-5 is administered individually. The instrument is untimed, and starting points based on chronological age allow for quick administration (10-15 minutes). Examiners should be familiar with the testing materials and have experience working with individuals in the age group being tested, but extensive examiner training is not necessary. If the PPVT-5 is administered along with the EVT-3, then the PPVT-5 should be administered first. The stimulus book is an easel-style book with each page displaying four pictures in a quadrant. Each picture is numbered (1-4) at the bottom. The record form includes a cover page with identifying information (e.g., name, age), raw scores and summary scores, and a graphical profile. Training and test items are listed with the target word on the record form. Examinees are instructed that they will hear a target word and that they can either point to the picture of the target word or indicate the number corresponding to the picture of the target word. Scoring is indicated on the record form by circling the number that the examinee indicates either from gesture or verbal response. The correct answer is indicated on the record form in red. The examiner can then indicate the accuracy of the answer at the time of administration. If the examinee does not respond, then the item is coded as incorrect and "NR" is circled, indicating there was no verbal or gestural response. A basal is established by three consecutive correct responses. A ceiling is established by six consecutive incorrect responses. Because responses are scored as the examinee answers, testing ends once the ceiling has been reached.

The raw score is based on the total number of errors subtracted from the total number of items attempted. Tables are provided in the appendix of the test manual to convert raw scores to standard scores. In addition, the appendix provides the confidence intervals, percentile ranks, normal curve equivalents, and stanines, all of which are transferred to the front page of the record form. The graphical profile provides an additional view of the examinee's performance. The last page of the record form provides space to compare PPVT-5 scores over time and to compare performance on the PPVT-5 with performance on the EVT-3. Tables are provided in the appendix of the test manual to evaluate whether changes in scores on the PPVT-5 or comparisons with EVT-3 scores are statistically significant.

DEVELOPMENT. New items were developed through a review of high-frequency words for young children and words that may be used in home, community, and school settings for older examinees. An item was considered new if the word had not been included in the PPVT–4 or if 50% or more of the images on its stimulus page were different or had been significantly modified from the PPVT–4. A total of 109 new items were embedded with 93 items from the PPVT–4 for the pilot study, which included 217 individuals with no known language disorder or hearing deficit ranging in age from 2 years 6 months to 21 years 11 months. The reported results from the pilot research were a bit vague indicating that "the majority of new items were familiar to the individuals who were presented them" (manual, p. 30). A total of 16 new items were added, and 26 items from the PPVT-4 were omitted. No specific information is provided to explain why items were omitted nor to which form the new items were added. In addition, no information was provided on whether the distribution of new items or omission of previous items was equal across age groups.

The examiner's manual provides information on interpreting quantitative scores (e.g., standard scores, growth scale values) from the PPVT-5. In addition, information on qualitative analyses was provided. The PPVT-5 was designed for further item analysis in the areas of home versus school vocabulary, vocabulary by part of speech, and STEM vocabulary. However, little information was provided as to how those distinctions were determined, and some words designated as "home" or "school" easily could be argued to belong in the other category. Without an explanation, it is unclear how helpful these additional analyses can be. Although information is provided regarding interpretation of scores, it is clear that although administration can be accomplished by an experienced but not expert test administrator, interpretation of results requires a much more thorough analysis by an expert in the field of language development.

TECHNICAL. The standardization study included 2,720 individuals ranging in age from 2 years 6 months to 90 years and older recruited from 44 states. Most age bands consisted of 100 individuals stratified by age, sex, race/ethnicity, geographic region, and parent/caregiver education level within 5% of Census distributions for race/ethnicity and parent/caregiver education level. Examiners included speech-language pathologists, psychologists, and individuals experienced with administering standardized tests. A total of 217 examiners completed and submitted practice test protocols that were evaluated prior to their participation in the standardization study. Start points were based on whether 90% or more of the examinees in a particular age group passed an item. Rasch ability scores were used to develop rules to establish basals and ceilings. Standard scores with a mean of 100 and a standard deviation of 15 were developed using inferential norming (Zhu & Chen, 2011).

Reliability. Reliability of the PPVT-5 was evaluated using three measures: internal consistency, alternate form reliability, and test-retest stability. Internal consistency was examined using the split-half method for both Forms A and B within each age band and resulted in very high coefficients (.94-.98). Internal consistency also was evaluated by providing standard error of measurement confidence intervals. SEMs ranged from 2.12 to 3.67, further indicating a high degree of reliability of the PPVT-5 scores.

Alternate form reliability was assessed by comparing the performance of 273 examinees who took both Forms A and B. Results were compared across three age bands. Although it is not clear how these age bands were determined, reliabilities between the two forms were high, with correlation coefficients ranging from .81 to .89.

Test-retest stability was examined in a study using only Form A in which 213 individuals were administered the PPVT-5 twice with approximately a one-month retest interval. Although the second administration resulted in higher average scores (as expected from practice), the correlation coefficients (corrected for variability) were high, ranging from .86 to .89.

Validity. Evidence of validity for the PPVT-5 score was established by reviewing the test content, its relationship to other variables, special group studies, and diagnostic accuracy. Test content was evaluated through literature review, users' feedback, and expert review. Feedback from test users and test developers from the test publisher's international offices was obtained. Interestingly, feedback was solicited from many international contacts but did not include a representative from Mexico. Given that the standardization sample comprised greater than 20% of individuals identifying as Hispanic, and that one of the stated goals of the current revisions was to create items that are familiar to a broader cultural background, it is unfortunate that a broader Hispanic perspective was not included. [Editor's note: The test publisher advised the Buros Center for Testing that a panel of 12 consultants, including four with expertise in Hispanic culture, reviewed the items to ensure their appropriateness regarding gender, ethnicity, regional differences, and varying socioeconomic levels.]

To examine the relationship of the PPVT-5 to other measures, including the EVT-3, PPVT-4,

Clinical Evaluation of Language Fundamentals–Fifth Edition (CELF-5), CELF Preschool-2, and Kaufman Test of Educational Achievement– Third Edition Brief (KTEA-3 Brief), smaller sub-studies were conducted. Other than the comparison with the EVT-3 (which was co-normed with the PPVT-5), the sample sizes of the smaller studies ranged from 56 participants (CELF Preschool-2) to 208 participants (KTEA-3 Brief). High correlation coefficients were found between the PPVT-5 and both the PPVT-4 (range = .76-.81) and the EVT-3 (range = .75-.77). The standard difference ranged from .10 to .33 with the PPVT-4 and was .01 with the EVT-3. The test authors suggest the higher outcome with the PPVT-4 may be due to differences in the normative population creating a broader range of ability in younger children on the PPVT-5. Moderate correlation coefficients were found between the PPVT-5 and the CELF-5 (.68-.73) and the CELF Preschool-2 (.61-.75). The PPVT-5 was also moderately correlated with the KTEA-3 Brief but with lower correlation coefficients (.42-.46) than were noted with some of the other measures.

Although the PPVT-5 was not designed to be a diagnostic test for different language delay disorders, performance on the PPVT-5 should be able to differentiate individuals with typical vocabulary development from different clinical subgroups whose receptive vocabulary may be delayed. Multiple studies were conducted to ascertain whether PPVT-5 scores would differentiate typically developing individuals from those with language impairment, learning disability, autism spectrum disorder, and hearing impairment. In each study, the test author used a matched control and found that the PPVT-5 correctly discriminated between typically developing individuals and those with language delay, specific language impairment, specific learning disability in reading/writing, autism spectrum disorder, and hearing impairment with cochlear implants.

The test author further examined the data from the sub-studies on language delay, specific language impairment, and learning disability in reading/writing to explore whether scores on the PPVT-5 could identify individuals with a language disorder relying on both positive and negative predictive power models. Results suggested that the PPVT-5 has high sensitivity and specificity and therefore can be used to identify individuals with language delay when used with other measures.

COMMENTARY AND SUMMARY. PPVT-5 is a norm-referenced assessment of receptive vocabulary of individuals ages 2 years 6 months to 90 years and older that can be completed in about 15 minutes. Because the PPVT-5 is conormed with the EVT-3, administration of the two tests provides a snapshot of both receptive and expressive vocabulary. The standardization sample sufficiently represents current U.S. demographic trends. Although there are some concerns with the sample used in the sub-studies in terms of size and age distribution, the standardization study described in the examiner's manual provides sufficient evidence of reliability and validity. The PPVT-5 is not meant to be a diagnostic tool. Like its predecessors, it is best used as an initial screening for vocabulary development or used in conjunction with other measures of language ability.

REVIEWER'S REFERENCE

Zhu, J., & Chen, H. (2011). Utility of inferential norming with smaller sample sizes. *Journal of Psychoeducational Assessment, 29*(6), 570-580.

[118]

Pearman Personality Integrator.

Purpose: Designed as "a measure of personality that gauges one's natural state (i.e., what is most comfortable) and one's everyday environment (i.e., what is most often demonstrated)."

Population: Ages 18 and older.

Publication Date: 2015.

Administration: Individual or group.

Restricted Distribution: Certification or pre-qualification required.

Parts, 2: Pearman Personality; Pearman FlexIndex.

Price Data: Available from publisher.

Time: 20-30 minutes for completion.

Comments: Administered and scored online; user's handbook only available online.

Author: Roger R. Pearman.

Publisher: Multi-Health Systems, Inc.

a) PEARMAN PERSONALITY.

Scores, 42: 14 Circle Scores: Natural Overall Attitude (Extraversion or Introversion), Demonstrated Overall Attitude (Extraversion or Introversion), Natural Overall Perceiving (Sensing or Intuiting), Demonstrated Overall Perceiving (Sensing or Intuiting), Natural Overall Judging (Thinking or Feeling), Demonstrated Overall Judging (Thinking or Feeling), Natural Extraverted Perceiving (Extraverted Intuiting or Extraverted Sensing), Demonstrated Extraverted Perceiving (Extraverted Intuiting or Extraverted Sensing), Natural Introverted Perceiving (Introverted Intuiting or Introverted Sensing), Demonstrated Introverted Perceiving (Introverted Intuiting or Introverted Sensing), Natural Extraverted Judging (Extraverted Feeling or Extraverted Thinking), Demonstrated Extraverted Judging (Extraverted Feeling or Extraverted Thinking), Natural Introverted Judging (Introverted Feeling or Introverted Thinking), Demonstrated Introverted

Judging (Introverted Feeling or Introverted Thinking); 28 Average Scores: Natural Extraversion, Demonstrated Extraversion, Natural Introversion, Demonstrated Introversion, Natural Sensing, Demonstrated Sensing, Natural Intuiting, Demonstrated Intuiting, Natural Thinking, Demonstrated Thinking, Natural Feeling, Demonstrated Feeling, Natural Extraverted Sensing, Demonstrated Extraverted Sensing, Natural Introverted Sensing, Demonstrated Introverted Sensing, Natural Extraverted Intuiting, Demonstrated Extraverted Intuiting, Natural Introverted Intuiting, Demonstrated Introverted Intuiting, Natural Extraverted Thinking, Demonstrated Extraverted Thinking, Natural Introverted Thinking, Demonstrated Introverted Thinking, Natural Extraverted Feeling, Demonstrated Extraverted Feeling, Natural Introverted Feeling, Demonstrated Introverted Feeling.
b) PEARMAN FLEXINDEX.
Scores, 6: Proactivity, Composure, Connectivity, Variety-Seeking, Rejuvenation, Total FlexIndex.

Review of the Pearman Personality Integrator by KARL N. KELLEY, Professor of Psychology, North Central College, Naperville, IL:

DESCRIPTION. Building on Jung's (1921) theory of personality types, Pearman has developed a modified view of understanding how personality types function in different environments. Pearman's Personality Integrator keeps the core architecture of Jung's model intact. Like Jung, Pearman suggests that a primary attitude (introversion-extraversion) directs an individual's energy either internally or externally. Then, there are two functions that mediate the expression of this energy. The perceiving function (sensing-intuition) directs energy toward concrete details or abstract possibilities, whereas the judging function (thinking-feeling) mediates decisions based on logic or values. Pearman's model suggests that the primary attitude influences the functions to create 14 scales or Pearman Personality types: Overall Attitude (Extraversion, Introversion); Overall Perceiving (Sensing, Intuiting); Overall Judging (Thinking, Feeling); Extraverted Perceiving (Extraverted Sensing, Extraverted Intuiting); Introverted Perceiving (Introverted Sensing, Introverted Intuiting); Extraverted Judging (Extraverted Feeling, Extraverted Thinking); Introverted Judging (Introverted Feeling, Introverted Thinking).

Expanding on Jung's model, Pearman measures both natural (the personality type) and demonstrated (the actual behaviors) qualities. The natural is who we are, and the demonstrated is what we do. Pearman argues that we are most effective and feel the least psychological strain when there is congruence between our natural qualities and demonstrated behaviors.

In addition to the Pearman Personality types, the test also includes a FlexIndex. Because situational demands often require us to modify our behaviors, this test measures five unique dimensions of plasticity: Proactivity (ability to anticipate future outcomes); Composure (self-control and patience); Connectivity (forming and using beneficial relationships); Variety-Seeking (openness to new opportunities for growth and development); Rejuvenation (ability to use positive coping strategies). The composite of these five dimensions is represented in a Total FlexIndex, which represents an individual's overall flexibility, agility, and resilience.

The goal of this test is to provide individuals with insights that will help them understand and improve overall functioning while reducing psychological strain. This test also provides a structure for developing new strategies for coping with ever-changing environments. The test focuses on employee and leadership development within organizations, but there is a wide range of other possible applications. These other areas include academic (student success and retention), teams (athletic), and clinical (vocational, relationship, psychotherapy).

DEVELOPMENT. The Pearman Personality Integrator was primarily developed to improve employee functioning and to develop organizational leaders. Specific examples of applications include employee development, change management, conflict resolution, leadership development, executive coaching, and succession planning. Although there are many other possible applications of this test, the individual and coaching reports focus on workplace situations.

The test, which is divided into three sections, can be completed online in approximately 30 minutes. The first section collects basic demographic information about the client. The next section focuses on assessing Pearman Personality types. In this section, clients respond to a series of item pairs that ask, "How natural is it for you to...?" and "How often do you...?". Responses are recorded using a sliding scale with anchors at *very unnatural* and *very natural* (for natural state) and from *never* to *always* (for demonstrated behaviors). The third section evaluates flexibility by using questions where responses are recorded using a fixed-choice Likert scale with anchors at *never* and *always*.

Two interpretative reports are produced, one for a client and one for a coach. Test users choose a Workplace Lens or a Leadership Lens for interpreting the report, depending on the context of the assessment. The client report explains the theoretical structure of the Pearman Personality type and the FlexIndex. The coach report includes suggestions about how to interpret and use the information. A structured action plan also may be created for the client report, and commitment to development worksheets and guides for providing feedback are available for coaches.

TECHNICAL.

Standardization. The normative sample of 2,400 participants matched the 2010 U.S./Canada census distribution for employed individuals for age, gender, race, and geographic region. All participants were professionals (working/retired) or students 18 years of age or older working toward a professional career. The data for the normative phase were collected and analyzed between 2014 and 2015. In the final sample, 77.8% held a bachelor's degree or higher, and 74.1% were employed full time.

Reliability. The Pearman Personality Integrator includes 28 scales, 14 natural and 14 demonstrated. All scales yielded moderate or high internal reliability. Alpha coefficients for the natural scales ranged from .61 to .88 and for the demonstrated scales from .61 to .87. Test-retest reliability data were collected for 115 individuals using a 2- to 4-week testing interval. For the natural scales, these test-retest reliability coefficients ranged from .68 to .87 (all $p < .001$). The coefficients for the demonstrated scales ranged from .58 to .83 (all $p < .001$).

The five scales on the Pearman FlexIndex also yielded moderate to high internal consistency. Alpha coefficients ranged from .74 to .86. The FlexIndex 2- to 4-week test-retest correlations ranged from .69 to .82 (all $p < .001$).

Validity. The construct evidence of validity of this test was assessed by comparing scores with scores from the Myers-Briggs Type Indicator, Form M (Briggs & Myers, 1998) and the HEXACO Personality Inventory (Lee & Ashton, 2004). Based on a sample of 377 employed individuals, the overlap between MBTI and Pearman Personality score types ranged from 68.4% to 86.1%. There also were statistically significant correlations between Pearman scores and logically consistent HEXACO dimensions. Specifically, Pearman Attitude correlated with HEXACO Extraversion ($r = .41$, $p < .001$); Pearman Perceiving correlated with HEXACO Openness to Experience ($r = .40$, $p < .001$); and Pearman Judging correlated with HEXACO Emotionality ($r = .30$, $p < .01$). In addition, those reporting smaller differences between natural and demonstrated scales reported significantly higher levels of job success, job satisfaction, and relationship satisfaction.

The FlexIndex was supported using both exploratory and confirmatory factor analyses. In examining outcomes, those reporting higher overall FlexIndex scores also reported significantly higher levels of job success, job satisfaction, and relationship satisfaction.

This test also would appear to avoid adverse impact. Although there were some statistically significant gender differences, all of the Cohen's *d* values were very small (median Cohen's d = .09), indicating a minimally significant effect. In most cases, women's scores were higher than men's scores. In addition, the proportion of Black or Hispanic participants scoring in the average or above average range equaled or exceeded that of White participants.

COMMENTARY. The Pearman Personality Integrator produces a complex report with a wide range of applications. Because of the complexity of the model, administrators need a considerable amount of training to use this instrument effectively. Fortunately, there is a great deal of support and training available. The technical manual is comprehensive, well-organized, and clear. Of note is the helpful structure provided to plan the overall assessment process. This process includes a clear definition of the various stakeholders and examples of potential ethical dilemmas. In addition, there are 17 training partners offering certifications in eight countries. (Nine training partners are in the United States.)

The reports are well designed and easy to read. This test provides individuals and coaches with a great deal of information. The conclusion of the report states, "You have been provided with a vast amount of information about your Pearman Personality type and your FlexIndex skills." However, through a liberal use of well-designed graphs and clearly written descriptions with examples, it is possible to understand the information. The report recommends taking time to think about the scores and to develop ideas about how to use the information. To assist both the individual and the coach, the reports end with a worksheet to develop an action plan and a statement to commit to personal development.

The results of this test also can be used with the Emotional Quotient Inventory 2.0 (EQ-i

2.0; Multi-Health Systems, Inc., 2011; 19:62), a measure of emotional intelligence published by the same company. The EQ-i 2.0 measures five composite dimensions (Self-Perception, Self-Expression, Interpersonal, Decision Making, and Stress Management) and an overall well-being indicator (Happiness). This information can further help individuals and coaches develop strategies for maximizing effectiveness and well-being.

SUMMARY. The Pearman Personality Indicator is a robust test with a large and active community of users based on Jung's (1921) theory of personality types. It extends Jung's model by measuring personality in terms of natural (personality type) and demonstrated (behavioral) aspects, with the assumption being that the more congruent these qualities, the more likely one will be successful and experience less strain. In addition, the FlexIndex provides information on an individual's flexibility in responding to ever-changing situational demands. For both assessments, the clients are given a structured worksheet to create an action plan to use the assessment information. Coaches are also provided with reports that can be used in overall employee and leadership development. The test can also be linked to the EQ-i 2.0 measure of emotional intelligence.

Although the test is complex, results are clearly explained in the reports. Coaches have access to a well-designed technical manual and 17 training partners offering certifications in the interpretation and use of this test. In addition, there is an online resource center that includes access to a variety of articles, papers, webinars, slide decks, and other information about the theory and use of this tool.

REVIEWER'S REFERENCES

Briggs, K. C., & Myers, I. B. (1998). Myers-Briggs Type Indicator, Form M. Palo Alto, CA: Consulting Psychologists Press.

Jung, C. G. (1921). *Psychological types*. Princeton, NJ: Bollingen Press.

Lee, K., & Ashton, M. C. (2004). Psychometric Properties of the HEXACO Personality Inventory. *Multivariate Behavioral Research, 39*, 329–358.

Multi-Health Systems, Inc. (2011). Emotional Quotient Inventory 2.0. Toronto, Ontario: Author.

Review of the Pearman Personality Integrator by RICHARD R. REILLY, Professor Emeritus, Stevens Institute of Technology, Hoboken, NJ:

DESCRIPTION. Per the test manual, the Pearman Personality Integrator consists of two assessment components. The Pearman Personality "assesses an individual's personality patterns according to personality type theory, while the Pearman FlexIndex section assesses the skills and abilities needed to function effectively within and outside of an individual's personality" (manual, p. 7). Both sections of the Pearman Personality Integrator are administered online.

The Pearman Personality includes 30 paired items. For each item pair, respondents are asked to indicate how natural it is for them to perform a specific behavior using a sliding scale with five anchors ranging from *very unnatural* to *very natural* (natural scales). For the same item pair, respondents are then asked to indicate how often they perform the behavior using a sliding scale with five anchors ranging from *never* to *always* (demonstrated behavior scales). The Pearman Personality is based on Jungian theory that individual psychology can be described by four forms of perceiving (extraverted sensing, introverted sensing, extraverted intuiting, and introverted intuiting) and four forms of judging (extraverted thinking, introverted thinking, extraverted feeling, and introverted feeling).

The Pearman FlexIndex includes 37 items, each of which is rated on a 6-point frequency scale. The Pearman FlexIndex measures five factors: Proactivity, Composure, Connectivity, Variety-Seeking, and Rejuvenation. Per the manual, the Pearman Personality Integrator "allows individuals to understand their full range of personality functioning, as well as how their flexibility and agility skills enable them to operate effectively within and outside of their preferred personality type" (p. 12).

The Pearman Personality Integrator is a level B assessment, meaning that interpretation should be made by a "qualified psychologist, certified individual, or other professional with a master's level course in tests and measurements" (manual, p. 14). The test authors recommend that the measure be used as part of a larger evaluation process that includes a variety of other assessment methods. Although the reading level is pitched at seventh grade according to the Flesch-Kincaid Grade Level Formula, the test manual recommends that respondents be at least 18 years of age. The manual provides extensive detail on the interpretation and application of the results. Among the applications noted are employee development, change management, conflict management, and leadership development and coaching.

DEVELOPMENT. Development of the Pearman Personality measure began with the generation of a large pool of items designed to measure the eight Jungian dimensions and the FlexIndex factors noted above. Experts in personality reviewed and sorted the items into the various categories. A pilot version included 85 item pairs for the Pearman Personality section and 105 items for the FlexIndex.

The pilot version was administered to a sample of 486 participants. A subset of these also completed the Myers-Briggs Type Indicator (MBTI). Item analyses and factor analyses were used to eliminate poorly performing items. After the pilot analysis some new items were written, and a panel of experts reviewed the items and assigned them to factors. The next phase included a revised version with 56 item pairs for Pearman Personality. The number of FlexIndex item pairs in this version is unclear as the test manual says 54 items were retained, and two to six new items were added to each subscale. This version was administered to a normative sample of 2,400 adults selected to match census data for the United States and Canada. Data analysis included "an array of advanced data analytic techniques" (manual, p. 139). Based on these analyses, the final scales were developed.

TECHNICAL. Several different analyses examined the reliability of the Pearman Personality scales. Alpha coefficients for the natural scales ranged from .61 to .88. Alpha coefficients for the demonstrated scales were similar and ranged from .61 to .87. It should be noted that 10 of the 14 scales were based on six items with the remaining four scales based on 12 items each. Internal consistencies for the FlexIndex were higher and ranged from .74 to .86. The overall FlexIndex score, based on all 37 items, had an alpha coefficient of .92. Test-retest reliability was estimated based on a sample of 115 respondents who were assessed twice, 2 to 4 weeks apart. The test-retest reliabilities ranged from .68 to .87 for the natural scales and from .58 to .83 for the demonstrated scales. A second sample tested 8 to 12 weeks apart found test-retest correlations from .45 to .77 for the natural scales and from .48 to .75 for the demonstrated scales. Test-retest reliabilities were examined on the FlexIndex for the same two samples and ranged from .69 to .82 for the first sample and from .69 to .78 for the second sample.

Validity for the Pearman Personality was assessed with a number of different methods. Content validity was assessed by the review of items by expert judges as described above during the development stage. The Pearman scales were correlated with the scales from the MBTI and the HEXACO Personality Inventory (Lee & Ashton, 2004). In a sample of 377 employed respondents, the classifications by type were compared for the Pearman and the MBTI. Results showed a significant degree of overlap between the Pearman and MBTI classifications. The Pearman scores were correlated with scores on the HEXACO Personality Inventory using a sample of 101 employed adults. Correlations were modest with the strongest correlation of .41 obtained for the Extraversion-Introversion scale on the Pearman and the Extraversion scale on the HEXACO. Respondents in the normative sample were asked to provide self-reported job success, job satisfaction, and relationship satisfaction ratings. The highest correlations between the Pearman and the self-reported criteria were obtained for the Extraversion-Introversion scale, ranging from .09 to .16. Correlations between the self-reported criteria and the other Pearman scales were quite low, and in most cases non-significant. Overall scores on the Pearman were compared for individuals who reported their organizational level (executives, senior managers, managers, non-management). Results showed that higher average responses were obtained for those in higher organizational levels. Effect sizes were relatively modest for most of the scales. For the FlexIndex an exploratory factor analysis (EFA) was performed on data from half of the normative sample, and a confirmatory factor analysis (CFA) was performed on the other half. The EFA yielded the five factors noted above in the description. The CFA showed a good fit to the factor model identified in the EFA. The FlexIndex scores were correlated with scores on the Emotional Quotient Inventory 2.0 and the Coping Inventory for Stressful Situations. The pattern of correlations indicated reasonable construct validity for the FlexIndex.

COMMENTARY. Because the Pearman Personality is based on Jungian type theory, research on the validity of the most widely used measure of Jungian types is relevant. McCrae and Costa (1989) failed to find evidence that the MBTI measures truly distinct types. Indeed, support for the existence of distinct personality types is lacking (Costa, Herbst, McCrae, Samuels, & Ozer, 2002). Pittenger (2005) notes that the available evidence fails to support the validity and utility of the MBTI. Asendorpf (2003) found only a few cases where the MBTI configural types added incremental validity to the NEO-FFI. Other critiques by Druckman and Bjork (1991) and Boyle (1995) question the validity of the MBTI. Of course, the Pearman is not the MBTI, but it is based on a similar theory and the notion that distinct personality types can be identified and that there is utility and validity to these classifications. Although the Pearman has been developed with extensive research, the evidence for the validity or utility of the Pearman for the purposes outlined in the test manual is not impressive. The FlexIndex was developed as a separate set of measures not related to Jungian theory and again was carefully developed. However, more evidence of external validity is needed to support the use of these measures. As noted above, the Pearman Personality scales showed modest correlations with the HEXACO Index, a well-researched instrument. Because some of the HEXECO scales differ from the highly endorsed Five-Factor Model of Personality, further examination of the relationship between the Pearman and the Five-Factor model would be an important additional basis on which to judge the construct validity of the Pearman. A similar comment could be made with regard to the FlexIndex.

SUMMARY. The Pearman Personality Integrator is a multidimensional personality assessment instrument that includes two sections. The Pearman Personality assesses types based on Jungian theory, and the FlexIndex assesses five personality factors. The test manual details the extensive research in developing both instruments. However, more construct- and criterion-related evidence of validity is needed to support the use of this instrument.

REVIEWER'S REFERENCES

Asendorpf, J. B. (2003). Head-to-head comparison of the predictive validity of personality types and dimensions. *European Journal of Personality, 17,* 327-346.

Boyle, G. J. (1995). Myers-Briggs Type Indicator (MBTI): Some Psychometric Limitations. *Australian Psychologist, 30,* 71-74.

Costa, P. T., Jr., Herbst, J. H., McCrae, R. R., Samuels, J. & Ozer, D. J. (2002). The replicability and utility of three personality types. *European Journal of Personality, 16*(S1). S73-S87.

Druckman, D., & Bjork, R. A. (Eds.). (1991). *In the mind's eye: Enhancing human performance.* Washington, DC: National Academy Press.

Lee, K., & Ashton, M. C. (2004). Psychometric properties of the HEXACO Personality Inventory. *Multivariate Behavioral Research, 39,* 329-358.

McCrae, R. R., & Costa, P. T., Jr. (1989). Reinterpreting the Myers-Briggs Type Indicator from the perspective of the five-factor model of personality. *Journal of Personality, 57,* 17-40.

Pittenger, D. J. (2005). Cautionary comments regarding the Myers-Briggs Type Indicator. *Consulting Psychology Journal: Practice and Research, (57)*3, 210-221.

[119]

Personality Assessment Screener–Observer.

Purpose: "Designed to provide a brief informant-based screening of information relevant to various clinical problems and to target areas where follow-up assessment might be needed."
Population: Ages 18 and older.
Publication Date: 2018.
Acronym: PAS-O.
Scores, 11: Negative Affect, Acting Out, Health Problems, Psychotic Features, Social Withdrawal, Hostile Control, Suicidal Thinking, Alienation, Alcohol Problem, Anger Control, Total.
Administration: Individual or group.
Price Data, 2020: $176 per complete kit including manual (143 pages) with fast guide, 25 response forms, and 25 score summary and profile forms; $63 per manual (includes fast guide); $58 per 25 response forms; $58 per 25 score summary and profile forms.
Time: Approximately 5 minutes for administration.
Comments: An adaptation of the Personality Assessment Screener (T9:1523) for obtaining informant reports.
Author: Leslie C. Morey.
Publisher: Psychological Assessment Resources, Inc.

Review of the Personality Assessment Screener–Observer by CARL ISENHART, Psychologist, Phoenix VA Health Care System, Phoenix, AZ:

DESCRIPTION. The Personality Assessment Screener–Observer (PAS-O) is a rapid-screening questionnaire designed for an informant to provide clinical information about a client who has taken either the Personality Assessment Screener (PAS) or the Personality Assessment Inventory (PAI). The instrument uses 22 items to cover 10 elements (i.e., domains: e.g., Negative Affect, Acting Out) and also provides a total score that can be compared with the client's PAS or PAI scores. It takes about 5 minutes to complete by an informant who has known the client for at least 2 years, who is at least 18 years of age, and who has at least a fourth-grade reading level. It is assumed that the informant has the physical, emotional, and cognitive ability to use the PAS-O to make the ratings. The measure can be administered in either individual or group format by personnel who are trained to administer rating scales. Interpretation of the instrument requires a trained professional, and the PAS-O should never be used on its own for diagnostic or treatment decisions.

To administer the PAS-O, the informant uses an answer sheet to rate the degree to which each statement applies to the client using the following key: F-*false, not at all true*; ST-*slightly true*; MT-*mainly true*; and VT-*very true.* The scores for the 10 elements and the total score are tallied and converted to a P score, which was developed for the PAS and represents the likelihood that a given score would indicate a problematic profile on the PAI if it were to be given to the client. For example, a PAS-O P score of 50 indicates that about 50% of those with that PAS-O scale score would have a problematic PAI if it were to be administered. The P score is calculated from the positive predictive values from the standardization sample (including both clinical and community groups).

If the client has taken the PAS, then the degree and character of problems can be compared between the client's PAS profile and the informant's ratings on the PAS-O. This procedure allows the clinician to calculate the exact amount of convergence or discrepancy between the two sets of scores. There are four comparison scores, each of which is transformed to a T score with a mean of 50 and a standard deviation of 10. A Score Summary and Profile Form is used to calculate these scores and to determine the degree to which these scores deviate from normative expectations. Typically, a two or more standard deviation different from the mean would be considered a "marked departure." The first comparison score is the raw difference score, which is calculated by subtracting the informant's raw scores from the client's PAS raw scores. A positive difference means the client responded in a more severe direction on the PAS than what the informant rated on the PAS-O. Likewise, a negative difference means the client responded in a less severe direction than the informant. The second comparison score is the absolute difference score, which is the unidirectional absolute difference between the client's and informant's scores, where the absolute difference is determined between the two sets of scores. The third comparison score is the global dissimilarity score, which is an overall assessment of disagreement between the PAS and PAS-O profiles and is calculated by summing the absolute difference scores for each of the 10 elements. Fourth, there is the configural similarity Q-correlation (interpreted like any correlation coefficient with a range of +1 to -1), which involves a complex, 15-step process that reflects the convergence of the form of the PAS and PAS-O displays. Finally, if the client has taken the PAI, the test manual provides a conversion table that allows for the PAS (which comprises 22 items embedded in the PAI) to be calculated and compared to the observer's ratings on the PAS-O.

DEVELOPMENT. The PAS-O items are the same items that make up the PAS, only the items are formatted to the third person (i.e., from "I" statements to "he/his" or "she/her"). The 22 PAS items were determined to be the most predictive items of problematic scores on the PAI. The PAS was developed to be a self-report, brief assessment of a client's clinical problems, and the PAS-O was designed to obtain observer-based information on the same dimensions.

TECHNICAL. The PAS-O was developed from the PAS, and there are independent sources that support the technical aspects of the PAS, which provides some technical foundation for the PAS-O (Creech, Evardone, Braswell, & Hopwood, 2010; Edens, Penson, Smith, & Ruchensky, 2019; Kelley, Edens, & Douglas, 2018; Kelley, Edens, & Morey, 2017; Porcerelli et al., 2012).

Standardization. There were two normative samples, a community sample and a clinical sample. In both samples, the target/client completed the PAI, and the informant completed the PAS-O. The community sample consisted of 252 dyads, all of whom were 18 years of age or older. They were recruited from urban and rural areas of 18 states with the goal of being representative of age, race, and gender according to the 2015 U.S. Census. The clinical sample consisted of 201 participants whose informants completed the PAS-O. The clients in this sample represented a number of diagnoses/problem areas and were receiving some level of outpatient mental health services. The standardized scores described above for convergence and discrepancy were developed from the combined clinical and community samples. The test manual provides the demographic and descriptive statistics for the community, clinical, and combined samples that include the mean, standard deviation, skewness, and kurtosis for the PAS and PAS-O Total and element scores. The test manual reported that gender, race/ethnicity, and age each had a minor influence on the degree of convergence between the client and observer scores.

Reliability. Alpha coefficients for the Total scores from the community, clinical, and combined samples were .79, .77, and .84, respectively. The lowest alpha coefficients across all three samples were reported for Hostile Control (ranging from .16 to .33) whereas the highest coefficients were reported for Suicidal Thinking in the clinical group (.86) and Social Withdrawal in the community and combined samples (.85 and .87, respectively). The test author also reported the use of "cross-informant correlation" as a measure of correspondence between the client and observer, and it was noted that typical coefficients from the research literature range from .25 to .45. Cross-informant correlation coefficients for the PAS/PAS-O scores were .75 for the Total score and an average of .57 for the 10 element scores, which demonstrate reliable rater agreement. Similar results were reported comparing the PAI full-scale/PAS-O Total scores where the average correlation coefficient was .50.

Validity. Based on the treating clinician's primary diagnosis, the clinical sample was divided into eight broad categories of disorders (e.g., anxiety disorder, anger issues). In all eight of the diagnostic/problem areas, evidence of validity was demonstrated by showing, using z-scores, that compared to the community sample the clinical sample was rated as having more difficulties on the Total score and almost all of the element scores. Discriminant validity evidence was presented by showing that the observer's ratings of a specific element correlated higher with the client's self-reported rating in that same element when compared to the client's ratings on the other elements.

COMMENTARY. The PAS-O is a brief screening instrument that provides a way to obtain informant information about a client's psychological functioning. It was developed from the PAS, which has established itself as a solid screening instrument and was itself developed from the PAI, a well-established objective assessment of psychological distress. The PAS-O can be used to assess an observer's perception of the client's problem areas and provides a number of scores that can be used to assess the level of discrepancy between the observer and the client. The reliability measures are strong (internal consistency and cross-informant correlation), and there are data to support the instrument's discriminant validity and ability to identify differences between community and clinical samples. Administration, scoring, and interpretation are straightforward. One caution concerns the observer's ability to provide objective and unbiased judgments in making the ratings. In addition, just as with any client responding to an assessment instrument, the observer needs to be evaluated to assure that he or she is free from interpersonal (e.g., feelings of resentment or antipathy toward the client), mental, emotional, or cognitive issues that could influence ratings.

SUMMARY. The PAS-O is a rapid-screening questionnaire designed for an informant to provide clinical information about a client who has taken either the Personality Assessment Screener (PAS) or the Personality Assessment Inventory (PAI). It covers 10 elements (i.e., problem areas) and also provides a total score that can be compared with the client's PAS or PAI scores. Given the brief administration time and the instrument's straightforward scoring and interpretation, the PAS-O would be a good supplement to any PAS or PAI administration. The concept of an informant using an objective assessment tool to supplement a client's responses is clever and hopefully will stimulate the development of similar observer rating forms for other assessment instruments.

REVIEWER'S REFERENCES

Creech, S. K., Evardone, M., Braswell, L., & Hopwood, C. J. (2010). Validity of the Personality Assessment Screener in veterans referred for psychological testing. *Military Psychology, 22,* 465-473.

Edens, J. F., Penson, B. N., Smith, S. T., & Ruchensky, J. R. (2019). Examining the utility of the Personality Assessment Screener in three criminal justice samples. *Psychological Services, 16,* 664-674.

Kelley, S. E., Edens, J. F., & Douglas, K. S. (2018). Concurrent validity of the Personality Assessment Screener in a large sample of offenders. *Law and Human Behavior, 42,* 156-166.

Kelley, S. E., Edens, J. F., & Morey, L. C. (2017). Convergence of self-reports and informant reports on the Personality Assessment Screener. *Assessment, 24,* 999-1007.

Porcerelli, J. H., Kurtz, J. E., Cogan, R., Markova, T., & Mickens, L. (2012). Personality Assessment Screener in a primary care sample of low-income urban women. *Journal of Personality Assessment, 94,* 262-266.

Review of the Personality Assessment Screener–Observer by SEAN REILLEY, Licensed Psychologist, Eastern State Hospital, Lexington, KY:

DESCRIPTION. The Personality Assessment Screener–Observer (PAS-O) is a new informant-based adaptation of the brief, objective questionnaire the Personality Assessment Screener (PAS). The PAS-O, much like the PAS, is a rapid screen for problems in 10 areas common in mental disorders and in individuals seeking clinical treatment. The PAS-O provides informant-based data using third-person worded versions of all 22 items from the PAS, which themselves were drawn from the Personality Assessment Inventory. PAS-O screening data provided from an adult knowledgeable about the client (e.g., significant other/spouse, family member, therapist) can be directly compared to the client's self-report using the PAS (22 items) or PAI (344 items). The PAS-O is intended to be completed by an adult rater independently from the client undergoing assessment and requires the informant to be at least 18 years of age, have a minimum of a fourth-grade reading level, to have known the client for at least two years, and typically be a native English speaker.

The PAS-O is administered face to face either in an individual or group session by technicians or supervisees of a licensed mental health professional or by the latter professional. It takes approximately 5 minutes to complete the 22 items and provide some brief information about the rater (e.g., nature and length of time in their relationship with the client). Of note, PAS-O responses for male clients being rated appear on the left side of the response form while responses for female clients being rated appear on the right side of the PAS-O response form. Similar to the PAS and PAI, informants completing the PAS-O rate each item using a 4-point scale ranging from *false, not at all true* to *very true.* A ballpoint pen or pencil is required for responding to items so that responses on the answer sheet are adequately transferred to the underlying scoring sheet. The PAS-O is scored by hand using directions found in the test manual, in an accompanying Fast Guide, and on the scoring form. Each PAS-O item receives a score ranging from 0 to 3 on the scoring form. Raw scores for specific PAS-O items that are denoted by non-shaded areas on the scoring form are summed to form 10 element scores (Negative Affect [NA], Acting Out [AO], Health Problems [HP], Psychotic Features [PF], Social Withdrawal [SW], Hostile Control [HC], Suicidal Thinking [ST], Alienation [AN], Alcohol Problem [AP], Anger Control [AC]) and a Total score. Similar to the PAS, the 10-element scores and Total PAS-O scores are converted to a standardized P score that reflects a level of probable risk that the client will report clinically significant responses on the PAI. Each of the P scores and their level of probable risk can be plotted on an interpretation grid on the top portion of the scoring sheet. If the client has completed the PAS and/or the PAI, four broad groups of metrics (raw difference, absolute difference, global similarity, configural similarity) can be calculated on a separate Score Summary and Profile Form to evaluate the convergence of client and informant ratings. Scores from these metrics are standardized into T scores and plotted as Dynamic Comparison Profiles on the profile form to facilitate evaluation.

DEVELOPMENT. The PAS-O was developed to enhance the psychological assessment process for adults by offering a brief, informant-based version of the PAS. A conceptual approach to scale development was undertaken wherein the clinical goal was to provide comparable screening data to augment the client's self-report or for clinical situations in which the client is unwilling or unable to describe his or her behavior across 10 clinical domains. The 22 items of the PAS that were maximally predictive of the broad range of problematic scores on the PAI were re-worded into the third person on the PAS-O using pronoun changes. One exception to this approach was made for the fourth PAS-O item in which an adjective was removed to reduce rating ambiguity.

Unique in the process of PAS-O development was the desire to evaluate clinical screening data for convergence from dyads of adult community-dwelling individuals as well as informant reports concerning clients involved in mental health treatment who had completed the PAI or PAS. To do so, four new metrics (raw difference, absolute difference, global similarity, and the configural similarity Q-correlation), which were guided in part by research by Cronbach and Gleser (1953), were developed for the PAS-O. These metrics allow the user to evaluate the global dissimilarity of dyad scores as well as the pattern, scatter, and clinical elevation of the Total score and individual problem areas or elements in a standardized fashion. Finally, the PAS-O, similar to the PAS, utilizes a transformation of raw scores to P scores to reflect the likelihood in the standardization sample that the client would be expected to report a problem on the PAI suggestive of clinically significant difficulties. No pilot or validation studies are reported in the PAS-O manual prior to collection of data from the standardization samples.

TECHNICAL. A combined standardization sample of 705 adults ranging in age from 18 to 88 was used for the PAS-O that included 252 community dyads (504 individuals) and a clinical group (201 adults) in outpatient treatment for varying clinical diagnoses. No clinical inpatients were included in the standardization sample, and a higher percentage of outpatients with schizophrenia and anxiety disorders diagnoses were reported compared to the PAI normative sample. The community group was strategically sampled from 18 states representing urban and rural areas of the United States and differed only slightly in education relative to the 2015 Census data. Community dwelling pairs were required to know each other for at least 1 month, although analyses with PAS-O scores and longer lengths of relationships yielded minimal to small effects. In the community sample, 49.2% of raters were spouses or intimate partners who were living together compared to 20.9% in the clinical group. Relatives not living in the same household made up the largest percentage of raters in the clinical sample (46.8%) compared to 13.1% in the community sample. Readability analyses using the Flesch-Kincaid method yielded a 3.6 grade level for the PAS-O consistent with a suggested fourth-grade reading level for the PAS-O, PAS, and PAI. Descriptive statistics indicate PAS-O informant scores for both community (lower scores on six of 10 elements) and clinical (lower scores on three of 10 elements; no difference on seven of 10 elements) groups were generally lower than client reports (PAS) and scores from the PAI normative standardization sample. The PAS-O clinical group, however, had higher scores relative to the community group as would be expected.

Estimates of temporal stability for the PAS-O as well as the impact of repeated measurements across a clinical treatment course are not reported in the PAS-O manual. Internal consistency estimates for the Total PAS-O score in the community (coefficient alpha = .79) and clinical (coefficient alpha = .77) groups are acceptable and similar to reported PAS Total score estimates. Elemental level internal consistency estimates would be expected to be impacted by short scale length, although six of 10 elements in both community and clinical samples exceeded an alpha coefficient of .60; the HC element had low reliability in both samples for the PAS-O, but is noted to be higher on the PAS. Global dissimilarity, one of the four new convergent metrics, achieved a minimally acceptable coefficient of .60 for internal consistency (coefficients were .62 in the community sample and .68 in the clinical sample). In terms of interrater reliability, cross informant correlations for PAS/PAS-O scores for the combined standardization sample are higher for the PAS-O Total score (correlation coefficient was .75) as well as for nine of 10 elements (correlation coefficients ranging from .37 to .69) compared to reported coefficients of .25 to .45 for other instruments in a meta-analysis cited in the test manual. Additionally, when a second rater was employed for a subsample of 53 participants in the community group, the PAS-O Total score (correlation coefficient of .55) and six of 10 elements demonstrated coefficients that exceeded the expected comparisons of .25 to .45, albeit, they were reduced in comparison to the first informant rater/client correlations.

Initial PAS-O and PAI correlations with impression management indicators on the PAI indicated discrepancies between client/informant may be related to underreporting by the client in outpatient clinical settings. In terms of convergent metrics, raw difference total scores and absolute difference total scores yielded moderate informant/client correlations with modest to moderate correlations at the element level. The global dissimilarity difference score yielded moderate to strong informant/client correlations. Evidence for discriminant validity is provided in the form of expected lower correlations between PAS/PAS-O scores for different elements relative to the same element. However, a few unexpected correlations emerged for the second rater/client off-diagonal correlations. For content evidence of validity, exploratory factor analyses of the PAS-O using the combined standardization sample are reported using principal components analysis with varimax rotation. The factor analysis yielded a similar underlying structure to that of the PAS at the elemental level for six of 10 elements (ST, AP, PF, HP, and two of three item loadings for NA and AO). However, some elements (SW, AN) and remaining items from NA and HC elements combined to form a unique common factor, and one AO item did not load significantly on any of the aforementioned factors. Regarding predictive validity evidence, PAS-O correlations with PAI scores typically yielded moderate to strong correlations with PAI scale scores involving similar clinical concepts, although lower correlation coefficients were noted for the PF element of the PAS-O and PAI clinical scales assessing positive symptoms of psychosis.

Sensitivity for the PAS-O in the combined standardization sample reached 90.9%, and specificity reached 99.0%, although the cut score that maximized these outcomes yielded moderate sensitivity (71.7%) and specificity (71.2%). The receiving operator characteristic curve for the PAS-O yielded a 0.757 estimate for PAI elevations. Diagnosis-based comparisons are also reported for the clinical outpatient sample. Generally, higher PAS-O scores were reported for focal elements as would be expected (e.g., the AP element score was highest for a subsample of clinical outpatients with an alcohol use disorder diagnosis). The outpatient group of individuals with schizophrenia had a higher negative symptom element (SW) relative to a positive symptom score (PF), which was thought to be due to the outpatient nature of the clinical setting.

COMMENTARY. The PAS-O appears to be a potentially valuable, brief screening questionnaire that may enhance the psychological assessment process by contributing an informant-based report on 10 common areas of clinical problems. The major benefit of the PAS-O currently is direct comparability to PAS/PAI client reports of clinical problems using normed measures of self-informant discrepancies. No data for inpatient adults are yet available, thus the generalizability of the PAS-O at present is for outpatient screening purposes. The underlying factor structure of the PAS-O shares areas of significant convergence and divergence with the factor structure of the PAS, although the instruments differ mostly in terms of first- and third-person pronouns. Future validation work employing more advanced factor analytic or structural equational modeling techniques with a larger sample may allow for better latent variable modeling for the PAS-O with enhanced scale prediction.

SUMMARY. The test developer, to his credit, has produced a potentially valuable, informant-based adult screening questionnaire for 10 areas of clinical problems that yields data for direct comparisons to PAS/PAI client reports using normed self/informant discrepancies. In order for this instrument to become a gold standard, careful, continued validation work will be required to solidify the PAS-O factor structure for outpatient screening and to explore utility for additional inpatient and correctional settings in which high-stakes screening is useful. As a whole, the PAS-O is recommended for outpatient screening purposes at this time for 10 areas of clinical problems common to the PAS and PAI.

REVIEWER'S REFERENCE

Cronbach, L. J., & Gleser, G. C. (1953). Assessing similarity between profiles. *Psychological Bulletin, 50*(6), 456-473.

[120]

Physiological Screening Test.

Purpose: Designed for athletic trainers and sports dieticians to use with collegiate athletes to identify those who may be at risk for eating disorders or disordered eating.
Population: Female collegiate athletes.
Publication Date: 2010.
Acronym: PST.
Scores: OK versus Eating Disorder/Disordered Eating.
Administration: Individual.
Price Data, 2020: $39.95 per manual (2010, 116 pages) and CD; scoring conducted by the authors for an additional fee.
Time: (15-20) minutes.
Comments: Title on test form is Physiologic Aspects of Eating Behaviors Questionnaire; developed "for those with a physiological background and who have less or no familiarity with psychological principles (or the DSM manuals) and have not been trained accordingly; Athletic Milieu Direct Questionnaire (see 12, this volume) is a companion test for sport psychologists.
Authors: David R. Black, Larry J. Leverenz, Daniel C. Coster, Laurie J. Larkin, and Rachel A. Clark.
Publisher: Healthy Learning.

Review of the Physiological Screening Test by JAMES P. DONNELLY, Professor, Department of Counseling & Human Services, Director of Measurement & Statistics, Institute for Autism Research, Canisius College, Buffalo, NY:

DESCRIPTION. The Physiological Screening Test (PST) was developed to provide a screening level assessment of the likelihood of an eating disorder or disordered eating (ED/DE) in female college athletes between the ages of 18 and 25. The test has 25 items, including four demographic questions, six self-report items, seven physical measurements, and eight interview questions. Because of the physical measures (e.g., blood pressure), screening must be completed by a trained professional (e.g., athletic trainer). The test takes 15-20 minutes to administer with an estimated reading level of eighth grade. Scores are entered into an Excel spreadsheet and sent via postal mail or email to one of the test developers, who scores the measure and returns the spreadsheet with results classifying the cases in terms of probability of ED, DE, or "OK." Scoring is said to take 7-10 days and includes a fee (amount unspecified but described as "minimal"; manual, p. 30). The test manual includes two CDs, one with the measure and spreadsheet, the other with a video describing test development and procedures for conducting a screening. The test manual and related documentation (e.g., National Athletic Trainers Association position statement on eating disorders in athletes; Bonci et al., 2008) emphasize that the test provides initial screening, not diagnosis.

DEVELOPMENT. The test manual provides an overview of clinical issues, sample protocols for comprehensive care, and guidance on test administration. Test development is described in an article by Black, Larkin, Coster, Leverenz, and Abood (2003). The test developers indicated that their goal was to meet the need for a screening test for eating disorders specifically for female collegiate athletes. Further, they sought to provide a measure that would incorporate self-report, interview, and physical measurements in part to reduce bias due to reliance strictly on self-report as is true in many alternative measures. Content for the items was derived from relevant literature, including physiological models of eating disorders to inform choice of physical measures, and experts who provided input on items as well as review of the initial measure.

The initial set of 44 items was included in a battery with two comparison measures, the Eating Disorders Inventory-2 (EDI-2) and the Bulimia Test-Revised (BT-R) along with the criterion measure, a clinical interview (Eating Disorder Examination). Participants included 148 NCAA Division I athletes in nine sports and three related activities (two forms of dance and cheerleading). Item analysis included t-test comparison of item means by the dichotomous criterion of Eating Disordered/Disordered Eating (ED/DE) or not based on the Eating Disorder Examination outcome, item-total correlations, alpha coefficients, and discriminant function analysis.

TECHNICAL. The sample was described as female athletes in various sports enrolled in a large Midwestern university with an average age of about 20 years. Physical measurements such as height and weight were listed, but no other demographic information was reported. The test authors noted that generalizability would be enhanced by a replication study with a nationally representative sample of Division I, II, and III athletes, but no such replication seems to have been completed in the nearly two decades since publication. It is unclear whether the statistical model derived from the development sample remains the basis of scoring and classification.

Test-retest reliability was reported to be .85 after a 2-week interval with a convenience sample of 45 female athletes, including a mixed group of college and high school participants. Internal consistency reliability was estimated in the process of item analysis, but no overall internal consistency or other reliability estimate of the final measure total score was reported by Black et al. (2003) nor included in the test manual.

The Eating Disorder Examination was used to classify participants according to diagnostic categories of the *Diagnostic and Statistical Manual of Mental Disorders (DSM*; 3rd ed., rev.; 4th ed.; American Psychiatric Association, 1987, 1994), which comprised the Eating Disordered (ED) group. Disordered Eating (DE) was coded by the presence of two major and two minor criteria from diagnostic categories (e.g., fear of weight gain in anorexia, purging episodes in bulimia). The ED and DE codes were used to contrast with non-ED/DE participants classified as "OK." These codes were then used to compare the PST with the EDI-2 and BT-R results on nine indicators of test accuracy (sensitivity, specificity, false positive rate, false negative rate, positive predictive value, negative predictive value, yield, accuracy, and validity—a combination of sensitivity and specificity). The PST values exceeded the other two tests on seven of the nine indicators, including sensitivity (86.5) and specificity (77.7).

COMMENTARY. The PST has several strong features, including the multimethod assessment model, the specificity of the purpose, relatively quick administration, the initial indicators of screening efficacy relative to other tests, and the potential to be an effective component of a comprehensive program of prevention and treatment. Several limitations are apparent as well. Psychometric limitations include minimal reliability estimation and reliance on the original sample for item analysis as well as estimates of validity. Black et al. (2003) noted that other screening options exist if qualified test administrators are not available, including a test developed by several of the same investigators (the Athletic Milieu Direct Questionnaire; AMDQ; Nagel, Black, Leverenz, & Coster, 2000; see 12, this volume). Black et al. (2003) suggested that a second screening of an athlete with the AMDQ would be advantageous. This may be true, but there are no published studies testing this procedure. Further, based on comparison of sample characteristics in the two measures, it appears that the same participants were used in the development of both the PST and the AMDQ, a point that, if true, further underlines the importance of replication. Replication would be very valuable not only to provide some measure of confidence in the measure's psychometric properties and possible revision of items, but also because the criterion measure and *DSM* have been revised in the interim, as have standards for test development and reporting (American Educational Research Association, American Psychological Association, & National Council on Measurement in Education, 2014). In addition to replication, there appears to be an opportunity to analyze precision of measurement (i.e., standard errors and confidence intervals) because a single statistician has been conducting all scoring of the measure since its inception and may have accumulated a substantial database. Further, in the interim since the original scale development, web-based scoring has become widely utilized. Practical advantages of this approach would include reduced time in scoring and follow-up with student athletes. Providing immediate feedback while in the presence of the student athlete might significantly enhance the likelihood that next steps in assessment would be completed as soon as possible. In situations that include the potential for such serious health conditions, efficiency of care protocols is clearly important.

SUMMARY. The Physiological Screening Test provides screening for the likely presence of eating disorders in female college athletes, a population in which problematic eating behavior may be more likely than students in general. The test must be administered by someone trained to obtain physical measures such as an athletic trainer, and it is scored via submission of a spreadsheet to a statistician who was a developer of the test. Replication was recommended by the test developers and would be most valuable in providing additional reliability and validity estimates and perhaps greater precision. Despite the absence of replication and other limitations noted, the PST can be used as a screening instrument by an appropriately trained professional in the context of a comprehensive program such as the one recommended by the National Athletic Trainers Association to provide early identification and treatment of a very significant behavioral health issue in female athletes.

REVIEWER'S REFERENCES

American Educational Research Association, American Psychological Association, & National Council on Measurement in Education. (2014). *Standards for educational and psychological testing.* Washington, DC: American Educational Research Association.

American Psychiatric Association. (1987). *Diagnostic and statistical manual of mental disorders* (3rd ed., rev.). Washington, DC: Author.

American Psychiatric Association. (1994). *Diagnostic and statistical manual of mental disorders* (4th ed.). Washington, DC: Author.

Black, D. R., Larkin, L. J. S., Coster, D. C., Leverenz, L. J., & Abood, D. A. (2003). Physiologic Screening Test for eating disorders/disordered eating among female collegiate athletes. *Journal of Athletic Training, 38,* 286-297.

Bonci, C. M., Bonci, L. J., Granger, L. R., Johnson, C. L., Malina, R. M., Milne, L. W., ... Vanderbunt, E. M. (2008). National Athletic Trainers' Association position statement: Preventing, detecting, and managing disordered eating in athletes. *Journal of Athletic Training, 43,* 80-108.

Nagel, D. L., Black, D. R., Leverenz, L. J., & Coster, D. C. (2000). Evaluation of a screening test for female college athletes with eating disorders and disordered eating. *Journal of Athletic Training, 35,* 431-440.

Review of the Physiological Screening Test by FRANCIS STASKON, Senior Analyst, Walgreen Co., Deerfield, IL:

DESCRIPTION. The Physiological Screening Test (PST) is an instrument designed for detecting eating disorder/disordered eating (ED/DE) among female athletes between the ages of 18 and 25. The test authors suggest it is possible to detect these disorders early and to provide a clinical intervention, thereby reducing possible harmful consequences. The test authors recommend that testing be repeated after a couple of weeks to help identify false negatives and false positives. Eating disorders is operationalized in the test manual according to the *Diagnostic and Statistical Manual of Mental Disorders* (4th ed., text rev.; *DSM-IV-TR;* American Psychiatric Association [APA], 2000), as is the concept of disordered eating. The test manual includes a CD-ROM containing printable copies of the PST, the full manual, and an Excel file formatted for data entry of results per test taker; also, a DVD includes videos explaining the PST, demonstrating administration of physical measures in the test, and coverage of related literature.

The PST is designed to be administered individually by trained personnel. It contains 25 items (four demographic items, six questionnaire items, seven physical measures, and eight interview questions). A total score is generated from the responses to 22 items, representing 13 variables proposed to distinguish ED, DE, and OK ("okay") patient types. The physiologic terms address signs and symptoms of dizziness, abdominal bloating, abdominal pain/cramps, frequency of bowel movement, stool consistency, and regularity of menstrual cycle. Responses are based on rating scales (with 3, 5, or 6 categories). Skinfold measures are taken at four locations (triceps, abdomen, suprailium, and thigh) in 0.2mm units, repeated three times per site. Another set of measures is required for calculating a waist-to-hip ratio; and a set of questions is included regarding exercise, parotid gland size, menstrual history, and weight history with numeric coding. Finally, blood pressure is taken in two positions (supine and standing) for detecting orthostatic hypotension. The administration manual states that the PST is at an eighth-grade reading level with total time to complete of no more than 20 minutes.

A total score interpretation is based on assigned posterior probability values that represent the likelihood that a given score designates the athlete with a possible eating disorder as compared to the calibration data (i.e., other screened athletes from convenience samples). Scores that have a posterior probability higher than 50% for the given category designate the category of the screening result (OK or ED/DE). The assessor has the option to adjust judgments on fractional scores around the 50th percentile in either direction. The assessor also has the option to create customized cutoff values depending upon the characteristics of the given case. An additional interpretation is suggested for distinguishing ED from DE as well as OK. A posterior probability is provided per subcategory. Probabilities are independent and sum to one. The subcategory assigned (ED or DE) is based on the category with the highest score probability value, which may be less than 50%, and these types could be summed to designate the screening as indicating *not OK* if posterior probabilities are all the same value. A posterior probability calculator is provided with the Excel file on the included CD, or for a non-disclosed fee from contacts listed in the test manual.

No percentile scores are provided, but the test manual includes a section on how one can use a pseudo percentile criterion for a group of athletes screened in a given setting by ranking the probabilities obtained per screening. In addition, one may apply a baseline prevalence rate for percent of participants with a likely eating disorder as the cut-point percentile for the given data. This practice is not endorsed by the test authors, and no other guidance is provided on this unendorsed ranking of athletes per screening pool.

DEVELOPMENT. As stated by Black et al. (2003), eating disorders among female athletes was a growing topic in the literature and drew comment from athletic and sports medicine personnel as an important concern. The test developers proposed that detecting eating disorders with a screener that included physiologic items would be a reliable and valid screening device. Items had content that included physiologic signs and symptoms of eating disorder/disordered eating in athletes based on supporting literature and recommendations from experts. The test developers argue that response bias was minimized in a physiologically based test because some items are reported measurements not easily manipulated or distorted for social desirability. However, no empirical evidence about response bias is provided in the test manual or cited in related publications.

TECHNICAL. A cross-sectional epidemiological study (Black et al., 2003) serves as a convergent validity study for the PST with comparisons to the Eating Disorders Inventory (EDI), the Bulimia Test-Revised (BT-R) screening tests, and the Eating Disorder Examination (EDE) structured interview. Sport, club, and dance athletes (N = 148) from 12 different teams from a Midwestern university attended two sessions to complete the measures. Scores on the EDI, BT-R, and PST were compared to the EDE classifications using a discriminant analysis. Item analysis required an alpha coefficient of at least .60 and an item-total correlation of at least .40 among items of the same type (e.g., physiologic questions vs. physiologic measures). Six questionnaire items were summed as a subscale in the discriminant function. Discriminant function coefficients did not need to be significant as long as the sign of the coefficient suggested evidence of content validity. General criteria of 80% sensitivity and 75% specificity were used for the final solutions. The test manual presents the sensitivity of the PST to be about 90% and specificity to be about 80%, where false positive rates are at 23%, and false negative rates are around 14%. In Black et al. (2003), yield was at 30.3%, accuracy at 80.7% and validity at 63.9%, with the PST comparing favorably to similar statistics for the EDI and BT-R. Estimated prevalence of ED/DE was at 35%, with twice as many classified as DE rather than ED (Black et al., 2003).

COMMENTARY. The validation of the PST was based on convenience samples with limited demographic variation and location. Joy, Kussman, and Nattiv (2016) report a lower prevalence of eating disorders among female collegiate students at 20%, and a higher prevalence among those in lean sports (25%). Rate differences are influenced not only by a limited validation sample, but also by revisions of eating disorder diagnoses in *DSM-5* (APA, 2013). Three disorders (avoidant/restrictive food intake disorder, rumination disorder, and pica) have been added, and binge eating disorder is now a formal diagnosis (Smink, van Hoeken, & Hoek, 2013). Given that the PST is based on the prior *DSM* criteria of eating disorders, it is likely that the calculated posterior probabilities to interpret screening results no longer reflect the actual likelihoods of signaling a disorder, at least as recognized currently, and leave out possible distinctions among the original ED/DE symptoms.

Another dated aspect of the PST is how obtaining the physiologic measures is standardized in a protocol that requires manual measurements and assessor training. There is now widespread use of digital instruments, cell phone apps, and wearable devices from which such measurements may be obtained. The test manual states blood pressure should be in accordance with American Heart Association (AHA) procedures. However, AHA recommendations were revised in 2019 (Muntner et al., 2019), addressing not only changes in diagnostic values but also the many new methods for taking blood pressure. In addition, there have yet to be established measurement standards of orthostatic vital signs for detecting orthostatic hypotension, where a clinical review established significant variations in practice (Emergency Nurses Association, 2015).

The PST gained some recognition and recommendation for screening American female athletes for eating disorders (Wagner, Erickson, Tierney, Houston, & Welch Bacon, 2016). However, the PST was not included along with other screeners in the National Athletic Trainers' Association (Bonci et al., 2008) position statement, nor the American College of Sports Medicine "female athlete triad" position statement (Nattiv et al., 2007). Finally, the PST does not appear to have much in the way of validation studies beyond the initial reliability and validity evidence presented in Black et al. (2003) and the test manual. The convenience sample of Midwestern university students and convergent comparisons with dated measures (all based on *DSM-III-R* and *DSM-IV* taxonomy) lead to concerns about the validity and utility of PST scores, given the cost of training for individually based assessments. Newer approaches have established online or app screening with updated criteria (Fitzsimmons-Craft et al., 2019). [Editor's note: The test authors report a participation rate of 84.5% of the university's eligible female athletes. They note that they attempted a census of all athletes but were advised some would not participate out of concern over losing scholarships or eligibility if their participation indicated an at-risk status.]

SUMMARY. In general, eating disorders have a detrimental effect on sport performance, mainly by negatively impacting qualities of muscular fitness (i.e., aerobic, musculoskeletal, flexibility, and motor), that are not completely restored with nutritional rehabilitation and weight regain (El Ghoch, Soave, Calugi, & Dalle Grave, 2013). Screeners such as the PST can aid in the detection of eating disorders. However, the field has developed since the creation of the PST, which was validated on a relatively small and demographically limited sample and with convergent measures derived from taxonomies from earlier editions of the *DSM*. The initial promise of this screener should be revived by addressing changes in diagnostic categories and advances in digital technology and by conducting a more robust validation study to address possible cultural influences.

REVIEWER'S REFERENCES

American Psychiatric Association. (2013). *Diagnostic and statistical manual of mental disorders.* (5th ed.). Washington, DC: Author.

American Psychiatric Association. (2000). *Diagnostic and statistical manual of mental disorders.* (4th ed., text rev.). Washington, DC: Author.

Black, D. R., Larkin, L. J. S., Coster, D. C., Leverenz, L. J., & Abood, D. A. (2003). Physiologic Screening Test for eating disorders/disordered eating among female collegiate athletes. *Journal of Athletic Training, 38,* 286-297.

Bonci, C. M., Bonci, L. J., Granger, L. R., Johnson, C. L., Malina, R. M., Milne, L. W., ... Vanderbunt, E. M. (2008). National Athletic Trainers' Association position statement: Preventing, detecting, and managing disordered eating in athletes. *Journal of Athletic Training, 43,* 80-108.

El Ghoch, M. E., Soave, F., Calugi, S., & Grave, R. (2013). Eating disorders, physical fitness and sport performance: A systematic review. *Nutrients, 5,* 5140-5160. doi:10.3390/nu5125140

Emergency Nurses Association Clinical Practice Guidelines Committee (2015). Clinical practice guidelines: Orthostatic vital signs. Retrieved from https://www.ena.org/practice-resources/resource-library/clinical-practice-guidelines

Fitzsimmons-Craft, E. E., Firebaugh, M., Graham, A. K., Eichen, D. M., Monterubio, G. E., Balantekin, K. N., ... Wilfley, D. E. (2019). State-wide university implementation of an online platform for eating disorders screening and intervention. *Psychological Services, 16*(2), 239-249.

Joy, E., Kussman, A., & Nattiv, A. (2016). 2016 update on eating disorders in athletes: A comprehensive narrative review with a focus on clinical assessment and management. *British Journal of Sports Medicine, 50,* 154-162. doi:10.1136/bjsports-2015-095735

Muntner, P., Shimbo, D., Carey, R. M., Charleston, J. B., Gaillard, T., ... Wright, J. T., Jr. (2019). Measurement of blood pressure in humans: A scientific statement from the American Heart Association. *Hypertension, 75,* e35-e66.

Nattiv, A., Loucks, A. B., Manore, M. M., Sanborn, C. F., Sundgot-Borgen, J., & Warren, M. P. (2007). The female athlete triad. *Medicine & Science in Sports & Exercise, 39,* 1867-1882. doi:10.1249/mss.0b013e318149f111

Smink, F. R. E., van Hoeken, D., & Hoek, H. W. (2013). Epidemiology, course, and outcome of eating disorders. *Current Opinion in Psychiatry, 26,* 543–548. doi:10.1097/YCO.0b013e328365a24f

Wagner, A. J., Erickson, C. D., Tierney, D. K., Houston, M. N., & Welch Bacon, C. E. (2016). The diagnostic accuracy of screening tools to detect eating disorders in female athletes. *Journal of Sport Rehabilitation, 25,* 395-398. doi:10.1123/jsr.2014-0337

[121]

Picture Interest Career Survey, Second Edition.

Purpose: Designed as a "language-free, self-report vocational interest inventory."

Population: Ages 10-65.

Publication Dates: 2007-2011.

Acronym: PICS-2.

Scores, 6: Realistic, Investigative, Artistic, Social, Enterprising, Conventional.

Administration: Individual or group.

Price Data, 2020: $66.95 per 25 surveys; administrator's guide (2011, 18 pages) may be downloaded at no charge.

Time: [15] minutes.

Comments: Self-administered, self-scored, and self-interpreted.

Author: Robert P. Brady.

Publisher: JIST Career Solutions, a division of Kendall Hunt.

Cross References: For reviews by Sheri Bauman and Julia Y. Porter of the original edition, see 18:94.

Review of the Picture Interest Career Survey, Second Edition by JAMES ATHANASOU, Associate Professor, University of Sydney, Maroubra, New South Wales, Australia:

DESCRIPTION. The Picture Interest Career Survey, 2nd edition (PICS-2) is offered in the tradition of reading-free vocational interest inventories. This assessment of activity preferences can be administered to individuals or groups and is suitable for a wide age range from adolescents onward. It is suitable for non-readers with some explanation and assistance. The stated aim of PICS-2 is to provide a basis for exploring careers.

The inventory comprises 36 items that each include choosing among pictures of people in three work environments. These pictures are activities and do not necessarily represent specific occupations. Users are asked to circle the picture that is most interesting to them. Each choice is classified into one of Holland's (1997) six vocational interest types, namely Realistic (R), Investigative (I), Artistic (A),

Social (S), Enterprising (E), and Conventional (C). Scores on each category can range from 0 to 18. One's overall occupational interest is then derived as a code that comprises the three highest interest scores. Occupations consistent with the highest letter or highest two letters are listed in the separate *PICS Career Locator*, which is found on the test publisher's website. Users also may access other major career resources, such as those from the U.S. Occupational Information Network (O*NET).

DEVELOPMENT. The PICS-2 is an ipsative assessment of interests and takes advantage of a format that separates vocational preferences. As such, it embodies the idea that preferences are relative and involve a choice from alternatives—albeit imperfect and constrained (Kuder, 1977). It contrasts with the modern *zeitgeist* of summative Likert ratings or checklists of individual items (Athanasou, 2011). Regrettably, the administrator's guide contains only partial information on how the test was developed, although to be fair it builds upon the experience of the earlier 2007 edition.

TECHNICAL. The administrator's guide provides considerable validity data mainly in the form of a congruence index developed for the Holland classification of vocational interests. Concurrent evidence of validity is the clear focus. Data are provided from adult vocational rehabilitation clients, and the results from the PICS-2 compare favorably with a person's present or most recent occupation.

The potential influence of gender stereotypes in the PICS-2 illustrations were examined by using pictures with opposite gender workers, and results were reported as congruent with current careers. The claim in the administrator's guide that the pictures can be described to those with visual impairments, however, is probably drawing a questionable conclusion and is not supported by any evidence. Content evidence of validity was also evaluated through analysis of the images. All six vocational types are said to be represented equally in the 108 images. To further investigate the content evidence of validity of each picture, the item-total correlation for each picture with its respective scale might be examined in future revisions.

There is no standardization sample with norms for the PICS-2. The measure is presented as an idiographic assessment, but it might still have been relevant to report results from different educational, demographic or occupational groups as a basis for comparison. Although the stated age range is 10-65 years, the administrator's guide refers mainly to adult samples. Interscale correlations should probably have been cited; as the PICS-2 is an ipsative measure, these intercorrelations should average at -1/(m-1) or around -0.2, where m is the number of scales. At present, it appears there are insufficient data to support the scale's use with younger groups.

Concurrent evidence of validity in the form of comparisons with other assessments was not reported. For instance, the equivalence of the PICS-2 to interest inventories such as Holland's Self-Directed Search or Vocational Preference Inventory (see Holland, 1997) or the U.S. Department of Labor's O*NET Interest Profiler (National Center for O*NET Development, n.d.) needs to be established to bolster faith in the value of PICS-2 as a substitute measure.

Alternate-form reliability was evaluated by comparing the first and second editions of the PICS. The median Spearman rank-order correlation was an impressive .94 with one group of working adults (N = 34) and .92 for a larger group of students (N = 92). Test-retest stability was not evaluated.

COMMENTARY. The administration of the PICS-2 is very simple. Scoring is intended to be completed by the user but might be complex for some individuals who are not familiar with paper-and-pencil assessments. There are descriptions of the six Holland types on the last page of the assessment booklet to aid interpretation, but some guidance is still probably needed. The user is also encouraged to list all six Holland codes in order from highest to lowest and to focus on "the three highest scored interest areas," but the accompanying career locator lists only one-letter or two-letter combinations. To be fair, the three-letter codes would find application in other career resources.

True use of the Holland vocational typology should also take into account factors such as (a) the differentiation of the profile of scores across the six categories (whether there are clear peaks in interests), (b) the consistency of the three highest interests in terms of the Holland hexagonal typology (whether the highest scores are adjacent, alternate, or opposite on the hexagon), (c) congruence with educational or vocational situations, and (d) one's identity (or clarity of vocational decidedness, situation, and exploration). Accordingly, this reviewer considers that interpretation is best left to professional users rather than laypersons as it is not merely a matter of looking at the highest score(s).

Finally, it is not an easy task to present interest items in a visual format, and a number of drawings may be difficult for users to interpret. Indeed, several pictures may even require the user to read some words in order to make meaning of the picture.

SUMMARY. Notwithstanding the observations presented in this review, the PICS-2 fills a gap in interest assessment. Whereas reading-free measures have been used mainly with special needs groups in the past, the PICS-2 is also designed for a general population. It is presented in a colorful and easy-to-use format that meets the goal stated on the cover of the test booklet, namely: "The Picture Interest Career Survey (PICS) is a quick, visual way for you to identify your occupational interest areas. You can then use your PICS results to explore careers that match those interests." The PICS-2 offers users an alternative approach to assessing the Holland vocational interest typology and allows them to access databases on occupations that are coded according to the RIASEC types. It will find greatest application in vocational counseling and vocational rehabilitation settings where many standardized inventories are complex, time consuming, and lacking in face validity or relevance for client groups. The PICS-2 will find application in place of paper-and-pencil measures of interest that rely upon reading, and for this reason, further development and enhancement are encouraged.

REVIEWER'S REFERENCES

Athanasou, J. A. (2011). Advantages and disadvantages of the different inventoried approaches to assessing career interests. *Australian Journal of Career Development, 20*(1), 53-62.

Holland, J. L. (1997). *Making vocational choices: A theory of vocational personalities and work environments* (3rd ed.). Odessa, FL: Psychological Assessment Resources.

Kuder, G. F. (1977). *Activity interests and occupational choice*. Chicago, IL: Science Research Associates.

National Center for O*NET Development. (n.d.). O*NET Interest Profiler. *O*NET Resource Center*. Retrieved from https://www.onetcenter.org/IP.html#overview

Review of the Picture Interest Career Survey, Second Edition by ZANDRA S. GRATZ, Professor of Psychology, Kean University, Union, NJ:

DESCRIPTION. As reported in the administrator's guide (manual), the Picture Interest Career Survey, 2nd Edition (PICS-2) is a self-report interest inventory that captures interests relative to Holland's (1959) themes (Realistic, Investigative, Artistic, Social, Enterprising, and Conventional (RIASEC). It is recommended for ages 10 to 65 and is reported to be language free. PICS-2 comprises 36 forced-choice items; each item includes three pictures that were developed to represent general work activities rather than specific occupations. The survey was designed to "help users discover what kinds of work they want to do and in what setting" (manual, p. 9). Across items, 18 pictures depict each RIASEC theme; pictures equally include activities involving people, data, things, and ideas. The PICS-2 may be administered individually or in group settings.

For each item, respondents are instructed to circle the picture they find most interesting. To facilitate scoring, the test booklet is arranged in such a way that alongside each item is the RIASEC theme associated with each picture. Instructions include generating scores by RIASEC theme, which may then be summed and graphed as well as ordered from highest to lowest.

To aid in interpretation, available online is the *PICS Career Locator* (JIST Works, n.d.) and *PICS Career Planning Worksheet* (JIST Works, 2007). The *Career Locator* lists job titles linked to each RIASEC theme as well as combinations of two themes, so individuals can review listings related to their strongest theme as well as the combination of their two strongest themes. The *Planning Worksheet* is a grid with columns labeled job title, education required, projected earnings, job outlook, my applicable skills, and my next step. Both resources also refer respondents to other web sites such as the *Occupational Outlook Handbook* (Bureau of Labor Statistics, U.S. Department of Labor, 2017).

DEVELOPMENT. Sparse information is reported as to the development of the original PICS and therefore the development of PICS-2. As noted in the manual, the focus of PICS-2 is on Holland's themes. The manual indicates that the PICS began with two research versions, each with gender-specific pictures. High congruence was reported between versions, regardless of the test taker's gender, and based on these results, one form was developed with depictions of varied genders. The manual also indicates high congruence was found between the PICS and current career "regardless of ethnic, racial, cultural or age differences" (manual, p. 14). However no data are presented to support this conclusion. As noted in the manual, based on feedback relative to the original PICS, five items were edited for PICS-2; neither the specific items nor the nature of the revisions was identified.

TECHNICAL. Presented in the manual are summaries of 12 studies completed for the original PICS. As noted in a prior review, although supportive results were achieved relative to reliability and validity, the sample sizes were too small to be persuasive (Porter, 2010). An additional five studies listed in the manual were conducted between the publication of PICS and PICS-2. Across these studies, support for concurrent criterion evidence of validity of PICS was noted. However, as before, these studies were based on small samples (244 across all studies) and involved the original PICS. Thus, as before, the extent to which these studies may be used as evidence of the efficacy of PICS-2 is not clear.

Content validation of PICS-2 follows that of PICS in that it follows Holland's themes and theory of career choice. New to this version was the revision of five items; according to the test manual, three judges with backgrounds in "either career assessment, counseling psychology, or career development" (manual, p. 9) agreed that the new items were appropriate replacements for the original items. As already noted, no details regarding the revisions were provided; specific information relative to the credentials of the judges also was not provided.

Concurrent criterion evidence of validity of PICS-2 is based on two studies, one with 35 employed adults and the other with 92 vocational/technical students. Each study reported congruence between participants' three top PICS-2 themes and that of their work or training environment. Alternate-form reliability was estimated by administering PICS and PIC-2. Limited information is presented regarding how the study was conducted, but it appears both forms were completed in one session. Given the similar sample sizes, the study may have involved the same participants as those in the concurrent criterion evidence of validity studies. Themes were rank ordered, and Spearman's rho was computed; coefficients were large (.92 for the student group and .94 for the group of working adults) and support the equivalency of the forms. No evidence of stability over time was offered.

The manual cites studies that depict the universality of personality and Holland's codes (e.g., Holland, 1992; McCrae and Costa, 1997). However, no data are offered to support the universality of PICS-2 data by any dimension, including gender, age, or race.

COMMENTARY. The PICS-2 is relatively easy to administer and score. The manual offers an effective depiction of Holland's themes and provides references for those who wish to learn more. Studies of the PICS-2 are limited. Although studies suggest that the original PICS and PICS-2 are equivalent, the applicability of research using the original PICS to that of PICS-2 is not clear.

Although considered a measure that requires no reading, some item choices have words within the drawings. For example, some illustrations of people sitting at desks have identifying words written on the office doors. Being able to read the words may be necessary to determine the appropriate work setting and therefore Holland's theme attribution.

Also of concern, the manual suggests that the test is appropriate for persons ages 10 to 65, but no data are reported for persons younger than 16. Beyond this limitation, only overall age and gender numbers were reported for studies using the PICS-2. Information on other variables, such as race, are needed. Also, no studies were reported comparing PICS-2 performance by any demographic variable, including age, race, or gender.

Congruence measures across theme scores were used to generate concurrent evidence of validity, which may inflate some of the results reported. Congruence scores do not reflect actual scores; rather, they are based on the three highest-rated themes. The actual scores within each theme may vary (see Arnold, 2004). That is, persons with the same three-letter code may have different absolute scores on each theme. Providing information relative to the score ranges among those designated by each theme may prove useful. Also, the *PICS Career Locator* lists jobs and education by individual theme and top two themes; studies of congruence are based on top three themes.

No data are presented relative to the distribution of persons across themes. That is, the number of persons whose high score falls within each theme, based on PICS-2, is not offered, nor is it provided for any combination of themes; thus it is not clear the extent to which the research samples reflect persons across all six RIASEC codes.

SUMMARY. If the test user's goal is to help clients identify their Holland's theme typology, PICS-2 has the potential to be helpful. However, more and expanded research relative to the reliability and validity of PICS-2 results is necessary. In so doing greater description of research methods should be shared and include analysis of reliability and validity by participant demographics such as age, gender, and race. Also, research sample information by RIASEC theme may prove helpful. These suggestions may help to establish greater confidence in the efficacy of the PICS-2. For potential users in need of more specific, targeted job/career information, PICS-2 may be of limited benefit. For this purpose, other measures such as the Reading-Free Vocational Interest Inventory: 2 (Becker, 2000) may provide more useful information.

REVIEWER'S REFERENCES

Arnold, J. (2004). The congruence problem in John Holland's theory of vocational decisions. *Journal of Occupational and Organizational Psychology, 77*, 95-113. doi:org/10.1348/096317904322915937

Becker, R. (2000). Reading-Free Vocational Interest Inventory: 2. Columbus, OH: Elbern.

Bureau of Labor Statistics, U.S. Department of Labor. (2017). *Occupation Outlook Handbook*. Retrieved from https://www.bls.gov/ooh

Holland, J. L. (1959). A theory of vocational choice. *Journal of Counseling Psychology, 6*, 35-45.

Holland, J. L. (1992). Making vocational choices: A theory of vocational personalities and work environments. Odessa, FL: Psychological Assessment Resources.

JIST Works. (n.d.). *PICS Career Locator*. Retrieved from https://jist.com/wp-content/uploads/2016/05/pics_career_locator_3.pdf

JIST Works. (2007). *PICS Career Planning Worksheet*. Retrieved from https://jist.com/wp-content/uploads/2016/05/pics-career-planning-worksheet.pdf

McCrae, R. R., & Costa, P. T., Jr. (1997). Personality trait structure as a human universal. *American Psychologist, 52*, 509-516.

Porter, J. (2010). [Test review of the Picture Interest Career Survey]. In R. A. Spies, J. F. Carlson, & K. F. Geisinger (Eds.), *The eighteenth mental measurements yearbook*. Lincoln, NE: Buros Institute of Mental Measurements.

[122]

Piers-Harris Self-Concept Scale, Third Edition.

Purpose: Designed as a "self-reported measure of self-concept (i.e., description and evaluation of one's own behavior and attitudes)."

Population: Ages 6 through 22 years.

Publication Dates: 1969-2018.

Acronym: Piers-Harris 3.

Scores, 9: Behavioral Adjustment, Freedom From Anxiety, Happiness and Satisfaction, Intellectual and School Status, Physical Appearance and Attributes, Social Acceptance, Total, plus 2 validity scales (Response Bias, Inconsistent Responding).

Administration: Individual.

Price Data, 2020: $164 per kit (print or online), including manual (2018, 91 pages) and 25 forms or online uses; $89 per manual (print or digital); $75 per 25 print forms or online uses.

Foreign Language Edition: Form available in Spanish.

Time: 10-15 minutes for administration.

Comments: Administered and scored online or via printed form.

Authors: Ellen V. Piers (scale and manual), Dale B. Harris (scale), Shirag K. Shemmassian (scale and manual), and David S. Herzberg (scale and manual).

Publisher: Western Psychological Services.

Cross References: For reviews by Mary Lou Kelley and Donald P. Oswald of the previous edition titled Piers-Harris Children's Self-Concept Scale, Second Edition, see 16:188; see also T5:1991 (108 references) and T4:2030 (123 references); for reviews by Jayne H. Epstein and Patrick J. Jeske of an earlier edition, see 9:960 (38 references); see also T3:1831 (107 references), 8:646 (95 references); and T2:1326 (10 references); for a review by Peter M. Bentler of the original edition, see 7:124 (8 references).

Review of the Piers-Harris Self-Concept Scale, Third Edition by CHRISTOPHER A. SINK, Professor and Batten Chair, Counseling and Human Services, MELANIE BURGESS, PhD Counseling Student, and DANIELLE WINTERS, PhD Counseling Student, Old Dominion University, Norfolk, VA:

DESCRIPTION. The self-report 58-item Piers-Harris Self-Concept Scale, Third Edition (Piers-Harris 3) is an update of an earlier version (Piers-Harris 2) that estimates total self-concept and six related domains: Behavioral Adjustment (BEH), Freedom From Anxiety (FRE), Happiness and Satisfaction (HAP), Intellectual and School Status (INT), Physical Appearance and Attributes (PHY), and Social Acceptance (SOC). The measure, which is untimed, can be administered in 10 to 15 minutes to early elementary-age children through young adults in a variety of settings (e.g., schools, clinics, hospitals, community agencies). The test form is available in both English and Spanish. Items should be understandable to examinees with at least a first-grade reading ability, and for those respondents who may not be able to complete the measure independently, administrators may read aloud the test items.

Besides expanding the age range of possible respondents from 7 to 18 years (Piers-Harris 2) to 6 to 22 years, the Piers-Harris 3 includes other substantial advancements. These include adding new items that address respondents' perceptions of bullying, social isolation, and body image; revising items to enhance readability; and adding online administration and scoring options. The test manual provides updated norms based on a nationally representative standardization sample and further research evidence of the measure's clinical validity with respondents with diagnosable conditions, including attention-deficit/hyperactive disorder (ADHD), autism spectrum disorder (ASD), depressive disorder, eating disorder, specific learning disorder (SLD), and trauma- or stressor-related disorder.

The Piers-Harris 3 can be used alongside other instruments to potentially identify, diagnose, and classify externalizing (e.g., conduct) and internalizing (e.g., depressive, anxiety) disorders. Information gained from the scale typically is used to plan and monitor interventions/treatments related to self-concept, as well as in research studies and program evaluation.

The test manual provides straightforward guidelines for interpreting Total and domain scale T scores (M = 50, SD = 10). The Total T score is understood in one of three ways: (a) no more than 39 reflects a respondent with *very low* to *low* self-concept; (b) scores from 40 to 59 indicate an *average* level of self-concept; and (c) scores 60 or greater suggest a *high* to *very high* general self-concept. T scores for the six domain scales are interpreted as follows: ≤ 39 are in the *low* and *very low* range; 40–55 are average and low average; and ≥ 56 are in the *above average* range. To aid in interpretation, standard errors of measurement are presented for domain scores, and T scores can be converted to percentile ranks. Standard scores and percentile ranks can be plotted on a profile sheet as a way to graphically display respondent information.

To further inform accuracy of score interpretation, the Piers-Harris 3 includes several relevant indices. First, the Response Bias (RES) index is a validation metric to identify respondents with tendencies to agree or disagree with items, regardless of content. This index accounts for the number of positive and negative responses with higher RES scores indicating positive response bias and lower RES scores indicating negative response bias. Second, the Inconsistent Response (INC) index can be used to recognize response patterns that pose a threat to validity, including administrator error in coding responses and respondent issues (e.g., limited rapport with the test administrator, motivation, and understanding of questionnaire items). The test authors address the importance of identifying positive exaggeration in interpretation of scores. Particularly, Total scores more than 1.5 standard deviations above the mean (i.e., ≥ 66) should be interpreted cautiously and may represent social desirability responding or the lack of realistic self-appraisal. Negative exaggeration is relatively rare, especially in children and adolescents.

Test users should have training and experience in the basic principles of psychological and educational assessment, test interpretation, and self-concept.

DEVELOPMENT. Item development for the Piers-Harris 3 began with a survey of a large sample of Piers-Harris 2 users. They suggested possible item revisions or deletion of statements that were outdated or lacked clarity. From this process, the test authors added new items to supplement existing ones, particularly in the social acceptance and physical self-concept domains. Subsequently, the standardization study included a 92-item research form with 15 revised items and 17 new items. Items with the strongest psychometric properties were retained, resulting in the final 58-item form, 62% of which were from the Piers-Harris 2, 19% were revised, and 19% were new. Researchers conducted a confirmatory factor analysis with a sample including more than 1,300 individuals ages 6 to 22, which resulted in an adequate fitting six-factor model.

In addition to the standardized sample, researchers collected data from a clinical sample of 233 individuals with specific learning disorders, attention-deficit/hyperactivity disorder, trauma- or stressor-related disorders, depressive disorder, autism spectrum disorders, and eating disorders. Each clinical sample was compared to a control group of non-clinical cases from the standardization sample, matched on age, gender, and ethnicity. To investigate potential group differences on test scores, MANOVAs were conducted. All but one (trauma- or stressor-related disorders) of these multivariate analyses indicated that Piers-Harris 3 scores were significantly lower in clinical groups compared to their non-clinical control groups. Overall, the authors suggested that individuals with clinical disorders experience lower self-concept compared to their typically developing peers.

TECHNICAL. The test authors reported that Piers-Harris 3 standardization data were representative of the U.S. population in terms of gender, socioeconomic status (i.e., head-of-household education level), race/ethnicity, and geographic region. The standardization sample included more than 1,300 individuals recruited from elementary, middle, and high schools, as well as colleges throughout the United States with consistent distribution across the age range. Individuals with mild disabilities that did not prevent participation in mainstream activities also were included in the sample.

Internal consistency and test-retest reliability are clearly summarized in the test manual. Internal consistency was assessed using alpha coefficients for the Total score and the domain scales. Coefficients for the Total score were excellent, ranging from .90 to .94. Alpha coefficients for the domain scales varied from acceptable to excellent: BEH (.68 to .81), FRE (.75 to .85), HAP (.63 to .85), INT (.72 to .80), PHY (.67 to .82), and SOC (.74 to .84). Test-retest reliability studies were conducted using 129 participants with time intervals ranging from 8 to 15 days and averaging 1.5 weeks. Adjusted stability coefficients for the Total score were excellent at .96 with an effect size (i.e., standard difference) of .14. Adjusted test-retest coefficients for the domain scales were excellent as well, ranging from .89 to .95 with effect sizes ranging from .01 to .12.

Construct validity evidence was examined using intercorrelations and factor structure. Domain scales demonstrated moderate to strong correlations with the Total score (.61 to .74) and weak to moderate correlations with each other (.24 to .62). Exploratory factor analysis was conducted on the previous version of this instrument, yielding the six dimensions. Researchers conducted a confirmatory factor analysis on the Piers-Harris 3 using both the standardization sample and the clinical sample to determining whether the data fit the hypothesized six-factor structure. A chi-square difference test determined that the six-factor model significantly improved model fit in comparison to a one-factor model. Next, researchers analyzed the level of equivalence between the Piers-Harris 3 and the Piers-Harris 2. Effect sizes (*d*) ranged from .04 to .31, and corrected correlation coefficients ranged from .82 to .98, suggesting measurement equivalence between the two instruments. Additionally, researchers examined correlations between the Piers-Harris 3 and the Tennessee Self-Concept Scale, Second Edition (TSCS:2) with a sample of 34 individuals independent from the standardization sample. Total scores on the Piers-Harris 3 and TSCS:2 correlated at .73. Anticipated correlations were moderate to moderately strong, with most correlations ranging from the .60s to .70s. Lastly, the Piers-Harris 3 was examined in relation to the Risk Inventory and Strengths Evaluation (RISE) with a subset of 47 participants from the standardization sample. Total scores on the Piers-Harris 3 and the RISE correlated at .68. All theoretically anticipated correlations were moderate, with most correlation coefficients ranging from the .40s to .60s. Divergent evidence of validity was demonstrated through positive self-concept Piers-Harris 3 scores correlating negatively with RISE subscales that represent conceptual opposites. Most correlation coefficients ranged from the -.30s to -.60s.

COMMENTARY. The Piers-Harris 3, like its predecessor, is a relatively brief, easy to score (by hand or electronically) measure for assessing self-concept and related domains in children, adolescents, and young adults. Because of its strong psychometric properties, the measure is informative for human services professionals (e.g., teachers, school counselors, educational psychologists, mental health clinicians) to screen English or Spanish-speaking respondents for potential behavioral and emotional problems associated with low self-concept. With appropriate caution and skill, the test also can be used as a diagnostic tool, particularly when practitioners want to assess students or clients at risk for various disorders (e.g., ADHD, ASD, SLD). In this diagnostic function, the Piers-Harris 3 should be administered with other relevant and validated instruments. Relatedly, Piers-Harris 3 findings can be used in clinical practice efficacy studies and program evaluations. To obtain a more nuanced view of examinees' self-concept and to augment the interpretation of total self-concept score, administrators should analyze respondents' domain-specific standard scores and percentile ranks.

The test manual is well organized, understandable, and provides numerous practical examples to assist practitioners with the assessment process and score interpretation. Validity and reliability information is adequately summarized, giving users assurance that the measure is appropriate for multiple settings and client groups. The standardization sample is comprehensive and representative of children and youth in North America. The use of the Piers-Harris 3 in varying cultural and linguistic contexts must be undertaken with appropriate caution.

SUMMARY. The Piers-Harris 3 is an expedient and well-constructed screening measure that appraises total self-concept and six related domains, including Behavioral Adjustment, Freedom From Anxiety, Happiness and Satisfaction, Intellectual and School Status, Physical Appearance and Attributes, and Social Acceptance. Moreover, when used in conjunction with other tests, the Piers-Harris 3 has diagnostic value for appraising respondents for possible disorders (e.g., ASD, ADHD). The self-report questionnaire is brief, easy-to-score, and flexible in its applicability. It can be administered in school, clinical, and other settings with respondents ranging in age from 6 to 22. The measure is psychometrically sound, with the test manual providing sufficient evidence for the reliability and validity of scores. Finally, the Piers-Harris 3 can be deployed as an outcome variable in research studies and program evaluations.

Review of the Piers-Harris Self-Concept Scale, Third Edition by CLAUDIA R. WRIGHT, Professor Emerita, California State University, Long Beach, Long Beach, CA:

DESCRIPTION. The Piers-Harris Self-Concept Scale, Third Edition (Piers-Harris 3) is a newly revised 58-item self-report measure of behaviors and attitudes designed for children, adolescents, and young adults (ages 6 through 22). As with previous versions, the Piers-Harris 3 rests on the premise that self-concept is a multidimensional construct from which six domain scales have been derived: Behavioral Adjustment (BEH, 10 items); Freedom from Anxiety (FRE, eight items); Happiness and Satisfaction (HAP, 11 items); Intellectual and School Status (INT, 12 items); Physical Appearance and Attributes (PHY, six items); and Social Acceptance (SOC, 11 items). The sum of the six domain scales yields a total score (TOT, 58 items) providing an overall estimate of self-concept. Two validity scale scores, Response Bias and Inconsistent Responding, are calculated from selected item comparisons.

The Piers-Harris 3 was developed to address criticisms pertaining to items shared across domain scales affecting the reliability and validity of test scores (Piers-Harris 2; see 16:188). Data are collected using either paper forms or the test publisher's online platform. The Piers-Harris 3 AutoScore (paper) Form offers flexibility for individual or group administration, simplifies the scoring procedure, and organizes responses by domain scales with clear directions for calculating scale scores and plotting profiles. Response options are "Yes" if the item applies to the examinee and "No" if it does not. For each scale, the higher the score, the more positive the examinee's perceived self-concept. Raw scores are converted to normalized T scores (*M* = 50, *SD* = 10) and percentile ranks to facilitate comparisons across domain scales. The test manual provides guidance for interpreting T scores in both table and narrative forms; instructive sample case studies; strategies for answering questions and minimizing distractions; and special directions for examinees with difficulty reading independently at the first-grade level, with visual limitations, or who are more proficient in Spanish and request the Spanish version.

DEVELOPMENT. Preparation for the standardization study involved a review of Piers-Harris 2 items for content, readability, redundancy, and ambiguity resulting in wording changes to 15 items and the addition of 17 new content items (e.g., bullying and social isolation). The 15 revised items were included on the scale along with the originally worded items. They, along with the 17 new items combined with the original 60-item Piers-Harris 2 to create the 92-item form administered to the standardization sample (*N* = 1,373). From these data, 58 items met psychometric criteria and were retained to create the Piers-Harris 3: 36 items (62%) were original Piers-Harris 2 items; 11 items (19%) were revised Piers-Harris 2 items; and 11 items (19%), were new. Names for five of the six domain scales remained the same, and the sixth, Popularity, with added content, was changed to Social Acceptance (SOC).

Examinees were recruited from primary and secondary schools and colleges across the United States: ages 6-22 years; 52.4% female, 47.6% male; 49.5% White, 23.7% Hispanic, 15.9% Black, 4.7% Asian, 6.2% Other; SES (education level for head-of-household), 34.8% held a 4-year college degree or higher, 28.8% some college, 24.2% high school graduate, 12.2%, no high school; Northeast (*n* = 257, 18.7%), South (*n* = 530, 38.6%), Midwest (*n* = 268, 19.5%), West (*n* = 318, 23.2%). The distributions of these potential moderator variables were consistent with U.S. Census data reported over a 5-year period (U.S. Bureau of the Census, 2017). Stratification of norms across moderator variables was rejected, citing small differences with no practical significance.

TECHNICAL. The reliability of Piers-Harris 3 scores was examined using internal consistency estimates of reliability (coefficient alpha), test-retest reliability, and equivalent forms. Alpha coefficients were high for the Total score (.92) for the entire standardization sample and across eight age groupings (range = .90-.94; ages = 6-7, 8-9, 10-11, 12-13, 14-15, 16-17, 18-19, 20-22; *n*s = 151-215). Alpha coefficients for domain scale scores were moderate across age groups: BEH (.75, range .68-.81); FRE (.78, range .75-.85); HAP (.78, range .63-.85); INT (.77, range .72-.80); PHY (.76, range .67-.82); SOC (.80, range .74-.84). For test-retest reliability, a subset of 129 examinees participated in two testing sessions over an interval ranging from 8 to 15 days (*M* = 1.5 weeks). Strong average corrected test-retest correlations and small effect sizes (*d*) for TOT (*r* = .96; average *d* = .14) and the domain scales (*r* = .93, range = .89-.95; average *d* = .07, range = .01-.12) confirmed statistically insignificant changes between the testing sessions. Support was found for the reliability of equivalent forms (paper and electronic versions) for a subset of 93 examinees who completed both versions: TOT (*r* = .96; average *d* = .01) and for the domain scales (*r* = .95, range = .91-.97; average *d* = .02, range = 0.0-0.07).

Evidence of validity for Piers-Harris 3 scores was examined using construct and concurrent validity methods as well as comparisons of clinical and matched-control groups. Regarding construct evidence, interscale correlations revealed moderate correlation coefficients between TOT and domain scale scores (.61-.74) and low to moderate correlation coefficients among domain scales (.24-.62), supporting their independent interpretation. A confirmatory factor analysis of data obtained from two independent samples revealed the predicted six-factor model was a better fit for differentiating among hypothesized dimensions of self-concept than a one-factor model: Standardization sample (N = 1,373): $\chi^2(15)$ = 1,610.77, $p < .001$; Clinical groups (N = 233): $\chi^2(15)$ = 299.80, $p < .001$.

Regarding concurrent evidence, correlations were examined between T scores on the Piers-Harris 3 and on each of two instruments: Tennessee Self-Concept Scale, Second Edition (TSCS:2; see 13:320 for a summary of construct and concurrent validity evidence), a well-known self-concept scale; and the newly developed Risk Inventory and Strengths Evaluation (RISE; Goldstein & Herzberg, 2019; see 140, this volume), designed to assess interpersonal and mental health risks and social-emotional strengths in adolescents and young adults.

Piers-Harris 3 and TSCS:2 were administered to a small, independent sample (N = 34): ages = 7-22, M = 13.9, SD = 4.8; 35.3% female, 64.7% male; White 38.2%, Black 3.2%, 38.2% Hispanic, 20.4% Other; 58.8% a 4-year college degree or higher and 29.5% a high school degree or less. Corrected correlations between T scores for TSCS:2 Total Self Concept and the seven Piers-Harris 3 scales yielded low to moderate concurrence: TOT = .73, BEH = .39, FRE = .63, HAP = .74, INT = .62, PHY = .61, SOC = .68. A similar pattern was observed between Piers-Harris 3 domain subscales and five TSCS:2 self-concept subscales: BEH with Family = .40, HAP with Personal = .67, INT with Academic/Work = .76, PHY with Physical = .63, SOC with Social = .68. Four domain scales loaded on more than one TSCS:2 subscale suggesting conceptual overlap: FRE with Physical = .68, Moral = .55, Personal = .59, Social = .60; HAP with Personal = .67, Physical = .66, Social = .76; PHY with Physical = .63, Moral = .58; SOC with Physical = .76, Moral = .66, Personal = .66, Social = .68.

Concurrent evidence of validity was examined using Piers-Harris 3 and RISE T scores employing a small subset (n = 47) from the standardization sample: ages = 12-20, M = 14.4, SD = 2.0; 55.3% female, 44.7% male; 51.1% White, 29.8% Hispanic, 19.1% Other; 72.3% a 4-year college degree or higher and 12.8% a high school degree or less. RISE contains six Risk subscales and three index scales (RISE Index, Risk Summary Scale, and Strength Summary Scale). Moderate corrected correlation coefficients were obtained between Piers-Harris 3 TOT and RISE Index T scores (.68); and between domain scales and RISE scales and subscales: TOT and Self-Confidence (.58); SOC and Interpersonal Skill (.47); BEH, HAP, and SOC with the Strength Summary Scale (.41, .41, .46, respectively). Divergent validity evidence was observed for the RISE Risk Summary Scale with TOT (-.68), BEH (-.68), FRE (-.53), HAP (-.41); and for RISE Risk subscales: BEH with Eating/Sleeping Problems (-.52) and Bullying/Aggression (-.44); FRE with Eating/Sleeping Problems (-.47) and Suicide/Self-Harm (-.40); and HAP with Suicide/Self-Harm (-.41).

To study the ability of Piers-Harris 3 scores to distinguish between individuals with and without diagnosed clinical disorders (see American Psychiatric Association, 2013), 233 participants were selected based on diagnostic criteria (e.g., current clinical diagnosis and treatment status). Each clinical case was matched on age, gender, and ethnicity to a nonclinical control selected from the standardization sample. Data were analyzed using multivariate analysis of variance (MANOVA) and effect size (d). Six clinical groups were formed with the following findings:

Specific learning disorder (SLD: n = 61, 26.2%; ages = 7-19, M = 11.85, SD = 3.0; 41% female, 59% male; 36.1% White, 34.4% Black, 26.2%, Hispanic, 3.2% Other). For the SLD group, TOT M = 39.1, SD = 9.3 (Control, TOT M = 51.3, SD = 10.8), cohort d comparisons were as predicted: a small d suggested little SLD effect on self-concept for PHY = 0.33; while medium to large ds indicated an SLD effect lowering perception of self-concept in socio-emotional and intellect-school status domains: TOT = 1.22, BEH = 1.13, FRE = 0.63, HAP = 0.77, INT = 1.21, SOC = 0.91.

Attention-deficit/hyperactivity disorder (ADHD: n = 56, 24.0%; ages = 6-22, M = 13.5, SD = 4.5; 33.9% female, 66.1% male; 30.4% White, 48.2% Black, 17.9% Hispanic, 3.6% Other). For the ADHD group, TOT M = 41.3, SD = 10.7 (Control TOT M = 51.1, SD = 9.3), medium to large ds pointed to an ADHD effect lowering perceived self-concept in behavioral, intellect-school status, and social-emotional domains: TOT = 0.97, BEH = 0.78, HAP = 0.83, INT = 0.96, SOC = 0.63.

Trauma- or stressor-related disorders (TSD: *n* = 44, 18.9%; ages = 6-22, *M* = 14.6, *SD* = 3.9; 50% female, 50% male; 15.9% White, 50% Black, 29.5% Hispanic, 4.5% Other); 59.1% diagnosed with post-traumatic stress disorder (PTSD), 40.9% with an adjustment disorder. Overall, for the TSD group, TOT *M* = 41.0, *SD* = 12.6 (Control, TOT *M* = 47.9, *SD* = 11.3), medium *d*s suggested lower perceived self-concept in behavioral, socio-emotional, and intellect-school status: TOT = 0.58, BEH = 0.60, HAP = 0.53, INT = 0.64. SOC = 0.58.

Depressive disorder (*n* = 29, 12.4%; ages 6-18, *M* = 15.1, *SD* = 3.0; 69.0% female, 31% male; 51.7% White, 20.7% Black, 24.1% Hispanic, 3.4% Other); 62.1% diagnosed with major depressive disorder, 24.1% with disruptive mood dysregulation disorder, and 13.8% with persistent depressive disorder. Overall, for the depressive disorder group, TOT *M* = 38.9, *SD* = 13.7 (Control, TOT *M* = 49.8, *SD* = 8.6), medium to large *d*s indicated lower perceived self-concept in socio-emotional, intellect-school status, and body image domains: TOT = 0.95, FRE = 0.78, HAP = 0.72, INT = 0.59., PHY = 0.94, SOC = 0.95.

Autism spectrum disorder (ASD; *n* = 28, 12.0%; ages = 6-22, *M* = 11.3, *SD* = 4.3; 21.4% female, 78.6% male; 82.1% White, 7.1% Black, 3.6% Hispanic, 7.1% Other). For the ASD group, TOT *M* = 42.0, *SD* = 9.4 (Control, TOT *M* = 50.2, *SD* = 9.4), medium to large *d*s indicated lower perceived self-concept in intellect-school status and social acceptance domains: TOT = 0.87, FRE = 0.75, INT = 1.39, SOC = 0.61.

Eating disorders (*n* = 15, 6.4%; ages = 10-20, *M* = 15.6, *SD* = 3.0; 73.3% female, 26.7% male; 46.7% White, 6.7% Black, 20.0% Hispanic, and 26.7% Other); 53.3% diagnosed with anorexia nervosa, 20% binge eating disorder, 13.3% bulimia nervosa, 6.7% avoidant/restrictive food intake disorder, and 6.7% pica. Overall, for the eating disorder group, TOT *M* = 27.4, *SD* = 10.5 (Control, TOT *M* = 45.7, *SD* = 9.8), large *d*s emphasized lower perceived self-concept across behavioral, socio-emotional, and body image domains: TOT = 1.80, BEH = 2.08, FRE = 0.74, HAP = 1.68, INT = 1.09, PHY = 1.48, SOC = 1.37.

COMMENTARY. Caution is warranted in interpreting concurrent validity findings relying on small samples, notably TSCS:2 (*N* = 34) and RISE (*n* = 47), both with proportions of moderator variables differing from the standardization sample. Regarding the Spanish version, because no relevant data were provided in the test manual and because the Piers-Harris 3 is said to be administered worldwide, early publication of current psychometric studies involving the Spanish version is encouraged.

SUMMARY. Concerns raised about the Piers-Harris 2 (see 16:188) have been addressed with the development of the Piers-Harris 3 by expanding the age range, updating norms, and adding new psychometric studies that support test-retest reliability, construct evidence of validity, and concurrent evidence of validity of test scores. Self-concept comparisons between clinical and matched control cohorts offer tentative support for identifying individuals at risk for a variety of disorders (e.g., eating disorders, SLD, and ADHD), and, if employed with multiple data sources, Piers-Harris 3 scores could be useful for monitoring interventions.

REVIEWER'S REFERENCES

American Psychiatric Association. (2013). *Diagnostic and statistical manual of mental disorders* (5th ed.). Washington, DC: Author.

Goldstein, S., & Herzberg, D. S. (2019). Risk Inventory and Strengths Evaluation. Torrance, CA: Western Psychological Services.

U.S. Bureau of the Census. (2017). American Community Survey 5-Year Estimates–Public Use Microdata Sample, 2011-2015. Retrieved from http://dataferrett.census.gov/The DataWeb/index.html

[123]

Porteus Maze Test [2017 Manual Revision].

Purpose: "Designed to examine an individual's ability and tendency to use planning strategies, behavioral inhibition and mental alertness in novel and concrete situations."

Population: Ages 3 and older.

Publication Dates: 1914-2017.

Scores, 3: Test Age, Test Quotient, Qualitative Score.

Administration: Individual.

Forms: 13 mazes.

Price Data, 2020: $160 per test kit including manual (2017, 27 pages), 13 mazes (100 copies of each), and 25 scoring sheets; $30 per manual; $30 per 25 scoring sheets; $30 per 100 maze copies (maze levels sold separately); $27 per test training DVD.

Time: Approximately 5 minutes per maze.

Comments: Mazes, which are from the Vineland Revision, have not changed; manual has been updated.

Author: Stanley D. Porteus.

Publisher: Stoelting Co.

Cross References: See T5:2010 (24 references), T4:2051 (25 references), 9:965 (19 references), T3:1853 (34 references), 8:224 (25 references), and T2:518 (52 references); for reviews by Richard F. Docter and John L. Horn, and excerpted reviews by William D. Altus, H. B. Gibson, D. C. Kendrick, and Laurance F. Shaffer, see 7:419 (67 references); see also 6:532 (38 references) and 5:412 (28 references); for reviews by C. M. Louttit and Gladys C. Schwesinger, see 4:356 (56 references).

Review of the Porteus Maze Test [2017 Manual Revision] by SCOTT A. NAPOLITANO, Associate Professor of Practice, Department of Educational Psychology, University of Nebraska–Lincoln, Lincoln, NE:

DESCRIPTION. The Porteus Maze Test [2017 Manual Revision] is designed to assess planning strategies, behavioral inhibition, decision making and mental alertness in individuals ages 3 and older. The test authors claim that, more recently, the test has been used to examine impulsiveness and features associated with attention-deficit/hyperactivity disorder. Although the test manual was updated in 2017, it does not appear that any changes have been made to the test or the standardization sample since about 1915.

The test materials consist of a series of 13 increasingly difficult mazes that the examinee must complete. A test scoring sheet provides directions for calculating the test scores, and a training DVD provides information related to test development, administration, and interpretation.

Administration of the mazes is not complicated, and the directions for administration are straightforward. The test manual explains three score types: Test Age, Qualitative Score, and Test Quotient. The Qualitative Score is designed to reflect deficits the examinee demonstrates in the skills measured by the test. The Test Quotient is a norm-referenced standard score with a mean of 100 and a standard deviation of 15.

DEVELOPMENT. The Porteus Maze Test was originally developed and standardized in 1914. After some modifications in the scoring procedures, the test was standardized with another sample that extended the age range to include high school students. Current scoring procedures were based on both samples. The test manual does not describe the underlying theoretical framework of the test or what and why changes were made to the new manual. Additionally, there is no discussion of how the mazes were developed originally. The test manual notes that Porteus believed the test "afforded an excellent means of: examining the foresight to anticipate, the mental alertness to [*sic*] needed to plan, and the prudence to deal with new stimuli and situations" (manual, p. 1).

TECHNICAL. The test was originally standardized with a sample of 1,000 children ages 3 to 12 years. The test manual states that after the initial standardization procedure, modifications were made, and the test was administered to an additional 1,255 children in order to extend the age range to 14. Following this procedure, the test was then administered to groups of high school students ages 13 to 19. The test manual states that the test was standardized on a diverse group. However, other than listing some nationalities, no details arc provided.

Limited information concerning reliability is provided in the test manual. A reliability study by Krikorian and Bartok (1998) reported an alpha coefficient of .81. The test authors state that the Porteus Maze Test demonstrates practice effects when administered more than one time. The test manual does not report test-retest data, per se. However, the manual reports that when the test is given a second time, "a portion of the individuals will improve by varying degrees, while others may show little, or no, improvement at all" (manual, p. 6).

The test manual presents limited validity evidence to support the use of the Porteus Maze Test for the purposes stated in the manual. A reference is made to early work by Porteus in the 1910s and 1920s that examined the relationship between social capacity and the test. The test manual reports average correlation coefficients between Porteus Maze Test scores and social capacity were .68 for males and .76 for females. Another area the manual includes as validity evidence is a comparison of Porteus Maze Test scores and industrial ability. A .67 correlation coefficient is reported for males, and a .75 correlation coefficient is reported for females. A study from the 1990s is also cited that reported a correlation coefficient of .38 between scores on the Porteus Maze Test and the Self Ordered Pointing Test. Additionally, the test manual discusses how some research suggests the Porteus Maze Test is useful for measuring executive functioning, visuo-spatial skills, impulse control with drug users, and antisocial personality disorder.

COMMENTARY. The Porteus Maze Test [2017 Manual Revision] is quick and relatively easy to administer and score. Although the test manual is new, there is no description of changes that were made. No specific information regarding the normative sample for the test is reported with the exception of ages, number of individuals in the sample, and a list of seven nationalities that were represented in the sample in some way. This makes it impossible to adequately assess the quality of the sample and the validity of the test for use with specific populations. The test development procedures are not described in detail, nor is the theoretical model supporting the test use. Overall, very limited reliability and validity data are provided. Improved reliability and validity evidence is needed for the Porteus Maze Test [2017 Manual Revision] to be useful for its intended purposes.

SUMMARY. The Porteus Maze Test was designed as a measure of planning, behavioral inhibition, and mental alertness. More recently, including in the 2017 manual revision, the test has been promoted as a measure of executive functioning and attention. The test has some significant weaknesses that limit its usefulness. In terms of test development, there is not an adequate explanation of the theoretical model of the test, nor is there a description of the test development procedures. The norms need to be updated and strengthened significantly, or at the very least, more detailed information regarding the most recent normative sample is needed to properly evaluate the test. Additionally, the test needs to demonstrate improved reliability and validity evidence to make it a psychometrically sound instrument. Unfortunately, with so many serious limitations, the Porteus Maze Test [2017 Manual Revision] cannot be recommended for clinical use at this time.

REVIEWER'S REFERENCE

Krikorian, R., & Bartok, J. A. (1998). Developmental data for the Porteus Maze Test. *The Clinical Neuropsychologist, 12*(3), 305-310.

Review of the Porteus Maze Test [2017 Manual Revision] by NORA M. THOMPSON, Licensed Psychologist, Board Certified–Clinical Neuropsychology, Private Practice–Cascade Neuropsychological Services, Edmonds, WA:

DESCRIPTION. The Porteus Maze Test [2017 Manual Revision] consists of a series of 13 pencil-and-paper mazes that range in difficulty from simple to complex. The test consists of the recently updated 25-page manual (contained in a vinyl report cover with white binding bar), a training DVD, scoring sheets, and pads containing each of the mazes. Examinees are tasked with tracing their way through each maze with a pencil without entering any blocked alleys. The Porteus Maze Test was designed to measure planning and behavioral inhibition in individuals ages 3 years and older. The test is nonverbal; in other words, it is performance based (i.e., pencil and paper) rather than requiring a verbal response. A Test Age score is calculated based on the number of mazes successfully completed, with partial credit given for some mazes completed on a second trial. A standardized score is derived based on the examinee's chronological age and obtained Test Age. A Qualitative Score also can be calculated using weighted error scores derived from a variety of specific types of errors (e.g., crossed line, cut corner).

DEVELOPMENT. The Porteus Maze Test [2017 Manual Revision] is the fourth variant of the original Porteus Maze Test (Porteus, 1959), the others being the Vineland Revision, the Porteus Maze Extension, and the Porteus Maze Supplement (Lezak, Howieson, & Loring, 2004). The mazes contained in the current Porteus Maze Test are taken from the Vineland Revision; only the test manual was updated in 2017.

Unlike previous versions of the test, the Porteus Maze Test [2017 Manual Revision] imposes a time limit of 5 minutes per maze, although the examinee is not informed of this detail. Also, the moment an error is made, the examinee is stopped, and the maze is removed. The manual authors report that these administration and scoring changes more effectively control for examinees who rush through the maze, making many errors but completing the maze quickly. Instead, examinees are given an opportunity to realize their errors and adapt their approach to subsequent mazes. Although this change makes intuitive sense, there is no description of the process the test developers used to determine the efficacy of the 5-minute time limit, nor is research presented (e.g., pilot data) supporting this approach to errors.

TECHNICAL. The description of the normative sample is vague, referring primarily to uncited research conducted on the original version of the Porteus Maze Test from 1914. The reader is left wondering whether the norm-referenced standardized scores presented in the test manual are based on data collected approximately 100 years ago. The revised manual states that the original standardization sample contained children "from many different nationalities" (p. 3), which are then listed. There are no data presented on the number of children in each age group or nationality. Likewise, there are no data presented on the race, ethnicity, or socioeconomic status of the normative sample.

The test manual provides little clear, up-to-date information regarding reliability. Internal reliability data from a 1998 study of the Vineland Revision form of the mazes (Krikorian & Bartok, 1998) are summarized in the test manual. This study reported an alpha coefficient of .81, reflecting good internal consistency. The sample used for calculating this estimate is not described in the test manual. Reference is made to a .95 reliability coefficient for the original version of the Porteus Mazes, although the type of reliability studied, the methodology of the study, and the demographic characteristics of the children included in the study are not presented. No test-retest reliability data are presented, although this is arguably a more complicated issue for a maze test where learning can affect performance after a short time period.

A variety of data is presented in the test manual to support the validity of the Porteus Maze Test as a measure of executive function, specifically of planning and impulse control. Neuropsychological studies have demonstrated moderate correlations with other measures of executive function. Studies using the original version of the test demonstrated strong relationships to social capacity (.64 for males, .76 for females) and employment success (.67 for males, .75 for females). The mazes have been studied in individuals with antisocial personality disorder and substance abuse disorders, as well as patients with a variety of brain disorders, such as Alzheimer's disease and traumatic brain injury. There are no data presented regarding the validity of the Porteus Maze Test across racial, ethnic, or cultural groups.

COMMENTARY. The Porteus Maze Test has a long history in the research literature from the fields of neuropsychology and personality as a measure of planning and behavioral inhibition in children and adults. As drawn from this research, the predictive validity of the test is strong across a variety of ages and patient populations relative to specific functional outcome variables. Clearly the test measures important aspects of human mental ability, that is, planning and behavioral inhibition.

Yet the Porteus Maze Test [2017 Manual Revision], while attempting to address weaknesses in previous versions of the test, continues to lack critical technical data. Sadly, this reviewer is not the first to raise such a criticism of the technical attributes of the test (Docter, 1972, and Horn, 1972). Notably, the test manual does not describe the characteristics of the normative sample used to generate standardized scores, which the potential test user needs in order to weigh the evidence of validity of the test scores for their particular population. It is not even clear whether the standardization data are based on the current version of the test. Only one referenced study addresses reliability (i.e., internal consistency), and that study was conducted using a previous version of the test. There are no data supporting the 5-minute time limit per maze or the impact of the current administration procedures on test scores. Although the test has been administered in a variety of countries and cultures, no data are presented to support the validity of the test scores for groups that vary in race, ethnicity, socioeconomic status, or culture. In the absence of this essential information, clinicians are encouraged to consider alternative measures such as select subtests from the NEPSY–II—Second Edition (children) and the Delis-Kaplan Executive Function System (children and adults).

SUMMARY. The Porteus Maze Test [2017 Manual Revision] has great potential to become a useful instrument in the assessment of planning and behavioral inhibition in children and adults. A large body of research supports the predictive validity of the Porteus Maze Test in a variety of neurological conditions and personality types in both children and adults. Whereas the Porteus Maze Test [2017 Manual Revision] is suitable for use in research settings, the test cannot be recommended for the purpose of individual diagnosis or clinical decision making due to critical limitations in the technical data. The demographic characteristics of the normative sample are not presented, leaving users unable to determine whether the test is appropriate to use validly with their particular populations. It is hoped that the test authors will address these shortcomings by means of thorough standardization procedures. Until then, clinicians are advised to use alternative nonverbal measures of planning and behavioral inhibition.

REVIEWER'S REFERENCES

Docter, R. F. (1972). [Test review of The Porteus Maze Test]. In O. K. Buros (Ed.), *The seventh mental measurements yearbook*. Highland Park, NJ: The Gryphon Press.

Horn, J. L. (1972). [Test review of The Porteus Maze Test]. In O. K. Buros (Ed.), *The seventh mental measurements yearbook*. Highland Park, NJ: The Gryphon Press.

Krikorian, R., & Bartok, J. A. (1998). Developmental data for the Porteus Maze Test. *The Clinical Neuropsychologist, 12*(3), 305-310.

Lezak, M. D., Howieson, D. B., & Loring, D. W. (2004). *Neuropsychological Assessment* (4th ed.). New York, NY: Oxford University Press.

Porteus, S. D. (1959). *The Maze Test and clinical psychology*. Palo Alto, CA: Pacific Books.

[124]

PostConcussion Executive Inventory.

Purpose: "Designed to assess and monitor changes in a student's cognitive and emotional regulation following concussion."

Population: Ages 5-18.

Publication Date: 2018.

Acronym: PCEI.

Administration: Individual.

Forms, 2: Parent, Self-Report.
Price Data, 2020: $149 per kit, including technical manual (2018, 56 pages), 25 parent forms, 25 self-report forms, 25 parent concussion recovery profile forms, and 25 self-report concussion recovery profile forms; $29 per technical manual; $39 per 25 forms (parent or self-report); $29 per 25 concussion recovery profile forms (parent or self-report).
Time: Less than 5 minutes for completion of each form.
Comments: Developed using items from the Behavior Rating Inventory of Executive Function, Second Edition (BRIEF2; see 18, this volume); part of the ConcussTrack™ family of products.
Authors: Gerard A. Gioia and Peter K. Isquith.
Publisher: Psychological Assessment Resources, Inc.
a) PARENT FORM
Population: Parents/guardians of children ages 5-18.
Scores, 6: 4 Retrospective-Adjusted Post-Injury Difference (RAPID) scores: Working Memory, Emotional Control, Initiate, Total RAPID; 2 validity scales: Negativity, Infrequency.
b) SELF-REPORT FORM
Population: Ages 11-18.
Scores, 6: 4 Retrospective-Adjusted Post-Injury Difference (RAPID) scores: Working Memory, Emotional Control, Task Completion, Total RAPID; 2 validity scales: Negativity, Infrequency.

Review of the PostConcussion Executive Inventory by SHAWN K. ACHESON, Clinical Neuroscience Services of WNC, Durham, NC:

DESCRIPTION. The PostConcussion Executive Inventory (PCEI) is a component of the ConcussTrack family of instruments. It is a brief (~5 minute) paper-and-pencil checklist of executive dysfunction symptoms that occur commonly following concussion or mild traumatic brain injury (mTBI) in children and adolescents ages 5 to 18. It was developed by two of the authors of the Behavior Rating Inventory of Executive Function (BRIEF). There is a 19-item self-report form for ages 11 to 18 and a 21-item parent report form for ages 5 to 18. The measure consists of three symptom scales (Working Memory, Emotional Control, and Task Completion [self-report]/Initiate [parent report]) and two validity scales (Negativity and Infrequency). The latter is a critical feature unavailable on many rating inventories. Another valuable feature is that the PCEI attempts to track symptom change from the week prior to injury to the present time (past week).

Scoring is performed using a tear-away carbonless top copy revealing reporter responses on the scoring sheets. From there it is a relatively simple process of calculating post-injury scores, retrospective baseline scores, and the Retrospective-Adjusted Post-Injury Difference (RAPID) score. The RAPID score is interpreted on a semi-quantitative clinical basis. That is, the RAPID score is considered clinically meaningful if it falls at the 80% or 90% range based on commonly used reliable change indices and corresponding confidence intervals. This measure is designed to be used repeatedly during the course of recovery from concussion/mTBI for children and adolescents.

DEVELOPMENT. The PCEI was developed in an incremental process beginning with items comprising the original BRIEF parent and self-report forms. Expert clinician ratings were used to identify items thought to be maximally sensitive to concussion, and items were retained based on expert discussion and consensus. Items and scales were further culled to better align with the BRIEF2 following its publication, and individual items were subjected to rigorous evaluation. Factor analysis was used to derive and confirm scale membership.

TECHNICAL. As mentioned above, the PCEI uses a reliable change index (RCI) to assess change in functioning from pre-injury to post-injury. As such, the clinical utility of this instrument does not rely on norm-referenced scores. The RCI criteria were developed using an archived database containing clinical data on students ages 5 to 18. Data were collected from parents and adolescents who had been seen across three visits (parents: Visit 1 n = 1,668; Visit 2 n = 1,010; Visit 3 n = 228; adolescents [ages 11–18]: Visit 1 n = 1,229; Visit 2 n = 824; Visit 3 n = 187). Both the parent group and the adolescent (self-report) group completed the PCEI at every visit.

At each visit, with three notable exceptions, internal consistency reliability coefficients were generally adequate to good (.64 to .89) for most of the parent and self-report scales among asymptomatic children and adolescents. Internal consistency reliability estimates for the parent report Initiate scale at Visits 1 and 2 were .50 and .44, respectively. For the self-report Emotional Control scale at Visit 2, internal consistency reliability was only .21. Among the symptomatic children and adolescents, internal consistency reliability was adequate to excellent (.75 to .93) for all scales at all time points. Test-retest reliability was expectedly low for parent and self-report measures among asymptomatic children and adolescents due to the restricted range of RAPID scores. Among those in the symptomatic sample, test-retest reliability was higher and associated with greater reductions in the RAPID score from Visit 1 to Visit 2. Interrater reliability of RAPID scores between parent and self-report forms demonstrated moderate agreement at Visit 1 for the asymptomatic sample (correlation coefficients were .37 to .48). Interrater reliability declined at Visits 2 and 3 due to restricted range of declining RAPID scores. Interrater reliability was moderate and significant ($p < .01$) at all visits for the symptomatic sample (correlation coefficients were .30 to .51).

Content validity evidence was well established by the work of expert clinicians and all items having been derived from a well-established measure of executive function (the BRIEF). Construct validity evidence was demonstrated using principal factor analysis, which yielded acceptable factor loadings of each item on each scale for both the parent and self-report forms. Only one item appeared to cross load on the Task Completion and Working Memory scales for the self-report measure. Thirty-one of the thirty-four factor loadings were 0.599 or higher. Evidence of convergent and discriminant validity was established with the PostConcussion Symptom Inventory (PCSI) using parent and self-report measures.

COMMENTARY. Despite the generally positive conclusions to be drawn from the details outlined above, a number of concerns and limitations must be carefully considered. There appear to be no data reported concerning the representativeness of the development sample beyond the reported age and gender distribution. It is important to note that this measure, as the name implies, focuses on the effect of concussion on executive function. Deficits in executive function following concussion, although common, are but one element in a suite of cognitive changes. Those cognitive changes are in turn but one element in a broader set of changes following concussion/mTBI that include changes in physical, cognitive, emotional, and sleep functioning. The lead author also co-authored the PostConcussion Symptom Inventory (2nd Edition), which assesses this broader set of changes. The incremental validity of drilling down into executive functioning is not well established but should be. Rules for scoring missing responses and handling negative RAPID scores are potentially critical and deserve inclusion on the score sheet, not just in the test manual.

Somewhat minor concerns include the layout and implementation of the PCEI. Both the self-report and parent forms require the individual to read the item and scan across the page to the far right columns to complete Part 1 (retrospective baseline ratings). Then, respondents are asked to back up toward the middle of the page to complete Part 2 (post-injury rating). This task was difficult enough for a caffeine-free 54-year-old reviewer; surely there is a better approach for concussed 11-year-olds. Indeed, the entire instrument could have been developed as a single page tear-off form and scored with a simple spreadsheet from the test publisher. Moreover, an app on a client's phone/tablet linked to a provider to deliver the data could have accomplished all of this and saved some trees.

Perhaps the most concerning issue involves the repeated assessment of baseline function across visits. This focus raises serious concern regarding retrospective (good ol' days) bias. It would have been valuable to report a single retrospective baseline at Visit 1 and use that baseline at all subsequent visits to calculate the RAPID score. If there is any change or improvement in baseline performance, it would only serve to prolong the appearance of symptoms across time and might perpetuate treatment or lead to iatrogenesis. It is hard to imagine what value there is in repeating a retrospective baseline, especially as the delay between that baseline and subsequent visits becomes longer.

SUMMARY. The PCEI is a brief measure of post-concussive executive dysfunction designed to assess change over the course of recovery. Like many of the instruments developed by this esteemed team, it offers solid psychometric qualities and good reliability. There is more than sufficient data to establish validity for its intended purpose. In this case, however, there is room to question its incremental validity and the process and implementation of the instrument. I look forward to the PCEI v2.0.

Review of the PostConcussion Executive Inventory by ALAN SMERBECK, Associate Professor, Department of Psychology, Rochester Institute of Technology, Rochester, NY:

DESCRIPTION. The PostConcussion Executive Inventory (PCEI) is a survey instrument derived from the Behavior Rating Inventory of Executive Function (BRIEF/BRIEF-2; Gioia, Isquith, Guy, & Kenworthy, 2000; Gioia, Isquith, Guy, & Kenworthy, 2015) to evaluate the severity of concussion symptoms and track recovery. It includes two parallel questionnaires: a 21-item parent form for caretakers of children ages 5-18 and a 19-item self-report for youth ages 11-18. Respondents rate how often each behavior is a problem on a 5-point Likert scale from *almost never* to *almost always*. Ratings are provided twice for each behavior: a retrospective baseline (RBL) for the week before the injury and a post injury (PI) report for the past week. The carbonless paper form transfers responses to a scoring sheet. No items are reverse scored. For each item, the RBL is subtracted from the PI to yield a rating of how much the symptom has worsened since the injury, called a Retrospective-Adjusted Post-Injury Difference (RAPID) score. RAPID scores can be summed to create three scales (Working Memory, Emotional Control, and Initiate/Task Completion) and a Total composite. Both forms also contain two validity scales (Infrequency and Negativity).

RAPID scores are interpreted using reliable change indices (RCIs). RCIs use the correlation between two variables to allow the examiner to determine whether an observed difference likely reflects true score, as opposed to error, variance. Differences less than the RCI cutoff are non-significant. If the difference meets or exceeds the cutoff, there is 80% (or 90%) certainty of a true score difference. To assess symptoms caused by concussion, cut points are provided for the difference between PI and RBL scores (i.e., RAPID scores) for Visits 1, 2, and 3+. To assess recovery over time, RAPID scores from multiple visits are transferred to a separate Concussion Recovery Profile Form. The difference between each pair of RAPID scores (e.g., Visit 1 Initiate RAPID vs. Visit 2 Initiate RAPID) is then compared to an RCI cut point. Tables are provided on the form for comparing Visits 1 and 2, Visits 2 and 3, and any other pair of visits using the Visits 2 and 3 cut points.

DEVELOPMENT. The PCEI scales and items are derived from the original BRIEF (Gioia et al., 2000) and BRIEF-2 (Gioia et al., 2015), using only items included on both forms. Expert consensus from five neuropsychologists was used to select scales and constituent items most likely to be sensitive to acute concussion. Items that failed to show a large, significant difference between RBL and PI ratings were removed, as were those that lacked good fit within a factor. The test manual reports that all items were written at a fifth-grade reading level. RCIs were derived from a sample of children with concussion presenting at a hospital specialty clinic who completed neurocognitive performance tests and survey measures at the first post-injury visit, after which they returned up to two additional times. The test authors generated RCIs using the Iverson method to answer two questions: whether the child's pre- and post-injury functioning differ (i.e., RAPID scores within a visit) and whether the child's post-injury impairment was declining (e.g., Visit 1 RAPID vs. Visit 2 RAPID). Cut points for within-visit RAPID scores were derived from the asymptomatic group only. Cut points for comparison across visits were based on both the symptomatic and asymptomatic groups.

TECHNICAL.

Sample. A total of 1,668 parent reports and 1,229 self-reports were completed at Visit 1. No information is given about the injury characteristics (e.g., severity, presence of prior concussions). The symptomatic subgroup is described as having a confirmed diagnosis based on current clinical criteria. The asymptomatic group is described as having cognitive and balance testing equal to baseline, no other neurological symptoms, and no elevations on the Post-Concussion Symptom Inventory (PCSI; Sady, Vaughan, & Gioia, 2014). At Visit 1, there were 1,255 parent reports in the symptomatic group and 964 self-reports. The asymptomatic group included 413 participants and 265 self-reports at Visit 1. Of the parents at Visit 1, 60.6% returned for Visit 2; 22.6% of the Visit 2 parent sample returned for Visit 3. Of the Visit 1 self-report group, 67.0% returned for Visit 2, and 22.7% of the Visit 2 sample returned for Visit 3. The smallest subsample is the symptomatic self-report group at Visit 3 (n = 93). The test manual lists demographics for participants at each of the three time points, split into asymptomatic and symptomatic groups, with separate columns for the parent and self-report groups. These tables indicate the gender ratio as well as the means and standard deviations for age and days post-injury. Most gender percentages are roughly balanced (between 40% and 60%), but some asymptomatic group subsamples are more than 60% male, and the Visit 3 symptomatic subsample is more than 60% female. The sample is predominantly adolescent, as the self-report sample is 73.7% of the total sample at Visit 1. No data are provided about race/ethnicity, socioeconomic status, region, or other demographic variables.

Reliability. For all reliability values, coefficients are stratified by parent/self-report, asymptomatic/symptomatic status, and visit number. The range of responses in the asymptomatic group is restricted, limiting correlations, including reliability coefficients. Internal consistency reliability coefficients for the Total composite range from .75 (Visit 1, parent, asymptomatic) to .93 (occurring three times in the symptomatic group), with a median of .90. Scale coefficients range from .21 to .92 with a median of .81 across the symptomatic and asymptomatic groups. All coefficients below .70 come from the asymptomatic group; the symptomatic median is .87. Test-retest reliability is based on the correlation between Visit 1 and Visit 2, which were 17.2 days apart on average. Total composite coefficients were .55 to .60 for both self-report groups and the parent symptomatic group; the parent asymptomatic group value was .06. Scale coefficients for the symptomatic group fall between .40 and .59. Asymptomatic scale coefficients range from -.01 to .61. Interrater reliability is assessed by comparing parent and self-report ratings. In the asymptomatic group, coefficients for the Total composite range from .24 to .48, with scale coefficients between .04 and .44. For the symptomatic samples, the range of coefficients for the Total composite is .46 to .48, with subscale coefficients between .30 and .51.

Validity. Content evidence of validity is demonstrated by building on an established instrument (BRIEF/BRIEF2), using expert consensus in development, and retaining items empirically demonstrated to be sensitive to concussion-related change. With regard to internal structure, the test manual provides factor analytic data for both the parent and self-report forms, demonstrating that scale items load well onto their respective factors, and that the three scales intercorrelate. The PCEI scales yield the expected pattern of correlations with two existing concussion scales: the PCSI (Sady et al., 2014) and the Concussion Learning Assessment and School Survey, 3rd Edition (Burns, Snedden, & Gioia, 2018). The instrument's sensitivity to concussion is demonstrated by the statistically significant differences between the symptomatic group's means for Visit 1 RBL and PI. The PCEI is shown to be sensitive to recovery by the symptomatic group's RAPID means and standard deviations across Visits 1 through 3, which show the expected decline over time, although some changes are small or non-significant.

COMMENTARY. This measure is an interesting and useful assessment that targets an underserved population. There are, however, some concerns. First, the test manual acknowledges the biases inherent in retrospective reporting but argues that these are minimized when rating the very recent past. This is a plausible argument that would be bolstered by evidence. Second, the PCEI interpretation of cut points muddies the distinction between statistical and clinical significance. The term *clinical significance* refers to changes that have "importance, relevance, or meaning" (Porta, 2014, p. 261). *Statistical significance* differentiates random variation from real score change, whereas *clinical significance* is established by reference to an external construct, such as adaptive functioning or quality of life. RCIs are measures of statistical, not clinical, significance. However, the test manual repeatedly refers to score differences that exceed the RCI cut points using terms such as "clinically meaningful difference," or "clinically important difference worthy of attention" (p. 23), which could confuse users as to the distinction.

Third, it is unclear whether low-to-negligible correlations can form the basis for valid RCIs. The within-visit RAPID cut points are based solely on the asymptomatic sample. The test manual does not provide the correlations between the RBL and PI for this group, but it does give correlations comparing the asymptomatic sample's Visit 1 and Visit 2 RAPID, with many coefficients indistinguishable from zero. An RCI is a way of assessing whether two scores are farther apart than would be expected given the strength of the predictive relationship between them. If the predictive relationship does not exist, the RCI may be less meaningful for interpretation. This leads to the final concern: Important information is omitted from the test manual. For example, a table of the asymptomatic group's correlations between RBL and PI would have been extremely useful, as would means and standard deviations for each subgroup at each time point. Similarly, more detailed inclusion/exclusion criteria and demographic information would help assess the representativeness of the sample, as would the distribution of ages. Although the test is for children as young as 5, the sample used to develop the RCI and cut points is mostly adolescent. Whether early elementary children were included in sufficient numbers to determine that the psychometric properties were invariant by age is not known.

SUMMARY. The PCEI provides clinicians with a quick, easily administered tool for assessing executive function impairment secondary to concussion in children and adolescents. In the manual's introduction, the test authors convincingly argue the importance of detecting and managing concussion symptoms as decisions are made about return to school and athletics. The test manual is brief (56 pages), and although it is well organized, it omits some information that would help to judge the instrument's psychometric sufficiency and applicability. Nonetheless, the PCEI offers clinicians a novel way to quantify executive function changes following concussion.

REVIEWER'S REFERENCES

Burns, A. R., Snedden, T. R., & Gioia, G. A. (2018). Reliability and validity of the Concussion Learning Assessment and School Survey (CLASS): A measure assessing academic problems following concussion [Abstract]. *Journal of the International Neuropsychological Society, 24, Suppl. 1*, 45.

Gioia, G. A., Isquith, P. K., Guy, S. C., & Kenworthy, L. (2000). Behavior Rating Inventory of Executive Function. Lutz, FL: Psychological Assessment Resources.

Gioia, G. A., Isquith, P. K., Guy, S. C., & Kenworthy, L. (2015). Behavior Rating Inventory of Executive Function, Second Edition. Lutz, FL: Psychological Assessment Resources.

Porta, M. (Ed.). (2014). *A dictionary of epidemiology* (6th ed.). New York, NY: Oxford University Press.

Sady, M. D., Vaughan, C. G., & Gioia, G. A. (2014). Psychometric characteristics of the Postconcussion Symptom Inventory in children and adolescents. *Archives of Clinical Neuropsychology, 29*, 348-363.

[125]

Psychological Capital Questionnaire.

Purpose: Designed to "measure an individual's psychological capital."
Population: Working adults.
Publication Date: 2014.
Acronym: PCQ.
Scores, 4: Hope, Efficacy, Resilience, Optimism.
Administration: Individual or group.
Forms, 3: Self-Rater, Rater, Self-Rater Short.
Price Data, 2020: $50 per PDF manual (41 pages); $60 per paper manual; $75 per Multi-rater Report; $200 per Group Report: Multi-rater; $100 per Trainer's Guide for Developing Psychological Capital; $15 per Individual Report: Self Form; $15 per Report About Me: Self Form; $200 per Group Report: Self Form; $4 per Transform Survey Hosting: Multi-rater ($100 set up fee); $2 per Transform Survey Hosting: Self Form (minimum purchase of 20); $2 per Transform Survey Hosting: Rater Form (minimum purchase of 20); $2 per Remote Online Survey License (minimum purchase of 50); $2 per License to Reproduce (minimum purchase of 50).
Foreign Language Editions: Both Self and Rater Forms are available in Finnish, French, Greek, Malay, Spanish; Self Form available in Arabic, Cambodian, Chinese, Dutch, French (Canada), German, Hebrew, Hungarian, Indonesian, Japanese, Korean, Lithuanian, Norwegian, Persian, Polish, Portuguese, Portuguese (Brazil), Slovenian, Thai, Turkish, and Urdu.
Time: [10-15] minutes.
Authors: Fred Luthans, Bruce J. Avolio, and James B. Avey.
Publisher: Mind Garden, Inc.

Review of the Psychological Capital Questionnaire by KATE HATTRUP, Professor of Psychology, San Diego State University, San Diego, CA:

DESCRIPTION. The Psychological Capital Questionnaire (PCQ) is a 24-item group or individually administered measure of four dimensions of psychological capital (PsyCap), namely Hope, Efficacy, Resilience, and Optimism. Respondents can rate their own psychological capital or that of others by responding to items presented either online or via paper and pencil. A 12-item version is also available for self-ratings only. A 6-point Likert forced-choice rating scale is used, with anchors ranging from *strongly disagree* to *strongly agree*.

The test manual does not provide detailed instructions for test administrators, including time limits and information about the purposes of the test. Basic written instructions are provided for respondents, indicating that they should respond to items according to how they feel "right now." Most respondents can probably complete the measure within 10 to 15 minutes.

A scoring protocol is provided, indicating which items should be reverse scored and which items are averaged for each of the four subdimensions. Each dimension is measured by a different set of six items. The 12-item version of the PCQ includes four items that measure Hope, two items that measure Optimism, and three items each for Efficacy and Resilience. A total score, measuring overall PsyCap, can be formed by averaging across all of the items.

DEVELOPMENT. In developing the PCQ, the authors sought to identify dimensions of positive organizational behavior that met the following criteria: (a) grounded in theory and research, (b) measured validly, (c) "state-like" and d) susceptible to development rather than "trait-like" or highly stable, and (d) related to workplace attitudes and behaviors. Thus, in developing the PCQ, the authors did not set out to develop a measure of a specific a priori construct, but rather sought to identify existing constructs that fit a domain defined by their inclusion criteria.

Existing measures of the four dimensions that met the inclusion criteria were identified and adapted to create the 24-item PCQ (Luthans, Avolio, Avey, & Norman, 2007). These measures were (a) Hope (Snyder et al., 1996); (b) Efficacy (Parker, 1998); (c) Optimism (Scheier & Carver, 1985); and Resilience (Wagnild & Young, 1993). Evidence of the reliability and validity of these other measures can be found in the literature. Items from each of these measures were selected on the basis of face and content validity, and then adapted to the workplace context by including the words "at work" and by asking the participants to describe how they think about themselves "right now."

Development of the shorter, 12-item, version of the PCQ was described by Avey, Avolio, and Luthans (2011). Items for the PCQ-12 were selected on the basis of factor loadings and the items' contribution to internal consistency reliability. The numbers of items retained for each dimension were meant to reflect, in part, the assumed dimensionality of each component; Hope, for example, consists of agency and perceived pathways, and so it was measured with four items, whereas the other dimensions were each measured with either two or three items.

PsyCap is conceptually defined not only by the specific dimensions, but also by the shared variance among the dimensions. Luthans et al. (2007) explain that this shared variance represents one's "positive appraisal of circumstances and probability for success based on motivated effort and perseverance" (p. 550). Empirically, the test manual reports that studies have found that an overall PsyCap score was more strongly and consistently related to work-relevant attitudes and performance than were the individual dimension scores.

TECHNICAL. Norms are not provided in the test manual for the PCQ or the PCQ-12. Means and standard deviations also are not provided in the manual, making it difficult to interpret individual obtained scores. A review by Dawkins, Martin, Scott, and Sanderson (2013) showed that means varied from 2.92 to 5.25 across 29 samples, with standard deviations ranging from .41 to .86. The test manual provides no guidance as to how specific observed scores are to be interpreted nor to what constitutes a high or low score on the measure. The manual also fails to provide guidance about whether scores are comparable across groups defined by age, gender, occupation, or ethnicity.

As noted in the test manual, Luthans et al. (2007) calculated internal consistency reliabilities for the four dimensions and the composite PsyCap in four samples. Alpha coefficients were generally acceptable, with only two falling below .70: Hope (.72, .75, .80, .76); Efficacy (.75, .84, .85, .75); Resilience (.71, .71, .66, .72); Optimism (.74, .69, .76, .79); and overall PsyCap (.88, .89, .89, .89). The two dimensions with alphas below .70 are the two that include negatively worded items, which can sometimes reduce internal consistency.

Luthans et al. (2007) also calculated retest reliability in a sample of 174 management students who completed the PCQ at three points in time over the course of 4 weeks. After disattenuating for internal reliability, the retest coefficient was .52 for PsyCap, supporting the interpretation of PsyCap as a state-like construct, whereas retest coefficients were .76 and .87 for Conscientiousness and core self-evaluations, respectively.

PsyCap is presumed to represent a higher order factor that results from combining the dimensions Hope, Efficacy, Resilience, and Optimism. The test manual summarizes results reported by Luthans et al. (2007), who claim to have tested this higher-order structure with confirmatory factor analyses (CFAs), and the relevant table of fit indices is provided in the manual. However, the table does not show fit indices for a hierarchical model with four lower-order factors loading on a higher-order PsyCap factor; instead, fit indices are provided for a four-factor model. (Moreover, the degrees of freedom [df] in the table are unexpected; for example, a single-factor model with 24 items would imply 252 df for the CFA, but the table lists 238 df.)

The manual summarizes results of several studies that investigated discriminant validity of PsyCap relative to other measures, and a table of correlations reported by Luthans et al. (2007) is reproduced. The highest correlation shown in the table between PsyCap and other constructs is with core self-evaluations (r = .60), which, after correcting for internal consistency unreliability, reaches .71. The same study, however, reported that PsyCap explained unique variance in job satisfaction and organizational commitment after controlling for Extraversion, Conscientiousness, and core self-evaluations. Another study reported in the manual (Peterson, Luthans, Avolio, Walumbwa, & Zhang, 2011) found lower correlations between PsyCap and Core Self-Evaluations across three time periods (r = .16, .25, .49).

The manual summarizes results from a number of studies that have reported significant correlations between the dimensions of PsyCap and job performance and workplace attitudes, and also between overall PsyCap scores and individual workplace outcomes. A meta-analysis by Avey, Reichard, Luthans, and Mhatre (2011) reported that across 51 independent studies, the overall evidence is supportive of positive correlations between PsyCap and job satisfaction, organizational commitment, employee well-being, organizational citizenship behavior, and job performance and negative correlations between PsyCap and employee cynicism, turnover intentions, stress/anxiety, and deviance.

The meta-analysis by Avey et al. (2011) also reported higher correlations between PsyCap and positive workplace outcomes in U.S. samples than in non-U.S. samples and higher correlations in the service industry than in manufacturing. No other evidence of differences in test scores or in their criterion-related evidence of validity is provided in the test manual.

COMMENTARY. The PCQ is a short and easy-to-administer measure of dimensions of positive organizational psychology. Its development, which was based on identifying and adapting items for existing measures that met several psychometric inclusion criteria, generally ensures a certain degree of psychometric quality of the resulting measure. However, the fact that PsyCap emerged from a set of inclusion criteria for specific subdimensions rather than from an a priori model of positive organizational behavior means that the higher-order factor measured by a composite of all of the items must be considered carefully. Although an interpretation of the higher-order factor is offered in the test manual, empirical evidence of the implied factor structure is not as strong as it should be. Furthermore, because other specific dimensions may eventually be found that also meet the inclusion criteria, the interpretation of higher order PsyCap is open to revision.

Because the PCQ measures a state-like construct, it is less appropriate for use in employee selection than measures that assess stable traits. The manual describes how training interventions might be designed to increase PsyCap among employees, with the expectation that improvements in PsyCap might then translate into positive individual and organizational outcomes. However, the lack of normative data in the manual means that practitioners would have difficulty interpreting PCQ scores in any particular context.

SUMMARY. The PCQ measures multidimensional state-like constructs as well as trait-like ones that reflect positive organizational behavior, using items that were adapted from existing measures of Hope, Efficacy, Resilience, and Optimism. Empirical evidence largely supports the internal consistency of the PCQ and its correlation with a host of variables relevant in the workplace. Psychological capital has attracted considerable attention in the literature. Until normative data are provided, along with additional empirical evidence to support its practical value, however, the PCQ is best applied in research contexts where the interpretation of specific score levels is not an important goal.

REVIEWER'S REFERENCES

Avey, J. B., Avolio, B. J., & Luthans, F. (2011). Experimentally analyzing the impact of leader positivity on follower positivity and performance. *The Leadership Quarterly, 22*, 282-294.

Avey, J. B., Reichard, R. J., Luthans, F., & Mhatre, K. H. (2011). Meta-analysis of the impact of positive psychological capital on employee attitudes, behaviors, and performance. *Human Resource Development Quarterly, 22*(2), 127-152.

Dawkins, S., Martin, A., Scott, J., & Sanderson, K. (2013). Building on the positives: A psychometric review and critical analysis of the construct of Psychological Capital. *Journal of Occupational and Organizational Psychology, 86*(3), 348-370.

Luthans, F., Avolio, B. J., Avey, J. B., & Norman, S. M. (2007). Positive psychological capital: Measurement and relationship with performance and satisfaction. *Personnel Psychology, 60*, 541-572.

Parker, S. K. (1998). Enhancing role breadth self-efficacy: The roles of job enrichment and other organizational interventions. *Journal of Applied Psychology, 83*, 835-852.

Peterson, S. J., Luthans, F., Avolio, B. J., Walumbwa, F. O., & Zhang, Z. (2011). Psychological capital and employee performance: A latent growth modeling approach. *Personnel Psychology, 64*, 427-450.

Scheier, M. F., & Carver, C. S. (1985). Optimism, coping, and health: Assessment and implications of generalized outcome expectancies. *Health Psychology, 4*, 219-247.

Snyder, C. R., Sympson, S. C., Ybasco, F. C., Borders, T. F., Babyak, M. A., & Higgins, R. L. (1996). Development and validation of the State Hope Scale. *Journal of Personality and Social Psychology, 70*, 321-335.

Wagnild, G. M., & Young, H. M. (1993). Development and psychometric evaluation of the resilience scale. *Journal of Nursing Measurement, 1*(2), 165-178.

Review of the Psychological Capital Questionnaire by DOUG LEIGH, Professor, Pepperdine University, and ZECCA LEHN, Independent Researcher, Huntington Beach, CA:

DESCRIPTION. The Psychological Capital Questionnaire (PCQ) is a 24-item measure designed to gauge individuals' positive psychological states in the workplace across four domains: Hope, Efficacy, Resilience, and Optimism. The test developers do not indicate the age range for which the instrument is appropriate; however, it presumably is designed to be completed by employed adults. The developers do not provide metrics regarding the readability of the PCQ; an analysis conducted by these reviewers via Microsoft Word for Mac version 15.39 yields a Flesch-Kincaid Grade Level score of 6.3. The test manual does not include an estimate of how long the PCQ takes to administer; according to the test publisher's website, it should take 10-15 minutes.

The technical manual indicates that the PCQ may be administered to individuals or groups and that it can be purchased and distributed in print or online. The instrument is available as a self-rated form, as well as in a format for completion by associates of the individual in question (i.e., multirater format). A 12-item short form also is available. As the psychometric properties of the latter two versions of the instrument are not addressed in the technical manual, this review pertains solely to the self-rated form of the PCQ.

Responses are made on a 6-point Likert-type scale concerning the degree to which respondents agree with 24 statements about how they think about themselves at the moment. The response scale is constructed in a balanced format, ranging from *strongly disagree* (scored 1) to *strongly agree* (scored 6).

Neutral evaluations are not possible as the scale is forced choice. Items are not counterbalanced but rather are assembled in four sequential groups of six items per each of the four measured dimensions. The construct underlying each group of items is not revealed to respondents during their completion of the instrument. Total scores for each of the four dimensions are calculated as the average of responses to each group of six items.

Three items are reverse scored: two in the Optimism subscale and one in the Resilience scale. The technical manual does not specify whether these three items were so developed as checks of response set or for other reasons. All items must be completed in order to obtain interpretable scores, though this point is not indicated in the instructions to respondents.

As no information regarding the interpretation of one's scores is provided outside of the technical manual, the PCQ is presumably intended to be proctored in organizational settings or used for research purposes. Even then, no interpretative guidance is provided in the technical manual beyond the assertion that higher scores indicate a greater presence of the construct measured by each of the four subscales.

DEVELOPMENT. The developers provide rather extensive information regarding the conceptual origins of the PCQ across various sections of the technical manual. They first assert the value of positive organizational behavior—"positive oriented human resource strengths and psychological capacities" (Luthans, 2002, p. 59)—in advancing various desirable workplace behaviors. The developers indicate that four aspects of positive organizational behavior—Hope, Efficacy, Resilience, and Optimism (abbreviated "HERO")—taken together represent a "higher order core construct called 'psychological capital' (PsyCap)" (manual, p. 2). Implications of this assertion are discussed in the Technical section, below.

The developers also summarize a hypothetical path model highlighting the components of a "PsyCap training model," an intervention intended as a "positive impact on employees' rated work-performance" (manual, p. 13). A graphical representation of this intervention appears to suggest two antecedents for each factor within HERO. The test developers offer some evidence of these claims from prior literature; however, these do not appear to have been examined empirically, and the PCQ itself does not appear to reflect these dichotomies.

TECHNICAL. The developers discuss the origins of the PCQ's 24 items by describing the development of the instrument's four subordinate constructs. Based on these constructs of PsyCap, six items were selected from each of four previously published measures "based on content and face validity" (manual, p. 19).

The developers discuss various studies through which evidence of the psychometric properties of the PCQ was developed. However, information about the participants and sample sizes appears incomplete in the test manual, in which one study's sample is described simply as "students" and another's is described as "employees" (p. 20). The only sample size provided is 404, indicated in a footnote to a table within the technical manual. Citations are included to the original publications where readers presumably can find additional information.

PsyCap is discussed in the technical manual as a "superordinate construct" (p. 19) comprising the four HERO constructs. A confirmatory factor analysis is reported to have "supported the high-order factor structure for the overall PsyCap measure" (manual, p. 19). The data presented, however, do not appear to substantiate the claim that the four constructs operate as second-order factors to a superordinate construct of PsyCap. Of the five models tested (including one four-factor model and three three-factor models), the one-factor model that included all 24 items performed the poorest, with the RMSEA above the commonly accepted threshold of 0.05, the CFI below the threshold of 0.95 and the SRMR above the threshold of 0.05 (McCoach, Gable, & Madura, 2003). Nevertheless, of the models tested, the four-factor baseline solution yielded the smallest χ^2 with the fewest degrees of freedom, the smallest RMSEA, largest CFI (though not over 0.95), and the smallest SRMR (though not under 0.05). Intercorrelations among the four scales were moderate, ranging from .26 between Optimism and Efficacy to .58 between Resilience and Hope.

Discussing the discriminant and convergent validity of the PCQ, the developers report that PCQ was not meaningfully related to age, education, or the Big Five factors of Agreeableness, Openness, and Neuroticism, and that it was correlated with core self-evaluations, Extraversion, and Conscientiousness. The developers provide evidence of discriminant validity between PsyCap and perceived employability, creativity and authentic leadership, and authentic leadership and positive work climate, all of which bear more salient likeness to the PsyCap construct. In their discussion of criterion-related evidence of validity, the developers indicate that the PCQ demonstrates an association with job satisfaction and affective organizational commitment.

Alpha reliability coefficients of the PCQ's four scales are reported for the "student" and "employee" samples as ranging from .66 to .89, which are considered to be sufficient evidence for claims of reliability by this reviewer (but see Lance, Butts, & Michels, 2006). Internal consistency for Optimism and Resilience tended to be slightly lower (each with coefficients slightly below .70 in one of the four pilot studies), though neither deviated substantially from coefficients obtained for Hope and Efficacy. The developers also report correlations between PsyCap and increasing core self-evaluations over three time periods, though why the evaluations increase over time is unclear based on information presented in the test manual.

COMMENTARY. Three aspects regarding the psychometric properties of the PCQ merit further discussion. First, regarding the development and selection of items, it appears that the items included in the final version of the instrument were not selected through a process in which a large pool of items were initially developed, with only those possessing the strongest evidence of reliability and validity advanced for candidacy in the final version of the instrument. Instead, test developers chose to include items from previously published instruments. This approach is unusual in that factor analysis of such data is typically used to inform decisions regarding which items to retain, which to revise, and which to delete (Flynn & Pearcy, 2001). Additional information regarding normed measures of central tendency and dispersion of scores is also critical in future iterations of the technical manual in order to interpret respondents' scores.

Second, the pilot studies that were conducted are not described in sufficient detail for meaningful interpretation of the findings that are presented. Missing from the technical manual is information such as the setting of each study, the demographics of the participants, the criteria used to include or exclude potential participants, the minimum sample size necessary for the inferential analyses conducted (typically determined via a priori power analysis), and the handling of non-response or incomplete data. Presumably such information might be addressed in source articles cited by the developers, but the lack of such information in the technical manual is somewhat disconcerting for those who may be considering the PCQ for research purposes. In addition, given that the PCQ appears intended for working adults, it is not clear why the instrument was pilot tested with students at all, unless they, too, were employed.

Lastly, as noted above, the veracity of the claim that a superordinate construct of overall PsyCap exists seems dubious. This conclusion is not to say that the four constructs measured by the PCQ do not possess sufficient evidence of validity and reliability in their own right, only that the assertion of a second-order model does not seem to be borne out by the developers' own findings. That no scoring method is provided to calculate overall PsyCap further suggests that the four HERO factors are not subordinate to overall PsyCap, but rather are oblique factors in their own right.

SUMMARY. The PCQ appears to possess sufficient evidence of internal consistency reliability and validity of the construct-oriented type—as well as a literature-supported conceptual base—for organizational use, and perhaps for research purposes as well. The technical manual is rather diffuse, however, in the sense that it seeks to present a large amount of information, often without related content being grouped together by subject matter. Better would be to segment its contents, such as its theoretical origins, item development, pilot testing, and evidence of reliability and validity in contiguous blocks of text. Additionally, whereas the manual provides considerable detail to assertions regarding the conceptual forbearers of PsyCap, as well as literature-supported claims of its correlates with various measures of workplace performance, but it does not provide similar detail evidencing the developers' assertions of the PCQ's psychometric adequacy.

The lack of information regarding the development and selection of items, pilot testing, and claims about the superordinate construct of PsyCap should be addressed in the next iteration of the technical manual. Additionally, information regarding the convergent evidence of validity of the PCQ with other extant measures of Hope, Efficacy, Resilience, and Optimism would bolster the developers' argument regarding its validity and reliability, as would information regarding its fitness in settings outside of the United States.

REVIEWERS' REFERENCES

Flynn, L. R., & Pearcy, D. (2001). Four subtle sins in scale development: Some suggestions for strengthening the current paradigm. *International Journal of Market Research, 43*(4), 409-423.

Lance, C. E., Butts, M. M., & Michels, L. C. (2006). The sources of four commonly reported cutoff criteria: What did they really say? *Organizational Research Methods*, 9(2), 202-220.

Luthans, F. (2002). Positive organizational behavior: Developing and managing psychological strengths. *Academy of Management Executive*, *16*(1), 57-72.

McCoach, D. B., Gable, R. K., & Madura, J. P. (2013). Instrument development in the affective domain: *School and corporate applications* (3rd ed.). New York, NY: Springer.

Wallis, C. (2005, January 17). The new science of happiness. *Time*, *165*(3), A2-A9.

[126]

Psychological Distress Profile.

Purpose: Designed as a self-report screening measure of psychological distress.
Population: Ages 18 and older.
Publication Date: 2015.
Acronym: PDP.
Scores, 5: Depression, Hopelessness, Anxiety, Anger, Total.
Administration: Individual or group.
Price Data, 2020: $50 per PDF manual (41 pages); $60 per paper manual; $15 per Individual Report; $15 per Report About Me; $2.50 per Transform Survey Hosting (minimum purchase of 50); $2.50 per Remote Online Survey License (minimum purchase of 50); $2.50 per License to Reproduce (minimum purchase of 50).
Time: (5-10) minutes.
Comments: Title on test form is How I Feel Questionnaire; administered online or via paper and pencil.
Authors: Gary Elkins and Aimee Johnson.
Publisher: Mind Garden, Inc.

Review of the Psychological Distress Profile by JOSEPH C. KUSH, Professor, and STEFANIE GRABAN, Graduate Assistant, Duquesne University, Pittsburgh, PA:

DESCRIPTION. The Psychological Distress Profile (PDP) is a 20-question scale designed to determine psychological distress in terms of Depression, Anxiety, Hopelessness, and Anger. The purpose of the scale is to create a short method for the self-reporting of distress that can be administered easily and without any specialized knowledge. The PDP manual describes the instrument and how to score and interpret it.

The PDP can be completed online or through paper and pencil administration in a variety of clinical settings and is intended for adults ages 18 and older. The PDP is designed to be easy and fast for respondents, with clear and concise instructions and normally can be completed in 5 to 10 minutes. It should be completed by the respondent, although people with severe handicaps or people who cannot read English well may need assistance. Directions suggest that the respondent should not be experiencing any kind of excessive physical or mental health conditions at the time of completion. Before completing the scale, the respondent should be given some time to look over the scale and answer several informational questions. Following the completion of the scale, the respondent should be debriefed, and any questions about the PDP should be answered.

The PDP begins with several general and demographic questions asking for information on gender, race, marital status, and education. Also included in the demographic section are questions about the respondent's history of anxiety, depression, anger, self-harm, suicide, substance abuse, and psychiatric hospitalization. Next, the respondent completes the "How I Feel Questionnaire," which consists of 20 items that are answered based on how he or she is feeling at the present time. Questions are scored on a 5-point Likert scale, with anchors of 1: *strongly disagree,* 3: *neutral,* and 5: *strongly agree.*

The PDP manual includes an easy to understand scoring guide. To obtain a total score for each construct, corresponding item raw scores are added to produce the four subscale scores and the Total score. Tables are provided so that scores can then be transformed to T scores and percentile ranks that can be compared with the general adult population.

DEVELOPMENT. The PDP was developed and validated from responses of 525 men and 533 women (N = 1,058) with sample data collected in three groups (ns = 307; 161; 530). The authors note that they attempted to create a diverse sample, although true random sampling "was not feasible" (manual, p. 10). Participants were recruited through Amazon's Mechanical Turk (MTurk) program, an online data collection tool. To be included as a participant, each person had to be at least 18 years old, a U.S. resident, and have a 90% task approval rate for their previous human intelligence tasks completed on MTurk. Anyone with a history of psychosis, cognitive impairments (i.e., dementia or delirium), or reading impairments that made them unable to complete the PDP or the consent documents, was excluded from the process.

The participants selected were 19 to 81 years old and, according to the test authors, represented all major ethnic groups. Information regarding socioeconomic status was not reported in the technical manual and remains a potential confound. Means, standard deviations, and alpha coefficients are presented by gender for each of the three sample groups. To examine possible demographic differences on the PDP, the test authors divided participants from the third sample group according to age: 18-27, 28-43, 44-60, and 61-81, and separated respondents by gender. Means and standard deviations are reported for each of these subgroups.

The PDP was constructed based on steps outlined by Loevinger (1957). First, an item pool of approximately 100 questions was generated by the test authors. After removing redundant items and confusing questions, the scale was sent to experts for their review. Three psychologists rated the items and selected the most descriptive items. The result was 54 remaining items. Second, the 54-item form was administered to a sample of 307 adults (i.e., the first sample group). Participants were from around the United States and ranged in age from 19 to 79. Finally, a principal component analysis reduced the scale to the current 20-item format.

TECHNICAL. Reported internal consistency for the 20-item scale is good across all subscales, and for males and females, with alpha coefficients ranging from .87 to .95. Subscale intercorrelations were calculated for men and women separately and are also adequate with coefficients ranging from .52 to .88. It can be expected that people experiencing psychological distress may experience many or all of the PDP constructs (Depression, Hopelessness, Anxiety, and Anger) at one time, so it is logical that the constructs are correlated. This is most strongly shown in the correlation coefficients obtained between Depression and Hopelessness, which were .88 for women and .86 for men. Additionally, the technical manual provides interitem correlations across each of the 20 questions demonstrating that each of the PDP items are correlated with one another. Finally, although it might be argued that the construct of psychological distress is transitory, the stability of the scale cannot be determined as the technical manual offers no evidence of any type of test-retest correlations, even over a brief interval such as 1 or 2 weeks.

Regarding convergent and divergent evidence of validity, the technical manual presents a number of correlations between the PDP and other clinical scales apparently administered to the third sample group (n = 529). For example, the Depression construct of the PDP produced a moderate correlation (r = .87) with the Beck Depression Inventory-II (BDI–II; Beck, Steer, & Brown, 1996). Similarly, the PDP Hopelessness subscale correlated .82 with the Beck Hopelessness Scale (BHS; Beck & Steer, 1988b). Additionally, moderate correlation coefficients of .68 and .85 were found between the PDP Anger subscale and the State-Trait Anger Expression Inventory–2 (STAXI–2; Spielberger, 1999) and between the PDP Anxiety subscale and the Beck Anxiety Inventory (BAI; Beck & Steer, 1988a), respectively. The test manual also reports moderate subscale correlations with several other scales (e.g., Balanced Inventory of Psychological Mindedness, Nyklíček & Denollet, 2009; Kessler 6, Kessler et al., 2002).

Results from an exploratory principal component analysis are also reported based on results from the third sample group (n = 530). This analysis used a principal components analysis with an oblique rotation. The results indicated a three-factor solution, accounting for 58.1% of variance. Depression and Hopelessness combined to form the first factor with Anger and Anxiety loading as expected and producing the second and third factors. The test manual contains no discussion of why this analysis found support for only three factors when the scale claims to assess four discrete factors.

Next, a series of analyses was performed for subgroupings of the population. To determine whether there were differences between psychologically stressed participants and non-stressed participants, independent t-tests were conducted comparing PDP performance with self-reporting to the Distress Thermometer (Roth et al., 1998). Results produced significant differences for each construct of the PDP, but results for false positives and false negatives were not reported.

Finally, t-tests were also conducted to determine whether there were differences between genders and across ethnic groups. Regarding gender, the only significant difference was in Anxiety with women producing a slightly elevated score. When comparing Caucasian, Hispanic, Black, Asian, and Others, an ANOVA produced no significant differences among any of the groups on any of the four subscales.

COMMENTARY. Currently, there are a number of instruments that are widely used to evaluate distress and assess dimensions of several unitary constructs (e.g., BDI–II; BAI; BHS; STAXI–2; and State-Trait Anxiety Inventory, Spielberger, Gorsuch, & Lushene, 1970). Additionally, a number of brief inventories are available to evaluate symptoms of psychological distress such as Four-Dimensional Symptom Questionnaire (Terluin, 1996), Screening Tool for Psychological Distress (Young, Ignaszewski, Fofonoff, & Kaan, 2007), Symptom Assessment Scale (Aoun, Monterosso, Kristjanson, & McConigley, 2011), and Kessler Psychological Distress Scale and its shortened six-item form (Kessler et al., 2002).

In this regard, it is difficult to ascertain how the PDP distinguishes itself from existing scales. The PDP is easy to use, and respondents should have no difficulty completing the scale. The test authors have made preliminary attempts to validate the PDP against known mental health inventories. As with many of these other inventories, the self-report nature of the scale may not accurately reflect respondents' mental health. As a result, the PDP should be used in conjunction with other measures.

The PDP may be a good screening tool for professionals to use to quickly assess the overall level of distress in their clients. However, because the answers are self-reported and the scale is so brief, it will also be necessary to supplement the PDP with more comprehensive measures that are more fully validated. As no test-retest reliability data are reported, the PDP should not be used to assess respondent growth or declines in psychological distress. Similarly, it is recommended that only the Total score of the PDP be used until additional factor analytic data can be collected. Finally, future research with the PDP, whether by the test authors or by independent researchers, should clearly describe the demographic characteristics of the sample to better ascertain the generalizability of the findings.

SUMMARY. The Psychological Distress Profile is a quick and easy to complete scale that is designed to determine a respondent's levels of Depression, Hopelessness, Anxiety, and Anger. The advantage of a brief scale can also be its greatest limitation; it is difficult to expect a self-report scale to reliably and accurately assess four discrete components of psychological distress with only 20 questions in a single 5-minute administration period. The PDP presents acceptable internal consistency reliability. Short- or long-term stability of the instrument is not reported. Similarly, while some proposed subscales of the PDP produced moderate correlations with other standardized measures, the evidence for construct validity reported in the technical manual does not align with the structure of the instrument (i.e., evidence for three factors was found, yet four factors are included) and it is recommended that only the Total score of the PDP be used even within the screening process.

REVIEWERS' REFERENCES

Aoun, S. M., Monterosso, L., Kristjanson, L. J., & McConigley, R. (2011). Measuring symptom distress in palliative care: Psychometric properties of the Symptom Assessment Scale (SAS). *Journal of Palliative Medicine, 14*(3), 315-321.

Beck, A. T., & Steer, R. A. (1988a). Beck Anxiety Inventory. San Antonio, TX: The Psychological Corporation.

Beck, A. T., & Steer, R. A. (1988b). Beck Hopelessness Scale. San Antonio, TX: The Psychological Corporation.

Beck, A. T., Steer, R. A., & Brown, G. K. (1996). Beck Depression Inventory—II. San Antonio, TX: The Psychological Corporation.

Kessler, R. C., Andrews, G., Colpe, L. J., Hiripi, E., Mroczek, D. K., Normand, S.-L. T., ... Zaslavsky, A. M. (2002). Short screening scales to monitor population prevalences and trends in non-specific psychological distress. *Psychological Medicine, 32*(6), 959-976.

Loevinger, J. (1957). Objective tests as instruments of psychological theory [Monograph]. *Psychological Reports, 3*(3), 635-694.

Nyklíček, I., & Denollet, J. (2009). Development and evaluation of the Balanced Index of Psychological Mindedness (BIPM). *Psychological Assessment, 21*(1), 32-44.

Roth, A. J., Kornblith, A. B., Batel-Copel, L., Peabody, E., Scher, H. I., & Holland, J. C. (1998). Rapid screening for psychologic distress in men with prostate carcinoma: A pilot study. *Cancer, 82*(10), 1904-1908.

Spielberger, C. D. (1999). State Trait Anger Expression Inventory–2. Lutz, FL: Psychological Assessment Resources.

Spielberger, C. D., Gorsuch, R. L., & Lushene, R. (1970). State-Trait Anxiety Inventory. Menlo Park, CA: Mind Garden.

Terluin, B. (1996). De Vierdimensionale Klachtenlijst (4DKL). Een vragenlijst voor het meten van distress, depressie, angst en somatisatie [The Four-Dimensional Symptom Questionnaire (4DSQ): A questionnaire to measure distress, depression, anxiety, and somatization]. *Huisarts Wet., 39*, 538-547.

Young, Q.-R., Ignaszewski, A., Fofonoff, D., & Kaan, A. (2007). Brief screen to identify 5 of the most common forms of psychosocial distress in cardiac patients: Validation of the Screening Tool for Psychological Distress. *The Journal of Cardiovascular Nursing, 22*(6), 525-534.

Review of the Psychological Distress Profile by GLORIA M. WORKMAN, Adjunct Assistant Professor, Center for the Study of Traumatic Stress, Uniformed Services University, Bethesda, MD:

DESCRIPTION. The Psychological Distress Profile (PDP) is a brief self-report multidimensional measure developed to assess the presence of psychological distress in adults. The PDP was designed to serve as a psychological distress screening instrument for use in the general population, in clinical settings, or for research purposes. The PDP comprises 20 items and assesses four distinct domains of psychological distress (i.e., Depression, Hopelessness, Anxiety, and Anger). The PDP can be administered on paper or online, and it can be completed in 5 to 10 minutes. The test developers indicate the test is suitable for adults ages 18 years and older who have an eighth-grade reading level or higher. The inventory includes an optional PDP fact sheet that contains demographic questions and items about the respondent's history of mental health problems and treatment.

The test manual provides concise and easy to follow instructions for administration, scoring, and interpretation. When completing the PDP, the respondent is instructed to select the response that best describes his/her current feelings by indicating the level of agreement or disagreement with each of the 20 statements using a 5-point scale (i.e., *strongly disagree* = *1; disagree* = *2; neutral* = *3; agree* = *4;* and *strongly agree* = *5*). A scoring guide and profile sheet are provided to facilitate scoring and interpretation. The examiner calculates scores for a Depression scale, a Hopelessness scale, an Anxiety scale, an Anger scale, and an overall psychological distress scale. Responses are weighted, and higher scores indicate a higher level of psychological distress. Scores on each scale range from 5 to 25. Scoring of the individual scales involves summing the five corresponding items to obtain raw scores for each domain. A Total psychological distress score can be computed by summing scores from all 20 items. Once the raw scores have been calculated for all scales and the Total score, corresponding percentile ranks and T-score equivalents can be obtained. The test manual includes a table of recommended cutoff scores (range: *minimal* to *severe*) for each construct assessed.

DEVELOPMENT. The PDP was developed in a three-step test development process originally proposed by Loevinger (1957, 1972). The first step involved generating a preliminary item pool that used the theoretical framework articulated by Veit and Ware (1983) for content development. The second part of this development phase involved a two-step process of refinement of items. Approximately 100 items were generated initially; subsequently, this item pool was reduced to 80 items to ensure clarity of items and removal of redundant items. The remaining items were then reviewed by three doctoral level psychologists to select the most descriptive and theoretically relevant items. The next stage of scale development involved creating preliminary scales that reflected high internal consistency with each distress component. This process resulted in the selection and administration of a 54-item experimental form of the PDP.

An initial sample (N = 307) for the experimental form of the PDP was recruited from workers on Amazon's Mechanical Turk (MTurk) platform. According to the test developers, the participants were recruited from across the United States and ranged in age from 19 to 79. No information is provided regarding ethnic and racial distribution, educational level, or marital status of this initial sample, which included 160 men and 147 women. Additionally, no information is provided regarding the payment made for responding to the PDP. Correlational analyses were conducted using the Kessler-6, a validated screening measure of psychological distress (Kessler et al., 2002). A principal component analysis was also conducted to examine items. In the final stage of development, the PDP scale was reduced to 20 items based on best theoretical fit and factor loadings.

TECHNICAL.

Standardization. The normative sample for the PDP included the initial sample described above plus two additional samples also recruited using MTurk. The total sample consisted of 525 men and 533 women (N = 1,058). The participants were U.S. residents who had a 90% task approval rate for their work with MTurk and ranged in age from 19 to 81. Individuals who reported a history of psychosis, cognitive impairment, severe learning disabilities, or a non-American Internet protocol address were excluded from the sample. Although the test developers report that diverse ethnic groups were well represented in the normative sample, no details are provided about the racial or ethnic distribution. The rationale for presenting the normative sample as three separate samples was not provided, nor was the discrepancy in sample size explained. (Table 1 in the manual presents 465 men, and the 60 missing are not accounted for.) Using a subset of the normative data, younger females (ages 18-27) were found to have higher mean scores on all four scales of the PDP compared to older females (ages 28-81). Older adults (ages 61-81) had the lowest means across the four subscales compared to younger age groups (ages 18-27, ages 28-43, and ages 44-60). It is unclear whether the differences reported are statistically significant, as no information is provided about the statistical analyses conducted to compare these means. No gender differences were reported across the four PDP scales.

Reliability. Coefficient alpha was computed for each of the PDP subscales. The instrument was administered to a subsample of the normative sample (i.e., Sample 2, N = 161; Sample 3, N = 530). Internal consistency reliability estimates were calculated for men and women across the four scales (i.e., Depression, Hopelessness, Anxiety, and Anger). Alpha coefficients ranged from .87 to .95 and were similar across samples and genders. Correlations between subscales ranged from r = .52 to .88 with high correlations between the Depression and Hopelessness scales, as expected.

Validity. Convergent and divergent evidence of validity were assessed for the PDP. Support for convergence and divergence of the PDP scales was provided in a multitrait matrix. The PDP ratings demonstrated high levels of convergence when compared to other well-established screening instruments of depression, anxiety, and anger. The PDP Depression subscale yielded the highest correlation coefficient with the Beck Depression Inventory-II (.87, p < .01). The PDP Anxiety subscale showed the strongest correlation with the Beck Anxiety Inventory (r = .85, p < .01), and the PDP

Hopelessness subscale demonstrated the strongest correlation with the Beck Hopelessness Inventory (r = .82, p < .01). The PDP Anger subscale was significantly correlated with the State Anger scale of the State Trait Anger Expression Inventory-2, (r = .68, p < .01).

The test developers conducted several independent samples t-tests to evaluate the differences between distressed respondents and non-distressed respondents. Participants were categorized in one of two groups (distressed versus non-distressed) based on their scores from the Distress Thermometer (Roth, Kornblith, Batel-Copel, Peabody, Scher, & Holland, 1998). Findings support significant differences between the two groups (distressed, N = 231 and non-distressed, N = 298) on each of the four domains. Independent samples t-tests were also conducted to evaluate differences between a distressed group (N = 133) and a non-distressed group (N = 399) as determined by a single self-identification distress item. Results indicated significant differences between the distressed and non-distressed participants on all four constructs. The test developers reported the statistical analyses were conducted with a sample of 530 participants (i.e., Sample 3), but they do not clarify why the sample sizes vary (N = 529 and N = 532).

COMMENTARY. The PDP is a quick and easy screening tool. The test manual provides clear instructions on the scoring and interpretation of the PDP. Its strengths include its brevity, rapid administration, and straightforward scoring procedure. Although some sections of the test manual are well written and clear, other sections would benefit from further clarification, greater detail regarding the standardization process, expansion of the theoretical model supporting the test, reorganization of chapters, and removal of redundancies. The test authors describe the PDP as a self-report screener of multidimensional psychological distress designed for individuals seen in a primary care or counseling setting or for research purposes. This questionnaire was developed using a convenience sample of MTurk workers and has not been validated for use with the general population, and therefore may introduce selection bias and not be appropriate for this population. Although the test developers have taken preliminary steps to cross-validate the screener, further test development is warranted. Next steps for test development could include obtaining a nationally representative sample of the general population, using the gold standard structured clinical interview, and including sensitivity and specificity analyses where possible.

SUMMARY. In its current state, the PDP is an exploratory brief self-report multidimensional measure of psychological distress that has promising psychometric properties. However, its utility in screening for general psychological distress in a wide array of health settings is uncertain. Interested readers may wish to compare the PDP to the Distress Questionnaire-5 (DQ-5; Batterham et al., 2017), which has been evaluated against several other psychological distress measures and found to be a superior performing scale.

REVIEWER'S REFERENCES

Batterham, P. J., Sunderland, M., Slade, T., Calear, A. L., & Carragher, N. (2017). Assessing distress in the community: Psychometric properties and crosswalk comparison of eight measures of psychological distress. *Psychological Medicine, 48*, 1316-1324.

Kessler, R. C., Andrews, G., Colpe, L. J., Hiripi, E., Mroczek, D. K., Normand, S.-L. T., ... Zaslavsky, A. M. (2002). Short screening scales to monitor population prevalences and trends in non-specific psychological distress. *Psychological Medicine, 32*, 959-976.

Loevinger, J. (1957). Objective tests as instruments of psychological theory [Monograph]. *Psychological Reports, 3*(3), 635-694.

Loevinger, J. (1972). Some limitations of objective personality tests. In J. N. Butcher (Ed.), *Objective personality assessment: Changing perspectives* (pp. 45-58). Oxford, England: Academic Press.

Roth, A. J., Kornblith, A. B., Batel-Copel, L., Peabody, E., Scher, H. I., & Holland, J. C. (1998). Rapid screening for psychologic distress in men with prostate carcinoma: A pilot study. *Cancer, 82*(10), 1904-1908.

Veit, C. T., & Ware, J. E., Jr. (1983). The structure of psychological distress and well-being in general populations. *Journal of Consulting and Clinical Psychology, 51*(5), 730-742.

[127]

Psychological Screening Inventory–2.

Purpose: Designed "to meet the need for a brief mental health screening device in situations where time and professional labor may be at a premium," such as in community clinics, referral agencies, counseling offices, hospitals, and courts.

Population: Ages 16 and older.

Publication Dates: 1973-2010.

Acronym: PSI-2.

Scores, 33: 6 Basic Screening Scales (Alienation, Social Nonconformity, Discomfort, Expression, Defensiveness, Depression), 21 Brief Content Scales (Close Relationship Difficulties, Low Self-Esteem, Depressive Feelings, Thought Disorder, Paranoid, Isolated/Alone/Alienated, Odd/Unusual Experiences, Stimulus-Seeking/Risk-Taking, Dysfunctional Childhood Home, Careless/Irresponsible/Impulsive, Undercontrol, Aggression/Anger, Childhood Conduct Disorder, Antisocial Characteristics, Fatigue/Low Energy, Health Problems, Anxious Feelings, Memory/Concentration Problems, Somatic Anxiety Symptoms, Likes to Perform, Verbal/Socially Outgoing), 6 Misrepresentation Scales (Symptom Overendorsement, Erroneous Psychiatric Stereotype, Endorsement of Excessive Virtue, Endorsement of Superior Adjustment, Random Responding, Health Problem Overstatement).

Administration: Individual or group.

Price Data, 2020: $105 per examination kit including technical manual (2010, 106 pages), 5 question/answer

sheets, 5 profile sheets, scoring template, and 1 online password; $26 per technical manual; $76 per testing kit including 25 question/answer sheets and 25 profile sheets; $62 per scoring template; $7 per online test including administration, scoring, and report (volume discounts available).
Foreign Language Editions: Translations available in Arabic, Danish, Hebrew, Japanese, Polish, Slovak, and Spanish.
Time: 15-20 minutes for administration.
Author: Richard I. Lanyon.
Publisher: SIGMA Assessment Systems, Inc.
Cross References: See T5:2115 (6 references), T4:2159 (20 references), 9:1015 (2 references), and T3:1931 (18 references); for a review by Stephen L. Golding of the original edition, see 8:654 (32 references); see also T2:1342 (7 references).

Review of the Psychological Screening Inventory-2 by EDWARD E. GOTTS, MultiTED Associates, Madison, IN:

DESCRIPTION. The Psychological Screening Inventory-2 (PSI-2) updates and expands the Psychological Screening Inventory (PSI; Golding, 1978). PSI-2's purpose is to screen for mental disorders and problems in persons ages 16 and older. Its results provide guidance as to whether additional assessment is needed. It is intended for use in situations in which dissimulation is not a significant concern. Its author offers it as a cost-effective instrument that imposes minimal response burden and is non-threatening to examinees. Contemporary community norms are based on a diverse opportunity sample (N = 1,046). Individual testing and scoring occur online; group testing uses paper forms. The PSI-2 manual indicates that completing the inventory should take 15 to 20 minutes for most respondents. The test manual, however, cautions examiners to allow as much time as needed and to minimize time pressure.

The PSI-2 reuses the original 130 PSI items to detect the presence of mental disorder or problems. It screens using traditional general categories of mental disorder: psychoses, neuroses, and psychopathy. One scale represents each category as follows: Alienation (Al) for psychoses, Discomfort (Di) for neuroses, and Social Nonconformity (Sn) for psychopathic tendencies. PSI-2 also retains two other PSI scales: Expression (Ex) to sample the personality trait of extraversion-introversion and Defensiveness (De) to detect response distortions due to over- and under-reporting. No particular theoretical framework is emphasized.

Several new features appear in PSI-2. First, nine items were added to represent Depression (Dp). They are interspersed among the original 130 items, bringing the total number of items to 139. Second, the PSI response format of *false/true* was expanded in PSI-2 to four options: *definitely false, slightly false, slightly true,* and *definitely true.* Third, the following six Misrepresentation Scales were developed to supplement the Defensiveness (De) scale: Random Responding (Ra), Health Problem Overstatement (HPO), Symptom Overendorsement (SOE), Erroneous Psychiatric Stereotype (EPS), Endorsement of Excessive Virtue (EEV), and Endorsement of Superior Adjustment (ESA). Fourth, 21 Brief Content Scales were prepared, using the full pool of 139 items. The result of these changes is that the PSI-2 contains 28 new scales plus the original five, for a total of 33 screening scales.

The PSI-2 is administered to individuals online. After being registered by the examiner to complete the measure, the respondent is instructed by the examiner and online text to respond on screen to lists of self-referenced statements by selecting one of the four ratings mentioned above. Items then appear on screen in lists of 10 at a time. After responding to each list of 10 statements, the respondent indicates that he or she is finished. At that time the program either advances to the next list or requests that the respondent complete any unrated items before continuing. This process continues until the 139 PSI-2 items are rated. After all items are rated, the examiner obtains a machine-generated printed summary of results. The examiner may discuss the results with the examinee but does not provide a copy of the screening inventory, and no information appears on screen that reveals or suggests the psychological meaning of the listed items. In this way, the inventory avoids influencing respondents beyond whatever meaning the individual items convey to them. Interpretive activity takes place later between examiner and examinee.

DEVELOPMENT. All items of the PSI were retained in the PSI-2 to preserve the potential to compare it to PSI's norming data obtained from a four-state sample of 1,000 non-clinical cases. Further, for making inferences to the PSI-2, this strategy makes available a body of published research previously completed using the PSI. This literature is referenced and discussed in the PSI-2 manual. Hence, the PSI-2 was developed by beginning with the original 130 PSI items, five scales, and norms. The PSI lacked a depression scale, which was needed to complete this as a mental health screening device. During related health research, three items each were selected to index depressed affect, guilt/self-blame, and motor retardation. These items formed a single factor that is the Depression (Dp) scale. Manual Chapter 3 explains construction of the nine-item Dp scale and all the other new PSI-2 scales. Six Misrepresentation Scales were added in the PSI-2 in recognition of multiple strategies that examinees may pursue that distort responses to the original five Basic Scales. Symptom Overendorsement (SOE) and Erroneous Psychiatric Stereotype (EPS) were prepared to represent faking bad; Endorsement of Superior Adjustment (ESA) and Endorsement of Excessive Virtue (EEV) were prepared to represent faking good. Random Responding (Ra) and Health Problems Overstatement (HPO) complete the Misrepresentation Scales. Evidence of these scales' validity was established by factor analysis with selected MMPI-2 scales, and these analyses appear in Manual Chapter 4.

The test author prepared 21 Brief Content Scales by examining clusters of the 139 items that share similar item content. He then treated them like subscales. He saw identifying these areas separately as leading to hypotheses to be evaluated further, beyond what the Basic Scales provide. Because their brevity limits each of the 21 scale reliabilities, only extreme scores need be heeded.

Another innovation in the PSI-2 is the adoption of the 4-point rating scale in place of the false-true format of the PSI. The purpose of this change was to increase the instrument's reliability by increasing the total number of data points on each scale while retaining the cost-effectiveness of a brief screening instrument. By keeping *false* and *true* as anchoring points in this expansion, the test author intended to preserve continuity for maximum PSI comparability. If this effort succeeded, he reasoned, extrapolations could be made from PSI's four-state norms, as well as from several published PSI studies.

Contemporary norms for the PSI-2 are based on a sample of 1,046 community-dwellers ages 17-85 years, 61% from Arizona, with the balance being a mix from 30 other states. Of the total, 502 examinees were males (mean age 37.1 years), and 544 were females (mean age 36.0 years). Males' average level of schooling was 15.3 years; the average level for females was 15.2 years. Mean scores for the six Basic Screening Scales are tabled in the PSI-2 manual by age, gender, educational level, ethnicity, and geographic place of residence.

TECHNICAL. Norms for the PSI-2 scales are derived from the community-based sample of 1,046. Further useful norms come from the PSI's Basic Screening Scales from its four-state sample of 1,000. Neither set of norms is based on a national probability sample. This means that age, ethnicity, gender, education, and geographic location are not nationally representative in either the PSI or PSI-2 norms. Despite these limitations, data from the combined samples appear to be a source of useful findings for the Basic Screening Scales, provided that the PSI-2 is used for screening and not for diagnosis or classification. Putting the PSI-2 into perspective, it should be noted that its author does not represent the measure as a test, but rather as a screening procedure. The availability of its 28 newly added scales may fascinate and mislead less experienced users to confuse it with a test. As with all other screening instruments, it is to be interpreted within its limitations.

Correlations between the five Basic Screening Scales of the PSI and the PSI-2 with a sample of 103 undergraduates ranged from .85 to .95. Test-retest studies were run separately for the PSI-2 and PSI. After a mean interval of 6 days, in a sample of 200 undergraduates, the PSI-2 Basic Screening Scales' test-retest reliability coefficients ranged from .81 to .94. Test-retest reliability coefficients for the PSI Basic Screening Scales after a mean delay of 10 days ranged from .73 to .89, also in a sample of undergraduates. Item analyses used alpha coefficients to estimate internal consistency of the PSI-2's Basic Screening Scales in the normative sample. Four of the six scales had coefficients ranging from .80 to .88; the remaining two, Alienation (Al) and Defensiveness (De), yielded coefficients of .61. Manual Chapter 3 attributes lower internal consistency of Al and De to their greater content heterogeneity. Internal consistency analyses of the PSI's five Basic Screening Scales, apparently using members of its norming sample, used Kuder-Richardson Formula 20. Results yielding coefficients of .62 and .51 for Al and De, respectively; coefficients for Sn, Di, and Ex ranged from .72 to .85.

Evidence of PSI's validity for mental health screening was shown when separate analyses compared T scores from the five Basic Screening Scales for samples of psychiatric inpatients, incarcerated offenders, mental health outpatients, and the norming group of 1,000 non-patients. Golding (1978) questioned its adequacy, in terms of its validity and reliability, for assigning persons to treatments.

Using a totally different approach, evidence of validity for the PSI-2 was evaluated, first, by having undergraduates identify adults in the community whom they knew well. Of the identified adults, 171 who were contacted agreed to participate anonymously in a study requiring them to complete the PSI-2, which they did. Second, the PSI-2 author created a rating scale with 21 paired statements (42 items) to represent aspects of the Basic Screening Scales and the Basic Content Scales in two ways: One of the paired representations described a characteristic of one of the scales whereas another item clearly represented its opposite. These pairs comprised the scale for undergraduates to use in rating the familiar adults. Third, undergraduates then evaluated those adults familiar to each of them, using ratings of 0-3 to indicate the degree to which each descriptor was like or opposite to the adult respondent. Fourth, correlation coefficients were computed between ratings and adult responses to corresponding items of the PSI-2. Significant correlations were found for all 21 Brief Content Scale items: for four scales $p < .01$, and for the remaining 17 scales $p < .001$. Because the manual does not clearly present PSI-2's validity study, the presentation above was written to clarify its steps.

COMMENTARY. The PSI-2 is based on American English and has reportedly been translated into seven other languages. Its author acknowledged his awareness that the standard for creating a valid translation calls for back translation. This was done only for an Arabic translation. One of four Spanish translations is described as being more carefully constructed; it too lacks back translation. Recognized norms are not established, except for one Spanish version on a non-clinical sample of Costa Rican adolescents. Realistically, the PSI-2 remains a screening procedure for English-speaking Americans. In emergency situations, an existing translation might be used, but with no assurance of its accuracy. Another concern is that the reading difficulty level of the PSI-2 items was not studied, despite the manual's assertion that items were written at a grade-school level.

The PSI-2 expanded its scope from five to 33 scales, all without undermining its claim to be a brief screening device. A second of its claims is that it is cost-effective. Considering the modest per user cost of administration and scoring, this aim is supported. Effort cost also has been contained by using only 139 items and by linking its expanded answer choices to *false-true* anchor points. The four-choice response format further removes, for more exacting respondents, the difficulty of being forced to decide between *false* and *true* when those choices seem to say either too much or too little. Thus, response effort is lessened. Third, its claim to reduce intentional response distortion is supported by Misrepresentation Scales. Fourth, its claim to support "specific decisions" and to answer "specific questions" (manual, p. 1) is not fully supported by its normative data. Strong claims of specificity appear to overreach the usual meaning and intent of a screening procedure.

The internal organization of the manual switches between the PSI and PSI-2, frequently creating challenges for the reader. Use of the PSI-2 manual, hence, requires extra attention to its rapid changes and overlaps. This complexity is magnified by 28 added scales that deserve fuller explication. By attributing derivative validity from the PSI to the PSI-2, the manual's scattered organization requires extra reader effort to follow its twists and turns. For example, Manual Chapter 2 redirects users first to study Chapters 3 and 4. For these reasons, a comprehensive review of the PSI-2 can only be attempted here. Before adopting and using PSI-2, readers are well advised to study its manual closely.

The reader may feel inconvenienced by the test author's frequent passing mention of studies whose content he does not fully disclose or discuss. The citations seem to be intended as a kind of proof. This style of documentation forces the reader to accept the test author's conclusions, to ignore them, or to consult the original publications. Finding those publications is not always possible, as is seen by examining the author's references to two of his own studies that he cites as: [(2009) "Manuscript in preparation"], whereas the manual itself bears a 2010 copyright. This reviewer later located the first of those references. It eventually was published in 2010. The second may have been published in 2012 with a differently arranged attribution of authorship; that possibility could not be confirmed.

In preparing the PSI-2, the test author deserves to be acknowledged for his creativity in adding a useful Depression scale comprising nine items, and, from a total of just 139 items, deriving six Misrepresentation Scales and 21 Content Scales, all linking clearly to the original Basic Screening Scales. His is a rare accomplishment.

SUMMARY. The Psychological Screening Inventory-2 (PSI-2) is a brief mental health screening instrument that captures the meanings of 33 conceptually designed scales. In general, the reliability and validity of its component scales are sufficient to support their application for screening and making referrals for further assessment. Administration and scoring of the PSI-2 are completed online at modest expense. The measure is intended to screen persons 16 years and older from the general population for whom intentional response distortion is not a particular concern. Examinee response burden is light. The PSI-2 improves upon its predecessor, the PSI, in a number of ways. The PSI-2 and PSI were normed using multi-state opportunity samples of non-clinical persons. Individually and collectively, the norming samples do not approximate a national probability sample. A large number of related studies have been published and are referenced in the manual. The PSI-2 is shown by its author to meet nearly all of the screening objectives for which it was designed.

REVIEWER'S REFERENCE

Golding, S. L. (1978). [Test review of Psychological Screening Inventory]. In O. K. Buros (Ed.), *The eighth mental measurements yearbook.* Highland Park, NJ: The Gryphon Press.

Review of the Psychological Screening Inventory-2 by RICHARD R. REILLY, Professor Emeritus, Stevens Institute of Technology, Hoboken, NJ:

DESCRIPTION. The Psychological Screening Inventory-2 (PSI-2) is a revision of the original PSI developed over 30 years ago by Richard I. Lanyon as a brief mental health screening device to be used in situations where time and professional labor may be at a premium. The PSI was a 130-item test designed to be used by professionals in mental health screening settings including community clinics and referral agencies, college counseling offices, hospitals and other medical facilities, and courts. According to the test manual, "The PSI was intended only as a screening device, to be used in detecting persons who might profitably receive more intensive attention" (p. 1).

The original PSI included five Basic Screening Scales, the first three of which represented traditional general categories of mental disorder: Alienation, for major psychiatric disorder; Social Nonconformity, for significant antisocial characteristics; and Discomfort, for general psychological distress. Two additional scales were Expression, designed to measure extroversion/introversion, and Defensiveness, designed to assess the general extent to which a respondent might have misrepresented his or her characteristics. The PSI-2 includes these original scales and adds a measure of Depression, increasing the number of items to 139. Six additional scales developed from the original items and designed to assess different types of misrepresentation also are included in the PSI-2. These include Symptom Overendorsement, Erroneous Psychiatric Stereotype, Endorsement of Excessive Virtue, Endorsement of Superior Adjustment, Random Responding, and Health Problem Overstatement. The PSI-2 also includes 21 Brief Content Scales each consisting of four to nine items. These scales measure specific characteristics such as Close Relationship Difficulties, Low Self-Esteem, and Aggression/Anger. The PSI-2 items are stated in the first person and utilize a 4-point rating scale: *definitely false, slightly false, slightly true,* and *definitely true.*

The PSI-2 is a B-level assessment, which the test publisher indicates requires a minimum of a master's degree in a field with relevance for psychological adjustment and mental health as well as knowledge of psychometrics and individual differences. According to the test author, the use of the PSI-2 for hiring and placement decisions should be explored only by persons with doctorates and a thorough grounding in psychological measurement. Use for this purpose should be approached cautiously because of the possibility of legal constraints. Administration is straightforward and typically takes 15-20 minutes. Items are written at the grade-school level. It is recommended that administrators read the instructions aloud and answer any questions that respondents might have. An online platform is used for both administration and scoring. The administration platform includes a prompt if all items on a page have not been answered. The scoring system generates a report presenting scores for all scales using a T-score format.

DEVELOPMENT. The original PSI was developed based on several considerations beginning with the traditional framework involving three categories of mental disorder: major psychiatric disorder (psychotic), general distress (neurotic), and antisocial characteristics (character disorder). A second consideration was prompted by the emergence of extroversion/introversion in studies using item pools designed to measure personality or psychopathology. A final consideration was the desire to include a measure of over- or under-reporting.

Scale construction followed a multi-stage procedure. A "universe of content" (manual, p. 1) was developed for each area, and twice as many items as would be needed were written for each category. Item selection for the Alienation, Social

Nonconformity, and Defensiveness scales was based on criterion versus control group comparisons. Measures of internal consistency and factor analyses were used to develop the Discomfort and Expression scales. Whereas the PSI employed a *true/false* response format, the 4-point scale described above was selected for the PSI-2 items to improve reliability and allow the revised scales to be equivalent to the original measure. The PSI-2 added a Depression scale based on the Multidimensional Health Profile (Ruehlman, Lanyon, & Karoly, 1998, 1999). The Depression scale was based on factor analytic work on nine items that resulted in a single factor for depression. The 21 Brief Content Scales were developed using principal components analysis on the 139 items in three data sets: the normative samples for the PSI and the PSI-2 and a third sample collected from 194 individuals in forensic settings. Components were retained if the component was similar across all three samples. The Misrepresentation Scales were developed based on research that showed that the assessment of misrepresentation is best done with individual measures that directly address the specific type of misrepresentation being attempted. The Symptom Overendorsement and Erroneous Psychiatric Stereotype scales were developed to detect faking bad by comparing the responses of a sample of 100 undergraduates when taking the test honestly versus taking the test under instructions to deliberately endorse psychopathology or malingering. The Endorsement of Superior Adjustment was constructed to detect faking good using a similar procedure. The Endorsement of Excessive Virtue scale, also to detect faking good, was developed by first having 15 expert judges designate items that reflected excessive virtue and then comparing the percentage endorsement for judges to that of respondents in the original PSI normative sample (N = 1,000). Items that differed by at least 40 percentage points were retained for the scale. The remaining two Misrepresentation Scales, Random Responding and Health Problem Overstatement, were constructed separately.

TECHNICAL. Norms for the PSI-2 were developed in 2006-2007 based on responses of 1,046 participants ages 17-85. The sample included 502 males and 544 females with an average age of 36.5 years and an average of 15.3 years of education. Participants lived in communities in 31 states, but 61% of the sample lived in Arizona. Of the 637 participants who reported ethnicity, 538 were Caucasian.

The technical manual includes extensive analyses addressing reliability and validity evidence. Test-retst reliabilities, based on a retest interval averaging 6 days, are at acceptable levels for all scales. (Coefficients ranged from .81 to .94.) Internal consistency estimates are somewhat lower. Alpha coefficients for the Alienation and Defensiveness scales are .61, lower than test-retest reliability. This may be due to item heterogeneity within these scales rather than true error of measurement. The pattern of intercorrelations between the major scales and a separate factor analysis support construct evidence of validity of the PSI-2 scores. Item response theory was applied to normative data for the various scales in the PSI and the PSI-2 and showed smaller standard errors of measurement for scales in the PSI-2. The assessment of criterion-related validity evidence was accomplished with a series of studies comparing individuals diagnosed or being treated for the relevant psychiatric disorders with a normative sample that served as a control group. Evidence of validity for the three major mental disorder scales included Cohen's d, a measure of effect size; ROC analysis, which allows assessment of accuracy across the range of possible cut scores; sensitivity, or the proportion of correctly identified individuals with a psychiatric disorder; specificity, or the proportion of correctly identified individuals without a psychiatric disorder; and positive and negative predictive power. Positive predictive power is the probability that a person above the cut score is a member of the target group. Negative predictive power is the probability that a person below the cut score is a member of the control group. All of the results support the validity of the PSI-2 scores. The results for predictive power, sensitivity, and specificity were computed with the assumption of a base rate of .20 for the target group and specific cutoffs corresponding to a T score of 60. With the exception of the Random Responding scale, the validity of the Misrepresentation Scales was examined by comparing responses when respondents were asked to fake in the intended direction vs. responding honestly. Correlations with the MMPI F Scale and two other measures of response inconsistency provided evidence for the validity of the Random Responding scale.

COMMENTARY. The technical manual for the PSI-2 could serve as an exemplar for test developers. It is well organized and comprehensive and demonstrates a keen understanding of psychometric methodology. In addition to what is presented in the test manual, an extensive body of published research supports the scale development and the reliability and evidence of validity of the measures within the PSI-2. Recommendations for administration and interpretation follow sound professional guidelines. The computerized administration and scoring make the PSI-2 a quick and relatively inexpensive initial screen. Given the emphasis on cost-effectiveness, future revisions of the test manual might include an analysis comparing the cost benefits of using the PSI-2 as an initial screen with other alternatives such as diagnostic interviews.

SUMMARY. The PSI-2 is a revision of the PSI and is designed to be a brief mental health screening device. The revision assesses three traditional categories of mental disorder: Alienation, Social Nonconformity, and Discomfort as well as Expression and Defensiveness. Twenty-one Brief Content Scales and six Misrepresentation Scales also have been included. The test manual provides extensive technical data supporting the reliability of the instrument and offering evidence of validity for the scores generated by it. Guidelines for administration and interpretation follow excellent standards of professional practice. The PSI-2 is recommended for use as a screening device for persons who might gain from additional assessment or attention.

REVIEWER'S REFERENCES

Ruehlman, L. S., Lanyon, R. I., & Karoly, P. (1998). *Multidimensional Health Profile: Professional manual.* Odessa, FL: Psychological Assessment Resources.

Ruehlman, L. S., Lanyon, R. I., & Karoly, P. (1999). Development and validation of the Multidimensional Health Profile. Part I: Psychosocial functioning. *Psychological Assessment, 11,* 166-176.

[128]

Quick Informal Assessment, Fourth Edition.

Purpose: Designed to "assess a student's proficiency in English."
Population: Students in kindergarten through adults.
Publication Dates: 1997-2015.
Acronym: QIA.
Scores: Total score only.
Administration: Individual.
Parts, 2: Oral, Literacy.
Forms: 6 alternate forms, A-F, for each part.
Price Data: Available from publisher.
Foreign Language Edition: Spanish version available.
Time: Administration time not reported.
Comments: Literacy assessment administered to students who score at Levels III through V on Oral test and who are in Grade 2 or above; oral performance can be categorized using English Language Development (ELD) standards (Levels I-V), California English Language Development (CA ELD) standards (Emerging Entering, Emerging Exiting, Expanding Entering, Expanding Exiting, Bridging), and World-Class Instructional Design and Assessment (WIDA) standards (Entering, Emerging, Developing, Expanding, Bridging-Reaching); for the literacy assessment, performance may be classified according to five levels of language proficiency (Pre-writing, Word Writing, Sentence Writing, Narrative Writing, Advanced Writing).
Authors: Constance O. Williams.
Publisher: CW Educational Enterprises.
Cross References: For reviews by Alan Garfinkel and Alfred P. Longo of the original edition, see 13:250.

Review of the Quick Informal Assessment, Fourth Edition by GABRIEL DELLA-PIANA, Professor Emeritus in Educational Psychology, College of Education, University of Utah, Salt Lake City, UT:

DESCRIPTION. The Quick Informal Assessment (QIA), which is in its fourth edition, is intended, as the title indicates, as an informal, teacher-administered, individual assessment of student proficiency in English (and other languages not reviewed here) with accuracy and speed. The test consists of two parts (Oral and Literacy) with six alternate forms in English and may be used at kindergarten through adult levels. The writing assessment (Literacy) is based on the Oral language section score and grade level of the student.

The Oral section consists of a story starter in the form of a picture. The examiner shows the picture to the examinee and may also introduce the story with a provided prompt. The prompt is followed by 20 questions, with five levels and four questions at each level, as the student looks at the picture. Questions focus on identifying parts of the picture, what is happening in the picture, what actions were taken by the main character, and so on. Acceptable responses appear to the right of each question and are to be scored with a plus (+) or minus (-). If a student gets three out of four responses correct at one level, the examiner proceeds to the next level. The proficiency level is the highest level at which the examinee answered at least three of the four questions correctly. If the examinee reaches the final question on the Oral portion of the assessment, the examiner writes the student's response on a separate sheet of paper so that scoring can take into account various aspects of the response such as grammatical correctness, accuracy, complexity, spontaneity, and developmental appropriateness. Based on Common Core State Standards, a QIA Language Proficiency Chart is provided for classification of English language development into one of three levels:

emerging, expanding, and bridging. Classifications are not intended to be fixed; regrouping may occur throughout the year. Test results are intended to guide instruction and the amount of scaffolding needed for students.

The Literacy section of the QIA is used for students who score at Levels 3 through 5 on the Oral test and who are in Grade 2 or above. The test author recommends that the same form be used as was used for the Oral test. Thus, the Literacy test form is one page with a small version of the picture and a paragraph to be read by the student as a prompt for a second paragraph to be written by the student. The starter paragraph repeats the description of the picture (i.e., the prompt) that was given to the student in the Oral section followed by an instruction to "write what you think will happen next." Thus, each student has the form that matches the one he or she had for the Oral section. The Literacy portion may be administered individually or in a group. Scoring is based on two rubrics. The first rubric consists of five levels: Pre-writing, Word Writing, Sentence Writing, Narrative Writing, and Advanced Writing. The second rubric also has five levels of proficiency for each of three categories: Vocabulary Usage (Word/Phrase Level), Language Forms and Conventions (Sentence Level), and Linguistic Complexity.

The examiner's manual contains instructions for administration and scoring and the test forms. A separate picture booklet includes color pictures printed on card stock for Forms A-F.

DEVELOPMENT. Although there is no separate section in the test manual on development of the instrument, the test author notes that this edition incorporated teacher feedback from the third edition, test questions have been aligned across the six alternate forms, various standards (based on research and Common Core Standards) have been "taken into account" (manual, p. 1), and updated art work reflects diversity of students in the schools.

TECHNICAL. The QIA is an informal assessment intended to supplement standardized measures. The test manual does not include formal technical data on standardization. The manual also does not contain reliability data, and no formal validity data are presented or discussed under those headings. Reliability, though not to be ignored, may be considered less important with a measure that is repeated by the teacher and by a process where levels are not fixed but rather are assumed as temporary with opportunity for the student to advance.

COMMENTARY. The QIA provides a useful set of informal assessment materials for an experienced teacher with knowledge of the subject matter and some assessment skill and knowledge to use to supplement other more formal standardized tests with validity and reliability evidence. The test manual does not suggest training for administration, scoring, interpretation, and use of the measure. However, training is seen by this reviewer as essential for administration, scoring, and use. At a minimum, teachers might form a group to do that self-training as peers. The test author's claim that the QIA is easy to administer without standardization data is speculative. The levels of QIA Oral Language Proficiency are based on previous research and Common Core Standards with a chart having reasonable specificity. The writing rubrics are also reasonably specific. Content validity as a representation of a domain may be inferred from this information, although it is not specifically analyzed and reported.

SUMMARY. The QIA is an informal assessment tool that teachers with a background in literacy and assessment may find useful for informal placement, progress monitoring, and instructional insights if not formal guides. This reviewer, however, suggests that a team of teachers work together to train themselves or find someone to assist them in administration, scoring, interpretation, and use of the data. This process should be approached as a challenging task.

Review of the Quick Informal Assessment, Fourth Edition by KEVIN B. JOLDERSMA, Senior Psychometrician, The American Board of Emergency Medicine, East Lansing, MI:

DESCRIPTION. The Quick Informal Assessment (QIA) is an English language proficiency assessment of Oral communication and Literacy. Each of the six Oral assessment forms consists of 20 open-ended questions. The six Literacy assessment forms consist of a single prompt that requires a short written response. Language proficiency is reported at five different levels that are cross mapped to three state and U.S. national proficiency descriptors.

The test is designed to be administered, scored, and interpreted by classroom teachers in an English language learning environment. Answers for the Oral assessment are entered and scored in real time. If a student does not pass a given level by responding to three out of four questions correctly, the test is concluded. No timing guidelines are provided.

The Literacy test is administered if an examinee scores at least Level 3 on the Oral assessment and is in second grade or higher. Students are given a single written prompt that contains a scenario and asks the examinee to write what comes next. Scores may be generated using a holistic rating facilitated by two possible rubrics. One rubric is unique to the QIA and provides five holistic descriptors of writing samples; the other details writing characteristics found at five levels used in several state and U.S. English language proficiency assessments. It is unclear whether the QIA writing rubric levels are intended to parallel the levels used in the Oral assessment or nationally accepted ELP levels.

In addition to the two testing components, teachers are supplied with two instructional aids. The English Verb Clock details the expected morphological and syntactic developmental cycle as students progress from early stages of English language acquisition toward integration and potentially exiting an English language development program. The second piece of supplemental material is a table containing 12 suggested activities for learners at various stages of development.

DEVELOPMENT. The fourth edition of the QIA updates the prior QIA to align better with the Common Core State Standards and to reflect increased student diversity in the test's artwork. As a criterion-referenced test, the QIA was developed to be a shorter and faster test of the Common Core English language proficiency standards than some longer measures that require more time to administer and score.

Materials provided for review by the test developer included an examiner's manual and accompanying test picture booklet. Minimal information regarding initial test development is available. The test manual discusses the difference between Basic Interpersonal Communication Skills (BICS) and Cognitive Academic Language Proficiency (CALP; Cummins, 1989), but it does not indicate how these concepts are operationalized in the QIA items or the levels it assigns. The Level 1 questions on the Oral assessment seem to represent BICS, but not even the Level 5 questions appear to address CALP.

TECHNICAL. Although not explicitly stated in the test manual, the QIA is a criterion-referenced test aligned to state and U.S. national standards in English language development. No information is provided about piloting the test or assessing item alignment to the cited standards. Although the process of linking to the related performance standards is not detailed, there is apparent care in the selection of specific verbs and morphological structures indicative of each level within the standards.

There is no technical information regarding the reliability of scores nor the seemingly arbitrary decision to use three out of four correct responses as the passing criterion for each level of the Oral section. The ability of four items to determine success or failure at each level of the assessment is dubious. The use of a single writing prompt to evaluate writing skills also would seem prone to possible misclassification.

In terms of appropriate test use, the test manual indicates that the test is intended as (a) a teacher-friendly measure (proficiency level), (b) an interim placement tool (while waiting for standardized test results), (c) a progress monitoring tool, (d) a student grouping tool, (e) a formative assessment, or (f) a language dominance test when combined with the QIA administered in other languages. Evidence of the relationship between test scores and any of these use cases is not presented. Care has been taken to present examinees with a diverse set of relatable, everyday pictures. There is not, however, evidence to suggest that test use across gender, racial, ethnic, or cultural groups is equivalent.

COMMENTARY. The two subtests do well to contain the paired receptive and productive skills for each form of communication. The Oral test implicitly involves a listening and speaking component, and the Literacy test contains both a reading and writing element.

On the Oral component, the test authors indicate that most questions are intended to elicit a specific verb form from the learner. Although these verb forms might be elicited from the learner incidentally, one could easily see answering the questions without mirroring the appropriate morphological form. The questions are intended to expose knowledge of basic vocabulary to verb tenses ranging in sophistication from simple present tense to past perfect conditional. The test authors cite Beck, McKeown, and Kucan (2013) as their rationale for having three tiers of vocabulary requirements but make no apparent connection to this work in the tasks or test questions.

Using verb forms and vocabulary leveling as a proxy for language proficiency has fallen into disfavor somewhat as task-based instruction (Long, 2015) has gained popularity. Although the test may be intended to focus on morphological complexity, grammaticality, and vocabulary sophistication, the tasks completed by the examinee might better be classified as recognition of objects, counting, describing a picture, language-mirroring, or inference about next steps (creative storytelling). National standards, including those cited in this assessment, also have made this shift toward making more task-oriented claims about what learners can do with language rather than providing superficial evidence of linguistic features. The apparent judgment of the QIA to value linguistic features over effective communication is unfortunate. In addition, placing value judgments on academic language being more sophisticated than social communication may say more about cultural or social values than about linguistic progression or language proficiency.

Within the Literacy component, the test authors indicate that the test should be taken by students in Grades 2 and up who score at least Level 3 or above on the Oral assessment. The assessment clearly involves a blend of reading comprehension and writing skills. The writing prompts assess not only the ability to read a scenario, but also to understand instructions, to relate to the picture and understand what is happening, and to invent a story about what will happen next. Teachers are asked to assess the writing sample in terms of vocabulary, sentence formation and conventions, and linguistic complexity. Each of these subdomains has five levels of proficiency; it is unclear what teachers should do in terms of the overall level if results are inconsistent.

Overall, the test authors indicate that the test is suitable for children in kindergarten through adults. It is difficult to believe that the same questions will function equally well across such a disparate group of test takers. In addition, this test appears to walk the difficult line between assessment and instructional tool without committing to one purpose.

SUMMARY. The QIA was designed to be a rapid and informal assessment of language proficiency across multiple domains (listening, speaking, reading, and writing) for use by classroom teachers in an English language learning environment. The test meets its goal of providing an instrument for loosely grouping students for instructional purposes. Many of the other suggested uses of the test do not have data to support these use cases. Given that there is little evidence to support effective use of the QIA, it is not recommended that this test be used for high stakes decision-making.

REVIEWER'S REFERENCES

Cummins, J. (1989). *Empowering minority students.* Sacramento, CA: California Association for Bilingual Education.

Beck, I. L., McKeown, M. G., & Kucan, L. (2013). *Bringing words to life: Robust vocabulary instruction* (2nd ed.). New York, NY: Guilford Press.

Long, M. (2015). *Second language acquisition and task-based language teaching.* Hoboken, NJ: Wiley-Blackwell.

[129]

Quick Interactive Language Screener™.

Purpose: "Designed to evaluate whether children are making language progress appropriate for their age group."
Population: Ages 3-0 to 5-11.
Publication Date: 2017.
Acronym: QUILS™.
Scores, 4: Vocabulary, Syntax, Process, Overall.
Administration: Individual.
Price Data, 2020: $99.95 per annual subscription including digital manual (144 pages), quick start guide, online screener access, student reports, parent reports, group reports, and language development activities and tips; $29.95 per print manual.
Time: 15-20 minutes for administration.
Comments: Administered and scored online.
Authors: Roberta Michnick Golinkoff, Jill de Villiers, Kathy Hirsh-Pasek, Aquiles Iglesias, and Mary Sweig Wilson.
Publisher: Paul H. Brookes Publishing Co., Inc.

Review of the Quick Interactive Language Screener by KATHLEEN ASPIRANTI, Assistant Professor, Youngstown State University, Youngstown, OH:

DESCRIPTION. The Quick Interactive Language Screener (QUILS) was developed to assess vocabulary, syntax, and language acquisition skills in young children. The QUILS is a screening instrument designed to quickly and easily identify children ages 3 through 5 in need of further, more extensive assessment. The goal of the QUILS is to provide a culturally fair, electronic screener that assesses whether a child's language development within the areas of Vocabulary, Process, and Syntax is appropriate for his/her age. There are three 16-item areas measured for a total of 48 items. The Vocabulary area measures knowledge of nouns, verbs, prepositions, and conjunctions. The Syntax area addresses knowledge of *wh*-questions, past tense, prepositional phrases, and embedded clauses. The Process area examines noun learning, adjective learning, verb learning, and converting active voice to passive voice.

The QUILS takes 15-20 minutes to administer via touchscreen tablet or computer. All items are presented using audio instructions and pictures or videos with three to four multiple-choice pictorial responses. Before administration, a seven-item language questionnaire is given to the child's parent or caregiver to determine English language proficiency. The child must be proficient in English in order to be eligible to take the QUILS; a bilingual English-Spanish version of the QUILS (QUILS: ES) is in development, according to the test publisher. Results are calculated via the computer software and are reported as raw scores, standard scores, and percentile ranks. Normative tables are provided in the user's manual. Student brief and detailed reports, parent reports, and group reports for multiple students are available through the computer software.

DEVELOPMENT. The user's manual lists four phases in the development of the QUILS: item development, first item tryout, second item tryout, and creation of the final version. Items were developed using three guiding principles. First, words or linguistic structures that would be biased for certain dialects (e.g., African American English, Southern White English) were avoided. Second, items had to be easily represented using static or animated visual display. Third, the items developed were significant in both English and Spanish language acquisition to allow the QUILS and the QUILS: ES to be compatible. Pilot testing of each item occurred during the item development phase within laboratory settings, but minimal information about this process was provided in the user's manual.

During the first item tryout phase, artists drew all items for consistency. Ninety-six items (half vocabulary, half syntax) were given to 306 examinees (3-5 years old) in Massachusetts, Delaware, and Pennsylvania. Test-order, Rasch, and differential item functioning (DIF) analyses were conducted to identify the best 60 items of the original pool of 96.

During the second item tryout phase, the 60-item screener was given to 674 examinees ages 3-5 years in Massachusetts, Delaware, Pennsylvania, Florida, and Nebraska. Reliability and validity analyses were conducted during this phase. After the second item tryout phase, Rasch and DIF analyses were completed, and 48 items were identified for inclusion in the final version of the QUILS.

TECHNICAL.

Standardization. The normative sample included 415 children ages 3-5 (mean age 4.5, 48.7% male) from five states who were dominant in English. Children with reported visual or hearing difficulties were excluded from the sample, but the presence of other disabilities was not reported. The majority of children were from low socioeconomic status families (61.2%). Only 43.6% of the sample included data on race.

Reliability. The QUILS provides evidence of reliability through test-retest, internal consistency, and interrater methods. Test-retest reliability was estimated by giving the QUILS twice to 75 children with an interval of 3-5 weeks for "nearly all" children (manual, p. 101). Reliability coefficients were .71 for Vocabulary, .73 for Syntax, .69 for Process, and .83 for the Overall score. Internal consistency, evaluated using coefficient alpha, was .79 for the Vocabulary and Syntax areas and .87 for the Process area. Interrater reliability concerns are minimized through automated administration and scoring. Standard scores at different testing sites were compared, and no dissimilarities were found between the different testers or testing sites.

Validity. Evidence of validity was provided as construct evidence. To examine construct evidence of validity, Rasch analyses were conducted on each area of the QUILS and on the screener overall. Although the user's manual indicates that "Fit statistics... were close to the expected value of 1" (p. 103), no actual data were provided. Infit mean-squares were calculated, and the values were reported to fall between -0.7 and 1.3, although actual scores were not provided.

Construct evidence was further evaluated during the second item tryout phase. During this phase, 40 children were given the Auditory Comprehension subtest of the Preschool Language Scales, Fifth Edition (PLS-5; Zimmerman, Steiner, & Pond, 2011), 44 children were given Form A of the Peabody Picture Vocabulary Test, Fourth Edition (PPVT-4; Dunn & Dunn, 2007), and 77 children were given both the PPVT-4 and the PLS-5. Scores on these assessments were compared to scores on the QUILS. Scores on the PPVT-4 correlated significantly with QUILS scores in the Vocabulary area (r = .67), Syntax area (r = .54), Process area (r = .58), and Overall (r = .67). Scores on the PLS-5 correlated significantly with QUILS scores in the Vocabulary area (r = .59), Syntax area (r = .54), Process area (r = .62), and Overall (r = .65). No validity studies examining content or criterion evidence of validity were reported in the test manual.

COMMENTARY. The reviewers evaluated several children with the QUILS using a tablet and found the screener easy to administer. The 3-year-old boy thought the screener was a fun game, but the 5-year-old girl appeared less engaged. The touchscreen interface was simple for the children to understand. The brief report and parent report were straightforward, and the detailed report provided the test taker's responses to all items. Children are recommended for further evaluation if scores fall below the 25th percentile, and other recommendations and resources are available through the QUILS website. Several helpful case studies are provided within the test manual.

The QUILS appears to be a useful, relatively quick, and simple tool to screen young children's language abilities. The user's manual contains all pertinent information, but several areas, such as the description surrounding the development of the items, could be expanded. Information on pilot studies was limited. Many schools screen students three times a year; however, with only one form of the QUILS available, practice effects could occur with repeated use. The availability of one form only also makes it difficult to rescreen children who may have had invalid results the first time. Additionally, normative data are not available for students with disabilities, and demographic data regarding race are available for only half of the sample. Therefore, scores obtained by students with disabilities or from racial minority groups should be interpreted with caution. Another concern is that reliability and validity data were collected during the second item tryout phase, rather than with the final version of the QUILS. It is not clear whether the reliability and validity data were based on all 60 items in the second item tryout phase or only the 48 items included in the final version.

SUMMARY. The QUILS was designed to quickly and easily screen the language abilities of young children. This assessment seems to meet its goal of measuring vocabulary, syntax, product, and the process of learning new vocabulary. Convincing evidence of test-retest and internal consistency reliability was established. Construct evidence of validity was presented, but additional evidence would increase the confidence test users may have in the use of QUILS scores. The screener provides cut scores in order to identify children in need of further language assessment; however, the normative sample should have included students with disabilities. Overall, this instrument can be recommended for use as a screener and will be useful to identify children in need of further assessment.

REVIEWER'S REFERENCES

Dunn, L. M., & Dunn, D. M. (2007). Peabody Picture Vocabulary Test, Fourth Edition. Minneapolis, MN: Pearson.

Zimmerman, I. L., Steiner, V. G., & Pond, R. E. (2011). Preschool Language Scales, Fifth Edition. San Antonio, TX: Psychological Corporation.

Review of the Quick Interactive Language Screener by MAURA JONES MOYLE, Associate Professor, Marquette University, Milwaukee, WI:

DESCRIPTION. The Quick Interactive Language Screener (QUILS) is an individually administered language screening tool for children ages 3-0 to 5-11. Its purposes are to monitor children's language development relative to their age and to identify children who would benefit from a comprehensive language evaluation. The QUILS is designed to assess the aspects of language that are predictive of later academic success (i.e., vocabulary and syntax) as well as process dimensions of language. The screener assesses language comprehension (i.e., it does not assess expressive language). The rationale for focusing on language comprehension versus language production is that young children often are reticent to interact verbally with adults, but they will usually participate in receptive language tasks (e.g., pointing at pictures). Also, delays in language comprehension tend to be better predictors of persistent language impairment than delays in expressive language (e.g., Leonard, 2014).

The QUILS is intended for English speakers only. A bilingual English-Spanish version of the QUILS is in development (QUILS: English-Spanish, or QUILS: ES). The QUILS provides a Language Questionnaire completed by parents that assists in determining whether the child is mostly monolingual and therefore a candidate for screening with the QUILS.

The QUILS assesses the products of linguistic knowledge, or what children have learned about vocabulary and syntax. In addition, it assesses language processes, or how quickly children learn new words and how well they generalize syntactic information. The test authors explain that assessing both linguistic products and processes helps reduce bias against children who speak nonmainstream forms of English. Assessing processes also assists in identifying children with normal language learning abilities who may exhibit delays in language development due to lack of exposure to rich language models.

The QUILS uses digital technology for administration and scoring. The screener can be delivered via a tablet, laptop, or desktop computer. Touchscreen capabilities are preferred, but a mouse can be used for responding. A reliable internet connection is required. According to the user's manual, the QUILS takes 15 to 20 minutes to administer. Testing may be paused but should be completed within 2 weeks. The QUILS can be administered by adults with no special training. The role of the adult is to set up a student record, ensure the child is familiar with using a touchscreen (or mouse), and provide the child with a brief set of directions to get the assessment started. Once it begins, additional directions and practice items are provided by the screener. The adult monitors children's responses during the practice items and may provide additional guidance to ensure the child understands how to make a selection. The test items are then delivered automatically in a standardized manner. Adults monitor children's attention to the screener because items cannot be repeated at will. Adults also encourage children to respond if they are hesitant (e.g., "Make your best guess."), and provide general reinforcement if needed (e.g., "Keep going!").

Each content area of the QUILS (Vocabulary, Syntax, Process) contains 16 items, for a total of 48 items. Once a child completes the screener, the QUILS software automatically records and scores responses and is capable of generating various types of reports. The reports provide standard scores and percentile ranks relative to the child's age for the three content areas and the Overall score. The report options include three types of student reports (i.e., the Student Brief Report, the Student Detailed Report, and a Status Over Time Report), a parent report, and two types of group reports.

The QUILS uses a cut score of the 25th percentile to identify children who should be referred for follow-up assessment. This cut score was chosen based on the clinical judgment and experience of the test development team.

DEVELOPMENT. The QUILS was developed over 5 years in four phases. The first phase was item development. A team of experts in child development, linguistics, and other related fields chose items that assess language skills known to develop in children between 3-0 and 5-11. Items were designed to avoid cultural bias for speakers of African American English and other non-mainstream dialects. Items were also chosen if they could be represented visually and if they had equal significance in English and Spanish in order to facilitate development of the QUILS: ES. Following pilot testing, those items that were too easy or too difficult or that did not reflect increasing skill development (i.e., response accuracy did not increase with age) were omitted. The next phases were the first and second item tryouts. In the first item tryout children were administered 96 items. Rasch and differential item functioning (DIF) analyses were completed, and the 60 best items (e.g., items that correlated with age) were identified. The second item tryout then identified the best 48 items using similar analyses as in the first item tryout. The fourth phase resulted in the final version of the QUILS, which contains the best 48 items after the first two item tryouts. These items were found to have good discriminative power across the range of abilities in the normative sample and were unbiased in terms of gender.

TECHNICAL. The QUILS was normed on 415 children ages 3-0 to 5-11 with no reported visual or hearing difficulties and who were English dominant. Children were screened in child care centers, Head Start programs, preschools, and kindergarten classrooms in the states of Massachusetts, Pennsylvania, Delaware, Florida, and Nebraska. The majority of children in the normative sample were from families of low socioeconomic status (61.2%). Data for race were reported for 43.6% of the sample. Of these children, 57.8% were White, 31.6% were African American, and 8.8% were multiracial. Fewer than 1% were Asian, and 1% were other races.

Information describing the validity and reliability of the QUILS is provided in the user's manual. First, the test authors address evidence of construct validity, which relates to the degree to which the test measures what it is designed to measure. The test authors discuss the theoretical perspectives and empirical knowledge of preschool language development that were used to guide the design of the QUILS. In addition, Rasch modeling was used to ensure internal integrity of the screener.

Convergent evidence of validity was examined by administering the QUILS and the Peabody Picture Vocabulary Test, Fourth Edition (PPVT-4; Dunn & Dunn, 2007) to 116 preschool children. Pearson correlation coefficients between the QUILS and the PPVT-4 were significant and of moderate strength (r = .54-.67) for the three area scores (Vocabulary, Syntax, Process) and the Overall score. In addition, 112 children were administered the QUILS and the Preschool Language Scales, Fifth

Edition (PLS-5; Zimmerman, Steiner, & Pond, 2011). Correlations were significant and of moderate strength (r = .54-.65). The test authors concluded that these results provide evidence for the validity of using scores from the QUILS as measures of children's language development.

The test authors conducted three types of analyses to estimate reliability of the QUILS. Test-retest reliability was estimated by re-administering the QUILS to a group of 75 children. The time interval between test administrations ranged from 3 to 5 weeks. The Overall QUILS scores exhibited a strong correlation between administrations (r = .83). The three area scores demonstrated moderate to strong correlations across administrations (r = .69-.73). Internal consistency reliability was calculated using coefficient alpha for the three content areas and the Overall score. The values ranged from .79 to .93, indicating that the items measure a unidimensional construct within each area of the screener and for the Overall score.

COMMENTARY. The QUILS is a well designed screener of language comprehension in preschool children. It is easy to administer and automatically generates standard scores, percentile ranks, and a variety of reports. Administration and use of the QUILS appears to be feasible in early childhood education settings, provided the settings have access to tablets or computers and an internet connection. The screener itself is presented in a game-like format using colorful graphics and regular breaks with encouraging animation for positive reinforcement. The characters included in the illustrations are diverse in terms of age, ethnicity, and ability. The administration time of 15 to 20 minutes might be long for some preschoolers, but the screener can be paused and resumed. The items cannot be repeated on demand, so an adult needs to be present to ensure the child is attending to the tasks. The test authors provide evidence supporting the validity and reliability of the QUILS scores and their uses. The normative sample is diverse, although demographic information regarding race was available for only 43.6% of the sample. The majority of children in the normative sample (61.2%) were from low income backgrounds.

SUMMARY. The Quick Interactive Language Screener (QUILS) is an individually administered screening tool of language comprehension skills for English-speaking children ages 3-0 to 5-11. The QUILS assesses vocabulary and syntax and examines both language products and processes. Its purpose is to monitor children's language development and ensure they are progressing as expected for their age. Children who fall below the cutoff score may benefit from a comprehensive language evaluation. The QUILS is based on current theoretical perspectives and empirical knowledge of preschool language development. Evidence supporting its validity and reliability as a language screener is provided.

REVIEWER'S REFERENCES

Dunn, L. M., & Dunn, D. M. (2007). Peabody Picture Vocabulary Test, Fourth Edition. Minneapolis, MN: Pearson.

Leonard, L. B. (2014). *Children with specific language impairment.* Cambridge, MA: MIT Press.

Zimmerman, I. L., Steiner, V. G., & Pond, R. E. (2011). Preschool Language Scales, Fifth Edition. San Antonio, TX: Psychological Corporation.

[130]

Quick Neurological Screening Test–3rd Edition, Revised.

Purpose: Designed to assess "motor planning and control, and integration of sensory information" and "to quantify, over time, the presence and extent of NSS [neurological soft signs] that may be of clinical importance."
Population: Ages 5 and older.
Publication Dates: 1974-2017.
Acronym: QNST-3R.
Scores, 14: Figure Recognition and Production, Palm Form Recognition, Eye Tracking, Sound Patterns, Finger to Nose, Thumb and Finger Circle, Rapidly Reversing Repetitive Hand Movements, Arm and Leg Extension, Tandem Walk, Stand on One Leg, Skipping, Left-Right Discrimination, Behavioral Irregularities, Total.
Administration: Individual.
Price Data, 2020: $125 per complete kit including manual (2017, 87 pages), 25 record forms, and 25 remedial guidelines forms; $65 per manual; $40 per 25 record forms; $20 per 25 remedial guidelines forms.
Time: (20) minutes.
Comments: May be completed in more than one session.
Authors: Margaret C. Mutti, Nancy A. Martin, Norma V. Spalding, and Harold M. Sterling.
Publisher: Academic Therapy Publications.
Cross References: For reviews by Bradley Merker and Shawn Powell of the third edition, see 19:139; for a review by Edward E. Gotts of the second revised edition, see 14:306; see also T5:2141 (1 reference) and T4:2183 (3 references); for a review by Russell L. Adams of an earlier edition, see 9:1027.

Review of the Quick Neurological Screening Test–3rd Edition, Revised by RIK CARL D'AMATO, Distinguished International Research Professor in School Psychology and Clinical Neuropsychology, the Chicago School of Professional Psychology, Chicago,

IL, and ELIZABETH M. POWER, Department of School Psychology, the College of Saint Rose, Albany, NY:

[The first reviewer would like to acknowledge the equal contributions of the second reviewer.]

DESCRIPTION. The Quick Neurological Screening Test– 3rd Edition, Revised (QNST-3R) is an individually administered tool designed to screen for neurological soft signs (NSS) in persons ages 5 to 80+ years. The test authors suggest that it is useful in reliably assessing, over time, the presence and extent of deficits in sensory processing and in motor planning and control. There is one form of the test, which has been adapted from traditional neurological exams and developmental scales. The assessment begins with a warm-up task that provides an opportunity for building rapport and making qualitative observations; this is not a scored section. The remainder of the assessment consists of 11 tasks and two additional items that score left-right skills and fine/gross motor behavior. A section of the test manual includes special educators as targeted users of this assessment. One would hope that an assessment similar to that of a neurological evaluation would be intended for use only by trained and knowledgeable practitioners.

Administration instructions are clear and easy to follow. The QNST-3R takes 20 minutes to administer and approximately 10 minutes to score. Raw scores are computed for each task, and a Total score is derived by summing the task scores. To obtain the raw score for each task, the examiner totals the number of error points. Multiple errors are described, and examinees score 0, 1, or 3 depending on the error. On some tasks, the examinee can only obtain a score of 0 or 3; there are no details as to why a score of 2 is not an option. The Total score indicates errors made by the examinee (i.e., number of NSS observed during the tasks). The QNST-3R uses the following functional categories based on the examinee's percentile rank: no discrepancy, moderate discrepancy, and severe discrepancy.

DEVELOPMENT. The QNST-3R is the latest edition of the QNST, which was first developed in 1974. The tasks used in the original assessment appear similar to those used in standard neurological exams. The assessment evolved to include clarifications of instructions and scoring (QNST-II), standardization using a national sample, and a wider age range (QNST-3). The test authors developed the QNST-3R to improve administration and scoring guidelines, as well as to reconsider certain tasks. Although the authors report a reanalysis of data, a date as to when this occurred is not provided. Following the re-analysis, one task (Double Simultaneous Stimulation of Hand and Cheek) was eliminated, and another task (Hand Skill) was converted to a warm-up task. The test manual provides limited information on the original QNST, as well as the second and third editions. The test authors briefly describe soft signs in normal development, as well as those in populations with learning disabilities, autism, attention-deficit/hyperactivity disorder (ADHD), schizophrenia, and Alzheimer's disease.

TECHNICAL. The re-analysis of the QNST-3R used the same standardization sample as the QNST-3, which included 1,158 individuals ages 5-97 years. The QNST-3 standardization involved 50 examiners and was conducted at 43 sites in 22 states across the United States at public, private, and parochial schools; clinics; and private practices. The standardization edition of the QNST-3 was administered individually to each participant. The test manual includes little information as to how the examiners were trained to use the tool. The sample appears to closely approximate demographics of the U.S. population according to the U.S. Bureau of the Census (2010). However, considering that the same sample used for the QNST-3 was used for this version, these reviewers consider these norms somewhat dated. The test authors provided demographic information regarding gender, ethnicity, education level, region, age range, disability type, and geographical area (e.g., rural, urban).

In order to evaluate reliability, the test authors considered measures of internal consistency and temporal stability (test-retest reliability). Previous reviewers expressed concern with the tool's reliability, specifically lack of mention of interrater reliability. Unfortunately, the QNST-3R is no exception; there is no mention of interrater reliability in the test manual. Internal consistency was examined using coefficient alpha and McDonald's omega coefficients. Results demonstrated acceptable internal consistency, except for with individuals ages 20-59, where the reported coefficients were below .70. The test authors suggest that results for this age group should be interpreted with caution. Test-retest reliability coefficients ranged from .53 and .93, with large effect sizes over a 12- to 21-day interval. The test authors note that the results from the QNST-3R are stable over time; however, there is no discussion provided for lower (i.e., .53) test-retest reliability coefficients.

Four types of validity evidence were provided for the QNST-3R: evidence based on content, evidence based on diagnostic accuracy, evidence based on relationships to performance on other assessments, and evidence based on relationships to other variables, such as age and disability group status. It is unclear when the validity evidence was collected. Evidence based on content is apparent in that items on the QNST-3 are more difficult for the youngest and oldest individuals when compared to others, for example, in the age bracket of 20-59 years. Scores from the QNST-3R were compared to scores on several other assessments, such as the Bruininks-Oseretsky Test of Motor Proficiency, Second Edition and the Bender Visual-Motor Gestalt Test, Second Edition. No significant correlations between the QNST-3R and other described assessments were observed, indicating that the QNST-3R measures skills that are distinct from the motor and cognitive skills assessed by the comparison tests, thus offering evidence of divergence. The comparison of these tests to the QNST-3R seems odd at best, given that they measure different abilities.

COMMENTARY. The QNST-3R is a brief and easy test to administer. Directions are clear and easy to understand. The assessment appears to have good face validity, though evidence for other forms of validity may be questionable. Although a tool is needed for assessing potential NSS across development, the current measure cannot be recommended for clinical use at this time. It seems apparent that the test authors did not make a great deal of change to this revision, and newer versions of the test appear to have perpetuated certain problems associated with earlier versions. The same sample was used for norming purposes as had been used in the previous edition. The test authors did not appear to consider reviews from Merker and Funk (2014) and from Powell (2014), who raised concerns about reliability and validity evidence. In future revisions, the authors would do well to ensure that examiners with appropriate expertise are used. Additionally, case studies should be provided to better guide users.

SUMMARY. The QNST-3R was designed to be an individually administered measure of NSS in persons ages 5 to 80+ years. This tool is meant to be used as a screening instrument, but it is problematic given the audiences to which it is offered. The QNST-3R was adapted from traditional neurological exams and allows for examiners to assess abilities such as motor maturity and development, gross and fine motor control, spatial organization, and more. Other instruments may better meet the goal of providing a quick screening for neurological soft signs. Considering issues related to validity evidence, and given that the test authors did not compare the measure to other measures that screen for NSS, this assessment cannot be recommended for use at this time.

REVIEWERS' REFERENCES

Merker, B., & Funk, B. A. (2014). [Review of the Quick Neurological Screening Test, 3rd edition]. In J. F. Carlson, K. F. Geisinger, & J. L. Jonson (Eds.), *The nineteenth mental measurements yearbook* (pp. 580-583). Lincoln, NE: Buros Center for Testing.

Powell, S. (2014). [Review of the Quick Neurological Screening Test, 3rd edition]. In J. F. Carlson, K. F. Geisinger, & J. L. Jonson (Eds.), *The nineteenth mental measurements yearbook* (pp. 583-585). Lincoln, NE: Buros Center for Testing.

Review of Quick Neurological Screening Test–3rd Edition, Revised by ANITA M. HUBLEY, Professor of Measurement, Evaluation, and Research Methodology, and SEAN MAXEY, Graduate Student of Counseling Psychology, University of British Columbia, Vancouver, British Columbia, Canada:

DESCRIPTION. The Quick Neurological Screening Test–3rd Edition, Revised (QNST-3R) is an individually administered, standardized screen for neurological soft signs (NSS), which are motor and sensory skills that "reflect both developmental and neurological processes" (manual, p. 7). The QNST-3R consists of a warm-up activity and 13 tasks. Tasks 12 (Left-Right Differences) and 13 (Behavioral Irregularities) are based on earlier tasks. The test manual describes the purpose of each task, materials needed, administration instructions, observational considerations, and scoring criteria. Photographs or drawings are occasionally presented to illustrate errors. As each task is completed, the examiner circles any observed errors listed on the record form. Correct performance is scored 0. Errors are each assigned 1 or 3 points. Task scores are the sum of the error scores, and the Total score is the sum of the task scores. The maximum Total score is 123 for individuals ages 5 to 7, 126 for those ages 8 to 9, and 129 for those ages 10 and older. Task and total raw scores are converted into one of three functional categories based on cutoffs at the 5th and 25th percentiles. The QNST-3R takes approximately 20 minutes to administer and 10 minutes to score. It is intended for use "by education and health professionals such as psychologists, rehabilitation specialists, occupational therapists, and special educators" (manual, p. 9).

DEVELOPMENT. The original QNST was published in 1974, with a focus on early school-age children; minor revisions were made in 1978.

A second edition with changes to the instructions and scoring was published in 1998, and a third edition published in 2012 reported new standardization data with a national sample ranging in age from 4 to 97 years. For the 2017 QNST-3R, the literature on NSS was updated; the record form, administration, and scoring procedures were revised; and the standardization sample was re-analyzed. As a result, one task was eliminated and another task became a warm-up task given limited score variability, poor reliability, and low relevance to current NSS assessment. The only statement about the development of QNST-3R tasks is that they were "adapted from traditional neurological exams and developmental scales" (manual, p. 8).

TECHNICAL. The QNST-3R standardization sample consisted of 1,158 individuals ages 5 to 97 years. Data collection occurred in schools, clinics, and private practices by 50 examiners (mostly occupational therapists, rehabilitation specialists, and supervised graduate students) in 22 U.S. states and aimed to approximate the 2010 U.S. Census demographics. All data screening, data entry, and electronic scoring took place at the test publisher's office.

Item analyses showed that most tasks were quite easy across age groups. Item discrimination values were well over the .20 cutoff for most tasks and age groups; exceptions were Task 12 for ages 5 and 6-7 (.06 and .19) and Task 13 for ages 20-59 (.09). Alpha coefficients for the QNST-3R ranged from .41 to .84, and McDonald's omega coefficients ranged from .54 to .89, with coefficients unacceptably low for ages 20-59 and borderline for ages 5 and 12-19. Test-retest corrected reliability estimates obtained after a 12- to 21-day interval (15-day average) with 56 individuals ages 6-19 ranged from .70 to .93 for most tasks (Total score = .90), but were unacceptably low for Tasks 12 (r = .53) and 13 (r = .59).

Evidence of validity based on test content was limited to the inclusion of tasks commonly used in basic neurological assessments and research. Expected developmental effects that NSS should decrease with age through adolescence, remain stable through adulthood, and possibly increase in late older age were generally supported. Known-groups evidence comparing groups with and without attention-deficit/hyperactivity disorder, learning disabilities, autism spectrum disorder, and dementia, using a matched-pairs design, found individuals with each of these conditions scored significantly higher than their matched peers. Test-criterion evidence (i.e., sensitivity, specificity) was reported separately for three age groups (ages 5-7, 8-9, and 10 and over) at the 95th and 75th percentiles. Unfortunately, the criterion used to determine the a priori presence of NSS was not stated. Given that the quality of the criterion is critical for this type of evidence, the usefulness of the presented validity evidence could not be judged. Relationships between scores on the QNST-3R and scores on other tests measuring related constructs (e.g., motor skills, design copy, cognitive ability) were conducted with individuals ages 5 or 6 to 19 years from the standardization sample who had a variety of disabilities. Cohen's kappa values were low (.18 to .26) and nonsignificant. The test authors' claim that these results were expected because the other assessments did not measure the exact same sets of skills as the QNST-3R is not convincing to these reviewers.

COMMENTARY. The QNST-3R manual is well written, and the record form is nicely organized. Instructions and scoring for the tasks are mostly clear, with excellent, detailed advice provided. No rationale was provided for assigning different points to errors, and it is not clear how "errors" such as refusing to complete a task or characteristics such as social withdrawal, anxiety, and defensiveness (i.e., Task 13) are related to NSS (see also Gotts, 2001; Merker & Funk, 2014). Although examinee handedness is observed and noted during the warm-up task, always starting administration with the right hand might disadvantage left-handed examinees. The reviewers strongly recommend that the differing maximum possible task and total raw scores be checked and clearly presented on the record form as we obtained slightly different values from those stated in the manual (p. 62). Finally, the test manual would benefit from the inclusion of case studies (see also Merker & Funk, 2014) and some commentary on the provided remedial guidelines.

The large standardization sample is a relative strength of the QNST-3R, but there is a notable lack of representation from states in the midwestern and northwestern regions of the country. In addition, the age distribution of the sample is skewed toward younger examinees. Of the total sample of 1,158, 72.8% were ages 5 to 19; 15.9% were ages 20 to 59; and 11.3% were ages 60 to 97 (see also Powell, 2014).

There is limited reliability evidence. Internal consistency estimates were satisfactory for some age groups (ages 6-11 and 60-97) but not for others.

Test-retest reliability evidence, which was available only for individuals ages 6-19, was adequate for most tasks but not for Tasks 12 and 13. Evidence for interrater reliability with samples of intended test users is missing but essential (see also Adams, 1985; Merker & Funk, 2014). Scoring of errors is a subjective process, and scoring instructions for some tasks (e.g., Tasks 4 and 8) are not straightforward.

Of the five sources of validity evidence discussed in the *Standards for Educational and Psychological Testing* (American Educational Research Association, American Psychological Association, & National Council on Measurement in Education, 2014), only limited evidence based on test content and relationships to other variables was available for the QNST-3R. Current test content evidence is weak. Test content evidence using neurologists as subject matter experts to evaluate the relevance of the tasks and associated errors and intended test users as practical experts to evaluate the clarity and ease of administration and scoring instructions is critical. Validity evidence based on developmental effects and known-group differences was generally supportive whereas relationships between the QNST-3R and tests measuring related constructs were not. Test-criterion evidence was poorly reported and thus could not be adequately judged. Use of a clearly stated quality criterion is essential. Test-criterion evidence should have been reported for more than just three age groups given identified developmental differences in NSS. Prevalence of NSS in the sample as well as positive and negative predictive values should also be reported, along with a more nuanced discussion of the results.

A critical concern with the QNST-3R is the lack of a clear conceptual and operational definition for the construct of NSS. What are the critical dimensions or aspects of NSS? This information is needed to determine whether the QNST-3R qualifies as a "measure" (Bollen & Diamantopoulos, 2017a, p. 587). Does the QNST-3R consist of reflective indicators, causal-formative indicators, or composite-formative indicators? This determination will impact the reliability and validity evidence that is most appropriate to gather and what to expect from those findings given that most classical test theory and item response theory analyses assume one is working with reflective indicators (Bollen & Diamantopoulos, 2017a, 2017b; Hardin, 2017).

SUMMARY. The creation of standardized indicators for NSS for use by non-neurologists is an interesting concept. What is unclear is whether the QNST-3R consists of reflective, causal-formative, or composite-formative indicators, which impacts the reliability and validity evidence one collects and what one expects from this evidence. The test manual is well written, and the record form is well laid out. The standardization sample for the QNST-3R is large but consists mostly of individuals younger than 20 years. There is limited and mixed reliability and validity evidence for the QNST-3R. Most critically, interrater reliability evidence and strong test content evidence are missing whereas test-criterion evidence was presented in such a way that it could not be properly evaluated. More theoretical work on the construct of interest (NSS) and stronger psychometric evidence are needed before the QNST-3R can be recommended for clinical use.

REVIEWERS' REFERENCES

Adams, R. L. (1985). [Review of the Quick Neurological Screening Test, Revised Edition]. In J. V. Mitchell, Jr. (Ed.), *The ninth mental measurements yearbook* (Vol. 2, pp. 1256-1258). Lincoln, NE: Buros Institute of Mental Measurements.

American Educational Research Association, American Psychological Association, & National Council on Measurement in Education. (2014). *Standards for educational and psychological testing*. Washington, DC: American Educational Research Association.

Bollen, K. A., & Diamantopoulos, A. (2017a). In defense of causal-formative indicators: A minority report. *Psychological Methods, 22*, 581-596.

Bollen, K. A., & Diamantopoulos, A. (2017b). Notes on measurement theory for causal-formative indicators: A reply to Hardin. *Psychological Methods, 22*, 605-608.

Gotts, E. E. (2001). [Review of the Quick Neurological Screening Test, 2nd Revised Edition]. In B. S. Plake & J. C. Impara (Eds.), *The fourteenth mental measurements yearbook* (pp. 979-981). Lincoln, NE: Buros Institute of Mental Measurements.

Hardin, A. (2017). A call for theory to support the use of causal-formative indicators: A commentary on Bollen and Diamantopoulos (2017). *Psychological Methods, 22*, 597-604.

Merker, B., & Funk, B. A. (2014). [Review of the Quick Neurological Screening Test, 3rd edition]. In J. F. Carlson, K. F. Geisinger, & J. L. Jonson (Eds.), *The nineteenth mental measurements yearbook* (pp. 580-583). Lincoln, NE: Buros Center for Testing.

Powell, S. (2014). [Review of the Quick Neurological Screening Test, 3rd edition]. In J. F. Carlson, K. F. Geisinger, & J. L. Jonson (Eds.), *The nineteenth mental measurements yearbook* (pp. 583-585). Lincoln, NE: Buros Center for Testing.

[131]

Rating Scale of Impairment.

Purpose: "Designed to measure functional limitations across a range of life areas."

Population: Ages 5-18.

Publication Date: 2016.

Acronym: RSI.

Administration: Individual or group.

Levels, 2: 5-12 years, 13-18 years.

Forms, 2: Teacher, Parent.

Price Data, 2020: $348 per hand scored kit including manual (216 pages) and 25 of each form [Teacher (5-12 Years), Teacher (13-18 Years), Parent (5-12 Years), and Parent (13-18 years)]; $419 per online kit including automatic scoring and report generation; $102 per manual; $67 per 25 forms (specify rater and age); $3.75 per online form.

Foreign Language Editions: Spanish forms available.

Comments: Computer administration and scoring available.

Authors: Sam Goldstein and Jack A. Naglieri.

Publisher: Multi-Health Systems, Inc.

a) 5-12 YEARS.

1) Teacher Form.

Scores, 4: School, Social, Mobility, Total.

Time: (5) minutes.

2) *Parent Form.*

Scores, 6: School, Social, Mobility, Domestic, Family, Total.

Time: (10) minutes.

b) 13-18 YEARS.

1) Teacher Form.

Scores, 4: School, Social, Mobility, Total.

Time: (5) minutes.

2) Parent Form.

Scores, 7: School/Work, Social, Mobility, Domestic, Family, Self-Care, Total.

Time: (10) minutes.

Review of the Rating Scale of Impairment by GERALD TINDAL, Castle-McIntosh-Knight Professor, College of Education, University of Oregon, Eugene, OR:

DESCRIPTION. The Rating Scale of Impairment (RSI) provides a summary rating of impairment by teachers and parents in three domains of School (10 items), Social (10 items), and Mobility (9 items) with two additional domains for parents that consist of Domestic (7 items), and Family (5 items) with yet another domain (Self-Care, 8 items) for parents of adolescents. Impairment is defined in the test manual as "a reduced ability to meet the demands of life because of a psychological, physical, or cognitive condition" (p. 6).

Both parent and teacher forms include positive statement endings to the question "During the past four weeks, how often has this student/your child…?" The Teacher Form includes 29 statements. Parent Forms include 41 and 49 statements for children (5-12 years) and youth (13-18 years), respectively. The rating values are *never*, *rarely*, *sometimes*, *often*, *very often*, and *always*. A score sheet is used with values transcribed into the domains for summation into subtotals. The form also includes a conversion table for transforming the raw scores into T scores (for domains and the Total Score), confidence intervals (90% or 95%), percentile ranks, and classifications.

"The RSI offers three report options (with or without computerized scoring): The Interpretive Report, the Progress Monitoring and Treatment Effectiveness Report, and the Comparative Report" (manual, p. 20). These reports differ in purpose, administrations, and sources with a single administration for the first option, multiple administrations (up to four by the same rater) for the second option, and up to five different raters for the last option. The technical manual includes chapters addressing an overview introduction, measurement of impairment, administration and scoring, interpretation, development, standardization, reliability, and validity.

DEVELOPMENT. The RSI was developed from 2007 through 2014 with an initial pilot study used to create forms for a normative study. "The preliminary content was determined by a comprehensive review of current research literature, as well as the authors' experience in the conceptualization and assessment of impairment" (manual, p. 41). Final scale construction was based on sampling students in the two age groups stratified by gender, race/ethnicity, region, parental education level, and clinical status. Extensive information is presented from two exploratory factor analyses (EFAs) using principal axis factoring and oblimin rotation and then two confirmatory factor analyses separately for each of the four forms. Once the final RSI forms were finalized, a Spanish translation was developed.

TECHNICAL. This section is based on information presented in three chapters of the technical manual concerning standardization, reliability, and validity. Data collection occurred from 2012 to 2014 and included 8,000 ratings from parents and teachers in all 50 states for both paper-pencil and computer-based administrations (which were not significantly different in outcomes). From this sample, 2,800 ratings were included in developing norms, with 800 for each form (i.e., parent and teacher). The norm sample was balanced or stratified to reflect percentages from the 2010 U.S. Census for the following: age (5-18), gender, race-ethnicity, region (Northeast, Midwest, South, and West), parental education level (five levels from no high school to graduate or professional degree), and eligibility for special education services (approximately 11.7%). Extensive tables are used in the test manual to display the percentages of these characteristics.

In analyzing trends in outcomes on the RSI with the normative sampling plan, the test authors found (a) statistically main effects of gender in the 13- to 18-year-old group for two scales on the parent form and all scales on the teacher form, and (b) statistically significant main effects of gender in the 5- to 12-year-old group for all but one scale (Mobility). Negligible age differences were found between RSI scores, and therefore scores were collapsed into two age groups (5-12 and 13-18). The norms themselves reflect a linear transformation of raw scores into T scores with a mean of 50 and standard deviation of 10.

Several different types of reliability estimates were calculated. Internal consistency was described using alpha coefficients for each RSI score (School/Work, Social, Mobility, Domestic, Family, Self-Care, and Total Score), broken down by teacher and parent form, as well as age group for both a clinical and normative sample. Most coefficients were above .80 with median alphas ranging from .85 to .89. Test-retest reliability and stability were evaluated with approximately 150-200 teachers and parents completing the RSI on two separate administrations over a 2- to 4-week period. Across all forms, the range of correlation coefficients was .85 to .97. The difference between scores reflected the stability of the instrument, with 84% to 99% of the scores within +/- 10 T-score points. Interrater reliability (agreement between two raters) was evaluated, with both age forms collapsed due to the small sample size. The correlation coefficients for the RSI scales ranged from .65 to .85 on the Parent Form and from .56 to .59 on the Teacher Form with Total Score coefficients of .87 and .77, respectively. Stability was examined as the difference in T scores, with 76% to 92% of the scores on the Parent Form and 73% to 82% of the scores on the teacher form, within +/- 10 T score points on the two administrations.

Perhaps the most important type of validity evidence is content, which was based on a "comprehensive review of current research literature as well as the authors' clinical experience on the conceptualization and assessment of function impairment" (manual, p. 79). In addition, the test authors mapped item domains to the World Health Organization's (WHO) International Classification of Functioning (ICF). For each RSI scale, a table displays the definition, an example item, and the ICF domain.

In evaluating validity by clinical diagnosis, both mean score differences and number of diagnoses are used to argue that the RSI can be used in making inferences of impairment. For example, significant differences were noted when two groups of children and youth were compared (with age groups collapsed): those previously diagnosed with a disorder (attention-deficit/hyperactivity disorder, autism spectrum disorder, anxiety-depression, intellectual disability, and physical disability) versus a random sample of those from the general population. The test authors report that those with clinical diagnoses obtained scores near or above 60, whereas those from the general population obtained RSI scores of 50 on both parent and teacher forms with substantial effect sizes in various domains (School/Work, Social, Domestic, Family, Self-Care, and Mobility). Furthermore, the number of diagnosed clinical disorders and/or medical problems (from 1 to 4+) was highly related to the score on the RSI, reflecting monotonic linear increase between these measures (with impairment scores increasing as the number of diagnoses increased).

An extensive number of analyses are reported depicting the relationship between scores on the RSI and other measures. Correlation coefficients between the RSI and the Barkley Functional Impairment Scale for Children and Adolescents ranged from .55 to .67 for the child age group (5-12) and from .63 to .71 for the youth age group (13-18). The RSI and the Children's Global Assessment Scale demonstrated correlation coefficients that ranged from -.34 to -.51. With the Conners Comprehensive Behavior Rating Scales and the RSI, the correlation coefficients varied considerably, from .12 to .57. The median correlation coefficients between the Adaptive Behavior Assessment System–II (ABAS-II) and the RSI ranged from -.42 to -.61 for ABAS-II scales and from -.50 to -.59 for the Total Composite. With the Devereux Student Strengths Assessment and the RSI, the median coefficients ranged from -.60 to -.73. With the Comprehensive Executive Function Inventory and the RSI, the median correlation coefficients ranged from -.57 to -.72 for scale scores and from -.70 to -.84 for the full scale score. The correlation of the Woodcock-Johnson III Tests of Achievement with the RSI yielded coefficients with medians that ranged from -.23 to .00. Finally, the median correlation coefficients between the Cognitive Assessment System and the RSI ranged from -.07 to .03. Extensive tables present these correlation coefficients, broken out by demographics and RSI age groups and domains.

Construct evidence of validity is documented through the analysis of the factor loadings and invariance across demographic groups (gender, age, race-ethnicity, and clinical status). Group differences in domain scores are also reported by race-ethnicity with both the children and youth groups. The test authors report similar (consistent) factor structures across gender, age groups, races/ethnicities, and clinical statuses. Finally, correlations between raters (parents and teachers) yielded coefficients that ranged from .42 to .55 for the scale scores and .50 to .54 for the Total Score.

COMMENTARY. The RSI provides a convenient way to classify levels of impairment exhibited in any of several life functions by children and youth. Classification options are *no impairment* to *mild impairment*, *moderate impairment*, and *considerable impairment*. Several specific cautions must be observed when using this instrument.

First, it is important to bear in mind which special education disability classifications were sampled during the test development process as well as which disabilities were not. Seven disability classifications were sampled, but other health impaired, emotional disturbance, and communication disorder were not among those sampled. In addition, the percentages for various interactions of variables in the standardization sample are precariously low (e.g., age, by parent educational level, by race/ethnicity).

Second, the emphasis placed on factor analysis to provide construct evidence of validity is questionable. Although the test authors also develop some additional construct evidence by examining generalizability across demographic groups and consistency of scores across raters, this reviewer believes the evidence offered could be more substantial. The content (construct) of the instrument is described as reflecting current research and the test authors' extensive experience. Neither conjecture can be refuted, calling into question the scientific justification supporting the instrument. Although the theoretical framework supporting the test that is described in an earlier chapter of the test manual appears strong, this reviewer regards test authors' experience as justification to be insufficient.

Finally, some portions of the discussion related to validity reflect a dated conception, as these portions suggest validity is a feature of the test, rather than an inference drawn about test scores and their interpretation and use in decision making. Outside of the chapter on validity, the test authors mention validity in the context of score interpretation. A more explicit and clear focus on the validation of test inferences, rather than test features, would be appropriate in the chapter devoted to validity evidence.

SUMMARY. The RSI provides information about functional impairment in different areas of life as experienced by children and youth. Its use in medical and mental health contexts allows clinicians to compare an individual's level of functioning to norms derived from a nationally representative group. Use of this instrument to assess functional impairment should be accompanied by the consideration of other variables and information from the client's life to make such inferences.

Review of the Rating Scale of Impairment by GLORIA M. WORKMAN, Adjunctive Assistant Professor, Center for the Study of Traumatic Stress, Department of Psychiatry, Uniformed Services University, Bethesda, MD:

DESCRIPTION. The Rating Scale of Impairment (RSI) offers a transdiagnostic overview of functional impairment in school-aged children and adolescents ages 5 to 18 with suspected psychological, physical, or cognitive disorders. The RSI provides multi-informant measures of impairment across a range of life domains and can assist clinicians in the development of individualized treatment plans, diagnostic selection, and monitoring of program intervention effectiveness. This behavioral rating assessment offers six scales (i.e., School or Work, Social, Mobility, Domestic, Family, and Self-Care) to help identify specific areas of functional impairment. Parents or teachers can complete the instrument. Questionnaire materials include parent and teacher rating forms and a technical manual.

General administration instructions, detailed scoring guidelines, and specific interpretation guidelines are provided in the test manual. The RSI profile contains the following six factors plus a Total Score: School or Work, Social, Mobility, Domestic, Family, and Self-Care. The number of items on each scale varies depending on the type of rater (i.e., parent or teacher) and the age of the ratee (i.e., child or adolescent). Parent and teacher ratings are based on observed behavior of the child/adolescent during the past 4 weeks. Scoring options include paper-and-pencil format or online administration. A QuickScore form is available for use in the pencil-and-paper scoring option and makes scoring easy. Raw scores for each scale are determined by adding endorsement values within each scale. Raw scale scores may be prorated if no more than one item is omitted from each scale. Scale scores are then converted to T scores, percentile ranks, and classifications using a conversion table provided in the test materials. The Total raw score is derived by summing T scores from each of the six RSI scales and using the conversion table to determine T score, percentile rank, and classification. The Total Score may not be computed if any of the scale scores are missing. The RSI items and instructions require at least a sixth-grade reading level. The RSI can be completed in 5-10 minutes and is also available in Spanish. Although the RSI Total Score provides a global level of impairment, test users are encouraged to focus on the six scales of functioning and impairment. The test developers offer three types of online reports to assist in the interpretation of the individual child/adolescent's RSI scores in comparison to the normative sample, across administrations to monitor changes in scores, and across raters to examine differences in ratings.

DEVELOPMENT. The RSI was developed over several years (2007-2014) and published in 2016. In designing the RSI, the test developers sought a multi-informant impairment assessment tool for children/adolescents and included both parent and teacher forms.

The initial item content for the RSI was determined by conducting a comprehensive literature review on this topic in conjunction with the test developers' theoretical understanding of impairment. The content structure was subsequently aligned with the key domains of functioning described in the International Classification of Functioning, Disability and Health by the World Health Organization (WHO) (ICF; WHO, 2001). Age specific items were created for children and adolescents across eight separate domains (i.e., academic, communication, interpersonal, mobility, domestic, organization, mental and physical health, and self-care). The initial pool of impairment items was further divided according to behaviors typically observed by either parents or teachers. This process resulted in two parent forms (ages 6-13 and 13-18) and two teacher forms (ages 6-13 and ages 13-18).

A pilot study was conducted with a sample of parents (N = 587) and teachers (N = 433). The rated children/adolescents were from both the general population and clinical groups (i.e., attention-deficit/hyperactivity disorder, conduct disorder, oppositional defiant disorder, learning disability, mood disorder, pervasive developmental disorder, anxiety disorder, intellectual disability, medical disability, and physical disability). Item discrimination analyses were performed between the nonclinical group and the clinical group.

The RSI pilot items were further analyzed for inclusiveness, clarity, and relevance, and this review resulted in a reduction of RSI items. Test developers also extended the age range downward to include 5-year-olds. The modified RSI forms developed for the normative study included 127 impairment items for younger children (ages 5-12) Parent Form, 96 items for the younger children (ages 5-12) Teacher Form, 124 items for adolescents (ages 13-18) Parent Form, and 95 items for adolescents (ages 13-18) Teacher Form.

The next step of scale development involved collecting data from normative and clinical samples. The test developers collected 2,800 ratings from a normative sample of parents and teachers and these RSI ratings were used to generate norms for the instrument.

A series of exploratory and confirmatory factor analyses were performed on the pooled data from the normative and clinical samples. Data from the normative and clinical samples were split in half to perform an initial series of item-level exploratory factor analyses followed by a second series of confirmatory factor analyses. Several items were excluded from the item pool, and some factor solutions were revised based on these analyses and further deliberation by the test developers. The findings reveal that a five-factor structure provided the best fit on the child (ages 5-12) Parent Form, six factors for the adolescent (ages 13-18) Parent Form, and three factors for both Teacher Forms (ages 5-12 and ages 13-18). The multidimensional factor solution of each RSI version remained constant across variables and supported a multifaceted construct. The final version of the RSI scales included 41 items for the child (ages 5-12) Parent Form, 49 items for the adolescent (ages 13-18) Parent Form, and 29 items for each of the Teacher Forms (ages 5-12 and ages 13-18).

The RSI provides a Total Score that is derived by adding the T scores of the scales. This method of computing the Total Score was selected to guarantee that each of the RSI scales is equally weighted despite the varying number of items per version (i.e., Child Parent Form [41 items], Adolescent Parent Form [49 items], and Teacher Forms [29 items]). The RSI Total Score provides an overall estimate of impairment that should be interpreted in conjunction with the individual RSI scales. Although the Total Score is a global representation of impairment, the RSI scales provide useful information about specific domains of impairment when there is variability among separate scales.

Spanish forms are available for the RSI. The Spanish translations were developed following the completion of the English RSI forms. The RSI questions, demographic items, and instructions were translated from English to Spanish by two Spanish-speaking school psychologists. After a collaborative review, the most representative translations were then back-translated into English. The process of reconciling translation involved having the translators review the translation for content and for language discrepancies. According to the test manual, final adjustments were made to the RSI Spanish forms to ensure comprehension and clarity. No specific information is provided regarding adjustments made for cultural differences in Spanish-speaking populations.

TECHNICAL.

Standardization. Standardization sample data were collected from 50 U.S. states over a 2-year period and included more than 8,000 ratings. The normative samples consisted of 2,800 ratings across the different versions with 800 for each of the RSI child forms (i.e., parent and teacher) and 600 for each of the RSI adolescent forms (i.e., parent and teacher). Data collection utilized two methods of administration (i.e., paper-and-pencil and online). The demographic variables of age and gender were evenly balanced in the normative samples. Additionally, a stratified sampling plan was used to ensure the distributions of race/ethnicity were stratified by geographic region and parental educational level. The normative samples also included ratings of children/adolescents with a clinical diagnosis or who were eligible for special education services. According to the test developers, the normative samples closely matched the 2010 U.S. Census Bureau demographic data. The test manual contains additional detailed information about procedures used to develop norms for each RSI form.

Reliability. The reliability of the RSI was supported using internal consistency, test-retest, and interrater reliability evidence. Internal consistency was estimated using alpha coefficients for the RSI scales and the Total Score. Median alpha coefficients for the RSI scales in the normative samples were .85 and .89 (ages 5-12, Parent Form/Teacher Form) and .85 and .91 (ages 13-18, Parent Form/Teacher Form). Median coefficients for the clinical samples were .85 and .92 (ages 5-12, Parent Form/Teacher Form) and .88 and .92 (ages 13-18, Parent Form/Teacher Form). The median alpha coefficients for the Total Score were identical (.95) across the normative and clinical samples. Test-retest reliability was assessed over a 2- to 4-week period (controlling for age and gender) using a general population sample. For the RSI scales, corrected coefficients ranged from .85 to .97 (all $p < .001$); for the Total Score, corrected coefficients ranged from .89 to .96 (all $p < .001$). The effect of time across administrations was not significant. The stability of the RSI T scores was estimated by computing the differences between Rating 1 and Rating 2 in the test-retest samples, and the results confirm the stability of this measure across administrations as 84% to 99.3% of the differences fell within one standard deviation. Interrater reliability was calculated by looking at the agreement between two parents' or two teachers' ratings of the same child/adolescent. The time interval between parent or teacher ratings varied (range 0 to 31 days). Corrected interrater reliability coefficients for RSI scales ranged from .65 to .85 (all $p < .001$) for parent raters and from .56 to .59 (all $p < .001$) for teacher raters. Corrected interrater reliability coefficients for the RSI Total Score were .77 and .87 (teachers and parents, respectively; both $p < .001$). The consistency between raters was also assessed, and results provide support for interrater consistency.

Validity. The test manual provides evidence of validity from several sources. Content evidence of validity was derived from multiple sources—a comprehensive literature review, the developers' theoretical understanding of functional impairment, and alignment with the structure of the World Health Organization's International Classification of Functioning (WHO, 2001). To examine criterion-related evidence, the developers conducted a series of analyses of covariance (ANCOVAs) to compare RSI scores from the general population sample with RSI scores from clinical groups. Observed differences in RSI scores were in the expected direction and statistically significant. Statistical significance of group differences was observed for all scores on both parent and teacher ratings ($p < .001$). The effect sizes of group membership ranged from small to large across parent and teacher forms. Ratings on RSI scales for children/adolescents with various diagnoses revealed a different pattern of scores compared to children/adolescents from the general population sample. RSI scores for children/adolescents in the clinical sample were also evaluated according to number of clinical diagnoses. Overall, functional impairment scores rose as the number of diagnoses increased. Criterion-related evidence of validity was further assessed by examining the relationship between the RSI and other measures of impairment. Findings showed the RSI was strongly correlated with the Barkley Functional Impairment Scale for Children and Adolescents (Barkley, 2012) (child sample corrected $r = .55$ to .67; adolescent sample corrected $r = .63$ to .71) and moderately correlated with the Children's Global Assessment Scale (Shaffer et al., 1983) (child sample corrected r = -.37 to -.45; adolescent sample corrected r = -.34 to -.51). The relationships between the RSI and several other psychological measures was evaluated, and the pattern of findings provides criterion-related evidence of validity. Construct evidence of validity was demonstrated by investigating the underlying factor structure of the RSI through a series of exploratory and confirmatory factor analyses. Test authors provide evidence of the generalizability of the RSI factor structure across demographic groups and raters. Consistency in performance across genders, age groups, races/ethnicities, clinical statuses, and raters was supported.

COMMENTARY. The RSI is a relatively easy measure to use, score, and interpret and offers useful information for assessing functional impairment in children and adolescents across several life areas. Its key strength is that it is a norm-referenced, empirically based assessment tool based on a nationally representative sample that can assist clinicians in the identification of functional impairment in important domains and improve treatment planning, diagnostic decisions and monitoring of effectiveness of treatment interventions. Detailed and easy-to-follow instructions for administering, scoring, and interpreting the RSI are provided in the test manual. The developers also include useful and lengthy explanations of the various statistical methods used in the development of this instrument. The information in the test manual provides strong evidence that the RSI yields scores that provide reliable and valid means of assessing functional impairment in children and adolescents. An important limitation of the Spanish RSI is the apparent lack of professional translators used for the translation of the RSI into Spanish (American Psychological Association, 2017). The Spanish RSI version would benefit from a more structured and systematic translation process that includes a team of professional translators, a team of Spanish-speaking school psychologists who will serve as reviewers, and cross-validation of the Spanish RSI with diverse Spanish-speaking populations within the United States.

SUMMARY. The RSI is a multi-informant measure designed to measure functional impairment across diverse areas of daily functioning for children and adolescents ages 5 through 18. Rigorous scientific methods were used to develop the RSI, and it is supported by a body of reliability and validity evidence. Administration is easy with paper-and-pencil or simple online formats. Test authors position it as a valuable measure of impairment to be used with symptom-based approaches as part of a comprehensive assessment. The RSI has potential utility in multiple settings (e.g., school evaluations, clinical practices, and justice systems). Limited information regarding the reliability and validity of the RSI Spanish version is provided. As such, caution should be exercised when drawing conclusions from the RSI Spanish forms.

REVIEWER'S REFERENCES

American Psychological Association. (2017). *Multicultural guidelines: An ecological approach to context, identity, and intersectionality.* Retrieved from http://www.apa.org/about/policy/multicultural-guidelines.pdf

Barkley, R. A. (2012). Barkley Functional Impairment Scale—Children and Adolescents. New York, NY: Guilford Press.

Shaffer, D., Gould, M. S., Brasic, J., Ambrosini, P., Fisher, P., Bird, H., & Aluwahlia, S. (1983). A children's global assessment scale (CGAS). *Archives of General Psychiatry, 40,* 1228-1231.

World Health Organization. (2001). *International Classification of Functioning, Disability and Health: ICF.* World Health Organization. Retrieved from http://www.who.int/classifications/icf/en/

[132]

Raven's Progressive Matrices 2, Clinical Edition.

Purpose: Designed as a nonverbal assessment of general cognitive ability, specifically "eductive ability, which ... involves the ability to think clearly and solve complex problems."

Population: Ages 4-0 to 90-11.

Publication Dates: 1938-2018.

Acronym: Raven's 2.

Scores: Total score only.

Administration: Individual or group

Forms, 3: Digital Long Form, Digital Short Form, Paper Form.

Price Data, 2020: $350 per Q-global (web-based) test kit including manual (2018, 78 pages), scoring template, 25 answer sheets, test booklet, and 1-year unlimited score report on Q-global; $110 per manual (digital or print); $3.50 per digital administration and score report; $40 per score report 1-year subscription; $315 per paper-and-pencil test kit including manual, scoring template, 25 answer sheets, and test booklet; $80 per test booklet; $75 per 25 answer sheets; $50 per scoring template.

Comments: "An integrated revision of the series of the Raven's Progressive Matrices, including Raven's Coloured Progressive Matrices, Raven's Standard Progressive Matrices, and Raven's Advanced Progressive Matrices"; administered via paper and pencil or digitally.

Author: Pearson.

Publisher: Pearson.

a) DIGITAL LONG FORM.

Time: 30-minute time limit for ages 4-0 to 8-11; 45-minute time limit for ages 9-0 to 90-11.

Comments: Contains "millions of unique parallel item sets that are randomly assembled from a large item bank"; if an Internet connection and computers are available "and examinees are comfortable taking a digital test, it is best practice to use the digital forms."

b) DIGITAL SHORT FORM.

Time: 20-minute time limit.

Comments: 24-item short form for use "when testing time is the main concern."

c) PAPER FORM.

Time: 30-minute time limit for ages 4-0 to 8-11; 45-minute time limit for ages 9-0 to 90-11.

Comments: "Parallel to the randomly assembled item sets of the Digital Long Form"; for use if an Internet connection and computers are not available or "if examinees are not comfortable taking a digital test."

Cross References: See T5:2163 (356 references), T4:2208 (260 references), 9:1007 (67 references), T3:1914 (200 references), 8:200 (190 references), T2:439 (122 references), and 7:376 (194 references); for a review by Morton Bortner of the Progressive Matrices (1963), see 6:490 (78 references); see also 5:370 (62 references); for reviews by Charlotte Banks, W. D. Wall, and George Westby of an earlier edition (1951), see 4:314 (32 references); for reviews by Walter C. Shipley and David Wechsler of an earlier edition (1943), see 3:258 (13 references); for a review by T. J. Keating of the original edition, see 2:1417 (8 references).

Review of Raven's Progressive Matrices 2, Clinical Edition by ALBERT M. BUGAJ, Department of Psychology, University of Wisconsin—Green Bay, Green Bay, WI:

DESCRIPTION. A nonverbal test of general cognitive ability, Raven's Progressive Matrices 2, Clinical Edition (Raven's 2) updates and combines three earlier versions of the instrument: Raven's Standard Progressive Matrices (SPM; Raven, 1938), Raven's Coloured Progressive Matrices (CPM; Raven, 1947), and Raven's Advanced Progressive Matrices (APM; Raven, 1962). Raven's 2 is intended as a screening tool, for reevaluation of individuals (e.g., psychiatric patients), and for research. It is also intended for individuals with limited language proficiency, impaired communication ability, and individuals from culturally diverse populations. It can be administered to groups or individuals. The manual points out that the test should not be used alone to make diagnoses or for educational placements and that it should not replace more comprehensive measures of cognitive ability, such as the Wechsler scales (Wechsler, 2008; Wechsler, 2014).

The instrument, designed for use with individuals from ages 4:0 to 90:11, exists in two formats, paper and digital. The hand-scored paper format consists of 60 items arranged in five sets of 12 items. Test takers ages 4:0 to 8:11 and 80:0 to 90:11 complete sections A, B, and C. Those between those two age ranges complete sections B through E. The time limit for the paper form is 30 minutes for those ages 4:0 to 8:11, and 45 minutes for those who are older.

A short form of the digital test includes 24 items for all age groups and has a time limit of 20 minutes. The digital long form contains 36 items for ages 4:0 through 8:11 (30-minute limit), 48 items for ages 9:0 to 79:11 (45 minutes), and 36 items for ages 80:0 to 90:11 (45 minutes). The digital, web-based test is scored using the test publisher's online platform. Unlike the paper version, the digital formats involve a discontinue rule. After Item 11, testing ceases after six consecutive incorrect responses. The digital form is based on a test bank containing 329 items. Each time the Raven's 2 is administered online, the item bank generates a unique test.

The test can be administered by individuals with a bachelor's degree in psychology, education, counseling, or speech and occupational therapy, although specialized training is needed. Only individuals with professional training in psychological assessment can interpret the test results. Examiners can familiarize themselves with digital administration of the test via a practice link on the test publisher's website.

A table found in the test manual is used to convert the raw score obtained on the Raven's 2 to an ability score, which places an individual's test performance on a common, equal interval scale. Using other tables in the manual, the examiner can convert the ability score to several age-based normative scores. These include a standard score with a mean of 100 (SD = 15), percentile ranks, stanines, normal curve equivalents, and age equivalents.

DEVELOPMENT. Item development commenced with an intensive review of matrix-type items. Potential items were analyzed in terms of type, difficulty, problem solving logic, confounding variables, and proposed response choices. A team of color experts reviewed the items using software simulating the effects of color blindness.

Further refinement of the item pool occurred in "assessment labs," comprising 17 to 38 participants who provided responses to 420 potential test items. Participants commented on flaws in item logic and design, color usage, visual acuity, and potential cultural bias. Items were analyzed for item difficulty, discrimination, and distractor functioning. As a result of the labs, some items were eliminated, and others revised.

Next, 12 pilot tests consisting of 40 to 50 items per test were constructed from 425 unique items. The forms were linked by common items spread across levels of difficulty. The pilot forms were digitally administered to 1,307 individuals ages 4:0 to 90:11. Approximately 100 participants completed each form. Results were analyzed using classical test theory and item response theory statistics, although no statistics are reported in the test manual. Based on the results, 10 forms consisting of 43 to 50 items per form were developed for standardization purposes.

All standardization forms were administered digitally to 2,275 examinees, with 35% of the group taking their form individually and the remainder tested in small groups. Within the standardization sample, 100 individuals were tested in each of 21 age bands from 4:0 to 69:11. The age band of 70:0 to 79:11 included 112 participants, and 63 individuals ages 80:0 to 90:11 were included. The three oldest age groups (i.e., 65 years and older) consisted of more women than men, in keeping with the general population of the United States. For the younger groups, equal numbers of males and females were tested. The group was further stratified to be representative of U.S. Census demographics in terms of race/ethnicity, education level, and geographic region. About 6.5% of the normative group consisted of individuals from special populations, such as individuals with learning disabilities, autism spectrum disorder, and the gifted and talented, again in keeping with Census statistics.

Norms for the Raven's 2 are based on ability scores, rather than raw scores. These scores were derived using the one-parameter Rasch item response theory model. Standard score norms were developed via the method of inferential norming (Wilkins, Rolfhus, Weiss, & Zhu, 2005). Age equivalent scores were derived by identifying the ability score that corresponded to a standard score of 100 for each normative age group. An ability score that was identified in two successive age groups was assigned to the younger group. An ability score found in three adjacent groups was assigned to the middle group.

TECHNICAL.

Reliability. Because a unique digital form is generated with each usage, internal consistency of the digital format was examined via a Monte Carlo study using IRT-based marginal reliability (Dmitrov, 2003). The study resulted in very low standard deviations for the reliability coefficients for both the long and short forms, .002-.005 for the former, and .006 for the latter, indicating a high degree of internal consistency. Marginal reliability coefficients for each group in the normative sample, for both the digital and paper forms, were high, ranging from .79 to .90.

Test-retest reliability was examined for the digital and paper forms, again using a diverse sample (n = 239) in terms of education, race/ethnicity, gender, and geographic location in the United States. Retests were administered from 21 to 64 days after the initial testing (mean = 36.4). Pearson correlations were determined based on the entire group tested and within four different age ranges. Coefficients for the two digital and the paper forms were reasonably high, ranging from .78 to .89.

Validity. Concurrent evidence of validity for the Raven's 2 was determined by examining the correlation of the test's scores with those on a variety of other measures. Sample sizes in these studies were adequate, typically ranging from 91 to 109, although one, utilizing the Wide Range Achievement Test, Fifth Edition (WRAT5; Wilkinson & Robertson, 2017; see 185, this volume), involved 161 participants. The demographic mix of participants in each study was similar to that used in the examinations of reliability. Three studies looked at the relationship between the Raven's 2 (all forms) and its earlier iterations (the CPM, SPM, and APM). Correlations were high, between .71 and .78. Scores on the three Raven's 2 forms also were compared to scores on the Naglieri Nonverbal Ability Test—Third Edition (NNAT3; Naglieri, 2016; see 99, this volume). Scores from the digital forms (r = .70 in both cases) and the paper form (r = .77) correlated well. The Raven's 2 correlated well with the nonverbal scale of the Kaufman Brief Intelligence Test, Second Edition (KBIT-2; Kaufman & Kaufman, 2004; 17:102) with coefficients from .70 to .75 depending on the Raven's form being used, but correlations were, as expected, lower for the verbal scale of the KBIT-2 (.43 to .50). Similar results occurred regarding the completely "verbal" WRAT5. Depending on the Raven's form being administered, correlations ranged from .43 to .62.

Three studies examined the utility of the Raven's 2 in testing the intelligence of special populations. These were the intellectually gifted, individuals with intellectual disabilities, and individuals receiving services for limited English proficiency. Scores from each of these groups were compared with scores from separate randomly selected samples from the normative group matched according to age, gender, race/ethnicity, and education. Results indicated that the individuals identified as gifted scored 13 to 14 points higher than the comparison group on each form of the Raven's 2 ($ps < .01$), whereas the individuals with intellectual disabilities scored 24 to 28 points lower than the comparison groups on each form ($ps < .01$). Scores of English language learners were not significantly different from those of the comparison groups.

COMMENTARY. Testing materials for the Raven's 2 paper form are well-designed. The test booklet is clearly printed, durable, and of a convenient size and shape. The manual is extremely well-written and presents a wealth of material in a clear manner. The theoretical basis of Raven's 2 and the revision process are covered in a thorough manner. The process of administering the paper and digital forms is described clearly and in detail. Discussion of the validity and reliability of scores resulting from this instrument is comprehensive. Overall, the Raven's 2 test materials and manual are of excellent quality.

Development of items for the Raven's 2 followed a rigorous process. A thorough examination of the statistical reliability and validity of test scores was performed, and the resultant test scores proved to have excellent characteristics in both areas. Especially important is the test's correlation to its previous editions, demonstrating that the Raven's 2 possesses the same properties of tests with a 70-year history. Also significant is the test's relationship to other instruments measuring cognitive ability.

SUMMARY. The Raven's 2 has been shown to possess strong reliability and validity. Because it exists in both paper and digital formats, the usability of the test is also high. The Raven's 2 can be highly recommended as a research tool and as a screening device for both the general population and for diverse groups.

REVIEWER'S REFERENCES

Dmitrov, D. M. (2003). Marginal true-score measures and reliability for binary items as a function of their IRT parameters. *Applied Psychological Measurement, 27*(6), 440-458.

Kaufman, A. S., & Kaufman, N. L. (2004). Kaufman Brief Intelligence Test, Second Edition. Bloomington, MN: NCS Pearson.

Naglieri, J. A. (2016). *Naglieri Nonverbal Ability Test*—Third Edition. Bloomington, MN: NCS Pearson.

Raven, J. C. (1938). Standard Progressive Matrices. Oxford: Oxford Psychologists Press.

Raven, J. C. (1947). Coloured Progressive Matrices. West Los Angeles, CA: Western Psychological Services.

Raven, J. C. (1962). Advanced Progressive Matrices. London, England: Lewis.

Wechsler, D. (2008). Wechsler Adult Intelligence Scale—Fourth Edition. Bloomington, MN: NCS Pearson.

Wechsler, D. (2014). Wechsler Intelligence Scale for Children—Fifth Edition. Bloomington, MN: NCS Pearson.

Wilkins, C., Rolfhus, E., Weiss, L., & Zhu, J. (2005, April). A simulation study comparing continuous and traditional norming with small sample sizes. *Paper Presented at the Annual Meeting of the American Educational Research Association.* Montreal, Canada.

Wilkinson, G. S., & Robertson, G. J. (2017). Wide Range Achievement Test, Fifth Edition. Bloomington, MN: NCS Pearson.

Review of the Raven's Progressive Matrices 2, Clinical Edition by DANIEL L. GADKE, Associate Professor of School Psychology, and MARGARET B. POWELL, School Psychology Doctoral Candidate, Mississippi State University, Mississippi State, MS:

DESCRIPTION. The Raven's Progressive Matrices 2, Clinical Edition (Raven's 2) is a nonverbal assessment designed to quickly and accurately estimate an individual's general cognitive ability, specifically eductive ability. According to the test manual, eductive ability involves the capacity to think clearly and solve complex problems. The test requires minimal verbal instruction and no spoken or written responses, which the authors suggest minimizes potential impact from language skills and cultural background. The Raven's 2 can be administered when time is limited and only an estimate of general cognitive ability is required. Additionally, the Raven's 2 is appropriate for mass screenings in settings such as schools, correctional facilities, military recruiting centers, and employment placement centers. This assessment is designed for individuals ages 4 years 0 months to 90 years 11 months.

The Raven's 2 includes three forms: a digital long form, a digital short form, and a paper form. Additional test components include a test manual, test booklet, answer sheet, and scoring template for paper administration. Depending on the form and the age of the individual, examinees are allowed 20, 30, or 45 minutes to complete the test. Older children and adults may be tested in groups of any size, but children age 7 or younger are encouraged to be tested individually or in groups of four or fewer. Both digital forms involve a discontinue rule whereas the paper form does not. Digital forms are scored automatically. For paper administration, total raw scores are calculated by counting the number of correct answers. Total raw scores can be converted into ability scores based on the item set administered. Ability scores can then be converted into standard scores with confidence intervals, percentile ranks, normal curve equivalents, stanines, and age equivalent scores, as well as descriptive classifications ranging from *extremely low* to *extremely high*.

DEVELOPMENT. The Raven's Progressive Matrices (RPM) was developed to assess the component of *g* known as eductive ability through the use of progressive matrices. According to the test authors, solving progressive matrices requires cognitive functions such as perception and attention to visual detail, inductive reasoning, fluid intelligence, broad visual intelligence classification and spatial ability, simultaneous processing, and working memory. This was the theoretical basis behind the development of the RPM and subsequently the Raven's 2. In developing the Raven's 2, the test authors focused on creating new items, enhancing test security, and controlling item exposure rate. Additionally, the revision includes updated normative information, new reliability and validity evidence, increased user-friendliness, and an extension of the age range. The 3-year research program that led to the publication of the Raven's 2 involved six stages: conceptual development, item development, assessment labs, pilot testing, standardization, and final evaluation and assembly.

Overall, the test authors did a thorough job of detailing the development of the Raven's 2. During conceptual development, focus groups and surveys were employed in schools and clinics, and a team that the authors referred to as experts in cognitive psychology, psychological measurement, and clinical assessment development helped to set revision goals. The authors of the Raven's 2 did not include further information about who took part in these focus groups and surveys. Item development began with a review of existing matrix-type items. The test authors indicated that research on relevant tests was used to assess the expected difficulty and range of new test items. Assessment labs were then used to create the new item bank and to evaluate the new items using convenience samples. Eight digital assessment labs with 17 to 38 participants in each were conducted to test a total of 420 items and provide comments on item logic and design, use of colors, visual acuity, and potential cultural bias. Participants' responses were analyzed for item difficulty, discrimination, and distractor functioning, which led to some items being dropped or modified for pilot testing. Twelve pilot test forms were assembled with a total of 425 unique items across forms, and a total of 1,307 individuals ages 4:0 to 90:11 participated. Pilot items were analyzed using classical item analysis and item response theory, and items that did not perform well were considered for removal or revision for the standardization stage.

TECHNICAL. The normative sample for the Raven's 2 included 2,275 individuals ages 4:0 to 90:11. The sample was collected using a stratified sampling plan with data from the U.S. Census Bureau (2015) to ensure representative percentages of people were included along the variables of age, gender, race/ethnicity, education level, and geographic region. Children with special education classifications were included to more accurately represent the population of school-age children. The test authors report that proportions of the sample were representative across all of the above-mentioned variables according to the U.S. Census Bureau (2015).

Reliability was evaluated using IRT-based marginal reliability rather than traditional internal consistency reliability methods. The marginal reliability coefficients of the digital long form and the paper form were characterized by the test authors as either good (.80s) or excellent (.90s) across all age groups. Marginal reliability coefficients for the digital short form were lower, at .79 for ages 4 and 7, but averaging .80 overall, which the test authors reported was considered to be good. Test-retest reliability was calculated to measure stability of scores over time. Test-retest intervals ranged from 21 to 64 days with a mean interval of 36 days. The authors reported the standard scores possess good to excellent stability across time for all ages. The stability coefficients corrected for the normative sample's variability ranged from .78 to .89 across ages, which were either equivalent to or higher than most of the test-retest reliability coefficients previously reported for previous Raven's measures. Overall, it appears that the Raven's 2 is a reliable measure.

The test authors sought to demonstrate the validity of the Raven's 2 as a measure of general cognitive ability through content-oriented evidence, evidence regarding cognitive processes, and evidence based on relationships with other measures. For content validity, the authors stated internal and external expert item reviews were conducted at each research stage to ensure adequate content coverage and relevance; however, no further detail was provided on how this was accomplished. Similarly, to provide validity evidence that examinees use the expected cognitive processes when responding to Raven's 2 items, the authors reported that internal and external experts were used to identify and eliminate any factors such as those involving design, color, or misleading distractors, that may have invoked irrelevant response processes. Additionally, analyses of item distractors, the discontinue rule, and testing time were performed to identify and control irrelevant factors, although little to no detail was included as to how this was accomplished.

Finally, the test authors attempted to demonstrate validity by comparing scores between the Raven's 2 and its predecessors, other cognitive ability measures, and a measure of achievement. Standard scores from the Raven's 2 were highly correlated with those from the RPM, indicating they measure the same construct. Additionally, standard scores from the Raven's 2 were highly correlated with those from the Naglieri Nonverbal Ability Test—Third Edition (NNAT3) and the nonverbal portion of the Kaufman Brief Intelligence Test, Second Edition (KBIT-2). However, the correlation between the Raven's 2 and the KBIT-2 Verbal score were in the moderate range, indicating that somewhat different traits may be involved. As expected, correlation coefficients between the scores of the Raven's 2 and the Wide Range Achievement Test, Fifth Edition (WRAT-5) were in the moderate range as well. Overall, based on the data presented, it appears that the Raven's 2 is a valid measure of general cognitive ability.

COMMENTARY. The Raven's 2 is a brief and easy-to-administer assessment of general cognitive ability, specifically eductive ability. Although the Raven's 2 would not be appropriate when a full measure of intellectual ability is required, the measure would be useful as an estimate of general intellectual ability or for screening purposes to determine whether a more in-depth evaluation is needed. With both paper and digital administration options, the Raven's 2 can be easily administered to a wide variety of populations in several different settings. Although the Raven's 2 is considered a nonverbal assessment, directions are given in a verbal manner for both the paper and digital forms, decreasing the usability with those who are not language proficient, who have communication-related disabilities, or who are from culturally diverse populations. Time limits range from 20 to 45 minutes; however, the paper form does not include a discontinue rule, which could increase random guessing rates and unnecessary testing time. Scoring is relatively easy, although the scoring process does involve converting scores two different times, increasing the possibility of scoring error. Data provided by the Raven's 2 authors suggest that the Raven's 2 generates both reliable and valid scores.

SUMMARY. The Raven's 2 was designed to measure general cognitive ability nonverbally in individuals ages 4 years 0 months to 90 years 11 months. The Raven's 2 underwent extensive development procedures to adequately address changes to the original RPM, including increasing user friendliness, updating the normative sample, and creating a new test item bank. Data support the Raven's 2 as a reliable and valid measure for estimating general cognitive ability.

[133]

REACH Survey.

Purpose: Designed as a school-level assessment of students' development of skills and attitudes associated with academic motivation.
Population: Students in Grades 6 to 12.
Publication Dates: 2005-2017.
Scores, 32: Relationships (Believe in Them, Expect Their Best, Grow From Failure, Voice, Mutual Respect, Guide, Inspire, Connect Sparks to Learning), Effort (Mastery vs. Performance Orientation, Belief in Malleable Intelligence, Academic Self-Efficacy), Aspirations (Goal Orientation, Future-Mindedness, Internal Locus of Control), Cognition (Focus, Academic Delayed Gratification, Positivity in the Face of Challenge), Heart (Spark Development, Spark Sharing, Transfer of Experience), School Climate, Sense of Belonging at School, Discrimination in School, Interesting and Engaging Instruction, Culturally Inclusive and Affirming Instruction, Influence of External Factors on Effort in School, Overall REACH.
Administration: Group.
Forms: Abbreviated version available.
Price Data, 2020: $300 per site report including strategies guidebook (2017, 184 pages) and 100 surveys; $300 per aggregate report (encompassing multiple sites); $150 per individual data file of all youth surveyed; $2.50 per survey in excess of 100.
Time: Average of 20 minutes for completion of survey.
Comments: User's guide (2016, 40 pages) available for download from survey publisher's website; data analyzed and report provided by survey publisher; minimum of 30 surveys required for report.
Authors: Search Institute (survey and user's guide); Kent Pekel (strategies guidebook).
Publisher: Search Institute.

Review of the REACH Survey by CHRISTINE DiSTEFANO, Professor, Educational Research and Measurement, University of South Carolina, Columbia, SC:

DESCRIPTION. The REACH Survey is part of a resource system targeted to educators, teachers, researchers, and other stakeholders with the purpose of strengthening academic motivation for students in Grades 6 to 12. Products and services offered as part of the REACH system include options for executing a survey, reviewing strategy workshops (online), planning schoolwide implementation, and conducting onsite professional development. The REACH Survey assesses five dimensions important to adolescents' academic motivation: Relationships (strengthening developmental relationships with peers and adults), Effort (use of strategies to be more successful in school), Aspirations (positive visions of future self), Cognition (use of metacognition strategies), and Heart (understanding personal values and interests). The REACH Framework operationalizes the focal dimensions and provides literature supporting the importance of each dimension as part of the framework. The REACH Standards provide milestones (one per dimension) that students should pass as they improve to enhance academic motivation. The REACH Strategies Guidebook provides scripted activities and suggestions for classroom teachers to improve students' competency in each of the five areas. Finally, the REACH Survey includes 85 questions that assess each of the five REACH dimensions as well as other factors important to students' motivation and school perseverance. In addition to the full survey, an abbreviated 53-item version is available.

The REACH Survey is written at an approximately sixth-grade reading level and can be completed in 30 minutes for middle school students and 20 minutes for high school students. The survey is administered and scored online by the test publisher. Feedback is provided to schools in a report that includes information across all the questions encompassed in the survey and an executive summary that captures key findings.

According to the user's guide, the survey is focused on measuring the "relationships and social and emotional skills that youth need to succeed in school and life" (p. 3). The user's guide provides detailed information to assist educators with planning and implementing a study in their school, including questions for guiding the purpose of the study, goals and outcomes to be achieved, sampling strategies, and suggested sample sizes needed for stable results. Sample parent consent letters and suggestions for reporting findings also are included. The user's guide states that the REACH Survey was revised and updated in 2016; however, no information about the revisions or updates is included in the guide.

Survey items are rated on a 5-point Likert scale, on which all anchors are labeled. The anchor categories change depending on the stem and include agreement (*strongly disagree* to *strongly agree*), concordance with a statement (*not at all like me* to *very much like me*), relating statements to teachers at the school (*not at all like my teachers* to *very much like my teachers*), and frequency of occurrence (*never* to *very often*). The frequent label switches require students to pay attention to the questions/stems, which may be difficult for younger students and poor readers, especially given the survey's length. It was not clear which survey items were related to each of the five REACH areas assessed. A sample report was provided to show what information may be presented to schools. Scores (overall and by domain) were presented and discussed, but it was not clear how these values were constructed.

DEVELOPMENT. Development of the REACH System began in 2013. The components included in the system were constructed from multiple sources such as an extensive literature review, synthesis of results from published studies, and new analysis of existing data collected over the previous 25 years by the test publisher. After operationalization and support of the REACH components (Relationships, Effort, Aspirations, Cognition, and Heart), the system was tested through workshops and discussions with relevant stakeholders. At the same time, the REACH Survey was constructed and revised through three pilot administrations. After each iteration, the survey was reviewed, psychometric properties were examined, and revisions were made to improve the scale. The construction of the REACH System was also informed by a large-scale pilot study conducted during the 2015-2016 academic year in four middle schools in Minnesota. The development process resulted in the construction of the REACH Strategies Guidebook and the REACH Survey.

The REACH Strategies Guidebook is an approximately 200-page manual that provides in-depth information about student motivation and how this construct relates to student academic success and other important characteristics such as well-being and resilience. The tools and techniques in the guidebook are described as "the result of three years of applied research and development" (Pekel, 2017, p. 11). The Strategies Guidebook serves as a "playbook" for schools to use when implementing the REACH System and provides a strong framework for bringing the materials directly into the classroom. For example, reflection questions, sample school plans, and interactive activities (anchor activities) are provided. Each anchor activity also includes plans to reinforce interactions with students in the classroom. The REACH Strategies Guidebook is described as the "outcome of our work to date, but is only a starting point for efforts to develop a powerful and scalable strategy for strengthening academic motivation" (Pekel, 2017, p. 11). Thus, the guidebook is a work in progress that will be further refined in future iterations of the REACH System.

TECHNICAL. The REACH Strategies Guidebook provides a strong research-based introduction for the components included in the REACH Framework. Many scholarly studies are cited to support the importance of the areas included as necessary elements of student motivation, relations of student motivation to other important aspects for youth, and the usefulness of the interventions. Although not detailed technical information, the information provides research support for the areas included with the REACH System.

A technical summary was provided for review to support the psychometric properties associated with the survey scores. Data used in the calculations are reported to have been provided from a sample of 602 high school students from one locale in Minnesota. The summary is very brief (five pages) and discusses both the "full" and abbreviated surveys. No information about the scores (e.g., subscale scores, total scores, how to interpret values) is provided.

The technical summary document includes a "soft" discussion of psychometric analyses conducted to support the scores from the REACH Survey. Analyses included examinations of reliability and construct and predictive evidence of validity. For each section, the information is interpreted for practitioners in a short paragraph titled "Why it matters." Coefficients are cited (e.g., coefficient alpha values presented for the range of subscales); however, the procedures conducted are discussed tangentially. Given that only a technical summary was provided, and not a technical manual, there is limited information available to interpret or to use in score interpretation. What is provided is summarized generally and interpreted for the user (e.g., "Our theory was shown to be supported by the actual data, using generally accepted model fit criteria," p. 3) without actual values available for interpretation. Summary values for the reliability and predictive coefficients are presented and are generally in acceptable regions and of appropriate values.

A brief summary of information related to the abbreviated REACH Survey also is provided. However, the psychometric information presented is even more limited than that for the full REACH Survey. No numbers at all are presented in this section, just a descriptive discussion.

COMMENTARY. The REACH System is a detailed framework designed to improve student motivation for middle and high school students. Five areas (Relationships, Effort, Aspirations, Cognition, and Heart) are targeted through summary activities, focused discussion questions, and a survey for student participants. Strengths of the system include detailed anchor activities that can be brought into the classroom without much adaptation or revision needed by teachers or school personnel. There are multiple anchor activities presented for each of the REACH areas, additional reflection questions, and sample plans for administering a school-wide system. The REACH Survey includes full and abbreviated forms to use with students. The psychometric information available to review was limited, with only summary values provided. In some areas, only qualitative description was provided, and actual values were not available for evaluation. The survey was hard to understand in terms of how the survey items mapped to the focal REACH constructs. Also, no information regarding how the instrument is scored was included in the technical summary or the user's guide.

SUMMARY. The REACH System is a comprehensive program and assessment framework designed to improve youths' academic motivation. The materials presented may help schools incorporate activities into the classroom with a goal of changing student motivation through discussion and reflection. The activities are nicely designed. The full survey, however, seems cumbersome (especially for younger middle school students), and the materials presented do not provide adequate psychometric information to warrant comfort with a comprehensive evaluation of soundness. Overall, the REACH System may help schools that want to devote effort to improving students' academic motivation through the activities as part of a school-wide program.

REVIEWER'S REFERENCE

Pekel, K. (2017). *The REACH strategies guidebook.* Minneapolis, MN: Search Institute.

Review of the REACH Survey by CHRISTOPHER A. SINK, Professor and Batten Chair, Counseling and Human Services, and WAYNE HANDLEY, Doctoral Student in Counselor Education and Supervision, Old Dominion University, Norfolk, VA:

DESCRIPTION. Based on the five-component REACH conceptual framework, the REACH Survey is a self-report, norm-referenced assessment for middle school and high school respondents (Grades 6 through 12; age range not specified). Essentially, the instrument assesses students' perceptions related to their motivation and perseverance levels and various social-emotional-cultural factors that may influence academic achievement and related outcomes. According to the materials provided to the reviewers by the survey publisher (Search Institute), there are several versions of the instrument varying in length. The online format has either 85 (Search Institute, 2016d, p. 3) or 88 (Pekel, 2017, pp. 182-183) items and is self-administered. There is also a 103-item pencil-and-paper version administered in group settings (Search Institute, 2017). Finally, a 53-item (Search Institute, 2016d, p. 3) or 58-item (Search Institute, 2016c, p. 58) version is available largely for middle school students. It is unclear how the abbreviated version is administered. Regardless of the format, respondents will need 20 to 30 minutes to complete the survey.

Though the precise number of items per domain is not specified in the user's guide, the primary domains appraised by the 88-item REACH Survey (see REACH Strategies Guidebook; Pekel, 2017) are Relationships (25 items; students' experiences with beneficial relationships with teachers), Effort (8 items; how students perceive their own intelligence and ability), Aspirations (10 items; students' perceptions of their own maximum potential), Cognition (10 items; metacognition and students' ability to defer gratification), and Heart (10 items; the ability of students to identify and understand what they love to do; develop, share, and leverage their "sparks," p. 183). The REACH Survey (Pekel, 2017) also provides schools with data on student perceptions in these areas: school climate (4 items), sense of belonging in schools (3 items), perception of discrimination in school (3 items), degree to which instruction is interesting and engaging (6 items), degree to which instruction is culturally inclusive and affirming (3 items), degree to which teachers encourage students to respect other cultures (1 item), and degree to which factors outside the school influence effort in school (5 items).

The only required testing materials are either the hard copy of the survey and a writing utensil or a computer/tablet with Internet access and the appropriate link sent from the test publisher. The survey link is accessible through a web browser, email, or school portal. Hard copy survey data must be entered into the online portal for scoring. The amount of time school staff needs to allocate for this task was not specified. Whereas the instructions for test administration are provided in the user's guide and readily understandable, the qualifications to be a REACH examiner are not clearly stated. Test monitors can be educators and related personnel. Within a few weeks of receiving the data, the Search Institute completes the scoring, interprets the findings, and provides the school with a detailed report, which can be used as formative or summative information. Assistance with understanding the findings in more depth can be obtained using the paper and online documentation from the test publisher.

DEVELOPMENT. The development and technical characteristics of the REACH Survey are largely summarized in the REACH Survey Technical Report (Search Institute, 2016b) and the Technical Summary (Search Institute, 2016c). Other Search Institute publications reiterate, and in some cases, add to this information. Across the sources, the documentation inadequately addresses the measure's development, psychometrics, theoretical underpinnings, and conceptual framework. Particulars on item development, selection, and content validity are severely lacking.

The Technical Summary (Search Institute, 2016c) states that the Search Institute began the survey creation process in 2013 with "an iterative cycle of measure development, testing, revision, testing, and revision" that included field work with educators (p. 2). The original pool of potential items was approximately 200. Through a series of four pilot studies (Search Institute, 2016a) that included exploratory and confirmatory factor analyses, the measure was gradually revised, and the total number of items was pared down. Initial respondents included more than 5,000 students from eight high schools and 14 middle schools. Pilot study respondents' demographic characteristics were very sparsely reported. The Technical Summary reported substantial racial/ethnic, gender, and socioeconomic diversity, but actual frequencies were not tabled. The Technical Summary also mentioned a final pilot study (no date provided) conducted with 602 Minnesota high school students in Grades 9-12. Demographic characteristics of this sample were specified: 53% female and non-White, and approximately 40% of the respondents were from families with economic challenges. Regrettably, pertinent psychometric findings related to this sample were not reported.

The REACH Survey Technical Report (Search Institute, 2016b) outlines several studies that attempted to demonstrate the validity and reliability of the REACH Survey. However, these reviewers found the presentation of the findings challenging to decipher in relationship to the research reported in the Technical Summary (Search Institute, 2016c) discussed above. This latter document, although not entirely coherently presented, yields some evidence for the usefulness of the measure to assess the REACH conceptual framework with middle and high school students. In short, the user's guide and technical documents offered insufficient information on the measure's development and theoretical grounding for its constructs and accompanying scales.

TECHNICAL. For the purposes of norming the different versions of the REACH Survey, the standardization process and sample characteristics were inadequately documented and explained. Specifically, as mentioned above, the technical documentation was sparse. Some background information about the samples was provided; however, essential data on the total standardization sample were not tabled or narratively conveyed. In other words, pertinent descriptive statistics, including frequency distributions, were missing. The samples' age, gender, grade levels, race/ethnicity, languages spoken, geographic region, free or reduced lunch status (a proxy indicator of socioeconomic status), and special needs status should have been reported. Whether the samples were comparable to that of the U.S. population is unknown. No details were communicated regarding the characteristics of the participating schools.

Survey item variability, reliability (internal consistency and stability), and validity (predictive and construct) are considered in several documents with little attention to clarity, detail, or overall organization. Given the unorthodox way of reporting these technical data, the reviewers focused on the limited information presented in the Technical Summary. To reiterate, details related to the samples examined for the measure's psychometric properties were largely absent. First, for the longer version of the REACH Survey, the Technical Summary indicates that there is sufficient evidence in student response patterns (item variability) allowing for differentiated score interpretations. In other words, the scales appeared to be able to distinguish lower from higher level perceptual scores. However, the standard errors of measurement (*SEM*s) for subtest and total scores were not included, making score interpretation imprecise. Second, internal consistency estimates (alpha coefficients) for the five principal domains (Relationships, Effort, Aspirations, Cognition, and Heart) were largely very good to strong, ranging from .80s to .90s. For each domain's subdimensions, the alphas were somewhat lower but adequate (.70s to .90s). Third, stability (test-retest) coefficients using intraclass correlations were computed using data from 73 students (71% female; 58% middle school age; 59% White) over a 1-week interval. Resulting coefficients were more than adequate, ranging from the .70s to the .90s for the survey's total score and the five major domains. Fourth, construct evidence of validity was examined through confirmatory factor analyses (CFA) on various pilot study samples. Though specifics are not reported, the derived CFA fit indices suggested an adequate match between student data and the underlying REACH structural model. Fifth, the measure's predictive evidence of validity was determined by correlating its scores with student grades and various measures of school experiences and barriers to perseverance. Summary findings are reported. For example, significant but low correlations (*r*s = .10s-.20s) were found between REACH measures and student GPA. Other unspecified statistical analyses were conducted showing that students were far more likely to have a B+ grade point average if they had at least adequate level scores on total REACH, and on the Effort, Cognition, and Heart dimensions. Largely low-moderate to strong correlations (64% of the correlations ranged from .30 to .80) were reported between various measures of school experiences (e.g., student perceptions of school climate, emotional belonging, cultural affirmation and respect, quality of instruction) and REACH scores. Higher survey scores were negatively associated with measures of perceived discrimination and obstacles to perseverance. Correlations were not detailed.

The psychometric properties of the abbreviated REACH Survey are minimally elucidated (no numerical data) in the Technical Summary. According to the document, each motivation subcategory associated with the five major domains comprises one or two items that are purportedly reliable and valid (construct/factorial and predictive). Finally, the shorter version had similar respondent means by gender, race/ethnicity, and "financial strain" (Search Institute, 2016c) as the longer survey.

COMMENTARY. The REACH Survey in its multiple formats is designed to measure variables associated with student academic motivation and persistence as a function of the developmental relationships between middle and high school teachers and students. It does so by providing student self-report scores in five major dimensions and other social/environmental areas linked with student learning. A total survey score is also calculated. Group-administered hard copy (103 items) and web-based (approximately 85 items) versions are offered. An abbreviated survey is an option for middle school students. Scoring and interpretation are done by the test publisher, and reports can be tailored to the school's requests (e.g., individual or group results). Results are then used by school personnel to develop and implement relevant curricular and instructional strategies. Educator-friendly support manuals (e.g., Strategies Guidebook) are available to assist with recommended changes. The measure appears to be theoretically grounded and has a body of research supporting it; however, the evidence of reliability and validity that is summarized in the technical documentation is insufficient. Moreover, limited information is presented on the survey development and the norming processes as well as the standardization sample. The Technical Summary should include details on these topics as well as on the various survey formats, administration, and scoring and interpretation. Given these technical deficiencies, the REACH Survey should not be used for purposes other than providing educators with low-stakes information on student perceptions of their own motivation and persistence and related school variables. Any school or classroom modifications based on the results should be done with appropriate caution and tentativeness.

SUMMARY. The SEARCH Institute created a self-report survey that is easy to administer and score. Increasing its utility with children and youth in Grades 6-12, there are multiple formats to choose from. REACH Survey dimensions appraise various important student-related variables associated with learning and development. The online version seems to be the most serviceable option for schools, as it provides external, professional-level scoring and data analysis services, taking much of the workload off test administrators. Additionally, the user's guide and Strategies Guidebook are relatively easy to follow, particularly for school personnel who possess limited experience with test administration. However, at present, there is no widely published information validating the broad educational claims made in the user's guide or the Strategies Guidebook. Moreover, given that the psychometric and other technical data supporting the different versions of the REACH Survey are inadequately presented in the accompanying materials, educators should use the results in a very circumscribed way. Student perceptions should always be viewed in light of personal, school, and family contexts. Scores are only tentative indicators, and overall school reports should be viewed with some caution.

REVIEWERS' REFERENCES

Pekel, K. (2017). *The REACH strategies guidebook: Approaches and activities to strengthen academic motivation.* Minneapolis, MN: Search Institute.

Search Institute. (2016a). *A portrait of any school students: Based on the results from the REACH Survey.* Minneapolis, MN: Author.

Search Institute. (2016b, February 1). *REACH Survey technical report.* Minneapolis, MN: Author.

Search Institute. (2016c, March). *Technical summary: Search Institute's REACH survey.* Minneapolis, MN: Author. Retrieved from http://www.searchinstitute.org/sites/default/files/a/REACH-Survey-Tech-Summary.pdf

Search Institute. (2016d, September). *User guide for the REACH Survey.* Minneapolis, MN: Author.

Search Institute. (2017). *The REACH Survey.* Minneapolis, MN: Author.

[134]

Reading GOALS Series for Adult Basic Education.

Purpose: Designed "to assess Adult Basic Education (ABE) learners' reading comprehension skills so that their progress in meeting educational goals can be evaluated."

Population: Students in Adult Basic Education and Adult Secondary Education programs as well as other instructional programs that assess reading comprehension.

Publication Dates: 2018-2019.

Acronym: Reading GOALS.

Scores: Total score only.

Administration: Individual or group.

Levels, 4: A, B, C, D.

Forms, 9: 2 parallel forms for each level (901R, 902R, 903R, 904R, 905R, 906R, 907R, 908R) plus reading appraisal (900R).

Price Data, 2020: $45 per administration manual (2018, 34 pages) with answer keys, scoring information, and administration directions; $100 per 25 test booklets (specify level and form number); $190 per set of 5 of each test booklet (40 total); $350 per set of 10 of each test booklet (80 total); $68 per 100 general purpose answer sheets.

Time: 30 minutes for administration of reading appraisal (paper and pencil); 15 minutes for administration of reading appraisal (digital); 10 minutes for administration of optional writing screener; 60 minutes for administration of Level A; 75 minutes for administration of Levels B-D (all times are approximate).

Comments: Computer administration available; designed to replace the CASAS Life and Work Reading Assessments (T9:374).

Authors: CASAS.

Publisher: CASAS.

Review of the Reading GOALS Series for Adult Basic Education by SUSAN N. KUSHNER BENSON, Associate Professor of Educational Research, Assessment, and Evaluation, University of Akron, Akron, OH:

DESCRIPTION. The Reading GOALS Series (Greater Opportunities for Adult Learning Success) is a reading comprehension curriculum and assessment series used with adult basic education learners. The Reading GOALS Series was developed and is maintained by CASAS (Comprehensive Adult Student Assessment System), and is a new test series designed to replace the Life and Work Reading Assessment series. CASAS is a nonprofit organization that focuses on curriculum and assessment across basic skill areas such as reading comprehension, mathematics, writing, listening and speaking for non-English learners, workforce development, and preparation for citizenship. With a focus on the adult learner and workforce development, CASAS is used nationally and internationally by federal and state government agencies, business and industry, community colleges, education and training providers, correctional facilities, and technical programs (CASAS, 2015).

Reading GOALS consists of four reading comprehension tests that measure how adult basic learners (ABE) progress across the six educational functioning level (EFL) definitions that are outlined by the National Reporting System (NRS). The levels range from *Beginning ABE Literacy* to *High Adult Secondary Education*. Each reading test includes a parallel form for a total of eight tests. The initial set of parallel forms (Forms 901/902) has 39 multiple-choice items per form, and the remaining three sets of parallel forms (Forms 903/904, 905/906, and 907/908) have 40 questions. Easy-to-interpret tables are provided for converting raw scores to scale scores, and these tables also clearly align scores with NRS EFL levels as well as the recommended next test level. All forms are available in paper and computer-based formats. A 28-item reading appraisal (Form 900) is also available in paper and computer-based formats and is used as a placement measure. Test materials include an administration manual and a technical manual.

DEVELOPMENT. The development process is succinctly and clearly illustrated as a flow chart in the technical manual. A seven-step process was used to develop the test: (1) test specification, (2) item development, (3) stage 1 item evaluation, (4) field testing, (5) stage 2 item evaluation, (6) form construction, and (7) form evaluation. In addition, steps involved in test maintenance (periodic review, item bank expansion, review of forms, and updating the technical manual) are included in the flow chart. In the 133-page narrative that follows, test developers provide a comprehensive and thorough explanation of the development process, providing extensive documentation and often citing research to substantiate their decision-making process. The test maintenance process is described and documented in an additional 20 pages. As would be expected with assessments that measure mastery of learning standards, the development process emphasized the development of a table of test specifications and creating and evaluating individual test items.

TECHNICAL.

Standardization. Various examinee samples were used during the development and field-testing process. Test developers provided demographic data to demonstrate that examinees represented the target population of diverse learners across the United States. Demographic information included the state in which the field testing took place, gender, ethnicity, years of education, and language. According to the test developers, sample participants represented the adult learner population of interest.

Reliability. The test developers report estimates of internal consistency and alternate-forms reliability. Coefficient alpha was used to estimate internal consistency; values ranged from .80 to .94 across all eight forms. The higher alpha values were reported for the lower test levels (i.e., beginning basic and low intermediate), and the lower alphas were reported for higher test levels (i.e., low adult secondary and high adult secondary). Given that all tests in the series have virtually the same number of items, test developers should have speculated about factors that may have influenced the descending values of alpha as the difficulty of the tests increased. Pearson correlations were reported as estimates of alternate-forms reliability and ranged from .79 to .92. Similar to estimates of internal consistency, alternate-forms reliability decreased as the difficulty of the tests increased.

Validity. The *Standards for Educational and Psychological Testing* (American Educational Research Association, American Psychological Association, & National Council on Measurement in Education, 2014) were used as the basis for describing evidence of validity. Within the psychometric community, these criteria are considered the framework with which instruments should be developed and evaluated. Five sources of validity evidence are identified and discussed in the *Standards*: (1) evidence based on test content, (2) evidence based on response processes, (3) evidence based on internal structure, (4) evidence based on relations to other variables, and (5) evidence for validity and consequences of testing.

The test developers report content, construct, and criterion-related evidence of validity. Although the test developers quote the 2014 edition of the *Standards* in their narrative about content evidence (technical manual, p. 162), they list the earlier 1999 edition of the *Standard*s in the reference list for this chapter. (The 2014 *Standards* do appear in reference lists for other chapters.) Although the evidence of validity provided by the test developers is comprehensive, the lack of continuity within the manual and the lack of alignment with the *Standards* contribute to a disjointed narrative.

Regarding content evidence of validity, the test developers clearly and unequivocally demonstrated the alignment of test questions with the intended domain of reading comprehension. Four distinct validity studies are described in this section of the technical manual, including empirical item response theory (IRT) data and the use of focus group reviews by a panel of experts comprising the GOALS technical advisory board. The content evidence of validity is compelling.

The test developers provide other evidence to substantiate validity in a later section of the test manual; however, this evidence is disjointed because the test developers do not align this discussion with the *Standards*. For example, the test developers devote two pages to the discussion of construct evidence of validity. The *Standards* no longer refer to the concept of construct validity as a distinct type of evidence. What the test developers identify as construct evidence is conceptualized in the *Standards* as evidence based on internal structure (Reading GOALS factor structure) and evidence of relationships with other variables (correlation of Reading GOALS scores with other measures). Furthermore, the test developers conducted several studies to demonstrate what they refer to as criterion-related validity. Instead, this evidence should be reported in a manner consistent with the *Standards* and referred to as evidence of the test's relationship to other variables. Disorganized narrative aside, Reading GOALS proficiency classifications were found to correlate with two large scale measures of adult learner's reading competency: Educational Testing Service's HiSet reading assessment and the Data Recognition Corporation's Test of Adult Basic Education (TABE). Finally, Reading GOALS classifications correlated with teacher evaluations of learner reading levels.

COMMENTARY. The test developers should be commended for the depth and quality of evidence provided to support the psychometric attributes of the Reading GOALS Series, particularly and appropriately related to content evidence of validity. The test administration manual is clearly written and organized. Consequently, individuals who are responsible for administering the Reading GOALS Series will find the test administration, scoring, and interpretation process straightforward. In contrast, individuals charged with making decisions about *selecting* the Reading GOALS are likely to find the 333-page technical manual unwieldy. Sections of the manual lack page numbers, nullifying the use of the table of contents. Instead of the brief cursory summaries at the end of each section, an introduction at the beginning of each section would make it easier to navigate through the dense narrative. Finally, the test developers should pay closer attention to the *Standards for Educational and Psychology Testing* (AERA, APA, & NCME, 2014) and correctly align their discussion of validity with the *Standards*.

SUMMARY. Overall, the Reading GOALS Series for Adult Basic Education is a psychometrically sound instrument that can be used with confidence in adult education programs. Test administrators will appreciate the logic, clarity, and comprehensiveness of the test administration manual.

REVIEWER'S REFERENCES

American Educational Research Association, American Psychological Association, & National Council on Measurement in Education. (2014). *Standards for educational and psychological testing*. Washington, DC: American Educational Research Association.

CASAS. (2015). *What is CASAS?* Retrieved from https://www.casas.org/docs/pagecontents/whatiscasas.pdf

Review of Reading GOALS Series for Adult Basic Education by KATHLEEN QUINN, Professor Emerita of Education, Holy Family University, and Former Director, Fall and Spring Reading Clinic, Bensalem, PA:

DESCRIPTION. Reading GOALS Series for Adult Basic Education is a series of tests designed to measure reading comprehension of adult basic education (ABE) and adult secondary education (ASE) learners as well as others in English as second language and workforce development programs. It can be administered and scored using a computer or in paper format. The reading appraisal test (Form 900R) consists of 28 multiple-choice items (four choices for each item) in order to determine which level (A [Forms 901R and 902R], B [903R and 904R], C [905R and 906R], or D

[907R and 908R]) to use with new test takers. An optional 10-minute, one-item writing screening is also available to assist with placement. There are two parallel forms for each level with Level A, Forms 901R and 902R, having 39 items and a 60-minute administration time and all other levels and forms having 40 items each and 75-minute administration times.

The Reading GOALS Series provides the user with a total scaled score that is matched with the National Reporting System (NRS) Educational Functioning Levels (EFLs). Scaled scores of 203 and below indicate an NRS EFL of 1 or *beginning literacy*; scores from 204 to 216 are equivalent to EFL 2 or *beginning basic*; scores from 217 to 227 are EFL 3 or *low intermediate*; scores from 228 to 238 are EFL 4 or *high intermediate*; scores from 239 to 248 are EFL 5 or *low adult secondary*; and scores of 249 and above are EFL 6 or *high adult secondary*.

DEVELOPMENT. The Reading GOALS Series was developed over a 4-year period (2013-16) and included a needs assessment from agencies that were using Comprehensive Adult Student Assessment Systems' (CASAS) previous test, CASAS Life and Work Reading Assessment. The Reading GOALS Series uses the same scale as this test but has new content.

The Reading GOALS Series focuses on alignment with the college and career readiness standards (CCRS) for adult education and the NRS EFLs and performance standards. CASAS also included the NRS submission guidelines, the *Standards for Educational and Psychological Testing* (American Educational Research Association, American Psychological Association, & National Council on Measurement in Education, 2014), principles of universal design, Coxhead's academic word list, and Webb's depth of knowledge framework in developing item content. Care was taken to include current materials like emails and website content as well as workforce materials like signs, charts, and advertisements in the items. The Flesch-Kincaid readability formula and the Lexile framework were used to determine readability and text complexity. The reading comprehension construct used by Alderson is the primary source for item structure so that only reading—and not listening or writing—is being evaluated, and all items are considered to be text dependent. Content becomes increasingly challenging as levels increase and emphasis is expanded to higher level comprehension and more academic vocabulary. Draft items were evaluated for accessibility, bias, diversity, clarity, and content by subject matter experts, all of whom are listed in the technical manual.

The main purpose of the Reading GOALS Series is to assess reading comprehension and measure progress over time. It is recommended that 70-100 hours of instruction and at least 4 months take place between administrations for pre-post assessment, with a maximum of four administrations per year even though no item is repeated in any of the forms/levels.

Items were initially evaluated for level of difficulty, relevance of topics, and formats by 30-50 agencies using observations, interviews, and "classical item statistics" (manual, p. 27), which led to revisions. Then, first phase pilot testing was done by embedding two to four non-scored items into the CASAS Life and Work Reading Assessments administered to 100 or more ABE and ASE learners. This analysis resulted in a second phase of revisions. In phase two, there were 59 agencies (from 11 states and the District of Columbia) and 256,100 students who participated.

Rasch item calibration using WINSTEPS eliminated any items with mean square infit or outfit greater than 2.0. The difficulty values for items (p-values) ranged from .15 and .85 with point-biserial correlations of at least .30, and high and low group discrimination of .30 or above. At that time, each level had one form with 50 items except for Level D, which had two forms.

After 1,170 items were reviewed for fairness and sensitivity by a panel of subject matter experts, 96 items were revised, and 270 were eliminated, with 640 items making the final cut. All of the final items measure one or more of the CCR reading standards, and almost all of the final items met the minimum criterion for point-biserial correlations (.25) and were in the expected p-value range (.15 to .85) except one item on Level A, Form 901, which had a p-value of .86.

TECHNICAL. Scaled scores are used to place students into appropriate NRS EFLs and to measure their progress after intervention occurs. Cut scores were established using the bookmark standard setting method using the panel of subject matter experts who asked themselves, "Does a typical minimally competent candidate at a given performance level have at least a 50% chance of answering this questions correctly?" (manual, p. 227). Whenever an expert answered "no," a bookmark was placed on that item. Impact data of 62,853 ABE and ASE students from California were compared to ABE students classified into each NRS EFL for 2014-2015. Standard error values (+/- 2 SE) were then used to determine cut scores with *low adult secondary* having much larger numbers occurring than the other five classifications.

Reliability evidence is provided by examining parallel forms from 809 students who took the test within a 7-day period without any interventions occurring. Reliability coefficients ranged from .79 to .92. Classification consistency across levels ranged from 70% to 85% regardless of which form was administered first. Correlation coefficients ranged from .76 to .90 with an overall agreement of 78%, $r = .81$.

Test developers suggested examining possible effects between paper and computer administration by giving both formats to each examinee is impractical in an adult education context. Instead, a differential item functioning (DIF) analysis was conducted for two separate groups, with the computer-based group as the reference group and the paper-based group as the focal group. Using Mantel-Haenszel DIF detection for all levels, "no discernible differences between the two delivery modes were detected" (manual, p. 281). Internal consistency was evaluated for each form with alpha coefficients ranging from .80 to .94 and item reliability coefficients ranging from .92 to .96.

As evidence of validity based on test content, the test authors noted that the Reading GOALS Series was developed, evaluated, and reviewed by subject matter experts in the fields of ABE, ASE, and literacy. To examine the relationship between the Reading GOALS Series and other variables, results were compared to those from the Hi-Set Language Arts—Reading Test. One hundred students took both tests, and an overall bivariate correlation of .46 was observed. In another study, existing data for 10,615 students were used to compare results from the Test for Adult Basic Education (TABE) and the CASAS Life and Work Reading Assessments (the predecessor to the Reading GOALS Series). The resulting correlation coefficient was .69 ($p < .001$). The developers stated that they are designing a new study that will compare the most recent TABE with the Reading GOALS Series. A teacher feedback study also found that the Reading GOALS Series classification and the teachers' classification of students ($N = 201$) into NRS EFLs were in exact agreement from 25% to 75% of the time ($r = .56$) and agreement within one level from 72.5% to 100% of the time.

To support the use of an overall score, a principal components analysis was conducted using 1,416 students' results. This analysis found that one factor explained from 16.17% to 32.02% of the variance for all forms with all meeting the 20% threshold except Forms 905, 907, and 908, which were slightly below the 20% threshold.

COMMENTARY. Although easy and efficient to administer and score, the user should be aware of specific issues that are of concern such as limited concurrent evidence regarding validity until the aforementioned study comparing the TABE with the Reading GOALS Series is conducted. In addition, most of the participants and agencies in the studies took place in California, and samples were not always representative of the 2014-2015 national ABE/ASE data. African Americans and Whites were often underrepresented, and Asians and Hispanics were often overrepresented (see manual, p. 284).

The test authors provided a wealth of information regarding test development, rationale, use, and security, and they also included detailed information on the subject matter experts. More information on readability and text complexity is needed. Specifically, a chart with a list of the Flesch-Kincaid and Lexile framework levels and averages for each passage and form is recommended. When this reviewer calculated levels for a passage from each level, it was found that the Level C and D passages examined had very similar readability levels.

SUMMARY. The Reading GOALS Series is an easily administered and scored test of reading comprehension for use with ABE and ASE students that is clearly linked with NRS EFLs and CCRS. The alternate forms provide a method to assess student progress over time. More information is needed on convergent and classification evidence of validity, balanced representation to match NRS ABE/ASE demographic data, and more detailed information on the readability and text complexity of each passage and form. As this test is used more widely in replacing the CASAS Life and Work Reading Assessments, continued data collection and analysis should be reported in order to support both validity and reliability.

REVIEWER'S REFERENCE

American Educational Research Association, American Psychological Association, & National Council on Measurement in Education. (2014). *Standards for educational and psychological testing.* Washington, DC: American Educational Research Association.

[135]

Receptive, Expressive & Social Communication Assessment–Elementary.

Purpose: Designed for "assessing functional communication deficits and social behaviors over a broad range of children."

Population: Children ages 5-0 to 12-11 with suspected social communication deficits.

Publication Date: 2015.

Acronym: RESCA-E.

Scores, 13 to 18: Receptive Language [Comprehension of Vocabulary, Comprehension of Oral Directions, Comprehension of Stories and Questions, Comprehension of Basic Morphology and Syntax (supplemental), Executing Oral Directions, (supplemental)], Expressive Language [Expressive Labeling of Vocabulary, Expressive Skills for Describing and Explaining, Narrative Skills, Expressive Use of Basic Morphology and Syntax (supplemental)], Social Communication [Comprehension of Body Language and Vocal Emotion, Social and Language Inference, Situational Language Use, Elicited Body Language (supplemental)], Social Communication Inventory (supplemental), Overall Score.

Administration: Individual.

Price Data, 2020: $525 per kit including administration manual (135 pages), technical manual (77 pages), receptive language test plates, expressive language and social communication test plates, 20 record forms, 20 social communication inventories, 20 picture worksheets, administration CD, accessories, and carrying bag; $105 per receptive language test plates; $105 per expressive language and social communication test plates; $80 per 20 record forms; $75 per technical manual; $60 per administration manual; $25 per 20 social communication inventories; $20 per administration CD; $15 per 20 picture worksheets.

Time: Approximately 60 minutes for administration of core subtests and 15-20 minutes for scoring.

Comments: Subtests may be administered individually or in combination; testing may be completed in more than one session; examiner must supply CD or MP3 player, voice recorder, and trash can for administration.

Authors: Patricia Hamaguchi and Deborah Ross-Swain.

Publisher: Academic Therapy Publications.

Review of the Receptive, Expressive & Social Communication Assessment–Elementary by CONNIE THERIOT (ENGLAND), Professor, Counseling Program, Lincoln Memorial University, Harrogate, TN:

DESCRIPTION. According to the test authors, "The Receptive, Expressive & Social Communication Assessment–Elementary (RESCA-E) is a comprehensive assessment that provides information about a child's receptive, expressive, and social language development, in addition to social communication behaviors" (technical manual, p. 9). Its design is specific for use with children ages 5-0 to 12-11 who exhibit functional language deficits and delays in social communication skills. Examiners, typically speech-language pathologists, school psychologists, and learning specialists, must be qualified to interpret psychometric scores and understand the limitations of the results.

The RESCA-E materials are enclosed in a well-constructed carrying case and include crayons, toys, picture worksheet, audio CD, Receptive Language Test Plates book, and Expressive Language and Social Communication Test Plates book, as well as administration and technical manuals. The examiner must provide a CD or MP3 player, voice recorder and trash can.

The RESCA-E has three core areas (Receptive Language, Expressive Language, and Social Communication) with three core subtests for each. Each core area also has at least one supplemental subtest for a total of 13 subtests included in the measure. The "subtests assess skills in four language domains: semantics, pragmatics, morphology, and syntax" (technical manual, p. 23). It takes approximately 60 minutes to administer the core subtests and 15 minutes to score. The manual and record forms provide clear instructions for selection of age-appropriate items for each subtest. Basal and ceiling rules are set for some subtests; others require administration of all items. The test authors suggest that flexibility in administration is appropriate depending on the scope and intended use of the results.

Subtest raw scores are converted to scaled scores with a mean of 10 and a standard deviation of 3. Subtest scaled scores are added to obtain core scores and the Overall score. The appendix of the administration manual includes percentile ranks, age equivalent scores, and critical difference scores.

DEVELOPMENT. Several previous versions of the RESCA-E were field tested prior to the preparation of the final printed version. The piloted version with 370 items was administered to a national sample of 526 children, including 67 diagnosed with expressive language disorder, receptive language disorder, social communication disorder, or autism spectrum disorder. Following item and factor analyses as well as a bias review, the norming version of the RESCA-E was created.

The norm sample included 825 children ages 5-0 to 12-11 from 30 states and Puerto Rico. Demographic information presented in the test manual shows the sample to be representative of the U.S. population according to the 2010 Census. Item difficulty analyses conducted with the norming version generally indicated that item difficulty values increased with age, and item discrimination indices reflected good overall discrimination for all subtests. Differential item functioning (DIF) analyses were conducted to examine group differences by gender, residence (urban-suburban vs. rural), and ethnicity (African American, Caucasian, Asian American, and Hispanic origin). Of the final 297 items that make up the RESCA-E, logistic regression procedures found 31 that showed statistically significant levels of DIF. The effect size of 30 of those items was determined to be negligible, and the items were retained. One item that had a moderate effect size for Hispanic versus non-Hispanic examinees was examined by an item-review panel and also retained.

TECHNICAL. Reliability was examined using alpha coefficients. Strong internal consistency estimates were observed for all core areas and the Overall score. Subtest coefficients for students in the 11- and 12-year ranges were somewhat lower; therefore, use of confidence intervals for these students is recommended when reporting results. Over an average interval of 15 days, test-retest coefficients "provide compelling evidence that results from the RESCA-E are stable over time" (technical manual, p. 41). Interrater reliability estimates from two studies were strong, with correlation coefficients ranging from .83 to .97. Standard errors of measurement or confidence intervals are available in an appendix of the administration manual.

The RESCA-E validity evidence includes test content, comparisons to other assessments, and relationships with other variables. Validity evidence associated with test content is based on the selection of items typically aligned with the intended construct. Content validity evidence based on confirmatory factor analysis is consistently strong for all factors of the RESCA-E: Receptive Language, Expressive Language, and Social Communication. To compare the RESCA-E with another assessment based on similar constructs, the Oral and Written Language Scales, Second Edition (OWLS-II) was used. Results show no significant difference between the means, and correlation coefficients demonstrated moderate to large effect sizes. The third type of validity evidence was based on relationships to other variables, specifically age and clinical diagnosis. First, test authors expected RESCA-E scores to increase with age because many of the items on the measure tap into developmental skills. As expected, all correlations were statistically significant between RESCA-E scores and chronological age. Second, using a matched-pairs design, children with autism spectrum disorder, social communication disorder, or other intellectual or developmental disability were matched with children who had no diagnoses. Results indicate that children with no diagnoses scored significantly higher than their matched peers with identified disorders.

COMMENTARY. Highlights of the RESCA-E include an abundance of empirical data to support the utility of the assessment instrument. One distinctive characteristic of the RESCA-E is the inclusion of an audio tape with stimuli tapping emotions, in which the examinee must point to the picture that epitomizes that emotion. Examinees must respond to both a verbal prompt and a visually dynamic facial expression of emotion to determine the subtle meaning of the message. Research by Recio, Wilhelm, Sommer, and Hildebrandt (2017) illustrates this ability to determine dynamic facial expressions of emotions by stating individual differences in the ability to recognize emotion from faces are related to the amounts of sensory resources available in two brain systems: those dedicated to the processing of affective information—namely, the encoding of valence categories—and also those dedicated to perceptual processing per se—namely, the encoding of (non-emotional) changes in facial features over time (p. 379).

This research provides additional evidence to support RESCA-E as an efficacious method for assessing pragmatic language functioning. The true measure of RESCA-E's utility lies in its ability to translate assessment results into intervention strategies to alleviate challenges experienced by children with social language disorders.

SUMMARY. The RESCA-E is designed to provide information about a child's receptive, expressive, and social language development as well as social communication behaviors. The test authors include assessment of subskills, such as "comprehension of body language, facial expressions, and vocal emotion" (technical manual, p. 10). An observational tool, the Social Communication Inventory, can be used to gather information about real-world social communication and behaviors. These unique qualities make the RESCA-E a comprehensive tool to assess the complex nature of language for children struggling with everyday social exchanges within a variety of settings. It is an empirically validated measure of pragmatic and socially contextual aspects of communication.

REVIEWER'S REFERENCE

Recio, G., Wilhelm, O., Sommer, W., & Hildebrandt, A. (2017). Are event-related potentials to dynamic facial expressions of emotion related to individual differences in the accuracy of processing facial expressions and identity? *Cognitive, Affective, & Behavioral Neuroscience, 17*(2), 364-380. doi:10.3758/s13415-016-0484-6

Review of the Receptive, Expressive & Social Communication Assessment–Elementary by LAUREEN J. McINTYRE, Speech-Language Pathologist and Associate Professor of Educational Psychology & Special Education, University of Saskatchewan, Saskatoon, Saskatchewan, Canada:

DESCRIPTION. The Receptive, Expressive & Social Communication Assessment–Elementary (RESCA-E) is an individually administered test designed to provide a comprehensive assessment of children's (5-0 to 12-11 years of age) social communication behaviors and receptive, expressive, and social language development that allows for the examination of a broad range of relevant functional and social language skills. Core subtests are estimated to take approximately 60 minutes to administer, and testing may be extended to more than one session (e.g., for younger children, to reduce examinee fatigue).

Administration instructions and allowable prompts for subtests are clear, easy to follow, and printed on the provided test plates. Prior to testing, the examiner calculates the examinee's chronological age to determine the norms table to use in interpreting test results. Some subtests have age-designated starting points and basal and ceiling rules whereas other subtests require all items to be administered. The examiner must provide three items not included in the kit (CD or MP3 player, voice recorder, and trash can). Four types of scores are derived from the examinee's raw scores: scaled scores, standard scores, percentile ranks, and age equivalents. The Social Communication Inventory (SCI) observational instrument allows an examinee's specific social communication and behaviors in real-world settings to be noted and progress tracked over time.

DEVELOPMENT. The intentionality model of language acquisition (Bloom, Tinker, & Scholnick, 2001) was used in developing the RESCA-E because it "posits that language learning is an inherently social process that develops through the ongoing tension between two core constructs: engagement and effort" (technical manual, p. 12). The test authors considered two necessary components of social communication (receptive language and expressive language) and examined social communication from three perspectives (language learning, social cognition, and executive function) because an individual must develop and integrate these skills across these domains to become competent in this area. However, detailed definitions of these constructs and an outline of how the test items map onto each component of the operational definitions of these constructs were not provided in the technical manual. Two earlier versions of the test underwent field testing with small samples of children in select U.S. sites. Additional tasks were added and items or subtests removed (e.g., items that proved difficult to score, provided inconsistent responses, or demonstrated differential item functioning [DIF]). The test was renamed the RESCA-E and piloted on a national sample of 526 children (370 items, nine core and four supplemental subtests; 61 items in Social Communication Inventory).

TECHNICAL.

Standardization. A sample of 825 children—409 girls, 409 boys, and seven whose gender was not reported—was administered the norming version of the RESCA-E (298 items). Participants were 5-0 to 12-11 years of age and lived across select states in four major regions of the United States (North Central, Northeast, South, and West). There are no Canadian norms for this test. The test authors reported that the demographics of the norming sample closely approximated the U.S. population. Most participants (about 77%) were White, 13% were Black, and about 4% were Asian American. Approximately 27% of participants were Hispanic. Only one child, or 0.12% of the sample, was American Indian/Alaska native compared with 1.31% of the U.S. population; three participants (0.36% of the sample) were Native Hawaiian/Pacific Islander compared with 0.25% of the population. A sample of 400 children (202 girls and 198 boys from 5-0 to 12-11 years of age) was administered the norming version of the SCI (31 items). Item analyses resulted in three redundant items being removed. Group differences were tested across gender, ethnicity, and Hispanic origin, and results indicated no evidence of DIF for any SCI item. The test authors concluded, "The SCI is a bias-free test in terms of gender, ethnicity, and Hispanic origin" (technical manual, p. 55).

Reliability evidence. Average internal consistency estimates were reported for individual subtests across eight age groupings. Alpha coefficients ranged from .77 to .89 for subtests and from .91 to .93 for core scores. These values were said to "demonstrate strong evidence for internal consistency" (technical manual, p. 40). However, the test authors reported one value of less than .70 in the 11-year-old group for the supplemental expressive subtest and three values below .70 in the 12-year-old group (one core and one supplemental receptive subtest, and one core social communication subtest). Therefore, the test authors recommended using confidence intervals when reporting results for these age groups. Alpha coefficients for the SCI were calculated for eight age groups and ranged from .94 to .98 with a value of .97 for the overall sample.

Test-retest reliability was evaluated using corrected (for range restriction) correlations for subtest scaled scores and core and overall standard scores. Values ranged from .59 to .95 and from .93 to .99, respectively (n = 56; average interval = 15 days). The test authors felt these values provided compelling evidence for this test's stability over time. Two interrater reliability studies were conducted: (1) two examiners independently scored three subtests from 20 randomly selected completed protocols (correlation coefficients ranged from .83 to .97); and (2) two examiners scored the results of one core receptive and one core social communication subtest (n = 20; coefficients were .83 and .89). These values were felt to provide "strong evidence that the RESCA-E can be scored reliably from one examiner to another" (technical manual, p. 43). Reliability evidence for the SCI was also collected using t-tests to compare the consistency of professional/parent ratings (i.e., mean scaled scores) on 16 completed forms. Findings suggested no significant differences between scores. However, no statistically significant relationships were found between parent and professional scores using Pearson product-moment correlations. The test authors felt this "could be the result of the small sample size and variations in a child's behavior between environments (e.g., school vs. home)" (technical manual, p. 58), and advised that multiple ratings of a child's social communication behavior across different settings should be collected.

Validity evidence. Confirmatory factor analysis was used to evaluate item fit for the three core language areas, and "results indicated that the model significantly fit the data" [Bentler comparative fit index or CFI of .951; root mean square error of approximation or RMSEA of .088] (technical manual, p. 49). Exploratory factor analysis evaluated the SCI's item and content structure, and it was reported items "combine to measure skills related to social communication skills in a child's environment" [factor loadings ranging from 0.60 to 0.79] (technical manual, p. 60).

Comparisons of examinees' RESCA-E scores (n = 13; Receptive Language Core/Social Communication Core; n = 21 Expressive Language Core/Social Communication Core) to their previous scores on the Oral Expression and Listening Comprehension Scales of the Oral and Written Language Scales, Second Edition (OWLS-II; Carrow-Woolfolk, 2011) were completed. The test authors reported "no significant differences between means were found and corrected correlation coefficients had moderate to very large effect sizes ... [suggesting] individuals had similar scores on comparable components of the RESCA-E and the OWLS-II" (technical manual, p. 49).

The test authors also considered the relationship of RESCA-E results to other variables (i.e., age, disability) and reported: "All subtest correlations were statistically significant and effect sizes ranged from moderate to large" [ranging from .43 to .69] (technical manual, p. 50); and "All Core and Overall Score correlations were statistically significant, with large effect sizes [ranging from .61 to .69]" (technical manual, p. 52). This suggested a strong association between test scores and chronological age. Assuming RESCA-E scores would be lower for children with a diagnosed disability than those who are typically developing, a matched-pairs design tested these assumptions (i.e., means and t-test analyses compared diagnosis versus no diagnosis, but same age, gender, ethnicity, and Hispanic origin). The test authors reported: individuals diagnosed with learning disabilities (LD), autism spectrum disorder (ASD), social communication disorder (SCD), intellectual disabilities (ID), or developmental disabilities (DD) scored significantly lower than matched peers on the Overall score of RESCA-E; individuals with LD, ASD, or SCD scored significantly lower than matched peers on all three cores; individuals with ID or DD scored significantly lower on the Receptive Language Core; individuals with attention-deficit/hyperactivity disorder did not perform significantly lower on three cores and Overall score than matched peers. Assuming SCI scores would be lower for children with ASD or SCD than for those who are typically developing, a matched-pairs design (i.e., means and t-test analyses compared 16 children with diagnoses with 16 children with no diagnosis, but same age, gender, and ethnicity) indicated significantly lower scaled scores for children with ASD or SCD than for matched peers.

COMMENTARY. The RESCA-E shows promise as a test that professionals can use to assess children's receptive, expressive, and social communication language skills that contribute to social communication competence. It encompasses language skill assessments in areas relevant for navigating and succeeding in the social environment of the classroom (i.e., narrative language skills, understanding and following real-world directions), and provides opportunities for professionals/parents to observe and report children's strengths and areas of need related to their social communication skills in everyday environments (i.e., classroom or at home). The test authors rightly caution professionals to use a body of evidence and not isolated data from just this test to determine the presence of a language or social communication disorder. However, this caution should also be extended to interpreting results for students from diverse backgrounds. Specifically, norms and reliability and validity evidence can be strengthened by including a larger sample that is more geographically (i.e., additional U.S. states, Canada), ethnically, and culturally diverse because a wider variety of children from diverse backgrounds are being educated in today's classrooms. And while high coefficient alpha values can be used to indicate adequate internal consistency, these values do not necessarily indicate a test's constructs have been adequately represented by selected test items (Crocker & Algina, 1986; McCrae, Kurtz, Yamagata, & Terracciano, 2011). Providing detailed definitions of test constructs and an outline of how test items map onto each of the components of the operational definitions of these constructs, would help to address these concerns. Validity evidence can also be strengthened by comparing test results to other frequently used comprehensive language assessments.

SUMMARY. The RESCA-E was created to assess language skills identified by the test authors as contributing to a child's social communication competence. This test has the potential to provide professionals a more holistic picture of a child's receptive, expressive, and social communication language skill development in home and school environments, which would be valuable in both identifying and addressing students' language needs. The test's norms and provided reliability and validity evidence appear adequate but could be strengthened to improve the utility of interpretations that are made from this test's results.

REVIEWER'S REFERENCES

Bloom, L., Tinker, E., & Scholnick, E. (2001). The intentionality model and language acquisition: Engagement, effort, and the essential tension in development. *Monographs of the Society for Research in Child Development, 66*(4) 1-101.

Carrow-Woolfolk, E. (2011). Oral and Written Language Scales, Second Edition: Listening Comprehension and Oral Expression. Torrance, CA: Western Psychological Services.

Crocker, L., & Algina, J. (1986). *Introduction to classical and modern test theory*. Orlando, FL: Holt, Rinehart and Winston.

McCrae, R. R., Kurtz, J. E., Yamagata, S., & Terracciano, A. (2011). Internal consistency, retest reliability, and their implications for personality scale validity. *Personality and Social Psychology Review, 15*, 28-50. doi:10.1177/1088868310366253

[136]

Reiss Motivation Profile for Self-Discovery.

Purpose: Designed to measure individual motivation across 16 domains.
Population: Ages 12 and older.
Publication Date: 2013.
Acronym: RMP.
Scores, 16: Acceptance, Curiosity, Eating, Family, Honor, Idealism, Independence, Order, Physical Activity, Power, Romance, Saving, Social Contact, Status, Tranquility, Vengeance.
Administration: Individual or group.
Forms, 6: Self-Discovery, Business, School, Children, Sports, Relationships.
Price Data: Available from publisher.
Foreign Language Editions: Various translations for each profile available from test publisher.
Time: 10-15 minutes for administration.
Comments: Scored online; online administration available.
Author: Steven Reiss.
Publisher: IDS Publishing.

a) REISS MOTIVATION PROFILE–BUSINESS VERSION.
Population: Working adults.
Scores, 16: Same as above with Beauty scale substituted for Romance scale.

b) REISS SCHOOL MOTIVATION PROFILE.
Population: Students ages 12 and older.
Acronym: RSMP.
Scores, 13: Acceptance, Curiosity, Family, Honor, Idealism, Independence, Order, Physical Activity, Power, Social Contact, Status, Tranquility, Vengeance.

c) REISS MOTIVATION PROFILE FOR CHILDREN.
Population: Ages 4 to 11.
Acronym: RMP-Child.
Scores, 10: Achievement, Attention, Belonging, Citizenship, Competition, Order, Physical Activity, Self Esteem, Tranquility, Understanding.
Comments: Two raters recommended; at least one rater must be a teacher.

d) REISS MOTIVATION PROFILE FOR SPORTS.
Population: Athletes and sports teams.
Scores, 14: Acceptance, Curiosity, Eating, Expedience, Family, Idealism, Interdependence, Order, Physical

Activity, Power, Social Contact, Status, Tranquility, Vengeance.
e) REISS MOTIVATION PROFILE–RELATIONSHIPS.
Population: Ages 16 and older.
Scores, 16: Acceptance, Curiosity, Eating, Family, Honor, Idealism, Independence, Order, Physical Activity, Power, Romance, Saving, Social Contact, Status, Tranquility, Vengeance.
Comments: Incompatibility Index included; requires profiles completed by two individuals.

Review of the Reiss Motivation Profile for Self-Discovery by DEBORAH L. BANDALOS, Professor of Assessment and Measurements, and ELIZABETH M. SPRATTO, Assessment Consultant, James Madison University, Harrisonburg, VA:

DESCRIPTION. The Reiss Motivation Profile (RMP) for Self-Discovery is a self-report measure of the extent to which an individual values 16 basic human needs, or motives: Acceptance, Curiosity, Eating, Family, Honor, Idealism, Independence, Order, Physical Activity, Power, Romance, Saving, Social Contact, Status, Tranquility, and Vengeance. It is based on the test author's theory that everyone experiences these 16 motives to some degree but prioritizes them differently. The test author posits that individuals' behaviors are predictable by their patterns of strength or weakness across the 16 motives. The RMP consists of eight items for each of the 16 motives, for a total of 128 items that respondents rate on a 7-point scale of -3 (*strongly disagree*) to 3 (*strongly agree*). The RMP appears easy to administer either individually or in a group setting. However, scoring procedures are not published; users must submit responses for online scoring.

The test author outlines many possible uses of the RMP in the book *The Reiss Motivation Profile* (2013), which explicates the theory underlying the instrument and serves as its manual. Part III of the book contains chapters suggesting uses in the areas of self-discovery, leadership training, executive coaching, conflict resolution, hiring, career counseling, and marketing. Each of these uses is illustrated by case studies or, in the case of career counseling, the test author's conjectures on the likely motivations of those in various occupations. In other publications, the author suggests clinical uses in applied behavior analysis, cognitive behavioral analysis, and counseling (Reiss & Havercamp, 1998), and as a supplement to personality tests (Havercamp & Reiss, 2003). However, no empirical evidence is provided to support these uses. As stated in the *Standards for Educational and Psychological Testing* (American Educational Research Association [AERA], American Psychological Association [APA], & National Council on Measurement in Education [NCME], 2014), test developers have the responsibility to present such evidence.

The focus of this review is the Reiss Motivation Profile (RMP) for Self-Discovery. The original RMP has been adapted into several additional versions designed for use in other contexts. These are: the Reiss Motivation Profile for Business; the Reiss School Motivation Profile; the Reiss Motivation Profile for Wellness; the Reiss Motivation Profile for Sports; the Reiss Relationship Profile; and the Reiss Profile IDD. The latter profile is completed by caregivers of individuals with intellectual and developmental disabilities.

DEVELOPMENT. The test author conducted a comprehensive scale development process, beginning with an extensive literature review to identify possible motivations. Based on this review, he created an initial item pool of 328 items, which was then reviewed by "colleagues, relatives, and friends" (Reiss & Havercamp, 1998, p. 98) who presumably had some familiarity with motivation theory. The scale subsequently went through four revisions in which items were deleted, changed, or added on the basis of a series of factor analyses. In a final confirmatory factor analysis (CFA), the test author reported support for a model with 15 factors (Reiss & Havercamp, 1998), although the results of this analysis are not reported in sufficient detail for this finding to be verified. The author reports (Reiss, 2013) conducting another CFA after adding the 16th factor, Saving, to the scale and states that this model provided a moderate fit to the data. It should be noted that most of the reliability and validity studies reported appear to have been conducted on the 15-factor RMP. The test author reported low to moderate correlations of scores from all 16 of the RMP scales with scores on the Marlowe-Crowne Social Desirability Scale (correlations ranged from .01 to .39), indicating minimal effects of socially desirable responding.

TECHNICAL. The test author reports that, since the summer of 2013, norms based on a sample of "about 60,000 people" from North America, Germany, and Holland have been used, and that norms are now reported separately for gender, age, and culture (Reiss, 2013, p.157). No further information on this sample is provided, so its makeup is not clear. It is also not clear which age ranges or cultural groups are included as the normative data are not provided. In a note included with the review materials the test author noted that a renorming of the RMP on 79,888 people from 23 countries on three continents (Asia, Europe, and North America) had just been completed. No further information on this sample was provided.

Because scores from the 16 scales are interpreted separately, the internal consistency of these scales is important. The test author reports the results of two studies of internal consistency for each scale, with the exception of Saving, which had not been developed at the time these studies were conducted. Thus, no information on internal consistency is available for the Saving scale. For the other 15 scales, values of coefficient alpha ranged from .79 to .94 (median = .88) for a sample of 311 undergraduate students, and from .74 to .92 (median = .82) for a separate sample of 398 respondents obtained from a variety of sources (a high school and college, a nursing home, a church group, professionals attending a seminar on developmental disabilities, and a Kiwanis Club). Because the RMP motivations are considered to be trait-like, the test author also reports values of test-retest reliability coefficients obtained from a sample of 123 undergraduate students over a 4-week interval. Correlation coefficients ranged from .69 to .88 (median = .81).

The test author provides several types of validity evidence, including evidence based on internal structure and evidence based on relations with external variables. Evidence for the internal structure of the RMP scales was obtained through factor analyses, both exploratory and confirmatory. The majority of these analyses were conducted on the 15-factor version of the RMP (i.e., excluding the Saving scale). Reiss does not provide complete tables of loadings for these analyses, although values of selected loadings are given in Reiss and Havercamp (1998). These loadings are reasonably high, overall, but it is difficult to judge the results in the absence of the full table of loadings. Reiss and Havercamp also conducted a CFA on a separate sample, but report only the RMSEA value of .047. Although this value is suggestive of a good fit to the data, it is not possible to judge the results without more information. Reiss (2013, p. 160) reports the results of a second CFA conducted on the full 16-factor scale but does not provide values of loading coefficients or other parameter estimates. Fit index values are mixed in their support for the 16-factor model (RMSEA = .053; NNFI = .894), and again, more information is needed to judge the fit of this model.

Evidence based on relations with external variables is provided in the form of group comparisons and correlations of RMP scale scores with those of other scales. Results of these analyses are in the expected directions. For the group comparisons, Reiss compared scores of various groups expected to have high scores on one or more of the RMP scales to those of a comparison group. The latter group consisted of the combined samples from previous EFA and CFA studies. The largest effect sizes were found for comparisons of this group to a group of 65 fraternity and sorority members on Status scores ($d = .92$); to a group of 71 athletes on Physical Activity scores ($d = 1.21$); to a group of 49 Protestant seminary students on Independence scores ($d = .77$) and Idealism scores ($d = .77$); and to a group of 52 college philosophy majors on Curiosity scores ($d = 1.06$). All of these comparisons were in the expected directions.

COMMENTARY. The RMP appears easy for respondents to complete, although it cannot be self-scored. The test author conducted an extensive and appropriate scale development process, resulting in reliability coefficients (both internal consistency and test-retest) that are moderate to high. In theory, the scale can be used in many different settings (e.g., business, relationship counseling). However, although the test author reports a wide variety of validity studies, no evidence is presented to support the specific uses suggested. As stated in the *Standards for Educational and Psychological Testing* (AERA, APA, & NCME, 2014), "A rationale should be presented for each intended interpretation of test scores for a given use, together with a summary of the evidence and theory bearing on the intended interpretation" (Standard 1.2, p. 23). The absence of such information makes it difficult for potential users to know whether an intended use is appropriate. There also are not sufficient data presented from the factor analyses to determine whether the internal structure of the scale is supported, and in fact, the majority of the factor analytic and reliability studies did not use the final 16-factor scale (the Saving factor was left out). Finally, although the norming samples are large and, according to the test author, diverse, no information on the makeup of these samples or their mean scores is provided. Similarly, although it appears that subgroup norms are available, no information is provided on these.

These reviewers note that many of these issues could be addressed simply by providing more information about already-existing data and analyses, and we urge the test author to do so. In addition, we encourage the author to conduct additional validity studies focused on the appropriateness of the specific uses suggested for the RMP.

SUMMARY. The Reiss Motivation Profile for Self-Discovery was designed to assess respondents' levels of 16 basic psychological needs. On the surface it appears that the scale may meet this goal, and if so could be useful in business, counseling, and other settings. However, the lack of information supporting the full 16-factor structure of the original scale and of validity evidence for use of the RMP in specific contexts limits its usefulness. Until such additional information is provided in the test manual, practitioners are advised to obtain their own evidence for intended uses and interpretations.

REVIEWERS' REFERENCES

American Educational Research Association, American Psychological Association, & National Council on Measurement in Education. (2014). *Standards for Educational and Psychological Testing.* Washington, DC: American Educational Research Association.

Havercamp, S. M., & Reiss, S. (2003). A comprehensive assessment of human strivings: Test-retest reliability and validity of the Reiss Profile. *Journal of Personality Assessment, 81,* 123-132.

Reiss, S. (2013). *The Reiss Motivation Profile: What motivates you?* Worthington, OH: IDS Publishing.

Reiss, S., & Havercamp, S. M. (1998). Toward a comprehensive assessment of fundamental motivation: Factor structure of the Reiss Profiles. *Psychological Assessment, 10,* 97-106.

Review of the Reiss Motivation Profile for Self-Discovery by JAMES P. VAN HANEGHAN, Professor of Counseling and Instructional Sciences, University of South Alabama, Mobile, AL:

DESCRIPTION. The Reiss Motivation Profile (RMP) for Self-Discovery is a 128-item self-report scale for adolescents and adults concerning the importance of 16 basic needs. The RMP is the core scale reflecting the theoretical model of needs proposed by Reiss (2013). Reiss and colleagues have also derived variations on the scale for business, sports, couples, and other applications. Depending on the purpose, all or only a subset of the original scales are included in the analysis. Although these are presented as different assessments, the assessments all depend on the validity of Reiss's core model and refer to the evidence supporting the RMP to undergird their validity.

For each of the 16 basic needs there are eight self-report items rated on 7-point Likert scales. The first scale is Acceptance. Reiss (2008, 2013) reported that high Acceptance scores reflect a lack of self-confidence and the need for acceptance by others. Curiosity reflects intellectual curiosity. Eating reflects value for eating and food. The Family scale addresses the importance of family. The Honor scale addresses the importance of character and integrity. The Idealism scale reflects value for social justice. The Independence scale reflects a value for self-reliance. The Order scale reflects value for organization and planning. The Physical Activity scale reflects value for engaging in physical exercise. The Power scale reflects an interest in having control over others. The Romance scale reflects an interest in sex and beauty. The Savings scale reflects an interest in collecting money or other items. The Social Contact scale reflects an interest in being with and engaging with others. The Status scale reflects an interest in being respected for one's place in society or an organization. The Tranquility scale reflects an interest in avoiding anxiety-producing situations. The Vengeance scale reflects the desire to confront those who are perceived to have done something against the respondent.

The raw scores on the test are transformed into standard scores using norming data that have been collected over the years. The test is scored online, and a profile of scores is produced. Scores in the top or bottom 20% are construed as showing stronger values in one direction or another. In theory, the assessment should be interpreted in conjunction with a qualified "master" who understands the assessment. However, details on this process are not well-specified, and there is no discussion of administration qualifications by Reiss (2013). Several uses of the scores and reconfiguration of the scale to address different domains are presented in the test manual to show the potential utility of the instrument in addressing relationships, sports, and business. For example, a comparison of a couple's scores can be used in relationship counseling. Mismatches within couples are purported to be indicative of potential sources of conflict. Variations of the scale constructed for school children and individuals with intellectual disabilities taking into account the developmental level and the appropriateness of scales were also developed.

DEVELOPMENT. The initial items were generated from reviews of prior conceptualizations of needs and the researchers' own additions. After several iterations and factor analytic studies, the test developers were able to produce the 16 eight-item scales. They bolstered their factor analytic studies with several concurrent validity and known-groups validity analyses. As they began to use the scale in practical contexts, they began to develop ways of using the scales in different domains (making a few adjustments such as changing Romance to Beauty in the Business version). Also, in some cases they reiterated the development process for new scales for children and those with intellectual disabilities.

TECHNICAL. The standardization samples and norming of the test have been proprietary. Although some initial norming samples were described, current norm samples are not described in detail. The test publisher provided information that the test was currently being renormed based on a sample of 79,888 test takers worldwide. Reiss (2013) reported that there were separate norms by gender, age, and culture. However, there are no specifics about the process used to create them nor any suggestions about why they should be used. Cut scores for high or low values were developed based on the norm sample percentiles, but the meaningfulness of high or low scores is presumed to be consequential without studies reported that support their use. IRT analysis of items and scales might provide more insight into how well the scales provide meaningful information. As suggested by the current American Educational Research Association (AERA), American Psychological Association (APA), and National Council on Measurement in Education (NCME) testing standards (2014, p. 129), this largely proprietary norming process and cut score determination would benefit from an independent review to support its adequacy.

The primary evidence of the validity of scales comes from two sources. One is the factor analytic work demonstrating that the items make up 16 correlated factors. The second source of evidence is concurrent validity studies. Correlations with the Big Five personality traits as measured by the NEO-PI-R, the Myers-Briggs Type Indicator, and several comparisons for known groups whose scores should be different based on the theory proposed. Most of the reported correlation coefficients were in the .20's and .30's. According to the test author, there were moderate to large differences for known groups. For example, philosophy majors scored higher on Curiosity (Cohen's d = 1.06). Studies that examined divergent and discriminant evidence of validity would strengthen the validity argument of the theoretical model.

Internal consistency and test-retest forms of reliability were presented (Reiss, 2015). Internal consistency (i.e., alpha) coefficients ranged from .74 to .92 (median .82) in a sample of 398 "racially diverse adolescents and adults" (Reiss, 2015). These values can be considered acceptable for research and using the test in exploratory ways; however, some may not be strong enough for consequential decision making. Four-week test-retest reliability coefficients were generally acceptable (values ranged from .69 to .88) in a sample of 123 undergraduates. Reiss found little to no evidence of social desirability effects. The RMP scales were mostly uncorrelated with the Marlowe-Crowne Social Desirability Scale (Reiss, 2015). Thus, the scales show some levels of internal consistency and stability. However, there are no data on the scores' long-term stability. The theory predicts some stability in the scores over long periods of time. Evidence of long-term test-retest stability is required to support this claim.

COMMENTARY. The efficacy of the RMP depends on the strong theoretical basis that undergirds its application. Although initial work on validity has been done, the theory has not been rigorously examined. Claims about universality and stability have not been strongly substantiated empirically. Such claims require analysis relative to evolutionary psychological theories and behavior genetics. Further, the implications of low and high scores discussed in the test manual are sometimes overly simplistic, assume a linear binary scaling of the attribute, and represent only a small sampling of the implications. Most of the evidence presented on group differences represents differences between known groups with little consideration of situational or other differences that address the complex interactions of situational, personality, and other factors that determine behavior (e.g., see Mischel & Shoda, 1995). Studies that take into account these complexes of variables are necessary to help stretch the theoretical basis.

Another concern is the lack of longitudinal research. Reiss (2013) makes a theoretical argument for the stability of these needs across adulthood without offering an empirical basis for this claim. Further, evidence needs to be presented in the research literature on the applications in business, sports, relationship counseling, and career counseling. Although there are some initial studies and apparently a great deal of practical work (e.g., see Reiss, 2008), there are few peer reviewed studies of these applications. For example, we know little about the consequential use in business settings. Would an employer have validity evidence to support rejection of an otherwise qualified applicant whose needs score did not match their organization? There are no studies of differential item or test functioning.

Evidence of successful use in various domains is presented by the test publisher. However, beyond the basic set of studies done early on to establish validity, most evidence comes from case studies.

Finally, there is the more mundane but important work of building an acceptable testing manual. There is a great deal of information missing from the book that serves as the manual that is important for administering and interpreting the test. For example, there are some case examples, but there are no samples of the profiles that are generated from the online scoring of the test for users to examine. The information in Reiss (2013) is helpful and provides some of the evidence needed, but the documentation needs to be more systematically structured in the format of a well-organized test manual. The documentation fails to meet several AERA/APA/NCME standards.

SUMMARY. Overall, there is a need to help build a stronger basis for the RMP and its applications. Many of the uses are promising, but a stronger and more public evidence base is needed. Further, the test manual needs to be better organized and more informative. Finally, evidence to establish consequential validity for the RMP's uses is needed, as are studies to determine how the needs interact with situational, personality, demographic, and cultural factors.

REVIEWER'S REFERENCES

American Educational Research Association, American Psychological Association, & National Council on Measurement in Education. (2014). *Standards for educational and psychological testing.* Washington, DC: American Educational Research Association.

Mischel, W. & Shoda, Y. (1995). A cognitive-affective system theory of personality: Reconceptualizing invariances in personality and the role of situations. *Psychological Review, 102,* 246–268. http://dx.doi.org/10.1037/0033-295X.102.2.246

Reiss, S. (2008). *The normal personality: A new way of thinking about people.* New York, NY: Cambridge University Press.

Reiss, S. (2013). *The Reiss Motivation Profile®: What motivates you?* Worthington, OH: IDS Publishing.

Reiss, S. (2015). *The Reiss Motivation Profile®: Reliability and validity.* Unpublished manuscript, The Ohio State University, Columbus, OH.

[137]

Reynolds Adaptable Intelligence Test–Nonverbal.

Purpose: Designed as "an assessment of nonverbal intelligence that ... requires almost no motor coordination or visual-motor skill."
Population: Ages 10 to 75.
Publication Date: 2016.
Acronym: RAIT-NV.
Scores, 3: Nonverbal Analogies, Sequences, Nonverbal Intelligence Index.
Administration: Individual or group.
Price Data, 2020: $180 per complete kit including professional manual (114 pages), fast guide (30 pages), 10 reusable item booklets, 50 answer sheets, 50 score summary forms, and scoring key; $75 per professional manual with fast guide; $28 per 50 answer sheets; $28 per 50 score summary forms; $64 per 10 reusable item booklets, $5 per scoring key.
Time: Maximum time allowed is 7 minutes for Nonverbal Analogies and 10 minutes for Sequences. Battery can be administered in approximately 20 minutes.
Comments: Test contains the two subtests that comprise the Fluid Intelligence Index of the Reynolds Adaptable Intelligence Test (20:147).
Author: Cecil R. Reynolds.
Publisher: Psychological Assessment Resources, Inc.

Review of the Reynolds Adaptable Intelligence Test-Nonverbal by THOMAS J. GROSS, Assistant Professor, Psychology Department, College of Education and Behavioral Sciences, Western Kentucky University, Bowling Green, KY:

DESCRIPTION. The Reynolds Adaptable Intelligence Test-Nonverbal (RAIT-NV) was developed from the Reynolds Adaptable Intelligence Test (RAIT) subtests for the Fluid Intelligence Index (FII), which is named the Nonverbal Intelligence Index (NVII) on the RAIT-NV. The RAIT-NV was normed for individuals from 10 years 0 months to 75 years of age. The RAIT-NV includes a professional manual and fast guide that give a test overview and administration and scoring information. Item books, answer sheets, scoring key overlay, and score summary forms are also included. Administration instructions require examinees to read the instructions silently and inform the examiner when they are finished; however, reading out loud and pointing by the examiner are allowed for examinees who are unable to read. There are general instructions, as well as individual subtest instructions. The test author recommends that examiners have formal training in assessment and knowledge of cognitive evaluation.

Two subtests comprise the NVII. The Nonverbal Analogies (NVA) subtest has 52 items and a 7-minute time limit. The task requires examinees to choose the best picture that fits a pictorial analogy. The Sequences (SEQ) subtest has 43 items and a 10-minute time limit. This subtest has examinees select a picture that best completes a series of pictures. Both subtests have a multiple-choice format, and the overlay is used to hand score the answer sheet. Raw scores are converted to T scores for each subtest, based on age, and the sum of the T scores is used to find the NVII standard score. An appendix in the professional manual provides 90% and 95% confidence intervals, percentile ranks, stanine scores, *z* scores, and normal curve equivalents. Age equivalents up to 19 years are provided, but the test author advises against their use. For each age group in the normative sample, statistical significance levels between NVA and SEQ subtest score discrepancies are included in the test manual with the percentage of difference scores.

DEVELOPMENT. The primary goal for developing the RAIT-NV was to provide a means to administer a traditional paper-and-pencil assessment of nonverbal intelligence to individuals or groups. The purpose of this goal was to have a reliable and valid intellectual assessment for examinees who might face environmental or personal setbacks that would impair their verbal skills. A secondary goal was to eliminate confounds related to cultural/linguistic biases through item reviews, and to provide multiple and conceptually equitable forms of instructions during administration. Further, the test author provides a means for comparing a change in NVII standard scores from administration from one time period to another. Much of the RAIT-NV development is discussed as a portion of the RAIT development. The test author reported piloting items and versions of the RAIT using classical test theory, Rasch analyses, and expert reviews to assess items. This approach is consistent with that described in previous reviews of the RAIT (see Floyd & Singh, 2014; Suppa, 2014).

TECHNICAL. The RAIT-NV used the RAIT standardization sample of 2,124 individuals divided into 23 age groups from 10 to 75 years. The range of ages in each group varied from 6 months to 10 years; age and group sizes ranged from 71 to 120 individuals. Within the sample, 484 participants completed the booklet version of the RAIT, and 1,640 completed the computer version. No differences between groups were found; still, the RAIT-NV can be administered only in booklet form. The standardization sample was selected to match the 2010 U.S. Census population statistics through stratified random sampling.

Raw scores were weighted within age groups based on gender, ethnicity, and educational attainment or parent's educational attainment for those 10 to 20 years of age. Continuous norming procedures were used to adjust raw score distributions and calculate subtest T scores for the NVA and SEQ at each age range. The NVII was created by using the cumulative frequency distribution of the summed subscale T scores to create a standard score scale with a mean of 100 and standard deviation of 15. The confidence intervals were calculated using an estimated true score and the standard error of estimate. The simple difference method was used to calculate the statistical significance of difference scores. It was observed that approximately 30 to 50% of the discrepancy scores were one or more standard deviations from the mean, dependent on age group (manual, Appendix I).

Regarding reliability, the median alpha coefficients were .89 for NVA (range = .84 to .93), .86 for SEQ (range .81 to .92), and .93 for NVII (range = .89 to .96). Test-retest reliability was assessed with 132 participants (10 to 20 years of age, n = 45; 21 to 40 years of age, n = 40; 41 to 75 years of age, n = 47) over a period of 18 to 34 days. Uncorrected and disattenuated (corrected for alpha) coefficients, respectively, for the total sample were .77 and .84 for NVA, .74 and .83 for SEQ, and .81 and .86 for NVII. The range for the uncorrected coefficients was .73 to .80 for NVA, .68 to .83 for SEQ, and .75 to .87 for NVII. The range of disattenuated coefficients was .81 to .89 for NVA, .77 to .97 for SEQ, and .80 to .92 for NVII. Correlations between the NVA and SEQ subtests were not readily apparent.

The test author reported that the RAIT-NV is designed to measure "nonverbal or fluid intelligence" (manual, p. 40). A principal component analysis using varimax rotation for the RAIT norming sample indicated that the NVA and SEQ subtests loaded onto a single factor with factor loadings of .91 and .81, respectively. External validity was assessed by correlating the RAIT-NV NVII and subtest scores with scores on other standardized tests and job industry and job training level as well as comparing performance across clinical groups. Correlations between RAIT-NV subtests and other standardized measures' subtests are provided.

In relation to other assessments of intelligence, the NVII was significantly correlated with the Test of General Reasoning Ability (TOGRA) General Reasoning Index (GRI) at .90. The TOGRA is a derivative test of the RAIT, as well. Correlations between the NVII and the Wechsler Intelligence Scale for Children—Fourth Edition (WISC-IV; n = 29) were significant for the Full Scale IQ (FSIQ) score (.51), Processing Speed Index (.52), and the Perceptual Reasoning Index (PRI; .43). Correlations between the NVII and the Wechsler Adult Intelligence Scale—Fourth Edition (WAIS-IV; n = 28) were significant only for the PRI (.44). Correlations (n = 51) between the NVII and Reynolds Intellectual Assessment Scales (RIAS) Verbal Intelligence Index (VIX; .65), Nonverbal Intelligence Index (NIX; .36), Composite Intelligence Index (CIX; .60), and an optional Composite Memory Index (CMX; .56) were statistically significant. The Wonderlic Personnel Test total score significantly correlated with the NVII (.71), as did the Beta III IQ score (.72).

The relationships of the NVII scores (n = 66) with tests of academic achievement were consistent across the Wide Range Achievement Test 4 (WRAT4) Reading Composite (.43) and the Test of Irregular Word Reading Efficiency (TIWRE) Reading Efficiency Index (.40). The author reported median and mean NVII scores by job industry and found that the NVII correlated significantly (.31; n = 372) with the complexity of professions as outlined by the O*NET Job Zones (National Center for O*NET Development, n.d.).

Seven clinical groups were identified: intellectual disability (n = 52), traumatic brain injury (n = 39), stroke (n = 32), dementia (n = 24), hearing impaired (n = 28), learning disability (10 to 17 years of age, n = 22; 18 to 50 years of age, n = 29), and attention-deficit/hyperactivity disorder (10 to 17 years of age, n = 28; 18 to 50 years of age, n = 34). Comparisons of means between the clinical groups and matched samples from the normative set were conducted with independent t-tests for the NVA, SEQ, and NVII scores. Overall, the matched groups had an NVII standard score of approximately 100 (range = 98 to 103), an NVA T score of approximately 51 (range = 50 to 54), and SEQ approximately T = 50 (range = 48 to 52); however, matched sample standard deviations were not provided. In sum, the clinical groups had lower mean scores than the respective matched groups; however, no effect sizes were provided.

COMMENTARY. The RAIT-NV is a brief and straightforward assessment that may be administered and scored with little effort on the part of the professional examiner. Test administrators should be aware that the RAIT-NV requires individuals to complete their own answer sheets, which could be difficult for younger individuals or those with intellectual or motor impairments. Also, many of the items on the NVA and some of the items on the SEQ subtests do require culturally specific knowledge (e.g., information about specific sports), which might limit generalization. General guidelines are provided for both verbal and nonverbal administration; there are no detailed instructions in the test manual regarding how to gesture nonverbal instructions.

The RAIT-NV was developed with a sample that closely approximates the 2010 U.S. Census; however, with projected changes in U.S. demographics (e.g., Colby & Ortman, 2015) the test developers could consider updating the standardization sample. Nonetheless, the summaries provided by the test developer indicate the RAIT-NV is generally reliable. The external evidence of validity of the RAIT-NV and the related subscales might need clarification. The NVII appears to estimate some form of overall intellectual functioning, but associations with overall intelligence scores varied by test. Although a comparison test such as the Wonderlic could be conceptualized as a measure of fluid abilities, it is more likely a measure of general intelligence (Hicks, Harrison, & Engle, 2015). Similarly, relationships between the NVII and other measures of fluid intelligence seem inconsistent. For example, the NVII has significant correlations with PRI on the WISC-IV and WAIS-IV but a larger correlation with the RIAS VIX than NIX. Those administering the RAIT-NV should consider reviewing the NVA and SEQ correlations with other test batteries' subtests to appraise subtest validity independently. In consideration of the populations of individuals with disabilities, it appears that the scores were consistently lower than the matched sample. Still, it is difficult to discern the magnitude of the differences as it was unclear how family-wise error was addressed in the means comparisons, and the omission of the matched groups' standard deviations makes independently calculating effect sizes difficult.

SUMMARY. The RAIT-NV succeeds in being a short duration test that can be completed in paper-and-pencil form by a wide age range of individuals. It could be useful as a screener of intellectual functioning but might need to be used in conjunction with other measures. The RAIT-NV is likely insufficient to be used for discriminating clinical and non-clinical groups until more information regarding differences between these groups is explored, such as sensitivity and specificity.

REVIEWER'S REFERENCES

Colby, S. L., & Ortman, J. M. (2015). *Projections of the size and composition of the U.S. population: 2014 to 2060: Population estimates and projections.* Current Population Reports, P25-1143. Washington, DC: U.S. Census Bureau.

Floyd, R. G., & Singh, L. J. (2017). [Test review of the Reynolds Adaptable Intelligence Test]. In J. F. Carlson, K. F. Geisinger, & J. L. Jonson (Eds.), *The twentieth mental measurements yearbook* (pp. 605-607). Lincoln, NE: Buros Center for Testing.

Hicks, K. L., Harrison, T. L., & Engle, R. W. (2015). Wonderlic, working memory capacity, and fluid intelligence. *Intelligence, 50,* 186-195. doi:10.1016/j.intell.2015.03.005

National Center for O*NET Development. (n.d.). *O*NET Online.* Retrieved from https://www.onetonline.org/help/online/zones

Suppa, C. H. (2017). [Test review of the Reynolds Adaptable Intelligence Test]. In J. F. Carlson, K. F. Geisinger, & J. L. Jonson (Eds.), *The twentieth mental measurements yearbook* (pp. 607-609). Lincoln, NE: Buros Center for Testing.

Review of the Reynolds Adaptable Intelligence Test–Nonverbal by RONALD A. MADLE, Retired School Psychologist (formerly Shikellamy School District and Penn State University), Lewisburg, PA:

DESCRIPTION. The Reynolds Adaptable Intelligence Test–Nonverbal (RAIT-NV) uses visual analogies and visual sequences to measure intelligence in individuals from 10-0 to 75-11 years. It was formed from the Fluid Intelligence Index (FII) of its parent assessment, the comprehensive Reynolds Adaptive Intelligence Test (RAIT). Stated applications include clinical assessment for individuals with various disabilities (e.g., learning disabilities, intellectual disabilities, autism spectrum disorder, neuropsychological impairments), human resources testing, and testing second language learners. It is not appropriate for individuals with significant visual or visual-perceptual impairments.

The RAIT-NV test kit includes 10 color item booklets and pads of 50 answer sheets and score summary forms with a see-through scoring key, a professional manual, and a fast guide. The test has 95 items across the Nonverbal Analogies (NVA) and Sequences (SEQ) subtests, with an overall Nonverbal Intelligence Index (NVII). Many individuals can learn to administer the test with the guidance of an appropriately qualified person. It can be administered to groups or individuals using a conventional paper-and-pencil format. All items have five multiple-choice options.

After silently reading the test instructions and sample items in the test booklet, the examinee begins the 20-minute-long test. Answers are recorded by filling in bubbles, although dictated responses are permissible. Items can be skipped and returned to within each section, there is no penalty for guessing, and scratch paper may be used. Alternate instructions are presented for examinees with secondary disabilities (e.g., reading, hearing, motor impairments) or second language learners. Even though the subtests have time limits, they are quite generous.

Objective scoring is completed on the score summary form, which includes demographic information, raw and standard subtest scores and the NVII, and significance of differences between subtests. The reverse side provides space for plotting subtest and index scores and for recording reliability of changes across administrations. Subtest raw scores are converted to T scores (mean = 50; standard deviation = 10), which are summed to obtain the NVII standard score using the traditional standard score metric (mean = 100; standard deviation = 15) with the associated confidence interval and percentile rank. Score descriptors are *significantly below/above average, moderately below/above average, below/above average,* and *average,* with *average* being 90-109 and all other intervals at 10-point increases or decreases.

In addition to providing fairly standard interpretive advice, the test author recommends accounting for the Flynn Effect by subtracting 0.3 standard score units from the obtained NVII for each year after the test standardization.

DEVELOPMENT. The RAIT-NV was developed as part of the RAIT, a comprehensive, flexible intellectual assessment that can be administered in individual or group formats. One hundred sixty-five items (86 NVA and 79 SEQ) were developed, reviewed, and piloted. In the first pilot study three groups of 150 people took selected subtests. Item difficulty, item discrimination, and item bias (DIF) statistics were derived from classical test theory and item response theory. The revised test, with NVA and SEQ items reduced to 72 and 68, respectively, was submitted to a second field test. A second sample of individuals (n = 397) was divided into two groups who took either odd-numbered or even-numbered items. Following the same analyses as in the first pilot, score means, standard deviations, and distributions were computed and items sorted by difficulty. A final analysis of item foil effectiveness and possible biases was completed before items were finalized for the standardization version.

TECHNICAL.

Standardization. The final RAIT standardization form included 52 NVA items and 43 SEQ items. At this point, time limits were assigned (7 minutes and 10 minutes for NVA and SEQ, respectively). There were no basal or ceiling rules, and each participant completed as many items as possible within the time limits assigned.

From July 2011 to November 2012 standardization data were collected in 40 states using both computer and paper-and-pencil administrations. A total of 2,124 people (484 booklet and 1,640 computer) across 23 age groups completed the standardization version. A multivariate analysis of covariance found no differences between the two administration methods, permitting use of all data in the norms.

Distributions on gender, ethnicity, and education level were consistent with the 2010 U.S. Census. Geographically the South and West were somewhat overrepresented, but there were no significant differences in scores across regions. A statistical weighting procedure was used to achieve a near-perfect match with the Census figures.

Besides the subtest and index scores the final norm tables include 90% and 95% confidence intervals, percentiles, stanines, *z* scores, normal curve equivalents, age equivalents, discrepancy scores, and reliable change scores.

Reliability. Content sampling (internal consistency) and time sampling reliability information is provided in the test manual. Interscorer reliability was not assessed due to the objective multiple-choice test format.

Coefficient alpha for the NVII was a very respectable .93, and for the NVA and SEQ scales, values were .89 and .86, correspondingly. Age group coefficients ranged from .81 to .96, with all NVII coefficients between .89 and .96. Most subtest alpha values were in the mid- to high .80s and considered acceptable for making decisions about individuals.

Test score stability was examined in 132 individuals from ages 10 to 75 with an average retest interval of 24.5 days (range = 18 to 34 days). The corrected stability coefficient for the total group was .86, with NVA and SEQ being .84 and .83, respectively. When three separate age groups are examined, the reliability for the 10- to 20-year-old group is somewhat weaker than that for the older groups (.77 to .81). Relatively small gains in scores across time (about three points) were noted.

Validity. The manual presents multiple types of evidence of validity. Test content included expert review of the item content and developmental sequencing of items by difficulty, as well as the internal consistency of the scales found in the reliability studies.

Principal components analyses explored the relationships among variables. A principal components analysis suggested either a two- or three-factor solution for the original RAIT, with the three-factor solution being chosen. Factor 2, or the Fluid Intelligence Index (which is the same as the NVII), had the strongest relationship to *g*. This finding was considered strong justification for breaking out the RAIT-NV as a stand-alone test.

The RAIT-NV was correlated with several measures of intelligence and achievement to provide convergent and divergent evidence of validity. Comparisons with the Test of General Reasoning Ability (.90; Reynolds, 2014), Wonderlic Personnel Test (.71; Wonderlic, 2002), and the Beta III (.72; Kellogg & Morton, 1999) showed a strong relationship between their overall scores typical of correlations between measures of *g*.

Further comparisons are reported between the Wechsler Intelligence Scale for Children—Fourth Edition (WISC-IV: Wechsler, 2003), Wechsler Adult Intelligence Scale—Fourth Edition (WAIS-IV; Wechsler, 2008), and Reynolds Intellectual Assessment Scales (RIAS; Reynolds & Kamphaus, 2003). The NVII correlated moderately with the Perceptual Reasoning Index (.43), Processing Speed Index (.52), and Full Scale IQ (.51) on the WISC-IV (n = 29). When 28 adults were administered the WAIS-IV and the RAIT-NV, a moderate correlation was found with the Perceptual Reasoning Index (.44). All other correlations with these two measures were not significant. Finally, the NVII was found to have moderate to strong correlations with each RIAS index in a sample of 51 individuals.

Correlations between the RAIT-NV and achievement measures showed moderately strong results on the Word Reading subtest of the Wide Range Achievement Test 4 (.44; Wilkinson & Robertson, 2006) and the Test of Irregular Word Reading Efficiency (.40; Reynolds & Kamphaus, 2007).

Finally, scores were examined for individuals in various clinical groups. Scores were as expected. For example, the intellectually disabled group had a mean NVII of 64.67 with similar results on the two subtests. Other groups examined (traumatic brain injury, stroke, dementia, hearing impaired, learning disabilities, and attention-deficit/hyperactivity disorder) also showed expected levels of impairment.

COMMENTARY AND SUMMARY. Overall, the RAIT-NV appears to be a useful test that has built on the solid foundation of its parent, the RAIT. It is easily administered and scored across a wide age range. Norms tables show good floor and ceiling scores at all ages with adequate or better item gradients. The RAIT-NV's psychometric characteristics are moderate to strong, although intercorrelations with some Wechsler index scores seem more typical of IQ-achievement correlations. Important, however, are consistently strong correlations with measures of fluid intelligence.

Clinically, there are sufficient floors and ceilings to permit classification of individuals as intellectually disabled or mentally gifted. As with other cognitive tests, however, it would not be possible to discriminate at the more impaired levels of intellectual disability.

The RAIT-IV should prove particularly useful in any setting where an efficient (especially group-administered) measure of intellectual functioning, especially fluid ability, is needed.

REVIEWER'S REFERENCES

Kellogg, C. E., & Morton, N. W. (1999). Beta III. San Antonio, TX: Pearson.
Reynolds, C. R. (2014). Test of General Reasoning Ability. Lutz, FL: Psychological Assessment Resources.
Reynolds, C. R., & Kamphaus, R. W. (2003). Reynolds Intellectual Assessment Scales. Lutz, FL: Psychological Assessment Resources.
Reynolds, C. R., & Kamphaus, R. W. (2007). Test of Irregular Word Reading Efficiency. Lutz, FL: Psychological Assessment Resources.
Wechsler, D. (2003). Wechsler Intelligence Scale for Children—Fourth Edition. San Antonio, TX: Pearson.
Wechsler, D. (2008). Wechsler Adult Intelligence Scale—Fourth Edition. San Antonio, TX: Pearson.
Wilkinson, G. S., & Robertson, G. J. (2006). Wide Range Achievement Test 4. Lutz, FL: Psychological Assessment Resources.
Wonderlic, E. F. (2002). Wonderlic Personnel Test. Libertyville, IL: Wonderlic.
U.S. Census Bureau. (2010). *Current population survey, March 2010.* Washington, DC: U.S. Department of Commerce.

[138]

Reynolds Intellectual Assessment Scales, Second Edition and Reynolds Intellectual Screening Test, Second Edition.

Purpose: Designed to assess verbal and nonverbal intelligence as well as memory and speeded processing.
Population: Ages 3-94.
Publication Dates: 1998-2015.
Administration: Individual.
Price Data, 2020: $688 per RIAS-2/RIST-2 comprehensive kit including professional manual (2015, 341 pages) with fast guide, 25 RIAS-2 record forms, 25 RIAS-2 response forms, 25 RIST-2 record forms, RIAS-2/RIST-2 stimulus book 1, RIAS-2 stimulus book 2, RIAS-2 stimulus book 3, and RIAS-2 stimulus book 4; $169 per manual; $119 per RIAS-2/RIST-2 stimulus book 1; $138 per RIAS-2 stimulus book 2; $138 per RIAS-2 stimulus book 3; $30 per RIAS-2 stimulus book 4; $93 per 25 RIAS-2 record forms; $30 per 25 RIAS-2 response forms; $63 per 25 RIST-2 record forms.
Authors: Cecil R. Reynolds and Randy W. Kamphaus.
Publisher: Psychological Assessment Resources, Inc.

a) REYNOLDS INTELLECTUAL SCREENING TEST, SECOND EDITION.
Purpose: Designed "to produce a single composite score that is an indicator of risk for intellectual impairment."
Acronym: RIST-2
Scores, 3: Guess What, Odd-Item Out, RIST-2 Index.
Time: 10-15 minutes for administration.
Comments: A "separate use for the RIST-2" is to obtain "an overall estimate of intelligence [when that is] all that is needed."

b) REYNOLDS INTELLECTUAL ASSESSMENT SCALES, SECOND EDITION.
Purpose: Designed as "an individually administered test of intelligence...with conormed, supplemental measures of memory and processing speed."
Acronym: RIAS-2.
Scores, 13: Verbal Intelligence Index (Guess What, Verbal Reasoning), Nonverbal Intelligence Index (Odd-Item Out, What's Missing), Composite Intelligence Index, Composite Memory Index (Verbal Memory, Nonverbal Memory), Speeded Processing Index (Speeded Naming Task, Speeded Picture Search).
Time: 40-45 minutes for administration of complete battery.

Cross References: For reviews by Bruce A. Bracken and Gregory Schraw of the original edition, see 16:213.

Review of the Reynolds Intellectual Assessment Scales, Second Edition and Reynolds Intellectual Screening Test, Second Edition by LEAH M. NELLIS, Dean and Professor, School of Education, Indiana University Kokomo, Kokomo, IN, and BRANDON J. WOOD, Doctoral Student, Indiana State University, Terre Haute, IN:

DESCRIPTION. The Reynolds Intellectual Assessment Scales, Second Edition (RIAS-2) is an individually administered, standardized test of intelligence based on the Cattell-Horn model of intelligence and designed for individuals ages 3 to 94 years. It was developed to assess overall cognitive functioning of individuals with emotional and/or mental illness, identify neuropsychological and memory impairments, and rule out intellectual disability. The Reynolds Intellectual Screening Test, Second Edition (RIST-2) can be used to understand an individual's risk for an intellectual impairment.

The RIAS-2 consists of four core subtests designed to measure different aspects of verbal and nonverbal intelligence. The Verbal Intelligence Index (VIX), composed of two subtests, reflects crystallized and verbal reasoning ability. The remaining two core subtests compose the Nonverbal Intelligence Index (NIX), reflecting fluid intelligence and overall nonverbal reasoning capabilities. Complete administration of the four core subtests takes approximately 20-25 minutes. The VIX and NIX combine to form the Composite Intelligence Index (CIX), which is an estimate of global intelligence.

In addition to the four core subtests, the RIAS-2 includes two supplementary memory subtests and two supplementary speeded processing subtests. The two memory subtests, which form the Composite Memory Index (CMX), provide estimates of an individual's verbal and nonverbal memory ability and can be administered in approximately 10-15 minutes. The two speeded processing subtests, which were designed to minimize the need for fine motor coordination, form the Speeded Processing Index (SPI), and can be used to assess an individual's reaction time and decision speed. Administration time of the two speeded processing subtests is approximately 5-10 minutes. According to the test manual, the RIAS-2 does not include information from the CMX or SPI in the general intelligence composite due to the limited correlation with important outcomes such as childhood academic achievement and adult occupational performance (Dodonova & Dodonov, 2012). Test authors caution against the use of both instruments for individuals with visual impairments.

The RIST-2, which consists of two of the RIAS-2 core subtests, is a screening measure of intelligence. The RIST-2 has its own record form, and total administration time is only approximately 10-15 minutes. An overall RIST-2 Index score is calculated. RIAS-2 and RIST-2 subtest raw scores are converted to T scores and then to index and composite scores. Other approaches to describing test results, such as confidence intervals, percentile ranks, and age-equivalents can be calculated for each index.

DEVELOPMENT. The RIAS-2 is an updated edition of the original Reynolds Intellectual Assessment Scales (RIAS; Reynolds & Kamphaus, 2003). Guided by the Cattell-Horn model of intelligence (Horn & Cattell, 1966), the RIAS-2 was primarily developed to provide a reliable and valid measurement of "*g*" and its two primary components, crystallized intelligence and fluid intelligence. Subtest selection for the RIAS-2 focused on eliminating excessive clinician time spent in assessment-related activities. Thus, RIAS-2 subtests are noted to be brief tasks that are regarded as strongly correlated with more extensive and detailed measures of general intelligence. Subtests also were selected with the goal of eliminating or reducing dependence on examinees' motor coordination, visual-motor speed, and reading ability. The addition of speeded processing subtests and the corresponding index was in response to feedback from clinicians using the RIAS.

Additional changes included increasing the ceiling, removing controversial subtest items, adding new content, and updating norms. To arrive at the standardized edition of the RIAS-2, the authors considered expert and bias panel comments. Five experts, who were culturally diverse and represented different areas of expertise, reviewed assessment items to evaluate each item's content and quality. Pilot testing was conducted with a national sample of 160 individuals representing various age ranges, genders, races, ethnicities, and educational levels. As a result, four items were revised, and five items from the Nonverbal Memory subtest were replaced. After item revisions and replacements, each subtest item was sorted by item difficulty according to each item's *p* value, which represented the percentage of individuals who responded to the subtest item correctly.

TECHNICAL. The normative sample for the RIAS-2 and RIST-2 included 2,154 participants, ages 3 to 94, from 32 states across the country yielding a sample reportedly representative of the U.S. population according to gender, ethnicity, education level, and region based on the 2012 U.S. Census. Individuals with sensory and neurological impairments and/or mental illnesses were included in the sample at percentages representative of the general population. The sample was stratified by age representing 24 age groups (3-19 years [1-year spans], 20-29 years, 30-39 years, 40-49 years, 50-59 years, 60-69 years, 70-79 years, and 80-94 years).

According to the examiner's manual, internal consistency reliability of the RIAS-2 subtests was investigated using coefficient alpha. All of the alpha coefficients for the RIAS-2 subtest scores were .80 or higher for every age group. Reliability estimates for all RIAS-2 indexes have median values, across age groups, that equal or exceed .90. The RIST-2 composite yielded a median standard error of measurement of 4.37 and a median internal consistency coefficient of .92. The reliability of the RIAS-2 and RIST-2 was reported to be strong with respect to many demographic variables (e.g., age, gender, ethnicity).

Test-retest data over a period of 7 to 43 days (median = 18 days) were presented for 97 individuals ages 3 to 72 years. Corrected test-retest coefficients ranged from .72 to .99 for RIAS-2 subtests and from .83 to .97 for index scores. Scorer differences were investigated by two members of the test publisher's staff independently scoring 35 randomly selected completed protocols. Subtest raw scores were correlated yielding coefficients of .99 for three subtests and 1.00 for five subtests.

Validity is discussed in terms of the theory-based, logic-based, and empirically based evidence used to support the interpretations and uses of test scores. Evidence is presented based on test content, response processes, internal structure, relationship to external variables, and test consequences. First, test authors provide evidence of validity for the RIAS-2 and the RIST-2 by aligning the development, structure, and utility of subtests and composites with cognitive theories such as Carroll's (1993) three-stratum theory and the Cattell-Horn (Horn & Cattell, 1966) model. Subtests were developed to be similar in format to those with a long history in the field of intelligence and psychological assessment and consistent with empirical and expert judgment. Expert review was used to investigate fairness and functioning of the items for individuals from diverse backgrounds and genders. Statistical analyses were used to retain subtests and items with high reliability and discriminability.

Item-total correlations demonstrated a positive correlation of .40 or above between each item and its corresponding subtest. Exploratory factor analyses were conducted for four age groups of the normative sample, and most tests yielded factor loadings of .43 or higher on the first factor (*g*) across all age levels. Loadings on two- and three-factor solutions exceeded the criterion of .90 across gender and ethnic groups. According to the test authors, confirmatory factor analyses provided evidence of the four indexes. The relationship between RIAS-2 scores and external variables was also explored. Subtest and index scores of the RIAS-2 and RIAS were described as "significant and correlated at comparable magnitudes" (manual, p. 113) with coefficients between .71 and .93. Correlations between the RIAS-2 indexes and the FSIQ from the Wechsler Intelligence Scale for Children—Fourth Edition ranged from .58 to .77 with significant correlations between meaningful subtest pairs and composites. In examining test consequences, test authors reported that evidence indicated a lack of cultural bias in the RIAS-2 for male and female examinees, Whites, African Americans, and Hispanics. In an attempt to investigate the sensitivity of the RIAS-2 to examinees purposefully exaggerating symptoms, a sample of unimpaired individuals were coached to "fake bad" when completing the RIAS-2, and scores were investigated. Collectively, these reviewers believe that evidence supports the validity of both instruments.

COMMENTARY. The RIAS-2 is similar in look and feel to the original RIAS; however, the new edition responds to two particular practitioner requests (i.e., the addition of the Speeded Processing Index and modified ceiling rules). The test manual also includes recently updated norms. The RIAS-2 is currently available from the test publisher in different product configurations, which allows for flexibility in purchasing for practitioners. All the information necessary to administer the RIAS-2 and RIST-2 (e.g., administration instructions, start points, end rules, reversal rules, time limits, verbal prompts) is included on the record forms. The delivery of each subtest and the transition between subtests is extremely easy, especially because administration of the subtests does not require the use of manipulatives or audio sources. No technology is required to score either the RIAS-2 or RIST-2. After raw scores are derived, they can be converted to standard scores within minutes. All conversion tables are located at the end of the examiner's manual in one centralized place. One limitation of the RIAS-2 is that it does not provide subtests that measure all *g* areas of the Cattell-Horn-Carroll (CHC) theory (McGrew, 2005). Clinicians using a cross-battery approach for specific learning disability evaluations may need to select a different or additional assessment tool to evaluate all areas of cognitive performance. The representativeness of the normative sample is a strength of the RIAS-2 and RIST-2.

SUMMARY. The RIAS-2, as a measure of general intellectual development, and the RIST-2, as a screening measure of general intelligence, can be administered to a wide age range of individuals. The RIAS-2 is useful as a time-efficient yet reliable measure of general intelligence and its two primary components (verbal and nonverbal intelligence). The RIST-2, which combines information from one verbal and one nonverbal subtest, can be used to estimate one's risk for intellectual impairment quickly. Given the various uses for the RIST-2 and the RIAS-2 (e.g., understanding the degree of intellectual disability; identifying individual giftedness; and assessing individuals with cognitive, physical, orthopedic, neuropsychological, and memory impairments), independent validation efforts are needed to supplement the existing psychometric support.

REVIEWERS' REFERENCES

Carroll, J. B. (1993). *Human cognitive abilities: A survey of factor analytic studies.* New York, NY: Cambridge University Press.

Dodonova, Y. A., & Dodonov, Y. S. (2012). On choosing a model for estimating the individual differences in latent growth trajectories. *Psikhologicheskie Issledovaniya, 6,* 1-7.

Horn, J. L., & Cattell, R. B. (1966). Refinement and test of the theory of fluid and crystallized general intelligences. *Journal of Educational Psychology, 57,* 253-270.

McGrew, K. S. (2005). The Cattell-Horn-Carroll theory of cognitive abilities: Past, present, future. In D. P. Flanagan & P. L. Harrison (Eds.), *Contemporary intellectual assessment: Theories, tests, and issues* (2nd ed., pp. 136-181). New York, NY: Guilford.

Reynolds, C. R., & Kamphaus, R. W. (2003). Reynolds Intellectual Assessment Scales and the Reynolds Intellectual Screening Test. Lutz, FL: Psychological Assessment Resources.

Review of the Reynolds Intellectual Assessment Scales, Second Edition and Reynolds Intellectual Screening Test, Second Edition by SANDRA WARD, Professor of Education, The College of William & Mary, Williamsburg, VA:

DESCRIPTION. The Reynolds Intellectual Assessment Scales, Second Edition (RIAS-2) is a norm referenced, individually administered intelligence test for ages 3 to 94. According to the test authors, the structure of the RIAS-2 emphasizes the measurement of "*g*" or general intelligence as well as verbal and nonverbal intelligence. Subtests were developed to reflect fluid and crystallized intelligence. According to the test manual, the RIAS-2 measures primary intellectual functions and can be used for the purposes of diagnosis and educational placement decisions. The authors provide a strong rationale for these uses that is supported by cited research. The Reynolds Intellectual Screening Test, Second Edition (RIST-2) is a screening measure of general intelligence for the purposes of identifying individuals at-risk of intellectual impairment who may benefit from a comprehensive intellectual assessment. The test authors appropriately emphasize that the RIST-2 is not to be used for making classification decisions.

The RIAS-2 includes four intelligence scale subtests that comprise the Composite Intelligence Index (CIX). Two of these subtests combine to form the Verbal Intelligence Index (VIX), and two of these subtests make up the Nonverbal Intelligence Index (NIX). The supplementary Composite Memory Index (CMI) and Speeded Processing Index (SPI) require the administration of four additional subtests. The RIST-2 is comprised of two subtests from the RIAS-2—one subtest each from the VIX and the NIX—that combine to produce a single composite score.

The test materials are attractive, well organized, and easy to use. Directions for administration are clear and straightforward in the manual, and the Fast Guide is a useful reference that summarizes the RIAS-2 and RIST-2 purpose, administration guidelines, and scoring procedures. The necessary materials, instructions, and scoring rules for each subtest also are presented in the record form for easy reference. The four CIX subtests can be administered in approximately 20-25 minutes. The CMX subtests take an additional 10-15 minutes, and the SPI subtests require 5-10 minutes. The RIST-2 takes 10-15 minutes to administer. The RIAS-2 can be administered by psychologists, educational diagnosticians, and other professionals in related fields who have formal training in assessment. User qualifications for the RIST-2 are more lenient because interpretation of a screener is simpler.

Procedures for hand-scoring the RIAS-2 and RIST-2 are easy to follow. Total raw scores for subtests are converted to T scores using appropriate tables in the test manual. For the indexes, sums of T scores are converted to composite standard scores that have a mean of 100 and standard deviation of 15. The examiner can obtain percentile ranks, confidence intervals, T scores, *z*-scores, normal curve equivalents, and stanincs in addition to the composite scores. There are sections of the record form to compute score discrepancies and reliable change for the indexes. Although the hand-scoring is straightforward, the use of computer scoring through the test publisher's online platform will facilitate the scoring process and reduce the chance of clerical errors.

The test authors provide a hierarchical model of interpretation for the RIAS-2 that is consistent with best practice, and their recommended interpretation of index scores is based on reliability and validity evidence presented in the manual. Information on interpretation is supplemented with useful case studies. With respect to the RIST-2, the authors recommend using the composite standard score.

DEVELOPMENT. The development of the RIAS-2 reflected the test authors' intent to provide a practical, reliable, and valid measure of "*g*" (general intelligence) across developmental levels. Their theoretical model restricted the two major components of *g* to verbal and nonverbal intelligence, which approximate the theoretical constructs of crystallized and fluid intelligence, respectively. Memory and processing speed subtests comprise separate indexes, and they are not considered in the measurement of *g*. A goal of the RIAS-2 included development of verbal and nonverbal processing speed subtests and a Speeded Processing Index. Additionally, the authors updated item content, extended the floor and ceiling, and updated norms.

The test manual provides a summary of the development and technical merits of the RIAS-2. The RIAS-2 is based mostly on items from the RIAS, but the RIAS-2 includes new items and motor-reduced processing speed subtests that are based on user feedback and results of a market research survey of RIAS users. The re-evaluation of core RIAS subtests resulted in revision, removal, and/or creation of items to update language and reflect societal advances. Items were added to increase the range of item difficulty.

Pilot testing of the RIAS-2 included a national sample of 160 individuals across four age groups. A larger sample was collected from specific ethnic groups to analyze gender and racial bias. The authors appropriately used both classical test theory and Rasch analyses to select items with varied difficulty that did not display bias based on gender and ethnicity. In addition, the feedback from expert reviewers was considered in final item selection.

Based on pilot test analyses and expert panel input, the standardization edition of the RIAS-2 was created. The national standardization sample of the RIAS-2 provided the final data for the same item analyses that were performed on the pilot data. After the removal of nine items and ordering of the items by difficulty, the basal and ceiling rules were established. The development of the RIST-2 is the same as for the RIAS-2 given that the RIST-2 is a subset of two RIAS-2 subtests.

TECHNICAL. The standardization sample of the RIAS-2 and RIST-2 consisted of 2,154 individuals between the ages of 3 and 94 years from 32 states that represented four regions of the United States. The sample was stratified to match the 2012 U.S. Census data for gender, ethnicity, educational level (parent or adult individual), and geographic region. Although the standardization sample closely matched the 2012 U.S. Census, a post-stratification weighting procedure was used to create a closer match. The data presented in the test manual indicated that the standardization sample closely matched the 2012 update of U.S. Census figures for gender, ethnicity, and educational level. With respect to geographic regions, there was an overrepresentation of individuals from the Northeast and Midwest and an underrepresentation of individuals from the South and West. A comparison of the mean scores by region revealed no differences, indicating that the slight regional misrepresentation should not impact the norms. One drawback of the standardization sample, in the opinion of this reviewer, is that all age groups but one contain fewer than 100 individuals (n = 78-99; the 5-year-old group includes 100 participants).

Norms for the RIAS-2 and RIST-2 were created using a continuous norming procedure that is helpful in mitigating the effects of sampling irregularities across a large age range. The norms are appropriately derived, and the multitude of available standardized score options should meet the needs of most examiners.

Considerable evidence for the reliability of the RIAS-2 and RIST-2 is presented in the test manual. The internal consistency reliability coefficients reported in the test manual are sufficient for the intended purpose of the RIAS-2. The alpha coefficient for the CIX exceeded .90 for all age groups. The alpha coefficients for the VIX and NIX ranged from .88 to .95 for all age groups. Coefficients for the CMX ranged from .86 to .96, and the alpha coefficient for the SPI was .99 across all groups. The median coefficient alpha value for the RIAS-2 subtests was at least .81 across age groups, and all the subtest alpha coefficients equaled or exceeded .80. The lower reliability for subtests suggests that interpretation should be based on composite scores. Standard errors of measurement are provided for age groupings, which is appropriate given the slight differences in reliability over the age range of the instrument. Test-retest reliability for the RIAS-2 was examined in a study of 97 cases with a median test-retest interval of 18 days. Test-retest reliability for the indexes ranged from .83 (SPI) to .97 (VIX). Subtest stability coefficients ranged from .72 to .99 over the same period. These coefficients are sufficient, but the sample upon which they are based was small. The test authors estimated practice effects for the RIAS-2 indexes and found them consistent with reported practice effects of other cognitive measures. A study of interscorer agreement across two independent examiners showed near perfect agreement for the subtests, supporting the clarity of administration and scoring procedures.

The test authors provided extensive evidence for the validity of the RIAS-2 that supports its use. They detailed extensively how their validation evidence meets the suggestions in the *Standards for Educational and Psychological Testing* (AERA, APA, & NCME, 2014). The authors provided evidence of validity based on theory, test content, response process, internal structure, relations with outside measures, and consequences of testing.

The sections on theory, test content, and response process are based on the premise that the RIAS-2 is a strong measure of g with both verbal and nonverbal components. These authors presented credible arguments for how the RIAS-2 subtests matched the theoretical expectations in each area. The sections addressing internal structure and relations with outside measures presented statistical evidence for the validity of the instrument.

Both exploratory and confirmatory factor analyses are presented as evidence for the internal structure. The exploratory analyses tended to suggest a three-factor solution, but a two-factor solution was also viable. It would have been helpful for the authors to include information on total explained variability with each analysis to facilitate comparisons of the various models. Exploratory analyses for subgroups demonstrated that the solutions are stable by gender and ethnicity. In a series of confirmatory factor analyses (CFA), 14 models were tested using the entire standardization sample. The models varied by the number of hypothesized constructs and the number of RIAS-2 subtests included. Although the authors provided a considerable number of tables and diagrams to present their results, making comparisons among models is difficult given that they vary on two dimensions. This section of the test manual would be strengthened by more description of the models and the logic behind them as well as how they were compared. Additionally, the authors used a target value for the RMSEA (.10) that is considered acceptable instead of the value (.05) that indicates a good fit. It is noteworthy that most of the models tested do not reach the level of good fit.

Relations to external variables included the examination of relationships of the RIAS-2 with age, the original RIAS, other measures of intelligence, measures of academic achievement, and a measure of memory. These studies tended to support the validity of the RIAS-2 with correlations being moderate in magnitude and in the correct direction. Several of the analyses were based on sample sizes less than 100, so representativeness may be of concern. Additionally, the speed-based subtests demonstrated low correlations with the external variables in several instances. In addition to these correlational studies, the comparison of the clinical groups to matched comparison groups from the standardization sample demonstrated differences in the expected direction. Again, the sample sizes representing the clinical groups were small and may call into question their representativeness.

Validity evidence for the RIST-2 depends heavily on the subscale evidence presented for the RIAS-2. The summary of the relevant validity data for the RIST-2 generally supports the use of the RIST-2 as a screening device for general intelligence. The authors detailed the appropriate use and described potential cut scores that can be used as indicators for full evaluation.

COMMENTARY. The RIAS-2 is a useful measure of general intelligence for ages 3-94 that can be used as part of a comprehensive assessment to make diagnostic and educational placement decisions. The RIST-2 can be used as a screening measure of general intelligence to identify individuals at risk for intellectual impairment. The test authors used a sound theoretical model and applied accepted standards in the instrument's development. The RIAS-2 and RIST-2 are well standardized. The reliability data support the recommended uses of the instruments with coefficient alpha values that exceed the recommended values for individual decision making and screening decisions. Validity evidence for the RIAS-2 and RIST-2 is sufficient to support their intended uses. Models tested in the confirmatory factor analyses provided an acceptable fit with an RMSEA target value of .10. With respect to model selection and preference, the test authors allowed that other models might be viable and preferred, but they presented main arguments and information based on their preferences.

SUMMARY. The RIAS-2 is a brief, four-subtest measure of g that includes the components of crystallized and fluid intelligence. Supplemental subtests can be administered to assess memory and processing speed. The technical adequacy of the instrument, including standardization and reliability is robust. Although support for validity is strong, this reviewer's most salient criticism is the authors' selection of a model for interpretation that is certainly acceptable, matches their preferences, and may have the strongest empirical backing across all age groups, but other models might also be viable. The RIAS-2 is a useful instrument to assess intellectual level across a wide age range. The RIST-2, a subset of RIAS-2 subtests, appears to be a viable screening measure for general intelligence.

REVIEWER'S REFERENCE

American Educational Research Association (AERA), American Psychological Association (APA), & National Council on Measurement in Education (NCME). (2014). *Standards for educational and psychological testing*. Washington, DC: AERA.

[139]

Reynolds Interference Task.

Purpose: Designed to assess "complex speeded processing, primarily involving te application of inhibition and attention-shifting."

Population: Ages 6-94.

Publication Date: 2017.

Acronym: RIT.

Scores, 4-8: Object Interference, Color Interference, Discrepancy, Total; optional: Object Interference Errors,

Object Interference Time to Completion, Color Interference Errors, Color Interference Time to Completion.
Administration: Individual.
Price Data, 2020: $103 per kit including professional manual (107 pages), fast guide, 25 examiner record forms, and stimulus book; $47 per professional manual and fast guide; $28 per stimulus book; $28 per 25 examiner record forms.
Time: 30 seconds for Object Interference subtest; 60 seconds for Color Interference.
Comments: Stopwatch or timer required for administration; co-normed with the Reynolds Intellectual Assessment Scales, Second Edition (see 138, this volume).
Authors: Cecil R. Reynolds and Randy W. Kamphaus.
Publisher: Psychological Assessment Resources, Inc.

Review of the Reynolds Interference Task by DAVID M. HULAC, Associate Professor, University of Northern Colorado, Greeley, CO:

DESCRIPTION. The Reynolds Interference Task (RIT) is a brief measure of complex processing speed consisting of a pair of tests that require test takers to quickly provide responses while inhibiting a prepotent response. The first test, Object Interference (OI), which lasts 30 seconds, requires participants to name an object with distracting words printed over it. The 60-second Color Interference (CI) test is a Stroop-like test in which words for various colors are printed in other-colored fonts. The test taker is instructed to name the colors while inhibiting a desire to read the words. The tasks are designed to measure two neuropsychological constructs of inhibition and attention-shifting, which are related to executive functioning. In addition to subtest scores for OI and CI, a Total Correct Index (TCI) is calculated and provides an overall indication of complex processing speed. The RIT was co-normed with the Reynolds Intellectual Assessment Scales, Second Edition (RIAS-2) to provide additional information on an individual's cognitive functioning.

DEVELOPMENT. Items for the OI subtest were selected as being one syllable words that represent common animals. For the CI subtest, common color names were selected and are also one syllable words. The items were reviewed by five experts who represented a variety of different racial and ethnic groups. The test is speeded, in that its developers created a large number of items to ensure that no participant in the pilot group would be able to finish the subtest in the amount of time allowed. Once the test was administered to a pilot sample representing different ages and racial/ethnic groups, the test authors conducted analyses to ensure that items were free from bias. Similarly, they conducted analyses on each age group to ensure no floor or ceiling effects.

TECHNICAL. The standardization sample includes groups of approximately 80-90 children and adolescents of each age between 6 and 19. There were also approximately 80 adult participants in each group ages 20-29, 30-39, 40-49, 50-59, 60-69, 70-79, and 80-94. In each group, there was an approximately equal number of males and females consistent with the U.S. demographic data for age and gender, the oldest groups had more women than men. The racial and geographical representation of the sample was weighted to match the 2012 U.S. Census. A continuous norming procedure was used to smooth out sampling irregularities.

Reliability information was collected to examine consistency of results across item samples, examiners, and time. Coefficient alpha estimates for OI, CI, and TCI all exceeded .90, suggesting a high degree of internal consistency. Corrected test-retest reliability coefficients (.77 for OI, .80 for CI, .82 for TCI) were also provided for a group of 69 individuals with a median retest interval of 19 days. The lowest estimates of test-retest reliability were observed for the 6- to 17- year-old sample, with corrected estimates for the OI test of .49 and for the CI test of .78. Thus, users would want to exercise great caution in interpreting only the OI test for children and adolescents.

Validity evidence was provided by examining the internal structure of the test as well as relationships with other tests. Intercorrelations between the subtests were moderate (correlation coefficients ranged from .47 to .52), meaning they are related, but interpretation of differences between the subtests may be useful. Low correlations with the Wechsler Intelligence Scale for Children—Fourth Edition and the Wechsler Adult Intelligence Scale—Fourth Edition suggest that constructs measured by the RIT are substantially different from those assessed by the Wechsler tests mentioned. Further construct validity evidence derives from an examination of scores from the following clinical samples: stroke, dementia, hearing impaired, intellectual disability, traumatic brain injury, general learning disability, attention-deficit/hyperactivity disorder (ADHD), and gifted. The mean TCI scores of those in the stroke, dementia, hearing impaired, intellectual disability, and general learning disability groups were significantly below those of matched group samples ($p < .05$), as were the scores of children with traumatic brain injury and children with ADHD. It should be noted that the professional manual does not provide any information on the predictive validity of the examination for distinguishing or correctly classifying individuals in different groups. In other words, sensitivity and specificity data are not provided. Finally, the test authors conducted a simulation of malingering that indicated that the test is not susceptible to malingering when appropriate detection criteria are applied.

COMMENTARY. The RIT is a reasonably reliable measure of speeded cognitive processing, response inhibition, and attention-shifting. These skills are not typically included in a standard measure of intellectual ability, and correlation coefficients suggest that the constructs measured by the RIT and standard intelligence tests are moderately different. The administration time of less than 2 minutes means that the test can be administered quickly. Because the test is relatively new, there is not much external research supporting validity evidence for the instrument. Additional research on the RIT should determine how well the test improves diagnostic accuracy.

Review of the Reynolds Interference Task by STEVEN R. SHAW, Associate Professor of Counselling and Educational Psychology, McGill University, Montreal, QC, Canada:

DESCRIPTION. The Reynolds Interference Task (RIT) is an individually administered neuropsychological test of complex speeded information processing appropriate for persons ages 6 to 94 years. The RIT is a measure of speeded processing with an additional layer of cognitive complexity: inhibition and attention shifting. The test minimizes fine motor control and motor speed, which is a potentially confounding factor in many other tests. The RIT is suggested as a good measure to monitor recovery from traumatic brain injury (TBI), stroke, and central nervous system disease patients, and for assessing deteriorations in suspected dementia. The RIT also may be useful in assessing other factors that are consistent with slow speed of information processing such as attention-deficit/hyperactivity disorder (ADHD) with sluggish cognitive tempo, learning disabilities, and depression.

The RIT consists of two subtests and a composite index. Object Interference consists of a grid of pictures of common animals with words printed over the pictures. Examinees are asked to name the animal under the word rather than the word itself over a 30-second period. Color Interference consists of a grid of color words (e.g., blue, black, green), which are printed in different colored ink. The examinees are asked to name the color of the ink rather than the word itself—very much like the well-known Stroop Color and Word Test (Golden & Freshwater, 1978)—in a 60 second period. Total administration time is approximately 5 minutes. The Total Correct Index (TCI) is a standard score that provides a summary estimate of the complex speeded processing involving the application of inhibition and attention shifting to make simple decisions and discriminations. Scores provided include age-adjusted T scores and age equivalents for both subtests as well as percentile ranks, z scores, T scores, normal curve equivalents, and stanines for the TCI. In addition, confidence intervals (90% and 95%) may be determined using a table provided in the test manual.

DEVELOPMENT. Items for Object Interference were developed using single-syllable words for common animals. Likewise, for the Color Interference subtest, common single-syllable color words were selected. Initial items were pilot tested on 121 individuals. All items were submitted to experts from a variety of culture and language backgrounds for review of content. These professionals were asked to evaluate whether any of the stimuli had clear bias or were offensive to individuals of differing genders, ethnicities, and religious backgrounds.

TECHNICAL.

Standardization. The RIT was co-normed with the Reynolds Intellectual Assessment Scales, Second Edition (RIAS-2; Reynolds & Kamphaus, 2015; see 138, this volume). The sample consisted of 1,824 participants from 32 states. The standardization sample is representative of the U.S. population in terms of gender, ethnicity, education level, and geographic region as defined by the 2012 U.S. Census Bureau. Potential examinees were screened for the following exclusionary criteria: color blindness, uncorrected hearing loss or visual impairment, history of traumatic brain injury, epilepsy, ADHD, schizophrenia, and current use of prescription medication. Persons with diagnoses of other psychiatric disorders were included if the percentage of the disorder in the sample did not exceed the proportion of the disorder found in the general U.S. population based on prevalence statistics provided in the *Diagnostic and Statistical Manual of Mental Disorders* (5th ed.; American Psychiatric Association, 2013).

Reliability. The internal consistency reliability of the RIT subtests was investigated using coefficient alpha. Alpha reliability coefficients for the subtest scores are reported for the 21 age groups from the total standardization sample. All alpha coefficients for the RIT subtest scores are .91 or higher for every age group. The median alpha reliability estimate for each subtest across age is equal to or higher than .93. Median reliability for Object Interference is .93, for Color Interference .96, and for Total Correct Index .96. The median standard error of measurement of the TCI is 3.00.

Stability was estimated by the test–retest method. The sample consisted of 69 participants ages 6 to 72 years. The interval between the two test administrations ranged from 7 to 43 days with a median test–retest interval of 19 days. For the entire sample, stability coefficients (corrected for attention) range from .77 (Object Interference) to .82 (Total Correct Index). There are modest practice effects ranging from approximately three T-score points for the subtests and approximately five standard score points for the TCI. However, for the 25 participants age 6 to 17 years the stability coefficient for Object Interference (.49 corrected) is substantially lower than those for the other age groups.

Validity. The professional manual provides extensive validity data. Although the RIT is a brief test, comprising only two subtests, the internal structure is consistent with theoretical models of speeded information processing and remains consistent from ages 6 through 94. Concurrent validity evidence is assessed with six different studies involving the Wechsler Intelligence Scale for Children Fourth Edition WISC-IV (WISC-IV; Wechsler, 2003; N = 79), the Wechsler Adult Intelligence Scale-Fourth Edition (WAIS-IV; Wechsler, 2008; N = 68), the Academic Achievement Battery Comprehensive Form (Messer, 2014; N = 211), the Feifer Assessment of Reading (Feifer & Gerhardstein Nader, 2015; N = 122), Reynolds Intellectual Assessment Scales, Second Edition (Reynolds & Kamphaus, 2015; N = 1,824), and the Child and Adolescent Memory Profile (Sherman & Brooks, 2015; N = 124). A general pattern emerges that Processing Speed Indices on the WISC–IV and WAIS–IV demonstrate the strongest correlations with the TCI. Correlations are mixed and not significant between WISC–IV and WAIS–IV subtests and Object Interference with the exception of Symbol Search on the WAIS-IV (r = .30, $p < .05$). Those same subtests are mostly statistically significant at a low to moderate level for Color Interference. Because the RIT is co-normed with the RIAS–2, among other factors, all the indices on the RIAS–2 demonstrate statistically significant, but modest, correlations with the TCI. Of special note is the Speeded Processing Index on the RIAS–2, which is correlated with the TCI at .58.

Multiple clinical samples were assessed to determine the utility of the RIT. Samples of persons with stroke, dementia, and hearing impairment, children with intellectual disabilities, children and adults with TBI, children and adults with learning disabilities, children and adults with ADHD, and persons with giftedness were all assessed using small samples. In every case, results were in the expected direction. An additional measure asked participants in a study (N = 40) to simulate malingering on the RIT and respond to the Test of Memory Malingering (TOMM; Tombaugh, 1996). The RIT, using criteria specified by the TOMM, accurately identified 100% of simulated malingerers.

Because there are few measures of complex speed of information processing available, it is difficult to make an overall judgment on the validity of the RIT for a variety of purposes; the presentation of relevant evidence seems reasonable and largely supportive of the validity of this measure.

COMMENTARY. Providing high-quality psychometric information for neuropsychological tests has always been a challenge due to the high costs and resource intensive nature of validating a test. By co-norming the RIT with the RIAS-2, the test authors have piggybacked a high quality standardization sample and multiple validity studies with a test that is in much wider use. The result is a reliable and well-standardized test that goes above and beyond many narrow-band neuropsychological assessments in psychometric support. The RIT is a well-developed measure of speeded processing.

SUMMARY. The Reynolds Interference Task (RIT) presents as a complex speed of information processing measure. This is a narrow-band test with limited clinical utility. However, there are a variety of clinical situations in which a well-normed and well-developed test of complex speed of information processing can be useful. Dementia, TBI, and complex ADHD are examples. Moreover, the Color Interference subtest is indistinguishable from the Stroop Color and Word Test (Golden & Freshwater, 1978), yet with improved and updated norms. The RIT is an effective addition to a neuropsychological battery.

REVIEWER'S REFERENCES

American Psychiatric Association. (2013). *Diagnostic and statistical manual of mental disorders* (5th ed.). Washington, DC: Author.

Feifer, S. G., & Gerhardstein Nader, R. (2015). Feifer Assessment of Reading. Lutz, FL: Psychological Assessment Resources.

Golden, C. J., & Freshwater, S. M. (1978). Stroop Color and Word Test. Wood Dale, IL: Stoelting.

Messer, M. A. (2014). Academic Achievement Battery Comprehensive Form. Lutz, FL: Psychological Assessment Resources.

Reynolds, C. R., & Kamphaus, R. W. (2015). Reynolds Intellectual Assessment Scales, Second Edition. Lutz, FL: Psychological Assessment Resources.

Sherman, E. M. S., & Brooks, B. L. (2015). Child and Adolescent Memory Profile. Lutz, FL: Psychological Assessment Resources.

Tombaugh, T. (1996). Test of Memory Malingering. North Tonawanda NY: Multi-Health Systems.

Wechsler, D. (2003). Wechsler Intelligence Scale for ChildrenFourth Edition. San Antonio, TX: Pearson.

Wechsler, D. (2008). Wechsler Adult Intelligence ScaleFourth Edition). San Antonio, TX: Pearson.

[140]

Risk Inventory and Strengths Evaluation.

Purpose: Designed to assess "risky behavior and psychological strengths" across home, school, and community settings.
Population: Ages 9 through 25 years.
Publication Date: 2019.
Acronym: RISE.
Administration: Individual.
Forms, 3: Self, Parent, Teacher.
Price Data, 2020: $267 per kit (print or online), including manual (153 pages) and 25 of each form; $89 per manual (print or digital); $15 per 5 forms or online uses (parent, teacher, or self-report).
Foreign Language Edition: Forms available in Spanish.
Comments: Administered online or via printed forms.
Authors: Sam Goldstein and David S. Herzberg.
Publisher: Western Psychological Services.

a) SELF FORM.
Population: Ages 12-25.
Scores, 14: Bullying/Aggression, Delinquency, Eating/Sleeping Problems, Sexual Risk, Substance Abuse, Suicide/Self-Harm, Emotional Balance, Interpersonal Skill, Self-Confidence, Risk Summary Scale, Strength Summary Scale, RISE Index, Inconsistent Responding, Impression Management.
Time: 10-15 minutes for administration.

b) PARENT FORM.
Population: Parents of individuals ages 9-18.
Scores, 14: Same as *a*) above.
Time: 10-15 minutes for administration.

c) TEACHER FORM.
Population: Teachers of individuals ages 9-18.
Scores, 6: Emotional Balance, Interpersonal Skill, Self-Confidence, Risk Summary Scale, Strength Summary Scale, RISE Index.
Time: 7-10 minutes for administration.

Review of the Risk Inventory and Strengths Evaluation by MICHELE CASCARDI, Professor, and HANNAH SCHORPP, Graduate Student and Adjunct Professor, Department of Psychology, William Paterson University, Wayne, NJ:

DESCRIPTION. The Risk Inventory and Strengths Evaluation (RISE) measures risky behaviors and psychological strengths of children, adolescents, and emerging adults (ages 9-25 years) who have been referred for learning and/or behavior problems. RISE may be used in clinical and educational settings for treatment planning and as an outcome measure to evaluate gains in social and emotional skills and reductions in risky behaviors. It is available in paper and online formats, as well as in English and Spanish languages. Data may be collected from three sources: self, parent, and teacher. The Self and Parent forms each have 66 items; the Teacher Form, which excludes a detailed assessment of risky behavior, has 36 items. Informants rate the frequency of youth behaviors in the prior 4 weeks on a 6-point scale from *never* to *always*. Teachers may administer and score the RISE; however, the test authors recommend that professionals who have appropriate graduate coursework and field experience in testing interpret scores and plan treatments.

There are three Primary Summary scales: Risk Summary for high-risk behaviors, Strength Summary for psychological strengths, and RISE Index, a composite of strengths and risks. There also are subscales for more detailed assessment: three Strength subscales for Self, Parent, and Teacher forms: Emotional Balance, Interpersonal Skill, and Self-Confidence; and six Risky Behavior subscales for Self and Parent forms: Bullying/Aggression, Delinquency, Eating/Sleeping Problems, Sexual Risk, Substance Abuse, and Suicide/Self-Harm. The Self and Parent forms have two validity scales: Inconsistent Responding and Impression Management.

DEVELOPMENT. RISE is based on a biopsychosocial model of psychological adaptation and development and is designed to evaluate risks and strengths associated with positive adult outcomes. The initial pilot study for RISE included 163 items based on outcome studies of youth engaging in high-risk behaviors and prospective research on psychological characteristics predictive of positive mental health and functional outcomes. Pilot data included Self (n = 322), Parent (n = 209), and Teacher (n = 208) Forms from students in regular education classrooms in eight U.S. communities. Exploratory factor analysis and Rasch analysis eliminated 50 items.

Raw scores for the Primary scales and Strength subscales are converted to T scores for comparison to norm reference groups. Raw score cutoffs are used for Risk subscales as they measure low-frequency behaviors and norm reference groups are not available. Each form also has critical items differentiating between clinical and normative samples.

TECHNICAL.

Standardization. The RISE has been evaluated in normative and clinical samples. The normative sample included 1,380 youth and young adults ages 12-25 years enrolled in full-time, general education classrooms from 20 states in all U.S. Census regions, as well as 1,005 parents and 1,000 teachers. Participants represented the U.S. Census data for gender, race/ethnicity, and education. The clinical sample included 270 youth and young adults ages 12-25 years from 11 states in all U.S. Census regions recruited from private practices, local clinics, and community agencies, as well as 185 parents and 152 teachers.

Reliability. The RISE exhibits good to excellent internal consistency in the normative and clinical samples for the Primary scales (alpha coefficients ranged from .90 to .97), Strength subscales (coefficients ranged from .73 to .92), and most Risk subscales (coefficients ranged from .70 to .92). Internal consistency was less strong for the Risk subscales Eating/Sleeping Problems (Parent Form) and Sexual Risk (Self Form). Test-retest reliability was examined over a 2-week period using a subsample of the normative sample. RISE scales were stable, with estimates ranging from .84 to .94 for Primary scales and from .81 to .88 for Strength subscales. The Self Form had higher stability for Risk subscales (coefficients ranged from .75 to .89) than the Parent Form (coefficients ranged from .55 to .85).

Validity.

Construct Evidence. Confirmatory factor analysis supported a two-factor model of Risk and Strengths. The correlation of Risk subscales to the Risk Summary scale was moderately high for the Parent Form (coefficients from .72 to .89) and Self Form (coefficients from .66 to .77). The Strength subscales correlated very highly with the Strength Summary scale for Parent, Teacher, and Self forms (coefficients from .91 to .96).

Concurrent Evidence. Concurrent evidence of validity was evaluated with four measures of risky behavior, psychological adaptation, and social/emotional functioning: Adaptive Behavior Assessment System, Third Edition (ABAS-3); Piers-Harris Self-Concept Scale, Third Edition (Piers-Harris 3); Behavior Assessment System for Children, Third Edition (BASC-3), and Conners Comprehensive Behavior Rating Scales (Conners CBRS).

The RISE showed strong evidence of concurrent validity with the ABAS-3. Risk and Strength Summary scores were correlated in expected directions with adaptive domains and the General Adaptive Composite (*r*s ranged from -.25 to -.46 and from .46 to .75, respectively) for all forms. Patterns of association were similar for Strength subscales, although the correlations between Emotional Balance and the ABAS-3 domains were weaker for the Teacher Form than for the Self and Parent forms. Adaptive skills important for social interaction were correlated with Risk subscales on the Parent Form (*r*s ranged from -.19 to -.48), but adaptive skills were not associated with Risk subscales on the Self Form. There was mixed evidence of concurrent validity with self-concept (Piers-Harris 3) for the Self Form with Risk Summary and subscales (*r*s ranged from -.01 to -.68) and Strength Summary and subscales (*r*s ranged from .00 to .58).

On the Self Form, the Risk Summary scale was positively correlated with BASC-3 School Problems, Internalizing Problems, Inattention/Hyperactivity, and the Emotional Symptoms Index (*r*s = .46 to .71) and negatively correlated with Personal Adjustment (r = -.58). The Strength Summary scale was negatively correlated with School Problems, Internalizing Problems, and Inattention/Hyperactivity (rs = -.12 to -.21) and positively correlated with Personal Adjustment (r = .44) and Emotional Symptoms Index (r = .09). Risk subscales had the strongest correlations with Sensation Seeking (*r*s = .33 to .53). Patterns of association for the BASC-3 and the Parent Form were similar, although the magnitudes of association were larger, with some exceptions. On the Parent Form, Conduct Problems and Hyperactivity were correlated with Risk subscales (*r*s = .36 to .82). The pattern of association with BASC-3 for the Strength Summary scale and subscales on the Teacher Form were similar to those on the Self and Parent forms.

The Risk Summary scale on the Self Form was positively correlated with Conners CBRS scales (r = .34 to .67), and the RISE Index scale was negatively correlated with Conners CBRS scales (r = -.31 to -.57). Risk subscales were positively correlated with Conners CBRS scales for Aggressive Behaviors

(r = .44 to .80), Hyperactivity/Impulsivity (r = .44 to .57), Violence Potential (r = .43 to .81), Academic Difficulties (r = .25 to .39), and Physical Symptoms (r = .16 to .67). The pattern of associations on the Risk subscales was mostly similar for the Self and Parent forms. The Strength Summary scale and subscales on the Parent and Teacher forms also were negatively correlated with Conners CBRS scales (rs ranged from -.41 to -.75 and -.24 to -.68, respectively).

Validity with Clinical Groups. The RISE Summary scales and subscales discriminate between at-risk or clinical groups and matched controls. When youth in a caseload of an organization working in underserved or gang-affected communities (i.e., At-Risk youth) were compared to matched controls, At-Risk youth scored significantly higher on all RISE scales and subscales with very large effect sizes (d = 1.13 to 2.09) for the Parent Form, and moderate to large effect sizes for the Self Form (d = 0.41 to 1.27) and Teacher Form (d = 0.30 to 2.86). Effect sizes for the Gang Membership group (i.e., youth who were reported to be in a gang at the time of assessment) were also large for all Summary scales and subscales on the Parent Form (d = 0.95 to 2.18), except for Eating/Sleeping Problems (d = 0.29) compared to matched controls. For the Self Form, the effect sizes for differences between the Gang Membership group and matched controls were moderate to large with larger effect sizes for Risk subscales (d = 0.67 to 1.96) than the Strength subscales (d = 0.33 to 0.62). In contrast, the effect sizes for the Teacher Form were larger for the Strength subscales (d = 1.97 to 2.38) and Strength Summary scale (d = 2.30) than for the Risk Summary scale (d = 0.15).

When compared to matched controls, youth in the Suicidality group and the Depression group demonstrated similar patterns. For the Parent and Self forms generally, effect sizes for RISE Summary scales and subscales were large (d = 0.78 to 1.89 and d = .67 to 2.40, respectively). Effect sizes were notably smaller for externalizing risky behavior such as Bullying/Aggression, Delinquency, Sexual Risk, and Substance Abuse (d = 0.06 to 0.19) on the Parent Form; Bullying/Aggression and Substance Abuse (d = 0.29 to 0.38) on the Self Form (Suicidality group); and Bullying/Aggression, Substance Abuse, Delinquency, and Sexual Risk (d = 0.33 to 0.36) on the Self Form (Depression group). For the Teacher Form, all effect sizes were large (d = 1.07 to 2.51).

RISE Summary scales discriminated attention-deficit/hyperactivity disorder (ADHD) and autism spectrum disorder (ASD) groups compared to matched controls on expected risky behavior and strengths with moderate to large effect sizes (d = 0.47 to 1.11). There was more variability for differences on certain Risk subscales. For example, youth ADHD and ASD groups were more likely to evidence problems with Eating/Sleeping than matched controls, but the groups did not differ from matched controls on other areas of risky behavior such as Bullying/Aggression, Delinquency, or Sexual Risk. In addition, youth with ASD were more likely than matched controls to evidence problems in Suicide/Self-Harm.

Differences between matched controls and those reporting eating disorders or substance abuse were evaluated for the Self Form only. Overall, effect sizes for eating disorders and substance abuse were large for RISE scales and subscales (d = 0.91 to 4.18 and d = 0.67 to 2.81, respectively), except for Delinquency in the Eating Disorders group (d = 0.26).

COMMENTARY. The RISE has undergone considerable development and validation, and the test manual provides evidence of reference group norms, reliability, and validity. It is easy to use with multiple informants. Although the test authors do not recommend a standardized method for integrating reports from youth, parents, and teachers, information from multiple informants provides assessment of problem areas in different contexts.

SUMMARY. The RISE is a short, straightforward measure to assess strengths and risky behaviors in children, adolescents, and young adults. The measure is available in English and Spanish. Although interpretation of test data should be completed by a graduate-level mental health provider, the test may be administered by teachers and classroom aides. The measure has documented strong psychometric properties, and it has been validated for use with multiple clinical populations. This measure can be an effective tool in treatment planning and monitoring outcomes for at-risk youth.

Review of Risk Inventory and Strengths Evaluation by MICHAEL P. McCREERY, Associate Professor, University of Nevada, Las Vegas, Las Vegas, NV:

DESCRIPTION and DEVELOPMENT. The Risk Inventory and Strengths Evaluation (RISE) consists of three rating forms used to assess risky behavior and psychological strengths across home, school, and community settings for ages 9-25 years. Forms are available for ratings by parents (66 items; ages 9-18), self (66 items; ages 12-25), and teachers (36 items; ages 9-18).

All forms are available in English and Spanish in print and digital formats. The test authors report that RISE has been designed as a core component of a comprehensive clinical assessment of individuals referred for learning and behavioral problems and that it is intended for both educational and clinical settings.

All RISE forms consist of three broad measures: Risk Summary Scale, Strength Summary Scale, and the RISE Index (total composite). Three strength subscales (Emotional Balance, Interpersonal Skill, and Self-Confidence) also are included on each form. The Parent and Self forms include the six risk subscales (Bullying/Aggression, Delinquency, Eating/Sleeping Problems, Sexual Risk, Substance Abuse, and Suicide/Self-Harm). All forms contain critical items designed to aid in determining the severity of risky behavior and the need for immediate intervention. In addition, the Parent and Self forms include two response validity scales (Inconsistent Responding and Impression Management).

TECHNICAL. Following standardization in which more than 4,000 forms were collected across 20 states, the normative sample was selected to match U.S. Census data according to gender, race/ethnicity, parents' educational level, and geographic region. The sample includes 1,005 Parent Forms; 1,380 Self Forms; and 1,000 Teacher Forms. Data also were obtained from clinical samples of at-risk youth, gang membership, suicidality, depression, attention deficit/hyperactivity disorder, autism spectrum disorder, eating disorders, and substance abuse.

Internal consistency estimates were reported for the three RISE forms for both the normative and the general clinical samples. Coefficients were largest for the composite scales, as would be expected, with values ranging from .90 to .97 for the normative sample and from .92 to .97 for the full clinical sample. Coefficients for the Strength subscales ranged from .78 to .89 for the normative sample and from .73 to .92 for the full clinical sample. For the Risk subscales, coefficients for the Parent form ranged from .76 to .95 for the normative sample and from .69 to .95 for the full clinical sample. For the Self form, coefficients ranged from .64 to .94 for the normative sample and from .74 to .91 for the full clinical sample.

Standard errors of measurement (*SEM*s) are reported in T-score units (M = 50, SD = 10) for the composite scales (1.73 to 3.16) and the Strength subscales (3.32 to 4.69). *SEM*s are not reported for the Risk subscale scores, which are interpreted using raw score cutoffs rather than T scores because of the relatively infrequent occurrence of these behaviors in the population.

Test-retest reliability coefficients were reported for each of the composite scales and subscales. The test-retest interval was approximately two weeks and based on samples drawn from the standardization study (Parent Form, n = 53; Self Form, n = 75; Teacher Form, n = 67). Test-retest reliability estimates for the composite scales ranged from .87 to .94 for the Parent Form, from .84 to .89 for the Self Form, and from .86 to .87 for the Teacher form. Coefficients for the Strength subscales ranged from .86 to .88 for the Parent Form, from .81 to .85 for the Self Form, and from .82 to .87 for the Teacher Form. Finally, reliability coefficients for the Risk subscales ranged from .55 to .85 for the Parent Form and from .75 to .89 for the Self Form. As a reminder, the Teacher Form does not include the Risk subscales.

Content validity evidence was examined through an early pilot study and during standardization as expert feedback was solicited regarding item content and relevance. Structural validity was examined using factor analysis, interscale correlations, and item-to-scale correlations. Concurrent validity evidence was examined through comparisons of scores between the RISE and the Adaptive Behavior Assessment System, Third Edition (ABAS-3); the Behavior Assessment System for Children, Third Edition; the Conners Comprehensive Behavior Rating Scales; and the Piers-Harris Self-Concept Scale, Third Edition. In the two samples studied (*ns* = 44 and 47), scores on the RISE generally correlated as expected with the above measures with one exception: Scores on the RISE Self Form produced nonsignificant correlations with those on the ABAS-3, a norm-referenced, adaptive skills assessment.

RISE scores also were validated through comparisons of scores between the clinical groups identified above and demographically matched control groups of typically developing individuals. The test manual reports that scores discriminated between the clinical and control groups in expected directions and with statistically significant effect sizes.

COMMENTARY. RISE is a new norm-referenced assessment published in 2019. Despite the short history of the measure, the authors have engaged in a commendable level of effort to examine the efficacy of each form, both in terms of the standardization process and the reliability of the scores. Moreover, the authors provide a considerable degree of detail with regard to administration and score interpretation. Because of internal consistency indicators (e.g., Self-Form: Sexual Risk subscale for ages 19-25, alpha = .64) or test-retest estimates (e.g., Parent-Form: Substance Abuse subscale, alpha = .56) not all form-subscale combinations may be suitable for specific age groups.

SUMMARY. Risk Inventory and Strengths Evaluation (RISE) is a newly developed norm-referenced instrument designed to assess risky behaviors and psychological strengths of referred populations in educational and clinical settings. The test manual is well organized, and the option of print or digital English and Spanish versions is an asset. Generally, the technical data demonstrate that the instrument could be considered when developing a comprehensive assessment plan. However, technical limitations associated with some form/Risk subscale combinations may limit usefulness until additional modifications can occur.

[141]

Risk Type Compass.

Purpose: Designed to assess the ways individuals behave in risk-oriented situations by assignment to one of eight distinctive Risk Types based on personality.
Population: Adults.
Publication Date: 2016.
Scores, 3: Risk Type, Risk Attitude, Risk Tolerance Index.
Administration: Individual.
Forms: Short form available.
Price Data, 2020: £35 per individual report; £275 per Team Report, plus £35 per person.
Time: Administration time not reported.
Comments: Administered online; various reports available including Personal, Investor, Financial Advisor, Risk Type, and Team.
Author: Geoff Trickey.
Publisher: Psychological Consultancy Limited [United Kingdom].

Review of the Risk Type Compass by DAVID J. PITTENGER, Interim Associate Vice President for Outreach and Dean of the Graduate College, Marshall University, Huntington, WV:

DESCRIPTION. The Risk Type Compass is designed to assess an individual's level of risk tolerance and attitude toward taking risks. According to the test publisher, the impetus for developing the test was the United Kingdom's creation of regulations governing those who offer financial advice to investors of securities and other financial instruments. Specifically, the investment strategies proffered should match the client's tolerance for or aversion to risk, with more speculative tactics employed with those willing to accept the risk and conservative plans suggested for those averse to potential losses.

The test attempts to determine the extent of risk propensity among employees as well as financial consultants and their clients. As a generality, the publisher of the test does not define risk in the pejorative; instead, the test authors present the tendency to take risks as a desirable trait in some settings and counterproductive in others. The guiding assumption for the design of the test is that assessment of and response to risk reflects general personality characteristics of the individual. Moreover, the test authors presume that risk propensity is not a single trait, as the behavior represents a range of personality constructs including, among others, anxiety, gullibility, impulsivity, and thrill-seeking. In total, the test authors believe that any risk assessment plan must begin by examining the propensity of people given the responsibility to offer advice and act on behalf of the agency.

The test is an online instrument consisting of a series of statements that the individual rates as being either an accurate or inaccurate characterization of his or her behavior. The test takes about 15 to 20 minutes to complete. The test authors developed the questions to assess the components of the five-factor model of personality: Openness to Experience, Conscientiousness, Extraversion, Agreeableness, and Neuroticism. The test manual devotes several pages to reviewing the contemporary literature that examines the association between each of the five personality traits and risk behavior and tolerance.

The test manual presents a factor analysis of the test showing four dominant factors: Calm, Emotional, Daring, and Measured. Other than the sample size (n = 328), the test manual presents little information about the population sampled, the version of the test used, and other methodological and statistical information necessary to evaluate fully the merits of the analysis. Moving forward, the test authors posit that the Calm and Emotional traits represent one continuum whereas the Daring and Measured traits represent an orthogonal trait continuum. Using these trait dimensions, the test authors created two additional dimensions for a total of eight trait types. These types are Excitable/Deliberate, Intense/Composed, Wary/Adventurous, and Prudent/Carefree. Although the risk type profile uses an eight-type taxonomy to describe a person, the test also reports the relative position of the individual along the dimension. For example, the report for one person may result in the classification Adventurous and at an extreme level whereas another person may receive the designation Wary but closer to the median of the dimension.

The report for an individual respondent includes several graphics showing his or her risk propensity. The first graphic is a circle whose circumference represents the eight risk types and a dot that represents the individual's relative position between the opposing types. The second illustration is a pie chart showing risk likelihood for recreation, health and safety, finances, reputation, and social activity. The third graphic presents a simple line extending from low to high risk propensity. Along the axis are points representing each of the risk types—Wary at the low-risk extreme and Adventurous at the high-risk extreme. A separate point shows the individual's placement along with a colored bar representing the confidence interval associated with the person's score. Finally, the report includes some generalized phrases about the person's likely behavior related to risk taking.

Those purchasing the test may select from several available reports including a financial advisor report of his or her clients, a report for the individual investor, and various individual and group reports. The test publisher suggests that the group reports will allow managers or other human services personnel to better understand personality dynamics with small teams of 25 or fewer employees to ensure appropriate oversight of the group regarding risk management.

DEVELOPMENT. The creation of the test began when the Financial Conduct Authority of the United Kingdom began to require financial consultants to determine their clients' willingness to assume financial risk when purchasing various financial products. With this directive and a review of the contemporary literature, the test authors decided to use the five-factor model as the empirical foundation for the creation of the test.

Although the test is described in the manual preface as a fourth edition, the test manual does not describe how the test items were created and selected for this or earlier versions of the instrument. [Editor's note: The test publisher clarified that "fourth edition" refers to the publication of the digital technical manual and not to the test itself.] The current manual does, however, present the results of a large sample (n = 7,072) of participants who completed the test and whose responses were considered valid. There is scant information regarding specific characteristics of the sample beyond age, gender, ethnicity, and area of employment for the proportion of respondents who chose to provide this information. The test manual does provide the results of a second factor analysis of an expanded sample (n = 7,264), which appears to confirm the original factor structure consisting of the four traits identified in an earlier analysis.

TECHNICAL. Internal reliability coefficients are reported in the test manual for the four personality factors as .80 for Calm, .75 for Emotional, .84 for Daring, and .81 for Measured, as well as for the two personality scales, Calm:Emotional (.87) and Daring:Measured (.85). In addition, a split-half reliability analysis was conducted on a large sample (n = 10,793). Correlation coefficients were computed between the two halves of the two scales, Calm:Emotional and Daring:Measured. The uncorrected coefficients were .82 and .79, respectively, and .80 for the combined scale. When corrected for scale length via the Spearman-Brown prophecy formula, the coefficients were .90, .89, and .89, respectively. Temporal stability of the test scores was examined using a sample of 56 participants, 84% of whom completed the test twice within a 1- to 4-week interval. The maximum interval length was 53 days. Reliability coefficients were .91 for the Calm:Emotional scale and .93 for the Daring:Measured scale.

Evidence of test score validity is presented in the test manual in the form of correlational studies that examined the extent of the association between the two scales of the Risk Type Compass scores and other measures of personality. Correlation coefficients were reported between the Risk Type Compass scores and scores obtained on comparable scales from the Profile:Match (coefficients ranged from .41 to .48, all significant at $p < .01$) and the Hogan Personality Inventory (coefficients were -.26 and .34, both significant at $p < .01$). Additional comparisons with the Hogan Development

Survey and the Hogan Personality Inventory Safety Competencies yielded several significant correlation coefficients that were generally found to be in the expected directions but more variable in magnitude. In addition, the test authors provide general descriptions of patterns of risk propensity among various large categories of employment. However, readers of the test manual hoping to see how test scores correspond with employee performance or other measures of actual risk-taking behaviors (i.e., to provide predictive evidence of validity) may need to wait for another edition of the test manual.

COMMENTARY. It may well be reasonable to assume that there is a link between personality and risk propensity, a matter that appears to be borne out in current research examining the five-factor model. It may be equally reasonable to assume that the Risk Type Compass represents a focused derivative of the five-factor model by assessing risk specifically. Less obvious, however, is the extent to which the Risk Type Compass provides useful insight beyond that afforded by other measures of personality, that its assessment of risk propensity provides a stable measure of individuals' behavior across time and consistent across settings, and that there are eight unique risk types that allow meaningful qualitative and quantitative distinctions between those who are Carefree and those who are Adventurous. Although such a difference may occur, empirical evidence is needed to conclude that these are mutually exclusive categories. Indeed, when looking at the Risk Comfort Zone graphic, one sees that many of the types are adjacent on the scale.

A final point relates to the Risk Attitude graph for individual reports. The pie chart is a notorious graphic for its inability to offer nuanced information about the underlying data. Imagine for a moment that a person is categorized as Wary, the opposite of Adventurous. This report uses the same sized pie chart divided into the same domains as the Risk Comfort Zone report. However, the two charts cannot be interpreted in the same manner, as one offers normative information and one offers ipsative information. Specifically, the Risk Attitude graph conveys intra-individual differences in preference for risk taking in each domain. It does not indicate actual risk taken. Even so, the use of two graphics that are so similar in appearance may lead to misunderstandings by test users.

SUMMARY. It is indeed wise to ask that those with fiduciary responsibility understand the risk that investors are willing to take with their money. Similarly, it would be wise for financial advisors to steer clients toward or away from risky investments given other important characteristics such as the investor's age, income, and financial obligations. Tests such as the Risk Type Compass may serve a useful purpose if results initiate a genuine dialogue between the advisor and client regarding short- and long-term investment strategies. Similarly, the results of the test could help coworkers better understand why their colleagues behave as they do. The question is the extent to which one needs a personality inventory to initiate these conversations.

It is also an interesting question to determine the extent to which personality traits can presage a person's propensity for caution or risk across many domains of behavior. The Risk Type Compass may well prove to be a useful predictive tool but will require further empirical analysis to ensure conventional assessment of reliability and validity to verify the prognostics provided by the test results.

Review of the Risk Type Compass by ROMEO VITELLI, Psychologist, Private Practice, Toronto, Ontario, Canada:

DESCRIPTION. The Risk Type Compass is an online measure designed to identify individual propensity for risk, both in terms of deeply rooted personality qualities and attitudes relating to risk-taking. Developed as part of an ongoing project into the study of the psychology of risk taking, this test compass reflects a unique approach to measuring the fears and anxieties surrounding risk and how it can be effectively managed.

First developed by Geoff Trickey and a team of U.K. researchers, the Risk Type Compass was originally intended to measure risk appetite of investors for financial companies seeking to comply with U.K. regulations. This led to a comprehensive research project examining prominent models of personality and risk taking including the five-factor model and the Hexaco Model of Personality. The developers also drew on the work of Bailard, Biehl, and Kaiser (1986) and later researchers to identify a four-factor model of risk-taking that became the basis for the Risk Type Compass.

In its current form, the Risk Type Compass provides two bipolar scales: the Calm:Emotional scale measuring fearfulness and the Daring:Measured scale, which measures impulsivity. Based on the scale scores, there are four "pure" risk types: Intense (i.e., emotional, sensitive to criticism, pessimistic); Prudent (i.e., self-controlled, focused, orderly); Composed (i.e., resilient, unemotional, tolerant); Carefree (i.e., spontaneous, unpredictable, challenging of authority). There are also four complex risk types that occur when two pure risk types merge and react. They are: Wary (i.e., methodical, vigilant, conservative); Deliberate (i.e., systematic, self-confident, optimistic); Adventurous (i.e., impulsive, fearless, willing to challenge convention); Excitable (i.e., spontaneous, emotional, potentially unpredictable).

Along with these eight risk types, there is also an Axial Group for individuals who cannot be easily classified into the other risk types. Though technically a typology, the Risk Type Compass allows test takers to be measured across all risk dispositions to reflect how individuals can incorporate many different characteristics.

Because our willingness to take risks is shaped by personality factors, personal experiences, and individual circumstances, the Risk Type Compass distinguishes between risk types, which remain stable over time, and risk attitudes, which are subject to change. There is also a third measure, the Risk Tolerance Index, providing an overall score concerning an individual's tolerance for risk.

The Risk Type Compass is completed online by test takers answering a series of questions relating to risk awareness and tolerance in a range of settings. The test can be completed in 20 minutes in a single sitting; examinees also have the option to pause the test and complete it later. Immediate feedback is provided in the form of a nine-page personal report that can be sent by email for the test taker to review.

The personal report includes a comprehensive review of the test taker's risk type, attitudes toward risk, and risk tolerance. For balance, the report also includes positive and negative aspects of the test taker's risk type as well as the different risk domains to which a risk taker might be exposed (health and safety, recreational, financial, reputational, and social). The report concludes with a summary page outlining the results in a graphic form.

Along with the personal report, the results of the Risk Type Compass can be provided in additional formats depending on the different needs of the test client. These options include team reports providing team leaders with risk results for individual team members, an investor report for individual investors, and a financial advisor report providing feedback on client management.

DEVELOPMENT. The Risk Type Compass was first developed by Psychological Consultancy Limited at the request of a prominent U.K. financial services company as a way to assess investment risk in their clientele. To comply with U.K. financial regulations, the company needed to assess individual client risk appetites prior to making investment recommendations.

Based on their review of risk personality literature, Geoff Trickey and the Psychological Consultancy Limited team identified key risk themes, which they then tested using an initial sample of 328 adults in a wide variety of occupations. Factor analysis yielded a four-factor risk theme model, which became the basis for the Risk Type Compass and its two bipolar scales: Calm:Emotional and Daring:Measured.

The four-factor solution gave rise to the idea of a compass model for the assessment, allowing for use in multiple settings. With the two bipolar scales presented as conceptually orthogonal, the original Risk Type Compass was expanded to its current structure with four pure risk types and four complex risk types. Additional scales measuring risk type and attitudes were developed and added as well as validated. A validity scale was incorporated into the Risk Type Compass to assess response consistency.

Since its initial development, the Risk Type Compass has been administered to thousands of individuals in different industries, permitting comparison of findings across a wide range of industries. Cross-sectional studies allow comparison of Risk Type Compass results for Baby Boomers as well as members of Generations X and Y. This allows for the Risk Type Compass to be used as a resource in hiring decisions and financial settings.

TECHNICAL. The standardization study results evaluating the internal consistency and test-retest reliability of the Risk Type Compass are presented in the test manual.

Internal reliability coefficients for the four personality factors identified by factor analysis (Calm, Emotional, Measured, and Daring) and the two Risk Type Compass scales (Calm:Emotional and Daring:Measured) range from .75 to .87, far exceeding the unofficial benchmark of .70 and indicating consistent measurement of the underlying item themes. Further evidence for this conclusion is shown by the standard errors of measurement for the Risk Type Compass scales of 6.79 and 6.18, respectively. Using data from 10,793 test participants, split-half analysis of the Risk Type Compass scales indicated strong correlations between the two halves of the Calm:Emotional and Daring:Measured scales (Spearman-Brown corrected coefficients of .90 and .89, respectively). Interitem correlations of each of the items included in the different subthemes also are presented and reflect the four Risk Type Compass factors.

A test-retest analysis was conducted using data from 56 participants who took the Risk Type Compass twice with a maximum interval of 53 days. Correlations were .91 for the Calm:Emotional scale and .93 for the Daring:Measured scale.

Reliability data were also collected for the Risk Type Compass short form (36 items), which reflected the internal reliability findings of the longer form (72 items) despite fewer items being used, indicating the short form's value as a parallel measure.

Construct validation of the Risk Type Compass was carried out by comparing it to Profile:-Match, a five-factor model personality measure developed and published by Psychological Consultancy Limited for assessing worker competence. The Hogan Personality Inventory (HPI) was also used to permit direct comparison of the Risk Type Compass with five-factor personality models as applied in occupational assessment.

Validity research results are provided comparing the Risk Type Compass Daring:Measured and Calm:Emotional scales with the HPI Prudence scale (measuring conscientiousness and self-discipline) and Adjustment scale (measuring confidence and self-esteem). Individuals scoring high on Adjustment were more likely to fall at the Calm end of the Calm:Emotional scale whereas Prudence scale scores were strongly correlated with the Measured end of the Daring:Measured scale. Similar analyses using other instruments such as the Hogan Personality Inventory Safety Competencies and the Hogan Motives, Values, Preferences Inventory (MVPI) provide additional validation evidence for the Pure and Complex Risk Types of the Risk Type Compass.

The Risk Type Compass manual also provides risk profiles for different occupations including IT professionals, police officers, engineers, auditors, and air traffic controllers as well as risk level differences as determined by level of seniority and job type. By showing the value of the Risk Type Compass in discriminating between potential candidates, the test authors demonstrate its effectiveness as a tool in employee selection, recruitment, and job training.

COMMENTARY. The Risk Type Compass fills an important niche for the assessment of risk tolerance in occupational settings. Designed to be used on the individual level as well as in assessing teams and entire organizations, it can be applied in a wide variety of occupational and organizational settings. Although risk type is still a relatively new concept with only limited research to date measuring its utility in different industries, the extensive research results described in the Risk Type Compass manual demonstrate its potential value as an important tool for risk management in various settings. The test manual also provides a good overview of the history and development of the test as well as how it potentially can be adapted to new applications over time. As the test authors point out, there are few situations in which risk is not a consideration and, as one of the few test instruments currently available for measuring risk tolerance and attitudes, the Risk Type Compass can play an important role in occupational psychology and human resources research.

SUMMARY. The Risk Type Compass is an online measure designed to identify individual propensity for risk, both in terms of deeply rooted personality qualities and attitudes. The test can be completed in 20 minutes in a single sitting, though takers also have the option to pause the test and complete it in a later session. Immediate feedback is provided in the form of a nine-page personal report that can be sent by email for the test taker to review. Alternative report formats are also available. With extensive reliability and validity research data, as well as comprehensive norms based on a large U.K. sample, the Risk Type Compass fills an important niche for the assessment of risk tolerance in occupational settings as well as being a valuable tool for clinical use and research.

REVIEWER'S REFERENCE

Bailard, T. E., Biehl, D. L., & Kaiser, R. W. (1986). *Personal money management* (5th ed.). Chicago, IL: Science Research Associates.

[142]

Rorschach Performance Assessment System.

Purpose: Designed "as an evidence-focused" system for administering, coding, and interpreting responses to the Rorschach inkblot task, a performance-based task used to identify personality characteristics.

Population: Clinical patients.

Publication Date: 2011.

Acronym: R-PAS.

Scores: Variables interpreted in 5 domains: Administration Behaviors and Observations, Engagement and

Cognitive Processing, Perception and Thinking Problems, Stress and Distress, Self and Other Representation.
Administration: Individual.
Price Data, 2020: $349.99 per new user kit including manual (2011, 548 pages), 10 administration booklets, administration binder, inkblots, 5 clinical protocols, and 5 interpretive guides in briefcase; $119.99 per inkblot set; $99.99 per spiral-bound print manual (volume discounts available); $89.99 per digital manual; $75 per 25 scoring forms; $34.99 per 10 portrait administration booklets (44 pages); $29.99 per 10 landscape administration booklets (28 pages); $22.99 per 25 color location charts; $22.99 per administration binder; $11.75 per clinical protocol (volume discounts available).
Foreign Language Editions: Various translations available from test publisher.
Time: Approximately 60 minutes for administration.
Comments: Each domain interpreted consists of scores derived from variables unique to the respective domain. Raw scores for some variables are determined by simply counting specific behaviors (e.g., rotation of the stimulus cards) while others require addition, subtraction, and/or the calculation of percentages based on codes assigned to the examinee's responses before converting them to percentile ranks and standard scores. Online scoring available.
Authors: Gregory J. Meyer, Donald J. Viglione, Joni L. Mihura, Robert E. Erard, and Philip Erdberg.
Publisher: Rorschach Performance Assessment System, LLC.

Review of the Rorschach Performance Assessment System by SAMUEL JUNI, Professor, New York University, New York City, NY:

DESCRIPTION. The Rorschach consists of 10 horizontally symmetrical cards (approximately 6.5 X 9.5 inches) with various combinations of black, white, and colors, arguably measuring organicity, cognitive style, personality, psychopathology, and interpersonal functioning. Examinees describe what they see, responses are coded (following clarification inquiry), and codes are interpreted in complex computational algorithms. Major coding foci include (among others) location, color, various shading derivate, synthetic variations, perspective, and distinct content categories. Serious doctoral programs may require a year or more of training to achieve Rorschach testing competence.

DEVELOPMENT. The overall test and its use have evolved from phenomenological a priori truisms toward empirically validated, evidence-based, operationalized approaches. First introduced by Hermann Rorschach in 1921 as a semi-intuitive, subjectively interpreted endeavor, the test was subsequently structured and formalized by a number of more objective systems devised by key diagnosticians. These systems were then subjected to a potpourri of theoretical analyses as well as isolated reliability and validity efforts and more organized validation research studies. Subsequently, John Exner critically and selectively synthesized what he deemed to be the most cogent, salient, and validated elements from these systems to yield the Comprehensive System (CS). The CS dominated the field for a number of decades and became synonymous with Rorschach testing in clinical psychology. Upon Exner's death, members of Exner's Rorschach Research Council continued refining and changing aspects of the system, yielding the (still evolving) R-PAS, which has inherited the CS mantle as the primary evidence-based manifestation of the Rorschach technique. The most noted R-PAS coding changes are the deletion of Form-dominant components from non-color determinant coding, the elimination of 10 traditional content categories, and the addition of three thematic codes for aggressive content, implicit dependency, and object representations.

The remainder of this review is best viewed as a continuation of the 2001 Buros review of the Exner Comprehensive System (CS) Rorschach approach (Hess, Zachar, & Kramer, 2001), concurring with the overall analysis and evaluation and its positive recommendation of the instrument as a reliable and valid projective test. The R-PAS is an elaborative adaptation of Exner's effort. No new variables or codes were created for the R-PAS, which selected variables used by others, "either in previous systems for scoring the Rorschach or as independently coded variables" (manual, p. 441). Most of the codes are taken directly from the CS books (which function as the Exner manual) and related CS-based studies. The corresponding standardization, validity, and reliability data are evaluated in the 2001 review. This review highlights positive features of the R-PAS as well as its problems and issues—some of which were inherited from previous Rorschach systems—and critically evaluates how these and other challenges are dealt with in the R-PAS. Therefore this review can be seen as a running commentary on the current version of the instrument, focusing on specific nuances of R-PAS administrative, coding, and interpretive approaches and also on issues in these domains that the R-PAS shares with (and has inherited from) the systems that preceded it. For more comprehensive pointed critical comparisons between the systems, see Gurley (2017) and Bram and Yalof (2018).

Projective testing is designed to elicit conscious and unconscious cognitive, emotional, and personality factors that are either inaccessible to or censored by an examinee. As an alternative to free association tasks (which are most susceptible to distortion and self-censoring), projective testing is less obvious in its intention, as it is sometimes presented as a creative effort involving imagination. Among the purest projective tasks are figure drawings and Card 16 of the TAT (which is totally blank). Although the Rorschach was designed as random inkblots, it quickly became apparent that there are specific "pulls" due to various aspects of the inkblots (e.g., shapes, colors, shading) that predispose respondents to verbalize specific themes and focus on specific determinants. Thus, elicited projective material is superimposed on a context with various cognitive and emotional constraints, yielding a pattern interpretable as a dynamic blueprint of the examinees' internal determinants in a variety of contextual scenarios.

For many decades, the Rorschach reigned in diagnostics as a projective technique (i.e., based upon the premise that responses entail the projection of unconscious material). Such techniques allow the examiner to deduce psychodynamic and personality determinants to which the respondent does not usually have access (and is certainly not eager to share). Nominally, the test manual cites the classic Rorschach systematizers (with the notable exception of Marguerite Hertz) as the theoretical bases for the test. The R-PAS conforms to the current "politically correct" zeitgeist in psychiatry that eschews psychodynamic diagnostics and personality assessment in favor of curtailed behavior style descriptions, as systematized in the *Diagnostic and Statistical Manual of Mental Disorders, Fifth Edition* (*DSM-5*; American Psychiatric Association, 2013) despite backlash from some espousing a psychodynamic perspective (*Lingiardi & McWilliams, 2017*).

Accordingly, the R-PAS extends Exner's efforts to downplay projective aspects of the Rorschach. Personality appears occasionally as a watered-down construct, as the R-PAS reformulates the Rorschach, instead, as a measure of "personality in action" anchored to performance and information processing. What emerges is (another) measure that purportedly entails behavioral observations and self-reporting to bring it in line with behaviorally linked criteria and concepts. Problem solving is heralded while feelings and emotions are restricted to ancillary Content Analyses, instead of what some would view as their rightful place among non-Form determinants. Use of the test to infer the examinee's typical stance toward the environment is not mentioned.

However, this test is still rooted in the nebulous domain bridging subjective, intuitive judgments and respectable psychometrics, as it was designed in the *Einfühlung* tradition where the examiner-analyst (with an allegedly flawless ego) steps into the examinee's shoes to determine whether responses are consistent with objective reality or normal personality. (Note the vestiges of this stance, for example, in the R-PAS introduction to the client: "I want to see it the way you did" [manual, p. 19].) Many of the constructs and indices remain inherently not operationalizable.

This review includes challenges to, questions, and demurrals about, some psychometric, administrative, coding, and interpretive aspects of the test. It is stressed, however, that given the small number of these considerations as compared to the large number of formulations, which—admirably—make sense and are clearly defined, the outlined factors likely will not negatively affect the interpretability of any of the scores to a significant extent. At most, they will increase slightly the magnitude of the error term in the equations (or raise the threshold for a "hit"), which may modestly diminish reliability. Thus, the issues outlined should be viewed as ranging from suggested changes to limited circumscribed critiques, but not as clinically significant flaws in the instrument.

TECHNICAL. Rorschach manuals are plenty, and they vary in their intent and scope. The R-PAS manual falls on the continuum between the Exner CS multi-book super-manual (Exner, 1986, 1991; Exner & Weiner, 1995) and Gurley's (2017) barebones "Essentials" guide, albeit significantly closer to the former in its comprehensiveness. Exner is a difficult read, with different parts appearing to be written by different associates, graduate students, or committees. The presentation is choppy, inconsistent, and difficult to assimilate, especially because partial information on some of the constructs must be culled from various sections. In addition, the volumes were written gradually as the system was developed and perfected, leading to frequent contradictions. Incomplete definitions yield reliability kinks, as much is left to the judgment of the examiners and scorers. The single R-PAS volume, by contrast, is well organized, and clarity was obviously a key goal in its design. Its technical manual is not extensive. This is reasonable, because the system is totally based on previous measures for which studies examining validity and reliability are already published in the literature. However, the validational approach of the manual, which entails collapsing psychometric data from various sources that vary in their administration and scoring, may be unwarranted.

Scoring indices have been updated from their statistically elementary modes by utilizing appropriate percentiles and standard scores (mean of 100 and standard deviation of 15). More scores—all collated from scattered published sources—have been added (Complexity, Space Integration, Space Reversal, Oral Dependency Language, Mutuality of Autonomy, Ego Impairment Index, and Aggressive Content).

Norms, reliability, validity, and standardization of the R-PAS depend on similar efforts taken from studies undertaken with the CS. Their evaluation is a major aspect of the 2001 Rorschach review (Hess, Zachar, & Kramer, 2001). Additional efforts cited in the R-PAS manual entail R-Optimized modeling procedures applied to previous CS data. These extract projected patterns from non-R-PAS administrations to make the protocols resemble R-PAS protocols. This procedure (arguably of questionable legitimacy) was used to investigate interrater reliability and yielded 125 protocols that were then analyzed along with 50 protocols that were actually administered according to the R-PAS guidelines. Reliability results are excellent (most indices in the .80s to .90s, with the lowest outlier being .69). In addition, mean interrater reliability indices were high for the six new PAS codes.

Virtually all Rorschach scoring systems that have evolved through the years contend with the balance between maintaining some of the less-definable constructs while stressing those that are definable and objectively measured. The R-PAS represents a remarkable effort to stay as close to the latter effort in tailoring precise administration and scoring algorithms yielding relatively solid valid and reliable measures and indices. As a result, however, a number of babies have been discarded with the bathwater. This is unfortunate, because the validity and reliability data are far from conclusive, with many based on scattered findings from studies with wide variations in administration and scoring computations. Nonetheless, the R-PAS is still the best system out there, especially for training and standardization purposes. This reviewer hopes that future editions will reincorporate some of the potentially powerful indices that have been discarded in the validity-reliability housecleaning efforts to gain admittance for the Rorschach to the cadre of personality measures in vogue with the current psychometric zeitgeist. A good start might be along the lines of *DSM-5*'s ancillary section of *Emerging Measures and Models*.

COMMENTARY.

Administration. The explicit stance of administration is that it is client-directed (i.e., "It's up to you"). This is belied, however, by a variety of subtle and overt structural overlays and persistent questioning designed to constrain and direct the client toward specific response goals (e.g., "What about it makes it look like ..." [manual, p. 18]). Thus, despite the verbal dodges suggested for examiners to employ, the test cannot rightly be viewed as non-directed. The instruction "What might this be?" suggests (perhaps disturbingly) to examinees that there is actually a correct response. (That suggestion has some merit because this is how Reality Testing is evaluated via the Form Quality tables.) Moreover, regardless of the scoring system used, administration of the Rorschach involves a host of seemingly benign messages (ranging from verbal dodges to blatant misinformation, particularly regarding the questions whether there are *correct* versus *incorrect* responses) that essentially misrepresent the nature of the test and its interpretation by omission and commission.

The "It's up to you" stance toward the client is overly stressed throughout the administrative guidelines of the R-PAS manual. When a client refutes or withdraws a response, there is no specific instruction for the examiner to comply and omit the response from the record. Relatedly, when a respondent offers a choice of options, this reviewer finds the most advisable approach is to code these as multiple responses rather than asking the client in any way to choose between them.

The criteria to determine whether complex responses should be regarded as one or multiple responses are not as definitive as they might be. They need clarification and more precise algorithms. The manual details precise administration and scoring algorithms yielding relatively solid valid and reliable measures and indices. Certainly, many of these algorithms made sense in the formative Rorschach history to avoid multiple coding and scoring options that would tax the resources (particularly time) of the professional interpreting the protocol. With the advent of automated systems to compute alternate indices and ratios, mutually exclusive coding rules that require *this-or-that* decisions are superfluous; moreover, they result in the loss of potentially relevant data.

Examiners who select the R-Optimized approach for administration employ *prompts* and *pulls* that encourage respondents to produce an optimal number (18-27) of responses to achieve protocols that are more uniform in length. However, the pulls sometimes rob the protocol of potentially significant projective material. This reviewer questions whether such limitations are appropriate. Relatedly, the logic of recording a *pull* if a respondent voluntarily hands the card back after four responses is not intuitively understandable. In the same vein, more guidance is needed for the Clarification Phase when respondents offer new responses and refuse to stick with their original responses. This often presents a difficult challenge for examiners. Finally, this reviewer's experience supports Bram's (2010) observation that R-Optimized procedures can be most disruptive for a fragile patient.

Several practical suggestions regarding administration are in order. For training purposes, more examiner guidance is needed for the Clarification Phase when respondents discard original responses and offer new ones as replacements. In terms of user-friendliness, instructions and discussions about location designations would be more understandable if card illustrations in the manual were presented in color for the chromatic cards. To avoid cluttered transcriptions in recording the administration protocol, there is no need to begin each verbalization of the respondent by *R*; it should be the default. Moreover, the examiner's verbalizations could be in parentheses, rather than requiring that each be preceded by *E*. Finally, examiners should record and score responses with an eraser- equipped pencil rather than the recommended pen.

Coding and Interpretation. As a rule, most of the traditional Rorschach clinical indices, especially those reflected in Exner's system, remain in the R-PAS (although some were renamed or modified). Notwithstanding the overall integrity of the R-PAS, this reviewer believes that some constructs were excluded inappropriately, some features could use additional clarification, some inadequacies need correction, and some unelaborated constructs should be refined. Following are comments and critiques of specific nuances; some of these are aimed at particular aspects of the R-PAS as such, whereas others pertain to features the R-PAS adopted uncritically from earlier Rorschach systems.

The manual usually calls for coding down (i.e., choosing the most problematic or pathological code) in cases where there are multiple coding options, albeit with notable exceptions where coding up is mandated. The differential logic is unelaborated, however, and consistency would be more prudent.

In terms of omissions, this reviewer finds the absence of several important clinical diagnostic clusters from the CS (i.e., Perseveration, Depression, and Obsessiveness) problematic. Also noted is that Color Naming and Color Projection, variables that contributed to the CS measure of emotional functioning (which appeared under the Affect heading of the structural summary), have been dropped in the R-PAS. Color Projection is a clinically blatant index of emotional lability. Its exclusion from R-PAS is a mistake. It is also not prudent to discard coding for Color Naming, although its clinical significance is less marked. These omissions engender significant limitations in diagnostics and in the interpretation of a key personality factor, respectively.

Maintaining past patterns, R-PAS limits the computation of the Affective Ratio to the last three cards only. Ignoring the color demands of Cards II and III, though consistent with the Rorschach tradition, is not addressed in the manual and is indefensible both phenomenologically and conceptually.

The omission of the degree of Form Dominance when scoring Reflection is very sensible, because few clinicians understand this elusive construct in combination with Reflection. However, the omission of the Form determinant component from Shading, Achromatic Color, Texture, Vista, and Reflection codes represents a grave error from a clinical and diagnostic perspective, especially from the Ego Psychology perspective of Kleiger (1997). Indeed, just as in the case of responses with color as a determinant, the degree of Form Dominance informs us about the level of ego involvement or cognition that mediates the experience of different affects represented by shading and achromatic determinants.

Occasional inadequate clarifications in the manual may confuse users and yield reliability problems, especially those with little previous Rorschach experience. In location coding, dealing with a response that combines two large detail locations requires more pointed guidance. The criteria in movement coding are also unclear at times. Specifically, the algorithm for Active versus Passive Inanimate Movement coding leaves room for error. Consider, for example, a flowing river, where there is active energy, but it is not supplied by the river itself.

The nuances of Space can be challenging to the user. Contrasting the Rorschach cards with Ruben Vase-Faces, the R-PAS authors argue that the white cardstock of the former is "clearly ground upon which Rorschach painted figure [*sic*]" (p. 69). This is not easily understood. Moreover, the notion of determining relative emphasis (or prominence) of space in determining Reversal coding is too subjective and not likely to be mastered uniformly, which will inevitably render the Space construct unreliable. It is more troubling yet that the R-PAS suggests using the sequence of response elements to inform such coding—a mode eschewed by Rorschachers as a rule—which is unjustified. The latter is reminiscent of Rorschach trainees who mistakenly decide on Color versus Form Dominance of a response based on verbalization sequence, which has consistently been deemed clinically irrelevant.

The detailed algorithms required to compute scores, ratios, and complexity adjustments basically force users to rely on computerized software. Indeed, some standard score plotting cannot be done by hand at all using conversion data provided in the manual (Diener, 2013).

A number of the coding and scoring algorithms require preemptive decisions by the examiner to choose only one aspect of a response while discarding the others. This is a profound error. It makes more sense to include all data and then use weighted formulae to consider each of the aspects differentially, all the while adding a special indicator signifying multiple coding, which would give the scoring program the option of coding up, coding down, or including all codes following the multiple regression paradigm. Moreover, adding a special code indicator for multiple Blends (where more than one determinant accounts for a given response) would give the scoring program the option to condense and discard redundant data when warranted.

Occasionally, precise coding decision rules defy the intent of the respective construct. For example, not coding a face with eyes and a mouth as Space-Reversal for Card I (p. 71) is incorrect if one indeed sees the spaces as actual facial parts (in contrast to the place where those parts would be). The reversal code appears warranted in such cases.

It is inappropriate that Mutuality of Autonomy Pathology is coded for a *smashed bug* (p. 51) despite the fact that there is no indication that this was due to an intentional act. Moreover, such coding is inconsistent with the general rule that historical data (i.e., events that occurred before the time narrative of the actual response) are not considered in the coding process.

Because of the initial card design, the Pair and Reflection codes were always limited to horizontal symmetry. However, since these codes are presumed to measure self-reflection and narcissist determinants, why not consider including these codes even if they are based on vertical symmetry? Arguably, such responses are especially potent because they are not elicited by card symmetry and are therefore more projectively based.

The Form Dimension construct, especially as it contrasts with Vista, is explored very well in the manual. The decision flowchart has as its origin the detailed variations of Shading-derived Vista manifestations. Once Shading components are ruled out, Form Dimension is then deemed an acceptable code. In addition, Form Dimension is defined exclusively based on size differentials or partial item blocking. From an artistic perspective, the latter definition has a glaring omission because non-Shading dimensionality can be visually represented by the convergence or divergence of parallel contours (e.g., tracks seen as going off perpendicular to the card as they converge). This yields merely three exclusive criteria for Form Dimension and simplifies the differential algorithm between Vista versus Form Dimension coding (obviating the need for the detailed positive coding analysis for Vista presented in the manual). Namely, one begins by determining whether dimensionality is perceived based on size differential or partial item blocking or parallel divergence/convergence (which warrants a Form Dimension code). Once these are ruled out, one may code Vista as a default, without determining positively that the dimensionality is Shading-derived.

The differential discussion in the manual on determining whether unclear dark or black objects are to be coded as Shading or Achromatic Color—an issue that often introduces random error variations into Rorschach protocols—is as impressive as it is thorough. However, an elementary and foolproof variance-reduction tool for trainees and seasoned examiners alike is suggested: Would the adjective change if more light were to shine into the picture? If so, the coding should be for Shading. If not, Achromatic Color should be coded.

The R-PAS features Oral Dependent Language as a thematic code. This index is derived from Masling's most impressive research findings. Psychometrically, it would have been prudent to separate out oral versus dependent language, which would make the measure more suitable for clinicians not strongly identified with traditional Freudian theory. In addition, the choice of limiting oneself to language versus themes (which, for example, qualifies a *tuning fork* to be coded in this category) is not conceptually defensible. Most puzzling, however, is the seemingly arbitrary decision to limit thematic coding solely to orality while ignoring the remaining fixation measures (specifically anal, sadistic, phallic, and genital), which were explored methodically in follow-up studies by Masling's proteges (including this reviewer and his students).

It should be self-evident that using the Rorschach with colorblind examinees is absurd. Yet, aside from a singular dated questionable study (Corsino, 1985) claiming that colorblind respondents *merely* show a decrement of Pure Color responses, nary a word can be found on this inadequacy. In this reviewer's experience, all determinants related to Color, Achromatic Color, and Shading (including their derivatives and correlates such as Vista and Form Dimension) show anomalous distributions for colorblind people. In fact, it is clear to many psychological evaluators that almost all current intelligence tests—where colorization of stimuli and response materials is consistently featured—disenfranchise colorblind examines and usually underestimate their abilities. When this issue is addressed (albeit rarely, as it has been in the case of the Wechsler tests), it is typically brushed off with unconvincing statistics and ineffective accommodations. Given the avowed commitment to diversity that defines the current politically correct stance of psychology, the insensitivity of the psychological assessment endeavor to nearly 10% of its constituency is remarkable indeed.

SUMMARY. The R-PAS is a well-developed instrument, which is remarkable for a projective measure. It is as user-friendly as an instrument with such complexity and sophistication can be. The psychometric features—including standardization, validity, and reliability—are well presented and at acceptable levels. Administration, coding, and interpretation instructions and algorithms are relatively clear. Constructs—many of which can be abstruse and difficult to understand—are adequately operationalized. The procedures in the manual are admirably annotated for seasoned Rorschachers as a resource guide, while also featuring sufficient examples and thoughtfully designed practice exercises for trainees. The automated scoring option seems adequate, on par with the Rorshcach Interpretive Assistance Program (RIAP) versions developed for the original CS. The test quality is high and surpassing any alternate versions. It is definitely recommended.

REVIEWER'S REFERENCES

American Psychiatric Association (2013). *Diagnostic and statistical manual of mental disorders* (5th ed.). Washington, DC: Author.

Bram, A. D. (2010). The relevance of the Rorschach and patient-examiner relationship in treatment planning and outcome assessment. *Journal of Personality Assessment, 92,* 91-115.

Bram, A. D., & Yalof, J. (2018). Two contemporary Rorschach systems: Views of two experienced Rorschachers on the CS and R-PAS. *Journal of Projective Psychology & Mental Health, 25,* 35-43.

Corsino, B. V. (1985). Color blindness and Rorschach color responsivity. *Journal of Personality Assessment, 49,* 533-534.

Diener, M. J. (2013, Winter). Focus on clinical practice—Review of 'An introduction to the Rorschach Performance Assessment System (R-PAS).' *Independent Practitioner,* 12-14.

Exner, J. E., Jr. (1986). *The Rorschach: A comprehensive system, Volume 1: Basic foundations* (2nd ed.). New York, NY: Wiley.

Exner, J. E., Jr. (1991). *The Rorschach: A comprehensive system, Volume 2: Interpretation* (2nd ed.). New York, NY: Wiley.

Exner, J. E., Jr. & Weiner, I. B. (1995). *The Rorschach: A comprehensive system, Volume 3: Assessment of children and adolescents* (2nd ed.). New York, NY: Wiley.

Gurley, J. R. (2017). *Essentials of Rorschach assessment: Comprehensive system and R-PAS.* Hoboken, NJ: Wiley.

Hess, A. K., Zachar, P., & Kramer, J. (2001). [Review of the Rorschach]. In B. S. Plake & J. C. Impara (Eds.), *The fourteenth mental measurements yearbook* (pp. 1033-1038). Lincoln, NE: Buros Institute of Mental Measurements.

Kleiger, J. H. (1997). Rorschach shading responses: From a printer's error to an integrated psychoanalytic paradigm. *Journal of Personality Assessment, 69,* 342-364.

Lingiardi, V., & McWilliams, N. (Eds.). (2017). *Psychodynamic diagnostic manual* (2nd ed.) (PDM-2). New York, NY: Guilford Press.

Yalof, J. (2017, March 9). CS or R-PAS: The travails of a Rorschach ambitendent. Rorschach Performance Assessment System (R-PAS). *R-PAS Newsletter,* 22.

Review of the Rorschach Performance Assessment System by STEVEN V. ROUSE, Professor of Psychology, Pepperdine University, Malibu, CA:

DESCRIPTION. Following the model of John Exner's Comprehensive System (CS; Exner, 1974, 1986, 1993, 2003), the Rorschach Performance Assessment System (R-PAS) was developed to encourage the use of administration, scoring, and interpretation methods for the Rorschach inkblot method that had documented evidence of validity and clinical utility. Because some of the CS scores and indices had been criticized as having insufficient validity for applied use, members of the Rorschach Research Council systematically reviewed published and unpublished research data in order to evaluate the value of commonly used Rorschach variables. The resulting Rorschach assessment system retains CS variables with published empirical support, removes unsubstantiated variables, and introduces new variables and procedures that have evidence of strengthening the Rorschach-based assessment of personality.

R-PAS administration can take two different forms. First, a non-directive approach similar to the method used for the CS includes both a Response Phase and a Clarification Phase, allowing the administrator to gain information necessary to code responses to each inkblot but without imposing constraints on the respondent. Because this method can result in extreme variability in the number of responses a respondent provides (which negatively affects assessment validity), an R-Optimized administration method was developed as a second approach. In order to achieve an optimal "R" value (that is, an optimal overall number of responses provided in an assessment), respondents are encouraged to provide two or three responses for each of the 10 cards using a "prompt for two, pull after four" rule. If respondents provide only one perception for a card, they are encouraged to mention a second or third item they see in the inkblot; if respondents provide four perceptions for an inkblot, they are subtly encouraged to return the card. Regardless of the administration approach used, the ease of R-PAS administration is enhanced by user-friendly response recording booklets. Each booklet provides ample room to record four responses for each card, with diagrams of each inkblot to mark the locations for each perception.

Response coding is similar to the coding used in the CS, with every response coded for location, content, determinant, and form quality. Additional codes are marked when relevant, such as Space Integration and Incongruous Combinations. Although test users familiar with the CS will need to adjust to a few changes, transition from CS coding to R-PAS coding is smooth.

Once protocols have been coded, the R-PAS allows for either hand-scoring or use of an online scoring program, resulting in approximately 60 empirically supported variables of clinical relevance. Whether scored by hand or with the online system, each of these scores is plotted in reference to the standardization sample. For protocols scored online, an interpretive guide is available for an extra cost, providing both general interpretive comments and case-specific inferences for each variable.

DEVELOPMENT. The R-PAS shows clear lines of continuity that connect it to the CS. Therefore, the development process did not require the creation of a large number of new procedures or variables. Rather, the process was one of evaluating published and unpublished empirical research, retaining some variables, modifying others, adding a small number of new variables, and eliminating those with questionable validity or utility. Meta-analytic validation data, especially data reported by Mihura, Meyer, Dumitrascu, and Bombel (2013), were influential in guiding decisions for retaining, modifying, or eliminating each variable. The R-PAS manual provides a 17-page table to document the rationale for retaining and modifying approximately 60 variables, along with a six-page table explaining the rationale for eliminating approximately 30 variables that had been included in previous editions of the CS or that had been proposed by other Rorschach researchers but had insufficient empirical justification.

TECHNICAL.

Standardization. Once an assessment protocol has been coded and scored, raw scores are converted to standardized scores using data from an international sample of 1,396 nonpatient adult respondents from 13 different countries who had all taken the Rorschach using standard CS administration procedures. The respondents represent a diversity of race, educational attainment, age, marital status, and gender. To provide an appropriate standardization sample for respondents who complete the R-PAS using R-Optimized procedures, a sample of 640 protocols was statistically adjusted to control for the number of responses given to each card; the manual provides an in-depth and clear explanation of this statistical modelling process, and both the rationale and process are compelling. As documented in the test manual, the difference in standardized score based on using the standard normative sample or the R-Optimized modelled sample is negligible for the majority of the variables. For six variables, however, non-negligible differences in means or standard deviations support the importance of selecting the most relevant standardization sample.

Reliability. Interrater agreement for the R-PAS variables appears to be strong. For the 60 variables obtained in an R-Optimized administration, only five had interrater correlation coefficients lower than .70, four had coefficients between .70 and .79, 14 had coefficients between .80 and .89, and the remaining 37 had coefficients at or above .90. However, reliability of scores relies on standardized methods of initially coding the R-PAS protocols; therefore, even if interrater reliability is documented for raters involved in the assessment development project, the real-world reliability might be substantially lower if test users do not code assessment protocols using the same standardized method.

Validity. As described above, the variables included in the R-PAS represent a compilation of Rorschach-based variables that have documented empirical validation support. Nevertheless, these range from variables with such strong validation evidence that they could be used with confidence in applied settings to those that should be used in a more tentative manner due to less compelling validation evidence. For this reason, approximately half of the R-PAS variables are designated as "Page 1" variables, presented on the front of the R-PAS profile sheet, indicating the strongest levels of validation evidence. The back of the profile sheet presents the remaining "Page 2" variables, indicating a greater need to be used cautiously, especially in high-stakes applied settings. Both pages include variables relevant to such domains as cognitive processing, emotionality, and social processes, but the two-page organization both implicitly and explicitly brings greater attention to those variables that can be used most confidently in applied assessment settings.

COMMENTARY. John Exner's development of the Rorschach Comprehensive System (CS) was historic. With wide inconsistency in the method's administration, scoring, and interpretation (ranging from well-validated to unsubstantiated), his approach modelled scientific empiricism, integrating those aspects that promoted psychometric strength in personality assessment. As evidenced by three revisions, he did not consider the CS to be a finished product but rather expected Rorschach users to continue to modify and improve the method. And, in fact, critics continued to argue that some of the variables in this system still lacked sufficient validity for applied use (e.g., Lilienfeld, Wood, & Garb, 2000).

With the development of the Rorschach Performance Assessment System (R-PAS), Meyer and colleagues continue to show commitment to scientific empiricism, allowing meta-analytic data to guide the retention, revision, and elimination of specific Rorschach-based variables. However, balanced with this empiricism was a recognition of the flaws that had been highlighted in the Comprehensive System; clearly, the criticisms leveled against the CS were in mind when developing R-PAS, and this resulted in a stronger assessment system. For example, Lilienfeld et al. (2000) criticized the variability of R (that is, in the number of responses on Rorschach protocols) in the CS; the R-PAS allows for R-Optimized administration, which remains relatively nondirective but results in a more standardized protocol length. Lilienfeld et al. (2000) criticized interrater reliability estimates below .80 for many of the CS variables and indices; the R-PAS boasts high interrater reliability and promotes real-world consistency of coding by requiring R-PAS normative data collectors to demonstrate coding proficiency. Lilienfeld et al. (2000) criticized the CS for including variables that did not possess enough validity to be used for applied purposes; the R-PAS variables were selected on the basis of meta-analytic validation studies, and even after variables were determined to be sufficiently validated for inclusion they were categorized as "Page 1" (i.e., those variables with enough validation evidence to be used for applied purposes) or "Page 2" (i.e., variables for which additional validation data would be needed for use in high-stakes applied settings) in order to promote the most valid use of the assessment system. Clearly, the R-PAS was developed with both the strengths and weaknesses of the CS in mind.

SUMMARY. Following the tradition of Exner's Comprehensive System, the Rorschach Performance Assessment System provides Rorschach users with an empirically grounded compilation of the strongest aspects of Rorschach use. Test users will benefit from a psychometrically improved assessment system. Those who have been trained to use the Comprehensive System will easily transition to the R-PAS.

REVIEWER'S REFERENCES

Exner, J. E., Jr. (1974). *The Rorschach: A comprehensive system, Vol. 1: Basic foundations.* New York, NY: Wiley.

Exner, J. E., Jr. (1986). *The Rorschach: A comprehensive system, Vol. 1: Basic foundations* (2nd ed.). New York, NY: Wiley.

Exner, J. E., Jr. (1993). *The Rorschach: A comprehensive system, Vol. 1: Basic foundations* (3rd ed.). New York, NY: Wiley.

Exner, J. E., Jr. (2003). *The Rorschach: A comprehensive system, Vol. 1: Basic foundations* (4th ed.). Hoboken, NJ: Wiley.

Lilienfeld, S. O., Wood, J. M., & Garb, H. N. (2000). The scientific status of projective techniques. *Psychological Science in the Public Interest, 1,* 27-66.

Mihura, J. L., Meyer, G. J., Dumitrascu, N., & Bombel, G. (2013). The validity of individual Rorschach variables: Systematic reviews and meta-analyses of the Comprehensive System. *Psychological Bulletin, 139,* 548-605.

[143]

Safe and Civil Schools' Climate and Safety Surveys.

Purpose: "Designed to capture features of the school environment and climate that can be targeted in improvement efforts and monitored over time."

Population: Elementary and secondary school students, parents, and staff.

Publication Dates: 1985-2018.
Scores: Individual item results only.
Administration: Group.
Forms, 5: Student (Grades 2-8), Student (Grades 6-12), Elementary Staff, Secondary Staff, Parent.
Price Data, 2020: $1 per student including student survey, staff survey, and parent survey ($200 minimum per school).
Foreign Language Edition: Student and parent surveys available in Spanish.
Time: Administration time not reported.
Comments: Administered online.
Author: Randy Sprick.
Publisher: Ancora Publishing.

Review of the Safe and Civil Schools' Climate and Safety Surveys by RIC BROWN, Adjunct Faculty, St. Johns University and Northern Arizona University, Professor Emeritus, California State University, Sacramento, CA:

DESCRIPTION. In the *Technical Adequacy of Safe and Civil Schools' Climate and Safety Surveys* document, four of the five instruments are noted to be of a formative nature to capture aspects of a school environment and climate. A brief overview of the rationale for such surveys is presented (although the references are beyond 5 years old). In the student and staff surveys, four scales are said to be embedded: Policies and Expectations, Climate and Safety, Engagement, and Problems. Thus, assessment of climate is considered across different vantage points and contexts. All items are presented (75 plus for staff, 55 plus for students and 35 plus for parents) in a 5-choice Likert-style format. The surveys are to be completed anonymously; providing demographic information is optional.

DEVELOPMENT. The original release of the staff perception surveys occurred in 1985. In 1988, the student surveys were released. The technical adequacy document notes that the student and staff surveys have been implemented in more than 1,000 schools, which has led to re-wording, deletion, and addition of new items with continual revision processes occurring. Currently, the surveys are delivered online. Although the material sent for review included a parental survey on the climate and safety topic, there were neither technical data nor developmental data regarding the parental survey presented in the technical adequacy documentation.

TECHNICAL. The sample described in the technical document was from a large Midwest, urban school district with 3,600 staff surveys and 23,000 student surveys administered in the fall of 2015. According to the document, approximately 30% of the students were White, 26% were Hispanic/Latino, about 18% were Black/African American, 5% were Asian, 11% were Other, and 9% did not specify. For the staff sample, more than 70% were White, about 10% were Hispanic/Latino and about 5% were Black/African American. More than two thirds of the staff members were certified teachers.

A factor analysis was performed using these data with more than adequate sample sizes for factor stability. All procedures used for the factor analysis were appropriate and reported clearly including factor retention, item retention, and factor loadings. Twelve tables are presented showing factor loadings for the scales noted previously for both staff and students.

Reliability data are presented in the form communalities done as part of the factor analysis for the two student surveys and the two staff surveys. Those numbers ranged from .40 to .80. In addition, a table is presented displaying alpha coefficients for four of the scales. Those coefficients ranged from .81 to .95.

In sum, the technical adequacy of the four scales discussed in the technical document has been demonstrated. In the commentary below, some related technical issues regarding reading level required of the students, perspectives required for respondents, and placement of demographic information are raised.

COMMENTARY. These surveys were developed and revised in the mid-to-late 1980s before the horrific massacre at Columbine High School in 1999 followed by more school shootings such as Sandy Hook and Parkland. Thus, the relevance of a school safety scale developed so long ago should be questioned for use in 2020 and beyond.

The surveys might be useful for general discussions of school climate, but a good school principal regularly interacting with staff, meeting with parents, and walking around talking to students should have a good assessment of the issues contained in these surveys. Thus, it is likely that these inventories would confirm what the principal and teachers already know. In today's school climate, the bigger concern is more about safety from gun violence (Lindle, 2019) with schools moving to threat assessment and safety upgrades (Jagodzinski, 2019) such as fencing, single points of entry, bullet proof glass, bollards, and so forth.

Bullying in person was certainly an issue in 1985, but cyberbullying (Cox-Wingo & Poirier,

2019) on various social media platforms was not yet a problem when this scale was initially published and revised.

Some questions might be raised regarding the reading level for the student surveys, especially for Grades 2-8. Words and phrases such as *tolerated, respectfully,* and *keeping track of assignments* might be difficult for younger children. In addition, while many children in elementary schools take tests where they choose the correct answer from among a list of answers (i.e., multiple-choice questions), the maturity needed to distinguish varying levels of agreement may not be present. Additionally, a survey exceeding 55 questions may be a challenge for young children and even teens. The survey for students in Grade 6-12 appears to reflect settings (e.g., locker rooms, parking lots) and situations particular to the older students.

Staff are asked about their perceptions of how students feel. If the staff member has had no incidences justifying a response, then is their response based on hearsay? The "no opinion" option is not an appropriate response for instances where a staff member has never experienced the situation noted in the question. For example, if one strongly agrees that staff members treat students fairly, does that mean everyone does or that most do? Does agree mean most, but not all? Is it a question regarding numbers who do or a general feeling about the school?

There were no technical data presented regarding the parent survey. In that survey, the prompts are written in the third person (e.g., Students generally feel ...). Responses therefore require speculation about other students. A more appropriate question might begin "My child ...," thus requiring minimal speculation regarding other children.

One might question requiring demographic information prior to responding to the survey content. Would a parent, staff member, or student feel uncomfortable about providing this information and thus not complete the survey? Putting demographic questions after content might be more appropriate. Although the authors indicate the demographic questions are optional, they are not specifically labeled as such. Instead, respondents may select an option such as "I prefer not to answer."

SUMMARY. This measure represents a case in which the developers designed and validated several surveys for students, staff, and parents in the mid-1980s regarding school safety and climate. Although the technical adequacy of the surveys (except for the parent survey for which no data were presented) is well documented, the content itself may be past its prime (Young, Walker, & Harris, 2019). The test developers note that the surveys have been revised and expanded since they were first published, but details of these changes are not included in the test materials. As noted previously, today's school safety issues are dramatically different from those 20 or more years ago. In our current climate of school violence, are these the instruments that will make the case for school safety improvements? Users of the scale need to be aware of exactly what the scales are intended to measure rather than simply rely on what the titles imply.

REVIEWER'S REFERENCES

Cox-Wingo, V., & Poirier, S. (2019). Bullying and mental health. In R. Papa (Ed.), *School violence in international contexts: Perspectives from educational leaders without borders.* New York, NY: Springer.

Jagodzinski, C. L. (2019). School safety upgrades and perceptions of safety protocols in prevention of school shootings. In R. Papa (Ed.), *School violence in international contexts: Perspectives from educational leaders without borders.* New York, NY: Springer.

Lindle, J. C. (2019). School leaders' caring for place while addressing fear, moral panic, and control. In R. Papa (Ed.), *School violence in international contexts: Perspectives from educational leaders without borders.* New York, NY: Springer.

Young, J. K., Walker, S., & Harris, S. (2019). Investigation of Texas educator response trainings for serious violence from outside intruders. In R. Papa (Ed.), *School violence in international contexts: Perspectives from educational leaders without borders.* New York, NY: Springer.

Review of the Safe and Civil Schools' Climate and Safety Surveys by R. W. KAMPHAUS, Professor and Dean, University of Oregon, Eugene, OR:

DESCRIPTION. The Safe and Civil Schools' Climate and Safety Surveys include a set of student, teacher, and parent self-report forms designed to assess characteristics of a school's climate. The results are used to identify areas of climate improvement. The surveys are also intended for repeated use as progress monitoring measures. Five survey forms are available: Staff Survey (Elementary), Staff Survey (Secondary), Student Survey Grades 2-8, Student Survey Grades 6-12, and Parent Survey. On paper, the forms differ in length from four to seven pages. All survey administration and data summarization are conducted online.

The staff surveys are anonymous. The first page of the two staff surveys includes instructions for completion and space for the staff member to enter the name of the school, the respondent's ethnicity, and the respondent's role in the school ("noncertified" personnel, "certified" professionals who are not serving as classroom teachers, and classroom teachers at various grade levels). Respondents may elect not to provide information about either their role or race/ethnicity. There are 78 items on the elementary survey and 83 for the secondary survey. Both forms include an opportunity to offer comments. The items are arranged by content category into the following sections: (a) student safety, (b) student interaction, (c) student and staff interaction, (d) communication of rules for student behavior and class procedures, (e) student's feelings toward the school, (f) perceptions of parent's and family's experiences with the school, (g) staff interactions and behavior management/disciplinary practices, and (h) potential problems at the school. The number of items within each category varies from four to 21 indicators. The sentence length of the indicators also varies, ranging from sentences of five or six words to those with 20 to 25 words. Each item requires the respondent to elect one of the following response options: *strongly agree, agree, disagree, strongly disagree,* or *no opinion.* The final set of times on each form–Section H–is marked differently. The response options for these items are *not a problem, minor problem, moderate problem, serious problem,* or *no opinion.*

The student surveys are formatted similarly to one another. Demographic information about the student includes the name of the school, the student's gender identification, school grade, and race/ethnicity. The instructions are similar, and response options for each indicator are virtually identical to those on the staff surveys. The rating category *minor problem* is changed to *small problem,* and *serious problem* is changed to *big problem.* The forms are shorter overall: 58 items for Grades 2-8 and 63 items for Grades 6-12. The student surveys do not contain items from Section F (perceptions of parent's and family's experiences), and only one item from Section G (staff interactions and behavior management/disciplinary practices) is included on both forms. A comments section is also included. The sentence length of the indicators is generally shorter than for the staff form, which should enhance readability for young students. The readability of some of the words on the Grades 2-8 survey, however, may be challenging for some second and third graders. Examples of potentially challenging words for young children include *respectfully, cliques* (although a parenthetical explanation of the term is included), and *disruptions.* A readability index for the items was not found in the materials provided nor was information about adaptations for children or youth who are English language learners.

The parent survey includes space on the front page to record the name of the child's school, "family" race/ethnicity, and the number of "boys" and "girls" the parent has attending the school. The response options for the 37 items are the same as for the staff survey. Sections A through E are briefer versions of the same content included on the staff surveys. Questions from Section C on the staff forms (students' interactions with each other) are not included, and—as is the case with the student surveys—there are no Section F items. Section G covers the same content as Section H on the staff surveys.

Scoring and interpretation guidelines are provided at the test publisher's website. This website provides two video tutorials: How to Use Online Reports and Data Analysis Example. The reports available online include four "Standard Reports": Progress Report, Survey Results, Survey Comments, and Possible Problems. An additional four Student Reports are available: By Gender, By Grade Level, By Race/Ethnicity, and Custom Filter. The four "Staff/Student/Parent Survey Comparisons" reports are Categories, Rank Order Report, Possible Problems Rank Order Report, and Category Summaries. Finally, a Year-to-Year Survey Comparisons report is provided.

The multiple reporting functions and uses of results are described well in the instructional videos. There are numerous methods described for interpreting the ratings of the individual items and identification of specific problems for intervention/prevention. The interpretive focus is almost exclusively on items and, to a lesser extent, category level interpretations. The instructional videos, for example, demonstrate how visual inspection of respondent endorsement percentages of response options may be used to identify categories and individual items that may need to be addressed and to identify whether those areas need to be addressed differentially by grade level, gender, race/ethnicity, and respondent group (e.g., primarily for staff, students, parents, or all three). Aggregate or composite scores were not described in the video tutorials, although total scores for categories for the staff and student surveys were used to report reliability data that are discussed below in this review. The score used for all interpretation is the percentage of response option endorsements for a given item.

DEVELOPMENT. The survey development procedures and technical properties are described in a document titled "Technical Adequacy of Safe and Civil Schools' Climate and Safety Surveys" (undated). This 14-page document provides information about development, reports the results of a factor-analytic study, includes alpha coefficients for the staff and student forms, and presents a table of items and content within four scales (Policies and Expectations, Climate and Safety, Engagement, and Problems).

The surveys have been in use since staff surveys were first released in 1985, followed by student surveys in 1988. The content of the surveys was designed to assess "school-wide problems and features of the school environment that may not be evident from other data sources" (technical document, p. 2). The report also indicates that data from more than 1,000 schools have been used to inform item deletion and revision as well as the creation of new items. A detailed record of these item improvements is not provided, nor is information about the expertise of the individuals who engaged in the item development process, or the theoretical or empirical considerations used in item development, revision, and deletion. Studies of item information functions, differential item functioning, or item interdependence are not provided.

TECHNICAL. Internal consistency estimates are provided for the four scales within the four student and staff forms. The alpha coefficients range from the low .80s to the mid .90s. No reliability evidence is provided for the parent survey. Neither are reliability data provided for the A through H categories, nor is score stability assessed using test-retest reliability. Given that much of the interpretation is at the item level, some information about the stability of these ratings is necessary for providing support for making inferences based on item responses.

The factor-analytic study is based on a large sample of 900 students and staff members at both the elementary and secondary levels. These samples were selected from a larger pool of approximately 23,000 available surveys. The survey items were subjected to an exploratory factor analysis with oblique rotation, and scree plots were used to identify factor loadings on four factors that correspond to three of the scales identified earlier. Items on the Problems scale were not included in the analysis due to the nature of the content. The analysis resulted in a small number of items being removed due to their lack of contribution to the measurement of any of the three factors. Factor loadings are reported. There is no indication whether the factor-analytic study has been subjected to peer review. Evidence regarding criterion-related, differential, or other construct validation studies was not included in the report, nor were data provided regarding fairness of item, category, or total scores.

COMMENTARY. The intended uses of the Safe and Civil Schools' Climate and Safety Surveys is only evident when reviewing the online instructional videos for users. Education staff and student responses to the Likert response options for individual items are, essentially, the scores upon which inferences are made. The central within-survey score inference being made is the identification of climate problems in a school building that warrant intervention or prevention. Cross-survey comparisons are used to identify subgroup differences for items within a school (i.e., grade, gender, race/ethnicity, and rater).

It could be argued that because the inferences are very limited, little psychometric evidence is required to support use of the Safe and Civil Schools' Climate and Safety Surveys. Inferences about individual students, teachers, or classrooms are not made. In effect, the unit of analysis is the school building, or perhaps a group of schools. Individuals, therefore, are not identified for intervention, prevention, or classification purposes (e.g., special education or mental health diagnosis). Schools, however, are classified as needing intervention, needing more or less intensive intervention based on the number of problem items identified, or as improved based on using the surveys as progress assessments or evaluation assessments (i.e., posttests). Psychometric evidence is required to support these school-based inferences.

At the time of this writing, reliability and validity evidence that supports the use of the Safe and Civil Schools' Climate and Safety Surveys is insufficient. Given this state of affairs, users of the surveys are basing their decisions to use them on their experiences using the measures; colleagues' recommendations or experiences; or training provided by the publisher, authors, online videos, or their representatives.

It could very well be that reliability and validity evidence will be supportive of the item interpretations advised. The developers of the Safe and Civil Schools' Climate and Safety Surveys are advised to hasten their reliability and validity research efforts. Fortunately, the developers appear to have ready access to a relatively large dataset that could be used to facilitate this research program.

SUMMARY. The Safe and Civil Schools' Climate and Safety Surveys purport to measure important and timely constructs that are of grave concern to American society. In this sense, the developers were prescient. In order to maximize the use of the measures, however, considerable psychometric research is necessary. If the developers make maximum use of the large dataset that they describe in their factor-analytic study, they could quickly close the gap between evidence and the application of their measures. The accumulation of this psychometric evidence is given more urgency because of the timeliness of current societal concerns about school safety, in particular.

[144]

The SCERTS Model: A Comprehensive Educational Approach for Children with Autism Spectrum Disorders.

Purpose: "Criterion-referenced" assessment designed as a "multidisciplinary approach to enhancing communication and social-emotional abilities" of people with autism spectrum disorders and related disabilities.
Population: People of all ages with autism spectrum disorders and related disabilities.
Publication Date: 2006.
Acronym: SCERTS Model.
Scores: 3 Communication Stages: Social Partner, Language Partner, Conversational Partner; 3 domains: Social Communication (Joint Attention, Symbol Use), Emotional Regulation (Mutual Regulation, Self-Regulation), Transactional Support (Interpersonal Support, Learning Support); 8 Social-Emotional Growth Indicators: Happiness, Sense of Self, Sense of Other, Active Learning and Organization, Flexibility and Resilience, Cooperation and Appropriateness of Behavior, Independence, Social Membership and Friendships.
Administration: Individual.
Forms: 3 SCERTS Assessment Process (SAP)-Report Forms (Social Partner, Language Partner, Conversational Partner); 3 SAP-Observation Forms (Social Partner, Language Partner, Conversational Partner); 3 SAP Summary Forms (Social Partner, Language Partner, Conversational Partner).
Price Data, 2020: $124.95 per two-volume manual (344 pages, 400 pages) set.
Time: 120-240 minutes for observation, depending on communication stage.
Comments: An ongoing curriculum-based assessment, planning, and implementation model.
Authors: Barry M. Prizant, Amy M. Wetherby, Emily Rubin, Amy C. Laurent, and Patrick J. Rydell.
Publisher: Paul H. Brookes Publishing Co., Inc.

Review of The SCERTS Model: A Comprehensive Educational Approach for Children with Autism Spectrum Disorders by STEFAN C. DOMBROWSKI, Professor, School Psychology Program, and ALICIA GIALANELLA, School Psychology Graduate Student, Rider University, Lawrenceville, NJ:

DESCRIPTION. The SCERTS Model is not a traditional norm-referenced standardized assessment instrument. Rather, it is an approach to assessment and intervention on behalf of children with autism spectrum disorder (ASD) that uses curriculum-based measurement of social, emotional, and communication functioning that links directly to interventions for children in the preschool and elementary school period. The SCERTS Model is multidisciplinary in nature requiring input from numerous stakeholders including speech-language pathologists, psychologists, psychiatrists, paraprofessionals, educators, and caregivers. The program is designed to support the development of individuals with ASD and their families within the social contexts of everyday school and home routines. The authors of the SCERTS Model state that the model was created out of a need for a developmental, social-pragmatic focused educational approach for individuals with ASD. It was not intended by its authors to be used as a clinical/educational diagnostic tool; rather, it was developed for the purpose of intervention planning once a child has been determined to be eligible for disability services (i.e., an individualized education plan [IEP] or individualized family service plan [IFSP]).

The SCERTS framework is built on, and assesses, three domains: Social Communication ("SC"), Emotional Regulation ("ER"), and Transactional Support ("TS"). SCERTS attempts to evaluate social communication skills and subsequently assist children with ASD display joint attention and symbol use to increase joy and trust in communicating and playing with others. The goal of the Emotional Regulation domain is to develop a child's ability to adapt to and cope with daily challenges to maintain a well-regulated state conducive to learning, attending to information, and engaging with others. Lastly, Transactional Support assesses interpersonal and language supports, as well as supports to families, professionals, and other service providers, that are necessary for learning within and across daily social contexts.

The SCERTS Model contains two volumes. Volume I: Assessment, comprises research foundations including developmental context, provides in-depth descriptions and objectives of the three SCERTS domains, and explores the utility of the model across different settings. Included is the SCERTS Assessment Process (SAP), which is supported by nearly two dozen informal forms and checklists for gathering information and monitoring progress. Detailed instructions covering SAP overview, implementation, and criteria for the rating forms are provided. All assessment forms are available in an appendix and may be photocopied. The assessment process requires conducting multiple observations of a child across contexts and using multiple raters. In addition, several interviews and questionnaires are to be completed and are subsequently linked to intervention. The SAP informal forms and checklists assess a child's capacity in the social communication, emotional regulation and transactional support domains. The authors suggest that items on the SAP contained in Volume I are rooted in the developmental psychology literature and the various developmental milestones that have been documented for children with and without disabilities. The SAP is linked to the SCERTS Model intervention curriculum in Volume II.

Volume II: Program Planning and Intervention, provides instruction on how to set individualized goals for children based on SAP results while linking goals across the three SCERTS domains. Volume II discusses how to help students reach those goals with appropriate activities and through the implementation of transactional supports. Additionally, Volume II examines how to use the SCERTS Model across three communication stages (Social Partner, Language Partner, Conversational Partner) in intervention planning and implementation.

DEVELOPMENT. The authors state that the hallmark of the SCERTS Model is its developmental, social-pragmatic focus consistent with evidence-based practice developed by researchers both within and outside of the field of ASD (National Research Council, 2001; Prizant & Rubin, 1999). Research and established education/intervention approaches on communication functions, positive behavior support models, child development, learning styles, and family-centered practice influenced the development of the SCERTS Model in creating a program that would accurately address communication ability, social skills, and emotional regulation in individuals with ASD. Additionally, the authors aligned the SCERTS Model with the recommendations made by the National Research Council of the National Academy of Sciences based on the council's review of 20 years of research regarding the education of children with ASD (National Research Council, 2001).

Although the SCERTS Model was originally published in 2006, and the curriculum in Volume II has been widely used, Morgan et al. (2018) recently conducted the first randomized clinical trial in a school setting that compared the SCERTS intervention to other autism training modules (ATM). The three-year study was implemented with a cluster sample comprising a heterogeneous group of 197 students with ASD across 60 schools in Florida and California. Findings showed higher levels of classroom active engagement based on social interaction for the SCERTS group compared to the ATM group. Higher outcomes on measures of adaptive communication, executive functioning, and social skills with small effect sizes (Cohen's d = 0.31-0.45) also were observed among the SCERTS group when compared to the ATM group. These preliminary findings provide a degree of support for the effectiveness of the SCERTS Model in being able to improve the social, communication, and emotional regulation abilities of children with ASD when implemented by teachers in a classroom setting.

TECHNICAL. Technical information (e.g., norming, reliability, validity) is unavailable in the SCERTS manual.

COMMENTARY. The SCERTS Model is a curriculum-based social, emotional, and communication assessment program for children with ASD that is linked with specific short- and long-term intervention goals. It does not offer technical information (e.g., reliability, validity) that is commonly found in the manuals of norm-referenced assessments and in some curriculum-based measures. However, the theoretical basis of the model is extensively documented in the manual. Additional discussion regarding the empirical effectiveness of the SCERTS Model would be worthwhile given the widespread use and popularity of the program. Strengths include the consideration of the child's functioning across multiple settings, contexts, and partners, which is key in gaining a comprehensive understanding of a child. The model offers an in-depth developmental assessment of social, emotional, and communication based milestones. Both the assessment and intervention guides are thorough and clearly delineated with straightforward language and multiple case examples provided throughout. Intervention goals for the three domains of the SCERTS framework are linked from assessment to intervention implementation. In totality, the SCERTS Model is well-conceptualized, thoroughly detailed, and offers a formalized but flexible approach to intervention planning.

Although the SCERTS Model has several strengths, one concern is that its approach to assessment (via the SAP) may be unrealistic for several reasons. First, one of the strengths of the SCERTS Model—its comprehensiveness and rich detail—may also serve as a reason the model may not be widely adopted. The learning curve will be fairly steep given the comprehensiveness of the model. Second, the amount of time it takes to complete an assessment may be a deterrent in a school-based setting where resources are scarce. There are many observations, interviews, and rating forms involved. Third, given the comprehensive approach to understanding and helping children with ASD across settings and partners, the curriculum may not be fully implemented without a supportive team of school-based professionals, teachers, and caregivers. If all parties are unable or unwilling to implement the necessary supports as recommended by the SCERTS Model, the effectiveness of the SCERTS curriculum will be diminished.

SUMMARY. The SCERTS Model aims to support the development of individuals with autism spectrum disorder (ASD) and their families through a comprehensive assessment and intervention-planning approach. The SCERTS Model can serve as a useful tool in profiling the strengths and weaknesses of a child with ASD, setting improvement goals, and planning and implementing appropriate interventions. Due to the lack of technical properties and the curriculum-based, criterion-referenced nature of the measure, it would be inappropriate to rely heavily upon the SCERTS Model for purposes of clinical diagnosis. However, given the comprehensiveness of the assessment approach, it may be useful for this purpose when used within the context of a comprehensive evaluation. The model is best used for intervention planning, as its assessment process is directly linked to such planning. Overall, the SCERTS Model should be a consideration for practitioners who work with children with ASD. It has been widely used for many years, and the first clinical randomized study provides promising results of a positive impact of the SCERTS Model among children with ASD when implemented in a school setting. Additional studies investigating the effectiveness of the SCERTS Model for intervention planning are needed.

REVIEWERS' REFERENCES

Morgan, L., Hooker, J. L., Sparapani, N., Reinhardt, V. P., Schatschneider, C., & Wetherby, A. M. (2018). Cluster randomized trial of the classroom SCERTS intervention for elementary students with autism spectrum disorder. *Journal of Consulting and Clinical Psychology, 86*(7), 631-644. doi:10.1037/ccp0000314

National Research Council. (2001). *Educating children with autism.* Washington, DC: The National Academies Press.

Prizant, B. M., & Rubin, E. (1999). Contemporary issues in interventions for autism spectrum disorders: A commentary. *Journal of the Association for Persons with Severe Handicaps, 24,* 199-208.

Review of The SCERTS Model: A Comprehensive Educational Approach for Children with Autism Spectrum Disorders by CONNIE THERIOT (ENGLAND), Professor of Graduate Education, Counseling Department, Lincoln Memorial University, Harrogate, TN:

DESCRIPTION. The acronym SCERTS represents the three domains subsumed in the SCERTS Model—Social Communication (SC), Emotional Regulation (ER), and Transactional Support (TS). The manual for The SCERTS Model: A Comprehensive Educational Approach for Children with Autism Spectrum Disorders consists of two volumes. Volume I, Assessment, provides "detailed information about developmental sequences and priorities for each domain" (manual I, p. ix). Volume II, Program Planning and Intervention, describes model implementation in home, school, and community settings. The volume offers guidance for prioritizing goals and implementing practices included in the Transactional Support domain, such as how to link Transactional Support goals with Social Communication and Emotional Regulation goals. Volume II also provides several vignettes about individual children and their families for each of the three major developmental stages used in the model. The vignettes include examples of forms completed during the SCERTS Assessment Process. Quality indicators are included to address program planning and assessment.

DEVELOPMENT. SCERTS is an educational model developed by Prizant, Wetherby, Rubin, and Laurant. The authors provide detailed reviews of other modalities employed with persons with autism spectrum disorders (ASD). They present the strengths and weaknesses of each of these modalities and note that the SCERTS Model "is not exclusionary of other practices or approaches" (manual I, p. 13); rather it is designed to address the limitations of other models. SCERTS incorporates practices from other approaches including Applied Behavior Analysis (ABA), TEACCH (Treatment and Education of Autistic and related Communication-handicapped Children), and RDI (Relationship

Development Intervention). The SCERTS Model differs most notably from the focus of traditional ABA by promoting child-initiated communication in everyday activities. SCERTS is most concerned with helping children with autism to achieve authentic progress, defined as the ability to learn and spontaneously apply functional and relevant skills in a variety of settings and with a variety of partners.

The basic tenets of the SCERTS Model are as follows: to address the core developmental challenges associated with ASD within the context of the natural environment of both child and family and to attempt to match developmental strengths and weaknesses to demonstrate consistency with teaching strategies. The test authors derived these basic tenets from theory; clinical and educational data; and knowledge of current practices, social rules, and empirical data. The objective is to measure change and progress in ecologically valid ways.

The SCERTS Model is a values-based modality that is respectful of both the child's and family's values and quality of life. The model incorporates functional communication; addresses interrelationships among the cognitive, social-emotional, sensory, and motor domains; and seeks to enhance the emotional regulatory capacities of persons with ASD. The model also incorporates a transactional approach specific to a child's strengths and weaknesses and emphasizes natural routines in home, school, and community environments. The goal of the assessor is to establish positive relationships with the child and the family, using family members as experts about the child.

The SCERTS Model identifies challenges that affect aspects of Social Communication such as "joint attention," or interacting socially in various contexts, and "symbol use," demonstrating an understanding of shared meanings in communication and play (manual I, p. 21). The Assessment volume of the SCERTS manual provides a comprehensive examination of the development of social communication. Topics include initial spontaneous communication, following turns and topics in conversation, using more sophisticated nonverbal and symbolic language, recognizing and repairing communication breakdowns, and responding to verbal and nonverbal cues of partner communication.

Emotional Regulation (mutual regulation, self-regulation) is also central to the SCERTS Model. The model's authors identify five critical dimensions identified as areas of difficulty for children with ASD. These areas include the abilities to read and understand social-emotional cues, perceive the intensity of the emotion and link meaning to these emotions, react to the partner's emotional expression, encourage or discourage certain behaviors based on cultural values and norms of a situation, and recover from dysregulation across varied contexts.

The authors refer to emotional regulation as fostering "flow," that is, striving to achieve a "state in which a person experiences focus, deep concentration, and productive engagement with a particular experience or activity (social or nonsocial) and a sense of control, motivation, and satisfaction in that experience" (manual I, p. 70). The SCERTS Model supports the development of a variety of flexible regulatory capacities to provide the framework for children with ASD. To prevent dysregulation, the SCERTS Model suggests reducing uncertainty by providing information about changes throughout the day (discussion or pictures). However, when needed, immediate support may include other methods such as providing sensory input to allow the child to engage in a regulating activity or to remove the child from the dysregulating activity.

The undergirding of the SCERTS Model is Transactional Support (interpersonal support, learning support) implemented by a team, such as environmental accommodations and learning supports (schedules or visual organizers). Eight Social-Emotional Growth Indicators—Happiness, Sense of Self, Sense of Other, Active Learning and Organization, Flexibility and Resilience, Cooperation and Appropriateness of Behavior, Independence, and Social Membership and Friendships—are also addressed.

TECHNICAL. The SCERTS Assessment Process (SAP) involves criterion-referenced measurement of a child's performance on developmental tasks. Specific assessment criteria are provided for three stages of communication development: Social Partner, Language Partner, and Conversational Partner. The assessment is curriculum-based and linked to the SCERTS Model curriculum, which addresses how to implement practices across various contexts. The second volume of the SCERTS manual provides vignettes with completed SAP forms. Typical standardization, reliability, and validity measures are not included in the manuals. Instead, most technical data rely on comparisons of the efficacy of other approaches and critical reviews in published literature. Specifically the authors state the SCERTS Model "is rooted in theory and research on child development as well as theory and research addressing the very nature of ASD" (manual I, p. 110). Support for the utility of the SCERTS Model is "the documentation of meaningful change through the collection of clinical and educational data" (manual I, p. 110). The SCERTS Model is "supported by empirical evidence from developmental and contemporary behavioral research on children with ASD and related disabilities" (manual I, p. 110). Addressing treatment fidelity and efficacy are the bedrocks of the model.

COMMENTARY. The SCERTS Model presents a comprehensive analysis of current treatment options used with children diagnosed with ASD. Although limited empirical research on the model is provided, the authors indicate that the SCERTS Model is consistent with the National Research Council's recommendations and instructional priorities regarding ASD, namely, "functional spontaneous communication" (2001, p. 6). The authors identify strengths and weaknesses of other models based on the priorities that each approach emphasizes, "e.g., initiated social communication versus compliance training, behavior management versus emotional regulation" (manual I, p. 114). Molteni, Guldberg, and Logan (2013) recommend further research to determine how professionals cooperate over time and how the SCERTS Model integrates in regular school settings. Shepherd, Landon, Goedeke, Ty, and Csako (2018), state that because parents rather than clinicians assess the everyday interventions, strict adherence to protocols may be lacking and further conclude, "More research is required to determine the child symptom profiles that predict positive responses to interventions, to ensure that the child is receiving the best of care" (p. 9). Goin-Kochel, Mackintosh, and Myers (2009) emphasize that intervention efficacy is largely dependent on parental commitment to particular therapies and that children with ASD, like all children, grow and develop as part of everyday life. Given the findings of these researchers, the SCERTS Model would benefit from additional empirical verification.

SUMMARY. The SCERTS Model was developed to provide a systematic and flexible approach for caregivers and professionals to work together to improve interactions of individuals with ASD. Manual I is highly informative and comprehensive. The principles contained within the SCERTS Model support flexibility and focus on teamwork among professionals and family members to effect positive change in the child's educational life plan. The model relies on long-term commitment among all members. Through a series of vignettes, Manual II promotes authentic progress, namely, the ability to learn and spontaneously apply meaningful and purposeful activities that provide both functional and relevant skills in a variety of settings and with a variety of partners.

REVIEWER'S REFERENCES

Goin-Kochel, R. P., Mackintosh, V. H., & Myers, B. J. (2009). Parental reports on the efficacy of treatments and therapies for their children with autism spectrum disorders. *Research in Autism Spectrum Disorders, 3,* 528-537.

Molteni, P., Guldberg, K., & Logan, N. (2013). Autism and multidisciplinary teamwork through the SCERTS Model. *British Journal of Special Education, 40*(3), 137-145.

National Research Council. (2001). *Educating children with autism.* Washington, DC: The National Academies Press.

Shepherd, D., Landon, J., Goedeke, S., Ty, K., & Csako, R. (2018). Parents' assessments of their child's autism-related interventions. *Research in Autism Spectrum Disorders, 50,* 1-10.

[145]

Screening Assessment for Gifted Elementary and Middle School Students, Third Edition.

Purpose: Designed "to identify students who are gifted and/or talented in intellectual and academic abilities."

Population: Ages 5-14.

Publication Dates: 1987-2019.

Acronym: SAGES-3.

Scores, 7: Reasoning Ability (Nonverbal Reasoning, Verbal Reasoning), Academic Ability (Language Arts/Social Studies, Mathematics/Science), General Ability.

Administration: Individual or group.

Levels, 2: Grades K-3, Grades 4-8.

Price Data, 2020: $346 per kit including examiner's manual (2019, 163 pages), 10 of each response booklet for Grades K–3 (Nonverbal Reasoning, Language Arts/Social Studies, Verbal Reasoning, and Mathematics/Science), 10 of each response booklet for Grades 4–8 (Nonverbal Reasoning, Language Arts/Social Studies, Verbal Reasoning, and Mathematics/Science), 50 K–3 examiner record forms, 50 4–8 examiner record forms, and scoring transparency; $69 per manual; $23 per 10 Nonverbal Reasoning or Verbal Reasoning response booklets (Grades K–3 or Grades 4–8); $27 per 10 Language Arts/Social Studies or Mathematics/Science response booklets (Grades K–3 or Grades 4–8); $31 per 50 examiner record forms (Grades K–3 or Grades 4–8); $15 per scoring transparency.

Time: 15-30 minutes for administration of each subtest; 60-120 minutes for administration of all subtests.

Comments: Subtests may be used separately; for young students, subtests can be administered on different days.

Authors: Susan K. Johnsen and Anne L. Corn.

Publisher: PRO-ED.

Cross References: For reviews by Carolyn M. Callahan and Howard M. Knoff of the second edition, see 15:219; see T5:2328 (1 reference); for reviews by Lewis R. Aiken and Susana Urbina of the Screening

Assessment for Gifted Elementary Students—Primary, see 12:349; for a review by E. Scott Huebner of the original edition, see 10:327.

Review of the Screening Assessment for Gifted Elementary and Middle School Students, Third Edition by LUCY BARNARD-BRAK, Associate Professor, University of Alabama, and JENNIFER JOLLY, Professor, University of Alabama, Tuscaloosa, AL:

DESCRIPTION. The third edition of the Screening Assessment for Gifted Elementary and Middle School Students (SAGES-3) and its preceding editions were developed to screen and identify students for potential giftedness. Based on the recommendations by reviewers and feedback from test users, improvements and changes were incorporated into the SAGES-3. As there is no consensus regarding the definition of giftedness (Worrell, Subotnik, Olszewski-Kubilius, & Dixon, 2019), the test authors provide current definitions that are often referenced including those from the U.S. Department of Education's Office of Educational Research and Improvement (1993), the No Child Left Behind Act (2002), the National Association for Gifted Children (2010), and the Every Student Succeeds Act (2015). These definitions of giftedness all are based upon intellectual or academic ability or potential in these areas. The test authors acknowledge that other criteria beyond intellectual and academic abilities define giftedness yet report that the majority of states include intellectual and academic abilities as part of their definitions of giftedness.

The SAGES-3 can be administered to a group or individually. The test is not timed. It is suggested that administrators allow 15–20 minutes for each subtest and 1 to 2 hours for the entire test. Depending on students' needs, individual subtests can be administered over several days. The test also can be administered to groups no larger than 30. The SAGES-3 has two forms, one for children in kindergarten through third grade (i.e., K-3) and another for children in fourth through eighth grade. Directions for administration and scoring were revised for clarity, and the test authors recommend that examiners possess some formal training in administering and interpreting assessment data. The SAGES-3 consists of four subtests: Nonverbal Reasoning; Language Arts/Social Studies; Verbal Reasoning; and Mathematics/Science. Subtest scores as well as composite scores for Reasoning Ability, Academic Ability, and General Ability are reported as standard scores referred to as indexes with a mean of 100 and a standard deviation of 15.

DEVELOPMENT. The SAGES-3 is the third edition of this assessment. Prior reviews of the second edition were conducted (e.g., Callahan, 2003; Knoff, 2003). These reviews provided critique that led to subsequent revisions culminating in the SAGES-3. The SAGES-3 clarified its definition of giftedness and added a Verbal Reasoning subtest. The SAGES-3 has a new and expanded normative sample. The third edition also examines and clarifies issues surrounding floors, ceilings, and item gradient.

TECHNICAL. The normative sample was relatively large (n = 808 for K-3; n = 1,023 for Grades 4-8) and nationally representative according to age, race, Hispanic status, gender, and parent education. Evidence for test reliability was established via satisfactory values for the internal consistency of scores, test-retest reliability, and interscorer reliability. The evidence for validity was a combination of content evidence, criterion-related evidence, and construct evidence.

In examining for the presence of differential item functioning according to subgroups, the authors used a significance level of 0.001, which appears to be quite stringent and resulted in limited ability to detect items for bias. The test authors argue that a Bonferroni correction would have resulted in an even lower level of significance given the high number of comparisons. However, more contemporary methods for adjusting for a potentially inflated Type I error rate that accompany the multiple comparisons of differential item functioning analyses exist (e.g., Benjamini & Hochberg, 1995; DeMars, 2010; Li, Brooks, & Johanson, 2012). The test authors should consider re-performing differential item functioning analyses using more contemporary methods in order to more accurately detect potential test bias. On the subtest/composite level, it appears that the differences between White and Black/African American samples ranged from small to medium/moderate (d = -.19 to -.55). Cohen's d values of .20, .50, and .80 and larger may be considered small, medium, and large, respectively (Cohen, 1988). As a result, these small to medium gaps between White and Black/African American students on the subtest/composite level could be further narrowed with updated differential item functioning analyses at the item level.

Additionally, the authors applied a two-parameter logistic item response theory model to the data. A three-parameter logistic model would have permitted them to examine for the presence of guessing and to incorporate this degree of guessing into the analyses. Guessing is a typical occurrence in cognitive ability testing using multiple choice as the response format. For the confirmatory factor analyses, the authors do not explain why subtests—rather than items—were used as indicators.

Criterion measures were provided for both SAGES-3: K–3 and SAGES-3: 4–8. For K-3 the following measures were used: the Cognitive Abilities Test, Form 6; the Wechsler Preschool and Primary Scale of Intelligence–Fourth Edition; and the Young Children's Achievement Test–Second Edition (YCAT-2). For Grades 4–8, the Detroit Test of Learning Abilities–Fifth Edition, the Universal Nonverbal Intelligence Test–Group Abilities Test (UNIT-GAT), and the Woodcock-Johnson IV Tests of Achievement were all used. Some of the correlations between the criterion measures and the SAGES-3 were lower than might be expected for a tool that measures cognitive and academic abilities. For instance, on the kindergarten through third grade form, the correlation between scores on the YCAT-2 and scores on the Mathematics/Science subtest was .56. For Grades 4-8, the correlation between the UNIT-GAT Full Scale Index and the SAGES-3 Nonverbal Reasoning subtest was .57. The authors cite the Hopkins (2002) guidelines in interpreting both *d* values and correlation values. Hopkins (2002) is a non-peer-reviewed website source that discusses effect sizes generally without the context of the consequences of cognitive and academic ability testing. Overall, there was, however, sufficient concurrent evidence of validity between the SAGES-3 and an appropriate and robust selection of measures.

COMMENTARY. The SAGES-3 is a useful measure to help identify giftedness in students as it can be administered individually or as a group. The SAGES-3 provides unique interpretive guidelines by which to associate scores with likelihood of giftedness with five categories ranging from *very likely to be gifted* to *very unlikely to be gifted*. Notably, the individual administration of the SAGES-3 makes use of ceiling rules (i.e., missing three of five consecutive items as a stopping point) that permits a time-efficient means of testing. For group testing, all items are administered. More sophisticated statistical techniques need to be used to assess differential item functioning in order to detect test bias. A higher standard for concurrent evidence of validity should also be applied across the subtests and composites. With the increasing Latinx student populations, the development of a Spanish language version of the SAGES-3 should be considered. This may be a strength of the SAGES-3 as the score differences between Hispanic and non-Hispanic student samples were generally smaller than the score differences between Black/African American and White student samples.

With regard to diagnostic accuracy, the authors discuss the importance of area under the curve (AUC) values in performing receiver operating characteristic (ROC) analyses but report incomplete information (e.g., lacking standard errors or *p*-values) regarding AUC values. Sensitivity and specificity values at different cut points were reported, and sensitivity and specificity were discussed in the test manual as being equally important. Yet, given that the SAGES-3 is a screening tool, sensitivity values are typically recommended to be weighed over and above specificity values in order not to miss any false negatives at the screening stage (Lalkhen & McCluskey, 2008).

SUMMARY. The SAGES-3 provides a reasonably sufficient measure of cognitive and academic ability with accompanying guidelines for identifying potential giftedness. Additionally, the SAGES-3 improves upon the SAGES-2 by providing a more robust normative sample as well as the additional subtest of Verbal Reasoning among other revisions. The unique contribution of the SAGES-3 is in providing guidelines for potential giftedness via a corresponding likelihood of giftedness in addition to assessing intellectual and academic abilities. Based on the changes made to this edition of SAGES, the instrument provides a reliable and valid measure in assessing potential giftedness.

REVIEWERS' REFERENCES

Benjamini, Y., & Hochberg, Y. (1995). Controlling the false discovery rate: A practical and powerful approach to multiple testing. *Journal of the Royal Statistical Society: Series B (Methodological)*, *57*(1), 289-300.

Callahan, C. M. (2003). [Test review of the Screening Assessment for Gifted Elementary and Middle School Students, Second Edition]. In B. S. Plake, J. C. Impara, & R. A. Spies (Eds.), *The fifteenth mental measurements yearbook*. Retrieved from http://marketplace.unl.edu/buros/

Cohen, J. (1988). *Statistical power analysis for the behavioral sciences* (2nd ed.). Hillsdale, NJ: Laurence Erlbaum Associates.

DeMars, C. E. (2010). Type I error inflation for detecting DIF in the presence of impact. *Educational and Psychological Measurement*, *70*(6), 961-972.

Hopkins, W. G. (2002). A scale of magnitudes for effect statistics. Retrieved from http://www.sportsci.org/resource/stats/effectmag.html

Knoff, H. M. (2003). [Test review of the Screening Assessment for Gifted Elementary and Middle School Students, Second Edition]. In B. S. Plake, J. C. Impara, & R. A. Spies (Eds.), *The fifteenth mental measurements yearbook*. Retrieved from http://marketplace.unl.edu/buros/

Lalkhen, A. G., & McCluskey, A. (2008). Clinical tests: Sensitivity and specificity. *Continuing Education in Anaesthesia, Critical Care & Pain, 8*(6), 221–223. doi:10.1093/bjaceaccp/mkn041

Li, Y., Brooks, G. P., & Johanson, G. A. (2012). Item discrimination and type I error in the detection of differential item functioning. *Educational and Psychological Measurement*, *72*(5), 847-861.

Worrell, F. C., Subotnik, R. F., Olszewski-Kubilius, P., & Dixson, D. D. (2019). Gifted students. *Annual Review of Psychology, 70*, 551–576.

Review of the Screening Assessment for Gifted Elementary and Middle School Students, Third Edition by SARAH BONNER, Associate Professor, Hunter College, City University of New York, New York City, NY:

DESCRIPTION. The Screening Assessment for Gifted Elementary and Middle School Students, Third Edition (SAGES-3) is an updated edition of SAGES-2. The test has two levels, Grades K-3 and Grades 4-8. Each level has four multiple-choice subtests: Nonverbal Reasoning, Mathematics/Science, Language Arts/Social Studies, and Verbal Reasoning. Subtest scores are combined to form three composite scores: Reasoning Ability, Academic Ability, and General Ability. The test authors identify four principal uses of scores: (1) to identify students for gifted and talented classes that emphasize reasoning and academics; (2) to screen students from a large general pool or to use as a second-level screening instrument for students nominated for inclusion into a gifted program; (3) to reveal students' relative strengths and weaknesses related to intellectual (reasoning) and academic abilities; and (4) for research about giftedness.

No specific certification or training is required to administer the test, which can be administered to groups of up to 30 (15 for younger students) or individually over a period of days. However, some experience in administering tests and interpreting test scores is recommended. Not all subtests need to be administered, although without administering all four, the General Ability composite cannot be obtained. The subtests are untimed; the estimated time to administer a subtest is up to 30 minutes. The number of items per subtest ranges from 26 to 40. Most items are read aloud to students, who mark their answers to the items directly in the test booklet. Testing procedures include instructions for when to stop individual administration or score a ceiling for group-administered tests. Subtest scores are converted to index scores, which are interpreted as percentile ranks with confidence intervals. The sums of index scores are used to generate the composites. Reasoning Ability is the sum of Verbal and Nonverbal Reasoning subtest indices; Academic Ability is the sum of Mathematics/Science and Language Arts/Social Studies subtests, and General Ability is the sum of all four subtests. Directions for test administration (with administrator scripts) and scoring are clear.

DEVELOPMENT. The development and rationale for each subtest in the SAGES-3 is provided separately; in other words, no rationale is provided for operationalizing giftedness in terms of these particular subdomains or for excluding subdomains suggested by the definitions cited in the test manual, such as creative or productive thinking. No information is provided about whether item content review was provided by experts in the field of giftedness or in the relevant domains.

The method of analogies is relied upon in both the Nonverbal and Verbal Reasoning subtests. The rationale for operationalizing the measurement of these constructs as analogic reasoning is based on theories of intelligence and empirical evidence of item discrimination. For Nonverbal Reasoning items, the test manual states that items were selected to have content that is purported to be "least affected by cultural factors" (p. 53). However, some items may be culturally dated or prone to multiple interpretations from the pictures. For both Nonverbal and Verbal Reasoning subtests, items were selected from an item bank based on item analysis of scores from two samples of gifted students (K-3, n = 1,096; Grades 4-6, n = 928). Demographic information about these samples is not provided; furthermore, it is not clear when these data were collected. The Verbal Reasoning subtest is an addition to the current edition of the test, but the size of the sample for the item analyses is the same across all subtests.

The other two subtests combine academic content domains that are traditionally treated as separate: Language Arts/Social Studies and Mathematics/Science. In each case, the authors make an argument about contemporary trends in disciplinary integration, embodied in the Common Core State Standards (CCSS). The authors provide alignment tables of the subtest items with Common Core strands and national standards in social studies. Interestingly, the alignment tables for the subtests show that no items on K-3 and only one item on Grades 4-8 are aligned to standards in both domains. The rationale for combining mathematics and science is similarly based on the CCSS, as well as on Next Generation Science Standards. The alignment tables for the subtests show that two items on K-3 and two items on Grades 4-8 are aligned to standards in both science and mathematics. No information was provided about who performed the alignment study and how it was conducted. Items appear to have been selected from the same samples of students as in the Nonverbal and Verbal Reasoning subtests, although it is stated that some items on the Language Arts/Social Studies subtest are new to this edition.

TECHNICAL.

Standardization. SAGES-3 was normed on a sample of 1,831 individuals from 25 states. The number of students per grade level ranged from 151 to 189. Professionals self-selected to be part of the norming study and were certified as field examiners based on their expertise and access to potential examinee pools. No information was provided about how students within an examinee's pool were selected for the norming study or the number of students per school. The sampling plan was designed to be representative of the U.S. school-age population. According to tables comparing characteristics of the sample with population characteristics, the sample was representative in most respects. Students with disabilities were underrepresented. The number and type of schools (public, private, charter) were not stated.

Continuous norming procedures were used to generate the index scores, which were standardized with a mean of 100 and a standard deviation of 15. Based on the index scores, the test authors derived percentile ranks and confidence intervals. However, no information was provided about the distributions of the data in the norming sample. Even with continuous norming of non-normal data, norming errors can arise, especially for extreme scores (see Lenhard, Lenhard, Suggate, & Segerer, 2018). Therefore, information about the distribution of scores in the norming sample should have been provided.

Reliability. The evidence about reliability of SAGES-3 includes internal consistency evidence (coefficient alpha), test-retest, and estimates of random rater error. Internal consistency is high across age levels for General Ability (.94 to .98) and is above .90 for Academic Ability and Reasoning Ability with the exception of Academic Ability for 6-year-olds (alpha = .87). Alpha falls below .90 on several subtests, particularly with younger children. A test-retest study for SAGES-3 was conducted with a small number of students (53 for K-3 and 60 for Grades 4-8) with a 2-week interval between administrations. The sample was primarily White and gifted. The size and non-representative nature of this sample makes it nearly impossible to interpret whether similar stability would be found with other groups. Test-retest reliability coefficients are reported with and without correction for restriction of range. The uncorrected coefficients for the composite scores range from .85 to .96. The uncorrected coefficients for the subtest scores range from .69 (Verbal Reasoning, ages 9-0 to 11-11) to .93 (Language Arts/Social Studies, ages 5-0 to 7-11).

To study consistency in scoring, two members of the test publisher's research staff independently scored a random sample of 50 student test forms and obtained a correlation coefficient of .97. Scoring was not studied in field settings.

Validity. As evidence of the internal structure of the SAGES-3, a confirmatory factor analysis was performed. The CFA yielded a one-factor solution, which was interpreted as representing the General Ability latent trait. The fit indices are generally adequate (except for RMSEA = .13 on the K-3 test). No factorial evidence is presented for the interpretation of the two separate composite scores, or for the individual subtest scores. High internal consistency coefficients are not evidence of unidimensionality. Based on the table of zero-order correlations between subtests, it appears that the academic and reasoning subtests are all correlated with one another to similar degrees.

Analyses for ceiling effects are reported. For all composites and subtests, ceilings are very high.

DIF analyses were performed using a fixed DIF detection threshold of .001 adjusted for multiple comparisons to control Type I error. No large DIF effects are reported. Significant differences are reported between Black students and matched samples of White students and between Hispanic students and White students on both subtests and composite scores on both the K-3 and Grades 4-8 tests. Effect sizes up to .5 standard deviations (r = -.26) were observed in the comparison between Black students and White students.

Correlations with a variety of other achievement and aptitude tests used as criterion measures are moderate to high; these are based on small sample studies. The samples have quite different demographics; therefore, it is hard to interpret the results of these studies. Diagnostic accuracy at multiple post-hoc cut scores are provided using IQ values as a criterion. Post-hoc data-based cut scores should always be verified using a cross-validation sample. The sensitivity of the SAGES-3 at the recommended cut scores was quite low in some instances; even for General Ability (the most reliable composite), as many as 35% of Grades 4-8 students who are truly gifted might be ruled out from further assessment with a recommended cut score of 122 (20% at 120).

COMMENTARY. SAGES-3 makes improvements over the previous edition. New and representative norms are provided for interpreting scores. New items are added to eliminate possible ceiling effects, and high ceilings are demonstrated for all composites and subtests. Internal consistency is generally a strength, with the exception of Academic Ability for younger children, which does not meet common standards for individual decision-making.

However, there continue to be concerns about SAGES-3. Of greatest concern is the validity of the test scores in terms of internal structure or dimensionality. Any dimensions that yield scores for interpretation should be validated. The intended use of subtest scores is vague in the manual. If they are to be used, their use should be clarified, and their validity argument(s) should be better-supported. The argument for the integration of Language Arts and Social Studies, or Mathematics and Science, is not strong. A panel should evaluate integrated content (not alignment to separate standards), and factorial analysis should demonstrate the unidimensionality of the subtests. Most of the interpretations seem to rely on the composites, but structural validity evidence for Academic Ability and Reasoning Ability was not presented. In terms of construct evidence of validity, it is a concern that the construct of giftedness may be underrepresented on SAGES-3 due to the reliance on analogies in the Reasoning Ability subtests and exclusion of other dimensions of giftedness.

Another problem is that test-retest information is based on a non-representative sample and is not likely to generalize; stability over time is a particular issue with younger children. Also, the false negative error rates of 15-25% (depending on cut score) when comparing SAGES-3 diagnostic accuracy with IQ values indicate that large numbers of children who qualify for gifted services will be ruled out under this test, even if it is used only as a screening instrument.

SUMMARY. SAGES-3 is a multiple-choice instrument to identify or screen for giftedness among students in kindergarten through eighth grade. Pluses are that it can be group administered and that professional scoring is not required. However, the test does not show strong enough psychometric evidence, particularly as regards validity, to support its use as an instrument for identification of giftedness. The General Ability composite is quite reliable and appears to capture factors associated with giftedness such as analogic reasoning and academic ability. Using the General Ability composite score, SAGES-3 could easily fit into a screening battery for giftedness.

REVIEWER'S REFERENCE

Lenhard, A., Lenhard, W., Suggate, S., & Segerer, R. (2018). A continuous solution to the norming problem. *Assessment, 25*(1), 112-125.

[146]

Self-Report Psychopathy Scale 4th Edition.

Purpose: Designed as a self-report measure to "allow researchers to examine psychopathy through the lens of the PCL [Psychopathy Checklist] structural model."
Population: Ages 18 and older.
Publication Date: 2016.
Acronyms: SRP 4; SRP 4:SF.
Scores, 7: Factor 1 (Interpersonal, Affective), Factor 2 (Lifestyle, Antisocial), Total.
Administration: Individual or group.
Forms, 2: Long, Short.
Price Data, 2020: $198 per kit including manual (2016, 213 pages), 25 self-report forms, and 25 self-report short forms; $83 per manual; $67 per 25 forms (specify long or short).
Time: Typically completed in less than 12 minutes (3-10 minutes for short form) with 10 minutes or less for scoring.
Comments: "The first official self-report version of Hare's PCL-R." "The SRP 4 is designed primarily for use in a research capacity. It is not intended to diagnose specific individuals or to make high-stakes criminal justice decisions."
Authors: Delroy L. Paulhus, Craig S. Neumann, and Robert D. Hare.
Publisher: Multi-Health Systems, Inc.
Cross References: For reviews by Shawn K. Acheson and Joshua W. Payne and by D. Joe Olmi of the Hare Psychopathy Checklist–Revised: 2nd Edition, see 16:101; see also T5:1174 (1 reference); for reviews by Solomon M. Fulero and Gerald L. Stone of The Hare Psychopathy Checklist—Revised, see 12:177 (5 references); see also T4:1127 (3 references).

Review of the Self-Report Psychopathy Scale 4th Edition by GEOFFREY L. THORPE, Professor Emeritus of Psychology, University of Maine, Orono, ME:

DESCRIPTION. Published in 2016, the Self-Report Psychopathy Scale 4th Edition (SRP 4) is the latest addition to the series of professionally completed protocols and self-report instruments originally designed by Robert Hare in the 1980s. The package consists of the 64-item SRP 4 questionnaire, the 29-item Short Form (SRP 4:SF), and a technical manual. The SRP 4 as presented to respondents has two front and back face-sheets that provide the instructions, the items, and the response options to be marked. Each item is rated by circling the appropriate number on a 5-point Likert scale ranging from *strongly disagree* (1) to *strongly agree* (5). With most items, agreement endorses psychopathic traits, but some items are phrased in the other direction and scored in reverse. Examiners score the SRP 4 by removing the face-sheets with the test items and responses to reveal a copy of the respondent's item ratings, scoring instructions, a scoring grid, a profile page with raw score to T score conversion table, and a scale scoring summary table.

DEVELOPMENT. In Hare's model, psychopathy—or psychopathic behavior—comprises a set of interpersonal, affective, impulsive, and social deviance elements (Acheson & Payne, 2005). Specifically, his measures assess such personality features as exploitative and callous attitudes and lack of empathy in addition to poorly regulated and delinquent behavior (Olmi, 2005). Current diagnostic criteria for the related construct of antisocial personality disorder place greater emphasis on social deviance and criminality, arguably to improve interrater reliability: Professionals conducting initial interviews and records reviews in clinical settings may be more likely to agree on how many arrests an interviewee has had than on his or her levels of disconstraint or deficiencies in empathy. The broader construct of psychopathy is not a formal diagnosis, though it "encompasses clinical features of several personality disorders" (DeMatteo, Fairfax-Columbo, & Scully, 2017, p. 2744).

Hare and his colleagues have incrementally refined their assessment of psychopathy by pursuing two approaches in parallel. The first, beginning in 1980 with a 22-item checklist and progressing to the Psychopathy Checklist-Revised (PCL-R; Hare, 1991) and the PCL-R 2nd Edition (Hare, 2003), calls for trained professionals to score items by "integrating extensive interview and collateral information according to specified criteria" (SRP 4 manual, p. 2). The second, which has progressed through first (SRP-I, 1985), second (SRP-II, 1989), experimental (SRP-E, 2007), and third (SRP-III, 2009) editions before culminating in the SRP 4, uses the self-report format. The test authors claim to have established that, despite the different formats, the same factor structure underpins the PCL-R and the SRP 4, supporting the designation of four first-order scales (Interpersonal Exploitation, Callous Affect, Erratic Lifestyle, and Antisocial Behavior facets) constituting the two second-order factors (Interpersonal/Affective and Lifestyle/Antisocial). Because the four facets are intercorrelated, they can be summed to produce a Total Score.

Traditionally, users of the professionally administered PCL-R have been required to undertake special training in interviewing and interpretive procedures, but the SRP 4 authors argue that its self-report-based Total Score may stand alone as a reliable and valid indicator of psychopathy.

TECHNICAL. The SRP 4 was standardized with four large samples of respondents: 638 from the general community in Oregon, 788 college undergraduates in Texas, 304 male offenders from a correctional facility in Wisconsin, and 389 university undergraduates (mostly female) from Belgium. Because of the large sample sizes, statistical comparisons included effect sizes in addition to significance testing. The sample distributions were essentially normal, with some exceptions. Notably, the Antisocial Behavior facet showed a positive skew in the non-offender samples with, as expected, fewer respondents than usual at the high end of the scale (strikingly evident among the 28 frequency distributions presented in the test manual). The sample differences were largely attributable to higher scores in the offender sample, with large effect sizes for practically all comparisons.

The PCL-R was the validation criterion for the SRP 4 tests. Confirmatory factor analysis and structural equation modeling supported a four-factor structure of the SRP 4 that echoed that of the PCL-R and in which each of the facets could be treated as a unidimensional factor. The test developers sought to establish the SRP 4's psychometric properties at the scale and item levels, employing item response theory methodology to assess item-to-factor relationships. That in turn required demonstrations of unidimensionality in the content domain of each scale.

Internal consistency estimates were strong, particularly for Total Scores, for which alpha coefficients ranged from .89 to .92 in the four samples. In a sample of 48 students, the test-retest correlation was also strong: With 10 weeks intervening between the first and second test administrations, the coefficient was .82.

Construct evidence of validity was demonstrated in the equivalent factor structure of the PCL-R and the SRP 4, and also by the finding that, in the forensic sample, those defined as psychopathic by scoring 30 or above on the PCL-R also showed higher scores on the SRP 4 scales, almost always with large effect sizes. Predictive evidence of validity was shown when students scoring high on the SRP-III (which was nearly identical to the SRP 4) were found to be more likely than others to cheat on exams and plagiarize term papers. Discriminant validity emerged from correlations with other measures assessing similar or differing concepts such as narcissism, sadism, and Machiavellianism.

The test manual provides numerous figures and tables that summarize the data from the standardization samples in considerable detail. The psychometric properties of the SRP 4:SF are reported to be very similar to those of the SRP 4 on all scales. The test authors argue that short forms derived from modern test theory modeling may show stronger properties than the longer originals (see also Thorpe & Favia, 2012).

The self-report format of these tests invites questions about respondents' credibility. The developers addressed this concern by citing data that show negative correlations between SRP scores and measures of malingering and impression management. Professionally appraised PCL-R protocols produce similar negative correlations. Individuals with high scores for psychopathy do not necessarily dissemble and may even flaunt their antisocial worldview in some contexts.

COMMENTARY. Hare's PCL-R has been widely accepted as the gold standard in the assessment of psychopathy, but the previous requirements for special training and exhaustive interviewing and records perusal may have limited its applicability. In that context, news of the availability of the SRP 4 and its short form as acceptable self-report forms would be cause for celebration among test users who assess the construct in forensic settings (conducting pre-sentence risk evaluations, for example). The test developers state that: "[A]mong self-report instruments, the SRP 4 is the measure of choice for assessing psychopathy in both basic *and applied settings*" (manual, p. 1, emphasis added), but their position on appropriate applications is later qualified: "The SRP 4 is designed primarily for use in ... research" and "is not intended to diagnose specific individuals or to make high-stakes criminal justice decisions" (p. 4). Professionals using the SRP 4 and its short form may have to resolve some ambiguity in the tests' intended applications.

Protocols that assess the risk of reoffending in sex offenders and in violent offenders in general have included PCL-R scores in the list of coded elements. The Violence Risk Appraisal Guide (VRAG) and the Sex Offender Risk Appraisal Guide (SORAG; Harris, Rice, Quinsey, & Cormier, 2015) both use the PCL-R as one of the 12 (VRAG) or 14 (SORAG) scored elements, and in each case the PCL-R score is given greater weight than the other components; it has the strongest correlation with total scores. In the Violence Risk Appraisal Guide—Revised (VRAG-R; Harris et al., 2015) only the Antisocial Behavior facet of the PCL-R is scored. If future research were to support replacement of the PCL-R by the SRP 4 or its short form there would be economies of time and effort in completing the risk appraisal guides.

SUMMARY. The SRP 4 and the SRP 4:SF represent the latest additions to the family of tests of psychopathy created and developed by Hare and his colleagues over several decades. Classical test theory and item response theory methodologies have established the sound psychometric properties of these new self-report tests, which have strong links to the well-established and widely used PCL-R. The test developers make a well-reasoned case for the potential utility of these tests to assess psychopathy in basic and applied settings but are cautious about the tests' suitability for use with individuals in forensic settings until further research has placed this application on a secure empirical foundation.

The SRP 4 and the SRP 4:SF are recommended as convenient, efficient, and readily accessible self-report measures of psychopathy with robust psychometric properties and an impressive developmental pedigree.

REVIEWER'S REFERENCES

Acheson, S. K., & Payne, J. W. (2005). [Test review of Hare Psychopathy Checklist-Revised: 2nd Edition.] In R. A. Spies & B. S. Plake (Eds.), *The sixteenth mental measurements yearbook*. Retrieved from http://marketplace.unl.edu/buros/

DeMatteo, D., Fairfax-Columbo, J., & Scully, M. (2017). Psychopathy. In A. Wenzel (Ed.), *The SAGE encyclopedia of abnormal and clinical psychology* (Vol. 5, pp. 2744-2748). Thousand Oaks, CA: SAGE Publications.

Hare, R. D. (1991). *Manual for the Psychopathy Checklist–Revised*. Toronto, ON: Multi-Health Systems.

Hare, R. D. (2003). *Hare Psychopathy Checklist–Revised (PCL-R) 2nd edition: Technical manual*. Toronto, ON: Multi-Health Systems.

Harris, G. T., Rice, M. E., Quinsey, V. L., & Cormier, C. A. (2015). *Violent offenders: Appraising and managing risk* (3rd ed.). Washington, DC: American Psychological Association.

Olmi, D. J. (2005). [Test review of Hare Psychopathy Checklist-Revised: 2nd Edition.] In R. A. Spies & B. S. Plake (Eds.), *The sixteenth mental measurements yearbook*. Retrieved from http://marketplace.unl.edu/buros/

Thorpe, G. L., & Favia, A. (2012). *Data analysis using item response theory methodology: An introduction to selected programs and applications*. https://digitalcommons.library.umaine.edu/psy_facpub/20/

Review of the Self-Report Psychopathy Scale 4th Edition by JAMES M. WOOD, Professor of Psychology, University of Texas at El Paso, El Paso, TX:

DESCRIPTION. The Self-Report Psychopathy Scale 4th edition (SRP 4) is a 64-item self-report questionnaire designed to measure the same constructs as the well-known Hare Psychopathy Check List–Revised (PCL-R; Hare, 1991, 2003). The SRP 4 has seven scales, each corresponding to a scale of the PCL-R.

First, the SRP 4 yields a Total Score, a global measure of psychopathic personality calculated from all 64 items. Second, the SRP 4 has four 16-item facet scales, reflecting the four intercorrelated first-order factors that emerged from factor analyses of the SRP 4 items. These facet scales are (a) Interpersonal Exploitation (Exploitation), reflecting a tendency to manipulate and take advantage of others; (b) Callous Affect (Callous), reflecting low empathy and a lack of concern for other people; (c) Erratic Lifestyle (Erratic), reflecting a self-seeking and irresponsible lifestyle; and (d) Antisocial Behavior (Antisocial; sometimes referred to as the Criminal Tendency facet), reflecting criminal activities and other serious violations of norms and rules. Third, the SRP 4 has two factor scales that represent the two second-order factors that underlie the four facet scales. These factor scales are named simply Factor 1 (calculated by summing the Exploitation and Callous scores) and Factor 2 (calculated by summing the Erratic and Antisocial scores).

The SRP 4 has an abbreviated form with a similar format, the 29-item Self-Report Psychopathy Scale 4th Edition Short Form (SRP 4:SF), with seven scales that correspond to those of the full SRP 4. The items on the SRP 4 and SRP 4:SF use a Likert-like response format with response options ranging from 1 (*strongly disagree*) to 5 (*strongly agree*). The SRP 4 is intended for use with individuals 18 years of age and older. Items are written at a fifth-grade reading level. The SRP 4 can usually be administered in less than 15 minutes and scored by hand in less than 10. The SRP 4:SF can be administered in 3 to 10 minutes.

DEVELOPMENT. Psychopathy is a dimension of personality characterized by several negative traits, including irresponsibility, egocentricity, callousness, exploitation of others, and antisocial behaviors. In the 1980s, Hare (1980, 1985b) developed a structured clinical instrument, the Psychopathy Check List (PCL), to assess psychopathy in forensic settings. After conducting a structured interview and reviewing file data, a clinician rated the respondent on 22 criteria (i.e., behaviors and personality traits characteristic of psychopathy). These ratings were summed to yield a PCL Total Score that reflected the respondent's level of psychopathy. The PCL was later revised as the Psychopathy Check List–Revised (PCL-R; Hare 1991, 2003), with the number of psychopathy criteria reduced to 20.

Hare refined his conceptualization of psychopathy over several decades and modified the PCL-R accordingly. In the 1990s, Hare (1991) separated the criteria of the PCL-R into two factors: Factor 1, reflecting interpersonal and affective features of psychopathy, and Factor 2, reflecting impulsive and antisocial behaviors. Later Hare (2003) subdivided Factor 1 into the facets now known as Callous Affect and Interpersonal Manipulation and Factor 2 into the facets of Erratic Lifestyle and Antisocial Behaviors.

While creating the original PCL in the 1980s, Hare (1985a) also developed the SRP, an unpublished 29-item self-report instrument to measure psychopathy. As the PCL-R was updated to reflect Hare's new conceptualizations, so was the SRP. Hare, Harpur, and Hemphill (1989) developed the 60-item SRP-II with subscales parallel to Factor 1 and Factor 2 of the PCL-R. Several versions of the SRP, now known collectively as the SRP Experimental (SRP E), were later developed to incorporate the four facets of the PCL-R and eliminate some items measuring anxiety or its absence. Eventually a 64-item version, the SRP-III, was developed but not published (Paulhus, Hemphill, & Hare, 2009). After minor changes in item wording, this 64-item version was released as the SRP 4 and published with an extensive technical manual.

TECHNICAL. Research findings regarding the psychometric properties of the SRP 4 and SRP 4:SF are summarized in the SRP 4 test manual and in a review by Sellbom, Lilienfeld, Fowler, and McCrary (2018).

Standardization. Tables in the manual present means and standard deviations for all SRP 4 and SRP 4:SF scales in three North American reference samples: (a) a Community reference sample (N = 638) of adults in Oregon, (b) a College reference sample (N = 788) of undergraduates in Texas, and (c) an Offender reference sample (N = 304) from a correctional facility in Wisconsin. The test manual does not explain how the samples were constructed, but random sampling does not appear to have been used, and the reference groups do not seem representative of definable populations. For instance, the Community reference sample was 98.2% White with an average age of 49.2 years.

Reliability. The internal reliability of SRP 4 scales as reported in its manual range from acceptable to excellent. In the three reference samples, alpha coefficients ranged from .89 to .92 for the Total Score, .80 to .89 for Factor 1, and .83 to .85 for Factor 2. For the facets, coefficient alpha was consistently above .70. Other researchers have reported similar positive findings regarding internal reliability (Gordts, Uzieblo, Neumann, Van den Bussche, & Rossi, 2017; Sandvik et al., 2012; Tew, Harkins, & Dixon, 2015; Wilson, Miller, Zeichner, Lynam, & Widiger, 2011).

Relevant to the evaluation of internal reliability, the test manual reports confirmatory factor analyses (CFA) of data from the three reference samples and a fourth sample of European college students. In each sample, the SRP 4 items fell onto four clearly defined factors corresponding to the predicted four facets of the test. However, about eight of the items loaded weakly on their predicted factors. CFAs by other researchers have generally reported similar results, confirming that the SRP 4 has four factors but that some of its items load poorly on these factors (see review by Boduszek & Debowska, 2016). In terms of fit indices for the 64-item measure, results were mixed, with the fit value for the incremental fit index falling short of the accepted standard, and the absolute and parsimony fit indices suggesting the four-factor model accounts adequately and parsimoniously for item covariances.

The test manual reports that the temporal stability of SRP 4 scores ranges from good to very good, with test-retest reliability coefficients of .82 for the Total Score and .70 to .85 for facet scores over an interval of 10 weeks. Similar positive findings regarding temporal stability have been reported by Gordts et al. (2017).

The test manual also provides information regarding internal reliability for the short form of the test, the SRP 4:SF. In the three SRP 4 reference samples, alpha coefficients ranged from .82 to .89 for the SRP 4:SF Total Score, from .73 to .86 for Factor 1, and from .71 to .78 for Factor 2. The average alpha values were generally acceptable (> .70) for the Manipulation and Erratic facets, but not for the Callous and Antisocial facets (for other studies of internal reliability, see Gordts et al., 2017 and Tew et al., 2015).

Validity. This section of the review reports on the validity of the SRP 4 and the nearly identical 64-item version of the SRP-III, but not earlier versions of the test. For succinctness, the SRP-III and SRP 4 will both be referred to here as the "SRP 4."

Extensive evidence indicates that the SRP 4 Total Score provides a valid measure of psychopathy. First, the Total Score has been shown to correlate moderately (r = .30 to .44) with psychopathy scores on the PCL-R (Kelsey, Rogers, & Robinson, 2015; Sandvik et al., 2012; Tew et al., 2015). Second, as shown in a study by Wilson et al. (2011), the SRP 4 Total Score demonstrates good convergence (.70 to .80) with the total scores of other well-known self-report psychopathy tests, including the Psychopathic Personality Inventory–Revised (Lilienfeld & Widows, 2005), the Levenson Self-Report Psychopathy Scale (Levenson, Kiehl, & Fitzpatrick, 1995), and the Elemental Psychopathy Assessment (Lynam et al., 2011). Third, several researchers have found that the Total Score is related to antisocial and aggressive behaviors and attitudes (Debowska, Boduszek, Kola, & Hyland, 2014; Jones & Paulhus, 2010; Neal & Sellbom, 2012; Williams, Nathanson, & Paulhus, 2010).

The validity of scores from the SRP 4 Antisocial and Erratic facets is well supported by research findings. Most researchers have found a moderate correlation (r > .45) between the SRP 4 Antisocial facet and the PCL-R Antisocial facet and a correlation almost as large (r > .40) between the SRP 4 Erratic facet and the PCL-R Erratic facet (Kelsey et al., 2015; Sandvik et al, 2012; Tew et al., 2015). Other evidence of convergence has also been reported (Gordts et al., 2017; Neal & Sellbom, 2012; Seibert, Miller, Few, Zeichner, & Lynam, 2011; Wilson et al., 2011).

Test scores from SRP 4 Manipulation and Callous facets have fared less well in validity studies. Researchers have generally found that these two facets correlate only weakly (r < .30) with their corresponding PCL-R facets (Kelsey et al., 2015; Sandvik et al, 2012; Tew et al., 2015). Furthermore, the SRP 4 Manipulation and Callous facets appear to have lower correlations with their corresponding PCL-R facets than with the PCL-R Erratic and Antisocial facets, suggesting problematic discriminant validity. However, several studies have found support for the convergent evidence of validity for test scores from these two SRP 4 facet scales (Gordts et al., 2017; Neal & Sellbom, 2012; Sandvik et al., 2012; Seibert et al., 2011; Watt & Brooks, 2012; Wilson et al., 2011).

Evidence of validity for SRP 4 Factor 1 and Factor 2 scores has received virtually no attention from researchers and is barely touched on in the test manual. Regarding validity evidence for scores from the abbreviated SRP 4:SF, Tew et al. (2015) reported that the SRP 4:SF Total Score correlated .96 with the SRP 4 Total Score and .40 with the PCL-R Total Score. The SRP 4:SF Erratic and Antisocial facets correlated about .90 with their corresponding SRP facets and about .40 with their corresponding PCL-R facets, whereas the SRP 4:SF Manipulation and Callous facets correlated about .93 with their corresponding SRP facets but only about .19 with the corresponding PCL-R facets. Findings from this study and others (Bettison, Mahmut, & Stevenson, 2013; Declercq, Carter & Neumann, 2015; Gordts et al., 2017; Neumann & Pardini, 2014) suggest that SRP 4:SF scores have approximately the same evidence of validity as their corresponding SRP 4 scores.

COMMENTARY. The SRP 4 was developed by leading experts on psychopathy and related dimensions of dark personality. The test is set apart from similar self-report measures because its scales were designed to reflect the same dimensions of psychopathy as the iconic PCL-R.

The SRP 4 Total Score is the test's most successful feature. It is highly correlated ($r > .70$) with other leading self-report measures of psychopathy, and moderately correlated ($r = .30$ to $.44$) with the Total Score of the PCL-R. Researchers who need only a global self-report measure of psychopathy would do well to consider the SRP 4 Total Score or the SRP 4:SF Total Score. Both have well-documented evidence of validity and are relatively short compared with most global self-report measures of psychopathy.

The SRP 4 facet scores are more problematic. The Erratic and Antisocial facet scores correlate at acceptable levels with their corresponding facets on the PCL-R, but the Manipulation and Callous facet scores do not. Researchers interested in exploring the PCL-R facets using self-report measures will find the SRP 4 facet scales to be only partially adequate for that purpose. The validity of the SRP 4 factor scales has barely been examined, so use of these scales cannot presently be recommended.

The SRP 4 manual provides scant information about its three reference groups, but clearly they do not constitute representative samples from identifiable populations. The use of these groups for normative comparisons or to calculate T scores is not recommended.

Finally, it should be emphasized that, although the SRP 4 has potential as a research tool, its use in applied settings for forensic and clinical evaluations is problematic. The test lacks adequate norms, and its classifications of psychopaths correspond poorly to classifications based on the PCL-R (Kelsey et al., 2015). Furthermore, as the test manual warns, the SRP 4 is vulnerable to positive response bias and likely to give misleading results when respondents have an incentive to present themselves in an unrealistically favorable light.

SUMMARY. The SRP 4 is a self-report instrument designed to measure the same features of psychopathy as the well-known PCL-R. It has been partly successful in achieving that goal. The SRP 4 Total Score provides a reliable and valid global self-report measure of psychopathy that is moderately correlated with the PCL-R Total Score. The abbreviated version of this scale, the SRP 4:SF, is highly correlated with its parent scale, achieves similar levels of validity, and has the advantage of being very short compared with other global measures of psychopathy. Scores from two of the SRP 4 facet scales (Erratic, Antisocial) correlate reasonably well with their corresponding PCL-R facets, but the other two (Manipulation, Callous) do not, and their discriminant validity is poor. The SRP 4 lacks adequate norms and may yield misleading results when respondents are motivated to represent themselves in an unrealistically positive light. Although the SRP 4 is likely to prove valuable in research, its use in forensic and clinical evaluations is not recommended.

REVIEWER'S REFERENCES

Bettison, T. M., Mahmut, M. K., & Stevenson, R. J. (2013). The relationship between psychopathy and olfactory tasks sensitive to orbitofrontal cortex function in a non-criminal student sample. *Chemosensory Perception, 6,* 198-210.

Boduszek, D., & Debowska, A. (2016). Critical evaluation of psychopathy measurement (PCL-R and SRP-III/SF) and recommendations for future research. *Journal of Criminal Justice, 44,* 1-12.

Debowska, A., Boduszek, D., Kola, S., & Hyland, P. (2014). A bifactor model of the Polish version of the Hare Self-Report Psychopathy Scale. *Personality and Individual Differences, 69,* 231-237.

Declercq, F., Carter, R., & Neumann, C. S. (2015). Assessing psychopathic traits and criminal behavior in a young adult female community sample using the Self-Report Psychopathy Scale. *Journal of Forensic Science, 60,* 928-935.

Gordts, S., Uzieblo, K., Neumann, C., Van den Bussche, E., & Rossi, G. (2017). Validity of the Self-Report Psychopathy Scales (SRP-III Full and Short Versions) in a community sample. *Assessment, 24,* 308-325.

Hare, R. D. (1980). A research scale for the assessment of psychopathy in criminal populations. *Personality and Individual Differences, 1,* 111-119.

Hare, R. D. (1985a). Comparison of procedures for the assessment of psychopathy. *Journal of Consulting and Clinical Psychology, 53,* 7-16.

Hare, R. D. (1985b). *The Psychopathy Checklist.* Unpublished manuscript, University of British Columbia, Vancouver, BC, Canada.

Hare, R. D. (1991). The Hare Psychopathy Checklist-Revised. Toronto, Ontario, Canada: Multi-Health Systems.

Hare, R. D. (2003). Hare Psychopathy Checklist-Revised: 2nd Edition. Toronto, Ontario, Canada: Multi-Health Systems.

Hare, R. D., Harpur, T. J., & Hemphill, J. F. (1989). *Scoring Pamphlet for the Self-Report Psychopathy Scale: SRP-II.* Unpublished document, Simon Fraser University, Vancouver, Canada.

Jones, D. N., & Paulhus, D. L. (2010). Different provocations trigger aggression in narcissists and psychopaths. *Social Psychological and Personality Science, 1,* 12-18.

Kelsey, K. R., Rogers, R., & Robinson, E. V. (2015). Self-report measures of psychopathy: What is their role in forensic assessments? *Journal of Psychopathology and Behavioral Assessment, 37,* 380-391.
Levenson, M. R., Kiehl, K. A., & Fitzpatrick, C. M. (1995). Assessing psychopathic attributes in a non-institutionalized population. *Journal of Personality and Social Psychology, 68,* 151-158.
Lilienfeld, S. O., & Widows, M. (2005). *Manual for the Psychopathic Personality Inventory—Revised (PPI-R).* Lutz, FL: Psychological Assessment Resources.
Lynam, D. R., Gaughan, E. T., Miller, J. D., Miller, D. J., Mullins-Sweatt, S., & Widiger, T. A. (2011). Assessing the basic traits associated with psychopathy: Development and validation of the Elemental Psychopathy Assessment. *Psychological Assessment, 23,* 108-124.
Neal, T. M. S., & Sellbom, M. (2012) Examining the factor structure of the Hare Self-Report Psychopathy Scale. *Journal of Personality Assessment, 94,* 244-253.
Neumann, C. S., & Pardini, D. (2014). Factor structure and construct validity of the Self-Report Psychopathy (SRP) Scale and the Youth Psychopathic Traits Inventory (YPI) in young men. *Journal of Personality Disorders, 28,* 419-433.
Paulhus, D. L., Hemphill, J. F., & Hare, R. D. (2009). *Manual for the Self-Report Psychopathy (SRP-III) scale.* Unpublished document, University of British Columbia, Vancouver, Canada.
Sandvik, A. M., Hansen, A. L., Kristensen, M. V., Johnsen, B. H., Logan, C., & Thornton, D. (2012). Assessment of psychopathy: Intercorrelations between Psychopathy Checklist Revised, Comprehensive Assessment of Psychopathic Personality–Institutional Rating Scale, and Self-Report of Psychopathy Scale—III, *International Journal of Forensic Mental Health, 11,* 280-288.
Seibert, L. A., Miller, J. D., Few, L. R., Zeichner, A., & Lynam, D. R. (2011). An examination of the structure of self-report psychopathy measures and their relations with general traits and externalizing behaviors. *Personality Disorders: Theory, Research, and Treatment, 2,* 193-208.
Sellbom, M., Lilienfeld, S. O., Fowler, K. A., & McCrary, K. L. (2018). The self-report assessment of psychopathy: Challenges, pitfalls, and promises. In C. J. Patrick (Ed.), *Handbook of Psychopathology* (2nd ed., 211-258). New York, NY: Guilford Press.
Tew, J., Harkins, L., & Dixon, L. (2015). Assessing the reliability and validity of the Self-Report Psychopathy Scales in a UK offender population. *The Journal of Forensic Psychiatry and Psychology, 26,* 166-184.
Watt, B. D., & Brooks, N. S. (2012). Self-report psychopathy in an Australian community sample. *Psychiatry, Psychology and Law, 19,* 389-401.
Williams, K. M., Nathanson, C., & Paulhus, D. L. (2010). Identifying and profiling scholastic cheaters: Their personality, cognitive ability, and motivation. *Journal of Experimental Psychology: Applied, 16,* 293-307.
Wilson, L., Miller, J. D., Zeichner, A., Lynam, D. R., & Widiger, T. A. (2011). An examination of the validity of the Elemental Psychopathy Assessment: Relations with other psychopathy measures, aggression, and externalizing behaviors. *Journal of Psychopathology and Behavioral Assessment, 33,* 315-322.

[147]

Shaywitz DyslexiaScreen.

Purpose: Designed to help teachers identify students at risk for reading difficulties.
Population: Students in Grades K-3.
Publication Dates: 2016-2018.
Scores: Total score only.
Administration: Individual.
Forms, 4: 0-3, corresponding to student's grade level.
Price Data, 2020: $49 per manual (2018, 38 pages); $1 per administration and report.
Time: Fewer than 5 minutes for administration.
Comments: Screening form completed by teacher; available only in digital format.
Author: Sally E. Shaywitz.
Publisher: Pearson.

Review of the Shaywitz DyslexiaScreen by ALICE CORKILL, Department Chair, University of Nevada, Las Vegas, Las Vegas, NV:

DESCRIPTION. The Shaywitz DyslexiaScreen is designed for use by classroom teachers to screen young children (ages 5:0 through 9:11) for dyslexia. Four forms of the DyslexiaScreen are available. Form 0 is for students in kindergarten, ages 5:0 to 6:11; Form 1 is for first graders, ages 6:0 to 7:11; Form 2 is for second graders, ages 7:0 to 8:11; and Form 3 is for third graders, ages 8:0 to 9:11. Each form includes 10 items with the exception of Form 1, which includes 12 items. The DyslexiaScreen takes less than 5 minutes to complete. Classroom teachers review each DyslexiaScreen item with a specific child in mind and identify the frequency of the DyslexiaScreen item behavior displayed by the child in question. DyslexiaScreen items address language and academic behaviors, academic mastery levels, learning problems, and grade progression likelihood. The test administrator records responses to each item using the test publisher's online platform. Various Likert-type scales are used in the item responses. On Form 1, for example (the form this reviewer examined), Items 1 through 6 used a 6-point scale (*never, rarely, sometimes, often, almost always, always*); Items 7 and 8 used a different 6-point scale (*definitely likely, very likely, moderately likely, moderately unlikely, very unlikely, not at all likely*); Item 9 used a 5-point scale (*highest, high, middle, low, lowest*); and the final three items used another 5-point scale (*superior, above average, average, below average, lowest 1-2 in class*). A "Teacher's Quick Guide for Item Rating" appears in the online test manual and includes behavioral examples associated with each item on each form.

The DyslexiaScreen is computer-scored, and a four-page report is delivered. The Individual Report includes student information, any additional comments the test administrator may have included before responding to the DyslexiaScreen items, a score summary that indicates whether the examinee is at risk for dyslexia, a summary of the results, suggested next steps for the student in question, suggestions for additional screening and further assessment, intervention and progress monitoring recommendations, a list of strategies for family and/or caregivers, and a list of the items and responses for which the student met the criteria for being at risk for dyslexia. Students are identified overall as *at risk* or *not at risk* for dyslexia. The Group Report includes the same information (minus the item responses) collated for a larger number of students.

Professionals who wish to administer and interpret the results from the DyslexiaScreen should have appropriate training in using clinical assessments.

DEVELOPMENT. The DyslexiaScreen includes a subset of items from the Multigrade

Inventory for Teachers (MIT). The test developer used data from the Connecticut Longitudinal Study (e.g., Shaywitz, Fletcher, Holahan, & Shaywitz, 1992) to select items from the MIT with point-biserial correlations greater than .30 with student group status (dyslexia or typical) for potential inclusion on the DyslexiaScreen. Through a series of analyses that were not well described in the test manual, four forms were developed. No rationale or description is provided that identifies the correspondence of items on the four forms to the content domains the DyslexiaScreen claims to address (e.g., language and academic behaviors, academic mastery levels, learning problems, and grade progression likelihood). In addition, there is no explanation for why Form 1 requires 12 items to address the same content that is addressed by 10 items on the other three forms. The test manual indicates that cut scores were established but does not clearly describe the method/procedure used.

TECHNICAL.

Standardization. The DyslexiaScreen was normed as part of the Connecticut Longitudinal Study. The Connecticut study was employed to determine whether students with dyslexia could be distinguished from non-dyslexia diagnosed students from a cognitive/academic perspective. In the Connecticut study, 414 students (52% female) were followed from Grades 1 through 12 (entering kindergarten in 1983). The students in this sample were predominantly White (85%) with parents who had at least a high school education (86%; of this 29% had some college or technical school, and 29.5% had a bachelor's degree). At Grades 2 and 4, scores from the Woodcock-Johnson Psycho-Educational Battery and the Wechsler Intelligence Scale for Children–Revised were used to identify students with dyslexia. Data from the Connecticut study sample were used to determine the cut score for the DyslexiaScreen. The cut score was then validated through a national sample (n = 279) that did not closely match the Connecticut study sample (e.g., national sample: 61.7% White; 44.1% had some college or technical school). These data were used to validate the cut score. (See the "Validity Evidence" section below in this review.)

Reliability. Internal consistency reliability (coefficient alpha) values range from .87 to .97 for the four DyslexiaScreen forms based on raw scores or dichotomous items. Sample sizes for the reliability values were not reported in the test manual. [Editor's note: The test publisher advised the Buros Center for Testing that the sample used was the same as that of the validation sample described above.]

Validity Evidence. Validity evidence for the survey included comparing DyslexiaScreen classifications (*at risk* or *not at risk*) with scores from the Reading Skills, the Word Reading, and the Pseudoword Decoding subtests of the Wechsler Individual Achievement Test—Third Edition (WIAT-III) subtests (Forms 0 and 1) and comparing DyslexiaScreen classifications with scores from a WIAT-III Dyslexia Index composite score (Forms 2 and 3). Examinees with scores below 85 on WIAT-III measures were placed into a dyslexia group; a non-dyslexia group was also identified for comparison. Students in the dyslexia group demonstrated significantly higher mean scores across all forms of the DyslexiaScreen compared to the non-dyslexia group. Validity evidence provided using the national sample described in the "Standardization" section of this review demonstrates that DyslexiaScreen scores correlate negatively with a variety of appropriate WIAT-III subtest scores. Correlation coefficients between the WIAT-III subtests and scores on Forms 0 and 1 ranged from -.56 to -.74; correlations with Forms 2 and 3 ranged from -.54 to -.80. In addition, validity evidence suggests that classroom teachers were able to use the DyslexiaScreen to identify students at risk for dyslexia with 70% to 100% accuracy.

COMMENTARY AND SUMMARY. The Shaywitz DyslexiaScreen is a quick, relatively easy, and cost-effective screening method ($1 per administration and report; $49 per manual at the time of this writing) for determining whether a child ages 5:0 to 9:11 is at risk for dyslexia as long as the ultimate goal is to refer children identified as *at risk* for additional testing or intervention services. The utility of the DyslexiaScreen relies heavily on a classroom teacher's subjective observations of children in the classroom and the teacher's ultimate ability to translate those observations into accurate ratings for the 10 or 12 items on the instrument. Little information was provided as to how the DyslexiaScreen items were selected, and no explanation was provided as to which items address each dyslexia-related content area (although one could easily speculate, at least with respect to some of the items). In addition, no information was provided as to why Form 1 required 12 items to determine dyslexia risk as opposed to the 10 items included on the other three forms. Printing a copy of the "Teacher's Quick Guide for Item Rating" from the online resources before beginning may facilitate navigation between the online rating form and the guide. The DyslexiaScreen administrator does not score the student responses; thus, potential scoring errors are minimized. The score summary (either *at risk* or *not at risk* for dyslexia) is clear. The information provided in the report is clear and fairly easy to understand. This reviewer was allotted one trial with the DyslexiaScreen and was easily able to develop a set of responses for an *at risk* result. The report reviewed, therefore, provided a series of strategies or suggested activities for working with an at-risk child. There was no evidence of research to support the included strategies either in the report or in the test manual. In addition, no evidence of research use of the DyslexiaScreen was provided the test manual.

REVIEWER'S REFERENCE

Shaywitz, B. A., Fletcher, J. M., Holahan, J. M., & Shaywitz, S. E. (1992). Discrepancy compared to low achievement definitions of reading disability: Results from the Connecticut Longitudinal Study. *Journal of Learning Disabilities, 25*(10), 639-648. doi:10.1177/002221949202501003

Review of the Shaywitz DyslexiaScreen by KAREN MACKLER, District Psychologist, Lawrence Public Schools, Lawrence, NY:

DESCRIPTION. The Shaywitz DyslexiaScreen is a rating scale completed by teachers of children in kindergarten through third grade. The scale was developed by Dr. Sally Shaywitz, who has long been associated with reading and reading disorders and is perhaps best known for her book *Overcoming Dyslexia* (2003). The test author asserts that the rating scale is an excellent tool for identifying children who are at risk for reading difficulties or dyslexia.

The checklist is brief and takes less than 5 minutes to complete for each student. It is only available digitally, through the test publisher's online platform. It also can be found as part of Pearson's Universal Screening application. Administration and scoring are completed via computer; the scale cannot be accessed on mobile devices. The measure may be completed remotely after invitation. The rater needs an ID number, full name, and date of birth for each child being rated. Individual and group reports are available. Results yield an *at risk* or *not at risk* designation. Research for the measure is based on the Connecticut Longitudinal Study (Ferrer et al., 2015).

Cut scores are available for each form based on the normative sample. Form 0 has 10 items and is for kindergarten students ages 5:0–6:11; Form 1 has 12 items and is for students in Grade 1 ages 6:0–7:11; Form 2 has 10 items and is for second graders ages 7:0–8:11; Form 3 also has 10 items and is for Grade 3 students ages 8:0–9:11.

Like the scale itself, the test manual is also available only through the test publisher's online platform. Also available is a quick guide for raters, which gives examples and guidelines for answering the questions. For example, if the rater is asked whether the student shows interest in reading material, the guide gives a description of what this question means and an example of what the behavior might look like, which is quite helpful to the user.

DEVELOPMENT. The Shaywitz DyslexiaScreen was developed in response to requirements regarding the identification of dyslexia in young children. The Cassidy Senate Resolution 576 (2016) included a definition of dyslexia as an unexpected difficulty in reading, despite good skills in higher cognitive functions such as reasoning, critical thinking, and problem solving.

Research by Ferrer, Shaywitz, Holahan, Marchione, & Shaywitz (2010) posits that developmental dyslexia impacts around 20% of school-aged children and is the most common disability seen within schools. Lerner's research (1989) suggests that 80% of children with a classification of a learning disability have dyslexia. The impact of this research is staggering, as these figures have implications for school achievement well past early childhood and into adolescence. The achievement gap persists through high school for children with dyslexia (Ferrer et al., 2015). Given these statistics, providing interventions at a young age is of paramount importance.

The Individuals with Disabilities Education Act (IDEA, 1997, 2004) requires that states identify, find, and evaluate all children who may need intervention to prevent and remediate disabilities. The Every Student Succeeds Act (ESSA, 2015) also mandates the use of evidence-based assessments to find and identify children at risk for dyslexia and other learning issues. Given these mandates, the Shaywitz DyslexiaScreen was developed to assist clinicians in assessing children at risk for reading problems, so that early intervention practices may be put into place.

The Shaywitz DyslexiaScreen rating scale was developed by taking items from the Multigrade Inventory for Teachers (MIT; Agronin, Holahan, Shaywitz, & Shaywitz, 1992), a 60-item questionnaire that was given to students' teachers at the end of the grade as part of the Connecticut

Longitudinal Study (Ferrer et al., 2015). Data were collected regarding activity, attention, adaptability, social behavior, language, and academics in the classroom. In Grades 1 and 2, teachers also were asked to provide more academic data regarding decoding, reading comprehension, arithmetic concepts, calculation, and written expression. These data were reviewed, and specific questions were selected for the Shaywitz DyslexiaScreen based on the point-biserial correlation for each prospective question with group membership (typical or dyslexia), which (as detailed below) was assigned using results from the Woodcock-Johnson Psycho-Educational Battery (Woodcock & Johnson, 1977) and the Wechsler Intelligence Scale for Children–Revised (Wechsler, 1974). Items with a .30 correlation or higher were held for further analysis.

The questions that remained were organized into scales and assessed for sensitivity, specificity, and internal consistency. Sensitivity indicates the proportion of students diagnosed with dyslexia that are classified as *at risk* by the teachers on the screener; specificity indicates the proportion of students who are typical readers and who were not found to be in the at-risk category on the screener. The resulting scale includes dichotomized items that were endorsed that differentiated between groups, with higher scores indicating a greater likelihood of dyslexia. The final scale was put through signal detection analyses. Receiver operating characteristic (ROC) analyses were performed, and the areas under the ROC curve were estimated for each scale. The final scale for each form represented the strongest combination of sensitivity, specificity, and reliability. Final item selection yielded 10 questions for Forms 0, 2, and 3, and 12 questions for Form 1. Cut scores are four or more items endorsed on Forms 0 and 2 and six or more items endorsed on Forms 1 and 3. Based upon analyses conducted with a national validity sample, adjustments were made to the original scale that was created using the data obtained from the Connecticut sample.

TECHNICAL. The Connecticut study involved 414 school-aged children who were entering kindergarten in 1983. The original sample is not reflective of the demographics of the country, as the sample was 85% White, 11.8% African American, and 1.9% Hispanic. Students were assessed yearly using the Woodcock-Johnson Psycho-Educational Battery (Woodcock & Johnson, 1977), specifically subtests comprising the Reading Cluster: Letter-Word Identification, Word Attack, and Passage Comprehension. Cognitive functioning was assessed every other year using the full-scale battery from the Wechsler Intelligence Scale for Children–Revised (Wechsler, 1974). Using the standard scores for the children at Grades 2 and 4, a student could be identified as being in the dyslexia group due to either low achievement (Reading Cluster standard score lower than 90 [25th percentile]) or a discrepancy criterion (Reading Cluster scores 1.5 standard deviations below predicted score based on Full Scale IQ score). All other children were placed into the typical group.

In 2016 and 2017, an attempt was made to validate the cut scores obtained from the Connecticut study sample. Small numbers of students were assessed from various parts of the Midwest, South, and West, including Nebraska, Illinois, North Carolina, California, and Hawaii (Total N = 279). The sample included students with previous diagnoses including attention-deficit/hyperactivity disorder (ADHD), autism spectrum disorder, seizure disorder, and reading disability, which may affect the findings. However, the Shaywitz DyslexiaScreen correctly identified all but one participant with a previous reading disability diagnosis as being at risk for dyslexia. The demographics of the additional groups were more diverse than the Connecticut group, with much larger percentages of Hispanics (10.7%-15.4%) and Other (7.5%-21.4%) groups represented across forms, although Whites continued to represent the largest group (47.6%-74.6%) in each sample.

Using the national validation sample, classification consistency was assessed for Forms 0 and 1 (kindergarten and first grade) by comparing classification on the Shaywitz DyslexiaScreen with scores on subtests from the Wechsler Individual Achievement Test, Third Edition (WIAT-III; Wechsler, 2009). Kindergarten students were tested on the Early Reading Skills subtest to assess phonological awareness, letter knowledge, and early word recognition. First grade students were assessed on the Word Reading and Pseudoword Decoding subtests, which measure word recognition skills and phonological decoding of nonsense words. The test authors chose a standard score of 85 or below on any of these subtests to consider a student part of the dyslexia group. For students in Grades 2 and 3, classification consistency was assessed by comparing the rating on the DyslexiaScreen with scores obtained on the Dyslexia Index of the WIAT-III. This index is composed of the Oral Reading Fluency,

Spelling, and Pseudoword Decoding subtests. A standard score below 85 on this index resulted in classification of at risk for dyslexia. The test authors also screened for intellectual disabilities. Those who scored within a significantly low range on a test of reasoning were excluded from the sample.

Comparisons between the dyslexia group and the nonclinical group indicated that mean raw scores on the DyslexiaScreen for those identified in the dyslexia group in kindergarten and Grade 1 were significantly higher than those in the nonclinical group with corresponding lower scores on tests of achievement. Similar results were evidenced by the second- and third-grade students.

Sensitivity and specificity analyses using the national validity sample indicate that the Shaywitz DyslexiaScreen has value as a screening instrument in its ability to differentiate between those at risk for dyslexia and those who would not be considered at risk. Results suggest moderately high sensitivity and specificity for Forms 0 and 1 and high sensitivity and moderately high specificity for Forms 2 and 3. Correct classifications were made for 71% of the kindergarten students, 85% of the Grade 1 students, 80% of the Grade 2 students, and 85% of the Grade 3 students. Sensitivity ranged from 70% for Grade 1 to 100% for Grade 2, and specificity ranged from 71% for kindergarten to 88% for Grade 1.

Correlations were calculated between scores on the Shaywitz DyslexiaScreen and the WIAT-III. For students in kindergarten and Grade 1, strong negative correlations were found between raw scores on the Shaywitz DyslexiaScreen and standard scores obtained on the WIAT-III Early Reading Skills, Word Reading, and Pseudoword Decoding subtests. Coefficients were -.56 between Form 1 and both WIAT-III Work Reading and Pseudoword Decoding and -.74 between Form 0 and WIAT-III Early Reading Skills. Similarly, correlation coefficients between Shaywitz DyslexiaScreen scores and WIAT-III subtest scores for students in Grades 2 and 3 ranged from -.54 to -.80.

Finally, internal consistency assesses the degree to which the questions on the scale correlate highly with one another. Coefficient alpha internal consistency reliability coefficients for each of the screener forms ranged from very good—in the high .80s—to the .90s, which this reviewer considers excellent. The reliability levels increase as the grade level of the student increases. Coefficients range from .87 for Form 0 to .95 for Form 3.

COMMENTARY. Given the resurgence of interest in dyslexia in school-aged children, the idea of a brief rating scale to discern preliminarily the presence of dyslexia is of interest. Given Dr. Shaywitz's status in the field of reading disabilities, the idea of her assisting in the diagnosis of dyslexia holds considerable promise. However, this reviewer questions whether a skilled clinician would become aware of responses to various items that suggest dyslexia to such an extent that the clinician would know that the risk threshold had been reached without using a computer to complete the scale or to generate a report. In other words, observation of the student and progress monitoring might give a clinician the same information as the screener.

That being said, the screener was developed using actual longitudinal data, and the statistics are sound. In and of itself, the Shaywitz DyslexiaScreen is worthy of its intent. As the test author states, this measure is seen as one piece of a broader evaluative process. Noteworthy are the guidelines for raters to use when answering the questions. A rater may second guess what the question is asking or desire to provide remediation for a student and so seek to answer in a skewed manner. The provided guidelines steer raters toward fidelity of response. This feature could be helpful to new teachers who do not have the experience of seeing which children progress naturally through the process of reading development. The guidelines are embedded in the online rating form, but making a printout for raters may also be beneficial.

If used to assist in determining which students should have targeted interventions or additional assessment in the area of phonological processing, then the screener will serve a necessary purpose. Used as a full class screener, the Shaywitz DyslexiaScreen could be helpful in setting up groups for multitiered systems of support (MTSS).

The individual reports generated are somewhat wordy and could be improved for parents. The demographics of the original Connecticut study are somewhat problematic, as they are not representative of the country. Attempts to rectify this sample deficiency with nationwide validity studies showed results that mostly matched the original data, and, where they did not, changes were made.

In places where MTSS or even response to intervention and progress monitoring are not used, this screening tool becomes more important to help identify children who may be at risk for reading difficulties. The data supporting lifelong achievement gaps should continue to push clinicians in the direction of early identification and intervention. This tool would be quite helpful in that regard.

SUMMARY. The Shaywitz DyslexiaScreen is a brief rating scale that could assist in the early identification of children with potential reading difficulties. Once a student is identified as at risk, targeted interventions may be developed and implemented. The screener could be particularly helpful to novice teachers and clinicians and for helping parents understand some of the specific difficulties a child has and what should be done at home to support the efforts in school. Users should be aware that the manual and rating scales are available only in digital format.

REVIEWER'S REFERENCES

Agronin, M. E., Holahan, J. M., Shaywitz, B. A., & Shaywitz, S. E. (1992). The Multi-Grade Inventory for Teachers (MIT): Scale development, reliability, and validity of an instrument to assess children with attentional deficits and learning disabilities. In S. E. Shaywitz & B. A. Shaywitz (Eds.), *Attention deficit disorder comes of age: Toward the twenty-first century* (pp. 89-116). Austin, TX: PRO-ED.

Every Student Succeeds Act, Pub. L. No. 114-95 1177 (2015).

Ferrer, E., Shaywitz, B. A., Holahan, J. M., Marchione, K., & Shaywitz, S. E. (2010). Uncoupling of reading and IQ over time: Empirical evidence for a definition of dyslexia. *Psychological Science, 21*(1), 93-101. doi:10.1177/0956797609354084

Ferrer, E., Shaywitz, B. A., Holahan, J. M., Marchione, K. E., Michaels, R., & Shaywitz, S. E. (2015). Achievement gap in reading is present as early as first grade and persists through adolescence. *The Journal of Pediatrics, 167*(5), 1121-1125. doi:10.1016/j.jpeds.2015.07.045

Individuals With Disabilities Education Act, 20 U.S.C.A. 1400 *et seq.* (1997).

Individuals With Disabilities Education Act, 20 U.S.C.A. 1400 *et seq.* (2004).

Lerner, J. W. (1989). Educational interventions in learning disabilities. *Journal of the American Academy of Child & Adolescent Psychiatry, 28*(3), 326-331. doi:10.1097/00004583-198905000-00004

S. Res. 576, 114 Cong. (2016) https://www.congress.gov/bill/114th-congress/senate-resolution/576/text

Shaywitz, S. E. (2003). *Overcoming dyslexia: A new and complete science-based program for reading problems at any level.* New York, NY: Knopf.

Wechsler, D. (1974). Wechsler Intelligence Scale for Children—Revised. New York, NY: The Psychological Corporation.

Wechsler, D. (2009). Wechsler Individual Achievement Test, Third Edition. Bloomington, MN: NCS Pearson.

Woodcock, R. W., & Johnson, M. B. (1977). The Woodcock-Johnson Psycho-Educational Battery. Allen, TX: DLM Teaching Resources.

[148]

Social Cognition.

Purpose: Designed to assess "relevant neuropsychological constructs of social perception to identify potential difficulties in this domain."
Population: Ages 16-90.
Publication Date: 2009.
Subtests, 3: Social Perception, Faces, Names.
Administration: Individual.
Price Data, 2020: $261.70 per kit including manual (136 pages), social perception audio (flash drive), social perception emotion card, stimulus book, 25 record forms, faces cards, and memory grid; $54.60 per 25 record forms.
Time: Administration time not reported.
Comments: The Social Cognition test was published as part of the Advanced Clinical Solutions for WAIS-IV and WMS-IV, but is available as a free-standing component.
Authors: Pearson.
Publisher: Pearson.

a) SOCIAL PERCEPTION.
Purpose: Designed to measure "cognitive skills associated with the understanding of social communication."
Population: Ages 16-90.
Scores, 4: Affect Naming, Prosody, Pairs, Social Perception.
Comments: Requires the use of auditory stimulus, provided on flash drive.
b) FACES [supplemental].
Purpose: Designed to measure "face discrimination and recognition with immediate learning and delayed recall conditions."
Population: Ages 16-90.
Scores, 4: Faces I, Faces II, Faces Content, Faces Spatial.
c) NAMES [supplemental].
Purpose: Designed to measure "face-name association, face-activity association, and incidental recall for facial expression of emotion."
Population: Ages 16-69.
Scores, 5: Names I, Names II, Names Proper Names, Names Activity, Names II Emotion.

Review of Social Cognition by ANITA M. HUBLEY, Professor of Measurement, Evaluation, and Research Methodology, and ROBERT RUDDELL, Graduate Student of Counseling Psychology, University of British Columbia, Vancouver, British Columbia, Canada:

DESCRIPTION. A measure of social cognitive processing, Social Cognition is composed of three independent subtests that, according to the test publisher's website, take 35-45 minutes to administer. The primary subtest, Social Perception, screens for "cognitive skills associated with the understanding of social communication" (manual, p. 1). It consists of three tasks. Affect Naming requires examinees to identify the expressed emotion in faces. In Prosody-Face Matching, examinees identify the face (out of six options) with the expression that best matches the emotional tone of a recorded voice. In Prosody-Pair Matching, examinees identify the prosody of the recorded voice by selecting the best picture (out of four options) of two individuals communicating. Examinees are also asked to identify the emotion being expressed, if the tone of the voice changes the meaning of the content and, if so, the speaker's real intent.

The Faces subtest assesses face discrimination and recognition as well as spatial recall. Examinees are shown a 4 x 4 grid on which 10 faces are shown for 10 seconds. When presented with an empty grid, examinees must select those faces from 20 face cards and correctly place them on the grid on four learning trials and a 10- to 15-minute delayed recall trial. The Names subtest measures visual-verbal associative learning of face, name, and activity, as well as incidental recall of facial expression of emotion. In this subtest, examinees are presented with pictures of 10 children, one at a time, and told their first and last names, and their favorite activity. For two faces, the examinee makes up the names and activities. Examinees are required to recall this information for all 10 faces on three learning trials and a 10- to 15-minute delayed recall trial.

DEVELOPMENT. Social Cognition was developed as part of the Advanced Clinical Solutions (ACS) for the Wechsler Adult Intelligence Scale—Fourth Edition (WAIS—IV) and the Wechsler Memory Scale—Fourth Edition (WMS—IV). The test manual does not describe the Social Cognition test in the context of the six ACS components (e.g., effort, reliable change scores, premorbid functioning) designed to complement the WAIS—IV and WMS—IV. A review of the ACS by Chu, Lai, Xu, and Zhou (2012) is helpful in this regard. Beyond stating that the Social Cognition subtests were developed "based on neuropsychological research that suggests affect recognition and face processing abilities are primary to understanding deficits in social functioning commonly observed in individuals with developmental, neuropsychiatric, and neurological disorders" (manual, p. 1), few details are provided about the rationale behind the selection of the specific tasks, emotions, faces, number of response options, and so forth. Some details are provided separately by Suchy and Holdnack (2013).

TECHNICAL. The Social Perception subtest was standardized alongside a subset of the WAIS—IV standardization sample; its normative sample consisted of 800 examinees ages 16-90 years presented in eight age groups of 100 each. The sample was stratified for age, sex, race/ethnicity, and education level using 2005 data from the U.S. Census Bureau. The Faces and Names subtests were standardized as part of the WMS-IV national tryout phase. The Faces normative sample consisted of 348 examinees ages 16-90 years presented in eight age groups of 30-60 participants each, whereas the Names normative sample was limited to six groups between the ages of 16 and 69 years. Inferential norming was used to obtain percentile ranks that were converted to smoothed standard scores (M = 10, SD = 3, range = 1-19) for all scores except Names II Emotion. If both the Social Perception subtest and WAIS-IV are administered, three contrast scaled scores that evaluate the examinee's performance on Social Perception, controlling for his or her general ability, verbal comprehension, or perceptual reasoning, can be obtained.

Internal consistency estimates of reliability across all eight age groups and overall ranged from .53 to .87 for the four Social Perception scores, from .72 to .95 for the four Faces scores, and from .86 to .95 for the four Names scores. Reliability estimates based on 15 clinical subgroups (e.g., traumatic brain injury, mild intellectual disability, schizophrenia, autistic disorder) for Social Perception scores, four clinical subgroups for Faces scores, and three clinical subgroups for Names scores ranged from .70 to .98, with nearly all exceeding .80. Test-retest reliability estimates were available only for Social Perception subtest scores (N = 143); intervals ranged from 12 to 82 days (M = 23 days). Reliability estimates, corrected for the variability of the normative sample, ranged from .60 to .83. Interscorer agreement, using two trained independent scorers for both clinical and normative cases, was 98-99%. Kandalaft et al. (2012) reported alpha coefficients ranging from .70 to .96 for the four Social Perception scores in a mixed clinical/control sample.

Very limited content evidence of validity was provided in the test manual. Reference was made to comprehensive literature and expert reviews as well as customer and expert panel feedback during the early research phases, but no details were provided. With respect to response processes evidence, the test authors reported having used "extensive literature reviews, expert consultation, and empirical evaluations" (manual, p. 63); however, they provided only two examples of such evidence. In the first example, child and adult actors were coached and provided with scenarios to achieve accurate expressions of emotions; their faces were rated by healthy adults for identification, intensity, and believability of the emotion being expressed. In the second example, verbal responses in the Social Perception Pairs condition were reviewed to establish rules for scoring.

Relations to other variables evidence was examined only for the Social Perception subtest. These scores were correlated with WAIS-IV, WMS-IV, and Wechsler Individual Achievement Test—Second Edition (WIAT-II) scores; most validity coefficients were in the low range for the WAIS-IV (subtests: .12 to .46; composites: .19 to .46), WMS-IV (subtests: .12 to .33; indexes: .20 to .40), and WIAT-II (subtests: .01 to .58; composites: .14 to .50). Social Perception scores were also correlated with scores from the Adaptive Behavior Assessment System-Second Edition (ABAS-II) in a variety of small normal and clinical samples; correlations were in the low range for normal aging (subtests: |.01| to |.34|; composites: .02 to .23), mild cognitive impairment (subtests: |.02| to |.32|; composites: |.01| to |.18|), and mild intellectual disability (subtests: .07 to .43; composites: .14 to .38) groups, low to moderate in a moderate intellectual disability group (subtests: .07 to .66; composites: .19 to .58), and mostly moderate in a traumatic brain injury group (subtests: .05 to .67; composites: .32 to .60), as one might expect.

Extensive comparisons were made between clinical groups and controls on the Social Perception subtest, and a few comparisons were made for the Faces and Names subtests. Sample sizes ranged from 14 to 115; nearly all were less than 50. The findings generally matched what one might expect and thus provided supportive evidence of validity.

Kandalaft et al. (2012) examined validity evidence based on relationships to other variables for the Social Perception total and subtest scores in a mixed clinical/control sample. In these reviewers' opinion, correlations with five other social cognition measures (.06 to .61) and a discriminant processing speed measure (.12 to .31) provided mixed support and may help further understanding of the distinct aspects of social cognitive processing tapped by the Social Perception subtests. It is unfortunate that the less-than-satisfactory reliability estimates for some measures may have attenuated some validity coefficients. Findings were mixed when comparing Social Perception subtest scaled scores among healthy controls and individuals diagnosed with Asperger syndrome or schizophrenia.

COMMENTARY. The Social Cognition subtests appear to be well designed. The administration and scoring instructions are clear and easy to follow as are the record form and stimulus book. The normative sample for the Social Perception subtest appears to be excellent in terms of age range, sample size, and U.S. Census stratification, whereas the normative samples for the Faces and Names subtests are very good but smaller and less well stratified. Test users also need to be aware of the more limited age range of norms for Names.

Overall, reliability evidence was mixed. Internal consistency evidence tended to range from adequate to excellent for nearly all Social Cognition tasks from clinical samples and for the Social Perception Prosody-Pair Matching task, and the Faces and Names subtests from the normative sample. For the other three Social Perception tasks, however, internal consistency evidence tended to be less than adequate in the normative sample, and could attenuate validity coefficients. Test-retest reliability evidence was limited but moderate to good. Interscorer agreement was very high. The reporting of reliability studies was incomplete. Sample sizes were not reported for the clinical samples. No age range was given for the test-retest sample, and test-retest intervals ranged widely. No information was provided about the scorers who participated in the interscorer reliability study or the level of training that was provided.

Although the *Standards for Educational and Psychological Testing* (American Educational Research Association, American Psychological Association, & National Council on Measurement in Education, 2014) was referenced, a confusing mix of language reflecting both older and more modern conceptualizations of validity was used in the test manual. Response processes evidence of validity was weak and says little about the degree to which "examinees engaged in the expected cognitive process when responding to subtest tasks" (manual, p. 63). Relations to other variables evidence was poorly presented and is of limited value in its present form. Presenting tables of correlations without a priori descriptions of expected theoretical patterns and relative magnitudes of relationships between particular subtest scores and scores from specific convergent and discriminant measures makes it difficult to evaluate whether there is truly any support for the intended score inferences. The Social Perception subtest and the other tests were not always administered on the same day, which could negatively impact validity coefficients. In these reviewers' opinion, many findings were described as though they were exploratory in nature rather than confirming or disconfirming expectations regarding the validity of inferences. The comparisons made between clinical groups and controls provided good support for validity. Even so, test users must be aware of potential limitations related to these samples and the lack of reliability evidence in some of these studies. Adding a single summary table of the results for all clinical groups to the manual would be useful. Finally, the manual would benefit from the inclusion of case studies as seen in several chapters of Holdnack et al.'s (2013) book.

SUMMARY. Tests of social cognitive processing have great potential value in clinical practice, and the Social Cognition subtests appear to be well designed, flexible, and promising measures. More information needs to be provided about the development of the test. The normative data, especially for the Social Perception subtest, are a strength. Greater attention needs to be paid to obtaining a variety of reliability and validity evidence for all of the subtests and adequately reporting that evidence in the manual. At present, the test manual presents limited, mixed, and at times poorly reported reliability and validity evidence to support the inferences made from Social Cognition scores. More theoretical and psychometric evidence is needed before this test can be recommended for clinical use.

REVIEWER'S REFERENCES

American Educational Research Association, American Psychological Association, & National Council on Measurement in Education. (2014). *Standards for educational and psychological testing*. Washington, DC: American Educational Research Association.

Chu, Y., Lai, M. H. C., Xu, Y., & Zhou, Y. (2012). Review of Advanced Clinical Solutions for WAIS-IV and WMS-IV. *Journal of Psychoeducational Assessment, 30*, 520-524. doi:10.1177/0734282912442868

Holdnack, J. A., Drozdick, L. W., Weiss, L. G., & Iverson, G. L. (Eds.). *WAIS-IV, WMS-IV, and ACS: Advanced clinical interpretation* [Academic Press digital version]. doi:10.1016/B978-0-12-386934-0.00012-2

Kandalaft, M. R., Didehbani, N., Cullum, C. M., Krawczyk, D. C., Allen, T. T., Tamminga, C. A., & Chapman, S. B. (2012). The Wechsler ACS Social Perception subtest: A preliminary comparison with other measures of social cognition. *Journal of Psychoeducational Assessment, 30*, 455-465. doi:10.1177/0734282912436411

Suchy, Y., & Holdnack, J. A. (2013). Assessing social cognition using the ACS for WAIS-IV and WMS-IV. In J. A. Holdnack, L. W. Drozdick, L. G. Weiss, & G. L. Iverson (Eds.), *WAIS-IV, WMS-IV, and ACS: Advanced clinical interpretation* [Academic Press digital version]. doi:10.1016/B978-0-12-386934-0.00008-0

Review of Social Cognition by SCOTT A. NAPOLITANO, Associate Professor of Practice, Educational Psychology Department, University of Nebraska–Lincoln, Lincoln, NE:

DESCRIPTION. The Social Cognition test is an individually administered test that includes three subtests: Social Perception, Faces, and Names. The test is designed to provide a direct measure of social cognition functioning in individuals from 16 years to 90 years.

The three subtests are administered independently and assess several aspects of face processing and social cognition. The primary subtest is Social Perception. This subtest is described as an overall screening subtest that measures deficits in social perception that can occur with many psychological disorders. It uses both auditory and visual stimuli and includes three parts: Affect Naming, Prosody-Face Matching, and Prosody-Pair Matching. Two supplemental subtests—Faces and Names—also are included in Social Cognition. The Faces subtest measures both face memory and spatial memory, allowing for a comparison of the two constructs. The Names subtest measures multiple aspects of memory including face memory, verbal learning, affect recognition, and affect recall.

The administration instructions are clearly described and easy to follow. Additionally, the test manual, protocols and materials are well developed and easy to use. The test yields several types of scores. Standard scores with a mean of 10 and a standard deviation of 3 are used for the Social Perception, Names, and Faces subtests. Contrast scores are used for comparisons of index scores from the Wechsler Adult Intelligence Scale—Fourth Edition (WAIS-IV; Wechsler, 2008) and scaled scores from the Social Cognition test. Finally, for the Names II Emotion task, the test authors have used cumulative percentage bands to represent the scores.

DEVELOPMENT. The Social Cognition test was developed along with the WAIS-IV and the Wechsler Memory Scale—Fourth Edition (WMS—IV; Wechsler, 2009) to provide a direct measure of social cognition. The test manual reports that social cognition traditionally has been inferred from performances on subtests from the WAIS-IV. Creating a more direct assessment method was the impetus for the development of the Social Cognition test. The Social Cognition test is grounded in neuropsychological research that has identified affect recognition and face processing abilities as key components of social functioning. Based on this research, the subtests included in the Social Cognition test were designed to measure these constructs.

TECHNICAL. The Social Cognition test was standardized along with the WAIS—IV and a national tryout of the WMS—IV. The Social Perception subtest normative sample included 800 participants ages 16 to 90. The sample was divided into eight age groups: 16-19, 20-29, 30-39, 40-49, 50-59, 60-69, 70-79, and 80-90. The Faces and Names subtests normative sample included 348 participants. The Faces sample was divided into the same eight age groups, and the Names subtest was divided into six groups, ages 16-69. The 2005 U.S. Census data provided the basis for stratification along age, sex, race/ethnicity, and education levels.

Reliability evidence is presented in the areas of internal consistency, test-retest stability, and interscorer agreement. Additionally, the test manual provides information on standard errors of measurement to facilitate the calculation of confidence intervals. In terms of internal consistency, the manual reports reliability coefficients calculated with split-half and alpha methods. The subtest coefficients range from .69 to .94 averaged across all age groups, indicating moderate to high internal consistency. In terms of test-retest reliability, information is reported on 143 examinees who were administered the Social Perception subtest on two occasions. The average time between administrations was 23 days. The test manual reports corrected stability coefficients between the two test times that ranged from .60 to .83 (corrected for variability of the normative sample), with small increases in performance over time. Test-retest data were not obtained on the Faces and Names subtests. In terms of interscorer agreement, all of the Social Cognition test subtests were scored by two separate individuals. The interscorer agreement was very high, with correlation coefficients ranging from .98 to .99.

The test manual describes a process of establishing content evidence of validity that included literature reviews, expert review, and consultation. Based on this information, items were modified and final test items were chosen to evaluate the specified constructs. The test authors also used a process that examined the response process of individuals taking the test. Additionally, the Social Perception subtest was compared to four external measures including measures of intellectual functioning, memory, academic achievement, and behavior. The Faces and Names subtests were not included in the concurrent validity studies. All of the subtests were included in some studies with special populations including individuals with a variety of psychiatric, developmental, and neurological disorders. Overall, the test authors reported that the Social Perception subtest demonstrated low to moderate correlations with general cognitive ability (coefficients ranged from .28 to .46 for full-scale intelligence) and memory functioning (coefficients ranged from .20 to .40 for memory indices). Based on these findings, the test authors concluded that the Social Perception subtest measures skills not measured by common tests of memory or intellectual functioning.

COMMENTARY. The Social Cognition test is a well-designed individually administered test of a wide range of social cognition abilities. The administration and scoring procedures are thoroughly described and easy to follow. Strengths of the test are the standardization sample and the fact that it was standardized along with the WAIS—IV and WMS-IV. The test also demonstrated good reliability in multiple areas. Validity evidence of test scores is an area that would benefit from additional studies, particularly in terms of convergent evidence. No studies were presented that compared the Social Cognition test with other measures of similar constructs, which would be beneficial in further examining evidence of validity. Additionally, the Faces and Names subtests were not included in the concurrent validity studies, but no explanation was provided for their exclusion. The large number of special populations included in the validity evaluation is definitely a strength of the test.

SUMMARY. The Social Cognition test is an individually administered test that was developed to provide a more direct measure of a broad range of abilities important to social functioning. This test does meet this goal and does fill an important void in this area of standardized testing. The test is also well developed and has sound psychometric properties. The inclusion of some additional validity studies in the future will make the test even more useful and sound. Given all of the positive factors outlined above, the test will be a positive addition to the assessment field.

REVIEWER'S REFERENCES

Wechsler, D. (2008). Wechsler Adult Intelligence Scale-Fourth Edition. San Antonio, TX: Pearson.

Wechsler, D. (2009). Wechsler Memory Scale-Fourth Edition. San Antonio, TX: Pearson.

[149]

Social-Emotional Developmental Age Level.

Purpose: Designed as "a behavioural assessment scale that aims to establish an individual's level of social-emotional development."

Population: Children and adults with a developmental age between birth and 14 years.

Publication Date: 2015.

Acronym: SEDAL.

Scores, 19: Social Development (Social Independence, Moral Development, Impulse Control, Initiating Contact, Self-Awareness in Social Contexts, Social Assessment Skills, Social Skills, Relating to Authority, Social Aspects of Sexual Development), Emotional Development (Emotional Independence, Moral Development, Impulse Control, Self Image, Sense of Reality, Fears, Regulation of Emotions), Developmental Age.

Administration: Individual.

Price Data, 2020: £309 per kit including manual (2015, 74 pages), 25 scoring booklets, and scoring program; £59 per manual; £99 per 25 scoring booklets; £185 per scoring program.

Foreign Language Editions: Originally published in Dutch; German version available.

Time: Administration time not reported.

Authors: Joop Hoekman, Aly Miedema, Bernard Otten, and Jan Gielen.

Publisher: Hogrefe Ltd [United Kingdom].

Review of the Social-Emotional Developmental Age Level by ABIGAIL BAXTER, Professor, Department of Leadership and Teacher Education, University of South Alabama, Mobile, AL:

DESCRIPTION. The Social-Emotional Developmental Age Level (SEDAL) is a translation of a Dutch tool, the ESSEON-R. It assesses the social and emotional developmental level of neurotypical individuals up to age 14 and individuals with disabilities functioning in this age range. It contains 152 items: 76 items assess Social Development, and 76 items assess Emotional Development. Within each domain, items are separated into dimensions; there are nine dimensions within the Social Development scale and seven within the Emotional Development scale. Some dimensions are represented in both domains (e.g., self-awareness, morality); others are unique to one domain (e.g., social assessment skills, regulation of emotions). Within each domain, items are grouped in age categories that span 6-month periods from birth to 3 years, 12 months from 3 to 10 years, and 2 years from 10 to 14 years. Not all of the dimensions are addressed in each age range (e.g., moral development is not assessed prior to the 18-month to 2-year age band).

SEDAL administration requires a professional examiner who is knowledgeable about child development. No additional training is required. The SEDAL is completed with one or multiple informants who know the individual well. It is not clear from the test materials whether informants are interviewed or complete the scoring book on their own. All 152 items must be rated as either *characteristic* or *not characteristic* of the examinee's behavior over the previous 3 months. An estimated administration time is not provided.

SEDAL scores include developmental ages for Social and Emotional domains and an overall (social-emotional) Developmental Age score. Hand or computer scoring is available. With hand scoring the examiner starts at item 76 on each subscale and identifies two consecutive age categories where 50% or more of the items were rated as *characteristic*. The upper limit of the age category is the domain developmental age. The SEDAL Developmental Age is the mean of the two domain developmental ages. Qualitative analyses investigate the pattern of ratings. The included scoring program allows for a choice of language (Dutch, German, or English) and contains six input screens where scoring booklet ratings are entered. Although not explicitly stated in the test manual, it appears that the scoring program provides reports that include domain, dimension, and item-level analyses.

DEVELOPMENT. The SEDAL emerged for behavioral assessment of children's social and emotional development. Its theoretical underpinnings are in developmental psychology and eclectic. Although many researchers and practitioners do not regard social and emotional development as independent constructs or behaviors, the SEDAL separates development in these two domains.

The SEDAL is an English translation of the ESSEON-R. Changes involved with the ESSEON-R include emphasizing more collaboration with informants, developing a useful scoring method, clarifying age ranges to aid interpretation, refining item wording, and developing qualitative analysis procedures. Test items consist of observable everyday behaviors that reflect developmental understandings. Potential items were drawn from behavioral descriptions in developmental psychology, social interaction, and education research as well as the test authors' experiences with individuals with developmental delays. The original item pool was 350 items. The current 152 items represent a culling of items based on fit; spread across domains, ages, and dimensions; ease of observation of the behavior; and clarity of expression.

Forty-seven professionals from the Netherlands and Flanders assessed item clarity and age category placement as well as each age category's comprehensiveness. This process led to the refinement of 28 items in the Social Development domain and 27 items in the Emotional Development domain as well as the movement of some items to different age categories (eight in Social Development, five in Emotional Development). From the test manual it is unclear whether the items were in Dutch or English.

TECHNICAL.

Standardization. The ESSEON-R was developed using a sample of "indigenous European children" (manual, p. 5), but no demographic characteristics or sample sizes are reported. Age placement of items was based on feedback from 47 professionals in the Netherlands and Flanders. As this process was completed for the ESSEON-R, it is difficult to judge the adequacy of the standardization for the SEDAL.

Reliability. Reliability and validity data are based on the ESSEON-R. Data were collected from multiple sources. Reliability of the Developmental Age, developmental ages for the two domains, and individual SEDAL items was assessed using interrater and test-retest procedures. Fifty-nine individuals with intellectual disabilities were evaluated by two examiners. Correlations of the two examiners' domain and Developmental Age scores as well as absolute differences between the raters were calculated. Pearson correlation coefficients ranged from .88 to .95 for the domain and Developmental Age scores. The absolute difference in scores for the two examiners ranged from 1.0 to 1.4 years (with standard deviations larger than the means). This result argues against absolute score interrater reliability. No data are presented concerning the reliability of individual items.

Kappa was used to compare the two examiners' ratings of *characteristic* or *not characteristic* for each item in a sample of 58 individuals. (It is unclear whether the sample is the same as that used for the Pearson correlations.) Data are presented at the domain and dimension level but not for individual items: Kappa could not be calculated for two items in the Emotional Development domain. The average reported kappas all meet Cicchetti and Sparrow's (1981) "sufficient" criteria.

Test-retest reliability was assessed in 25 individuals with intellectual disabilities and using a retest interval of 4 weeks. Significant positive relationships existed (r = .89-.97); however, absolute differences in domain and Developmental Age scores varied from .7 years to 1.2 years, and standard deviation differences were relatively large. The average kappa per domain and dimensions were "good" or better (Cicchetti & Sparrow, 1981). Item-level test-retest reliability evidence is not presented.

Standard errors of measurement for the domain and Developmental Age scores ranged from .8 years to 1.5 years, and the 90% confidence intervals for them ranged from 1.3 years to 2.5 years.

Validity. For concurrent evidence of validity, the Social Development and Emotional Development ages of 116 participants (no further details are provided) were correlated, yielding a coefficient of .89. Obtained scores were compared to scores on the Scale for Social Competence (SRZ), the SRZ Social Skills subscale, the Vineland Z, and the Vineland Z Socialisation subscale. Pearson correlation coefficients ranged from .74 to .81. Developmental ages were also compared to measures of cognitive ability (i.e., Raven's Coloured Progressive Matrices and Psychoeducational Profile-Revised). Again, significant correlations were found between the domain and Developmental Age scores and scores on the Raven's (r = .61-.64) and the Psychoeducational Profile-Revised (r = .60-.80) suggesting a relationship between the obtained Social and Emotional development ages and cognitive ability.

Discriminant evidence of validity was assessed by comparing SEDAL domain and Developmental Age scores to scores on the Challenging Behavior Scale for the Mentally-Disabled. These analyses indicated non-significant correlations of very small magnitude (r = .05-.06) indicating that the two tools measured different concepts.

COMMENTARY. The SEDAL assesses two important aspects of development in children and individuals with developmental disabilities: social development and emotional development. There are significant concerns related to the development and norming of the SEDAL and the instrument's psychometric characteristics. The SEDAL is based upon the "social-emotional development of indigenous European children" (manual, p. 5). This limits its usefulness because research has illuminated the large role played by culture in social and emotional development (Immordino-Yang & Yang, 2017; Immordino-Yang, Yang, & Damasio, 2016; Rubin, 1998; Sharma & Fischer, 1998). Information about individuals involved in the development and refinement of the SEDAL is not sufficient. SEDAL scores represent age equivalents based on research literature and professional judgments of 47 practitioners. No norming was used to validate the age scores. Reliability analyses were conducted with a relatively small sample of individuals with intellectual disabilities. Intraclass correlations would provide better reliability estimates than Pearson correlations (Shrout & Fleiss, 1979). It is unclear who participated in validity analyses. Tests of cognitive ability were used to demonstrate concurrent validity. Finally, the SEDAL is a translation of the ESSEON-R into English (British). The wording of some individual items appears stilted in American English (e.g., "person of trust," "contrary behavior"). Information about the translation process is not provided, so it is unclear that guidelines for translating and adapting tests (International Test Commission, 2017) were followed. Psychometric data for the SEDAL are not provided as separate from the ESSEON-R.

SUMMARY. The SEDAL assesses social and emotional development in children up to age 14 and individuals with intellectual disabilities. There is not enough information available in the test manual to understand the test development process nor the SEDAL's psychometric characteristics. There are concerns that it may be a simple translation of a tool developed for a more limited population that is being extended to different populations without sufficient data to support the reliability or validity of the generalization. Although the developmental level of an individual's social and emotional skills can be assessed with the SEDAL, more useful information may be obtained from measures of adaptive behavior and/or behavior that assess how the individual uses his/her social and emotional skills in real life settings.

REVIEWER'S REFERENCES

Cicchetti, D. V., & Sparrow, S. A. (1981). Developing criteria for establishing interrater reliability of specific items: Applications to assessment of adaptive behavior. *American Journal of Mental Deficiency, 86,* 127-137.

Immordino-Yang, M. H., & Yang, X-F. (2017). Cultural differences in the neural correlates of social-emotional feelings: An interdisciplinary, developmental perspective. *Current Opinions in Psychology, 17,* 34-40. doi:10.1016/j.copsyc.2017.06.008

Immordino-Yang, M. H., Yang, X-F., & Damasio, H. (2016). Cultural modes of expressing emotions influence how emotions are experienced. *Emotion, 16,* 1033-1039. doi:10.1037/emo0000201

International Test Commission. (2017). *International Test Commission guidelines for translating and adapting tests.* Retrieved from: https://www.intestcom.org/files/guideline_test_adaptation_2ed.pdf

Rubin, K. H. (1998). Social and emotional development from a cultural perspective. *Developmental Psychology, 34,* 611-615. doi:10.1037/0012-1649.34.4.611

Sharma, D. & Fischer, K. W. (1998). Socioemotional development across cultures: Context, complexity, and pathways. *New directions for Child and Adolescent Development, 1998(80),* 3-20. doi:10.1002/cd.23219988003

Shrout, P. E., & Fleiss, J. L. (1979). Intraclass correlation: Uses in assessing rater reliability. *Psychological Bulletin, 86,* 420–428.

Review of the Social-Emotional Developmental Age Level by LAURIE FORD, Associate Professor, and ANGELINA LEE, PhD Candidate, School Psychology, University of British Columbia, Vancouver, Canada:

DESCRIPTION. The Social-Emotional Developmental Age Level (SEDAL) is an English translation of the Dutch behavioral assessment scale *Social Emotionele Ontwikkelingsniveau-Revisie* (ESSEON-R). The SEDAL "aims to establish an individual's level of social-emotional development" (manual, p. 5) and allows systematic comparison of observed behavior of an individual with the behavior of similar-aged peers with typical development. Designed for use with children and adults with an intellectual disability (developmental age of 0 to 14 years 11 months), it may be useful for others with developmental delay or disorder, psychological or psychiatric disorder/problems, sensory impairment and/or communication disorder, and learning disability/difficulties with developmental levels in this range. The 152-item scale is divided into two domains, Social Development and Emotional Development (76 items each domain), that fall into one or more theoretically based dimensions organized by developmental phases (age ranges) in 6-, 12-, and 24-month intervals. Dimensions in the Social Development domain are Social Independence, Moral Development, Impulse Control, Initiating Contact, Self-Awareness in Social Contexts, Social Assessment Skills, Relating to Authority, and Social Aspects of Sexual Development. Within the Emotional Development domain, dimensions include Emotional Independence, Moral Development, Impulse Control, Self-Image, Sense of Reality, Fears, and Regulation of Emotions. Given the connectedness of many of the dimensions, many items contribute to more than one dimension.

The SEDAL is administered and scored by a qualified professional (e.g., pediatrician, psychiatrist, psychologist) who has expertise in the normative process of child development to use as a framework, in consultation with informants (e.g., parents, caregivers, educators) who have daily contact with the individual and in-depth knowledge of the individual's behavior in various situations. Direct observation by those completing the rating is not required. When completing the scoring booklet, each item describing behavior is marked either *characteristic* or *not characteristic* depending on whether the description is representative of the individual's behavior during the previous 3 months. Scoring criteria in the two areas are outlined in the test manual and scoring booklet. Assessors are encouraged to use their clinical judgment and interpretation of informants' descriptions of the individual's behavior and to refer to the developmental phases provided in the scoring booklet as well as the guidelines provided in the test manual. Some floor and ceiling effects are noted at the beginning (0 years) and end (14 years) of the SEDAL. No further information is provided about administration such as length of time or method (e.g., structured or semi-structured interview format).

The test authors indicate that the SEDAL is most efficiently scored using the scoring software program (included on a USB card), which generates results at the domain, dimension, and item levels, and determines a developmental age level for each domain and computes the SEDAL Developmental Age, or the mean of the developmental ages of both domains. Developmental age levels also can be determined via hand-scoring by working backward from the last item of each domain and identifying the highest age of the highest age category of two consecutive age categories with 50% or more of the items scored as *characteristic*. Additional qualitative information can be interpreted by examining patterns and discrepancies at the domain, dimension, and item levels. Developmental age on the SEDAL is defined as the age at which a certain set of behaviors are manifested by at least 50% of children in the normative sample.

Interpretation is aided by sections of the reports from the scoring program. The test authors caution that the SEDAL is an aid to diagnosis that should be used in conjunction with results from other assessments, clinical observations, and consultation with parents/caregivers and educators. Collaboration with appropriate informants in the assessment of social-emotional development is critical.

DEVELOPMENT. The SEDAL was originally developed as the ESSEON, its Dutch predecessor, in 2000 to address the gap in behavioral assessment of social-emotional development. The original scale went through a number of revisions with repeated testing in educational and clinical practice before the ESSEON-R was translated into the SEDAL in 2011 and its most recent version in 2015. A German translation, the SEN, is also available.

The SEDAL is founded on the concept of continuity in development. According to the test authors, this is a combination of different phases of development from a continuous course. Social functioning and emotional functioning were treated as interconnected but distinct developmental domains, in addition to moral, psychosexual, and self-development as dimensions in social and emotional contexts. The SEDAL domains are hypothetical rather than statistically supported. However, the test authors posit that the domains "provide a structurally, qualitatively and practically useful framework based on theoretical constructs and practitioner insight" (manual, p. 42). The 152 items were refined from a pool of about 350 items derived from behavioral descriptions in developmental psychology literature on interaction and education, as well as the test authors' clinical experience in working with children and adults with developmental delays. The items and the age categories assigned to each item were revised following suggestions by a research group consisting of 47 professionals, including a pediatrician, parents, primary and secondary school teachers, childcare workers, and professionals in special education from the Netherlands and Belgium.

TECHNICAL. The technical information on the English version of the test (the SEDAL) is very limited with most information provided in the technical manual deriving from the 2007 Dutch version (ESSEON-R). Information is provided for the Social Development and the Emotional Development domains and SEDAL items, but technical information for the dimension level is limited to kappa values used to evaluate interrater reliability. What this reviewer found misleading is that the introductory paragraph to the psychometric chapter indicates the focus is the ESSEON-R, but the SEDAL is referred to in the chapter as well. The test authors indicate that the psychometric information provided is from masters' theses with the ESSEON-R. No information on the standardization sample for the Dutch version or the English version was found in the test manual.

Reliability. Interrater reliability coefficients were reported as .91, .88, and .95 for the Social Development domain, Emotional Development domain, and the Developmental Age, respectively, based on a study involving 59 individuals with intellectual disabilities, each of whom was evaluated by two examiners. In addition, the examiners' ratings on each item (as characteristic or not characteristic) were compared to determine kappa values (kappa %) at domain and dimension levels. Average kappa % for the Social Development domain was 63.9 (and ranged from 60.4 to 72.0 across dimensions) and 62.0 for the Emotional Development domain (ranging from 54.6 to 67.2 across dimensions). Test-retest reliability coefficients were reported as .89, .95, and .97 for the Social Development domain, Emotional Development domain, and the Developmental Age, respectively, based on a study involving 25 individuals with intellectual disabilities, each of whom was retested four weeks after the Dutch version of the measure was initially completed. Correlation coefficients ranged from .89 to .97.

Validity. Concurrent evidence of validity derives from a study of 116 individuals with intellectual disabilities who completed the Dutch version of the measure as well as the Scale for Social Competence and the Vineland Z. Moderately high correlation coefficients were reported, with values ranging from .74 to .81. In addition, Social Development and Emotional Development ages were compared to scores obtained from two measures of cognitive ability, the Raven's Coloured Progressive Matrices and the Psychoeducational Profile—Revised. Significant correlations of moderate magnitude were noted, with coefficients for the Raven's ranging from .61 to .64 and for the Psychoeducational Profile—Revised from .60 to .80.

COMMENTARY. The SEDAL is based on strong developmental theory and has good face validity and subsequently should hold promise as a measure of social and emotional functioning for individuals with intellectual disabilities. The authors provide detailed descriptive information, anchored in strong developmental theory, regarding the domains and dimensions measured by the SEDAL. Members of the advisory panel for item development were from Belgium and the Netherlands. However, simply taking a test that was developed for use in another language (and context) and translating it into English does not meet the standards for appropriate use of a test for the purpose of decision making without strong caution and reservation. The test authors provide no information on the process of translation, a critical first step in test adaptation. Further, psychometric information on the English version of the test is not provided. The psychometric information reported is on the Dutch version of the test (ESSEON-R), and that information is limited. Procedures for completing the scoring booklet are also sparse. It is unclear whether items are read to informants directly or whether the test is administered as an interview or by semi-structured or other informal means. Scoring software (provided with the test) is strongly recommended by the test authors but did not work on the Macintosh computer operating system these reviewers tried as part of this review. Given the other measures available to examine social and emotional development with English-speaking clients and the significant psychometric difficulties with this version of the measure, it is difficult to support its use in its present form.

SUMMARY. The English version of the ESSEON-R, the SEDAL, is anchored in well-supported developmental theory. A number of thesis studies provide some support for the ESSEON-R in Dutch. However, no information on the translation process for the English measure (SEDAL), the English standardization sample, reliability, and validity of the English version is provided. Further, the administration procedures are not clear, and the scoring options do not appear to work with Macintosh operating systems. In its current version, the test does not have the support needed for the intended purpose stated by its authors; to aid in the diagnosis of social and emotional difficulties in individuals with intellectual disabilities. Extreme caution in its use is recommended.

[150]

Social Language Development Test–Adolescent: Normative Update.

Purpose: Designed to assess the "continued refinement of social language abilities that occurs during adolescence" in order to identify "students with social language impairments."

Population: Ages 12-0 to 17-11.
Publication Dates: 2010-2017.
Acronym: SLDT-A: NU.
Scores, 6: Making Inferences, Interpreting Social Language, Problem Solving, Social Interaction, Interpreting Ironic Statements, Social Language Development Index.
Administration: Individual.
Price Data, 2020: $212 per kit including manual (2017, 87 pages), picture book, 25 record booklets, scoring standards and example responses book, and audio recordings; $77 per manual; $53 per picture book; $42 per 25 record booklets; $40 per scoring standards and example responses book.
Time: Approximately 45 minutes for administration.
Comments: Audio recordings can be accessed on the test publisher's website.
Authors: Linda Bowers, Rosemary Huisingh, and Carolyn LoGiudice.
Publisher: PRO-ED.

Review of the Social Language Development Test–Adolescent: Normative Update by CHRISTINE DiSTEFANO, Professor of Educational Research and Measurement, University of South Carolina, Columbia, SC:

DESCRIPTION. The Social Language Development Test–Adolescent: Normative Update (SLDT-A: NU) is designed to assess the competence of social language ability and development of these skills during adolescence. The test is appropriate to use with adolescents ages 12 years 0 months through 17 years 11 months who speak English and are able to follow directions. The SLDT-A: NU measures five skills important to appropriate social language development during adolescence: making correct inferences; interpreting social language; solving problems with peers; taking someone's perspective; and understanding idioms, irony, and sarcasm. The instrument may be used to identify adolescents who lag behind peers in social language development as well as to determine the degree to which the individual is deficient. The test may also be used to identify strengths and weaknesses of an individual's language competency.

The SLDT-A: NU should be administered by a qualified examiner who is trained in assessment, scoring, and interpretation of results and who has knowledge of language evaluation. The test includes two main components, a picture book and the *Scoring Standards and Example Responses Book*. The materials are used to yield scores on five subtests: Making Inferences, Interpreting Social Language, Problem Solving, Social Interaction, and Interpreting Ironic Statements. The picture book is used for the Making Inferences subtest. The book consists of color photographs of persons expressing various emotions. To respond, examinees take the perspective of a person in the photograph and describe what the person is thinking, using cues from the picture for support. Prompts for the remaining four subtests are contained in the Scoring Standards book, where scenarios or questions are posed to the examinee. In addition, the SLDT-A: NU includes audio recordings available online so examinees can listen and respond to the Interpreting Ironic Statements subtest items. Each subtest contains 12 stimuli, for a total of 60 items on the instrument. Testing time for the SLDT-A: NU is approximately 45 minutes.

For scoring, contextual examples are provided in the Scoring Standards book to assist examiners in evaluating responses to each stimulus. Items are scored with a "1" if the response is appropriate and a "0" if the response is incorrect or off-target. Individual item scores (0/1) are summed to create raw scores for each subtest, which are then converted into percentile ranks and scaled scores using age-based norms. The five subtest scores are summed to create one overall score, the Social Language Development Index. Both the subtest scaled scores and the index score may be compared to score ranges that provide a descriptive term (ranging from *impaired or delayed* to *gifted or very advanced*) to describe social language status.

DEVELOPMENT. The original version of the SLDT-A was published in 2010. The SLDT-A: NU (2017) is a normative update, not a revision of the instrument. Thus, content of the items was not changed across forms; only a new sample, reflective of 2016 U.S. demographics, was analyzed. This process included rebalancing the original data set by increasing numbers of children from underrepresented demographic subgroups and reducing numbers from overrepresented subgroups. Additional changes to the SLDT-A: NU included (a) reporting scaled scores for subtests (M = 10, SD = 3); (b) recalculating the total score based on subtest scaled scores (M = 100, SD = 15); (c) reanalyzing or newly analyzing psychometric information (e.g., item analyses, reliability, validity, sensitivity, item bias); and (d) revising and reorganizing the examiner's manual.

TECHNICAL. The SLDT-A: NU normative sample includes scores from 868 adolescents across 42 states collected between the spring and fall of 2009. Information reported in the test manual shows that the normative update was closely aligned with 2016 U.S. demographics, with the exception of a larger percentage of children in the SLDT-A: NU sample having specific language impairment (SLI) or autism spectrum disorder (ASD). Details in the test manual provide a breakdown of the normative update sample by age and geographic region, gender, race, and Hispanic status.

SLDT-A: NU subtest and composite scores were examined for reliability evidence by age using three different methods. Internal consistency estimates, via coefficient alpha, were appropriate, ranging from .74 to .90 for subtests and roughly .95 for the composite score. Internal consistency estimates were also provided for demographic subgroups (gender, race, Hispanic status, exceptionality status). Values by subgroup again ranged from .74 to .90 for subtests and roughly .95 for the composite. Test-retest reliability was determined across an approximately two-week interval for a sample of 74 adolescents, with reliability coefficients (corrected for effects of range) of .85 and higher for all subtests and .96 to .98 for index scores. Finally, interscorer reliability was examined by correlating scores from 10 trained examiners across 10 test forms. The average coefficient across items for all subtests was .85. In general, all reliability information was at acceptable (or higher) levels (Bandalos, 2018).

The SLDT-A: NU authors performed extensive evaluations of validity, including examinations of evidence derived from test content/format, analysis of test bias, sensitivity analysis, and criterion validity analysis (i.e., differences between known groups). These methods are widely used to support construct validity (Benson, 1998). First, a detailed rationale was provided for selecting test items, including an operational definition of each subtest and how items fit with the skill to be assessed. The conventional item analysis included calculations of classical test theory based indices of item difficulty and item discrimination, with results provided by subtest and age. Concerning item discrimination, median point-biserial correlation coefficients were .36 to .65, illustrating a moderate correlation between items. The median item difficulty (percentage of adolescents answering the item correctly) was .54 to .85, with lower difficulty levels (i.e., harder items) observed for 12-year-olds. Finally, differential item functioning (DIF) was examined by subgroups of gender, Black adolescents vs. White adolescents, Asian/Pacific Islander examinees vs.

White examinees, and Hispanic vs. non-Hispanic students. Using mean differences among matched samples, effect size measures showed no more than two subtests with small levels of DIF.

Test developers assessed the ability of the SLDT-A: NU to accurately detect students previously diagnosed with severe social language problems. Developers expected the measure to differentiate students with ASD, which is characterized by social language difficulty, from typically developing students. In contrast, developers did not expect students with SLI, which is characterized by language difficulties that may or may not involve social communication, to be differentiated from typically developing students. Results from sensitivity analyses appeared to support these theories. In addition, mean difference scores between clinical subgroups and normally developing students (matched for age and other demographic factors), illustrated large effect sizes between groups of students with and without ASD and moderate effect sizes between groups with and without SLI, suggesting acceptable evidence of known groups validity for the SLDT-A: NU to identify adolescents with social language disorders.

Finally, internal structure was assessed using confirmatory factor analysis, where all five subtests loaded on a unidimensional factor, Social Language Development. Results suggested good model-data fit and high factor loadings. Correlations among subtests illustrated that the subtests were related, but non-overlapping, with correlation coefficients ranging between .53 and .70.

COMMENTARY. The SLDT-A: NU features a normative update while retaining its original items to provide more current and relevant demographic comparisons aligned with 2016 U.S. population figures. The instrument may be used to identify adolescents with social language impairment, allowing for intervention and remediation if necessary. Strengths of the test include five distinct areas of social language development assessed by the instrument and prompts/pictures that are likely to engage examinees. Other strengths include relatively low cost for materials, age-based norms, easy scoring procedures, and standardized score information to facilitate interpretation. The psychometric information provides acceptable levels of reliability and validity using a representative normative population; however, some samples used in comparative analyses are very small (e.g., 21) and thus, results should be interpreted with caution. The test manual provides sufficient details for administration and interpretation, as well as subtest-specific error patterns that may emerge during responding and remediation strategies to address deficiencies.

SUMMARY. The SLDT-A: NU provides a normative update to the instrument, allowing for more relevant demographic comparisons. Items consist of prompts for examinees to engage in while taking the test. The psychometric information provided in the examiner's manual largely supports sufficient levels of reliability and validity. The ideas presented in the test manual for assistance and remediation by subtest will be very helpful for practitioners to intervene with adolescents exhibiting social language impairment. The test meets its goal of providing an instrument that may be used to assess the quality and development of social language ability of adolescents.

REVIEWER'S REFERENCES

Bandalos, D. L. (2018). *Measurement theory and applications for the social sciences.* New York, NY: Guilford Press.

Benson, J. (1998). Developing a strong program of construct validation: A test anxiety example. *Educational Measurement: Issues and Practice, 17*(1), 10-17.

Review of Social Language Development Test–Adolescent: Normative Update by JULIA Y. PORTER, National Certified Counselor, National Certified School Counselor, Mississippi Licensed Professional Counselor, Ocean Springs, MS:

DESCRIPTION. The Social Language Development Test–Adolescent: Normative Update (SLDT-A: NU) uses five subtests to examine five skills that have been identified through research as important to the development of adolescent social language: (a) Making Inferences, (b) Interpreting Social Language, (c) Problem Solving, (d) Social Interaction, and (e) Interpreting Ironic Statements. The SLDT-A: NU comes as a test kit that includes an examiner's manual, a step-by-step scoring and example response manual, a picture book used with the Making Inferences subtest, an examiner record booklet that includes 60 items (12 per subtest), and a web link to access audio recordings, which are used with the Interpreting Ironic Statements subtest. The SLDT-A: NU is designed to be administered in a paper-and-pencil format individually to adolescents ages 12 years 0 months (12:0) to 17 years 11 months (17:11) who speak English and who are able to follow directions. The examiner reads aloud each item, and the respondent answers verbally. The examiner writes down each response verbatim and assigns a score to the response. Administration time is approximately 45 minutes. Although the

SLDT-A: NU is not timed, after 10 seconds, the examiner encourages the respondent to answer. The examiner does not provide feedback during the administration but may ask for clarification.

The test examiner interprets an individual's responses based on instructions from the SLDT-A: NU *Scoring Standards and Example Responses Book* and assigns a 1 (correct) or 0 (incorrect) to each response. Not answering an item also results in a score of 0. Responses are totaled for each of the five subtests and converted to standard scores using tables provided in the examiner's manual. A composite Social Language Development Index (mean of 100 and standard deviation of 15) is calculated by summing the subtest scaled scores. Results are reported as raw scores, age equivalents, percentile ranks, scaled scores (mean of 10, standard deviation of 3), and a composite index score. Scaled scores and index scores fall into one of seven categories: *impaired or delayed* (scaled: 1-3, index < 70), *borderline impaired or delayed* (scaled: 4-5, index: 70-79), *below average* (scaled: 6-7, index: 80-89), *average* (scaled: 8-12, index: 90-109), *above average* (scaled: 13-14, index: 110-119), *superior* (scaled: 15-16, index 120-129), and *gifted or very advanced* (scaled 17-20, index: > 129).

Suggested uses for the SLDT-A: NU include helping to identify adolescents who have deficits in social language development, helping to determine strengths and weaknesses of an individual's social language development, and providing a research instrument for studying social language development in adolescents.

DEVELOPMENT. First published in 2010, the test examines social learning development in adolescents based on the "system of rules that guides speakers in communicating effectively" (manual, p. 1). Research indicates that effective communication skills are correlated with the ability to get along with peers, with academic achievement, and with successful employment. The 60 items included on the SLDT-A: NU were selected through research reviews and confirmed through statistical analysis.

In 2014, a normative update to rebalance the demographic subgroups to reflect the demographic characteristics of the current population was begun. Data reported in this 2017 update reflect results of this research, which used demographic characteristics from 2016 for school-aged adolescents. Research on the SLDT-A: NU is ongoing, and current studies include additional validity studies.

TECHNICAL. The SLDT-A: NU was normed on a nationally representative sample of 868 students (12 years, n = 201; 13 years, n = 177; 14 years, n = 151; 15 years, n = 102; 16 years, n = 117; 17 years, n = 120) from 42 states in the United States. Tables are provided in the examiner's manual broken down by age with information about the norm sample's geographic region (Northeast 17%, South 38%, Midwest 22%, West 23%), gender (males 50%, females 50%), race (White 77%, Black/African American 18%, Asian/Pacific Islander 4%, Other < 1%), Hispanic status (yes 21%, no 79%), and exceptionality status (specific language impairment 6%, autism spectrum disorder 5%, other/special education 9%). Scaled scores are provided to allow comparisons across subtests for an individual's performance. The most reliable score from the SLDT-A: NU for diagnosis or determining intervention or placement is the Social Language Development Index, which includes the sums of the scaled scores for the subtests.

Test floors and ceilings were examined based on standards proposed by Bracken (1987). Statistical analyses indicate that the average subtest floors were all excellent, which indicates the SLDT-A: NU subtests adequately assess low social language ability. Floor composite index scores were also excellent. Subtest ceilings ranged from poor to fair, indicating that subtest scores should be interpreted with caution when evaluating upper levels of social communication ability. Composite ceilings ranged from fair to very good for respondents ages 12:0 to 15:11.

Discrepancy analyses were used to determine values for the differences between subtest scaled scores that are statistically significant and clinically significant. Correlation coefficients (coefficient alpha composite .95, test-retest composite .96, and scorer difference composite .85), which were calculated to examine reliability, produced high reliability estimates.

Evidence of validity was evaluated using content-description (qualitative), criterion-prediction (quantitative), and construct-identification (quantitative) methods. No statistically significant difference was found between male and female performance, Black/African American and non-Black/African American performance, Asian/Pacific Islander performance and non-Asian/Pacific Islander performance, and Hispanic and non-Hispanic performance. Results indicate that the SLDT-A: NU has little or no systematic bias related to gender, race, or ethnicity. The examiner's manual contains detailed information including tables that report the results of statistical analyses.

COMMENTARY. The SLDT-A: NU was developed carefully based on research using stringent test development procedures. Two manuals included as part of the test kit are easy to read; provide a detailed explanation of instrument development and validation procedures; and give detailed instructions for administering, scoring, and interpreting the SLDT-A: NU. The manuals should be especially helpful for new test administrators. Also included in the examiner's manual are specific remediation strategies that could be useful in helping adolescents develop social language skills. These strategies can be used in individual sessions or in group sessions.

Examiners will need to practice administering and scoring the SLDT-A: NU before using it. The test developers suggest formal assessment training and administering the SLDT-A: NU at least three times for practice. Assessment results should be used along with clinical judgment, results from additional assessments, and consultation with other professionals to determine diagnoses and interventions for individuals.

A limitation is that the cause of respondents' social language development deficits is not identified by the SLDT-A: NU. Test developers recommend caution in making diagnostic decisions using SLDT-A: NU results. Another limitation may be the test examiner's ability to accurately classify responses that do not fit within the examples provided in the test manuals.

SUMMARY. A paper-and-pencil assessment instrument that takes approximately 45 minutes to complete, the SLDT-A: NU is administered individually to adolescents ages 12:0 to 17:11. The 60 items on the SLDT-A: NU measure verbal and nonverbal communication skills developed during adolescence that are critical for peer interactions, academic performance, and careers. Formal training in assessment is recommended before use. Assessment results provide information about the current social communication skills of an individual. These data may be helpful in identifying adolescents who would benefit from intervention programs to improve their social communication skills.

REVIEWER'S REFERENCE

Bracken, B. A. (1987). Limitations of preschool instruments and standards for minimal levels of technical adequacy. *Journal of Psychoeducational Assessment, 4*, 313-326.

[151]

Social Language Development Test–Elementary: Normative Update.

Purpose: Designed "to identify children who are having difficulty in social communication."
Population: Ages 6-0 to 11-11.
Publication Dates: 2008-2017.
Acronym: SLDT-E: NU.
Scores, 5: Making Inferences, Interpersonal Negotiation, Multiple Interpretations, Supporting Peers, Social Language Development Index.
Administration: Individual.
Price Data, 2020: $212 per kit including manual (2017, 80 pages), picture book, 25 record booklets, and Scoring Standards and Example Responses Book (2017, 48 pages); $77 per manual; $53 per picture book; $42 per 25 record booklets; $40 per Scoring Standards and Example Responses Book.
Time: Approximately 45 minutes for administration.
Authors: Linda Bowers, Rosemary Huisingh, and Carolyn LoGiudice.
Publisher: PRO-ED.

Review of the Social Language Development Test–Elementary: Normative Update by JORGE E. GONZALEZ, Professor, and JACQUELINE ANDERSON, Doctoral Student in School Psychology, University of Houston, Houston, TX:

DESCRIPTION. The Social Language Development Test–Elementary: Normative Update (SLDT-E: NU) is an individually administered norm-referenced English language test of social language development in children ages 6 years 0 months through 11 years 11 months that takes approximately 45 minutes to administer. According to the test authors, the normative update reduced the size of overrepresented subgroups and increased the size of underrepresented groups by rebalancing an existing data set. In addition to the normative update, other changes included the following: (a) realignment of demographic characteristics of the normative sample to reflect those of the U.S. school-age population as reported in the *Statistical Abstract of the United States* (ProQuest, 2014); (b) addition of scaled scores that have a mean of 10 and standard deviation of 3; (c) recalculation of the total score to a composite score called the Social Language Development Index; (d) new item and bias analyses to support evidence of content-description validity; (e) new reliability and validity studies with attention to diagnostic accuracy; and (f) substantial revision and expansion of the test manual to provide additional information on administration.

According to the test authors, the test has three major purposes: to identify children whose social language development lags significantly behind their peers and to evaluate the degree of observed delay, to examine patterns of social language strengths and weaknesses, and for use as a research tool for those who study social language development in children. The test materials include an examiner's manual with descriptive information about the test as well as scoring instructions and psychometric properties. Also included is a picture book, examiner's record booklets, and a scoring standards book that includes example responses.

The test is composed of four subtests and a composite score that measure social language abilities. The subtests include Making Inferences, a measure of children's ability to infer what someone in a picture is thinking; Interpersonal Negotiation, a measure of the ability to imagine a conflictual situation between two peers and to infer the perspective of each character; Multiple Interpretations, a measure that requires demonstration of flexible thinking by interpreting a photo from two different, albeit plausible perspectives; and Supporting Peers, a measure that assesses the ability to adopt different perspectives in a given situation and to provide positive and/or supportive reactions.

The test authors suggest that test results may be useful in intervention planning and as a tool for research purposes. All items in the test are administered with the examiner reading out loud verbatim items from the examiner's booklet. For each item, detailed scoring guidelines and examples of acceptable answers are provided. If a child's answer is unclear, the examiner is permitted to ask, "What else can you tell me?" The examiner record booklet has five sections: Identifying Information, Subtest Performance, Composite Performance, Descriptive Terms (ranging from *impaired or delayed* to *gifted or very advanced*), and Record of Item Performance. The SLDT-E: NU produces normative scores as age equivalents, percentile ranks, subtest scaled scores, and a composite index score. The test now includes the Social Language Development Index, described as a direct linear transformation of the sum of subtest scaled scores with a mean of 100 and a standard deviation of 15. The test authors suggest it is the most useful of the scores as it represents the basic constructs embodied in the test and is highly reliable.

DEVELOPMENT. The normative update was developed using a sample of 1,002 participants from 26 states. The data were collected by 609 American Speech-Language Hearing-Association certified speech-language pathologists who registered as test examiners between 2007 and 2008. According to the test authors, the sample was nationally representative and stratified according to selected demographic categories (i.e., geographic region, race, Hispanic status, and gender). According to the test authors, the rationale underlying test content and format was driven by four demonstrations of content-description validity: providing an underlying rationale for test content, detailed rationale for selection of items, validity of items supported by item analyses, and bias analyses. The test authors consulted the empirical literature about social development, pragmatics, interpersonal interaction skills, and social cognition to support the rationale that developmentally notable changes in social cognition and social problem solving occur as children enter adolescence, thus establishing a rationale for measuring social cognition from ages 6 through 11.

Conventional item analyses using item discrimination indices with point-biserial correlation techniques produced median item discriminating powers ranging from .38 for age 7 Multiple Interpretations to .62 for age 6 Interpersonal Negotiation. Median item difficulty at six age intervals ranged from .40 for age 6 Multiple Interpretations to .77 for age 11 Making Inferences. Differential item functioning analysis comparisons for male versus female, African American versus non-African American, and Hispanic versus non-Hispanic revealed 11 item comparisons to be statistically significant at the .001 level. However, further analyses indicated negligible effect sizes for all the comparisons and therefore the differences were not meaningful. Demographic subgroup comparisons revealed that subtest scores for all subgroups fell within the average range, thus providing evidence of the fairness of the test for mainstream and non-mainstream subgroups. Across all comparisons with the control sample standard differences ranged from small to trivial, suggesting that scores on the test possessed little to no bias.

TECHNICAL.

Reliability. Alpha coefficients for the SLDT-E: NU were calculated at six age intervals for the subtests and composite score using data from the updated norms. With the exception of one subtest, average alpha coefficients for each age interval exceeded .80. (Coefficients for Multiple Interpretations ranged from .74 to .79.) Alpha coefficients for selected groups ranged from .79 for Multiple Interpretations (male, White, other race, Hispanic status "no," and specific language impairment [SLI]) to .96 for the Social Language Development Index (Asian/Pacific Islander and autism spectrum disorder [ASD]). Over an interval of approximately two weeks, test-retest reliability coefficients for subtests ranged from .67 for Multiple Interpretations in Ages 6 through 8 (*n* = 46) to .92 for Making Inferences in ages 9 through 11 (*n* = 50). For the combined test-retest sample (*N* = 96), the coefficient for the Social Language Development Index was .89. Standard errors of measurement (*SEM*s) were calculated for subtests (average *SEM* of 1) and the Social Language Development Index (average *SEM* of 4).

Validity. Criterion-prediction evidence of validity was examined via diagnostic accuracy analyses. Such analyses document the precision with which test scores accurately predict students who are known to possess difficulties in social language and do so without excessive false positives. Two groups were studied: children with SLI and children with ASD. Results showed that when using a cutoff score of 90, the test's diagnostic accuracy met or exceeded minimum recommended standards. In examining construct-identification evidence of validity, the test authors reported studying the relationship between test scores and age, differences among groups (ASD, SLI, and other special education), subtest interrelationships, factor analyses, and item validity. Moderate correlation coefficients were observed between subtests and age, an outcome that offers construct-identification evidence of validity. Regarding comparisons of the three exceptionality groups (SLI, ASD, other special education) on the SLDT-E: NU, results showed all groups performed as expected. In examining subtest interrelationships, scaled scores of the entire normative sample were correlated, yielding coefficients ranging from .38 to .54 with a median of .52. This result suggests subtests measure related but not identical aspects of social language. Adding to the construct-identification evidence of validity, factor analyses revealed that all items loaded on a single factor, supporting the validity of the SLDT-E: NU composite score.

COMMENTARY. In examining the scaled scores, it is notable that the test authors report floor and ceiling effects for some subtests at various ages. They characterize all observed effects as mild, although some appear to occur across a wide range of ages (e.g., the Multiple Interpretations subtest demonstrated mild floor effects across all ages and mild ceiling effects from ages 7 years 0 months through 11 years 11 months). The test authors indicate that scores at the extreme ability ranges (low, high) should be interpreted with caution as they may fail to provide sufficient ability information at these ranges. These reviewers would add that scores for populations that differ in marked ways from the normative populations (e.g., Asian) should be interpreted with caution and only in the presence of a multimethod assessment protocol. Best practices dictate a multimethod approach in most assessments, especially when diagnostic and/or instructional decisions may result. The SLDT-E: NU does add a reliable and valid tool to any armamentarium involved in assessing multiple dimensions of language development. The Multiple Interpretations subtest seemed to be the most problematic of the scales, with lower discriminating power, lower item difficulty estimates, lower alpha coefficients, and lower test-retest estimates.

SUMMARY. The SLDT-E: NU was designed to be an individually administered measure of social language development that is of particular use in evaluating social language competence and/or incompetence, for planning instruction and intervention programs as part of comprehensive evaluation, and for use in research. The test appears to be reliable and valid for its intended purposes. Some caution is warranted in interpreting scores of the Multiple Interpretations subtest for some age groups.

REVIEWERS' REFERENCE

ProQuest. (2014). *ProQuest statistical abstract of the United States, 2015.* Bethesda, MD: Bernan.

Review of the Social Language Development Test–Elementary: Normative Update by CHAD M. GOTCH, Assistant Professor of Educational Psychology, and DUSTIN S. J. VAN ORMAN, Doctoral Student, Washington State University, Pullman, WA:

DESCRIPTION. The Social Language Development Test–Elementary: Normative Update (SLDT-E: NU) aims to allow children to demonstrate development in social language comprehension and expression. It is designed for ages 6 through 11 years, particularly those who may have social language deficits (e.g., individuals with an intellectual disability or autism spectrum disorder [ASD]). The intended uses of the test are to: (a) help identify children with deficits relative to peers in social language development and assess the degree of the deficit; (b) identify patterns of strengths and weaknesses in social language development; and (c) advance understanding of social language development in children in research settings.

The SLDT-E: NU is individually administered, requiring about 45 minutes that may be split across multiple sessions. Examinees should be able to speak English and understand directions. Examiners should be speech language pathologists, school psychologists, educational diagnosticians, and related professionals with formal training in assessment and evaluation of language.

The test manual provides a thorough description of each of the test domains and descriptions of error patterns to support examiner judgment in scoring each item. A *Scoring Standards and Example Responses* book also provides examples of correct and incorrect responses. Items within subtests are scored 0 or 1 (Making Inferences and Multiple Interpretations), 0 to 3 (Interpersonal Negotiation), and 0 to 4 (Supporting Peers) and summed within domains to obtain raw scores. The examiner then references tables in the test manual to convert raw scores to scaled subtest scores (M = 10, SD = 3). These conversions are made for 1-year age bands from 6 through 8 years, then a 3-year band for 9 through 11 years. The four subtest scaled scores are then summed and converted to a Social Language Development Index composite score (M = 100, SD = 15). Subtest and composite scores are matched to descriptive terms (e.g., *gifted or very advanced, average, impaired or delayed*), and can be converted to percentile ranks. Subtest raw scores also may be converted to age equivalents and percentile ranks.

DEVELOPMENT. The test manual includes an informal account of item development, situated within a perspective that effective communication requires pragmatic evaluation, which involves self-reflection, verbal mediation, response inhibition, and behavior direction that is developed through experience (Gallagher, 1999). The test authors identify Norris and Hoffman's (1993) three contexts in which language occurs: (a) settings and participants, (b) topics and purposes, and (c) nonverbal cues and figurative language. The authors describe reviewing empirical and theoretical articles on social language and reference personal experiences with item development in the context of spoken language assessment. Age 6 years was determined a suitable entry point for the measurement of social language, and items of increasing complexity were developed such that a diversity of correct and incorrect responses was achieved. Changes for this normative update include: a new norm sample stratified by demographic characteristics to represent the U.S. school-aged population, the addition of scaled scores for subtests, recalculation of the total score, new technical documentation (e.g., item analyses, item bias studies, content description, diagnostic accuracy analyses), and a reorganization of the test manual.

TECHNICAL.

Standardization. The normative sample comprises 1,002 children from 26 states representing all major regions of the United States. A stratified sampling approach ensured a close match to the national school-aged population on gender, race, and special needs (e.g., specific language impairment, ASD) across 1-year age bands of 155 to 176 examinees. There is a slight underrepresentation of children identified as Hispanic (19% in the norm sample vs. 23% nationwide), which, given the age of the examinees and nationwide trends in English learners (Musu-Gillette et al., 2017), could reflect the need for examinees to be able to communicate in English.

Reliability. Internal consistency reliability is provided via coefficient alpha for 1-year age intervals. Observed estimates range from .92 to .95 for the Social Language Development Index and from .74 to .95 across subtests. There is no discernible relationship between internal consistency and age, gender, race, Hispanic label, or students receiving special services. Test-retest reliability estimates were obtained from a sample of 96 children who completed the test at an approximately two-week interval. Observed estimates were .89 for the Social Language Development Index, .93 for Making Inferences, .87 for Interpersonal Negotiation, .69 for Multiple Interpretations, and .70 for Supporting Peers. Finally, the test manual states that 10 trained examiners scored 10 random tests and reports a correlation coefficient of .84 as a form of interscorer agreement.

Validity. The test manual addresses evidence for validating score inferences based on analyses of item functioning, potential impact on racial/ethnic subgroups, sensitivity/specificity, relationships to other variables, and test structure. Basic item analysis showed median point-biserial correlations ranging from .38 to .62 and median item difficulties ranging from .40 to .77 across subtests and age. There was a noticeable trend that indicated items were more difficult for younger children than older children. Differential item functioning analyses (female vs. male, African American vs. non-African American,

Hispanic vs. non-Hispanic) found no pattern of favored subgroup. Further, effect sizes for the flagged items were negligible. Subtest and composite scores were compared for particular subgroups (female vs. male, African American vs. White, Asian/Pacific Islander vs. White, Hispanic vs. non-Hispanic) via *t* tests and effect sizes. Three comparisons—female vs. male on Supporting Peers and the Social Language Development Index, African American vs. White on Interpersonal Negotiation—were significant at the $p < .05$ level or better. Cohen's *d* effect sizes across all comparisons ranged from a magnitude of 0.02 to 0.34. Sensitivity/specificity analyses employing cut scores between 90 and 94 on the composite score returned values greater than .80 for both sensitivity and specificity with a ROC/AUC value of .91 for an ASD diagnosis. For specific language impairment, the same range of cut scores produced specificity indices above .80, but sensitivity indices were between .50 and .61. The ROC/AUC was .76. Known-group comparisons found significantly lower performances for children with ASD (*d*s = -1.24 to 1.92 across subtests and composite), a specific language impairment (*d*s = -0.38 to -0.95), and receiving special education services (*d*s = -0.36 to -1.23). Subtest intercorrelations ranged from .38 to .54. A principal components analysis using subtest scaled scores suggested a single composite score.

COMMENTARY. The test manual successfully argues the merit of looking at language development through a lens that complements traditional foci of comprehension and phonics. The domain targeted by test items has been clearly and purposefully defined against literature in the field. There is some question, however, of the extent to which the test content captures a pragmatic perspective of language versus a measurement of social cognitive skills. Submitting items to an expert panel review for quantitative ratings (e.g., Polit & Tatano Beck, 2006) against the theoretical framework could strengthen confidence in the relevance and representativeness of the test's content.

Recommendations for examiner credentials, a fairly robust and representative norm sample, item functioning analyses, and direct, conventional scoring procedures all support an inference that SLDT-E: NU scores can accurately represent different levels of development in the domains targeted by the items. No analysis of response processes is referenced in the test manual, however. An analysis of examinee cognition via think-aloud protocol could be beneficial, particularly for the Making Inferences subtest, which relies on arguably narrow interpretations of what constitutes a correct answer. Estimates of validity show sufficient magnitude to support an inference that SLDT-E: NU scores serve as legitimate representations of the relevant assessment universe for research purposes and low-stakes decisions about an individual (Nunnally & Bernstein, 1994). Relative to other available options for reporting interrater agreement (e.g., Gwet, 2014), the interscorer agreement analysis presented is weak. Results of known-group comparisons and sensitivity/specificity analyses signal initial support that SLDT-E: NU scores relate to other variables in a theory-consistent manner. A more robust examination of test structure (e.g., via confirmatory factory analysis) is warranted. Finally, the examination of disparate impact across subgroups via mean comparisons provides initial support that use of the SLDT-E: NU will avoid negative unintended consequences.

SUMMARY. The intended uses of the SLDT-E: NU are broad, covering both clinical and research uses. The set of validation efforts presented in the test manual provides confidence that the SLDT-E: NU employs reasonably well-functioning items and that subtest and composite scores broadly represent development of children 6 through 11 years old. Interpretation of these scores, however, is less clear. From a practical standpoint, the SLDT-E: NU appears most capable of serving within an assessment of a child for an ASD diagnosis. The test could be useful in identifying children with a specific language impairment or other need for special services, but its contribution would not be as strong for these aims. In terms of the second and third intended uses of the test, a critical examination of test content and scoring interpretations is warranted before providing strong recommendation that the SLDT-E: NU can be used to identify strengths and weaknesses and advance understanding of social language development.

REVIEWERS' REFERENCES

Gallagher, T. M. (1999). Interrelationships among children's language, behavior, and emotional problems. *Topics in Language Disorders, 19,* 1-15.

Gwet, K. L. (2014). *Handbook of inter-rater reliability* (4th ed.). Gaithersburg, MD: Advanced Analytics.

Musu-Gillette, L., de Brey, C., McFarland, J., Hussar, W., Sonnenberg, W., & Wilkinson-Flicker, S. (2017). *Status and trends in the education of racial and ethnic groups 2017* (NCES 2017-051). U.S. Department of Education, National Center for Education Statistics. Washington, DC. Retrieved from http://nces.ed.gov/pubsearch

Norris, J., & Hoffman, P. (1993). *Whole language intervention for school-age children.* San Diego, CA: Singular.

Nunnally, J. C., & Bernstein, I. H. (1994). *Psychometric theory* (3rd ed.). New York, NY: McGraw-Hill.

Polit, D. F., & Tatano Beck, C. (2006). The content validity index: Are you sure you know what's being reported? Critique and recommendations. *Research in Nursing and Health, 29,* 489–497. https://doi.org/10.1002/nur.20147

[152]

Social Profile.

Purpose: Designed "for observational assessment of the behavioral interactions of activity groups as a whole or of individuals within an activity group."
Publication Date: 2013.
Acronym: SP.
Administration: Individual or group.
Forms, 2: Children, Adult/Adolescent.
Price Data, 2020: $140 per manual (2013, 95 pages) containing flash drive with downloadable and writable versions of both forms and group participation social observation sheet (membership discounts available).
Time: Administration time not reported.
Comments: "The [profile] may be scored either by an individual or, preferably, through discussion, with the group jointly identifying its social participation skill levels." Typically administered after at least 30 minutes of group observation; assessment may occur in one session or across extended periods.
Author: Mary V. Donohue.
Publisher: AOTA Press.

a) CHILDREN.
Population: Ages 18 months to 11 years.
Scores, 10: 3 Levels (Parallel, Associative, Basic Cooperative) in each of 3 constructs (Activity Participation, Social Interaction, Group Membership and Roles) plus Average Summary Score.

b) ADULT/ADOLESCENT.
Population: Ages 12 and older.
Scores, 16: 5 Levels (Parallel, Associative, Basic Cooperative, Supportive Cooperative, Mature) in each of 3 constructs (Activity Participation, Social Interaction, Group Membership and Roles) plus Average Summary Score.

Review of the Social Profile by ALBERT M. BUGAJ, Department of Psychology, University of Wisconsin–Green Bay, Green Bay, WI:

DESCRIPTION. Intended for use by therapists, group leaders, and teachers, the Social Profile (SP) is designed to assess cooperation within groups or the level of interaction expressed by individuals within a group. The test manual includes two forms of the SP, a version for use with children ages 18 months to 11 years, and an adult/adolescent version for older individuals. The test manual provides full instructions for performing observations and scoring. Case studies serve as examples of using the SP. All forms and scoring sheets are available in the test manual itself and can be printed from a memory card provided in the manual.

The theoretical basis of the SP rests on Parten's (1932) analysis of children's play behavior and Mosey's (1968; 1986) revision of Parten's work. The SP arranges social behavior on a developmental continuum of social interaction with five levels. At the parallel level, individuals do not interact with one another but simply play or work side-by-side. The mature level represents the highest form of interaction, in which group members interact harmoniously and effectively to achieve goals. In between lie the associative, basic cooperative, and supportive cooperative levels, each with increasing degrees of goal activity. The test manual indicates individuals may exhibit behaviors at several levels. Interaction type also may differ based on the setting.

Rating interactions expressed by a group commences with a half-hour long observation. Notes are taken using an observation sheet provided in the test manual and on the memory card. Eight areas of interaction are observed (cooperation, norms, roles, communication, activity behaviors, power and leadership, motivation and attraction, and goals). Thirty-nine Likert scales (26 on the children's form) are completed based on the observations. The scales are grouped in three areas: Activity Participation, Social Interaction, and Group Membership and Roles. Specific items are linked to specific levels of interaction. A score of 0 on these scales indicates these behaviors were *never* observed; 5 indicates they occurred *always*. Scores within each level for each area are averaged, and these averages are then transferred to a summary sheet, on which they are again averaged (i.e., the areas Activity Participation, Social Interaction, and Group Membership and Roles, are averaged for the parallel level, then the associative level, and so on). These results also may be graphed. Interpretation of the average scores determines the level of cooperation within the group, or of an individual if the analysis is performed at that level.

DEVELOPMENT. Construction of the SP commenced with the observation of preschool groups in 36 sessions in eight metropolitan and suburban settings. Elementary and middle school children were observed on playgrounds and in gymnasiums, lunchrooms, and classroom art groups in nine rural, suburban, and city settings. Junior high and high school students were observed in similar settings along with sports fields and clubs. The number of junior high and high school groups observed is not reported in the test manual, nor is that for elementary/middle school students. The test manual states that the elementary and middle school children were in metropolitan New York and New Jersey; the geographic location of the other age groups is not specified. No observations of adult-aged groups are reported. These observations resulted in the development of 252 potential items.

Eleven experienced psychosocial activity group leaders rated the items for clarity and appropriateness. After the review, the number of items was reduced to 166. Repetitious and nonessential items were then removed, resulting in the current children and adult forms. Feedback provided by observers and self-scorers in senior community groups indicated the length of the instrument was manageable, and the Likert scales easy to use. Based on the feedback, some wording was changed to make the phrasing more familiar, and a question was introduced at the beginning of each item grouping to create greater focus in making observations.

TECHNICAL. The 39 items were field-tested by observing 21 groups (total *n* = 242) in five preschools. Statistical analysis indicated a moderate level of internal consistency with an alpha coefficient of .71. After two additional analyses, all items were retained. The same study found that parallel behavior, the earliest form of interaction, was displayed most frequently among 2- and 3-year-olds. Analysis of variance and correlational analyses revealed increasing levels of more mature interaction that were significantly related to increasing age, as predicted by the theories of Parten (1932) and Mosey (1968).

Subsequent factor analysis of the same set of data demonstrated the data were arranged in three factors corresponding to the three levels of interaction observed in the group. A factor analysis of the data collected via observations of 15 groups of preschoolers (*n* not indicated in the test manual) resulted in four factors, the final factor involving supportive cooperative behaviors, the fourth level in the model. Cluster analysis performed on this data set further indicated the independent structures measured by the instrument. Two further factor analytic studies, both using preschool children, also found factor structures in keeping with the theoretical basis of the SP.

A study with adult groups examined construct evidence of validity. Thirty psychiatric patients were observed first on admission to occupational therapy groups and unit services and again after about 30 days had elapsed. Statistical analyses indicated significantly increasing SP scores over time, as predicted.

Three studies examined interrater reliability. One study examined 15 preschool groups using an earlier longer form (252 items) of the scale; the second study examined 21 occupational therapy groups in a psychiatric unit; and the final study assessed 14 preschool, adolescent, and senior care center groups. For the first study, interrater reliability coefficients were moderate (.58 to .80) to moderately high (.71 to .90) for basic cooperative and parallel behaviors, respectively. Coefficients for the second and third studies, which involved the 39-item form, were .80 and .88, respectively. One study examined the test-retest reliability of the SP, finding a correlation coefficient of .75 over a 4-week period.

COMMENTARY. Questions must be raised regarding the SP, although it rests on a sound theoretical basis, beginning with the test manual itself. The manual could be better organized. Rather than providing the reader with the theoretical background of the test, the manual commences with a detailed description of the instrument. Not until Chapter 2 is the background of the test provided. Reversing the order of these chapters would make the description of the instrument easier to read and provide the reader with an important theoretical context.

Although the theoretical basis of the SP is clearly and logically explained, providing substantial construct evidence of validity for the instrument, a greater degree of greater clarity is required. For example, the test manual refers to Bandura's (1977) social learning theory but does not clearly explain the link between Parten's work and that of Bandura. Reference is made to a study examining changes in social participation through social learning, but that does not mean the concepts are theoretically similar. The test manual also links social learning theory to Vygotsky's thoughts on child development, referring to the 1978 publication *Mind in Society*. However, Bandura's concept of social learning via modeling and Vygotsky's ideas are quite different. Whereas Bandura refers to modeling (or the copying) of another person's behavior, Vygotsky believed children's thought processes develop through such processes as dialogue and the internalization of speech (van der Veer & Zavershneva, 2018). Vygotsky's ideas also predate Bandura by about 50 years: The 1978 publication is a translation and compilation of several sources (Yasnitsky, 2010).

At least two clerical mishaps occur in the chapter describing the development of the SP. In the first, reference is made to a section within the chapter titled "Analysis of Internal Consistency Reliability of Items." This would seem to refer to the section titled "Analysis of Items' Internal

Consistency Reliability." In the second instance, the text on page 18 refers to a correlation coefficient of .8805 between 2- and 3-year-olds and parallel-level behaviors, whereas the value reported in an accompanying table is -.8805. So, the text reports a positive correlation, whereas the table shows a (theoretically correct) negative relationship.

Chapter 3 is also somewhat disorganized. For example, it begins with a description of the preschool children studied during the initial development of the instrument. The examination of the internal consistency of the final version is then discussed. It is not until after this that the construction of that final version is described. The chapter would flow more logically if the two sections were reversed.

Turning to the development of the SP, adequate procedures were followed during item development. However, pretesting seems to be limited to groups consisting of children and high school students. No pretesting appears to have been performed with adult groups. Further, the demographic characteristics of the samples tested are not reported. Although mention is made that the preschoolers observed during the initial development of the SP came from "various cultural and socioeconomic backgrounds" (p. 15), it is not known whether they were stratified to include a good gender balance and individuals from diverse populations. This is also true of the studies of the internal consistency and factor structure of the SP. Although these studies do attest to the validity and reliability of the SP with children and teens, further testing of the instrument's properties regarding adults and diverse populations should be performed.

One study with adult psychiatric patients in occupational therapy did demonstrate significant improvements in social interaction over a 30-day period. However, this study lacked comparison groups performing non-social activities or no activities. Thus, it is not possible to assess how much change may have occurred due to processes other than the interaction during the therapy sessions. (See Keppel & Zedeck, 1989, pp. 445-448 for a discusson of this topic in research design.)

SUMMARY. The SP appears to possess a sound theoretical basis and should prove useful as a measurement tool in groups consisting of children and high school students. The SP can be recommended only as a research tool with adults due to the limited testing of that age group during development. It also must be used with caution when working with diverse populations. If used in clinical settings to measure change, it must be used with great caution until further examinations of its properties are made using adult participants.

REVIEWER'S REFERENCES

Bandura, A. (1977). *Social learning theory.* New York, NY: General Learning Press.

Daniels, H. (2012). Dialectic and dialogic: The essence of a Vygotskian pedagogy. *Cultural-Historical Psychology, 8*(3), 70-79.

Keppel, G., & Zedeck, S. (1989). *Data analysis for research designs: Analysis of variance and multiple regression/correlation approaches.* New York, NY: W. H. Freeman.

Mosey, A. C. (1968). Recapitulation of ontogenesis: A theory for practice of occupational therapy. *American Journal of Occupational Therapy, 22,* 426-438.

Mosey, A. C. (1986). *Psychosocial components of occupational therapy.* New York, NY: Raven Press.

Parten, M. B. (1932). Social participation among pre-school children. *Journal of Abnormal and Social Psychology, 27,* 243-269.

van der Veer, R., & Zavershneva, E. (2018). The final chapter of Vygotsky's *Thinking and Speech. Journal of the History of the Behavioral Sciences, 54*(2), 101-116.

Vygotsky, L. S. (1978). *Mind in Society.* Cambridge, MA: Harvard University Press.

Yasnitsky, A. (2010). Guest editor's introduction: "Archival revolution" in Vygotskian studies? Uncovering Vygotsky's archives. *Journal of Russian & East European Psychology, 48*(1), 3-13.

Review of the Social Profile: Assessment of Social Participation in Children, Adolescents, and Adults by LYNN SHELLEY, Professor and Chair, Department of Psychology, Westfield State University, Westfield, MA:

DESCRIPTION. The Social Profile: Assessment of Social Participation in Children, Adolescents, and Adults (SP) is a descriptive assessment of social interaction in an activity group that provides a description of the developmental and functional level of the group or an individual in the group. Groups, such as families, clubs, teams, community groups, or therapeutic groups are observed while performing a task for a minimum of 30 minutes. There is a children's version and an adult/adolescent version, so the age range is 18 months and up. The children's version yields a description of three developmental levels of social interaction that fall on an ordinal scale (parallel, associative, and basic cooperative); the adult/adolescent version examines the same three levels, plus two more (supportive cooperative and mature). Therapists, health professionals, teachers, or other group leaders can use the SP to evaluate the developmental level of the social interactions of an individual in the group, or of the entire group, and the adult/adolescent version also can be scored by high-functioning group members. The test manual suggests scoring can be done by an individual or through group discussion. The SP can be used once or repeatedly, thus permitting changes in behavior to be monitored over time and making the SP useful for clinical evaluation, evaluating treatment over time, or research purposes such as outcome studies.

For the adult/adolescent version, 39 items are used to rate the frequency of specific behaviors on a Likert-type scale (0 = *never,* 5 = *always*). Items span three topics (Activity Participation, Social

Interaction, and Group Membership and Roles). Within the topics are one to four items for the five increasingly mature levels of interaction (parallel, associative, basic cooperative, supportive cooperative, and mature). The children's version has 26 Likert-type items that span the same three topics. Within those topics, two to four items rate three levels of interaction (parallel, associative, basic cooperative). The SP manual describes how to compute scores and provides case examples. With both versions, an average for each level is obtained within each topic. From those averages, an average for each topic can be obtained (and if desired, plotted onto a graph). The adult/adolescent version yields 15 averages, and the children's version yields nine averages, so a profile of social functioning is obtained. Scoring is done by hand. Information about the amount of time necessary to complete items and compute scores is not provided in the test manual and will vary depending upon experience and amount of discussion.

DEVELOPMENT. There is a strong theoretical foundation for the SP, and although Donohue adopts an eclectic theoretical approach to growth and development, she relies extensively on the work of Parten (1932) and Mosey (1986) in the area of social interaction and group processes as well as subsequent empirical work exploring those theories (e.g., Dyer & Moneta, 2006; Field, 1984). This strong theoretical foundation, combined with extensive observation of various-aged groups of typically developing children and adolescents, forms the foundation of the items and subscales, which were field tested with both preschool and adult groups and adapted based on that fieldwork. Early versions of the scale contained more than 250 items, but item analyses and expert judges eventually pared the numbers to their current levels. Thorough descriptions of fieldwork, instrument development, and psychometric properties are described in the test manual and other published research (e.g., Donohue, 2003, 2005, 2007).

TECHNICAL.

Reliability. During instrument development, internal consistency of the shortened scale was explored using data from 21 preschool groups. An alpha coefficient of .71 was observed, and it was determined that no further items needed to be removed (Donohue, 2003). Adequate test-retest reliability was demonstrated using the children's version with an interval of 4 weeks between assessments (r = .75). Interrater reliability was explored using longer versions of the scale during instrument development as well as with the final version. Across two studies of the final version, 32 raters working in pairs observed 21 adult psychiatric groups; 14 adult community groups; and 14 preschool, adolescent, and senior-center groups and found acceptable levels of consistency with intraclass correlation coefficients of .80 for psychiatric groups and .88 for preschool and senior center groups. However, another study using an earlier, longer form of the scale with preschoolers resulted in a range of correlation coefficients comparing scores of two observers for parallel, associative, and basic cooperative levels that yielded tremendous variation for all behavior levels (.05 to .90). The associative level demonstrated the lowest coefficients (.05 to .22). Recent research not described in the test manual has yielded better interrater reliability values when using a weighted formula for computing an overall Social Profile (Bonsaksen, Donohue, & Milligan, 2016). The test authors strongly recommend that test users have a clear understanding of the constructs prior to using the instrument and that they initially work in pairs to establish adequate interrater reliability.

Validity. During instrument development, evidence of validity was considered in several ways. The test author explored content evidence of validity by having 11 expert judges evaluate items for their utility and importance, and the judges critiqued the five group-level concepts. Consequently, some items were removed and wording of labels changed. Prior to the elimination of items, exploratory factor analysis and cluster analysis were conducted to explore construct validity and found factors that corresponded to the theorized conceptual levels (Donohue, 2005). Because the five group levels are theorized to represent a developmental pathway, construct validity also was explored by examining the five group-level concepts across age in preschoolers ages 2 to 5 years using analysis of variance and correlations within age groups (Donohue, 2003). Ratings for parallel, associative, and basic cooperative scores followed the pattern that would be predicted by Mosey (1968) and Parten (1932), and profiles illustrated how children progress through the groups and increasingly engage in multiple levels simultaneously, indicating an increasingly complex developmental pattern across age.

Sensitivity of the instrument was explored by using the instrument pre- and post-treatment of adult psychiatric patients participating in occupational therapy groups (Donohue, Hanif, & Wu

Berns, 2011, as cited in the test manual). The SP successfully detected differences over a 1-month time span.

COMMENTARY. There are several strengths and unique features of the SP. The instrument has a very strong theoretical foundation, and the SP is an exciting tool to further explore the theory. Another strength and interesting feature of this instrument is that it can be used across the lifespan, used repeatedly, and used with individuals at various levels of functioning, making it ideal for developmental studies. The children's version goes up to 11 years of age, and the adult/adolescent version begins at 12 years, but it is unclear why this age was chosen as the cut point, and there does not appear to be enough research around the transition ages. The two instruments overlap, so it may be beneficial to attempt the adult/adolescent version with younger children, such as those ages 6 to 11 years, to see whether instances of more advanced interactions occur.

The instrument is fairly quick and easy to administer and score, but administration instructions tend to be unclear, and for some issues, missing. A nice feature of the SP is that it can be used with many types of groups performing just about any type of activity. However, the test manual lacks guidance about what group members should be instructed prior to the observation period. Nor is there a place on the scoring sheet to record the number of group members nor the activity performed. Clearer instructions and more items on the scoring sheets that describe the context and group members are necessary.

Similarly, there is little guidance about types of activity groups to observe to elicit optimal group performance. The scoring sheet states: "Choose an activity group session typical for this group that is at an average level of participation for the group or for an individual being observed in the group" (manual, p. 75). But, type of activity can impact the profile. Appropriate interactions can vary for different activities, so different profiles will be more or less likely to occur depending on the activity undertaken. Some guidance can be extrapolated from the case examples, but activity type is important for users to consider when interpreting outcomes.

The test manual states the SP can be scored "by an individual, or, preferably through discussion, with the group jointly identifying its social participation skill levels" (p. 2). But there are neither instructions about how to facilitate group scoring, nor case examples of group scoring, and group scoring was not described in the validity and reliability studies. Given the large variability in interrater reliability coefficients, group scoring should be undertaken with care.

The steps taken during instrument development to explore reliability and validity were impressive. There are some concerns about interrater reliability for some of the subscales, but the test author, who suggests adequate practice and working in teams, acknowledges this issue. Overall the case examples are helpful, but the actual scoring sheets lack detailed instructions and do not prompt for the collection of all relevant information. This is a bit surprising given the impressive work developing these versions and the otherwise thoroughness of the test manual.

SUMMARY. The SP yields a descriptive profile of the social functioning and developmental status of a group as a whole or an individual within a group. It is a useful tool for both clinical and research purposes that can be used by any type of group leader. This instrument fills a niche where there are no similar instruments with as strong a theoretical foundation, and it makes a unique contribution to the arsenal of existing tools.

REVIEWER'S REFERENCES

Bonsaksen, T., Donohue, M. V., & Milligan, R. M. (2016). Occupational therapy students rating the social profile of their educational group: Do they agree? *Scandinavian Journal of Occupational Therapy, 23*(6), 477–484.

Donohue, M. V. (2003). Group profile studies with children: Validity measures and item analysis. *Occupational Therapy in Mental Health, 19,* 1-23.

Donohue, M. V. (2005). Social Profile: Assessment of validity and reliability with preschool children. *Canadian Journal of Occupational Therapy, 72*(3), 164–175.

Donohue, M. V. (2007). Interrater reliability of the Social Profile: Assessment of community and psychiatric group participation. *Australian Occupational Therapy Journal, 54*(1), 49–58.

Donohue, M. V., Hanif, H., & Wu Berns, L. (2011). An exploratory study of social participation in occupational therapy groups. *Mental Health Special Interest Section Quarterly, 34*(4), 1-4.

Dyer, S., & Moneta, G. B. (2006). Frequency of parallel, associative, and cooperative play in British children of different socioeconomic status. *Social Behavior and Personality: An International Journal, 34*(5), 587–592.

Field, T. (1984). Play behaviors of handicapped children who have friends. In T. Field, J. L. Roopnarine, & M. Segal (Eds.), *Friendships in normal and handicapped children* (pp. 153-162). Norwood, NJ: Ablex.

Mosey, A. C. (1986). *Psychosocial components of occupational therapy.* New York, NY: Raven Press.

Parten, M. B. (1932). Social participation among pre-school children. *Journal of Abnormal and Social Psychology, 27,* 243-269.

[153]

SPECTRA: Indices of Psychopathology.

Purpose: Designed to provide "an integrated hierarchical assessment of psychopathology from (lower order) clinical constructs, up through multiple spectra, as well as critical information about cognitive and adaptive capacity."

Population: Ages 18 and older.

Publication Date: 2018.

Acronym: SPECTRA.

Scores, 21: 12 clinical scales in 3 spectra: Internalizing Spectrum (Depression, Anxiety, Social Anxiety,

Post-Traumatic Stress), Externalizing Spectrum (Alcohol Problems, Drug Problems, Severe Aggression, Antisocial), Reality-Impairing Spectrum (Psychosis, Paranoid Ideation, Manic Activation, Grandiose Ideation); 3 supplemental scales: Cognitive Concerns, Psychosocial Functioning, Suicidal Ideation; General Psychopathology Index; Profile Classification Index; 1 validity scale: Infrequency.
Administration: Individual or group.
Price Data, 2020: $164 per introductory kit including manual (96 pages), fast guide (14 pages), 5 reusable item booklets, 25 response booklets, 25 score summary/profile forms, and certificate for 5 online scoring reports; $54 per manual (including fast guide); $54 per 25 response booklets; $54 per 25 score summary/profile forms; $26 per 5 reusable item booklets; $3 per online administration or online score report (minimum 5).
Time: 15-20 minutes for administration.
Authors: Mark A. Blais and Samuel Justin Sinclair.
Publisher: Psychological Assessment Resources, Inc.

Review of SPECTRA: Indices of Psychopathology by ASHRAF KAGEE, Professor of Psychology, Stellenbosch University, Stellenbosch, South Africa:

DESCRIPTION. SPECTRA: Indices of Psychopathology is a 96-item self-administered instrument that measures psychopathology and functioning. The measure consists of 12 clinical scales that assess various dimensions of mental distress, namely, Depression, Anxiety, Social Anxiety, Post-Traumatic Stress, Alcohol Problems, Severe Aggression, Antisocial Behavior, Drug Problems, Psychosis, Paranoid Ideation, Manic Activation, and Grandiose Ideation.

The scales are based on clinical utility and their relationship to three spectra, namely, Internalizing, Externalizing, and Reality-Impairing, which together comprise the General Psychopathology Index. This general index provides a measure of the total burden of psychopathology. By organizing mental distress in an integrated way, the SPECTRA can be used to assess psychopathology at the level of specific clinical constructs, at the level of broader spectra, and at a more global level.

The SPECTRA also includes three supplemental scales that assess Cognitive Concerns, Psychosocial Functioning, and Suicidal Ideation. The scale has an Infrequency Index consisting of three items that are infrequently endorsed by respondents and a Protocol Classification Index that reflects the number of indices that are endorsed above a critical level.

Persons who administer and score the SPECTRA are not required to have any formal training in psychology or psychometrics. However, they should be familiar with the instrument manual to address questions from test takers that may arise during test administration. Interpretation, on the other hand, requires professional training in psychopathology and functioning, such as that which would be provided in a postgraduate degree program in clinical or counseling psychology, as well as training in the ethics of psychological testing.

The SPECTRA may be used for clinical applications such as assessing or treating individual patients to identify specific indicators of psychopathology with a view to diagnosis and treatment planning. It is available for use in a range of clinical settings, including inpatient and outpatient clinics, hospitals, schools, and forensic settings.

The instrument may also be used in research settings to understand global measures of psychopathology. The test authors recommend that the SPECTRA be interpreted in a systematic multistep process to improve clinical precision and to minimize the error that may be associated with variability in interpretation.

DEVELOPMENT. The SPECTRA was developed and standardized as a broad measure of psychopathology and functioning in adults over the age of 18. The test authors conducted a literature review to identify lower-order constructs that would serve as markers for the three higher-order psychopathology spectra (Internalizing, Externalizing, and Reality-Impairing). This process yielded 15 potential lower-order constructs, five for each of the higher-order constructs. Test authors generated a pool of 10 to 12 items for each lower-order construct, yielding a total of 174 items. Following an expert review for clarity and construct relevance by an expert panel, the item pool was reduced to 110 items.

The 110-item version of the scale was administered to a mixed sample of clinical and non-clinical participants. These were 495 college students from a large midwestern university and 149 psychiatric patients receiving treatment in the northeastern United States. The psychometric properties of the scale were then determined, specifically to assess item-scale convergence (in which strong correlations are expected to occur between items from a given scale and the respective/parent scale) and item-scale divergence (in which weaker correlations are expected to occur between items from a given scale and all other/non-parental scales). Some strong cross-scale correlations were obtained, findings that diminished both convergence and divergence, and prompted the test developers to reduce the total number of items to 74 (on 12 scales) and to rework the content of several scales.

The 74-item version of the scale was administered to a second sample of 130 clinical patients and 502 college students. The latter sample also completed several additional instruments in order to provide concurrent evidence of validity. Item-scale convergence improved, with resultant coefficients ranging from .45 to .76. Similarly, item-scale divergence improved such that all items on six scales yielded significantly higher correlation coefficients with their respective parent scale than with other scales. For the remaining six scales, only two items correlated more strongly with a non-parental scale. Principal components analysis of the scale produced 16 components with eigenvalues greater than 1.00. The most appropriate solution yielded 12 components that were interpretable as capturing the 12 SPECTRA scales. Most items demonstrated factor loadings above .40 on their expected scale. The 12 components explained 62% of the item-level variance.

Finally, additional items were added to the 74-item scale to yield the 96-item version. These items make up the supplemental scales Suicidal Ideation, Cognitive Concerns, and Psychosocial Functioning and the embedded Infrequency validity scale.

The test materials consist of an item booklet, a response booklet, a professional manual, a score summary form, and a fast guide. The item booklet presents 96 items, and the respondent is asked, "How true are the following statements about you?" Items are written at a fourth-grade reading level. The respondent records his or her responses in the response booklet in which response options are presented on a 5-point Likert-type scale: *not at all true* (NT); *a little bit true* (AT); *moderately true* (MT); *quite true* (QT); and *completely true* (CT).

TECHNICAL. The standardization sample included 1,062 adults ages 18-91 years who were representative of the U.S. population for age, gender, race/ethnicity, level of education, and geographic region. Data were collected in 2013. An older adult comparison group was made up of 272 members of the standardization sample ages 60 and older. Finally, a college student comparison group was formed by combining data from 91 members of the standardization sample and 337 additional college students.

Internal consistency indicators for the SPECTRA are generally high. Median alpha coefficients across scales, spectra, and the General Psychopathology Index were .86 (overall range .66 to .96), .83 (overall range .68 to .94), and .79 (overall range .27 to .96) for the standardization, college, and older adults samples, respectively. For the Externalizing and Reality-Impairing spectra, mean interitem correlation coefficients range between .12 and .31, indicating that the scales tap independent content. Values for the Internalizing spectrum range from .39 to .53. Test-retest reliability coefficients for the scales range from .73 to .96, with the exception of the Drug Problems scale (r = .63), with minimal mean change in scores indicating good consistency over time (N = 62; 1- to 2-week interval).

The SPECTRA has shown favorable concurrent validity with a range of measures such as the Patient Health Questionnaire, Alcohol Use Disorders Identification Test, and various subscales selected from Section III of the Emerging Measures and Models of the *Diagnostic and Statistical Manual of Mental Disorders* (5th ed.; American Psychiatric Association, 2013). All SPECTRA scales were significantly correlated with their target scale and 10 of the 12 yielded correlation coefficients greater than .50, indicating both significant and meaningful associations with these scales.

COMMENTARY. The SPECTRA is easy to administer and relatively straightforward to interpret, with good visual appeal to both administrators and test takers. It may be especially useful to generalist practitioners seeking to understand a patient's psychological status at first blush. As such, it may be of use as an intake assessment instrument in clinical practice settings as it yields useful summary data for patients.

The SPECTRA may be less useful in specialist clinics as the data it yields have quite a broad range that deal with several dimensions of psychological distress. Studies of sensitivity and specificity of the instrument against a gold standard have not been reported and thus the measure may be less appropriate for diagnostic purposes and more appropriate for gaining a sense of the chief problems affecting individuals seeking psychological help in a clinical setting, or in generating valid and reliable data in a research setting.

One or two items are double-barreled, in that they ask about two things while allowing only a single response. However, these are kept to a minimum and in general the items are easy to understand by anyone with a basic level of reading.

SUMMARY. The SPECTRA is a 96-item self-administered instrument that measures psychopathology and functioning. It consists of 12 clinical scales that assess various dimensions of mental distress. The SPECTRA is best suited for use by mental health professionals trained in psychometric assessment and the ethics of psychological testing. The items cover several dimensions of psychopathology. Important advantages are its relative brevity, ease of use, and user-friendliness. It has demonstrated high internal consistency and good convergent validity with other instruments.

REVIEWER'S REFERENCE

American Psychiatric Association. (2013). *Diagnostic and statistical manual of mental disorders* (5th ed.). Washington, DC: Author.

Review of SPECTRA: Indices of Psychopathology by PETER ZACHAR, Professor of Psychology, Auburn University Montgomery, Montgomery, AL:

DESCRIPTION. The SPECTRA: Indices of Psychopathology is a 96-item instrument whose development was inspired by the quantitative model of psychopathology (Kotov et al., 2017). As implemented in this instrument, the quantitative model organizes the domain of psychopathology into three coherent spectra: Internalizing (INT), Externalizing (EXT), and Reality-Impairing (RI).

The quantitative model is hierarchical. Above the three spectra, at the highest level of the hierarchy, lies the General Psychopathology Index (GPI). Lower down on the hierarchy within each spectrum are symptom clusters that frequently co-occur. There is good evidence that higher rates of co-occurrence within the INT and EXT spectra reflect a shared genetic vulnerability among those disorders (Krueger, 1999). Conditions within a spectrum may also benefit from similar treatment strategies.

Under the Internalizing spectrum are constructs for Depression, Anxiety, Social Anxiety, and Post-Traumatic Stress. Under the Externalizing spectrum are constructs for Alcohol Problems, Drug Problems, Severe Aggression, and Antisocial (behaviors). Under the less coherent Reality-Impairing spectrum are constructs for Psychosis, Paranoid Ideation, Manic Activation, and Grandiose Ideation. This spectrum likely includes personality trait variance that spans the normal and the abnormal.

Consistent with the behavioral genetic roots of spectrum models, the general psychopathology construct represents a vulnerability to psychopathology across the board (Caspi et al., 2014). According to one interpretation of the quantitative model, people with complex and severe symptom presentations should score higher on general psychopathology. Very complex cases would have elevated scores in more than one spectrum, complex cases elevated scores in one spectrum only, and simpler cases no spectra elevations, but an elevation on a lower order scale.

In addition, the SPECTRA has supplemental scales for Suicidal Ideation, Cognitive Concerns, and level of Psychosocial Functioning. There are also two brief validity checks, but the SPECTRA lacks the sophisticated validity checks found in other instruments.

The main purposes of the SPECTRA are to efficiently screen for common psychopathological symptom clusters with which patients 18 years or older may present in both general clinical and neuropsychological settings, and to aid in understanding co-occurring symptom clusters. For patients and research participants, the items are easy to read and completing the whole instrument should not be a burden.

Anchored by 5-point Likert scales, the SPECTRA can be scored by hand or computer. Scoring the SPECTRA by hand is more ponderous than it is for other widely used psychological instruments, which potentially increases the risk for scoring errors. Because there are only five to eight items on each lower order scale, even one error could alter the results. Consequently, this reviewer recommends the computer scoring option.

DEVELOPMENT. The quantitative approach to psychopathology is based on factor analytic models that seek to map out an empirically based structure for the domain of psychopathology. Internalizing and Externalizing are highly replicated factors. Reality-Impairing is a factor that sometimes emerges depending on which symptoms are included in the item set. The vulnerability to psychopathology construct is also called the p factor, but its validity is subject to debate (van Bork, Epskamp, Rhemtulla, Borsboom, & van der Maas, 2017). Factor analytic models of psychopathology can be more or less complex with both Internalizing and Externalizing sometimes being split into two or more factors, but a parsimonious three-factor model is statistically and theoretically plausible.

Rather than being derived through factor analysis, the SPECTRA scales were rationally defined based on previous research in the factor analytic tradition. The test authors began with a three-factor model, developed preliminary lower order scales for each factor, and then refined them psychometrically. The goal of the development process was to enhance internal consistency and simple structure. As a result, the items on each scale are correlated with each other, and items are more correlated with their own scale than with the other scales. During the development process, four of the preliminary scales were combined to make two scales and one preliminary scale was dropped, resulting in 12 lower-order scales in the final version. These scales were replicated in an exploratory principal components analysis. Information about how the supplemental scales were developed was not included in the test manual.

TECHNICAL. For the standardization sample, the test authors contracted with a marketing and research firm called Knowledge Networks to obtain a sample that is representative of the U.S. population with respect to age, gender, race/ethnicity, educational attainment, and geographical region. The final sample incudes 1,062 individuals ranging in age from 18 to 91. The test authors selected 272 people age 60 and older from the full sample to create an older adult comparison sample. They also combined a subset of college students from the full sample with additional data to create a 428-person college student comparison sample. Non-normalized T scores are available for the full standardization sample as well as for the older adult and college student comparison samples. Consistent with current trends in test development, the normative sample is composed of both males and females.

Internal consistency indices are very good for the full sample, especially given the low number of items on each scale. Test-retest reliability is only appropriate for constructs that should be stable over time, which is not always the case with constructs related to psychopathology. One, however, would expect stability over the 1- to 2-week period assessed by the test authors. These test-retest coefficients using Pearson correlations are also good. The Internalizing spectrum and its subscales' reliabilities are uniformly excellent.

The test manual presents copious validity information. Most importantly, this rationally developed instrument has the structure that the quantitative model of psychopathology says it should have. The scales within each spectrum correlate as expected, and the three-factor structure of the instrument was replicated with an exploratory factor analysis. It was also validated with a confirmatory factor analysis, which indicated that the Internalizing factor is the most valid of the three. Numerous other validity coefficients assessing concurrent correlations with external criteria are also supportive. One of the tables indicates that the developers also obtained concurrent correlations with tests commonly used in neuropsychological settings, but most of the results are not reported in the test manual.

COMMENTARY. The test authors made a prediction about future practices in modeling psychopathology that looks to have been prescient and, as a result, they are ahead of the game with this instrument. A close competitor would be the Minnesota Multiphasic Personality Inventory–2–Restructured Form® (Ben-Porath & Tellegen, 2008), which is more sophisticated, but harder to use. With respect to the MMPI indices overall, the parsimonious SPECTRA would be a more competitive instrument if it contained a somatic symptom scale on the internalizing spectrum. In the near future, however, the test authors may have to worry about competing with another free test being constructed by the leaders of the quantitative psychopathology movement, who have formed the Hierarchical Taxonomy of Psychopathology (HiTOP) Consortium (Krueger, Kotov, Watson, & Zimmerman, 2018).

A strength of the SPECTRA that is not promulgated in its marketing strategy is that the SPECTRA is largely in conformity with constructs classified in the *Diagnostic and Statistical Manual of Mental Disorders* (5th ed.; *DSM-5*; American Psychiatric Association, 2013). What the SPECTRA adds to the *DSM-5* is an empirically based organization of many common *DSM-5* constructs. Its use of the *DSM* makes the SPECTRA familiar and coherent in a way that instruments with arbitrary collections of scales are not.

The marketing plan emphasizes the instrument's dimensionality, but the SPECTRA is dimensional in the way that most psychological tests are dimensional, not dimensional in the sense of being antagonistic to *DSM* constructs. With respect to its dimensions, the SPECTRA primarily samples only the pathological range of the constructs it assesses, and low scores have no interpretation. This is what makes it easy to use, but as a result, it is not fully representative of dimensional models.

One of the strengths of the test manual can be found in its suggestions for how to implement the quantitative model of psychopathology in clinical settings. One relative weakness of the manual is that it does not sequence information in a user-friendly way, as one would do as an instructor. In more than one place, a reader has to skip ahead in the manual to make sense of what she or he is reading.

One trade-off with being a parsimonious and easy to use measure is that as an instrument for use in psychological assessment, the SPECTRA is descriptively thin. Unlike many broadband tests of personality and psychopathology, the SPECTRA did not consider time-honored clinical theories as a background to its development. This can be seen as a disadvantage or an advantage, depending on one's perspective. At the very least, to fill out the quantitative model of psychopathology, the SPECTRA could be supplemented with a personality measure that coheres with the factor analytic tradition.

SUMMARY. The SPECTRA is a parsimonious and easy to use measure of the three-factor model of psychopathology. Its hierarchical approach with one global factor, three coherent spectra, and common *DSM* constructs offers an empirically based and coherent model of the domain of psychopathology. Once a person presents for treatment, this instrument would readily help differentiate more from less complex cases and offers a conceptual framework for thinking about the co-morbidities present in the more complex cases.

REVIEWER'S REFERENCES

American Psychiatric Association. (2013). *Diagnostic and statistical manual of mental disorders* (5th ed.). Washington, DC: Author.

Ben-Porath, Y. S., & Tellegen, A. (2008). Minnesota Multiphasic Personality Inventory–2–Restructured Form®. Minneapolis, MN: University of Minnesota Press.

Caspi, A., Houts, R. M., Belsky, D. W., Goldman-Mellor, S. J., Harrington, H., Israel, S., ... Moffitt, T. E. (2014). The p factor: One general psychopathology factor in the structure of psychiatric disorders? *Clinical Psychological Science, 2*, 119-137.

Kotov, R., Krueger, R. F., Watson, D., Achenbach, T. M., Althoff, R. R., Bagby, R. M., ... Zimmerman, M. (2017). The Hierarchical Taxonomy of Psychopathology (HiTOP): A dimensional alternative to traditional nosologies. *Journal of Abnormal Psychology, 126*, 454-477.

Krueger, R. F. (1999). The structure of common mental disorders. *Archives of General Psychiatry, 56*, 921-926.

Krueger, R. F., Kotov, R., Watson, D., & Zimmerman, J. (2018). Progress in achieving quantitative classification of psychopathololgy. *World Psychiatry, 17*, 282-293.

van Bork, R., Epskamp, S., Rhemtulla, M., Borsboom, D., & van der Maas, H. L. J. (2017). What is the p-factor of psychopathology? Some risks of general factor modeling. *Theory & Psychology, 27*, 759-773.

[154]

SSIS™ Social-Emotional Learning Edition.

Purpose: "Designed for evaluating and improving social-emotional learning skills in children and adolescents."
Population: Students in preschool through Grade 12.
Publication Dates: 2008-2017.
Acronym: SSIS SEL.
Administration: Individual or group.
Parts, 3: Screening/Progress Monitoring Scales; Teacher, Parent, and Student Forms; Classwide Intervention Program.
Price Data, 2020: $341 per kit including digital manual (2017, 139 pages), digital intervention program manual (2017, 294 pages), 25 online reports (includes administration; choice of parent, teacher, or student form), and 25 online progress monitoring reports (includes administration); $121 per manual; $135.50 per intervention program manual; $60 per 1-year scoring subscription (volume pricing available); $51.75 per 25 forms (administration only; parent, teacher, or student); $47.25 per 25 progress monitoring forms (administration only); $3.50 per online report (includes administration; choice of parent, teacher, or student); $2 per online screening/progress monitoring report (includes administration).
Comments: Computer administration available; computer scored; individual and group-level reports available.
Authors: Frank M. Gresham and Stephen N. Elliott.
Publisher: Pearson.

a) SCREENING/PROGRESS MONITORING SCALES.
Purpose: Designed as a teacher-completed, class-based rating form for assessing student-based strengths and improvement areas.
Scores, 10: Social-Emotional Composite (Self-Awareness, Self-Management, Social Awareness, Relationship Skills, Responsible Decision Making, Total), Academic Functioning Composite (Motivation to Learn, Reading Skills, Mathematics Skills, Total).
Time: 30-45 minutes for evaluation of up to 25 students.
Comments: Criterion-referenced; assesses social-emotional learning competencies identified by the Collaborative for Academic, Social, and Emotional Learning (CASEL).

b) TEACHER, PARENT, AND STUDENT FORMS.
Purpose: Designed to provide "different viewpoints on the social-emotional functioning of a student."
Scores, 7-8: SEL Composite (Self-Awareness, Self-Management, Social Awareness, Relationship Skills, Responsible Decision Making, Total), Core Skills, Academic Competence (Teacher form only).
Foreign Language Editions: Parent and student forms available in Spanish.
Time: 10 minutes or less for administration.
Comments: Student form for ages 8 and older.

c) CLASSWIDE INTERVENTION PROGRAM.
Comments: Provides weekly lesson plans for teaching social-emotional skills as well as intervention resources.

Cross References: For reviews by Beth Doll and Kristin Jones and by Jeanette Lee-Farmer and Joyce Meikamp of the Social Skills Improvement System Rating Scales, see 18:125; for information regarding the Social Skills Rating System, see T5:2452 (24 references); for reviews by Kathryn M. Benes and Michael Furlong and by Mitchell Karno of the Social Skills Rating System, see 12:362 (10 references); see also T4:2502 (4 references).

Review of the SSIS™ Social-Emotional Learning Edition by REBECCA GOKIERT, Associate Professor, Faculty of Extension, University of Alberta, and CHELSEA DURBER, Ph.D. Candidate, Department of Educational Psychology, University of Alberta, Edmonton, Alberta, Canada:

DESCRIPTION. The SSIS™ Social-Emotional Learning Edition (SSIS SEL) has two main purposes: (1) to assess and monitor students' progress in five core competencies articulated by the Collaborative for Academic, Social, and Emotional Learning (CASEL, 2015) and three academic areas; and (2) to teach students key social-emotional skills through an intervention program. The SSIS SEL can be used as a classroom-based universal screening tool and as a monitoring tool to evaluate changes over time during the multi-week intervention. The SSIS SEL can be used with children and youth ages 3 to 18 years, but the intervention is recommended for those between the ages of 4 and 14. The SSIS SEL Edition is made up of the Screening/Progress Monitoring Scales; Teacher, Parent, and Student Forms; and the Classwide Intervention Program (CIP).

The Screening/Progress Monitoring Scales is a classroom assessment for up to 25 students that takes 30-45 minutes to complete. Students are rated on each of the competencies using a 5-point scale. Scores ranging from 3 to 5 indicate *proficiency*, a score of 2 indicates *emerging skills*, and a score of 1 indicates *limited skills*. The measure produces a Social-Emotional Composite score, which is the sum of the five core CASEL competencies (Self-Awareness, Self-Management, Social Awareness, Relationship Skills, and Responsible Decision Making), and an Academic Functioning Composite, which is the sum of Motivation to Learn, Reading Skills, and Mathematic Skills.

The teacher, parent, and student forms produce the same composite and subscale scores as the Screening/Progress Monitoring Scales as well as a Core Skills scale score and an Academic Competence scale score (for the teacher form only). These forms take 10-20 minutes to complete. Norm-referenced standard scores are provided for the composite and scale scores for each questionnaire and can be generated from the general norm group or a gender-specific norm group. The scores can be interpreted as follows: *average* (standard score 85-115), *below average* (70-84), and *above average* (116-130). Scores of 69 or below are considered *well below average;* scores of 131 or higher are considered *well above average*. The test authors provide very detailed scoring and interpretation instructions as well as a case example.

The Classwide Intervention Program (CIP) is a comprehensive complementary developmental curriculum focused on 23 social-emotional skills that represent the five core CASEL competencies. The CIP can be used to teach students social-emotional skills. The CIP is made up of 23 units; each unit is structured as a lesson plan that describes a social-emotional skill, has specific learning objectives, identifies resources, and has three lessons (PowerPoint slide presentations). When the SSIS SEL Edition is purchased, the user is provided with access to online resources that can be downloaded and tailored to the students' learning environment.

The SSIS SEL Edition materials are all available in English; the parent and student forms are also available in Spanish. The assessment and forms can be administered and scored using the test publisher's online platform.

DEVELOPMENT. The SSIS SEL Edition is based on its predecessor, the SSIS Rating Scales and SSIS Performance Screening Guide. The test authors wanted to bring the SSIS SEL Edition in line with a robust literature around SEL, including the CASEL competencies. The development of the SSIS SEL Edition was guided by several goals, which are detailed in the test manual. The domains of the Screening/Progress Monitoring Scales were selected based on the five CASEL competencies; three academic areas of the previous Performance Screening Guide; and an iterative review by the authors, development staff, and experienced users of the past version to develop and refine the items and associated behavioral descriptions. Five teachers participated in a Q-sort procedure and perfectly sorted 25 behavioral performance descriptors onto the five SEL competencies (Elliott, Davies, Frey, Gresham, & Cooper, 2018). The teacher, parent, and student forms were taken from the original SSIS and reviewed for relevancy to the SEL competencies. Data from the standardization were used to statistically examine the item-to-SEL competencies. Item-scale correlations were calculated, and items with the highest item-scale correlations were retained for further confirmatory factor analysis (CFA).

TECHNICAL. Much of the technical information provided for the SSIS SEL Edition is based on the original standardization sample that was gathered in 2006-2007. However, the test authors have recently published manuscripts with additional validity and reliability evidence (see Elliot et al., 2018; Gresham, Elliot, Metallo, Byrd, Wilson, & Cassidy, 2018).

Standardization. Data from the SSIS Rating Scales standardization project were used to develop the SSIS SEL teacher, parent, and student forms. The standardization sample consisted of 4,700 children ages 3 through 18 years from 115 sites across 36 states. The standardization sample was based on U.S. Census data from 2006 and was designed to have equal gender representation and to match the Census figures with regard to race/ethnicity, socioeconomic status (mother's education level), and geographic location. Special education placement was also controlled. The test authors used three norm groups: a preschool group (ages 3-5 years) and two school-aged groups (ages 5-12 and 13-18). During the standardization process, data were collected for further reliability and validity studies (e.g., internal consistency, test-retest, and interrater reliability; convergent/discriminant, concurrent, and validity evidence based on clinical groups). The standardization goals, process, and reliability and validity studies are described fully in the SSIS SEL manual.

Reliability. The test authors report internal consistency using coefficient alpha for the Screening/Progress Monitoring Scales and the teacher, parent, and student forms. Reliability estimates were provided for each of the forms across the three normative samples (3-5 years, 5-12 years, and 13-18 years); by gender; and, in some cases, for the Spanish sample. Coefficients for the teacher form ranged from .70 to .97 (no Spanish sample). For the parent form, coefficients ranged from .74 to .96 for the normative sample and from .69 to .96 for the Spanish sample. Student form coefficients ranged from .70 to .95 for the normative sample and from .70 to .96 for the Spanish sample. Overall, the coefficient alpha values are in the adequate to excellent range.

The test authors also examined test-retest reliability of the teacher form using a sample of 144 individuals who completed this form twice, approximately 1.5 months apart. The corrected reliability coefficients were mostly in the low .80s. Students (n = 127) between the ages of 8 and 18 years completed the student form twice, approximately two months apart with corrected reliability coefficients ranging from the mid .70s to the low .80s. A sample of 115 individuals completed the parent form twice, approximately two months apart, yielding corrected reliability coefficients that were generally in the upper .70s and mid .80s. Across all forms, mean scores between administrations were similar, and most effect sizes (i.e., standard differences) were below .10, which indicates that each form is stable over the testing interval. Elliot et al. (2018) calculated reliability estimates for the Screening/Progress Monitoring Scales using a sample of 268 Australian students from preschool to Grade 3 and obtained excellent alpha coefficients for the Social-Emotional Composite (.91) and the Academic Functioning Composite (.90). Additionally, Elliot et al. had 12 teachers complete the scales at two time points (one month apart), and test-retest correlations for the composites and the scales ranged from .70 to .91.

The test authors evaluated interrater reliability for the teacher and parent forms using samples from the standardization project (54 individuals were rated by two teachers, and 110 individuals were rated by two caregivers). Corrected reliability coefficients ranged from .38 to .71. Overall, the Screening/Progress Monitoring Scales and the teachers, parent, and student forms demonstrate adequate reliability. Gresham et al. (2018) recently examined interrater agreement across rater pairs in two samples. The first sample consisted of 168 students in Grades 3-12 who had parent, teacher, and self ratings. The second sample consisted of 164 students with ratings by two raters in a similar role (two caregivers or two teachers). Overall, significant interrater correlations indicated that pairs of different raters had greater than chance levels of agreement. Pairs of similar raters (teacher-teacher or teacher-parent) had higher correlation coefficients than pairs of dissimilar raters (parent-student or teacher-student).

Validity. The test authors provide several sources of validity evidence under the main categories of content, construct, intercorrelation, convergent, discriminant, and criterion validity. The authors effectively describe, using accessible language, how they gathered validity evidence and how to interpret each table of results. Content evidence is demonstrated by grounding the SSIS SEL in the social-emotional learning framework proposed by CASEL (2012). Through a card sort method (described above), five teachers were able to perfectly match items to the five SEL competencies. To provide evidence for the constructs measured, item-scale correlations and scale intercorrelations were calculated. Not surprising, intercorrelations among scale scores are high, as are correlations between the scale scores and the SEL Composite. The correlations among scale scores from the teacher, parent, and student forms are presented in the test manual. Overall, correlations between forms are low to moderate, with the highest correlations between the teacher and parent forms when compared to combinations of other forms. An explanation of CFA and differential item functioning (DIF) is provided in the Development section of the test manual and is descriptive in nature with limited information on the factor loadings and on items that demonstrated DIF and were dropped from the current forms. For information on the DIF analyses and outcomes, a review of Gresham and Elliot (2008) and the original SSIS manual is recommended.

To demonstrate convergent evidence of validity, the SSIS SEL Edition scales were compared against other measures of emotional functioning such as the previous SSIS edition (Gresham & Elliot, 2008), the Behavior Assessment System for Children–Second Edition (BASC-2), and the Vineland Adaptive Behavior Scales, Second Edition (Vineland-II). Correlations between the SSIS SEL Edition scales and the previous SSIS teacher, parent, and student forms are high, with correlations between the student forms higher than those for the parent and teacher forms. The BASC-2 parent, teacher, and self-report forms (composite scales and subscales) were compared to the SSIS SEL teacher, parent, and student forms' composite and subscales. The highest positive correlations were found between the SSIS SEL subscale and composite scores and the Adaptive Skills (teacher, parent) and Personal Adjustment (student) composites on the BASC-2 (teacher form r = .68-.82; parent form r = .41-.76; student form r = .31-.54). The Vineland-II and the SSIS SEL parent and teacher forms were compared, yielding low to moderate coefficients for both parents (range = .01 to .52) and teachers (range = .30 to .75). Discriminant evidence of validity is provided in comparing the SSIS SEL to Externalizing, Internalizing, School Problems, and Maladaptive Behavior on the BASC-2 and the Vineland-II. For the comparison to the BASC-2, all correlations were negative or negligible (teacher form r = -.78 to -.21; parent form r = -.64 to .09; student form r = -.41 to -.09). Similar results were found for the parent form when compared to the Vineland II (r = -.25 to .07).

The SEL competencies for the teacher, parent, and student forms were compared using a sample of children diagnosed with autism spectrum disorder and a matched control group. The clinical sample scored significantly lower than the control group on all SEL competencies for the teacher and parent forms. The student form had similar trends; however, the sample size was considerably lower (41 and 50 for the teacher and parent forms compared to nine for the student form).

COMMENTARY. The SSIS SEL Edition is a comprehensive assessment and intervention system for identifying and improving social-emotional learning skills in children ages 3 to 18 years. The SSIS SEL Edition is based on the SSIS Rating Scales and SSIS Performance Screening Guide and draws its theoretical strength from its grounding in the social-emotional learning framework proposed by CASEL (2012). This tool was normed according to several factors based on Census population trends and for three major age bands that reflect the age range of the SSIS SEL. Although the test authors presented detailed standardization information, using a more current version of the Census would present a more accurate depiction of population trends. Administration, scoring, and interpretation are relatively easy as detailed instructions are provided in the test manual, and an online scoring and reporting system is available. The reliability evidence is convincing, with internal consistency estimates in the adequate to excellent ranges. Two recently published articles indicated good test-retest and interrater reliability estimates (Elliot et al., 2018; Gresham et al., 2018). Finally, evidence of validity is provided across several categories, but these estimates are generally in the low to moderate ranges.

SUMMARY. In sum, the SSIS SEL Edition is an assessment and intervention system for children ages 3-18 years. The test manual provides strong reliability and adequate validity evidence to support the social-emotional inferences that are generated from the SSIS SEL Edition teacher, parent, and student forms. The Classwide Intervention Program (CIP) provides a comprehensive curriculum that can be used by teachers to support social-emotional learning skills that are identified through the Screening/Progress Monitoring Scales and the teacher, parent, and student forms. The tool demonstrates some utility in discriminating between typically developing children and those with autism spectrum disorder. The tool is recommended for use; however, additional reliability and validity evidence with updated Census data and for distinct clinical groups would further enhance its utility.

REVIEWERS' REFERENCES

Collaborative for Academic, Social, and Emotional Learning. (2012). *2013 CASEL guide: Effective social and emotional learning programs (Preschool and elementary school edition).* Chicago, IL: Author.

Collaborative for Academic, Social, and Emotional Learning. (2015). *2015 CASEL guide: Effective social and emotional learning programs–middle and high school edition.* Chicago, IL: Author.

Elliott, S. N., Davies, M. D., Frey, J. R., Gresham, F., & Cooper, G. (2018). Development and initial validation of a social emotional learning assessment for universal screening. *Journal of Applied Developmental Psychology, 55*, 39-51.

Gresham, F. M., & Elliott, S. N. (2008). *Social Skills Improvement System Rating Scales manual.* Bloomington, MN: Pearson.

Gresham, F. M., Elliott, S. N., Metallo, S., Byrd, S., Wilson, E., & Cassidy, K. (2018). Cross-informant agreement of children's social-emotional skills: An investigation of ratings by teachers, parents, and students from a nationally representative sample. *Psychology in the Schools, 55*(2), 208-223.

Review of the SSIS™ Social-Emotional Learning Edition by RENÉE M. TOBIN, Professor of Psychological Studies in Education, Temple University, Philadelphia, PA, and MICHAEL MATTA, Adjunct Professor of Psychological Diagnosis, University of Milano-Bicocca, Milan, Italy:

DESCRIPTION. The SSIS™ Social-Emotional Learning Edition (SSIS SEL) is a comprehensive system of rating and monitoring scales and an intervention program focused on social-emotional skills and learning abilities. The SSIS SEL rating scales are designed to offer "different viewpoints on the social-emotional functioning of a student" (manual, p. 3), by offering rapid screening and monitoring measures.

Teachers, parents, and students complete different forms of the rating scales. Each form requires respondents to evaluate the items on 4-point scales from *not true* to *very true* (for the student form) or from *never* to *almost always* (for the teacher and parent forms). The student form requires respondents to decide how true each item is of the student's own behavior, whereas the teacher and the parent forms require respondents to answer based on the frequency of observations of the student's behavior during the previous two months. Teachers are instructed to complete the form after they have had 3 to 4 weeks of experience with the student. Similarly, parents/guardians are required to have had regular observations and interactions with the child for about a month before completing the form.

Different colors help to distinguish the three forms. The green student form is a 46-item measure that can be administered individually or in groups in 10 to 20 minutes. It is suitable for students who are 8 years and older. The purple parent form consists of 51 items and requires the same amount of time to complete. The blue teacher form consists of 58 items and also takes 10 to 20 minutes to complete. All three forms assess five social-emotional skills: Self-Awareness, Self-Management, Social Awareness, Relationship Skills, and Responsible Decision Making. Additionally, an SEL Composite is computed as well as a validity scale (i.e., Response Pattern Index). On the teacher form, seven items regarding student motivation and performance combine to form an Academic Competence scale.

The Screening/Progress Monitoring Scales is a classroom-based, criterion-referenced instrument that allows for tracking students' weaknesses, strengths, and improvements across the skills evaluated by the rating scales. The Screening/Progress Monitoring Scales can be completed by teachers only; 30-45 minutes are needed to assess an entire class of 25 students.

The Classwide Intervention Program (CIP) provides weekly lessons for teaching social-emotional skills. It is a six-step program that addresses the five domains of social-emotional competence identified by the Collaborative for Academic, Social, and Emotional Learning (CASEL). The intervention includes activities with digital and paper materials best suited for youth ages 4 to 14 years.

DEVELOPMENT. The SSIS SEL represents a thorough revision of the previous editions of the system, which were the SSIS Rating Scales and the SSIS Performance Screening Guide. The domains assessed by the Rating Scales were selected from the five SEL competencies identified by CASEL.

The SSIS SEL teacher, parent, and student forms are products of the revision of the SSIS Rating Scales. Most of the items that belonged to the Social Skills and Problem Behavior scales were retained and reorganized to align with CASEL's five SEL competencies based on author, development staff, and user feedback. A confirmatory factor analysis (CFA) was conducted for each rating scale form. After considering item loadings and modification indexes, a new CFA was performed to test the final structure of the scales. The Flesch-Kincaid Grade Level Index was used to establish the readability of two rating scale forms. The student form requires a second-grade reading level, whereas the parent form requires a fifth-grade reading level. The student and parent forms are available in English and in Spanish.

A different approach was used to develop the Screening/Progress Monitoring Scales. Specifically, a Q-sort procedure was used to determine the placement of items within the five SEL scales. The test authors created 25 behavioral descriptors based on the rating levels of each SEL competency. Then, five teachers were asked to assign each item to one of the five competencies, and an agreement of 100% was found.

TECHNICAL.

Standardization. The SSIS SEL Rating Scales were normed using data collected in 2006 and 2007 for the previous edition of the test. Demographic targets were based on 2006 U.S. Census figures (U.S. Census Bureau, 2006). The three rating scales were standardized based on data collected from 4,550 students, specifically, 800 students, 2,800 parents, and 950 teachers. Statistical norms were created based on three age groups (i.e., 3–5, 5–12, and 13–18 years). Interestingly, data were collected from 5-year-old children in two different settings—preschool and school-aged programs—to allow for the comparison of target children to those in the standardization sample depending on whether the child is enrolled in preschool or school-age programs. The sample contained equal numbers of males and females, and data matched the U.S. population by considering the distribution of ethnicity/race, mother's education level, and geographic area.

Scores were standardized with a mean of 100 and a standard deviation of 15. Thus, scores lower than 85 may progressively indicate weaknesses in one or more social-emotional skill domains.

Reliability. Reliability was examined using three methods. Internal consistency was assessed using alpha coefficients. Coefficients for the three rating scales ranged from adequate to excellent by forms, norm group, and age level. The student form yielded the lowest values, whereas the teacher form yielded the strongest ones. Alpha coefficients for the Screening/Progress Monitoring Scales were excellent (.91 and .90, respectively, for the Social-Emotional Composite and the Academic Functioning Composite), and they were part of a larger peer-reviewed publication (Elliott, Davies, Frey, Gresham, & Cooper, 2018). Test-retest reliability was examined using a representative subgroup (n = 266) of the normative sample, and corrected coefficients ranged from .78 to .91, from .78 to .85, and from .73 to .83 for teacher, parent, and student forms, respectively. The mean interval between the two ratings was one month for the monitoring scales, and from 43 to 66 days for the rating scales. Finally, interrater reliability was tested for the rating scales (teacher and parent forms only). A mean interval of about two months passed between the two ratings. For the teacher form, corrected coefficients ranged from .38 to .68. For the parent form, corrected coefficients ranged from .47 to .71. Results for the Self-Awareness scale for both forms and the Responsible Decision Making scale for the teacher form were insufficient (.38, .47, and .46, respectively) with this sample.

Validity evidence. Validity was examined for the rating scales only through three methods. Score intercorrelations for each form supported that SEL domains were significantly related to one another, and each of them was strongly related to the SEL Composite. Correlations between forms were low overall, ranging from .09 to .39.

Correlations between the SSIS SEL and the previous edition of the test (Gresham & Elliott, 2008) were strong. In contrast, its correlations with the Behavior Assessment System for Children–Second Edition and the Vineland Adaptive Behavior Scales, Second Edition ranged from low (.00) to moderate (.82); these values are consistent with results that usually emerge from multiple forms of behavioral tests.

Finally, analyses were conducted to examine comparisons between responses about a group of children with autism spectrum disorder (ASD) and a matched comparison group. Multiple t-tests showed that children with ASD exhibited significantly lower scores on each scale on all the rating scale forms.

COMMENTARY. The SSIS SEL has some important strengths. Social-emotional skills represent key predictors of individual long-term outcomes at school and within interpersonal relationships. The measures can be administered easily, and the three forms provide a more comprehensive view of functioning. The Screening/Progress Monitoring Scales allow for the consideration of individual patterns over time. Assessing these skills about every four weeks provides a valuable opportunity for teachers who wish to put in place tailored and personalized interventions. Moreover, these reviewers commend the test authors for creating a detailed intervention program consisting of role-playing activities and video vignettes that aim to stimulate students' participation to address SEL areas in need of improvement.

Overall, the SSIS SEL Edition offers strong tools for assessing and intervening with youth. It is built on an established foundation of research and maps well onto current approaches to SEL development (e.g., the CASEL competency domains). As with all measures, the SSIS SEL Edition has some minor theoretical and methodological weaknesses. One potential issue is the comparison group for the teacher form. That is, this form explicitly requires teachers to complete the form by comparing the target child's behavior to the behavior of the rest of the class, leading to context-dependent ratings. With these instructions, it is likely that the same child would obtain different scores if she or he were in a different class or school. These reviewers also recommend caution when interpreting results of the Self-Awareness scale because of its consistently low values across multiple reliability estimates. Moreover, limited information about the CFA was provided. The procedure that the test authors followed to create the scales is not clear, and this might affect the scores' interpretation. Finally, the test authors did not provide scoring keys that would allow hand-scoring, presumably because of the online administration and scoring procedures detailed in the test manual. Given that the manual contains almost 70 pages of tables, this omission of tables with which to convert raw data into standard scores is puzzling.

SUMMARY. The SSIS SEL is a comprehensive system that was designed for assessing students' social-emotional skills from multiple viewpoints. It also provides detailed intervention programs for SEL skill development and allows for the measurement of changes over time. The test meets its goals of offering a rapid tool for screening purposes and an impressive variety of activities to promote the development of social-emotional competencies and relationships in school-based settings. Moreover, external validity was sufficiently tested, and significant relationships were found with other standardized tests. Analyses of factor structure were briefly presented. Ratings rely on observations of children's overt behavior and are context dependent.

These reviewers recommend the use of the Screening/Progress Monitoring Scales, the rating forms, and the Classwide Intervention Program for an integrated approach that addresses individual areas in need of improvement and allows for the examination of behavioral patterns over time.

REVIEWERS' REFERENCES

Elliott, S. N., Davies, M. D., Frey, J. R., Gresham, F., & Cooper, G. (2018). Development and initial validation of a social emotional learning assessment for universal screening. *Journal of Applied Developmental Psychology, 55,* 39-51. https://doi.org/10.1016/j.appdev.2017.06.002

Gresham, F. M., & Elliott, S. N. (2008). *Social Skills Improvement System: Rating Scales manual.* Bloomington, MN: Pearson.

U.S. Census Bureau (2006). *Current Population Survey, March 2006.* Washington, DC: Author.

[155]

Star Early Literacy® [2018 Manual].

Purpose: "A computer-adaptive assessment instrument designed to measure the early literacy skills of beginning readers."

Population: Students in prekindergarten through Grade 3.

Publication Dates: 2001-2018.

Scores, 52: Proficiency ratings in 10 subdomains: Alphabetic Principle, Concept of Word, Visual Discrimination, Phonemic Awareness, Phonics, Structural Analysis, Vocabulary, Sentence-Level Comprehension, Paragraph-Level Comprehension, Early Numeracy; proficiency ratings for 41 skill sets; Overall Score.

Administration: Individual or Group.

Price Data: Price information available from publisher for a one-time school fee (based on each school/district's specific needs) plus an annual subscription cost per student.

Time: Less than 10 minutes on average to administer each assessment.

Comments: Administered aurally by computer; reports norm-referenced scores and criterion-referenced scores; software includes report capabilities (e.g., diagnostic reports); capable of sharing databases with other Renaissance Learning software; data hosted by test publisher; may be administered as often as weekly for progress monitoring; information regarding complete system requirements available from test publisher; technical manual (2018, 125 pages) available via test publisher's website.

Author: Renaissance Learning, Inc.

Publisher: Renaissance Learning, Inc.

Cross References: For reviews by Theresa Graham and Sandra B. Ward of the original edition, see 15:240.

Review of Star Early Literacy® [2018 Manual] by HYESUN LEE, Assistant Professor of Psychology, California State University Channel Islands, Camarillo, CA:

DESCRIPTION. Star Early Literacy is a computer-adaptive test designed to assess early literacy skills in students from pre-kindergarten through Grade 3. With the revision of the previous edition that assessed seven literacy domains, the current edition evaluates proficiency in three broad domains: Word Knowledge and Skills, Comprehension Strategies and Constructing Meaning, and Numbers and Operations. The three domains include 10 blueprint subdomains related to 41 skill sets or concepts aligned with state standards including the Common Core State Standards (CCSS). The domain of Numbers and Operations was added in 2011. The computer-adaptive nature of the test, measuring each student's literacy level through 27 items selected based on his or her performance on previous items, brings the advantages of easy administration and relatively short testing time (less than 10 minutes), while allowing for repeated measurement to assess student growth (10 or more administrations per year). The selected test items and instructions along with graphics and animations are presented through "a neutral, un-accented American English voice" (technical manual, p. 21). The 27 multiple-choice items with three options each are distributed into Sections A (14 items with short audio segments), B (eight items with longer audio segments), and C (five numeracy items). No more than three items are from the same skill set. Before the test session starts, an instructional video is shown to present how to answer questions using a mouse, keyboard, or tablet. Then proficiency in using the response device is checked through example questions. To demonstrate proficiency, students must provide three consecutive correct answers, each within 5 seconds. Instructions for acquiring help are provided if difficulty in using the device is detected. Before the actual test, students also need to correctly answer three of five practice questions. Failure to pass the practice session prompts students to see the instructor for help.

Star Early Literacy provides scaled, norm-referenced, and criterion-referenced scores to help teachers monitor student progress and provide literacy instructions and interventions for students' current needs. The test provides two types of scaled scores: Star Early Literacy scaled scores and unified scaled scores. The Star Early Literacy scaled scores, nonlinear transformations of score estimates based on the Rasch model, range from 300 to 900. Scale transformations are provided to assist interpretation of scores, aiming for alignment with age (e.g., the scale score of 500 matches the performance of 5-year-olds). To meet the need of a unified assessment for growth trajectories from early literacy to reading skills, a common scale for Star Early Literacy and Star Reading has been used since the 2017-2018 school year as an optional scale. The Early Literacy unified score scale ranges from 200 to 1100. For norm-referenced scores, percentile ranks, normal curve equivalent scores, and grade equivalents based on the 2017 norms are available. Also, student growth percentiles (SGPs) are available for measuring a student's relative growth compared to other students from the same grade with a similar score history (i.e., academic peers). For criterion-referenced scores, proficiency categories such as *Emergent Reader, Transitional Reader,* and *Probable Reader* are provided based on scaled scores. Additionally, subdomain scores, skill set scores, and an Estimated Oral Reading Fluency score are provided. Subdomain and skill set scores represent the expected percentage of items correct if all items were administered and are estimated by fitting a Rasch model. Estimated Oral Reading Fluency is the estimated number of words that a student can read correctly per minute on text appropriate for one's grade level.

DEVELOPMENT. The test manual provides the hierarchical structure of content specification used for item development. As of January 2018 the operational pool included 3,424 items for nine early literacy subdomains and one early numeracy subdomain measuring 133 literacy skills and 12 numeracy skills. After initial pilot testing in 2000, the development of new items has continued through "dynamic calibration," a process whereby field testing items are included in actual testing sessions. Thus, randomly selected students may be administered additional items that result in an increase of 1 to 2 minutes of testing time. The calibration results of field testing items are used only for item analyses, thus not counted toward students' scores. Regarding the test design, screen layout, including text size and graphics, are well designed to reduce construct-irrelevant factors as much as possible. Thorough test security features seem to be implemented for the protection of test content as well as the confidentiality of individual test results.

TECHNICAL.

Standardization. The 2017 norms were developed based on samples of K–3 students who took the Star Early Literacy, Star Reading, or both to represent the full range of literacy development between Aug. 15, 2014, and June 30, 2015. Stratified samples of 1,428,592 students for the fall norms and 998,490 for the spring norms were selected to meet the national population characteristics including student demographics and school characteristics. Overall, the norming samples appear to represent national demographics well, but not school characteristics. For discrepancies found in sample characteristics, post stratification weights were applied for the estimation of Rasch scores. For the development of SGP norms, scores from more than 933,000 students from Grades K–3 were used. Detailed information was not provided in the technical manual regarding the SGP norms.

Reliability. Generic, split-half, and test-retest reliability coefficients along with standard errors of measurement were reported for both scaled and unified scores using the 2015–2016 school year data. Generic reliability estimates were computed using mean squared conditional standard errors of measurement from IRT estimation. The generic, split-half, and test-retest reliability coefficients for scaled scores ranged from .82 to .91, from .83 to .91, and from .56 to .85, respectively. The generic, split-half, and test-retest reliability coefficients for unified scores ranged from .81 to .87, from .83 to .90, and from .58 to .85, respectively. The average intervals for test-retest reliability ranged from 77 to 101 days. Reliability coefficients were computed based on average sample sizes of 90,000 (generic); 18,896 (split-half); and 19,500 (test-retest) for each grade.

Validity. The test manual includes new validation studies conducted in 2012 with data from the 2011 edition. To provide evidence that Star Early Literacy measures early literacy skills that improve with age and schooling, average scaled scores were computed for each age group and grade. Increasing score patterns were noted, as presented in two summary tables provided in the test manual. Evidence based on relations to other variables was examined using teachers' ratings of students' mastery of literacy skills (n = 6,708). The correlation coefficients ranged from .46 to .60, and the graphical display provided in the test manual shows that scaled scores correspond well to the mastery of skills. Because there was a change in the number of early numeracy items in the 2011 edition, the factor structure was also examined in 2012. An exploratory factor analysis based on data from 6,785 students who took both previous and current editions showed the existence of one general factor, indicating that the numeracy items measure the same construct as other items. Finally, dimensionality assessments were conducted with 10 subdomain scores through exploratory (n = 23,807) and confirmatory (n = 55,521) factor analyses for each grade. Combining the scree plots and model fit indices (e.g., CFI, GFI, and NFI close to 1.00 and RMSEA close to .08), unidimensionality was confirmed.

Although evidence from other validation studies (e.g., relationships with reading, literacy, and readiness assessment scores, meta-analyses of correlation coefficients from the validation studies, and sensitivity and specificity for instructional decisions) was included in the test manual, those studies were based on data from the 2001 edition. Because the test authors report, "The current and original versions are measuring highly related, but not identical, constructs" (manual, p. 72), a caution should be noted related to the authors' later statement that test users have reason "to accept evidence of the validity of those earlier versions as being applicable to the current version as well" (manual, p. 79). To ensure valid score interpretations, more validation studies for the current edition are needed. In relation to test fairness, intensive content reviews seem to have been conducted for initial pilot items. However, psychometric measures such as differential item functioning (DIF) analyses were not reported in the technical manual for either the initial item pool or current field test items. [Editor's note: The test publisher advised the Buros Center for Testing that DIF analyses were conducted and are included in a separate technical report.]

COMMENTARY. The Star Early Literacy test is a user-friendly assessment for measuring early literacy skills. The short testing time would be an especially attractive feature for both relatively young students and teachers. A wide variety of available scores will aid teachers in identifying student's needs and planning instructions. To monitor students' performance trajectories from early literacy to reading skills, the addition of unified scores seems useful. However, there is a lack of key information about the derivation of equating coefficients for transforming Star Early Literacy Rasch scores to the Star Reading Rasch scores; the test manual mentions only that a linear equating procedure from Kolen and Brennan (2004) was employed for the transformation of scores. Those familiar with equating procedures might be able to assume the adoption of the single group design for the derivation of equating coefficients: 1.5572 and 5.2275. However, it is still not clear which data were used for the derivation and what the sample sizes were. In addition, considering that Star Early Literacy is a large-scale testing program with ample opportunities to access empirical testing data, one may question why no psychometric evidence for test fairness was presented. To appropriately screen operational/field items showing substantive differences in psychometric characteristics among subgroups of test takers, thus potentially resulting in adverse impact on test results, statistical examinations including DIF analyses would be a crucial step to prevent unintended consequences. A review of a previous version of Star Early Literacy (Graham, 2003) also pointed out that there may be potential advantages for students with more computer experience. Thus, psychometric investigations in addition to content experts' reviews are strongly recommended to ensure test fairness and valid score interpretations.

SUMMARY. Star Early Literacy is an aurally administered computer-adaptive test composed of 27 multiple-choice items measuring early literacy skills. Test results obtained through a short testing time may be useful for teachers to quickly assess students' literacy skills and make instructional plans for students' needs. However, cautious interpretations of scaled and unified scores for different subgroups of test takers should be observed due to the lack of evidence for test fairness and insufficiency of available validity evidence for the current edition of the test.

REVIEWER'S REFERENCES

Graham, T. (2003). [Test review of STAR Early Literacy]. In B. S. Plake, J. C. Impara, & R. A. Spies (Eds.), *The fifteenth mental measurements yearbook*. Lincoln, NE: Buros Institute of Mental Measurements.

Kolen, M. J., & Brennan, R. L. (2004). *Test equating, scaling, and linking: Methods and practices* (2nd ed.). New York, NY: Springer.

Review of Star Early Literacy® [2018 Manual] by KATHLEEN QUINN, Professor Emerita of Education, Former Director, Fall and Spring Reading Clinic, Holy Family University, Philadelphia, PA:

DESCRIPTION. Star Early Literacy is an aurally computer-administered and computer-adaptive assessment of early literacy skills. The test consists of 27 multiple- choice items (three choices for each item) covering three broad domains (Word Knowledge and Skills, Comprehension Strategies and Constructing Meaning, and Numbers and Operations) that are divided into 10 subdomains (Alphabetic Principle, Concept of Word, Visual Discrimination, Phonemic Awareness, Phonics, Structural Analysis, Vocabulary, Sentence-Level Comprehension, Paragraph-Level Comprehension, and Early Numeracy). It is designed for use with children in Grades Pre-K through 3. The assessment takes place entirely online using a computer or tablet. Testing begins after training to be sure the students know how to use a mouse, keyboard, or touchscreen and can follow the directions for listening to each item, selecting among the three choices provided via clicking or touching the screen, and then clicking or touching the word "Next" at the bottom of the screen. If the student is not successful during the training session (getting three questions in a row correct), the testing stops. When taking this test in the role of student, it was found that the training items were not related to the skills being tested but only to the ability of the student to master the computer/electronic aspects of taking the test. After completing the training and a short practice session, the adaptive nature of the test begins. On average, testing time is less than 10 minutes.

Star Early Literacy provides the user with both norm-referenced and criterion-referenced scores including scaled scores, unified scaled scores (which are linked with the Star Reading assessment for continuity and consistency and are new to this edition), percentile ranks, grade equivalents, proficiency ratings (based on subdomains and skill sets), and literacy classifications (scaled scores below 675 = *Emergent Reader;* scores of 675-774 = *Transitional Reader;* scores 775 and above = *Probable Reader*). In addition, student growth percentiles and estimated oral reading fluency can be obtained, although no specifics are provided as to which items contribute to this latter score. Scoring and reports are generated automatically.

DEVELOPMENT. Star Early Literacy was developed to screen beginning readers in a group setting while providing information about their overall pre-reading (Pre-K-K), transitional (1-2) and probable (3) reading ability as well as information about student need for intervention and to assess growth over time. The test manual suggests that students be screened two to five times per year and that those in need of intervention can be given the test as frequently as weekly for progress monitoring. Because of its adaptive nature and large item bank (more than 3,400 items), the test manual states that it is very unlikely that the student will be tested on the same item more than once.

State standards, curriculum materials, and the Common Core State Standards were used by early learning consultants to develop the content and items for the original prototype, which was administered to 1,500 children in Pre-K to Grade 2 to determine their ability to respond to non-adaptive items and interface with the computer and/or tablet. Teacher input and reaction was also taken into account. As a result, 2,929 items were selected and calibrated (using IRT methodology to establish a continuous scale of difficulty) with approximately 600 items per grade (Pre-K-3). This process used data from a large sample of 32,493 students in Grades Pre-K-3 in 300 schools across the United States. The content was also reviewed to ensure fairness, eliminate bias, and have a balance of gender usage (such as names, nouns, and pronouns) as well as a variety of subjects and topics. Readability was checked for sentence length and number of words (Pre-K-1 = maximum of 10 words per sentence; Grades 2-3 = maximum of 12 words per sentence).

There was no mention in the technical manual of who the experts/consultants were or how these readability criteria were established.

TECHNICAL. Normative data were collected from 1,893,599 K-3 students in 50 states and the District of Columbia who took either Star Early Literacy or Star Reading from August 2014 through June 2015. These data were used to establish fall and spring norms for both tests so that overlapping scaled scores, unified scaled scores, and growth norms could be established. This aspect of the norming project was important because many schools use both Star Early Literacy and Star Reading. Demographic data were stratified by geographic region, school size and location, socioeconomic status (SES; four categories), gender, and race/ethnicity. The sample was weighted to represent U.S. student population statistics based on 2013-14 data from the National Center for Educational Statistics (NCES) and 2016 data from Market Data Retrieval (MDR).

Reliability evidence derives from the 2015-2016 school year data. Generic and split-half reliability coefficients offer evidence of internal consistency. For the Star Early Literacy unified scale, the overall coefficients based on a sample of 450,000 students from Pre-K to Grade 3 were .91 (ranging from .81 to .87) and .92 (ranging from .83 to .90), respectively. For the Star Early Literacy scaled scores, the overall coefficients were .91 for both estimates (ranging from .83 to .91) across grade levels and based on a sample of 450,000 students distributed evenly across grade levels. Test-retest reliability coefficients were reported for the unified scale and scaled scores (n = 97,500 students, distributed evenly across grade levels) with average retest intervals ranging from 77 to 101 days (82 days, overall). Reliability coefficients ranged from .58 to .85 (.85 overall) and from .56 to .85 (.82 overall) for the Star Early Literacy unified scale and scaled scores, respectively. In addition, standard errors of measurement are reported by grade level and overall based on a sample of 450,000 students distributed evenly across grades. For the unified scale scores, values hovered tightly around 30. For the scaled scores, values ranged between the high 30s and high 40s.

Validity is discussed by the test publisher as "the extent that there are evidentiary data to support claims as to what the test measures; interpretation of its scores; and the uses for which it is recommended or applied" (technical manual, p. 48). The test publisher provides evidence to support validity of test scores by examining the relationship between age/grade during internal research conducted in 2001 and 2012. Although the test authors provide evidence that scores tend to increase with age and grade, they do not report statistical significance for these differences. Both concurrent (all correlated assessments taking place within 2 months of the Star Early Literacy test) and predictive (all correlated assessments taking place more than 2 months after the Star Early Literacy test) validity studies were conducted and involved correlating Star Early Literacy scores with a variety of other early reading assessments such as the Brigance K&1 Screen, DIBELS, Gates-MacGinitie Reading Test, and GRADE (18 total plus an author-developed teacher rating checklist). Average validity coefficients ranged from .52-.77, with overall concurrent validity coefficients averaging .59 and overall predictive validity coefficients averaging .58. Meta-analysis of these results indicates an overall validity coefficient of .60 and a standard error of measurement of .02 at the 95% confidence interval. In addition, evidence of technical adequacy for informing screening and progress monitoring decisions was positively reviewed by the Center for Response to Intervention (CRTI) and the National Center on Intensive Intervention (NCII), both funded by the U.S. Department of Education.

Findings from a relatively small (n = 71 from one school) predictive validity study (Clemens et al., 2015) suggest that Star Early Literacy demonstrates statistically significant, though moderate, evidence of validity (35-38% variance) for predicting year-end reading ability in kindergarteners. When an individually administered, paper and pencil measure of letter naming and sound naming were combined with Star Early Literacy, 58% of the variance was explained when predicting year-end kindergarten reading ability. Similar findings were reported for predicting end of first grade reading ability by combining Star Early Literacy with word reading fluency (61% of the variance was explained). Both of these combinations also resulted in far fewer false positives and false negatives regarding students identified as at risk (i.e., those scoring below the 40th percentile).

The basis for item selection and item analysis is thoroughly provided in the Star Early Literacy technical manual. To support the use of the Overall Score, a factor analysis was implemented and indicated one factor for all items in each domain and subdomain including Early Numeracy.

COMMENTARY. Although Star Early Literacy appears easy and efficient to administer and score in most cases, the user should be aware of specific issues that might arise such as difficulty with the technology and young students' ability to follow directions independently, especially when giving this test to a whole class at once. When this reviewer observed a small group of kindergarteners taking the test, some lower-functioning students appeared to have difficulty maintaining attention and interest; several students were challenged by the use of the mouse and headsets. Such issues could impact their performance and scores.

Further use of outside sources of evidence in future editions, such as the study by Clemens et al. (2015), is needed to support the use of Star Early Literacy for predictive validity and progress monitoring, again, especially for students who function in the lower classification levels of Star Early Literacy. Use of supplementary, individually administered tests in specific areas of need and those areas of reading that are not assessed by Star Early Literacy, such as oral reading fluency, higher order listening, and reading comprehension, should be combined with Star Early Literacy to provide more accurate and in-depth analysis of student needs and interventions.

SUMMARY. Star Early Literacy is a somewhat easily administered measure that provides an efficient screening assessment of pre-reading skills for students in Grades K-3. (Potential challenges exist if administering to beginning kindergarteners and entire classes.) It may not be as useful for predicting which students may need further intervention after the end of first grade unless combined with more individualized, specific measures of word reading, oral reading fluency, and comprehension (Clemens et al., 2015). For the most part, the psychometric properties and development of Star Early Literacy are sound and thorough. This test could provide a quick and helpful measure of initial pre-reading ability that can then be used to determine which students need further assessment and intervention.

REVIEWER'S REFERENCE

Clemens, N. H., Hagan-Burke, S., Luo, W., Cerda, C., Blakely, A., Frosch, J., . . . Jones, M. (2015). The predictive validity of a computer-adaptive assessment of Kindergarten and First-Grade reading skills. *School Psychology Review, 44*, 76-97.

[156]

Star Math® [2018 Manual].

Purpose: A computer-adaptive assessment designed to align to national and state curriculum standards in mathematics.

Population: Students in Grades K-12.

Publication Dates: 1998-2018.

Scores: Assesses skills in 4 domains: Numbers & Operations, Algebra, Geometry & Measurement, Data Analysis/Statistics/Probability.

Administration: Individual or Group.

Price Data: Price information available from publisher for a one-time school fee (based on each school/district's specific needs) plus an annual subscription cost per student.

Time: Average completion time of 15-25 minutes, depending on grade level.

Comments: Reports norm-referenced scores (percentile ranks, normal curve equivalents, grade equivalents) and criterion-referenced scores; software includes report capabilities (e.g., diagnostic reports); capable of sharing databases with other Renaissance Learning software; data hosted by the test publisher; information regarding system requirements available from test publisher; technical manual (2018, 178 pages) available via test publisher's website; shorter Star Math Progress Monitoring version also available.

Author: Renaissance Learning, Inc.

Publisher: Renaissance Learning, Inc.

Cross References: For reviews by Mary L. Garner and G. Michael Poteat of an earlier version titled STAR Math, Version 2.0, see 16:234; for reviews by Joseph C. Ciechalski and Cindy M. Walker of the original version, see 15:241.

Review of Star Math® [2018 Manual] by R. J. de AYALA, Professor, Department of Educational Psychology, University of Nebraska-Lincoln, Lincoln, NE:

DESCRIPTION. Two versions of Star Math are available. Both versions are administered as fixed-length adaptive tests and can provide feedback on students' instructional math levels relative to national norms. Neither is intended for use in "high-stakes" situations.

The first version is the 24-item Star Math 2 Progress Monitoring test. This version is targeted at progress monitoring. Star Math, Version 2.0 (renamed Star Math Progress Monitoring test) was reviewed by Garner (2005) and Poteat (2005) in *The Sixteenth Mental Measurements Yearbook.*

The second is a comprehensive 34-item standards-based assessment that is aligned with state and national curriculum standards. This test differs from Star Math, Version 2.0 not only in length, but also in its organization and its use of a test bank of more than 6,200 items that cover 790 skills. This review is focused on the 34-item Star Math test.

This fixed-length adaptive test tailors the test to each student's achievement level. By adapting the test to an examinee, items that are either too easy or too difficult are not administered, thereby reducing examination time while maintaining domain coverage. Fifty percent of over 16 million examinees completed the examination in about 25 minutes or less; 95% completed the test in 39 minutes or less.

The test consists of six item blocks with each block comprising a blend of items from four domains: (1) Numbers and Operations; (2) Algebra; (3) Geometry and Measurement; and (4) Data Analysis, Statistics and Probability. Content is "spiraled" to ensure content balancing and an ability estimate based on a broad range of content. The test is administered on an internet-connected computer or tablet with or without a brief practice test. For a specific skill, a calculator or formula reference sheet is available alongside the item. Examinees are given 3 minutes to answer a question, a default that can be extended to 6 minutes as an accommodation. Additionally, read-aloud audio guidance is available. If the allotted time is exceeded, the examinee's response is treated as incorrect and the next item is administered. Each examinee is alerted when there are 15 seconds remaining in the allotted time. If need be, a test administration can be paused and resumed at a later time.

The management system permits report generation at the student level, for specific subgroups, or for a combination of subgroups (e.g., English language learners who are eligible for free/reduced lunch). All of the items, student test scores, test content, and export files are encrypted. Additional security features include restriction of computer access to the system, username/password, and the use of permission groups. Because the test may be administered multiple times within a year, the system tracks the items administered to each examinee. An item will not be administered to an examinee more than once within a 75-day period.

DEVELOPMENT. The assessment utilizes mathematical standard resources such as the Common Core State Standards, the National Assessment of Educational Progress (NAEP), the Trends in International Mathematics and Science Study (TIMSS), and the National Council of Teachers of Mathematics, to name a few. From these resources a skills list was iteratively developed in consultation with mathematicians, educators, and psychometricians. The result was 790 skills representing 54 skill sets. For content development these skills were organized into domains (Numbers and Operations; Geometry and Measurement; Algebra; Data Analysis, Statistics and Probability). Each item in the bank is aligned to one skill. Item creation involved consideration of multiple factors (e.g., cognitive load, grade level vocabulary, reading level, sentence level and structure). Each item is designed to be presentable without the need to scroll and to be free of stereotypes, references to religious holidays/activities, inappropriate information, and negative construction.

TECHNICAL. Adaptive testing administers items targeted to an examinee's current ability estimate. The examinee's item response leads to a series of progressively more accurate ability estimates. The test's first item is one with a difficulty level that is relatively easy for students at the examinee's grade level. Specifically, the item is one that a typical student one or two grade levels below grade placement is expected to answer correctly 85% of the time; this default may be overridden to use students' math instructional level. Subsequent items are selected so that the examinee is expected to respond correctly 67% of the time given his or her current ability estimate; items previously administered to the examinee within the past 75 days are not administered to that examinee. Given the item pool size, multiple items satisfy these criteria. Thus, the item is randomly selected from the set of potential items, thereby minimizing presenting the same item too many times.

Item pool replenishment is accomplished by randomly embedding 1-5 new tryout items into administered adaptive tests to collect response data for (dynamic) calibration; these items are not used for estimating an examinee's math proficiency. Proficiency estimation is calculated by maximum likelihood estimation. Because this approach cannot be used until an examinee has correctly and incorrectly answered two items, a Bayesian modal estimation approach is used initially.

Star Math's norming was based on 1.9 million students across Grades 1-12 from 50 states and the District of Columbia. Standard Rasch scale scores are transformed and reported on a Unified scale that is common to all Star assessments. The Unified scale ranges from 200 to 1,400 with Star Math falling in the 600-1,400 region; conditional standard errors of measurement are 18-19 across Grades 1-12.

The dimensionality analyses (CFA, EFA) showed good fit to a unidimensional model at each grade band: K-2, 3-5, 6-8, and 9-12. This unidimensionality permits the use of the Rasch model as the instrument's psychometric foundation. After estimating item difficulty and performing fit analyses, content reviewers examine each item to determine whether the item should be retained. To be retained, items need to meet five criteria (e.g., Rasch item fit, item-total correlation > .62).

The IRT-based "generic" reliability estimates for the Star Math test ranged from .90 to .95 with split-half and alternate-form reliability estimates of .89-.94 and .74-.84, respectively. Concurrent and predictive validity evidence involved comparisons of Star Math scores with those from 73 standardized examinations (e.g., Iowa Test of Basic Skills). With regard to concurrent validity evidence, average correlation coefficients were .64-.75 (Grades 1-6) and .56-.74 (Grades 7-12). Predictive validity correlations using a 60-day lag between administrations yielded mean correlations of .55-.74 (Grades 1-6) and .65-.77 (Grades 7-12). A meta-analysis of the concurrent and predictive correlations by grade level showed validity coefficients of .71-.78 (Grades 3-12); for Grades 1 and 2 the coefficients were .56 and .63, respectively. Overall predictive proficiency classification accuracies ranged from 76% to 91%; 83% of the criterion tests had values that were 83% to 89%.

COMMENTARY. The development of Star Math is sound. The clearly written technical manual presents the skill sets and skills organized by domains, calibration information, reliability, dimensionality analyses, validity evidence, and conversion tables (e.g., for grade equivalency).

From an item response theory perspective, maximum information for proficiency estimation occurs when an item is selected so an examinee has a 50% chance of correctly responding to the item. In contrast, Star Math uses a 67% criterion. As a result, item selection is not maximally informative for ability estimation; however, the student's psychological experience may be more positive with a 67% criterion rather than a 50% criterion. Additionally, as a test of fixed length rather than variable length, some examinees will be estimated more accurately than others. This reviewer could not find justification for why the 34-item length was chosen. It was unclear whether the inclusion of new items for dynamic calibration affects test length. Other considerations are the inability of an examinee to revisit a previously answered item and whether there is a single mathematical proficiency across Grades 1 through 12. The grade-by-grade dimensionality analyses showed unidimensionality within grades; however, this does not mean the unidimensional math proficiency construct in first grade is the same as the one in 12th grade. Thus, making comparisons across grades may not be advisable.

Although the test's blueprint shows that some questions require interpreting information, some classroom teachers may find the use of a multiple-choice item format in lieu of an open-ended response format to be a limitation. For these individuals the test can be used to complement teacher-developed, open-ended item format tests and to provide breadth of coverage for a wide range of grades. In this way, the teacher obtains valuable information about a student's misconceptions while simultaneously receiving information from Star Math about how the student could be expected to perform on standardized tests (e.g., the overall classification accuracy with the ACT Mathematics test was 89%). Thus, Star Math may be used to aid in fine-tuning instruction to improve performance on high-stakes instruments and to predict performance on high-stakes tests.

SUMMARY. Star Math is a sound fixed-length adaptive mathematics test based on the Rasch psychometric model. Reliability estimates show that scores have acceptable to high levels of consistency. The validity coefficients indicate considerable evidence supporting its use for assessing mathematics. Moreover, the management system provides a district-wide database for comparing student math proficiency within and across schools as well as nationally. The test provides useful math proficiency information for its intended audience (students, teachers, and administrators). However, proficiency comparisons across a wide range of grades (e.g., second and 10th) may not be advisable.

REVIEWER'S REFERENCES

Garner, M. L. (2005). [Test review of STAR Math®, Version 2.0]. In R. A. Spies & B. S. Plake (Eds.), *The sixteenth mental measurements yearbook*. Retrieved from http://marketplace.unl.edu/buros/

Poteat, G. M. (2005). [Test review of STAR Math®, Version 2.0]. In R. A. Spies & B. S. Plake (Eds.), *The sixteenth mental measurements yearbook*. Retrieved from http://marketplace.unl.edu/buros/

Review of Star Math® [2018 Manual] by BRIAN F. FRENCH, Professor of Educational Psychology, Washington State University, Pullman, WA:

DESCRIPTION. Star Math, a computer adaptive test (CAT) for students in Grades 1 to 12, is nested in a suite of early literacy, reading, and mathematics assessments. Star Math provides teachers and administrators with a student's mathematical ability estimate. As in previous iterations, the product continues to provide a 24-item CAT, requiring an average of 14 minutes to complete. A new generation 34-item CAT, a state and national standards-based assessment requiring an average of 25 minutes to complete, is also available. The former is said to be used for (a) tracking growth, (b) providing a quick estimate of a student's math instructional level, and (c) screening and progress-monitoring; the latter provides (a) normative information, (b) information to guide instruction, and (c) information to administrators to predict later performance and identify needs of various groups. This unidimensional assessment differs from its predecessor by providing a longer assessment option, reorganized content, an expanded item pool from 1,900 to 6,200 items, and a dynamic item calibration process.

Items focus on four broad domains (i.e., Numbers and Operations; Algebra; Geometry & Measurement; and Data Analysis, Statistics & Probability) with 54 skill sets and 790 skills. Many scaled scores are available including an Enterprise score and a Unified score, which is scaled to apply to all assessments in the Star suite. Also available are grade equivalents, percentile ranks, normal curve equivalents, growth percentile scores, and a grade placement score. The Enterprise score, the original Star Math score, is available while the transition to the Unified score occurs over time.

All testing, reporting, and data management occurs in an online management system with security features to protect the test content and confidentiality of results. Access levels can be controlled and monitored with flexible access points (e.g., teacher's home, principal's office) and many reporting options for both disaggregated (e.g., student level, groups and subgroups) and aggregated (e.g., school, district) data. The online interface appears effective and is flexible regarding how a student interacts with the CAT (keyboard, mouse, touch screen, tablet). Both the technical manual and the administration manual are well-written, comprehensive, easy to read and follow, and available online.

DEVELOPMENT. Star Math, published originally in 1998 and again in 2002 and 2011, appears to adapt to new state and national curricula and standards with frequent updates. The major differences with the latest version are the expansion of the item pool, the availability of the short and long forms (24 and 34 items), increased skill coverage, and enhanced online platform functions. Item development was clearly defined via a test blueprint, including an item revision process to ensure item quality, and was guided by many resources such as Common Core State Standards for Mathematics, the National Council of Teachers of Mathematics, the National Assessment of Educational Progress, and the Third International Mathematics and Science Study. Item quality was examined both empirically (e.g., item analysis via item response theory) and via expert panel reviews. Item writing guidelines, distractor choices, and attention to items reflecting curricular materials were accounted for in both the short and long forms. Guidelines are available for calculator and formula reference sheet use as well as for read-aloud protocols for accommodating students with certain needs. Star Math items were calibrated via Rasch modeling on cycles of data collected in the 2008, 2009, and 2010 school years from more than 1.5 million students with a range of 520 to over 58,000 responses per item (median responses = 2,561). In an example calibration of 2,743 items, 36% percent met inclusion criteria. The remaining 64% percent were not included in the CAT pool. Additional information about the calibration and fit of the remaining items was not clear. A new Unified score (range = 600 to 1400) was developed and introduced to provide a common scale for the Star Math and Reading assessments.

TECHNICAL. Normative information is available for test scores and growth scores (i.e., distributions of test score changes over time). The 2017 norms are based on data (N > 3.5 million) collected during the 2014-2015 school year in both the fall and spring from Grades 1 to 12 under standard administration conditions. A post-stratified sample (N = 1,917,271) was created from the customer database to best represent the U.S. student population on the key variables of geographic region, district socioeconomic status, district/school size, grade, and math ability. Students represented 11,313 schools in 50 states with 406,809 tested in both the fall and the spring. The sample approximates national estimates within a 6% range, although some categories may be overrepresented (e.g., town school nationally = 11.7% vs. town school in the sample = 18.2%; White students nationally = 49.6% vs. White students in the sample = 56.1%) and underrepresented (e.g., high SES nationally = 31.1% vs high SES in the sample = 21.0%). The student growth percentiles are based on a sample of 5.4 million records and are updated periodically. Final normative scores were based on the weighted Rasch ability estimates to account for key demographic characteristics and increase representativeness of the sample. These scores are transformed to the Unified and Enterprise scores.

Reliability. Score reliability and measurement precision estimates are reported in the form of (a) generic, (b) split-half, (c) alternate forms/test-retest, and (d) the conditional standard error of measurement for both the 34- and the 24-item tests. Generic reliability estimates are from the IRT calibration, defined as 1 minus (error variance divided by total score variance), and are considered upper bound estimates of internal consistency for this CAT. Across grades, the generic values for the 34-item test ranged from .90 to .95, with a value of .97 across the total sample. The split-half reliability estimates, obtained from correlations of odd and even item splits and corrected by the Spearman-Brown formula, ranged from .89 to .94 across grades with an overall value of .97. Alternate-forms/test-retest reliability estimates were obtained by correlating student scores from being tested twice with no overlapping items, given the CAT environment. The average time between testing ranged from 84 days to 112 days, and estimates ranged from .74 to .84 with a value of .94 across all grades. The average conditional standard errors for the Unified and the Enterprise scores ranged from 18 to 19 and 29 to 30, respectively, where differences in values reflect differences in the scales. The same types of reliability and measurement precision are provided for the 24-item progress monitoring CAT. The ranges of the generic, split-half, and alternate-forms/test-retest reliability estimates were .85 to .95, .86 to .96, and .67 to .91, respectively, across grades and the total sample. The range of the CSEM was greater for the Unified (23-24) and Enterprise (38-39) scores, with the difference likely due to the 10-item length difference.

Validity. Several components of validity evidence exist. Content evidence of validity is strongly grounded in current state standards, expert panel reviews, and a clearly articulated test blueprint. Internal structure evidence was provided via exploratory and confirmatory factor analyses for four grade bands and supported the unidimensional structure. Evidence of validity also was provided through many correlations (> 320) with other measures of mathematics achievement with the expectation of strong and positive relationships. This expectation was met with correlations across grades ranging from .56 to .75. Predictive relationships (> 400) were also examined with values ranging from .55 to .77. Lower values with predictive relationships are expected compared to concurrent values due to the passage of time associated with predictive relationships. Measures employed represented popular mathematics assessments (e.g., California Achievement Test) and many state assessments. A meta-analysis summarized validity coefficients (N = 747) across 12 grades with a range of .56 (Grade 1) to .78 (Grade 6), with an average of .76. Correlations were presented for state level Smarter Balanced Assessment Consortium tests (range .86 to .90) and Partnership for Assessment for Readiness for College and Careers tests (range .77 to .86). In addition, accuracy of the Star Math scores in predicting student proficiency on such tests across Grades 3 to 8 ranged from 89% to 92%, with sensitivity and specificity across these grades ranging from 57% to 71% and from 94% to 98%, respectively. Evidence to support score use for progress monitoring consisted of the slope of improvement or a trend line for students retested as many as 10 times a year with resulting correlations ranging from .92 to .94.

COMMENTARY. Star Math improves over its predecessors. The amount of data collected is impressive, the online platform and management system function well, and the supporting information is strong. The psychometric information documented in the technical manual generally supports intended score uses. The reliability and validity information follows the classical checklist approach instead of a more current validity argument framework focused on score inferences. The majority of reliability estimates meet standards for score use for individual decisions or research purposes (e.g., Nunnally & Bernstein, 1994). The validity evidence is strong for supporting content, test structure, and correlations with student level data. The balance between specificity and sensitivity for indicating proficiency could be improved. Moreover, it appears the majority of the evidence provided in the technical manual is for the 34-item assessment, not the 24-item assessment, leaving the user to draw generalities between the two versions. That said, the amount of validity evidence is an improvement from the previous version. Glaring omissions from the technical manual are the lack of attention to fairness issues, including differential item functioning, measurement invariance, and support for score functioning across groups as well as evidence for score use at the aggregate levels. The reviewer notes that the test publisher provided a separate technical report regarding differential item functioning analysis during the review process. This is necessary but insufficient evidence to address fairness issues. Clear next steps are to build a clear validity framework tied to the intended uses and to build evidence to support progress monitoring and fairness. Such work will point to where gaps exist in the current validity argument.

SUMMARY. Star Math is well designed for the intended purpose of obtaining a quick estimate of mathematical ability of students in Grades 1-12. The increased access to the online testing environment that is flexible for administration (mouse, keyboard, touch screen) and help that is easy to access (online chat) is appealing and reflects current assessment trends. The online management system with multiple access points and data options can be useful from the teacher level to state-level administrators. The technical manual includes adequate documentation of the development of the assessment; reliability and validity evidence presented in the manual supports score use for a quick assessment of math ability, but less so for monitoring progress. Additional information to support intended score uses (e.g., adjusting instruction, predicting grade level, identifying needs of groups, scoring meaning beyond the student level) is needed. Past criticisms (Poteat, 2005; Walker, 2003) have commented on the high price of the assessment. It was disappointing to see the cost information removed, and this reviewer could not obtain an estimate when contacting the company directly. This reviewer finds the Star Math assessment of value as a data point in evaluating a student's mathematics level but hesitates to recommend it as a progress monitoring tool, for unqualified use for all groups in the absence of fairness evidence, or for decision making at aggregate levels.

REVIEWER'S REFERENCES

Nunnally, J. C., & Bernstein, I. H. (1994). *Psychometric theory.* (3rd ed.) New York, NY: McGraw-Hill.

Poteat, G. M. (2005). [Review of the STAR Math®, Version 2.0.] In R. A. Spies & B. S. Plake (Eds.), *The sixteenth mental measurements yearbook.* Retrieved from http://marketplace.unl.edu/buros/

Walker, C. M. (2003). [Review of the STAR Math.] In B. S. Plake, J. C. Impara, & R. A. Spies (Eds.), *The fifteenth mental measurements yearbook* (pp. 866-868). Lincoln, NE: Buros Institute of Mental Measurements.

[157]

Star Reading® [2018 Manual].

Purpose: A computer-adaptive test designed to align to national and state curriculum standards in reading and language arts.

Population: Students in Grades K-12.

Publication Dates: 1996–2018.

Scores: Assesses skills in 5 domains: Word Knowledge and Skills, Comprehension Strategies and Constructing Meaning, Analyzing Literary Text, Understanding Author's Craft, Analyzing Argument and Evaluating Text.

Administration: Individual or Group.

Price Data: Price information available from publisher for a one-time school fee (based on each school/district's specific needs) plus an annual subscription cost per student.

Time: 15-20 minutes for administration.

Comments: Reports norm-referenced scores (percentile ranks, normal curve equivalents, grade equivalents) and criterion-referenced scores (instructional reading levels); software includes report capabilities (e.g., diagnostic reports); capable of sharing databases with other Renaissance Learning software; data hosted by the test publisher; information regarding system requirements available from test publisher; technical manual (2018, 188 pages) available via test publisher's website; Star Reading Progress Monitoring version is available as a 25-item measure of reading comprehension.

Author: Renaissance Learning, Inc.

Publisher: Renaissance Learning, Inc.

Cross References: For reviews by Lori Nebelsick-Gullett and by Betsy B. Waterman and David M. Sargent of a previous version titled STAR Reading Version 2.2, see 15:242; for reviews by Theresa Volpe-Johnstone and Sandra Ward of the original edition, see 14:368.

Review of Star Reading® [2018 Manual] by MICHAEL HARWELL, Professor, Department of Educational Psychology, University of Minnesota, Minneapolis, MN:

DESCRIPTION. The Star Reading assessments (2018) provide estimates of a student's reading comprehension, reading achievement relative to national norms, and growth in reading comprehension and achievement over time. Star Reading is a computer-adaptive test designed to be aligned with national and state curriculum standards in reading for U.S. students in Grades K-12. Star Reading is not intended to be a high-stakes test like those linked to mastery of state reading standards, but the test is used in potentially high-stakes decisions such as identifying students at risk for reading difficulties or screening for reading deficiencies. The frequency with which the test is administered is guided by its purpose: For progress-monitoring, students will take Star Reading frequently (e.g., weekly) whereas for screening purposes, the test publisher recommends students take the test two to five times per school year. Feedback to educators is immediate, and student scores on previous administrations of the test are tracked by the software. Both norm-referenced and criterion-referenced scores are available via score reports designed for school staff and parents.

Test administration requires a computer or tablet with internet access for each student and a username and password to log on. A test administration manual that includes URLs for supporting documents guides educators planning to administer the Star Reading test. For example, a technical recommendations document provides information about computer requirements such as internet connections, browsers, and firewalls. Security features include limitations on the computers students can access, categorizing educators into user permission groups with different levels of access, and the fact that students generally respond to different sets of items. A practice session provides students with some familiarity with the computer interface and applies a benchmark of three correctly answered questions. Student who cannot meet the benchmark have their sessions terminated because they are not prepared to take the test. A student who answers three questions correctly is taken to the actual test items. Because the use of computer-adaptive testing with younger students may pose special challenges, Star Reading suggests introducing these students to the test a few days before the actual testing using a "how to" video available online.

Two versions of Star Reading are available: A 25-item test of reading comprehension often used for progress monitoring in programs such as response to intervention that takes approximately 10 minutes to complete, and a 34-item test that serves a similar purpose but assesses a greater breadth of reading skills, takes approximately 20 minutes to complete, and is aligned with national and state reading standards. Items are presented on a plain white screen and typically consist of individual sentences or text passages with characteristics students are asked about. Adaptive branching is used in which students initially are presented with an item whose difficulty level is below what is typical for their grade. A correct response prompts the introduction of a more difficult item, and an incorrect response prompts a less difficult item. In general students in Grades K-2 who fail to respond to an item within 60 seconds are timed out, as are students in Grades 3-12 who do not respond within 45 seconds, although students may take longer to complete the test with the agreement of the test administrator. (Timed-out items are scored as incorrect.) A proprietary Bayesian-modal item response theory (IRT) procedure is used to estimate a student's reading proficiency after each item response until the student answers at least one item correctly and one incorrectly; a proprietary maximum likelihood IRT estimation procedure is then used.

DEVELOPMENT. Star Reading is based on 36 blueprint skills organized into five blueprint domains (Word Knowledge and Skills, Comprehension Strategies and Constructing Meaning, Analyzing Literary Text, Understanding Author's Craft, and Analyzing Argument and Evaluating Text). Each item is designed to assess specific skills within these blueprints. The steps of developing the test are reported in some detail in the technical manual and included (a) using reading and assessment experts to identify blueprint skills drawing on resources such as the National Council of Teachers of English Principles of Adolescent Literacy Reform and Common Core Standards for Language Arts, (b) developing grade-appropriate items reflecting these skills using teams of content and writing experts, (c) field-testing items and analyzing the resulting data using Rasch IRT models, and (d) convening a panel of experts to review field-testing results to identify appropriate items based on their measurement properties, content coverage, readability, and fairness. Items for the 2018 version of Star Reading are used to generate scores forming the Unified scale: This scale places current and previous Star Reading scaled scores from the Enterprise scale on a common scale that facilitates comparisons across grades and time.

Information reported for the calibration samples used in the development of Star Reading items shows they were large (at least 15,000 students per grade) and generally approximated the national school population, although no evidence of the representation of special education and English language learner (ELL) students is reported. The Star Reading Accommodations FAQ document states that the computer-adaptive nature of Star Reading makes it suitable for students with disabilities such as limited vision and hearing and that the test can be administered in Spanish for Grades 1-8, but no evidence of the impact of accommodations on test scores is provided.

TECHNICAL. Two kinds of norms accompany Star Reading: test score norms and student growth norms, both of which are based on samples exceeding 18,000 students per grade in a school year. Norming samples generally approximated national school population characteristics such as gender and race as well as school enrollment, location, and type of school (public, non-public), although, again, the representation of special education and ELL students is not provided. Outcomes available for students include their instructional reading level (reading level at which a student can recognize words and comprehend written instructions with some assistance); grade equivalent; oral fluency score, which estimates a student's ability to read words quickly and accurately; percentile rank; normal curve equivalent; lexile score; and growth percentile, characterizing students' linear growth in reading relative to their peers. These scores are clearly defined in the Report Interpretation Guide.

Test documents provide evidence of the psychometric prowess of Star Reading for the Unified scale. Generic and split-half reliabilities reported by grade exceeded .91, and alternate-forms reliabilities ranged from .81 to .88. Conditional standard errors of measurement are also reported by grade. Substantial evidence of validity is presented including content evidence, predictive evidence, construct evidence, and concurrent evidence, mostly in tables of correlations between Star Reading and other tests. Correlations between Star Reading scores and state test scores add important validity evidence given the incorporation of reading standards in Star Reading, as does a meta-analysis of correlations of Star Reading with other tests. Evidence of the classification accuracy of Star Reading compared to state reading and language arts tests that categorize each student's reading proficiency into one of a small number of categories and evidence of the validity of the progress monitoring component based on growth (change) over time, is also provided.

COMMENTARY. Previous reviews of Star Reading have generally been positive but also expressed concerns about the way items were written, incomplete validity evidence, and norms for younger students. The current version of Star Reading seems largely to have addressed these concerns, particularly with regard to validity evidence, while maintaining strengths noted in previous reviews including clearly defining the intended uses of the test, strong development and technical features, and supporting materials that are well written and accessible to a wide audience of educators. The developers of Star Reading could have devoted additional resources to reassure educators that a student's computer literacy will have little or no effect on their performance. The assumption appears to be that students are technologically savvy enough to master the use of a computer or tablet with modest practice. Perhaps this assumption is correct given that 86% of children ages 3-18 used the internet at home in 2015 (McFarland et al., 2018). Nonetheless some educators may wonder whether computer literacy impacts the scores of younger students, those with no home computer, or those without internet access at home. Star Reading also appears to assume test administrators possess sufficient computer literacy to adequately respond to test-related challenges. For example, there is nothing in the test materials that speaks to test administrators responding to computer issues such as login difficulties, warning messages about firewalls, or student questions about the properties of a mouse or tablet. Allaying these kinds of concerns would have been relatively easy.

SUMMARY. Overall the Star Reading assessments represent a computer-adaptive testing system that should be a valuable addition to school districts seeking multipurpose tools to improve student reading. The supporting documentation is well written, and the technical work underlying Star Reading is strong. Two areas needing attention are the documentation of representation of special education and ELL students in Star Reading norms and information that speaks to the impact of computer literacy on student scores and the ability of test administrators to respond to computer issues.

REVIEWER'S REFERENCES

McFarland, J., Hussar, B., Wang, X., Zhang, J., Wang, K., Rathbun, A., ... Bullock Mann, F. (2018). *The Condition of Education 2018* (NCES 2018-144). U.S. Department of Education. Washington, DC: National Center for Education Statistics. Retrieved from https://nces.ed.gov/pubsearch/pubsinfo.asp?pubid=2018144

U. S. Department of Education. (2012). *Improving the measurement of socioeconomic status for the National Assessment of Educational Progress: A theoretical foundation* (NCES 2013-009). Washington, DC: Author. Retrieved from https://nces.ed.gov/nationsreportcard/pdf/researchcenter/socioeconomic_factors.pdf

Review of Star Reading® [2018 Manual] by THANOS PATELIS, Principal Scientist at Human Resources Research Organization and Research Scholar at Fordham University, New York City, NY:

DESCRIPTION. Star Reading is a computer-adaptive test (CAT) designed to measure reading achievement of students in Grades K-12. There is a comprehensive version of the test comprising 34 items and taking less than 20 minutes to administer and a shorter version comprising 25 items taking less than 10 minutes to administer. The stated purposes of both versions are to (a) provide an estimate of reading comprehension of students, (b) assess reading achievement in comparison to national norms, and (c) provide a means of tracking student performance longitudinally. The longer version is reported by the test developers to measure reading skills in more depth. The technical manual suggests scores can be used to predict performance on high-stakes tests and to inform instruction but cautions against using these measures for high-stakes uses such as student retention, promotion, and accountability.

DEVELOPMENT. The current version represents the third generation of Star Reading and incorporates a standards-based approach to its foundation. The conceptual framework represents five domains, 10 skills sets, 36 general skills, and more than 470 discrete skills reported to align with national and state curriculum standards in reading and language arts that include the Common Core State Standards. Item development involved adherence to these skills, readability, cognitive load, content differentiation, and presentation. To achieve fairness of the items, the technical manual indicated there were goals established to meet demographic and contextual balance. Additionally, the technical manual listed five declarations of what aspects were found to be balanced and fair. However, the method and evidence supporting these declarations were not provided in the technical manual. Items were calibrated by collecting responses online by embedding uncalibrated items within tests administered and then predicting the item difficulty parameter for each item to the previous Star Reading Rasch ability estimates. Previous calibrations for Star Reading Version 2 were done using a large and apparently nationally representative sample of students. Linking to Star Reading Version 1 was done using an equipercentile method. Items are delivered using computer-adaptive methodology. A proprietary Bayesian-modal item response theory (IRT) estimation method was used for scoring, and a proprietary maximum likelihood IRT estimation procedure was used to develop scaled scores. Evidence of differential item functioning (DIF) was not found in the technical manual, but the test publisher provided a separate technical document that included DIF analyses for the following comparisons: males versus females, Caucasians versus African Americans, Caucasians versus American Indians, Caucasians versus Asians, and Caucasians versus Hispanics.

TECHNICAL.

Standardization. Two sets of norms are available that represent test score norms and growth norms. Test score norms were produced in the 2017-18 school year for Star Early Literacy and Star Reading with separate fall and spring norms for Grades K-12. The norms were based on existing examinees selected using post-stratification procedures by geographic region, district socioeconomic status, and district/school size to ensure the norm samples were representative of the K-12 U.S. student population. The final norming samples comprised 2,786,680 examinees in the fall norms group and 1,855,730 examinees in the spring norms group with all coming from 50 states and 18,113 schools. Based on the information provided in the technical manual, the distributions by U.S. region, school enrollment, district socioeconomic status, and location were fairly well represented with a few exceptions: slight underrepresentation in the Northeast; from suburban and urban schools; schools with less than 200 enrollment; schools with 500 or more enrollment; and schools in districts with higher socioeconomic status and slight overrepresentation in the Southeast; from rural and town locations; schools with enrollments between 200 and 499; and schools in districts with lower socioeconomic status students.

Descriptive statistics of weighted student performance on the Unified and Enterprise scaled scores were provided for fall and spring by grade. The sample characteristics for fall and spring norming samples were similar. Growth norms were provided representing student growth percentiles (SGPs). SGPs were reported as percentile ranks representing the degree of growth in comparison to how other examinees who started at the same level changed in performance.

Reliability. Various sources of evidence for reliability and conditional standard errors of measurement were provided for the 34-item Star Reading test and the 25-item Star Reading progress monitoring test for both the Star Reading scale score and the Unified scale score. Internal consistency is referred to in the technical manual as "generic reliability" and defined as the proportion of error over total variance subtracted from one after error was calculated as the average of the squared standard error for each person's test score from the 2015-2016 administration. Split-half reliability also was calculated by separating odd and even numbered questions, calculating the correlation between the scores of the two halves, and using the Spearman-Brown formula to estimate the reliability for the full test. Alternate-form/test-retest reliability was calculated by administering two forms to the same examinee after an average of 96 days overall.

These three sets of reliability estimates were calculated for examinees in each grade and across all examinees. The number of examinees used for calculating the so-called generic reliability estimates and the split-half estimates for each grade were quite large, ranging from 15,583 in Grade 1 to 16,575 in Grade 10 with a total of 193,644. For calculating the alternate-form/test-retest reliability, 70,000 examinees were used for each grade representing Grades 1 to 12 for a total of 840,000 examinees. The average latency between administrations ranged from 77 days in Grade 3 to 117 days in Grade 11 for an average of 96 days across all grade levels. For each grade, the generic reliability estimates ranged from .94 to .96 on the Unified scale and from .93 to .95 on the Enterprise scale, representing high levels. The split-half reliabilities ranged from .94 to .96 on the Unified scale and from .91 to .95 on the Enterprise scale, also representing high levels. The alternate-form/test-retest reliabilities using a time latency between administrations showed values that ranged from .82 in Grade 1 to .88 in Grades 7 to 9, which showed strong stability over the 77- to 117-day average time interval across grades.

Based on the same samples of students from the 2015-2016 administration, the average conditional standard error of measurement ranged from 16 to 17 for each grade with a standard deviation of 1.1 to 2.8 in a grade on the Unified scale. The global standard error of measurement, based on the overall internal consistency of the test and the standard deviation of the test scores at each grade level on the Unified scale, ranged from 16 to 18. On the Enterprise scale, the average conditional standard error of measurement ranged from 21 to 71 for each grade with a standard deviation of 13.0 to 31.1 in a grade. The global standard error of measurement ranged from 27 to 78 across the grades.

Validity. Validity evidence in support of the use of Star Reading scores as an estimate of reading comprehension was provided and represented a variety of sources. Content evidence of validity was based on the argument that the content of the item bank represented the target content specifications and the reliance on the content balancing specifications of the adaptive test delivery platform to the five test blueprint domains of (a) Word Knowledge and Skills, (b) Comprehension Strategies and Constructing Meaning, (c) Analyzing Literary Text, (d) Analyzing Argument and Evaluating Text, and (e) Understanding the Author's Craft. The domain of Analyzing Argument and Evaluating Text was not present for tests given in Grades K-3. Evidence for internal structure of the Star Reading test was based on exploratory and confirmatory factor analyses showing that one factor existed. Additionally, results of item-level factor analyses of the combined Star Reading and the Degrees of Reading Power (DRP) tests in Grades 3, 5, 7, and 10 were reported to have one large factor emerge. The bulk of the validity evidence represented relations to other tests using a variety of tests (almost 40) and approaches that included concurrent and predictive analyses as well as analyses of classification accuracy. Several hundred correlation coefficients between Star Reading and the various other tests by grade showed substantial uncorrected correlations that ranged from .65 to .80. Meta-analysis results of the 789 correlation coefficients between Star Reading and other test scores showed an overall estimate of .79 with a standard error of 0.001. Classification accuracy studies with several state tests was shown to be 83% to 87% across grades with the Area Under the Curve (AUC) based on receiver operating characteristic (ROC) curves at .90 for all grades. Disaggregated classification and AUC statistics were provided by race/ethnicity in comparison to six state achievement tests showing overall classification rates that ranged from 67% for Black, non-Hispanic examinees to 82% for Asian/Pacific Islander students. Additionally, the AUC statistics were mostly above .80 except for four grade-by-ethnicity groupings that were greater than .50.

Additional evidence was provided to support the purpose of the Star Reading as a means of monitoring student progress. Evidence regarding the reliability of the change in student performance for at-risk students was provided. Star Reading reliability of the slope characteristics across administrations were at/above .93 for each grade, except for Grade 1 where the correlation was .76. Additionally, as evidence for use in progress monitoring, the technical manual indicated that multiple forms are readily available (being a computer adaptive test); test time is efficient at 15-20 minutes; and adequate growth can be specified by using the student growth percentiles, the linkages to state assessment performance levels, and/or normative information. A study was referenced in the technical manual that suggested reliable progress monitoring could be made within five Star Reading administrations with suggestions for the duration of Star Reading progress monitoring based on grade level.

COMMENTARY. The information and directions provided in the Star Reading manuals are extensive, well written, and easy to use. The reading domain and skills are clearly specified. Substantial technical and empirical evidence is provided to support the use of STAR Reading scores as intended. There is evidence needed to support the use of STAR Reading with various groups of students and in making claims of performance over time.

SUMMARY. Star Reading is a computer-adaptive reading test for students in Grades K-12. There is a comprehensive version of the test comprising 34 items and taking less than 20 minutes to administer and a shorter version comprising 25 items and taking less than 10 minutes to administer. The stated purposes of both versions are to (a) provide an estimate of reading comprehension of students, (b) assess reading achievement in comparison to national norms, and (c) provide a means of tracking student performance longitudinally. Star Reading represents a clearly articulated set of reading domains and skills with the five major domains being Word Knowledge and Skills, Comprehension Strategies and Constructing Meaning, Analyzing Literary Text, Understanding the Author's Craft, and Analyzing Argument and Evaluating Text. The extensive item bank and the abundance of technical and empirical information support the intended uses. Efforts to gather evidence to support the use of scores by various student groups and to substantiate claims about progress should continue.

[158]

STAR Reading Test, 2nd Edition, 2014 Update [New Zealand].

Purpose: Designed to "supplement the assessments that teachers make about their students' progress and achievement in reading."
Population: Students in Years 3-9 in New Zealand schools.
Publication Dates: 2000-2013.
Acronym: STAR.
Administration: Group.
Levels, 4: Years 3-4, Years 5-6, Years 7-8, Year 9.
Price Data, 2020: NZ$66 per starter kit for Years 3-6 including teacher's manual, one of each test booklet, and marking keys; NZ$92 per starter kit for Years 3-8 including teacher's manual, one of each test booklet, and marking keys; NZ$55 per starter kit for Years 7-9 including teacher's manual, one of each test booklet, and marking keys; NZ$31 per teacher's manual; NZ$19.50 per marking keys for Years 3-4 and 5-6; NZ$25 per marking keys for Years 7-9; NZ$15.60 per 10 test booklets.
Comments: "Each STAR test has been designed with a particular year level in mind. However, each of the new STAR tests can be used productively with students at two or more year levels." Years 3-4, 5-6, and 7-8 each have 3 tests of increasing difficulty (i.e., A, B, C); 2nd edition tests published in 2011, update applies only to manual.
Authors: Warwick Elley, Hilary Ferral, and Verena Watson.
Publisher: New Zealand Council for Educational Research.

a) YEARS 3-4.
Population: Students in Years 3-4 in New Zealand schools.
Scores, 5: Word Recognition, Sentence Comprehension, Paragraph Comprehension, Vocabulary, Total.
Levels, 3: A, B, C.
Time: (30) minutes.

b) YEARS 5-6.
Population: Students in Years 5-6 in New Zealand schools.
Scores, 5: Word Recognition, Sentence Comprehension, Paragraph Comprehension, Vocabulary, Total.
Levels, 3: A, B, C.
Time: (30) minutes.

c) YEARS 7-8.
Population: Students in Years 7-8 in New Zealand schools.
Scores, 7: Word Recognition, Sentence Comprehension, Paragraph Comprehension, Vocabulary, Language of Advertising, Reading of Different Text Types, Total.
Levels, 3: A, B, C.
Time: (40) minutes.

d) YEAR 9.
Population: Students in Year 9 in New Zealand schools.
Scores, 7: Word Recognition, Sentence Comprehension, Paragraph Comprehension, Vocabulary, Language of Advertising, Reading of Different Text Types, Total.
Time: (40) minutes.

Cross References: For a review by John W. Young of an earlier edition titled STAR Supplementary Tests of Achievement in Reading, see 15:243.

Review of the STAR Reading Test, 2nd Edition, 2014 Update by KATHLEEN D. ALLEN, Professor of Education and Counseling Psychology, Saint Martin's University, Lacey, WA:

DESCRIPTION. The purpose of the STAR Reading Test is to provide standardized supplemental assessments that align with specific aspects of New Zealand's national standards (Ministry of Education, 2010) for students in Years 3-9 (approximately ages 8-14). Each test is divided into four subtests, with two additional subtests in Years 7-9. The four subtests administered at all levels are (a) Word Recognition, a multiple-choice assessment where students select the best word (from four choices) to describe a picture; (b) Sentence Comprehension, a modified cloze assessment where students choose from four words to complete the blank space in a sentence; (c) Paragraph Comprehension, a constructed response cloze assessment with multiple blank spaces in a paragraph where students write words that make sense in the context of the paragraph (word suggestions are included for Years 3-4); and (d) Vocabulary Range, a multiple-choice assessment where students choose from four words to find the best synonym for a highlighted word in a sentence. Two additional subtests are administered to Years 7-9: (a) The Language of Advertising, a selected word assessment where students select the most "emotive" (persuasive) word in a sentence; and (b) Reading Different Text Types, a multiple-choice, selected-phrase assessment where the prompt is a paragraph for a specific writing genre (i.e., a fairy tale, recipe, diary, or weather report) and students select from three phrases embedded in the paragraph that would typify the writing genre of the prompt.

The Teacher Manual provides explicit directions for each subtest to standardize test administration. All subtests are timed and designed to be administered to a group of students. Teachers select the appropriate test forms that match each student's reading achievement level. Administration time for the entire STAR Reading assessment is 30 minutes for students in Years 3-6 and 40 minutes for students in Years 7-9. Students write the answers directly in test booklets and teachers calculate the raw scores using provided marking key booklets. The Teacher Manual includes a conversion table to convert raw scores into scale scores and stanines, as well as a sample STAR student report. Teachers can also use the New Zealand Council for Educational Research (NZCER) as a resource to create reports. The components of the STAR Reading Test are the Teacher Manual, three marking keys (Years 3-4, Years 5-6, and Years 7-9), three student booklets for Years 3-4 (test forms A, B, and C), three student booklets for Years 5-6 (test forms A, B, and C), three student booklets for Years 7-8 (test forms A, B, and C), and one student booklet for Year 9 (test form A).

DEVELOPMENT.

Theoretical framework. The original version of the STAR Reading test was developed between 1999 and 2003. Development of both the original and revised versions of the test were funded by the NZCER to assess three aspects of reading from New Zealand's national education standards: thinking critically about texts, making meaning of texts, and learning the code of written language (Ministry of Education, 2010). The code of written language (including the skills of knowledge of how words work, knowledge of phoneme-grapheme relationships, automatic recognition of high frequency words) is evaluated with the Word Recognition and Sentence Comprehension subtests. Students must be able to decode the provided words using their knowledge of phoneme-grapheme relationships and how words work to determine the correct answers. To address the evaluation of automatic recognition of high frequency words, entries for the Word Recognition subtest were selected from high frequency lists (Croft & Mapa, 1988) and a dictionary (Shallcrass, 1994) commonly used in the New Zealand primary (elementary) schools. Making meaning of texts (including the skills of use of background knowledge, use of vocabulary knowledge, knowledge of how language is structured, knowledge about literacy, and use of comprehension strategies) is evaluated with the Paragraph Comprehension and Vocabulary Range subtests. Students must be able to access prior learning—their lexicon of words, syntax, and semantics—and use context clues to determine the correct answers. Thinking critically about texts (including the skills of analyzing texts and bringing critical awareness to texts) is evaluated with The Language of Advertising and Reading Different Text Types subtests. Students must be able to analyze phrases to determine the writing genre and critically read sentences to select the most persuasive word.

Task development. The second edition of the STAR Reading Test was created to update the theory basis for the test, make suggested scoring direction revisions for clarity, and improve scale score accuracy. Scale scores for the STAR Reading Test are calculated using the Rasch measurement model (Rasch, 1980). This model allows for the transcription of raw test scores into scale scores. For accurate results, each student must be tested at his or her own reading achievement level. Therefore, the test authors developed new test forms for different reading achievement levels. This step was performed to improve scale score accuracy and reduce the ceiling effect in scores of advanced readers. Most of the test items have been revised since the original edition of the STAR Reading Test was published. New items were pilot tested in a small number of schools. After analysis, 19 tests were constructed for a national trial. A post-stratification was conducted to eliminate bias due to unequal numbers of students in quintile or school size groups. Stanines were calculated using norming sample data. The results from this trial were used to construct the 10 test forms for specific reading achievement levels.

TECHNICAL.

Standardization. The norming sample for the test's second edition trial was representative of the New Zealand national population at each reading achievement level. The sampling rate was based on statistical data from the country's Ministry of Education to match the intended population. The norming sample included 70 schools and 7,581 students. It was stratified according to school quintile and size to achieve a variation of setting (urban or rural), ethnic diversity, and type of school. In the analysis of gender, girls scored a bit higher than boys at all levels, but this difference only accounted for about 1 percent of the total score variance. No specific data on different ethnic or cultural groups are included.

Reliability. The internal consistency between test items was calculated with the norming sample and the trial tests using coefficient alpha. The resulting reliability coefficients (alpha = .93–.96, M = 28.8–59.6, SD = 9.7–19.2) indicate a high level of internal consistency.

Validity. The match between the theoretical framework and the purpose of the test provides content evidence of validity. The Teacher Manual describes how each aspect of the designated New Zealand national standards are assessed in the subtests. Additionally, the test items were reviewed by NZCER employees, teachers, and literacy specialists before the pilot testing. The "consequential validity" of the test is addressed in the Teacher Manual. Results of the STAR Reading Test can be used for measuring growth over a specific time period, setting goals, identifying student needs, creating student groups, selecting students for enrichment programs, and comparing performance levels. In addition, the subtest scores can aid in instructional planning for groups or individual students. The Teacher Manual also contains suggestions for using the data from the STAR Reading Test to begin a "line of investigation" (p. 27) of specific student needs and provides ideas for instruction aligned with those needs.

COMMENTARY. Revisions and additions made for the second edition of STAR Reading were adequately tested with a pilot study and subsequent trials. The Teacher Manual is thorough and includes clear instructions for administration and scoring and technical information as well as information on the application of test results to classroom planning and instruction. Because many of the test items are purposefully designed to access the background knowledge of students in New Zealand, some vocabulary words, spellings, names, and places would be unfamiliar to students in other countries. Therefore, the STAR Reading Test results would probably not be generalizable internationally and should not be used for research or student assessment outside of New Zealand.

SUMMARY. The STAR Reading Test seems to be an effective assessment for students in New Zealand. It is based on a sound theoretical model and appears to have internal consistency reliability as well as content, construct, and consequential evidence of validity. Predictive evidence of validity could be gathered as well with the correlation between student needs from the "line of investigation" and subtest scores. The tests are easy to administer, and it takes students less than an hour to complete all the subtests. Scoring can be done by the teacher, which makes this test less expensive than many other national standardized tests. Although currently a pencil-and-paper test, the STAR Reading Test could be adapted for computer administration, although the subtest times might need to be altered and it would only be feasible for schools with the technology resources for group administration.

REVIEWER'S REFERENCES

Croft, A. C., & Mapa, L. (1998). *Spell-Write: An aid to writing and spelling* (2nd ed.). Wellington, New Zealand: New Zealand Council for Educational Research.

Ministry of Education. (2010). *The literacy learning progressions.* Wellington, New Zealand: Learning Media Limited.

Rasch, G. (1980). *Probabilistic models for some intelligence and attainment tests* (2nd ed.). Chicago, IL: University of Chicago Press.

Shallcrass, J. (Ed.). (1994). *The New Zealand Oxford primary school dictionary.* Auckland, New Zealand: Oxford University Press.

Review of the STAR Reading Test, 2nd Edition, 2014 Update by SANDRA WARD, Professor of Education, The College of William & Mary, Williamsburg, VA:

DESCRIPTION. The STAR Reading Test, 2nd Edition, 2014 Update is a standardized, group-administered instrument developed to assess aspects of reading that inform teachers about students' mastery of skills in the following areas: learning the code of written language, making meaning of texts, and thinking critically about texts. The test authors suggest that the instrument should be used to supplement assessments made by teachers regarding reading achievement of students across Years 3-9 in New Zealand schools. No age span is provided in the test materials. The measure consists of 10 tests that are arranged in order of difficulty for Years 3-4, 5-6, 7-8, and Year 9. Each level has three tests of increasing difficulty (A, B, and C), except for Year 9, which has a single test. Years 3-6 include four subtests (Word Recognition, Sentence Comprehension, Paragraph Comprehension, and Vocabulary Knowledge). Years 7-9 include two additional subtests (Language of Advertising and Reading of Different Text Types).

Directions for administration and scoring are straightforward and easy to follow. Group administration time is approximately 30 minutes for Years 3-6 and approximately 40 minutes for Years 7-9. Although the test manual states that teachers can administer any of the tests at any time of year, the test authors suggest that teachers will obtain more useful data if the tests are given at the indicated times. Students write their answers directly in the test booklets. Teachers use marking keys in the answer booklets to score the students' tests. Schools also can use New Zealand Council for Educational Research (NZCER) scoring services for results and reports. Correct answers are summed for raw scores on each subtest, then subtest scores are added to obtain a total test score. The total score is converted to a STAR scale score called star units. Star units range from 10 to 175 for Years 3-9 and represent equal intervals, which enables the teacher to compare student gains from year to year. Tables are provided to convert the total test scores to stanines to make comparisons to other instruments and appropriate norm groups. The logic for identifying the proper norm table for stanines is problematic because all forms were normed in Term 1, and there are no direct norms for other terms of the school year. The test authors recommend looking at the next year's norms for an assessment conducted in Term 4 because that is the closest comparison point. For midyear assessments, the authors indicate that there is no good choice of norms. For each subtest, the mean (average score for reference group), typical range, and critical score are provided; however, the source of derivation of these values is not adequately described.

DEVELOPMENT. According to the test authors, the purpose of the 2014 update was to make use of the STAR more straightforward for teachers. No data or items were changed from the second edition published in 2011. The changes made for the 2014 update represented revisions of the manual and the reporting forms to improve administration and interpretation. Specifically, the authors changed the section on the use of stanines.

The second edition of the STAR (2011) was created to match the revised New Zealand standards and the needs expressed by teachers. The original subtests of the STAR were retained, but most items were new to the second edition. These items were tested, and the scales developed in a multistage process using Rasch measurement principles. An original set of items was developed and tested on a small sample of schools. The test authors created 19 linked tests from the items that were identified as suitable in the first stage. These tests were administered to students from a stratified random sample of schools. The analysis of these results led the authors to retain, modify, or remove items from the pool. The retained and modified items were then used to create 10 tests targeted to year levels. These tests were used in the norming study from which the final tests were constructed. The use of Rasch measurement is an appropriate method to identify items and develop scales. However, the test authors provide no substantial description of the number of items tested or the specific indicators that were used to identify poor items. There is no mention of any item bias analyses used in the development process.

TECHNICAL. The data for the standardization of the STAR, 2nd Edition (2011) were obtained through a stratified, random sample of schools. The stratification variables for the sample were school decile and school size. Participating schools were asked to test a number of classes of students based on the school size. The test authors argue that this method produced a sample that represented New Zealand students in terms of ethnic diversity, school type, and urbanicity. No data are presented to demonstrate that the sample matches the population on these characteristics, and this reviewer believes it is unlikely that the employed sampling method would produce such a sample.

The test authors provide only internal consistency estimates of reliability (coefficient alpha) for the 10 tests from the norming trial. The reliability coefficients exceed .90 indicating that all tests have sufficient reliability to make the type of interpretations recommended by the test authors. No test-retest or Rasch estimates of reliability are provided even though the test authors present reliability in terms of stability and used Rasch methods to construct the scales. Standard errors for the scales are presented in separate tables, but no explanation is provided on how they were calculated.

The authors provide minimal support for the validity of the STAR, 2nd Edition. The authors present an argument for the content match of the items to the New Zealand standards. The judgment of literacy specialists and teachers is mentioned, but no data are provided on the number, composition, or agreement of these panels. Evidence is presented that indicates that performance on all of the tests correlates with age as expected. The data provided on differences based on gender show that the STAR, 2nd Edition scores differ between males and females. It is not indicated whether the reported differences are statistically significant, but the differences are reported as being usual for reading achievement instruments. Typical validity evidence such as correlations with other similar measures, subtest correlations, and factor analyses are not reported. Additionally, there are no studies with special populations or evidence that the instrument can lead to appropriate interventions.

COMMENTARY. The STAR, 2nd Edition, 2014 Update is a brief, group administered test designed for teachers to assess reading skills across Years 3-9 in New Zealand schools. The changes made for the 2014 update represented revisions of the manual and the reporting forms to improve administration and interpretation. Administration and scoring are straightforward. Users are encouraged to use the total scale score called star units to assess student gains across time. The use of stanines is discouraged because the logic for identifying the proper norm table for stanines is problematic given that all the forms were normed in Term 1. Although mean scores, typical ranges, and critical scores are provided, the source of these scores is not explained.

In the development of the 2014 update, no data or items were changed from the STAR, 2nd Edition published in 2011. The authors appropriately used Rasch measurement techniques to identify items and develop scales, but they do not provide sufficient description of the indicators used to select items. Additionally, there is no mention of the use of differential item functioning (item bias) analyses in the test's development.

There is no evidence presented to support the degree to which the standardization sample is representative of students in New Zealand schools, so the use of stanines for comparisons of performance to other instruments is somewhat questionable. Internal consistency reliability coefficients are strong and support the use of the instrument; however, the test authors provide no evidence of test-retest stability. Support for validity of the STAR, 2nd Edition is insufficient. Content was developed to match the New Zealand reading standards, and data indicated that scale scores correlate appropriately with age. Correlations with similar measures, subtest correlations, and factor analyses were not reported.

SUMMARY. The STAR, 2nd Edition, 2014 Update is a standardized, group-administered instrument for schools in New Zealand that teachers can use to track students' mastery of reading skills over time. Based on the data provided regarding the technical adequacy of the instrument, users should use the instrument cautiously. The STAR, 2nd Edition, 2014 Update should be used in conjunction with other assessments to measure reading achievement and make instructional decisions. Reliability data support the internal consistency of the measure, but information on stability is lacking. Evidence for validity is provided, but is insufficient. Although scale scores appropriately increase with age and content was developed to match the national standards, no information is provided to support the structural, criterion, or consequential evidence of validity of the instrument.

[159]

Student Language Scale (SLS) Screener for Language & Literacy Disorders.

Purpose: Designed to "gather multi-informant input from parents, teachers, students, and others regarding a school-age student's language/literacy skills and other strengths and needs."

Population: Ages 6-18 years.

Publication Date: 2018.

Acronym: SLS.

Scores: Risk for Language/Literacy Disorder.

Administration: Individual or group.

Price Data, 2020: $79.95 per kit including user's manual (75 pages), 50 forms, and quick start guide; $49.95 per manual; $34.95 per 50 forms.

Time: 1-3 minutes for completion.

Comments: Companion to the Test of Integrated Language and Literacy Skills™ (TILLS; 20:181); can be used as a stand-alone tool or with other assessments.

Authors: Nickola Wolf Nelson, Barbara M. Howes, and Michele A. Anderson.

Publisher: Paul H. Brookes Publishing Co., Inc.

[159] Student Language Scale (SLS) Screener for Language & Literacy Disorders

Review of the Student Language Scale (SLS) Screener for Language & Literacy Disorders by KAREN L. GISCHLAR, Associate Professor, and ALICIA GIALANELLA, Graduate Student, School Psychology Program, Rider University, Lawrenceville, NJ:

DESCRIPTION. The Student Language Scale (SLS) Screener for Language & Literacy Disorders is an evidence-based questionnaire and screening tool designed to examine a school-age student's language/literacy skills, strengths, and needs from multiple perspectives, including teachers, parents, and students themselves. The scale, which compares teacher and parent ratings of individual students to cut scores, is intended to be used as a screening tool for language/literacy disorders (LLD). Scores obtained from the scale can be used in deciding whether a student should undergo a comprehensive evaluation. Additionally, the SLS provides information about a student's strengths and needs from teacher and parent input that can be used to enhance instruction and school-home communication for students of all abilities. Student ratings cannot be used for screening, but they can contribute qualitative information for use in discussions about student needs and priorities.

The SLS is a one-page form consisting of a 12-item rating scale, an ability checklist, and a priority question. Items 1-8 of the rating scale correspond to the eight constructs assessed by the Test of Integrated Language and Literacy Skills (TILLS; Nelson, Plante, Helm-Estabrooks, & Hotz, 2016; 20:181), developed concurrently with the SLS, whereas Items 9-12 represent related social/cognitive skills. Scores on the items range from 1 (*not good*) to 7 (*very good*); ratings less than 5 on any two of the first eight items are considered "failing" and indicate a potential LLD requiring a comprehensive evaluation. The TILLS was designed for use as a diagnostic tool for LLD and is recommended for administration to students who have "failed" the screening to determine eligibility for special services, as required by the Individuals with Disabilities Education (Improvement) Act. For students already receiving special education services, the SLS can aid individual education program teams in identifying areas to target for instruction. In addition, when building the home-school connection, parent and student ratings can be particularly beneficial in understanding each party's perspectives regarding the student and how he or she performs across environments. Finally, the SLS is a useful tool for identifying those at-risk students who have not met the fail criteria but who would benefit from intervention.

The second section of the SLS is the ability checklist of skills, which represents both language and non-language skills areas. Raters are asked to check the areas that are easiest for the student on the first list and then to check those that are hardest for the student from the same set of choices in a duplicated checklist. In this manner, there is input on areas of strength as well as areas of concern. The final section of the SLS is the open-ended priority question that asks the rater to record the one area believed to be most important in helping the student to achieve at school. This format allows for personal meanings to be reflected through a wide variety of possible responses. Overall, the SLS is useful in determining a student's strengths and needs, particularly in regard to LLD, by gaining input from teachers, parents, and students, enabling a comprehensive picture of the student's abilities.

Most teachers, parents, and students should be able to complete the SLS independently after a brief explanation of its purpose. Administrators should emphasize that there are no correct or incorrect answers and that informants should complete all three sections. If necessary, assistance can be given to individuals who need help in understanding or reading the form. This may be the case with younger children or with individuals who have difficulty reading or understanding English. An interpreter or scribe, an oral interview, or various other accommodations may be necessary for these individuals. Teachers at any grade level from 1-12 can complete the SLS either for an individual student or as a screening tool for an entire class. If a primary goal of using the SLS is to establish greater school-home communication, teachers can complete a form for each student and send forms home for parents to complete and bring to parent-teacher conferences. Teachers also could administer the SLS as a classroom activity to gain student perspectives.

DEVELOPMENT. In the early stages of development of the SLS, the scale's authors considered how ethnographic interviewing is used in the schools to gain multiple perspectives of a student's development and progress. The test authors then outlined the key constructs to be assessed by the scale by referring to the language levels-by-modalities model used for the TILLS, which was concurrently normed with the SLS.

Once content items were developed across the constructs, a panel of interdisciplinary scientific experts and parents was formed to provide input on the cultural-linguistic appropriateness of the items for a diverse population of students and families. Following try-outs with preliminary versions of the SLS, the scale was administered as part of the broader TILLS standardization research, which included 1,900 students ages 6 through 18 years. The students in the standardization sample were assigned to groups including Normal Language Group, Language Learning Disabilities Group, Language and Literacy Risk Group, and three additional groups of Students in Special Populations (children identified as having an autism spectrum disorder, being deaf or hard of hearing, or having a mild intellectual developmental disability). Group assignment was determined through demographic information obtained for each student participant.

Preliminary versions of the scale were piloted before the final version was published. One of the earliest versions was the Language and Literacy Questionnaire (LLQ). The LLQ consisted of a 52-item rating scale consistent with the advice of the scientific experts consulted by the test authors. The measure incorporated an orthogonal set of questions that asked about the student's abilities across tasks that corresponded to all four communication modalities (listening, speaking, reading, writing) at each language level. After this version of the LLQ was piloted, the test authors conducted qualitative focus groups with teachers, parents, and students. The consensus was that the LLQ was too long. Quantitative data also revealed low correlations between LLQ items and preliminary TILLS performance measures as well as inconsistent performance and wavering validity on certain questions. Therefore, the test authors revised the form to include 12 items and rewrote questions to be simple, clear, and consistent with the TILLS model. This scale was used in TILLS standardization research and was called the Student Rating Scale (SRS). The SRS was eventually renamed the SLS to distinguish this scale from others, with no changes to content. Separate exploratory factor analyses were conducted for teachers, parents, and students, revealing a two-factor model following oblique rotation. Consistent with the TILLS, Items 1-8 of the 12-item rating scale loaded onto the first factor, namely language/literacy skills, whereas Items 9-12 loaded onto the second construct of cognitive/social skills across all three informant groups (interfactor correlations of .68 for teachers, .61 for parents, and .60 for students).

TECHNICAL. As noted by the test authors, the validity of SLS results for the purpose of screening depends on how accurately the scale predicts which students are likely to have language/literacy disorders. A screening tool should be able to differentiate students with a high risk of the disorder in question from those with a low risk. To evaluate evidence of validity for the SLS, the test authors sought to determine a pass/fail cut score that would maximize sensitivity and specificity. Sensitivity was based on the criterion that 80% or more of students identified by other measures to have an LLD would fail the screener. Conversely, specificity was based on the criterion that 80% or more of students identified as not having an LLD would pass the screener.

To determine the optimal cut score, test developers tested the criterion of two or more of the first eight items receiving a rating less than 5. Results indicated that teacher ratings of lower than 5 on two or more of the first eight items on the scale correctly identified 61 of the 66 students (92%) with documented LLD, 182 of the 203 students (90%) without known disorders, and 41 of 48 students (85%) considered at risk for the development of an LLD. Likewise, parent ratings demonstrated acceptable sensitivity and specificity. Specifically, parent ratings correctly identified 203 of 239 students (85%) with known LLD and 1,065 of 1,290 students (83%) without known disorders. Parent ratings for the at-risk group correctly identified only 122 of 192 students (64%), suggesting that parents may not be able to identify accurately the children included in this group. Finally, student self-ratings on the first eight items of the SLS resulted in percentages that fell below the 80% criterion, rendering them invalid for use in screening.

A second means of evaluating validity evidence for the SLS, receiver operating characteristic (ROC) curve analysis, was employed to evaluate the scale's screening accuracy for teacher, parent, and student ratings. A ROC curve is a graphical plot that compares the true positive rate against the false positive rate at different cut scores (sensitivity by 1-specificity). A more discriminative instrument with the most precise cut scores will produce a sharper curve with maximum area under the curve. A less discriminative instrument, on the other hand, will produce a flatter curve with smaller values for the area under the curve. Consistent with the results of the other analyses described for the SLS, the values for the areas under the curve were highest for teacher ratings (.94), next highest for parent ratings (.89), and smallest for student ratings (.74). These findings support the validity of teacher and parent ratings for the purpose of making pass/fail screening decisions with the SLS.

Finally, the test authors examined concurrent validity of the scale for the purpose of gathering input for evaluation and planning through binary correlations of data from subsets of informant (i.e., teacher, parent, and student) ratings with theoretically aligned composite scores on the TILLS. Although all correlation coefficients were statistically significant, only the teacher and parent ratings correlated highly enough with TILLS scores to be useful. The student ratings correlated weakly with test scores, but the test authors suggested that they may be valuable when taken at face value in understanding how a student perceives his/her abilities. These findings suggest that the SLS yields results that are valid for use as a screener of language and literacy disorders and to provide information about strengths and weaknesses for evaluation and planning when used with teachers and, to a lesser degree, parents.

To evaluate the reliability of the SLS, the authors calculated internal reliability via coefficient omega for each of the three types of raters (teachers, parents, and students). Coefficient omega was selected over the more commonly used coefficient alpha because of the brevity of the scale, although alpha was calculated for comparison with omega. Coefficient omega was .96 for teachers, .94 for parents, and .84 for students. Alpha values were nearly identical. These findings suggest strong internal consistency of the SLS.

Intrarater reliability, which is similar to test-retest reliability, also was calculated for teacher, parent, and student informants at intervals of less than 6 months. As with the other analyses, teachers demonstrated the highest consistency in ratings across time with an interclass correlation coefficient of .92. Coefficients were .83 for parents and .61 for students. Although the intrarater reliability coefficient for the student sample was moderate, an interesting pattern emerged for this group's ratings. Findings suggested that students were more consistent in rating their cognitive and social skills (i.e., the last four items on the scale) than they were in rating their own language and literacy skills (the first eight items on the scale).

A final measure of reliability, interrater, evaluated the extent of agreement of ratings between dyads formed from the three groups (teachers, parents, and students). Binary correlations for all group combinations were moderately strong and statistically significant. The strongest correlation (.75) was between the teacher and parent ratings, whereas the teacher-student (.61) and the parent-student (.66) comparisons evidenced weaker relationships. The test authors caution that although it can be assumed that the three classes of raters all would have awareness of a child's language and literacy skill difficulties, the differing environments and experiences with the child might impact the rater's perspective. In sum, the SLS presents validity and reliability data that provide support for its use as a screening tool with input for planning.

COMMENTARY. The SLS manual is well organized and clearly written. Technical terminology is explained in such a way that the content is readily accessible to the reader. Further, the test manual includes information regarding psychometric properties, including ROC analyses, that demonstrate adequate sensitivity and specificity for using the SLS as a screener. The scale itself is brief and should be easy for most raters to complete in a few minutes' time. Completed example scales and explanations are included at the back of the test manual to aid interpretation of results.

One concern with reliability and validity evidence regards the description of the sample. The scale authors note that the majority of the 1,900 students ages 6 through 18 years included in the TILLS standardization research participated in the SLS study. These students were assigned to one of six groups: (a) Normal Language Group; (b) Language Learning Disabilities Group; (c) Language and Literacy Risk Group; or (d) one of three groups of Students in Special Populations. Group membership was decided with predefined inclusion criteria. However, there is no information regarding numbers of students by gender, age, or ethnicity. These data may be available in the TILLS manual, but given that the test authors contend that the SLS can be used as a stand-alone measure, they should have been included in the SLS manual as well. It is important for an evaluator to know whether assessment tools, including informant rating scales, are valid for the population being tested.

The test manual notes that the SLS can be used in deciding whether a comprehensive evaluation is warranted for a child. Although the scale can be completed by teachers, parents, and children, analyses suggest that teacher ratings are the best source for decision-making. Thus, a teacher form should always be completed in conjunction with a parent form. The manual also notes that evaluators can look for patterns among informants by placing "completed SLS forms side by side." Certainly, caution should be exercised in conducting this type of "eyeball analysis." Finally, the test manual suggests that the SLS can be used to monitor change over time to observe whether teacher and parent ratings are stable, improving, or declining. However, there is no mention of the scale's sensitivity to growth. An evaluator should not use the SLS as the sole measure of a student's progress. Rather, evidence-based language and literacy progress monitoring tools should be used for this purpose.

SUMMARY. The SLS provides evidence for being a reliable tool that generates scores appropriate for use as a screener for language and literacy disorders among school-age youth. It appears to be easy to complete and should not take too much of a teacher's or parent's time. However, the evaluator should explore the sample of children and families represented in the standardization sample before deciding to use the scale with individuals; this information is lacking in the SLS manual.

REVIEWERS' REFERENCE

Nelson, N. W., Plante, E., Helm-Estabrooks, N., & Hotz, G. (2016). Test of Integrated Language and Literacy Skills. Baltimore, MD: Paul H. Brookes.

Review of the Student Language Scale (SLS) Screener for Language & Literacy Disorders by ROSALIE MARDER UNTERMAN, Associate Professor/Clinical Director, Graduate Program Speech-Language Pathology, Touro College School of Health Sciences, Brooklyn, NY:

DESCRIPTION. The Student Language Scale (SLS) Screener for Language & Literacy Disorders is an evidence-based questionnaire/screening tool used to gather information about a student's language/literacy skills as well as other strengths and needs. The screener was designed to gain information from teachers, parents, and students regarding language and literacy skills of school-age children ages 6-0 to 18-11 to be used for referral for further evaluation, to evaluate and plan activities for students with special needs, and to improve the quality of school-home communication.

The SLS consists of a user's manual, a tablet of 50 Student Language Scale forms and a quick start guide. Forms are completed by a teacher, parent/caregiver, or even the student and include 12 items to rate using a 7-point scale ranging from *not good* (1) to *very good* (7). Performance is evaluated in comparison to skills of peers according to the following instruction: "Compared with other students of the same age, circle the number to show how good this student is at ...." Areas rated include understanding school vocabulary, sound/word capabilities for reading and spelling, listening comprehension and spoken expression of stories, reading comprehension and written formulation of stories, and cognitive and social skills. In addition, the rater indicates activities, such as art, music, and sports that are "easiest" and "hardest" for the student. Finally, an open-ended question is asked about helping the student succeed in school.

As a screening tool, if two or more of the first eight questions are rated less than 5, then follow-up testing with the co-developed Test of Integrated Language and Literacy Skills (TILLS; Nelson, Plante, Helm-Estabrooks, & Hotz, 2016; 20:181) and other appropriate procedures would be recommended for an in-depth assessment of language/literacy. The questions also provide additional information for developing effective teaching and allow for communication between the school and home environments.

DEVELOPMENT. The Student Language Scale was developed to gather information of the type that could be obtained from ethnographic interviews of teachers, parents, and students. This information would then be utilized as a precursor to assessment and intervention. The key constructs to be rated refer to the language levels-by-modalities model of the TILLS. Content areas were developed in consultation with a panel of interdisciplinary experts and parents to allow for a diverse population of parents and students. Student participants were assigned to groups as per identification of a disorder by a multidisciplinary school-based team or a private practitioner. Disorders identified were language impairment, reading disorder, dyslexia, or specific learning disability in oral and/or written language. Three primary groups were assigned: Normal Language Group, Language Learning Disabilities Group, and Language and Literacy Risk Group. Three additional groups from special populations also were included: autism spectrum disorder, deaf or hard of hearing, and mild intellectual developmental disability. The SLS was used as part of the TILLS standardization research, with sample and separate exploratory factor analyses performed for teachers, parents, and students. A pattern of two factors was evident, with Items 1-8 reflecting the primary language/literacy construct, and Items 9-12 reflecting the second factor of cognitive/social skills.

TECHNICAL. As reported by the test authors, quantitative data were collected from 2010 to 2015 in conjunction with standardization research on the TILLS. More than 1,900 students (ages 6-18 years) were tested, and information was gathered from teachers and parents as well. Validation studies examined whether the screener could accurately identify students at risk for the disorder in question. Test developers sought a cut score that would maximize sensitivity (based on the criterion that 80% or more of students identified by other measures to have LLD should fail the screening test) and specificity (based on the criterion that 80% or more of the students identified as not having language/literacy disorders should pass the screening test). Passing the screening would indicate low risk. Scores of 5 or above generally were found to be associated with typical development, and scores of 4 or below were associated with other indicators of language/literacy disorder or risk. Thus, the cutoff of two or more scores of less than 5 on the first eight questions of the scale was established for failing the screening. When using teacher ratings to detect LLD, sensitivity of 92% and specificity of 90% were reported by the test authors; values for parent ratings were 85% and 83%, respectively.

SLS scores also were correlated with corresponding composite and total scores from the TILLS to examine concurrent evidence of validity. Correlation coefficients between SLS scores for Items 1-8 and TILLS total scores were statistically significant ($p < .001$) for teachers, parents, and students. Coefficients for teachers and parents were .75 and .61, respectively. Although the correlation between student self-ratings and the TILLS total score was statistically significant, the test authors reported that the resulting coefficient of .33 indicated they should be interpreted with caution.

Reliability of SLS scores was examined using several methods. Although internal consistency traditionally is evaluated and reported as coefficient alpha, the test authors noted that assessments with more items tend to have higher values for coefficient alpha. An alternative statistic, coefficient omega, was used because it is less affected by length. For the 12-item scale, coefficient omega was .96 for teachers, .94 for parents, and .84 for students. The test authors compared these results with coefficient alpha values and found they were nearly identical, indicating strong internal reliability. Intra-rater (test-retest) reliability was measured by calculating interclass correlations over a period of less than 6 months. Teachers showed the highest correlation coefficient (.92), parents second (.83), and students third (.61), although it was noted that students were more consistent in rating cognitive and social skills than language and literacy skills. A third measure of reliability, interrater reliability, is more difficult to measure when comparing assessments of multiple types of informants (teachers, parents, and students). Binary correlations were calculated (intraclass correlations) between pairs of raters and found to be moderately strong (.75) for teachers and parents and weaker, although still moderately strong (.61), for teachers and students.

COMMENTARY. The SLS Screener for Language & Literacy Disorders is a quick, easily administered screener for language/literacy disorders in school-age children. Items describe the TILLS model of sound/word and sentence/discourse levels across oral and written modalities. The user's manual is written in a clear manner, and instructions are concise. Administration time is 1-3 minutes. With the 2-5-8 cutoff (two or more scores below 5 on the first eight items), the scale provides a simple way of determining the need for further testing. The scale's authors also note that if Items 3 and 4 are the lowest ones scored (below 5), further evaluation should include assessment for dyslexia. By incorporating a checklist of the student's abilities as well as a motivational question, the test authors allowed for increased use of the results for further evaluation, planning, and parent involvement.

SUMMARY. The SLS Screener for Language & Literacy Disorders (SLS) is an individually administered screener that is easily completed by teachers, parents, and students. The screener indicates the need for further assessment using the Test of Integrated Language and Literacy Skills (TILLS), which follows the model of sound/word and sentence/discourse levels across oral and written modalities.

REVIEWER'S REFERENCE

Nelson, N. W., Plante, E., Helm-Estabrooks, N., & Hotz, G. (2016). Test of Integrated Language and Literacy Skills. Baltimore, MD: Paul H. Brookes.

[160]

Suicide Assessment Manual for Inmates.

Purpose: Designed as "a clinical checklist of risk factors ... to guide evaluators through important information and

variables that should be assessed to determine an inmate's risk for institutional suicide" within the next 24 hours.
Population: Individuals admitted to pretrial remand facility.
Publication Date: 2006.
Acronym: SAMI.
Scores: No formal scores; assessment of 20 risk factors leads to ratings for Imminent Risk of Suicide (High, Medium, Low), Monitoring Recommended (Yes, No, Frequency), and Refer to Mental Health (Yes, No).
Administration: Individual.
Price Data, 2020: CAD70 per manual (84 pages), which includes rating form.
Time: Administration time not reported.
Comments: Item scores are not added, and no cutoffs are used to determine high, medium, or low risk.
Author: Patricia A. Zapf.
Publisher: Mental Health, Law, and Policy Institute, Simon Fraser University [Canada].

Review of the Suicide Assessment Manual for Inmates by ROCHELLE CADE, Associate Professor, University of Mary Hardin-Baylor, Belton, TX:

DESCRIPTION. The Suicide Assessment Manual for Inmates (SAMI) is a rating scale used to assess an inmate's risk for suicide in a pretrial facility or remand center within the next 24 hours. The 84-page spiral-bound manual includes five sections of content (Overview, Literature Review, Preliminary Research, SAMI, and SAMI Rating Form) that are conveniently separated by tabs. The SAMI section of the manual includes 20 risk factors, a brief rationale for each factor, from two to eight questions an assessor may ask for each risk factor, scoring criteria, and notes for the evaluator to consider. The 20 items on the SAMI are rated on a 3-point scale, with a score of 0 associated with *low* risk, 1 associated with a *moderate* risk, and 2 associated with an *increased* risk for suicide. Assessors complete a two-page rating form while discussing the interview questions with the inmate. Scoring criteria are included for each risk factor. Although the author states in the overview section of the manual the scores on each of the 20 individual items are "*not* to be added up" (manual, p. 2), assessors will note that the rating form includes a space labeled "grand total" following the rating of individual items. This format suggests that the scores are to be totaled. Below the grand total space on the rating form, assessors circle whether imminent risk of suicide is high, medium, or low. Assessors are not given scoring instructions or guidance on making this determination, as the SAMI author states in the overview that there are "*no* cutoffs that are used to determine high, medium, or low risk" (manual, p. 2). Assessors are then asked to determine whether monitoring is recommended (yes/no), what the frequency of monitoring should be (24 hours or 15 minutes), and whether a referral for mental health services is warranted (yes/no). The rating form concludes with the assessor's comments or other recommendations, date and time the SAMI was completed with the inmate, and the assessor's signature.

There are no specific qualifications for administering or scoring the SAMI as the manual states that the assessment is "suited to assist any mental health professional" (p. 2). The manual states that such assessment does involve professional skill and judgment, as the assessor makes the final determination of the inmate's level of suicide risk, actions to be taken, and referral for mental health services.

DEVELOPMENT. The literature review tab in the manual contains the identification and summarization of 22 variables related to risk for suicide in general as well as in jails and prison settings. Only 20 of these variables (marital status, history of drug or alcohol abuse, psychiatric history, history of suicide attempts, history of institutional suicide attempts, family history of suicide, arrest history, history of impulsive behavior, high profile crime or position of respect, current intoxication, concern about other major life problems, feelings of hopelessness or excessive guilt, psychotic symptoms/thought disorder, depressive symptomatology, stress and coping, social support, recent significant loss, suicidal ideation, suicidal intent, and suicide plan) were included as items on the SAMI. Two of the variables identified, age and sex, were not included by the instrument's author due to their lack of predictive validity. There is no other information about the review of literature such as how the literature review was conducted, which search terms or databases were used, and how articles were selected for inclusion and exclusion in the review. Additionally, there was no explanation as to why the literature was not limited to suicide risk factors or variables for prisoners or inmates or the specific time frame of 24 hours after admission to a pretrial or other correctional setting. There is also no explanation as to how the risk factors were developed into the suggested relevant questions the evaluator asks the inmate.

TECHNICAL. The preliminary research tab in the SAMI manual contains descriptive information for 138 male inmates who completed the SAMI as part of an intake evaluation with a nurse and psychology student to help determine placement in the facility. The maximum score on the SAMI is 40; the scores for the sample ranged from 1 to 20 (M = 6.82, SD = 3.9). A majority of the sample (87%) had no history of suicide attempts. A higher percentage (96%) of inmates reported no history of institutional suicide attempts. Of note, no data were reported on the number of inmates who had been incarcerated previously, either in jail or prison. Additionally, 91% of the inmates reported no family history of suicide. In addition to descriptive information, point-biserial correlations of the SAMI total scores and category of risk for suicide (low, medium, high), referral to mental health services (yes/no), and need for monitoring (yes/no) were reported. Although the correlation between SAMI total score and referral for mental health services was strong and positive (r = .75), the correlation between SAMI total score and category of risk for suicide was positive, yet weak (r = .25). This section of the assessment manual also provides results from an exploratory factor analysis that resulted in a six-factor solution (Affective Disturbance, Suicide History, Current Cognitive State, Current Situational Variables, Impulsivity, and Support and Coping). Following the factor analysis, correlation coefficients are presented between SAMI factor scores and suicide risk (low, medium, high), referral to mental health services (yes/no), and need for monitoring (yes/no). Correlations between the six-factor solution and suicide risk ranged from a low of .01 (Factor 5 Impulsivity) to the highest for Factor 3 (Current Cognitive State) of .58. There are two significant issues in the preliminary research. First, the overview section of the SAMI manual clearly states SAMI scores are not to be added, so it is unclear as to why the author used total scores in the correlation with risk for suicide. Second, the introductory paragraph of the preliminary research section indicates the risk for suicide is a "perceived" risk, not an actual risk of suicide as no data are presented related to inmates' suicidal ideation, attempts, or completion after their first 24 hours in the facility (manual, p. 19). Thus, the SAMI's ability to predict inmate actual risk of suicide is unknown.

COMMENTARY. The SAMI is a rating scale that provides a structure for professionals to evaluate an inmate's risk for suicide within 24 hours of admission to a pretrial facility. Preliminary research included descriptive data for 138 male inmates, the majority of whom had no history of suicide attempts or family history of suicide. No data for female inmates were included in the SAMI manual. Assessors utilizing the SAMI will find relatively simple instructions for scoring the 20 items. However, assessors will find no guidance on how scores on individual items (or the grand total score) should inform their decision making related to inmate suicide risk level, frequency of monitoring, or referral for mental health services. In addition to this limitation, the SAMI manual provides limited evidence of the validity of the rating scale, the most notable being the lack of concurrent validity with other established measures of suicide risk or predictive validity of actual suicide attempts or completions of inmates within 24 hours of admission to a pretrial facility.

SUMMARY. The SAMI is a 20-item rating scale used to assess an inmate's risk for suicide. Assessors will likely appreciate the user-friendly manual and relatively straightforward administration and individual item scoring on the rating form. However, assessors are left with little guidance on how the scores relate to level of suicide risk, perceived or actual, and this limits the SAMI's clinical utility. A lack of reliability information and more substantial psychometric support for the validity of the SAMI limit its research utility.

Review of the Suicide Assessment Manual for Inmates by GEOFFREY L. THORPE, Professor Emeritus of Psychology, University of Maine, Orono, ME:

DESCRIPTION. The Suicide Assessment Manual for Inmates (SAMI) describes the development of a 20-item rating form to guide clinical assessments of the risk of suicide in criminal defendants who have been remanded to residential facilities pretrial. The items form a clinical checklist of risk factors, the essential variables to be assessed in predicting the likelihood of an incarcerated defendant's committing suicide within 24 hours. Scores on the 20 items are not summated, and there is no overall classification of risk. Each item stands alone and is scored on a 3-point scale in which 0 is associated with a *low risk* for suicide, 1 with *moderate risk,* and 2 with *increased risk.* The test manual supplies several suggested relevant questions for each item, each phrased as a question for the respondent (for example, "Have you ever attempted suicide?"). However, the SAMI does not simply provide the format for a semi-structured interview. Evaluators are cautioned to be aware of the undependability of self-reported information and are urged to seek collateral evidence from clinical records and other sources. Noting the importance of documentation of evaluations of suicide risk, the test author suggests that rating protocols are helpful in the preparation of reports and progress notes and in confirming that a suitably wide-ranging assessment was conducted. She states: "The SAMI was not developed to act as a predictor of suicide risk. The final assessment of suicide risk is left to the professional conducting the evaluation" (manual, p. 3).

The material received from the SAMI publisher consists of an 84-page spiral-bound booklet that includes the sections Overview, Literature Review, Preliminary Research, the SAMI (a description of and rationale for each of the 20 risk factors with instructions and notes on scoring), References, and the SAMI Rating Form.

DEVELOPMENT. The author of the SAMI argues that structured clinical guidelines for suicide risk assessment of remanded inmates are needed because suicide is the leading cause of death in jails and is more common in the incarcerated than in the general population. The SAMI was developed from the results of a literature review on suicide in both populations that identified 22 essential correlates, 20 of which appear in the rating form. Age and sex are not included because neither variable has shown consistent predictive validity for suicide among the incarcerated, informally illustrated by the observation that most detainees who kill themselves are young and male, as indeed are most detainees.

Each of the 20 risk factors listed in the SAMI Rating Form is the subject of a brief literature review. The shortest of these is for Item 9, high profile crime or (defendant's) position of respect, consisting of two sentences and including one reference; the longest is for Item 20, suicide plan, with three paragraphs and seven citations. No reference is more recent than 2006, the SAMI's publication date. All 20 item descriptors can be seen in the results of an exploratory factor analysis presented in the Preliminary Research section of the manual.

The SAMI was administered during an intake evaluation to 138 incarcerated male defendants (age range 20 to 70) in British Columbia in 2001 and 2002. A principal component analysis with varimax rotation produced six factors. Marital status emerged as a strong factor in itself if seven factors were extracted, but it did not load on any other factor. Factor 1, Affective Disturbance, had loadings ranging from .574 to .877 and consisted of five items: concern about other major life problems, depressive symptoms, recent significant loss, feelings of hopelessness or excessive guilt, and stress and (lack of) coping (skills). Factor 2, Suicide History, had loadings ranging from .553 to .789 and consisted of five items: suicide plan, family history of suicide, history of institutional suicide attempts, history of suicide attempts, and suicidal intent. Factor 3, Current Cognitive State, had loadings of .754 and .838 and consisted of two items: psychotic symptoms or thought disorder and suicidal ideation. Factor 4, Current Situational Variables, had loadings of .887 and .863 and consisted of two items: current intoxication and high-profile crime or position of respect. Factor 5, Impulsivity, had loadings ranging from .622 to .790 and consisted of three items: arrest history, substance abuse history, and history of impulsive behavior. Factor 6, Support and Coping, had loadings of .687 and .663 and consisted of two items: (lack of) social support and psychiatric history.

TECHNICAL. The technical information provided in the SAMI booklet does not fall into the categories associated with traditional tests. The material in the Preliminary Research section is presented under the headings Scoring Frequencies, Relations Between SAMI Total Scores and Relevant Variables, Factor Analysis, Correlations Between SAMI Factor Scores and Relevant Variables, and Regression Analyses, with a final paragraph on Limitations. (SAMI total scores are used in the test manual's research section but are not intended for use by clinical evaluators.)

The Scoring Frequencies subsection tabulates, for each item, the percentage of scores falling into each item category (0, 1, and 2). For example, the frequencies for Item 7: arrest history are 0, *low risk* ("inmate has been arrested between 1-3 times"), 23%; 1, *moderate risk* ("inmate has been arrested 4 or more times"), 37%; and 2, *increased risk* ("inmate is a first-time offender"), 40%. The descriptors for the categories in Item 7 reflect the bimodal distribution of suicide peaks identified in the research literature and the observation that members of the moderate and increased risk groups tend to become suicidal at different times. First-time arrestees are more likely than those with four or more arrests to become suicidal shortly after their admission to the facility. For a few items the frequencies for Category 2, *increased risk,* are found to be just 1%; these are high-profile crime or position of respect, current intoxication, and psychotic symptoms or thought disorder. For two of the items assumed to be highly relevant to suicide assessment, the frequencies were: Item 19, suicidal intent: 0, 99%; 1, 1%; and 2, 0%; and Item 20, suicide plan: 0, 97%; 1, 3%; and 2, 0%.

Correlation coefficients are listed for the relationships between SAMI total scores and category of risk for suicide (low, medium, or high), referral to mental health services, and assessed need for monitoring. Values ranged from .25 (total score and risk category) to .75 (total score and referral to mental health services). Scores on the first three factors derived from the principal component analysis showed significant correlations with those three variables. No information is given regarding how those other variables were defined or the degree to which, if at all, decisions about risk, referrals, and monitoring were informed by SAMI total scores or factor scores.

The results of regression analyses entering (1) age, marital status, and Factors 1 through 6, and (2) age and each of the 20 SAMI items were tabulated, and predictors were identified for mental health referral and risk. No commentary on those results was offered.

COMMENTARY. The test author's claims for the SAMI are modest. It is not presented as a traditional test supported by formal data on reliability, validity, and standardization. The SAMI is a manual that includes a rating form with items derived from the results of literature reviews on potential risk factors. Responses to the 20 items are not aggregated to produce a total score, and there are no cutoff scores signifying levels of risk with associated specification of indices of selectivity and specificity. Each item stands alone and produces a three-component risk classification of *low, moderate,* or *increased*. The SAMI is described by its author as a rating scale, a clinical checklist, a guide, a framework, and an *aide-mémoire* that provides a structure for evaluations. She denotes the research section of the test manual as preliminary and as providing descriptive information and acknowledges that "a major limitation" of the data is the absence of demonstrated predictive validity: Item scores have not been compared with outcomes such as absence of suicidal behavior, suicide attempts, or death by suicide. A further potential limitation, derived from inspection of the data on scoring frequencies, is that the preliminary research sample did not include inmates reporting suicidal intent or plans.

Because of the limited scope of the SAMI, it seems neither fair nor appropriate to hold it to the standards of traditional test development. It is not presented as a test. The author makes it clear throughout the manual that the rating form is a compilation of pertinent areas of enquiry relevant to suicide risk assessment. Each item was drawn from a review of the relevant literature that guided item selection and informed the categorization of response options. The arrest history item provides an example of the author's care in establishing the scoring categories in view of epidemiological information reported in the literature: The three response options are not scaled intuitively but take into account the bimodal peaks of suicide frequency in defendants remanded for the first time versus those with more than three arrests, and the different timeframes in which the critical behavior occurs in those groups of defendants.

That said, the rating form items could of course be studied more definitively with a much larger multisite sample that includes defendants with suicidal ideation and plans. Factors derived from analyses with the new sample could form scales for potential development as tests with data collected on interrater reliability, test-retest reliability, internal consistency, predictive validity, normative data, and information on selectivity and specificity with certain cutoff scores. If such scales could be shown to possess properties of monotonicity and unidimensionality, then a polytomous item response theory-based analysis could be conducted to establish the relationship of each item to the construct measured by the scale itself and to examine the contribution made by each of the three response options to the information provided by the item. For example, an item for which the intermediate scoring category (1) does not register empirically could be recast for dichotomous scoring. Further development of the SAMI along such lines could add significantly to its utility for healthcare professionals evaluating the risk of suicide in newly remanded defendants.

SUMMARY. The SAMI summarizes information on the development of a rating scale to assist clinical evaluators in preparing short-term suicide risk assessments of remanded criminal defendants. The 20 rating form items were drawn from literature reviews, and scoring criteria and suggestions for questions for a semi-structured interview are provided. Data from preliminary research on a sample of 138 male inmates include response frequencies, the results of a principal component analysis, and correlations of SAMI items, factor scores, and total scores with suicide risk categories, referrals for mental health care, and monitoring. The SAMI is not presented as a test with traditional psychometric data on reliability, validity, and standardization with normative groups. The rating form and its supporting literature reviews and scoring guidelines serve as a convenient compendium of risk factors to evaluate in the clinical assessment of short-term suicide risk among remanded defendants. The SAMI as it stands could represent a preliminary step toward the development of a formal test or tests following research with larger samples and the provision of data from traditional psychometric explorations.

[161]

Supports Intensity Scale–Adult Version.

Purpose: Designed to "measure the relative intensity of support that each person with intellectual disability or related developmental disabilities needs to fully participate in community life."
Population: Individuals ages 16-64 with intellectual or closely related developmental disabilities.
Publication Dates: 2004-2015.
Acronym: SIS-A.
Scores, 9: Home Living, Community Living, Lifelong Learning, Employment, Health and Safety, Social, Support Needs Index, Exceptional Medical Needs, Exceptional Behavioral Needs.
Administration: Individual.
Price Data, 2020: $155 per user's manual (2015, 136 pages) and 25 interview forms; $50 per 25 interview forms; $190 per 100 interview forms; $20 per 25 annual review protocols; $120 per manual.
Time: (120-150) minutes.
Comments: Structured interview format.
Authors: James R. Thompson, Brian R. Bryant, Robert L. Schalock, Karrie A. Shogren, Marc J. Tassé, Michael L. Wehmeyer, Edward M. Campbell, Ellis M. (Pat) Craig, Carolyn Hughes, David A. Rotholz.
Publisher: American Association on Intellectual and Developmental Disabilities.
Cross References: For reviews by Sandra A. Loew and David J. Pittenger of an earlier edition, see 16:238.

Review of the Supports Intensity Scale–Adult Version by CARRIE R. JACKSON, Professor of School Psychology, Youngstown State University, Youngstown, OH:

DESCRIPTION. The Supports Intensity Scale–Adult Version (SIS–A) consists of three sections: Section 1, Exceptional Medical and Behavioral Support Needs, which assesses support needs across 19 medical conditions and 13 problem behaviors; Section 2, the Support Needs Index, which assesses life activities through 49 items focusing on Home Living, Community Living, Lifelong Learning, Employment, Health and Safety, and Social Activities; and Section 3, the Supplemental Protection and Advocacy Scale, which evaluates support needs with respect to self-determination and civil rights. The SIS-A is administered by a qualified interviewer via structured interview with two or more respondents who are familiar with the individual being assessed. Respondents should know the individual being rated for at least three months and should have recently observed the individual in each environment for extended periods of time. The individual being rated also may serve as a respondent to the interview.

Section 1, Exceptional Medical and Behavioral Support Needs, allows for the identification of specific medical and behavioral concerns. In the Exceptional Medical Support Needs portion, interview respondents are asked to rate each item for the individual being assessed with respect to the following question: "What is the significance of the following medical conditions for this person in regard to extra support required?" (manual, p. 9). Each of the 19 Exceptional Medical Support Needs items is rated on a scale of 0 (*no support needed*) to 2 (*extensive support needed*). Items that do not pertain to the individual being rated are given a 0 as well. In the Exceptional Behavioral Support Needs portion, respondents are asked to rate each of the 12 items for the individual being assessed with respect to the following question: "What is the significance of the following challenging behaviors for this person with regard to extra support required?" (manual, p. 10). Exceptional Behavioral Support Needs items are rated 0 if the individual being rated does not engage in the behavior, 1 if the individual engages in the behavior and needs some extra support, and 2 if the individual displays the behavior and requires significant extra support. Individuals who receive a rating of 2 on one or more medical or behavioral items and those whose total score is more than 5 for either medical or behavioral needs are considered to have more intense support needs than other individuals.

Section 2, the Support Needs Index, yields standard scores. Section 2 comprises 49 items focusing on life activities divided into six support domains/subscales (Home Living Activities, Community Living Activities, Lifelong Learning

Activities, Employment Activities, Health and Safety Activities, and Social Activities). Each item is rated on a 5-point scale with respect to type of support ("What extraordinary support would enable him or her to be successful in the activity?"), frequency that support is needed ("How often would extraordinary support be needed to enable him or her to be successful in the activity?"), and daily support time required ("How much total daily support time would be needed to enable the individual to be successful in the activity?"). The type of support needed is rated 0 if no support is needed, 1 if the individual requires monitoring, 2 if verbal/gestural prompting is needed, 3 if the individual requires partial physical assistance, and 4 if full physical assistance is needed. Frequency of support is rated 0 if the individual requires extraordinary support less than once per month or not at all, 1 if support is required more than once a month but not weekly, 2 if support is required at least weekly but not daily, 3 if support is needed more than once per day but not hourly, and 4 if support is required hourly to allow for participation in the activity. The test authors note that all rating options do not apply to all of the items. Daily support time required is rated 0 if no time is required, 1 if less than 30 minutes of support are provided per day, 2 if 30 minutes to 2 hours of support are provided daily, 3 if supports are needed for at least 2 hours but for no more than 4 hours daily, and 4 if supports are needed for 4 or more hours daily. The following maximum scores are possible for the Support Needs Index subscales: Home Living Activities–92 points, Community Living Activities–91 points, Lifelong Learning Activities–104 points, Employment Activities–87 points, Health and Safety Activities–94 points, and Social Activities–93 points. Raw scores are converted to normalized standard scores (*M* = 10, *SD* = 3) and subscale percentile ranks. The activity subscale standard score may be converted to the Support Needs Index scale score (composite standard score; *M* = 100, *SD* = 15) with an accompanying Support Needs Index scale percentile rank. The Support Needs Profile (a visual graph that represents an individual's support needs on the six life activity subscales) can be created by plotting an individual's scores on the interview form.

Items in Section 3, The Supplemental Protection and Advocacy Scale, also are scored according to the type and frequency of support as well as the daily support time required. Section 3 contains eight items pertaining to protection and advocacy activities. Raw scores for each item are ranked from highest to lowest; the four highest raw scores in this section are recorded on the SIS-A Profile. Although scores from this scale do not contribute to an individual's SIS-A standard score, they provide information with respect to self-determination and civil rights.

The interview may be conducted individually or in small groups for individuals ages 16 to 64 years and is untimed. The expected time needed to administer and score the interview is from 2 to 2.5 hours. Administration requires a writing utensil and interview form. The interview form is used to record responses to interview questions and to score each item. The test authors recommend that examiners possess at least a bachelor's degree and be working in the human service field with individuals with developmental disabilities. In some cases, examiners who have experience conducting individual assessments and possess knowledge of testing principles may be considered qualified to serve as an interviewer. The user's manual provides item descriptions, technical information, normative data, and scoring examples.

The developers of the SIS-A indicate that this instrument may serve as a tool to enhance decision making within the person-centered planning (PCP) process regarding the types and intensities of supports required for individuals with developmental disabilities "to promote meaningful engagement in a variety of life activities" (manual, p. 69). The SIS-A provides the PCP team a means of examining life experiences and outcomes, assessing needs for support, developing individual support plans (ISPs), implementing and monitoring ISPs, and evaluating ISPs. At the organizational/system level, the SIS-A may contribute to decision-making and quality management, such as resource allocation.

DEVELOPMENT. The SIS-A was developed to assist planning teams in examining the intensity of supports necessary to meet the needs of individuals with developmental disabilities who inherently exhibit medical conditions and challenging behaviors requiring unique supports. In updating the Supports Intensity Scale (SIS; Thompson et al., 2004), the authors of the SIS-A expanded descriptions of items to enhance clarity and consistency, and rearranged items between sections to enhance interviewer knowledge at the start of administration.

TECHNICAL. Although the original Supports Intensity Scale was widely adopted and positively reviewed, the SIS-A, which uses the same items, rating scales, scoring methodology, and normative information as its predecessor, incorporates additional research to provide further evidence of reliability and validity. The SIS-A uses norms from the SIS, which were based on 1,306 individuals from 33 states and two Canadian provinces. Data were collected in 2002. The normative sample was obtained by sending letters to colleagues working with individuals with intellectual and developmental disabilities and requesting they recruit potential interviewers. Additional interviewers were contacted through the American Association on Intellectual and Developmental Disabilities (AAIDD) member database. Participants were solicited from all 50 states, and a total of 68 professionals ultimately administered the SIS-A.

Internal consistency was estimated using coefficient alpha, which was found to be very high. With one exception, all coefficients were above .90 for subscales; means across ages were ≥ .94. Using Pearson product-moment correlations, subscale scores were determined to be unrelated to the age or gender of the rated individual. As a result, these two variables were not considered in later analysis. Test-retest and interrater reliability were also examined; variable interrater results were found, leading the test authors to conclude that the SIS-A is an acceptable tool for planning (though not for diagnostic) purposes. Interscorer reliability was estimated through the analysis of reliability coefficients for each subscale and the Support Needs Index. Reliability estimates were found to be extremely high (.997) for all subscales and the Support Needs Index.

Evidence of content validity was developed by thoroughly reviewing the current literature, applying Q-sort methodology to assign items into the most applicable support domains, and piloting an initial version of the scale. The literature review yielded 130 potential items taken from approximately 1,500 sources. The Q-sort methodology was applied by asking 74 professionals to categorize these 130 potential items into 12 support domains. As a result of the Q-sort, eight of the 12 support domains were retained, and two of those eight domains were renamed. Four field tests were then conducted to identify the best items and to refine the SIS-A. Evidence of content validity was provided in the form of item discrimination coefficients, which ranged from .53 to .82, providing validation for the subscale scores.

Evidence of criterion-related validity was established by having raters provide a rating of an individual's support needs based on a 5-point Likert scale prior to completing the SIS-A. SIS-A scores and Likert scale ratings were intercorrelated; results for all coefficients exceeded the minimal level (.35) that the test developers considered necessary to support criterion-related validity.

Evidence of construct validity was demonstrated by selecting constructs contributing to test performance, generating a hypothesis for each construct, and evaluating each hypothesis. Analysis of coefficients indicated that significant differences among age groups did not exist on the SIS-A, offering construct evidence in the form of age differentials. Evidence of construct validity was also demonstrated via a correlation matrix of the subscale and composite normative scores. In comparing the SIS-A subscale scores to available intelligence test scores, construct evidence was demonstrated by a significant inverse relationship between SIS-A scores and scores on tests of cognitive ability. The SIS-A was compared to other measures of adaptive behavior (Inventory for Client and Agency Planning and Vineland Adaptive Behavior Scale), which also yielded evidence for construct validity. In addition, this analysis demonstrated that the SIS-A measures a unique construct from other measures of adaptive behavior and intelligence. Evidence of construct validity was also evaluated in group differentiation studies by examining mean standard scores; that is, individuals with greater support needs should be scored significantly higher on the SIS-A than individuals with fewer support needs. Finally, item validity was examined by correlating scores on individual items with total scores on the SIS-A. Median item-total correlations ranged from .53 to .82.

Updated research since the SIS was published indicates that internal consistency reliability remained as high as was initially found, even with a larger sample obtained through online data collection. Construct validity evidence also remained at acceptable levels when examined using data from the larger sample. Interrater reliability was found to be enhanced by providing professionals with formal training on the instrument.

COMMENTARY. Person-centered planning is of great importance for individuals with intellectual and other developmental disabilities, and the SIS-A may serve as a useful tool in this process. The SIS-A has a large normative base and is quickly and easily scored, though the time required to complete the interview (2 to 2.5 hours) is intensive, especially considering that a minimum of two interviews should be completed per individual being rated. The normative sample approximates the geographical distribution of the U.S. population, as data were collected from 33 states, though samples of convenience were used to recruit participants, and the norms have not been updated since the original SIS normative data were collected in 2002. The test developers suggest the SIS-A yields information that is unique (i.e., different from other measures of adaptive behavior), though little detail is given as to what differences exist. The user's manual could be enhanced by providing interviewers with concrete examples of how to incorporate the information yielded by the SIS-A into ISPs, as the test authors indicate that it is the responsibility of the interviewer to integrate and interpret the information that is generated by this tool. Subsequent to the original SIS publication, formal training was found to enhance the reliability of scores from the measure, but such training is not required for use. Including concrete examples of interpretation and analysis of SIS-A results in the test materials could improve interrater reliability and test-retest reliability outcomes.

SUMMARY. The SIS-A authors have succeeded in improving upon the original SIS, which studies have found to provide valid information regarding the needs of individuals with developmental disabilities (Wehmeyer, Chapman, Little, Thompson, Schalock, & Tassé, 2009; Weiss, Lunsky, Tassé, & Durbin, 2009). The utility of the SIS in determining appropriate supports for individuals with severe mental illness also has been demonstrated in psychiatric populations (Jenaro, Cruz, del Carmen Perez, Flores, & Vega, 2011). Additionally, a study by Chou, Lee, Chang, and Yu (2013) showed that the SIS may be used effectively as an aid in planning for resource allocation for individuals with intellectual disabilities in Taiwan, suggesting it may prove a valuable tool globally.

REVIEWER'S REFERENCES

Chou, Y.-C., Lee, Y.-C., Chang, S., & Yu, A. P. (2013). Evaluating the Supports Intensity Scale as a potential assessment instrument for resource allocation for persons with intellectual disability. *Research in Developmental Disabilities, 34*(6), 2056-2063.

Jenaro, C., Cruz, M., del Carmen Perez, M., Flores, N. E., & Vega, V. (2011). Utilization of the Supports Intensity Scale with psychiatric populations: Psychometric properties and utility for service delivery planning. *Archives of Psychiatric Nursing, 25*(5), e9-e17.

Thompson, J. R., Bryant, B. L., Campbell, E. M., Craig, E. M., Hughes, C. M., Rotholz, D. A., ... Wehmeyer, M. L. (2004). Supports Intensity Scale. Washington, DC: AAMR American Association on Mental Retardation.

Wehmeyer, M., Chapman, T. E., Little, T. D., Thompson, J. R., Schalock, R., & Tassé, M. J. (2009). Efficacy of the Supports Intensity Scale (SIS) to predict extraordinary support needs. *American Journal on Intellectual and Developmental Disabilities, 114*(1), 3-14.

Weiss, J. A., Lunsky, Y., Tassé, M. J., & Durbin, J. (2009). Support for the construct validity of the Supports Intensity Scale based on clinician rankings of need. *Research in Developmental Disabilities, 30*(5), 933-941.

Review of the Supports Intensity Scale—Adult Version by KATHLEEN TORSNEY, Professor of Psychology, William Paterson University, Wayne, NJ:

DESCRIPTION. The Supports Intensity Scale—Adult Version (SIS-A) is an assessment for evaluating the individual level of support needs for persons with intellectual disabilities or related developmental disabilities. The measure is a structured interview that is conducted with two or more individuals who are well acquainted with the target individual, who is between the ages of 16 and 64. The instrument could be used with older or younger individuals, if no other measure is available, to assess support needs. A Supports Intensity Scale—Children's Version (SIS-C; see 162, this volume) is also available for children ages 5 through 16. The test authors indicate that the measure is to be used with person-centered treatment planning so that people with disabilities can have the most appropriate individualized support plans. The SIS-A assesses the degree of support that the person with intellectual disabilities and related developmental disabilities requires to partake in community activities. The measure can be administered individually or with small groups of people who are familiar with the target individual. Respondents should know the individual for at least 3 months. Some individuals may be their own respondents and therefore advocate for themselves. The structured interview typically lasts 2-2.5 hours. The administrator should possess at least a baccalaureate degree and be employed in a field serving persons with intellectual and developmental disabilities (IDD).

There are three sections of the SIS–A that assess aspects of support needs. Section 1, Exceptional Medical and Behavioral Support Needs, includes 19 medical conditions and 13 problem behaviors. Section 2 is the Support Needs Index, which evaluates life activities through 49 items that are grouped into six domains with norm-referenced scores: Home Living Activities, Community Living Activities, Lifelong Learning Activities, Employment Activities, Health and Safety Activities, and Social Activities. Section 3 is the Supplemental Protection and Advocacy Scale, which appraises the amount of support needed for eight activities related to protecting civil rights and promoting self-determination.

Raw scores on the Support Needs Index subscales are converted to standard scores (M = 10, SD = 3) and percentile ranks. Subscale standard scores are summed and converted to the Support Needs Index standard score (*M* = 100, *SD* = 15) and a percentile rank.

DEVELOPMENT. The SIS-A was developed to provide a measure of the supports needed by individuals with intellectual and developmental disabilities. A better understanding of the supports an individual needs in order to participate in community activities can inform funding and treatment planning. The measure is built on the social-ecological model of intellectual disabilities, which holds that the impact of an intellectual disability is primarily a mismatch between the person's competencies and the demands of the settings and activities accompanying participation in society. This model acknowledges that persons with intellectual disabilities have deficits in intelligence and in adaptive behavior but emphasizes the importance of support needs in the daily life of the individual.

The SIS-A expands upon the success of the SIS (Thompson et al., 2004). The test authors received feedback that the SIS could be re-designed so that there would be a version for adults and one for children. The SIS-A contains the same items and scales as the SIS, and the normative sample has not been updated. The SIS-A manual includes information from research conducted since the publication of the SIS, including data that was collected using the SIS Online, which allows for quick and efficient data collection.

TECHNICAL.

Standardization. Normative data for the SIS, which extend to the SIS-A, were based on 1,306 individuals in 33 states and two Canadian provinces. The test authors sent letters to individuals working with persons with IDD in all 50 states, and each interviewer was asked to assess between 5 and 20 persons. A total of 68 professionals conducted interviews for the norm sample. Of the interviewers, European Americans made up 88% of the group, African Americans 9%, and other groups the remaining 3%. Regarding the standardization sample, 56% of participants were female (44% were male), 51% were ages 30-49, 52% had estimated intelligence levels between 36 and 69, 47% had mild or moderate adaptive behavior levels, and 40% had severe or profound adaptive behavior levels. As far as other sample demographics, 80% were European Americans, 14% were African Americans, 3% were Hispanic Americans, 1% were Native Americans, and < 1% were Asian Americans. In addition to the intellectual disability, 95% of the sample were diagnosed with mental retardation, and 37% had a psychiatric disability, with 29% of the sample living in a small group home (< 7 residents) and 53% being employed in supported or sheltered employment. Regarding languages, 97% of the sample spoke English, 1% spoke Spanish, and 2% spoke another language. Finally, 81% of the sample resided in an urban environment and 19% lived in a rural area.

Reliability. Coefficients of internal consistency ranged from .86 to .99 across all age groups for the six subscales and the composite of the Support Needs Index. Test-retest reliability was examined with 106 persons with IDD in Illinois ranging in age from 21 to 83 years. Two interviews with the same rater were conducted approximately three weeks apart and yielded corrected correlation coefficients ranging from .74 for Community Living Activities to .94 for Social Activities. Interrater reliability estimates ranged from a corrected coefficient of .55 for Lifelong Learning Activities and Employment Activities to .90 for Home Living activities.

Thompson, Tassé, and McLaughlin (2008) examined reliability in three conditions: inter-respondent, inter-interviewer, and mixed interrater (different respondents with different interviewers). Interviewers in the study had received at least a half-day of formal training on administering and scoring the SIS-A. Reliability coefficients exceeded .45 for all subscales across conditions, and median coefficients hovered close to .80 for each of the three conditions. Three subscales demonstrated coefficients between .47 and .54 in the inter-interviewer or mixed interrater condition or both: Lifelong Learning Activities, Employment Activities, and Social Activities. Slightly lower correlation coefficients were observed in the mixed interrater condition, although these values improved compared to those obtained with the original SIS, suggesting that stronger reliability evidence occurs when interviewers are suitably trained.

Validity. Validity evidence related to the SIS-A's content was developed through a comprehensive literature review, Q-sort, field tests, and item analyses. The literature and the Q-sort offer qualitative support for the content validity of the measure. In an item analysis, item discrimination ranged from .53 for Health and Safety Activities of 16- to 19-year-olds to .82 for Employment Activities of 60- to 69-year-olds and 16- to 19-year-olds. Regarding criterion-related evidence, the test authors asked readers to rate support needs on a 5-point Likert scale before completing the SIS-A, and all coefficients were significant and were above .35, suggesting acceptable criterion-related validity. The test authors noted that construct evidence of validity was obtained through evaluations of age differentiation, intercorrelation of SIS-A scores, relationship of the SIS-A to tests of intelligence, and relationship of the SIS-A to measures of adaptive behavior. A study examining whether SIS-A rankings estimated support needs made by independent clinicians for 50 persons with IDD in Ontario (Weiss, Lunsky, Tassé, & Durbin, 2009) found significant differences between the low need, medium need, and high need groups.

COMMENTARY. The SIS-A is built on the success of the Supports Intensity Scale (2004) which was designed to determine not only the supports that an individual might need but also the intensity of those supports. The test authors note that the SIS-A can be used to assist individuals in treatment planning as well as to foster resource allocation and strategic planning. However, the norm group is not consistent with the percentages of Hispanic and Asian individuals in the United States. To illustrate, the U.S. Census data show that approximately 18% of the population is Hispanic; however, only 3% of the normative sample was Hispanic. In addition, according to the U.S. Census, about 6% of Americans are of Asian descent, and less than 1% of the normative sample was Asian American. Therefore, one should exercise caution when interpreting results for individuals of Hispanic or Asian background and recognize that estimates of resource allocation and planning may be similarly affected by the lack of representativeness in the norm population. The test manual urges interviewers to be "sensitive to cultural characteristics" (p. 6), but it does not specify how cultural factors such as economic background, ethnicity, or gender might affect responses on the measure. A more explicit description of how expression of support needs could be affected by cultural characteristics should be included in the test manual.

SUMMARY. The SIS-A is a very well designed and useful tool for assessing support needs for persons with intellectual and other developmental disabilities. It was developed from the successful SIS assessment which was geared for adults and children. Having a specific assessment for adults allows for questions that more specifically explore the nature of support needs for adults with IDD. The norms are limited for persons with Hispanic or Asian backgrounds, and the manual could more explicitly outline how the interviewer would assess cultural and ethnic factors. Overall, the SIS-A is a very good measure for understanding the support needs that a person with IDD requires in order to effectively and meaningfully participate in community activities.

REVIEWER'S REFERENCES

Thompson, J. R., Bryant, B. L., Campbell, E. M., Craig, E. M., Hughes, C., Rotholz, D. A., ... Wehmeyer, M. L. (2004). Supports Intensity Scale. Washington, DC: AAMR American Association on Mental Retardation.

Thompson, J. R., Tassé, M. J., & McLaughlin, C. A. (2008). Interrater reliability of the Supports Intensity Scale. *American Journal on Mental Retardation 113*(3). 231-237.

Weiss, J. A., Lunsky, Y., Tassé, M. J., & Durbin, J. (2009). Support for the construct validity of the Supports Intensity Scale based on clinician rankings of need. *Research in Developmental Disabilities, 30*(5), 933-941. doi:10.1016/j.ridd.2009.01.007

[162]

Supports Intensity Scale–Children's Version.

Purpose: Designed as a standardized measure to assess the intensity of support needs of children with intellectual or developmental disabilities.

Population: Individuals ages 5-16 with intellectual or closely related developmental disabilities.

Publication Date: 2016.

Acronym: SIS-C.

Scores, 10: Exceptional Medical Needs, Exceptional Behavioral Needs, Home Life, Community & Neighborhood, School Participation, School Learning, Health & Safety, Social, Advocacy, Support Needs Index.

Administration: Individual.

Price Data: Available from publisher.

Time: Administration time not reported.

Comments: Structured interview format; information must be collected from at least 2 respondents.

Authors: James R. Thompson, Michael L. Wehmeyer, Carolyn Hughes, Karrie A. Shogren, Hyojeong Seo, Todd D. Little, Robert L. Schalock, Rodney E. Realon, Susan R. Copeland, James R. Patton, Edward A. Polloway, Debbie Shelden, Shea Tanis, and Marc J. Tassé.

Publisher: American Association on Intellectual and Developmental Disabilities.

Review of the Supports Intensity Scale—Children's Version by CATHERINE A. FIORELLO, Professor of School Psychology, Temple University, and SOFIA PHAM, Postdoctoral Fellow of Behavioral Psychology, Westchester Institute for Human Development, Temple University, Philadelphia, PA:

DESCRIPTION. The Supports Intensity Scale–Children's Version (SIS-C) is a norm-referenced, standardized assessment used to assess children's support needs based on information provided by at least two respondents through a structured interview. The test authors note that the scale can be administered by someone with a baccalaureate degree who works or has worked with children with intellectual disabilities. The SIS-C is intended to evaluate students ages 5 through 16 for the purpose of informing placement decisions and intervention planning. Interviewers can include psychologists, speech and language pathologists, and social workers, among others.

Interviewers should gather information from at least two respondents who have known the child for at least three months and who have observed the child recently and for long periods of time. They should include respondents who have observed the child in relevant settings and may include the child. The test authors recommend interviewing respondents together, as it is more efficient and may be more conducive to gathering critical information. The interviewer must use his or her clinical judgment to determine appropriate ratings for the child based on the respondents' input. The SIS-C consists of two sections: Exceptional Medical and Behavioral Needs and Support Needs Index Scale. For the medical and behavioral needs section, interviewers are instructed to rate how much support is required for 31 items (18 pertaining to medical needs and 13 pertaining to behavioral needs) on a 3-point Likert-type scale (*no support needed* = 0 to *extensive support needed* = 2). The Support Needs Index Scale is normed and consists of seven subscales: Home Life, Community and Neighborhood, School Participation, School Learning, Health and Safety, Social, and Advocacy. Interviewers are instructed to rate the type of support, frequency of support, and daily support time, as compared to typically developing children of the same age, on a 5-point Likert-type scale. The overall index score is calculated by averaging the mean ratings of the seven subscales. Subscale normative scores have a mean of 10 and standard deviation (*SD*) of 3, whereas the overall index score has a mean of 100 and *SD* of 15, with higher scores indicating more intensive needs.

DEVELOPMENT. A pool of candidate items was obtained from the Supports Intensity Scale–Adult Version (SIS-A). A task force examined the current literature to determine additional support areas needed for the SIS-C. There were initially 75 candidate items, and 61 items were retained after a Q-Sort procedure with 51 raters. A focus group of experts finalized the pilot version of the SIS-C. This version was piloted by 52 interviewers who provided feedback on items and their administration and scoring, which resulted in minor edits. The resulting field-test version was used to collect normative data.

TECHNICAL.

Standardization. The sample employed for development of the SIS-C consisted of 4,015 children ages 5 through 16. The sample represents children from 23 states who were receiving state developmental disability services and school services. Interviewers were primarily White (72.0%) and female (81.3%). A total of 12,050 respondents were interviewed by 694 interviewers. Respondents included primarily family members and teachers, with some direct service providers, paraprofessionals, case managers, friends, and others.

The norms for the SIS-C are based on a sample of 4,015 children diagnosed with intellectual disability and co-occurring related developmental disabilities. The sample was stratified by age (2-year cohorts) and intellectual ability (*mild, moderate,* and *severe/profound*). The children's IQs were reported by respondents instead of measured directly by the interviewer. Adaptive behaviors were used to estimate intellectual functioning for 129 cases when respondents could not provide the information. Multiple imputation was used for 82 cases with missing IQ estimates.

The racial background of participants in the normative sample is roughly proportionate to the U.S. population. However, descriptive statistics and comparisons of scores across race are not provided, nor did the test authors provide evidence to suggest that this measure is invariant across racial groups.

Reliability. Coefficients alpha and omega were used to estimate internal consistency. Values across age levels exceeded .90 for each subscale, which indicates that the scores have adequate internal consistency reliability across age groups. Coefficient omega values also were reported because each cluster of items did not have equal factor loadings on the total score. Resulting coefficient omega values were similar to the alpha values.

Test-retest reliability analyses were conducted based on a sample of 39 children and 27 interviewers with an average of 20 days (range = 7 to 88 days) between interviews. The Pearson correlation coefficients for the subscales ranged from .86 to .93 with a coefficient of .94 for the overall score. These findings provide support for the stability of SIS-C scores among children with intellectual disabilities. The SIS-C target age range is 5 through 16 years. However, the test-retest sample consisted of individuals ages 6 to 21, which may have introduced some error if the stability of the SIS-C varies based on the child's age.

Three conditions were used to analyze interrater reliability: inter-interviewer, inter-respondent, and mixed. Pearson correlation coefficients ranged from .69 to .95 for subscales in all three conditions and from .86 to .93 for the total index score, providing good to excellent support for interrater reliability.

Validity. In addition to conducting a systematic review of the SIS-A, an extant literature review, a Q-sort procedure, a pilot test, and a final field-test, the test authors used structural equation modeling to examine content validity evidence. The test authors sufficiently demonstrated item discrimination for each latent factor.

To provide construct evidence, the test authors showed that SIS-C scores were moderately related to age, IQ, and adaptive behavior scores. This result suggests that the SIS-C measures a construct that is closely related to, but distinct from, IQ and adaptive behaviors. Additionally, the test authors conducted correlational analyses between subscales to support the notion that different areas of support needs are interdependent. In examining the factor structure of the SIS-C, the test authors conducted measurement invariance testing across six age groups (5-6, 7-8, 9-10, 11-12, 13-14, and 15-16) to determine whether the structure remained stable across age. Fit indices were within acceptable ranges for these analyses, suggesting the SIS-C can be used to assess children with intellectual disability across age groups.

Because of the lack of a gold-standard measure of children's support needs within the population of individuals with intellectual disabilities, the test authors examined criterion-related validity by asking respondents to estimate children's need for support in each area on a 5-point Likert-type scale prior to completing the SIS-C. The respondents' ratings were significantly correlated with SIS-C scores across age cohorts. The test authors also compared ratings for 142 adolescents who completed both the SIS-A and SIS-C and found significant correlations between the scores of the two measures.

COMMENTARY. The test authors provide clear guidelines on how the structured interviews should be conducted as well as how to use results to guide intervention planning and placement decisions. The test authors sufficiently demonstrated the reliability and evidence of validity of the SIS-C. Despite the lack of existing measurement tools available to evaluate evidence of criterion-related validity and construct validity, the test authors employed a variety of sophisticated statistical methods to ensure that the tool accurately and reliably assessed the support needs of children with intellectual disabilities across age groups and ability levels. Overall, the SIS-C is a useful tool for evaluating the needs of children with intellectual disabilities.

The test authors state that anyone with a baccalaureate degree who works or has worked with children with intellectual disabilities is qualified to administer the SIS-C. Because ratings rely heavily on clinical judgment, it is crucial to ensure that interviewers are adept at conducting structured interviews and interpreting results. Although the test authors provided three hours of training to field testers for norming the instrument, they do not call for all interviewers to receive formal training on assessing children with intellectual disabilities prior to administering the SIS-C. Further, the test authors did not mention the need for interviewers to have knowledge of typically developing children even though the interviewers are expected to judge how much more support children with intellectual disabilities need when compared to typically developing children.

The normative sample is generally broad and representative. Regarding the normative process, there are a few limitations. First, IQ level was reported by respondents instead of measured directly. Respondents may not have reported accurate scores, which may have impacted how the sample was stratified. Second, evidence for measurement invariance and descriptive statistics across racial groups were not presented. Although the sample was demographically representative, the majority of the sample was White. It is unclear whether reliability and validity evidence generalizes to minority groups. Lastly, the sample used to demonstrate test-retest reliability included participants older than the target population for the SIS-C.

SUMMARY. The SIS-C is a structured interview tool that was designed to evaluate the intensity of support needs for children with intellectual disabilities. This tool allows service providers to make informed decisions about placement and intervention, for it is one of the few norm-referenced measures of support needs that has been validated for this population. Although this tool has strong evidence of validity and reliability, the accuracy of ratings relies heavily on clinical judgment. As such, the person administering this assessment should have formal training in the assessment of children with intellectual disabilities as well as typically developing children.

Review of the Supports Intensity Scale–Children's Version by CARLEN HENINGTON, Professor of Educational and School Psychology, Mississippi State University, Mississippi State, MS:

DESCRIPTION. The Supports Intensity Scale–Children's Version (SIS-C) is based on a supports paradigm in which intellectual disabilities (ID) and related developmental disabilities (IDD) are considered a "state of functioning" (manual, p. 1) rather than a deficit. The SIS-C is norm-referenced and assesses the level of children's (5-16 years) pattern of support needs relative to those of a representative standardization sample. The goal is to obtain fair, uniform information indicating the supports (including assistive technology) needed for success.

The child's support needs are assessed via interviews conducted by an administrator who uses clinical judgment to rate the items presented in two sections. Section 1 includes medical and behavioral support needs;

Section 2 provides an overall perspective of needs. Section 1's medical component assesses needs in four areas: (a) respiratory care (e.g., inhalation therapy); (b) feeding assistance (e.g., tube feeding); (c) skin care (e.g., positioning, wound care); and (d) other exceptional medical care (e.g., seizure management). Section 1's behavioral component assesses need level (*none, some,* or *extensive support needed*) for: (a) external behavior (e.g., emotional outbursts); (b) self-directed behavior (e.g., self-injury); (c) sexual behavior (e.g., sexual aggression); and (d) other exceptional behavioral concerns (e.g., elopement). Section 2, the Supports Needs Index (SNI) includes 61 activity items and yields seven subscale scores: (a) Home Life (e.g., chores, toileting); (b) Community and Neighborhood (e.g., compliance with community standards/rules); (c) School Participation (e.g., transportation, co-curricular activities); (d) School Learning (e.g., academic skills and completion); (e) Health and Safety (e.g., aches and pains, self-protection); (f) Social (e.g., managing relationships and routine changes); and (g) Advocacy (e.g., taking action, goal attainment). Detailed descriptions of each item are provided in the test manual, which also discusses differences between the SIS-C and other adaptive behavior measures.

During administration, the interviewer obtains demographic information and ratings from multiple respondents who have known the child for at least 3 months and have observed him or her in one or more environments for an extended time (several hours per setting). Interviews (preferably face-to-face) may be conducted individually, in a group, or both. (Field testing was completed using both individual and group interviews.) Respondents' perspectives are then collectively assigned a rating by the interviewer and may not specifically align with some conceptualizations of respondents.

Questions are grouped by subscales with a brief cue for each item (e.g., completes chores) as measured by questions that provide a sentence stem describing a hypothetical behavior or activity followed by three sentence endings to assess the level of support in three categories: (a) type (*none, monitoring, prompting, partial physical assistance, full physical assistance*); (b) frequency (*negligible, infrequently, frequently, very frequently, always*); and (c) daily support time (*none, less than 30 minutes, 30 minutes to less than 2 hours, 2 hours to less than 4 hours, 4 hours or more*). Based on the collective input from respondents, who may include the child, responses are rated by the interviewer on a scale of 0 to 4, with less support receiving lower scores. The interviewer must reconcile contradictory information to determine the appropriate score for each item. Administrators/interviewers should have a baccalaureate degree and experience in providing services for children with ID as well as effective interviewing and decision-making skills.

Scoring the SIS-C is straightforward. Scores on Sections 1 and 2 are used to identify the likelihood of greater services needed for a child and in which areas. For Section 1, results from each area (medical needs, behavioral needs) are totaled and transferred to the Scoring Form and Profile located within the protocol. Instructions for interpreting results are on the scoring form. Instructions for scoring Section 2 also are straightforward with the level of support in the three categories (type, frequency, and time) totaled for each item (range = 0-12). Then, a mean rating is calculated for each of the seven subscales, and subscale mean ratings are averaged for the overall mean rating. A standard score and a standardized percentile rank are determined for each of the subscales (M = 10, SD = 3) and the overall Support Needs Index composite (M = 100, SD = 15) using age-based normative tables in the test manual. The standard scores for each subscale and the Support Needs Index are graphed on the profile form.

DEVELOPMENT. The SIS-C, developed by the American Association on Intellectual and

Developmental Disabilities (AAIDD), was constructed to reflect the support needs of children and youth based upon the existing adult version (SIS-A) and a literature search. An expert panel selected 61 items for inclusion, and a pilot test was conducted in three states (Illinois, North Carolina, Tennessee) with children ages 5-16 years. Unclear or confusing items were noted, resulting in minor edits. Then, a sample of 4,015 individuals, stratified by age cohort in 2-year increments and by commonly used classifications of students with ID (i.e., *mild, moderate, severe/profound*) were selected for a field test involving 694 interviewers of more than 12,000 respondents. The children were predominately male (67.5%) and White (55.9%) or Black (20.4%) with English as their primary language (57.3%). Along with ID, 53% had a secondary diagnosis of autism spectrum disorder, and 40% had a secondary diagnosis of developmental delay. Most individuals in the normative sample (94.4%) resided at home.

Normative scores were generated using a pre-modeling technique (i.e., parceling by summing or averaging items; Little, 2013), and procedures outlined by Seo, Little, Shogren, and Lang (2016) were applied to identify sets of items for each support construct of the seven subscales. The test authors explain that unequal distributions of composite scores across the bands indicate "the influence of age on support needs, showing that older students had fewer support needs than younger children" (manual, p. 73).

TECHNICAL. Internal consistency estimates for the subscales and the total sample exceeded .90, indicating strong internal consistency. Standard deviations showed some variability due to the constraint applied to latent variances for some age groups; standard error of measurement at the manifest level ranged from .15 to .26 for subtests across age groups. To examine test-retest reliability, interviews were conducted on two occasions regarding 39 children with an average of 20.12 days between interviews. Resultant reliability coefficients ranged from .86 to .94. For interrater reliability, a comparison of results obtained via inter-interviewers, inter-respondents and mixed-inter-raters was completed with approximately 30 children. Coefficients ranged from .69 to .95 for subscales and from .87 to .93 for the SNI. Taken together, these four indicators of reliability show that SIS-C scores were highly consistent across the procedures.

Four types of validity evidence were also reported. Content and factorial evidence showed measurement properties are highly similar across age groups. To assess criterion-related evidence, the test authors used a definition from Little (2013) that stated for structural equation models with multiple constructs, all potential relationships among the constructs can be evidence of criterion validity. Therefore, correlations between subscale scores and a set of two respondents who indicated the needs of an individual on a Likert scale can be viewed as evidence of criterion validity. In the case of the SIS-C, all such comparisons yielded correlation coefficients greater than .35. Additionally, scores for 142 individuals, ages 15-21 years, on the SIS-C and the SIS-A were compared; correlation coefficients ranged between .76 and .84 for those subtests in both measures. Thus, in this reviewer's opinion, criterion-related evidence of validity was adequate.

Evidence of construct validity was examined across age cohorts by comparing support needs and adaptive behavior scores, yielding coefficients that ranged from .33 to .62 (all significant at $p < .001$), with the lowest correlations generally for the 7- to 8-year age cohort and higher correlations for younger and older age cohorts. These values offer support for construct evidence and also show that the measurement is different from those assessing only adaptive behavior. Although numerous tables and graphics providing evidence of the various analyses were presented, no peer reviewed publications examining reliability and validity of the SIS-C were cited.

COMMENTARY. The SIS-C is an excellent tool to meet the identified goal of determining the support needs of an individual across medical and behavioral realms. A strength is the relatively brief, but comprehensive, assessment across respondents that results in a useful tool for planning and programming for individuals with a variety of disabilities with a range of impact.

SUMMARY. The test developers have produced a useful tool for those who seek to provide support to individuals with a range of disabilities and support needs. The materials are user friendly, and administration and scoring are straightforward. Resulting reading profiles offer information on the type, frequency, and requisite time needed for supports in seven critical areas typically reviewed during a meeting to develop plans for an individual with disabilities. There is a need for additional validation to show that the type of planning resulting from the use of the SIS-C leads to improved outcomes for children and stakeholder satisfaction.

REVIEWER'S REFERENCES

Little, T. D. (2013). *Longitudinal structural equation modeling: Methodology in the social sciences*. New York, NY: Guilford.

Seo, H., Little, T. D., Shogren, K. A., & Lang, K. M. (2016). On the benefits of latent variable modeling for norming scales: The case of the Supports Intensity Scale—Children's Version. *International Journal of Behavioral Development, 40*, 373-384. doi:101177/0165025416671612

[163]

Systematic Analysis of Language Transcripts 16.

Purpose: Clinical software designed to assess language acquisition and disorders through the use of language samples.
Population: Students in prekindergarten through Grade 12.
Publication Dates: 2009-2016.
Acronym: SALT 16.
Scores: 8 variables in Standard Measures Report: Transcript Length, Intelligibility, Narrative/Expositor/Persuasion Structure, Syntax/Morphology, Semantics, Discourse, Verbal Facility, Errors.
Administration: Individual.
Price Data: Available from publisher.
Foreign Language & Other Editions: Bilingual Spanish/English and Australian databases available.
Time: Unlimited.
Authors: Jon F. Miller and Aquiles Iglesias (software); Jon F. Miller, Karen Andriacchi, and Ann Nockerts (clinician's guide).
Publisher: SALT Software, LLC.
Cross References: For reviews by Abigail Baxter and Kathy L. Shapley of the 2010 English Version, see 19:164; for reviews by Jeanette W. Farmer and by Tiffany L. Hutchins and Michael S. Cannizzaro of the 2010 Bilingual SE Version, see 19:163.

Review of the Systematic Analysis of Language Transcripts 16 (SALT 16) by MONICA GORDON-PERSHEY, Associate Professor, School of Health Sciences, Cleveland State University, Cleveland, OH:

DESCRIPTION. The Systematic Analysis of Language Transcripts 16 (SALT 16) is a software package designed to assess the linguistic characteristics of samples of spoken or written language. Examiners transcribe language samples into the software, then computational analyses provide measures of the complexity of the language sample. The software can be used with any language sample in English or Spanish.

The analyses performed by the SALT 16 program provide standard measures of language performance in eight categories: Transcript Length, Intelligibility, Narrative/Expository/Persuasion Structure, Syntax/Morphology, Semantics, Discourse, Verbal Facility, and Errors. The website for SALT Software, LLC (http://www.saltsoftware.com) states that SALT research and development have been ongoing since the 1980s.

Contemporaneous with the development of the software over four decades, the researchers built multiple reference databases that allow users to compare language samples obtained to language samples from several thousand speakers ages 2 years 8 months through 18 years 9 months. The SALT databases function as a repository of information on the measurement of the development of language length and complexity in childhood and adolescence.

This language sample analysis software is intended for use by speech-language pathologists (SLPs) as a clinical instrument for the identification of language delays or disorders, and as a research and educational tool. The SALT 16 provides a detailed computational analysis of language content, form, and use, the three main areas of language competence upon which clinical assessments of deficit are determined. Samples are analyzed for their content (i.e., semantics, word usage), form (syntax, morphology), and use (the overall purpose and structure as revealed by elements of pragmatics, discourse, exposition, and narration). The results furnish an indicator of expressive language strengths and weaknesses and may be used to characterize the nature of an examinee's language deficits as involving semantic, syntactic, and/or pragmatic elements.

The computerized assessments are intended to be used along with other forms of language sample analysis that SLPs prepare manually (see Walden, Gordon-Pershey, & Paul, 2014 for a description) and with standardized tests of language development and performance.

Because the SALT 16 software can be used to analyze any language sample, it follows that it can be used with any language sampling elicitation materials and procedures that an examiner administers. The SALT website offers self-paced training courses that provide advice on choosing elicitation materials and sampling contexts that are compatible with the specifications of the SALT analyses. Guidelines describe how to elicit language samples that are consistent with the software's analytic properties and that are reliable across examinees and for retesting individuals. The website offers a variety of suggested materials to elicit story narration, exposition, and retelling that are based on children's literature (for example, *Frog, Where Are You?* by Mercer Mayer, *A Porcupine Named Fluffy* by Helen Lester, and *Doctor DeSoto* by William Steig). Elicitation kits that provide wordless versions of these picture books are for sale on the website. Wordless books allow a child to produce an open-ended story in response to the pictures.

Scoring procedures entail accurate inputting of the language sample into the SALT 16 software. Online transcription training courses teach how to input language samples using the conventions of the SALT annotation system, which differs from standard sentence punctuation and which accounts for speech features such as intelligibility, pauses, interruptions, and overlapping speech. Several guide sheets and examples are available online to facilitate accurate transcription input. The SALT Software company offers a transcription service that will input any digital audio or video file for a fee.

Scores are presented on the Standard Measures Report, which summarizes eight main language variables, each with several subcomponents: (a) Transcript Length, which includes the total number of utterances, a list of all words spoken, total number of completed words, and elapsed time in minutes; (b) Intelligibility, which includes the percentage of intelligible utterances; (c) Narrative/Expository/Persuasion, which offers scores for these language structures based on a variety of indicators (for example, narration includes character development, plot, and other properties of narrative structure); (d) Syntax/Morphology, which includes the mean length of utterance in words and in morphemes based on analysis of Communication Units (C-units; each unit is composed of an independent clause with its modifiers) and a Subordination Index (a ratio of the number of main and subordinate clauses to the number of C-units, yielding a measure of syntactic complexity based on the embedding of subordinate noun, adjective, or adverbial clauses); (e) Semantics, which includes the number of total words, the number of different words, the number of different word roots, and the ratio of different words to total words (known as the Type Token Ratio); (f) Discourse, which includes the mean turn length in words, the number of utterances within overlapping speech, number of utterances interrupted by another speaker, and number of times the speaker interrupted another speaker; (g) Verbal Facility, which reports words per minute, ratio of words to mazes (i.e., filled pauses, false starts, repetitions, and reformulations), the number of pauses within and between utterances, and number of abandoned utterances; and (h) Errors, which includes the number and percentage of utterances with errors or omissions. The SALT Software website offers multiple explanatory pages and rubrics for interpreting the many scores obtained within the Standard Measures Report. These eight categories offer raw scores and percentages for the examinee's performance, without comparisons to other individuals.

To compare an individual's performance to that of others, the SALT reference databases offer transcripts of speakers engaged in play, conversation, narrative, narrative story retell, exposition, and persuasion. The reference samples were gathered in Wisconsin, California, Utah, New Zealand, Australia, and Edmonton, Alberta, Canada, and represent English monolingual speakers, Spanish monolinguals, and English-Spanish bilinguals. Online analysis aids suggest how to interpret an examinee's performance relative to peer performance.

DEVELOPMENT. The original SALT software was designed to replicate the complex manual tasks of categorizing, counting, and summarizing linguistic features. Each SALT software version refined the mechanisms for inputting and coding data for tabulation and summarization. Concurrent to the improvement of the software, the SALT developers gathered language samples that would reflect a normative array of language behaviors in children and adolescents. Heilmann, Miller, and Nockerts (2010) reported on the development of several language sample databases that contained transcripts from more than 6,000 speakers. The SALT website includes a resource list of articles published since 2004 that pertain to use of SALT software for research and clinical purposes or that describe the creation of the SALT transcript databases.

TECHNICAL. Reliability of the SALT software is dependent upon the reliability of the user. The software recognizes only the transcriptions and the codes that the user inputs. If a user is not consistent in inputting and coding, or if multiple users do not input and code similarly, the resulting reports will not be reliable. The guide sheets posted on the SALT website are intended to support consistent inputting and coding practices.

Best practices for interpreting SALT summary reports dictates that users compare the reports generated to other sources of data, such as standardized test scores. A document on the SALT website titled "Using SALT to Assess the Common Core Grades K-12" compares the SALT elicitation protocols, language measures, and reports to selected Common Core State Standards for English Language

Arts in the category of Speaking and Listening. This document can help SALT users determine whether the items on the summary reports reflect the language skills necessary to meet the Common Core State Standards.

The SALT authors report that the SALT language transcript databases offer reliable and valid evidence of the normative development of language. Participant characteristics and the procedures used in the Wisconsin and California studies are posted on the SALT website.

COMMENTARY. The usefulness of the SALT software is that it can reduce the labor intensiveness of manual forms of language sample analysis. The software provides consistent calculations of language features and detailed summary reports, and the data displays are easy to read. Any language sample, either spoken or written, can be analyzed. The elicitation materials offered by the SALT developers provide a degree of reliability across conditions, examinees, and examiners.

SUMMARY. The SALT software meets the intended purposes of providing detailed language sample analyses. The results furnish an indicator of expressive language strengths and weaknesses and may be used to characterize the nature of an examinee's language deficits.

REVIEWER'S REFERENCES

Heilmann, J. J., Miller, J. F., & Nockerts, A. (2010). Using language sample databases. *Language, Speech, and Hearing Services in Schools, 41*, 84-95.

Miller, J. F., Andriacchi, K., & Nockerts, A. (Eds.). (2015). *Assessing language production using SALT software: A clinician's guide to language sample analysis*. Middleton, WI: SALT Software, LLC.

Walden, P. R., Gordon-Pershey, M., & Paul, R. (2014). Communication sampling procedures. In R. Paul (Ed.), *Introduction to clinical methods in communication disorders* (3rd ed., pp. 117-174). Baltimore, MD: Paul H. Brookes.

Review of the Systematic Analysis of Language Transcripts 16 by PATRICIA A. PRELOCK, Professor and Dean, College of Nursing and Health Sciences, University of Vermont, Burlington, VT:

DESCRIPTION. The Systematic Analysis of Language Transcripts (SALT) is in its second, revised edition as software designed to support clinicians and researchers in the language sample analysis process. The release of the latest version of the SALT software and clinician's guide to language analysis (SALT 16) addresses language sampling across the lifespan (Miller, Andriacchi, & Nockerts, 2015; Miller & Iglesias, 2015). The SALT program includes an installation and resource guide and a clinician's guide to language sample analysis as well as a website (www.saltsoftware.com) for additional information about training courses and other available materials.

The installation and resource guide provides instructions for downloading the SALT 16 software for both Windows and Mac computers, creating a virtual Windows environment for Mac users. Clear instructions are provided for both Windows and Mac installations. The clinician's guide or reference book, *Assessing Language Production Using SALT Software: A Clinician's Guide to Language Sample Analysis*, provides a comprehensive explanation for eliciting, transcribing, analyzing, and interpreting language samples as well as a discussion of language assessment in bilingual populations and applications of SALT using case studies. The reference book also contains several databases and scoring options that can be used by clinicians and researchers to make comparisons among clinical, neurotypical, and bilingual populations.

Language sample analysis is one of the few ways to truly capture a communicator's functional language use in a variety of settings. The SALT software makes the analysis of language samples more consistent, efficient, and reliable as it standardizes the language sampling process from selecting the context for collecting the sample to interpreting the results. Over the last 50 years, language sampling and analysis have evolved from a descriptive approach to children's language to a criterion-referenced approach that uses data from the developmental literature. Language sample analysis has some key components that highlight its value. First, it is flexible, allowing numerous ways to analyze a sample of language at the syntactic, semantic, and discourse levels regardless of individuals' cognitive ability or their first language. Second, it is repeatable such that language samples can be collected at any time and over time to assess change in language performance. Third, it is authentic as performance evaluated via language sampling derives from language used in the natural environment; it also correlates with more standard measures of oral narratives and reading comprehension. Fourth, language sample analysis is accountable in that it can measure language "at all levels and at frequent intervals" (Miller et al., 2015, p. 5). Finally, language sample analysis aligns with expectations for measuring students' outcomes as part of the Common Core State Standards. With all the value described for language sample analysis, implementation challenges do exist, so computer technology has emerged as a solution. The SALT software program is one of those solutions, automating the analysis process and using available databases for comparison.

SALT 16 provides practical solutions to three primary areas of challenge in implementing language sample analysis: time, consistency, and interpretation. Analyzing a language sample using the SALT program takes seconds rather than hours, which are typically associated with analysis. The SALT program ensures consistency as elicitation protocols and transcription format are provided so the same sample type, length, and transcription rules are used across samples. The SALT databases include data from more than 7,000 typical speakers so clinicians and researchers can compare individual clinical samples to age- or grade-matched peers. Research by SALT developers has provided important information about mean length of utterance, number of different words, number of total words, number of words per minute, length of samples, and contexts that are more difficult and that influence the length of the sample (e.g., narration, conversation with adults, or during play) and the complexity of language.

The SALT website (www.saltsoftware.com) also includes several products or materials that can be used to elicit language samples. For example, the website includes a story retell elicitation kit, an expository and persuasion elicitation kit, and a frog story elicitation kit. Several online training courses are available as is a forum where questions can be posted.

DEVELOPMENT. The development of the SALT databases came from a number of research studies with typically developing participants of varying age, gender, socioeconomic status and geographic locations. The databases include samples from play, conversation, narrative storytelling (in which students select a story or retell a story), expository, persuasion, bilingual Spanish/English story retell and unique story, monolingual Spanish retell, story generation from pictures, the Gilliam Narrative Tasks, and New Zealand/Australia databases (including conversation, story retell, personal narrative, and expository).

TECHNICAL. The SALT 16 draws its comparison data from more than 7,000 samples of language representing a diverse demographic of children and adolescents from a series of research studies with typical populations.

Reliability. The reliability of transcription using the SALT transcript protocol is high, with agreement ranging from 90 to 100% indicating transcribers followed the expected transcription protocol (Heilmann et al., 2008). Test-retest paradigms also yielded high reliability coefficients for samples collected within a 2-week period. In these studies there was some variability across transcripts but little impact on the aspects of language being measured (Heilmann et al., 2008).

Validity. As previously discussed, SALT software is a responsive approach to the challenges of analyzing language samples, which are the most ecologically valid method of evaluating a child's language. The software program uses databases representing a range of demographic characteristics giving it broad use for comparing language samples. The reference guide also describes what constitutes a valid language sample, coaches clinicians on the materials needed to elicit the best samples, provides guides on ways to facilitate the most natural sample of a child's language, and offers a basic protocol for transcription.

COMMENTARY. The SALT 16 software program is an invaluable tool for clinicians and researchers who wish to analyze a sample of language in a time efficient and consistent manner. Transcription time averages about 40 minutes whereas the analysis through the SALT software takes only a few seconds. The resulting analysis allows for comparisons with similar groups and contexts for elicitation. Collaborations with researchers have advanced the utility of the tool to bilingual populations including Spanish (Miller et al., 2006), French (Thordardottir, 2005), and Turkish (Acarlar & Johnston, 2006), with a growing number of other language experts considering the utility of SALT for their populations. The reference manual provides a comprehensive description of the constructs used in the analysis process, offers guidance on selecting comparison groups, and gives examples of cases for application of the constructs and the databases. Miller and colleagues' (2015) chapter on interpreting language samples facilitates the clinician's ability to create communication profiles for their students related not only to observed delays (e.g., reduced mean length of utterance and number of words) but also likely to difficulties with word retrieval (e.g., pauses, word repetitions), organization of narratives (e.g., nonspecific referencing, missing characters), deficits in discourse (e.g., overlapping speech and interruptions), low semantic content (e.g., talking around a topic, using pronouns in place of specific nouns), and language disorders where performance is significantly different from what would be expected for age-matched peers. In addition to more traditional language sample analysis, the SALT software also has the ability to assess written language and dysfluent motor speech production because its codes can be customized for the specific purposes of the clinician or researcher (DiVall-Rayan, Miller, Andriacchi, & Nockerts, 2015).

SUMMARY. Knowing that language impairments take on many forms, language sample analysis is an important component in the assessment process as it gives insight into the overall language ability of children in their daily communicative interactions. The SALT software advances clinicians' and researchers' ability to analyze language samples in a quick, efficient, and consistent manner (Price, Hendricks, & Cook, 2010). Although the initial transcription of samples requires time (30 to 40 minutes) and a thorough understanding of the required transcription protocol, the actual analysis is quick and can be used to create a communication profile for individual children. SALT 16 appears to have established a reliable transcription process and valid tool with a significant database of typical language samples giving the tool broad utility for performance comparison. A number of research studies have used SALT to describe the language of children and adolescents across different elicitation contexts confirming its value in defining language strengths and challenges and identifying differences among comparator populations and conversational contexts (Guo & Eisenberg, 2015; Gusewski & Rojas, 2017; Heilmann & Malone, 2014; Heilmann, Miller, Nockerts, & Dunaway, 2010; Heilmann, Nockerts, & Miller, 2010; Miller, Andriacchi, & Nockerts, 2016).

REVIEWER'S REFERENCES

Acarlar, F., & Johnston, J. (2006). Computer-based analysis of Turkish child language: Clinical and research applications. *Journal of Multilingual Communication Disorders, 4*(2), 78-94.

DiVall-Rayan, J., Miller, J. F., Andriacchi, K., & Nockerts, A. (2015). Additional applications of SALT. In J. F. Miller, K. Andriacchi, & A. Nockerts (Eds.), *Assessing language production using SALT software: A clinician's guide to language sample analysis* (pp. 137-161). Middleton, WI: SALT Software, LLC.

Guo, L.-Y., & Eisenberg, S. (2015). Sample length affects the reliability of language sample measures in 3-year-olds: Evidence from parent-elicited conversational samples. *Language, Speech, and Hearing Services in Schools, 46,* 141-153.

Gusewski, S., & Rojas, R. (2017). Tense marking in the English narrative retells of dual language preschoolers. *Language, Speech, and Hearing Services in Schools, 48,* 183-196.

Heilmann, J., & Malone, T. O. (2014). The rules of the game: Properties of a database of expository language samples. *Language, Speech, and Hearing Services in Schools, 45,* 277-290.

Heilmann, J., Miller, J. F., Iglesias, A., Fabiano-Smith, L., Nockerts, A., & Digney Andriacchi, K. (2008). Narrative transcription accuracy and reliability in two languages. *Topics in Language Disorders, 28*(2), 178-188.

Heilmann, J., Miller, J. F., Nockerts, A., & Dunaway, C. (2010). Properties of the narrative scoring scheme using narrative retells in young school-age children. *American Journal of Speech-Language Pathology, 19,* 154-166.

Heilmann, J., Nockerts, A., & Miller, J. F. (2010). Language sampling: Does the length of the transcript matter? *Language, Speech, and Hearing Services in Schools, 41,* 393-404.

Miller, J. F., Andriacchi, K., & Nockerts, A. (Eds.). (2015). *Assessing language production using SALT software: A clinician's guide to language sample analysis.* Middleton, WI: SALT Software, LLC.

Miller, J. F., Andriacchi, K., & Nockerts, A. (2016). Using language sample analysis to assess spoken language production in adolescents. *Language, Speech, and Hearing Services in Schools, 47,* 99-112.

Miller, J. F., Heilmann, J., Nockerts, A., Iglesias, A., Fabiano, L., & Francis, D.J. (2006). Oral language and reading in bilingual children. *Journal of Learning Disabilities Research & Practice, 21*(1), 30-43.

Miller, J. F., & Iglesias, A. (2015). *Systematic Analysis of Language Transcripts (SALT): Research Version 16* [Computer Software]. Madison, WI: SALT Software, LLC.

Price, L. H., Hendricks, S., & Cook, C. (2010). Incorporating computer-aided language sample analysis into clinical practice. *Language, Speech, and Hearing Services in Schools, 41,* 206-222.

Thordardottir, E. T. (2005). Early lexical and syntactic development in Quebec French and English: Implications for cross-linguistic and bilingual assessment. *International Journal of Language & Communication Disorders, 40,* 243-278.

[164]

Systematic Screening for Behavior Disorders, Second Edition.

Purpose: Designed as a universal screener for identifying students with either externalizing or internalizing behavior problems and disorders.
Population: Students in preschool through Grade 9.
Publication Dates: 1990-2014.
Acronym: SSBD.
Administration: Group.
Price Data, 2020: $225 per portfolio, including administrator's guide (2014, 210 pages), 1 CD with technical manual, 10 classroom screening packets Grades 1-9, and 2 classroom screening packets PreK-K; $10 per screening packet, including 1 copy Stage 1 screening form, 3 copies Stage 2 Screening for Externalizing Students form, and 3 copies Stage 2 Screening for Internalizing Students form.
Time: (45) minutes for each stage.
Comments: Completed via pencil and paper or online; rankings completed by teacher at each stage.
Authors: Hill M. Walker, Herbert H. Severson, and Edward G. Feil.
Publisher: Ancora Publishing.

a) STAGE 1.
Scores: 2 rankings: Internalizing, Externalizing.
b) STAGE 2.
1) *PreK-K.*
Scores, 4: Critical Events Index, Aggressive Behavior Scale (for externalizers), Social Interaction Scale (for internalizers), Combined Frequency Index for Adaptive and Maladaptive Behavior.
2) *Grades 1-9.*
Scores, 2: Critical Events Index, Combined Frequency Index for Adaptive and Maladaptive Behavior.

Cross References: See T5:2607 (1 reference); for reviews by Mary Lou Kelley and by Leland C. Zlomke and Robert Spies of an earlier edition, see 13:313.

Review of the Systematic Screening for Behavior Disorders, Second Edition by CARRIE A. CHAMP MORERA, Coordinator of Admissions Assessment, Milton Hershey School, Hershey, PA:

DESCRIPTION. The Systematic Screening for Behavior Disorders, Second Edition (SSBD 2nd ed.) is a systematic universal screening system used to identify students in prekindergarten through Grade 9 who are at risk for externalizing and internalizing behavior concerns. In addition to identifying behavior concerns, the measure is used to determine referrals for and eligibility for special education services and provides access to interventions and/or other specialized services and supports. The test authors state that the goals of the SSBD 2nd ed. include the following: universal behavior screening for all students in elementary and middle school grades, identification of social-emotional needs and adaptive behaviors that contribute to positive school success and peer relationships, identification of critical behaviors and maladaptive behaviors that are disruptive to the student and classroom, short-term evaluation of school interventions, progress monitoring, and identification of students who are most at risk for school dropout.

Because the SSBD 2nd ed. is a universal screener, every student in a given group has the opportunity to be identified as having externalizing or internalizing behavior problems. Externalizing behaviors are defined by the test authors as "all behavior problems that are directed outwardly by the student toward the external social environment" (administrator's guide, p. 4), whereas internalizing behaviors are defined as "all behavior problems that are directed inwardly (i.e., away from the external social environment) and represent problems with self" (administrator's guide, p. 4).

To begin the two-stage screening procedure, teachers complete two separate, but parallel, protocols, one for externalizing behaviors and one for internalizing behaviors. Two slightly different forms are available depending on the grade levels of the students being screened—Grades PreK-K and Grades 1-9. In Stage 1, the teacher identifies five students who are judged to be most at risk for externalizing behavior problems and five students who are judged to be most at risk for internalizing behavior problems based on the definitions and examples on the protocols. Then, the teacher rank orders the students from most severe to least severe in exhibiting the respective behaviors. The three highest ranked students in each category proceed to Stage 2; however, the same student cannot be identified in both categories. During Stage 2, the teacher completes a Critical Events Index form and a Combined Frequency Index for Adaptive and Maladaptive Behavior form for the three students previously identified in each group. Additionally, for the PreK-K group, the teacher completes an Aggressive Behavior Scale for the highest ranked students in the externalizing group and a Social Interaction Scale for the highest ranked students in the internalizing group. The Critical Events Index lists 33 serious behaviors for students in Grades 1-9 and 15 such behaviors for students in prekindergarten or kindergarten. On the forms, the teacher marks whether the behavior indicated in each item occurred. The Combined Frequency Index for Adaptive and Maladaptive Behavior form (23 items for Grades 1-9; 17 items for PreK-K) as well as the Aggressive Behavior Scale (nine items) comprise lists of behaviors in which the teacher rates the extent to which the behavior occurs using a Likert scale from 1 (*never*) to 5 (*frequently*). The Social Interaction Scale (eight items) is rated from 1 (*never*) to 7 (*frequently*).

After the forms are completed, the scores are totaled for each scale. The measure allows for a simple conversion of raw scores to percentile ranks, risk categories (moderate risk, high risk, extreme risk; no risk is an option for PreK-K students), and standard scores. Conversion tables for scores obtained by students in Grades 1-9 are provided separately for externalizers and internalizers. Additional tables are provided for nonranked control students on the Critical Events Index, Adaptive Behavior Scale, and Maladaptive Behavior Scale. Item means and standard deviations are provided in separate tables. It is notable that the norm group for Grades 1 to 9 includes all students in these grades for their respective categories previously mentioned, whereas the norm group for Grades Pre-K to K compares female students with other girls in prekindergarten and kindergarten and male students with other males in these same grades.

The administration and training instructions are clear. Instructions and training are provided in various formats including in the test manual, online videos, and PowerPoint slides, which can be printed from the accompanying CD. Instructional and training materials also cover the purpose of the SSBD, scoring, interpretation and SSBD school applications. The test manual provides chapters on getting started with the SSBD, administration and staff training, scoring steps, and interpretation. Case studies offer information on how to use the SSBD as part of a comprehensive screening process.

The SSBD 2nd ed. also references supplemental tools that are available as part of the Screening, Identification, and Mentoring System (SIMS).

These tools include the SIMS Behavior Observation Codes and the School Archival Records Search (SARS). The SIMS portfolio, which includes the SSBD 2nd ed., offers progress monitoring and a standardized way to quantify students' behavior and academic performance. These tools need to be purchased separately.

DEVELOPMENT. The SSBD 2nd ed. is both a revised version and extension of the original SSBD developed in 1990. The SSBD and SSBD 2nd ed. were developed through three well-planned and carefully researched phases. Phase 1 consisted of the initial development of the SSBD instruments, during which several prototypes were evaluated for interrater reliability, test-retest reliability, and sensitivity. Phase 2 focused on validation and field-testing of the measures over a 4-year period. At this point, trial testing was conducted to evaluate (a) the psychometric characteristics of the SSBD, (b) teacher accuracy in contrasting groups of students with whom the instrument is intended to be used, and (c) teachers' perceptions and acceptance of the screening procedures. Finally, Phase 3 included applied work and further research to extend the applicability of the SSBD to additional populations, which were expanded to include Grades pre-kindergarten and kindergarten, as well as Grades 7-9. The test authors describe several validation studies in the technical manual to support the validity and reliability of the SSBD 2nd ed. for use with pre-kindergarten and kindergarten students. Furthermore, initial research findings support the use of this instrument in Grades 7-9, but additional research needs to be conducted.

TECHNICAL. A separate technical manual is included on a CD with the SSBD 2nd ed. kit. The standardization sample for the SSBD 2nd ed. consisted of more than 11,000 students from Grades 1-6 with nearly 7,000 of these cases added to the original norm group in 2013. In addition, data for the norm samples were obtained from students in prekindergarten to Grade 9 from various sites across the United States. Data from the norm group for the original SSBD were retained for the revised instrument as multiple research studies subsequently conducted align closely with the original norms.

Demographic characteristics of the normative sample are described and include gender, ethnicity, grade, age, and income. The subsample of PreK-K students included those in regular and special education or specialized services. Percentile ranks, T scores, and risk categories were developed for the SSBD 2nd ed. This reviewer regards these scores as the most useful for comparison purposes in educational assessment.

Overall, the SSBD 2nd ed. appears to provide a reliable assessment of externalizing and internalizing behavior disorders in students from PreK through Grade 9. The evidence offered in support of reliability documents good internal consistency, test-retest reliability, and sufficient interrater agreement. The test authors provided extensive empirical evidence to support the measure's item, factorial, discriminant, criterion-related, concurrent, and predictive validity. Comprehensive statistical analyses and studies have been conducted with this instrument. Two follow-up measures, the SIMS Behavior Observation Codes and the SARS, were used as part of the validation effort of the SSBD 2nd ed. and can be used to obtain more specific information about the behaviors of students identified as being at risk based on results obtained from the SSBD 2nd ed.

COMMENTARY. The SSBD 2nd ed. is an enhancement to the original SSBD. A strength of the SSBD 2nd ed. is that it has been normed over multiple years with over 11,000 cases representing the nation as a whole with considerable research completed on the instrument validating its use. It is an improvement over the previous version as two screening stages make the instrument concise, as opposed to three stages utilized previously. The previous third stage is still available as an optional and separate tool that emphasizes progress monitoring. The SSBD 2nd ed. has been expanded to reach a wider range of students, Grades PreK-9, making it an attractive screening system for school districts. Furthermore, online and print versions of the SSBD are available so users have a choice of administration format. The online version automatically generates school, district, and individual student reports for those at risk of internalizing and externalizing behavior problems. A CD is included with the kit, which includes reproducible forms for scoring and interpretation. Finally, in the SSBD 2nd ed. manual, a section is provided that lists resources for next steps, including interventions and assessments.

Extensive research on the SSBD has been conducted by the test authors and other researchers, which continues to have a positive effect on the evolution of the SSBD. The instrument may prove useful for evaluating social competence, ADHD behaviors, and behavioral pathology in general education students. In addition to universal screening, the SSBD 2nd ed. appears to provide information that may facilitate intervention planning for students who demonstrate specific behavioral problems.

In terms of improvement, additional research studies on the use of the SSBD 2nd ed. with middle school students should be conducted to further support its use for this population. On a related note, the test authors may wish to explore the use of this instrument with Grades 10-12. This instrument would then cover the entire elementary, middle, and high school population.

This instrument is suited for use in classrooms, schools, and school districts. For practitioners evaluating individual students who already have been referred or practitioners who evaluate individual students outside of the school setting, this instrument would not be appropriate as its administration depends on ratings of a group of students. In these cases, individually administered broadband standardized norm-referenced assessments, such as the Behavior Assessment System for Children, Third Edition (BASC-3; Reynolds & Kamphaus, 2015) or the Child Behavior Checklist from the Achenbach System of Empirically Based Assessment (ASEBA; Achenbach, 2015) would be most appropriate.

SUMMARY. Overall, the SSBD 2nd ed. is an adequately standardized and clinically sound measure of universal screening for externalizing and internalizing risk. It can be used for Grades PreK through 9, which is an expanded range from the original version. The test authors provide thorough guidelines for training and administration. It is a cost-effective measure that can be used with classrooms and schools to quickly identify students at risk for behavioral difficulties. The SSBD 2nd ed. allows for early identification, resulting in the potential for early intervention and improved outcomes for students.

REVIEWER'S REFERENCES

Achenbach, T. M. (2015). Achenbach System of Empirically Based Assessment. Burlington, VT: ASEBA Research Center for Children, Youth, and Families.

Reynolds, C. R., & Kamphaus, R. W. (2015). Behavior Assessment System for Children, Third Edition. San Antonio, TX: Pearson.

Review of the Systematic Screening for Behavior Disorders, Second Edition by CYNTHIA A. ROHRBECK, Associate Professor of Psychology, and CATHERINE G. COOGAN, Clinical Psychology Doctoral Student, The George Washington University, Washington, DC:

DESCRIPTION. The Systematic Screening for Behavior Disorders, Second Edition (SSBD 2nd ed.) is a teacher completed two-stage universal screening measure for Pre-K to ninth-grade students who are high on externalizing or internalizing symptoms. Test developers recommend that students be screened at least twice each school year. In addition to identifying children who should be referred for intervention, the measure also may be used for program evaluation and research. The measure is packaged in a cardboard book/box that fastens with Velcro and includes the administrator's guide (manual), SSBD Stages 1 and 2 worksheets, and a CD that includes the technical manual, reproducible scoring and reporting forms, and PowerPoint presentations about the measures for teachers and staff.

Compared to the first edition of the SSBD, the SSBD 2nd edition includes students in PreK-K classrooms and Grades 7-9. Online and print versions are now available. The second edition of the SSBD has two screening stages, in contrast to the first edition, which had three. However, the second edition SSBD can be used in conjunction with the Screening, Identification, and Monitoring System (SIMS) and the School Archival Records Search (SARS) as optional "Stage 3 measures" that provide additional information for intervention and referral. The creators of the SSBD also created the SIMS and SARS.

In Stage 1, the teacher (either individually or in a group setting) identifies the five students in the classroom who are judged to demonstrate the highest level of externalizing symptoms and the five students judged to demonstrate the highest level of internalizing symptoms (based on definitions provided) and ranks the students in each group. Students can be ranked in only one group (either externalizing or internalizing). In Stage 2, in-depth ratings of the top three ranked students in each category are completed. Screening forms include a Critical Events Index (33 *Yes/No* low frequency but serious adjustment problem items that are added together) and a Combined Frequency Index (23 items reflecting adaptive and maladaptive behaviors using a Likert scale from 1 [*never*] to 5 [*frequently*], also added together) for students in Grades 1-9. Stage 2 for PreK-K students includes a shorter 15-item Critical Events Index (with *Yes/No* responses that are added together). As with the older students, a Combined Frequency Index (of an Adaptive Student Behavior Scale and a Maladaptive Behavior Scale with a total of 17 items with Likert scale responses from 1 [*never*] to 5 [*frequently*] added together) is also completed. In addition, students ranked high on externalizing symptoms are rated on an Aggressive Behavior Scale (containing nine items on a Likert scale from 1 [*never*] to 5 [*always*], and students ranked high in internalizing symptoms are rated on a Social Interaction Scale (containing eight items with Likert scale responses from 1 [*never*] to 7 [*frequently*]. Stage 2 can be completed online or on paper. Identifying and rating students in Stage 1 and Stage 2 is estimated to take approximately 45 minutes. Two of the critical events on the Critical Events Index require mandatory reporting across all ages if endorsed because they are indicators of possible physical abuse.

The test authors recommend that someone other than the original teacher score the Stage 2 measures. For students in Grades 1-9, decision rules about whether each student meets "risk criteria" (or qualifies for intervention) depends on his or her score on the Critical Events Index (if 0, then no, if 4 or higher for students ranked high on internalizing symptoms, then yes, or if 5 or higher for students ranked high on externalizing symptoms, then yes). For students with critical events scores between those numbers (0-3 or 0-4), a combination of the Critical Events Index score and the adaptive and maladaptive behavior scales score is used. For students in PreK-K, decisions about individuals at risk are based on a combination of scores on (a) the PreK-K Critical Events Index, (b) the Combined Frequency Index, and (c) the Social Interaction Scale (for students ranked high on internalizing symptoms) or the Aggressive Behavior Scale (for students ranked high on externalizing behaviors).

The SSBD manual includes tables for converting raw scores to T scores and norms for the two large grade groups (PreK-K and 1-9). Norms by sex are also available for PreK-K students. The test manual includes guidelines for interpretation, guidance for explaining results to parents, several case studies, and intervention recommendations.

DEVELOPMENT. In adapting the SSBD for use with preschool age students, the Critical Events Index was shortened. For students ranked high on externalizing symptoms, an emphasis on the frequency and intensity of disruptive behaviors was accomplished by moving some of the critical events items to an Aggressive Behavior Scale with Likert scale responses from 1 to 5. For students ranked high on internalizing symptoms, the Social Interaction Scale was added. The Combined Frequency Index includes a shorter adaptive behavior scale and maladaptive behavior scale than those used with students in Grades 1-9; some items reflecting academic performance and peer relationships were eliminated. The Combined Frequency Index is completed for both groups of preschoolers.

TECHNICAL. Technical information about the SSBD is included in the technical manual on the SSBD CD and is also available online. The manual includes initial development information based on 4,463 students from Grades 1-6 for the first edition. Scores from an additional 6,743 students in Grades 1-6 from 10 sites and collaborators were added in 2012-13. As shown in an appendix of the technical manual, the recent scores were similar to the original norms; thus, the test developers retained the original cutoffs for additional screening or intervention. The test developers note that Stage 2 score profiles appear similar across five ethnic groups and conclude that norms by ethnicity are unnecessary.

The technical manual includes new norms for children in PreK–K. That sample included 2,853 students in Stage 1 and 1,401 participants in Stage 2 from eight states—California, Kentucky, Louisiana, Nebraska, New Hampshire, Oregon, Texas, and Utah. Additional demographic information is available for this younger group (e.g., age, ethnicity, family income levels), compared to the Grades 1-6 sample. A substantial portion of the PreK-K sample (58%) had family incomes categorized as low (less than $15,000/year or Head Start eligible). The sample was 54% male and 69% White (as identified by their teachers). In the PreK-K sample, interrater reliability coefficients (i.e., kappa) between teachers and assistant teachers ranged from .42 to .70 in Stage 1. In Stage 2, kappa coefficients ranged from .48 to .79. Test-retest kappa coefficients were as low as .25 for children high on internalizing scores, which may be expected over a 6-month period. Evidence of concurrent and discriminant validity is provided.

The technical manual does not include a standardization sample for Grades 7-9. It refers to two studies in which the SSBD was used with students in Grades 7-9 but does not report demographics of those samples. In one study, students who had been identified in the SSBD Stage 1 screening had more office disciplinary referrals and lower GPAs than the general population (Caldarella, Young, Richardson, Young, & Young, 2008). At Stage 2, internal consistency estimates ranged from .54 to .90 and interrater reliability correlations (kappa) between teachers ranged from .58 to .60. The test authors note the need for additional reliability and validity information for Grades 7-9. At this time, it appears that the original norms for Grades 1-6 are being used for Grades 1-9.

COMMENTARY. The SSBD 2nd ed. is a two-stage teacher screener for PreK to ninth-grade students high in externalizing or internalizing behaviors. A comprehensive test packet is strengthened by clear definitions of behavior problems, PowerPoint slides for training, and additional technical material. Because teachers must rank the highest five students for both externalizing and internalizing behaviors, children with internalizing disorders will not be overlooked. Important critical items include some that may trigger mandatory reporting.

The numbers of children ranked (five at Stage 1) and rated (three at Stage 2) appears arbitrary. In some schools/classrooms there may be fewer or more students who would fit an at-risk category. In addition, teachers may find it frustrating to be limited to the identification of five students in the externalizing and five in the internalizing groups, with no overlap between the two. Because not all children are ranked on both dimensions, there might be sex or ethnic biases (e.g., girls may be ranked as high in internalizing problems; African-American or Latino students may have a disproportionate amount of disciplinary referrals compared to White students; Skiba et al., 2011). Stage 2 scoring is complicated, particularly for the PreK-K students with rating forms and Likert scale responses that vary between students high on internalizing behaviors and those high on externalizing behaviors. When students have multiple teachers, presumably frequently in the upper grades, there is not a clear recommendation about which teacher should identify students. There may not be psychometric advantages to the SSBD over other student rating instruments (e.g., the Child Behavior Checklist in the Achenbach System of Empirically Based Assessment, the Behavior Assessment System for Children) that could also serve as a "stage 2" assessment for identified at-risk students. Current SSBD norms do not appear to include students in Grades 7-9. In this reviewer's opinion, further breakdown of norms by grade (not just a Grade 1-6 grouping) may be worth consideration, in addition to norms by sex and ethnicity.

SUMMARY. The Systematic Screening for Behavior Disorders (SSBD 2nd ed.) is a teacher-completed universal screening measure for PreK to ninth-grade students at risk for externalizing or internalizing problems. It enables the identification of students demonstrating either internalizing or externalizing symptoms. The second edition expands the age range and adds support for the measure's reliability and the validity of its scores and their uses. Standardization (normative) data remain limited, especially for the older grades.

REVIEWERS' REFERENCES

Caldarella, P., Young, E. L., Richardson, M. J., Young, B. J., & Young, K. R. (2008). Validation of the Systematic Screening for Behavioral Disorders in middle and junior high school. *Journal of Emotional and Behavioral Disorders, 16*, 105-117. https://doi.org/10.1177/1063426607313121

Skiba, R. J., Horner, R. H., Chung, C. G., Rausch, M. K., May, S. L., & Tobin, T. (2011). Race is not neutral: A national investigation of African American and Latino disproportionality in school discipline. *School Psychology Review, 40*, 85-107. https://doi.org/10.1057/978-1-137-51257-4

[165]

TAPS-4: A Language Processing Skills Assessment.

Purpose: "Designed to provide information about language processing and comprehension skills across three intersecting areas: phonological processing, auditory memory, and listening comprehension."
Population: Ages 5-0 through 21-11.
Publication Dates: 1985-2018.
Acronym: TAPS-4.
Scores, 15: Phonological Processing Index (Word Discrimination, Phonological Deletion, Phonological Blending, Syllabic Blending [supplemental]), Auditory Memory Index (Number Memory Forward, Word Memory, Sentence Memory, Number Memory Reversed [supplemental]), Listening Comprehension Index (Processing Oral Directions, Auditory Comprehension, Auditory Figure-Ground [supplemental]), Overall Score.
Administration: Individual.
Price Data, 2020: $205 per kit including manual (2018, 157 pages), 25 record forms, and administration CD; $80 per manual; $85 per 25 record forms; $40 per administration CD.
Time: 60-90 minutes for administration; 15-20 minutes for scoring.
Comments: "Examiners may administer single subtests as part of a larger test battery, one or two indices, or the entire assessment"; formerly titled Test of Auditory Perceptual Skills and Test of Auditory Processing Skills.
Authors: Nancy Martin, Rick Brownell, and Patricia Hamaguchi.
Publisher: Academic Therapy Publications.
Cross References: For reviews by Timothy R. Konold and Rebecca Blanchard and by Dolores Kluppel Vetter of the Test of Auditory Processing Skills—Third Edition, see 18:137; for reviews by Annabel J. Cohen and by Anne R. Kessler and Jaclyn B. Spitzer of the Test of Auditory-Perceptual Skills, see 13:324 (2 references).

Review of the TAPS-4: A Language Processing Skills Assessment by HYESUN LEE, Assistant Professor of Psychology, California State University Channel Islands, Camarillo, CA:

DESCRIPTION. The TAPS-4: A Language Processing Skills Assessment is "designed to provide information about language processing and comprehension skills across three intersecting areas" (manual, p. 7) and "can help identify ongoing or previously undiagnosed higher order language difficulties" (manual, p. 11). While retaining the three main index areas (Phonological Processing, Auditory Memory, and Listening Comprehension) from the TAPS-3, the TAPS-4 subtests have been restructured: fewer subtests for the Auditory Memory Index and Overall score, three new subtests (Processing Oral Directions, Auditory Figure-Ground, and Syllabic Blending), and consolidation of two subtests (Auditory Comprehension and Auditory Reasoning) into one (Auditory Comprehension). Both the Phonological Processing Index and the Auditory Memory Index comprise three subtests and one supplemental subtest. The Listening Comprehension Index consists of two subtests and one supplemental subtest.

The TAPS-4 is individually administered by speech pathologists, school psychologists, and learning specialists trained to assess language skills. The target population is English-speaking individuals ages 5 years 0 months through 21 years 11 months who live in the United States. Testing time is 60-90 minutes to administer and 15-20 minutes to score. The TAPS-4 may be scored by hand or through the test publisher's online scoring and reporting system. Six subtests are administered using a CD or downloadable audio file. The test manual states that the TAPS-4 can be administered either as a whole test battery or as individual subtests. Detailed instructions and guidelines for test administration, scoring, and interpretation of results are provided in the test manual. For multiple administrations, a 4- to 6-month interval is recommended to reduce the impact of practice effects.

Four types of scores are available for subtests, indices, and the Overall score: scaled scores (M = 10, SD = 3), standard scores (M = 100, SD = 15), percentile ranks, and age equivalents. Tables for converting raw scores to scaled scores and percentile ranks are provided in three-month intervals for ages 5 and 6, six-month intervals for ages 7 through 10, and one-year intervals for ages 11 through 21. In addition, conversion tables from summed scaled scores for each index to standard scores; from standard scores to other metrics such as z scores, T scores, and stanines; and from raw scores to age equivalents are provided. Standard errors of measurement (*SEM*s) and confidence intervals (CIs) also are provided for each age group. Critical values for difference scores for subtests and indices are provided for each age group at an alpha level of .05. Tables showing the difference scores at which 10%, 5%, and 1% of the normative sample would have been identified are provided using all age groups.

DEVELOPMENT. Focusing on higher-order language skills that are critical for the development of effective listening and communication abilities, the TAPS-4 is based on the framework of the Cattell-Horn-Carroll theory, which describes language and memory skills in relation to cognitive abilities. Whereas earlier versions of the TAPS were intended to measure auditory perceptual or processing skills, which are one component of oral language processing, the current version corresponds to the recent evolution in the understanding of language processing as an aspect of cognitive ability. Existing TAPS items and subtests were revised, and new subtests were created through a review process with professionals in psychology and speech pathology combined with literature reviews and users' feedback. The test manual thoroughly describes procedures used for field testing (N = 266) and pilot testing (N = 646) and explains how results were used to develop and evaluate items for the final version of the TAPS-4. Classical test theory and differential item functioning (DIF) analyses also were used for the final selection of 248 items. Overall, psychometric procedures together with expert reviews seem to have been appropriately employed for the development of the TAPS-4.

TECHNICAL.

Standardization. The norming sample (N = 2,023) was collected from 40 states and closely represents national demographics (i.e., gender, race/ethnicity, education level, and region including residential characteristics). The number of individuals for each age group was comparably proportioned across 17 groups from ages 5 to 21. The test manual presents not only demographic information but also details about locations and sites where data were collected. The test authors reported collecting information about household income, but that information was not included in the test manual. The table for summary descriptive statistics for each age group based on raw scores is informative, especially data related to the performance of each age group that shows a consistent pattern of improvement on each subtest with age. However, the test authors did not explain clearly why the three main indices, which are the sum of subtests, showed the same increasing pattern as demonstrated in the subtests only after medians were smoothed.

Reliability. Internal consistency, test-rest, and interrater reliability estimates were reported along with *SEMs* and CIs. Alpha coefficients for the Overall score (ranging from .87 to .96) and index scores (ranging from .67 to .94) appear acceptable. Some subtests showed alpha coefficients below .70 for multiple age groups: Number Memory Reversed yielded alpha coefficients lower than .70 in age groups from 5 through 12, and coefficients for Word Discrimination, Phonological Deletion, and Auditory Comprehension were below .70 in age groups from 14 through 21. It should be noted that the alpha value was .09 for Word Discrimination in the age 21 group. The test manual suggests that a ceiling effect could be the reason for low internal consistency. However, considering the fact that the overall difficulty for Word Discrimination was at or above .95 from ages 10 to 21, a question arises about why the alpha coefficient fluctuated from .09 to .77 in that age range.

Coefficients for test-retest reliability with an average interval of 16 days were above .90 for Overall and index scores, and above .70 for subtest scores, except for Processing Oral Directions, when a correction was applied for range restriction. However, Word Discrimination showed a coefficient of .38 without correction. Considering that item exposure may affect the results of test-retest analyses as acknowledged in the test manual, the sample size for the test-retest reliability study was relatively small (n = 87), and some demographic groups were not well represented (e.g., 3.5% for the Black/African American group, 2.3% for 8- and 15-year-olds). Re-examination of test-retest reliability is recommended to support test stability.

Regarding interrater reliability, relatively high intraclass correlation coefficients were found for the three subtests requiring judgment from examiners; intraclass coefficients ranged from .97 to .99 (n = 30). As expected, the same pattern detected in the results for internal consistency was revealed in *SEMs* and CIs (e.g., relatively large *SEMs* and CIs for Word Discrimination) because the alpha coefficients were used for the computations.

Validity. Validity evidence was examined in terms of test content, internal structure, and relations with other variables. As noted in a review of the TAPS-3 (Konold & Blanchard, 2010), there is still a lack of information about how content validity was examined in the TAPS-4. To examine whether the structure of three main indices fit the data well, both exploratory and confirmatory factor analyses were conducted. The exploratory factor analysis extracted three factors. However, based on the findings from the confirmatory factor analysis that the three main index scores loaded highly on the Overall score factor, a comparison of model fit with a one-factor model would be suggested to support the need for three index scores. Additional validity evidence was provided based on relations between TAPS-4 subtest, index, and Overall scores and (a) those from the Clinical Evaluation of Language Fundamentals—Fifth Edition (CELF-5), and (b) chronological ages. Correlations between scores from the TAPS-4 and CELF-5 ranged from .61 to .79 (n = 17), and those with age ranged from .47 to .77 (n = 2,023). The test developers also examined whether TAPS-4 scores differentiate individuals with disabilities from those without. The results demonstrated that the TAPS-4 detected language processing challenges well among those with disabilities such as learning disability (n = 29), specific language impairment (n = 27), and hearing impairment (n = 37); significant score differences in the three index scores and the Overall score were found between those with and without disabilities. As addressed in the test manual, validation is an ongoing process; thus, continuous efforts to provide validity evidence would lend credence to decisions made using TAPS-4 scores.

COMMENTARY. The TAPS-4 is designed based on the current theoretical framework of language processing in speech-language pathology and audiology and is intended to measure oral language processing skills under the context of linguistic and cognitive abilities. Detailed guidelines for administering the TAPS-4 and illustrative examples for scoring will help practitioners to use it with ease. Record forms are user-friendly for recording and scoring responses and effective for presenting results; the front and back of the form include tables to display test results based on the five available score metrics along with CIs for subtest, index, and Overall scores. The test manual systematically organizes and presents information practitioners need in order to evaluate the processes used for test development, standardization, and research studies for reliability and validity, resulting in better understanding of the TAPS-4. Regarding psychometric properties, some of the TAPS-4 subtests showed poor reliability. An additional concern may be placed in relation to the psychometric conversion process. Considering that each age group has its own conversion table from raw scores to other metrics, sample sizes of slightly over or under 100 individuals in each age group may not be large enough to ensure psychometrically reliable processes for score derivation. Finally, it was not clearly explained when the supplemental subtests should be administered.

SUMMARY. The TAPS-4 measures language processing and comprehension skills in three main areas of Phonological Processing, Auditory Memory, and Listening Comprehension using eight subtests and three supplemental subtests. Speech-language pathologists, psychologists, learning specialists, and professionals in relevant areas may consider using the TAPS-4 to obtain information about aural language processing skills in individuals ages 5 through 21. The assessment is easy to administer and score, and the record form is effective for presenting test results. However, because of low reliability coefficients reported for some subtests, caution should be taken when interpreting results. Considering that smoothing was employed for the derivation of scaled subtest scores for each age group and that raw score distributions are heterogeneous across subtests and age groups, caution should be taken when interpreting age-specific scaled subtest scores, as different age groups and subtests may have been differentially affected by the smoothing process. In addition, this reviewer recommends using TAPS-4 scores along with other resources for decision-making purposes.

REVIEWER'S REFERENCE

Konold, T. R., & Blanchard, R. (2010). [Test review of the Test of Auditory Processing Skills–Third Edition]. In R. A. Spies, J. F. Carlson, & K. F. Geisinger (Eds.), *The eighteenth mental measurements yearbook*. Lincoln, NE: Buros Institute of Mental Measurements.

Review of the TAPS-4: A Language Processing Skills Assessment by DIANE L. WILLIAMS, Professor, Department of Communication Sciences and Disorders, The Pennsylvania State University, University Park, PA:

DESCRIPTION. The TAPS-4 is an individually administered measure of language processing for children, adolescents, and young adults ages 5 through 21 years. It comprises 11 subtests: three for Phonological Processing, three for Auditory Memory, and two for Listening Comprehension with one additional supplemental subtest for each of the three areas. The Phonological Processing subtests assess word discrimination, phonological deletion, phonological blending, and syllabic blending. The Auditory Memory subtests assess memory for numbers forward, memory for words, memory for sentences, and memory for numbers in reverse order. The Listening Comprehension subtests assess processing of oral directions, auditory comprehension for passages of varying levels of complexity, and auditory comprehension when challenged with background noise (Auditory Figure-Ground subtest). The test authors suggest these areas may help identify underlying factors that lead to difficulties in reading and writing.

The TAPS-4 can be administered in its entirety, one or two of the indices can be administered, or one or more of the subtests may be administered to assess specific areas. Testing may occur in more than one session. Administration time will vary depending on the number of subtests administered with complete administration estimated to require 60-90 minutes.

The administration procedures as presented in the test manual are well organized and clearly written. Administration of all subtests begins with Item 1. Ceiling rules for subtests are clearly explained in the test manual and are provided on the test protocol at the beginning of each subtest. The first six subtests are administered using pre-recorded stimuli (available on CD or as downloadable audio files). Other subtests are administered orally by the examiner. Detailed administration instructions including specific directions to give the examinee, scoring criteria, and ceiling rules are provided within the test protocol.

Criteria for scoring of each item for the calculation of raw scores are given on the test protocol. Additional scoring guidelines and samples for the Processing Oral Directions and Auditory Figure-Ground subtests are provided as appendices in the test manual. Norms are available for converting raw scores to scaled scores for each of the primary and supplemental subtests and to standard scores for the Phonological Processing, Auditory Memory, and Listening Comprehension indices as well as for the Overall score. Subtest scaled scores are based on a population distribution with a mean of 10 and a standard deviation of 3. Standard scores are based on a population distribution with a mean of 100 and a standard deviation of 15. Additional available statistical measures include confidence intervals, percentile ranks, age-equivalent scores, and difference scores (for comparisons of different subtest scores and index scores).

DEVELOPMENT. In earlier versions, the TAPS was described as a test of auditory processing. However, current conceptualization of auditory processing is more narrowly defined as a set of behaviors focused on lower-order skills such as sound localization, auditory discrimination, and auditory pattern recognition (Medwetsky, 2011). Accordingly, the test authors have reconceptualized the TAPS as a measure of language processing. The test authors state that the TAPS-4 is based on the Cattell-Horn-Carroll theory of cognitive abilities, specifically, the broad areas of Short-Term Memory, Auditory Processing, and Comprehension-Knowledge.

Consistent with this reconceptualization, three new subtests were created: Processing Oral Directions, Auditory Figure-Ground, and Syllabic Blending. The first two are parallel subtests to measure understanding of orally presented language with and without competing background noise. Other revisions from the TAPS-3 included the elimination or revision of problematic test items and the creation of new items for the subtests that were retained. A previously separate subtest, Auditory Reasoning, was collapsed into the retained subtest of Auditory Comprehension. The new subtests were field tested with 226 individuals, 5 through 21 years of age, in 11 states. Revisions were made based on the information gathered.

The complete pilot version of the TAPS-4, consisting of 11 subtests with 381 items, was then administered to a national sample of 646 individuals ages 5 through 21. The sample included 95 individuals with diagnoses of "learning disability, ADHD [attention-deficit/hyperactivity disorder], auditory processing impairment, specific language impairment, and hearing impairment" (manual, p. 45). After data collection, item analysis was conducted, and scoring rules were developed for the new subtests. Classical test theory techniques were used to assess item difficulty, and items were reordered for five of the subtests. Ceiling rules were established for the nine subtests that have ceilings. In addition, "items were assessed for bias using differential item functioning" (manual, p. 45). Items that were problematic, that is, were difficult to score, elicited inconsistent responses, or appeared to be biased, were removed.

TECHNICAL. The standardization sample for the TAPS-4 consisted of 2,023 individuals (45% males; 55% females), ages 5 years 0 months through 21 years 11 months from 194 sites in 40 states across the United States. Each year of age represented from 4.10% to 7.07% of the overall sample. Distribution of race/ethnicity, level of parental education, and geographical distribution mirrored that for the country as a whole. The sample also included 381 individuals with disabilities including specific learning disability/dyslexia, ADHD, auditory processing disorder, specific language impairment, and cochlear implant/hearing impairment.

Internal consistency was reported for the subtest, index, and Overall scores for each year of the norming sample. The majority of these values were in the acceptable range with a few notable exceptions; low alpha values appeared to be due to ceiling effects for older individuals for specific subtests.

A sample of 87 individuals was used to estimate test-retest reliability of the TAPS-4 using correlation coefficients. The evidence indicated that individual subtest, index, and Overall scores were strongly associated on the two test administrations. However, most scores increased significantly upon the second administration (14 to 21 days after the first one). The test authors suggested that this was due to practice effects and cautioned that the test should not be routinely re-administered after a short period.

Because several of the subtest items required the examiner to make judgments by applying scoring guidelines, interrater reliability was evaluated for these items. Intraclass correlation coefficients for those subtests were high, ranging from .97 to .99, suggesting that scoring criteria were clear and could be consistently applied by different examiners.

Evidence for validity included exploratory and confirmatory factor analyses that suggested the subtests of the TAPS-4 loaded onto the expected factors and the data were consistent with a three-factor solution. The TAPS-4 demonstrated concurrent evidence of validity when its scores were compared with those from the Clinical Evaluation of Language Fundamentals—Fifth Edition (CELF-5; Wiig, Semel, & Secord, 2013; 20:43); both measures were administered to a small sample of 17 individuals. A moderate to large positive relationship between the TAPS-4 scores and chronological age provided support for the assumption that the test evaluates developmental skills. Evidence of validity for the

TAPS-4 was further demonstrated by the pattern of performance of individuals in the normative sample who had diagnosed disabilities.

COMMENTARY. The standardization sample was geographically, racially, and ethnically diverse. Notably, it included individuals with various disabilities. Some of the TAPS-4 subtests overlap with other measurement instruments for phonological processing (e.g., the Elision subtest from the Comprehensive Test of Phonological Processing–Second Edition [CTOPP-2; Wagner, Torgesen, Rashotte, & Pearson, 2013; 20:60]), for number memory (e.g., Memory for Digits on the CTOPP-2 or Digit Span Forward and Digit Span Backward on the Test of Integrated Language and Literacy Skills [Nelson, Plante, Helm-Estabrooks, & Hotz, 2016; 20:181]), and for sentence memory (e.g., Recalling Sentences on the CELF-5). However, the TAPS-4 includes distinct subtests that focus on other aspects of phonological processing (i.e., Word Discrimination and Phonological Blending), auditory memory (i.e., Word Memory), and listening comprehension (i.e., the Processing Oral Directions subtest, which requires a verbal response to a spoken sentence rather than a nonverbal pointing response; the Auditory Comprehension subtest, which requires a response to orally presented linguistic information of increasing length and/or complexity). Measures of test-retest reliability, interrater reliability, and internal consistency indicate that the TAPS-4 yields reliable scores. Factor analyses support the assertion that the TAPS-4 is based on three discrete abilities (phonological processing, auditory memory, and listening comprehension) and is consistent with the theoretical model on which it was designed. The manual is well organized with provision of information about the theoretical basis of the TAPS-4, step-by-step instructions, clearly described scoring criteria, and technical information about item selection and test construction. Caution must be taken with some of the subtests due to possible ceiling effects for adolescents and young adults. The test also should not be re-administered within a short period of time due to practice effects that occurred for several of the subtests.

SUMMARY. The TAPS-4 is intended to identify underlying factors that may be affecting performance with reading and writing or to reveal higher-order language difficulties. The test can be reliably administered and scored. Evidence of validity supports the underlying theoretical structure of this instrument as a measure of phonological processing, auditory memory, and listening comprehension. The TAPS-4 would be particularly useful with individuals 5 through 21 years of age who are suspected of having difficulties with language processing and comprehension that may not have been identified with other measures of receptive and expressive language. The TAPS-4 also may be helpful in determining specific areas of weakness in language processing (i.e., phonological vs. memory vs. comprehension).

REVIEWER'S REFERENCES

Medwetsky, L. (2011). Spoken language processing model: Bridging auditory and language processing to guide assessment and intervention. *Language, Speech, and Hearing Services in Schools, 42,* 286-296.

Nelson, N. W., Plante, E., Helm-Estabrooks, N., & Hotz, G. (2016). Test of Integrated Language and Literacy Skills. Baltimore, MD: Paul H. Brookes.

Wagner, R. K., Torgesen, J. K., Rashotte, C. A., & Pearson, N. A. (2013). Comprehensive Test of Phonological Processing–Second Edition. Austin, TX: PRO-ED.

Wiig, E. H., Semel, E., & Secord, W. A. (2013). Clinical Evaluation of Language Fundamentals—Fifth Edition. San Antonio, TX: Pearson.

[166]

Teaching Pyramid Infant-Toddler Observation Scale for Infant-Toddler Classrooms, Research Edition.

Purpose: "Designed to measure the fidelity of implementation of practices associated with the Pyramid Model in center-based infant and toddler care settings."

Population: Teachers and classrooms for infants and toddlers (birth to 3 years).

Publication Date: 2019.

Acronym: TPITOS™.

Scores: 13 Items: Teacher Provides Opportunities for Communication and Building Relationships; Teacher Demonstrates Warmth and Responsivity to Individual Children; Teacher Promotes Positive Peer Interactions; Teacher Promotes Children's Active Engagement; Teacher Is Responsive to Children's Expression of Emotions and Teaches About Feelings; Teacher Communicates and Provides Feedback About Developmentally Appropriate Behavioral Expectations; Teacher Responds to Children in Distress and Manages Challenging Behaviors; Teacher Uses Specific Strategies or Modifications for Children with Disabilities/Delays or Who Are Dual Language Learners; Teacher Conveys Predictability Through Carefully Planned Schedule, Routines, and Transitions; Environment Is Arranged to Foster Social-Emotional Development; Teacher Collaborates with His or Her Peers to Support Children's Social-Emotional Development; Teacher Has Effective Strategies for Engaging Parents in Supporting Their Children's Social-Emotional Development and Addressing Challenging Behaviors; Teacher Has Effective Strategies for Communicating with Families and Promoting Family Involvement in the Classroom; plus Item Indicators and Red Flags.

Administration: Individual teachers and classrooms.

Parts, 2: Observation, Interview.

Price Data, 2020: $90 per set including professional manual (118 pages) and 5 forms; $55 per manual; $35 per 5 forms.
Time: 120 minutes for observation (minimum); 20 minutes for teacher interview; 30-45 minutes for scoring.
Comments: Test publisher strongly recommends that users of the instrument become certified by completing a training program.
Authors: Kathryn M. Bigelow, Judith J. Carta, Dwight W. Irvin, and Mary Louise Hemmeter.
Publisher: Paul H. Brookes Publishing Co., Inc.

Review of the Teaching Pyramid Infant-Toddler Observation Scale for Infant-Toddler Classrooms, Research Edition by STEPHANIE M. CURENTON, Associate Professor, and CRISTINA GRANDA, Consulting Research Assistant, Boston University, Boston, MA:

DESCRIPTION. Teaching Pyramid Infant-Toddler Observation Scale for Infant-Toddler Classrooms, Research Edition (TPITOS) was intended for classrooms in educational or childcare centers with any combination of infants (birth to 18 months old) and toddlers (19 to 36 months old). It is designed to assess fidelity to the Pyramid Model, a multi-tiered social-emotional framework, and is similar in structure and format to the preschool version of the measure, Teaching Pyramid Observation Tool (TPOT™; Hemmeter, Fox, & Synder, 2014; 20:173). To administer TPITOS, a trained and certified rater records information on the target teacher during a 2-hour classroom observation and a 20-minute follow-up interview. There are three categories of measurement: Observation, Interview, and ratings of Red Flags. The Observation and Interview portions consist of 13 scored items, informed by 78 indicator behaviors. In Items 1–7, each indicator behavior is scored as *yes, no,* or *N/A* (*not applicable*) based on observations during at least three of four different routines: free play, structured group activity, care routines, and outdoor activities. In Items 8–13, each indicator behavior is in the same manner based on the entire observation period. Item scores are determined by the percentage of indicator behavior scores marked *yes* out of all indicator behaviors scored. *N/A* scores are excluded from the total count of indicator behaviors scored. The Red Flag measurement consists of 11 scored items, each of which provides example and non-example behaviors for a rater to determine a *yes* or *no* score on the item for the teacher, and in some instances, for the classroom. Specifically, four items measure behaviors at the classroom level, six items measure behaviors at the teacher level, and one item measures behavior at the teacher level or the classroom level. This process yields a Red Flag score for both the teacher and the classroom, determined by the percentage of items scored *yes* out of the total indicator behaviors scored.

Multiple TPITOS assessments of different teachers working in the same classroom or program can serve as measures of competencies of a teaching team and provide data to support professional development, identify strengths and areas to enhance, and monitor growth in these competencies. For research purposes, the TPITOS can be used to assess fidelity to Pyramid Model practices alone or as part of a pre/post intervention implementation evaluation.

DEVELOPMENT. The Pyramid Model (Hemmeter, Ostrosky, & Fox, 2006) is based on empirical evidence of teaching practices that promote early social-emotional competence and discourage challenging behaviors. The framework is based on three progressive intervention tiers or, a multi-tiered system of supports: universal promotion, secondary prevention, and tertiary intervention. Because the structure and rating system of the TPITOS and TPOT are so similar, they can be used in combination, with TPITOS used in classrooms for children ages birth to 3 and TPOT used in classrooms for children ages 3-5. Compared to the TPOT, TPITOS differs in three key aspects: (1) the teachers being evaluated must work with children between birth and 36 months of age; (2) the sole focus is on the practices that promote "nurturing and responsive caregiving relationships and high quality, supportive environments" (manual, p. 1) at the universal rather than secondary or tertiary levels of the Pyramid Model; and (3) the items align with recommendations of infant-toddler care practices from the Division of Early Childhood and infant-toddler modules developed by the Center on the Social and Emotional Foundations for Early Learning.

A prototype of TPITOS underwent field testing and iterative revisions through a national collaborative network of infant-toddler professionals, including coaches, supervisors, program administrators, and researchers. However, the manual does not provide specific references related to the testing or implementation of the prototype TPITOS. The manual also does not address how indicators in the TPITOS compare with those in other measures of infant-toddler care quality such as the Infant/Toddler Environment Rating Scale, the Quality of Caregiver–Child Interactions for Infants and Toddlers (Q-CCIIT), the Classroom Assessment Scoring System (CLASS Infant and CLASS Toddler), or state-level Quality Rating and Improvement Systems.

TECHNICAL. No information is provided in the TPITOS manual on the samples that were used to refine and test the final version of this measurement. The only reliability measure mentioned in the manual is the interrater reliability that training participants must reach to be certified in using the TPITOS. On the second day of training, after watching one 2-hour classroom observation followed by a teacher interview, participants must achieve at least 80% interobserver agreement with a master coder. Although there are published studies evaluating the validity of the TPOT, there are no such studies for the TPITOS.

COMMENTARY AND SUMMARY. The TPITOS is a classroom observation measure that fills a unique niche in the early childhood field. However, the measure's uniqueness also may be viewed as a weakness in that it is tied to a specific intervention strategy and conceptual model used during teaching practices with infants and toddlers. If teachers have not been explicitly trained in this model, then the measure would not be a valid or useful assessment of their teaching practices. Several training options are available for those interested in using the Pyramid Model. Practitioners such as administrators, coaches, supervisors, and teachers who are learning to implement the model can access training both online and in person. Those who want to use the TPITOS for research or evaluation purposes must attend in-person reliability training. Both types of trainings have associated fees, but there are free webinars available that provide basic information about the model and its importance.

The TPITOS manual and accompanying score sheets provide clear and detailed instructions for use, and the ability to rate behaviors across classroom activities (care routines, outside, free play, structured group) is a strength. The measure allows for the collection of data using multiple sources and methods (e.g., interviews, observations); however, scoring across these multiple data sources can be complicated.

The manual includes several useful features, such as (a) instructions for using spreadsheets (available on the test publisher's website) for entering scores, tracking progress, and creating graphic representations; (b) case studies that provide detailed examples of practice in the field; (c) appendices of abbreviations, indicators that may be scored *N/A* under specific circumstances, and criteria for indicators that measure frequency; (d) references to additional resources, websites, and readings related to the Pyramid Model; and (e) a frequently asked questions section that may address questions that remain after finishing the manual.

One limitation is that some behaviors that may not have been observed, namely specific strategies with dual language learners, can still be coded via interviews even if the teacher demonstrated no classroom practices related to this area. This lack of attention to the specific care and educational needs of dual language learners, as well as a neglect of culture overall, is a weakness of the measure. Some items, such as those that call for specific nonverbal facial expressions (e.g., smiling) or tone of voice to indicate the valence of one's emotions (smiling or tone of voice) may not function the same across cultures.

Given the specificity of the TPITOS to the Pyramid Model, these reviewers recommend using the measure only for those programs and teachers implementing this system. Educational and childcare programs that operate from conceptual frameworks and programmatic structures other than the Pyramid Model have additional options and may want to consider the Q-CCIIT (developed for the Administration for Children and Families, U.S. Department of Health and Human Services), the CLASS Infant, and the CLASS Toddler.

REVIEWERS' REFERENCES

Hemmeter, M. L., Fox, L., & Synder, P. S. (2014). Teaching Pyramid Observation Tool (TPOT™) for Preschool Classrooms, Research Edition. Baltimore, MD: Paul H. Brookes Publishing Co.

Hemmeter, M. L., Ostrosky, M., & Fox, L. (2006). Social and emotional foundations for early learning: A conceptual model for intervention. *School Psychology Review, 35*(4), 583-601.

Review of the Teaching Pyramid Infant-Toddler Observation Scale for Infant-Toddler Classrooms, Research Edition by LYNN SHELLEY, Professor and Chair, Department of Psychology, Westfield State University, Westfield, MA:

DESCRIPTION. The Teaching Pyramid Infant-Toddler Observation Scale for Infant-Toddler Classrooms, Research Edition (TPITOS; pronounced *tippy toes*) is an observational tool designed to assess the fidelity of implementation of practices associated with the Pyramid Model in infant-toddler care settings. The Pyramid Model proposes tiers of evidence-based practices that share the goals of promoting social-emotional competence of young children and of addressing challenging behaviors (Fox, Dunlap, Hemmeter, Joseph, & Strain, 2003). Tier 1 promotes the universal implementation of practices that foster high-quality, supportive environments and nurturing and responsive caregiving relationships. The TPITOS assesses implementation of this tier, specifically in infant-toddler group care settings.

The TPITOS determines the extent to which caregiver behaviors in the infant-toddler classroom are consistent or inconsistent with the model. It can be used once or repeatedly; thus, it can compare implementation of the model pre- and post-training. The measure also can be part of professional development or training that identifies strengths and weaknesses, it can be used sporadically to prevent drift from previously learned practices, and it can be used in program evaluation.

During a 2-hour observation period that should include multiple routines (free play, structured group activities, care routines, and outdoor activities), trained observers score 13 observation items, each with multiple indicators (78 total indicators). Items are broadly conceptualized, and indicators are behaviorally operationalized. Indicators are scored *yes, no,* or *not applicable* based on the observation. If there was no opportunity to observe certain indicators, questions are provided that can be asked after the observation during a 15-20 minute interview. There are also 11 Red Flags that are coded as present (*yes*) or absent (*no*). Red Flags are practices inconsistent with the Pyramid Model.

The TPITOS manual provides background information on the model and includes examples of how to use the measure for professional development. It also provides clear elaborations of definitions and scoring criteria. Scoring sheets are thorough, intuitive, and easy to follow. Indicators under the first seven items are scored across four possible routines (free play, structured group, care routines, and outdoors). The overall value for each indicator is the value given most frequently for that indicator. For example, if an indicator had yes for three routines and no for one routine, the overall value would be yes. The manual provides instructions about how to resolve ties, but trained observers' expert judgment is important in these instances. Yes responses for Red Flags are summed. Item scores are computed as the percentage of indicators scored yes. Scoring can be completed by hand or by using an Excel spreadsheet provided with the package. The spreadsheets aid tremendously in summarizing the data and provide useful graphs and summary information (for a single teacher, multiple teachers, classrooms, and across assessments). The total amount of time required for scoring is 30-45 minutes.

It is highly recommended that only certified TPITOS assessors use the instrument. Certification includes completing reliability training and obtaining 80% agreement with master TPITOS coders. Training typically involves attendance at a 2-day workshop, and it is recommended that certification be renewed on a regular basis.

DEVELOPMENT. The TPITOS is part of a framework that promotes empirically supported practices that aid social-emotional competence and address challenging behavior during early childhood. The Pyramid Model has previously been implemented in classrooms with children ages 2 to 5 years; the Teaching Pyramid Observation Tool (TPOT; Hemmeter, Fox, & Snyder, 2014; 20:173) has been used to assess the fidelity of adherence to the model in preschool classrooms and to provide feedback to teachers and program administrators. The TPITOS is designed for early childhood educators working with children from birth to 3 years old, and the items focus solely on nurturing and responsive caregiving relationships and high-quality supportive environments. The manual provides an extensive description of the theoretical foundation for the scale, but this research edition provides little to no information about the development of the instrument beyond one paragraph stating that it underwent significant field testing over a period of years (manual, p. 8).

TECHNICAL. Given the experience of the instrument developers, the impressive work done to develop the Pyramid Model, the years of work by the National Center for Pyramid Model Innovations, and the thoroughness of the use and scoring sections of the TPITOS manual, the manual is surprisingly sparse with respect to addressing the *Standards for Educational and Psychological Testing* (American Educational Research Association, American Psychological Association, & National Council on Measurement in Education, 2014). No information is provided about the psychometric properties of the instrument. Other than a recommendation that users of the instrument achieve a certain level of interrater reliability, no other forms of reliability are mentioned in the manual, nor is there evidence that the reliability of the instrument was explored or that validity studies were conducted. Because this is a research edition of the instrument, it is expected that this limitation will be addressed. A description of the development and psychometric properties of the TPOT exists (Snyder, Hemmeter, Fox, Bishop, & Miller, 2013); thus, it is hoped similar studies will be planned for the TPITOS. For now, important unanswered questions remain.

COMMENTARY. There are several strengths and unique features of the TPITOS, Research Edition. The Pyramid Model framework in which the TPITOS is situated has a strong basis in theory and promotes evidence-based practices. The objectives of the model are clearly defined, attainable, and easily measured. This model can build a common language among teachers, and the Red Flags are a valuable way to highlight teacher behaviors that require immediate attention. The scoring sheet and user's manual are clear and user friendly, the time necessary for each assessment is reasonable (about 2.5 hours), the information yielded is easy to understand and use, and the developers offer extensive support for practitioners on the Pyramid Model website. Additionally, the instrument has multiple uses ranging from professional development to program evaluation.

The TPITOS also has a unique relationship to the TPOT. There is evidence to suggest training in the Pyramid Model can effectively change teachers' behavior with preschool children and that those changes can be maintained, as determined by the TPOT (Hemmeter, Hardy, Schnitz, Adams, & Kinder, 2015). However, the degree to which those classroom behaviors translate into changes in children's functioning has yet to be demonstrated, as does evidence that the same findings would be made using the TPITOS with teachers in classrooms for younger children. Thus, although the Pyramid Model and practices recommended are undoubtedly empirically based, the next step in research—examining the longitudinal effectiveness of this program—has yet to be done.

The TPITOS developers strongly recommended that users of the measure become certified to use the scale. Although the manual is clear and easy to use, quality observations and accurate scoring are the bedrock of this instrument. There are tremendous subtleties in infant and toddler behaviors, and often there are no opportunities to observe a behavior or there are several opportunities observed with different reactions all in one observation period. Reliably managing the unpredictability of such situations is paramount to the utility of TPITOS scores. Certification programs are offered at a reasonable price and on a fairly regular schedule. The manual states that certified users are not qualified to train others. Thus, districts with small budgets or those in rural areas may find getting individuals trained to be challenging. Additionally, although the TPITOS is available through its publisher for a very reasonable price, it is also available online from several mass market merchants, thereby sending a mixed message about who should have access to and use the instrument.

SUMMARY. The Pyramid Model for Promoting Social Emotional Competence in Infants and Young Children and the framework that includes the TPITOS is an up-to-date model that encompasses appropriate objectives. It includes training and establishing systems and policies that will decrease disparities in discipline, promote family engagement, promote inclusion, and, most importantly, encourage data-driven decisions. The TPITOS has the potential to be an excellent tool for determining fidelity to the practices the model proposes. However, at this time, using the TPITOS, Research Edition implies acceptance of and faith in an instrument with no evidence provided that demonstrates validity or reliability. This is an exciting instrument that stands to be the leader in the field. It is important to recognize that this research edition still needs more research; yet, any tool for use with infant and toddler teachers with an acronym pronounced *tippy toes* was clearly developed by creative individuals and thus deserves a chance.

REVIEWER'S REFERENCES

American Educational Research Association, American Psychological Association, & National Council on Measurement in Education. (2014). *Standards for educational and psychological testing*. Washington, DC: American Educational Research Association.

Fox, L., Dunlap, G., Hemmeter, M. L., Joseph, G. E., & Strain, P. S. (2003). The Teaching Pyramid: A model for supporting social competence and preventing challenging behavior in young children. *Young Children, 58*(4), 48–52.

Hemmeter, M. L., Fox, L., & Snyder, P. (2014). *Teaching Pyramid Observation Tool (TPOT™) for Preschool Classrooms, Research Edition manual.* Baltimore, MD: Paul H. Brookes Publishing Co.

Hemmeter, M. L., Hardy, J. K., Schnitz, A. G., Adams, J. M., & Kinder, K. A. (2015). Effects of Training and Coaching with Performance Feedback on Teachers' Use of "Pyramid Model" Practices. *Topics in Early Childhood Special Education, 35*(3), 144-156.

Snyder, P. A., Hemmeter, M. L., Fox, L., Bishop, C. C., & Miller, M. D. (2013). Developing and Gathering Psychometric Evidence for a Fidelity Instrument: The Teaching Pyramid Observation Tool–Pilot Version. *Journal of Early Intervention, 35*(2), 150–172.

[167]

Test of Adolescent/Adult Word Finding–Second Edition.

Purpose: Designed as a "diagnostic tool for assessing word finding skills."

Population: Ages 12-80.

Publication Dates: 1989-2016.

Acronym: TAWF-2.

Score: Total score only.
Administration: Individual.
Forms, 2: Complete, Brief.
Price Data, 2020: $405 per complete kit including examiner's manual (2016, 157 pages), Word Finding Assessment Picture Book, Comprehension Check Picture Book, and 25 record forms; $84 per manual; $138 per Word Finding Assessment Picture Book; $121 per Comprehension Check Picture Book; $62 per 25 record booklets.
Time: 20-30 minutes for administration of Complete Test; 10-15 minutes for Brief Test.
Comments: "Both the Complete Test and the Brief Test consist of two assessment components: the standardized assessment and the informal assessment."
Author: Diane J. German.
Publisher: PRO-ED.
Cross References: See T5:2667 (1 reference); for reviews by Ronald B. Gillam and Richard E. Harding of the original edition, see 12:391.

Review of the Test of Adolescent/Adult Word Finding–Second Edition by KATHLEEN D. ALLEN, Professor of Education and Counseling Psychology, Saint Martin's University, Lacey, WA:

DESCRIPTION. The Test of Adolescent/Adult Word Finding–Second Edition (TAWF-2) is designed to assess the word finding ability of examinees ages 12 to 80. This assessment may be administered as a Complete Test (80 items) or a Brief Test (28 items). Five sections comprise both versions of the test: (a) Picture Naming: Nouns, (b) Sentence Completion Naming, (c) Picture Naming: Verbs, (d) Picture Naming: Word Groups, and (e) Comprehension Check. According to the examiner's manual, the formal and informal data from the TAWF-2 can be used in diagnosing word finding difficulties for people with learning, speech, reading, or memory impairments and support the development of individualized and targeted interventions.

The TAWF-2 kit contains the Comprehension Check Picture Book, Word Finding Assessment Picture Book, examiner record booklets, and an Examiner's Manual. The examiner's manual provides testing environment requirements and basic testing guidelines as well as detailed instructions for the standardized and informal sections of the test. The complete battery of tests (formal and informal) requires 20 to 30 minutes to administer. The Brief Test requires 10 to 15 minutes. All tests are individually administered using the picture books for oral prompts and directions. Raw scores are recorded in the examiner record booklet. The total raw score for the naming portion is converted to an index score (the Word Finding Index) and an associated percentile rank using tables in the examiner's manual. The Comprehension Check raw score is compared to a benchmark score to determine whether the examinee actually knows the words that could not be named. If the raw score is less than the benchmark score, the examiner administers the informal assessments instead of calculating the Word Finding Index. Formal training on the TAWF-2 is not required for administration and scoring, but the test author suggests that the examiner have experience in speech-language or psychoeducational assessment.

DEVELOPMENT.

Theoretical framework. According to the psycholinguistic research presented in the examiner's manual, the process of single word finding occurs at three levels. First, conceptual repository is the long-term memory retrieval of all of the word's attributes (category, function, location, and perception). Second, lexical representation is the long-term memory retrieval of the word's semantic (meaning), syntactic (grammar), morphological (word structures), and phonological (speech sound units) features. Third, speech motor program is the ability to formulate a mental plan for articulation and then to pronounce the word correctly (Rapp & Goldrick, 2006; Roelofs, 2000). In the TAWF-2, the ability to recall an already known word is assessed with different word recall contexts (Picture Naming and Sentence Completion) and forms (Picture Naming: Nouns, Picture Naming: Verbs, and Picture Naming: Word Groups). The failure to efficiently recall an already known word usually stems from either (a) the inability to recall the semantic and syntactic features (lexical representation) that correspond to the word's attributes (conceptual repository) or (b) the inability to recall the word's morphological and/or phonological features (lexical representation). This inability can occur for various reasons, such as having inefficient long-term memory retrieval or an insufficient vocabulary. To analyze the reason for word recall failure, TAWF-2 includes informal assessments and the Comprehension Check. Data are collected on phonemic cueing, word substitutions, error patterns, delayed response time, gestures, extraneous verbalizations, and articulation.

Task development. The Test of Adolescent/Adult Word Finding (TAWF; 1990) was designed using the Rasch latent trait test construction model (Wright & Stone, 1979) to compare an examinee's vocabulary knowledge with their ability to efficiently retrieve words from their long-term memory as measured by speed and accuracy. The TAWF-2 was created to improve the test's administration, to add new information for validity and interpretation of data, and to update the normative sample and theoretical model.

TECHNICAL.

Standardization. The norming sample for the TAWF-2 comprised 1,710 examinees between the ages of 12 and 80 years from 28 U.S. states and four geographic regions of the United States. The stratification of the sample by region, gender, race, Hispanic status, exceptionality status, educational attainment, and household income reflects the statistical percentages as reported by the U.S. Census Bureau in 2011.

Reliability. Internal consistency reliability is calculated with coefficient alpha using the entire norming sample divided into 10 age intervals for the Complete Test and the Brief Test (the normative sample consists of 11 age groups; ages 18 and 19 are combined for the reliability analyses). The resulting reliability coefficients for the Complete Test (.85-.91) and for the Brief Test (.67-.81) indicate an acceptable level of consistency among test items. The internal consistency reliability coefficient is also calculated on the selected demographics of race and gender. These coefficients (.79-.91 for the Complete and Brief tests) also indicate acceptable reliability. Test-retest reliability was estimated using 58 participants (27 school age and 31 adults) in Illinois and Texas. Specific characteristics of gender, race, Hispanic status, and exceptionality of the sample population are provided. In the 2-week test-retest study, baseline scores for the combined sample for the Complete Test (M = 102, SD = 14) and Brief Test (M = 103, SD = 14) were compared to subsequent scores for the Complete Test (M = 112, SD = 11) and the Brief Test (M = 108, SD = 10). Resulting correlation coefficients (Complete Test corrected r = .95, Brief Test corrected r = .94) were very strong. For interscorer reliability, 50 tests were selected at random from the standardization sample and scored by two trained staff members from the test publishing company. The correlation of the resulting scores (.99) signifies high agreement.

Validity. Content evidence of validity of the TAWF-2 is provided through the citation of research and theory support for selection of the words, utilizing pictures and words as a stimulus for single word retrieval, using speed as measurement, and the informal assessments (delayed responses, phonemic cueing, imitation, substitution analysis, and secondary behavioral characteristics). In addition, quantitative item analyses using the norming sample provides effectual data on item discrimination, item difficulty, and item bias. To provide criterion-related evidence of validity, scores from the TAWF-2 were correlated with scores from the first edition of the TAWF and three other assessments that measure the criteria of expressive vocabulary and word association. The resulting coefficients (.47-.85) for the Brief and Completes tests indicate a moderate to very large magnitude of correlation. A binary classification analysis of the test's sensitivity and specificity to determine whether examinees are at risk for word finding difficulties yielded evidence of predictive validity (Complete Test = .82, Brief Test = .84 classification accuracy). To provide construct-related evidence of validity, the test author analyzed score differences between examinees with and without word-finding difficulties, studied the relationship between Complete Test scores and Brief Test scores, and conducted a factor analysis (item-total correlations) and item total correlations.

COMMENTARY. The theoretical base of the TAWF-2 aligns well with current psycholinguistic research on lexical knowledge and memory, which substantiates its construct evidence of validity. This test also has criterion, content, and predictive evidence of validity. Internal consistency, test-retest, and interscorer reliability are thoroughly analyzed using the norming sample, which reflects current statistical percentages and includes stratification of relevant population characteristics. Information in the examiner's manual clearly states that enough data are gathered to aid in an initial diagnosis of word-finding impairment and to help determine whether the reason is situated in the lexical or cognitive realm. Quantitative assessment helps to determine whether an examinee has a word-finding impairment, and qualitative assessments allow the examiner to help determine the reason for word-recall failure. The use of both qualitative and quantitative measures adds to the test's value as a diagnostic tool. Because the purpose of the TAWF-2 is to assist in diagnostic assessment, it does not provide sufficient data to generate a targeted specific individualized intervention plan.

SUMMARY. The TAWF-2 has a sound research base relating both to the theoretical construct and its test design. The test author provides thorough evidence of reliability and validity. The use of both quantitative and qualitative assessment allows for identification of examinees experiencing word-finding difficulties and analysis of possible reasons for this impairment. Resulting data can provide an initial goal for intervention, but are only marginally useful for designing a specifically targeted plan. However, this limitation does not diminish the power of the TAWF-2 as an excellent diagnostic tool for word finding and the technical soundness of this test.

REVIEWER'S REFERENCES

Rapp, B., & Goldrick, M. (2006). Speaking words: Contributions of cognitive neuropsychological research. *Cognitive Neuropsychology, 23*(1), 39-73.

Roelofs, A. (2000). WEAVER++ and other computational models of lemma retrieval and word-form encoding. In L. Wheeldon (Ed.), *Aspects of language production* (pp. 71-114). New York, NY: Psychology Press.

Wright, B. D., & Stone, M. H. (1979). *Best test design.* Chicago, IL: MESA Press.

Review of the Test of Adolescent/Adult Word Finding–Second Edition by MONICA GORDON-PERSHEY, Associate Professor, School of Health Sciences, Cleveland State University, Cleveland, OH:

DESCRIPTION. The Test of Adolescent/Adult Word Finding–Second Edition (TAWF-2) is an individually administered assessment of word-finding skills intended for use by speech-language pathologists and similar professionals to test adolescents and adults ages 12 to 80 years. Word finding is familiar to many people as the "tip of the tongue" phenomenon: a speaker has a word in mind, but cannot recall or say the word instantaneously. This problem becomes an indicator of a language disorder when it occurs frequently, is difficult to self-correct, and/or impairs one's ability to communicate. Word finding deficits are common in aphasia, dementia, specific learning disabilities, and attention-deficit disorders.

The TAWF-2 consists of 80 standardized items within four subtests: Picture Naming: Nouns (24 items, naming a single picture of commonplace items); Sentence Completion Naming (13 items, filling in a blank, e.g., Dogs can dig using their _____); Picture Naming: Verbs (19 items, naming the action pictured using the present progressive tense, e.g., "climbing" steps, and past tense, e.g., "climbed"); and Picture Naming: Word Groups (24 items, naming items in a group). The standardized Comprehension Check verifies that errors did not occur due to lack of word comprehension.

A standardized 28-item Brief Test is included for use when a shorter test is advantageous. Examiners record test performance using a handwritten scoring booklet. The Complete Test takes 20 to 30 minutes, and the Brief Test takes 10 to 15 minutes.

Five informal assessments assist in diagnosis: (a) phonemic cueing determines whether word finding can be stimulated when the examiner says the first sound of a target word; (b) substitution analysis explores whether an error affects a semantic or a phonemic property of the word; (c) imitation reveals examinees' ability to repeat words spoken by the examiner; (d) secondary-characteristic analyses explore whether examinees gesture or verbalize awareness of their deficits; (e) delayed response records when examinees take 4 or more seconds to respond.

Scoring entails awarding one point for each correct response produced in less than 4 seconds. A scoring guide offers some alternative responses for some of the items. If an examinee says "uh" or "um" or another filler word and then produces a correct response, the response is scored as incorrect. Self-corrections also are scored as incorrect.

Performance is compared to a standardization sample for 11 age ranges (in 1-year increments from 12-19 years and then ages 20-39, 40-59, and 60-80). Raw scores for the complete test are converted into percentile ranks and a Word Finding Index based on accuracy and speed that ranges from less than 70 to greater than 129. The index has seven descriptive levels, from *very strong* to *very weak*. Index scores below 90 are in the bottom 25% and indicate a word-finding problem. Subtest scores are not interpreted separately.

The examiner's manual provides approximately 20 pages of explanatory material for interpreting performance on the five informal assessments. A flowchart depicts how to use error patterns to differentially diagnose types of word-finding deficits.

DEVELOPMENT. The TAWF-2 is a revision of the National College of Education Test of Adolescent/Adult Word Finding (German, 1990). The TAWF-2 is based upon a theoretical model of word retrieval that postulates three sequential skills of cognitive, linguistic, and motor performance: (1) the conceptual repository, (2) lexical representations of words, and (3) speech motor programming.

The conceptual repository represents the long-term memory storage of concepts associated with a word. Speakers mentally represent items, actions, and conceptual properties (for example, the perceptual attributes of what an item looks like). These concepts activate a word's lexical features: its lemma and lexeme. The word's lemma includes its semantic and syntactic features, and the word's lexeme includes its morphological and phonological features. The lemma and lexeme trigger the mental construction of a motor plan for articulating the word, and the plan is then carried out by moving the physical structures that produce speech. When this process occurs without interruption, a speaker can find words with accuracy and efficiency.

The theoretical model of word-finding errors proposes three error types. The first type is failure to access the lemma, although the conceptual repository is activated. Sometimes a word with similar meaning is produced, such as "music" for "tune." The second type is when the lexeme cannot be found, and the speaker may say something like "I don't have the word right now." The third type is when an unintended lexeme is produced, as in "string" instead of "spring," or a partial or inaccurate lexeme is spoken, as in "bocuers" for "binoculars."

TECHNICAL. The TAWF-2 was standardized using a sample of 1,710 persons from 28 states, ages 12 to 80 years. Stratified sampling reflected the 2011 U.S. Census regarding geographic region, gender, race, Hispanic status, exceptionality status, education, and income.

The examiner's manual reports various indices for the entire normative sample and various age ranges. Average coefficient alpha values across age groups for internal consistency were .88 for the Complete Test and .76 for the Brief Test. Alphas for racial and gender subgroups ranged from .79 to .91. The standard errors of measurement (*SEM*), which are used to determine confidence intervals for the Word Finding Index per age range, were 5 or 6 for the Complete Test and 7, 8, or 9 for the Brief Test. Test-retest reliability over a 2-week period for 27 examinees under age 18 was .98 for the Complete Test and .93 for the Brief Test; for 31 examinees ages 18 and over coefficients were .94 for the Complete Test and .96 for the Brief Test. To obtain interscorer reliability, two staff members employed by the test publisher scored 50 randomly selected protocols with a reliability coefficient of .99.

Content evidence of validity was based upon prior research that employed naming tasks to demonstrate word finding. Target words were selected based on the frequency of use and their semantic categories (sports, fruits, vegetables, instruments, animals, body parts) and had from two to 10 phonemes and one to four syllables. The criterion that naming must occur in under 4 seconds was suggested by past studies. The informal analyses emanated from research on clinical practices.

The TAWF-2 item analysis yielded point-biserial correlations for the scores for each age range to determine each item's discriminating power, with .20 being the typical minimum satisfactory correlation. The median discriminating power over all ages for the Complete Test was .27, and .29 for the Brief Test (due to the smaller number of items). The range of item difficulty values, as identified by the number of examinees who passed an item, is generally acceptable at 15-85%. The median difficulty for the Complete Test was 85%, and 82% for the Brief Test. Item analysis methods were applied to a pool of 327 items, based upon the performance of a group of 233 typical examinees and nine examinees with word-finding deficits. The results of these analyses resulted in reducing the pool to 100. Performance of the standardization sample identified 20 items with lower comprehensibility, familiarity, culture and gender fairness, and discriminatory ability. The 80 remaining items were assessed for racial or gender bias using logistic regression models.

To establish criterion-related evidence of validity, three other standardized naming tests were given to 25 to 99 members of the standardization sample. These scores correlated with the Word Finding Index at .47 to .85.

Sensitivity and specificity of the test were discerned by applying receiver operating characteristics/area under the curve analyses, yielding a sensitivity index of .93 and a specificity index of .82. Construct-related evidence of validity for word finding was explored through a factor analysis, with a single factor accounting for .70 of the variance.

COMMENTARY. The critical factor in diagnosing a deficit in word finding is the accurate identification of this deficit as opposed to some other deficit(s). The theoretical model appears adequate for explaining how a speaker may fail to retrieve a word. However, questions arise about how well the construct of word finding can be directly evidenced by skill in naming. The test does not explore the word finding problems that occur in the context of daily communication.

Moreover, false positives are possible when a speaker is penalized for saying "um" before speaking. This interjection may not always signify word finding, as it could arise from speech disfluency, shyness, slower processing time, unfamiliarity, deliberation, or mere habit. Scoring self-corrections as errors might also defeat the purpose of testing for functional word-finding skills because in daily living, a self-corrected response can be functional.

Measurement accuracy is a concern. The *SEM* and the confidence intervals for the Brief Test could reduce the score accuracy by almost one-third.

SUMMARY. The TAWF-2 may assist in determining an individual's word-finding skills and potential for interventions. The informal analyses provide information that may guide therapy targets, such as increasing naming speed, responding to phonemic cues, or imitating target words. The test is applicable to diverse clinical populations and is useful for differentiating semantic versus phonemic paraphasic errors.

REVIEWER'S REFERENCE

German, D. J. (1990). National College of Education Test of Adolescent/Adult Word Finding. Austin, TX: PRO-ED.

[168]

Test of Early Language Development–Fourth Edition.

Purpose: Designed "to identify children who have oral language problems and determine the degree of their problems."
Population: Ages 3-0 to 7-11.
Publication Dates: 1981-2018.
Acronym: TELD-4.
Scores, 3: Receptive Language, Expressive Language, Spoken Language Index.
Administration: Individual.
Forms, 2: A, B.
Price Data, 2020: $434 per kit including manual (2018, 142 pages), picture book for Forms A and B, 25 Form A record booklets, 25 Form B record booklets, and access to online scoring software; $161 per picture book; $115 per manual; $79 per 25 record booklets (Form A or Form B).
Time: 15-40 minutes for administration, depending on child's age and ability.
Comments: Online scoring and reporting available.
Authors: Wayne P. Hresko, D. Kim Reid, and Donald D. Hammill.
Publisher: PRO-ED.
Cross References: For reviews by Sherwyn P. Morreale and Philip A. Backlund and by Hoi K. Suen of the third edition, see 14:388; see also T5:2680 (19 references) and T4:2749 (6 references); for reviews by Javaid Kaiser and David A. Shapiro of the second edition, see 12:393 (4 references); for reviews by Janice Arnold Dale and Elizabeth M. Prather of the original edition, see 9:1250 (1 reference).

Review of the Test of Early Language Development–Fourth Edition by TIFFANY L. HUTCHINS, Associate Professor, University of Vermont, Burlington, VT, and MICHAEL S. CANNIZZARO, Associate Professor, University of Vermont, Burlington, VT:

DESCRIPTION. The Test of Early Language Development–Fourth Edition (TELD-4) is intended as a brief and easily administered norm-referenced test to assess the oral language abilities of children ages 3 years 0 months to 7 years 11 months. According to the test authors, the TELD-4 can be used to identify children with oral language problems and to determine the degree of their difficulties, to qualify children for services, to identify language strengths and weaknesses, to monitor treatment progress, and to conduct research.

TELD-4 administration takes 15-40 minutes depending on the examinee's age and language proficiency. The test is divided into Receptive and Expressive Language subtests with alternate forms to allow for repeated measurement. The TELD-4 package contains an examiner's manual, a picture book, and a package of record booklets. The manual provides a description of the test's development, administration, and scoring as well as the standardization process. The picture book is an easel-style flip book of color illustrations that depict everyday objects and activities as well as people who represent a range of racial backgrounds. The record booklet is self-contained in that it captures the necessary identifying information about the examinee, provides space to record all scores, and includes all prompts and scoring instructions to facilitate administration.

The Receptive and Expressive Language subtests yield raw, age equivalent, percentile rank, and standard index scores (M = 100, SD = 15) as well as percentile ranks. Subtest index scores are summed to form a composite from which the Spoken Language Index standard score and a percentile rank are derived. Seven descriptive terms associated with variable performance are included to characterize the level of language function (i.e., *impaired or delayed, borderline impaired or delayed, below average, average, above average, superior, gifted or very advanced*).

DEVELOPMENT. Changes to the TELD-4 were based on formal and informal feedback from users of the previous version (TELD-3). Major purposes of the revision included adding items to eliminate floor and ceiling effects and inappropriate item gradients, collecting all new normative data that were representative of a U.S. sample, conducting new and rigorous studies of reliability and validity, assessing test items for bias, and including an online scoring feature to facilitate report generation.

TECHNICAL.

Standardization. The TELD-4 was standardized on a sample of 1,074 children (ages 3 years 0 months through 7 years 11 months) representing

32 states and 292 ZIP codes across the five major regions of the continental United States. Data for child age (in 1-year intervals) are stratified by region, child gender, race, Hispanic status, highest parental education level, and household income. These data conform to national expectations as reported in the *ProQuest Statistical Abstract of the United States 2016* (ProQuest, 2016). Whether children were exposed to more than one language in the home and whether children were speakers of African American Vernacular English (AAVE) is not reported. The standardization sample represented children vis-à-vis exceptionality status (e.g., gifted and talented, intellectual disability, developmental delay, speech/language impairment); each group comprised 1% to 6% of the sample.

Reliability. The TELD-4 was evaluated for several forms of reliability. Alpha coefficients for each age interval for the Receptive and Expressive Language subtests and the composite score ranged from .93 to .98, suggesting that items have a high degree of interrelatedness. A similar result was obtained for alpha coefficients for the selected subgroupings of gender, race/ethnicity, and exceptionality status, which was taken as evidence that "the TELD-4 is equally reliable for all the subgroups" and that the test "contains little or no bias relative to these groups" (manual, pp. 36-37). However, these conclusions are questionable. Not only is alpha affected by test length (the TELD-4 has a relatively large number of items) but also, when used in isolation, alpha is not an adequate measure of internal consistency or multidimensionality, and it does not inform questions about the reliability of a test to produce trustworthy data (e.g., Schmitt, 1996; Sijtsma, 2009).

Alternate forms concurrent reliability was evaluated for Forms A and B of the TELD-4 using a subsample (n = 312) that was similar to the standardization sample on all demographic variables. Pearson correlation coefficients, corrected for range effects, ranged from .81 to .92 (in a negatively skewed distribution of coefficients) suggesting a high degree of correspondence between the two forms of the test. Alternate forms predictive reliability was also evaluated. For these comparisons, Forms A and B were administered at two points in time. (Interval was approximately two weeks.) Corrected Pearson correlation coefficients ranged from .61 to .93 (in a negatively skewed distribution of coefficients), suggesting a relatively high degree of reliability.

Test-retest reliability was evaluated using two subsamples (one for Form A and one for Form B; total n = 82) that were similar to the standardization sample on all demographic variables. The test-retest interval was approximately two weeks. (Range and mean are not specified.) Pearson correlation coefficients for the Receptive and Expressive Language subtests and composite scores for the combined sample ranged from .86 to .91, suggesting good temporal stability.

Interscorer reliability was evaluated using two trained raters who independently scored 50 TELD-4 protocols drawn randomly from the normative sample. All correlation coefficients between the scores from the two raters were .99, indicating high agreement between two scorers who are calculating scores from previously administered protocols. No data are offered to evaluate the measure's inter-examiner or inter-administrator reliability, which would be helpful given that proper administration requires good familiarity with the testing procedures and the fact that some items on the TELD-4 can yield ambiguous data (described below).

Validity. Content evidence of validity can be evaluated theoretically and empirically. With regard to the former, the TELD-4 is intended to tap only the semantic and morphosyntactic receptive and expressive language domains. Within these domains, content was chosen that had been "used successfully to understand, to screen, and to instruct young children" (manual, p. 44). Yet, a brief description of how item content is relevant to the intended construct(s) and tied to the goals of the test would be helpful. Although some professionals will understand the goal of many TELD-4 items on their face, this is not true for all professionals or for all items. These reviewers recommend that each item be explicitly tethered to a construct (or subconstructs) so users can better judge the adequacy of the TELD-4's content coverage, relevance, and balance.

With regard to empirical demonstrations of content validity, the TELD-4 items were evaluated using item discrimination and item difficulty. All analyses yielded results that satisfy rigorous standards of psychometric assessment. TELD-4 floor, ceiling, and item gradients were also evaluated. The adequacy of the floors and ceilings were found to be excellent, and the item gradients were sensitive for detecting minor fluctuations in examinees' abilities.

Analyses of test bias were conducted to compare the performance of various groups of test takers. Differential item functioning analysis was conducted with the following groups: female versus male, Black/African American versus non-Black/African American, and Hispanic versus non-Hispanic. Other analyses compared mean scores of demographic subgroups (Black/African American, Asian/Pacific Islander, Hispanic) to those of White/non-Hispanic examinees. Results (including tests of statistical and clinical significance) yielded non-significant results or significant results that were trivial or small in magnitude. This led the test authors to conclude that TELD-4 scores possess "little or no bias" (p. 52) vis-à-vis gender and the categories of race/ethnicity that were explored.

Criterion-related evidence of validity was assessed by correlating TELD-4 scores with several established tests (or subtests) designed to assess receptive and expressive language. All Pearson correlation coefficients were in the moderate to high range (.50 to .85) with magnitudes described in the test manual as large or very large, results that would be expected if TELD-4 scores provide valid indicators of early receptive and expressive semantic and morphosyntactic development.

To examine identification accuracy, the test authors conducted analyses to explore the utility of various cut scores. According to the test manual, using cut scores as low as 85 and as high as 92, the TELD-4 meets or exceeds "the minimum standards for diagnostic accuracy for sensitivity and specificity (indexes ranged from .75 to .95 and from .59 to 1.00, respectively) and receiver operating characteristics/area under the curve values (range .80 to .99)" (p. 65). Although these results are highly encouraging, because the reported analyses collapsed across age, it is unknown whether classification accuracy is consistent across ages. Given the concern involving the use of a 1-year interval for a construct that develops rapidly in young children, identification accuracy by child age should be reported. In addition, the inclusion of children with oral-language problems in the normative sample may limit sensitivity because mild cases may be missed (Peña, Spaulding, & Plante, 2006).

Guided by the sound reasoning that receptive and expressive language abilities will increase in children with development, TELD-4 scores were correlated with age (again, using 1-year intervals). Pearson correlation coefficients for the receptive and expressive subtests for Forms A and B ranged from .63 to .70, which, in these reviewers' opinion, are smaller than expected and leave half or more of the variation in TELD-4 scores unexplained. The age interval of 1 year may be problematic, particularly for younger children for whom more rapid development (and more variation within the normal range of functioning) occurs. The test authors should consider conducting analyses using continuous age data, which should have the benefit of increasing sensitivity and identification accuracy.

Several contrasted groups comparisons were conducted to further explore construct evidence of validity. Differences were expected and observed when TELD-4 scores for typically developing children were compared to those for children with articulation disorder (presumably because articulation disorder often accompanies language disorder), children with learning disability, children with language impairment, children with developmental delay, and children with autism spectrum disorder. Finally, intercorrelated TELD-4 scores and TELD-4 scores correlated with measures of school achievement, reading ability, and intelligence provided additional evidence in support of construct validity.

COMMENTARY. As noted above, the content of the TELD-4 has fair face validity, but a brief description of how item content is relevant to the intended construct(s) and tied to the goals of the test would be helpful. Here, "content" also includes the nature of the stimulus materials, and it should be noted that performance on TELD-4 items is differentially affected by chance (e.g., many items require a dichotomous response, the number of distractors in the stimulus book vary by item as does the influence of processes of elimination), which also should be taken up in a broader description of content validity.

By accepted standards and guidelines, the statistical evidence in support of the TELD-4 is strong. Nevertheless, additional analyses should be conducted to address concerns related to inter-examiner reliability and identification accuracy. With regard to inter-examiner reliability, without more formal guidance than is currently provided, some items on the TELD-4 may yield ambiguous data (e.g., items that call for a narrative response) that may introduce undue inter-examiner error. With regard to identification accuracy, suggestions for a future revision include (1) reporting sensitivity and specificity by age, and (2) exploring ways to improve accuracy even more by removing children who have language disorders from the normative sample.

The new standardization sample is relatively large, and stratification of variables for all demographic factors provides compelling evidence for a representative sample. Because they are highly relevant to the construct of receptive and expressive language, demographic variables that could be added in a future revision include language exposure in the home (and bilingualism). The proportion of children who are speakers of AAVE should be reported along with recommended modifications for use with children with linguistically diverse backgrounds.

Finally, some TELD-4 items may not be fair indicators of receptive and expressive semantic and morphosyntactic development for children who have a motor impairment (because several items call for a motor response), a visual impairment (because several items require viewing the stimulus book), or pragmatic language deficits (because some items require non-literal interpretation of language and a sophisticated understanding of the pragmatics of the test-taking situation). Thus, these reviewers encourage the test developers to describe the limitations of the TELD-4 for use with certain populations and to develop standardized child-friendly instructions that explain what children are going to be asked to do and why they are being asked to do it.

SUMMARY. The changes to the TELD-4 reflect the test authors' goals for eliminating floor and ceiling effects and inappropriate item gradients, collecting new normative data to ensure the representativeness of the sample, and conducting a wide range of psychometric assessments. The test authors were highly successful in these endeavors. The strengths of the TELD-4 include its carefully constructed and representative normative sample and its generally strong psychometric support. The TELD-4 examiner's manual is well organized and accessible, and users will find the majority of test items easy to administer and score. Additional analyses are recommended to address questions about inter-examiner reliability and to strengthen claims for identification accuracy, especially for the youngest children for whom this test was designed. The TELD-4 can be recommended as a screen for receptive and expressive semantic and morphosyntactic development and as part of a more comprehensive assessment battery to aid in the identification of children with language disorders. Its use with children with motor impairment, visual impairment, or pragmatic deficits is questionable.

REVIEWERS' REFERENCES

Peña, E. D., Spaulding, T. J., & Plante, E. (2006). The composition of normative groups and diagnostic decision making: Shooting ourselves in the foot. *American Journal of Speech-Language Pathology, 15*, 247-254.

ProQuest. (2015). *ProQuest statistical abstract of the United States 2016: The national data book.* Bethesda, MD: Bernan.

Schmitt, N. (1996). Uses and abuses of coefficient alpha. *Psychological Assessment, 8*(4), 350-353.

Sijtsma, K. (2009). On the use, the misuse, and the very limited usefulness of Cronbach's alpha. *Psychometrika, 74*(1), 107-120.

Review of the Test of Early Language Development–Fourth Edition by ROSALIE MARDER UNTERMAN, Associate Professor/Clinical Director, Graduate Program Speech-Language Pathology, Touro College School of Health Sciences, Brooklyn, NY:

DESCRIPTION. The Test of Early Language Development–Fourth Edition (TELD-4) is an individually administered norm-referenced screening test that measures oral language proficiency of individuals ages 3-0 through 7-11. The test was designed to assess spoken language relating to language features, such as semantics, syntax, and morphology, as well as language systems in receptive and expressive groupings.

The TELD-4 materials include an examiner's manual, a picture book, and examiner record booklets for each form (A and B). Each form comprises two subtests. The Receptive Language subtest includes semantic and syntax/morphology items to assess children's understanding of spoken language. The Expressive Language subtest includes semantic and syntax/morphology items to assess knowledge generally thought to be important to children (name and age) as well as sentence repetition, responses to questions, and sentence-construction items. The estimated administration time is 15-40 minutes.

Subtest raw scores are converted to normative scores including age equivalents, percentile ranks, and index scores with a mean of 100 and standard deviation of 15. This allows the examiner to make comparisons between subtests. Subtest index scores are summed and converted to the Spoken Language Index and a percentile rank. Confidence intervals are provided for subtest and composite scores. Descriptive terms corresponding to the index scores range from *impaired or delayed* to *gifted or very advanced.*

DEVELOPMENT. The Test of Early Language Development (TELD) was published in 1981 and provided a quick and easily administered screening test for identifying a spoken (oral) language problem in young children. There have been three previous editions (1981, 1991, 1999). The structure of the test was changed substantially in the third edition. The purpose remained to provide a norm-referenced score for general language, but scores for the Receptive Language and Expressive Language subtests were added. Concerns were noted regarding adequate evaluation of children in the upper and lower age ranges; stratification of normative data by age, gender, geographic region, ethnicity and race; wording of test items; and clarification of instructions.

The TELD-4 was developed in 2018 and addressed concerns raised about previous editions. Items were added to eliminate floor and ceiling effects, new normative data were collected from a sample of more than 1,000 students ages 3 through 7, and the demographic characteristics of the sample were stratified by age to conform with the projected U.S. school-aged population for 2016. New studies were conducted for reliability, test bias, and criterion-prediction validity. Administration and scoring procedures were clarified.

TECHNICAL. As reported by the test authors, normative data were collected from a sample of 1,074 students ages 3-0 through 7-11 residing in 32 states and 292 ZIP codes. The sample data were weighted to ensure representativeness and to increase the size of underrepresented groups. Reported demographics included geographic region, gender, race, Hispanic status, exceptionality status, educational level of parents, and household income level. Examiners were professionals with qualifications in special education, psychology, or a related field; experience in test administration; and access to examinees.

Reliability was evaluated via coefficient alpha, alternate forms (immediate administration), test-retest, alternate forms (delayed administration), and scorer difference. Content sampling error (internal consistency reliability) was investigated using coefficient alpha. Five age intervals were used, and coefficients were averaged using Fisher's *z*-transformation technique. All coefficients for the subtests and the composite exceeded .90. Averaged across ages, the coefficient for the Spoken Language composite was .97 for both forms. Alternate forms (immediate administration) examined content sampling error. Index scores for Forms A and B were correlated at five age intervals, resulting in correlation coefficients ranging from .81 to .88 for Receptive Language and Expressive Language and from .87 to .92 for the Spoken Language composite. These results indicate strong alternate form reliability. Test-retest reliability was evaluated using two groups (ages 3-5 years [n = 49]; ages 6-7 years [n = 33]) and a retest interval of approximately two weeks. For the younger group, correlation coefficients were .87-.90 for the subtests and .92 for the composite on both forms. Coefficients for the older group were slightly lower, ranging from .80 to .85 for the subtests with composite coefficients of .90 and .81 for Forms A and B, respectively. Alternate forms (delayed administration) estimated test error relating to both content and time sampling using the same sample as that used for the test-retest analysis. Correlation coefficients for the combined sample were .66-.85 for the subtests and .81-.88 for the composite. Finally, scorer difference reliability was examined with resulting coefficients above .90.

Three types of evidence of validity were discussed: content-description, criterion-prediction, and construct-identification. Regarding content-description validity, many of the items on the TELD-4 had been on previous editions of the test, with additional items added at the lower and upper age ranges to eliminate floor and ceiling effects. Language tests and developmental inventories were used for rationale and choice of stimuli. Analyses of item discrimination and difficulty were used in choosing to retain test stimuli. Test floors were examined for accurate identification of individuals with very low ability, and analysis of composites indicated floors were adequate. Ceilings were examined for identification of individuals with very high ability, and it was found that composite ceilings were excellent. Item gradients were adequate because normative tables were smoothed so small changes in raw score did not result in larger changes in standard scores.

Criterion-prediction evidence derived from comparisons of the TELD-4 and five criterion measures: Bankson Expressive Language Test—Third Edition (BELT-3), Preschool Language Scale—Fifth Edition (PLS-5), Test for Auditory Comprehension of Language—Fourth Edition (TACL-4), Test of Expressive Language (TEXL), and Young Children's Achievement Test—Second Edition (YCAT-2). The corrected correlation coefficients ranged from .50 (large) to .85 (very large), supporting the idea that TELD-4 scores provide valid measures of spoken language. Additionally, the standard scores were similar to other tests of spoken language.

Construct-identification validity was assessed with a three-step procedure: identifying six constructs that could account for test performance, generating hypotheses on the basis of the constructs, and supporting the hypotheses with logical or empirical methods. Relationship with age was indicated with correlation coefficients of raw score means increasing with student age. Differences among groups were examined by comparing individuals with disabilities, such as intellectual impairment, with those without such disabilities, such as students enrolled in gifted programs. Expected differences were noted for the two groups; then specific subgroups were examined. Articulation disorder was examined with groups matched on age, race, ethnicity, and gender; spoken language ability was significantly lower than in the matched group. Students diagnosed with learning disabilities also scored lower on the TELD-4 than the control sample, consistent with results seen in other tests (TACL-4, TEXL). Students diagnosed with language impairments, developmental delay, and autism spectrum disorder also were compared with a matched non-impaired group; large effect sizes were observed for the subtests and the composite. Relationship to reading was examined by correlating TELD-4 scores with those from five reading assessments. Correlation coefficients between the TELD-4 Spoken Language Index and the index scores from the reading tests ranged from .52 to .71, providing evidence of construct-identification validity of the test scores. The test authors discussed the relationship to academic achievement and correlated TELD-4 scores with those from the YCAT-2, demonstrating relationships between TELD-4 scores and writing and spoken language.

Two studies were provided for analysis of test bias: differential item functioning analysis (item level) and subgroup performance (subtest and composite score levels). Items were analyzed and comparisons made for three groups (male vs. female, Black/African American vs. non-Black/ African American, and Hispanic vs. non-Hispanic). Three item comparisons were statistically significant at the .001 level, but they were further examined for content, and it was found that the differences were not meaningful, suggesting that the TELD-4 items had little or no systematic bias with regard to gender, race, or ethnicity.

COMMENTARY. The Test of Early Language Development—Fourth Edition (TELD-4) is a quick, easily administered screening test for identifying a spoken (oral) language problem. The examiner's manual is very detailed and clearly written. Instructions for the examiner are concise and clear regarding administration and scoring. Scoring can be completed manually or by using the test publisher's online scoring and reporting system (included with the kit). Administration time is not excessive, allowing relatively rapid assessment of skills. Scoring is not difficult and can be completed quickly. The TELD-4 provides four types of normative scores: age equivalents, percentile ranks, subtest index scores, and a composite index score. Age equivalents are referred to as spoken language ages, with raw score points as the basis for age equivalents.

Although described as an assessment of spoken language, one should consider that this instrument largely stresses grammar and vocabulary. It involves auditory memory and working memory but does not assess these specific skills. Aspects of spoken language such as phonology, relevant for students with language disorders, are not considered. It has been noted that care needs to be taken in test interpretation because there may be many factors contributing to a student's score. Considering the questions and vocabulary, the possibility of under-identification may exist.

SUMMARY. The TELD-4 is an individually administered norm-referenced screener of oral language proficiency. It is an easily administered instrument with clear instructions and interpretation information. Various aspects of language proficiency are assessed using Receptive and Expressive Language subtests that assess semantics, syntax, and morphology. Because this is a screening test, results would best be used as part of professional clinical observation and judgment.

[169]

Test of Early Reading Ability—Fourth Edition.

Purpose: Designed to help identify "children who have significant problems in reading development and to determine the degree of their problems."
Population: Ages 4-0 to 8-11.
Publication Dates: 1981-2018.
Acronym: TERA-4.
Scores, 4: Alphabet, Conventions, Meaning, General Reading Index.
Administration: Individual.
Forms, 2: A, B.
Price Data, 2020: $394 per complete kit including examiner's manual (2018, 128 pages), picture book, 25 examiner record forms for Form A, 25 examiner record forms for Form B, and reader; $97 per examiner's manual; $171 per picture book; $63 per 25 examiner record forms (Form A or Form B).
Time: 15-45 minutes for administration.
Comments: Online scoring available.
Authors: D. Kim Reid, Wayne P. Hresko, and Donald D. Hammill.
Publisher: PRO-ED.

Cross References: For reviews by Sharon H. deFur and Lisa F. Smith of the third edition, see 15:259; see T5:2682 (13 references) and T4:2751 (2 references); for reviews by Michael D. Beck and Robert W. Hiltonsmith of the second edition, see 11:429 (1 reference); for reviews by Isabel L. Beck and Janet A. Norris of the original edition, see 9:1253.

Review of the Test of Early Reading Ability—Fourth Edition by KAREN L. GISCHLAR, Associate Professor, and ALICIA GIALANELLA, Graduate Student, School Psychology Program, Rider University, Lawrenceville, NJ:

DESCRIPTION. The Test of Early Reading Ability—Fourth Edition (TERA-4) is designed to measure the reading ability of young children, particularly those in preschool to second grade (ages 4-0 through 8-11 years). An individually administered and norm-referenced test, the TERA-4 includes three subtests—Alphabet, Conventions, and Meaning—that combine to form a composite score, the General Reading Index. The Alphabet subtest measures the child's knowledge of letters, including the ability to distinguish between letters and non-letters; recognize letters in different fonts; associate letters with speech sounds; identify initial and final sounds in printed words; count sounds and syllables in printed words; and read pseudowords. The Conventions subtest assesses the child's familiarity with common orthographic rules, such as book handling skills and knowledge of pictographs, logograms, numerals, symbols, and punctuation marks. Finally, the Meaning subtest is a measure of the child's ability to name letters of the alphabet, read basic sight words, and comprehend print.

The TERA-4 can be used for a number of purposes, including: (a) to identify children with reading problems and to determine the degree of those problems, (b) to recognize a child's reading strengths and weaknesses, (c) to help qualify children for special interventions, (d) to monitor progress within intervention programs, (e) to serve as a research measure, and (f) to accompany other assessment techniques in a comprehensive evaluation. The test authors caution that the TERA-4 should not be used solely in instructional decision-making and planning. Rather, the test should be used in conjunction with criterion-referenced tests, authentic assessment, direct observation, and informal surveys.

The test is appropriate for children who primarily speak American English and should be given only by those who have received some formal training in assessment administration, scoring, and interpretation. Testing time ranges from 15 minutes to approximately 45 minutes, depending on the number of breaks a child requires and the entry points used. For all three subtests, the basal and ceiling rules are three consecutive items correct and three consecutive items incorrect, respectively. One point is recorded for each correct response, and a zero is recorded for each incorrect response. The evaluator should encourage the child to progress fairly rapidly through the test; extra time may be allotted for children who are slow to produce responses. If a child fails to respond within 15 seconds of the presentation of an item, a response should be encouraged. If no response is forthcoming, the item should be scored as incorrect.

Once the TERA-4 has been administered, the examiner should convert raw scores to standard scores. This can be accomplished either by using the tables in the test manual, or by using the optional online scoring system. Once standard scores have been derived, the examiner can then use the tables or software to identify the corresponding normative scores, which include age equivalents and percentile ranks. Also included in the test manual are descriptive terms that correspond to the range of scaled scores (i.e., *impaired or delayed* to *gifted or very advanced*). The test authors note that the obtained results estimate a child's reading ability at a given time in a particular situation and that the clinician should gather information about the child beyond the TERA-4 scores prior to making a decision regarding instructional placement.

DEVELOPMENT. The TERA was developed in 1981 with updates in 1989, 2001, and most recently in 2018 with publication of the TERA-4. With each new edition, the test authors have collected new normative data, enhanced reliability and validity information through additional analyses, and made improvements to the test. Further, for each update, the authors have refined the measure to address critiques.

From the start, the TERA has been grounded in research that examines the development of reading skills in young children. As the authors note, in the early 1980s when the test was first published, researchers were only beginning to study how very young children learn to read. The TERA-4 incorporates more recent studies that examine the components of early reading, including those conducted by leaders in the field. Additionally, the authors have considered other instruments, instructional materials, and scope and sequence charts for early childhood, kindergarten, and first grade in the development of test items. A number of early childhood curricula were reviewed for content in constructing new items for the TERA-4.

The TERA-4 retains many of the items from earlier editions of the test, but additional items were added at the lower and upper age ranges to eliminate floor and ceiling effects. As the authors note, a test's standard scores must have adequate floors, ceilings, and item gradients to be clinically useful. All new items were checked for appropriate vocabulary syntax against published word lists and established developmental scales. Additionally, with the TERA-4, differential item functioning and subgroup performance analyses were conducted to detect possible biases at the item, subtest, and composite levels. Bias is said to exist when children from different gender or racial groups who have the same ability level perform differently on the same item. Results of the analyses revealed little to no systematic bias with regard to gender, race, or ethnicity.

With the TERA-4, an online scoring and reporting system was introduced. The online system offers a quick, efficient way to convert raw scores to standard scores, generate percentile ranks, identify intraindividual differences, and obtain a summary report. Furthermore, use of the software helps to reduce human error in applying basal and ceiling rules and in accurately calculating scores.

TECHNICAL. The TERA-4 was normed on a sample consisting of 1,025 children ages 4-0 through 8-11 years residing in 29 states and 271 ZIP codes. Testing was conducted from spring 2013 through fall 2015. The normative sample matched the percentages reported in *ProQuest Statistical Abstracts of the United States 2016* and the *Digest of Education Statistics 2015* on the characteristics of geographic region, gender, race, Hispanic status, exceptionality status, parental education, and household income. However, some groups were over- or under-represented in the initial data collection, so approximately 7% of the final TERA-4 normative data were weighted to ensure fair representation of diverse groups. A linking sample was used concurrently to norm the parallel Form B. All examinees were tested with Form A, and 350 participants were randomly chosen to take both TERA-4 forms. The linking sample demographics also approximated those of the U.S. population. Administration effects within the linking sample were controlled by counterbalancing the order of the test-form presentation.

Five types of reliability data are reported in the TERA-4 manual: internal consistency (coefficient alpha), alternate forms (immediate administration), test-retest, alternate forms (delayed administration), and scorer difference. Alpha coefficients were derived for five age intervals and were notably high, with the average subtest coefficients exceeding .90 and the average for the composite reaching .98 for both forms. Alternate-forms reliability (immediate administration) was calculated by giving both forms to a group of 350 children within one testing session, with half taking Form A first and the other half taking Form B first. Alternate-forms reliability coefficients across all ages were .80-.89 for subtests and .90-.96 for the General Reading Index, demonstrating high equivalency across forms. Test-retest reliability was investigated using two samples of children (N = 124) across 10 states with 2 weeks between testing sessions. Results were indicative of moderate to strong test-retest reliability, with results for subtests ranging from .80 to .98 when corrected for effects of range. All coefficients for the composite score exceeded .90. The same children who participated in the test-retest analyses were used to examine alternate-forms reliability (delayed administration). Results were lower on this index with coefficients for subtests ranging from .59 to .95 when corrected for range, although the reliability coefficients for the composite score were .88 or higher. Lastly, scorer difference was examined by having two members of the test publisher's research staff independently score 50 TERA-4 protocols randomly chosen from the normative sample. The scorings were correlated and results yielded high reliability, with coefficients above .90 for all subtest and index scores. Although this result provides evidence of interscorer agreement, additional raters and raters more typically found in practice, would have strengthened this finding.

The validity of TERA-4 scores as measures of young children's reading ability was investigated using three types of evidence: content-description, criterion-prediction, and construct-identification. Content-description evidence was demonstrated in four ways by the test authors. First, the rationale underlying the test's content and format was provided by citing previous editions of the test, established scales, and existing research. Second, the process of conventional item analysis used during test construction was described. Third, analyses of floors, ceilings, and item gradients were conducted. Finally, the process of identifying biased items was described in detail for selected demographic subgroups. The majority of the effect sizes in the bias studies were trivial, indicating that the items on the TERA-4 are likely a fair, representative set.

Next, a series of criterion-prediction studies was conducted by correlating scores from the TERA-4 with those from other measures of reading ability, including the Early Reading Assessment, Test of Silent Contextual Reading Fluency-Second Edition, Test of Silent Reading Efficiency and Comprehension, and Test of Silent Word Reading Fluency-Second Edition. Correlation coefficients were .74-.93 when corrected for restricted range, which are considered to be large and provide supportive evidence that the TERA-4 does, indeed, measure the construct of general reading ability. Additionally, the test authors explored the diagnostic accuracy of the TERA-4 by using various cutoff points that corresponded to cutoff scores used by school systems. A cut score of 92 was determined to maximize sensitivity and specificity.

Finally, construct-identification evidence was examined by first recognizing variables (e.g., age, learning disability in reading, language impairment) that may account for test performance. The test authors generated hypotheses (e.g., raw scores should increase with age) and verified them through empirical or logical methods. Results indicated that all hypotheses were supported. Through exploratory principal components analyses, the three subtests were shown to load onto a single factor, presumably general reading ability. Altogether, these reviewers believe the TERA-4 demonstrated evidence of validity as a measure of general reading ability. Therefore, it may be useful for the purpose of clinical assessment and diagnosis when used within the context of a comprehensive evaluation alongside other measures.

COMMENTARY. The TERA-4 appears to be easy to administer, score, and interpret. The test manual clearly explains how to determine entry points and basal and ceiling levels and provides sample protocols for illustration. Also included at the front of the manual is a bulleted list of basic testing procedures that should be helpful to the examiner. The directions for administration should be readily understood by trained professionals. All needed materials are included in the kit and are clearly marked as Form A or Form B. At the back of the manual are a protocol and interpretive report for an example student that should further guide the examiner in interpreting and reporting TERA-4 results.

Notably, the test authors have included criticisms of earlier editions of the test in the manual and explained how each updated version has addressed those concerns. The TERA-4 appears to include the most extensive reliability and validity studies to date, and it also demonstrates little to no bias with regard to gender, race, or ethnicity for items and subtests. The addition of the online scoring and reporting system reduces the chance of human error in converting scores and aids the examiner in interpretation.

The test authors should be commended for openly addressing criticisms of the TERA with each new edition. A recommendation for a future edition of the test is to omit the age equivalent scores. Although concerns about the use of these scores were raised by others reviewing past editions of the TERA, the test authors contend that they have no choice but to include them, given that most school districts require their use. However, age equivalent scores rarely add value to an evaluation of a child's skills and, often, add confusion. Age equivalent scores are not necessarily indicative of relative age-group development or performance but are often misinterpreted as if they are, which can be detrimental to children scoring at the extremes. Rather than feeling pressured to include these scores, the authors may want to consider using a new edition of the test as an opportunity to educate school professionals on the pitfalls of reporting them.

Additionally, the test authors note that one purpose of the TERA-4 is to "document children's progress in reading" (manual, p. vii). However, the test manual provides no direction for using the test as a progress monitoring tool. A new edition of the test should instruct the user how long to wait between test administrations and whether to use alternate forms in documenting the effectiveness of a reading program or intervention. Additionally, because it is important to conduct formative assessments while a child receives intervention, the authors may want to consider either including progress monitoring tools or pointing the examiner toward other quality measures published for this purpose.

SUMMARY. The TERA-4 demonstrates strong reliability and validity for its intended purpose. The test appears to be easy to administer and interpret and is a valuable tool to use as part of a comprehensive evaluation of a young child suspected of having a learning disability in reading. Users should be cautioned about the pitfalls of using age equivalent scores; rather, percentile ranks should be considered in decision making.

Review of the Test of Early Reading Ability—Fourth Edition by AMY N. SCOTT, Associate Professor in the Counseling and School Psychology Program, University of the Pacific, Stockton, CA:

DESCRIPTION. The Test of Early Reading Ability—Fourth Edition (TERA-4) is designed to assess the reading skills of children ages 4 through 8 years. There are two forms (Form A and Form B) that each have three subtests (Alphabet, Conventions, and Meaning). The three subtests are combined to yield an overall composite score, the General Reading Index. According to the test manual, total testing time takes 15-45 minutes. Items that are answered correctly are scored as "1," and items that are answered incorrectly or have no response within 15 seconds are scored "0." Suggested entry points are provided, and basal and ceiling rules are three correct items or three incorrect items, respectively, or until the first or last item of the test has been administered. The Conventions subtest has an additional administration rule in that all students ages 4-6 are administered Items 1-14, and basal and ceiling rules begin at Item 15. On this subtest, children older than 6 who do not achieve a basal at their entry point should be administered items in reverse until the child reaches Item 14. Then, if needed, Items 1-14 are administered in numerical order. The test authors encourage use of the online scoring and reporting system, as item level scores can be entered, and the scoring program checks for correct application of basal and ceiling rules. Alternatively, the test may be scored manually. The Examiner Record Booklet contains five sections: Identifying Information, Subtest Performance, Composite Performance, Descriptive Terms, and Record of Item Performance. Normative scores include age equivalents, percentile ranks, subtest scaled scores, and composite index score.

DEVELOPMENT. The Test of Early Reading Ability was originally developed in 1981. It was designed to examine three important skills that develop in young children: "learning the alphabet, discovering the arbitrary orthographic conventions used to read and write English, and finding meaning in print" (manual, p. vii). The authors' goal was to design a test that measured emergent reading skills; it was not their goal to assess phonological awareness or oral vocabulary, as there are other tests on the market more appropriate for assessing those skills. The current edition, the TERA-4, incorporated concerns and recommendations from previous reviews and test users along with the authors' ideas for continued improvement of the test, including a norm sample that is representative of the United States; "stringent" fidelity processes; studies on test bias, as well as floors, ceilings, and item gradients; more studies with larger samples to provide evidence of reliability and validity; and the ability to score the test manually or use an online scoring system.

TECHNICAL. The standardization sample consisted of 1,025 children ages 4 years 0 months to 8 years 11 months who were from 29 states and represented the nation on a variety of demographic levels as of 2016. The sample ranged from a low of 153 4-year-olds to a high of 241 6-year-olds.

Reliability was examined using coefficient alpha, alternate forms (immediate administration), test-retest, alternate forms (delayed administration), and scorer differences. Coefficient alpha ranged from a low of .88 to a high of .97 across the three subtests for each age level. The General Reading Index coefficient alpha ranged from .96 to .98 across age levels with an average of .98. The alternate-forms reliability (immediate administration) across the three subtests ranged from .80 to .89 at various ages with coefficients for the General Reading Index ranging from .90 to .96 across ages and averaging .92 for the total sample. Test-retest reliability was conducted after a 2-week interval using two samples, one ages 4-5 and the other ages 6-8 years. Test-retest reliability was not as strong at the subtest level for the 6- to 8-year-old group as it was for the group of 4- and 5-year-olds: average coefficients for subtests ranged from .89 to .97 in the younger group and from .83 to .85 in the older group. At both age levels, the General Reading Index was strong with a reliability coefficient of .96 for the younger sample and .94 for the older sample. Alternate forms reliability (delayed administration) was conducted with the same sample as the test-retest sample with Form A and Form B administered in counterbalanced order. Similar to the test-retest results, there were differences by age level. On average, the delayed administration was less reliable for the older group of children with coefficients ranging from .65 to .80 on the subtests compared to .82 to .95 for the younger children.

Overall, the alternate form reliability for the General Reading Index was .89 (older) and .93 (younger) with a coefficient of .91 for the combined sample. Interscorer reliability ranged from .96 to .99 when 50 randomly chosen forms were independently scored by two members of the test publisher's staff.

Three types of validity evidence are discussed in detail in the test manual: content description, criterion prediction, and construct identification. In terms of content, the authors provide qualitative information for how the TERA items have been historically identified, and they list specific tests that were reviewed for content prior to developing the fourth edition. A conventional item analysis was also conducted revealing acceptable item discrimination. Subtest and composite floors and ceilings were examined and determined to be more than adequate at all ages, except for the ceiling at the upper limit of the test (ages 8-9 to 8-11) in which the average subtest ceiling was poor. Item difficulty gradients were smoothed such that a single raw score point difference did not result in more than 1 scaled score point or 5 standard score points (one-third of a standard deviation) increase/decrease. Differential item functioning was examined for gender and ethnicity (White, Black/African American, Hispanic, Asian/Pacific Islander). The magnitude of the difference between groups was determined to be trivial across subtests and the composite with the exception of a small difference on the Meaning subtest where females outperformed males and White children outperformed Black/African American children.

The TERA-4 was correlated with other tests of reading to determine the criterion-prediction evidence of validity. The index scores for each test were compared to the TERA-4 General Reading Index and the results indicated "very large" or "nearly perfect" correlations, indicating that the tests appear to measure the same construct, which is assumed to be general reading ability. The test authors also conducted a diagnostic accuracy analysis revealing that a cut score of 92 on the composite score was predictive of diagnosing a learning disability.

In terms of construct identification validity, the raw scores increase as students become older. The authors also compared subtest and composite scores with selected subgroups of individuals with known exceptionalities and disabilities; correlations were in the expected direction. Additionally, the TERA-4 was correlated with measures of academic achievement, spoken language, and intelligence; the correlations were all in the expected direction. Subtest intercorrelations yielded coefficients of .60 to .71. Because each subtest is purported to measure different reading skills, a high correlation was not expected. A factor analysis revealed that items load on a single factor, providing evidence that the General Reading Index is a valid score.

COMMENTARY. The TERA-4 has continued to improve since its first version. Given the reliability and validity studies, as well as the authors' goal of developing a test to measure emergent reading skills, this test may be best for students ages 4-6 years. Although the Alphabet, Conventions, and Meaning subtests may be predictive of later reading difficulties, the test does not measure phonemic awareness, which is a skill highly predictive of reading difficulties in school-aged children. The TERA-4 is easy to administer and score. It is appropriate for preschool and early elementary school students who may need additional intervention in the area of reading, as it may help target skills not assessed by other tests. It is a measure that would easily accommodate a pre-test/post-test designed research study on emergent reading skills given that there are two forms of the test. Additional research should be conducted examining the cut score of 92 to predict a learning disability, as a standard score of 92 is within the average range, and some practitioners may have difficulty diagnosing a disability using a score within the average range.

SUMMARY. The TERA-4 is a measure designed to assess emergent reading skills for children ages 4-8 years. It is easy to administer and score. The test manual includes appropriate studies demonstrating improved reliability and validity over previous versions of the test.

[170]

Test of Gross Motor Development—Third Edition.

Purpose: Designed to "assess gross motor skill performance."
Population: Ages 3 through 10.
Publication Dates: 1985-2019.
Acronym: TGMD-3.
Scores, 3: Locomotor, Ball Skills, Gross Motor Index.
Administration: Individual.
Price Data, 2020: $150 per kit including 25 examiner record forms and examiner's manual (2019, 110 pages); $60 per 25 record forms; $90 per manual.
Time: 15-20 minutes for administration.
Comments: Examiner must supply equipment including several balls, a light plastic paddle, two cones or markers, a plastic bat, a batting tee, and tape.

Author: Dale A. Ulrich.
Publisher: PRO-ED.
Cross References: For reviews by Libby G. Cohen and G. Michael Poteat of the second edition, see 15:261; see T5:2689 (2 references) and T4:2762 (2 references); for reviews by Linda K. Bunker and Ron Edwards of the original edition, see 10:370.

Review of the Test of Gross Motor Development—Third Edition by ILYSE O'DESKY, Associate Professor and Clinical Neuropsychologist, and ZANDRA GRATZ, Professor of Psychology, Kean University, Cranford, NJ:

DESCRIPTION. The Test of Gross Motor Development—Third Edition (TGMD-3) is a norm-referenced measure of gross motor skills in children ages 3 years 0 months through 10 years 11 months. The test includes two subtests: Locomotor and Ball Skills. The Locomotor subtest evaluates skills involving balance and coordination of the entire body. Specific skills assessed within the Locomotor subtest include running, galloping, hopping, skipping, jumping to the side, and sliding. The Ball Skills subtest evaluates eye-hand and eye-foot coordination. Within the Ball Skills subtest, assessments include striking a ball by hand and with a paddle, dribbling with one hand, catching a ball with two hands, kicking a stationary ball, and throwing both overhand and underhand. Each of the 13 performance assessments has three to five behavioral components. Each behavioral component is scored 0 or 1, and each performance assessment requires two trials. Materials for assessments must be supplied by the examiner and include such things as a batting tee, traffic cones, and various size balls.

The test author lists five uses for the TGMD-3: identifying children whose gross motor development is behind their peers, planning instruction, assessing individual progress, evaluating programs, and supporting research. Although it is noted in the test manual that children may be tested individually or in small groups of two to four, it is difficult to envision being able to accurately score performance in a small group setting. Test administration time is estimated to be 15 to 20 minutes. Record forms provide clear descriptions and detailed instructions as to the materials/space required, directions for the examiner, and behavioral criteria by which to evaluate a child's performance. The manual further defines the criteria for each performance via text and picture and provides an example of how the TGMD-3 may be used in planning instruction. Raw scores on the subtests are converted to scaled scores, age equivalents, and percentile ranks. Subtest scores are combined to form a Gross Motor composite.

DEVELOPMENT. The original TGMD was published in 1985 and, as described in the test manual, was developed to identify specific aspects of movement and to offer, in addition to normative data, support for instructional planning. The TGMD was revised in response to comments (e.g., Bunker, 1989), and, as a result, the TGMD-2 (2000) had norms separated by gender and were considered a better representation of the population. Moreover, in response to practitioner feedback, some items were changed. Reactions of reviewers of the TGMD-2 were mixed (Cohen, 2003; Poteat, 2003). As noted by the test author, the current TGMD-3 was changed based on practitioners' and reviewers' comments to include greater attention to the development and interpretation of psychometric indicators as well as to modify specific items.

TECHNICAL. The normative sample included 100 to 126 children of each year of age from 3 to 10. Generally, the norm sample parallels that of the U.S. school-aged population. The exception to this statement concerns exceptionality status, where approximately 13% of the normative sample is so identified as compared to 34% nationally. The test author indicated that the norm sample was weighted in such a manner as to increase the representativeness of the sample and to increase the relative sample size of underrepresented groups. The author indicated difficulty in the standardization process to obtain participants from underrepresented groups but did not explain the nature of the difficulty nor the efforts made to recruit participants from these groups. Also not shared were the characteristics of the original sample (pre-weighting). The manual provides normative data for 12 age groupings by gender. Also provided is the percentage of the normative sample that mastered each of the 13 behavioral assessments by age and gender.

Coefficient alpha estimates of reliability were computed on the entire norm sample; by age group, coefficients ranged from .87 to .93 for Locomotor skills and .84 to .90 for Ball Skills. Coefficient alpha estimates of the composite score ranged from .91 to .95. Also noted were coefficient alpha estimates for several subgroups including gender, race/ethnicity, and selected exceptionality categories; these coefficients fell between .93 and .97. The demographic details of the subgroups used in these analyses were not supplied. Test-retest estimates, with a 1-week interval were generated using a sample of 105 children. Both corrected (for range effects) and uncorrected coefficients were provided for three age groupings (3:0-5:11, 6:0-7:11, and 8:0-10:11). In that corrected scores may be overestimates (Schmitt, 1996), this review focuses on uncorrected coefficients. For the Locomotor subtest, uncorrected coefficients ranged from .74 to .88. For Ball Skills, test-retest estimates ranged from .80 to .87. Across ages, the uncorrected reliability estimate was .92 for the composite. Interrater reliability estimates were obtained by using videotaped assessments of 10 children and five raters with a 2-week interval. Strong evidence of rater consistency was reported by subtest and overall (interrater r = .96; intrarater r = .98). In summary, there appears to be substantial evidence as to the reliability of the TGMD-3.

Three experts established content considerations of validity. Changes across editions included returning the "Skip" item from the first edition to the third (instead of "Leap"). This change was based on feedback that children with autism spectrum disorder could leap but not skip, and this lack influenced their likely qualification for services. Floors and ceilings were examined and appear reasonable. Bias examinations across behavioral assessments identified statistically significant differences across genders (four items) and ethnicities (eight items). The test author concluded based on item review and small effect size associated with the differences that these items did not pose a threat to their equitable use. However, no specific data were provided.

Criterion evidence of validity was examined via correlations between the TGMD-3 and the prior edition (TGMD-2) as well as the Movement Assessment Battery for Children, 2nd edition (MABC-2). Correlations between the TGMD-2 and the TGMD-3 were .81 for Locomotor, .85 for Ball Skills/Object Control, and .87 for the composite. Correlations between the TGMD-3 and the MABC-2 were for the most part significant, although low in the opinions of these reviewers. The test author aptly suggested that the limited correlation between these measures was the result of differences in the mode and definition of the skills assessed.

Diagnostic aspects of validity were examined with a sample of children diagnosed with either cognitive impairment or autism, each matched to a non-diagnosed sample. Although the TGMD-3 performed well, evidence to support the test author's suggestion that the results were underestimated due to errors in identifying diagnosed and non-diagnosed individuals was not provided. Potential users may find it helpful to review the data in the test manual, which include the distribution of hits and false negatives/positives at several cutoff scores.

Construct evidence of validity included significant correlations between both Locomotor and Ball Skills scores with age for both males and females. In addition, significant differences for each subtest and composite between samples with selected disorders and typically developing samples were found. Furthermore, factor analysis confirms the factor structure of performance assessments by subscale. Although the study of validity is ongoing, sufficient evidence of validity was provided.

COMMENTARY. Overall, the TGMD-3 appears to be a suitable measure of gross motor development and has fared favorably in comparative analyses (Wiart & Darrah, 2001). More information/research would be helpful as to the reasons for and impact of item changes made across editions. In addition, much of the psychometric information is based on the entire norm sample, but limited information as to its demographics are available, and extensive information is available only for the weighted sample. Beyond this, additional information and research relative to the examination of bias may prove useful. Also suggested is that the videotaped administrations used in the qualifying of field examiners for use in developing the technical data be made available to potential users to ensure the integrity of TGMD-3 scores.

From the point of view of the examiner, the instructions for each task are depicted clearly. While the manual indicates the overall composite score should be used to determine someone's gross motor ability, a more detailed item analysis makes it possible for the teacher to devise drills to improve specific motor skills. Moreover, the detailed analysis of specific skills allows for the development of goals for a child's individualized education program. The TGMD-3 allows for an objective assessment of a child's progress as opposed to a subjective assessment by a teacher comparing the student to his or her classmates. Although the manual indicates that the age equivalent scores were provided "reluctantly," in this instance, these scores are often the most useful to explain to parents the level at which their child is performing.

A major advantage of the test is that it appears to be engaging for the student. It is likely that the evaluator would have good compliance on the part of the examinee during the evaluation. Indeed, if a child is not compliant on what appears to be a fun activity, there is a higher likelihood that there is a weakness present, whether motor or other processing problem, barring other explanations such as the child is tired or not feeling well. Although the TGMD-3 is not a test that can be easily used by a clinician in a private practice in that it requires a 60' x 30' space with a wall (manual, p. 8), it would be useful for assessing gross motor skills in a school or physical rehabilitation setting as well as in private preschools.

SUMMARY. The TGMD-3 appears to be a viable tool to help identify those whose gross motor development may not be typical and to assess their progress. Although more data may prove useful, those data provided give confidence in the use of the TGMD-3.

REVIEWERS' REFERENCES

Bunker, L. K. (1989). [Test review of Test of Gross Motor Development]. In J. C. Conoley & J. J. Kramer (Eds.), *The tenth mental measurements yearbook* (pp. 843-845). Lincoln, NE: Buros Institute of Mental Measurements.

Cohen, L. G. (2003). [Test review of Test of Gross Motor Development–Second Edition]. In B. S. Plake, J. C. Impara, & R. A. Spies (Eds.), *The fifteenth mental measurements yearbook* (pp. 946–948). Lincoln, NE: Buros Institute of Mental Measurements.

Poteat, G. M. (2003). [Test review of Test of Gross Motor Development–Second Edition]. In B. S. Plake, J. C. Impara, & R. A. Spies (Eds.), *The fifteenth mental measurements yearbook* (pp. 948-950). Lincoln, NE: Buros Institute of Mental Measurements.

Schmitt, N. (1996). Uses and abuses of coefficient alpha. *Psychological Assessment, 8,* 350-353.

Wiart, L., & Darrah, J. (2001). Review of four tests of gross motor development. *Developmental Medicine & Child Neurology, 43,* 279–285.

[171]

Test of Language Development–Primary: Fifth Edition.

Purpose: Designed "to assess children's spoken language ability within a semantic, grammatic, and phonological context."

Population: Ages 4-0 through 8-11.

Publication Dates: 1977-2019.

Acronym: TOLD-P:5.

Scores, 15: 9 subtest scores: Picture Vocabulary, Relational Vocabulary, Oral Vocabulary, Syntactic Understanding, Sentence Imitation, Morphological Completion, Word Discrimination (Supplemental), Phonemic Analysis (Supplemental), Word Articulation (Supplemental); 6 composite scores: Listening, Organizing, Speaking, Grammar, Semantics, Spoken Language.

Administration: Individual.

Price Data, 2020: $405 per complete kit including examiner's manual (2019, 185 pages), picture book, 25 examiner record forms, and online scoring and reporting; $115 per examiner's manual; $179 per picture book; $111 per 25 examiner record forms.

Time: 35-50 minutes for administration of the six core subtests; approximately 30 minutes for administration of supplemental subtests.

Comments: The test publisher recommends administering core subtests and supplemental subtests in separate sessions.

Authors: Phyllis L. Newcomer and Donald D. Hammill.

Publisher: PRO-ED.

Cross References: For reviews by Maura Jones Moyle and Steven Long and by Loraine J. Spenciner of the fourth edition, see 20:183; for reviews by Ronald A. Madle and Gabrielle Stutman of the third edition, see 14:390; see also T5:2695 (72 references) and T4:2768 (21 references); for reviews by Linda Crocker and Carol E. Westby of the second edition, see 11:437 (20 references).

Review of the Test of Language Development–Primary: Fifth Edition by DENISE A. FINNERAN, Assistant Professor, and NANCY C. GULLATT, Professor of Speech Pathology, Department of Communication Sciences and Disorders, University of Oklahoma Health Sciences Center, Oklahoma City, OK:

DESCRIPTION. The Test of Language Development–Primary: Fifth Edition (TOLD-P:5) is an individually administered and comprehensive measure of oral language ability for Standard American English-speaking children, ages 4 through 8 years. The TOLD-P:5 is designed to identify children performing below peers in oral language, to identify a child's strengths and weaknesses in language, to document progress during intervention, and to provide a measure of language for research purposes.

The TOLD-P:5 provides a linguistic assessment in the core areas of semantics (Picture Vocabulary [PV], Relational Vocabulary [RV], Oral Vocabulary [OV]) and grammar (Syntactic Understanding [SU], Sentence Imitation [SI], Morphological Completion [MC]). These core subtests are used to determine composite (i.e., index) scores for Listening (PV, SU), Organizing (RV, SI), Speaking (OV, MC), Grammar (SU, SI, MC), Semantics (PV, RV, OV), and Spoken Language (all six core subtests). The phonological component is addressed in three supplemental subtests: Word Discrimination (WD), Phonemic Analysis (PA), and Word Articulation (WA).

The test authors report that the major revisions to this fifth edition of the test include the following: (a) normative data collected between 2015 and 2018 that are representative of the 2017 U.S. population; (b) studies of subtest floors, ceilings, and item gradients to document "excellent ability across all ages and ability levels to not only measure students' spoken language ability but also detect minor fluctuations in those abilities" (manual,

p. xiv); (c) studies of test bias to document "little or no bias in regard to gender, race, or ethnicity" (p. xiv); (d) studies to document validity, sensitivity, and specificity, and (e) online scoring and reporting system included.

The TOLD-P:5 is designed to be administered by professionals with formal assessment training. The subtests are not timed. The six core subtests can be completed in one session within 35 to 50 minutes. The three supplemental subtests take around 30 minutes to complete and should not be administered at the same time as the core subtests. The two subtests that comprise the Listening composite and the supplemental Word Articulation subtest use a picture book. This book consists of full-color drawings but does not contain tabs to guide the examiner to the appropriate subtest stimuli. The subtests used for the Organizing and Speaking composites and the Word Discrimination and Phonemic Awareness subtests are presented orally with no visual stimuli.

The examiner's manual contains chapters on the linguistic features included in the theoretical framework, administration and scoring, interpretation of findings, and test development. Normative tables are provided in appendices. Subtest raw scores are converted to scaled scores (mean = 10; standard deviation = 3) and descriptive terms are provided (e.g., *below average, superior*). As with other assessment tools from the test publisher, *average* is applied to scaled scores of 8 through 12. Composite (index) scores are calculated using the sum of scaled scores, and the test manual provides appendices for the associated composite (index) scores (mean = 100; standard deviation = 15). The descriptive term *average* is assigned to composite (index) scores of 90 through 110. Subtest and composite raw scores are converted to percentile ranks and age equivalents. The test authors recommend using composite scores in assessment and provide a way to prorate the Spoken Language Index if a core subtest is not completed. The test publisher's online scoring and report system provides electronic scoring and report generation.

DEVELOPMENT. The TOLD-P:5, like previous test versions, was designed using a two-dimensional model of language. This model includes linguistic features (semantics, grammar, phonology) and linguistic systems (listening, organizing, speaking). The test authors describe the target linguistic features in the first chapter as an introduction to the test. In the chapter on test validity the test authors describe how they examined TOLD-P:5 normative data for test bias. These studies included children who fell within the normal range for their chronological age. The dichotomous groups used for these analyses involved gender (female versus male), and "minority subgroups" (manual, p. 72; Black/African American, Asian/Pacific Islander, Hispanic, American Indian/Alaska Native). The test authors report that the study of item-level differences across subgroup revealed "little or no systematic bias in regard to gender, race, and Hispanic status" (p. 71). The other study involved a comparison of subgroups at the subtest and composite levels. The test authors report that these analyses revealed little or no bias for gender or for the minority subgroups tested. They also report that the subtest and composite scores for the TOLD-P:5 were excellent for the test floors (important for identifying children with lower levels of language ability) and test ceilings (important for identifying children with high levels of language ability).

TECHNICAL. The TOLD-P:5 was normed on 1,007 children in 2015 through 2018 from 31 states in the continental United States. The demographics of the sample were representative of the nation as a whole for the year 2017 in terms of gender, geographic region, race, Hispanic ethnicity, exceptionality status, family income, and education level of parents. As with previous versions, the test manual does not provide information on languages (other than English) or dialects (other than Standard American English) in the normative sample for the TOLD-P:5. The test authors report that approximately 19% of the sample had an identified disorder. As suggested by Moyle and Long (2017) in a review of a previous version of this test, the inclusion of people with the target disability in a normative sample may reduce diagnostic sensitivity of a test for mild cases (Peña, Spaulding, & Plante, 2006).

The test authors present three types of evidence to demonstrate reliability of the TOLD-P:5: internal consistency, test-retest, and scorer difference. They consider coefficients of .80 to be minimally reliable and of .90 and higher to be the most desirable. The TOLD-P:5 demonstrated internal consistency with average alpha coefficients across the age ranges exceeding .80 for all subtests. Test-retest reliability was evaluated using two samples of children (172 children in total) with testing approximately two weeks apart. Reliability estimates for all but one subtest were above .80

with a majority falling above .90. This indicates acceptable to excellent test-retest reliability. Scorer difference reliability was examined using two raters who independently scored 50 TOLD-P:5 record booklets randomly drawn from the normative sample. Correlation coefficients were greater than .90 for all subtests and composite (index) values. As noted by Moyle and Long (2017), the method would be more rigorous if the raters had scored actual responses during testing.

The test authors present evidence for three types of test validity: content-description validity, criterion-prediction validity, and construct-identification validity. Content-description validity is addressed with an analysis of items, floors and ceilings, and item gradients, and by presenting a rationale for items and formats for each subtest.

Criterion-prediction evidence of validity was examined by correlating TOLD-P:5 scores with scores from eight oral language measures: the Clinical Evaluation of Language Fundamentals—Fifth Edition (Wiig, Semel, & Secord, 2013), the Test for Auditory Comprehension of Language—Fourth Edition (Carrow-Woolfolk, 2014), the Test of Early Language Development—Fourth Edition (Hresko, Reid, & Hammill, 2018), the Bankson Expressive Language Test—Third Edition (Bankson, Mentis, & Jagielko, 2018), the Test of Language Development–Primary: Fourth Edition (Newcomer & Hammill, 2008), the Test of Language Development–Intermediate: Fifth Edition (Hammill & Newcomer, 2019), the Test of Expressive Language (Carrow-Woolfolk & Allen, 2014), and the Spoken Language subtest of the Young Children's Achievement Test—Second Edition (Hresko, Peak, Herron, & Hicks, 2018). The average correlation coefficients between the TOLD-P:5 composites and the criterion tests ranged from .84 to .94 (very large to nearly perfect, based on guidelines from Hopkins, 2002). There was a wider range of coefficient values for the TOLD-P:5 subtests; these are presented in an appendix of the test manual.

Construct-identification evidence of validity "relates to the degree to which underlying traits of a test can be identified and the extent to which these traits reflect the theoretical model on which the test is based" (manual, p. 92). The test authors confirmed all assumptions made based on the theoretical framework. These included a positive correlation between TOLD-P:5 raw scores and chronological age, a positive correlation between TOLD-P:5 standard scores and related measures (academic achievement, intelligence, other TOLD-P:5 standard scores), and differing TOLD-P:5 performance among diagnostic groups.

Diagnostic accuracy was reported using three indices: sensitivity (correct identification of children with language problems), specificity (correct identification of children without language impairments), and receiver operating characteristic/area under the curve (ROC/AUC; overall diagnostic accuracy). The test authors report that all indices meet "the minimum standards for diagnostic accuracy ... when used to differentiate children with low spoken language ability from those in matched samples" (manual, p. 91).

COMMENTARY. Overall, the TOLD-P:5 is an omnibus language assessment that is easy to administer and score. This tool is designed for speakers of Standard American English only. The test manual is well organized and nicely laid out, although readability is affected by the paper gloss. The composite scores and subtests are described with varying levels of detail with some inconsistency in terminology for the Word Articulation subtest (referred to as both an assessment of articulation and of phonology). The record booklet is nicely organized and easy to read with most spoken instruction prompts printed in red. Rules for ceilings and repetitions are presented, although the location of this information varies across subtests. There are clear rules regarding probes for all but the Oral Vocabulary subtest. Scoring guidelines are clear, although the rationale for Morphological Completion subtest scoring could be clearer given that some items on this subtest could elicit alternate responses that are semantically and/or pragmatically appropriate. Most of the color drawings are clear representations, although there are some pictures with excessive visual distractors (lines, colors), and some that appear outdated.

SUMMARY. The TOLD-P:5 is a receptive and expressive omnibus English language assessment for Standard American English-speaking children ages 4:0 through 8:11 years. The test is in its fifth version and its authors continue to improve and update content. Overall the test is user-friendly with clear instructions and scoring. The evidence suggests that the TOLD-P:5 yields scores that are reliable and lead to valid uses. When testing children who use nonmainstream English, the Diagnostic Evaluation of Language Variation–Norm Referenced (Seymour, Roeper, & de Villiers, 2018) is a more appropriate language assessment. Test interpretation for bilingual and nonmainstream English-speaking children should be balanced with other more culturally appropriate assessments.

REVIEWERS' REFERENCES

Bankson, N. W., Mentis, M., & Jagielko, J. R. (2018). Bankson Expressive Language Test—Third Edition. Austin, TX: PRO-ED.

Carrow-Woolfolk, E. (2014). Test for Auditory Comprehension of Language—Fourth Edition. Austin, TX: PRO-ED.

Carrow-Woolfolk, E., & Allen, E. A. (2014). Test of Expressive Language. Austin, TX: PRO-ED.

Hopkins, W. G. (2002). A scale of magnitudes for effect statistics. In A new view of statistics. Retrieved July 14, 2005, from http://www.sportsci.org/resource/stats/effectmag.html

Hresko, W. P., Peak, P. K., Herron, S. R., & Hicks, D. L. (2018). Young Children's Achievement Test—Second Edition. Austin, TX: PRO-ED.

Hresko, W. P., Reid, D. K., & Hammill, D. D. (2018). Test of Early Language Development—Fourth Edition. Austin, TX: PRO-ED.

Moyle, M. J., & Long, S. (2017). [Test review of Test of Language Development–Primary: Fourth Edition]. In J. F. Carlson, K. F. Geisinger, & J. L. Jonson (Eds.), *The twentieth mental measurements yearbook*. Lincoln, NE: Buros Center for Testing.

Hammill, D. D., & Newcomer, P. L. Test of Language Development–Intermediate: Fifth Edition. Austin, TX: PRO-ED.

Newcomer, P. L., & Hammill, D. D. (2008). Test of Language Development–Primary: Fourth Edition. Austin, TX: PRO-ED.

Peña, E. D., Spaulding, T. J., & Plante, E. (2006). The composition of normative groups and diagnostic decision making: Shooting ourselves in the foot. American Journal of Speech-Language Pathology, 15, 247-254.

Seymour, H. N., Roeper, T. W., & de Villiers, J. (2018). Diagnostic Evaluation of Language Variation—Norm Referenced. Sun Prairie, WI: Ventris Learning.

Wiig, E. H., Semel, E., & Secord, W. A. (2013). Clinical Evaluation of Language Fundamentals—Fifth Edition. San Antonio, TX: Pearson.

Review of the Test of Language Development–Primary: Fifth Edition by MILDRED MURRAY-WARD, Professor of Education, Retired, California State University, Stanislaus, Turlock, CA:

DESCRIPTION. The Test of Language Development–Primary: Fifth Edition (TOLD-P:5) is the current edition of the TOLD, first published in 1977. The TOLD-P:5 is an individually administered assessment designed to identify children's oral language difficulties and the degrees of those difficulties. The test authors indicate that the TOLD-P:5 can be used to identify children with oral communication difficulties, to determine strengths and weaknesses in linguistic abilities, to document progress of children in prescribed remedial or therapeutic programs, and to provide a measure of oral language development for researchers studying children's language.

The TOLD-P:5 comprises nine subtests organized into six core subtests and three supplemental subtests. The subtests are combined into a two-dimensional model: linguistic features and linguistic systems. Linguistic features has three components: Semantics (Picture Vocabulary [PV], Relational Vocabulary [RV], and Oral Vocabulary [OV]); Grammar (Syntactic Understanding [SU], Sentence Imitation [SI], and Morphological Completion [MC]); and Phonology (Word Discrimination [WD], Phonemic Analysis [PA], and Word Articulation [WA]). Linguistic systems also involves three components: Listening (PV, SU, and WD); Organizing (RV, SI, and PA); and Speaking (OV, MC, and WA). The subtests are combined into six composite areas: Listening (PV, SU); Organizing (RV, SI); Speaking (OV, MC); Grammar (SU, SI, MC); Semantics (PV, RV, OV); and Spoken Language (an overall composite using all six core subtests). The remaining composite, Phonology (WD, PA, and WA), is considered supplemental and is not used in the Spoken Language composite. The reason for excluding these subtests from the Spoken Language Composite is explained in the test manual, but their actual use is not specified.

Test materials include an examiner's manual, examiner record booklets, and a picture book. Online scoring and reporting are included. The examiner's manual provides a detailed discussion of the test's theoretical and historical development, subtest descriptions, scoring directions, and test development procedures. The cover of the examiner record booklet contains four areas. In Section 1, the child's name, date tested, birth date, age, gender, grade level, school name, and examiner name and title are listed. In Section 2, the core subtest raw scores are recorded and converted to age equivalents, percentile ranks, and scaled scores (mean of 10; *SD* of 3). Confidence intervals can be calculated, and a descriptive term for the child's performance is recorded. In Section 3, the core scaled scores are summed into their respective composite scores and converted to percentile ranks and index scores (mean of 100; *SD* of 15) with confidence intervals and descriptive terms for the scores. In Section 4, the descriptive terms for scaled and index scores are noted. Clear directions and a completed sample help guide the examiner in administration, recording responses, and converting scores. Estimated testing times are 30-50 minutes for the core subtests and 30 minutes for the supplemental subtests. The picture book provides stimulus pictures to be used in the PV, SU, and WA subtests. The online scoring and reporting system is clearly described in the examiner's manual. The system allows for entry of test data, conversion of subtest or total raw scores to other score forms, identification of intra-individual differences, and production of a score summary and narrative report.

DEVELOPMENT. The TOLD-P:5 is the fifth edition of this test. As each version of the TOLD was developed, its authors addressed issues raised by reviewers of prior editions. The theoretical framework of the TOLD-P:5 is clearly described and referenced in the first chapter of the test manual. Each subtest is also described and well documented. Changes in the TOLD over the five versions include: introduction of composite scores, additional subtests, detailed descriptions of test rationale and interpretation of results, more representative norming samples, larger samples for reliability studies, more reliability and validity evidence, removal of floor and ceiling effects, inclusion of standard errors of measurement, additional information on examiner qualifications, and confidence intervals added to the examiner record booklet.

TECHNICAL.

Normative Sample. The test authors included detailed descriptions of the norming sample (N = 1007), which was designed to match the *Digest of Educational Statistics 2015* and *ProQuest Statistical Abstract of the United States 2017* statistics on geographic regions, gender, race, ethnicity, exceptionality status, parent educational, and household income. Overall, the sample appears to be representative.

Reliability. The TOLD-P:5 authors provide reliability evidence for internal consistency, test-retest reliability (test score stability), and scorer difference for each age group tested. The test authors describe the rationale for each procedure, established practices, and standards for evaluating the results. Internal consistency reports involved alpha coefficients for the core and supplementary subtests and composite scores for groups defined by age, gender, ethnicity/race, and disability status. Average coefficients were all above .80, and the alpha coefficients for composite scores were all near or above .90.

Score stability was assessed using a test-retest procedure (2-week interval) using groups defined by age, gender, ethnicity/race, and exceptionality. Reliability coefficients ranged from .75 to .99, with most in the .90 range. Scorer difference reliability involved two of the test publisher's staff members who independently scored 50 randomly selected protocols from the norming sample. The resulting correlation coefficients were .90 or higher. Taken together, the results provide evidence that the TOLD-P:5 is a reliable measure, with well-integrated content, stable scores, and consistent scoring results.

Validity. The TOLD-P:5 authors provide evidence of content-description, criterion-prediction, and construct-identification validity. Content-description validity evidence was provided through examination of the content and how it assesses the content domain, individual item analyses, floor and ceiling effects, item gradients, and item bias. The test authors describe the theoretical basis and sources of content for each subtest. They also explain the rationale for the selection of specific content, such as the source and choice of words from word lists. Next, they list other tests with similar item formats. Finally, they present evidence of item discrimination, item difficulty, floor and ceiling gradients, and analysis of test bias to assure that the content accurately reflects the test domain. The evidence gathered supports the notion that the test items do accurately assess the content domain.

Because the TOLD-P:5 is intended to identify children with linguistic problems, determine the nature of those problems, and document progress in interventions, criterion-prediction validity is of special concern. To assess criterion-prediction validity evidence for the test, the authors examined the correlation of TOLD-P:5 scores with established tests and the test's ability to differentiate among children with known levels of spoken language development. Correlations between composite scores on the TOLD-P:5 and eight other oral language assessments were found to be in the .67 (large) to .99 (nearly perfect) range. In addition, differences between scores on tests measuring the same oral language components as the TOLD-P:5 composite scores were explored using dependent samples t-tests. Differences in scores for the six composites and other measures of these composites resulted in 28 comparisons. Of the 28 score comparisons, 22 had very small or trivial differences. Finally, the accuracy of TOLD-P:5 classifications of children with and without spoken language disorders was examined by determining the degree to which the TOLD-P:5 accurately predicted those children with a diagnosed specific language impairment (sensitivity index or true positives) and those without such an impairment (specificity index or true negatives). Using a cutoff score of 87 and a sample of 110 children, the test's sensitivity index was .82, accurately predicting 45 of the 55 children with a language impairment. The test's specificity index of .78 showed the score accurately predicted 43 of the 55 children with no language impairment.

Construct-identification validity involves examining the degree to which the test truly reflects the theoretical model on which the test was based. Seven constructs involving the developmental and specific nature of spoken language development were examined: relationship between

TOLD-P:5 scores and age, degree to which the TOLD-P:5 differentiated among groups of people with below-average spoken language, correlation of TOLD-P:5 scores with achievement, correlation of TOLD-P:5 scores with intelligence measures, degree to which TOLD-P:5 subtests correlate with each other, degree to which the subtests relate to the test constructs, and degree to which the items on a subtest correlate with other items in that subtest. Results indicate that TOLD-P:5 scores do increase with age, children with different diagnoses attained different Spoken Language scores in expected patterns, TOLD-P:5 scores were strongly correlated with achievement and intelligence scores, factor analysis supported the organization of TOLD-P:5 subtests to the composites, and item discrimination indices revealed that the individual test items are highly correlated with the total test scores.

COMMENTARY. The TOLD-P:5 is a comprehensive measure of oral language development in young children. The test consists of nine distinct subtests, organized into two dimensions. Of the nine subtests, six are organized into five composites as well as an overall composite. The role of the six subtests is clear; however, the role of the three supplemental subtests is never specified. The test is not difficult to administer, but it does require a trained examiner.

The history of the five TOLD assessments is comprehensive and clear. The theoretical foundations of the TOLD-P:5 are well documented, as are the extensive revisions, based on prior test reviews and implemented by the test authors. Evidence of item development, norming, reliability, and validity studies is extensive and quite comprehensive, as is the evidence and rationale for the various studies and criteria for evaluating the results. Of particular note are the studies on criterion-related validity, because this assessment is part of the evidence used to identify children with oral language difficulties, to make remedial and programmatic decisions about those children, and to monitor their progress.

This reviewer recommends two changes. First, review the inclusion of the supplemental tests. The test authors note that they are not included in the composites, but they make no mention of how they should be used. If they are to be used, that information should be provided to test users. Second, review the picture book items. Some of the illustrations are dated (such as the clock face), and the level of abstraction varies considerably from identification of an item in isolation (an airplane) to roles or actions of people in context (a judge making a decision). Some, such as the judge making decisions, could be beyond the experience of some children.

SUMMARY. The TOLD-P:5 is an individual assessment of oral language development. It is well grounded in a theoretical framework and should be a useful tool in identifying children with oral communication difficulties, determining strengths and weaknesses in linguistic abilities, documenting progress of children in prescribed remedial or therapeutic programs, and providing a measure of oral language development for researchers studying children's language. The test displays extensive evidence of high-quality item development, sound norming, and reliability and validity. Of particular note is the criterion-validity evidence so important in the process of identifying, diagnosing, and monitoring children in oral language development.

[172]

Test of Memory and Learning–Senior Edition.

Purpose: Designed to "sample a variety of memory functions that are of clinical and theoretical interest for adults from 55 years through 89 years of age."
Population: Ages 55 to 89.
Publication Date: 2012.
Acronym: TOMAL-SE.
Scores, 9 to 14: 9 core battery scores: Verbal Memory Index (Object Recall, Memory for Stories, Word List Learning), Nonverbal Memory Index (Facial Memory, Visual Sequential Memory, Memory for Location), Composite Memory Index; 5 supplemental scores: Delayed Recall Index (Facial Memory Delayed, Memory for Stories Delayed, Object Recall Delayed), Learning Index.
Administration: Individual.
Price Data, 2017: $235 per kit including manual (115 pages), picture book, 25 record booklets, and 15 chips; $109 per scoring and reporting software; $102 per picture book; $75 per manual; $47 per 25 record booklets; $10 per 15 chips.
Time: 30-35 minutes for administration of core battery; additional 8-12 minutes required for administration of delayed recall subtests.
Comments: Upward extension and adaptation of the Test of Memory and Learning–Second Edition (18:143).
Authors: Cecil R. Reynolds and Judith K. Voress.
Publisher: PRO-ED.

[Editor's note: After these reviews were completed, the test publisher advised the Buros Center for Testing that this test is out of print.]

Review of the Test of Memory and Learning–Senior Edition by JOHN J. BRINKMAN, Professor of Psychology and Counseling, and EMILY LAUTZENHEISER, Assistant Professor of Psychology and Counseling, University of Saint Francis, Fort Wayne, IN:

DESCRIPTION. The Test of Memory and Learning-Senior Edition (TOMAL-SE) is an individually administered assessment of verbal and nonverbal memory and learning for English-speaking individuals ages 55-89. The test authors suggest that the assessment may best evaluate memory processes for patients who present with clinical issues related to memory and learning, including neurological disorders such as dementia, stroke, and traumatic brain injury. The test authors emphasize that the TOMAL-SE does not assess long-term memory or incidental memory, and they recommend a separate independent evaluation for patients who present with difficulties related to daily memory or learning problems.

Working memory, spatial memory, delayed recall, and learning are evaluated by the TOMAL-SE's six core subtests, three delayed recall subtests, and three indexes. The six core subtests are Facial Memory, Memory for Stories, Word List Learning, Visual Sequential Memory, Object Recall, and Memory for Location. The three delayed recall subtests are Facial Memory Delayed, Memory for Stories Delayed, and Object Recall Delayed. The three indexes are the Verbal Memory Index, Nonverbal Memory Index, and Composite Memory Index. Additionally, two supplementary indexes may be computed: the Learning Index and the Delayed Recall Index.

The TOMAL-SE consists of an examiner record booklet, a picture book, an examiner's manual, and 15 chips for the Facial Memory and Memory for Location subtests. The TOMAL-SE is available only in paper format and is hand scored. The TOMAL-SE's indexes are scaled to a standard score with a mean of 100 and a standard deviation of 15; subtests are scaled to a standard score with a mean of 10 and a standard deviation of 3. Identifying information and all raw, scaled, and index scores are recorded on the first two pages of the record booklet, along with percentile rank and descriptive terms for the index scores. Concise instructions for test administration are provided for each subtest in the record booklet, with more detailed information available in the examiner's manual. The test authors recommend that when administering and scoring the TOMAL-SE, particular attention should be paid to specific instructions for each subtest, as well as floor effects in certain populations (e.g., individuals with dementia), and minimum number of trials required for some subtests.

DEVELOPMENT. The TOMAL-SE was developed over the course of five years to be a reliable assessment of memory and learning in individuals ages 55 through 89. It is intended to provide a thorough assessment of memory and learning from a clinical standpoint, while also being sensitive to examinee fatigue, lack of cooperation, motor deterioration, limited attention span, and visual limitations. The TOMAL-SE's items were derived from the Test of Memory and Learning (TOMAL), which assesses memory and learning abilities of children and adolescents. The test authors explain that the TOMAL-SE's subtests were developed through the combined experience of the test authors, comprehensive literature reviews, and test tryouts. They also explain that the subtests underwent independent task analyses and two factor analyses, which they suggest established that memory is the underlying construct of the TOMAL-SE. Additionally, the TOMAL-SE underwent an item analysis that demonstrated appropriate item selection via discrimination coefficients and difficulty percentages.

TECHNICAL. The TOMAL-SE normative sample was chosen to align with the 2010 U.S. Census for individuals ages 55-89. Individuals from 15 U.S. states were included in the sample of 428 individuals. The sample approximated Census demographics with regard to gender, region, race, Hispanic status, family income, and educational attainment. Women were overrepresented (62% female), and Asians were underrepresented (< 1% in the sample compared to 4% of the 2010 U.S. Census). The test authors acknowledged that representation by geographic region was "somewhat off" but reported that "older adults from one geographic region should perform similarly to older adults from another geographic region" (manual, p. 55). The test authors also provided information related to living arrangements of the sample (e.g., 65% lived alone or with family; 26% lived in senior housing).

Reliability was assessed via internal consistency estimates (alpha coefficients), test-retest reliability across a 2-week period, and interscorer reliability. Internal consistency was calculated across six age groups. Alpha coefficients for the subtests ranged from .73 to .99 and for the indexes from .91 to .97, demonstrating generally acceptable internal reliability. Age did not appear to affect the internal reliability of the measures. Standard errors of measurement for the indexes ranged from 3 to 5; the subtests' standard error of measurement ranged from 0 to 2.

Alpha coefficients also were reported by gender and ethnicity, as well as for three clinical groups (i.e., dementia, psychiatric, and stroke). The dementia, psychiatric, and stroke sample groups were small, ranging from 8 to 24 participants, and no demographic information was provided. Overall, alpha coefficients were consistently strong for gender (.79 to .98) and for European Americans and African Americans (.80 to .98). The dementia group demonstrated highly variable coefficients across subtests (e.g., .24 for Facial Memory and .96 for Memory for Stories Delayed). However, index coefficients were more consistent (.73 to .94).

The test-retest reliability sample comprised 35 individuals, primarily White/European American (60%) females (74%) with a less-than-Bachelor's-degree education (80%). Corrected coefficients from this sample were strong across a 2-week period (.80 to .99).

Limited information was provided to support interscorer reliability. Fifty pairs of completed protocols were randomly selected from the normative sample and scored independently by one test author and one member of the test publisher's staff. A brief summary of scores demonstrated reliability coefficients consistently in the .90s. It should be noted that the only demographic information provided for this sample was an age band of 65-83 years.

Validity evidence was based on five sources including test content, response processes, internal structure, relationships to external variables, and consequences of testing. Validity evidence related to test content and response processes was described as being dependent upon the original TOMAL and largely described the development of the TOMAL-SE. Evidence related to internal structure was derived from item and factor analyses. Item analysis was conducted using the normative sample with results confirming the internal characteristics of the test items. Factor analyses using correlation matrices derived from standard scores for the total sample provided factor solutions that, according to the test authors, were highly stable and consistent with the original TOMAL and the TOMAL-2.

Evidence based on relationships to external variables was demonstrated via correlations with age as well as to four other assessments: the Test of Verbal Conceptualization and Fluency (TVCF), the Reynolds Intellectual Screening Test (RIST), the Test of Irregular Word Reading Efficiency (TIWRE), and the Wide Range Assessment of Memory and Learning-Second Edition (WRAML2). The evidence regarding the external variable of age demonstrated consistency of scores across gender and ethnicity, with scores for all groups decreasing with age. When the TOMAL-SE was compared to the four other similar assessments (N = 32), correlation coefficients ranged from small to very large, with the highest consistent degree of correlation occurring with the TOMAL-SE's Composite indexes, rather than subtests, as expected. For consequences of testing, delta values for the subtests were calculated and demonstrated that gender, race, and ethnicity had little to no effect on the TOMAL-SE's results.

COMMENTARY. The TOMAL-SE is a well-designed assessment of memory and learning in individuals between the ages of 55 and 89. As the test authors suggest, it is one of the only assessments specifically developed to clinically assess memory and learning in older individuals. Its use is strengthened by its predecessors, the TOMAL and TOMAL-2, both of which are established tests of memory and learning. Additionally, it provides a thorough, comprehensive measure of memory and learning that is sensitive to examinees with specific needs (e.g., fatigue, lack of cooperation, limited attention span).

Although the TOMAL-SE is a well-designed assessment of memory and learning, additional information and training should be considered. Limited information was available regarding the norming population. Norming and psychometric data were vague and limited by underrepresented populations and small sample sizes. Also, small sample sizes were reported with limited information about the sample groups (i.e., the clinical groups). Additionally, while the test authors state that examiners who administer the TOMAL-SE "should have some basic knowledge of the neurobiology of memory" (manual, p. 8), interpretation guidelines provided in the examiner's manual speak to a need for a more advanced understanding of neuropsychology. Similarly, the authors advised examiners to consider the examinee's age, developmental status, and education level when interpreting subtest and index results, but no instructions or data are provided as to how to interpret or scale any of the scores against those metrics except age. Therefore, the TOMAL-SE may require more training and/or coursework than is described in the test manual.

SUMMARY. The TOMAL-SE is an individually administered test designed to assess verbal and nonverbal memory and learning in individuals ages 55-89. The assessment adequately measures four areas of memory and learning including working memory, spatial memory, delayed recall, and learning. Despite some of the small clinical sample sizes used, psychometric properties have been adequately established. The strength of the TOMAL-SE lies in its ability to assess older adults who present with clinical issues related to memory and learning, including neurological disorders such as dementia, stroke, and traumatic brain injury.

Review of the Test of Memory and Learning–Senior Edition by MARC A. SILVA, James A. Haley Veterans Hospital, Mental Health and Behavioral Sciences Service, Tampa, FL:

DESCRIPTION. The Test of Memory and Learning–Senior Edition (TOMAL-SE) is a standardized memory test battery designed for individuals ages 55-89 and intended for use in assessing dementia, stroke, traumatic brain injury, and other central nervous system conditions that impact learning and memory. The TOMAL-SE contains six core subtests and three supplementary subtests. For the experienced examiner, administration time for the core battery is approximately 30 minutes; the supplementary subtests add another 8-12 minutes.

Core Subtests. Facial Memory is a seven-item subtest in which examinees are shown a page with black-and-white photos of faces for several seconds. The next page contains the same photos intermixed amongst distractors. Examines indicate which faces they recognize. In Memory for Stories, examinees listen to and repeat back two short stories. Word List Learning is a five-trial subtest in which examinees listen to and repeat back a 10-item word list. Visual Sequential Memory is a six-item subtest in which examinees are shown a page with a series of geometric designs arranged in a row. On the following page, the designs are rearranged. Examinees are asked to indicate the order in which designs originally appeared. Object Recall is a five-trial subtest in which examinees are shown a page with 15 pictures of common objects and are asked to recall the objects after each trial. Memory for Location is a 13-item subtest in which examinees are shown a 3 x 4 grid (six items) and a 4 x 4 grid (seven items) with dots marking specific locations. After each item, examinees are shown a blank grid and are asked to recall the location of each dot.

Supplementary Subtests. Facial Memory Delayed is a recognition subtest in which examinees are shown 40 pictures and asked to indicate whether each picture was shown during the core Facial Memory subtest. In Memory for Stories Delayed, examinees are asked to recall details from the Memory for Stories subtest. Object Recall Delayed is a recognition subtest in which examinees are shown 40 pictures and asked to indicate whether the picture was shown during Object Recall.

Correct responses receive 1 point, and failed or omitted items receive 0 points. Three subtests have unscored practice items designed to ensure comprehension of task instructions. The nine subtest total scores are each converted into scaled scores (M = 10; SD = 3) that contribute to five index scores (M = 100; SD = 15) that include the following: Composite Memory Index (all six core subtests), Verbal Memory Index (three core subtests), Nonverbal Memory Index (three core subtests), Learning Index (the two core subtests with multiple learning trials), and a Delayed Recall Index (the three supplementary subtests).

The TOMAL-SE kit contains the examiner's manual, stimulus book, 15 chips (used during two core subtests), and 25 record forms. The examiner's manual contains information on TOMAL-SE development, subtest descriptions, administration and scoring instructions, psychometric data, interpretive guidance, and score transformation tables. The record forms contain administration and scoring instructions including discontinue rules, plus space for recording and plotting test scores.

DEVELOPMENT. As stated in the test manual, the TOMAL-SE is an adaptation and upward extension of the TOMAL-Second Edition, which was published in 2007. The upper age range was extended to 89 (from 60). Administration time was decreased to reduce the impact of fatigue on performance. Many existing visual memory tests require fine motor control, which is often impaired in older adults; however, graphomotor demand is minimized on the TOMAL-SE.

Development of the TOMAL-SE occurred over five years. Content was adapted from previous versions of the TOMAL, which was initially intended to measure memory in children and adolescents, then was revised to include young and middle-age adults, and most recently extended for use with older adults. Content was selected to reflect both verbal and visual memory, based on a neurobiological conceptual framework. Upon piloting, some items were eliminated. No further information on item development and selection is provided in the test materials.

TECHNICAL.

Standardization. The TOMAL-SE was standardized on 428 individuals ages 55-89 from 15 states across the United States and recruited between 2008 and 2009. Their demographic makeup closely matched that of the U.S. population based on 2010 U.S. Census data. No information is provided on whether normative sample participants were screened for injuries or diseases affecting the central nervous system. The test authors note that 65% were living independently or with family, 26% were in senior housing, 7% were in nursing homes or assisted living facilities, and 2% were living in other housing arrangements. The TOMAL-SE was also administered to three clinical subgroups comprising 48 individuals ages 57-89 and diagnosed with dementia (n = 8), stroke (n = 24), and psychiatric disturbance (n = 16).

Per the test manual, a continuous norming procedure was used to develop standardized scores. Percentile ranks were derived and converted to standard scores for each age band. Tables for converting subtest raw scores to standard scores and percentile ranks are presented for six age bands: 55-64, 65-69, 70-74, 75-79, 80-84, and 85-89. Tables for converting the sum of scaled scores to index scores and percentile ranks are included in an appendix in the test manual.

Reliability. For the total sample, internal consistency indices for subtests ranged from .81 (Facial Memory) to .98 (Object Recall Delayed), and among the indexes from .94 (Nonverbal Memory Index) to .97 (Composite Memory Index). Across the six age bands, internal consistency estimates were high across subtests, ranging from .73 to .99; all composites exceeded .90. Among the clinical subgroups, internal consistency estimates were high for most subtests (median = .85) and all composite scores (median = .94). The modal standard error of measurement index at the subtest level was 1 (range 0-2). At the composite level, standard errors of measurement indices ranged from 3 to 5. Test-retest reliability, estimated with a sample of 35 participants who completed the TOMAL-SE twice across a 2-week period, yielded coefficients of .80 and higher across all age bands. Interscorer reliability was assessed by having two individuals independently score 50 protocols that were randomly selected from the normative sample; reliability coefficients ranged from .93 to .99 for indices and .91 to .99 for subtests.

Validity. Per the test manual, TOMAL-SE content was reviewed by five clinical neuropsychologists; at least four of the five ranked memory as the most salient cognitive feature for all subtests. Factor analysis resulted in a two-factor solution but diverged from the authors' verbal/nonverbal classification of subtests. Rather, Visual Sequential Memory and Memory for Location loaded on one factor, whereas Object Recall and the remaining core subtests loaded on a second factor. Correlation coefficients (corrected for range effects and attenuation) between TOMAL-SE indexes and the Screening Memory Index from the Wide Range Assessment of Memory and Learning, Second Edition (Sheslow & Adams, 2003) ranged from .75 to .87. Correlations with an intellectual screening measure yielded corrected coefficients ranging from .65 to .85. Correlations with a fluency test demonstrated corrected coefficients that ranged from .47 to .73. Construct validity was supported by comparing the standardization and clinical samples on TOMAL-SE performance, the latter of which scored approximately 1 standard deviation below the former.

COMMENTARY. Key strengths of the TOMAL-SE include content coverage spanning verbal and visual modalities in a relatively brief administration time. Verbal and visual memory constructs were partially supported by factor analysis. Visual test materials are contained in a single stimulus book for ease of use. Also, visual tests rely on a recognition format and circumvent the need for fine hand-motor control.

Test administration and scoring is generally straightforward with a few exceptions. For example, on some subtests, the orientation of the stimulus book may make it difficult to reconcile examinee responses with the record form. The examiner must mentally rotate the stimulus book and examinee responses to correspond to the scoring form. Also, the pages in the stimulus book can be difficult to turn, which is concerning for test items with exposure time limits.

Because assessing delayed recall is a key component of memory evaluation and is a sensitive indicator of dementia (Welsh, Butters, Hughes, Mohs, & Heyman, 1992), it is curious that the delayed recall subtests are supplementary. The test demonstrates adequate reliability and some evidence that supports validity of its scores; however, discriminant validity evidence is relatively weaker.

The test manual presents insufficient data on test performance among clinical groups, and independent research on the TOMAL-SE is needed.

SUMMARY. The TOMAL-SE was designed to be a brief, individually administered measure of memory, designed for use with older adults. It meets its goal of suitability for older adults given relatively brief administration time and reduced reliance on fine motor control. It has strong reliability, but further evidence of its validity (particularly convergent/discriminant validity evidence using measures of memory and other cognitive functions, as well as validation in persons with brain injury, dementia, and other diseases affecting the central nervous system) is needed. Clinicians should consider using established measures such as the Wechsler Memory Scale—Fourth Edition (Weschler, 2009) until further research supporting the TOMAL-SE is available.

REVIEWER'S REFERENCES

Sheslow, D., & Adams, W. (2003). Wide Range Assessment of Memory and Learning, Second Edition. San Antonio, TX: Pearson.

Wechsler, D. (2009). Wechsler Memory Scale—Fourth Edition. San Antonio, TX: Pearson.

Welsh, K. A., Butters, N., Hughes, J. P., Mohs, R. C., & Heyman, A. (1992). Detection and staging of dementia in Alzheimer's disease: Use of the neuropsychological measures developed for the Consortium to Establish a Registry for Alzheimer's Disease. *Archives of Neurology, 49*, 448-452.

[173]

Test of Narrative Language–Second Edition.

Purpose: Designed to assess "comprehension and production of connected speech used to tell stories."
Population: Ages 4-0 to 15-11.
Publication Dates: 2004-2017.
Acronym: TNL-2.
Scores, 3: Comprehension, Production, Narrative Language Ability Index.
Administration: Individual.
Price Data, 2020: $201 per kit including manual (2017, 136 pages), picture book, and 25 record booklets; $81 per picture book; $75 per manual; $59 per 25 record booklets.
Time: 15-30 minutes for administration; 20-30 minutes for scoring.
Comments: Digital audio recorder required for administration.
Authors: Ronald B. Gillam and Nils A. Pearson.
Publisher: PRO-ED.
Cross References: For reviews by Abigail Baxter and Gabriele van Lingen of the original edition, see 16:247.

Review of the Test of Narrative Language—Second Edition by KATHLEEN ASPIRANTI, Assistant Professor, Youngstown State University, Youngstown, OH:

DESCRIPTION. The Test of Narrative Language—Second Edition (TNL-2) is an updated version of the Test of Narrative Language (TNL) that was developed to examine the narrative language abilities of children ages 4-0 through 15-11. The TNL-2 provides a comprehensive measure of a child's ability to understand and tell stories. The goal of the TNL-2 is to assess the comprehension and production of narrative language through scripted stories, personal stories, and fictional stories. The TNL-2 purports to identify children who have narrative language or pragmatic disorders, to recognize discrepancies between narrative comprehension and production, to monitor progress in narrative language that results from language interventions, and to evaluate narrative language in research studies. The test consists of 109 items across six tasks: three in the Comprehension subtest and three in the Production subtest. Each subtest consists of three story types: a narrative script with a picture, a personal story with sequenced pictures, and a fictional story with a picture. Examiners must have some formal training in language development and assessment.

With no time limits, the TNL-2 takes 15-30 minutes to administer. An additional 20-30 minutes are needed for scoring. It is recommended that examiners audio record the testing session to make scoring easier and more reliable. The TNL-2 is administered using a picture book with verbal stimuli for each task and an examiner record booklet for the examiner to administer and score tasks. Scores on oral narratives are calculated by the number of specific ideas provided by the child and do not require the examiner transcription. Tables are provided in the examiner's manual that provide detailed scoring criteria for each task. Scoring is completed by hand with standard scores, percentile ranks, and age equivalents provided for the Comprehension subtest, Production subtest, and total Narrative Language Ability Index (NLAI). In addition, standard errors of measurement (*SEM*s) at 10 age intervals are provided. The record form includes a space for listing the corresponding *SEM*.

DEVELOPMENT. In developing the TNL-2, the test authors indicated that the basic elements of the TNL were maintained. A detailed rationale for the content and format of the test is included in the validity section of the examiner's manual. The specific theoretical models of narrative language development are described and matched to each task of the TNL-2. Specific rationale for the content of each subtest is also provided. However, information about pilot testing new items is lacking. As the TNL-2 is an update from the TNL, its authors indicated several improvements based on feedback and research but did not elaborate on said feedback or research. Improvements noted include updated norms with a larger and more diverse normative sample, a wider range of standardization ages (4 through 15 instead of 5 through 12), pictorial supports for all tasks, updated pictures, an increase of the number of items to expand the floor and ceiling of each task, updated scoring systems for oral narratives, and updated evidence of reliability and validity.

TECHNICAL.

Standardization. Normative sample data were collected with the following standardization measures in place: Only experienced examiners administered the TNL-2; signed parental permission was obtained for each child; audio recordings of each administration were analyzed for fidelity; and electronic data were submitted to integrity checks. The normative sample consisted of 1,310 children ages 4-0 through 15-11 from 21 states and 162 ZIP codes. When compared to U.S. Census data (ProQuest, 2015; Snyder, deBrey, & Dillow, 2016), the normative sample was relatively representative of the population regarding geographic region, gender, race, Hispanic status, parental education level, family income level, and exceptionality status.

Reliability. Evidence of reliability was provided for the TNL-2 through internal consistency reliability, test-retest reliability, and interscorer reliability data. Alpha coefficients were calculated to estimate the internal consistency of each subtest and the NLAI for each age group and ranged from .73 (11-year-olds, Comprehension subtest) to .94 (6-year-olds, NLAI). Average alpha coefficients were .81 for the Comprehension subtest, .87 for the Production subtest, and .90 for the NLAI. *SEM*s for 10 age intervals were also provided for each subtest and the NLAI with modal *SEM*s of 1 for both the Comprehension and Production subtests and 5 for the NLAI. Alpha coefficients were reported for both subtests and the NLAI for selected gender, race, and exceptionality subgroups. Reported values were ≥ .93, ≥ .92, and ≥ .74, respectively.

Test-retest reliability was evaluated through a sample of 58 children using an interval of approximately two weeks. Reliability coefficients were .85 for the Comprehension subtest, .82 for the Production subtest, and .93 for the NLAI. Interscorer reliability was examined through two individuals independently scoring 50 random TNL-2 test protocols. Correlations for interscorer agreement were .99 for the Comprehension subtest, Production subtest, and NLAI. Overall, the reliability coefficients provide evidence for acceptable levels of internal consistency, test-retest, and interscorer reliability.

Validity. Extensive evidence of validity is provided through content-description, criterion-prediction, and construct-identification validity evidence. As mentioned above, the test manual includes extensive description of the rationale used to create the format and items for the TNL-2. Point-biserial correlations were used to determine item discrimination. The median item discrimination coefficients for each subtest ranged from .20 to .34 across the range of ages for which the test is intended, which are satisfactory levels for item discrimination. Item difficulty was examined through the percentage of examinees that pass a specific item. The median difficulty of Comprehension items ranged from .20 to .80, whereas the median difficulty of Production items ranged from .12 to .62. The items are more difficult for younger children than for older children.

Test bias was analyzed using differential item functioning (DIF) analysis for each item. There were no items with moderate or large effect sizes when comparisons were made between selected subgroups of examinees. Demographic subgroup comparisons were conducted for mean subtest and composite standard scores of several subgroups. Mean scores were comparable across all subgroups with NLAI scores ranging from 93 for Hispanic examinees to 103 for Asian/Pacific Islander examinees. The magnitudes of any comparison group differences were small based on effect size measures using Cohen's *d* and effect size *r*, and described further in the examiner's manual.

Criterion-prediction evidence of validity was evaluated through correlations of the TNL-2 with the Systematic Analysis of Language Transcripts software analysis (SALT; Miller, Andriacchi, & Nockerts, 2011). Analyses of the number of different words (NDW), mean length of utterance (MLU), and narrative structure score (NSS) were conducted for 142 children ages 5-12. These scores were correlated with the TNL-2 subtest and NLAI scores and yielded moderate coefficients for the Comprehension subtest (*r* ranged from .38 to .47) and large coefficients for the Production subtest (*r* ranged from .49 to .70) and the NLAI (*r* ranged from .53 to .66). Diagnostic accuracy analysis was provided through receiver operating characteristic/area under the curve (ROC/AUC) analyses, which yielded an area under the curve of .97. A cutoff index score of 92 provided the best sensitivity and specificity for children with a previous diagnosis of a language learning disability (LLD) with sensitivity and specificity values of .92, indicating that the TNL-2 is capable of discriminating between individuals with and without LLDs.

Construct-identification evidence of validity was evaluated through several procedures. Each subtest correlated at a large or very large magnitude with the age of the examinee, and, using data from the entire normative sample, subtest scores demonstrated a correlation coefficient of .62. Analyses of scores from different subgroups are provided and extensively discussed, with mean differences from primary parental language, school achievement, and five exceptionality subgroups (gifted and talented, attention-deficit/hyperactivity disorder, articulation disorder, learning disability, language impairment). Finally, confirmatory factor analysis was conducted with large to very large factor loadings on each task. Overall, there is vast evidence for the validity of test results from the TNL-2.

COMMENTARY. The TNL-2 is an updated version of the original TNL and provides new standardization with a large, diverse sample with demographic characteristics representative of the U.S. population. This is an improvement from the TNL, which included a limited normative sample. Additional items to increase the floor and ceiling of each task were included, thereby improving the reliability of scores for struggling and advanced examinees. The TNL-2 also has provided more evidence of validity for its use as a diagnostic assessment to identify children with language impairment or language-based learning disabilities. The test authors indicate that the TNL-2 should be used in conjunction with other measures if used for identification purposes, and with a 6.8% rate of false positives at the recommended cutoff score of 92, these reviewers agree with this statement. Additionally, the test authors suggest the TNL-2 could be used to help diagnose social communication disorder, but this must be interpreted with great caution as criteria to diagnose social communication disorder have not been empirically validated (Swineford, Thurm, Baird, Wetherby, & Swedo, 2014).

The materials are adequate for administering and scoring the TNL-2, and scoring criteria are explained in depth through tables available in the examiner's manual. Although the test authors provide a description of the theoretical knowledge behind narrative language, pilot data and information about the development of specific new items are lacking. The current reviewers administered the TNL-2 to several children of various ages to examine the face validity of the test when administered to children. The TNL-2 was easy to administer but took some time to score, particularly the Production subtests. All three children found the test fun, were able to follow directions, and understood the purpose of the tasks. Overall, the TNL-2 seemed to accurately reflect each child's narrative language ability. The children felt the test was enjoyable and were open to taking the test again at a later date when asked.

SUMMARY. The TNL-2 is a norm-referenced test that measures a child's ability to understand and tell stories. It evaluates narrative language abilities of children ages 4 through 15. The test was developed using a sound theory of language development and extensive reliability and validity measures. The TNL-2 is a welcome update to the TNL, providing a larger standardization sample, revised pictures and tasks, and additional items. However, in order to diagnose language disabilities, this test should be used in conjunction with other measures of language and/or child development.

REVIEWER'S REFERENCES

Miller, J. F., Andriacchi, K., & Nockerts, A. (2011). *Assessing language production using SALT software: A clinician's guide to language sample analysis.* Middleton, WI: SALT Software.

ProQuest. (2015). *ProQuest statistical abstract of the United States 2015: The national data book.* Bethesda, MD: Bernan Press.

Snyder, T. D., deBrey, C., & Dillow, S. A. (2016). *Digest of educational statistics 2014* (NCES 2016-006). Washington, DC: National Center for Education Statistics, Institute of Education Sciences, U.S. Department of Education.

Swineford, L. B., Thurm, A., Baird, G., Wetherby, A. M., & Swedo, S. (2014). Social (pragmatic) communication disorder: A research review of this new DSM-5 diagnostic category. *Journal of Neurodevelopmental Disorders, 6*(1), 41.

Review of the Test of Narrative Language—Second Edition by LISSA POWER deFUR, Professor, Communication Sciences and Disorders, and Director, Speech, Hearing, and Learning Services, Longwood University, Farmville, VA:

DESCRIPTION. The Test of Narrative Language—Second Edition (TNL-2) is an individually administered test that aims to measure children's ability to both understand and tell stories. It includes three types of stories: scripts, personal narratives, and fictional narratives. It is based on the concept of narrative language, that is, stories that present relationships between characters and actions and are organized with a plot structure. The TNL-2 is designed for four uses: (a) identifying children with narrative language and/or social disorders; (b) identifying whether there is a discrepancy between narrative comprehension and production; (c) documenting progress; and (d) measuring narrative language in research. The target population is individuals ages 4 years 0 months through 15 years 11 months. The assessment requires audio taping children's responses for scoring accuracy. Administration time is approximately 15 to 30 minutes.

DEVELOPMENT. The process of revising and re-standardizing the Test of Narrative Language (TNL), originally published in 2004, began in 2012. Normative data, gathered between 2013 and 2015, used a sample conforming to the U.S. population (as reported by the U.S. Census Bureau). This sample was larger than that for the TNL. In addition to updating normative data, the TNL-2 developers revised the pictures to be more engaging, increased the number of items on the comprehension tasks by adding items for both younger and older children, and revised the scoring system to facilitate the scoring process. Most notably, reliability and validity data were updated, addressing a concern with the TNL. This extensive section of the test manual includes a discussion of the diagnostic accuracy of the TNL-2.

The TNL-2 is based on the literature regarding narratives, using research from the fields of linguistics, psychology, and speech-language pathology. Narratives include both comprehension and production, and both modalities are assessed in this test. The test is designed to uncover the typical difficulties students with language disorders and learning disabilities have with narratives, as described in the research. The TNL-2 seeks to identify such comprehension difficulties as drawing inferences, remembering story elements, and understanding the gist of the story. The TNL-2 examines production difficulties at both the macrostructure and microstructure levels. These include the child's ability to reference characters and story contexts, to use grammar propositions, and to organize the story (macrostructure). At the microstructure level, the TNL-2 is designed to identify children's vocabulary restrictions, use of complex sentences, and ability to tie the story together.

The TNL-2 is structured to assess children's abilities in three types of stories: scripts, personal-like narratives, and fiction-like narratives. These stories represent six tasks, with both comprehension and production for each of the six stories. Scoring results in two subtest scores (Comprehension and Production) and a total score (Narrative Language Ability Index; NLAI).

TECHNICAL. The standardization sample for TNL-2 included 1,310 children ages 4 years 0 months through 15 years 11 months, residing in 21 states and 162 ZIP codes. The sample was designed to reflect geographic region, gender, race, Hispanic status, family income, educational level of the parents, and exceptionality status that are representative of the United States as a whole.

The consistency with which the TNL-2 measures both comprehension and production narrative language skills is reflected in respectable reliability coefficients. Test-retest reliability was examined using a sample of children (n = 58) across the age range of the test, who completed the TNL-2 twice over an interval of about two weeks. The test authors' analyses revealed corrected test-retest reliability coefficients that exceeded .82 for the subtests and a coefficient of .99 for NLAI. Interscorer reliability estimates were .99 for the TNL-2 subtests and index. Therefore, the TNL-2 meets the standard of reliability, and test users can have confidence in the results.

Evidence of validity for the TNL-2 includes content-description, criterion-prediction, and construct-identification. With reference to content-description evidence, the TNL-2 was developed by focusing on the research-based rationale for the assessment and contemporary models of narrative language. The formats of the subtests were developed based on the characterizations of children's narratives as discussed in the research literature. The test authors conducted two studies of test bias to detect possible bias at the item, subtest, and composite score levels. These analyses revealed little to no bias for any subgroup (gender, black/African American, Asian/Pacific Islander, or Hispanic).

Criterion-prediction evidence, the ability of the assessment to predict an individual's performance, means that a test should correlate strongly with established measures of comparable abilities and accurately differentiate among persons with better than average or delayed abilities. The TNL-2 was found to correlate most strongly with the Narrative Structure Score (NSS) of the Systematic Analysis of Language Transcripts software (SALT; Miller, Andriacchi, & Nockerts, 2011), a well-researched instrument for measuring children's production of narratives. Correlation coefficients for the NSS and the Comprehension subtest, the Production subtest, and the NLAI were .47, .70, and .66, respectively. In the area of diagnostic accuracy, the test authors compared performance on the TNL-2 using children identified by school personnel as having a language learning disorder and students with no known language or literacy deficits. To the extent that these school diagnoses were accurate, the TNL-2 demonstrated strong sensitivity (ability to correctly identify children with significant difficulties in narrative language) and strong specificity (ability to correctly identify children without significant difficulties in narrative language), with corresponding indices of .92 for both indicators of diagnostic accuracy.

Construct-identification evidence, or the degree to which the traits reflect the theoretical model the TNL-2 is based upon, appears strong. Specifically, the TNL-2 demonstrated construct-identification evidence through its demonstration that narrative language raw scores increased with increases in participants' ages, that different aspects of narrative language assessed correlate with one another (the test manual reports an intercorrelation coefficient of .62 between the scaled scores of the subtests), that the TNL-2 results correlate with data on school achievement (Catts, Nielsen, Bridges, Liu, & Bontempo, 2015), and that the measure differentiates among groups that have above and below average language skills (extensive evidence provided in the test manual).

The thorough standardization analysis demonstrates high levels of reliability and validity for the TNL-2.

COMMENTARY. The TNL-2 is a valuable tool for assessing narrative language in children, from upper preschool age through adolescence. It is more time efficient than completing a language sample analysis, making it a valuable tool for professionals investigating children's narrative language. It has a strong theoretical base and represents a research-based construct, building on the test authors' thorough analysis of the literature on narrative development. The lead author, Ronald Gillam, has completed much of the seminal work in language disorders, including in the area of narrative language. The revision of the first edition includes a normative sample that reflects the U.S. population well in terms of geography, gender, race, family income, and parent education. A larger norm group would be desirable, especially in the areas of students with exceptionalities.

Notably, the TNL-2 has strong specificity and sensitivity, making it a useful tool to differentiate between children who have narrative language impairments and those who do not. This makes it an exceptionally important part of an assessment battery used for school personnel during the evaluation for determining eligibility for special education. In addition, the test is designed to be useful for monitoring progress. This feature will similarly be useful to school teams in documenting a child's progress toward meeting individualized educational program goals.

The test administration directions are clear, and the test is easy to administer. The revision addresses prior concerns regarding the ability to discern scripted directions by using different color fonts. The picture plates are colorful and unambiguous, understandable to children of diverse backgrounds. The examiner record booklet is easy to navigate with clearly marked instructions. Detailed scoring criteria are given for the subtest tasks, which is exceptionally useful on an assessment measure such as this when uniform responses are not feasible.

SUMMARY. The TNL-2 is designed to be an individually administered measure of narrative language. It is not designed to be a stand-alone measure of language comprehension and production and will need to be used with additional assessments. The TNL-2 focuses on production and comprehension of scripts, personal narratives, and fictional narratives. It has strong reliability indices and evidence of validity, especially in terms of identifying children with narrative language impairment (sensitivity) and those without (specificity). It is strongly correlated with another well-known measure of narrative language. It is a valuable tool for clinicians who need to identify children with narrative language deficits and is equally useful for monitoring progress in intervention.

REVIEWER'S REFERENCES

Catts, H. W., Nielsen, D. C., Bridges, M. S., Liu, Y. S., & Bontempo, D. E. (2015). Early identification of reading disabilities within an RTI framework. *Journal of Learning Disabilities, 48,* 281-297.

Miller, J. F., Andriacchi, K., & Nockerts, A. (2011). *Assessing language production using SALT software: A clinician's guide to language sample analysis.* Middleton, WI: SALT Software.

[174]

Test of Premorbid Functioning.

Purpose: Designed to "estimate an individual's premorbid [pre-injury] cognitive and memory functioning."
Population: Ages 16-90.
Publication Dates: 2001-2009.
Acronym: TOPF.
Scores: Total score only.
Administration: Individual.

Price Data, 2020: $215.50 per Q-global kit including manual (2009, 104 pages), 25 record forms, and word card; $104.10 per manual; $54.60 per 25 record forms; $15.30 per word card.
Time: Less than 10 minutes for completion.
Comments: A revision of the Wechsler Test of Adult Reading.
Author: Pearson.
Publisher: Pearson.
Cross References: For reviews by Nora M. Thompson and Sandra Ward of the original edition titled Wechsler Test of Adult Reading, see 16:268.

Review of the Test of Premorbid Functioning by SALLY KUHLENSCHMIDT, Professor of Psychology, Western Kentucky University, Bowling Green, KY:

DESCRIPTION. The purpose of the Test of Premorbid Functioning (TOPF) is to estimate what the cognitive functioning and memory of a person was before an injury or traumatic brain event. This estimate can then be compared to current functioning and used to make diagnoses and develop treatment plans. This test is designed to be used with clients ages 16 to 90 who have a range of neurological difficulties. It is a revision of the Wechsler Test of Adult Reading (WTAR).

The TOPF kit includes one Q-global score report for each of the 25 protocols as well as a manual and stimulus word card. Q-global is the test publisher's online scoring and interpretation service. Little information is provided in the test kit about this system, such as whether and where data are stored. Information about the system is available on the test publisher's website. Scoring must be completed online, and a level C qualification is required for purchase.

Instructions for administration appear both in the test manual and on the protocol. The protocol includes a demographic checklist for ages 20 to 90, the TOPF stimulus word list, and a footnote referring the examiner to the test manual for a demographic checklist for examinees ages 16-19. The words on the stimulus card are printed in a large font. Instructions for the test takers are to be read aloud and appear both in the test manual and on the protocol. After a serics of demographic questions the examiner presents a laminated card with 70 words (36 on one side and 34 on the other in two columns). The words are ordered from least to most difficult and have nonobvious pronunciations. Prompts are allowed if the respondent goes too quickly or gives two pronunciations. If the examinee does not respond within approximately 30 seconds, an incorrect response is recorded. Testing is discontinued after five incorrect pronunciations. The test can be completed in a few minutes by a high functioning individual.

Scoring requires preparation, as some of the words have multiple options for pronunciation. The test manual refers the examiner to the online Merriam-Webster or American Heritage Dictionaries (without citations) for audio of acceptable pronunciations.

The TOPF provides a standard score (M = 100, SD = 15) percentile rank, standard error of measurement, and descriptive label. The TOPF was developed with the fourth editions of the Wechsler Adult Intelligence Scale (WAIS-IV) and the Wechsler Memory Scale (WMS-IV). The Q-global report provides comparisons between actual and predicted TOPF, WAIS-IV, and WMS-IV scores along with significance and base rates. The test manual provides two case studies in the Appendices and a sample score report on the publisher's website.

The test authors provide models for estimating pre-morbid functioning using demographic information and TOPF score for two age groups (16 to 19 and 20 to 90). The prediction models are simple demographics only (all ages) complex demographics (ages 20 to 90), TOPF only, and TOPF with each type of demographic model.

DEVELOPMENT. The TOPF was renamed from the prior measure (WTAR) to reduce confusion about the test purpose. Reading was chosen as an ability stable over the lifespan and more resistant to neurological insult than other abilities. The test authors provide minimal information about how the test items were selected, stating that there is some overlap with prior similar measures.

To narrow relevant variables for prediction, the test authors repeatedly conducted hierarchical multiple regression with backward selection, dropping nonsignificant variables. The final set was used for the prediction models. TOPF scores can be predicted from the demographics (e.g., R^2 = .42 for ages 20 to 90) as can the WAIS-IV and WMS-IV index scores. The test manual breaks down each index by prediction model and age groups. For example, for ages 16 to 19 the best model for the Full Scale IQ (FSIQ) was simple demographics with TOPF score (R^2 = .46). For ages 20 to 90, the best model for the FSIQ was the complex demographics with TOPF score (R^2 = .61). A discussion of incremental validity of the TOPF is absent.

TECHNICAL. The TOPF was standardized with the WAIS-IV and WMS-IV, and the test manual refers readers to those manuals for information on the sample. For a number of the Age by Education Level groups there were zero persons in the sample to reflect the Asian population. Despite efforts to improve the prediction range the test is still best for scores from about 59 to 130.

Split-half reliability estimates ranged from .96 to .99 across 13 unevenly distributed age groupings from 16 to 90. Split-half reliability coefficients were .97 or higher for the following special groups: Alzheimer's, mild cognitive impairment, traumatic brain injury, temporal lobectomy, major depressive disorder (MDD), autism spectrum disorder, Asperger's disorder, and attention-deficit/hyperactivity disorder (ADHD). Test-retest stability was evaluated for 293 examinees (3-week average interval). Correlation coefficients ranged from .89 to .95 for four age groups.

Correlations show the strongest relationships (especially for years of education and occupation) to the more verbal WAIS-IV and WMS-IV indices. There were different patterns for minority groups, including negative correlations between TOPF scores and being African-American or Hispanic. Correlations are low for ages 16 to 19. Correlations with the Wechsler Individual Achievement Test-Second Edition (N = 93, ages 16 to 19) found the TOPF correlated most strongly with subtests that assess verbal skills, such as the Reading Composite (r = .82) and the Written Language Composite (r = .70) but was also a fair predictor of Mathematics and Oral Language (both r = .63).

In a concurrent validity study (N = 2,152 ages 16 to 90) the TOPF demonstrated the strongest correlations with the WAIS-IV Verbal Comprehension Index (r = .75) and the FSIQ (r = .70), with lower coefficients observed with the Working Memory Index (r = .61), Perceptual Reasoning Index (r = .50), and Processing Speed Index (r = .37). Similar but lower correlations were found in another study with 16-year-olds and the Wechsler Intelligence Scale for Children, Fourth Edition.

The test authors examined the TOPF with the eight special groups used in the reliability analysis (e.g., Alzheimer's; N = 22 to N = 61). They concluded that for those with brain injury or dementia, scores on the TOPF are likely affected by the disease process and that only the demographic information should be used to predict premorbid functioning. The predictions were better for those with MDD, Asperger's disorder, and ADHD.

COMMENTARY. The strengths of the TOPF include fast and easy administration, a national sample tied to intelligence and memory measures, reliable scores, basic validity information, and a thorough analysis of various models for predicting premorbid functioning. Areas for improvement include the demographic questionnaire, administration of the TOPF, interpretation for specific populations, incremental validity, and clarity on how to choose a prediction model given the research data.

Given the central role of demographics for prediction there is relatively little attention given to gathering and recording this information, including lack of direction on the interview and what information is critical to obtain. There is no protocol space for complex responses, such as for a person who was fostered or adopted. Nor is it clear how to record when the client qualifies for several of the choices, such as several ethnicities. The user is referred to the WAIS-IV for definitions of geographic regions. There is no discussion of disabilities impacting educational attainment. These issues become pressing for those with long histories such as older clients.

Some items need updating, such as choices for *sex* (APA Style prefers *gender*) and *occupation*. *Occupation* presents a number of difficulties (e.g., a ranking of jobs that has *not in labor force* falling in the high middle of the scale above *skilled trade/public safety* whereas *unemployed* is almost at the bottom). Discussion of occupation and education carry implicit societal messages about the value of the individual that might lead a respondent to perform less effectively on the reading task (Steele & Aronson, 1995). Clinicians might consider whether to collect demographic information after the word reading test to avoid influencing performance.

A final category of questions was puzzling. The TOPF asks several questions about current life even though the measure is for premorbid functioning. Are these questions concerned with life immediately prior to the trauma of interest or events on the day of testing? There is an item about sleep the night before the test (to assess fatigue), but sleep patterns change over the lifespan and across circumstances, so interpretation is challenging and no guidance is provided. To assess cognitive reserve, a few questions about physical activity are provided but with no further interpretative guidance. Some items require more judgment in selecting an option (e.g., the quality of one's elementary school, which the examinee may have attended decades ago). A person who lives on a farm, in a nursing facility, or has moved many times may have difficulty meaningfully identifying the wealth of his or her neighborhood. The quality of the prediction models likely could be improved with greater precision in writing, more nuanced options, and clearer instructions.

The reading task would benefit from some changes as well. The stimulus card includes the full name of the test, which might be intimidating to examinees. Examples of incorrect responses would be helpful as well as direction concerning regional accents. Those with physical disabilities may need additional time to articulate the words on the reading task. It would be helpful to have guidelines on what level of articulation challenge invalidates the test results.

The TOPF appears to be less effective for clients 16 to 19 and for minority groups. The prediction models that include the TOPF score are not recommended by the test authors for those with chronic neurological disorders. Developing prediction models using clinical samples would be helpful. Providing incremental validity data would help clinicians judge the value of adding the TOPF to their toolkit.

Clinicians may find interpretation challenging given the multitude of prediction models. Presenting models by age and providing occasional summaries might help. The availability of a simple, accurate tool for estimating premorbid functioning is desirable, but there is still work to do.

SUMMARY. The TOPF requires reading words with nonobvious pronunciations in order to predict premorbid functioning. Demographic information contributes substantially to the multiple prediction models provided. Norm groups are available for ages 16 to 90 and are linked to the WAIS-IV and WMS-IV. Demographic data collection needs improvement. The prediction models including the TOPF are not recommended by the test authors for those with chronic neurological disorders or injuries.

REVIEWER'S REFERENCE

Steele, C., & Aronson, J. (1995). Stereotype threat and the intellectual test performance of African Americans. *Journal of Personality and Social Psychology, 69*, 797–811. https://doi.org/10.1037/0022-3514.69.5.797

Review of the Test of Premorbid Functioning by MARC A. SILVA, James A. Haley Veterans Hospital, Mental Health and Behavioral Sciences Service, Tampa, FL, and ERIN BRENNAN, Doctoral Student, University of South Florida, Department of Educational and Psychological Studies, Tampa, FL:

DESCRIPTION. The Test of Premorbid Functioning (TOPF) is a 70-item measure intended to estimate premorbid intelligence and memory in persons ages 16-90 years. Administration time is less than 10 minutes (PsychCorp, 2018). Examinees are shown an 8.5 x 11 inch card containing 70 printed words with irregular grapheme-to-phoneme translation. They are asked to pronounce each word beginning with Item 1. The test is discontinued following five consecutive errors.

The record form contains administration and scoring instructions, phonetic pronunciations for each word, and space to record demographic information. The test manual directs examiners to dictionary websites for acceptable audio pronunciations. Correct responses each receive 1 point. Total raw scores are converted to standardized scores with a mean of 100 and a standard deviation of 15. Demographics and/or standardized TOPF scores are imputed into regression equations to generate predicted IQ and index scores on the fourth editions of the Wechsler Adult Intelligence Scale (WAIS-IV) and Wechsler Memory Scale (WMS-IV). There are separate regression equations for ages 16-19 and 20-90. Examiners choose to base predictions on demographics alone, TOPF score alone, or demographics plus TOPF score combined. (The test manual recommends the latter.) The test manual provides little guidance on when to select the TOPF-only predictive model, which is associated with larger estimation error for most indices. Using demographics only to predict premorbid cognitive scores is suggested if there is a statistically significant difference between actual and predicted TOPF scores.

For examinees ages 20-90, simple or complex demographics models are available. The simple model includes sex, geographic region, education, race/ethnicity, and occupation. The complex model includes additional factors such as neighborhood affluence and exercise frequency. For examinees ages 16-19, only a simple demographics model is permitted, which omits occupation and includes parent rather than examinee education.

The TOPF is available as a standalone test or bundled with the Advanced Clinical Solutions for WAIS-IV and WMS-IV package. Both contain the test manual, word card, record forms, and computerized scoring. Examiners should have graduate-level training and experience in standardized clinical assessment, although trained technicians and research assistants may administer and score the TOPF under supervision.

DEVELOPMENT. The TOPF is a revision of the Wechsler Test of Adult Reading (WTAR; Psychological Corporation, 2001). Like their predecessors, the National Adult Reading Test (NART; Nelson, 1982) in England, and the American Version (AMNART; Grober, Sliwinsk, & Korey, 1991), the WTAR and TOPF require pronunciation of words with irregular grapheme-to-phoneme conversion. Word reading relies on prior exposure and learning, rather than knowledge of phonemic rules. This reading recognition paradigm assumes that word reading is less vulnerable to decline following neurological insult than other cognitive abilities. The TOPF was conormed with the WAIS-IV and WMS-IV. (The WTAR was conormed with the third editions.)

The TOPF expands upon the WTAR in several ways. The number of test items was increased by 20, with emphasis on more difficult items. Demographics were expanded: The highest educational level was increased, and occupational status and geographic region were added. Also, the TOPF uses equipercentile equating to transform TOPF age-adjusted standard scores to WAIS-IV and WMS-IV equated scores prior to entry into regression equations. Per the TOPF manual, these changes resulted in improved prediction range and prediction accuracy. The test manual provides detail about the characteristics of the standardization sample, the methodological technique behind the prediction models, and psychometric characteristics. Examiners should be aware that computerized scoring is required to obtain predicted IQ and memory scores, as predicted scores are not available in the test manual.

TECHNICAL.

Standardization. Per the test manual, there are two premorbid prediction samples: one for predicting premorbid intellectual functioning, derived from the WAIS-IV standardization sample (N = 2,152), and one for predicting premorbid memory functioning, derived from the WMS-IV standardization sample (N = 1,242). Oversampling of racial/ethnic minorities and persons with low and high educational attainment was conducted. Thus, the prediction samples deviate from the demographic makeup of the U.S. population but ensure representation of these groups (White, African American, Hispanic, Asian, and persons with low and high educational attainment).

Reliability. Internal consistency of TOPF scores was excellent. Split-half reliability was similar across age groups with an average coefficient of .98 in both the premorbid prediction sample and among special clinical groups (e.g., mild cognitive impairment, traumatic brain injury). Standard error of measurement ranged from 1.50 to 3.00 across age groups (M = 2.28). Test-retest stability was examined in a subset of 293 examinees administered the TOPF twice across a 3-week interval. Stability was high (corrected r = .93). Mean score change was ≤ 1 point, indicating minimal practice effect.

Validity. The test manual did not address content evidence of validity. Information on item selection was unavailable. No data were presented comparing the TOPF with other measures of premorbid function such as the NART and the AMNART. However, an independent study (Berg, Durant, Banks, & Miller, 2016) reported poor agreement between the TOPF and the Word Reading subtest from the Wide Range Achievement Test 4.

Convergent and discriminant evidence were supported by comparing results from the TOPF with scores from the Wechsler Individual Achievement Test, Second Edition in a sample of 93 examinees ages 16-19. Correlations with the Reading Composite (r = .82) and related subtests such as Spelling (r = .79) and Word Reading (r = .77), were higher than correlations with nonreading indices (e.g., r = .63 with Mathematics Composite).

The TOPF more strongly predicts intellectual functioning than it does memory. The TOPF correlation with the WAIS-IV FSIQ was .70. Correlation coefficients of the TOPF with WAIS-IV composites ranged from .37 (Processing Speed Index) to .75 (Verbal Comprehension Index). In contrast, correlations with WMS-IV indices yielded coefficients that ranged from .36 (Visual Memory Index) to .47 (Visual Working Memory Index).

Construct evidence of validity was supported via clinical group performance comparisons; predicted versus actual performance discrepancies were larger for persons with Alzheimer's dementia than they were for persons with mild cognitive impairment, for example. There is some evidence that the TOPF may underestimate IQ in clinical samples (Alioto, Hoyman, Posecion, Holt, & Zeiner, 2015).

COMMENTARY. The TOPF is brief, and administration is straightforward. Examiners should familiarize themselves with pronunciations of the words prior to using the TOPF. The test kit does not include an audio recording of acceptable pronunciations. Rather, examiners are directed to dictionary websites for audio clips. Although easily accessible via computer or smart phone, different websites have slight variations in pronunciation that may influence scoring. It may behoove examiners to sample audio clips widely to avoid penalizing examinees unfairly.

The TOPF in certain ways improves upon the WTAR. Psychometrically, its reliability and validity evidence are comparable to the WTAR. The normative sample now includes previously omitted groups (e.g., Asians) and increased representation of persons at the upper and lower extremes of educational attainment. The use of equipercentile equating reduces problems such as regression to the mean.

The test was lengthened by 20 words, with an expanded ceiling. Although this potentially lengthens administration time, this change is coupled with a shortened discontinue rule of five rather than 12 consecutively failed items, which will perhaps reduce frustration of examinees who are struggling.

The TOPF combined with demographics provides better estimates of premorbid functioning than either the TOPF or demographics alone. However, the demographics-only prediction model is indicated in cases of expressive aphasia and reading disorders, as TOPF scores will be influenced by these conditions. Notably, the complex demographics option provides marginally better predictive accuracy beyond simple demographics. This minimal value added may not be worth the time investment to collect the additional demographic information. Finally, the TOPF is most appropriately used as a predictor of premorbid intelligence (FSIQ and VCI in particular) because the predictive accuracy of memory indices is considerably lower. Other limitations include scant evidence of item selection and validity based on test content. There is a need for independent research validating the TOPF in various clinical groups.

SUMMARY. Premorbid functioning estimation assists clinicians with evaluating whether brain injury or disease has resulted in cognitive decline. The TOPF has utility as a measure of premorbid cognition, particularly intellectual functioning. The TOPF combined with demographics provides better predictive accuracy than either one alone in most cases. Unusually low TOPF scores may underestimate premorbid ability, and demographic predictions are more appropriate in select circumstances. Although the WTAR and TOPF are similar in many respects regarding reliability and validity, the latter is a more suitable choice due to extended predictive range, expanded representation of subgroups, and the shift in clinical assessment from the third to the fourth edition of the WAIS.

REVIEWERS' REFERENCES

Alioto, A., Hoyman, L., Posecion, L., Holt, H., & Zeiner, H. (2015). Comparison of Advanced Clinical Solutions Test of Premorbid Functioning and "best performance method" in estimating baseline intellectual functioning [Abstract]. *Archives of Clinical Neuropsychology, 30,* 598. doi:10.1093/arclin/acv047.299

Berg, J.-L., Durant, J., Banks, S. J., & Miller, J. B. (2016). Estimates of premorbid ability in a neurodegenerative disease clinic population: Comparing the Test of Premorbid Functioning and the Wide Range Achievement Test, 4th Edition. *The Clinical Neuropsychologist, 30,* 547-557. doi:10.1080/13854046.2016.1186224

Grober, E., Sliwinsk, M., & Korey, S. R. (1991). Development and validation of a model for estimating premorbid verbal intelligence in the elderly. *Journal of Clinical and Experimental Neuropsychology, 13,* 933-949.

Nelson, H. E. (1982). *National Adult Reading Test: Test manual.* Windsor, United Kingdom: NFER-Nelson.

PsychCorp. (2018). Test of Premorbid Functioning (TOPF). Retrieved January 5, 2018, from https://www.pearsonclinical.com/psychology/products/100001946/test-of-premorbid-functioning.html?origsearchtext=topf

[175]

Test of Semantic Reasoning.

Purpose: Designed "to measure children's depth of vocabulary knowledge without relying on expressive language skills (e.g., defining or describing words)."
Population: Ages 7 through 17.
Publication Date: 2016.
Acronym: TOSR.
Scores: Total score only.
Administration: Individual.
Price Data, 2020: $175 per kit including manual (77 pages), test plates, and 25 record forms; $80 per test plates; $55 per manual; $40 per 25 record forms.
Time: Approximately 20 minutes to administer and 5 minutes to score.
Comments: May be completed in more than one session.
Authors: Beth Lawrence and Deena Seifert.
Publisher: Academic Therapy Publications.

Review of the Test of Semantic Reasoning by MARY BOYLE, Professor of Communication Sciences & Disorders, Montclair State University, Montclair, NJ:

DESCRIPTION. The Test of Semantic Reasoning (TOSR) is designed to examine semantic skills, particularly depth of vocabulary knowledge, in children and adolescents ages 7 to 17 without requiring oral or written responses. The test authors define vocabulary depth as the extent of semantic representations a person has for each known word. Others have defined vocabulary depth as involving precision and multiplicity of meaning, collocational use of words, morphological knowledge about word structure, and use of a word in different contexts (Li & Kirby, 2015; Tannenbaum, Torgesen, & Wagner, 2005). The TOSR focuses on the last part of the definition: Each targeted semantic concept is represented photographically in four contexts. The test authors chose the term *semantic reasoning* to convey the process of analyzing the relationship among words or pictures to infer the meaning of a new word. The authors state that an individual must integrate visual processing, inferential thinking, and deductive reasoning to choose the one word from four choices that best represents the commonality among the photographs.

The TOSR was designed to be administered by speech-language pathologists, clinical psychologists, school psychologists, learning specialists, and others trained to assess language skills. Testing can be completed in approximately 20 minutes, and results can be scored in 5 minutes. Although the test can be completed in a single session, the test authors suggest using more than one testing session for younger children or for individuals who demonstrate fatigue, resistance, or negative behavior.

Materials consist of a test manual, a 90-item test plates booklet, and a record form for recording and scoring performance. Instructions for administering and scoring the test are straightforward, and the materials are easy to manipulate during testing. The test manual provides complete instructions for administration and scoring. Directions for administering the test (e.g., the starting items for specific chronological ages, how to establish basals and ceilings) are also summarized on the record form. Correct answers for each item are printed in bold on the record form, and items are scored 1 if correct or 0 if incorrect.

The test plates booklet is a spiral binder that can be set up so the picture plate is visible to the test taker and a page containing the corresponding instructions or prompts is visible to the examiner. One demonstration item and one practice item are to be administered before starting the test proper. Instructions for administering these items are provided in the test manual and duplicated in the test plates booklet. For each of the 90 test items, the prompt "Which word goes with all four pictures?" and the four printed words for that test item are on the side of the test plates booklet facing the examiner, while the test taker sees the plate with the four pictures and the four printed words for that item.

The total raw score is the number of items that the test taker answers correctly plus items preceding the basal item. The total raw score is converted to a standard score, a percentile rank, and an age-equivalent using the appropriate age table contained in an appendix to the test manual. The test manual also provides 90% and 95% confidence intervals for the standard score for each age. The record form provides space to record the raw score, the standard score, either the 90% or 95% confidence interval associated with the standard score, the percentile rank, and the age-equivalent.

DEVELOPMENT. The test authors developed the TOSR to allow measurement of a child's depth of vocabulary knowledge without requiring an oral or written response. They cite research that reported a strong relationship between word knowledge and reading comprehension as supporting the need for a test to examine vocabulary depth. They assert that requiring oral or written responses may confound results if the test taker has impairments in language formulation or word retrieval.

The test authors focused on theories of vocabulary development and reasoning skills in developing the TOSR. They relate the notion of vocabulary depth to the process of extended mapping, which is involved in learning words. Upon first exposure to a word, children make a guess about the word's meaning based on the context in which they hear it, a process called fast mapping. As they are exposed to the word over time and in different contexts, they develop a deeper, more nuanced understanding of the word's meaning, a process called extended mapping. Children use clues from the environmental or textual context to deepen their understanding of an already-acquired word or to infer the meaning of an unfamiliar word. The TOSR requires individuals to use inductive reasoning to identify similarities among the four pictures on the test plate. Then, they must apply deductive reasoning, using their knowledge about the meanings of the four printed words, to infer the connection between one of the printed words and the four images.

Potential items for the TOSR were selected from several published word lists using criteria of grade level, number of nuanced meanings, and ease of visual representation. A 118-item version of the TOSR was piloted on 376 children ages 6 years 0 months (6-0) to 18 years 11 months (18-11), including 29 individuals with diagnoses that included learning disabilities, specific language impairment, and attention-deficit/hyperactivity disorder. After items were eliminated for bias or inadequate discrimination, models were tested for reliability. A 90-item model that maximized the range of item difficulty across the age span was chosen for norming. The 90 items underwent assessment for item difficulty, item discrimination, and item bias. All 90 items were retained.

TECHNICAL. The standardization sample for the TOSR consisted of 1,117 English-speaking children and adolescents ages 7-0 to 17-11 living in the United States. The sample was representative of the U.S. population as reported in the 2010 Census in terms of gender, ethnicity, Hispanic origin, parent education level, region of the country (North Central, Northeast, South, or West), and urban/suburban versus rural dwelling. The sample included 114 individuals with disabilities. The disabilities included specific language impairment, learning disability, autism, and attention-deficit/hyperactivity disorder. Some of the individuals with disabilities had more than one disability, but the number of such individuals is not reported. Raw score means, standard deviations, and smoothed medians for each age group are provided.

Coefficient alpha was used to estimate internal consistency of test items for each age range. Coefficients above .90 were obtained for each range, and Fisher's average of all of the values was .96. This suggests that the TOSR demonstrates strong internal consistency.

Stability, or test-retest reliability, was assessed for 86 individuals who were tested a second time 13 to 24 days after initial testing. To assess whether there was a statistically significant difference between the mean scores of the sample at the two test times, a *t*-test was performed, although no information on the type of *t*-test was provided—presumably it was the paired-sample formula. Of concern, a significant difference was found between the test sessions, which indicates that the scores in the second session increased above levels that would be expected by chance variation. The test authors state that this increase in scores indicates that a practice effect occurred. They speculate that waiting 4 to 6 months before re-testing will "reduce any practice effects" (manual, p. 43). However, they do not provide any data demonstrating that a longer time period would, in fact, decrease or eliminate practice effects. This poses problems regarding interpretation of changes in the TOSR results of an individual over time because an evaluator cannot be sure whether changes in the score are due to true changes in an individual's semantic reasoning, due to practice effects, or due to poor stability of the test.

Regarding test-retest correlation results, the test authors report that coefficients were "corrected for range effects" (manual, p. 43). Generally, correlation coefficients are corrected for range *restriction* (not "range effects"), which is expected to underestimate a correlation's strength. There are several methods of correcting for range restriction, but the test authors do not disclose which method they used or why that method was chosen. It is possible that the test authors conflated the terms *range restriction* and *attenuation effects* when they used the term *range effects*, but these are two separate matters. Attenuation effects occur when a test is unreliable, which may be the case with the TOSR given the statistically significant difference in scores from the first to the second test session. However, the test authors do not discuss correcting the correlation coefficient for attenuation effects. Methods to correct for attenuation effects are different from methods used to correct for range restriction.

The authors did not disclose what statistic they used to assess test-retest correlation, but since they reported the results as *r*, it appears that they used the Pearson product-moment correlation. Many statisticians suggest that the intraclass correlation coefficient, rather than the Pearson product-moment correlation, be used to assess test-retest stability because the Pearson statistic cannot detect systematic error (Weir, 2005). The test authors report that the uncorrected correlation coefficient for the TOSR was .73 and that the corrected correlation coefficient was .94. Correlation coefficients of .70 or above are generally considered to be acceptable.

The test authors report the standard error of measurement *(SEM)* by age, along with the associated 90% and 95% confidence intervals. However, it is not clear whether the *SEM* was calculated using the uncorrected or corrected correlation coefficient. Because of the lack of clarity concerning the rationale or methodology for calculating the corrected correlation coefficient, the *SEMs* should be interpreted with caution.

The methods used in developing the TOSR provide content evidence of validity. To assess its concurrent validity, the TOSR was compared to the Receptive One-Word Picture Vocabulary Test, 4th Edition (ROWPVT-4; Martin & Brownell, 2010), a norm-referenced assessment of receptive vocabulary breadth. Because there is no other test that assesses vocabulary depth without requiring oral or written responses, the comparison to the ROWPVT-4 is reasonable. Twenty individuals took both tests. The test authors report that there was no statistically significant difference in the scores of the two tests ($t(19) = 2.03, p = 0.057$). However, given the small sample size, it is possible that no difference was found because of insufficient power. This possibility is supported by the fact that the probability value was close to being statistically significant. The test authors report uncorrected ($r = .91$) and corrected ($r = .72$) correlation coefficient values that suggest a strong relationship between scores on the two tests.

COMMENTARY. The TOSR is a test that shows promise in assessing an aspect of semantic knowledge in children and adolescents that is not addressed by other assessments. Its strengths include careful development and its ability to tap semantic reasoning ability without confounding results by requiring oral or written responses. In future development of the TOSR, the authors might consider improving the psychometric properties in several ways. First, it is important to verify their speculation that an interval of 4 to 6 months before re-testing will eliminate the practice effects that were evident with their norming sample. If they cannot demonstrate that test results are stable from one administration to another, then it is not possible to use the TOSR to assess semantic reasoning ability (or change in that ability) with confidence. Additionally, the preferred intraclass correlation coefficient (rather than the Pearson product-moment correlation) should be used to assess test-retest stability. In this regard, the rationale and methodology for correcting the correlation coefficient should be clearly reported, and the coefficient used to calculate the *SEM* should be clearly indicated.

SUMMARY. The TOSR was designed to measure a child's depth of vocabulary knowledge without requiring an oral or written response. This aspect of semantic knowledge is not currently addressed by other assessments. However, several aspects of the test need attention, including a re-evaluation of test-retest reliability after a longer interval between sessions than was used with the standardization sample and clear, transparent reporting of the rationale and methodology used to calculate reliability of the measurement.

REVIEWER'S REFERENCES

Li, M., & Kirby, J. R. (2015). The effects of vocabulary breadth and depth on English reading. *Applied Linguistics, 36*, 611-634.

Martin, N. A., & Brownell, R. (2011). Receptive One-Word Picture Vocabulary Test, 4th Edition. Novato, CA: Academic Therapy Publications.

Tannenbaum, K. R., Torgesen, J. K., & Wagner, R. K. (2005). Relationships between world knowledge and reading comprehension in third-grade children. *Scientific Studies of Reading, 10*, 381-398.

Weir, J. P. (2005). Quantifying test-retest reliability using the intraclass correlation coefficient and the SEM. *Journal of Strength Conditioning and Resistance, 19*, 231-240.

Review of the Test of Semantic Reasoning by DIANA B. NEWMAN, Associate Professor (Retired), Communication Disorders, Southern Connecticut State University, New Haven, CT:

DESCRIPTION. The Test of Semantic Reasoning (TOSR) is an individually administered standardized assessment for use with individuals 7-17 years of age that measures the breadth and depth of vocabulary knowledge and the ability to reason using semantic information. The breadth of vocabulary is defined as the number of words in one's lexicon, surface-level knowledge of the word. The depth of vocabulary refers to how well words are known including forms, nuanced meanings, and uses in context.

The TOSR requires the individual to visually evaluate four color photographs representing a single word in a variety of contexts and infer the connection. After listening to four word choices, also printed along the bottom of each page, the examinee responds orally or points to the one word the four images represent. Rather than measuring only the number of words understood, the student's nuanced understanding of vocabulary is also assessed. The test format necessitates the use of two types of fluid semantic reasoning skills: inductive reasoning and deductive reasoning.

The evaluator should be a speech-language pathologist, clinical psychologist, school psychologist, learning specialist, or other professional with training in measuring language skills. It is reported that administration typically takes 20 minutes (basal and ceiling rules are provided) with an additional 5 minutes required for scoring; norm referenced scores are determined.

DEVELOPMENT. The TOSR was derived from a technology-based vocabulary instruction approach developed by the two authors in 2014. The approach uses semantic reasoning to determine not only the breadth of vocabulary knowledge, as is the more common practice in assessment, but the depth as well.

Target words were selected from several educational resources according to grade level, number of nuanced meanings, and ease of visual representation. Following field-testing of these initial items, a TOSR pilot version with 118 items split into two overlapping forms of 79 items each was developed and administered to a national sample of 376 individuals. Item difficulty and item discrimination were assessed, with a 90-item model then chosen for norming.

TECHNICAL. The norming sample of 1,117 individuals was stratified by age, gender, race/ethnicity, geographic and metro region, parent/caregiver education, and disability according to the 2010 U.S. Census and similar to the population to whom the TOSR may be administered.

The test manual reports that the majority of the 78 examiners were speech-language pathologists or school psychologists, though learning specialists, reading specialists, and other qualified educational professionals also participated. Examiners were encouraged to administer the test to individuals formally identified with a specific diagnosis that might affect academic performance; thus the norming validity studies included data from these individuals.

Reliability was evaluated using measures of internal consistency and test-retest stability. The internal consistency of test scores was examined using alpha coefficients, which were found to be large; the average alpha coefficient was 0.96. Reliability coefficients and standard errors of measurement were used to determine confidence intervals at 90% and 95% and are presented in the normative tables. Reliability was also examined using test-retest coefficients. The corrected test-retest correlation coefficient was .94, with a "nearly perfect effect size" (manual, p. 43). However, although the scores were stable over time, there was a significant increase in scores between the first and second administrations (conducted 13 to 24 days apart). Therefore, it was suggested that in order to reduce any practice effects, there be at least 4 to 6 months between the initial administration and re-administration.

Evidence of validity was based on content, relationship to performance on another assessment, and relationship to variables of age and disability group status. Validity based on test content included item performance analyzed by classical test analysis procedures and differential item functioning; both were completed in the pilot phase and revised as necessary before the norming phase. Validity was also suggested when comparing the test scores to performance on the Receptive One-Word Picture Vocabulary Test, 4th Edition (Martin & Brownell, 2010). A significant corrected correlation, .72, with a "very large effect size" (manual, p. 48) was found, indicating that the TOSR was measuring the number of lexical entries (breadth of receptive vocabulary). Evidence of validity was also established through testing assumptions of the underlying construct. First, in the normative sample, the correlation between the TOSR raw scores and age was statistically significant (r = .75) with a very large effect size. Further, research has found vocabulary to increase with age; TOSR raw scores showed a developmental progression with age. Additionally, the test manual cites literature that has found individuals with learning disabilities and/or language impairment to have vocabulary deficits. Matched-pairs design showed mean differences and t-test analyses for examinees with clinical diagnoses and matched examinees without diagnoses.

COMMENTARY. Research findings indicate that the development of both the breadth and depth of vocabulary are necessary for academic success, the latter especially for strong reading comprehension. Vocabulary measures are an integral part of a language evaluation of a school-aged student; a standardized measure that assesses both breadth and depth of word understanding is an important part of the battery. However, in present day practice, the robustness (depth) of word knowledge is typically assessed with an expressive task such as providing word definitions or synonyms (McGregor, Sheng, & Ball, 2007). The TOSR is the first standardized measure to assess both the breadth and depth of vocabulary knowledge without requiring an oral or written response. Further, not only does the TOSR provide valuable information about the examinee's word knowledge but also of that individual's higher-order thinking and reasoning skills in the semantics domain; such skills gradually increase and become more refined with typical development (e.g., Badger & Shapiro, 2012; Godwin, Matlen, & Fisher, 2012).

The test authors are to be commended for thinking outside the box in designing the TOSR. By using pictures instead of oral or written responses, the playing field has been leveled for the very population for whom these tests are developed (e.g., those with language impairments or learning difficulties). However, it must be kept in mind that performance on the TOSR does rely on either the student's auditory memory or reading skills. Specifically, only one repetition of the word choices is allowed though the words are also printed along the bottom of the page. Therefore, a problem may arise if the examinee has limitations in both auditory working memory and reading. That is, four unrelated words may be too demanding for some individuals to recall and process. The young examinee or in fact, any individual who cannot remember nor read the words, may be at a disadvantage; a poor score may incorrectly be interpreted as weak vocabulary knowledge or semantic reasoning. Caution then must be taken in interpreting test scores of such students.

The test authors provide detailed rationale and references to the research literature in support of the development of the TOSR. However, evidence of validity of the TOSR's scores is limited, especially concerning the depth of vocabulary. (Only validity evidence comparing the TOSR to a test breadth of vocabulary breadth is presented.) Although the TOSR is the only norm-referenced test that measures the depth of vocabulary knowledge without requiring an oral or written response, correlations with other established tests measuring the same construct even with a different format, would have provided additional strength to the psychometric properties of the test. The TOSR is still of value to the practitioner, but given the limited evidence for validity, it is of utmost importance that other vocabulary assessments, including criterion–referenced measures, also be used. In fact, the test authors recognize the limitations of the TOSR as only one measure of vocabulary knowledge and state the test should not be the sole instrument by which to determine a diagnosis concerning vocabulary.

SUMMARY. It is important for the professional to have available a norm-referenced, comprehensive measure of vocabulary knowledge, that is, one that goes beyond simply measuring the number of words known (lexical knowledge) but also examines the deeper understanding of words. The literature suggests that pictures are an excellent source of semantic information (McGregor, Sheng, & Ball, 2007). The TOSR's unique use of pictures rather than oral or written responses fills a need for a measure of deep understanding of vocabulary that can be administered to those with expressive language difficulties. Additionally by its format, the test also offers information about the examinee's semantic reasoning skills (inductive reasoning and deductive reasoning). The TOSR would be a helpful addition to a battery of language assessment instruments used with school-aged children.

REVIEWER'S REFERENCES

Badger, J. R., & Shapiro, L. R. (2012). Evidence of a transition from perceptual to category induction in 3- to 9-year-old children. *Journal of Experimental Child Psychology, 113,* 131–146. https://doi.org/10.1016/j.jecp.2012.03.004

Godwin, K. E., Matlen, B. J., & Fisher, A. V. (2012). Development of category-based reasoning in 4- to 7-year-old children: The influence of label co-occurrence and kinship knowledge. *Journal of Experimental Child Psychology, 115,* 74-90. doi:10.1016/j.jecp.2012.11.008

Martin, N. A., & Brownell, R. (2011). Receptive One-Word Picture Vocabulary Scale, 4th Edition. Novato, CA: Academic Therapy Publications.

McGregor, K. K., Sheng, L., & Ball, T. (2007). Complexities of expressive word learning over time. *Language, Speech, and Hearing Services in Schools, 38,* 353-364. doi:10.1044/0161-1461(2007/037)

[176]

Test of Variables of Attention (Version 9.0).

Purpose: Designed to evaluate "attention and inhibitory control" to "aid in the assessment of attention deficits."
Population: Ages 4 to 80+.
Publication Dates: 1988-2017.
Acronym: T.O.V.A.
Scores, 9: Response Time Variability, Response Time, Response Sensitivity, Commissions, Omissions, Anticipatory Responses, Post-Commission Response Time, Multiple Responses, Attention Comparison.
Subtests, 2: Auditory T.O.V.A. (ages 6 and older), Visual T.O.V.A.
Administration: Individual.
Price Data, 2020: $895 per kit including manual (2017, 165 pages), clinical manual (2017, 49 pages), visual and auditory tests, USB device, microswitch, installation guide, installation CD and USB flash drive, 5 test credits, and accessory cables; $395 per TOVA 7 or 8 change kit; $15 per test credit (volume discounts available).
Foreign Language Editions: Available in Dutch, French, German, Hebrew, Korean, Spanish, and Swedish.
Time: 10.8 minutes (timed) for ages 4 to 5.5 years; 21.6 minutes (timed) for examinees older than 5.5 years.
Comments: T.O.V.A. 9 is not an upgrade to T.O.V.A. 8, but rather is a new software installation and set of hardware; T.O.V.A. 7 and 8 users may order a T.O.V.A. 9 change kit and return existing hardware.
Authors: Lawrence M. Greenberg (clinical manual), Chris Holder (clinical manual), Carol L. Kindschi (clinical manual), Tammy Dupuy (clinical manual and user's manual), Scott Swalwell, Sr. (user's manual), and Andrew Greenberg (user's manual).
Publisher: The TOVA Company.
Cross References: For reviews by Sandra Loew and by Susan C. Whiston and Harrison Kane of Version 7.03, see 14:394; see also T5:2720 (2 references); for reviews by Rosa A. Hagin and Peter Della Bella and by Margot B. Stein of an earlier version, see 13:336 (1 reference).

Review of the Test of Variables of Attention (Version 9.0) by STEVEN R. SHAW, Associate Professor of Educational and Counselling Psychology, McGill University, Montréal, QC, Canada:

DESCRIPTION. The Test of Variables of Attention (Version 9.0; T.O.V.A.) is an individually administered computerized test developed to assess attention and response inhibition in typically developing and clinical populations. The T.O.V.A. is commonly used in conjunction with other clinical tools and diagnostic tests in neuropsychological and psychological evaluations.

The T.O.V.A. consists of software and hardware that is compatible with both Windows and Mac operating systems. The T.O.V.A. presents auditory and visual stimuli through an existing desktop or laptop computer. High-quality monitors and speakers are required for visual and auditory stimuli presentation. Responses are recorded with a microswitch that is part of the test kit. Installation is simple and well developed. Upon administration, T.O.V.A. test results are saved, downloaded, and scored online.

The T.O.V.A. kit includes installation and boot media on a USB drive, the T.O.V.A. USB device, a 6-foot USB cable, the T.O.V.A. microswitch, a 6-foot stereo audio cable, a 6-foot VGA (video) cable, user's manual, and clinical manual. The user's manual consists of installation and administration information. The clinical manual consists of definitions of attention-deficit/hyperactivity disorder (ADHD), interpretive clinical suggestions, and sample reports. Technical information on reliability, validity, and standardization is not reported in either manual but is available in a professional manual (Leark, Dupuy, Greenberg, Kindschi, & Hughes, 2016) available online at the test publisher's website. In addition, because the T.O.V.A. is scored online, order forms for purchasing test credits are provided. Five test credits are included with a purchased test kit.

This testing method is a 21.6-minute computerized auditory and visual continuous performance test (CPT). Test instructions can be read on the computer monitor by the examinee and are presented audibly in a multimedia approach. Options are available for presenting instructions in multiple languages. The task is to press the button on the microswitch as fast as possible when a small square is at the top of the presentation and not to press the button when the small square is near the bottom. For the auditory test, the button is to be pressed as quickly as possible when a high note is presented and not pressed when a low note is presented.

The T.O.V.A. yields five major scores. Response Time Variability is a measure of the variability in examinee's response time for accurate responses; that is, consistency of response speed. Response Time is the average time for an examinee to respond correctly to a target. Errors of Commission occur when the examinee fails to inhibit responding and incorrectly responds to a nontarget. Errors of Omission are when the examinee does not respond to the designated target when the target is presented. D prime is a response discriminative ability score reflecting the ratio of hits to false alarms. D prime measures the accuracy of the target (signal) and nontarget (noise) and can be interpreted as a measure of perceptual sensitivity.

DEVELOPMENT. The CPT paradigm was introduced in the 1950s and has been commonly used in experimental psychology. This paradigm began to evolve from laboratory to clinical settings with the rise of microcomputers in the 1970s and 1980s. The development of non-alphanumeric, non-sequential, and randomly presented stimuli tasks measured with laboratory-grade tools providing precise, direct, and objective assessment of attention and response inhibition progressed significantly. Development of norms and a wide variety of validity studies have continued to improve the test. The current version is T.O.V.A. 9.0.

TECHNICAL.

Standardization. The preliminary normative data for the Visual T.O.V.A. were collected from randomly selected classrooms in Grades 1, 3, 5, 7, and 9. All participants were students in suburban public schools in or near Minneapolis, Minnesota. The ages of the children sampled ranged from 6 to 16 years. Nearly all of the children (99%) were identified as Caucasian. Participants were excluded if they met any of the following criteria: a deviant classroom behavior rating defined by a score of greater than two standard deviations from the mean on the Connors Parent Teacher Questionnaire, Abbreviated Form; use of psychoactive medication; or receiving special education services. All testing was done in the morning to control for possible diurnal effects. Additional samples were collected from students ages 4 and 5 and ages 16 to 19 to increase the age range for the T.O.V.A. The additional samples were also collected in or around Minneapolis, Minnesota. The total sample size was 1,340. For adult participants, 250 individuals ages 20 and older were tested. The sample consisted of undergraduate students in three Minnesota liberal arts colleges and persons residing in nearby communities; 99% of the sample identified as Caucasian.

Normative data for the Auditory T.O.V.A. consisted of 2,551 participants recruited from elementary and high schools in the Minneapolis area. Again, 99% of the sample was Caucasian. Exclusionary criteria were the same as for the Visual T.O.V.A. The age group for the Auditory T.O.V.A. ranged from 6 to 19 years. The professional manual notes that the auditory version was too difficult for children ages 4 and 5. In addition, the professional manual notes that there are limited normative data available for the adult sample. Therefore, testing with adult samples is considered experimental for the auditory version.

Reliability. As for all timed tests, many traditional metrics for assessing consistency are not appropriate for the T.O.V.A. For each of the five variables (omission, commission, response time, response time variability, D prime) and two conditions (stimulus infrequent and stimulus frequent), trials were divided into four quarters, and correlation coefficients were calculated among quarters for all variables across both conditions. Coefficients tended to be lowest in errors of omission (range was from .70 to .72) and highest for response time (range was from .93 to .95).

Temporal stability of the T.O.V.A. involved multiple studies. Most relevant is a study involving 31 children with a mean age of 10 years and standard deviation of 2.6 years. They were administered the T.O.V.A. and then had a second administration 90 minutes later. The purpose of this time interval was to determine whether the T.O.V.A. is useful for assessing the effects of stimulant medication for children with ADHD. Correlation coefficients ranged from .70 (omissions) to .87 (response time variability). There were significant practice effects in commission scores and response time. A second study took place using a 1-week interval involving 33 children with a mean age of 10.1 years with a standard deviation of 2.5 years. Correlation coefficients ranged from .74 (commission) to .87 (response time variability). There were significant effect sizes in commission as scores on the second testing were approximately 12 points higher on the second administration for both the 90-minute and 1-week retest intervals. Overall, there is reasonable evidence for temporal stability of the T.O.V.A., yet there are significant practice effects that need to be considered during interpretation.

Overall, evidence of reliability is difficult to interpret as there are multiple studies that use a variety of samples with differing demographic characteristics. Nonetheless, the overall picture is of a reasonably reliable measure.

Validity. A variety of validity studies are presented in the professional manual that support the ability of multiple variables on the T.O.V.A. to differentiate between children with ADHD and typically developing children. Most of the reported studies do not differentiate ADHD from other psychiatric diagnoses. An exception is a series of studies that used the T.O.V.A. variables to differentiate between children with ADHD and those with conduct disorder. The T.O.V.A. was effective in differentiating these two populations. A potential complicating factor is that T.O.V.A. variables, especially omission, are significantly correlated with general mental ability in children (Hurford et al., 2017). This is not surprising given that attention is a cognitive ability. However, this relationship needs to be considered when interpreting T.O.V.A. data and when formulating diagnostic impressions of ADHD in children with differing cognitive abilities. There is evidence that the T.O.V.A. can be used effectively with multiple ethnic groups, yet no formal investigations of bias were reported. In addition, the T.O.V.A. is sensitive in response to psychotropic medication (Peskin et al., 2016). Although there are dozens of studies evaluating validity evidence for a variety of factors, the validity of T.O.V.A. scores for making unique contributions to clinical decision-making above and beyond checklists and direct observations has not been established.

COMMENTARY. The T.O.V.A. 9.0 is a version of the widely used CPT paradigm from experimental psychology. As a clinical instrument, the T.O.V.A. correlates positively with other measures of attention and measures of executive function. Impairments in attention are nonspecific symptoms of ADHD, dementia, major depressive disorders, learning disabilities, anxiety disorders, and other neurological impairments and psychiatric diagnoses. The variables measured by the T.O.V.A. do not represent functional impairment nor any of the symptoms required for making a diagnosis. The clinical manual discusses the criteria for ADHD contained in the *Diagnostic and Statistical Manual of Mental Disorders* (5th ed.; American Psychiatric Association, 2013) and suggests that the T.O.V.A. may be included in a diagnostic workup for ADHD. However, none of the criteria for diagnosing ADHD are related to the variables measured by the T.O.V.A. Rather, T.O.V.A. metrics are nonspecific correlates of the behaviors required for diagnosis of ADHD. The clinical utility of the T.O.V.A. can be questioned as to whether results add important information for diagnosis, and no information is provided that indicates T.O.V.A. results reliably lead to specific effective treatments. However, the T.O.V.A. can be used to evaluate medication effects on attention and impulse control in an experimental, but not functional, environment. T.O.V.A. could be a measure used for elderly populations to identify dementia, yet the normative sample for adults is not sufficient to support the clinical utility of

T.O.V.A. for elderly populations (Braverman et al., 2010). Although its authors suggest that the T.O.V.A. provides a fully objective assessment of attention, the non-representative standardization sample, incomplete reports of internal reliability, and challenges to the diagnostic utility of this measure make its clinical usefulness extremely limited. The T.O.V.A. remains a useful research tool.

SUMMARY. The T.O.V.A. is based on the CPT paradigm commonly used in experimental psychology, and its authors claim it provides an objective measure of attention and impulse control. Reliability and validity evidence is somewhat scattered, with some evidence appearing in multiple published studies, and is not provided in the purchased test kit. However, the online availability of the professional manual coupled with a brief search of literature yields many studies using and evaluating the T.O.V.A. Although the T.O.V.A. may have a variety of useful purposes, diagnosis, per se, is not among them.

REVIEWER'S REFERENCES

American Psychiatric Association. (2013). *Diagnostic and statistical manual of mental disorders* (5th ed.). Washington, D.C.: Author.

Hurford, D. P., Fender, A. C., Boux, J. L., Swigart, C. C., Boydston, P. S., Butts, S. R.,...Pike, M. E. (2017). Examination of the effects of intelligence on the Test of Variables of Attention for elementary students. *Journal of Attention Disorders, 21*, 929–937.

Leark, R. A., Dupuy, T. R., Greenberg, L. M., Kindschi, C. L., & Hughes, S. J. (2016). *T.O.V.A. professional manual: Test of Variables of Attention Continuous Performance Test.* Los Alamitos, CA: The T.O.V.A. Company.

Peskin, M., Sommerfeld, E., Basford, Y., Rozen, S., Zalsman, G., Weizman, A., & Manor, I. (2016). Continuous performance test is sensitive to a single methylphenidate challenge in preschool children with ADHD. *Journal of Attention Disorders.* Advance online publication. doi:10.1177/1087054716680075

Review of the Test of Variables of Attention (Version 9.0) by JENNIFER M. STRANG, Neuropsychologist, Washington DC Veterans Affairs Medical Center, Washington, DC:

DESCRIPTION. The Test of Variables of Attention, Version 9.0 (T.O.V.A. 9) is a computerized measure of attention and inhibitory control intended to aid in the assessment of attention deficits, such as those that characterize attention-deficit/hyperactivity disorder (ADHD). It is a culture- and language-free continuous performance test (CPT) that measures multiple components of visual and auditory information processing and is intended for use in normal and clinical populations, ages 4 to 80+ years. The test authors assert that the T.O.V.A. provides an objective assessment to be interpreted in conjunction with a full clinical history and behavior rating scales, thus providing a comprehensive evaluation of attention disorders. Version 9.0 is not an upgrade from Version 8, but rather includes the following changes: (a) it now has FDA clearance; (b) there are several minor user interface and Windows software compatibility fixes; and (c) there are changes to the clinical manual to reflect indications for use.

The T.O.V.A 9 kit includes a clinical manual, a user's manual, and an array of custom hardware. The clinical manual provides a brief description of the test, updated information on ADHD and the fifth edition of the *Diagnostic and Statistical Manual of Mental Disorders* (American Psychiatric Association, 2013), a description of T.O.V.A. variables, and an interpretive guide with illustrative sample reports. The user's manual provides detailed information about installing and using the T.O.V.A. The hardware includes an audio-video interface device, a push-button controller called the microswitch, a USB stick, and a variety of cables. The examiner is instructed to connect the hardware to a computer before installing the software. T.O.V.A. 9 offers two modes of hardware setup: external audio/video (EAV) and precision test environment (PTE). In EAV mode, the examiner connects the computer's video cable to the T.O.V.A. interface device and then connects the interface device to the computer's external monitor. However, the only type of video connection the device offers is VGA, which is obsolete and has been dropped from products by virtually all PC manufacturers. The Lenovo IdeaPad laptop that we were using has no VGA port, so we were unable to connect the hardware in EAV mode.

We next tried to connect the T.O.V.A. 9 hardware in PTE mode. In this mode, the interface device connects to a computer via a USB cable. This approach appeared promising initially; however, documentation contains a warning that the PTE mode is not intended for use with computers running Windows 8 or Windows 10, and "would probably not function correctly." Our test system ran Windows 10, but, lacking other options, we attempted to connect the hardware and perform the installation anyway, which failed. The PTE mode appears to be a heavyweight, low-level installation that essentially replaces the computer's native operating system while the T.O.V.A. 9 is being administered. It requires the examiner to reboot the computer before use so that it can boot into PTE instead of Windows.

As a last resort, we attempted to install T.O.V.A. 9 in PTE mode on an Apple MacBook Pro running Mac OS X Sierra (v.10.12.6). This attempt also was unsuccessful. Although the software appeared to install without any problems, we were unable to boot the system into PTE mode from either the supplied CD or the USB stick. Upon contacting the company to inquire about the lack of support for modern hardware and operating systems, we were informed that in the test creators' opinion, older hardware offers greater timing precision, which is essential to produce accurate results.

Once one is able to install and operate the T.O.V.A. successfully, administration is straightforward. While seated in front of the computer, the examinee listens to a set of instructions presented via computer audio or read aloud by the examiner, illustrated by photos and a short sample of the test. The examinee takes a 2-minute practice test followed by the actual test, which lasts for 21.6 minutes for examinees ages 6 to 80+ years and 10.8 minutes for examinees ages 4 and 5. In the visual T.O.V.A, examinees distinguish between two geometric figures—targets and nontargets—presented in two target-frequency conditions: stimulus infrequent (vigilance mode) and stimulus frequent (high response demand mode). Examinees are instructed to press the microswitch as quickly as possible after seeing the target stimulus and to do nothing (i.e., not press the switch) when they see the nontarget. Similarly, in the auditory T.O.V.A., examinees distinguish between two tones–a high note and a low note–presented in the two different stimulus conditions. In the professional manual, not included in the T.O.V.A. 9 kit but available online, there is considerable detail regarding appropriate test environment, testing procedures, and proper use of the T.O.V.A.

The primary variables include Response Time Variability (consistency of response time), Response Time (processing time taken to respond correctly to a target), D prime (d', ratio of hit rate to false alarm rate), Errors of Commission (incorrect response to a target; a measure of impulsivity and/or disinhibition), and Errors of Omission (lack of response to a target; a measure of focus and vigilance). Secondary variables include anticipatory responses (a response to stimuli before the examinee could have processed the information), post-commission response time (response time when a target immediately follows a commission error), and multiple responses (unclear what this measures).

DEVELOPMENT. The T.O.V.A. was created in 1966 as an outcome measure in research examining the effects of three classes of medication in the treatment of children with hyperkinetic disorder. In contrast to other CPTs, the stimuli were non-alphanumeric, non-sequential, and randomly (but infrequently) presented. Over the years, several modifications have been made, including the development of the microswitch, inclusion of tallies of anticipatory responses and commission errors as measures of performance validity, development of self-scoring computer algorithms, incorporation of an auditory T.O.V.A., expansion of the normative base, and other technical updates to improve timing accuracy.

TECHNICAL. The Visual T.O.V.A. normative sample comprised 1,340 children ages 4-19 and 250 adults ages 20 and older. As discussed in previous reviews in *The Fourteenth Mental Measurements Yearbook* (Plake & Impara, 2001), the adult sample is relatively small, with cell sizes ranging from 4 to 39 participants. Additionally, minority populations and geographic locations are not well represented, as 99% of participants were Caucasians from rural and suburban Minnesota. The Auditory T.O.V.A. normative sample comprised 2,551 children ages 6-19 years. There also is a small adult sample (N = 129), and the test authors advise T.O.V.A. users to consider the auditory version to be experimental for adults.

The professional manual cites studies of both internal consistency and test-retest reliability within normative and ADHD clinical samples. In the normative sample, Pearson correlation coefficients (r) were computed for all variables across the two target frequency conditions. Internal consistency reliability estimates appear acceptable, with the highest coefficients for response time, ranging from .89 to .98, and the lowest coefficients for d', ranging from .52 to .82. In a 2008 study (Llorente et al.) that examined internal consistency for an ADHD clinical sample ($57 \le n \le 63$), reliability coefficients ranged from .53 to .94. The test manual also cites two studies examining test-retest reliability. The initial study of a sample of 49 children diagnosed with ADHD (Llorente et al., 2001) revealed moderate test-retest correlation coefficients (.51 to .82) from baseline through four months, which the test authors explain is not unexpected, as one would expect greater variability of performance with individuals diagnosed with ADHD than with normal controls. In the second study (Leark, Wallace, & Fitzgerald, 2004), two test-retest intervals–a 90-minute period and a 1-week period–were examined with samples of normal controls. Correlation coefficients ranged from .70 to .87 and from .74 to .87, respectively.

Studies evaluating criterion evidence of validity for Visual T.O.V.A. scores are discussed in the professional manual in detail. Criterion evidence is of particular importance with the T.O.V.A., which purports to distinguish between non-clinical and attention-disordered populations. Indeed, results from several studies found that the T.O.V.A. distinguishes between ADHD groups, other clinical groups, and normal controls. Additional studies of sensitivity and specificity, factor analysis, and discriminant analysis provide further support for the validity of Visual T.O.V.A. Data related to construct evidence of validity for Auditory T.O.V.A. scores also are presented with support for the sustained attention construct of the omission score. Discriminant function analyses and studies investigating the use of the T.O.V.A. with non-English-speaking groups and special populations (e.g., deaf children, gifted children) provide additional validity data.

COMMENTARY and SUMMARY. The T.O.V.A. 9 is a CPT intended to aid in the assessment of attention disorders. It is not an upgrade from Version 8, but rather now has FDA clearance, minor user interface and Windows software compatibility fixes, and changes to the clinical manual to reflect indications for use. Its strengths include the use of culture- and language-free stimuli; objective assessment of multiple components of visual and auditory information processing to obtain a full picture of attentional functioning; embedded validity measures; and acceptable evidence of criterion validity. On the other hand, as mentioned in previous reviews, normative data are derived from a predominantly Caucasian, geographically restricted sample, limiting its use with diverse populations. Furthermore, the adult normative sample is small, particularly for the Auditory T.O.V.A., which is recommended for experimental use only. Most significantly, the T.O.V.A. 9 is unusable with modern hardware and operating systems. To address this problem, the company offers an option to purchase a refurbished laptop computer with an older operating system, a solution that is inadequate and impractical for many examiners.

T.O.V.A. 9's lack of support for hardware and operating environments likely to be found in most contemporary offices and clinics, especially those lacking dedicated Information Technology staff, diminishes whatever diagnostic advantages it offers and may make it unsuitable for many examiners working today. The developers are strongly urged to invest the resources necessary to bring their product to current technological standards.

REVIEWER'S REFERENCES

American Psychiatric Association. (2013). *Diagnostic and statistical manual of mental disorders* (5th ed.). Washington, D.C.: Author.

Leark, R. A., Wallace, D. R., & Fitzgerald, R. (2004). Test-retest reliability and standard errors of measurement for the Test of Variables of Attention (T.O.V.A.) with healthy school aged children. *Assessment, 11*, 285-289.

Llorente, A. M., Amado, A. J., Voigt, R. G., Berretta, M. C., Fraley, J. K., Jensen, C. L., & Heird, W. C. (2001). Internal consistency, temporal stability, and reproducibility of the Test of Variables of Attention in children with attention-deficit/hyperactive disorder. *Archives of Clinical Neuropsychology, 16*, 535-546.

Llorente, A. M., Voigt, R., Jensen, C. L., Fraley, J. K., Heird, W. C., & Rennie, K. M. (2008). The Test of Variables of Attention (TOVA): Internal consistency (Q1 vs. Q2 and Q3 vs. Q4) in children with attention deficit/hyperactivity disorder (ADHD). *Child Neuropsychology, 14*, 314-322.

Plake, B. S., & Impara, J. C. (Eds.). (2001). *The fourteenth mental measurements yearbook.* Lincoln, NE: Buros Institute of Mental Measurements.

[177]

Test of Visual Perceptual Skills, 4th Edition.

Purpose: Designed to assess "visual-perceptual abilities without requiring a motor response."
Population: Ages 5-0 to 21-11.
Publication Dates: 1982-2017.
Acronym: TVPS-4.
Scores, 8: 7 subtests: Visual Discrimination, Visual Memory, Spatial Relationships, Form Constancy, Sequential Memory, Visual Figure-Ground, Visual Closure; Overall Score.
Administration: Individual.
Price Data, 2020: $205 per kit including manual (2017, 96 pages), test plates, and 25 record forms; $85 per test plates; $75 per manual; $45 per 25 record forms.
Time: Approximately 30 minutes to administer and 5-10 minutes to score.
Comments: Subtests may be administered separately; may be completed in more than one session; online scoring and reporting available.
Author: Academic Therapy Publications.
Publisher: Academic Therapy Publications.
Cross References: For reviews by Phillip L. Ackerman and Brian F. French of the third edition, see 18:146; see T5:2724 (13 references); for reviews by Nancy A. Busch-Rossnagel and Joseph W. Denison of an earlier edition titled Test of Visual-Perceptual Skills (Non-Motor), see 9:1276.

Review of the Test of Visual Perceptual Skills, 4th Edition by ESTHER STAVROU, Associate Clinical Professor in School-Clinical Child Psychology, Ferkauf Graduate School of Psychology, Yeshiva University, Bronx, NY:

DESCRIPTION. The Test of Visual Perceptual Skills, 4th Edition (TVPS-4) is an individually administered test of visual-perceptual abilities that does not require a motor response. It is designed for individuals ages 5 through 21 years and is described in the test manual as appropriate for use by occupational therapists, psychologists, educational specialists, optometrists, and other professionals for diagnostic and research purposes.

The TVPS-4 consists of seven subtests, which can be administered separately or as a group: Visual Discrimination, Visual Memory, Spatial Relationships, Form Constancy, Sequential Memory, Visual Figure-Ground, and Visual Closure. Each subtest consists of two unscored sample items and 18 test items. The TVPS-4 is untimed, and the stimuli are presented as black-and-white figures in an easel-backed flip book. As in previous versions of the TVPS, a multiple-choice format is used. Examinees can either point to the chosen image or verbally respond with the number beneath their answer.

The administration directions are clear and easy to follow. Each subtest begins with two practice items, and the examinee is provided with feedback on his or her performance. All materials are conveniently contained in one stimulus book. However, the tasks are somewhat monotonous, and the materials are not very engaging. Thus, it may be difficult to sustain the attention and interest of some students over the seven subtests, particularly since administration of all subtests requires approximately 30 minutes. Scoring is simple, and raw scores are converted to subtest scaled scores and an Overall standard score. Confidence intervals, percentile ranks, and age-equivalents are provided. Although the test developers appropriately urge users to interpret age-equivalent scores with caution, they are prominently reported on the record form. A table for converting standard scores to other metrics, including T scores, stanines and normal curve equivalents also is available.

DEVELOPMENT. The TVPS-4 is the latest revision of the TVPS, initially authored by Dr. Morrison F. Gardner. Critical reviews and feedback from users of the TVPS-3 were used to enhance the fourth edition. In addition to updated and expanded norms, 14 new images were added at the lower end of the test to improve its sensitivity at younger ages or for more impaired children.

According to the test publishers, Scheiman's model for visual information processing (2011) and the Cattell-Horn-Carroll (CHC) theory of intelligence provide the context for understanding the skills assessed by the TVPS-4. By describing the TVPS-4 in the context of CHC theory, the publishers address previous criticisms (Ackerman, 2010) about the absence of information in the test manual explaining the construct of visual-perceptual abilities as it relates to other nonverbal or spatial abilities and how it fits within a wider network of abilities.

TECHNICAL. The available age norms are based on a sample of 1,790 individuals ages 5 through 21. The demographic characteristics of the normative sample are only roughly representative of the United States population when compared to the 2010 U.S. Census data. Broad regions of the United States were generally represented, but only 28 states were sampled and in 12 of those states, testing was conducted at only one site. The age breakdown of the sample is somewhat uneven, varying in size from 94 participants at age 5 to 141 at age 9. Norms for ages 18 to 19 and 20 to 21 are combined into 2-year groups. Black/African American examinees are under-represented in the sample (9.6% vs. 14.3% in the population) and Whites and Asian-Americans are over-represented. The American Indian/Alaska Native group is very small (.5%), even when considering the small proportion of the U.S. population (1.26%) that this group comprises. It is notable that there were no sites sampled in Alaska. Disparities were also noted for parental education, with an over-representation of individuals with higher parental education and under-representation of individuals from lower parental education backgrounds. An improvement over previous editions is the inclusion of individuals with a variety of disabilities.

Reliability of the TVPS-4 is addressed through examination of internal consistency and temporal stability. Internal consistency for the Overall score and subtests is reported in the form of alpha coefficients. The alpha coefficient for the Overall score was .94 when averaged across ages. In addition, at each age the coefficients were above .90, indicating strong internal consistency. For the seven subtests, the alpha coefficients ranged from .68 (Sequential Memory) to .81 (Spatial Relationships) when averaged across ages. However, for some ages the correlations go as low as .43. Because 19 of the 105 subtest alpha coefficients are below .70, the test publisher recommends the use of confidence intervals when reporting subtest scores. However, given the low reliability for some subtests it would be questionable to administer and interpret single subtests as suggested.

Test-retest stability was examined by retesting 71 children from the standardization sample 14 to 25 days after the first administration. The retest sample was a non-representative group, with the majority of students being White (84.5%) and female (71.8%), and all residing in urban/suburban areas. The test-retest coefficient for the Overall score was

.97 with an average gain of three points on retest, reflecting potential practice or learning effects. The test publisher recommends that the TVPS-4 not be administered earlier than four to six months after the last administration to minimize these practice effects. The corrected (for range restriction) correlations for the individual subtests ranged from .46 (Sequential Memory) to .81 (Spatial Relationships). The children were retested by the same examiner, which may inflate stability since examiner factors, such as examiner errors or differences in administration are not taken into account. Standard errors of measurement for the Overall score ranged from 3.04 to 4.42 depending on the age group; therefore, examiners should consider using age-based confidence intervals, which are conveniently included in the test manual. The standard errors used to calculate the confidence intervals were based on the various values of coefficient alpha, rather than the stability coefficients.

As content evidence of validity for the TVPS-4, the test manual authors present item difficulty, item discrimination, and item reliability analyses. (Others would generally consider such information as construct evidence of validity.) Average item difficulty values generally increased with age with some exceptions, particularly after age 18. Construct evidence of validity was also offered through a comparison of the TVPS-4 with the Motor-Free Visual Perception Test-4, which measures similar constructs. In a small (n = 32), non-representative sample, the means were roughly equivalent, and scores from the two tests were highly correlated (.90). Exploratory and confirmatory factor analyses are used to support the structure of the scale. Results of the factor analyses "suggested that a single factor best described the overall set of skills and abilities examined by the test" (manual, p. 58). Finally, validity support was provided by comparing the performance of children with and without disabilities on the TVPS-4. According to the test developers, learning disabilities and autism spectrum disorders are often associated with visual-perceptual difficulties, and thus children with these diagnoses would be expected to score lower than matched controls without disabilities. Similarly, children with attention-deficit/hyperactivity disorder would not be expected to demonstrate differences in performance. These hypotheses were supported during the standardization and development of the test, but further independent studies with larger and more representative samples are required. Furthermore, the learning disabled group is not adequately specified. Because the diagnosis "learning disabled" encompasses various disorders, not all learning disabled children are necessarily expected to demonstrate visual-perceptual difficulties. The test developers encourage further studies by users of the TVPS-4 in this section of the test manual, which concludes with a curious statement: "The data presented in this section provides a foundation of evidence to support the validity of the TVPS-4 as an instrument to use in evaluating vocabulary development" (manual, p. 63). The connection with vocabulary development in this statement is unclear.

COMMENTARY. The test developers have acknowledged problems with prior editions of the TVPS and have taken steps to address many of them. For example, they have used feedback from users to add more items at the lower levels. In addition they have tried to address Ackerman's (2010) criticism related to the absence of information in the TVPS-3 manual explaining the construct of visual perception and how it relates to other similar or broader abilities. In addition, clinical samples were included in the new standardization group. The TVPS-4 manual includes detailed and straightforward information regarding administration and scoring. Critical values are provided in the manual to allow for comparison of scores on the various subtests along with base rates for score differences. However, guidance for interpretation of these score comparisons is not provided, and given the low reliability of some of the subtests, test users may want to avoid these comparisons.

SUMMARY. The TVPS-4 is easily administered and scored and can provide clinicians with a useful way to screen for visual-perceptual skills. Whereas more time-efficient tests are available, such as the Bender Visual-Motor Gestalt Test, Second Edition (16:30) or the Beery VMI (19:14), the advantage of the TVPS-4 is the absence of a motor requirement. This difference is useful when examinees have motor disabilities or when trying to rule out fine-motor difficulties when assessing visual perception. The standardization sample of the TVPS-4 is only roughly representative of the U.S. population with some disparities in representation at different ages, parental education level, and race/ethnicity. Even as a screening instrument, only the Overall score has adequate reliability to be interpreted with confidence. The subtests, particularly the Sequential Memory subtest, are not considered reliable enough on their own to be interpreted individually even for screening or research purposes.

Preliminary validation studies are provided by the test publisher, and further independent validation studies are needed. For instance, given that the CHC model was described as a context for understanding visual-perceptual abilities, studies examining how the TVPS-4 scores correspond to measures of relevant CHC factors would be helpful. As cautioned by the test developers, the TVPS-4 should not be used in isolation to diagnose a visual-perceptual disorder. However, the test has a useful place within the context of a comprehensive evaluation including other tests, behavioral observations, interviews, and work samples.

REVIEWER'S REFERENCES

Ackerman, P. L. (2010). [Test review of the Test of Visual Perceptual Skills, 3rd Edition]. In R. A. Spies, J. F. Carlson, & K. F. Geisinger (Eds.), *The eighteenth mental measurements yearbook* (pp. 658-660). Lincoln, NE: Buros Institute of Mental Measurements.

Scheiman, M. (2011). *Understanding and managing vision deficits: A guide for occupational therapists* (3rd ed.). Thorofare, NJ: Slack.

Review of the Test of Visual Perceptual Skills, 4th Edition by CAROLYN H. SUPPA, Licensed Psychologist, Charleston, WV, and LAURA M. SUPPA, Optometrist, Charleston Vision Source, Charleston, WV:

DESCRIPTION. The Test of Visual Perceptual Skills, 4th Edition (TVPS-4) is an individually administered multiple-choice assessment of visual-perceptual abilities that does not require complex motor responses such as copying. It is intended for English-speaking children, adolescents, and young adults ages 5 through 21 living in the United States and assesses abilities relating to identifying visual features, integrating visual information with other sensory systems, and interpreting and attaching meaning to this information. The TVPS-4 is "designed for both diagnostic and research purposes" (manual, p. 7) for use by professionals in clinical and research settings working with medical, developmental, and learning conditions.

Seven subtests—Visual Discrimination, Visual Memory, Spatial Relationships, Form Constancy, Sequential Memory, Visual Figure-Ground, and Visual Closure—are administered using 126 black-and-white line drawings (18 items per subtest), most of which were retained from the TVPS-3. Two lower-level items per test have been added based on analysis of scaled scores and TVPS-3 user feedback "to expand the range of easier items and to improve the discriminative ability of the test for younger or more impaired individuals" (manual, p. 12). To minimize the testing burden due to additional test items and expanded age range from the previous version's age limit of 18, there are uniform age-based start points suggested for each subtest for individuals 12 years and older as well as basal and ceiling rules. These and other administration instructions, including scripts, are clearly written in the test manual. Single subtests may be selected for specific assessments, and testing may be performed in more than one session. The test requires approximately 30 minutes to administer in its entirety. The manual instructs administrators to provide the subtest prompt after 45 seconds and to note extended response times that may indicate underlying difficulties. The back of the record form provides space for such notes and other behavioral observations.

Scoring time is reported as 5 to 10 minutes, and performance is easily recorded on an explicit record form. Online scoring and reporting services are available. Scaled scores corresponding by age to subtest raw scores are provided, and the sum of scaled scores is converted to a standard score from which percentile ranks, normal curve equivalents, T scores, scaled scores, and stanines may be derived. Subtest difference scores may be calculated for the potential identification of specific visual-perceptual problems, and the test manual includes subtest comparison instructions and critical values. In case of statistically significant difference scores, the manual states that "it is highly recommended to further assess for the practical significance" and encourages the examiner "to analyze subtest performance then use clinical judgment and best practice guidelines when making decisions about reporting the Overall score" (manual, p. 33). The TVPS-4 does not provide for the derivation of optional index scores that are a part of the previous edition (TVPS-3).

DEVELOPMENT. The TVPS-4 manual provides an overview of two theoretical perspectives of visual-perceptual skill development and processes on which the assessment is based: Scheiman's model of vision and the Cattell-Horn-Carroll (CHC) theory of cognitive abilities. The TVPS-4 focuses on the visual analysis skill set within the visual information processing component of Scheiman's model. Visual analysis skills are defined as awareness of distinctive features of visual forms and "part-whole and visual imagery abilities" and include four component skills: visual discrimination, visual figure ground, visual closure, and visual memory and visualization (manual, p. 8). The test manual states that although the CHC theory "is not specifically a theory or model of visual perception," the inclusion of "visual-processing skills as one aspect of a broader understanding of cognitive abilities" and the increasing use of CHC by various fields of psychology "to understand ability and organize assessment" (manual, p. 8) support its use. The domain-specific cognitive ability of visual processing skills is described as including "the visual analysis skills identified in Scheiman's model" as well as "a number of other skills, such as length estimation, and closure speed" (manual, p. 9). Of the 11 narrow visual processing skills, the TVPS-4 is said to measure three: visualization, flexibility of closure, and visual memory, according to two citations provided in the test manual. The manual recognizes the importance of visual-receptive skills in understanding visual perception and provides a cautionary statement regarding the possible need to assess visual-receptive function components of the ocular system "whenever there are concerns about visual processing" (manual, p. 9). An updated discussion of risks for visual-perceptual problems associated with certain medical, developmental, and learning conditions is presented and provides some research suggesting that lower visual-perceptual skills place individuals at higher risk for academic, social, and occupational challenges.

TECHNICAL. The TVPS-4 final standardization sample consisted of 1,790 individuals ages 5 years 0 months through 21 years 11 months living in 28 states. Testing was individually conducted by occupational therapists or school psychologists at 81 schools or private professional practices with normally developing individuals and a percentage of individuals "who had been formally identified with a specific diagnosis that might affect visual-perceptual skills" (manual, p. 39). Demographic characteristics—including gender, ethnicity, Hispanic origin, parent education, geographic region of the country, rural/urban location, and disability status—of the normative sample and their relation to the U.S. population are presented and described as closely approximating U.S. Census data from 2010.

Alpha coefficients were computed to assess internal consistency of test items for subtest scores and the Overall score at each age range of the norming sample. Average subtest values ranged from .68 to .81 across age ranges with values of individual subtests for specific ages ranging from .43 to .90. The Overall score average was .94. Overall results suggest evidence for internal consistency of the TVPS-4, although 19 of the 105 coefficient alpha values for individual ages at the subtest level were below .70. Therefore, the test manual recommends the use of confidence intervals when reporting and interpreting subtest scores and results.

Test-retest reliability was investigated by retesting 71 individuals from the norming study after an average of 17 days. Demographics of this sample are presented but lack diversity in several areas. Reported test-retest reliability coefficients ranging from .46 to .81 for subtests and .97 for the Overall score are stated as providing evidence for temporal stability. Standard errors of measurement are provided for scaled and standard scores by age for the subtest scores and the overall scale.

Content/construct evidence of validity as presented in the test manual includes the use of most items from previous test versions and factor analyses, which suggest that all abilities assessed by the TVPS-4 load onto a single factor. Item bias analyses were conducted on various groups in the normative sample including gender, residence, and ethnicity. Items with significant levels of differential item functioning (DIF) were reviewed by an unidentified item-review panel, and individual item response percentages were calculated. This step led to a determination that DIF results were "likely due to chance," and thus the items that were flagged were included in the test (manual, p. 38). Other evidence such as item review by experts or skill mapping are not presented in the test manual.

Convergent evidence of validity was provided by comparing scores from the TVPS-4 with scores from the Motor-Free Visual Perception Test-4 using 34 individuals from the norming sample. Results showed no significant mean differences and a significant correlation (corrected for range restriction) between scores on both tests. To examine evidence of the test authors' assumptions regarding the underlying construct in terms of improving visual-perceptual skills with age, statistically significant correlations between raw scores and age in the normative sample are reported. Also, results from an analysis examining score differences between individuals in a diagnostic group and matched controls are presented. The manual concludes that these data provide "a foundation of evidence" to support the validity of using the TVPS-4 to evaluate vocabulary development (manual, p. 63), but it does not elaborate on an applied rationale for this statement.

COMMENTARY. The two models employed as theoretical foundations for the TVPS-4 are purported to provide an updated, functional, and "clinically and educationally relevant context for understanding the skills assessed by the TVPS-4" (manual, p. 8). Further discussion is needed to provide insight into the reasons for and applications of the use of this visual-cognitive component of visual perception, the differentiation of and uses for these subtests in clinical and research settings, and how test items continue to relate to updated theoretical perspectives. Although the TVPS-4 does not require complex motor skills, it does require a degree of receptive language skills and the ability to respond through pointing or speaking. Research for the support of this assessment method and its uses with certain populations needs further discussion.

The test manual states that "there is increasing recognition of the importance of early identification of visual-perceptual challenges" (manual, p. 13) and that updated review of the literature on visual processing is presented to support "cross-professional communication" (manual, p. 5). Even though the manual references the TVPS-4 as "the latest update of one of the most consistently used assessments in pediatric occupational therapy practice" (manual, p. 13), research evidence from this or other practical applications such as vision therapy in developmental optometric practice is not presented. Further research-based practice applications for use of the TVPS-4 are needed to recommend its use over other assessments for the identification of those at risk for educational, social, and occupational challenges, particularly in regard to diagnostic purposes referenced in the test manual (p. 7).

It is evident that the TVPS-4 has made strides to address criticisms of the previous edition such as expanding the age range, adding a uniform age-based start point to all subtests for individuals 12 years and older, providing subtest difference scores calculations, increasing demographic information on the normative sample, eliminating indices due to a lack of psychometric information, and providing subtest comparison information. These revisions improved some psychometric properties that have increased the utility of TVPS-4 for research purposes. However, reviews of earlier versions of the TVPS also question the theoretical basis for its use as well as whether validity evidence presents any rationale for using this test over others. Unfortunately, validity evidence has not been improved enough in the TVPS-4 to support its use. Further discussion of the connection between theoretical context and subtest selection and development and of how the TVPS-4 differs from other available assessments is needed. The test manual does provide adequate cautions against using the TVPS-4 as the sole source of data.

SUMMARY. The TVPS-4 is designed as an individually administered multiple-choice assessment of visual perceptual skills without requiring the use of complex motor skills for English-speaking children, adolescents, and young adults ages 5 to 21. Administration, scoring, and interpretation instructions are clearly detailed in the test manual. The test is easy to use, taking approximately 30 minutes to administer and 5-10 minutes to score. The authors of the TVPS-4 have made efforts to address criticisms of the previous edition; however, the lack of additional theoretical, validity, or research evidence to support the use of its visual-cognitive model of visual perception and concerns regarding the use of subtest difference scores do not support the use of the TVPS-4 for any specific research or clinical purpose, particularly with regard to diagnosis.

REVIEWERS' REFERENCES

Ackerman, P. L. (2010). [Test review of Test of Visual Perceptual Skills, 3rd Edition]. In R. A. Spies, J. F. Carlson, & K. F. Geisinger (Eds.), *The eighteenth mental measurements yearbook.* Retrieved from http://marketplace.unl.edu/buros/

French, B. F. (2010). [Test review of Test of Visual Perceptual Skills, 3rd Edition]. In R. A. Spies, J. F. Carlson, & K. F. Geisinger (Eds.), *The eighteenth mental measurements yearbook.* Retrieved from http://marketplace.unl.edu/buros/

[178]

Transition-to-Work Inventory, Third Edition.

Purpose: Designed to "measure a person's leisure interests in order to help him or her turn these interests into possible employment opportunities, a small-business enterprise, or a home-based business."
Population: Job seekers.
Publication Dates: 2004-2012.
Acronym: TWI.
Scores, 16: Agriculture and Natural Resources, Architecture and Construction, Arts and Communication, Business and Administration, Education and Training, Finance and Insurance, Government and Public Administration, Health Science, Hopsitality/Tourism/Recreation, Human Service, Information Technology, Law and Public Safety, Manufacturing, Retail and Wholesale Sales and Service; Scientific Research/Engineering/Mathematics, Transportation/Distribution/Logistics.
Administration: Group.
Price Data, 2020: $69.95 per 25 inventories; administrator's guide (2012, 14 pages) available as free download from publisher's website.
Time: (20-25) minutes.
Comments: Self-administered and self-scored.
Author: John J. Liptak.
Publisher: JIST Career Solutions, a division of Kendall Hunt.

No review available. This test does not meet review criteria established by the Buros Center for Testing that call for at least minimal technical and development information.

[179]

Trauma Symptom Checklist for Children Screening Form/Trauma Symptom Checklist for Young Children Screening Form.

Purpose: Designed to screen for symptoms of trauma.
Population: Ages 3 to 17.
Publication Dates: 2016-2018.
Scores, 2: General Trauma, Sexual Concerns.
Administration: Individual or group.
Price Data, 2020: $74 per complete kit including technical paper (2018, 14 pages) and 25 screening form answer sheets (specify children or young children); $4 per technical paper; $71 per 25 answer sheets (specify children or young children).
Foreign Language Edition: Both forms are available in Spanish.
Time: Approximately 5 minutes for administration and scoring of either form.
Comments: Each form contains a subset of items from its respective full length form; if the child is between ages 8 and 12, both screening forms should be administered when possible; if only one screening form can be administered for an 8- to 12-year-old, then the clinician should decide whether the child or the (nonabusive) caretaker would be most appropriate to complete the form.
Authors: John Briere (forms and technical paper) and Jeffrey N. Wherry (technical paper).
Publisher: Psychological Assessment Resources, Inc.

a) TRAUMA SYMPTOM CHECKLIST FOR CHILDREN SCREENING FORM.
Purpose: Designed to evaluate "self-reported trauma symptoms in children."
Population: Ages 8 to 17.
Acronym: TSCC Screening Form.

b) TRAUMA SYMPTOM CHECKLIST FOR YOUNG CHILDREN SCREENING FORM.
Purpose: Designed to evaluate trauma symptoms in children via parent/caretaker report.
Population: Ages 3 to 12.
Acronym: TSCYC Screening Form.

Cross References: For reviews by Karen Mackler and Terry A. Stinnett of the Trauma Symptom Checklist for Young Children, see 17:191; for reviews by Gregory J. Boyle and Chockalingam Viswesvaran of the Trauma Symptom Checklist for Children, see 15:269.

Review of the Trauma Symptom Checklist for Children Screening Form/Trauma Symptom Checklist for Young Children Screening Form by JOHN A. MILLS, Professor of Psychology, Indiana University of Pennsylvania, Indiana, PA:

DESCRIPTION. The Trauma Symptom Checklist for Children Screening Form (TSCC Screening Form) and the Trauma Symptom Checklist for Young Children Screening Form (TSCYC Screening Form) are individually or group administered measures of trauma symptoms in children and adolescents. The author indicates that the measures (TSCC Screening Form administered to 8- to 17-year-olds, TSCYC Screening Form administered to parents/caregivers of 3- to 12-year-olds) evaluate symptoms of trauma in children who may have been exposed to a wide variety of trauma with the intention of making a better referral to services than can be made with an intake interview alone. The test author describes the problems professionals experience when needing to make referrals that are based solely on interviews, which often are subjective and non-standardized and require substantial training in symptom detection. These problems tend to place undue emphasis on the manifest severity of an event or obvious features of a response (Wherry, Huey, & Medford, 2015). Because of these pressures, there is a demand for efficient and psychometrically sound measures to screen children for possible referral for further assessment and intervention.

If the child is between 8 and 12 years old (an area of overlap between the two measures), the clinician must decide whether the child or a caregiver would be a better respondent. The clinician should be suitably qualified in the ethical administration, scoring, and interpretation of psychological tests. In addition, all child advocacy center (CAC) and other professionals who are approved by the test publisher and who have been screened and trained may administer the instrument with proper supervision. The measure may be administered individually or in groups, in each case ensuring that comfort and privacy are assured. Scoring is completed through the response blank, with a scoring sheet conveniently attached under the response blank. Raw scores for the two scales are derived separately and recorded on age- and gender-normed charts on the same form. For the quality of the score, no more than one item can be omitted, so the clinician may need to work with the examinee to complete items. Scores plotted in the *shaded* area of a profile section on the scoring chart are consistent with clinical concern. Any child with any screening score in these areas should be referred for further assessment or intervention.

DEVELOPMENT. The TSCC and TSCYC Screening Forms were developed by taking items from the original TSCC and TSCYC (Briere, 1996 and Briere, 2005, respectively) that demonstrated the best psychometric properties. Specifically, items were selected that best predicted overall trauma and sexual-related symptoms in normative samples. The TSCC and TSCYC Screening Forms both include two subscales, General Trauma (12 items) and Sexual Concerns (eight items). The test author states that it is not useful to demand further diagnosis-related specificity in a screening measure. Spanish screening forms were developed by translating the forms and back-translating them with bilingual judges and content-qualified judges.

TECHNICAL. The test author reports that the TSCC and TSCYC Screening Forms can be completed and scored in 5 minutes and provide scores for General Trauma and Sexual Concerns.

Standardization. Clinical cutoffs on the TSCC and TSCYC Screening Forms were established on the basis of psychometric theory and an emphasis on identifying individuals at risk. This approach is more conservative than cutoffs for the longer measures from which the screening forms were derived. This care is exemplified by the provision that a single reported symptom on the Sexual Concerns scale of the TSCYC Screening Form prompts a referral decision for 3- and 4-year-old females because of the low base rate of such manifestations in young children and the possible significance of their appearance.

Norms. The author reports that TSCC Screening Form data were acquired from the self-reports of 3,955 children ages 8 to 17 years from three nonclinical samples in different locales. Two of the nonclinical samples were *not* administered the sexually related questions (n = 3,708). Also in the context of the TSCC and TSCYC data collection, caretaker reports from 750 children were collected from a sample that was demographically stratified to match the 2002 U.S. Census figures. The overall nonclinical sample provided a reasonably representative sample of the general population for gender and race/ethnicity, and additional detailed information about this sample is available in the TSCC and TSCYC professional manuals (Briere, 1996 and Briere, 2005, respectively).

Detailed reliability and validity information about the screening forms is presented in a technical paper and in supporting research reports. Reliability estimates and validity evidence were derived from both the TSCC and TSCYC Screening Form normative samples in addition to a sample of children presenting to an urban CAC. Internal consistency estimates (alpha coefficients) were presented for the TSCC and TSCYC Screening Form scales, and all indices were described by the test author as falling in the good to excellent range with an overall mean alpha coefficient of .79. Because the number of 3- to 4-year-olds in the CAC sample was too small for useful evaluation, that group was not included in the analysis. Test-retest reliability data were from 33 children in the TSCYC Screening Form normative sample and indicated an adequate degree of consistency (r = .80 across an interval of 1 to 13 days). Comparable data for the TSCC were not presented, and no explanation for this omission was offered. Reliability and validity of the Spanish versions of the full TSCYC and TSCC have been studied, and references for those reports were provided in the screening form technical paper.

The test author makes the reasonable argument that the connection between the screening forms and the full-scale versions is relevant to arguments for validity. The validity of the TSCC and TSCYC have been supported in prior works, so the high correlations between relevant components of the screening forms and the full-scale versions are presented (in tabular form) as evidence that the screening forms strongly represent the related domains from the full-scale versions. These data included the aforementioned limitation associated with the lack of an adequate sample of 3- to 4-year-olds from the CAC sample.

COMMENTARY. It is clear that the efficient and effective screening of children for symptoms of trauma is a laudable goal. The TSCC and TSCYC Screening Forms are based on well-established and larger measures and appear to have promising psychometric properties. There are some areas of relative weakness in the psychometric data, but support for reliability and validity are reasonably strong. The test author is careful to discuss the professional context of this assessment method, and the arguments for clinical utility are strong. The author also is careful to warn the potential user that the measures cannot be used as evidence of factual history. However, the rationale for clinical cutoffs is skillfully couched in the context of identifying children who need further assessment or intervention.

SUMMARY. The Trauma Symptom Checklist for Children Screening Form and the Trauma Symptom Checklist for Young Children Screening Form are psychometrically sound measures of trauma symptoms in children ages 3 to 17 that were derived from previously established longer forms of each measure. Each measure provides clinical cutoff scores on separate scales of General Trauma (12 items) and Sexual Concerns (eight items). Clinicians evaluating children ages 8–12 years decide whether to administer the TSCYC Screening Form (to a caregiver) or to administer the TSCC Screening Form (directly to the child). The measures should be administered at times that are appropriate to recall potential traumatic experiences, bearing in mind the possible connection between disclosure and reaction to trauma and the experience of assessment. The measures are convenient to score and provide suitably normed scores for General Trauma and Sexual Concerns. Clinical cutoff scores are established at one standard deviation above the mean to maximize the likelihood of identifying a symptomatic abused child. A positive result should lead directly to a treatment referral or more in-depth assessment.

REVIEWER'S REFERENCES

Briere, J. (1996). Trauma Symptom Checklist for Children. Lutz, FL: Psychological Assessment Resources.

Briere, J. (2005). Trauma Symptom Checklist for Young Children. Lutz, FL: Psychological Assessment Resources.

Wherry, J. N., Huey, C. C., & Medford, E. A. (2015). A national survey of child advocacy directors regarding knowledge of assessment, treatment referral, and training needs in physical and sexual abuse. *Journal of Child Sexual Abuse, 24,* 280-299.

Review of the Trauma Symptom Checklist for Children Screening Form/Trauma Symptom Checklist for Young Children Screening Form by CARL J. SHEPERIS, Dean of the College of Education and Human Development, Texas A&M University-San Antonio, and MARIYA T. DAVIS, Assistant Professor of Special Education, Texas A&M University-San Antonio, San Antonio, TX:

DESCRIPTION. The Trauma Symptom Checklist for Children Screening Form (TSCC Screening Form) and the Trauma Symptom Checklist for Young Children Screening Form (TSCYC Screening Form) are designed to quickly identify symptoms of trauma, including physical and sexual abuse, in children and adolescents. The TSCC Screening Form (ages 8 to 17) is a self-report instrument for children, and the TSCYC Screening Form is a caregiver report for children ages 3 to 12. The screening forms, which can be administered in either individual or group situations, each consist of two subscales: (a) General Trauma (GT), with 12 items; and (b) Sexual Concerns (SC), with eight items. The GT subscale is scored separately from the SC subscale because sexual symptoms tend to be specific to childhood sexual abuse, and non-sexual symptoms reflect general abuse-related impact.

The administration instructions are clear and easy to follow. For the TSCC Screening Form, the examinee answers each of the 20 questions regarding things children sometimes think, feel, or do by indicating how often it happens to them. For the TSCYC Screening Form, the caregiver answers 20 questions regarding things children sometimes do, feel, or experience by indicating how often it happened in the last month. Examinees respond by circling answers on a scale of 0 to 3 for the TSCC Screening Form, and on a scale of 1 to 4 for the TSCYC Screening Form.

A scoring sheet is used to calculate the GT and SC raw scores by transferring the circled item scores to the corresponding lines. Then, the scores for Items 1-12 are added to obtain the GT raw score, and the scores for Items 13-20 are added to obtain the SC raw score. Next, the raw scores are plotted on the screening form profile by marking an X on the corresponding tick mark as appropriate for the child's gender and age. Elevated scores indicate a need for further assessment. It should be noted that there can be no more than one missing item response in order to generate a valid GT or SC score. The clinical cutoff scores for the scales are set at one standard deviation above the mean based on applied psychometric theory.

Each screening form takes approximately 5 minutes for administration and scoring. Both forms should be interpreted by a professional who possesses (a) a degree, certificate, or license to practice in the field of health care; and (b) appropriate training and experience with clinical behavioral assessment instruments.

DEVELOPMENT. The TSCC Screening Form and TSCYC Screening Form were derived from the Trauma Symptom Checklist for Children (TSCC; Briere, 1996) and the Trauma Symptom Checklist for Young Children (TSCYC; Briere, 2005), respectively. Both the English and Spanish versions of the screening forms were created by selecting items from the TSCC and the TSCYC that best predicted overall trauma and sexual-related symptomatology.

TECHNICAL. In developing the TSCC Screening Form the author used data from the same TSCC sample of 3,955 children between the ages of 8 and 17 that were gathered between 1994 and 1995. The sample comprised 52% female and 48% male participants with adequate representation of White (41%), Black/African American (28%), and Hispanic (20%) individuals. The manual for the screening forms, which was published as a technical paper, did not include other demographic data. Instead, the author of the instrument referred users to the original TSCC manual for additional information.

The normative data for the TSCYC Screening Form were derived from the 2002 sample of 750 caregivers used for the long form of the TSCYC. The racial composition of the sample differed from the TSCC sample with 62% White, 16% Hispanic, 16% Black/African American, and 6% Asian or other participants. According to the test author, the sample was nearly evenly distributed across each age. As such, the sample for each age was based on approximately 75 parent reports. This is a relatively low sample size for each age represented. Once again, the test author referred readers to the original TSCYC manual for more detailed information. Thus, the manual for the screening forms lacked sufficient detail for a test user to determine the appropriateness of the process or the representativeness of the samples.

In order to evaluate reliability and validity evidence the test author gathered additional data from a sample of 268 children between the ages of 8 and 17 who were referred to a single child advocacy center in 2016. The demographic data of this sample differed from the original standardization sample for the TSCC, in that the new sample included participants, 90.3% of whom were female, from the following racial backgrounds: Hispanic (56.3%), White (16.8%), Black/African American (22.8%), and other (4.1%). The test author examined the sample of 268 children separately from the original sample drawn between 1994 and 1995 for purposes of calculating reliability and validity and then reported averages across the samples.

The additional sample for the reliability and validity study of the TSCYC Screening Form was also demographically different from the original sample of the TSCYC. In this case, the sample included 176 caretakers of children between the ages of 3 and 12 (80.1% female) from the following racial backgrounds: Hispanic (51.7%), White (14.2%), Black/African American (30.1%), and other (4%). The test author calculated reliability and validity data in the same manner as that used for the TSCC Screening Form.

Internal consistency estimates (alpha coefficients) for the TSCC Screening Form and the TSCYC Screening Form were reported to have a mean of .79. The test author excluded data from caretakers of 3- to 4-year-olds in the child advocacy center sample because the sample was too small, making it difficult to assess fully the internal consistency of the TSCYC Screening Form for the youngest age group. Across samples (normative and clinical) and genders, alpha coefficients ranged from .85 to .91 and from .62 to .84 for the GT and SC subscales, respectively, on the TSCC Screening Form. Across samples and genders, alpha coefficients ranged from .76 to .89 and from .60 to .87 for the GT and SC subscales, respectively, on the TSCYC Screening Form. The author also reported test-retest reliability estimates (r = .80; p < .001) for the TSCYC Screening Form based on data from 33 participants in the normative sample over a time period ranging between 1 and 13 days.

In evaluating overall construct evidence of the shortened forms of the two instruments, the test author elected to examine correlations between scores on the screening forms and scores on the original full-scale instruments. The author reported an average correlation coefficient of .95 between the General Trauma scale on the TSCC Screening Form and the Total score on the full-scale TSCC (minus the Sexual Concerns scale). The mean correlation between the TSCC Screening Form Sexual Concerns scale and the TSCC Sexual Concerns scale was reported to be r = .95. The mean correlation between the TSCYC Screening Form General Trauma scale and the TSCYC Total score (minus the Sexual Concerns scale) was reported as r = .93. Similarly, the correlation coefficient between the Sexual Concerns scales on the screening and full-length forms was reported to be .94. Again, 3- and 4-year-olds from the child advocacy center sample were excluded from the calculations. The resulting correlation coefficients are not unexpected and, by themselves, provide only partial insight into the construct validity of the instruments.

Although the test manual indicates that it represents technical data for the Spanish versions of the TSCC Screening Form and the TSCYC Screening Form, there was no information provided about the standardization process. The test author did not provide information about the reliability and validity of the Spanish versions of the screening forms.

COMMENTARY. The TSCC Screening Form and the TSCYC Screening Form are brief measures designed to identify symptoms of trauma through either caregiver reports for children ages 3 to 12 or through self-reports for children ages 8-17. The key strengths of these two instruments are that they are derived from two full-scale measures that have been shown to have adequate reliability and validity. The scoring process for these instruments is straightforward and easy to complete. Although these instruments are easy to administer and easy to score, there are a number of concerns about these short forms, including the lack of adequate information about the development of the instruments, confusing information about the reliability and validity evaluations, and the ages of participants in the original standardization samples. In developing short forms of existing tests, it is customary to compare results obtained on the short form to those obtained on the full-length form to assess the extent to which the shorter form yields the same or similar information about the test takers. Greater correspondence between the two forms indicates that the short form may be used in place of the full-length form, at least for some test purposes, such as screening. However, these types of comparisons need not be the only evidence of validity provided, and additional sources of evidence would strengthen the validity argument for the TSCC Screening Form and the TSCYC Screening Form. Additional validity evidence should be gathered on the screening forms with larger clinical samples representing current U.S. Census data. In addition to gathering additional evidence, future iterations of the test manual should include clearer descriptions of the instrument development process and more detailed information on the interpretation of results (e.g., case studies).

SUMMARY. The TSCC Screening Form and the TSCYC Screening Form were designed to be brief measures for identifying trauma symptomology in children ages 3 to 17. The author of these instruments relied heavily upon the data from the original full-scale versions and did not conduct enough evaluation of the screening forms. As such, there is a need for further study of the instruments and revised manuals before they can be fully recommended. Further, because the test manual lacked information about the Spanish screening forms' standardization process and technical properties, they could not be evaluated for clinical use.

REVIEWERS' REFERENCES

Briere, J. (1996). Trauma Symptom Checklist for Children. Lutz, FL: Psychological Assessment Resources.

Briere, J. (2005). Trauma Symptom Checklist for Young Children. Lutz, FL: Psychological Assessment Resources.

[180]

Universal Nonverbal Intelligence Test–Group Abilities Test.

Purpose: Designed as "a nonverbal screener of reasoning (i.e., general cognitive) ability."
Population: Ages 5-0 through 21-11 years.
Publication Date: 2019.
Acronym: UNIT-GAT.
Scores, 3: Analogic Reasoning, Quantitative Reasoning, Full Scale.
Administration: Individual or group.
Price Data, 2020: $219 per complete kit including examiner's manual (138 pages), 25 response booklets, 25 record forms, and scoring transparencies; $71 per examiner's manual; $71 per 25 response booklets; $47 per 25 record forms; $15 per scoring transparency (Analogic Reasoning or Quantitative Reasoning).
Time: 10-minute time limit for each subtest; approximately 30 minutes total for administration.
Authors: Bruce A. Bracken and R. Steve McCallum.
Publisher: PRO-ED.

Review of the Universal Nonverbal Intelligence Test–Group Abilities Test by DOREEN W. FAIRBANK, Professor, Psychology and Social Work Department, Meredith College, Raleigh, NC:

DESCRIPTION. The Universal Nonverbal Intelligence Test–Group Abilities Test (UNIT-GAT) is a nonverbal screening test of reasoning ability that consists of two subtests: Analogic Reasoning and Quantitative Reasoning. The results are reported as a Full Scale index (a composite score), derived from a combination of the subtests. UNIT-GAT may be administered in a group or individual setting with students ages 5 years 0 months to 21 years 11 months. The test is designed for students who are verbally uncommunicative; have English as a second language; are from different cultures; or exhibit a disability that affects auditory reception, verbal expression, language development, or overall general communication. The test authors believe the UNIT-GAT is a "culturally sensitive, psychometrically validated screener for individuals who cannot be assessed fairly with conventional language-loaded tests" (manual, p. 1).

The UNIT-GAT test kit includes the examiner's manual; administration at a glance laminated card with the test administration script; examinee response booklets (test items); examinee record forms (scoring information, examinee responses, test session validity checklist, and notes/observations); and scoring transparencies. Any professional with group assessment experience including teachers, social workers, counselors, and psychologists can administer the UNIT-GAT. Professionals with appropriate training and experience in intellectual testing and score interpretation who follow the *Standards for Educational and Psychological Testing* (American Educational Research Association,

American Psychological Association, & National Council on Measurement in Education, 2014) should interpret the results of the test.

The manual provides excellent instructions for preparation and test administration, including information on room conditions, material needs, time limits, determining whether to administer the test in a group or individual setting, and the student response format. Each item is presented in a matrix format with the examinee selecting one of four responses that best completes a two- or four-matrix analogy. Analogic Reasoning is administered first, followed by Quantitative Reasoning. Before each subtest, the examiner demonstrates several examples followed by the examinee completing several practice items to ensure task comprehension. The examinee starts at Item 1 (regardless of age) and continues as fast as possible without skipping any items. The time limit for each subtest is 10 minutes. Analogic Reasoning comprises 73 items, and Quantitative Reasoning has 78 items. The manual estimates the test should not take longer than 30 minutes for the total administration and should be completed during one session. There are two test recording formats depending on age. Examinees ages 5-8 record responses directly below each item in the examinee response booklet, whereas ages 9 through 21 record responses on a separate examinee record form using a bubble sheet format. If the examiner believes that an older examinee's performance may be negatively affected by using the examinee record form, the examinee can record his/her answers in the examinee response booklet.

Examinee information and results are recorded in four sections on the front page of the record form. Section 1 provides space to record identifying information about the student. Section 2 provides space for raw scores, scaled scores, percentile ranks, confidence intervals, and descriptive classifications (determined in Section 3) for both Analogic Reasoning and Quantitative Reasoning. Also included is space for recording the sum of scaled scores and the Full Scale index score with the corresponding percentile rank, confidence interval, and descriptive classification. The descriptive classifications presented in Section 3 are based on seven scaled score intervals (ranging from 1-3 to 17-20) and seven index score intervals (ranging from < 70 to > 129). For each interval, a descriptive term (from *very delayed* to *very superior*) is provided. Section 4 displays the Interpretation of Subtest Performance and includes a pairwise subtest comparison to determine whether the difference between the two subtests' scaled scores is statistically significant.

Each item is scored 1 for a correct response or 0 for incorrect, skipped, or multiple responses. A discontinuation rule is applied if three items in a row are incorrect. Every item attempted after that is scored as 0. The test manual clearly describes how to transform raw scores into standard scores. A scoring transparency is included to help score the items.

DEVELOPMENT. The UNIT-GAT was developed as a nonverbal measure of the combination of analogic (fluid) and quantitative (crystalized) reasoning ability to provide a valid estimate of "general intelligence" for the purpose of screening individuals for possible placement in gifted or special needs programs (manual, p. 1). The UNIT-GAT was designed to reduce the differences or bias found in a language-dependent test, as it requires limited receptive language and no expressive language skills. The sample and practice items also decrease the need for receptive language, although test-taking instructions continue to be read to examinees. The authors focused on testing reasoning abilities that are expected to be based less on educational experience and previous knowledge, thus providing a more culturally fair assessment instrument.

TECHNICAL.

Standardization. Normative data were collected from 2013 to 2017 from 1,605 students in 31 states. Two percent of the normative data was weighted to help ensure a representative sample. The examiner's manual displays the demographic characteristics of the normative sample against the percentage of the corresponding demographic in the U.S. school-age population for each of the following areas: geographic region, gender, race, Hispanic status, exceptionality status, household income, and educational attainment of parents. The normative sample appears to be quite representative of the U.S. population. After UNIT-GAT was developed, a pilot phase was conducted with assessment professionals and consultants with diverse cultural, ethnic, and racial backgrounds. An additional phase was included during test standardization; a separate group of professionals examined the items for any type of bias or items that may appear to be offensive to a particular group. The results from this development phase and statistical procedures demonstrate that the UNIT-GAT is fairly free from systematic bias.

Reliability. Evidence of reliability was clearly demonstrated through three types of reliability: internal consistency, test-retest, and scorer consistency. Coefficient alpha was used to demonstrate internal consistency for both subtests at 15 different age intervals. The range for Analogic Reasoning was from .88 to .95 with an average across ages of .93; coefficients for Quantitative Reasoning ranged from .86 to .94 with an average of .92. The Full Scale composite had an average alpha coefficient of .95. Test-retest reliability estimates were calculated using a sample of 136 students tested twice over a period that averaged 18.5 days. Coefficients were .67 for Analogic Reasoning, .71 for Quantitative Reasoning, and .78 for the composite. Scorer consistency was examined with 50 complete protocols each scored by two members of the test publisher's staff. A resulting coefficient of .99 was observed for both subtests and the composite.

Validity. Evidence of validity was demonstrated using content-description evidence of validity (item analysis; analysis of floors, ceilings, and item gradients; and differential item functioning analysis with subgroup mean-difference comparisons), criterion-prediction evidence of validity, and construct-identification evidence of validity. Item analysis was used throughout development until each item reached the criterion to be accepted on the final measure. Criterion-prediction evidence of validity was presented using four other intelligence measures, both verbal and nonverbal. Each correlation coefficient demonstrated strong criterion correlations as evidence of validity, suggesting the UNIT-GAT can be used with confidence as a screening measure of intelligence. A confirmatory factor analysis supported the structural design of the UNIT-GAT and provided construct evidence of validity.

COMMENTARY. The UNIT-GAT accomplishes the authors' goals of developing a nonverbal, culturally sensitive screening assessment with strong psychometric properties. The degree of development and testing to ensure fairness and reduce systematic bias is a major strength of the UNIT-GAT. Although the test provides a quick, valid screening for gifted and special needs eligibility and placement, it should not be used as the only information for eligibility and/or placement. The method of recording examinee responses (ages 9-21) could be considered a weakness. More accurate results may occur if all students were allowed to record answers on the test booklet rather than transcribing to a different form using a bubble format. Because the test is strictly timed, this format may hinder the older examinee, resulting in lower scores.

SUMMARY. The UNIT-GAT was developed to provide a non-verbal screening test of reasoning ability that quickly measures intelligence while demonstrating strong psychometric properties. UNIT-GAT appears to be a culturally sensitive assessment for students who are verbally uncommunicative, non-English speakers, or have difficulty with language-loaded assessments. Reasoning ability is measured through analogic and quantitative items with a Full Scale composite score being produced. The normative sample, standardization procedures, and evidence of reliability and validity presented in the test manual demonstrate rigorous investigations that should provide an examiner with confidence when using this screening assessment.

REVIEWER'S REFERENCE

American Educational Research Association, American Psychological Association, & National Council on Measurement in Education. (2014). *Standards for educational and psychological testing.* Washington, DC: American Educational Research Association.

Review of the Universal Nonverbal Intelligence Test–Group Abilities Test by M. DAVID MILLER, Professor of Research and Evaluation Methods, University of Florida, Gainesville, FL:

DESCRIPTION. The Universal Nonverbal Intelligence Test–Group Abilities Test (UNIT-GAT) is a nonverbal group-administered screener of reasoning ability for ages 5-21. The test includes two subtests: Analogic Reasoning and Quantitative Reasoning. Analogic Reasoning requires solving analogies in a matrix format. Quantitative Reasoning requires solving mathematical problems. The UNIT-GAT also reports a Full Scale composite.

The UNIT-GAT can be used to measure cognitive limitations or strengths and the degree of the strengths and limitations. It is intended for examinees who have difficulty processing verbal aspects of intelligence tests. The test is meant to be especially useful for examinees with speech, language, or hearing impairments; those from different cultural backgrounds; those with limited English proficiency; and those with serious emotional disturbance or physical disabilities.

The test can be administered and interpreted by educators and related professionals with experience administering group assessments. The examiner's manual provides clear guidelines for examiner qualifications and skills needed, conditions of administration, and administration instructions for the assessment to be administered verbally.

Examinees ages 5-8 are instructed to record their responses directly in the response booklet, which also contains the test items, whereas test takers ages 9-21 record answers on a separate bubble sheet. Students are allowed 10 minutes to complete each subtest.

Raw scores for the subtests are converted to norm-referenced scores including scaled scores, percentile ranks, and age equivalents. The sum of the subtest scaled scores is converted into the Full Scale composite index, and percentile ranks can be derived. Seven descriptive classifications ranging from *very delayed* to *very superior* correspond to subtest scaled scores and the composite score. No rationale is provided in the test manual for the cutoffs used to establish the classifications. Examples for interpreting the scores are provided in the test manual.

DEVELOPMENT. The UNIT-GAT was developed with validity considerations guiding the process. The test authors aimed to create a cross-cultural assessment of both fluid and crystalized intelligence that could be used as a general cognitive ability screener. The test is based on theoretical assumptions and developmental components that were used in the development of the individually administered Universal Nonverbal Intelligence Test–Second Edition (UNIT2; Bracken & McCallum, 2016; see 181, this volume), from which the UNIT-GAT was adapted. According to the test manual, "many of the items in the UNIT-GAT were retained from the UNIT2," but the exact number is not specified.

The scores are based on normative data of 1,605 participants collected from 31 states from 2013 to 2017. The data represented the four Census regions of the United States and approximately mirrored national data on geographic region, gender, race, Hispanic status, exceptionality status, household income, and parents' educational level. To further describe the normative sample, data are stratified by age for each of the variables above (except exceptionality status), and several three-way interactions (e.g., age by gender by parent education) are presented. Some of the three-way interactions result in cells too small for any meaningful interpretation of the sample, particularly small race groups such as Asian/Pacific Islanders or American Indian/Alaska Natives.

TECHNICAL. The UNIT-GAT was comprehensive in the technical data collected. The data include extensive consideration of the three foundational components of the *Standards for Educational and Psychological Testing* (American Educational Research Association [AERA], American Psychological Association [APA], & National Council on Measurement in Education [NCME], 2014)—validity, reliability, and fairness. Within each foundational component, multiple studies were conducted.

Validity. Many types of evidence of validity are reported with a strong emphasis on content, group differences, criterion correlations, and internal structure. The content evidence process is broadly described and includes the rationale for the test's content and format, results of item discrimination and item difficulty analyses, and discussion of floors and ceilings. Evidence is strong overall; however, there is no evidence of external review of the content during or after test development. Future studies should include external reviewers for content evidence of validity. In addition, item analyses based on classical test theory show that the median item difficulty and item discrimination results were good for the 15 age intervals presented. However, because individual item statistics are not reported, prospective test users can be sure only that the *typical* item statistics work well.

Because the UNIT-GAT is intended to serve the needs of examinees who cannot be fairly assessed with conventional language-loaded tests, group differences are a core issue. Consequently, the validity evidence includes differential item functioning (DIF) analyses and comparisons of group mean differences on each subtest and the composite. The DIF analyses include an adjustment for the large number of items and groups being analyzed by setting the Type I error rate at .001. With this error rate almost no items are identified with DIF for gender, race, or ethnicity. Mean differences for gender, race, and ethnicity after adjusting for geographic region, age, and other demographic variables show the test has similar scores for gender and small differences for race and ethnicity relative to similar verbal assessments.

Relationships with multiple criteria also provide strong evidence for the validity of UNIT-GAT scores. The UNIT-GAT Full Scale composite shows moderate to large positive correlations (.29-.82) with similar assessments including the UNIT2, the Detroit Tests of Learning Abilities–Fifth Edition, the Wechsler Intelligence Scale for Children–Fifth Edition, and the Naglieri Nonverbal Ability Test–Second Edition as well as with reading achievement tests. The assessment also has strong positive relationships with IQ and chronological age. Mean differences are in the expected directions for students in the following groups: gifted/talented, emotional/behavioral disorder, limited English proficient, deaf/hard of hearing, attention-deficit/hyperactivity disorder, learning disability, low-functioning autism, and intellectual disability/developmental delay.

Finally, evidence is provided of the internal structure of the assessment. Confirmatory factor analyses show reasonable fit for five age groups and for the total sample.

Reliability. The UNIT-GAT has high internal consistency (coefficient alpha). Average internal consistency coefficients across age categories are .93, .92, and .95 for Analogic Reasoning, Quantitative Reasoning, and the composite, respectively. Internal consistency is also high for each gender, racial, ethnic, and exceptionality group. Test-retest reliability (stability) was not as high as internal consistency, with subtest reliabilities for age groups ranging from .57 to .79 for Analogic Reasoning and from .52 to .86 for Quantitative Reasoning. The range for the composite was higher, from .63 to .86. Thus, the stability of the assessment over a short time period (average 18.5 days) was only moderate. Interscorer consistency was high (.99) when two members of the test publisher's staff independently scored 50 record forms drawn at random.

Fairness. Extensive fairness studies were conducted including expert reviews, psychometric analyses, comparative analyses of matched groups, and comparisons of the factor structure. Reviews of all items and procedures for potential bias were conducted by internal and external reviews including those by consultants to the test publishers who were described as quite diverse. Similar reviews had also been completed for the UNIT2 with which many items are shared. On the basis of the expert reviews, the test authors concluded that the UNIT-GAT content is fair to test takers regardless of background and dispositions. Statistical analyses, including comparison analyses, show that some differences do occur. However, there are other group comparisons where no differences occur. These differences suggest that the test does generate some group differences, but the differences are relatively small compared to other tests, particularly verbal intelligence tests.

COMMENTARY. The UNIT-GAT provides a valid and reliable measure of intelligence that is nonverbal and presumably culturally sensitive. The assessment provides extensive and strong psychometric evidence that is consistent with the *Standards for Educational and Psychological Testing* (AERA, APA, & NCME, 2014) with emphasis on validity, reliability, and fairness. The preponderance of evidence supports the validity, reliability, and fairness of the UNIT-GAT for its proposed uses. However, there are several issues that need to be examined in future studies of the test. First, the moderate test-retest reliability coefficients raise concerns about the stability of a characteristic that is usually assumed to be consistent over time. Second, some of the mean differences across groups suggest some potential issues with fairness. However, the groups (e.g., Black/African American, limited English proficient) with lower scores typically score lower on intelligence tests, and the magnitude of the difference on the UNIT-GAT is less than that typically found in verbal intelligence assessments. Third, the reviews leading to content evidence of validity were conducted by the test developers themselves and the authors of the UNIT-GAT and not by independent, external reviewers. The content judgments are probably reasonable and suggest the validity of UNIT-GAT scores; nonetheless, users should review the content themselves as external reviewers until such studies are reported.

SUMMARY. The UNIT-GAT was developed as a nonverbal intelligence test to provide a screening tool for general cognitive ability. The manual for the assessment provides a wide range of psychometric studies, which largely confirm the validity, reliability, and fairness of the assessment's use as a measure of reasoning ability. The psychometric evidence also focuses broadly on issues of testing examinees ages 5 to 21 with special needs, including emotional/behavioral disorders, limited English proficiency, hearing impairments, attention-deficit/hyperactivity disorder, learning disability, low-functioning autism, and intellectual disability/developmental delay. The assessment provides a strong measure with the main limitation being moderate stability over time.

REVIEWER'S REFERENCES

American Educational Research Association, American Psychological Association, & National Council on Measurement in Education. (2014). *Standards for educational and psychological testing.* Washington, DC: American Educational Research Association.

Bracken, B. A., & McCallum, R. S. (2016). Universal Nonverbal Intelligence Test–Second Edition. Austin, TX: PRO-ED.

[181]

Universal Nonverbal Intelligence Test–Second Edition.

Purpose: Designed to "assess general intelligence and three foundational cognitive abilities."

Population: Ages 5 through 21.

Publication Dates: 1998-2016.

Acronym: UNIT2.
Scores, 13: 6 subtest scores (Symbolic Memory, Nonsymbolic Quantity, Analogic Reasoning, Spatial Memory, Numerical Series, Cube Design), 7 composite scores (Memory, Reasoning, Quantitative, Abbreviated Battery IQ, Standard Battery with Memory, Standard Battery Without Memory, Full Scale IQ).
Administration: Individual.
Price Data, 2020: $839 per complete kit with case including examiner's manual (2016, 260 pages), 3 stimulus books, 25 record forms, 16 response chips, 2 response grids, 9 cubes, response mat, 10 symbolic memory cards and Administration at a Glance card in canvas case; $726 per kit without case; $132 per examiner's manual; $73 per 25 record forms; $209 per Online Scoring and Reporting System (includes 1 year starter subscription with unlimited scoring and reports for up to 5 users); $73 per annual renewal.
Time: 10-15 minutes for administration of Abbreviated Battery; approximately 30 minutes for Standard Battery; approximately 45 minutes for Full Scale Battery.
Authors: Bruce A. Bracken and R. Steve McCallum.
Publisher: PRO-ED.
Cross References: For a review by Deborah L. Bandalos of the original edition, see 14:404.

Review of the Universal Nonverbal Intelligence Test-Second Edition by VINCENT C. ALFONSO, Dean, School of Education, ADRIANA WISSEL, Assistant Professor, KATHY LE, Master's in Clinical Mental Health Counseling, and CLAIRE SEEGER, Master's in Clinical Mental Health Counseling, School of Education, Gonzaga University, Spokane, WA:

DESCRIPTION. The Universal Nonverbal Intelligence Test-Second Edition (UNIT2), developed by Bruce A. Bracken and R. Steve McCallum and published in 2016, is a nonverbal measure of general intelligence and three foundational cognitive abilities (i.e., memory, fluid reasoning, and quantitative reasoning) for individuals ages 5 years 0 months to 21 years 11 months. It is a collection of individually administered nonverbal tasks that includes the following subtests: Symbolic Memory, Nonsymbolic Quantity, Analogic Reasoning, Spatial Memory, Numerical Series, and Cube Design. The test authors report that the UNIT2 is a particularly useful measure for individuals who may experience difficulties with speech, language, or hearing; possess color-vision deficiencies; come from diverse backgrounds; or are verbally uncommunicative.

The examiner communicates expected task demands to the examinee using eight universal hand and body gestures. One point is awarded for each correct answer. For examinees 8 years of age or older, one point is also awarded for each unadministered item preceding the first item passed by the examinee to yield an age-appropriate score.

On the Symbolic Memory subtest, the youngest examinees (ages 5–7 years) select one of several options that correspond to a human figure, whereas older examinees (ages 8–21 years) recreate a sequence of human figures using response cards after viewing the sequence for 5 seconds. The Nonsymbolic Quantity subtest requires examinees to determine which one of the responses presented best fits an incomplete conceptual or numerical analogy, sequence, or problem. On the Analogic Reasoning subtest, each item is an incomplete conceptual or geometric analogy presented in a matrix format. The examinee must complete the analogy by pointing to one of four response options. The Spatial Memory subtest requires the youngest examinees to select one or two of three options presented that match a stimulus figure. Older examinees view a random pattern of green and/or black dots presented on a grid for 5 seconds and must recreate the spatial pattern. The Numerical Series subtest presents an array of numbers or mathematical symbols that create a perceptual match or complete a quantitative series. The examinee determines which of the response options best completes the incomplete series. The Cube Design subtest involves the presentation, matching, and/or direct reproduction of two-color, abstract geometric designs. The younger examinees match one of three or four options to a stimulus design, whereas older examinees view a stimulus design and then reconstruct the design directly on the stimulus book or response mat.

The test manual follows a standard and clear format for presenting each subtest that includes a brief description, a list of materials needed, instructions for arranging the materials, starting and stopping points, instructions for administering the items, scoring criteria, and any special age considerations. The UNIT2 can be administered in 10–45 minutes (10–15 minutes for Abbreviated Battery; 30 minutes for Standard Battery; 45 minutes for Full Scale Battery). Recording examinee performance is organized within the Examiner Record form, a form that also provides space for notes and observations. The UNIT2 produces four types of normative scores—subtest scaled scores, composite indexes, percentile ranks, and age equivalents—and one category (or descriptive classification). When interpreting results, examiners are encouraged first to interpret the global intelligence score, followed by construct-specific scores, and, finally, subtest performance.

DEVELOPMENT. The first edition of the UNIT (Bracken & McCallum, 1998) was designed to assess the general intelligence and cognitive abilities of school-aged participants. The test was administered nonverbally to accommodate all students in which language and verbal abilities may be a barrier for assessment outcomes. The authors chose two constructs—reasoning and memory—to assess intelligence. Reasoning allows individuals to recognize relationships and infer appropriate conclusions, whereas memory allows retention and retrieval of new information. The six subtests, either symbolic (measures concept abilities) or nonsymbolic (measures performance abilities), resulted in scores for memory, fluid reasoning, and quantitative reasoning. The test authors argue that intelligence is derived from the ability to problem solve using these abilities. This theoretical understanding creates a hierarchical model with general intelligence at the top, followed by memory and reasoning.

In the revision of the UNIT, two subtests were removed (i.e., Object Memory and Mazes) due to redundancy and poor psychometric qualities. The pilot study for the revision also deemed the subtests unnecessary. Two new subtests (Nonsymbolic Quantity and Numerical Series) were added to assess quantitative reasoning more thoroughly. The age limit was extended to 21 years 11 months, allowing all high school and some college-aged participants to be assessed. A new normative sample was used to provide norms consistent with the current demographics of the United States. The fairness of the assessment was advanced by working to eliminate any language bias, creating multiple scores, assessing cognitive abilities rather than acquired knowledge, reducing emphasis on speed, and presenting multiple activities to increase interest. The nonverbal approach of the UNIT2 should not be confused as an assessment for measurement of nonverbal intelligence, but as a nonverbal assessment of intelligence.

According to McCallum and Bracken (in press) the theoretical organization of the UNIT2 is "consistent with portions of several instruments that adopt the Cattell–Horn–Carroll [CHC] model of cognitive abilities." This model or theory underlies implicitly or explicitly every major intelligence test in the United States (cf. Carroll, 1993, 1997; Schneider & McGrew, in press). As supported by the work of Flanagan, Ortiz, and Alfonso (2017), the authors of the UNIT2 seem to have captured several CHC broad abilities on their test, which is consistent with the field of intelligence testing today.

Some new features of the UNIT2 include the following: a normative sample with an upward extension of normative tables, studies of reliability and validity, and quantitative subtests to replace two former subtests. Enhanced features include a nonverbal stimulus-and-response administration format, various batteries, wide breadth of use with exceptional students, a fair assessment of culturally and linguistically different examinees, reduced situational sources of test bias, and full-color stimuli, manipulatives, and pointing response modes to engage examinees.

TECHNICAL. Information regarding the technical characteristics of the UNIT2 was gathered primarily from the test manual and from McCallum and Bracken (in press). The standardization sample consisted of 1,603 individuals from 33 states across the United States. Testing was conducted during the period 2010-2015. Geographically, the states in the South made up 39% of the sample, followed by the West (23%), the Midwest (22%), and the Northeast (16%). The sex of the individuals in the sample was 51% male and 49% female. White individuals made up approximately 75% of the sample followed by Black/African American (16%), Asian/Pacific Islander (5%), two or more (4%), and American Indian/Eskimo/Aleut (2%). Individuals identified as Hispanic made up 20% of the sample.

With regard to the exceptionality status of individuals in the sample, the following percentages are reported in the examiner's manual: gifted and talented (6%), intellectual disability (3%), deaf/hard of hearing (2%), language impairment (2%), learning disability (5%), attention-deficit/hyperactivity disorder (4%), and autism spectrum disorder (4%). Age divisions for norms tables are the following: 3 months for ages 5 through 9 years, 6 months for ages 10 through 14 years, 1 year for ages 15 through 17 years, and 4 years for ages 18 through 21 years. The test authors state that standardization sample data "show close matches to U.S. census figures for the relevant demographic categories and exceptionalities. Examiners can have confidence that scores from their examinees are compared to a representative sample" (manual, p. 100).

Reliability was demonstrated via coefficient alpha. The averaged internal consistency reliability coefficients using Fisher's z-transformation for subtests and composites across the age span ranged from .89 for the Spatial Memory subtest to .98 for the Standard Battery Without Memory and Full Scale Battery composites. All internal consistency reliability coefficients for each subtest and composite at each 1-year age interval were .84 or higher. The average standard error of measurement (*SEM*) for each subtest and each composite ranged from .60 to 1.04 and from 2.12 to 3.97, respectively.

Test-retest reliability was assessed with a sample of 199 individuals (divided into four groups), ages 9–21 years, across 13 states with a mean intervening testing time of 17.8 days. The test-retest sample was 52% male, 48% female; 80% White, 8% African/American, 4% Asian/Pacific Islander, and 2% American Indian/Eskimo/Aleut. Twenty-percent were of Hispanic background, and 30% had a disability/exceptionality. Corrected subtest stability coefficients for the combined sample ranged from .75 (Spatial Memory) to .94 (Cube Design). Corrected composite stability coefficients for the combined sample ranged from .85 (Abbreviated Battery) to .93 (Standard Battery Without Memory and Full Scale Battery). All stability coefficients for the combined sample were .75 or higher.

Interscorer reliability was assessed with two publisher staff members who were familiar with the test's scoring procedures. They independently scored 50 complete UNIT2 test records. Results of the two scorings were correlated; coefficients for all scores ranged from .98 to .99.

The floors for the UNIT2 subtests are adequate beginning at age 7 years; several subtests do not have adequate floors below 7 years. Practitioners should use caution in interpretation of subtest scores for young individuals (i.e., less than 7 years of age). The floors for UNIT2 composites are adequate across the age range of the test. Most subtests and composites evidence adequate ceilings. Exceptions are the Numerical Series subtest beginning at age 11 years 6 months, the Analogic Reasoning and Cube Design subtests beginning at age 14 years, and the Nonsymbolic Quantity subtests beginning at age 14 years 6 months.

Content-description evidence of validity was established via the development goals for the instrument, conventional item analysis procedures, and differential item functioning analyses. Development goals for the UNIT2, as well as the rationale for the content and format of the subtests and items, are detailed in the examiner's manual.

Regarding conventional item analysis, the authors state that they used traditional procedures to delete items that did not meet criteria that are well established in the field. As a result, "unsatisfactory items ... were deleted from the experimental version of the test before the UNIT2 was normed. The items that satisfied the item discrimination and item difficulty criteria were placed in easy-to-difficult order, and the test was normed" (manual, p. 125). Median discriminating powers and median item difficulties are found in the examiner's manual.

Differential item functioning (DIF) analysis was used to provide additional support for the validity of the UNIT2. The test authors provide a good explanation of the DIF procedures used for all items in each of the UNIT2 subtests and compared three dichotomous groups (male vs. female, African-American vs. non-African-American, Hispanic vs. non-Hispanic). Logistic regression of all items for all subtests was applied to all identified groups. Results revealed no systematic bias for gender, race, or ethnicity.

Criterion-prediction evidence of validity was assessed via correlations with seven criterion measures as well as comparisons of means and standard deviations and diagnostic accuracy analyses (including sensitivity and specificity indexes). Details of the studies that were conducted are found in the examiner's manual. According to McCallum and Bracken (in press), "These studies indicate that the UNIT2 is a sound measure of global intelligence, but it may not be strongly correlated with measures of processing speed—speed was a factor downplayed in the UNIT and UNIT2 because processing speed is not valued in many cultures, at least to the extent it is valued in the mainstream U.S. culture." This argument may be worth exploring further, however, as some believe that processing speed largely impacts learning, particularly with school-aged youth.

Construct-identification evidence of validity was demonstrated using a three-step procedure. First, the authors identified several constructs presumed to account for test performance. Second, they generated hypotheses based on the identified constructs. Third, these "hypotheses were verified by logical or empirical methods" (manual, p. 153). Analyses of the UNIT2 subtests and composites included relationship to age, difference between groups, relationship to academic achievement, relationships among the subtests and composites, confirmatory factor analysis, and item validity. Clear and thorough details of all analyses regarding construct-identification evidence of validity are provided in the examiner's manual.

Finally, Bracken and McCallum dedicate a chapter of the manual to a discussion of fairness or the degree to which a test is not biased. They discuss the rationale for the UNIT2 model of fairness, internal test characteristics, analysis of subtest and composite fairness, and the degree to which nonverbal tests may be free of cultural and linguistic content. The test authors concluded that although some group differences in intelligence occur, these differences are smaller than differences reported for tests that are more language-based. This chapter is well written in the opinion of these reviewers, may serve as an educational tool for novice examiners, and may be used as a model for other instruments.

COMMENTARY. Using an adaptation of Alfonso and Flanagan's (2009) criteria for evaluating the adequacy of the technical characteristics of preschool assessment instruments, these reviewers offer the following comments regarding the technical rigor of the UNIT2. The standardization sample characteristics are generally adequate to good because the sample consisted of 1,000–2,000 persons overall, normative data were collected relatively recently, age divisions of norm tables are small for younger ages, and the normative group represents the U.S. population on five or more important demographic variables (according to U.S. Census data found in ProQuest, 2014). Regarding internal consistency reliability, nearly all subtests and composites across the age range of the test demonstrate what these reviewers consider at least adequate coefficients (i.e., .80 or higher). The test-retest reliability sample (overall $N = 199$) is adequate along with most reliability coefficients, but the age range of the test-retest sample is inadequate (i.e., spans more than 2 years). The length of the test-retest interval is good (i.e., less than 3 months). Almost all subtest and composite floors and ceilings across the age span of the test are adequate; thus, the UNIT2 can discriminate among persons of very low or very high ability. In general, the validity of the UNIT2 appears to be more than adequate as a beginning point. The test authors provide three ample strands of adequate quality validity evidence that are consistent with the *Standards for Educational and Psychological Testing* (American Educational Research Association, American Psychological Association, & National Council on Measurement in Education, 2014). As with all tests, additional validity evidence is suggested for the UNIT2.

SUMMARY. The UNIT2 offers practitioners an updated tool for assessing general intelligence for individuals for whom the use of language may serve as a barrier—those with language differences, language delay, and hearing impairment, among others. The UNIT2 remains simple in appearance and delivery, and most subtests reflect those of the UNIT. The manipulatives and pictures remain useful for keeping examinees of a variety of ages engaged and attend to various learning styles. Revised norms and some modernization of subtests help examiners gain a deeper understanding of respondents' true abilities. While ongoing assessment of validity and reliability is recommended, current psychometrics indicate the UNIT2 is a satisfactory nonverbal assessment of several cognitive abilities for a diverse population.

REVIEWERS' REFERENCES

Alfonso, V. C., & Flanagan, D. P. (2009). Assessment of preschool children. In B. A. Mowder, F. Rubinson, & A. E. Yasik (Eds.), *Evidence-based practice in infant and early childhood psychology* (pp. 129-166). New York, NY: Wiley.

American Educational Research Association, American Psychological Association, & National Council on Measurement in Education. (2014). *Standards for educational and psychological testing*. Washington, DC: American Educational Research Association.

Bracken, B. A., & McCallum, R. S. (1998). Universal Nonverbal Intelligence Test. Austin, TX: PRO-ED.

Carroll, J. B. (1993). *Human cognitive abilities: A survey of factor-analytic studies*. Cambridge, England: Cambridge University Press.

Carroll, J. B. (1997). The three-stratum theory of cognitive abilities. In D. P. Flanagan, J. L. Genshaft, & P. L. Harrison (Eds.), *Contemporary intellectual assessment: Theories, tests, and issues* (pp. 122–130). New York, NY: Guilford.

Flanagan, D. P., Ortiz, S. O., & Alfonso, V. C. (2017). *Cross-battery assessment software system 2.0* (X-BASS 2.0). Hoboken, NJ: Wiley.

McCallum, R. S., & Bracken, B. A. (in press). Universal Nonverbal Intelligence Test 2: A multidimensional nonverbal alternative for cognitive assessment. In D. P. Flanagan & E. M. McDonough (Eds.), *Contemporary intelligence assessment: Theories, tests, and issues* (4th ed., pp. xxx–xxx). New York, NY: Guilford.

ProQuest. (2014). *ProQuest statistical abstract of the United States, 2014* (2nd ed.). Bethesda, MD: Bernan.

Schneider, W. J., & McGrew, K. S. (in press). The Cattell-Horn-Carroll model of intelligence. In D. P. Flanagan & E. M. McDonough (Eds.), *Contemporary intellectual assessment: Theories, tests, and issues* (4th ed., pp. xxx–xxx). New York, NY: Guilford.

Review of the Universal Nonverbal Intelligence Test–Second Edition by SHANI D. CARTER, Professor of Business, Wagner College, Staten Island, NY:

DESCRIPTION. The Universal Nonverbal Intelligence Test–Second Edition (UNIT2) is an individually administered measure to assess general intelligence and three foundational cognitive abilities (i.e., memory, fluid reasoning, and quantitative reasoning) by administration of six tests: Symbolic Memory, Nonsymbolic Quantity, Analogic Reasoning, Spatial Memory, Numerical Series, and Cube Design. It is designed for ages 5 through 21.

The test authors state it will be useful to practitioners to identify cognitive limitations and strengths, particularly among people with limited English proficiency, or people with speech and language impairments, emotional disturbance, or physical disabilities. The exams are conducted via attractive, multicolored flip charts requiring examinees to view graphics and then to place green and black response cards or chips in workspaces indicating their answers, or to use green and white cubes to duplicate a design. For example, for Symbolic Memory, examinees first view a green or black graphic of a man, woman, or child, and then must place a card containing the same colored graphic in the work space. For Nonsymbolic Quantity, examinees are shown black-and-white dominos and must choose which domino of a set of four matches the example based on the location of a red question mark.

Each of the six tests has 26 to 56 questions ranging in difficulty from elementary to expert, allowing all examinees the opportunity to have at least several correct responses while also allowing advanced examinees to have a challenge.

Examiners document responses in a 16-page record form and use an appendix in the examiner's manual to convert raw scores to scaled scores based on the age of the examinee. Using the scaled scores, examiners can easily determine which of the seven classifications from *very delayed* to *very superior* an examinee is when compared to population norms.

The examiner's manual contains extensive background information on test development, psychometric properties, and examiner instructions. Different instructions are provided for different age groups (i.e., 5 to 7; 8 to 21). Examiners must have extensive training and practice prior to administering the exams.

DEVELOPMENT. In developing the UNIT2, the test authors sought to use extensive feedback to improve the UNIT, which was published in 1998 to measure intelligence via problem-solving ability. The review of the intelligence literature and the psychometric literature provided in the test manual is extensive and appropriate. Each of the three foundational cognitive abilities is reviewed as an independent construct with appropriate literature. Memory is measured by Symbolic Memory and Spatial Memory. Fluid reasoning is measured by Analogic Reasoning and Cube Design. Quantitative reasoning is measured by Nonsymbolic Quantity and Numerical Series.

Compared to the UNIT of 1998, the UNIT2 eliminated two subtests (mazes and object memory) and added two subtests on quantitative reasoning to measure the added facet of intelligence (i.e., quantitative). The maximum age was increased from 17 years to 21 years, and the subtests were revised to allow a greater range of scores for the lowest-functioning examinees. The six resulting subtests were piloted and then standardized.

TECHNICAL. The standardization sample included 1,603 examinees from across the United States. The sample population was representative of the U.S. population on major demographic characteristics (e.g., region, gender, race, household income, parent's educational level) but over-sampled for some disabilities (e.g., hearing impairment, intellectual disability).

Coefficient alpha values ranged from .84 to .98 for the subtests based on age, gender, and race of the examinee, with nearly all alpha coefficients being above .90. Test-retest reliability at an average of 17.8 days (N = 199) for the subtests ranged from .67 to .97 depending on subtest and age. Interscorer reliability using two scorers and 50 tests ranged from .98 to .99 based on subtest.

Correlation coefficients were calculated to provide criterion-related evidence of validity for predicting scores on seven other intelligence tests (N = 33 to 546). The comparison tests were: UNIT; Cognitive Assessment System-Second Edition (CAS2); Wechsler Intelligence Scale for ChildrenFourth Edition (WISC-IV); Stanford-Binet Intelligence Scales, Fifth Edition (SB5); Comprehensive Test of Nonverbal Intelligence-Second Edition (CTONI-2); Woodcock-Johnson III Tests of Cognitive Abilities-Third Edition (WJ III); and Universal Multidimensional Abilities Scale (UMAS). In many cases, the correlations between related subtests were very high (e.g., WISC-IV and UNIT2 memory correlation = .70). The correlations with the CAS2 were lowest, and the correlations with the CTONI-2 and WISC-IV were highest.

Test scores by demographic groups (i.e., age, race, gender) were examined, as were scores by primary clinical diagnosis or exceptionality (e.g., gifted and talented; articulation disorder; language impairment, ADHD; hearing impairment; autism; visual impairment). Scores were found to be appropriate based on the group measured compared to national norms or demographically matched samples on similar tests.

Estimated correlations between the UNIT2 Standard and Full Scale Batteries and measures of academic achievement ranged from .54 to .79.

COMMENTARY. The UNIT2 is a highly accurate measure of facets of intelligence that was found to be fair across many demographic characteristics such as race, gender, and intellectual impairment. It is based upon an extensive review of decades of literature in intelligence and psychometrically based measurement. It has been rigorously evaluated for use across populations, and extensively validated against similar exams. Like these other tests, it must be administered to individuals by highly trained administrators, which will be time-consuming and costly.

Although many of the questions require identification of red or green objects (which are colors that people with color-vision deficiencies sometimes cannot identify), the test color scheme was approved by an optometrist with expertise in color-vision deficiencies after validation with people with color-vision deficiencies. The test was normed on the U.S. population, and therefore is appropriate for use only with the U.S. population. Caution should be exercised when examining people with limited mobility because the questions require examinees to move cards, chips, or cubes to answer questions. Further, the examiner instructions regarding various types of nonverbal communication (e.g., nodding) are appropriate for the United States but may be inappropriate for examinees from other countries (e.g., India and Mexico). The test authors acknowledge that "no gestures are truly universal" and that using gestures instead of verbal directions "may not completely eliminate potential linguistic or cultural bias" (manual, p. 15).

SUMMARY. The UNIT2 was designed to be an individually administered measure of several facets of intelligence that would be of use to educators and psychologists who wish to determine the intellectual functioning level of examinees. The test meets its goal of aligning with generally accepted definitions of facets of intelligence. Nevertheless, the test has several drawbacks that limit its usefulness with color-blind examinees and with examinees from outside the United States.

[182]

Vineland Adaptive Behavior Scales–Third Edition.

Purpose: Designed to assess adaptive behavior, "the performance of daily activities required for personal and social sufficiency," across the life-span.
Population: Birth-90+.
Publication Dates: 1935-2016.
Acronym: Vineland-3.
Administration: Individual.
Forms, 7: Comprehensive Teacher, Domain-Level Teacher, Comprehensive Parent/Caregiver, Domain-Level Parent/Caregiver, Comprehensive Interview with item-level probes, Comprehensive Interview with no item-level probes, Domain-Level Interview.
Price Data, 2020: $444.50 per online comprehensive forms kit including manual (2016, 362 pages), 1-year subscription to online scoring, and 25 copies of each form; $389.50 per hand-scored comprehensive forms kit including manual and 25 copies of each form; $156 per manual (print or digital); $60 per 1-year online scoring subscription.
Foreign Language Edition: Parent/Caregiver Forms available in Spanish.
Comments: Computer administration and scoring available.
Authors: Sara S. Sparrow, Domenic V. Cicchetti, and Celine A. Saulnier.
Publisher: Pearson.

a) PARENT/CAREGIVER.
Purpose: Designed to assess adaptive behavior via parent/caregiver report.

1) Comprehensive Parent/Caregiver Form.
Population: Birth-90+.
Scores, 13 to 18: 9 subdomain scores in 3 domains: Communication (Receptive, Expressive, Written), Daily Living Skills (Personal, Domestic, Community), Socialization (Interpersonal Relationships, Play and Leisure, Coping Skills); 2 optional subdomain scores in 1 optional domain: Motor Skills (Gross Motor, Fine Motor); 2 optional Maladaptive Behavior scores: Internalizing, Externalizing; Adaptive Behavior Composite.
Time: 10-25 minutes to complete core domains, depending on age; 2-4 minutes to complete optional Motor Skills domain (ages birth-9 years only); 2-3 minutes to complete optional Maladaptive Behavior domain (ages 3 and older only).

2) *Domain-Level Parent/Caregiver Form.*
Population: Ages 3-90+.
Scores, 4 to 7: 3-4 domain scores: Communication, Daily Living Skills, Socialization, Motor Skills (optional); 2 optional Maladaptive Behavior scores: Internalizing, Externalizing; Adaptive Behavior Composite.
Time: 10-15 minutes to complete core domains; 2-3 minutes to complete optional Motor Skills domain (ages 3-9 only); 2-3 minutes to complete optional Maladaptive Behavior domain.

b) TEACHER.
Purpose: Designed to assess "adaptive behavior in the school (including preschool) or structured daycare setting."

1) Comprehensive Teacher Form.
Population: Ages 3-21.
Scores, 13 to 18: 9 subdomains scores in 3 domains: Communication (Receptive, Expressive, Written), Daily Living Skills (Personal, Numeric, School Community), Socialization (Interpersonal Relationships, Play and Leisure, Coping Skills); 2 optional subdomain scores in 1 optional domain: Motor Skills (Gross Motor, Fine Motor); 2 optional Maladaptive Behavior scores: Internalizing, Externalizing; Adaptive Behavior Composite.
Time: 10-20 minutes to complete core domains, depending on age; 1-2 minutes to complete optional

Motor Skills domain (ages 3-9 only); 1-2 minutes to complete optional Maladaptive Behavior domain.

2) *Domain-Level Teacher Form.*

Population: Ages 3-21.

Scores, 4 to 7: 3-4 domain scores: Communication, Daily Living Skills, Socialization, Motor Skills (optional); 2 optional Maladaptive Behavior scores: Internalizing, Externalizing; Adaptive Behavior Composite.

Time: 8-10 minutes to complete core domains; 1-2 minutes to complete optional Motor Skills domain (ages 3-9 only); 1-2 minutes to complete optional Maladaptive Behavior domain.

c) INTERVIEW FORMS.

Purpose: Designed to assess adaptive behavior via a semistructured interview.

1) *Comprehensive Interview Form (with and without probes).*

Population: Birth-90+.

Scores, 13 to 18: 9 subdomain scores in 3 domains: Communication (Receptive, Expressive, Written), Daily Living Skills (Personal, Domestic, Community), Socialization (Interpersonal Relationships, Play and Leisure, Coping Skills); 2 optional subdomain scores in 1 optional domain: Motor Skills (Gross Motor, Fine Motor); 2 optional Maladaptive Behavior scores: Internalizing, Externalizing; Adaptive Behavior Composite.

Time: 20-40 minutes to complete core domains, depending on age; 2-5 minutes to complete optional Motor Skills domain (ages birth-9 years only); 3-4 minutes to complete optional Maladaptive Behavior domain (ages 3 and older only).

2) *Domain-Level Interview Form.*

Population: Ages 3-90+.

Scores, 4 to 7: 3-4 domain scores: Communication, Daily Living Skills, Socialization, Motor Skills (optional); 2 optional Maladaptive Behavior scores: Internalizing, Externalizing; Adaptive Behavior Composite.

Time: 23-27 minutes to complete core domains; 2-3 minutes to complete optional Motor Skills domain (ages 3-9 only); 2-3 minutes to complete optional Maladaptive Behavior domain.

Cross References: For reviews by Stephanie Stein and Keith F. Widaman of the second edition, see 18:150; see T5:2813 (156 references) and T4:2882 (62 references); for a review by Jerome M. Sattler of an earlier edition, see 10:381 (9 references); for a review by Iris Amos Campbell of an earlier Survey Form and Expanded Form, see 9:1327 (8 references); see also T3:2557 (38 references), 8:703 (23 references), T2:1428 (50 references), P:281 (21 references), 6:194 (20 references), and 5:120 (15 references); for reviews by William M. Cruickshank and Florence M. Teagarden of an earlier edition titled Vineland Social Maturity Scale, see 4:94 (21 references); for reviews by C. M. Louttit and John W. M. Rothney and an excerpted review of the Vineland Social Maturity Scale, see 3:107 (58 references); for reviews by Paul H. Furfey, Elaine F. Kinder, and Anna S. Starr of the Vineland Social Maturity Scale: Experimental Form B, see 1:1143.

Review of the Vineland Adaptive Behavior Scales—Third Edition by KAREN T. CAREY, Provost, University of Alaska Southeast, Juneau, AK:

DESCRIPTION. The Vineland Adaptive Behavior Scales—Third Edition (Vineland-3) is an individually administered assessment of adaptive behavior. Three forms are available online or on paper and include the Interview Form, the Parent/Caregiver Form, and the Teacher Form. All information comes from a third party, as the individual being evaluated does not participate in the assessment. The Teacher Form is designed for individuals from 3 to 21 years of age, and the Interview and Parent/Caregiver Forms are designed for individuals from birth to 90+. All three forms are available in a Comprehensive version and a shorter Domain-Level version.

The Vineland-3 is designed to assess three domains of adaptive behavior: Communication, Daily Living Skills, and Socialization. Two optional domains of Motor Skills and Maladaptive Behavior also may be assessed. Subdomains available on the Comprehensive Forms are Receptive, Expressive, and Written for the Communication domain; Personal, Domestic/Numeric, and Community/School Community (Daily Living Skills domain); Interpersonal Relationships, Play and Leisure, and Coping Skills (Socialization domain); Fine Motor Skills and Gross Motor Skills (Motor Skills domain); and Internalizing, Externalizing, and Critical Items (Maladaptive Behavior domain). Written, Domestic/Numeric, and Community/School Community are designed for individuals ages 3 and older; Coping Skills is designed for individuals ages 2 and older; Gross and Fine Motor are designed for individuals ages birth through 9; and Maladaptive subdomains are designed for ages 3 to adult. All other subdomains may be administered for anyone between birth and 90+.

Subdomain raw scores are converted to *v*-scale scores that range from 1 to 24 with a mean of 15 and a standard deviation of 3. Domain scores and the overall Adaptive Behavior Composite are converted to standard scores with a mean of 100 and a standard deviation of 15. Domain scores can range from 20 to 140. Multi-rater comparisons can be made between teachers and parents/caregivers, and item-level comparisons are available. On the Comprehensive Form, intervention guidance is provided for each subdomain. An overall profile can be plotted for both domain and subdomain scores.

As the Vineland-3 is based on third-party responses, informants can note whether their responses represent estimates or actual observations of ability. If fewer than 15% of the item scores in a domain or subdomain are estimated, the test authors note that the section probably is not compromised. If 15% to 25% of the scores are estimates, the domain or subdomain score should be interpreted with caution, and if estimates are above 25%, the score should not be interpreted.

DEVELOPMENT. The Vineland-3 was developed in response to feedback from users of the Vineland-II, including concerns about the time required for administration. Basal and ceiling rules have now been established for the Comprehensive Parent/Caregiver and Teacher Forms, and the briefer Domain-Level Forms were added. For the Interview Form, a new online administration option is available, and items with related content are grouped on a single screen, shortening the administration time. For children ages 3 to 9, the Comprehensive Interview Form and the Comprehensive Teacher Form take about the same amount of time to administer as the Vineland-II forms, whereas the Comprehensive Parent/Caregiver Form takes "substantially less time than the Vineland-II Parent/Caregiver Rating Form" (manual, p. 7).

Unlike the Vineland-II, which had the same wording and norms for both the Survey Interview Form and the Parent/Caregiver Rating Form, the Vineland-3 Parent/Caregiver Form contains items written at a lower reading level (i.e., fifth-grade) than the Interview Form and separate norms. Other changes from the Vineland-II include updated content, the addition of suggested interview questions and probes for the Interview Form, a subdomain name change on the Teacher Form (from *Academic* to *Numeric*), and some item scoring changes.

TECHNICAL. The Vineland-3 Interview and Parent/Caregiver Forms were standardized on 2,560 individuals from birth to 90+ representative of the U.S. population and drawn from the four geographic regions specified by the Census: West, North Central, Northeast, and South. The Teacher Form included 1,415 students from ages 3 to 18. Mother's education level was used to approximate an individual's socioeconomic status, and the norming population was matched for specified special education categories based on 2012-2013 figures from the National Center for Education Statistics. Race/ethnicity was reported as African American, Asian, Hispanic, White, or Other.

The methods used to assess reliability of the Vineland-3 were the same for all forms. Internal consistency was estimated using coefficient alpha, and coefficients are reported for each age group. For the Interview Form, average coefficients for domains and subdomains and the Adaptive Behavior Composite ranged from .83 to .98; for the Parent/Caregiver Form, coefficients ranged from .90 to .99; and for the Teacher Form, the range was .87 to .99. Test-retest reliability coefficients over a 12- to 35-day interval and corrected for range restrictions ranged from .56 to .92 on the Interview Form, from .60 to .94 on the Parent/Caregiver Form, and from .62 to .93 on the Teacher Form. Corrected inter-interviewer reliability coefficients for 96 individuals ages 0-20 ranged from .61 to .84. Interrater reliability coefficients ranged from .38 to .94 for the Parent/Caregiver Form (N = 148) and from .22 to .91 for the Teacher Form (N = 141).

Evidence of validity was based on test content, special study groups, and comparisons to other assessment tools. Content evidence was assessed through examination of items by experts and users of the Vineland-II. Mean scores across the ages were compared for each of the three forms and demonstrate the expected developmental trends over the age range. Special study groups included individuals with developmental delays, intellectual disabilities, autism spectrum disorder, hearing impairments, and visual impairments. Scores from the special study groups were compared to those from matched controls using paired-samples t-tests and mean differences. Groups with intellectual or developmental disabilities had poorer adaptive functioning (mean difference of Adaptive Behavior Composite scores was -1.74 to -4.92), and the autism spectrum disorder sample had higher Maladaptive Behavior domain scores (mean difference of -5.76 to -2.29). The hearing-impaired group scored lower in the Communication domain (mean difference of 4.75 to 11.10), and the visually impaired group scored lower on all domains compared to matched controls (mean difference of 11.31 to 17.00).

Correlational analyses were conducted with the Vineland-II, the Bayley Scales of Infant and Toddler Development—Third Edition (17:17), and the Adaptive Behavior Assessment System–Third Edition (20:5). With the Vineland II, corrected coefficients for the Interview Form ranged from .31 to .87; for the Parent/Caregiver Form, corrected coefficients ranged from .14 to .78; and for the Teacher Form, corrected coefficients ranged from

.37 to .91. Moderate to high correlations were obtained between the domain and Adaptive Behavior Composite scores of the Comprehensive Parent/Caregiver Form and the Adaptive Behavior domain score on the Bayley-3 (Communication domain r = .81, Daily Living Skills domain r = .67, Motor Skills domain r = .67, Adaptive Behavior Composite r = .76). The Parent/Caregiver and Teacher Forms were compared with age-specific forms of the ABAS-3 and yielded moderate to high correlations for the overall scores of both assessments (r = .75 to .88).

COMMENTARY. The Vineland-3 is a useful tool for assessing adaptive behavior across the age ranges. The addition of a computerized form allows basal and ceiling levels to be determined automatically and allows for the addition of possible interview questions and probes for the examiner. The fifth-grade reading level is a much-needed addition for the Parent Form, making the measure much more user friendly.

SUMMARY. The Vineland Adaptive Behavior Scales—Third Edition has been updated and revised to address concerns raised over the years with the Vineland-II.

Review of the Vineland Adaptive Behavior Scales—Third Edition by JEREMY R. SULLIVAN, Professor and Chair of Educational Psychology, University of Texas at San Antonio, San Antonio, TX:

DESCRIPTION. The Vineland Adaptive Behavior Scales—Third Edition (Vineland-3) represents the latest revision of these long-standing and popular measures of adaptive behavior (previous editions include Sparrow, Balla, & Cicchetti, 1984; Sparrow, Cicchetti, & Balla, 2005). The purpose of the scales is to provide a comprehensive assessment of adaptive behavior that contributes to the evaluation of individuals with intellectual and developmental disabilities. The test authors define the adaptive behavior construct as "the performance of daily activities required for personal and social sufficiency" (manual, p. 10), and the Vineland-3 purports to measure the examinee's performance in these areas, as rated by informants who are familiar with the individual. There are three forms of the test. The Interview Form is completed by a professional who interviews a parent or other caregiver about the examinee's adaptive behavior. The Parent/Caregiver Form is a behavior rating scale completed by a parent or other caregiver. Both the Interview and Parent/Caregiver Forms provide norms for ages birth to 90+ years. The Interview Form has the advantage of providing more detailed and elaborate descriptions of the examinee's adaptive behavior, as examiners ask open-ended questions and request specific examples to help them arrive at their ratings of each behavior. The Parent/Caregiver Form includes the same behaviors, but the respondent completes the rating scale on his or her own, without the opportunity to provide detailed descriptions of the examinee's functioning. The Teacher Form is a questionnaire completed by the examinee's teacher or similar school staff member, and provides norms for ages 3 to 21.

Each of the three forms includes a Comprehensive version and a Domain-Level version; the Comprehensive versions include a greater number of items, as well as subdomains, to provide more detailed information about the examinee's functioning. On the Comprehensive Forms, the domains (and subdomains) include Communication (Receptive, Expressive, and Written), Daily Living Skills (Personal, Domestic/Numeric, and Community/School Community), and Socialization (Interpersonal Relationships, Play and Leisure, and Coping Skills). Optional domains include Motor Skills (Gross Motor, Fine Motor) and Maladaptive Behavior (Internalizing, Externalizing; Critical Items). The most global score on the Vineland-3 is the Adaptive Behavior Composite (ABC), which is based on scores from the Communication, Daily Living Skills, and Socialization domains. The Domain-Level Forms provide scores for Communication, Daily Living Skills, and Socialization in addition to the ABC but have fewer items than the Comprehensive Forms and therefore do not provide subdomain scores.

Each form can be administered using the test publisher's online platform, or with a paper-and-pencil record form. New users of the Vineland-3 will likely need the most guidance and practice when learning to administer the Interview Form because the examiner must use a conversational style and open-ended questions to elicit descriptions of the examinee's typical behavior and then score each item based on these responses. The Interview Form response book includes sample language to illustrate how the examiner may ask about each behavior, and more detailed scoring criteria for many items are included in appendices to the test manual. Using these suggested questions is optional (i.e., examiners can develop their own ways to elicit the necessary information, and additional follow-up questioning may be necessary for some items), but new users likely will appreciate having this option while they are learning to use the test. Start points, item scoring, and basal and ceiling rules will be familiar to examiners with training in cognitive and academic assessment.

Vineland-3 items ask respondents to rate the frequency with which the examinee performs various behaviors, when appropriate, without prompting or assistance. Each form uses a 3-point response scale. The paper-and-pencil forms can be scored by hand, and the test manual provides step-by-step directions for converting raw scores to norm-referenced scores such as standard scores, confidence intervals, and percentile ranks. Subdomain scores are converted to *v*-scores, which are norm-referenced scores with a mean of 15 and a standard deviation of 3. Domain scores and the ABC are converted to standard scores with a mean of 100 and standard deviation of 15. The score report form includes tables to examine ipsative strengths and weaknesses. The norms tables required for these score conversions are located in appendices online rather than in the test manual; the test authors explain that this decision was made to reduce the length/weight of the manual. This reviewer was able to find the appendices easily through a Google search, and given that the norms tables are combined into a 525-page document, the decision to separate these from the physical manual makes sense.

Standard scores on the ABC and domain scales range from 20 to 140, meaning there is a much wider range of scores below the mean, which is consistent with the test's purpose of distinguishing different levels of deficits in adaptive behaviors. The test manual includes discussion of how Vineland-3 results can inform diagnostic decision-making—specifically when considering diagnoses of developmental delay, intellectual disability, and autism spectrum disorder—in addition to intervention planning. The test manual also provides a detailed description of how the Vineland-3 is different from the Vineland-II, so users familiar with the previous version can quickly familiarize themselves with the changes.

DEVELOPMENT. The process of content development began with reviewing item content from the previous version of the Vineland. Items were revised, added, or deleted based on user feedback about the Vineland-II and in response to suggestions from expert reviewers. All forms were subjected to usability analyses by appropriate professionals, who provided additional feedback on the items, scoring criteria, and administration. Pilot testing was then conducted to help select the best-performing items to include on the final versions (based on bias analysis and other statistical indices) and to establish the basal and ceiling rules for each form. Overall, the revision process is described in sufficient detail in the manual, and the test authors took appropriate and deliberate steps to identify the optimal items for the final versions of the Vineland-3 forms. The Parent/Caregiver Form is available in Spanish, but the test manual does not provide information about how this version was developed.

TECHNICAL.

Standardization. Almost all standardization data were collected using the online versions of the Vineland-3 forms. Standardization data were gathered from parents/caregivers who provided responses on behalf of 2,560 individuals ages birth to late adulthood, and from teachers who provided responses on behalf of 1,415 students ages 3 to 18 (the norms for age 18 are also used for students ages 19 to 21). The norm samples were gathered to reflect the 2014 U.S. Census data and also to represent various disability categories. The test manual provides detailed tables describing these samples. In general, demographic characteristics of the sample adequately match those of the U.S. Census.

Reliability. Score reliability was assessed with internal consistency, test-retest reliability, and interrater reliability analyses. With regard to internal consistency, reliability coefficients and standard errors of measurement are provided for the different age groupings for each of the Vineland-3 forms. On the Comprehensive Interview Form, average coefficients across age are in the .90s for the domain scores and range from .83 to .95 for the subdomains. These coefficients are only slightly lower on the Domain-Level Form. Internal consistency coefficients are lower for the youngest age groups (sometimes as low as the .20s and .30s), due to limited score variability at the youngest ages. On the Comprehensive Parent/Caregiver Form, average coefficients across age are in the high .90s for the domain scores and range from .92 to .97 for the subdomains. These coefficients are only slightly lower on the Domain-Level Form. On the Comprehensive Teacher Form, average coefficients across age are in the .90s for the domain scores and range from .89 to .96 for the subdomains. These coefficients are only slightly lower on the Domain-Level Form. Across all forms, internal reliability coefficients for the ABC averaged across age are consistently in the high .90s.

Test-retest reliability was assessed using test-retest correlation coefficients; Cohen's *d* was used to assess the standard difference between mean scores on first testing and mean scores on second testing. Results for the Interview Form (*N* = 248) were mixed, with some scores showing strong stability over time while others had *d* values in the .30s and .40s. Test-retest results for the Parent/Caregiver Form (*N* = 194) were similar to the Interview Form results, with a few *d* values in the .20s to .40s, but overall suggesting consistent scores over time. Generally speaking, similar results were found for scores on the Teacher Form (*N* = 123). Test-retest intervals for the three forms were 12 to 35 days.

In terms of interrater reliability, two interviewers administered the Interview Form independently, with the same respondent reporting on the same examinee (*N* = 96). In general, the standardized difference scores were pretty low (although two were in the .20s), suggesting that the two interviewers rated the examinees' behaviors similarly. Two caregivers rated the same examinee using the Parent/Caregiver Form (*N* = 148). Corrected reliability coefficients were generally acceptable, with a few exceptions that are lower than expected. Further, some of the coefficients for the ABC were lower than desired, ranging from .69 to .93 depending on age group and form (Comprehensive vs. Domain-Level). Two teachers rated the same students using the Teacher Form (*N* = 141). Corrected reliability coefficients are generally lower than those for the interviewer and parent/caregiver ratings, suggesting that teachers did not respond as consistently with one another as did the other raters.

Validity. The test manual describes several types of evidence for validity to support potential uses and interpretations of the Vineland-3 scales; this review will be selective due to space constraints. First, evidence based on test content and structure includes the historical significance of the three core domains (Communication, Daily Living Skills, and Socialization), which have been included on the previous versions of the Vineland and which continue to be prioritized in contemporary conceptualizations of adaptive behavior and intellectual disability. Additional evidence is provided by the test development procedures described previously (e.g., expert review of item content). Intercorrelations among scales are used to provide evidence for the structure of the Vineland-3, and subdomain correlations tend to be higher within domains than between domains (although this is not always the case).

Performance of clinical groups is used to provide evidence of the clinical or diagnostic utility of Vineland-3 scores. When comparing mean scores of clinical groups with those of matched control groups, Vineland scores were able to differentiate behavioral functioning among samples of children with developmental delay, intellectual disability, and autism spectrum disorder, with each of these groups showing expected mean differences (i.e., greater deficits in adaptive behavior) compared to the control groups. This pattern was observed across the Interview, Parent/Caregiver, and Teacher forms. As is often the case with clinical group studies, some of the sample sizes were small, but the results are consistent enough across form, age, and clinical groups to be compelling.

The test authors examined relations with other measures including the Adaptive Behavior Assessment System–Third Edition (ABAS-3; 21:5) and the Bayley Scales of Infant and Toddler Development–Third Edition (Bayley-III; 17:17). Results generally show moderate to strong correlations among scales measuring similar constructs, although this is not always the case. For example, with the Parent/Caregiver Form, scores on the Communication, Socialization, and Motor Skills domains were highly correlated with their corresponding scales on the Bayley-III. On the other hand, correlations between the Parent/Caregiver scales and the ABAS-3 parent rating forms were not as consistently strong. Similar results were found for the Teacher Form correlated with the ABAS-3 teacher rating forms, suggesting that these two tests conceptualize and measure adaptive behavior in their own ways even though there is overlap in the constructs measured.

COMMENTARY. Given the high-stakes nature of the decisions made with adaptive behavior scales (e.g., diagnosis of intellectual and developmental disabilities), it is critical for these measures to be developed with close attention to psychometric properties. For the most part, the Vineland-3 meets this high standard and will likely be as widely used as its predecessors. The test provides a comprehensive assessment of adaptive behaviors that are highly relevant to everyday functioning and allows examiners to compare ratings from multiple informants and develop hypotheses about discrepant ratings (e.g., setting characteristics). Item-level analysis, while not having adequate reliability for diagnostic decision-making, is likely useful for intervention planning, as each item describes a behavior that could be targeted for intervention or remediation. The addition of sample language for each interview item likely will make it easier for examiners to learn how to use the Interview Form.

The test manual provides detailed administration, scoring, and technical information. This information may be a lot for new users of the Vineland to digest, and novices may want to attend a professional development workshop to help orient them to the nuances of the test (e.g., interpreting *v*-scale scores, employing the conversational style of questioning required by the Interview Form).

The Vineland-3 is strengthened by the addition of the Domain-Level Forms, which were developed in response to feedback about the Vineland-II requesting reduced administration times. Many users will appreciate this development, and the Domain-Level Forms may be sufficient for classification decisions or triennial re-evaluations. At the same time, the Comprehensive Forms may be preferred when the results will be used to develop interventions for the individual because these forms provide the more specific subdomain scores that may be especially helpful in intervention planning.

Although evidence for internal consistency is strong (especially for the domain scores and ABC), it may have been useful to conduct separate internal consistency analyses with the clinical samples to see how consistent items/scores are for individuals with diagnosed disorders or disabilities. Finally, whereas the Vineland-II manual included confirmatory factor analytic data to support the test structure, the Vineland-3 manual does not report any factor analyses. Intercorrelation matrices are used to provide support for the structure of the domain and subdomain scales, but factor analysis could have provided additional information.

SUMMARY. The Vineland-3 is an important test as classification systems have placed increasing importance on adaptive behavior (in conjunction with assessment of cognitive abilities) when diagnosing intellectual disability. Unlike measures of cognitive functioning, there are not many contemporary standardized, norm-referenced measures of adaptive behavior available for professionals. The Vineland and ABAS are the most familiar and widely used norm-referenced contemporary measures of adaptive behavior. Correlations with the ABAS scales reported in the Vineland-3 manual suggest these two tests measure the construct differently; more research is needed to inform for which clinical purposes one may be more appropriate than the other. In the meantime, the Vineland-3 will be a valuable option for school psychologists, clinical psychologists, and developmental pediatricians who need to assess adaptive behavior when diagnosing intellectual and developmental disabilities.

REVIEWER'S REFERENCES

Sparrow, S. S., Balla, D. A., & Cicchetti, D. V. (1984). Vineland Adaptive Behavior Scales. Circle Pines, MN: American Guidance Service.

Sparrow, S. S., Cicchetti, D. V., & Balla, D. A. (2005). Vineland Adaptive Behavior Scales, Second Edition. Bloomington, MN: Pearson.

[183]

Watson-Barker Listening Test [Revised Video Version Form E and Form F].

Purpose: Designed to assess listening comprehension abilities.
Population: Ages 18 and older.
Publication Dates: 1984-2011.
Acronym: WBLT.
Scores, 6: Evaluating Message Content, Understanding Meaning in Conversations, Understanding and Remembering Lectures, Evaluating Emotional Meanings in Messages, Following Instructions and Directions, Total.
Administration: Group.
Forms: E, F.
Price Data, 2020: $299.99 per kit, including facilitator guide (2011, 50 pages), DVD, and 20 self-scoring answer sheets; $37.95 per 50 answer sheets.
Time: (40) minutes per form.
Comments: Administered via DVD.
Authors: Kittie W. Watson, Larry L. Barker, Charles V. Roberts, Rick Bommelje, and John D. Roberts.
Publisher: Innolect, Inc.
Cross References: For reviews by James R. Clopton and Joseph P. Stokes of an earlier edition, see 10:384.

No review available. This test does not meet review criteria established by the Buros Center for Testing that call for at least minimal technical and development information.

[184]

Wechsler Intelligence Scale for Children—Fifth Edition, Spanish.

Purpose: Designed for assessing general intelligence in children who live in the United States and speak primarily Spanish.
Population: Spanish-speaking children in the United States (including Puerto Rico), ages 6-0 through 16-11.
Publication Dates: 2005-2017.
Acronym: WISC-V Spanish.
Scores, 27: 5 Primary Index scores: Verbal Comprehension Index (Similarities, Vocabulary), Visual Spatial

Index (Block Design, Visual Puzzles), Fluid Reasoning Index (Matrix Reasoning, Figure Weights), Working Memory Index (Digit Span, Picture Span), Processing Speed Index (Coding, Symbol Search); 7 Ancillary Index scores: Verbal (Expanded Crystallized) Index (Similarities, Vocabulary, Information, Comprehension), Expanded Fluid Index–3 (Matrix Reasoning, Figure Weights, Arithmetic), Quantitative Reasoning Index (Figure Weights, Arithmetic), Auditory Working Memory Index (Digit Span, Letter-Number Sequencing), Nonverbal Index (Block Design, Visual Puzzles, Matrix Reasoning, Figure Weights, Picture Span, Coding), General Ability Index (Similarities, Vocabulary, Block Design, Matrix Reasoning, Figure Weights), Cognitive Proficiency Index (Digit Span, Picture Span, Coding, Symbol Search); Full Scale IQ: Verbal Comprehension (Similarities, Vocabulary, [allowable substitutions: Information or Comprehension]), Visual Spatial (Block Design [allowable substitution: Visual Puzzles], Fluid Reasoning (Matrix Reasoning, Figure Weights [allowable substitution: Arithmetic]), Working Memory (Digit Span [allowable substitutions: Picture Span or Letter-Number Sequencing]), Processing Speed (Coding [allowable substitution: Symbol Search]).
Administration: Individual.
Price Data, 2020: $1,300 per complete kit including manual (2017, 206 pages), technical and interpretive manual (2014, 288 pages), stimulus books 1-3, 25 record forms, 25 response booklets, symbol search scoring key, coding scoring key, and block design set; $275 per stimulus book 1, 2, or 3; $250 per technical and interpretive manual; $250 per manual; $135 per 25 record forms; $90 per 25 response booklets; $46 per block set; $40 per 1-year online scoring subscription; $2.15 per online score report.
Time: Average administration time to obtain the FSIQ is 54 minutes; average administration time to obtain the 5 Primary Index scores is 71 minutes.
Comments: Adaptation of Wechsler Intelligence Scale for Children—Fifth Edition (WISC-V; 20:205); Full Scale IQ is the only composite score that allows subtest substitutions; only one substitution permitted. Computer administration and scoring available.
Author: David Wechsler.
Publisher: Pearson.

Review of the Wechsler Intelligence Scale for Children—Fifth Edition, Spanish by JEFFERY P. BRADEN, Professor of Psychology, Dean, College of Humanities and Social Sciences, North Carolina State University, Raleigh, NC:

DESCRIPTION. The Wechsler Intelligence Scale for Children—Fifth Edition, Spanish (WISC-V Spanish) is an adaptation of the English-language Wechsler Intelligence Scale for Children—Fifth Edition (WISC-V). As such, it contains all of the tests and components of the WISC-V except for the complementary index scales and their subtests (i.e., Naming Speed Literacy, Naming Speed Quantity, Immediate Symbol Translation, Delayed Symbol Translation, and Recognition Symbol Translation are not included). A tablet interface for test administration is available from the test publisher, as is computerized scoring, but this reviewer did not have the opportunity to review them, nor are data about them provided in the WISC-V Spanish materials.

Test materials include spiral-bound easels and consumable booklets. Easels provide items (for examinee view) on one side and directions in Spanish on the back for the examiner. The materials are colorful, durable, and easy to use. Consumable answer booklets provide monochromatic symbols, require examinees to use a pencil, and come with templates to ease scoring. Consumable record forms (Protocolos) are well designed (if complex) and helpful to capture examinee responses. The overview of test administration is clear and easy to follow.

DEVELOPMENT. The WISC-V Spanish is broadly intended to provide access to the WISC-V to Spanish-speaking examinees. The goals of the WISC-V are available in the *WISC-V Technical and Interpretive Manual* (Wechsler, 2014), which is included with the WISC-V Spanish materials, and has been reviewed elsewhere (Benson, 2017; Keith, 2017). On page 9 of the *WISC-V Spanish Manual* (Wechsler, 2017), the author states that the measure can be used to "obtain a comprehensive assessment of general intellectual functioning"; "identify intellectual giftedness, intellectual disability, and cognitive strengths and weaknesses"; "serve as a guide for treatment planning and placement decisions"; and "provide invaluable clinical information for neuropsychological evaluation and research purposes." Appendices in the *WISC-V Spanish Manual* include information allowing examiners to identify statistically reliable versus base-rate differences among scores and composites. A new feature (not available in the previous WISC-IV Spanish) allows examiners to adjust verbal scores for the examinee's immersion in English-speaking culture on an array of acculturation variables independent of parental socioeconomic status (SES). This feature is available only for computer-scored results; this reviewer did not have the ability to independently review outcomes beyond the description provided in Appendix D of the test manual.

TECHNICAL.

Standardization. The WISC-V Spanish is not a re-norming of the WISC-V with Spanish-speaking children; rather, the developers used an equating sample (*N* = 220) to establish equivalence between the WISC-V and the WISC-V Spanish. Although many examiners may assume re-norming is preferable to equating, there are advantages to equating beyond being less expensive than norming, including maintaining continuity of score meaning across the English and Spanish forms. The *WISC-V Spanish Manual* does a good job of explaining how and why the equating was conducted, although solid understanding of item response theory (IRT) is required to fully follow the discussion. Three points stand out: First, the equating sample (although small) is broadly representative of Spanish-speaking children in the United States; second, subtests with language-reduced content (e.g., Block Design, Figure Weights) were not equated or adjusted; and third, data were collected from two clinical samples (representing high and low ability examinees). Finally, although the developers used blind back-translation procedures to generate Spanish items and directions from the original English source, they occasionally substituted words when the translated (Spanish) word functioned differently from its source (English) counterpart to maximize item performance (i.e., the new word functioned more like the source word in terms of difficulty, bias, etc.).

Reliability. Internal consistency estimates for individual subtests, composites, and indexes are all good to excellent and are generally similar to reliability indices reported for the WISC-V. The subtests and indexes maintained good to excellent values in both clinical samples as well.

Validity. The WISC-V Spanish provides evidence regarding relations with other variables in three forms: (1) a comparison between the equating sample and matched controls from the (English) WISC-V normative group; (2) a sample (*N* = 83) of students given both the WISC-V Spanish and its predecessor (the WISC-IV Spanish), and (3) two clinical samples of high (*N* = 30) and low (*N* = 40) cognitive ability. The results of these analyses mostly support expectations. That is, there are few statistically or clinically significant differences between the equating and matched normative sample; performance on the WISC-V Spanish and the WISC-V was correlated reasonably well and showed only a few clinically meaningful differences; and examinees in high and low ability groups had high and low (respectively) scores and indexes. Some caveats include direct comparisons that showed students taking the WISC-V Spanish scored lower on two subtests (Block Design and Visual Puzzles) and one index (Visual-Spatial) than their (English-speaking) matched counterparts. Examinees taking the Spanish versions of the WISC-IV and WISC-V scored higher on the WISC-IV Working Memory Index and subtests than the parallel WISC-V index and subtests. However, most evidence was supportive that the WISC-V Spanish behaved as expected in normative and clinical samples, and with one other measure (the WISC-IV Spanish). What is most startling, however, is the dearth of other validity evidence provided in support of the claims made for the test.

COMMENTARY. The WISC-V Spanish reflects the best and worst of the Wechsler tradition. On the positive side, strong technical expertise underpins an attractive, practical battery of subtests that appeals to examinees and examiners alike. The available evidence suggests the new version performs largely as its predecessors, and the gradual adaptation of the instrument in response to research on cognitive abilities with each successive revision should comfort those wanting incremental improvements in a familiar tool.

On the negative side, the WISC-V Spanish (and the WISC-V) maintain a tradition of making claims without supporting data or mentioning research contrary to claims, as required by the *Standards for Educational and Psychological Testing* (American Educational Research Association [AERA], American Psychological Association [APA], & National Council on Measurement in Education [NCME], 1999; 2014). Although such shortcomings are common among most tests of cognitive ability (Braden & Niebling, 2012), it is remarkable that the publishers of the WISC-V Spanish and WISC-V continue this disappointing tradition. Specifically, the WISC-V Spanish makes two broad claims without providing any supportive evidence: (1) that test results are helpful in revealing neuropsychological processes, and (2) that test results are useful in selecting and planning treatments. The forms of evidence needed to support these claims are, respectively, evidence of response processes and evidence of test consequences. Neither type of evidence is provided in the *WISC-V Spanish Manual* (Wechsler, 2017). Furthermore, the *WISC-V Technical and Interpretive Manual* (Wechsler, 2014) is nearly as silent; barely a page discussing (but not providing supportive evidence of) response processes appears on pages 70-71 of the technical manual, and a scant half page is devoted to test consequences (again, only describing the issue but not providing supportive evidence; technical manual, p. 147). In contrast, two forms of evidence (internal structure and relations with other variables) receive abundant attention (pp. 71-147). Although the copious presentation of factor analyses, correlations, and other data is impressive, it is irrelevant to the claims made for the clinical value of testing. This reviewer could find no study directly linking test results to neurological processes, nor demonstrating that test data improve clinical or educational outcomes, within the test materials.

A problem related to the absence of evidence supporting claims is the failure to recognize and include contrary evidence when making claims. For example, the *WISC-V Spanish Manual* (Wechsler, 2017) asserts, "The Boston Process Approach to neuropsychological assessment ... is as important as a quantitative evaluation of scores" (p. 5). No mention is made of the decades of research, beginning with Meehl (1954/1996) and continuing into the present century (Grove & Lloyd, 2006), that consistently shows adding qualitative clinical judgment to test score interpretation is (much) more likely to erode than improve validity. Likewise, literature showing there is no evidence of cognitive test results leading to better outcomes in educational or clinical settings is ignored (e.g., Braden & Shaw, 2009), as are the potential deleterious effects of labeling children as having a disability. Although it would be unfair to publishers to expect them to be responsible for changing these realities, their failure to recognize and report them is contrary to obligations outlined in contemporary test standards (AERA, APA, & NCME, 2014).

Finally, the WISC-V Spanish also sustains the tradition of failing to bring sound science or evidence to the issue of test accommodations. On page 12, the *WISC-V Spanish Manual* says any accommodations "should be documented." It goes on to say, "Professionals who assess the child's functioning should rely on clinical judgment to evaluate the effects of such modified procedures on test scores" (p. 12). However, the guidelines for general test administration and scoring state, "It is *imperative* [emphasis in the original] that you adhere to the administration, recording, and scoring procedures detailed in the Stimulus Books and this manual" (p. 15). Besides being confusing, the discussion is misleading, as it fails to inform the examiner which skills are target skills (and therefore should not be changed), versus those that are access skills (and can/should be changed to accommodate disabilities). The use of "clinical judgment" as a basis for determining test accommodations is clearly contradicted by available research, U.S. federal educational policy, and contemporary test standards. Most distressingly for me, the manual (p. 12) cites this reviewer's own work (Braden, 2003) as support for their unusual and contradictory claims. The misunderstanding of that work does little to encourage confidence in the treatment of test accommodations.

SUMMARY. Examiners seeking a Spanish-language version of the WISC-V should be largely satisfied with the WISC-V Spanish. Its materials, norms, and technical data are consistent with previous versions and represent an incremental improvement in aligning a practical test of cognitive abilities with contemporary research on the structure of mental abilities. Furthermore, the available data largely support the assumption that results from the WISC-V Spanish can be understood in the same manner that WISC-V results are understood. However, examiners seeking direct (rather than circumstantial) evidence to satisfy claims that the WISC-V Spanish improves neuropsychological understanding or enhances outcomes for examinees will be disappointed. The dearth of evidence to support such claims is not unique to the WISC-V Spanish; although it is a ubiquitous feature of most cognitive tests, its absence (despite claims of clinical and educational utility) is deeply disappointing.

REVIEWER'S REFERENCES

American Educational Research Association, American Psychological Association, & National Council on Measurement in Education. (1999). *Standards for educational and psychological testing*. Washington, DC: American Educational Research Association.

American Educational Research Association, American Psychological Association, & National Council on Measurement in Education. (2014). *Standards for educational and psychological testing*. Washington, DC: American Educational Research Association.

Benson, N. F. (2017). [Test review of Wechsler Intelligence Scale for Children—Fifth Edition]. In J. F. Carlson, K. F. Geisinger, & J. L. Jonson (Eds.), *The twentieth mental measurements yearbook*. Lincoln, NE: Buros Center for Testing.

Braden, J. P. (2003). Accommodating clients with disabilities on the WAIS-III and WMS. In D. S. Tulsky et al. (Eds.), *Use of the WAIS-III/WMS in clinical practice* (pp. 451-486). San Diego, CA: Academic Press.

Braden, J. P., & Niebling, B. C. (2012). Using the joint test standards to evaluate the validity evidence for intelligence tests. In D. P. Flanagan and P. L. Harrison (Eds.), *Contemporary intellectual assessment: Theories, tests, and issues* (3rd ed., pp. 739-757). New York, NY: Guilford.

Braden, J. P., & Shaw, S. R. (2009). Intervention validity of cognitive assessment: Knowns, unknowables, and unknowns. *Assessment for Effective Intervention, 34*(2), 106-115.

Grove, W. M., & Lloyd, M. (2006). Meehl's contribution to clinical versus statistical prediction. *Journal of Abnormal Psychology, 115*(2), 192-194.

Keith, T. Z. (2017). [Test review of Wechsler Intelligence Scale for Children—Fifth Edition]. In J. F. Carlson, K. F. Geisinger, & J. L. Jonson (Eds.), *The twentieth mental measurements yearbook*. Lincoln, NE: Buros Center for Testing.

Meehl, P. E. (1996). *Clinical versus statistical prediction: A theoretical analysis and a review of the evidence*. Northvale, NJ: Jason Aronson. (Original work published 1954)

Wechsler, D. (2014). *WISC-V Technical and interpretive manual*. Bloomington, MN: PsychCorp.

Wechsler, D. (2017). *WISC-V Spanish manual*. Bloomington, MN: PsychCorp.

Weiss, L. G., Munoz, M. R., & Prifitera, A. (2016). Testing Hispanics with WISC-V and WISC-IV Spanish. In L. G. Weiss, D. H. Saklofske, J. A. Holdnack, & A. Prifitera (Eds.), *WISC-V assessment and interpretation: Scientist-practitioner perspectives* (pp. 215-236). San Diego, CA: Elsevier.

Review of the Wechsler Intelligence Scale for Children—Fifth Edition, Spanish by MICHAEL S. MATTHEWS, Professor of Gifted Education, Department of Special Education and Child Development, University of North Carolina at Charlotte, Charlotte, NC:

DESCRIPTION. The Wechsler Intelligence Scale for Children—Fifth Edition, Spanish (WISC-V Spanish) is an adaptation of the widely used Wechsler Intelligence Scale for Children—Fifth Edition that has been equated for scoring purposes with the English-language WISC-V. It is an individually administered measure of intellectual ability that is designed for children ages 6:0 through 16:11 who speak primarily Spanish and are living in the United States. It may be administered in either pencil-and-paper or digital format, with average administration time ranging from 54 to 71 minutes.

The WISC-V Spanish assumes the examiner already has some familiarity with the original WISC-V and the appropriate training required to use it. Administration conditions are standardized; clear and detailed instructions are provided to explain administration procedures and potential errors the examiner should avoid. Whereas a trained technician can administer and score the various subtests under supervision, the test manual notes that results should be interpreted only by individuals with formal graduate-level or professional training in psychological assessment.

Eleven of the 14 subtests in the WISC-V Spanish (Block Design, Similarities, Matrix Reasoning, Digit Span, Coding, Vocabulary, Symbol Search, Information, Letter-Number Sequencing, Comprehension, and Arithmetic) are retained from the earlier WISC-IV Spanish. The remaining three (Figure Weights, Visual Puzzles, and Picture Span) are new subtests developed for and drawn from the English-language WISC-V. Administration of the 10 primary subtests allows an examiner to derive the Full Scale IQ, all primary index scores, and three of the ancillary index scores; the other four ancillary index scores require the administration of additional subtests. A maximum of one substitution, of seven permissible subscale replacements, may be allowable under specific circumstances as detailed in the *WISC-V Spanish Manual.*

Subtest raw scores are converted to scale scores with a mean of 10 and standard deviation of 3. Subtest scale scores in turn are combined in a variety of ways to yield the Full Scale IQ score (with five domains), plus a variety of primary indices (five scales, each based on two subscales) and ancillary index scores (seven scales, based on two to six subscales). Notably, the manual also allows for process observations, which in the English version of this measure are presented via a separate version (i.e., Wechsler Intelligence Scale for Children–Fifth Edition, Integrated; see review by Matthews & Foley-Nicpon, 2017). Test manuals and administration instructions are in English; Spanish passages necessary for administration (including prompting, error correction, etc.) are listed in a different font and color to make them easier to locate.

The complete test kit includes the *WISC-V Spanish Manual*, the *WISC-V Technical and Interpretive Manual* (2014; this is the same for English and Spanish versions), blocks for the Block Design subtest, three stimulus books, templates and a search key for scoring the Coding and Symbol Search subtests, 25 response booklets for the Coding and Symbol Search subtests, and 25 record forms for tabulating responses on the remaining subscales.

DEVELOPMENT. The theoretical background for the WISC-V Spanish follows that of the WISC-V, as this Spanish version was deliberately designed to be equivalent in the responses and processes evoked, scores produced, and constructs measured. Because the WISC-V has been well documented elsewhere, this reviewer has focused on developments that show potential for informing the education of high-ability children such as the academically gifted population; these learners from Spanish-speaking backgrounds are severely under-identified in most schools, likely in part due to assessment-related issues (e.g., Matthews & Farmer, 2017; Matthews & Kirsch, 2011; Matthews & Peters, 2018).

One unique new feature of the WISC-V Spanish is that in recognition of the diversity of the Spanish-speaking population in the United States, an appendix to the test manual offers optional procedures for adjusting verbal scores based on the examinee's language and environmental background. Whereas its predecessor, the WISC-IV Spanish, allowed for such adjustments on the basis of years of education in the United States (i.e., acculturation) and parent education levels, the current version offers a more sophisticated approach based in recalibration of scale scores using multiple regression techniques. (Unfortunately, this adjustment is only available with online scoring and not for paper format administrations.) Predictor variables in 11 areas are gathered from parents using a questionnaire and then used to adjust the child's index scores on the Verbal Comprehension Index and Verbal Expanded Crystallized Index. The test manual provides a cover letter and copies of this questionnaire in both English- and Spanish-language versions. Crucially, this adjustment may increase, decrease, or leave unchanged the child's ability estimate. The test manual emphasizes that scores adjusted in this manner do not represent the child's intellectual ability or more accurate normative information; rather, they estimate the degree to which environmental and personal variables may have influenced the child's performance.

TECHNICAL.

Standardization. Because of its close relationship to the WISC-V, development of the WISC-V Spanish paralleled the procedures used in the previously developed English-language version. Initially, conceptual development and review by experts representing a variety of Spanish-speaking cultural backgrounds and dialects led to an initial revision containing only those six subtests revised in translation, plus one other that was not revised. A small-scale pilot test with 30 examinees was conducted to evaluate the adequacy of these translated items and instructions, the equivalency of the item content, and any other related issues.

In a subsequent equating stage, a stratified sample of 220 examinees, representative of the U.S. Spanish-speaking population ages 6:0 to 16:11, was used to equate the WISC-V Spanish with the WISC-V English norming sample (N = 2,200) using a combination of item response theory and equipercentile equating methods. Small samples of students with mild intellectual disability (n = 8) and high cognitive ability (n = 6 who scored at or above the 98th percentile on a standardized measure of achievement, or had obtained a Full Scale IQ score ≥ 1 standard deviation above the mean) were included within the equating sample to ensure representation of the full range of cognitive abilities. The test manual notes that because of the equating procedures, no manual conversion of composite norms or age equivalents is required between the Spanish and English versions.

Reliability. Split-half reliability was calculated for three age bands and also for all ages using the equating sample. Reliability coefficients ranged from what this reviewer considers acceptable (.72) to excellent (.96), with averages for 10 of the 16 reported scales falling at or above .90. Split-half coefficients were mostly in the same range for the two special groups (high cognitive ability and mild intellectual disability) as well, though the sample sizes for these groups were very small.

Test-retest stability does not appear to have been evaluated separately with the Spanish-speaking equating sample; the test manual refers to data reported previously for the English-language version.

Validity. Validity evidence for the WISC-V Spanish was not collected separately. The *WISC-V Spanish Manual* states, "Because the WISC-V Spanish has been subjected to equating procedures, the same evidence [as reported for the WISC-V] supports WISC-V Spanish validity" (p. 91). Face validity appears strong, as mean performance of the equating sample is not meaningfully different from mean performance on the same subtests and composite scales across the Spanish and English versions; most differences have trivial effect sizes.

Scores from a clinical sample of 30 children in a high cognitive ability group were uniformly higher, as would be expected, than those from a matched comparison group from the equating sample. Likewise, a group identified as students with mild intellectual disability (n = 40) scored lower than those in their matched control group. Both of these comparisons lend some preliminary support for the validity of the WISC-V Spanish.

Finally, 83 members of the equating sample were administered both the WISC-V Spanish and the WISC-IV Spanish in counterbalanced order to compare performance on the two measures. Correlations were acceptable across all scales and indices, ranging from .54 to .89 with most coefficients in the .70 range.

COMMENTARY. The WISC-V Spanish is a complex instrument, with substantial variation across subtests in terms of reversal rules, timing, prompting, acceptable response variations, and other aspects of administration. The addition of another language necessarily complicates the use of this measure in comparison to its English equivalent. Substantial practice, some degree of Spanish language proficiency, and perhaps additional specialized training likely will be needed in order to administer this measure proficiently. As someone with just enough command of Spanish to have communicated effectively with second graders in the course of research a number of years ago, this reviewer is encouraged that the level of Spanish proficiency needed to administer and interpret feedback from the WISC-V Spanish appears to be moderate.

There has been a relatively high trust placed in the equating process in establishing or supporting the reliability, validity, and scoring of the WISC-V Spanish. Samples used in developing this version are much smaller than those used in corresponding development of the earlier English-language version of the WISC-V. While IRT and the other equating procedures are robust, additional evidence supporting equivalence and more stand-alone studies of the WISC-V Spanish would further bolster user confidence in this otherwise very promising measure.

An additional strength of the WISC-V Spanish is the opportunity it offers to derive language- environment adjusted scores. While the manual specifically notes (p. 183) that "adjusted scores have not been validated for gifted identification" or for making other classifications of children who speak Spanish, such adjustment seems like it would have strong potential for reversing the well-documented under-representation of Spanish-speaking and bilingual children in gifted education programing in U.S. schools (e.g., Matthews & Kirsch, 2011). The inclusion of the high cognitive ability special group study also supports the appropriateness of using the WISC-V Spanish with students who show the potential for being identified as gifted or academically talented.

SUMMARY. The WISC-V Spanish is overall a thoughtfully developed measure that is built on the strong foundation of the WISC-V. Though complex, it offers a psychometrically sound and valuable tool for understanding intellectual abilities among the diverse population of Spanish-speaking students who attend U.S. schools. The WISC-V Spanish will likely be an important tool in efforts to increase the accuracy of educational decisions for Spanish-speaking and bilingual students, to promote equity in access to appropriate educational services, and to reduce performance gaps among high-achieving learners who may not be accurately assessed using even the best instruments available in English alone.

REVIEWER'S REFERENCES

Matthews, M. S., & Farmer, J. (2017). Predicting academic achievement growth among low-income Mexican American learners using dynamic and static assessments. *Australasian Journal of Gifted Education, 26*(1), 5-21. https://doi.org/10.21505/ajge.2017.0002

Matthews, M. S., & Foley-Nicpon, M. (2017). [Test review of the Wechsler Intelligence Scale for Children-Fifth Edition, Integrated]. In J. F. Carlson, K. F. Geisinger, & J. L. Jonson (Eds.), *The twentieth mental measurements yearbook* (pp. 871-874). Lincoln, NE: Buros Center for Testing.

Matthews, M. S., & Kirsch, L. (2011). Evaluating gifted identification practice: Aptitude testing and linguistically diverse learners. *Journal of Applied School Psychology, 27*, 155-180. doi:10.1080/15377903.2011.565281

Matthews, M. S., & Peters, S. J. (2018). Methods to increase the identification rate of students from traditionally underrepresented populations for gifted services. In S. I. Pfeiffer, E. Shaunessy-Dedrick, & M. Foley-Nicpon (Eds.), *APA handbook of giftedness and talent* (pp. 317-332). Washington, DC: American Psychological Association.

[185]

Wide Range Achievement Test, Fifth Edition.

Purpose: Designed to measure "the basic academic skills of word reading, spelling, math computation, and sentence comprehension."
Population: Ages 5-85+.
Publication Dates: 1940-2017.
Acronym: WRAT5.
Scores, 5: Spelling, Math Computation, Reading Composite (Word Reading, Sentence Comprehension, Total).
Administration: Individual.
Forms, 2: Parallel forms: Blue, Green.
Price Data, 2020: $425 per complete kit including manual (2017, 115 pages), norms book, 25 record forms (Blue and Green), 25 response booklets (Blue and Green), 25 sentence comprehension forms (Blue and Green), sentence comprehension card set, word reading/spelling card set, and 1-year online scoring subscription; $49.25 per manual; $74 per norms book; $60 per 25 record forms and response booklets (Blue or Green); $58.75 per 25 sentence comprehension forms (Blue or Green); $40 per 1-year online scoring subscription (3- and 5-year subscriptions available); $16 per sentence comprehension card set; $16 per reading/spelling card set; $2.20 per online score report.
Time: 10-25 minutes for administration of all four subtests to younger examinees (Grades K-3); 30-40 minutes for administration to older examinees.
Comments: Online scoring and reporting available; subtests may be administered separately; certain parts/subtests may be administered in small groups of up to five examinees; Sentence Comprehension subtest is not administered to examinees in kindergarten (5-year-olds).
Authors: Gary S. Wilkinson and Gary J. Robertson.
Publisher: Pearson.
Cross References: For reviews by Kathryn E. Hoff and Mark E. Swerdlik and by Darrell L. Sabers and Amy M. Olson of the fourth edition, see 18:157; see T5:2879(237 references); for reviews by Linda Mabry and Annie W. Ward of the third edition, see 12:414 (111 references); see also T4:2956 (121 references); for reviews by Elaine Clark and Patti L. Harrison of the revised edition (1984), see 10:389 (161 references); for reviews by Paula Matuszek and Philip A. Saigh of the 1978 edition, see 9:1364 (103 references); see also T3:2621 (249 references), 8:37 (117 references), and T2:50 (35 references); for reviews by Jack C. Merwin and Robert L. Thorndike of the revised edition (1965), see 7:36 (49 references); see also 6:27 (15 references); for reviews by Paul Douglas Courtney, Verner M. Sims, and Louis P. Thorpe of the 1946 edition, see 3:21.

Review of the Wide Range Achievement Test, Fifth Edition by MARK A. ALBANESE, Director of Testing and Research, National Conference of Bar Examiners, Professor Emeritus, University of

Wisconsin-Madison, and JUAN CHEN, Research Psychometrician, National Conference of Bar Examiners, Madison, WI:

DESCRIPTION. The Wide Range Achievement Test, Fifth Edition (WRAT5) is designed to measure the fundamental academic skills of individuals ranging in age from 5 to 85+ quickly and easily. Scores of the WRAT5 are intended to be used to provide initial screening for academic weaknesses, to evaluate individuals' basic academic skills to make placement decisions, to monitor academic growth overtime, to serve as part of more comprehensive batteries to support diagnostic and placement decisions, and to measure academic achievement for research purposes.

The WRAT5 consists of four subtests: Word Reading (including 15 letter reading items in Part 1 and 55 word reading items in Part 2), Spelling (including name writing and 13 letter writing items in Part 1 and 42 word spelling items in Part 2), Math Computations (including 15 oral math items in Part 1 and 40 math computation items in Part 2), and Sentence Comprehension (including 50 items). The WRAT5 includes two parallel forms (i.e., Blue Form and Green Form) that are considered to be interchangeable. The authors of the previous edition (i.e., WRAT4) suggested combining the parallel forms in a single administration to obtain a more comprehensive observation of examinees' performance; however, this strategy is not mentioned in the WRAT5 manual.

Administration of the WRAT5 requires examinees' oral responses to items in Word Reading, Part 1 of Math Computation (except for two items that require examinees to show certain numbers of fingers), and Sentence Comprehension. Examinees' written responses are required in Spelling and Part 2 of Math Computation. The Sentence Comprehension subtest is not administered to individuals age 5 or to kindergarteners. The test authors state that examiners can choose to administer any single subtest separately or any combination of subtests and are free to determine the administration order of subtests. However, it is important to note that the standardization process was conducted based only on administration of all four subtests in the suggested order. The test authors also state that Part 2 of the Math Computation subtest and the Spelling subtest can be administered in small groups (up to five examinees) to save administration time; however, there are no step-by-step instructions for administration to small groups in the test manual, and the standardization process did not include small group administration. There is no time limit for taking the WRAT5 except for Part 2 of the Math Computation subtest, which requires examinees to answer as many of the items as they can within 15 minutes. Typically, administration of all WRAT5 subtests takes 10 to 25 minutes for examinees between kindergarten and Grade 3 and 30 to 40 minutes for older examinees between Grade 4 and Grade 12+. Administration guidelines and directions for the subtests are clear and straightforward.

Multiple scores are derived for each of the four subtests. After examiners calculate the raw score (i.e., number correct) for each subtest, the corresponding norm-referenced (based on age or grade) standard scores can then be obtained from the conversion tables in the *WRAT5 Norms Book*. The standard scores for Word Reading and Sentence Comprehension can be combined to obtain a Reading composite standard score. The standard scores are scaled to have a mean of 100 and a standard deviation of 15, ranging from 55 to 145. Critical values of two levels of confidence intervals (90% and 95%) are also provided for each subtest and the Reading composite in the norms book. Alternative scores, including percentile ranks, grade equivalents, normal curve equivalents, and stanines also are derived for the WRAT5 subtests. Additionally, the WRAT5 provides growth scale values (GSVs) to measure examinees' performance change over time. According to the test authors, GSVs are linearly transformed from the Rasch Ability Scale Scores (RASS) and do not include negative scores, which some test users might find difficult to understand. Besides the traditional hand scoring, the test publisher's Q-global web-based platform is introduced for more efficient, accurate and comprehensive scoring and score reporting.

DEVELOPMENT. Users will find a number of changes in the WRAT5. Items and scoring rules now reflect the differences in examinees' knowledge across school curricula and geographic regions. For example, both uppercase and lowercase letters are included in Part 1 of Word Reading, and scoring does not require examinees to write answers in the simplest form in Math Computation unless explicitly stated. Content coverage has been expanded to improve clinical utility (e.g., some old Math Computation items that cover the same math skill were replaced with new items that measure a different math skill). Items have been shortened and simplified by removing vague, outdated, or other distracting elements to reduce administration time and to remove construct-irrelevant factors. Administration has been simplified and streamlined through incorporating updated rules to determine the starting point, to reverse, and to discontinue the test administration. For example, administration of Part 2 of the Word Reading and Spelling subtests and administration of the Sentence Comprehension subtest are discontinued when examinees respond incorrectly to five consecutive items; previously, the number of incorrect responses needed for discontinuation was 10 for Part 2 of Word Reading and Spelling and seven for Sentence Comprehension. Also, the starting point of the Sentence Comprehension subtest now is based on grade level, rather than on Word Reading scores.

TECHNICAL.

Standardization. The WRAT5 includes two normative samples: an age norm sample consisting of 2,355 examinees between 5 years 0 months and 85 years 11 months and a grade norm sample consisting of 2,150 examinees in Grades K-12. Around 66% of examinees in the age norm sample were from the grade norm sample. A stratified sampling plan ensured the norms were representative of the U.S. population in terms of educational level, race/ethnicity, geographic region, and sex. The normative samples also included a group of examinees (1.3%) with mild intellectual disability and a group of gifted individuals (1.2%). The normative sample data were used to conduct item analyses, evaluate administration and scoring rules, equate parallel forms, create raw to standard score conversions, and derive alternative scores.

Reliability. The internal consistency of the WRAT5 subtests and the Reading composite was estimated by odd-even split-half correlations. Coefficients range from the upper .80s to the .90s. The test manual also reports the standard errors of measurement (*SEM*s) derived from the split-half reliability coefficients. Corrected alternate-form correlations range from .88 to .94 for the Word Reading, Spelling, and Math Computation subtests and the Reading composite and from .76 to .85 for the Sentence Comprehension subtest. These values probably are satisfactory, although the Sentence Comprehension subtest reliabilities were lower and should be interpreted in light of these lower values. The interscorer reliabilities for the Sentence Comprehension subtest are excellent with a percent agreement of 99.4% for the Blue Form and 99.6% for the Green Form.

Validity. Examiner and expert feedback and analysis of data collected from examinees serve as the main content arguments for the validity of the WRAT5. However, no detailed explanation of the processes and results from the analyses are provided in the documentation. For example, the authors do not provide the test specifications for each subtest and how the items map to these specifications, nor do they report item analysis results that support the inclusion/exclusion of specific items. The absence of such information weakens the content argument for the validity of the WRAT5.

The construct argument for validity is based upon intercorrelations among the four subtests and between the subtests and the Reading composite. In general, higher correlations were obtained between subtests that share similar constructs (e.g., correlation between Word Reading and Spelling was .75 for ages 5-18) and lower correlations between subtests that measure different constructs (e.g., correlation between Math Computation and Sentence Comprehension was .57 for ages 5-18), providing convergent and discriminant evidence of validity, respectively.

Concurrent evidence of validity is based upon correlations with other similar instruments, including the WRAT4, Wechsler Individual Achievement Test–Third Edition (WIAT-III), Wechsler Abbreviated Scale of Intelligence–Second Edition (WASI-II), and Wechsler Intelligence Scale for Children–Fifth Edition (WISC-V). Correlations between the WRAT5 and the achievement tests (WRAT4 and WIAT-III) are generally higher than those between the WRAT5 and other cognitive ability tests (WASI-II and WISC-V), providing evidence that the WRAT5 is better defined as an achievement test than an ability test (a criticism of the WRAT4 in the 2010 review by Sabers and Olson).

Support for the clinical utility and validity of the WRAT5 is based upon data collected from four special groups—those identified as having reading disorder (*N* = 71), math disorder (*N* = 47), or mild intellectual disability (*N* = 52) and those identified as academically gifted (*N* = 64)—each compared to matched controls. The results supported the WRAT5's ability to differentiate the special groups from their corresponding matched control groups; however, the authors explicitly point out that these samples may not be representative and that WRAT5 scores alone "should never be used as the sole criteria for identification or diagnostic purposes" (manual, p. 53).

COMMENTARY. The WRAT in its various editions has existed for more than 70 years, evidently serving a vital function for its users. The updated administration instructions and scoring rules for the WRAT5 further shorten the administration time. Old items were revised to eliminate construct-irrelevant factors or were replaced by new items to expand content coverage and ensure broader utility of the test. The WRAT5 also embraces new technology with a web-based scoring tool for more convenient scoring and score reporting. Although not mentioned in the test manual, the WRAT5 can now be administered and scored using the test publisher's interactive online platform. The test manual provides detailed steps and examples for basic and extended interpretation of the WRAT5 scores. Instructions for interpreting growth scale values and analyses for diagnostic purposes (e.g., ability-achievement discrepancy analysis) are also provided.

Despite the strengths mentioned above, a cautionary note is needed. The authors report using a common-person IRT method for equating the Blue and Green forms; however, it is unclear whether they used the WINSTEPS software and the Rasch model in equating as they did for item analyses. Assuming that the Rasch model was used, more information about equating is needed including the following: the specific common-person Rasch model equating method that was used (e.g., method based on item difficulties or method based on person abilities as proposed in Masters, 1985); the degree to which the data conformed to the Rasch model; whether misfit items or examinees with particularly implausible performances were removed from equating. In addition, the equating procedure was validated using data from the grade norm sample; however, neither the validation process nor the detailed validation results are presented.

The test authors suggest incorporating precision information for more accurate interpretation of individual examinees' standard scores through building confidence intervals. The critical values, calculated based on the *SEM*s, for computing the confidence intervals for each subtest and the Reading composite are provided in the norms book for each age or grade group. The same set of critical values is used for both Blue and Green forms. It is unclear whether one test form or some equated combined version was used in computing these *SEM*s and confidence intervals. In addition, it would be preferable if a more precise conditional standard error of measurement (CSEM), which is unique for each score point, were calculated and used for computing confidence intervals of individual score points.

The authors provide the predicted WRAT5 standard scores obtained from regression of the WISC-V and WASI-II ability standard scores and use them for conducting ability-achievement discrepancy analysis to identify individuals with a specific learning disability. However, with the regression equation being based upon 97 examinees who took the WISC-V and 98 who took the WASI-II, the stability of the coefficients for making accurate predictions is a concern.

SUMMARY. The WRAT5 is a very brief and easy-to-use assessment suitable for use in research and as a quick evaluation of individuals' basic academic achievements. Considering the limitations in reporting validity evidence and the potential for other psychometric issues, one should be cautious when making medium- and especially high-stakes decisions such as placement (e.g., academic or vocational) and diagnostic (e.g., identifying academically gifted individuals or persons with a learning disability) decisions.

REVIEWERS' REFERENCES

Masters, G. N. (1985). Common-person equating with the Rasch model. *Applied Psychological Measurement, 9*(1), 73-82.

Sabers, D. L., & Olson, A. M. (2010). [Test review of Wide Range Achievement Test 4]. In R. A. Spies, J. F. Carlson, & K. F. Geisinger (Eds.), *The eighteenth mental measurements yearbook* (pp. 719-721). Lincoln, NE: Buros Institute of Mental Measurements.

Review of the Wide Range Achievement Test, Fifth Edition by GREGORY J. CIZEK, Guy B. Phillips Distinguished Professor of Educational Measurement and Evaluation, University of North Carolina-Chapel Hill, Chapel Hill, NC:

DESCRIPTION. The Wide Range Achievement Test, Fifth Edition (WRAT5) is the fourth revision of an academic skills screener introduced in 1946. The aim of the WRAT5 is straightforward: to measure "basic academic skills...for individuals ranging from kindergarten (age 5) through grade 12 and adulthood (ages 18–85+)." The WRAT5 is described in the test manual as "a quick, simple, psychometrically sound measure of foundational academic skills" (manual, p. 1).

Those basic academic skills comprise Sentence Comprehension, Word Reading, Spelling, and Math Computation components. The latter three subtests each contain two parts: Word Reading consists of Letter Reading and Word Reading; Spelling consists of Letter Writing and Spelling; and Math Computation consists of Oral Math and Math

Computation. Part 1 of each area is the starting subtest administered to younger examinees or older examinees who do not meet a criterion score on Part 2. A Reading composite score is based on performance on the Word Reading and Sentence Comprehension subtests.

The materials comprising the WRAT5 are clear and concise. Parallel forms of the test (blue, green) were developed by including common items across Part 1 of the two forms and performing a common-persons linking. Materials for each form consist of two-sided, 8.5 x 11" cards with items for the Sentence Comprehension and Word Reading subtests; an examinee response recording form for the Spelling and Math Computation subtests; an administrator recording form for the Sentence Comprehension subtest; and an administrator recording form for the Math Computation, Spelling, and Word Reading subtests that also includes an overall score summary. All information relevant to understanding the purpose of the WRAT5, administering and scoring the test, interpreting test results, and all technical information are provided in the WRAT5 manual; a compendium of tables for converting raw scores on each subtest to standard scores is provided in a companion document, the *WRAT5 Norms Book*. The primary measurement purpose of the WRAT5 is as a norm-referenced test. A standard slate of standard scores is provided, including percentile ranks, normal curve equivalent scores, stanines, grade equivalent scores, and growth scale values. All normative information provided is for national (U.S.) comparison groups by age and grade level.

The WRAT5 is intended to be individually administered. Some allowance is made for group administration of the Part 2 Math Computation and Spelling subtests; however, the materials and directions all suggest individual administration as the preferred approach. Administration of the WRAT5 should take 10-25 minutes for examinees in Grades K-3, and 30-40 minutes for older examinees (Grade 4 through adults).

Administration of the WRAT5 is fairly straightforward, but includes a few rules for identifying appropriate start points based on the grade level of the examinee, reverse rules, and discontinue rules that dictate when a subtest should be terminated. Finally, although the test manual prescribes a fixed order for subtest administration, it also indicates that test administrators are free to depart from the recommended sequence.

All items comprising the WRAT5 are of a supply-type format in which the test administrator directs an examinee to say the name of a letter, pronounce a word, spell a dictated word, supply a word, count aloud, solve orally presented mathematics problems, or perform mathematics computations. Users can choose between paper-and-pencil administration and tablet-based administration using the test publisher's interactive platform, and between hand scoring and the test publisher's web-based scoring service.

A wide range of uses is suggested for the WRAT5. They include: obtaining estimates of achievement and screening for achievement weaknesses in reading, mathematics, and spelling; making educational placement decisions; monitoring academic progress; contributing to a comprehensive psychoeducational or neuropsychological assessment; and research uses. It should be noted that the "wide range" of the test's title refers to intended application across examinees from very young to very old ages, and perhaps to the wide range of potential uses, but not to a wide range of achievement constructs.

DEVELOPMENT. The WRAT5 has a similar look and feel to its predecessor, the WRAT4 (Wilkinson & Robertson, 2006). Limited information on specific development procedures is found in the fifth edition manual. The most extensive documentation for the new edition relates to the new norming sample, procedures, and results.

In terms of content and administration, the test authors identify the main differences between the fourth and fifth editions as greater skill coverage in the Math Computation and Sentence Comprehension subtests; simplified administration; revised scoring rules; and shortened testing time accomplished via the elimination of routing tasks and the need for some prompts, reduction in the number of sample items, and revision of discontinue criteria for some subtests. Changes such as the reduction in the number of sample items are easily seen; other changes such as the claimed expansion of skill coverage in Math Computation are more difficult to perceive. For example, expansion of the Math Computation domain is said to include the addition of attention to skills in geometry, inequalities, roots, and exponents, but the specifics of these additions are not documented, so users cannot readily identify which skills have been added or the rationale for their inclusion.

As part of the redevelopment process, the manual indicates that small-sample cognitive labs were conducted to investigate the appropriateness and functioning of new items and to evaluate those items for potential bias. Additionally, a larger scale pilot test was conducted to evaluate all of the changes described previously, to generate data on item difficulty, and to investigate possible cultural bias. On one hand, although the findings from these preliminary evaluations are not provided, the results were presumably incorporated into the final versions and contribute to enhanced validity of WRAT5 scores. On the other hand, some specific changes are described in the test manual. For example, to account for variation in how young readers learn, alphabet letters presented to young examinees in the Letter Reading task were included as uppercase characters in the fourth edition; in the fifth edition, approximately half of the letters are now presented as lowercase. Additionally, scoring rules for this subtest were revised so that, for example, an examinee is credited for naming a letter by saying its name or by saying the sound that it makes.

Other specific changes include simplified prompts for the Spelling subtest; changes for the Math Computation subtest that include expanded domain coverage and revised item formats (from vertical to horizontal presentation); and revised scoring rules. Revisions to the Sentence Comprehension subtest included reducing the number of syllables in words, the overall sentence length, and the difficulty of the vocabulary used.

TECHNICAL. The test manual and norms book provide clear and accessible documentation of important technical information for gauging the overall quality of the instrument.

Norms. Essential characteristics of any norm-referenced measurement procedure are that information on the comparison group is relevant, representative, and recent. As approximately 10 years have passed since publication of the WRAT4, it is reasonable that updated standardization should take place and new norms be produced for the WRAT5.

The norms group for the fifth edition was selected to comprise children and adults ages 5-85, stratified according to current U.S. Census data on education (four levels), race/ethnicity (five groups), region (four groups), sex (two genders), age (six levels), and grade (two levels). Norms data were collected between April 2016 and April 2017 and involved 222 test administrators across 41 states. Age-based norms were obtained from a sample of 2,355 examinees ages 5 years 0 months to 85 years 11 months. Norm intervals, which range from 3 months to 10 years, are smaller for younger examinees and wider for older examinees. The grade-level norms group (a subset of the age norms group) consisted of 2,150 examinees across Grades K-12. Fall, winter, and spring norms were developed.

Administration of the WRAT5 yields a raw score on each subtest. These scores are converted via look-up tables into standard scores with means of 100 and standard deviations of 15. The standard scores are the basis for deriving age- and grade-level percentile ranks, normal curve equivalents, and stanines. Raw scores are used for determining grade equivalents and growth scale values. Accurate information is provided regarding appropriate interpretation of these scores, including exhortation to apply confidence intervals based on the standard error of measurement as a way of discouraging rigid interpretations of point estimates. The test manual includes clear directions on how to manually compute raw scores, obtain derived scores, and interpret results; however, the process likely would be less error-prone and more efficient if the publisher's automated scoring system were used. The test authors appropriately caution users to rely on growth scale values over grade-equivalent scores when making inferences about progress. The growth scale values provide equal interval measurement across the age/grade levels and are described as providing "similar information at the Rasch Ability Scaled Scores (RASS) reported for the WRAT4" (manual, p. 67).

Validity. Validity evidence provided for the WRAT5 is limited. The intended purpose of the test seems to be as a measure of knowledge and skills learned in, or necessary for, school success. Concerning evidence based on test content, the test manual asserts that what is measured are "the basic academic skills of word reading, spelling, math computation, and sentence comprehension" (manual, p. 1). Those skills appear to have remained fairly constant over the 50+ years of WRAT editions; however, scant information is provided on how these skills were identified or how the specific content was determined. A review of the items suggests that the test might actually measure somewhat of an amalgam of learned academic skills and general cognitive ability. Even accepting the WRAT5 as a strict achievement measure, content-based interpretations of scores must be tentative. For example, the Reading composite likely suffers from construct under-specification: examinees' actual reading or comprehension is not measured so much as is the ability to provide a sensible missing word in a given sentence and to pronounce single words. Although the Math Computation subtest *does* require mathematical computations, the content domain for the computations is not specified and—perhaps in an attempt to avoid language loading or to reduce testing time—the mathematics problems are what is sometimes called *naked math,* devoid of context. Overall, it seems reasonable to question whether the skills included in the WRAT5 are still relevant and whether the constructs implied by the subtest names are accurate.

The evidence supporting WRAT5 score interpretations consists of several sources. First, some judgmental procedures were conducted by an internal advisory team to review test content for appropriateness and sensitivity concerns related to sex, race/ethnicity, socioeconomic status (SES), language, and culture. A similar evaluation was conducted by reviewers from Canada, England, Australia, Brazil, and India for use by English speaking examinees in those countries. A list of reviewer names is provided, but no other specifics on procedures or results is presented.

Evidence based on internal structure comprises evidence of internal consistency (described in the next section on Reliability) and intercorrelations between WRAT5 subtests computed on the age-based norms group. As would be hypothesized, correlations among subtests most dissimilar in content coverage were the weakest (e.g., among test takers ages 5-18 years, the correlation between the Reading composite and Math Computation was .52), whereas correlations between more content-similar subtests were stronger (e.g., the correlation between the Reading composite and Sentence Comprehension was .92).

Evidence based on relationships among variables was also gathered, primarily involving the correlations between WRAT5 scores and scores on well-known achievement or ability measures using modest but diverse samples; WRAT5 correlates (and sample sizes) included the WRAT4 (n = 105), the Wechsler Individual Achievement Test–Third Edition (WIAT-III; n = 105), the Wechsler Abbreviated Scale of Intelligence–Second Edition (WASI-II; n = 98), and the Wechsler Intelligence Scale for Children–Fifth Edition (WISC-V; n = 97). The correlations were as would be expected although, interestingly, scores on the WRAT5 appeared to correlate about as strongly with scores on the WRAT4 (a similar achievement measure) as with a different achievement measure (the WIAT-III) and traditional ability measures (the WASI-II and the WISC-V). It should be noted that the manual authors state that the correlation between WRAT5 scores and other achievement test scores are higher than those with cognitive ability test scores. Additional data collections were conducted to examine the diagnostic accuracy of the WRAT5 with respect to four special groups: students identified as having a specific learning disorder in reading or in mathematics, students with mild intellectual disability, and those identified as academically gifted. Although the sample sizes used were very small (ns = 47-71), mean differences between the special groups and matched examinees not so identified were as predicted.

Finally, the WRAT5 manual contains a section titled "Evidence Based on Consequences of Testing" (p. 56). The manual indicates that "continued research evaluating the use of the WRAT5 ... is expected to provide further evidence that the results of the WRAT5 contribute to beneficial consequences for examinees" (manual, p. 56). It is not clear what is meant by "further evidence" since this reviewer did not find any evidence regarding test consequences presented in the test manual.

Reliability. Three kinds of reliability information are available for the WRAT5. Internal consistency evidence was derived using examinee ability estimates from the norming samples and an odd-even split-half procedure. For age-based scores, the subtest reliability estimates were generally quite high, ranging from .85 (e.g. Math Computation, age 5) to .96 (e.g., Word Reading, age 6). As would be expected due to the greater number of items included, values for the Reading composite were higher, ranging from .93 (20- to 24-year-olds) to .98 (6-year-olds). Internal consistency estimates for grade-based scores were only slightly lower.

Alternate-forms reliability evidence was gathered based on a subsample of examinees who were administered both WRAT5 forms in a counterbalanced design between 0 and 28 days apart. The correlations between scores on the two forms were generally high across all ages (ranging from .78 for Sentence Comprehension to .90 for Spelling); however, the age levels strata seemed overly broad. The three age levels (and sample sizes) were as follows: 5-17 years (n = 194), 18-34 years (n = 103) and 35-85+ years (n = 120); as a result, it is impossible for users to gauge with certainty the alternate-forms reliability for any specific age level.

Interscorer reliability is provided for the Sentence Comprehension subtest; for that subtest, test administrators must judge the acceptability of examinees' responses with respect to the scoring criteria provided. Interscorer reliability was calculated using 100 random cases (50 for each form) selected from the norming sample that were scored by three trained scorers. Interscorer agreements for both forms were above .99.

COMMENTARY. The technical manual for the WRAT5 lists six key features of the new edition: brief testing time; flexible configuration; user-friendly administration and scoring; reliability, validity, and clinical utility; representative norms; and fairness for diverse gender, ethnic, and SES backgrounds. Sufficient evidence exists regarding accomplishment of the first three of those goals: the test can be given in less than 30 minutes for most examinees; administration is straightforward (especially when the examiner gains familiarity with the start, reverse, and stopping rules); scoring is not complicated (especially when the computerized scoring option is chosen); and WRAT5 materials are well designed and easy to use.

Evidence regarding the last three goals suggests somewhat less success. Adequate information—and adequately high reliability evidence—is provided, but information on development of the WRAT5 and validity information are extremely limited. Much additional information would be necessary for users to judge the adequacy of content included in the WRAT5. Other than statements about internal reviews, no information is provided related to differential item functioning analyses or other procedures that might have been used to enhance fairness. Correlations between the WRAT5 and other measures seem typical for associations observed between other cognitive measures, but they do not provide clear, compelling evidence about the intended meaning or uses of WRAT5 scores. Given the modest changes in content from prior editions, detail on the WRAT5's content foundation might be generalized from documentation from a previous edition, but there is a history of fairly sparse information in this key area. One reviewer of the WRAT3 noted that, "Although the WRAT has undergone several revisions it is basically the same test it was originally. ... The greatest problem with all editions of the WRAT is that there is really NO validity evidence" (Ward, 1995, p. 1110). Another reviewer went further, observing that there was "insufficient evidence of validity or reliability" (Mabry, 1995, p. 1110). A review of the WRAT4 used characterizations such as "minimal," "limited," and "inadequate" to describe the evidence and samples used to investigate validity (Hoff & Swerdlik, 2010, pp. 718-719), although another review observed that "the reliability and validity evidence [for the WRAT4] ... surpasses that of many small tests" (Sabers & Olson, 2010, p. 720).

Overall, it is somewhat discouraging that, aside from the commendable collection of updated standardization data, the authors of the WRAT5 did not use the occasion of a new edition to document more fully the case for validity of WRAT5 scores. Perhaps most fundamentally, the primary intended interpretations supported by WRAT5 scores remain unclear. No compelling case has been made to refute Sabers's and Olson's (2010) observation with respect to the fourth edition: "The most serious problems ... are not with technical or psychometric issues, but rather in determining what purpose it serves and tailoring it more specifically to that purpose" (p. 721).

SUMMARY. The WRAT5 has some commendable features. The latest edition still provides a quick, dependable measure of a limited range of knowledge and skills deemed important for academic success across a wide range of examinee ages and grade levels. The most noteworthy feature of the WRAT5 is the updated and representative norms. Revisions in terms of content, format, administration, and scoring procedures are all modest, but reasonable and likely to make testing more efficient and accurate. Updated reliability information is provided; reliability analyses show at least moderate to strong internal consistency, alternate-forms reliability, and interscorer reliability.

Validity evidence is least well developed for the WRAT5. Correlations between WRAT5 scores and other measures are of the order that would be expected between nearly any pair of school ability/achievement tests. Reported mean differences between selected special groups and matched controls would also be expected on nearly any cognitive measure (e.g., examinees identified as having a reading disability performed, on average, worse than those not so identified). No content evidence of validity is provided, although modest evidence based on internal structure supports the subtest configuration and claims of the WRAT5.

The authors of the WRAT5 provide well-advised cautions on its use. It is best used as a quick, norm-referenced measure of a limited set of foundational academic skills. It is most useful in situations where WRAT5 performance is combined with other relevant information to inform decisions to refer examinees for more in-depth evaluation, placement decisions, and academic progress monitoring. The authors appropriately warn users that "scores on the WRAT5 should never be used as the sole criteria for identification or diagnostic purposes" (manual, p. 53). When other reliable, valid sources of information are in short supply, the WRAT5 should provide moderately accurate and dependable information on relative standing of examinees with respect to limited literacy and numeracy skills across a broad range of ages and grade levels.

REVIEWER'S REFERENCES

American Educational Research Association, American Psychological Association, & National Council on Measurement in Education. (2014). *Standards for educational and psychological testing.* Washington, DC: American Educational Research Association.

Hoff, K. E., & Swerdlik, M. E. (2010). [Test review of Wide Range Achievement Test 4]. In R. A. Spies, J. F. Carlson, & K. F. Geisinger (Eds.), *The eighteenth mental measurements yearbook* (pp. 716-719). Lincoln, NE: Buros Institute of Mental Measurements.

Mabry, L. (1995). [Test review of Wide Range Achievement Test 3]. In J. C. Conoley & J. C. Impara (Eds.), *The twelfth mental measurements yearbook* (pp. 1108-1110). Lincoln, NE: Buros Institute of Mental Measurements.

Sabers, D. L., & Olson, A. M. (2010). [Test review of Wide Range Achievement Test 4]. In R. A. Spies, J. F. Carlson, & K. F. Geisinger (Eds.), *The eighteenth mental measurements yearbook* (pp. 719-721). Lincoln, NE: Buros Institute of Mental Measurements.

Ward, A. W. (1995). [Test review of Wide Range Achievement Test 3]. In J. C. Conoley & J. C. Impara (Eds.), *The twelfth mental measurements yearbook* (pp. 1110-1111). Lincoln, NE: Buros Institute of Mental Measurements.

Wilkinson, G. S., & Robertson, G. J. (2006). *WRAT4 professional manual.* Lutz, FL: Psychological Assessment Resources.

[186]

Woodcock-Muñoz Language Survey III.

Purpose: Designed to provide "a broad sampling of academic language proficiency in the areas of listening, speaking, reading, writing, and comprehension."
Population: Ages 3-0 through 22-11.
Publication Dates: 1993-2017.
Acronym: WMLS III.
Scores, 22: 8 test scores: Analogies, Oral Comprehension, Picture Vocabulary, Oral Language Expression, Letter-Word Identification, Passage Comprehension, Dictation, Written Language Expression; 14 cluster scores: Listening, Speaking, Broad English Oral Language, Basic English Oral Language, Applied English Oral Language, Reading, Writing, Broad Reading and Writing, Basic Reading and Writing, Applied Reading and Writing, Comprehension, Broad English Language Ability, Basic English Language Ability, Applied English Language Ability.
Administration: Individual.
Forms, 3: English A, English B, Spanish.
Price Data, 2020: $1,095.29 per English A and Spanish complete kit including manual (2017, 225 pages), English and Spanish test books, 25 Form A test records with scoring licenses, 25 Spanish test records with scoring licenses, and 50 response booklets; $615.33 per individual form complete kit (specify Form A, B, or Spanish); $78.20 per 25 test records with scoring licenses (specify Form A, B, or Spanish), $25.96 per 25 response books (specify Form A, B, or Spanish).
Foreign Language Edition: Spanish form available.
Time: 60-75 minutes for administration of all 8 tests on one form.
Comments: Co-normed with the Woodcock-Johnson IV (20:207); may be used for evaluating English and/or Spanish language proficiency; when administered in both English and Spanish, performance can be compared to determine oral language dominance. "Examiners who administer the WMLS English forms need to be fluent and literate in English ... those who administer the WMLS III Spanish Form need to be fluent and literate in Spanish." Score reports must be generated using test publisher's online platform.
Authors: Richard W. Woodcock, Criselda G. Alvarado, Mary L. Ruef, and Fredrick A. Schrank.
Publisher: Riverside Insights.
Cross References: For reviews by James Dean Brown and Salvador Hector Ochoa of the 2005 revision, see 17:202; for reviews by Linda Crocker and Chi-Wen Kao of the original edition, see 13:364.

Review of the Woodcock-Muñoz Language Survey III by BETH DOLL, University of Nebraska–Lincoln, Lincoln, NE:

DESCRIPTION. The Woodcock-Muñoz Language Survey III (WMLS III) is a set of 16 individually administered tests of academic language proficiency including eight tests that are administered and completed in English and eight tests that are administered and completed in Spanish. The English and Spanish forms follow an identical structure with two tests each of listening, speaking, reading, and writing. The two listening tests (analogies and an oral cloze task) provide an aggregate measure of language-based knowledge and comprehension. Two speaking tests (picture vocabulary and an oral expression task) provide an aggregate measure of language expression. Two reading tasks (letter-word identification and passage comprehension) describe reading achievement, and two writing tasks (writing to dictation and written words/sentences/passages) describe written language achievement.

The WMLS III provides a broad measure of academic language proficiency in English and/or in Spanish to use in making key educational decisions or conducting educational research. Intended for use primarily in school settings, the WMLS III is best suited for describing a student's dominance in academic English or Spanish, growth or change in academic English or Spanish language ability, eligibility for bilingual educational services, or readiness for English-only instruction. WMLS III results also may contribute to assessments of students' instructional needs or learning disabilities, or to research or evaluation related to language development in either or both languages. Two parallel forms are available for the WMLS III English tests, whereas a single form is available for the WMLS III Spanish tests. The English and Spanish forms of the WMLS III can be administered together or separately, depending on the decisions that the results will be used to make. The English form must be administered and scored by an examiner who is fluent in English, and the Spanish form must be administered and scored by an examiner who is fluent in Spanish; consequently, the two forms will often be administered by two different examiners.

The WMLS III manual emphasizes that this is a measure of academic language proficiency as opposed to conversational fluency in a language. This distinction is important for school-based applications. Academic language specifically describes proficiency in the concise and sometimes abstract vocabulary that underlies schooling and facility with the complex, formal grammatical structures used to understand and express complicated ideas.

Test records and response booklets purchased with the WMLS III kit provide a record of responses and a table for converting raw scores to age equivalent and grade equivalent scores. Raw scores are then entered into an online scoring and reporting program that converts these results into *W* scores from which are derived a variety of proficiency (criterion-referenced) and standard (norm-referenced) scores. Derived proficiency scores include the *W* Difference Score, describing difference between the examinee's *W* score and the median *W* score of the norm-reference group; a Relative Proficiency Index, representing the degree to which the examinee's *W* score falls above or below the average for the reference group; and a Language Proficiency Level, describing the progression of language acquisition from initial development through advanced proficiency. Derived norm-referenced scores include standard scores with a mean of 100 and a standard deviation of 15, as well as *T* scores, *z* scores, normal curve equivalents and percentile ranks.

The online scoring and reporting program is necessary for the use of the WMLS III, and its access is strictly limited by the number of test record booklets that have been purchased. In addition to the scoring analysis, the online site provides audio files for test administration, training videos, and other resources. Online scoring is useful in protecting the integrity of score derivation, but because it is the only scoring option, it also ensures that users of the WMLS III are dependent on access to the online program in order to derive usable results from any administration. Thc online program is password-protected to users authorized by the purchaser of test record forms. Use of the program is not entirely intuitive but clicking on a Resources tab accesses video tutorials that explain the various facets of the program. Results of the profile analysis can be saved as a report for parents or teachers or as an uninterpreted data record. Roster reports for multiple administrations across multiple examinees can be saved in a spreadsheet format.

The WMLS III is a comprehensive, individually administered standardized measure; assessment materials include an administration easel, test forms, and audio files that are available in the online scoring and reporting program. Examiners are expected to follow strict administration procedures, and three features of the WMLS III kit are designed to ensure that this is the case. First, the WMLS III easels include well-designed prompts and scripts that clearly guide examiners through standard administration of the tests. Useful suggestions are provided for accommodating examinees with visual impairments, hearing impairments, or attentional impairments. Second, the test manual includes extensive examiner training guidelines and practice exercises, and third, the online scoring and reporting program incorporates error-checking to catch data entry errors and force their correction. Examiners qualified to administer and interpret the WMLS III should have knowledge and experience in language assessment as well as the use of standardized measures to make educational decisions.

DEVELOPMENT. The WMLS III is a significant revision of its predecessor, the Woodcock-Muñoz Language Survey—Revised (WMLS-R; Woodcock, Munoz-Sandoval, Ruef, & Alvarado, 2005). With this revision, modifications were made in the tests and tasks, the language proficiency levels, and the standardization and norms. The WMLS III's simplified cluster composition was organized around listening, speaking, reading, and writing by the addition of three new tests (Oral Comprehension, Oral Language Expression, and Written Language Expression) and the elimination of two WMLS-R tests (Understanding Directions, and Story Recall). Whereas the WMLS-R had used the familiar Cognitive Academic Language Proficiency (CALP) levels, the WMLS III language proficiency levels were developed from accumulated research to provide a more accurate emphasis on the *academic* language needed to succeed in school classrooms.

The WMLS III was co-normed with the Woodcock-Johnson IV (WJ IV; Schrank, McGrew, & Mather, 2014) using a two-phase procedure. In Phase 1, the reconceptualization of the test blueprint prompted the creation and psychometric evaluation of new items, item scaling, and norming for the English language tests. Because the two measures were normed together between 2009 and 2012 and because there were items in common to both measures, it was possible to create common *W* scores for the WMLS III English and the WJ IV, such that scores from the two measures can be directly compared. The norming sample for Phase 1 included more than 7,000 participants ranging in age from 2 to 80 years, and representative of the U.S. population by geographic region, community type, gender, country of birth, ethnicity, and parent education. For specific information about the norming study, the WMLS III manual refers users to the WJ IV Technical Manual (McGrew, LaForte, & Schrank, 2014), which is available online.

Development of both the English and Spanish language versions of the WMLS III occurred in Phase 2. First, additional items were written and piloted in both English and Spanish, and the Oral Language Expression test was added to the battery. Between 25% and 35% of Spanish items were direct translations of the English items. Then, all retained items were calibrated in 2016 using two samples: 1,055 native English-speaking examinees and 1,041 native Spanish-speaking examinees who were representative of all regions of the United States.

Importantly, 93% of the WMLS III Spanish sample were residents of the United States unlike the WMLS-R sample, which had been drawn predominantly from other Spanish-speaking nations. Regarding country of ethnic origin, 83% of the native speakers of Spanish were of Mexican origin as opposed to origins from Cuba, Puerto Rico, or other Central or South American territories or nations. No information is provided about the degree to which the Spanish calibration sample included bilingual as compared to monolingual Spanish participants.

Calibrated items were used to equate the Spanish with the English forms of the WMLS III and to flag and eliminate items when item difficulty varied substantially by gender or ethnicity. Simultaneously, outside experts reviewed all calibrated items for offensive language, stereotypes, or potential bias. Validated test items were assembled into the final test forms.

The six WMLS III language proficiency levels include two levels of language proficiency and four levels of language development and emerging proficiency. These are based on a thoughtful and evidence-based revision of the more familiar CALP (cognitive academic language proficiency) levels that had been used in the WMLS-R. The revised levels were drafted from a review of research related to the time needed to acquire proficiency relative to native-speaking peers and prominent state exit and entry standards for language instruction education programs. These levels were then reviewed and validated by a committee of experts in bilingual education.

TECHNICAL. The WMLS III items, calibration, scaling, and norm development employed the Rasch single-parameter logistic test model (Rasch, 1980). The *W* scale underlying the WMLS III scores is a direct transformation of the Rasch logit scale and places examinee ability and item difficulty on a common scale in which a *W* score of 500 represents the difficulty level at which 50% of fourth graders would complete the item successfully.

Technical properties of the WMLS III are reported in the test manual for the English form only, and a review of resources from the WMLS III online site provided no additional information about technical properties of the Spanish form. Internal consistency reliability estimates for the WMLS III English tests was strong, consistently falling above .75 for individual tests across all age groups and ranging from .87 to .99 for cluster scores. Validity analyses of the WMLS III English forms show that the item difficulty curves followed optimal and predicted patterns. Concurrent validity studies reported moderate correlation coefficients (.47 to .81) between the English tests and other recognized language scales: the Comprehensive Assessment of Spoken Language (Carrow-Woolfolk, 1999) and the Oral and Written Language Scales (Carrow-Woolfolk, 1995). Correlations also are reported between the WMLS III English reading and writing tests and related subtests of the Kaufman Test of Educational Achievement—

Second Edition (Kaufman & Kaufman, 2004) and the Wechsler Individual Achievement Test—Third Edition (Wechsler, 2009).

COMMENTARY. The WMLS III is a revision of the respected WMLS-R and provides a comprehensive norm-referenced measure of academic language. Like its predecessor, the WMLS III is a statistically sophisticated measure that implements some of the most recent advances in measurement science. It retains the WMLS-R's emphasis on Spanish and English forms, co-norming with the most recent WJ test and use of Rasch-based *W* scores linked to item difficulty and examinee ability. The WMLS III improves on the WMLS-R in a number of respects: The test's norms are updated, it uses a simplified and conceptually elegant structure to better reflect academic language, it introduces refined language proficiency levels that are more consistent with decisions related to language instruction education programs, and the Spanish form is based on a calibration sample comprised predominantly of U.S. residents. These refinements are responsive to emerging research and practice in language and education.

Administration and scoring of the WMLS III is now entirely dependent upon access to the online scoring and reporting program, introducing new technology requirements for internet access, adequate sound systems (for the audio administration files), and file format compatibility. Users will need to budget for these ongoing costs of adopting the measure in addition to the initial purchase costs.

It is troubling that there is very little information about the technical properties of the WMLS III Spanish form, particularly because a prominent use of the measure will be educational planning for growing numbers of English language learner and bilingual students. The test manual clarifies that a technically sound calibration procedure was used to equate the Spanish and English forms. Nevertheless, use of the Spanish form and comparison of scores from the Spanish and English forms requires more specific information to verify the internal consistency of the Spanish tests, other indices of reliability and validity of the Spanish tests, and the reliability and validity of comparisons.

Even while the WMLS III was under development, new evidence has emerged that comparisons of Spanish speaking students' expressive and receptive language might differ depending on the student's status as bilingual or monolingual and depending on the test used. In one study, bilingual students performed more poorly than monolingual students on vocabulary measures from both WMLS-R Spanish and WMLS-R English forms (Gibson, Jarmulowicz, & Kimbrough Oller, 2018). As a second example, Schmidtke (2017) found that vocabulary tests underestimated bilingual students' true verbal ability even when examinees were tested in both languages and each language was compared to monolingual norms. These results suggest that it is particularly important for users to know the proportion of bilingual and monolingual speakers who were included in the norming groups and to use caution when interpreting results for bilingual students.

Other evidence suggests that differences in the difficulty of the WMLS III tests may depend on the Spanish speakers' country of origin. Sandilos et al. (2015) documented significant differences in Spanish dialects and vocabulary for U.S. residents from various countries of origin and found significant differences in WMLS-R English performance for some origins. Because the predominant country of origin in the Spanish calibration study was Mexico, examiners will need to be cautious when interpreting WMLS III Spanish scores of students whose country of origin is not Mexico.

SUMMARY. The WMLS III English tests provide a comprehensive assessment of academic language that can be used for diverse, important educational decisions. The WMLS Spanish tests have been thoughtfully developed, but the test manual provides limited evidence of their technical soundness. Substantial additional evidence is needed for the reliability and validity of the WMLS Spanish tests and the validity of comparisons between the Spanish and English results.

REVIEWER'S REFERENCES

Carrow-Woolfolk, E. (1995). Oral and Written Language Scales. Torrance, CA: Western Psychological Services.

Carrow-Woolfolk, E. (1999). Comprehensive Assessment of Spoken Language. Torrance, CA: Western Psychological Services.

Gibson, T. A., Jarmulowicz, L., & Kimbrough Oller, D. (2018). Difficulties using standardized tests to identify the receptive expressive gap in bilingual children's vocabularies. *Bilingualism: Language and Cognition, 21*(2), 328-339.

Kaufman, A. S., & Kaufman, N. L. (2004). Kaufman Test of Educational Achievement—Second Edition. San Antonio, TX: Pearson.

McGrew, K. S., LaForte, E. M., & Schrank, F. A. (2014). *Technical manual. Woodcock-Johnson IV*. Rolling Meadows, IL: Riverside.

Sandilos, L. E., Lewis, K., Komaroff, E., Scheffner Hammer, C., Scarpino, S. E., Lopez, L., ... Goldstein, B. (2015). Analysis of bilingual children's performance on the English and Spanish versions of the Woodcock-Munoz Language Survey–R (WMLS-R). *Language Assessment Quarterly, 12* (4), 386-408. doi:10.1080/15434303.2015.1100198

Schmidtke, J. (2017). Home and community language proficiency in Spanish-English early bilingual university students. *Journal of Speech, Language, and Hearing Research, 60*, 2879-2890.

Schrank, F. A., McGrew, K. S., & Mather, N. (2014). Woodcock-Johnson IV. Rolling Meadows, IL: Riverside.

Wechsler, D. (2009). Wechsler Individual Achievement Test—Third Edition. San Antonio, TX: Pearson.

Woodcock, R. W., Muñoz-Sandoval, A. F., Ruef, M. L., & Alvarado, C. G. (2005). Woodcock-Muñoz Language Survey–Revised. Itasca, IL: Riverside.

Review of the Woodcock-Muñoz Language Survey III by SANDRA I. PLATA-POTTER, Assistant Professor, Early Childhood Education, University of Mount Olive, Mount Olive, NC:

DESCRIPTION. The Woodcock-Muñoz Language Survey III (WMLS III) is a "set of individually administered tests that provides a broad sampling of academic language proficiency in the areas of listening, speaking, reading, writing, and comprehension" (manual, p. 1) for English and/or Spanish speakers. The WMLS III is designed to evaluate language proficiency of individuals ages 3 years 0 months through 22 years 11 months. Language proficiency is assessed using eight tests in three categories: listening and speaking/escuchar y hablar, reading and writing/leer y escribir, and cross-domain clusters/compuestos entre dominios. The tests are (a) Analogies/Analogías, (b) Oral Comprehension/Comprensión oral, (c) Picture Vocabulary/Vocabulario sobre dibujos, (d) Oral Language Expression/Expresión de lenguaje oral, (e) Letter-Word Identification/Identificación de letras y palabras, (f) Passage Comprehension/Comprensión de textos, (g) Dictation/Dictado, and (h) Written Language Expression/Expresión de lenguaje escrito. Each test can be administered individually or combined to provide cluster scores. To determine language dominance for bilingual speakers, the comparative language index (CLI) can be used to compare the examinee's performance in the respective language tasks.

The test booklet is an easel format with tabs for quick location of content that facilitates administration of the test. When set up, critical information for the administrator of the test faces the examiner. One test (Oral Comprehension/Comprensión oral) requires examinees to listen to an audio recording and provide the missing word in the sentence heard. The audio file is accessed through the WMLS III online scoring and reporting system. The test manual provides detailed information about the test, administration and scoring procedures, and scores and interpretation as well as information regarding norming, reliability, training guidelines, and practice exercises. Administration and scoring procedures are provided for each individual test and include information about starting points and basal and ceiling rules. The comprehensive manual is quite extensive in terms of the information provided.

DEVELOPMENT. The test manual states the WMLS III is a "significant revision of the Woodcock-Muñoz Language Survey-Revised" (manual, p. 5). The WMLS III contains five of the seven tests from the WMLS-R (Analogies/Analogías, Picture Vocabulary/Vocabulario sobre dibujos, Letter-Word Identification/Identificación de letras y palabras, Passage Comprehension/Comprensión de textos, and Dictation/Dictado) and adds three new ones (Oral Comprehension/Comprensión oral, Oral Language Expression/Expresión de lenguaje oral, and Written Language Expression/Expresión de lenguaje escrito). Test developers had two goals for the new version. The first was to better coordinate how "users assess the listening, speaking, reading, and writing domains of language" (manual, p. 5), and the second was to provide each domain with one test of foundational skills and one test of foundational knowledge. The design of the WMLS III is such that not only is quantitative information collected, but some qualitative information (e.g., examinee's language exposure in home, school, and community; native language; academic language instruction; examinee's test behavior) can be collected as well.

Development occurred in two phases. Phase 1 consisted of conceptualizing the specifications for the master plan, creating and evaluating new items, and norming. Six goals were specified for Phase 2 (e.g., increase the number of items for both English and Spanish, revise test items and artwork, collect additional data for validity). These tasks were carried out immediately following the completion of Phase 1.

TECHNICAL. The norming and calibration processes are discussed in-depth in the test manual. Care was taken to closely follow professional standards explicated in the *Standards for Educational and Psychological Testing* (American Educational Research Association, American Psychological Association, & National Council on Measurement in Education, 2014). The norming sample (n = 7,416) was drawn from 46 states and the District of Columbia. The test manual provides numerous tables with descriptive information concerning demographic characteristics of the sample (e.g., age, grade). Moreover, the WMLS III was co-normed with the Woodcock-Johnson IV. The Rasch single-parameter logistic model was used for calibration, equating, and scaling. The test manual includes a detailed explanation of how the model was applied to the WMLS III.

Reliability estimates are provided for individual tests and cluster scores for the WMLS III English. Split-half coefficients were calculated and corrected using the Spearman-Brown formula. Standard errors of measurement for each test also are reported in the test manual.

The *Standards for Educational and Psychological Testing* also were applied to the validation process for the WMLS III. Evidence to support validity is provided regarding test development, scoring, and interpretation. Intercorrelations between tests and clusters are reported as well as correlations obtained between scores from the WMLS III and other measures of oral language, achievement, and language proficiency.

COMMENTARY. Akin to comments made about the WMLS-R in a previous review (Ochoa, 2007), the WMLS III consists of a robust application of psychometric properties. In general, the test manual provides a depth of detailed information for the user to be sufficiently informed about the test's purpose, administration, and interpretation. The test user is provided with much detail on how to administer and score the test. Scoring is conducted online, and test administrators have the added option of customizing score reports.

The WMLS III manual states there are two test forms (Form A and Form B) in English and one form (Form A) in Spanish. This reviewer found little to no information in the test materials regarding Form B. Although the test manual makes mention of two forms in various places, no examples of the forms were found in the test manual.

SUMMARY. The level of due diligence put into the development of the WMLS III is noteworthy. In addition to the English and Spanish assessments, test users also have the option to obtain a comparative language index that combines information from English and Spanish administrations. The test manual is comprehensive and durable; however, the thickness of the paper makes it somewhat difficult to manage. A helpful suggestion would be to add tabs to delineate the chapters.

REVIEWER'S REFERENCES

American Educational Research Association, American Psychological Association, & National Council on Measurement in Education. (2014). *Standards for educational and psychological testing.* Washington, DC: American Educational Research Association.

Ochoa, S. H. (2007). [Test review of Woodcock-Muñoz Language Survey—Revised]. In K. F. Geisinger, R. A. Spies, J. F. Carlson, & B. S. Plake (Eds.), *The seventeenth mental measurements yearbook.* Retrieved from http://marketplace.unl.edu.buros/

[187]

The WORD Test 3 Elementary.

Purpose: Designed to assess expressive vocabulary and semantics.
Population: Children ages 6 and older.
Publication Dates: 1981-2014.
Scores, 7: Associations, Synonyms, Semantic Absurdities, Antonyms, Definitions, Flexible Word Use, Total.
Administration: Individual.
Price Data, 2020: $168 per complete kit including examiner's manual (2014, 197 pages) and 20 test forms; $45 per 20 forms.
Time: (30) minutes.
Authors: Linda Bowers, Rosemary Huisingh, Carolyn LoGiudice, and Jane Orman.
Publisher: PRO-ED.
Cross References: For a review by Darrell L. Sabers and Huaping Sun of the second edition, see 17:203; see also T5:2911 (6 references) and T4:2983 (2 references); for reviews by Mavis Donahue and Nambury S. Raju of the original edition, see 9:1393.

Review of the WORD Test 3 Elementary by WILLIAM D. SCHAFER, Affiliated Professor (Emeritus), University of Maryland College Park, College Park, MD:

DESCRIPTION. The WORD Test 3 Elementary is designed to aid diagnosis of strengths and weaknesses in vocabulary usage to help teachers and parents/guardians understand students' skill sets as well as to recommend intervention strategies. It is intended for children ages 6 through 11 for whom English is their primary language.

The test is intended to be administered individually by a clinician. Each subtest consists of 15 items, all of which are presented to each child, and scoring of each item is completed as the test is administered. Raw scores are the sums of the item scores on the various tasks, with a total raw score also determined. The six subtests are as follows:

Associations. Each item consists of four words, one of which is semantically unrelated to the other three. To receive credit for the item, the child must correctly identify the unrelated word and explain why it does not fit with the others. This task is intended to assess, in part, the child's ability to categorize words and to use those categories.

Synonyms. Each item is a word for which the child must supply a synonym. This task is intended to assess semantic usage as well as the ability to express words with similar meaning.

Semantic Absurdities. Each item is an absurd statement, and the child is asked to repair the incongruity. The intent is to assess the ability to recognize meaning, identify semantic conflict, and resolve the conflict with an appropriate substitution.

Antonyms. The child is asked to supply a word with an opposite meaning to the word in each item. This task is intended to assess the ability to supply words with the same semantic usage but with opposite meaning.

Definitions. The items are words for which the child is to supply definitions. This task is intended to assess ability to identify semantic attributes, to choose which attributes are relevant, and to express the meaning of the target word without using it.

Flexible Word Use. Each item is a word with several meanings. The child is asked to supply two meanings. The intent is to assess the ability to recall and express multiple definitions for words that may be used in several ways.

DEVELOPMENT. The original WORD Test was introduced in 1981 to assist clinicians assessing deficiencies in semantic abilities and expressive vocabulary in order to plan interventions. It consisted of six subtests, five of which were dichotomously scored (Synonyms, Semantic Absurdities, Antonyms, Definitions, and Multiple Definitions) and one that was scored on a 0-1-2 scale (Associations). A revision (The WORD Test 2) appeared in 2004 and consisted of six dichotomously scored scales with a new name, Flexible Word Use, in place of Multiple Definitions, and Associations scored dichotomously.

The WORD Test 3 is a revision of The WORD Test 2. Several items were revised to reflect modern terminology in classrooms. An effort was also made to enhance the norms available for the test.

The WORD Test 3, like its predecessors, focuses on words that are used less frequently than daily but that do appear in several types of written texts as opposed to having only specialized usage. The various subtests correspond with activities associated with acquiring new vocabulary as described in the test manual.

TECHNICAL.

Standardization. The normative sample was said to represent 2004 Census data according to gender, race, education, placement, and socioeconomic status. Children (n = 1,302) ages 6-11 years from 43 states were included. Normative data are presented in 6-month increments for ages 6:0 to 11:11, resulting in sample sizes of 102-117 for each of the 12 intervals. Raw scores are converted to percentile ranks and standard scores with a mean of 100 and a standard deviation of 15.

Reliability. Reliability was examined in four ways: test-retest, internal consistency, standard error of measurement (*SEM*), and scorer agreement.

Test-retest reliability coefficients were calculated for a sample of 153 participants within 6-month age ranges, resulting in sample sizes ranging from 8 to 17. The test-retest interval was not specified in the test manual. The correlations are reasonably high, ranging from .18 for Associations, ages 10:6-10:11, to .97 for Antonyms, ages 9:6-9:11. Of the 72 test-retest reliability coefficients reported for the subtests by age levels, 61 (84.7%) were .70 or higher and only three were below .50. The test-retest coefficients for the total test within age ranges varied from .82 to .97.

Kuder-Richardson 20 (KR20) coefficients were also calculated for 6-month age ranges, presumably for the entire normative sample. These coefficients ranged from .58 (Semantic Absurdities, 11:6-11:11) to .85 (Flexible Word Use, 8:0-8:5).

Standard errors of measurement (SEMs) were calculated for standard scores by task and for the total test. For tasks, *SEM*s ranged from .37 (Antonyms, 9:6-9:11) to 2.22 (Synonyms, 6:6-6:11). For the total test, the range was 2.19 (ages 9:6-9:11) to 6.78 (ages 9:0-9.5).

Six raters re-scored a sample of 15 test forms to evaluate scorer agreement. Agreement across the 90 items for the 15 pairs of raters varied from 90% to 96%.

Validity. Validity evidence was examined by calculating item-task point-biserial correlations by age, by calculating task and total test intercorrelations by age, and by comparing scoring levels for typical vs. language disordered children, for males vs. females, for various races and ethnicities, and for race-socioeconomic status interactions.

For Associations, the median point-biserial across all age ranges ranged from .21 to .58. For Synonyms the range was .33 to .68. The range for Semantic Absurdities was from .27 to .56. For Antonyms, the range was from .38 to .66. The range for Definitions was from .37 to .67. For Flexible Word Use the range was from .52 to .72.

The task-task intercorrelations across all age levels ranged from .63 (Flexible Word Use with Semantic Absurdities) to .81 (Antonyms with Synonyms; Definitions with Synonyms). The across-age task-total test correlations ranged from .86 (Associations; Semantic Absurdities) to .92 (Definitions). The task-task intercorrelations across all ages ranged from .33 to .80. For the 6-month age ranges, the task-task intercorrelations were as follows: for ages 6:0-6:5, the range was from .47 to .79; for ages 6:6-6:11 from .43 to .74; for ages 7:0-7:5 from .46 to .76; for ages 7:6-7:11 from .46 to .76; for ages 8:0-8:5 from .53 to .80; for ages

8:6-8:11 from .54 to .77; for ages 9:0-9:5 from .47 to .74; for ages 9:6-9:11 from .33 to .67; for ages 10:0-10:5 from .51 to .74; for ages 10:6-10:11 from .51 to .75; for ages 11:0-11:5 from .54 to .76; and for ages 11:6-11:11 from .40 to .69. The task-total test intercorrelations across all ages ranged from .66 to .91. The within-age task-total test intercorrelations were as follows: for ages 6:0-6:5, the range was from .77 to .91; for ages 6:6-6:11 from .75 to .89; for ages 7:0-7:5 from .79 to .89; for ages 7:6-7:11 from .76 to .89; for ages 8:0-8:5 from .80 to .88; for ages 8:6-8:11 from .75 to .91; for ages 9:0-9:5 from .80 to .89; for ages 9:6-9:11 from .73 to .85; for ages 10:0-10:5 from .80 to .87; for ages 10:6-10:11 from .75 to .88; for ages 11:0-11:5 from .75 to .89; and for ages 11:6-11:11 from .66 to .86.

Differences between typically developing and language disordered children were studied within age ranges using *t*-tests. The .01 level of significance was used throughout. For ages 6:0-6:5, 6:6-6:11, 7:0-7:5, and 8:0-8.5, the total test and five subtests reached statistical significance; only Flexible Word Use did not. For ages 7:6-7:11 and 8:6-8:11, all seven tests reached statistical significance. In all comparisons, score differences were in the predicted direction, with typically developing students obtaining higher mean scores than language disordered students.

Mean differences between males and females were evaluated using *t*-tests within the 12 age ranges for each of the six tasks and overall, resulting in 84 tests. None of these *t*-test results reached statistical significance at the .05 level.

Differences for race (Caucasian, African-American, Hispanic, or Latino) were tested at each of the 12 age ranges for each of the six tasks, resulting in 72 *F*-tests. None was statistically significant at the .01 level with the exception of Semantic Absurdities at ages 7:0-7:5, Definitions at ages 7:6-7:11, Associations and Synonyms at ages 9:0-9:5, and Associations at ages 9:6-9:11.

Interactions between race and SES were studied for each task at each age range, resulting in 72 two-way analyses of variance. In no case was the interaction statistically significant at the .01 level.

Utility. The examiner's manual is attractive and easy to read. For each task, the examiner is to present an example item and briefly discuss the student's response. That is followed by the task's items and accompanied by a list of correct and incorrect responses. Judgment is needed for unlisted responses.

Raw scores are generated as the exam is given. Tables are then used to translate the raw scores to within-age percentile ranks and standard scores, which are presented graphically on the answer sheet. The test manual recommends the results be used to identify student strengths and weaknesses, recommend additional testing, recommend intervention strategies, help appropriate adults understand the examinee's expressive vocabulary skills, and recommend means of vocabulary acquisition at school and in the home. For each task, there is a discussion about interpreting errors and designing interventions based on them.

COMMENTARY. The domain of the test could use elaboration. It is not clear whether this six-factor structure of language competence is well accepted or whether there are competing structures of language ability that exist as alternates.

The words on the test, themselves, are the content of its tasks. The basis for their choice is not developed in the manual. No judgment seems possible one way or the other about how well they represent their respective domains.

The total-test Kuder-Richardson (KR20) coefficients ranged from .92 to .96 within age ranges. Because the subtests have only 15 items each, small coefficients are reasonable; the full test, with 90 items, can be expected to demonstrate coefficients in the middle .90s as does The WORD Test 3 Elementary.

Particularly for the individual tasks, the reliability coefficients do not seem sufficient to support individual interpretation of the results of the test as profiles. Clinicians are urged to use the test's outcomes as suggestive rather than diagnostic and to gather further evidence before implementing or recommending instructional approaches based on the results. The emphasis in the test manual on interpreting profiles rather than overall scores could lead an educator to plan an intervention based on chance results. On the other hand, the interventions discussed in the manual all seem desirable regardless of student needs.

Although the reported analyses are generally supportive of the validity of test scores, it should be noted that they are based on small sample sizes. Also, the test authors argue from non-significance in the manual. However, non-significance can often be explained by low power in small-*n* studies; it should be incumbent on the test authors to conduct a power analysis before using non-significance as a supportive finding. Additionally, the approach the test authors used to address nonorthogonality in the two-way analyses of variance due to non-proportional sample sizes should be noted.

A concern regarding the scorer study should be raised. It is not clear from the test manual what information the scorers actually used. During testing, correct responses are scored correct, but the child's responses are written for incorrect responses; this suggests that raters may only have seen those student responses that were judged incorrect, and that there could have been no basis to judge a correct initial item score to have been a scoring error. Nor could the re-scorers have probed examinee responses when they felt the messages being received were unclear, as could the original examiners. These factors could artificially increase rater correlations.

There is no discussion of relationships with other variables. For example, as an assessment of expressive vocabulary, one wonders how this test's results would compare with another test of expressive vocabulary as well as with a test of receptive vocabulary, for which the correlation should be lower.

Also missing is consequential evidence. How has the test been used? What outcomes were recommended? Were they successful? Did the users feel the test was worth the resources needed to administer it? It would be helpful if the test authors were to develop evidence demonstrating that the test supports effective decision making about instruction.

There are several other improvements that could enhance this test. At the outset, the test authors could develop a cognitive model of expressive vocabulary; what elements does it have, why does it consist of those, and what does it not include? That model could be used to generate the subtests and also could be used to generate a sampling plan leading to the specific items for each of them. Norms could be generated for well-described and appropriately sampled populations of adequate size. Concurrent evidence of validity could be studied with a multi-trait, multi-method approach using other tests of expressive vocabulary, tests of similar traits such as receptive vocabulary, tests of more tangentially similar traits such as school grades, and unrelated variables such as height or weight. Finally, the suggestions given for additional instruction for low-scoring children should be based on evidence generated from documented studies of their effectiveness.

The instructions for administration are not always clear. Different examiners could easily differ in the ways they implement the protocol. For example, in the Semantic Absurdities subtest, the examiner is to leave the last word out on a second reading, but the target word is not always the last word. Also of concern is how the examiner should introduce each subtest when the child is confused by the one example given for each.

Norms are available for ages less than 12. Students who did not use English proficiently were excluded from the normative population. The development of norms was emphasized in the revision. According to the manual, the norming population was intended to reflect the national school population, with some exceptions (e.g., students with hearing loss and non-verbal students were omitted). The norming examiners were 392 speech-language pathologists who selected examinees to match demographic profiles communicated by the study authors. The test manual is silent on whether and, if so, how the examiners were to avoid selecting examinees from among their client populations who may be expected already to exhibit a bias in their semantic abilities.

The norms are translated into tables that are used by examiners to establish age-equivalent scores as well as standard scores. All norms are calculated using children restricted to 6-month age ranges, so the sizes of the relevant norming groups are far less than the size of the norming population, ranging from 102 to 117. At a minimum, the test authors might consider smoothing the norms across the age ranges; indeed, there are inconsistencies across the age ranges in the tables, such that at times the standard score for a raw score increases as age increases.

SUMMARY. The WORD Test 3 Elementary is a careful attempt to assess an important diagnostic set of traits that can interfere with effective instruction. The norming study is more ambitious than was available in the past, but the sample is not representative of a clearly defined population. The test does appear to be reasonable in suggesting avenues of exploration to a clinician who is working with learning issues in an elementary age student but should not be used in the absence of supporting evidence from other sources.

REVIEWER'S REFERENCES

Donahue, M. (1985). [Test review of The WORD Test]. In J. V. Mitchell, Jr. (Ed.), *The ninth mental measurements yearbook*. Retrieved from http://marketplace.unl.edu/buros/

Sabers, D. L., & Sun, H. (2007). [Test review of The WORD Test 2: Elementary]. In K. F. Geisinger, R. A. Spies, J. F. Carlson, & B. S. Plake (Eds.), *The seventeenth mental measurements yearbook*. Retrieved from http://marketplace.unl.edu/buros

Review of The WORD Test 3 Elementary by JEFFREY H. SNOW, Associate Professor of Pediatrics/ Pediatric Neuropsychologist, Department of Pediatrics, University of Arkansas for Medical Sciences, Little Rock, AR:

DESCRIPTION. The WORD Test 3 Elementary is an individually administered measure designed to assess vocabulary and semantic skills. The test authors indicate that children need to understand semantic concepts among words in order to progress with such skills as reading comprehension. They further report that this measure can be useful in structuring therapy. The measure is designed for children ages 6-0 through 11-11. The test comprises six subtests that are as follows: Associations, Synonyms, Semantic Absurdities, Antonyms, Definitions, and Flexible Word Use. Each subtest is composed of 15 items, all of which are administered to the child. For the Associations subtest, the child must select the one semantically unrelated word from among four words. For the Synonyms subtest, the child is to provide a one-word synonym for each test item. In Semantic Absurdities, the child must recognize incongruity within a presented statement. The Antonyms subtest requires the child to provide a one-word opposite for each test item. For the Definitions subtest, the child must provide the meaning of each test item. The Flexible Word Use subtest requires the child to express two different meanings for each test item.

The administration instructions are clearly written and easy to follow. The only material required for test administration is the test form, although the examiner's manual provides example answers and is needed for scoring the measure. The fact that there is no basal or ceiling for the subtests makes administration easy. The test authors indicate that about 30 minutes is required for administration.

DEVELOPMENT. The test authors note that there has been a growing body of literature showing the importance of development of language skills and the effect this has on children's classroom performance and functioning in other environments. These findings prompted them to develop an update to the second edition of this test. The second version of this test was released in 2004, and the authors wanted to provide updated norms and remove or change items that were no longer valid. A guiding principle for this measure is that children's ability to understand word meaning increases their expressive and receptive language skills. As the test authors note, children with weak vocabulary skills and other language difficulties struggle with academic and social development. They report that this measure provides information that can help structure intervention, particularly for children from less stimulating environments. The test authors indicate this test also can provide a means to evaluate a child's progress with therapy and other intervention.

TECHNICAL. The test authors used demographic information from the 2004 Census for standardization. The sample consisted of 1,302 children selected from 43 states. The age range was 6-0 through 11-11. Data from an additional 367 children who were identified with a language disorder were used in a validity study. There was broad ethnicity with Caucasian (66%), African American (13%), Hispanic (17%), and other groups (4%) represented. The children were from all socioeconomic status (SES) levels that were evenly divided across high, middle, and low income levels and were enrolled in regular and/or special education. The children selected with individualized education plans received instruction in both the regular and special education classrooms. The standardization data collection ran from February 2014 to May 2014.

The standardization study showed 6-month intervals were sensitive to vocabulary development. The test manual provides means, medians, and standard deviations for raw score values for each age level, subtest, and the total test. Male-female comparisons for each subtest and the total test at each age level were calculated using *t*-tests. This analysis yielded three significant differences, and the test authors report that this finding supports using the combined male-female norms. The test manual provides tables with the following data: number of participants, means, medians, and standard deviations for each task and total test by age; age equivalents of raw scores for each task and total test; and raw scores, percentile ranks, and standard score values for each task and total test by age.

In terms of reliability, the test authors report test-retest reliability coefficients and standard errors of measurement (*SEM*s) for each subtest and total test by age. The interval between test sessions is not specified. Values are provided at 6-month intervals. Coefficients for subtests ranged from .18 to .97. The median values for each subtest ranged from .77 to .86. Coefficients for the total test ranged from .82 to .97 with a median value of .91. The *SEM*s for each subtest ranged from .41 to 2.22 with median values ranging from .92 to 1.46. The *SEM*s for the total test ranged from 2.19 to 6.78 with a median value of 4.10.

The test authors also report internal consistency estimates of reliability using KR20 coefficients and interscorer coefficients. Internal consistency values for the subtests ranged from .58 to .85 with the median values from .68 to .82. The values for the total test ranged from .92 to .96 with a median value of .94. The test authors examined interscorer reliability by selecting 15 test forms randomly and having each scored by six speech-language pathologists. Each clinician scored all of the items on the test. The test authors calculated the percent agreement among the six speech-language pathologists. The percentages ranged from 90% to 96% with a median of 94%.

The test authors report data to support the validity of the WORD Test 3 scores and their uses. In one study, randomly selected participants from the normative sample were compared with a mixed matched sample of participants identified with a language disorder. The test authors used *t*-test comparisons. The results show that all but four of the differences were statistically significant ($p < .01$ level). Results for the Flexible Word Use subtest did not reach statistical significance for four of the 12 age groups. In another analysis, the relationship among the six subtests was examined using correlations. The correlation coefficients were generally moderate, and the test authors interpreted this as showing that the subtests assess separate language functions but are still part of a general language construct.

Data are presented examining racial and SES differences in test performance. The test authors randomly selected samples of Caucasian, African American, and Hispanic children, and the percentage of participants passing each item across the three groups was compared using *z*-test comparisons. The results showed 14% of the 3,240 *z*-tests were significant and randomly distributed. The test authors then examined subtest performance using chi square tests. For each group, children above and below the subtest median and 75th percentile were compared. The results showed three of 144 chi square statistics reached significance. An analysis of variance (ANOVA) comparing number correct for each subtest was conducted and 6% reached significance. Finally, the test authors used a two-factor ANOVA to investigate racial/SES differences. These data showed 56 of 72 comparisons were not statistically significant, and none of the race by SES interactions reached significance. The test authors interpret all of the data to show that the test is free from racial bias.

COMMENTARY. The WORD Test 3 Elementary is a relatively brief measure that assesses different aspects of language function. The test is easy to administer and requires only the protocol and test manual. The fact that there is not a basal or ceiling within each subtest makes administration easy but does present risks with children administered this measure. Younger children or those with a significant language disorder may become frustrated early on given the number of items they will likely miss. This can affect their effort on later subtests. The reliability data are solid, although the test authors do not report the interval between testing for the test-retest data. The validity information is good, although additional studies outside of the normative sample should be completed. This test will be particularly useful for speech-language pathologists or child psychologist/pediatric neuropsychologists who need more specific information concerning language functions.

SUMMARY. The WORD Test 3 Elementary is an individually administered test designed to assess vocabulary and semantic skills with children. The data do support that this test assesses different aspects of language functions as well as a general language construct. The test manual is clear and straightforward, and the test is easy to administer and score. Additional validity evidence from different clinical samples would be useful, but clinicians can be confident in using this measure.

[188]

Work Motivation Scale.

Purpose: Designed to assist "individuals in career development and planning by helping them understand their work motives and values and apply that understanding to their career choices and preferred work environment."
Population: Ages 13-65.
Publication Dates: 2002-2008.
Acronym: WMS.
Scores, 12: Survival and Safety Motives (Earnings and Benefits, Working Conditions), Affiliation Motives (Coworker Relations, Supervisor Relations), Self-Esteem Motives (Task Orientation, Managing Others), Fulfillment Motives (Mission Orientation, Success Orientation).
Administration: Individual or group.
Price Data, 2020: $61.95 per 25 scales; administrator's guide (2008, 16 pages) may be downloaded at no charge.
Time: Administration time not reported.

Author: Robert P. Brady.
Publisher: JIST Career Solutions, a division of Kendall Hunt.
Cross References: For reviews by Alan C. Bugbee, Jr. and Bert A. Goldman of an earlier version titled Work Orientation Values Survey, see 17:204.

Review of the Work Motivation Scale by JAMES T. AUSTIN, Program Lead for Assessment Services for Center on Education and Training for Employment, The Ohio State University, Columbus, OH:

DESCRIPTION. Work Motivation Scale (WMS) materials state, on the cover of the instrument, that scores can "identify key work values and motives," which then can be used "to improve career satisfaction and success." The WMS is a 32-item scale with 5-point Likert responses that can be administered in group or individual settings; it consists of a colorful six-page booklet and a 15-page administrator's guide, both copyrighted 2008. The WMS represents a revision by Robert P. Brady of his Work Orientation and Values Survey (WOVS; 2002). The WOVS was reviewed in *The Seventeenth Mental Measurements Yearbook* by Bugbee (2007) and by Goldman (2007). This review, therefore, adds an evaluation of progress made by the developer and publisher since those reviews appeared.

The stated purposes are to measure and identify eight key work values and four work motives (each comprised of two work values). Featured on the cover of the booklet are two of the constructs measured (work values, motives) and two key outcomes (career satisfaction and success). Target populations are adolescent and adult job seekers and incumbents, with separate norms provided for youth and adults. Intended uses involve self- or counselor-directed career planning. These features, taken together, establish a framework for developing and evaluating validity evidence to support score interpretations related to career satisfaction and occupational choice. The administrator's guide is free to download from the publisher's website.

Scoring is a six-step process that can be completed by the test taker (although this reviewer could not find guidance for what ages self-scoring would be inappropriate). The capability of self-scoring with comparisons to norms makes the scale one that can be used with youth and adult populations, although reading levels could affect quality of responses.

DEVELOPMENT. Construct definition is a crucial step in the development and validation of any measure. Underlying assumptions of the scale seem to be related to theories published after 1950 (Ginzberg, Ginsburg, Axelrad, & Herma, 1951; Super, 1957; Super & Bohn, 1970). Those theories have evolved, and new theories are available. The theory of work adjustment proposed by Dawis and Lofquist (1984), for example, is a framework that provides a work importance measure (Minnesota Importance Questionnaire); the Occupational Information Network (O*NET) also offers a measure derived from the theory of work adjustment framework. Carlstrom and Hughey (2014) provide a useful tutorial on exploring work values. The literature review in the WMS administrator's guide was expanded by adding sources that appeared from 2002 to 2008 and broadened by adding citations to industrial-organizational psychology research.

The WMS represents a minor revision of a previous instrument (WOVS), occurring just after the 2007 reviews by Bugbee and Goldman, which establishes a lens for viewing the WMS in terms of responsiveness to the two reviews. According to those reviewers, there was insufficient detail on scale development. A new subscale (four items measuring Success Orientation) is described in greater detail in this version; the focus was clearly operational and not conceptual-theoretical in terms of the guiding framework of career development. In particular, the following sequence was described: (1) a pool of 16 possible items was created and mixed with eight non-relevant items; (2) the combined pool of 24 items was presented to a panel of counseling and psychology experts ($n = 4$), who were asked to judge the motive category for each of the items in the pool; (3) results indicated a coefficient of agreement of .98 for the pool of 16 items (the specific measure was not given); and (4) four of the 16 items were selected for the 2008 revision that produced the WMS, although the basis for their selection was not provided (for example, item-total correlations with motive category or construct).

TECHNICAL. Technical information about the WMS is provided in the sections of the administrator's guide on validity, reliability, and normative information. Validity is important for establishing evidence supporting scale score interpretations. Reliability indices support the consistency and precision of responses (and may limit criterion-related evidence of validity). Norms are important aids for interpreting scores. These desiderata are discussed in order.

Validity is claimed for WMS score interpretations under content and criterion (concurrent) evidence of validity. Content evidence of validity was claimed for the earlier WOVS, which provided seven of the eight constructs, based on complete agreement of three content experts about item-construct match attributed to the original version's administrator's guide. New evidence was provided in the development of the Success Orientation construct as follows: the 16 newly developed Success Orientation items were combined with eight other motive category items (perhaps the same set of 24 items presented to the expert panel, but it is unclear) and administered to 20 working adults. The split-half reliability estimate, corrected by Spearman-Brown, was .89. The claim at the end of this section was that results "suggested strong validity and reliability had been established for the four new Success Orientation items" (administrator's guide, p. 4).

Concurrent/criterion evidence of validity was provided through a sample of 62 working adults who provided scale responses and their significant others who were asked to respond on the WMS from the perspective of the focal respondent. All paired *t*-test results for participant and significant other for the four motive categories and the eight subordinate constructs were non-significant. This suggests only that there were no statistically significant average differences. This design, however, may not provide the type of evidence needed to support the claims of the developer that scores can be used to "improve career satisfaction." No convergent evidence was proposed for validity, which could be evaluated by correlating WMS scores with measures that claim to assess similar constructs as noted above (O*NET Work Importance Profiler and the Theory of Work Adjustment Minnesota Importance Questionnaire).

Reliability evidence is provided in the administrator's guide for one split-half and two test-retest samples. Split-half estimates were computed from a sample of 62 working adults (described only by age range [20-60 years] and mean [38.2 years]). Coefficients ranged from .60 (Earnings and Benefits) to .89 (Managing Others). Test-retest reliability results from two studies indicated ranges of .71 to .91 (N = 42 community college students) and .79 to .93 (N = 26 volunteer sample of adult participants). The studies reportedly occurred during consecutive months (i.e., February and March 2007, August and September 2007), but precise retest intervals were not provided. Standard errors of measurement for raw scores and T scores were presented in the administrator's guide for both youth and adults. The logic of using a standardized score was not provided, a point noted by previous reviewers, but logic could be developed based on the norm-referenced model.

Normative information is provided in the guide for youth and adults. Specifically, two tables in the guide provide normative information for value constructs (eight) and motive categories (four) based on a sample of 453 youth; two tables for adults provide similar information, although the sample size is more limited (n = 142). Although the current norm tables are based on a larger sample than the WOVS and added samples of youth, the sample population was limited to three Midwestern states and not well described except for age range (possibly a convenience sample, with numerous individuals thanked in the administrator's guide for assisting in data collection). No norms are provided based on gender or ethnicity.

COMMENTARY. To what extent did the developer respond to the critiques from Bugbee and from Goldman in this revision, undertaken after their 2007 reviews? There is some new literature cited, a broadening of the citations to include organizational and human resource considerations. A new subscale was developed and described in better detail. Additional data collection did occur, especially in much larger normative samples (600+ responses compared to 74 noted in the 2007 reviews). The problematic aspect remains that samples are not well described, and therefore less confidence can be placed in the results.

SUMMARY. In evaluating this revision, it is important to judge the extent to which the developer was effectively motivated by the critiques in an earlier volume of the Mental Measurements Yearbook series (2007).

Although there were some changes including a more expansive and updated literature review, it is difficult to follow the logic among the citations. Adding research and theory from industrial-organizational psychology is helpful given the focus on values and motives in the workplace. There is a consistent rooting of this scale and its predecessor, the WOVS, in the work of Ginzberg et al. (1951) and Super (1957), but attention to more recent work in this area would help support the constructs developed. Evidence tends to support reliability (split-half, test-retest), but confidence is lower because of the small samples, which are described variably. Some validity evidence for content and concurrent relationships is provided, but convergent strategies should be conducted to estimate relationships with better-established instruments (e.g.,

Minnesota Theory of Work Adjustment, O*NET Work Importance Profiler). The test developer could increase confidence in the external relationships of the scale with outcome-based studies across school, work, or sports settings.

There has been little published research that uses the WMS, other than that of the author-developer, so this reviewer believes that usage must occur in practice settings where it is incumbent on developers and users to temper claims for score interpretation with the boundaries of the empirical support. This scale, therefore, could be improved in its foundation, development, evidence, and technical qualities.

REVIEWER'S REFERENCES

Brady, R. P. (1972). *An examination of selected variables affecting the vocational development of elementary school children.* (Doctoral dissertation, University of Cincinnati, 1971.) Dissertation Abstracts International, 32(7), 3681-3682 (University Microfilms, 72-2958).

Bugbee, A. C., Jr. (2007). [Test review of Work Orientation and Values Survey]. In K. F. Geisinger, R. A. Spies, J. F. Carlson, & B. S. Plake (Eds.), *The seventeenth mental measurements yearbook* (pp. 880-882). Lincoln, NE: Buros Institute of Mental Measurements.

Carlstrom, A. H., & Hughey, K. F. (2014). Exploring work values: Helping students articulate their good (work) life. *NCADA Journal, 34*(2), 5-15.

Dawis, R., & Lofquist, L. H. (1984). *A psychological theory of work adjustment.* Minneapolis, MN: University of Minnesota Press.

Ginzberg, E., Ginsburg, S. W., Axelrad, S., & Herma, J. L. (1951). *Occupational choice: An approach to a general theory.* New York, NY: Columbia University Press.

Goldman, B. A. (2007). [Test review of Work Orientation and Values Survey]. In K. F. Geisinger, R. A. Spies, J. F. Carlson, & B. S. Plake (Eds.), *The seventeenth mental measurements yearbook* (pp. 882-883). Lincoln, NE: Buros Institute of Mental Measurements.

Super, D. E. (1957). *The psychology of careers.* New York, NY: Harper.

Super, D. E., & Bohn, M. J. (1970). *Occupational psychology.* Belmont, CA: Wadsworth.

Review of the Work Motivation Scale by JEFFREY A. JENKINS, Professor of Justice Studies, Roger Williams University, Bristol, RI:

DESCRIPTION. The Work Motivation Scale (WMS) is a revision of the Work Orientation Values Scale (WOVS), first published in 2002. Its name was changed in 2008 to better reflect the use of the instrument in assisting individuals to "understand their work motives ... and apply that understanding to their career choices and preferred work environment" (administrator's guide, p. 1). Like its predecessor, the WMS was developed to assist counselors and workplace administrators in examining the work motives and values of individuals. It is a self-report measure that was designed to be an easy to use and interpret survey of respondents' motives concerning their work or work interests.

The WMS is composed of 32 items intended to measure four categories of work motives: Survival and Safety Motives, Affiliation Motives, Self-Esteem Motives, and Fulfillment Motives. Survival and Safety Motives are described as the desire for adequate wages, favorable benefits, and a safe and secure work environment. Affiliation Motives involve acceptance by and cooperation with coworkers and supervisors. Self-Esteem Motives are those related to a need for challenging and meaningful work and the opportunity for responsibility and achievement. Fulfillment Motives relate to an individual's opportunities in the workplace to achieve their highest potential.

Each of these categories consists of two value scales (called *constructs* in the administrator's guide), measured by four items per scale. Survival and Safety Motives consists of the Earnings and Benefits scale and the Working Conditions scale. The Earnings and Benefits scale reflects the importance an individual places on salary, vacation, and other work benefits; the Working Conditions scale involves the value individuals place on the physical work environment and availability of resources to accomplish their work.

Affiliation Motives consists of the Coworker Relations and Supervisor Relations scales. Coworker Relations involves the need for collaboration and participation in coworker activities. The Supervisor Relations scale involves the need to satisfy one's supervisor and gain recognition from doing so.

Self-Esteem Motives consists of the Task Orientation and Managing Others scales. Task Orientation measures the importance of planning and focusing on the job at hand, and Managing Others relates to whether individuals value the performance of their department or other work unit and desire opportunities to supervise others.

Finally, the Fulfillment Motives category consists of Mission Orientation and Success Orientation scales. Mission Orientation is the desire to participate in work that clearly contributes to the "big picture" for the organization. Success Orientation involves accomplishing one's career goals using work to achieve potential.

The 32 items are all answered using a 5-point Likert-type scale on which a respondent indicates *very important* (5 points), *important* (4 points), *somewhat important* (3 points) *of little importance* (2 points), or *not important* (1 point) to a characteristic or aspect of work in response to the question "How important is each of these to you in your work?" The items are presented as short descriptive phrases. Each item is shown on the response form in a different color that corresponds to the value it represents. Responses to each item are recorded by circling the number on the rating scale that corresponds to the respondent's view of the importance of each item to his or her work.

After rating each of the items, respondents total their ratings for the four items within each of the eight value scales. These totals are then placed upon a profile that allows respondents to examine the relative importance of the eight value constructs. Respondents are then asked to find the three value scales with the highest scores. Next, respondents calculate motive scores by summing the two value scores that comprise each of the four work motives and find the two highest motive scores. Using the highest value scores and motive scores, respondents are asked to consider (and write down) their minimum acceptable and preferred work values (e.g., minimum earnings and preferred earnings). These results presumably serve as the basis for career exploration. Instructions for scoring are printed on the instrument itself, and the administrator's guide also provides assistance with scoring and tips for interpretation.

DEVELOPMENT. The precursor to the WMS, the WOVS, was developed in recognition of the central role played by motives and values in career development and occupational choice. Based on vocational theory and research stretching back to the 1950s, the WMS seeks to relate the desire for productive and satisfying work to the values and motives a person brings to the work setting. Although the administrator's guide provides a useful summary of some of this literature, it does not specifically discuss how the instrument was designed or the items developed and written.

As a revision of the WOVS, the WMS was expanded to include a new scale, Success Orientation, which replaced the Time Orientation scale from the previous edition, and the classification scheme placing each of the scales within one of the four work motives and calculating associated scores was adopted. Development of the Success Orientation scale involved creating a pool of 16 new items reflecting the construct. These items were mixed with other items from the WOVS and presented to a panel of four experts who identified them with near-perfect agreement as reflecting Fulfillment Motives. These 16 items were then included along with eight other items from the WOVS in a pilot test administered to a sample of 20 working adults. The split-half reliability of this research instrument was found to be .89, and four items were selected to represent Success Orientation (as well as Fulfillment Motives) in the WMS.

TECHNICAL. The administrator's guide notes that the content evidence of validity for the items comprising the seven value scales carried over to the WMS from the WOVS was established by a study involving agreement among three experts that the original items measured the value scale construct it was intended to assess. It is also stated in the administrator's guide that the development process and pilot testing of the additional four items measuring Success Orientation support the content validity of this new scale.

The guide also contains a brief description of the validity of the WMS based on a sample of working adults and their significant others. The significant others were asked to complete the instrument "as if they were the participants" (administrator's guide, p. 4). Paired *t*-tests were conducted between the participant and significant other groups for each of the value and motives scales, resulting in no significant differences between the groups. This finding is presented as support for concurrent evidence of validity.

Internal consistency and test-retest reliability were examined for the WMS. Split-half reliability estimates for each scale were provided for a sample of 63 working adults and showed Spearman-Brown correlation coefficients of .60 to .89. Test-retest reliability coefficients—apparently over a 1- to 2-month interval—were provided for a sample of 42 college students (r = .71 to .91) and a sample of 26 adults (r = .79 to .93). Tables of norms for a sample of youths (n = 453) and adults (n = 142) showing raw scores and T scores are also presented in the administrator's guide. In addition, tables reporting the standard errors of measurement for youths and adults are included. Aside from a note indicating that urban, suburban, rural, and small-town schools participated in the norming study, no further information is provided about either the youth or adult samples, their representativeness, or how the study was conducted.

COMMENTARY. The WMS appears useful as a brief measure of career orientation. The instrument is easy to use by both test administrators and respondents in the career counseling setting. Scoring is straightforward, and interpretation of the scale results does not require specialized training, though an understanding of the role of values and motives in decision making would be beneficial to users.

Although the revisions in the WMS involving the addition of work motives scales may be warranted, these additional scale scores are summations of the seven original scales plus the new Success Orientation scale. This manner of scoring may be theoretically justified, but no construct evidence of validity is presented to support it or to support the claim that the instrument measures both value constructs and work motives. Moreover, the discussion in the administrator's guide reporting criterion-related evidence of validity does not explain how the reported study, in which participants responded to the WMS as if they were their significant others, constitutes an adequate criterion to support the criterion-related evidence of validity for the instrument. Given this uncertainty regarding the validity of the scale scores, the instrument may serve as an exploratory tool, but it should not be considered a definitive measure of values or motives relating to work as individuals explore their occupational options.

The split-half reliability coefficients reported are generally high for this type of instrument, and the estimation of reliability in different samples that include participants in different occupations and different stages of their work life is to be commended. It is not clear, however, why norms are presented when no reference is made to interpreting scale scores using such norms, or why the norms tables include T scores, when neither the instrument itself nor the administrator's guide refers to calculating or interpreting T scores in practice.

SUMMARY. The WMS is a revision of the WOVS, including a change of the instrument's name. Like its predecessor, it is intended to be used in career counseling and to help individuals understand their work motives and values. As such, it reliably measures eight values and four work motives that the values reflect. The content validity evidence of the items on the WMS appears to be supported; the construct evidence and criterion-related evidence of validity of both the values scale scores and the motives scale scores are less clear. Caution should therefore be used regarding over-reliance on the scales to make individual decisions about career interests.

[189]

The Work Self-Efficacy Inventory.

Purpose: Designed to "measure job behaviors referring to beliefs in one's command of the social requirements necessary for success in the workplace."
Population: Working adults.
Publication Date: 2010.
Acronym: WS-Ei.
Scores, 8: Learning, Problem Solving, Pressure, Role Expectations, Teamwork, Sensitivity, Work Politics, Overall Work Self-Efficacy.
Administration: Individual or group.
Forms, 2: Form A (self version), Form B (performance version).
Price Data, 2020: $50 per PDF manual (48 pages); $60 per paper manual; $15 per Individual Report: Self Form; $15 per Report About Me: Self Form; $200 per Group Report: Self Form; $2.50 per Transform Survey Hosting: Self Form (minimum purchase of 20); $2.50 per Remote Online Survey License or License to Reproduce (minimum purchase of 50).
Time: Approximately 10 minutes for administration of Form A and 5 minutes for administration of Form B.
Author: Joseph A. Raelin.
Publisher: Mind Garden, Inc.

Review of the Work Self-Efficacy Inventory by SHANI D. CARTER, Professor of Business, Wagner College, Staten Island, NY:

DESCRIPTION. The Work Self-Efficacy Inventory (WS-Ei) is an individually or group administered measure of self-report or other-report of seven dimensions of self-efficacy (i.e., Learning, Problem Solving, Pressure, Role Expectations, Teamwork, Sensitivity, and Work Politics) and performance designed for adults. High scores on dimensions indicate areas that can "lead to both personal goal accomplishment and individual performance" (manual, p. 47). Low scores on dimensions point to behaviors that can be used to enhance those dimensions in order to improve performance.

For Form A, the self-report, the examinee is given a single-page, black-and-white survey consisting of 30 items. Using the prompt, "Thinking about your most recent work experience, how confident are you in your ability to," the examinee responds to items such as knowing what is expected of them in various contexts. The instrument uses a 5-point scale (i.e., *not at all*, *a little*, *a moderate amount*, *a lot*, *completely*). There are four to six items for each of the seven dimensions.

For Form B, a performance-based measure, the examinee (or the other rater) is given a single-page, black-and-white survey consisting of eight items that purport to measure dimensions of performance that indicate self-efficacy. Using the prompt, "Thinking about your (his or her) most recent work experience, how successful have you (has [name of person]) been," the examinee (or other) responds to items such as knowing work expectations during recent work experiences. The instrument uses the same 5-point scale. There is one item for each of the seven dimensions and one for the composite scale.

For Form A, for scoring purposes, examinees or administrators calculate a mean score for each of the seven dimensions and a mean score for the 30 items, with the range of possible scores being 1 to 5 for each dimension. Examinees or administrators then compare the scores to those of the normative sample and convert raw scores to T scores with a mean of 50 and a standard deviation of 10. This step enables examinees to see how their scores compare to scores for 2,628 other people. The T scores can be plotted on a histogram to create a visualization of how examinees compare to the norming group. Examinees interpret their scores by considering the definitions of the dimensions and descriptions of activities to undertake to improve the dimensions of self-efficacy.

The administration instructions for the instrument are clear and easy to follow, as is the instrument itself, which is written at the undergraduate level. The test author states it should take 10 to 15 minutes to complete the instrument, which seems appropriate based on the instrument's content.

DEVELOPMENT. The WS-Ei was developed to help employees and supervisors identify employees' self-efficacy, which "can lead to both personal goal accomplishment and individual performance" (manual, p. 47).

The author relied heavily upon relevant literature, in particular the scale-development literature, supplemented by dozens of journal articles from top journals and texts examining construction of self-efficacy and motivation scales and theories of self-efficacy and self-confidence. The literature review is comprehensive and appropriate, albeit dated, because the vast majority of references cited were published in 2002 or earlier.

The description of the item development process is quite detailed. For each of the seven dimensions (i.e., Learning, Problem Solving, Pressure, Role Expectations, Teamwork, Sensitivity, and Work Politics), the test author cited literature to provide a theoretical basis for the dimension along with a review of existing scales that measure the dimension. All items were taken from existing scales or developed by consulting existing scales.

The author began with a pool of 95 items and used ratings from 21 expert judges to sort the items into dimensions, resulting in the retention of 85 items in nine dimensions. The author piloted the scale on 415 undergraduates and used exploratory and confirmatory factor analyses to decrease the number of items to 36 across nine dimensions with two to six items each. Coefficient alpha for the nine dimensions ranged from .69 to .87.

A second study was conducted using the 36 items in nine dimensions with a sample of 214 continuing education students. Confirmatory factor analysis results suggested that there should be five dimensions, but because two dimensions (i.e., Working under Pressure and Role Expectations) contained three items each, the author added two items to each dimension from the original set of items. This addition resulted in a total of 40 items, but the author did not explain how the added items were selected or how the number of items was pared down to the final 30 items used in the WS-Ei.

TECHNICAL. Detailed validity and reliability statistics are not provided for the final version of the instrument. Test-retest and interrater reliability analyses were not provided, so the assertion that self-efficacy is a dispositional trait, and not an emotional state, is not supported in the view of this reviewer.

It is not possible to state whether the dimensions in the final version of the instrument have internal consistency or whether the dimensions are independent. The final version of the instrument consisting of 30 items was examined for validity and reliability using 1,638 undergraduates, but factor loadings and coefficient alpha for the dimensions are not provided. The test author stated "all items loaded on the first factor ... explaining 38.5% of the total variance" and "factor coefficients ranged from .383 to .710" (manual, p. 19). Coefficient alpha for the entire scale was reported as .94.

The author provided a correlation matrix of the seven dimensions, which showed only one correlation was less than .30 (i.e., Problem Solving and Role Expectations, r = .28), while about one third (i.e., 8 of 21) of the correlations were above .50. These high correlations cast doubt upon the author's assertion that the dimensions are independent constructs.

The author also provided results of analysis of comparison of the seven subscale dimensions with the performance ratings of 36 employee-supervisor pairs to determine whether the scale is useful as a predictor of job performance. Although many of the correlations were significant at the .05 level and were above .30, to this reviewer no pattern of the correlations appeared showing any dimension of self-efficacy having a strong relationship to a single aspect of performance or vice-versa. These results further reinforce the doubt of the test author's assertion that the dimensions are independent constructs. It is possible that there are too few items per dimension for the dimensions to be measured accurately without Type I and Type II errors, given that six of the seven dimensions contain only four items each.

The test author conducted an Equal Employment Opportunity Commission (EEOC) analysis using a sample of 260 middle managers, analyzing scores by race and ethnicity (i.e., African American, White, Hispanic/Latino; Native American/Alaskan) and by gender. The author provided only summary statistics for the groups (i.e., percent of group that scored at or above the 30th percentile on general population norms), and demonstrated that each group passed the EEOC 4/5 rule of thumb for adverse impact. It would be preferable, however, for the author to provide raw scores on each dimension for each group to demonstrate whether any dimensions of the instrument are likely to cause adverse impact. Analysis was not provided to indicate whether mean score differences between men and women or between different racial or ethnic groups were statistically significant. Geographic location and demographic characteristics such as age, gender, and race are not provided for any of the analyses except the EEOC analysis, which included race/ethnicity and gender.

COMMENTARY. The WS-Ei is a relatively brief, easy-to-administer, and easy-to-interpret measure of the self-report or other-report of seven dimensions of self-efficacy or performance (i.e., Learning, Problem Solving, Pressure, Role Expectations, Teamwork, Sensitivity, and Work Politics).

Its key strengths are that it is based on a wealth of relevant literature and that the instrument is simple to use. In addition, it can be self-administered and self-scored, allowing employees and job seekers to reflect upon their strengths and weaknesses in private. Scoring is simple, consisting of calculating means of 30 items in groups of four to six on a scale of 1 to 5.

Additional reliability and validity work is needed to establish stability of scores, independence of the seven dimensions via factor analysis, and the relationship of the dimensions to scales produced by other authors. Data are not provided to support the assertion that the seven dimensions are independent.

The WS-Ei also has not been rigorously evaluated for use across populations, and data on the validity and reliability for different populations are lacking. Raw scores and norms should be provided for demographic characteristics such as age, gender, race, and educational level so employees can have a framework from which to interpret scores.

SUMMARY. The WS-Ei was designed to be an individually or group administered measure of self-efficacy that would be of use to employees in determining how to use different behaviors to increase self-efficacy with the goal of improving their performance. The instrument meets its goal of measuring a single construct of self-efficacy, but, unfortunately, the independence of the seven dimensions is not supported by data, so using the instrument to measure independent dimensions is not recommended.

Review of The Work Self-Efficacy Inventory by JANET V. SMITH, Assistant Vice President for Institutional Assessment, Pittsburg State University, Pittsburg, KS:

DESCRIPTION. The Work Self-Efficacy Inventory (WS-Ei) is a quick and easy inventory designed to measure confidence and success in a range of key job behaviors and abilities. These areas include learning, problem solving, dealing with pressure, understanding and managing role expectations, teamwork, sensitivity to others, and managing work politics. As such, the WS-Ei assesses soft skills related to social requirements of successful workplace behaviors. In addition to these seven specific areas, the measure also addresses overall work self-efficacy. There are two forms of the test. The self-version, or Form A, is a 30-item self-report measure of confidence in one's own abilities. Respondents are asked to consider their most recent work experience and rate their confidence in specific work-related behaviors on a 5-point Likert scale, ranging from *not at all confident* to *completely confident*. The performance version, or Form B, is an eight-item performance-based measure that can be completed by others, with a single item addressing each of the identified work areas of the 30-item inventory. According to the test manual, Form B also can be self-administered. Rather than asking about level of confidence, the respondent is asked to consider recent work experience and rate level of success in each work efficacy area, also on a 5-point Likert scale, ranging from *not at all successful* to *completely successful*.

The WS-Ei takes approximately 10 minutes to complete and is available in both pencil-and-paper and web-based versions. According to the manual, the test is particularly useful for new or prospective workers. No age range is specified nor is a minimum reading level provided; however, test items appear very straightforward. The test is scored by simply summing responses for each subscale and dividing by the number of subscale items in order to derive the mean. The test manual provides a table for conversion of raw scores into T scores.

The manual suggests a number of applications for the WS-Ei, including professional and personal development and as a tool for performance feedback, managerial encouragement, and 360-degree feedback. The manual also briefly notes it may be useful to administer both self and other versions of Form B in order to compare self and rater evaluations of performance.

DEVELOPMENT. The WS-Ei is based on both review of literature on self-efficacy and empirical data. A major component of the development of each scale was review of existing scales relevant to each dimension, with many items adapted for use from existing scales. Items developed through review of the literature were subject to expert judge analysis and factor analysis, resulting in 36 items retained from an original pool of 95 potential items. The test manual does not detail how the final 30 items were selected. Exploratory factor analysis showed high factor loadings onto single scales for most test items, although many subscales show a high level of intercorrelation.

TECHNICAL. Psychometric data provided in the test materials are quite sparse. A single set of norms is provided, based on what appears to be a collection of samples totaling 2,628 respondents. No information is provided regarding the nature of this normative sample, beyond sample size. Regarding reliability of the instrument, a number of coefficient alpha reliability coefficients are provided. The internal consistency reliability of the full scale was estimated to be .94 in a sample of 1,638 undergraduate students. Subscale reliability coefficients are also provided for the 36-item version. Information regarding validity is quite limited. A factor-analytic study with the sample of 1,638 sophomore undergraduates reportedly yielded factor coefficients ranging from .383 to .710, but no details of specific factor loadings are provided. The test manual reports findings from one validity study involving correlations between the seven WS-Ei subscale scores and performance ratings for a group of 36 middle managers, with multiple significant correlations showing promising support for the instrument. No other information regarding the study is provided. Finally, the manual reports findings related to the Equal Employment Opportunity Commission (EEOC) 4/5ths compliance rule, indicating no adverse findings with use of the instrument. However, of the 260 participants in the study, some minority groups had as few as two or five participants, making it difficult to draw firm conclusions.

The test manual contains a section devoted to ongoing research and poses several research questions as well as identifies a limited number of studies using the WS-Ei. Findings appear promising, but insufficient detail is provided to evaluate results.

All technical information provided appears to apply to Form A only, with no mention of Form B, either in terms of development or psychometric properties.

COMMENTARY. The WS-Ei is very user-friendly, both from the perspective of the test taker and the test user. It is quick to administer, and scoring is quite simple. Conceptually, the test covers a number of dimensions of perceived self-efficacy and perceived performance in a range of key job behaviors and abilities related to social requirements of successful workplace behaviors. Currently, more complete psychometric data, especially relating to validity, are lacking. Although normative data are provided, there is limited information provided regarding demographics of the normative sample, making it impossible to evaluate representativeness of norms. In addition, the very limited validity data presented are based on use with student populations or involve inadequate sample sizes and are again lacking in detail. The test author recognizes need for additional validity studies and encourages further research using the instrument. Of note, information about test development references a 36-item instrument, whereas the actual WS-Ei Form A is comprised of only 30 items. The reason for this discrepancy is unclear.

SUMMARY. Overall, the WS-Ei shows promise for use in evaluating a number of important work-related soft skills, but lack of adequate psychometric data makes it difficult to recommend use of this instrument at this time. Users are especially cautioned regarding normative data, as insufficient data are available to evaluate their potential for use. Rather, at this time, the test may be used for self-reflection and to generate useful discussion regarding job behaviors and abilities, but test data should not be used for evaluation or decision-making purposes until psychometric properties are more fully established.

[190]

Work Values Inventory.

Purpose: "A career exploration and job selection tool developed to assess an individual's work values ... [or] standards that determine an individual's attitude, choices, and actions related to the workplace."
Population: Ages 18 and older.
Publication Date: 2016.
Acronym: WVI.
Scores, 9: Achievement, Relationships, Independence, Working Conditions, Support, Recognition; 3 diagnostic indicators (Profile Elevation, Differentiation, Commonness).
Administration: Individual or group.
Price Data, 2020: $160 per introductory kit including professional manual (65 pages), fast guide, 25 assessment booklets, 25 score summary sheets, and 25 occupations indexes; $71 per professional manual and fast guide; $71 per 25 occupations indexes; $56 per 25 assessment booklets; $27 per 25 score summary sheets.
Time: (10) minutes.
Comments: "Developed to capture the six constructs of the O*NET Work Values model."
Authors: Melissa A. Messer and Jennifer A. Greene.
Publisher: Psychological Assessment Resources, Inc.

Review of the Work Values Inventory by DOUG LEIGH, Professor, Pepperdine University, and ZECCA LEHN, Independent Researcher, Huntington Beach, CA:

DESCRIPTION. The Work Values Inventory (WVI) is a 61-item measure designed to gauge the degree of importance that individuals place in six work values: Achievement, Independence, Support, Relationships, Working Conditions, and Recognition. The test authors indicate that the instrument is appropriate for individuals 18 years of age or older, with items written at a seventh-grade level.

The questionnaire may be self-administered, scored, and interpreted in an individual or group setting, with scoring optionally conducted by career counseling professionals. Responses are made on a 4-point Likert-type scale concerning the degree to which the respondent values 60 workplace opportunities related to the instrument's six constructs. A final item solicits whether the respondent answered honestly to the preceding 60 questions, accompanied by the options *yes* or *no*. The test developers indicate that the WVI takes about 10 minutes to complete and 5 minutes to score, which appears to be a reasonable approximation. Subsequent interpretation of these scores and their implications for vocational exploration through accompanying materials might be expected to require an additional 30 or more minutes per completed instrument.

If self-administered, the WVI consists of four activities: completing the instrument, scoring and identifying one's highest three work values, reviewing all six work values, and exploring jobs the respondent may wish to consider. Several websites are suggested as resources for further exploration. Additional activities are possible when the WVI is administered by a career counseling professional: determination of percentile ranks for each of the six work values and calculation and interpretation of Profile Elevation (sum score of all values), Differentiation (numeric range of highest minus lowest work value), and Commonness (frequency with which a respondent's top three work values were also present among a sample with which the WVI was standardized).

Completion. The instrument is formatted as a consumable eight-page paper booklet, with items appearing un-counterbalanced in six groups of 10 items. The 4-point response scale represents unbalanced construction, as three options are associated with positively valuing the workplace opportunities described (*somewhat, highly,* and *very highly*) and one option reflecting *not valued.* Respondents complete the WVI by circling one of these four response options.

Scoring. All items must be completed in order to obtain interpretable scores. Total scores for each of the six work values are calculated by counting the number of *somewhat value, highly value,* and *very highly value* responses in each block of 10 items. Somewhat, highly, and very highly value responses are weighted (x1, x2, x3, respectively) then summed for each of the work values to produce six total scores. Items rated *not valued* are excluded from scoring (that is, they are essentially scored as zero). After obtaining the six scores, respondents are instructed to list their top three work values in rank order. Should two or three values be tied, respondents are instructed to break the tie by ranking the Achievement scale highest, followed by Independence, Support, Relationships, Working Conditions, and Recognition. In the case of four or more tied work values, respondents are instructed to re-rate their responses to all items in scales with tied results.

Overview of the Six Work Values. A section in the assessment booklet titled "What Are Work Values?" variously describes them as needs, preferences, related to satisfaction, and related to jobs in which one might excel or be a good fit. Respondents are provided a description of the six work values, two "facets" associated with each, and examples of jobs said to capitalize on each value.

Jobs to Consider. As "Next Steps," respondents are encouraged to "explore your interests, and think about which skills and abilities are your strongest." They are also advised to consult an accompanying booklet, the WVI Occupations Index, which lists various occupations by their highest-rated work value. The index is organized first by highest-ranked work value, then requisite education level, then alphabetically. Eight-digit codes from the U.S. Department of Labor's Occupational Information Network (O*NET) database are provided. Second and third highest-ranked work values from the O*NET database are also provided in the index.

DEVELOPMENT. Based on the six constructs of the O*NET Content Model, two subconstructs (called *facets* by the test developers) were first developed. Eight to 10 items were developed for each of these 12 facets, with some items revised based on feedback from an expert panel of unstated size and identity. This process yielded an initial item pool of 104 items.

Items were administered to a standardization sample of 526 individuals employed in one of eight O*NET job families indicated as being "common" (manual, p. 21) among the Bureau of Labor Statistics's (BLS) 23 major occupational groups. The rationale for selecting these occupational groups is not explained in the test manual. Whereas these occupational groups represent approximately 50% of U.S. employment tracked by the BLS, only four are among the largest employers in the country (Bureau of Labor Statistics, 2017). Approximately two-thirds of the sample was recruited through an unnamed online survey sampling company. The means of recruitment for the remaining 172 respondents is not indicated.

The sample ranged from 18 to 70 years of age and was said to be "closely matched to the U.S. population according to gender and race/ethnicity" (manual, p. 21). This appears to be the case, given tables in the test manual comparing the sample to the U.S. population by race and gender (p. 22). Additionally, the sample appeared skewed toward those with higher education (48.3% in the sample possessed 16+ years of education vs. 22.4% in the general U.S. population in 2014, when the norms were calculated; U.S. Census Bureau, n.d.).

TECHNICAL. Upon pilot testing the draft WVI with the sample described above, summary statistics were calculated for each of the instrument's six scales. Independent samples *t*-tests compared gender differences on each scale, and no significant differences were found. The statistical approach used is somewhat inappropriate given the inflation of the family-wise error rate (Kirk, 1994) that is created by six *t*-tests. Correlations of each of the six scales with age by gender, education level, and race/ethnicity did not reveal any meaningful trends. However, no data are provided for correlations across the six scales by gender and age separately, so interpretation of those effects is not possible. Further confounding this matter, neither age nor gender is solicited on the WVI, making such interpretations impossible by anyone other than test takers themselves (who do not have access to the requisite technical manual).

After pilot testing, the item pool was reduced to 10 items for each of the six scales in the WVI (five per each subconstruct or facet), for a total of 60 items. The rationale for selecting two facets for each of the six constructs is not explained in the test manual, nor is the decision to have an equal number of items in each facet beyond it being "for consistency across the scales" (manual, p. 21).

Alpha reliability coefficients for each of the six scales were above .70. Test-retest reliability among a group of 58 individuals over a 1- to 5-week period ranged from .82 to .95. No explanation is provided for the 4-week variance in time of retesting.

Intercorrelations of the instrument's six scales are bifurcated by gender but not presented overall nor disaggregated by other demographics. The majority of reported intercorrelations were moderate, ranging from .50 to .60.

Convergent evidence of validity is presented regarding the relationship of responses on the WVI and results from the Self-Directed Search (SDS), the NEO Personality Inventory-3 (NEO-PI-3), the Working Styles Assessment (WSA), and the Test of General Reasoning Ability (TOGRA). Whereas the SDS and WSA concern career exploration, the NEO-PI-3 and TOGRA do not, calling into question their utility as indicators of convergent validity. Surprisingly, correlations between the WVI and the Work Importance Locator—a freely available career exploration tool developed by O*NET (National Center for O*NET Development, n.d.; McCloy et al., 1999) that has well-established evidence of reliability and validity—were not explored by the test developers.

The developers point to prior work in which work values were assigned to occupations included in the O*NET database, but they do not indicate the number of raters (which was six, as determined from Rounds, Armstrong, Liao, Lewis, & Rivkin, 2008) and appear to erroneously indicate that the raters were job incumbents. (They were actually graduate students in counseling psychology.)

In their discussion of "construct validity" (manual, p. 28), no factor-analytic findings—the most typical means of developing arguments for such claims of validity (McCoach, Gable, & Madura, 2013)—are reported. Instead, the concordance of the highest three work values for each of the eight major occupational groups represented in the standardization sample are reported. The percentage of agreement was then determined between these three work values and those previously established by O*NET (Rounds, et al., 2008). At best, this method provides minimal evidence regarding the WVI's concurrent evidence of validity (Mislevy & Rupp, 2010), and perhaps less so, its construct evidence of validity.

Lastly, the developers report their efforts to establish concurrent evidence of validity. They indicate that occupational title and level of job satisfaction was simultaneously solicited from the standardization sample (n = 526). Occupational titles were then matched to the WVI Occupations Index when possible, resulting in a sample size of 297. Individuals who reported being extremely satisfied or very satisfied with their jobs (n = 196) were then compared with those who reported being somewhat satisfied or not at all satisfied (n = 101). The test authors report that, "It can be assumed that an individual's top work values can help to identify occupations that he or she is likely to find satisfying" (manual, p. 30). However, this belief does not appear to be substantiated by the developers' findings. Among those whose highest WVI-ranked work value matched one of the O*NET work values associated with their occupation, 63% reported being satisfied, and 59% reported being unsatisfied, a difference of 4%. A similar difference is reported when at least two of three highest WVI-ranked work values matched an O*NET work value for the respondent's occupation (54% satisfied vs. 50% unsatisfied). Beyond the negligible differences in these findings, the exclusion of more than 40% of the standardization sample from this process because their occupations could not be matched to the Occupations Index calls into question how data from these individuals could have been used in any of the aforementioned analyses. Whether this finding is an oversight or a fundamental error in the recruitment process is unclear.

COMMENTARY. The three highest work values for all eight of the major occupational groups represented in the standardization sample were Achievement, Independence, and Support, leaving these reviewers to wonder what role the other three work values—Relationships, Working Conditions, and Recognition—serve. This result is especially puzzling because half of the occupations recommended in the Occupational Index presume that one of these three work values was rated highest by a respondent. Regarding re-rating of items in some cases of ties, it would seem that such a process is unlikely to be feasible when the instrument is administered by counseling professionals, because the respondents likely would not be present to do so once the counselor undertakes to score and interpret the respondents' completed assessments.

Regarding the facets that make up the work values, they appear to be based on 100 "interests" indexed by O*NET that have since been superseded. (O*NET has since adopted "corresponding needs" related to work values.) Additionally, as of 2017, the O*NET framework is under revision by the Office of Management and Budget. These developments call into question the ability of the WVI to accurately reflect its underlying model.

SUMMARY. The Work Values Inventory might serve as a platform for initiating informal conversations with job seekers regarding the occupations that could merge their values with those of the occupations available to them. However, as a tool for researchers or counseling professionals, it cannot be endorsed at this time. The theoretical basis of O*NET appears to be sound; however, further development of the WVI is required. More pertinently, given the questionable operationalization of the O*NET schema, caution is advised in using the WVI for employee selection, which is one of the potential uses advocated by the test developers.

REVIEWERS' REFERENCES

Bureau of Labor Statistics. (2017). Employment by major occupational group. Retrieved from https://www.bls.gov/emp/tables/emp-by-major-occupational-group.htm

Kirk, R. E. (1994). *Experimental design: Procedures for the behavioral sciences.* Pacific Grove, CA: Brooks/Cole.

Kline, R. B. (2013). *Beyond significance testing* (2nd ed.). Washington, DC: American Psychological Association.

McCloy, R., Waugh, G., Medsker, G., Wall, J., Rivkin, D., & Lewis, P. (1999). Development of the O*NET Paper-and-Pencil Work Importance Locator. National Center for O*NET Development. Retrieved from https://www.onetcenter.org/dl_files/DevWIL.pdf

McCoach, D. B., Gable, R. K., & Madura, J. P. (2013). *Instrument development in the affective domain: School and corporate applications.* New York, NY: Springer.

Mislevy, J. L., & Rupp, A. A. (2010). Concurrent validity. In N. J. Salkind (Ed.), *Encyclopedia of research design.* Thousand Oaks, CA: SAGE. doi:10.4135/9781412961288.n67

National Center for O*NET Development. (n.d.). Work Importance Locator (WIL and Work Importance Profiler (WIP). *O*NET Resource Center*. Retrieved from https://www.onetcenter.org/WIL.html

Rounds, J., Armstrong, P. I., Liao, H.-Y., Lewis, P., & Rivkin, D. (2008). Second generation occupational value profiles for the O*NET system: Summary. National Center for O*NET Development. Retrieved from https://www.onetcenter.org/dl_files/SecondOVP_Summary.pdf

U.S. Census Bureau. (n.d.). Educational attainment in the United States: 2014. Retrieved from https://www.census.gov/data/tables/2014/demo/educational-attainment/cps-detailed-tables.html

Review of the Work Values Inventory by PHILIP J. MOBERG, Associate Professor, Northern Kentucky University, Highland Heights, KY:

DESCRIPTION. The Work Values Inventory (WVI) is an individual- or group-administered measure of six work values for use with adults 18 years of age or older in career counseling or personnel selection settings. Clear instructions precede 60 self-descriptive statements representing needs and preferences for work roles, relationships, outcomes, environments, and job characteristics. Examinees respond by rating how much they value each activity or behavior (i.e., *not valued, somewhat valued, highly valued,* and *very highly valued*). Completion time is estimated at 10 minutes, with individual scores computed by the examinee or a professional examiner.

Raw scores may be converted into percentile ranks, graphically plotted on a score summary sheet, and compared to norms reported in the test manual. Professional examiners, such as career counselors, may compute three additional scores for diagnostic purposes: Profile Elevation (sum of scores), Differentiation (high minus low score), and Commonness (percent of top three work values for comparison to female and male norms). To identify occupations sharing similar value patterns, examinees follow directions provided in the assessment booklet to compare their scores with those characterizing 1,300 occupations listed in the WVI Occupations Index (Messer & Greene, 2016), a booklet provided to examinees. Test takers are instructed to refer to the U.S. Department of Labor's Occupational Information Network (O*NET) website to explore specific occupations.

The WVI manual contains chapters describing (a) theoretical foundations and potential applications, (b) development and standardization, (c) administration and scoring, (d) reliability and validity evidence, and (e) use and interpretation. Appendices report percentile ranks for WVI scale scores and normative data for the three diagnostic scores.

DEVELOPMENT. The test authors developed the WVI by applying the O*NET Content Model (U.S. Department of Labor, n.d.) as an organizing framework. The O*NET Content Model characterizes individual occupations along six dimensions: (a) worker characteristics, (b) workforce characteristics, (c) experience requirements, (d) occupational requirements, (e) worker requirements, and (f) occupational information. Worker characteristics includes four domains: worker abilities, occupational interests, work styles, and work values. The WVI focuses on six work values, measuring preferences for Achievement, Independence, Recognition, Relationships, Support, and Working Conditions.

For the six values constructs, the WVI authors wrote eight to 10 items to represent each of two facets per construct, for a total of 16 to 20 items for every construct. An undescribed expert panel rated each item based on (a) item quality, (b) construct representativeness, (c) face validity and relevance, and (d) potential bias. Based on advice from the expert panel, some items were modified or deleted, and a 104-item version of the scale was created for administration to a standardization sample. Following analyses of standardization sample data, five items were retained for each facet, resulting in the final 60-item scale.

The WVI standardization sample (N = 526), which also served as the normative sample, was selected to reflect population gender and race/ethnicity distributions reported in the 2014 U.S. Census. Females (n = 264) and males (n = 262) ranged in age from 18 to 70 years. When divided into four race/ethnic groups (i.e., Caucasian, African-American, Hispanic, Other) and then further subdivided into three age groups (i.e., 18-24, 25-39, and 40-70 years), the mean differences between sample and population percentages across 12 comparisons were 0.86% for males and 0.58% for females.

The sample included individuals employed in eight O*NET occupation groups: business (8.4%), computer and mathematics (10.3%), healthcare support (11.4%), education and library (10.3%), management (26.0%), administrative support (12.4%), protective services (11.2%), and sales-related (10.1%). The types of organizations (e.g., public, private, education, government, military, manufacturing, retail, service) represented in the sample are not indicated. This information would enhance confidence when interpreting generalizability.

TECHNICAL.

Norms. To establish norms and evaluate subgroup distinctions, the test authors compared mean scores of males and females on the six work values scales. Examination of t-test results revealed no statistically significant gender differences. Within genders, the authors examined correlations between age and work values but did not specify in the test manual whether age was treated as a categorical or continuous variable. Only the work value of Independence correlated significantly with age, a relationship attributed by the test authors to increasing desire for autonomy with progressive maturity. No other work value correlated significantly with age, educational level, or race-ethnicity group.

Reliability. Evidence of internal consistency, test-retest, and interscorer reliability is reported. Using coefficient alpha, the test authors examined internal consistency reliability in the standardization sample for separate and combined gender groups subdivided into three age groups (i.e., 18-24, 25-39, and 40-70 years). Reliability coefficients ranged from .81 for male (ages 25-39) values toward Working Conditions to .95 for female (ages 18-24) values toward Relationships. For the six value scales, gender differences in alpha coefficients ranged from .00 to .04, demonstrating strong similarity of reliability.

Test-retest reliability was evaluated by administering the WVI to 25 females and 33 males twice with a 1- to 5-week intervening period. Coefficients for scales ranged from .82 to .95. Paired-samples *t*-tests of first and second administration means produced no significant differences.

Interscorer reliability was assessed by examining the consistency of two trained research assistants who independently scored 20 protocols randomly drawn from the standardization sample. Of the 20 cases, 85% were assigned the correct scale score by both scorers, 100% were assigned the top work value, and 90% were assigned the correct rank order of values, reflecting strong agreement between scorers.

"Internal" Evidence of Validity. By examining relations among work values in the standardization sample, the test authors concluded that the six value dimensions represent correlated, rather than distinct, constructs. Intercorrelations ranged from .51 to .72 for females and from .46 to .71 for males, with an absolute mean difference in magnitude for parallel coefficients of .02.

Unambiguous evidence of validity based on internal structure is not provided because no factor-analytic results are reported. Rather than examine the initial item pool using an exploratory factor analysis to determine the extent to which the items formed six related dimensions, the test authors employed an undescribed expert panel to evaluate the items based on four criteria (i.e., item quality, construct representativeness, face validity and relevance, and potential bias or other problems). Thus, the extent to which the WVI items represent six discrete, but overlapping, constructs is unclear. Empirical evidence of internal structure is needed to support the authors' assertion and expert panel's judgment that six distinct value constructs are represented by items comprising the WVI.

"External" Evidence of Validity. The authors assessed face validity during the development process via ratings by an expert panel. An informative perspective could be obtained if examinees, rather than experts, were asked to indicate the extent to which the value items reflected the intended constructs. Respondent beliefs about the extent to which WVI items assess personal values is likely to impact individual responses and could be illuminating.

Convergent Evidence of Validity. The authors assessed convergent validity by examining correlations of WVI work values with interest, personality, work style, and general reasoning constructs. Correlations of WVI work values with Holland's occupational personality interests (i.e., Realistic, Investigative, Artistic, Social, Enterprising, Conventional), measured by the Self-Directed Search (SDS; Holland & Messer, 2013), are reported by gender. However, only five of 72 reported correlations were statistically significant, in part because sample sizes were small (female n = 22, male n = 30).

Also reported by gender are correlations of WVI work values with the "Big Five" personality constructs (i.e., Neuroticism, Extraversion, Openness, Agreeableness, Conscientiousness) representing Digman's Five-Factor Model and measured by the NEO Personality Inventory–3 (NEO-PI-3; McCrae & Costa, 2010). Again, in part because sample sizes were comparatively small (female n = 22, male n = 30), only seven of 60 reported correlations were statistically significant.

The test authors further report by gender the correlations of WVI work values with 18 working styles grouped into five domains (i.e., Drive, Interpersonal Skill, Adjustment, Responsibility, and Problem-Solving Skill) measured by the Working Styles Assessment (WSA; Messer & Ureksoy, 2014). With these slightly larger samples (female n = 32, male n = 31), 80 of 216 correlation coefficients were statistically significant. Because sample sizes involved in the foregoing research produce unstable results, the test authors would be well advised to generate additional, definitive evidence of work value relations with all three sets of constructs.

Finally, using a combined gender sample (n = 62), the authors report means and standard deviations for WVI work values across three levels of reasoning ability as measured by the Test of General Reasoning Ability (TOGRA; Reynolds, 2014). The authors divided TOGRA scores into three groups: General Reasoning Index (GRI) below 100 (n = 17), GRI from 100 to 110 (n = 28), and GRI above 110 (n = 17). Post-hoc tests revealed a statistically significant difference only on the WVI Recognition scale. Because neither a rationale for establishing criterion groups nor norms for the GRI are provided, interpretation is hampered. A more informative strategy might be to separate subsample groups by one-half of a standard deviation to clearly distinguish between low, moderate, and high standing on the reasoning construct.

Concurrent Evidence of Validity. The authors obtained current occupational titles from incumbents in the standardization sample (n = 297), then divided these participants into two groups, those extremely/very satisfied and those somewhat/not at all satisfied with their occupations. Using frequency distributions, the authors compared participants' highest-ranked work value with the primary work value of their occupations. For the satisfied group, 63% matched highest work value with their occupation's primary value, and 54% matched two or more work values. For the dissatisfied group, 59% matched highest work value with their occupation's primary value, and 50% matched two or more work values. Unfortunately, this evidence (63% vs. 59% and 54% vs. 50%) does not distinguish persuasively between satisfied and dissatisfied groups and prompts discriminant validity concerns.

COMMENTARY. The WVI meets its goal of assessing characteristics of occupational personality (e.g., attitudes, behaviors, feelings, likes/dislikes, preferences, tendencies, and values) that have the potential to relate to work attitudes and behaviors. Several conceptual, methodological, and empirical issues obscure interpretation and undermine application.

Although the authors assert that the WVI's structure is derived from the O*NET model of occupational values, the method used to identify dimensional structure underlying the initial items did not include an exploratory or confirmatory factor analysis. In the absence of empirical evidence, concern arises about the assertion that the rationally developed items represent six distinct but correlated constructs.

Regarding interpretation, the test manual describes two facets that make up each value scale and recommends that professionals examine facet scores when interpreting values, but scoring instructions are not provided. Because the reader must refer to the assessment booklet for a list of items that constitute each facet, the authors should consider including facet definitions and a list of items that constitute each facet in the manual itself to facilitate reference and interpretation.

Validity is a concern for the WVI. Although convergent validity was evaluated separately for gender groups by examining correlations with six SDS occupational interests and five normal personality dimensions, both samples included only 52 individuals (22 females and 30 males). Additional data are needed to enhance confidence in these findings. Similarly, evidence of convergent validity relating values to work styles produced 216 correlations based on a sample of 32 females and 31 males. Again, additional data are needed to establish stable evidence of these relationships.

Evidence of internal consistency reliability, which was estimated using results from the entire standardization sample (N = 526), is very strong: above .90 for five of the six value scales and above .80 for the remaining scale. However, evidence of test-retest reliability is based on a sample of only 58 individuals, and evidence of interscorer reliability is based on a classification sample of only 20 cases.

SUMMARY. The WVI is an individual or group-administered measure of six work values for use with adults over age 18 years in career exploration and personnel selection. It is written at a seventh-grade level with scoring performed by either the test taker or a professional examiner. To ensure appropriate use, the test authors recommend that test users understand measurement theory, interest inventories, and occupations.

The WVI is easily administered and offers promise for use in occupational exploration and career counseling settings. Use in personnel selection settings is premature, however, because empirical evidence linking work values to in-role, extra-role, adaptive, expert, or counterproductive job performance is not provided. It should not be used in this fashion at this time.

Because the standardization sample consists primarily of incumbents working in professional and semiprofessional, white-collar occupations, generalizability is limited to similar population groups. Although occupational groups are described broadly in the test manual, the specific types of organizations and industries represented in the standardization sample are not. The concern is that values may vary in public versus private sector jobs. Thus, the level of occupations represented is not known (e.g., healthcare support occupations) nor are organizational types. Confidence in the generalizability of the WVI would be enhanced if occupational level and organizational type for the standardization sample were described. The authors intend the WVI to inform decisions about career path, college major, and personnel selection, but the lack of internal structural and construct evidence of validity prompts concerns, particularly regarding support for selection decisions.

REVIEWER'S REFERENCES

Holland, J. L., & Messer, M. A. (2013). Self-Directed Search, 5th Edition. Lutz, FL: Psychological Assessment Resources.

McCrae, R. R., & Costa, P. T., Jr. (2010). NEO Personality Inventory-3. Lutz, FL: Psychological Assessment Resources.

Messer, M. A., & Greene, J. A. (2016). Work Values Inventory Occupations Index. Lutz, FL: Psychological Assessment Resources.

Messer, M. A., & Ureksoy, H. (2014). Working Styles Assessment. Lutz, FL: Psychological Assessment Resources.

Reynolds, C. R. (2014). Test of General Reasoning Ability. Lutz, FL: Psychological Assessment Resources.

U.S. Department of Labor. (n.d.). The O*NET Content Model. Retrieved from https://www.onetcenter.org/dl_files/ContentModel_DetailedDesc.pdf

[191]

Young Children's Achievement Test–Second Edition.

Purpose: Designed to measure "achievement abilities ... with respect to those skills and abilities that ensure success in school."
Population: Ages 4 through 7.
Publication Dates: 2000-2018.
Acronym: YCAT-2.
Scores, 6: General Information, Mathematics, Reading, Writing, Spoken Language, Early Achievement Index.
Administration: Individual.
Forms, 2: Parallel forms A and B.
Price Data, 2020: $392 per complete kit including examiner's manual (2018, 139 pages), picture book, 25 Form A examiner record booklets, 25 Form B examiner record booklets, 25 Form A student response forms, and 25 Form B student response forms; $81 per manual (print or digital); $99 per picture book (print or digital); $67 per 25 examiner record booklets (Form A or Form B); $39 per 25 student response forms (Form A or Form B).
Time: 30-50 minutes for administration.
Authors: Wayne P. Hresko, Pamela K. Peak, Shelley R. Herron, and Deanna L. Hicks.
Publisher: PRO-ED.
Cross References: For reviews by Russell N. Carney and Susan J. Maller of the original edition, see 15:285.

Review of the Young Children's Achievement Test–Second Edition by SUSAN BROOKHART, Professor Emerita, Duquesne University, Pittsburgh, PA:

DESCRIPTION. The Young Children's Achievement Test–Second Edition (YCAT-2) is an individually administered test of academic achievement for children ages 4 years 0 months through 7 years 11 months. According to the examiner's manual, the YCAT-2 has three principal uses: (1) to identify children who are significantly below their peers in important learning and information processing abilities, for example for placement decisions or to help document the need for services; (2) to document academic progress or gains and identify a student's strengths and weaknesses; and (3) to serve as a measure in research projects.

The YCAT-2 (2018) is a revision of the YCAT, originally published in 2000. As did its predecessor, the YCAT-2 has five subtests: General Information, Math, Reading, Writing, and Spoken Language. The five subtests can be combined to create a composite score called the Early Achievement Index. The examiner's manual (p. 4) states that the Early Achievement Index is more reliable and valid than individual subtest scores, and "will most likely indicate whether a child will have significant challenges in his or her early years."

Unlike its predecessor, the YCAT-2 has two forms (A and B). The manual (p. ix) explains that a second form was developed for use in evaluating the effects of instruction. That is, the YCAT-2 "can be used in test-teach-test situations."

There are 178 items in the five subtests, although students do not take all of them. Subtest items are ordered, and entry points for each subtest are given by age. Directions are given for establishing basal (three correct answers in a row) and ceiling (three incorrect answers in a row) levels. Items are scored 1 or 0 (correct or incorrect); all items below the basal are scored as correct, and all items above the ceiling are scored as incorrect. Raw scores are then converted to age equivalent scores, scaled scores, and percentile ranks (with confidence interval). A chart allows the examiner to attach one of seven descriptive terms to subscale performance, based on the scaled score. Descriptive terms range as follows: *impaired or delayed, borderline impaired or delayed, below average, average, above average, superior,* and *gifted or very advanced.*

DEVELOPMENT. The test developers produced the first edition of the YCAT for the same purposes as the YCAT-2. They reviewed other early childhood achievement tests, generated an item pool, and used traditional item analysis measures to select the YCAT items.

To their credit, the test authors considered previous reviews of the YCAT when they developed the YCAT-2, as well as suggestions from users and their own ideas. The following are additions/improvements made in developing the YCAT-2: new normative data; the creation of an alternate form (Form B) to facilitate test-teach-test designs and a linking study to link Form A to Form B; new test bias studies using updated methodology; new studies of item floors, ceilings, and gradients for both subtest and composite scores; and additional validity studies.

TECHNICAL.

Standardization. The YCAT-2 norming sample included 846 children ages 4 years 0 months through 7 years 11 months. The sample is statistically representative of the U.S. school-aged population with respect to geography, gender, race, Hispanic status, exceptionality status, and family income. Data were collected by qualified examiners from 2012 through 2016. All students in the norming sample took Form A. A randomly assigned subset of examinees (n = 207) took both Form A and Form B, and this linking sample also was representative of the U.S. population.

Four types of normative scores are calculated: age equivalents for subtest scores, percentile ranks for both subtest and composite scores, scaled scores for subtests, and a composite index. The examiner's manual presents tables for converting raw scores to these normative scores.

The examiner's manual gives directions for interpreting subtest scores and the composite Early Achievement Index. The manual also provides directions for pairwise subtest comparisons including a chart that lists both statistically significant differences and clinically meaningful differences between subtest scores. Additionally, the manual supplies directions for ipsative subtest comparisons (comparing a child's score on a given subtest with that child's mean score on all five subtests) to identify self-referenced relative strengths and weaknesses. Examiners who wish to do ipsative subtest comparisons should ensure they refer to the publisher's corrections; the first printing of the manual contained errors in this section.

Reliability. Several methods of analyzing reliability were employed. Internal consistency was reported for each subtest and the composite by form, age, gender, and ethnicity. Values for the subtests were generally high, especially considering the age of the children, and ranged from .81 to .98, with most values in the .90s. The average alpha value for the composite was .97.

Alternate forms reliability was also investigated. Corrected correlations for alternate forms, immediate administration, across all ages ranged from .63 to .84. The corrected correlation for alternate forms, immediate administration, for the composite score was .89. Corrected correlations for alternate forms, delayed (approximately two weeks) administration, across all ages ranged from .53 to .78. The corrected correlation for alternate forms, delayed administration, for the composite score was .78.

Test-retest reliability was calculated for both forms, at approximately a two-week interval. Corrected correlations for test-retest reliability, across all ages and both forms, ranged from .57 to .81. The corrected correlation for test-retest reliability for the composite score was .80.

Interscorer reliability was studied with two of the test publisher's research staff members independently scoring 50 randomly selected YCAT-2 examiner record booklets. Correlations between the two scorers' results were high (.94 to .99 for the subtests, with most values at .98, and .98 for the composite).

Validity. The examiner's manual presents a large amount of evidence of the validity of the YCAT-2. A rationale and references are provided for the overall structure and content of the test. Conventional item analysis (item difficulty and discrimination) were used to select well-functioning items, and tables of those results are displayed. Analysis of the subtests' and composite's floor, ceiling, and item gradients demonstrate that the test can measure the full range of student ability. Test bias was studied with both differential item functioning and demographic subgroup comparisons, and the test was found to be appropriately free of bias.

Concurrent evidence of validity was studied by correlating the YCAT-2 subtest and composite scores with scores on the Woodcock-Johnson III Tests of Achievement and the Test of Language Development—Primary: Fifth Edition. This reviewer considered correlations as being high (.73-.95).

Diagnostic accuracy analyses (sensitivity: correctly identifying students with a disability related to low achievement; specificity: correctly identifying students who do not have a disability; and receiver operating characteristic/area under the curve analysis: the average sensitivity for all possible values of specificity) were conducted on samples of students for whom specific learning disability and cognitive impairment status was known and matched samples of non-disabled children, with positive results.

Construct validity evidence took several forms. YCAT-2 scores were found to be related to age, exceptionality (specific learning disability, language impairment, and cognitive impairment), reading ability, language development, and intelligence, as predicted. Confirmatory factor analysis demonstrated that a model positing that the Early Achievement Index (the composite) has a five-factor structure (the subtests) is plausible. Finally, item-test correlations were high, another indicator of the internal structure of the test.

COMMENTARY. The YCAT-2 examiner's manual is clearly written. The examiner record booklets for both Form A and Form B are clear and easy to use. The picture book for Forms A and B presents attractive and readable material for children. The book contains content in the form of verbal and numerical material as well as pictures, depending on the item.

This reviewer was impressed with the amount of study, careful work, and positive results reported for the YCAT-2. The second edition has made clear improvements from the first edition, and very much to the authors' credit, they used feedback from the first edition in the revision process. This reviewer has only one criticism, and that relates to the treatment of validity evidence, specifically, the lack of studies to support the intended uses specified for the test.

The examiner's manual names three types of validity (p. 49): content-description validity, criterion-prediction validity, and construct-identification validity. The authors cite Anastasi and Urbina (1997) for the terms and suggest their framework is compatible with that presented in current measurement textbooks and the *Standards for Educational and Psychological Testing* (American Educational Research Association, American Psychological Association, & National Council on Measurement in Education, 2014). In fact, views of validity have shifted somewhat over the past few decades, and validity is currently considered to be a unitary concept (Messick, 1989). Different uses require different arguments, supported with evidence (Kane, 2006). The *Standards* describe five types of evidence (evidence based on test content, response processes, internal structure, relations to other variables, and the validity and consequences of testing) that can be mustered to support the validity of using a test for a particular purpose. The YCAT-2 has three of these (test content, internal structure, and relations to other variables), although the discussion in the validity chapter of the manual is not differentiated by the purpose being validated (the three intended uses of the YCAT-2) but by "type of validity" (manual, p. 49).

The use of an outdated framework for validity is more than an academic quibble here because it led to a misguided decision. The only major suggestion made by reviewers of the YCAT first edition that the test publisher did *not* take in developing the YCAT-2 was to conduct a predictive validity study to support the primary purpose for the test, namely to identify children who are significantly below their peers in order to provide appropriate instruction and interventions. The authors did not perform such a study, saying, "On this point, we take the position that one purpose of administering the YCAT is to identify preschool students who are already behind peers in academic ability so that interventions may begin immediately. In our efforts to encourage the immediate use of interventions, we have developed multiple forms of the test so that it may be used pre- and postintervention" (manual, p. viii). If the authors had used a contemporary framework for validity based on test use rather than types of validity, the need for predictive evidence to back up the claim that students identified by the YCAT-2 as in need of assistance actually do benefit from that assistance would have been more obvious. Instead, as their position shows, the authors essentially left the task of validating that primary use to the practitioners and recommended that a second administration of the same test be used as the criterion for showing achievement benefits.

Another intended use also calls for supporting evidence. The test's second purpose, measuring and documenting educational progress, could better be supported if a study of longitudinal use of the YCAT-2 in fact produced meaningful learning trajectories for students.

SUMMARY. The YCAT-2 is an individually administered test of skills that ensure success in school. It is designed to be administered to children 4 years 0 months through 7 years 11 months and used to identify students developing below their peers and recommend interventions, document educational growth, and/or serve as a measure in research. Evidence for the test's development and standardization, and of its reliability and validity, are strong and clearly presented in the examiner's manual. Based on this evidence, the test can be recommended for use for any of these purposes. However, this reviewer would like to see a reframing of the validation information to more persuasively support an argument for the intended uses of identifying the need for educational services and for measuring and documenting growth.

REVIEWER'S REFERENCES

American Educational Research Association, American Psychological Association, & National Council on Measurement in Education. (2014). *Standards for educational and psychological testing*. Washington, DC: AERA.

Anastasi, A., & Urbina, S. (1997). *Psychological testing* (7th ed.). Upper Saddle River, NJ: Prentice Hall.

Kane, M. T. (2006). Validation. In R. L. Brennan (Ed.), *Educational measurement* (4th ed., pp. 17-64). Westport, CT: Praeger.

Messick, S. (1989). Validity. In R. L. Linn (Ed.), *Educational measurement* (3rd ed., pp. 13-103). New York, NY: Macmillan.

Review of Young Children's Achievement Test–Second Edition by OKAN BULUT, Associate Professor of Measurement, Evaluation, and Data Science, University of Alberta, Edmonton, Alberta, Canada:

DESCRIPTION. The Young Children's Achievement Test–Second Edition (YCAT-2) is an individually administered test of academic abilities and skills deemed important for young children's success in schools. According to the examiner's manual, the YCAT-2 is suitable for preschool, kindergarten, and first-grade children (ages 4 years 0 months through 7 years 11 months) who can speak American English. A complete kit of the YCAT-2 includes the examiner's manual, student response forms, examiner record booklets for two parallel forms (i.e., Form A and Form B), and a picture book comprising different pictures for Forms A and B. Based on the test authors' description, 30 to 50 minutes are required for a complete test administration.

The YCAT-2 yields five scores from the subtests of General Information, Mathematics, Reading, Writing, and Spoken Language. Raw scores (i.e., the number of correctly answered items) for the subtests can be converted to age equivalent scores, scaled (i.e., standard) scores, and percentile ranks using tables provided in the examiner's manual. In addition to subtest scores, there is a composite score called the Early Achievement Index, which is the sum of scaled scores for the five subtests. The Early Achievement Index also can be converted to a percentile rank. Furthermore, a table in the record booklet allows the examiner to interpret scaled scores for both subtests and the composite in descriptive terms (e.g., *impaired or delayed, below average, above average, superior*).

DEVELOPMENT. The YCAT-2 is an updated version of the first edition of the Young Children's Achievement Test (YCAT) created by Hresko, Peak, Herron, and Bridges in 2000. In the examiner's manual, the authors provide a brief discussion of the literature supporting the need for measuring young children's early academic abilities. Furthermore, the authors mention that the YCAT-2 can be used for (a) identifying children whose learning and information processing abilities are significantly below their peers, (b) documenting children's academic progress, and (c) serving as a measure in research projects on children's academic achievement.

TECHNICAL.

Standardization. The norm sample for the YCAT-2 consisted of 846 children (ages 4 years 0 months through 7 years 11 months) residing in 25 states across the United States. The entire sample was administered Form A, and a subset of the sample (n = 207) was also administered Form B. The order of administration was counterbalanced, and forms typically were administered one day apart. Data collection was completed between 2012 and 2016. The tables in the examiner's manual show that the sample was representative of the U.S. school-age population (based on the 2017 Census data) in terms of several demographic characteristics such as geographical region, gender, race, family income, and parental education.

Reliability. Five types of reliability were reported. For internal consistency, coefficient alpha values were reported for each subtest and the composite (i.e., Early Achievement Index) at four age intervals, ranging from .81 (General Information, age 7, Form B) to .98 (composite, age 4, Form B). The alpha values for General Information and Writing were mostly in the mid to high .80s, whereas the alpha values were mostly around .90 or higher for the other subtests. In addition, the alpha values for seven demographic subgroups were mostly in the mid .90s. For both test forms, test-retest reliability (approximately two-week interval) was calculated using two samples of children: ages 4-0 through 5-11 (n = 62) and ages 6-0 through 7-11 (n = 88). The test authors did not describe the sampling procedure for the test-retest sample. The corrected test-retest reliability coefficients ranged from .47 (General Information, ages 6-0 to 7-11, Form B) to .89 (Reading, ages 6-0 to 7-11, Form B). Forms A and B mostly yielded different test-retest reliability values. The corrected alternate-form reliability between Forms A and B (using the initial data collection) ranged from .60 to .90 for the subtests and from .86 to .93 for the composite across four age intervals. The corrected alternate-form reliability coefficients for delayed administration using the test-retest sample were mostly in the .70s and .80s. Overall, the test-retest results suggest that the two forms may not be strictly parallel regarding their psychometric properties. Lastly, two members of the test publisher's research staff independently scored a random sample of 50 YCAT-2 examiner record booklets from the norm sample. The correlation between the two scorers (higher than .90) was used to conclude adequate scorer reliability for the YCAT-2. The authors did not comment on the generalizability of this finding for the population of all YCAT-2 examiners, including those who may not be as well trained with the measure.

Validity. The authors presented content, criterion-related, and construct evidence of validity of the YCAT-2 in the examiner's manual. To collect content evidence of validity, the test authors reviewed the existing YCAT items and created new items based on the recent literature on early childhood achievement (e.g., tests, inventories, curriculum materials, and reports). The authors also conducted conventional item analysis and concluded that the test items satisfied the requirements to serve as content evidence of validity. Lastly, differential item functioning (DIF) was investigated for the YCAT-2 items using the logistic regression method, and it was reported that none of the items indicated significant bias with regard to race, gender, or Hispanic status. This implausible finding was most likely due to using a strict significance level (.001) in the DIF analyses.

To obtain criterion-related evidence of validity, correlational analyses were conducted between scores from the YCAT-2 and the Woodcock-Johnson III Tests of Achievement (n = 45). Results ranged from .76 to .95 for similar subtest areas and from .71 to .87 for the composite. Furthermore, the correlation between the spoken language subtest in the YCAT-2 and the Test of Language Development-Primary: Fifth Edition (n = 34) was .73. In addition, non-significant differences between average scaled scores from the YCAT-2 and the other achievement tests were used to justify the close alignment between the tests.

Although the test authors aimed to investigate diagnostic accuracy of the YCAT-2 in identifying children with low academic achievement, their analyses solely focused on diagnosis of students with learning disabilities (n = 23) and cognitive impairments (n = 39). Several cutoff scores were reported for accurate classifications of learning disability and cognitive impairment using the YCAT-2, but the authors did not provide clear guidelines on which cutoff scores are more appropriate. Overall, there was no evidence regarding predictive validity of the YCAT-2.

There is a variety of construct evidence of validity in the examiner's manual. Construct evidence of validity included (a) correlations of the YCAT-2 scores with age that ranged from .65 to .81; (b) statistically significant comparisons of the average scores from children without disabilities and contrast groups (i.e., children with learning disability, cognitive impairment, or language impairment); (c) moderate to large correlations between the YCAT-2 scores and various measures of reading, language, and intelligence; and (d) subtest intercorrelations that ranged from .44 to .66. In addition, the results of confirmatory factor analysis (CFA) indicate that there is a single factor (i.e., composite) underlying the skills measured by the five subtests of the YCAT-2. However, CFA was not used to evaluate construct evidence of validity of individual subtests (e.g., General Information, Math, and Reading) separately.

COMMENTARY. As the second edition of the YCAT, the YCAT-2 also aims to measure academic abilities essential for children in preschool through first grade. The YCAT-2 manual is well-structured and easy to follow for examiners. Test administration and scoring guidelines are straightforward. The test materials, especially the picture book, are attractive and engaging for children. With the new edition, the test authors addressed most concerns raised by the reviewers of the first edition, such as lack of details in reliability and DIF analyses (e.g., Carney, 2003; Maller, 2003). Also, the YCAT-2 contains new items aligned with the current literature on academic abilities in young children. Comprehensive analyses supporting both reliability and validity appear to be a strength. Although the authors included an alternative form (Form B) in the YCAT-2 for test-teach-test situations, the lack of strict parallelism between the forms appears to be a drawback for this purpose. Diagnostic accuracy analyses should have focused on predicting school failure instead of diagnosing learning disability and cognitive impairments.

SUMMARY. The YCAT-2 is a test of academic abilities and skills deemed important for English-speaking children ages 4-0 to 7-11 years.

After its first edition, the YCAT-2 continues to be an effective tool for measuring young children's academic abilities accurately at different age levels and for identifying children whose academic abilities are significantly behind their peers.

REVIEWER'S REFERENCES

Carney, R. N. (2003). [Test review of the Young Children's Achievement Test]. In B. S. Plake, J. C. Impara, & R. A. Spies (Eds.), *The fifteenth mental measurements yearbook* (pp. 1036-1039). Lincoln, NE: Buros Institute of Mental Measurements.

Hresko, W. P., Peak, P. K., Herron, S. R., & Bridges, D. L. (2000). Young Children's Achievement Test. Austin, TX: PRO-ED.

Maller, S. J. (2003). [Test review of the Young Children's Achievement Test]. In B. S. Plake, J. C. Impara, & R. A. Spies (Eds.), *The fifteenth mental measurements yearbook* (pp. 1039-1042). Lincoln, NE: Buros Institute of Mental Measurements.

[192]

Youth and Program Strengths Survey.

Purpose: Designed as a group-level "assessment of the strengths, supports, and noncognitive factors that are essential for young people's success in life" as well as the factors that make up a high-quality youth program.
Population: Students in Grades 4-12.
Publication Dates: 2005-2016.
Acronym: YAPS Survey.
Scores, 8: Physical and Psychological Safety; Providing Appropriate Structure; Providing Supportive Relationships; Providing Opportunities to Belong; Building Positive Social Norms; Supporting Efficacy and Mattering; Providing Opportunities for Skill-Building; Integrating Family, School, and Community Efforts.
Administration: Group.
Price Data, 2020: $300 per site report, including up to 100 surveys; $2.50 per additional survey (beyond the included 100); $300 per aggregate report (encompassing multiple sites); $150 per individual data file of all youth surveyed.
Time: 20 minutes or less for completion.
Comments: User's guide (September, 2016, 50 pages) available for download from survey publisher's website; data analyzed and report provided by survey publisher; minimum of 30 surveys required for report; online administration available and includes the 58-item Developmental Assets Profile (see 47, this volume).
Author: Search Institute.
Publisher: Search Institute.

Review of the Youth and Program Strengths Survey by CLAUDIA R. WRIGHT, Professor Emerita, California State University, Long Beach, Long Beach, CA:

DESCRIPTION. The Developmental Assets Profile (DAP) and the Out of School Time Program Quality Survey are administered together under the new title Youth and Program Strengths Survey (YAPS). The focus of this review is on the program quality portion; the DAP is reviewed separately (see 47, this volume). The 40-item YAPS Program Quality scale is a self-report measure designed for youth (Grades 4-12) to assess their perceptions of staff-related support and program opportunities they experience as participants in a specific setting involving school- or community-based out-of-school-time (OST) activities.

The purpose of this instrument is to provide OST program developers and administrators information about the effectiveness of programmatic objectives from the perspective of the program participants. The YAPS Program Quality scale is made up of eight scales that total 37 items: Physical and Psychological Safety (two items), Appropriate Structure (six items), Supportive Relationships (eight items), Opportunities to Belong (three items), Positive Social Norms (three items), Support for Efficacy and Mattering (seven items), Opportunities for Skill-Building (five items); and Integration of Family, School, and Community Efforts (three items). An additional three items address the amount of exposure to the target program and other OST programs. Response options vary by the nature of the question. For example, 5-point Likert scales are used to assess (a) an examinee's level of agreement (*strongly disagree* to *strongly agree*) with selected item statements; and (b) how often (*never* to *very often*) an examinee perceives encouragement to participate in program activities. Survey administrators are reminded to make accommodations for examinees with special needs as well as to take into consideration the reading level proficiencies of examinees and to provide reading support or additional time when required.

Data analyses are performed and reported to OST program personnel by the survey publisher. Results can be organized by individual responses and subgroups as well as customized to include specific program components. Reports include a demographic profile and detailed explanations for each of the eight scale scores that are clearly presented in jargon-free, informative narratives along with supporting charts and tables to facilitate interpretation of findings. Although it is apparent that raw scores are converted to facilitate comparisons across scales and that the possible total score for each scale is 40, no information was found in the survey materials regarding the metric by which this conversion was made.

DEVELOPMENT. To clarify the evolution of the 40-item YAPS Program Quality scale, the previous version of Search Institute's current full YAPS Survey represents a revision of a briefer measure called the Developmental Assets and Life Experiences Profile, which contained only seven program quality items (Search Institute, 2017). Two pilot studies were employed to examine the reliability and validity of this instrument's test scores. The first study was conducted in 2009 with a national sample of 1,200 15-year-olds (Scales, Roehlkepartain, & Benson, 2010); the second was conducted in 2011 with a sample of 474 children in Grades 4-6 who were enrolled in Salvation Army youth development centers, who were administered the measure after appropriate wording changes were made to adjust the reading level (Scales, Fraher, & Andress, 2011). Moderately high internal consistency estimates of reliability (alpha coefficients) were reported for total test scores for the teen sample (alpha = .87, Scales et al., 2010) and for the Salvation Army sample (alpha = .89, Scales et al., 2011).

Of interest to test developers was use of the Developmental Assets and Life Experiences Profile to examine concurrent youth development outcomes (e.g., positive emotions, hopeful purpose, civic engagement, and school success) as a function of participation in a high-quality OST program. (In this case, the youth development centers were operated by the Salvation Army.) Although not stated, it is assumed that the perceived quality of a program was classified as either high or low depending upon an examinee's response to selected items. Data analyses revealed weak concurrent validity evidence for test scores between participation in high-quality programs and the five outcome measures: positive emotions (r = .39), hopeful purpose (r = .22), civic engagement (r = .34), and school success (r = .26), all $p \leq .001$; and avoiding violence (r = .10, $p \leq .05$). Further, logistic regression analyses were applied to generate the following odds ratios (Exp[B]) using program quality to predict the odds of a particular outcome: positive emotions (2.41), hopeful purpose (1.59), civic engagement (3.31), and school success (1.72), all $p \leq .001$; avoiding violence (1.27, $p \leq .05$). It was tentatively concluded that participants in a high-quality OST program were 3 times more likely to make contributions to their community and 2 times more likely to hold positive emotions than those who participate in lower-quality programs. By 2014, following an extensive review of the literature and with particular reliance on the National Research Council's 2002 report on Community Programs for Youth (National Research Council and Institute of Medicine, 2002), the test developers modified the instrument by including with the seven original items an additional 33 program quality elements to enhance content and construct types of evidence of validity (Search Institute, 2016; 2017) resulting in the 40-item YAPS Program Quality scale, which is the focus of this review.

TECHNICAL. Pilot data were obtained for the YAPS Program Quality scale, which includes the 33 additional items expanding the content related to program quality. However, no information is provided in the survey materials regarding characteristics of the sample. With respect to the internal consistency reliability of test scores, moderate to strong alpha coefficients ranging from .74 to .91 (*mdn* = .835) were reported for the eight scales: Physical and Psychological Safety (.75); Appropriate Structure (.91); Supportive Relationships (.88); Opportunities to Belong (.83); Positive Social Norms (.74); Support for Efficacy and Mattering (.84); Opportunities for Skill-Building (.87); and Integration of Family, School, and Community Efforts (.82). No additional psychometric findings were reported for the Program Quality scale.

COMMENTARY. It is this reviewer's opinion that the use of YAPS Program Quality scale scores would be strengthened by including predictive and criterion-related evidence of validity. Because the survey authors look forward (e.g., "A high-quality OST program is one that can protect young people from risk and promote their resilience and thriving" [Search Institute, 2017, p. 4]), particular emphasis upon the predictive validity of test scores would be most informative.

SUMMARY. The 40-item Youth and Program Strengths Survey offers a promising assessment of examinees' perceptions of their experiences as participants in settings involving school- or community-based out-of-school-time (OST) youth activities. As the instrument is relatively new and expected to be used worldwide, additional psychometric studies across demographics and across types of OST groups would contribute to its usefulness.

REVIEWER'S REFERENCES

National Research Council and Institute of Medicine. (2002). *Community programs to promote youth development.* Washington, DC: National Academies Press.

Scales, P. C., Fraher, K., & Andress, S. (2011). *The Salvation Army-Search Institute youth asset development initiative: Report on 2011 administration of the Development Assets and Life Experiences Profile.* Minneapolis, MN: Search Institute.

Scales, P. C., Roehlkepartain, E. C., & Benson, P. L. (2010). *Teen voice 2010: Relationships that matter to America's teens.* Richfield and Minneapolis, MN: Best Buy Children's Foundation and Search Institute.

Search Institute. (2016). *User guide for the Youth and Program Strengths Survey.* Minneapolis, MN: Author.

Search Institute. (2017). *A youth report on program quality at Search Institute sample: Based on the results from Search Institute's Youth and Program Strengths (YAPS) Survey.* Minneapolis, MN: Author.

Review of the Youth and Program Strengths Survey by SHARON ZUMBRUNN, Associate Professor of Educational Psychology, Virginia Commonwealth University, Richmond, VA:

DESCRIPTION. The Youth and Program Strengths Survey (YAPS) is a 40-item questionnaire that provides the participants of out-of-school programs an opportunity to assess the quality of the program as well as the ways in which the program provides essential factors for their success in life. The online survey is intended to be administered by those coordinating an out-of-school program for youth in Grades 4-12 to the participants in their programs. Across the survey, Likert-type items range from *strongly disagree* to *strongly agree* or from *never* to *very often*. The YAPS allows program participants to share their perspectives on the program in the following categories: Physical and Psychological Safety (two items); Appropriate Structure (six items); Supportive Relationships (eight items); Opportunities to Belong (three items); Positive Social Norms (three items); Support for Efficacy and Mattering (seven items); Opportunities for Skill Building (five items); and Integration of Family, School, and Community Efforts (three items). Three additional dosing items involve attendance in the program and others like it.

The YAPS is accompanied by a detailed user guide that maps out how to design, plan, and prepare for administering the survey (which also includes the Developmental Assets Profile, reviewed separately [see 47, this volume]); how to conduct the study; and how to interpret, use, and communicate the findings with stakeholders of the program. Some possible uses for this survey suggested by the YAPS Survey user guide are to obtain baseline information about a program, learn about youth perspectives on a program, improve or monitor improvements of a program, build awareness of an issue, or meet requirements for funding sources. Scoring is provided by the survey publisher after data from the survey have been collected, and a detailed analysis and report are returned to the program. Survey purchase includes this analysis for one assessment; provision of the results may take up to two weeks depending on time of year and number of participants surveyed. Scored analysis provides helpful information for each subcategory in the survey including a description of the subcategory and results by overview, histogram, table for demographic cohorts, and table for item-by-item responses.

DEVELOPMENT. The YAPS measure grew from the national Teen Voice study of 15-year-olds (Scales, Roehlkepartain, & Benson, 2010). Core items of the original version were based on the work of Roth and Brooks Gunn (2003) who looked at 48 programs in the categories of competence, confidence, connections, character, and caring. In 2011, the YAPS was reworded to be appropriate for the reading level of students in Grades 4–6, and in 2014, the survey was expanded to include the eight categories reported in the National Research Council report (2002) on community programs for youth. This report provides eight "features of positive youth development settings" (National Research Council and Institute of Medicine, 2002, pp. 90-91) with descriptors and opposite poles, which this survey assesses. The YAPS gathers the perspectives of the youth involved in the programs about these eight features rather than relying on the observations of outsiders to the program or leaders of the program.

TECHNICAL. Little detail is provided regarding standardization of the YAPS; norms for the survey are not provided. A sample report titled A Youth Report on Program Quality includes a section ("Interpreting Your Survey Results") that states, "Though it can be interesting to compare your results to others [the survey publisher's] experience in working with communities is that it can be distracting and counterproductive" (p. 7). The survey publisher suggests instead that analyzing the specific context and goals of the program is much more valuable when looking at the results.

Three pilot samples were used to establish evidence for reliability and precision. The initial national samples included 1,200 15-year-old youth and then nearly 500 fourth to sixth grade youth to whom the re-worded version for a lower reading level was administered. Additional demographic information for these samples was not included in the survey materials. The survey was updated in 2014 to include a more robust version of the construct, but information on the sample used for the pilot of this version was not provided. Further, specific information regarding the steps undertaken to select final items was not made available. Data collection and analysis procedures were not provided for any of the pilot studies. Alpha coefficients were reported as estimates of internal consistency for each of the eight categories. All estimates fell within acceptable to very good ranges with coefficients of .74 to .91. No test-retest information was provided to establish additional reliability. Overall, reliability evidence is lacking as outlined in the *Standards for Educational and Psychological Testing* (American Educational Research Association [AERA], American Psychological Association [APA], & National Council on Measurement in Education [NCME], 2014).

Evidence to support the validity of the YAPS is limited. Some content evidence of validity is provided. Within the sample report, tables are presented that align the individual items with the eight principles intended to be measured. The survey authors also attempted to provide concurrent evidence of validity. Specifically, they report findings from a study examining youth development outcomes related to a high-quality youth program, though qualifications for this program being labeled "high quality" were not provided (user guide, p. 45). No evidence is provided to demonstrate convergent or discriminant evidence of validity. Predictive evidence of validity is provided in the form of correlations between program quality and positive outcomes. However, this information should be interpreted with caution, as the sample used for this evidence could be different from the sample of another group, which could affect generalizability of the finding. The user guide suggests that the YAPS can be administered every three months and could be used to show growth within a program; however, no evidence of reliability or validity for this use was provided. Evidence to substantiate validity of the YAPS is lacking (AERA, APA, & NCME, 2014).

COMMENTARY. The YAPS attempts to measure the effectiveness of youth development programs—an endeavor that is no doubt important. A key strength of the YAPS is that it includes items that likely align with several critical aspects of quality programs, although effectiveness of programs depends on more than the positive perspectives in the eight categories addressed in this survey. Funding for these programs often depends on positive outcomes, and the tables presented in the technical overview document attempt to provide such evidence; however, evidence for long-term positive outcomes from a youth development program also depends on staff training, funding support, and many other variables not assessed in this survey. Although the eight principles in this survey are well-founded, research on out-of-school programs also shows the complex nature of studying them and following up for outcome data because of their diversity in nature (Durlak, Weissberg, & Pachan, 2010).

Another key strength of the YAPS is that it provides programs with a detailed report specifying youth participants' perspectives of areas of strength and growth for the program to consider in improvement planning. The survey authors state that the report "provides a positive road map and recommendations to guide [administrators] in proactive and focused planning and improvement based on your results" (sample report, p. 5). Although the authors provide thoughtful guidance about structuring discussions with multiple stakeholders to consider the personalized reports, it should be noted that explicit recommendations related to concrete strategies that programs can implement to strengthen focus areas are not included in the report. The YAPS authors might consider providing research-based improvement strategies for each of the targeted areas to further guide programs.

More transparency is needed to describe the development of this scale. Greater description of the process used to develop the questionnaire and more detail related to relevant characteristics of the students who participated in the development process have implications for establishing generalizability and validity. Further, the validity evidence provided was limited. Revision of these sections is strongly recommended.

Additional pilot testing, independent uses of this survey, and transparency in samples used for these studies would benefit the evidence for reliability and validity for this questionnaire. Only two pilot tests were reported, and the demographics of both included only ages of participants. Finally, this guide does an impressive job at guiding program leaders through the process of administering the YAPS; however, potential users should take into account that adhering to the steps will take a considerable amount of time to plan and implement.

SUMMARY. The results of the YAPS could provide valuable information to youth development programs by connecting participant perspectives on the work being done within programs to concrete principles provided by the Community Programs to Promote Youth Development. Whereas it is a strength that this survey gives voice to the participants in these programs, it is also a limitation acknowledged by the survey authors. The YAPS should be used with caution until reliability and validity evidence are established.

REVIEWER'S REFERENCES

American Educational Research Association, American Psychological Association, & National Council on Measurement in Education. (2014). *Standards for educational and psychological testing*. Washington, DC: American Educational Research Association.

Durlak, J. A., Weissberg, R. P., & Pachan, M. (2010). A meta-analysis of after-school programs that seek to promote personal and social skills in children and adolescents. *American Journal of Community Psychology, 45*(3), 294-309.

National Research Council and Institute of Medicine. (2002). *Community programs to promote youth development.* Washington, DC: National Academies Press.

Roth, J. L., & Brooks-Gunn, J. (2003). Youth development programs: Risk, prevention and policy. *Journal of Adolescent Health, 32*(3), 170-182.

Scales, P. C., Roehlkepartain, E. C., & Benson, P. L. (2010). *Teen voice 2010: Relationships that matter to America's teens.* Richfield and Minneapolis, MN: Best Buy Children's Foundation and Search Institute.

TESTS TO BE REVIEWED FOR THE TWENTY-SECOND MENTAL MEASUREMENTS YEARBOOK

By the time each new Mental Measurements Yearbook *reaches publication, the staff at the Buros Center has already collected many new and revised tests destined to be reviewed in the next* Mental Measurements Yearbook. *Following is a list of tests that meet the review criteria and that will be reviewed, along with additional tests published and received in the coming months, in* The Twenty-Second Mental Measurements Yearbook.

Aprenda: La Prueba de Logros en Español, Tercera Edición
Arizona Battery for Communication Disorders of Dementia-Second Edition

Classic Learning Test
Clinical Assessment of Articulation and Phonology-Second Edition
Comprehensive Trail-Making Test-Second Edition

DIBELS 8th Edition-Dynamic Indicators of Basic Early Literacy Skills-8th Edition

Gibson Test of Cognitive Skills
Group Embedded Figures Test [Second Edition Manual]

The Impact Message Inventory-Circumplex
Inwald Personality Inventory-2

Measure of Engagement, Independence, and Social Relationships, Research Edition

Millon Adolescent Clinical Inventory-II
Minnesota Multiphasic Personality Inventory-3

Personality Disorder Adjective Check List
PostConcussion Symptom Inventory-2

Sixteen Personality Factor Questionnaire, Sixth Edition
Slosson Intelligence Test-Fourth Edition
Social Skills Inventory [Second Edition Manual]

Test of Language Development-Intermediate: Fifth Edition
Trails-X

Visual Skills Appraisal, 2nd Edition

Wechsler Individual Achievement Test, Fourth Edition

TESTS REQUESTED BUT NOT RECEIVED

The staff of the Buros Center for Testing endeavors to acquire copies of every new or revised commercially available test. Descriptions of all tests are included in Tests in Print *and reviews for all tests that meet our review criteria are included in* The Mental Measurements Yearbook. *A comprehensive search of multiple sources of test information is ongoing, and test materials are regularly requested from publishers. Many publishers routinely provide review copies of all new test publications. However, some publishers refuse to provide materials and others advertise tests long before the tests are actually published. Following is a list of test titles that have been requested but not yet provided.*

Abel Assessment for Sexual Interest–3 for Men and Women
Abel Assessment for Sexual Interest–2 for Boys and Girls
The Abel-Blasingame Assessment for Individuals with Intellectual Disabilities
Abilities Forecaster
Ability Test
Acadience Reading Diagnostic: Phonemic Awareness & Word Reading and Decoding
Acadience Reading K-6
Acadience Reading Survey
Access Reading Test, Second Edition
Accuracy Level Test
AccuRater
AccuVision
ACER General Ability Tests (AGAT)
ACER Select
Achiever
ACT Assessment
The ACT Survey Services [Revised]
ACTFL Listening Proficiency Test
ACTFL Oral Proficiency Interview
ACTFL Reading Proficiency Test
ACTFL Writing Proficiency Test
Acumen Leadership WorkStyles
Acumen Team Skills
Acumen Team WorkStyles
Adaptiv Resilience Factor Inventory
Adaptive Behavior Evaluation Scale, Revised Second Edition
Adaptive Matrices Test
Adaptive Tachistoscopic Traffic Perception Test
Admitted Student Questionnaire and Admitted Student Questionnaire Plus
Adolescent Coping Scale, Second Edition
The Adolescent Multiphasic Personality Inventory
Adolescent Self-Report and Projective Inventory
Adult Critical Threat Assessment
Adult Health Nursing
Adult Life Skills
Adult Measure of Essential Skills
Adult Reading Test
Adult Temperament Questionnaire, Second Edition [2017]
Adult Youth Engagement Survey
Advanced Management Tests
The Advanced Problem Solving Tests
Affective Go/No-go
Agentic Leadership Questionnaire
Aggression Assessment Method
Aggressive Driving Behavior
Aggressive Incidents Scale (AIS)
AIMSweb Plus
Alcoholic Selection Procedure
Allied Health Aptitude Test
Analytical Aptitude Skills Evaluation
Analytical Reasoning Skills Battery
Apperceptive Personality Test
Applicant Potential Test
Applied Technology Series
Aprenda: La Prueba de Logros en Español, Tercera Edición
Aptitude Assessment
Aptitude Test Battery for Pupils in Standards 6 and 7
Aptitude Tests Portfolio
The Arabic Speaking Test
The Area Coordinator Achievement Test
Arizona Basic Assessment and Curriculum Utilization System for Young Handicapped Children
Armed Services Vocational Aptitude Battery [Revised]
Arno Profile System
ASI Resident Assessment for Juvenile Justice
Asperger's Disorder Assessment Scale
Assertiveness Style Profile
Assessing Barriers to Education
Assessing Levels of Comprehension
Assessing Semantic Skills Through Everyday Themes
Assessment of Collaborative Tendencies [Revised]
Assessment of Competencies and Traits
Assessment of Dual Diagnosis
Assessment of Functional Living Skills
Assessment of Grandparenting Style
Assessment of Organizational Readiness for Mentoring
Assessment of Sound Awareness and Production

Child-Focused Toddler and Infant Experiences: Revised Form
Child Health Nursing
Child Health Questionnaire
Child Observation Record (COR) for Infants and Toddlers
Children's Interaction Matrix
Children's Self-Report and Projective Inventory
Children's Assessment of Participation and Enjoyment/Preferences for Activities of Children
Children's Depression Scale, Third Edition
Children's Progress Academic Assessment
Choice Reaction Time
CITE Learning Styles Instrument
Citizenship
CLEP Education Assessment Series
Clerical Series Test Modules
Clerical Test Battery
Clifton StrengthFinder
Clinical Assessment of Interpersonal Relationships
Cloze Reading Tests 1-3, Second Edition
Coaching Competencies Questionnaire
Coaching Effectiveness Profile
Cognitive (Intelligence) Test: Nonverbal
Cognitive Abilities Test, Form 8
The Cognitive Assessment of Minnesota
Cognitive Linguistic Quick Test-Plus
Cognitive Performance Test (CPT)
Cognitive Stability Index
Cognitive, Linguistic and Social-Communicative Scales
Cognitrone
College Entrance Test
College Majors Scorecard
College Portfolio Builder
College Success
Collegiate Assessment of Academic Proficiency (CAAP)
Collegiate Assessment of Academic Proficiency [Revised]
Colorado Malingering Tests
Colorado Neuropsychology Tests
Common Instrument Suite
The Communication Behaviors Inventory II
Communication Checklist-Adult
Communication Checklist-Self-Report
Communication Competency Assessment Instrument
Communication Effectiveness Profile
Communication Independence Profile for Adults
Communication Style Inventory
Community College Student Experiences Questionnaire, Second Edition
Community Health Nursing
Compass
COMPASS Managerial Practices Profile
Competency-Based Position Analysis
Composite International Diagnostic Interview
Comprehensive Nursing Achievement Test for Practical Nursing Students
Comprehensive Nursing Achievement-PN
Comprehensive Nursing Achievement-RN
Comprehensive Personality Analysis
Comprehensive Test of Adaptive Behavior--Revised
Comprehensive Testing Program III
Computer-Based Test of English as a Foreign Language and Test of Written English
The Computer Category Test
Computer Optimized Multimedia Intelligence Test
Computer Programmer Ability Battery
The Concise Learning Styles Assessment
Concussion Resolution Index
Conflict Style Instrument
Continuous Visual Recognition Task
Controller Staff Selector
Copeland Symptom Checklist for Attention Deficit Disorders, Adult Version
Copeland Symptom Checklist for Attention Deficit Disorders, Child and Adolescent Version
Coping Inventory for Stressful Situations, Second Edition
Coping Scale for Adults, Second Edition
COPS Interest Inventory (1995 Revision)
COPSystem Picture Inventory of Careers
COR Advantage
Core Abilities Assessment
Core Concepts Promotional Exam Series
Core Values Index
Corporate Communication Assessment
Corrections Promotional Exams
Corsi-Block-Tapping-Test
Counterproductive Behavior Index
Courageous Leadership Profile
Creating a Great Place to Learn
Creative Response Evaluation
Creativity Questionnaire
Creativity/Innovation Effectiveness Profile
Criterion-Referenced Articulation Profile
Criterion Test of Basic Skills-2
Criterion Validated Written Tests for Firefighter [Revised]
Critical Thinking in Clinical Nursing Practice-PN
Critical Thinking in Clinical Nursing Practice-RN
Critical Thinking Test
Cultural Diversity and Awareness Profile
Customer Care Ability Test
Customer Satisfaction Practices Tool
Customer Service Commitment Profile
Customer Service Listening Skills Exercise
Customer Service Profile
Customer Service Simulator
Customer Service Skills Profile
Customer Service Survey
Customer Service Styles
Customer Support Test

Dark Triad of Personality at Work (TOP)

Data Entry and Data Checking Tests
Data Entry Test
Dealing With Conflict Instrument
DecideX
Decision Style Profile
Delayed Matching to Sample
Dementia Questionnaire for People with Learning Disabilities
Denison Leadership Development Survey
Denison Organizational Culture Survey
Detailed Assessment of Speed of Handwriting
Determination Test
Determination Test for Children
Developmental Eye Movement Test
Developmental Reading Assessment, 2nd Edition PLUS
Developmental Reading Assessment, Third Edition
Developmental Therapy Rating Inventory of Teacher Skills
Devereux Student Strengths Assessment-High School Edition
Diagnostic Assessment for the Severely Handicapped II
Diagnostic Evaluation of Articulation and Phonology, U.K. Edition
Diagnostic Evaluation of Articulation and Phonology, U.S. Edition
The Diagnostic Inventory of Personality and Symptoms
Diagnostic Mathematics Profiles
Diagnostic Online Mathematics Assessment (DOMA)
Diagnostic Prescriptive Assessment
Diagnostic Readiness Test-PN
Diagnostic Readiness Test-RN
The Diana Screen
Differential Aptitude Tests for Guidance
Differential Aptitude Tests for Schools
Differential Aptitude Tests for Selection
Differential Assessment of Autism & Other Developmental Disorders
Differential Attention Test
Differential Screening Test for Processing
Differential Stress Inventory
Dimensions of Excellence Scales [1991 Edition]
Dimensions of Self-Concept, Form W
Dimensions of Success
Discovering Diversity Profile
Discovery Leadership Profile
DISCStyles
Dispatch Supervisor Promotional Exam
Disruptive Behavior Rating Scale
Diversity & Cultural Awareness Profile
Diversity Survey
The Dot Counting Test
Double Labyrinth Test
Draw A Person Questionnaire
Drug/Alcohol Attitude Survey
Dynamic Assessment and Intervention: Improving Children's Narrative Abilities
Dynamic Loewenstein Occupational Therapy Cognitive Assessment (DLOTCA Battery)
Dynamic Loewenstein Occupational Therapy Cognitive Assessment for Geriatric Use (DLOTCA)
Dynamic Occupational Therapy Cognitive Assessment for Children
Dyslexia Portfolio
Dyslexia Screener
Dyslexia Screening Test-Junior
Dyslexia Screening Test-Secondary

Early Functional Communication Profile
Early Literacy Diagnostic Test
Early Repetition Battery
Early Years Easy Screen
ECHOS Early Childhood Observation System
Edinburgh Reading Tests [2002 Update]
Edinburgh Reasoning Series
Educational Assessment of School Youth for Occupational Therapists
Educational Development Series--Revised Edition
Educational Interest Inventory II
Efron Visual Acuity Test
Electronics and Instrumentation Technician
eMeasures of Vocabulary Growth
Emerging Leader Profile
Emerging Literacy & Language Assessment
Emo Questionnaire [Revised]
Emotion Recognition Task
Emotional and Behavior Problem Scale Second Edition: Renormed
Emotional Competence Inventory--University Edition
Emotional Intelligence Appraisal: Me Edition
Emotional Intelligence Appraisal: Multi-Rater and 360 Editions
Emotional Intelligence Profile
Emotional Intelligence Skills Assessment
Emotional Intelligence Style Profile
Emotional Quotient Scale for Children
Emotional Quotient Scale for Employee
Emotional Smarts!
Employability Competency System (ECS) Reading and Math
Employee Adjustment Survey
Employee Empowerment Survey
Employee Evaluation of Management Survey
Employee Opinion Survey
Empowerment Development Gauge and Evaluation
Empowerment Management Inventory
EMT-Basic
EMT-Intermediate
Entrepreneur EDGE
Entrepreneurial Aptitude Profile
Entry Level Police Officer Examination
Essential Skills Screener
The Ethical Type Indicator
Everyday Life Activities: Photo Series (ELA)

Everyday Memory Survey
eWrite Online Writing Assessment
Exam Preparation Inventory
Examining for Aphasia--Fourth Edition
Express Assessments
The Expressive Language Test, Second Edition
Expressive Language Test-2: Normative Update
Extended DISC
Eysenck Personality Scales

Facial Recognition
Facilitation Skills Inventory
Faculty Survey of Student Engagement
Family Child Care Program Quality Assessment
Family Crisis Oriented Personal Evaluation Scales
Family Evaluation Form
Family History Analysis
Farnsworth Lantern Color Vision Test
Fieldwork Performance Evaluation for the Occupational Therapy Student
Fifteen Factor Questionnaire
Fiteen Factor Questonnaire Plus
Filipino Family Relationship Scale
Filipino Professional/Technical Employee Needs Inventory
Financial Literacy Inventory
Fire Engineer
Fire Inspector and Senior Fire Inspector
Fire Service Administrator (Battalion Chief)
Fire Service Administrator (Captain) 574
Fire Service Administrator (Chief) 578
Fire Service Administrator (Deputy Chief)
Fire Service Supervisor (Sergeant, Lieutenant)
Fire Service Supervisor Exams
Firefighter Driver/Engineer Promotional Exam
Firefighter Examinations 275.1 and 275.2
Firefighter Test: B-4
Firefighter Test: B-3
Flicker/Fusion Frequency
Flynt/Cooter Comprehensive Reading Inventory-2
Following Instructions Test
Form CR (Creativity)
Form L (Learning How You Learn)
Formative Assessment System for Teachers (FAST)
Foundations of Nursing
Four-Lenses Assessment
Four Sigma Qualifying Test
FourSight Thinking Profile
French Reading Comprehension Tests
The French Speaking Test
Functional Analysis of Behavior
Functional Assessment for Multiple Causality
Functional Assessment of Communication Skills for Adults (ASHA-FACS)
Functional Communication Profile--Revised
Functional Hearing Inventory
Functional Independence Skills Handbook
Functional Language Assessment and Intervention Sourcebook
The Functional Time Estimation Questionnaire
Further Education Reasoning Test

Gardner Social (Maturity) Developmental Scale
Gates-MacGinitie Reading Test, Second Canadian Edition
General Clerical Test-Revised
General Education Performance Index
General Health Questionnaire
General Interest Structure Test
General Reasoning Test
Genos Emotional Intelligence Multi-Rater Assessment
The German Speaking Test
Gifted Evaluation Scale--Third Edition
Global Executive Leadership Inventory
Global Mindset Inventory
Global Perspective Inventory
Goal/Objective Setting Profile
Gold
Golden Personality Type Profiler
Graded Naming Test
The Graduate and Management Problem Solving Series
Graduate Appraisal Questionnaire
Graduate Reasoning Test
Group Diagnostic Reading Aptitude and Achievement Tests, Intermediate Form
Group Literacy Assessment
Group Mathematics Test, Third Edition
Group Perceptions Inventory
Group-Level Team Assessment

Halstead Russell Neuropsychological Evaluation System, Revised
Hamilton Anatomy of Risk Management
Hand Tool Dexterity Test
Hare P-Scan Research Version 2
Harvard Trauma Questionnaire
Health and Illness: Adult Care
Healthcare Employee Productivity Report
HELP Strands (Hawaii Early Learning Profile)
The HELP Test-Elementary
Herrmann Brain Dominance Instrument [Revised]: Thinking Styles Assessment
High Performing Organizations Assessment
The Highlands Ability Battery
The Highly Effective Meeting Profile
Hill Interaction Matrix [Revised]
Hilson Adolescent Profile--Version S
Hilson Career Satisfaction Index
Hilson Life Adjustment Profile
Hilson Safety/Security Risk Inventory
The Hindi Proficiency Test
Hiskey-Nebraska Test of Learning Aptitude [Renormed]
Hodder Group Reading Tests 1-3
Hogan Business Reasoning Inventory

Holistic Student Assessment
Honesty Survey
Honesty Test
Hopkins Symptom Checklist-25
Human Job Analysis

ICD-10 Checklists
ICT Self-Rating Scale
Identi-fi
In-Law Relationship Scale
Individual Growth and Development Indicators of Early Literacy, Second Edition (IGDIs)
Individual Growth and Development Indicators of Early Numeracy, Second Edition (IGDIs)
Individualized Mathematics Program
Infant-Toddler Program Quality Assessment
Influence Style Indicator
Influencing Skills Index
The Influencing Skills Inventory
Influencing Skills Profile
Influencing Strategies and Styles Profile
The Influencing Style Clock
Informal Reading Inventory: Preprimer to Twelfth Grade, 8th Edition
Information and Communications Technology Literacy Assessment
Initial Assessment: An Assessment for Reading, Writing and Maths [New Version]
Insight Pre-School
Insight Primary
Insight Secondary
Insights Discovery
IntegriTEST
Integrity Inventory
Integrity Survey
Intelligence Structure Battery
Intercultural Communication Inventory
Intercultural Development Inventory (IDI v3)
Interest-A-Lyzer Family of Instruments [manual and all 6 interest assessments]
Internal Customer Service Survey
Interpersonal Trust Surveys, Self, Revised Second Printing
InterSurvS
Interview Style Inventory
Inventory for Assessing a Biblically Based World-view of Cultural Competence Among Healthcare Professionals
Inventory for Assessing the Process of Cultural Competence Among Healthcare Professionals--Revised
Inventory for Assessing the Process of Cultural Competence Among Healthcare Professionals--Student Version
Inventory for Personality Assessment in Situations
Inventory of Classroom Style and Skills (INCLASS)
Inventory of Driving Related Personality Traits
Inventory of Gambling Situations
Inventory of Leadership Styles
Inventory of Program Stages of Development
Inventory of Religious Activities and Interests
Inwald Survey 5
Inwald Survey 8
IS Manager/Consultant Skills Evaluation
I-7 Impulsiveness Questionnaire

The Janus Competency Identification & Assessment System
The Japanese Speaking Test
Job Observation and Behavior Scale: Opportunity for Self-Determination
Job Requirements Questionnaire
Job Skills Training Needs Assessment
Job Values Inventory
Job-O Enhanced
Jonico Questionnaire
Jordan Dyslexia Assessment/Reading Program
Judgement
Judgment of Line Orientation
Jung type Indicator
Junior Scholastic Aptitude Test Battery (Standard 5)
Juvenile Treatment Outcome

The Kaufman Speech Praxis Test for Children
Kendrick Assessment Scales of Cognitive Ageing
Kilmann-Covin Organizational Influence Survey
Kilmanns Personality Style Instrument
Kilmanns Team-Gap Survey
Kilmanns Time-Gap Survey
Kindergarten Readiness Checklists for Parents
Kindergarten Readiness Test-Larson [2014 Edition]
Kohlman Evaluation of Living Skills--Third Edition
Kuder Career Interests Assessment
Kuder Career Search
Kuder Skills Assessment
Kuder Skills Confidence Assessment
Kuder Skills Confidence Assessment-A
Kuder Work Values Assessment

Langdon Adult Intelligence Test
Language Assessment for Grades 3 & 4
Language Assessment Scales, Reading and Writing
Language-Free Programmer/Analyst Aptitude Test
Language Processing Test-Revised
LAS Links Second Edition Placement Test
Law Enforcement Investigator Exam
Law School Survey of Student Engagement
Leader Action Profile
Leader Behavior Analysis II for Team Leaders
Leadership Competency Inventory [Revised]
Leadership Development Profile
Leadership Development Report
Leadership Development Series
Leadership Effectiveness Profile
Leadership Motivation Inventory
Leadership Qualities Scale
Leadership Skills Test

Learning & Study Strategies Inventory (LASSI) for Learning Online
Learning Accomplishment Profile System
Learning Climate Questionnaire
Learning Disability Evaluation Scale, Renormed Second Edition
Learning Styles Inventory, Version III
Leatherman Leadership Questionnaire II
Legendary Service Leader Assessment
Level of Service Inventory-Revised: Screening Version
Life Skills Inventory
Lifespace Access Profile
Lifestyle Questionnaire [Selby MillSmith]
Light Industrial Skills Test
LinguiSystems Articulation Test: Normative Update
Linking Skills Index
Linking Skills Profile
Listening & Literacy Index
The Listening Comprehension Test 2
Listening Comprehension Test-Adolescent: Normative Update
Listening Effectiveness Profile
Literacy Probe 7-9
Lockout/Tagout
Lore Leadership Assessment II
Lowenstein Occupational Therapy Cognitive Assessment Battery [Second Edition]

Magellan 6
Maintenance Planner
Making a Terrific Career Happen (MATCH)
Management Behavior Assessment Test
Management Development Questionnaire [The Psychological Corporation]
Management Effectiveness Profile
Management Practices Inventory II
Management Skills and Styles Assessment
Management Training Needs Analysis
Management/Impact
The Managerial and Professional Profiles
Managing Performance
Mann Assessment of Swallowing Ability (MASA)
MAP (Measuring and Assessing Individual Potential)
Marriage Assessment Inventory
Marshalla Oral Sensorimotor Test
Maternity and Child Health Nursing
Maternity Infant Nursing
Math GOALS
Math Grade-Placement Tests
The Math Inventory
Mathematical Achievement Test
Mathematics in Practice
Matson Evaluation of Drug Side-Effects
Matson Evaluation of Social Skills for Individuals with Severe Retardation
Matson Evaluation of Social Skills in Youngsters-II
The McQuaig System
Me and My World
Measured Success
Measurement, Reading, & Arithmetic
Measures in Health Psychology Portfolio
Measures of Guidance Impact
Mechanical Ability Test
Mechanical Reasoning Ability Test
Mechanical-Technical Perceptive Ability
Medical College Admission Test
Meeting Effectiveness Questionnaire
MEGA Risk Assessment Tool
Member Satisfaction Survey
Mental Health Concepts
Mentoring Dynamics Survey Online
Metric Assessment of Personality
MFaCTs: Mathematics Fluency and Calculation Tests-Elementary
MFaCTs: Mathematics Fluency and Calculation Tests-Secondary
Michigan English Language Assessment Battery
Michigan Screening Profile of Parenting
Michigan State Suggestibility Profiles
Middle Years Ability Test
Mill Hill Vocabulary Scales
Miller Emotional Maturity Scale
Miller Self-Concept Scale
Miller Stress Scale
MindStreams
Mini International Neuropsychiatric Interview
Minnesota Cognitive Acuity Screen
Minnesota Developmental Programming System Behavioral Scales
Montgomery Assessment of Vocabulary Acquisition
Moray House Tests
Motivation Questionnaire
Motor Performance Series
Motor Screening Task
Movement ABC
Movement Assessment Battery for Children--Second Edition
The MSFI College of Law Admission Test
Multi-Digit Memory Test
Multi-Dimensional Pain Scale
Multidimensional Personality Questionnaire
Multidimensional Verbal Intelligence Test
Multi-Level Management Surveys
Multi-Motive Grid
Multi-Tasking Ability Test
Multiphasic Environmental Assessment Procedure [1998 Revision]
Myself as a Learner Scale Digital

National Basic Abilities Test
National Correctional Office Selection Inventory
The National Corrections Officer Selection Test
National Criminal Justice Officer Selection Inventory-Integrity

National Firefighter Selection Inventory
The National Firefighter Selection Test & National Firefighter Selection Test--Emergency Medical Services
The National First- and Second-Line Supervisor Tests
The National Police Officer Test [Revised]
National Public Safety Dispatcher Selection Inventory
NCTE Cooperative Test of Critical Reading and Appreciation
Negotiation Style Instrument
Neitz Test of Color Vision
Nelson Assessment: Mathematics
Network Technician Staff Selector
Networking & Relationship Building Profile
The New Jersey Test of Children's Reasoning
The New Jersey Test of Reasoning [Adult Version]
New Non-Reading Intelligence Tests 1-3
New Salford Sentence Reading Test
New Workers Inventory
Next Generation Ability Tests
NOCTI Experienced Worker Assessments
NOCTI Job Ready Assessments
Non-verbal IQ Test
Non-Verbal Learning Test
Normative Adaptive Behavior Checklist--Revised
Norris-Ryan Argument Analysis Test
NSight Aptitude/Personality Questionnaire
Numeracy Progress Tests
Numerical Computation Test
Nursing Care During Childbearing and Nursing Care of the Child
Nursing Care in Mental Health and Mental Illness
Nursing Care of Adults, Parts I, II, and III
Nursing Care of Children
Nursing the Childbearing Family

O'Connor Finger Dexterity Test
O'Connor Tweezer Dexterity Test
O*Net Ability Profiler
Objective Achievement Motivation Test
Occupational Interest Profile
Occupational Personality Profile
Occupational Preference Inventory
Occupational Therapy Driver Off-Road Assessment Battery
Occupational: Administrative Personnel
Occupational: Customer Service
Odor Memory Test
Office Systems Battery
Ohio Vocational Competency Assessment
Older Adult Cognitive Screener
Online Sales Effectiveness Profile
Ontario Numeracy Assessment Package
Ontario Writing Assessment
The Opportunities-Obstacles Profile
Oral Communication Battery
Organisational Transitions
Organizational Assessment Survey
Organizational Climate Survey
Organizational Courage Assessment
Organizational Focus Questionnaire
Organizational Survey System

Pacesetter
Paediatric Index of Emotional Distress
Pair Behavioral Style Instrument
Paramedic
Parent as a Teacher Inventory [2012 Revision]
Parent-Child Interaction Feeding & Teaching Scales
Parental Involvement in Education Scale
Parenting Needs Inventory for Parents
Parolee Inventory
Partner Power Profile
Partnering Development Assessment
P.A.S.S. III Survey
Paternal Role Survey
Pathognomonic Scale
Pathways to Independence, Second Edition
Patriarch
PCA Checklist for Computer Access
Pediatric Performance Validity Test Suite (PdPVTS)
Pediatric Symptoms Checklist
Peer Relations Assessment Questionnaires-Revised (PRAQ-R)
The Perceived Efficacy and Goal Setting System
Perception and Attention Functions
PERFORM Rating Scale
Performance Coaching
Performance Management Assessment System
Performance On-Line
Performance Skills Quality Teams Assessment
Performer
Peripheral Perception
Perseveration Test
Personal Effectiveness Profile
Personal Interest and Values Survey
Personal Listening Profile
Personal Profile Analysis
Personal Stress & Well-being Assessment
The Personality Preference Profile
Personality Questionnaire
Personality Style at Work Assessment
Personnel Security Standards Psychological Questionnaire
Personnel Selection Inventory
Pharmacology in Clinical Nursing
Phoneme Factory Phonology Screener
Phonics Early Reading Assessment
Phonological Awareness & Reading Profile
Phonological Awareness Literacy Screening 1-3 (PALS 1-3)
Phonological Awareness Literacy Screening-K (PALS-K)
Phonological Awareness Literacy Screening-PreK (PALS-PreK)
The Phonological Awareness Profile
The Phonological Awareness Test 2
Phonological Awareness Test-2: Normative Update

Physical Assessment
Pictorial Inventory of Careers [Revised]
Picture Interest Exploration Survey
Pictured Feelings Instrument
Pikunas Adult Stress Inventory
PIP Developmental Charts, Second Edition
PLAN [Revised]
The Play Observation Scale [2001 Revision]
Plotkin Index
PM Benchmark Kit
PN Fundamentals
PN Pharmacology
Police Administrator (Assistant Chief) 566
Police Administrator (Captain) 565
Police Administrator (Chief) 568
Police Administrator (Lieutenant) 564
Police Candidate Background Self-Report
Police Corporal/Sergeant Examination 562 and 563
Police Officer Examinations 175.1 and 175.2
Police Officer Morale Survey
Police Officer: A-2
Police Radio Dispatcher
Polymath Intellectual Ability Scale
Portland Digit Recognition Test [Revised]
Positive and Negative Syndrome Scale [Revised]
Positivity Test
Post-Heroic Leadership
POWER
Power and Performance Measures-Revised
The Praxis Series: Professional Assessments for Beginning Teachers
Pre High School Placement Test (Pre-HSPT)
Pre-Admission Examination-PN
Pre-Admission Examination-RN
Pre-Post Inventory [Behavior Data Systems, Ltd.]
Pre-Referral Intervention Manual, Fourth Edition
Predictive Early Assessment: Reading Language
Predictive Index
The Predictive Reading Profile
Predictive Sales Survey
The Preferred Leader Assessment
The Preliminary Hindi Proficiency Test
The Preliminary Japanese Speaking Test
Premenstrual Assessment Form
The Preschool Behavioral and Emotional Rating Scale
Preschool Development Inventory
Preschool Evaluation Scale, Second Edition
Preschool Visual-Motor Integration Assessment
The Press Test [Revised]
The Prevue Assessment
Primary Reading Test
Primary WRAP--Writing and Reading Assessment Profile
PROBE 2
Probity/Honesty Inventory
Problem Situation Inventory
Problem-Solving & Decision-Making Profile
Professional Profile
Profile of Learning Styles [GL Assessment England]
Profile of Personal Development Needs
Profile of Preschool Learning and Developmental Readiness (ProLADR)
PROFILE:MATCH2
Progress in English
Progress in Maths 4-14
Progress in Maths 6-14 Digital
Progress in Reading Assessment
Progressive Achievement Tests in Mathematics, Fourth Edition
Progressive Achievement Tests in Reading, Fourth Edition (PAT-R 4)
Progressive Achievement Tests in Science (PATScience)
Progressive Achievement Tests in Written Spelling, Punctuation and Grammar (PAT-SPG)
Proof Reading Test
Propensity to Leave a Job
ProWrite
Psychiatric Mental Health Nursing
Psycho-Moral and Self-Regulation Scale
Pulse Surveys

QbCheck
QbTest
QO2 Profile [Opportunities/Obstacles Quotient]
QPASS: The Quick Psycho-Affective Symptoms Scan
Qualitative Reading Inventory
Quality Customer Service Assessment
Quality Customer Service Test
Quality Effectiveness Profile
Quality Healthcare Employee Inventory
Quality of Communication Life Scale (ASHA-QCL)
Questionnaire Concerning Reaction to Pain
Questionnaire for the Determination of Suicide Risk
Questionnaire on Functional Drinking
Questions About Behavior Function
Questions About Behavior Function-Mental Illness
Quick Assessments for Neurogenic Communication Disorders
Quotient ADHD System

Racial Attitude Survey
Radio Operator and Senior Radio Operator
Rahim Social Intelligence Test (Observer & Self-Rating)
Randot Stereotests
RAPID Reading Assessment for Prescriptive Instructional Data
Rate Level Test
Reaction Test
Reading Efficiency Level Battery
Reading Efficiency Level Test
Reading Grade-Placement Tests
The Reading Inventory
Reading Now
Reading Observation Scale
Reading Power Essentials

Reading Progress Scale
Reading Style Inventory 2000
Ready School Assessment
Real Estate Instructor Examination
Reasoning 5-7 Test Series
Recovery Attitude and Treatment Evaluation
Recruitment Personality Test
Reid Report [29th Edition]
Reinstatement Review Inventory-II
Reiss Screen for Maladaptive Behavior
The Relationship Report Card
Relationship Selling Skills Inventory
Restaurant Manager Assessment Report
Retail Skills Test
Retail Store Manager Staff Selector
Right-Left Orientation
Risk Choice
The Risk for Sexual Violence Protocol (RSVP)
The Roberts Personality and Motivation Questionnaire
The Roberts Workstyles Profiler
Rookwood Driving Battery
Rossetti Infant-Toddler Language Scale
Rothwell Miller Values Blank
Rumble's Quest

Safety Effectiveness Profile
Sage Vocational Assessment System
Sales Effectiveness Profile
Sales Indicator
Sales Profile
Sales Skills Profile
Salford Sentence Reading Test (Revised)
Saville Consulting Wave
Scales for Service and Client Orientation
Scholastic Proficiency Test---Higher Primary Level
School Child Stress Scale
School Diversity Inventory
School Readiness Tests for Blind Children
Science Research Temperament Scale
Science, Social Studies, and Mathematics Academic Reading Test (SSSMART)
Scoreboard
Screening for Central Auditory Processing Difficulties
The Screening Tool of Feeding Problems
Secondary Level Assessment
Secondary Reading Assessment Inventory
Secord Contextual Articulation Test
Self-Assessment and Program Review for Positive Behavior Interventions and Supports
Self-Directed Learning Readiness Scale [Revised]
Self-Directed Team Assessment
Self-Image Profile for Adults
Self-Perceptions Inventory [2006 Revision]
Seligman Attributional Style Questionnaire
SELweb EE
SELweb LE
Senior South African Individual Scale--Revised
Sensomotor Coordination
SEPO (Serial Position) Test for the Detection of Guilty/Special Knowledge
Serial Digit Learning
Servant Leadership Inventory Forms A&B
Service Ability Inventory for the Healthcare Industry
Service First
Service Skills Indicator
Severe Impairment Battery-Short Form
Sexual Abuse Interview for the Developmentally Disabled
Sexual Violence Risk-20 (SVR-20) Version 2
SF-12: Physical and Mental Health Summary Scales
SF-36: Physical and Mental Health Summary Scales
Shore Handwriting Screening for Early Handwriting Development
The Shorr Couples Imagery Test
The Shorr Parent/Child Imagery Test
SigmaRadius 360° Feedback
Signal-Detection
Simulated Oral Proficiency Interview
Simultaneous Capacity/Multi-Tasking
Single Word Reading Test 6-16
Situational Leadership II Leadership Skills Assessment
Situational Leadership [Revised]
Six Factor Automated Vocational Assessment System
16+ PersonalStyle Profile
SkillCheck Professional Plus
Skills Navigator
Skills Pointer
Skills Profiler
Slosson Auditory Perceptual Skill Screener
Slosson Diagnostic Math Screener
Slosson Intelligence Test--Primary
Slosson Oral Reading Test--Revised 3
Slosson Phonics and Structural Analysis Test
Slosson Visual Perceptual Skill Screener
Slosson Visual-Motor Performance Test
Slosson Written Expression Test
Slosson-Diagnostic Math Screener
Smell Threshold Test
Social Communication Questionnaire
Social Competency Rating Form
Social Emotional Evaluation
Social Performance Survey Schedule
Social Use of Language Programme: Revised Edition
Somatic Inkblot Series
Spanish Articulation Measures--Revised Edition
Spanish Language Assessment Procedures, Third Edition
The Spanish Speaking Test
Spanish Test for Assessing Morphologic Production
Spatial Orientation
Special Abilities Scales
Special Needs Assessment Profile Infant Check
Special Needs Assessment Profile-Behavior
Speech and Language Checklists PLUS
Speech and Language Evaluation Scale, Second Edition
Spousal Assault Risk Assessment Guide, Version 3

StabiliTEST
Staff Burnout Scale for Police and Security Personnel
Stages of Concern Questionnaire
Stalking Assessment and Management (SAM)
Stanford English Language Proficiency Test 2
STAR Supplementary Tests of Achievement in Reading
Step One Survey
Strategic Acceleration Quotient Assessment
Strategic Leadership Type Indicator
Stress Management Questionnaire [Revised]
Stress Mastery Questionnaire
Structured Clinical Interview for DSM-5
Structured Interview for Disorders of Extreme Stress & Traumatic Antecedents Questionnaire--Self Report
Structured Observations of Sensory Integration-Motor
Structured Photographic Articulation Test-3 Featuring Dudsberry (SPAT-D 3)
Student Aspiration Inventory
Student Educational Assessment Screening
Student Self-Concept Scale
Super's Work Values Inventory-Revised
Supervisory Aptitude Test
Supervisory Proficiency Tests
Supervisory Skills Inventory
Supervisory Skills Questionnaire, Fifth Edition
Supervisory Skills Test
The Supplementary Shorr Imagery Test
SureHire
Survey of Beliefs
Survey of Implementation
Survey of Organizations
Survey of Student Resources & Assets
Sutherland Phonological Awareness Test, Revised
System for Testing and Evaluation of Potential
System of Interactive Guidance Information, Plus
Systematic Assessment of Voice

TABE Complete Language Assessment System-English
Tajma Personality Profile
Tangent Screen
TapDance
Targeted Prediction
Teacher and Student Technology Surveys
Teacher Performance Assessment
Teacher Performance Assessment [2006 Revision]
Team Assessment System
Team Charter Checkup
Team Climate Inventory
Team Culture Analysis
Team Dimensions Profile
Team Effectiveness Inventory
Team Empowerment Practices Test
Team Leader Competencies
Team Leader Skills Assessment
Team Management Index
Team Management Profile
Team Member Behavior Analysis
Team Performance Assessment
Team Performance Index
Team Performance Profile
Team Performance Questionnaire
Team Skills Indicator
Team Success Profile
Team-Review Survey
Teambuilding Effectiveness Profile
Technology and Internet Assessment
Telemarketing Ability Test
Temperament Comparator [Revised]
Temporal Orientation
TerraNova Online
Test Alert (Test Preparation)
Test of Academic Achievement Skills-Revised
Test of Adult Literacy Skills
Test of Assessing Secondary Completion
Test of Auditory Reasoning and Processing Skills
Test of English Language Learning (TELL)
Test of Everyday Attention for Children, Second Edition
Test of Grocery Shopping Skills
Test of Inductive Reasoning Principles
Test of Oral Reading and Comprehension Skills
Test of Pictures/Forms/Letters/Numbers Spatial Orientation and Sequencing Skills
Test of Problem Solving 2--Adolescent
Test of Problem Solving 3: Elementary: Normative Update
Test of Relational Concepts: Norms for Deaf Children
Test of Semantic Skills--Intermediate
Test of Semantic Skills--Primary
Test of Silent Reading Skills
Test of Verbal Conceptualization and Fluency
Test of Visual-Motor Skills--Upper Level
Tests of Adult Basic Education 11&12 (TABE 11&12)
Tests of Reading Comprehension, Second Edition
Tests of Reading Comprehension, Third Edition
The Texas Oral Proficiency Test
Theological School Inventory
360° Assessment and Development
360° By Design
360° Feedback Assessment
Thurston Cradock Test of Shame
Time Management Effectiveness Profile
Time Management Inventory
Time Mastery Profile
Time-Movement Anticipation
Titmus Stereo Fly Test
Tools for Assessment and Development of Visual Skills
Toronto Alexithymia Scale (TAS-20)
Total Brain
Total Quality Management Survey
Training Needs Assessment for Modern Leadership Skills
Training Needs Assessment Test
Training Proficiency Scale
Transition Behavior Scale, Third Edition
Truck Driver Inventory
TRUSTEE

Trustworthiness Attitude Survey
The Two Cultures Test
Two-Hand Coordination
Types of Work Index
Types of Work Profile

Undergraduate Assessment Program: Business Test
Urban District Assessment Consortium's Alternative Accountability Assessments
USES General Aptitude Test Battery for the Deaf

Valpar Computerized Ability Test
Value Assessment Scale
Value Development Index [Form A, Form B, Form C]
Values and Motives Questionnaire
Vanderbilt Assessment Scales
Verbal Dyspraxia Profile
Victim Index
Video-Based Law Enforcement Exam
Vienna Risk-Taking Test Traffic
Vigilance
Violence Ideation and Suicidality Treatment Algorithm
Visual Analogue Scales
Visual Form Discrimination
Visual Memory Test
Visual Pursuit Test
Visualization
The Vocabulary Gradient Test
Vocational Interest, Experience and Skill Assessment (VIESA), 2nd Canadian Edition

Warehouse/Plant Worker Staff Selector
What About You?
What's my Coaching Style?
What's my Communication Style?
What's my Leadership Style?
What's my Learning Style?
What's my Selling Style?
What's my Style?
What's my Team Member Style?
What's my Time Style?
Window on Work Values Profile
Wisconsin Personality Disorders Inventory-IV
Wonderlic Interactive Skills Evaluations, Keyboard and Office Skills
Wonderlic Interactive Skills Evaluations, Software Skills
Wonderlic Personnel Test and Scholastic Level Exam
Word Analysis Diagnostic Tests
Word Processing Aptitude Battery
The WORD Test 2-Adolescent
Words List
Work Expectations Profile
Work Habits, Attitudes and Productivity Scale [Employee and Student Editions]
Work Performance Series
Work Personality Profile & Computer Report
Work Preference Questionnaire [1990 Revision]
Work-Readiness Cognitive Screen
Work Skills Series Manual Dexterity
Work Team Simulator
Workforce Learning Systems--Reading and Math
Workforce Skills Certification System (WSCS)
Working and Organizational Motivation Inventory
Working Memory Rating Scale
Workplace Ergonomics Profile
Workplace Essentials Profile
Workplace Personality Inventory II
Workplace Personality Profile
Workplace Skills Survey--Form E
Workplace Speaking
WPS Electronic Tapping Test
Writing and Reading Assessment Profile (WRAP)
Written Language Observation Scale

Xyting In Sight

York Assessment of Reading for Comprehension (YARC Secondary)
Youth Outcomes Battery

ZooU

DISTINGUISHED REVIEWERS

Based on the recommendation of our National Advisory Council, the Buros Center for Testing is now making special recognition of the long-term contributions made by individual reviewers to the success of the Mental Measurements Yearbook *series. To receive the "Distinguished Reviewer" designation, an individual must have contributed to six or more editions of this series beginning with* The Ninth Mental Measurements Yearbook. *The first list below includes those who have now achieved Distinguished Reviewer status by their contribution to six or more editions as of the current* Twenty-First Mental Measurements Yearbook. *The second list includes those reviewers who qualified with their contribution to an earlier volume of the* Mental Measurements Yearbook *series (those who also reviewed in* The Twenty-First Mental Measurements Yearbook *are indicated with an asterisk). By virtue of their long-term service, all these individuals exemplify an outstanding dedication in their professional lives to the principles of improving the science and practice of testing.*

Shawn K. Acheson
Kathleen Allen
James A. Athanasou
Abigail Baxter
Roger A. Boothroyd
Jeffery P. Braden
Gary L. Canivez
Anthony T. Dugbartey
Zandra S. Gratz
Carl Isenhart
Timothy R. Konold
S. Kathleen Krach
Jody L. Kulstad**
Jennifer N. Mahdavi
Brad M. Merker
Leah M. Nellis
Arturo Olivarez, Jr.
Michael J. Scheel
Christopher A. Sink
Janet V. Smith
Romeo Vitelli
Georgette P. Yetter
Suzanne Young

**Distinguished as of *The Twentieth Mental Measurements Yearbook*

DISTINGUISHED REVIEWERS FROM PREVIOUS MENTAL MEASUREMENTS YEARBOOKS

(* Also reviewed for *The Twenty-First Mental Measurements Yearbook*)

*Phillip L. Ackerman
Caroline M. Adkins
*Mark Albanese
John O. Anderson
*Jeffrey A. Atlas
*James T. Austin
Stephen N. Axford
Patricia A. Bachelor
Laura L. B. Barnes
Phillip G. Benson
Ronald A. Berk
*Frank M. Bernt
Brian F. Bolton
Gregory J. Boyle
*Susan M. Brookhart
James Dean Brown
*Ric Brown
*Albert M. Bugaj
*Michael B. Bunch
Linda K. Bunker
Carolyn M. Callahan
*Karen T. Carey
Janet F. Carlson
JoEllen V. Carlson
*Russell N. Carney
C. Dale Carpenter
*Tony Cellucci
*Mary "Rina" Mathai Chittooran
Joseph C. Ciechalski
*Gregory J. Cizek
*Mary M. Clare
*Collie Wyatt Conoley
*Alice J. Corkill
Merith Cosden
*Andrew A. Cox
Kevin D. Crehan
*Rik Carl D'Amato
Ayres G. D'Costa
Gary J. Dean
Sharon H. deFur

Gerald E. DeMauro
*Beth Doll
George Engelhard, Jr.
*Connie T. England
Deborah B. Erickson
*Doreen Ward Fairbank
Robert Fitzpatrick
*Rosemary Flanagan
John W. Fleenor
Stephen J. Freeman
Michael J. Furlong
Robert K. Gable
Ronald J. Ganellen
John S. Geisler
Bert A. Goldman
*Theresa Graham Laughlin
J. Jeffrey Grill
Thomas W. Guyette
Richard E. Harding
Patti L. Harrison
*Michael R. Harwell
*Kate Hattrup
Theodore L. Hayes
*Sandra D. Haynes
*Carlen Henington
Allen K. Hess
Robert W. Hiltonsmith
*Thomas P. Hogan
*Anita M. Hubley
*David P. Hurford
*Jeffrey A. Jenkins
Kathleen M. Johnson
*Samuel Juni
*Ashraf Kagee
*Randy W. Kamphaus
*Michael G. Kavan
Timothy Z. Keith
Mary Lou Kelley
*Jean Powell Kirnan
Howard M. Knoff
*Joseph C. Kush
*Matthew E. Lambert
Suzanne Lane
Aimée Langlois
Joseph G. Law, Jr.
Frederick T. L. Leong
S. Alvin Leung
Cederick O. Lindskog
*Steven H. Long
*Ronald A. Madle
Cleborne D. Maddux
Koressa Kutsick Malcolm
*Rebecca J. McCauley
Frederic J. Medway
Joyce Meikamp
William B. Michael
*M. David Miller
Patricia L. Mirenda
Judith A. Monsaas
Kevin L. Moreland
Paul M. Muchinsky
*Mildred Murray-Ward
Anthony J. Nitko
Janet A. Norris
Salvador Hector Ochoa
Judy Oehler-Stinnett
D. Joe Olmi
Gretchen Owens
Steven Ira Pfeiffer
James W. Pinkney
*David J. Pittenger
*Julia Y. Porter
G. Michael Poteat
Shawn Powell
Nambury S. Raju
Paul Retzlaff
Cecil R. Reynolds
Bruce G. Rogers
*Cynthia A. Rohrbeck
Michael J. Roszkowski
Darrell L. Sabers
Vincent J. Samar
Jonathan Sandoval
Eleanor E. Sanford-Moore
William I. Sauser, Jr.
Diane J. Sawyer
*William D. Schafer
Gregory Schraw
Gene Schwarting
*Steven R. Shaw
Eugene P. Sheehan
*Jeffrey K. Smith
Lisa F. Smith
Loraine J. Spenciner
Jayne E. Stake
*Stephanie Stein
Terry A. Stinnett
Richard B. Stuart
Gabrielle Stutman
Hoi K. Suen
Mark E. Swerdlik
*Nora M. Thompson
*Gerald Tindal
Roger L. Towne
Michael S. Trevisan
John J. Vacca
Wilfred G. Van Gorp
*James P. Van Haneghan
*Chockalingam Viswesvaran
*Sandra B. Ward
T. Steuart Watson
*Keith F. Widaman
*Martin J. Wiese
*William K. Wilkinson
*Claudia R. Wright
James E. Ysseldyke
*Peter Zachar
Sheldon Zedeck

CONTRIBUTING TEST REVIEWERS

SHAWN K. ACHESON, Clinical Neuroscience Services of WNC, Durham, NC

PHILLIP L. ACKERMAN, Professor of Psychology, Georgia Institute of Technology, Atlanta, GA

SANDRA T. ACOSTA, Associate Professor of Bilingual Education, Educational Psychology, Texas A&M University, College Station, TX

MARK A. ALBANESE, Director of Testing and Research, National Conference of Bar Examiners, Professor Emeritus, University of Wisconsin-Madison, Madison, WI

VINCENT C. ALFONSO, Dean, School of Education, Gonzaga University, Spokane, WA

KATHLEEN D. ALLEN, Professor of Education and Counseling Psychology, Saint Martin's University, Lacey, WA

DAVID ALPIZAR, doctoral candidate, Educational Psychology, Washington State University, Pullman, WA

JACQUELINE ANDERSON, Doctoral Student in School Psychology, University of Houston, Houston, TX

LILITH ANTINORI, Graduate Student in Clinical Psychology, The George Washington University, Washington, DC

ANDREA ANTONIUK, Graduate Student in School and Clinical Child Psychology, Educational Psychology, University of Alberta, Edmonton, AB, Canada

KATHLEEN ASPIRANTI, Assistant Professor, Youngstown State University, Youngstown, OH

MICHELLE ATHANASIOU, Professor of School Psychology, University of Northern Colorado, Greeley, CO

JAMES ATHANASOU, Associate Professor, University of Sydney, Maroubra, New South Wales, Australia

JEFFREY A. ATLAS, Director, Mental Health Services, SCO Family of Services, Queens, NY

JAMES T. AUSTIN, Program Lead for Assessment Services for Center on Education and Training for Employment, The Ohio State University, Columbus, OH

JORDAN AUSTIN, Doctoral Student, University of North Carolina, Greensboro, Greensboro, NC

DEBORAH L. BANDALOS, Professor of Assessment and Measurements, James Madison University, Harrisonburg, VA

LUCY BARNARD-BRAK, Associate Professor, University of Alabama, Tuscaloosa, AL

SHERI BAUMAN, Professor of Counseling, Department of Disability and Psychoeducational Studies, University of Arizona, Tucson, AZ

ABIGAIL BAXTER, Professor, Department of Leadership and Teacher Education, University of South Alabama, Mobile, AL

A. ALEXANDER BEAUJEAN, Associate Professor of Psychology and Neuroscience, Baylor University, Waco, TX

LEIGH J. BEGLINGER, Department of Adult Neuropsychology, St. Luke's Rehabilitation Hospital, Boise, ID

SARA BENDER, Associate Professor of Psychology, Central Washington University, Ellensburg, WA

NICHOLAS F. BENSON, Associate Professor of School Psychology, Baylor University, Waco, TX

FRANK BERNT, Professor of Teacher Education, Saint Joseph's University, Philadelphia, PA

MICHAEL BIBENS, Ph.D. Student, Oklahoma State University Center for Health Sciences, Tulsa, OK

WARREN BOBROW, President, All About Performance LLC, Los Angeles, CA

JANE E. BOGAN, Associate Professor of Education, Wilmington College, Wilmington, OH

KATHY J. BOHAN, Associate Professor of Educational Psychology-School Psychology, Northern Arizona University, Flagstaff, AZ

SARAH BONNER, Associate Professor, Hunter College, City University of New York, New York City, NY

ROGER A. BOOTHROYD, Professor, Department of Mental Health Law and Policy, Louis de la Parte Florida Mental Health Institute, College of Behavioral and Community Sciences, University of South Florida, Tampa, FL

MARGARET P. BOYER, Doctoral Student, University of California-Santa Barbara, Santa Barbara, CA

MARY BOYLE, Professor of Communication Sciences & Disorders, Montclair State University, Montclair, NJ

JEFFERY P. BRADEN, Professor of Psychology, Dean, College of Humanities and Social Sciences, North Carolina State University, Raleigh, NC

ERIN BRENNAN, doctoral student, University of South Florida, Department of Educational and Psychological Studies, Tampa, FL
JOHN J. BRINKMAN, Professor of Psychology and Counseling, University of Saint Francis, Fort Wayne, IN
SUSAN BROOKHART, Professor Emerita, Duquesne University, Pittsburgh, PA
RIC BROWN, Adjunct Faculty, St. Johns University and Northern Arizona University, Professor Emeritus, California State University, Sacramento, CA
BETHANY A. BRUNSMAN, Assessment/Evaluation Specialist, Lincoln Public Schools, Lincoln, NE
ALBERT M. BUGAJ, Department of Psychology, University of Wisconsin–Green Bay, Green Bay, WI
ERIC S. BUHS, Associate Professor of Educational Psychology, University of Nebraska-Lincoln, Lincoln, NE
OKAN BULUT, Associate Professor of Measurement, Evaluation, and Data Science, University of Alberta, Edmonton, Alberta, Canada
MICHAEL B. BUNCH, Senior Vice President, Measurement Incorporated, Durham, NC
MELANIE BURGESS, PhD Counseling Student, PhD Counseling Student, Old Dominion University, Norfolk, VA
ROCHELLE CADE, Associate Professor, University of Mary Hardin-Baylor, Belton, TX
MICHAEL CAHILL, Assistant Provost, Regis University, Denver, CO
GARY L. CANIVEZ, Professor of Psychology, Department of Psychology, Eastern Illinois University, Charleston, IL
MICHAEL S. CANNIZZARO, Associate Professor, University of Vermont, Burlington, VT
KAREN T. CAREY, Provost, University of Alaska Southeast, Juneau, AK
RUSSELL N. CARNEY, Professor Emeritus of Psychology, Missouri State University, Springfield, MO
CATHLEEN CARNEY THOMAS, Assistant Professor, Communication Disorders and Sciences, Indiana State University, Terre Haute, IN
SHANI D. CARTER, Professor of Business, Wagner College, Staten Island, NY
MICHELE CASCARDI, Professor, Department of Psychology, William Paterson University, Wayne, NJ
TONY CELLUCCI, Professor and Director of the ECU Psychological Assessment and Specialty Services (PASS) Clinic, East Carolina University, Greenville, NC
SAMANTHA CHACE, Doctoral Student in Counseling Psychology, Auburn University, Auburn, AL
CARRIE A. CHAMP MORERA, Coordinator of Admissions Assessment, Milton Hershey School, Hershey, PA
JUAN CHEN, Research Psychometrician, National Conference of Bar Examiners, Madison, WI
MARY (RINA) M. CHITTOORAN, Associate Professor, School of Education, Saint Louis University, St. Louis, MO
GREGORY J. CIZEK, Guy B. Phillips Distinguished Professor of Educational Measurement and Evaluation, University of North Carolina-Chapel Hill, Chapel Hill, NC
MARY M. CLARE, Professor Emerita, Lewis & Clark College, Portland, OR
D. ASHLEY COHEN, Forensic Neuropsychologist, CogniMetrix, San Jose, CA
DANA R. CONNOR, Staff Neuropsychologist, Henry Ford Health System, Detroit, MI
COLLIE W. CONOLEY, Professor, University of California-Santa Barbara, Santa Barbara, CA
CATHERINE G. COOGAN, Clinical Psychology Doctoral Student, The George Washington University, Washington, DC
ALICE CORKILL, Department Chair, University of Nevada, Las Vegas, Las Vegas, NV
DAMIEN C. CORMIER, Associate Professor of Educational Psychology, University of Alberta, Edmonton, AB, Canada
McKENNA COSOTTILE, Postdoctoral Fellow, Geisinger Health System, Danville, PA
KATHY L. COUFAL, Professor, Speech-Language Pathology, University of Nebraska-Omaha, Omaha, NE
ANDREW A. COX, Professor Emeritus, Counseling, Rehabilitation, and Interpreter Training, Troy University, Phenix City, AL
MICHAEL K. CRUCE, Nationally Certified School Psychologist, Educational Service Unit #6, Milford, NE
STEPHANIE M. CURENTON, Associate Professor, Boston University, Boston, MA
RIK CARL D'AMATO, Distinguished International Research Professor in School Psychology and Clinical Neuropsychology, the Chicago School of Professional Psychology, Chicago, IL
PRISCILLA M. DANIELSON, Speech/Language Pathologist and AT/AAC Specialist, Linguistic Solutions, LLC, Royal Oak, MD
KAIYLA DARMER, Doctoral Student, Temple University, Philadelphia, PA
MARIAH N. DAVIS, Doctoral Student of School Psychology, Temple University, Philadelphia, PA
MARIYA T. DAVIS, Assistant Professor of Special Education, Texas A&M University-San Antonio, San Antonio, TX
R. J. de AYALA, Professor, University of Nebraska-Lincoln, Lincoln, NE
GABRIEL DELLA-PIANA, Professor Emeritus in Educational Psychology, College of Education, University of Utah, Salt Lake City, UT
LEAH DEMBITZER, Assistant Professor, Concordia College-New York, Bronxville, NY
SHARI L. DeVENEY, Associate Professor of Special Education and Communication Disorders, University of Nebraska at Omaha, Omaha, NE

CHRISTINE DiSTEFANO, Professor, Educational Research and Measurement, University of South Carolina, Columbia, SC

BETH DOLL, University of Nebraska–Lincoln, Lincoln, NE

STEFAN C. DOMBROWSKI, Professor, School Psychology Program, Rider University, Lawrenceville, NJ

JAMES P. DONNELLY, Professor, Department of Counseling & Human Services, Director of Measurement & Statistics, Institute for Autism Research, Canisius College, Buffalo, NY

ANTHONY T. DUGBARTEY, Adjunct Associate Professor, Department of Psychology, University of Victoria, Victoria, British Columbia, and Forensic Psychiatric Services Commission, Victoria, British Columbia, Canada

CHELSEA DURBER, Ph.D. Candidate, Department of Educational Psychology, University of Alberta, Edmonton, Alberta, Canada

ROBIN L. EDGE, Associate Professor, Brooks Rehabilitation Department of Communication Sciences and Disorders, Jacksonville University, Jacksonville, FL

CONNIE THERIOT ENGLAND, Professor, Counseling Program, Lincoln Memorial University, Harrogate, TN

JOSEPH R. ENGLER, Associate Professor of School Psychology, Gonzaga University, Spokane, WA

CAROL EZZELLE, Director, Psychometrics, National Board for Professional Teaching Standards, Arlington, VA

DOREEN W. FAIRBANK, Professor, Psychology and Social Work Department, Meredith College, Raleigh, NC

RYAN L. FARMER, Assistant Professor, Oklahoma State University, Stillwater, OK

RACHEL FENTON, graduate student in clinical psychology, The George Washington University, Washington, DC

DENISE A. FINNERAN, Assistant Professor, Department of Communication Sciences and Disorders, University of Oklahoma Health Sciences Center, Oklahoma City, OK

CATHERINE A. FIORELLO, Professor of School Psychology, Temple University, Philadelphia, PA

AGNES FLANAGAN, Graduate Student in School and Clinical Child Psychology, Educational Psychology, University of Alberta, Edmonton, AB, Canada

ROSEMARY FLANAGAN, Independent Practice, Garden City, NY

RANDY G. FLOYD, Professor of Psychology, University of Memphis, Memphis, TN

LAURIE FORD, Associate Professor, School Psychology, University of British Columbia, Vancouver, BC, Canada

BRIAN F. FRENCH, Professor of Educational Psychology, Washington State University, Pullman, WA

DANIEL L. GADKE, Associate Professor of School Psychology, Mississippi State University, Mississippi State, MS

MAURICIO A. GARCIA-BARRERA, Associate Professor, Department of Psychology, University of Victoria, B.C., Canada

MARY L. GARNER, Professor Emeritus of Mathematics, Kennesaw State University, and Visiting Assistant Professor of Mathematics, Oglethorpe University, Atlanta, GA

CARLTON S. GASS, Neuropsychologist, TMH Physicians Partners Neurology Specialists, Tallahassee Memorial Healthcare, Tallahassee, FL

ALICIA GIALANELLA, Graduate Student, School Psychology Program, Rider University, Lawrenceville, NJ

KAREN L. GISCHLAR, Associate Professor, School Psychology Program, Rider University, Lawrenceville, NJ

REBECCA GOKIERT, Associate Professor, Faculty of Extension, University of Alberta, Edmonton, Alberta, Canada

JORGE E. GONZALEZ, Professor, School Psychology, University of Houston, Houston, TX

MONICA GORDON PERSHEY, Associate Professor, School of Health Sciences, Cleveland State University, Cleveland, OH

CHAD M. GOTCH, Assistant Professor of Educational Psychology, Washington State University, Pullman, WA

EDWARD E. GOTTS, MultiTED Associates, Madison, IN

STEFANIE GRABAN, Graduate Assistant, Duquesne University, Pittsburgh, PA

THERESA GRAHAM LAUGHLIN, Adjunct Faculty, Nebraska Methodist College of Nursing, Omaha, NE

CRISTINA GRANDA, Consulting Research Assistant, Boston University, Boston, MA

ZANDRA S. GRATZ, Professor of Psychology, Kean University, Union, NJ

THOMAS J. GROSS, Assistant Professor, Psychology Department, College of Education and Behavioral Sciences, Western Kentucky University, Bowling Green, KY

NANCY C. GULLATT, Professor of Speech Pathology, Department of Communication Sciences and Disorders, University of Oklahoma Health Sciences Center, Oklahoma City, OK

GRANT A. HACHERL, School Psychology Graduate Assistant, Psychology Department, College of Education and Behavioral Sciences, Western Kentucky University, Bowling Green, KY

JOHN D. HALL, Professor of Psychology and Counseling, Arkansas State University, State University, AR

WAYNE HANDLEY, Doctoral Student in Counselor Education and Supervision, Old Dominion University, Norfolk, VA

MICHAEL HARWELL, Professor, Department of Educational Psychology, University of Minnesota, Minneapolis, MN

KATE HATTRUP, Professor of Psychology, San Diego State University, San Diego, CA

JOHN K. HAWLEY, Engineering Psychologist, U.S. Army Research Laboratory, Ft. Bliss Field Element, Ft. Bliss, TX

LESLIE R. HAWLEY, Research Assistant Professor, Nebraska Center for Research on Children, Youth, Families and Schools, University of Nebraska-Lincoln, Lincoln, NE

SANDRA HAYNES, Chancellor, Washington State University Tri Cities, Richland, WA

CARLEN HENINGTON, Professor of Educational and School Psychology, Mississippi State University, Mississippi State, MS

ANNA HICKEY, Assistant Professor of Clinical Pediatrics, SIU School of Medicine, Springfield, IL

THOMAS P. HOGAN, Emeritus Professor of Psychology, University of Scranton, Scranton, PA

JANET HOUSER, Provost and Professor, Regis University, Denver, CO

ANITA M. HUBLEY, Professor of Measurement, Evaluation, and Research Methodology, University of British Columbia, Vancouver, British Columbia, Canada

DAVID M. HULAC, Associate Professor, University of Northern Colorado, Greeley, CO

DAVID P. HURFORD, Director of the Center for Research, Evaluation and Awareness of Dyslexia and Professor, Psychology and Counseling, Pittsburg State University, Pittsburg, KS

TIFFANY L. HUTCHINS, Associate Professor, University of Vermont, Burlington, VT

IHEOMA U. IRUKA, Chief Research Innovation Officer and Director, HighScope Educational Research Foundation, Ypsilanti, MI

CARL ISENHART, Psychologist, Phoenix VA Health Care System, Phoenix, AZ

CARRIE R. JACKSON, Professor of School Psychology, Youngstown State University, Youngstown, OH

ELLEN L. JACOBS, Director, Reading and Speech Clinic, Baker City, OR

JEFFREY A. JENKINS, Professor of Justice Studies, Roger Williams University, Bristol, RI

KEVIN B. JOLDERSMA, Senior Psychometrician, The American Board of Emergency Medicine, East Lansing, MI

JENNIFER JOLLY, Professor, University of Alabama, Tuscaloosa, AL

STEPHANIE JOSEPH, Doctoral Student, Temple University, Philadelphia, PA

SAMUEL JUNI, Professor, New York University, New York City, NY

ASHRAF KAGEE, Professor of Psychology, Stellenbosch University, Stellenbosch, South Africa

RUPA KALAHASTHI, Graduate Student in Clinical Psychology, The George Washington University, Washington, DC

RANDY W. KAMPHAUS, Professor and Dean, University of Oregon, Eugene, OR

ESTHER KAUFMANN, Senior Lecturer and Researcher, University of Zurich (Switzerland), Institute of Education, Zurich, Switzerland

MICHAEL G. KAVAN, Professor of Family Medicine and Professor of Psychiatry, Associate Dean for Student Affairs, Creighton University School of Medicine, Omaha, NE

ASHLEY KEENER, PhD, Research Assistant, Oklahoma State University Center for Health Sciences, Tulsa, OK

KARL N. KELLEY, Professor of Psychology, North Central College, Naperville, IL

RYAN J. KETTLER, Associate Professor, Rutgers, The State University of New Jersey, New Brunswick, NJ

RICHARD T. KINNIER, Professor of Counseling and Counseling Psychology, Arizona State University, Tempe, AZ

JEAN POWELL KIRNAN, Professor of Psychology, The College of New Jersey, Ewing, NJ

ANNETTE S. KLUCK, Assistant Provost for Women's Initiatives and Professor of Counseling Psychology, Auburn University, Auburn, AL

TIMOTHY R. KONOLD, Professor of Research, Statistics, and Evaluation, University of Virginia, Charlottesville, VA

LARRY KORTERING, Professor of Special Education, Appalachian State University, Boone, NC

S. KATHLEEN KRACH, Assistant Professor of School Psychology, Florida State University, Tallahassee, FL

SALLY KUHLENSCHMIDT, Professor of Psychology, Western Kentucky University, Bowling Green, KY

JOSEPH C. KUSH, Professor, Duquesne University, Pittsburgh, PA

SUSAN N. KUSHNER BENSON, Associate Professor of Educational Research, Assessment, and Evaluation, University of Akron, Akron, OH

MATTHEW E. LAMBERT, Private Practice, Granbury, TX

EMILY LAUTZENHEISER, Assistant Professor of Psychology and Counseling, University of Saint Francis, Fort Wayne, IN

KATHY LE, Master's in Clinical Mental Health Counseling, School of Education, Gonzaga University, Spokane, WA

ANGELINA LEE, PhD Candidate, School Psychology, University of British Columbia, Vancouver, Canada

HYESUN LEE, Assistant Professor of Psychology, California State University Channel Islands, Camarillo, CA

ZECCA LEHN, Independent Researcher, Huntington Beach, CA

DOUG LEIGH, Professor, Pepperdine University, Huntington Beach, CA

ADAM LEKWA, Assistant Research Professor, Rutgers, the State University of New Jersey, New Brunswick, NJ
MELANIE E. LEUTY, Associate Professor, Department of Psychology, University of Southern Mississippi, Hattiesburg, MS
ANNABEL W. LI, Graduate Student, University of Northern Colorado, Greeley, CO
HONGLI LI, Assistant Professor, Georgia State University, Atlanta, GA
JIEHAN LI, Graduate Student in Research and Evaluation Methods, University of Florida, Gainesville, FL
STEVEN H. LONG, Associate Professor, Marquette University, Milwaukee, WI
WILLIAM LORIÉ, Principal, Capital Metrics, Washington, DC
JUSTIN A. LOW, Associate Professor of Counseling and School Psychology, University of the Pacific, Stockton, CA
YE LUO, Assistant Professor, Department of Counseling and Higher Education, College of Education, University of North Texas, Denton, TX
ELIZABETH E. MacDOUGALL, Associate Professor of Psychology and Counseling, Hood College, Frederick, MD
KAREN MACKLER, District Psychologist, Lawrence Public Schools, Lawrence, NY
RONALD A. MADLE, Retired School Psychologist (formerly Shikellamy School District and Penn State University), Lewisburg, PA
JENNIFER N. MAHDAVI, Professor of Special Education, Sonoma State University, Rohnert Park, CA
DENISE E. MARICLE, Professor, Doctoral Program in School Psychology, Texas Woman's University, Denton, TX
MICHAEL MATTA, Adjunct Professor of Psychological Diagnosis, University of Milano-Bicocca, Milan, Italy
MICHAEL S. MATTHEWS, Professor of Gifted Education, Department of Special Education and Child Development, University of North Carolina at Charlotte, Charlotte, NC
SEAN MAXEY, Graduate Student of Counseling Psychology, University of British Columbia, Vancouver, British Columbia, Canada
REBECCA J. McCAULEY, Professor, Department of Speech and Hearing Science, The Ohio State University, Columbus, OH
MICHAEL P. McCREERY, Associate Professor, University of Nevada, Las Vegas, Las Vegas, NV
BRITTANY McGEEHAN, Doctoral Candidate in School Psychology, Texas Woman's University, Denton, TX
RYAN J. McGILL, Assistant Professor of School Psychology, William & Mary School of Education, Williamsburg, VA
LAUREEN J. McINTYRE, Speech-Language Pathologist and Associate Professor of Educational Psychology & Special Education, University of Saskatchewan, Saskatoon, Saskatchewan, Canada
TAMARA McKENZIE-HARTMAN, Defense and Veterans Brain Injury Center, James A. Haley VA Hospital, Tampa, FL
PATRICK J. McNICHOLAS, Doctoral Candidate, University of Memphis, Memphis, TN
TAWNYA MEADOWS, Pediatric Psychologist, Geisinger Health System, Danville, PA
KENNETH MELNICK, Associate Professor in the Communication Sciences and Disorders Department, Worcester State University, Worcester, MA
BRADLEY MERKER, Division Head, Neuropsychology, Henry Ford Health System, Detroit, MI
M. DAVID MILLER, Professor of Research and Evaluation Methods, University of Florida, Gainesville, FL
JOHN A. MILLS, Professor of Psychology, Indiana University of Pennsylvania, Indiana, PA
RAMA K. MISHRA, Neuropsychologist, Addictions and Mental Health, Medicine Hat Regional Hospital, Alberta, Canada
PHILIP J. MOBERG, Associate Professor, Northern Kentucky University, Highland Heights, KY
KIRK MOCHRIE, Doctoral Candidate in Clinical Health Psychology at East Carolina University, Greenville, NC
MAURA JONES MOYLE, Associate Professor, Marquette University, Milwaukee, WI
MILDRED MURRAY-WARD, Professor of Education, Retired, California State University, Stanislaus, Turlock, CA
SCOTT A. NAPOLITANO, Associate Professor of Practice, Department of Educational Psychology, University of Nebraska–Lincoln, Lincoln, NE
LEAH M. NELLIS, Dean and Professor, School of Education, Indiana University Kokomo, Kokomo, IN
DIANA B. NEWMAN, Associate Professor (Retired), Communication Disorders, Southern Connecticut State University, New Haven, CT
ILYSE O'DESKY, Associate Professor of Psychology, Kean University, Union, NJ; Chief of Psychology, Saint Barnabas Medical Center, Livingston, NJ; Director, Neuropsychological Testing Center, Springfield, NJ
KATHERINE O'NEIL, Doctoral Student in Counseling Psychology, Auburn University, Auburn, AL
ARTURO OLIVÁREZ, JR., Professor, Educational Leadership & Foundations Department, University of Texas at El Paso, El Paso, TX
TRACY L. PASKIEWICZ, Lecturer, School Psychology Program, University of Massachusetts-Boston, Boston, MA
THANOS PATELIS, Principal Scientist at Human Resources Research Organization and Research Scholar at Fordham University, New York City, NY
RHEA PAUL, Professor and Chair, Department of Communication Disorders, Sacred Heart University, Fairfield, CT

CHELSEA PEARSALL, Graduate Assistant, Department of Psychology, William Paterson University, Wayne, NJ

LAURA L. PENDERGAST, Associate Professor, Temple University, Philadelphia, PA

LISA L. PERSINGER, Assistant Professor, Northern Arizona University, Flagstaff, AZ

SOFIA PHAM, Postdoctoral Fellow of Behavioral Psychology, Westchester Institute for Human Development, Temple University, Philadelphia, PA

ROCHELLE PICARDO, Master's Student, School Psychology, University of British Columbia, Vancouver, BC, Canada

DAVID J. PITTENGER, Interim Associate Vice President for Outreach and Dean of the Graduate College, Marshall University, Huntington, WV

SANDRA I. PLATA-POTTER, Assistant Professor, Early Childhood Education, University of Mount Olive, Mount Olive, NC

NATALIE POLITIKOS, Associate Professor, Department of Psychology, University of Hartford, West Hartford, CT

JULIA Y. PORTER, National Certified Counselor, National Certified School Counselor, Mississippi Licensed Professional Counselor, Ocean Springs, MS

HEATHER POTTS, Advanced Doctoral Student, Syracuse University, Psychology Intern, SIU School of Medicine, Springfield, IL

DEBORAH M. POWELL, Associate Professor, University of Guelph, Guelph, Ontario, Canada

MARGARET B. POWELL, School Psychology Doctoral Candidate, Mississippi State University, Mississippi State, MS

ELIZABETH M. POWER, Assistant Professor, Department of School Psychology, the College of Saint Rose, Albany, NY

LISSA POWER deFUR, Professor, Communication Sciences and Disorders, and Director, Speech, Hearing, and Learning Services, Longwood University, Farmville, VA

PATRICIA A. PRELOCK, Professor and Dean, College of Nursing and Health Sciences, University of Vermont, Burlington, VT

KATHLEEN QUINN, Professor Emerita of Education, Holy Family University, and Former Director, Fall and Spring Reading Clinic, Bensalem, PA

GLEN E. RAY, Professor of Psychology, Auburn University at Montgomery, Montgomery, AL

SEAN REILLEY, Licensed Psychologist, Eastern State Hospital, Lexington, KY

RICHARD R. REILLY, Professor Emeritus, Stevens Institute of Technology, Hoboken, NJ

CYNTHIA A. ROHRBECK, Associate Professor of Psychology, The George Washington University, Washington, DC

STEVEN V. ROUSE, Professor of Psychology, Pepperdine University, Malibu, CA

LINDA RUAN, Doctoral Candidate in School Psychology, Temple University, Philadelphia, PA

ROBERT RUDDELL, Graduate Student of Counseling Psychology, University of British Columbia, Vancouver, British Columbia, Canada

SAMANTHA RUSHWORTH, M.S., Temple University, Philadelphia, PA

RICHARD RUTH, Associate Professor of Clinical Psychology, The George Washington University, Washington, DC

MEAGAN RYAN, Clinical Psychology Doctoral Student, The George Washington University, Washington, DC

LIA SANDILOS, Assistant Professor, Temple University, Philadelphia, PA

WILLIAM D. SCHAFER, Affiliated Professor (Emeritus), University of Maryland College Park, College Park, MD

MICHAEL J. SCHEEL, Professor, Educational Psychology, University of Nebraska-Lincoln, Lincoln, NE

CHARLES A. SCHERBAUM, Professor of Psychology, Baruch College, City University of New York, New York, NY

HANNAH SCHORPP, Graduate Student and Adjunct Professor, Department of Psychology, William Paterson University, Wayne, NJ

STEPHEN T. SCHROTH, Professor of Early Childhood Education/Gifted & Creative Education and Graduate Programs Director, Towson University, Towson, MD

AMY N. SCOTT, Associate Professor in the Counseling and School Psychology Program, University of the Pacific, Stockton, CA

CLAIRE SEEGER, Master's in Clinical Mental Health Counseling, School of Education, Gonzaga University, Spokane, WA

NATASHA SEGOOL, Associate Professor, Department of Psychology, University of Hartford, West Hartford, CT

STEVEN R. SHAW, Associate Professor of Counselling and Educational Psychology, McGill University, Montreal, QC, Canada

LYNN SHELLEY, Professor and Chair, Department of Psychology, Westfield State University, Westfield, MA

CARL J. SHEPERIS, Dean of the College of Education and Human Development, Texas A&M University-San Antonio, San Antonio, TX

DONNA S. SHEPERIS, Associate Professor, Department of Counseling, Palo Alto University, Los Altos, CA

MARK D. SHRIVER, Professor, Psychology, Munroe-Meyer Institute, University of Nebraska Medical Center, Omaha, NE

MARK E. SIBICKY, Professor of Psychology, Marietta College, Marietta, OH

MARC A. SILVA, James A. Haley Veterans Hospital, Mental Health and Behavioral Sciences Service, Tampa, FL

CHRISTOPHER A. SINK, Professor and Batten Chair, Counseling and Human Services, Old Dominion University, Norfolk, VA
AMY SKINNER, Doctoral Candidate in School Psychology, Texas Woman's University, Denton, TX
ALAN SMERBECK, Assistant Professor of Psychology, Rochester Institute of Technology, Rochester, NY
JANET V. SMITH, Assistant Vice President for Institutional Assessment, Pittsburg State University, Pittsburg, KS
JEFFREY K. SMITH, Professor of Education, University of Otago, Dunedin, New Zealand
JEFFREY H. SNOW, Associate Professor of Pediatrics, University of Arkansas for Medical Sciences, Little Rock, AR
ELIZABETH M. SPRATTO, Assessment Consultant, James Madison University, Harrisonburg, VA
FRANCIS STASKON, Senior Analyst, Walgreen Co., Deerfield, IL
ESTHER STAVROU, Associate Clinical Professor in School-Clinical Child Psychology, Ferkauf Graduate School of Psychology, Yeshiva University, Bronx, NY
STEPHANIE STEIN, Department Chair, Central Washington University, Ellensburg, WA
KRISTEN STODDARD, Doctoral Student, University of Northern Colorado, Greeley, CO
JENNIFER M. STRANG, Neuropsychologist, Washington DC Veterans Affairs Medical Center, Washington, DC
KARA M. STYCK, Assistant Professor of School Psychology, Department of Psychology, Northern Illinois University, Dekalb, IL
JEREMY R. SULLIVAN, Professor and Chair of Educational Psychology, University of Texas at San Antonio, San Antonio, TX
SAMANTHA DEHAAN SULLIVAN, Advanced Doctoral Student, Illinois State University and Practicum Student, SIU School of Medicine, Springfield, IL
CAROLYN H. SUPPA, Licensed Psychologist, Charleston, WV
LAURA M. SUPPA, Optometrist, Charleston Vision Source, Charleston, WV
SUSAN M. SWEARER, Willa Cather Professor of Educational Psychology, University of Nebraska–Lincoln, Lincoln, NE
NORA M. THOMPSON, Licensed Psychologist, Board Certified - Clinical Neuropsychology, Private Practice - Cascade Neuropsychological Services, Edmonds, WA
TRACY THORNDIKE, Associate Professor of Special Education and Education Leadership, Western Washington University, Bellingham, WA
GEOFFREY L. THORPE, Professor Emeritus of Psychology, University of Maine, Orono, ME
GERALD TINDAL, Castle-McIntosh-Knight Professor, College of Education, University of Oregon, Eugene, OR
REBECCA J. TIPTON, Graduate Student, Baylor University, Waco, TX
RENÉE M. TOBIN, Professor of Psychological Studies in Education, Temple University, Philadelphia, PA
ALLYSON K. TOPPS, Doctoral Candidate, University of Memphis, Memphis, TN
KATHLEEN TORSNEY, Professor of Psychology, William Paterson University, Wayne, NJ
ROSALIE MARDER UNTERMAN, Associate Professor/Clinical Director, Graduate Program Speech-Language Pathology, Touro College School of Health Sciences, Brooklyn, NY
JAMES P. VAN HANEGHAN, Professor of Counseling and Instructional Sciences, University of South Alabama, Mobile, AL
DUSTIN S. J. VAN ORMAN, Doctoral Student, Washington State University, Pullman, WA
MATT VASSAR, Clinical Assistant Professor of Psychiatry and Behavioral Sciences, Oklahoma State University Center for Health Sciences, Tulsa, OK
NINA E. VENTRESCO, Graduate Student, Lehigh University, Bethlehem, PA
ALBERT VILLANUEVA-REYES, Program Director & Professor of Speech-Language Pathology, Gannon University, Ruskin, FL
CHOCKALINGAM VISWESVARAN, Professor of Psychology, Florida International University, Miami, FL
ROMEO VITELLI, Psychologist, Private Practice, Toronto, Ontario, Canada
SANDRA WARD, Professor of Education, The College of William & Mary, Williamsburg, VA
COLE WAYANT, Doctoral Candidate, Oklahoma State University Center for Health Sciences, Tulsa, OK
CAROL WESTBY, Consultant, Bilingual Multicultural Services, Inc., Albuquerque, NM
JENNA M. WHITE, Graduate Student, School Psychology, Gonzaga University, Spokane, WA
KEITH F. WIDAMAN, Distinguished Professor of the Graduate Division, University of California, Riverside, CA
MARTIN J. WIESE, School Psychologist, Lincoln Public Schools, Lincoln, NE
WILLIAM K. WILKINSON, Consultant Psychologist, Boleybeg, Galway, Republic of Ireland
DIANE L. WILLIAMS, Professor, Department of Communication Sciences and Disorders, The Pennsylvania State University, University Park, PA
DANIELLE WINTERS, PhD Counseling Student, Old Dominion University, Norfolk, VA
ADRIANA WISSEL, Assistant Professor, in Clinical Mental Health Counseling, School of Education, Gonzaga University, Spokane, WA
EDWARD WITT, Manager, Walgreen Co., Deerfield, IL
BRANDON J. WOOD, Doctoral Student, Indiana State University, Terre Haute, IN

JAMES M. WOOD, Professor of Psychology, University of Texas at El Paso, El Paso, TX

KATHERINE MARSHALL WOODS, Assistant Professor of Clinical Psychology, The George Washington University, Washington, DC

GLORIA M. WORKMAN, Adjunctive Assistant Professor, Center for the Study of Traumatic Stress, Department of Psychiatry, Uniformed Services University, Bethesda, MD

CLAUDIA R. WRIGHT, Professor Emerita, California State University, Long Beach, Long Beach, CA

GEORGETTE YETTER, Associate Professor, School Psychology, Oklahoma State University, Stillwater, OK

ESTHER H. YI, Doctoral Student in School Psychology, Department of Psychology, Northern Illinois University, Dekalb, IL

SUZANNE YOUNG, Professor of Educational Research, University of Wyoming, Laramie, WY

PETER ZACHAR, Professor of Psychology, Auburn University Montgomery, Montgomery, AL

BO ZHANG, Professor, Department of Educational Psychology, University of Wisconsin-Milwaukee, Milwaukee, WI

MENGYAO ZHANG, Research Psychometrician, National Conference of Bar Examiners, Madison, WI

SHARON ZUMBRUNN, Associate Professor of Educational Psychology, Virginia Commonwealth University, Richmond, VA

INDEX OF TITLES

This title index lists all the tests included in The Twenty-First Mental Measurements Yearbook. *Citations are to test entry numbers, not to pages (e.g., 54 refers to test 54 and not page 54). Test numbers along with test titles are indicated in the running heads at the top of each page, whereas page numbers, used only in the Table of Contents but not in the indexes, appear at the bottom of each page. Superseded titles are listed with cross references to current titles, and alternative titles are also cross referenced.*

Some tests in this volume were previously listed in Tests in Print IX *(2016). An* (N) *appearing immediately after a test number indicates that the test is a new, recently published test, and/or that it has not appeared before in any Buros Center publication other than* Tests in Print IX. *An* (R) *indicates that the test has been revised or supplemented since last included in a Buros publication. An asterisk (*) indicates the test did not meet review criteria. In these cases, the test description appears, but no reviews are available.*

INDEX OF ACRONYMS

This Index of Acronyms refers the reader to the appropriate test in The Twenty-First Mental Measurements Yearbook. *In some cases tests are better known by their acronyms than by their full titles, and this index can be of substantial help to the person who knows the former but not the latter. Acronyms are listed only if the author or publisher has made substantial use of the acronym in referring to the test, or if the test is widely known by the acronym. A few acronyms are registered trademarks (e.g., SAT); where this is known to us, only the test with the registered trademarks is referenced. There is some danger in the overuse of acronyms. However, this index, like all other indexes in this work, is provided to make the task of identifying a test as easy as possible. All numbers refer to test numbers, not page numbers.*

AAB: Academic Achievement Battery, 1
ABDS: Adaptive Behavior Diagnostic Scale, 2
ABLLS-R: Assessment of Basic Language and Learning Skills–Revised (The), 10
ADEPT-15: Adaptive Employee Personality Test, 3
ADHD SOC: Attention Deficit Hyperactivity Disorder School Observation Code, 13
ALEKS PPL: ALEKS PPL (Placement, Preparation and Learning), 6
AMDQ: Athletic Milieu Direct Questionnaire, 12
APPSI-2: Assessment for Persons With Profound or Severe Impairments–Second Edition, 9
Arizona-4: Arizona Articulation and Phonology Scale, Fourth Revision, 8
ASC: Assessment of Story Comprehension, 11
AWS: Areas of Worklife Survey [Fifth Edition Manual], 7

BASC-3 Flex Monitor: BASC-3 Flex Monitor, 16
Batería IV: Batería IV Woodcock-Muñoz™, 17
Batería IV APROV: Batería IV Woodcock-Muñoz™, 17
Batería IV COG: Batería IV Woodcock-Muñoz™, 17
BELT-3: Bankson Expressive Language Test–Third Edition, 14
BESA: Bilingual English-Spanish Assessment, 21
BIOS: Bilingual English-Spanish Assessment, 21
BRIEF2: Behavior Rating Inventory of Executive Function, Second Edition, 18
Brown EF/A Scales: Brown Executive Function/Attention Scales, 22
BSCTS-CA: Barkley Sluggish Cognitive Tempo Scale—Children and Adolescents, 15

C DFS: Flow Scales, 66
C FSS: Flow Scales, 66
CADL-3: Communication Activities of Daily Living–Third Edition, 35
CAPs: Clinical Assessment of Pragmatics, 33
CAS-II: Cognistat [2016 Manual], 34
CASD-SF: Checklist for Autism Spectrum Disorder-Short Form, 28
CASL-2: Comprehensive Assessment of Spoken Language, Second Edition, 37
CEFI Adult: Comprehensive Executive Function Inventory Adult, 38
CEI: Career Exploration Inventory: A Guide for Exploring Work, Leisure, and Learning, Fifth Edition, 26
CEI-EZ: Career Exploration Inventory EZ, Second Edition, 27
CHAS-24: Clarity Well-Being Measures, 31
CHELLO: Child/Home Early Language & Literacy Observation Tool, 29
COACH: Choosing Outcomes & Accommodations for Children (COACH): A Guide to Educational Planning for Students with Disabilities, Third Edition, 30
COAST: California Older Adult Stroop Test, 23
COPE: Coping Operations Preference Enquiry, 40
COPES: Community Oriented Programs Environment Scale [Fourth Edition Manual], 36
COVR: Classification of Violence Risk, 32
CPAC-S: Contextual Probes of Articulation Competence—Spanish, 39
CRI: Coping Resources Inventory [Revised], 41
CriSS: Crisis Stabilization Scale, 42

CLASSIFIED SUBJECT INDEX

The Classified Subject Index classifies all tests included in The Mental Measurements Yearbook *into 18 major categories: Achievement, Behavior Assessment, Developmental, Education, English and Language, Fine Arts, Foreign Languages, Intelligence and General Aptitude, Mathematics, Miscellaneous, Neuropsychological, Personality, Reading, Science, Sensory-Motor, Social Studies, Speech and Hearing, and Vocations. This Classified Subject Index for the tests reviewed in* The Twenty-First Mental Measurements Yearbook *includes tests in 14 of the 18 available categories. (The categories of Fine Arts, Foreign Languages, Science, and Social Studies had no representative tests in this volume.) Each category appears in alphabetical order, and tests are ordered alphabetically within each category. Each test entry includes test title, population for which the test is intended, and the test entry number in* The Twenty-First Mental Measurements Yearbook. *All numbers refer to test numbers, not to page numbers. Brief suggestions for the use of this index are presented in the introduction, and definitions of the categories are provided at the beginning of this index.*

Achievement

Tests that measure acquired knowledge across school subject content areas. Included here are test batteries that measure multiple content areas and individual subject areas not having separate classification categories. (Note: Some batteries include both achievement and aptitude subtests. Such batteries may be classified under the categories of either Achievement or Intelligence and Aptitude depending upon the principal content area.)

See also Fine Arts, Intelligence and General Aptitude, Mathematics, Reading, Science, and Social Studies.

Behavior Assessment

Tests that measure general or specific behavior within educational, vocational, community, or home settings. Included here are checklists, rating scales, and surveys that measure observer's interpretations of behavior in relation to adaptive or social skills, functional skills, and appropriateness or dysfunction within settings/situations.

Developmental

Tests that are designed to assess skills or emerging skills (such as number concepts, conservation, memory, fine motor, gross motor, communication, letter recognition, social competence) of young children (0-7 years) or tests which are designed to assess such skills in severely or profoundly disabled school-aged individuals. Included here are early screeners, developmental surveys/profiles, kindergarten or school readiness tests, early learning profiles, infant development scales, tests of play behavior, social acceptance/social skills, and preschool psychoeducational batteries. Content specific screeners, such as those assessing readiness, are classified by content area (e.g., Reading).

See also Neuropsychological and Sensory-Motor.

Education

General education-related tests, including measures of instructional/school environment, effective schools/teaching, study skills and strategies, learning styles and strategies, school attitudes, educational programs/curriculae, interest inventories, and educational leadership.

Specific content area tests (i.e., science, mathematics, social studies, etc.) are listed by their content area.

English and Language

Tests that measure skills in using or understanding the English language in spoken or written form. Included here are tests of language proficiency, applied literacy, language comprehension/development/proficiency, English skills/proficiency, communication skills, listening comprehension, linguistics, and receptive/expressive vocabulary. (Tests designed to measure the mechanics of speaking or communicating are classified under the category Speech and Hearing.)

Fine Arts

Tests that measure knowledge, skills, abilities, attitudes, and interests within the various areas of fine and performing arts. Included here are tests of aptitude, achievement, creativity/talent/giftedness specific to the Fine Arts area, and tests of aesthetic judgment.

Foreign Languages

Tests that measure competencies and readiness in reading, comprehending, and speaking a language other than English.

Intelligence and General Aptitude

Tests that measure general acquired knowledge, aptitudes, or cognitive ability and those that assess specific aspects of these general categories. Included here are tests of critical thinking skills, nonverbal/verbal reasoning, cognitive abilities/processing, learning potential/aptitude/efficiency, logical reasoning, abstract thinking, creative thinking/creativity; entrance exams and academic admissions tests.

Mathematics

Tests that measure competencies and attitudes in any of the various areas of mathematics (e.g., algebra, geometry, calculus) and those related to general mathematics achievement/proficiency. (Note: Included here are tests that assess personality or affective variables related to mathematics.)

Miscellaneous

Tests that cannot be sorted into any of the current MMY categories as listed and defined above. Included here are tests of handwriting, ethics and morality, religion, driving and safety, health and physical education, environment (e.g., classroom environment, family environment), custody decisions, substance abuse, and addictions.

See also Personality.

Neuropsychological

Tests that measure neurological functioning or brain-behavior relationships either generally or in relation to specific areas of functioning. Included here are neuropsychological test batteries, questionnaires, and screening tests. Also included are tests that measure memory impairment, various disorders or decline associated with dementia, brain/head injury, visual attention, digit recognition, finger tapping, laterality, aphasia, and behavior (associated with organic brain dysfunction or brain injury).

See also Developmental, Intelligence and General Aptitude, Sensory-Motor, and Speech and Hearing.

Personality

Tests that measure individuals' ways of thinking, behaving, and functioning within family and society. Included here are projective and apperception tests, needs inventories, anxiety/depression scales; tests assessing substance use/abuse (or propensity for abuse), risk taking behavior, general mental health, emotional intelligence, self-image/-concept/-esteem, empathy, suicidal ideation, schizophrenia, depression/hopelessness, abuse, coping skills/stress, eating disorders, grief, decision-making, racial attitudes; general motivation, attributions, perceptions; adjustment, parenting styles, and marital issues/satisfaction.

For content-specific tests, see subject area categories (e.g., math efficacy instruments are located in Mathematics). Some areas, such as substance abuse, are cross-referenced with the Personality category.

Reading

Tests that measure competencies and attitudes within the broadly defined area of reading. Included here are reading inventories, tests of reading achievement and aptitude, reading readiness/early reading ability, reading comprehension, reading decoding, and oral reading. (Note: Included here are tests that assess personality or affective variables related to reading.)

Science

Tests that measure competencies and attitudes within any of the various areas of science (e.g., biology, chemistry, physics), and those related to general science achievement/proficiency. (Note: Included here are tests that assess personality or affective variables related to science.)

Sensory-Motor

Tests that are general or specific measures of any or all of the five senses and those that assess fine or gross motor skills. Included here are tests of manual dexterity, perceptual skills, visual-motor skills, perceptual-motor skills, movement and posture, laterality preference, sensory integration, motor development, color blindness/discrimination, visual perception/organization, and visual acuity.

See also Neuropsychological and Speech and Hearing.

Social Studies

Tests that measure competencies and attitudes within the broadly defined area of social studies. Included here are tests related to economics, sociology, history, geography, and political science, and those related to general social studies achievement/proficiency. (Note: Also included here are tests that assess personality or affective variables related to social studies.)

Speech and Hearing

Tests that measure the mechanics of speaking or hearing the spoken word. Included here are tests of articulation, voice fluency, stuttering, speech sound perception/discrimination, auditory discrimination/comprehension, audiometry, deafness, and hearing loss/impairment.

See also Developmental, English and Language, Neuropsychological, and Sensory-Motor.

Vocations

Tests that measure employee skills, behaviors, attitudes, values, and perceptions relative to jobs, employment, and the work place or organizational environment. Included here are tests of management skill/style/competence, leader behavior, careers (development, exploration, attitudes); job- or work-related selection/admission/entrance tests; tests of work adjustment, team or group processes/communication/effectiveness, employability, vocational/occupational interests, employee aptitudes/competencies, and organizational climate.

See also Intelligence and General Aptitude, and Personality and also specific content area categories (e.g., Mathematics, Reading).

ACHIEVEMENT

BEHAVIOR ASSESSMENT

DEVELOPMENTAL

EDUCATION

ENGLISH AND LANGUAGE

INTELLIGENCE AND GENERAL APTITUDE

MATHEMATICS

MISCELLANEOUS

NEUROPSYCHOLOGICAL

PERSONALITY

READING

SENSORY-MOTOR

SPEECH AND HEARING

VOCATIONS

PUBLISHERS DIRECTORY AND INDEX

This directory and index gives the names and test entry numbers of all publishers represented in The Twenty-First Mental Measurements Yearbook. *Current addresses are listed for all publishers for which this is known. This directory and index also provides telephone and FAX numbers and e-mail and Web addresses for those publishers who responded to our request for this information. Please note that all test numbers refer to test entry numbers, not page numbers. Publishers are an important source of information about catalogs, specimen sets, price changes, test revisions, and many other matters.*

Academic Therapy Publications
20 Leveroni Court
Novato, CA 94949-5746
Telephone: 800-422-7249
FAX: 415-883-3720
E-mail: customerservice@academictherapy.com
Web: www.academictherapy.com
Tests: 69, 98, 130, 135, 165, 175, 177

American Association on Intellectual and Developmental Disabilities
8403 Colesville Road, Suite 900
Silver Spring, MD 20910
Telephone: 202-387-1968
FAX: 202-387-2193
E-mail: books@aaidd.org
Web: www.aaidd.org
Tests: 51, 161, 162

American Occupational Therapy Association, Inc.
6116 Executive Boulevard, Suite 200
Bethesda, MD 20852-4929
Telephone: 800-792-2682
FAX: 301-652-6611
E-mail: praota@aota.org
Web: www.aota.org
Test: 152

Ancora Publishing
21 West 6th Avenue
Eugene, OR 97401
Telephone: 866-542-1490
FAX: 541-345-1507
Web: www.ancorapublishing.com
Tests: 67, 68, 143, 164

Aon Hewitt
199 Water Street, 11th Floor
New York, NY 10038
Telephone: 212-479-4236
Web: www.aon.com/human-capital-consulting
Test: 3

Aperture Education
100 Main Street, Suite 201
Fort Mill, SC 29715
Telephone: 844-685-2499
E-mail: info@apertureed.com
Web: apertureed.com
Test: 50

Assessio
P.O. Box 470 54
SE 100 74
Sweden
E-mail: info@assessio.se
Web: www.assessio.com
Tests: 88, 95

Ballard & Tighe, Publishers
471 Atlas Street
Brea, CA 92821
Telephone: 800-321-4332
FAX: 714-255-9828
E-mail: info@ballard-tighe.com
Web: www.ballard-tighe.com
Tests: 79, 80, 81

Behavior Analysts, Inc.
311 Lennon Lane, Suite A
Walnut Creek, CA 94598
Telephone: 925-210-9378
FAX: 925-210-0436
Web: www.partingtonbehavioranalysts.com
Test: 10

CASAS
5151 Murphy Canyon Road, Suite 220
San Diego, CA 92123-4339
Telephone: 858-292-2900
FAX: 858-292-2910
E-mail: casas@casas.org
Web: www.casas.org
Test: 134

Center for Applied Linguistics
4646 40th Street, NW
Washington, DC 20016-1859
Telephone: 202-362-0700
FAX: 202-363-7204
E-mail: aea@cal.org
Web: www.cal.org
Test: 19

Checkmate Plus, Ltd.
P.O. Box 696
Stony Brook, NY 11790-0696
Telephone: 800-779-4292
FAX: 631-360-3432
E-mail: info@checkmateplus.com
Web: www.checkmateplus.com
Test: 13

Clarity Health Assessment Systems, Inc.
100 Easy Street, Unit 5744
Carefree, AZ 85377
Telephone: 203-434-2399
E-mail: info@measurewithclarity.com
Web: measurewithclarity.com
Test: 31

Cognistat, Inc.
P.O. Box 460
Fairfax, CA 94978
Telephone: 800-922-5840
FAX: 514-336-6537
E-mail: info@cognistat.com
Web: www.cognistat.com
Test: 34

Creative Solutions Press LLC
3724 Capilano Drive
West Lafayette, IN 47906
Telephone: 765-807-2467
FAX: 765-746-2306
Web: www.creativesolutionspress.com
Test: 12

CW Educational Enterprises
460 Olive Street
Menlo Park, CA 94025
Telephone: 650-324-3434
E-mail: connieoliv@sbcglobal.net
Web: www.cwellresources.com
Test: 128

Griffith University
Mt. Gravatt Campus
M07 Room 2.17
176 Messines Ridge Road
Mount Gravatt, Queensland 4122
Australia
Telephone: 61 7 37356425
E-mail: k.freiberg@griffith.edu.au
Web: www.realwell.org.au
Test: 115

Guilford Press
370 Seventh Avenue, Suite 1200
New York, NY 10001-1020
Telephone: 800-365-7006
FAX: 212-966-6708
E-mail: info@guilford.com
Web: www.guilford.com
Tests: 4, 15

Healthy Learning
P.O. Box 1828
Monterey, CA 93942
Telephone: 888-229-5745
FAX: 831-372-6075
E-mail: info@healthylearning.com
Web: www.healthylearning.com
Test: 120

Hogrefe Ltd
Hogrefe House
Albion Place
Oxford OX1 1QZ
United Kingdom
Telephone: +44 (0)1865 797920
FAX: +44 (0)1865 797949
E-mail: publishing@hogrefe.co.uk
Web: www.hogrefe.co.uk
Tests: 44, 54, 92, 101, 149

Hogrefe Publishing Corp.
361 Newbury Street, Fifth Floor
Boston, MA 02115
Telephone: 857-800-2002
E-mail: publishing@hogrefe.com
Web: us.hogrefe.com
Test: 59

IDS Publishing Corporation
P.O. Box 389
Worthington, OH 43085
Telephone: 614-885-2323
FAX: 614-885-2323
E-mail: ids@idspublishing.com
Web: www.idspublishing.com
Test: 136

Innolect, Inc.
2764 Pleasant Road #11503
Fort Mill, SC 29708-7299
Telephone: 803-396-8500
E-mail: innolect@innolectinc.com
Web: www.innolectinc.com
Test: 183

JIST Career Solutions, a division of Kendall Hunt
4050 Westmark Drive
Dubuque, IA 52004
Telephone: 800-228-0810
E-mail: corpinfo@kendallhunt.com
Web: jist.com
Tests: 26, 27, 83, 109, 110, 121, 178, 188

Kaplan Early Learning Company
1310 Lewisville-Clemmons Road
P.O. Box 67
Lewisville, NC 27023-0609
Telephone: 800-334-2014
E-mail: info@kaplanco.com
Web: www.kaplanco.com
Test: 49

The Leadership Challenge, A Wiley Brand
989 Market Street
San Francisco, CA 94103-1741
Telephone: 866-888-5159
E-mail: leadership@wiley.com
Web: www.leadershipchallenge.com
Tests: 56, 86

Mac Keith Press
Second Floor, Rankin Building
139-143 Bermondsey Street
London SE1 3UW
United Kingdom
Telephone: +44 (0)20 3958 3547
E-mail: admin@mackeith.co.uk
Web: www.mackeith.co.uk
Test: 102

McGraw-Hill Education
2 Penn Plaza, 20th Floor
New York, NY 10121
E-mail: aleksppl.inquiry@mheducation.com
Web: www.mheducation.com
Test: 6

Mental Health, Law, and Policy Institute
Simon Fraser University
8888 University Drive
Burnaby, British Columbia V5A 1S6
Canada
Telephone: 877-585-9933
FAX: 604-669-0145
E-mail: info@proactive-resolutions.com
Web: members.psyc.sfu.ca/labs/mhlpi/publications
Tests: 82, 160

Mind Garden, Inc.
707 Menlo Avenue, Suite 120
Menlo Park, CA 94025
Telephone: 650-322-6300
FAX: 650-322-6398
E-mail: info@mindgarden.com
Web: www.mindgarden.com
Tests: 7, 23, 36, 40, 41, 42, 61, 62, 65, 66, 87, 104, 125, 126, 189

Multi-Health Systems, Inc.
P.O. Box 950
North Tonawanda, NY 14120-0950
Telephone: 800-456-3003
FAX: 888-540-4484
E-mail: customerservice@mhs.com
Web: www.mhs.com
Tests: 38, 71, 89, 113, 118, 131, 146

National Institutes of Health
625 N. Michigan Avenue, Suite 2700
Chicago, IL 60611
Telephone: 312-503-3453
E-mail: help@NIHToolbox.org
Web: healthmeasures.net/explore-measurement-systems/nih-toolbox
Tests: 105, 106, 107, 108

New Zealand Council for Educational Research
Education House West
178-182 Willis Street
Box 3237
Wellington 6011
New Zealand
Telephone: 00 64 4 384 7939
FAX: 00 64 4 384 7933
E-mail: sales@nzcer.org.nz
Web: www.nzcer.org.nz
Test: 158

Paul H. Brookes Publishing Co., Inc.
P.O. Box 10624
Baltimore, MD 21285-0624
Telephone: 800-638-3775
FAX: 410-337-8539
Web: www.brookespublishing.com
Tests: 11, 21, 29, 30, 43, 74, 129, 144, 159, 166

Pearson
19500 Bulverde Road
San Antonio, TX 78259
Telephone: 800-627-7271
FAX: 800-232-1223
E-mail: pearsonassessments@pearson.com
Web: www.pearsonassessments.com
Tests: 16, 20, 22, 24, 52, 58, 70, 85, 99, 111, 117, 132, 147, 148, 154, 174, 182, 184, 185

PRO-ED
8700 Shoal Creek Boulevard
Austin, TX 78757-6897
Telephone: 800-897-3202
FAX: 800-397-7633
E-mail: info@proedinc.com
Web: www.proedinc.com
Tests: 2, 9, 14, 35, 39, 46, 57, 75, 100, 145, 150, 151, 167, 168, 169, 170, 171, 172, 173, 180, 181, 187, 191

Psychological Assessment Resources, Inc.
16204 N. Florida Avenue
Lutz, FL 33549-8119
Telephone: 800-331-8378
FAX: 800-727-9329
E-mail: custsupp@parinc.com
Web: www.parinc.com
Tests: 1, 18, 32, 53, 63, 64, 78, 84, 91, 97, 116, 119, 124, 137, 138, 139, 153, 179, 190

Psychological Consultancy Limited
8 Mount Ephraim
Tunbridge Wells TN4 8AS
United Kingdom
Telephone: 44 (0)1892 559 540
FAX: 44 (0)1892 522 096
E-mail: info@psychological-consultancy.com
Web: www.psychological-consultancy.com
Test: 141

Psychology Foundation of Australia
University of New South Wales, Upper Campus
Psychology Office, Matthews Building
High Street, Kensington
Sydney, New South Wales 2052
Australia
E-mail: psychology@unsw.edu.au
Web: www2.psy.unsw.edu.au/groups/dass
Test: 45

Renaissance Learning, Inc.
P.O. Box 8036
Wisconsin Rapids, WI 54495-8036
Telephone: 800-338-4204
FAX: 715-424-4242
E-mail: answers@renaissance.com
Web: www.renaissance.com
Tests: 155, 156, 157

Riverside Insights
One Pierce Place Suite 900
Itasca, IL 60143
Telephone: 800-323-9540
E-mail: inquiry@riversideinsights.com
Web: www.riversideinsights.com
Tests: 17, 186

Rorschach Performance Assessment System, LLC
P.O. Box 12699
Toledo, OH 43606
Telephone: 567-316-0056
Web: r-pas.org
Test: 142

Routledge Psychology
711 3rd Ave, 8th Floor
New York, NY 10017
Telephone: 212-216-7800
FAX: 212-564-7854
E-mail: psychology@routledge.com
Web: www.routledge.com/psychology
Test: 25

SALT Software, LLC
414 D'Onofrio Drive
Madison, WI 53719
Telephone: 888-440-7258
FAX: 608-237-2220
E-mail: sales@saltsoftware.com
Web: www.saltsoftware.com
Test: 163

The SASSI Institute
201 Camelot Lane
Springville, IN 47462
Telephone: 800-726-0526
FAX: 800-546-7995
E-mail: sassi@sassi.com
Web: sassi.com
Test: 5

Schoolhouse Educational Services, LLC
1052 Forest Oak Drive, Suite 200
Onalaska, WI 54650
Telephone: 608-787-5636
E-mail: cpps@psychprocesses.com
Web: www.schoolhouseeducationalservices.com
Test: 90

Search Institute
3001 Broadway Street NE #310
Minneapolis, MN 55413
Telephone: 800-888-7828
FAX: 612-376-8955
E-mail: info@searchinstitute.org
Web: www.search-institute.org
Tests: 47, 133, 192

SIGMA Assessment Systems, Inc.
P.O. Box 610757
Port Huron, MI 48061-0757
Telephone: 800-265-1285
FAX: 800-361-9411
E-mail: SIGMA@SigmaAssessmentSystems.com
Web: www.sigmaassessmentsystems.com
Tests: 55, 96, 127

Stoelting Co.
620 Wheat Lane
Wood Dale, IL 60191-1164
Telephone: 800-860-9775
FAX: 630-860-9775
E-mail: psychtests@stoeltingco.com
Web: www.stoeltingco.com/psychologicaltesting.html
Tests: 28, 77, 103, 123

Stuttering Therapy Resources, Inc.
8005 Spectrum Drive
McKinney, TX 75070
Telephone: 844-478-8883
FAX: 844-478-8883
E-mail: info@stutteringtherapyresources.com
Web: www.stutteringtherapyresources.com
Test: 114

Teachers College Press
1234 Amsterdam Avenue
New York, NY 10027
Telephone: 212-678-3929
FAX: 212-678-4149
E-mail: tcpress@tc.columbia.edu
Web: www.teacherscollegepress.com
Tests: 60, 76

The TOVA Company
222 Anthes Avenue, Suite 101
Langley, WA 98260
Telephone: 800-729-2886
FAX: 800-452-6919
E-mail: info@tovatest.com
Web: www.tovatest.com
Test: 176

University of Minnesota Press
Test Division, University of Minnesota Press
111 Third Avenue South, Suite 290
Minneapolis, MN 55401-2520
Telephone: 612-627-1963
FAX: 612-627-1980
Web: www.upress.umn.edu/test-division
Tests: 93, 94

VG Press
595 W. Granada Boulevard, Suite H
Ormond Beach, FL 32174
Telephone: 386-677-3995
Web: www.nbfe.net
Test: 73

VORT Corporation
P.O. Box G
Menlo Park, CA 94026
Telephone: 888-757-8678
FAX: 650-327-0747
E-mail: sales@vort.com
Web: www.vort.com
Test: 72

Western Psychological Services
625 Alaska Avenue
Torrance, CA 90503-5124
Telephone: 800-648-8857
FAX: 424-201-6950
E-mail: customerservice@wpspublish.com
Web: www.wpspublish.com
Tests: 8, 33, 37, 48, 112, 122, 140

Work Life Help
E-mail: ekossek@purdue.edu; hammerl@ohsu.edu
Test: 62

INDEX OF NAMES

This index indicates whether a citation refers to authorship of a test, a test review, or a reviewer's reference for a specific test. Numbers refer to test entries, not to pages. The abbreviations and numbers following the names may be interpreted as follows: "test, 73" indicates authorship of test 73; "rev, 86" indicates authorship of a review of test 86; "ref, 45" indicates a reference in one of the "Reviewer's References" sections for test 45. Reviewer names mentioned in cross references are also indexed.

SCORE INDEX

This Score Index lists all the scores, in alphabetical order, for all the tests included in The Twenty-First Mental Measurements Yearbook. *Because test scores can be regarded as operational definitions of the variable measured, sometimes the scores provide better leads to what a test actually measures than the test title or other available information. The Score Index is very detailed, and the reader should keep in mind that a given variable (or concept) of interest may be defined in several different ways. Thus the reader should look up these several possible alternative definitions before drawing final conclusions about whether tests measuring a particular variable of interest can be located in this volume. If the kind of score sought is located in a particular test or tests, the reader should then read the test descriptive information carefully to determine whether the test(s) in which the score is found is (are) consistent with reader purpose. Used wisely, the Score Index can be another useful resource in locating the right score in the right test. As usual, all numbers in the index are test numbers, not page numbers.*